2015

CATHOLIC ALMANAC

D0167807

Our Sunday Visitor Publishing Division
Our Sunday Visitor, Inc.
Huntington, Indiana 46750

OUR SUNDAY VISITOR'S CATHOLIC ALMANAC
2015 EDITION

STAFF

Greg Erlandson
Editor-in-Chief

Matthew E. Bunson, D.Min., K.H.S.
General Editor

Murray W. Hubley
Production Editor

Cathy Dee
Web Editor

Contributors to the 2015 Edition
Gerald Korson
Rev. Ronald Roberson, C.S.P. .
Russell Shaw

Carrie Bannister, Assistant
Amanda Falk, Design

ACKNOWLEDGMENTS: Catholic News Service, for coverage of news and documentary texts; *The Documents of Vatican II*, ed. W. M. Abbott (Herder and Herder, America Press: New York 1966), for quotations of Council documents; *Annuario Pontificio* (2014); *Statistical Yearbook of the Church* (2012); *L'Osservatore Romano* (English editions); *The Official Catholic Directory* — Excerpts of statistical data and other material, reprinted with permission of *The Official Catholic Directory*, © 2014 by Reed Reference Publishing, a division of Reed Publishing (USA) Inc. Trademark used under license from Reed Publishing (Nederland) B.V.; *The Papal Encyclicals*, 5 vols., ed. C. Carlen (Pierian Press, Ann Arbor, MI); Newsletter of the U.S. Bishops' Committee on the Liturgy; The United States Catholic Mission Assoc. (3029 Fourth St. N.E., Washington, DC 20017), for U.S. overseas-mission compilations and statistics; *Catholic Press Directory* (2014); *Annuaire Directoire*, Canadian Conference of Catholic Bishops, for latest available Canadian Catholic statistics; other sources as credited in particular entries.
Special thanks are owed to Secretariat for Pro-Life Activities, USCCB; Canadian Conference of Catholic Bishops; and Rev. Jorge Francisco Vázquez Moreno, adjunct secretary of the Conferencia del Episcopado Mexicano.

2015 Catholic Almanac

Editorial Note: Comments, corrections, and suggestions should be addressed to the editorial offices of the *Catholic Almanac*: 200 Noll Plaza, Huntington, IN 46750; (800) 348-2440; E-mail: almanac@osv.com.

Visit us online at www.CatholicAlmanac.com, and at the Our Sunday Visitor website at www.OSV.com.

CONTENTS

PART ONE: NEWS AND EVENTS
Year in Review:
September 2013-August 2014 5
Deaths 51
News in Depth:
Pope Francis 55
Papal Trips 2013-2014
Assisi, Italy (Oct. 4, 2013)..................56
The Holy Land (May 24-26, 2014) 57
South Korea (Aug. 13-18, 2014)..................63
News and Documents:
Francis and the Invocation for Peace...........67
Pope Francis and the Sex Abuse Crisis 67
New Cardinals.....................................70
Canonizations of Popes John Paul II
and John XXIII...............................71
Holy See Finances 73
Apostolic Exhortation: *Evangelii Gaudium*..75
Beatification of Pope Paul VI..................76
International News 2013-14:
Christians in Iraq..............................77
Synod of Bishops................................79
National News 2013-14:
Religious Liberty and the HHS Mandate 82
Update on the Sex Abuse Scandal 82
Life Issues 2013-14 83
United States Conference of
Catholic Bishops:
Meetings of U.S. Bishops 2013-14
November 12-13, 2013..........................86
June 10-14, 2014..............................86

PART TWO: THE TEACHINGS
OF THE CATHOLIC CHURCH
Doctrine of the Catholic Church:
Catechism of the Catholic Church 87
Lumen Gentium 89
Pope, Teaching Authority, Collegiality 92
Revelation.......................................93
The Bible...96
Apostles and Evangelists 105
Apostolic Fathers, Fathers, Doctors 106
Creeds...109
Christian Morality 110
Moral Teachings of Pope John Paul II........112
Catholic Social Doctrine 114
Social Doctrine Under Pope John Paul II...115
Social Encyclicals of Pope John Paul II
and Pope Benedict XVI.........................115
Socio-Economic Statements by Bishops....118
Blessed Virgin Mary 119
Redemptoris Mater 121
Apparitions of the Blessed Virgin Mary.....123
Third Secret of Fatima..........................124
The Code of Canon Law.........................125
Glossary.................................... 128
The Church Calendar 161
Table of Movable Feasts 164
2015 Calendar 165
Holy Days and Other Observances..........171
Liturgical Life of the Church 175
Mass, Eucharistic Sacrifice, Banquet 178
Liturgical Developments..........................182
New Translation of the Order of the Mass...183

Summorum Pontificum 187
The Sacraments of the Church................. 190
Baptism..191
Confirmation.....................................192
Eucharist 192
Penance..195
Anointing of the Sick 196
Holy Orders 196
Matrimony...198
Communion of Saints 204
Saints — Patrons and Intercessors............211
Canonization and Beatifications, 2013-14 215

PART THREE: THE CHURCH UNIVERSAL
Dates, Events in Catholic History.............. 218
Ecumenical Councils 228
The Papacy and the Holy See:
Pope Francis 231
Pope Benedict XVI................................232
Popes of the Catholic Church 233
Popes of the Twentieth Century 238
Pope St. John Paul II 243
Papal Encyclicals — 1740 to Present 245
Canonizations by Leo XIII and Successors....250
Beatifications by Pope St. John Paul II 252
Beatifications by Benedict XVI 254
Beatifications by Pope Francis 255
Roman Curia 255
Vatican City State 261
Diplomatic Activities of the Holy See 264
Representatives of the Holy See................264
Diplomats to the Holy See 268
U.S.-Holy See Relations 269
Pontifical Academies 271
Hierarchy of the Catholic Church............. 273
Synod of Bishops.................................275
College of Cardinals.............................276
Cardinals' Biographies..........................276
Categories of Cardinals..........................294
Consistores 295
Distribution of Cardinals 296
Cardinal Electors................................297
Cardinals in the U.S.............................297
Deceased Cardinals 2013-2014....................297
The Universal Church
The Church Throughout the World...........298
Catholic World Statistics 335
Episcopal Conferences 336
International Catholic Organizations 340
Eastern Catholic Churches 343
Jurisdictions and Faithful......................344
Eastern Catholic Churches in U.S............348
Byzantine Divine Liturgy.........................348
Code of Canons of the Eastern Churches...351
The Catholic Church in the U.S.
Chronology of U.S. Catholic History..........352
U.S. Catholic History 358
Missionaries to the Americas 363
Franciscan Missions 365
Church-State Relations in the U.S. 366
Catholics in the U.S. Government.............371
United States Hierarchy:
Jurisdictions, Hierarchy, Statistics 373
Ecclesiastical Provinces..........................373

Archdioceses, Dioceses,
Archbishops, Bishops..............................374
Chancery Offices 384
Cathedrals in the United States................387
Basilicas in the United States....................389
Shrines and Places of Interest, U.S. 390
Biographies of American Bishops 394
Bishop Brothers 417
U.S. Bishops Overseas...............................417
Deceased Bishops, 2013-2014 418
Retired/Resigned U.S. Prelates 418
American Bishops of the Past 419
United States Conference
of Catholic Bishops............................... 420
State Catholic Conferences........................422
Cultural Diversity in the Church................ 424
Hispanic Catholics in the U.S. 424
African-American Catholics in the U.S. 426
Asian and Pacific Islander in the U.S..........428
Native-American Catholics..........................428
Pastoral Care of Migrants, Refugees, and
Travelers...429
Missionary Activity of the Church 429
U.S. Catholic Mission Association 430
Statistics of the Church in the U.S.
U.S. Statistics and Summary......................432
Percentage of Catholics
in the Total U.S. Population 433
Catholic Population, U.S.............................435
Receptions into the Church, U.S. 439
The Catholic Church in Canada................ 441
Ecclesiastical Jurisdictions of Canada........442
Canadian Conference of Catholic Bishops ...445
Canadian Shrines 446
Statistical Summary 447
The Catholic Church in Mexico 449
Ecclesiastical Jurisdictions of Mexico 451
Mexican Conference of Catholic Bishops.....455
Statistical Summary 455

PART FOUR: THE LIFE OF THE CHURCH IN
THE WORLD
Consecrated Life:
Institutes of Consecrated Life....................458
Religious Institutes of Men in the U.S........458
Membership, Religious Institutes of Men.....467
Religious Institutes of Women 468
Membership, Religious Institutes
of Women...486
Organizations of Religious 489
Secular Institutes 489
Third Orders 493
Apostolates and Ministries:
Laity in the Church 494
Special Apostolates and Groups................495
Catholic Youth Organizations 496
Campus Ministry.......................................497
Associations, Movements, Societies 498
Catholic Social Services 508
Facilities for Retired and Aged Persons 511
Facilities for Disabled Children, Adults 520
Retreats, Spiritual Renewal Programs........525
Education:
Legal Status of Catholic Education............532
Education Vouchers...................................532
Ex Corde Ecclesiae..................................533

Catholic School Statistics Summary 534
Catholic Schools and Students in U.S. 535
Catholic Universities, Colleges in U.S. 539
Diocesan, Interdiocesan Seminaries...........544
World and U.S. Seminary Statistics.............546
Pontifical Universities 547
Ecclesiastical Faculties...............................548
Pontifical Universities, Institutes in Rome ...550
Catholic Communications:
Catholic Press Statistics.............................551
Newspapers, Magazines, Newsletters.......551
Books 564
Canadian Catholic Publications..................565
International Catholic Periodicals................566
Catholic News Agencies............................566
Radio, Television, Theatre 567
Film (includes "best lists")........................569
Roman Catholic Internet Sites...................569
Developments in Communications 570
Message of the Holy Father
for World Communications Day 570
Pontifical Honors and Awards....................571
Pontifical Orders.......................................571
Ecclesiastical Orders.................................572
2014 Catholic Press Awards 573
2014 Christopher Awards...........................575
Ecumenism, Interreligious Dialogue:
Ecumenism...576
Pope Francis (2013-)................................576
Pope Benedict XVI (2005-2013) 578
Vatican II Decree.......................................578
Directory on Ecumenism 579
Ecumenical Agencies.................................580
International Bilateral Commissions...........582
U.S. Ecumenical Dialogues 583
Common Declarations 583
Ecumenical Statements 586
Separated Eastern Churches:
The Orthodox Church 588
Eastern Ecumenism 589
The Orthodox Churches,
Notable Developments...........................590
Relations with the Oriental
Orthodox Churches 592
Relations with the Polish National
Catholic Church......................................593
Reformation Churches:
Leaders and Doctrines of the
Reformation...595
Protestant Churches in the U.S. 596
Anglican-Roman Catholic Final Report 600
Anglican-Catholic Relations.......................600
Joint Declaration on Justification...............603
Interreligious Dialogue:
Judaism..605
Catholic-Jewish Relations 605
We Remember: A Reflection on
the Shoah 607
Papal Statements......................................607
Millennium Events 608
International Liaison Committee..................609
Islam 611
Hinduism and Buddhism............................615

Index 617

Year In Review September 2013 to August 2014

SEPTEMBER 2013

VATICAN

Appeal for Peace in Syria On Sept. 4, Pope Francis continued his appeal for prayer and fasting for an end to the bloody civil war in Syria. The pope made the call at the end of his general audience. The statement ended with the declaration, "May the cry for peace be raised strongly throughout the earth!" It was followed by the meeting in the Vatican the next day of the Vatican's Diplomatic Corps to discuss the situation in Syria. The gathered diplomats heard an address from Abp. Dominique Mamberti, Secretary for Relations with States, who said, "The Pope's heartbroken appeal gives voice to the desire for peace that rises from every part of the earth, from the heart of all men of good will. In the concrete historical situation, marked by violence and wars in many places, the Pope's voice is raised at a particularly grave and delicate moment in the long Syrian conflict, which has already witnessed too much suffering, devastation and sorrow, to which are added the many innocent victims of the attacks of last Aug. 21, which aroused horror and concern in global public opinion because of the consequences of the possible use of chemical weapons."

Letter to Putin On Sept. 5, it was reported that as the representatives of the G20 summit were preparing to meet, Pope Francis had sent a letter to Russian President Vladimir Putin, the host of the summit in St. Petersburg, Russia. In his letter, the Holy Father thanked the G20 for its work to bring international economic and financial reform, but he added, "the world economy will only develop if it allows a dignified way of life for all human beings, from the eldest to the unborn child, not just for citizens of the G20 member states but for every inhabitant of the earth, even those in extreme social situations or in the remotest places...From this standpoint, it is clear that, for the world's peoples, armed conflicts are always a deliberate negation of international harmony, and create profound divisions and deep wounds which require many years to heal."

The pope also called on the summit participants to resist armed conflict and to work to bring peace in Syria and promote international stability. He declared, "The leaders of the G20 cannot remain indifferent to the dramatic situation of the beloved Syrian people which has lasted far too long, and even risks bringing greater suffering to a region bitterly tested by strife and needful of peace. To the leaders present, to each and every one, I make a heartfelt appeal for them to help find ways to overcome the conflicting positions and to lay aside the futile pursuit of a military solution. Rather, let there be a renewed commitment to seek, with courage and determination, a peaceful solution through dialogue and negotiation of the parties, unanimously supported by the international community. Moreover, all governments have the moral duty to do everything possible to ensure humanitarian assistance to those suffering because of the conflict, both within and beyond the country's borders."

President of Bolivia On Sept. 6, Pope Francis welcomed President Evo Morales of Bolivia to the Apostolic Palace in the Vatican. After the meeting, President Morales had a session with Card. Tarcisio Bertone, the Vatican Secretary of State and Abp. Dominique Mamberti, secretary for Relations with States. According to a communique released by the Holy See, the meeting between Francis and Morales discussed a variety of issues, including the economic and social problems in South America. The communique added, "Mention was then made of the decisive contribution of the Catholic Church in Bolivia in the fields of education, healthcare, support for families and welfare provision for children and the elderly."

Papal Plea for Peace On Sept. 7, Pope Francis held a Day of Fasting and Prayer for Peace in Syria and throughout the world that was attended by more than 100,000. In a four-hour service in the Vatican, he presided over the praying of the rosary Eucharistic adoration and gave a reflection on the question, "Am I really my brother's keeper?" His answer was a definitive "Yes!" He added that, "we bring about the rebirth of Cain in every act of violence and in every war. All of us! And even today we continue this history of conflict between brothers, even today we raise our hands against our brother. Even today, we let ourselves be guided by idols, by selfishness, by our own interests, and this attitude persists. We have perfected our weapons, our conscience has fallen asleep, and we have sharpened our ideas to justify ourselves. As if it were normal, we continue to sow destruction, pain, death! Violence and war lead only to death, they speak of death! Violence and war are the language of death!"

The vigil also included the opportunity for people to go to confession, the recitation of the Angelus, the presentation of the beloved Marian image of the "*Salus Populi Romani*" (health of the Roman people), the Office of Readings and Eucharistic benediction.

Letter to Non-Believers On Sept. 11, Pope Francis published a letter addressed to Eugenio Scalfari, the founder of the Italian newspaper "*La Repubblica*," in which he reached out in dialogue and charity to non-believers. The letter was a reply to several questions on faith and belief that had been published in July. The pope wrote, in part, "Faith, for me, was born from an encounter with Jesus. A personal encounter that touched my heart and gave me a direction and a new meaning to my existence. But at the same time it was a meeting that was made possible by the community of faith which I lived in and through which I found access to the intelligence of the Sacred Scripture, to the new life that flows like gushing water from Jesus through the Sacraments, to the fraternity with all and to the service of the poor, true image of the Lord. Without the Church, I believe, I would not have encountered Jesus, while being aware that the immense gift that is faith is preserved in the fragile clay vessels of our humanity." He went on to discuss the issues of conscience and sin and the existence of an absolute Truth.

Nuncio under Investigation On Sept. 13, the Holy See's Press Office under Fr. Federico Lombardi, S.J., confirmed that the Vatican would cooperate fully with authorities in the Dominican Republic in their investigation into Abp. Józef Wesolowski and whether he engaged in improper sexual conduct while serving in the country. Upon learning of the accusation against the diplomat, the Vatican Secretariat of State recalled the nuncio, suspended him from his post, and launched its own investigation with the Congregation for the Doctrine of the Faith. Moreover, diplomatic immunity for the nuncio was not invoked. The former nuncio was subsequently placed on canonical trial and removed from all ministry.

Beatification of "Gaucho Priest" On Sept. 16, Pope Francis expressed his joy at the beatification Fr. José Gabriel Brochero, the famed "Gaucho Priest" of Argentina who was also a beloved Servant of the Poor and Sick. In a letter to Abp. José María Arancedo, president of the Argentine Episcopal Conference, the Holy Father said that Fr. Brochero was a "shepherd who had the smell of his sheep." He added, "I imagine the good priest Brochero on his mule, travelling along the barren and desolate roads of the 200 square kilometres that made up his parish, searching for your great-grandparents, your great-great-grandparents, to ask if they needed anything and to invite them to do the spiritual exercises of St. Ignatius of Loyola. He knew every corner of the parish. He did not stay in the sacristy combing his sheep. Fr. Brochero brought Jesus to each family. He would visit them with an image of the Virgin and a prayer book with the Word of God, the things he needed to celebrate Mass each day. They would invite him around to chat, and Brochero would talk to them in a way that everyone understood, that came from his heart, his faith and the love he had for Jesus."

Pope Francis Writes Imam On Sept. 17, Pope Francis sent a message to the Imam Ahmed al-Tayyeb, the great Imam of the Islamic University al-Azhar, in Cairo, Egypt, to reiterate his abiding respect "for Islam and Muslims" and his commitment to fostering "understanding among Christians and Muslims in the world, to build peace and justice." The letter was delivered by the apostolic nuncio to Egypt, Abp. Jean-Paul Gobel.

Renewed Appeal for Peace On Sept. 18, Pope Francis reiterated his plea for a peaceful resolution to the crisis in Syria and urged all combatants to resolve the civil strife through dialogue and negotiation. The pope made the appeal his general audience and was timed to anticipate the "International Day for Peace" marked by the United Nations a few days later. The pope taught, "May peace, a gift from Christ, forever reside in our hearts and support the aims and actions of the leaders of the Nations and all men of good will. Let us all be committed to encouraging efforts for a diplomatic and political solution in the seedbeds of war that remain a cause for concern." He then mentioned Syria specifically.

An End to Nuclear Proliferation On Sept. 18, Abp. Dominique Mamberti, the Vatican Secretary for Relations with States, addressed the International Atomic Energy Agency (IAEA), in Vienna, Austria, and appealed for the international community to work for an end to the proliferation of nuclear weapons. He urged technical cooperation among the countries of the world and noted the 50th Anniversary of the papal encyclical "*Pacem in Terris*" of Pope St. John XXIII, saying, "Even though written 50 years ago, these words seem to reflect the beginning of the 21st century, where there are still States possessing nuclear weapons, not all of which are signatories to the NPT (Non-Proliferation Treaty), while the possibility of nuclear terrorism is very real. We should ask ourselves whether we really live in a more secure and safer world today compared with that of a few decades ago." He went on to call for "Nuclear-weapon-free zones are the best example of trust, confidence and affirmation that peace and security are possible without possessing nuclear weapons."

Interview with the Jesuits On Sept. 20, the major Jesuit publications around the world published a remarkable interview between Pope Francis and the Jesuit Fr. Antonio Spadaro, editor in chief of the Jesuit Italian journal, "*La Civilta Cattolica*." The interview was published in several Jesuit journals, including "*America*" magazine and created a major media moment because of the frank comments of the pope but also because of much of what he said was taken out of context by secular and even some Catholic press and bloggers. The interview was wide-ranging and included the focus on God's loving mercy, discernment, proclaiming the Gospel in a broken world, seeing the Church as a field hospital, and helping people everywhere to see a simple but powerful and transforming Gospel message.

Pope in Sardinia On Sept. 22, Pope Francis paid a visit to the Italian island of Sardinia and gave his encouragement to the inhabitants who have long suffered economic hardships. The pontiff visited The Shrine of Our Lady of Bonaria and celebrated an open-air Mass in Cagliari. During his homily the pope said, "Sardinia, this beautiful region of yours, has for a long time suffered from many situations of poverty, which is also accentuated by its geographical isolation. The loyal cooperation of everyone is necessary, with the commitment of the heads of institutions — including the Church — to secure fundamental rights to persons and families and make a more fraternal and solidary society grow; to secure the right to work, the right to provide bread for your family, bread earned by work!"

He went on to encourage the Sardinians in their struggles and urged them not to give up hope.

Pope Francis had a special message for young Sardinians, telling them to trust in Christ. "Trust in Jesus," he said, "and when I say this, I want to be sincere and say to you: I do not come here to sell you an illusion. I come here to say: there is a Person who can carry you through: trust in Him!...When it seems that all is still and stagnant, when personal problems disturb us, social unease does not find the necessary solutions, we must not give up. The path is Jesus: let him embark with us and let us set out to sea with Him! Everything changes with Jesus."

Social Communications On Sept. 23, Pope Francis addressed the participants of the Plenary Assembly of the Pontifical Council for Social Communications, who had gathered in Rome to reflect on the theme: "The Internet and the Church." In speaking to Catholic communicators, the pontiff stressed the importance of using the resources of the Church to evangelize the digital continent and to foster for those in that forum an encounter with Christ. "In the last few decades," the pope said, "various means of communication have evolved significantly, but the Church's concern remains the same, taking on new forms and expressions...Do not be afraid to be this presence, expressing your Christian identity as you become citizens of this environment. A Church that follows this path learns how to walk with everybody!"

Benedict XVI and an Atheist Mathematician On Sept. 25, it was reported that Pope emeritus Benedict XVI had written Piergiorgio Odifreddi, a professor of mathematics at the University of Turin and an avowed atheist; excerpts were published in the Italian newspaper "*La Repubblica.*" The letter was a response to Odifreddi's 2011 book "*Caro Papa, ti scrivo*" ("Dear Pope, I am writing you") which was itself a reply to then Joseph Ratzinger's famous 1968 book "Introduction to Christianity." In the letter, the retired pope thanked Odifreddi "for having carefully attempted to engage my book and thus my faith," even though elements of the work left him perplexed because of "a certain aggressiveness and recklessness in argumentation."

The letter was especially significant because of Benedict's forceful rejection of Odifreddi's comments on the sexual abuse of minors by the clergy. "I have never tried to cover these things up," Benedict wrote. "That the power of evil should penetrate so deeply into the inner world of the faith is for us a painful fact (*una sofferenza*) that, on the one hand, we must endure, while, on the other hand, we must at the same time do all we can to see that these kinds of things do not happen again. It is no comfort to know that, according to sociological research, the percentage of priests guilty of these crimes is no higher than that in other similar professions." In addition, he rejected the biased perspective of the professor, adding, "If it is not right to be silent about evil in the Church, neither must one be silent about the bright trail of goodness and purity that the Christian faith has traced through the centuries."

Nevertheless, Benedict praised Odifreddi, writing, "I greatly appreciate the fact that you, through your engagement with my 'Introduction to Christianity,' sought such an open dialogue with the faith of the Catholic Church and that, despite all the differences in what is central, convergences are not lacking."

Blessed John XXIII and Blessed John Paul II to be Canonized On Sept. 30, it was announced that Pope Francis would preside over the canonizations of both Blessed John Paul II and Blessed John XXIII on Sunday, April 27, 2014, Divine Mercy Sunday, in Rome. The announcement confirmed what had been rumored, including the fact that possible plans for a canonization in the fall or winter would be put off until the spring to accommodate the travel of the several million expected pilgrims and that he had waived the requirement of a second miracle in the case of John XXIII. A second miracle had been confirmed for John Paul II, the miraculous healing of a Costa Rican woman.

GENERAL AUDIENCES
Sept. 4, 2013
Sept. 11, 2013, The Church is Our Mother
Sept. 18, 2013
Sept. 25, 2013

INTERNATIONAL
International Day of Charity On Sept. 5, the United Nations officially commemorated the anniversary of Bl. Mother Teresa of Calcutta by declaring Sept. 5 as the International Day of Charity. According to a communique issued by the UN, "On this International Day of Charity, the United Nations invites all Member States and all international and regional organizations, as well as civil society, including non-governmental organizations and individuals, to commemorate the day in an appropriate manner, by encouraging charity, including through education and public awareness-raising activities." Blessed Mother Teresa died on Sept. 5, 1997 and was beatified on Oct. 19, 2003 by St. John Paul II.

Cuban Bishops Pastoral Letter On Sept. 15, the bishops of Cuba issued a pastoral letter to the Cuban people, "*La Esperanza No Defrauda*," taking as its theme the virtue of hope and focusing on the importance of hope in the face of such tumultuous change in the island in the last 20 years. The document was released two decades after the famous pastoral letter from the bishops in 1993, "Love Hopes for Everything." The bishops of Cuba noted that, "although Cuba has changed in the last years and the present is not like the past years, a new generation of Cubans lives with the firm hope that the future be better than the present."

"One of Us" Campaign On Sept. 17, it was announced that the "One of Us Initiative" had secured more than 1.2 million signatures for their campaign seeking "juridical protection of the dignity, the right to life and of the integrity of every human being from conception in the areas of EU competence in which such protection is of particular importance." The 4th General Assembly of the European Citizen's Initiative made the announcement and called once again for the European Union to ban financing all activities that results in the destruction of human embryos.

Latin Bishops Meet in Rome On Sept. 17, the Conference of Latin Bishops in Arab Regions (CELRA) began their ordinary meeting in Rome, bringing together representatives of the Latin dioceses in the Middle East, Egypt, and Somalia. The bishops and representatives focused their agenda on the Year of Faith and the 50th Anniversary of the Second Vatican Council, but special attention was paid to the severe on-going crisis in the region — especially in Syria — and the flight of Christians from the Middle East.

British Confessions On Sept. 18, the Catholic Bishops' Conference of England and Wales released the results of a new survey that found a significant increase in the number of people going to confessions in Great Britain. According to the new survey, there has been an increase in the use of the sacrament of penance reported by 65% of all dioceses and archdioceses; the primary cause for the increase is said to be the influence of the 2010 papal visit by then Pope Benedict XVI and the current influence of Pope Francis. The campaign, The Light is ON for YOU promoting confession in pubs and shopping malls has been able to tap into the increase, and various dioceses have added the number of hours that confessions are available for the penitents.

NATIONAL

Bishops Oppose Military Intervention On Sept. 5, Card. Timothy Dolan of New York, president of the U.S. Conference of Catholic Bishops (USCCB), and Bp. Richard E. Pates of Des Moines, chairman of the USCCB Committee on International Justice and Peace, sent a letter to every member of Congress, urging them to resist military intervention in the Syrian civil war and to work instead for a negotiated settlement. The bishops wrote, "the conflict in Syria will only be resolved through a negotiated political settlement," while condemning the catastrophic loss of life, believed to number more than 100,000; more than two million have been forced to leave the country and perhaps as many as four million were driven from their homes. The bishops added, "Our focus is on the humanitarian catastrophe unfolding in Syria and on saving lives by ending the conflict, not fueling it...we ask the United States to work urgently and tirelessly with other governments to obtain a cease-fire, initiate serious negotiations, provide impartial humanitarian assistance, and encourage efforts to build an inclusive society in Syria that protects the rights of all its citizens, including Christians and other minorities."

Immigration Reform On Sept. 9, dioceses across the United States marked a day of raising public awareness about immigration and the need for authentic immigration reform. Abp. José Gomez of Los Angeles and chairman of the U.S. Conference of Catholic Bishops' Committee on Migration wrote, "Now is the time for Catholics to let their elected officials know that they support immigration reform. We are an immigrant Church and an immigrant nation. The Church has grown with the nation and since the beginning has helped integrate immigrants into our culture and economy...Right now, our immigration system is broken. As a result, families are being broken apart and millions of people, including children, are being hurt. We need immigration reform to help our nation live up to its beautiful promise of equality and dignity for all people."

Chinese-American Catholics On Sept. 13, Bp. Randolph Calvo, chairman of the Subcommittee on Asian and Pacific Island Affairs of the U.S. Conference of Catholic Bishops (USCCB) celebrated the 25th anniversary of the U.S. Catholic China Bureau Conference and the recent publication of the first parallel translation of the Old Testament in English and Chinese. He wrote, "These efforts show the continued growth and strengthening of the faith among Chinese Americans. It helps the Church around the world to understand the history and struggles of the Catholic Church in China...In the Year of Faith, our hope is to see a greater number of Chinese Catholics growing in their faith, teaching their children about Jesus and spreading the word of God." According to the 2010 U.S. Census, Chinese Americans are the largest Asian group in the U.S., although the number of Chinese Catholics remains small, estimated at close to 350,000.

HHS Mandate Fight On Sept. 17, Card. Timothy M. Dolan of New York and president of the U.S. Conference of Catholic Bishops' (USCCB) issued a statement reiterating the opposition of the bishops to the U.S. Department of Health and Human Services (HHS) mandate in the Affordable Care Act that requires employers to cover contraception, abortifacients, and sterilization in their insurance plans. He wrote, "We are united in our resolve to continue to defend our right to live by our faith, and our duty to serve the poor, heal the sick, keep our apostolates strong and faithful, and insure our people." He added that the so-called final rule still suffered from the same three basic problems: "Its narrow definition of 'religious employer' reduces religious freedom to the freedom of worship by dividing our community between houses of worship and ministries of service; Its second-class treatment of those great ministries — the so-called 'accommodation' — leaves them without adequate relief; Its failure to offer any relief to for-profit businesses run by so many of our faithful in the pews."

Conscience Protection On Sept. 27, Card. Seán O'Malley of Boston, chair of the USCCB Committee on Pro-Life Activities, and Abp. William Lori of Baltimore, head of the Ad Hoc Committee for Religious Liberty, sent a letter to the members of the U.S. Senate and House of Representatives calling on them to pass the Health Care Conscience Rights Act (H.R. 940/S. 1204). The prelates wrote: "Protection for conscience rights in health care is of especially great importance to the Catholic Church, which daily contributes to the welfare of U.S. society through schools, social services, hospitals and assisted living facilities. These institutions, which have been part of the Church's ministry since the earliest days of our country, arose from religious convictions. They should not be told by government to abandon or compromise those convictions in order to continue serving their own employees or the neediest Americans. Nor should individual Catholics or others be told they cannot legally purchase or provide health coverage unless they violate their conscience." Referring to the infamous HHS Mandate from the U.S. Department of Health and Human Services (HHS) that compels virtually all employers to include contraception, sterilization, and abortifacients in health plans, the bishops wrote, "The mandate includes drugs and devices that can act against a human life after fertilization, implicating our moral teaching on abortion as well as contraception. We make our plea as religious leaders who strongly support universal access to health care. Such access is threatened by Congress's continued failure to protect the right of conscience. Those who help provide health care, and those who need such care for themselves and their families, should not be forced to choose between preserving their religious and moral integrity and participating in our health care system."

OCTOBER 2013

VATICAN

"La Repubblica" On Oct. 1. The Italian newspaper *"La Repubblica"* published an interview with Pope Francis conducted by the paper's atheist co-founder, Eugenio Scalfari. Conducted in the Domus Sanctae Marthae, the pope's Vatican residence, the interview was wide-ranging and was the subject of considerable misrepresentations in the media, especially regarding the pontiff's views of proselytism and narcissism. The interview was also highlighted by the pope's exchange with the atheist editor on issues of belief and faith. [For more details, see under **Special Reports**.]

IOR Annual Budget On Oct. 1, the Holy See's Institute for Works of Religion (IOR) published its first ever annual budget report, the first in the Institute's 125 year history. The 100 page report provided business activities and financial statements for 2012 and the first 8 months of 2013 and represented the Vatican's effort to introduce transparency into the Holy See's entire financial system. In June 2013, Pope Francis established a Pontifical Commission to gather reliable information on the various activities of the IOR. According to the president of the IOR, Ernst von Freyburg, the report seeks to explain the mission, activities, corporate governance, and the ongoing reform program of the Institute.

International Day of Older Persons On Oct. 2, the Pontifical Council for Health Care Ministry issued a statement from its president, Abp. Zygmunt Zimowski, on the value of the life of the elderly. He wrote: "This international day constitutes an important occasion, destined to assume ever greater relevance, considering that there are estimated to be over 600 million older people in the world, and that the progressive ageing of the world population could, within a decade, bring this figure to over a billion elderly people. Therefore we are all called to collaborate everywhere, Christians and persons of good will, in the pursuit of a juster and more equitable society, enriched also by the effective participation of those who are at times considered 'not useful' or even as a 'burden,' but who may instead offer a contribution based on the experience and wisdom acquired throughout life... In many societies in so-called 'rich' countries, ensuring that the elderly are and remain 'co-protagonists' in social life means, in addition, facing the reality of increasing longevity, due to various factors including the growth of knowledge in medical and scientific fields. This longevity cannot, therefore, simply be a question of greater survival time, but should rather be accorded its due value in a respectful and appropriate manner, starting with the wishes and characteristics of the elderly and considering the context to which they belong."

Council of Cardinals On Oct. 3, it was reported that the Council of Cardinals meeting at the Vatican were focused chiefly on the reform of the Roman Curia and that they would be doing much more than merely revising or updating the apostolic constitution *"Pastor Bonus."* Rather, a thoroughgoing reform is needed extending across all of the dicasteries, including the Secretariat of State, with the potential innovations of a *Moderator Curiae* (Moderator of the Curia) and a far greater role for lay people in the central government of the Church.

Pope Francis in Assisi On Oct. 4, Pope Francis visited Assisi and met with the poor and the forgotten while calling on the faithful to emulate the example of St. Francis of Assisi. The pope regularly spoke off the cuff and touched on the image of the Church stripping herself of worldliness. He also visited the Seraphic Institute for Disabled Children in Assisi. [See also **Special Reports**.]

King Letsie III of Lesotho On Oct. 7, Pope Francis received King Letsie III of Lesotho, along with his wife, Queen Masenate Mohato Seeiso in the Vatican Apostolic Palace. The king and queen had subsequent meetings with Card. Tarcisio Bertone, Vatican Secretary of State, and Abp. Dominique Mamberti, Secretary for Relations with States. According to a communique released by the Holy See, the Holy Father and the King of Lesotho discussed the on-going collaboration between the State and the Church, most so regarding the importance of religious freedom. "Appreciation was expressed for the commitment of the Sovereign and the Government to prioritizing health care and education, and for the significant ecclesial contribution in the fields of charity, justice and peace."

Extraordinary Synod of Bishops On Oct. 8, Pope Francis announced that he would convoke an Extraordinary Synod of Bishops to be held from Oct. 5-18, 2014, at the Vatican. The synod would gather on the theme "The Pastoral Challenges of the Family in the Context of the Evangelization." In a press conference for the announcement, Fr. Federico Lombardi, S.J., head of the Holy See Press Office, said, "It is important that the Church move forward together as a community, in reflection and prayer, and decide on common pastoral orientations dealing with the most important aspects of our life together — particularly on the family — under the guidance of the Pope and the bishops. The convening of this Extraordinary Synod is a clear indication of this direction."

Catholicity On Oct. 9, Pope Francis used his ongoing Catechesis on the Creed during his weekly general audience to teach on the Catholicity of the Church. He taught: "The Church is Catholic because it is the space, the home in which the entire faith is announced, in which the salvation that is brought to us by Christ is offered to all. The Church allows us to encounter the mercy of God that transforms us because Jesus Christ is present in it, it gives the true confession of faith, the fullness of the sacramental life, the authenticity of the ordained ministry. In the Church, each one of us finds what is necessary to believe, to live as Christians, to become saints, to walk in every place and in every age."

New Vatican City Law On Oct. 9, the Pontifical Commission for Vatican City State passed a new law that enforces new measures for full financial transparency. Titled Law Number XVIII, it advances reforms begun under Pope Benedict XVI and continuing under Pope Francis. The law implements the rules enumerated by Pope Francis in a *motu proprio* released last August and that reaffirmed the Holy See's commitment to resisting money laundering and the international financing of terrorism; the foundation for the reforms were established by Pope Benedict in his own 2010 *motu proprio*.

Immaculate Heart of Mary On Oct. 13, Pope Francis celebrated the presence of the famed image of Our Lady of Fatima, that was brought to Rome from Portugal for the pope's consecration of the world to the Immaculate Heart of Mary. Francis carried out the consecration before a crowd of an estimated 200,000 pilgrims and began the ceremony with a Marian catechesis. The event was marked by vigils at 10 Marian Shrines worldwide, including Aparecida in Brazil and Luján in Argentina, Lourdes in France, Czestochowa in Poland and Banneux in Belgium, as well as shrines in Nazareth in Israel, Nairobi in Kenya, Akita in Japan, Vailankanny in India and Washington in the United States.

Knights of Columbus On Oct. 10, Pope Francis met with the Board of Directors of the Knights of Columbus during an audience at the Vatican Apostolic Palace. The Holy Father used the audience to thank the Knights for their prayers throughout his pontificate and for their support of the Holy See. The pope added, "This support finds particular expression in the Vicarius Christi Fund, which is an eloquent sign of your solidarity with the Successor of Peter in his concern for the universal Church, but it is also seen in the daily prayers, sacrifices and apostolic works of so many Knights in their local Councils, their parishes and their communities."

President of Croatia On Oct. 10, Pope Francis welcomed President Ivo Josipovic of Croatia to the Vatican Apostolic Palace; the president then met with Card. Tarcisio Bertone, the Vatican Secretary of State, and Abp. Dominique Mamberti, Secretary for Relations with States. A communique was issued by the Holy See Press Office after the meetings that stressed Croatia's Catholic tradition and the diplomatic relations that were "consolidated by four current Agreements promoting collaboration between the Church and the State for the common good of Croatian society." The communique added, "The Parties went on to express their satisfaction at the entry of Croatia into the European Union and several themes of common interest emerged. Mention was made of the challenges that the country must face during the current economic crisis, as well as the regional context, with special reference to the situation of Croatians in Bosnia and Herzegovina."

European Parliament President On Oct. 11, Pope Francis met with Martin Schulz, President of the European Parliament at the Vatican Apostolic Palace. The visit coincided with the publication of an essay written by him to commemorate the 25th anniversary of Blessed Pope John II's visit to the European Parliament 25 years ago. In the article, Schulz wrote, "Twenty-five years ago, on this same day, John Paul II delivered before the European Parliament meeting in Strasbourg an inspirational speech. Today, for the European Parliament, it would be a great honor to hear again the message of the Holy Father, his words of foresight, solidarity, and hope." In a press conference, Fr. Federico Lombardi, Vatican press spokesman said, that President Schulz had renewed an invitation to the Holy Father to speak to the European Parliament and that their discussions had covered a variety of topics, including poverty, immigration, youth unemployment, the "throwaway" culture and the economic crises in Europe and the world. After the audience, President Schulz issued his own statement: "Whether we look at the protection of refugees in the Mediterranean, the fight against poverty and social exclusion or improving the prospects of young people both within and outside the EU, these are subjects on which we share similar views and on which we can join forces."

Malnutrition is a Scandal On Oct. 16, Pope Francis marked World Food Day by sending a message to the United Nations Food and Agriculture Organization (FAO) that spoke of the crisis of hunger and malnutrition faced by so many around the world and terming it a scandal. He wrote: "It is a scandal that there is still hunger and malnutrition in the world. It is not just a question of responding to immediate emergencies, but of

addressing together, in all areas, a problem that challenges our personal and social conscience, to achieve a just and lasting solution."

President Mahmoud Abbas On Oct. 17, Pope Francis welcomed Mahmoud Abbas, President of the Palestinian Authority, at the Vatican. This was the first meeting between the two, and Abbas' delegation included the mayor of Bethlehem and the Palestinian ambassador in Italy. After the meeting with the Pope, President Abbas met with Abp. Dominique Mamberti, Vatican Secretary for Relations with States. In a notable exchange of gifts, the pontiff gave Abbas a pen, and Abbas said: "I hope to sign the peace treaty with Israel with this pen." The Holy Father replied by saying, "Soon, soon." The meeting was held in the Library in the Vatican. As for Abbas, he gave the pontiff a picture made up of four tiles with a drawing of Bethlehem, and the first Bible printed in Palestine. President Abbas also invited the Holy Father to the Holy Land.

Vatican Television Center On Oct. 18, Pope Francis sent a message to mark the 30th Anniversary of the Vatican Television Center (CTV). The message was sent to CTV director, Msgr. Dario Edoardo Viganò, and was read at a conference celebrating the founding of the television center. The pope wrote that the Center "contributes to bringing the Church closer to the world, bridging distances, taking the word of God to millions of Catholics, even to places where often professing one's faith is a courageous choice." Francis noted also that the founding coincided with another important date: the 50th anniversary of the decree of the Second Vatican Council, "*Inter Mirifica*," the conciliar document on Social Communications. He added, "During these decades technology has advanced at great speed, creating unexpected and interconnected networks. It is necessary to maintain the evangelical perspective in this type of 'global communication highway' in presenting events, your approach must be not worldly, but ecclesial...This requires a special responsibility, a great capacity for interpreting reality in a spiritual light. Effectively, the events in the life of the Church have a special character: they are governed by a logic that is not primarily that of, so to say, 'worldly' categories, and precisely for this reason it is not easy to interpret and communicate them to a broad and varied public...Thanks to the images [it transmits], CTV walks alongside the Pope in bringing Christ to the many forms of solitude of contemporary man, even reaching sophisticated technological peripheries. In this, your mission, it is important to remember that the Church is present in the world of communication, in all its varied expressions, first and foremost to lead people to the encounter with Jesus Christ."

New U.S. Ambassador On Oct. 21, Kenneth F. Hackett, the new U.S. Ambassador to the Holy See, formally presented his credentials to Pope Francis at the Vatican Apostolic Palace. Amb. Hackett was nominated to the post by President Barack Obama in June and had served as president of Catholic Relief Services (CRS) for 18 years. According to a statement issued by the U.S. Embassy to the Holy See, the new ambassador stressed to the pontiff the United States' commitment to engaging religious leaders in addressing "critical global issues." It added, "The Vatican and the Holy Father have the ability to influence world events in a positive way through the calling of faith and they will continue to be important partners in future collaboration. In my time at CRS, I had the personal joy of being involved in efforts to alleviate some of the conditions Pope Francis talks about — poverty, refugees, migration — and I believe there is much we can continue to do together to work further toward promoting human dignity."

Holy See and Hungary On Oct. 21, the Holy See and Hungary signed an agreement modifying the 1997 Concordat on the financing of the public service and religious activity in Hungary of the Catholic Church and several other financial issues The agreement was signed at the Hungarian parliament in Budapest by Abp. Alberto Bottari de Castello, apostolic nuncio to Hungary and deputy Prime Minister of Hungary Zsolt Semjén. The agreement modifies the existing concordat of 1997, in the context of new legislation linked to the Basic Law of Hungary, promulgated in 2011 that regulates financial issues pertaining the teaching of religion in schools, Catholic higher education institutions, the restoration and conservation of religious art and monuments and works of art owned by ecclesiastical bodies, as well as the disposition of taxes that are distributed to the Church.

President of Equatorial Guinea On Oct. 25, Pope Francis welcomed the president of the Republic of Equatorial Guinea, Teodoro Obiang Nguema Mbasogo, to the Vatican. The president later had a meeting with Abp. Dominique Mamberti, secretary for Relations with States. According to a communique issued by the Holy See, the meetings were cordial and covered a variety of issues, including the Church's contributions to the human, social and cultural development of Equatorial Guinea. The session with Abp. Mamberti also encompassed the exchange of instruments for the ratification of an agreement between the Holy See and the Republic of Equatorial Guinea for diplomatic relations between the Church and the State, signed in the city of Mongomo in 2012 that confirms the legal status of the Church and her Institutions and regularizes canonical marriage, places of worship, educational institutions and spiritual assistance to Catholics in hospitals and prisons.

Burmese Nobel Laureate On Oct. 29, Pope Francis received Aung San Suu Kyi, the Burmese Nobel Peace Laureate and famed dissident at the Vatican. The Nobel laureate was in the midst of a European visit and was made an honorary citizen of Rome. Fr. Federico Lombardi, S.J., director of the Holy See Press Office, spoke with journalists after the meeting, noting that there was "a great feeling of harmony and accord between the Holy Father and this symbolic figure of the Asian world."

General Audiences

Oct. 2, 2013
Oct. 9, 2013
Oct. 16, 2013
Oct. 23, 2013
Oct. 30, 2013

INTERNATIONAL

Estonia joins Bishops' Conferences On Oct. 3, the Council of European Bishops' Conferences (CCEE) plenary assembly approved the request from the bishops of Estonia that their episcopal conference be accepted as a member of the Council. With Estonia joining the council, the CCEE now includes the presidents of the 33 bishops' conferences of Europe; in addition there are the archbishop of Luxembourg, the archbishop of the Principality of Monaco, the Maronite Archbishop

of Cyprus, the Bishop of Chisinau (Moldova), the Eparchial Bishop of Mukachevo and the Apostolic Administrator of Estonia; the President of the Bishops' Conference of Kazakhstan and the Latin Patriarch of Jerusalem also participate.

Legion of Christ On Oct. 7, Card. Velasio De Paolis, pontifical delegate for the Legion of Christ and Regnum Christi, announced that an extraordinary general chapter for the Legion would be held in January, to be concluded at the end of February, with the task of continuing the reform of the Legion and Regnum Christi and to implement a new constitution. De Paolis was appointed pontifical delegate by Pope Benedict XVI in 2010 to oversee the complete reform of the Legion in the aftermath of the horrendous scandals involving its founder, Fr. Marcial Maciel. In a letter announcing the general chapter, Card. De Paolis wrote: "The moment has come to summon the Extraordinary General Chapter indicated by the Holy Father. I thought that it would be good to announce it on the day that the Church celebrates the memory of St. Francis of Assisi. Let us place this important event under the protection of the Poverello of Assisi. It comes at the conclusion of a long journey of spiritual renewal and effort revising the Constitutions... It is useful to remember that this Chapter's 'main tasks will be the election of a new Government for the Institute and the approval of the new Constitutions' (letter of His Holiness Pope Francis, June 19, 2013), which will have to be presented to the Holy Father. Other questions will be considered according to a list of issues approved by the chapter fathers themselves, in the degree to which there is time available."

Australian Reforms On Oct. 8, the bishops of Australia announced that they had approved a reform agenda for the handling of abuse cases involving clergy. The entire programs of reforms would be presented in the first half of 2014, and proposals included: appointing independent compensation commissioners to determine payments to victims; appointment of lay and independent experts to strengthen the Church's National Committee of Professional Standards; the introduction of an independent national board to develop and administer national child protection standards; providing more rigorous assessment, monitoring, auditing and enforcement of Toward Healing practices; and introducing greater transparency through public reporting by both the new national board and the Toward Healing process.

Crisis for Global Christians On Oct. 17, the UK office of Catholic Charity Aid to the Church in Need issued a report on the state of persecution of Christians in 30 countries around the world, including Afghanistan, China, Laos, Pakistan, Vietnam and Zimbabwe. Titled "Persecuted and Forgotten?," the report was issued at a meeting in the Houses of Parliament and documented the severe situation facing Christians and the departure of Christian communities from their native regions. According to the report, in two-thirds of the countries where persecution of Christians was most severe, the problems grew appreciably worse, and in the Middle East, the Christian population was in danger of extinction. It also documented attacks on churches, pressure to convert to Islam or abandon the faith, mob violence against Christian homes, the abduction and rape of Christian girls and anti-Christian propaganda in all phases of life. In addition, anti-Christian persecution is prevalent in other regions, such as North Korea and China.

Canadian Venerable On Oct. 18, it was announced that Marie-Élisabeth Turgeon, founder of the Sisters of Our Lady of the Holy Rosary (Congrégation des Sœurs du Saint-Rosaire) had been declared venerable, meaning that the Holy See had recognized her as having led a life of heroic virtue. Born in 1840 in Beaumont, south of Quebec City, she is the first person from the Archdiocese of Rimouski to receive the title venerable. She died in 1881. Her cause for canonization was introduced in the Archdiocese of Rimouski in 1989, and the decree opening the canonical inquiry was signed on Nov. 15, 1990.

Coptic Church Under Attack On Oct. 22, two masked gunmen on motorcycles attacked a wedding in the Coptic Orthodox Church of Our Lady in Hadra, Egypt, killing 4 and injuring 12 people. Among the dead was a 9-year-old child. The attack was part of a growing number of violent acts against Christians in Egypt since the fall of President Mohammed Morsi and the political defeat of the Muslim Brotherhood.

German Bishop Removed On Oct. 23, the Holy See Press Office issued a statement that Pope Francis had temporarily removed Bp. Franz-Peter Tebartz-van Elst of Limburg, pending an investigation into claims of excessive expenditures for his episcopal residence. Controversy had erupted when it was disclosed that the German bishop had spent around €31 million ($42 million) for the construction of a new residence and adjoining offices. It was also announced that a Commission has been set up by the German Episcopal Conference to investigate the entire affair and that during the period of inquiry, Rev. Wolfgang Rösch would serve as Vicar General.

Sisters Declared Venerable On Oct. 31, the Congregation for the Causes of Saints announced that several nuns, including the Irish founder of the Presentation Sisters, have been declared venerable. The announcement declared that Pope Francis had authorized the recognition of the heroic virtue for Honoria "Nano" Nagle (Joan of God, 1728-1784), as well as Celestina Bottego, foundress of the Xaverian Missionary Sisters of Mary (1895-1980), and Olga della Madre di Dio (born Olga Maria Fortunata Gugelmo), Italian professed nun of the Congregation of the Daughters of the Church (1910-1943). The decree also noted the recognition of the martyrdom of Anton Durcovici of Iai, Romania (1888-1951), who was martyred in Sighet prison, Bucharest, Romania.

NATIONAL

Colorado Bishops on Immigration On Oct. 1, Abp. Samuel J. Aquila of Denver and Bp. Michael J. Sheridan of Colorado Springs, and Apostolic Administrator of Pueblo, released a joint statement articulating a Catholic framework for the controversial debate on immigration reform. Titled "Immigration and Our Nation's Future," the letter is 3,000-words and discusses seven moral principles, based on Catholic social teaching, that should be used to inform the debate.

The bishops stressed that they were not in any way political or advocating any political party or position, rather, they sought to inform the discussion. "America," they wrote, "needs to reform its immigration laws across the board, but establishing the specifics of those new regulations is the job of lawmakers, not pastors…God is both infinitely just and merciful and the immigration situation America is facing requires the wise application of both justice and mercy." The seven principles were: The principle of the common good; the universal destination of the world's resources and the right to private property; the dignity and rights of all migrants should be respected and protected; the creation of nations and the right to control borders are legitimate; the right to emigrate and respect for local laws; refugees and asylum seekers should be afforded protection; and authentic integration of immigrants and the enforcement of laws.

Bishops Write on the Budget On Oct. 1, the bishops of three committees of the U.S. Conference of Catholic Bishops (USCCB) called on Congress to fulfill the basic role of government. The letters were sent to the House and Senate by Abp. José Gomez of Los Angeles (chair of the USCCB Committee on Migration), Bp. Stephen Blaire of Stockton (chairs the Committee on Domestic Justice and Human Development) and Bp. Richard Pates of Des Moines (chair of the Committee on International Justice and Peace), and declared: "In 2011, we welcomed bipartisan action which averted a federal government shutdown and the hardship that would have come with failure to reach agreement."

Parish Diversity Oct. 11 In a new report by the Center for Applied Research in the Apostolate (CARA), the diversity of parishes in the U.S. is increasingly diverse, with some 38% estimated to be multicultural. The report was commissioned by the Secretariat of Cultural Diversity in the Church of the U.S. Conference of Catholic Bishops (USCCB) and estimates there are approximately 6,700 multicultural parishes in the country, many located in the South and West. CARA found that multicultural parishes average 1,445 registered households, compared to 1,168 for parishes in general, and three in ten U.S. parishes (29 percent or 5,000) celebrate at least one Mass a month in a language other than English or Latin. Other findings included: approximately 42.5 million U.S. residents who self-identify as non-Hispanic white are Catholic; 29.7 million U.S. residents who self-identify as Hispanic or Latino are estimated to be Catholic; approximately 3.6 million U.S. residents who self-identify as Asian, Native Hawaiian, or Pacific Islander are estimated to be Catholic, representing about 20% of this race and ethnicity; approximately 2.9 million U.S. residents who self-identify as black, African American, African or Afro-Caribbean are estimated to be Catholic; and 535,500 U.S. residents who self-identify as American Indian or Alaskan Native are estimated to be Catholic.

NOVEMBER 2013

VATICAN

DVD on Eucharistic Adoration On Nov. 7, the Congregation for Divine Worship and the Discipline of the Sacraments announced that it would publish together with HM Television a new DVD to teach the importance of Eucharistic Adoration. The second on a series of four videos, the DVD is entitled: "From the Visible to the Invisible" and covers a variety of important aspects of Adoration. The program was supported by Cardinal Antonio Cañizares Llovera, Prefect of the Congregation for Divine Worship and the Discipline of the Sacraments, and stressed in an interview included in the DVD that, "A new evangelization implies bringing mankind to recognize God as God. Not just any god, but the God who has revealed Himself to us in the person of Jesus Christ, in the Incarnate Word, who has manifested the fullness of this revelation in His own death and resurrection. And to live this, one must live it in Adoration."

Church in the Republic of Chad On Nov. 7, it was announced that the Holy See and the Republic of Chad had signed an agreement delineating the legal status of the Catholic Church in Chad. The agreement was made in the country's capital city of Yamena and was signed on behalf of the Holy See by Abp. Jude Thaddeus Okolo, apostolic nuncio in Chad, and by Moussa Faki Mahamat, minister of Foreign Affairs and African Integration for the Republic of Chad. There are more than 900,000 Catholics living in Chad, some 10% of the country's population.

Costa Rican President On Nov. 8, Pope Francis welcomed the President of the Republic of Costa Rica, Laura Chinchilla Miranda, at the Apostolic Palace in the Vatican. Following the meeting, President Miranda had a session with Abp. Dominique Mamberti, secretary for Relations with States. According to a communique from the Vatican, the meeting between Miranda and Francis was very cordial, and the two discussed the pressing social issues that need collaboration between the Church and Costa Rica. Common attention was given to the defense of life and the protection of the environment. It added, "Particular attention was paid to the possibility of working towards a future Agreement between the Holy See and the Republic of Costa Rica in order to strengthen bilateral relations for the good and the development of the country. Finally, the focus turned to the regional situation and to certain international problems, emphasising the importance of commitment to peace-building."

"Latinitas" On Nov. 8, it was announced that the Holy See would launch a new journal, "*Latinitas*," dedicated to the language of Latin. The periodical would be published by the Pontifical Academy Latinitas, instituted by Pope Benedict XVI in 2012, and would have three sections: scientific ("*Historica et philologica*"); "*Humaniora*," dedicated to contemporary literature in Latin and "*Ars docendi*," issues of teaching classical languages and cultures, ranging from antiquity to the present day. The articles were to be published in Italian and other languages as well as Latin. There would also be a volume with an appendix in Latin with "*Breves de Academiae vita notitiae*," a summary of the activities of the academy, the "*Argumenta*," abstracts of the contributions to the journal and a practical "*Index universus*."

Appeal for Peace in Syria On Nov. 13, Pope Francis used the end of his general audience to make a renewed appeal for an end to the bloody strife in Syria. The pope declared, "It is with great sadness that I have learnt of the mortar attack two days ago in Damascus in which several children were killed on the way home from school, along with the driver of their bus. Other children were injured. Please, let us pray with all our strength that these tragedies may never again happen!"

President Giorgio Napolitano On Nov. 14, Pope Francis made his first official visit to the President of Italy, Giorgio Napolitano at the Quirinale Palace in Rome. The pontiff was accompanied by Abp. Dominique Mamberti, Secretary for Relations with States, Card. Agostino Vallini, Vicar General of His Holiness for the Diocese of Rome, and Abp. Adriano Bernardini, apostolic nuncio to Italy. Pope Francis gave Napolitano a gift of two bronze statues from Italian artist Guido Veroi. He said to the Italian president, "Already in these first eight months of my petrine service I have been able to experience from you, Mr. President, many gestures of attention. They are added to the many [gestures] that you have progressively manifested, during your first seven years, toward my predecessor Benedict XVI. To him, I wish to address in this time our thoughts and affection, recalling his visit to the Quirinale, where in that occasion he described as 'the symbolic home of all Italians.' Paying a visit to this place, so rich in symbols and history, ideally I would like to knock on the doors of each inhabitant of the country, when the roots of my earthly family lie, and offer the word of the Gospel, healing and always new, to all… The main task of the Church is to bear witness to God's mercy and to encourage a generous response of solidarity to open up a future of hope; because where hope grows, there is an increase in energy and commitment to the construction of a more human and just social and civil order, and new potential emerges for healthy and sustainable development."

"Hermeneutic of Continuity" On Nov. 15, Pope Francis sent a letter to Abp. Agostino Marchetto, a former Secretary of the Pontifical Council for the Pastoral Care of Migrants and Itinerant People and one of the Church's leading scholars on Vatican II, regarding his book, "The Second Vatican Ecumenical Council: A Counterpoint for the History of the Council." The work is considered one of the strongest arguments for the principle of interpreting the Council through the "hermeneutic of continuity and reform" against a "hermeneutic of rupture." The letter was originally sent on Oct. 7, 2013, but was made public in Nov. 12, to mark the public release of the work published by the Libreria Editrice Vaticana (LEV), entitled "Papal Primacy and Episcopate: From the First Millennium to the Second Ecumenical Vatican Council — Studies in Honor of Archbp. Agostino Marchetto." The Holy Father wrote in part, "Once I said to you, dear Msgr. Marchetto, and today I wish to repeat it, that I consider you the best interpreter of Vatican Council II. I know that it is a gift of God, but I also know that you have made it fructify."

Globalized Uniformity On Nov. 18, Pope Francis used his daily Mass at the Casa Santa Marta in the Vatican to decry the dangers of what he termed the "Spirit of Adolescent Progressivism" and the "globalization of hegemonic uniformity" that comes from the spirit of worldliness. The pope cited the failure of the people in the Old Testament to remain faithful to God and his Covenants: "They believe that to go forward in any type of choice was better than to remain in the habits of fidelity. This is called apostasy, adultery." This apostasy is a fruit of the devil, and the people are drawn to pagan practices which leads not to "the beautiful globalization of unity of all Nations, each one with their own customs, instead it is the globalization of hegemonic uniformity, it is the single thought. And this sole thought is the fruit of worldliness." This globalization happens today, and the pontiff noted, "Because the spirit of worldliness exists, even today it takes this desire to be progressive on the single thought. If one was found with the Book of the Covenant and if anyone obeyed that Law, the King's sentence would condemn him to death: and this we have read in the newspapers, this month. These people have negotiated the faithfulness to their Lord; these people, moved by the spirit of the world, have negotiated their own identity, they have negotiated their belonging to a people, a people that God loves so much, that God wants as His people."

Financial Information Authority On Nov. 18, Pope Francis approved a *motu proprio* giving formal structure to the Vatican's Financial Information Authority (FIA). In a communique released by the Holy See Press Office, the authority will work to strengthen the financial framework of the Vatican's finances and will strive to prevent illegal activities in finances. It added, "the Statutes distinguish the role and functions of the President, the Board of Directors and the Directorate, so as to ensure that the F.I.A. may fulfill even more adequately its institutional functions in full autonomy and independence and in a manner consistent with the institutional and legal framework of the Holy See and the Vatican City State. In addition, the new Statutes establish a specific office for prudential supervision, providing it with the necessary professional resources."

Patriarchs and Major Archbishops On Nov. 21, Pope Francis met with the Patriarchs and Major Archbishops of the Oriental Churches who were in Rome for the Plenary Assembly of the Congregation for the Eastern Churches. Speaking to the gathered leaders, the Holy Father declared, "You are 'watchful guardians of communion and servants of ecclesial unity.' This unity, which you are called to realize in your Churches, responding to the gift of the Spirit, finds its natural and full expression in 'indefectible union with the Bishop of Rome,' rooted in the ecclesiastica communio, which you received on the day after your election."

President Vladimir Putin On Nov. 25, Pope Francis welcomed Russian President Vladimir Putin to the Vatican Apostolic Palace; it was the first meeting between the Russian leader and the Holy Father. A communique released by the Holy See described the discussions as cordial and covering a wide variety of topics, including the strife in the Middle East, especially in Syria, as well as the letter sent by the pope to the participants of the G20 Summit in St. Petersburg. The communique added, "They underlined the urgent need to end the violence and to bring necessary humanitarian assistance to the population, as well as promoting concrete initiatives for a peaceful solution to the conflict, which privileges the path of negotiation and involves the various ethnic and religious components, recognizing their indispensable role in society." There was no announcement or expectation of a papal trip to Russia in the near future.

Closing the Year of Faith On Nov. 25, Pope Francis brought a close to the Year of Faith with a Mass in St. Peter's Square on the Solemnity of Christ the King. The Year of Faith was originally opened by Pope Benedict XVI, and Pope Francis expressed his thanks to the pope emeritus for the decision to hold the year. The Mass was also significant as it marked the first public display of a reliquary containing bone fragments of St. Peter taken from the tomb of Peter re-discovered in 1942 during excavations beneath St. Peter's Basilica.

"Evangelii Gaudium" On Nov. 26, Pope Francis officially promulgated his first apostolic exhortation, "*Evangelii Gaudium*" ("The Joy of the Gospel"), focusing on the New Evangelization and "the theme of the proclamation of the Gospel in the contemporary world." The exhortation develops the major themes presented by the bishops at last year's Synod on the New Evangelization, but it was written from the unique perspective of Pope Francis and reflected many of his key themes. [For details, see under **News in Depth**.]

"Year of Consecrated Life" On Nov. 29, Pope Francis announced that 2015 would be dedicated to Consecrated Life. The pontiff made the announcement during the 82nd General Assembly of the Union of Superior Generals. The pope said to the Superiors, "A radical approach is required of all Christians, but religious persons are called upon to follow the Lord in a special way: They are men and woman who can awaken the world."

General Audiences
Nov. 6, 2013
Nov. 13, 2013
Nov. 20, 2013
Nov. 27, 2013

INTERNATIONAL
Nunciature Attacked On Nov. 5, the apostolic nunciature in Damascus, Syria, was attacked when a single mortar was fired at the third floor. While casualties or injuries were reported, the attack highlighted the dangers faced by the Vatican diplomats in the Middle East, in particular in the wake of the decision by the nuncio, Abp. Mario Zenari to remain in service in the midst of the civil war raging in the country

Massacre of Syrian Christians On Nov. 5, the town of Sadad, Syria, suffered a bloody massacre of Christians, the worst loss of life since the start of the Syrian civil war. Syriac Orthodox Metropolitan of Homs and Hama, Abp. Selwanos Boutros Alnemeh decried the attack by Islamic gunmen that left 45 civilians dead, including several women and children. The gunmen also held some 1,500 families hostages while many more Christians fled for their lives. Churches and homes were damaged.

European Bishops On Nov. 7, the members of the Council of European Bishops completed their meeting in Trieste, Italy, and stressed the need for evangelization. A statement issued by the bishops stressed that as "charity is a constitutive part and a response of faith of every Christian, it needs the community so as not to lose its ecclesial character. Nor is it possible to think of charity as an activity of the Church entrusted to a specific structure. The local parishes, in fact, testify to a great diversity and models which respond to the needs of the reality in which they find themselves. At the same time, the bishop is always more conscious of his role in guiding, governing and controlling his charitable bodies."

Israeli Demolition On Nov. 6, Patriarch Fouad Twal, the Latin Patriarch of Jerusalem, protested Israel's demolition of a Church-owned property in East Jerusalem, calling it a breach of international law and an act of vandalism. The property belonged to a Muslim family, and it was bulldozed by Israeli security forces; the family was left homeless. The patriarch noted that it was owned by the patriarchate and that no word had been given by authorities prior to the demolition. The event was significant as it marked the first time that the Israeli government had demolished property belonging to the Church.

One of Us Campaign On Nov. 8, it was announced that the European Citizen Initiative One of Us had drawn to a close after securing 1.8 million signatures, making it the greatest success for the Pro-Life effort to date and that 20 countries had secured the minimum number of signatures required by the European Commission for a formal protest of the EU policy of destroying human embryos. The Initiative One of Us sought to reaffirm the status of the human embryo as "One of Us." It declared: "No budget allocation will be made for the funding of activities that destroys human embryos, or that presumes their destruction." The European Commission would be compelled to adopt a formal response, although it is under no legal obligation to propose legislation.

Angola Bishops On Nov. 8, the plenary assembly of the Bishops Conference of Angola and São Tomé (CEAST) completed its work and issued a statement in defense of life as sacred "from conception" because and against the dangers of abortion for the region. In a pastoral message issued at the end of the plenary assembly, the bishops declared about life, "no human being can claim the right to suppress it under any pretext...parents, friends, educators and health care operators should not recommend or facilitate abortion...they should encourage the acceptance of a new life, regardless of the circumstances in which it was conceived." The bishops added: "abortion is a disregard for the fundamental values of Angolan society...Possible decriminalization of abortion would be a real attack on national security and to our survival as a people. In fact, as experts of population policy say, "procreation determines the future of nations. We remind everyone that Angola has been a Christian country for centuries. Therefore, it is expected that Parliament, elected by a large majority of Christians and mainly composed of believers, fulfil the duty to respect the wishes of their voters."

Ukrainian Anniversary On Nov. 8, the clergy of the Ukrainian Greek Catholic Church (UGCC) and the Ukrainian Orthodox Church-Kyivan Patriarchate (UOC-KP) issued a joint appeal to the faithful of Ukraine to mark the 80th anniversary of the infamous Holodomor, the deliberate famine caused by Josef Stalin and the communist regime then in power. The famine killed millions, and the Ukrainian clergy called on all believers to pray for those who died.

Syrian Children Killed On Nov. 13, five children were killed in a mortar attack on a Christian primary school in Damascus; the attack also wounded 27 others. The St. John Damascene primary school in the district of Al-Qassaa in Damascus, was bombarded by mortar rounds, part of an escalating series of attacks on the Christians in Syria in the midst of the bloody civil war. The apostolic nuncio was attacked by a mortar on Nov. 5.

Belgian Euthanasia On Nov. 13, leaders of the Christian, Muslim and Jewish communities in Belgium issued a joint communique opposing the legalization of euthanasia for minors suffering from incurable diseases. The statement declared, "Euthanasia of the most fragile persons is inhuman and destroys the foundations of our society. It is a denial of the dignity of these persons and leaves them to the judgment, that is, the arbitrariness of the one who decides. The issue of euthanizing children has been debated in the Senate for several years in Belgium, advancing the agenda of euthanizing the elderly or emancipated minors (beginning at 15) that was approved in 2002. The parameters for such acts range from a prognosis of irreversible sickness, "unbearable" physical or psychic suffering or a grave incurable sickness. In Europe, euthanasia is currently legal in Belgium, Holland, Luxembourg and Switzerland.

Typhoon Yolanda On Nov. 15, Card. Luis Antonio Tagle, Archbishop of Manila, called for a day of prayer and fasting for the victims of Hurricane Yolanda that made landfall in the Philippines on Nov. 8 and caused severe damage because of its 195 mph winds. The typhoon was one of the most severe on record, and Card. Tagle sought to draw attention to the material and also the spiritual toll of the disaster. Called a "Day of Lament and Hope: Solidarity in Prayer," the day was intended to be one praying and standing in solidarity with those "who are suffering, grieving and confused because of the successive calamities that affected the country." Card. Tagle led a prayer service in the parish of San Fernando de Dialo in Manila.

Bombing in Beirut On Nov. 19, more than 20 people were killed and nearly 150 wounded in south Beirut when an apparent suicide bomber set off an explosion that was then followed by a car bomb. The bombing took place near the Iranian Embassy in Beirut, and among the victims was the cultural attaché of the Iranian Embassy. The entire region has experienced a severe increase in violence in the last several years.

NATIONAL

Special Olympics On Nov. 7, Catholic Relief Services (CRS), the charity organization of the U.S. Bishops' Conference announced that it would be partnering with the Special Olympics International to expand services for those with intellectual disabilities in developing countries. The new partnership was marked officially at CRS' world headquarters in Baltimore, and the chairman of Special Olympics, Timothy Shriver, said of the children who will be helped, "They and their families have not been adequately or proportionately represented in development strategies, interventions, funding or goals. This partnership will help address that urgent need."

U.S. Bishops on Employment On Nov. 4, Bp. Stephen Blaire of Stockton, chairman of the U.S. Conference of Catholic Bishops' Committee on Domestic Justice and Human Development; Abp. Salvatore Cordileone of San Francisco, chairman of the USCCB Subcommittee for the Promotion and Defense of Marriage, and Abp. William Lori of Baltimore, chairman of the USCCB Ad

Hoc Committee for Religious Liberty issued a letter to the U.S. Senate discussing the reasons why the Bishops' Conference were opposed to the Employment Non-Discrimination Act of 2013 (ENDA). In the letter, the bishops declared, "Work is fundamental to that dignity." They added that "the Catholic Church has consistently stood with workers in this country and continues to oppose unjust discrimination in the workplace. No one should be an object of scorn, hatred, or violence for any reason, including his or her sexual inclinations."

The bishops' letter added that ENDA goes beyond prohibiting unjust discrimination and poses several problems. It notes, for example, that the bill: (1) lacks an exception for a "bona fide occupational qualification," which exists for every other category of discrimination under Title VII of the Civil Rights Act, except for race; (2) lacks a distinction between homosexual inclination and conduct, thus affirming and protecting extramarital sexual conduct; (3) supports the redefinition of marriage, as state-level laws like ENDA have been invoked in state court decisions finding marriage discriminatory or irrational; (4) rejects the biological basis of gender by defining "gender identity" as something people may choose at variance with their biological sex; and (5) threatens religious liberty by punishing as discrimination the religious or moral disapproval of same-sex sexual conduct, while protecting only some religious employers.

Illinois Same-Sex "Marriage" On Nov. 6, Illinois became the 15th U.S. state to legalize same-sex "marriage," when the State House approved legislation with a vote of 61-54. Illinois governor, Pat Quinn, promised to sign the legislation. In response to the legislation, the Illinois Catholic Conference issued a statement that said the "decision by Illinois lawmakers to change the definition of marriage not only goes against the common consensus of the human race — which understands that nature tells us that marriage is the union of one man and one woman — but it also undermines an institution that is the cornerstone of a healthy society. The optimal condition in which to raise children is a home that includes both a mother and father, since women and men are not interchangeable."

Nuncio Addresses the Bishops On Nov. 11, Abp. Carlo Maria Viganó, the apostolic nuncio to the United States, addressed the U.S. Conference of Catholic Bishops (USCCB) at the start of their Fall General Assembly in Baltimore, Maryland. In his remarks, the nuncio said, "I urge you, my brothers, to preserve a spirit of real unity among yourselves and, of course, with the successor of Peter, trusting in the way he sees best to live out his mission to mankind. Unity expressed in a real, prayer-filled communion of mind and heart is the only way we will remain strong and be able to face whatever the future may hold for us." He also encouraged the USCCB to be genuine in their witness of divine love. [For the text of the address, see under the USCCB coverage in **News in Depth.**

U.S. Bishops' President On Nov. 12, Abp. Joseph Kurtz of Louisville, was elected president of the U.S. Conference of Catholic Bishops (USCCB)

during the bishops' annual fall General Assembly, in Baltimore, Maryland. Kurtz had served as vice president of USCCB since 2010, during the tenure of Card. Timothy Dolan as president. Card. Daniel DiNardo of Galveston-Houston was elected USCCB vice president. Abp. Kurtz was elected president on the first ballot with 125 votes, while Card. DiNardo was elected vice president on the third ballot by 147-87 in a runoff vote against Abp. Charles Chaput of Philadelphia. Other chairmen were elected for a variety of other committees.

Liturgical Votes On Nov. 12, the U.S. Conference of Catholic Bishops (USCCB) approved five liturgical issues presented by the Committee on Divine Worship during the annual Fall General Assembly in Baltimore, Maryland. The approved topics included the use of the Mexican missal to draft the U.S. Spanish-language missal with appropriate adaptations, adaptations to the marriage ceremony and proposed English-language translations of the Order of Celebrating Marriage and the Order of Confirmation. The bishops approved the Order of Celebrating Marriage, and the final translation from the International Committee on English in the Liturgy (ICEL), includes some prayers and rites not previously included in the first edition and also four adaptations to the Order of Celebrating Marriage, including the option of an alternative forms of vows (already an option in the current Rite), the option of moving the Nuptial Blessing to follow the Prayer of the Faithful during Mass, the option to include a Litany of the Saints (including the invocation of many married saints) at the beginning of the Marriage Rite and translating into English the Hispanic cultural adaptations of the Exchange of Coins and the Blessing and Placing of the Lazo or Veil over the couple during the nuptial blessing.

Marriage in Hawaii On Nov. 15, Hawaii became the next U.S. state to have its legislature approve legislation for same-sex marriage. The law was then signed by the governor. Abp. Salvatore Cordileone of San Francisco, chairman of the U.S. Bishops' Subcommittee for the Promotion and Defense of Marriage, responded to the news by issuing a statement that saidn, in part, "The decision in Hawaii is disappointing and shows the need for rebuilding a culture of the family in our country. Changing the meaning of marriage in the law does not promote the common good or protect authentic rights.

HHS Mandate On Nov. 26, the U.S. Supreme Court agreed to hear two cases challenging the federal government's HHS mandate that forces religious employers to provide insurance that covers abortion-inducing drugs, sterilizations and contraception. The two cases were *Sebelius v. Hobby Lobby Stores, Inc.* (10th Circuit Court of Appeals) and *Conestoga Wood Specialties v. Sebelius* (3rd Circuit Court of Appeals). The two circuit courts reached different verdicts on the question of whether for-profit secular corporations possess free exercise rights and could therefore be exempted from the mandate. The case was eventually decided in June 2014 by the Supreme Court in favor of the plaintiffs.

DECEMBER 2013

VATICAN

King Abdullah II On Dec. 3, King Abdullah II of Jordan received Abp. Dominique Mamberti, Vatican Secretary for Relations with States in Amman. The meeting was intended to foster further good relations between Jordan and the Holy See. A communique after the meeting declared, "The meeting also touched on efforts to achieve peace between the Palestinians and Israelis based on the two-state solution which would see an independent Palestinian state established on Palestinian national soil with East Jerusalem its capital living in peace and security alongside Israel."

Council of Cardinals On Dec. 3, the Council of Cardinals appointed by Pope Francis in September to assist the reform of the Roman Curia began its second set of meetings in the Vatican. The eight members began their session by concelebrating the Holy Father's daily Mass at Casa Santa Marta. According to Fr. Federico Lombardi, S.J., director of the Holy See Press Office, the Cardinals continued their initial work by examining the Congregation for Divine Worship and the Discipline of Sacraments. It was also revealed that the Cardinals will likely not propose a mere revision of the Apostolic Constitution *"Pastor Bonus"* of Pope St. John Paul II but a brand new apostolic constitution.

Nativity Scene On Dec. 4, it was reported that a Neapolitan nativity scene and a Christmas tree from Bavaria, Germany, would be used to decorate St. Peter's Square for the Christmas season. The nativity scene was created in the workshop of "Cantone & Costabile." The scene had the title of "Francis 1223–Francis 2013" and was given to Card. Crescenzio Sepe, Abp. of Naples, who then offered it to Pope Francis. The Christmas tree was from Bavaria, and was a gift from the community of Waldmünchen.

Commission for Protection of Minors On Dec. 5, Pope Francis announced the formal creation of a special commission for the protection of children. Established at the urging of the eight-member Council of Cardinals, especially one of its members, Card. Sean O'Malley, the commission would have the task of advising Pope Francis on the Holy See's commitment to the protection of children and in pastoral care for victims of abuse. Card. O'Malley in a press conference added, the commission would also help formulate new initiatives and would work with episcopal conferences and religious congregations. The commission was subsequently given its membership in March. [For other details, see under **News in Depth**.]

Nelson Mandela On Dec. 6, Pope Francis sent a telegram to Pres. Jacob Zuma of South Africa in which he expressed his condolences at the passing of former Pres. Nelson Mandela who died at the age of 95. The pontiff wrote, "It was with sadness that I learned of the death of former President Nelson Mandela, and I send prayerful condolences to all the Mandela family, to the members of the government and to all the people of South Africa."

Christ in the Digital Age On Dec. 9, Pope Francis gave an address to the plenary assembly of the Pontifical Council for the Laity under the theme "Proclaiming Christ in the Digital Era." The pope said, "Faced with philosophies of great depth and an educational method of exceptional value, but infused with pagan elements, the Fathers did not shy away from comparison, nor did they compromise with any ideas contrary to their faith. Instead, they were able to recognize and assimilate the most elevated concepts, transforming them from within in the light of the Word of God. They implemented St. Paul's call to 'test everything, hold on to the good.'"

President Denis Sassou N'Guesso On Dec. 9, Pope Francis welcomed Pres. Denis Sassou N'Guesso of the Republic of Congo to the Vatican Apostolic Palace. The president went on to meet with Abp. Pietro Parolin, Vatican Secretary of State. In a communique issued by the Holy See, the pope and president discussed the role of the Church in the country, humanitarian situations, and mutual concern regarding the rise of tensions in the face of fundamentalism.

Statue of the Immaculate Conception On Dec. 9, Pope Francis made his sixth visit to the Basilica of St. Mary Major in Rome since his election in March. The pontiff commemorated the Feast of the Immaculate Conception by venerating a statue of the Blessed Mother that is found in the Piazza di Spagna and that was consecrated in 1857. The Holy Father declared in his prayer, "Holy and Immaculate Virgin, to You, the honor of our people and caring guardian of our city, we turn with confidence and love...Awaken in us all a renewed desire for holiness: in our word shine forth the splendor of truth, in our works resound the hymn of charity, in our body and in our hearts dwell purity and chastity, in our life may the beauty of the Gospel always be present."

Moneyval Report On Dec. 10, Moneyval, the body that assesses the work of European member States in respecting anti-money laundering laws and guidelines gave its approval to the report issued by the Vatican City State with updates on the steps taken to combat terrorism financing and money laundering. In a communique, Msgr. Antoine Camilleri, Under Secretary for Relations with States, and Head of the Delegation of the Holy See and Vatican City State to Moneyval, stated in a communique, "The adoption of the Progress Report confirms the significant efforts undertaken by the Holy See and the Vatican City State to strengthen its legal and institutional framework. The Holy See is fully committed to continuing to improve further the effective implementation of all necessary measures to build a well functioning and sustainable system aimed at preventing and fighting financial crimes."

"Person of the Year 2013" On Dec. 11, "TIME" magazine announced that it had named Pope Francis "Person of the Year." The magazine declared that it had chosen to honor the pontiff because of his extraordinary humility and compassion, adding, "In a very short time, a vast, global, ecumenical audience has shown a hunger to follow him. For pulling the papacy out of the palace and into the streets, for committing the world's largest faith to confronting its deepest needs and for balancing judgment with mercy, Pope Francis is TIME's 2013 Person of the Year." Fr. Federico Lombardi, S.J., Vatican spokesman, said "It is a positive sign that one of the most prestigious acknowledgements in the field of the international press has been attributed to one who proclaims spiritual, religious and moral values in the world, and who speaks effectively in favor of peace and greater justice."

Human Trafficking On Dec. 12, Pope Francis met with 16 new non-resident ambassadors and one diplomatic representative who presented their credential letters at the Vatican Apostolic Palace and condemned human trafficking as "a crime against humanity." The pontiff added that human trafficking, "affects the most vulnerable people in society: women, children, the disabled, the poorest and those who come from situations of family or social disintegration…This cannot continue. It constitutes a grave violation of the human rights of the victims and an offense to their dignity, as well as a defeat for the global community. All persons of good will, whether they profess a religion or not, cannot allow these women, these men and these children to be treated as objects, deceived, violated, often repeatedly sold, for various purposes, and at the end either killed or ruined physically and mentally, to end up discarded and abandoned. It is shameful."

Christmas Tree On Dec. 13, Pope Francis met with a group of Bavarian pilgrims who had made the journey to Rome for the lighting of the Christmas tree in St. Peter's Square. The tree was given to the Holy See by Vatican by the Bavarian town of Waldmünchen. The pontiff thanked them for the gift and used the encounter to speak of Christmas. "Even today," he said, "Jesus continues to dispel the darkness of error and sin, to bring humanity the joy of the blazing light of God, of which the Christmas tree is a sign and reminder. Let us be wrapped by the light of His truth, because 'the joy of the Gospel fills the hearts and the lives of all who encounter Jesus.'"

Curia Officials and Confession On Dec. 16, it was reported that Pope Francis had given his personal directive to the cardinals and archbishops heading the dicasteries of the Roman Curia to assist every day in hearing confessions at Santo Spirito in Sassia, a church near the Vatican. The church, right off of the Via della Conciliazione and near the Borgo Santo Spirito, was dedicated to the Divine Mercy devotion.

"La Stampa" Interview On Dec. 16, the Italian newspaper, La Stampa, published a wide ranging interview with Pope Francis, including the Christmas season, plan for a visit to the Holy Land, and the idea that his teachings have caused some to question whether he is a "Marxist." The interview was conducted by the veteran Vaticanista, Andrea Tornielli. The pontiff described Christmas as a time of tenderness. "When Christians forget about hope and tenderness," he said, "they become a cold Church, that loses its sense of direction and is held back by ideologies and worldly attitudes, whereas God's simplicity tells you: go forward, I

am a Father who caresses you." He added, "The Bible clearly shows that God's main virtue is that He is love. He waits for us; he never tires of waiting for us. He gives us the gift and then waits for us. This happens in the life of each and every one of us. There are those who ignore him. But God is patient and the peace and serenity of Christmas Eve is a reflection of God's patience toward us." Francis also noted a possible trip to the Holy Land, noting his desire to meet with Bartholomew, Patriarch of Constantinople, and to commemorate this 50th anniversary of the historic meeting between Pope Paul VI and Athenagoras in Jerusalem in 1964.

Birthday Gift On Dec. 18, Pope Francis' favorite soccer team from Argentina visited the Vatican. The team from Buenos Aires, San Lorenzo de Almagro, presented the pontiff with a replica of the Inicial Championship Cup and jersey at the end of the pope's weekly general audience. San Lorenzo won the cup this year, the first time since 2007. When he served in Argentina, Cardinal Bergoglio was an avid fan of the team, served as its chaplain, and held the membership card no. 88235N-0. The gifts were presented by the club's vice-president, Marcelo Tinelli, to mark Francis' 77th birthday on Dec. 17. The team was founded by a Salesian priest, Fr. Lorenzo Massa, who started a team in the poor section of the Almagro quarter, and young Jorge Bergoglio went to their games frequently. As a priest, he regularly said Mass for the squad. Pope Francis said to the team, "I especially greet the San Lorenzo football team, who won the Championship last Sunday and have brought the Cup here. Thank you very much."

Christmas Visit On Dec. 23, Pope Francis paid a visit to Pope Emeritus Benedict XVI at the former pope's residence at the Mater Ecclesiae Monastery in Vatican City. According to a statement issued by the Holy See Press Office, the pontiff visited Benedict to extend his Christmas greetings. The communique added, "After a brief prayer together in the Chapel, they met for a private meeting that lasted roughly 30 minutes in a room in the residence." Francis also met with the members of the Pope Emeritus' household, including Abp. Georg Gänswein, prefect of the Papal Household and personal secretary of Benedict XVI and the Memores Domini, lay members of the lay ecclesial movement of Communion and Liberation who care for the Pope Emeritus' household.

Midnight Mass On Dec. 24, Pope Francis celebrated the Solemnity of the Nativity of the Lord with a Mass in the Vatican Basilica. He used his homily to speak about the passage in Isaiah (9:1): "The people who walked in darkness have seen a great light." He used the passage to contrast the light and dark in our own lives, teaching, "In our personal history too, there are both bright and dark moments, lights and shadows. If we love God and our brothers and sisters, we walk in the light; but if our heart is closed, if we are dominated by pride, deceit, self-seeking, then darkness falls within us and around us. "Whoever hates his brother — writes the Apostle John — is in the darkness; he walks in the darkness, and does not know the way to go, because the darkness has blinded his eyes"

(1 Jn 2:11). A people who walk, but as a pilgrim people who do not want to go astray."

Urbi et Orbi On Dec. 25, Pope Francis delivered the traditional *Urbi et Orbi* address for Christmas Day in St. Peter's Square. The pontiff spoke of "the song of the angels," imploring, "I ask everyone to share in this song: it is a song for every man or woman who keeps watch through the night, who hopes for a better world, who cares for others while humbly seeking to do his or her duty." He then spoke of authentic peace that can be achieved through "the Child in the manger, Child of peace, our thoughts turn to those children who are the most vulnerable victims of wars, but we think too of the elderly, to battered women, to the sick... Wars shatter and hurt so many lives!

"Too many lives have been shattered in recent times by the conflict in Syria, fueling hatred and vengeance. Let us continue to ask the Lord to spare the beloved Syrian people further suffering, and to enable the parties in conflict to put an end to all violence and guarantee access to humanitarian aid. We have seen how powerful prayer is! And I am happy today too, that the followers of different religious confessions are joining us in our prayer for peace in Syria. Let us never lose the courage of prayer! The courage to say: Lord, grant your peace to Syria and to the whole world. And I also invite non-believers to desire peace with that yearning that makes the heart grow: all united, either by prayer or by desire. But all of us, for peace."

General Audiences
Dec. 4, 2013
Dec. 11, 2013
Dec. 18, 2013

INTERNATIONAL
Secular Intolerance On Dec. 3, a report was released by the Observatory on Intolerance and Discrimination Against Christians in Europe that documented the increasing secular intolerance in Europe. Dr. Martin Kugler, a member of the Observatory, declared in a press release that in 2010, 84 percent of secular attacks in France were against Christian sites. The center also detailed that there are currently 41 laws impacting Christian practice found in Western Europe and that the restrictions ranged from freedom of conscience, freedom of expression, freedom of assembly to parental rights and discriminatory equality policies.

Dutch Churches On Dec. 3, a report on the future of churches in the Netherlands painted a distressing picture. The "Future of Religious Heritage" details that an estimated 600-700 churches in the Netherlands will be decommissioned by 2018, a reality caused by declining numbers of worshippers and calls on concerned people of all faiths to work together to preserve the structures, part of the need to preserve religious sites across Europe.

Zimbabwe Reforms On Dec. 3, the bishops of Zimbabwe, in cooperation with the members of the Society of Jesus in the country made a public appeal for genuine reform in the country. The plea was made in a pastoral letter that decried the absence of real change in the wake of the recent elections and lamented that "there are no visible prospects for improvement in the spheres of life in Zimbabwe that cry for restoration to give people hope for a better life." The country suffers from endemic poverty and political corruption.

Belgian Euthanasia On Dec. 3, the Belgian Senate's Justice and Social Affairs Committee approved a draft bill that would permit euthanasia for children. The decision meant that the whole Belgian Parliament would be able to vote on the bill which was expected to pass. The proposed legislation permitted would allow the euthanasia of terminally-ill minors under the pretext that they can decide for themselves and that they are in "unbearable pain." Their parents' approval would also be required.

Legion of Christ On Dec. 5, the Legion of Christ issued a letter from Fr. Sylvester Heereman L.C., the Legion's acting general director, to all members that restated and reiterated the commitment of the Legion to prevent and resist the evils of sexual abuse. The communication included a report on the failures of the Legion to deal in the past and what the Legion is doing to deal with current cases. Fr. Heereman wrote, "When we confront the reality of sexual abuse, it is helpful to keep certain complementary values in mind: compassion and solidarity with the victims, the responsibility to protect people who are under our pastoral care, the right of the accused to a due process, the promotion and defense of justice, and — keeping in mind that sexual abuse is a behavior that will never be tolerated — mercy and support of our brothers who are guilty of this crime."

Fr. Heereman likewise gave an accounting of the work of the Outreach Commission that had been established to care for the victims of the late founder Fr. Marcial Maciel as well as a an assessment of the way the allegations had been handled in the past. The report found that of the 35 Legion priests had been accused of sexual abuse of minors, 14 were acquitted, 9 were found guilty (including the founder), 2 were ineligible for canonical investigation when the allegation was presented, 10 were still under review; of the 6 superiors (including the founder) accused of sexually abusing adults under their authority, 3 were acquitted (imprudent behavior, not crimes; 1 freely accepted restrictions on ministry as a precaution), 3 were found guilty, including the founder. In all, less than 1% of the 1,133 priests ordained in the history of the Legion have been found guilty of sexual abuse, and less than 4% of Legionary priests have been accused of sexual misconduct.

Irish Embassy On Dec. 5, the Irish government announced its intention to reopen its embassy to the Holy See, although it was likely that such a move would likely comprise the use of the Irish Embassy to Italy serving also as the location for the embassy to the Holy See. A similar structure is used by several other governments, including the United Kingdom, Israel, and the Netherlands. The government closed the embassy in 2011 as part of its wider criticism of the Holy See and the Church and was vehemently opposed by many in the country and sparked a campaign called "Ireland Stand Up" to reopen the longstanding diplomatic post. The move was also seen as an effort of the government to circumvent Church opposition to its extreme decisions to relax abortion laws and call for a referendum on same-sex "marriage."

Irish Sex Abuse Progress On Dec. 10, the Fourth Tranche of the Reviews of Safeguarding practices undertaken by the Church in Ireland was released, and the report found that considerable progress had been made in numerous dioceses, including the Archdioceses of Armagh, and Cashel & Emly. The report also found progress, with a few exceptions, in the implementation of norms and safeguards

Lebanese Nuns Kidnapped On Dec. 10, it was announced that the government of Lebanon was working to secure the release of a group of Orthodox nuns who were apparently kidnapped by Islamist insurgents in the Syrian town of Maaloula. The Lebanese government was being represented by the head of its security ministry, General Abbas Ibrahim, who was also working to secure the release of Orthodox bishops Boulos Yazigi and Youhanna Ibrahim who were abducted in April. An additional appeal for the nuns' release was made by the United Nations Secretary General Ban Ki-Moon that said, in part, "The Secretary-General joins in the appeals for their safety and well-being, and that of all persons who may be detained against their will in Syria." Pope Francis also made a call for their release during his general audience on Dec. 4.

Ukrainian Unrest On Dec. 11, Major Abp. Sviatoslav Shevchuk, abp. of Kiev and the members of the permanent synod of the Ukrainian Greek-Catholic Church condemned police actions against protesters in Kiev's "Independence Square," and "the action directed towards restricting civil liberties, especially the freedom of expression and peaceful civic manifestation of the citizens of Ukraine." The members also rejected all violence in the on-going civil strife in the country. The upheaval led to a massive protest in Independence Square in Kiev, including night-time protests, during which police and interior ministry special forces launched an attack on the protesters.

Latin Patriarch On Dec. 19, the Latin Patriarch of Jerusalem, Abp. Fouad Twal, issued his annual Christmas Message in which he reminded the faithful not to forget the agony occurring in Syria; he also confirmed what had long been rumored, that Pope Francis would visit the Holy Land in May. The patriarch wrote, "Christmas leads the eyes of the world to look towards Bethlehem," but, he added, "At this time, we cannot forget the inhabitants of Syria, and among them the refugees in our neighboring countries, as well as all those around the world." He also wrote about the on-going conflict between the Israelis and Palestinians, but he also thanked Israeli authorities for their assistance in the closing events of the Year of Faith.

Somali Christmas Ban On Dec. 26, the government of Somalia banned the celebration of Christmas for the first time in the country's history. The directive was issued by the Ministry of Justice and Religious Affairs and was announced by Sheikh Mohammed Khayrow Aden, director general of the ministry, along with Sheikh Ali Dhere, director of Religious Matters. They reminded Muslims that Christmas celebrations were prohibited in the country and that police and authorities would punish violators. The ban extended to hotels and public places.

NATIONAL

Hunger Campaign On Dec. 19, the Commission for International Justice and Peace of the U.S. Conference of Catholic Bishops announced that it was joining together with Pope Francis and Caritas Internationalis to fight global hunger. The campaign, "One Human Family, Food for All," was scheduled to begin on Dec. 10 and was inaugurated with a Mass celebrated by Bp. Richard Pates, chairman of the bishops' Committee at the USCCB headquarters in Washington, D.C. In a press release, Bp. Pates and Abp. Thomas Wenski, chairman of the USCCB Committee on Domestic Justice and Human Development, applauded the work of Pope Francis, saying, "Since his election, Pope Francis has challenged Catholics and all people to go beyond the boundaries of their own lives and encounter the poor and marginalized. As legislators in Washington deliberate how to allocate budget resources to the many people who are hungry, both in our country and around the world, this campaign gives all of us an opportunity to turn awareness into action."

Human Trafficking On Dec. 12, the U.S. Conference of Catholic Bishops (USCCB) Committee on Migration announced that Feb. 8 would be an annual day of prayer for survivors and victims of human trafficking. The day was chosen because it is the feast day of St. Josephine Bakhita, who was kidnapped as a child and sold into slavery in Sudan. She also lived as a slave in Italy but eventually was given her freedom. Thereafter, she became a woman religious and was a living symbol of the war against slavery. In a press release, Bp. Eusebio Elizondo, M.Sp.S., aux. bp. of Seattle and chairman of the Committee wrote, "On that day, we will lift our voices loudly in prayer, hope, and love for trafficking victims and survivors. If just one person realizes from this day that they or someone they know is being trafficked, we will have made a difference."

Protect Marriage On Dec. 13, Abp. Salvatore Cordileone of San Francisco, chairman of the U.S. Conference of Catholic Bishops' Subcommittee for the Promotion and Defense of Marriage, and Abp. William Lori of Baltimore, chairman of the Ad Hoc Committee for Religious Liberty, spoke in favor of the Marriage and Religious Freedom Act (S. 1808) introduced in the U.S. Senate by Senator Mike Lee and voiced their support of the companion Marriage and Religious Freedom Act introduced by Rep. Raúl Labrador in the U.S. House of Representatives in Sept. 2013. Abp. Cordileone said, "The fact that this very important non-discrimination bill has now been introduced in the Senate is quite encouraging. As with the House bill, the Marriage and Religious Freedom Act introduced in the Senate would prohibit the federal government from discriminating against religious believers who hold to the timeless truth that marriage is the union of one man and one woman."

JANUARY 2014

VATICAN

Solemnity of Mary, Mother of God On Jan. 1, Pope Francis celebrated the Mass of the Solemnity of Mary, Mother of God in the Octave of Christmas and the celebration of the 47th World Day of Peace on the theme, "Fraternity, Foundation and Pathway to Peace." In his homily, he said, "The Mother of God. This is the first and most important title of Our Lady. It refers to a quality, a role which the faith of the Christian people, in its tender and genuine devotion to our heavenly Mother, has understood from the beginning...Mary has always been present in the hearts, the piety and above all the pilgrimage of faith of the Christian people."

Papal Attendees According to a Communique Issued by the Prefecture of the Papal Household On Jan. 2, Since Pope Francis' election on March 13, 2013, more than 6,600,000 faithful have attended the general audiences (1,548,500), private audiences (87,400), liturgical celebrations in the Vatican Basilica and in St. Peter's Square (2,282,000), Angelus and Regina Coeli (2,706,000). The Household noted as well that those numbers comprise solely those events that took place within the Vatican, and do not include other events such as apostolic visits to spots in Rome or papal trips beyond the Eternal City or Italy. The estimated total number of faithful who have attended those papal events is estimated at 6,623,000. In 2012, an estimated 2.3 million pilgrims and visitors attended the Vatican events of Pope Benedict XVI, and 2.5 million in 2011. In other reports, the Vatican announced that 5.5 million people visited the Vatican Museums in 2013.

"Anthropological Regression" On Jan. 3, Pope Francis was reported as saying to describing proposed legislation in Malta to permit same-sex marriages as an "anthropological regression." The exchange was reported in the Italian publication *Avvenire* and was between the pontiff and Aux. Bp. of Malta Charles J. Scicluna. According to the report, the pope was saddened by the news, especially as the legislation would permit same sex couples to adopt. The phrase was used by the pontiff as far back as 2010 when he was still the Abp. of Buenos Aires and was published in his book with Rabbi Abraham Skorka, "On Heaven and Earth."

Mass at the Gesù On Jan. 3, Pope Francis celebrated Mass at the Gesù, the mother-church of the Jesuits and declared Peter Faber, S.J., a saint through equivalent canonization. Faber was one of the founders of the Society of Jesus, and he was long venerated for his holiness although never officially canonized. In his homily, the pope said, "We Jesuits want to be honored with the name of Jesus, under the military banner of the cross, and that means: to have the same feelings of Christ. It means doing what He did, and with the same sentiments He had, with the sentiments of His heart. Each of us, the Jesuits, who follow Jesus should be willing to empty himself, to be men who do not live in a self-centered way because the center of the Society is Christ and His Church."

Limiting Monsignors On Jan. 7, Pope Francis instituted a change in the use of the title of "monsignor," mandating that it should be granted only to priests who have reached the age of 65 years of age. The declaration was issued by the Secretariat of State and was sent to the world's episcopal conferences through the nunciatures in each country. It stated, "in the world's dioceses, the only ecclesiastical title henceforth to be conferred shall be 'chaplain of His Holiness,' to which the appellation, 'monsignor,' shall correspond. The title shall be conferred only upon priests who have reached the age of 65." Until now, diocesan priests under the age of 65 were eligible for the title, granted at the request of their bishops.

The decree added that the use of the title "monsignor" in connection with certain major offices and in cases where there is a maintained cultural practice (i.e., for bishops or the vicar general of the diocese) "remains unchanged."

Further, regarding the Roman Curia, the decree states, "no change has been made either in the titles or in the use of the appellation 'monsignor,' these being connected to the offices entrusted, and to the service performed." The statement added, the new rule "has no retroactive effect" and that those "who received a title in the past, keep it." It is believed that the change has been made by Pope Francis as part of his desire for a simplification of Church life and titles. Traditionally, the titles have been of three grades: apostolic protonotary; honorary prelate of His Holiness; and chaplain of His Holiness.

Chinese Media On Jan. 7, it was announced that the "China International News Forum," comprised of 50 representatives from media and diplomatic associations in the People's Republic of China had chosen Pope Francis to be third among the top ten most important people in the world for 2013. The list also included Pres. of Iran, Hassan Rouhani, the Pres. of Russia, Vladimir Putin and the former Egyptian President, Mohammed Morsi. This was the first time that a pope or even a religious personality had ever appeared on the list.

Papal Ushers On Jan. 10, Pope Francis met with the "*Sediari Pontifici*," or Papal Ushers, marking a tradition dating back to the 14th century. Traditionally, the ushers were responsible for carrying the pope in the *sedia gestatoria*, the elevated papal throne. The ushers were greeted by the pontiff in the Consistory Hall in the Vatican Apostolic Palace, and Francis asked them to serve with humility and simplicity, adding, "In your daily work too, you have the opportunity to emulate these characteristics of the Son of God, Who 'did not come to be served, but to serve.' Experienced with this interior attitude, work can be transformed into an apostolate, a valuable opportunity for communicating the joy of being Christians to all you encounter...I offer you my warmest wishes for peace; I guarantee my prayers for you, and count on yours on my behalf."

New Cardinals On Jan. 13, Pope Francis made public the list of the new members of the College of Cardinals who were to be installed at a Consistory on Feb. 22. The pontiff made the announcement at the end of his recitation of the Angelus. The list of the new members of the College included:

Abp. Pietro Parolin, the Vatican Secretary of State; Abp. Lorenzo Baldisseri, Secretary General of the Synod; Abp. Gerhard Ludwig Müller, abp. emeritus of Regensburg and Prefect of the Congregation for the Doctrine of the Faith, Abp. Beniamino Stella, Prefect of the Congregation for the Clergy, Abp. Vincent Gerard Nichols of Westminster (Great Britain); Abp. Leopoldo José Brenes Solórzano of Managua (Nicaragua), Abp. Gérald Cyprien Lacroix of Québec (Canada); Abp. Jean-Pierre Kutwa of Abidjan (Ivory Coast); Abp. Orani João Tempesta, O.Cist. of Rio de Janeiro (Brazil); Abp. Gualtiero Bassetti of Perugia-Città della Pieve (Italy); Abp. Mario Aurelio Poli of Buenos Aires (Argentina); Abp. Andrew Yeom Soo jung of Seoul (Korea); Abp. Ricardo Ezzati Andrello, S.D.B. of Santiago de Chile (Chile); Abp. Philippe Nakellentuba Ouédraogo of Ouagadougou (Burkina Faso); Abp. Orlando B. Quevedo, O.M.I., of Cotabato (Philippines); Bp. Chibly Langlois of Les Cayes (Haiti).

Several retired prelates were also named: Abp. Loris Francesco Capovilla, titular abp. of Mesembria; Abp. Fernando Sebastián Aguilar, C.M.F., abp. emeritus of Pamplona; and Abp. Kelvin Edward Felix, abp. emeritus of Castries, in the Antilles. [For details, see under **News in Depth.**]

Diplomatic Corps On Jan. 13, Pope Francis held the traditional papal address to the Diplomatic Corps accredited to the Holy See and urged the diplomats to remember that fraternity and peace are first established in the family. The pontiff quoted his message for the World Day of Peace, declaring, "This is the message of the Crib, where we see the Holy Family, not alone and isolated from the world, but surrounded by shepherds and the Magi, that is by an open community in which there is room for everyone, poor and rich alike, those near and those afar. In this way we can appreciate the insistence of my beloved predecessor Benedict XVI that 'the language of the family is a language of peace.'" Addressing the on-going situation in the Middle East, the pope declared his intention to visit the Holy Land and to promote reconciliation and peace, even as he lamented the deplorable conditions faced by Christians in the region: "The exodus of Christians from the Middle East and North Africa continues to be a source of concern. They want to continue to be a part of the social, political and cultural life of countries which they helped to build, and they desire to contribute to the common good of societies where they wish to be fully accepted as agents of peace and reconciliation."

Holy See and Cameroon On Jan. 13, the Holy See announced that it had reached an agreement with the government of Cameroon regulating relations between the Church in Cameroon. According to a communique issued by the Holy See, the agreement was signed at the Ministry of Foreign Affairs of the Republic of Cameroon in the capital Yaoundé. The communique added, "The agreement, which consists of nine articles, regulates the relationship between the Church and the State who, within a framework of the independence and autonomy of both parties, undertake to work together for the moral, spiritual and material wellbeing of the

human person and for the promotion of the common good. It will come into effect upon signing, in accordance with article 9 of the same Agreement."

New IOR Commission On Jan. 15, Pope Francis appointed new members to the Commission of Cardinals overseeing the Institute for the Works of Religion (IOR), known commonly as the Vatican Bank. The new members were: Card. Christoph Schönborn, O.P., abp. of Vienna; Card. Thomas Christopher Collins, abp. of Toronto; Card. Jean-Louis Tauran, president of the Pontifical Council for Interreligious Dialogue; Card. Santos Abril y Castilló, archpriest of the Papal Basilica of St Mary Major; and Card.-designate Pietro Parolin, the Vatican Secretary of State. The only previous member who remained on the commission was Card. Tauran.

Msgr. Georg Ratzinger Turns 90 On Jan. 16, Msgr. Georg Ratzinger celebrated his 90th birthday with his brother, Pope Emeritus Benedict XVI, at the pope emeritus' Mater Ecclesiae residence in the Vatican Gardens. The brothers celebrated Mass, shared a Bavarian breakfast, and then attended an afternoon concert. The concert was organized in Msgr. Ratzinger's honor, and was attended by Card.-designate Gerhard Ludwig Müller, prefect of the Congregation for the Doctrine of the Faith, Abp. George Gänswein, private secretary to Benedict XVI, and Vatican spokesman Fr. Federico Lombardi, S.J.

Former Vatican Official Charged On Jan. 21, the Holy See announced that Msgr. Nunzio Scarano, a former Vatican official who had been arrested by Italian authorities in July for allegedly attempting to transport 20 million euros on a private jet from Switzerland into Italy, was charged with additional crimes of alleged money laundering. The Vatican spokesman, Fr. Federico Lombardi, S.J., told journalists that the Holy See was cooperating with Italian authorities in the investigation.

President Francois Hollande On Jan. 24, Pope Francis welcomed French President Francois Hollande to the Apostolic Palace in the Vatican. President Hollande also met with Card.-designate Pietro Parolin, the Vatican Secretary of State, and Abp. Dominique Mamberti, Secretary for Relations with States and then attended a luncheon at the French Embassy to the Holy See for the French members of the Secretariat of State. Hollande extended an invitation to the pontiff to visit France and pledged France's support in helping the Christians of the Middle East.

Catholic Universities On Jan. 30, Pope Francis had an audience with the Board of Trustees of the University of Notre Dame and reminded them of the importance of an "uncompromising witness" of Catholic universities to the teachings of the Church. The Holy Father's audience was part of the formal launching of the University's Rome Center. He said, "From its founding, Notre Dame University has made an outstanding contribution to the Church in your country through its commitment to the religious education of the young and to serious scholarship inspired by confidence in the harmony of faith and reason in the pursuit of truth and virtue. Conscious of the critical importance of this apostolate for the new evangelization, I express my gratitude for the commitment which Notre Dame University has shown over the years to supporting and strengthening Catholic elementary and secondary school education throughout the United States."

The pope added, "Essential in this regard is the uncompromising witness of Catholic universities to the Church's moral teaching, and the defense of her freedom, precisely in and through her institutions, to uphold that teaching as authoritatively proclaimed by the magisterium of her pastors."

Ecclesiastical Heraldry On Jan. 30, the Holy See announced the publication of a manual on ecclesiastical heraldry in the Catholic Church. The book was authored by Card. Andrea Cordero Lanza di Montezemolo and Fr. Antonio Pompili and was published by Libreria Editrice Vaticana, the Vatican publishing house. It includes coverage of the history and norms for heraldry in the Church, the design of shields, and the so-called grammar and sytax of coats of arms in the Church.

Congregation for the Doctrine of the Faith On Jan. 31, Pope Francis met in an audience with the members of the Congregation for the Doctrine of the Faith. The pope thanked them for their labors on behalf of the Church, especially in the area of dealing with clergy sexual abuse. The pope declared, "Think of the welfare of children and the young, who in the Christian community must always be protected and supported in their human and spiritual growth. In this sense, the possibility is being looked into of connecting the specific Commission for the Protection of Minors, which I have established, to your dicastery. I hope it will be an example for all those who wish to promote the welfare of children."

General Audiences

Jan. 8, 2014
Jan. 15, 2014
Jan. 22, 2014
Jan. 29, 2014

INTERNATIONAL

Legionaries of Christ On Jan. 9, Card. Velasio de Paolis, C.S., the Pontifical Delegate for the Legionaries of Christ, urged the members of the congregation to advance their renewal during the opening Mass of the Legion's Extraordinary General Chapter. The Chapter was intended to create a new constitution and establish new leadership for the Legion. The Cardinal, however, reminded the members that this was only a part of the wider process of reform. He also spoke about the tragic legacy of the founder, Fr. Marciel Maciel, noting, "Suffering has purified you, matured you and made you experience God's grace and love, who has called you to share in the mystery of redemption through the cross and through sorrow. You have participated in the pain of those who have suffered because of some members of the Legion. You have chosen the only way the Gospel knows for the redemption of evil: not escape, not rejection, not the condemnation of others, but participation, solidarity, and love that enters into sin and sorrow so as to redeem them

from the inside."

Cardinal Reinhard Marx on Capitalism On Jan. 10, *L'Osservatore Romano* published an interview with Card. Reinhard Marx, abp. of Munich, on the topic of capitalism and the need to focus always on the poor and marginalized and the dignity of the human person. He said, "Capitalism should not become the model of society because [...] it does not take into account individual destinies, the weak and the poor," although he stressed that Catholics should not reject the market economy, "which is necessary and sensible, but it must serve man." Nor, Marx observed, should Catholic despise the rich. Rather, material goods are merely a means to an end and cannot represent the true meaning of life.

Iranian Christians On Jan. 15, four Christians in Iran were arrested for praying together in a house on New Years' Day. According to Fides News Agency, the Christians, Sara Rahimi-Nejad, Mostafa Nadri, Majid Sheidaei, and George Isaiah, were praying together in a house in the city of Karaj when they were arrested by state police. The arrest was joined by other incidents involving the persecution of Christians during Christmas by Iranian authorities.

Egypt's New Constitution On Jan. 17, Egyptian voters approved by an overwhelming majority the country's new constitution. The constitution was promoted and supported by the Christians of Egypt who were pleased by the new constitution, especially as it bans political parties based on religion and grants key protections to the minority Christians in the country. The referendum was approved by nearly 90 percent of the people and was protested and boycotted by the Muslim Brotherhood whose head, the Islamist President Mohammed Morsi, was removed by a military coup. Christians not only will have legal rights, but they will be permitted to build churches without restrictions as well.

Medjugorje Investigation On Jan. 20, it was announced that the international commission assembled by the Vatican to investigate the events at Medjugorje would be submitting its findings to the Congregation for the Doctrine of the Faith (CDF). According to the Holy See Press Office, the commission, created by the Congregation for the Doctrine of the Faith in 2010, and presided by Card. Camillo Ruini had completed its work and would be presenting its results to the Congregation. The commission made up of cardinals, bishops, theologians, and various experts, and the members examined the apparitions that had started in 1981 and that subsequently have drawn pilgrims from all over the world. The communique added that the CDF would then examine the findings and make a final determination.

Ireland's Embassy to the Holy See On Jan. 21, it was announced that the government of Ireland would reopen its embassy to the Holy See. Tánaiste Eamon Gilmore, Ireland's foreign minister, declared that the reopening would be part of a wider embassy building program. The announcement stated that the new embassy to the Holy See would be housed in a separate building from the Irish embassy to Italy in the Villa Spada, the premises of the old Vatican embassy, and is expected to be more modest. Abp. Charles Brown, apostolic nuncio to Ireland, said in a statement: "I am very pleased by the announcement of the Irish Government regarding the reopening of a residential Embassy of Ireland to the Holy See, and the appointment of a resident Ambassador. It is an excellent decision for the people of Ireland and will be beneficial to Ireland in making its distinctive and important contribution to international relations. We are all grateful to those who worked so hard to make this day possible."

Don Alvaro Beatification On Jan. 22, it was announced that Pope Francis had approved a miracle and had issued the formal decree of the Congregation for the Causes of the Saints clearing the way for the beatification of Venerable Bp. Alvaro del Portillo. The bishop was the direct successor to St. Josemaría Escrivá as the prelate of Opus Dei. He was scheduled for beatification in his native Madrid, on Sept. 27. Bp. Javier Echevarría, Prelate of Opus Dei, declared, "In this moment of profound joy, I wish to thank Pope Francis for his decision to proceed with the beatification of this bishop who loved and served the Church so much. From now on, let us entrust to the soon-to-be Blessed Alvaro the intentions of the Holy Father: the apostolic renewal and service to God of all Christians, the care and support of the needy, the upcoming synod on the family, the holiness of priests."

Boko Haram Attack On Jan. 29, the Islamist terror organization Boko Haram attacked a Catholic Church in Nigeria, killing an estimated 26 people. According to Fides News Agency, members of Boko Haram attacked the church in the village of Waga Chakawa in northern Nigeria in the middle of Sunday Mass with firearms and explosives. On the same day, the militants attacked two other villages, killing 54 people.

NATIONAL

State Marriage Laws On Jan. 13, Abp. Salvatore Cordileone of San Francisco, chairman of the U.S. Conference of Catholic Bishops' Subcommittee for the Promotion and Defense of Marriage, issued a statement that saluted the introduction on Jan. 9, of the bipartisan State Marriage Defense Act of 2014 (H.R. 3829) in the U.S. House of Representatives by Rep. Randy Weber (R-TX). He wrote, "The State Marriage Defense Act is a necessary piece of legislation that will prevent the federal government from unjustly disregarding, in certain instances, state marriage laws concerning the definition of marriage."

Urging the U.S. House of Representatives to pass the Act, Abp. Cordileone added, "State marriage laws defining marriage as the union of one man and one woman deserve respect by the federal government. This bill does that. I, therefore, strongly encourage the House of Representatives to pass the State Marriage Defense Act."

9 Days for Life On Jan. 16, the Committee on Pro-Life Activities of the U.S. Conference of Catholic Bishops urged Catholics to participate in a novena from Jan. 18-26 to observe the 41st anniversary

of the *Roe v. Wade* Supreme Court decision that legalized abortion in the United States. In a statement, Card. Sean O'Malley, head of the committee, noted, "By our participation in these 9 Days for Life, as we call upon the Lord for the healing and conversion of our nation and those impacted by the culture of death, we are also reminded — through the very act of prayer — of our beautiful dependence on God and His deep love for each of us." The novena would be promoted through all possible means, including text, e-mail, and social media. In Washington, DC, the annual March for Life was held on Jan. 22, the anniversary date of the decision.

U.S. Bishops and Human Dignity On Jan. 17, Abp. Thomas Wenski of Miami and Bp. Richard Pates of Des Moines, Iowa, chairs of the Committees on Domestic Justice and Human Development and International Justice and Peace of the U.S. Conference of Catholic Bishops, issued a letter to the chairs and ranking members of the Senate Committee on Finance and the House Committee on Ways and Means urging them to respect human dignity in forming federal policies. They wrote, "While the USCCB does not take positions for or against particular trade agreements, we would like to take this opportunity to offer principles for your consideration that defend human life and dignity, protect the environment and public health, and promote justice and peace in our world."

March for Life On Jan. 22, several hundred thousand marchers braved the cold in Washington, D.C., to mark the 41st anniversary of the infamous 1973 Supreme Court decision, *Roe vs. Wade*, that legalized abortion in the U.S. Since that decision, more than 55 million babies have been aborted. Marchers gathered at several locations in Washington, DC, and heard addresses by prominent Catholic leaders. They then gathered and marched in the capital. As was expected, the secular media paid little attention to the March.

U.S. Embassy Anniversary On Jan. 23, Ken Hackett, the U.S. Ambassador to the Holy See, and Abp. Dominique Mamberti, the Vatican Secretary for Relations with States, marked the 30th anniversary of the formal establishment of diplomatic relations between the Holy See and the United States.

The celebration was held at the Palazzo della Cancelleria, in Rome. Abp. Mamberti observed, "May the friendship and cooperation between the Holy See and the United States of America be ever more strengthened within the family of nations in order that the world may progress in building peace, justice and fraternity."

Rolling Stone On Jan. 28, the American magazine, *Rolling Stone* published a full feature on Pope Francis and placed his picture on the cover. The pontiff was depicted with the caption: "The times, they are a-changin'." The story marked yet another secular publication focusing on or honoring the pope with stories. "TIME" magazine honored Francis as "Person of the Year."

The article in *Rolling Stone* was notable for its expected progressive bias but nevertheless was a significant milestone on the media's coverage of the pope and the modern papacy.

FEBRUARY 2014

VATICAN

Samoan Head of State On Feb. 3, Pope Francis welcomed Tui Atua Tupua Tamasese Efi, the O le Ao o le Malo ("head of state") of the Independent State of Samoa to the Apostolic Palace in the Vatican. The pontiff and Samoan leader discussed a variety of issues, including aspects of Samoan social and economic life and the wider situation in the Pacific. Following his session with the pope, Tamasese Efi met with Card.-elect Pietro Parolin, Vatican Secretary of State, and Abp. Dominique Mamberti, Secretary for Relations with States.

Prayer For Consecrated Life On Feb. 3, Pope Francis used his weekly Angelus address to focus on the importance of praying for those in consecrated life, marking the Day of Consecrated Life. He spoke of the way that consecrated life is a gift, adding, "This gift of ourselves to God regards every Christian because we are all consecrated to him through our baptism. We are all called to offer ourselves to the Father with Jesus and like Jesus, making a generous gift of our lives, in the family, at work, in service to the Church, in works of mercy... There is great need of these presences that reinforce and renew the commitment to spread the Gospel, Christian education, charity toward the neediest, contemplative prayer; the commitment to human formation, the spiritual formation of young people and of families; the commitment to justice and peace in the human family."

U.N. Committee On Feb. 5, the Holy See officially responded to the inflammatory observations and recommendations by the United Nations Committee on the Rights of the Child that criticized the Vatican for supposedly failing to protect children from abuse and that included recommendations that the Church change her teachings on homosexuality and abortion. The official statement declared, "The Committee is particularly concerned that in dealing with allegations of child sexual abuse, the Holy See has consistently placed the preservation of the reputation of the Church and the protection of the perpetrators above children's best interests, as observed by several national commissions of inquiry." In reply to the suggestion that the Church adapt teachings to meet the demands of the committee, the Holy See expressed disappointment for what it saw as "an attempt to interfere with Catholic Church teaching on the dignity of the human person and in the exercise of religious freedom."

Fr. Federico Lombardi, S.J., Holy See spokesman, expressed regret for the report and added, "The United Nations is a reality that is very important to humanity today. The Holy See has always provided strong moral support to the United Nations as a meeting place among all the nations, to foster peace in the world and the growth of the community of peoples in harmony, mutual respect and mutual enrichment. Countless documents and addresses of the Holy See at [the UN's] highest levels and the intense participation of the Holy See's representatives in the activities of many UN bodies attest to this." Nevertheless, the report's recommendations "have not taken adequate account of the responses, both written and oral, given by the representatives of the Holy See. Those who have read and heard these answers do not find proportionate reflections of them in the document of the committee, so as to suggest that it was practically already written, or at least already in large part blocked out before the hearing."

Archbishop Chaput On Feb. 7, the Holy See announced that Pope Francis had confirmed Card. Stanislaw Rylko as president of the Pontifical Council for the Laity, and Bp. Josef Clemens as secretary and had named Abp. Charles Chaput of Philadelphia to the same council.

Abp. Gänswein and Benedict XVI On Feb. 10, Abp. Georg Gänswein, personal secretary to Pope emeritus Benedict XVI and Prefect of the Papal Household gave an interview to Reuters in which he said that the retired pope had no regrets about resigning the papacy and was "at peace with himself and I think he is even at peace with the Lord." He added that the pope emeritus was still present in the Church, adding, "His mission now, as he once said, is to help the Church and his successor, Pope Francis, through prayer. This is his first and most important task.

Catholic Education On Feb. 13, Pope Francis addressed the participants of the plenary session of the Congregation for Catholic Education that was meeting in Rome. He stressed the importance of maintaining the identity of Catholic universities and uniting it with the 50th anniversary of the Second Vatican Council declaration "*Gravissimum Educationis*" and the 25th anniversary of the Apostolic Constitution "*Ex Corde Ecclesiae*." The pontiff taught, "Jesus began to proclaim the good news of the 'Galilee of the people,' a crossroads of people, diverse in terms of race, culture and religion. This context resembles today's world, in certain respects. The profound changes that have led to the ever wider diffusion of multicultural societies require those who work in the school or university sector to be involved in educational itineraries involving comparison and dialogue, with a courageous and innovative fidelity that enables Catholic identity to encounter the various 'souls' of multicultural society."

American Jewish Institute On Feb. 13, Pope Francis held a private audience with the American Jewish Institute and urged the members to continue the progress in dialogue. The Holy Father also thanked the members for their work on behalf of promoting "dialogue and fraternity" between Jews and Catholics. The pontiff discussed the 50th Anniversary of *Nostra Aetate*, the Second Vatican Council's declaration on dialogue with other religions, saying, "This foundation is theological, and not simply an expression of our desire for reciprocal respect and esteem. Therefore, it is important that our dialogue be always profoundly marked by the awareness of our relationship with God."

Engaged Couples On Feb. 14, Pope Francis met with some 25,000 young people, engaged couples preparing for marriage, during a special St. Valentine's day audience. Organized by the Pontifical Council for the Family, the audience included music and dancing before the Holy Father's arrival. The pope urged the couples to make a definitive commitment. "Just as the love of God is stable and forever," the pope said, "so we would want the love that is the foundation of the family to be stable and forever. We cannot let ourselves be overcome by the 'throwaway culture.'" The pope also stressed the importance of "courtesy," "thank you," and "I'm sorry."

Council of Cardinals On Feb. 17, the Council of Cardinals appointed by Pope Francis to serve as key advisors to the pontiff held their third meeting to discuss reform of the economic and organizational structures of the Roman Curia and other key offices of the Holy See. This meeting also included discussions of the Apostolic Constitution *"Pastor Bonus"* issued by Pope John Paul II in 1988 to reform the Roman Curia. The eight council members concelebrated Mass with the Holy Father at Casa Santa Marta in Vatican City.

Argentinian Passport On Feb. 18, it was announced that Pope Francis had renewed his Argentinian passport and national identity card, even though he was also intending to retain a Vatican passport. In a surprise to media, the pope had his photo taken, his fingerprints scanned, and his signature recorded. Additionally, it was reported that the pontiff paid for the passport and identity card himself, as noted by the Argentinian embassy. The passport is valid from Febr. 14, 2014 until Feb. 14, 2029, and was issued with his baptismal name: Jorge Mario Bergoglio.

Extraordinary Consistory of Cardinals On Feb. 20, Pope Francis began the Extraordinary Consistory for the College of Cardinals at which he elevated new members to the Sacred College. The pontiff also held several meetings with the members, focusing much of the discussion on the Synod of Bishops in October under the theme of "The Pastoral Challenges of the Family in the Context of the New Evangelization."

Papal Video On Feb. 21, Pope Francis was presented in a private video recording for his longtime friend, Anglican Episcopal Bishop Tony Palmer, that was played at a gathering of Kenneth Copeland Ministries, a Protestant ministry based in Texas. In the message, the pope urged the Protestants to work for Christian unity and to fulfill the yearning that "this separation comes to an end and gives us communion. I am nostalgic (yearning), of that embrace that the Holy Scripture speaks of when Joseph's brothers began to starve from hunger, they went to Egypt, to buy, so that they could eat. We have lot of cultural riches, and religious riches. And we have diverse traditions. But we have to encounter one another as brothers. We must cry together like Joseph did. These tears will unite us. The tears of love." He added, "Let us allow our nostalgia (yearning) to grow, because this will propel us to find each other, to embrace one another. And together to worship Jesus Christ as the only Lord of History... And let us pray to the Lord that He unites us all. Come on, we are brothers. Let's give each other a spiritual hug and let God complete the work that he has begun. And this is a miracle; the miracle of unity has begun."

Mass with New Cardinals On Feb. 24, Pope Francis concelebrated Mass with 19 new cardinals after installing the new members of the College of Cardinals the day before in St. Peter's Basilica. The pope used the occasion to remind the 19 new cardinals that they are entering the Church of Rome, not a royal court; he added that they must be led by the Holy Spirit: "By his creative and renewing power, the Spirit always sustains the hope of God's People as we make our pilgrim way through history, and ... he always supports the witness of Christians…In the Gospel Jesus also speaks to us of holiness, and explains to us the new law, his law. He does this by contrasting the imperfect justice of the scribes and Pharisees with the higher justice of the Kingdom of God…Dear brother Cardinals," continued the Pope, "the Lord Jesus and mother Church ask us to witness with greater zeal and ardour to these ways of being holy. It is exactly in this greater self-gift, freely offered, that the holiness of a Cardinal consists. We love, therefore, those who are hostile to us; we bless those who speak ill of us; we greet with a smile those who may not deserve it. We do not aim to assert ourselves; we oppose arrogance with meekness; we forget the humiliations that we have endured. May we always allow ourselves to be guided by the Spirit of Christ, who sacrificed himself on the Cross so that we could be 'channels' through which his charity might flow. This is the attitude of a Cardinal, this must be how he acts. A Cardinal — I say this especially to you — enters the Church of Rome, my brothers, not a royal court"

Cardinal Pell to Rome On Feb. 24, the Holy See announced that Pope Francis had appointed Card. George Pell of Sydney as prefect of the new Secretariat for the Economy, an office to oversee the reforms and restructuring of Vatican finances. The secretariat was the result of the recommendations by the Pontifical Commission for Reference on the Organization of the Economic- Administrative Structure of the Holy See (COSEA) that were approved by both the Council of Cardinals created by Francis to advise his reform of the Roman Curia and the Committee of Cardinals that oversees Holy See finances. The Secretariat was structured to implement policies established by a new Council for the Economy, a 15-member Council composed of eight cardinals or bishops from around the world and seven international lay experts. Card Pell henceforth will report to the Council for the Economy.

Haitian President On Feb. 24, Pope Francis welcomed Haitian President Michael Joseph Martelly to the Apostolic Palace in the Vatican. The two discussed the major issues facing Haiti, especially the recovery from the terrible earthquake of 2010. Pres. Martelly had come to Rome to celebrate the elevation to the cardinalate of Haiti's first Cardinal, Bp. Chibly Langlois of Les Cayes. According to a communique from the Vatican Press Office, the meeting stressed "the good relations between Haiti and the Holy See, and the Parties focused in particular on the precious contribution made by the Church in the country, especially in the fields of education and healthcare, as well as in charitable sectors. Mention was also made of the importance of continuing efforts for the rebuilding of the country, and for promoting sincere dialogue between various institutions for reconciliation and the common good, both domestically and at an international level." Martelly also met with Card. Secretary of State Pietro Parolin and Abp. Dominique Mamberti, secretary for Relations with States.

Paul VI Miracle On Feb. 26, it was announced that a panel of theologians from the Congregation for the Causes of Saints had approved a miracle through the intercession of Venerable Pope Paul VI. The miracle reportedly involved the healing in utero of a child in California in the 1990s. The child's mother had been urged to have an abortion because the child was feared to be suffering from various ailments. She refused, and a friend brought a prayer card and a small piece of one of Paul's vestments. [For other details, see under **News in Depth**.]

Pontifical Commission for Latin America On Feb. 28, Pope Francis received members of the Pontifical Commission for Latin America who were visiting Rome for their Plenary Assembly under the theme of "Educational Emergency and the Transmission of the Faith to Latin American Youth." In his address, the pope spoke of the importance of handing on the faith, especially to young people, seeing in the example of Jesus Christ. He said, "The Holy Mother Church is convinced that the best teacher for the young is Jesus Christ. She wishes to instil in them these same sentiments, showing them how beautiful it is to live as He did, banishing selfishness and allowing oneself to be drawn by the beauty of goodness...We must not abandon the young, or leave them at the roadside; they have a great need to feel valued in their dignity, surrounded by affection, and understood."

Speaking of dialogue, the pontiff spoke of Christ's encounter with the rich young man's concerns, saying, "Jesus listened, without condemning; he was without prejudice, he did not speak about the usual things. In the same way, the young want to feel at home in Church. Not only must the Church open her doors to them; she must actively seek them... They must hear that Christ is not a character in a novel, but a living person, who wants to share their irrepressible desire for life, commitment, and dedication. If we content ourselves with offering them mere human comfort, we let them down. It is important to offer them the best we have: Jesus Christ, His Gospel, and with Him, a new horizon, which enables them to face life with coherence, honesty and high-mindedness."

General Audience

Feb. 5, 2014
Feb. 12, 2014
Feb. 19, 2014
Feb. 26, 2014

INTERNATIONAL

Crisis in Aleppo On Feb. 3, Aid to the Church in Need sent out an urgent appeal for help to assist the many in need in the Syrian city of Aleppo and that an aid package had been assembled to assist them. The emergency aid totaled €190,000 (£156,900 and more than $200,000) and would be used to assist the wounded and repair the damage done to homes especially with the deepening of winter. Aid to the Church in Need is an international Catholic charity that functions under the direction of the Holy See to assist those suffering in the Church around the world.

Marches Across Europe On Feb. 3, hundreds of thousands of Catholics and people of conscience marched across the major cities of Europe in defense of marriage and the traditional family. Marches were held in Paris, Lyon, Brussels, Bucharest, Madrid, Warsaw and Rome, with the individual marches ranging from 20,000 to more than half a million. The largest demonstration was held in Paris, where estimates put the size of the crowd at more than 500,000 under the wider theme of "*La Manif Pour Tous*" ("Protest for Everyone"). The Parisian march was especially in protest of the radical legislation and enactments under French President François Hollande, including the recent law allowing same-sex "marriage," in vitro fertilization, and other manipulations of traditional family life and gender.

Lunacek Report On Feb. 5, the European Parliament approved the so-called Lunacek Report, a document that would require EU member states to embrace a radical agenda for promoting "gender" ideology. The bill was approved by a margin of 394 votes in favor, contrary to 176 against and 72 abstentions. The so-called "Roadmap for LGBTI Rights" would impose coercive regulations to insure regulations against perceived homophobia and discrimination on the grounds of sexual orientation and gender identity. The report also mandated that European states to "register and investigate hate crimes" and prohibit "incitement to hatred on grounds of sexual orientation and gender identity."

Pro-Family Victory On Feb. 5, owing to massive protests in France, the government of Pres. François Hollande postponed its plans to implement a radical and highly controversial family law that would have legalized assisted procreation for lesbian couples or surrogate motherhood for homosexual men who wanted children. Protests in Paris were estimated to have drawn more than 500,000. The protests came at a time when Hollande's government was reaching new levels of unpopularity owing to its radical social and economic agenda.

Legionaries of Christ On Feb. 6, Fr. Eduardo Robles Gil, L.C., a 61 year-old Mexican member of the Legion was elected the new General Director of the community. The Mexican priest is best known for his work with abuse victims of the Legion's late founder, Fr. Marcial Maciel. He succeeded Fr. Silvester Heereman, L.C. who becomes one of the Legion's general councillors. The election was seen as a vital next step in the reform and renewal of the Legion, especially under the guidance of Cardinal Velasio De Paolis, C.S. who had been overseeing the process that has included dealing with massive charges of abuse

Belgian Euthanasia On Feb. 14, the Belgian House of Representatives gave its final approval to a bill passed by the Belgian Senate in November that would extend the country's euthanasia law to children under 18. The bill was supported by 86 members, with 44 voting against, and 12 abstentions. The law allows children with terminal diseases and ailments in "pain" to be killed if their parents agree and a psychiatrist or psychologist can determine that they are fully conscious of the decision. There were massive protests in the country, led by the bishops of the country and a large group of pediatricians.

Kidnapped Christians On Feb. 18, members of the Syrian opposition to the government of Pres. Bashar al-Assad of Syria called for the release of Christians who had been kidnapped; the plea was made at the Geneva II Peace Conference by Sheikh Mohammad Abdel-Hady al-Yaaqubi who asked "all Islamic militants to immediately release all those who are unjustly detained against their will, especially the innocent bishops, nuns and monks."

Ban on Belgian Adoptions On Feb. 18, the Russian Parliament asked their country's foreign ministry to examine the law recently approved by the Belgian government that would permit child euthanasia and determine if Belgium should be prohibited from having its citizens adopt Russian minors. The concern of Russian legislators was a direct consequence of the Belgian law, especially as Russian lawmakers and many other were concerned that children adopted by Belgian citizens might be at risk from the law that allowed parents to put their children to death in the face of what was described in the law as "great pain" from various diseases and ailments.

Anglican Ordinariates On Feb. 20, the heads of the three Anglican Ordinariates — the ecclesiastical structures established under Pope Benedict XVI to permit Anglican converts to enter into full communion in the Church while allowing the retention of some Anglican practices — met together for the first time. The three heads were: Msgr. Keith Newton, Ordinary of the Personal Ordinariate of Our Lady of Walsingham in the United Kingdom; Msgr. Jeffrey Steenson, Ordinary of the Personal Ordinariate of the Chair of St Peter in the United States; and Msgr. Harry Entwistle, Ordinary of the Personal Ordinariate of Our Lady of the Southern Cross in Australia. The three ordinaries met with the Prefect of the Congregation for the Doctrine of the Faith, Card.-designate Gerhard Ludwig Müller, and other officials there, to forge closer ties and bring them up to date on the progress being made by the ordinariates.

Anti-Homosexuality Bill On Feb. 24, Pres. Yoweri Museveni signed a bill that brought tough restrictions on homosexual behavior, including possible arrest for some homosexual acts and prison terms for offenders. The decision to approve the law came after the Ugandan government and legislature declared an unwillingness to be compelled to confirm to Western conceptions of morality. In a statement, Pres. Museveni declared, "I would like to discourage the USA government from taking the line that passing this law will 'complicate our valued relationship' with the USA as Pres. Obama said. Countries and societies should relate with each other on the basis of mutual respect and independence in decision making. 'Valued relationship' can-

not be sustainably maintained by one society being subservient to another society. There are a myriad acts the societies in the West do that we frown on or even detest. We, however, never comment on those acts or make them preconditions for working with the West.

NATIONAL

Guttmacher Study On Feb. 5, the pro-abortion Guttmacher Institute released a report that the abortion rate was at its lowest since 1973 and the legalization of abortion by the infamous Supreme Court decision of *Roe vs. Wade*. Despite the good news regarding the declining abortion rate, the Institute claimed: Half of pregnancies among American women are unintended, and four in 10 of these are terminated by abortion; twenty-one percent of all pregnancies (excluding miscarriages) end in abortion; since 1973, nearly 53 million legal abortions have occurred; around half of American women will experience an unintended pregnancy by age 45; and at 2008 abortion rates, one in 10 women will have an abortion by age 20, one in four by age 30 and three in 10 by age 45.

Mental Illness Pastoral Letter On Feb. 17, the bishops of New York State published a pastoral letter speaking about people who suffer mental illness. Titled, "'For I am Lonely and Afflicted': Toward a Just Response to the Needs of Mentally Ill Persons," the letter looks to Our Lord as the role model in the treatment of those suffering from mental illness, saying, "we must reject the twin temptations of stereotype and fear, which can cause us to see mentally ill people as something other than children of God, made in His image and likeness, deserving of our love and respect." The letter likewise noted that less than 5% of violent acts are committed by people with mental illness and that mental illness places a burden on family members and is a cross to bear. The bishops taught, "Our Judeo-Christian tradition calls us to be witnesses of God's love and mercy and to be instruments of hope for these individuals. Let us be clear, it is our duty and the duty of every pastor, every chaplain, every religious education director and Catholic school principal, and all others in positions of Church leadership at every level to welcome with openness and affection those men, women and children who are afflicted with any form of mental illness and to integrate them into the life of the Church to the fullest extent possible."

Constitutional Amendment On Feb. 20, Abp. Salvatore Cordileone of San Francisco sent a letter to Rep. Tim Huelskamp (R-KS) expressing his support for the federal Marriage Protection Amendment (H. J. Res. 51) introduced by the Congressman in the U.S. House of Representatives. The archbishop wrote, "The amendment would secure in law throughout the country the basic truth known to reason that marriage is the union of one man and one woman... An amendment to the U.S. Constitution is the only remedy in law against this judicial activism that may ultimately end with federal judges declaring that the U.S. Constitution requires states, and consequently the federal government, to redefine marriage."

MARCH 2014

VATICAN

Prayer for Vocations On Mar. 3, Pope Francis used his homily at morning Mass at the Casa Santa Marta to call on Catholics to pray for vocations. The pontiff used the day's Gospel reading from St. Mark and the encounter between Jesus and the rich young man, where Our Lord was asked, "Good teacher, what must I do to inherit eternal life?" In looking at the young man, Francis compared his situation to the struggle of young people to discern their own vocation. He declared, "We should pray so that the heart of these young people can be emptied, emptied from other interests, from other loves, so that the heart can become free," he said. "And this is the prayer for vocations: 'Lord, send us, send us nuns, send us priests, defend them from idolatry, from the idolatry of vanity, from the idolatry of pride, from the idolatry of power, from the idolatry of money.' And our prayer is to prepare these hearts to be able to follow Jesus closely."

Peace in Ukraine On Mar. 3, Pope Francis used his Angelus to call for peace in the Ukraine. The Holy Father said, "I ask you to continue to pray for Ukraine, which finds itself in a delicate situation. While it is my wish that the citizens of the country strive to overcome misunderstandings and to build the future of the nation together, I make a heartfelt appeal to the international community to support every initiative on behalf of dialogue and harmony."

Gardens at Castel Gandolfo On Mar. 3, the director of the Vatican Museums announced that Pope Francis had decided to open the gardens of the Pontifical Villa at Castel Gandolfo "where the splendor of art and the glory of nature co-exist in admirable equilibrium" to the public. The gardens would be open from Monday through Saturday mornings, with a 90-minute guided tour of the gardens, in Italian or English.

Prime Minister of Romania On Mar. 3, Pope Francis welcomed the Romanian Prime Minister Victor Ponta to the Vatican Apostolic Palace. In a communique issued by the Holy See, the two discussed themes such as education and family life, as well as relations with the Romanian Orthodox Patriarchate. The communique added, "In considering the potential of the Catholic Church for contributing to the common good of society as a whole, other open questions were discussed regarding the Catholic community in Romania." The Prime Minister also met with Card. Pietro Parolin, Vatican Secretary of State and Abp. Dominique Mamberti, Secretary for Relations with States.

Cardinal Loris Capovilla On Mar. 3, Card. Angelo Sodano, the dean of the College of Cardinals, bestowed the red hat on 98-year-old Loris Francesco Capovilla, enrolling him in the Sacred College of Cardinals. Owing to problems with his health and his advanced age, Card. Capovilla was not able to be present at the Feb. 22 consistory. He was assigned the titular see of Santa Maria in Trastevere, a distinct honor for the one-time secretary to Pope St. John XXIII.

Pope Francis Magazine On Mar. 4, Mondadori, Italy's largest book and magazine publisher, would begin publishing a full-color magazine on the pope, "*Il Mio Papa*," with an initial print run of 3 million copies. In a press release, the publisher noted the immense popularity of the pope whose election has spurred a global increase in interest in ethical, moral, and religious topics. The magazine would be heavy with photographs of the pontiff and cover his writings, speeches and travels, with a weekly section devoted to the non-profit charity ONLUS.

Corriere della Sera On Mar. 5, the Italian newspaper *Corriere della Sera* published an interview with Pope Francis to mark the first year of his pontificate. The interview was conducted by editor-in-chief Ferruccio de Bortoli, and covered a broad range of topics, including how Pope Francis sees himself, his relationship with Pope emeritus Benedict XVI and the ideological labels that are often used to describe him. The pontiff said about the near mythology that has developed around him, "To paint the Pope as if he were some kind of Superman, a sort of star, is offensive. The Pope is a man who laughs, cries, sleeps well and has friends like everyone else. He is a normal person." Regarding Pope emeritus Benedict, Francis observed, "He is discreet, humble, he does not want to bother…His wisdom is a gift from God. Some would have wanted him to retire to a Benedictine abbey far from the Vatican. And I thought of grandparents, who with their wisdom and counsel give strength to the family and should not end up in a retirement home." On political labels, the Holy Father rejected any idea that he is some kind of a Marxist, noting that he "never shared the Marxist ideology because it is not true, but I know many good people who have professed Marxism."

Priests of Rome On Mar. 6, Pope Francis met with the pastors and priests of the Diocese of Rome. He spoke to them on a variety of topics, stressing especially mercy in the life of priestly ministry. He said, "Let us ask ourselves what mercy means for a priest, allow me to say for us priests. For us, for all of us! Priests are moved to compassion before the sheep, like Jesus, when he saw the people harassed and helpless, like sheep without a shepherd. Jesus has the "bowels" of God, Isaiah speaks about it very much: he is full of tenderness for the people, especially for those who are excluded, that is, for sinners, for the sick who no one takes care of…. Thus, in the image of the Good Shepherd, the priest is a man of mercy and compassion, close to his people and a servant to all. This is a pastoral criterion I would like to emphasize strongly: closeness. Closeness and service, but closeness, nearness!... Whoever is wounded in life, in whatever way, can find in him attention and a sympathetic ear…. The priest reveals a heart especially in administering the Sacrament of Reconciliation; he reveals it by his whole attitude, by the manner in which he welcomes, listens, counsels and absolves…. But this comes from how he experiences the Sacrament firsthand, from how he allows himself to be embraced by God the Father in Confession and remains in this embrace…. If one experiences this in one's own regard, in his own heart, he can also give it to others in his ministry. And I leave you with the question: How do I confess? Do I allow myself to be embraced? A great priest from Buenos Aires comes to mind, he is younger than I, he is around the age of 72…. Once he came to see me. He is a great confessor: there are always people waiting in line for him there…. The majority of priests confess to him… He is a great confessor. And once he came to see me: "But Father…."; "Tell me"; "I have a small scruple, because I know that I forgive too much!"; "Pray… if you forgive too much…" And we spoke about mercy. At a certain point he said to me: "You know, when I feel this scruple keenly, I go to the chapel, before the Tabernacle, and I say to Him: Excuse me, but it's Your fault, because it is you who has given me the bad example! And I go away at peace…." It is a beautiful prayer of mercy! If one experiences this in his own regard in Confession, in his own heart, he is able to give it to others. The priest is called to learn this, to have a heart that is moved. Priests who are — allow me to say the word — "aseptic," those "from the laboratory," all clean and tidy, do not help the Church. Today we can think of the Church as a "field hospital." Excuse me but I repeat it, because this is how I see it, how I feel it is: a "field hospital." Wounds need to be treated, so many wounds! So many wounds! There are so many people who are wounded by material problems, by scandals, also in the Church.... People wounded by the world's illusions.... We priests must be there, close to these people."

No Christianity Without a Cross On Mar. 6, Pope Francis used his homily for morning Mass at the Casa Santa Marta by reflecting on the Gospel of Luke and Jesus' call to follow Him by reminding Christians that "Without the Cross, there is no Christian. The pontiff added, "If anyone wishes to come after me, he must deny himself and take up his cross daily and follow me...There is always this path that He has done first: the path of humility, also the path of humiliation, to destroy Himself, and then rise again. But, this is the path, the Christian style. Without the Cross, there is no Christian. The Christian style takes the cross of Jesus and goes forward. Not without the cross, not without Jesus."

Spiritual Exercises On Mar. 9, the first Sunday of Lent, the Pope and the Roman Curia began their spiritual exercises for Lent. The meditations were led by Fr. Angelo De Donatis, parish priest of San Marco Evangelista in Campidoglio. The theme for the exercises was "the purification of the heart," and they were conducted at the Casa del Divin Maestro in Ariccia, just outside of Rome.

World Council of Churches On Mar. 7, Pope Francis met a delegation from the World Council of Churches headed by General Sec. Rev. Dr. Olav Fykse Tveit, a Norwegian Lutheran theologian. The pope spoke to the group, declaring, "I wish all of you a warm welcome and I thank Doctor Tveit for his words to me on your behalf. This meeting marks one more stage, an important one, in the long-standing and fruitful relationship between the Catholic Church and the World Council of Churches. The Bishop of Rome is grateful to you for the work you are doing in support of Christian unity. From its inception, the World Council of Churches has contributed greatly to making all Christians aware that our divisions represent a serious obstacle to the witness of the Gospel in the world. We cannot be resigned to these divisions as if they were merely an inevitable part of the historical experience of the Church. If Christians ignore the call to unity which comes to them from the Lord, they risk ignoring the Lord himself and the salvation he offers through his Body, the Church: 'There is salvation in no one else, for there is no other name ... by which we must be saved' (Acts 4:12). Relations between the Catholic Church and the World Council of Churches, developing since the Second Vatican Council, have brought us to a sincere ecumenical cooperation and to an ever increasing 'exchange of gifts' between the different communities by overcoming mutual misunderstanding.

"The path to full and visible communion is still today an uphill struggle. The Spirit encourages us, however, not to be afraid, not to allow ourselves to be satisfied with the progress we have made in recent decades, but to move forward in trust. Prayer is fundamental on this journey. Only with a spirit of humble and unceasing prayer will we be able to have the necessary foresight, discernment and motivation to serve the human family in all its struggles and needs, both spiritual and material. Dear brothers and sisters, I assure you of my prayers that during your meeting with the Pontifical Council for Promoting Christian Unity it will be possible to find the most effective way for us to advance together on this path. May the Spirit of the Lord sustain every one of you and your families, your colleagues at the World Council of Churches and all those who have the cause of Christian unity at heart. Pray also for me that the Lord may permit me to be a docile instrument of his will and a servant of unity. May the peace and grace of the Lord accompany all of you."

Lay Ecclesial Bodies On Mar. 10, Pope Francis sent a letter to a Congress organized by the Vicariate of Rome and held at the Pontifical Lateran University under the theme of "The mission of Christian laypeople in the city." The pope wrote, "The lay faithful, by virtue of their Baptism, are agents in the work of evangelization and human promotion," he said. "Incorporated in the Church, each member of the People of God is inseparably disciple and missionary. We must always depart from this common root of ours, as sons and daughters of the Mother Church. As a result of this common belonging to the Church and participation in her mission, it is important that parishes and lay ecclesial bodies are not opposed to each other.

"The latter, with their variety and dynamic quality, are a resource for the Church, projecting into different environments and sectors of social life; but it is good for them to maintain a vital link to the organic pastoral ministry of the diocese and the parishes, so as not to construct a partial reading of the Gospel or to uproot themselves from the Mother Church. I recommend that you make habitual use of the Compendium of the Social Doctrine of the Church, a complete and valuable tool. With the help of this 'compass,' I encourage you to work for the social inclusion of the poor, always offering religious and spiritual attention to them as a priority."

President Cristina Fernandez de Kirchner On Mar. 17, Pope Francis welcomed President Cristina Fernandez de Kirchner to his residence at Casa Santa Marta in Vatican City. In a communique issued by the Holy See Press Office, the meeting was described as having "the aim of presenting to the Holy Father the greetings, wishes and affection of the Argentine people to commemorate the anniversary of the first year of his pontificate. The pope met with her privately after his encounter with her delegation and then had lunch with her. It was also anticipated that Pres. Kirchner would give the Holy Father his Argentinian passport and identification card that he renewed last month.

"24 Hours for the Lord" On Mar. 24, after reciting the Angelus prayer, Pope Francis asked the faithful to celebrate "24 hours for the Lord," to be held on March 28 and 29. The pope instructed that St. Peter's Basilica would be open on the 28th and various other churches in Rome would remain open throughout the night for prayer and confession. The idea emerged out of the Synod on the New Evangelization, where bishops from around the world stressed the importance of the Sacrament of Reconciliation.

Protection of Minors On Mar. 24, the Holy See announced that Pope Francis had named the members of the recently created Pontifical Commission for the Protection of Minors. The new members are: Catherine Bonnet, a French child psychiatrist; Marie Collins, an

Irish abuse victim; Baroness Sheila Hollins, a member of the House of Lords and former president of the Royal College of Psychiatrists and the British Medical Association; Card. Seán O'Malley, abp. of Boston and a member of the Council of Cardinals; Claudio Papale, a lay canon lawyer; Hanna Suchocka, former Polish prime minister (1992-93), minister of justice (1997-2000) and ambassador to the Holy See (2001-13); Fr. Humberto Miguel Yañez, an Argentine Jesuit moral theologian and former student of then Fr. Jorge Mario Bergoglio; and Fr. Hans Zollner, a German Jesuit and chair of the steering committee of the Center for Child Protection at the Institute of Psychology at the Pontifical Gregorian University.

German Resignation On Mar. 26, the Holy See announced that Pope Francis had accepted the resignation of Bp. Franz-Peter Tebartz-van Elst of Limburg, in the wake of an investigation into the construction of a new episcopal residence. It was learned that the bishop had spent an estimated €31 million ($42 million) on the construction of a new residence and offices, although much of the spending had been approved by his predecessor. The German bishop was placed on administrative leave at the start of the investigation by the Congregation of Bishops.

President Barack Obama On Mar. 27, Pope Francis welcomed U.S. President Barack Obama to the Vatican Apostolic Palace. The first meeting between Pope Francis and the U.S. President, the encounter was carried out in several stages, including a formal session in the palace, followed by a private conversation that lasted nearly 50 minutes. In a communiqué issued by the Holy See Press Office the Holy Father and President exchanged views on "international themes" and the hope that "there would be respect for humanitarian and international law and a negotiated solution between the parties involved...In the context of bilateral relations and cooperation between Church and State, there was a discussion on questions of particular relevance for the Church in that country, such as the exercise of the rights to religious freedom, life and conscientious objection, as well as the issue of immigration reform."

Pres. Obama presented the Holy Father with a variety of seeds from the White House garden in a chest made of leather and also wood from the Basilica of the National Shrine of the Assumption of the Blessed Virgin Mary, one of the oldest Catholic cathedrals in the U.S. Pope Francis gave the president two medallions. The first was made of hand-coated fused bronze and depicted an angel "embracing and bringing together the northern and southern hemispheres of the earth, while overcoming the opposition of a dragon," signifying "A World of Solidarity and Peace Founded on Justice." The second medallion was a replica of a medallion commemorating the laying of the first stone of the north colonnade of St. Peter's Basilica designed by Gian Lorenzo Bernini. In addition, Francis gave a copy of his apostolic exhortation, "*Evangelii Gaudium*." The president and his delegation later met with Card. Pietro Parolin, Vatican Secretary of State.

Former Vatican Bank Chief Cleared On Mar. 28, Ettore Gotti Tedeschi, the former president of the Institute for Religious Works, or Vatican bank, was cleared of money-laundering charges by the Criminal Court of Rome. The Italian financier was fired in May 2012 after the bank's board issued a no-confidence vote and a nine point list of personal and professional failings.

General Audiences
March 5, 2014
March 19, 2014
March 26, 2014

INTERNATIONAL

Venezuelan Violence On Mar. 12, it was reported that churches in the city of Caracas, Venezuela, were attacked as part of the political unrest and the government's harsh response. According to Fides New Agency, Msgr. Victor Hugo Basabe, undersecretary of the Episcopal Conference of Venezuela, informed reporters attacks took place in areas where the violence was severe, and the attacks even took place during Mass. Most incidents were of vandalism and sacrilege against the churches. Upheaval has grown significantly worse in the country under Pres. Nicolás Maduro, successor to the late president Hugo Chávez who was himself a bitter opponent of the Church.

Human Trafficking On Mar. 17, it was announced that representatives of the world's major religions had agreed to form the "Global Freedom Network" with the aim of eradicating human trafficking by 2020. The agreement was signed at the Vatican in cooperation with the Walk Free Foundation. A joint statement signed by the representatives "underscores the searing personal destructiveness of modern slavery and human trafficking and calls for urgent action by all other Christian Churches and global faiths. Modern slavery and human trafficking are crimes against humanity. The physical, economic and sexual exploitation of men, women and children condemns 30 million people to dehumanization and degradation. Every day we let this tragic situation continue is a grievous assault on our common humanity and a shameful affront to the consciences of all peoples. Any indifference to those suffering exploitation must cease. We call to action all people of faith and their leaders, all governments and people of goodwill, to join the movement against modern slavery and human trafficking and support the Global Freedom Network."

Syrian Crisis On Mar. 19, Syrian Chaldean Bp. Antoine Audo of Aleppo, President of Caritas Syria, discussed the severe crisis in Syria at a Caritas Syria meeting held in Lebanon. The bishop warned against the immense toll the conflict was taking on the psychological and emotional stability of the people. He additionally lauded the work of Caritas. Speaking of the emotional crisis, the bishop noted, "In addition to food parcels, health care and relief to the poor, we have identified two new fields of action: psycho-social assistance and the help to engage young Syrians in micro-work projects, especially in villages and in the countryside. We have decided to take this new direction linked to work and psycho-social assistance. But this also requires time and training. Our operators had never imagined having to cope with a humanitarian commitment of this magnitude."

NATIONAL
Israeli-Palestinian Conflict On Mar. 3, Jewish, Christian and Muslim national leaders met in Washington, D.C. in support of a two-state peace

agreement between Israel and Palestine. The group sent a letter to Secretary of State John Kerry under the title of the National Interreligious Leadership Initiative for Peace in the Middle East (NILI), in which they urged a two-state peace agreement, declaring, "We believe the coming months are critical to achieving a negotiated two-state peace agreement. "We also would urge you to meet personally with religious leaders on the ground in Jerusalem, most importantly including leaders of the Council of Religious Institutions in the Holy Land (CRIHL). While we know that some in our communities will oppose any compromises as leaders of NILI we support benchmark principles and practical ideas developed in earlier official and informal negotiations that provide possible elements for necessary compromises on key issues that could be acceptable to majorities of Israelis and Palestinians." Catholic members of the group included, Card. Theodore McCarrick, retired archbishop of Washington; Bp. Richard E. Pates of Des Moines, Iowa, chairman of the U.S. bishops' Committee on International Justice and Peace; and Bp. Denis Madden, auxiliary bishop of Baltimore and chairman of the U.S. bishops' Committee on Ecumenical and Interreligious Affairs.

Defense of Marriage On Mar. 3, Abp. Salvatore Cordileone of San Francisco, chairman of the U.S. Conference of Catholic Bishops' Subcommittee for the Promotion and Defense of Marriage, gave his public endorsement to the State Marriage Defense Act of 2014 (S. 2024) introduced in the U.S. Senate by Sen. Ted Cruz. A companion bill (H.R. 3829) was introduced in the U.S. House of Representatives by Rep. Randy Weber. Abp. Cordileone wrote that the Department of Justice is the most recent federal agency "to use a 'place of celebration' rule rather than a 'place of domicile' rule when determining the validity of a marriage for purposes of federal rights, benefits, and privileges. By employing a 'place of celebration' rule, these agencies have chosen to ignore the law of the state in which people reside in determining whether they are married. The effect, if not the intent, of this choice is to circumvent state laws defining marriage as the union of one man and one woman." Abp. Cordileone called on the U.S. Senate to pass the State Marriage Defense Act of 2014.

"Second Chance Act" On Mar. 4, Abp. Thomas Wenski of Miami and Fr. Larry Snyder, the chairman of the U.S. Bishops' Committee on Domestic Justice and Human Development and the president of Catholic Charities USA sent a letter to the chairs and ranking members of the House and Senate Judiciary Committees supporting the Second Chance Act. The letter stated, "Those who return to our communities from incarceration face significant challenges. These include finding housing and stable employment, high rates of substance abuse, physical and mental health challenges and social isolation. The Second Chance Act supports much needed programs in government agencies and nonprofit organizations that provide employment assistance, substance abuse treatment, housing, family programming, mentoring, victim support and other services to individuals returning to the community from prison or jail."

Fulton Sheen Miracle On Mar. 6, the board of medical experts that advises the Congregation for the Causes of Saints had agreed unanimously that the healing of a stillborn baby is indeed inexplicable medically and should be attributed to the intercession of Venerable Fulton Sheen. The child in question had been stillborn and was not breathing for more than an hour in September 2010. Breathing was restored after 61 minutes and made a full recovery. If approved by a board of theologians, the miracle will be presented to Pope Francis for formal approval, clearing the way for Sheen's beatification.

Pope Francis Poll On Mar. 6, the Pew Research Center published its poll on the popularity of Pope Francis. Its findings revealed that the pontiff has a favorability rating among the vast majority of American Catholics and that 71% think he represents a "major change in direction" for the Church. According to Pew, the poll also revealed the so-called Francis Effect, finding that some 40% of American Catholics were praying more regularly, although there were limited increases in the sacrament of reconciliation or Mass attendance.

Pew reported, "There also is broad consensus among Catholics that Francis represents a major change in direction for the church, and that this is a change for the better. Large majorities of men and women, Catholics in all adult age groups, and both regular Mass attenders and more infrequent Mass-goers express this view."

Majority Oppose Abortion On Mar. On Mar. 7, CNN published a poll that found that a strong majority of Americans (58%) want restrictions on abortion, with 38% of Americans favoring abortion being legal in only a few circumstances. Some 27% want abortion legal in all circumstances, while 20% want it illegal in all circumstances. Only 13% favor abortion being legal in most circumstances. In addition, the poll also found that most Americans (56%) continue to oppose public funding for abortion, while only 39% favor public funding for abortions.

U.S. Supreme Court Hears Arguments On Mar. 26, the U.S. Supreme Court heard arguments in the controversial lawsuit relating to the HHS Mandate involving the religious rights of business owners. Two family-owned businesses, Hobby Lobby and Conestoga Wood, had sued to resist the mandate that compels employers to include sterilization, contraceptives and abortion-inducing drugs in their employee health plans coverage. The court heard a related issue on the applicability of the Religious Freedom Restoration Act (RFRA) that protects religious liberty to business owners in the operation of their for-profit corporations.

Sex Abuse Prevention According to a report released on Mar. 28 by the Center for Applied Research in the Apostolate (CARA) at Georgetown University, "2013 Survey of Allegations and Costs: A Summary Report for the Secretariat of Child and Youth Protection, United States Conference of Catholic Bishops," U.S. dioceses and religious orders in 2013 increased what they spent on child protection by more than 50 percent.

APRIL 2014

VATICAN

"A Most Beautiful Thing" On Apr. 2, Pope Francis used his general audience to discuss the sacrament of marriage, teaching that the married couple is itself the image of God, that the sacrament "leads us to the heart of the design of God, that is a design of covenant with his people, with all of us, a design of communion" and that "the image of God is the married couple." The pontiff also gave practical advice to couples, including the reality that married life brings challenges, including money, work and children. He added that couples "quarrel — it is always so in marriage — sometimes even plates fly. However, we must not become sad because of this; the human condition is like this. And the secret is that love is stronger from the moment there is quarreling, so I always advise spouses: Never end a day when you quarreled without making peace. Always! And it is not necessary to call the United Nations to come to one's home to make peace. A small gesture, a caress, a hello is sufficient! And until tomorrow — and tomorrow one begins again. And this is life; it must be carried forward thus, carried forward with the courage of wanting to live it together. And this is great, it is beautiful! Married life is a most beautiful thing and we must guard it always, protect the children." He noted as well several key words that "must be in the home": "please, thank you, sorry [*permesso, grazie, scusa*] – three magical words."

Queen of England On Apr. 3, Pope Francis welcomed Queen Elizabeth II of England to the Apostolic Palace in the Vatican and greeted her in English, with the word "Welcome." The Queen visited with her husband, the Duke of Edinburgh, and her royal entourage. It was noted that she was 20 minutes late and apologized for the lateness of her lunch with Italian President Napolitano. The two exchanged several gifts, including Pope Francis' gift of an orb, representing the world, with a silver cross of St. Edward on top, for the Queen's new grandson. He also presented her with a copy of the Decree of Saint Edward the Confessor, King of England, who died in 1066 and was canonized by Pope Alessandro III in 1161 with the title of "Confessor." He was the last Anglo-Saxon king before the Norman Conquest in 1066, although Harold Godwinson also claimed the throne of England. The Queen gave the pontiff a chest of typical English items from her many estates, including Buckingham Palace, Sandringham in Norfok, Windsor Castle and the Castle of Balmoral in Scotland.

Human Trafficking On Apr. 10, Pope Francis addressed the participants of the Second International Conference "Combating Human Trafficking: Church and Law Enforcement in Partnership" that was completing its work of two days. The pontiff called the conference "a sign: it is a sign of the Church and a sign of men and women of good will who want to cry out, 'Enough!'" The conference marked the coming together of Vatican and international Law Enforcement Agencies to fight human trafficking. Organized by the Bishops' Conference of England and Wales, the conference was chaired by Card. Vincent Nichols of Westminster. Pope Francis added, "Human trafficking is an open wound on the body of contemporary society, a scourge upon the body of Christ. It is a crime against humanity. The very fact of our being here to combine our efforts means that we want our strategies and areas of expertise to be accompanied and reinforced by the mercy of the Gospel, by closeness to the men and women who are victims of this crime." At the end of the conference, a communique was issued by the Holy See noting that a declaration had been approved calling on all law enforcement to develop an effective strategy against human trafficking, marked the commitment of senior law enforcement officials within the international community "to eradicate the scourge of this serious criminal activity, which abuses vulnerable people. This conference is part, of a process where we work together on the international stage to develop strategies in prevention, pastoral care and re-integration, placing the victim at the centre of all we do."

Institute for the Works of Religion On Apr. 7, the Holy See Press Office issued a communique announcing that Pope Francis had approved the proposed reform structure for the Institute for the Works of Religion (IOR). The plan was developed by representatives of the Pontifical Referring Commission to the IOR (CRIOR), the Pontifical Commission for Reference on the Organization of the Economic- Administrative Structure of the Holy See (COSEA), the IOR's Commission of Cardinals and the IOR Board of Superintendence. The statement declared "The IOR will continue to serve with prudence and provide specialized financial services to the Catholic Church worldwide," the statement read. It continued, "The valuable services that can be offered by the Institute assist the Holy Father in his mission as universal pastor and also aid those institutions and individuals who collaborate with him in his ministry."

Official Logo for Papal Visit On Apr. 8, officials from Korea and Rome announced the official logo and motto for Pope Francis' planned visit to Korea from Aug. 14-18. The official motto will be: "Arise! Shine, for your light has come, the glory of the Lord has dawned upon you" (Isaiah 60:1). According to a statement from Holy See, the logo would consist of a flame, with the shape of a boat to embody the motto. The color blue and red of the flame were intended to signify the separation of the Korean Peninsula, North and South, even whole pointing toward the hope for eventual reunification. The boat also was supposed to resemble the waves and the blade of a knife, commemorating the sacrifice of the martyrs who gave foundation to the Church in Korea. The light blue color signified the mercy of God, as wide as the ocean. Pope Francis was scheduled to become the first pope to visit Korea since Pope St. John Paul II visited the peninsula 25 years ago.

Papal Apology On Apr. 11, Pope Francis gave an address to the International Catholic Child Bureau and issued an official apology for the harm done to children by priests guilty of sexual abuse. The International Catholic Child Bureau is a French non-profit organization founded in 1948 working to protect children's rights. The pope saluted the work of the Bureau and then asked forgiveness for the evil done by "all the evil that some priests — quite a few, quite a few in number, not in comparison with the totality — to take charge and ask for forgiveness for the harm they have done because of sexual abuses of children…The Church is conscious of this harm, which is a personal, moral harm of their own, but men of the Church. And we are not going to take a step back in regard to the treatment of these problems and of the sanctions that must be in place; on the contrary, I think we must be very strong; one does not fool around with children."

Pope and Seminarians On Apr. 15, Pope Francis met with a group of seminarians from the Pontifical Leonine College of Anagni, a regional seminary for the dioceses around Rome. He spoke about what he termed were "half priests." The pope said, "We have so many, so many half way priests. It is a sorrow, that they do not succeed in reaching the fullness. They have something about them of employees, a bureaucratic dimension and this does no good to the Church. I advise you, be careful that you do not fall into this! You are becoming pastors in the image of Jesus, the Good Shepherd, to be like Him and in His person in the midst of his flock, to feed his sheep."

Easter Triduum On Apr. 17, Pope Francis marked the Easter Triduum with major liturgies, starting with Holy Thursday and the Chrism Mass in Saint Peter's Basilica. During this Mass, the pontiff blessed the chrism oil used for baptism, confirmation, Holy Orders. Francis also celebrated the Mass of the Lord's Supper at the Don Carlo Gnocchi Foundation of St. Mary of Providence Center, located in the Casalotti Boccea section of Rome, for the care of the elderly and the disabled. Pope Francis washed the feet of several patients. Last year, the pope celebrated his first Holy Thursday Mass as pope at Rome's Casal del Marmo prison, where he washed the feet of the inmates. On Good Friday, he presided over the Celebration of the Lord's Passion in St. Peter's Basilica and then journeyed to the Roman Colosseum for the Stations of the Cross. There, he meditated on the reflections on the Way of the Cross, using reflections composed by Abp. Giancarlo Maria Bregantini of Campobasso-Boiano, Italy. On Holy Saturday, Francis celebrated the Easter Vigil Mass in St. Peter's Square. The next morning, he celebrated Easter Mass in St. Peter's Square. Following the Easter Mass, Francis delivered the traditional *Urbi et Orbi* (to the city [Rome] and to the world) blessing. The Holy Father spoke about the reality that in Jesus, "love has triumphed over hatred, mercy over sinfulness, goodness over evil, truth over falsehood, life over death. That is why we tell everyone: 'Come and see!' In every human situation, marked by frailty, sin and death, the Good News is no mere matter of words, but a testimony to unconditional and faithful love: it is about leaving ourselves behind and encountering others, being close to those crushed by life's troubles, sharing with the needy, standing at the side of the sick, elderly and the outcast... 'Come and see!': Love is more powerful, love gives life, love makes hope blossom in the wilderness."

Papal Phone Call Reports On Apr. 24, a brief media storm erupted over reports that the pope had called an Argentine woman and discussed her marital situation. Pope Francis supposedly telephoned Jaqui Lisbona of St. Lawrence, Argentina, who had written to the Holy Father after her pastor told her that she could not receive the Sacrament because she was not validly married to Julio Sabetta, who was divorced and civilly remarried. The pope supposedly told her that she could receive Communion, although there was no mention of the claim in the Facebook post made by Lisbona about the call. It was generally acknowledged that Lisbona had talked with the pope, it was not clear at all what the pontiff had actually said to her. Holy See spokesman Fr. Federico Lombardi, S.J., dismissed media reports that the phone conversation contained some deviation from Church teaching, noting, "That which has been communicated in relation to this matter, outside the scope of personal relationships, and the consequent media amplification, cannot be confirmed as reliable, and is a source of misun-

derstanding and confusion."

Message for Vesakh On Apr. 24, Card. Jean-Louis Tauran and Fr. Miguel Ángel Ayuso Guixot, president and secretary of the Pontifical Council for Interreligious Dialogue, issued the 2014 message to Buddhists marking the festival of Vesakh. The message for 2014 had the theme, "Buddhists and Christians: Together Fostering Fraternity," stressing, "Each one of us is called to be an artisan of peace, by uniting and not dividing, by extinguishing hatred and not holding on to it, by opening paths to dialogue and not by constructing new walls! Let us dialogue and meet each other in order to establish a culture of dialogue in the world, a culture of encounter!" [See under **Ecumenism and Interreligious Dialogue** for full coverage.]

Albanian Prime Minister On Apr. 24, Pope Francis welcomed Edi Rama, the prime minister of Albania, to the Vatican Apostolic Palace. In a statement from the Holy See, the meeting was cordial, and "the Parties remarked upon the good relations between the Holy See and the Republic of Albania, and focused on themes of common interest regarding the relations between the ecclesial and civil communities, including interreligious dialogue and the contribution of the Church to the common good of Albanian society." The prime minister subsequently met with Cardinal Secretary of State Pietro Parolin and Abp. Dominique Mamberti, Secretary for Relations with States.

John XXIII and John Paul II Canonized On Apr. 27, Divine Mercy Sunday, Pope Francis canonized Pope St. John XXIII and Pope St. John Paul II. It was estimated that several million people had arrived in Rome to mark the event. Pope emeritus Benedict XVI, who beatified John Paul II and was a witness in the process of canonization for his predecessor, also attended. Pope Francis used his homily to speak of the wounds of Christ, teaching, "The wounds of Jesus are a scandal, a stumbling block for faith, yet they are also the test of faith. That is why on the body of the risen Christ the wounds never pass away: they remain, for those wounds are the enduring sign of God's love for us. They are essential for believing in God. Not for believing that God exists, but for believing that God is love, mercy and faithfulness." He declared that John XXIII and John Paul II "were not afraid to look upon the wounds of Jesus, to touch his torn hands and his pierced side. They were not ashamed of the flesh of Christ, they were not scandalized by him, by his cross." He added, that they "lived through the tragic events of that century, but they were not overwhelmed by them. For them, God was more powerful; faith was more powerful — faith in Jesus Christ the Redeemer of man and the Lord of history; the mercy of God, shown by those five wounds, was more powerful; and more powerful too was the closeness of Mary our Mother." [For full coverage see under **News in Depth**.]

Prime Minister of Ukraine On Apr. 28, Pope Francis welcomed the prime minister of Ukraine, Arseniy Yatsenyuk, to the Apostolic Palace in the Vatican. In a communiqué issued by the Holy See, the meetings were cordial and centered on the relations between the Holy See and Ukraine, with a special eye on the difficult political and military situation facing Ukraine. There was also some discussion of the challenges facing the Churches and religious organizations in the region. Following the session with the pontiff, the prime minister met with the Cardinal Secretary of State Pietro Parolin and the

Secretary for Relations with States, Abp. Dominique Mamberti.

Vatican Bank Reform On Apr. 28, it was announced that the Supervisory Commission of Cardinals overseeing the reforms to the Institute for the Works of Religion (commonly called the Vatican Bank) had ended its discussions with guidelines for moving forward. Among the decisions was to meet three times a year or as frequently as circumstances required. The commission had been established by Pope Benedict XVI to assist with the reform of the Bank and the restoration of its credibility in the face of various scandals. The commission was then revised by Pope Francis, who replaced most of its members. The new commission included the Secretary of State, Card. Pietro Parolin, Card. Santos Abril y Castello, Card. Christoph Schoenborn and Card. Thomas Collins. The only holdover was Card. Jean-Louis Tauran.

General Audiences

April 2, 2014
April 9, 2014
April 16, 2014
April 23, 2014, "Why do you seek the living among the dead?"
April 30, 2014

INTERNATIONAL

Vandalism at a Marian Shrine On Apr. 4, Patriarch Fouad Twal, Latin Patriarch of Jerusalem, condemned an attack on the Marian shrine of Our Lady at Deir Rafat, near Jerusalem; the act was believed to be the responsibility of Israeli extremists and was condemned by officials of the Israeli government. The patriarch declared to the charitable organization Aid to the Church in Need, "We condemn these attacks in the strongest terms."

Dutch Missionary Priest Killed On Apr. 7, a Dutch Jesuit priest, Fr. Frans van der Lugt, was murdered in the Syrian city of Homs while working in his garden. The Jesuit had served in Syria since 1967 and was shepherd to a small Christian community that had been trying to survive in the midst of the terrible fighting in the city. Fr. Adolfo Nicolás, superior general of the Society of Jesus, said of the priest, "He always spoke of peace and reconciliation and opened his door to all who asked for his help, regardless of race or religion. We hope and ask the Lord that his sacrifice bear fruits of peace and that it may be a further incentive to silence the weapons and put aside hatred."

Philippine Supreme Court Upholds Law On Apr. 8, The Philippines Supreme Court upheld the constitutionality of a controversial "Reproductive Health" (RH) law that allows universal access to contraceptives, birth control and intrauterine devices (IUD), and enforces "sexual education" for children starting at the 5th grade. The court, nevertheless, struck down penalties against health care providers who refuse to provide contraception on the basis of religious beliefs, birth control for minors without parental consent and punishments against public officials who are unwilling to support the law. Abp. Socrates Villegas of Lingayen Dagupan, who is also president of the Philippine episcopal conference, issued a statement on the decision stating, "The Church must continue to uphold the sacredness of human life, to teach always the dignity of the human person and to safeguard the life of every human person from conception to natural death. Although the Supreme Court has upheld the constitutionality of the RH law, it has truly watered down the RH law and consequently upheld the importance of adhering to an informed religious conscience even among government workers. It has also stood on the side of the rights of parents to teach their children... Through 2,000 years, the Church has lived in eras of persecution, authoritarian regimes, wars and revolutions. The Church can continue its mission even with such unjust laws. Let us move on from being an RH-law-reactionary-group to truly Spirit empowered disciples of the Gospel of life and love. We have a positive message to proclaim."

Religious Freedom Law On Apr. 11, Thein Sein, president of Myanmar requested the Parliament of Myanmar to review a new religious freedom law that would place restrictions on interfaith marriages, conversions and polygamy, and that would also approve birth control for the country. The law was seen as an effort to concretize the special status of Buddhism in Myanmar and to limit the growth of other religions in the majority Buddhist culture. In a statement, Abp. Charles Maung Bo of Yangon expressed his unhappiness with the proposed law arguing that the state should not interfere with the rights of individuals to choose their own religion.

Maltese Same-Sex Civil Unions On Apr. 3, the government of Malta officially legalized same-sex unions and also adoption by homosexual couples. The decision, made by the government of Prime Minister Joseph Muscat of the Labour Party, was pushed through the Maltese legislature despite the solid majority opposition of the Maltese people; a mere one-fifth of the population was in favor of same-sex adoptions. Bp. Charles Scicluna, auxiliary bishop of Malta, gave an interview to The Malta Independent newspaper, observing, "This does not reflect the order established by God in creation and may expose the children, eventually entrusted to such adoptive parents, to adverse effects. This goes against the principle that the best interests of the child should be the paramount concern in legislation. It is hoped that this principle will remain paramount whenever the new law is applied."

Good Friday in Cuba On Apr. 17, the Communist government of Cuba under Pres. Raúl Castro officially declared Good Friday to be a national holiday. The move marked the continued progress of the Church in securing official recognition of religious holidays in the aftermath of the 2012 visit to the island country by Pope Benedict XVI. The pope had made the initial request during his journey to Cuba and his meeting with Castro. That same year, on Apr. 6, the officially atheist regime recognized Good Friday, the first such recognition since the start of the Community regime under Fidel Castro in the 1950s. In 2013, the Cuban government allowed religious services to be broadcast, and with the new decree, Cubans will mark Good Friday as an official holiday and a day off for all workers.

David Cameron and Christianity On Apr. 17, British Prime Minister David Cameron sparked a national debate in the United Kingdom with his observations in an article published in the *Anglican Church Times*. Cameron declared, "I believe we should be more confident about our status as a Christian country, more ambitious about expanding the role of faith-based organizations, and, frankly, more evangelical about a faith that compels us to get out there and make a difference to people's lives." He added that he had experienced the healing power of religion in his own life, believed that Great Britain remains a Christian country, and that Christianity could have a transformative impact on the "Spiritual, physical, and moral" state of contemporary culture against the increasingly "secular age" that brings demands of strict neutrality for religion in public life.

The comments were attacked immediately by the usual militant atheists, progressives and secularists in the media, while some others also saw the comments as an effort to repair relations with many Britons who were shocked by Cameron's sudden embrace of same-sex marriage. He was nevertheless defended by Abp. Justin Welby of Canterbury and Catholic bishops, including Bp. Kieran Conry of Arundel and Brighton, who told the *Daily Telegraph*, "I think people will be glad to see the Gospel getting back into politics — or explicitly back into politics, it is there in a lot of what the Government tries to do, in looking after people."

NATIONAL

Mass at the US-Mexico Border On Apr. 1, Card. Seán O'Malley of Boston and members of the U.S. Conference of Catholic Bishops' Committee on Migration made their way to the U.S.-Mexico border to commemorate the loss of life among those striving to reach the U.S., to tour the border and to draw public attention to the plight of immigrants. The cardinal and other bishops celebrated Mass and placed a wreath at the border wall in Nogales, Arizona, to remember those immigrants who have died on their way to the country. The idea received its inspiration from Pope Francis who celebrated Mass at Lampedusa, an island off the Italian coast, to bring the world's attention to the plight of the millions of immigrants across the globe. He threw a wreath into the Mediterranean Sea to remember those who had died trying to reach Europe.

U.S. Aid to Philippines On Apr. 9, $24.5 million had been collected to assist the victims of Typhoon Haiyan that struck the Pacific country in November 2013 and caused catastrophic damage, including damage to 600,000 homes and displacing or impacting some 12 million people. The money was approved by the U.S. Conference of Catholic Bishops' (USCCB) Administrative Committee Meeting and would include both humanitarian relief and long-term church reconstruction needs. Abp. Dennis M. Schnurr of Cincinnati, chairman of the USCCB Committee on National Collections, declared, "Both humanitarian and Church needs are significant. When the delegation visited the Philippines in early February, they were able to see the needs first-hand. I spoke with Archbishop Coakley, who was in the delegation, and we agreed to recommend an even split of the collection to the Administrative Committee."

Colorado Legislation On Apr. 10, the Archdiocese of Denver publicly denounced a bill in the Colorado legislature that would create what the state's Catholic conference described as "a 'fundamental right' to not only abortion, but also to other things defined as 'reproductive healthcare' in this bill," according to Jenny Kraska, director of the State Catholic Conference. In a statement, Kraska observed that "proponents of this bill state that this bill will be the first of its kind in the country...It's very broadly written and therefore has the potential to be broadly interpreted. It has the potential to overturn and make null and void good laws like parental notification for children who want to get an abortion." Abp. Samuel Aquila of Denver subsequently held a prayer service at the State Capitol to pray for an end to the proposed legislation, warning in an open letter to "supporters of life" that, "This over-reaching piece of legislation would essentially shut down any attempt to pass life-affirming legislation in Colorado ever again."

ARC-USA Statement Release On Apr. 24, the Anglican-Roman Catholic Dialogue in the United States (ARC-USA) concluded a six-year round of dialogue with the release of "Ecclesiology and Moral Discernment: Seeking a Unified Moral Witness," a statement that was approved at the meeting of the committee from Feb. 24-25, 2014, at Virginia Theological Seminary in Alexandria, Virginia. The meeting in Virginia was chaired by Bp. John Bauerschmidt of the Episcopal Diocese of Tennessee.

The document focused chiefly on two issues: migration/immigration and same sex relations; there were stark differences in the areas of moral theology, but the report also noted some important areas of commonality.

The differences in theology were discussed openly, especially in the area of a Magisterium, with the document declaring, "The absence of an authoritative universal magisterium among the churches of the Anglican Communion marks a signal difference in the structure of teaching authority."

FOCUS Wins Injunction On Apr. 25, the Fellowship of Catholic University Students secured an injunction from a federal court to halt enforcement of the HHS Mandate that would require employers to provide contraception, sterilization and abortion-inducing drugs to employees. The U.S. District Court for the District of Colorado issued the preliminary injunction. FOCUS employs more that 400 employees and was represented by the Alliance Defending Freedom (ADF).

In a statement, Alliance Senior Counsel Michael J. Norton said, "In America, we don't try to separate what people do from what they believe. Faith-based organizations should be free to operate according to the faith they espouse and live out on a daily basis. If the administration can punish Christian ministries simply because they want to abide by their faith, there is no limit to what other freedoms it can take away. The court was right to block enforcement of this unconstitutional mandate against FOCUS."

MAY 2014

VATICAN

Crucifixion of Christians On May 2, Pope Francis expressed his anguish over the plight of Christians in Syria and said that he wept upon learning that some Christians had been crucified for their faith. The pontiff made the comments during his homily at morning Mass in Casa Santa Marta. The pope lamented, "I cried when I saw reports on the news of Christians crucified in a certain country, that is not Christian. Still today there are these people who kill and persecute, in the name of God."

Council for the Economy On May 2, Pope Francis addressed the members of the Pontifical Council for the Economy, speaking about its role in the reform of the Roman Curia. The pontiff said, "The Holy See feels called to actuate this mission, taking into account especially its responsibility to the universal Church. Moreover, these changes will reflect the desire to put into action the necessary reform of the Roman Curia to serve better the "*fidelis dispensator et prudens.*" The endeavor will not be simple and requires courage and determination. A new mentality of evangelical service should be established in the different administrations of the Holy See. The Council for the Economy plays a significant role in this process of reform. It has the task to oversee the economic management and to supervise the structures and the administrative and financial activities of these administrations. It carries out its activity in close relationship with the Secretariat for the Economy. I take advantage of the occasion to thank Card. Pell also for his effort, for his work, and also for his Australian "rugby-er" tenacity. Thank you, Eminence!"

President of Angola On May 2, Pope Francis welcomed Pres. José Eduardo dos Santos of Angola to the Vatican Apostolic Palace. In a communiqué issued by the Holy See, the pontiff and president discussed "the legal state of the Catholic Church in the country," the communiqué stated. "In this context, reference was also made to the important contribution offered by the Catholic Church to the country through its educational and healthcare institutions." After the meeting, the president met with Card. Pietro Parolin, the Vatican Secretary of State.

New Swiss Guards On May 5, Pope Francis held an audience for the new recruits of the Pontifical Swiss Guard who were sworn in the next day. The pontiff told them, "Your uniform is an evocative trait of the Swiss Guard and attracts the attention of the people. Remember that it is not the uniform, but rather he who wears it, who must be noted for his kindness, his spirit of welcome, for his charitable attitude toward all. Consider this also in your relations between yourselves, according importance, also in your community life…With your special service, you are called upon to offer serene and joyful Christian witness to whoever arrives in the Vatican to visit St. Peter's Basilica and to meet the Pope."

Pope Paul VI's Beatification On May 11, it was announced that a miracle had been approved by the Congregation for the Causes of Saints attributed to the intercession of Pope Paul VI. The approval cleared the way for the beatification of the late pope at the Vatican on Oct. 19, 2014, by Pope Francis. Born Giovanni Battista Montini in 1897, Pope Paul VI served as pontiff in the tumultuous decade after the end of the Second Vatican Council. He died in 1978.

Q&A with Seminarians On May 13, Pope Francis held a question and answer session with seminarians from all over the world who are studying in Rome's pontifical colleges (including the North American College for Americans). The pontiff answered a variety of questions on the priesthood and consecrated life, focusing on authentic formation that does not stress exclusively academic formation for the priestly life but the four pillars of the spiritual, academic, pastoral and human. He stressed being organized in studies and in ministry and being vigilant. "The ideal," he said, "is to end the day tired. … But with a good tiredness, not a reckless tiredness, that is harmful to your health over time."

Financial Information Authority On May 19, the L'Autorità di Informazione Finanziaria (AIF) (Financial Information Authority) issued its annual report on the activities and supervision of financial information for the prevention of and combating money laundering and the financing of terrorism (Year II, 2013). The report found "a significant strengthening of the legal and institutional framework of the Holy See and Vatican City State to effectively combat financial crime, an institutionalization of international collaboration of the competent authority of the Holy See with its foreign counterparts, and a massively improved performance in monitoring potential financial wrongdoing…The Evaluation conducted by Moneyval, the Committee of Experts on the Evaluation of Anti-Money Laundering Measures and the Financing of Terrorism of the Council of Europe, in December 2013, and our statistics allow us to say that today we have a proper and equivalent system in place to prevent and fight financial crime. A system that is well in line with international standards."

Pope Francis' Visit to the Holy Land On May 24, Pope Francis visited the Holy Land from May 24-26 on his apostolic visit to the holy places since his election. The journey was intended especially to commemorate the 50th anniversary of Pope Paul VI's historic encounter in Jerusalem with Patriarch Athenagoras, an event that was seen as a watershed moment in the history of ecumenism.

The pontiff arrived in Amman, Jordan, on May 24, where he met with King Abdullah II and the Jordanian Queen and then Mass at the International Stadium in Amman. He then visited the Baptismal Site at Bethany beyond the Jordan and met with refugees and disabled young people in the Latin church at Bethany beyond the Jordan. On May 25, Francis departed Jordan by helicopter for Bethlehem where he was greeted by Pres. Mahmoud Abbass president of the State of Palestine at the presidential Palace in Bethlehem. He then said Mass in Manger Square in Bethlehem and recited the Regina Coeli with an allocution. Following the Mass, the Holy Father had lunch with families from Palestine in the Franciscan convent of Casa Nova in Bethlehem, visited the Grotto of the Nativity in Bethlehem, and met with Children from the refugee Camps of Deheisheh, Aida, and Beit Jibrin at the Phoenix Center of the Deheisheh Refugee Camp. After a farewell at the helicopter port of Bethlehem, Francis traveled to Ben Gurion International Airport in Tel Aviv and from there went to Jerusalem.

That evening, the Holy Father met with the Ecumenical Patriarch of Constantinople at the Apostolic Delegation in Jerusalem and signed a joint declaration. They then held a formal ecumenical meeting on the occasion of the 50th anniversary of the meeting in Jerusalem between Pope Paul VI and Patriarch Athenagoras in the Basilica of the Holy Sepulcher. He had dinner with the Patriarchs and Bishops and the Papal Household at the Latin Patriarchate in Jerusalem

On May 26, 2014, the pontiff visited the Grand Mufti of Jerusalem in the building of the Great Council on the Esplanade of the Mosques. He then visited the famed Western Wall in Jerusalem and placed a wreath at Mount Herzl in Jerusalem before going to the Yad Vashem Museum in Jerusalem that documents the Holocaust. He next met with the two chief rabbis at Heichal Shlomo Center in Jerusalem, before heading to the Jerusalem Great Synagogue and then a courtesy meeting with Shimon Peres, the President of the State of Israel at the Presidential Residence in Jerusalem. Soon after, Francis met with Benjamin Netanyahu, the Prime Minister of Israel at the Notre Dame Center in Jerusalem, followed by lunch there with the Papal Household and entourage. Next came a private visit to the Ecumenical Patriarch of Constantinople at the building next to the Orthodox church of Viri Galilei on the Mount of Olives and then a meeting with priests, men and women religious and seminarians in the church of Gethsemane at the foot of the Mount of Olives. That afternoon, Francis celebrated Mass with the ordinaries of the Holy Land in the room of the Cenacle in Jerusalem. He departed Israel soon after from Ben Gurion International Airport in Tel Aviv. [For details, see under **News in Depth**.]

UN Committee Against Torture On May 25, the United Nations Committee for the Convention Against Torture (CAT) released an advance unedited version of its Concluding Observations on the Initial Report of the Holy See. The Vatican responded by noting that the report had recognized that the Holy See had made many "serious and substantial reforms on its procedures that further advance the principles and objectives of the CAT" and that the committee had likewise acknowledged "extensively the good faith efforts of the Holy See to comply with and advance the CAT, to institute reforms to prevent sexual abuse, and to compensate and facilitate the care and healing of the victims of sexual abuse."

According to the report, the committee "did not find the Holy See in violation of the CAT, and acknowledges that the Holy See and Catholic dioceses and religious orders have instituted important efforts to prevent sexual abuse." The committee additionally "appreciates the open and constructive dialogue with the high-level delegation of the Holy See and notes that many Catholic dioceses and religious orders have provided financial settlements to victims of sexual abuse. Finally, the Conclusions do not assert that the Church's efforts to protect the unborn are a form of torture or cruel, inhuman or degrading treatment or punishment under the CAT, thus safeguarding the fundamental human right of freedom of religion and opinion and the protection and promotion of human life."

Papal Press Conference On May 26, during his flight back to Italy from his trip to the Holy Land, Pope Francis held a 90-minute press conference with reporters that covered a variety of topics, including the upcoming Synod of Bishops, the reforms of the Vatican, priestly celibacy, and the sex abuse scandal. The pontiff also discussed his upcoming trips to Asia, including Sri Lanka and the Philippines in January next year.

Addressing the sex abuse scandal, he reiterated that the Church must have a "zero tolerance" approach to clerical abuse, but he also made international news by announcing that he would meet with several abuse victims in early June and that he was also punishing bishops who had failed in that area. He used strong language on the crisis, comparing clergy sexual abuse to "celebrating a Black Mass."

The Pope was asked about clerical celibacy — which is often erroneously connected by reporters and media to the causes of clergy sexual abuse. He told reporters that the "door is always open" to ending mandatory priestly celibacy as it is not a dogma of the faith, but he also appreciates it a "great deal" and believes it is "a gift for the Church."

Asked about the issue of the Church's pastoral care of the divorced and remarried, Francis noted that the upcoming Synod of Bishops on the Family would look at whole range of issues facing the family in the modern world. He said, "What I didn't like, was what some people, within the Church as well, said about the purpose of the Synod: that it intends to allow remarried divorcees to take communion, as if the entire issue boiled down to a case."

Asked about the possibility that he might resign some day, he replied candidly that he would "do what the Lord tells me to do" and "pray and try to follow God's will." He noted that Benedict XVI had "opened the door" to the possibility, he said, but "whether there will be others, only God knows. I believe that if a bishop of Rome feels he is losing his strength, he must ask himself the same questions Pope Benedict XVI did."

General Audiences
May 7, 2014
May 14, 2014
May 21, 2014

INTERNATIONAL
Canadian March for Life On May 8, tens of thousands of pro-life Canadians marched in Ottawa to promote the Culture of Life. They received a message from Pope Francis, sent through the Cardinal Secretary of State, Card. Pietro Parolin to Card. Gérald Cyprien Lacroix, abp. of Québec and Primate of the Church in Canada. Card. Lacroix read the message to the throng that had assembled in front of Parliament Hill. The papal message read: "His Holiness Pope Francis is pleased to greet everyone taking part in the 17th National March for Life in Ottawa, and he assures them of his spiritual closeness as they give witness to the God-given dignity, beauty and value of human life. He prays that this event foster greater respect for the inviolable right to life of each person from conception to natural death and support the efforts of all who labor to ensure that this fundamental human right receives adequate legal protection. To the organizers and participants, and in particular to those who aid women in crisis pregnancies and their children, the Holy Father cordially imparts his Apostolic Blessing as a pledge of joy and peace in the risen Lord."

Joint Appeal On May 15, participants in a colloquium in Amman, Jordan, issued a joint appeal for greater cooperation, improved education for children, and urged the international community to work for the release of recently kidnapped Nigerian schoolgirls. The colloquium was organized by the Jordanian government and was held under the joint leadership of Jordan's Prince El Hassan bin Talal, founder and president of the Royal Institute for Interfaith Studies, and Card. Jean-Louis Tauran, president of the Pontifical Council for Interreligious Dialogue. The participants issued a declaration of common points of agreement, including: the fundamental institutions for the education of children and youth are the family and the school; the importance of proper religious education, in particular for the transmission of religious and moral values; the necessary consideration of the dignity of the human person, especially in educational institutions; there is widespread disregard for the international provisions aimed at guaranteeing the effective respect of fundamental human rights, in particular religious freedom; the most urgent challenges are the peaceful resolution of current conflicts, the eradication of poverty and the promotion of the spiritual and moral dimension of life; the conviction that religion is not the cause of conflicts, but rather inhumanity and ignorance; consequently integral education is essential; and many recalled that religions, properly understood and practiced, are not causes of division and conflicts but rather a necessary factor for reconciliation and peace. The group also issued a proposed "Cultural Decalogue" for education: 1) Never renounce intellectual curiosity; 2) Have intellectual courage, instead of intellectual cowardice; 3) Be humble and not intellectually arrogant; 4) Practice intellectual empathy, instead of closed-mindedness; 5) Observe intellectual integrity; 6) Keep your intellectual autonomy; 7) Persevere in the face of surrounding superficiality; 8) Trust reason; 9) Be fairminded and not intellectually unfair; and 10) Consider pluralism as richness, not a threat.

Meriam Ibrahim On May 15, what soon became an international case of religious freedom that was almost universally ignored by the mainstream western press, Meriam Yahia Ibrahim Ishag, 27, a Christian, was convicted of apostasy by a Sudanese court in the Khartoumarea district of Haj Yousef and sentenced to death if she did not recant. Born to a family with a Muslim father, Ibrahim was actually raised in the Christian Orthodox faith by her mother as her father was absent. Ibrahim was likewise ordered to receive 100 lashes for adultery because of her marriage to a Christian South Sudanese man, Daniel Wani. According to the interpretation of Sharia or Islamic law by the Sudanese, such a marriage is deemed adultery. The sentences were handed down despite the fact that Ibrahim was expecting a child to be born in the coming weeks. She was subsequently imprisoned with her 20-month-old son at Omdurman Women's Prison near Khartoum. The court decision was condemned by a number of Western embassies in Sudan.

On May 19, international appeals were expressed calling for her release, including by members of the British Parliament. On May 27, she gave birth to a daughter while in prison. The events regarding her fate continued to play out into June. [See International News in June for other details.]

Abortion in Colombia On May 6, the Senate of Colombia unanimously voted that there is no so-called "right to abortion" in the country. The decision was hailed by Pro-Life advocates who had fought a furious lobbying by international abortion rights advocates. The issue emerged as part of a debated bill, law 244/2013, that was intended to protect female victims of sexual violence but that excluded language to establish abortion as a right. The proposed law was seen initially as a valuable legal statement of justice for victims of sexual violence, especially as a result of armed conflict. Article 13 of the bill, however, sought to establish abortion as a right by stipulating that victims of rape must have access to abortion, thereby establishing in Colombia the legal precedent for abortion on demand. The Pro-Life movement, seeing

through the legal technicality of the article, asked for the Senate to reconsider the provision. The final version of the bill omitted the reference, using less stringent language. The Colombian Constitution includes Article 11 stating that the "right to life is inviolable." Abortion has been allowed in the country since 2006, under the specific circumstances of pregnancy as the result of rape or incest; when the health or life of the mother is endangered; or the fetus is unlikely to survive or suffers fetal malformation.

European Education On May 19, a gathering of European Bishops and Catholic School Leaders completed four days of meetings in Sarajevo to assess Catholic Education in Europe. The Congress was organized by the School section of the "Catechesis, School and University" Consilium Conferentiarum Episcoporum Europe or Council of the Bishops' Conferences of Europe (CCEE) Commission, and by the European Committee for Catholic Education (CEEC), in collaboration with the Catholic Bishops' Conference of Bosnia and Herzegovina (BK BiH) and brought together 70 bishops and national educational directors; it was officially convened by the CCEE and CEEC under the leadership of Cardinal Vinko Puljic, abp. of Sarajevo. The gathering discussed all of the major issues facing Catholic education in Europe including the struggle against secularism, the dangers of a sense of personal isolation for teachers, and creating a learning atmosphere that is beneficial for authentic learning. Central to Catholic education, the Congress emphasized teaching all disciplines in light of the Gospel and making available to students what it called the "heritage of the Gospel" (the unique contribution that the Gospel provides to knowledge and culture). Focus was also placed on Catholic identity in schools.

Canadian Pro-Life March On May 22, tens of thousands of Pro-Life marchers gathered in Toronto at Parliament Hill for the 17th Pro-life National March. Canadian organizers have noted with pleasure the increase in attendance every year. They were joined by Card. Thomas Collins of Toronto and Card. Gérald Lacroix of Quebec, along with other Catholic and Anglican bishops. Card. Lacroix read a message from Pope Francis, signed by the Holy See's Secretary of State, Card. Pietro Parolin: "He, [the Pope] prays that this event fosters greater respect for the inviolable right to life of each person from conception to natural death and support the efforts of all who labour to ensure that this fundamental human right receives adequate legal protection. To the organizers and participants, and in particular to those who aid women in crisis pregnancies and their children, the Holy Father cordially imparts his Apostolic Blessing as a pledge of joy and peace in the risen Lord."

European Commission On May 28, the European Commission, called the Barroso Commission, officially vetoed the Citizens' Initiative "UN DE NOUS / ONE OF US" that had called for an end to the European Union funding the destruction of human embryos. The petition had been signed by two million people, the largest such collection of signatures in the history of the EU. The petition specifically requested that the EU research budget no longer be used to finance projects that involve or pre-suppose the destruction of human embryos and that modifications be made to EU regulations. The European Citizens' Initiative (ECI), a process for citizen participation created by the Treaty of Lisbon, allows a million citizens to take the initiative of introducing a legislative proposal in the European institutions. In a statement, the

ONE OF US Committee declared, "While each initiative draft is controlled upstream by the Commission before being open to signature, the Barroso Commission claims to possess the right of veto downstream, against initiatives having yet successfully obtained the required popular support. Such veto power is illegitimat and anti-democratic since politically, it is the European Legislature that may give a verdict on the content of the Initiative, and not the Commission, otherwise, the ECI mechanism would be meaningless." The Committee planned to appeal the undemocratic and biased decision before the Court of Justice in Luxembourg.

Increasing Euro-Skepticism On May 28, Card. Reinhard Marx of Munich, head of the Commission of the Bishops' Conferences of the European Community (COMECE), expressed his worry about the growing level of Euro-Skepticism, a rejection of the idea of the European Union and European integration and the rise of populist, nationalist, and xenophobic movements and political parties. In a statement on the recent European elections, Card. Marx observed, "A large majority of the citizens who participated in the European elections voted for pro-European candidates. In the years to come this will allow the European Parliament to continue its work for the common good of all Europeans with dedicated and competent women and men. A matter of concern is the significant increase of support for parties which reject the project of European integration. A number of them were even able to secure a majority of votes in some Member States including France, Denmark and the United Kingdom. Some of these parties are not only populist but nationalistic and xenophobic. Such positioning is unacceptable for Christians and is a threat to the peaceful coexistence of the peoples of our continent."

Belgians Euthanized On May 28, *Sudpresse*, Belgium's chief French-speaking newspaper, issued a report on the number of Belgians who had been euthanized in 2013. The results found a sharp increase in the number killings: 1,816 cases of euthanasia were reported in 2013; 1,432 were killed in 2012, an increase of 26.8%. The newspaper reported that there are 150 cases of euthanasia per month in Belgium or, even more telling, 5 people euthanized a day. Of the 1,816 cases, 51.7% were males and 48.3% were female. A majority (53.5%) were between the ages of 70 and 90, 21% were over 90.

NATIONAL

Harvard Black Mass On May 13, Catholics and people of goodwill expressed relief that a Satanic Black Mass scheduled for the previous night in Cambridge, Mass., had been apparently canceled. The Harvard Extension Cultural Studies Club had originally planned to host the sacrilegious and blasphemous ceremony at the Queens Head pub in Memorial Hall on the Harvard campus in Cambridge, and the decision to allow the viciously anti-Catholic and historically criminal and bloody mockery of the Mass sparked an immense outcry across the country. A petition to halt the Black Mass was signed by 60,000 people in the region and was supported by the Harvard Student Catholic Association and Card. Seán O'Malley, abp. of Boston. The president of Harvard, Drew Faust said in a statement, "It is deeply regrettable that the organizers of this event, well aware of the offense they are causing so many others, have chosen to proceed with a form of expression that is so flagrantly disrespectful and inflammatory." Nevertheless, the Harvard head permitted the sacrilege to go forward on the claim of the value of free expression on campus. The Archdiocese of Boston held a Holy Hour and Eucharistic Procession at the local St. Paul's Church on the same evening as the originally scheduled Black Mass. It was attended by several thousand people, including Pres. Faust. The event, while the source of great anguish to Catholics, served to galvanize Catholics in the heavily secularized area of Boston and gave great encouragement to Catholic students at Harvard University.

Family Meeting Theme On May 14, Abp. Charles Chaput of Philadelphia announced the official theme for the September 2015 World Meeting of Families in Philadelphia: "Love is Our Mission: The Family Fully Alive." The archbishop made the announcement with Abp. Vincenzo Paglia, president of the Pontifical Council for the Family, who was visiting the archdiocese to advance preparations for the meeting next year. Abp. Chaput declared: "When we first realized that Archbishop Paglia's visit to Philadelphia would occur near the time that we planned to share the theme for the 2015 World Meeting of Families, it seemed only appropriate that we ask him to be part of this moment. Each World Meeting of Families has a theme from which all content and programming flows. Key note addresses, breakout sessions, and panels are developed on a wide variety of topics that all connect back to the central theme. In Milan in 2012 the theme of the world meeting was 'The Family: Work and Celebration.' As we began to discuss what the theme in Philadelphia would be, we took inspiration from this place, its history and its spirit. As many of you know from our history books, William Penn founded this colony as a holy experiment-an example to the nations. His Charter of Privileges guaranteed religious freedom to all. Pennsylvania welcomed Quakers, Lutherans, Anglicans, Presbyterians, Baptists, Mennonites and dozens of other congregations as well as Catholics and Jews. Colonial Philadelphia was a blueprint for democracy. It was founded upon liberty and tolerance. Surely there were tensions that arose as customs and languages weren't necessarily shared, but as we know Philadelphians, even today, strive to find what unites rather than divides us. We specially chose this place, which overlooks Independence Mall for the announcement of our theme today because it is a beautiful reflection of why Philadelphia will be an extraordinary host to the World Meeting of Families, and hopefully, a place to welcome Pope Francis...

"Ladies and gentleman, the theme for the World Meeting of Families – Philadelphia 2015 is, 'Love is Our Mission: The Family Fully Alive.'"

Immigration Reform On May 29, Abp. Thomas Wenski of Miami and the chair of the U.S. Conference of Catholic Bishops' Committee on Migration celebrated a Mass for immigrants and their families at St. Peter's Catholic Church on Capitol Hill. Abp. Wenski also concelebrated Mass at the U.S.-Mexico border on Apr. 1 with other bishops, including Cardinal Seán O'Malley. He spoke during the Mass on Capitol Hill about praying for political leaders and the hope that they might find the courage to enact genuine immigration reform. He said in his homily, "Our immigration system is a stain on the soul of our nation. As a moral matter, it must be changed. We must pray that our elected officials recognize this and have the courage to reform." He then visited with a group of young immigrants and heard stories about the impact of deportations on families.

JUNE 2014

VATICAN

Charismatic Movement On June 2, Pope Francis attended a gathering of the Charismatic Movement at Rome's Olympic Stadium and spoke to the more than 50,000 in attendance from 55 countries. The had come to mark the 37th Annual National Convocation of "Renewal in the Spirit" heard encouraging words form the pontiff. He told them to "remember that the Church was born to go forth that morning of Pentecost, so go forth onto the streets and evangelize, proclaim the Gospel...Do not cage the Holy Spirit! Evangelization, spiritual ecumenism, attention to the poor and needy, and welcome to the marginalized.

"Globalization of Indifference" On June 2, Pope Francis sent a message to a meeting organized by the Pontifical Council "Cor Unum" intended to gather together various charitable organizations and offices to deal with the growing humanitarian crisis in Syria. In his message, the pontiff observed, "We must accept with great sorrow that the Syrian crisis has not been resolved, but instead continues, and there is the risk of growing accustomed to it: of forgetting the victims claimed on a daily basis, the unspeakable suffering, the thousands of refugees, which include the elderly and children, who suffer and at times die of hunger and of diseases causes by the conditions of war. This indifference is harmful! Once again we must repeat the name of this illness that does so much damage in today's world: the globalization of indifference."

Prime Minister of Japan On June 6, Pope Francis welcomed Japanese Prime Minister Shinzo Abe to the Apostolic Palace in the Vatican. According to a Vatican communiqué, "During the cordial discussions, the good relations between Japan and the Holy See were evoked, as well as the understanding and collaboration between the Church and State in the fields of education, social welfare and healthcare." The prime minister also met with the Cardinal Secretary of State Pietro Parolin, and Abp. Dominique Mamberti, secretary for Relations with States.

Vatican Finances On June 6, Pope Francis made significant changes to the Financial Intelligence Authority that oversees the Holy See's financial operations. The pontiff replaced the essentially all Italian board with a group of international experts, including an American. The members of the new board were: Juan C. Zarate, a U.S. senior adviser at the Center for Strategic and International Studies and visiting lecturer at Harvard Law School; Maria Bianca Farina, a senior Italian administrator at the Italian postal system's investment and insurance divisions and an expert in tax audits and investment management; Marc Odendall, a Swiss-based philanthropist and former chairman of the International Ethics Board of EDHEC Business School; and Joseph Yubaraj Pillay, chairman of the Council of Presidential Advisers of the Republic of Singapore and of Tiger Airways Holdings. The pope also promoted Italian Tommaso Di Ruzza, formerly a study assistant at the FIA, to be the agency's "ad interim" vice-director. The overall head of the Financial Intelligence Authority is Swiss lawyer Rene Bruelhart.

International Cooperation On June 9, the newly restructured Vatican Financial Information Authority that oversees Vatican Finances issued a statement entitled the "AIF Strengthens International Cooperation: Memoranda of Understanding with the U.K., France and Four More Countries." The statement read, in part: "L'Autorità Informazione Finanziaria (AIF), the Financial Intelligence Unit of the Holy See and Vatican City State, has formalized its bilateral cooperation with the U.K., France and four other countries with Memoranda of Understanding signed during the Plenary Meeting of the Egmont Group held in Peru. The Memoranda were signed with the Financial Intelligence Units of the U.K., France, Malta, Romania, Poland and Peru by the Director of AIF, Rene Bruelhart. [See under News in Depth for other details.]

Francis, Abbas, and Peres Pray for Peace On June 8, Pope Francis hosted an Invocation for Peace in the Vatican Gardens where he welcomed Presidents Shimon Peres of Israel and Mahmoud Abbas of the Palestinian Authority and thus fulfilled a pledge made during his pilgrimage to the Holy Land. The three were joined by Ecumenical Patriarch Bartholomew I at the Casa Santa Marta in Vatican City and were then taken by a van to the Vatican Gardens where they were joined by their respective delegations. The Invocation began with the plea: "May the Lord grant us peace! We are gathered here, Israelis and Palestinians, Jews, Christians and Muslims, to offer our prayer for peace for the Holy Land and for all its inhabitants."

The Invocation had three parts, with pleas for peace from the Jewish, Christian, and Muslim representatives. The Holy Father, President Peres, and President Abbas all spoke briefly. Francis taught, "Our world is a legacy bequeathed to us from past generations, but it is also on loan to us from our children: our children who are weary, worn out by conflicts and yearning for the dawn of peace, our children who plead with us to tear down the walls of enmity and to set out on the path of dialogue and peace, so that love and friendship will prevail. Many, all too many, of those children have been innocent victims of war and violence, saplings cut down at the height of their promise. It is our duty to ensure that their sacrifice is not in vain. The memory of these children instills in us the courage of peace, the strength to persevere undaunted in dialogue, the patience to weave, day by day, an ever more robust fabric of respectful and peaceful coexistence, for the glory of God and the good of all. Peacemaking calls for courage, much more so than warfare. It calls for the courage to say yes to encounter and no to conflict: yes to dialogue and no to violence; yes to negotiations and no to hostilities; yes to respect for agreements and no to acts of provocation; yes to sincerity and no to duplicity. All of this takes courage, it takes strength and tenacity." [For full coverage, see under News in Depth.]

Pope and FIFA World Cup On June 12, Pope Francis sent a message to the participants of the FIFA World Cup 2014 urging them to remember that sports tournaments are "not only a game but also an opportunity for dialogue, comprehension and mutual human enrichment. Sport is not only a form of entertainment, but also — and above all I would say — a tool for communicating values that promote the good of the human person and help to build a more peaceful and fraternal society...Let us think of loyalty, perseverance, friendship, sharing, solidarity. In fact, there are many values and attitudes fostered by football that are not only important on the field, but in all aspects of life, especially in building peace. Sport is a school for peace — it teaches us how to build peace."

Canonizations On June 12, it was announced that Pope Francis would preside over the canonizations of six blessed on the feast of Christ the King on Sunday, Nov. 23. The six new saints would be: Giovanni Antonio Farina (1803-1888), an Italian bishop and founder the Institute of the Sisters Teachers of Saint Dorothy, Daughters of the Sacred Hearts; Kuriakose Elias Chavara (1805-1871), a Syro-Malabar priest in India and founder of the Carmelites of Mary Immaculate; Ludovico of Casoria (1814-1885), an Italian Franciscan priest and founder of the Gray Sisters of St. Elizabeth; Nicola Saggio (Nicola da Longobardi, 1650-1709), an Italian oblate of the Order of Minims; Euphrasia Eluvathingal (1877-1952), an Indian Carmelite of the Syro-Malabar Church; and Amato Ronconi (1238-1304), an Italian, Third Order Franciscan and founder a hospital for poor pilgrims.

Interview with Spanish Newspaper On June 13, the leading newspaper of Barcelona, Spain, "*La Vanguardia*," published a wide-ranging interview with Pope Francis. The topics ranged from the Popemobile to the legacy and true record of his predecessor Pope Pius XII to the thorny Spanish issue of Catalonian independence. The pontiff also discussed some of his key themes of unemployment among young people and creating an unjust throwaway culture.

Ratzinger Prize On June 17, it was announced that the 2014 Ratzinger Prize for theology had been given to a woman for the first time. Card. Camillo Ruini announced that French professor Anne-Marie Pelletier, the prize's first female winner, and Polish priest and scholar, Professor Waldemar Chrostowski, the first Polish winner, would be the recipients for the year. Professor Pelletier, 69, is an expert in hermeneutics and biblical exegesis, while Msgr. Chrostowski, 63, is a Scripture scholar and expert on Catholic-Jewish dialogue. The Ratzinger Prize includes an award of $87,000. It was started in 2010 and is referred to as the "Nobel Prize in Theology."

Pope Visits Calabria On June 21, Pope Francis visited the Diocese of Cassano all'Jonio in the Calabrian province of Cosenza, Italy's southernmost region outside the island of Sicily. It is a region that suffers from chronic economic problems, high unemployment, and the presence of the Mafia. The pope began his visit by going to the Rosetta Sisca penitentiary of Castrovillari where he was welcomed by Bp. Nunzio Galantino, bishop emeritus of the diocese and secretary general of the Italian Episcopal Conference, and by the mayor of the city, Domenico Lo Polito. He later spoke to the Calabrian priests and reminded them to be joyful and happy, to embrace the "joy of being priests" and to remember that "Jesus makes us see if we are working as good agents, or as ...'employees.'"

In his closing Mass, the pontiff had very strong words for the Mafia and created a media frenzy when he used the word excommunicate to describe the way that Mafia bosses had removed themselves from the Church by their terrible acts. The Holy Father talked about the Mafia the closing Mass at the Piana di Sibari, Calabria's largest plain. He said, "When adoration of the Lord is substituted by adoration of money, the road to sin opens to personal interest ... When one does not adore the Lord, one becomes an adorer of evil, like those who live by dishonesty and violence."

Papal Diplomat Laicized On June 27, the Holy See Press Office announced that Abp. Jozef Wesolowski, a former papal diplomat had been found guilty of sexually abusing minors and had been forcibly laicized after a trial by the Congregation for the Doctrine of the Faith. The one-time apostolic nuncio to the Dominican Republic was told that he had "two months in which to make an eventual appeal." The Holy See had recalled Wesolowski in August of 2013 after Pope Francis learned that the nuncio had been accused of sexually abusing teenage boys in the Dominican Republic. The former diplomat also faces possible extradition to Poland and the Dominican Republic, and the Holy See announced it would not resist any such legal efforts.

Instrumentum Laboris On June 27, the Holy See announced that the Synod of Bishops had issued its working document for the upcoming Synod on the Family, scheduled for October. The document, termed an *Instrumentum Laboris*, was the result of the global consultation and questionnaire on pastoral issues facing the family in modern life and included such major topics as same-sex "marriage," reception of the sacraments for divorced and remarried couples, and openness to life. The 75-page document was divided into three parts: the Gospel of the Family, the Pastoral Program for the Family in Light of New Challenges, and openness to life and the responsibility of parents in the upbringing of their children. [For full coverage, see under **News in Depth**.]

Spanish King and Queen On June 30, Pope Francis welcomed the newly crowned King Felipe VI and Queen Letizia of Spain to the Vatican Apostolic Palace. King Juan Carlos, the former ruler of Spain, had met with Francis in April and had announced soon after that he would abdicate in favor of his American-educated son. Pope Francis and the King and Queen of Spain met privately for almost 45 minutes. After the meeting, the King and Queen had a session with the Vatican Secretary of State, Card. Pietro Parolin.

General Audiences

June 4, 2014
June 11, 2014
June 18, 2014
June 25, 2014

INTERNATIONAL

U.K. Midwives and Abortion On June 3, the British health system approved a new set of guidelines that would allow for the first time midwives and nurses in Great Britain to supervise in performing abortions. Previously, midwives and nurses were permitted to participate in some areas, but the new rules would permit them to administer the drugs used for medical abortions. A doctor would need only to approve the procedure. Pro-Life leaders expressed alarm at the development, especially as it would represent a severe perversion of the traditional function of midwives.

Catholic-Orthodox Forum On June 5, the participants in a five-day forum in the IV European Catholic-Orthodox dialogue in Minsk released a final statement that included a nine-point message. The forum was held in the capital of Belarus, at the invitation of the Patriarchal Exarch of all Belarus, Metropolitan Pavel of Minsk and Sluzk, while the Catholic Church was represented Card. Peter Erdo, President of the Episcopal Conference of Europe. The message said, in part, "Our message — participants wrote — wants to be first of all a sign of joy and hope ... we know that many are suffering and are in search of a word that gives sense to their life. Indeed where Christian faith and morality have been dismissed, a feeling of emptiness leads many to despair and nihilism. The Church offers consistent values by incorporating humanity in Christ, the source of all true values."

Christian Dead in Mosul Abp. Amel Nona, the Chaldean archbishop of Mosul declared to the Catholic charity Aid to the Church in Need that the last Christians had left the city in the face of the seizure of Mosul by the barbaric Islamist forces of ISIS (Islamic State of Iraq and Syria) that had captured whole stretched of Iraq and Syria and was bringing death and genocidal treatment of Christians. ISIS, which also calls itself the Islamic State, brought staggering suffering and brutality to the city, informing Christians that they could flee, convert, or be killed. There were reports of mass executions, crucifixions, and torture of men, women, and children. The Nineveh plains, home to a number of ancient Christian villages, were soon also overrun. The significance of the fall of Mosul was that for the first time in literally 1,600 years, the Mass was not celebrated.

Syrian Destruction On June 19, Patriarch Gregory III Laham told the annual meeting of the Holy Synod of the Melkite Greek Catholic Church that some 91 churches had been damaged or destroyed during the terrible fighting in Syria, including 37 Melkite Catholic Churches. He noted as well that whole parts of the Syrian population had been forced to flee the country because of the bloodshed. The patriarch observed, "Lebanon is in crisis, the presidency of the republic is vacant, beloved Iraq is back again to fire and blood. We hope that Egypt quickly regains its stability and security with its new president, to whom we express all our good wishes for him to lead his country to that stability and security to which it aspires. What can be said about Syria, which is in its fourth year of bloody crisis, a real way of the cross for an entire nation, a country where people and buildings are devastated? Let us never forget the suffering of our brothers and sisters in the Holy Land and the Israeli-Palestinian conflict that engenders the whole region's crises. We thank our Pope Francis for his concern, his appeals and all his initiatives for peace in our region and in every one of our countries."

Iraq Rescue Plan On June 23, the Catholic bishops of Iraq concluding their meeting in Baghdad where they agreed to a "rescue plan" for Christianity in the country and expressed growing alarm at the bloody attacks on Christians at the hands of ISIS that had cause renewed displacement of the Christian populations. The bishops recognized the catastrophe of Christianity in Iraq, noting that the Christian population had declined had declined from 1.5 million in the late 1980s to barely 300,000 today. Especially heartbreaking was the news that the Christian population of Mosul was extinct through death or flight and that for the first time in 1,600 years Mass was not being said.

Mariam Ibrahim On June 24, Marian Ibrahim, the Christian woman who had been sentenced to death for apostasy by a Sudanese court was finally released by authorities and then promptly re-arrested at the airport while trying to leave the country. She and her husband Daniel Wani, and their children, were detained and interrogated at the national security headquarters in Khartoum on the spurious charges of having forged documents. At the time of her "conviction," she was expecting her second child and subsequently gave birth while in prison. On July 26, she was released by authorities and sought refuge in the American embassy in Khartoum.

NATIONAL

Philadelphia Archdiocese Files Suit On June 4, the Archdiocese of Philadelphia and affiliated charities filed suit in federal court to block enforcement of portions of the Affordable Care Act, specifically the infamous HHS Mandate. The statement declared, "Charitable entities related to the Archdiocese of Philadelphia, along with the Archdiocese itself, filed suit late yesterday in Federal court against the U. S. Department of Health and Human Services, the U. S. Department of Labor, and the U. S. Department of the Treasury as well as their respective Secretaries. Grounded on the Religious Freedom Restoration Act and the First Amendment, the action asks the court to block enforcement of portions of the Affordable Care Act (ACA) that force religious employers to provide contraceptive services that violate Catholic belief. The charitable entities argue that ACA regulations force them to violate their religious convictions by either directly supplying, or cooperating in the process to supply, services that gravely conflict with Catholic belief. The court filing disputes the Government's power to order Catholic entities to offer or cooperate in such services. Dozens of similar cases have been filed nationwide. Various courts have already recognized that the Affordable Care Act imposes a burden on sincerely held religious beliefs. Relief was recently granted in the Western District of Pennsylvania to the Dioceses of Pittsburgh and Erie."

Immigration Reform On June 5, the president of the United States Conference of Catholic Bishops, Abp. Joseph Kurtz of Louisville issued a statement on immigration reform. It read, "In his first message to mark the World Day of Migrants, Pope Francis wrote: 'Every human being is a child of God! He or she bears the image of Christ! We ourselves need to see, and then to enable others to see, that migrants and refugees do not only represent a problem to be solved, but are brothers and sisters to be welcomed, respected, and loved.' In this spirit, I call upon our political leaders to reform our nation's broken immigration system. The time to act is now. As pastors, we see the human consequences of this broken system each day in our parishes and social service programs, as families are separated, migrant workers are exploited, and our fellow human beings risk everything to find a better life for themselves and the ones they love. Our nation should no longer tolerate an unjust system. We will pray for and work with members of Congress so that they might reform our immigration laws in a manner that properly balances the protection of human rights with the rule of law. And as we approach our General Assembly next week in New Orleans, I would ask my brother bishops to join me in offering our prayers, works, and joys of that meeting for the intention that the human dignity of all immigrants be fully respected, that they may be treated, truly, as 'brothers and sisters to be welcomed, respected, and loved.'"

St. Louis Archbishop Controversy On June 11, the archdiocese of St. Louis issued a statement in response to media reports seriously misrepresenting the testimony of Abp. Robert Carlson in a clergy sex abuse case at which he was deposed. The statement sought to clarify the actual testimony and refute the specious headlines being printed in the media. The statement read in part, "This statement is intended to clear up confusion generated by the release on June 9, 2014, of a videotaped deposition of Abp. Robert J. Carlson, Archbishop of St. Louis. This deposition was taken in a lawsuit for damages pending in a Minnesota state court relating to events that occurred more than 30 years ago in Minnesota. Neither Abp. Carlson nor the Archdiocese of St. Louis is a party to this case. Further, the Archbishop has been previously deposed by the same Plaintiff's counsel on at least three separate prior occasions in the 1980s focused on the activities of the same priest that he was again asked about last month — 27 years later. Recent inaccurate and misleading reporting by certain media outlets has impugned Abp. Carlson's good name and reputation. During a press conference held on June 9, 2014, Plaintiff's lawyer strategically took Abp. Carlson's response to a question out of context and suggested that the Archbishop did not know that it was a criminal offense for an adult to molest a child. Nothing could be further from the truth. Contrary to what is being reported, Abp. Carlson is and has been a leader in the Church when it comes to recognizing and managing matters of sexual abuse involving the clergy. As far back as 1980, then-Father Carlson wrote 'This behavior cannot be tolerated' in a memo referencing a priest's abusive actions (Exhibit 301 of this case)."

Phoenix Priests Attacked On June 12, Fr. Kenneth Walker, 28, associate pastor of Mater Misericordiae (Mother of Mercy) Mission Church on Phoenix, AZ, was attacked along with the pastor, Fr. Joseph Terra, 56, during a burglary. Fr. Walker died in the hospital. A popular young priest, Fr. Walker had just celebrated the second anniversary of his ordination to the priesthood as a member of the Priestly Fraternity of St. Peter. The diocese of Phoenix issued a statement, declaring, "We are stunned and deeply saddened to learn of the tragic assault. We ask that people offer prayers for both priests, the religious community, their families and the parish."

Francis invited to Philadelphia On June 12, the Bishops of the United States officially invited Pope Francis to the World Meeting of Families in Philadelphia scheduled for Sept. 22-27, 2015. The letter, approved by the bishops at their spring meeting in New Orleans and signed by the president of the United States Conference of Catholic Bishops, Abp. Joseph Kurtz of Louisville, read: "Assembled in New Orleans at our spring plenary meeting, we the Catholic Bishops of the United States look forward with joyful anticipation to the Eighth World Meeting of Families that is scheduled to take place in Philadelphia in September 2015. This event will be an occasion for Catholics from around the world to reflect on family life, and the role that families can play in strengthening our society and our Catholic faith.

"We wish to take this opportunity to warmly invite Your Holiness to grace us with your presence at this event. We have no doubt that the participants would be deeply honored, and would receive with gratitude your pastoral reflections on the meaning of the family.

"It is our fervent hope, Your Holiness, that you will favorably consider our invitation to visit us in the United States. Your presence would not only add significance to the World Meeting of Families, but also serve to deepen the bonds of affection that our faithful and many other Americans share with you as Bishop of Rome."

Fulton Sheen Miracle On June 18, it was announced that the seven-member theological commission serving the Congregation for the Causes of Saints had unanimously agreed that a recently investigated miracle involving a child should be attributed to the intercession of the Venerable Servant of God Archbishop Fulton Sheen.

The child in question involved a stillborn baby born in September 2010 who was not breathing for more than an hour. Inexplicably, the child began breathing and recovered fully. The decision by the theological commission was the next step in the validation of the miracle following the approval of the miracle in March by the commission of Vatican medical experts. The committee of cardinals and bishops who advise the Congregation will next examine the case and give their recommendation to Pope Francis.

Unaccompanied Child-Immigrants On June 25, the bishops of Texas issued a statement regarding the flood of unaccompanied minors making their way to the United States across the U.S.-Mexican border. The statement said in part: "Texas' Catholic Bishops are deeply concerned about the increasing number of unaccompanied children and mothers from Central America and Mexico who are crossing into the United States through our state. Some of these children, as young as four years of age, are reportedly being held in crowded conditions in Customs and Border Protection detention facilities until they can be processed and accepted into a temporary living shelter. So far this year, some 47,000 unaccompanied minors have been apprehended, with estimates that the number could grow to 90,000 by the end of September."

Supreme Court Pro-Life Decision On June 26, the U.S. Supreme Court struck down a 2007 Massachusetts law that created a "buffer zone" around the state's abortion clinics. But that severely limited access to abortion clinics for members of the Pro-Life case seeking to counsel women considering an abortion. The Justices ruled unanimously in *McCullen v. Coakley* in finding that the Massachusetts law violates the First Amendment. As it was written the law specifically targeted members of the Pro-Life movement by establishing a 35-foot "no-pro-life" speech zone outside abortion clinics and prohibiting them from "enter[ing] or remain[ing] on a public way or sidewalk adjacent" to a stand-alone abortion facility." The law was no applied equally as it permitted those encouraging women to have abortion unlimited access to the women. The law also allowed police to arrest and charge any person engaged in pro-life advocacy, including speaking, praying, wearing t-shirts, hats, or buttons, displaying signs, leafleting, or even making consented approaches to women or others entering the abortion clinic.

Hobby Lobby Decision On June 30, in a fiercely ideologically divided decision, the U.S. Supreme Court reached a 5-4 decision regarding the so-called Hobby Lobby case against the HHS Mandate that required businesses to provide contraception coverage to employers, including sterilization and abortion-inducing drugs. The Court found that family owned businesses could claim religious exemption from the mandate. A narrow majority of the court found that the Obama administration had not proven that mandate is the least restrictive means of advancing its interest in guaranteeing the provision of free access to contraception in health insurance plans. In addition, the Court also concluded that the 1993 Religious Freedom Restoration Act requires that closely held companies receive the same accommodation granted by the administration to nonprofit organizations that object to the mandate on religious grounds. Justices Roberts, Scalia, Thomas, and Kennedy voted for the majority while Justices Ginsburg, Breyer, Sotomayor, and Kagan dissenting. [See under **News in Depth** for complete coverage.]

JULY 2014

VATICAN

Holy See's Permanent Representative to UN On July 2, it was announced that Pope Francis had appointed Abp. Bernadito Auza to succeed Abp. Francis Chullikatt as the Holy See's permanent representative to the United Nations in New York. From the Philippines, Abp. Auza, 55, has served as apostolic nuncio to Haiti and is a long-time Vatican diplomat. He is the first Filipino to represent the Holy See at the UN. The archbishop also served in Bulgaria and Albania and worked in the second section of the Secretariat of State from 1999 to 2006. He was an official at the Holy See's mission at the UN in New York before being sent to Haiti as nuncio. His time in Haiti included work to assist the relief efforts in the wake of the devastating earthquake in 2010.

Official Logo and Prayer for WYD 2016 On July 3, the Vatican released the official logo and prayer for the 2016 World Youth Day in Krakow, Poland. The logo and prayer were unveiled at a press conference held by Krakow's metropolitan archbishop, Card. Stanislaw Dziwisz. The logo was created by Monika Rybczynska, 28, and utilizes a geographical outline of Poland, along with a cross, while a yellow circle marks the position of Krakow; the flame of divine mercy emerges from the cross, and the colors in the logo of blue, red, and yellow, signify the official colors of Krakow and its coat of arms. The text of the prayer reads:

"God, merciful Father, in your Son, Jesus Christ, you have revealed your love and poured it out upon us in the Holy Spirit, the Comforter, We entrust to you today the destiny of the world and of every man and woman.

We entrust to you in a special way young people of every language, people and nation: guide and protect them as they walk the complex paths of the world today and give them the grace to reap abundant fruits from their experience of the Krakow World Youth Day.

Heavenly Father, grant that we may bear witness to your mercy. Teach us how to convey the faith to those in doubt, hope to those who are discouraged, love to those who feel indifferent, forgiveness to those who have done wrong and joy to those who are unhappy. Allow the spark of merciful love that you have enkindled within us become a fire that can transform hearts and renew the face of the earth.

Mary, Mother of Mercy, pray for us. St. John Paul II, pray for us."

International Association of Exorcists On July 4, the Holy See granted its formal approval to the International Association of Exorcists. The decree was issued the Congregation for Clergy and granted official recognition of a worldwide group of 230 exorcists from 30 countries. The association was founded in Italy in 1991 by Fr. Gabriel Amorth, the famed exorcist in Rome.

First Woman Rector On July 4, it was announced that the Congregation for Catholic Education, under the presidency of Card. Zenon Grocholewski, had appointed Sr. Mary Melone as rector of the Pontifical University Antonianum, the pontifical university run by the Order of Friars Minor. She will not only be the first woman rector of a Roman pontifical university but was the first woman to obtain a permanent position as a professor on the theology faculty of the Roman university; she was also the school's first female dean. She is a member of the Franciscan Sisters of Blessed Angelina.

Francis Visits Molise On July 5, Pope Francis vis-

ited the Italian region of Molise in southern Italy, to bring support and encouragement to the archdiocese of Campobasso-Bojano. He first met local business leaders at the University of Molise in Campobasso and spoke about the crisis of unemployment and the problems faced by families because of economic problems. He then said Mass in the old Romagnoli stadium of Campobasso, and used his homily to stress the need "to put the dignity of the human person at the center of every perspective and every action. Other interests, even if legitimate, are secondary."

Francis then met with some 20,000 young people from the dioceses of Molise and Abruzzo at the Shrine of Castelpetroso in southern Italy, urging them to see what is most important in life. He said, "Contemporary society and its prevailing cultural models — the 'culture of the provisional' — do not provide a climate conducive to the formation of stable life choices with solid bonds, built on the rock of love and responsibility rather than on the sand of emotion…This feeds superficiality in taking responsibility because in the depths of the soul they risk being regarded as something from which we can still be free." The pontiff called on them to walk to the future with Jesus because, "Alone we cannot do it. Faced with the pressure of events and fashions, we will not be able to find the right path, and even if we could find it, we would not have enough strength to persevere, to deal with the climbs and unforeseen obstacles. And here comes the invitation of the Lord Jesus: "If you want ... follow me." He invites us to accompany us on the journey." The pope later met with detainees at the Administrative House of Isernia and gave a talk to a crowd in Isernia where he spoke about Pope St. Celestine V, the pontiff who resigned in 1294 for the good of the Church.

Pope Meet with Abuse Victims On July 6 and 7, Pope Francis met with six abuse victims in the Vatican in what was reportedly a very emotional encounter. The pope invited the victims, two from England, two from Germany, and one from Ireland, to stay at the Casa Santa Marta. He greeted them after dinner on the 6th and then had breakfast with them. He also celebrated Mass for them and delivered a homily in which he apologized powerfully for their suffering. The pope then met with the victims in a series of individual sessions that took up most of the morning and into the afternoon. According to Fr. Federico Lombardi, S.J., Director of the Holy See Press Office, the victims expressed "their profound gratitude to the Holy Father." Lombardi added, "The Pope spent much time with them, which reflected his intention to listen and to understand." [See also under **News in Depth**.]

Holy See Finances On July 8, a press conference was held by the director of the Holy See Press Office, Fr. Federico Lombardi, S.J., regarding the release of the consolidated financial statement of the Holy See and the financial statement of the Governorate of Vatican City State. The statement found that there was a surplus of some 10 million euros. The Holy See ended the year 2013 with a deficit of 24,470,549 euros, "due principally to negative fluctuations deriving from the valuation of gold, to the value of around 14 million euros." The administration of the Governorate, "autonomous, and independent of contributions from the Holy See," ended 2013 with a profit of 33,040,583 euros, an increase of around 10 million euros compared to last year. [See under **News in Depth** for other details.]

Vatican Bank On July 8, the Institute for Works of

Religion (IOR), commonly called the Vatican Bank, released its financial statements for 2013 in which it documented the completion of its first phase of a wider reform. Ernst von Freyberg, outgoing IOR president, stressed that the institute had focused on making itself "compliant with financial regulation, safer and more transparent, so as to create options for the Holy Father to decide on the future of the Institute. Through this work we have laid the ground for a new team to make the IOR a truly outstanding service provider in Catholic finance. Nevertheless, the IOR's reforms proved costly, so that profits fell in 2013 to 2.9 million euros, from 86.6 million euros in 2012. [See under **News in Depth** for other details.]

Peace in the Holy Land On July 13, Pope Francis called on the faithful to pray for peace in the Holy Land after reciting the Angelus prayer in St. Peter's Square. He spoke of the 'Invocation for Peace' on June 8 with Patriarch Bartholomew, Presidents Shimon Peres of Israel and Mahmoud Abbas of the Palestinian Authority, saying, "Some might think that such a meeting took place in vain. But no, because prayer helps us not to allow ourselves to be overcome by evil, nor resign ourselves to violence and hatred taking over dialogue and reconciliation."

"La Repubblica" Interview On July 13, Fr. Federico Lombardi, S.J., head of the Holy See Press Office issued a statement regarding an article on Pope Francis published in the Italian daily newspaper, La Repubblica. The statement read: "In the Sunday edition of "*La Repubblica*" an article by Eugenio Scalfari was prominently featured relating a recent conversation that took place with Pope Francis. The conversation was very cordial and most interesting and touched principally upon the themes of the plague of sexual abuse of minors and the Church's attitude toward the mafia. However, as it happened in a previous, similar circumstance, it is important to notice that that words that Mr. Scalfari attributes to the Pope, 'in quotations' come from the expert journalist Scalfari's own memory of what the Pope said and is not an exact transcription of a recording nor a review of such a transcript by the Pope himself to whom the words are attributed. We should not or must not speak in any way, shape or form of an interview in the normal use of the word, as if there had been a series of questions and answers that faithfully and exactly reflect the precise thoughts of the one being interviewed. It is safe to say, however that the overall theme of the article captures the spirit of the conversation between the Holy Father and Mr. Scalfari while at the same time strongly restating what was said about the previous 'interview' that appeared in La Repubblica: the individual expressions that were used and the manner in which they have been reported, cannot be attributed to the Pope. Let me state two particular examples. We must take into consideration two affirmations that have drawn much attention and that are not attributed to the Pope. The first is that among pedophiles are also "some cardinals"; and the second regarding celibacy: 'I will find solutions.' In the article published in La Repubblica, these two affirmations are clearly attributed to the Pope but curiously, the quotations were opened at the beginning but were not closed at the end. We must ask ourselves why the final quotations are not present: is this an omission or explicit recognition that this is an attempt to manipulate some naïve readers?"

Papal Lunch On July 25, Pope Francis surprised Vatican staff and workers by appearing suddenly at the Vatican canteen and getting his own lunch on a tray. The pope got into line like any other staff member and sat with various workers during the lunch.

Papal Interview On July 28, the Argentinian magazine "*Viva*," a supplement of the newspaper El Clarín, published an interview with Pope Francis marking the first 500 days of his pontificate. As with other papal interviews, the discussion ranged over a variety of topics and touched on many of the key themes important to this pope. The pontiff was especially notable in providing "10 points for happiness." He said, "The Romans have a saying, which can be taken as a point of reference, they say: 'Campa e lascia campà' ...live and let live. That's the first step to peace and happiness." His remaining points were: "giving oneself to others"; "moving quietly," citing the Argentine novel "Don Segundo Sombra," written by Ricardo Güiraldes in which a man reminisces about his youth, with life like a rocky stream, but as he got older, he became a running river and was "quietly peaceful; playing with children and the importance of a healthy culture of leisure; the importance of sharing Sundays with family; helping young people find employment; looking after nature; rapidly forgetting the negative; respecting those who think differently; and actively seeking peace.

Pope visits Caserta On July 28, Pope Francis visited the southern Italian city of Caserta and met with the priests of the region. He encouraged them to be creative in their vocations when asked by one priest, "How can we overcome the existential crisis born of the linguistic, semantic and cultural revolution in evangelical witness?" He urged them as well to be examples of unity, noting, "This cannot be done speaking badly about each other. The unity of bishops is important to the unity of the Church...The bishops must be in agreement in unity, but not in uniformity. Each one has his charisma; each one has his way of thinking and his point of view." He went on to recommend that central to a diocesan priest's spirituality is the relationship with the bishop and with the rest of the priests, a difficult task he acknowledged, especially in the face of things like gossip, adding, "The devil knows that this seed bears fruit, and he sows it well." The Holy Father then met with a friend of his, an evangelical pastor, Rev. Giovanni Traettino in Caserta and used the occasion of the visit to issue an apology to Pentecostals for any Catholics who might have persecuted them in the past. He spoke to a crowd of some 200, Pentecostals from across Italy, the United States, and Argentina and told them, "I don't understand a Christian who stands still! I don't understand a Christian who doesn't walk. A Christian must walk."

INTERNATIONAL

Anglican Women Bishops On July 14, Anglican Church of England at its general synod in York, England, voted overwhelmingly to allow the ordination of women bishops. Under pressure from members of Parliament and Abp. Justin Welby, abp. of Canterbury, who had threatened to dissolve the synod should it fail to approve the measure, the synod granted permission to begin ordaining women bishop after what is expected to be the immediate approval of Parliament. A similar measure had been defeated nearly two years ago by a narrow vote. The vote was expected not only to complicate Catholic-Anglican dialogue but would certainly create further divisions within the worldwide Anglican Communion. Abp. Welby tried to reassure the conservative and traditional members of the CofE and the worldwide Anglican Communion that respect would be given to their objections, but it was unclear how that provision would function. The Catholic Bishops' Conference of England and Wales issued in response to the vote under the signature of Abp. Bernard Longley, Chairman of the Department for Dialogue and Unity, stating: "The Catholic Church remains fully committed to its dialogue with the Church of England and the Anglican Communion. For the Catholic Church, the goal of ecumenical dialogue continues to be full visible ecclesial communion. Such full ecclesial communion embraces full communion in the episcopal office. The decision of the Church of England to admit women to the episcopate therefore sadly places a further obstacle on the path to this unity between us. Nevertheless we are committed to continuing our ecumenical dialogue, seeking deeper mutual understanding and practical cooperation wherever possible. We note and appreciate the arrangement of pastoral provision, incorporated into the House of Bishops' Declaration and the amending Canon passed by the General Synod, for those members of the Church of England who continue to hold to the historic understanding of the episcopate shared by the Catholic and Orthodox Churches. At this difficult moment we affirm again the significant ecumenical progress which has been made in the decades since the Second Vatican Council and the development of firm and lasting friendships between our communities. We rejoice in these bonds of affection and will do all we can to strengthen them and seek together to witness to the Gospel in our society."

No Right to Same-Sex "Marriage" On July 18, the European Court of Human Rights ruled that no right to same-sex "marriage" can be imposed by the EU on member states; it added further that to do so would be a breach of the European Convention on Human Rights. The ruling, delivered by the court at Strasbourg, reiterated in the Convention, Article 12 "enshrines the traditional concept of marriage as being between a man and a woman [and] cannot be construed as imposing an obligation on the Contracting States to grant access to marriage to same-sex couples." The decision was a severe blow to progressive advocates of same-sex "marriage" in the EU who had been arguing that such form of marriage are a "fundamental right."

Mafia Appeal On July 18, Card. Paolo Romeo, abp. of Palermo issued an appeal for all citizens and institutions to work against the evil presence of the Mafia. The prelate used the feast of Santa Rosalia Tuesday to urge the people of Palermo, the capital of Sicily, to root out the pernicious influence of organized crime. He declared, "Faith is not a tranquilizer for consciousness. We are aware that our faith is absolutely incompatible with the mafia and criminal systems that disfigure."

Christians in Iraq On July 21, the Patriarch of the Chaldean Catholic Church, Patriarch Louis Raphaël I Sako, issued a letter addressed to all people of good-will in which he warned that Iraq was heading to utter disaster. He warned that the threat of Islamists in the country was poised to bring terrible ruin to the minority groups and would have dire consequences for the unity of the country. "Iraq," he wrote, "is heading to a humanitarian, cultural, and historical disaster." He noted especially the horrifying treatment of the Christians in the city of Mosul at the hands of the Islamic State of Iraq and Syria (ISIS). He wrote, "It is shameful that Christians are being rejected, expelled and diminished. It is obvious that this would have disastrous consequences on the coexistence between the majority and the minorities, even among Muslims themselves, in the near and long term. Hence, Iraq is heading to a humanitarian, cultural, and historical disaster. Therefore we call unto them, a warm, brotherly, urgent and serious call, and we appeal to our fellow Iraqis who support them to reconsider their strategy, and respect the unarmed innocent people, of all ethnicities, religions and sects. The Quran commands respect to the innocent, and does not call to seize the property of people forcibly, it calls on helping the widow, the orphan, the destitute and the defenseless, and even recommend to help the seventh neighbor."

The rise of ISIS in the last months has led to mass killings of Christians, including documented crucifixions, torture, beheadings of children, rape and mutilation of Christian women, and the forced marriage of Christian girls as young as nine years old to Islamist soldiers. The churches of Mosul and the surrounding villages and town on the Nineveh Plain have been desecrated, pillaged, and destroyed or turned into mosques, and the fleeing Christian and religious minority population driven into the surrounding deserts where many died from exhaustion, the heat, and lack of food and water. In addition, Shi'ites, Yazidis, and Shabaks, have fled from the ISIS forces who have also destroyed Shi'ite mosques and shrines. On July 21, the office of UN Secretary-General Ban Ki-Moon issued a statement condemning ISIS attacks on all religions as a crime against humanity. The statement condemned "in the strongest terms the systematic persecution of minority populations in Iraq by Islamic State [of Iraq and Syria] and associated armed groups…any systematic attack on the civilian population or segments of the civilian population, because of their ethnic background, religious beliefs or faith may constitute a crime against humanity." Western countries issued various types of condemnations, but for the most part Western media was silent for weeks on the genocide being perpetrated against the Christians and religious minorities.

Day for Life On July 27, Catholics and other concerned about the Culture of Life in the United Kingdom and Ireland received a special message from Pope Francis, signed by Vatican Secretary of State Card. Pietro Parolin as they marked The Day for Life in honor of the dignity of human life. The message from Pope Francis read: "As the Church in England, Ireland, Scotland and Wales celebrates the 2014 Day for Life, the Holy Father expresses his confidence that this annual witness to the sanctity of God's gift of life will inspire the faithful, and young Catholics in particular, to combat the culture of death, not only by working to ensure adequate legal protection for the fundamental human right to life, but also by seeking to bring the merciful love of Christ as a life-giving balm to those troubling 'new forms of poverty and vulnerability' (cf. *Evangelii Gaudium*, No. 210) which are increasingly evident in contemporary society. To all involved in the Day for Life celebrations, His Holiness imparts his Apostolic Blessing as a pledge of wisdom, joy and peace in the Risen Lord."

Mariam Ibrahim On July 24, the Sudanese woman Mariam Meriam Yahia Ibrahim Ishag was at last able to leave Sudan and fly to Italy, with the help of the Italian and American governments. The departure from Sudan marked an end to a tortured saga that had started with her arrest on charges of blasphemy and her receiving a death sentence in May for being a Christian. She gave birth to a daughter in prison and was released on June 24 at the order of a Sudanese appeals court. The following day, however, as she and her family attempted to leave the country, she was re-arrested. Two days later, she was released and took refuge in the United States embassy in Khartoum with her family. Negotiations with the Sudanese government at last enable her to leave Sudan, and on July 24, Ibrahim, her husband, Daniel Wani, and their children flew to Rome on an Italian government plane, accompanied by Italy's deputy foreign minister, Lapo Pistelli. She was welcomed at Rome's Ciampino airport by Italy's Prime Minister, Matteo Renzi, and was then taken to the Vatican where she and her family had a private audience with Pope Francis at the Casa Santa Marta. The family subsequently flew to the United States, and they took up residence in New Hampshire.

NATIONAL

Oklahoma Black Mass On July 3, Abp. Paul Coakley of Oklahoma City expressed genuine outrage at the announcement that a Satanic Black Mass would be held on Sept. 21 at the Oklahoma City Civic Center. The archbishop issued a statement condemning the decision of the Civic Center to grant permission. He wrote: "For more than 1 billion Catholics worldwide and more than 200,000 Catholics in Oklahoma, the Mass is the most sacred of religious rituals. It is the center of Catholic worship and celebrates Jesus Christ's redemption of the world by his death and resurrection. In particular, the Eucharist — which we believe to be the body, blood, soul and divinity of Jesus Christ — is the source and summit of our faith. That's why we're astonished and grieved that the Civic Center would promote as entertainment and sell tickets for an event that is very transparently a blasphemous mockery of the Mass. The 'Black Mass' that is scheduled for the Civic Center in September is a satanic inversion and distortion of the most sacred beliefs not only of Catholics, but of all Christians."

Baton Rouge Seal of Confession On July 8, the Diocese of Baton Rouge in Louisiana issued a statement in response to a Louisiana Supreme Court decision that a priest should break the seal of confession. The court decision stemmed from the case of a girl who was sexually molested by an adult male and allegedly discussed the crime with a priest in confession. The Diocese of Baton Rouge and the priest, Fr. Jeff Bayhi, were named defendants in a lawsuit that alleges that Fr. Bayhi advised her not to report the incident. The diocesan statement read: "By matter of policy, the Roman Catholic Diocese of Baton Rouge does not normally comment on pending legal cases, especially when the plaintiff files the case under seal. The Church respects the request for sealing of the record and will not make statements. However, in the instant case, even though the district court record is under seal, the opinion issued by the Court of Appeals for the First Circuit in Baton Rouge and the Writ opinion by the Supreme Court of Louisiana are not under seal. Since those two opinions are public record and the media has contacted the Church for comment, we provide this statement of the position of the Catholic Church and Fr. Jeff Bayhi. The issue as it relates to the 'Church defendants' (Fr. Bayhi and the Diocese of Baton Rouge) attacks the seal of confession and the attempt by the plaintiffs to have the court compel testimony from the priest, Fr. Bayhi, as to whether or not there were confessions and, if so, what the contents of any such confessions were… A foundational doctrine of the Roman Catholic Church for thousands of years mandates that the seal of confession is absolute and inviolable. Pursuant to his oath to the Church, a priest is compelled never to break that seal. Neither is a priest allowed to admit that someone went to confession to him. If necessary, the priest would have to suffer a finding of contempt in a civil court and suffer imprisonment rather than violate his sacred duty and violate the seal of confession and his duty to the penitent… This matter cuts to the core of the Catholic faith, and for a civil court to inquire as to whether or not a factual situation establishes the Sacrament of Confession is a clear and unfettered violation of the Establishment Clause of the Constitution of the United States. This matter is of serious consequence to all religions, not just the Catholic faith. The statutes involved in this matter address "sacred communications" which are confidential and are exempt from mandatory reporting. In other words, Protestant ministers, Jewish Rabbis, clergy of the Muslim religion, etc., all counsel and receive sacred communication of a confidential nature which are covered by these statutes.

Executive Order On July 23, Abp. William E. Lori of Baltimore, Chairman of the Ad Hoc Committee for Religious Liberty and Bp. Richard J. Malone of Buffalo, Chairman of the Committee on Laity, Marriage, Family Life and Youth issued a statement on Pres. Obama's July 21 executive order prohibiting federal government contractors from what the Administration deems "sexual orientation" and "gender identity" discrimination and to forbid "gender identity" discrimination in the employment of federal employees. The statement read: "Today's executive order is unprecedented and extreme and should be opposed. In the name of forbidding discrimination, this order implements discrimination. With the stroke of a pen, it lends the economic power of the federal government to a deeply flawed understanding of human sexuality, to which faithful Catholics and many other people of faith will not assent.

As a result, the order will exclude federal contractors precisely on the basis of their religious beliefs. More specifically, the Church strongly opposes both unjust discrimination against those who experience a homosexual inclination and sexual conduct outside of marriage, which is the union of one man and one woman. But the executive order, as it regards federal government contractors, ignores the inclination/conduct distinction in the undefined term 'sexual orientation.'

"As a result, even contractors that disregard sexual inclination in employment face the possibility of exclusion from federal contracting if their employment policies or practices reflect religious or moral objections to extramarital sexual conduct. The executive order prohibits "gender identity" discrimination, a prohibition that is previously unknown at the federal level, and that is predicated on the false idea that "gender" is nothing more than a social construct or psychological reality that can be chosen at variance from one's biological sex. This is a problem not only of principle but of practice, as it will jeopardize the privacy and associational rights of both federal contractor employees and federal employees.

"For example, a biological male employee may be allowed to use the women's restroom or locker room provided by the employer because the male employee identifies as a female. In an attempt to avoid these needless conflicts, states that have passed "sexual orientation" or "gender identity" prohibitions have overwhelmingly included protections for religious employers. "

AUGUST 2014

Global Day of Prayer for Peace in Iraq On Aug. 6, Catholics around the world took part in a world day of prayer for peace, marking the Feast of the Transfiguration. The day of prayer was intended to pray for an end to the immense violence, suffering, and bloodshed in Iraq, especially in the face of the persecution of Christians by the Islamic State. The prayer for the day was composed by Patriarch Louis Raphael I Sako, Patriarch of the Chaldeans in Iraq:
"Lord, The plight of our country is deep and the suffering of Christians is severe and frightening. Therefore, we ask you Lord to spare our lives, and to grant us patience, and courage to continue our witness of Christian values with trust and hope.
Lord, peace is the foundation of life; Grant us the peace and stability that will enable us to live with each other without fear and anxiety, and with dignity and joy. Glory be to you forever."
Cardinal Mueller on Marriage On Aug. 7, Card. Gerhard Mueller, the prefect of the Congregation for the Doctrine of the Faith discussed the authentic Catholic understanding of the Sacrament of Marriage in a new book organized as an interview with Spanish journalist Carlos Granados, director of the Biblioteca de Autores Cristianos in Madrid. The book, *The Hope of the Family*, looks closely at the poor understanding of marriage; the English-language edition was to be published by Ignatius Press. The German cardinal has been an outspoken defender of the Church's teachings on marriage, in particular in the lead up to the Extraordinary Synod on the Family in October 2014, and he has lamented especially the impact of individualism in society on the appreciation of the indissolubility of marriage.
Cardinal Filoni Sent to Iraq On Aug. 8, it was announced that Pope Francis was sending Card. Fernando Filoni, prefect of the Congregation for the Evangelization of Peoples, as his personal envoy to Iraq to assure Christians and other minorities suffering persecution by ISIS, the Islamic State, and to meet with Iraqi officials about the deteriorating conditions in the country. Filoni had served previously as apostolic nuncio to Iraq from 2001 to 2006, during the most chaotic years in the region in the aftermath of the U.S. invasion in 2003. A communiqué issued by the Holy See read, "In light of the grave situation in Iraq, the Holy Father has nominated Card. Fernando Filoni, prefect of the of the Congregation for the Evangelization of Peoples, as his personal envoy to express his spiritual closeness to the populations that are suffering and to carry to them the solidarity of the Church."
"You Cannot Make War in the Name of God!" On Aug. 10, Pope Francis concluded his Sunday Angelus with another appeal for peace in Iraq and Gaza. He said, "The news coming from Iraq leaves us in disbelief and dismay: thousands of people, including many Christians, brutally driven from their homes; children dead from thirst and hunger during the escape; women who are abducted; people slaughtered; violence of

every kind; destruction everywhere, destruction of homes, destruction of religious, historical and cultural patrimonies. All this greatly offends God and greatly offends humanity. You cannot bring hatred in the name of God. You cannot make war in the name of God!"
Pope Francis in Korea The Holy Father visited South Korea from Aug. 13-18, officially to celebrate the 6th World Youth Day in Asia and to beatify124 Korean martyrs. The trip was an opportunity for the pontiff to give encouragement to the Church not just in Korea but across the whole of Asia. On Aug. 15, the pontiff said Mass on the Solemnity of the Assumption in Daejeon World Cup Stadium and then met with young Asians at the Shrine of Solmoe. The next day, he visited the Shrine of the Martyrs at Seo So mun, and celebrated the Mass of Beatification of Paul Yun Ji-Chung and 123 companions, martyrs, at the gate of Gwanghwamun in Seoul. On Aug. 17, he met with the bishops of Asia in the Sanctuary of Haemi and celebrated Mass for the 6th Asian Youth Day in Haemi Castle. The following day, he celebrated Mass for Peace and Reconciliation in Myeong-dong Cathedral in Seoul. [For full coverage, see under **News in Depth**.]

General Audiences

August 6, 2014

INTERNATIONAL

Pope Lifts Suspension On Aug. 5, Pope Francis officially lifted the suspension of a Nicaraguan priest who had been suspended by Pope John Paul II for his embrace of radical liberation theology and political involvement with the Marxist Sandinista government of Nicaragua. Fr. Miguel d'Escoto Brockmann, a now 81-year-old Maryknoll priest had been suspended "*a divinis*" in the 1980s. The priest accepted the suspension in obedience and refrained pastoral ministry, although he remained a member of the Maryknoll Congregation. The pope's decision stemmed form the request by the priest to be permitted to celebrate the Eucharist before his death.
Iraqi Patriarch On Aug. 7, Patriarch Louis Raphael Sako, president of the Bishops' Conference of Iraq and Patriarch of the Chaledean Catholics, issued an urgent message, through the Catholic charity Aid to the Church in Need, urging help for Iraq's Christians in the wake of the seizure of the Nineveh Plain by the forces of ISIS. The message read: "The ISIS militants attacked with mortars most of the villages of the plain of Nineveh, during the night of 6th-7th of August and now they are controlling the area. The Christians, about 100,000, horrified and panicked, fled their villages and houses [with] nothing but the clothes on their backs. An exodus, a real via crucis, Christians are walking on foot in Iraq's searing summer heat towards the Kurdish cities of Erbil, Duhok and Soulaymiyia, the sick, the elderly, infants and pregnant women among them. They are facing a human catastrophe and risk a real genocide. They need water, food, shelter…Regarding the churches and church properties in the villages now being

occupied by the ISIS militants, we have reports of destruction and desecration. The old manuscripts and documents (1500) are being burnt. As evident to all, the Central Government is incapable of enforcing law and order in this part of the country. There are also doubts about the capacity of the Kurdistan Region alone to defend the fierce advance of the jihadists. Clearly, there is a lack of cooperation between the Central Government and the Regional Autonomous Government. This "vacuum" is profited by the ISIS to impose their rule and terror. There is a need of international support and a professional, well equipped army. The situation is going from bad to worse. We appeal with sadness and pain to the conscience of all and all people of good will and the United Nations and the European Union, to save these innocent persons from death."

NATIONAL

Catholic Adoption Agencies On Aug. 1, Abp. Salvatore J. Cordileone of San Francisco, chairman of the USCCB Subcommittee for the Promotion and Defense of Marriage, Abp. William E. Lori of Baltimore, chairman of the Ad Hoc Committee for Religious Liberty, and Abp. Thomas G. Wenski of Miami, chairman of the Committee on Domestic Justice and Human Development, issued a letter in support of the Child Welfare Provider Inclusion Act of 2014, introduced on July 30 by Rep. Mike Kelly (R-PA) in the U.S. House of Representatives and Sen. Mike Enzi (R-WY) in the U.S. Senate. The archbishops noted that "the Act would prohibit federal and state officials in the administration of federally funded child welfare services from excluding child welfare providers simply because of the providers' religious beliefs or moral convictions."

Meriam Ibrahim Arrives in the U.S. On Aug. 1, Mariam Ibrahim, the Sudanese woman who had been arrested in Sudan and sentenced to death of supposed apostasy against Islam, ended her long ordeal by arriving in the United States via Italy. Released from Sudanese captivity, she and her family, including her husband, Daniel Wani, and her two young children, Martin, 18 months old, and Maya, born two months ago in prison, had flown to Rome through the efforts of the Vatican, Italian, and U.S. governments; while there, she met briefly with Pope Francis. It was expected that Ibrahim would remain in the United States.

Prayer to Stop a Black Mass On Aug. 4, Abp. Paul Coakley of Oklahoma City issued a public letter calling on Catholics and all people of goodwill to pray for the cancellation of a Black Mass planned for Sunday, Sept. 21, at the Civic Center Music Hall in Oklahoma City. He wrote: "Even though tickets are being sold for this event as if it were merely some sort of dark entertainment, this Satanic ritual is deadly serious. It is a blasphemous and obscene inversion of the Catholic Mass. Using a consecrated Host obtained illicitly from a Catholic church and desecrating it in the vilest ways imaginable, the practitioners offer it in sacrifice to Satan. This terrible sacrilege is a deliberate attack on the Catholic Mass as well as the foundational beliefs of all Christians. It mocks Our Lord Jesus Christ, whom we Catholics believe is truly present under the form of bread and wine in the Holy Eucharist when it has been consecrated by a validly ordained priest. In spite of repeated requests, there has been no indication that the City intends to prevent this event from taking place…Since it seems this event will not be cancelled, I am calling on all Catholics of the Archdiocese of Oklahoma City to counteract this challenge to faith and decency through prayer and penance. Specifically, I am asking that the Prayer to St. Michael the Archangel be included at the conclusion of every Mass, beginning on the Feast of the Transfiguration of the Lord (Aug. 6) and continuing through the Feast of the Archangels (Sept. 29). I invite all Catholics to pray daily for divine protection through the intercession of this heavenly patron who once defeated Lucifer in his rebellion against the Almighty and who stands ready to assist us in this hour of need. Secondly, I am asking that each parish conduct a Eucharistic Holy Hour with Benediction to honor Christ's Real Presence in the Holy Eucharist, between the Solemnity of the Assumption of the Blessed Virgin Mary (Aug. 15) and Sept. 21, to avert this proposed sacrilege. Finally, I invite all Catholics, Christians and people of good will to join me in prayer for a Holy Hour, outdoor Eucharistic Procession and Benediction…"

Knights of Columbus On Aug. 7, Pope Francis sent a letter to the Knights of Columbus through his written on Pope Francis' behalf by his secretary of state, Card. Pietro Parolin, on the occasion of the Knights' Supreme Convention, in Orlando, FL. The pope wrote in part: "The theme of this year's Supreme Convention — You Will All Be Brothers: Our Vocation to Fraternity — is one particularly close to the Holy Father's heart. Faith teaches us that, created in the image and likeness of the triune God and redeemed by Christ's sacrifice of atonement, the Church is called to be a community of brothers and sisters who accept and care for one another and serve as a leaven of reconciliation and unity for the whole human family. In the complex social and ecclesial situation of late nineteenth century America, this vocation found particular expression in principles of faith, fraternity and service which guided the establishment of the Knights of Columbus. The fidelity of the Knights to these high ideals has not only ensured the continued vitality of your Order, but has also contributed, and continues to contribute, to the mission of the Church at every level and, in particular, to the universal ministry of the Apostolic See. For this, His Holiness is profoundly grateful." The Knights also pledged $500,000 in relief for the Christians in Iraq and promised to match an additional $500,000 in donations from the public.

Pray for Iraq On Aug. 8, Bp. Richard E. Pates of Des Moines, Iowa, chairman of the Committee of International Justice and Peace of the U.S. Conference of Catholic Bishops (USCCB), issued a letter asking U.S. bishops to invite the people of their dioceses to pray for peace in Iraq on Sunday, Aug. 17. The text of a prayer written by the Chaldean Catholic Patriarch of Iraq, Louis Raphael Sako, was proposed for use.

DEATHS — AUGUST 2013 TO AUGUST 2014

Agre, Cardinal Bernard Agre, 88, June 9, 2014, abp. of Abidjan from 1994-2006; a native of Abidjan, he was ordained a priest in 1953 and studied in Rome at the Pontifical Urbanian University; appointed bp. of Man in 1969, he was transferred to Yamoussoukro and then to Abidjan in 1994; he was named a Cardinal in 2001; in the Ivory Coast, he was a strong voice for peace and a smooth democratic transition of power in the face of various military coups, especially between 1998 and 2000.

Allain, Gov. William, 85, Dec. 2, Governor of Mississippi from 1984 to 1988, the state's only Catholic governor. Born near Natchez, MS, he attended the University of Notre Dame and earned a law degree from the University of Mississippi School of Law. He served in the United States Army infantry in the Korean War, and after the war practiced law in Natchez, MS, until his appointment as assistant state attorney general in 1962. Elected state attorney general in 1979, he was elected governor in 1984. As governor, he promoted consumer protection and promoted women and minorities to state boards and offices. He was a daily communicant, even as governor.

Bartolucci, Cardinal Domenico, 96, Nov. 11, 2013, long-time director of the Sistine Chapel Choir. Born in Borgo San Lorenzo, Italy, he entered the seminary of Florence and ordained to the priesthood in 1939. He earned a diploma in composition and orchestra direction from the Florence Conservatory of Music and went to Rome in 1942 for advanced studies in music. He helped direct the choir at the Basilica of St. John Lateran and then became choir director at the Basilica of St. Mary Major and an instructor at the Pontifical Institute for Sacred Music. In 1952, he became the assistant director of the Sistine Chapel Choir and director in 1956. He formed the Sistine Chapel boys' choir and took the group on international tours. He retired in 1997, but he continued composing music, including "Benedictus," in honor of then Pope Benedict XVI. He was named a Cardinal in November 2010.

Boland, Bishop Raymond J., 82, Feb. 27, 2014, bp. of Birmingham from 1988-1993 and bp. of Kansas City-St. Joseph from 1993 to 2005. Born in County Tipperary, Ireland, and raised in County Cork, he studied at Christian Brothers College in Cork, the National University of Ireland in Dublin and All Hallows Missionary College in Drumcondra, and as ordained a priest of the Archdiocese of Washington in 1957. During his service in Washington, he was a pastor, secretary for Catholic education, chancellor, vicar general and moderator of the curia; he also coordinated Pope John Paul II's 1979 visit to Washington. Named bp. of Birmingham, he was ordained a bishop on March 25, 1988, and moved to Kansas City-St. Joseph five years later. He retired to Ireland. His brother Kevin was ordained a priest of the diocese of Savannah and was the bishop there from 1995-2011.

Brenner, Mother Antonia, 86, Oct. 17, 2013, a one-time socialite in Beverly Hills who became a woman religious and founded the Eudist Servants of the 11th Hour. Born Mary Clark, she gave up wealth and comfort to serve prisoners at the La Mesa Penitentiary in Tijuana in 1965; after her children were grown, she she moved into the prison, sleeping in a cell in the women's wing. She then founded the Eudist Servants of the 11th Hour, for older women, in 1997 to work with prisoners in the United States.

Caldecott, Stratford, 60, July 17, noted Catholic author; born in London, he studied at Dulwich College and Oxford University where he earned a Masters Degree and there met Léonie Richards, whom he married in 1977; a convert in 1980 (followed by his wife in 1983), he wrote about his conversion in *The Path to Rome* and *The Beauty of God's House: Essays in Honor of Stratford Caldecott*; he worked for years as a senior editor at Routledge, HarperCollins, and T&T Clark, but in the early 1990s he and his wife founded the Centre for Faith & Culture in Oxford; in 2001 they founded the journal "Second Spring"; he served on the editorial boards of *Communio*, *The Chesterton Review*, and *Oasis*; he also wrote and edited books on J.R.R. Tolkien, the seven Sacraments, the historian Christopher Dawson, the Book of Revelation, and liturgical reform and wrote in a host of magazines, including *Touchstone*, *This Rock*, *Parabola*, the *Chesterton Review*, *The Imaginative Conservative*, the *Catholic Herald*, *The Tablet*, and the *National Catholic Register*; he received an honorary doctorate in Sacred Theology from the Pontifical John Paul II Institute at the Catholic University of America in 2013, and was to be awarded posthumously the 15th Paideia Prize "for lifetime contribution to classical education and the cultivation of wisdom and virtue" by the CiRCE Institute in 2015; before his death, family members and friends launched the #CapForStrat campaign, in which numerous actors playing superheroes in Hollywood films sent messages of support to him, as he was a long-time fan of the cinematic genre.

Carles Gordo, Cardinal Ricardo, 87, Dec. 17, 2013, abp. of Barcelona from 1990 to 2004 and a cardinal from 1994. Born in Valencia, Spain, he was ordained to the priesthood in 1951 and was long a pastor, youth minister and chaplain to a young Catholic worker's group. Named bp. of Tortosa in 1969, he was promoted to Barcelona by Pope John Paul II, who named his Cardinal priest in 1994.

Ce, Cardinal Marco, 88, May 12, 2014, patriarch of Venice from 1978 to 2002. Born to a family of farmers near Cremona, in northern Italy, he was ordained to the priesthood at the age of 22 and then taught dogmatic theology and sacred Scripture. He remained a noted biblical scholar and gave the Lenten retreat for Pope Benedict XVI in 2006 on the Gospel of Mark. Rector of the diocesan seminary of Cremona, he was named an aux. bp. of Bologna in 1970. In 1978, he was appointed as successor to Albino Luciani who had been elected Pope John Paul I. He was named a Cardinal by Pope John Paul II in 1979.

Clancy, Cardinal Edward Bede, 90, Aug. 3, 2014, abp. of Sydney, Australia, from 1988-2001 and the leading prelate in the country; a native of Lithgow, Australia, he was ordained a priest in 1949 and studied in Rome at the Pontifical Urban University and then the Pontifical Biblical Institute, where he earned a degree in sacred Scripture; app. titular bp. of Ard Carna and aux. bp. of Sydney in 1973 and then abp. of Canberra and Goulburn in 1978; named abp. of Sydney in 1983, he was made a cardinal in 1988, with the titular church of Holy Mary of Vallicella.

Daly, Bishop James J., 92, Oct. 14, 2013, aux. bp. of Rockville Centre from 1977 to 1996. Born in the Bronx and raised in Queens, he was ordained a priest of the diocese of Brooklyn in 1948 and served in the Brooklyn diocese and then Rockville Centre as an assistant pastor and at the diocesan seminary, Immaculate Conception. Ordained an aux. bp. for Rockville Centre in 1977, he served on the Administrative Committee of the U.S. Bishops' Conference and on the National Advisory Council.

Delly, Cardinal Emmanuel-Karim, 86, Apr. 8, 2014, Patriarch of the Chaldeans from 2003 to 2012, and a Cardinal from 2007. Born in Telkaif, near Mosul, he was ordained to the priesthood in Rome in 1952 and earned a master's degree in philosophy from the Pontifical Urbanian University and a doctorate in theology and another in canon law from the Pontifical Lateran University. Ordained an aux. bp. of Babylon in 1962, he attended the last three sessions of the Second Vatican Council. Appointed titular abp. of Kaskar dei Caldie in 1967, he was retired at the time of his election as Chaldean Archbishop of Baghdad in 2003. He served as patriarch during the difficult years after the U.S. invasion of Iraq in 2003 and the terrible suffering faced by Iraqi Christians.

Denton, Rear Adm. Jeremiah, 89, Mar. 29, 2013, Navy admiral and flight captain during the Vietnam War who was captured in 1965 and held prisoner for more than seven-and-a-half years. Born in Mobile, AL, he studied at Spring Hill College and then the U.S. Naval Academy at Annapolis, MD. He later studied at the National Defense University, the Naval War College and George Washington University. During his time as a POW, he was imprisoned at the Hoa Lo Prison, nicknamed the "Hanoi Hilton." He received two Air Medals, two Purple Hearts, the Distinguished Flying Cross and the Combat Action Ribbon. He retired from the Navy in 1977 with the rank of rear admiral and served from 1980 to 1986 as a U.S. senator from Alabama. A devout Catholic, he attributed his survival to his Catholic faith and wrote about his ordeal in his book, *When Hell Was In Session.*

Donnelly, Bishop Robert W., 83, July 21, 2014, auxiliary bishop of Toledo from 1984-2006; a native of Toledo, he was ordained a priest for the diocese in May 1957 and held a variety of posts until his appointment titular bp. of Garba and aux. bp. of Toledo on Mar. 14, 1984; ord. a bishop on May 3, 1984, he retired on May 30, 2006.

Foley, Thomas, 84 Oct. 18, 2013, Speaker of the House of Representatives from 1989 to 1995. Born in Spokane, WA, he studied at Gonzaga University and the University of Washington, earning bachelor of arts degree in 1951. In 1957, he earned a law degree. He entered private practice after law school, and in 1958 began working in the Spokane County prosecutor's office as a deputy prosecuting attorney. He also taught at Gonzaga University Law School from 1958 to 1959, and in 1960, he joined the office of the State of Washington Attorney General. In 1961, he joined the staff of the United States Senate Committee on Interior and Insular Affairs as assistant chief clerk and special counsel. He left this post to run for Congress in 1964. He represented Washington's 5th congressional district for the next 30 years as a Democratic member and was House speaker from 1989 until early 1995. He was the first sitting speaker since the Civil War to lose a re-election bid, which he did in November 1994, part of the Republican sweep in the 1994 elections. He served as the United States Ambassador to Japan from 1997 to 2001 under President Bill Clinton. While a Catholic, he earned much criticism for his support of abortion.

Gossman, Bishop F. Joseph, 83, Aug. 12, 2013, bp. of Raleigh from 1975 to 2006 who was noted for his commitment to social justice and also presided over the rapid growth of the diocese. Born in Baltimore, MD, he was ordained a priest for Baltimore in 1955 after studies at St. Mary's Seminary in Baltimore and the Pontifical North American College in Rome. He then earned a doctorate in canon law at The Catholic University of America, Washington, and served as an assistant pastor, cathedral administrator, vice chancellor, tribunal official and St. Mary's Seminary professor. He was named an aux. bp. of Baltimore in 1968 at 38, making him one of the youngest bishops in the world. Appointed bishop of Raleigh in 1975, he embarked on a program of expansion for the diocese as the Catholic population increased four-fold during his episcopacy. He was noted for his work on social justice issues, including immigration, economic justice and opposition to the death penalty.

Gros, Brother Jeffrey, 75, Aug. 12, 2013, Christian Brother, leading expert in ecumenism, and a long-time official with the U.S. Conference of Catholic Bishops. Born John Jefferson Gros in Memphis, TN, he entered the novitiate of the Christian Brothers in 1955 and professed his final vows in 1963. He received a bachelor's degree from St. Mary's University of Minnesota, a master's degree in theology from Marquette University, and a doctorate in theology from Fordham University. He held a variety of posts in ecumenism, including director of Faith and Order for the National Council of Churches, distinguished professor of ecumenical and historical theology at Memphis Theological Seminary, dean of the Institute for Catholic Ecumenical Leadership, president of the Society for Pentecostal Studies, consultant to the Archdiocese of Chicago's Office of Ecumenical and Interreligious Affairs, an adjunct professor at Catholic Theological Union in Chicago, and associate director for the Secretariat for Ecumenical and Interreligious Affairs for the USCCB. He also was a participant in countless ecumenical initiatives with religious groups and was a respected international speaker and writer.

Harrington, Father Daniel J., 73, Feb. 7, 2014, Jesuit priest and one of the world's leading New Testament scholars. Born in Arlington, MA, he entered the Jesuit novitiate in Gloucester in 1958 and studied at the Weston School of Theology and then Ancient Near Eastern languages at Harvard University, where he earned a doctorate; he also studied at Hebrew University and the Ecole Biblique in Jerusalem. Ordained a priest in 1971, he briefly taught sacred Scripture at St. Mary of the Lake Seminary in IL and then joined the faculty of Weston Jesuit School of Theology in 1972. He authored more than 60 books on Scripture, served as the general editor of New Testament Abstracts, and wrote "The Word" column for *America* magazine for three years.

Hensgen, Sister Caroleen, 98, Oct. 15, 2013, a member of the School Sisters of Notre Dame and the first woman to be appointed superintendent of schools for a U.S. Catholic diocese. Born in St. Louis, she entered the congregation of the School Sisters of Notre Dame from St. Ann in Normandy, MO, and professed her first vows in 1935. She earned a bachelor's degree in Latin and English in 1944 and a master's in Latin in 1949 from St. Louis University and then taught elementary grades at St. Francis Solanus in Quincy, IL, in 1933 and from 1940 to 1948 junior and secondary schools in St. Louis and Belleville, IL. From 1948 to 1967, she was principal at several high schools was then superintendent of elementary schools for the diocese of Dallas from 1967 to 1991.

She then served as education consultant for the diocese from 1991 to 1993 and conducted educational research from 1993 to 2002.

Lourdusamy, Cardinal D., Simon, 90, June 2, 2014, Indian Cardinal, the first Asian to hold a major post in the Roman Curia, and prefect of the Congregation for the Oriental Churches from 1985 to 1991. Born in Kalleri, he was ordained a priest of Pondicherry in 1951 after studies at St. Agnes's Minor Seminary in Cuddalore, and St. Peter's Pontifical Seminary, Bangalore. He then earned a doctorate in canon law at the Pontifical Urbaniana University with highest honors. After service in the archdiocese of Pondicherry and Cuddalore, he was appointed an aux. bp. of Bangalore in 1962. In 1964, he was named coadjutor abp. of Bangalore, acceding to the see in 1968. In 1973, he was sent to Rome to serve as sec. of the Congregation for the Propagation of the Faith. He held the post until 1985 when he was promoted to prefect of the Congregation of the Oriental Churches. A Cardinal from 1985, he served as protodeacon from 1993 to 1996. He retired in 1991.

Lyne, Bishop Timothy J., 94, Sept. 25, 2013, aux. bp. of Chicago from 1983 to 1995. A native of Chicago, IL, he studied at Quigley Preparatory Seminary and the University of St. Mary of the Lake and Mundelein Seminary, where he earned an M.A. and a licentiate in Sacred Theology. Ordained a priest for Chicago in 1943, he was named an aux. bp. under Card. Bernardin and served under every succeeding archbishop and held a variety of posts, including vicar for senior priests from 1988 to 2013.

Marchisano, Cardinal Francesco, 85, July 27, 2014, Italian Cardinal and one of the great caretakers of the Vatican's artistic and cultural patrimony; born in Racconigi, Italy, he was ordained a priest in 1952; ord. titular bp. of Populonia, in 1989, he served with great distinction as president of the Pontifical Commission of Sacred Archeology, the Pontifical Commission for the Cultural Patrimony of the Church, and then archpriest of the Patriarchal Vatican Basilica and vicar general for the State of Vatican City, and president of the Fabric of St. Peter, from 2002-2006; he was also in charge of the Permanent Commission for the Care of the Historical and Artistic Monuments of the Holy See from 2003-2009; named a cardinal in 2003, with the deaconry, St. Lucy of Gonfalone, he retired in 2009.

Mazombwe, Cardinal Medardo, 81, Aug. 29, 2013, abp. of Lusaka from 1996 to 2006 and a Cardinal from 2010. Born in Chundamira, Zambia, he was ordained to the priesthood in 1960. Named bp. of Chipata in 1970, he was promoted to the rank of abp. of Lusaka in 1996. Over the years, he served as pres. of Zambia's Episcopal Conference (1972–1975; 1988–1990; 1999–2002) and chair of the regional conferences under Association of Member Episcopal Conferences in Eastern Africa (A.M.E.C.E.A.) from 1979–86). He became internationally known for his effort to secure Zambia's debt cancellation through the Jubilee Zambia Campaign that finally succeeded in 2005.

McCormack Bishop William J., aux. bp. of New York from 1986 to 2001. A native of New York City, he attended Portsmouth Abbey High School in Rhode Island, where he was friends with Robert F. Kennedy, the future U.S. attorney general, U.S. senator from New York, and presidential candidate. Ordained a priest for New York in 1959, he served in various assignments, including director of the office of World Justice and Peace and vice chancel-

lor. From 1964 to 1970, he was the archdiocesan director of the Society for the Propagation of the Faith and on the society's board of directors from 1964-70. From 1980 to 2001, he served as national director of the Society and was active internationally. He was also chair of the U.S. Bishops' Committee on World Missions and member of the committees on Justice and Peace, Social Development, and International Policy.

McDonald, Bishop Andrew J., 90, Apr. 1, 2014, bp. of Little Rock from 1972 to 2000. Born in Savannah, he entered the minor seminary of St. Charles College in Catonsville, MD, and then completed his studies at St. Mary Seminary in Baltimore. Ordained in 1948, he then earned a doctorate in canon law from the Pontifical Lateran University in Rome. After service in the diocese of Savannah, he was named bp. of Little Rock. As bishop, he worked to implement the Second Vatican Council, encouraged a variety of lay movements, including Cursillo, Search, Catholic Charismatic Renewal, Marriage Encounter, and Retrouvaille, and focused on social justice issues.

Melady, Thomas P., 86, Jan. 6, 2014, U.S. Ambassador to the Holy See and many other posts. Born in Norwich, CT, he served in the U.S. Army during the last stages of World War II and went on to earn degrees from Duquesne University and The Catholic University of America and later taught at St. John's University. He served from 1959 to 1967 as the president of the Africa Service Institute and was an adjunct professor at Fordham University from 1966 to 1969. He was later chairman of Seton Hall University and a consultant to the National Urban League, taught at George Washington University, and was president of Sacred Heart University in Connecticut from 1976 to 1986. He served as an ambassador to Burundi (1969) and Uganda (1972) under President Richard Nixon, and then ambassador to the Holy See under President George H.W. Bush from 1989 to 1993, including the first year of the administration of President Bill Clinton. He was the author of 17 books, including *Profiles of African Leaders, Idi Amin Dada: Hitler in Africa* and *The Ambassador's Story*, and more than 180 articles.

Molinari, Father Paolo, 90, May 2, 2014, Italian Jesuit priest and renowned postulator (or promoter) of causes of sainthood. He entered the Jesuits in 1942 and was ordained a priest in 1953. He began working on the causes of saints in 1957 and served as the official postulator for the causes Jesuits and many other until his official retirement in 2010. Among the most notable causes were the Martyrs of England and Wales, St. Philippine Duchesne, and St. Kateri Tekakwitha. In all, he concluded the processes for a staggering 39 causes of beatification or canonization, with a total number of 150 blesseds or saints. He was also president of the Vatican's College of Postulators, professor of theology at the Pontifical Gregorian University in Rome, and an adviser to several popes.

Policarpo, Cardinal Jose da Cruz, 78, Mar. 12, 2014, patriarch of Lisbon, from 1998 to 2013 and the respected leader of the Church in Portugal. Born in Alvorninha, Portugal, he studied at the minor seminaries of Santarem and Almada and then Christ the King Seminary in Olivais. Ordained a priest in 1961, he was sent to Rome for further studies at the Pontifical Gregorian University. From 1963 to 1968, he taught at the minor seminary at Penafirme, Portugal and then from 1970 at the Portuguese

Catholic University; he was also rector of the Olivais seminary. Named an aux. bp. of Lisbon in 1978, he was appointed coadjutor of the archdiocese in 1997 and acceded to the see the next year. Named a Cardinal in 2001, he was briefly considered papabili (or a candidate) in the 2005 conclave that elected Pope Benedict XVI.

Quinn, Bishop A. James, 81, Oct. 18, 2013, aux. bp. of Cleveland from 1983 to 2008. A Cleveland native, he was ordained a priest in 1958 and held a variety of assignments until his appointment as an auxiliary bishop in 1983. He served as vicar for the western region of the Cleveland diocese and was noted for his pastoral care of the Catholics in the suburbs and Lorain County. He also served as a member of the boards of Laity in Support of Retired Priests, the Poor Clare Nuns of Cleveland foundation, and the First Friday Forum of Lorain County. He retired in 2008.

Seigenthaler, John, 86, July 11, 2014, famed journalist and civil rights advocate; a native of Nashville, he was first moved to become involved with civil rights while attending Father Ryan High School; he served in the Air Force and then attended the George Peabody College for Teachers in Nashville; instead of teaching, he entered journalism at newspaper, *The Tennessean* and went on to win numerous journalism awards; he became a close friend of Robert Kennedy and edited Kennedy's book, *The Enemy Within*; he worked on the campaign of John F. Kennedy and served as an aide to Attorney General Robert Kennedy where he was extremely active in the civil rights movement; he also worked for Robert's ill-fated presidential campaign in 1968; aside from serving as editor of *The Tennessean*, he was founding editorial director of *USA Today*.

Stoeger, Father William R., 70, Mar. 24, 2014, Jesuit priest and staff scientist for the Vatican Observatory Research Group in Tucson, AZ. Born in Torrance, CA, he entered the Jesuit order at Los Gatos in 1961 and studied Spring Hill College in Mobile, AL, the University of California Los Angeles, and Cambridge University in England where he received a doctorate in astrophysics. At Cambridge, he worked with Stephen Hawking, the renowned British theoretical physicist and cosmologist. He also studied at the Jesuit School of Theology at Berkeley and was ordained a Jesuit priest in 1972, along with his brother, Jack. After teaching gravitational physics at the University of Maryland, he joined the staff of the Vatican Observatory in Arizona, specializing in theoretical cosmology, high-energy astrophysics, and interdisciplinary studies.

Thompson, Bishop David B., 90, Nov. 24, 2013, bp. of Charleston from 1990-1999; born in Philadelphia, he earned a bachelor's degree and a master's in history at St. Charles Borromeo Seminary in Wynnewood, PA, and was ordained a priest for Philadelphia on May 27, 1950. He studied at The Catholic University of America in Washington and earned a licentiate in canon law; after holding a variety of posts, he was named the founding principal of Notre Dame High School in Easton, PA, in 1957 and became famous for the Notre Dame "Bandstand" in 1957 that attracted such notables as Paul Anka, Frankie Avalon, Chubby Checker, Connie Francis and Annette Funicello; appointed coadjutor bp. of Charleston in April 1989, he acceded to the see in 1990; he opposed flying the Confederate flag over the Statehouse and gambling, and issued the 1992 pastoral letter, "Our Heritage – Our Hope."

Cardinal Edmund C. Szoka, 1927-2014

American Cardinal Edmund C. Szoka died on Aug. 20, 2014, at the age of 86, in Novi, MI. A native of Grand Rapids, MI, he grew up in a working class Polish-American neighborhood. Called to the priesthood, he studied at St. Joseph's Seminary in Grand Rapids, Sacred Heart Major Seminary in Detroit, and then St. John's Provincial Seminary in Plymouth, MI. Ordained a priest on June 5, 1954, he was sent to Rome to earn a doctorate in canon law at the Pontifical Urban University. He then served as secretary to Bishop Noa of Marquette, whom he accompanied to the first session of the Second Vatican Council in 1962. On July 20, 1971, he was ordained the first bishop of the diocese of Gaylord, in Michigan. Ten years later, he was promoted to become archbishop of Detroit. On June 28, 1988, Pope St. John Paul II named him to the College of Cardinals, with the titular church of Sts. Andrew and Gregory al Monte Celio. In 1990, he was appointed President of the Prefecture for Economic Affairs of the Holy See with the task of reforming Vatican finances. He held the post with great success until 1997 when he was named President of the Pontifical Commission for the Vatican City State, the committee that oversees the administration of the Vatican City. 1997-2006. His tenure extended across the pontificates of John Paul II and Benedict XVI. He resigned his post in 2006. Pope Francis sent a telegram to Abp. Allen H. Vigneron of Detroit, expressing his condolences and "recalling with gratitude the late Cardinal's tireless episcopal ministry in Gaylord and Detroit, and his years of service to the Apostolic See and the Vatican City State."

Deceased Cardinals 2013-2014

The following Cardinals died between Aug. 2013 and Aug. 2014. For their individual obituaries, see above.

Agre, Cardinal Bernard Agre, 88, June 9, 2014, abp. of Abidjan from 1994-2006.

Bartolucci, Cardinal Domenico, 96, Nov. 11, 2013, long-time director of the Sistine Chapel Choir.

Carles Gordo, Cardinal Ricardo, 87, Dec. 17, 2013, abp. of Barcelona from 1990-2004 and a cardinal from 1994.

Ce, Cardinal Marco, 88, May 12, 2014, patriarch of Venice from 1978-2002.

Clancy, Cardinal Edward Bede, 90, Aug. 3, 2014, abp. of Sydney, Australia, from 1988-2001.

Delly, Cardinal Emmanuel-Karim, 86, Apr. 8, 2014, Patriarch of the Chaldeans from 2003-2012.

Lourdusamy, Cardinal D., Simon, 90, June 2, 2014, Indian Cardinal, the first Asian to hold a major post in the Roman Curia, and prefect of the Congregation for the Oriental Churches from 1985-1991.

Marchisano, Cardinal Francesco, 85, July 27, 2014, Italian Cardinal and one of the great caretakers of the Vatican's artistic and cultural patrimony.

Mazombwe, Cardinal Medardo, 81, Aug. 29, 2013, abp. of Lusaka from 1996-2006.

Policarpo, Cardinal Jose da Cruz, 78, Mar. 12, 2014, patriarch of Lisbon, from 1998-2013.

Szoka, Cardinad C., 86, Aug. 20, 2014, abp. of Detroit from 1981-1990 and long-time Vatican official.

News in Depth

POPE FRANCIS

Pope Francis completed his first year as head of the Church on March 13, and his first 12 months revealed a deeply pastoral pope who is proclaiming God's loving mercy revealed in Jesus Christ, who is challenging the faithful to become "spirit-filled evangelizers" in the world, and who is a humble and joy-filled reformer faithful to his namesake, St. Francis of Assisi.

A surprising pope The arrival of Card. Jorge Mario Bergoglio as Pope Francis on the loggia of St. Peter's Basilica on the evening of March 13, 2013, remains one of the most unanticipated events in the modern life of the Church. His shocking election was not an accident of history, nor was it simply a case of the last man standing. He had received many votes in the 2005 conclave, and his reputation among the cardinalate quietly had increased in the eight years of Pope Benedict XVI's pontificate. His address to his fellow cardinals on the day before the conclave was a perfect manifesto of reform and spiritual renewal that resonated.

As Card. Timothy Dolan of New York told ABC's "This Week" last December, "What we were after was a good pastor with a track record of solid administration but fatherly warm, tender care for the sheep, for his people. And, boy, we got that on steroids with Pope Francis."

The newly elected Pope Francis proceeded to fulfill the mandate given to him by the college. But what was evident on the loggia of St. Peter's was that this new pope was going to be very different.

A new style Pope Francis spent his first year using traditional settings for teachings — general audiences, homilies and speeches — but he also embraced all new forms of media, from Twitter to the first papal "selfie," to lead the Church firmly onto the digital continent. He showed masterful gifts for touching hearts and minds, across cultures, faiths and backgrounds, with practical — even blunt — language and poignant gestures. Taken together, he demonstrated a new form of papal communication.

In an interview with Vatican Radio in April last year, Abp. Claudio Maria Celli, head of the Pontifical Council for Social Communications, observed, "Do you remember how the pope was embracing a young handicapped boy, placing his cheek near to the cheek of the boy? No words, but that was the only way to communicate something to that boy ... Pope Francis is not only touching the intellectual aspect, but is touching the heart and the imagination."

The impact of his first year on the wider world has been dramatic. As Card. Dolan said on "This Week," "This pope has successfully, finally, shat-

tered the caricature ... that the Church is kind of mean and dour and always saying 'no,' and always telling us what we can't do, and always telling us why we should be excluded. He's saying, 'no, come on in, the Church is about warmth and tenderness.'"

Ironically, Pope Francis initially expressed reluctance to grant interviews with the world press. This changed dramatically with his 90-minute press conference on the flight back to Rome from Rio de Janeiro last July. The interview included the now famous line, "Who am I to judge?" that was supposedly in answer to a question about homosexuality (but was more a pastoral reply to a question regarding a priest with a troubled background) and sparked a media frenzy. Subsequent interviews, such as the one in Jesuit journals, and with the atheist editor Eugenio Scalfari of the Italian newspaper *La Repubblica*, caused similar storms of controversy over his supposed comments about abortion, proselytizing and the Church's relationship with atheists.

The secular press slipped into its customary habit of spinning the pope's words as a call for homosexual marriage, married priests, a Catholic crusade against capitalism and an end to the Church's condemnation of abortion and contraception. Pope Francis wants none of these things, but for all of the spin, the secular press was touched by the humble pontiff. *Rolling Stone* magazine gave him a lengthy, albeit egregious cover story; *Esquire* magazine named him the "Best Dressed Man of 2013"; and *Time* magazine honored him as Person of the Year. In explaining *Time*'s choice, editor Nancy Gibbs wrote, "The heart is a strong muscle; he's proposing a rigorous exercise plan. And in a very short time, a vast, global, ecumenical audience has shown a hunger to follow him."

For Pope Francis, this media outreach is not an end in itself but assists him in advancing the key themes of his first year as pope. He has sparked what is being called the "Francis Effect" — the return of Catholics to the Church and the implementation of the New Evangelization in the real world. Crucial to the "Francis Effect" are the themes of mercy, encounter and movement.

Walking the walk When asked the first question in the Jesuit journals interview — "Who is Jorge Mario Bergoglio?" — the pope replied "I am a sinner." Cognizant of his own sins, Pope Francis said when he took possession of the Basilica of St. John Lateran last April, "Jesus shows us this merciful patience of God so that we can regain confidence, hope — always!"

He returned repeatedly to this throughout the first year, proclaiming that we can trust always in God's mercy and love.

Mercy, however, is found in having a deeply personal encounter with Jesus Christ. Pope Francis wrote in *Evangelii Gaudium* ("The Joy of the Gospel"), his first apostolic exhortation on the New Evangelization released in November, "I invite all Christians, everywhere, at this very moment, to a renewed personal encounter with Jesus Christ, or at least an openness to letting him encounter them."

Through his gestures he gave enduring examples of mercy and encounter: embracing Vinicio Riva, the man with ulcerating disfigurements; wading into the crowds in Rio de Janeiro during World Youth Day in July; or inviting a child with Down syndrome to ride in the popemobile.

Pope Francis added repeatedly in his first year that a Church standing still will grow old. Mercy and encounter must be carried out into the world, to what he calls the outskirts.

Pope Francis insists every member of the Church — "nourished by the light and strength of the Holy Spirit" — has a role to play, and there is no room for negativity and pessimism. He laments in the apostolic exhortation, "There are Christians whose lives seem like Lent without Easter."

Reform and renewal From the start of his pontificate, Pope Francis has stood in continuity with Pope Emeritus Benedict's desires to bring reform and renewal, an undertaking that is for the entire Church, from individual Catholics to parishes and dioceses — even the papacy itself.

For Pope Francis, a particular focus is the reform of the Curia, the central government of the Church. In April, he created an advisory council of eight cardinals (including the American Sean O'Malley of Boston) that is expected to propose sweeping changes to the institutional structure of the Holy See. The pope also established several commissions to improve Vatican financial transparency and to continue Pope Benedict's efforts to end clergy sexual abuse.

His words for the faithful are just as dramatic. He has called on Catholics not be a "Mr. and Mrs. Whiner," "querulous and disillusioned pessimists" with faces like "a pickled pepper." He is the first pope to warn against being "sourpusses" in a papal document.

As for Pope Francis himself, he has spent the year faithful to his namesake's humble service and joy. He lives in the Casa Santa Marta, a hotel in the Vatican, eschewed the traditional papal summer vacation at Castel Gandolfo and invited homeless men to his 77th birthday dinner in December.

Of all the images of Francis during his first papal year, though, the most emblematic were the times of laughter and of joy. He seems to be having a great time as pope — not in a frivolous or self-serving sense, but in the way of the joy-filled Christian. As he said in a recent homily, the Christian style is joy — "the joy of Jesus, which always forgives and helps."

Cardinal Dolan said it best. In his first year, Francis has become the "world's parish priest."

PAPAL TRIPS, 2013-2014

Assisi, Italy, October 4, 2013

Pope Francis visited Assisi, Italy — the birthplace of his papal namesake, St. Francis — on Oct. 4, in an opportunity for him to highlight several key themes of his pontificate, including mercy, the renunciation of worldliness, discernment and the embrace of Christ in poverty — especially poverty in spirit — to change the world.

The journey to Assisi on *il Poverello*'s feast day included elements that have become standard for the pope as he proclaims his themes, such as meetings with disabled and sick children and the poor and an audience with young people.

Francis is particularly gifted in gestures and images, and the meeting with the sick and disabled at the sports field of the Serafico Institute of Assisi was filled with poignant moments of mercy, most so as he embraced and kissed young people and their caregivers on the cheek and gave each of them the Sign of the Cross on their foreheads.

He then set aside a prepared talk in favor of a powerful off-the-cuff meditation on the scars of Christ that he compared to the suffering of the sick.

"A Christian adores Jesus, seeks Jesus, knows how to recognize the scars of Jesus. When Jesus rose he was beautiful. He didn't have his wounds on his body, but he wanted to keep the scars, and he brought them with him to heaven," he said. "The scars of Jesus are here, and they are in heaven before the Father. We care for the scars of Jesus here, and he from heaven shows us his scars and tells all of us, 'I am waiting for you.'"

Stripping away worldliness Pope Francis prayed at the tombs of Sts. Francis and Clare and before the cross of San Damiano, but he also made it a point to pray privately in St. Francis' hovel and to speak at the archbishop's residence where 800 years ago St. Francis stripped off his fine clothes, renounced all wealth and embraced the call of radical poverty.

Precious Gift "In the name of St. Francis, I say to you: I haven't gold or silver to give you, but something much more precious, the Gospel of Jesus. Go forward with courage! ... Be witnesses of the Faith with your life: Bring Christ into your homes, proclaim him among your friends, welcome him and serve him in the poor."

The prayer at the hovel, and his pastoral encounter with the poor at the archbishop's residence, both stressed the pontiff's call on the whole Church to strip away all forms of worldliness and emulate *il Poverello*'s poverty, which itself was rooted in the servant humility of Jesus. Once again, Francis spoke extemporaneously on the cross as the ultimate sign of Christ's humility.

In recent interviews, the pope has talked about the need for the Church to be engaged with the world, but in Assisi he reminded its members not to succumb to the spirit of the world, described by the pope as "the leprosy, the cancer of society and the cancer of the revelation of God and the enemy of Jesus." This spirit, he warned, leads to vanity, arrogance and pride and the grave sin of idolatry.

For the Christian, the cross, humility and the rejection of the spirit of the world are vital for authentic progress; otherwise, Francis taught, "we become pastry shop Christians ... like nice sweet things but not real Christians."

Peace of Christ The imagery of stripping away worldliness and putting on Christ was carried forward in the papal Mass in the piazza before the Basilica of St. Francis. Being a Christian, Pope Francis declared, "means having a living relationship with the person of Jesus; it means putting on Christ, being conformed to him."

The journey of St. Francis to Christ began with the gaze of the crucified Jesus whose cross "speaks to us of love, the love of God incarnate, a love which does not die, but triumphs over evil and death. When we let the crucified Jesus gaze upon us, we are re-created, we become 'a new creation.'"

To be a follower of Christ, Francis noted, is to find true peace, "the peace that Christ alone can give, a peace which the world cannot give. Many people, when they think of St. Francis, think of peace; very few people, however, go deeper. What is the peace which Francis received, experienced and lived, and which he passes on to us? It is the peace of Christ, which is born of the greatest love of all, the love of the cross."

The pope then stressed that Franciscan peace is not something saccharine. "Hardly!" the pope proclaimed, "That is not the real St. Francis! Nor is it a kind of pantheistic harmony with forces of the cosmos ... That is not Franciscan either! It is not Franciscan, but a notion that some people have invented! The peace of St. Francis is the peace of Christ."

Pope Francis then held a raucous audience with young people in front of the Basilica of Santa Maria degli Angeli in Assisi. The pope answered questions about marriage, discerning a vocation and justice, and he urged the youth to have the courage to get married and have families. In between moments of laughter, he reminded them that Christian marriage is a "real vocation, just like priesthood and religious life are.

"Two Christians who marry each other have recognized in their love story the Lord's call, the vocation to form one flesh, one life from the two, male and female," he said. "It takes courage to start a family."

He added that they should be open also to the vocations of the priesthood and the religious life and that celibacy or virginity for the kingdom of heaven was the vocation that Jesus lived. He acknowledged that priesthood and the religious life do bring the giving up of marriage and a family, but he assured them that "virginity for the kingdom of God is not a 'no,' it's a 'yes.' Discerning a vocation requires hearing God's voice, which can only be accomplished through regular prayer that comes from a familiar relationship with the Lord and is "like keeping the window of our life open so that he can make his voice heard."

Speaking on justice, Pope Francis called on young people to work for societies that are mutually just

and peaceful.

"The Gospel," he taught, "doesn't have to do only with religion, but with the human person, the whole person, and with the world, society and human civilization."

The pope gave the young people and the whole Church one final lesson regarding St. Francis. As we all set out to work for evangelization and authentic justice, we should, he said, "look at St. Francis. ... Francis made the Faith grow and renewed the Church; at the same time, he renewed society, making it more fraternal, but always with the Gospel."

The Holy Land, May 24-26, 2014

Pope Francis, on the second apostolic journey of his pontificate, traveled to the Holy Land. Pope Francis visited the Holy Land on his first apostolic visit to the holy places since his election. The journey was intended especially to commemorate the 50th anniversary of Pope Paul VI's historic encounter in Jerusalem with Patriarch Athenagoras, an event that was seen as a watershed moment in the history of ecumenism.

Program

• Meeting with the Authorities of the Kingdom of Jordan (Amman, May 24, 2014)

• Holy Mass at the Amman International Stadium (May 24, 2014)

• Meeting with refugees and young people with disabilities in the Latin Church in Bethany beyond the Jordan (May 24, 2014)

• Meeting with Palestinian Authorities (Bethlehem, May 25, 2014)

• Holy Mass in Manger Square in Bethlehem (May 25, 2014)

• Regina Coeli Prayer (Bethlehem, May 25, 2014)

• Greeting to children of the refugee camp of Dheisheh, Aida and Beit Jibrin at the Phoenix Center of Dheisheh refugee camp (Bethlehem, May 25, 2014)

• Welcoming ceremony at the Tel Aviv Ben Gurion International Airport (Tel Aviv, May 25, 2014)

• Common Declaration of Pope Francis and the Ecumenical Patriarch Bartholomew I; Private meeting with the Ecumenical Patriarch of Constantinople at the Apostolic Delegation of Jerusalem (May 25, 2014)

• Ecumenical Celebration on the occasion of the 50th anniversary of the meeting in Jerusalem between Pope Paul VI and Patriarch Athenagoras (Jerusalem, Basilica of the Holy Sepulchre, May 25, 2014)

• Visit to the Grand Mufti of Jerusalem in the building of the Great Council on the Esplanade of the Mosques (Jerusalem, May 26, 2014)

• Visit to the Yad Vashem Memorial in Jerusalem (May 26, 2014)

• Courtesy visit to the two chief rabbis of Israel at Heichal Shlomo Center in Jerusalem, next to the Jerusalem Great Synagogue (Jerusalem, May 26, 2014)

• Courtesy visit to the President of the State of Israel in the Presidential Residence (Jerusalem, May 26, 2014)

• Meeting with priests, religious and seminarians in the Church of Gethsemane at the foot of the Mount of Olives (Jerusalem, May 26, 2014)

• Holy Mass with the Ordinaries of the Holy Land

and the Papal Entourage (Room of the Cenacle in Jerusalem, May 26, 2014)
• Press Conference of the Holy Father during the return flight from the Holy Land (May 26, 2014)

Excerpts from Addresses and Homilies
(Complete texts of papal addresses, remarks and homilies can be found at www.vatican.va.)
• **Meeting with the Authorities of the Kingdom of Jordan (Amman, 24 May 2014)**
Jordan has offered a generous welcome to great numbers of Palestinian and Iraqi refugees, as well as to other refugees from troubled areas, particularly neighboring Syria, ravaged by a conflict which has lasted all too long. Such generosity merits, Your Majesty, the appreciation and support of the international community. The Catholic Church, to the extent of its abilities, has sought to provide assistance to refugees and those in need, especially through Caritas Jordan.

While acknowledging with deep regret the continuing grave tensions in the Middle East, I thank the authorities of the Kingdom for all that they are doing and I encourage them to persevere in their efforts to seek lasting peace for the entire region. This great goal urgently requires that a peaceful solution be found to the crisis in Syria, as well as a just solution to the Israeli-Palestinian conflict.

I take this opportunity to reiterate my profound respect and esteem for the Muslim community and my appreciation for the leadership of His Majesty the King in promoting a better understanding of the virtues taught by Islam and a climate of serene coexistence between the faithful of the different religions. You are known as a man of peace and a peacemaker: thank you! I am grateful that Jordan has supported a number of important initiatives aimed at advancing interreligious dialogue and understanding between Jews, Christians and Muslims. I think in particular of the Amman Message and the support given within the United Nations Organization to the annual celebration of World Interfaith Harmony Week.

I would also like to offer an affectionate greeting to the Christian communities welcomed by this Kingdom, communities present in this country since apostolic times, contributing to the common good of the society of which they are fully a part. Although Christians today are numerically a minority, theirs is a significant and valued presence in the fields of education and health care, thanks to their schools and hospitals. They are able to profess their faith peaceably, in a climate of respect for religious freedom. Religious freedom is in fact a fundamental human right and I cannot fail to express my hope that it will be upheld throughout the Middle East and the entire world. The right to religious freedom "includes on the individual and collective levels the freedom to follow one's conscience in religious matters and, at the same time, freedom of worship... [it also includes] the freedom to choose the religion which one judges to be true and to manifest one's beliefs in public" (*Ecclesia in Medio Oriente*, No. 26). Christians consider themselves, and indeed are, full citizens, and as such they seek, together with their Muslim fellow citizens, to make their own particular contribution to the society in which they live.
• **Holy Mass in Manger Square in Bethlehem (25 May 2014) Regina Coeli Prayer (Bethlehem, 25 May 2014)**
What a great grace it is to celebrate the Eucharist in the place where Jesus was born! I thank God and I thank all of you who have welcomed me on my pilgrimage:

President Mahmoud Abbas and the other civil authorities; Patriarch Fouad Twal and the other bishops and ordinaries of the Holy Land, the priests, the good Franciscans, the consecrated persons and all those who labor to keep faith, hope and love alive in these lands; the faithful who have come from Gaza and Galilee, and the immigrants from Asia and Africa. Thank you for your welcome!

The Child Jesus, born in Bethlehem, is the sign given by God to those who awaited salvation, and he remains forever the sign of God's tenderness and presence in our world. The angel announces to the shepherds: "This will be a sign for you: you will find a child..."

Today too, children are a sign. They are a sign of hope, a sign of life, but also a "diagnostic" sign, a marker indicating the health of families, society and the entire world. Wherever children are accepted, loved, cared for and protected, the family is healthy, society is more healthy and the world is more human. Here we can think of the work carried out by the Ephpheta Paul VI institute for hearing and speech impaired Palestinian children: it is a very real sign of God's goodness. It is a clear sign that society is healthier.

To us, the men and women of the 21st century, God today also says: "This will be a sign for you," look to the child...

The Child of Bethlehem is frail, like all newborn children. He cannot speak and yet he is the Word made flesh who came to transform the hearts and lives of all men and women. This Child, like every other child, is vulnerable; he needs to be accepted and protected. Today, too, children need to be welcomed and defended, from the moment of their conception.

Sadly, in this world, with all its highly developed technology, great numbers of children continue to live in inhuman situations, on the fringes of society, in the peripheries of great cities and in the countryside. All too many children continue to be exploited, maltreated, enslaved, prey to violence and illicit trafficking. Still too many children live in exile, as refugees, at times lost at sea, particularly in the waters of the Mediterranean. Today, in acknowledging this, we feel shame before God, before God who became a child.

And we have to ask ourselves: Who are we, as we stand before the Child Jesus? Who are we, standing as we stand before today's children? Are we like Mary and Joseph, who welcomed Jesus and care for him with the love of a father and a mother? Or are we like Herod, who wanted to eliminate him? Are we like the shepherds, who went in haste to kneel before him in worship and offer him their humble gifts? Or are we indifferent? Are we perhaps people who use fine and pious words, yet exploit pictures of poor children in order to make money? Are we ready to be there for children, to "waste time" with them? Are we ready to listen to them, to care for them, to pray for them and with them? Or do we ignore them because we are too caught up in our own affairs?

"This will be a sign for us: you will find a child..." Perhaps that little boy or girl is crying. He is crying because he is hungry, because she is cold, because he or she wants to be picked up and held in our arms... Today too, children are crying, they are crying a lot, and their crying challenges us. In a world which daily discards tons of food and medicine there are children, hungry and suffering from easily curable diseases, who cry out in vain. In an age which insists on the protection of minors, there is a flourishing trade in weapons which end up in the hands of child-soldiers, there is a ready market for goods produced by the slave labor of small children. Their cry is stifled: the cry of these children is stifled! They must fight, they must work, they cannot cry! But their mothers cry for them, as modern-day Rachels: they weep for their children, and they refuse to be consoled (cf. Mt 2:18).

"This will be a sign for you": you will find a child. The Child Jesus, born in Bethlehem, every child who is born and grows up in every part of our world, is a diagnostic sign indicating the state of health of our families, our communities, our nation. Such a frank and honest diagnosis can lead us to a new kind of lifestyle where our relationships are no longer marked by conflict, oppression and consumerism, but fraternity, forgiveness and reconciliation, solidarity and love.

• **Common Declaration of Pope Francis and the Ecumenical Patriarch Bartholomew I; Private meeting with the Ecumenical Patriarch of Constantinople at the Apostolic Delegation of Jerusalem (May 25, 2014).**

1. Like our venerable predecessors Pope Paul VI and Ecumenical Patriarch Athenagoras who met here in Jerusalem 50 years ago, we too, Pope Francis and Ecumenical Patriarch Bartholomew, were determined to meet in the Holy Land "where our common Redeemer, Christ our Lord, lived, taught, died, rose again, and ascended into Heaven, whence he sent the Holy Spirit on the infant Church" (Common communiqué of Pope Paul VI and Patriarch Athenagoras, published after their meeting of Jan. 6, 1964). Our meeting, another encounter of the Bishops of the Churches of Rome and Constantinople founded respectively by the two Brothers the Apostles Peter and Andrew, is a source of profound spiritual joy for us. It presents a providential occasion to reflect on the depth and the authenticity of our existing bonds, themselves the fruit of a grace-filled journey on which the Lord has guided us since that blessed day of 50 years ago.

2. Our fraternal encounter today is a new and necessary step on the journey toward the unity to which only the Holy Spirit can lead us, that of communion in legitimate diversity. We call to mind with profound gratitude the steps that the Lord has already enabled us to undertake. The embrace exchanged between Pope Paul VI and Patriarch Athenagoras here in Jerusalem, after many centuries of silence, paved the way for a momentous gesture, the removal from the memory and from the midst of the Church of the acts of mutual excommunication in 1054. This was followed by an exchange of visits between the respective Sees of Rome and Constantinople, by regular correspondence and, later, by the decision announced by Pope John Paul II and Patriarch Dimitrios, of blessed memory both, to initiate a theological dialogue of truth between Catholics and Orthodox. Over these years, God, the source of all peace and love, has taught us to regard one another as members of the same Christian family, under one Lord and Saviour, Jesus Christ, and to love one another, so that we may confess our faith in the same Gospel of Christ, as received by the Apostles and expressed and transmitted to us by the Ecumenical Councils and the Church Fathers. While fully aware of not having reached the goal of full communion, today we confirm our commitment to continue walking together towards the unity for which Christ our Lord prayed to the Father so "that all may be one" (Jn 17:21).

3. Well aware that unity is manifested in love of God and love of neighbor, we look forward in eager anticipation to the day in which we will finally partake together in the Eucharistic banquet. As Christians, we are called to prepare to receive this gift of Eucharistic communion, according to the teaching of St. Irenaeus of Lyon (*Against Heresies*, IV,18,5, PG 7,1028), through the confession of the one faith, persevering prayer, inner conversion, renewal of life and fraternal dialogue. By achieving this hoped for goal, we will manifest to the world the love of God by which we are recognized as true disciples of Jesus Christ (cf. Jn 13:35).

4. To this end, the theological dialogue undertaken by the Joint International Commission offers a fundamental contribution to the search for full communion among Catholics and Orthodox. Throughout the subsequent times of Popes John Paul II and Benedict the XVI, and Patriarch Dimitrios, the progress of our theological encounters has been substantial. Today we express heartfelt appreciation for the achievements to date, as well as for the current endeavours. This is no mere theoretical exercise, but an exercise in truth and love that demands an ever deeper knowledge of each other's traditions in order to understand them and to learn from them. Thus we affirm once again that the theological dialogue does not seek a theological lowest common denominator on which to reach a compromise, but is rather about deepening one's grasp of the whole truth that Christ has given to his Church, a truth that we never cease to understand better as we follow the Holy Spirit's promptings. Hence, we affirm together that our faithfulness to the Lord demands fraternal encounter and true dialogue. Such a common pursuit does not lead us away from the truth; rather, through an exchange of gifts, through the guidance of the Holy Spirit, it will lead us into all truth (cf. Jn 16:13).

5. Yet even as we make this journey towards full communion we already have the duty to offer common witness to the love of God for all people by working together in the service of humanity, especially in defending the dignity of the human person at every stage of life and the sanctity of family based on marriage, in promoting peace and the common good, and in responding to the suffering that continues to afflict our world. We acknowledge that hunger, poverty, illiteracy, the inequitable distribution of resources must constantly be addressed. It is our duty to seek to build together a just and humane society in which no-one feels excluded or emarginated.

6. It is our profound conviction that the future of the human family depends also on how we safeguard – both prudently and compassionately, with justice and fairness – the gift of creation that our Creator has entrusted to us. Therefore, we acknowledge in repentance the wrongful mistreatment of our planet, which is tantamount to sin before the eyes of God. We reaffirm our responsibility and obligation to foster a sense of humility and moderation so that all may feel the need to respect creation and to safeguard it with care. Together, we pledge our commitment to raising awareness about the stewardship of creation; we appeal to all people of goodwill to consider ways of living less wastefully and more frugally, manifesting less greed and more generosity for the protection of God's world and the benefit of His people.

7. There is likewise an urgent need for effective and committed cooperation of Christians in order to safeguard everywhere the right to express publicly one's faith and to be treated fairly when promoting that which Christianity continues to offer to contemporary society and culture. In this regard, we invite all Christians to promote an authen-

tic dialogue with Judaism, Islam and other religious traditions. Indifference and mutual ignorance can only lead to mistrust and unfortunately even conflict.

8. From this holy city of Jerusalem, we express our shared profound concern for the situation of Christians in the Middle East and for their right to remain full citizens of their homelands. In trust we turn to the almighty and merciful God in a prayer for peace in the Holy Land and in the Middle East in general. We especially pray for the Churches in Egypt, Syria, and Iraq, which have suffered most grievously due to recent events. We encourage all parties regardless of their religious convictions to continue to work for reconciliation and for the just recognition of peoples' rights. We are persuaded that it is not arms, but dialogue, pardon and reconciliation that are the only possible means to achieve peace.

9. In an historical context marked by violence, indifference and egoism, many men and women today feel that they have lost their bearings. It is precisely through our common witness to the good news of the Gospel that we may be able to help the people of our time to rediscover the way that leads to truth, justice and peace. United in our intentions, and recalling the example, fifty years ago here in Jerusalem, of Pope Paul VI and Patriarch Athenagoras, we call upon all Christians, together with believers of every religious tradition and all people of good will, to recognize the urgency of the hour that compels us to seek the reconciliation and unity of the human family, while fully respecting legitimate differences, for the good of all humanity and of future generations.

10. In undertaking this shared pilgrimage to the site where our one same Lord Jesus Christ was crucified, buried and rose again, we humbly commend to the intercession of the Most Holy and Ever Virgin Mary our future steps on the path towards the fullness of unity, entrusting to God's infinite love the entire human family. " May the Lord let his face shine upon you, and be gracious to you! The Lord look upon you kindly and give you peace!" (Num 6:25-26).

• **Ecumenical Celebration on the occasion of the 50th anniversary of the meeting in Jerusalem between Pope Paul VI and Patriarch Athenagoras (Jerusalem, Basilica of the Holy Sepulchre, May 25, 2014)**

In this Basilica, which all Christians regard with the deepest veneration, my pilgrimage in the company of my beloved brother in Christ, His Holiness Bartholomaios, now reaches its culmination. We are making this pilgrimage in the footsteps of our venerable predecessors, Pope Paul VI and Patriarch Athenagoras, who, with courage and docility to the Holy Spirit, made possible, fifty years ago, in this holy city of Jerusalem, an historic meeting between the Bishop of Rome and the Patriarch of Constantinople. I cordially greet all of you who are present. In a special way I express my heartfelt gratitude to those who have made this moment possible: His Beatitude Theophilos, who has welcomed us so graciously, His Beatitude Nourhan Manoogian and Father Pierbattista Pizzaballa.

It is an extraordinary grace to be gathered here in prayer. The empty tomb, that new garden grave where Joseph of Arimathea had reverently placed Jesus' body, is the place from which the proclamation of the resurrection begins: "Do not be afraid; I know that you are looking for Jesus who was crucified. He is not here, for he has been raised, as he said. Come, see the place where he lay. Then go quickly and tell his disciples, 'He has been raised from the dead'" (Mt 28:5-7). This proclamation, confirmed by the testimony of those to whom the risen Lord appeared, is the heart of the Christian message, faithfully passed down from generation to generation, as the Apostle Paul, from the very beginning, bears witness: "I handed on to you as of first importance what I in turn had received: that Christ died for our sins in accordance with the Scriptures, and that he was buried, and that he was raised on the third day in accordance with the Scriptures" (1 Cor 15:3-4). This is the basis of the faith which unites us, whereby together we profess that Jesus Christ, the only-begotten Son of the Father and our sole Lord, "suffered under Pontius Pilate, was crucified, died and was buried; he descended into hell; on the third day he rose again from the dead" (Apostles' Creed). Each of us, everyone baptized in Christ, has spiritually risen from this tomb, for in baptism all of us truly became members of the body of the One who is the Firstborn of all creation; we were buried together with him, so as to be raised up with him and to walk in newness of life (cf. Rom 6:4).

Let us receive the special grace of this moment. We pause in reverent silence before this empty tomb in order to rediscover the grandeur of our Christian vocation: we are men and women of resurrection, and not of death. From this place we learn how to live our lives, the trials of our Churches and of the whole world, in the light of Easter morning. Every injury, every one of our pains and sorrows, has been borne on the shoulders of the Good Shepherd who offered himself in sacrifice and thereby opened the way to eternal life. His open wounds are like the cleft through which the torrent of his mercy is poured out upon the world. Let us not allow ourselves to be robbed of the basis of our hope, which is this: Christòs anesti! Let us not deprive the world of the joyful message of the resurrection! And let us not be deaf to the powerful summons to unity which rings out from this very place, in the words of the One who, risen from the dead, calls all of us "my brothers" (cf. Mt 28:10; Jn 20:17).

Clearly we cannot deny the divisions which continue to exist among us, the disciples of Jesus: this sacred place makes us even more painfully aware of how tragic they are. And yet, fifty years after the embrace of those two venerable Fathers, we realize with gratitude and renewed amazement how it was possible, at the prompting of the Holy Spirit, to take truly significant steps towards unity. We know that much distance still needs to be travelled before we attain that fullness of communion which can also be expressed by sharing the same Eucharistic table, something we ardently desire; yet our disagreements must not frighten us and paralyze our progress. We need to believe that, just as the stone before the tomb was cast aside, so too every obstacle to our full communion will also be removed. This will be a grace of resurrection, of which we can have a foretaste even today. Every time we ask forgiveness of one another for our sins against other Christians and every time we find the courage to grant and receive such forgiveness, we experience the resurrection! Every time we put behind us our longstanding prejudices and find the courage to build new fraternal relationships, we confess that Christ is truly risen! Every time we reflect on the future of the Church in the light of her vocation to unity, the dawn of Easter breaks forth! Here I reiterate the hope already expressed by my predecessors for a continued dialogue with all our brothers and sisters in Christ, aimed at finding a means of exercising the specific ministry of the Bishop of Rome which, in fidelity to his mission, can be open to a new situation and can be, in the present context, a service of love and of communion acknowledged by all (cf. JOHN PAUL II, *Ut Unum Sint*, Nos. 95-96).

Standing as pilgrims in these holy places, we also remember in our prayers the entire Middle East, so frequently and lamentably marked by acts of violence and conflict. Nor do we forget in our prayers the many other men and women who in various parts of our world are suffering from war, poverty and hunger, as well as the many Christians who are persecuted for their faith in the risen Lord. When Christians of different confessions suffer together, side by side, and assist one another with fraternal charity, there is born an ecumenism of suffering, an ecumenism of blood, which proves particularly powerful not only for those situations in which it occurs, but also, by virtue of the communion of the saints, for the whole Church as well. Those who kill, persecute Christians out of hatred, do not ask if they are Orthodox or Catholics: they are Christians. The blood of Christians is the same.

• **Visit to the Grand Mufti of Jerusalem in the building of the Great Council on the Esplanade of the Mosques (Jerusalem, May 26, 2014)**

I am grateful for the opportunity to meet with you in this sacred place. I thank you for the courteous invitation you have extended to me and, in particular, I wish to thank the Grand Mufti and the President of the Supreme Muslim Council.

Following in the footsteps of my predecessors, and in particular the historic visit of Pope Paul VI fifty years ago, the first visit of a Pope to the Holy Land, I have greatly desired to come as a pilgrim to the places which witnessed the earthly presence of Jesus Christ. But my pilgrimage would not be complete if it did not also include a meeting with the people and the communities who live in this Land. I am particularly happy, therefore, to be with you, dear Muslim faithful, brothers.

At this moment I think of Abraham, who lived as a pilgrim in these lands. Muslims, Christians and Jews see in him, albeit in different ways, a father in faith and a great example to be imitated. He became a pilgrim, leaving his own people and his own house in order to embark on that spiritual adventure to which God called him.

A pilgrim is a person who makes himself poor and sets forth on a journey. Pilgrims set out intently toward a great and longed-for destination, and they live in the hope of a promise received (cf. Heb 11:8-19). This was how Abraham lived, and this should be our spiritual attitude. We can never think ourselves self-sufficient, masters of our own lives. We cannot be content with remaining withdrawn, secure in our convictions. Before the mystery of God we are all poor. We realize that we must constantly be prepared to go out from ourselves, docile to God's call and open to the future that he wishes to create for us.

In our earthly pilgrimage we are not alone. We cross paths with other faithful; at times we share with them a stretch of the road and at other times we experience with them a moment of rest which refreshes us. Such is our meeting today, for which I am particularly grateful. It is a welcome and shared moment of rest, made possible by your hospitality, on the pilgrimage of our life and that of our communities. We are experiencing a fraternal dialogue and exchange which are able to restore us and offer us new strength to confront the common challenges before us.

Nor can we forget that the pilgrimage of Abraham was also a summons to righteousness: God wanted him to witness his way of acting and to imitate him. We too wish to witness to God's working in the world, and so, precisely in this meeting, we hear deep within us his summons to work for peace and justice, to implore these gifts in prayer and to learn from on high mercy, magnanimity and compassion.

• **Visit to the Yad Vashem Memorial in Jerusalem (May 26, 2014)**

"Adam, where are you?" (cf. Gn 3:9). Where are you, o man? What have you come to? In this place, this memorial of the Shoah, we hear God's question echo once more: "Adam, where are you?" This question is charged with all the sorrow of a Father who has lost his child. The Father knew the risk of freedom; he knew that his children could be lost… yet perhaps not even the Father could imagine so great a fall, so profound an abyss! Here, before the boundless tragedy of the Holocaust, That cry – "Where are you?" – echoes like a faint voice in an unfathomable abyss…

Adam, who are you? I no longer recognize you. Who are you, o man? What have you become? Of what horror have you been capable? What made you fall to such depths?

Certainly it is not the dust of the earth from which you were made. The dust of the earth is something good, the work of my hands. Certainly it is not the breath of life which I breathed into you. That breath comes from me, and it is something good (cf. Gn 2:7).

No, this abyss is not merely the work of your own hands, your own heart… Who corrupted you? Who disfigured you? Who led you to presume that you are the master of good and evil? Who convinced you that you were god? Not only did you torture and kill your brothers and sisters, but you sacrificed them to yourself, because you made yourself a god.

Today, in this place, we hear once more the voice of God: "Adam, where are you?"

From the ground there rises up a soft cry: "Have mercy on us, O Lord!" To you, O Lord our God, belongs righteousness; but to us confusion of face and shame (cf. Bar 1:15).

A great evil has befallen us, such as never happened under the heavens (cf. Bar 2:2). Now, Lord, hear our prayer, hear our plea, save us in your mercy. Save us from this horror.

Almighty Lord, a soul in anguish cries out to you. Hear, Lord, and have mercy! We have sinned against you. You reign for ever (cf. Bar 3:1-2). Remember us in your mercy. Grant us the grace to be ashamed of what we men have done, to be ashamed of this massive idolatry, of having despised and destroyed our own flesh which you formed from the earth, to which you gave life with your own breath of life. Never again, Lord, never again!

"Adam, where are you?" Here we are, Lord, shamed by what man, created in your own image and likeness, was capable of doing.

Remember us in your mercy.

• **Courtesy visit to the President of the State of Israel in the Presidential Residence (Jerusalem, May 26, 2014)**

I am grateful to you, Mr President, for your kind and sage words of greeting and your warm welcome. I am happy to be able to meet you once again, this time in Jerusalem, the city which preserves the Holy Places dear to the three great religions which worship the God who called Abraham. The Holy Places are not monuments or museums for tourists, but places where communities of believers daily express their faith and culture, and carry out their works of charity. Precisely for this reason, their sacred character must be perpetually maintained and protection given not only to the legacy of the past but also to all those who visit these sites today and to those who will visit them in the future. May Jerusalem be truly the City of Peace! May her identity and her sacred character, her universal religious and cultural significance shine forth as a treasure for all mankind! How good it is when pilgrims and residents enjoy free access to the Holy Places and can freely take part in religious celebrations.

Mr. President, you are known as a man of peace and a peacemaker. I appreciate and admire the approach you have taken. Peacemaking demands first and foremost respect for the dignity and freedom of every human person, which Jews, Christians and Muslims alike believe to be created by God and destined to eternal life. This shared conviction enables us resolutely to pursue peaceful solutions to every controversy and conflict. Here I renew my plea that all parties avoid initiatives and actions which contradict their stated determination to reach a true agreement and that they tirelessly work for peace, with decisiveness and tenacity.

There is likewise need for a firm rejection of all that is opposed to the cultivation of peace and respectful relations between Jews, Christians and Muslims. We think, for example, of recourse to violence and terrorism, all forms of discrimination on the basis of race or religion, attempts to impose one's own point of view at the expense of the rights of others, anti-Semitism in all its possible expressions, and signs of intolerance directed against individuals or places of worship, be they Jewish, Christian or Muslim.

A variety of Christian communities live and work in the State of Israel. They are an integral part of society and participate fully in its civic, political and cultural affairs. Christians wish, as such, to contribute to the common good and the growth of peace; they wish to do so as full-fledged citizens who reject extremism in all its forms and are committed to fostering reconciliation and harmony.

The presence of these communities and respect for their rights – as for the rights of all other religious groups and all minorities – are the guarantee of a healthy pluralism and proof of the vitality of democratic values as they are authentically embodied in the daily life and workings of the State.

• **Holy Mass with the Ordinaries of the Holy Land and the Papal Entourage (Room of the Cenacle in Jerusalem, May 26, 2014)**
It is a great gift that the Lord has given us by bringing us together here in the Upper Room for the celebration of the Eucharist. I greet you with fraternal joy and I wish to express my affection to the Oriental Catholic Patriarchs who have taken part in my pilgrimage during these days. I want to thank them for their significant presence, particularly dear to me and I assure them of a special place in my heart and in my prayers. Here, where Jesus shared the Last Supper with the apostles; where, after his resurrection, he appeared in their midst; where the Holy Spirit descended with power upon Mary and the disciples, here the Church was born, and she was born to go forth. From here she set out, with the broken bread in her hands, the wounds of Christ before her eyes, and the Spirit of love in her heart.

In the Upper Room, the risen Jesus, sent by the Father, bestowed upon the apostles his own Spirit and with his power he sent them forth to renew the face of the earth (cf. Ps 104:30).

To go forth, to set out, does not mean to forget. The Church, in her going forth, preserves the memory of what took place here; the Spirit, the Paraclete, reminds her of every word and every action, and reveals their true meaning.

The Upper Room speaks to us of service, of Jesus giving the disciples an example by washing their feet. Washing one another's feet signifies welcoming, accepting, loving and serving one another. It means serving the poor, the sick and the outcast, those whom I find difficult, those who annoy me.

The Upper Room reminds us, through the Eucharist, of sacrifice. In every Eucharistic celebration Jesus offers himself for us to the Father, so that we too can be united with him, offering to God our lives, our work, our joys and our sorrows… offering everything as a spiritual sacrifice.

The Upper Room also reminds us of friendship. "No longer do I call you servants – Jesus said to the Twelve – but I have called you friends" (Jn 15:15). The Lord makes us his friends, he reveals God's will to us and he gives us his very self. This is the most beautiful part of being a Christian and, especially, of being a priest: becoming a friend of the Lord Jesus, and discovering in our hearts that he is our friend.

The Upper Room reminds us of the Teacher's farewell and his promise to return to his friends: "When I go… I will come again and will take you to myself, that where I am you may be also" (Jn 14:3). Jesus does not leave us, nor does he ever abandon us; he precedes us to the house of the Father, where he desires to bring us as well.

The Upper Room, however, also reminds us of pettiness, of curiosity – "Who is the traitor?" – and of betrayal. We ourselves, and not just others, can reawaken those attitudes whenever we look at our brother or sister with contempt, whenever we judge them, whenever by our sins we betray Jesus.

The Upper Room reminds us of sharing, fraternity, harmony and peace among ourselves. How much love and goodness has flowed from the Upper Room! How much charity has gone forth from here, like a river from its source, beginning as a stream and then expanding and becoming a great torrent. All the saints drew from this source; and hence the great river of the Church's holiness continues to flow: from the Heart of Christ, from the Eucharist and from the Holy Spirit.

Lastly, the Upper Room reminds us of the birth of the new family, the Church, our holy Mother the hierarchical Church established by the risen Jesus; a family that has a Mother, the Virgin Mary. Christian families belong to this great family, and in it they find the light and strength to press on and be renewed, amid the challenges and difficulties of life. All God's children, of every people and language, are invited and called to be part of this great family, as brothers and sisters and sons and daughters of the one Father in heaven.

These horizons are opened up by the Upper Room, the horizons of the Risen Lord and his Church.

From here the Church goes forth, impelled by the life-giving breath of the Spirit. Gathered in prayer with the Mother of Jesus, the Church lives in constant expectation of a renewed outpouring of the Holy Spirit. Send forth your Spirit, Lord, and renew the face of the earth (cf. Ps 104:30)!

• **Press Conference of the Holy Father during the return flight from the Holy Land (May 26, 2014)**
On his return flight to Rome after his hectic trip to the Holy Land, Pope Francis held a highly noteworthy press

conference with reporters, including the surprise announcement that he would meet with a group of sex abuse victims and celebrate Mass for them in the near future, perhaps in early June, and that he is open to retiring from the papacy.

As the Catholic and secular media learned last July on the flight from Rio de Janeiro to Rome after his attendance at World Youth Day, the pope's journey home is potentially as newsworthy as the trip itself. The flight from Tel Aviv to Rome proved no exception.

As he did on the Brazil flight, Pope Francis made himself available to reporters on board the papal plane for an impromptu press conference. Attention focused on the sex abuse scandal, upcoming papal journeys and a possible new wrinkle to the challenges facing Vatican finances.

In responding to questions about the Church's handling of the sex abuse scandal, Pope Francis reiterated his firm commitment to a "zero tolerance" policy for abuse, but he also revealed two surprising developments. The first was his planned meeting with victims, and the second was that at least four bishops currently are under Vatican scrutiny with regard to the scandal.

As he has in the past, Francis used strong language for abusers. He called the abuse of children by priests "an ugly crime," a "very grave" problem and a betrayal of the Body of Christ. Instead of bringing children to holiness, such a priest, Pope Francis declared, abuses them and gives them problems that last a lifetime.

He compared the actions of abuser priests to the celebration of a black mass, the Satanic ritual involving the desecration of the Eucharist. In December last year, the Holy Father established an unprecedented Pontifical Commission for the Protection of Minors with the task of advising him on the Church's efforts to protect children and offer pastoral care for victims of abuse. He named its first eight members in March, including four women. One of them, the Irish lay woman Marie Collins, was herself a victim of clergy sexual abuse as a girl in the 1960s.

As an unmistakable sign of outreach to victims, Pope Francis stated that he would meet soon with six to eight sex abuse victims from various countries, including Germany, England and Ireland, and would celebrate a private Mass for them in the Casa Santa Marta, the Vatican hotel where he resides. This will be Pope Francis' first encounter with a group of victims, although he met with Collins in May.

In a second surprise, the pope announced that three unnamed bishops currently are being investigated by the Vatican for their activities related to the scandal and another has been found guilty and will be facing punishment. The pope did not elaborate as to whether they are under investigation for personal actions of abuse or if they had failed to handle cases properly.

Critics of the Church's handling of the scandal often have focused on the issue of possible penalties for bishops who fail to hold abusers accountable, and Pope Francis seems determined to make bishops accountable. He said to reporters that in Argentina there is a euphemism for the special treatment of some officials, calling them "daddy's boys." The pope said sternly, "On this problem, there can't be any daddy's boys," meaning that no one should be safe from punishment when it comes to clergy sexual abuse.

Another topic of scandal discussed was the reported mishandling of some 15 million euro (approximately $20.5 million) belonging to the Institute for the Works of Religion, commonly called the Vatican Bank. The Vatican has tried to cope with several financial scandals over past years and has worked to implement global requirements for financial

transparency and fraud prevention. The current problem, however, has greater potential ramifications because of concerns that Card. Tarcisio Bertone, Vatican Secretary of State from 2006 to 2013, might be involved.

Pope Francis has moved quickly since his election to launch wide-ranging reforms in the area of Vatican finances, including the creation of a commission to improve oversight of the Vatican Bank and to fight against fraud. When asked what the biggest challenge so far has been to implementing reform, he replied that "the first challenge is me," but he was remarkably candid about the inquiry into the money, saying, "It is something under study; it is not clear. Perhaps it is the truth, but at this moment it's not definitive. It is under study, to be fair." He also stressed the continuing importance of effective reforms, noting, "while there will always be sinners, it's important to try not to increase their number."

Francis also announced that he would visit the Philippines and Sri Lanka next January. With an apostolic voyage already planned for Korea in August, the pontiff is making very manifest that promoting the Catholic Faith in Asia is a major priority for his pontificate.

He is also concerned for the plight of Christians in Asia and around the world, with a focus on religious liberty. "There are martyrs, today, Christian martyrs," he lamented. "And in some places you cannot carry the crucifix or cannot have a Bible. You cannot teach the Catechism to children, today! And I think — and I believe I am not mistaken — that at this time there are more martyrs than in the early days of the Church."

As for his own possible retirement, Francis seems quite willing to consider it under the right circumstances, pointing to Pope Emeritus Benedict as a role model both for him and all future popes. "We need to look at him as an institution: he opened a door, the door of emeritus popes," Francis declared. "Only God knows if there will be others, but the door is open." He added on a personal note that if the day comes, "I will do what the Lord tells me to do. ... But I believe that Benedict XVI was not a unique case."

South Korea, August 13-18, 2014

Pope Francis, on the third apostolic journey of his pontificate, traveled to South Korea. Pope Francis visited Korea. The primary reason for the visit was to celebrate the 6th Asian Youth Day, although Francis also presided over the beatification of Paul Yun Ji-Chung and 123 martyr companions. He likewise gave encouragement to the Church in Korea and promoted the process of reconciliation between North and South Korea.

Program

• Meeting with the Authorities in Chungmu Hall at the "Blue House" (Seoul, Aug. 14, 2014)

• Meeting with the Bishops of Korea in the headquarters of the Korean Episcopal Conference (Seoul, Aug. 14, 2014)

• Holy Mass on the Solemnity of the Assumption in the World Cup Stadium of Daejeon (Aug. 15, 2014)

• Prayer of the Angelus Domini (Daejeon, Aug. 15, 2014)

• Meeting with the Asian youth at the Shrine of Solmoe (Aug. 15, 2014)

• Holy Mass for the Beatification of Paul Yun Ji-Chung and 123 martyr companions at Gwanghwamun Gate (Seoul, Aug. 16, 2014)

• Meeting with the religious communities of Korea at

the Training Center "School of Love" in Kkottongnae (Aug. 16, 2014)
• Meeting with the leaders of the Apostolate of the laity at the Spirituality Centre (Kkottongnae, Aug. 16, 2014)
• Meeting with the Bishops of Asia at the Shrine of Haemi (Aug. 17, 2014)
• Closing Holy Mass of the 6th Asian Youth Day (Haemi Castle, Aug. 17, 2014)
• Holy Mass for Peace and Reconciliation at Myeong-dong Cathedral (Seoul, Aug. 18, 2014)

Excerpts from Addresses and Homilies

(*Complete texts of papal addresses, remarks and homilies can be found at www.vatican.va.*)

• Meeting with the Authorities in Chungmu Hall at the "Blue House" (Seoul, Aug. 14, 2014)

It is a great joy for me to come to Korea, the land of the morning calm, and to experience not only the natural beauty of this country, but above all the beauty of its people and its rich history and culture. This national legacy has been tested through the years by violence, persecution and war. But despite these trials, the heat of the day and the dark of the night have always given way to the morning calm, that is, to an undiminished hope for justice, peace and unity. What a gift hope is! We cannot become discouraged in our pursuit of these goals which are for the good not only of the Korean people, but of the entire region and the whole world.

I wish to thank President Park Geun-hye for her warm welcome. I greet her and the distinguished members of the government. I would like to acknowledge also the members of the diplomatic corps, and all those present who by their many efforts have assisted in preparing for my visit. I am most grateful for your hospitality, which has immediately made me feel at home among you.

My visit to Korea is occasioned by the Sixth Asian Youth Day, which brings together young Catholics from throughout this vast continent in a joyful celebration of their common faith. In the course of my visit I will also beatify a number of Koreans who died as martyrs for the Christian faith: Paul Yun Ji-chung and his 123 companions. These two celebrations complement one another. Korean culture understands well the inherent dignity and wisdom of our elders and honors their place in society. We Catholics honor our elders who were martyred for the faith because they were willing to give their lives for the truth which they had come to believe and by which they sought to live their lives. They teach us how to live fully for God and for the good of one another.

A wise and great people do not only cherish their ancestral traditions; they also treasure their young, seeking to pass on the legacy of the past and to apply it to the challenges of the present. Whenever young people gather together, as on the present occasion, it is a precious opportunity for all of us to listen to their hopes and concerns. We are also challenged to reflect on how well we are transmitting our values to the next generation, and on the kind of world and society we are preparing to hand on to them. In this context, I think it is especially important for us to reflect on the need to give our young people the gift of peace.

This appeal has all the more resonance here in Korea, a land which has long suffered because of a lack of peace. I can only express my appreciation for the efforts being made in favor of reconciliation and stability on the Korean peninsula, and to encourage those efforts, for they are the only sure path to lasting peace. Korea's quest for peace is a cause close to our hearts, for it affects the stability of the entire area and indeed of our whole war-weary world.

The quest for peace also represents a challenge for each of us, and in a particular way for those of you dedicated to the pursuit of the common good of the human family through the patient work of diplomacy. It is the perennial challenge of breaking down the walls of distrust and hatred by promoting a culture of reconciliation and solidarity. For diplomacy, as the art of the possible, is based on the firm and persevering conviction that peace can be won through quiet listening and dialogue, rather than by mutual recriminations, fruitless criticisms and displays of force.

• Holy Mass for the Beatification of Paul Yun Ji-Chung and 123 martyr companions at Gwanghwamun Gate (Seoul, Aug. 16, 2014)

Today we celebrate this victory in Paul Yun Ji-chung and his 123 companions. Their names now stand alongside those of the holy martyrs Andrew Kim Taegon, Paul Chong Hasang and companions, to whom I just paid homage. All of them lived and died for Christ, and now they reign with him in joy and in glory. With Saint Paul, they tell us that, in the death and resurrection of his Son, God has granted us the greatest victory of all. For "neither death, nor life, nor angels, nor principalities, nor things present, nor things to come, nor powers, nor height, nor depth, nor anything else in all creation, will be able to separate us from the love of God in Christ Jesus our Lord" (Rom 8:38-39).

The victory of the martyrs, their witness to the power of God's love, continues to bear fruit today in Korea, in the Church which received growth from their sacrifice. Our celebration of Blessed Paul and Companions provides us with the opportunity to return to the first moments, the infancy as it were, of the Church in Korea. It invites you, the Catholics of Korea, to remember the great things which God has wrought in this land and to treasure the legacy of faith and charity entrusted to you by your forebears.

In God's mysterious providence, the Christian faith was not brought to the shores of Korea through missionaries; rather, it entered through the hearts and minds of the Korean people themselves. It was prompted by intellectual curiosity, the search for religious truth. Through an initial encounter with the Gospel, the first Korean Christians opened their minds to Jesus. They wanted to know more about this Christ who suffered, died, and rose from the dead. Learning about Jesus soon led to an encounter with the Lord, the first baptisms, the yearning for a full sacramental and ecclesial life, and the beginnings of missionary outreach. It also bore fruit in communities inspired by the early Church, in which the believers were truly one in mind and heart, regardless of traditional social differences, and held all things in common (cf. Acts 4:32).

This history tells us much about the importance, the dignity and the beauty of the vocation of the laity. I greet the many lay faithful present, and in particular the Christian families who daily by their example teach the faith and the reconciling love of Christ to our young. In a special way, too, I greet the many priests present; by their dedicated ministry they pass on the rich patrimony of faith cultivated by past generations of Korean Catholics.

Today's Gospel contains an important message for all of us. Jesus asks the Father to consecrate us in truth, and to protect us from the world.

First of all, it is significant that, while Jesus asks the Father to consecrate and protect us, he does not ask him to take us out of the world. We know that he sends his disciples forth to be a leaven of holiness and truth in the world: the salt of the earth, the light of the world. In this, the martyrs show us the way.

Soon after the first seeds of faith were planted in this land, the martyrs and the Christian community had to choose between following Jesus or the world. They had heard the Lord's warning that the world would hate them because of him (Jn 17:14); they knew the cost of discipleship. For many, this meant persecution, and later flight to the mountains, where they formed Catholic villages. They were willing to make great sacrifices and let themselves be stripped of whatever kept them from Christ – possessions and land, prestige and honor – for they knew that Christ alone was their true treasure.

So often we today can find our faith challenged by the world, and in countless ways we are asked to compromise our faith, to water down the radical demands of the Gospel and to conform to the spirit of this age. Yet the martyrs call out to us to put Christ first and to see all else in this world in relation to him and his eternal Kingdom. They challenge us to think about what, if anything, we ourselves would be willing to die for...

Today is a day of great rejoicing for all Koreans. The heritage of Blessed Paul Yun Ji-chung and his companions – their integrity in the search for truth, and their fidelity to the highest principles of the religion which they chose to embrace, and their testimony of charity and solidarity with all – these are part of the rich history of the Korean people. The legacy of the martyrs can inspire all men and women of good will to work in harmony for a more just, free and reconciled society, thus contributing to peace and the protection of authentically human values in this country and in our world.

• **Meeting with the Bishops of Asia at the Shrine of Haemi (Aug. 17, 2014)**

On this vast continent which is home to a great variety of cultures, the Church is called to be versatile and creative in her witness to the Gospel through dialogue and openness to all. This is the challenge before you! Dialogue, in fact, is an essential part of the mission of the Church in Asia (cf. *Ecclesia in Asia*, 29). But in undertaking the path of dialogue with individuals and cultures, what should be our point of departure and our fundamental point of reference, which guides us to our destination? Surely it is our own identity, our identity as Christians. We cannot engage in real dialogue unless we are conscious of our own identity. We can't dialogue, we can't start dialoguing from nothing, from zero, from a foggy sense of who we are. Nor can there be authentic dialogue unless we are capable of opening our minds and hearts, in empathy and sincere receptivity, to those with whom we speak. In other words, an attentiveness in which the Holy Spirit is our guide. A clear sense of one's own identity and a capacity for empathy are thus the point of departure for all dialogue. If we are to speak freely, openly and fruitfully with others, we must be clear about who we are, what God has done for us, and what it is that he asks of us. And if our communication is not to be a monologue, there has

to be openness of heart and mind to accepting individuals and cultures. Fearlessly, for fear is the enemy of this kind of openness.

The task of appropriating and expressing our identity does not always prove easy, however, since – being sinners – we will always be tempted by the spirit of the world, which shows itself in a variety of ways. I would like to point to three of these. One is the deceptive light of relativism, which obscures the splendor of truth and, shaking the earth beneath our feet, pulls us toward the shifting sands of confusion and despair. It is a temptation which nowadays also affects Christian communities, causing people to forget that in a world of rapid and disorienting change, "there is much that is unchanging, much that has its ultimate foundation in Christ, who is the same yesterday, and today, and forever" (*Gaudium et Spes*, No. 10; cf. Heb 13:8). Here I am not speaking about relativism merely as a system of thought, but about that everyday practical relativism which almost imperceptibly saps our sense of identity.

A second way in which the world threatens the solidity of our Christian identity is superficiality, a tendency to toy with the latest fads, gadgets and distractions, rather than attending to the things that really matter (cf. Phil 1:10). In a culture which glorifies the ephemeral, and offers so many avenues of avoidance and escape, this can present a serious pastoral problem. For the ministers of the Church, it can also make itself felt in an enchantment with pastoral programs and theories, to the detriment of direct, fruitful encounter with our faithful, and others too, especially the young who need solid catechesis and sound spiritual guidance. Without a grounding in Christ, the truths by which we live our lives can gradually recede, the practice of the virtues can become formalistic, and dialogue can be reduced to a form of negotiation or an agreement to disagree. An agreement to disagree... so as not to make waves... This sort of superficiality does us great harm.

Then too, there is a third temptation: that of the apparent security to be found in hiding behind easy answers, ready formulas, rules and regulations. Jesus clashed with people who would hide behind laws, regulations and easy answers... He called them hypocrites. Faith by nature is not self-absorbed; it "goes out." It seeks understanding; it gives rise to testimony; it generates mission. In this sense, faith enables us to be both fearless and unassuming in our witness of hope and love. St. Peter tells us that we should be ever ready to respond to all who ask the reason for the hope within us (cf. 1 Pt 3:15). Our identity as Christians is ultimately seen in our quiet efforts to worship God alone, to love one another, to serve one another, and to show by our example not only what we believe, but also what we hope for, and the One in whom we put our trust (cf. 2 Tm 1:12).

Once again, it is our living faith in Christ which is our deepest identity, our being rooted in the Lord. If we have this, everything else is secondary. It is from this deep identity – our being grounded in a living faith in Christ – it is from this profound reality that our dialogue begins, and this is what we are asked to share, sincerely, honestly and without pretence, in the dialogue of everyday life, in the dialogue of charity, and in those more formal opportunities which may present themselves. Because Christ is our life (cf. Phil 1:21), let us speak "from him and of him" readily and without hesitation or fear. The simplicity of his word becomes evident in the simplicity of our lives, in the simplicity of our communication, in the simplicity of our works of loving service to our brothers and sisters.

I would now touch on one further aspect of our Christian identity. It is fruitful. Because it is born of, and constantly nourished by, the grace of our dialogue with the Lord and the promptings of his Spirit, it bears a harvest of justice, goodness and peace. Let me ask you, then, about the fruits which it is bearing in your own lives and in the lives of the communities entrusted to your care. Does the Christian identity of your particular Churches shine forth in your programs of catechesis and youth ministry, in your service to the poor and those languishing on the margins of our prosperous societies, and in your efforts to nourish vocations to the priesthood and the religious life? Does it make itself felt in their fruitfulness? This is a question I raise, for each of you to think about.

Finally, together with a clear sense of our own Christian identity, authentic dialogue also demands a capacity for empathy. For dialogue to take place, there has to be this empathy. We are challenged to listen not only to the words which others speak, but to the unspoken communication of their experiences, their hopes and aspirations, their struggles and their deepest concerns. Such empathy must be the fruit of our spiritual insight and personal experience, which lead us to see others as brothers and sisters, and to "hear," in and beyond their words and actions, what their hearts wish to communicate. In this sense, dialogue demands of us a truly contemplative spirit of openness and receptivity to the other. I cannot engage in dialogue if I am closed to others. Openness? Even more: acceptance! Come to my house, enter my heart. My heart welcomes you. It wants to hear you.

• Closing Holy Mass of the 6th Asian Youth Day (Haemi Castle, Aug. 17, 2014)

The glory of the martyrs shines upon you! These words – a part of the theme of the Sixth Asian Youth Day – console and strengthen us all. Young people of Asia: you are the heirs of a great testimony, a precious witness to Christ. He is the light of the world; he is the light of our lives! The martyrs of Korea – and innumerable others throughout Asia – handed over their bodies to their persecutors; to us they have handed on a perennial witness that the light of Christ's truth dispels all darkness, and the love of Christ is gloriously triumphant. With the certainty of his victory over death, and our participation in it, we can face the challenge of Christian discipleship today, in our own circumstances and time.

The words which we have just reflected upon are a consolation. The other part of this Day's theme – Asian Youth! Wake up! – speaks to you of a duty, a responsibility. Let us consider for a moment each of these words.

First, the word "Asian." You have gathered here in Korea from all parts of Asia. Each of you has a unique place and context where you are called to reflect God's love. The Asian continent, imbued with rich philosophical and religious traditions, remains a great frontier for your testimony to Christ, "the way, and the truth and the life" (Jn 14:6). As young people not only in Asia, but also as sons and daughters of this great continent, you have a right and a duty to take full part in the life of your societies. Do not be afraid to bring the wisdom of faith to every aspect of social life!

As Asians too, you see and love, from within, all that is beautiful, noble and true in your cultures and traditions. Yet as Christians, you also know that the Gospel has the power to purify, elevate and perfect this heritage. Through the presence of the Holy Spirit given you in Baptism and sealed within you at Confirmation, and in union with your pastors, you can appreciate the many positive values of the diverse Asian cultures. You are also able to discern what is incompatible with your Catholic faith, what is contrary to the life of grace bestowed in Baptism, and what aspects of contemporary culture are sinful, corrupt, and lead to death.

Returning to the theme of this Day, let us reflect on a second word: "Youth." You and your friends are filled with the optimism, energy and good will which are so characteristic of this period of life. Let Christ turn your natural optimism into Christian hope, your energy into moral virtue, your good will into genuine self-sacrificing love! This is the path you are called to take. This is the path to overcoming all that threatens hope, virtue and love in your lives and in your culture. In this way your youth will be a gift to Jesus and to the world.

As young Christians, whether you are workers or students, whether you have already begun a career or have answered the call to marriage, religious life or the priesthood, you are not only a part of the future of the Church; you are also a necessary and beloved part of the Church's present! You are Church's present! Keep close to one another, draw ever closer to God, and with your bishops and priests spend these years in building a holier, more missionary and humble Church, a holier, more missionary and humble Church, a Church which loves and worships God by seeking to serve the poor, the lonely, the infirm and the marginalized.

In your Christian lives, you will find many occasions that will tempt you, like the disciples in today's Gospel, to push away the stranger, the needy, the poor and the broken-hearted. It is these people especially who repeat the cry of the woman of the Gospel: "Lord, help me!". The Canaanite woman's plea is the cry of everyone who searches for love, acceptance, and friendship with Christ. It is the cry of so many people in our anonymous cities, the cry of so many of your own contemporaries, and the cry of all those martyrs who even today suffer persecution and death for the name of Jesus: "Lord, help me!" It is often a cry which rises from our own hearts as well: "Lord, help me!" Let us respond, not like those who push away people who make demands on us, as if serving the needy gets in the way of our being close to the Lord. No! We are to be like Christ, who responds to every plea for his help with love, mercy and compassion.

Finally, the third part of this Day's theme – "Wake up!" – This word speaks of a responsibility which the Lord gives you. It is the duty to be vigilant, not to allow the pressures, the temptations and the sins of ourselves or others to dull our sensitivity to the beauty of holiness, to the joy of the Gospel. Today's responsorial psalm invites us constantly to "be glad and sing for joy". No one who sleeps can sing, dance or rejoice. I don't like to see young people who are sleeping. No! Wake up! Go! Go Forward! Dear young people, "God, our God, has blessed us!" (Ps 67:6); from him we have "received mercy" (Rom 11:30). Assured of God's love, go out to the world so that, "by the mercy shown to you", they – your friends, co-workers, neighbors, countrymen, everyone on this great continent – "may now receive the mercy of God" (cf. Rom 11:31). It is by his mercy that we are saved.

Dear young people of Asia, it is my hope that, in union with Christ and the Church, you will take up this path, which will surely bring you much joy. Now, as we approach the table of the Eucharist, let us turn to our Mother Mary, who brought Jesus to the world. Yes, Mother Mary, we long to have Jesus; in your maternal affection help us to bring him to others, to serve him faithfully, and to honor him in every time and place, in this country and throughout Asia. Amen.

NEWS AND DOCUMENTS

Francis and the Invocation for Peace

On the evening of June 8, an unlikely quartet walked through the Vatican Gardens, making international headlines just by being together.

Pope Francis welcomed Presidents Shimon Peres of Israel and Mahmoud Abbas of Palestine to what the Vatican termed an Invocation for Peace, held in the Vatican Gardens. The idea of the gathering was first proposed by the pontiff during his recent visit to the Holy Land and was readily accepted by both sides.

The event consisted of public and private gatherings, with Presidents Peres and Abbas first meeting at the Domus Sanctae Marthae, the Vatican guesthouse, with Pope Francis and Patriarch Bartholomew I of Constantinople.

After brief conversation, they traveled together by van to the Vatican Gardens, where they were awaited by respective delegations, including Card. Pietro Parolin the Vatican Secretary of State, rabbis, imams, ambassadors and officials from the Holy See, Israel and Palestine.

The ceremony began in English, with the statement: "We have gathered here, Israelis and Palestinians, Jews, Christians and Muslims, so that each of us can express his or her desire for peace for the Holy Land and for all who dwell there."

The Invocation was held in three parts, with representatives speaking according to the chronological order of the three faiths: Judaism, Christianity and Islam.

Each part was structured around three moments. The first consisted of an expression of praise to God "for His gift of creation and for His having created us as members of the human family." The second asked pardon from God "for the times that we have failed to act as brothers and sisters and for our sins against Him and against our fellow men and women." The third implored God to grant "the gift of peace to the Holy Land and to enable us to be peacemakers." Each of the moments was framed by a brief musical interlude.

The Christian part was recited in English, Italian and Arabic and was notable for a prayer of penance from Pope St. John Paul II.

Following the three parts of prayer, Pope Francis and the two presidents each made an invocation for peace.

"Our children grow weary, worn out by conflicts … our children who plead with us to tear down the walls of enmity and to set out on the path of dialogue and peace," Pope Francis said.

Peres said, "From Jerusalem I have come to call for Shalom, Salaam, Peace. Peace between nations, peace between Faiths, peace between people, peace for our children."

Abbas declared, "We ask you O lord for peace in the Holy Land, Palestine and Jerusalem, together with its people. We call on you to make Palestine and Jerusalem in particular a secure land for all believers, a place of prayer and worship for the followers of the three monotheistic religions."

The pope and the presidents, along with Patriarch Bartholomew, then exchanged a sign of peace, and Pope Francis and the two presidents planted an olive tree together as a symbol of peace.

In the days leading up to the event, there was considerable confusion in the press both to the particulars of the service and its objectives.

The Vatican Press office, as well as Catholic leaders from the region, sought to clarify that the Invocation for Peace was not supposed to be an occasion for negotiations, nor was it to be a high profile prayer service. Rather, it was a time for key figures in the Middle East to come together to pray for peace at the urging of Pope Francis. When he made the initial invitation, the pontiff said it would be a "heartfelt prayer to God for the gift of peace." It was deliberately low key, held in the verdant Vatican Gardens — and not in St. Peter's Basilica.

In a press conference on June 6, Fr. Pierbattista Pizzaballa, O.F.M., the Custos of the Holy Land, described the encounter as purely religious and intended to provide space to allow people to stand back from the conflict and "recreate a desire for change." There was no expectation of immediate solutions to the complex problems of the Middle East, but Pizzaballa said that it might reopen a path of dialogue and allow people to dream of a world where peace is actually possible.

Vatican officials additionally stressed the crucial point that the Invocation for Peace would bring members of three different religions "together for prayer, but not prayer together," as is prescribed by recently published guidelines from the Pontifical Council for Inter-religious Dialogue, the Holy See office in charge of outreach to other faiths.

The invocation was solemn, quiet and indeed low key. It was a rare occasion to allow the power of prayer to enter into the peace process and demonstrated that in the midst of long and bitter conflict, both sides can find common ground in a plea to God for reconciliation and peace. What comes next remains to be seen.

Pope Francis and the Sex Abuse Crisis

One of the tasks that Pope Francis has inherited from Pope Emeritus Benedict XVI was continuing the progress of the Church in combatting clergy sexual abuse. The last year demonstrated the degree to which the pontiff took his duty seriously. The pontiff established a commission to advise him in dealing with the crisis, and in July, he had a dramatic meeting with sex abuse victims in the Vatican.

Commission for the Protection of Minors

On Dec. 5, he announced that he would establish a first-ever papal commission for child protection.

The new commission will advise the pontiff on

the Church's efforts to protect children and offer pastoral care for victims of abuse.

Card. Seán Patrick O'Malley, archbishop of Boston and a member of the eight-member Council of Cardinals, and Jesuit Fr. Federico Lombardi, the director of the Holy See Press Office, formally announced the creation of the commission at a Vatican news conference.

Fr. Lombardi said the idea originated during a Dec. 4 meeting between the pope and his Council of Cardinals, which serves as counsel to the pope and which was in Rome Dec. 3-5 for meetings. Francis not only liked the idea but announced the formation of the new commission the next morning.

In addressing the surprised members of the media, Card. O'Malley stressed two important aspects of the commission. First, it represents continuity with Pope Benedict's labors to end clergy sexual abuse and bring genuine reform in that area. Second, the commission will have clearly delineated objectives, including formulating new suggestions for initiatives across the entire Church.

Card. O'Malley, whose work in Boston has earned him great credibility in confronting the sexual abuse crisis, noted that the commission will work to further steps in the Church's labors against clergy sexual abuse that gained momentum under Pope Benedict. Even before becoming pope, then-Card. Joseph Ratzinger in 2001 lobbied to have Pope John Paul II assign responsibility to the Congregation for the Doctrine of the Faith (CDF) to oversee all of the cases worldwide and was crucial in the promulgation that same year of the apostolic letter titled Sacramentorum Sanctitatis Tutela ("The Safeguarding of the Sacraments") that confirmed the CDF's responsibility for disciplinary review and action regarding violations associated with abuse and that reserved to the CDF the responsibility for reviewing sexual violations "committed by a cleric with a minor below the age of 18 years."

The new commission was welcomed by bishops. Abp. Joseph E. Kurtz of Louisville, Ky., president of the U.S. Conference of Catholic Bishops, released a statement praising the commission.

"The announcement of this initiative reflects a broad-based approach that considers changes in Vatican procedures in dealing with clerics accused of abuse, seminary training for future priests, and other pastoral efforts to address this horrific problem," Abp. Kurtz wrote. "This international effort is particularly welcome as we have come to learn that this tragedy affects many, if not all, parts of the world."

He also supported the 2002 Dallas Charter by the U.S. bishops and the imposition of the Essential Norms, by which dioceses created safe environments for children, launched a "zero tolerance" policy regarding abuse and worked to improve the formation of priests and the seminary system. The results have been dramatic as the audits by the National Review Board have found that in recent years the numbers of annually reported cases of sexual abuse of minors in the entire Church in the United States have declined to single digits.

Unquestionably, enormous advances have been made in child protection, screening and the way that the Church handles cases both in terms of civil and ecclesiastical law. The task now for the Church is to maintain that vigilance but also to push ahead with providing ongoing pastoral care to the victims and enforcing Pope Benedict's 2011 directive that all of the bishops' conferences around the world establish formal guidelines for dealing with clerical sex abuse.

The commission is a significant next step to formalize what is now a worldwide effort at prevention and pastoral care, but it is intended to collaborate rather than dictate. The CDF has a long-established track record over cases in the Church, while the directive is still very much a work in progress. For example, at the start of 2013 nearly one-quarter of the globe's dioceses were not in compliance.

The commission will help provide clarity, encouragement and practical assistance to the world's bishops, but Card. O'Malley stressed that its primary purpose is pastoral. It will study the effectiveness of present programs for the protection of children and assistance to victims, and it will then consider suggestions for new initiatives "on the part of the Curia, in collaboration with bishops, episcopal conferences, religious superiors and conferences of religious superiors."

This does not mean that the new commission will interfere with or assume any of the current authority of the Congregation for the Doctrine of the Faith over cases, nor will it supersede the responsibility of local bishops for overseeing the protection of children in their respective dioceses. As Card. O'Malley observed, that "competence lies with bishops," and the Holy See desires only "to be helpful and help to identify best practices."

He was asked whether the commission would deal with the issue of accountability on the part of bishops in reporting cases of abuse to civil authorities and replied that the question has yet to be addressed.

The commission's planned composition will also reflect its pastoral orientation. It will likely be very international and have 12 members described by Card. O'Malley as "persons suited to the systematic implementation of these new initiatives, including laypersons, religious and priests with responsibilities for the safety of children, in relations with the victims, in mental health, in the application of the law, etc."

But what does this new commission tell us about Pope Francis and how will it impact the lives of average Catholics? Francis has not spoken frequently about the issue, but the commission represents his desire to look at new ways of insuring a safe environment for children and providing genuine healing to victims. It reveals further the willingness of the pope to accept practical advice from his Council of Cardinals — made up of several members who have dealt with the crisis in their own archdioceses.

The commission's efforts may also be seen on the parish level with improved training for those in pastoral ministry to recognize signs of abuse and in the way that dioceses everywhere cooperate better with civil authorities and embrace new innovations in screening and psychological tests for prospective seminarians.

On March 22, Pope Francis named the first members of an unprecedented papal commission for child protection.

The eight members are from all over the globe, but four are women and one, Irish lay woman Marie Collins, was also a victim of clergy sexual abuse as a girl in the 1960s. Another notable appointment is Card. Seán Patrick O'Malley, archbishop of Boston.

In all, there are three members of the clergy and five laypeople, including the four women. All have impressive reputations in areas such as child psychology, childhood development, law and the care of victims of sexual abuse. Though the members are from eight different countries, seven hail from Europe or the United States, where the crisis has been especially severe. Ireland, in particular, is still coming to grips with the dimensions of the abuse. Pope Francis did not appoint a head of the commission, instead apparently wants to provide the members with their own room for decisions.

In a Vatican press conference announcing the new commission, Vatican spokesman Jesuit Fr. Federico Lombardi, S.J., explained that it is expected to work quickly to set up its final structure, clarify the full scope of its responsibilities and canvass for names of additional candidates, especially from other continents and countries.

Card. O'Malley stressed in December that the commission's primary purpose is pastoral, and it will neither interfere with any of the current authority of the Congregation for the Doctrine of the Faith that has jurisdiction over the cases of abuse around the world, nor impinge on the obligation of bishops to oversee the protection of children in their respective dioceses. Lombardi added, "the Commission will take a multi-pronged approach to promoting youth protection, including: education regarding the exploitation of children; discipline of offenders; civil and canonical duties and responsibilities; and the development of best practices as they have emerged in society at large."

In defending the authentic record of the Church, Lombardi quoted both of Francis' predecessors, Pope Blessed John Paul II and Pope Emeritus Benedict XVI, citing Benedict's address to the Irish bishops in 2006 at which the pontiff recommitted the Church to safeguard minors and "to establish the truth of what happened in the past, to take whatever steps are necessary to prevent it from occurring again, to ensure that the principles of justice are fully respected and, above all, to bring healing to the victims and to all those affected by these egregious crimes."

In a recent interview with the Italian daily newspaper *Corriere della Sera*, Francis readily acknowledged the wounds caused by the scandal even as he noted that the abuse of children is widespread all over the world. And, Francis said, the "Church is perhaps the only public institution to have acted with transparency and responsibility. No other has done more. And the Church is the only one to be attacked."

While criticized by some pundits for sounding defensive in the interview, Francis is deeply committed to carrying forward the reforms. Lombardi told reporters, "Pope Francis has made clear that the Church must hold the protection of minors amongst her highest priorities."

Council members The earnestness of the pope is made manifest with his choices for the commission, starting especially with the Dublin-born lay woman Marie Collins, who was herself a victim of sexual abuse and is today an international leader in the effort to protect children and bring justice for survivors. She assisted the Archdiocese of Dublin in setting up its Child Protection Service in 2003, was a founding trustee of an advocacy and counselling support group for abuse survivors and gave her name to the Marie Collins Foundation, a UK charity for helping children who suffer sexual abuse and exploitation via Internet and mobile technologies.

Collins brings the vital perspectives to the commission of a survivor of abuse by the clergy, of the failure of Church authorities to hear properly the voices of victims and the needs of those recovering from the ordeal.

Card. O'Malley — already part of the eight-member Council of Cardinals that advises the pope — has a long track record in dealing with the scandal, especially in Boston, and has a strong pastoral touch.

Catherine Bonnet, a French child psychologist, has been a powerful and even prophetic voice in France and across Europe about the effect of sexual abuse and the sexual exploitation of children.

Fr. Humberto Miguel Yáñez, an Argentinian Jesuit, is head of the moral theology department at the Pontifical Gregorian University in Rome. He has known Francis for many years and even had him as a professor during studies at a Jesuit Argentine college.

Baroness Sheila Hollins, a former president of the Royal College of Psychiatrists and currently the president of the British Medical Association, was recently named to the House of Lords and is ranked among Britain's foremost specialists in child development and disability issues for children.

Claudio Papale, an Italian lay jurist, is a noted expert in canon (or Church) law and moral offenses and teaches at Rome's Pontifical Urbaniana University.

Hanna Suchocka, prime minister of Poland from 1992-1993 under the presidency of Lech Walesa, is currently Poland's ambassador to the Holy See and a member of the Pontifical Academy of Social Sciences in the Vatican. She also served as minister of justice and attorney general of Poland and is widely respected in the areas of human rights and international law.

Another Jesuit, German Father Hans Zollner, is academic vice rector of the Gregorian University and head of its Institute of Psychology. He was one of the key figures in organizing a landmark international symposium in early 2012 in Rome focusing on clergy sexual abuse under the title, "Toward Healing and Renewal" and at which Marie Collins was a speaker.

Francis has kept a significant promise to maintain momentum in combatting clergy sexual abuse by filling the first seats of the new commission with serious and credible members. He is also demonstrating a collaborative style and openness to voices from outside the halls of the Vatican, especially those of women. In this new commission, we may be seeing a glimpse of what Francis intends in the full reform of the Roman Curia that is coming later this year.

Francis Meets With Victms The intense meeting between Pope Francis and victims of clergy sexual abuse in early July at the Vatican marked a new chapter in the Church's response to the tragic scandal that has been part of Catholic life for more than a decade.

Pope St. John Paul II worked in his last years to help the Church craft an adequate response to clergy sex abuse, even as he was criticized by some for the long delay in galvanizing the Church's resources. He was aided in the reform process by then-Card. Joseph Ratzinger who, after becoming Pope Benedict XVI in 2005, moved swiftly to investigate and then punish Fr. Marcial Maciel Degollado, founder of the Legionaries of Christ, on charges of horrendous sexual abuse and misconduct and to implement international norms for dealing with cases.

Francis thus came to the papacy in March 2013 with a proven system in place for handling abuse, certainly in the United States. The result of the reforms in the United States has been striking as the annual audits of dioceses over the last years have shown a decline in new cases of abuse to the low single digits, a sea change from the early 2000s.

The question now to be asked is where the Church's response goes from here, especially under Francis?

The pope certainly is continuing the efforts of the recent popes to deal with the crisis, but he has also put his own stamp on the Church's pastoral approach to victims.

The pontiff is committed to following the laws of the Church in removing abusers as part of what he has repeatedly described as a "zero-tolerance" policy. In his homily at Mass with the victims of abuse at the Casa Santa Marta on July 7, the pope said, "There is no place in the Church's ministry for those who commit these abuses, and I commit myself not to tolerate harm done to a minor by any individual, whether a cleric or not. All bishops must carry out their pastoral ministry with the utmost care in order to help foster the protection of minors, and they will be held accountable."

Francis referenced this willingness to act against bishops during his in-flight press conference returning from the Holy Land at the end of May.

And he moved sharply and transparently in removing the apostolic nuncio to the Dominican Republic, Abp. Jozef Wesolowski, when he was charged with sex abuse. Wesolowski was recalled by the Vatican, tried by the Congregation for the Doctrine of the Faith and laicized in June. He may also be extradited to the Dominican Republic or Poland. This was an unprecedented trial, and it is likely that similar steps will follow with other bishops in the future.

Institutionally, Francis assured the victims that the Church would "continue to exercise vigilance in priestly formation," and that he is dedicated to developing better policies and procedures for the protection of minors and for the training of Church personnel.

"We need to do everything in our power," he said, "to ensure that these sins have no place in the Church."

Just as significant, Francis is determined to expand the Church's pastoral care of victims. Last December, he established the Commission for the Protection of Minors and filled it in March with genuinely serious leaders in dealing with the crisis, including Card. Séan O'Malley of Boston and the Irish woman Marie Collins, who was abused as a girl. The commission will advise the pope on ways to improve the Church's approach to the problem, with a particular eye on bettering pastoral care and concern.

One of the keys for Francis in this pastoral solicitude is to meet with victims, something certain to become a regular feature of Francis' more expansive outreach. Pope Benedict XVI met six times during his pontificate with those who had been abused, including a session during his 2008 visit to the United States.

Francis, however, gave several days to the victims. He celebrated Mass for them, shared several meals with them and then spent almost 3 1/2 hours meeting with them one-on-one. Dismissed by the usual critics as a "publicity stunt," the sessions were described by Jesuit Fr. Federico Lombardi, the Vatican spokesman, as "a very profound, spiritual and kind dialogue with a pastor." Look for Francis to hold additional encounters, including one during his anticipated visit to the United States next year. For average Catholics, the pontificate of Pope Francis is a renewed opportunity to tell the truth of what is being done to prevent abuse and especially to care for the victims. And the pope is showing the way in the need to redouble our commitment to resist what he calls "execrable acts of abuse which have left lifelong scars" and to promote healing for the abused. There are still many victims in need of our prayers and attention.

NEW CARDINALS

During his Sunday Angelus Jan. 12, Pope Francis named 19 new cardinals-designate and announced that a consistory would be held on Feb. 22 for their formal induction into the College of Cardinals. This will be the first such consistory for the pope since his election last year and gives a clear indication of Pope Francis' priorities for the college.

While the pope took no revolutionary steps, he did increase the total number of cardinals to 218, and the number of cardinal electors (those under the age of 80 and eligible to vote in a conclave) to 122, thus setting aside briefly the limit of 120 electors established by Pope Paul VI. Two current cardinal electors, however, will turn 80 in March, meaning the number of electors will return soon to the limit. Pope John Paul II also exceeded the limit several times. There are also three new cardinals over the age of 80 whose appointment is in recognition of their service to the Church. One of them, Abp. Loris Capovilla, 98, was secretary to Blessed John XXIII.

Geographic expansion In one notable innovation, Pope Francis named new members from places that have never had a cardinal. Bp. Chibly Langlois of Les Cayes is the first cardinal from Haiti, while Abp. Orlando Quevedo is the first cardinal from the Archdiocese of Cotabato in the Philippines. In Italy, Pope Francis passed over the long-standing cardinal-headed sees of Venice and Turin to give the red hat to Abp. Gualtiero Bassetti of Perugia-Città della Pieve.

The list is immediately striking in several other regards. First, Pope Francis is clearly seeking to internationalize the college further, in much the same way as previous popes, especially Popes Pius XII, Paul VI and Blessed John Paul II. In all, there are eight cardinals from Europe, five from Latin America, two from Africa, two from Asia, one from North America and one from the Caribbean. There are no new cardinals from the United States. Pope Francis is looking at Latin America as a priority. Five of the new cardinals-designate are from Latin America or the Caribbean, increasing by a third the number of Latin American cardinals and acknowledging that some 40 percent of the world's Catholics are located there.

But Pope Francis is also concerned with having a college that represents the universal Church and that can speak powerfully and prophetically to the entire world. For that reason, two choices were quite significant — the African Abp. Philippe Ouédraogo of Ouagadougou, Burkina Faso, and the Haitan Bp. Langlois. These two new cardinals come from some of the poorest countries in the world and will give additional voice within the college to the painful and pressing concerns of the vast numbers who live in poverty.

Pope Francis did not significantly reduce the numbers and influence of European and North American cardinals and Italians in particular, as there will be six new European cardinal electors, including one from Great Britain, Vincent Nichols the archbishop of Westminster; four from Italy; and one from Canada, the archbishop of Québec, Gérard Lacroix. Three of the Italians are in posts in the Roman Curia, which traditionally bring automatic appointment to the college, such as the Italian Abp. Pietro Parolin, the recently named Secretary of State, and another European, the German Gerhard Ludwig Müller, currently the prefect of the Congregation for the Doctrine of the Faith. Curial cardinals continue to represent 34 percent of the cardinal electors, and Italians are still 24 percent. Nevertheless, Francis' curial choices are officials he trusts the most to push ahead with his reforms. He has relied heavily in his first year on the institution of the Secretariat of State to begin his reform of the Vatican establishment.By appointing Abp. Parolin and several other officials who come out of the Secretariat, the pope is cementing their prominence in his pontificate.

Pope Francis is looking for a global Church to be reflected in the college, but he is also relying on experienced Vatican hands for reform of the papal government. He seeks a college that mirrors his own key concerns, and given the fact that there will be dozens of cardinals turning 80 during the next few years, he is poised to transform the membership and shape directly the election of his successor.

The New Cardinals

Archbishop Pietro Parolin, 59, Vatican Secretary of State, Italy.

Archbishop Lorenzo Baldisseri, 73, general secretary of the Synod of Bishops, Italy.

Archbishop Gerhard Müller, 66, prefect of the Congregation for the Doctrine of the Faith, Germany.

Archbishop Beniamino Stella, 72, prefect of the Congregation for Clergy, Italy.

Archbishop Vincent Nichols, 68, archbishop of Westminster, Great Britain.

Archbishop Leopoldo Brenes Solórzano, 64, archbishop of Managua, Nicaragua.

Archbishop Gèrald Lacroix, I.S.P.X., 56, archbishop of Québec, Canada.

Archbishop Jean-Pierre Kutwa, 68, archbishop of Abidjan, Ivory Coast.

Archbishop Orani João Tempesta, O.Cist., 63, archbishop of São Sebastião do Rio de Janeiro, Brazil.

Archbishop Gualtiero Bassetti, 71, archbishop of Perugia-Città della Pieve, Italy.

Archbishop Mario Poli, 66, archbishop of Buenos Aires, Argentina.

Archbishop Andrew Yeom Soo-jung, 70, archbishop of Seoul, South Korea.

Archbishop Ricardo Ezzati Andrello, S.D.B., 72, archbishop of Santiago, Chile.

Archbishop Philippe Ouédraogo, 68, archbishop of Ouagadougou, Burkina Faso.

Archbishop Orlando Quevedo, O.M.I., 74, archbishop of Cotabato, Philippines.

Bishop Chibly Langlois, 55, bishop of Les Cayes, Haiti.

Cardinals over the age of 80

Archbishop Loris Capovilla, 98, former secretary to Pope Blessed John XXIII and prelate of Loreto, Italy.

Archbishop Fernando Sebastián Aguilar, C.M.F., 84, archbishop emeritus of Pamplona, Spain.

Archbishop Kelvin Felix, 81, archbishop emeritus of Castries, Saint Lucia, Antilles

Titular Churches for the New Cardinals

The following is a list of the titular or diaconate churches assigned by Pope Francis to the new cardinals created during the ordinary public consistory:

Cardinal Pietro Parolin, title of Santi Simone e Giuda Taddeo a Torre Angela

Cardinal Lorenzo Baldisseri, diaconate of Sant'Anselmo all'Aventino

Cardinal Gerhard Ludwig Muller, diaconate of Sant'Agnese in Agone

Cardinal Beniamino Stella, diaconate of Santi Cosma e Damiano

Cardinal Vincent Gerard Nichols, title of Santissimo Redentore e Sant'Alfonso in via Merulana

Cardinal Leopoldo Jose Brenes Solorzano, title of San Gioacchino ai Prati di Castello

Cardinal Gerald Cyprien Lacroix, I.S.P.X., title of San Giuseppe all'Aurelio

Cardinal Jean-Pierre Kutwa, title of Sant'Emerenziana a Tor Fiorenza

Cardinal Orani Joao Tempesta, O.Cist., title of Santa Maria Madre della Provvidenza a Monte Verde

Cardinal Gualtiero Bassetti, title of Santa Cecilia

Cardinal Mario Aurelio Poli, title of San Roberto Bellarmino

Cardinal Andrew Yeom Soo-Jung, title of San Crisogono

Cardinal Ricardo Ezzati Andrello, S.D.B., title of Santissimo Redentore a Valmelania

Cardinal Philippe Nakellentuba Ouedraogo, title of Santa Maria Consolatrice al Tiburtino

Cardinal Orlando B. Quevedo, O.M.I., title of Santa Maria "Regina Mundi" a Torre Spaccata

Cardinal Chibly Langlois, title of San Giacomo in Augusta

Cardinal Loris Francesco Capovilla, title of Santa Maria in Trastevere

Cardinal Fernando Sebastian Aguilar, C.M.F., title of Sant'Angela Merici

Cardinal Kelvin Edward Felix, title of Santa Maria della Salute a Primavalle.

CANONIZATIONS OF POPES JOHN PAUL II AND JOHN XXIII

On Apr. 27, Divine Mercy Sunday, Pope Francis canonized Pope St. John XXIII (1958-63) and Pope St. John Paul II (1978-2005). It was estimated that several million people had arrived in Rome to mark the event. Pope emeritus Benedict XVI, who beatified John Paul II and was a witness in the process of canonization for his predecessor, also attended. It was the first time two popes were canonized on the same day.

The Holy See had announced July 5 that Pope Francis had approved the canonization of two of the most beloved popes of the last century, Blessed John XXIII and Blessed John Paul II.

While the announcement that a second miracle had been approved for Pope John Paul was anticipated, the news that Pope Francis had cleared the way for Pope John to be declared a saint without a second miracle was entirely unexpected.

The decision to proceed without the traditional second miracle certainly falls within Pope Francis' authority as supreme pontiff. Nor would a double canonization be entirely unheard of. In 2000, Pope John Paul beatified both Popes Blessed Pius IX and John XXIII in the same ceremony.

Best known for his summoning of the Second Vatican Council (1962-65), Pope John — born Angelo Giuseppe Roncalli — was also revered for his good nature, wit, common sense and, above all, his holiness. His autobiography, *Journal of a Soul*, is considered a spiritual classic.

His cause for canonization was opened in 1967 with the blessing of his successor, Pope Paul VI.

Speaking about Pope Francis' decision to proceed with a canonization without the second typically required miracle, Vatican Press spokesman Jesuit Fr. Federico Lombardi pointed out that it was the pope's will that the sanctity of the great pontiff who summoned Vatican II be recognized. Fr. Lombardi added that a canonization without a second miracle is still valid, given that a miracle verified by the Congregation for Saints' Causes led to his beatification in 2000. He also pointed to ongoing discussions among theologians and experts about whether it is necessary to have two distinct miracles for beatification and canonization, and then there is the pope's right to dispense with a second miracle.

In the case of Pope John Paul, calls for his canonization began literally at the time of his death in 2005. At his funeral, there were chants of "santo subito" (Italian for "saint immediately"), and within days of his own election as Pope John Paul's successor, Pope Benedict XVI waived the customary five-year waiting period to begin a cause.

Pope John Paul was beatified on May 1, 2011, after the Congregation for Saints' Causes approved the miraculous cure of a French nun suffering from Parkinson's disease. The reported second miracle was of Floribeth Mora Diaz, a Costa Rican woman who inexplicably recovered from a cerebral aneurism on the day of John Paul's beatification and after praying for his intercession. His formal canonization will be the fastest in modern history.

Some in the media have speculated that the two canonizations are intended to provide theological "balance" between the supposedly liberal Pope John and the conservative Pope John Paul. Far more significant is the continuing backdrop of the 50th anniversary of Vatican II. Both popes were figures in the council's labors — Pope John convoked it and then-Bishop Karol Wojtyla of Krakow, Poland, the future John Paul II, took part as a member of a new generation of bishops who supported the pope's aspirations for reform and renewal, aggiornamento, in the Church.

Lionized by many in the media and some Church circles for what they see as opening the door to the purported "liberalization" of the Church, Pope John in truth had a clear vision for the council, one in which the unchanging and badly needed teachings of the Faith could be presented in ways that the modern world could best understand.

That vision was very much a component in the papal program of Pope John Paul, who devoted considerable effort in his pontificate to the authentic implementation of the council's decrees. This included the important 1985 Synod of Bishops that looked at the proper interpretation of the council. In this regard, the two new pontiff

saints represent a vital source of continuity with the contemporary papal magisterium, including the New Evangelization and the teachings of Popes Benedict XVI and Francis, including Pope Francis' newly released encyclical, *Lumen Fidei* ("The Light of Faith").

The following is the text of Pope Francis' homily for the canonization Mass:

"At the heart of this Sunday, which concludes the Octave of Easter and which St. John Paul II wished to dedicate to Divine Mercy, are the glorious wounds of the risen Jesus.

He had already shown those wounds when he first appeared to the Apostles on the very evening of that day following the Sabbath, the day of the resurrection. But, as we have heard, Thomas was not there that evening, and when the others told him that they had seen the Lord, he replied that unless he himself saw and touched those wounds, he would not believe. A week later, Jesus appeared once more to the disciples gathered in the Upper Room. Thomas was also present; Jesus turned to him and told him to touch his wounds. Whereupon that man, so straightforward and accustomed to testing everything personally, knelt before Jesus with the words: "My Lord and my God!" (Jn 20:28).

The wounds of Jesus are a scandal, a stumbling block for faith, yet they are also the test of faith. That is why on the body of the risen Christ the wounds never pass away: they remain, for those wounds are the enduring sign of God's love for us. They are essential for believing in God. Not for believing that God exists, but for believing that God is love, mercy and faithfulness. Saint Peter, quoting Isaiah, writes to Christians: "by his wounds you have been healed" (1 Pt 2:24, cf. Is 53:5).

Saint John XXIII and Saint John Paul II were not afraid to look upon the wounds of Jesus, to touch his torn hands and his pierced side. They were not ashamed of the flesh of Christ, they were not scandalized by him, by his cross; they did not despise the flesh of their brother (cf. Is 58:7), because they saw Jesus in every person who suffers and struggles. These were two men of courage, filled with the parrhesia of the Holy Spirit, and they bore witness before the Church and the world to God's goodness and mercy.

They were priests, and bishops and popes of the twentieth century. They lived through the tragic events of that century, but they were not overwhelmed by them. For them, God was more powerful; faith was more powerful – faith in Jesus Christ the Redeemer of man and the Lord of history; the mercy of God, shown by those five wounds, was more powerful; and more powerful too was the closeness of Mary our Mother.

In these two men, who looked upon the wounds of Christ and bore witness to his mercy, there dwelt a living hope and an indescribable and glorious joy (1 Pt 1:3,8). The hope and the joy which the risen Christ bestows on his disciples, the hope and the joy which nothing and no one can take from them. The hope and joy of Easter, forged in the crucible of self-denial, self-emptying, utter identification with sinners, even to the point of disgust at the bitterness of that chalice. Such were the hope and the joy which these two holy popes had received as a gift from the risen Lord and which they in turn bestowed in abundance upon the People of God, meriting our eternal gratitude.

This hope and this joy were palpable in the earliest community of believers, in Jerusalem, as we have heard in the Acts of the Apostles (cf. 2:42-47). It was a community which lived the heart of the Gospel, love and mercy, in simplicity and fraternity.

This is also the image of the Church which the Second Vatican Council set before us. John XXIII and John Paul II cooperated with the Holy Spirit in renewing and updating the Church in keeping with her pristine features, those features which the saints have given her throughout the centuries. Let us not forget that it is the saints who give direction and growth to the Church. In convening the Council, St. John XXIII showed an exquisite openness to the Holy Spirit. He let himself be led and he was for the Church a pastor, a servant-leader, guided by the Holy Spirit. This was his great service to the Church; for this reason I like to think of him as the the pope of openness to the Holy Spirit.

In his own service to the People of God, St. John Paul II was the pope of the family. He himself once said that he wanted to be remembered as the pope of the family. I am particularly happy to point this out as we are in the process of journeying with families towards the Synod on the family. It is surely a journey which, from his place in heaven, he guides and sustains.

May these two new saints and shepherds of God's people intercede for the Church, so that during this two-year journey toward the Synod she may be open to the Holy Spirit in pastoral service to the family. May both of them teach us not to be scandalized by the wounds of Christ and to enter ever more deeply into the mystery of divine mercy, which always hopes and always forgives, because it always loves."

HOLY SEE FINANCES

One of the largest tasks undertaken by Pope Francis in his first year and a half as pope has been the reform of Vatican Finances. 2014 saw massive reforms launched in this area, in particular the creation of the Secretariat of the Economy, with Card. George Pell of Sydney appointed as its new prefect.

On Feb. 24, Pope Francis issued a papal document, called a *motu proprio, Fidelis Dispensator et Prudens*, establishing a new coordinating agency for the economic and administrative affairs of the Holy See and the Vatican City State. The document followed the motu proprio approving the new statutes of the Financial Intelligence Authority in Nov. 2013, but the new reforms were even more sweeping, creating a new Secretariat for the Economy with authority over all economic and administrative activities within the Holy See and the Vatican City State. To head the new office, he appointed the Australian Card. George Pell, a member of the Council of Cardinals.

The reforms were sparked by the flurry of scandals that regrettably marked a good part of the pontificate of Pope Benedict XVI, and that pontiff set in motions a process of reform that Francis has carried forward with great determination.

As for the Secretariat, the motu proprio stipulated that Card. Pell, would work with the Pontifical Commission for Reference on the Organization of the Economic-Administrative Structure of the Holy See (COSEA) to complete and then implement the reforms. The new structure was the fruit of recommendations made by Council of Cardinal advisors and the Committee of 15 Cardinals that oversee the financial affairs of the Holy See to accept the proposed reforms suggested by the Pontifical Commission for Reference on the Organization of the Economic-Administrative Structure of the Holy See (COSEA), that was initially created by Pope Francis in July 2013. COSEA recommended changes to simplify and consolidate existing management structures and improve coordination and oversight across the Holy See and Vatican City State and adopting more formal accounting standards and generally accepted financial management and reporting practices.

The Holy See Press Office issued a communiqué on Feb. 24, 2014, on the creation of the new secretariat. It read:

The Holy Father today announced a new coordination structure for economic and administrative affairs of the Holy See and the Vatican State.

Today's announcement comes after the recommendations of the rigorous review conducted by the Pontifical Commission for Reference on the Organization of the Economic- Administrative Structure of the Holy See (COSEA) were considered and endorsed by both the Council of 8 Cardinals established to advise the Holy Father on governance and the Committee of 15 Cardinals which oversees the financial affairs of the Holy See.

COSEA recommended changes to simplify and consolidate existing management structures and improve coordination and oversight across the Holy See and Vatican City State. COSEA also recommended more formal commitment to adopting accounting standards and generally accepted financial management and reporting practices as well as enhanced internal controls, transparency and governance.

The changes will enable more formal involvement of senior and experienced experts in financial administration, planning and reporting and will ensure better use of resources, improving the support available for various programs, particularly our works with the poor and marginalized.

The changes announced by the Holy Father include:

1. Establishment of a new Secretariat for the Economy which will have authority over all economic and administrative activities within the Holy See and the Vatican City State. The Secretariat will be responsible, among other things, for preparing an annual budget for the Holy See and Vatican City State as well as financial planning and various support functions such as human resources and procurement. The Secretariat will also be required to prepare detailed financial statements of the Holy See and Vatican State.

2. The Secretariat for the Economy will implement policies determined by a new Council for the Economy – a 15 member Council comprised of 8 Cardinals or Bishops, reflecting various parts of the world and seven lay experts of different nationalities with strong professional financial experience. The Council will meet on a regular basis and to consider policies and practices and to prepare and analyze reports on the economic-administrative activities of the Holy See.

3. The Secretariat for the Economy will be headed by a Cardinal Prefect reporting to the Council for the Economy. He will be supported by a Secretary-General in the management of day to day activities.

4. The Holy Father has appointed Card. Pell, the current Archbishop of Sydney, Australia, to the role of Prefect of the Secretariat for the Economy. Details for Card. Pell are attached.

5. New arrangements also include the appointment of an Auditor-General, appointed by the Holy Father who

will be empowered to conduct audits of any agency of the Holy See and Vatican City State at any time.

6. The changes will confirm the role of APSA as the Central bank of the Vatican with all the obligations and responsibilities of similar institutions around the world.

7. The AIF will continue to undertake its current and critical role of prudential supervision and regulation of activities within the Holy See and Vatican City State.

The Prefect of the new Secretariat for the Economy has been asked to start work as soon as possible. He will prepare the final statutes and other related matters with the assistance of any necessary advisors and will work with COSEA to complete the implementation of these changes approved by the Holy Father.

Meanwhile, the Holy See pushed ahead with other financial reforms, including a major change to the Vatican's Financial Intelligence Authority (AIF), the body that monitors the Vatican's financial operations. The all-Italian panel was replaced by a new group of international experts, including Juan C. Zarate, a U.S. senior adviser at the Center for Strategic and International Studies and visiting lecturer at Harvard Law School; Maria Bianca Farina, a senior Italian administrator at the Italian postal system's investment and insurance divisions; Marc Odendall, a Swiss-based philanthropist and former financier who has served as chairman of the International Ethics Board of EDHEC Business School; Joseph Yubaraj Pillay, chairman of the Council of Presidential Advisers of the Republic of Singapore and of Tiger Airways Holdings. Pope Benedict XVI had established the Financial Intelligence Authority in late 2010 to oversee Vatican financial operations. The authority is headed by Swiss lawyer Rene Bruelhart.

On June 9, the AIF announced that it had issued a memoranda of understanding with the United Kingdom, France and several other countries. The statement read:

A Memorandum of Understanding (MOU) is standard practice and formalizes the cooperation and exchange of financial information to fight money laundering and combat terrorist financing across borders between the competent authorities of both countries. It is based on the model Memorandum of Understanding prepared by the Egmont Group, the global organization of national Financial Intelligence Units, and contains clauses on reciprocity, permitted uses of information and confidentiality.

"Becoming a member of the Egmont Group last year was a major step toward strengthening the international cooperation of the Holy See and supporting the global efforts to fight Money Laundering and the Financing of Terrorism," said Bruelhart. "The signing of these latest MOUs shows that we are continuously expanding our network of cooperation, and will further facilitate our joint efforts."

AIF became a member of the Egmont Group in July of 2013, and has already signed MOUs with the Financial Intelligence Units of Australia, Belgium, Cyprus, Germany, Italy, the Netherlands, Slovenia, Spain and the United States. AIF is the competent authority of the Holy See/Vatican City State to fight money laundering and the financing of terrorism. It was established in 2010.

On July 8, the Holy See Press Office held a press conference releasing the Vatican's 2013 financial statements. The two financial statements, revealed a surplus of some10 million euros; the consolidated financial statement for the Holy See for the year 2013 closed with a deficit of 24,470,549 euros, due principally to negative fluctua-

tions deriving from the valuation of gold, to the value of around 14 million euros. The administration of the Governorate of Vatican City ended 2013 with a profit of 33,040,583, an increase of around 10 million compared to 2012. The following communiqué was issued:

Financial Statements for 2013: Consolidated Financial Statement of the Holy See and the Governorate of Vatican City State

During the meeting of the Council of the Economy on Saturday 5 July, the Prefecture for Economic Affairs of the Holy See, as is customary at this time of year, presented a report of the two main budgets for 2013: the consolidated financial statement of the Holy See and the financial statement of the Governorate of Vatican City State.

The data included in these statements may be summarised as follows:

The consolidated financial statement for the Holy See for the year 2013 closes with a deficit of 24,470,549, due principally to negative fluctuations deriving from the valuation of gold, to the value of around 14 million. Although evaluative elements and therefore not actualised, according to the accounting principles based on the criterion of prudence contained in the "Regulations for the Preparation of the Financial Statements of the Holy See," they were recorded among the negative components in the overview of financial management.

The most significant categories of expenditure at those regarding personnel costs (2,886 persons on Dec. 31, 2013), a net sum of around 125 million, and the payment of taxes which affect the real estate sector, approximately 15 million.

Contributions made pursuant to canon 1271 of the Code of Canon Law – i.e., the economic support offered by ecclesiastical circumscriptions throughout the world to maintain the service the Roman Curia offers to the universal Church – passed from 22,347,426 in 2012 to 22,435,359, thus remaining substantially stable.

The Institute for Works of Religion (IOR), as it does each year, offered the Holy Father a significant sum in support of his apostolic and charitable ministry. For 2013 this was a sum of 50,000,000.

Considering the overall combined results of the two Financial Statements, as is usual, 2013 closes with a profit of around 10 million.

The Council for the Economy, after hearing the Report, made the following declaration:

· "The Council has been informed by the Prefecture for Economic Affairs of the budgets relating to 2013, and has taken note of the declaration by the External Auditor, according to whom 'in all the most important aspects, the financial position of Vatican City State as of Dec. 31, 2013 and the results of transactions relating to the year 2013 comply with the current accounting principles of the regulations of Vatican City State.' On this basis, the Council has approved the 2013 Budget and invites the Secretariat for the Economy to work towards further alignment of Vatican accounting principles with international standards."

Note on the IOR contribution: Since the Annual Report of the IOR published this morning makes reference to a contribution of 54 million, it is to be noted that, like last year, 50 million were destined for the Holy See budget, and the other 4 million for other works (in 2012 these included, for example, donations to the Fund for the support of cloistered monasteries, the Amazon Fund, the Fund to support the Churches of the former Soviet Union).

On the same day as the consolidated financial statement, the official report was issued on the financial state of the Institute for Works of Religion, the so-called Vatican Bank, with the impact of recent reforms apparent in the report. The Bank had completed its first its first phase of reform, and Ernst von Freyberg, IOR president, noted that the institute focused on making itself "compliant with financial regulation, safer and more transparent, so as to create options for the Holy Father to decide on the future of the Institute. Through this work we have laid the ground for a new team to make the IOR a truly outstanding service provider in Catholic finance." Nevertheless, the reforms were costly, and profits fell in 2013 to 2.9 million euros, from 86.6 million euros in 2012.

On July 9, Card. Pell held a press conference at which he announced several new major initiatives for Vatican reform. The reforms were approved after careful consultation with COSEA and were approved by the Council for the Economy and the Council of Cardinals, as well as by the Holy Father. The changes included the establishment of a small Project Management Office (PMO), led by Mr. Danny Casey formerly Business Manager of the Sydney archdiocese. The major changes were in four main areas:

The Ordinary Section of APSA was transferred to the Secretariat for the Economy. The remaining staff of APSA would begin to focus exclusively on its role as a Treasury for the Holy See and the Vatican City State.

The Council for the Economy appointed a technical committee to study the situation of the Pension Fund and to make proposals to the Council for the Economy before the end of the year. The Council recognized and acknowledged that the pensions being paid today and for the next generation are safe but the fund needs to ensure there are sufficient funds for future generations in a changing environment.

A committee was appointed to propose reforms for the Vatican Media. The committee will publish a report and a reform plan within the next 12 months after considering the COSEA report. The members of the committee come from Vatican staff and from senior international experts. The senior international experts were: Lord Christopher Patten (UK, will act as President of the committee), Mr. Gregory Erlandson (USA), Ms. Daniela Frank (Germany), Fr. Eric Salobir OP (France), Ms. Leticia Soberon (Spain, Mexico), and Mr. George Yeo (Singapore). Vatican staff were: Mons. Paul Tighe (Secretary of the Pontifical Council for Social Communications, will act as Secretary of the committee), Giacomo Ghisani (Vatican Radio), Mons. Carlo Maria Polvani (Secretariat of State), Mons. Lucio Adrián Ruiz (Vatican Internet Service) and Prof. Giovanni Maria Vian (*L'Osservatore Romano*).

The Vatican Bank (IOR) would begin the next stage of reform, under the new leadership of Jean-Baptiste de Franssu, who became President of the IOR on July 9, 2014. Phase Two would include: strengthening the business foundation for IOR; gradually shifting assets under management to a newly created, central Vatican Asset Management (VAM), in order to overcome duplication of efforts in this field among Vatican institutions; focusing IOR on financial advice and payment services for clergy, congregations, dioceses and lay Vatican employees.

APOSTOLIC EXHORTATION: *EVANGELII GAUDIUM*

Pope Francis released his apostolic exhortation *Evangelii Gaudium* ("The Joy of the Gospel"), on Nov. 26, the first document of his pontificate to reflect almost completely the pope's own mind.

Though *Lumen Fidei* ("The Light of Faith"), released in July, was Pope Francis' first published work, that document primarily was inherited from Pope Emeritus Benedict XVI. "The Joy of the Gospel," though, is all Francis.

Vision of evangelization Spread out over five chapters and 51,000 words, "The Joy of the Gospel" is an intensely pastoral meditation on the New Evangelization that calls Catholics "to believe once again in the revolutionary nature of love and tenderness."

In it, Pope Francis reflects on the need for a loving personal encounter with Jesus Christ, the essential place of joy in evangelization, the crises in the contemporary world, the demand to love the poor, unity in the Church, the authentic role of women in the Church, the evils of abortion and other threats to human dignity and the need for creating "spirit-filled evangelizers." Interestingly, rather than merely analyzing the work that resulted from last year's Synod of Bishops on the New Evangelization, the exhortation very much contains Francis' own vision for evangelization.

"I invite all Christians, everywhere, at this very moment, to a renewed personal encounter with Jesus Christ," he writes, and he urges repeatedly for Catholics to be joyful in evangelizing. Far from saying, as some have claimed in recent months, that Catholics should not evangelize, Francis insists that every member of the Church has a role to play, and that there is no room for negativity and pessimism. He laments, "There are Christians whose lives seem like Lent without Easter. ... An evangelizer must never look like someone who has just come back from a funeral!"

Marian Example In *Evangelii Gaudium*, Pope Francis calls for the creation of what he terms "spirit-filled evangelizers," meaning "evangelizers fearlessly open to the working of the Holy Spirit." And the model par excellence is Mary, Mother of Evangelization.

"Today," Francis concludes, "we look to her and ask her to help us proclaim the message of salvation to all and to enable new disciples to become evangelizers in turn."

Likewise, he calls on Catholics "to abandon the complacent attitude that says: 'We have always done it this way.' I invite everyone to be bold and creative in this task of rethinking the goals, structures, style and methods of evangelization in their respective communities." He also warns against "spiritual worldliness," which is marked by the two extremes of "a purely subjective faith" or "a narcissistic and authoritarian elitism."

In contrast, he writes that the Church's evangelizing "has to concentrate on the essentials, on what is most beautiful, most grand, most appealing and at the same time most necessary. In this basic core, what shines forth is the beauty of the saving love of God made manifest in Jesus Christ who died and rose from the dead."

Missionary approach And this requires an ecclesial renewal that cannot be deferred. He describes a dream of a missionary impulse that transforms everything, "something much more in the line of an evangelical discernment. It is the approach of a missionary disciple, an approach 'nourished by the light and strength of the Holy Spirit' and that remembers always that evangelization is "first and foremost the Lord's work, surpassing anything which we can see and understand." Such renewal is for the entire Church, however, from individual Catholics to parishes and dioceses, and even the papacy itself.

Francis is not calling for some chaotic or haphazard campaign. "A Church which 'goes forth,'" he writes, "is a Church whose doors are open. Going out to others in order to reach the fringes of humanity does not mean rushing out aimlessly into the world." Faithful to the Second Vatican Council, he teaches, "today's vast and rapid cultural changes demand that we constantly seek ways of expressing unchanging truths in a language which brings out their abiding newness."

Toward that end, he takes a sober look at the modern world and gives a strong "no" to an economy of exclusion, the new idolatry of money, a financial system that rules rather than serves, inequality that spawns violence and a sterile pessimism. In sum, he writes, "the dignity of each human person and the pursuit of the common good are concerns which ought to shape all economic policies." Citing Jesus' example of poverty and love for the forgotten and marginalized, Pope Francis wants a "Church which is poor and for the poor."

'Spiritual desertification' Pope Francis also warns that "the culture of prosperity deadens us" and lists other grave challenges, such as the priority that is given to "the outward, the immediate, the visible, the quick, the superficial and the provisional"; the proliferation of new religious movements — from fundamentalism to a spirituality without God; the process of secularization that reduces the faith and the Church to the sphere of the private and personal; and the profound cultural crisis of the modern family, which will be the focus of the Extraordinary Synod of Bishops next October.

He uses the vivid term of "spiritual desertification" to describe the results of trying "to build a society without God or to eliminate their Christian roots." He adds that there is need for "an encounter between faith, reason and the sciences with a view to developing new approaches and arguments on the issue of credibility, a creative apologetics which would encourage greater openness to the Gospel on the part of all."

End to fighting factions Francis diagnoses the failure of Catholics to respond to cultural challenges not through "an excess of activity, but rather activity undertaken badly" and that can lead to discouragement and despair. "A tomb psychology develops and slowly transforms Christians into mummies in a museum," he cautions, adding such an outlook "is a defeatism which turns us into querulous and disillusioned pessimists, sourpusses."

Here he encourages the Church toward unity by saying, "No to warring among ourselves." Francis touches on that war in several ways. He reiterates that "reservation of the priesthood to males ... is not a question open to discussion, but it can prove especially divisive if sacramental power is too closely identified with power in general." Similarly, he notes that "when properly understood, cultural diversity is not a threat to Church unity," and he reminds the faithful that "popular piety enables us to see how the Faith, once received, becomes embodied in a culture and is constantly passed on."

And for those who claim that Francis has demoted the Church's teachings on abortion, he strongly condemns the destruction of "unborn children, the most defenseless and innocent among us." He adds bluntly, however, that "we have done little to adequately accompany women in very difficult situations, where abortion appears as a quick solution to their profound anguish."

BEATIFICATION OF POPE PAUL VI

The Vatican issued a formal announcement May 10 that Pope Paul VI, pope from 1963 to 1978, would be beatified by Pope Francis on Oct. 19. The pope who is best known for his 1968 encyclical *Humanae Vitae* that defended and restated Church teaching on contraception will be beatified during the closing Mass of the Extraordinary Synod of Bishops on the Family that was announced by Pope Francis last year.

Pope Francis approved the beatification of his predecessor when he signed a decree on May 9 recognizing a miracle attributed to the intercession of Pope Paul, a traditionally vital requirement for beatification and a key step toward canonization. A second miracle is next required by the current norms, although Francis waived the need for a second miracle when he chose to canonize Pope St. John XXIII on April 27, with Pope St. John Paul II. Pope Paul will join a growing list of recent popes who have been beatified or canonized, or who are the subjects of ongoing causes for canonization.

In Pope Paul's case, his cause for canonization began in May 1993 when Pope John Paul II approved the start of the diocesan investigation for the late pope who was born Giovanni Battista Montini in 1897 in the northern Italian region of Brescia. In December 2012, Pope Benedict XVI approved the declaration of Pope Paul as someone who had led a life of "heroic virtue" and granted the late pontiff the title of venerable. The cause then awaited confirmation of a miracle to clear the way for beatification. That miracle proved a very fitting one.

In February, theologians at the Congregation for the Causes of Saints signed off on a proposed miracle that had taken place back in the 1990s in California. It involved an unborn child who was diagnosed with a variety of medical problems, including a damaged bladder and anhydramnios (the absence of fluid in the amniotic sac). As the doctors concluded the child would be born with severe disabilities and probably brain damage, they urged the mother to have an abortion. She refused, and a friend of the family, a nun, reportedly placed a photograph of Pope Paul VI and a small piece of cloth from one of his vestments on the woman's stomach and asked for his intercession. The child was born in the 39th week inexplicably in perfect health, and doctors continued to track his normal development for more than a decade. The Holy See started its official inquiry into the case in 2003. Medical experts concluded their assessments last December that the survival and recovery of the child were truly inexplicable.

The miracle is considered especially poignant given Pope Paul's heroic role in reaffirming the Church's teachings on contraception and the sanctity of procreation and married life with *Humanae Vitae*. That once controversial encyclical is seen today as powerfully prophetic, in particular Paul's warnings that a contraceptive culture "could open wide the way for marital infidelity and a general lowering of moral standards" and the threat of the state imposing the use of contraception on everyone.

Pope Paul's teachings are viewed as clearly relevant to the work of the Extraordinary Synod on the Family that will be held in Rome from Oct. 5-19 to study the challenging issues facing modern family life. Paul established the Synod of Bishops in September 1965 to encourage unity and consultation between the popes and the bishops of the world.

Ordained a priest in 1920, the future pope was recruited two years later for service in the Vatican Secretariat of State and became a trusted secretary to Cardinal Eugenio Pacelli, who was elected Pope Pius XII in 1939. During World War II, Montini helped organize a massive effort to assist refugees, including an information service for family members to find their missing loved ones. Appointed archbishop of Milan in 1954, he was named a cardinal by St. John XXIII in 1958 and was a key supporter of the Second Vatican Council (1962-65). Elected to succeed John in 1963, he brought the council to a conclusion and then spent the rest of his pontificate struggling to implement its reforms. To lead by example, he simplified the protocols of the ornate papal court, declared a Year of Faith for

1967-68, issued the Credo of the People of God and memorably gave away a papal tiara as a sign of his concern for the poor. It is on permanent display in the Basilica of the National Shrine of the Immaculate Conception in Washington, D.C.

Paul became the first pope in the modern era to travel internationally. He made a historic visit to Jordan and Israel in January 1964, and his nine trips in all included India, the United Nations and New York, the Shrine of Our Lady of Fatima in Portugal, Turkey, Colombia and Bermuda, Switzerland, Uganda and Iran, Pakistan and Asia. During a visit to the Philippines in 1970, he escaped an assassination attempt by a knife-wielding assailant. He also appointed cardinals from all over the world and wrote about the dangers to the human person through globalization and unequal economic development in the encyclical *Populorum Progressio* in 1967. The encyclical was much praised by Pope Benedict XVI in his 2009 encyclical *Caritas in Veritate.*

Paul's last years were noted for his immense suffering as he labored to guide the Church through the storms of cultural upheaval, political unrest and frequent dissent against Church teachings. He bore the trials with fortitude and joy and called for an end to war and violence right up to his passing at the papal summer villa at Castel Gandolfo on Aug. 6, 1978, at the age of 80.

INTERNATIONAL NEWS 2013-2014

Christians in Iraq

One of the most underreported stories of 2014 has been the genocide committed against the Christians of Syria and Iraq, in particular because of the rise of the Islamist State by the members of ISIS (or ISIL), the Islamic State of Iraq and Syria that seized a vast stretch of territory across the Syrian and Iraqi desert. ISIS has established what it terms an Islamic State, a Caliphate that will, ostensibly, be ruled under Sharia law.

ISIS captured the northern Iraqi city of Mosul – a longstanding Christian center in the country – in June and committed unspeakable atrocities against the Christian population, especially women and children, including mass crucifixions, torture, beheadings, rape, and forced marriages of Christian girls as young as nine to Islamist fighters. Churches were burned and desecrated, relics destroyed, and ancient texts were defiled. By the end of the purge, during which Christians were told to convert, leave, or die, Mass was no longer said in the city; it marked the first time Mass was not celebrated in Mosul in some 1,800 years. ISIS also destroyed Shi'ite mosques

The anti-Christian campaign expanded in the next weeks as ISIS surged into the Nineveh Plain surrounding Mosul as Christians and other minority groups, including Shi'ites, Yazidis, and Shabaks, were driven north into the Kurdish held territories where they hoped to find safety. The Christians and others fled with literally the clothes on their backs and without food or water.

On July 21, the Chaldean Catholic Patriarch Louis Raphaël I Sako issued a letter addressed to

all people of good-will in which he warned that Iraq was heading to utter disaster. The full text of Patriarch Sako's letter follows, English translation by AsiaNews:

To the people of conscience and good will in Iraq and the world,

To the voice of the moderates, our Muslim brothers and sisters in Iraq and the world,

To all concerned about the continuation of Iraq as a nation for all its citizens,

To all leaders, thinkers, and human rights activists,

To all defenders of the dignity of the human person and the freedom of religions,

Peace and God's Mercy!

The takeover of the Islamist jihadists of Mosul and their announcement of an Islamic state, and after days of composure and anticipation, the situation had turned negative on the Christians of the city and surrounding areas. The first signs of this reversal were the kidnapping of the two nuns and three orphans who were released after 17 days. We were encouraged by this development and we considered it a glimmer of hope, and a breakthrough. Only to be surprised by the latest developments, the Islamic state issued a statement calling on Christians openly to convert to Islam, and either pay Jizya without specifying a ceiling, or leave their city and their homes, with their clothes only, without any luggage, and issued a "fatwa" that the homes will become the property to the Islamic state. They have marked the letter "N" on the homes of Christians for "Nazarenes"!!! As they have marked on the homes of Shiites with the letter (R) for "Rejectors." Who knows what is holding in the coming days as the laws of the Islamic state is based on what they claim to be the Sharia law, including the redefinition of identities on the basis of religion and sectarianism.

These requirements offend Muslims and the reputation of Islam, which says "you have your religion and we have ours," and "There is no compulsion in religion," and it is in contradiction of a thousand and four hundred years of history and a lifetime of the Islamic world, and coexistence with different religions and different peoples, east and west, respecting their beliefs and living in fraternity. The Christians and in particular in our East, and since the advent of Islam, have shared together sweet and bitter memories, their bloods were mixed in defense of their rights and their land, and together they built, cities, civilization and heritage. It is shameful that Christians are being rejected, expelled and diminished. It is obvious that this would have disastrous consequences on the coexistence between the majority and the minorities, even among Muslims themselves, in the near and long term. Hence, Iraq is heading to a humanitarian, cultural, and historical disaster.

Therefore we call unto them, a warm, brotherly, urgent and serious call, and we appeal to our fellow Iraqis who support them to reconsider their strategy, and respect the unarmed innocent people, of all ethnicities, religions and sects. The Quran commands respect to the innocent, and does not call to seize the property of people forcibly, it calls on helping the widow, the orphan, the destitute and the defenseless, and even recommend to help the seventh neighbour. We also call on Christians in the region to adopt rationality and acumen, and calculate their options well and understand what is planned for the area, and come together in love and think through together and in solidarity to build confidence in themselves and their neighbours, gathering around their church, being patient, enduring and praying until the storm passes.

+ Louis Raphael I Sako, Patriarch of
the Chaldean Catholic Church

On July 21, the office of U.N. Secretary-General Ban Ki-Moon issued a statement condemned ISIS attacks on all religions as a crime against humanity, "in the strongest terms the systematic persecution of minority populations in Iraq by Islamic State [of Iraq and Syria] and associated armed groups." He added, "any systematic attack on the civilian population or segments of the civilian population, because of their ethnic background, religious beliefs or faith may constitute a crime against humanity."

The U.S. State Department made similar statements of condemnation, but the vast majority of Western media outlets were silent for weeks as the tragedy in Mosul and then the Nineveh Plain unfolded.

On July 22, Islamists seized Mar (Saint) Behnam, a fourth-century monastery in the town of Qaraqosh in northern Iraq. The monks were ordered to leave the monastery on foot with nothing but their clothes. They were rescued by Kurdish peshmerga fighters who drove them to safety in Kurdistan. The monstery was then looted and the relics and sacred texts were destroyed and defiled.

On July 23, Pope Francis telephoned the Patriarch of the Syriac Catholic Church Ignatius Youssef III Younan to assure him of his prayerful solidarity. The pope used his weekly Angelus blessing to offer prayers for Iraqi Christians who "are persecuted, chased away, forced to leave their houses without the possibility of taking anything with them."

On July 24, Patriarch Sako issued an appeal, with the leaders of the Chaldean, Syrian Orthodox, Syrian Catholic, and Armenian Bishops in northern Iraq, for the Iraqi government to take steps against ISIS and prevent a catastrophe for the nation. They likewise urged the government to protect the brutally treated Christian minorities. A similar appeal for international aid and assistance was issued the next day by the Archbishops of Mosul. The appeal read: "We, the Archbishops of Mosul, coming from all the denominations gathered in Erbil/Ankawah, headed by His Beatitude Patriarch Raphael Louis I Sako, are shocked, in pain, and worried about what happened to the innocent Christians of Mosul because of their religion. It is a crime against humanity, as the UN Secretary General Mr. Ban Ki-moon said, and 'a shameful stain that should not be tolerated' as the Secretary General of the Arab League Mr. Nabil Alaraby called it. It's a crime in and of itself – a blatant persecution that we condemn and denounce. We call on all people of conscience in Iraq and the world to put pressure on to the militants to stop the destruction of churches and monasteries and the burning of manuscripts and relics from our Christian heritage, which are also a priceless Iraqi and global heritage. What has been said about an agreement between the militants and churchmen is completely untrue, because what has happened is an unmitigated crime that cannot be denied or justified!"

Pope Francis announced on Aug. 8 that he would be sending a personal envoy to Iraq to reassure Christians and other minorities of his spiritual closeness and the Church's solidarity and to meet with Iraqi leaders to urge them to promote stability and an end to the threat of ISIS. Card. Fernando Filoni, prefect of the Congregation for the Evangelization of Peoples and former apostolic nuncio to Iraq during the Iraq War, was chosen for the mission. A communiqué issued by the Vatican stated, "In light of the grave situation in Iraq, the Holy Father has nominated Card. Fernando Filoni, prefect of the of the Congregation for the Evangelization of Peoples, as his personal envoy to express his spiritual closeness to the populations that are suffering and to carry to them the solidarity of the Church."

That same day, Card. Leonardo Sandri, prefect of the Congregation for the Eastern Churches, spoke out on behalf of the Christians in Iraq and Syria and appealed for humanitarian intervention in the region.

Pope Francis has spoken repeatedly both in public addresses and in social media about the situation, including an emotional appeal on July 20, in which he said:

"[O]ur brothers and sisters are persecuted, they are pushed out, forced to leave their homes without the opportunity to take anything with them. To these families and to these people I would like to express my closeness and my steadfast prayer. Dearest brothers and sisters so persecuted, I know how much you suffer, I know that you are deprived of everything. I am with you in your faith in Him who conquered evil! May the God of peace create in all an authentic desire for dialogue and reconciliation. Violence is not conquered with violence. Violence is conquered with peace! Let us pray in silence, asking for peace; everyone, in silence.... Mary Queen of peace, pray for us!"

On Aug. 8, the chairman of the Committee of International Justice and Peace of the U.S. Conference of Catholic Bishops (USCCB), Bp. Richard E. Pates of Des Moines, asked the U.S. bishops to invite the people of their dioceses to pray for peace in Iraq on Aug. 17. He also sent out the text of a prayer written by Patriarch Sako:

Lord,
The plight of our country
is deep and the suffering of Christians
is severe and frightening.
Therefore, we ask you Lord
to spare our lives, and to grant us patience,
and courage to continue our witness of Christian values
with trust and hope.
Lord, peace is the foundation of life;
Grant us the peace and stability that will enable us
to live with each other without fear and anxiety,
and with dignity and joy.
Glory be to you forever.

Pope Francis, on Aug. 10, made another appeal for peace in Iraq and Gaza before ending his Angelus address. He said, "The news coming from Iraq leaves us in disbelief and dismay: thousands of people, including many Christians, brutally driven from their homes; children dead from thirst and hunger during the escape; women who are abducted; people slaughtered; violence of every kind; destruction everywhere, destruction of homes, destruction of religious, historical and cultural patrimonies. All this greatly offends God and greatly offends humanity. You cannot bring hatred in the name of God. You cannot make war in the name of God!" He then asked the pilgrims in St. Peter's Square for a moment of silence and prayer.

The United States at last began surgical airstrikes against ISIS units threatening Kurdistan in the first week of August. Air operations were open-ended, but the strikes were far too late to prevent the near extinction of Christianity in much of northern Iraq and the start of a humanitarian disaster.

Synod of Bishops

The Vatican's Oct. 8 announcement that Pope Francis would convene an extraordinary general assembly of the Synod of Bishops next October — on "the pastoral challenges of the family in the context of evangelization" — raised two immediate questions. First, how will the impending reforms of the Synod of Bishops impact the deliberations and work of the bishops? And second, would the issue of divorced and remarried Catholics be discussed under the wider theme of family and marriage in the modern world?

The urgency of the synod was made clear by the director of the Holy See Press Office, Jesuit Fr. Federico Lombardi, when he said in a press conference, "It is very important that an extraordinary synod has been convoked on the theme of the pastoral care of the family. This is the way in which the pope intends to promote reflection and to guide the path of the community of the Church, with the responsible participation of the episcopate from different parts of the world."

Pope Francis drove home the importance of the gathering to him personally by going to the offices of the synod's general secretariat near the Vatican and taking part in some of the two days of preparatory discussions held just before the official announcement. Customarily, the officials would meet with the pope in the Apostolic Palace and his participation would be limited.

Effects of reforms

The Synod of Bishops was inaugurated by Pope Paul VI in 1965 with the intention of fostering close cooperation between the pope and the world's bishops in dealing with questions and situations facing the Church or to deliberate on essential points of doctrine and procedure in the life of the Church. Topics for previous synods have included evangelization, catechetics, penance and reconciliation, the Eucharist and the role of the laity in the Church.

This will be only the third extraordinary synod convoked by a pope. The two previous extraordinary synods, in 1969 and 1985, looked at the relationship of bishops and priests and the implementation of the Second Vatican Council (on its 20th anniversary), respectively. There have been 13 so-called ordinary synods — such as the one convened last year in Rome on the New Evangelization.

Extraordinary Gathering

"Extraordinary" synods are summoned to deal with some urgent matter of concern to the pope and have a shorter time for preparation. The number of participants for the Oct. 5-19, 2014, synod will be smaller, perhaps no more than 200, than for ordinary synods, although it can be expected that Pope Francis also will invite lay experts on family life and marriage in addition to the usual cardinals, heads of the world's bishops' conferences and officials from various Vatican offices.

This third extraordinary synod comes at the time when the synod itself has been slated for potentially extensive reforms under Pope Francis, and it was a topic of considerable discussion by the eight-person Council of Cardinals recently established by the pope to oversee the reorganization and renewal of the entire Roman Curia.

There have been complaints for some years that the synod's proceedings are too cumbersome and inefficient, there are too many speeches and the final statements are largely prepared with little input from the actual participants. The Council of Cardinals had its first formal meeting with Francis at the start of October, and it is expected that a full set of reforms for the synod will emerge over the next months.

Notably, the official charged with carrying out the reforms in a practical sense was a long-time Vatican official, Abp. Lorenzo Baldisseri, who was appointed the new General Secretary of the Synod of Bishops only last September after years in the Congregation of Bishops. How the synod performs next year will give a major clue as to the seriousness and overall effectiveness of Francis' wider reform agenda for the Roman Curia.

Pastoral care for divorced

The other immediate question that emerged regarding the extraordinary synod is whether attention will be paid to the pastoral crisis of such large numbers of Catholics who have been divorced or are divorced and civilly remarried. Parishes and dioceses continue to grapple with the best ways to provide proper pastoral care, especially to those Catholics who are divorced and remarried without an annulment and therefore may not present themselves to receive the Eucharist.

There have been recent efforts, most notably in the Archdiocese of Freiburg, Germany, to explore potential guidelines to assist divorced and remarried Catholics in receiving Communion.

The announcement of the synod clearly was meant to discourage any movement on this issue ahead of the gathering next year.

As Fr. Lombardi said, "It is right that the Church should move as a community in reflection and prayer, and that she takes common pastoral directions in relation to the most important points — such as the pastoral of the family — under the guidance of the pope and the bishops. The convocation of the extraordinary Synod clearly indicates this path.

"In this context," he stressed, "the proposal of particular pastoral solutions by local persons or offices carries the risk of engendering confusion. It is opportune to emphasize the importance of following a path in full communion with the ecclesial community."

A matter of mercy

Before his election as pope, then-Card. Jorgé Mario Bergoglio spoke frequently about the need for an effective ministry to the divorced that fosters a genuine sense of belonging and participation even for those unable to receive Communion. His concern, however, is not a radical departure from the papal teachings of recent pontiffs, including Blessed John Paul II and Pope Emeritus Benedict XVI. In 2012, during the World Meeting of Families in Milan, Pope Benedict taught, "Their suffering is great and yet we can only help parishes and individuals to assist these people to bear the pain of divorce ... the Church loves them, but it is important they should see and feel this love."

Pope Francis addressed the very issue of divorced Catholics during his in-flight press conference returning to Italy from World Youth Day in Rio de Janeiro, Brazil, in July. He said bluntly that he wants the synod to address the crisis within the larger context of the entire pastoral area of marriage and also desires an examination of what can be an overly complex and lengthy annulment process.

"We are moving toward a somewhat deeper pastoral care of marriage," he said, reiterating the theme of mercy as central to that pastoral care, even for the divorced and remarried.

"The Church is a mother, and she must travel this path of mercy," he added. "And find a form of mercy for all."

On Nov. 5, officials of the Holy See released an official preparatory document for the October 2014 Extraordinary Synod of Bishops, which has as its theme "the pastoral challenges of the family in the context of evangelization."

The preparatory document establishes many of the key topics for deliberations by the bishops, including "The Church and the Gospel on the Family"; "The Plan of God, Creator and Redeemer"; and "The Church's Teaching on the Family." The attention of the media, however, was understandably more focused on the last part of the document — a questionnaire on the main challenges facing the family today.

Questionnaire

Below are several questions excerpted from the Vatican's preparatory document. Each bishops' conference was given a copy along with a request to turn in an assessment of these questions by January 2014. (OSV invited readers to offer their own answers to at feedback@osv.com, and selected responses were printed in a later issue.)

Some media outlets presented the 39 questions as a way for the Vatican to poll Catholics on whether the Church should change its teachings on divorce and remarriage, cohabitation, same-sex marriage, abortion and contraception. Such unfounded speculation was dismissed immediately by the Vatican, but it also demonstrated a failure on the part of many reporters and commentators to read the actual questions.

The questionnaire seeks to assess the current levels of knowledge and acceptance of the Church's teachings on marriage and the family and various cultural obstacles to their adherence. The questions are intended to allow "the particular Churches to participate actively in the preparation of the Extraordinary Synod, whose purpose is to proclaim the Gospel in the context of the pastoral challenges facing the family today."

The questions are divided into several pastoral categories, such as "The Diffusion of the Teachings on the Family in Sacred Scripture and the Church's Magisterium"; "Marriage according to the Natural Law"; "Pastoral Care in Certain Difficult Marital Situations"; "On Unions of Persons of the Same Sex"; and "The Openness of the Married Couple to Life." A final section asks about other challenges and proposals that should be discussed.

Better understanding

Catholics are not asked whether the Church should change its teachings. For example, on the issue of couples being open to life, the questions ask, "What knowledge do Christians have today of the teachings of *Humanae Vitae* ("On Human Life") on responsible parenthood? Are they aware of how morally to evaluate the different methods of family planning? Could any insights be suggested in this regard pastorally?" The follow-up asks, "Is this moral teaching accepted? What aspects pose the most difficulties in a large majority of couple's accepting this teaching?"

Sending out questions in preparation for an upcoming synod is also hardly unprecedented. In the lead up to the 2012 Synod of Bishops on the New Evangelization, 30 questions were distributed to the world's bishops on all phases of evangelization in the modern world.

Card. Peter Erdö, the archbishop of Esztergom-Budapest in Hungary, who was appointed by Pope Francis in September as the relator of the upcoming synod, stressed at a Nov. 5 press conference that the questions seek simply to provide a better understanding of current levels of knowledge and attitudes as the bishops do their work.

There is no plan, he declared, to make decisions based on public opinion. "Certainly the doctrine of the magisterium must be the basis of the common reasoning of the synod," Card. Erdö said.

Submitting results The Hungarian cardinal will help guide the synod in its deliberations, working closely with the synod's new general secretary, Abp. Lorenzo

Baldisseri, who was appointed last month. They noted that the questionnaire would be distributed to the world's episcopal conferences, which will then be free to disseminate them as they see fit, including distributing them to parishes. Individual Catholics are also encouraged to respond on their own and send the questionnaire to the Vatican, if they wish.

The episcopal conferences are expected to organize the collected data from individual dioceses and archdioceses and present summaries to the Synod Secretariat, the commission in charge of the preparations for the synod. The secretariat will then incorporate the results in the working document, called the *Instrumentum Laboris*, for the synod itself. The bishop's conferences were asked to submit their summaries to the General Secretariat by the end of January 2014.

Instrumentum Laboris

On June 26, the Vatican issued a working document, called an *instrumentum laboris*, for the October 2014 extraordinary Synod of Bishops on the family that was announced by Pope Francis last year to deal with the pressing "pastoral challenges of the family in the context of evangelization." The document sets the agenda for the discussions among the bishops who will gather in Rome, and rather than focusing exclusively on the issue of the divorced and remarried as many in the media had assumed, the bishops instead will confront a vast array of problems, challenges and concerns.

In November, the synod's leadership under then-Abp. (now Card.) Lorenzo Baldisseri sent out 39 questions to the world's episcopal conferences to assess the knowledge and acceptance of the Church's teachings on marriage and the family and various cultural obstacles to their adherence. The responses informed the key topics for the synod, although some media outlets erroneously interpreted the questions as a way for the Vatican to poll Catholics on whether the Church should change her teachings on divorce and remarriage and sexual morality.

Discussion topics

As with any working document for a synod, the 75-page instrumentum is very straightforward. The discussion of family life is presented in three parts: "Communicating the Gospel of the Family in Today's World," "The Pastoral Program for the Family in Light of New Challenges" and "An Openness to Life and Parental Responsibility in Upbringing." Beneath the general sounding categories, the bishops' agenda covers some of the most important and controversial challenges for the modern family, such as abortion, contraception, same-sex marriage, and divorced and remarried Catholics. The bishops are realistic in their assessment but not pessimistic.

The first part, for example, considers the Church's teachings on God's plan for marriage and the family, but it notes the diverse acceptance of Church teaching and some of the reasons for the difficulty in their acceptance among the faithful, most so on moral issues. Based on survey results, there is "a want of an authentic Christian experience, namely, an encounter with Christ on a personal and communal level," as well as assorted conflicts and influences, from the mass media to the hedonistic culture caused by "selfish liberalization of morals" and what Pope Francis decries is a "'culture of waste' and a 'culture of the moment.'"

The tone becomes even more sober in the second part,

with its focus on pastoral challenges facing the family, "such as the crisis of faith, critical internal situations, external pressures and other problems."

The bishops see the urgency of what they term the "crisis in faith and family." This crisis entails "the break-up and breakdown of families," the effect of long work hours and poor wages, violence and abuse, wars, migration, consumerism and individualism, and disparity of cult. Even more urgent are the "difficult pastoral situations" that touch on the thorniest and most controverted aspects of the Church's encounter with modernity: cohabitation, separated and divorced couples, divorced and remarried Catholics — including how the Church handles marriage cases — teen and single mothers, canonically irregular situations, non-believers or non-practicing Catholics who wish to marry, same-sex unions and transmission of the Faith to children in those unions.

Marital issues

In speaking forthrightly about the whole situation of divorced and separated Catholics as well as the divorced and remarried, the instrumentum notes the various responses from around the world that better pastoral care is badly needed. And while much of the conversation in recent months has been about divorced and remarried Catholics, the document laments that more attention must be given to separated and divorced persons who have not remarried. "Oftentimes," the document says, "these people seem to have the added suffering of not being given proper care by the Church and thus overlooked."

Tied closely to divorce and remarriage are the many responses requesting that the canonical processing of marriage cases be streamlined.

At the same time, the instrumentum gives voice to those urging caution in streamlining or reducing the process. There is concern whether it is possible to deal with this matter through a judicial process only, that there might be injustices and errors, the possible impression that "the indissolubility of the sacrament is not respected" or "the mistaken idea that an annulment is simply 'Catholic divorce.'" There is, nevertheless, a wide consensus for better pastoral training for those involved in any ministry to the divorced and separated.

A diagnosis

On the issue of the shifting definition of marriage in modern society, the document declares that while every episcopal conference opposes same-sex legislation, the bishops also are striving to find "balance between the Church's teaching on the family and a respectful, non-judgmental attitude toward people living in such unions."

Pope Francis wants the deliberations at the synod to be open and for the bishops to participate actively in discussions. The instrumentum, then, is not the end of deliberations but a diagnosis of the present situation with some clear directions based on the questions sent around the whole Church.

The survey was valuable, and it points to the need to preach the Gospel of the family in the present day, crafting a better response to the new challenges and assisting "parents in developing a mentality of openness to life."

A reading of the instrumentum reveals no call for changing the teachings of the Church but making those teachings more faithful. For very good reason, then, the extraordinary synod has been entrusted to the Holy Family, which "is to be contemplated in every family situation so as to draw light, strength and consolation."

NATIONAL NEWS 2013-2014

Religious Liberty and the HHS Mandate

On June 30, the U.S. Supreme Court handed down a decision regarding the so-called HHS Mandate that requires businesses to provide contraception coverage to employers, including sterilization and abortion-inducing drugs.

The 5-4 decision cut along fiercely ideological lines and was specific to the two cases of *Sebelius v. Hobby Lobby Stores, Inc.* (10th Circuit Court of Appeals) and *Conestoga Wood Specialties v. Sebelius* (3rd Circuit Court of Appeals). The two circuit courts reached different verdicts on the question of whether for-profit secular corporations possess free exercise rights and could therefore be exempted from the mandate.

The high court had agreed to hear the cases in Nov. 2013.

In Jan. 2014, it was announced that Dominos Pizza founder Tom Monaghan had succeeded in securing an emergency motion for a Temporary Restraining Order (TRO) to halt enforcement of the controversial HHS mandate on the grounds of the mandate's violation of the employer's First Amendment religious rights. The mandate, part of the Affordable Care Act – so-called Obamacare – and took effect Jan. 1, 2013. The Thomas More Law Center (TMLC) filed the motion, and U.S. District Judge Lawrence Zatkoff ruled in favor of the motion, citing the government's failure to "satisfy its burden of showing that its actions were narrowly tailored to serve a compelling interest."

As of early January, there were more than 40 separate lawsuits challenging the HHS mandate, including suits from Hobby Lobby, Wheaton College, East Texas Baptist University, Houston Baptist University, Belmont Abbey College, Colorado Christian University, the Eternal Word Television Network (EWTN), Ave Maria University, and Our Sunday Visitor.

The decision by SCOTUS in June pertained only to the Hobby Lobby and Conestoga cases, and the court found that family owned businesses could claim religious exemption from the mandate. A narrow majority of the court found that the Obama administration had not proven that mandate is the least restrictive means of advancing its interest in guaranteeing the provision of free access to contraception in health insurance plans. In addition, the Court also concluded that the 1993 Religious Freedom Restoration Act requires that closely held companies receive the same accommodation granted by the administration to nonprofit organizations that object to the mandate on religious grounds. As has been the case for a number of years, the decision cut along ideological lines, with Justices Alito, Roberts, Scalia, Thomas, and Kennedy voting for the majority while Justices Ginsburg, Breyer, Sotomayor, and Kagan dissenting.

The day of the ruling, Abp. Joseph E. Kurtz of Louisville, president of the U.S. Conference of Catholic Bishops, and Abp. William E. Lori of Baltimore, chairman of the U.S. bishops' Ad Hoc Committee for Religious Liberty, released a statement:

"We welcome the Supreme Court's decision to recognize that Americans can continue to follow their faith when they run a family business. In this case, justice has prevailed, with the Court respecting the rights of the Green and Hahn families to continue to abide by their faith in how they seek their livelihood, without facing devastating fines. Now is the time to redouble our efforts to build a culture that fully respects religious freedom.

"The Court clearly did not decide whether the so-called 'accommodation' violates RFRA when applied to our charities, hospitals and schools, so many of which have challenged it as a burden on their religious exercise. We continue to hope that these great ministries of service, like the Little Sisters of the Poor and so many others, will prevail in their cases as well."

Update on the Sex Abuse Scandal
By Russell Shaw

In 2013 new allegations of sex abuse of children by U.S. Catholic clergy were the fewest since 2004, when the annual collection of these figures began. According to the Center for Applied Research in the Apostolate (CARA), 457 victims made 464 allegations against 352 offenders during the year.

But most of the alleged incidents occurred several decades ago, and only 10 of them in 2013, with the largest number occurring between 1970 and 1979. Three-fourths of the alleged offenders have died by now or have left or been removed from ministry. Three hundred seventy of the allegations were judged credible. Ten incidents involved persons who are currently minors.

These numbers are contained in the 2013 Survey of Allegations and Costs: A Summary Report for the Secretariat of Child and Youth Protection, United States Conference of Catholic Bishops. Preparation and publication of these annual reports are required by the U.S. bishops' Charter for the Protection of Children and Young People.

The latest report, released March 28, showed that the abuse scandal cost American dioceses $108,954,109 during the year covered. That brought the total cost between 2004 and 2012 to $2,744,881,843 – $2,351,903,157 for dioceses and eparchies and $392,978,686 for religious institutes. The figures include settlements ($61.1 million in 2013), therapy for victims ($6.1 million), attorneys' fees ($28.9 million), support for offenders ($10.4 million), and miscellaneous other costs ($2.4 million).

The document noted a 50% increase over 2012 in spending for child protection by dioceses and religious institutes. A major reason for the rise, said Deacon Bernard Nojadera, director of the USCCB child and youth protection secretariat, was the cost of updated checks on the backgrounds of Church personnel required at five-year intervals by the bishops' charter.

The report also provided results of the annual compliance audit of dioceses conducted by StoneBridge Business Partners. (The Diocese of Lincoln, Neb., and three Eastern eparchies refused to participate.) The audit showed outreach and support being provided to 340 new abuse survivors and family members as well as continued support for another 1,843 previously being assisted.

The auditors found 4,645,700 children—94.6% of the potential total—have received safe environment training. Similar training has been given to 35,914 priests (99.6%), 16,129 deacons (99.7%), 6,360 candidates for ordination (99.5%), 167,953 educators (99.5%), 251,146 other Church employees (98.6%), and 1,902,143 volunteers (98%).

Abp. Joseph E. Kurtz of Louisville, president of USCCB, said the efforts reflected in the report "remain essential priorities for our Church."

As usual, however, he progress reflected in the report was frequently overshadowed by other developments.

In February, the Diocese of Helena, Mont. became the 11th U.S. diocese to file for chapter 11 bankruptcy protection in response to financial pressures arising from abuse cases. The diocese listed $33.6 million in liabilities against $16 million in assets, not counting parishes, schools, and other separately incorporated Catholic institutions. A court was to distribute $15 million in diocesan funds to victims.

Earlier, in November 2013 and January 2014 the Diocese of Gallup, N.M., and the Diocese of Stockton, Calif. had become the ninth and tenth respectively to declare bankruptcy.

Payouts during the year included the following.

The Diocese of Santa Rosa, Calif. in July paid $3.5 million to a victim. The payment was one of the largest ever to an individual.

In June, it was disclosed that a court-appointed arbitrator the previous March had ordered the Diocese of Kansas City, Mo. to pay an additional $1.1 million to victims of a local priest, Shawn Ratigan, for failing to follow its own abuse guidelines. That brought to $3.75 million the settlement costs in the case of Ratigan, who currently is serving a 50-year prison sentence on child pornography charges. The diocese said the arbitrator had exceeded his authority and challenged the order in court.

Also in June, the Archdiocese of Seattle settled 30 claims of sexual abuse by Christian Brothers at two area high schools for $12.5 million.

The Archdiocese of Chicago in February reached a $3.2 million settlement with a man claiming abuse by ex-priest Daniel McCormack. The archdiocese had earlier settled other suits brought by men alleging abuse by McCormack.

In February, too, the Archdiocese of Los Angeles paid $13 million to 17 people claiming abuse by priests. That brought to $740 million the cost of settlements to the archdiocese.

The year also brought a series of events in the Archdiocese of St. Paul and Minneapolis, where more than 40 lawsuits have been filed in cases involving local priests.

In July, a district judge ordered a court trial, starting Sept. 22, in a case involving a former priest named Thomas Adamson. The archdiocese, which at the time—the 1970s—was headed by the late Abp. John R. Roach, is charged with negligence in giving Adamson a parish assignment despite abuse charges against him in the nearby Diocese of Winona, where he served before coming to St. Paul and Minneapolis.

In another, unrelated development, Abp. John C. Nienstedt, the present Archbishop of St. Paul and Minneapolis, has become a target of allegations of inappropriate sexual relations of men dating back four decades. Calling the charges "entirely false," Abp. Nienstedt directed the hiring of an independent law firm to investigate the allegations and make a report.

In July, the archdiocese's former chancellor for canonical matters, Jennifer M. Haselberger, filed a lengthy memorandum claiming her concerns about sex abuse were "ignored, dismissed, or the emphasis was shifted to what was best for the priest involved." Aux. Bp. Andrew Cozzens said her recollections were "not always shared by others." And in a deposition made public in June, retired Abp. Harry Flynn, a former chairman of the U.S. bishops' committee on sex abuse, said that in his years as head of the archdiocese, 1995-2008, he had delegated the handling of abuse-related issues to others.

In Philadelphia, meanwhile, a former official of the Philadelphia archdiocese responsible for clergy assignments was released from prison when an appeals court in December 2013 unanimously overturned his conviction for child endangerment. Msgr. William J. Lynn had served 18 months for endangering a 10-year-old boy whom the former priest alleged to have abused him denied abusing. Philadelphia District Attorney Seth Williams said he planned to appeal the ruling that freed Msgr. Lynn.

LIFE ISSUES 2013-2014

By Gerald Korson

As the fall of 2013 approached, pro-life advocates across the United States were expressing optimism for the future of the cause after a string of successes in state legislatures. Forty-nine of 50 states had enacted some new restriction on abortion, and hopes were running high for some inertia in defense of life at the national level. While the ensuing 12 months surely brought additional reasons to celebrate, there were setbacks and disappointments as well in both the statehouses and the courts.

Much of the life-issues debate centered upon the Affordable Care Act, the Obama administration's healthcare reform initiative, and its onerous requirement that employers — even the vast majority of religious-affiliated employers — provide coverage for contraceptives and certain abortifacient drugs in their employee benefits plans.

Other Court and Legislative Action

One of the frequently seen arguments by abortion advocates today is to loosen the minimum qualifications required of abortion providers. In a number of states, "pro-choice" forces have fought laws or proposals requiring physicians who perform abortions to have admitting privileges at a local hospital; in others, they have argued that nurse practitioners and physician assistants should be able to perform abortions without a physician present. Still others oppose the enforcement of basic standards for the cleanliness and equipment used in abortion clinics. In the name of making abortion more available, such initiatives simply make abortion more dangerous for the mother who chooses to abort her child.

After California Gov. Jerry Brown signed a bill into law in October 2013 permitting trained non-physicians to perform first-trimester abortions and loosening building regulations for abortion clinics, the president of the California Catholic Conference issued a statement critical of the move, saying it would increase the number of abortions and risk the lives of women. "We oppose abortion, and until it becomes illegal, we will oppose measures which expand it — especially when it is at the expense of the girls and women undergoing the procedure," said Aux. Bp. Gerald E. Wilkerson of Los Angeles. He noted the change in law would create a "two-tier health system" since the clinics that would operate under such reduced standards would cater primarily to women who are poor and cannot afford better qualified care.

The state of Texas could almost be described as Ground Zero for abortion debate in recent years. In October 2013, an appeals court let stand a state law requiring abortion doctors to have admitting privileges at a nearby hospital, overruling a district court judge's opinion issued three days earlier. In November, the U.S. Supreme Court upheld the Texas laws in a 5-4 vote.

The ruling effectively shut down one-third of the state's thirty-six abortion clinics. According to Texas Right to Life, Planned Parenthood in testimony before the appeals court "conceded that at least 210 women in Texas annually must be hospitalized after seeking an abortion." The group further reported that witnesses on both sides of the question "testified that some of the women who are hospitalized after an abortion have complications that require an OB/GYN specialist's treatment." Admitting-privileges provisions had previously been blocked by courts in Alabama, Mississippi, North Dakota and Wisconsin.

Also in November, there was a setback in the neighboring state of Oklahoma: The nation's high court declined to consider a challenge to an Oklahoma Supreme Court ruling that overturned a 2010 state law requiring women to get an ultrasound before going through with an abortion. Calling the U.S. Supreme Court's refusal "gravely disappointing," Abp. Paul S. Coakley of Oklahoma City said that "providing a woman who faces an unexpected pregnancy with additional information about her child in the form of an ultrasound and medical description" is a service that helps women avoid exploitation toward a particular agenda. It was the second pro-life rebuff in Oklahoma that month: The U.S. Supreme Court previously had declined to review another state Supreme Court decision that a major portion of Oklahoma's abortion law was unconstitutional because it effectively bans all drug-induced abortions.

To the west, voters in Albuquerque, New Mexico, rejected a ballot measure that would have banned late-term abortions after 20 weeks of pregnancy except to save the mother's life. Albuquerque was targeted for the pro-life initiative because it has a clinic that performs late-term abortions. The proposal generated much debate about whether or not the fetus can feel pain.

In March 2014, a similar measure fell to defeat in West Virginia when Gov. Earl Ray Tomblin vetoed the Pain-Capable Unborn Child Protection act, which also would have prohibited most abortions after the 20-week mark. The act had the support of medical evidence that unborn children can indeed feel pain at 20 weeks.

In April, Democrats in the Colorado Senate decided to spike an abortion bill that the state's Catholic conference had called "radical." The bill effectively would have made abortion a fundamental right in the state. After the Colorado bishops and Senate Republicans put up stiff opposition, the "pro-choice" senators decided to abandon the measure rather than fight a losing battle. The bill, S.B. 175, had been compared to a state version of the "Freedom of Choice Act," a proposal to entrench abortion "rights" that has been introduced in the U.S. Congress periodically without success since 1989.

Several pro-life measures have been introduced in the U.S. Congress in 2014. One of these, the No Taxpayer Funding for Abortion Act (H.R. 7), would apply the principles of the 1976 Hyde Amendment to federal health programs, including the Affordable Care Act. The Hyde Amendment prohibits the use of taxpayer dollars to supply federal subsidies to any part of a benefits package that includes elective abortions. H.R. 7 also requires that health care providers fully disclose the extent of their abortion coverage, including any abortion surcharges required of premium payers.

Card. Sean P. O'Malley of Boston, who chairs the U.S. bishops' Committee on Pro-Life Activities, praised the legislation, saying that "the federal government should not use its funding power to support elective abortion, and should not force taxpayers to subsidize this violence." The bill, which was introduced by Rep. Chris Smith (R-N.J.) and Rep. Dan Lipinski (D-Ill.), passed the House but was largely symbolic as it was not expected to receive Senate approval.

In June, U.S. Rep. Steven Palazzo (R-Mass.) introduced the Every Child is a Blessing Act (H.R. 4698), which is designed to prevent "wrongful birth" lawsuits — cases filed by parents who say they would have aborted their child if they had known he or she would be born with a disability. The bill protects disabled children from discrimination and from the suggestion that they would have been better off dead. "The concept that a violent prenatal death by abortion is preferable to life with a disability is incompatible with, and corrosive to, fundamental disability-rights principles," said Douglas Johnson, legislative director of National Right to Life, in a letter to Palazzo.

The Affordable Care Act and the HHS mandate are seen by many as vehicles for eroding once-sacred conscience protections for persons of religious faith. Among these critics is Dr. John Brehany, executive director and ethicist at the Catholic Medical Association, who told an August 2013 medical conference that the health care reform package — informally referred to as "Obamacare" — "muddies the picture" on conscience clauses that once exempted health-care professionals and institutions from playing any part in procedures such as abortion and sterilization. "While Obamacare itself does have a couple of conscience-protection provisions built in, the fact is, if you look at the big picture, which are the old federal laws and what was achieved from 1973 to 2004, we are now missing some important protections, and we are now vague on how these old laws will carry forward into the future," Brehany said.

A couple of high-profile cases involving judgments of "brain death" revealed conflicts between the medical definition of death and the rights of family members to continue treatment and care. In Oakland, Calif., 13-year-old Jahi McMath was declared brain dead after severe complications from surgery for sleep apnea. A death certificate was issued in December 2013, but the family won a court order allowing them to transfer Jahi to another facility, where she was still receiving care at press time. Meanwhile, in Texas, 33-year-old Marlise Munoz collapsed at home and suffered brain death in November 2013. Because she was pregnant, she was kept on life support as required by Texas law in an effort to help her 10-week-old unborn child survive until viability. Her husband sued for and won the right to disconnect his wife's life support, and Munoz died in late January 2014. Opinion even among leading Catholic ethicists is mixed in both cases.

Euthanasia has received legal sanction in several European nations, and as of June 2014 it was poised to reach the North American continent. By a vote of 94-22, he National Assembly in the Canadian province of Quebec has passed a "dying with dignity" bill that mirrors existing euthanasia laws in Belgium. It was not clear what action, if any, the federal Canadian government would take in response. For its part, Belgium last February expanded its euthanasia law to allow terminally ill children to be put to death if they request it themselves and their parents and doctors also consent.

Back in the United States, there is a growing movement seeking the right to assisted suicide in the state of New Mexico. In January 2014, a judicial court judge in Albuquerque ruled that terminally ill, mentally competent patients have the right to request a physician's help in committing suicide. The state's Catholic bishops condemned the ruling. "Our laws are meant to protect life," the bishops said. "The Catholic Church teaches that we are stewards of life, and in heeding God's command, 'Thou shall not kill' ... we recognize that we cannot dispose of life. ... Physicians and other caregivers have the obligation to maintain life and to relieve pain." Quoting the *Catechism of the Catholic Church*, they added: "Voluntary cooperation in suicide is contrary to the moral law."

Popular support for capital punishment in the United States continued to erode amid continued concerns about the fallibility of the judicial system and the humaneness of the methods of execution. "Botched executions" continue to be reported. In July 2014, Joseph Wood suffered needlessly during a lethal injection in Arizona, leading some observers to characterize the event as "cruel and unusual punishment"; in April, Clayton Lockett experienced obvious pain and distress at his lethal injection in Oklahoma and later died of cardiac arrest.

"How we treat criminals says a lot about us as a society," Abp. Coakley of Oklahoma said after the latter incident. "We certainly need to administer justice with due consideration for the victims of crime, but we must find a way of doing so that does not contribute to the culture of death, which threatens to completely erode our sense of the innate dignity of the human person and of the sanctity of human life from conception to natural death."

Catholic pharmacists have been urged not to cooperate in providing the drugs needed for the states to carry out lethal injections. "As Catholic people of faith, we ask that you not only consider the ethical codes breached when pharmacists use their training and tools to facilitate state-sponsored killings, but also consider the profound moral codes that call upon all of us to respect the sacred dignity of every God-given human life," said a May 2014 letter to the American Pharmacists Association that was signed by a number of Catholic leaders who oppose the death penalty. "All producers of the primary drugs necessary for state-sponsored killings have banned their products from use in executions. States intent on carrying out executions have now turned to compounding pharmacists to obtain drugs that have and will, painfully or slowly, cause the death of the recipient."

In February, a pharmacy in Tulsa, Okla., had refused to provide pentobarbital, a lethal drug, for the execution of Michael Taylor, who was on death row in Missouri. The state of Missouri found a new supplier of the drug, and Taylor was put to death on schedule.

Earlier that year, in March, Glenn Ford was released from Louisiana's death row after 30 years when his conviction was overturned.

The Catholic Church always supports efforts to end the death penalty and to treat capital criminals with clemency. The bishops unfailingly throw their support behind proposals to end capital punishment at the state level. When a bill was introduced in the New Hampshire legislature to outlaw executions, Bp. Peter A. Libasci of Manchester spoke openly in its favor, saying the death penalty "publicly validates the very act of taking a human life. The death penalty does not help the criminal to understand the magnitude of what he or she has done; it reinforces, instead, the terrifying notion that there is, ultimately, no sacrilege in the taking of human life."

Even in the case of notorious criminals, the Church opposes the death penalty when other means, such as secure incarceration, are available to protect society from harm. In February 2014, the Conference of Major Superiors of Men issued a statement urging "restorative justice" rather than capital punishment for 20-year-old Dzhokhar Tsarnaev, one of the men involved in the fatal bomb attack during the 2013 Boston Marathon. "The truth is that the death penalty fails to humanize our lives," the CMSM statement said. "The love is about increasingly becoming a people of empathy, compassion and the courage to transcend our destructive habits." Likewise, in August 2013, Abp. Timothy M. Broglio of the Archdiocese of Military Services openly opposed capital punishment for Army Maj. Nidal Hasan, who was sentenced to death that month in the 2009 massacre that killed 13 persons at Fort Hood, Texas. "The Church teaches that unjustified killing is wrong in all circumstances. That includes the death penalty," Abp. Broglio said in a statement.

MEETINGS OF U.S. BISHOPS 2013-2014

November 12-13, 2013

The Bishops of the United States Catholic Conference in Baltimore, gathered for their Nov. 12-13 fall general meeting.

Agenda:

The bishops acted on a variety of issues:

• Issued a "Special Message" on the HHS Mandate.

• Sent a message of solidarity and support for the people of the Philippines in the wake of Typhoon Haiyan and heard a report on the work of Catholic Relief Services.

• Approved the drafting of a formal statement on pornography to be issued from the entire body of bishops.

• Approved five liturgical items presented by the Committee on Divine Worship, including the use of the Mexican missal to draft the U.S. Spanish-language missal with appropriate adaptations, adding adaptations to the marriage ceremony and on proposed English-language translations of the Order of Celebrating Marriage and the Order of Confirmation.

• Approved the addition of a new staff person to the Secretariat of Pro-Life Activities to work on a national level with the post-abortion ministry Project Rachel.

• Approved a budget for 2014 and a 3% increase in the diocesan assessment for 2015.

• Heard a report from Abp. Salvatore J. Cordileone of San Francisco, chairman of the Subcommittee on the Promotion and Defense of Marriage on the U.S. Supreme Court's ruling against Defense of Marriage Act (DOMA) and the U.S. Senate's passage of the Employment Non-Discrimination Act.

• The Subcommittee on the Church in Latin America approved $2.46 Million for 164 grants to 20 countries in Latin America and the Caribbean.

• Received an update on the reconstruction work accomplished in Haiti.

• Elected a number of officers and committee heads including: Abp. Joseph Kurtz of Louisville as president of the USCCB and Cardinal Daniel DiNardo of Galveston-Houston as vice president; Abp. George Lucas of Omaha as chairman of the Committee of Catholic Education; Coadjutor Abp. Bernard A. Hebda of Newark, New Jersey, to the Committee on Canonical Affairs and Church Governance; Bp. Mitchell T. Rozanski,

auxiliary bishop of Baltimore, to the Committee on Ecumenical and Interreligious Affairs; Abp. Leonard Blair of Hartford to the Committee on Evangelization and Catechesis; Bp. Oscar Cantú of Las Cruces to the Committee on International Justice and Peace; Bp. Edward Burns of Juneau to the Committee on Child and Youth Protection; Bp. Arthur Serratelli of Paterson as chair of the Committee on Divine Worship to replace Cardinal DiNardo.

June 10-14, 2014

The Bishops gathered for their annual Spring Assembly from June 10-13, 2014, in New Orleans, LA.

They acted on the following issues:

The public sessions of the meetings took place June 11 and the morning of June 12 before the bishops went into executive session.

• Heard a report by the National Review Board on the progress that has been made in efforts to protect children from sexual abuse.

• Heard a report aid to typhoon victims in the Philippines.

• Approved a three-year extension of the Ad Hoc Committee on Religious Liberty.

• Approved a limited revision of the 2007 statement "Forming Consciences for Faithful Citizenship" and the draft of a new introductory note for it. The revision and draft will be presented for a vote by the U.S. bishops at their annual fall assembly in November.

• Voted to permit the Committee on Clergy, Consecrated Life and Vocations to seek a renewed recognitio, or approval, from the Vatican for the National Directory for the Formation, Ministry and Life of Permanent Deacons in the United States.

• Officially invited Pope Francis to attend the World Meeting of Families in September 2015 in Philadelphia.

• Heard from Helen Alvare, law professor at George Mason University Law School, in Arlington, Virginia, on the link between new evangelization and poverty.

• Heard from Brad Wilcox, associate professor of sociology and director of the National Marriage Project at the University of Virginia, on marriage and the economy.

Doctrine of the Catholic Church

THE CATECHISM OF THE CATHOLIC CHURCH

By Russell Shaw

"The Catechism of the Catholic Church ... is a statement of the Church's faith and of Catholic doctrine, attested to or illumined by Sacred Scripture, the Apostolic Tradition and the Church's Magisterium. I declare it to be a sure norm for teaching the faith and thus a valid and legitimate instrument for ecclesial communion."

Thus Pope John Paul II in the Apostolic Constitution *Fidei Depositum* ("The Deposit of Faith") formally presented the first official catechism or compendium of doctrine for the universal Church to have been published since the 16th century.

Fidei Depositum is dated Oct. 11, 1992, the 30th anniversary of the opening of the Second Vatican Council (1962-65), and that date is significant. The predecessor of the *Catechism of the Catholic Church* is the Roman Catechism or Catechism of the Council of Trent, which was published by Pope St. Pius V in 1566 following the great reforming council held from 1545 to 1563. As the Roman Catechism sets forth the doctrine of the Church in light of the Council of Trent, so the Catechism of the Catholic Church sets forth the Church's teaching against the background of Vatican Council II.

History of the Catechism

In development since 1986, the definitive text of the *Catechism of the Catholic Church* was officially approved by Pope John Paul on June 25, 1992, with Dec. 8 the date of formal promulgation.

Nine separate drafts of the *Catechism* were prepared. The document was written in French. In November 1989, the commission of cardinals sent a draft text to all the bishops of the world asking for their comments and suggestions. Although this consultation produced a reaction generally favorable to the text, more than 24,000 individual amendments were submitted by the bishops, and these were reviewed by the commission, and helped to shape the further revision of the document.

The pope in *Fidei Depositum* described the *Catechism* as "a sure and authentic reference text" both for the teaching of Catholic doctrine and particularly for the preparation of local catechisms; he said the *Catechism* was presented to "all the Church's Pastors and the Christian faithful" with these ends in view. Other purposes mentioned included helping Catholics to deepen their knowledge of the faith, supporting ecumenical efforts by "showing carefully the content and wondrous harmony of the Catholic faith," and providing authoritative answers to anyone who wishes to know "what the Catholic Church believes."

Structure and Contents of the Catechism

The *Catechism* adopts the four-fold division of the *Roman Catechism*. The four parts or "pillars" deal with the Creed; the Sacred Liturgy, with special emphasis on the sacraments; the Christian way of life, analyzed according to the Ten Commandments; and prayer, considered in the framework of the petitions of the Our Father.

Describing this organizational scheme, Pope John Paul said: "The four parts are related one to another: the Christian mystery is the object of faith (first part); it is celebrated and communicated in liturgical actions (second part); it is present to enlighten and sustain the children of God in their actions (third part); it is the basis of our prayer, the privileged expression of which is the Our Father, and it represents the object of our supplication, our praise and our intercession (fourth part)."

The pope also stressed the Christocentric nature of Christian faith as it is presented in the *Catechism*. "In reading the *Catechism of the Catholic Church* we can perceive the wonderful unity of the mystery of God, his saving will, as well as the central place of Jesus Christ, the only-begotten Son of God, sent by the Father, made man in the womb of the Blessed Virgin Mary by the power of the Holy Spirit, to be our Savior. Having died and risen, Christ is always present in his Church, especially in the sacraments; he is the source of our faith, the model of Christian conduct, and the Teacher of our prayer."

The text of the *Catechism of the Catholic Church*, with extensive cross-references and sectional summaries, consists of 2,865 numbered paragraphs. Passages in large print set out its more substantive contents, while passages in small print provide background information and explanations; there are numerous cross-references in the margins directing readers to other passages that treat the same theme or related themes. Among the features of the *Catechism* are the "In Brief" sections found throughout, which sum up the teaching of the preceding unit.

OUTLINE OF THE CATECHISM

Prologue (1-25)

The nature of catechesis is described, along with the aim of the present *Catechism* and its intended readership, its structure, its use, and the desirability of adaptations for different cultures, age groups, etc.

Part One: The Profession of Faith (26-1065)

Section One discusses the nature of faith. "Faith is man's response to God, who reveals himself and gives himself to man, at the same time bringing man a superabundant light as he searches for the ultimate meaning of his life. Thus we shall consider first that search (Chapter One), then the divine Revelation by which God comes to meet man (Chapter Two), and finally the response of faith (Chapter Three)" (26). The topics discussed include knowledge of God; Divine Revelation and its transmission; Sacred Scripture; and faith as the human response to God. "We do not believe in formulas, but in those realities they express, which faith allows us to touch.... All the same, we do approach these realities with the help of formulations of the faith which permit us to express the faith and to hand it on, to celebrate it in community, to assimilate and live on it more and more" (170).

Section Two deals with the profession of Christian faith, with the treatment organized according to the articles of the Creed. The Creed used is the Apostles' Creed; its "great authority," says the *Catechism*, quoting St. Ambrose, arises from its being "the Creed of the Roman Church, the See of Peter, the first of the apostles" (194). Among the doctrines covered in the three chapters of this section are the Trinity, creation, the angels, the creation of man, original sin, the Incarnation, the virgin birth, redemption, the Resurrection of Christ, the work of the Holy Spirit, the Church, the hierarchical constitution of the Church, the communion of saints, the Virgin Mary as Mother of Christ and Mother of the Church, the resurrection of the dead, judgment, heaven, and hell. "[T]he Creed's final 'Amen' repeats and confirms its first words: 'I believe.' To believe is to say 'Amen' to God's words, promises and commandments; to entrust oneself completely to him who is the 'Amen' of infinite love and perfect faithfulness. The Christian's everyday life will then be the 'Amen' to the 'I believe' of our baptismal profession of faith" (1064).

Part Two: The Celebration of the Christian Mystery (1066-1690)

Section One considers the sacramental economy. It explains that in this present "age of the Church," begun on Pentecost, "Christ now lives and acts in his Church, in a new way appropriate to this new age. He acts through the sacraments in what the common Tradition of the East and the West calls 'the sacramental economy'... the communication (or 'dispensation') of the fruits of Christ's Paschal Mystery in the celebration of the Church's 'sacramental' liturgy" (1076). Topics treated here are the Paschal Mystery and its sacramental celebration.

Section Two covers the seven sacraments of the Church. "Christ instituted the sacraments of the new law.... The seven sacraments touch all the stages and all the important moments of Christian life: they give birth and increase, healing and mission to the Christian's life of faith. There is thus a certain resemblance between the stages of natural life and the stages of the spiritual life" (1210). The presentation is organized in four chapters. These are: the sacraments of Christian initiation (Baptism, Confirmation, the Eucharist) in chapter one; the sacraments of healing (Penance and Reconciliation, the Anointing of the Sick) in chapter two; the "sacraments at the service of communion" (Holy Orders and Matrimony) in chapter three; and sacramentals and Christian funerals in chapter four.

Part Three: Life in Christ (1691-2557)

Section One is entitled "Man's Vocation: Life in the Spirit." Its three chapters discuss the dignity of the human person, the human community, and "God's Salvation: Law and Grace" (the moral law, grace and justification, the Church as teacher of moral truth). "Catechesis has to reveal in all clarity the joy and the demands of the way of Christ.... The first and last point of reference of this catechesis will always be Jesus Christ himself, who is 'they way, and the truth, and the life'" (1697-1698).

Section Two reflects on the contents of Christian moral life. The treatment is organized according to the Ten Commandments, with a chapter devoted to each commandment and its concrete applications. While the commandments admit of what is traditionally called light matter (venial sin), nevertheless, the text says: "Since they express man's fundamental duties towards God and towards his neighbor, the Ten Commandments reveal, in their primordial content, grave obligations. They are fundamentally immutable, and they oblige always and everywhere. No one can dispense from them. The Ten Commandments are engraved by God in the human heart" (2072).

Part Four: Christian Prayer (2558-2865)

Section One considers prayer in Christian life, underlining the relationship of this topic to the rest of the *Catechism*: "The Church professes this mystery [of faith] in the Apostles' Creed (Part One) and celebrates it in the sacramental liturgy (Part Two), so that the life of the faithful may be conformed to Christ in the Holy Spirit to the glory of God the Father (Part Three). This mystery, then, requires that the faithful believe in it, that they celebrate it, and that they live from it in a vital and personal relationship with the living and true God. This relationship is prayer" (2558). The section then discusses the "revelation of prayer" in the Old Testament and now in the age of the Church, the tradition of prayer, and the life of prayer (kinds of prayer, problems and perseverance in prayer).

Section Two presents an extended reflection on the Our Father, considered as the model of prayer. Quoting Tertullian, the *Catechism* says: "The Lord's Prayer 'is truly the summary of the whole Gospel.' 'Since the Lord ... after handing over the practice of prayer, said elsewhere, 'Ask and you will receive,' and since everyone has petitions which are peculiar to his circumstances, the regular and appropriate prayer [the Lord's Prayer] is said first, as the foundation of further desires'" (2761).

Reception of the Catechism

Following the publication of the *Catechism of the Catholic Church*, Pope John Paul established an Interdicasterial Commission for the Catechism, under the chairmanship of Cardinal Ratzinger, responsible for overseeing translations of the volume and reviewing and approving suggested changes in the text. The commission approved the English translation of the *Catechism* in February 1994, and it was published on June 22 of that year — in the United States, under the auspices of the National Conference of Catholic Bishops.

Pope John Paul presented the *editio typica* or normative Latin version of the *Catechism* in a formal ceremony on Sept. 8, 1997.

The following day, Cardinal Ratzinger presented the *editio typica* at a Vatican news conference. At the same time, he also introduced more than a hundred changes which had been approved for incorporation into the text. Most of the changes were of a minor, editorial nature. The most important was in paragraphs 2265-2267 of the *Catechism*, where the treatment of capital punishment had been strengthened to reflect the discussion of the same topic in Pope John Paul's 1995 encyclical letter *Evangelium Vitae* (*"The Gospel of Life"*).

In the United States, the National Conference of Catholic Bishops in 1994 established an Ad Hoc Committee to Oversee the Use of the Catechism. It has an office and staff at NCCB headquarters in Washington, DC. The committee reviews and approves materials that seek to make substantial direct use of the text of the *Catechism of the Catholic Church*, and also reviews catechetical series for their conformity with the *Catechism*. In addition, the committee was mandated to conduct a feasibility study of a national catechism or catechetical series for the United States.

Compendium of the Catechism

On June 28, 2005, Pope Benedict XVI issued a *motu proprio* for the approval and publication of the *Compendium of the Catechism of the Catholic Church*. The Holy Father declared in his *motu proprio*:

"The *Compendium*, which I now present to the Universal Church, is a faithful and sure synthesis of the *Catechism of the Catholic Church*. It contains, in concise form, all the essential and fundamental elements of the Church's faith, thus constituting, as my Predecessor had wished, a kind of *vademecum* which allows believers and non-believers alike to behold the entire panorama of the Catholic faith.

"In its structure, contents and language, the *Compendium* faithfully reflects the *Catechism of the Catholic Church* and will thus assist in making the Catechism more widely known and more deeply understood."

The Introduction to the *Compendium*, written by Joseph Cardinal Ratzinger prior to his election as pope, described the process by which the text came about, namely to realize more fully the potential of the *Catechism* and to provide a synthesis of the vast treasure of its teachings. Then Cardinal Ratzinger noted its three principal characteristics: "the close reliance on the *Catechism of the Catholic Church*; the dialogical format; the use of artistic images in the catechesis."

Like the *Catechism*, the Compendium offers four parts, corresponding to the fundamental laws of life in Christ. Part one is "The Profession of Faith"; part two is "The Celebration of the Christian Mystery"; part three is "Life in Christ"; and the fourth part is "Christian Prayer."

DOGMATIC CONSTITUTION ON THE CHURCH — *LUMEN GENTIUM*

Following are excerpts from the first two chapters of the "Dogmatic Constitution on the Church" (*Lumen Gentium*) promulgated by the Second Vatican Council. They describe the relation of the Catholic Church to the Kingdom of God, the nature and foundation of the Church, the People of God, the necessity of membership and participation in the Church for salvation. Additional subjects in the constitution are treated in other *Almanac* entries.

I. MYSTERY OF THE CHURCH

By her relationship with Christ, the Church is a kind of sacrament or sign of intimate union with God, and of the unity of all mankind (No. 1).

He (the eternal Father) planned to assemble in the holy Church all those who would believe in Christ. Already from the beginning of the world the foreshadowing of the Church took place. She was prepared for in a remarkable way throughout the history of the people of Israel and by means of the Old Covenant. Established in the present era of time, the Church was made manifest by the outpouring of the Spirit. At the end of time she will achieve her glorious fulfillment. Then all just men from the time of Adam, "from Abel, the just one, to the last of the elect," will be gathered together with the Father in the universal Church (No. 2).

When the work which the Father had given the Son to do on earth (cf. Jn 17:4) was accomplished, the Holy Spirit was sent on the day of Pentecost in order that he might forever sanctify the Church, and thus all believers would have access to the Father through Christ in the one Spirit (cf. Eph 2:18).

The Spirit dwells in the Church and in the hearts of the faithful as in a temple (cf. 1 Cor 3:16; 6:19).... The Spirit guides the Church into the fullness of truth (cf. Jn 16:13) and gives her a unity of fellowship and service. He furnishes and directs her with various gifts, both hierarchical and charismatic, and adorns her with the fruits of His grace (cf. Eph 4:11-12; 1 Cor 12:4; Gal 5:22). By the power of the Gospel he makes the Church grow, perpetually renews her, and leads her to perfect union with her Spouse (No. 4).

Foundation of the Church

The mystery of the holy Church is manifest in her very foundation, for the Lord Jesus inaugurated her by preaching the Good News, that is, the coming of God's Kingdom, which, for centuries, had been promised in the Scriptures.... In Christ's word, in his works, and in his presence this Kingdom reveals itself to men.

The miracles of Jesus also confirm that the Kingdom has already arrived on earth.

Before all things, however, the Kingdom is clearly visible in the very Person of Christ, Son of God and Son of Man.

When Jesus rose up again after suffering death on the cross for mankind, he manifested that he had been appointed Lord, Messiah, and Priest forever (cf. Acts 2:36; Heb 5:6; 7:17-21), and he poured out on his disciples the Spirit promised by the Father (cf. Acts 2:33). The Church, consequently, equipped with the gifts of her Founder and faithfully guarding his precepts receives the mission to proclaim and to establish among all peoples the Kingdom of Christ and of God. She becomes on earth the initial budding forth of that Kingdom. While she slowly grows, the Church strains toward the consummation of the Kingdom and, with all her strength, hopes and desires to be united in glory with her King (No. 5).

Figures of the Church

In the Old Testament the revelation of the Kingdom had often been conveyed by figures of speech. In the same way the inner nature of the Church was now to be made known to us through various images.

The Church is a sheepfold ... a flock ... a tract of land to be cultivated, the field of God ... his choice vineyard ... the true vine is Christ ... the edifice of God ... the house of God ... the holy temple (whose members are) living stones ... this holy city ... a bride ... our Mother ... the spotless spouse of the spotless Lamb ... an exile (No. 6).

In the human nature which he united to himself, the Son of God redeemed man and transformed him into a new creation (cf. Gal 6:15; 2 Cor 5:17) by overcoming death through his own death and resurrection. By communicating his Spirit to his brothers, called together from all peoples, Christ made them mystically into his own body.

In that body, the life of Christ is poured into the believers, who, through the sacraments, are united in a hidden and real way to Christ who suffered and was glorified. Through baptism we are formed in the likeness of Christ.

Truly partaking of the body of the Lord in the breaking of the eucharistic bread, we are taken up into communion with him and with one another (No. 7).

One Body in Christ

As all the members of the human body, though they are many, form one body, so also are the faithful in Christ (cf. 1 Cor 12:12). Also, in the building up of Christ's body there is a flourishing variety of members and functions. There is only one Spirit who distributes his different gifts for the welfare of the Church (cf. 1 Cor 12:1-11). Among these gifts stands out the grace given to the apostles. To their authority, the Spirit himself subjected even those who were endowed with charisms (cf. 1 Cor 14). The head of this body is Christ (No. 7).

Mystical Body of Christ

Christ, the one Mediator, established and ceaselessly sustains here on earth his holy Church, the community of faith, hope, and charity, as a visible structure. Through her he communicates truth and grace to all. But the society furnished with hierarchical agencies and the Mystical Body of Christ are not to be considered as two realities, nor are the visible assembly and the spiritual community, nor the earthly Church and the Church enriched with heavenly things. Rather they form one interlocked reality which is comprised of a divine and a human element. For this reason, this reality is compared to the mystery of the incarnate Word. Just as the assumed nature inseparably united to the divine Word serves him as a living instrument of salvation, so, in a similar way, does the communal structure of the Church serve Christ's Spirit, who vivifies it by way of building up the body (cf. Eph 4:16).

This is the unique Church of Christ which in the Creed we avow as one, holy, catholic, and apostolic. After his Resurrection our Savior handed her over to Peter to be shepherded (Jn 21:17), commissioning him and the other apostles to propagate and govern her (cf. Mt 28:18, ff.). Her he erected for all ages as "the pillar and mainstay of the truth" (1 Tm 3:15). This Church, constituted and organized in the world as a society, subsists in the Catholic Church, which is governed by the successor of Peter and by the bishops in union with that successor, although many elements of sanctification and of truth can be found outside of her visible structure. These elements, however, as gifts properly belonging to the Church of Christ, possess an inner dynamism toward Catholic unity.

The Church, embracing sinners in her bosom, is at the same time holy and always in need of being purified, and incessantly pursues the path of penance and renewal.

The Church, "like a pilgrim in a foreign land, presses forward, announcing the cross and death of the Lord until he comes" (cf. 1 Cor 11:26) (No. 8).

II. THE PEOPLE OF GOD

At all times and among every people, God has given welcome to whosoever fears him and does what is right (cf. Acts 10:35). It has pleased God, however, to make men holy and save them not merely as individuals without any mutual bonds, but by making them into a single people, a people which acknowledges him in truth and serves him in holiness. He therefore chose the race of Israel as a people unto himself. With it he set up a covenant. Step by step he taught this people by manifesting in its history both himself and the decree of his will, and by making it holy unto himself. All these things, however, were done by way of preparation and as a figure of that new and perfect covenant which was to be ratified in Christ.

Christ instituted this New Covenant, that is to say, the New Testament, in his blood (cf. 1 Cor 11:25), by calling together a people made up of Jew and Gentile, making them one, not according to the flesh but in the Spirit.

This was to be the new People of God ... reborn ... through the Word of the living God (cf. 1 Pt 1:23). from water and the Holy Spirit (cf. Jn 3:5-6) ... "a chosen race, a royal priesthood, a holy nation, a purchased people. You who in times past were not a people, but are now the People of God" (1 Pt 2:9-10).

That messianic people has for its head Christ. Its law is the new commandment to love as Christ loved us (cf. Jn 13:34). Its goal is the Kingdom of God, which has been begun by God himself on earth, and which is to be further extended until it is brought to perfection by him at the end of time.

This messianic people, although it does not actually include all men, and may more than once look like a small flock, is nonetheless a lasting and sure seed of unity, hope, and salvation for the whole human race. Established by Christ as a fellowship of life, charity, and truth, it is also used by him as an instrument for the redemption of all, and is sent forth into the whole world as the light of the world and the salt of the earth (cf. Mt 5:13-16).

Israel according to the flesh ... was already called the Church of God (Neh 13:1; cf. Nm 20:4; Dt 23:1, ff.). Likewise the new Israel ... is also called the Church of Christ (cf. Mt 16:18). For he has bought it for himself with his blood (cf. Acts 20:28), has filled it with his Spirit, and provided it with those means which befit it as a visible and social unity. God has gathered together as one all those who in faith look upon Jesus as the author of salvation and the source of unity and peace, and has established them as the Church, that for each and all she may be the visible sacrament of this saving unity (No. 9).

Priesthood

The baptized, by regeneration and the anointing of the Holy Spirit, are consecrated into a holy priesthood.

[All members of the Church participate in the priesthood of Christ, through the common priesthood of the faithful. See **Priesthood of the Laity**.]

Though they differ from one another in essence and not only in degree, the common priesthood of the faithful and the ministerial or hierarchical priesthood are nonetheless interrelated. Each of them in its own special way is a participation in the one priesthood of Christ (No. 10).

It is through the sacraments and the exercise of the virtues that the sacred nature and organic structure of the priestly community is brought into operation (No. 11). (*See* **Role of the Sacraments**.)

Prophetic Office

The holy People of God shares also in Christ's prophetic office. It spreads abroad a living witness to him, especially by means of a life of faith and charity and by offering to God a sacrifice of praise.... The body of the faithful as a whole, anointed as they are by the Holy One (cf. Jn 2:20, 27), cannot err in matters of belief. Thanks to a supernatural sense of faith which characterizes the People as a whole, it manifests this unerring quality when, "from the bishops down to the last member of the laity," it shows universal agreement in matters of faith and morals.

God's People accepts not the word of men but the very Word of God (cf. 1 Thes 2:13). It clings without fail to the faith once delivered to the saints (cf. Jude 3), penetrates it more deeply by accurate insights, and applies it more thoroughly to life. All this it does under the lead of a sacred teaching authority to which it loyally defers.

It is not only through the sacraments and Church ministries that the same Holy Spirit sanctifies and leads the People of God.... He distributes special graces among the faithful of every rank. By these gifts he makes them fit and ready to undertake the various tasks or offices advantageous for the renewal and upbuilding of the Church. These charismatic gifts ... are to be received with thanksgiving and consolation, for they are exceedingly suitable and useful for the needs of the Church.

Judgment as to their genuineness and proper use belongs to those who preside over the Church, and to whose special competence it belongs ... to test all things and hold fast to that which is good (cf. 1 Thes 5:12; 19-21) (No. 12).

All Are Called

All men are called to belong to the new People of God. Wherefore this People, while remaining one and unique, is to be spread throughout the whole world and must exist in all ages, so that the purpose of God's will may be fulfilled. In the beginning God made human nature one. After his children were scattered, he decreed that they should at length be united again (cf. Jn 11:52). It was for this reason that God sent his Son.... that he might be Teacher, King, and Priest of all, the Head of the new and universal People of the sons of God. For this God finally sent his Son's Spirit as Lord and Lifegiver. He it is who, on behalf of the whole Church and each and every one of those who believe, is the principle of their coming together and remaining together in the teaching of the apostles and in fellowship, in the breaking of bread and in prayers (cf. Acts 2:42) (No. 13).

One People of God

It follows that among all the nations of earth there is but one People of God, which takes its citizens from every race, making them citizens of a Kingdom which is of a heavenly and not an earthly nature. For all the faithful scattered throughout the world are in communion with each other in the Holy Spirit.... the Church or People of God foster(s) and take(s) to herself, insofar as they are good, the ability, resources and customs of each people. Taking them to herself, she purifies, strengthens, and ennobles them.... This characteristic of universality which adorns the People of God is a gift from the Lord himself. By reason of it, the Catholic Church strives energetically and constantly to bring all humanity with all its riches back to Christ its Head in the unity of his Spirit.

In virtue of this catholicity each individual part of the Church contributes through its special gifts to the good of the other parts and of the whole Church. Thus through the common sharing of gifts. The whole and each of the parts receive increase.

All men are called to be part of this catholic unity of the People of God. And there belong to it or are related to it in various ways, the Catholic faithful as well as all who believe in Christ, and indeed the whole of mankind. For all men are called to salvation by the grace of God (No. 13).

The Catholic Church

This sacred Synod turns its attention first to the Catholic faithful. Basing itself upon sacred Scripture and tradition, it teaches that the Church is necessary for salvation. For Christ, made present to us in his Body, which is the Church, is the one Mediator and the unique Way of salvation. In explicit terms he himself affirmed the necessity of faith and baptism (cf. Mk 16:16; Jn 3:5) and thereby affirmed also the necessity of the Church, for through baptism as through a door men enter the Church. Whosoever, therefore, knowing that the Catholic Church was made necessary by God through Jesus Christ, would refuse to enter her or to remain in her could not be saved.

They are fully incorporated into the society of the Church who, possessing the Spirit of Christ, accept her entire system and all the means of salvation given to her, and through union with her visible structure are joined to Christ, who rules her through the Supreme Pontiff and the bishops. This joining is effected by the bonds of professed faith, of the sacraments, of ecclesiastical government, and of communion. He is not saved, however, who, though he is part of the body of the Church, does not persevere in charity. He remains indeed in the bosom of the Church, but only in a "bodily" manner and not "in his heart."

Catechumens who, moved by the Holy Spirit, seek with

explicit intention to be incorporated into the Church, are by that very intention joined to her. Mother Church already embraces them as her own (No. 14).

Other Christians, The Unbaptized

The Church recognizes that in many ways she is linked with those who, being baptized, are honored with the name of Christian, though they do not profess the faith in its entirety or do not preserve unity of communion with the successor of Peter.

We can say that in some real way they are joined with us in the Holy Spirit, for to them also he gives his gifts and graces, and is thereby operative among them with his sanctifying power (No. 15).

Finally, those who have not yet received the Gospel are related in various ways to the People of God. In the first place there is the people to whom the covenants and the promises were given and from whom Christ was born according to the flesh (cf. Rom 9:4-5). On account of their fathers, this people remains most dear to God, for God does not repent of the gifts he makes nor of the calls he issues (cf. Rom 11:28-29).

But the plan of salvation also includes those who acknowledge the Creator. In the first place among these are the Moslems. Nor is God himself far distant from those who in shadows and images seek the unknown God.

Those also can attain to everlasting salvation who through no fault of their own do not know the Gospel of Christ or his Church, yet sincerely seek God and, moved by grace, strive by their deeds to do his will as it is known to them through the dictates of conscience. Nor does divine Providence deny the help necessary for salvation to those who, without blame on their part, have not yet arrived at an explicit knowledge of God, but who strive to live a good life, thanks to his grace. Whatever goodness or truth is found among them is looked upon by the Church as a preparation for the Gospel. She regards such qualities as given by him who enlightens all men so that they may finally have life. (No. l6).

THE POPE, TEACHING AUTHORITY, COLLEGIALITY

The Roman Pontiff — the successor of St. Peter as the bishop of Rome and head of the Church on earth — has full and supreme authority over the universal Church in matters pertaining to faith and morals (teaching authority), discipline and government (jurisdictional authority).

The primacy of the pope is real and supreme power. It is not merely a prerogative of honor — that is, of his being regarded as the first among equals. Neither does primacy imply that the pope is just the presiding officer of the collective body of bishops. The pope is the head of the Church.

Catholic belief in the primacy of the pope was stated in detail in the dogmatic constitution on the Church, *Pastor Aeternus*, approved in 1870 by the fourth session of the First Vatican Council. Some elaboration of the doctrine was made in the Dogmatic Constitution on the Church which was approved and promulgated by the Second Vatican Council Nov. 21, 1964. The entire body of teaching on the subject is based on Scripture and tradition and the centuries-long experience of the Church.

Infallibility

The essential points of doctrine concerning infallibility in the Church and the infallibility of the pope were stated by the Second Vatican Council in the Dogmatic Constitution on the Church, as follows:

"This infallibility with which the divine Redeemer willed his Church to be endowed in defining a doctrine of faith and morals extends as far as extends the deposit of divine revelation, which must be religiously guarded and faithfully expounded. This is the infallibility which the Roman Pontiff, the head of the college of bishops, enjoys in virtue of his office, when, as the supreme shepherd and teacher of all the faithful who confirms his brethren in their faith (cf. Lk 22:32), he proclaims by a definitive act some doctrine of faith or morals. Therefore his definitions, of themselves, and not from the consent of the Church, are justly styled irreformable, for they are pronounced with the assistance of the Holy Spirit, an assistance promised to him in blessed Peter. Therefore they need no approval of others, nor do they allow an appeal to any other judgment. For then the Roman Pontiff is not pronouncing judgment as a private person. Rather, as the supreme teacher of the universal Church, as one in whom the charism of the infallibility of the Church herself is individually present, he is expounding or defending a doctrine of Catholic faith.

"The infallibility promised to the Church resides also in the body of bishops when that body exercises supreme teaching authority with the successor of Peter. To the resultant definitions the assent of the Church can never be wanting, on account of the activity of that same Holy Spirit, whereby the whole flock of Christ is preserved and progresses in unity of faith.

"But when either the Roman Pontiff or the body of bishops together with him defines a judgment, they pronounce it in accord with revelation itself. All are obliged to maintain and be ruled by this revelation, which, as written or preserved by tradition, is transmitted in its entirety through the legitimate succession of bishops and especially through the care of the Roman Pontiff himself.

"Under the guiding light of the Spirit of truth, revelation is thus religiously preserved and faithfully expounded in the Church. The Roman Pontiff and the bishops, in view of their office and of the importance of the matter, strive painstakingly and by appropriate means to inquire properly into that revelation and to give apt expression to its contents. But they do not allow that there could be any new public revelation pertaining to the divine deposit of faith" (No. 25).

Authentic Teaching

The pope rarely speaks *ex cathedra* — that is, "from the chair" of St. Peter — for the purpose of making an infallible pronouncement. More often and in various ways he states authentic teaching in line with Scripture, tradition, the living experience of the Church, and the whole analogy of faith. Of such teaching, the Second Vatican Council said in its Dogmatic Constitution on the Church (No. 25):

"Religious submission of will and of mind must be shown in a special way to the authentic teaching authority of the Roman Pontiff, even when he is not speaking *ex cathedra*. That is, it must be shown in such a way that his supreme magisterium is acknowledged with reverence, the judgments made by him are sincerely adhered to, according to his manifest mind and will. His mind and will in the matter may be known chiefly either from the character of the documents, from his frequent repetition of the same doctrine, or from his manner of speaking."

Bishops "are authentic teachers, that is, teachers endowed with the authority of Christ, who preach to the people committed to them the faith they must believe and put into practice. By the light of the Holy Spirit, they make that faith clear, bringing forth from the treasury of revelation new things and old (cf. Mt 13:52), making faith bear fruit and vigilantly warding off any errors which threaten their flock (cf. 2 Tm 4:1-4).

"Bishops, teaching in communion with the Roman Pontiff, are to be respected by all as witnesses to divine and Catholic truth. In matters of faith and morals, the bishops speak in the name of Christ and the faithful are to accept their teaching and adhere to it with a religious assent of soul."

Magisterium — Teaching Authority

Responsibility for teaching doctrine and judging orthodoxy belongs to the official teaching authority of the Church.

This authority is personalized in the pope, the successor of St. Peter as head of the Church, and in the bishops together and in union with the pope, as it was originally committed to Peter and to the whole college of apostles under his leadership. They are the official teachers of the Church.

Others have auxiliary relationships with the magisterium: theologians, in the study and clarification of doctrine; teachers — priests, religious, lay persons — who cooperate with the pope and bishops in spreading knowledge of religious truth; the faithful, who by their sense of faith and personal witness contribute to the development of doctrine and the establishment of its relevance to life in the Church and the world.

The magisterium, Pope Paul VI noted in an address at a general audience Jan. 11, 1967, "is a subordinate and faithful echo and secure interpreter of the divine word." It does not reveal new truths, "nor is it superior to sacred Scripture." Its competence extends to the limits of divine revelation manifested in Scripture and tradition and the living experience of the Church, with respect to matters of faith and morals and related subjects. Official teaching in these areas is infallible when it is formally defined, for belief and acceptance by all members of the Church, by the pope, acting in the capacity of supreme shepherd of the flock of Christ; also, when doctrine is proposed and taught with moral unanimity of bishops with the pope in a solemn collegial manner, as in an ecumenical council, and/or in the ordinary course of events. Even when not infallibly defined, official teaching in the areas of faith and morals is authoritative and requires religious assent.

The teachings of the magisterium have been documented in creeds, formulas of faith, decrees and enactments of ecumenical and particular councils, various kinds of doctrinal statements, encyclical letters and other teaching instruments. They have also been incorporated into the liturgy, with the result that the law of prayer is said to be a law of belief.

Collegiality

The bishops of the Church, in union with the pope, have supreme teaching and pastoral authority over the whole Church in addition to the authority of office they have for their own dioceses.

This collegial authority is exercised in a solemn manner in an ecumenical council and can be exercised in other ways as well, "provided that the head of the college calls them to collegiate action, or at least so approves or freely accepts the united action of the dispersed bishops that it is made a true collegiate act."

This doctrine is grounded on the fact that: "Just as, by the Lord's will, St. Peter and the other apostles constituted one apostolic college, so in a similar way the Roman Pontiff as the successor of Peter, and the bishops as the successors of the apostles are joined together."

Doctrine on collegiality was stated by the Second Vatican Council in the Dogmatic Constitution on the Church (Nos. 22 and 23).

(For coverage of the *Role of Mary in the Mystery of Christ and the Church,* Chapter VIII, *Lumen Gentium,* see the section on the Blessed Virgin Mary.)

REVELATION

Following are excerpts from the "Dogmatic Constitution on Divine Revelation" (*Dei Verbum*) promulgated by the Second Vatican Council. They describe the nature and process of divine revelation, inspiration and interpretation of Scripture, the Old and New Testaments, and the role of Scripture in the life of the Church.

I. REVELATION ITSELF

God chose to reveal himself and to make known to us the hidden purpose of his will (cf. Eph. 1:9) by which through Christ, the Word made flesh, man has access to the Father in the Holy Spirit and comes to share in the divine nature (cf. Eph 2:18; 2 Pt 1:4). Through this revelation, therefore, the invisible God (cf. Col 1:15; 1 Tm 1:17). speaks to men as friends (cf. Ex 33:11; Jn 15:14-15) and lives among them (cf. Bar 3:38) so that he may invite and take them into fellowship with himself. This plan of revelation is realized by deeds and words having an inner unity: the deeds wrought by God in the history of salvation manifest and confirm the teaching and realities signified by the words, while the words proclaim the deeds and clarify the mystery contained in them. By this revelation then, the deepest truth about God and the salvation of man is made clear to us in Christ, who is the Mediator and at the same time the fullness of all revelation (No. 2).

God from the start manifested himself to our first parents. Then after their fall his promise of redemption aroused in them the hope of being saved (cf. Gn 3:15), and from that time on he ceaselessly kept the human race in his care, in order to give eternal life to those who perseveringly do good in search of salvation (cf. Rom 2:6-7). He called Abraham in order to make of him a great nation (cf. Gn 12:2). Through the patriarchs, and after them through Moses and the prophets, he taught this nation to acknowledge himself as the one living and true God and to wait for the Savior promised by him. In this manner he prepared the way for the Gospel down through the centuries (No. 3).

Revelation in Christ

Then, after speaking in many places and varied ways through the prophets, God "last of all in these days has spoken to us by his Son" (Heb 1:1-2). Jesus perfected revelation by fulfilling it through his whole work of making himself present and manifesting himself: through his words and deeds, his signs and wonders, but especially through his death and glorious resurrection from the dead and final sending of the Spirit of truth. Moreover, he confirmed with divine testimony what revelation proclaimed: that God is with us to free us from the darkness of sin and death, and to raise us up to life eternal.

The Christian dispensation, therefore, as the new and definitive covenant, will never pass away, and we now await no further new public revelation before the glorious manifestation of our Lord Jesus Christ (cf. 1 Tm 6:14; Ti 2:13) (No. 4).

II. TRANSMISSION OF REVELATION

God has seen to it that what he had revealed for the salvation of all nations would abide perpetually in its full integrity and be handed on to all generations. Therefore Christ the Lord, in whom the full revelation of the supreme God is brought to completion (cf. 2 Cor 1:20; 3:16; 4:6), commissioned the apostles to preach to all men that Gospel which is the source of all saving truth and moral teaching, and thus to impart to them divine gifts. This Gospel had been promised in former times through the prophets, and Christ himself fulfilled it and promulgated it with his own lips. This commission was faithfully fulfilled by the apostles who, by their oral preaching, by example, and by ordinances, handed on what they had received from Christ or what they had learned through the prompting of the Holy Spirit. The commission was fulfilled, too, by those apostles and apostolic men who under the inspiration of the same Holy Spirit committed the message of salvation to writing (No. 7).

Tradition

But in order to keep the Gospel forever whole and alive within the Church, the apostles left bishops as their successors, "handing over their own teaching role" to them. This sacred tradition, therefore, and sacred Scripture of both the Old and the New Testament are like a mirror in which the pilgrim Church on earth looks at God (No. 7).

The apostolic preaching, which is expressed in a special way in the inspired books, was to be preserved by a continuous succession of preachers until the end of time. Therefore the apostles, handing on what they themselves had received, warn the faithful to hold fast to the traditions which they have learned. Now what was handed on by the apostles includes everything which contributes to the holiness of life, and the increase in faith of the People of God; and so the Church, in her teaching, life, and worship, perpetuates and hands on to all generations all that she herself is, all that she believes (No. 8).

Development of Doctrine

This tradition which comes from the apostles develops in the Church with the help of the Holy Spirit. For there is a growth in the understanding of the realities and the words which have been handed down. This happens through the contemplation and study made by believers through the intimate understanding of spiritual things they experience, and through the preaching of those who have received through episcopal succession the sure gift of truth. For, as the centuries succeed one another, the Church constantly moves forward toward the fullness of divine truth until the words of God reach their complete fulfillment in her.

The words of the holy Fathers witness to the living presence of this tradition, whose wealth is poured into the practice and life of the believing and praying Church. Through the same tradition the Church's full canon of the sacred books is known, and the sacred writings themselves are more profoundly understood and unceasingly made active in her; ... and the Holy Spirit, through whom the living voice of the Gospel resounds in the Church, and through her, in the world, leads unto all truth those who believe and makes the word of Christ dwell abundantly in them (cf. Col 3:16) (No. 8).

Tradition and Scripture

Hence there exist a close connection and communication between sacred tradition and sacred Scripture. For both of them, flowing from the same divine wellspring, in a certain way merge into a unity and tend toward the same end. For sacred Scripture is the word of God inasmuch as it is consigned to writing under the inspiration of the divine Spirit. To the successors of the apostles, sacred tradition hands on in its full purity God's word, which was entrusted to the apostles by Christ the Lord and the Holy Spirit. Thus, led by the light of the Spirit of truth, these successors can in their preaching preserve this word of God faithfully, explain it, and make it more widely known. Consequently, it is not from sacred Scripture alone that the Church draws her certainty about everything which has been revealed. Therefore both sacred tradition and sacred Scripture are to be accepted and venerated with the same sense of devotion and reverence (No. 9).

Sacred tradition and sacred Scripture form one sacred deposit of the word of God, which is committed to the Church (No. 10).

Teaching Authority of Church

The task of authentically interpreting the word of God, whether written or handed on, has been entrusted exclusively to the living teaching office of the Church, whose authority is exercised in the name of Jesus Christ. This teaching office is not above the word of God, but serves it, teaching only what has been handed on ... it draws from this one deposit of faith everything which it presents for belief as divinely revealed.

It is clear, therefore, that sacred tradition, sacred Scripture, and the teaching authority of the Church ... are so linked and joined together that one cannot stand without the others, and that all together and each in its own way under the action of the one Holy Spirit contribute effectively to the salvation of souls (No. 10).

III. INSPIRATION, INTERPRETATION

Those revealed realities contained and presented in sacred Scripture have been committed to writing under the inspiration of the Holy Spirit. Holy Mother Church, relying on the belief of the apostles, holds that the books of both the Old and New Testament in their entirety, with all their parts, are sacred and canonical because, having been written under the inspiration of the Holy Spirit (cf. Jn 20:31; 2 Tm 3:16; 2 Pt 1:19-21, 3:15-16) they have God as their author and have been handed on as such to the Church herself. In composing the sacred books, God chose men and, while employed by him, they made use of their powers and abilities, so that, with him acting in them and through them, they, as true authors, consigned to writing everything and only those things which he wanted (No. 11).

Inerrancy

Therefore, since everything asserted by the inspired authors or sacred writers must be held to be asserted by the Holy Spirit, it follows that the books of Scripture must be acknowledged as teaching firmly, faithfully, and without error that truth which God wanted put into the sacred writings for the sake of our salvation. Therefore "all Scripture is inspired by God and useful for teaching, for reproving, for correcting, for instruction in justice; that the man of God may be perfect, equipped for every good work" (2 Tm 3:16-17) (No. 11).

Literary Forms

However, since God speaks in sacred Scripture through men in human fashion, the interpreter of sacred Scripture, in order to see clearly what God wanted to communicate to us, should carefully investigate what meaning the sacred writers really intended, and what God wanted to manifest by means of their words.

The interpreter must investigate what meaning the sacred writer intended to express and actually expressed in particular circumstances as he used contemporary literary forms in accordance with the situation of his own time and culture. For the correct understanding of what the sacred author wanted to assert, due attention must be paid to the customary and characteristic styles of perceiving, speaking, and narrating which prevailed at the time of the sacred writer, and to the customs men normally followed at that period in their everyday dealings with one another (No. 12).

Analogy of Faith

No less serious attention must be given to the content and unity of the whole of Scripture, if the meaning of the sacred texts is to be correctly brought to light. The living tradition of the whole Church must be taken into account along with the harmony which exists between elements of the faith. All of what has been said about the way of interpreting Scripture is subject finally to the judgment of the Church, which carries out the divine commission and ministry of guarding and interpreting the word of God (No. 12).

IV. THE OLD TESTAMENT

In carefully planning and preparing the salvation of the whole human race, the God of supreme love, by a special dispensation, chose for himself a people to whom he might entrust his promises. First he entered into a covenant with Abraham (cf. Gn 15:18) and, through Moses, with the people of Israel (cf. Ex 24:8). To this people which he had acquired for himself, he so manifested himself through words and deeds as the one true and living God that Israel came to know by experience the ways of God with men. The plan of salvation, foretold by the sacred authors, recounted and explained by them, is found as the true word of God in the books of the Old Testament: these books, therefore, written under divine inspiration, remain permanently valuable (No. 14).

Principal Purpose

The principal purpose to which the plan of the Old Covenant was directed was to prepare for the coming both of Christ, the universal Redeemer, and of the messianic Kingdom. Now the books of the Old Testament, in accordance with the state of mankind before the time of salvation established by Christ, reveal to all men the knowledge of God and of man and the ways in which God deals with men. These books show us true divine pedagogy (No. 15).

The books of the Old Testament with all their parts, caught up into the proclamation of the Gospel, acquire and show forth their full meaning in the New Testament (cf. Mt 5:17; Lk 24:27; Rom 16:25-26; 2 Cor 3:14-16) and in turn shed light on it and explain it (No. 16).

V. THE NEW TESTAMENT

The word of God is set forth and shows its power in a most excellent way in the writings of the New Testament. For when the fullness of time arrived (cf. Gal 4:4), the Word was made flesh and dwelt among us in the fullness of grace and truth (cf. Jn 12:32). This mystery had not been manifested to other generations as it was now revealed to his holy apostles and prophets in the Holy Spirit (cf. Eph 3:4-6), so that they might preach the Gospel, stir up faith in Jesus, Christ and Lord, and gather the Church together. To these realities, the writings of the New Testament stand as a perpetual and divine witness (No. 17).

The Gospels and Other Writings

The Gospels have a special preeminence for they are the principal witness of the life and teaching of the incarnate Word, our Savior.

The Church has always and everywhere held and continues to hold that the four Gospels are of apostolic origin. For what the apostles preached afterwards they themselves and apostolic men, under the inspiration of the divine Spirit, handed on to us in writing: the foundation of faith, namely, the fourfold Gospel, according to Matthew, Mark, Luke, and John (No. 18).

The four Gospels ... whose historical character the Church unhesitatingly asserts, faithfully hand on what Jesus Christ, while living among men, really did and taught for their eternal salvation until the day he was taken up into heaven (see Acts 1:1-2). Indeed, after the ascension of the Lord the apostles handed on to their hearers what he had said and done. The sacred authors wrote the four Gospels, selecting some things from the many which had been handed on by word of mouth or in writing, reducing some of them to a synthesis, explicating some things in view of the situation of their churches, and preserving the form of proclamation but always in such fashion that they told us the honest truth about Jesus. For their intention in writing was that we might know "the truth" concerning those matters about which we have been instructed (cf. Lk 1:2-4) (No. 19).

Besides the four Gospels, the canon of the New Testament also contains the Epistles of St. Paul and other apostolic writings, composed under the inspiration of the Holy Spirit. In these writings those matters which concern Christ the Lord are confirmed, his true teaching is more and more fully stated, the saving power of the divine work of Christ is preached, the story is told of the beginnings of the Church and her marvelous growth, and her glorious fulfillment is foretold (No. 20).

VI. SCRIPTURE IN CHURCH LIFE

The Church has always venerated the divine Scriptures just as she venerates the body of the Lord. She has always regarded the Scriptures together with sacred tradition as the supreme rule of faith, and will ever do so. For, inspired by God and committed once and for all to writing, they impart the word of God himself without change, and make the voice of the Holy Spirit resound in the words of the prophets and apostles. Therefore, like the Christian religion itself, all the preaching of the Church must be nourished and ruled by sacred Scripture (No. 21).

Easy access to sacred Scripture should be provided for all the Christian faithful. That is why the Church from the very beginning accepted as her own that very ancient Greek translation of the Old Testament which is named after 70 men (the Septuagint); and she has always given a place of honor to other translations, Eastern and Latin, especially the one known as the Vulgate. But since the word of God should be available at all times, the Church with maternal concern sees to it that suitable and correct translations are made into different languages, especially from the original texts of the sacred books. And if, given the opportunity and the approval of Church authority, these translations are produced in cooperation with the separated brethren as well, all Christians will be able to use them (No. 22).

Biblical Studies, Theology

The constitution encouraged the development and progress of biblical studies "under the watchful care of the sacred teaching office of the Church."

It also noted: "Sacred theology rests on the written word of God, together with sacred tradition, as its primary and perpetual foundation," and that "the study of the sacred page is, as it were, the soul of sacred theology" (Nos. 23, 24).

(*See separate article,* **Interpretation of the Bible,** p.103.)

THE BIBLE

The Canon of the Bible is the Church's official list of sacred writings. These works, written by men under the inspiration of the Holy Spirit, contain divine revelation and, in conjunction with the tradition and teaching authority of the Church, constitute the rule of Catholic faith. The Canon was fixed and determined by the tradition and teaching authority of the Church.

The Catholic Canon

The Old Testament Canon of 46 books is as follows.

• **The Pentateuch**, the first five books: Genesis (Gn), Exodus (Ex), Leviticus (Lv), Numbers (Nm), Deuteronomy (Dt).

• **Historical Books**: Joshua (Jos), Judges (Jgs), Ruth (Ru) 1 and 2 Samuel (Sm), 1 and 2 Kings (Kgs), 1 and 2 Chronicles (Chr), Ezra (Ezr), Nehemiah (Neh), Tobit (Tb), Judith (Jdt), Esther (Est), 1 and 2 Maccabees (Mc).

• **Wisdom Books**: Job (Jb), Psalms (Ps), Proverbs (Prv), Ecclesiastes (Eccl), Song of Songs (Song), Wisdom (Wis), Sirach (Sir).

• **The Prophets**: Isaiah (Is), Jeremiah (Jer), Lamentations (Lam), Baruch (Bar), Ezekiel (Ez), Daniel (Dn), Hosea (Hos), Joel (Jl), Amos (Am), Obadiah (Ob), Jonah (Jon), Micah (Mi), Nahum (Na), Habakkuk (Hb), Zephaniah (Zep), Haggai (Hg), Zechariah (Zec) Malachi (Mal).

The New Testament Canon of 27 books is as follows.

• **The Gospels**: Matthew (Mt), Mark (Mk), Luke (Lk), John (Jn).

• **The Acts of the Apostles** (Acts).

• **The Pauline Letters**: Romans (Rom), 1 and 2 Corinthians (Cor), Galatians (Gal), Ephesians (Eph), Philippians (Phil), Colossians (Col), 1 and 2 Thessalonians (Thes) 1 and 2 Timothy (Tm), Titus (Ti), Philemon (Phlm), Hebrews (Heb).

• **The Catholic Letters**: James (Jas), 1 and 2 Peter (Pt), 1, 2, and 3 John (Jn), Jude (Jude).

• **Revelation** (Rv).

Developments

The Canon of the Old Testament was firm by the fifth century despite some questioning by scholars. It was stated by a council held at Rome in 382, by African councils held in Hippo in 393 and in Carthage in 397 and 419, and by Innocent I in 405.

All of the New Testament books were generally known and most of them were acknowledged as inspired by the end of the second century. The Muratorian Fragment, dating from about 200, listed most of the books recognized as canonical in later decrees. Prior to the end of the fourth century, however, there was controversy over the inspired character of several works — the Letter to the Hebrews, James, Jude, 2 Peter, 2 and 3 John and Revelation. Controversy ended in the fourth century and these books, along with those about which there was no dispute, were enumerated in the canon stated by the councils of Hippo and Carthage and affirmed by Innocent I in 405.

The Canon of the Bible was solemnly defined by the Council of Trent in the dogmatic decree *De Canonicis Scripturis,* Apr. 8, 1546.

Hebrew and Other Canons

The Hebrew Canon of sacred writings was fixed by tradition and the consensus of rabbis, probably by about 100 A.D. by the Synod or Council of Jamnia and certainly by the end of the second or early in the third century. It consists of the following works in three categories.

• **The Law** (Torah): the five books of Moses: Genesis, Exodus, Leviticus, Numbers, Deuteronomy.

• **The Prophets**: former prophets — Joshua, Judges, 1 and 2 Samuel, 1 and 2 Kings; latter prophets — Isaiah, Jeremiah, Ezekiel, and 12 minor prophets (Hosea, Joel, Amos, Obadiah, Jonah, Micah, Nahum, Habakkuk, Zephaniah, Haggai, Zechariah, Malachi).

• **The Writings**: 1 and 2 Chronicles, Ezra, Nehemiah, Job, Psalms, Proverbs, Ecclesiastes, Song of Songs, Ruth, Esther, Daniel.

This Canon, embodying the tradition and practice of the Palestine community, did not include a number of works contained in the Alexandrian version of sacred writings translated into Greek between 250 and 100 B.C. and in use by Greek-speaking Jews of the Dispersion (outside Palestine). The rejected works, called apocrypha and not regarded as sacred, are: Tobit, Judith, Wisdom, Sirach, Baruch, 1 and 2 Maccabees, the last six chapters of Esther and three passages of Daniel (3:24-90; 13; 14). These books have also been rejected from the Protestant Canon, although they are included in Bibles under the heading "*Apocrypha.*"

The aforementioned books are held to be inspired and sacred by the Catholic Church. In Catholic usage, they are called deuterocanonical because they were under discussion for some time before questions about their canonicity were settled. Books regarded as canonical with little or no debate were called protocanonical. The status of both categories of books is the same in the Catholic Bible.

The Protestant Canon of the Old Testament is the same as the Hebrew.

The Old Testament Canon of some separated Eastern churches differs from the Catholic Canon. Christians are in agreement on the Canon of the New Testament.

Languages

Hebrew, Aramaic and Greek were the original languages of the Bible. Most of the Old Testament books were written in Hebrew. Portions of Daniel, Ezra, Jeremiah, Esther, and probably the books of Tobit and Judith were written in Aramaic. The Book of Wisdom, 2 Maccabees and all the books of the New Testament were written in Greek (although there are traditions that Matthew's Gospel may have been based in part on materials in Aramaic).

Manuscripts and Versions

The original writings of the inspired authors have been lost. The Bible has been transmitted through ancient copies called manuscripts and through translations or versions.

Authoritative Greek manuscripts include the Sinaitic and Vatican manuscripts of the fourth century and the Alexandrine of the fifth century A.D. The Septuagint and Vulgate translations are in a class by themselves.

The Septuagint version, a Greek translation of the Old Testament for Greek-speaking Jews, was begun about 250 and completed about 100 B.C. The work of several Jewish translators at Alexandria, it differed from the Hebrew Bible in the arrangement of books and included several, later called deuterocanonical, which were not acknowledged as sacred by the community in Palestine.

The Vulgate was a Latin version of the Old and New Testaments produced from the original languages by St. Jerome from about 383 to 404. It became the most widely used Latin text for centuries and was regarded as basic long before the Council of Trent designated it as authentic and suitable for use in public reading, controversy, preaching and teaching. Because of its authoritative character, it became the basis for many translations into other languages. A critical revision was completed by a pontifical commission in 1977.

Hebrew and Aramaic manuscripts of great antiquity and value have figured more significantly than before in recent scriptural work by Catholic scholars, especially since their use was strongly encouraged, if not mandated, in 1943 by Pius XII in the encyclical *Divino Afflante Spiritu.*

The English translation of the Bible in general use among Catholics until well into the 20th century was the Douay-Rheims, so-called because of the places where it was prepared and published, the New Testament at Rheims in 1582 and the Old Testament at Douay in 1609. The translation was made from the Vulgate text. As revised and issued by Bp. Richard Challoner in 1749 and 1750, it became the standard Catholic English version for about 200 years.

A revision of the Challoner New Testament, made on the basis of the Vulgate text by scholars of the Catholic Biblical Association of America, was published in 1941 in the United States under the sponsorship of the Episcopal Committee of the Confraternity of Christian Doctrine.

New American Bible

A new translation of the entire Bible, the first ever made directly into English from the original languages under Catholic auspices, was projected in 1944 and completed in the fall of 1970 with publication of the *New American Bible.* The Episcopal Committee of the Confraternity of Christian Doctrine sponsored the NAB. The translators were members of the Catholic Biblical Association of America and scholars of other faiths. The typical edition was produced by St. Anthony Guild Press, Paterson, NJ.

The *Jerusalem Bible*, published by Doubleday & Co., Inc., is an English translation of a French version based on the original languages.

Biblical translations approved for liturgical use by the National Conference of Catholic Bishops and the Holy See are the *New American Bible* (1970 edition), the *Revised Standard Version-Catholic Edition*, and the *Jerusalem Bible* (1966).

The Protestant counterpart of the *Douay-Rheims Bible* was the *King James Bible*, called the *Authorized Version* in England. Originally published in 1611 and in general use for more than three centuries, its several revisions include the *Revised Standard Version* and the *New Revised Standard Version.*

Biblical Federation

In November 1966, Pope Paul VI commissioned the Secretariat for Promoting Christian Unity to start work for the widest possible distribution of the Bible and to coordinate endeavors toward the production of Catholic-Protestant Bibles in all languages.

The World Catholic Federation for the Biblical Apostolate, established in 1969, sponsors a program designed to create greater awareness among Catholics of the Bible and its use in everyday life.

The U. S. Center for the Catholic Biblical Apostolate is related to the Secretariat for Pastoral Research and Practices, National Conference of Catholic Bishops, 3211 Fourth St. N.E., Washington, DC, 20017.

APOCRYPHA

In Catholic usage, Apocrypha are books which have some resemblance to the canonical books in subject matter and title but which have not been recognized as canonical by the Church. They are characterized by a false claim to divine authority; extravagant accounts of events and miracles alleged to be supplemental revelation; material favoring heresy (especially in "New Testament" apocrypha); minimal, if any, historical value. Among examples of this type of literature itemized by J. McKenzie, S.J., in *Dictionary of the Bible* are: the Books of Adam and Eve, Martyrdom of Isaiah, Testament of the Patriarchs, Assumption of Moses, Sibylline Oracles; Gospel of James, Gospel of Thomas, Arabic Gospel of the Infancy, History of Joseph the Carpenter; Acts of John, Acts of Paul, Acts of Peter, Acts of Andrew, and numerous epistles.

Books of this type are called "pseudepigrapha" by Protestants.

In Protestant usage, some books of the Catholic Bible (deuterocanonical) are called apocrypha because their inspired character is rejected.

DEAD SEA SCROLLS

The Qumran Scrolls, popularly called the Dead Sea Scrolls, are a collection of manuscripts, all but one of them in Hebrew, found since 1947 in caves in the Desert of Juda west of the Dead Sea.

Among the findings were a complete text of Isaiah dating from the second century B.C., more or less extensive fragments of other Old Testament texts (including the deuterocanonical Tobit), and a commentary on Habakkuk. Until the discovery of these materials, the oldest known Hebrew manuscripts were from the A.D. 10th century.

Also found were messianic and apocalyptic texts, and other writings describing the beliefs and practices of the Essenes, a rigoristic Jewish sect.

The scrolls, dating from about the first century before and after Christ, are important sources of information about Hebrew literature, Jewish history during the period between the Old and New Testaments, and the history of Old Testament texts. They established the fact that the Hebrew text of the Old Testament was fixed before the beginning of the Christian era and have had definite effects in recent critical studies and translations of the Old Testament. Together with other scrolls found at Masada, they are still the subject of intensive study.

BOOKS OF THE BIBLE

Old Testament Books

Pentateuch

The Pentateuch is the collective title of the first five books of the Bible. Substantially, they identify the Israelites as Yahweh's Chosen People, cover their history from Egypt to the threshold of the Promised Land, contain the Mosaic Law and Covenant, and disclose the promise of salvation to come. Principal themes concern the divine promise of salvation, Yahweh's fidelity and the Covenant. Work on the composition of the Pentateuch was completed in the sixth century.

Genesis: The book of origins, according to its title in the Septuagint. In two parts, covers: religious prehistory, including accounts of the origin of the world and man, the original state of innocence and the fall, the promise of salvation, patriarchs before and after the deluge, the Tower of Babel narrative, genealogies (first 11 chapters); the covenant with Abraham and patriarchal history from Abraham to Joseph (balance of the 50 chapters). Significant are the themes of Yahweh's universal sovereignty and mercy.

Exodus: Named with the Greek word for departure, is a religious epic which describes the oppression of the 12 tribes in Egypt and their departure, liberation or passover therefrom under the leadership of Moses; Yahweh's establishment of the covenant with them, making them his chosen people, through the mediation of Moses at Mt. Sinai; instructions concerning the tabernacle, the sanctuary and Ark of the Covenant; the institution of the priesthood. The book is significant because of its theology of liberation and redemption. In Christian interpretation, the Exodus is a figure of baptism.

Leviticus: Mainly legislative in theme and purpose, contains laws regarding sacrifices, ceremonies of ordination and the priesthood of Aaron, legal purity, the holiness code, atonement, the redemption of offerings and other subjects. Summarily, Levitical laws provided directives for all aspects of religious observance and for the manner in which the Israelites were to conduct themselves with respect to Yahweh and each other. Leviticus was the liturgical handbook of the priesthood.

Numbers: Taking its name from censuses recounted at the beginning and near the end, is a continuation of Exodus. It combines narrative of the Israelites' desert pilgrimage from Sinai to the border of Canaan with laws related to and expansive of those in Leviticus.

Deuteronomy: The concluding book of the Pentateuch, recapitulates, in the form of a testament of Moses, the Law and much of the desert history of the Israelites; enjoins fidelity to the Law as the key to good or bad fortune for the people; gives an account of the commissioning of Joshua as the successor of Moses. Notable themes concern the election of Israel by Yahweh, observance of the Law, prohibitions against the worship of foreign gods, worship of and confidence in Yahweh, the power of Yahweh in nature. The Deuteronomic Code or motif, embodying all of these elements, was the norm for interpreting Israelite history.

Joshua, Judges, Ruth

Joshua: Records the fulfillment of Yahweh's promise to the Israelites in their conquest, occupation and division of Canaan under the leadership of Joshua. It also contains an account of the return of Transjordanian Israelites and of a renewal of the Covenant. It was redacted in final form probably in the sixth century or later.

Judges: Records the actions of charismatic leaders, called judges, of the tribes of Israel between the death of Joshua and the time of Samuel, and a crisis of idolatry among the people. The basic themes are sin and punishment, repentance and deliverance; its purpose was in line with the Deuteronomic motif, that the fortunes of the Israelites were related to their observance or non-observance of the Law and the Covenant. It was redacted in final form probably in the sixth century.

Ruth: Named for the Gentile (Moabite) woman who, through marriage with Boaz, became an Israelite and an ancestress of David (her son, Obed, became his grandfather). Themes are filial piety, faith and trust in Yahweh, the universality of messianic salvation. Dates ranging from c. 950 to the seventh century have been assigned to the origin of the book, whose author is unknown.

Historical Books

These books, while they contain a great deal of factual material, are unique in their preoccupation with presenting and interpreting it, in the Deuteronomic manner, in primary relation to the Covenant on which the nation of Israel was founded and in accordance with which community and personal life were judged.

The books are: Samuel 1 and 2, from the end of Judges (c. 1020) to the end of David's reign (c. 961); Kings 1 and 2, from the last days of David to the start of the Babylonian exile and the destruction of the Temple (587); Chronicles 1 and a major theological work for the 21st century that has had center stage since the mid-20th century 2, from the reign of Saul (c. 1020-1000) to the return of the people from the exile (538); Ezra and Nehemiah, covering the reorganization of the Jewish community after the exile (458-397); Maccabees 1 and 2, recounting the struggle against attempted suppression of Judaism (168-142).

Three of the books listed below — Tobit, Judith, and Esther — are categorized as religious novels.

Samuel 1 and 2: A single work in concept and contents, containing episodic history of the last two Judges, Eli and Samuel, the establishment and rule of the monarchy under Saul and David, and the political consequences of David's rule. The royal messianic dynasty of David was the subject of Nathan's oracle in 2 Sm. 7. The books were edited in final form probably late in the seventh century or during the exile.

Kings 1 and 2: Cover the last days of David and the career of Solomon, including the building of the Temple and the history of the kingdom during his reign; stories of the prophets Elijah and Elisha; the history of the divided kingdom to the fall of Israel in the North (721) and the fall of Judah in the South (587), the destruction of Jerusalem and the Temple. They reflect the Deuteronomic motif in attributing the downfall of the people to corruption of belief and practice in public and private life. They were completed probably in the sixth century.

Chronicles 1 and 2: A collection of historical traditions interpreted in such a way as to present an ideal picture of one people governed by divine law and united in one Temple worship of the one true God. Contents include genealogical tables from Adam to David, the careers of David and Solomon, coverage of the kingdom of Judah to the exile, and the decree of Cyrus permitting the return of the people and rebuilding of Jerusalem. Both are related to and were written about 400 by the same author, the Chronicler, who composed Ezra and Nehemiah.

Ezra and Nehemiah: A running account of the return of the people to their homeland after the exile and of practical efforts, under the leadership of Ezra and Nehemiah, to restore and reorganize the religious and political community on the basis of Israelite traditions, divine worship and observance of the Law. Events of great significance were the building of the second Temple, the building of a wall around Jerusalem and the proclamation of the Law by Ezra. This restored community was the start of Judaism. Both are related to and were written about 400 by the same author, the Chronicler, who composed Chronicles 1 and 2.

Tobit: Written in the literary form of a novel and having greater resemblance to wisdom than to historical literature, narrates the personal history of Tobit, a devout and charitable Jew in exile, and persons connected with him, viz., his son Tobiah, his kinsman Raguel and Raguel's daughter Sarah. Its purpose was to teach people how to be good Jews. One of its principal themes is patience under trial, with trust in divine Providence which is symbolized by the presence and action of the angel Raphael. It was written about 200.

Judith: Recounts, in the literary form of a historical novel or romance, the preservation of the Israelites from conquest and ruin through the action of Judith. The essential themes are trust in God for deliverance from danger and emphasis on observance of the Law. It was written probably during the Maccabean period.

Esther: Relates, in the literary form of a historical novel or romance, the manner in which Jews in Persia were saved from annihilation through the central role played by Esther, the Jewish wife of Ahasuerus; a fact commemorated by the Jewish feast of Purim. Like Judith, it has trust in Divine Providence as its theme and indicates that God's saving will is sometimes realized by persons acting in unlikely ways. It may have been written near the end of the fourth century.

Maccabees 1 and 2: While related to some extent because of common subject matter, are quite different from each other.

The first book recounts the background and events of the 40-year (175-135) struggle for religious and political freedom led by Judas Maccabeus and his brothers against the Hellenist Seleucid kings and some Hellenophiles among the Jews. Victory was symbolized by the rededication of the Temple. Against the background of opposition between Jews and Gentiles, the author equated the survival of belief in the one true God with survival of the Jewish people, thus identifying religion with patriotism. It was written probably near the year 100.

The second book supplements the first to some extent, covering and giving a theological interpretation to events from 180 to 162. It explains the feast of the dedication of the Temple, a key event in the survival of Judaism which is commemorated in the feast of Hanukkah; stresses the primacy of God's action in the struggle for survival; and indicates belief in an afterlife and the resurrection of the body. It was completed probably about 124.

Wisdom Books

With the exceptions of Psalms and the Song of Songs, the titles listed under this heading are called "wisdom books" because their purpose was to formulate the fruits of human experience in the context of meditation on sacred Scripture and to present them as an aid toward understanding the problems of life. Hebrew wisdom literature was distinctive from pagan literature of the same type, but it had limitations; these were overcome in the New Testament, which added the dimensions of the New Covenant to those of the Old. Solomon was regarded as the archetype of the wise man.

Job: A dramatic, didactic poem consisting mainly of several dialogues between Job and his friends concerning the mystery involved in the coexistence of the just God, evil and the suffering of the just. It describes an innocent man's experience of suffering and conveys the truth that faith in and submission to God rather than complete understanding, which is impossible, make the experience bearable; also, that the justice of God cannot be defended by affirming that it is realized in this world. Of unknown authorship, it was composed between the seventh and fifth centuries.

Psalms: A collection of 150 religious songs or lyrics reflecting Israelite belief and piety dating from the time of the monarchy to the post-Exilic period, a span of well over 500 years. The psalms, which are a compendium of Old Testament theology, were used in the temple liturgy and for other occasions. They were of several types suitable for the king, hymns, lamentations, expressions of confidence and thanksgiving, prophecy, historical meditation and reflection, and the statement of wisdom. About one-half of them are attributed to David; many were composed by unknown authors.

Proverbs: The oldest book of the wisdom type in the Bible, consisting of collections of sayings attributed to Solomon and other persons regarding a wide variety of subjects including wisdom and its nature, rules of conduct, duties with respect to one's neighbor, the conduct of daily affairs. It reveals many details of Hebrew life. Its nucleus dates from the period before the exile. The extant form of the book dates probably from the end of the fifth century.

Ecclesiastes: A treatise about many subjects whose unifying theme is the vanity of strictly human efforts and accomplishments with respect to the achievement of lasting happiness; the only things which are not vain are fear of the Lord and observance of his commandments. The pessimistic tone of the book is due to the absence of a concept of afterlife. It was written by an unknown author probably in the third century.

Song of Songs: A collection of love lyrics reflecting various themes, including the love of God for Israel and the celebration of ideal love and fidelity between man and woman. It was written by an unknown author after the exile.

Wisdom: Deals with many subjects including the reward of justice; praise of wisdom, a gift of Yahweh proceeding from belief in him and the practice of his Law; the part played by him in the history of his people, especially in their liberation from Egypt; the folly and shame of idolatry. Its contents are taken from the whole sacred literature of the Jews and represent a distillation of its wisdom based on the law, beliefs and traditions of Israel. The last of the Old Testament books, it was written in the early part of the first century before Christ by a member of the Jewish community at Alexandria.

Sirach: Resembling Proverbs, is a collection of sayings handed on by a grandfather to his grandson. It contains a variety of moral instruction and eulogies of patriarchs and other figures in Israelite history. Its moral maxims apply to individuals, the family and community, relations with God, friendship, education, wealth, the Law, divine worship. Its theme is that true wisdom consists in the Law. (It was formerly called Ecclesiasticus, the Church Book, because of its extensive use by the Church for moral instruction.) It was written in Hebrew between 200 and 175, during a period of strong Hellenistic influence, and was translated into Greek after 132.

The Prophets

These books and the prophecies they contain "express judgments of the people's moral conduct, on the basis of the Mosaic alliance between God and Israel. They teach sublime truths and lofty morals. They contain exhortations, threats, announcements of punishment, promises of deliverance. In the affairs of men, their prime concern is the interests of God, especially in what pertains to the Chosen People through whom the Messiah is to come; hence their denunciations of idolatry and of that externalism in worship which exclude the interior spirit of religion. They are concerned also with the universal nature of the moral law, with personal responsibility, with the person and office of the Messiah, and with the conduct of foreign nations" (*The Holy Bible*, Prophetic Books, CCD Edition, 1961; Preface). There are four major (Isaiah, Jeremiah, Ezekiel, Daniel) and twelve minor prophets (distinguished by the length of books), Lamentations and Baruch. Earlier prophets, mentioned in historical books, include Samuel, Gad, Nathan, Elijah, and Elisha.

Before the exile, prophets were the intermediaries through whom God communicated revelation to the people. Afterwards, prophecy lapsed and the written word of the Law served this purpose.

Isaiah: Named for the greatest of the prophets whose career spanned the reigns of three Hebrew kings from 742 to the beginning of the seventh century, in a period of moral breakdown in Judah and threats of invasion by foreign enemies. It is an anthology of poems and oracles credited to him and a number of followers deeply influenced by him. Of special importance are the prophecies concerning Immanuel (6 to 12), including the prophecy of the virgin birth (7:14). Chapters 40 to 55, called Deutero-Isaiah, are attributed to an anonymous poet toward the end of the exile; this portion contains the Songs of the Servant. The concluding part of the book (56-66) contains oracles by later disciples. One of many themes in Isaiah concerned the saving mission of the remnant of Israel in the divine plan of salvation.

Jeremiah: Combines history, biography and prophecy in a setting of crisis caused by internal and external factors, viz., idolatry and general infidelity to the Law among the Israelites and external threats from the Assyrians, Egyptians and Babylonians. Jeremiah prophesied the promise of a new covenant as well as the destruction of Jerusalem and the Temple. His career began in 626 and ended some years after the beginning of the exile. The book, the longest in the Bible, was edited in final form after the exile.

Lamentations: A collection of five laments or elegies over the fall of Jerusalem and the fate of the people in exile, written by an unknown eyewitness. They convey the message that Yahweh struck the people because of their sins and reflect confidence in his love and power to restore his converted people.

Baruch: Against the background of the already-begun

exile, it consists of an introduction and several parts: an exile's prayer of confession and petition for forgiveness and the restoration of Israel; a poem praising wisdom and the Law of Moses; a lament in which Jerusalem, personified, bewails the fate of her people and consoles them with the hope of blessings to come; and a polemic against idolatry. Although ascribed to Baruch, Jeremiah's secretary, it was written by several authors, probably in the second century.

Ezekiel: Named for the priest-prophet who prophesied in Babylon from 593 to 571, during the first phase of the exile. To prepare his fellow early exiles for the impending fall of Jerusalem, he reproached the Israelites for past sins and predicted woes to come upon them. After the destruction of the city, the burden of his message was hope and promise of restoration. Ezekiel had great influence on the religion of Israel after the exile.

Daniel: The protagonist is a young Jew, taken early to Babylon where he lived until about 538, who figured in a series of edifying stories which originated in Israelite tradition. The stories, whose characters are not purely legendary but rest on historical tradition, recount the trials and triumphs of Daniel and his three companions, and other episodes including those concerning Susannah, Bel, and the Dragon. The book is more apocalyptic than prophetic: it envisions Israel in glory to come and conveys the message that men of faith can resist temptation and overcome adversity. It states the prophetic themes of right conduct, divine control of men and events, and the final triumph of the kingdom. It was written by an unknown author in the 160s to give moral support to Jews during the persecutions of the Maccabean period.

Hosea: Consists of a prophetic parallel between Hosea's marriage and Yahweh's relations with his people. As the prophet was married to a faithless wife whom he would not give up, Yahweh was bound in Covenant with an idolatrous and unjust Israel whom he would not desert but would chastise for purification. Hosea belonged to the Northern Kingdom of Israel and began his career about the middle of the eighth century. He inaugurated the tradition of describing Yahweh's relation to Israel in terms of marriage.

Joel: Is apocalyptic and eschatological regarding divine judgment, the Day of the Lord, which is symbolized by a ravaging invasion of locusts, the judgment of the nations in the Valley of Josaphat and the outpouring of the Spirit in the messianic era to come. Its message is that God will vindicate and save Israel, in view of the prayer and repentance of the people, and will punish their enemies. It was composed about 400.

Amos: Consists of an indictment against foreign enemies of Israel; a strong denunciation of the people of Israel, whose infidelity, idolatry and injustice made them subject to divine judgment and punishment; and a messianic oracle regarding Israel's restoration. Amos prophesied in the Northern Kingdom of Israel, at Bethel, in the first half of the eighth century; chronologically, he was the first of the canonical prophets.

Obadiah: A 21-verse prophecy, the shortest and one of the sternest in the Bible, against the Edomites, invaders of southern Judah and enemies of those returning from the exile to their homeland.

It was probably composed in the fifth century.

Jonah: A parable of divine mercy with the theme that Yahweh wills the salvation of all, not just a few, men who respond to his call. Its protagonist is a disobedient prophet; forced by circumstances beyond his control to preach penance among Gentiles, he is highly successful in his mission but baffled by the divine concern for those who do not belong to the Chosen People. It was written after the exile, probably in the fifth century.

Micah: Attacks the injustice and corruption of priests, false prophets, officials and people; announces judgment and punishment to come; foretells the restoration of Israel; refers to the saving remnant of Israel. Micah was a contemporary of Isaiah.

Nahum: Concerns the destruction of Nineveh in 612 and the overthrow of the Assyrian Empire by the Babylonians.

Habakkuk: Dating from about 605-597, concerns sufferings to be inflicted by oppressors on the people of Judah because of their infidelity to the Lord. It also sounds a note of confidence in the Lord, the Savior, and declares that the just will not perish.

Zephaniah: Exercising his ministry in the second half of the seventh century, during a time of widespread idolatry, superstition and religious degradation, he prophesied impending judgment and punishment for Jerusalem and its people. He prophesied too that a holy remnant of the people (*anawim*, mentioned also by Amos) would be spared. Zephaniah was a forerunner of Jeremiah.

Haggai: One of the first prophets after the exile, Haggai in 520 encouraged the returning exiles to reestablish their community and to complete the second Temple (dedicated in 515), for which he envisioned greater glory, in a messianic sense, than that enjoyed by the original Temple of Solomon.

Zechariah: A contemporary of Haggai, he prophesied in the same vein. A second part of the book, called Deutero-Zechariah and composed by one or more unknown authors, relates a vision of the coming of the Prince of Peace, the Messiah of the Poor.

Malachi: Written by an anonymous author, presents a picture of life in the post-Exilic community between 516 and the initiation of reforms by Ezra and Nehemiah about 432. Blame for the troubles of the community is placed mainly on priests for failure to carry out ritual worship and to instruct the people in the proper manner; other factors were religious indifference and the influence of doubters who were scandalized at the prosperity of the wicked. The vision of a universal sacrifice to be offered to Yahweh (1:11) is interpreted in Catholic theology as a prophecy of the sacrifice of the Mass. Malachi was the last of the minor prophets.

DATES of the OLD TESTAMENT

c. 1800 – c. 1600 B.C.: Period of the patriarchs (Abraham, Isaac, Jacob).

c. 1600: Israelites in Egypt.

c. 1250: Exodus of Israelites from Egypt.

c. 1210: Entrance of Israelites into Canaan.

c. 1210 – c. 1020: Period of the Judges.

c. 1020 – c. 1000: Reign of Saul, first king.

c. 1000 – c. 961: Reign of David.

c. 961 – 922: Reign of Solomon. Temple built during his reign.

922: Division of the Kingdom into Israel (North) and Judah (South).

721: Conquest of Israel by Assyrians.

587-538: Conquest of Judah by Babylonians.

Babylonian Captivity and Exile: Destruction of Jerusalem and the Temple, 587. Captivity ended with the return of exiles, following the decree of Cyrus permitting the rebuilding of Jerusalem.

515: Dedication of the second Temple.

458–397: Restoration and reform of the Jewish religious and political community; building of the Jerusalem wall, 439. Leaders in the movement were Ezra and Nehemiah.

168–142: Period of the Maccabees; war against Syrians.

142: Independence granted to Jews by Demetrius II of Syria.

135–37: Period of the Hasmonean dynasty.

63: Beginning of Roman rule.

37–4: Period of Herod the Great.

NEW TESTAMENT BOOKS

Gospels

The term "Gospel" is derived from the Anglo-Saxon *god-spell* and the Greek *euangelion*, meaning good news, good tidings. In Christian use, it means the good news of salvation proclaimed by Christ and the Church, and handed on in written form in the Gospels of Matthew, Mark, Luke and John.

The initial proclamation of the coming of the kingdom of God was made by Jesus in and through his Person, teachings and actions, and especially through his Passion, death and resurrection. This proclamation became the center of Christian faith and the core of the oral Gospel tradition with which the Church spread the good news by apostolic preaching for some 30 years before it was committed to writing by the Evangelists.

Nature of the Gospels

The historical truth of the Gospels was the subject of an instruction issued by the Pontifical Commission for Biblical Studies Apr. 21, 1964.

• The sacred writers selected from the material at their disposal (the oral Gospel tradition, some written collections of sayings and deeds of Jesus, eyewitness accounts) those things which were particularly suitable to the various conditions (liturgical, catechetical, missionary) of the faithful and the aims they had in mind, and they narrated these things in such a way as to correspond with those circumstances and their aims.

• The life and teaching of Jesus were not simply reported in a biographical manner for the purpose of preserving their memory but were "preached" so as to offer the Church the basis of doctrine concerning faith and morals.

• In their works, the Evangelists presented the true sayings of Jesus and the events of his life in the light of the better understanding they had following their enlightenment by the Holy Spirit. They did not transform Christ into a "mythical" Person, nor did they distort his teaching. Passion narratives are the core of all the Gospels, covering the suffering, death and resurrection of Jesus as central events in bringing about and establishing the New Covenant. Leading up to them are accounts of the mission of John the Baptizer and the ministry of Jesus, especially in Galilee and finally in Jerusalem before the Passion. The infancy of Jesus is covered by Luke and Matthew with narratives inspired in part by appropriate Old Testament citations.

Matthew, Mark and Luke, while different in various respects, have so many similarities that they are called Synoptic; their relationships are the subject of the Synoptic Problem.

Matthew: Written probably between 80 and 100 for Jewish Christians with clear reference to Jewish background and identification of Jesus as the divine Messiah, the fulfillment of the Old Testament. Distinctive are the use of Old Testament citations regarding the Person, activity and teaching of Jesus, and the presentation of doctrine in sermons and discourses.

Mark: Most likely the first of the Gospels, dating from about 70. Written for Gentile Christians, it is noted for the realism and wealth of concrete details with which it reveals Jesus as Son of God and Savior more by his actions and miracles than by his discourses. Theologically, it is less refined than the other Gospels.

Luke: Written about 75 for Gentile Christians. It is noted for the universality of its address, the insight it provides into the Christian way of life, the place it gives to women, the manner in which it emphasizes Jesus' friendship with sinners and compassion for the suffering.

John: Edited and arranged in final form probably between 90 and 100, this is the most sublime and theological of the Gospels, and is different from the Synoptics in plan and treatment. Combining accounts of signs with longer discourses and reflections, it progressively reveals the Person and mission of Jesus — as Word, Way, Truth, Life, Light — in line with the purpose, "to help you believe that Jesus is the Messiah, the Son of God, so that through this faith you may have life in his name" (Jn 20:31). There are questions about the authorship but no doubt about the Johannine authority and tradition behind the Gospel.

Acts of the Apostles

Written by Luke about 75 as a supplement to his Gospel. It describes the origin and spread of Christian communities through the action of the Holy Spirit from the resurrection of Christ to the time when Paul was placed in custody in Rome in the early 60s.

Letters (Epistles)

These letters, many of which antedated the Gospels, were written in response to existential needs of the early Christian communities for doctrinal and moral instruction, disciplinary action, practical advice, and exhortation to true Christian living.

Pauline Letters

These letters, which comprise approximately one-fourth of the New Testament, are primary and monumental sources of the development of Christian theology. Several of them may not have had Paul as their actual author, but evidence of the Pauline tradition behind them is strong.

The letters to the Colossians, Philippians, Ephesians and Philemon have been called the "Captivity Letters" because of a tradition that they were written while Paul was under house arrest or another form of detention.

Romans: Written about 57, probably from Corinth, on the central significance of Christ and faith in him for salvation, and the relationship of Christianity to Judaism; the condition of mankind without Christ; justification and the Christian life; duties of Christians.

Corinthians 1: Written near the beginning of 57 from Ephesus to counteract factionalism and disorders, it covers community dissension, moral irregularities, marriage and celibacy, conduct at religious gatherings, the Eucharist, spiritual gifts (charisms) and their function in the Church, charity, the resurrection of the body.

Corinthians 2: Written later in the same year as 1 Cor, concerning Paul's defense of his apostolic ministry, and an appeal for a collection to aid poor Christians in Jerusalem.

Galatians: Written probably between 54 and 55 to counteract Judaizing opinions and efforts to undermine his authority, it asserts the divine origin of Paul's authority and doctrine, states that justification is not through Mosaic Law but through faith in Christ, insists on the practice of evangelical virtues, especially charity.

Ephesians: Written probably between 61 and 63, mainly on the Church as the Mystical Body of Christ.

Philippians: Written between 56 and 57 or 61 and 63 to warn the Philippians against enemies of their faith, to urge them to be faithful to their vocation and unity of belief, and to thank them for their kindness to him while he was being held in detention.

Colossians: Written probably while he was under house arrest in Rome from 61 to 63, to counteract the influence of self-appointed teachers who were watering down doctrine concerning Christ. It includes two highly important Christological passages, a warning against false teachers, and an instruction on the ideal Christian life.

Thessalonians 1 and 2: Written within a short time of each other probably in 51 from Corinth, mainly on doctrine concerning the *Parousia*, the second coming of Christ.

Timothy 1 and 2, Titus: Written between 65 and 67, or perhaps in the 70s, giving pastoral counsels to Timothy and Titus, who were in charge of churches in Ephesus and Crete, respectively. 1 Tm emphasizes pastoral responsibility for preserving unity of doctrine; 2 Tm describes Paul's imprisonment in Rome.

Philemon: A private letter written between 61 and 63 to a wealthy Colossian concerning a slave, Onesimus, who had escaped from him; Paul appealed for kind treatment of the man.

Hebrews: Dating from sometime between 70 and 96, a complex theological treatise on Christology, the priesthood and sacrifice of Christ, the New Covenant, and the pattern for Christian living. Critical opinion is divided as to whether it was addressed to Judaeo or Gentile Christians.

Catholic Letters

These seven letters have been called "catholic" because it was thought for some time, not altogether correctly, that they were not addressed to particular communities.

James: Written sometime before 62 in the spirit of Hebrew wisdom literature and the moralism of Tobit. An exhortation to practical Christian living, it is also noteworthy for the doctrine it states on good works and its citation regarding anointing of the sick.

Peter 1 and 2: The first letter may have been written between 64 and 67 or between 90 and 95; the second may date from 100 to 125. Addressed to Christians in Asia Minor, both are exhortations to perseverance in the life of faith despite trials and difficulties arising from pagan influences, isolation from other Christians and false teaching.

John 1: Written sometime in the 90s and addressed to Asian churches, its message is that God is made known to us in the Son and that fellowship with the Father is attained by living in the light, justice and love of the Son.

John 2: Written sometime in the 90s and addressed to a church in Asia, it commends the people for standing firm in the faith and urges them to perseverance.

John 3: Written sometime in the 90s, it appears to represent an effort to settle a jurisdictional dispute in one of the churches.

Jude: Written probably about 80, it is a brief treatise against erroneous teachings and practices opposed to law, authority and true Christian freedom.

Revelation

Written in the 90s along the lines of Johannine thought, it is a symbolic and apocalyptic treatment of things to come and of the struggle between the Church and evil combined with warning but hope and assurance to the Church regarding the coming of the Lord in glory.

INTERPRETATION OF THE BIBLE

According to the Dogmatic Constitution on Divine Revelation (*Dei Verbum*) issued by the Second Vatican Council, "the interpreter of Sacred Scripture, in order to see clearly what God wanted to communicate to us, should carefully investigate what meaning the sacred writers really intended, and what God wanted to manifest by means of their words" (No. 12).

Hermeneutics, Exegesis

This careful investigation proceeds in accordance with the rules of hermeneutics, the normative science of biblical interpretation and explanation. Hermeneutics in practice is called exegesis.

The principles of hermeneutics are derived from various disciplines and many factors which have to be considered in explaining the Bible and its parts. These include: the original languages and languages of translation of the sacred texts, through philology and linguistics; the quality of texts, through textual criticism; literary forms and genres, through literary and form criticism; cultural, historical, geographical and other conditions which influenced the writers, through related studies; facts and truths of salvation history; the truths and analogy of faith.

Distinctive to biblical hermeneutics, which differs in important respects from literary interpretation in general, is the premise that the Bible, though written by human authors, is the work of divine inspiration in which God reveals his plan for the salvation of men through historical events and persons, and especially through the Person and mission of Christ.

Textual, Form Criticism

Textual criticism is the study of biblical texts, which have been transmitted in copies several times removed from the original manuscripts, for the purpose of establishing the real state of the original texts. This purpose is served by comparison of existing copies; by application to the texts of the disciplines of philology and linguistics; by examination of related works of antiquity; by study of biblical citations in works of the Fathers of the Church and other authors; and by other means of literary study.

Since about 1920, the sayings of Christ have been a particular object of New Testament study, the purpose being to analyze the forms of expression used by the Evangelists in order to ascertain the words actually spoken by him.

Literary Criticism

Literary criticism aims to determine the origin and kinds of literary composition, called forms or genres, employed by the inspired authors. Such determinations are necessary for decision regarding the nature and purpose and, consequently, the meaning of biblical passages. Underlying these studies is the principle that the manner of writing was conditioned by the intention of the authors, the meaning they wanted to convey, and the then-contemporary literary style, mode or medium best adapted to carry their message — e.g., true history, quasi-historical narrative, poems, prayers, hymns, psalms, aphorisms, allegories, discourses. Understanding these media is necessary for the valid interpretation of their message.

Literal Sense

The key to all valid interpretation is the literal sense of biblical passages. Regarding this matter and the relevance to it of the studies and procedures described above, Pius XII wrote the following in the encyclical *Divino Afflante Spiritu:*

"What the literal sense of a passage is, is not always as obvious in the speeches and writings of ancient authors of the East as it is in the works of our own time. For what they wished to express is not to be determined by the rules of grammar and philology alone nor solely by the context; the interpreter must, as it were, go back wholly in spirit to those remote centuries of the East and with the aid of history, archeology, ethnology, and other sciences accurately determine what modes of writing, so to speak, the authors of that ancient period would be likely to use and in fact did use. In explaining the Sacred Scripture and in demonstrating and proving its immunity from all error [the Catholic interpreter] should make a prudent use of this means, determine to what extent the manner of expression or literary mode adopted by the sacred writer may lead to a correct and genuine interpretation; and let him be convinced that this part of his office cannot be neglected without serious detriment to Catholic exegesis."

The literal sense of the Bible is the meaning in the mind of and intended by the inspired writer of a book or passage of the Bible. This is determined by the application to texts of the rules of hermeneutics. It is not to be confused with word-for-word literalism.

Typological Sense

The typological sense is the meaning which a passage has not only in itself but also in reference to something else of which it is a type or foreshadowing. A clear example is the account of the Exodus of the Israelites: in its literal sense, it narrates the liberation of the Israelites from death and oppression in Egypt; in its typical sense, it foreshadowed the liberation of men from sin through the redemptive death and resurrection of Christ. The typical sense of this and other passages emerged in the working out of God's plan of salvation history. It did not have to be in the mind of the author of the original passage.

Accommodated Senses

Accommodated, allegorical and consequent senses are figurative and adaptive meanings given to books and passages of the Bible for moral and other purposes. Such interpretations involve the danger of stretching the literal sense beyond proper proportions. Hermeneutical principles require that interpretations like these respect the integrity of the literal sense of the passages in question.

In the Catholic view, the final word on questions of biblical interpretation belongs to the teaching authority of the Church. In other views, generally derived from basic principles stated by Martin Luther, John Calvin and other reformers, the primacy belongs to individual judgment acting in response to the inner testimony of the Holy Spirit, the edifying nature of biblical subject matter, the sublimity and simplicity of the message of salvation, the intensity with which Christ is proclaimed.

Biblical Studies

The first center for biblical studies, in some strict sense of the term, was the School of Alexandria, founded in the latter half of the second century. It was noted for allegorical exegesis. Literal interpretation was a hallmark of the School of Antioch.

St. Jerome, who produced the Vulgate, and St. Augustine, author of numerous commentaries, were the most important figures in biblical studies during the patristic period. By the time of the latter's death, the Old and New Testament canons had been stabilized. For some centuries afterwards, there was little or no progress in scriptural studies, although commentaries were written, collections were made of scriptural excerpts from the writings of the Fathers of the Church, and the systematic reading of Scripture became established as a feature of monastic life.

Advances were made in the 12th and 13th centuries with the introduction of new principles and methods of scriptural analysis stemming from renewed interest in Hebraic studies and the application of dialectics.

By the time of the Reformation, the Bible had become the first book set in movable type, and more than 100 vernacular editions were in use throughout Europe.

The Council of Trent

In the wake of the Reformation, the Council of Trent formally defined the Canon of the Bible; it also reasserted the authoritative role of tradition and the teaching authority of the Church as well as Scripture with respect to the rule of faith. In the heated atmosphere of the 16th and 17th centuries, the Bible was turned into a polemical weapon; Protestants used it to defend their doctrines, and Catholics countered with citations in support of the dogmas of the Church. One result of this state of affairs was a lack of substantial progress in biblical studies during the period.

Rationalists from the 18th century on and later Modernists denied the reality of the supernatural and doctrine concerning inspiration of the Bible, which they generally regarded as a strictly human production expressive of the religious sense and experience of mankind. In their hands, the tools of positive critical research became weapons for biblical subversion. The defensive Catholic reaction to their work had the temporary effect of alienating scholars of the Church from solid advances in archeology, philology, history, textual and literary criticism.

Catholic Developments

Major influences in bringing about a change in Catholic attitude toward use of these disciplines in biblical studies were two papal encyclicals and two institutes of special study, the *École Biblique*, founded in Jerusalem in 1890, and the Pontifical Biblical Institute established in Rome in 1909. The encyclical *Providentissimus Deus*, issued by Leo XIII in 1893, marked an important breakthrough; in addition to defending the concept of divine inspiration and the formal inspiration of the Scriptures, it encouraged the study of allied and ancillary sciences and techniques for a more fruitful understanding of the sacred writings. The encyclical *Divino Afflante Spiritu*, by Pope Pius XII 50 years later, gave encouragement for the use of various forms of criticism as tools of biblical research. A significant addition to documents on the subject is "The Interpretation of the Bible in the Church," published by the Pontifical Biblical Commission in November 1993. It presents an overview of approaches to the Bible and probes the question: "Which hermeneutical theory best enables a proper grasp of the profound reality of which Scripture speaks and its meaningful expression for people today?"

The documents encouraged the work of scholars and stimulated wide communication of the fruits of their study.

Great changes in the climate and direction of biblical studies have occurred in recent years. One of them has been an increase in cooperative effort among Catholic, Protestant, Orthodox and Jewish scholars. Their common investigation of the Dead Sea Scrolls is well-known. Also productive has been the collaboration of Catholics and Protestants in turning out various editions of the Bible.

The development and results of biblical studies in this century have directly and significantly affected all phases of the contemporary renewal movement in the Church. Their influence on theology, liturgy, catechetics, and preaching indicate the importance of their function in the life of the Church.

On Sept. 30, 2010, Pope Benedict XVI issued *Verbum Domini: a Post-Synodal Apostolic Exhortation on the Word of God in the Life and Mission of the Church.*

APOSTLES AND EVANGELISTS

The Apostles were the men selected, trained, and commissioned by Christ to preach the Gospel, to baptize, to establish, direct and care for his Church as servants of God and stewards of his mysteries. They were the first bishops of the Church.

St. Matthew's Gospel lists the Apostles in this order: Peter, Andrew, James the Greater, John, Philip, Bartholomew, Thomas, Matthew, James the Less, Jude, Simon, and Judas Iscariot. Matthias was elected to fill the place of Judas. Paul became an Apostle by a special call from Christ. Barnabas was called an Apostle.

Two of the Evangelists, John and Matthew, were Apostles. The other two, Luke and Mark, were closely associated with the apostolic college.

Andrew: Born in Bethsaida, brother of Peter, disciple of John the Baptist, a fisherman, the first Apostle called; according to legend, preached the Gospel in northern Greece, Epirus and Scythia, and was martyred at Patras about 70; in art, is represented with an X-shaped cross, called St. Andrew's Cross; is honored as the patron of Russia and Scotland; Nov. 30.

Barnabas: Originally called Joseph but named Barnabas by the Apostles, among whom he is ranked because of his collaboration with Paul; a Jew of the Diaspora, born in Cyprus; a cousin of Mark and member of the Christian community at Jerusalem, influenced the Apostles to accept Paul, with whom he became a pioneer missionary outside Palestine and Syria, to Antioch, Cyprus, and southern Asia Minor; legend says he was martyred in Cyprus during the Neronian persecution; June 11.

Bartholomew (Nathaniel): A friend of Philip; according to various traditions, preached the Gospel in Ethiopia, India, Persia, and Armenia, where he was martyred by being flayed and beheaded; in art, is depicted holding a knife, an instrument of his death; Aug. 24 (Roman Rite), Aug. 25 (Byzantine Rite).

James the Greater: A Galilean, son of Zebedee, brother of John (with whom he was called a "Son of Thunder"), a fisherman; with Peter and John, witnessed the raising of Jairus's daughter to life, the transfiguration, the agony of Jesus in the Garden of Gethsemane; first of the Apostles to die, by the sword in 44 during the rule of Herod Agrippa; there is doubt about a journey legend says he made to Spain and also about the authenticity of relics said to be his at Santiago de Compostela; in art, is depicted carrying a pilgrim's bell; July 25 (Roman Rite), Apr. 30 (Byzantine Rite).

James the Less: Son of Alphaeus, called "Less" because he was younger in age or shorter in stature than James the Greater; one of the Catholic Epistles bears his name; was stoned to death in 62 or thrown from the top of the temple in Jerusalem and clubbed to death in 66; in art, is depicted with a club or heavy staff; May 3 (Roman Rite), Oct. 9 (Byzantine Rite).

John: A Galilean, son of Zebedee, brother of James the Greater (with whom he was called a "Son of Thunder"), a fisherman, probably a disciple of John the Baptist, one of the Evangelists, called the "Beloved Disciple"; with Peter and James the Greater, witnessed the raising of Jairus's daughter to life, the transfiguration, the agony of Jesus in the Garden of Gethsemane; Mary was commended to his special care by Christ; the fourth Gospel, three Catholic Epistles, and Revelation bear his name; according to various accounts, lived at Ephesus in Asia Minor for some time and died a natural death about 100; in art, is represented by an eagle, symbolic of the sublimity of the contents of his Gospel; Dec. 27 (Roman Rite), May 8 (Byzantine Rite).

Jude Thaddeus: One of the Catholic Epistles, the shortest, bears his name; various traditions say he preached the Gospel in Mesopotamia, Persia, and elsewhere, and was martyred; in art, is depicted with a halberd, the instrument of his death; Oct. 28 (Roman Rite), June 19 (Byzantine Rite).

Luke: A Greek convert to the Christian community, called "our most dear physician" by Paul, of whom he was a missionary companion; author of the third Gospel and Acts of the Apostles; the place — Achaia, Bithynia, Egypt — and circumstances of his death are not certain; in art, is depicted as a man, a writer, or an ox (because his Gospel starts at the scene of temple sacrifice); Oct. 18.

Mark: A cousin of Barnabas and member of the first Christian community at Jerusalem; a missionary companion of Paul and Barnabas, then of Peter; author of the Gospel which bears his name; according to legend, founded the Church at Alexandria, was bishop there and was martyred in the streets of the city; in art, is depicted with his Gospel and a winged lion, symbolic of the voice of John the Baptist crying in the wilderness, at the beginning of his Gospel; Apr. 25.

Matthew: A Galilean, called Levi by Luke and John and the son of Alphaeus by Mark, a tax collector, one of the Evangelists; according to various accounts, preached the Gospel in Judea, Ethiopia, Persia and Parthia, and was martyred; in art, is depicted with a spear, the instrument of his death, and as a winged man in his role as Evangelist; Sept. 21 (Roman Rite), Nov. 16 (Byzantine Rite).

Matthias: A disciple of Jesus whom the faithful 11 Apostles chose to replace Judas before the Resurrection; uncertain traditions report that he preached the Gospel in Palestine, Cappadocia or Ethiopia; in art, is represented with a cross and a halberd, the instruments of his death as a martyr; May 14 (Roman Rite), Aug. 9 (Byzantine Rite).

Paul: Born at Tarsus, of the tribe of Benjamin, a Roman citizen; participated in the persecution of Christians until the time of his miraculous conversion on the way to Damascus; called by Christ, who revealed himself to him in a special way; became the Apostle of the Gentiles, among whom he did most of his preaching in the course of three major missionary journeys through areas north of Palestine, Cyprus, Asia Minor, and Greece; 14 epistles bear his name; two years of imprisonment at Rome, following initial arrest in Jerusalem and confinement at Caesarea, ended with martyrdom, by beheading, outside the walls of the city in 64 or 67 during the Neronian persecution; in art, is depicted in various ways with St. Peter, with a sword, in the scene of his conversion; June 29 (with St. Peter), Jan. 25 (Conversion).

Peter: Simon, son of Jonah, born in Bethsaida, brother of Andrew, a fisherman; called Cephas or Peter by Christ who made him the chief of the Apostles and head of the Church as his vicar; named first in the listings of Apostles in the Synoptic Gospels and the Acts of the Apostles; with James the Greater and John, witnessed the raising of Jairus's daughter to life, the transfiguration, the agony of Jesus in the Garden of Gethsemane; was the first to preach the Gospel in and around Jerusalem and was the leader of the first Christian community there; established a local church in Antioch; presided over the Council of Jerusalem in 51; wrote two Catholic Epistles to the Christians in Asia Minor; established his see in Rome where he spent his last years and was martyred by crucifixion in 64 or 65 during the Neronian persecution; in art, is depicted carrying two keys, symbolic of his primacy in the Church; June 29 (with St. Paul), Feb. 22 (Chair of Peter).

Philip: Born in Bethsaida; according to legend, preached the Gospel in Phrygia where he martyeded by crucifixion; May 3 (Roman Rite), Nov. 14 (Byzantine Rite).

Simon: Called the Cananean or the Zealot; according to legend, preached in various places in the Middle East and suffered martyrdom by being sawed in two; in art, is depicted with a saw, the instrument of his death, or a book, symbolic of his zeal for the Law; Oct. 28 (Roman Rite), May 10 (Byzantine Rite).

Thomas (Didymus): Notable for his initial incredulity regarding the Resurrection and his subsequent forthright confession of the divinity of Christ risen from the dead; according to legend, preached the Gospel in places from the Caspian Sea to the Persian Gulf and eventually reached India where he was martyred near Madras; Thomas Christians trace their origin to him; in art, is depicted kneeling before the risen Christ, or with a carpenter's rule and square; feast, July 3 (Roman Rite), Oct. 6 (Byzantine Rite).

* * *

Judas: The Gospels record only a few facts about Judas, the Apostle who betrayed Christ. The only non-Galilean among the Apostles, he was from Carioth, a town in southern Judah. He was keeper of the purse in the apostolic band. He was called a petty thief by John. He voiced dismay at the waste of money, which he said might have been spent for the poor, in connection with the anointing incident at Bethany. He took the initiative in arranging the betrayal of Christ. Afterwards, he confessed that he had betrayed an innocent man and cast into the Temple the money he had received for that action. Of his death, Matthew says that he hanged himself; the Acts of the Apostles states that he swelled up and burst open; both reports deal more with the meaning than the manner of his death — the misery of the death of a sinner.

The consensus of speculation over the reason why Judas acted as he did in betraying Christ focuses on disillusionment and unwillingness to accept the concept of a suffering Messiah and personal suffering of his own as an Apostle.

APOSTOLIC FATHERS, FATHERS, DOCTORS OF THE CHURCH

The writers listed below were outstanding and authoritative witnesses to authentic Christian belief and practice, and played significant roles in giving them expression.

Apostolic Fathers

The Apostolic Fathers were Christian writers of the first and second centuries whose writings echo genuine apostolic teaching. Chief in importance are: St. Clement (d. c. 97), bishop of Rome and third successor of St. Peter in the papacy; St. Ignatius (50-c. 107), bishop of Antioch and second successor of St. Peter in that see, reputed to be a disciple of St. John; St. Polycarp (69-155), bishop of Smyrna and a disciple of St. John. The authors of the Didache and the Epistle of Barnabas are also numbered among the Apostolic Fathers.

Other early ecclesiastical writers included: St. Justin,

martyr (100-165), of Asia Minor and Rome, a layman and apologist; St. Irenaeus (130-202), bishop of Lyons, who opposed Gnosticism; and St. Cyprian (210-258), bishop of Carthage, who opposed Novatianism.

Fathers and Doctors

The Fathers of the Church were theologians and writers of the first eight centuries who were outstanding for sanctity and learning. They were such authoritative witnesses to the belief and teaching of the Church that their unanimous acceptance of doctrines as divinely revealed has been regarded as evidence that such doctrines were so received by the Church in line with apostolic tradition and Sacred Scripture. Their unanimous rejection of doctrines branded them as heretical. Their writings, however, were not necessarily free of error in all respects.

The greatest of these Fathers were: Sts. Ambrose, Augustine, Jerome, and Gregory the Great in the West; Sts. John Chrysostom, Basil the Great, Gregory of Nazianzus, and Athanasius in the East.

The Doctors of the Church were ecclesiastical writers of eminent learning and sanctity who have been given this title because of the great advantage the Church has derived from their work. Their writings, however, were not necessarily free of error in all respects.

Albert the Great, St. (c. 1200-1280): Born in Swabia, Germany; Dominican; bishop of Regensburg (1260-1262); wrote extensively on logic, natural sciences, ethics, metaphysics, Scripture, systematic theology; contributed to development of Scholasticism; teacher of St. Thomas Aquinas; canonized and proclaimed doctor, 1931; named patron of natural scientists, 1941; called *Doctor Universalis, Doctor Expertus*; Nov. 15.

Alphonsus Liguori, St. (1696-1787): Born near Naples, Italy; bishop of Saint Agatha of the Goths (1762-1775); founder of the Redemptorists; in addition to his principal work, *Theologiae Moralis*, wrote on prayer, the spiritual life and doctrinal subjects in response to controversy; canonized, 1839; proclaimed doctor, 1871; named patron of confessors and moralists, 1950; Aug. 1.

Ambrose, St. (c. 340-397): Born in Trier, Germany; bishop of Milan (374-397); one of the strongest opponents of Arianism in the West; his homilies and other writings — on faith, the Holy Spirit, the Incarnation, the sacraments and other subjects — were pastoral and practical; influenced the development of a liturgy at Milan which was named for him; Father and Doctor of the Church; Dec. 7.

Anselm, St. (1033-1109): Born in Aosta, Piedmont, Italy; Benedictine; archbishop of Canterbury (1093-1109); in addition to his principal work, *Cur Deus Homo*, on the atonement and reconciliation of man with God through Christ, wrote about the existence and attributes of God and defended the *Filioque* explanation of the procession of the Holy Spirit from the Father and the Son; proclaimed doctor, 1720; called Father of Scholasticism; Apr. 21.

Anthony of Padua, St. (1195-1231): Born in Lisbon, Portugal; first theologian of the Franciscan Order; preacher; canonized, 1232; proclaimed doctor, 1946; called Evangelical Doctor; June 13.

Athanasius, St. (c. 297-373): Born in Alexandria, Egypt; bishop of Alexandria (328-373); participant in the Council of Nicaea I while still a deacon; dominant opponent of Arians whose errors regarding Christ he refuted in *Apology Against the Arians*, Discourses against the Arians and other works; Father and Doctor of the Church; called Father of Orthodoxy; May 2.

Augustine, St. (354-430): Born in Tagaste, North Africa; bishop of Hippo (395-430) after conversion from Manichaeism; works include the autobiographical and mystical *Confessions, City of God*, treatises on the Trinity, grace, passages of the Bible and doctrines called into question and denied by Manichaeans, Pelagians, and Donatists; had strong and lasting influence on Christian theology and philosophy; Father and Doctor of the Church; called Doctor of Grace; Aug. 28.

Basil the Great, St. (c. 329-379): Born in Caesarea, Cappadocia, Asia Minor; bishop of Caesarea (370-379); wrote three books; *Contra Eunomium*, in refutation of Arian errors; a treatise on the Holy Spirit; many homilies; and several rules for monastic life, on which he had lasting influence; Father and Doctor of the Church; called Father of Monasticism in the East; Jan. 2. **Bede the Venerable, St.** (c. 673-735): Born in Northumberland, England; Benedictine; in addition to his principal work, *Ecclesiastical History* of the English Nation (covering the period 597-731), wrote scriptural commentaries; regarded as probably the most learned man in Western Europe of his time; called Father of English History; May 25.

Bernard of Clairvaux, St. (c. 1090-1153): Born near Dijon, France; abbot; monastic reformer, called the second founder of the Cistercian Order; mystical theologian with great influence on devotional life; opponent of the rationalism brought forward by Abélard and others; canonized, 1174; proclaimed doctor, 1830; called Mellifluous Doctor because of his eloquence; Aug. 20.

Bonaventure, St. (c. 1217-1274): Born near Viterbo, Italy; Franciscan; bishop of Albano (1273-1274); cardinal; wrote *Itinerarium Mentis in Deum, De Reductione Artium ad Theologiam, Breviloquium*, scriptural commentaries, additional mystical works affecting devotional life, and a life of St. Francis of Assisi; canonized, 1482; proclaimed doctor, 1588; called Seraphic Doctor; July 15.

Catherine of Siena, St. (c. 1347-1380): Born in Siena, Italy; member of the Third Order of St. Dominic; mystic; authored a long series of letters, mainly concerning spiritual instruction and encouragement, to associates, and *Dialogue*, a spiritual testament in four treatises; was active in support of a crusade against the Turks and efforts to end war between papal forces and the Florentine allies; had great influence in inducing Gregory XI to return himself and the Curia to Rome in 1377, to end the Avignon period of the papacy; canonized, 1461; proclaimed the second woman doctor, Oct. 4, 1970; Apr. 29; named a co-patroness of Europe, with St. Edith Stein and St. Bridget of Sweden, on Oct. 1, 1999.

Cyril of Alexandria, St. (c. 376-444): Born in Egypt; bishop of Alexandria (412-444); wrote treatises on the Trinity, the Incarnation and other subjects, mostly in refutation of Nestorian errors; made key contributions to the development of Christology; presided at the Council of Ephesus, 431; proclaimed doctor, 1882; June 27.

Cyril of Jerusalem, St. (c. 315-386): Bishop of Jerusalem from 350; vigorous opponent of Arianism; principal work, *Catecheses*, a pre-baptismal explanation of the creed of Jerusalem; proclaimed doctor, 1882; Mar. 18.

Ephraem, St. (c. 306-373): Born in Nisibis, Mesopotamia; counteracted the spread of Gnostic and Arian errors with poems and hymns of his own composition; wrote also on the Eucharist and Mary; proclaimed doctor, 1920; called Deacon of Edessa and Harp of the Holy Spirit; June 9.

Francis de Sales, St. (1567-1622): Born in Savoy; bishop of Geneva (1602-1622); spiritual writer with strong influence on devotional life through treatises such as *Introduction to a Devout Life*, and *The Love of God*; canonized, 1665; proclaimed doctor, 1877; patron of Catholic writers and the Catholic press; Jan. 24.

Gregory Nazianzen, St. (c. 330-c. 390): Born in Arianzus, Cappadocia, Asia Minor; bishop of Constantinople (381-390); vigorous opponent of Arianism; in addition to five theological discourses on the Nicene Creed and the Trinity for which he is best known, wrote letters and poetry; Father and Doctor of the Church; called the Christian Demosthenes because of his eloquence and, in the Eastern Church, the Theologian; Jan. 2.

Gregory I, the Great, St. (c. 540-604): Born in Rome; pope (590-604): wrote many scriptural commentaries, a compendium of theology in the *Book of Morals* based on Job, Dialogues concerning the lives of saints, the immortality of the soul, death, purgatory, heaven and hell, and fourteen books of letters; enforced papal supremacy and established the position of the pope vis-á-vis the emperor; worked for clerical and monastic reform and the observance of clerical celibacy; Father and Doctor of the Church; Sept. 3.

Hilary of Poitiers, St. (c. 315-368): Born in Poitiers, France; bishop of Poitiers (c. 353-368); wrote *De Synodis*, with the Arian controversy in mind, and *De Trinitate*, the first lengthy study of the doctrine in Latin; introduced Eastern theology to the West; contributed to the development of hymnology; proclaimed doctor, 1851; called the Athanasius of the West because of his vigorous defense of the divinity of Christ against Arians; Jan. 13.

Hildegard of Bingen, St. (1098-1179) German mystic and abbess, called the "Sibyl of the Rhine" because of her many visions; she wrote the *Scivias*, a collection of visions, divided into three books; other works included hymns, scientific treatises, letters, and theological writings; given equivalent canonization by Pope Benedict XVI, she was proclaimed a doctor in 2012; Sept. 17.

Isidore of Seville, St. (c. 560-636): Born in Cartagena, Spain; bishop of Seville (c. 600-636); in addition to his principal work, *Etymologiae*, an encyclopedia of the knowledge of his day, wrote on theological and historical subjects; regarded as the most learned man of his time; proclaimed doctor, 1722; Apr. 4.

Jerome, St. (c. 343-420): Born in Stridon, Dalmatia; translated the Old Testament from Hebrew into Latin and revised the existing Latin translation of the New Testament to produce the Vulgate version of the Bible; wrote scriptural commentaries and treatises on matters of controversy; regarded as Father and Doctor of the Church from the eighth century; called Father of Biblical Science; Sept. 30.

John Chrysostom, St. (c. 347-407): Born in Antioch, Asia Minor; archbishop of Constantinople (398-407); wrote homilies, scriptural commentaries and letters of wide influence in addition to a classical treatise on the priesthood; proclaimed doctor by the Council of Chalcedon, 451; called the greatest of the Greek Fathers; named patron of preachers, 1909; called Golden-Mouthed because of his eloquence; Sept. 13.

John Damascene, St. (c. 675-c. 749): Born in Damascus, Syria; monk; wrote *Fountain of Wisdom*, a three-part work including a history of heresies and an exposition of the Christian faith, three discourses against the Iconoclasts, homilies on Mary, biblical commentaries, and treatises on moral subjects; proclaimed doctor, 1890;

called Golden Speaker because of his eloquence; Dec. 4.

John of the Cross, St. (1542-1591): Born in Old Castile, Spain; Carmelite; founder of Discalced Carmelites; one of the greatest mystical theologians, wrote *The Ascent of Mt. Carmel*; *The Dark Night of the Soul*, *The Spiritual Canticle*, *The Living Flame of Love*; canonized, 1726; proclaimed doctor, 1926; called Doctor of Mystical Theology; Dec. 14.

John of Ávila, St. (1500-1569) Apostle of Andalusia, a Spanish mystic reformer, and preacher, the patron of priests in Spain; Jewish-born near Toledo, he initially prepared for missionary work in Mexico, but he was sent to revive the faith in Andalusia; renowned for his sermons, he was an ardent proponent of clerical reform; canonized in 1970 by Pope Paul VI; proclaimed doctor in 2012; May 10.

Lawrence of Brindisi, St. (1559-1619): Born in Brindisi, Italy; Franciscan (Capuchin); vigorous preacher of strong influence in the post-Reformation period; 15 tomes of collected works include scriptural commentaries, sermons, homilies and doctrinal writings; canonized, 1881; proclaimed doctor, 1959; July 21.

Leo I, the Great, St. (c. 400-461): Born in Tuscany, Italy; pope (440-461); wrote the *Tome* of Leo, to explain doctrine concerning the two natures and one Person of Christ, against the background of the Nestorian and Monophysite heresies; other works included sermons, letters and writings against the errors of Manichaeism and Pelagianism; was instrumental in dissuading Attila from sacking Rome in 452; proclaimed doctor, 1574; Nov. 10.

Peter Canisius, St. (1521-1597): Born in Nijmegen, Holland; Jesuit; wrote popular expositions of the Catholic faith in several catechisms which were widely circulated in 20 editions in his lifetime alone; was one of the moving figures in the Counter-Reformation period, especially in southern and western Germany; canonized and proclaimed doctor, 1925; Dec. 21.

Peter Chrysologus, St. (c. 400-450): Born in Imola, Italy; served as archbishop of Ravenna (c. 433-450); his sermons and writings, many of which were designed to counteract Monophysitism, were pastoral and practical; proclaimed doctor, 1729; July 30.

Peter Damian, St. (1007-1072): Born in Ravenna, Italy; Benedictine; cardinal; his writings and sermons, many of which concerned ecclesiastical and clerical reform, were pastoral and practical; proclaimed doctor, 1828; Feb. 21.

Robert Bellarmine, St. (1542-1621): Born in Tuscany, Italy; Jesuit; archbishop of Capua (1602-1605); wrote *Controversies*, a three-volume exposition of doctrine under attack during and after the Reformation, two catechisms and the spiritual work, *The Art of Dying Well*; was an authority on ecclesiology and Church-state relations; canonized, 1930; proclaimed doctor, 1931; Sept. 17.

Teresa of Jesus (Ávila), St. (1515-1582): Born in Ávila, Spain; entered the Carmelite Order, 1535; in the early 1560s, initiated a primitive Carmelite reform which greatly influenced men and women religious, especially in Spain; wrote extensively on spiritual and mystical subjects; principal works included her *Autobiography*, *Way of Perfection*, *The Interior Castle*, *Meditations on the Canticle*, *The Foundations*, *Visitation of the Discalced Nuns*; canonized, 1622; proclaimed first woman doctor, Sept. 27, 1970; Oct. 15.

Thérèse of Lisieux, St. (1873-1897): Born in Alençon, Normandy, France; entered the Carmelites at Lisieux in 1888, lived for only nine more years, dying on September

30, 1897 from tuberculosis. Trusting completely in God, a path she described as the "little way," she lived a seemingly ordinary life of a nun, but her spiritual advancement was such that her superiors instructed her to write an autobiography in 1895 (*The Story of a Soul*). One of the most popular and respected saints throughout the 20th century, she was canonized on May 17, 1925. Pope John Paul II declared her the third woman doctor on Oct. 20, 1997, in the letter *Divini amoris scientia*; her relics also toured the United States, attracting huge crowds, Sept.–Oct. 2013.

Thomas Aquinas, St. (1225-1274): Born near Naples, Italy; Dominican; teacher and writer on virtually the whole range of philosophy and theology; principal works were *Summa contra Gentiles*, a manual and systematic defense of Christian doctrine, and *Summa Theologiae*, a new (at that time) exposition of theology on philosophical principles; canonized, 1323; proclaimed doctor, 1567; called *Doctor Communis, Doctor Angelicus*, the Great Synthesizer because of the way in which he related faith and reason, theology and philosophy (especially that of Aristotle), and systematized the presentation of Christian doctrine; named patron of Catholic schools and education, 1880; Jan. 28.

CREEDS

Creeds are formal and official statements of Christian doctrine. As summaries of the principal truths of faith, they are standards of orthodoxy and are useful for instructional purposes, for actual profession of the faith and for expression of the faith in the liturgy.

The classical creeds are the Apostles' Creed and the Creed of Nicaea-Constantinople. Two others are the Athanasian Creed and the Creed of Pius IV.

Apostles' Creed

Text: *I believe in God, the Father almighty, Creator of heaven and earth.*

And in Jesus Christ, his only Son, our Lord; who was conceived by the Holy Spirit, born of the Virgin Mary, suffered under Pontius Pilate, was crucified, died, and was buried. He descended into hell; the third day he arose again from the dead; he ascended into heaven, sits at the right hand of God, the Father almighty; from thence he shall come to judge the living and the dead.

I believe in the Holy Spirit, the holy Catholic Church, the communion of saints, the forgiveness of sins, the resurrection of the body, and life everlasting. Amen.

Background: The Apostles' Creed reflects the teaching of the Apostles but is not of apostolic origin. It probably originated in the second century as a rudimentary formula of faith professed by catechumens before the reception of baptism. Baptismal creeds in fourth-century use at Rome and elsewhere in the West closely resembled the present text, which was quoted in a handbook of Christian doctrine written between 710 and 724. This text was in wide use throughout the West by the ninth century. The Apostles' Creed is common to all Christian confessional churches in the West, but is not used in Eastern Churches.

Nicene Creed

The following translation of the Latin text of the Creed was prepared by the International Committee on English in the Liturgy.

Text: *I believe in one God, the Father almighty, maker of heaven and earth, of all things visible and invisible.*

I believe in one Lord Jesus Christ, the Only Begotten Son of God, born of the Father before all ages.

God from God, Light from Light, true God from true God, begotten, not made, consubstantial with the Father; through him all things were made.

For us men and for our salvation he came down from heaven, and by the Holy Spirit was incarnate of the Virgin Mary, and became man.

For our sake he was crucified under Pontius Pilate, he suffered death and was buried, and rose again on the third day in accordance with the Scriptures.

He ascended into heaven and is seated at the right hand of the Father.

He will come again in glory to judge the living and the dead and his kingdom will have no end.

I believe in the Holy Spirit, the Lord, the giver of life, who proceeds from the Father and the Son, who with the Father and the Son is adored and glorified, who has spoken through the prophets.

I believe in one, holy, catholic and apostolic Church.

I confess one Baptism for the forgiveness of sins and I look forward to the resurrection of the dead and the life of the world to come. Amen

Background: The Nicene Creed (Creed of Nicaea-Constantinople) consists of elements of doctrine contained in an early baptismal creed of Jerusalem and enactments of the Council of Nicaea (325) and the Council of Constantinople (381).

Its strong trinitarian content reflects the doctrinal errors, especially of Arianism, it served to counteract. Theologically, it is much more sophisticated than the Apostles' Creed.

Since late in the fifth century, the Nicene Creed has been the only creed in liturgical use in the Eastern Churches. The Western Church adopted it for liturgical use by the end of the eighth century.

The Athanasian Creed

The Athanasian Creed, which has a unique structure, is a two-part summary of doctrine concerning the Trinity and the Incarnation-Redemption bracketed at the beginning and end with the statement that belief in the cited truths is necessary for salvation; it also contains a number of anathemas or condemnatory clauses regarding doctrinal errors. Although attributed to St. Athanasius, it was probably written after his death, between 381 and 428, and may have been authored by St. Ambrose. It is not accepted in the East; in the West, it formerly had place in the Roman-Rite Liturgy of the Hours and in the liturgy for the Solemnity of the Holy Trinity.

Creed of Pius IV

The Creed of Pius IV, also called the Profession of Faith of the Council of Trent, was promulgated in the bull *Injunctum Nobis*, Nov. 13, 1564. It is a summary of doctrine defined by the council concerning: Scripture and tradition, original sin and justification, the Mass and sacraments, veneration of the saints, indulgences, the primacy of the See of Rome. It was slightly modified in 1887 to include doctrinal formulations of the First Vatican Council.

CHRISTIAN MORALITY

By Fr. Alfred McBride, O.Praem.

"Incorporated into Christ by Baptism, Christians are 'dead to sin and alive in Christ Jesus ... '" (Rom 6:11).

CHRISTIAN MORALITY IS LIFE IN CHRIST

The third part of the *Catechism* focuses on Christian morality. After the Creed as faith professed, and sacraments as faith celebrated, the *Catechism* turns our attention to the faith lived. It deals with this issue in two major sections. The first section establishes the context for Christian morality. The second section analyzes the ten commandments. This approach preserves the *Catechism's* resolute insistence on the primacy of God's initiative through Revelation, salvation, and grace followed by our human response in faith, celebration, and Christian witness. Hence morality does not begin with the rules but with the call to life in Christ and the Holy Spirit. Covenant love comes first, then the response of Christian affection in the life of the commandments. This saves us both from legalism and from piety without practical witness.

The following excerpt from the *Catechism of the Catholic Church* sets the vision for the Christian moral life:

LIFE IN CHRIST

1691 "Christian, recognize your dignity and, now that you share in God's own nature, do not return to your former base condition by sinning. Remember who is your head and of whose body you are a member. Never forget that you have been rescued from the power of darkness and brought into the light of the Kingdom of God."[1]

1692 The Symbol of the faith confesses the greatness of God's gifts to man in his work of creation, and even more in redemption and sanctification. What faith confesses, the sacraments communicate: by the sacraments of rebirth, Christians have become "children of God,"[2] "partakers of the divine nature."[3] Coming to see in the faith their new dignity, Christians are called to lead henceforth a life "worthy of the gospel of Christ."[4] They are made capable of doing so by the grace of Christ and the gifts of his Spirit, which they receive through the sacraments and through prayer.

1693 Christ Jesus always did what was pleasing to the Father,[5] and always lived in perfect communion with him. Likewise Christ's disciples are invited to live in the sight of the Father "who sees in secret,"[6] in order to become "perfect as your heavenly Father is perfect."[7]

1694 Incorporated into Christ by Baptism, Christians are "dead to sin and alive to God in Christ Jesus" and so participate in the life of the Risen Lord.[8] Following Christ and united with him,[9] Christians can strive to be "imitators of God as beloved children, and walk in love"[10] by conforming their thoughts, words and actions to the "mind ... which is yours in Christ Jesus,"[11] and by following his example.[12]

1695 "Justified in the name of the Lord Jesus Christ and in the Spirit of our God,"[13] "sanctified ... [and] called to be saints,"[14] Christians have become the temple of the Holy Spirit.[15] This "Spirit of the Son" teaches them to pray to the Father[16] and, having become their life, prompts them to act so as to bear "the fruit of the Spirit"[17] by charity in action. Healing the wounds of sin, the Holy Spirit renews us interiorly through a spiritual transformation.[18] He enlightens and strengthens us to live as "children of light" through "all that is good and right and true."[19]

1696 The way of Christ "leads to life"; a contrary way "leads to destruction."[20] The Gospel parable of the two ways remains ever present in the catechesis of the Church; it shows the importance of moral decisions for our salvation: "There are two ways, the one of life, the other of death; but between the two, there is a great difference."[21]

1697 Catechesis has to reveal in all clarity the joy and the demands of the way of Christ.[22] Catechesis for the "newness of life"[23] in him should be:

• a catechesis of the Holy Spirit, the interior Master of life according to Christ, a gentle guest and friend who inspires, guides, corrects, and strengthens this life;

• a catechesis of grace, for it is by grace that we are saved and again it is by grace that our works can bear fruit for eternal life;

• a catechesis of the beatitudes, for the way of Christ is summed up in the beatitudes, the only path that leads to the eternal beatitude for which the human heart longs;

• a catechesis of sin and forgiveness, for unless man acknowledges that he is a sinner he cannot know the truth about himself, which is a condition for acting justly; and without the offer of forgiveness he would not be able to bear this truth;

• a catechesis of the human virtues which causes one to grasp the beauty and attraction of right dispositions toward goodness;

• a catechesis of the Christian virtues of faith, hope, and charity, generously inspired by the example of the saints; a catechesis of the twofold commandment of charity set forth in the Decalogue;

• an ecclesial catechesis, for it is through the manifold exchanges of "spiritual goods" in the "communion of saints" that Christian life can grow, develop, and be communicated.

1698 The first and last point of reference of this catechesis will always be Jesus Christ himself, who is "the way, and the truth, and the life."[24] It is by looking to him in faith that Christ's faithful can hope that he himself fulfills his promises in them, and that, by loving him with the same love with which he has loved them, they may perform works in keeping with their dignity: "I ask you to consider that our Lord Jesus Christ is your true head, and that you are one of his members. He belongs to you as the head belongs to its members; all that is his is yours: his spirit, his heart, his body and soul, and all his faculties. You must make use of all these as of your own, to serve, praise, love, and glorify God. You belong to him, as members belong to their head. And so he longs for you to use all that is in you, as if it were his own, for the service and glory of the Father."[25] "For to me, to live is Christ."[26]

Footnotes

1. St. Leo the Great, *Sermo* 22 in nat. Dom. 3: PL 54, 192C. [2] Jn 1:12; 1 Jn 3:1. [3] 2 Pt 1:4. [4] Phil 1:27. [5] Cf. Jn 8:29. [6] Mt 6:6. [7] Mt 5:48. [8] Rom 6:11 and cf. 6:5; cf. Col 2:12. [9] Cf. Jn 15:5. [10] Eph 5:1-2. [11] Phil 2:5. [12] Cf. Jn 13:12-16. [13] 1 Cor 6:11. [14] 1 Cor 1:2. [15] Cf. 1 Cor 6:19. [16] Cf. Gal 4:6. [17] Gal 5:22,25. [18] Cf. Eph 4:23. [19] Eph 5:8,9. [20] Mt 7:13; cf. Dt 30:15-20. [21] Didache 1, 1: SCh 248, 140. [22] Cf. John Paul II, CT 29. [23] Rom 6:4. [24] Jn 14:6. [25] St. John Eudes, *Tract. de admirabili corde Jesu*, 1, 5. [26] Phil 1:21.

THE TEN COMMANDMENTS

Any discussions of the commandments should begin with the scene at Sinai where God gave them to us. Read Ex 19:3-6; 20:1-17. The first event is a covenant experience. God tells Moses how much he has loved the Israelites, is delivering them from slavery by "raising them up on eagles' wings," and is bringing them to freedom. God then offers them a binding covenant of love. He will be their only God and they will be his chosen people. It's like a marriage experience, an exchange of vows between God and Israel.

The next section shows God telling them how to live out the love they have pledged. He gives them the Ten Commandments as the means to live the covenant, to express the love they have promised. The *Catechism* points out that the Ten Commandments are privileged expressions of the natural law, made known to us by reason as well as Divine Revelation. We are obliged in obedience to observe these laws of love, both in serious and light matters. Love is in the details as well as the large matters. We must remember that what God has commanded, he makes possible by his grace.

Jesus set the tone for understanding the importance of the commandments. When a rich young man came to him and asked him what he should do to enter eternal life, Jesus replied, "if you wish to enter into life, keep the commandments" (Mt 19:17). In another case, someone asked him which were the greatest commandments, Jesus replied, "you shall love the Lord, your God, with all your heart, with all your soul, and with all your mind. This is the greatest and first commandment. The second is like it: You shall love your neighbor as yourself" (Mt 22:37-39). The first three commandments deal with Christ's call to God with all our being. The last seven commandments show us how to love our neighbors as we love ourselves.

The following excerpt from the *Catechism of the Catholic Church* shows how Jesus taught the importance of the Ten Commandments:

"Teacher, what must I do . . .?"

2052 "Teacher, what good deed must I do, to have eternal life?" To the young man who asked this question, Jesus answers first by invoking the necessity to recognize God as the "One there is who is good," as the supreme Good and the source of all good. Then Jesus tells him: "If you would enter life, keep the commandments." And he cites for his questioner the precepts that concern love of neighbor: "You shall not kill, You shall not commit adultery, You shall not steal, You shall not bear false witness, Honor your father and mother." Finally Jesus sums up these commandments positively: "You shall love your neighbor as yourself."[1]

2053 To this first reply Jesus adds a second: "If you would be perfect, go, sell what you possess and give to the poor, and you will have treasure in heaven; and come, follow me."[2] This reply does not do away with the first: following Jesus Christ involves keeping the Commandments. The Law has not been abolished,[3] but rather man is invited to rediscover it in the person of his Master who is its perfect fulfillment. In the three synoptic Gospels, Jesus' call to the rich young man to follow him, in the obedience of a disciple and in the observance of the Commandments, is joined to the call to poverty and chastity.[4] The evangelical counsels are inseparable from the Commandments.

2054 Jesus acknowledged the Ten Commandments, but he also showed the power of the Spirit at work in their let-

ter. He preached a "righteousness [which] exceeds that of the scribes and Pharisees"[5] as well as that of the Gentiles. [6] He unfolded all the demands of the Commandments. "You have heard that it was said to the men of old, 'You shall not kill.' ... But I say to you that every one who is angry with his brother shall be liable to judgment."[7]

2055 When someone asks him, "Which commandment in the Law is the greatest?"[8] Jesus replies: "You shall love the Lord your God with all your heart, and with all your soul, and with all your mind. This is the greatest and first commandment. And a second is like it: You shall love your neighbor as yourself. On these two commandments hang all the Law and the prophets."[9] The Decalogue must be interpreted in light of this twofold yet single commandment of love, he fullness of the Law: "The commandments: 'You shall not commit adultery, You shall not kill, You shall not steal, You shall not covet,' and any other commandment, are summed up in this sentence: 'You shall love your neighbor as yourself.' Love does no wrong to a neighbor; therefore love is the fulfilling of the law."[10]

Footnotes

[1] Mt 19:16-19. [2] Mt 19:21. [3] Cf. Mt 5:17. [4] Cf. Mt 19:6-12,21,23-29. [5] Mt 5:20. [6] Cf. Mt 5:46-47. [7] Mt 5:21-22. [8] Mt 22:36. [9] Mt 22:37-40; cf. Dt 6:5; Lv 19:18. [10] Rom 13:9-10.

In the traditional Catholic enumeration and according to Dt. 5:6-21, the Commandments are:
1. "I, the Lord, am your God You shall not have other gods besides me. You shall not carve idols."
2. "You shall not take the name of the Lord, your God, in vain."
3. "Take care to keep holy the Sabbath day."
4. "Honor your father and your mother."
5. "You shall not kill."
6. "You shall not commit adultery."
7. "You shall not steal."
8. "You shall not bear dishonest witness against your neighbor."
9. "You shall not covet your neighbor's wife."
10. "You shall not desire your neighbor's house or field, nor his male or female slave, nor his ox or ass, nor anything that belongs to him" (summarily, his goods).

Another version of the Commandments, substantially the same, is given in Ex 20:1-17.

The traditional enumeration of the Commandments in Protestant usage differs from the above. Thus: two commandments are made of the first, as above; the third and fourth are equivalent to the second and third, as above, and so on; and the 10th includes the ninth and 10th, as above.

Love of God and Neighbor

The first three of the commandments deal directly with man's relations with God, viz.: acknowledgment of one true God and the rejection of false gods and idols; honor due to God and his name; observance of the Sabbath as the Lord's day.

The rest cover interpersonal relationships, viz.: the obedience due to parents and, logically, to other persons in authority, and the obligations of parents to children and of persons in authority to those under their care; respect for life and physical integrity; fidelity in marriage, and chastity; justice and rights; truth; internal respect for faithfulness in marriage, chastity, and the goods of others.

Perfection in Christian Life

The moral obligations of the Ten Commandments are complemented by others flowing from the twofold law of love, the whole substance and pattern of Christ's teaching, and everything implied in full and active membership and participation in the community of salvation formed by Christ in his Church. Some of these matters are covered in other sections of the *Almanac* under appropriate headings.

Precepts of the Church

The purpose of the precepts of the Church, according to the *Catechism of the Catholic Church*, is "to guarantee to the faithful the indispensable minimum in the spirit of prayer and moral effort, in the growth and love of God and neighbor" (No. 2041).

1. Attendance at Mass on Sundays and holy days of obligation. (Observance of Sundays and holy days of obligation involves refraining from work that hinders the worship due to God.)
2. Confession of sins at least once a year. (Not required by the precept in the absence of serious sin.)
3. Reception of the Eucharist at least during the Easter season (in the U.S., from the first Sunday of Lent to Trinity Sunday).
4. Keep holy the holy days of obligation.
5. Observance of specified days of fasting and abstinence.

There is also an obligation to provide for the material needs of the Church.

CATHOLIC MORAL TEACHINGS OF POPE JOHN PAUL II

On Aug. 6, 1993, Pope John Paul II published his tenth encyclical, Veritatis Splendor *("The Splendor of the Truth") regarding the fundamental truths of the Church's moral teachings. On Mar. 25, 1995, he published his eleventh encyclical,* Evangelium Vitae *("The Gospel of Life"), concerning the value and inviolability of human life. The following material is adapted from* The Encyclicals of John Paul II, *with the kind permission of Most Rev. J. Michael Miller, C.S.B.*

Veritatis Splendor ("The Splendor of the Truth")

On Aug. 6, 1993, John Paul II signed his 10th encyclical, *Veritatis Splendor,* regarding certain fundamental truths of the Church's moral teaching.[1] Undoubtedly it is the pope's most complex and most discussed document. Since its publication, the encyclical has generated a great deal of comment in the media and among theologians. This is not surprising, since *Veritatis Splendor* is the first-ever papal document on the theological and philosophical foundations of Catholic moral teaching. In this encyclical the pope affirms that divine revelation contains "a specific and determined moral content, universally valid and permanent" (§37.1), which the Magisterium has the competence to interpret and teach.

Six years before, in the apostolic letter *Spiritus Domini* (1987), John Paul had publicly announced his intention to publish a document that would treat "more fully and more deeply the issues regarding the very foundations of moral theology" (§5.1). For several reasons the encyclical's preparation took longer than was first anticipated. First, the pope widely consulted bishops and theologians throughout the world, and various drafts were drawn up. Second, he thought that it was fitting for the encyclical "to be preceded by the *Catechism of the Catholic Church,* which contains a complete and systematic exposition of

Christian moral teaching" (§5.3). The *Catechism,* published in 1992, gives a full presentation of the Church's moral doctrine, including that on particular questions, and expounds it in a positive way. *Veritatis Splendor,* on the other hand, limits itself to dealing with the fundamental principles underlying all moral teaching.

But why does John Paul think that an encyclical on moral issues will serve the Church and the world on the threshold of the third millennium? According to him, reflection on the ethical implications of Christian faith, lived from the beginning as the "way" (Acts 22:4), belongs to the full proclamation of the Gospel. Moreover, he is convinced that society is in the throes of a *"crisis of truth"* (§32.2). This crisis has the "most serious implications for the moral life of the faithful and for communion in the Church, as well as for a just and fraternal social life" (§5.2).

The deChristianization of many cultures involves not only a loss of faith but also *"a decline or obscuring of the moral sense"* (§106.2). This new moral situation brings with it "the *confusion between good and evil,* which makes it impossible to build up and to preserve the moral order" (§93.1). The ethical bewilderment of some Catholics has led to "the spread of numerous doubts and objections of a human and psychological, social and cultural, religious and even properly theological nature, with regard to the Church's moral teachings" (§4.2). In an increasingly secular world, believers are "making judgments and decisions [that] often appear extraneous or even contrary to those of the Gospel" (§88.2). Moreover, dissent from Catholic moral teaching often entails "an overall and systematic calling into question of traditional moral doctrine" (§4.2). Thus, as a service to the ethical and spiritual welfare of individuals and cultures, John Paul addresses the basic moral principles handed down by the Christian Tradition.

In order to meet his goal, the pope responds in a constructive way to the contemporary moral crisis by proclaiming "the splendor of the truth." When he announced the forthcoming publication of *Veritatis Splendor,* he described the encyclical's purpose: "It reaffirms the dignity of the human person, created in God's image, and proposes anew the genuine concept of human freedom, showing its essential and constitutive relationship with the truth in accordance with Christ's words: 'The truth will make you free!' (Jn 8:32)."[2] On another occasion, John Paul said that he intended the encyclical to be "a proclamation of truth and a hymn to freedom: values felt strongly by contemporary man and deeply respected by the Church."[3] His primary aim, then, is not to censure specific dissident moral opinions but to proclaim that Christ is "the true and final answer to the problem of morality" (§85).

John Paul sets several specific objectives for the encyclical. First, he wishes "*to reflect on the whole of the Church's moral teaching,* with the precise goal of recalling certain fundamental truths of Catholic doctrine which, in the present circumstances, risk being distorted or denied" (§4.2, cf. §30.1). Second, he aims to show the faithful "the inviting splendor of that truth which is Jesus Christ himself" (§83.2). Christ alone is the answer to humanity's questions, "the only response fully capable of satisfying the desire of the human heart" (§7.1). Third, if the present crisis is to be successfully resolved, the Magisterium must authoritatively discern "*interpretations of Christian morality which are not consistent with 'sound teaching'* (2 Tm 4:3)" (§29.4, cf. §27.4). This pastoral discernment of the pope and bishops is necessary as a way of assuring "*the right of the faithful* to receive Catholic doctrine in its purity and integrity" (§113.2).

The pope addresses *Veritatis Splendor* specifically to his brother bishops. He intends them to be the first, but not exclusive, recipients of the encyclical. John Paul reminds them of their responsibility to safeguard and find "ever new ways of speaking with love and mercy" about *"the path of the moral life"* (§3.1,2).

John Paul II's training in ethics and moral theology is clearly evident in *Veritatis Splendor*. The encyclical's exposition is sometimes highly technical, especially in its analyses and responses to opinions contrary to Church teaching. While some commentators have voiced disagreement about the accuracy of the pope's descriptions of the ethical positions with which he disagrees, they respect his desire to be fair-minded. As we shall see, whenever John Paul deals with an opinion he disagrees with, he first takes great pains to point out what is positive in the view. Only after doing this does he then examine its weaknesses. When unmasking theological and philosophical ideas incompatible with revealed truth, he scrupulously avoids imposing "any particular theological system, still less a philosophical one" (§29.4).

Throughout the encyclical the pope repeatedly draws inspiration from the Bible. Chapter one, structured around the encounter of Jesus with the rich young man (Mt 19:16-21), establishes a biblical foundation for fundamental moral principles. In this chapter the pope wishes to apply the theological method proposed by the Second Vatican Council: "Sacred Scripture remains the living and fruitful source of the Church's moral doctrine" (§28.2, cf. §5.3). Chapter two, on the other hand, uses Scripture chiefly to corroborate positions advanced on the basis of the natural moral law. The beginning of chapter three returns to a more biblical approach; it discusses discipleship in terms of the Paschal Mystery and of martyrdom as the supreme expression of following Christ.

More so than in his other encyclicals, in *Veritatis Splendor* John Paul relies considerably on the teaching of St. Thomas Aquinas, referring to him directly at least 20 times, and on the teaching of St. Augustine, citing him 16 times. The pope also mines extensively the documents of Vatican II, especially *Gaudium et Spes*, which he cites more than 25 times. Except for one reference to St. Alphonsus Liguori and a single direct citation of John Henry Newman, the pope mentions no moral philosopher or theologian after the Middle Ages.

Footnotes

[1] *Acta Apostolicae Sedis*, 85 (1993), 1133-1228. [2] *Angelus*, Oct. 3, 1993, *L'Osservatore Romano*, 40 (1993), 1. [3] *Angelus*, Oct. 17, 1993, *L'Osservatore Romano*, 42 (1993), 1.

Evangelium Vitae ("The Gospel of Life")

"The *Gospel of life* is at the heart of Jesus' message" (§1.1). With these words Pope John Paul II begins his eleventh encyclical, *Evangelium Vitae*, published on Mar. 25, 1995.[1] He aptly chose the feast of the Annunciation, which celebrates Mary's welcoming of the Son of God who took flesh in her womb, to issue a document dedicated to the value and inviolability of human life. By taking up the cause of the "great multitude of weak and defenseless human beings" (§5.4), especially unborn children and those at the end of life, the pope continues the defense of human dignity dealt with in his three social encyclicals. *Evangelium Vitae* is an anguished and vigorous response to *"scientifically and systematically programmed threats"* against life (§17.2), assaults which have repercussions on Church teaching, touching upon "the core of her faith in the redemptive Incarnation of the Son of God" (§3.1).

For John Paul II, the cause of life is the cause of the Gospel entrusted to the Church, which is duty-bound to raise her voice in the defense of life. His encyclical is a "pressing appeal addressed to each and every person, in the name of God: *respect, protect, love and serve life, every human life!*" (§5.5).

Preparations for the encyclical began in Apr. 1991, when the pope called a special meeting in Rome of the College of Cardinals to discuss current threats to human life. After their deliberations, the cardinals asked him "to reaffirm with the authority of the Successor of Peter the value of human life and its inviolability" (§5.1). As a first response to their request, the pope wrote a personal letter to every bishop, seeking contributions to the planned document. They replied with valuable suggestions, and he incorporated many of their proposals into the encyclical. *Evangelium Vitae*, then, is the fruit of genuine episcopal collegiality. By taking an active part in its preparation, the bishops "bore witness to their unanimous desire to share in the doctrinal and pastoral mission of the Church with regard to the *Gospel of life*" (§5.2).

Unlike *Veritatis Splendor*, which was directed primarily to bishops, John Paul intends *Evangelium Vitae* to be read also by the lay faithful, indeed by all people of good will. Concern for the sacredness of human life is not just a matter for Catholics. "The value at stake," writes the pope, "is one which every human being can grasp by the light of reason" (§101.2). The essential truths of the Gospel of life "are written in the heart of every man and woman," echoing in every human conscience "from the time of creation itself" (§29.3). He insists that anyone who is sincerely open to truth and goodness can discover "the sacred value of human life from its very beginning until its end, and can affirm the right of every human being to have this primary good respected to the highest degree" (§2.2).

The encyclical's style is typically Wojtylan. It intersperses rigorous analysis with prayers and exhortations. As can be seen from the more than 300 biblical quotations and references, Scripture accompanies the pope's presentation from start to finish, giving *Evangelium Vitae* an inspirational tone and familiar style. He also relies heavily on the Church Fathers. The 18 patristic quotations that appear in the encyclical reinforce the truths that God is the origin of life, that human beings share in divine life, and that Jesus gave his life so that others might live. As is customary, John Paul frequently cites the documents of the Second Vatican Council — here, more than 25 times. He also makes use of the *Catechism of the Catholic Church*, citing it on 10 occasions.

Of particular significance in *Evangelium Vitae* are the pope's three authoritative doctrinal pronouncements: on the direct and voluntary killing of innocent human life (cf. §57.4), on abortion (cf. §62.3), and on euthanasia (cf. §65.3). In each of these formal statements John Paul recalls, through his ordinary magisterium, that a specific proposition is taught infallibly by the ordinary and universal Magisterium of the College of Bishops in communion with the Successor of Peter. He does not, therefore, call upon the charism which belongs to the Petrine ministry to teach infallibly, as this was defined at the First Vatican Council (1870). Rather, the pope "confirms" or "declares" (as in the case of abortion) a doctrine already taught by the bishops as belonging to the Catholic faith. Thus, there is nothing "new" in the Pope's affirmations, but merely the reiteration of teaching about which a consensus exists in the Episcopal College.

Footnotes: [1] *Acta Apostolicae Sedis,* 87 (1995), 401-522.

CATHOLIC SOCIAL DOCTRINE

Nature of the Doctrine

Writing in *Christianity and Social Progress*, Pope John XXIII made the following statement about the nature and scope of the Church's social doctrine as stated in the encyclicals in particular and related writings in general:

"What the Catholic Church teaches and declares regarding the social life and relationships of men is beyond question for all time valid.

"The cardinal point of this teaching is that individual men are necessarily the foundation, cause, and end of all social institutions insofar as they are social by nature, and raised to an order of existence that transcends and subdues nature.

"Beginning with this very basic principle whereby the dignity of the human person is affirmed and defended, Holy Church — especially during the last century and with the assistance of learned priests and laymen, specialists in the field — has arrived at clear social teachings whereby the mutual relationships of men are ordered. Taking general norms into account, these principles are in accord with the nature of things and the changed conditions of man's social life, or with the special genius of our day. Moreover, these norms can be approved by all."

Background

While social concerns have always been a part of the Church's teachings, Catholic social doctrine has been the subject of much consideration since the end of the last century and has been formulated in a progressive manner in a number of authoritative documents starting with the encyclical *Rerum Novarum* ("On Capital and Labor") issued by Leo XIII in 1891. Owing to its significance, the encyclical was called by Pope John XXIII the *magna carta* of Catholic social doctrine.

Other outstanding examples are the encyclicals: *Quadragesimo Anno* ("On Reconstruction of the Social Order") by Pius XI in 1931; *Mater et Magistra* ("Christianity and Social Progress") and *Pacem in Terris* ("Peace on Earth"), by John XXIII in 1961 and 1963, respectively; *Populorum Progressio* ("Development of Peoples"), by Paul VI in 1967; *Laborem Exercens* ("On Human Work"), *Sollicitudo Rei Socialis* ("On Social Concerns") and *Centesimus Annus* ("The 100th Year") by John Paul II in 1981, 1987 and 1991, respectively. Among many other accomplishments of ideological importance in the social field, Pius XII made a distinctive contribution with his formulation of a plan for world peace and order in Christmas messages from 1939 to 1941, and in other documents.

Of particular significance to the contemporary application of social doctrine are the document *Gaudium et Spes* (Pastoral Constitution on the Church in the Modern World) issued by the Second Vatican Council and Pope John Paul II's encyclical letters, *Laborem Exercens* ("On Human Work"), *Sollicitudo Rei Socialis* ("On Social Concerns"), and *Centesimus Annus* ("The 100th Year").

These documents represent the most serious attempts in modern times to systematize the social implications of divine revelation as well as the socially relevant writings of the Fathers and Doctors of the Church. Their contents are theological penetrations into social life, with particular reference to human rights, the needs of the poor and those in underdeveloped countries, and humane conditions of life, freedom, justice and peace. In some respects, they read like juridical documents; essentially, however, they are Gospel-oriented and pastoral in intention.

Gaudium et Spes

Gaudium et Spes ("Pastoral Constitution on the Church in the Modern World") was the last document issued by Vatican Council II (Dec. 7, 1965). The document has as its purpose to search out the signs of God's presence and meaning in and through the events of this time in human history. Accordingly, it deals with the situation of men in present circumstances of profound change, challenge and crisis on all levels of life. It is evenly divided into two main parts: the Church's teaching on humanity in the modern era and urgent problems of the times.

Part One

The first part begins: "The joys and the hopes, the griefs and the anxieties of this age" (No. 1) — a clear indication that the Council Fathers were aware both of the positive nature of the modern world and its many dangers and travails. Further, the council places great emphasis throughout on the human existence, a stress that was quite innovative in its presentation: "According to the almost unanimous opinion of believers and unbelievers alike, all things on earth should be related to man as their center and crown" (No. 12). Having developed an analysis of humanity, the document then offered a thorough summary of traditional Church teaching on human life, complete with discussion of sin, the union of body and soul, and the moral conscience.

There is, as well, a genuinely realistic appraisal of contemporary society, noting the pervasiveness of atheism, adding that its spread can be attributed in part to the fault and carelessness of those within the Church whose actions and failures "must be said to conceal rather than reveal the authentic face of God and religion" (No. 19). Toward the fuller understanding of the place of the Church in the modern world, *Gaudium et Spes* emphasizes the harmony that should exist between the Catholic faith and scientific progress because "earthly matters and the concerns of faith derive from the same God" (No. 36). This does not mean, however, that there ought to be no qualifying elements or restraints to science; the Council Fathers add to this positive statement the provision that such research, "within every branch of learning," must be "carried out in a genuinely scientific manner and in accord with moral norms" (No. 36). Finally, the first part makes an ecumenical gesture, noting that the Church "holds in high esteem the things which other Christian Churches or ecclesial communities have done..." (No. 40).

Part Two

Part Two offers the practical application of the Church's teaching and message enunciated in Part One. Most pressing is the council's concern for the family, and its treatment of family life and marriage is the most detailed and extensive in the history of the councils of the Church. This leads to study of the deeply troubling presence of contraception. The council reiterates Church instruction in an affirmation of opposition to contraception that would receive even fuller expression in three years in the encyclical *Humanae Vitae*. In the matter of abortion, the document states clearly: "... from the moment of its conception life must be guarded with the greatest care, while abortion and infanticide are unspeakable crimes" (No. 51). In its study of culture, in which the council reminds all humanity that culture and civilization are creations of man, it points out his responsibility over it and his duty to seek that which is above, which entails an "obligation to work with all men in constructing a more human world" (No. 57). Here we have a powerful preface or introduction to the next concerns voiced in *Gaudium et Spes*: the questions of economic life, political systems, and war. In building upon earlier social encyclicals, *Gaudium et Spes* discusses economics as vital to human progress and social development, striking the important balance (developed so masterfully in the later writings of Pope John Paul II) between the rights of an individual to possess goods and the obligation to aid the poor (Nos. 63-72). While declaring the autonomous and independent nature of the Church and politics, the Council Fathers do acknowledge: "There are, indeed, close links between earthly affairs and those aspects of man's condition which transcend this world. The Church herself employs the things of time to the degree that her own proper mission demands" (No. 76). The document goes on to state that "the arms race is an utterly treacherous trap for humanity" (No. 81) and "It is our clear duty, then, to strain every muscle as we work for the time when all war can be completely outlawed by international consent" (No. 82).

SOCIAL DOCTRINE UNDER POPE JOHN PAUL II

Throughout his pontificate, Pope John Paul II traveled the globe speaking out on all matters of the Church's social teachings and wrote a number of important encyclicals that are reflective not only of the Church's traditions of social doctrine but that sought to utilize the teachings of the faith to offer specific points of reflection and solutions to the many pressing problems of the late 20th century. Rooted in Christian anthropology and Tradition, Scripture, and Magisterium, John Paul's writings encompassed economic ethics, the rights and dignity of the worker, the primacy of the human person, the place of the family in society and the Church, and the integrative teachings of the Church in the areas of moral and pastoral theology. The three main expressions of his social teachings were the encyclicals: *Laborem Exercens* (1981); *Sollicitudo Rei Socialis* (1987); and *Centesimus Annus* (1991).

SOCIAL ENCYCLICALS OF POPE JOHN PAUL II AND POPE BENEDICT XVI

The following material on the encyclicals of John Paul II is adapted from The Encyclicals of John Paul II, *with the kind permission of the Most Rev. J. Michael Miller, C.S.B.*

Laborem Exercens

Fascinated as he is by commemorative events, Pope John Paul II marked the ninetieth anniversary of Leo XIII's *Rerum Novarum* (1891) by publishing his first social encyclical, *Laborem Exercens*, on Sept. 14, 1981.[1] Before

him, Pius XI in *Quadragesimo Anno* (1931), John XXIII in *Mater et Magistra* (1961), and Paul VI in *Octogesima Adveniens* (1971) had observed the anniversary of Leo's ground-breaking encyclical with documents of their own.

Laborem Exercens is a very personal document. The encyclical has solid roots in the pope's own experience as a worker. It reflects his familiarity with various worlds of work: in mines and factories, in artistic and literary production, in scholarship and pastoral ministry. More particularly, *Laborem Exercens* has its origins in the long debate carried on by the Archbishop of Kracow with Marxist intellectuals. The topics chosen, which include the struggle between capital and labor, ownership of the means of production, and solidarity, as well as the terminology of the encyclical, bear ample witness to this background of controversy. Here, however, he is less concerned with economic systems than with the human person as a "worker." Furthermore, John Paul intended his letter to encourage the Solidarity union movement, which in the early 1980s was the primary motor for effecting social and political change in a Poland under a totalitarian regime.

The style of encyclical is distinctively Wojtylan. It reveals the pope's preference for combining a phenomenological description of experience with philosophical-theological meditation. While he cites the Second Vatican Council's *Gaudium et Spes*, John Paul never directly quotes from any previous social encyclical, not even from *Rerum Novarum*. The encyclical's footnotes are almost entirely biblical, indicating that its primary inspiration is Sacred Scripture. As in his two previous encyclicals, *Redemptor Hominis* (1979) and *Dives in Misericordia* (1980), the pope relies heavily upon the plastic and descriptive language of the Bible, especially from the opening chapters of Genesis, to develop his theme. The encyclical unfolds the meaning of the human vocation to work in light of the biblical text on "subduing the earth" (cf. Gn 1:28). This call to exercise dominion is to be carried out by those created "in the image of God" (Gn 1:27) through their work, which the pope qualifies as "*one of the characteristics that distinguish* man from the rest of creatures" (preface).

Unlike earlier social encyclicals which dealt with a wide range of different questions, *Laborem Exercens* is sharply focused. John Paul chooses a very specific theme — the dignity and role of human work — and explores its many ramifications: "Through work man must earn his daily bread and contribute to the continual advance of science and technology and, above all, to elevating unceasingly the cultural and moral level of the society within which he lives in community with those who belong to the same family" (preface). At the present moment, he believes, the world is faced with important choices. It is "on the eve of new developments in technological, economic, and political conditions which, according to many experts, will influence the world of work and production no less than the industrial revolution of the last century" (§1.3).

A crisis in the meaning of human work is a crucial factor contributing to society's current plight. "Work, as human issue, is at the very center of the 'social question' " (§2.1). Moreover, the pope adds, "human work is *a key*, probably *the essential key*, to the whole social question" (§3.2). It is a problem with ramifications which extend beyond the so-called "working class"; the dimensions of the crisis are universal. Therefore he does not confine his encyclical to a reflection on the work only of industrial or agricultural workers. Instead, he extends it to encompass the work done by every sector of society: management, white-collar workers, scientists, intellectuals, artists, women in the home. "Each and every individual, to the proper extent and in an incalculable number of ways, takes part in the giant process whereby man 'subdues the earth' through his work" (§4.4). To use a favorite expression of the pope's, the world's "workbench" includes all those who labor for their daily bread — all men and women.

As in his two previous encyclicals, John Paul takes up the "way" of the human person, this time with regard to his fundamental activity of work. *Laborem Exercens* is yet another chapter in the pope's book on Christian anthropology. Moreover, since work is a great gift and good for humanity, his tone throughout the encyclical is constructive and exhortatory.

Footnote

1. *Acta Apostolicae Sedis,* 73 (1981), 577-647.

Sollicitudo Rei Socialis

Although signed on Dec. 30, 1987, Pope John Paul II's encyclical "on social concern" was not officially published until Feb. 19, 1988.[1] Like *Laborem Exercens* (1981), this second social encyclical commemorates a previous papal document. *Sollicitudo Rei Socialis* marks the twentieth anniversary of Paul VI's *Populorum Progressio* (1967). But more than merely recalling the relevance and doctrine of Pope Paul's encyclical, it highlights new themes and responds to the problems of development in the Third World which had emerged in the intervening 20 years.

John Paul writes as a teacher, explaining why the proclamation of the Church's social doctrine belongs to her evangelizing mission. He also writes as an informed witness to the increasing injustice and poverty in the world. Lastly, he writes as a defender of human dignity and inalienable rights, and of every person's transcendent vocation to communion with the Triune God.

In some ways *Sollicitudo Rei Socialis* echoes *Laborem Exercens* (1981). John Paul's use of Sacred Scripture, for example, is similar in that he frequently quotes from the opening chapters of Genesis. The differences between the two social encyclicals, however, are noteworthy. Whereas in *Laborem Exercens* (1981) the pope never directly cites *Rerum Novarum* (1891), the encyclical of Leo XIII which it commemorates, throughout *Sollicitudo Rei Socialis* John Paul quotes or refers to *Populorum Progressio* more than forty times. It is his constant point of reference. Second, to support his presentation, the pope marshals statements taken from earlier writings and discourses of his own pontificate, as well as the social teaching of the Second Vatican Council expressed in *Gaudium et Spes.* Third, more than in any other encyclical, John Paul makes use of documents published by the Roman Curia. Especially notable are his six references to the *Instruction on Christian Freedom and Liberation* (1986) issued by the Congregation for the Doctrine of the Faith. He also cites two publications of the Pontifical Commission "Iustitia et Pax": *At the Service of the Human Community: An Ethical Approach to the International Debt Question* (1986) and *The Church and the Housing Problem* (1987).

While *Sollicitudo Rei Socialis* perceptively analyzes the economic, political, social, and cultural dimensions of world development, its perspective is primarily ethical and theological. John Paul rereads *Populorum Progressio* through a moral-spiritual lens. His main concern is to form the consciences of individual men and women, to help them in their task of promoting authentic development "in the light of faith and of the Church's Tradition" (§41.7).

Footnote

1. *Acta Apostolicae Sedis,* 80 (1988), 513-586.

Centesimus Annus

Pope John Paul II issued his ninth encyclical, *Centesimus Annus,* on May 1, 1991.[1] Not surprisingly, the pope chose to mark the centenary of Leo XIII's *Rerum Novarum* (1891) with a document of his own. In the four years since the signing of *Sollicitudo Rei Socialis* (1987) the Berlin Wall had collapsed, and in the light of this event John Paul offers his "rereading" of *Rerum Novarum.* His purpose is twofold. He wishes to recall Leo's contribution to the development of the Church's social teaching and to honor the popes who drew upon the encyclical's "vital energies" in their social teaching.

Centesimus Annus has some interesting peculiarities. First, among all John Paul's encyclicals, it relies the least on citing Sacred Scripture. Its few biblical references are primarily exhortatory or illustrative. For his sources the pope depends mostly on *Rerum Novarum* and on the social encyclicals of his predecessors, as well as on earlier documents and discourses of his own Magisterium. Second, much of the encyclical's content is conditioned by current geopolitical affairs. Indeed, the encyclical reads as if the pope had *Rerum Novarum* in one hand and a diary of the 1989 events sweeping eastern Europe in the other.

Despite the opinions of some commentators, John Paul's primary interest is not to pass judgment on either failed socialism or contemporary capitalism. Above all, in keeping with his desire to articulate a Christian anthropology, he recalls the need for Catholic social doctrine to have a *"correct view of the human person* and of his unique value" (§11.3). Without such a view, he believes, it is impossible to solve today's social, economic, and political problems. The Church's distinctive contribution to meeting these challenges is her vision of the transcendent dignity of the human person created in God's image and redeemed by Christ's blood.

The pope's rereading of Leo XIII encompasses three time frames: "looking back" at *Rerum Novarum* itself, "looking around" at the contemporary situation, and "looking to the future" (§3.1). In looking back, John Paul confirms the enduring principles of Leo's encyclical, principles that belong to the Church's doctrinal inheritance. His "pastoral solicitude" also impels the pope to analyze recent political events from the perspective of the Gospel "in order to discern the new requirements of evangelization" (§3.5).

Even more clearly than in his two previous social encyclicals, *Laborem Exercens* (1981) and *Sollicitudo Rei Socialis* (1987), John Paul clearly distinguishes the authentic doctrine contained in the Church's social teaching from the analysis of contingent historical events. This analysis, he states, "is not meant to pass definitive judgments, since this does not fall *per se* within the Magisterium's specific domain" (§3.5). Whatever comes within the doctrinal sphere, however, "pertains to the Church's evangelizing mission and is an essential part of the Christian message" (§5.5).

Footnote

Acta Apostolicae Sedis, 83 (1991), 793-867.

Caritas in Veritate

On July 7, 2009, Pope Benedict XVI issued the third encyclical since his election in 2005 and his first social encyclical, *Caritas in Veritate* (Love in Truth). Within hours of its publication, media outlets and pundits weighed in with their own interpretations of what the Holy Father had written or what they thought the pontiff really meant to say. Some saw in the encyclical a rejection of capitalism, others a call for a one-world government to regulate corporations. Still others saw a demand for the environment to become the main priority for the Church's theologians. There is always a tendency to impose upon a major papal document what we want to see in it, but through a proper understanding of Pope Benedict and the goals he has set for the Church, it is possible to appreciate his true hopes for *Caritas in Veritate*.

Pope Benedict chose for his third encyclical a concern for the Church that is very much in tune with the "signs of the times." In the face of a global financial meltdown, the pope reiterates Catholic social teaching and then makes even more manifest the essential links between truth, the moral good, and the real world. As he writes, "Each person finds his good by adherence to God's plan for him, in order to realize it fully: in this plan, he finds truth, and through adherence to this truth he becomes free" (CV, Introduction). The love of truth is symphonic in the way that the pontiff makes a direct link between scientific and technological progress with the imposition of a culture of death on the developing world. The encyclical, of course, does not propose technical solutions to the vast social problems of the contemporary world as these lie outside the competence of the Magisterium of the Church. Still, it offers principles that are crucial to building human development, if the world has the wisdom to listen.

The foundation for this remarkable project is Benedict's wider concern about applying the social teachings of the Church. For some years, there has been a tendency by some theologians to think that there are two functional and rival approaches in Catholic social doctrine, one rooted in the time before the Second Vatican Council and a better one that came afterward. For Benedict, Catholics must have a commitment to continuity in Church teachings. There is only one Catholic social teaching – not two – and to make his point, he quotes from every social encyclical since Leo XIII's *Rerum Novarum* in 1891 and quotes Pope John Paul II that "there is a single teaching, consistent and at the same time ever new" (*Sollicitudo Rei Socialis*, 3). This permits Benedict to pull together the whole framework of Catholic social thought, especially its pillars of the defense of human dignity, of solidarity, and of subsidiarity as they apply to human development.

The encyclical does not merely repeat the thought of previous popes. Rather, the pontiff builds on the legacy of his predecesssors and applies the timeless teachings of the Church in a timely way. Even as he restates traditional Catholic social thought, the pontiff makes several significant innovations, such as the link between the culture of life and human development and the connection between justice and concern for the environment.

The world situation of today, the pope declares, is clearly one of increasing globalization, a shrinking of the earth in the face of advances of communication, travel, and technology. This is an opportunity for the whole global community, but it brings with it grave social and economic imbalances that can be remedied only by genuine reform and moral and cultural renewal. Business decisions and finance cannot be separated from the priority of the human person. Here continuity again becomes crucial. Where Pope John XXIII stressed peace in his 1958 social encyclical *Pacem in Terris*, and Pope Paul VI urged justice in his 1967 social encyclical *Populorum Progressio*, Pope Benedict ties them to the defense of human life in every form.

The encyclical makes the link "between life ethics and social ethics" (No. 15), especially in its tribute to the late Pope Paul VI's prophetic encyclicals *Populorum Progressio* and *Humanae Vitae* (1968). In *Populorum Progressio*, Paul VI anticipated the problems that have attended globalization, and in *Humanae Vitae*, he predicted with searing accuracy the long-term social effects of a contraceptive culture. Reflecting on both of these earlier documents, *Caritas in Veritate* proclaims that true development must encompass the rights of all human persons, including the unborn. The Holy Father notes that economic development and humanitarian aid from the West are too often accompanied by the imposition of dehumanizing programs and exploitation of labor and natural resources, but they can also entail an obligation to embrace of the culture of death through the same toxic reproductive and technological policies that are eroding the social fabric of the first world. Benedict XVI argues that not only do abortion, contraception, and euthanasia inherently trample upon the dignity of the human person and responsible human freedom, they are bad economics because of the strains they places on social welfare systems and labor resources, not to mention the wider impoverishment of culture. The Pope writes, "Openness to life is at the center of true development. When a society moves toward the denial or suppression of life, it ends up no longer finding the necessary motivation and energy to strive for man's true good" (No. 28). There is also a practical economic advantage to this openness. Populous nations are able to emerge from poverty in part because of the talents of their people, while one-time prosperous nations that are plagued by falling birth rates witness strains on social welfare systems, increased costs, and dwindling "brain pool."

Human development, most so in light of globalization, is a reminder that we are deeply and innately connected to each other. Pope Benedict describes this reality when he calls upon all people to remember that "the development of peoples depends above all on a recognition that the human race is a single family." The decisions that are made in board rooms in the first world have a direct impact upon the lives and the destinies of men, women, and children in far flung corners of the earth. By thinking and acting in solidarity with the poor, the helpless, and the developing parts of the world, we will be able to embrace "the interconnection between the impetus toward the unification of humanity and the Christian ideal of a single family of peoples in solidarity and fraternity" (No. 13).

The Pope also examines the principle of subsidiarity, the idea that the most people can be helped when functions of government are handled at a more immediate or local level. A key teaching in Catholic social thought, subsidiarity rejects the dangers of the vast social welfare state in favor of a real development that does not lose focus on the human person. There are those who claimed that the encyclical condemned capitalism and called for a socialist model for global economic management. Such claims were made falsely about Pope John Paul II's encyclical *Centessimus Annus*, and they were just as erroneous regarding *Caritas in Veritate*. Benedict calls for proper government intervention in the economy when needed, but he also demands a thorough reform of the United Nations and the "economic institutions and international finance."

Likewise, the connection between the development of people and the environment has long-term consequences for everyone. Nature is a gift from God that signifies "a design of love and truth" (No. 48), meaning that humanity has an obligation to use it responsibly. That entails the proper use of energy resources and with a sense of solidarity that reflects the vision of a human family. Technologically advanced societies must find ways to reduce their energy consumption, encourage new and alternative forms of energy, and assist developing societies with their own energy needs. The imperative is to establish decisively what the pontiff terms "the overall moral tenor of society," and the environment is related to the culture of life. The pope writes, "The book of nature is one and indivisible: it takes in not only the environment but also life, sexuality, marriage, the family, social relations: in a word, integral human development. Our duties toward the environment are linked to our duties toward the human person, considered in himself and in relation to others. It would be wrong to uphold one set of duties while trampling on the other" (No. 51). While a complicated and lengthy document, the pope's social encyclical is a welcome opportunity to meditate in a new way on the priorities of the current pontificate. The Holy Father is not proposing some supposed middle way between capitalism and socialism. In restating eloquently the clear development of Catholic social teachings from *Rerum Novarum* in 1891 to *Quadragesimo Anno* in 1940, to *Populorum Progressio*, and then to *Sollicitudo Rei Socialis* in 1987 and *Centessimus Annus*, Pope Benedict is reminding the world that the Church offers only one Way: Christ, who is the Way, the Truth, and the Life.

SOCIO-ECONOMIC STATEMENTS BY U.S. BISHOPS

Over a period of nearly 80 years, the bishops of the United States have issued a great number of socio-economic statements reflecting papal documents in a U.S. context.

One such statement, entitled "Economic Justice for All: Social Teaching and the U.S. Economy" was issued in November, 1986. Its contents are related in various ways with the subsequently issued encyclical letter, *Centesimus Annus*. Principles drawn from the bishops' document are given in the following excerpt entitled "A Catholic Framework for Economic Life." Another significant statement, entitled "The Harvest of Justice Is Sown in Peace" (1993) follows.

A Catholic Framework for Economic Life

As followers of Jesus Christ and participants in a powerful economy, Catholics in the United States, are called to work for greater economic justice in the face of persistent poverty, growing income gaps and increasing discussion of economic issues in the United States and around the world. We urge Catholics to use the following ethical framework for economic life as principles for reflection, criteria for judgment and directions for action. These principles are drawn directly from Catholic teaching on economic life.

1. The economy exists for the person, not the person for the economy.

2. All economic life should be shaped by moral principles. Economic choices and institutions must be judged by how they protect or undermine the life and dignity of the human person, support the family and serve the common good.

3. A fundamental moral measure of an economy is how the poor and vulnerable are faring.

4. All people have a right to life and to secure the basic necessities of life (e.g., food, clothing, shelter, education, health care, safe environment, economic security).

5. All people have the right to economic initiative, to productive work, to just wages and benefits, to decent working conditions as well as to organize and join unions or other associations.

6. All people, to the extent they are able, have a corresponding duty to work, a responsibility to provide for the needs of their families and an obligation to contribute to the broader society.

7. In economic life, free markets have both clear advantages and limits; government has essential responsibilities and limitations; voluntary groups have irreplaceable roles, but cannot substitute for the proper working of the market and the just policies of the state.

8. Society has a moral obligation, including governmental action where necessary, to assure opportunity, meet basic human needs and pursue justice in economic life.

9. Workers, owners, managers, stockholders and consumers are moral agents in economic life. By our choices, initiative, creativity and investment, we enhance or diminish economic opportunity, community life and social justice.

10. The global economy has moral dimensions and human consequences. Decisions on investment, trade, aid and development should protect human life and promote human rights, especially for those most in need wherever they might live on this globe.

The Harvest of Justice Is Sown in Peace

The National Conference of Catholic Bishops, at a meeting Nov. 17, 1993, issued a statement entitled "The Harvest of Justice Is Sown in Peace," marking the 10th anniversary of their earlier pastoral letter, "The Challenge of Peace: God's Promise and Our Response."

The Challenge of Peace

"The challenge of peace today is different, but no less urgent" than in 1983, and the threat of global nuclear war "may seem more remote than at any time in the nuclear age." Questions of peace and war, however, cannot be addressed "without acknowledging that the nuclear question remains of vital political and moral significance."

The statement outlines an agenda for action to guide future advocacy efforts of the bishops' national conference. It also urges that the cause of peace be reflected constantly in liturgical prayers of petition, preaching and Catholic education at all levels.

Confronting the temptation to isolationism in U.S. foreign policy is among "the major challenges peacemakers face in this new era."

Factors in a vision for peace include a commitment to the universal common good and recognition of the imperative of human solidarity.

Nonviolent revolutions in some countries "challenge us to find ways to take into full account the power of organized, active nonviolence."

With respect to just war criteria, the statement says that "important work needs to be done in refining, clarifying and applying the just war tradition to the choices facing our decision-makers in this still violent and dangerous world."

Subjects of concern include humanitarian intervention, deterrence, conscientious objection and the development of peoples.

Presumption against Force

"Our conference's approach, as outlined in 'The Challenge of Peace,' can be summarized in this way:

"1) In situations of conflict our constant commitment ought to be, as far as possible, to strive for justice through nonviolent means.

"2) But when sustained attempts at nonviolent action fail to protect the innocent against fundamental injustice, then legitimate political authorities are permitted as a last resort to employ limited force to rescue the innocent and establish justice."

Lethal Force

"Whether lethal force may be used is governed by the following criteria:

• "Just cause: Force may be used only to correct a grave, public evil, i.e., aggression or massive violation of the basic rights of whole populations.

• "Comparative justice: While there may be rights and wrongs on all sides of a conflict, to override the presumption against the use of force, the injustice suffered by one party must significantly outweigh that suffered by the other.

• "Legitimate authority: Only duly constituted public authorities may use deadly force or wage war.

• "Right intention: Force may be used only in a truly just cause and solely for that purpose.

• "Probability of Success: Arms may not be used in a futile cause or in a case where disproportionate measures are required to achieve success.

• "Proportionality: The overall destruction expected from the use of force must be outweighed by the good to be achieved.

• "Last Resort: Force may be used only after all peaceful alternatives have been seriously tried and exhausted.

"These criteria [of just war], taken as a whole, must be satisfied in order to override the strong presumption against the use of force."

Just War

"The just-war tradition seeks also to curb the violence of war through restraint on armed combat between the contending parties by imposing the following moral standards for the conduct of armed conflict:

• "Noncombatant Immunity: Civilians may not be the object of direct attack, and military personnel must take due care to avoid and minimize indirect harm to civilians.

• "Proportionality: In the conduct of hostilities, efforts must be made to attain military objectives with no more force than is militarily necessary and to avoid disproportionate collateral damage to civilian life and property.

• "Right Intention: Even in the midst of conflict, the aim of political and military leaders must be peace with justice so that acts of vengeance and indiscriminate violence, whether by individuals, military units or governments, are forbidden."

Structures for Justice and Peace

Quoting an address given by Pope John Paul in Aug. 1993 in Denver, the statement said:

" 'The international community ought to establish more effective structures for maintaining and promoting justice and peace. This implies that a concept of strategic interest should evolve which is based on the full development of peoples – out of poverty and toward a more dignified existence, out of injustice and exploitation toward fuller respect for the human person and the defense of universal rights.'

"As we consider a new vision of the international community, five areas deserve special attention: (1) strengthening global institutions; (2) securing human rights; (3) promoting human development; (4) restraining nationalism and eliminating religious violence; and (5) building cooperative security."

Humanitarian Intervention

"Pope John Paul, citing the 'conscience of humanity and international humanitarian law,' has been outspoken in urging that 'humanitarian intervention be obligatory where the survival of populations and entire ethnic groups is seriously compromised. This is a duty for nations and the international community.' He elaborated on this right and duty of humanitarian intervention in his 1993 annual address to the diplomatic corps (accredited to the Holy See): "'Once the possibilities afforded by diplomatic negotiations and the procedures provided for by international agreements and organizations have been put into effect, and that [sic], nevertheless, populations are succumbing to the attacks of an unjust aggressor, states no longer have a 'right to indifference.' It seems clear that their duty is to disarm this aggressor if all other means have proved ineffective. The principles of the sovereignty of states and of noninterference in their internal affairs — which retain all their value — cannot constitute a screen behind which torture and murder may be carried out.'"

THE BLESSED VIRGIN MARY

ROLE OF MARY IN THE MYSTERY OF CHRIST AND THE CHURCH

The following excerpts are from Chapter VIII of the Second Vatican Council's "Constitution on the Church," Lumen Gentium.

Preface

Wishing in his supreme goodness and wisdom to effect the redemption of the world, "when the fullness of time came, God sent his Son, born of a woman, that we might receive the adoption of sons" (Gal 4:4-5). "He for us men, and for our salvation, came down from heaven, and was incarnate by the Holy Spirit from the Virgin Mary." This divine mystery of salvation is revealed to us and continued in the Church, which the Lord established as his own body. In this Church, adhering to Christ the head and having communion with all his saints, the faithful must also venerate the memory "above all of the glorious and perpetual Virgin Mary. Mother of our God and Lord Jesus Christ." (52)

At the message of the angel, the Virgin Mary received the Word of God in her heart and in her body, and gave Life to the world. Hence, she is acknowledged and honored as being truly the Mother of God and Mother of the Redeemer. Redeemed in an especially sublime manner by reason of the merits of her Son, and united to him by a close and indissoluble tie, she is endowed with the supreme office and dignity of being the Mother of the

Son of God. As a result, she is also the favorite daughter of the Father and the temple of the Holy Spirit. Because of this gift of sublime grace, she far surpasses all other creatures, both in heaven and on earth.

At the same time, however, because she belongs to the offspring of Adam, she is one with all human beings in their need for salvation. Indeed, she is "clearly the Mother of the members of Christ since she cooperated out of love so that there might be born in the Church the faithful, who are members of Christ their head. Therefore, she is also hailed as a pre-eminent and altogether singular member of the Church, and as the Church's model and excellent exemplar in faith and charity. Taught by the Holy Spirit, the Catholic Church honors her with filial affection and piety as a most beloved Mother. (53)

This sacred synod intends to describe with diligence the role of the Blessed Virgin in the mystery of the Incarnate Word and the Mystical Body. It also wishes to describe the duties of redeemed mankind toward the Mother of God, who is the Mother of Christ and Mother of men, particularly of the faithful.

The synod does not, however, have it in mind to give a complete doctrine on Mary, nor does it wish to decide those questions which have not yet been fully illuminated by the work of theologians. (54)

II. The Role of the Blessed Virgin in the Economy of Salvation

The Father of mercies willed that the consent of the pre-destined Mother should precede the Incarnation so that, just as a woman contributed to death, so also a woman should contribute to life. This contrast was verified in outstanding fashion by the Mother of Jesus. She gave to the world that very Life which renews all things, and she was enriched by God with gifts befitting such a role.

It is no wonder, then, that the usage prevailed among the holy Fathers whereby they called the Mother of God entirely holy and free from all stain of sin, fashioned by the Holy Spirit into a kind of new substance and new creature. Adorned from the first instant of her conception with the splendors of an entirely unique holiness, the Virgin of Nazareth is, on God's command, greeted by an angel messenger as "full of grace" (cf. Lk 1:28). To the heavenly messenger she replies: "Behold the handmaid of the Lord; be it done to me according to thy word" (Lk 1:38).

By thus consenting to the divine utterance, Mary, a daughter of Adam, became the Mother of Jesus. Embracing God's saving will with a full heart and impeded by no sin, she devoted herself totally as a hand-maid of the Lord to the person and work of her Son. In subordination to him and along with him, by the grace of almighty God she served the mystery of redemption.

Rightly, therefore, the holy Fathers see her as used by God not merely in a passive way but as cooperating in the work of human salvation through free faith and obedience. (56)

This union of the Mother with the Son in the work of salvation was manifested from the time of Christ's virginal conception up to his death. It is shown first of all when Mary, arising in haste to go a major theological work for the 21st century that has had center stage since the mid-20th century to visit Elizabeth, was greeted by her as blessed because of her belief in the promise of salvation, while the precursor leaped for joy in the womb of his mother (cf. Lk 1:41-45). This association was shown also at the birth of our Lord, who did not diminish his Mother's virginal integrity but sanctified it, when the Mother of God joyfully showed her first-born Son to the shepherds and the Magi.

When she presented him to the Lord in the Temple, making the offering of the poor, she heard Simeon fore-telling at the same time that her Son would be a sign of contradiction and that a sword would pierce the Mother's soul, that out of many hearts thoughts might be revealed (cf. Lk 2:34-35). When the Child Jesus was lost and they had sought him sorrowing, his parents found him in the temple, taken up with things which were his Father's business. They did not understand the reply of the Son. But his Mother, to be sure, kept all these things to be pondered over in her heart (cf. Lk 2:41-51). (57)

In the public life of Jesus, Mary made significant appearances. This was so even at the very beginning, when she was moved with pity at the marriage feast of Cana, and her intercession brought about the beginning of the miracles by Jesus the Messiah (Cf. Jn 2:1-11). In the course of her Son's preaching, she received his praise when, in extolling a kingdom beyond the calculations and bonds of flesh and blood, he declared blessed (cf. Mk 3:35 par.; Lk 11:27-28) those who heard and kept the word of the Lord as she was faithfully doing (cf. Lk 2:19,51).

Thus, the Blessed Virgin advanced in her pilgrimage of faith and loyally persevered in her union with her Son unto the cross. There she stood, in keeping with the divine plan (cf. Jn 19:25), suffering grievously with her only-begotten Son. There she united herself with a maternal heart to his sacrifice, and lovingly consented to the immolation of this Victim whom she herself had brought forth. Finally, the same Christ Jesus dying on the cross gave her as a mother to his disciple. This he did when he said: "Woman, behold your son" (Jn 19:26-27). (58)

But since it pleased God not to manifest solemnly the mystery of the salvation of the human race until he poured forth the Spirit promised by Christ, we see the apostles before the day of Pentecost "continuing with one mind in prayer with the women and Mary, the Mother of Jesus, and with his brethren" (Acts 1:14). We see Mary prayerfully imploring the gift of the Spirit, who had already overshadowed her in the Annunciation.

Finally, preserved free from all guilt of original sin, the Immaculate Virgin was taken up body and soul into heavenly glory upon the completion of her earthly sojourn. She was exalted by the Lord as Queen of all, in order that she might be the more thoroughly conformed to her Son, the Lord of lords (cf. Rv 19:16) and the conqueror of sin and death. (59)

III. The Blessed Virgin and the Church

We have but one Mediator, as we know from the words of the Apostle: "For there is one God, and one Mediator between God and men, himself man, Christ Jesus, who gave himself as a ransom for all" (1 Tm 2:5-6). The maternal duty of Mary toward men in no way obscures or diminishes this unique mediation of Christ, but rather shows its power. For all the saving influences of the Blessed Virgin on men originate, not from some inner necessity, but from the divine pleasure. They flow forth from the superabundance of the merits of Christ, rest on his mediation, depend entirely on it, and draw all their power from it. In no way do they impede the immediate union of the faithful with Christ. Rather, they foster this union. (60)

In an utterly singular way, she (Mary) cooperated by her obedience, faith, hope and burning charity in the Savior's work of restoring supernatural life to souls. For this reason she is a mother to us in the order of grace. (61)

This maternity of Mary in the order of grace began with the consent which she gave in faith at the Annunciation and which she sustained without wavering beneath the cross. This maternity will last without interruption until the eternal fulfillment of all the elect. For, taken up to heaven, she did not lay aside this saving role, but by her manifold acts of intercession continues to win for us gifts of eternal salvation.

By her maternal charity, Mary cares for the brethren of her Son who still journey on earth surrounded by dangers and difficulties until they are led to their happy fatherland. Therefore, the Blessed Virgin is invoked by the Church under the titles of Advocate, Auxiliatrix, Adjutrix and Mediatrix. These, however, are to be so understood that they neither take away nor add anything to the dignity and efficacy of Christ the one Mediator.

For no creature could ever be classed with the Incarnate Word and Redeemer. But, just as the priesthood of Christ is shared in various ways both by sacred ministers and by the faithful; and as the one goodness of God is in reality communicated diversely to his creatures: so also the unique mediation of the Redeemer does not exclude but rather gives rise among creatures to a manifold cooperation which is but a sharing in this unique source.

The Church does not hesitate to profess this subordinate role of Mary. She experiences it continuously and commends it to the hearts of the faithful so that, encouraged by this maternal help, they may more closely adhere to the Mediator and Redeemer. (62)

Through the gift and role of divine maternity, Mary is united with her Son, the Redeemer, and with his singular graces and offices. By these, the Blessed Virgin is also intimately united with the Church. As St. Ambrose taught, the Mother of God is a model of the Church in the matter of faith, hope and charity, and perfect union with Christ. For in the mystery of the Church, herself rightly called Mother and Virgin, the Blessed Virgin stands out in eminent and singular fashion as exemplar of both virginity and motherhood. (63)

In the most holy Virgin, the Church has already reached that perfection whereby she exists without spot or wrinkle (cf. Eph 5:27). Yet, the followers of Christ still strive to increase in holiness by conquering sin. And so they raise their eyes to Mary who shines forth to the whole community of the elect as a model of the virtues. Devotedly meditating on her and contemplating her in the light of the Word made man, the Church with reverence enters more intimately into the supreme mystery of the Incarnation and becomes ever increasingly like her Spouse. (64)

The Church in her apostolic work looks to her who brought forth Christ, conceived by the Holy Spirit and born of the Virgin, so that through the Church Christ may be born and grow in the hearts of the faithful also. The Virgin Mary in her own life lived as an example of that maternal love by which all should be fittingly animated who cooperate in the apostolic mission of the Church on behalf of the rebirth of men. (65)

IV. Devotion to the Blessed Virgin in the Church

Mary was involved in the mystery of Christ. As the most holy Mother of God she was, after her Son, exalted by divine grace above all angels and men. Hence, the Church appropriately honors her with special reverence. Indeed, from most ancient times the Blessed Virgin has been venerated under the title of "God-bearer." In all perils and needs, the faithful; have fled prayerfully to her protection. Especially after the Council of Ephesus the cult of the people of God toward Mary wonderfully increased in veneration and love, in invocation and imitation, according to her own prophetic words: "All generations shall call me blessed; because he who is mighty has done great things for me" (Lk 1:48).

As it has always existed in the Church, this cult (of Mary) is altogether special, Still, it differs essentially from the cult of adoration which is offered to the Incarnate Word, as well as to the Father and the Holy Spirit. Yet, devotion to Mary is most favorable to this supreme cult. The Church has endorsed many forms of piety toward the Mother of God, provided that they were within the limits of sound and orthodox doctrine. These forms have varied according to the circumstances of time and place, and have reflected the diversity of native characteristics and temperament among the faithful. While honoring Christ's Mother, these devotions cause her Son to be rightly known, loved and glorified, and all his commands observed. Through him all things have their beginning (cf. Col 1:15-16) and in him "it has pleased (the eternal Father) that all his fullness should dwell" (Col 1:19). (66)

This most holy synod deliberately teaches this Catholic doctrine. At the same time, it admonishes all the sons of the Church that the cult, especially the liturgical cult, of the Blessed Virgin, be generously fostered. It charges that practices and exercises of devotion toward her be treasured as recommended by the teaching authority of the Church in the course of centuries.

This synod earnestly exhorts theologians and preachers of the divine word that, in treating of the unique dignity of the Mother of God, they carefully and equally avoid the falsity of exaggeration on the one hand and the excess of narrow-mindedness on the other.

Let the faithful remember, moreover, that true devotion consists neither in fruitless and passing emotion, nor in a certain vain credulity. Rather, it proceeds from the true faith, by which we are led to know the excellence of the Mother of God, and are moved to a filial love toward our Mother and to the imitation of her virtues. (67)

REDEMPTORIS MATER

Redemptoris Mater (*Mother of the Redeemer*), Pope John Paul II's sixth encyclical letter, was a "reflection on the role of Mary in the mystery of Christ and on her active and exemplary presence in the life of the Church." The letter was published Mar. 25, 1987.

Central to consideration of Mary is the fact that she is the Mother of God (*Theotokos*), since by the power of the Holy Spirit she conceived in her virginal womb and brought into the world Jesus Christ, the Son of God, who is of one being with the Father and the Holy Spirit.

Mary was preserved from original sin in view of her calling to be the Mother of Jesus. She was gifted in grace beyond measure. She fulfilled her role in a unique pilgrimage of faith. She is the Mother of the Church and the spiritual mother of all people.

The following excerpts are from the English text

provided by the Vatican and circulated by the CNS Documentary Service, *Origins*, Apr. 9, 1987 (Vol. 16, No. 43). Subheads have been added. Quotations are from pertinent documents of the Second Vatican Council.

Mary's Presence in the Church

Mary, through the same faith which made her blessed, especially from the moment of the Annunciation, is present in the Church's mission, present in the Church's work of introducing into the world the kingdom of her Son.

This presence of Mary finds as many different expressions in our day just as it did throughout the Church's history. It also has a wide field of action: through the faith and piety of individual believers; through the traditions of Christian families or "domestic churches," of parish and missionary communities, religious institutes and dioceses; through the radiance and attraction of the great shrines where not only individuals or local groups, but sometimes whole nations and societies, even whole continents, seek to meet the Mother of the Lord, the one who is blessed because she believed, is the first among believers, and therefore became the Mother of Emmanuel.

This is the message of the land of Palestine, the spiritual homeland of all Christians, because it was the homeland of the Savior of the world and of his Mother.

This is the message of the many churches in Rome and throughout the world which have been raised up in the course of the centuries by the faith of Christians. This is the message of centers like Guadalupe, Lourdes, Fátima and others situated in the various countries. Among them, how could I fail to mention the one in my own native land, Jasna Gora? One could perhaps speak of a specific "geography" of faith and Marian devotion which includes all of these special places of pilgrimage where the people of God seek to meet the Mother of God in order to find, within the radius of the maternal presence of her "who believed," a strengthening of their own faith.

Mary and Ecumenism

"In all of Christ's disciples the Spirit arouses the desire to be peacefully united, in the manner determined by Christ, as one flock under one shepherd." The journey of the Church, especially in our own time, is marked by the sign of ecumenism: Christians are seeking ways to restore that unity which Christ implored from the Father for his disciples on the day before his passion.

Christians must deepen in themselves and each of their communities that "obedience of faith" of which Mary is the first and brightest example.

Christians know that their unity will be truly rediscovered only if it is based on the unity of their faith. They must resolve considerable discrepancies of doctrine concerning the mystery and ministry of the Church, and sometimes also concerning the role of Mary in the work of salvation.

Mary, who is still the model of this pilgrimage, is to lead them to the unity which is willed by their one Lord, and which is so much desired by those who are attentively listening to what "the Spirit is saying to the churches" today.

A Hopeful Sign

Meanwhile, it is a hopeful sign that these churches and ecclesial communities are finding agreement on fundamental points of Christian belief, including matters relating to the Virgin Mary. For they recognize her as the Mother of the Lord and hold that this forms part of our faith in Christ, true God and true man. They look to her who at the foot of the cross accepted as her son the Beloved Disciple (John), the one who in his turn accepted her as his Mother.

On the other hand, I wish to emphasize how profoundly the Catholic Church, the Orthodox Church and the ancient churches of the East feel united by love and praise of the *Theotokos*. Not only "basic dogmas of the Christian faith concerning the Trinity and God's Word made flesh of the Virgin Mary were defined in ecumenical councils held in the East," but also in their liturgical worship "the Eastern Christians pay high tribute, in very beautiful hymns, to Mary ever-Virgin. God's most holy Mother."

The churches which profess the doctrine of Ephesus proclaim the Virgin as "true Mother of God" since "our Lord Jesus Christ, born of the Father before time began according to his divinity, in the last days he himself, for our sake and for our salvation, was begotten of Mary the Virgin Mother of God according to his humanity." The Greek Fathers and the Byzantine tradition, contemplating the Virgin in the light of the Word made flesh, have sought to penetrate the depth of that bond which unites Mary, as the Mother of God, to Christ and the Church. The Virgin is a permanent presence in the whole reality of the salvific mystery.

Marian Mediation

The Church knows and teaches with St. Paul that there is only one mediator: "For there is one God, and there is one mediator between God and men, the man Christ Jesus, who gave himself as a ransom for all" (1 Tm 2:5-6). "The maternal role of Mary toward people in no way obscures or diminishes the unique mediation of Christ, but rather shows its power." It is mediation in Christ.

The Church knows and teaches that "all the saving influences of the Blessed Virgin on mankind originate from the divine pleasure. They flow forth from the superabundance of the merits of Christ, rest on his mediation, depend entirely on it and draw all their power from it. In no way do they impede the immediate union of the faithful with Christ. Rather, they foster this union." This saving influence is sustained by the Holy Spirit, who, just as he overshadowed the Virgin Mary when he began in her the divine motherhood, in a similar way constantly sustains her solicitude for the brothers and sisters of her Son.

Mediation and Motherhood

In effect, Mary's mediation is intimately linked with her motherhood. It possesses a specifically maternal character, which distinguishes it from the mediation of the other creatures who in various and always subordinate ways share in the one mediation of Christ, although her own mediation is also a shared mediation. In fact, while it is true that "no creature could ever be classed with the Incarnate Word and Redeemer," at the same time "the unique mediation of the Redeemer does not exclude but rather gives rise among creatures a manifold cooperation which is but a sharing in this unique source." Thus "the one goodness of God is in reality communicated diversely to his creatures."

Subordinate Mediation

The teaching of Vatican II presents the truth of Mary's mediation as "a sharing in the one unique source that is the mediation of Christ himself." Thus we read: "The Church does not hesitate to profess this subordinate role of Mary. She experiences it continuously and commends it to the hearts of the faithful so that, encouraged by this maternal help, they may more closely adhere to the

Mediator and Redeemer."

This role is at the same time special and extraordinary. It flows from her divine motherhood and can be understood and lived in faith only on the basis of the full truth of this motherhood. Since by virtue of divine election Mary is the earthly Mother of the Father's consubstantial Son and his "generous companion" in the work of redemption, "she is a Mother to us in the order of grace." This role constitutes a real dimension of her presence in the saving mystery of Christ and the Church.

Mary is honored in the Church "with special reverence. Indeed, from most ancient times the Blessed Virgin Mary has been venerated under the title of 'God-bearer.' In all perils and needs, the faithful have fled prayerfully to her protection." This cult is altogether special; it bears in itself and expresses the profound link which exists between the Mother of Christ and the Church. As Virgin and Mother, Mary remains for the Church a "permanent model." It can therefore be said that, especially under this aspect, namely, as a model or rather as a "figure," Mary, present in the mystery of Christ, remains constantly present also in the mystery of the Church. For the Church too is "called mother and virgin," and these names have a profound biblical and theological justification.

Mary and Women

This Marian dimension of Christian life takes on special importance in relation to women and their status. In fact, femininity has a unique relationship with the Mother of the Redeemer, a subject which can be studied in greater depth elsewhere.... The figure of Mary of Nazareth sheds light on womanhood as such by the very fact that God, in the sublime event of the incarnation of his Son, entrusted himself to the ministry, the free and active ministry, of a woman.

... Women, by looking to Mary, find in her the secret of living their femininity with dignity and of achieving their own true advancement. In the light of Mary, the Church sees in the face of women the reflection of a beauty which mirrors the loftiest sentiments of which the human heart is capable: the self-offering totality of love; the strength that is capable of bearing the greatest sorrows; limitless fidelity and tireless devotion to work; the ability to combine penetrating intuition with words of support and encouragement.

APPARITIONS OF THE BLESSED VIRGIN MARY

The Bessed Virgin Mary has appeared historically in places all over the world. Eight of the best-known apparitions are described.

Banneux, near Liège, Belgium: Mary appeared eight times between Jan. 15 and Mar. 2, 1933, to an 11-year-old peasant girl, Mariette Beco, in a garden behind the family cottage in Banneux. She called herself the Virgin of the Poor, and has since been venerated as Our Lady of the Poor, the Sick, and the Indifferent. A small chapel was blessed Aug. 15, 1933. Approval of devotion to Our Lady of Banneux was given in 1949 by Bp. Louis J. Kerkhofs of Liège, and a statue of that title was solemnly crowned in 1956.

Beauraing, Belgium: Mary appeared 33 times between Nov. 29, 1932, and Jan. 3, 1933, to five children in the garden of a convent school in Beauraing. A chapel was erected on the spot. Reserved approval of devotion to Our Lady of Beauraing was given Feb. 2, 1943, and final approbation July 2, 1949, by Bp. Charue of Namur (d. 1977).

Fátima, Portugal: Mary appeared six times between May 13 and Oct. 13, 1917, to three children (Lucia dos Santos, 10, who became a Carmelite nun, died in 2005; Francisco Marto, 9, who died in 1919; and his sister Jacinta, 7, who died in 1920; Jacinta and Francisco were beatified by Pope John Paul II in 2000) in a field called Cova da Iria near Fátima. She recommended frequent recitation of the Rosary; urged works of mortification for conversion of sinners; called for devotion to herself under the title of her Immaculate Heart; asked that the people of Russia be consecrated to her under this title, and that the faithful make a Communion of reparation monthly on the first Saturday.

The apparitions were declared worthy of belief in Oct. 1930, and devotion to Our Lady of Fátima was authorized under the title of Our Lady of the Rosary. In Oct. 1942, Pius XII consecrated the world to Mary under the title of her Immaculate Heart. Ten years later, in the first apostolic letter addressed directly to the peoples of Russia, he consecrated them in a special manner to Mary. For more on the Third Secret of Fátima, see below.

Guadalupe, Mexico: Mary appeared four times in 1531 to an Indian, Juan Diego (beatified in 1990 and canonized in 2002), on Tepeyac hill outside of Mexico City, and instructed him to tell Bishop Zumarraga of her wish that a church be built there. The bishop complied with the request about two years later, after being convinced of the genuineness of the apparition by the evidence of a miraculously painted life-size figure of the Virgin on the mantle of the Indian. The mantle bearing the picture has been preserved and is enshrined in the Basilica of Our Lady of Guadalupe. The shrine church, originally dedicated in 1709 and subsequently enlarged, has the title of basilica.

Benedict XIV, in a 1754 decree, authorized a Mass and Office under the title of Our Lady of Guadalupe for celebration on Dec. 12, and named Mary the patroness of New Spain. Our Lady of Guadalupe was designated patroness of Latin America by St. Pius X in 1910 and of the Americas by Pius XII in 1945.

La Salette, France: Mary appeared as a sorrowing and weeping figure Sept. 19, 1846, to two peasant children, Melanie Matthieu, 15, and Maximin Giraud, 11, at La Salette. The message she confided to them, regarding the necessity of penance, was communicated to Pius IX in 1851 and has since been known as the "secret" of La Salette. Bp. de Bruillard of Grenoble declared in 1851 that the apparition was credible, and devotion to Mary under the title of Our Lady of La Salette was authorized. A Mass and Office with this title were authorized in 1942. The shrine church was given the title of minor basilica in 1879.

Lourdes, France: Mary, identifying herself as the Immaculate Conception, appeared 18 times between Feb. 11 and July 16, 1858, to 14-year-old Bernadette Soubirous (canonized in 1933) at the grotto of Massabielle near Lourdes. Her message concerned the necessity of prayer and penance for the conversion of peoples. Mary's request that a chapel be built at the grotto and spring was fulfilled in 1862. Devotion under the title of Our Lady of Lourdes was authorized, and a Feb. 11 feast commemorating the apparitions was instituted by Leo XIII. St. Pius X extended this feast throughout the Church in 1907. The Church of Notre Dame was made a basilica in 1870, and the Church of the Rosary was built later. The underground Church of St. Pius X, with a capacity of 20,000 persons, was consecrated Mar. 25, 1958. Plans were announced in 1994 for renovation and reconstruction of the Lourdes sanctuary.

Notre Dame du Laus, France: Mary appeared to the

young girl Benôite Rencurel between 1664 and 1718. After four months of daily apparitions starting in May 1664, the Virgin Mary asked Rencurel to build a church and a sanctuary to receive priests. The apparitions received formal approval on May 4, 2008, after years of study by theologians. The shrine is located in the French Alps, near the southeastern French town of Gap.

Our Lady of the Miraculous Medal, France: Mary appeared three times in 1830 to Catherine Labouré (canonized in 1947) in the chapel of the motherhouse of the Daughters of Charity of St. Vincent de Paul, Rue de Bac, Paris. She commissioned Catherine to have made the medal of the Immaculate Conception, now known as the Miraculous Medal, and to spread devotion to her under this title. In 1832, the medal was struck.

Other approved apparitions include Pontmain, France (1871), Knock, Ireland (1879), and Akita (1984).

THE THIRD SECRET OF FÁTIMA

Courtesy Vatican Information Service.

On June 26, 2000, the Holy See Press Office issued the document "The Message Of Fátima" that had been prepared by the Congregation for the Doctrine of the Faith and carried the signatures of Card. Joseph Ratzinger and Abp. Tarcisio Bertone S.D.B., respectively prefect and secretary of the congregation.

The document, which is over 40 pages long, was published in English, French, Italian, Spanish, German, Portuguese and Polish. It was made up of an introduction by Abp. Bertone; the first and second parts of the "secret" of Fátima in Sr. Lucia's original text dated Aug. 31, 1941, and addressed to the bishop of Leiria-Fátima, and a translation; the photostatic reproduction of the original manuscript of the third part of the "secret" and a translation; John Paul II's letter to Sr. Lucia dated Apr. 19, 2000, and a translation; a summary of Sr. Lucia's conversation with Abp. Bertone and Bp. Serafim de Sousa Ferreira e Silva of Leiria-Fátima which took place on Apr. 27, 2000, in the Carmel Monastery of St. Teresa of Coimbra, Portugal; the words of Cardinal Secretary of State Angelo Sodano at the end of the beatification of Jacinta and Francisco on May 13, 2000; a theological commentary by Card. Ratzinger.

In his introduction, Abp. Bertone affirms that "Fátima is undoubtedly the most prophetic of modern apparitions.... In 1917 no one could have imagined all this: the three '*pastorinhos*' of Fátima see, listen and remember, and Lucia, the surviving witness, commits it all to paper when ordered to do so by the Bishop of Leiria and with Our Lady's permission."

He continues: "The third part of the 'secret' was written ... on Jan. 3, 1944. There is only one manuscript, which is here reproduced photostatically. The sealed envelope was initially in the custody of the Bishop of Leiria. To ensure better protection for the 'secret' the envelope was placed in the secret archives of the Holy Office on Apr. 4, 1957. The Bishop of Leiria informed Sr. Lucia of this."

The secretary of the Congregation for the Doctrine of the Faith indicates that "according to the records of the Archives, the Commissary of the Holy Office, Fr. Pierre Paul Philippe, O.P., with the agreement of Card. Alfredo Ottaviani, brought the envelope containing the third part of the 'secret of Fátima' to Pope John XXIII on Aug. 17, 1959. 'After some hesitation,' His Holiness said: 'We shall

wait. I shall pray. I shall let you know what I decide.' In fact Pope John XXIII decided to return the sealed envelope to the Holy Office and not to reveal the third part of the 'secret.' Paul VI read the contents with the Substitute, Abp. Angelo Dell'Acqua, on Mar. 27, 1965, and returned the envelope to the Archives of the Holy Office, deciding not to publish the text. John Paul II, for his part, asked for the envelope containing the third part of the 'secret' following the assassination attempt on May 13, 1981," and this was given to Abp. Eduardo Martinez Somalo, Substitute of the Secretariat of State, on July 18 of the same year. On Aug. 11 it was returned to the Archives of the Holy Office.

"As is well known," added Abp. Bertone, "Pope John Paul II immediately thought of consecrating the world to the Immaculate Heart of Mary and he himself composed a prayer for what he called an 'Act of Entrustment' which was to be celebrated in the Basilica of St. Mary Major on June 7, 1981."

"In order to respond more fully to the requests of 'Our Lady,' the Holy Father desired to make more explicit during the Holy Year of the Redemption the Act of Entrustment of June 7, 1981, which had been repeated in Fátima on May 13, 1982."

"Sr. Lucia," continued the archbishop, "personally confirmed that this solemn and universal act of consecration corresponded to what Our Lady wished. Hence any further discussion or request is without basis."

Sr. Lucia had already hinted at the interpretation of the third part of the "secret" in a letter to the Holy Father dated May 12, 1982. That letter is also published in the document.

Finally, Abp. Tarcisio Bertone indicates that "the decision of His Holiness Pope John Paul II to make public the third part of the 'secret' of Fátima brings to an end a period of history marked by tragic human lust for power and evil, yet pervaded by the merciful love of God and the watchful care of the Mother of Jesus and of the Church."

TRANSLATION OF THE THIRD SECRET OF FÁTIMA

On June 26, 2000, the Holy See issued the complete translation of the original Portuguese text of the third part of the secret of Fátima, revealed to the three shepherd children at Cova da Iria-Fátima on July 13, 1917, and committed to paper by Sr. Lucia on Jan. 3, 1944:

"I write in obedience to you, my God, who command me to do so through his Excellency the Bishop of Leiria and through your Most Holy Mother and mine.

"After the two parts which I have already explained, at the left of Our Lady and a little above, we saw an Angel with a flaming sword in his left hand; flashing, it gave out flames that looked as though they would set the world on fire; but they died out in contact with the splendor that Our Lady radiated toward him from her right hand: pointing to the earth with his right hand, the Angel cried out in a loud voice: 'Penance, Penance, Penance!' And we saw in an immense light that is God: 'something similar to how people appear in a mirror when they pass in front of it' a Bishop dressed in White 'we had the impression that it was the Holy Father.' Other Bishops, Priests, men and women Religious going up a steep mountain, at the top of which there was a big Cross of rough-hewn trunks as of a cork-tree with the bark; before reaching there the Holy Father passed through a big city half in ruins and half trembling with halting step, afflicted with pain and sorrow, he prayed for the souls of the corpses he met on his way; having reached the top of the mountain, on his knees at the foot of the big Cross he was killed by a group of soldiers who fired bullets and arrows at him, and in the same way there died one after another the other Bishops, Priests, men and women Religious, and various lay people of different ranks and positions. Beneath the two arms of the Cross there were two Angels each with a crystal aspersorium in his hand, in which they gathered up the blood of the Martyrs and with it sprinkled the souls that were making their way to God."

EVENTS AT MEDJUGORJE

The alleged apparitions of the Blessed Virgin Mary to six young people of Medjugorje, Bosnia-Herzegovina, have been the source of interest and controversy since they were first reported in June 1981, initially in the neighboring hillside field, subsequently in the village church of St. James and even in places far removed from Medjugorje.

Reports say the alleged visionaries have seen, heard, and even touched Mary during visions, and that they have variously received several or all of 10 secret messages related to coming world events and urging a quest for peace through penance and personal conversion. An investigative commission appointed by former local Bp. Pavao Zanic of Mostar-Duvno reported in Mar. 1984 that the authenticity of the apparitions had not been verified. He called the apparitions a case of "collective hallucination" exploited by local Franciscan priests at odds with him over control of a parish.

Former Abp. Frane Franic of Split-Makarska, on the other hand, said in Dec. 1985: "Speaking as a believer and not as a bishop, my personal conviction is that the events at Medjugorje are of supernatural inspiration." He based his conviction on the observations of spiritual benefits related to the reported events, such as the spiritual development of the six young people, the increases in Mass attendance and sacramental practice at the scene of the apparitions, and the incidence of reconciliation among people.

On Jan. 29, 1987, the bishops of Yugoslavia declared: "On the basis of research conducted so far, one cannot affirm that supernatural apparitions are involved" at Medjugorje. Currently, the events at Medjugorje are under on-going investigation by the Holy See to determine their authenticity. Nevertheless, the site of Medjugorje remains a popular destination for Catholic pilgrims from Europe and the United States. On Mar. 17, 2010, the Vatican announced that it was launching a formal inquiry into Medjugorje under the authority of the Congregation for the Doctrine of the Faith.

THE CODE OF CANON LAW

Canon Law is the term that denotes the body of laws governing the Catholic Church. The name is derived from the Greek word *kanon* (rule, i.e., rule of practical direction), which, from the fourth century, was used to denote the ordinances and regulations promulgated by the various Church councils that were convened to discuss problems or important topics. The actual term "canon law" (*ius canonicum*) came into use in the 1100s and was intended to differentiate ecclesiastical law from civil law (*ius civile*).

History of Canon Law

In a practical sense, the laws and regulations began to take shape as early as apostolic times and were evident in their nascent form in the Didache, the Didscalia and the Apostolic Tradition. Owing to the persecution of the Church, however, there was little effort to gather laws together, and certainly less time was devoted to systematizing them.

The fourth century brought the Church freedom from persecution and the resulting rapid growth in membership that was a concomitant of the favors bestowed upon the faith by the rulers of the Roman Empire. New laws were naturally needed and desired. Local regulations were soon established through the decrees of the councils, although these most often had only a local authority and adherence. The general (or ecumenical) councils made laws for the whole Church, and the custom developed of carrying on the decrees of previous assemblies by having them read before the start of a new council. Collections of these laws or canons were then undertaken, but these did not bear the weight of being an official code as they were gathered under private authority.

The earliest efforts at collecting Church laws were centered around the private compilation of the decrees of the Eastern councils to which were added those of the Western Church. The councils of the African Church also made lasting contributions, the most significant coming out of the Seventeenth Council of Carthage (419), which accepted the book of canons later adopted into the canon law of both the Eastern and Western Churches. An official Code of Canon Law was recognized in the seventh century under the Isidorian Collection. Other important influences were the writings of monks in England and Ireland. The monks compiled lists of sins and various offenses to which confessors applied the proper fines or penances. The resulting books were called Penitentials, and they offer scholars an invaluable glimpse into the state of Church law in early medieval England and the development of moral theology.

The Carolingian Reforms of the Church under Charlemagne facilitated the enactment of much legislation that was beneficial to the faith, but it also signaled a long period of secular interference in ecclesiastical affairs. Two by-products of this lay intrusion were the creation of the forged but interesting False Decretals (collections of false canons and decrees of the popes used to falsify the Church's position) and the application of legal arguments by Churchmen that could protect the Church from abuse. Efforts at revitalization would become heightened under the Gregorian Reform, in particular with the reign of Pope St. Gregory VII (1073-1085). From that time, throughout the Middle Ages, laws from the Church would be centered in and produced by the papacy, assisted in running the administration of the Church by the Roman Curia.

Gradually, legal experts collected the decrees of popes, enactments of councils, and sources of older, ancient canons. To these were added glosses, or commentaries, to assist in the teaching of the details of the subject. Still, the study of canon law was severely handicapped by the sheer number of collections, the contradiction between many points of law, and the inability to find specific laws because of the chronological arrangements of the material. Thus can be seen the major significance of the *Decretum* of Gratian, published around 1148 in Bologna. Compiled by the legal expert Gratian, the *Decretum* (in full, *Concordantia discordantum canonum*) was not a formal collection of canons but sought to provide a juridical system for its readers. Toward this end, though, Gratian examined (and excerpted) virtually every canon ever published. The *Decretum* was quickly adopted as the textbook of canon law, despite the fact that it was a private collection and not codified.

Over the next centuries, the popes added to the body of laws by giving rulings to those questions posed to them by bishops from around the Church. These decretal letters were then brought together and, for purposes of comprehensiveness, added to the *Decretum Gratiani*. The most important of these was the *Liber extra*, the collection made by St. Raymond Peñafort for Pope Gregory IX. This received official approval and was to be a vital source for the *Corpus Juris Canonici*. Other remarkable contributors to canon law in the late Middle Ages were Zenzelinus de Cassanis, Jean Chappuis, Guido de Baysio, John the Teuton (or Joannes Teutonicus), Stephen of Tournai, and most of all, Joannes Andreae (d. 1348).

Considerable activity was initiated by the Council of Trent (1545-1563), which sought to reform and reinvigorate the Church in the wake of the Protestant Reformation. The same century brought the formation in 1588 of the Sacred Congregation of the Curia by Pope Sixtus V (r. 1585-1590), which became the main means of implementing new laws and examining facets of established ones.

The final decision to codify the laws of the Church was made by Pope St. Pius X who, in 1903, issued *Arduum*, the *motu proprio* ordering the complete reform and codification of all canon law. It was completed and promulgated in 1917 as the *Codex Juris Canonici*, the first official guide to the laws of the Catholic Church. A new Code of Canon Law was issued by Pope John Paul II in 1983, the final result of a call for a new code dating back to Pope John XXIII (r. 1958-1963) and continued by Pope Paul VI (r. 1963-1978).

The 1983 Code of Canon Law

Pope John Paul II promulgated a revised Code of Canon Law for the Latin Rite on Jan. 25, 1983, with the apostolic constitution *Sacrae Disciplinae Legis* ("Of the Sacred Discipline of Law") and ordered it into effect as of the following Nov. 27. Promulgation of the Code marked the completion of the last major reform in the Church stemming from the Second Vatican Council.

The 1983 Code of Canon Law replaced the one which had been in effect since 1918. The new Code incorporates into law the insights of Vatican Council II. These 1,752 canons focus on the People of God and the threefold ministries of sanctifying, teaching and governance. Also included are general norms, temporalities, sanctions and procedures.

Guiding Principles

When Pope John XXIII announced on Jan. 25, 1959, that he was going to convoke the Second Vatican Council, he also called for a revision of the existing Code of Canon Law. His successor, Paul VI, appointed a commission for this purpose in 1963 and subsequently enlarged it. The commission, which began its work after the conclusion of the Council in 1965, was directed by the 1967 Synod of Bishops to direct its efforts in line with 10 guiding principles. The bishops said the revised Code should:

- be juridical in character, not just a set of broad moral principles;
- be intended primarily for the external forum (regarding determinable fact, as opposed to the internal forum of conscience);
- be clearly pastoral in spirit;
- incorporate most of the faculties bishops need in their ministry;
- provide for subsidiarity or decentralization;
- be sensitive to human rights;
- state clear procedures for administrative processes and tribunals;
- be based on the principle of territoriality;
- reduce the number of penalties for infraction of law;
- have a new structure.

The commission carried out its mandate with the collegial collaboration of bishops all over the world and in consultation and correspondence with individuals and experts in canon law, theology, and related disciplines. The group finished its work in 1981 and turned its final draft over to Pope John Paul II at its final plenary meeting in October of that year.

Features

The revised code is shorter (1,752 canons) than the one it replaced (2,414 canons) and has a number of important features:

It is more pastoral and flexible, as well as more theologically oriented than the former Code. It gives greater emphasis than its predecessor to a number of significant facets and concepts in church life.

In the apostolic constitution with which he promulgated the Code, Pope John Paul II called attention to its nature and some of its features, as follows:

Prime Legislative Document

"Since this is so, it seems clear enough that the Code in no way has its scope to substitute for faith, grace, the charisms, and especially charity in the life of the Church of the faithful. On the contrary, its end is rather to create such order in ecclesial society that, assigning primacy to love, grace and charisms, it at the same time renders more active their organic developments in the life both of the ecclesial society and of the individuals belonging to it. Inasmuch as it is the Church's prime legislative document, based on the juridical and legislative heritage of revelation and tradition, the Code must be regarded as the necessary instrument whereby due order is preserved in both individual and social life and in the Church's activity. Therefore, besides containing the fundamental elements of the hierarchical and organic structure of the Church, laid down by her divine Founder and founded on apostolic or at any rate most ancient tradition, and besides outstanding norms concerning the carrying out of the task mandated to the Church herself, the Code must also define a certain number of rules and norms of action."

Suits the Nature of the Church

"The instrument the Code is fully suits the Church's nature, for the Church is presented, especially through the magisterium of the Second Vatican Council, in her universal scope, and especially through the Council's ecclesiological teaching. In a certain sense, indeed, this new Code may be considered as a great effort to transfer that same ecclesiological or conciliar doctrine into canonical language. And, if it is impossible for the image of the Church described by the Council's teaching to be perfectly converted into canonical language, the Code nonetheless must always be referred to that very image, as the primary pattern whose outline the Code ought to express as well as it can by its own nature.

"From this derive a number of fundamental norms by which the whole of the new Code is ruled, of course within the limits proper to it as well as the limits of the very language befitting the material.

"It may rather be rightly affirmed that from this comes that note whereby the Code is regarded as a complement to the magisterium expounded by the Second Vatican Council.

"The following elements are most especially to be noted among those expressing a true and genuine image of the Church: the doctrine whereby the Church is proposed as the People of God and the hierarchical authority is propounded as service; in addition, the doctrine which shows the Church to be a 'communion' and from that lays down the mutual relationships which ought to exist between the particular and universal Church and between collegiality and primacy; likewise, the doctrine whereby all members of the People of God, each in the manner proper to him, share in Christ's threefold office of priest, prophet and king; to this doctrine is also connected that regarding the duties and rights of the Christian faithful, particularly the laity; then there is the effort which the Church has to make for ecumenism."

Code Necessary for the Church

"Indeed, the Code of Canon Law is extremely necessary for the Church ... The Church needs it for her hierarchichal and organic structure to be visible: so that exercise of the offices and tasks divinely entrusted to her, especially her sacred power and administration of the sacraments, should be rightly ordered; so that mutual relations of the Christian faithful may be carried out according to justice based on charity, with the rights of all being safeguarded and defined; so that we may then prepare and perform our common tasks, and that these, undertaken in order to live a Christian life more perfectly, may be fortified by means of the canonical laws.

"Thus, canonical laws need to be observed because of their very nature. Hence it is of the greatest importance that the norms be carefully expounded on the basis of solid juridical, canonical and theological foundations."

BOOKS OF THE CODE

Book I, General Norms (Canons 1-203): Canons in this book cover Church laws, in general, custom and law, general decrees and instructions, administrative acts, statutes, physical and juridical persons, juridical acts, the power of governing, ecclesiastical offices, prescription (statutes of limitations), the reckoning of time.

Book II, The People of God (Canons 204-746): Canons in Part I cover the obligations and rights of all the faithful, the obligations and rights of lay persons, sacred ministers and clerics, personal prelatures and associations of the faithful.

Canons in Part II cover the hierarchic constitution of the Church under the headings: the supreme authority of the Church and the college of bishops, diocesan churches and the authority constituted in them, councils of diocesan churches and the internal order of diocesan churches.

Canons in Part III cover institutes of consecrated life and societies of apostolic life.

Book III: The Teaching Office of the Church (Canons 747-833): Canons under this heading cover: the ministry of the divine word, the missionary action of the Church, Catholic education, the instruments of social communication and books in particular, and the profession of faith.

Book IV, The Sanctifying Office of the Church (Canons 834-1252): Canons under this heading cover each of the seven sacraments – baptism, confirmation, the Eucharist, penance, anointing of the sick, holy orders and matrimony; other acts of divine worship including sacramentals, the Liturgy of the Hours, ecclesiastical burial; the veneration of saints, sacred images and relics, vows and oaths.

Book V, Temporal Goods of the Church (Canons 1254-1310): Canons under this heading cover: the acquisition and administration of goods, contracts, the alienation of goods, wills and pious foundations.

Book VI, Sanctions in the Church (Canons 1311-1399): Canons in Part I cover crimes and penalties in general: the punishment of crimes in general, penal law and penal precept, persons subject to penal sanctions, penalties and other punishments, the application and cessation of penalties.

Canons in Part II cover penalties for particular crimes: crimes against religion and the unity of the Church; crimes against the authority of the Church and the liberty of the Church; the usurpation of Church offices and crimes in exercising office; false accusation of a confessor; crimes against special obligations; crimes against human life and liberty; a general norm regarding the punishment of external violations of divine law not specifically covered in the Code.

Book VII, Procedures (Canons 1400-1752): Judicial proceedings are the principal subjects of canons under this heading: tribunals and their personnel, parties to proceedings, details regarding litigation and the manner in which it is conducted, special proceedings – with emphasis on matrimonial cases.

Glossary

A

Abbacy Nullius: A non-diocesan territory whose people are under the pastoral care of an abbot acting in general in the manner of a bishop.

Abbess: The female superior of a monastic community of nuns; e.g., Benedictines, Poor Clares, some others. Elected by members of the community, an abbess has general authority over her community but no sacramental jurisdiction.

Abbey: *See* **Monastery**.

Abbot: The male superior of a monastic community of men religious; e.g., Benedictines, Cistercians, some others. Elected by members of the community, an abbot has ordinary jurisdiction and general authority over his community. Eastern Rite equivalents of an abbot are a hegumen and an archimandrite. A regular abbot is the head of an abbey or monastery. An abbot general or archabbot is the head of a congregation consisting of several monasteries. An abbot primate is the head of the modern Benedictine Confederation.

Abiogenesis: The term used to describe the spontaneous generation of living matter from non-living matter.

Ablution: A term derived from Latin, meaning washing or cleansing, and referring to the cleansing of the hands of a priest celebrating Mass, after the offering of gifts; and to the cleansing of the chalice with water and wine after Communion.

Abnegation: The spiritual practice of self-denial (or mortification), in order to atone for past sins or in order to join oneself to the passion of Christ. Mortification can be undertaken through fasting, abstinence, or refraining from legitimate pleasure.

Abortion: Abortion is not only "the ejection of an immature fetus" from the womb, but is "also the killing of the same fetus in whatever way at whatever time from the moment of conception it may be procured." (This clarification of Canon 1398, reported in the Dec. 5, 1988, edition of *L'Osservatore Romano*, was issued by the Pontifical Council for the Interpretation of Legislative Texts — in view of scientific developments regarding ways and means of procuring abortion.) Accidental expulsion, as in cases of miscarriage, is without moral fault. Direct abortion, in which a fetus is intentionally removed from the womb, constitutes a direct attack on an innocent human being, a violation of the Fifth Commandment. A person who procures a completed abortion is automatically excommunicated (Canon 1398 of the *Code of Canon Law*); also excommunicated are all persons involved in a deliberate and successful effort to bring about an abortion. Direct abortion is not justifiable for any reason, e.g.: therapeutic, for the physical and/or psychological welfare of the mother; preventive, to avoid the birth of a defective or unwanted child; social, in the interests of family and/or community. Indirect abortion, which occurs when a fetus is expelled during medical or other treatment of the mother for a reason other than procuring expulsion, is permissible under the principle of double effect for a proportionately serious reason; e.g., when a medical or surgical procedure is necessary to save the life of the mother. Such a procedure should not be confused with the purportedly "medical" procedure of the partial-birth abortion, a particularly cruel form of abortion.

Abrogation: The Abolition or elimination of a law by some official action. In Canon Law, abrogation occurs through a direct decree of the Holy See or by the enactment of a later or subsequent law contrary to the former law.

Absolute: (1) A term in philosophy, first introduced at the end of the 18th century and used by Scholasticism, that signifies the "perfect being" (i.e., God), who relies upon no one for existence. Modern philosophical thought has added two new concepts: a) the Absolute is the sum of all being; b) the Absolute has no relationship with any other things; the Absolute is thus unknowable. These concepts are agnostic and contrary to Catholicism, which holds that God is the cause of all being (and hence not the sum) and is knowable by his creatures, at least in part. (2) Certain truths, revealed by God, which are unchanging.

Absolution, Sacramental: The act by which bishops and priests, acting as agents of Christ and ministers of the Church, grant forgiveness of sins in the sacrament of penance. The essential formula of absolution is: "I absolve you from your sins; in the name of the Father, and of the Son, and of the Holy Spirit. Amen." The power to absolve is given with ordination to the priesthood and episcopate. Priests exercise this power in virtue of authorization (faculties) granted by a bishop, a religious superior or canon law. Authorization can be limited or restricted regarding certain sins and penalties or censures. In cases of necessity, and also in cases of the absence of their own confessors, Eastern and Latin Rite Catholics may ask for and receive sacramental absolution from an Eastern or Latin Rite priest; so may Polish National Catholics, according to a Vatican decision issued in May 1993. Any priest can absolve a person in danger of death; in the absence of a priest with the usual faculties, this includes a laicized priest or a priest under censure. (*See* additional entry under **Sacraments**, pp. 190, 185.)

Abstinence: 1. The deliberate deprivation by a person of meat or of foods prepared with meat on those days prescribed by the Church as penitential (Ash Wednesday, Good Friday, and all Fridays of the year which are not solemnities — in the United States, not all Fridays of the year but only the Fridays of Lent). Those 14 years of age and above are bound by the discipline. (2) Sexual abstinence is the willing refrain from sexual intercourse;

total abstinence is observed in obedience to the Sixth Commandment by single persons and couples whose marriages are not recognized by the Church as valid; periodic abstinence or periodic continence is observed by a married couple for regulating conception by natural means or for ascetical motives.

Adoration: The highest act and purpose of religious worship, which is directed in love and reverence to God alone in acknowledgment of his infinite perfection and goodness, and of his total dominion over creatures. Adoration, which is also called latria, consists of internal and external elements, private and social prayer, liturgical acts and ceremonies, and especially sacrifice.

Adultery: Marital infidelity. Sexual intercourse between a married person and another to whom one is not married, a violation of the obligations of the marital covenant, chastity and justice; any sin of impurity (thought, desire, word, action) involving a married person who is not one's husband or wife has the nature of adultery.

Advent Wreath: A wreath of laurel, spruce, or similar foliage with four candles which are lighted successively in the weeks of Advent to symbolize the approaching celebration of the birth of Christ, the Light of the World, at Christmas. The wreath originated among German Protestants.

Agape: A Greek word, meaning love, love feast, designating the meal of fellowship eaten at some gatherings of early Christians. Although held in some places in connection with the Mass, the agape was not part of the Mass, nor was it of universal institution and observance. It was infrequently observed by the fifth century and disappeared altogether between the sixth and eighth centuries.

Age of Reason: (1) The time of life when one begins to distinguish between right and wrong, to understand an obligation and take on moral responsibility; seven years of age is the presumption in church law. (2) Historically, the 18th century period of Enlightenment in England and France, the age of the Encyclopedists and Deists. According to a basic thesis of the Enlightenment, human experience and reason are the only sources of certain knowledge of truth; consequently, faith and revelation are discounted as valid sources of knowledge, and the reality of supernatural truth is called into doubt and/or denied.

Aggiornamento: An Italian word having the general meaning of bringing up to date, renewal, revitalization, descriptive of the processes of spiritual renewal and institutional reform and change in the Church; fostered by the Second Vatican Council.

Agnosticism: A theory which holds that a person cannot have certain knowledge of immaterial reality, especially the existence of God and things pertaining to him. Immanuel Kant, one of the philosophical fathers of agnosticism, stood for the position that God, as well as the human soul, is unknowable on speculative grounds; nevertheless, he found practical imperatives for acknowledging God's existence, a view shared by many agnostics. The First Vatican Council declared that the existence of God and some of his attributes can be known with certainty by human reason, even without divine revelation. The word agnosticism was first used, in the sense given here, by T. H. Huxley in 1869.

Agnus Dei: A Latin phrase, meaning Lamb of God. (1) A title given to Christ, the Lamb (victim) of the Sacrifice of the New Law (on Calvary and in Mass). (2) A prayer said at Mass before the reception of Holy Communion. (3) A sacramental. It is a round paschal-candle fragment blessed by the pope. On one side it bears the impression of a lamb, symbolic of Christ. On the reverse side, there may be any one of a number of impressions; e.g., the figure of a saint, the name and coat of arms of the reigning pope. The *agnus dei* may have originated at Rome in the fifth century. The first definite mention of it dates from about 820.

Akathist Hymn: The most profound and famous expression of Marian devotion in churches of the Byzantine Rite. It consists of 24 sections, 12 of which relate to the Gospel of the Infancy and 12 to the mysteries of the Incarnation and the virginal motherhood of Mary. In liturgical usage, it is sung in part in Byzantine churches on the first four Saturdays of Lent and in toto on the fifth Saturday; it is also recited in private devotion. It is of unknown origin prior to 626, when its popularity increased as a hymn of thanksgiving after the successful defense and liberation of Constantinople, which had been under siege by Persians and Avars. *Akathist* means "without sitting," indicating that the hymn is recited or sung while standing. Pope John Paul II, in a decree dated May 25, 1991, granted a plenary indulgence to the faithful of any rite who recite the hymn in a church or oratory, as a family, in a religious community or in a pious association — in conjunction with the usual conditions of freedom from attachment to sin, reception of the sacraments of penance and the Eucharist, and prayers for the intention of the pope (e.g., an Our Father, the Apostles' Creed and an aspiration). A partial indulgence can be gained for recitation of the hymn in other circumstances.

Alchemy: Ancient mystical science, defined in its strictest sense as the transmuting of base metals into gold; it is considered a predecessor of chemistry. Alchemy is a truly old field of study, found among the Egyptians, Chinese, Greeks, and Indians, transmitted by tradition and often secret writings to the Arabs, Byzantines, and Europeans. It was called during the Middle Ages the "Great Work" or the "Art," and its study entailed complex experimentation with large numbers of compounds, elixirs, and elements. The aim was to find the elixir that could add to the life-span – perhaps even obtain immortality – through the elixir vitae, the Philosopher's Stone that could transmute metals into gold. While the Church condemned false alchemists, especially those who preyed upon the gullible, a number of major Church figures either examined alchemy or were reputed alchemists themselves. St. Thomas Aquinas discussed it in his *Summa Theologiae* and was the reputed author of several alchemy treatises. So too were St. Albertus Magnus (with the dubious work *De Alchimia*), Roger Bacon, Arnold of Villanova, Vincent of Beauvais, and Pope John XXII. That pontiff issued the bull *Spondent quas non exhibent* in 1317 against dishonest alchemists.

Alleluia: An exclamation of joy derived from Hebrew, "All hail to him who is, praise God," with various use in the liturgy and other expressions of worship.

Allocution: A formal type of papal address, as distinguished from an ordinary sermon or statement of views.

Alms: An act, gift or service of compassion, motivated by love of God and neighbor, for the help of persons in need; an obligation of charity, which is measurable by the ability of one person to give assistance and by the degree of another's need. Almsgiving, along with prayer and fasting, is regarded as a work of penance as well as an exercise of charity. (*See* **Mercy, Works of**, p. 148.)

Alpha and Omega: The first and last letters of the Greek alphabet, used to symbolize the eternity of God (Rv 1:8) and the divinity and eternity of Christ, the beginning and end of all things (Rv 21:6; 22:13). Use of the letters as a monogram of Christ originated in the fourth century or earlier.

Amen: A Hebrew word meaning truly, it is true. In the Gospels, Christ used the word to add a note of authority to his statements. In other New Testament writings, as in Hebrew usage, it was the concluding word to doxologies. As the concluding word of prayers, it expresses assent to and acceptance of God's will.

Anamnesis: A prayer recalling the saving mysteries of the death and resurrection of Jesus, following the consecration at Mass in the Latin Rite.

Anaphora: A Greek term for the Canon or Eucharistic Prayer of the Mass.

Anathema: A Greek word with the root meaning of cursed or separated and the adapted meaning of excommunication, used in church documents, especially the canons of ecumenical councils, for the condemnation of heretical doctrines and of practices opposed to proper discipline.

Anchorite: A kind of hermit living in complete isolation and devoting himself exclusively to exercises of religion and severe penance according to a rule and way of life of his own devising. In early Christian times, anchorites were the forerunners of the monastic life. The closest contemporary approach to the life of an anchorite is that of Carthusian and Camaldolese hermits.

Angels: Purely spiritual beings with intelligence and free will whose name indicates their mission as servants and messengers of God. They were created before the creation of the visible universe. Good angels enjoy the perfect good of the beatific vision. They can intercede for persons. The doctrine of guardian angels, although not explicitly defined as a matter of faith, is rooted in long-standing tradition. No authoritative declaration has ever been issued regarding choirs or various categories of angels: seraphim, cherubim, thrones, dominations, principalities, powers, virtues, archangels and angels. Archangels commemorated in the liturgy are: Michael, leader of the angelic host and protector of the synagogue; Raphael, guide of Tobiah and healer of his father; Gabriel, angel of the Incarnation. Fallen angels, the chief of whom is called the Devil or Satan, rejected the love of God and were therefore banished from heaven to hell. They can tempt persons to commit sin.

Angelus: A devotion which commemorates the Incarnation of Christ. It consists of three versicles, three Hail Marys and a special prayer, and recalls the announcement to Mary by the Archangel Gabriel that she was chosen to be the Mother of Christ, her acceptance of the divine will, and the Incarnation (Lk 1:26-38). The Angelus is recited in the morning, at noon and in the evening. The practice of reciting the Hail Mary in honor of the Incarnation was introduced by the Franciscans in 1263. The *Regina Caeli*, commemorating the joy of Mary at Christ's Resurrection, replaces the Angelus during the Easter season.

Anger (Wrath): Passionate displeasure arising from some kind of offense suffered at the hands of another person, frustration or other cause, combined with a tendency to strike back at the cause of the displeasure; a violation of the Fifth Commandment and one of the capital sins if the displeasure is out of proportion to the cause and/or if the retaliation is unjust.

Anglican Orders: Holy orders conferred according to the rite of the Anglican Church, which Leo XIII declared null and void in the bull *Apostolicae Curae*, Sept. 13, 1896. The orders were declared null because they were conferred according to a rite that was substantially defective in form and intent, and because of a break in apostolic succession that occurred when Matthew Parker became head of the Anglican hierarchy in 1559. In making his declaration, Pope Leo cited earlier arguments against validity made by Julius III in 1553 and 1554 and by Paul IV in 1555. He also noted related directives requiring absolute ordination, according to the Catholic ritual, of convert ministers who had been ordained according to the Anglican Ordinal.

Anglican Use Parishes: In line with Vatican-approved developments since 1980, several Anglican use parishes have been established in the United States with the right to continue using some elements of Anglican usage in their liturgical celebrations. A Vatican document dated Mar. 31, 1981, said: "In June, 1980, the Holy See, through the Congregation for the Doctrine of the Faith, agreed to the request presented by the bishops of the United States of America in behalf of some clergy and laity formerly or actually belonging to the Episcopal (Anglican) Church for full communion with the Catholic Church. The Holy See's response to the initiative of these Episcopalians includes the possibility of a 'pastoral provision' which will provide, for those who desire it, a common identity reflecting certain elements of their own heritage."

Animals: Creatures of God, they are entrusted to human stewardship for appropriate care, use for human needs, as pets, for reasonable experimentation for the good of people. They should not be subject to cruel treatment.

Annulment: A decree issued by an appropriate Church authority or tribunal that a sacrament or ecclesiastical act is invalid and therefore lacking in all legal or canonical consequences.

Antichrist: The "deceitful one," the "antichrist" (2 Jn 7), adversary of Christ and the kingdom of God, especially in the end time before the second coming of Christ. The term is also used in reference to anti-Christian persons and forces in the world.

Antiphon: (1) A short verse or text, generally from Scripture, recited in the Liturgy of the Hours before and after psalms and canticles. (2) Any verse sung or recited by one part of a choir or congregation in response to the other part, as in antiphonal or alternate chanting.

Anti-Semitism: A prejudice against Jews, and often accompanied by persecution. The prejudice has existed historically from the time of the ancient Persian Empire and survives even to the present day. It has been condemned consistently by the Church as being in opposition to scriptural principles and Christian charity.

Apologetics: The science and art of developing and presenting the case for the reasonableness of the Christian faith, by a wide variety of means including facts of experience, history, science, philosophy. The constant objective of apologetics, as well as of the total process of pre-evangelization, is preparation for response to God in faith; its ways and means, however, are subject to change in accordance with the various needs of people and different sets of circumstances.

Apostasy: (1) The total and obstinate repudiation of the Christian faith. An apostate automatically incurs a penalty of excommunication. (2) Apostasy from orders is the unlawful withdrawal from or rejection of the obligations of the clerical state by a man who has received major orders. An apostate from orders is subject to a canonical penalty. (3) Apostasy from the religious life occurs when a Religious with perpetual vows unlawfully leaves the community with the intention of not returning, or actually remains outside the community without permission. An apostate from religious life is subject to a canonical penalty.

Apostolate: The ministry or work of an apostle. In Catholic usage, the word is an umbrella-like term covering all kinds and areas of work and endeavor for the service of God and the Church and the good of people. Thus, the apostolate of bishops is to carry on the mission of the Apostles as pastors of the People of God: of priests, to preach the word of God and to carry out the sacramental and pastoral ministry for which they are ordained; of religious, to follow and do the work of Christ in conformity with the evangelical counsels and their rule of life; of lay persons, as individuals and/or in groups, to give witness to Christ and build up the kingdom of God through practice of their faith, professional competence and the performance of good works in the concrete circumstances of daily life. Apostolic works are not limited to those done within the Church or by specifically Catholic groups, although some apostolates are officially assigned to certain persons or groups and are under the direction of church authorities. Apostolate derives from the commitment and obligation of baptism, confirmation, holy orders, matrimony, the duties of one's state in life, etc.

Apostolic Succession: Bishops of the Church, who form a collective body or college, are successors to the Apostles by ordination and divine right; as such they carry on the mission entrusted by Christ to the Apostles as guardians and teachers of the deposit of faith, principal pastors and spiritual authorities of the faithful. The doctrine of apostolic succession is based on New Testament evidence and the constant teaching of the Church, reflected as early as the end of the first century in a letter of Pope St. Clement to the Corinthians. A significant facet of the doctrine is the role of the pope as the successor of St. Peter, the vicar of Christ and head of the college of bishops. The doctrine of apostolic succession means more than continuity of apostolic faith and doctrine; its basic requisite is ordination by the laying on of hands in apostolic succession.

Archives: Documentary records, and the place where they are kept, of the spiritual and temporal government and affairs of the Church, a diocese, church agencies like the departments of the Roman Curia, bodies like religious institutes, and individual parishes. The collection, cataloguing, preserving, and use of these records are governed by norms stated in canon law and particular regulations. The strictest secrecy is always in effect for confidential records concerning matters of conscience, and documents of this kind are destroyed as soon as circumstances permit.

Ark of the Covenant: The sacred chest of the Israelites in which were placed and carried the tablets of stone inscribed with the Ten Commandments, the basic moral precepts of the Old Covenant (Ex 25: 10-22;37:1-9). The Ark was also a symbol of God's presence. The Ark was probably destroyed with the Temple in 586 B.C.

Asceticism: The practice of self-discipline. In the spiritual life, asceticism — by personal prayer, meditation, self-denial, works of mortification, and outgoing interpersonal works — is motivated by love of God and contributes to growth in holiness.

Ashes: Religious significance has been associated with their use as symbolic of penance since Old Testament times. Thus, ashes of palm blessed on the previous Sunday of the Passion are placed on the foreheads of the faithful on Ash Wednesday to remind them to do works of penance, especially during the season of Lent, and that they are dust and unto dust will return. Ashes are a sacramental.

Aspergillum: A vessel or device used for sprinkling holy water. The ordinary type is a metallic rod with a bulbous tip which absorbs the water and discharges it at the motion of the user's hand.

Aspersory: A portable metallic vessel, similar to a pail, for carrying holy water.

Aspiration (Ejaculation): Short exclamatory prayer; e.g., My Jesus, mercy.

Atheism: Denial of the existence of God, finding expression in a system of thought (speculative atheism) or a manner of acting (practical atheism) as though there were no God. The Second Vatican Council, in its Pastoral Constitution on the Church in the Modern World (*Gaudium et Spes*, Nos. 19 to 21), noted that a profession of atheism may represent an explicit denial of God, the rejection of a wrong notion of God, an affirmation of man rather than of God, an extreme protest against evil. It said that such a profession might result from acceptance of such propositions as: there is no absolute truth; man can assert nothing, absolutely nothing, about God; everything can be explained by scientific reasoning alone; the whole question of God is devoid of meaning.

Atonement: The redemptive activity of Christ, who reconciled man with God through his Incarnation and entire life, and especially by his suffering and Resurrection. The word also applies to prayer and good works by which persons join themselves with and take part in Christ's work of reconciliation and reparation for sin.

Attributes of God: Perfections of God. God possesses — and is — all the perfections of being, without limitation. Because he is infinite, all of these perfections are one, perfectly united in him. Because of the limited power of human intelligence, divine perfections — such as omnipotence, truth, love, etc. — are viewed separately, as distinct characteristics, even though they are not actually distinct in God.

Authority, Ecclesiastical: The authority exercised by the Church, and particularly by the pope and the bishops; it is delegated by Jesus Christ to St. Peter. This authority extends to all those matters entrusted to the Apostles by

Christ, including teaching of the Faith, the liturgy and sacraments, moral guidance, and the administration of discipline.

Avarice (Covetousness): A disorderly and unreasonable attachment to and desire for material things; called a capital sin because it involves preoccupation with material things to the neglect of spiritual goods and obligations of justice and charity.

Ave Maria: See **Hail Mary**, p. 143.

B

Baldacchino: A canopy over an altar.

Baptism: *See* **Sacraments**, p. 190.

Beatification: A preliminary step toward canonization of a saint. It begins with an investigation of the candidate's life, writings and heroic practice of virtue, and, except in the case of martyrs and exceptional circumstances, the certification of one miracle worked by God through his or her intercession. If the findings of the investigation so indicate, the pope decrees that the Venerable Servant of God may be called Blessed and may be honored locally or in a limited way in the liturgy. Additional procedures lead to canonization (*see* separate entry), chiefly the certification of a second miracle.

Beatific Vision: The intuitive, immediate and direct vision and experience of God enjoyed in the light of glory by all the blessed in heaven. The vision is a supernatural mystery.

Beatitude: A literary form of the Old and New Testaments in which blessings are promised to persons for various reasons. Beatitudes are mentioned 26 times in the Psalms, and in other books of the Old Testament. The best known Beatitudes — identifying blessedness with participation in the kingdom of God and his righteousness, and descriptive of the qualities of Christian perfection — are those recounted in Mt 5:3-12 and Lk 6:20-23. The Beatitudes are of central importance in the teaching of Jesus.

Benedictus: The canticle or hymn of Zechariah at the circumcision of St. John the Baptist (Lk 1:68-79). It is an expression of praise and thanks to God for sending John as a precursor of the Messiah. The Benedictus is recited in the Liturgy of the Hours as part of the Morning Prayer.

Biglietto: A papal document of notification of appointment to the cardinalate.

Biretta: A stiff, square hat with three ridges on top worn by clerics in church and on other occasions.

Blasphemy: Any internal or external expression of hatred, reproach, insult, defiance or contempt with respect to God and the use of his name, principally, and to the Church, saints and sacred things, secondarily; a serious sin, directly opposed to the second commandment. Blasphemy against the Spirit is the deliberate refusal to accept divine mercy, rejection of forgiveness of sins and of the promise of salvation. The sin that is unforgivable because a person refuses to seek or accept forgiveness.

Blessing: Invocation of God's favor, by official ministers of the Church or by private individuals. Blessings are recounted in the Old and New Testaments, and are common in the Christian tradition. Many types of blessings are listed in the Book of Blessings of the Roman Ritual. Private blessings, as well as those of an official kind, are efficacious.

Blessings are imparted with the Sign of the Cross and appropriate prayer.

Bride of Christ: A metaphorical title that denotes the intimate union that Christ enjoys with his Church; the title is mentioned specifically in the NT (2 Cor 11:2).

Brief, Apostolic: A papal letter, less formal than a bull, signed for the pope by a secretary and impressed with the seal of the Fisherman's Ring. Simple apostolic letters of this kind are issued for beatifications and with respect to other matters.

Bull, Apostolic: Apostolic letter, a solemn form of papal document, beginning with the name and title of the pope (e.g., John Paul II, Servant of the Servants of God), dealing with an important subject, sealed with a *bulla* or red-ink imprint of the device on the *bulla*. Bulls are issued to confer the titles of bishops and cardinals, to promulgate canonizations, to proclaim Holy Years and for other purposes. A collection of bulls is called a *bullarium*.

Burial, Ecclesiastical: Interment with ecclesiastical rites, a right of the Christian faithful. The Church recommends burial of the bodies of the dead, but cremation is permissible if it does not involve reasons against Church teaching. Ecclesiastical burial is in order for catechumens; for unbaptized children whose parents intended to have them baptized before death; and even, in the absence of their own ministers, for baptized non-Catholics unless it would be considered against their will.

Burse, Financial: A special fund maintained by a diocese, religious institute, or private foundation usually endowed by a private benefactor; it often has the purpose of making possible the education of candidates for the priesthood.

C

Calumny (Slander): Harming the name and good reputation of a person by lies; a violation of obligations of justice and truth. Restitution is due for calumny.

Calvary: A knoll about 15 feet high just outside the western wall of Jerusalem where Christ was crucified, so called from the Latin *calvaria* (skull) which described its shape.

Canon: A Greek word meaning rule, norm, standard, measure. (1) The word designates the Canon of Sacred Scripture, which is the list of books recognized by the Church as inspired by the Holy Spirit. (2) The term also designates the canons (Eucharistic Prayers, anaphoras) of the Mass, the core of the eucharistic liturgy. (3) Certain dignitaries of the Church have the title of Canon, and some religious are known as Canons. (*See* **Bible**, p. 96.)

Canonization: An infallible declaration by the pope that a person, who died as a martyr and/or practiced Christian virtue to a heroic degree, is now in heaven and is worthy of honor and imitation by all the faithful. [For details, see **Process of Canonization** under **Communion of Saints**, p. 204; *See also* **Beatification, Saints, Canonizations by Leo XIII and His Successors**, p. 251.]

Canon Law: *See* under **Canon Law**, p. 125.

Canticle: A scriptural chant or prayer differing from the psalms. Three of the canticles prescribed for use in the Liturgy of the Hours are: the *Magnificat*, the Canticle of Mary (Lk 1:46-55); the *Benedictus*, the Canticle of

Zechariah (Lk 1:68-79); and the *Nunc Dimittis*, the Canticle of Simeon (Lk 2:29-32).

Capital Punishment: Punishment for crime by means of the death penalty. The political community, which has authority to provide for the common good, has the right to defend itself and its members against unjust aggression and may in extreme cases punish with the death penalty persons found guilty before the law of serious crimes against individuals and a just social order. Such punishment is essentially vindictive. Its value as a crime deterrent is a matter of perennial debate. The prudential judgment as to whether or not there should be capital punishment belongs to the civic community. The U.S. Supreme Court, in a series of decisions dating from June 29, 1972, ruled against the constitutionality of capital punishment except in specific cases and with appropriate consideration, with respect to sentence, of mitigating circumstances of the crime. Pope John Paul II, in his encyclical letter *Evangelium Vitae* ("The Gospel of Life"), wrote: "There is a growing tendency, both in the Church and in civil society, to demand that it (capital punishment) be applied in a very limited way or even that it be abolished completely." Quoting the *Catechism of the Catholic Church*, the pope wrote: " 'If bloodless means are sufficient to defend human lives against an aggressor and to protect public order and the safety of persons, public authority must limit itself to such means, because they better correspond to the concrete conditions of the common good and are more in conformity to the dignity of the human person.'"

Capital Sins: Sins which give rise to other sins: pride, avarice, lust, wrath (anger), gluttony, envy, sloth.

Cardinal Virtues: The four principal moral virtues are prudence, justice, temperance and fortitude.

Casuistry: In moral theology, the application of moral principles to specific cases. Casuistry can be of assistance because it takes the abstract and makes it practical in a particular situation. It has definite limitations and does not replace the conscience in the decision-making process; additionally, it must be aligned with the cardinal virtue of prudence.

Catacombs: Underground Christian cemeteries in various cities of the Roman Empire and Italy, especially in the vicinity of Rome; the burial sites of many martyrs and other Christians.

Catechesis: The whole complex of church efforts to make disciples of Christ, involving doctrinal instruction and spiritual formation through practice of the faith.

Catechism: A systematic presentation of the fundamentals of Catholic doctrine regarding faith and morals. Sources are Sacred Scripture, tradition, the magisterium (teaching authority of the Church), the writings of Fathers and Doctors of the Church, liturgy. The new *Catechism of the Catholic Church*, published Oct. 11, 1992, consists of four principal sections: the profession of faith, (the Creed), the sacraments of faith, the life of faith (the Commandments) and the prayer of the believer (the Lord's Prayer). The 16th century Council of Trent mandated publication of the *Roman Catechism*. Catechisms such as these two are useful sources for other catechisms serving particular needs of the faithful and persons seeking admission to the Catholic Church.

Catechumen: A person preparing in a program (catechumenate) of instruction and spiritual formation for baptism and reception into the Church. The Church has a special relationship with catechumens. It invites them to lead the life of the Gospel, introduces them to the celebration of the sacred rites, and grants them various prerogatives that are proper to the faithful (one of which is the right to ecclesiastical burial). (*See* **Rite of Christian Initiation of Adults**, under **Baptism**, p. 192.)

Cathedra: A Greek word for chair, designating the chair or seat of a bishop in the principal church of his diocese, which is therefore called a cathedral.

Cathedraticum: The tax paid to a bishop by all churches and benefices subject to him for the support of episcopal administration and for works of charity.

Catholic: A Greek word, meaning universal, first used in the title Catholic Church in a letter written by St. Ignatius of Antioch about 107 to the Christians of Smyrna.

Celebret: A Latin word, meaning "Let him celebrate," the name of a letter of recommendation issued by a bishop or other superior stating that a priest is in good standing and therefore eligible to celebrate Mass or perform other priestly functions.

Celibacy: The unmarried state of life, required in the Roman Church of candidates for holy orders and of men already ordained to holy orders, for the practice of perfect chastity and total dedication to the service of people in the ministry of the Church. Celibacy is enjoined as a condition for ordination by church discipline and law, not by dogmatic necessity. In the Roman Church, a consensus in favor of celibacy developed in the early centuries while the clergy included both celibates and men who had been married once. The first local legislation on the subject was enacted by a local council held in Elvira, Spain, about 306; it forbade bishops, priests, deacons and other ministers to have wives. Similar enactments were passed by other local councils from that time on, and by the 12th century particular laws regarded marriage by clerics in major orders to be not only unlawful but also null and void. The latter view was translated by the Second Lateran Council in 1139 into what seems to be the first written universal law making holy orders an invalidating impediment to marriage. In 1563 the Council of Trent ruled definitely on the matter and established the discipline in force in the Roman Church. Some exceptions to this discipline have been made in recent years. A number of married Protestant and Episcopalian (Anglican) clergymen who became converts and were subsequently ordained to the priesthood have been permitted to continue in marriage. Married men over the age of 35 can be ordained to the permanent diaconate. Eastern Church discipline on celibacy differs from that of the Roman Church. In line with legislation enacted by the Synod of Trullo in 692 and still in force, candidates for holy orders may marry before becoming deacons and may continue in marriage thereafter, but marriage after ordination is forbidden. Bishops of Eastern Catholic Churches in the U.S., however, do not ordain married candidates for the priesthood. Bishops of Eastern Catholic Churches are unmarried.

Cenacle: The upper room in Jerusalem where Christ ate the Las Supper with his Apostles.

Censer: A metal vessel with a perforated cover and suspended by chains, in which incense is burned. It is used at some Masses, Benediction of the Blessed Sacrament and other liturgical functions.

Censorship of Books: An exercise of vigilance by the Church for safeguarding authentic religious teaching. Pertinent legislation in a decree issued by the Congregation for the Doctrine of the Faith Apr. 9, 1975, is embodied in the Code of Canon Law (Book III, Title IV). The legislation deals with requirements for pre-publication review and clearance of various types of writings on religious subjects. Permission to publish works of a religious character, together with the apparatus of reviewing them beforehand, falls under the authority of the bishop of the place where the writer lives or where the works are published. Clearance for publication is usually indicated by the terms *Nihil obstat* ("Nothing stands in the way") issued by the censor and *Imprimatur* ("Let it be printed") authorized by the bishop. The clearing of works for publication does not necessarily imply approval of an author's viewpoint or his manner of handling a subject.

Censures: Sanctions imposed by the Church on baptized Roman Catholics 18 years of age or older for committing certain serious offenses and for being or remaining obstinate therein: (1) excommunication (exclusion from the community of the faithful, barring a person from sacramental and other participation in the goods and offices of the community of the Church), (2) suspension (prohibition of a cleric to exercise orders) and (3) interdict (deprivation of the sacraments and liturgical activities). The intended purposes of censures are to correct and punish offenders; to deter persons from committing sins which, more seriously and openly than others, threaten the common good of the Church and its members; and to provide for the making of reparation for harm done to the community of the Church. Censures may be incurred automatically (*ipso facto*) on the commission of certain offenses for which fixed penalties have been laid down in Church law (*latae sententiae*); or they may be inflicted by sentence of a judge (*ferendae sententiae*). Automatic excommunication is incurred for the offenses of abortion, apostasy, heresy and schism. Obstinacy in crime — also called contumacy, disregard of a penalty, defiance of Church authority — is presumed by law in the commission of offenses for which automatic censures are decreed. The presence and degree of contumacy in other cases, for which judicial sentence is required, is subject to determination by a judge. Absolution can be obtained from any censure, provided the person repents and desists from obstinacy. Absolution may be reserved to the pope, the bishop of a place, or the major superior of an exempt clerical religious institute. In danger of death, any priest can absolve from all censures; in other cases, faculties to absolve from reserved censures can be exercised by compe-

tent authorities or given to other priests. The penal law of the Church is contained in Book VI of the Code of Canon Law.

Ceremonies, Master of: One who directs the proceedings of a rite or ceremony during the function.

Chamberlain (*Camerlengo*): (1) the Chamberlain of the Holy Roman Church is a cardinal with special responsibilities, especially during the time between the death of one pope and the election of his successor; among other things, he safeguards and administers the goods and revenues of the Holy See and heads particular congregations of cardinals for special purposes. (*See* also **Papal Election**, p. 150.) (2) the Chamberlain of the College of Cardinals has charge of the property and revenues of the College and keeps the record of business transacted in consistories. (3) the Chamberlain of the Roman Clergy is the president of the secular clergy of Rome.

Chancellor: Notary of a diocese, who draws up written documents in the government of the diocese; takes care of, arranges and indexes diocesan archives, records of dispensations and ecclesiastical trials.

Chancery: (1) A branch of church administration that handles written documents used in the government of a diocese. (2) The administrative office of a diocese, a bishop's office.

Chant: A type of sacred singing. It is either recitative in nature with a short two-to-six tones for an accentus, or melodic in one of three styles (syllabic, neumatic, or melismatic).

Chapel: A building or part of another building used for divine worship; a portion of a church set aside for the celebration of Mass or for some special devotion.

Chaplain: A priest — or, in some instances, a properly qualified religious or lay person — serving the pastoral needs of particular groups of people and institutions, such as hospitals, schools, correctional facilities, religious communities, the armed forces, etc.

Chaplet: A term, meaning little crown, applied to a rosary or, more commonly, to a small string of beads used for devotional purposes; e.g., the Infant of Prague chaplet.

Chapter: A general meeting of delegates of religious orders for elections and the handling of other important affairs of their communities.

Charismatic Renewal: A movement which originated with a handful of Duquesne University students and faculty members in the 1966-67 academic year and spread from there to Notre Dame, Michigan State University, the University of Michigan, other campuses and cities throughout the U.S., and to well over 125 other countries. Scriptural keys to the renewal are: Christ's promise to send the Holy Spirit upon the Apostles; the description, in the Acts of the Apostles, of the effects of the coming of the Holy Spirit upon the Apostles on Pentecost; St. Paul's explanation, in the Letter to the Romans and 1 Corinthians, of the charismatic gifts (for the good of the Church and persons) the Holy Spirit would bestow on Christians; New Testament evidence concerning the effects of charismatic gifts in and through the early Church. The personal key to the renewal is baptism in the Holy Spirit. This is not a new sacrament but the personally experienced actualization of grace already sacramentally received, principally in baptism and confirmation. The experience of baptism in the Holy Spirit is often accompanied by the reception of one or more charismatic gifts. A characteristic form of the renewal is the weekly prayer meeting, a gathering which includes periods of spontaneous prayer, singing, sharing of experience and testimony, fellowship and teaching. (*See* also **Index**.)

Charisms: Gifts or graces given by God to persons for the good of others and the Church. Examples are special gifts for apostolic work, prophecy, healing, discernment of spirits, the life of evangelical poverty, here-and-now witness to faith in various circumstances of life. The Second Vatican Council made the following statement about charisms in the Dogmatic Constitution on the Church (No. 12): "It is not only through the sacraments and Church ministries that the same Holy Spirit sanctifies and leads the People of God and enriches it with virtues. Allotting his gifts 'to everyone according as he will' (1 Cor 12:11), he distributes special graces among the faithful of every rank. By these gifts he makes them fit and ready to undertake the various tasks or offices advantageous for the renewal and upbuilding of the Church, according to the words of the Apostle: 'The manifestation of the Spirit is given to everyone for profit' (1 Cor 12:7). These charismatic gifts, whether they be the most outstanding or the more simple and widely diffused, are to be received with thanksgiving and consolation, for they are exceedingly suitable and useful for the needs of the Church. Still, extraordinary gifts are not to be rashly sought after, nor are the fruits of apostolic labor to be presumptuously expected from them. In any case, judgment as to their genuineness and proper use belongs to those who preside over the Church, and to whose special competence it belongs, not indeed to extinguish the Spirit, but to test all things and hold fast to that which is good" (cf. 1 Thes 5:12; 19-21).

Charity: Love of God above all things for his own sake, and love of one's neighbor as oneself because and as an expression of one's love for God; the greatest of the three theological virtues. The term is sometimes also used to designate sanctifying grace.

Chastity: Properly ordered behavior with respect to sex. In marriage, the exercise of the procreative power is integrated with the norms and purposes of marriage. Outside of marriage, the rule is self-denial of the voluntary exercise and enjoyment of the procreative faculty in thought, word or action. The vow of chastity, which reinforces the virtue of chastity with the virtue of religion, is one of the three vows professed publicly by members of institutes of consecrated life.

Chirograph or Autograph Letter: A letter written by a pope himself, in his own handwriting.

Chrism: A mixture of olive or other vegetable oil and balsam (or balm), that is consecrated by a bishop for use in liturgical anointings: Baptism, Confirmation, Holy Orders, the blessing of an altar.

Christ: The title of Jesus, derived from the Greek translation *Christos* of the Hebrew term Messiah, meaning the Anointed of God, the Savior and Deliverer of his people. Christian use of the title is a confession of belief that Jesus is the Savior.

Christianity: The sum total of things related to belief in Christ — the Christian religion, Christian churches, Christians themselves, society based on and expressive of Christian beliefs, culture reflecting Christian values.

Christians: The name first applied about the year 43 to followers of Christ at Antioch, the capital of Syria. It was used by the pagans as a contemptuous term. The word applies to persons who profess belief in the divinity and teachings of Christ and who give witness to him in life.

Circumcision: A ceremonial practice symbolic of initiation and participation in the covenant between God and Abraham.

Circumincession: The indwelling of each divine Person of the Holy Trinity in the others.

Clergy: Men ordained to holy orders and commissioned for sacred ministries and assigned to pastoral and other duties for the service of the people and the Church. (1) Diocesan or secular clergy are committed to pastoral ministry in parishes and in other capacities in a particular church (diocese) under the direction of their bishop, to whom they are bound by a promise of obedience. (2) Regular clergy belong to religious institutes (orders, congregations, societies — institutes of consecrated life) and are so called because they observe the rule (*regula*, in Latin) of their respective institutes. They are committed to the ways of life and apostolates of their institutes. In ordinary pastoral ministry, they are under the direction of local bishops as well as their own superiors.

Clericalism: A term generally used in a derogatory sense to mean action, influence and interference by the Church and the clergy in matters with which they allegedly should not be concerned. Anticlericalism is a reaction of antipathy, hostility, distrust and opposition to the Church and clergy arising from real and/or alleged faults of the clergy, overextension of the role of the laity, or for other reasons.

Cloister: Part of a monastery, convent or other house of religious reserved for use by members of the institute. Houses of contemplative Religious have a strict enclosure.

Code: A digest of rules or regulations, such as the Code of Canon Law.

Code of Canon Law: *See* **Canon Law**, p. 125.

Collegiality: A term in use especially since the Second Vatican Council to describe the authority exercised by the College of Bishops. The bishops of the Church, in union with and subordinate to the pope — who has full, supreme and universal power over the Church which he can always exercise independently — have supreme teaching and pastoral authority over the whole Church. In addition to their proper authority of office for the good of the faithful in their respective dioceses or other jurisdictions, the bishops have authority to act for the good of the universal Church. This collegial authority is exercised in a solemn manner in an ecumenical council and can also be exercised in other ways sanctioned by the pope. Doctrine on collegiality was set forth by the Second Vatican Council in *Lumen Gentium* (the Dogmatic Constitution on the Church). (*See* separate entry, p. 189) By extension, the concept of collegiality is applied to other forms of participation and co-responsibility by members of a community.

Communicatio in Sacris: The reception of the Church's sacraments by non-members or the reception by Catholics of sacraments in non-Catholic Churches.

Communion of Saints: "The communion of all the faithful of Christ, those who are pilgrims on earth, the dead who are being purified, and the blessed in heaven, all together forming one Church; in this communion, the merciful love of God and his saints is always (attentive) to our prayers" (Paul VI, *Creed of the People of God*).

Communism: The substantive principles of modern communism, a theory and system of economics and social organization, were stated about the middle of the 19th century by Karl Marx, author of *The Communist Manifesto* and, with Friedrich Engels, *Das Kapital*. The elements of communist theory include: radical materialism; dialectical determinism; the inevitability of class struggle and conflict, which is to be furthered for the ultimate establishment of a worldwide, classless society; common ownership of productive and other goods; the subordination of all persons and institutions to the dictatorship of the collective; denial of the rights, dignity and liberty of persons; militant atheism and hostility to religion, utilitarian morality. Communism in theory and practice has been the subject of many papal documents and statements. Pius IX condemned it in 1846. Leo XIII dealt with it at length in the encyclical letter *Quod Apostolici Muneris* in 1878 and *Rerum Novarum* in 1891. Pius XI wrote on the same subject in the encyclicals *Quadragesimo Anno* in 1931 and *Divini Redemptoris* in 1937. These writings have been updated and developed in new directions by Pius XII, John XXIII, Paul VI and John Paul II.

Compline: The night prayer of the Church that completes the daily cursus (course) of the Liturgy of the Hours (Divine Office).

Concelebration: The liturgical act in which several priests, led by one member of the group, offer Mass together, all consecrating the bread and wine. Concelebration has always been common in churches of Eastern Rite. In the Roman Rite, it was long restricted, taking place only at the ordination of bishops and the ordination of priests. The Constitution on the Sacred Liturgy issued by the Second Vatican Council set new norms for concelebration, which is now relatively common in the Roman Rite.

Concordance, Biblical: An alphabetical verbal index enabling a user knowing one or more words of a scriptural passage to locate the entire text.

Concordat: A church-state treaty with the force of law concerning matters of mutual concern — e.g., rights of the Church, arrangement of ecclesiastical jurisdictions, marriage laws, education. Approximately 150 agreements of this kind have been negotiated since the Concordat of Worms in 1122.

Concupiscence: Any tendency of the sensitive appetite. The term is most frequently used in reference to desires and tendencies for sinful sense pleasure.

Confession: Sacramental confession is the act by which a person tells or confesses his sins to a priest who is authorized to give absolution in the sacrament of penance.

Confessor: A priest who administers the sacrament of penance. The title of confessor, formerly given to a category of male saints, was suppressed with publication of the calendar reform of 1969.

Confraternity: An association whose members practice a particular form of religious devotion and/or are engaged in some kind of apostolic work.

Congregation: (1) The collective name for the people who form a parish. (2) One of the chief administrative departments of the Roman Curia. (3) An unofficial term for a group of men and women who belong to a religious community or institute of consecrated life.

Conscience: Practical judgment concerning the moral goodness or sinfulness of an action (thought, word, desire). In the Catholic view, this judgment is made by reference of the action, its attendant circumstances and the intentions of the person to the requirements of moral law as expressed in the Ten Commandments, the summary law of love for God and neighbor, the life and teaching of Christ, and the authoritative teaching and practice of the Church with respect to the total demands of divine Revelation. A person is obliged: (1) to obey a certain and correct conscience; (2) to obey a certain conscience even if it is inculpably erroneous; (3) not to obey, but to correct, a conscience known to be erroneous or lax; (4) to rectify a scrupulous conscience by following the advice of a confessor and by other measures; (5) to resolve doubts of conscience before acting. It is legitimate to act for solid and probable reasons when a question of moral responsibility admits of argument (*See* **Probabiliorism** and **Probabilism,** p. 152).

Conscience, Examination of: Self-examination to determine one's spiritual state before God, regarding one's sins and faults. It is recommended as a regular practice and is practically necessary in preparing for the sacrament of penance. The particular examen is a regular examination to assist in overcoming specific faults and imperfections.

Consequentialism: A moral theory, closely associated with proportionalism and utilitarianism, that holds that the preferable action is one that brings about the best consequences. Preferred results, rather than the objective truth and intentionality, are the object of actions based on consequentialism. While traditional moral theology acknowledges that consequences are important in determining the rightness of an act, importance is also placed on the intrinsic morality of the act and the agent's intention.

Consistory: An assembly of cardinals presided over by the pope.

Constitution: (1) An apostolic or papal constitution is a document in which a pope enacts and promulgates law. (2) A formal and solemn document issued by an ecumenical council on a doctrinal or pastoral subject, with binding force in the whole Church; e.g., the four constitutions issued by the Second Vatican Council on the Church, liturgy, Revelation, and the Church in the modern world. (3) The constitutions of institutes of consecrated life and societies of apostolic life spell out details of and norms drawn from the various rules for the guidance and direction of the life and work of their members.

Consubstantiation: A theory which holds that the Body and Blood of Christ coexist with the substance of bread and wine in the Holy Eucharist. This theory, also called impanation, is incompatible with the doctrine of transubstantiation.

Contraception: Anything done by positive interference to prevent sexual intercourse from resulting in conception. Direct contraception is against the order of nature. Indirect contraception — as a secondary effect of medical treatment or other action having a necessary, good, non-contraceptive purpose — is permissible under the principle of the double effect. The practice of periodic continence is not contraception because it does not involve positive interference with the order of nature. (*See Humanae Vitae*, p. 199, other entries.)

Contrition: Sorrow for sin coupled with a purpose

of amendment. Contrition arising from a supernatural motive is necessary for the forgiveness of sin. (1) Perfect contrition is total sorrow for and renunciation of attachment to sin, arising from the motive of pure love of God. Perfect contrition, which implies the intention of doing all God wants done for the forgiveness of sin (including confession in a reasonable period of time), is sufficient for the forgiveness of serious sin and the remission of all temporal punishment due for sin. (The intention to receive the sacrament of penance is implicit — even if unrealized, as in the case of some persons — in perfect contrition.) (2) Imperfect contrition or attrition is sorrow arising from a quasi-selfish supernatural motive; e.g., the fear of losing heaven, suffering the pains of hell, etc. Imperfect contrition is sufficient for the forgiveness of serious sin when joined with absolution in confession, and sufficient for the forgiveness of venial sin even outside of confession.

Contumely: Personal insult, reviling a person in his presence by accusation of moral faults, by refusal of recognition or due respect; a violation of obligations of justice and charity.

Conversion: In a general sense, the turning away from someone or something and the moving toward another person or thing. In Christian belief, conversion is the embrace of Jesus Christ and a rejection of all that keeps one from God.

Corpus Iuris Canonici: *See* **Canon Law**, p. 125.

Council: A formal meeting of Church leaders, summoned by a bishop or appropriate Church leader, with the general purpose of assisting the life of the Church through deliberations, decrees, and promulgations. Different councils include: **diocesan** councils (synod), a gathering of the officials of an individual diocese; **provincial** councils, the meeting of the bishops of a province; **plenary** councils, the assembly of the bishops of a country; and **ecumenical** councils, a gathering of all the bishops in the world under the authority of the Bishop of Rome.

Counsels, Evangelical: Gospel counsels of perfection, especially voluntary poverty, perfect chastity and obedience, which were recommended by Christ to those who would devote themselves exclusively and completely to the immediate service of God. Religious (members of institutes of consecrated life) bind themselves by public vows to observe these counsels in a life of total consecration to God and service to people through various kinds of apostolic works.

Counter-Reformation: The period of approximately 100 years following the Council of Trent (1545-63), which witnessed a reform within the Church to stimulate genuine Catholic life and to counteract effects of the Reformation.

Covenant: A bond of relationship between parties pledged to each other. God-initiated covenants in the Old Testament included those with Noah, Abraham, Moses, Levi, David. The Mosaic (Sinai) covenant made Israel God's Chosen People on terms of fidelity to true faith, true worship, and righteous conduct according to the Decalogue. The New Testament covenant, prefigured in the Old Testament, is the bond people have with God through Christ. All people are called to be parties to this perfect and everlasting covenant, which was mediated and ratified by Christ. The marriage covenant seals the closest possible relationship between a man and a woman.

Creation: The production by God of something out of nothing. The biblical account of creation is contained in the first two chapters of Genesis.

Creator: God, the supreme, self-existing Being, the absolute and infinite First Cause of all things.

Creature: Everything in the realm of being is a creature, except God.

Cremation: The reduction of a human corpse to ashes by means of fire. Cremation is not in line with Catholic tradition and practice, even though it is not opposed to any article of faith. The Congregation for the Doctrine of the Faith, under date of May 8, 1963, circulated among bishops an instruction which upheld the traditional practices of Christian burial but modified anti-cremation legislation. Cremation may be permitted for serious reasons, of a private as well as public nature, provided it does not involve any contempt of the Church or of religion, or any attempt to deny, question, or belittle the doctrine of the resurrection of the body. In a letter dated Mar. 21, 1997, and addressed to Bp. Anthony M. Pilla, president of the National Conference of Catholic Bishops, the Congregation for Divine Worship and the Discipline of the Sacraments granted "a particular permission to the diocesan bishops of the United States of America. By this, local Ordinaries (heads of dioceses) are authorized . . . to permit that the funeral liturgy, including where appropriate the celebration of the Eucharist, be celebrated in the presence of the cremated remains instead of the natural body." Bp. Pilla asked bishops not to use this indult until appropriate texts and ritual directives are approved by the Vatican. (*See* **Burial, Ecclesiastical**).

Crib: Also Crèche, a devotional representation of the birth of Jesus. The custom of erecting cribs is generally attributed to St. Francis of Assisi, who in 1223 obtained from Pope Honorius III permission to use a crib and figures of the Christ Child, Mary, St. Joseph, and others, to represent the mystery of the Nativity.

Crosier: The bishop's staff, symbolic of his pastoral office, responsibility and authority; used at liturgical functions.

Crypt: An underground or partly underground chamber; e.g., the lower part of a church used for worship and/or burial.

Cura Animarum: A Latin phrase, meaning care of souls, designating the pastoral ministry and responsibility of bishops and priests.

Curia: The personnel and offices through which (1) the pope administers the affairs of the universal Church, the Roman Curia (*See* p. 255), or (2) a bishop the affairs of a diocese, diocesan curia. The principal officials of a diocesan curia are the vicar general of the diocese, the chancellor, officials of the diocesan tribunal or court, examiners, consultors, auditors, notaries.

Custos: A religious superior who presides over a number of convents collectively called a custody. In some institutes of consecrated life a custos may be the deputy of a higher superior.

D

Dean: (1) A priest with supervisory responsibility over a section of a diocese known as a deanery. The post-Vatican II counterpart of a dean is an episcopal vicar. (2) The senior or ranking member of a group.

Decision: A judgment or pronouncement on a

cause or suit, given by a church tribunal or official with judicial authority. A decision has the force of law for concerned parties.

Declaration: (1) An ecclesiastical document which presents an interpretation of an existing law. (2) A position paper on a specific subject; e.g., the three declarations issued by the Second Vatican Council on religious freedom, non-Christian religions, and Christian education.

Decree: An edict or ordinance issued by a pope and/or by an ecumenical council, with binding force in the whole Church; by a department of the Roman Curia, with binding force for concerned parties; by a territorial body of bishops, with binding force for persons in the area; by individual bishops, with binding force for concerned parties until revocation or the death of the bishop. The nine decrees issued by the Second Vatican Council were combinations of doctrinal and pastoral statements with executive orders for action and movement toward renewal and reform in the Church.

Dedication of a Church: The ceremony whereby a church is solemnly set apart for the worship of God. The custom of dedicating churches had an antecedent in Old Testament ceremonies for the dedication of the Temple, as in the times of Solomon and the Maccabees. The earliest extant record of the dedication of a Christian church dates from early in the fourth century, when it was done simply by the celebration of Mass. Other ceremonies developed later. A church can be dedicated by a simple blessing or a solemn consecration. The rite of consecration is generally performed by a bishop.

Deposit of the Faith: The body of saving truth, entrusted by Christ to the Apostles and handed on by them to the Church to be preserved and proclaimed. As embodied in Revelation and Tradition the term is very nearly coextensive with objective revelation, in that it embraces the whole of Christ's teaching. But the term of deposit highlights particular features of the apostolic teaching implying that this teaching is an inexhaustible store that rewards and promotes reflection and study so that new insights and deeper penetration might be made into the mystery of the divine economy of salvation. Although our understanding of this teaching can develop, it can never be augmented in its substance; the teaching is a divine trust that cannot be altered, modified, or debased. The term *depositum fidei* first entered official Catholic teaching with the Council of Trent, but its substance is well-attested in the Scriptures and the Fathers.

Despair: Abandonment of hope for salvation arising from the conviction that God will not provide the necessary means for attaining it, that following God's way of life for salvation is impossible, or that one's sins are unforgivable; a serious sin against the Holy Spirit and the theological virtues of hope and faith, involving distrust in the mercy and goodness of God and a denial of the truths that God wills the salvation of all persons and provides sufficient grace for it. Real despair is distinguished from unreasonable fear with respect to the difficulties of attaining salvation, from morbid anxiety over the demands of divine justice, and from feelings of despair.

Detraction: Revelation of true but hidden faults of a person without sufficient and justifying reason; a violation of requirements of justice and charity, involving the obligation to make restitution when this is possible without doing more harm to the good name of the offended party. In some cases, e.g., to prevent evil, secret faults may and should be disclosed.

Devil: (1) Lucifer, Satan, chief of the fallen angels who sinned and were banished from heaven. Still possessing angelic powers, he can cause such diabolical phenomena as possession and obsession, and can tempt men to sin. (2) Any fallen angel.

Devotion: (1) Religious fervor, piety; dedication. (2) The consolation experienced at times during prayer; a reverent manner of praying.

Devotions: Pious practices of members of the Church include not only participation in various acts of the liturgy but also in other acts of worship generally called popular or private devotions. Concerning these, the Second Vatican Council said in the Constitution on the Sacred Liturgy (*Sacrosanctum Concilium*, No. 13): "Popular devotions of the Christian people are warmly commended, provided they accord with the laws and norms of the Church. Such is especially the case with devotions called for by the Apostolic See. Devotions proper to the individual churches also have a special dignity. These devotions should be so drawn up that they harmonize with the liturgical seasons, accord with the sacred liturgy, are in some fashion derived from it, and lead the people to it, since the liturgy by its very nature far surpasses any of them." Devotions of a liturgical type are Exposition of the Blessed Sacrament, recitation of Evening Prayer and Night Prayer of the Liturgy of the Hours. Examples of paraliturgical devotion are a Bible Service or Vigil, and the Angelus, Rosary and Stations of the Cross, which have a strong scriptural basis.

Diocese: A particular church, a fully organized ecclesiastical jurisdiction under the pastoral direction of a bishop as local Ordinary.

Discalced: Of Latin derivation and meaning without shoes, the word is applied to religious orders or congregations whose members go barefoot or wear sandals.

Disciple: A term used sometimes in reference to the Apostles but more often to a larger number of followers (70 or 72) of Christ mentioned in Lk 10:1.

Disciplina Arcani: A Latin phrase, meaning discipline of the secret and referring to a practice of the early Church, especially during the Roman persecutions, to: (1) conceal Christian truths from those who, it was feared, would misinterpret, ridicule and profane the teachings, and persecute Christians for believing them; (2) instruct catechumens in a gradual manner, withholding the teaching of certain doctrines until the catechumens proved themselves of good faith and sufficient understanding.

Dispensation: The relaxation of a law in a particular case. Laws made for the common good sometimes work undue hardship in particular cases. In such cases, where sufficient reasons are present, dispensations may be granted by proper authorities. Bishops, religious superiors and others may dispense from certain laws; the pope can dispense from all ecclesiastical laws. No one has authority to dispense from obligations of the divine law.

Divination: Attempting to foretell future or hidden things by means of things like dreams, necromancy, spiritism, examination of entrails, astrology, augury, omens, palmistry, drawing straws, dice, cards, etc. Practices like these attribute to created things a power which belongs to God alone and are violations of the First Commandment.

Divine Praises: Fourteen praises recited or sung at Benediction of the Blessed Sacrament in reparation for sins of sacrilege, blasphemy and profanity. Some of these praises date from the end of the 18th century: *Blessed be God. / Blessed be his holy Name. / Blessed be Jesus Christ, true God and true Man. / Blessed be the Name of Jesus. / Blessed be his most Sacred Heart. / Blessed be his most Precious Blood. / Blessed be Jesus in the most holy Sacrament of the Altar. / Blessed be the Holy Spirit, the Paraclete. / Blessed be the great Mother of God, Mary most holy. / Blessed be her holy and Immaculate Conception. / Blessed be her glorious Assumption. / Blessed be the name of Mary, Virgin and Mother. / Blessed be St. Joseph, her most chaste Spouse. / Blessed be God in his Angels and in his Saints.*

Double Effect Principle: Actions sometimes have two effects closely related to each other, one good and the other bad, and a difficult moral question can arise: Is it permissible to place an action from which two such results follow? It is permissible to place the action, if: the action is good in itself and is directly productive of the good effect; the circumstances are good; the intention of the person is good; the reason for placing the action is proportionately serious to the seriousness of the indirect bad effect.

Doxology: (1) The lesser doxology, or ascription of glory to the Trinity, is the Glory be to the Father. The first part dates back to the third or fourth century, and came from the form of baptism. The concluding words, As it was in the beginning, etc., are of later origin. (2) The greater doxology, Glory to God in the highest, begins with the words of angelic praise at the birth of Christ recounted in the Infancy Narrative (Lk 2:14). It is often recited at Mass. Of early Eastern origin, it is found in the Apostolic Constitutions in a form much like the present. (3) The formula of praise at the end of the Eucharistic Prayer at Mass, sung or said by the celebrant while he holds aloft the paten containing the consecrated host in one hand and the chalice containing the consecrated wine in the other.

Dulia: A Greek term meaning the veneration or homage, different in nature and degree from that given to God, paid to the saints. It includes honoring the saints and seeking their intercession with God.

Duty: A moral obligation deriving from the binding force of law, the exigencies of one's state in life, and other sources.

E

Easter Controversy: A three-phase controversy over the time for the celebration of Easter. Some early Christians in the Near East, called Quartodecimans, favored the observance of Easter on the 14th day of Nisan, the spring month of the Hebrew calendar, whenever it occurred. Against this practice, Pope St. Victor I, about 190, ordered a Sunday observance of the feast. The Council of Nicaea, in line with usages of the Church at Rome and Alexandria, decreed in 325 that Easter should be observed on the Sunday following the first full moon of spring. Uniformity of practice in the West was not achieved until several centuries later, when the British Isles, in delayed compliance with measures enacted by the Synod of Whitby in 664, accepted the Roman date of observance. Unrelated to the controversy is the fact that some Eastern Christians, in accordance with traditional calendar practices, celebrate Easter at a different time than the Roman and Eastern Churches.

Easter Duty: The serious obligation binding Catholics of Roman Rite, to receive the Eucharist during the Easter season (in the U.S., from the first Sunday of Lent to and including Trinity Sunday).

Easter Water: Holy water blessed with special ceremonies and distributed on the Easter Vigil; used during Easter Week for blessing the faithful and homes.

Ecclesiology: Study of the nature, constitution, members, mission, functions, etc., of the Church.

Ecology: The natural environment of the total range of creation — mineral, vegetable, animal, human — entrusted to people for respect, care and appropriate use as well as conservation and development for the good of present and future generations.

Ecstasy: An extraordinary state of mystical experience in which a person is so absorbed in God that the activity of the exterior senses is suspended.

Economy, Divine: The fulfillment of God's plan of salvation. It was fully developed in his divine mind from eternity, and fully revealed in Jesus Christ. Before the Incarnation it was known only obscurely, but after the ascension of Christ and the coming of the Holy Spirit at Pentecost, it became the substance of apostolic preaching and is preserved in its integrity for each new generation.

Ecumenism: The movement of Christians and their churches toward the unity willed by Christ. The Second Vatican Council called the movement "those activities and enterprises which, according to various needs of the Church and opportune occasions, are started and organized for the fostering of unity among Christians" (Decree on Ecumenism, No. 4). Spiritual ecumenism, i.e., mutual prayer for unity, is the heart of the movement. The movement also involves scholarly and pew-level efforts for the development of mutual understanding and better interfaith relations in general, and collaboration by the churches and their members in the social area. (*See* **Index** for other entries.)

Elevation: The raising of the host after consecration at Mass for adoration by the faithful. The custom was introduced in the Diocese of Paris about the close of the 12th century to offset an erroneous teaching of the time which held that transubstantiation of the bread did not take place until after the consecration of the wine in the chalice. The elevation of the chalice following the consecration of the wine was introduced in the 15th century.

Encyclical: The highest form of papal teaching document. It is normally addressed to all the bishops and/or to all the faithful.

Envy: Sadness over another's good fortune because it is considered a loss to oneself or a detraction from one's own excellence; one of the seven capital sins, a violation of the obligations of charity.

Epiclesis: An invocation of the Holy Spirit, to bless the offerings consecrated at Mass; before the consecration in the Latin Rite, after the consecration in Eastern usage.

Epikeia: A Greek word meaning reasonableness and designating a moral theory and practice, a mild interpretation of the mind of a legislator who is prudently considered not to wish positive law to bind in certain circumstances.

Episcopate: (1) The office, dignity and sacramental powers bestowed upon a bishop at his ordination. (2) The body of bishops collectively.

Equivocation: (1) The use of words, phrases, or gestures having more than one meaning in order to conceal information which a questioner has no strict right to know. It is permissible to equivocate (have a broad mental reservation) in some circumstances. (2) A lie, i.e., a statement of untruth. Lying is intrinsically wrong. A lie told in joking, evident as such, is not wrong.

Eschatology: Doctrine concerning the last things: death, judgment, heaven and hell, and the final state of perfection of the people and kingdom of God at the end of time.

Eternity: The interminable, perfect possession of life in its totality without beginning or end; an attribute of God, who has no past or future but always is. Man's existence has a beginning but no end and is, accordingly, called immortal.

Ethics: Moral philosophy, the science of the morality of human acts deriving from natural law, the natural end of man, and the powers of human reason. It includes all the spheres of human activity — personal, social, economic, political, etc. Ethics is distinct from but can be related to moral theology, whose primary principles are drawn from divine revelation.

Euthanasia: Mercy killing, the direct causing of death for the purpose of ending human suffering. Euthanasia is murder and is totally illicit, for the natural law forbids the direct taking of one's own life or that of an innocent person. The use of drugs to relieve suffering in serious cases, even when this results in a shortening of life as an indirect and secondary effect, is permissible under conditions of the double-effect principle. It is also permissible for a seriously ill person to refuse to follow — or for other responsible persons to refuse to permit — extraordinary medical procedures even though the refusal might entail shortening of life.

Evangelization: Proclamation of the Gospel, the Good News of salvation in and through Christ, among those who have not yet known or received it; and efforts for the progressive development of the life of faith among those who have already received the Gospel and all that it entails. Evangelization is the primary mission of the Church, in which all members of the Church are called to participate.

Evolution: Scientific theory concerning the development of the physical universe from unorganized matter (inorganic evolution) and, especially, the development of existing forms of vegetable, animal and human life from earlier and more primitive organisms (organic evolution). Various ideas about evolution were advanced for some centuries before scientific evidence in support of the main-line theory of organic evolution, which has several formulations, was discovered and verified in the second half of the 19th century and afterwards. This evidence — from the findings of comparative anatomy and other sciences — confirmed evolution of species and cleared the way to further investigation of questions regarding the processes of its accomplishment. While a number of such questions remain open with respect to human evolution, a point of doctrine not open to question is the immediate creation of the human soul by God. For some time, theologians regarded the theory with hostility, considering it to be in opposition to the account of creation in the early chapters of Genesis and subversive of belief in such doctrines as creation, the early state of man in grace, and the fall of man from grace. This state of affairs and the tension it generated led to considerable controversy regarding an alleged conflict between religion and science. Gradually, however, the tension was diminished with the development of biblical studies from the latter part of the 19th century onwards, with clarification of the distinctive features of religious truth and scientific truth, and with the refinement of evolutionary concepts. So far as the Genesis account of creation is concerned, the Catholic view is that the writer(s) did not write as a scientist but as the communicator of religious truth in a manner adapted to the understanding of the people of his time. He used anthropomorphic language, the figure of days and other literary devices to state the salvation truths of creation, the fall of man from grace, and the promise of redemption. It was beyond the competency and purpose of the writer(s) to describe creation and related events in a scientific manner.

Excommunication: Severe ecclesiastical penalty imposed by the Church that excludes a member of the faithful from the wider community. Excommunication is today covered in its particulars by Canon 1331 of the new Code of Canon Law, promulgated in 1983. It exists in two contemporary forms, *ferendae sententiae* and *latae sententiae*. The former is a penalty imposed after a formal proceeding presided over by at least three judges. The latter is considered an automatic penalty for certain acts, including the procuring of a successful abortion (Canon 1398), the embrace of heresy (Canon 1364), violation of the Seal of Confession (Canon 1388), and the blasphemous and sacrilegious use of the Eucharist (Canon 1367). A person under the ban of excommunication is unable to take part in all ceremonies of public worship, especially the Eucharist, to receive or celebrate the sacraments, and to discharge any ecclesiastical offices, ministries, or functions. (See **Censures**).

Ex Opere Operantis: A term in sacramental theology meaning that the effectiveness of sacraments depends on the moral rectitude of the minister or participant. This term was applied to rites of the O.T. in contrast with those of the N.T. when it was first advanced in the thirteenth century.

Ex Opere Operato: A term in sacramental theology meaning that sacraments are effective by means of the sacramental rite itself and not because of the worthiness of the minister or participant.

Exorcism: (1) Driving out evil spirits; a rite in which evil spirits are charged and commanded on the authority of God and with the prayer of the Church to depart from a person or to cease causing harm to a person suffering from diabolical possession or obsession. The sacramental is officially administered by a priest delegated for the purpose by the bishop of the place. Elements of the rite include the Litany of Saints; recitation of the Our Father, one or more creeds, and other prayers; specific prayers of exorcism; the reading of Gospel passages and use of the Sign of the Cross. On Jan. 26, 1999, the Congregation for Divine Worship and the Discipline of the Sacraments published a new rite of exorcism in the Roman Ritual. (2) Exorcisms which do not imply the conditions of either diabolical possession or obsession form part of the ceremony of baptism and are also included in formulas for various blessings; e.g., of water.

Exposition of the Blessed Sacrament: "In churches where the Eucharist is regularly reserved, it is recommended that solemn exposition of the Blessed Sacrament for an extended period of time should take place once a year, even though the period is not strictly continuous. Shorter expositions of the Eucharist (Benediction) are to be arranged in such a way that the blessing with the Eucharist is preceded by a reasonable time for readings of the word of God, songs, prayers and a period for silent prayer." So stated Vatican directives issued in 1973.

F

Faculties: Grants of jurisdiction or authority by the law of the Church or superiors (pope, bishop, religious superior) for exercise of the powers of holy orders; e.g., priests are given faculties to hear confessions, officiate at weddings; bishops are given faculties to grant dispensations, etc.

Faith: In religion, faith has several aspects. Catholic doctrine calls faith the assent of the mind to truths revealed by God, the assent being made with the help of grace and by command of the will on account of the authority and trustworthiness of God revealing. The term faith also refers to the truths that are believed (content of faith) and to the way in which a person, in response to Christ, gives witness to and expresses belief in daily life (living faith). All of these elements, and more, are included in the following statement: " 'The obedience of faith' (Rom 16:26; 1:5; 2 Cor 10:5-6) must be given to God who reveals, an obedience by which man entrusts his whole self freely to God, offering 'the full submission of intellect and will to God who reveals' (First Vatican Council, Dogmatic Constitution on the Catholic Faith, Chap. 3), and freely assenting to the truth revealed by him. If this faith is to be shown, the grace of God and the interior help of the Holy Spirit must precede and assist, moving the heart and turning it to God, opening the eyes of the mind, and giving 'joy and ease to everyone in assenting to the truth and believing it'" (Second Council of Orange, Canon 7) (Second Vatican Council, Constitution on Revelation, *Dei Verbum*, No. 5). Faith is necessary for salvation.

Faith, Rule of: The norm or standard of religious belief. The Catholic doctrine is that belief must be professed in the divinely revealed truths in the Bible and tradition as interpreted and proposed by the infallible teaching authority of the Church.

Fast, Eucharistic: Abstinence from food and drink, except water and medicine, is required for one hour before the reception of the Eucharist. Persons who are advanced in age or suffer from infirmity or illness, together with those who care for them, can receive Holy Communion even if they have not abstained from food and drink for an hour. A priest celebrating two or three Masses on the same day can eat and drink something before the second or third Mass without regard for the hour limit.

Father: A title of priests, who are regarded as spiritual fathers because they are the ordinary ministers of baptism, by which persons are born

to supernatural life, and because of their pastoral service to people.

Fear: A mental state caused by the apprehension of present or future danger. Grave fear does not necessarily remove moral responsibility for an act, but may lessen it.

First Friday: A devotion consisting of the reception of Holy Communion on the first Friday of nine consecutive months in honor of the Sacred Heart of Jesus and in reparation for sin. (*See* **Sacred Heart, Promises.**)

First Saturday: A devotion tracing its origin to the apparitions of the Blessed Virgin Mary at Fátima in 1917. Those practicing the devotion go to confession and, on the first Saturday of five consecutive months, receive Holy Communion, recite five decades of the Rosary, and meditate on the mysteries for 15 minutes.

Fisherman's Ring: A signet ring (termed in Italian the *pescatorio*) engraved with the image of St. Peter fishing from a boat, and encircled with the name of the reigning pope. It is not worn by the pope. It is used to seal briefs, and is destroyed after each pope's death.

Forgiveness of Sin: Catholics believe that sins are forgiven by God through the mediation of Christ in view of the repentance of the sinner and by means of the sacrament of penance. (*See* **Penance, p.151; Contrition**, p. 136).

Fortitude: Courage to face dangers or hardships for the sake of what is good; one of the four cardinal virtues and one of the seven gifts of the Holy Spirit.

Forty Hours Devotion: A Eucharistic observance consisting of solemn exposition of the Blessed Sacrament coupled with special Masses and forms of prayer, for the purposes of making reparation for sin and praying for God's blessings of grace and peace. The devotion was instituted in 1534 in Milan. St. John Neumann of Philadelphia was the first bishop in the U.S. to prescribe its observance in his diocese. For many years in this country, the observance was held annually on a rotating basis in all parishes of a diocese. Simplified and abbreviated Eucharistic observances have taken the place of the devotion in some places.

Forum: The sphere in which ecclesiastical authority or jurisdiction is exercised. (1) External: Authority is exercised in the external forum to deal with matters affecting the public welfare of the Church and its members. Those who have such authority because of their office (e.g., diocesan bishops) are called ordinaries. (2) Internal: Authority is exercised in the internal forum to deal with matters affecting the private spiritual good of individuals. The sacramental forum is the sphere in which the sacrament of penance is administered; other exercises of jurisdiction in the internal forum take place in the non-sacramental forum.

Freedom, Religious: The Second Vatican Council declared that the right to religious freedom in civil society "means that all men are to be immune from coercion on the part of individuals or of social groups and of any human power, in such wise that in matters religious no one is to be forced to act in a manner contrary to his own beliefs. Nor is anyone to be restrained from acting in accordance with his own beliefs, whether privately or publicly, whether alone or in association with others, within due limits" of requirements for the common good. The foundation of this right in civil society is the "very dignity of the human person" (Declaration on Religious Freedom, *Dignitatis Humanae*, No. 2). The conciliar statement did not deal with the subject of freedom within the Church. It noted the responsibility of the faithful "carefully to attend to the sacred and certain doctrine of the Church" (No. 14).

Freemasons: A fraternal order that originated in London in 1717 with the formation of the first Grand Lodge of Freemasons. From England, the order spread to Europe and elsewhere. Its principles and basic rituals embody a naturalistic religion, active participation in which is incompatible with Christian faith and practice. Grand Orient Freemasonry, developed in Latin countries, is atheistic, irreligious and anticlerical. In some places, Freemasonry has been regarded as subversive of the state; in Catholic quarters, it has been considered hostile to the Church and its doctrine. In the United States, Freemasonry has been widely regarded as a fraternal and philanthropic order. For serious doctrinal and pastoral reasons, Catholics were forbidden to join the Freemasons under penalty of excommunication, according to church law before 1983. Eight different popes in 17 different pronouncements, and at least six different local councils, condemned Freemasonry. The first condemnation was made by Clement XII in 1738. Eastern Orthodox and many Protestant bodies have also opposed the order. In the U.S., there was some easing of the ban against Masonic membership by Catholics in view of a letter written in 1974 by Cardinal Franjo Seper, prefect of the Congregation for the Doctrine of the Faith. The letter was interpreted to mean that Catholics might join Masonic lodges which were not anti-Catholic. This was called erroneous in a declaration issued by the Doctrinal Congregation Feb. 17, 1981. The prohibition against Masonic membership was restated in a declaration issued by the Doctrinal Congregation Nov. 26, 1983, with the approval of Pope John Paul II, as follows. "The Church's negative position on Masonic associations remains unaltered, since their principles have always been regarded as irreconcilable with the Church's doctrine. Hence, joining them remains prohibited by the Church. Catholics enrolled in Masonic associations are involved in serious sin and may not approach Holy Communion. Local ecclesiastical authorities do not have the faculty to pronounce a judgment on the nature of Masonic associations which might include a diminution of the above-mentioned judgment." This latest declaration, like the revised Code of Canon Law, does not include a penalty of excommunication for Catholics who join the Masons. Local bishops are not authorized to grant dispensations from the prohibition. The foregoing strictures against Masonic membership by Catholics were reiterated in a report by the Committee for Pastoral Research and Practice, National Conference of Catholic Bishops, released through Catholic News Service June 7, 1985.

Free Will: The faculty or capability of making a reasonable choice among several alternatives. Freedom of will underlies the possibility and fact of moral responsibility.

Friar: Term applied to members of mendicant orders to distinguish them from members of monastic orders. (*See* **Mendicants**, p. 148.)

Fruits of the Holy Spirit: Charity, joy, peace, patience, kindness, goodness, generosity, gentleness, faithfulness, modesty, self-control, chastity.

Fruits of the Mass: The spiritual and temporal blessings that result from the celebration of the Holy Sacrifice of the Mass. The general fruits are shared by all the faithful, living and departed, while the special fruits are applied to the priest who celebrates it, to those for whose intention it is offered, and to all those who participate in its celebration.

Fundamental Option: The orientation of one's life either to God by obedience or against Him through disobedience. Catholic Tradition acknowledges that one free and deliberate act with knowledge renders one at odds with God. A prevalent and vague moral theory thus asserts that one act cannot change one's option to God — no matter how grave — unless the action comes from the person's "center." Pope John Paul II cautioned against this ambiguous position in the encyclical *Veritatis Splendor* (1993).

G

Gehenna: Greek form of a Jewish name, Gehinnom, for a valley near Jerusalem, the site of Moloch worship; used as a synonym for hell.

Genuflection: Bending of the knee, a natural sign of adoration or reverence, as when persons genuflect with the right knee in passing before the tabernacle to acknowledge the Eucharistic presence of Christ.

Gethsemani: A Hebrew word meaning oil press, designating the place on the Mount of Olives where Christ prayed and suffered in agony the night before he died.

Gifts of the Holy Spirit: Supernatural habits disposing a person to respond promptly to the inspiration of grace; promised by Christ and communicated through the Holy Spirit, especially in the sacrament of confirmation. They are: wisdom, understanding, counsel, knowledge, fortitude, piety, and fear of the Lord.

Glorified Body: The definitive state of humanity in eternity. The risen Christ calls humanity to the glory of his resurrection; this is a theological premise that presupposes that, like Christ, all of his brothers and sisters will be transformed physically.

Gluttony: An unreasonable appetite for food and drink; one of the seven capital sins.

God: The infinitely perfect Supreme Being, uncaused and absolutely self-sufficient, eternal, the Creator and final end of all things. The one God subsists in three equal Persons, the Father and the Son and the Holy Spirit. God, although transcendent and distinct from the universe, is present and active in the world in realization of his plan for the salvation of human beings, principally through Revelation, the operations of the Holy Spirit, the life and ministry of Christ, and the continuation of Christ's ministry in the Church. The existence of God is an article of faith, clearly communicated in divine Revelation. Even without this Revelation, however, the Church teaches, in a declaration by the First Vatican Council, that human beings can acquire certain knowledge of the existence of God and some of his attributes. This can be done on the bases of principles of reason and reflection on human experience. Non-revealed arguments or demonstrations for the existence of God have been developed from the principle of causality; the contingency of human beings and the universe; the existence of design, change and movement in the universe; human awareness of moral responsibility; widespread human testimony to the existence of God.

Goods of Marriage: Three blessings — children, faithful companionship, and permanence — that were first enumerated by St. Augustine in a work on marriage.

Grace: A free gift of God to persons (and angels), grace is a created sharing or participation in the life of God. It is given to persons through the merits of Christ and is communicated by the Holy Spirit. It is necessary for salvation. The principal means of grace are the sacraments (especially the Eucharist), prayer and good works. (1) **Sanctifying or habitual grace** makes persons holy and pleasing to God, adopted children of God, members of Christ, temples of the Holy Spirit, heirs of heaven capable of supernaturally meritorious acts. With grace, God gives persons the supernatural virtues and gifts of the Holy Spirit. The sacraments of baptism and penance were instituted to give grace to those who do not have it; the other sacraments, to increase it in those already in the state of grace. The means for growth in holiness, or the increase of grace, are prayer, the sacraments, and good works. Sanctifying grace is lost by the commission of serious sin. Each sacrament confers sanctifying grace for the special purpose of the sacrament; in this context, grace is called sacramental grace. (2) **Actual grace** is a supernatural help of God which enlightens and strengthens a person to do good and to avoid evil. It is not a permanent quality, like sanctifying grace. It is necessary for the performance of supernatural acts. It can be resisted and refused. Persons in the state of serious sin are given actual grace to lead them to repentance.

Grace at Meals: Prayers said before meals, asking a blessing of God, and after meals, giving thanks to God. In addition to traditional prayers for these purposes, many variations suitable for different occasions are possible, at personal option.

Guilt: The condition of an individual who has committed some moral wrong and is liable to receive punishment.

H

Habit: (1) A disposition to do things easily, given with grace (and therefore supernatural) and/or acquired by repetition of similar acts. (2) The garb worn by Religious.

Hagiography: Writings or documents about saints and other holy persons.

Hail Mary: A prayer addressed to the Blessed Virgin Mary; also called the *Ave Maria* (Latin equivalent of Hail Mary) and the Angelic Salutation. In three parts, it consists of the words addressed to Mary by the Archangel Gabriel on the occasion of the Annunciation, in the Infancy Narrative (*Hail Mary, full of grace, the Lord is with you,* Lk 1:28); the words addressed to Mary by her cousin Elizabeth on the occasion of the Visitation (*Blessed are you among women; Blessed is the fruit of your womb*; Lk 1-42); a concluding petition (*Holy Mary, Mother of God, pray for us sinners now and at the hour of our death. Amen.*). The first two salutations were joined in Eastern rite formulas by the sixth century, and were similarly used at Rome in the seventh century. Insertion of the name of Jesus at the conclusion of the salutations was probably made

by Urban IV about 1262. The present form of the petition was incorporated into the breviary in 1514.

Heaven: The state of those who, having achieved salvation, are in glory with God and enjoy the beatific vision. The phrase, kingdom of heaven, refers to the order or kingdom of God, grace, salvation.

Hell: The state of persons who die in mortal sin, in a condition of self-alienation from God which will last forever.

Heresy: The obstinate post-baptismal denial or doubt by a Catholic of any truth which must be believed as a matter of divine and Catholic faith (Canon 751, of the Code of Canon Law). Formal heresy involves deliberate resistance to the authority of God who communicates revelation through Scripture and tradition and the teaching authority of the Church. Heretics automatically incur the penalty of excommunication (Canon 1364 of the Code of Canon Law). Heresies have been significant not only as disruptions of unity of faith but also as occasions for the clarification and development of doctrine. Heresies from the beginning of the Church to the 13th century are described in **Dates and Events in Church History**, p. 218.

Hermeneutics: *See* under the section **Interpretation of the Bible**, p. 103.

Hermit: *See* **Anchorite**, p. 130.

Heroic Act of Charity: The completely unselfish offering to God of one's good works and merits for the benefit of the souls in purgatory rather than for oneself. Thus a person may offer to God for the souls in purgatory all the good works he performs during life, all the indulgences he gains, and all the prayers and indulgences that will be offered for him after his death. The act is revocable at will, and is not a vow. Its actual ratification depends on the will of God.

Heroic Virtue: The exemplary practice of the four cardinal virtues and three theological virtues; such virtue is sought in persons considered for sainthood.

Heterodoxy: False doctrine teaching or belief; a departure from truth.

Hierarchy: The hierarchy of order who carry out the sacramental, teaching, and pastoral ministry of the Church; the hierarchy consists of the pope, bishops, priests, and deacons; the pope and the bishops give pastoral governance to the faithful.

Holy Father: A title used for the pope; it is a shortened translation of the Latin title *Beatissimus Pater*, "Most Blessed Father" and refers to his position as the spiritual father of all the Christian faithful.

Holy Grail: A symbol of mystical veneration, perfection, and mystery that came to be identified as the chalice used by Christ at the Last Supper. The Holy Grail was a major element of medieval legend, lore, and literature, appearing variously as a cup, dish, a stone, or even a cauldron into which blood would drip from a bloody lance. It also became closely connected over time with the Arthurian legend. Scholars differ over the possible origins of the Grail legend, some proposing a Celtic or classical mythological origin, others a Christian or Oriental one. Gradually, however, the original elements were united with the tales told of the adventures of Joseph of Arimathea and the arrival of Christianity in the British Isles. The earliest Grail romance was composed around 1180 by Chrétien de Troyes in his *Perceval* or *Conte del*

Graal, the start of the great literary tradition that flourished in the late twelfth and early to mid-thirteenth centuries. Other famous Grail stories were written by Wolfram von Eschenbach (*Parzival*), Robert de Boron (*Roman de l'Estoire dou Graal*), and the 13th-century prose romance *L'Estoire del Saint Graal* (*History of the Holy Grail*).

Holy See: (1) The diocese of the pope, Rome. (2) The pope himself and/or the various officials and bodies of the Church's central administration at Vatican City — the Roman Curia — which act in the name and by authority of the pope.

Holy Spirit: God the Holy Spirit, third Person of the Holy Trinity, who proceeds from the Father and the Son and with whom he is equal in every respect; inspirer of the prophets and writers of sacred Scripture; promised by Christ to the Apostles as their advocate and strengthener; appeared in the form of a dove at the baptism of Christ and as tongues of fire at his descent upon the Apostles; soul of the Church and guarantor, by his abiding presence and action, of truth in doctrine; communicator of grace to human beings, for which reason he is called the sanctifier.

Holy Water: Water blessed by the Church and used as a sacramental, a practice which originated in apostolic times.

Holy Year: A year during which the pope grants the plenary Jubilee Indulgence to the faithful who fulfill certain conditions. For those who make a pilgrimage to Rome during the year, the conditions are reception of the sacraments of penance and the Eucharist, visits and prayer for the intention of the pope in the basilicas of St. Peter, St. John Lateran, St. Paul and St. Mary Major. For those who do not make a pilgrimage to Rome, the conditions are reception of the sacraments and prayer for the pope during a visit or community celebration in a church designated by the bishop of the locality. Pope Boniface VIII formally proclaimed the first Holy Year on Feb. 22, 1300, and the first three Holy Years were observed in 1300, 1350 and 1390. Subsequent ones were celebrated at 25-year intervals except in 1800 and 1850 when, respectively, the French invasion of Italy and political turmoil made observance impossible. Pope Paul II (1464-1471) set the 25-year timetable. In 1500, Pope Alexander VI prescribed the start and finish ceremonies — the opening and closing of the Holy Doors in the major basilicas on successive Christmas Eves. All but a few of the earlier Holy Years were classified as ordinary. Several — like those of 1933 and 1983-84 to commemorate the 1,900th and 1,950th anniversaries of the death and resurrection of Christ — were in the extraordinary category. Pope John Paul designated Jubilee Year 2000 to be a Holy Year ending the second and beginning the third millennium of Christianity.

Homosexuality: The condition of a person whose sexual orientation is toward persons of the same rather than the opposite sex. The condition is not sinful in itself. Homosexual acts are seriously sinful in themselves; subjective responsibility for such acts, however, may be conditioned and diminished by compulsion and related factors.

Hope: The theological virtue by which a person firmly trusts in God for the means and attainment salvation. The virtue was the subject of Pope Benedict XVI's encyclical, *Spe Salvi* in 2007.

Hosanna: A Hebrew word, meaning *O Lord, save, we pray*.

Host, The Sacred: The bread under whose appearances Christ is and remains present in a unique manner after the consecration which takes place during Mass. (*See* **Transubstantiation**, p. 159.)

Human Dignity: The inherent worth of all human persons as they are made in God's image and likeness and they alone — of all God's creatures on earth — have an immortal soul.

Humanism: A world view centered on man. Types of humanism which exclude the supernatural are related to secularism.

Humility: A virtue which induces a person to evaluate himself or herself at his or her true worth, to recognize his or her dependence on God, and to give glory to God for the good he or she has and can do.

Hyperdulia: The special veneration accorded the Blessed Virgin Mary because of her unique role in the mystery of Redemption, her exceptional gifts of grace from God, and her pre-eminence among the saints. *Hyperdulia* is not adoration; only God is adored.

Hypostatic Union: The union of the human and divine natures in the one divine Person of Christ.

I

Icons: Byzantine-style paintings or representations of Christ, the Blessed Virgin and other saints, venerated in the Eastern Churches where they take the place of statues.

Idolatry: Worship of any but the true God; a violation of the First Commandment.

IHS: In Greek, the first three letters of the name of Jesus — *Iota, Eta, Sigma*.

Immaculate Conception: The doctrine that affirms that "the Blessed Virgin Mary was preserved, in the first instant of her conception, by a singular grace and privilege of God omnipotent and because of the merits of Jesus Christ the Savior of the human race, free from all stain of Original Sin," as stated by Pope Pius IX in his declaration of the dogma, Dec. 8, 1854. Thus, Mary was conceived in the state of perfect justice, free from Original Sin and its consequences, in virtue of the redemption achieved by Christ on the cross.

Immortality: The survival and continuing existence of the human soul after death.

Imprimatur: *See* **Censorship of Books**, p. 134.

Impurity: Unlawful indulgence in sexual pleasure. (*See* **Chastity**, p. 135.)

Imputability: A canonical term for the moral responsibility of a person for an act that he or she has performed.

Incardination: The affiliation of a priest to his diocese. Every secular priest must belong to a certain diocese. Similarly, every priest of a religious community must belong to some jurisdiction of his community; this affiliation, however, is not called incardination.

Incarnation: (1) The coming-into-flesh or taking of human nature by the Second Person of the Trinity. He became human as the Son of Mary, being miraculously conceived by the power of the Holy Spirit, without ceasing to be divine. His divine Person hypostatically unites his divine and human natures. (2) The supernatural mystery coextensive with Christ from the moment of his human conception and continuing through his life on earth; his sufferings and death; his resurrection from the dead and ascension to glory with the Father; his sending, with the Father, of the Holy Spirit upon the Apostles and the Church; and his unending mediation with the Father for the salvation of human beings.

Incense: A granulated substance which, when burnt, emits an aromatic smoke. It symbolizes the zeal with which the faithful should be consumed, the good odor of Christian virtue, the ascent of prayer to God. An incense boat is a small vessel used to hold incense which is to be placed in the censer.

Incest: Sexual intercourse with relatives by blood or marriage; a sin of impurity and also a grave violation of the natural reverence due to relatives. Other sins of impurity desire, etc., concerning relatives have the nature of incest.

Inculturation: The correct and entirely appropriate adaptation of the Catholic liturgy and institutions to the culture, language, and customs of an indigenous or local people among whom the Gospel is first proclaimed. Pope John Paul II on Feb. 15, 1982, at a meeting in Lagos with the bishops of Nigeria proclaimed: "An important aspect of your own evangelizing role is the whole dimension of the inculturation of the Gospel into the lives of your people. The Church truly respects the culture of each people. In offering the Gospel message, the Church does not intend to destroy or to abolish what is good and beautiful. In fact, she recognizes many cultural values and, through the power of the Gospel, purifies and takes into Christian worship certain elements of a people's customs."

Index of Prohibited Books: A list of books which Catholics were formerly forbidden to read, possess or sell, under penalty of excommunication. The books were banned by the Holy See after publication because their treatment of matters of faith and morals and related subjects were judged to be erroneous or serious occasions of doctrinal error. Some books were listed in the Index by name; others were covered under general norms. The Congregation for the Doctrine of the Faith declared June 14, 1966, that the Index and its related penalties of excommunication no longer had the force of law in the Church. Persons are still obliged, however, to take normal precautions against occasions of doctrinal error.

Indifferentism: A theory that any one religion is as true and good — or false — as any other religion, and that it makes no difference, objectively, what religion one professes, if any. The theory is completely subjective, finding its justification entirely in personal choice without reference to or respect for objective validity. It is also self-contradictory, since it regards as equally acceptable — or unacceptable — the beliefs of all religions, which in fact are not only not all the same but are in some cases opposed to each other.

Indulgence: According to The Doctrine and Practice of Indulgences, an apostolic constitution issued by Paul VI Jan. 1, 1967, an indulgence is the remission before God of the temporal punishment due for sins already forgiven as far as their guilt is concerned, which a follower of Christ — with the proper dispositions and under certain determined conditions — acquires through the intervention of the Church. An indulgence is partial or plenary, depending on whether it does away with either part or all of the temporal punishment due for sin. Both types of indulgences can always be applied to the dead by way of suffrage; the actual disposition of indulgences applied to the dead rests with God. Only one plenary indulgence can be gained in a single day. The Apostolic Penitentiary

issued a decree Dec. 14, 1985, granting diocesan bishops the right to impart — three times a year on solemn feasts of their choice — the papal blessing with a plenary indulgence to those who cannot be physically present but who follow the sacred rites at which the blessing is imparted by radio or television transmission. In July 1986, publication was announced of a new and simplified *Enchiridion Indulgentiarum*, in accord with provisions of the revised Code of Canon Law. A revised manual was issued by the Holy See on Sept. 17, 2000.

Indult: A favor or privilege granted by competent ecclesiastical authority, giving permission to do something not allowed by the common law of the Church.

Infallibility: 1) The inability of the Church to err in its teaching, in that she preserves and teaches the deposit of truth as revealed by Christ; 2) The inability of the Roman Pontiff to err when he teaches *ex cathedra* in matters of faith or morals, and indicates that the doctrine is to be believed by all the faithful; and 3) the inability of the college of bishops to err when speaking in union with the pope in matters of faith and morals, agreeing that a doctrine must be held by the universal Church, and the doctrine is promulgated by the Pontiff.

Infused Virtues: The theological virtues of faith, hope, and charity; principles or capabilities of supernatural action, they are given with sanctifying grace by God rather than acquired by repeated acts of a person. They can be increased by practice; they are lost by contrary acts. Natural-acquired moral virtues, like the cardinal virtues of prudence, justice, temperance, and fortitude, can be considered infused in a person whose state of grace gives them supernatural orientation.

Inquisition: A tribunal for dealing with heretics, authorized by Gregory IX in 1231 to search them out, hear and judge them, sentence them to various forms of punishment, and in some cases to hand them over to civil authorities for punishment. The Inquisition was a creature of its time when crimes against faith, which threatened the good of the Christian community, were regarded also as crimes against the state, and when heretical doctrines of such extremists as the Cathari and Albigensians threatened the very fabric of society. The institution, which was responsible for many excesses, was most active in the second half of the 13th century.

Inquisition, Spanish: An institution peculiar to Spain and the colonies in Spanish America. In 1478, at the urging of King Ferdinand, Pope Sixtus IV approved the establishment of the Inquisition for trying charges of heresy brought against Jewish (*Marranos*) and Moorish (*Moriscos*) converts. It acquired jurisdiction over other cases as well, however, and fell into disrepute because of irregularities in its functions, cruelty in its sentences, and the manner in which it served the interests of the Spanish crown more than the accused persons and the good of the Church. Protests by the Holy See failed to curb excesses of the Inquisition, which lingered in Spanish history until early in the 19th century.

I N R I: The first letters of words in the Latin inscription atop the cross on which Christ was crucified: *(I)esus (N)azaraenus, (R)ex (I)udaeorum* — Jesus of Nazareth, King of the Jews.

Insemination, Artificial: The implanting of human semen by some means other than consummation of natural marital intercourse. In view of the principle that procreation should result only from marital intercourse, donor insemination is not permissible.

In Sin: The condition of a person called spiritually dead because he or she does not possess sanctifying grace, the principle of supernatural life, action and merit. Such grace can be regained through repentance.

Instruction: A document containing doctrinal explanations, directive norms, rules, recommendations, admonitions, issued by the pope, a department of the Roman Curia or other competent authority in the Church. To the extent that they so prescribe, instructions have the force of law.

Intercommunion, Eucharistic Sharing: The common celebration and reception of the Eucharist by members of different Christian churches; a pivotal issue in ecumenical theory and practice. Catholic participation and intercommunion in the Eucharistic liturgy of another church without a valid priesthood and with a variant Eucharistic belief is out of order. Under certain conditions, other Christians may receive the Eucharist in the Catholic Church. (*See* additional Intercommunion entry). Intercommunion is acceptable to some Protestant churches and unacceptable to others.

Interdict: A censure imposed on persons for certain violations of church law. Interdicted persons may not take part in certain liturgical services, administer or receive certain sacraments.

Intinction: A method of administering Holy Communion under the dual appearances of bread and wine, in which the consecrated host is dipped in the consecrated wine before being given to the communicant. The administering of Holy Communion in this manner, which has been traditional in Eastern-Rite liturgies, was authorized in the Roman Rite for various occasions by the Constitution on the Sacred Liturgy promulgated by the Second Vatican Council.

Irenicism: Peace-seeking, conciliation, as opposed to polemics; an important element in ecumenism, provided it furthers pursuit of the Christian unity willed by Christ without degenerating into a peace-at-any-price disregard for religious truth.

Irregularity: A permanent impediment to the lawful reception or exercise of holy orders. The Church instituted irregularities — which include apostasy, heresy, homicide, attempted suicide — out of reverence for the dignity of the sacraments.

J

Jehovah: The English equivalent of the Hebrew *Adonai* ("my Lord") used out of fear and reverence for the Holy Name of Yahweh. *Jehovah* uses the consonants YHWH and the vowels of *Adonai* (a, o, a). Scholars today maintain that *Jehovah* is a false derivation.

Jesus: The name of Jesus, meaning "God saves," expressing the identity and mission of the second Person of the Trinity become man; derived from the Aramaic and Hebrew Yeshua and Joshua, meaning Yahweh is salvation.

Jesus Prayer: A prayer of Eastern origin, dating back to the fifth century: *"Lord Jesus Christ, Son of God, have mercy on me (a sinner)."*

Judgment: (1) **Last or final judgment**: Final judgment by Christ, at the end of the world and the general resurrection. (2) **Particular judgment**: The judgment that takes place immediately after a person's death, followed by entrance into heaven, hell or purgatory.

Jurisdiction: Right, power, authority to rule. Jurisdiction in the Church is of divine institution; has pastoral service for its purpose; includes legislative, judicial and executive authority; can be exercised only by persons with the power of orders. (1) Ordinary jurisdiction is attached to ecclesiastical offices by law; the officeholders, called Ordinaries, have authority over those who are subject to them. (2) Delegated jurisdiction is that which is granted to persons rather than attached to offices. Its extent depends on the terms of the delegation.

Justice: One of the four cardinal virtues by which a person gives to others what is due to them as a matter of right. (*See* **Cardinal Virtues,** p. 133.)

Justification: The act by which God makes a person just, and the consequent change in the spiritual status of a person, from sin to grace; the remission of sin and the infusion of sanctifying grace through the merits of Christ and the action of the Holy Spirit.

K

Kenosis: A term from the Greek for "emptying" that denotes Christ's emptying of himself in his free renunciation of his right to divine status, by reason of the Incarnation, particularly as celebrated in the kenotic hymn (Phil 2:6-11), where it is said that Christ "emptied himself," taking the form of a slave, born in the likeness of man totally integrated with his divinity.

Kerygma: Proclaiming the word of God, in the manner of the Apostles, as here and now effective for salvation. This method of preaching or instruction, centered on Christ and geared to the facts and themes of salvation history, is designed to dispose people to faith in Christ and/or to intensify the experience and practice of that faith in those who have it.

Keys, Power of the: Spiritual authority and jurisdiction in the Church, symbolized by the keys of the kingdom of heaven. Christ promised the keys to St. Peter, as head-to-be of the Church (Mt 16:19), and commissioned him with full pastoral responsibility to feed his lambs and sheep (Jn 21:15-17), The pope, as the successor of St. Peter, has this power in a primary and supreme manner. The bishops of the Church also have the power, in union with and subordinate to the pope. Priests share in it through holy orders and the delegation of authority. Examples of the application of the Power of the Keys are the exercise of teaching and pastoral authority by the pope and bishops, the absolving of sins in the sacrament of penance, the granting of indulgences, the imposing of spiritual penalties on persons who commit certain serious sins.

Kingdom of God: God's sovereign lordship or rule over salvation history, leading to the eschatological goal of eternal life with God.

Koinonia: A term from the Greek word for "community, fellowship, or association" that was used by St. Luke for the fellowship of believers who worshipped together and held all their possessions in common (Acts 2:42-47); it is also used of fellowship with God (1 Jn 1:3, 6), with the Son (1 Cor 1:9), and with the Holy Spirit (2 Cor 13:13; Phil 2:1). St. Paul used *koinonia* to denote the intimate union of the believer with Christ and the community that exists among all the faithful themselves (Rom 15:26; 2 Cor 6:14).

L

Laicization: The process by which a man ordained to holy orders is relieved of the obligations of orders and the ministry and is returned to the status of a lay person.

Languages of the Church: The languages in which the Church's liturgy is celebrated. These include Ge'ez, Syriac, Greek, Arabic, and Old Slavonic in the Eastern Churches. In the West, there is, of course, Latin and the various vernaculars. The Eastern Rites have always had the vernacular. The first language in church use, for divine worship and the conduct of ecclesiastical affairs, was Aramaic, the language of the first Christians in and around Jerusalem. As the Church spread westward, Greek was adopted and prevailed until the third century when it was supplanted by Latin for official use in the West. In the Western Church, Latin prevailed as the general official language until the promulgation on Dec. 4, 1963, of the Constitution on the Sacred Liturgy (*Sacrosanctum Concilium*) by the second session of the Second Vatican Council. Since that time, vernacular languages have come into use in the Mass, administration of the sacraments, and the Liturgy of the Hours. Latin, however, remains the official language for documents of the Holy See, administrative and procedural matters.

Latria: Greek-rooted Latin term that refers to that form of praise due to God alone.

Law: An ordinance or rule governing the activity of things. (1) **Natural law**: Moral norms corresponding to man's nature by which he orders his conduct toward God, neighbor, society and himself. This law, which is rooted in human nature, is of divine origin, can be known by the use of reason, and binds all persons having the use of reason. The Ten Commandments are declarations and amplifications of natural law. The primary precepts of natural law, to do good and to avoid evil, are universally recognized, despite differences with respect to understanding and application resulting from different philosophies of good and evil. (2) **Divine positive law**: That which has been revealed by God. Among its essentials are the twin precepts of love of God and love of neighbor, and the Ten Commandments. (3) **Ecclesiastical law**: That which is established by the Church for the spiritual welfare of the faithful and the orderly conduct of ecclesiastical affairs. (*See* **Canon Law**, p. 125.) (4) **Civil law**: That which is established by a socio-political community for the common good.

Liberalism: A multiphased trend of thought and movement favoring liberty, independence and progress in moral, intellectual, religious, social, economic and political life. Traceable to the Renaissance, it developed through the Enlightenment, the rationalism of the 19th century, and modernist- and existentialist-related theories of the 20th century. Evaluations of various kinds of liberalism depend on the validity of their underlying principles. Extremist positions — regarding subjectivism, libertinarianism, naturalist denials of the supernatural, and the alienation of individuals and society from God and the Church — were condemned by Gregory XVI in the 1830s, Pius IX in 1864, Leo XIII in 1899, and St. Pius X in 1907. There is, however, nothing objectionable about forms of liberalism patterned according to sound principles of Christian doctrine.

Liberation Theology: Deals with the relevance of Christian faith and salvation — and, therefore, of the mission of the Church — to efforts for the promotion of human rights, social justice and human development. It originated in the religious, social, political and economic environment of Latin America, with its contemporary need for a theory and corresponding action by the Church, in the pattern of its overall mission, for human rights and integral personal and social development. Some versions of liberation theology are at variance with the body of church teaching because of their ideological concept of Christ as liberator, and also because they play down the primary spiritual nature and mission of the Church. Instructions from the Congregation for the Doctrine of the Faith — "On Certain Aspects of the Theology of Liberation" (Sept. 3, 1984) and "On Christian Freedom and Liberation" (Apr. 5, 1986) — contain warnings against translating sociology into theology and advocating violence in social activism.

Life in Outer Space: Whether rational life exists on other bodies in the universe besides earth, is a question for scientific investigation to settle. The possibility can be granted, without prejudice to the body of revealed truth.

Limbo: The limbo of the fathers was the state of rest and natural happiness after death enjoyed by the just of pre-Christian times until they were admitted to heaven following the Ascension of Christ.

Litany: A prayer in the form of responsive petition; e.g., St. Joseph, pray for us, etc. Examples are the litanies of Loreto (Litany of the Blessed Mother), the Holy Name, All Saints, the Sacred Heart, the Precious Blood, St. Joseph, Litany for the Dying.

Logos: A Greek term for "word, speech, or reason." It is most commonly identified with the title given to Jesus in John's Gospel, though not exclusive to that Gospel; In the N.T., however, the term reflects more the influence of Hellenistic philosophy: St. Paul uses logos as interchangeable with *sophia*, wisdom (1 Cor 1:24). The *Logos* is the Wisdom of God made manifest in the Son. As a name for the Second Person of the Trinity, the Incarnate Word, the term receives new meaning in the light of the life, death, and resurrection of Jesus Christ.

Loreto, House of: A Marian shrine in Loreto, Italy, consisting of the home of the Holy Family which, according to an old tradition, was transported in a miraculous manner from Nazareth to Dalmatia and finally to Loreto between 1291 and 1294. Investigations conducted shortly after the appearance of the structure in Loreto revealed that its dimensions matched those of the house of the Holy Family missing from its place of enshrinement in a basilica at Nazareth. Among the many popes who regarded it with high honor was John XXIII, who went there on pilgrimage Oct. 4, 1962. The house of the Holy Family is enshrined in the Basilica of Our Lady.

Love: A devotion to a person or object that has been categorized by Greek philosophy into four types: *storge* (one loves persons and things close to him); *philia* (the love of friends); *eros* (sexual love and that of a spiritual nature); *agape* (a self-giving to one in need). Christian charity is love, but not all love is true charity. The virtue was the subject of study by Pope Benedict XVI's 2005 encyclical *Deus Caritas Est*.

Lust: A disorderly desire for sexual pleasure; one of the seven capital sins.

M

Magi: In the Infancy Narrative of St. Matthew's Gospel (2:1-12), three wise men from the East whose visit and homage to the Child Jesus at Bethlehem indicated Christ's manifestation of himself to non-Jewish people. The narrative teaches the universality of salvation. The traditional names of the Magi are Caspar, Melchior and Balthasar.

Magisterium: The Church's teaching authority, instituted by Christ and guided by the Holy Spirit, which seeks to safeguard and explain the truths of the faith. The Magisterium is exercised in two ways. The extraordinary Magisterium is exercised when the pope and ecumenical councils infallibly define a truth of faith or morals that is necessary for one's salvation and that has been constantly taught and held by the Church. Ordinary Magisterium is exercised when the Church infallibly defines truths of the Faith as taught universally and without dissent; which must be taught or the Magisterium would be failing in its duty; is connected with a grave matter of faith or morals; and which is taught authoritatively. Not everything taught by the Magisterium is done so infallibly; however, the exercise of the Magisterium is faithful to Christ and what He taught.

Magnificat: The canticle or hymn of the Virgin Mary on the occasion of her visitation to her cousin Elizabeth (Lk 1:46-55). It is an expression of praise, thanksgiving and acknowledgment of the great blessings given by God to Mary, the Mother of the Second Person of the Blessed Trinity made Man. The *Magnificat* is recited in the Liturgy of the Hours as part of the Evening Prayer.

Martyr: A Greek word, meaning witness, denoting one who voluntarily suffered death for the faith or some Christian virtue.

Martyrology: A catalogue of martyrs and other saints, arranged according to the calendar. The *Roman Martyrology* contains the official list of saints venerated by the Church. Additions to the list are made in beatification and canonization decrees of the Congregation for the Causes of Saints.

Mass for the People: On Sundays and certain feasts throughout the year pastors are required to offer Mass for the faithful entrusted to their care. If they cannot offer the Mass on these days, they must do so at a later date or provide that another priest offer the Mass.

Materialism: Theory that holds that matter is the only reality, and everything in existence is merely a manifestation of matter; there is no such thing as spirit, and the supernatural does not exist. Materialism is incompatible with Christian doctrine.

Meditation: Mental, as distinguished from vocal, prayer, in which thought, affections, and resolutions of the will predominate. There is a meditative element to all forms of prayer, which always involves the raising of the heart and mind to God.

Mendicants: A term derived from Latin and meaning beggars, applied to members of religious orders without property rights; the members, accordingly, worked or begged for their support. The original mendicants were Franciscans and Dominicans in the early 13th century; later, the Carmelites, Augustinians, Servites and others were given the mendicant title and privileges, with respect to exemption from episcopal jurisdiction and wide faculties for preaching and administering the sacrament of penance. The practice of begging is limited at the pres-

ent time, although it is still allowed with the permission of competent superiors and bishops. Mendicants are supported by free will offerings and income received for spiritual services and other work.

Mercy, Divine: The love and goodness of God, manifested particularly in a time of need.

Mercy, Works of: Works of corporal or spiritual assistance, motivated by love of God and neighbor, to persons in need. (1) **Corporal works**: feeding the hungry, giving drink to the thirsty, clothing the naked, visiting the imprisoned, sheltering the homeless, visiting the sick, burying the dead. (2) **Spiritual works**: counseling the doubtful, instructing the ignorant, admonishing sinners, comforting the afflicted, forgiving offenses, bearing wrongs patiently, praying for the living and the dead.

Merit: In religion, the right to a supernatural reward for good works freely done for a supernatural motive by a person in the state of and with the assistance of grace. The right to such reward is from God, who binds himself to give it. Accordingly, good works, as described above, are meritorious for salvation.

Metanoia: A term from the Greek *metanoein* ("to change one's mind, repent, be converted") that is used in the NT for conversion. It entails the repentance of sin and the subsequent turning toward the Lord. *Metanoia* is fundamental to the Christian life and is necessary for spiritual growth.

Metaphysics: The branch of philosophy (from the Greek *meta* — after + *physika* — physics) dealing with first things, including the nature of being (ontology), the origin and structure of the world (cosmology), and the study of the reality and attributes of God (natural theology). Metaphysics has long been examined by Catholic philosophers, most especially in the writings of St. Augustine and St. Thomas Aquinas.

Millennium: A thousand-year reign of Christ and the just upon earth before the end of the world. This belief of the Millenarians, Chiliasts, and some sects of modern times is based on an erroneous interpretation of Rv 20.

Miracles: Observable events or effects in the physical or moral order of things, with reference to salvation, which cannot be explained by the ordinary operation of laws of nature and which, therefore, are attributed to the direct action of God. They make known, in an unusual way, the concern and intervention of God in human affairs for the salvation of men.

Mission: (1) Strictly, it means being sent to perform a certain work, such as the mission of Christ to redeem mankind, the mission of the Apostles and the Church and its members to perpetuate the prophetic, priestly and royal mission of Christ. (2) A place where: the Gospel has not been proclaimed; the Church has not been firmly established; the Church, although established, is weak. (3) An ecclesiastical territory with the simplest kind of canonical organization, under the jurisdiction of the Congregation for the Evangelization of Peoples. (4) A church or chapel without a resident priest. (5) A special course of sermons and spiritual exercises conducted in parishes for the purpose of renewing and deepening the spiritual life of the faithful and for the conversion of lapsed Catholics.

Modernism: The "synthesis of all heresies," which appeared near the beginning of the 20th century. It undermines the objective validity of religious beliefs and practices which, it contends, are products of the subconscious developed by mankind under the stimulus of a religious sense. It holds that the existence of a personal God cannot be demonstrated, the Bible is not inspired, Christ is not divine, nor did he establish the Church or institute the sacraments. A special danger lies in modernism, which is still influential, because it uses Catholic terms with perverted meanings. St. Pius X condemned 65 propositions of modernism in 1907 in the decree *Lamentabili* and issued the encyclical *Pascendi* to explain and analyze its errors.

Monastery: The dwelling place, as well as the community thereof, of monks belonging to the Benedictine and Benedictine-related orders like the Cistercians and Carthusians; also, the Augustinians and Canons Regular. Distinctive of monasteries are: their separation from the world; the enclosure or cloister; the permanence or stability of attachment characteristic of their members; autonomous government in accordance with a monastic rule, like that of St. Benedict in the West or of St. Basil in the East; the special dedication of its members to the community celebration of the liturgy as well as to work that is suitable to the surrounding area and the needs of its people. Monastic superiors of men have such titles as abbot and prior; of women, abbess and prioress. In most essentials, an abbey is the same as a monastery.

Monk: A member of a monastic order — e.g., the Benedictines, the Benedictine-related Cistercians and Carthusians, and the Basilians, who bind themselves by religious profession to stable attachment to a monastery, the contemplative life and the work of their community. In popular use, the title is wrongly applied to many men religious who really are not monks.

Monotheism: Belief in and worship of one God.

Morality: Conformity or difformity of behavior to standards of right conduct. (*See* **Moral Obligations**, p. 110; **Commandments of God**, p.111; **Precepts of the Church**, p. 112; **Conscience**, p. 136; **Law**, p. 147.)

Mortification: Acts of self-discipline, including prayer, hardship, austerities and penances undertaken for the sake of progress in virtue.

Motu Proprio: A Latin phrase designating a document issued by a pope on his own initiative. Documents of this kind often concern administrative matters.

Mystagogy: Experience of the mystery of Christ, especially through participation in the liturgy and the sacraments.

Mysteries of Faith: Supernatural truths whose existence cannot be known without revelation by God and whose intrinsic truth, while not contrary to reason, can never be wholly understood even after revelation. These mysteries are above reason, not against reason. Among them are the divine mysteries of the Trinity, Incarnation and Eucharist. Some mysteries — e.g., concerning God's attributes — can be known by reason without revelation, although they cannot be fully understood.

N

Natural Law: *See* **Law**, p. 147.

Natural Theology: The field of knowledge that relies upon human reason and the observation of nature, instead of revelation, to determine the existence and attributes of God.

Necromancy: Supposed communication with the dead; a form of divination.

Neo-Scholasticism: A movement begun in the late 19th century that had as its aim the restoration of Scholasticism for use in contemporary philosophy and theology. Great emphasis was placed upon the writings of such Scholastic masters as Peter Lombard, St. Albert the Great, St. Anselm, St. Bonaventure, Bl. John Duns Scotus, and especially St. Thomas Aquinas. The movement began at the Catholic University of Louvain, in Belgium, and then found its way into theological centers in Italy, France, and Germany. Particular attention was given to the philosophical and theological works of St. Thomas Aquinas, from which arose a particular school of neo-Thomism; the movement was strongly reinforced by Pope Leo XIII who issued the encyclical *Aeterni Patris* (1879) mandating that Scholasticism, in particular Thomism, be the foundation for all Catholic philosophy and theology taught in Catholic seminaries, universities, and colleges. Neo-Scholasticism was responsible for a true intellectual renaissance in 20th-century Catholic philosophy and theology. Among its foremost modern leaders were Jacques Maritain, Étienne Gilson, M. D. Chenu, Henri de Lubac, and Paul Claudel.

Nihil Obstat: *See* **Censorship of Books**, p. 134.

Non-Expedit: A Latin expression. It is not expedient (fitting, proper), used to state a prohibition or refusal of permission.

Novena: A term designating public or private devotional practices over a period of nine consecutive days; or, by extension, over a period of nine weeks, in which one day a week is set aside for the devotions.

Novice: A man or woman preparing, in a formal period of trial and formation called a novitiate, for membership in an institute of consecrated life. The novitiate lasts a minimum of 12 and a maximum of 24 months; at its conclusion, the novice professes temporary promises or vows of poverty, chastity and obedience. Norms require that certain periods of time be spent in the house of novitiate; periods of apostolic work are also required, to acquaint the novice with the apostolate(s) of the institute. A novice is not bound by the obligations of the professed members of the institute, is free to leave at any time, and may be discharged at the discretion of competent superiors. The superior of a novice is a master of novices or director of formation.

Nun: (1) Strictly, a member of a religious order of women with solemn vows (*moniales*). (2) In general, all women religious, even those in simple vows who are more properly called sisters.

Nunc Dimittis: The canticle or hymn of Simeon at the sight of Jesus at the Temple on the occasion of his presentation (Lk 2:29-32). It is an expression of joy and thanksgiving for the blessing of having lived to see the Messiah. It is prescribed for use in the Night Prayer of the Liturgy of the Hours.

O

Oath: Calling upon God to witness the truth of a statement. Violating an oath, e.g., by perjury in court, or taking an oath without sufficient reason, is a violation of the honor due to God.

Obedience: Submission to one in authority. General obligations of obedience fall under the Fourth Commandment. The vow of obedience professed by religious is one of the evangelical counsels.

Obsession, Diabolical: The extraordinary state of one

who is seriously molested by evil spirits in an external manner. Obsession is more than just temptation.

Occasion of Sin: A person, place, or thing that is a temptation to sin. An occasion may be either a situation that always leads to sin or one that usually leads to sin.

Octave: A period of eight days given over to the celebration of a major feast such as Easter.

Oils, Holy: The oils blessed by a bishop at the Chrism Mass on Holy Thursday or another suitable day, or by a priest under certain conditions. (1) The oil of catechumens (olive or vegetable oil), used at baptism; also, poured with chrism into the baptismal water blessed in Easter Vigil ceremonies. (2) Oil of the sick (olive or vegetable oil) used in anointing the sick. (3) Chrism (olive or vegetable oil mixed with balm), which is ordinarily consecrated by a bishop, for use at baptism, in confirmation, at the ordination of a priest and bishop, in the dedication of churches and altars.

Ontologism: A philosophical theory (the name is taken from the Greek for being and study) that posits that knowledge of God is immediate and intuitive; it stipulates further that all other human knowledge is dependent upon this. It was condemned in 1861 by Pope Pius IX. (*See* also **Ontology**.)

Ontology: A branch of metaphysics that studies the nature and relations of existence.

Oratory: A chapel.

Ordinariate: An ecclesiastical jurisdiction for special purposes and people. Examples are military ordinariates for armed services personnel (in accord with provisions of the apostolic constitution *Spirituali militum curae*, Apr. 21, 1986) and Eastern-Rite ordinariates in places where Eastern-Rite dioceses do not exist.

Ordination: The consecration of sacred ministers for divine worship and the service of people in things pertaining to God. The power of ordination comes from Christ and the Church, and must be conferred by a minister capable of communicating it.

Organ Transplants: The transplanting of organs from one person to another is permissible provided it is done with the consent of the concerned parties and does not result in the death or essential mutilation of the donor. Advances in methods and technology have increased the range of transplant possibilities in recent years.

Original Sin: The sin of Adam (Gn 2:8-3:24), personal to him and passed on to all persons as a state of privation of grace. Despite this privation and the related wounding of human nature and weakening of natural powers, original sin leaves unchanged all that man himself is by nature. The scriptural basis of the doctrine was stated by St. Paul in 1 Cor 15:21ff., and Rom 5:12-21. Original sin is remitted by baptism and incorporation in Christ, through whom grace is given to persons. Pope John Paul II, while describing original sin during a general audience Oct. 1, 1986, called it "the absence of sanctifying grace in nature which has been diverted from its supernatural end."

O Salutaris Hostia: The first three Latin words, *O Saving Victim*, of a Benediction hymn.

Ostpolitik: Policy adopted by Pope Paul VI in an attempt to improve the situation of Eastern European Catholics through diplomatic negotiations with their governments.

Oxford Movement: A movement in the Church of England from 1833 to about 1845 which had for its objective a threefold defense of the Church as a divine institution, the apostolic succession of its bishops, and the *Book of Common Prayer* as the rule of faith. The movement took its name from Oxford University and involved a number of intellectuals who authored a series of influential Tracts for Our Times. Some of its leading figures — e.g., F. W. Faber, John Henry Newman and Henry Edward Manning — became converts to the Catholic Church. In the Church of England, the movement affected the liturgy, historical and theological scholarship, the status of the ministry, and other areas of ecclesiastical life.

P

Paganism: A term referring to non-revealed religions, i.e., religions other than Christianity, Judaism, and Islam.

Palms: Blessed palms are a sacramental. They are blessed and distributed on the Sunday of the Passion in commemoration of the triumphant entrance of Christ into Jerusalem. Ashes of the burnt palms are used on Ash Wednesday.

Pange Lingua: First Latin words, *Sing, my tongue*, of a hymn in honor of the Holy Eucharist, used particularly on Holy Thursday and in Eucharistic processions.

Pantheism: Theory that all things are part of God, divine, in the sense that God realizes himself as the ultimate reality of matter or spirit through being and/or becoming all things that have been, are, and will be. The theory leads to hopeless confusion of the Creator and the created realm of being, identifies evil with good, and involves many inherent contradictions.

Papal Election: The pope is elected by the College of Cardinals during a secret conclave which begins no sooner than 15 days and no later than 20 days after the death of his predecessor. Cardinals under the age of 80, totaling no more than 120, are eligible to take part in the election by secret ballot. Election is by a two-thirds vote of participating cardinals. New legislation regarding papal elections and church government during a vacancy of the Holy See was promulgated by Pope John Paul II, Feb. 23, 1996, in the apostolic constitution *Universi Dominici Gregis* ("Shepherd of the Lord's Whole Flock").

Paraclete: A title of the Holy Spirit meaning, in Greek, Advocate, Consoler.

Parental Duties: All duties related to the obligation of parents to provide for the welfare of their children. These obligations fall under the Fourth Commandment.

Parish: A community of the faithful served by a pastor charged with responsibility for providing them with full pastoral service. Most parishes are territorial, embracing all of the faithful in a certain area of a diocese: some are personal or national, for certain classes of people, without strict regard for their places of residence.

Parousia: The coming, or saving presence, of Christ which will mark the completion of salvation history and the coming to perfection of God's kingdom at the end of the world.

Particular Church: A term used since Vatican II that denotes certain divisions of the Universal Church. Examples include dioceses, vicariates, and prelatures.

Paschal Candle: A large candle, symbolic of the risen Christ, blessed and lighted on the Easter Vigil and placed at the altar until Pentecost. It is ornamented with five large grains of incense, representing the wounds of Christ, inserted in the form of a cross; the Greek letters Alpha and Omega, symbolizing Christ the beginning and end of all things, at the top and bottom of the shaft of the cross; and the figures of the current year of salvation in the quadrants formed by the cross.

Paschal Precept: Church law requiring reception of the Eucharist in the Easter season (*See* separate entry) unless, for a just cause, once-a-year reception takes place at another time.

Passion of Christ: Sufferings of Christ, recorded in the four Gospels.

Pastor: An ordained minister charged with responsibility for the doctrinal, sacramental and related service of people committed to his care; e.g., a bishop for the people in his diocese, a priest for the people of his parish.

Pater Noster: The initial Latin words, *Our Father*, of the Lord's Prayer.

Patriarch: (1) The leaders of the Israelite tribes and heads of prominent families who appear in Genesis from Adam to Joseph. Among the most significant patriarchs of the Old Testament are Abraham, Isaac, and Jacob; the patriarchal narratives in Genesis associated with them constitute the prologue to Israel's salvation history, and the period during which they lived is known as the Age of the Patriarchs. It is noted that the title of patriarch that was used for David (Acts 2:29) was simply one of honor. (2) The head of a branch of the Eastern Church, corresponding to a province of the one-time Roman Empire. There are five official traditional patriarchal sees: Rome, Constantinople, Alexandria, Antioch, and Jerusalem. Presently, the autocephalous churches of the Orthodox Church comprise several of these traditional patriarchates.

Peace, Sign of: A gesture of greeting — e.g., a handshake — exchanged by the ministers and participants at Mass.

Pectoral Cross: A cross worn on a chain about the neck and over the breast by bishops and abbots as a mark of their office.

Penance or Penitence: (1) The spiritual change or conversion of mind and heart by which a person turns away from sin, and all that it implies, toward God, through a personal renewal under the influence of the Holy Spirit. Penance involves sorrow and contrition for sin, together with other internal and external acts of atonement. It serves the purposes of reestablishing in one's life the order of God's love and commandments, and of making satisfaction to God for sin. (2) Penance is a virtue disposing a person to turn to God in sorrow for sin and to carry out works of amendment and atonement. (3) The sacrament of penance and sacramental penance.

People of God: A name for the Church in the sense that it is comprised by a people with Christ as its head, the Holy Spirit as the condition of its unity, the law of love as its rule, and the kingdom of God as its destiny. Although it is a scriptural term, it was given new emphasis by the Second Vatican Council's Dogmatic Constitution on the Church (*Lumen Gentium*).

Perjury: Taking a false oath, lying under oath, a violation of the honor due to God.

Persecution, Religious: A campaign waged against a church or other religious body by persons and governments intent on its destruction. The best known campaigns of this type against the Christian Church were the Roman persecutions which occurred intermittently from about 54 to the promulgation of the Edict of Milan in 313. More Catholics have been persecuted in the 20th century than in any other period in history.

Personal Prelature: *See* under **Opus Dei**, p. 507.

Peter's Pence: A collection made each year among Catholics for the maintenance of the pope and his works of charity. It was originally a tax of a penny on each house, and was collected on St. Peter's day, whence the name. It originated in England in the 8th century.

Petition: One of the four purposes of prayer. In prayers of petition, persons ask of God the blessings they and others need.

Pharisees: Influential class among the Jews, referred to in the Gospels, noted for their self-righteousness, legalism, strict interpretation of the Law, acceptance of the traditions of the elders as well as the Law of Moses, and beliefs regarding angels and spirits, the resurrection of the dead and judgment. Most of them were laymen, and they were closely allied with the Scribes; their opposite numbers were the Sadducees. The Pharisaic and rabbinical traditions had a lasting influence on Judaism following the destruction of Jerusalem in A.D. 70.

Pious Fund: Property and money originally accumulated by the Jesuits to finance their missionary work in Lower California. When the Jesuits were expelled from the territory in 1767, the fund was appropriated by the Spanish Crown and used to support Dominican and Franciscan missionary work in Upper and Lower California. In 1842 the Mexican government took over administration of the fund, incorporated most of the revenue into the national treasury, and agreed to pay the Church interest of six percent a year on the capital so incorporated. From 1848 to 1967 the fund was the subject of lengthy negotiations between the U.S. and Mexican governments because of the latter's failure to make payments as agreed. A lump-sum settlement was made in 1967 with payment by Mexico to the U.S. government of more than $700,000, to be turned over to the Archdiocese of San Francisco.

Polytheism: Belief in and worship of many gods or divinities, especially prevalent in pre-Christian religions.

Poor Box: Alms-box; found in churches from the earliest days of Christianity.

Pope: A title from the Italian word *papa* (from Greek *pappas*, father) used for the Bishop of Rome, the Vicar of Christ and successor of St. Peter, who exercises universal governance over the Church.

Portiuncula: (1) Meaning little portion (of land), the Portiuncula is the chapel of Our Lady of the Angels near Assisi, Italy, which the Benedictines gave to St. Francis early in the 13th century. He repaired the chapel and made it the first church of the Franciscan Order. It is now enshrined in the Basilica of St. Mary of the Angels in Assisi. (2) The plenary Portiuncula Indulgence, or Pardon of Assisi, was authorized by Honorius III. Originally, it could be gained for the souls in purgatory only in the chapel of Our Lady of the Angels; by later concessions, it could be gained also in other Franciscan and parish churches. The indulgence (applicable to the souls in purgatory) can be gained from noon of Aug. 1 to midnight of Aug. 2, once each day. The conditions are, in addition to freedom from attachment to sin: reception of the sacraments of penance and the Eucharist on or near the day and a half; a visit to a parish church within the day and a half, during which the Our Father, the Creed and another prayer are offered for the intentions of the pope.

Positivism: The philosophy that teaches that the only reality is that which is perceived by the senses; the only truth is that which is empirically verified. It asserts that ideas about God, morality, or anything else that cannot be scientifically tested are to be rejected as unknowable.

Possession, Diabolical: The extraordinary state of a person who is tormented from within by evil spirits who exercise strong influence over his powers of mind and body. (*See* also **Exorcism**, p. 140.)

Postulant: One of several names used to designate a candidate for membership in a religious institute during the period before novitiate.

Poverty: (1) The quality or state of being poor, in actual destitution and need, or being poor in spirit. In the latter sense, poverty means the state of mind and disposition of persons who regard material things in proper perspective as gifts of God for the support of life and its reasonable enrichment, and for the service of others in need. It means freedom from unreasonable attachment to material things as ends in themselves, even though they may be possessed in small or large measure. (2) One of the evangelical counsels professed as a public vow by members of an institute of consecrated life. It involves the voluntary renunciation of rights of ownership and of independent use and disposal of material goods; or, the right of independent use and disposal, but not of the radical right of ownership. Religious institutes provide their members with necessary and useful goods and services from common resources. The manner in which goods are received and/or handled by religious is determined by poverty of spirit and the rule and constitutions of their institute.

Pragmatism: Theory that the truth of ideas, concepts and values depends on their utility or capacity to serve a useful purpose rather than on their conformity with objective standards; also called utilitarianism.

Prayer: The raising of the mind and heart to God in adoration, thanksgiving, reparation and petition. Prayer, which is always mental because it involves thought and love of God, may be vocal, meditative, private and personal, social, and official. The official prayer of the Church as a worshipping community is called the liturgy.

Precepts: Commands or orders given to individuals or communities in particular cases; they establish law for concerned parties. Preceptive documents are issued by the pope, departments of the Roman Curia and other competent authority in the Church.

Presence of God: A devotional practice of increasing one's awareness of the presence and action of God in daily life.

Presumption: A sin against hope, by which a person striving for salvation (1) either relies too much on his own capabilities or (2) expects God to do things which he cannot do, in keeping with his divine attributes, or does not will to do, according to his divine plan. Presumption is the opposite of despair.

Preternatural Gifts: Exceptional gifts, beyond the exigencies and powers of human nature, enjoyed by Adam in the state of original justice: immunity from suffering and death, superior knowledge, integrity or perfect control of the passions. These gifts were lost as the result of original sin; their loss, however, implied no impairment of the integrity of human nature.

Pride: Unreasonable self-esteem; one of the seven capital sins.

Prie-Dieu: A French phrase, meaning pray God, designating a kneeler or bench suitable for kneeling while at prayer.

Priesthood: (1) The *common priesthood* of the non-ordained faithful. In virtue of baptism and confirmation, the faithful are a priestly people who participate in the priesthood of Christ through acts of worship, witness to the faith in daily life, and efforts to foster the growth of God's kingdom. (2) The *ordained priesthood*, in virtue of the sacrament of orders, of bishops, priests and deacons, for service to the common priesthood.

Primary Option: The life-choice of a person for or against God which shapes the basic orientation of moral conduct. A primary option for God does not preclude the possibility of serious sin.

Prior: A superior or an assistant to an abbot in a monastery.

Privilege: A favor, an exemption from the obligation of a law. Privileges of various kinds, with respect to ecclesiastical laws, are granted by the pope, departments of the Roman Curia and other competent authority in the Church.

Probabiliorism: The moral system asserting that the more probable opinion of a varied set of acceptable positions regarding the binding character of a law should be accepted. If the reasons for being free from a law are more probably true, one is freed from the law's obligations. Probabiliorism, however, maintained that if it was probable that the law did not bind, one still had to follow it unless it was more probable that the law did not bind.

Probabilism: A moral system for use in cases of conscience which involve the obligation of doubtful laws. There is a general principle that a doubtful law does not bind. Probabilism, therefore, teaches that it is permissible to follow an opinion favoring liberty, provided the opinion is certainly and solidly probable. Probabilism may not be invoked when there is question of: a certain law or the certain obligation of a law; the certain right of another party; the validity of an action; something which is necessary for salvation.

Pro-Cathedral: A church used as a cathedral.

Promoter of the Faith (*Promotor fidei*): An official of the Congregation for the Causes of Saints, whose role in beatification and canonization procedures is to establish beyond reasonable doubt the validity of evidence regarding the holiness of prospective saints and miracles attributed to their intercession.

Prophecy: (1) The communication of divine revelation by inspired intermediaries, called prophets, between God and his people. Old Testament prophecy was unique in its origin and because of its ethical and religious content, which included disclosure of the saving will of Yahweh for the people, moral censures and warnings of divine punishment because of sin and violations of the Law and Covenant, in the form of promises, admonitions, reproaches and threats. Although Moses and other earlier figures are called prophets, the period of prophecy is generally dated from the early years of the monarchy to about 100 years after the Babylonian Exile. From that time on, the written Law and its interpreters supplanted the prophets as guides of the people. Old Testament prophets are cited in the New Testament, with awareness that God spoke through them and that some of their oracles were fulfilled in Christ. John the Baptist is the outstanding prophetic figure in the New Testament. Christ never claimed the title of prophet for himself, although some people thought he was one. There were prophets in the early Church, and St. Paul mentioned the charism of prophecy in 1 Cor 14:1-5. Prophecy disappeared after New Testament times. Revelation is classified as the prophetic book of the New Testament. (2) In contemporary non-scriptural usage, the term is applied to the witness given by persons to the relevance of their beliefs in everyday life and action.

Proportionalism: The moral theory that asserts that an action is judged on whether the evils resulting are proportionate to the goods that result. If the evils outweigh the goods, the act is objectionable; if the opposite is true, the act is permissible. Proportionalism differs from consequentialism in that the former admits that the inherent morality of the act and the agent's intention must also be considered. Proportionalism is rejected by critics as it does not offer an objective criterion for determining when evils are proportionate or disproportionate. It also fails to consider the intrinsic nature of human acts and does nothing to assist Christians to grow in virtue.

Province: (1) A territory comprising one archdiocese called the metropolitan see and one or more dioceses called suffragan sees. The head of the archdiocese, an archbishop, has metropolitan rights and responsibilities over the province. (2) A division of a religious order under the jurisdiction of a provincial superior.

Prudence: Practical wisdom and judgment regarding the choice and use of the best ways and means of doing good; one of the four cardinal virtues.

Punishment Due for Sin: The punishment which is a consequence of sin. It is of two kinds: (1) Eternal punishment is the punishment of hell, to which one becomes subject by the commission of mortal sin. Such punishment is remitted when mortal sin is forgiven. (2) Temporal punishment is a consequence of venial sin and/or forgiven mortal sin; it is not everlasting and may be remitted in this life by means of penance. Temporal punishment unremitted during this life is remitted by suffering in purgatory.

Purgatory: The state or condition of those who have died in the state of grace but with some attachment to sin, and are purified for a time before they are admitted to the glory and happiness of heaven. In this state and period of passive suffering, they are purified of unrepented venial sins, satisfy the demands of divine justice for temporal punishment due for sins, and are thus converted to a state of worthiness of the beatific vision.

Q

Quadragesima: From the Latin for fortieth, the name given to the forty penitential days of Lent.

Quinquennial Report: A report on the current state of a diocese that must be compiled and submitted by a bishop to the Holy See every five years in anticipation of the *ad liminal* visit.

Quinque Viae: From the Latin for the "five ways," the five proofs for the existence of God that were proposed by St. Thomas Aquinas in his *Summa Theologiae* (Part I, question 2, article 3). The five ways are: 1) all the motion in the world points to an unmoved Prime Mover; 2) the subordinate agents in the world imply the First Agent; 3) there must be a Cause Who is not perishable and Whose existence is underived; 4) the limited goodness in the world must be a reflection of Unlimited Goodness; 5) all things tend to become something, and that inclination must have proceeded from some Rational Planner.

R

Racism: A theory which holds that any one or several of the different races of the human family are inherently superior or inferior to any one or several of the others. The teaching denies the essential unity of the human race, the equality and dignity of all persons because of their common possession of the same human nature, and the participation of all in the divine plan of redemption. It is radically opposed to the virtue of justice and the precept of love of neighbor. Differences of superiority and inferiority which do exist are the result of accidental factors operating in a wide variety of circumstances, and are in no way due to essential defects in any one or several of the branches of the one human race. The theory of racism, together with practices related to it, is incompatible with Christian doctrine.

Rash Judgment: Attributing faults to another without sufficient reason; a violation of the obligations of justice and charity.

Rationalism: A theory which makes the mind the measure and arbiter of all things, including religious truth. A product of the Enlightenment, it rejects the supernatural, divine revelation, and authoritative teaching by any church.

Recollection: Meditation, attitude of concentration or awareness of spiritual matters and things pertaining to salvation and the accomplishment of God's will.

Relativism: Theory which holds that all truth, including religious truth, is relative, i.e., not absolute, certain or unchanging; a product of agnosticism, indifferentism, and an unwarranted extension of the notion of truth in positive science. Relativism is based on the tenet that certain knowledge of any and all truth is impossible. Therefore, no religion, philosophy or science can be said to possess the real truth; consequently, all religions, philosophies and sciences may be considered to have as much or as little of truth as any of the others.

Relics: The physical remains and effects of saints, which are considered worthy of veneration inasmuch as they are representative of persons in glory with God. Catholic doctrine proscribes the view that relics are not worthy of veneration. In line with norms laid down by the Council of Trent and subsequent enactments, discipline concerning relics is subject to control by the Congregations for the Causes of Saints and for Divine Worship and the Discipline of the Sacraments.

Religion: The adoration and service of God as expressed in divine worship and in daily life. Religion is concerned with all of the relations existing between God and human beings, and between humans themselves because of the central significance of God. Objectively considered, religion consists of a body of truth that is believed, a code of morality for the guidance of conduct, and a form of divine worship. Subjectively, it is a person's total response, theoretically and practically, to the demands of faith; it is living faith, personal engagement, self-commitment to God. Thus, by creed, code and cult, a person orders and directs his or her life in reference to God and, through what the love and service of God implies, to all people and all things.

Reliquary: A vessel for the preservation and exposition of a relic; sometimes made like a small monstrance.

Reparation: The making of amends to God for sin committed; one of the four ends of prayer and the purpose of penance.

Requiem: A Mass offered for the repose of the soul of one who has died in Christ. Its name is derived from the first word of the Gregorian (Latin) entrance chant (or Introit) at Masses for the dead: *Requiem aeternam dona eis, Domine* ("Eternal rest grant unto them, O Lord"). The revised Rite for Funerals refers to the requiem as the Mass of Christian Burial; however, it would not be uncommon to hear people employ the former usage.

Rescript: A written reply by an ecclesiastical superior regarding a question or request; its provisions bind concerned parties only. Papal dispensations are issued in the form of rescripts.

Reserved Censure: A sin or censure, absolution from which is reserved to religious superiors, bishops, the pope, or confessors having special faculties. Reservations are made because of the serious nature and social effects of certain sins and censures.

Restitution: An act of reparation for an injury done to another. The injury may be caused by taking and/or retaining what belongs to another or by damaging either the property or reputation of another. The intention of making restitution, usually in kind, is required as a condition for the forgiveness of sins of injustice, even though actual restitution is not possible.

Ring: In the Church a ring is worn as part of the insignia of bishops, abbots, et al.; by sisters to denote their consecration to God and the Church. The wedding ring symbolizes the love and union of husband and wife.

Ritual: A book of prayers and ceremonies used in the administration of the sacraments and other ceremonial functions. In the Roman Rite, the standard book of this kind is the Roman Ritual.

Rogito: The official notarial act or document testifying to the burial of a pope.

Rosary: A form of mental and vocal prayer centered on mysteries or events in the lives of Jesus and Mary. Its essential elements are meditation on the mysteries and the recitation of a number of decades of Hail Marys, each beginning with the Lord's Prayer. Introductory prayers may include the Apostles' Creed, an initial Our Father, three Hail Marys and a Glory be to the Father; each decade is customarily concluded with a Glory be to the Father; at the end, it is customary to say the Hail, Holy Queen and a prayer from the liturgy for the feast of the Blessed Virgin Mary of the Rosary. Traditionally, the Mysteries of the Rosary, which are the subject of medita-

tion, are: (1) Joyful — the Annunciation to Mary that she was to be the Mother of Christ, her visit to Elizabeth, the birth of Jesus, the presentation of Jesus in the Temple, the finding of Jesus in the Temple. (2) Sorrowful — Christ's agony in the Garden of Gethsemani, scourging at the pillar, crowning with thorns, carrying of the cross to Calvary, and crucifixion. (3) Glorious — the Resurrection and Ascension of Christ, the descent of the Holy Spirit upon the Apostles, Mary's Assumption into heaven and her crowning as Queen of angels and men.

The complete Rosary, called the Dominican Rosary, consists of 15 decades. In customary practice, only five decades are usually said at one time. Rosary beads are used to aid in counting the prayers without distraction. The Rosary originated through the coalescence of popular devotions to Jesus and Mary from the 12th century onward. Its present form dates from about the 15th century. Carthusians contributed greatly toward its development; Dominicans have been its greatest promoters. The fifteen mysteries were standardized by Pope Pius V in 1569.

In 2002, Pope John Paul II added five new mysteries dedicated to chapters from Jesus' public life. Titled the Mysteries of Light, they are: Christ's baptism in the Jordan River; Christ's self-revelation at the marriage of Cana; Christ's announcement of the kingdom of God with the invitation to conversion; Christ's Transfiguration, when he revealed his glory to his Apostles; and the institution of the Eucharist at the Last Supper as the sacramental expression of the paschal mystery. The pope asked that the Mysteries of Light be recited especially on Thursday.

S

Sabbath: The seventh day of the week, observed by Jews and Sabbatarians as the day for rest and religious observance.

Sacrarium: A basin with a drain leading directly into the ground; standard equipment of a sacristy.

Sacred Heart, Enthronement of the: An acknowledgment of the sovereignty of Jesus Christ over the Christian family, expressed by the installation of an image or picture of the Sacred Heart in a place of honor in the home, accompanied by an act of consecration.

Sacred Heart, Promises: Twelve promises to persons having devotion to the Sacred Heart of Jesus, which were communicated by Christ to St. Margaret Mary Alacoque in a private revelation in 1675.

Sacrilege: Violation of and irreverence toward a person, place or thing that is sacred because of public dedication to God; a sin against the virtue of religion. Personal sacrilege is violence of some kind against a cleric or religious, or a violation of chastity with a cleric or religious. Local sacrilege is the desecration of sacred places. Real sacrilege is irreverence with respect to sacred things, such as the sacraments and sacred vessels.

Sacristy: A utility room where vestments, church furnishings and sacred vessels are kept and where the clergy vest for sacred functions.

Sadducees: The predominantly priestly party among the Jews in the time of Christ, noted for extreme conservatism, acceptance only of the Law of Moses, and rejection of the traditions of the elders. Their opposite numbers were the Pharisees.

Saints, Cult of: The veneration, called *dulia*, of holy persons who have died and are in glory with God in heaven; it includes honoring them and petitioning them for their intercession with God. Liturgical veneration is given only to saints officially recognized by the Church; private veneration may be given to anyone thought to be in heaven. The veneration of saints is essentially different from the adoration given to God alone; by its very nature, however, it terminates in the worship of God. (*See* also **Dulia**, p. 139, and **Latria**, p. 147.)

Salvation: The liberation of persons from sin and its effects, reconciliation with God in and through Christ, the attainment of union with God forever in the glory of heaven as the supreme purpose of life and as the God-given reward for fulfillment of his will on earth. Salvation-in-process begins and continues in this life through union with Christ in faith professed and in action; its final term is union with God and the whole community of the saved in the ultimate perfection of God's kingdom. The Church teaches that: God wills the salvation of all men; men are saved in and through Christ; membership in the Church established by Christ, known and understood as the community of salvation, is necessary for salvation; men with this knowledge and understanding who deliberately reject this Church, cannot be saved. The Catholic Church is the Church founded by Christ. (*See* below, **Salvation outside the Church**.)

Salvation History: The facts and the record of God's relations with human beings, in the past, present and future, for the purpose of leading them to live in accordance with his will for the eventual attainment after death of salvation, or everlasting happiness with him in heaven. The essentials of salvation history are: God's love for all human beings and will for their salvation; his intervention and action in the world to express this love and bring about their salvation; the revelation he made of himself and the covenant he established with the Israelites in the Old Testament; the perfecting of this revelation and the new covenant of grace through Christ in the New Testament; the continuing action-for-salvation carried on in and through the Church; the communication of saving grace to people through the merits of Christ and the operations of the Holy Spirit in the here-and-now circumstances of daily life and with the cooperation of people themselves.

Salvation outside the Church: The Second Vatican Council covered this subject summarily in the following manner: "Those also can attain to everlasting salvation who through no fault of their own do not know the Gospel of Christ or his Church, yet sincerely seek God and, moved by grace, strive by their deeds to do his will as it is known to them through the dictates of conscience. Nor does divine Providence deny the help necessary for salvation to those who, without blame on their part, have not yet arrived at an explicit knowledge of God, but who strive to live a good life, thanks to his grace. Whatever good or truth is found among them is looked upon by the Church as a preparation for the Gospel. She regards such qualities as given by him who enlightens all men so that they may finally have life" (Dogmatic Constitution on the Church, *Lumen Gentium*, No. 16). These teachings were reiterated by the document issued by the Congregation for the Doctrine of the Faith, *Dominus Iesus*.

Sanctifying Grace: *See* **Grace**, p. 143.

Satanism: Worship of the devil, a blasphemous inversion of the order of worship which is due to God alone.

Scandal: Conduct which is the occasion of sin to another person.

Scapular: (1) A part of the habit of some religious orders like the Benedictines and Dominicans; a nearly shoulder-wide strip of cloth worn over the tunic and reaching almost to the feet in front and behind. Originally a kind of apron, it came to symbolize the cross and yoke of Christ. (2) Scapulars worn by lay persons as a sign of association with religious orders and for devotional purposes are an adaptation of monastic scapulars. Approved by the Church as sacramentals, they consist of two small squares of woolen cloth joined by strings and are worn about the neck. They are given for wearing in a ceremony of investiture or enrollment. There are nearly 20 scapulars for devotional use: the five principal ones are generally understood to include those of Our Lady of Mt. Carmel (the brown Carmelite Scapular), the Holy Trinity, Our Lady of the Seven Dolors, the Passion, the Immaculate Conception.

Scapular Medal: A medallion with a representation of the Sacred Heart on one side and of the Blessed Virgin Mary on the other. Authorized by St. Pius X in 1910, it may be worn or carried in place of a scapular by persons already invested with a scapular.

Scapular Promise: According to a legend of the Carmelite Order, the Blessed Virgin Mary appeared to St. Simon Stock in 1251 at Cambridge, England, and declared that wearers of the brown Carmelite Scapular would be the beneficiaries of her special intercession. The scapular tradition has never been the subject of official decision by the Church. Essentially, it expresses belief in the intercession of Mary and the efficacy of sacramentals in the context of truly Christian life.

Schism: Derived from a Greek word meaning separation, the term designates formal and obstinate refusal by a baptized Catholic, called a schismatic, to be in communion with the pope and the Church. The canonical penalty is excommunication. One of the most disastrous schisms in history resulted in the definitive separation of the Church in the East from union with Rome about 1054.

Scholasticism: The term usually applied to the Catholic theology and philosophy which developed in the Middle Ages. (*See* also **Neo-Scholasticism**, p. 149.)

Scribes: Hebrew intellectuals noted for their knowledge of the Law of Moses, influential from the time of the Exile to about A.D. 70. Many of them were Pharisees. They were the antecedents of rabbis and their traditions, as well as those o the Pharisees, had a lasting influence on Judaism following the destruction of Jerusalem in A.D. 70.

Scruple: A morbid, unreasonable fear and anxiety that one's actions are sinful when they are not, or more seriously sinful than they actually are. Compulsive scrupulosity is quite different from the transient scrupulosity of persons of tender or highly sensitive conscience, or of persons with faulty moral judgment.

Seal of Confession: The obligation of secrecy which must be observed regarding knowledge of things learned in connection with the confession of sin in the sacrament of penance. The seal covers matters whose revelation would make the sacrament burdensome. Confessors are prohibited, under penalty of excommunication, from making any direct revelation of confessional matter; this prohibition holds, outside of confession, even with respect to the person who made the confession unless the person releases the priest from the obligation. Persons other than confessors are obliged to maintain secrecy, but not under penalty of excommunication. General, non-specific discussion of confessional matter does not violate the seal.

Secularism: A school of thought, a spirit and manner of action which ignores and/or repudiates the validity or influence of supernatural religion with respect to individual and social life.

See: Another name for diocese or archdiocese.

Seminary: A house of study and formation for men, called seminarians, preparing for the priesthood. Traditional seminaries date from the Council of Trent in the middle of the 16th century; before that time, candidates for the priesthood were variously trained in monastic schools, universities under church auspices, and in less formal ways.

Sermon on the Mount: A compilation of sayings of Our Lord in the form of an extended discourse in Matthew's Gospel (5:1 to 7:27) and, in a shorter discourse, in Luke (6:17-49). The passage in Matthew, called the "Constitution of the New Law," summarizes the living spirit of believers in Christ and members of the kingdom of God. Beginning with the Beatitudes and including the Lord's Prayer, it covers the perfect justice of the New Law, the fulfillment of the Old Law in the New Law of Christ, and the integrity of internal attitude and external conduct with respect to love of God and neighbor, justice, chastity, truth, trust and confidence in God.

Seven Last Words of Christ: The Seven Last Words of Christ on the Cross were: (1) *"Father, forgive them; for they do not know what they are doing."* (Lk 23:34); (2) To the penitent thief: *"I assure you: today you will be with me in Paradise."* (Lk 23:24); (3) To Mary and his Apostle John: *"Woman, behold thy son! . . . Behold your mother."* (Jn 19:26); (4) *"Eli Eli, lama sabacthani* [*"My God, my God, why have you forsaken me?"*] (Mt 27:46; cf. Mk 15:34); (5) *"I thirst."* (Jn 19:28); (6) *"It is finished."* (Jn 19:30); (7) *"Father, into thy hands I commend my spirit."* (Lk 23:46).

Shrine, Crowned: A shrine approved by the Holy See as a place of pilgrimage. The approval permits public devotion at the shrine and implies that at least one miracle has resulted from devotion at the shrine. Among the best known crowned shrines are those of the Virgin Mary at Lourdes and Fátima. Shrines with statues crowned by Pope John Paul in 1985 in South America were those of Our Lady of Coromoto, patroness of Venezuela, in Caracas, and Our Lady of Carmen of Paucartambo in Cuzco, Peru.

Shroud of Turin: A strip of brownish linen cloth, 14 feet, three inches in length and three feet, seven inches in width, bearing the front and back imprint of a human body. A tradition dating from the 7th century, which has not been verified beyond doubt, claims that the shroud is the fine linen in which the body of Christ was wrapped for burial. The early history of the shroud is obscure. It was enshrined at Lirey, France, in 1354 and was transferred in 1578 to Turin, Italy, where it has been kept in the cathedral down to the present time. Scientific investigation, which began in 1898, seems to indicate that the markings on the shroud are those of a human body. The shroud, for the first time since 1933, was placed on public view from Aug. 27 to Oct. 8, 1978, and was seen by an estimated 3.3 million people. Scientists conducted intensive studies of it thereafter, finally determining that the material of the shroud dated from between 1260 and 1390. The shroud, which had been the possession of the House of Savoy, was willed to Pope John Paul II in 1983.

Sick Calls: When a person is confined at home by illness or other cause and is unable to go to church for reception of the sacraments, a parish priest should be informed and arrangements made for him to visit the person at home. Such visitations are common in pastoral practice, both for special needs and for providing persons with regular opportunities for receiving the sacraments. If a priest cannot make the visitation, arrangements can be made for a deacon or Eucharistic minister to bring Holy Communion to the homebound or bedridden person.

Sign of the Cross: A sign, ceremonial gesture or movement in the form of a cross by which a person confesses faith in the Holy Trinity and Christ, and intercedes for the blessing of himself or herself, other persons and things. In Roman-Rite practice, a person making the sign touches the fingers of the right hand to forehead, below the breast, left shoulder and right shoulder while saying: *"In the name of the Father, and of the Son, and of the Holy Spirit."* The sign is also made with the thumb on the forehead, the lips, and the breast. For the blessing of persons and objects, a large sign of the cross is made by movement of the right hand. In Eastern-Rite practice, the sign is made with the thumb and first two fingers of the right hand joined together and touching the forehead, below the breast, the right shoulder and the left shoulder; the formula generally used is the doxology, *"O Holy God, O Holy Strong One, O Immortal One."* The Eastern manner of making the sign was general until the first half of the 13th century; by the 17th century, Western practice involved the whole right hand and the reversal of direction from shoulder to shoulder.

Signs of the Times: Contemporary events, trends and features in culture and society, the needs and aspirations of people, all the factors that form the context in and through which the Church has to carry on its saving mission. The Second Vatican Council spoke on numerous occasions about these signs and the relationship between them and a kind of manifestation of God's will, positive or negative, and about subjecting them to judgment and action corresponding to the demands of divine revelation through Scripture, Christ, and the experience, tradition and teaching authority of the Church.

Simony: The deliberate intention and act of selling and/or buying spiritual goods or material things so connected with the spiritual that they cannot be separated therefrom; a violation of the virtue of religion, and a sacrilege, because it wrongfully puts a material price on spiritual things, which cannot be either sold or bought. In Church law, actual sale or purchase is subject to censure in some cases. The term is derived from the name of Simon Magus, who attempted to buy from Sts. Peter and John the power to confirm people in the Holy Spirit (Acts 8:4-24).

Sin: (1) Actual sin is the free and deliberate violation of God's law by thought, word or action. (a) **Mortal** sin — involving serious matter, sufficient reflection and full consent — results in the loss of sanctifying grace and alienation from God, and renders a person incapable of performing meritorious supernatural acts and subject to everlasting punishment. (b) **Venial** sin — involving less serious matter, reflection and consent — does not have such serious consequences. (2) **Original** sin is the sin of Adam, with consequences for all human beings. (*See* separate entry.)

Sins against the Holy Spirit: Despair of salvation, presumption of God's mercy, impugning the known truths of faith, envy at another's spiritual good, obstinacy in sin, final impenitence. Those guilty of such sins stubbornly resist the influence of grace and, as long as they do so, cannot be forgiven.

Sins, Occasions of: Circumstances (persons, places, things, etc.) which easily lead to sin. There is an obligation to avoid voluntary proximate occasions of sin, and to take precautions against the dangers of unavoidable occasions.

Sins That Cry to Heaven for Vengeance: Willful murder, sins against nature, oppression of the poor, widows and orphans, defrauding laborers of their wages.

Sister: Any woman religious, in popular speech; strictly, the title applies only to women religious belonging to institutes whose members never professed solemn vows. Most of the institutes whose members are properly called Sisters were established during and since the 19th century. Women religious with solemn vows, or belonging to institutes whose members formerly professed solemn vows, are properly called nuns.

Sisterhood: A generic term referring to the whole institution of the life of women religious in the Church, or to a particular institute of women religious.

Situation Ethics: A subjective, individualistic ethical theory which denies the binding force of ethical principles as universal laws and preceptive norms of moral conduct, and proposes that morality is determined only by situational conditions and considerations and the intention of the person. It has been criticized for ignoring the principles of objective ethics. (See also **Consequentialism,** p. 136, and **Proportionalism,** p. 153.)

Slander: Attributing to a person faults which he or she does not have; a violation of the obligations of justice and charity, for which restitution is due.

Sloth (Acedia): One of the seven capital sins; spiritual laziness, involving distaste and disgust for spiritual things; spiritual boredom, which saps the vigor of spiritual life. Physical laziness is a counterpart of spiritual sloth.

Sorcery: A kind of black magic in which evil is invoked by means of diabolical intervention; a violation of the virtue of religion.

Soteriology: The division of theology which treats of the mission and work of Christ as Redeemer.

Species, Sacred: The appearances of bread and wine (color, taste, smell, etc.) which remain after the substance has been changed at the Consecration of the Mass into the Body and Blood of Christ. (See **Transubstantiation,** p. 159.)

Spiritism: Attempts to communicate with spirits and departed souls by means of seances, table tapping, ouija boards, and other methods; a violation of the virtue of religion. Spiritualistic practices are noted for fakery.

Stational Churches, Days: Churches, especially in Rome, where the clergy and lay people were accustomed to gather with their bishop on certain days for the celebration of the liturgy. The 25 early titular or parish churches of Rome, plus other churches, each had their turn as the site of divine worship in practices which may have started in the third century. The observances were rather well developed toward the latter part of the 4th century, and by the fifth they included a Mass concelebrated by the pope and attendant priests. On some occasions, the stational liturgy was preceded by a procession from another church called a collecta. There were 42 Roman stational churches in the 8th century, and 89 stational services were scheduled annually in connection with the liturgical seasons. Stational observances fell into disuse toward the end of the Middle Ages. Some revival was begun by John XXIII in 1959 and continued by Paul VI and John Paul II.

Stations (Way) of the Cross: A form of devotion commemorating the Passion and death of Christ, consisting of a series of meditations (stations): (1) his condemnation to death, (2) taking up of the cross, (3) the first fall on the way to Calvary, (4) meeting his Mother, (5) being assisted by Simon of Cyrene and (6) by the woman Veronica who wiped his face, (7) the second fall, (8) meeting the women of Jerusalem, (9) the third fall, (10) being stripped and (11) nailed to the cross, (12) his death, (13) the removal of his body from the cross and (14) his burial. Depictions of these scenes are mounted in most churches, chapels and in some other places, beneath small crosses. A person making the Way of the Cross passes before these stations, or stopping points, pausing at each for meditation. If the stations are made by a group of people, only the leader has to pass from station to station. A plenary indulgence is granted to the faithful who make the stations, under the usual conditions: freedom from all attachment to sin, reception of the sacraments of penance and the Eucharist, and prayers for the intentions of the pope. Those who are impeded from making the stations in the usual manner can gain the same indulgence if, along with the aforementioned conditions, they spend at least a half hour in spiritual reading and meditation on the passion and death of Christ. The stations originated remotely from the practice of Holy Land pilgrims who visited the actual scenes of incidents in the Passion of Christ. Representations elsewhere of at least some of these scenes were known as early as the 5th century. Later, the stations evolved in connection with and as a consequence of strong devotion to the Passion in the 12th and 13th centuries. Franciscans, who were given custody of the Holy Places in 1342, promoted the devotion widely; one of them, St. Leonard of Port Maurice, became known as the greatest preacher of the Way of the Cross in the 18th century. The general features of the devotion were fixed by Clement XII in 1731.

Statutes: Virtually the same as **decrees** (See separate entry), they almost always designate laws of a particular council or synod rather than pontifical laws.

Stigmata: Marks of the wounds suffered by Christ in his crucifixion, in hands and feet by nails, and side by the piercing of a lance. Some persons, called stigmatists, have been reported as recipients or sufferers of marks like these. The Church, however, has never issued any infallible declaration about their possession by anyone, even in the case of St. Francis of Assisi whose stigmata seem to be the best substantiated and may be commemorated in the Roman-Rite liturgy. Ninety percent of some 300 reputed stigmatists have been women. Judgment regarding the presence, significance, and manner of causation of stigmata would depend, among other things, on irrefutable experimental evidence.

Stipend, Mass: An offering given to a priest for applying the fruits of the Mass according to the intention of the donor. The offering is a contribution to the support of the priest. The disposition of the fruits of the sacrifice, in line with doctrine concerning the Mass in particular and prayer in general, is subject to the will of God. Mass offerings and intentions were the subjects of a decree approved by John Paul II and made public Mar. 22, 1991: (1) Normally, no more than one offering should be accepted for a Mass; the Mass should be offered in accord with the donor's intention; the priest who accepts the offering should celebrate the Mass himself or have another priest do so. (2) Several Mass intentions, for which offerings have been made, can be combined for a "collective" application of a single Mass only if the previous and explicit consent of the donors is obtained. Such Masses are an exception to the general rule.

Stole Fee: An offering given on certain occasions; e.g., at a baptism, wedding, funeral, for the support of the clergy who administer the sacraments and perform other sacred rites.

Stoup: A vessel used to contain holy water.

Suffragan See: Any diocese, except the archdiocese, within a province.

Suicide: The taking of one's own life; a violation of God's dominion over human life. Ecclesiastical burial is denied to persons while in full possession of their faculties; it is permitted in cases of doubt.

Supererogation: Actions which go beyond the obligations of duty and the requirements enjoined by God's law as necessary for salvation. Examples of these works are the profession and observance of the evangelical counsels of poverty, chastity, and obedience, and efforts to practice charity to the highest degree.

Supernatural: Above the natural; that which exceeds and is not due or owed to the essence, exigencies, requirements, powers and merits of created nature. While human beings have no claim on supernatural things and do not need them in order to exist and act on a natural level, they do need them in order to exist and act in the higher order or economy of grace established by God for their salvation. God has freely given them certain things which are beyond the powers and rights of their human nature. Examples of the supernatural are: grace, a kind of participation by human beings in the divine life, by which they become capable of performing acts meritorious for salvation; divine revelation by which God manifests himself to them and makes known truth that is inaccessible to human reason alone; faith, by which they believe divine truth because of the authority of God who reveals it through Sacred Scripture and tradition and the teaching of his Church.

Suspension: A censure by which a cleric is forbidden to exercise some or all of his powers of orders and jurisdiction, or to accept the financial support of his benefices.

Syllabus, The: (1) When not qualified, the term refers to the list of 80 errors accompanying Pope Pius IX's encyclical *Quanta Cura*, issued in 1864. (2) The Syllabus of St. Pius X in the decree *Lamentabili*, issued by the Holy Office July 4, 1907, condemning 65 heretical propositions of modernism. This schedule of errors was followed shortly by that pope's encyclical *Pascendi*, the principal ecclesiastical document against modernism, issued Sept. 8, 1907.

Synod, Diocesan: Meeting of representative persons of a diocese — priests, religious, lay persons — with the bishop, called by him for the purpose of considering and taking action on matters affecting the life and mission of the Church in the diocese. Persons taking part in a synod have consultative status; the bishop alone is the legislator, with power to authorize synodal decrees. According to canon law, every diocese should have a synod every 10 years.

T

Tabernacle: The receptacle in which the Blessed Sacrament is reserved in churches, chapels, and oratories. It is to be immovable, solid, locked, and located in a prominent place.

Te Deum: The opening Latin words, Thee, God, of a hymn of praise and thanksgiving prescribed for use in the Office of Readings of the Liturgy of the Hours on many Sundays, solemnities and feasts.

Temperance: Moderation, one of the four cardinal virtues.

Temptation: Any enticement to sin, from any source: the strivings of one's own faculties, the action of the devil, other persons, circumstances of life, etc. Temptation itself is not sin. Temptation can be avoided and overcome with the use of prudence and the help of grace.

Thanksgiving: An expression of gratitude to God

for his goodness and the blessings he grants; one of the four ends of prayer.

Theism: A philosophy which admits the existence of God and the possibility of divine revelation; it is generally monotheistic and acknowledges God as transcendent and also active in the world. Because it is a philosophy rather than a system of theology derived from revelation, it does not include specifically Christian doctrines, like those concerning the Trinity, the Incarnation and Redemption.

Theodicy: From the Greek for God (theos) and judgment (dike), the study of God as he can be known by natural reason, rather than from supernatural revelation. First used by Gottfried Leibnitz (1646-1716), its primary objective is to make God's omnipotence compatible with the existence of evil.

Theological Virtues: The virtues which have God for their direct object: faith, or belief in God's infallible teaching; hope, or confidence in divine assistance; charity, or love of God. They are given to a person with grace in the first instance, through baptism and incorporation in Christ.

Theology: Knowledge of God and religion, deriving from and based on the data of divine Revelation, organized and systematized according to some kind of scientific method. It involves systematic study and presentation of the truths of divine Revelation in Sacred Scripture, tradition, and the teaching of the Church. Theology has been divided under various subject headings. Some of the major fields have been: dogmatic (systematic theology), moral, pastoral, historical, ascetical (the practice of virtue and means of attaining holiness and perfection), sacramental, and spiritual (higher states of religious experience). Other subject headings include ecumenism (Christian unity, interfaith relations), ecclesiology (the nature and constitution of the Church), and Mariology (doctrine concerning the Blessed Virgin Mary), etc.

Theotokos: From the Greek for God-bearer, the preeminent title given to the Blessed Mother in the Oriental Church. This title has very ancient roots, stretching as far back as the third century but it did not became official in the Church until the Council of Ephesus in 431.

Thomism: The philosophy based on St. Thomas Aquinas (1224/5-1274), which is mandated to be the dominant philosophy used in Catholic educational institutions. (See also **Neo-Scholasticism** and **Scholasticism**.)

Tithing: Contribution of a portion of one's income, originally one-tenth, for purposes of religion and charity. The practice is mentioned 46 times in the Bible. In early Christian times, tithing was adopted in continuance of Old Testament practices of the Jewish people, and the earliest positive Church legislation on the subject was enacted in 567. Catholics are bound in conscience to contribute to the support of their church, but the manner in which they do so is not fixed by law. Tithing, which amounts to a pledged contribution of a portion of one's income, has aroused new attention in recent years in the United States.

Titular Sees: Dioceses where the Church once flourished but which now exist only in name or title. Bishops without a territorial or residential diocese of their own; e.g., auxiliary bishops, are given titular sees. There are more than 2,000 titular sees; 16 of them are in the United States.

Transfinalization, Transignification: Terms coined to express the sign value of consecrated bread and wine with respect to the presence and action of Christ in the Eucharistic sacrifice and the spiritually vivifying purpose of the Eucharistic banquet in Holy Communion. The theory behind the terms has strong undertones of existential and "sign" philosophy, and has been criticized for its openness to interpretation at variance with the doctrine of transubstantiation and the abiding presence of Christ under the appearances of bread and wine after the sacrifice of the Mass and Communion have been completed. The terms, if used as substitutes for transubstantiation, are unacceptable; if they presuppose transubstantiation, they are acceptable as clarifications of its meaning.

Transubstantiation: "The way Christ is made present in this sacrament (Holy Eucharist) is none other than by the change of the whole substance of the bread into his Body, and of the whole substance of the wine into his Blood (in the Consecration at Mass), this unique and wonderful change the Catholic Church rightly calls transubstantiation" (encyclical *Mysterium Fidei* of Paul VI, Sept. 3, 1965). The first official use of the term was made by the Fourth Council of the Lateran in 1215. Authoritative teaching on the subject was issued by the Council of Trent.

Treasury of the Church: The superabundant merits of Christ and the saints from which the Church draws to confer spiritual benefits, such as indulgences.

Triduum: A three-day series of public or private devotions.

U-Z

Ultramontanism: The movement found primarily in France during the 19th century that advocated a strong sense of devotion and service to the Holy See. Generally considered a reaction to the antipapal tendencies of Gallicanism, its name was derived from the Latin for "over the mountains," a reference to the Alps, beyond which rested Rome and the Holy See.

Unction: From the Latin, ungere, meaning to anoint or smear, a term used to denote the Sacrament of the Sick (or the Anointing of the Sick); it was more commonly termed Extreme Unction and was given as an anointing to a person just before death.

Universal Law: See **Law**.

Urbi et Orbi: A Latin phrase meaning "To the City and to the World" that is a blessing given by the Holy Father. Normally, the first *Urbi et Orbi* delivered by a pontiff is immediately after his election by the College of Cardinals. This is a blessing accompanied by a short address to the crowds in St. Peter's Square and to the world; frequently, as with Pope John Paul II in 1978, it is delivered in as many languages as possible. The pope also delivers an *Urbi et Orbi* each year at Christmas and at Easter.

Usury: Excessive interest charged for the loan and use of money; a violation of justice.

Vagi: A Latin word meaning wanderers that is used to describe any homeless person with no fixed residence.

Veni Creator Spiritus: A Latin phrase, meaning "Come, Creator Spirit" that is part of a hymn sung to the Holy Spirit. The hymn invokes the presence of the Holy Spirit and was perhaps first composed by Rabanus Maurus (776-856). The hymn is commonly sung as part of the Divine Office, papal elections, episcopal consecrations, ordinations, councils, synods, canonical elections, and confirmations.

Venial Sin: See under **Sin**.

Veronica: A word resulting from the combination of a Latin word for true, vera, and a Greek word for image, eikon, designating a likeness of the face of Christ or the name of a woman said to have given him a cloth on which he caused an imprint of his face to appear. The veneration at Rome of a likeness depicted on cloth dates from about the end of the 10th century; it figured in a popular devotion during the Middle Ages, and in the Holy Face devotion practiced since the 19th century. A faint, indiscernible likeness said to be of this kind is preserved in St. Peter's Basilica. The origin of the likeness is uncertain, and the identity of the woman is unknown. Before the 14th century, there were no known artistic representations of an incident concerning a woman who wiped the face of Christ with a piece of cloth while he was carrying the cross to Calvary.

Vespers: From the Latin for evening, the evening service of the Divine Office, also known as Evening Prayer, or among Anglicans as Evensong.

Viaticum: Holy Communion given to those in danger of death. The word, derived from Latin, means provision for a journey through death to life hereafter.

Vicar Forane: A Latin term meaning "deputy outside" that is applied to the priest given authority by the local bishop over a certain area or region of the diocese.

Vicar General: A priest or bishop appointed by the bishop of a diocese to serve as his deputy, with ordinary executive power, in the administration of the diocese.

Vicar, Judicial: The title given to the chief judge and head of the tribunal of a diocese.

Virginity: Observance of perpetual sexual abstinence. The state of virginity, which is embraced for the love of God by religious with a public vow or by others with a private vow, was singled out for high praise by Christ (Mt 19:10-12) and has always been so regarded by the Church. In the encyclical *Sacra Virginitas*, Pius XII stated: "Holy virginity and that perfect chastity which is consecrated to the service of God is without doubt among the most perfect treasures which the founder of the Church has left in heritage to the society which he established." Paul VI approved in 1970 a rite in which women can consecrate their virginity "to Christ and their brethren" without becoming members of a religious institute. The *Ordo Consecrationis Virginum*, a revision of a rite promulgated by Clement VII in 1596, is traceable to the Roman liturgy of about 50

Virtue: A habit or established capability for performing good actions. Virtues are natural (acquired and increased by repeating good acts) and/or supernatural (given with grace by God).

Visions: A charism by which a specially chosen individual is able to behold a person or something that is naturally invisible. A vision should not be confused with an illusion or hallucination. Like other charisms, a vision is granted for the good of people; it should be noted, however, that they are not essential for holiness or salvation. Many saints throughout history have beheld visions, among them St. Thomas Aquinas, St. Teresa of Ávila, St. John of the Cross, and St. Francis of Assisi.

Vocation: A call to a way of life. Generally, the term applies to the common call of all persons, from God, to holiness and salvation. Specifically, it refers to particular states of life, each called a vocation, in which response is made to this universal call; viz., marriage, the religious life and/or priesthood, the single state freely chosen or accepted for the accomplishment of God's will. The term also applies to the various occupations in which persons make a living. The Church supports the freedom of each individual in choosing a particular vocation, and reserves the right to pass on the acceptability of candidates for the priesthood and religious life. Signs or indicators of particular vocations are many, including a person's talents and interests, circumstances and obligations, invitations of grace and willingness to respond thereto.

Vow: A promise made to God with sufficient knowledge and freedom, which has as its object a moral good that is possible and better than its voluntary omission. A person who professes a vow binds himself or herself by the virtue of religion to fulfill the promise. The best known examples of vows are those of poverty, chastity and obedience professed by religious (See **Counsels, Evangelical**, p. 137; individual entries). Public vows are made before a competent person, acting as an agent of the Church, who accepts the profession in the name of the Church, thereby giving public recognition to the person's dedication and consecration to God and divine worship. Vows of this kind are either solemn, rendering all contrary acts invalid as well as unlawful; or simple, rendering contrary acts unlawful. Solemn vows are for life; simple vows are for a definite period of time or for life. Vows professed without public recognition by the Church are called private vows. The Church, which has authority to accept and give public recognition to vows, also has authority to dispense persons from their obligations for serious reasons.

Witness, Christian: Practical testimony or evidence given by Christians of their faith in all circumstances of life — by prayer and general conduct, through good example and good works, etc.; being and acting in accordance with Christian belief; actual practice of the Christian faith.

Zeal: The expression of charity that permits one to serve God and others fully with the objective of furthering the Mystical Body of Christ.

Zucchetto: A small skullcap worn by ecclesiastics, most notably prelates and derived from the popular Italian vernacular term *zucca,* meaning a pumpkin, and used as slang for head. The Holy Father wears a white zucchetto made of watered silk; cardinals use scarlet, and bishops use purple. Priests of the monsignorial rank may wear black with purple piping. All others may wear simple black. The origins of the zucchetto are traced back to the early Middle Ages when clergy adopted a skullcap to provide a covering for the part of the head that had been shaved during tonsure. It was worn especially during the winter. The zucchetto worn by cardinals is also usually of silk.

The Church Calendar

The calendar of the Roman Church consists of an arrangement throughout the year of a series of liturgical seasons, commemorations of divine mysteries and commemorations of saints for purposes of worship.

The key to the calendar is the central celebration of the Easter Triduum, commemorating the supreme saving act of Jesus in his death and resurrection to which all other observances and acts of worship are related.

The purposes of this calendar were outlined in the Constitution on the Sacred Liturgy (*Sacrosanctum Concilium*, Nos. 102-105) promulgated by the Second Vatican Council.

"Within the cycle of a year ... (the Church) unfolds the whole mystery of Christ, not only from his incarnation and birth until his ascension, but also as reflected in the day of Pentecost, and the expectation of a blessed, hoped-for return of the Lord.

"Recalling thus the mysteries of redemption, the Church opens to the faithful the riches of her Lord's powers and merits, so that these are in some way made present at all times, and the faithful are enabled to lay hold of them and become filled with saving grace (No. 102).

"In celebrating this annual cycle of Christ's mysteries, holy Church honors with special love the Blessed Mary, Mother of God" (No. 103).

"The Church has also included in the annual cycle days devoted to the memory of the martyrs and the other saints (who) sing God's perfect praise in heaven and offer prayers for us. By celebrating the passage of these saints from earth to heaven the Church proclaims the paschal mystery as achieved in the saints who have suffered and been glorified with Christ; she proposes them to the faithful as examples who draw all to the Father through Christ, and through their merits she pleads for God's favors (No. 104).

"In the various seasons of the year and according to her traditional discipline, the Church completes the formation of the faithful by means of pious practices for soul and body, by instruction, prayer, and works of penance and mercy (No. 105)."

The Roman Calendar

Norms for a revised calendar for the Western Church as decreed by the Second Vatican Council were approved by Paul VI in the *motu proprio Mysterii Paschalis* dated Feb. 14, 1969. The revised calendar was promulgated a month later by a decree of the Congregation for Divine Worship and went into effect Jan. 1, 1970, with provisional modifications. Full implementation of all its parts was delayed in 1970 and 1971, pending the completion of work on related liturgical texts. The U.S. bishops ordered the calendar into effect for 1972.

The Seasons

Advent: The liturgical year begins with the first Sunday of Advent, which introduces a season of four weeks or slightly less duration with the theme of expectation of the coming of Christ. During the first two weeks, the final coming of Christ as Lord and Judge at the end of the world is the focus of attention. From Dec. 17 to 24, the emphasis shifts to anticipation of the celebration of his Nativity on the solemnity of Christmas.

Advent has four Sundays. Since the 10th century, the first Sunday has marked the beginning of the liturgical year in the Western Church. In the Middle Ages, a kind of pre-Christmas fast was in vogue during the season.

Christmas Season: The Christmas season begins with the vigil of Christmas and lasts until the Sunday after Jan. 6, inclusive.

The period between the end of the Christmas season and the beginning of Lent belongs to the ordinary time of the year. Of variable length, the pre-Lenten phase of this season includes what were formerly called the Sundays after Epiphany and the suppressed Sundays of Septuagesima, Sexagesima and Quinquagesima.

Lent: The penitential season of Lent begins on Ash Wednesday, which occurs between Feb. 4 and Mar. 11, depending on the date of Easter, and lasts until the Mass of the Lord's Supper (Holy Thursday). It has six Sundays. The sixth Sunday marks the beginning of Holy Week and is known as Passion (formerly called Palm) Sunday.

The origin of Lenten observances dates back to the fourth century or earlier.

Easter Triduum: The Easter Triduum begins with evening Mass of the Lord's Supper and ends with Evening Prayer on Easter Sunday.

Easter Season: The Easter season whose theme is resurrection from sin to the life of grace, lasts for 50 days, from Easter to Pentecost. Easter, the first Sunday after the first full moon following the vernal equinox, occurs between Mar. 22 and Apr. 25. The terminal phase of the Easter season, between the solemnities of the Ascension of the Lord and Pentecost, stresses anticipation of the coming and action of the Holy Spirit.

Ordinary Time: The season of Ordinary Time begins on Monday (or Tuesday if the feast of the Baptism of the Lord is celebrated on that Monday) after the Sunday following Jan. 6 and continues until the day before Ash Wednesday, inclusive. It begins again on the Monday after Pentecost and ends on the Saturday before the first Sunday of Advent. It consists of 33 or 34 weeks. The last Sunday is celebrated as the Solemnity of Christ the King. The overall purpose of the season is to elaborate the themes of salvation history.

The various liturgical seasons are characterized in part by the scriptural readings and Mass prayers assigned to each of them. During Advent, for example, the readings are messianic; during the Easter season, from the Acts of the Apostles, chronicling the Resurrection and the original proclamation of Christ by the Apostles, and from the Gospel of John; during Lent, baptismal and penitential passages. Mass prayers reflect the meaning and purpose of the various seasons.

Commemorations of Saints

The commemorations of saints are celebrated concurrently with the liturgical seasons and feasts of our Lord. Their purpose is to illustrate the paschal mysteries as reflected in the lives of saints, to honor them as heroes of holiness, and to appeal for their intercession.

In line with revised regulations, some former feasts were either abolished or relegated to observance in particular places by local option for one of two reasons: (1) lack of sufficient historical evidence for observance of the feasts; or, (2) lack of universal significance.

The commemoration of a saint, as a general rule, is observed on the day of death (*dies natalis*, day of birth to glory with God in heaven). Exceptions to this rule include the feasts of St. John the Baptist, who is honored on the day of his birth; Sts. Basil the Great and Gregory Nazianzen; and the brother Saints, Cyril and Methodius, who are commemorated in joint feasts. Application of this general rule in the revised calendar resulted in date changes of some observances.

Sundays and Other Holy Days

Sunday is the original Christian feast day and holy day of obligation because of the unusually significant events of salvation history which took place and are commemorated on the first day of the week viz., the Resurrection of Christ, the key event of his life and the fundamental fact of Christianity; and the descent of the Holy Spirit upon the Apostles on Pentecost, the birthday of the Church. The transfer of observance of the Lord's Day from the Sabbath to Sunday was made in apostolic times. The Mass and Liturgy of the Hours (Divine Office) of each Sunday reflect the themes and set the tones of the various liturgical seasons.

Holy days of obligation are special occasions on which Catholics who have reached the age of reason are seriously obliged, as on Sundays, to assist at Mass: they are also to refrain from work and involvement with business that impedes participation in divine worship and the enjoyment of appropriate rest and relaxation.

The holy days of obligation observed in the U.S. are: Christmas, the Nativity of Jesus, Dec. 25; Solemnity of Mary the Mother of God, Jan. 1; Ascension of the Lord; Assumption of Blessed Mary the Virgin, Aug. 15; All Saints' Day, Nov. 1; Immaculate Conception of Blessed Mary the Virgin, Dec. 8.

The precept to attend Mass is abrogated in the U.S. whenever the Solemnity of Mary, the Assumption, or All Saints falls on a Saturday or Monday (1991 decree of U.S. bishops; approved by Holy See July 4, 1992, and effective Jan. 1, 1993).

In addition to these, there are four other holy days of obligation prescribed in the general law of the Church which are not so observed in the U.S.: Epiphany, Jan. 6; St. Joseph, Mar. 19; Corpus Christi; Sts. Peter and Paul, June 29. The solemnities of Epiphany and Corpus Christi are transferred to a Sunday in countries where they are not observed as holy days of obligation.

Solemnities, Feasts, Memorials

Categories of observances according to dignity and manner of observance are: solemnities, principal days in the calendar (observance begins with Evening Prayer I of the preceding day; some have their own vigil Mass); feasts (celebrated within the limits of the natural day); obligatory memorials (celebrated throughout the Church); optional memorials (observable by choice).

Fixed observances are those that are regularly celebrated on the same calendar day each year.

Movable observances are those that are not observed on the same calendar day each year. Examples of these are Easter (the first Sunday after the first full moon following the vernal equinox), Ascension (40 days after Easter), Pentecost (50 days after Easter), Trinity Sunday (first after Pentecost), Christ the King (last Sunday of the liturgical year).

Weekdays, Days of Prayer

Weekdays are those on which no proper feast or vigil is celebrated in the Mass or Liturgy of the Hours (Divine Office). On such days, the Mass may be that of the preceding Sunday, which expresses the liturgical spirit of the season, an optional memorial, a votive Mass, or a Mass for the dead. weekdays of Advent and Lent are in a special category of their own.

Days of Prayer: Dioceses, at times to be designated by local bishops, should observe "days or periods of prayer for the fruits of the earth, prayer for human rights and equality, prayer for world justice and peace, and penitential observance outside of Lent." So stated the Instruction on Particular Calendars (No. 331) issued by the Congregation for the Sacraments and Divine Worship June 24, 1970.

These days are contemporary equivalents of what were formerly called ember and rogation days.

Ember days originated at Rome about the fifth century, probably as Christian replacements for seasonal festivals of agrarian cults. They were observances of penance, thanksgiving, and petition for divine blessing on the various seasons; they also were occasions of special prayer for clergy to be ordained. These days were observed four times a year.

Rogation days originated in France about the fifth century. They were penitential in character and also occasions of prayer for a bountiful harvest and protection against evil.

Days and Times of Penance

Fridays throughout the year and the season of Lent are penitential times.

Abstinence: Catholics in the U.S., from the age of 14 throughout life, are obliged to abstain from meat on Ash Wednesday, the Fridays of Lent and Good Friday. The law forbids the use of meat, but not of eggs, the products of milk or condiments made of animal fat. Permissible are soup flavored with meat, meat gravy and sauces. The obligation to abstain from meat is not in force on days celebrated as solemnities (e.g., Christmas, Sacred Heart).

Fasting: Catholics in the U.S., from the day after their 18th birthday to the day after their 59th birthday, are also obliged to fast on Ash Wednesday and Good Friday. The law allows only one full meal a day, but does not prohibit the taking of some food in the morning and evening, observing as far as quantity and quality are concerned approved local custom. The order of meals is optional, i.e., the full meal may be taken in the evening instead of at midday. Also: (1) The combined quantity of food taken at the two lighter meals should not exceed the quantity taken at the full meal; (2) The drinking of ordinary liquids does not break the fast.

Obligation: There is a general obligation to do penance for sins committed and for the remission of punishment resulting from sin. Substantial observance of fasting and abstinence, prescribed for the community of the Church, is a matter of serious obligation; it allows, however, for alternate ways of doing penance (e.g., works of charity, prayer and prayer-related practices, almsgiving).

Readings at Mass

Scriptural readings for Masses on Sundays and holy days are indicated under the appropriate dates in the calendar pages for the year 2014-15. The Year B cycle is prescribed for Sunday Masses in liturgical year 2015, Nov. 30, 2014 to Nov. 22, 2015. In Year B, most of the Gospel readings are from the Gospel of Mark. The Year C cycle is prescribed for Sunday Masses in liturgical year 2016.

The Year I weekday cycle is prescribed for 2015, from Nov. 29, 2014. The Year II cycle is prescribed for 2016.

Monthly Prayer Intentions

Intentions chosen and recommended by Pope Benedict XVI to the prayers of the faithful and circulated by the Apostleship of Prayer are given for each month of the calendar. Pope John Paul II expressed his desire that all Catholics make these intentions their own "in the certainty of being united with the Holy Father and praying according to his intentions and desires."

Celebrations in U.S. Particular Calendar

The General Norms for the Liturgical Year and the Calendar, issued in 1969 and published along with the General Roman Calendar for the Universal Church, noted that the calendar consists of the General Roman Calendar used by the entire Church and of particular calendars used in particular churches (nations or dioceses) or in families of religious.

The particular calendar for the U.S. contains the following celebrations. **January**: 4, Elizabeth Ann Seton; 5, John Neumann; 6, André Bessette; Day of Prayer for Unborn Children. **March**: 3, Katharine Drexel. **May**: 10, Damien DeVeuster; 15, Isidore the Farmer. **July**: 1, Bl. Junípero Serra; 4, Independence Day; 14, Kateri Tekakwitha. **August**: 18, Jane Frances de Chantal. **September**: 9, Peter Claver. **October**: 6, Bl. Marie-Rose Durocher; 19, Isaac Jogues and John de Brébeuf and Companions; 20, Paul of the Cross. **November**: 13, Frances Xavier Cabrini; 18, Rose Philippine Duchesne; 23, Bl. Miguel Agustín Pro; fourth Thursday, Thanksgiving Day. **December**: 9, Juan Diego; 12, Our Lady of Guadalupe.

TABLE OF MOVABLE FEASTS

| Year | Ash Wed. | Easter | Ascension | Pentecost | Weeks of Ordinary Time | | | | First Sunday of Advent |
| | | | | | Before Lent | | After Pentcst. | | |
					Weeks	Ends	Weeks	Begins	
2014	Mar. 5	Apr. 20	May 29	June 8	8	Mar. 4	25	June 9	Nov. 30
2015	Feb. 18	Apr. 5	May 14	May 24	6	Feb. 17	27	May 25	Nov. 29
2016	Feb. 10	Mar. 27	May 5	May 15	5	Feb. 9	28	May 16	Nov. 27
2017	Mar. 1	Apr. 16	May 25	June 4	8	Feb. 28	26	June 5	Dec. 3
2018	Feb. 14	Apr. 1	May 10	May 20	6	Feb. 13	28	May 21	Dec. 2
2019	Mar. 6	Apr. 21	May 30	June 9	8	Mar. 5	25	June 10	Dec. 1
2020	Feb. 26	Apr. 12	May 21	May 31	7	Feb. 25	26	June 1	Nov. 29
2021	Feb. 17	Apr. 4	May 13	May 23	6	Feb. 16	27	May 24	Nov. 28
2022	Mar. 2	Apr. 17	May 26	June 5	8	Mar. 1	25	June 6	Nov. 27
2023	Feb. 22	Apr. 9	May 18	May 28	7	Feb. 21	27	May 29	Dec. 3
2024	Feb. 14	Mar. 31	May 9	May 19	6	Feb. 13	28	May 20	Dec. 1
2025	Mar. 5	Apr. 20	May 29	June 8	8	Mar. 4	25	June 9	Nov. 30
2026	Feb. 18	Apr. 5	May 14	May 24	6	Feb. 17	27	May 25	Nov. 29
2027	Feb. 10	Mar. 28	May 6	May 16	5	Feb. 9	28	May 17	Nov. 28
2028	Mar. 1	Apr. 16	May 25	June 4	8	Feb. 29	26	June 5	Dec. 3
2029	Feb. 14	Apr. 1	May 10	May 20	6	Feb. 13	28	May 21	Dec. 2
2030	Mar. 6	Apr. 21	May 30	June 9	9	Mar. 7	25	June 10	Dec. 1
2031	Feb. 26	Apr. 13	May 22	June 1	7	Feb. 25	26	June 2	Nov. 30
2032	Feb. 11	Mar. 28	May 6	May 16	5	Feb. 11	28	May 17	Nov. 28
2033	Mar. 2	Apr. 17	May 26	June 5	8	Mar. 1	25	June 6	Nov. 27
2034	Feb. 22	Apr. 9	May 18	May 28	7	Feb. 21	27	May 29	Dec. 3
2035	Feb. 7	Mar. 25	May 3	May 13	5	Feb. 6	29	May 14	Dec. 2
2036	Feb. 27	Apr. 13	May 22	June 1	7	Feb. 26	26	June 2	Nov. 30
2037	Feb. 18	Apr. 5	May 14	May 24	6	Feb. 17	27	May 25	Nov. 29
2038	Mar. 10	Apr. 25	June 3	June 13	9	Mar. 9	24	June 14	Nov. 28
2039	Feb. 23	Apr. 10	May 19	May 29	7	Feb. 22	26	May 30	Nov. 27

2015 CALENDAR

January 2015

Universal: That those from diverse religious traditions and all people of good will may work together for peace.

Evangelization: That in this year dedicated to consecrated life, religious men and women may rediscover the joy of following Christ and strive to serve the poor with zeal.

1 Thurs. The Octave Day of the Nativity of the Lord; Solemnity of Mary, the Holy Mother of God. (Nm 6:22-27; Gal 4:4-7; Lk 2:16-21.)

2 Fri. Sts. Basil the Great and Gregory Nazianzus, bishops and Doctors of the Church; memorial.

3 Sat. Christmas Weekday, Most Holy Name of Jesus.

4 Sun The Epiphany of the Lord; solemnity. (Is 60:1-6; Eph 3:2-3a,5-6; Mt 2:1-12.)

5 Mon. St. John Neumann, bishop; memorial.

6 Tues. Christmas Weekday; St. André Bessette, religious; optional memorial.

7 Wed. Christmas Weekday; St. Raymond of Peñafort, priest; optional memorial.

8 Thurs. Christmas Weekday.

9 Fri. Christmas Weekday.

10 Sat. Christmas Weekday.

11 Sun The Baptism of the Lord; feast. (Is 42:1-4,6-7 or Is 55:1-11; Acts 10:34-38 or 1 Jn 5:1-9; Mk 1:7-11.)

12 Mon. Weekday (First Week in Ordinary Time).

13 Tues. Weekday. St. Hilary, bishop-doctor; memorial.

14 Wed. Weekday.

15 Thurs. Weekday.

16 Fri. Weekday.

17 Sat. St. Anthony; memorial.

18 Sun Second Sunday in Ordinary Time. (1 Sm 3:3b-10, 19; 1 Cor 6:13c-15a,17-20; Jn 1:35-42.)

19 Mon. Weekday.

20 Tues. Weekday. St. Fabian, pope-martyr; St. Sebastian, martyr; memorial.

21 Wed. St. Agnes, virgin and martyr; memorial.

22 Thurs. Day of Prayer for the Legal Protection of Unborn Children; memorial.

23 Fri. Weekday. St. Vincent, deacon and martyr; St. Marianne Cope, virgin; memorial.

24 Sat. St. Francis de Sales, bishop-doctor; memorial.

25 Sun Third Sunday of Ordinary Time. (Jon 3:1-5,10; 1 Cor 7:29-31; Mk 1:14-20.)

26 Mon. Sts. Timothy and Titus, bishops; memorial.

27 Tues. Weekday, St. Angela Merici, virgin; memorial.

28 Wed. St. Thomas Aquinas, priest and Doctor of the Church; memorial.

29 Thurs. Weekday.

30 Fri. Weekday.

31 Sat. St. John Bosco, priest; memorial.

Observances: Solemnity of the Mother of God, a holy day of obligation, and a papal message for the World Day of Peace, Jan. 1; ordination of bishops by the Pope on the Solemnity of the Epiphany, Jan. 6. Week of Prayer for Christian Unity, Jan. 18-25 concluding with celebration of the Conversion of St. Paul, Jan. 25; National Day of Prayer for Life and March for Life, in connection with the anniversary of the 1973 *Roe vs. Wade* and *Dole vs. Bolton* pro-abortion decisions of the U.S. Supreme Court, Jan. 21-22. Other celebrations in the month of January: Sts. Basil the Great and Gregory Nazianzus, Jan. 2; St. Elizabeth Ann Seton, Jan. 4; St. Anthony, Jan. 17; St. Francis De Sales, Jan. 24; St. Thomas Aquinas, Jan. 28; St. John Bosco, Jan. 31.

February 2015

Universal: That prisoners, especially the young, may be able to rebuild lives of dignity.

Evangelization: That married people who are separated may find welcome and support in the Christian community.

1 Sun Fourth Sunday in Ordinary Time. (Dt 18:15-20; 1 Cor 7:32-35; Mk 1:21-28.)

2 Mon. The Presentation of the Lord; feast

3 Tues. Weekday. St. Blaise, bishop-martyr; St. Ansgar, bishop; optional memorial.

4 Wed. Weekday.

5 Thurs. St. Agatha, virgin and martyr; memorial.

6 Fri. St. Paul Miki and Companions, martyrs; memorial.

7 Sat. Weekday.

8 Sun. Fifth Sunday in Ordinary Time. (Jb 7:1-4,6-7; 1 Cor 9:16-19,22-23; Mk 1:29-39.)

9 Mon. Weekday.

10 Tues. St. Scholastica, virgin, memorial.

11 Wed. Weekday.

12 Thurs. Weekday green

13 Fri. Weekday.

14 Sat. Sts. Cyril, monk, and Methodius, bishop; memorial.

15 Sun. Sixth Sunday in Ordinary Time. (Lv 13:1-2,44-46; 1 Cor 10:31-11:1; Mk 1:40-45.)

16 Mon. Weekday.

17 Tues. Weekday. The Seven Holy Founders of the Servite Order; optional memorial.

18 Wed. Ash Wednesday. (Jl 2:12-18; 2 Cor 5:20-6:2; Mt 6:1-6,16-18.)

19 Thurs. Thursday after Ash Wednesday.

20 Fri. Friday after Ash Wednesday.

21 Sat. Saturday after Ash Wednesday. St. Peter Damian, bishop-doctor, optional memorial.

22 Sun. First Sunday of Lent. (Gn 9:8-15; 1 Pt 3:18-22; Mk 1:12-15.)

23 Mon. Lenten Weekday. St. Polycarp, bishop and martyr; optional memorial.

24 Tues. Lenten Weekday.

25 Wed. Lenten Weekday.

26 Thurs. Lenten Weekday.

27 Fri. Lenten Weekday.

28 Sat. Lenten Weekday.

Observances:

The Presentation of the Child Jesus in the Temple, traditional day for the blessings of candles that will be used throughout the year. The Lenten Season begins with Ash Wednesday (Feb. 18) when ashes are blessed and imposed on the forehead of the faithful to remind them of their obligation to do penance for sins, to seek spiritual renewal by means of prayer, fasting and good works. Catholics are called to bear the trials and difficulties of everyday life. Optional memorial of St. Blasé, bishop-martyr, whose intercession is sought against ailments of the throat and other evils. Optional memorial of Our Lady of Lourdes which is also World Day of the Sick, a day of prayer, healing and anointing of those who are ill. Other celebrations in the month of February: St. Agatha, Feb. 5; St. Paul Miki and Companions, Feb. 6; St. Scholastic, Feb. 10; Sts. Cyril and Methodius, Feb. 14; the Chair of Saint Peter, Feb. 22.

March 2015

Universal: That those involved in scientific research may serve the well-being of the whole human person.

Evangelization: That the unique contribution of women to the life of the Church may be recognized always.

1 Sun. Second Sunday of Lent. (Gn 22:1-2,9a,10-13, 15-18; Rom 8:31b-34; Mk 9:2-10.)

2 Mon. Lenten Weekday.

3 Tues. Lenten Weekday. St. Katharine Drexel, virgin; optional memorial.

4 Wed. Lenten Weekday. St. Casimir; optional memorial.

5 Thurs. Lenten Weekday.

6 Fri. Lenten Weekday.

7 Sat. Lenten Weekday. Sts. Perpetua and Felicity, martyrs; optional memorial.

8 Sun. Third Sunday of Lent. (Ex 20:1-17 or 20:1-3,7-8, 12-17; 1 Cor 1:22-25; Jn 2:13-25.)

9 Mon. Lenten Weekday. St. Frances of Rome, religious; optional memorial.

10 Tues. Lenten Weekday.

11 Wed. Lenten Weekday.

12 Thurs. Lenten Weekday.

13 Fri. Lenten Weekday.

14 Sat. Lenten Weekday.

15 Sun. Fourth Sunday of Lent. (2 Chr 36:14-16,19-23; Eph 2:4-10; Jn 3:14-21.)

16 Mon. Lenten Weekday.

17 Tues. Lenten Weekday. St. Patrick, bishop; commemoration.

18 Wed. Lenten Weekday. St. Cyril of Jerusalem, bishop and Doctor of the Church; commemoration.

19 Thurs. St. Joseph, Spouse of the Blessed Virgin Mary; solemnity.

20 Fri. Lenten Weekday.

21 Sat. Lenten Weekday.

22 Sun. Fifth Sunday of Lent. (Jer 31:31-34; Heb 5:7-9; Jn 12:20-33.)

23 Mon. Lenten Weekday. St. Turibius of Mongrovejo, bishop; optional memorial.

24 Tues. Lenten Weekday.

25 Wed. The Annunciation of the Lord; solemnity.

26 Thurs. Lenten Weekday.

27 Fri. Lenten Weekday.

28 Sat. Lenten Weekday.

29 Sun. Palm Sunday; The Lord's Passion. (Mk 11:1-10 or Jn 12:12-16; Is 50:4-7/Phil 2:6-11; Mk 14:1-15:47 or 15:1-39.)

30 Mon. Monday of Holy Week.

31 Tues. Tuesday of Holy Week.

Observances:

Catholics are reminded of the serious obligation to fast and abstain on those appointed days during the Lenten season as well as the opportunity for other acts of mortification and sacrifice. Unless otherwise indicated, all memorials celebrated during Lent are treated as commemorations. Commemorations may be celebrated during the praying of the Divine Office at Lauds and Vespers as well as the Holy Mass. The Solemnity of St. Joseph, husband of Mary, is observed Mar. 19. The Solemnity of the Annunciation is observed Mar. 25.

April 2015

Universal: That people may learn to respect creation and care for it as a gift of God.

Evangelization: That persecuted Christians may feel the consoling presence of the Risen Lord and the solidarity of all the Church.

1 Wed. Wednesday of Holy Week.

2 Thurs. Holy Thursday. Chrism Mass; The Easter Triduum begins with the Mass of the Lord's Supper in the evening

3 Fri. Friday of the Passion of the Lord (Good Friday); fast and abstinence.

4 Sat. Holy Saturday; Easter Vigil.

5 Sun. Easter Sunday: Resurrection of the Lord; solemnity. (Acts 10:34a,37-43; Col 3:1-4 or 1 Cor 5:6b-8; Jn 20:1-9 or Mk 16:1-7; or, at an afternoon or evening Mass, Lk 24:13-35.)

6 Mon. Monday within the Octave of Easter.

7 Tues. Tuesday within the Octave of Easter.

8 Wed. Wednesday within the Octave of Easter.

9 Thurs. Thursday within the Octave of Easter.

10 Fri. Friday in the Octave of Easter.

11 Sat. Saturday in the Octave of Easter.

12 Sun. Second Sunday of Easter; Divine Mercy Sunday. (Acts 4:32-35; 1 Jn 5:1-6; Jn 20:19-31.)

13 Mon. Easter Weekday. St. Martin I, pope and martyr; optional memorial.

14 Tues. Easter Weekday.

15 Wed. Easter Weekday.

16 Thurs. Easter Weekday.

17 Fri. Easter Weekday.

18 Sat. Easter Weekday.

19 Sun. Third Sunday of Easter. (Acts 3:13-15,17-19; 1 Jn 2:1-5a; Lk 24:35-48.)

20 Mon. Easter Weekday.

21 Tues. Easter Weekday. St. Anselm, bishop and Doctor of the Church; optional memorial.

22 Wed. Easter Weekday.

23 Thurs. Easter Weekday. St. George, martyr; St. Adalbert, bishop and martyr; optional memorial.

24 Fri. Easter Weekday. St. Fidelis of Sigmaringen, priest and martyr; optional memorial.

25 Sat. St. Mark, evangelist; feast.

26 Sun. Fourth Sunday of Easter. (Acts 4:8-12; 1 Jn 3:1-2; Jn 10:11-18 .)

27 Mon. Easter Weekday.

28 Tues. Easter Weekday. St. Peter Chanel, priest and martyr; St. Louis Grignion de Montfort, priest.

29 Wed. St. Catherine of Siena, virgin and Doctor of the Church; memorial.

30 Thurs. Easter Weekday. St. Pius V, pope; optional memorial.

Observances:

Holy Week: Passion Sunday (Palm Sunday) begins these most solemn and holy celebrations of the Church Year. It is on this day that the Church blesses and distributes palms commemorating our Lord's triumphal entrance into Jerusalem and it is during this celebration that the Passion is read for the first time during Holy Week. Monday, Tuesday and Wednesday of Holy Week are preparatory days leading to the Sacred Triduum. The Sacred Triduum begins with the Mass of the Lord's Supper on Holy Thursday evening. Good Friday commemorates the Passion of Jesus. Easter Vigil which includes the Service of Light, Liturgy of the Word recounting salvation history, Liturgy of Christian Initiation. Easter Sunday is the day when the Holy Father delivers the traditional *Urbi et Orbi* address, to the City of Rome and to the World.

May 2015

Universal: That, rejecting the culture of indifference, we may care for our neighbors who suffer, especially the sick and the poor.

Evangelization: That Mary's intercession may help Christians in secularized cultures be ready to proclaim Jesus.

1 Fri. Easter Weekday. St. Joseph the Worker; optional memorial.

2 Sat. St. Athanasius, bishop-doctor; memorial.

3 Sun. Fifth Sunday of Easter. (Acts 9:26-31; 1 Jn 3:18-24; Jn 15:1-8.)

4 Mon. Easter Weekday.

5 Tues. Easter Weekday.

6 Wed. Easter Weekday.

7 Thurs. Easter Weekday.

8 Fri. Easter Weekday.

9 Sat. Easter Weekday.

10 Sun. Sixth Sunday of Easter. (Acts 10:25-26, 34-35, 44-48; 1 Jn 4:7-10; Jn 15:9-17.)

11 Mon. Easter Weekday.

12 Tues. Easter Weekday. Sts. Nereus and Achilleus, martyrs; St. Pancras, martyr ; optional memorial.

13 Wed. Easter Weekday. Our Lady of Fatima; optional memorial.

14 Thurs. The Ascension of the Lord; solemnity. Holy day of Obligation. (Acts 1:1-11; Eph 1:17-23 or Eph 4:1-13 or 4:1-7,11-13; Mk 16:15-20.)

15 Fri. Easter Weekday. St. Isidore; optional memorial.

16 Sat. Easter Weekday.

17 Sun. Seventh Sunday of Easter. (Acts 1:15-17,20a, 20c-26; 1 Jn 4:11-16; Jn 17:11b-19).

18 Mon. Easter Weekday. St. John I, pope and martyr; optional memorial.

19 Tues. Easter Weekday.

20 Wed. Easter Weekday. St. Bernardine of Siena, priest; optional memorial.

21 Thurs. Easter Weekday. St. Christopher Magallanes, priest, and companions, martyrs; optional memorial.

22 Fri. Easter Weekday. St. Rita of Cascia, religious; optional memorial.

23 Sat. Easter Weekday.

24 Sun. Pentecost Sunday; solemnity. (Acts 2:1-11; 1 Cor 12:3b-7,12-13 or Gal 5:16-25; Jn 20:19-23 or Jn 15:26-27; 16:12-15.)

25 Mon. Eighth Week in Ordinary Time. Weekday. St. Bede the Venerable, priest-doctor; St. Gregory VII, pope; St. Mary Magdalene de' Pazzi, virgin; optional memorial.

26 Tues. St. Philip Neri, priest; memorial.

27 Wed. Weekday. St. Augustine of Canterbury, bishop; optional memorial.

28 Thurs. Weekday.

29 Fri. Weekday.

30 Sat. Weekday.

31 Sun. The Most Holy Trinity; solemnity. (Dt 4:32-34, 39-40; Rom 8:14-17; Mt 28:16-20.)

Observances:

The Easter Sunday is completed with the celebration of the Feast of Pentecost, the gift of the Holy Spirit given to the apostles and the Church. The Feast of the Most Holy Trinity is celebrated on May 31; usually the Visitation of the Blessed Virgin Mary. The Solemnity of the Ascension celebrated May 14 (transferred to Sunday in some dioceses) is a Holy Day of Obligation. Also, May is traditionally dedicated to our Blessed Mother. Customary Marian devotions include the recitation of the Rosary and the Litany of Loretto, Marian processions, and the crowning of Mary.

June 2015

Universal: That immigrants and refugees may find welcome and respect in the countries to which they come.

Evangelization: That the personal encounter with Jesus may arouse in many young people the desire to offer their own lives in priesthood or consecrated life.

1 Mon. St. Justin, martyr; memorial. Ninth Week in Ordinary Time.

2 Tues. Weekday. Sts. Marcellinus and Peter, martyrs; optional memorial.

3 Wed. St. Charles Lwanga and Companions, martyrs; memorial.

4 Thurs. Weekday.

5 Fri. St. Boniface, bishop and martyr; memorial.

6 Sat. Weekday. St. Norbert, bishop; optional memorial.

7 Sun. The Most Holy Body and Blood of Christ (Corpus Christi); solemnity. (Ex 24:3-8 ; Heb 9:11-15 ; Mk 14:12-16, 22-26.)

8 Mon. Tenth Week in Ordinary Time. Weekday.

9 Tues. Weekday. St. Ephrem, deacon and Doctor of the Church; optional memorial.

10 Wed. Weekday.

11 Thurs. St. Barnabas, apostle; memorial.

12 Fri. The Most Sacred Heart of Jesus; solemnity.

13 Sat. Weekday. The Immaculate Heart of the Blessed Virgin Mary; St. Anthony of Padua, Priest and Doctor of the Church; optional memorial.

14 Sun. Eleventh Sunday in Ordinary Time. (Ez 17:22-24; 2 Cor 5:6-10; Mk 4:26-34.)

15 Mon. Weekday.

16 Tues. Weekday.

17 Wed. Weekday.

18 Thurs. Weekday.

19 Fri. Weekday. St. Romuald, abbot; optional memorial.

20 Sat. Weekday.

21 Sun. Twelfth Sunday in Ordinary Time. (Jb 38:1,8-11; 2 Cor 5:14-17; Mk 4:35-41.)

22 Mon. Weekday. St. Paulinus of Nola, bishop; Sts. John Fisher, bishop, and Thomas More, martyrs; optional memorial.

23 Tues. Weekday.

24 Wed. The Nativity of St. John the Baptist; solemnity.

25 Thurs. Weekday.

26 Fri. Weekday.

27 Sat. Weekday. St. Cyril of Alexandria, bishop and Doctor of the Church; optional memorial.

28 Sun. Thirteenth Sunday in Ordinary Time. (Wis 1:13-15; 2:23-24; 2 Cor 8:7,9,13-15; Mk 5:21-43 or 5:21-24, 35b-43.)

29 Mon. Sts. Peter and Paul, apostles; solemnity.

30 Tues. Weekday. The First Martyrs of the Holy Roman Church; optional memorial.

Observances:

The great feast and solemnity of the Trinity on May 31 is followed by the Feast the Body and Blood of Christ (Corpus Christi) celebrated on June 7. It is the custom in dioceses to gather for a Corpus Christi procession to venerate the Body of Christ at special altars prepared near the cathedral church. The procession concludes with Benediction. Also in June is the Feast of the Sacred Heart on June 12 and the Feast of Sts. Peter and Paul on June 29.

July 2015

Universal: That political responsibility may be lived at all levels as a high form of charity.

Evangelization: That, amid social inequalities, Latin American Christians may bear witness to love for the poor and contribute to a more fraternal society.

1 Wed. Weekday. Blessed Junípero Serra, priest; optional memorial.

2 Thurs. Weekday.

3 Fri. St. Thomas, apostle; feast.

4 Sat. Weekday. Proper Mass for Independence Day.

5 Sun. Fourteenth Sunday in Ordinary Time (Ez 2:2-5; 2 Cor 12:7-10; Mk 6:1-6a)

6 Mon. Weekday. St. Maria Goretti, virgin and martyr; optional memorial.

7 Tues. Weekday.

8 Wed. Weekday.

9 Thurs. Weekday. St. Augustine Zhao Rong, priest, and Companions, martyrs; optional memorial.

10 Fri. Weekday.

11 Sat. St. Benedict, abbot; memorial.

12 Sun. Fifteenth Sunday in Ordinary Time (Am 7:12-15; Eph 1:3-14 or 1:3-10; Mk 6:7-13)

13 Mon. Weekday. St. Henry ; optional memorial.

14 Tues. St. Kateri Tekakwitha, virgin; memorial.

15 Wed. St. Bonaventure, bishop and Doctor of the Church; memorial.

16 Thurs. Weekday. Our Lady of Mount Carmel; optional memorial.

17 Fri. Weekday.

18 Sat. Weekday. St. Camillus de Lellis, priest; optional memorial.

19 Sun. Sixteenth Sunday in Ordinary Time (Jer 23:1-6; Eph 2:13-18; Mk 6:30-34)

20 Mon. Weekday. St. Apollinaris, bishop and martyr.

21 Tues. Weekday. St. Lawrence of Brindisi, priest and Doctor of the Church; optional memorial.

22 Wed. St. Mary Magdalene; memorial.

23 Thurs. Weekday green. St. Bridget, religious.

24 Fri. Weekday. St. Sharbel Makhluf, priest; optional memorial.

25 Sat. St. James, apostle; feast.

26 Sun. Seventeenth Sunday in Ordinary Time (2 Kgs 4:42-44; Eph 4:1-6; Jn 6:1-15)

27 Mon. Weekday.

28 Tues. Weekday.

29 Wed. St. Martha; memorial.

30 Thurs. Weekday. St. Peter Chrysologus, bishop and Doctor of the Church; optional memorial.

31 Fri. St. Ignatius of Loyola, priest; memorial.

Observances:

Blessed Junípero Serra, whose optional memorial may be celebrated July 1, founded the California Missions. St. Thomas the Apostle is observed on July 3; St. Maria Goretti, July 6; St. Benedict, the founder of Western monasticism and patron saint of Europe, July 11; St. Kateri Tekakwitha, July 14; St. Bonaventure, called the second found of the Franciscan Order, July 15; St. Ignatius Loyola, founder of the Society of Jesus, July 31. Independence Day, July 4, is observed with a special Mass for celebration in the United States.

August 2015

Universal: That volunteers may give themselves generously to the service of the needy.

Evangelization: That setting aside our very selves we may learn to be neighbours to those who find themselves on the margins of human life and society.

1 Sat. St. Alphonsus Liguori, bishop and Doctor of the Church; memorial.

2 Sun. Eighteenth Sunday in Ordinary Time (Ex 16:2-4, 12-15 ; Eph 4:17, 20-24 ; Jn 6:24-35)

3 Mon. Weekday.

4 Tues. St. John Vianney, priest; memorial.

5 Wed. Weekday. The Dedication of the Basilica of St. Mary Major; optional memorial.

6 Thurs. The Transfiguration of the Lord; feast.

7 Fri. Weekday. St. Sixtus II, pope, and Companions, martyrs; St. Cajetan, priest; optional memorial.

8 Sat. St. Dominic, priest; memorial.

9 Sun. Nineteenth Sunday in Ordinary Time (1 Kgs 19:4-8; Eph 4:30-5:2; Jn 6:41-51)

10 Mon. St. Lawrence, deacon and martyr; feast.

11 Tues. St. Clare, virgin; memorial.

12 Wed. Weekday. St. Jane Frances de Chantal, religious; optional memorial.

13 Thurs. Weekday. Sts. Pontian, pope, and Hippolytus, priest, martyrs; optional memorial.

14 Fri. St. Maximilian Kolbe, priest and martyr; memorial.

15 Sat. Assumption of the Blessed Virgin Mary; solemnity. Not a Holy Day of Obligation this year.

16 Sun. Twentieth Sunday in Ordinary Time (Prv 9:1-6; Eph 5:15-20; Jn 6:51-58)

17 Mon. Weekday.

18 Tues. Weekday.

19 Wed. Weekday. St. John Eudes, priest; optional memorial.

20 Thurs. St. Bernard, abbot and Doctor of the Church; memorial.

21 Fri. St. Pius X, pope; memorial.

22 Sat. The Queenship of the Blessed Virgin Mary; memorial.

23 Sun. Twenty-First Sunday in Ordinary Time (Jos 24:1-2a, 15-17, 18b; Eph 5:21-32 or 5:2a, 25-32; Jn 6:60-69)

24 Mon. St. Bartholomew, apostle; feast.

25 Tues. Weekday. St. Louis; St. Joseph Calasanz, priest; optional memorial.

26 Wed. Weekday.

27 Thurs. St. Monica; memorial.

28 Fri. St. Augustine, bishop and Doctor of the Church; memorial.

29 Sat. The Passion of St. John the Baptist; memorial.

30 Sun. Twenty-Second Sunday in Ordinary Time (Dt 4:1-2, 6-8; Jas 1:17-18, 21b-22, 27; Mk 7:1-8, 14-15, 21-23)

31 Mon. Weekday.

Observances:

St. Alphonsus Liguori, doctor of the Church and moral theologian, Aug. 1; St. John Vianney, patron saint of parish priests, Aug. 4; The Feast of the Transfiguration of the Lord, Aug. 6; St. Dominic, founder of the Dominicans, Aug, 8; St. Clare, foundress of the Poor Clares, Aug. 11; The Feast of the Assumption of the Blessed Virgin Mary, Aug. 15; St. Bernard of Clairvaux, Aug. 20; St. Monica, Aug. 27 and her son St. Augustine, the doctor of grace and father of the Church, Aug. 28.

September 2015

Universal: That opportunities for education and employment may increase for all young people.

Evangelization: That catechists may give witness by living in a way consistent with the faith they proclaim.

1 Tues. Weekday.

2 Wed. Weekday.

3 Thurs. St. Gregory the Great, pope and Doctor of the Church; memorial.

4 Fri. Weekday.

5 Sat. Weekday.

6 Sun. Twenty-Third Sunday in Ordinary Time (Is 35:4-7a; Jas 2:1-5; Mk 7:31-37)

7 Mon. Weekday.

8 Tues. The Nativity of the Blessed Virgin Mary; feast.

9 Wed. St. Peter Claver, priest; memorial.

10 Thurs. Weekday.

11 Fri. Weekday.

12 Sat. Weekday. The Most Holy Name of Mary; optional memorial.

13 Sun. Twenty-Fourth Sunday in Ordinary Time (Is 50:5-9a; Jas 2:14-18; Mk 8:27-35.)

14 Mon. The Exaltation of the Holy Cross; feast.

15 Tues. Our Lady of Sorrows; memorial.

16 Wed. Sts. Cornelius, pope, and Cyprian, bishop, martyrs; memorial.

17 Thurs. Weekday. St. Robert Bellarmine, bishop and Doctor of the Church; optional memorial.

18 Fri. Weekday.

19 Sat. Weekday. St. Januarius, bishop and martyr; optional memorial.

20 Sun. Twenty-Fifth Sunday in Ordinary Time (Wis 2:12, 17-20; Jas 3:16-4:3; Mk 9:30-37)

21 Mon. St. Matthew, apostle and evangelist; feast.

22 Tues. Weekday.

23 Wed. St. Pius of Pietrelcina, priest; memorial.

24 Thurs. Weekday.

25 Fri. Weekday.

26 Sat. Weekday. Sts. Cosmas and Damian, Martyrs; optional memorial.

27 Sun. Twenty-Sixth Sunday in Ordinary Time (Nm 11:25-29; Jas 5:1-6; Mk 9:38-43, 45, 47-48)

28 Mon. Weekday. St. Wenceslaus, martyr; St. Lawrence Ruiz and Companions, martyrs; optional memorial.

29 Tues. Sts. Michael, Gabriel, and Raphael, archangels; feast.

30 Wed. St. Jerome, priest and Doctor of the Church; memorial.

Observances:

Birth of the Blessed Virgin Mary, Sept. 8; St. John Chrysostom, doctor of the Church, Sept. 13; Exaltation of the Holy Cross, Sept. 14; Our Lady of Sorrows, Sept. 15; St. Robert Bellarmine, doctor of the Church, Sept. 17. Padre Pio, Sept. 23.; St. Vincent de Paul, founder of the Vincentians and Daughters of Charity, Sept. 27; Sts. Michael, Gabriel, and Raphael, archangels, Sept. 29.; St. Jerome, Sept. 30. Labor Day is celebrated Sept. 3 with a special Mass.

October 2015

Universal: That human trafficking, the modern form of slavery, may be eradicated.

Evangelization: That with a missionary spirit the Christian communities of Asia may announce the Gospel to those who are still awaiting it.

1 Thurs. St. Thérèse of the Child Jesus, virgin and Doctor of the Church; memorial.

2 Fri. The Holy Guardian Angels; memorial.

3 Sat. Weekday.

4 Sun. Twenty-Seventh Sunday in Ordinary Time (Gn 2:18-24; Heb 2:9-11; Mk 10:2-16 or 10:2-12)

5 Mon. Weekday.

6 Tues. Weekday. St. Bruno, Priest; Blessed Marie-Rose Durocher, virgin; optional memorial.

7 Wed. Our Lady of the Rosary; memorial.

8 Thurs. Weekday.

9 Fri. Weekday. St. Denis, bishop, and Companions, martyrs; St. John Leonardi, priest; optional memorial.

10 Sat. Weekday.

11 Sun. Twenty-Eighth Sunday in Ordinary Time (Wis 7:7-11; Heb 4:12-13; Mk 10:17-30 or 10:17-27)

12 Mon. Weekday.

13 Tues. Weekday.

14 Wed. Weekday. St. Callistus I, pope-martyr; optional memorial.

15 Thurs. St. Teresa of Jesus, virgin-doctor; memorial.

16 Fri. Weekday. St. Hedwig, religious; St. Margaret Mary Alacoque, virgin; optional memorial.

17 Sat. St. Ignatius of Antioch, bishop-martyr; memorial.

18 Sun. Twenty-Ninth Sunday in Ordinary Time (Is 53:10-11; Heb 4:14-16; Mk 10:35-45 or 10:42-45)

19 Mon. Sts. John de Brébeuf and Isaac Jogues, priests, and Companions, martyrs; memorial.

20 Tues. Weekday. St. Paul of the Cross, priest; optional memorial.

21 Wed. Weekday.

22 Thurs. Weekday. St. John Paul II, pope; optional memorial.

23 Fri. Weekday. St. John of Capistrano, priest; optional memorial.

24 Sat. Weekday. St. Anthony Mary Claret, bishop; optional memorial.

25 Sun. Thirtieth Sunday in Ordinary Time (Jer 31:7-9; Heb 5:1-6; Mk 10:46-52)

26 Mon. Weekday.

27 Tues. Weekday.

28 Wed. Sts. Simon and Jude, apostles; feast.

29 Thurs. Weekday.

30 Fri. Weekday.

31 Sat. Weekday.

Observances:

St. Thérèse of the Child Jesus, Doctor of the Church, Oct.1; Guardian Angels Oct. 2; St. Francis of Assisi, founder of the Franciscan Order, while not celebrated this year, is usually Oct. 4; Pope St. John XXIII, is usually Oct. 11; St. Teresa of Jesus, Doctor of the Church, reformer of the Carmelite Order, Oct. 15; The North American Martyrs, Oct. 19. St. Paul of the Cross, founder of the Congregation of the Passion, Oct. 20. St. John Paul II, Oct. 22; Sts. Simon and Jude, Oct. 28. Mission Sunday is observed during the month, with appeals for prayer and financial support for persons and projects involved in the ministry of evangelization at home and abroad.

November 2015

Universal: That we may be open to encounter and dialogue with all, even those whose convictions differ from our own.

Evangelization: That pastors of the Church, with love for their flocks, may accompany them and enliven their hope.

1 Sun **All Saints;** solemnity. (Rv 7:2-4,9-14; 1 Jn 3:1-3; Mt 5:1-12a.)

2 Mon. The Commemoration of All the Faithful Departed (All Souls' Day).

3 Tues. Thirty-First Week in Ordinary Time. Weekday. St. Martin de Porres, religious; optional memorial.

4 Wed. St. Charles Borromeo, bishop; memorial.

5 Thurs. Weekday.

6 Fri. Weekday.

7 Sat. Weekday.

8 Sun. **Thirty-Second Sunday in Ordinary Time** (1 Kgs 17:10-16/Heb 9:24-28/Mk 12:38-44 or 12:41-44)

9 Mon. The Dedication of the Lateran Basilica; feast.

10 Tues. St. Leo the Great, pope-doctor; memorial.

11 Wed. St. Martin of Tours, bishop, memorial.

12 Thurs. St. Josaphat, bishop and martyr; memorial.

13 Fri. St. Frances Xavier Cabrini, virgin; memorial.

14 Sat. Weekday.

15 Sun. **Thirty-Third Sunday in Ordinary Time** (Dn 12:1-3; Heb 10:11-14, 18; Mk 13:24-32)

16 Mon. Weekday. St. Margaret of Scotland; St. Gertrude, virgin; optional memorial.

17 Tues. St. Elizabeth of Hungary, religious; memorial.

18 Wed. Weekday. The Dedication of the Basilicas of Sts. Peter and Paul, apostles; St. Rose Philippine Duchesne, virgin; memorial.

19 Thurs. Weekday.

20 Fri. Weekday.

21 Sat. Presentation of the Blessed Virgin Mary; memorial.

22 Sun. **Our Lord Jesus Christ, King of the Universe;** solemnity (Dn 7:13-14; Rv 1:5-8; Jn 18:33b-37)

23 Mon. Thirty-Fourth or Last Week in Ordinary Time. Weekday. St. Clement I, pope and martyr; St. Columban, abbot; Bl. Miguel Agustín Pro, priest and martyr; optional memorial.

24 Tues. St. Andrew Dung-Loc, priest, and Companions, martyrs; memorial.

25 Wed. Weekday. St. Catherine of Alexandria, virgin and martyr; optional memorial.

26 Thurs. Thanksgiving Day; Proper Mass.

27 Fri. Weekday.

28 Sat. Weekday.

29 Sun. **First Sunday of Advent** (Jer 33:14-16; 1 Thes 3:12-4:2; Lk 21:25-28, 34-36)

30 Mon. St. Andrew, apostle; feast.

Observances:

All Saints Day, Nov. 1; All Souls Day, Nov. 2; Frances Xavier Cabrini, foundress, first U.S. citizen-saint, Nov. 13; St. Albert the Great, Doctor of the Church, usually Nov. 15; Presentation of the Blessed Virgin Mary, Nov. 21; Christ the King, Nov. 23; Thanksgiving Day, Nov. 26; The beginning of the Church Year, the first Sunday of Advent, Nov. 29. The month of November is traditionally devoted to praying for our beloved dead. Masses for Dead are offered frequently throughout the month especially at cemeteries.

The annual fall meeting of the bishops of the United States takes place this month in Baltimore, MD. Its agenda covers a wide range of topics with particular attention given to doctrinal, pastoral and educational issues that impact the life of the Church in the United States.

December 2015

Universal: That all may experience the mercy of God, who never tires of forgiving.

Evangelization: That families, especially those who suffer, may find in the birth of Jesus a sign of certain hope.

1 Tues. Advent Weekday.

2 Wed. Advent Weekday.

3 Thurs. St. Francis Xavier, priest; memorial.

4 Fri. Advent Weekday. St. John Damascene, priest and Doctor of the Church; optional memorial.

5 Sat. Advent Weekday.

6 Sun. **Second Sunday of Advent** (Bar 5:1-9; Phil 1:4-6, 8-11; Lk 3:1-6)

7 Mon. St. Ambrose, bishop and Doctor of the Church; memorial.

8 Tues. The Immaculate Conception of the Blessed Virgin Mary. Patronal Feast day of the United States of America; solemnity; Holy Day of Obligation)

9 Wed. Advent Weekday. St. Juan Diego; optional memorial.

10 Thurs. Advent Weekday.

11 Fri. Advent Weekday. St. Damasus I, pope; optional memorial.

12 Sat. Our Lady of Guadalupe, feast.

13 Sun. **Third Sunday of Advent** (Zep 3:14-18a; Phil 4:4-7; Lk 3:10-18)

14 Mon. St. John of the Cross, priest and Doctor of the Church; memorial.

15 Tues. Advent Weekday.

16 Wed. Advent Weekday.

17 Thurs. Advent Weekday.

18 Fri. Advent Weekday.

19 Sat. Advent Weekday.

20 Sun. **Fourth Sunday of Advent** (Mi 5:1-4a; Heb 10:5-10; Lk 1:39-45)

21 Mon. Advent Weekday. St. Peter Canisius, priest and Doctor of the Church; optional memorial.

22 Tues. Advent Weekday.

23 Wed. Advent Weekday. St. John of Kanty; priest, optional memorial.

24 Thurs. Advent Weekday.

25 Fri. The Nativity of the Lord. Christmas; solemnity. Holy Day of Obligation (Vigil: Is 62:1-5; Acts 13:16-17, 22-25; Mt 1:1-25 or 1:18-25; Night: Is 9:1-6; Ti 2:11-14; Lk 2:1-14; Dawn: Is 62:11-12; Ti 3:4-7; Lk 2:15-20; Day: Is 52:7-10; Heb 1:1-6; Jn 1:1-18 or 1:1-5, 9-14.)

26 Sat. St. Stephen, The First Martyr; feast

27 Sun. **The Holy Family of Jesus, Mary and Joseph**; feast (Sir 3:2-6, 12-14 or 1 Sm 1:20-22, 24-28; Col 3:12-21 or 3:12-17 or 1 Jn 3:1-2, 21-24; Lk 2:41-52)

28 Mon. The Holy Innocents, martyrs; feast.

29 Tues. Fifth Day within the Octave of the Nativity of the Lord; St. Thomas Becket, bishop and martyr; optional memorial.

30 Wed. Sixth Day within the Octave of the Nativity of the Lord.

31 Thurs. Seventh Day within the Octave of the Nativity of the Lord. St. Sylvester I, pope; optional memorial.

Observances:

St. Francis Xavier, missionary, Dec. 3; Sts. John Damascene, Ambrose, John of the Cross, Peter Canisius,' Doctors of the Church; Immaculate Conception, Dec. 8; St. Juan Diego, Dec. 9; Our Lady of Guadalupe, Dec. 12; Birth of our Lord, Dec. 25; St. Stephen, proto-martyr, Dec. 26; St. John, apostle-evangelist, usually Dec. 27; Holy Family, Dec. 27.

HOLY DAYS AND OTHER OBSERVANCES

The following list includes the six holy days of obligation observed in the U.S. and additional observances of devotional and historical significance. The dignity or rank of observances is indicated by the terms: solemnity (highest in rank); feast; memorial (for universal observance); optional memorial (for celebration by choice).

All Saints, Nov. 1, Holy Day of Obligation, solemnity. Commemorates all the blessed in heaven, and is intended particularly to honor the blessed who have no special feasts. The background of the feast dates to the fourth century when groups of martyrs, and later other saints, were honored on a common day in various places. In 609 or 610, the Pantheon, a pagan temple at Rome, was consecrated as a Christian church for the honor of Our Lady and the martyrs (later all saints). In 835, Gregory IV fixed Nov. 1 as the date of observance.

All Souls, Commemoration of the Faithful Departed, Nov. 2. The dead were prayed for from the earliest days of Christianity. By the sixth century it was customary in Benedictine monasteries to hold a commemoration of deceased members of the order at Pentecost. A common commemoration of all the faithful departed on the day after All Saints was instituted in 998 by St. Odilo, of the Abbey of Cluny, and an observance of this kind was accepted in Rome in the 14th century.

Annunciation of the Lord (formerly, Annunciation of the Blessed Virgin Mary), Mar. 25, solemnity. A feast of the Incarnation which commemorates the announcement by the Archangel Gabriel to the Virgin Mary that she was to become the Mother of Christ (Lk 1:26-38), and the miraculous conception of Christ by her. The feast was instituted about 430 in the East. The Roman observance dates from the seventh century, when celebration was said to be universal.

Ascension of the Lord, movable observance held 40 days after Easter, holy day of obligation, solemnity. Commemorates the Ascension of Christ into heaven 40 days after his Resurrection from the dead (Mk 16:19; Lk 24:51; Acts 1:2). The feast recalls the completion of Christ's mission on earth for the salvation of all people and his entry into heaven with glorified human nature. The Ascension is a pledge of the final glorification of all who achieve salvation. Documentary evidence of the feast dates from early in the fifth century, but it was observed long before that time in connection with Pentecost and Easter.

Ash Wednesday, movable observance, six and one-half weeks before Easter. It was set as the first day of Lent by Pope St. Gregory the Great (590-604) with the extension of an earlier and shorter penitential season to a total period including 40 weekdays of fasting before Easter. It is a day of fast and abstinence. Ashes, symbolic of penance, are blessed and distributed among the faithful during the day. They are used to mark the forehead with the Sign of the Cross, with the reminder: "Remember you are dust, and to dust you will return," or "Turn away from sin and be faithful to the Gospel."

Assumption, Aug. 15, holy day of obligation, solemnity. Commemorates the taking into heaven of Mary, soul and body, at the end of her life on earth, a truth of faith that was proclaimed a dogma by Pius XII on Nov. 1, 1950. One of the oldest and most solemn feasts of Mary, it

has a history dating back to at least the seventh century when its celebration was already established at Jerusalem and Rome.

Baptism of the Lord, movable, usually celebrated on the Sunday after January 6, feast. Recalls the baptism of Christ by John the Baptist (Mk 1:9-11), an event associated with the liturgy of the Epiphany. This baptism was the occasion for Christ's manifestation of himself at the beginning of his public life.

Birth of Mary, Sept. 8, feast. This is a very old feast which originated in the East and found place in the Roman liturgy in the seventh century.

Candlemas Day, Feb. 2. See **Presentation of the Lord**.

Chair of Peter, Feb. 22, feast. The feast, which has been in the Roman calendar since 336, is a liturgical expression of belief in the episcopacy and hierarchy of the Church.

Christmas, Birth of Our Lord Jesus Christ, Dec. 25, holy day of obligation, solemnity. Commemorates the birth of Christ (Lk 2:1-20). This event was originally commemorated in the East on the feast of Epiphany or Theophany. The Christmas feast itself originated in the West; by 354 it was certainly kept on Dec. 25. This date may have been set for the observance to offset pagan ceremonies held at about the same time to commemorate the birth of the sun at the winter solstice. There are texts for three Christmas Masses at midnight, dawn, and during the day.

Christ the King, movable, celebrated on the last Sunday of the liturgical year, solemnity. Commemorates the royal prerogatives of Christ and is equivalent to a declaration of his rights to the homage, service and fidelity of all people in all phases of individual and social life. Pius XI instituted the feast Dec. 11, 1925.

Conversion of St. Paul, Jan. 25, feast. An observance mentioned in some calendars from the 8th and 9th centuries. Pope Innocent III (1198-1216) ordered its observance with great solemnity.

Corpus Christi (The Body and Blood of Christ), movable, celebrated on the Thursday (or Sunday, as in the U.S.) following Trinity Sunday, solemnity. Commemorates the institution of the Holy Eucharist (Mt 26:26-28). The feast originated at Liège in 1246 and was extended throughout the Church in the West by Urban IV in 1264. St. Thomas Aquinas composed the Liturgy of the Hours for the feast.

Cross, The Holy, Sept. 14, feast. Commemorates the finding of the Cross on which Christ was crucified, in 326 through the efforts of St. Helena, mother of Constantine; the consecration of the Basilica of the Holy Sepulchre nearly 10 years later: and the recovery in 628 or 629 by Emperor Heraclius of a major portion of the cross which had been removed by the Persians from its place of veneration at Jerusalem. The feast originated in Jerusalem and spread through the East before being adopted in the West. General adoption followed the building at Rome of the Basilica of the Holy Cross "in Jerusalem," so called because it was the place of enshrinement of a major portion of the cross of crucifixion.

Dedication of St. John Lateran, Nov. 9, feast. Commemorates the first public consecration of a church, that of the Basilica of the Most Holy Savior by Pope St. Sylvester about 324. The church, as well as the Lateran Palace, was the gift of Emperor Constantine. Since the 12th century it has been known as St. John Lateran, in honor of John the Baptist after whom the adjoining baptistery was named. It was rebuilt by Innocent X (1644-55), reconsecrated by Benedict XIII in 1726, and enlarged by Leo XIII (1878-1903). This basilica is regarded as the church of highest dignity in Rome and throughout the Roman rite.

Dedication of St. Mary Major, Aug. 5, optional memorial. Commemorates the rebuilding and dedication by Pope Sixtus III (432-40) of a church in honor of Blessed Mary the Virgin. This is the Basilica of St. Mary Major on the Esquiline Hill in Rome. An earlier building was erected during the pontificate of Liberius (352-66); according to legend, it was located on a site covered by a miraculous fall of snow seen by a nobleman favored with a vision of Mary.

Easter, movable celebration held on the first Sunday after the full moon following the vernal equinox (between Mar. 22 and Apr. 25), solemnity with an octave. Commemorates the Resurrection of Christ from the dead (Mk 16:1-7). The observance of this mystery, kept since the first days of the Church, extends throughout the Easter season which lasts until the feast of Pentecost, a period of 50 days. Every Sunday in the year is regarded as a "little" Easter. The date of Easter determines the dates of movable feasts, such as Ascension and Pentecost, and the number of weeks before Lent and after Pentecost.

Easter Vigil, called by St. Augustine the "Mother of All Vigils," the night before Easter. Ceremonies are all related to the Resurrection and renewal-in-grace theme of Easter: blessing of the new fire, procession with the Easter Candle, singing of the Easter Proclamation (Exsultet), Liturgy of the Word with at least three Old Testament readings, the Litany of Saints, blessing of water, baptism of converts and infants, renewal of baptismal promises, Liturgy of the Eucharist. The vigil ceremonies are held after nightfall on Saturday.

Epiphany of the Lord, Jan. 6 or (in the U.S.) a Sunday between Jan. 2 and 8, solemnity. Commemorates the manifestations of the divinity of Christ. It is one of the oldest Christian feasts, with an Eastern origin traceable to the beginning of the third century and antedating the Western feast of Christmas. Originally, it commemorated the manifestations of Christ's divinity — or Theophany — in his birth, the homage of the Magi, and baptism by John the Baptist. Later, the first two of these commemorations were transferred to Christmas when the Eastern Church adopted that feast between 380 and 430. The central feature of the Eastern observance now is the manifestation or declaration of Christ's divinity in his baptism and at the beginning of his public life. The Epiphany was adopted by the Western Church during the same period in which the Eastern Church accepted Christmas. In the Roman rite, commemoration is made in the Mass of the homage of the wise men from the East (Mt 2:1-12).

Good Friday, the Friday before Easter, the second day of the Easter Triduum. Liturgical elements of the observance are commemoration of the Passion and Death of Christ in the reading of the Passion (according to John), special prayers for the Church and people of all ranks, the veneration of the Cross, and a Communion service. The celebration takes place in the afternoon, preferably at 3:00 p.m.

Guardian Angels, Oct. 2, memorial. Commemorates the angels who protect people from spiritual and physical dangers and assist them in doing good. A feast in their honor celebrated in Spain in the 16th century was placed in the Roman calendar in 1615 and Oct. 2 was set as the date of observance. Earlier, guardian angels were honored liturgically in conjunction with the feast of St. Michael.

Holy Family, movable observance on the Sunday after Christmas, feast. Commemorates the Holy Family of Jesus, Mary and Joseph as the model of domestic society, holiness and virtue. The devotional background of the feast was very strong in the 17th century. In the 18th century, in prayers composed for a special Mass, a Canadian bishop likened the Christian family to the Holy Family. Leo XIII consecrated families to the Holy Family. In 1921, Benedict XV extended the Divine Office and Mass of the feast to the whole Church.

Holy Innocents, Dec. 28, feast. Commemorates the infants who suffered death at the hands of Herod's soldiers seeking to kill the child Jesus (Mt 2:13-18). A feast in their honor has been observed since the fifth century.

Holy Saturday, the day before Easter. The Sacrifice of the Mass is not celebrated, and Holy Communion may be given only as Viaticum. If possible the Easter fast should be observed until the Easter Vigil.

Holy Thursday, the Thursday before Easter. Commemorates the institution of the sacraments of the Eucharist and holy orders, and the washing of the feet of the Apostles by Jesus at the Last Supper. The Mass of the Lord's Supper in the evening marks the beginning of the Easter Triduum. Following the Mass, there is a procession of the Blessed Sacrament to a place of reposition for adoration by the faithful. Usually at an earlier Mass of Chrism, bishops bless oils (of catechumens, chrism, the sick) for use during the year. (For pastoral reasons, diocesan bishops may permit additional Masses, but these should not overshadow the principal Mass of the Lord's Supper.)

Immaculate Conception, Dec. 8, holy day of obligation, solemnity. Commemorates the fact that Mary, in view of her calling to be the Mother of Christ and in virtue of his merits, was preserved from the first moment of her conception from original sin and was filled with grace from the very beginning of her life. She was the only person so preserved from original sin. The present form of the feast dates from Dec. 8, 1854, when Pius IX defined the dogma of the Immaculate Conception. An earlier feast of the Conception, which testified to long-existing belief in this truth, was observed in the East by the eighth century, in Ireland in the ninth, and subsequently in European countries. In 1846, Mary was proclaimed patroness of the U.S. under this title.

Immaculate Heart of Mary, Saturday following the second Sunday after Pentecost, memorial. On May 4, 1944, Pius XII ordered this feast observed throughout the Church in order to obtain Mary's intercession for "peace among nations, freedom for the Church, the conversion of sinners, the love of purity and the practice of virtue." Two years earlier, he consecrated the entire human race to Mary under this title. Devotion to Mary under the title of her Most Pure Heart originated during the Middle Ages. It was given great impetus in the 17th century by the preaching of St. John Eudes, who was the first to celebrate a Mass and Divine Office of Mary under this title. A feast, celebrated in various places and on different dates, was authorized in 1799.

Joachim and Ann, July 26, memorial. Commemorates the parents of Mary. A joint feast, celebrated Sept. 9, originated in the East near the end of the sixth century. Devotion to Ann, introduced in the eighth century at Rome, became widespread in Europe in the 14th century; her feast was extended throughout the Latin Church in 1584. A feast of Joachim was introduced in the West in the 15th century.

John the Baptist, Birth of, June 24, solemnity. The precursor of Christ, whose cousin he was, was commemorated universally in the liturgy by the fourth century. He is the only saint, except the Blessed Virgin Mary, whose birthday is observed as a feast. Another feast, on Aug. 29, commemorates his passion and death at the order of Herod (Mk 6:14-29).

Joseph, Mar. 19, solemnity. Joseph is honored as the husband of the Blessed Virgin Mary, the patron and protector of the universal Church and workman. Devotion to him already existed in the eighth century in the East, and in the 11th in the West. Various feasts were celebrated before the 15th century when Mar. 19 was fixed for his commemoration; this feast was extended to the whole Church in 1621 by Gregory XV. In 1955, Pius XII instituted the feast of St. Joseph the Workman for observance May 1; this feast, which may be celebrated by local option, supplanted the Solemnity or Patronage of St. Joseph formerly observed on the third Wednesday after Easter. St. Joseph was proclaimed protector and patron of the universal Church in 1870 by Pius IX.

Michael, Gabriel and Raphael, Archangels, Sept. 29, feast. A feast bearing the title of Dedication of St. Michael the Archangel formerly commemorated on this date the consecration in 530 of a church near Rome in honor of Michael, the first angel given a liturgical feast. For a while, this feast was combined with a commemoration of the Guardian Angels. The separate feasts of Gabriel (Mar. 24) and Raphael (Oct. 24) were suppressed by the calendar in effect since 1970 and this joint feast of the three archangels was instituted.

Octave of Christmas, Jan. 1. See **Solemnity of Mary, Mother of God**.

Our Lady of Guadalupe, Dec. 12, feast (in the U.S.). Commemorates under this title the appearances of the Blessed Virgin Mary in 1531 to an Indian, Juan Diego, on Tepeyac hill outside Mexico City (see **Apparitions of the Blessed Virgin Mary**, p. 123). The celebration, observed as a memorial in the U.S., was raised to the rank of feast at the request of the National Conference of Catholic Bishops. Approval was granted in a decree dated Jan. 8, 1988.

Our Lady of Sorrows, Sept. 15, memorial. Recalls the sorrows experienced by Mary in her association with Christ: the prophecy of Simeon (Lk 2:34-35), the flight into Egypt (Mt 2:13-21), the three-day separation from Jesus (Lk 2:41-50), and four incidents connected with the Passion — her meeting with Christ on the way to Calvary, the crucifixion, the removal of Christ's body from the cross, and his burial (Mt 27:31-61; Mk 15:20-47; Lk 23:26-56; Jn 19:17-42). A Mass and Divine Office of the feast were celebrated by the Servites, especially, in the 17th century, and in 1814 Pius VII extended the observance to the whole Church.

Our Lady of the Rosary, Oct. 7, memorial. Commemorates the Virgin Mary through recall of the mysteries of the Rosary which recapitulate events in her life and the life of Christ. The feast was instituted in 1573 to commemorate a Christian victory by the Holy Alliance over the invading fleet of the Ottoman Empire at the Battle of Lepanto in 1571, and was extended throughout the Church by Clement XI in 1716.

Passion Sunday (formerly called Palm Sunday), the Sunday before Easter. Marks the start of Holy Week by recalling the triumphal entry of Christ into Jerusalem at the beginning of the last week of his life (Mt 21:1-9). A procession and other ceremonies commemorating this event were held in Jerusalem from very early Christian times and were adopted in Rome by the ninth century, when the blessing of palm for the occasion was introduced. Full liturgical observance includes the blessing of palm and a procession before the principal Mass of the day. The Passion, by Matthew, Mark or Luke, is read during the Mass.

Pentecost, also called Whitsunday, movable celebration held 50 days after Easter, solemnity. Commemorates the descent of the Holy Spirit upon the Apostles, the preaching of Peter and the other Apostles to Jews in Jerusalem, the baptism and aggregation of some 3,000 persons to the Christian community (Acts 2:1-41). It is regarded as the birthday of the Catholic Church. The original observance of the feast antedated the earliest extant documentary evidence from the third century.

Peter and Paul, June 29, solemnity. Commemorates the martyrdoms of Peter by crucifixion and Paul by beheading during the Neronian persecution. This joint commemoration of the chief Apostles dates at least from 258 at Rome.

Presentation of the Lord (formerly called Purification of the Blessed Virgin Mary, also Candlemas), Feb. 2, feast. Commemorates the presentation of Jesus in the Temple — according to prescriptions of Mosaic Law (Lv 12:2-8; Ex 13:2; Lk 2:22-32) — and the purification of Mary 40 days after his birth. In the East, where the feast antedated fourth century testimony regarding its existence, it was observed primarily as a feast of Our Lord; in the West, where it was adopted later, it was regarded more as a feast of Mary until the calendar in effect since 1970. Its date was set for Feb. 2 after the celebration of Christmas was fixed for Dec. 25, late in the fourth century. The blessing of candles, probably in commemoration of Christ who was the Light to enlighten the Gentiles, became common about the 11th century and gave the feast the secondary name of Candlemas.

Queenship of Mary, Aug. 22, memorial. Commemorates the high dignity of Mary as Queen of heaven, angels and men. Universal observance of the memorial was ordered by Pius XII in the encyclical *Ad Caeli Reginam*, Oct. 11, 1954, near the close of a Marian Year observed in connection with the centenary of the proclamation of the dogma of the Immaculate Conception and four years after the proclamation of the dogma of the Assumption. The original date of the memorial was May 31.

Resurrection. See **Easter**.

Sacred Heart of Jesus, movable observance held on the Friday after the second Sunday after Pentecost (Corpus Christi, in the U.S.), solemnity. The object of the devotion is the divine Person of Jesus, whose heart is the symbol of his love for all people — for whom he accomplished the work of Redemption. The Mass and Office now used on the feast were prescribed by Pius XI in 1929. Devotion to the Sacred Heart was introduced into the liturgy in the 17th century through the efforts of St. John Eudes who composed an Office and Mass for the feast. It was furthered as the result of the revelations of St. Margaret Mary Alacoque after 1675 and by the work of St. Claude de la Colombière, S.J. In 1765, Clement XIII approved a Mass and Office for the feast, and in 1856 Pius IX extended the observance throughout the Roman rite.

Solemnity of Mary, Mother of God, Jan. 1, holy day of obligation, solemnity. The calendar in effect since 1970, in accord with Eastern tradition, reinstated the Marian character of this commemoration on the octave day of Christmas. The former feast of the Circumcision, dating at least from the first half of the sixth century, marked the initiation of Jesus (Lk 2:21) in Judaism and by analogy focused attention on the initiation of persons in the Christian religion and their incorporation in Christ through baptism. The feast of the Solemnity supplants the former feast of the Maternity of Mary observed on Oct. 11.

Transfiguration of the Lord, Aug. 6, feast. Commemorates the revelation of his divinity by Christ to Peter, James and John on Mt. Tabor (Mt 17:1-9). The feast, which is very old, was extended throughout the universal Church in 1457 by Callistus III.

Trinity, The Holy, movable observance held on the Sunday after Pentecost, solemnity. Commemorates the most sublime mystery of the Christian faith, i.e., that there are Three Divine Persons — Father, Son and Holy Spirit — in one God (Mt 28:18-20). A votive Mass of the Most Holy Trinity dates from the seventh century; an Office was composed in the 10th century; in 1334, John XXII extended the feast to the universal Church.

Visitation, May 31, feast. Commemorates Mary's visit to her cousin Elizabeth after the Annunciation and before the birth of John the Baptist, the precursor of Christ (Lk 1:39-47). The feast had a medieval origin and was observed in the Franciscan Order before being extended throughout the Church by Urban VI in 1389. It is one of the feasts of the Incarnation and is notable for its recall of the Magnificat, one of the few New Testament canticles, which acknowledges the unique gifts of God to Mary because of her role in the redemptive work of Christ. The canticle is recited at Evening Prayer in the Liturgy of the Hours.

Liturgical Life of the Church

The nature and purpose of the liturgy, along with norms for its revision, were the subject matter of *Sacrosanctum Concilium* (the Constitution on the Sacred Liturgy) promulgated by the Second Vatican Council. The principles and guidelines stated in this document, the first issued by the Council, are summarized here and/or are incorporated in other Almanac entries on liturgical subjects.

Nature and Purpose of Liturgy

The paragraphs under this and the following subhead are quoted directly from *Sacrosanctum Concilium* (Constitution on the Sacred Liturgy).

"It is through the liturgy, especially the divine Eucharistic Sacrifice, that 'the work of our redemption is exercised.' The liturgy is thus the outstanding means by which the faithful can express in their lives, and manifest to others, the mystery of Christ and the real nature of the true Church" (No. 2).

"The liturgy is considered as an exercise of the priestly office of Jesus Christ. In the liturgy the sanctification of man is manifested by signs perceptible to the senses, and is effected in a way which is proper to each of these signs; in the liturgy full public worship is performed by the Mystical Body of Jesus Christ, that is, by the Head and his members.

"From this it follows that every liturgical celebration, because it is an action of Christ the priest and of his Body the Church, is a sacred action surpassing all others. No other action of the Church can match its claim to efficacy, nor equal the degree of it" (No. 7).

"The liturgy is the summit toward which the activity of the Church is directed; at the same time it is the fountain from which all her power flows. For the goal of apostolic works is that all who are made sons of God by faith and baptism should come together to praise God in the midst of his Church, to take part in her sacrifice, and to eat the Lord's Supper.

"From the liturgy, therefore, and especially from the Eucharist, as from a fountain, grace is channeled into us; and the sanctification of men in Christ and the glorification of God, to which all other activities of the Church are directed as toward their goal, are most powerfully achieved" (No. 10).

Full Participation

"Mother Church earnestly desires that all the faithful be led to that full, conscious, and active participation in liturgical celebrations which is demanded by the very nature of the liturgy. Such participation by the Christian people as 'a chosen race, a royal priesthood, a holy nation, a purchased people' (1 Pt 2:9; cf. 2:4-5), is their right and duty by reason of their baptism.

"In the restoration and promotion of the sacred liturgy, this full and active participation by all the people is the aim to be considered before all else; for it is the primary and indispensable source from which the faithful are to derive the true Christian spirit" (No. 14).

"In order that the Christian people may more securely derive an abundance of graces from the sacred liturgy, holy Mother Church desires to undertake with great care a general restoration of the liturgy itself. For the liturgy is made up of unchangeable elements divinely instituted, and elements subject to change. The latter not only may but ought to be changed with the passing of time if features have by chance crept in which are less harmonious with the intimate nature of the liturgy, or if existing elements have grown less functional.

"In this restoration, both texts and rites should be drawn up so that they express more clearly the holy things which they signify. Christian people, as far as possible, should be able to understand them with ease and to take part in them fully, actively, and as befits a community" (No. 21).

Norms

Norms regarding the reforms concern the greater use of Scripture; emphasis on the importance of the sermon or homily on biblical and liturgical subjects; use of vernacular languages for prayers of the Mass and for administration of the sacraments; provision for adaptation of rites to cultural patterns.

Approval for reforms of various kinds — in liturgical texts, rites, etc. — depends on the Holy See, regional conferences of bishops and individual bishops, according to provisions of law. No priest has authority to initiate reforms on his own. Reforms may not be introduced just for the sake of innovation, and any that are introduced in the light of present-day circumstances should embody sound tradition.

To assure the desired effect of liturgical reforms, training and instruction are necessary for the clergy, religious and the laity. The functions of diocesan and regional commissions for liturgy, music and art are to set standards and provide leadership for instruction and practical programs in their respective fields.

Most of the constitution's provisions regarding liturgical reforms have to do with the Roman rite. The document clearly respects the equal dignity of all rites, leaving to the Eastern Churches control over their ancient liturgies.

(For coverage of the Mystery of the Eucharist, *see* **The Mass**; other sacraments, *see* separate entries.)

Sacramentals

Sacramentals, instituted by the Church, "are sacred signs which bear a resemblance to the sacraments: they signify effects, particularly of a spiritual kind, which are obtained through the Church's intercession. By them men are disposed to receive the chief effect of the sacraments, and various occasions in life are rendered holy" (No. 60).

"Thus, for well-disposed members of the faithful, the liturgy of the sacraments and sacramentals sanctifies almost every event in their lives; they are given access to the stream of divine grace which flows from the paschal mystery of the passion, death, and resurrection of Christ, the fountain from which all sacraments and sacramentals draw their power. There is hardly any proper use of material things which cannot thus be directed toward the sanctification of men and the praise of God" (No. 61).

Some common sacramentals are priestly blessings, blessed palm, candles, holy water, medals, scapulars, prayers and ceremonies of the Roman Ritual.

Liturgy of the Hours

The *Liturgy of the Hours* (Divine Office) is the public prayer of the Church for praising God and sanctifying the day. Its daily celebration is required as a sacred obligation by men in holy orders and by men and women religious who have professed solemn vows. Its celebration by others is highly commended and is to be encouraged in the community of the faithful.

"By tradition going back to early Christian times, the *Divine Office* is arranged so that the whole course of the day and night is made holy by the praises of God. Therefore, when this wonderful song of praise is worthily rendered by priests and others who are deputed for this purpose by Church ordinance, or by the faithful praying together with the priest in an approved form, then it is truly the voice of the bride addressing her bridegroom; it is the very prayer which Christ himself, together with his Body, addresses to the Father" (No. 84).

"Hence all who perform this service are not only fulfilling a duty of the Church, but also are sharing in the greatest honor accorded to Christ's spouse, for by offering these praises to God they are standing before God's throne in the name of the Church their Mother" (No. 85).

Revised Hours

The *Liturgy of the Hours*, revised since 1965, was the subject of Pope Paul VI's apostolic constitution *Laudis Canticum*, dated Nov. 1, 1970. The master Latin text was published in 1971; its four volumes have been published in authorized English translation since May 1975.

One-volume, partial editions of the *Liturgy of the Hours* containing Morning and Evening Prayer and other elements, have been published in approved English translation.

The revised *Liturgy of the Hours* consists of:

• Office of Readings, for reflection on the word of God. The principal parts are three psalms, biblical and non-biblical readings.

• Morning and Evening Prayer, called the "hinges" of the *Liturgy of the Hours*. The principal parts are a hymn, two psalms, an Old or New Testament canticle, a brief biblical reading, Zechariah's canticle (the *Benedictus*, morning) or Mary's canticle (the *Magnificat*, evening), responsories, intercessions and a concluding prayer.

• Daytime Prayer. The principal parts are a hymn, three psalms, a biblical reading and one of three concluding prayers corresponding to the time of day.

• Night Prayer. The principal parts are one or two psalms, a brief biblical reading, Simeon's canticle (*Nunc Dimittis*), a concluding prayer and an antiphon in honor of Mary.

In the revised *Liturgy of the Hours*, the hours are shorter than they had been, with greater textual variety, meditation aids, and provision for intervals of silence and meditation. The psalms are distributed over a four-week period instead of a week; some psalms, entirely or in part, are not included. Additional canticles from the Old and New Testaments are assigned for Morning and Evening Prayer. Additional scriptural texts have been added and variously arranged for greater internal unity, correspondence to readings at Mass, and relevance to events and themes of salvation history. Readings include some of the best material from the Fathers of the Church and other authors, and improved selections on the lives of the saints.

The book used for recitation of the *Office* is the *Breviary*.

For coverage of the Liturgical Year, see **Church Calendar**.

Sacred Music

"The musical tradition of the universal Church is a treasure of immeasurable value, greater even than that of any other art. The main reason for this pre-eminence is that, as sacred melody united to words, it forms a necessary or integral part of the solemn liturgy.

"Sacred music increases in holiness to the degree that it is intimately linked with liturgical action, winningly expresses prayerfulness, promotes solidarity, and enriches sacred rites with heightened solemnity. The Church indeed approves of all forms of true art, and admits them into divine worship when they show appropriate qualities" (No. 112).

The constitution decreed:

• Vernacular languages for the people's parts of the liturgy, as well as Latin, may be used.

• Participation in sacred song by the whole body of the faithful, and not just by choirs, is to be encouraged and brought about.

• Provisions should be made for proper musical training for clergy, religious and lay persons.

• While Gregorian Chant has a unique dignity and relationship to the Latin liturgy, other kinds of music are acceptable.

• Native musical traditions should be used, especially in mission areas.

• Various instruments compatible with the dignity of worship may be used.

Gregorian Chant: A form and style of chant called Gregorian was the basis and most highly regarded standard of liturgical music for centuries. It originated probably during the formative period of the Roman liturgy and developed in conjunction with Gallican and other forms of chant. Pope St. Gregory I the Great's connection with it is not clear, although it is known that he had great concern for and interest in church music. The earliest extant written versions of Gregorian Chant date from the ninth century. A thousand years later, the Benedictines of Solesmes, France, initiated a revival of chant which gave impetus to the modern liturgical movement.

Sacred Art and Furnishings

"Very rightly the fine arts are considered to rank among the noblest expressions of human genius.

This judgment applies especially to religious art and to its highest achievement, which is sacred art. By their very nature both of the latter are related to God's boundless beauty, for this is the reality which these human efforts are trying to express in some way. To the extent that these works aim exclusively at turning men's thoughts to God persuasively and devoutly, they are dedicated to God and to the cause of his greater honor and glory" (No. 122).

The objective of sacred art is "that all things set apart for use in divine worship should be truly worthy, becoming, and beautiful, signs and symbols of heavenly realities. The Church has always reserved to herself the right to pass judgment upon the arts, deciding which of the works of artists are in accordance with faith, piety, and cherished traditional laws, and thereby suited to sacred purposes.

"Sacred furnishings should worthily and beautifully serve the dignity of worship" (No. 122).

According to the constitution:

• Contemporary art, as well as that of the past, shall "be given free scope in the Church, provided that it adorns the sacred buildings and holy rites with due honor and reverence" (No. 123).

• Noble beauty, not sumptuous display, should be sought in art, sacred vestments and ornaments.

• "Let bishops carefully exclude from the house of God and from other sacred places those works of artists which are repugnant to faith, morals, and Christian piety, and which offend true religious sense either by their distortion of forms or by lack of artistic worth, by mediocrity or by pretense.

• "When churches are to be built, let great care be taken that they be suitable for the celebration of liturgical services and for the active participation of the faithful" (No. 124).

• "The practice of placing sacred images in churches so that they may be venerated by the faithful is to be firmly maintained. Nevertheless, their number should be moderate and their relative location should reflect right order. Otherwise they may create confusion among the Christian people and promote a faulty sense of devotion" (No. 125).

• Artists should be trained and inspired in the spirit and for the purposes of the liturgy.

• The norms of sacred art should be revised. "These laws refer especially to the worthy and well-planned construction of sacred buildings, the shape and construction of altars, the nobility, location, and security of the Eucharistic tabernacle, the suitability and dignity of the baptistery, the proper use of sacred images, embellishments, and vestments" (No. 128).

RITES

Rites are the forms and ceremonial observances of liturgical worship coupled with the total expression of the theological, spiritual and disciplinary heritages of particular churches of the East and West.

Different rites have evolved in the course of church history, giving to liturgical worship and church life in general forms and usages peculiar and proper to the nature of worship and the culture of the faithful in various circumstances of time and place. Thus, there has been development since apostolic times in the prayers and ceremonies of the Mass, in the celebration of the sacraments, sacramentals and the Liturgy of the Hours, and in observances of the liturgical calendar. The principal sources of rites in present use were practices within the patriarchates of Rome (for the West) and Antioch, Alexandria and Constantinople (for the East). Rites are identified as Eastern or Western on the basis of their geographical area of origin in the Roman Empire.

Eastern and Roman Rites

Eastern rites are proper to Eastern Catholic Churches (see separate entry). The principal rites are Byzantine, Alexandrian, Antiochene, Armenian and Chaldean.

The Latin or Roman rite prevails in the Western Church. It was derived from Roman practices and the use of Latin from the third century onward, and has been the rite in general use in the West since the eighth century. Other rites in limited use in the Western Church have been the Ambrosian (in the Archdiocese of Milan), the Mozarabic (in the Archdiocese of Toledo), the Lyonnais, the Braga, and rites peculiar to some religious orders like the Dominicans, Carmelites and Carthusians.

The purpose of the revision of rites in progress since the Second Vatican Council is to renew them, not to eliminate the rites of particular churches or to reduce all rites to uniformity. The Council reaffirmed the equal dignity and preservation of rites as follows.

"It is the mind of the Catholic Church that each individual church or rite retain its traditions whole and entire, while adjusting its way of life to various needs of time and place. Such individual churches, whether of the East or the West, although they differ somewhat among themselves in what are called rites (that is, in liturgy, ecclesiastical discipline and spiritual heritage), are, nevertheless, equally entrusted to the pastoral guidance of the Roman Pontiff, the divinely appointed successor of St. Peter in supreme government over the universal Church. They are, consequently, of equal dignity, so that none of them is superior to the others by reason of rite."

Determination of Rite

Determination of a person's rite is regulated by Church law. Through baptism, a child becomes a member of the rite of his or her parents. If the parents are of different rites, the child's rite is decided by mutual consent of the parents; if there is lack of mutual consent, the child is baptized in the rite of the father. A candidate for baptism over the age of 14 can choose to be baptized in any approved rite. Catholics baptized in one rite may receive the sacraments in any of the approved ritual churches; they may transfer to another rite only with the permission of the Holy See and in accordance with other provisions of the Code of Canon Law.

MASS, EUCHARISTIC SACRIFICE AND BANQUET

Declarations of Vatican II

The Second Vatican Council made the following declarations among others with respect to the Mass:

"At the Last Supper, on the night when he was betrayed, our Savior instituted the Eucharistic Sacrifice of his Body and Blood. He did this in order to perpetuate the Sacrifice of the Cross throughout the centuries until he should come again, and so to entrust to his beloved spouse, the Church, a memorial of his death and resurrection: a sacrament of love, a sign of unity, a bond of charity, a paschal banquet in which Christ is consumed, the mind is filled with grace, and a pledge of future glory is given to us" (*Sacrosanctum Concilium*, Constitution on the Sacred Liturgy, No. 47).

"... As often as the Sacrifice of the Cross in which 'Christ, our Passover, has been sacrificed' (1 Cor 5:7) is celebrated on an altar, the work of our redemption is carried on. At the same time, in the sacrament of the Eucharistic bread the unity of all believers who form one body in Christ (cf. 1 Cor 10:17) is both expressed and brought about. All men are called to this union with Christ" (*Lumen Gentium*, Dogmatic Constitution on the Church, No. 3).

"... The ministerial priest, by the sacred power he enjoys, molds and rules the priestly people. Acting in the person of Christ, he brings about the Eucharistic Sacrifice, and offers it to God in the name of all the people. For their part, the faithful join in the offering of the Eucharist by virtue of their royal priesthood" (Ibid., No. 10).

Declarations of Trent

Among its decrees on the Holy Eucharist, the Council of Trent stated the following points of doctrine on the Mass.

1. There is in the Catholic Church a true sacrifice, the Mass instituted by Jesus Christ. It is the sacrifice of his Body and Blood, Soul and Divinity, himself, under the appearances of bread and wine.

2. This Sacrifice is identical with the Sacrifice of the Cross, inasmuch as Christ is the Priest and Victim in both. A difference lies in the manner of offering, which was bloody upon the Cross and is bloodless on the altar.

3. The Mass is a propitiatory Sacrifice, atoning for the sins of the living and dead for whom it is offered.

4. The efficacy of the Mass is derived from the Sacrifice of the Cross, whose superabundant merits it applies to men.

5. Although the Mass is offered to God alone, it may be celebrated in honor and memory of the saints.

6. Christ instituted the Mass at the Last Supper.

7. Christ ordained the Apostles priests, giving them power and the command to consecrate his Body and Blood to perpetuate and renew the Sacrifice.

ORDER OF THE MASS

The Mass consists of two principal divisions called the **Liturgy of the Word**, which features the proclamation of the Word of God, and the **Eucharistic Liturgy**, which focuses on the central act of sacrifice in the Consecration and on the Eucharistic Banquet in Holy Communion. (Formerly, these divisions were called, respectively, the **Mass of the Catechumens** and the **Mass of the Faithful**.) In addition to these principal divisions, there are ancillary introductory and concluding rites.

The following description covers the Mass as celebrated with participation by the people. This Order of the Mass was approved by Pope Paul VI in the apostolic constitution *Missale Romanum* dated Apr. 3, 1969, and promulgated in a decree issued Apr. 6, 1969, by the Congregation for Divine Worship. The assigned effective date was Nov. 30, 1969.

Introductory Rites

Entrance: The introductory rites begin with the singing or recitation of an entrance song consisting of one or more scriptural verses stating the theme of the mystery, season or feast commemorated in the Mass.

Greeting: The priest and people make the Sign of the Cross together. The priest then greets them in one of several alternative ways and they reply in a corresponding manner.

Introductory Remarks: At this point, the priest or another of the ministers may introduce the theme of the Mass.

Penitential Rite: The priest and people together acknowledge their sins as a preliminary step toward worthy celebration of the sacred mysteries.

This rite includes a brief examination of conscience, a general confession of sin and plea for divine mercy in one of several ways, and a prayer for forgiveness by the priest.

Glory to God: A doxology, a hymn of praise to God, sung or said on festive occasions.

Opening Prayer: A prayer of petition offered by the priest on behalf of the worshiping community.

I. Liturgy of the Word

Readings: The featured elements of this liturgy are readings of passages from the Bible. If three readings are in order, the first is usually from the Old Testament, the second from the New Testament (Letters, Acts, Revelation), and the third from one of the Gospels; the final reading is always a selection from a Gospel. The first reading(s) is (are) concluded with the formula, "The Word of the Lord" (effective Feb. 28, 1993; optional before that date), to which the people respond, "Thanks be to God." The Gospel reading is concluded with the formula, "The Gospel of the Lord," (effective as above), to which the people respond, "Praise to you, Lord Jesus Christ." Between the readings, psalm verses are sung or recited. A Gospel acclamation is either sung or omitted.

Homily: An explanation, pertinent to the mystery being celebrated and the special needs of the listeners, of some point in either the readings from sacred Scripture or in another text from the Ordinary or Proper parts of the Mass; it is a proclamation of the Good News for a response of faith.

Creed: The Nicene profession of faith, by priest and people, on certain occasions.

Prayer of the Faithful: Litany-type prayers of petition, with participation by the people. Called general intercessions, they concern needs of the Church, the salvation of the world, public authorities, persons in need, the local community.

II. Eucharistic Liturgy

Presentation and Preparation of Gifts: Presentation to the priest of the gifts of bread and wine, principally, by participating members of the congregation. Preparation of the gifts consists of the prayers and ceremonies with which the priest offers bread and wine as the elements of the sacrifice to take place during the Eucharistic Prayer and of the Lord's Supper to be shared in Holy Communion.

Washing of Hands: After offering the bread and wine, the priest cleanses his fingers with water in a brief ceremony of purification.

Pray, Brothers and Sisters: Prayer that the sacrifice to take place will be acceptable to God. The first part of the prayer is said by the priest; the second, by the people.

Prayer over the Gifts: A prayer of petition offered by the priest on behalf of the worshiping community.

Eucharistic Prayer

Preface: A hymn of praise, introducing the Eucharistic Prayer or Canon, sung or said by the priest following responses by the people. The Order of the Mass contains a variety of prefaces, for use on different occasions.

Holy, Holy, Holy; Blessed is He: Divine praises sung or said by the priest and people.

Eucharistic Prayer (Canon): Its central portion is the Consecration, when the essential act of sacrificial offering takes place with the changing of bread and wine into the Body and Blood of Christ. The various parts of the prayer, which are said by the celebrant only, commemorate principal mysteries of salvation history and include petitions for the Church, the living and dead, and remembrances of saints.

Doxology: A formula of divine praise sung or said by the priest while he holds aloft the chalice containing the consecrated wine in one hand and the paten containing the consecrated host in the other.

Communion Rite

Lord's Prayer: Sung or said by the priest and people.

Prayer for Deliverance from Evil: Called an embolism because it is a development of the final petition of the Lord's Prayer; said by the priest. It concludes with a memorial of the return of the Lord to which the people respond, "For the kingdom, the power, and the glory are yours, now and forever."

Prayer for Peace: Said by the priest, with corresponding responses by the people. The priest can, in accord with local custom, bid the people to exchange a greeting of peace with each other.

Lamb of God (*Agnus Dei*): A prayer for divine mercy sung or said while the priest breaks the consecrated host and places a piece of it into the consecrated wine in the chalice.

Communion: The priest, after saying a preparatory prayer, administers Holy Communion to himself and then to the people, thus completing the sacrifice-banquet of the Mass. (This completion is realized even if the celebrant alone receives the Eucharist.) On giving the Eucharist to each person under both species separately, the priest or eucharistic minister says, "The Body of Christ," "The Blood of Christ." The customary response is "Amen." If the Eucharist is given by intinction (in which the host is dipped into the consecrated wine), the priest says, "The Body and Blood of Christ." **Communion Song**: Scriptural verses or a suitable hymn sung or said during the distribution of Holy Communion. After Holy Communion is received, some moments may be spent in silent meditation or in the chanting of a psalm or hymn of praise.

Prayer after Communion: A prayer of petition offered by the priest on behalf of the worshiping community.

Concluding Rite

Announcements: Brief announcements to the people are in order at this time.

Dismissal: Consists of a final greeting by the priest, a blessing, and a formula of dismissal. This rite is omitted if another liturgical action immediately follows the Mass; e.g., a procession, the blessing of the body during a funeral rite.

Some parts of the Mass are changeable with the liturgical season or feast, and are called the proper of the Mass. Other parts are said to be common because they always remain the same.

Additional Mass Notes

Catholics are seriously obliged to attend Mass in a worthy manner on Sundays and holy days of obligation. Failure to do so without a proportionately serious reason is gravely wrong.

It is the custom for priests to celebrate Mass daily whenever possible. To satisfy the needs of the faithful on Sundays and holy days of obligation, they are authorized to say Mass twice (**bination**) or even three times (**trination**). Bination is also permissible on weekdays to satisfy the needs of the faithful. On Christmas every priest may say three Masses.

The **fruits of the Mass**, which in itself is of infinite value, are: **general**, for all the faithful; **special (ministerial)**, for the intentions or persons specifically intended by the celebrant; **most special (personal)**, for the celebrant himself. On Sundays and certain other days pastors are obliged to offer Mass for their parishioners, or to have another priest do so. If a priest accepts a stipend or offering for a Mass, he is obliged in justice to apply the Mass for the intention of the donor. Mass may be applied for the living and the dead, or for any good intention.

Mass can be celebrated in several ways: e.g., with people present, without their presence (privately), with two or more priests as co-celebrants (concelebration), with greater or less solemnity.

Some of the various types of Masses are: **for the dead** (Funeral Mass or Mass of Christian Burial, Mass for the Dead — formerly called Requiem Mass); **ritual**, in connection with celebration of the sacraments, religious profession, etc.; **nuptial**, for married couples, with or after the wedding ceremony; **votive**, to honor a Person of the Trinity, a saint, or for some special intention.

Places, Altars for Mass

The ordinary place for celebrating the Eucharist is a church or other sacred place, at a fixed or movable altar.

The altar is a table at which the Eucharistic Sacrifice is celebrated.

A fixed altar is attached to the floor of the church. It should be of stone, preferably, and should be consecrated. The Code of Canon Law orders observance of the custom of placing under a fixed altar relics of martyrs or other saints.

A movable altar can be made of any solid and suitable material, and should be blessed or consecrated.

Outside of a sacred place, Mass may be celebrated in an appropriate place at a suitable table covered with a linen cloth and corporal. An altar stone containing the relics of saints, which was formerly prescribed, is not required by regulations in effect since the promulgation Apr. 6, 1969, of *Institutio Generalis Missalis Romani*.

LITURGICAL VESTMENTS

In the early years of the Church, vestments worn by the ministers at liturgical functions were the same as the garments in ordinary popular use. They became distinctive when their form was not altered to correspond with later variations in popular style. Liturgical vestments are symbolic of the sacred ministry and add appropriate decorum to divine worship.

Mass Vestments

Alb: A body-length tunic of white fabric; a vestment common to all ministers of divine worship.

Amice: A rectangular piece of white cloth worn about the neck, tucked into the collar and falling over the shoulders; prescribed for use when the alb does not completely cover the ordinary clothing at the neck.

Chasuble: Originally, a large mantle or cloak covering the body, it is the outer vestment of a priest celebrating Mass or carrying out other sacred actions connected with the Mass.

Chasuble-Alb: A vestment combining the features of the chasuble and alb; for use with a stole by concelebrants and, by way of exception, by celebrants in certain circumstances.

Cincture: A cord which serves the purpose of a belt, holding the alb close to the body.

Dalmatic: The outer vestment worn by a deacon in place of a chasuble.

Stole: A long, band-like vestment worn by a priest about the neck and falling to about the knees. A deacon wears a stole over the left shoulder, crossed and fastened at his right side.

The material, form and ornamentation of the aforementioned and other vestments are subject to variation and adaptation, according to norms and decisions of the Holy See and concerned conferences of bishops. The overriding norm is that they should be appropriate for use in divine worship. The customary ornamented vestments are the chasuble, dalmatic and stole.

The minimal vestments required for a priest celebrating Mass are the alb, stole, and chasuble.

Liturgical Colors

The colors of outer vestments vary with liturgical seasons, feasts and other circumstances. The colors and their use are:

Green: For the season of ordinary time; symbolic of hope and the vitality of the life of faith.

Violet (Purple): For Advent and Lent; may also be used in Masses for the dead; symbolic of penance. (See below, Violet for Advent.)

Red: For the Sunday of the Passion, Good Friday, Pentecost; feasts of the Passion of Our Lord, the Apostles and Evangelists, martyrs; symbolic of the supreme sacrifice of life for the love of God.

Rose: May be used in place of purple on the Third Sunday of Advent (formerly called Gaudete Sunday) and the Fourth Sunday of Lent (formerly called Laetare Sunday); symbolic of anticipatory joy during a time of penance.

White: For the seasons of Christmas and Easter; feasts and commemorations of Our Lord, except those of the Passion; feasts and commemorations of the Blessed Virgin Mary, angels, saints who are not martyrs, All Saints (Nov. 1), St. John the Baptist (June 24), St. John the Evangelist (Dec. 27),

the Chair of St. Peter (Feb. 22), the Conversion of St. Paul (Jan. 25). White, symbolic of purity and integrity of the life of faith, may generally be substituted for other colors, and can be used for funeral and other Masses for the dead.

Options are provided regarding the color of vestments used in offices and Masses for the dead. The newsletter of the U.S. Bishops' Committee on the Liturgy, in line with No. 308 of the General Instruction of the Roman Missal, announced in July 1970: "In the dioceses of the U.S., white vestments may be used, in addition to violet (purple) and black, in offices and Masses for the dead."

On more solemn occasions, better than ordinary vestments may be used, even though their color (e.g., gold) does not match the requirement of the day.

Violet for Advent: Violet is the official liturgical color for the season of Advent, according to the September 1988 edition of the newsletter of the U.S. Bishops' Committee on the Liturgy. Blue was being proposed in order to distinguish between the Advent season and the specifically penitential season of Lent. The newsletter said, however, that "the same effect can be achieved by following the official color sequence of the Church, which requires the use of violet for Advent and Lent, while taking advantage of the varying shades which exist for violet. Light blue vestments are not authorized for use in the U.S."

Considerable freedom is permitted in the choice of colors of vestments worn for votive Masses.

Other Vestments

Cappa Magna: Flowing vestment with a train, worn by bishops and cardinals.

Cassock: A non-liturgical, full-length, close-fitting robe for use by priests and other clerics under liturgical vestments and in ordinary use; usually black for priests, purple for bishops and other prelates, red for cardinals, white for the pope. In place of a cassock, priests belonging to religious institutes wear the habit proper to their institute.

Cope: A mantle-like vestment open in front and fastened across the chest; worn by sacred ministers in processions and other ceremonies, as prescribed by appropriate directives.

Habit: The ordinary (non-liturgical) garb of members of religious institutes, analogous to the cassock of diocesan priests; the form of habits varies from institute to institute.

Humeral Veil: A rectangular vestment worn about the shoulders by a deacon or priest in Eucharistic processions and for other prescribed liturgical ceremonies.

Mitre: A headdress worn at some liturgical functions by bishops, abbots and, in certain cases, other ecclesiastics.

Pallium: A circular band of white wool about two inches wide, with front and back pendants, marked with six crosses, worn about the neck. It is a symbol of the fullness of the episcopal office. Pope Paul VI, in a document issued July 20, 1978, on his own initiative and entitled Inter Eximia Episcopalis, restricted its use to the pope and archbishops of metropolitan sees. In 1984, Pope John Paul II decreed that the pallium would ordinarily be conferred by the pope on the solemnity of Sts. Peter and Paul, June 29. The pallium is made from the wool of lambs blessed by the pope on the feast of St. Agnes (Jan. 21).

Rochet: A knee-length, white linen-lace garment of prelates worn under outer vestments.

Surplice: a loose, flowing vestment of white fabric

with wide sleeves. For some functions, it is interchangeable with an alb.

Zucchetto: A skullcap worn by bishops and other prelates.

SACRED VESSELS, LINENS
Vessels

Paten and Chalice: The principal sacred vessels required for the celebration of Mass are the paten (plate) and chalice (cup) in which bread and wine, respectively, are offered, consecrated and consumed. Both should be made of solid and noble material which is not easily breakable or corruptible. Gold coating is required of the interior parts of sacred vessels subject to rust. The cup of a chalice should be made of non-absorbent material.

Vessels for containing consecrated hosts (see below) can be made of material other than solid and noble metal — e.g., ivory, more durable woods — provided the substitute material is locally regarded as noble or rather precious and is suitable for sacred use.

Sacred vessels should be blessed, according to prescribed requirements.

Vessels, in addition to the paten, for containing consecrated hosts are:

Ciborium: Used to hold hosts for distribution to the faithful and for reservation in the tabernacle.

Luna, Lunula, Lunette: A small receptacle which holds the sacred host in an upright position in the monstrance.

Monstrance, Ostensorium: A portable receptacle so made that the sacred host, when enclosed therein, may be clearly seen, as at Benediction or during extended exposition of the Blessed Sacrament.

Pyx: A watch-shaped vessel used in carrying the Eucharist to the sick.

Linens

Altar Cloth: A white cloth, usually of linen, covering the table of an altar. One cloth is sufficient. Three were used according to former requirements.

Burse: A square, stiff flat case, open at one end, in which the folded corporal can be placed; the outside is covered with material of the same kind and color as the outer vestments of the celebrant.

Corporal: A square piece of white linen spread on the altar cloth, on which rest the vessels holding the Sacred Species — the consecrated host(s) and wine — during the Eucharistic Liturgy. The corporal is used whenever the Blessed Sacrament is removed from the tabernacle; e.g., during Benediction the vessel containing the Blessed Sacrament rests on a corporal.

Finger Towel: A white rectangular napkin used by the priest to dry his fingers after cleansing them following the offering of gifts at Mass.

Pall: A square piece of stiff material, usually covered with linen, which can be used to cover the chalice at Mass.

Purificator: A white rectangular napkin used for cleansing sacred vessels after the reception of Communion at Mass.

Veil: The chalice intended for use at Mass can be covered with a veil made of the same material as the outer vestments of the celebrant.

THE CHURCH BUILDING

A church is a building set aside and dedicated for purposes of divine worship, the place of assembly for a worshipping community. A Catholic church is the ordinary place in which the faithful assemble for participation in the Eucharistic Liturgy and other forms of divine worship.

In the early years of Christianity, the first places of assembly for the Eucharistic Liturgy were private homes (Acts 2:46; Rom 16:5; 1 Cor 16:5; Col 4:15) and, sometimes, catacombs. Church building began in the latter half of the second century during lulls in persecution and became widespread after enactment of the Edict of Milan in 313, when it finally became possible for the Church to emerge completely from the underground. The oldest and basic norms regarding church buildings date from about that time.

The essential principle underlying all norms for church building was reformulated by the Second Vatican Council: "When churches are to be built, let great care be taken that they be suitable for the celebration of liturgical services and for the active participation of the faithful" (*Sacrosanctum Concilium*, Constitution on the Sacred Liturgy, No. 124).

This principle was subsequently elaborated in detail by the Congregation for Divine Worship in a document entitled *Institutio Generalis Missalis Romani*, which was approved by Paul VI Apr. 3, 1969, and promulgated by a decree of the congregation dated Apr. 6, 1969. Coverage of the following items reflects the norms stated in Chapter V of the *Institutio*.

Main Features

Sanctuary: The part of the church where the altar of sacrifice is located, the place where the ministers of the liturgy lead the people in prayer, proclaim the word of God and celebrate the Eucharist. It is set off from the body of the church by a distinctive structural feature — e.g., elevation above the main floor — or by ornamentation. (The traditional communion rail, removed in recent years in many churches, served this purpose of demarcation.) The customary location of the sanctuary is at the front of the church; it may, however, be centrally located.

Altar: The main altar of sacrifice and table of the Lord is the focal feature of the sanctuary and entire church. It stands by itself, so that the ministers can move about it freely, and is so situated that they face the people during the liturgical action. In addition to this main altar, there may also be others; in new churches, these are ideally situated in side chapels or alcoves removed to some degree from the body of the church.

Adornment of the Altar: The altar table is covered with a suitable linen cloth. Required candelabra and a cross are placed upon or near the altar in plain sight of the people and are so arranged that they do not obscure their view of the liturgical action.

Seats of the Ministers: The seats of the ministers should be so arranged that they are part of the seating arrangement of the worshipping congregation and suitably placed for the performance of ministerial functions. The seat of the celebrant or chief concelebrant should be in a presiding position.

Ambo, Pulpit, Lectern: The stand at which scriptural lessons and psalm responses are read, the word of God preached, and the prayer of the faithful offered. It is so placed that the ministers can be easily seen and heard by the people.

Places for the People: Seats and kneeling benches (pews) and other accommodations for the people are so arranged that they can participate in the most appropriate way in the liturgical action and have freedom of movement for the reception of Holy Communion. Reserved seats are out of order.

Place for the Choir: Where it is located depends on the most suitable arrangement for maintaining the unity of the choir with the congregation and for providing its members maximum opportunity for carrying out their proper function and participating fully in the Mass.

Tabernacle: The best place for reserving the Blessed Sacrament is in a chapel suitable for the private devotion of the people. If this is not possible, reservation should be at a side altar or other appropriately adorned place. In either case, the Blessed Sacrament should be kept in a tabernacle, i.e., a safe-like, secure receptacle.

Statues: Images of the Lord, the Blessed Virgin Mary and the saints are legitimately proposed for the veneration of the faithful in churches. Their number and arrangement, however, should be ordered in such a way that they do not distract the people from the central celebration of the Eucharistic Liturgy. There should be only one statue of one and the same saint in a church.

General Adornment and Arrangement of Churches: Churches should be so adorned and fitted out that they serve the direct requirements of divine worship and the needs and reasonable convenience of the people.

Other Items

Ambry: A box containing the holy oils, attached to the wall of the sanctuary in some churches.

Baptistery: The place for administering baptism. Some churches have baptisteries adjoining or near the entrance, a position symbolizing the fact that persons are initiated in the Church and incorporated in Christ through this sacrament. Contemporary liturgical practice favors placement of the baptistery near the sanctuary and altar, or the use of a portable font in the same position, to emphasize the relationship of baptism to the Eucharist, the celebration in sacrifice and banquet of the death and resurrection of Christ.

Candles: Used more for symbolical than illuminative purposes, they represent Christ, the light and life of grace, at liturgical functions. They are made of beeswax. (See Index: Paschal Candle.)

Confessional, Reconciliation Room: A booth-like structure for the hearing of confessions, with separate compartments for the priest and penitents and a grating or screen between them. The use of confessionals became general in the Roman rite after the Council of Trent. Since the Second Vatican Council, there has been a trend in the U.S. to replace or supplement confessionals with small reconciliation rooms so arranged that priest and penitent can converse face-to-face.

Crucifix: A cross bearing the figure of the body of Christ, representative of the Sacrifice of the Cross.

Cruets: Vessels containing the wine and water used at Mass. They are placed on a credence table in the sanctuary.

Holy Water Fonts: Receptacles containing holy water, usually at church entrances, for the use of the faithful.

Sanctuary Lamp: A lamp which is kept burning continuously before a tabernacle in which the Blessed Sacrament is reserved, as a sign of the Real Presence of Christ.

LITURGICAL DEVELOPMENTS

The principal developments covered in this article are enactments of the Holy See and actions related to their implementation in the U.S.

Modern Movement

Origins of the modern movement for renewal in the liturgy date back to the 19th century. The key contributing factor was a revival of liturgical and scriptural studies. Of special significance was the work of the Benedictine monks of Solesmes, France, who aroused great interest in the liturgy through the restoration of Gregorian Chant. St. Pius X approved their work in a *motu proprio* of 1903 and gave additional encouragement to liturgical study and development.

St. Pius X did more than any other single pope to promote early first Communion and the practice of frequent Communion, started the research behind a revised breviary, and appointed a group to investigate possible revisions in the Mass.

The movement attracted some attention in the 1920s and '30s but made little progress.

Significant pioneering developments in the U.S. during the 1920s, however, were the establishment of the Liturgical Press, the beginning of publication of *Orate Fratres* (now *Worship*), and the inauguration of the League of the Divine Office by the Benedictines at St. John's Abbey, Collegeville, MN. Later events of influence were the establishment of the Pius X School of Liturgical Music at Manhattanville College of the Sacred Heart and the organization of a summer school of liturgical music at Mary Manse College by the Gregorian Institute of America. The turning point toward real renewal was reached during and after World War II.

Pius XII gave it impetus and direction, principally through the background teaching in his encyclicals on the Mystical Body (*Mystici Corporis Christi*, 1943), Sacred Liturgy (*Mediator Dei*, 1947), and On Sacred Music (*Musicae Sacrae*, 1955), and by means of specific measures affecting the liturgy itself. His work was continued during the pontificates of his successors. The Second Vatican Council, in virtue of *Sacrosanctum Concilium*, the Constitution on the Sacred Liturgy, inaugurated changes of the greatest significance.

Before and After Vatican II

The most significant liturgical changes made in the years immediately preceding the Second Vatican Council were the following:

1. Revision of the rites of Holy Week for universal observance from 1956.

2. Modification of the Eucharistic fast and permission for afternoon and evening Mass, in effect from 1953 and extended in 1957.

3. The Dialogue Mass, introduced in 1958.

4. Use of popular languages in administration of the sacraments.

5. Calendar-missal-breviary reform, in effect from Jan. 1, 1961.

6. Seven-step administration of baptism for adults, approved in 1962.

The Constitution on the Sacred Liturgy, *Sacrosanctum Concilium*, approved (2,174 to 4) and promulgated by the Second Vatican Council on Dec. 4, 1963, marked the beginning of a profound renewal in the Church's corporate worship. Implementation of some of its measures was ordered by Paul VI on Jan. 25, 1964, in the *motu proprio Sacram Liturgiam*. On Feb. 29, a special commission, the Consilium for Implementing the Constitution on the Sacred Liturgy, was formed to supervise the execution of the entire program of liturgical reform. Implementation of the program on local and regional levels was left to bishops acting through their own liturgical commissions and in concert with their fellow bishops in national conferences.

Liturgical reform in the U.S. has been carried out under the direction of the Liturgy Committee, National Conference of Catholic Bishops. Its secretariat, established early in 1965, is located at 3211 Fourth St. N.E., Washington, DC 20017.

Stages of Development

Liturgical development after the Second Vatican Council proceeded in several stages. It started with the formulation of guidelines and directives, and with the translation into vernacular languages of virtually unchanged Latin ritual texts. Then came structural changes in the Mass, the sacraments, the calendar, the Divine Office and other phases of the liturgy. These revisions were just about completed with the publication of a new order for the sacrament of penance in February 1974. A continuing phase of development, in progress from the beginning, involves efforts to deepen the liturgical sense of the faithful, to increase their participation in worship and to relate it to full Christian life.

RECENT DEVELOPMENTS

'Happy Are Those Who Are Called to His Supper'

On Nov. 14, 2006, during their fall general meeting in Baltimore, the Bishops of the United States, by a 201-24 vote with two abstentions, "'Happy Are Those Who Are called to His Supper': On Preparing to Receive Christ Worthily in the Eucharist," a statement on the preparation needed to receive Communion worthily.

The New English Translation of the Order of the Mass

On June 15, 2006, during their spring meeting in Los Angeles, the Bishops of the United States approved the new English translations of the Order of the Mass and adopted several U.S. adaptations. The new translation was approved by a vote of 173-29, and the American adaptations comprised of prayers or ritual instructions not contained in the original Latin version were approved by a vote of 184-8.

On Mar. 25, 2010, Card. Antonio Cañizares Llovera, Prefect of the Congregation for Divine Worship and the Discipline of the Sacraments, issued a letter granting approval, or "recognitio," of the proposed U.S. version of the new edition of the *Roman Missal*. The new translation was introduced officially with the start of Advent 2011.

The United States Conference of Catholic Bishops (USCCB) undertook extensive efforts to prepare the faithful for the changes. Catholic publishers also devoted a variety of resources to publish guides to the changes as well as charts and pew sheets for use by Catholics to familiarize themselves with the new translation, especially during Mass.

New U.S. Norms for Distribution of Communion Under Both Species

New norms for the distribution and reception of Communion under the outward signs of both bread and wine by Catholics in the U.S. were approved by the U.S. bishops on June 15, 2001, and confirmed by the Holy See on Mar. 22, 2002; they were subsequently published by Bp. Wilton D. Gregory of Belleville, IL, president of the USCCB.

The norms, which replace the U.S. bishops' 1984 directory titled "This Holy and Living Sacrifice," give specific directives regarding liturgical roles, sacred vessels and the rites to be followed in distributing Communion under both kinds.

The first section of the new norms provides a theological summary of the Church's teaching on Communion under both kinds, while the following section describes the authorized procedures by which such distribution can be accomplished at Mass.

The U.S. adaptations are to be incorporated into the new *General Instruction of the Roman Missal* and have the same force of law in the U.S. as the rest of the general instruction. The General Instruction of the recently revised *Roman Missal* permits bishops' conferences to provide norms for the distribution of Communion under both kinds, meaning under the outward signs of both bread and wine.

Included among the norms is an indult — or exception to the general requirement — from the Vatican Congregation for Divine Worship and the Sacraments that provides for the cleansing of sacred vessels by special eucharistic ministers. The indult was promulgated as "particular law" for the dioceses of the U.S. at the same time as the norms and it became effective on Apr. 7, 2002.

However, the Vatican congregation declined to approve an indult authorizing special ministers to assist with the distribution of the consecrated blood to other chalices during the singing of the "Lamb of God."

In the letter confirming the norms, the congregation also made clear that special eucharistic ministers, or indeed any communicant, may assist in the consumption of what remains of the blood after distribution of Communion has been completed.

Texts and Translations

The master texts of all documents on liturgical reform are in Latin. Effective dates of their implementation have depended on the completion and approval of appropriate translations into vernacular languages. English translations were made by the International Committee for English in the Liturgy.

The principal features of liturgical changes and the effective dates of their introduction in the U.S. are covered below under topical headings. (For expanded coverage of various items, especially the sacraments, see additional entries.)

On May 7, 2001, the Congregation for Divine Worship and the Sacraments issued the new instruction, *Liturgiam Authenticam* ("The Authentic Liturgy"). The instruction set stricter rules for the translation of Latin liturgical texts into other languages and bears the subtitle, "On the Use of Vernacular Languages in the Publication of the Books of the Roman Liturgy." The instruction was welcomed by then-NCCB president, Bp. Joseph A. Fiorenza of Galveston-Houston, who said that it reflects long consultations between the Vatican and English-speaking bishops, adding that "It is now our hope and expectation that there will be a much quicker approval of liturgical texts" by the Vatican. The instruction was subsequently debated at the bishops' meeting in November 2001.

General Instruction of the Roman Missal

In spring 2001, Pope John Paul II authorized the publication of an *editio typica tertia* of the *Missale Romanum*. The much anticipated revision included a new edition of the *Institutio Generalis Missalis Romani* (*General Instruction of the Roman Missal*). On Nov. 12, 2002, the Latin Church members of the United States Conference of Catholic Bishops approved a translation of the *Institutio Generalis Missalis Romani* prepared by the International Commission on English in the Liturgy. The translation was confirmed by the Congregation for Divine Worship and the Discipline of the Sacraments on Mar. 17, 2003. This translation of the *General Instruction of the Roman Missal* is the sole translation of the *Institutio Generalis Missalis Romani, editio typica tertia* for use in the dioceses of the United States of America. Concerning the new edition, Msgr. James P. Moroney, Executive Director of the USCCB Secretariat for the Liturgy, wrote in the Foreword:

"This revised *Institutio Generalis* possesses a unique role among all the documents on the liturgy. Like its preceding editions, it has been published in order to give life to a dream. It was the dream of reformers such as St. Hippolytus, St. Gregory, and St. Leo. It was the dream of Pope Paul VI and clearly remains the vision of Pope John Paul II, who calls us to 'an ever deeper grasp of the liturgy of the Church, celebrated according to the current books and lived above all as a reality in the spiritual order' (*Vicesimus Quintus Annus*, 1988, No. 14). Likewise, this dream is shared by the Bishops' Committee on the Liturgy and the United States Conference of Catholic Bishops that it serves. Finally, it is the vision of the Church itself: the dream of God's people joined to Christ in Baptism and made 'ever more holy by conscious, active, and fruitful participation in the mystery of the Eucharist' (*General Instruction of the Roman Missal*, No. 5)."

Redemptionis Sacramentum

On Apr. 23, 2004, the Congregation for Divine Worship and the Sacraments, in collaboration with the Congregation for the Doctrine of the Faith and at the request of Pope John Paul II issued the instruction "*Redemptionis Sacramentum*: On Certain Matters to Be Observed or to Be Avoided Regarding the Most Holy Eucharist." The instruction states:

"It is not at all the intention here to prepare a compendium of the norms regarding the Most Holy Eucharist, but rather, to take up within this Instruction some elements of liturgical norms that have been previously expounded or laid down and even today remain in force in order to assure a deeper appreciation of the liturgical norms; to establish certain norms by which those earlier ones are explained and complemented; and also to set forth for bishops, as well as for priests, deacons and all the lay Christian faithful, how each should carry them out in accordance with his own responsibilities and the means at his disposal."

The Mass

A new Order of the Mass, supplanting the one authorized by the Council of Trent in the 16th century, was introduced in the U.S. Mar. 22, 1970. It had been approved by Paul VI in the apostolic constitution *Missale*

Romanum, dated Apr. 3, 1969.

Preliminary and related to it were the following developments.

Mass in English: Introduced Nov. 29, 1964. In the same year, Psalm 42 was eliminated from the prayers at the foot of the altar.

Incidental Changes: The last Gospel (prologue of John) and vernacular prayers following Mass were eliminated Mar. 7, 1965. At the same time, provision was made for the celebrant to say aloud some prayers formerly said silently.

Rubrics: An instruction entitled *Tres Abhinc Annos*, dated May 4 and effective June 29, 1967, simplified directives for the celebration of Mass, approved the practice of saying the canon aloud, altered the Communion and dismissal rites, permitted purple instead of black vestments in Masses for the dead, discontinued wearing of the maniple, and approved in principle the use of vernacular languages for the canon, ordination rites, and lessons of the Divine Office when read in choir.

Eucharistic Prayers (Canons): The traditional Roman Canon in English was introduced Oct. 22, 1967. Three additional Eucharistic prayers, authorized May 23, 1968, were approved for use in English the following Aug. 15.

The customary Roman Canon, which dates at least from the beginning of the fifth century and has remained substantially unchanged since the seventh century, is the first in the order of listing of the Eucharistic prayers. It can be used at any time, but is the one of choice for most Sundays, some special feasts like Easter and Pentecost, and for feasts of the Apostles and other saints who are commemorated in the canon. Any preface can be used with it.

The second Eucharistic prayer, the shortest and simplest of all, is best suited for use on weekdays and various special circumstances. It has a preface of its own, but others may be used with it. This canon bears a close resemblance to the one framed by St. Hippolytus about 215.

The third Eucharistic prayer is suitable for use on Sundays and feasts as an alternative to the Roman Canon. It can be used with any preface and has a special formula for remembrance of the dead.

The fourth Eucharistic prayer, the most sophisticated of them all, presents a broad synthesis of salvation history. Based on the Eastern tradition of Antioch, it is best suited for use at Masses attended by persons versed in Sacred Scripture. It has an unchangeable preface.

Five additional Eucharistic prayers — three for Masses with children and two for Masses of reconciliation — were approved in 1974 and 1975, respectively, by the Congregation for the Sacraments and Divine Worship.

Use of the Eucharistic Prayers for Various Needs and Occasions, was approved by the U.S. bishops in 1994, confirmed by the appropriate Vatican congregations May 9, 1995, and ratified for use beginning Oct. 1, 1995.

Lectionary: A new compilation of scriptural readings and psalm responsories for Mass was published in 1969. The Lectionary contains a three-year cycle of readings for Sundays and solemn feasts, a two-year weekday cycle, and a one-year cycle for the feasts of saints, in addition to readings for a variety of votive Masses, ritual Masses and Masses for various needs. There are also responsorial psalms to follow the first readings and Gospel or alleluia versicles.

A second edition of the Lectionary, substantially the same as the first, was published in 1981. New features included an expanded introduction, extensive scriptural references and additional readings for a number of solemnities and feasts.

Volume One of a new Lectionary for the Mass was decreed by Bp. Anthony Pilla of Cleveland, then president of the NCCB, as permissible for use as of the first Sunday of Advent, Nov. 29, 1998. The first new Lectionary since 1973, Volume One contains the readings for Sundays, solemnities and feasts of the Lord. Volume Two, containing the readings for weekdays, feasts of saints, and various other occasions, was given final approval on June 19, 1998, by the NCCB but still required confirmation by the Holy See.

Sacramentary (Missal): The Vatican Polyglot Press began distribution in June 1970, of the Latin text of a new *Roman Missal*, the first revision published in 400 years. The English translation was authorized for optional use beginning July 1, 1974; the mandatory date for use was Dec. 1, 1974.

The Sacramentary is the celebrant's Mass book of entrance songs, prayers, prefaces and Eucharistic prayers, including special common sets of texts for various commemorations and intentions — dedication of churches, Mary, the apostles, martyrs, doctors of the Church, virgins, holy men and women, the dead, other categories of holy persons, administration of certain sacraments, special intentions.

Study of the Mass: The Bishops' Committee on the Liturgy, following approval by the National Conference of Catholic Bishops in May 1979, began a study of the function and position of elements of the Mass, including the Gloria, the sign of peace, the penitential rite and the readings. Major phases of the study have been completed, and work is still under way toward completion of the project.

Mass for Special Groups: Reasons and norms for the celebration of Mass at special gatherings of the faithful were the subject of an instruction issued May 15, 1969. Two years earlier, the U.S. Bishops' Liturgy Committee went on record in support of the celebration of Mass in private homes under appropriate conditions.

Sunday Mass on Saturday: The Congregation for the Clergy, under date of Jan. 10, 1970, granted the request that the faithful, where bishops consider it pastorally necessary or useful, may satisfy the precept of participating in Mass in the late afternoon or evening hours of Saturdays and the days before holy days of obligation. This provision is stated in Canon 1248 of the Code of Canon Law.

Bination and Trination: Canon 905 of the Code of Canon Law provides that local ordinaries may permit priests to celebrate Mass twice a day (bination), for a just cause; in cases of pastoral need, they may permit priests to celebrate Mass three times a day (trination) on Sundays and holy days of obligation.

Mass in Latin: According to notices issued by the Congregation for Divine Worship June 1, 1971, and Oct. 28, 1974: (1) Bishops may permit the celebration of Mass in Latin for mixed-language groups; (2) bishops may permit the celebration of one or two Masses in Latin on weekdays or Sundays in any church, irrespective of mixed-language groups involved (1971); (3) priests may celebrate Mass in Latin when people are not present; (4) the approved revised Order of the Mass is to be used in Latin as well as vernacular languages; (5) by way of exception, bishops may permit older and handicapped priests to use the Council of Trent's Order of the Mass in private celebration of the holy Sacrifice. (See Permission for **Tridentine Mass**.)

Mass Obligation Waived: The Congregation for Bishops approved July 4, 1992, a resolution of the U.S. bishops to waive the Mass attendance obligation for the holy days of Mary, the Mother of God (Jan. 1), the Assumption of Mary (Aug. 15) and All Saints (Nov. 1) when these solemnities fall on Saturday or Monday.

Inter-Ritual Concelebration: The Apostolic Delegation (now Nunciature) in Washington, DC, announced in June 1971 that it had received authorization to permit priests of Roman and Eastern rites to celebrate Mass together in the rite of the host church. It was understood that the inter-ritual concelebrations would always be "a manifestation of the unity of the Church and of communion among particular churches."

Ordo of the Sung Mass: In a decree dated June 24 and made public Aug. 24, 1972, the Congregation for Divine Worship issued a new *Ordo of the Sung Mass* — containing Gregorian chants in Latin — to replace the *Graduale Romanum*.

Mass for Children: Late in 1973, the Congregation for Divine Worship issued special guidelines for children's Masses, providing accommodations to the mentality and spiritual growth of pre-adolescents while retaining the principal parts and structures of the Mass. The Directory for Masses with Children was approved by Paul VI Oct. 22 and was dated Nov. 1, 1973. Three Eucharistic prayers for Masses with children were approved by the congregation in 1974; English versions were approved June 5, 1975. Their use, authorized originally for a limited period of experimentation, was extended indefinitely Dec. 15, 1980.

Lectionary for Children: A lectionary for Masses with children, with an announced publication date of September 1993, was authorized for use by choice beginning Nov. 28, 1993. A revised *Lectionary for Masses with Children* was approved by the bishops on Nov. 15, 2006 during their fall general meeting in Washington. The text must also be approved by the Vatican before it can be used in the liturgy in the United States. Assuming approval is given, it will replace the experimental children's Lectionary that has been in use since 1993. The new Lectionary includes stricter rules for its use.

Sacraments

The general use of English in administration of the sacraments was approved for the U.S. Sept. 14, 1964. Structural changes of the rites were subsequently made and introduced in the U.S. as follows.

Pastoral Care of the Sick: Revised rites, covering also administration of the Eucharist to sick persons, were approved Nov. 30, 1972, and published Jan. 18, 1973. The effective date for use of the provisional English prayer formula was Dec. 1, 1974. The mandatory effective date for use of the ritual, Pastoral Care of the Sick in English, was Nov. 27, 1983.

Baptism: New rites for the baptism of infants, approved Mar. 19, 1969, were introduced June 1, 1970.

Rite of Christian Initiation of Adults: Revised rites were issued Jan. 6, 1972, for the Christian initiation of adults — affecting preparation for and reception of baptism, the Eucharist and confirmation; also, for the reception of already baptized adults into full communion with the Church. These rites, which were introduced in the U.S. on the completion of English translation, nullified a seven-step baptismal process approved in 1962. On Mar. 8, 1988, the National Conference of Catholic Bishops was notified that the Congregation for Divine Worship had approved the final English translation of the Rite of Christian Initiation of Adults. The mandatory date for putting the rite into effect was Sept. 1, 1988.

Confirmation: Revised rites, issued Aug. 15, 1971, became mandatory in the U.S. Jan. 1, 1973. The use of a stole by persons being confirmed should be avoided, according to an item in the December 1984 edition of the Newsletter of the Bishops' Committee on the Liturgy. The item said: "The distinction between the universal priesthood of all the baptized and the ministerial priesthood of the ordained is blurred when the distinctive garb (the stole) of ordained ministers is used in this manner."

A decree regarding the proper age for confirmation, approved by the U.S. bishops in June 1993 was ratified by the Congregation for Bishops Feb. 8, 1994. The decree reads: "In accord with prescriptions of canon 891, the National Conference of Catholic Bishops hereby decrees that the sacrament of confirmation in the Latin rite shall be conferred between the age of discretion, which is about the age of seven, and 18 years of age, within the limits determined by the diocesan bishop and with regard for the legitimate exceptions given in canon 891, namely, when there is danger of death or where, in the judgment of the minister, grave cause urges otherwise." The decree became effective July 1, 1994, and continued in effect until July 1, 1999.

Special Ministers of the Eucharist: The designation of lay men and women to serve as special ministers of the Eucharist was authorized by Paul VI in an "Instruction on Facilitating Communion in Particular Circumstances" (*Immensae Caritatis*), dated Jan. 29 and published by the Congregation for Divine Worship Mar. 29, 1973. Provisions concerning them are contained in Canons 230 and 910 of the Code of Canon Law.

Qualified laypersons may serve as special ministers for specific occasions or for extended periods in the absence of a sufficient number of priests and deacons to provide reasonable and appropriate service in the distribution of Holy Communion, during Mass and outside of Mass (to the sick and shut-ins). Appointments of ministers are made by priests with the approval of the appropriate bishop.

The Newsletter of the U.S. Bishops' Committee on the Liturgy stated in its February 1988 edition: "When ordinary ministers (bishops, priests, deacons) are present during a Eucharistic celebration, whether they are participating in it or not, and are not prevented from doing so, they are to assist in the distribution of Communion. Accordingly, if the ordinary ministers are in sufficient number, special ministers of the Eucharist are not allowed to distribute Communion at that Eucharistic celebration." Pope John Paul II approved this decision and ordered it published June 15, 1987.

Holy Orders: Revised ordination rites for deacons, priests and bishops, validated by prior experimental use, were approved in 1970. The sacrament of holy orders underwent further revision in 1972 with the elimination of the Church-instituted orders of porter, reader, exorcist, acolyte and subdeacon, and of the tonsure ceremony symbolic of entrance into the clerical state. The former minor orders of reader and acolyte were changed from orders to ministries.

Matrimony: A revised rite for the celebration of marriage was promulgated by the Congregation for Divine Worship and the Discipline of the Sacraments Mar. 19, 1969, and went into effect June 1, 1970. A second typi-

cal edition of the order of celebration, with revisions in accord with provisions of the Code of Canon Law promulgated in 1983, was approved and published in 1990 (*Notitiae*, Vol. 26, No.6). The date for implementation was reported to be dependent on the completion of required translations and appropriate formalities.

Penance: Ritual revision of the sacraments was completed with approval by Pope Paul VI on Dec. 2, 1973, of new directives for the sacrament of penance or reconciliation. The U.S. Bishops' Committee on the Liturgy set Feb. 27, 1977, as the mandatory date for use of the new rite. The committee also declared that it could be used from Mar. 7, 1976, after adequate preparation of priests and people. The Holy See gave authorization in 1968 for the omission of any reference to excommunication or other censures in the formula of absolution unless there was some indication that a censure had actually been incurred by a penitent.

Additional Developments

Music: An instruction on Music in the Liturgy, dated Mar. 5 and effective May 14, 1967, encouraged congregational singing during liturgical celebrations and attempted to clarify the role of choirs and trained singers. More significantly, the instruction indicated that a major development under way in the liturgy was a gradual erasure of the distinctive lines traditionally drawn between the sung liturgy and the spoken liturgy, between what had been called the high Mass and the low Mass.

In the same year, the U.S. Bishops' Liturgy Committee approved the use of contemporary music, as well as guitars and other suitable instruments, in the liturgy. The Holy See authorized in 1968 the use of musical instruments other than the organ in liturgical services, "provided they are played in a manner suitable to worship."

On Nov. 14, 2008 the U.S. Bishops at the fall meeting approved new guidelines for the use of music in worship, English- and Spanish-language rituals for the celebration of weekday Liturgies of the Word, and revised Lectionary readings for Lent. The music document, "Sing to the Lord: Music in Divine Worship," was accepted by the bishops in a 183-22 vote, with three abstentions.

Calendar: A revised liturgical calendar approved by Paul VI Feb. 14 and made public May 9, 1969, went into effect in the U.S. in 1972. Since that time, memorials and feasts of beatified persons and saints have been added.

Communion in Hand: Since 1969, the Holy See has approved the practice of in-hand reception of the Eucharist in regions and countries where it had the approval of the appropriate episcopal conferences. The first grant of approval was to Belgium in May 1969. Approval was granted the U.S. in June 1977.

Liturgy of the Hours: The background, contents, scope and purposes of the revised *Divine Office*, called the *Liturgy of the Hours*, were described by Paul VI in the apostolic constitution *Laudis Canticum*, dated Nov. 1, 1970. A provisional English version, incorporating basic features of the master Latin text, was published in 1971. The four complete volumes of the Hours in English have been published since May 1975. One-volume, partial editions have also been published in approved form. Nov. 27, 1977, was set by the Congregation for Divine Worship and the National Conference of Catholic Bishops as the effective date for exclusive use in liturgical worship of the translation of the Latin text of the *Liturgy of the Hours* approved by the International Committee on English in the Liturgy.

Holy Week: The English version of revised Holy Week rites went into effect in 1971. They introduced concelebration of Mass, placed new emphasis on commemorating the institution of the priesthood on Holy Thursday, and modified Good Friday prayers for other Christians, Jews and other non-Christians.

The Congregation for Divine Worship released Feb. 20, 1988, a "Circular Letter concerning the Preparation and Celebration of the Easter Feasts." It called the feasts the "summit of the whole liturgical year," and criticized practices which dilute or change appropriate norms for their celebration. Singled out for blame for the abuse or ignorance of norms was the "inadequate formation given to the clergy and the faithful regarding the paschal mystery as the center of the liturgical year and of Christian life." The document set out the appropriate norms for the Lenten season, Holy Week, the Easter Triduum, Easter and the weeks following. It was particularly insistent on the proper celebration of the Easter Vigil, to take place after nightfall on Saturday and before dawn on Sunday.

Oils: The Congregation for Divine Worship issued a directive in 1971 permitting the use of other oils — from plants, seeds or coconuts — instead of the traditional olive oil in administering some of the sacraments. The directive also provided that oils could be blessed at other times than at the usual Mass of Chrism on Holy Thursday, and authorized bishops' conferences to permit priests to bless oils in cases of necessity.

Dancing and Worship: Dancing and worship was the subject of an essay which appeared in a 1975 edition of *Notitiae* (11, pp. 202-205), the official journal of the Congregation for the Sacraments and Divine Worship. The article was called a "qualified and authoritative sketch," and should be considered "an authoritative point of reference for every discussion of the matter."

The principal points of the essay were:
• "The dance has never been made an integral part of the official worship of the Latin Church."
• "If the proposal of the religious dance in the West is really to be made welcome, care will have to be taken that in its regard a place be found outside of the liturgy, in assembly areas which are not strictly liturgical. Moreover, the priests must always be excluded from the dance."

Mass for Deceased Non-Catholic Christians: The Congregation for the Doctrine of the Faith released a decree June 11, 1976, authorizing the celebration of public Mass for deceased non-Catholic Christians under certain conditions: "(1) The public celebration of the Masses must be explicitly requested by the relatives, friends, or subjects of the deceased person for a genuine religious motive. (2) In the Ordinary's judgment, there must be no scandal for the faithful."

Built of Living Stones: Art, Architecture, and Worship: At their November 2001 meeting in Washington, DC, the Bishops approved this document by the U.S. Bishops' Committee on the Liturgy; it replaces the document *Environment and Art in Catholic Worship* issued in March 1978.

Doxology: The bishops' committee called attention in August 1978, to the directive that the Doxology concluding the Eucharistic Prayer is said or sung by the celebrant (concelebrants) alone, to which the people respond, "Amen." **Churches, Altars, Chalices**: The Newsletter of the U.S. Bishops' Committee on the Liturgy reported in November 1978, that the Congregation for Divine Worship had given provisional approval of a new English translation for the rite of dedicating churches and altars, and of a new form for the blessing of chalices.

Eucharistic Worship: This was the subject of two documents issued in 1980. *Dominicae Coenae* was a letter addressed by Pope John Paul to bishops throughout the world in connection with the celebration of Holy Thursday; it was dated Feb. 24 and released Mar.18, 1980. It was more doctrinal in content than the "Instruction on Certain Norms concerning Worship of the Eucharistic Mystery" (*Inaestimabile Donum*, "The Priceless Gift"), which was approved by the Pope Apr. 17 and published by the Congregation for the Sacraments and Divine Worship May 23. Its stated purpose was to reaffirm and clarify teaching on liturgical renewal contained in enactments of the Second Vatican Council and in several related implementing documents.

Tridentine Mass: The celebration of Mass according to the 1962 typical (master) edition of the *Roman Missal* — the so-called Tridentine Mass — was authorized by Pope Benedict XVI under certain conditions according to the *motu proprio Summorum Pontificum*, issued on July 7, 2007. **See below.**

In a letter from the Congregation for Divine Worship, dated Oct. 3, 1984, Pope John Paul II wished to be responsive to priests and faithful who remained attached to the so-called Tridentine rite. The principal condition for the celebration was: "There must be unequivocal, even public, evidence that the priest and people petitioning have no ties with those who impugn the lawfulness and doctrinal soundness of the *Roman Missal* promulgated in 1970 by Pope Paul VI." (This, in particular, with reference to the followers of dissident Abp. Marcel Lefebvre.)

Six guidelines for celebration of the Tridentine Mass were contained in the letter regarding its "wide and generous" use, for two purposes: to win back Lefebvre followers and to clear up misunderstandings about liberal permission for use of the Tridentine rite. The letter, from the Pontifical Commission *Ecclesia Dei*, said in part:
• The Tridentine Mass can be celebrated in a parish church, so long as it provides a pastoral service and is harmoniously integrated into the parish liturgical schedule.
• When requested, the Mass should be offered on a regular Sunday and holy day basis, "at a central location, at a convenient time" for a trial period of several months, with "adjustment" later if needed.
• Celebrants of the Mass should make it clear that they acknowledge the validity of the postconciliar liturgy.
• Although the commission has the authority to grant use of the Tridentine rite to all groups that request it, the commission "would much prefer that such faculties be granted by the Ordinary himself so that ecclesial communion can be strengthened."
• While the new Lectionary in the vernacular can be used in the Tridentine Mass, as suggested by the Second Vatican Council, it should not be "imposed on congregations that decidedly wish to maintain the former liturgical tradition in its integrity."
• Older and retired priests who have asked permission to celebrate Mass according to the Tridentine rite should be given the chance to do so for groups that request it.

In March 2003, the Vatican Secretariat of State issued new rules allowing the old rite to be used under very strict conditions.

Summorum Pontificum

Pope Benedict XVI issued the Apostolic Letter in the form of a *motu proprio*, *Summorum Pontificum*, on July 7,

2007. The following is the text of the letter: It has always been the care of the Supreme Pontiffs until the present time, that the Church of Christ offer worthy worship to the Divine Majesty "for the praise and glory of his name" and "for the good of all his Holy Church."

As from time immemorial so in the future the principle shall be respected "according to which each particular Church must be in accord with the universal Church not only regarding the doctrine of the faith and sacramental signs, but also as to the usages universally handed down by apostolic and unbroken tradition. These are to be maintained not only so that errors may be avoided, but also so that the faith may be passed on in its integrity, since the Church's rule of prayer (*lex orandi*) corresponds to her rule of belief (*lex credendi*)."

Among Pontiffs who have displayed such care there excels the name of St. Gregory the Great, who saw to the transmission to the new peoples of Europe both of the Catholic faith and of the treasures of worship and culture accumulated by the Romans in preceding centuries. He gave instructions for the form of the Sacred Liturgy of both the Sacrifice of the Mass and of the Divine Office as was celebrated in the City. He made the greatest efforts to foster monks and nuns, who militating under the Rule of St. Benedict, in every place along with the proclamation of the Gospel by their life likewise exemplified that most salutary expression of the Rule "let nothing be given precedence over the work of God" (ch. 43). In this way the sacred liturgy according to the Roman manner made fertile not only the faith and piety but also the culture of many peoples. Moreover it is evident that the Latin Liturgy in its various forms has stimulated in the spiritual life very many saints in every century of the Christian age and strengthened in the virtue of religion so many peoples and made fertile their piety However, in order that the Sacred Liturgy might more efficaciously absolve its task, several others among the Roman Pontiffs in the course of the centuries have brought to bear particular concern, among whom St. Pius V is eminent, who with great pastoral zeal, at the exhortation of the Council of Trent, renewed the worship of the whole Church, ensuring the publishing of liturgical books amended and "restored according to the norm of the Fathers" and put them into use in the Latin Church It is clear that among the liturgical books of the Roman Rite the Roman Missal is eminent. It grew in the city of Rome and gradually down through the centuries took on forms which are very similar to those in vigor in recent generations.

"It was this same goal that as time passed the Roman Pontiffs pursued, adapting or establishing liturgical rites and books to new ages and then at the start of the present century undertaking a more ample restoration." It was in this manner that our Predecessors Clement VIII, Urban VIII, St Pius X, Benedict XV, Pius XII and the Blessed John XXIII acted.

In more recent time, however, the Second Vatican Council expressed the desire that with due respect and reverence for divine worship it be restored and adapted to the needs of our age. Prompted by this desire, our Predecessor the Supreme Pontiff Paul VI in 1970 approved for the Latin Church liturgical books restored and partly renewed, and that throughout the world translated into many vernacular languages, have been welcomed by the bishops and by the priests and faithful. John Paul II revised the third typical edition of the *Roman Missal*. Thus the Roman Pontiffs have acted so that "this liturgical

edifice, so to speak, ...might once again appear splendid in its dignity and harmony."

However in some regions not a small number of the faithful have been and remain attached with such great love and affection to the previous liturgical forms, which had profoundly imbued their culture and spirit, that the Supreme Pontiff John Paul II, prompted by pastoral concern for these faithful, in 1984 by means of a special Indult *Quattuor abhinc annos*, drawn up by the Congregation for Divine Worship, granted the faculty to use the *Roman Missal* published by John XXIII in 1962; while in 1988 John Paul II once again, by means of the motu proprio *Ecclesia Dei*, exhorted the bishops to make wide and generous use of this faculty in favor of all the faithful requesting it.

Having pondered at length the pressing requests of these faithful to our Predecessor John Paul II, having also heard the Fathers of the Consistory of Cardinals held on March 23, 2006, having pondered all things, invoked the Holy Spirit and placed our confidence in the help of God, by this present Apostolic Letter we DECREE the following:

Art. 1. The *Roman Missal* promulgated by Paul VI is to be regarded as the ordinary expression of the law of prayer (lex orandi) of the Catholic Church of Latin Rite, while the Roman Missal promulgated by St. Pius V and published again by Blessed John XXIII as the extraordinary expression of the law of prayer (*lex orandi*) and on account of its venerable and ancient use let it enjoy due honor. These two expressions of the law of prayer (*lex orandi*) of the Church in no way lead to a division in the law of prayer (*lex orandi*) of the Church, for they are two uses of the one Roman Rite.

Hence it is licit to celebrate the Sacrifice of the Mass in accordance with the typical edition of the Roman Missal promulgated by Blessed John XXIII in 1962 and never abrogated, as the extraordinary form of the Liturgy of the Church. The conditions laid down by the previous documents *Quattuor abhinc annos* and *Ecclesia Dei* for the use of this Missal are replaced by what follows:

Art. 2. In Masses celebrated without the people, any priest of Latin rite, whether secular or religious, can use the *Roman Missal* published by Pope Blessed John XXIII in 1962 or the *Roman Missal* promulgated by the Supreme Pontiff Paul VI in 1970, on any day except in the Sacred Triduum. For celebration in accordance with one or the other Missal, a priest does not require any permission, neither from the Apostolic See nor his own Ordinary.

Art. 3. If Communities or Institutes of Consecrated Life or Societies of Apostolic Life of either pontifical or diocesan rite desire to have a celebration of Holy Mass in accordance with the edition of the *Roman Missal* promulgated in 1962 in the conventual or "community" celebration in their own oratories, this is allowed. If an individual community or the entire Institute or Society wants to have such celebrations often or habitually or permanently, the matter is to be decided by the Major Superiors according to the norm of law and the particular laws and statutes.

Art. 4. With due observance of law, even Christ's faithful who spontaneously request it, may be admitted to celebrations of Holy Mass mentioned in art. 2 above.

Art. 5, § 1. In parishes where a group of faithful attached to the previous liturgical tradition exists stably, let the pastor willingly accede to their requests for the celebration of the Holy Mass according to the rite of the *Roman Missal* published in 1962. Let him see to it that the good of these faithful be harmoniously reconciled with ordinary pastoral care of the parish, under the governance of the bishop according to canon 392, avoiding discord and fostering the unity of the whole Church.

§ 2. Celebration according to the Missal of Blessed John XXIII can take place on weekdays, while on Sundays and on feast days there may be one such celebration.

§ 3. Let the pastor permit celebrations in this extraordinary form for faithful or priests who request it, even in particular circumstances such as weddings, funerals or occasional celebrations, for example pilgrimages.

§ 4. Priests using the Missal of Blessed John XXIII must be worthy and not impeded by law.

§ 5. In churches, which are neither parochial nor conventual, it is the rector of the church who grants the above-mentioned permission.

Art. 6. In Masses celebrated with the people according to the Missal of Blessed John XXIII, the Readings can be proclaimed even in the vernacular, using editions that have received the recognitio of the Apostolic See.

Art. 7. Where some group of lay faithful, mentioned in art. 5§1 does not obtain what it requests from the pastor, it should inform the diocesan bishop of the fact. The bishop is earnestly requested to grant their desire. If he cannot provide for this kind of celebration, let the matter be referred to the Pontifical Commission Ecclesia Dei.

Art. 8. A Bishop who desires to make provision for requests of lay faithful of this kind, but is for various reasons prevented from doing so, may refer the matter to the Pontifical Commission "Ecclesia Dei," which should give him advice and help.

Art. 9, § 1. Likewise a pastor may, all things duly considered, grant permission to use the older ritual in administering the Sacraments of Baptism, Matrimony, Penance and the Anointing of the Sick, as the good of souls may suggest.

§ 2. Ordinaries are granted the faculty to celebrate the sacrament of Confirmation using the former Roman Pontifical, as the good of souls may suggest.

§ 3. It is lawful for clerics in holy orders to use even the *Roman Breviary* promulgated by Blessed John XXIII in 1962.

Art 10. It is lawful for the local Ordinary, if he judges it opportune, to erect a personal parish according to the norm of canon 518 for celebrations according to the older form of the Roman rite or appoint a rector or chaplain, with due observance of the requirements of law.

Art. 11. The Pontifical Commission Ecclesia Dei, erected in 1988 by John Paul II, continues to carry out its function. This Commission is to have the form, duties and norm for action that the Roman Pontiff may wish to assign to it.

Art. 12. The same Commission, in addition to the faculties it already enjoys, will exercise the authority of the Holy See by maintaining vigilance over the observance and application of these dispositions.

Whatever is decreed by Us by means of this *Motu Proprio*, we order to be firm and ratified and to be observed as of Sept. 14 this year, the feast of the Exaltation of the Holy Cross, all things to the contrary notwithstanding.

Given at Rome, at St Peter's, on July 7, in the Year of Our Lord 2007, the Third of Our Pontificate.

+ BENEDICT XVI

1. *General Instruction of the Roman Missal*, third edition, 2002, No. 397

2. Pope John Paul II, ap. letter *Vicesimus quintus annus*,

Dec. 4, 1988, No. 3: AAS 81 (1989) p. 899.

3. Ibidem.

4. Pope St Pius X, *motu proprio Abhinc duos annos*, Oct. 23, 1913: AAS 5 (1913) 449-450; cf. Pope John Paul II, ap. letter *Vicesimus quintus annus*, Dec. 4, 1988, No. 3: AAS 81 (1989) p. 899

5. Cf. Pope John Paul II, *motu proprio Ecclesia Dei adflicta*, July 2, 1988, No. 6: AAS 80 (1988) p. 1498. (This unofficial translation has been prepared by the United States Conference of Catholic Bishops' Secretariat for the Liturgy. Only the Latin original of the Apostolic Letter may be considered the official text.)

Universae Ecclesia

On May 13, 2011, the Pontifical Commission "Ecclesia Dei" published the Instruction on the application of Benedict XVI's Apostolic Letter *motu proprio "Summorum Pontificum."* The document, approved by the Pope, was signed by Card. William Levada and Msgr. Guido Pozzo, respectively president and secretary of the Pontifical Commission "Ecclesia Dei."

Spanish: In accord with decrees of the Congregation for Divine Worship, Spanish was approved as a liturgical language in the U.S. (Jan. 19, 1985). The *texto unico* of the Ordinary of the Mass became mandatory in the U.S. Dec. 3, 1989. Spanish translations of Proper-of-the-Mass texts proper to U.S. dioceses were approved Mar. 12, 1990. An approved Spanish version of the Rite for the Christian Initiation of Adults was published in 1991. The Institute of Hispanic Liturgy opened its national office June 1, 1995, on the campus of The Catholic University of America in Washington.

Funeral Rites: A revised Order of Christian Funerals became mandatory in the U.S. Nov. 2, 1989.

Permission for the presence of cremated human remains in the funeral liturgy, including the Eucharist, was granted in 1997 to local bishops in the U.S. by the Congregation for Divine Worship and the Discipline of the Sacraments. Adaptations to existing rites are under study.

Popular Piety and Liturgy: The relation of popular piety to the liturgy was the subject of remarks by Pope John Paul II at a meeting with a group of Italian bishops Apr. 24, 1986. He said, in part:

"An authentic liturgical ministry will never be able to neglect the riches of popular piety, the values proper to the culture of a people, so that such riches might be illuminated, purified and introduced into the liturgy as an offering of the people."

Extended Eucharistic Exposition: In response to queries, the Secretariat of the U.S. Bishops' Committee on the Liturgy issued an advisory stating that liturgical law permits and encourages in parish churches:

• Exposition of the Blessed Sacrament for an extended period of time once a year, with consent of the local Ordinary and only if suitable numbers of the faithful are expected to be present;

• Exposition ordered by the local Ordinary, for a grave and general necessity, for a more extended period of supplication when the faithful assemble in large numbers.

With regard to perpetual exposition, this form is generally permitted only in the case of those religious communities of men or women who have the general practice of perpetual Eucharistic adoration or adoration over extended periods of time.

The Secretariat's advisory appeared in the June-July 1986 edition of the Newsletter of the Bishops' Committee on the Liturgy.

Native American Languages: The Newsletter of the U.S. Bishops' Committee on the Liturgy reported in December 1986, and May 1987, respectively, that the Congregation for Divine Worship had authorized Mass translations in Navajo and Choctaw. Lakota was approved as a liturgical language in 1989.

Communion Guidelines: In 1986 and again in 1996, the U.S. bishops' approved the insertion of advisories in missalettes and similar publications, stating that: (1) The Eucharist is to be received by Catholics only, except in certain specific cases; (2) To receive Communion worthily, a person must be in the state of grace (i.e., free of serious sin) and observe the eucharistic fast (See separate entry).

Unauthorized Eucharistic Prayers: The May 1987 Newsletter of the U.S. Bishops' Committee on the Liturgy restated the standing prohibition against the use of any Eucharistic Prayers other than those contained in the Sacramentary. Specifically, the article referred to the 25 unauthorized prayers in a volume entitled *Spoken Visions*.

Homilist: According to the Pontifical Commission for the Authentic Interpretation of Canon Law, the diocesan bishop cannot dispense from the requirement of Canon 767, par. 1, that the homily in the liturgy be reserved to a priest or deacon. Pope John Paul approved this decision June 20, 1987.

Concerts in Churches: In a letter released Dec. 5, 1987, the Congregation for Divine Worship declared that churches might be used on a limited basis for concerts of sacred or religious music, but not for concerts featuring secular music.

Blessings: A revised *Book of Blessings* was ordered into use beginning Dec. 3, 1989.

Litany of the Blessed Virgin Mary: "Queen of Families," a new invocation, was reported by the U.S. bishops in 1996, for insertion between "Queen of the Rosary" and "Queen of Peace."

Inclusive Language: "Criteria for the Evaluation of Inclusive Language Translations of Scriptural Texts Proposed for Liturgical Use" was issued by the U.S. bishops in November 1990. The criteria distinguish between non-use of vertical inclusiveness in references to God and use of horizontal, gender-inclusive terms (he/she, man/woman and the like) where appropriate in references to persons.

THE SACRAMENTS OF THE CHURCH

The sacraments are actions of Christ and his Church (itself a kind of sacrament) that signify grace, cause it in the act of signifying it, and confer it upon persons properly disposed to receive it. They perpetuate the redemptive activity of Christ, making it present and effective. They infallibly communicate the fruit of that activity — namely grace — to responsive persons with faith. Sacramental actions consist of the union of sensible signs (matter of the sacraments) with the words of the minister (form of the sacraments).

Christ himself instituted the seven sacraments of the New Law by determining their essence and the efficacy of their signs to produce the grace they signify.

Christ is the principal priest or minister of every sacrament; human agents — an ordained priest, baptized persons contracting marriage with each other, any person conferring emergency baptism in a proper manner — are secondary ministers. Sacraments have efficacy from Christ, not from the personal dispositions of their human ministers.

Each sacrament confers sanctifying grace for the special purpose of the sacrament; this is, accordingly, called sacramental grace. It involves a right to actual graces corresponding to the purposes of the respective sacraments.

Baptism, confirmation and the Eucharist are sacraments of initiation; penance (reconciliation) and anointing of the sick, sacraments of healing; order and matrimony, sacraments for service.

While sacraments infallibly produce the grace they signify, recipients benefit from them in proportion to their personal dispositions. One of these is the intention to receive sacraments as sacred signs of God's saving and grace-giving action. The state of grace is also necessary for fruitful reception of the Holy Eucharist, confirmation, matrimony, holy orders and anointing of the sick. Baptism is the sacrament in which grace is given in the first instance and original sin is remitted. Penance is the secondary sacrament of reconciliation, in which persons guilty of serious sin after baptism are reconciled with God and the Church, and in which persons already in the state of grace are strengthened in that state.

Role of Sacraments

The Second Vatican Council prefaced a description of the role of the sacraments with the following statement concerning participation by all the faithful in the priesthood of Christ and the exercise of that priesthood by receiving the sacraments (Dogmatic Constitution on the Church, *Lumen Gentium*, Nos. 10 and 11).

"The baptized by regeneration and the anointing of the Holy Spirit are consecrated into a spiritual house and a holy priesthood. Thus through all those works befitting Christian men they can offer spiritual sacrifice and proclaim the power of him who has called them out of darkness into his marvelous light (cf. 1 Pt 2:4-10).

"Though they differ from one another in essence and not only in degree, the common priesthood of the faithful and the ministerial or hierarchical priesthood (of those ordained to holy orders) are nonetheless interrelated. Each of them in its own special way is a participation in the one priesthood of Christ. The ministerial priest, by the sacred power he enjoys, molds and rules the priestly people. Acting in the Person of Christ, he brings about the Eucharistic Sacrifice, and offers it to God in the name of all the people. For their part, the faithful join in the offering of the Eucharist by virtue of their royal priesthood. They likewise exercise that priesthood by receiving the sacraments, by prayer and thanksgiving, by the witness of a holy life, and by self-denial and active charity.

"It is through the sacraments and the exercise of the virtues that the sacred nature and organic structure of the priestly community is brought into operation."

Baptism: "Incorporated into the Church through baptism, the faithful are consecrated by the baptismal character to the exercise of the cult of the Christian religion. Reborn as sons of God, they must confess before men the faith which they have received from God through the Church."

Confirmation: "Bound more intimately to the Church by the sacrament of confirmation, they are endowed by the Holy Spirit with special strength. Hence they are more strictly obliged to spread and defend the faith both by word and by deed as true witnesses of Christ."

Eucharist: "Taking part in the Eucharistic Sacrifice, which is the fount and apex of the whole Christian life, they offer the divine Victim to God, and offer themselves along with It. Thus, both by the act of oblation and through holy Communion, all perform their proper part in this liturgical service, not, indeed. all in the same way but each in that way which is appropriate to himself. Strengthened anew at the holy table by the Body of Christ, they manifest in a practical way that unity of God's People which is suitably signified and wondrously brought about by this most awesome sacrament."

Penance: "Those who approach the sacrament of penance obtain pardon from the mercy of God for offenses committed against him. They are at the same time reconciled with the Church, which they have wounded by their sins, and which by charity, example, and prayer seeks their conversion."

Anointing of the Sick: "By the sacred anointing of the sick and the prayer of her priests, the whole Church commends those who are ill to the suffering and glorified Lord, asking that he may lighten their suffering and save them (cf. Jas 5:14-16). She exhorts them, moreover, to contribute to the welfare of the whole People of God by associating themselves freely with the passion and death of Christ (cf. Rom 8:17; Col 1:24; 2 Tm 2:11-12; 1 Pt 4:13)."

Holy Orders: "Those of the faithful who are consecrated by holy orders are appointed to feed the Church in Christ's name with the Word and the grace of God."

Matrimony: "Christian spouses, in virtue of the sacrament of matrimony, signify and partake of the mystery of that unity and fruitful love which exists between Christ and his Church (cf. Eph 5:32). The spouses thereby help each other to attain to holiness in their married life and by the rearing and education of their children. And so, in their state and way of life, they have their own special gift among the People of God (cf. 1 Cor 7:7).

"For from the wedlock of Christians there comes the family, in which new citizens of human society are born. By the grace of the Holy Spirit received in baptism these are made children of God, thus perpetuating the People of God through the centuries. The family is, so to speak, the domestic Church. In it parents should, by their word and example, be the first preachers of the faith to their children. They should encourage them in the vocation which is proper to each of them, fostering with special care any religious vocation.

"Fortified by so many and such powerful means of salvation, all the faithful, whatever their condition or state, are called by the Lord, each in his own way, to that perfect holiness whereby the Father himself is perfect."

Baptism

Baptism is the sacrament of spiritual regeneration by which a person is incorporated in Christ and made a member of his Mystical Body, given grace, and cleansed of original sin. Actual sins and the punishment owed for

them are remitted also if the person baptized was guilty of such sins (e.g., in the case of a person baptized after reaching the age of reason). The theological virtues of faith, hope and charity are given with grace. The sacrament confers a character on the soul and can be received only once.

The matter is the pouring of water. The form is: "I baptize you in the name of the Father and of the Son and of the Holy Spirit."

The minister of solemn baptism is a bishop, priest or deacon, but in case of emergency anyone, including a non-Catholic, can validly baptize. The minister pours water on the forehead of the person being baptized and says the words of the form while the water is flowing. The water used in solemn baptism is blessed during the rite.

Baptism is conferred in the Roman rite by immersion or infusion (pouring of water), depending on the directive of the appropriate conference of bishops, according to the Code of Canon Law. The Church recognizes as valid baptisms properly performed by non-Catholic ministers. The baptism of infants has always been considered valid and the general practice of infant baptism was well established by the fifth century. Baptism is conferred conditionally when there is doubt about the validity of a previous baptism.

Baptism is necessary for salvation. If a person cannot receive the baptism of water described above, this can be supplied by baptism of blood (martyrdom suffered for the Catholic faith or some Christian virtue) or by baptism of desire (perfect contrition joined with at least the implicit intention of doing whatever God wills that people should do for salvation).

A sponsor is required for the person being baptized. (*See* **Godparents**, below).

A person must be validly baptized before he or she can receive any of the other sacraments.

Christian Initiation of Infants: Infants should be solemnly baptized as soon after birth as conveniently possible. Anyone may baptize an infant in danger of death. If the child survives, the ceremonies of solemn baptism should be supplied.

The sacrament is ordinarily conferred by a priest or deacon of the parents' parish.

Catholics 16 years of age and over who have received the sacraments of confirmation and the Eucharist and are practicing their faith are eligible to be sponsors or godparents. Only one is required. Two, one of each sex, are permitted. A non-Catholic Christian cannot be a godparent for a Catholic child, but may serve as a witness to the baptism. A Catholic may not be a godparent for a child baptized in a non-Catholic religion, but may be a witness.

"Because of the close communion between the Catholic Church and the Eastern Orthodox churches," states the 1993 Directory on Ecumenism, "it is permissible for a just cause for an Eastern faithful to act as godparent together with a Catholic godparent at the baptism of a Catholic infant or adult, so long as there is provision for the Catholic education of the person being baptized and it is clear that the godparent is a suitable one.

"A Catholic is not forbidden to stand as godparent in an Eastern Orthodox Church if he/she is so invited. In this case, the duty of providing for the Christian education binds in the first place the godparent who belongs to the church in which the child is baptized."

The role of godparents in baptismal ceremonies is secondary to the role of the parents. They serve as representatives of the community of faith and with the parents request baptism for the child and perform other ritual functions. Their function after baptism is to serve as proxies for the parents if the parents should be unable or fail to provide for the religious training of the child.

At baptism every child should be given a name with Christian significance, usually the name of a saint, to symbolize newness of life in Christ.

Christian Initiation of Adults: According to the *Ordo Initiationis Christianae Adultorum* ("Rite of the Christian Initiation of Adults") issued by the Congregation for Divine Worship on Jan. 6, 1972, and put into effect in revised form Sept. 1, 1988, adults are prepared for baptism and reception into the Church in several stages:

• An initial period of inquiry, instruction and evangelization.

• The catechumenate, a period of at least a year of formal instruction and progressive formation in and familiarity with Christian life. It starts with a statement of purpose and includes a rite of election.

• Immediate preparation, called a period of purification and enlightenment, from the beginning of Lent to reception of the sacraments of initiation — baptism, confirmation, Holy Eucharist — during ceremonies of the Easter Vigil. The period is marked by scrutinies, formal giving of the creed and the Lord's Prayer, the choice of a Christian name, and a final statement of intention.

• A mystagogic phase whose objective is greater familiarity with Christian life in the Church through observances of the Easter season and association with the community of the faithful, and through extended formation for about a year.

National Statutes for the Catechumenate were approved by the National Conference of Catholic Bishops Nov. 11, 1986, and were subsequently ratified by the Vatican.

The priest who baptizes a catechumen can also administer the sacrament of confirmation.

A sponsor is required for the person being baptized.

The Ordo also provides a simple rite of initiation for adults in danger of death and for cases in which all stages of the initiation process are not necessary, and guidelines for: (1) the preparation of adults for the sacraments of confirmation and Holy Eucharist in cases where they have been baptized but have not received further formation in the Christian life; (2) the formation and initiation of children of catechetical age.The Church recognizes the right of anyone over the age of seven to request baptism and to receive the sacrament after completing a course of instruction and giving evidence of good will. Practically, in the case of minors in a non-Catholic family or environment, the Church accepts them when other circumstances favor their ability to practice the faith – e.g., well-disposed family situation, the presence of another or several Catholics in the family. Those who are not in such favorable circumstances are prudently advised to defer reception of the sacrament until they attain the maturity necessary for independent practice of the faith.

Reception of Baptized Christians: Procedure for the reception of already baptized Christians into full communion with the Catholic Church is distinguished from the catechumenate, since they have received some Christian formation. Instruction and formation are provided as necessary, however; and conditional baptism is administered if there is reasonable doubt about the validity of the person's previous baptism.

In the rite of reception, the person is invited to join the community of the Church in professing the Nicene Creed and is asked to state: "I believe and profess all that the holy Catholic Church believes, teaches, and proclaims as

revealed by God." The priest places his hand on the head of the person, states the formula of admission to full communion, confirms (in the absence of a bishop), gives a sign of peace, and administers Holy Communion during a Eucharistic Liturgy.

Confirmation

Confirmation is the sacrament by which a baptized person, through anointing with chrism and the imposition of hands, is endowed with the fullness of baptismal grace; is united more intimately to the Church; is enriched with the special power of the Holy Spirit; is committed to be an authentic witness to Christ in word and action. The sacrament confers a character on the soul and can be received only once.

According to the apostolic constitution *Divinae Consortium Naturae*, dated Aug. 15, 1971, in conjunction with the *Ordo Confirmationis* ("Rite of Confirmation"): "The sacrament of confirmation is conferred through the anointing with chrism on the forehead, which is done by the imposition of the hand (matter of the sacrament), and through the words: '*N., receive the seal of the Holy Spirit, the Gift of the Father*'" (form of the sacrament). On May 5, 1975, bishops' conferences in English-speaking countries were informed by the Congregation for Divine Worship that Pope Paul VI had approved this English version of the form of the sacrament: "*Be sealed with the gift of the Holy Spirit.*"

The ordinary minister of confirmation in the Roman rite is a bishop. Priests may be delegated for the purpose. A pastor can confirm a parishioner in danger of death, and a priest can confirm in ceremonies of Christian initiation and at the reception of a baptized Christian into union with the Church.

Ideally, the sacrament is conferred during the Eucharistic Liturgy. Elements of the rite include renewal of the promises of baptism, which confirmation ratifies and completes, and the laying on of hands by the confirming bishop and priests participating in the ceremony.

"The entire rite," according to the *Ordo*, "has a twofold meaning. The laying of hands upon the candidates, done by the bishop and the concelebrating priests, expresses the biblical gesture by which the gift of the Holy Spirit is invoked. The anointing with chrism and the accompanying words clearly signify the effect of the Holy Spirit. Signed with the perfumed oil by the bishop's hand, the baptized person receives the indelible character, the seal of the Lord, together with the Spirit who is given and who conforms the person more perfectly to Christ and gives him the grace of spreading the Lord's presence among men."

A sponsor is required for the person being confirmed. Eligible is any Catholic 16 years or older who has received the sacraments of confirmation and the Eucharist and is practicing the faith. The baptismal sponsor, preferably, can also be the sponsor for confirmation. Parents may present their children for confirmation but cannot be sponsors.

In the Roman rite, it has been customary for children to receive confirmation within a reasonable time after first Communion and confession. There is a trend, however, to defer confirmation until later when its significance for mature Christian living becomes more evident. In the Eastern rites, confirmation is administered at the same time as baptism.

Eucharist

The Holy Eucharist is a sacrifice (*see* **The Mass**) and the sacrament in which Christ is present and is received under the appearances of bread and wine.

The matter is bread of wheat, unleavened in the Roman

rite and leavened in the Eastern rites, and wine of grape. The form consists of the words of consecration said by the priest at Mass: "This is my body. This is the cup of my blood" (according to the traditional usage of the Roman rite).

Only a priest can consecrate bread and wine so they become the body and blood of Christ. After consecration, however, the Eucharist can be administered by deacons and, for various reasons, by religious and lay persons.

Priests celebrating Mass receive the Eucharist under the species of bread and wine. In the Roman rite, others receive under the species of bread only, i.e., the consecrated host, though in some circumstances they may receive under the species of both bread and wine. In Eastern-rite practice, the faithful generally receive a piece of consecrated leavened bread which has been dipped into consecrated wine (i.e., by intinction).

Conditions for receiving the Eucharist, commonly called Holy Communion, are the state of grace, the right intention and observance of the Eucharistic fast.

The faithful of Roman rite are required by a precept of the Church to receive the Eucharist at least once a year, ordinarily during the Easter time. (*See* **Eucharistic Fast, Mass, Transubstantiation, Viaticum**.)

First Communion and Confession: Children are to be prepared for and given opportunity for receiving both sacraments (Eucharist and reconciliation, or penance) on reaching the age of discretion, at which time they become subject to general norms concerning confession and Communion. This, together with a stated preference for first confession before first Communion, was the central theme of a document entitled *Sanctus Pontifex* and published May 24, 1973, by the Congregation for the Discipline of the Sacraments and the Congregation for the Clergy, with the approval of Pope Paul VI.

What the document prescribed was the observance of practices ordered by St. Pius X in the decree *Quam Singulari* of Aug. 8, 1910. Its purpose was to counteract pastoral and catechetical experiments virtually denying children the opportunity of receiving both sacraments at the same time. Termination of such experiments was ordered by the end of the 1972-73 school year.

At the time the document was issued, two- or three-year experiments of this kind – routinely deferring reception of the sacrament of penance until after the first reception of Holy Communion – were in effect in more than half of the dioceses of the U.S. They have remained in effect in many places, despite the advisory from the Vatican.

One reason stated in support of such experiments is the view that children are not capable of serious sin at the age of seven or eight, when Communion is generally received for the first time, and therefore prior reception of the sacrament of penance is not necessary. Another reason is the purpose of making the distinctive nature of the two sacraments clearer to children.

The Vatican view reflected convictions that the principle and practice of devotional reception of penance are as valid for children as they are for adults, and that sound catechetical programs can avoid misconceptions about the two sacraments.

A second letter on the same subject and in the same vein was released May 19, 1977, by the aforementioned congregations. It was issued in response to the question:

"'Whether it is allowed after the declaration of May 24, 1973, to continue to have, as a general rule, the reception of first Communion precede the reception of the sacrament of penance in those parishes in which this practice developed in the past few years.'

"The Sacred Congregations for the Sacraments and Divine Worship and for the Clergy, with the approval of the Supreme Pontiff, reply: Negative, and according to the mind of the declaration.

"The mind of the declaration is that one year after the promulgation of the same declaration, all experiments of receiving first Communion without the sacrament of penance should cease so that the discipline of the Church might be restored, in the spirit of the decree, *Quam Singulari*."

The two letters from the Vatican congregations have not produced uniformity of practice in this country. Simultaneous preparation for both sacraments is provided in some dioceses where a child has the option of receiving either sacrament first, with the counsel of parents, priests and teachers. Programs in other dioceses are geared first to reception of Communion and later to reception of the Sacrament of Reconciliation.

Commentators on the letters note that: they are disciplinary rather than doctrinal in content; they are subject to pastoral interpretation by bishops; they cannot be interpreted to mean that a person who is not guilty of serious sin must be required to receive the sacrament of penance before (even first) Communion.

Canon 914 of the Code of Canon Law states that sacramental confession should precede first Communion.

Holy Communion under the Forms of Bread and Wine (by separate taking of the consecrated bread and wine or by intinction, the reception of the host dipped in the wine): Such reception is permitted under conditions stated in instructions issued by the Congregation for Divine Worship (May 25, 1967; June 29, 1970), the *General Instruction on the Roman Missal* (No. 242), and directives of bishops' conferences and individual bishops.

Accordingly, Communion can be administered in this way to: persons being baptized, received into communion with the Church, confirmed, receiving anointing of the sick; couples at their wedding or jubilee; religious at profession or renewal of profession; lay persons receiving an ecclesiastical assignment (e.g., lay missionaries); participants at concelebrated Masses, retreats, pastoral commission meetings, daily Masses and, in the U.S., Masses on Sundays and holy days of obligation.

A communicant has the option of receiving the Eucharist under the form of bread alone or under the forms of bread and wine. (*See* **New U.S. Norms in the Liturgy section**.)

Holy Communion More Than Once a Day: A person who has already received the Eucharist may receive it (only) once again on the same day only during a Eucharistic celebration in which the person participates. A person in danger of death who has already received the Eucharist once or twice is urged to receive Communion again as Viaticum. Pope John Paul approved this decision, in accord with Canon 917, and ordered it published July 11, 1984.

Holy Communion and Eucharistic Devotion outside of Mass: These were the subjects of an instruction (*De Sacra Communione et de Cultu Mysterii Eucharistici extra Missam*) dated June 21 and made public Oct. 18, 1973, by the Congregation for Divine Worship.

Holy Communion can be given outside of Mass to persons unable for a reasonable cause to receive it during Mass on a given day. The ceremonial rite is modeled on the structure of the Mass, consisting of a penitential act, a scriptural reading, the Lord's Prayer, a sign or gesture of peace, giving of the Eucharist, prayer and final blessing. Viaticum and Communion to the sick can be given by extraordinary ministers (authorized lay persons) with appropriate rites.

Forms of devotion outside of Mass are exposition of the Blessed Sacrament (by men or women religious, especially, or lay persons in the absence of a priest; but only a priest can give the blessing), processions and congresses with appropriate rites.

Intercommunion: Church policy on intercommunion was stated in an "Instruction on the Admission of Other Christians to the Eucharist," dated June 1 and made public July 8, 1972, against the background of the Decree on Ecumenism approved by the Second Vatican Council, and the Directory on Ecumenism issued by the Secretariat for Promoting Christian Unity in 1967, 1970 and 1993.

Basic principles related to intercommunion are:

• "There is an indissoluble link between the mystery of the Church and the mystery of the Eucharist, or between ecclesial and Eucharistic communion; the celebration of the Eucharist of itself signifies the fullness of profession of faith and ecclesial communion" (1972 Instruction).

• "Eucharistic communion practiced by those who are not in full ecclesial communion with each other cannot be the expression of that full unity which the Eucharist of its nature signifies and which in this case does not exist; for this reason such communion cannot be regarded as a means to be used to lead to full ecclesial communion" (1972 Instruction).

• The question of reciprocity "arises only with those churches which have preserved the substance of the Eucharist, the sacrament of orders and apostolic succession" (1967 Directory).

• "A Catholic cannot ask for the Eucharist except from a minister who has been validly ordained" (1967 Directory).

The policy distinguishes between separated Eastern Christians and other Christians.

With Separated Eastern Christians (e.g., Orthodox): These may be given the Eucharist (as well as penance and anointing of the sick) at their request. Catholics may receive these same sacraments from priests of separated Eastern churches if they experience genuine spiritual necessity, seek spiritual benefit, and access to a Catholic priest is morally or physically impossible. This policy (of reciprocity) derives from the facts that the separated Eastern churches have apostolic succession through their bishops, valid priests, and sacramental beliefs and practices in accord with those of the Catholic Church.

With Other Christians (e.g., members of Reformation-related churches, others): Admission to the Eucharist in the Catholic Church, according to the Directory on Ecumenism, "is confined to particular cases of those Christians who have a faith in the sacrament in conformity with that of the Church, who experience a serious spiritual need for the Eucharistic sustenance, who for a prolonged period are unable to have recourse to a minister of their own community and who ask for the sacrament of their own accord; all this provided that they have proper dispositions and lead lives worthy of a Christian." The spiritual need is defined as "a need for an increase in spiritual life and a need for a deeper involvement in the mystery of the Church and its unity."

Circumstances under which Communion may be given to other properly disposed Christians are danger of death, imprisonment, persecution, grave spiritual necessity coupled with no chance of recourse to a minister of their own community. Catholics cannot ask for the Eucharist from ministers of other Christian churches who have not been validly ordained to the priesthood.

Ecclesia de Eucharistia

On Apr. 17, 2002, Holy Thursday, during the Mass of the Lord's Supper, and within the liturgical setting of the beginning of the Paschal Triduum Pope John Paul II issued the 14th encyclical letter of his pontificate, *Ecclesia de Eucharistia*. The encyclical was intended to offer a theological reflection on the mystery of the Eucharist in its relationship with the Church.

Specifically, the pope uses the letter to reaffirm the traditional teaching of the Church on the real presence of Christ in the Eucharist, on the need for validly ordained ministers for its celebration, and on the importance of following the Church's liturgical norms.

The encyclical is organized into five chapters and a conclusion, beginning with the declaration: "The Church draws her life from the Eucharist. This truth does not simply express a daily experience of faith, but recapitulates the heart of the mystery of the Church. In a variety of ways she joyfully experiences the constant fulfillment of the promise." The Eucharistic Sacrifice is thus truly "the source and summit of the Christian life," as the Second Vatican Council proclaimed, and contains the Church's entire spiritual wealth: Jesus Christ, who offers himself to the Father for the redemption of the world. In celebrating this "mystery of faith," the Church presents the Paschal Triduum in a contemporary way, for men and women in every age.

Chapter One, "The Mystery of Faith," describes the sacrificial nature of the Eucharist which, through the ministry of the priest, makes sacramentally present at each Mass the body "given up" and the blood "poured out" by Christ for the salvation of the world.

Chapter Two, "The Eucharist Builds the Church," states that the Church "teaches that the celebration of the Eucharist is at the center of the process of the Church's growth."

Chapter Three, "The Apostolicity of the Eucharist and of the Church," notes that that just as the Church is apostolic so too is the Eucharist in three ways. First, "The Eucharist too has its foundation in the Apostles, not in the sense that it did not originate in Christ himself, but because it was entrusted by Jesus to the Apostles and has been handed down to us by them and by their successors. It is in continuity with the practice of the Apostles, in obedience to the Lord's command, that the Church has celebrated the Eucharist down the centuries." Second, "it is celebrated in conformity with the faith of the Apostles." Third, just as the full reality of Church does not exist without apostolic succession, so there is no true Eucharist without the bishop.

Chapter Four, "The Eucharist and Ecclesial Communion," teaches that "the culmination of all the sacraments in perfecting our communion with God the Father by identification with his only-begotten Son through the working of the Holy Spirit."

Chapter Five, "The Dignity of the Eucharistic Celebration" is concerned with the truthful celebration of the Eucharist enunciated in the previous chapter.

Chapter Six, "At the School of Mary, 'Woman of the Eucharist,'" offers a reflection on the analogy between the Mother of God, and the Church.

In his conclusion, the pontiff quotes his Apostolic Letter *Novo Millennio Ineunte* in stating, "it is not a matter of inventing a 'new program.' The program already exists: it is the plan found in the Gospel and in the living Tradition; it is the same as ever." Clearly, the implementation of this process of a renewed impetus in Christian living passes through the Eucharist. He concludes, "In the humble signs of bread and wine, changed into his body and blood, Christ walks beside us as our strength and our food for the journey, and he enables us to become, for everyone, witnesses of hope."

Sacramentum Caritatis

On Mar. 13, 2007, Pope Benedict XVI released the post-synodal apostolic exhortation, *Sacramentum Caritatis* ("The Sacrament of Charity"), a 131-page papal reflection on the discussions and suggestions made during the 2005 world Synod of Bishops on the Eucharist.

Penance

Penance is the sacrament by which sins committed after baptism are forgiven and a person is reconciled with God and the Church.

Individual and integral confession and absolution are the only ordinary means for the forgiveness of serious sin and for reconciliation with God and the Church.

(Other than ordinary means are perfect contrition and general absolution without prior confession, both of which require the intention of subsequent confession and absolution.)

A revised ritual for the sacrament – *Ordo Paenitentiae*, published by the Congregation of Divine Worship Feb. 7, 1974, and made mandatory in the U.S. from the first Sunday of Lent, 1977 – reiterates standard doctrine concerning the sacrament; emphasizes the social (communal and ecclesial) aspects of sin and conversion, with due regard for personal aspects and individual reception of the sacrament; prescribes three forms for celebration of the sacrament; and presents models for community penitential services.

The basic elements of the sacrament are sorrow for sin because of a supernatural motive, confession (of previously unconfessed mortal or grave sins, required; of venial sins also, but not of necessity), and reparation (by means of prayer or other act enjoined by the confessor), all of which comprise the matter of the sacrament; and absolution, which is the form of the sacrament.

The traditional words of absolution – *"I absolve you from your sins in the name of the Father, and of the Son, and of the Holy Spirit"* – remain unchanged at the conclusion of a petition in the new rite that God may grant pardon and peace through the ministry of the Church.

The minister of the sacrament is an authorized priest – i.e., one who, besides having the power of orders to forgive sins, also has faculties of jurisdiction granted by an ecclesiastical superior and/or by canon law.

The sacrament can be celebrated in three ways:

• For individuals, the traditional manner remains acceptable but is enriched with additional elements including: reception of the penitent and making of the Sign of the Cross; an exhortation by the confessor to trust in God; a reading from Scripture; confession of sins; manifestation of repentance; petition for God's forgiveness through the ministry of the Church and the absolution of the priest; praise of God's mercy, and dismissal in peace. Some of these elements are optional.

• For several penitents, in the course of a community celebration including a Liturgy of the Word of God and prayers, individual confession and absolution, and an act of thanksgiving.

• For several penitents, in the course of a community celebration, with general confession and general absolution. In extraordinary cases, reconciliation may be attained by general absolution without prior individual confession as, for example, under these circumstances: (1) danger of death, when there is neither time nor priests available for hearing confessions; (2) grave necessity of a number of penitents who, because of a shortage of confessors, would be deprived of sacramental grace or Communion for a lengthy period of time through no fault of their own. Persons receiving general absolution are obliged to be properly disposed and resolved to make an individual confession of the grave sins from which they have been absolved; this confession should be made as soon as the opportunity to confess presents itself and before any second reception of general absolution.

Norms regarding general absolution, issued by the Congregation for the Doctrine of the Faith in 1972, are not intended to provide a basis for convoking large gatherings of the faithful for the purpose of imparting general absolution, in the absence of extraordinary circumstances. Judgment about circumstances that warrant general absolution belongs principally to the bishop of the place, with due regard for related decisions of appropriate episcopal conferences.

Communal celebrations of the sacrament are not held in connection with Mass.

The place of individual confession, as determined by episcopal conferences in accordance with given norms, can be the traditional confessional or another appropriate setting.

A precept of the Church obliges the faithful guilty of grave sin to confess at least once a year.

The Church favors more frequent reception of the sacrament not only for the reconciliation of persons guilty of serious sins but also for reasons of devotion. Devotional confession – in which venial sins or previously forgiven sins are confessed – serves the purpose of confirming persons in penance and conversion.

Penitential Celebrations: Communal penitential celebrations are designed to emphasize the social dimensions of Christian life – the community aspects and significance of penance and reconciliation.

Elements of such celebrations are community prayer, hymns and songs, scriptural and other readings, examination of conscience, general confession and expression of sorrow for sin, acts of penance and reconciliation, and a form of non-sacramental absolution resembling the one in the penitential rite of the Mass.

If the sacrament is celebrated during the service, there must be individual confession and absolution of sin.

Recent Developments: On May 2, 2002, officials of the Roman Curia released a motu proprio by Pope John Paul II, *Misericordia Dei* ("Mercy of God, On Certain Aspects of the Celebration of the Sacrament of Penance"). The 15-page document called for a "vigorous revitalization" of the sacrament and asked bishops to adopt stricter observance on Church law's "grave necessity" requirement as a condition for the use of general absolution. It also requested that bishops' conferences submit national norms for general absolution to the Holy See for approval "as soon as possible."

In February 2003, the Bishops' Committee on the Liturgy and the Subcommittee for the Jubilee Year 2000 of the USCCB issued a new booklet, *Celebrating the Sacrament of Penance: Questions and Answers*. The booklet provides answers to some of the frequently asked questions about the Sacrament of Penance, including "Why Do We Need the Sacrament of Penance?" "What Happens in the Sacrament of Penance?" and "What is 'General Absolution'?" The booklet is intended for use in parishes during preparation for the Sacrament of Penance, as a resource for reflection on the sacrament during particular seasons such as Lent, and as a practical tool to aid penitents as they go to confession.

(*See* **Absolution, Confession, Confessional, Confessor,**

Contrition, Faculties, Forgiveness of Sin, Power of the Keys, Seal of Confession, Sin.)

Anointing of the Sick

This sacrament, promulgated by St. James the Apostle (Jas 5:13-15), can be administered to the faithful after reaching the age of reason who are in danger because of illness or old age. By the anointing with blessed oil and the prayer of a priest, the sacrament confers on the person comforting grace; the remission of venial sins and inculpably unconfessed mortal sins, together with at least some of the temporal punishment due for sins; and, sometimes, results in an improved state of health.

The matter of this sacrament is the anointing with blessed oil (olive oil, or vegetable oil if necessary) of the forehead and hands; in cases of necessity, a single anointing of another portion of the body suffices. The form is: "Through this holy anointing and his most loving mercy, may the Lord assist you by the grace of the Holy Spirit so that, when you have been freed from your sins, he may save you and in his goodness raise you up."

Anointing of the sick, formerly called extreme unction, may be received more than once, e.g., in new or continuing stages of serious illness. Ideally, the sacrament should be administered while the recipient is conscious and in conjunction with the sacraments of penance and the Eucharist. It should be administered in cases of doubt as to whether the person has reached the age of reason, is dangerously ill or dead.

The sacrament can be administered during a communal celebration in some circumstances, as in a home for the aged.

Holy Orders

Order is the sacrament by which the mission given by Christ to the Apostles continues to be exercised in the Church until the end of time; it is the sacrament of apostolic mission. It has three grades: episcopacy, priesthood and diaconate. The sacrament confers a character on the soul and can be received only once. The minister of the sacrament is a bishop.

Order, like matrimony but in a different way, is a social sacrament. As the Second Vatican Council declared in *Lumen Gentium*, the Dogmatic Constitution on the Church: "For the nurturing and constant growth of the People of God, Christ the Lord instituted in his Church a variety of ministries, which work for the good of the whole body. For those ministers who are endowed with sacred power are servants of their brethren, so that all who are of the People of God, and therefore enjoy a true Christian dignity, can work toward a common goal freely and in an orderly way, and arrive at salvation" (No. 18).

Bishop: The fullness of the priesthood belongs to those who have received the order of bishop. Bishops, in hierarchical union with the pope and their fellow bishops, are the successors of the Apostles as pastors of the Church: they have individual responsibility for the care of the local churches they serve and collegial responsibility for the care of the universal Church (*see* **Collegiality**). In the ordination or consecration of bishops, the essential form is the imposition of hands by the consecrator(s) and the assigned prayer in the preface of the rite of ordination.

"With their helpers, the priests and deacons, bishops have taken up the service of the community presiding in place of God over the flock whose shepherds they are, as teachers of doctrine, priests of sacred worship, and officers of good order" (No. 20).

Priests: A priest is an ordained minister with the power to celebrate Mass, administer the sacraments, preach and teach the word of God, impart blessings, and perform additional pastoral functions, according to the mandate of his ecclesiastical superior.

Concerning priests, the Second Vatican Council stated in *Lumen Gentium* (No. 28): "The divinely established ecclesiastical ministry is exercised on different levels by those who from antiquity have been called bishops, priests, and deacons. Although priests do not possess the highest degree of the priesthood, and although they are dependent on the bishops in the exercise of their power, they are nevertheless united with the bishops in sacerdotal dignity. By the power of the sacrament of orders, and in the image of Christ the eternal High Priest (Heb 5:1-10;7:24;9:11-28), they are consecrated to preach the Gospel, shepherd the faithful, and celebrate divine worship as true priests of the New Testament.

"Priests, prudent cooperators with the episcopal order as well as its aides and instruments, are called to serve the People of God. They constitute one priesthood with their bishop, although that priesthood is comprised of different functions."

In the ordination of a priest of Roman rite, the essential matter is the imposition of hands on the heads of those being ordained by the ordaining bishop. The essential form is the accompanying prayer in the preface of the ordination ceremony. Other elements in the rite are the presentation of the implements of sacrifice – the chalice containing the wine and the paten containing a host – with accompanying prayers.

Deacon: There are two kinds of deacons: those who receive the order and remain in it permanently, and those who receive the order while advancing to priesthood. The following quotation – from Vatican II's Dogmatic Constitution on the Church (*Lumen Gentium*, No. 29) – describes the nature and role of the diaconate, with emphasis on the permanent diaconate.

"At a lower level of the hierarchy are deacons, upon whom hands are imposed 'not unto the priesthood, but unto a ministry of service.' For strengthened by sacramental grace, in communion with the bishop and his group of priests, they serve the People of God in the ministry of the liturgy, of the word, and of charity. It is the duty of the deacon, to the extent that he has been authorized by competent authority, to administer baptism solemnly, to be custodian and dispenser of the Eucharist, to assist at and bless marriages in the name of the Church, to bring Viaticum to the dying, to read the sacred Scripture to the faithful, to instruct and exhort the people, to preside at the worship and prayer of the faithful, to administer sacramentals, and to officiate at funeral and burial services. (Deacons are) dedicated to duties of charity and administration.

"The diaconate can in the future be restored as a proper and permanent rank of the hierarchy. It pertains to the competent territorial bodies of bishops, of one kind or another, to decide, with the approval of the Supreme Pontiff, whether and where it is opportune for such deacons to be appointed for the care of souls. With the consent of the Roman Pontiff, this diaconate will be able to be conferred upon men of more mature age, even upon those living in the married state. It may also be conferred upon suitable young men. For them, however, the law of celibacy must remain intact" (No. 29).

The Apostles ordained the first seven deacons (Acts 6:1-6): Stephen, Philip, Prochorus, Nicanor, Timon,

Parmenas, Nicholas.

Former Orders, Ministries: With the revision of the sacrament of order which began in 1971, the orders of subdeacon, acolyte, exorcist, lector and porter were abolished because they and their respective functions had fallen into disuse or did not require ordination. The Holy See started revision of the sacrament of order in 1971. By virtue of an indult of Oct. 5 of that year, the bishops of the U.S. were permitted to discontinue ordaining porters and exorcists. Another indult, dated three days later, permitted the use of revised rites for ordaining acolytes and lectors.

To complete the revision, Pope Paul VI abolished Sept. 14, 1972, the orders of porter, exorcist and subdeacon; decreed that laymen, as well as candidates for the diaconate and priesthood, can be installed (rather than ordained) in the ministries (rather than orders) of acolyte and lector; reconfirmed the suppression of tonsure and its replacement with a service of dedication to God and the Church; and stated that a man enters the clerical state on ordination to the diaconate.

The abolished orders were:

• Subdeacon, with specific duties in liturgical worship, especially at Mass. The order, whose first extant mention dates from about the middle of the third century, was regarded as minor until the 13th century; afterwards, it was called a major order in the West but not in the East.

• Acolyte, to serve in minor capacities in liturgical worship; a function now performed by Mass servers.

• Exorcist, to perform services of exorcism for expelling evil spirits; a function which came to be reserved to specially delegated priests.

• Lector, to read scriptural and other passages during liturgical worship; a function now generally performed by lay persons.

• Porter, to guard the entrance to an assembly of Christians and to ward off undesirables who tried to gain admittance; an order of early origin and utility but of present insignificance.

Permanent Diaconate

Restoration of the permanent diaconate in the Roman rite – making it possible for men to become deacons permanently, without going on to the priesthood – was promulgated by Pope Paul VI June 18, 1967, in a document entitled *Sacrum Diaconatus Ordinem* ("Sacred Order of the Diaconate").

The Pope's action implemented the desire expressed by the Second Vatican Council for reestablishment of the diaconate as an independent order in its own right not only to supply ministers for carrying on the work of the Church but also to complete the hierarchical structure of the Church of Roman rite.

Permanent deacons have been traditional in the Eastern Church. The Western Church, however, since the fourth or fifth century, generally followed the practice of conferring the diaconate only as a sacred order preliminary to the priesthood, and of restricting the ministry of deacons to liturgical functions.

The pope's document, issued on his own initiative, provided:

• Qualified unmarried men 25 years of age or older may be ordained deacons. They cannot marry after ordination.

• Qualified married men 35 years of age or older may be ordained deacons. The consent of the wife of a prospective deacon is required. A married deacon cannot remarry after the death of his wife.

• Preparation for the diaconate includes a course of study and formation over a period of at least three years.

• Candidates who are not members of religious institutes must be affiliated with a diocese. Reestablishment of the diaconate among religious is reserved to the Holy See.

• Deacons will practice their ministry under the direction of a bishop and with the priests with whom they will be associated. (For functions, *see* the description of deacon, under **Holy Orders**.)

Restoration of the permanent diaconate in the U.S. was approved by the Holy See in October 1968. Shortly afterwards the U.S. bishops established a committee for the permanent diaconate, which was chaired by Bp. Edward U. Kmiec of Nashville in 1997. The current head of the Committee on Clergy, Consecrated Life and Vocations is Abp. Robert Carlson of St. Louis. The committee operates offices are at 3211 Fourth St. N.E., Washington, DC 20017. Fr. William S. McKnight, S.T.D. is executive director of the committee.

Status and Functions

The *2014 Official Catholic Directory* reports that in the U.S. there were a total of 18,089 permanent deacons (the highest total by far for any single country), a decrease of 32 from the previous year and an increase of 3,062 from 2004. Worldwide, there are currently 42,104 deacons, according to the 2012 edition of the *Annuarium Statisticum Ecclesiae* (the most recent edition).

Training programs of spiritual, theological and pastoral formation are based on guidelines emanating from the National Conference of Catholic Bishops.

Deacons have various functions, depending on the nature of their assignments. Liturgically, they can officiate at baptisms, weddings, wake services and funerals, can preach and distribute Holy Communion. Some are engaged in religious education work. All are intended to carry out works of charity and pastoral service of one kind or another.

The majority of deacons, the majority of whom are married, continue in their secular work. Their ministry of service is developing in three dimensions: of liturgy, of the word, and of charity. Depending on the individual deacon's abilities and preference, he is assigned by his bishop to either a parochial ministry or to another field of service. Deacons are active in a variety of ministries including those to prison inmates and their families, the sick in hospitals, nursing homes and homes for the aged, alienated youth, the elderly and the poor, and in various areas of legal service to the indigent, of education and campus ministry.

National Association of Diaconate Directors: Membership organization of directors, vicars and other staff personnel of diaconate programs. Established in 1977 to promote effective communication and facilitate the exchange of information and resources of members; to develop professional expertise and promote research, training and self evaluation; to foster accountability and seek ways to promote means of implementing solutions to problems. The association is governed by an executive board of elected officers. Officers include Deacons: Deacon Gerald DuPont, Chairman; Deacon Thomas R. Dubois, MPS, exec. dir. Contact: 2136 12th Street - Suite 105, Rockford, IL 61104; (815) 965-2100; www.nadd.org.

"A Portrait of the Permanent Diaconate"

In June 2013, the USCCB released "A Portrait of the Permanent Diaconate: A Study for the U.S. Conference of Catholic Bishops 2012-2013," prepared by the Center for Applied Research in the Apostolate (CARA). The report was the result of a national survey of the Office of the Permanent Diaconate in arch/dioceses and arch/eparchies in the United States that was commissioned by the Secretary of Clergy and Consecrated Life and Vocations of the U.S. Conference of Catholic Bishops. The major findings reported in part:

• The 183 Latin Rite arch/dioceses that responded to the questionnaire report a total of 12,756 permanent deacons. The two arch/eparchies that responded report a total of 38 permanent deacons. Extrapolating to include arch/dioceses and arch/eparchies that did not respond to the survey, it can be estimated that there are as many as 18,497 permanent deacons in the United States today

• Ninety-three percent of active deacons are currently married; four percent are widowers, and two percent never married. Ninety-five percent of active deacons are at least 50 years old; about a quarter are in their fifties; 43 percent are in their sixties; and 25 percent are 70 or older. Almost 90 percent of dioceses have a minimum age for deacon candidacy and half have a mandatory retirement age. In the U.S. the minimum age for ordination to the permanent diaconate is 35. The average minimum age for acceptance into a diaconate program is 33. Thirteen percent of dioceses have a mandatory retirement age of 70. Eighty percent mandate retirement at 75. Seventy-eight percent of active deacons are white. Fifteen percent are Hispanic or Latino, three percent are African American and three percent are Asian.

Ordination of Women

The Catholic Church believes and teaches that, in fidelity to the will of Christ, it cannot ordain women to the priesthood. This position has been set out over the last quarter-century in a series of authoritative documents published by or with the authority of Pope Paul VI and Pope John Paul II.

The first of these, *Inter Insigniores* ("Among the Characteristics"), was issued by the Congregation for the Doctrine of the Faith in October 1976. Its central statement is: "The Sacred Congregation for the Doctrine of the Faith judges it necessary to recall that the Church, in fidelity to the example of the Lord, does not consider herself authorized to admit women to priestly ordination."

In support of this, the document cited the constant tradition of the Church, the fact that Christ called only men to be Apostles and the continuation of this practice by the Apostles themselves, and the sacramental appropriateness of a male priesthood acting *in persona Christi*–in the person of Christ.

In light of continuing discussion, Pope John Paul II returned to the subject in the apostolic letter *Ordinatio Sacerdotalis* ("Priestly Ordination"), issued May 29, 1994: "Wherefore, in order that all doubt may be removed regarding a matter of great importance, a matter which pertains to the Church's divine constitution itself, in virtue of my ministry of confirming the brethren (cf. Lk 22.32) I declare that the Church has no authority whatsoever to confer priestly ordination on women and that this judgment is to be definitively held by all the Church's faithful."

The Congregation for the Doctrine of the Faith followed this on Oct. 28, 1995, with a response, published over the signature of its Prefect, Card. Joseph Ratzinger, to a bishop's inquiry concerning how "to be definitively held" should be understood. The response was:

"This teaching requires definitive assent, since, founded on the written Word of God and from the beginning constantly preserved and applied in the Tradition of the Church, it has been set forth infallibly by the ordinary and universal Magisterium (cf. Second Vatican Council, Dogmatic Constitution on the Church *Lumen Gentium*, 25, 2).

Concerning the possible ordination of women to the diaconate, the International Theological Commission in 2002 concluded that the permanent diaconate belongs to the sacrament of orders and thus is limited to men only.

MATRIMONY

Marriage Doctrine

The following excerpts, stating key points of doctrine on marriage, are from *Gaudium et Spes*, (Nos. 48 to 51) promulgated by the Second Vatican Council:

Conjugal Covenant

The intimate partnership of married life and love has been established by the Creator and qualified by his laws. It is rooted in the conjugal covenant of irrevocable personal consent.

God himself is the author of matrimony, endowed as it is with various benefits and purposes. All of these have a very decisive bearing on the continuation of the human race, on the personal development and eternal destiny of the individual members of a family, and on the dignity, stability, peace, and prosperity of the family itself and of human society as a whole. By their very nature, the institution of matrimony itself and conjugal love are ordained for the procreation and education of children, and find in them their ultimate crown.

Thus a man and a woman render mutual help and service to each other through an intimate union of their persons and of their actions. Through this union they experience the meaning of their oneness and attain to it with growing perfection day by day. As a mutual gift of two persons, this intimate union, as well as the good of the children, imposes total fidelity on the spouses and argues for an unbreakable oneness between them (No. 48).

Sacrament of Matrimony

Christ the Lord abundantly blessed this many-faceted love. The Savior of men and the Spouse of the Church comes into the lives of married Christians through the sacrament of matrimony. He abides with them thereafter so that, just as he loved the Church and handed himself over on her behalf, the spouses may love each other with perpetual fidelity through mutual self-bestowal.

Graced with the dignity and office of fatherhood and motherhood, parents will energetically acquit themselves of a duty which devolves primarily on them; namely, education, and especially religious education.

The Christian family, which springs from marriage as a reflection of the loving covenant uniting Christ with the Church, and as a participation in that covenant, will manifest to all men the Savior's living presence in the world, and the genuine nature of the Church (No. 48).

Conjugal Love

The biblical Word of God several times urges the betrothed and the married to nourish and develop their wedlock by pure conjugal love and undivided affection.

This love is an eminently human one since it is directed from one person to another through an affection of the will. It involves the good of the whole person. Therefore it can enrich the expressions of body and mind with a unique dignity, ennobling these expressions as special ingredients and signs of the friendship distinctive of marriage. This love the Lord has judged worthy of special gifts, healing, perfecting, and exalting gifts of grace and of charity.

Such love, merging the human with the divine, leads the spouses to a free and mutual gift of themselves, a gift proving itself by gentle affection and by deed. Such love pervades the whole of their lives. Indeed, by its generous activity it grows better and grows greater. Therefore it far excels mere erotic inclination, which, selfishly pursued, soon enough fades wretchedly away.

This love is uniquely expressed and perfected through the marital act. The actions within marriage by which the couple are united intimately and chastely are noble and worthy ones. Expressed in a manner which is truly human, these actions signify and promote that mutual self-giving by which spouses enrich each other with a joyful and a thankful will.

Sealed by mutual faithfulness and hallowed above all by Christ's sacrament, this love remains steadfastly true in body and in mind, in bright days or dark. It will never be profaned by adultery or divorce. Firmly established by the Lord, the unity of marriage will radiate from the equal personal dignity of wife and husband, a dignity acknowledged by mutual and total love.

The steady fulfillment of the duties of this Christian vocation demands notable virtue. For this reason, strengthened by grace for holiness of life, the couple will painstakingly cultivate and pray for constancy of love, largeheartedness, and the spirit of sacrifice (No. 49).

Fruitfulness of Marriage

Marriage and conjugal love are by their nature ordained toward the begetting and educating of children. Children are really the supreme gift of marriage and contribute very substantially to the welfare of their parents. God himself wished to share with man a certain special participation in his own creative work. Thus he blessed male and female, saying: "Increase and multiply" (Gn 1:28).

Hence, while not making the other purposes of matrimony of less account, the true practice of conjugal love, and the whole meaning of the family life which results from it, have this aim: that the couple be ready with stout hearts to cooperate with the love of the Creator and the Savior, who through them will enlarge and enrich his own family day by day.

Parents should regard as their proper mission the task of transmitting human life and educating those to whom it has been transmitted. They should realize that they are thereby cooperators with the love of God the Creator, and are, so to speak, the interpreters of that love. Thus they will fulfill their task with human and Christian responsibility (No. 50).

Norms of Judgment

They will thoughtfully take into account both their own welfare and that of their children, those already born and those who may be foreseen. For this accounting they will reckon with both the material and the spiritual conditions of the times as well as of their state in life. Finally, they will consult the interests of the family group, of temporal society, and of the Church herself.

The parents themselves should ultimately make this judgment in the sight of God. But in their manner of acting, spouses should be aware that they cannot proceed arbitrarily. They must always be governed according to a conscience dutifully conformed to the divine law itself, and should be submissive toward the Church's teaching office, which authentically interprets that law in the light of the Gospel. That divine law reveals and protects the integral meaning of conjugal love, and impels it toward a truly human fulfillment.

Marriage, to be sure, is not instituted solely for procreation. Rather, its very nature as an unbreakable compact between persons, and the welfare of the children, both demand that the mutual love of the spouses, too, be embodied in a rightly ordered manner, that it grow and ripen. Therefore, marriage persists as a whole manner and communion of life, and maintains its value and indissolubility, even when offspring are lacking — despite, rather often, the very intense desire of the couple (No. 50).

Love and Life

This Council realizes that certain modern conditions often keep couples from arranging their married lives harmoniously, and that they find themselves in circumstances where at least temporarily the size of their families should not be increased. As a result, the faithful exercise of love and the full intimacy of their lives are hard to maintain. But where the intimacy of married life is broken off, it is not rare for its faithfulness to be imperiled and its quality of fruitfulness ruined. For then the upbringing of the children and the courage to accept new ones are both endangered.

To these problems there are those who presume to offer dishonorable solutions. Indeed, they do not recoil from the taking of life. But the Church issues the reminder that a true contradiction cannot exist between the divine laws pertaining to the transmission of life and those pertaining to the fostering of authentic conjugal love.

Church Teaching

For God, the Lord of Life, has conferred on men the surpassing ministry of safeguarding life – a ministry which must be fulfilled in a manner which is worthy of men. Therefore from the moment of its conception life must be guarded with the greatest care, while abortion and infanticide are unspeakable crimes. The sexual characteristics of man and the human faculty of reproduction wonderfully exceed the dispositions of lower forms of life. Hence the acts themselves which are proper to conjugal love and which are exercised in accord with genuine human dignity must be honored with great reverence (No. 51).

Therefore when there is question of harmonizing conjugal love with the responsible transmission of life, the moral aspect of any procedure does not depend solely on the sincere intentions or on an evaluation of motives. It must be determined by objective standards. These, based on the nature of the human person and his acts, preserve the full sense of mutual self-giving and human procreation in the context of true love. Such a goal cannot be achieved unless the virtue of conjugal chastity is sincerely practiced. Relying on these principles, sons of the Church may not undertake methods of regulating procreation which are found blameworthy by the teaching authority of the Church in its unfolding of the divine law.

Everyone should be persuaded that human life and the task of transmitting it are not realities bound up with this world alone. Hence they cannot be measured or perceived only in terms of it, but always have a bearing on the eternal destiny of men (No. 51).

Humanae Vitae

Marriage doctrine and morality were the subjects of the encyclical letter *Humanae Vitae* ("Of Human Life"), issued by Pope Paul VI, July 29, 1968. *Humanae Vitae* was given reaffirmation and its teaching restated and defended by Pope John Paul II in his encyclical *Evangelium Vitae* (*The Gospel of Life*, 1995). Following are a number of key excerpts from *Humanae Vitae*, which was framed in the pattern of traditional teaching and statements by the Second Vatican Council.

Each and every marriage act ("*quilibet matrimonii usus*") must remain open to the transmission of life (No. 11).

Indeed, by its intimate structure, the conjugal act, while most closely uniting husband and wife, capacitates them for the generation of new lives according to laws inscribed in the very being of man and of woman. By safeguarding both these essential aspects, the unitive and the procreative, the conjugal act preserves in its fullness the sense of true mutual love and its ordination toward man's most high calling to parenthood (No. 12).

It is, in fact, justly observed that a conjugal act imposed upon one's partner without regard for his or her condition and lawful desires is not a true act of love, and therefore denies an exigency of right moral order in the relationships between husband and wife. Hence, one who reflects well must also recognize that a reciprocal act of love which jeopardizes the responsibility to transmit life — which God the Creator, according to particular laws, inserted therein — is in contradiction with the design constitutive of marriage and with the will of the Author of life. To use this divine gift, destroying, even if only partially, its meaning and its purpose, is to contradict the nature both of man and of woman and of their most intimate relationship, and therefore it is to contradict also the plan of God and his will (No. 13).

Forbidden Actions

The direct interruption of the generative process already begun, and, above all, directly willed and procured abortion, even if for therapeutic reasons, are to be absolutely excluded as licit means of regulating birth.

Equally to be excluded is direct sterilization, whether perpetual or temporary, whether of the man or of the woman. Similarly excluded is every action which, either in anticipation of the conjugal act, or in its accomplishment, or in the development of its natural consequences, proposes, whether as an end or as a means, to render procreation impossible.

To justify conjugal acts made intentionally infecund, one cannot invoke as valid reasons the lesser evil, or the fact that such acts would constitute a whole together with the fecund acts already performed or to follow later and hence would share in one and the same moral goodness. In truth, if it is sometimes licit to tolerate a lesser evil in order to avoid a greater evil or to promote a greater good, it is not licit, even for the gravest reasons, to do evil so that good may follow therefrom; that is, to make into the object of a positive act of the will something which is intrinsically disorder, and hence unworthy of the human person, even when the intention is to safeguard or promote individual, family or social well-being.

Consequently, it is an error to think that a conjugal act which is deliberately made infecund, and so is intrinsically dishonest, could be made honest and right by the ensemble of a fecund conjugal life (No. 14).

If, then, there are serious motives to space out births, which derive from the physical or psychological conditions of husband and wife, or from external conditions, the Church teaches that it is then licit to take into account the natural rhythms immanent in the generative functions, for the use of marriage in the infecund periods only, and in this way to regulate birth without offending earlier stated principles (No. 16).

Pastoral Concerns

We do not at all intend to hide the sometimes serious difficulties inherent in the life of Christian married persons; for them, as for everyone else, "the gate is narrow and the way is hard that leads to life." But the hope of that life must illuminate their way, as with courage they strive to live with wisdom, justice and piety in this present time, knowing that the figure of this world passes away.

Let married couples then, face up to the efforts needed, supported by the faith and hope which "do not disappoint because God's love has been poured into our hearts through the Holy Spirit, who has been given to us." Let them implore divine assistance by persevering prayer; above all, let them draw from the source of grace and charity in the Eucharist. And, if sin should still keep its hold over them, let them not be discouraged but rather have recourse with humble perseverance to the mercy of God, which is poured forth in the sacrament of penance (No. 25).

Marriage Laws

The Catholic Church claims jurisdiction over its members in matters pertaining to marriage. Church legislation on the subject is stated principally in 111 canons of the Code of Canon Law.

Marriage laws of the Church provide juridical norms in support of the marriage covenant. In 10 chapters, the revised Code covers: pastoral directives for preparing men and women for marriage; impediments in general and in particular; matrimonial consent; form for the celebration of marriage; mixed marriages; secret celebration of marriage; effects of marriage; separation of spouses; and convalidation of marriage.

Catholics are bound by all marriage laws of the Church. Non-Catholics, whether baptized or not, are not considered bound by these ecclesiastical laws except in cases of marriage with a Catholic. Certain natural laws, in the Catholic view, bind all men and women, irrespective of their religious beliefs; accordingly, marriage is prohibited before the time of puberty, without knowledge and free mutual consent, in the case of an already existing valid marriage bond, in the case of antecedent and perpetual impotence.

Formalities

These include, in addition to arrangements for the time and place of the marriage ceremony, doctrinal and moral instruction concerning marriage and the recording of data which verifies in documentary form the eligibility and freedom of the persons to marry. Records of this kind, which are confidential, are preserved in the archives of the church where the marriage takes place.

Premarital instructions are the subject matter of Pre-Cana Conferences.

Marital Consent

Matrimonial consent can be invalidated by an essential defect, substantial error, the strong influence of force and fear, the presence of a condition or intention against the nature of marriage.

Form of Marriage

A Catholic is required, for validity and lawfulness, to contract marriage – with another Catholic or with a non-Catholic – in the presence of a competent priest or deacon and two witnesses.

There are two exceptions to this law. A Roman-rite

Catholic (since Mar. 25, 1967) or an Eastern-rite Catholic (since Nov. 21, 1964) can contract marriage validly in the presence of a priest of a separated Eastern-rite Church, provided other requirements of law are complied with. With permission of the competent Roman-rite or Eastern-rite bishop, this form of marriage is lawful, as well as valid. (*See* **Eastern-rite Laws**, below.)

With these two exceptions, and aside from cases covered by special permission, the Church does not regard as valid any marriages involving Catholics which take place before non-Catholic ministers of religion or civil officials.

(An excommunication formerly in force against Catholics who celebrated marriage before a non-Catholic minister was abrogated in a decree issued by the Sacred Congregation for the Doctrine of the Faith on Mar. 18, 1966.)

The ordinary place of marriage is the parish of either Catholic party or of the Catholic party in case of a mixed marriage.

Church law regarding the form of marriage does not affect non-Catholics in marriages among themselves. The Church recognizes as valid the marriages of non-Catholics before ministers of religion and civil officials, unless they are rendered null and void on other grounds.

The canonical form is not to be observed in the case of a marriage between a non-Catholic and a baptized Catholic who has left the Church by a formal act.

Impediments

Diriment Impediments to marriage are factors that render a marriage invalid.

• Age, which obtains before completion of the 14th year for a woman and the 16th year for a man

• Impotency, if it is antecedent to the marriage and permanent (this differs from sterility, which is not an impediment)

• The bond of an existing valid marriage

• Disparity of worship, which obtains when one party is a Catholic and the other party is unbaptized

• Sacred orders

• Religious profession of the perpetual vow of chastity

• Abduction, which impedes the freedom of the person abducted

• Crime, variously involving elements of adultery, promise or attempt to marry, conspiracy to murder a husband or wife

• Blood relationship in the direct line (father-daughter, mother-son, etc.) and to the fourth degree inclusive of the collateral line (brother-sister, first cousins)

• Affinity, or relationship resulting from a valid marriage, in any degree of the direct line

• Public honesty, arising from an invalid marriage or from public or notorious concubinage; it renders either party incapable of marrying blood relatives of the other in the first degree of the direct line

• Legal relationship arising from adoption; it renders either party incapable of marrying relatives of the other in the direct line or in the second degree of the collateral line.

Dispensations from impediments: Persons hindered by impediments cannot marry unless they are dispensed therefrom in view of reasons recognized in canon law. Local bishops can dispense from the impediments most often encountered (e.g., disparity of worship) as well as others.

Decision regarding some dispensations is reserved to the Holy See.

Separation

A valid and consummated marriage of baptized persons cannot be dissolved by any human authority or any cause other than the death of one of the persons.

In other circumstances:

1. A valid but unconsummated marriage of baptized persons, or of a baptized and an unbaptized person, can be dissolved:

a. by the solemn religious profession of one of the persons, made with permission of the pope. In such a case, the bond is dissolved at the time of profession, and the other person is free to marry again.

b. by dispensation from the pope, requested for a grave reason by one or both of the persons. If the dispensation is granted, both persons are free to marry again.

Dispensations in these cases are granted for reasons connected with the spiritual welfare of the concerned persons.

2. A legitimate marriage, even consummated, of unbaptized persons can be dissolved in favor of one of them who subsequently receives the sacrament of baptism. This is the Pauline Privilege, so called because it was promulgated by St. Paul (1 Cor 7:12-15) as a means of protecting the faith of converts. Requisites for granting the privilege are:

a. marriage prior to the baptism of either person;

b. reception of baptism by one person;

c. refusal of the unbaptized person to live in peace with the baptized person and without interfering with his or her freedom to practice the Christian faith. The privilege does not apply if the unbaptized person agrees to these conditions.

3. A legitimate and consummated marriage of a baptized and an unbaptized person can be dissolved by the pope in virtue of the Privilege of Faith, also called the Petrine Privilege.

Civil Divorce

Because of the unity and the indissolubility of marriage, the Church denies that civil divorce can break the bond of a valid marriage, whether the marriage involves two Catholics, a Catholic and a non-Catholic, or non-Catholics with each other.

In view of serious circumstances of marital distress, the Church permits an innocent and aggrieved party, whether wife or husband, to seek and obtain a civil divorce for the purpose of acquiring title and right to the civil effects of divorce, such as separate habitation and maintenance, and the custody of children. Permission for this kind of action should be obtained from proper Church authority. The divorce, if obtained, does not break the bond of a valid marriage.

Under other circumstances – as would obtain if a marriage was invalid (see **Annulment**, below) – civil divorce is permitted for civil effects and as a civil ratification of the fact that the marriage bond really does not exist.

Annulment

This is a decision by a competent church authority – e.g., a bishop, a diocesan marriage tribunal, the Roman Rota – that an apparently valid marriage was actually invalid from the beginning because of the unknown or concealed existence, from the beginning, of a diriment impediment, an essential defect in consent, radical incapability for marriage, or a condition placed by one or both of the parties against the very nature of marriage.

Eastern-rite Laws

Marriage laws of the Eastern Church differ in several respects from the legislation of the Roman rite. The regulations in effect since May 2, 1949, were contained in the *motu proprio Crebre Allatae* issued by Pius XII the previous February.

According to both the Roman Code of Canon Law and the Oriental Code, marriages between Roman-rite Catholics and Eastern-rite Catholics ordinarily take place in the rite of the groom and have canonical effects in that rite.

Regarding the form for the celebration of marriages between Eastern Catholics and baptized Eastern non-Catholics, the Second Vatican Council declared:

"By way of preventing invalid marriages between Eastern Catholics and baptized Eastern non-Catholics, and in the interests of the permanence and sanctity of marriage and of domestic harmony, this sacred Synod decrees that the canonical 'form' for the celebration of such marriages obliges only for lawfulness. For their validity, the presence of a sacred minister suffices, as long as the other requirements of law are honored" (Decree on Eastern Catholic Churches, No. 18).

Marriages taking place in this manner are lawful, as well as valid, with permission of a competent Eastern-rite bishop.

The Rota

The Roman Rota is the ordinary court of appeal for marriage, and some other cases, which are appealed to the Holy See from lower church courts. Appeals are made to the Rota if decisions by diocesan and archdiocesan courts fail to settle the matter in dispute. Pope John Paul II, at annual meetings with Rota personnel, speaks about the importance of the court's actions in providing norms of practice for other tribunals.

Mixed Marriages

"Mixed Marriages" (*Matrimonia Mixta*) was the subject of a letter issued under this title by Pope Paul VI, on Mar. 31, 1970, and also a statement, "Implementation of the Apostolic Letter on Mixed Marriages," approved by the National Conference of Catholic Bishops on Nov. 16, 1970.

One of the key points in the bishops' statement referred to the need for mutual pastoral care by ministers of different faiths for the sacredness of marriage and for appropriate preparation and continuing support of parties to a mixed marriage.

Pastoral experience, which the Catholic Church shares with other religious bodies, confirms the fact that marriages of persons of different beliefs involve special problems related to the continuing religious practice of the concerned persons and to the religious education and formation of their children.

Pastoral measures to minimize these problems include instruction of a non-Catholic party in essentials of the Catholic faith for purposes of understanding. Desirably, some instruction should also be given the Catholic party regarding his or her partner's beliefs.

Requirements

The Catholic party to a mixed marriage is required to declare his (her) intention of continuing practice of the Catholic faith and to promise to do all in his (her) power to share his (her) faith with children born of the marriage by having them baptized and raised as Catholics. No declarations or promises are required of the non-Catholic party, but he (she) must be informed of the declaration and promise made by the Catholic.

Notice of the Catholic's declaration and promise is an essential part of the application made to a bishop for permission to marry a baptized non-Catholic, or a dispensation to marry an unbaptized non-Catholic.

A mixed marriage can take place with a Nuptial Mass. (The bishops' statement added this caution: "To the extent that Eucharistic sharing is not permitted by the general discipline of the Church, this is to be considered when plans are being made to have the mixed marriage at Mass or not.")

The ordinary minister at a mixed marriage is an authorized priest or deacon, and the ordinary place is the parish church of the Catholic party. A non-Catholic minister may not only attend the marriage ceremony but may also address, pray with and bless the couple.

For appropriate pastoral reasons, a bishop can grant a dispensation from the Catholic form of marriage and can permit the marriage to take place in a non-Catholic church with a non-Catholic minister as the officiating minister. A priest may not only attend such a ceremony but may also address, pray with and bless the couple.

"It is not permitted," however, the bishops' statement declared, "to have two religious services or to have a single service in which both the Catholic marriage ritual and a non-Catholic marriage ritual are celebrated jointly or successively."

Pastoral Ministry for Divorced and Remarried

Ministry to divorced and remarried Catholics is a difficult field of pastoral endeavor, situated as it is in circumstances tantamount to the horns of a dilemma.

At Issue

On the one side is firm church teaching on the permanence of marriage and norms against reception of the Eucharist and full participation in the life of the Church by Catholics in irregular unions.

On the other side are men and women with broken unions followed by second and perhaps happier attempts at marriage which the Church does not recognize as valid and which may not be capable of being validated because of the existence of an earlier marriage bond.

Factors involved in these circumstances are those of the Church, upholding its doctrine and practice regarding the permanence of marriage, and those of many men and women in irregular second marriages who desire full participation in the life of the Church.

Sacramental participation is not possible for those whose first marriage was valid, although there is no bar to their attendance at Mass, to sharing in other activities of the Church, or to their efforts to have children baptized and raised in the Catholic faith.

An exception to this rule is the condition of a divorced and remarried couple living in a brother-sister relationship.

There is no ban against sacramental participation by separated or divorced persons who have not attempted a second marriage, provided the usual conditions for reception of the sacraments are in order.

Unverified estimates of the number of U.S. Catholics who are divorced and remarried vary between 6 and 8 million.

Tribunal Action

What can the Church do for them and with them in pastoral ministry, is an old question charged with new urgency because of the rising number of divorced and remarried Catholics.

One way to help is through the agency of marriage tribunals charged with responsibility for investigating and settling questions concerning the validity or invalidity of a prior marriage. There are reasons in canon law justifying the Church in declaring a particular marriage null and void from the beginning, despite the short- or long-term existence of an apparently valid union.

Decrees of nullity (annulments) are not new in the history of the Church. If such a decree is issued, a man or woman is free to validate a second marriage and live in complete union with the Church.

The 2012 *Statistical Yearbook of the Church* (*Annuarium Statisticum Ecclesiae*, the most recent edition) reported in 2012 that U.S. tribunals issued 26,237 annulments (in ordinary and documentary processes). The canonical reasons were: invalid consent (21,521), impotence (4), other impediments (1,517), defect of form (4,022). Worldwide, 49,810 decrees or declarations of nullity were issued in 2012.

On Feb. 8, 2005, Vatican officials issued a new instruction for Church marriage tribunals that was intended clarify Church law, defend the sacrament of marriage, and ensure the efficiency that justice requires. The new handbook for Latin-rite diocesan and interdiocesan tribunals, *Dignitas Connubii* ("The Dignity of Marriage"), details clear procedures for accepting, investigating, assessing, and appealing marriage cases.

Reasons behind Decrees

Pastoral experience reveals that some married persons, a short or long time after contracting an apparently valid marriage, exhibit signs that point back to the existence, at the time of marriage, of latent and serious personal deficiencies which made them incapable of valid consent and sacramental commitment.

Such deficiencies might include gross immaturity and those affecting in a serious way the capacity to love, to have a true interpersonal and conjugal relationship, to fulfill marital obligations, or to accept the faith aspect of marriage.

Psychological and behavioral factors like these have been given greater attention by tribunals in recent years and have provided grounds for numerous decrees of nullity.

Decisions of this type do not indicate any softening of the Church's attitude regarding the permanence of marriage. They affirm, rather, that some persons who have married were really not capable of doing so.

Serious deficiencies in the capacity for real interpersonal relationship in marriage were the reasons behind a landmark decree of nullity issued in 1973 by the Roman Rota, the Vatican high court of appeals in marriage cases. Pope John Paul referred to such deficiencies – the "grave lack of discretionary judgment," incapability of assuming "essential matrimonial rights and obligations," for example – in an address Jan. 26, 1984, to personnel of the Rota.

The tribunal way to a decree of nullity regarding a previous marriage, however, is not open to many persons in second marriages — because grounds are either lacking or, if present, cannot be verified in tribunal process.

Unacceptable Solutions

One unacceptable solution of the problem, called "good conscience procedure," involves administration of the sacraments of penance and the Eucharist to divorced and remarried Catholics unable to obtain a decree of nullity for a first marriage who are living in a subsequent marriage "in good faith."

This procedure, despite the fact that it has no standing or recognition in church law, is being advocated and practiced by some priests and remarried Catholics.

This issue was addressed by the Congregation for the Doctrine of the Faith in a letter to bishops dated Oct. 14, 1994, and published with the approval of Pope John Paul II. The letter said in part:

"Pastoral solutions in this area have been suggested according to which divorced-and-remarried members of the faithful could approach holy Communion in specific cases when they considered themselves authorized according to a judgment of conscience to do so. This would be the case, for example, when they had been abandoned completely unjustly although they sincerely tried to save the previous marriage; or when they are convinced of the nullity of their previous marriage although (they are) unable to demonstrate it in the external forum; or when they have gone through a long period of reflection and penance; or also when for morally valid reasons they cannot satisfy the obligation to separate.

"In some places it has also been proposed that, in order objectively to examine their actual situation, the divorced-and-remarried would have to consult a prudent and experienced priest. This priest, however, would have to respect their eventual decision in conscience to approach holy Communion, without this implying an official authorization.

"In these and similar cases, it would be a matter of a tolerant and benevolent pastoral solution in order to do justice to the different situations of the divorced-and-remarried.

"Even if analogous solutions have been proposed by a few fathers of the Church and in some measure were practiced, nevertheless these never attained the consensus of the fathers and in no way came to constitute the common doctrine of the Church nor to determine her discipline. It falls to the universal magisterium, in fidelity to sacred Scripture and tradition, to teach and to interpret authentically the deposit of faith."

Conditions for Receiving Communion

Practically speaking, "when for serious reasons — for example, for the children's upbringing — a man and a woman cannot satisfy the obligation to separate," they may be admitted to Communion if "they take on themselves the duty to live in complete continence, that is, by abstinence from the acts proper to married couples. In such a case they may receive holy Communion as long as they respect the obligation to avoid giving scandal."

The teaching of the Church on this subject "does not mean that the Church does not take to heart the situation of those faithful who, moreover, are not excluded from ecclesial communion. She is concerned to accompany them pastorally and invite them to share in the life of the Church in the measure that is compatible with the dispositions of divine law, from which the Church has no power to dispense. On the other hand, it is necessary to instruct these faithful so that they do not think their participation in the life of the Church is reduced exclusively to the question of the reception of the Eucharist. The faithful are to be helped to deepen their understanding of the value of sharing in the sacrifice of Christ in the Mass, or spiritual communion, of prayer, of meditation on the word of God, and of works of charity and justice."

The Communion of Saints

THE DECLARATION OF CANONIZATION

Such a declaration is preceded by the process of beatification and another detailed investigation concerning the person's reputation for holiness, writings, and (except in the case of martyrs) a miracle ascribed to his or her intercession after death. The pope can dispense from some of the formalities ordinarily required in canonization procedures (equivalent canonization), as Pope John XXIII did in the canonization of St. Gregory Barbarigo on May 26, 1960. A saint is worthy of honor in liturgical worship throughout the universal Church. From its earliest years the Church has venerated saints. Public official honor always required the approval of the bishop of the place. Martyrs were the first to be honored. St. Martin of Tours, who died in 397, was an early non-martyr venerated as a saint. The earliest canonization by a pope with positive documentation was that of St. Ulrich (Uldaric) of Augsburg by John XV in 993. Alexander III reserved the process of canonization to the Holy See in 1171. In 1588 Sixtus V established the Sacred Congregation of Rites for the principal purpose of handling causes for beatification and canonization: this function is now the work of the Congregation for the Causes of Saints. The official listing of saints and blessed is contained in the Roman Martyrology (revised, updated, and published in 2002 by the Congregation for Divine Worship and the Discipline of the Sacraments) and related decrees issued after its last publication. *Butler's unofficial Lives of the Saints* (1956 and recently updated) contains 2,565 entries. The Church regards all persons in heaven as saints, not just those who have been officially canonized.

SAINTS OF THE CHURCH

Biographical sketches of additional saints and blesseds are found in other *Almanac* entries. See **Index**, under the name of each saint for the apostles, evangelists, Doctors of the Church, and Fathers of the Church. For beatification and canonization procedures, see those entries in the **Glossary** (p. 128).

An asterisk (*) with a feast date indicates that the saint is listed in the General Roman Calendar or the proper calendar for U.S. dioceses. For rank of observances, see listing in calendar for current year on preceding pages.

Adalbert (956-97): Born in Bohemia; bishop of Prague; Benedictine; missionary in Poland, Prussia and Hungary; martyred by Prussians near Danzig; Apr. 23.*

Adjutor (d. 1131): Norman knight; fought in First Crusade; monk-recluse after his return; Apr. 30.

Agatha (d. c. 250): Sicilian virgin-martyr; her intercession credited in Sicily with stilling eruptions of Mt. Etna; patron of nurses; Feb. 5.*

Agnes (d. c. 304): Roman virgin-martyr; martyred at age of 10 or 12; patron of young girls; Jan. 21.*

Aloysius Gonzaga (1568-91): Italian Jesuit; died while nursing plague-stricken; canonized 1726; patron of youth; June 21.*

Amand (d. c. 676): Apostle of Belgium; b. France; established monasteries throughout Belgium; Feb. 6.

Andre Bessette, (Bro. Andre) (1845-1937): Canadian Holy Cross Brother; prime mover in building of St. Joseph's Oratory, Montreal; beatified May 23, 1982; canonized Oct. 17, 2010. Jan. 6.

Andre Grasset de Saint Sauveur, Bl. (1758-92): Canadian priest; martyred in France, Sept. 2, 1792, during the Revolution; one of a group called the Martyrs of Paris who were beatified in 1926; Sept. 2.

Andrew Bobola (1592-1657): Polish Jesuit; joined Jesuits at Vilna; worked for return of Orthodox to union with Rome; martyred; canonized 1938; May 16.

Andrew Corsini (1302-73): Italian Carmelite; bishop of Fiesoli; mediator between quarrelsome Italian states; canonized 1629; Feb. 4.

Andrew Dung-Lac and Companions (d. 18th-19th c.): Martyrs of Vietnam. Total of 117 included 96 Vietnamese, 11 Spanish and 10 French missionaries (8 bishops; 50 priests, including Andrew Dung-Lac; 1 seminarian, 58 lay persons). Canonized June 19, 1988; inscribed in General Roman Calendar, 1989, as a memorial. Nov. 24.*

Andrew Fournet (1752-1834): French priest; co-founder with St. Jeanne Elizabeth Bichier des Anges of the Daughters of the Holy Cross of St. Andrew; canonized 1933; May 13.

Andrew Kim, Paul Chong and Companions (d. between 1839-67): Korean martyrs (103) killed in persecutions of 1839, 1846, 1866, and 1867; among them were Andrew Kim, the first Korean priest, and Paul Chong, lay apostle; canonized May 6, 1984, during Pope John Paul II's visit to Korea. Sept. 20.*

Angela Merici (1474-1540): Italian secular Franciscan; foundress of Company of St. Ursula, 1535, the first teaching order of women Religious in the Church; canonized 1807; Jan. 27.*

Angelico, Bl. (Fra Angelico; John of Faesulis) (1387-1455): Dominican; Florentine painter of early Renaissance; proclaimed blessed by John Paul II, Feb. 3, 1982; patron of artists; Feb. 18.

Anne Marie Javouhey, Bl. (1779-1851): French virgin; foundress of Institute of St. Joseph of Cluny, 1812; beatified 1950; July 15.

Ansgar (801-65): Benedictine monk; b. near Amiens; archbishop of Hamburg; missionary in Denmark, Sweden, Norway and northern Germany; apostle of Scandinavia; Feb. 3.*

Anthony (c. 251-c. 354): Abbot; Egyptian hermit; patriarch of all monks; established communities for hermits which became models for monastic life, especially in the

East; friend and supporter of St. Athanasius in the latter's struggle with the Arias; Jan. 17.*

Anthony Claret (1807-70): Spanish bishop; founder of Missionary Sons of the Immaculate Heart of Mary (Claretians), 1849; archbishop of Santiago, Cuba, 1851-57; canonized 1950; Oct. 24.*

Anthony Gianelli (1789-1846): Italian bishop; founded the Daughters of Our Lady of the Garden, 1829; bishop of Bobbio, 1838; canonized 1951; June 7.

Anthony Zaccaria (1502-39): Italian priest; founder of Barnabites (Clerks Regular of St. Paul), 1530; canonized 1897; July 5.*

Apollonia (d. 249): Deaconess of Alexandria; martyred during persecution of Decius; her patronage of dentists and those suffering from toothaches probably rests on tradition that her teeth were broken by her persecutors; Feb. 9.

Augustine of Canterbury (d. 604 or 605): Italian missionary; apostle of the English; sent by Pope Gregory I with 40 monks to evangelize England; arrived there 597; first archbishop of Canterbury; May 27.*

Bartolomea Capitania (1807-33): Italian foundress with Vincenza Gerosa of the Sisters of Charity of Lovere; canonized 1950; July 26.

Beatrice da Silva Meneses (1424-90): Foundress, b. Portugal; founded Congregation of the Immaculate Conception, 1484, in Spain; canonized 1976; Sept. 1.

Benedict Joseph Labré (1748-83): French layman; pilgrim-beggar; noted for his piety and love of prayer before the Blessed Sacrament; canonized 1883; Apr. 16.

Benedict of Nursia (c. 480-547): Abbot; founder of monasticism in Western Europe; established monastery at Monte Cassino; proclaimed patron of Europe by Paul VI in 1964; July 11.*

Benedict the Black (*il Moro*) (1526-89): Sicilian Franciscan; born a slave; joined Franciscans as lay brother; appointed guardian and novice master; canonized 1807; Apr. 3.

Bernadette Soubirous (1844-79): French peasant girl favored with series of visions of Blessed Virgin Mary at Lourdes (*see* **Lourdes Apparitions**); joined Institute of Sisters of Notre Dame at Nevers, 1866; canonized 1933; Apr. 16.

Bernard of Montjoux (or Menthon) (d. 1081): Augustinian canon; probably born in Italy; founded Alpine hospices near the two passes named for him; patron of mountaineers; May 28.

Bernardine of Feltre, Bl. (1439-94): Italian Franciscan preacher; a founder of *montes pietatis*; Sept. 28.

Bernardine of Siena (1380-1444): Italian Franciscan; noted preacher and missioner; spread of devotion to Holy Name is attributed to him; represented in art holding to his breast the monogram IHS; canonized 1450; May 20.*

Blase (d. c. 316): Armenian bishop; martyr; the blessing of throats on his feast day derives from tradition that he miraculously saved the life of a boy who had half-swallowed a fish bone; Feb. 3.*

Boniface (Winfrid) (d. 754): English Benedictine; bishop; martyr; apostle of Germany; established monastery at Fulda which became center of missionary work in Germany; archbishop of Mainz; martyred near Dukkum in Holland; June 5.*

Brendan (c. 489-583): Irish abbot; founded monasteries; his patronage of sailors probably rests on a legend that he made a seven-year voyage in search of a fabled paradise; called Brendan the Navigator; May 16.

Bridget (Brigid) (c. 450-525): Irish nun; founded religious community at Kildare, the first in Ireland; patron, with Sts. Patrick and Columba, of Ireland; Feb. 1.

Bridget (Birgitta) (c. 1303-73): Swedish mystic; widow; foundress of Order of Our Savior (Brigittines); canonized 1391; patroness of Sweden; named a co-patroness of Europe, with St. Edith Stein and St. Catherine of Siena, on Oct. 1, 1999; July 23.*

Bruno (1030-1101): German monk; founded Carthusians, 1084, in France; Oct. 6.*

Cabrini, Mother: *See* **Frances Xavier Cabrini.**

Cajetan (Gaetano) **of Thiene** (1480-1547): Italian lawyer; religious reformer; a founder of Oratory of Divine Love, forerunner of the Theatines; canonized 1671; Aug. 7.*

Callistus I (d. 222): Pope, 217-22; martyr; condemned Sabellianism and other heresies; advocated a policy of mercy toward repentant sinners; Oct. 14.*

Camillus de Lellis (1550-1614): Italian priest; founder of Camillians (Ministers of the Sick); canonized 1746; patron of the sick and of nurses; July 14.*

Casimir (1458-84): Polish prince; grand duke of Lithuania; noted for his piety; buried at cathedral in Vilna, Lithuania; canonized 1521; patron of Poland and Lithuania; Mar. 4.*

Cassian of Tangier (d. 298): Roman martyr; an official court stenographer who declared himself a Christian; patron of stenographers; Dec. 3.

Catherine Labouré (1806-76): French Religious; favored with series of visions soon after she joined Sisters of Charity of St. Vincent de Paul in Paris in 1830; first Miraculous Medal (*see* **Index**) struck in 1832 in accord with one of the visions; canonized 1947; Nov. 28.

Catherine of Bologna (1413-63): Italian Poor Clare; mystic, writer, artist canonized 1712; patron of artists; May 9.

Cecilia (2nd-3rd century): Roman virgin-martyr; traditional patroness of musicians; Nov. 22.*

Charles Borromeo (1538-84): Italian cardinal; nephew of Pope Pius IV; cardinal bishop of Milan; influential figure in Church reform in Italy; promoted education of clergy; canonized 1610; Nov. 4.*

Charles Lwanga and Companions (d. between 1885 and 1887): Twenty-two Martyrs of Uganda, many of them pages of King Mwanga of Uganda, who were put to death because they denounced his corrupt lifestyle; canonized 1964; first martyrs of black Africa; June 3.*

Charles of Sezze (1616-70): Italian Franciscan lay brother who served in humble capacities; canonized 1959; Jan. 6.

Christopher (3rd cent.): Early Christian martyr inscribed in Roman calendar about 1550; feast relegated to particular calendars because of legendary nature of accounts of his life; traditional patron of travelers; July 25.

Clare (1194-1253): Foundress of Poor Clares; b. at Assisi; was joined in religious life by her sisters, Agnes and Beatrice, and eventually her widowed mother Ortolana; canonized 1255; patroness of television; Aug. 11.*

Claude de la Colombiere (1641-82): French Jesuit; spiritual director of St. Margaret Mary Alacoque; instrumental in spreading devotion to the Sacred Heart; beatified, 1929; canonized May 31, 1992; Feb. 15.

Clement Hofbauer (1751-1820): Redemptorist priest, missionary; born in Moravia; helped spread Redemptorists north of the Alps; canonized 1909; Mar. 15.

Clement I (d. c. 100): Pope, 88-97; third successor of St. Peter; wrote important letter to Church in Corinth settling disputes there; venerated as a martyr; Nov. 23.*

Columba (521-97): Irish monk; founded monasteries in

Ireland; missionary in Scotland; established monastery at Iona which became the center for conversion of Picts, Scots, and Northern English; Scotland's most famous saint; patron saint of Ireland (with Sts. Patrick and Brigid); June 9.

Columban (545-615): Irish monk; scholar; founded monasteries in England and Brittany (famous abbey of Luxeuil), forced into exile because of his criticism of Frankish court; spent last years in northern Italy where he founded abbey at Bobbio; Nov. 23.*

Conrad of Parzham (1818-94): Bavarian Capuchin lay brother; served as porter at the Marian shrine of Altotting in Upper Bavaria for 40 years; canonized 1934; Apr. 21.

Contardo Ferrini, Bl. (1859-1902): Italian secular Franciscan; model of the Catholic professor; beatified 1947; patron of universities; Oct. 20.

Cornelius (d. 253): Pope, 251-53; promoted a policy of mercy with respect to readmission of repentant Christians who had fallen away during the persecution of Decius (*lapsi*); banished from Rome during persecution of Gallus; regarded as a martyr; Sept. 16 (with Cyprian).*

Cosmas and Damian (d. c. 303): Arabian twin brothers, physicians; martyred during Diocletian persecution; patrons of physicians; Sept. 26.*

Crispin and Crispinian (3rd cent.): Early Christian martyrs; said to have met their deaths in Gaul; patrons of shoemakers, a trade they pursued; Oct. 25.

Crispin of Viterbo (1668-1750): Capuchin brother; canonized June 20, 1982; May 21.

Cyprian (d. 258): Early ecclesiastical writer; b. Africa; bishop of Carthage, 249-58; supported Pope St. Cornelius concerning the readmission of Christians who had apostatized in time of persecution; erred in his teaching that baptism administered by heretics and schismatics was invalid; wrote *De Unitate*; Sept. 16 (with St. Cornelius).*

Cyril and Methodius (9th century): Greek missionaries, bothers; venerated as apostles of the Slavs; Cyril (d. 869) and Methodius (d. 885) began their missionary work in Moravia in 863; developed a Slavonic alphabet; used the vernacular in the liturgy, a practice that was eventually approved; declared patrons of Europe with St. Benedict, Dec. 31, 1980; Feb. 14.*

Damasus I (d. 384): Pope, 366-84; opposed Arians and Apollinarians; commissioned St. Jerome to work on Bible translation; developed Roman liturgy; Dec. 11.*

Damian: *See* Cosmas and Damian.

Damien of Molokai (d. 1889): The so-called leper priest of Molokai; originally from Belgium, Damien devoted over 20 years to the care of the lepers in Hawaii, ultimately dying from the same disease. He was beatified by Pope John Paul II in 1995 canonized on Oct. 11, 2009.

David (5th or 6th cent.): Nothing for certain known of his life; said to have founded monastery at Menevia; patron saint of Wales; Mar. 1.

Denis and Companions (d. 3rd cent.): Denis, bishop of Paris, and two companions identified by early writers as Rusticus, a priest, and Eleutherius, a deacon; martyred near Paris; Denis is popularly regarded as the apostle and a patron saint of France; Oct. 9.*

Dismas (1st cent.): Name given to repentant thief (Good Thief) to whom Jesus promised salvation (Lk. 23:40-43); regarded as patron of prisoners; Mar. 25 (observed on second Sunday of October in U.S. prison chapels).

Dominic (Dominic de Guzman) (1170-1221): Spanish priest; founded Order of Preachers (Dominicans), 1215, in France; preached against Albigensian heresy; a contemporary of St. Francis of Assisi; canonized 1234; Aug. 8.*

Dominic Savio (1842-57): Italian youth; pupil of St. John Bosco; died before his 15th birthday; canonized 1954; patron of choir boys; May 6.

Duns Scotus, John (d. 1308): Scottish Franciscan; theologian; advanced theological arguments for doctrine of the Immaculate Conception; proclaimed blessed; cult solemnly confirmed by John Paul II, Mar. 20, 1993; Nov. 8.

Dunstan (c. 910-88): English monk; archbishop of Canterbury; initiated reforms in religious life; counselor to several kings; considered one of greatest Anglo-Saxon saints; patron of goldsmiths, locksmiths, jewelers (trades in which he is said to have excelled); May 19.

Dymphna (dates unknown): Nothing certain known of her life; according to legend, she was an Irish maiden murdered by her heathen father at Gheel near Antwerp, Belgium, where she had fled to escape his advances; her relics were discovered there in the 13th century; since that time cures of mental illness and epilepsy have been attributed to her intercession; patron of those suffering from mental illness; May 15.

Edith Stein, St. (1891-1942): German Carmelite (Teresa Benedicta of the Cross); born of Jewish parents; author and lecturer; baptized in Catholic Church, 1922; arrested with her sister Rosa in 1942 and put to death at Auschwitz; beatified 1987, by Pope John Paul II during his visit to West Germany; was canonized by Pope John Paul II on Oct. 11, 1998, and named a co-patroness of Europe, with St. Bridget of Sweden and St. Catherine of Siena, on Oct. 1, 1999. Aug. 10.

Edmund Campion (1540-81): English Jesuit; convert 1573; martyred at Tyburn; canonized 1970, one of the Forty English and Welsh Martyrs; Dec. 1.

Edward the Confessor (d. 1066): King of England, 1042-66; canonized 1161; Oct. 13.

Eligius (c. 590-660): Bishop; born in Gaul; founded monasteries and convents; bishop of Noyon and Tournai; famous worker in gold and silver; Dec. 1.

Elizabeth Ann Seton (1774-1821): American foundress; convert, 1805; founded Sisters of Charity in the U.S.; beatified 1963; canonized Sept. 14, 1975; the first American-born saint; Jan. 4 (U.S.).*

Elizabeth of Hungary (1207-31): Became secular Franciscan after death of her husband in 1227; devoted life to poor and destitute; a patron of the Secular Franciscan Order; canonized 1235; Nov. 17.*

Elizabeth of Portugal (1271-1336): Queen of Portugal; b. Spain; retired to Poor Clare convent as a secular Franciscan after the death of her husband; canonized 1626; July 4.*

Emily de Rodat (1787-1852): French foundress of the Congregation of the Holy Family of Villefranche; canonized 1950; Sept. 19.

Emily de Vialar (1797-1856): French foundress of the Sisters of St. Joseph of the Apparition; canonized 1951; June 17.

Erasmus (Elmo) (d. 303): Life surrounded by legend; martyred during Diocletian persecution; patron of sailors; June 2.

Ethelbert (552-616): King of Kent, England; baptized by St. Augustine of Canterbury, 597; issued legal code; furthered spread of Christianity; Feb. 26.

Eusebius of Vercelli (283-370): Italian bishop; exiled from his see (Vercelli) for a time because of his opposition to Arianism; considered a martyr because of sufferings he endured; Aug. 2.*

Fabian (d. 250): Pope, 236-50; martyred under Decius; Jan. 20.*

Felicity: *See* **Perpetua and Felicity**.

Ferdinand III (1198-1252): King of Castile and Leon; waged successful campaigns against the Moors in Spain; founded university at Salamanca; canonized 1671; May 30.

Fiacre (Fiachra) (d. c. 670): Irish hermit; patron of gardeners; Aug. 30.

Fidelis of Sigmaringen (Mark Rey) (1577-1622): German Capuchin; lawyer before he joined the Capuchins; missionary to Swiss Protestants; stabbed to death by peasants who were told he was an agent of the Austrian emperor; Apr. 24.*

Frances of Rome (1384-1440): Italian model for housewives and widows; happily married for 40 years; after death of her husband in 1436 joined community of Benedictine Oblates she had founded; canonized 1608; patron of motorists; Mar. 9.*

Frances Xavier Cabrini (Mother Cabrini) (1850-1917): American foundress; b. Italy; founded the Missionary Sisters of the Sacred Heart, 1877; settled in the U.S. 1889; became an American citizen at Seattle 1909; worked among Italian immigrants; canonized 1946, the first American citizen so honored; Nov. 13 (U.S.).*

Francis Borgia (1510-72): Spanish Jesuit; joined Jesuits after death of his wife in 1546; became general of the Order, 1565; Oct. 10.

Francis Caracciolo (1563-1608): Italian priest; founder with Father Augustine Adorno of the Clerics Regular Minor (Adorno Fathers); canonized 1807; declared patron of Italian chefs, 1996; June 4.

Francis Fasani (1681-1742): Italian Conventual Franciscan; model of priestly ministry, especially in service to poor and imprisoned; canonized 1986; Nov. 27.

Francis of Assisi (Giovanni di Bernardone) (1181/82-1226): Founder of the Franciscans, 1209; received stigmata 1224; canonized 1228; one of best known and best loved saints; patron of Italy, Catholic Action and ecologists; Oct. 4.*

Francis of Paola (1416-1507): Italian hermit; founder of Minim Friars; Apr. 2.*

Francis Xavier (1506-52): Spanish Jesuit; missionary to Far East; canonized 1602; patron of foreign missions; considered one of greatest Christian missionaries; Dec. 3.*

Francis Xavier Bianchi (1743-1815): Italian Barnabite; acclaimed apostle of Naples because of his work there among the poor and abandoned; canonized 1951; Jan. 31.

Frederick (d. 838): Bishop and martyr, also called Friderich; July 18.

Frederick (d. 1121): Bishop of Liège, Belgium, believed poisoned by the count of Louvain; May 27.

Gabriel of the Sorrowful Mother (Francis Possenti) (1838-62): Italian Passionist; died while a scholastic; canonized 1920; Feb. 27.

Gaspar (Caspar) **del Bufalo** (1786-1836): Italian priest; founded Missionaries of the Precious Blood, 1815; canonized 1954; Jan. 2.

Gemma Galgani (1878-1903): Italian laywoman; visionary; subject of extraordinary religious experiences; canonized 1940; Apr. 11.

Genesius (d. c. 300): Roman actor; according to legend, was converted while performing a burlesque of Christian baptism and was subsequently martyred; patron of actors; Aug. 25.

Geneviève (422-500): French nun; a patroness and protectress of Paris; events of her life not authenticated; Jan. 3.

George (d.c. 300): Martyr, probably during Diocletian persecution in Palestine; all other incidents of his life, including story of the dragon, are legendary; patron of England; Apr. 23.*

Gerard Majella (1725-55): Italian Redemptorist lay brother; noted for supernatural occurrences in his life including bilocation and reading of consciences; canonized 1904; patron of mothers; Oct. 16.

Gertrude (1256-1302): German mystic; writer; helped spread devotion to the Sacred Heart; Nov. 16.*

Gregory VII (Hildebrand) (1020?-85): Pope, 1075-85; Benedictine monk; adviser to several popes; as pope, strengthened interior life of Church and fought against lay investiture; driven from Rome by Henry IV; died in exile; canonized 1584; May 25.*

Gregory Barbarigo (1626-97): Italian cardinal; noted for his efforts to bring about reunion of separated Christians; canonized 1960; June 18.

Gregory of Nyssa (c. 335-95): Bishop; theologian; younger brother of St. Basil the Great; Mar. 9.

Gregory Thaumaturgus (c. 213-68): Bishop of Neocaesarea; missionary, famed as wonder worker; Nov. 17.

Gregory the Illuminator (257-332): Martyr; bishop; apostle and patron saint of Armenia; helped free Armenia from the Persians; Sept. 30.

Hedwig (1174-1243): Moravian noblewoman; married duke of Silesia, head of Polish royal family; fostered religious life in country; canonized 1266; Oct. 16.*

Helena (250-330): Empress; mother of Constantine the Great; associated with discovery of the True Cross; Aug. 18.

Henry (972-1024): Bavarian emperor; cooperated with Benedictine abbeys in restoration of ecclesiastical and social discipline; canonized 1146; July 13.*

Herman Joseph (1150-1241): German Premonstratensian; his visions were the subjects of artists; writer; cult approved, 1958; Apr. 7.

Hippolytus (d. c. 236): Roman priest; opposed Pope St. Callistus I in his teaching about the readmission to the Church of repentant Christians who had apostatized during time of persecution; elected antipope; exiled to Sardinia; reconciled before his martyrdom; important ecclesiastical writer; Aug. 13* (with Pontian).

Hugh of Cluny (the Great) (1024-1109): Abbot of Benedictine foundation at Cluny; supported popes in efforts to reform ecclesiastical abuses; canonized 1120; Apr. 29.

Ignatius of Antioch (d. c. 107): Early ecclesiastical writer; martyr; bishop of Antioch in Syria for 40 years; Oct. 17.*

Ignatius of Laconi (1701-81): Italian Capuchin lay brother whose 60 years of religious life were spent in Franciscan simplicity; canonized 1951; May 11.

Ignatius of Loyola (1491-1556): Spanish soldier; renounced military career after recovering from wounds received at siege of Pampeluna (Pamplona) in 1521; founded Society of Jesus (Jesuits), 1534, at Paris; wrote *The Book of Spiritual Exercises*; canonized 1622; July 31.*

Irenaeus of Lyons (130-202): Early ecclesiastical writer; opposed Gnosticism; bishop of Lyons; traditionally regarded as a martyr; June 28.*

Isidore the Farmer (d. 1170): Spanish layman; farmer; canonized 1622; patron of farmers; May 15 (U.S.).*

Jane Frances de Chantal (1572-1641): French widow; foundress, under guidance of St. Francis de Sales, of Order of the Visitation; canonized 1767; Dec. 12* (General Roman Calendar); Aug. 18* (U.S.).

Januarius (Gennaro) (d. 304): Bishop of Benevento; martyred during Diocletian persecution; fame rests on liquefaction of some of his blood preserved in a phial at Naples, an unexplained phenomenon which has occurred regularly several times each year for over 400 years; Sept. 19.*

Jeanne Delanoue (1666-1736): French foundress of Sisters of St. Anne of Providence, 1704; canonized 1982; Aug. 16.

Jeanne (Joan) de Lestonnac (1556-1640): French foundress; widowed in 1597; founded the Religious of Notre Dame 1607; canonized 1947; Feb. 2.

Jeanne de Valois (Jeanne of France) (1464-1505): French foundress; deformed daughter of King Louis XI; was married in 1476 to Duke Louis of Orleans who had the marriage annulled when he ascended the throne as Louis XII; Jeanne retired to life of prayer; founded contemplative Annonciades of Bourges, 1504; canonized 1950; Feb. 5.

Jeanne-Elizabeth Bichier des Ages (1773-1838): French Religious; co-founder with St. Andrew Fournet of Daughters of the Cross of St. Andrew, 1807; canonized 1947; Aug. 26.

Jeanne Jugan, Bl. (1792-1879): French Religious; foundress of Little Sisters of the Poor; beatified Oct. 3, 1982; Aug. 30.

Jerome Emiliani (1481-1537): Venetian priest; founded Somascan Fathers, 1532, for care of orphans; canonized 1767; patron of orphans and abandoned children; Feb. 8.*

Joan Antida Thouret (1765-1826): French Religious; founded, 1799, congregation now known as Sisters of Charity of St. Joan Antida; canonized 1934; Aug. 24.

Joan of Arc (1412-31): French heroine, called The Maid of Orleans, La Pucelle; led French army in 1429 against English invaders besieging Orleans; captured by Burgundians the following year; turned over to ecclesiastical court on charge of heresy, found guilty and burned at the stake; her innocence was declared in 1456; canonized 1920; patroness of France; May 30.

Joaquina de Vedruna de Mas (1783-1854): Spanish foundress; widowed in 1816; after providing for her children, founded the Carmelite Sisters of Charity; canonized 1959; Aug. 28.

John I (d. 526): Pope, 523-26; martyr; May 18.*

John XXIII Pope from 1958-1963 best known for convoking the Second Vatican Council; canonized on Apr. 27, 2014; June 3.

John Baptist de la Salle (1651-1719): French priest; founder of Brothers of the Christian Schools, 1680; canonized 1900; patron of teachers; Apr. 7.*

John Berchmans (1599-1621): Belgian Jesuit scholastic; patron of Mass servers; canonized 1888; Aug. 13.

John (Don) Bosco (1815-88): Italian priest; founded Salesians, 1859, for education of boys; cofounder of Daughters of Mary Help of Christians for education of girls; canonized 1934; Jan. 31.*

John Capistran (1386-1456): Italian Franciscan; preacher; papal diplomat; canonized 1690; declared patron of military chaplains, Feb. 10, 1984. Oct. 23.*

John de Ribera (1532-1611): Spanish bishop and statesman; archbishop of Valencia, 1568-1611, and viceroy of that province; canonized 1960; Jan. 6.

John Eudes (1601-80): French priest; founder of Sisters of Our Lady of Charity of Refuge, 1642, and Congregation of Jesus-Mary (Eudists), 1643; canonized 1925; Aug. 19.*

John Fisher (1469-1535): English prelate; theologian; martyr; bishop of Rochester, cardinal; refused to recognize validity of Henry VIII's marriage to Anne Boleyn; upheld supremacy of the pope; beheaded for refusing to acknowledge Henry as head of the Church; canonized 1935; June 22 (with St. Thomas More).*

John Francis Regis (1597-1640): French Jesuit priest;

preached missions among poor and unlettered; canonized 1737; patron of social workers, particularly medical social workers, because of his concern for poor and needy and sick in hospitals; July 2.

John Gualbert (d. 1073): Italian priest; founder of Benedictine congregation of Vallombrosians, 1039; canonized 1193; July 12.

John Kanty (Cantius) (1395-1473): Polish theologian; canonized 1767; Dec. 23.*

John Leonardi (1550-1609): Italian priest; worked among prisoners and the sick; founded Clerics Regular of the Mother of God; canonized 1938; Oct. 9.*

John Nepomucene (1345-93): Bohemian priest; regarded as a martyr; canonized 1729; patron of Czechoslovakia; May 16.

John Nepomucene Neumann (1811-60): American prelate; b. Bohemia; ordained in New York 1836; missionary among Germans near Niagara Falls before joining Redemptorists, 1840; bishop of Philadelphia, 1852; first bishop in U.S. to prescribe Forty Hours devotion in his diocese; beatified 1963; canonized June 19, 1977; Jan. 5 (U.S.).*

John of Ávila (1499-1569): Spanish priest; preacher; ascetical writer; spiritual adviser of St. Teresa of Jesus (Ávila); canonized 1970; May 10.

John of Britto (1647-93): Portuguese Jesuit; missionary in India where he was martyred; canonized 1947; Feb. 4.

John of God (1495-1550): Portuguese founder; his work among the sick poor led to foundation of Brothers Hospitallers of St. John of God, 1540, in Spain; canonized 1690; patron of sick, nurses, hospitals; Mar. 8.*

John of Matha (1160-1213): French priest; founder of the Order of Most Holy Trinity, whose original purpose was the ransom of prisoners from the Muslims; Feb. 8.

John Ogilvie (1579-1615): Scottish Jesuit; martyr; canonized 1976, the first canonized Scottish saint since 1250 (Margaret of Scotland); Mar. 10.

John Paul II (1920-2005): Pope from 1978-2005; one of the longest serving popes in history; wrote a great number of encyclicals that examined the modern world, human dignity, and eternal moral truths; his more than 120 international trips were vital moments in modern Catholic history; beatified on May 1, 2011 and canonized on Apr. 27, 2014; Oct. 22.

John Vianney (Curé of Ars) (1786-1859): French parish priest; noted confessor, spent 16 to 18 hours a day in confessional; canonized 1925; patron of parish priests; Aug. 4.*

Josaphat Kuncevyc (1584-1623): Basilian monk; b. Poland; archbishop of Polotsk, Lithuania; worked for reunion of separated Eastern Christians with Rome; martyred by mob of schismatics; canonized 1867; Nov. 12.*

Josemaria Escrivá de Balaguer (1902-75) Priest and Founder of Opus Dei; the society was designed to promote holiness among individuals in the world; beatified in 1992 and canonized on Oct. 6, 2002; May 17.

Joseph Benedict Cottolengo (1786-1842): Italian priest; established Little Houses of Divine Providence (*Piccolo Casa*) for care of orphans and the sick; canonized 1934; Apr. 30.

Joseph Cafasso (1811-60): Italian priest; renowned confessor; promoted devotion to Blessed Sacrament; canonized 1947; June 23.

Joseph Calasanz (1556-1648): Spanish priest; founder of Piarists (Order of Pious Schools); canonized 1767; Aug. 25.*

Joseph of Cupertino (1603-63): Italian Franciscan; noted for remarkable incidents of levitation; canonized 1767; Sept. 18.

Joseph Pignatelli (1737-1811): Spanish Jesuit; left Spain when Jesuits were banished in 1767; worked for revival of the Order; named first superior when Jesuits were reestablished in Kingdom of Naples, 1804; canonized 1954; Nov. 28.

Juan Diego (16th cent.): Mexican Indian; convert; indigenous name according to tradition Cuauhtlatohuac ("The eagle who speaks"); favored with apparitions of Our Lady (*see* **Our Lady of Guadalupe**, p. 123) on Tepeyac hill; beatified, 1990; canonized July 30, 2002; Dec. 9* (U.S.).

Julia Billiart (1751-1816): French foundress; founded Sisters of Notre Dame de Namur, 1804; canonized 1969; Apr. 8.

Juliana Falconieri (1270-1341): Italian foundress of the Servite Nuns; the niece of St. Alexis Falconieri; canonized in 1737; June 19.

Justin de Jacobis (1800-60): Italian Vincentian; bishop; missionary in Ethiopia; canonized 1975; July 31.

Justin Martyr (100-65): Early ecclesiastical writer; Apologies for the Christian Religion, Dialog with the Jew Tryphon; martyred at Rome; June 1.*

Kateri Tekakwitha (1656-80): "Lily of the Mohawks." Indian maiden born at Ossernenon (Auriesville), N.Y.; baptized Christian, Easter, 1676, by Jesuit missionary Fr. Jacques de Lambertville; lived life devoted to prayer, penitential practices and care of sick and aged in Christian village of Caughnawaga near Montreal where her relics are now enshrined; beatified June 22, 1980 and canonized on Oct. 21, 2012; July 14.

Katharine Drexel, St. (1858-1955): Philadelphia-born heiress; devoted wealth to founding schools and missions for Indians and Blacks; foundress of Sisters of Blessed Sacrament for Indians and Colored People, 1891; beatified 1988; canonized on Oct. 1, 2000; Mar. 3* (U.S.).

Ladislaus (1040-1095): King of Hungary; supported Pope Gregory VII against Henry IV; canonized 1192; June 27.

Lawrence (d. 258): Widely venerated martyr who suffered death, according to a long-standing but unverifiable legend, by fire on a gridiron; Aug. 10.*

Lawrence (Lorenzo) **Ruiz and Companions** (d. 1630s): Martyred in or near the city of Nagasaki, Japan; Lawrence Ruiz, first Filipino saint, and 15 companions (nine Japanese, four Spaniards, one Italian and one Frenchman); canonized 1987; Sept. 28.*

Leonard Murialdo (1828-1900): Italian priest; educator; founder of Pious Society of St. Joseph of Turin, 1873; canonized 1970; Mar. 30.

Leonard of Port Maurice (1676-1751): Italian Franciscan; ascetical writer; preached missions throughout Italy; canonized 1867; patron of parish missions; Nov. 26.

Leopold Mandic (1866-1942): Croatian-born Franciscan priest, noted confessor; spent most of his priestly life in Padua, Italy; canonized 1983; July 30.

Louis IX (1215-70): King of France, 1226-70; participated in Sixth Crusade; patron of Secular Franciscan Order; canonized 1297; Aug. 25.*

Louis de Montfort (1673-1716): French priest; founder of Sisters of Divine Wisdom, 1703, and Missionaries of Company of Mary, 1715; wrote *True Devotion to the Blessed Virgin*; canonized 1947; Apr. 28.*

Louis Zepherin Moreau, Bl. (d. 1901): Canadian bishop; headed St. Hyacinthe, Que., diocese, 1876-1901; beatified 1987; May 24.

Louise de Marillac (1591-1660): French foundress, with St. Vincent de Paul, of the Sisters of Charity; canonized 1934; Mar. 15.

Lucy (d. 304): Sicilian maiden; martyred during

Diocletian persecution; one of most widely venerated early virgin-martyrs; patron of Syracuse, Sicily; invoked by those suffering from eye diseases; Dec. 13.*

Lucy Filippini (1672-1732): Italian educator, helped improve status of women through education; considered a founder of the Religious Teachers Filippini, 1692; canonized 1930; Mar. 25.

Madeleine Sophie Barat (1779-1865): French foundress of the Society of the Sacred Heart of Jesus; canonized 1925; May 25.

Malachy (1095-1148): Irish bishop; instrumental in establishing first Cistercian house in Ireland, 1142; canonized 1190; Nov. 3.

Marcellinus and Peter (d.c. 304): Early Roman martyrs; June 2.*

Margaret Clitherow (1556-86): English martyr; convert shortly after her marriage; one of Forty Martyrs of England and Wales; canonized 1970; Mar. 25.

Margaret Mary Alacoque (1647-90): French Religious; spread devotion to Sacred Heart in accordance with revelations made to her in 1675 (*see* **Sacred Heart,** p. 154); canonized 1920; Oct. 16.*

Margaret of Cortona (1247-97): Secular Franciscan; reformed her life in 1273 following the violent death of her lover; canonized 1728; May 16.

Margaret of Hungary (1242-70): Contemplative; daughter of King Bela IV of Hungary; lived a life of self-imposed penances; canonized 1943; Jan. 18.

Margaret of Scotland (1050-1093): Queen of Scotland; noted for solicitude for the poor and promotion of justice; canonized 1250; Nov. 16.*

Maria Goretti (1890-1902): Italian virgin-martyr; a model of purity; canonized 1950; July 6.*

Mariana Paredes of Jesus (1618-45): South American recluse; Lily of Quito; canonized, 1950; May 28.

Marianne Cope, See under **Missionaries to the Americas** (p. 363).

Marie-Leonie Paradis, Bl. (1840-1912): Canadian Religious; founded Little Sisters of the Holy Family, 1880; beatified 1984; May 4.

Marie-Rose Durocher, Bl. (1811-49): Canadian Religious; foundress of Sisters of Holy Names of Jesus and Mary; beatified 1982; Oct. 6* (in U.S.).

Martha (1st cent.): Sister of Lazarus and Mary of Bethany; Gospel accounts record her concern for homely details; patron of cooks; July 29.*

Martin I (d. 655): Pope, 649-55; banished from Rome by emperor in 653 because of his condemnation of Monothelites; considered a martyr; Apr. 13.*

Martin of Tours (316-97): Bishop of Tours; opposed Arianism and Priscillianism; pioneer of Western monasticism, before St. Benedict; Nov. 11.*

Mary Mazzarello (1837-81): Italian foundress, with St. John Bosco, of the Daughters of Mary Help of Christians, 1872; canonized 1951; May 14.

Mary Josepha Rossello (1811-81): Italian-born foundress of the Daughters of Our Lady of Mercy; canonized 1949; Dec. 7.

Mary Magdalen Postel (1756-1846): French foundress of the Sisters of Christian Schools of Mercy, 1807; canonized 1925; July 16.

Mary Magdalene (1st cent.): Gospels record her as devoted follower of Christ to whom he appeared after the Resurrection; her identification with Mary of Bethany (sister of Martha and Lazarus) and the woman sinner (Lk 7:36-50) has been questioned; July 22.*

Mary Magdalene dei Pazzi (1566-1607): Italian Carmelite nun; recipient of mystical experiences; canonized 1669; May 25.*

Mary Michaeli Desmaisières (1809-65): Spanish-born foundress of the Institute of the Handmaids of the Blessed Sacrament, 1848; canonized 1934; Aug. 24.

Maximilian Kolbe (1894-1941): Polish Conventual Franciscan; prisoner at Auschwitz who heroically offered his life in place of a fellow prisoner; beatified 1971, canonized 1982; Aug. 14.*

Methodius: *See* **Cyril and Methodius**.

Miguel Febres Cordero (1854-1910): Ecuadorean Christian Brother; educator; canonized 1984; Feb. 9.

Miguel Pro, Bl. (1891-1927): Mexican Jesuit; joined Jesuits, 1911; forced to flee because of religious persecution; ordained in Belgium, 1925; returned to Mexico, 1926, to minister to people despite government prohibition; unjustly accused of assassination plot against president; arrested and executed; beatified 1988. Nov. 23* (U.S.).

Monica (332-87): Mother of St. Augustine; model of a patient mother; her feast is observed in the Roman calendar the day before her son's; Aug. 27.*

Nereus and Achilleus (d.c. 100): Early Christian martyrs; soldiers who, according to legend, were baptized by St. Peter; May 12.*

Nicholas of Flüe (1417-87): Swiss layman; at the age of 50, with the consent of his wife and 10 children, he retreated from the world to live as a hermit; called Brother Claus by the Swiss; canonized 1947; Mar. 21.

Nicholas of Myra (4th cent.): Bishop of Myra in Asia Minor; one of most popular saints in both East and West; most of the incidents of his life are based on legend; patron of Russia; Dec. 6.*

Nicholas of Tolentino (1245-1305): Italian hermit; famed preacher; canonized 1446; Sept. 10.

Nicholas Tavelic and Companions (Deodatus of Aquitaine, Peter of Narbonne, Stephen of Cuneo) (d. 1391): Franciscan missionaries; martyred by Muslims in the Holy Land: canonized 1970; Nov. 14.

Norbert (1080-1134): German bishop; founded Canons Regular of Premontre (Premonstratensians, Norbertines), 1120; promoted reform of the clergy, devotion to Blessed Sacrament; canonized 1582; June 6.*

Odilia (d. c. 720): Benedictine abbess; according to legend she was born blind, abandoned by her family and adopted by a convent of nuns where her sight was miraculously restored; patroness of blind; Dec. 13.

Oliver Plunket (1629-81): Irish martyr; theologian; archbishop of Armagh and primate of Ireland; beatified 1920; canonized, 1975; July 1.

Pancras (d. c. 304): Roman martyr; May 12.*

Paola Frassinetti (1809-82): Italian Religious; foundress, 1834, of Sisters of St. Dorothy; canonized 1984; June 11.

Paschal Baylon (1540-92): Spanish Franciscan lay brother; spent life as door-keeper in various Franciscan friaries; defended doctrine of Real Presence in Blessed Sacrament; canonized 1690; patron of all Eucharistic confraternities and congresses, 1897; May 17.

Patrick (389-461): Famous missionary of Ireland; began missionary work in Ireland about 432; organized the Church there and established it on a lasting foundation; patron of Ireland, with Sts. Bridget and Columba; Mar. 17.*

Paul Miki and Companions (d. 1597): Martyrs of Japan; Paul Miki, Jesuit, and 25 other priests and laymen were martyred at Nagasaki; canonized 1862, the first canonized martyrs of the Far East; Feb. 6.*

Paul of the Cross (1694-1775): Italian Religious; founder of the Passionists; canonized 1867; Oct 19* (Oct. 20, U.S.*).

Paulinus of Nola (d. 451): Bishop of Nola (Spain); writer; June 22.*

Peregrine (1260-1347): Italian Servite; invoked against cancer (he was miraculously cured of cancer of the foot after a vision); canonized 1726; May 1.

Perpetua and Felicity (d. 203): Martyrs; Perpetua was a young married woman; Felicity was a slave girl; Mar. 7.*

Peter Chanel (1803-41): French Marist; missionary to Oceania, where he was martyred; canonized 1954; Apr. 28.*

Peter Fourier (1565-1640): French priest; co-founder with Alice LeClercq (Mother Teresa of Jesus) of the Augustinian Canonesses of Our Lady, 1598; canonized 1897; Dec. 9.

Peter Gonzalez (1190-1246): Spanish Dominican; worked among sailors; court chaplain and confessor of King St. Ferdinand of Castile; patron of sailors; Apr. 14.

Peter Julian Eymard (1811-68): French priest; founder of the Congregation of the Blessed Sacrament (men), 1856, and Servants of the Blessed Sacrament (women), 1864; dedicated to Eucharistic apostolate; canonized 1962; Aug. 2.*

Peter Nolasco (c. 1189-1258): Born in Langueduc area of present-day France; founded the Mercedarians (Order of Our Lady of Mercy), 1218, in Spain; canonized 1628; Jan. 31.

Peter of Alcantara (1499-1562): Spanish Franciscan; mystic; initiated Franciscan reform; confessor of St. Teresa of Jesus (Ávila); canonized 1669; Oct. 22 (in U.S.).

Philip Benizi (1233-85): Italian Servite; noted preacher, peacemaker; canonized 1671; Aug. 23.

Philip Neri (1515-95): Italian Religious; founded Congregation of the Oratory; considered a second apostle of Rome because of his mission activity there; canonized 1622; May 26.*

Philip of Jesus (1517-57): Mexican Franciscan; martyred at Nagasaki, Japan; canonized 1862; patron of Mexico City; Feb. 6.*

Pio, Padre (1887-1968): Pio da Pietrelcina (Francesco Forgione), and Italian Capuchin Franciscan, mystic and stigmatic; assisted souls from all over the world who came to him for counsel and guidance; canonized on June 16, 2002; Sept. 23.

Pius V (1504-72): Pope, 1566-72; enforced decrees of Council of Trent; organized expedition against Turks resulting in victory at Lepanto; canonized 1712; Apr. 30.*

Pius IX (d. 1878): Pope, 1846-78; the second longest pontiff in the history of the Church; defined the dogma of the Immaculate Conception and convoked Vatican Council I (1870-1871); Feb. 7.

Polycarp (2nd cent.): Bishop of Smyrna; ecclesiastical writer; martyr; Feb. 23.*

Pontian (d. c. 235): Pope, 230-35; exiled to Sardinia by the emperor; regarded as a martyr; Aug. 13 (with Hippolytus).*

Rafaela Maria Porras y Ayllon (1850-1925): Spanish Religious; founded the Handmaids of the Sacred Heart, 1877; canonized 1977; Jan. 6.

Raymond Nonnatus (d. 1240): Spanish Merced-arian; cardinal; devoted his life to ransoming captives from the Moors; Aug. 31.

Raymond of Peñafort (1175-1275): Spanish Dominican; confessor of Gregory IX; systematized and codified canon law, in effect until 1917; master general of Dominicans, 1238; canonized 1601; Jan. 7.*

Rita of Cascia (1381-1457): Widow; cloistered Augustinian Religious of Umbria; invoked in impossible and desperate cases; May 22.

Robert Southwell (1561-95): English Jesuit; poet; martyred at Tyburn; canonized 1970, one of the Forty English and Welsh Martyrs; Feb. 21.

Roch (1350-79): French layman; pilgrim; devoted life to care of plague-stricken; widely venerated; invoked against pestilence; Aug. 17.

Romuald (951-1027): Italian monk; founded Camaldolese Benedictines; June 19.*

Rose of Lima (1586-1617): Peruvian Dominican tertiary; first native-born saint of the New World; canonized 1671; Aug. 23.*

Scholastica (d. c. 559): Sister of St. Benedict; regarded as first nun of the Benedictine Order; Feb. 10.*

Sebastian (3rd cent.): Roman martyr; traditionally pictured as a handsome youth with arrows; martyred; patron of athletes, archers; Jan. 20.*

Seven Holy Founders of the Servants of Mary (Buonfiglio Monaldo, Alexis Falconieri, Benedict dell'Antello, Bartholomew Amidei, Ricovero Uguccione, Gerardino Sostegni, John Buonagiunta Monetti): Florentine youths who founded Servites, 1233, in obedience to a vision; canonized 1888; Feb. 17.*

Sharbel Makhlouf (1828-98): Lebanese Maronite monk-hermit; canonized 1977; Dec. 24.

Sixtus II and Companions (d. 258): Sixtus, pope 257-58, and four deacons, martyrs; Aug. 7.*

Stanislaus (1030-79): Polish bishop; martyr; canonized 1253; Apr. 11.*

Stephen (d. c. 33): First Christian martyr; chosen by the Apostles as the first of the seven deacons; stoned to death; Dec. 26.*

Stephen (975-1038): King; apostle of Hungary; welded Magyars into national unity; canonized 1083; Aug. 16.*

Sylvester I (d. 335): Pope 314-35; first ecumenical council held at Nicaea during his pontificate; Dec. 31.*

Tarcisius (d. 3rd cent.): Early martyr; according to tradition, was martyred while carrying the Blessed Sacrament to some Christians in prison; patron of first communicants; Aug. 15.

Teresa Margaret Redi (1747-70): Italian Carmelite; lived life of prayer and austere penance; canonized 1934; Mar. 11.

Teresa of Jesus Jornet Ibars (1843-97): Spanish Religious; founded the Little Sisters of the Abandoned Aged, 1873; canonized 1974; Aug. 26.

Teresa, Mother (1910-97): Sister, foundress of the Missionaries of Charity, and Nobel Prize winner; called Mother Teresa of Calcutta; beatified by Pope John Paul II on Oct. 19, 2003; Sept. 5.

Theodore Guérin: *See* under **Missionaries to the Americas** (p. 363).

Thérèse Couderc (1805-85): French Religious; foundress of the Religious of Our Lady of the Retreat in the Cenacle, 1827; canonized 1970; Sept. 26.

Thomas Becket (1118-70): English martyr; archbishop of Canterbury; chancellor under Henry II; murdered for upholding rights of the Church; canonized 1173; Dec. 29.*

Thomas More (1478-1535): English martyr; statesman, chancellor under Henry VIII; author of Utopia; opposed Henry's divorce, refused to renounce authority of the papacy; beheaded; canonized 1935; Pope John Paul II declared him patron of politicians on Oct. 31, 2000; June 22 (with St. John Fisher).*

Timothy (d. c. 97): Bishop of Ephesus; disciple and companion of St. Paul; martyr; Jan. 26.*

Titus (d. c. 96): Bishop; companion of St. Paul; recipient of one of Paul's epistles; Jan. 26.*

Titus Brandsma, Bl. (1881-1942): Dutch Carmelite priest; professor, scholar, journalist; denounced Nazi persecution of Jews; arrested by Nazis, Jan. 19, 1942; executed by lethal injection at Dachau, July 26, 1942; beatified 1985; July 26.

Valentine (d. 269): Priest, physician; martyred at Rome; legendary patron of lovers; Feb. 14.

Vicenta Maria Lopez y Vicuna (1847-96): Spanish foundress of the Daughters of Mary Immaculate for domestic service; canonized 1975; Dec. 26.

Vincent (d. 304): Spanish deacon; martyr; Jan. 22.*

Vincent de Paul (1581?-1660): French priest; founder of Congregation of the Mission (Vincentians, Lazarists) and co-founder of Sisters of Charity; declared patron of all charitable organizations and works by Leo XIII; canonized 1737; Sept. 27.*

Vincent Ferrer (1350-1418): Spanish Dominican; famed preacher; Apr. 5.*

Vincent Pallotti (1795-1850): Italian priest; founded Society of the Catholic Apostolate (Pallottines), 1835; Jan. 22.

Vincent Strambi (1745-1824): Italian Passionist; bishop; reformer; canonized 1950; Sept. 25.

Vitus (d.c. 300): Martyr; died in Lucania, southern Italy; regarded as protector of epileptics and those suffering from St. Vitus Dance (chorea); June 15.

Walburga (d. 779): English-born Benedictine Religious; belonged to group of nuns who established convents in Germany at the invitation of St. Boniface; abbess of Heidenheim; Feb. 25.

Wenceslaus (d. 935): Duke of Bohemia; martyr; patron of Bohemia; Sept. 28.*

Zita (1218-78): Italian maid; noted for charity to poor; patron of domestics; Apr. 27.

SAINTS — PATRONS AND INTERCESSORS

A patron is a saint who is venerated as a special intercessor before God. Most patrons have been so designated as the result of popular devotion and long-standing custom. In many cases, the fact of existing patronal devotion is clear despite historical obscurity regarding its origin. The Church has made official designation of relatively few patrons; in such cases, the dates of designation are given in parentheses in the list below. The theological background of the patronage of saints includes the dogmas of the Mystical Body of Christ and the Communion of Saints. Listed are patron saints of occupations and professions, and saints whose intercession is sought for special needs.

Academics: Thomas Aquinas.

Accomodations: Gertrude of Nivelles.

Accountants: Matthew.

Actors: Genesius.

Adopted children: Clotilde; Thomas More.

Advertisers: Bernardine of Siena (May 20, 1960).

Alcoholics: John of God; Monica.

Alpinists: Bernard of Montjoux (or Menthon) (Aug. 20, 1923).

Altar servers: John Berchmans.

Anesthetists: René Goupil.
Animals: Francis of Assisi.
Archaeologists: Damasus.
Archers: Sebastian.
Architects: Thomas, Apostle.
Art: Catherine of Bologna.
Artists: Luke, Catherine of Bologna, Bl. Angelico (Feb. 21, 1984).
Astronauts: Joseph Cupertino.
Astronomers: Dominic.
Athletes: Sebastian.
Authors: Francis de Sales.
Aviators: Our Lady of Loreto (1920), Thérèse of Lisieux, Joseph of Cupertino.
Bakers: Elizabeth of Hungary, Nicholas.
Bankers: Matthew.
Barbers: Cosmas and Damian, Louis.
Barren women: Anthony of Padua, Felicity.
Basket-makers: Anthony, Abbot.
Bees: Ambrose.
Birth: Margaret.
Beggars: Martin of Tours.
Blacksmiths: Dunstan.
Blind: Odilia, Raphael.
Blood banks: Januarius.
Bodily ills: Our Lady of Lourdes.
Bookbinders: Peter Celestine.
Bookkeepers: Matthew.
Booksellers: John of God.
Boy Scouts: George.
Brewers: Augustine of Hippo, Luke, Nicholas of Myra.
Bricklayers: Stephen.
Brides: Nicholas of Myra.
Bridges: John of Nepomucene.
Broadcasters: Gabriel.
Brushmakers: Anthony, Abbot.
Builders: Vincent Ferrer.
Bus drivers: Christopher.
Butchers: Anthony (Abbot), Luke.
Butlers: Adelelm.
Cabdrivers: Fiacre.
Cabinetmakers: Anne.
Cancer patients: Peregrine.
Canonists: Raymond of Peñafort.
Carpenters: Joseph.
Catechists: Viator, Charles Borromeo, Robert Bellarmine.
Catholic Action: Francis of Assisi (1916).
Catholic Press: Francis de Sales.
Chandlers: Ambrose, Bernard of Clairvaux.
Chaplains: John of Capistrano.
Charitable societies: Vincent de Paul (May 12, 1885).
Chastity: Thomas Aquinas.
Childbirth: Raymond Nonnatus; Gerard Majella.
Children: Nicholas of Myra.
Children of Mary: Agnes, Maria Goretti.
Choirboys: Dominic Savio (June 8, 1956), Holy Innocents.
Church: Joseph (Dec. 8, 1870).
Circus people: Julian the Hospitaller.
Clerics: Gabriel of the Sorrowful Mother.
Colleges: Thomas Aquinas.
Comedians: Vitus.
Communications personnel: Bernardine.
Confessors: Alphonsus Liguori (Apr. 26, 1950), John Nepomucene.
Converts: Helena; Vladimir.

Convulsive children: Scholastica.
Cooks: Lawrence, Martha.
Coopers: Nicholas of Myra.
Coppersmiths: Maurus.
Dairy workers: Brigid.
Dancers: Vitus.
Deaf: Francis de Sales.
Dentists: Apollonia.
Desperate situations: Gregory of Neocaesarea, Jude Thaddeus, Rita of Cascia.
Dietitians (in hospitals): Martha.
Diplomats: Gabriel.
Divorce: Helena.
Drug addiction: Maximilian Kolbe.
Dyers: Maurice, Lydia.
Dying: Joseph.
Ecologists: Francis of Assisi (Nov. 29, 1979).
Ecumenists: Cyril and Methodius.
Editors: John Bosco.
Emigrants: Frances Xavier Cabrini (Sept. 8, 1950).
Endurance: Pantaleon.
Engineers: Ferdinand III.
Epilepsy, Motor Diseases: Vitus, Willibrord.
Eucharistic congresses and societies: Paschal Baylon (Nov. 28, 1897).
Expectant mothers: Raymond Nonnatus, Gerard Majella.
Eye diseases: Lucy.
Falsely accused: Raymond Nonnatus.
Farmers: George, Isidore.
Farriers: John the Baptist.
Fathers: Joseph.
Firemen: Florian.
Fire prevention: Catherine of Siena.
First communicants: Tarcisius.
Fishermen: Andrew.
Florists: Thérèse of Lisieux.
Forest workers: John Gualbert.
Foundlings: Holy Innocents.
Friendship: John the Divine.
Fullers: Anastasius the Fuller, James the Less.
Funeral directors: Joseph of Arimathea, Dismas.
Gardeners: Adelard, Tryphon, Fiacre, Phocas.
Glassworkers: Luke.
Goldsmiths: Dunstan, Anastasius.
Gravediggers: Anthony, Abbot.
Greetings: Valentine.
Grocers: Michael.
Grooms: King Louis IX of France.
Hairdressers: Martin de Porres.
Happy meetings: Raphael.
Hatters: Severus of Ravenna, James the Less.
Headache sufferers: Teresa of Jesus (Ávila).
Heart patients: John of God.
Homeless: Margaret of Cortona; Benedict Joseph Labré.
Horses: Giles; Hippolytus.
Housekeepers: Zita.
Hospital administrators: Basil the Great, Frances X. Cabrini.
Hospitals: Camillus de Lellis and John of God (June 22, 1886), Jude Thaddeus.
Housewives: Anne.
Hunters: Hubert, Eustachius.
Infantrymen: Maurice.
Innkeepers: Amand, Martha, Julian the Hospitaller.
Innocence: Hallvard.
Invalids: Roch.

Janitors: Theobald.
Jewelers: Eligius, Dunstan.
Journalists: Francis de Sales (Apr. 26, 1923).
Jurists: John Capistran.
Laborers: Isidore, James, John Bosco.
Lawyers: Ivo (Yves Helory), Genesius, Thomas More.
Learning: Ambrose.
Librarians: Jerome.
Lighthouse keepers: Venerius (Mar. 10, 1961).
Linguists: Gottschalk.
Locksmiths: Dunstan.
Lost souls: Nicholas of Tolentino.
Lovers: Raphael; Valentine.
Lunatics: Christina.
Maids: Zita.
Marble workers: Clement I.
Mariners: Michael, Nicholas of Tolentino.
Medical record librarians: Raymond of Peñafort.
Medical social workers: John Regis.
Medical technicians: Albert the Great.
Mentally ill: Dymphna.
Merchants: Francis of Assisi, Nicholas of Myra.
Messengers: Gabriel.
Metal workers: Eligius.
Military chaplains: John Capistran (Feb. 10, 1984).
Millers: Arnulph, Victor.
Missions, foreign: Francis Xavier (Mar. 25, 1904), Thérèse of Lisieux (Dec. 14, 1927).
Missions, black: Peter Claver (1896, Leo XIII), Benedict the Black.
Missions, parish: Leonard of Port Maurice (Mar. 17, 1923).
Monks: Benedict of Nursia.
Mothers: Monica.
Motorcyclists: Our Lady of Grace.
Motorists: Christopher, Frances of Rome.
Mountaineers: Bernard of Montjoux (or Menthon).
Musicians: Gregory the Great, Cecilia, Dunstan.
Mystics: John of the Cross.
Notaries: Luke, Mark.
Nuns: Bridget.
Nurses: Camillus de Lellis and John of God (1930, Pius XI), Agatha, Raphael.
Nursing and nursing service: Elizabeth of Hungary, Catherine of Siena.
Orators: John Chrysostom (July 8, 1908).
Organ builders: Cecilia.
Orphans: Jerome Emiliani.
Painters: Luke.
Paratroopers: Michael.
Pawnbrokers: Nicholas.
Plumbers: Vincent Ferrer.
Pharmacists: Cosmas and Damian, James the Greater.
Pharmacists (in hospitals): Gemma Galgani.
Philosophers: Justin.
Physicians: Pantaleon, Cosmas and Damian, Luke, Raphael.
Pilgrims: James the Greater.
Plasterers: Bartholomew.
Poets: David, Cecilia.
Politicians: Thomas More
Poison sufferers: Benedict.
Policemen: Michael.
Poor: Lawrence, Anthony of Padua.
Poor souls: Nicholas of Tolentino.
Popes: Gregory I the Great.
Porters: Christopher.

Possessed: Bruno, Denis.
Postal employees: Gabriel.
Priests: Jean-Baptiste Vianney (Apr. 23, 1929).
Printers: John of God, Augustine of Hippo, Genesius.
Prisoners: Dismas, Joseph Cafasso.
Protector of crops: Ansovinus.
Public relations: Bernardine of Siena (May 20, 1960).
Public relations (of hospitals): Paul, Apostle.
Publishers: John the Divine.
Race relations: Martin de Porres.
Radiologists: Michael (Jan. 15, 1941).
Radio workers: Gabriel.
Refugees: Alban.
Retreats: Ignatius Loyola (July 25, 1922).
Rheumatism: James the Greater.
Saddlers: Crispin and Crispinian.
Sailors: Cuthbert, Brendan, Eulalia, Christopher, Peter Gonzalez, Erasmus, Nicholas.
Scholars: Bede the Venerable; Brigid.
Schools, Catholic: Thomas Aquinas (Aug. 4, 1880), Joseph Calasanz (Aug. 13, 1948).
Scientists: Albert (Aug. 13, 1948).
Sculptors: Four Crowned Martyrs.
Seamen: Francis of Paola.
Searchers of lost articles: Anthony of Padua.
Secretaries: Genesius.
Secular Franciscans: Louis of France, Elizabeth of Hungary.
Seminarians: Charles Borromeo.
Servants: Martha, Zita.
Shepherds: Drogo.
Shoemakers: Crispin and Crispinian.
Sick: Michael, John of God and Camillus de Lellis (June 22, 1886).
Silversmiths: Andronicus.
Singers: Gregory, Cecilia.
Single mothers: Margaret of Cortona.
Single women: Catherine of Alexandria.
Skaters: Lidwina.
Skiers: Bernard of Montjoux (or Menthon).
Social workers: Louise de Marillac (Feb. 12, 1960).
Soldiers: Hadrian, George, Ignatius, Sebastian, Martin of Tours, Joan of Arc.
Speleologists: Benedict.
Stamp collectors: Gabriel.
Stenographers: Genesius, Cassian.
Stonecutters: Clement.
Stonemasons: Stephen.
Stress: Walter of Portnoise.
Students: Thomas Aquinas.
Surgeons: Cosmas and Damian, Luke.
Swimmers: Adjutor.
Swordsmiths: Maurice.
Tailors: Homobonus.
Tanners: Crispin and Crispinian, Simon.
Tax collectors: Matthew.
Teachers: Gregory the Great, John Baptist de la Salle (May 15, 1950).
Telecommunications workers: Gabriel (Jan. 12, 1951).
Television: Clare of Assisi (Feb. 14, 1958).
Television workers: Gabriel.
Thieves: Dismas.
Theologians: Augustine, Alphonsus Liguori.
Throat ailments: Blase.
Torture victims: Alban; Eustachius; Regina; Vincent; Victor of Marseilles.

Toymakers: Claude.
Travelers: Anthony of Padua, Nicholas of Myra, Christopher, Raphael.
Travel hostesses: Bona (Mar. 2, 1962).
Truck drivers: Christopher.
Universities: Blessed Contardo Ferrini.
Veterinarians: Blaise.
Vocations: Alphonsus.
Whales: Brendan the Voyager.
Watchmen: Peter of Alcantara.
Weavers: Paul the Hermit, Anastasius the Fuller, Anastasia.
Wine merchants: Amand.
Wineries: Morand; Vincent.
Women in labor: Anne.
Workingmen: Joseph.
Writers: Francis de Sales (Apr. 26, 1923), Lucy.
Yachtsmen: Adjutor.
Young girls: Agnes.
Youth: Aloysius Gonzaga (1729, Benedict XIII; 1926, Pius XI), John Berchmans, Gabriel of the Sorrowful Mother.

Patron Saints of Places

Albania: Our Lady of Good Counsel.
Alsace: Odilia.
Americas: Our Lady of Guadalupe, Rose of Lima.
Angola: Immaculate Heart of Mary (Nov. 21, 1984).
Argentina: Our Lady of Lujan.
Armenia: Gregory Illuminator.
Asia Minor: John, Evangelist.
Australia: Our Lady Help of Christians.
Belgium: Joseph.
Bohemia: Wenceslaus, Ludmilla.
Bolivia: Our Lady of Copacabana, *"Virgen de la Candelaria."*
Borneo: Francis Xavier.
Brazil: Nossa Señora de Aparecida, Immaculate Conception, Peter of Alcantara.
Canada: Joseph, Anne.
Chile: James the Greater, Our Lady of Mt. Carmel.
China: Joseph.
Colombia: Peter Claver, Louis Bertran.
Corsica: Immaculate Conception.
Cuba: Our Lady of Charity.
Czechoslovakia: Wenceslaus, John Nepomucene, Procopius.
Denmark: Ansgar, Canute.
Dominican Republic: Our Lady of High Grace, Dominic.
East Indies: Thomas, Apostle.
Ecuador: Sacred Heart.
El Salvador: Our Lady of Peace (Oct. 10, 1966).
England: George.
Equatorial Guinea: Immaculate Conception (May 25, 1986).
Europe: Benedict (1964), Cyril and Methodius, co-patrons (Dec. 31, 1980); Sts. Catherine of Siena, Bridget of Sweden, and Edith Stein, co-patronesses (Oct. 1, 1999).
Finland: Henry.
France: Our Lady of the Assumption, Joan of Arc, Thérèse (May 3, 1944).
Germany: Boniface, Michael.
Gibraltar: Blessed Virgin Mary, "Our Lady of Europe" (May 31, 1979).
Greece: Nicholas, Andrew.
Holland: Willibrord.
Hungary: Blessed Virgin, "Great Lady of Hungary," Stephen, King.

Iceland: Thorlac (Jan. 14, 1984).
India: Our Lady of Assumption.
Ireland: Patrick, Brigid and Columba.
Italy: Francis of Assisi, Catherine of Siena.
Japan: Peter Baptist.
Korea: Joseph and Mary, Mother of the Church.
Lesotho: Immaculate Heart of Mary.
Lithuania: Casimir, Cunegunda.
Luxembourg: Willibrord.
Malta: Paul, Our Lady of the Assumption.
Mexico: Our Lady of Guadalupe.
Monaco: Devota.
Moravia: Cyril and Methodius.
New Zealand: Our Lady Help of Christians.
Norway: Olaf.
Papua New Guinea (including northern Solomon Islands): Michael the Archangel (May 31, 1979).
Paraguay: Our Lady of Assumption (July 13, 1951).
Peru: Joseph (Mar. 19, 1957).
Philippines: Sacred Heart of Mary.
Poland: Casimir, Cunegunda, Stanislaus of Krakow, Our Lady of Czestochowa.
Portugal: Immaculate Conception, Francis Borgia, Anthony of Padua, Vincent of Saragossa, George.
Russia: Andrew, Nicholas of Myra, Thérèse of Lisieux.
Scandinavia: Ansgar.
Scotland: Andrew, Columba.
Silesia: Hedwig.
Slovakia: Our Lady of Sorrows.
South Africa: Our Lady of Assumption (Mar. 15, 1952).
South America: Rose of Lima.
Solomon Islands: Blessed Virgin Mary, Most Holy Name of Mary (Sept. 4, 1991).
Spain: James the Greater, Teresa.
Sri Lanka (Ceylon): Lawrence.
Sweden: Bridget, Eric.
Tanzania: Immaculate Conception (Dec. 8, 1964).
United States: Immaculate Conception (1846).
Uruguay: Blessed Virgin Mary, *"La Virgen de los Treinte y Tres"* (Nov. 21, 1963).
Venezuela: Our Lady of Coromoto.
Wales: David.
West Indies: Gertrude.

Emblems, Portrayals of Saints

Agatha: Tongs, veil.
Agnes: Lamb.
Ambrose: Bees, dove, ox, pen.
Andrew: Transverse cross.
Anne, Mother of the Blessed Virgin: Door.
Anthony of Padua: Infant Jesus, bread, book, lily.
Augustine of Hippo: Dove, child, shell, pen.
Bartholomew: Knife, flayed and holding his skin.
Benedict: Broken cup, raven, bell, crosier, bush.
Bernard of Clairvaux: Pen, bees, instruments of the Passion.
Bernardine of Siena: Tablet or sun inscribed with IHS.
Blase: Wax, taper, iron comb.
Bonaventure: Communion, ciborium, cardinal's hat.
Boniface: Oak, ax, book, fox, scourge, fountain, raven, sword.
Bridget of Sweden: Book, pilgrim's staff.
Bridget of Kildare: Cross, flame over her head, candle.
Catherine of Ricci: Ring, crown, crucifix.
Catherine of Siena: Stigmata, cross, ring, lily.
Cecilia: Organ.
Charles Borromeo: Communion, coat of arms with

word "Humilitas."

Christopher: Giant, torrent, tree, Child Jesus on his shoulders.

Clare of Assisi: Monstrance.

Cosmas and Damian: A phial, box of ointment.

Cyril of Alexandria: Blessed Virgin holding the Child Jesus, pen.

Cyril of Jerusalem: Purse, book.

Dominic: Rosary, star.

Edmund the Martyr: Arrow, sword.

Elizabeth of Hungary: Alms, flowers, bread, the poor, a pitcher.

Francis of Assisi: Wolf, birds, fish, skull, the Stigmata.

Francis Xavier: Crucifix, bell, vessel.

Genevieve: Bread, keys, herd, candle.

George: Dragon.

Gertrude: Crown, taper, lily.

Gervase and Protase: Scourge, club, sword.

Gregory I (the Great): Tiara, crosier, dove.

Helena: Cross.

Ignatius of Loyola: Communion, chasuble, book, apparition of Our Lord.

Isidore: Bees, pen.

James the Greater: Pilgrim's staff, shell, key, sword.

James the Less: Square rule, halberd, club.

Jerome: Lion.

John Berchmans: Rule of St. Ignatius, cross, rosary.

John Chrysostom: Bees, dove, pen.

John of God: Alms, a heart, crown of thorns.

John the Baptist: Lamb, head on platter, skin of an animal.

John the Evangelist: Eagle, chalice, kettle, armor.

Josaphat Kuncevyc: Chalice, crown, winged deacon.

Joseph, Spouse of the Blessed Virgin: Infant Jesus, lily, rod, plane, carpenter's square.

Jude: Sword, square rule, club.

Justin Martyr: Ax, sword.

Lawrence: Cross, book of the Gospels, gridiron.

Leander of Seville: Pen.

Liberius: Pebbles, peacock.

Longinus: In arms at foot of the cross.

Louis IX of France: Crown of thorns, nails.

Lucy: Cord, eyes on a dish.

Luke: Ox, book, brush, palette.

Mark: Lion, book.

Martha: Holy water sprinkler, dragon.

Mary Magdalene: Alabaster box of ointment.

Matilda: Purse, alms.

Matthew: Winged man, purse, lance.

Matthias: Lance.

Maurus: Scales, spade, crutch.

Meinrad: Two ravens.

Michael: Scales, banner, sword, dragon.

Monica: Girdle, tears.

Nicholas: Three purses or balls, anchor or boat, child.

Patrick: Cross, harp, serpent, baptismal font, demons, shamrock.

Paul: Sword, book or scroll.

Peter: Keys, boat, cock.

Philip, Apostle: Column.

Philip Neri: Altar, chasuble, vial.

Rita of Cascia: Rose, crucifix, thorn.

Roch: Angel, dog, bread.

Rose of Lima: Crown of thorns, anchor, city.

Sebastian: Arrows, crown.

Simon Stock: Scapular.

Teresa of Jesus (Ávila): Heart, arrow, book.

Thérèse of Lisieux: Roses entwining a crucifix.

Thomas, Apostle: Lance, ax.

Thomas Aquinas: Chalice, monstrance, dove, ox, person trampled under foot.

Vincent de Paul: Children.

Vincent Ferrer: Pulpit, cardinal's hat, trumpet, captives.

CANONIZATIONS AND BEATIFICATIONS 2013-14

Pope Francis beatified and canonized the following individuals from Sept. 2013 to Aug. 2014. Included are the dates of the beatifications, as well as relevant biographical information.

BEATIFICATIONS

2013

José Gabriel del Rosario Brochero (1840-1914) An Argentine Catholic priest, called affectionately the "Gaucho priest." Ordained a priest in 1866, he served in various assignments but gave his life to the care of the people in the city of Córdoba and the valley Traslasierras. He built churches and schools, and made roads to help the poor and the needy. He was beatified in the small town of Córdoba in Argentina on Sept. 14, 2013, before a crowd estimated at 300,000.

Tommaso da Olera (1563-1631) An Italian Franciscan Capuchin friar, known as the "brother of the street" for his mendicant humility. A native of Bergamo, Italy, he entered the Capuchins at the age of 17 and made his profession in 1584 and became a beloved figure for his care of the poor and the sick and as a spiritual advisor to the Habsburgs, including Emperor Ferdinand II of Austria. He was beatified on Sept. 21, 2013, in Bergamo, Italy.

Miroslav Bulesic (1920-1947) A Croatian priest and martyr. Born in Cabrunici, a village in Istria (then part of Italy), he was called to the priesthood and studied in Rome at the Pontifical Gregorian University. After ordination, he served as a parish priest. In 1947, he tried to administer Confirmation against the wishes of local Communists and was beaten severely and then martyred by having his throat cut. He died forgiving his attackers. He was beatified on Sept. 28, 2013, in Istra, Croatia.

Rolando Rivi (1931-1945) An Italian priest and martyr. He entered the seminary at the age of 11 and was in the seminary throughout World War II in Modena, but he was forced to return home in 1944. He wore his cassock in the face of threats by Communist partisans and was tortured and murdered near Modena. His cassock was taken as a prize. He is the first seminarian to be beatified. He was beatified on Oct. 5, 2013, in Modena, Italy.

522 Spanish Martyrs (d. 1936-1939) The largest group of martyrs ever beatified, they were all victims of the brutality of the Spanish Civil War. All of the martyrs died for the faith and were bishops, priests and laypeople ranging in age from 16 to 78 and from all over the country. There were 33 separate causes all incorporated into the beatification. The ceremony of beatification was held on Oct. 13, 2013, in Tarragona, Spain.

Sándor István (1914-1953) A Hungarian printer, Salesian lay brother and martyr. A native of Hungary, he was serving as a teacher of the Catholic faith during the Communist era in Hungary and was arrested in 1952 for resisting atheism and as an enemy of the Communist regime. Condemned by a show trial, he was sentenced to death and executed as an enemy of the people and hanged on June 8, 1953 at Budapest, Hungary. He was beatified on Oct. 19, 2013, in Budapest.

Maria Theresia Bonzel (1830-1905) German woman religious and founder of the Sisters of St. Francis of Perpetual Adoration. She became a Franciscan tertiary by age 20 and desired to enter the religious life. After overcoming the opposition of her parents, she began with eight other women the Sisters of St. Francis and served as its head, taking the name Mother Maria Theresia. The community flourished and established houses all over the world, including the United States. She was beatified on Nov. 10, 2013, in Paderborn, Germany.

2014

Maria Cristina of Savoy (1812-1836) Italian first Queen consort of Ferdinand II of the Two Sicilies and the youngest daughter of King Victor Emmanuel I of Sardinia and Archduchess Maria Teresa of Austria-Este. Deeply prayerful and modest, she wed Ferdinand II of the Two Sicilies in 1832 and suffered his annoyance at her humility. She died at the age of 23, after having given birth five days before to her only child, Francis II of the Two Sicilies. She was beatified on Jan. 25, 2014, in Naples, Italy.

Giuseppe Girotti (1905-1945) An Italian Dominican priest and martyr. He entered the Dominicans and made his profession in 1923 and was ordained a priest in 1930. After extensive studies with a specialization in Scripture at the École Biblique in Jerusalem, he taught at the Dominican Theological Seminary at Turin, Italy. Arrested by the Nazis for helping Jews to escape the Holocaust, he was transferred to various camps and finally died at Dachau. He was noted in the camps for his care of fellow prisoners. He was beatified on Apr. 26, 2014, in Alba, Cuneo, Italy.

Anton Durcovici (1888-1951) A Romanian bishop and martyr. Called to the priesthood at a young age, he studied in Iasi and Bucharest, Romania, and then in Rome, where he earned two doctorates. Returning home, he was ordained a priest in 1910 and was assigned to teach at the Bucharest seminary. Appointed bishop of Iasi in 1947, he was arrested two years later by the Hungarian Communist regime and suffered torture, starvation and imprisonment until his death from harsh winter conditions. He was buried in an unmarked grave. Revered as a martyr, he was beatified on May 17, 2014.

Mario Vergara (1910-1950) and **Isidore Ngei Ko Lat** (1920-1950) Two martyrs in the region of Burma, modern Myanmar. Vergara was an Italian missionary priest of PIME. Ordained a priest in 1934, he was sent to Burma as a missionary and served in the mountains. Interred in 1940 by the British in India, he went back to Burma in 1946 and was slain by hostile local tribes with his devoted catechist Isidore Ngei Ko Lat, a Burmese seminarian and catechist. The two were beatified on May 24, 2014, in Aversa, Caserta, Italy.

Maria Esperanza Alhama (1893-1983) Founder of the Handmaids of Merciful Love in 1930 and the Sons of Merciful Love in 1951. Born in Santomera, Spain, she entered the Congregation of the Daughters of Calvary at the age of 21. In 1930, she started the Servants of the Merciful Love in Madrid and later founded the Sons of Merciful Love in Rome. Her later years were marked by mystical experiences of the Passion of Christ at Collevalenza , Umbria, where a sanctuary was established that attracted many visitors, including Pope St. John Paul II. She was beatified on May 31, 2014, at Perugia, Italy.

Paul Yun Ji-Chung and 123 companions (d. 1791-1888) A group of Korean Martyrs who died for the faith during the worst persecutions of the faith in the Korean kingdom. In all, more than 8,000 Christians died during the oppression; 103 were canonized in May 1984 under Pope St. John Paul II. The newest martyrs were beatified on Aug. 15, 2014, in Daejeon, South Korea, by Pope Francis during his visit to Korea to celebrate the Asian Youth Day.

Scheduled for Beatification in 2014

Giovannina Franks (1807-1872), Sept. 20, 2014, Como, Italy.

Alvaro del Portillo (1914-1994), Sept. 27, 2014, Madrid, Spain.

Teresa Demjanovich (1901-1927), Oct. 4, 2014, Newark, New Jersey, United States.

Francesco Zirano (1564-1603), Oct. 12, 2014, Sassari, Italy.

Pope Paul VI (d. 1978), Oct. 19, 2014, St. Peter's Square, Vatican City.

Maria Assunta Caterina Marchetti (1871-1948), Oct. 25, 2014, São Paulo, Brazil.

CANONIZATIONS

2013

Angela of Foligno (1248-1309) Mystic from Umbria, Italy, who spent most of her life in the town of Foligno. A member of a wealthy family, she adopted a severe life of austerity following the death of her husband. Later, she became a Franciscan tertiary and received a number of visions, particularly of the Lord's passion. The account of the visions, dictated by Angela's confessor, Friar Arnold, was published under the title *Liber Visionum et Instructionum*, earning notoriety as a profound expression of Franciscan spirituality. She was given an equivalent canonization on Oct. 9, 2013, in Vatican City.

2014

Peter Faber (1506-1546) One of the founders of the Society of Jesus with St. Ignatius Loyola and others. Born in what was then Savoy, he studied at the University of Paris, where he shared a room St. Francis Xavier. There he met Ignatius of Loyola and became part of the initial foundation of the Society of Jesus. Ordained in 1534, he took his vows at Montmartre on Aug. 15, that same year. He worked with St. Ignatius over the next years and placed himself at the service of the popes who used him to fight against the Protestant Reformation. He took part in the Diet of Worms and then the Diet of Ratisbon in 1541 and labored for renewal in the Church across Germany and then in Spain and Portugal. He served at the Council of Trent on behalf of Pope Paul III. Pope Francis announced Faber's equivalent canonization on the pope's own birthday, Dec. 17, 2013. Francis also gave thanks for Faber's canonization during Mass on Jan. 3, 2014, at the Church of the Gesù in Rome.

José de Anchieta (1534–1597) The Jesuit Apostle of Brazil. Born in San Cristobal de la Laguna, Spain, and a relative of St. Ignatius of Loyola, he entered the Society of Jesus at the age of 18 at Coimbra, Portugal, in 1551. He was sent to Brazil two years later and spent the 44 years there, founding missions, including Sao Paulo de Piratininga. In 1567, he was appointed superior of the Jesuit province of Brazil, and a decade later became the Jesuit provincial of Brazil. He was a thaumaturgist, healing many, and animals and birds came at his call. He died at Reritiba, Brazil, and the local tribes came in vast numbers to honor his passing. The bishop who preached at his funeral called him a first-ranked missionary. Pope John Paul II designated José de Anchieta as "this great son of Ignatius" at his beatification on June 22, 1980. He was given an equivalent canonization by Pope Francis on Apr. 3, 2014 in the Vatican.

Marie of the Incarnation Guyart (1599-1672) The founder of the Ursulines in Canada and the patroness of the Algonquin and Iroquois nations. Born in Tours, France, she married but was widowed and so joined the Ursuline convent in Tours and then sailed for Canada. On Aug. 1, 1639, she founded the oldest institution of learning for women in North America. Called the "Theresa of her time and of the New World," she worked among the Native Americans, especially the Algonquin and Iroquois. Bp. St. Francois de Montmorency-Laval approved the rule of her congregation in 1681. Pope John Paul II beatified Marie of the Incarnation Guyart on June 22, 1980; she was given an equivalent canonization on Apr. 2, 2014, by Pope Francis.

Francois-Xavier de Montmorency-Laval (1623-1708) A French missionary to Quebec and the first bishop of Canada. Born in Montigny-sur-Avre, France, he studied with the Jesuits and wanted to be a priest although there were long obstacles. Ordained in 1647, he was appointed vicar apostolic of Tongkin (modern Vietnam), in the Paris Foreign Mission Society at age 30, but never took up residence there because of the political and geographical conditions. In 1654, Francois resigned his position and spent four years at a hermitage in Caen. Pope Alexander VII (r. 1655-1667) appointed him vicar apostolic of New France in 1658, and on Dec. 8 of that year, Francois was consecrated a bishop. Shortly thereafter he set sail for Canada, reaching Quebec on June 16, 1659. He died in Quebec after three decades of tireless labors for the Canadian Church. Pope John Paul II beatified him on June 22, 1980; he was given equivalent canonization by Pope Francis on Apr. 2, 2014.

Pope John XXIII (1881-1963) for details, see under **Special Reports**.

Pope John Paul II (1920-2005) for details, see under **Special Reports**.

Scheduled for Canonization in 2014

The following were scheduled for canonization by Pope Francis on Nov. 23, 2014:

Kuriakose Elias Chavara, the Indian founder of the Carmelites of Mary Immaculate.

Euphrasia Eluvathingal, an Indian Carmelite sister and member of the Syro-Malabar Catholic Church.

Nicholas of Longobardi, an Italian friar of the Minim order.

Giovanni Antonio Farina, an Italian bishop of Vicenza and the founder of the Teaching Sisters of St. Dorothy.

Ludovico of Casoria, an Italian Franciscan priest who founded the Grey Franciscan Friars of Charity and the Grey Franciscan Sisters of St. Elizabeth

Amato Ronconi, an Italian lay Franciscan and founder of a hospice for the poor in Rimini, Italy.

Note on Equivalent Canonizations

Aside from the public proclamation of a saint by the pope, there is another type of canonization called an "equivalent canonization" (or *equipollent canonization*) in which the pope grants permission for the Universal Church to observe the veneration of a servant of God or blessed who has not yet been canonized. Established in 1632 by Pope Urban VIII, an equivalent canonization does not mean that the pope is bypassing the process of canonization or introducing some new cause for canonization. The Holy Father instead acts in recognition of a cause that is longstanding and of someone who is already held in great esteem by the faithful and enjoys fame for miraculous intercessions. For whatever reason, the cause of canonization was never completed. No formal canonization is needed, and the Pope only needs to sign a decree to make it official. Pope Benedict XVI used an equivalent canonization for Hildegard of Bingen in 2012, and Pope Francis has used it for Peter Faber, Angela de Foligno, José de Anchieta, Marie of the Incarnation and François-Xavier de Montmorency-Laval.

Pope Francis on Holiness

On Oct. 2, 2013, Pope Francis used his General Audience to speak of holiness and the Church. The following is an excerpt:

"In the Church, the God we encounter is not a merciless judge, but like the Father in the Gospel parable. You may be like the son who left home, who sank to the depths, farthest from the Gospel. When you have the strength to say: I want to come home, you will find the door open. God will come to meet you because he is always waiting for you, God is always waiting for you, God embraces you, kisses you and celebrates. That is how the Lord is, that is how the tenderness of our Heavenly Father is. The Lord wants us to belong to a Church that knows how to open her arms and welcome everyone, that is not a house for the few, but a house for everyone, where all can be renewed, transformed, sanctified by his love, the strongest and the weakest, sinners, the indifferent, those who feel discouraged or lost. The Church offers all the possibility of following a path of holiness, that is the path of the Christian: she brings us to encounter Jesus Christ in the Sacraments, especially in Confession and in the Eucharist; she communicates the Word of God to us, she lets us live in charity, in the love of God for all. Let us ask ourselves then, will we let ourselves be sanctified? Are we a Church that calls and welcomes sinners with open arms, that gives courage and hope, or are we a Church closed in on herself? Are we a Church where the love of God dwells, where one cares for the other, where one prays for the others?

"...What can I, a weak fragile sinner, do? God says to you: do not be afraid of holiness, do not be afraid to aim high, to let yourself be loved and purified by God, do not be afraid to let yourself be guided by the Holy Spirit. Let us be infected by the holiness of God. Every Christian is called to sanctity (cf. Dogmatic Constitution *Lumen Gentium*, Nos. 19-42); and sanctity does not consist especially in doing extraordinary things, but in allowing God to act. It is the meeting of our weakness with the strength of his grace, it is having faith in his action that allows us to live in charity, to do everything with joy and humility, for the glory of God and as a service to our neighbor. There is a celebrated saying by the French writer Léon Bloy, who in the last moments of his life, said: "The only real sadness in life is not becoming a saint." Let us not lose the hope of holiness, let us follow this path. Do we want to be saints? The Lord awaits us, with open arms; he waits to accompany us on the path to sanctity. Let us live in the joy of our faith, let us allow ourselves to be loved by the Lord... let us ask for this gift from God in prayer, for ourselves and for others."

Dates and Events in Catholic History

FIRST CENTURY

c. 33: First Christian Pentecost; descent of the Holy Spirit upon the disciples; preaching of St. Peter in Jerusalem; conversion, baptism and aggregation of some 3,000 persons to the first Christian community.

St. Stephen, deacon, was stoned to death at Jerusalem; he is venerated as the first Christian martyr.

c. 34: St. Paul, formerly Saul the persecutor of Christians, was converted and baptized. After three years of solitude in the desert, he joined the college of the apostles; he made three major missionary journeys and became known as the Apostle to the Gentiles; he was imprisoned twice in Rome and was beheaded there between 64 and 67.

39: Cornelius (the Gentile) and his family were baptized by St. Peter; a significant event signaling the mission of the Church to all peoples.

42: Persecution of Christians in Palestine broke out during the rule of Herod Agrippa; St. James the Greater, the first apostle to die, was beheaded in 44; St. Peter was imprisoned for a short time; many Christians fled to Antioch, marking the beginning of the dispersion of Christians beyond the confines of Palestine. At Antioch, the followers of Christ were called Christians for the first time.

49: Christians at Rome, considered members of a Jewish sect, were adversely affected by a decree of Claudius which forbade Jewish worship there.

51: The Council of Jerusalem, in which all the apostles participated under the presidency of St. Peter, decreed that circumcision, dietary regulations, and various other prescriptions of Mosaic Law were not obligatory for Gentile converts to the Christian community. The crucial decree was issued in opposition to Judaizers who contended that observance of the Mosaic Law in its entirety was necessary for salvation.

64: Persecution broke out at Rome under Nero, the emperor said to have accused Christians of starting the fire which destroyed half of Rome.

64 or 67: Martyrdom of St. Peter at Rome during the Neronian persecution. He established his see and spent his last years there after preaching in and around Jerusalem, establishing a see at Antioch, and presiding at the Council of Jerusalem.

70: Destruction of Jerusalem by Titus.

88-97: Pontificate of St. Clement I, third successor of St. Peter as bishop of Rome, one of the Apostolic Fathers. The First Epistle of Clement to the Corinthians, with which he has been identified, was addressed by the Church of Rome to the Church at Corinth, the scene of irregularities and divisions in the Christian community.

95: Domitian persecuted Christians, principally at Rome.

c. 100: Death of St. John, apostle and evangelist, marking the end of the Age of the Apostles and the first generation of the Church.

By the end of the century, Antioch, Alexandria and Ephesus in the East and Rome in the West were established centers of Christian population and influence.

SECOND CENTURY

c. 107: St. Ignatius of Antioch was martyred at Rome. He was the first writer to use the expression, "the Catholic Church."

112: Emperor Trajan, in a rescript to Pliny the Younger, governor of Bithynia, instructed him not to search out Christians but to punish them if they were publicly denounced and refused to do homage to the Roman gods. This rescript set a pattern for Roman magistrates in dealing with Christians.

117-38: Persecution under Hadrian. Many Acts of Martyrs date from this period.

c. 125: Spread of Gnosticism, a combination of elements of Platonic philosophy and Eastern mystery religions. Its adherents claimed that its secret-knowledge principle provided a deeper insight into Christian doctrine than divine revelation and faith. One gnostic thesis denied the divinity of Christ; others denied the reality of his humanity, calling it mere appearance (Docetism, Phantasiasm).

c. 144: Excommunication of Marcion, bishop and heretic, who claimed that there was total opposition and no connection at all between the Old Testament and the New Testament, between the God of the Jews and the God of the Christians; and that the Canon (list of inspired writings) of the Bible consisted only of parts of St. Luke's Gospel and 10 letters of St. Paul. Marcionism was checked at Rome by 200 and was condemned by a council held there about 260, but the heresy persisted for several centuries in the East and had some adherents as late as the Middle Ages.

c. 155: St. Polycarp, bishop of Smyrna and disciple of St. John the Evangelist, was martyred.

c. 156: Beginning of Montanism, a form of religious extremism. Its principal tenets were the imminent second coming of Christ, denial of the divine nature of the Church and its power to forgive sin, and excessively rigorous morality. The heresy, preached by Montanus of Phrygia and others, was condemned by Pope St. Zephyrinus (199-217).

161-80: Reign of Marcus Aurelius. His persecution, launched in the wake of natural disasters, was more violent than those of his predecessors.

165: St. Justin, an important early Christian writer, was martyred at Rome.

c. 180: St. Irenaeus, bishop of Lyons and one of the great early theologians, wrote *Adversus Haereses*. He stated that the teaching and tradition of the

Roman See was the standard for belief.

196: Easter Controversy, concerning the day of celebration — a Sunday, according to practice in the West, or the 14th of the month of Nisan (in the Hebrew calendar), no matter what day of the week, according to practice in the East. The controversy was not resolved at this time.

The *Didache*, whose extant form dates from the second century, is an important record of Christian belief, practice and governance in the first century.

Latin was introduced as a liturgical language in the West. Other liturgical languages were Aramaic and Greek.

The Catechetical School of Alexandria, founded about the middle of the century, gained increasing influence on doctrinal study and instruction, and interpretation of the Bible.

THIRD CENTURY

202: Persecution under Septimius Severus, who wanted to establish a simple common religion in the Empire.

206: Tertullian, a convert since 197 and the first great ecclesiastical writer in Latin, joined the heretical Montanists; he died in 230.

215: Death of Clement of Alexandria, teacher of Origen and a founding father of the School of Alexandria.

217-35: St. Hippolytus, the first antipope; he was reconciled to the Church while in prison during persecution in 235.

232-54: Origen established the School of Caesarea after being deposed in 231 as head of the School of Alexandria; he died in 254. A scholar and voluminous writer, he was one of the founders of systematic theology and exerted wide influence for many years.

c. 242: Manichaeism originated in Persia: a combination of errors based on the assumption that two supreme principles (good and evil) are operative in creation and life, and that the supreme objective of human endeavor is liberation from evil (matter). The heresy denied the humanity of Christ, the sacramental system, the authority of the Church (and state), and endorsed a moral code which threatened the fabric of society. In the 12th and 13th centuries, it took on the features of Albigensianism and Catharism.

249-51: Persecution under Decius. Many of those who denied the faith (*lapsi*) sought readmission to the Church at the end of the persecution in 251. Pope St. Cornelius agreed with St. Cyprian that *lapsi* were to be readmitted to the Church after satisfying the requirements of appropriate penance. Antipope Novatian, on the other hand, contended that persons who fell away from the Church under persecution and/or those guilty of serious sin after baptism could not be absolved and readmitted to communion with the Church. The heresy was condemned by a Roman synod in 251.

250-300: Neo-Platonism of Plotinus and Porphyry gained followers.

251: Novatian, an antipope, was condemned at Rome.

256: Pope St. Stephen I upheld the validity of baptism properly administered by heretics, in the Rebaptism Controversy.

257: Persecution under Valerian, who attempted to destroy the Church as a social structure.

258: St. Cyprian, bishop of Carthage, was martyred.

c. 260: St. Lucian founded the School of Antioch, a center of influence on biblical studies.

Pope St. Dionysius condemned Sabellianism, a form of modalism (like Monarchianism and Patripassianism). The heresy contended that the Father, Son and Holy Spirit are not distinct divine persons but are only three different modes of being and self-manifestations of the one God. St. Paul of Thebes became a hermit.

261: Gallienus issued an edict of toleration which ended general persecution for nearly 40 years.

c. 292: Diocletian divided the Roman Empire into East and West. The division emphasized political, cultural and other differences between the two parts of the Empire and influenced different developments in the Church in the East and West. The prestige of Rome began to decline.

FOURTH CENTURY

303: Persecution broke out under Diocletian; it was particularly violent in 304.

305: St. Anthony of Heracles established a foundation for hermits near the Red Sea in Egypt.

c. 306: The first local legislation on clerical celibacy was enacted by a council held at Elvira, Spain; bishops, priests, deacons and other ministers were forbidden to have wives.

311: An edict of toleration issued by Galerius at the urging of Constantine the Great and Licinius officially ended persecution in the West; some persecution continued in the East.

313: The Edict of Milan issued by Constantine and Licinius recognized Christianity as a lawful religion in the Roman Empire.

314: A council of Arles condemned Donatism, declaring that baptism properly administered by heretics is valid, in view of the principle that sacraments have their efficacy from Christ, not from the spiritual condition of their human ministers. The heresy was condemned again by a council of Carthage in 411.

318: St. Pachomius established the first foundation of the cenobitic (common) life, as compared with the solitary life of hermits in Upper Egypt.

325: Ecumenical Council of Nicaea (I). Its principal action was the condemnation of Arianism, the most devastating of the early heresies, which denied the divinity of Christ. The heresy was authored by Arius of Alexandria, a priest. Arians and several kinds of Semi-Arians propagandized their tenets widely, established their own hierarchies and churches, and raised havoc in the Church for several centuries. The council contributed to formulation of the Nicene Creed (Creed of Nicaea-Constantinople); fixed the date for the observance of Easter; passed regulations concerning clerical discipline; adopted the civil divisions of the Empire as the model for the jurisdictional organization of the Church.

326: With the support of St. Helena, the True Cross on which Christ was crucified was discovered.

337: Baptism and death of Constantine.

c. 342: Beginning of a 40-year persecution in Persia.

343-44: A council of Sardica reaffirmed doctrine formulated by Nicaea I and declared also that bishops had the right of appeal to the pope as the highest authority in the Church.

361-63: Emperor Julian the Apostate waged an unsuccessful campaign against the Church in an attempt to restore paganism as the religion of the Empire.

c. 365: Persecution of orthodox Christians under Emperor Valens in the East.

c. 376: Beginning of the barbarian invasion in the West.

379: Death of St. Basil, the Father of Monasticism in the East. His writings contributed greatly to the development of rules for the life of Religious.

381: Ecumenical Council of Constantinople (I). It condemned various brands of Arianism as well as Macedonianism, which denied the divinity of the Holy Spirit; contributed to formulation of the Nicene Creed; approved a canon acknowledging Constantinople as the second see after Rome in honor and dignity.

382: The Canon of Sacred Scripture, the official list of the inspired books of the Bible, was contained in the Decree of Pope St. Damasus and published by a regional council of Carthage in 397; the Canon was formally defined by the Council of Trent in the 16th century.

382-c. 406: St. Jerome translated the Old and New Testaments into Latin; his work is called the Vulgate version of the Bible.

396: St. Augustine became bishop of Hippo in North Africa.

FIFTH CENTURY

410: Visigoths under Alaric sacked Rome and the last Roman legions departed Britain. The decline of imperial Rome dates approximately from this time.

430: St. Augustine, bishop of Hippo for 35 years, died. He was a strong defender of orthodox doctrine against Manichaeism, Donatism and Pelagianism. The depth and range of his writings made him a dominant influence in Christian thought for centuries.

431: Ecumenical Council of Ephesus. It condemned Nestorianism, which denied the unity of the divine and human natures in the Person of Christ; defined *Theotokos* (Bearer of God) as the title of Mary, Mother of the Son of God made Man; condemned Pelagianism. The heresy of Pelagianism, proceeding from the assumption that Adam had a natural right to supernatural life, held that man could attain salvation through the efforts of his natural powers and free will; it involved errors concerning the nature of original sin, the meaning of grace and other matters. Related Semi-Pelagianism was condemned by a council of Orange in 529.

432: St. Patrick arrived in Ireland. By the time of his death in 461 most of the country had been converted, monasteries founded and the hierarchy established.

438: The Theodosian Code, a compilation of decrees for the Empire, was issued by Theodosius II; it had great influence on subsequent civil and ecclesiastical law.

451: Ecumenical Council of Chalcedon. Its principal action was the condemnation of Monophysitism (also called Eutychianism), which denied the humanity of Christ by holding that he had only one, the divine, nature.

452: Pope St. Leo the Great persuaded Attila the Hun to spare Rome.

455: Vandals under Geiseric sacked Rome.

484: Patriarch Acacius of Constantinople was excommunicated for signing the *Henoticon*, a document which capitulated to the Monophysite heresy. The excommunication triggered the Acacian Schism which lasted for 35 years.

494: Pope St. Gelasius I declared in a letter to Emperor Anastasius that the pope had power and authority over the emperor in spiritual matters.

496: Clovis, King of the Franks, was converted and became the defender of Christianity in the West. The Franks became a Catholic people.

SIXTH CENTURY

520: Irish monasteries flourished as centers for spiritual life, missionary training, and scholarly activity.

529: The Second Council of Orange condemned Semi-Pelagianism.

c. 529: St. Benedict founded the Monte Cassino Abbey. Some years before his death in 543 he wrote a monastic rule which exercised tremendous influence on the form and style of religious life. He is called the Father of Monasticism in the West.

533: John II became the first pope to change his name. The practice did not become general until the time of Sergius IV (1009).

533-34: Emperor Justinian promulgated the *Corpus Iuris Civilis* for the Roman world; like the Theodosian Code, it influenced subsequent civil and ecclesiastical law.

c. 545: Death of Dionysius Exiguus who was the first to date history from the birth of Christ, a practice which resulted in use of the B.C. and A.D. abbreviations. His calculations were at least four years late.

553: Ecumenical Council of Constantinople (II). It condemned the Three Chapters, Nestorian-tainted writings of Theodore of Mopsuestia, Theodoret of Cyrus and Ibas of Edessa.

585: St. Columban founded an influential monastic school at Luxeuil.

589: The most important of several councils of Toledo was held. The Visigoths renounced Arianism, and St. Leander began the organization of the Church in Spain.

590-604: Pontificate of Pope St. Gregory I the Great. He set the form and style of the papacy which prevailed throughout the Middle Ages; exerted great influence on doctrine and liturgy; was strong in support of monastic discipline and clerical celibacy; authored writings on many subjects. Gregorian Chant is named in his honor.

596: Pope St. Gregory I sent St. Augustine of Canterbury and 40 monks to do missionary work in England.

597: St. Columba died. He founded an important monastery at Iona, established schools and did notable missionary work in Scotland. By the end of the century, monasteries of nuns were common; Western monasticism was flourishing; monasticism in the East, under the influence of Monophysitism and other factors, was losing its vigor.

SEVENTH CENTURY

613: St. Columban established the influential monastery of Bobbio in northern Italy; he died there in 615.

622: The *Hegira* (flight) of Mohammed from Mecca to Medina signalled the beginning of

Islam which, by the end of the century, claimed almost all of the southern Mediterranean area.

628: Heraclius, Eastern Emperor, recovered the True Cross from the Persians.

649: A Lateran council condemned two erroneous formulas (Ecthesis and Type) issued by emperors Heraclius and Constans II as means of reconciling Monophysites with the Church.

664: Actions of the Synod of Whitby advanced the adoption of Roman usages in England, especially regarding the date for the observance of Easter. (See **Easter Controversy**, p. 139.)

680-81: Ecumenical Council of Constantinople (III). It condemned Monothelitism, which held that Christ had only one will, the divine; censured Pope Honorius I for a letter to Sergius, bishop of Constantinople, in which he made an ambiguous but not infallible statement about the unity of will and/or operation in Christ.

692: Trullan Synod. Eastern-Church discipline on clerical celibacy was settled, permitting marriage before ordination to the diaconate and continuation in marriage afterwards, but prohibiting marriage following the death of the wife thereafter. Anti-Roman canons contributed to East-West alienation.

During the century, the monastic influence of Ireland and England increased in Western Europe; schools and learning declined; regulations regarding clerical celibacy became more strict in the East.

EIGHTH CENTURY

711: Muslims began the conquest of Spain.

726: Emperor Leo III, the Isaurian, launched a campaign against the veneration of sacred images and relics; called Iconoclasm (image-breaking), it caused turmoil in the East until about 843.

731: Pope Gregory III and a synod at Rome condemned Iconoclasm, with a declaration that the veneration of sacred images was in accord with Catholic tradition.

Venerable Bede issued his *Ecclesiastical History of the English People*.

732: Charles Martel defeated the Muslims at Poitiers, halting their advance in the West.

744: The Monastery of Fulda was established by St. Sturmi, a disciple of St. Boniface; it was influential in the evangelization of Germany.

754: A council of more than 300 Byzantine bishops endorsed Iconoclast errors. This council and its actions were condemned by the Lateran synod of 769.

Stephen II (III) crowned Pepin ruler of the Franks. Pepin twice invaded Italy, in 754 and 756, to defend the pope against the Lombards. His land grants to the papacy, called the Donation of Pepin, were later extended by Charlemagne (773) and formed part of the States of the Church.

c. 755: St. Boniface (Winfrid) was martyred. He was called the Apostle of Germany for his missionary work and organization of the hierarchy there.

781: Alcuin was chosen by Charlemagne to organize a palace school, which became a center of intellectual leadership.

787: Ecumenical Council of Nicaea (II). It condemned Iconoclasm, which held that the use of images was idolatry, and Adoptionism, which claimed that Christ was not the Son of God by nature but only by adoption. This was the last council regarded as ecumenical by Orthodox Churches.

792: A council at Ratisbon condemned Adoptionism.

The famous *Book of Kells* ("The Great Gospel of Columcille") dates from the early eighth or late seventh century.

NINTH CENTURY

800: Charlemagne was crowned Emperor by Pope Leo III on Christmas Day.

Egbert became king of West Saxons; he unified England and strengthened the See of Canterbury.

813: Emperor Leo V, the Armenian, revived Iconoclasm, which persisted until about 843.

814: Charlemagne died.

843: The Treaty of Verdun split the Frankish kingdom among Charlemagne's three grandsons.

844: A Eucharistic controversy involving the writings of St. Paschasius Radbertus, Ratramnus and Rabanus Maurus occasioned the development of terminology regarding the doctrine of the Real Presence.

846: Muslims invaded Italy and attacked Rome.

847-52: Period of composition of the False Decretals, a collection of forged documents attributed to popes from St. Clement (88-97) to Gregory II (714-731). The Decretals, which strongly supported the autonomy and rights of bishops, were suspect for a long time before being repudiated entirely about 1628.

848: The Council of Mainz condemned Gottschalk for heretical teaching regarding predestination. He was also condemned by the Council of Quierzy in 853.

857: Photius displaced Ignatius as patriarch of Constantinople. This marked the beginning of the Photian Schism, a confused state of East-West relations which has not yet been cleared up by historical research. Photius, a man of exceptional ability, died in 891.

865: St. Ansgar, apostle of Scandinavia, died.

869: St. Cyril died and his brother, St. Methodius (d. 885), was ordained a bishop. The Apostles of the Slavs devised an alphabet and translated the Gospels and liturgy into the Slavonic language.

869-70: Ecumenical Council of Constantinople (IV). It issued a second condemnation of Iconoclasm, condemned and deposed Photius as patriarch of Constantinople and restored Ignatius to the patriarchate. This was the last ecumenical council held in the East. It was first called ecumenical by canonists toward the end of the 11th century.

871-c. 900: Reign of Alfred the Great, the only English king ever anointed by a pope at Rome.

TENTH CENTURY

910: William, duke of Aquitaine, founded the Benedictine Abbey of Cluny, which became a center of monastic and ecclesiastical reform, especially in France.

915: Pope John X played a leading role in the expulsion of Saracens from central and southern Italy.

955: St. Olga, of the Russian royal family, was baptized.

962: Otto I, the Great, crowned by Pope John XII, revived Charlemagne's kingdom, which became the Holy Roman Empire.

966: Mieszko, first of a royal line in Poland, was baptized; he brought Latin Christianity to Poland.

988: Conversion and baptism of St. Vladimir and the people of Kiev which subsequently became part of Russia.

993: John XV was the first pope to decree the official canonization of a saint — Bishop Ulrich (Uldaric) of Augsburg — for the universal Church.

997: St. Stephen became ruler of Hungary. He assisted in organizing the hierarchy and establishing Latin Christianity in that country.

999-1003: Pontificate of Sylvester II (Gerbert of Aquitaine), a Benedictine monk and the first French pope.

ELEVENTH CENTURY

1009: Beginning of lasting East-West Schism in the Church, marked by dropping of the name of Pope Sergius IV from the Byzantine diptychs (the listing of persons prayed for during the liturgy). The deletion was made by Patriarch Sergius II of Constantinople.

1012: St. Romuald founded the Camaldolese Hermits.

1025: The Council of Arras, and other councils later, condemned the Cathari (Neo-Manichaeans, Albigenses).

1027: The Council of Elne proclaimed the Truce of God as a means of stemming violence; it involved armistice periods of varying length, which were later extended.

1038: St. John Gualbert founded the Vallombrosians.

1043-59: Constantinople patriarchate of Michael Cerularius, the key figure in a controversy concerning the primacy of the papacy. His and the Byzantine synod's refusal to acknowledge this primacy in 1054 widened and hardened the East-West Schism in the Church.

1047: Pope Clement II died; he was the only pope ever buried in Germany.

1049-54: Pontificate of St. Leo IX, who inaugurated a movement of papal, diocesan, monastic and clerical reform.

1054: Start of the Great Schism between the Eastern and Western Churches; it marked the separation of Orthodox Churches from unity with the pope.

1055: Condemnation of the Eucharistic doctrine of Berengarius.

1059: A Lateran council issued new legislation regarding papal elections; voting power was entrusted to the Roman cardinals.

1066: Death of St. Edward the Confessor, king of England from 1042 and restorer of Westminster Abbey.

Defeat, at Hastings, of Harold by William, Duke of Normandy (later William I), who subsequently exerted strong influence on the life-style of the Church in England.

1073-85: Pontificate of St. Gregory VII (Hildebrand). A strong pope, he carried forward programs of clerical and general ecclesiastical reform and struggled against German King Henry IV and other rulers to end the evils of lay investiture. He introduced the Latin liturgy in Spain and set definite dates for the observance of ember days.

1077: Henry IV, excommunicated and suspended from the exercise of imperial powers by Gregory VII, sought absolution from the pope at Canossa. Henry later repudiated this action and in 1084 forced Gregory to leave Rome.

1079: The Council of Rome condemned Eucharistic errors (denial of the Real Presence of Christ

under the appearances of bread and wine) of Berengarius, who retracted.

1084: St. Bruno founded the Carthusians.

1097-99: The first of several Crusades undertaken between this time and 1265. Recovery of the Holy Places and gaining free access to them for Christians were the original purposes, but these were diverted to less worthy objectives in various ways. Results included: a Latin Kingdom of Jerusalem, 1099-1187; a military and political misadventure in the form of a Latin Empire of Constantinople, 1204-1261; acquisition, by treaties, of visiting rights for Christians in the Holy Land. East-West economic and cultural relationships increased during the period. In the religious sphere, actions of the Crusaders had the effect of increasing the alienation of the East from the West.

1098: St. Robert founded the Cistercians.

TWELFTH CENTURY

1108: Beginnings of the influential Abbey and School of St. Victor in France.

1115: St. Bernard established the Abbey of Clairvaux and inaugurated the Cistercian Reform.

1118: Christian forces captured Saragossa, Spain; the beginning of the Muslim decline in that country.

1121: St. Norbert established the original monastery of the Praemonstratensians near Laon, France.

1122: The Concordat of Worms (*Pactum Callixtinum*) was formulated and approved by Pope Callistus II and Emperor Henry V to settle controversy concerning the investiture of prelates. The concordat provided that the emperor could invest prelates with symbols of temporal authority but had no right to invest them with spiritual authority, which came from the Church alone, and that the emperor was not to interfere in papal elections. This was the first concordat in history.

1123: Ecumenical Council of the Lateran (I), the first of its kind in the West. It endorsed provisions of the Concordat of Worms concerning the investiture of prelates and approved reform measures in 25 canons.

1139: Ecumenical Council of the Lateran (II). It adopted measures against a schism organized by antipope Anacletus and approved 30 canons related to discipline and other matters; one of the canons stated that holy orders is an invalidating impediment to marriage.

1140: St. Bernard met Abelard in debate at the Council of Sens. Abelard, whose rationalism in theology was condemned for the first time in 1121, died in 1142 at Cluny.

1148: The Synod of Rheims enacted strict disciplinary decrees for communities of women Religious.

1152: The Synod of Kells reorganized the Church in Ireland.

1160: Gratian, whose *Decretum* became a basic text of canon law, died.

Peter Lombard, compiler of the Four Books of Sentences, a standard theology text for nearly 200 years, died.

1170: St. Thomas Becket, archbishop of Canterbury, who clashed with Henry II over church-state relations, was murdered in his cathedral.

1171: Pope Alexander III reserved the process of canonization of saints to the Holy See.

1179: Ecumenical Council of the Lateran (III). It enacted measures against Waldensianism and Albigensianism (see year 242 regarding Manichaeism), approved reform decrees in 27 canons, provided that popes be elected by a two-thirds vote of the cardinals.

1184: Waldenses and other heretics were excommunicated by Pope Lucius III.

THIRTEENTH CENTURY

1198-1216: Pontificate of Innocent III, during which the papacy reached its medieval peak of authority, influence and prestige in the Church and in relations with civil rulers.

1208: Innocent III called for a crusade, the first in Christendom itself, against the Albigensians; their beliefs and practices threatened the fabric of society in southern France and northern Italy.

1209: Verbal approval was given by Innocent III to a rule of life for the Order of Friars Minor, started by St. Francis of Assisi.

1212: The Second Order of Franciscans, the Poor Clares, was founded.

1215: Ecumenical Council of the Lateran (IV). It ordered annual reception of the sacraments of penance and the Eucharist; defined and made the first official use of the term transubstantiation to explain the change of bread and wine into the body and blood of Christ; adopted additional measures to counteract teachings and practices of the Albigensians and Cathari; approved 70 canons.

1216: Formal papal approval was given to a rule of life for the Order of Preachers, started by St. Dominic.

The Portiuncula Indulgence was granted by the Holy See at the request of St. Francis of Assisi.

1221: Rule of the Third Order Secular of St. Francis (Secular Franciscan Order) approved verbally by Honorius III.

1226: Death of St. Francis of Assisi.

1231: Pope Gregory IX authorized establishment of the Papal Inquisition for dealing with heretics. It was a creature of its time, when crimes against faith and heretical doctrines of extremists like the Cathari and Albigenses threatened the good of the Christian community, the welfare of the state and the very fabric of society. The institution, which was responsible for excesses in punishment, was most active in the second half of the century in southern France, Italy and Germany.

1245: Ecumenical Council of Lyons (I). It confirmed the deposition of Emperor Frederick II and approved 22 canons.

1247: Preliminary approval was given by the Holy See to a Carmelite rule of life.

1270: St. Louis IX, king of France, died. Beginning of papal decline.

1274: Ecumenical Council of Lyons (II). It accomplished a temporary reunion of separated Eastern Churches with the Roman Church; issued regulations concerning conclaves for papal elections; approved 31 canons.

Death of St. Thomas Aquinas, Doctor of the Church, of lasting influence.

1280: Pope Nicholas III, who made the Breviary the official prayer book for clergy of the Roman Church, died.

1281: The excommunication of Michael Palaeologus

by Pope Martin IV ruptured the union effected with the Eastern Church in 1274.

FOURTEENTH CENTURY

1302: Pope Boniface VIII issued the bull *Unam Sanctam*, concerning the unity of the Church and the temporal power of princes, against the background of a struggle with Philip IV of France; it was the most famous medieval document on the subject.

1309-77: For a period of approximately 70 years, seven popes resided at Avignon because of unsettled conditions in Rome and other reasons; see separate entry.

1311-12: Ecumenical Council of Vienne. It suppressed the Knights Templar and enacted a number of reform decrees.

1321: Dante Alighieri died a year after completing the *Divine Comedy*.

1324: Marsilius of Padua completed *Defensor Pacis*, a work condemned by Pope John XXII as heretical because of its denial of papal primacy and the hierarchical structure of the Church, and for other reasons. It was a charter for conciliarism (an ecumenical council is superior to the pope in authority).

1337-1453: Period of the Hundred Years' War, a dynastic struggle between France and England.

1338: Four years after the death of Pope John XXII, who had opposed Louis IV of Bavaria in a years-long controversy, electoral princes declared at the Diet of Rhense that the emperor did not need papal confirmation of his title and right to rule. Charles IV later (1356) said the same thing in a *Golden Bull*, eliminating papal rights in the election of emperors.

1347-50: The Black Death swept across Europe, killing perhaps one-fourth to one-third of the total population; an estimated 40 per cent of the clergy succumbed.

1374: Petrarch, poet and humanist, died.

1377: Return of the papacy from Avignon to Rome. Beginning of the Western Schism; see separate entry.

FIFTEENTH CENTURY

1409: The Council of Pisa, without canonical authority, tried to end the Western Schism but succeeded only in complicating it by electing a third claimant to the papacy; see Western Schism.

1414-18: Ecumenical Council of Constance. It took successful action to end the Western Schism involving rival claimants to the papacy; rejected the teachings of Wycliff; condemned Hus as a heretic. One decree — passed in the earlier stages of the council but later rejected — asserted the superiority of an ecumenical council over the pope (conciliarism).

1431: St. Joan of Arc was burned at the stake.

1431-45: Ecumenical Council of Florence (also called Basle-Ferrara-Florence). It affirmed the primacy of the pope against the claims of conciliarists that an ecumenical council is superior to the pope. It also formulated and approved decrees of union with several separated Eastern Churches — Greek, Armenian, Jacobite — which failed to gain general or lasting acceptance.

1438: The Pragmatic Sanction of Bourges was enacted by Charles VII and the French Parliament to curtail papal authority over the

Church in France, in the spirit of conciliarism. It found expression in Gallicanism and had effects lasting at least until the French Revolution.

1453: The fall of Constantinople to the Turks.

c. 1456: Gutenberg issued the first edition of the Bible printed from movable type, at Mainz, Germany.

1476: Pope Sixtus IV approved observance of the feast of the Immaculate Conception on Dec. 8 throughout the Church.

1478: Pope Sixtus IV, at the urging of King Ferdinand of Spain, approved establishment of the Spanish Inquisition for dealing with Jewish and Moorish converts accused of heresy. The institution, which was peculiar to Spain and its colonies in America, acquired jurisdiction over other cases as well and fell into disrepute because of its procedures, cruelty and the manner in which it served the Spanish crown, rather than the accused and the good of the Church. Protests by the Holy See failed to curb excesses of the Inquisition, which lingered in Spanish history until early in the 19th century.

1492: Columbus discovered the Americas.

1493: Pope Alexander VI issued a Bull of Demarcation which determined spheres of influence for the Spanish and Portuguese in the Americas.

The Renaissance, a humanistic movement which originated in Italy in the 14th century, spread to France, Germany, the Low Countries and England. A transitional period between the medieval world and the modern secular world, it introduced profound changes which affected literature and the other arts, general culture, politics and religion.

SIXTEENTH CENTURY

1512-17: Ecumenical Council of the Lateran (V). It stated the relation and position of the pope with respect to an ecumenical council; acted to counteract the Pragmatic Sanction of Bourges and exaggerated claims of liberty by the Church in France; condemned erroneous teachings concerning the nature of the human soul; stated doctrine concerning indulgences. The council reflected concern for abuses in the Church and the need for reforms but failed to take decisive action in the years immediately preceding the Reformation.

1517: Martin Luther signaled the beginning of the Reformation by posting 95 theses at Wittenberg. Subsequently, he broke completely from doctrinal orthodoxy in discourses and three published works (1519 and 1520); was excommunicated on more than 40 charges of heresy (1521); remained the dominant figure in the Reformation in Germany until his death in 1546.

1519: Zwingli triggered the Reformation in Zurich and became its leading proponent there until his death in combat in 1531.

1524: Luther's encouragement of German princes in putting down the two-year Peasants' Revolt gained political support for his cause.

1528: The Order of Friars Minor Capuchin was approved as an autonomous division of the Franciscan Order; like the Jesuits, the Capuchins became leaders in the Counter-Reformation.

1530: The Augsburg Confession of Lutheran faith was issued; it was later supplemented by the

Smalkaldic Articles, approved in 1537.

1533: Henry VIII divorced Catherine of Aragon, married Anne Boleyn, was excommunicated. In 1534 he decreed the Act of Supremacy, making the sovereign the head of the Church in England, under which Sts. John Fisher and Thomas More were executed in 1535. Despite his rejection of papal primacy and actions against monastic life in England, he generally maintained doctrinal orthodoxy until his death in 1547.

1536: John Calvin, leader of the Reformation in Switzerland until his death in 1564, issued the first edition of *Institutes of the Christian Religion*, which became the classical text of Reformed (non-Lutheran) theology.

1540: The constitutions of the Society of Jesus (Jesuits), founded by St. Ignatius of Loyola, were approved.

1541: Start of the 11-year career of St. Francis Xavier as a missionary to the East Indies and Japan.

1545-63: Ecumenical Council of Trent. It issued a great number of decrees concerning doctrinal matters opposed by the Reformers, and mobilized the Counter-Reformation. Definitions covered the Canon of the Bible, the rule of faith, the nature of justification, grace, faith, original sin and its effects, the seven sacraments, the sacrificial nature of the Mass, the veneration of saints, use of sacred images, belief in purgatory, the doctrine of indulgences, the jurisdiction of the pope over the whole Church. It initiated many reforms for renewal in the liturgy and general discipline in the Church, the promotion of religious instruction, the education of the clergy through the foundation of seminaries, etc. Trent ranks with Vatican II as the greatest ecumenical council held in the West.

1549: The first Anglican *Book of Common Prayer* was issued by Edward VI. Revised editions were published in 1552, 1559 and 1662 and later.

1553: Start of the five-year reign of Mary Tudor who tried to counteract actions of Henry VIII against the Roman Church.

1555: Enactment of the Peace of Augsburg, an arrangement of religious territorialism rather than toleration, which recognized the existence of Catholicism and Lutheranism in the German Empire and provided that citizens should adopt the religion of their respective rulers.

1558: Beginning of the reign (to 1603) of Queen Elizabeth I of England and Ireland, during which the Church of England took on its definitive form.

1559: Establishment of the hierarchy of the Church of England, with the consecration of Matthew Parker as archbishop of Canterbury.

1563: The first text of the 39 Articles of the Church of England was issued. Also enacted were a new Act of Supremacy and Oath of Succession to the English throne.

1570: Elizabeth I was excommunicated. Penal measures against Catholics subsequently became more severe.

1571: Defeat of the Turkish armada at Lepanto staved off the invasion of Eastern Europe.

1577: The Formula of Concord, the classical statement of Lutheran faith, was issued; it was, generally, a Lutheran counterpart of the canons of the Council of Trent. In 1580, along with other formulas of doctrine, it was included in the Book of Concord.

1582: The Gregorian Calendar, named for Pope Gregory XIII, was put into effect and was eventually adopted in most countries: England delayed adoption until 1752.

SEVENTEENTH CENTURY

1605: The Gunpowder Plot, an attempt by Catholic fanatics to blow up James I of England and the houses of Parliament, resulted in an anti-Catholic Oath of Allegiance.

1610: Death of Matteo Ricci, outstanding Jesuit missionary to China, pioneer in cultural relations between China and Europe.

Founding of the first community of Visitation Nuns by Sts. Francis de Sales and Jane de Chantal.

1611: Founding of the Oratorians.

1613: Catholics were banned from Scandinavia.

1625: Founding of the Congregation of the Mission (Vincentians) by St. Vincent de Paul. He founded the Sisters of Charity in 1633.

1642: Death of Galileo, scientist, who was censured by the Congregation of the Holy Office for supporting the Copernican theory of the sun-centered planetary system. The case against him was closed in his favor in 1992.

Founding of the Sulpicians by Jacques Olier.

1643: Start of publication of the Bollandist *Acta Sanctorum*, a critical work on lives of the saints.

1648: Provisions in the Peace of Westphalia, ending the Thirty Years' War, extended terms of the Peace of Augsburg (1555) to Calvinists and gave equality to Catholics and Protestants in the 300 states of the Holy Roman Empire.

1649: Oliver Cromwell invaded Ireland and began a severe persecution of the Church there.

1653: Pope Innocent X condemned five propositions of Jansenism, a complex theory which distorted doctrine concerning the relations between divine grace and human freedom. Jansenism was also a rigoristic movement which seriously disturbed the Church in France, the Low Countries and Italy in this and the 18th century.

1673: The Test Act in England barred from public office Catholics who would not deny the doctrine of transubstantiation and receive Communion in the Church of England.

1678: Many English Catholics suffered death as a consequence of the Popish Plot, a false allegation by Titus Oates that Catholics planned to assassinate Charles II, land a French army in the country, burn London, and turn over the government to the Jesuits.

1682: The four Gallican articles, drawn up by Bossuet, asserted political and ecclesiastical immunities of France from papal control. The articles, which rejected the primacy of the pope, were declared null and void by Pope Alexander VIII in 1690.

1689: The Toleration Act granted a measure of freedom of worship to other English dissenters but not to Catholics.

EIGHTEENTH CENTURY

1704: Chinese Rites — involving the Christian adaptation of elements of Confucianism, veneration of ancestors and Chinese terminology in religion — were condemned by Clement XI.

1720: The Passionists were founded by St. Paul of the Cross.

1724: Persecution in China.

1732: The Redemptorists were founded by St. Alphonsus Liguori.

1738: Freemasonry was condemned by Clement XII and Catholics were forbidden to join, under penalty of excommunication; the prohibition was repeated by Benedict XIV in 1751 and by later popes.

1760s: Josephinism, a theory and system of state control of the Church, was initiated in Austria; it remained in force until about 1850.

1764: Febronianism, an unorthodox theory and practice regarding the constitution of the Church and relations between Church and state, was condemned for the first of several times. Proposed by an auxiliary bishop of Trier using the pseudonym Justinus Febronius, it had the effects of minimizing the office of the pope and supporting national churches under state control.

1773: Clement XIV issued a brief of suppression against the Jesuits, following their expulsion from Portugal in 1759, from France in 1764 and from Spain in 1767. Political intrigue and unsubstantiated accusations were principal factors in these developments. The ban, which crippled the society, contained no condemnation of the Jesuit constitutions, particular Jesuits or Jesuit teaching. The society was restored in 1814.

1778: Catholics in England were relieved of some civil disabilities dating back to the time of Henry VIII, by an act which permitted them to acquire, own and inherit property. Additional liberties were restored by the Roman Catholic Relief Act of 1791 and subsequent enactments of Parliament.

1789: Religious freedom in the United States was guaranteed under the First Amendment to the Constitution.

Beginning of the French Revolution which resulted in: the secularization of church property and the Civil Constitution of the Clergy in 1790; the persecution of priests, religious and lay persons loyal to papal authority; invasion of the Papal States by Napoleon in 1796; renewal of persecution from 1797-1799; attempts to dechristianize France and establish a new religion; the occupation of Rome by French troops and the forced removal of Pius VI to France in 1798.

This century is called the age of Enlightenment or Reason because of the predominating rational and scientific approach of its leading philosophers, scientists and writers with respect to religion, ethics and natural law. This approach downgraded the fact and significance of revealed religion. Also characteristic of the Enlightenment were subjectivism, secularism and optimism regarding human perfectibility.

NINETEENTH CENTURY

1801: Concordat between Napoleon and Pope Pius VII is signed. It is soon violated by the Organic Articles issued by Napoleon in 1802.

1804: Napoleon crowns himself Emperor of the French with Pope Pius in attendance.

1809: Pope Pius VII was made a captive by Napoleon and deported to France where he remained in exile until 1814. During this time he refused to cooperate with Napoleon who sought to bring the Church in France under his own control, and other leading cardinals were imprisoned.

The turbulence in church-state relations in France at the beginning of the century recurred in connection with the Bourbon Restoration, the July Revolution, the second and third Republics, the Second Empire and the Dreyfus case.

1814: The Society of Jesus, suppressed since 1773, was restored.

1817: Reestablishment of the Congregation for the Propagation of the Faith (Propaganda) by Pius VII was an important factor in increasing missionary activity during the century.

1820: Year's-long persecution, during which thousands died for the faith, ended in China. Thereafter, communication with the West remained cut off until about 1834. Vigorous missionary work got under way in 1842.

1822: The Pontifical Society for the Propagation of the Faith, inaugurated in France by Pauline Jaricot for the support of missionary activity, was established.

1829: The Catholic Emancipation Act relieved Catholics in England and Ireland of most of the civil disabilities to which they had been subject from the time of Henry VIII.

1832: Gregory XVI, in the encyclical *Mirari Vos*, condemned indifferentism, one of the many ideologies at odds with Christian doctrine which were proposed during the century.

1833: Start of the Oxford Movement which affected the Church of England and resulted in some notable conversions, including that of John Henry Newman in 1845, to the Catholic Church.

Bl. Frederic Ozanam founded the Society of St. Vincent de Paul in France. The society's objectives are works of charity.

1848: *The Communist Manifesto*, a revolutionary document symptomatic of socio-economic crisis, was issued.

1850: The hierarchy was reestablished in England and Nicholas Wiseman made the first archbishop of Westminster. He was succeeded in 1865 by Henry Manning, an Oxford convert and proponent of the rights of labor.

1853: The Catholic hierarchy was reestablished in Holland.

1854: Pius IX proclaimed the dogma of the Immaculate Conception in the bull *Ineffabilis Deus*.

1858: The Blessed Virgin Mary appeared to St. Bernadette at Lourdes, France.

1864: Pius IX issued the encyclical *Quanta Cura* and the *Syllabus of Errors* in condemnation of some 80 propositions derived from the scientific mentality and rationalism of the century. The subjects in question had deep ramifications in many areas of thought and human endeavor; in religion, they explicitly and/or implicitly rejected divine revelation and the supernatural order.

1867: The first volume of *Das Kapital* was published. Together with the Communist First International, formed in the same year, it had great influence on the subsequent development of communism and socialism.

1869: The Anglican Church was disestablished in Ireland.

1869-70: Ecumenical Council of the Vatican (I).

It defined papal primacy and infallibility in a dogmatic constitution on the Church; covered natural religion, revelation, faith, and the relations between faith and reason in a dogmatic constitution on the Catholic faith.

1870-71: Victor Emmanuel II of Sardinia, crowned king of Italy after defeating Austrian and papal forces, marched into Rome in 1870 and expropriated the Papal States after a plebiscite in which Catholics, at the order of Pius IX, did not vote. In 1871, Pius IX refused to accept a Law of Guarantees. Confiscation of church property and hindrance of ecclesiastical administration by the regime followed.

1871: The German Empire, a confederation of 26 states, was formed. Government policy launched a *Kulturkampf* whose May Laws of 1873 were designed to annul papal jurisdiction in Prussia and other states and to place the Church under imperial control. Resistance to the enactments and the persecution they legalized forced the government to modify its anti-Church policy by 1887.

1878: Beginning of the pontificate of Leo XIII, who was pope until his death in 1903. Leo is best known for the encyclical *Rerum Novarum*, which greatly influenced the course of Christian social thought and the labor movement. His other accomplishments included promotion of Scholastic philosophy and the impetus he gave to scriptural studies.

1881: The first International Eucharistic Congress was held in Lille, France.

Alexander II of Russia was assassinated. His policies of Russification — as well as those of his two predecessors and a successor during the century — caused great suffering to Catholics, Jews and Protestants in Poland, Lithuania, the Ukraine and Bessarabia.

1882: Charles Darwin died. His theory of evolution by natural selection, one of several scientific highlights of the century, had extensive repercussions in the faith-and-science controversy.

1887: The Catholic University of America was founded in Washington, DC.

1893: The U.S. apostolic delegation was set up in Washington, DC.

TWENTIETH CENTURY

1901: Restrictive measures in France forced the Jesuits, Benedictines, Carmelites and other religious orders to leave the country. Subsequently, 14,000 schools were suppressed; religious orders and congregations were expelled; the concordat was renounced in 1905; church property was confiscated in 1906. For some years the Holy See, refusing to comply with government demands for the control of bishops' appointments, left some ecclesiastical offices vacant.

1903-14: Pontificate of St. Pius X. He initiated the codification of canon law, 1904; removed the ban against participation by Catholics in Italian national elections, 1905; issued decrees calling upon the faithful to receive Holy Communion frequently and daily, and stating that children should begin receiving the Eucharist at the age of seven, 1905 and 1910, respectively; ordered the establishment of the Confraternity of Christian Doctrine in all parishes throughout the world, 1905; condemned Modernism in the decree

Lamentabili and the encyclical *Pascendi*, 1907.

1908: The United States and England, long under the jurisdiction of the Congregation for the Propagation of the Faith as mission territories, were removed from its control and placed under the common law of the Church.

1910: Laws of separation were enacted in Portugal, marking a point of departure in church-state relations.

1911: The Catholic Foreign Mission Society of America — Maryknoll, the first U.S.-founded society of its type — was established.

1914: Start of World War I, which lasted until 1918.

1914-22: Pontificate of Benedict XV. Much of his pontificate was devoted to seeking ways and means of minimizing the material and spiritual havoc of World War I. In 1917 he offered his services as a mediator to the belligerent nations, but his pleas for settlement of the conflict went unheeded.

1917: The Blessed Virgin Mary appeared to three children at Fatima, Portugal.

A new constitution, embodying repressive laws against the Church, was enacted in Mexico. Its implementation resulted in persecution in the 1920s and 1930s.

Bolsheviks seized power in Russia and set up a communist dictatorship. The event marked the rise of communism in Russian and world affairs. One of its immediate, and lasting, results was persecution of the Church, Jews and other segments of the population.

1918: The Code of Canon Law, in preparation for more than 10 years, went into effect in the Western Church.

1919: Benedict XV stimulated missionary work through the decree *Maximum Illud*, in which he urged the recruiting and training of native clergy in places where the Church was not firmly established.

1920-22: Ireland was partitioned by two enactments of the British government which (1) made the six counties of Northern Ireland part of the United Kingdom in 1920 and (2) gave dominion status to the Irish Free State in 1922. The Irish Free State became an independent republic in 1949.

1922-39: Pontificate of Pius XI. He subscribed to the Lateran Treaty, 1929, which settled the Roman Question created by the confiscation of the Papal States in 1871; issued the encyclical *Casti connubii*, 1930, an authoritative statement on Christian marriage; resisted the efforts of Benito Mussolini to control Catholic Action and the Church, in the encyclical *Non abbiamo bisogno*, 1931; opposed various fascist policies; issued the encyclicals *Quadragesimo anno*, 1931, developing the social doctrine of Leo XIII's *Rerum novarum*, and *Divini Redemptoris*, 1937, calling for social justice and condemning atheistic communism; condemned anti-Semitism, 1937.

1926: The Catholic Relief Act repealed virtually all legal disabilities of Catholics in England.

1931: Leftists proclaimed Spain a republic and proceeded to disestablish the Church, confiscate church property, deny salaries to the clergy, expel the Jesuits and ban teaching of the Catholic faith. These actions were preludes to the civil war of 1936-1939.

1933: Emergence of Adolf Hitler to power in Germany. By 1935 two of his aims were clear, the elimination of the Jews and control of a single national church. Six million Jews were killed in the Holocaust. The Church was subject to repressive measures, which Pius XI protested futilely in the encyclical *Mit Brennender Sorge* in 1937.

1936-39: Civil war in Spain between the leftist Loyalist and the forces of rightist leader Francisco Franco The Loyalists were defeated and one-man, one-party rule was established. Many priests, religious and lay persons fell victim to Loyalist persecution and atrocities.

1939-45: World War II.

1939-58: Pontificate of Pius XII. He condemned communism, proclaimed the dogma of the Assumption of Mary in 1950, in various documents and other enactments provided ideological background for many of the accomplishments of the Second Vatican Council. (See **Twentieth Century Popes**, p. 241.)

1940: Start of a decade of communist conquest in more than 13 countries, resulting in conditions of persecution for a minimum of 60 million Catholics as well as members of other faiths.

Persecution diminished in Mexico because of nonenforcement of anti-religious laws still on record.

1950: Pius XII proclaimed the dogma of the Assumption of the Blessed Virgin Mary.

1957: The communist regime of China established the Patriotic Association of Chinese Catholics in opposition to the Church in union with the pope.

1958-63: Pontificate of Bl. John XXIII. His principal accomplishment was the convocation of the Second Vatican Council, the twenty-first ecumenical council in the history of the Church. (See **Twentieth Century Popes**, p. 241.)

1962-65: Ecumenical Council of the Vatican (II). It formulated and promulgated 16 documents — two dogmatic and two pastoral constitutions, nine decrees and three declarations — reflecting pastoral orientation toward renewal and reform in the Church, and making explicit dimensions of doctrine and Christian life requiring emphasis for the full development of the Church and the better accomplishment of its mission in the contemporary world.

1963-78: Pontificate of Paul VI. His main purpose and effort was to give direction and provide guidance for the authentic trends of church renewal set in motion by the Second Vatican Council. (See **Twentieth Century Popes**, p. 241.)

1978: The 34-day pontificate of John Paul I. Start of the pontificate of John Paul II; see **p. 246**.

1983: The revised Code of Canon Law, embodying reforms enacted by the Second Vatican Council, went into effect in the Church of Roman Rite.

1985: Formal ratification of a Vatican-Italy concordat replacing the Lateran Treaty of 1929.

1989-91: Decline and fall of communist influence and control in Middle and Eastern Europe and the Soviet Union.

1991: The Code of Canon Law for Eastern Churches went into effect.

1992: Approval of the new *Catechism of the Catholic Church*.

The Vatican officially closed the case against Galileo Galilei.

1994: Initiation of celebration preparations of the start of the third Christian millennium in the year 2000.

1997: Pope John Paul II issued an apology for any

anti-Semitism by Catholics; a conference on anti-Semitism was also held in Rome and a number of Catholic leaders in Europe issued apologies for historical anti-Semitism.

1998: Pope John Paul II visited Cuba and secured the release of over 300 political prisoners.

The Vatican issued a white paper on Anti-Semitism, entitled: *We Remember: A Reflection on the Shoah.*

Twentieth anniversary of the pontificate of Pope John Paul II; he became the longest reigning pontiff elected in the 20th century.

TWENTY-FIRST CENTURY

2000: The Catholic Church celebrated the Holy Year 2000 and the Jubilee; commencement of the third Christian millennium.

Pope John Paul II issued apology for the sinful actions of the Church's members in the past. Pope John Paul II traveled to the Holy Land in an historic visit.

2001: Pope John Paul II traveled to Greece and Syria. He also named 44 new members to the College of Cardinals in an unprecedented consistory.

On September 11, the World Trade Center was destroyed and the Pentagon attacked by Islamic terrorists who hijacked several planes and used them as weapons of mass destruction. The attacks launched a global war on terror.

2003: Pope John Paul II appealed for a peaceful resolution to the Iraq War. A coalition headed by the U.S. removed Saddam Hussein.

2004: In March, Pope John Paul II became the third longest reigning pontiff in history, surpassing Pope Leo XIII (r. 1878-1903).

2005: Pope John Paul II died on Apr. 2. Cardinal Joseph Ratzinger was elected pope on Apr. 19 and took the name Benedict XVI. His first encyclical, *Deus Caritas Est,* was issued on Dec. 25, 2005.

2009: Pope Benedict XVI visited the Holy Land.

2010: The sex abuse crisis expanded to Europe, with the scandal engulfing Germany, Belgium, and especially Ireland.

2013: Pope Benedict XVI became the first pope since Gregory XII in 1415 to renounce the papacy; Cardinal Jorge Mario Bergoglio of Argentina is elected as his successor and takes the name Francis. Francis is the first pontiff from Latin America, the first Jesuit, and the first non-European pope since the 8th century.

ECUMENICAL COUNCILS

An ecumenical council is an assembly of the college of bishops, with and under the presidency of the pope, which has supreme authority over the Church in matters pertaining to faith, morals, worship and discipline.

The Second Vatican Council stated: "The supreme authority with which this college (of bishops) is empowered over the whole Church is exercised in a solemn way through an ecumenical council. A council is never ecumenical unless it is confirmed or at least accepted as such by the successor of Peter. It is the prerogative of the Roman Pontiff to convoke these councils, to preside over them, and to confirm them" (Dogmatic Constitution on the Church, *Lumen Gentium,* No. 22).

Pope Presides

The pope is the head of an ecumenical council; he presides over it either personally or through legates. Conciliar decrees and other actions have binding force only when confirmed and promulgated by him. If a pope dies during a council, it is suspended until reconvened by another pope. An ecumenical council is not superior to a pope; hence, there is no appeal from a pope to a council.

Collectively, the bishops with the pope represent the whole Church. They do this not as democratic representatives of the faithful in a kind of church parliament, but as the successors of the Apostles with divinely given authority, care and responsibility over the whole Church.

All and only bishops are council participants with deliberative vote. The supreme authority of the Church can invite others and determine the manner of their participation.

Basic legislation concerning ecumenical councils is contained in Canons 337-41 of the Code of Canon Law. Basic doctrinal considerations were stated by the Second Vatican Council in the Dogmatic Constitution on the Church.

Background

Ecumenical councils had their prototype in the Council of Jerusalem in 51, at which the Apostles under the leadership of St. Peter decided that converts to the Christian faith were not obliged to observe all the prescriptions of Old Testament law (Acts 15). As early as the second century, bishops got together in regional meetings, synods or councils to take common action for the doctrinal and pastoral good of their communities of faithful. The expansion of such limited assemblies to ecumenical councils was a logical and historical evolution, given the nature and needs of the Church.

Emperors Involved

Emperors were active in summoning or convoking the first eight councils, especially the first five and the eighth. Among reasons for intervention of this kind were the facts that the emperors regarded themselves as guardians of the faith; that the settlement of religious controversies, which had repercussions in political and social turmoil, served the cause of peace in the state; and that the emperors had at their disposal ways and means of facilitating gatherings of bishops. Imperial actions, however, did not account for the formally ecumenical nature of the councils.

Some councils were attended by relatively few bishops, and the ecumenical character of several was open to question for a time. However, confirmation and de facto recognition of their actions by popes and subsequent councils established them as ecumenical.

Role in History

The councils have played a highly significant role in the history of the Church by witnessing to and defining truths of revelation, by shaping forms of worship and discipline, and by promoting measures for the ever-necessary reform and renewal of Catholic life. In general, they have represented attempts of the Church to mobilize itself in times of crisis for self-preservation, self-purification and growth.

The first eight ecumenical councils were held in the East; the other 13, in the West. The majority of separated Eastern Churches — e.g., the Orthodox — recognize the ecumenical character of the first seven councils, which formulated a great deal of basic doctrine. Other separated Eastern Churches acknowledge only the first two or first three ecumenical councils.

The 21 Councils

The 21 ecumenical councils in the history of the Church are listed below, with indication of their names or titles (taken from the names of the places where they were held); the dates; the reigning and/or approving popes; the emperors who were instrumental in convoking the eight councils in the East; the number of bishops who attended, when available; the number of sessions. Significant actions of the first 20 councils are indicated under appropriate dates in **Dates and Events in Church History.**

Nicaea I, 325: St. Sylvester I (Emperor Constantine I); attended by approximately 300 bishops; sessions held between May 20 or June 19 to near the end of August.

Constantinople I, 381: St. Damasus I (Emperor Theodosius I); attended by approximately 150 bishops; sessions held from May to July.

Ephesus, 431: St. Celestine I (Emperor Theodosius II); attended by 150 to 200 bishops; five sessions held between June 22 and July 17.

Chalcedon, 451: St. Leo I (Emperor Marcian); attended by approximately 600 bishops; 17 sessions held between Oct. 8 and Nov. 1.

Constantinople II, 553: Vigilius (Emperor Justinian I); attended by 165 bishops; eight sessions held between May 5 and June 2.

Constantinople III, 680-681: St. Agatho, St. Leo II (Emperor Constantine IV); attended by approximately 170 bishops; 16 sessions held between Nov. 7, 680, and Sept. 6, 681.

Nicaea II, 787: Adrian I (Empress Irene); attended by approximately 300 bishops; eight sessions held between Sept. 24 and Oct. 23.

Constantinople IV, 869-870: Adrian II (Emperor Basil I); attended by 102 bishops; six sessions held between Oct. 5, 869, and Feb. 28, 870.

Lateran I, 1123: Callistus II; attended by approximately 300 bishops; sessions held between Mar. 8 and Apr. 6.

Lateran II, 1139: Innocent II; attended by 900 to 1,000 bishops and abbots; three sessions held in April.

Lateran III, 1179: Alexander III; attended by at least 300 bishops; three sessions held between Mar. 5 and 19.

Lateran IV, 1215: Innocent III; sessions held between Nov. 11 and 30.

Lyons I, 1245: Innocent IV; attended by approximately 150 bishops; three sessions held between June 28 and July 17.

Lyons II, 1274: Gregory X; attended by approximately 500 bishops; six sessions held between May 7 and July 17.

Vienne, 1311-1312: Clement V; attended by 132 bishops; three sessions held between Oct. 16, 1311, and May 6, 1312.

Constance, 1414-1418: Gregory XII, Martin V; attended by nearly 200 bishops, plus other prelates and many experts; 45 sessions held between Nov. 5, 1414, and Apr. 22, 1418.

Florence (also called Basel-Ferrara-Florence), 1431-c. 1445: Eugene IV; attended by many Latin-Rite and Eastern-Rite bishops; preliminary sessions were held at Basel and Ferrara before definitive work was accomplished at Florence.

Lateran V, 1512-1517: Julius II, Leo X; 12 sessions held between May 3, 1512, and Mar. 6, 1517.

Trent, 1545-1563: Paul III, Julius III, Pius IV; 25 sessions held between Dec. 13, 1545, and Dec. 4, 1563.

Vatican I, 1869-1870: Pius IX; attended by approximately 800 bishops and other prelates; four public sessions and 89 general meetings held between Dec. 8, 1869, and Sept. 1, 1870.

VATICAN II

The Second Vatican Council, which was forecast by Pope John XXIII Jan. 25, 1959, was held in four sessions in St. Peter's Basilica.

Pope John convoked it and opened the first session, which ran from Oct. 11 to Dec. 8, 1962. Following John's death June 3, 1963, Pope Paul VI reconvened the council for the other three sessions which ran from Sept. 29 to Dec. 4, 1963; Sept. 14 to Nov. 21, 1964; Sept. 14 to Dec. 8, 1965.

A total of 2,860 Fathers participated in council proceedings, and attendance at meetings varied between 2,000 and 2,500. For various reasons, including the denial of exit from Communist-dominated countries, 274 Fathers could not attend.

The council formulated and promulgated 16 documents — two dogmatic and two pastoral constitutions, nine decrees and three declarations — all of which reflect its basic pastoral orientation toward renewal and reform in the Church. Given below are the Latin and English titles of the documents and their dates of promulgation.

Lumen Gentium (Dogmatic Constitution on the Church), Nov. 21, 1964.

Dei Verbum (Dogmatic Constitution on Divine Revelation), Nov. 18, 1965.

Sacrosanctum Concilium (Constitution on the Sacred Liturgy), Dec. 4, 1963.

Gaudium et Spes (Pastoral Constitution on the Church in the Modern World), Dec. 7, 1965.

Christus Dominus (Decree on the Bishops' Pastoral Office in the Church), Oct. 28, 1965.

Ad Gentes (Decree on the Church's Missionary Activity), Dec. 7, 1965.

Unitatis Redintegratio (Decree on Ecumenism), Nov. 21, 1964.

Orientalium Ecclesiarum (Decree on Eastern Catholic Churches), Nov. 21, 1964.

Presbyterorum Ordinis (Decree on the Ministry and Life of Priests), Dec. 7, 1965.

Optatam Totius (Decree on Priestly Formation), Oct. 28, 1965.

Perfectae Caritatis (Decree on the Appropriate Renewal of the Religious Life), Oct. 28, 1965.

Apostolicam Actuositatem (Decree on the Apostolate of the Laity), Nov. 18, 1965.

Inter Mirifica (Decree on the Instruments of Social Communication), Dec. 4, 1963.

Dignitatis Humanae (Declaration on Religious Freedom), Dec. 7, 1965.

Nostra Aetate (Declaration on the Relationship of

the Church to Non-Christian Religions), Oct. 28, 1965.

Gravissimum Educationis (Declaration on Christian Education), Oct. 28, 1965.

The key documents were the four constitutions, which set the ideological basis for all the others. To date, the documents with the most visible effects are those on the liturgy, the Church, the Church in the world, ecumenism, the renewal of religious life, the life and ministry of priests, the lay apostolate.

The main business of the council was to explore and make explicit dimensions of doctrine and Christian life requiring emphasis for the full development of the Church and the better accomplishment of its mission in the contemporary world.

Enactments of the Second Vatican Council have been points of departure for a wide variety of developments in the internal life of the Church and its mission in the world at large. Much effort has been made in the pontificate of Pope John Paul II to provide the interpretation and implementation of the conciliar documents with a more uniform and universal structure.

POPE BENEDICT XVI AND THE SECOND VATICAN COUNCIL

In December 2005, Pope Benedict XVI gave a reflection on the interpretation of Vatican II. The following are excerpts of his address:

The last event of this year on which I wish to reflect here is the celebration of the conclusion of the Second Vatican Council 40 years ago. This memory prompts the question: What has been the result of the Council? Was it well received? What, in the acceptance of the Council, was good and what was inadequate or mistaken? What still remains to be done? No one can deny that in vast areas of the Church the implementation of the Council has been somewhat difficult, even without wishing to apply to what occurred in these years the description that St. Basil, the great Doctor of the Church, made of the Church's situation after the Council of Nicea: he compares her situation to a naval battle in the darkness of the storm, saying among other things: "The raucous shouting of those who through disagreement rise up against one another, the incomprehensible chatter, the confused din of uninterrupted clamoring, has now filled almost the whole of the Church, falsifying through excess or failure the right doctrine of the faith..." (*De Spiritu Sancto*, XXX, 77; PG 32, 213 A; SCh 17 ff., p. 524).

We do not want to apply precisely this dramatic description to the situation of the post-conciliar period, yet something from all that occurred is nevertheless reflected in it. The question arises: Why has the implementation of the Council, in large parts of the Church, thus far been so difficult?

Well, it all depends on the correct interpretation of the Council or — as we would say today — on its proper hermeneutics, the correct key to its interpretation and application. The problems in its implementation arose from the fact that two contrary hermeneutics came face to face and quarreled with each other. One caused confusion, the other, silently but more and more visibly, bore and is bearing fruit.

On the one hand, there is an interpretation that I would call "a hermeneutic of discontinuity and rupture"; it has frequently availed itself of the sympathies of the mass media, and also one trend of modern theology. On the other, there is the "hermeneutic of reform," of renewal in the continuity of the one subject-Church which the Lord has given to us. She is a subject which increases in time and develops, yet always remaining the same, the one subject of the journeying People of God.

The hermeneutic of discontinuity risks ending in a split between the pre-conciliar Church and the post-conciliar Church. It asserts that the texts of the Council as such do not yet express the true spirit of the Council. It claims that they are the result of compromises in which, to reach unanimity, it was found necessary to keep and reconfirm many old things that are now pointless. However, the true spirit of the Council is not to be found in these compromises but instead in the impulses toward the new that are contained in the texts.

These innovations alone were supposed to represent the true spirit of the Council, and starting from and in conformity with them, it would be possible to move ahead. Precisely because the texts would only imperfectly reflect the true spirit of the Council and its newness, it would be necessary to go courageously beyond the texts and make room for the newness in which the Council's deepest intention would be expressed, even if it were still vague.

In a word: it would be necessary not to follow the texts of the Council but its spirit. In this way, obviously, a vast margin was left open for the question on how this spirit should subsequently be defined and room was consequently made for every whim....

The hermeneutic of dis-continuity is countered by the hermeneutic of reform, as it was presented first by Pope John XXIII in his Speech inaugurating the Council on Oct. 11, 1962 and later by Pope Paul VI in his Discourse for the Council's conclusion on Dec. 7, 1965.

Here I shall cite only John XXIII's well-known words, which unequivocally express this hermeneutic when he says that the Council wishes "to transmit the doctrine, pure and integral, without any attenuation or distortion." And he continues: "Our duty is not only to guard this precious treasure, as if we were concerned only with antiquity, but to dedicate ourselves with an earnest will and without fear to that work which our era demands of us...." It is necessary that "adherence to all the teaching of the Church in its entirety and preciseness..." be presented in "faithful and perfect conformity to the authentic doctrine, which, however, should be studied and expounded through the methods of research and through the literary forms of modern thought. The substance of the ancient doctrine of the deposit of faith is one thing, and the way in which it is presented is another...," retaining the same meaning and message (*The Documents of Vatican II*, Walter M. Abbott, S.J., p. 715).

The Papacy and the Holy See

POPE FRANCIS

Cardinal Jorge Mario Bergolgio, archbishop of Buenos Aires, Argentina, was elected Bishop of Rome and the 265th Successor of St. Peter as Supreme Pastor of the Universal Church on Mar. 13, 2013, after five ballots over two days. He chose the name Francis in honor of St. Francis of Assisi.

Pope Francis is the first non-European pope since 731, the first Jesuit to be elected, the first pope of the Western Hemisphere, the first of the Southern Hemisphere, and the first Latin American.

Early Life

Jorge Mario Bergoglio was born Dec. 17, 1936, in the working class Flores neighborhood of Buenos Aires, Argentina. The members of his family were considered "Porteños," the name used for the inhabitants of Buenos Aires who are largely second-or third-generation descendants from immigrants, with ties to the Old World. Being of Italian origin, they were also termed "Tanos," the local word for Italian immigrants. In the case of the Bergoglios, they were immigrants from Turin, in the Piedmont region of Italy. His father was Mario Bergoglio, a railway worker, and his mother Regina Sivori, a housewife who oversaw the early education of the family's five children. Bergoglio initially wanted to pursue a career in chemistry, but his academic hopes were slowed when he was teenager owing to an infection that led to the removal of a portion of his right lung. He eventually graduated in chemistry from the University of Buenos Aires and is said to have expressed hopes of being married. As a young man he was fond of the tango, Argentina's beloved traditional dance, and he has never lost his love for the San Lorenzo de Almagro soccer club of Buenos Aires. Ultimately, Bergoglio discerned that Christ was calling him to the priesthood and the Society of Jesus. His process of discernment was shaped by an experience of God's loving mercy on Sept. 21, 1953, on the feast of St. Matthew. He entered

Coat of Arms of Pope Francis

the Jesuit novitiate at Villa Devoto, Argentina, in 1958 and after a long period of formation, he was ordained to the priesthood on Dec. 13, 1969. Father Bergoglio took his final vows on April 22, 1973, and was elected provincial of Argentina that same year.

Father Bergoglio's time as provincial from 1973 to 1979 came at a challenging time for the Church. Many priests and religious in Latin America were being drawn to the theological movement of liberation theology, and very early on Father Bergoglio saw it as an aberration of the Church's authentic concern for the poor and the call to authentic justice rooted in the Gospel and nurturing an encounter with Jesus Christ.

From 1976 until 1983, with the fall of the military dictatorship that had ruled for decades, Argentina was plagued by the so-called "Guerra Sucia" ("Dirty War"), an era of brutal oppression and violence during which the regime killed between 13,000 and 30,000 citizens. The terrible events of the Dirty War impacted the life of Fr. Bergoglio. He had to walk a fine and dangerous line with the government. Some of his priests became targets of the dictatorship because of their associations with the guerillas and also their open opposition to the government. He urged the priests of the province not to give in to the temptation to take up arms and surrender their lives to violence and hatred, and regularly hid people on Church property to prevent their arrest, and once gave his own identity papers to a man who looked like him so that he could escape the country.

Completing his difficult tenure as provincial, Fr. Bergoglio settled back into teaching and a quiet life in academia. In 1980, he was named rector of the seminary in San Miguel, where he had studied. In 1986, he went to Germany to complete his doctorate, and on his return to Argentina continued to teach and serve as a spiritual director and confessor for the Society of Jesus in Córdoba. He also was well-known in the order for his expertise in Ignatian

Spirituality, the school of spirituality developed by St. Ignatius Loyola.

Bishop and Cardinal

On May 20, 1992, he was informed that he been appointed by Pope John Paul II as an auxiliary bishop of Buenos Aires and the titular bishop of Auca. Fr. Bergoglio was ordained a bishop on June 27, 1992. Bp. Bergoglio was named on June 3, 1997, to be the Coadjutor Archbishop of Buenos Aires. Card. Quarracino died the next year, and Abp. Bergoglio acceded to the see on Feb. 28, 1998. Pope John Paul II appointed him to the College of Cardinals Feb. 21, 2001, with the titular church in Rome of St. Robert Bellarmine.

From the start of his time as archbishop, Bergoglio made it clear that his lifelong commitment to the poor and his emphasis on humility and pastoral service were not going to end with his new office. He decided not to live in the traditional archbishop's residence but instead in a simple apartment next to the cathedral on the Plaza de Mayo in Buenos Aires. He fixed his own meals and famously took the bus and the subway to travel around the city.

Matching his humility in service is what Card. Bergoglio often called apostolic courage. In that sense, he was a prophetic voice as archbishop and was unafraid to stand firm in defending rights and dignity of the human person, speaking out against secularism and materialism, and proclaiming the authentic teachings of the Church in Argentina and Latin America.

Foreign Pastoral Visits

Brazil, July 22-29, 2013
Holy Land, May 24-26, 2014
South Korea, Aug. 13-18, 2014
Albania, Sept. 21, 2014

Canonizations and Beatifications

As of Aug. 15, 2014, Pope Francis' pontificate has witnessed the beatification of 843 Servants of God. Pope Francis has canonized 45 beati. The total number of blesseds and saints in his pontificate was 888.

Encyclicals and Other Writings

Pope Francis has issued one encyclical, *Lumen Fidei* ("The Light of Faith" in 2013). He also promulgated a post-synodal apostolic exhortation, *Evangelii Gaudium* ("The Joy of the Gospel" in 2013).

POPE BENEDICT XVI (2005-2013)

Cardinal Joseph Ratzinger of Germany, Prefect of the Congregation for the Doctrine of the Faith since 1981 and one the great theologians in the Church over the last 50 years, was elected Bishop of Rome and the 264th successor of St. Peter as Supreme Pastor of the Universal Church on Apr. 19, 2005, after four ballots over two days. He chose the name Benedict in honor of Pope Benedict XV, an advocate of peace, and St. Benedict of Nursia, who helped to resurrect civilization in Europe during the Dark Ages. Pope Benedict XVI was invested with the pallium, the symbol of his office, on Apr. 24, 2005, in ceremonies attended by more than 500,000 people in St. Peter's Square. At the time of his birthday in 2012, he became the sixth longest lived pope. Pope Leo XIII, who died at the age of 93 was the oldest living pontiff. On Feb. 28, 2013, at 8 p.m., he resigned the papacy. He was the first pope to renounce the papacy since 1415 and the resignation of Pope Gregory XII.

Early Life

Joseph Aloysius Ratzinger was born on Apr. 16, 1927, while the family was living in a three-story house in the little village of Marktl am Inn, situated in eastern Bavaria. His family moved several times in his early years owing to his father's opposition to the Nazis, and young Joseph was forced to join the Hitler Youth. He was adamantly opposed to the Nazis and made every effort to leave at the first opportunity. In 1939, he entered the minor seminary in Traunstein, his first step toward the priesthood. World War II forced a postponement of his studies, until 1945, when he re-entered the seminary with his brother, Georg. In 1947, he entered the *Herzogliches Georgianum*, a theological institute associated with the University of Munich. Finally, on June 29, 1951, both Joseph and his brother were ordained to the priesthood by Card. Faulhaber, in the Cathedral at Freising, on the Feast of Sts. Peter and Paul.

Continuing his theological studies at the University of Munich, he received his doctorate in theology in July 1953, with a thesis entitled *Volk und Haus Gottes in Augustins* *Lehre von der Kirche* ("The People and House of God in Augustine's doctrine of the Church"). He fulfilled a requirement for teaching at the university level by completing a book-length treatise, "The Theology of History in St. Bonaventure." On Apr. 15, 1959, he began lectures as a full professor of fundamental theology at the University of Bonn. From 1962-1965, he was present during all four sessions of the Second Vatican Council as a *peritus,* or chief theological advisor, to Card. Josef Frings of Köln (Cologne), Germany.

In 1963, he began teaching at the University of Münster, taking, in 1966, a second chair in dogmatic theology at the University of Tübingen. A wave of student uprisings swept across Europe in 1968, and Marxism quickly became the dominant intellectual system at Tübingen. He found the radicalized environment to be unacceptable, so in 1969 he moved back to Bavaria and took a teaching position at the University of Regensburg. There, he eventually became dean and vice president. He was also a member of the International Theological Commission of the Holy See from 1969 until 1980.

In 1972, together with Hans Urs von Balthasar, Henri De Lubac and others, he launched the Catholic theological journal *Communio,* a quarterly review of Catholic theology and culture. It has been said that this was done in response to the misinterpretation of the Second Vatican Council by various theologians, as represented by the theological journal *Concilium.*

Archbishop and Cardinal

On Mar. 24, 1977, Fr. Ratzinger was appointed Archbishop of Munich and Freising by Pope Paul VI. He was ordained a bishop on May 28, 1977, taking as his Episcopal motto a phrase from 3 John 8, *Cooperatores Veritatis* ("Fellow Worker in the Truth"). On June 27, 1977, he was elevated to Cardinal (Cardinal Priest) by Pope Paul VI, with the titular church of St. Mary of Consolation (in Tiburtina). In 1980, he was named by Pope John Paul II to chair the special Synod on the Laity. Shortly after that, the pope asked him to head the Congregation for Catholic Education. Card. Ratzinger declined, feeling he should not leave his post in Munich too soon. On Nov. 25, 1981, he accepted the post of the Prefect for the Congregation for the Doctrine of the Faith, becoming at the same time *ex officio* the President of the Pontifical Biblical Commission, and the International Theological Commission.

Card. Ratzinger was President of the Commission for the Preparation of the *Catechism of the Catholic Church*, and after six years of work (1986-92) he presented the new *Catechism* to the Holy Father. On Apr. 5, 1993, he was transferred to the order of Cardinal Bishops, with the suburbicarian see of Velletri-Signi. On Nov. 9, 1998, his election as Vice-Dean of the Sacred College of Cardinals was approved by Pope John Paul II, and the Holy Father approved his election as Dean of the College of Cardinals on Nov. 30, 2002, with the title of the suburbicarian See of Ostia added to that of Velletri-Segni.

Besides his prefecture at the Doctrine of the Faith, his curial memberships include: the Second Section of the Secretariat of State, the Congregation of Bishops, of Divine Worship and the Discipline of the Sacraments, of Catholic Education, of Evangelization of Peoples, for the Oriental Churches; and the Pontifical Councils for Christian Unity, for Culture (councils); as well as, the Commissions *Ecclesia Dei*, and for Latin America.

As Dean of the College he was a key figure during the *sede vacante* after the death of Pope John Paul II on April 2, 2005, and delivered the funeral homily for the deceased pontiff.

Foreign Pastoral Visits

2005: Cologne, Germany (World Youth Day), Aug. 18-21.
2006: Poland, May 25-28; Valencia, Spain, July 8-9; Munich, Germany, Sept. 9-14; Turkey, Nov. 28-Dec. 1.
2007: Brazil, May 9-14; Austria, Sept. 7-9.

2008: United States, Apr. 15-21; Sydney, Australia, July 12-21; France, Sept. 12-15.
2009: Cameroon and Angola, Mar. 17-23; Holy Land, May 8-15; Czech Republic, Sept. 26-28.
2010: Malta, Apr. 17-18; Portugal, May 11-14; Cyprus, June 4-6; England and Scotland, Sept. 16-19; Spain, Nov. 6-7.
2011: Croatia, June 4-5; Madrid, Spain, Aug. 18-21; Germany, Sept. 22-25; Benin, Nov. 18-20.
2012: Mexico and Republic of Cuba, Mar. 23-29; Lebanon, Sept. 14-16.

Canonizations and Beatifications

As of Feb. 28, 2013, Pope Benedict XVI's pontificate witnessed the beatification of 843 Servants of God. Pope Benedict XVI canonized 45 beati. The total number of blesseds and saints in his pontificate was 888.

Encyclicals and Other Writings

Cardinal Joseph Ratzinger at the time of his election as Pope Benedict XVI was one of the Church's greatest theologians and author of a vast body of writings. Since his election, he has issued several documents, including several *motu proprio* and apostolic letters. His first encyclical, *Deus Caritas Est*, was issued on Dec. 25, 2005. His second encyclical, *Spe Salvi*, released Nov. 30, 2007. On Mar. 13, 2007, he released the post-synodal apostolic exhortation, *Sacramentum Caritatis* ("The Sacrament of Charity"), a reflection on the discussions and suggestions made during the 2005 world Synod of Bishops on the Eucharist. In spring 2007, he also published his first book as pope, *Jesus of Nazareth*. The second volume was published in spring 2011. On July 7, 2007, he issued the long-awaited *Motu Proprio Summorum Pontificum*, on the "Roman liturgy prior to the reform of 1970." His third encyclical, *Caritas in Veritate*, was issued on July 7, 2009. On Sept. 30, 2010, he issued the post-synodal apostolic exhortation, *Verbum Domini*, on the Word of God in the Life and Mission of the Church.

POPES OF THE ROMAN CATHOLIC CHURCH

Information includes the name of the pope, in many cases his name before becoming pope, his birthplace or country of origin, the date of accession to the papacy, and the date of the end of reign that, in all but a few cases, was the date of death. Double dates indicate date of election and date of solemn beginning of ministry as Pastor of the universal Church. Source: *Annuario Pontificio*.

St. Peter (Simon Bar-Jona): Bethsaida in Galilee; d. c. 64 or 67.
St. Linus: Tuscany; 67-76.
St. Anacletus (Cletus): Rome; 76-88.
St. Clement: Rome; 88-97.
St. Evaristus: Greece; 97-105.
St. Alexander I: Rome; 105-115.
St. Sixtus I: Rome; 115-125.
St. Telesphorus: Greece; 125-136.
St. Hyginus: Greece; 136-140.
St. Pius I: Aquileia; 140-155.
St. Anicetus: Syria; 155-166.
St. Soter: Campania; 166-175.
St. Eleutherius: Nicopolis in Epirus; 175-189.
Up to the time of St. Eleutherius, the years indicated for the beginning and end of pontificates are not absolutely certain. Also, up to the middle of the 11th century, there are some doubts about the exact days and months given in chronological tables.

St. Victor I: Africa; 189-199.
St. Zephyrinus: Rome; 199-217.
St. Callistus I: Rome; 217-222.
St. Urban I: Rome; 222-230.
St. Pontian: Rome; July 21, 230, to Sept. 28, 235.
St. Anterus: Greece; Nov. 21, 235, to Jan. 3, 236.
St. Fabian: Rome; Jan. 10, 236, to Jan. 20, 250.
St. Cornelius: Rome; Mar. 251 to June 253.
St. Lucius I: Rome; June 25, 253, to Mar. 5, 254.
St. Stephen I: Rome; May 12, 254, to Aug. 2, 257.
St. Sixtus II: Greece; Aug. 30, 257, to Aug. 6, 258.
St. Dionysius: birthplace unknown; July 22, 259, to Dec. 26, 268.
St. Felix I: Rome; Jan. 5, 269, to Dec. 30, 274.
St. Eutychian: Luni; Jan. 4, 275, to Dec. 7, 283.
St. Caius: Dalmatia; Dec. 17, 283, to Apr. 22, 296.
St. Marcellinus: Rome; June 30, 296, to Oct. 25, 304.
St. Marcellus I: Rome; May 27, 308, or June 26, 308, to Jan. 16, 309.
St. Eusebius: Greece; Apr. 18, 309, to Aug. 17, 309 or 310.
St. Melchiades (Miltiades): Africa; July 2, 311, to Jan. 11, 314.
St. Sylvester I: Rome; Jan. 31, 314, to Dec. 31, 335.
(Most popes before St. Sylvester I were martyrs.)
St. Marcus: Rome; Jan. 18, 336, to Oct. 7, 336.
St. Julius I: Rome; Feb. 6, 337, to Apr. 12, 352.

Liberius: Rome; May 17, 352, to Sept. 24, 366.

St. Damasus I: Spain; Oct. 1, 366, to Dec. 11, 384.

St. Siricius: Rome; Dec. 15, or 22 or 29, 384, to Nov. 26, 399.

St. Anastasius I: Rome; Nov. 27, 399, to Dec. 19, 401.

St. Innocent I: Albano; Dec. 22, 401, to Mar. 12, 417.

St. Zosimus: Greece; Mar. 18, 417, to Dec. 26, 418.

St. Boniface I: Rome; Dec. 28 or 29, 418, to Sept. 4, 422.

St. Celestine I: Campania; Sept. 10, 422, to July 27, 432.

St. Sixtus III: Rome; July 31, 432, to Aug. 19, 440.

St. Leo I (the Great): Tuscany; Sept. 29, 440, to Nov. 10, 461.

St. Hilary: Sardinia; Nov. 19, 461, to Feb. 29, 468.

St. Simplicius: Tivoli; Mar. 3, 468, to Mar. 10, 483.

St. Felix III (II): Rome; Mar. 13, 483, to Mar. 1, 492. He should be called Felix II, and his successors of the same name should be numbered accordingly. The discrepancy in the numerical designation of popes named Felix was caused by the erroneous insertion in some lists of the name of St. Felix of Rome, a martyr.

St. Gelasius I: Africa; Mar. 1, 492, to Nov. 21, 496.

Anastasius II: Rome; Nov. 24, 496, to Nov. 19, 498.

St. Symmachus: Sardinia; Nov. 22, 498, to July 19, 514.

St. Hormisdas: Frosinone; July 20, 514, to Aug. 6, 523.

St. John I, Martyr: Tuscany; Aug. 13, 523, to May 18, 526.

St. Felix IV (III): Samnium; July 12, 526, to Sept. 22, 530.

Boniface II: Rome; Sept. 22, 530, to Oct. 17, 532.

John II: Rome; Jan. 2, 533, to May 8, 535. John II was the first pope to change his name. His given name was Mercury.

St. Agapitus I: Rome; May 13, 535, to Apr. 22, 536.

St. Silverius, Martyr: Campania; June 1 or 8, 536, to Nov. 11, 537 (d. Dec. 2, 537). St. Silverius was violently deposed in Mar. 537, and abdicated Nov. 11, 537. His successor, Vigilius, was not recognized as pope by all the Roman clergy until his abdication.

Vigilius: Rome; Mar. 29, 537, to June 7, 555.

Pelagius I: Rome; Apr. 16, 556, to Mar. 4, 561.

John III: Rome; July 17, 561, to July 13, 574.

Benedict I: Rome; June 2, 575, to July 30, 579.

Pelagius II: Rome; Nov. 26, 579, to Feb. 7, 590.

St. Gregory I (the Great): Rome; Sept. 3, 590, to Mar. 12, 604.

Sabinian: Blera in Tuscany; Sept. 13, 604, to Feb. 22, 606.

Boniface III: Rome; Feb. 19, 607, to Nov. 12, 607.

St. Boniface IV: Abruzzi; Aug. 25, 608, to May 8, 615.

St. Deusdedit (Adeodatus I): Rome; Oct. 19, 615, to Nov. 8, 618.

Boniface V: Naples; Dec. 23, 619, to Oct. 25, 625.

Honorius I: Campania; Oct. 27, 625, to Oct. 12, 638.

Severinus: Rome; May 28, 640, to Aug. 2, 640.

John IV: Dalmatia; Dec. 24, 640, to Oct. 12, 642.

Theodore I: Greece; Nov. 24, 642, to May 14, 649.

St. Martin I, Martyr: Todi; July, 649, to Sept. 16, 655 (in exile from June 17, 653).

St. Eugene I: Rome; Aug. 10, 654, to June 2, 657. St. Eugene I was elected during the exile of St. Martin I, who is believed to have endorsed him as pope.

St. Vitalian: Segni; July 30, 657, to Jan. 27, 672.

Adeodatus II: Rome; Apr. 11, 672, to June 17, 676.

Donus: Rome; Nov. 2, 676, to Apr. 11, 678.

St. Agatho: Sicily; June 27, 678, to Jan. 10, 681.

St. Leo II: Sicily; Aug. 17, 682, to July 3, 683.

St. Benedict II: Rome; June 26, 684, to May 8, 685.

John V: Syria; July 23, 685, to Aug. 2, 686.

Conon: birthplace unknown; Oct. 21, 686, to Sept. 21, 687.

St. Sergius I: Syria; Dec. 15, 687, to Sept. 8, 701.

John VI: Greece; Oct. 30, 701, to Jan. 11, 705.

John VII: Greece; Mar. 1, 705, to Oct. 18, 707.

Sisinnius: Syria; Jan. 15, 708, to Feb. 4, 708.

Constantine: Syria; Mar. 25, 708, to Apr. 9, 715.

St. Gregory II: Rome; May 19, 715, to Feb. 11, 731.

St. Gregory III: Syria; Mar. 18, 731, to Nov. 741.

St. Zachary: Greece; Dec. 10, 741, to Mar. 22, 752.

Stephen II (III): Rome; Mar. 26, 752, to Apr. 26, 757. After the death of St. Zachary, a Roman priest named Stephen was elected but died (four days later) before his consecration as bishop of Rome, which would have marked the beginning of his pontificate. Another Stephen was elected to succeed Zachary as Stephen II. (The first pope with this name was St. Stephen I, 254-57.) The ordinal III appears in parentheses after the name of Stephen II because the name of the earlier elected but deceased priest was included in some lists. Other Stephens have double numbers.

St. Paul I: Rome; Apr. (May 29), 757, to June 28, 767.

Stephen III (IV): Sicily; Aug. 1 (7), 768, to Jan. 24, 772.

Adrian I: Rome; Feb. 1 (9), 772, to Dec. 25, 795.

St. Leo III: Rome; Dec. 26 (27), 795, to June 12, 816.

Stephen IV (V): Rome; June 22, 816, to Jan. 24, 817.

St. Paschal I: Rome; Jan. 25, 817, to Feb. 11, 824.

Eugene I: Rome; Feb. (May) 824 to Aug. 827.

Valentine: Rome; Aug. 827, to Sept. 827.

Gregory IV: Rome; 827, to Jan. 844.

Sergius II: Rome; Jan. 844 to Jan. 27, 847.

St. Leo IV: Rome; Jan. (Apr. 10) 847, to July 17, 855.

Benedict III: Rome; July (Sept. 29), 855, to Apr. 17, 858.

St. Nicholas I (the Great): Rome; Apr. 24, 858, to Nov. 13, 867.

Adrian II: Rome; Dec. 14, 867, to Dec. 14, 872.

John VIII: Rome; Dec. 14, 872, to Dec. 16, 882.

Marinus I: Gallese; Dec. 16, 882, to May 15, 884.

St. Adrian III: Rome; May 17, 884, to Sept. 885. Cult confirmed June 2, 1891.

Stephen V (VI): Rome; Sept. 885, to Sept. 14, 891.

Formosus: Bishop of Porto; Oct. 6, 891, to Apr. 4, 896.

Boniface VI: Rome; Apr. 896 to Apr. 896.

Stephen VI (VII): Rome; May 896 to Aug. 897.

Romanus: Gallese; Aug. 897 to Nov. 897.

Theodore II: Rome; Dec. 897 to Dec. 897.

John IX: Tivoli; Jan. 898 to Jan. 900.

Benedict IV: Rome; Jan. (Feb.) 900 to July 903.

Leo V: Ardea; July 903 to Sept. 903.

Sergius III: Rome; Jan. 29, 904, to Apr. 14, 911.

Anastasius III: Rome; Apr. 911 to June 913.

Landus: Sabina; July 913 to Feb. 914.

John X: Tossignano (Imola); Mar. 914 to May 928.

Leo VI: Rome; May 928 to Dec. 928.

Stephen VII (VIII): Rome; Dec. 928 to Feb. 931.

John XI: Rome; Feb. (Mar.) 931 to Dec. 935.

Leo VII: Rome; Jan. 3, 936, to July 13, 939.

Stephen VIII (IX): Rome; July 14, 939, to Oct. 942.

Marinus II: Rome; Oct. 30, 942, to May 946.

Agapitus II: Rome; May 10, 946, to Dec. 955.

John XII (Octavius): Tusculum; Dec. 16, 955, to May 14, 964 (date of his death).

Leo VIII: Rome; Dec. 4 (6), 963, to Mar. 1, 965.

Benedict V: Rome; May 22, 964, to July 4, 966.

Confusion exists concerning the legitimacy of claims to the pontificate by Leo VIII and Benedict V. John XII was deposed Dec. 4, 963, by a Roman council. If this deposition was invalid, Leo was an antipope. If the deposition of John was valid, Leo was the legitimate pope and Benedict was an antipope.

John XIII: Rome; Oct. 1, 965, to Sept. 6, 972.

Benedict VI: Rome; Jan. 19, 973 to June 974.

Benedict VII: Rome; Oct. 974 to July 10, 983.

John XIV (Peter Campenora): Pavia; Dec., 983 to Aug. 20, 984.

John XV: Rome; Aug. 985 to Mar. 996.

Gregory V (Bruno of Carinthia): Saxony; May 3, 996, to Feb. 18, 999.

Sylvester II (Gerbert): Auvergne; Apr. 2, 999, to May 12, 1003.

John XVII (Siccone): Rome; June 1003 to Dec. 1003.

John XVIII (Phasianus): Rome; Jan. 1004, to July 1009.

Sergius IV (Peter): Rome; July 31, 1009, to May 12, 1012.

The custom of changing one's name on election to the papacy is generally considered to date from the time of Sergius IV. Before his time, several popes had changed their names. After his time, it became a regular practice, with few exceptions, e.g., Adrian VI and Marcellus II.

Benedict VIII (Theophylactus): Tusculum; May 18, 1012, to Apr. 9, 1024.

John XIX (Romanus): Tusculum; Apr. (May) 1024 to 1032.

Benedict IX (Theophylactus): Tusculum; 1032 to 1044.

Sylvester III (John): Rome; Jan. 20, 1045, to Feb. 10, 1045.

Sylvester III was an antipope if the forcible removal of Benedict IX in 1044 was not legitimate.

Benedict IX (second time): Apr. 10, 1045, to May 1, 1045.

Gregory VI (John Gratian): Rome; May 5, 1045, to Dec. 20, 1046.

Clement II (Suitger, Lord of Morsleben and Hornburg): Saxony; Dec. 24 (25), 1046 to Oct. 9, 1047.

If the resignation of Benedict IX in 1045 and his removal at the Dec. 1046, synod were not legitimate, Gregory VI and Clement II were antipopes.

Benedict IX (third time): Nov. 8, 1047, to July 17, 1048 (d. c. 1055).

Damasus II (Poppo): Bavaria; July 17, 1048, to Aug. 9, 1048.

St. Leo IX (Bruno): Alsace; Feb. 12, 1049, to Apr. 19, 1054.

Victor II (Gebhard): Swabia; Apr. 16, 1055, to July 28, 1057.

Stephen IX (X) (Frederick): Lorraine; Aug. 3, 1057, to Mar. 29, 1058.

Nicholas II (Gerard): Burgundy; Jan. 24, 1059, to July 27, 1061.

Alexander II (Anselmo da Baggio): Milan; Oct. 1, 1061, to Apr. 21, 1073.

St. Gregory VII (Hildebrand): Tuscany; Apr. 22 (June 30), 1073, to May 25, 1085.

Bl. Victor III (Dauferius; Desiderius): Benevento; May 24, 1086, to Sept. 16, 1087. Cult confirmed July 23, 1887.

Bl. Urban II (Otto di Lagery): France; Mar. 12, 1088, to July 29, 1099. Cult confirmed July 14, 1881.

Paschal II (Raniero): Ravenna; Aug. 13 (14), 1099, to Jan. 21, 1118.

Gelasius II (Giovanni Caetani): Gaeta; Jan. 24 (Mar. 10), 1118, to Jan. 28, 1119.

Callistus II (Guido of Burgundy): Burgundy; Feb. 2

(9), 1119, to Dec. 13, 1124.

Honorius II (Lamberto): Fiagnano (Imola); Dec. 15 (21), 1124, to Feb. 13, 1130.

Innocent II (Gregorio Papareschi): Rome; Feb. 14 (23), 1130, to Sept. 24, 1143.

Celestine II (Guido): Citta di Castello; Sept. 26 (Oct. 3), 1143, to Mar. 8, 1144.

Lucius II (Gerardo Caccianemici): Bologna: Mar. 12, 1144, to Feb. 15, 1145.

Bl. Eugene III (Bernardo Paganelli di Montemagno): Pisa; Feb. 15 (18), 1145, to July 8, 1153. Cult confirmed Oct. 3, 1872.

Anastasius IV (Corrado): Rome; July 12, 1153, to Dec. 3, 1154.

Adrian IV (Nicholas Breakspear): England; Dec. 4 (5), 1154, to Sept. 1, 1159.

Alexander III (Rolando Bandinelli): Siena; Sept. 7 (20), 1159, to Aug. 30, 1181.

Lucius III (Ubaldo Allucingoli): Lucca; Sept. 1 (6), 1181, to Sept. 25, 1185.

Urban III (Uberto Crivelli): Milan; Nov. 25 (Dec. 1), 1185, to Oct. 20, 1187.

Gregory VIII (Alberto de Morra): Benevento; Oct. 21 (25), 1187, to Dec. 17, 1187.

Clement III (Paolo Scolari): Rome; Dec. 19 (20), 1187, to Mar. 1191.

Celestine III (Giacinto Bobone): Rome; Mar. 30 (Apr. 14), 1191, to Jan. 8, 1198.

Innocent III (Lotario dei Conti di Segni); Anagni; Jan. 8 (Feb. 22), 1198, to July 16, 1216.

Honorius III (Cencio Savelli): Rome; July 18 (24), 1216, to Mar. 18, 1227.

Gregory IX (Ugolino, Count of Segni): Anagni; Mar. 19 (21), 1227, to Aug. 22, 1241.

Celestine IV (Goffredo Castiglioni): Milan; Oct. 25 (28), 1241, to Nov. 10, 1241.

Innocent IV (Sinibaldo Fieschi): Genoa; June 25 (28), 1243, to Dec. 7, 1254.

Alexander IV (Rinaldo, House of Ienne): Ienne (Rome); Dec. 12 (20), 1254, to May 25, 1261.

Urban IV (Jacques Pantal,on): Troyes; Aug. 29 (Sept. 4), 1261, to Oct. 2, 1264.

Clement IV (Guy Foulques or Guido le Gros): France; Feb. 5 (15), 1265, to Nov. 29, 1268.

Bl. Gregory X (Teobaldo Visconti): Piacenza; Sept. 1, 1271 (Mar. 27, 1272), to Jan. 10, 1276. Cult confirmed Sept. 12, 1713.

Bl. Innocent V (Peter of Tarentaise): Savoy; Jan. 21 (Feb. 22), 1276, to June 22, 1276. Cult confirmed Mar. 13, 1898.

Adrian V (Ottobono Fieschi): Genoa: July 11, 1276, to Aug. 18, 1276.

John XXI (Petrus Juliani or Petrus Hispanus): Portugal; Sept. 8 (20), 1276, to May 20, 1277.

There is confusion in the numerical designation of popes named John. The error dates back to the time of John XV.

Nicholas III (Giovanni Gaetano Orsini): Rome; Nov. 25 (Dec. 26), 1277, to Aug. 22, 1280.

Martin IV (Simon de Brie): France; Feb. 22 (Mar. 23), 1281, to Mar. 28, 1285.

The names of Marinus 1 (882-84) and Marinus II (942-46) were construed as Martin. In view of these two pontificates and the earlier reign of St. Martin I (649-55), this pope was called Martin IV.

Honorius IV (Giacomo Savelli): Rome; Apr. 2 (May

20), 1285, to Apr. 3, 1287.

Nicholas IV (Girolamo Masci): Ascoli; Feb. 22, 1288, to Apr. 4, 1292.

St. Celestine V (Pietro del Murrone): Isernia; July 5 (Aug. 29), 1294, to Dec. 13, 1294; d. May 19, 1296. Canonized May 5, 1313.

Boniface VIII (Benedetto Caetani): Anagni; Dec. 24, 1294 (Jan. 23, 1295), to Oct. 11, 1303.

Bl. Benedict XI (Niccolo Boccasini): Treviso; Oct. 22 (27), 1303, to July 7, 1304. Cult confirmed Apr. 24, l736.

Clement V (Bertrand de Got): France; June 5 (Nov. 14), 1305, to Apr. 20, 1314. (*First of Avignon popes.*)

John XXII (Jacques d'Euse): Cahors; Aug. 7 (Sept. 5), 1316, to Dec. 4, 1334.

Benedict XII (Jacques Fournier): France; Dec. 20, 1334 (Jan. 8, 1335), to Apr. 25, 1342.

Clement VI (Pierre Roger): France; May 7 (19), 1342, to Dec. 6, 1352.

Innocent VI (Etienne Aubert): France; Dec. 18 (30), 1352, to Sept. 12, 1362.

Bl. Urban V (Guillaume de Grimoard): France; Sept. 28 (Nov. 6), 1362, to Dec. 19, 1370. Cult confirmed Mar. 10, 1870.

Gregory XI (Pierre Roger de Beaufort): France; Dec. 30, 1370 (Jan. 5, 1371), to Mar. 26, 1378. (*Last of Avignon popes.*)

Urban VI (Bartolomeo Prignano): Naples; Apr. 8 (18), 1378, to Oct. 15, 1389.

Boniface IX (Pietro Tomacelli): Naples; Nov. 2 (9), 1389, to Oct. 1, 1404.

Innocent VII (Cosma Migliorati): Sulmona; Oct. 17 (Nov. 11), 1404, to Nov. 6, 1406.

Gregory XII (Angelo Correr): Venice; Nov. 30 (Dec. 19), 1406, to July 4, 1415, when he voluntarily resigned from the papacy to permit the election of his successor. He died Oct. 18, 1417. (*See* **Western Schism**, page 240.)

Martin V (Oddone Colonna): Rome; Nov. 11 (21), 1417, to Feb. 20, 1431.

Eugene IV (Gabriele Condulmer): Venice; Mar. 3 (11), 1431, to Feb. 23, 1447.

Nicholas V (Tommaso Parentucelli): Sarzana; Mar. 6 (19), 1447, to Mar. 24, 1455.

Callistus III (Alfonso Borgia): Jativa (Valencia); Apr. 8 (20), 1455, to Aug. 6, 1458.

Pius II (Enea Silvio Piccolomini): Siena; Aug. 19 (Sept. 3), 1458, to Aug. 14, 1464.

Paul II (Pietro Barbo): Venice; Aug. 30 (Sept. 16), 1464, to July 26, 1471.

Sixtus IV (Francesco della Rovere): Savona; Aug. 9 (25), 1471, to Aug. 12, 1484.

Innocent VIII (Giovanni Battista Cibo): Genoa; Aug. 29 (Sept. 12), 1484, to July 25, 1492.

Alexander VI (Rodrigo Borgia): Jativa (Valencia); Aug. 11 (26), 1492, to Aug. 18, 1503.

Pius III (Francesco Todeschini-Piccolomini): Siena; Sept. 22 (Oct. 1, 8), 1503, to Oct. 18, 1503.

Julius II (Giuliano della Rovere): Savona; Oct. 31 (Nov. 26), 1503, to Feb. 21, 1513.

Leo X (Giovanni de' Medici): Florence; Mar. 9 (19), 1513, to Dec. 1, 1521.

Adrian VI (Adrian Florensz): Utrecht; Jan. 9 (Aug. 31), 1522, to Sept. 14, 1523.

Clement VII (Giulio de' Medici): Florence; Nov. 19 (26), 1523, to Sept. 25, 1534.

Paul III (Alessandro Farnese): Rome; Oct. 13 (Nov. 3), 1534, to Nov. 10, 1549.

Julius III (Giovanni Maria Ciocchi del Monte): Rome; Feb. 7 (22), 1550, to Mar. 23, 1555.

Marcellus II (Marcello Cervini): Montepulciano; Apr. 9 (10), 1555, to May 1, 1555.

Paul IV (Gian Pietro Carafa): Naples; May 23 (26), 1555, to Aug. 18, 1559.

Pius IV (Giovan Angelo de' Medici): Milan; Dec. 25, 1559 (Jan. 6, 1560), to Dec. 9, 1565.

St. Pius V (Antonio-Michele Ghislieri): Bosco (Alexandria); Jan. 7 (17), 1566, to May 1, 1572. Canonized May 22, 1712.

Gregory XIII (Ugo Buoncompagni): Bologna; May 13 (25), 1572, to Apr. 10, 1585.

Sixtus V (Felice Peretti): Grottammare (Ripatransone); Apr. 24 (May 1), 1585, to Aug. 27, 1590.

Urban VII (Giambattista Castagna): Rome; Sept. 15, 1590, to Sept. 27, 1590.

Gregory XIV (Niccolo Sfondrati): Cremona; Dec. 5 (8), 1590, to Oct. 16, 1591.

Innocent IX (Giovanni Antonio Facchinetti): Bologna; Oct. 29 (Nov. 3), 1591, to Dec. 30, 1591.

Clement VIII (Ippolito Aldobrandini): Florence; Jan. 30 (Feb. 9), 1592, to Mar. 3, 1605.

Leo XI (Alessandro de' Medici): Florence; Apr. 1 (10), 1605, to Apr. 27, 1605.

Paul V (Camillo Borghese): Rome; May 16 (29), 1605, to Jan. 28, 1621.

Gregory XV (Alessandro Ludovisi): Bologna; Feb. 9 (14), 1621, to July 8, 1623.

Urban VIII (Maffeo Barberini): Florence; Aug. 6 (Sept. 29), 1623, to July 29, 1644.

Innocent X (Giovanni Battista Pamfili): Rome; Sept. 15 (Oct. 4), 1644, to Jan. 7, 1655.

Alexander VII (Fabio Chigi): Siena; Apr. 7 (18), 1655, to May 22, 1667.

Clement IX (Giulio Rospigliosi): Pistoia; June 20 (26), 1667, to Dec. 9, 1669.

Clement X (Emilio Altieri): Rome; Apr. 29 (May 11), 1670, to July 22, 1676.

Bl. Innocent XI (Benedetto Odescalchi): Como; Sept. 21 (Oct. 4), 1676, to Aug. 12, 1689. Beatified Oct. 7, 1956.

Alexander VIII (Pietro Ottoboni): Venice; Oct. 6 (16), 1689, to Feb. 1, 1691.

Innocent XII (Antonio Pignatelli): Spinazzola (Venosa); July 12 (15), 1691, to Sept. 27, 1700.

Clement XI (Giovanni Francesco Albani): Urbino; Nov. 23, 30 (Dec. 8), 1700, to Mar. 19, 1721.

Innocent XIII (Michelangelo dei Conti): Rome; May 8 (18), 1721, to Mar. 7, 1724.

Benedict XIII (Pietro Francesco Vincenzo Maria Orsini): Gravina (Bari); May 29 (June 4), 1724, to Feb. 21, 1730.

Clement XII (Lorenzo Corsini): Florence; July 12 (16), 1730, to Feb. 6, 1740.

Benedict XIV (Prospero Lambertini): Bologna; Aug. 17 (22), 1740, to May 3, 1758.

Clement XIII (Carlo Rezzonico): Venice; July 6 (16), 1758, to Feb. 2, 1769.

Clement XIV (Giovanni Vincenzo Antonio Lorenzo Ganganelli): Rimini; May 19, 28 (June 4), 1769, to Sept. 22, 1774.

Pius VI (Giovanni Angelo Braschi): Cesena; Feb. 15 (22), 1775, to Aug. 29, 1799.

Pius VII (Barnaba Gregorio Chiaramonti): Cesena; Mar. 14 (21), 1800, to Aug. 20, 1823.

Leo XII (Annibale della Genga): Genga (Fabriano); Sept. 28 (Oct. 5), 1823, to Feb. 10, 1829.

Pius VIII (Francesco Saverio Castiglioni): Cingoli; Mar. 31 (Apr. 5), 1829, to Nov. 30, 1830.

Gregory XVI (Bartolomeo Alberto-Mauro-Cappellari): Belluno; Feb. 2 (6), 1831, to June 1, 1846.

Bl. Pius IX (Giovanni M. Mastai-Ferretti): Senigallia; June 16 (21), 1846, to Feb. 7, 1878.

Leo XIII (Gioacchino Pecci): Carpineto (Anagni); Feb. 20 (Mar. 3), 1878, to July 20, 1903.

St. Pius X (Giuseppe Sarto): Riese (Treviso); Aug. 4 (9), 1903, to Aug. 20, 1914. Canonized May 29, 1954.

Benedict XV (Giacomo della Chiesa): Genoa; Sept. 3 (6), 1914, to Jan. 22, 1922.

Pius XI (Achille Ratti): Desio (Milan); Feb. 6 (12), 1922, to Feb. 10, 1939.

Pius XII (Eugenio Pacelli): Rome; Mar. 2 (12), 1939, to Oct. 9, 1958.

Bl. John XXIII (Angelo Giuseppe Roncalli): Sotto il Monte (Bergamo); Oct. 28 (Nov. 4), 1958, to June 3, 1963.

Paul VI (Giovanni Battista Montini): Concessio (Brescia); June 21 (30), 1963, to Aug. 6, 1978.

John Paul I (Albino Luciani): Forno di Canale (Belluno); Aug. 26 (Sept. 3), 1978, to Sept. 28, 1978.

Bl. John Paul II (Karol Wojtyla): Wadowice, Poland; Oct. 16 (22), 1978, to April 2, 2005.

Benedict XVI (Joseph Ratzinger): Marktl Am Inn, Germany; Apr. 19 (24), 2005, to Feb. 28, 2013.

Francis (Jorge Mario Bergoglio): Buenos Aires, Argentina; Mar. 13 (19), 2013.

ANTIPOPES

This list of men who claimed or exercised the papal office in an uncanonical manner includes names, birthplaces and dates of alleged reigns. Source: *Annuario Pontificio*.

St. Hippolytus: Rome; 217-235; was reconciled before his death.

Novatian: Rome; 251.

Felix II: Rome; 355 to Nov. 22, 365.

Ursinus: 366-367.

Eulalius: Dec. 27 or 29, 418, to 419.

Lawrence: 498; 501-505.

Dioscorus: Alexandria; Sept. 22, 530, to Oct. 14, 530.

Theodore: ended alleged reign, 687.

Paschal: ended alleged reign, 687.

Constantine: Nepi; June 28 (July 5), 767, to 769.

Philip: July 31, 768; retired to his monastery on the same day.

John: ended alleged reign, Jan. 844.

Anastasius: Aug. 855 to Sept. 855; d. 880.

Christopher: Rome; July or Sept. 903 to Jan. 904.

Boniface VII: Rome; June 974 to July 974; Aug. 984 to July 985.

John XVI: Rossano; Apr. 997 to Feb. 998.

Gregory: ended alleged reign, 1012.

Benedict X: Rome; Apr. 5, 1058, to Jan. 24, 1059.

Honorius II: Verona; Oct. 28, 1061, to 1072.

Clement III: Parma; June 25, 1080 (Mar. 24, 1084), to Sept. 8, 1100.

Theodoric: ended alleged reign, 1100; d. 1102.

Albert: ended alleged reign, 1102.

Sylvester IV: Rome; Nov. 18, 1105, to 1111.

Gregory VIII: France; Mar. 8, 1118, to 1121.

Celestine II: Rome; ended alleged reign, Dec. 1124.

Anacletus II: Rome; Feb. 14 (23), 1130, to Jan. 25, 1138.

Victor IV: Mar. 1138, to May 29, 1138; submitted to Pope Innocent II.

Victor IV: Montecelio; Sept. 7 (Oct. 4), 1159, to Apr. 20, 1164; he did not recognize his predecessor (Victor IV, above).

Paschal III: Apr. 22 (26), 1164, to Sept. 20, 1168.

Callistus III: Arezzo; Sept., 1168, to Aug. 29, 1178; submitted to Pope Alexander III.

Innocent III: Sezze; Sept. 29, 1179, to 1180.

Nicholas V: Corvaro (Rieti); May 12 (22), 1328, to Aug. 25, 1330; d. Oct. 16, 1333.

Four antipopes of the Western Schism:

Clement VII: Sept. 20 (Oct. 31), 1378, to Sept. 16, 1394.

Benedict XIII: Aragon; Sept. 28 (Oct. 11), 1394, to May 23, 1423.

Alexander V: Crete; June 26 (July 7), 1409, to May 3, 1410.

John XXIII: Naples; May 17 (25), 1410, to May 29, 1415. (Date of deposition by Council of Constance which ended the Western Schism; d. Nov. 22, 1419.)

Felix V: Savoy; Nov. 5, 1439 (July 24, 1440), to Apr. 7, 1449; d. 1451.

AVIGNON PAPACY

Avignon was the residence (1309-77) of a series of French popes (Clement V, John XXII, Benedict XII, Clement VI, Innocent VI, Urban V and Gregory XI). Prominent in the period were power struggles over the mixed interests of Church and state with the rulers of France (Philip IV, John II), Bavaria (Lewis IV), England (Edward III); factionalism of French and Italian churchmen; political as well as ecclesiastical turmoil in Italy, a factor of significance in prolonging the stay of popes in Avignon. Despite some positive achievements, the Avignon papacy was a prologue to the Western Schism that began in 1378.

GREAT WESTERN SCHISM

The Great Western Schism was a confused state of affairs that divided Christendom into two and then three papal obediences from 1378 to 1417.

It occurred some 50 years after Marsilius theorized that a general (not ecumenical) council of bishops and other persons was superior to a pope and nearly 30 years before the Council of Florence stated definitively that no kind of council had such authority.

It was a period of disaster preceding the even more disastrous period of the Reformation.

Urban VI, following the return of the papal residence to Rome after approximately 70 years at Avignon, was elected pope Apr. 8, 1378, and reigned until his death in 1389. He was succeeded by Boniface IX (1389-1404), Innocent VII (1404-1406) and Gregory XII (1406-1415). These four are considered the legitimate popes of the period.

Some of the cardinals who chose Urban pope, dissatisfied with his conduct of the office, declared that his election was invalid. They proceeded to elect Clement VII, who claimed the papacy from 1378 to

1394. He was succeeded by Benedict XIII.

Prelates seeking to end the state of divided papal loyalties convoked the Council of Pisa (1409) which, without authority, found Gregory XII and Benedict XIII guilty in absentia on 30-odd charges of schism and heresy, deposed them, and elected a third claimant to the papacy, Alexander V (1409-1410). He was succeeded by John XXIII (1410-1415).

The schism was ended by the Council of Constance (1414-1418). Although originally called into session in an irregular manner, the council, acquired authority after being convoked by Gregory XII in 1415. In its early irregular phase, it deposed John XXIII whose election to the papacy was uncanonical anyway. After being formally convoked, it accepted the abdication of Gregory in 1415 and dismissed the claims of Benedict XIII two years later, thus clearing the way for the election of Martin V on Nov. 11, 1417. The Council of Constance also rejected the theories of John Wycliff and condemned Jan Hus as a heretic.

POPES OF THE TWENTIETH CENTURY

LEO XIII

Leo XIII (Gioacchino Vincenzo Pecci) was born May 2, 1810, in Carpineto, Italy. Although all but three years of his life and pontificate were in the 19th century, his influence extended well into the 20th century.

He was educated at the Jesuit college in Viterbo, the Roman College, the Academy of Noble Ecclesiastics, and the University of the Sapienza. He was ordained in 1837.

He served as an apostolic delegate to two States of the Church, Benevento from 1838 to 1841 and Perugia in 1841 and 1842. Ordained titular archbishop of Damietta, he was papal nuncio to Belgium from Jan. 1843, until May 1846; in the post, he had controversial relations with the government over education issues and acquired his first significant experience of industrialized society.

He was archbishop of Perugia from 1846 to 1878. He became a cardinal in 1853 and chamberlain of the Roman Curia in 1877. He was elected to the papacy Feb. 20, 1878. He died July 20, 1903.

Canonizations: He canonized 18 saints and beatified a group of English martyrs.

Church Administration: He established 300 new dioceses and vicariates; restored the hierarchy in Scotland and set up an English, as contrasted with the Portuguese, hierarchy in India; approved the action of the Congregation for the Propagation of the Faith in reorganizing missions in China.

Encyclicals: He issued 86 encyclicals, on subjects ranging from devotional to social. In the former category were *Annum Sacrum*, on the Sacred Heart, in 1899, and 11 letters on Mary and the Rosary.

Social Questions: Much of Leo's influence stemmed from social doctrine stated in numerous encyclicals, concerning liberalism, liberty, the divine origin of authority; socialism, in *Quod Apostolici Muneris*, 1878; the Christian concept of the family, in *Arcanum*, 1880; socialism and economic liberalism, relations between capital and labor, in *Rerum Novarum*, 1891. Two of his social encyclicals were against the African slave trade.

Interfaith Relations: He was unsuccessful in unity overtures made to Orthodox and Slavic Churches. He declared Anglican orders invalid in the apostolic bull *Apostolicae Curae* Sept. 13, 1896.

International Relations: Leo was frustrated in seeking solutions to the Roman Question arising from the seizure of church lands by the Kingdom of Italy in 1870. He also faced anticlerical situations in Belgium and France and in the *Kulturkampf* policies of Bismarck in Germany.

Scholarship: In the encyclical *Aeterni Patris* of Aug. 4, 1879, he ordered a renewal of philosophical and theological studies in seminaries along scholastic, and especially Thomistic, lines, to counteract influential trends of liberalism and Modernism. He issued guidelines for biblical exegesis in *Providentissimus Deus* Nov. 18, 1893, and established the Pontifical Biblical Commission in 1902.

In other actions affecting scholarship and study, he opened the Vatican Archives to scholars in 1883 and established the Vatican Observatory.

United States: He authorized establishment of the apostolic delegation in Washington, DC, Jan. 24, 1893. He refused to issue a condemnation of the Knights of Labor. With a document entitled *Testem Benevolentiae*, he eased resolution of questions concerning what was called an American heresy in 1899.

ST. PIUS X

St. Pius X (Giuseppe Melchiorre Sarto) was born in 1835 in Riese, Italy. Educated at the college of Castelfranco and the seminary at Padua, he was ordained to the priesthood Sept. 18, 1858. He served as a curate in Trombolo for nine years before beginning an eight-year pastorate at Salzano. He was chancellor of the Treviso diocese from Nov. 1875, and bishop of Mantua from 1884 until 1893. He was cardinal-patriarch of Venice from that year until his election to the papacy by the conclave held from July 31 to Aug. 4, 1903.

Aims: Pius's principal objectives as pope were "to restore all things in Christ, in order that Christ may be all and in all," and "to teach (and defend) Christian truth and law."

Canonizations, Encyclicals: He canonized four saints and issued 16 encyclicals. One of the encyclicals was issued in commemoration of the 50th anniversary of the proclamation of the dogma of the Immaculate Conception of Mary.

Catechetics: He introduced a whole new era of religious instruction and formation with the encyclical *Acerbo Nimis* of Apr. 15, 1905, in which he called for vigor in establishing and conducting parochial programs of the Confraternity of Christian Doctrine.

Catholic Action: He outlined the role of official Catholic Action in two encyclicals in 1905 and 1906. Favoring organized action by Catholics themselves, he had serious reservations about interconfessional collaboration.

He stoutly maintained claims to papal rights in the anticlerical climate of Italy. He authorized bishops to relax prohibitions against participation by Catholics in some Italian elections.

Church Administration: With the *motu proprio*

Arduum Sane of Mar. 19, 1904, he inaugurated the work that resulted in the Code of Canon Law; the code was completed in 1917 and went into effect in the following year. He reorganized and strengthened the Roman Curia with the apostolic constitution *Sapienti Consilio* of June 29, 1908.

While promoting the expansion of missionary work, he removed from the jurisdiction of the Congregation for the Propagation of the Faith the Church in the United States, Canada, Newfoundland, England, Ireland, Holland and Luxembourg.

International Relations: He ended traditional prerogatives of Catholic governments with respect to papal elections, in 1904. He opposed anti-Church and anticlerical actions in several countries: Bolivia in 1905, because of anti-religious legislation; France in 1906, for its 1901 action in annulling its concordat with the Holy See, and for the 1905 Law of Separation by which it decreed separation of Church and state, ordered the confiscation of church property, and blocked religious education and the activities of religious orders; Portugal in 1911, for the separation of Church and state and repressive measures that resulted in persecution later.

In 1912 he called on the bishops of Brazil to work for the improvement of conditions among Indians.

Liturgy: "The Pope of the Eucharist," he strongly recommended the frequent reception of Holy Communion in a decree dated Dec. 20, 1905; in another decree, *Quam Singulari*, of Aug. 8, 1910, he called for the early reception of the sacrament by children. He initiated measures for liturgical reform with new norms for sacred music and the start of work on revision of the Breviary for recitation of the Divine Office.

Modernism: Pius was a vigorous opponent of "the synthesis of all heresies," which threatened the integrity of doctrine through its influence in philosophy, theology and biblical exegesis. In opposition, he condemned 65 of its propositions as erroneous in the decree *Lamentabili,* July 3, 1907; issued the encyclical *Pascendi* in the same vein, Sept. 8, 1907; backed both of these with censures; and published the Oath against Modernism in Sept. 1910, to be taken by all the clergy. Ecclesiastical studies suffered to some extent from these actions, necessary as they were at the time.

Pius followed the lead of Leo XIII in promoting the study of scholastic philosophy. He established the Pontifical Biblical Institute May 7, 1909.

His death, Aug. 20, 1914, was hastened by the outbreak of World War I. He was beatified in 1951 and canonized May 29, 1954. His feast is observed Aug. 21.

BENEDICT XV

Benedict XV (Giacomo della Chiesa) was born Nov. 21, 1854, in Pegli, Italy.

He was educated at the Royal University of Genoa and Gregorian University in Rome. He was ordained to the priesthood Dec. 21, 1878.

He served in the papal diplomatic corps from 1882 to 1907, as secretary to the nuncio to Spain from 1882 to 1887, as secretary to the papal secretary of state from 1887, and as undersecretary from 1901.

He was ordained archbishop of Bologna Dec. 22, 1907, and spent four years completing a pastoral visitation there. He was made a cardinal just three months before being elected to the papacy

Sept. 3, 1914. He died Jan. 22, 1922. Two key efforts of his pontificate were for peace and the relief of human suffering caused by World War I.

Canonizations: Benedict canonized three saints; one of them was Joan of Arc.

Canon Law: He published the Code of Canon Law, developed by the commission set up by St. Pius X, May 27, 1917; it went into effect the following year.

Curia: He made great changes in the personnel of the Curia. He established the Congregation for the Oriental Churches May 1, 1917, and founded the Pontifical Oriental Institute in Rome later in the year.

Encyclicals: He issued 12 encyclicals. Peace was the theme of three of them. In another, published two years after the cessation of hostilities, he wrote about child victims of the war. He followed the lead of Leo XIII in *Spiritus Paraclitus*, Sept. 15, 1920, on biblical studies.

International Relations: He was largely frustrated on the international level because of the events and attitudes of the war period, but the number of diplomats accredited to the Vatican nearly doubled, from 14 to 26, between the time of his accession to the papacy and his death.

Peace Efforts: Benedict's stance in the war was one of absolute impartiality but not of uninterested neutrality. Because he would not take sides, he was suspected by both the Allies and the Central Powers, and the seven-point peace plan he offered to all belligerents, Aug. 1, 1917, was turned down. The points of the plan were: recognition of the moral force of right; disarmament; acceptance of arbitration in cases of dispute; guarantee of freedom of the seas; renunciation of war indemnities; evacuation and restoration of occupied territories; examination of territorial claims in dispute.

Relief Efforts: Benedict assumed personal charge of Vatican relief efforts during the war. He set up an international missing persons bureau for contacts between prisoners and their families, but was forced to close it because of the suspicion of warring nations that it was a front for espionage operations. He persuaded the Swiss government to admit into the country military victims of tuberculosis.

Roman Question: Benedict prepared the way for the meetings and negotiations which led to settlement of the question in 1929.

PIUS XI

Pius XI (Ambrogio Damiano Achille Ratti) was born May 31, 1857, in Desio, Italy.

Educated at seminaries in Seviso and Milan, and at the Lombard College, Gregorian University and Academy of St. Thomas in Rome. He was ordained to the priesthood in 1879.

He taught at the major seminary of Milan from 1882 to 1888. Appointed to the staff of the Ambrosian Library in 1888, he remained there until 1911, acquiring a reputation for publishing works on paleography and serving as director from 1907 to 1911. He then moved to the Vatican Library, of which he was prefect from 1914 to 1918. In 1919, he was named apostolic visitor to Poland in Apr.

nuncio in June, and was made titular archbishop of Lepanto Oct. 28. He was made archbishop of Milan and cardinal June 13, 1921, before being elected to the papacy Feb. 6, 1922. He died Feb. 10, 1939.

Aims: The objective of his pontificate, as stated in the encyclical *Ubi Arcano*, Dec. 23, 1922, was to establish the reign and peace of Christ in society.

Canonizations: He canonized 34 saints, including the Jesuit Martyrs of North America, and conferred the title of Doctor of the Church on Sts. Peter Canisius, John of the Cross, Robert Bellarmine and Albertus Magnus.

Eastern Churches: He called for better understanding of the Eastern Churches in the encyclical *Rerum Orientalium* of Sept. 8, 1928 and developed facilities for the training of Eastern-Rite priests. He inaugurated steps for the codification of Eastern Church law in 1929. In 1935 he made Syrian Patriarch Tappouni a cardinal.

Encyclicals: His first encyclical, *Ubi Arcano*, in addition to stating the aims of his pontificate, blueprinted Catholic Action and called for its development throughout the Church. In *Quas Primas*, Dec. 11, 1925, he established the feast of Christ the King for universal observance. Subjects of some of his other encyclicals were: Christian education, in *Rappresentanti in Terra*, Dec. 31, 1929; Christian marriage, in *Casti Connubii*, Dec. 31, 1930; social conditions and pressure for social change in line with the teaching in *Rerum Novarum*, in *Quadragesimo Anno*, May 15, 1931; atheistic Communism, in *Divini Redemptoris*, Mar. 19, 1937; the priesthood, in *Ad Catholici Sacerdotii*, Dec. 20, 1935.

Missions: Following the lead of Benedict XV, Pius called for the training of native clergy in the pattern of their own respective cultures, and promoted missionary developments in various ways. He ordained six native bishops for China in 1926, one for Japan in 1927, and others for regions of Asia, China and India in 1933. He placed the first 40 mission dioceses under native bishops, saw the number of native priests increase from about 2,600 to more than 7,000, and the number of Catholics in missionary areas more than double from nine million.

In the apostolic constitution *Deus Scientiarum Dominus* of May 24, 1931, he ordered the introduction of missiology into theology courses.

Interfaith Relations: Pius was negative to the ecumenical movement among Protestants but approved the Malines Conversations, 1921-1926, between Anglicans and Catholics.

International Relations: Relations with the Mussolini government deteriorated from 1931 on, as indicated in the encyclical *Non Abbiamo Bisogno*, when the regime took steps to curb liberties and activities of the Church; they turned critical in 1938 with the emergence of racist policies. Relations deteriorated in Germany also from 1933 on, resulting finally in condemnation of the Nazis in the encyclical *Mit Brennender Sorge*, March 1937. Pius sparked a revival of the Church in France by encouraging Catholics to work within the democratic framework of the Republic rather than foment trouble over restoration of a monarchy. Pius was powerless to influence developments related to the civil war that erupted in Spain in July 1936, sporadic persecution and repression by the Calles

regime in Mexico, and systematic persecution of the Church in the Soviet Union. Many of the 10 concordats and two agreements reached with European countries after World War I became casualties of World War II.

Roman Question: Pius negotiated for two and a half years with the Italian government to settle the Roman Question by means of the Lateran Agreement of 1929. The agreement provided independent status for the State of Vatican City; made Catholicism the official religion of Italy, with pastoral and educational freedom and state recognition of Catholic marriages, religious orders and societies; and provided a financial payment to the Vatican for expropriation of the former States of the Church.

PIUS XII

Pius XII (Eugenio Maria Giovanni Pacelli) was born Mar. 2, 1876, in RomEducated at the Gregorian University and the Lateran University, in Rome, he was ordained to the priesthood Apr. 2, 1899.

He entered the Vatican diplomatic service in 1901, worked on the codification of canon law, and was appointed secretary of the Congregation for Ecclesiastical Affairs in 1914. Three years later he was ordained titular archbishop of Sardis and made apostolic nuncio to Bavaria. He was nuncio to Germany from 1920 to 1929, when he was made a cardinal, and took office as papal secretary of state in the following year. His diplomatic negotiations resulted in concordats between the Vatican and Bavaria (1924), Prussia (1929), Baden (1932), Austria and the German Republic (1933). He took part in negotiations that led to settlement of the Roman Question in 1929.

He was elected to the papacy Mar. 2, 1939. He died Oct. 9, 1958, at Castel Gandolfo after the 12th longest pontificate in history.

Canonizations: He canonized 34 saints, including Mother Frances X. Cabrini, the first U.S. citizen-saint.

Cardinals: He raised 56 prelates to the rank of cardinal in two consistories held in 1946 and 1953. There were 57 cardinals at the time of his death.

Church Organization and Missions: He increased the number of dioceses from 1,696 to 2,048. He established native hierarchies in China (1946), Burma (1955) and parts of Africa, and extended the native structure of the Church in India. He ordained the first black bishop for Africa.

Communism: In addition to opposing and condemning Communism on numerous occasions, he decreed in 1949 the penalty of excommunication for all Catholics holding formal and willing allegiance to the Communist Party and its policies. During his reign the Church was persecuted in some 15 countries that fell under communist domination.

Doctrine and Liturgy: He proclaimed the dogma of the Assumption of the Blessed Virgin Mary, Nov. 1, 1950 (apostolic constitution, *Munificentissimus Deus*).

In various encyclicals and other enactments, he provided background for the *aggiornamento* introduced by his successor, John XXIII: by his formulations of doctrine and practice regarding the Mystical Body of Christ, the liturgy, sacred music and biblical studies; by the revision of the Rites of Holy Week; by initiation of the work which led to the calendar-missal-breviary reform ordered into effect Jan. 1, 1961; by the first of several modifications of the Eucharistic fast; by extending the time of Mass to the evening. He instituted the feasts of Mary, Queen, and of St. Joseph the Worker, and clarified teaching concerning devotion to the Sacred Heart.

His 41 encyclicals and nearly 1,000 public addresses made Pius one of the greatest teaching popes. His concern in all his communications was to deal with specific points at issue and to bring Christian principles to bear on contemporary world problems.

Peace Efforts: Before the start of World War II, he tried unsuccessfully to get the contending nations — Germany and Poland, France and Italy — to settle their differences peaceably. During the war, he offered his services to mediate the widened conflict, spoke out against the horrors of war and the suffering it caused, mobilized relief work for its victims, proposed a five-point program for peace in Christmas messages from 1939 to 1942, and secured a generally open status for the city of Rome. He has been criticized in some quarters for not doing enough to oppose the Holocaust. This is a matter of historical debate, but it is a fact that through his direct intercession many thousands of Jews in Rome and Italy were saved from certain death, and he resisted wherever possible the threat of Nazism to human rights. Such were his contributions to assisting Jews that the rabbi of Rome, Dr. Abraham Zolli, was converted to Catholicism, and upon his death, Pius was praised by Golda Meir for his efforts. After the war, he endorsed the principles and intent of the U.N. and continued efforts for peace.

United States: Pius appointed more than 200 of the 265 American bishops resident in the U.S. and abroad in 1958, erected 27 dioceses in this country, and raised seven dioceses to archiepiscopal rank.

ST. JOHN XXIII

St. John XXIII (Angelo Roncalli) was born Nov. 25, 1881, at Sotto il Monte, Italy.

He was educated at the seminary of the Bergamo diocese and the Pontifical Seminary in Rome, where he was ordained to the priesthood Aug. 10, 1904.

He spent the first nine or 10 years of his priesthood as secretary to the bishop of Bergamo and as an instructor in the seminary there. He served as a medic and chaplain in the Italian army during World War I. Afterwards, he resumed duties in his own diocese until he was called to Rome in 1921 for work with the Society for the Propagation of the Faith.

He began diplomatic service in 1925 as titular archbishop of Areopolis and apostolic visitor to Bulgaria. A succession of offices followed: apostolic delegate to Bulgaria (1931-1935); titular archbishop of Mesembria, apostolic delegate to Turkey and Greece, administrator of the Latin vicariate apostolic of Istanbul (1935-1944); apostolic nuncio to France (1944-1953). On these missions, he was engaged in delicate negotiations involving Roman, Eastern Rite and Orthodox relations; the needs of people suffering from the consequences of World War II; and unsettling suspicions arising from wartime conditions.

He was made a cardinal Jan. 12, 1953, and three days later was appointed patriarch of Venice, the position he held until his election to the papacy Oct. 28, 1958. He died of stomach cancer June 3, 1963. His canonization was approved by Pope Francis in 2013.

John was a strong and vigorous pope whose influence far outmeasured both his age and the shortness of his time in the papacy. He was beatified by Pope John Paul II on Sept. 3, 2000 and canonized on Apr. 27, 2014 by Pope Francis.

Second Vatican Council: John announced Jan. 25, 1959, his intention of convoking the 21st ecumenical council in history to renew life in the Church, to reform its structures and institutions, and to explore ways and means of promoting unity among Christians. Through the council, which completed its work two and a half years after his death, he ushered in a new era in the history of the Church.

Canon Law: He established a commission Mar. 28, 1963, for revision of the Code of Canon Law. The revised Code was promulgated in 1983.

Canonizations: He canonized 10 saints and beatified Mother Elizabeth Ann Seton, the first native of the U.S. ever so honored. He named St. Lawrence of Brindisi a Doctor of the Church.

Cardinals: He created 52 cardinals in five consistories, raising membership of the College of Cardinals above the traditional number of 70; at one time in 1962, the membership was 87. He made the college more international in representation than it had ever been, appointing the first cardinals from the Philippines, Japan and Africa. He ordered episcopal ordination for all cardinals. He relieved the suburban bishops of Rome of ordinary jurisdiction over their dioceses so they might devote all their time to business of the Roman Curia.

Eastern Rites: He made all Eastern Rite patriarchs members of the Congregation for the Oriental Churches.

Ecumenism: He assigned to the Second Vatican Council the task of finding ways and means of promoting unity among Christians. He established the Vatican Secretariat for Promoting Christian Unity June 5, 1960. He showed his desire for more cordial relations with the Orthodox by sending personal representatives to visit Patriarch Athenagoras I June 27, 1961; approved a mission of five delegates to the General Assembly of the World Council of Churches which met in New Delhi, India, in Nov. 1961; and removed a number of pejorative references to Jews in the Roman-Rite liturgy for Good Friday.

Encyclicals: Of the eight encyclicals he issued, the two outstanding ones were Mater et Magistra ("Christianity and Social Progress"), in which he recapitulated, updated and extended the social doctrine stated earlier by Leo XIII and Pius XI; and Pacem in Terris ("Peace on Earth"), the first encyclical ever addressed to all men of good will as well as to Catholics, on the natural law principles of peace.

Liturgy: In forwarding liturgical reforms already begun by Pius XII, he ordered a calendar-missal-breviary reform into effect Jan. 1, 1961. He authorized the use of vernacular languages in the administration of the sacraments and approved giving Holy Communion to the sick in afternoon hours. He selected the liturgy as the first topic of major discussion by the Second Vatican Council.

Missions: He issued an encyclical on the missionary activity of the Church; established native hierarchies in Indonesia, Vietnam and Korea; and called on North American superiors of religious institutes to have one-tenth of their members assigned to work in Latin America by 1971.

Peace: John spoke and used his moral influence for peace in 1961 when tension developed over Berlin, in 1962 during the Algerian revolt from France, and later the same year in the Cuban missile crisis. His efforts were singled out for honor by the Balzan Peace Foundation. In 1963, he was posthumously awarded the U.S. Presidential Medal of Freedom.

BL. PAUL VI

Bl. Paul VI (Giovanni Battista Montini) was

born Sept. 26, 1897, at Concesio in northern Italy. Educated at Brescia, he was ordained to the priesthood May 29, 1920. He pursued additional studies at the Pontifical Academy for Noble Ecclesiastics and the Pontifical Gregorian University. In 1924 he began 30 years of service in the Secretariat of State; as undersecretary from 1937 until 1954, he was closely associated with Pius XII and was heavily engaged in organizing informational and relief services during and after World War II. He declined the offer of the cardinalate by Pope Pius XII.

Ordained archbishop of Milan Dec. 12, 1954, he was inducted into the College of Cardinals Dec. 15, 1958, by Pope John XXIII. Trusted by John, he was a key figure in organizing the first session of Vatican Council II and was elected to the papacy June 21, 1963, two days after the conclave began. He died of a heart attack Aug. 6, 1978.

Second Vatican Council: He reconvened the Second Vatican Council after the death of John XXIII, presided over its second, third and fourth sessions, formally promulgated the 16 documents it produced, and devoted the whole of his pontificate to the task of putting them into effect throughout the Church. The main thrust of his pontificate — in a milieu of cultural and other changes in the Church and the world — was toward institutionalization and control of the authentic trends articulated and set in motion by the council. He was scheduled to be beatified on Oct. 19, 2014.

Canonizations: He canonized 84 saints. They included groups of 22 Ugandan martyrs and 40 martyrs of England and Wales, as well as two Americans — Elizabeth Ann Bayley Seton and John Nepomucene Neumann.

Cardinals: He created 144 cardinals, and gave the Sacred College a more international complexion than it ever had before. He limited participation in papal elections to 120 cardinals under the age of 80.

Collegiality: He established the Synod of Bishops in 1965 and called it into session five times. He stimulated the formation and operation of regional conferences of bishops, and of consultative bodies on other levels.

Creed and Holy Year: On June 30, 1968, he issued a Creed of the People of God in conjunction with the celebration of a Year of Faith. He proclaimed and led the observance of a Holy Year from Christmas Eve of 1974 to Christmas Eve of 1975.

Diplomacy: He met with many world leaders, including Soviet President Nikolai Podgorny in 1967, Marshal Tito of Yugoslavia in 1971 and President Nicolai Ceausescu of Romania in 1973. He worked constantly to reduce tension between the Church and the intransigent regimes of Eastern European countries by means of a detente type of policy called Ostpolitik. He agreed to significant revisions of the Vatican's concordat with Spain and initiated efforts to revise the concordat with Italy. More than 40 countries established diplomatic relations with the Vatican during his pontificate.

Encyclicals: He issued seven encyclicals, three of which are the best known. In *Populorum Progressio* ("Development of Peoples") he appealed to wealthy countries to take "concrete action" to promote human development and to remedy imbalances between richer and poorer nations; this encyclical, coupled with other documents and related actions, launched the Church into a new depth of involvement as a public advocate for human rights and for humanizing social, political and economic policies. In *Sacerdotalis Caelibatus* ("Priestly Celibacy") he reaffirmed the strict observance of priestly celibacy throughout the Western Church. In *Humanae Vitae* ("Of Human Life") he condemned abortion, sterilization and artificial birth control, in line with traditional teaching and in "defense of life, the gift of God, the glory of the family, the strength of the people."

Interfaith Relations: He initiated formal consultation and informal dialogue on international and national levels between Catholics and non-Catholics — Orthodox, Anglicans, Protestants, Jews, Muslims, Buddhists, Hindus, and unbelievers. He and Greek Orthodox Patriarch Athenagoras I of Constantinople nullified in 1965 the mutual excommunications imposed by their respective churches in 1054.

Liturgy: He carried out the most extensive liturgical reform in history, involving a new Order of the Mass effective in 1969, a revised church calendar in 1970, revisions and translations into vernacular languages of all sacramental rites and other liturgical texts.

Ministries: He authorized the restoration of the permanent diaconate in the Roman Rite and the establishment of new ministries of lay persons.

Peace: In 1968, he instituted the annual observance of a World Day of Peace on New Year's Day. The most dramatic of his many appeals for peace and efforts to ease international tensions was his plea for "No more war!" before the U.N., Oct. 4, 1965.

Pilgrimages: A "Pilgrim Pope," he made pastoral visits to the Holy Land and India in 1964, the U.N. and New York City in 1965, Portugal and Turkey in 1967, Colombia in 1968, Switzerland and Uganda in 1969, and Asia, Pacific islands and Australia in 1970. While in Manila in 1970, he was stabbed by a Bolivian artist.

Roman Curia: He reorganized the central administrative organs of the Church in line with provisions of the apostolic constitution, *Regimini Ecclesiae Universae*, streamlining procedures for more effective service and giving the agencies a more international perspective by drawing officials and consultors from all over the world. He also instituted a number of new commissions and other bodies. Coupled with curial reorganization was a simplification of papal ceremonies.

JOHN PAUL I

John Paul I (Albino Luciani) was born Oct. 17, 1912, in Forno di Canale (now Canale d'Agordo) in northern Italy. Educated at the minor seminary in Feltre and the major seminary of the Diocese of Belluno, he was ordained to the priesthood July 7, 1935. He pursued further studies at the Pontifical Gregorian University in Rome and was awarded a doctorate in theology. From 1937 to 1947 he was vice rector of the Belluno seminary, where he taught dogmatic and moral theology, canon law and sacred art. Ordained bishop of Vittorio Veneto Dec. 27, 1958, he attended all sessions of the Second Vatican Council, participated in three assemblies of the Synod of Bishops (1971, 1974 and 1977), and was vice president of the Italian Bishops' Conference from 1972 to 1975. He was appointed archbishop and patriarch of Venice Dec. 15, 1969, and was inducted into the College of Cardinals Mar. 5, 1973.

He was elected to the papacy Aug. 26, 1978, on the fourth ballot cast by the 111 cardinals participating in the largest and one of the shortest conclaves in history. The quickness of his election was matched by the brevity of his pontificate of 33 days, during which he delivered 19 addresses. He died of a heart attack Sept. 28, 1978.

ST. JOHN PAUL II

Karol Josef Wojtyla was born May 18, 1920, in Wadowice, an industrial town near Cracow. He attended schools in Wadowice and in 1938 enrolled in the faculty of philosophy of the Jagiellonian University in Cracow, where he moved with his father. At the university he was active in the Studio 38 experimental theater group. In Oct. 1942, he began studies for the priesthood in the underground seminary maintained by Card. Adam Sapieha of Cracow. He was struck by an automobile Feb. 29, 1944, and hospitalized until Mar. 12. In Aug. of that year Card. Sapieha transferred him and the other seminarians to the Archbishop's Residence, where they lived and studied until war's end. Ordained a priest by the Cardinal on Nov. 1, 1946, he left Poland Nov. 15 to begin advanced studies in Rome at the Angelicum University (the Pontifical University of St. Thomas Aquinas). He subsequently earned doctorates in theology and philosophy and was a respected moral theologian and ethicist.

On July 4, 1958, Pope Pius XII named him auxiliary bishop to Abp. Eugeniusz Baziak, Apostolic Administrator of Cracow. Following Abp. Baziak's death in 1962, he became Vicar Capitular and then on Jan. 13, 1964, Abp. of Cracow. Abp. Wojtyla attended all four sessions of the Second Vatican Council, from 1962 to 1965, and helped draft Schema XIII, which became *Gaudium et Spes*, the Pastoral Constitution on the Church in the Modern World. He also contributed to *Dignitatis Humanae* (the "Declaration on Religious Freedom") and on the theology of the laity. Pope Paul VI created him a cardinal in the consistory of June 26, 1967, with the titular Roman church of S. Cesario in Palatio.

He was elected pope on Oct. 16, 1978. He was invested with the pallium, symbol of his office, on Oct. 22 in ceremonies attended by more than 250,000 people in St. Peter's Square. He was the first non-Italian pope since Adrian VI (1522-23) and the first Polish pope ever. At his election, he was the youngest pope since Pius IX (1846-78). On May 24, 1998, he became the longest-reigning pope elected in the 20th century, surpassing the 19 years, seven months and seven days of Pius XII (1939-58). (Leo XIII, who died in 1903, was pope for 25 years.) His pontificate was also the third longest in the history of the Church. He surpassed Pope Leo XIII (25 years, 5 months), and is behind only Bl. Pius IX (31 years, 7 months, 21 days) and St. Peter (precise dates unknown). His death on Apr. 2, 2005 at 9:37 p.m. in the Apostolic Palace in the Vatican came after two months of sharp decline from an infection. He was admitted to Gemelli Clinic, where he had been taken after the assassination attempt in 1981, on Jan. 30. His cause for canonization was opened soon after his passing as Pope Benedict XVI waived the customary five year waiting period. After confirmation of a miracle (a French nun was cured of Parkinson's Disease), the late pontiff was beatified in front of several million pilgrims at the Vatican on May 1, 2011. He was canonized on Apr. 27, 2014. His feast day is Oct. 22.

Foreign Pastoral Visits

He was the most-traveled pope in history. He covered over 750,000 miles during 104 pastoral visits outside Italy, over 146 within Italy, and 301 to the parishes of Rome. In all, he visited 129 countries and held talks with 1,022 heads of state or government. By the end of his pontificate, the Holy See had diplomatic relations with 174 states, as well as diplomatic relations with the European Union and Sovereign Military Order of Malta, and special relations with the Russian Federation and the PLO. His 104 trips outside Italy were as follows:

1979 Dominican Republic and Mexico, Jan. 5-Feb. 1; Poland, June 2-10; Ireland and the United States, Sept. 29-Oct. 7; Turkey, Nov. 28-30.

1980 Africa (Zaire, Congo Republic, Kenya, Ghana, Upper Volta, Ivory Coast), May 2-12; France, May 30-June 2; Brazil (13 cities), June 30-July 12; West Germany, Nov. 15-19.

1981 Philippines, Guam, and Japan, with stopovers in Pakistan and Alaska, Feb. 16-27.

1982 Africa (Nigeria, Benin, Gabon, Equatorial Guinea), Feb. 12-19; Portugal, May 12-15; Great Britain, May 28-June 2; Argentina, June 11-12; Switzerland, June 15; San Marino, Aug. 29; Spain, Oct. 31-Nov. 9.

1983 Central America (Costa Rica, Nicaragua, Panama, El Salvador, Guatemala, Belize, Honduras) and Haiti, Mar. 2-10; Poland, June 16-23; Lourdes, France, Aug. 14-15; Austria, Sept. 10-13.

1984 South Korea, Papua New Guinea, Solomon Islands, Thailand, May 12; Switzerland, June 12-17; Canada, Sept. 9-20; Spain, Dominican Republic, and Puerto Rico, Oct. 10-12.

1985 Venezuela, Ecuador, Peru, Trinidad and Tobago, Jan. 26-Feb. 6; Belgium, The Netherlands, and Luxembourg, May 11-21; Africa (Togo, Ivory Coast, Cameroon, Central African Republic, Zaire, Kenya, and Morocco), Aug. 8-19; Liechtenstein, Sept. 8.

1986 India, Feb. 1-10; Colombia and Saint Lucia, July 1-7; France, Oct. 4-7; Oceania (Australia, New Zealand, Bangladesh, Fiji, Singapore, and Seychelles), Nov. 18-Dec. 1.

1987 Uruguay, Chile, and Argentina, Mar. 31-Apr. 12; West Germany, Apr. 30-May 4; Poland, June 8-14; the United States and Canada, Sept. 10-19.

1988 Uruguay, Bolivia, Peru, and Paraguay, May 7-18; Austria, June 23-27; Africa (Zimbabwe, Botswana, Lesotho, Swaziland, and Mozambique), Sept. 10-19; France, Oct. 8-11.

1989 Madagascar, Reunion, Zambia, and Malawi, Apr. 28-May 6; Norway, Iceland, Finland, Denmark, and Sweden, June 1-10; Spain, Aug. 19-21; South Korea, Indonesia, East Timor, and Mauritius, Oct. 6-16.

1990 Africa (Cape Verde, Guinea Bissau, Mali, and Burkna Faso), Jan. 25-Feb. 1; Czechoslovakia, Apr. 21-22; Mexico and Curaçao, May 6-13; Malta, May 25-27; Africa (Tanzania, Burundi, Rwanda, and Ivory Coast), Sept. 1-10.

1991 Portugal, May 10-13; Poland, June 1-9; Poland and Hungary, Aug. 13-20; Brazil, Oct. 12-21.

1992 Africa (Senegal, The Gambia, Guinea), Feb. 10-26; Africa (Angola, São Tome, and Principe), June 4-10; Dominican Republic, Oct. 10-14.

1993 Africa (Benin, Uganda, Sudan), Feb. 2-10; Albania, Apr. 25; Spain, June 12-17; Jamaica, Mexico, Denver (United States), Aug. 9-15; Lithuania, Latvia, Estonia, Sept. 4-10.

1994 Zagreb, Croatia, Sept. 10.
1995 Philippines, Papua New Guinea, Australia, Sri Lanka, Jan. 12-21; Czech Republic and Poland, May 20-22; Belgium, June 3-4; Slovakia, June 30-July 3; Africa (Cameroon, South Africa, Kenya), Sept. 14-20; United Nations and United States, Oct. 4-8.
1996 Central America (Guatemala, Nicaragua, El Salvador), Feb. 5-11; Tunisia, Apr. 17; Slovenia, May 17-19; Germany, June 21-23; Hungary, Sept. 6-7; France, Sept. 19-22.
1997 Sarajevo, Apr. 12-13; Czech Republic, Apr. 25-27; Lebanon, May 10-11; Poland, May 31-June 10; France, Aug. 21-24; Brazil, Oct. 2-5.
1998 Cuba, Jan. 21-25; Nigeria, Mar. 21-23; Austria, June 19-21; Croatia, Oct. 3-4.
1999 Mexico, Jan. 22-25; St. Louis, United States, Jan. 26-27; Romania, May 2-5; Poland June, 5-17; Slovenia, Sept. 19; India, Nov. 6-7; Georgia, Nov. 8-9.
2000 Egypt and Mount Sinai, Feb. 24-26; Holy Land, March 20-26; Fátima, May 12-13.
2001 Greece, Syria, and Malta, May 4-9; Ukraine, June 23-27; Kazakstan and Armenia, Sept. 22-27.
2002 Azerbaijan and Bulgaria, May 22-26; Toronto, Canada, July 23-28; Guatemala City, July 29-30; Mexico City, July 31-Aug. 2; Poland, Aug. 16-19.
2003 Spain, May 3-4; Croatia, June 5-9; Bosnia-Herzegovina, June 22; Slovak Republic, Sept. 11-14.
2004 Switzerland, May 5-6; Lourdes, France, Aug. 15-16.

Encyclicals and Other Writings

Certainly he was the pope most prolific in literary output, having issued 14 encyclicals, 14 apostolic exhortations, 11 apostolic constitutions, 45 apostolic letters and 30 *motu proprio*.

Pope John Paul's first encyclical, *Redemptor Hominis* (1979), set the tone for and in general terms indicated the subject matter of many of the documents to follow. Among his other publications were: *Catechesi Tradendae*, a post-synodal apostolic exhortation on catechesis, 1979; apostolic letter proclaiming Sts. Cyril and Methodius, together with St. Benedict, patrons of Europe, 1980; post-synodal apostolic exhortation *Familiaris Consortio*, on the family, 1981; apostolic letter *Caritatis Christi*, for the Church in China, 1982; letter for the 500th anniversary of the birth of Martin Luther, 1983; apostolic letter *Salvifici Doloris* ("On the Christian Meaning of Suffering"), apostolic exhortation *Redemptionis Donum*, to men and women religious, apostolic letters *Redemptionis Anno*, on Jerusalem, and *Les Grands Mysteres*, on Lebanon, and post-synodal apostolic exhortation *Reconciliatio et Poenitentia* ("Reconciliation and Penance"), all 1984.

Also: apostolic letter *Dilecti Amici*, on the occasion of the United Nations' International Year of Youth, 1985; apostolic letter *Euntes in Mundum*, for the millennium of Christianity in Kievan Rus', and apostolic letter *Mulieris Dignitatem* ("On the Dignity and Vocation of Women"), all 1988; post-synodal apostolic exhortation *Christifideles Laici* ("The Lay Members of Christ's Faithful People") and apostolic exhortation *Redemptoris Custos* ("On St. Joseph"), 1989; post-synodal apostolic exhortation *Pastores Dabo Vobis* ("I Give You Shepherds"), 1992; "Letter to Families," for the International Year of the Family, "Letter on the International Conference on Population and Development" in Cairo, apostolic letter *Ordinatio Sacerdotalis* ("On Reserving Priestly Ordination to Men Alone"), apostolic letter *Tertio Millennio Adveniente*, on preparation for the Jubilee Year 2000, and "Letter to Children in the Year of the Family," all 1994.

Also: apostolic letter *Orientale Lumen* ("The Light of the East"), on Catholic-Orthodox relations, "Letter to Women," post-synodal apostolic exhortations *Ecclesia in Africa, Ecclesia in Asia*, and *Ecclesia in Europa*, and apostolic letter for the fourth centenary of the Union of Brest, all 1995; apostolic constitution *Universi Dominici Gregis* ("On the Vacancy of the Apostolic See and the Election of the Roman Pontiff"), post-synodal apostolic exhortation *Vita Consecrata* ("On the Consecrated Life and Its Mission in the Church and in the World"), and apostolic letter on the 350th anniversary of the Union of Uzhorod, all 1996; post-synodal apostolic exhortation, "A New Hope for Lebanon," 1997; *Incarnationis Mysterium*, Bull of Indiction of the Great Jubilee of the Year 2000, 1998; and the apostolic letter *Misericordia Dei* ("On Certain Aspects of the Celebration of the Sacrament of Penance"), 2002.

In his years as pope he published several books, including *Crossing the Threshold of Hope* (1994), *Gift and Mystery: On the Fiftieth Anniversary of My Priestly Ordination* (1996), and *Alzatevi, andiamo (Get Up, Let Us Go*, 2004), on the pontiff's 20 years as a bishop in Poland.

Issues and Activities

Communism: Many students of the complex fall of communism in Eastern Europe credit John Paul with a central role. His visits to his Polish homeland in 1979 (June 2-10) and 1983 (June 16-23) bolstered Polish Catholicism and kindled Polish resistance to communism, while his determined support for the Solidarity labor movement gave his countrymen a vehicle for their resistance. The result was a growing nonviolent liberation movement leading to the dramatic developments of 1989—the collapse of communist regimes, the emergence of democracy in Poland and other countries, the fall of the Berlin Wall, and, in time, to the breakup of the Soviet Union and the end of the Cold War. Dramatic in a much different way was the 1981 attempt on the Pope's life. At 5:19 p.m. on May 13, as he greeted crowds in St. Peter's Square before his Wednesday general audience, a Turkish terrorist named Mehmet Ali Agca shot John Paul at close range. Whether the assassin acted alone or at the behest of others—and which others—remain unanswered questions. Following a six-hour operation, John Paul was hospitalized for 77 days at Gemelli Hospital. He visited Ali Agca in the Rebibbia prison on Dec. 27, 1983.

Doctrinal Concerns: The integrity of Catholic doctrine was a major concern of Pope John Paul. On Nov. 25, 1981, he appointed Archbishop—later, Cardinal and Pope Benedict XVI—Joseph Ratzinger of Munich-Freising, a prominent theologian, Prefect of the Congregation for the Doctrine of the Faith. The congregation under Card. Ratzinger has published important documents on bioethics, liberation theology (1984 and 1986), the Church's inability to ordain women as priests, the latter affirming that the teaching on this matter has been "set forth infallibly" (1995), and same-sex unions (2003).

Catechism: One of Pope John Paul's most important initiatives was the *Catechism of the Catholic Church*. The idea for this up-to-date compendium was broached at the extraordinary assembly of the Synod of Bishops held in 1985 to evaluate the implementation of Vatican Council II. The pope approved, and the project went forward under a commission of cardinals headed by Card. Ratzinger. Published in 1992 by authorization of John Paul II (the original was in French, with the English translation appearing in 1994 and the authoritative Latin *editio typica* in 1997), this first catechism for the universal Church in four centuries is crucial to the hoped-for renewal of catechesis.

Canon Law: John Paul oversaw the completion of the revision of the Code of Canon Law begun in 1959 at the direction of Pope John XXIII. He promulgated the new code on Jan. 25, 1983; it went into effect on Nov. 27 of that year. In *Sacrae Disciplinae Leges*, the apostolic constitution accompanying the revised code, the pope says it has "one and the same intention" as Vatican Council II — whose convening John XXIII announced at the same time — namely, "the renewal of Christian living."

On Apr. 18, 1990, John Paul promulgated the Code of Canons for the Eastern Churches. Although particular sections of the Eastern code appeared at various times dating back to 1949, this was the first time an integrated code of law for the Eastern Churches had been issued in its entirety.

Ecumenical and Interreligious Relations: He was the first pope ever to visit a synagogue (Rome, April 1986) and the first to visit a mosque (Omayyad Great Mosque of Damascus, May 2001). Two of his major documents, the encyclical *Ut Unum Sint* and the apostolic letter *Orientale Lumen*, both published in 1995, deal with these matters.

The Holy See formally initiated diplomatic relations with the State of Israel at the level of apostolic nunciature and embassy on June 15, 1994. In Mar. 1998, the Commission for Religious Relations with the Jews published an important document on the roots of the World War II Jewish Holocaust entitled *We Remember: A Reflection on the Shoah.* In a letter dated Mar. 12 to the commission chairman, Card. Edward Idris Cassidy, the Pope expressed "fervent hope" that it would "help to heal the wounds of past misunderstandings and injustices."

On Sunday, Mar. 12, 2000, Pope John Paul II presided over a day of pardon for those sins committed by members of the Church over the centuries. The Holy Father issued a formal apology for the misdeeds of the members of the Church in the past, including a renewed apology for all anti-Semitic actions by Catholics. This apology was given even greater depth by the Holy Father's trip to the Holy Land in Mar. 2000. During his historic visit to Israel, the pope placed a written apology to the Jewish people in the Wailing Wall in Jerusalem. He made further efforts at ecumenical dialogue with the Orthodox Churches during his visits to Greece, Syria, and Ukraine in 2001 and at the Day of Prayer for Peace at Assisi in Jan. 2002.

Women's Concerns: Pope John Paul's insistence that, in fidelity to the will of Christ, the Church is unable to ordain women as priests put him at odds with some feminists, as did his opposition to abortion and contraception. But it is clear from his writings that he was unusually sensitive to women's issues, and he was a strong defender of women's dignity and rights, about which he often has spoken. In 1995 he appointed a woman, Professor Mary Ann Glendon of the Harvard University Law School, head of the Holy See's delegation to the fourth U.N. conference on women, held in Beijing Sept. 4-15, the first time a woman had been named to such a post.

World Affairs: At least since Jan. 1979, when he accepted a request for mediation in a border conflict between Argentina and Chile, John Paul II worked for peace in many parts of the world. He supported efforts to achieve reconciliation between conflicting parties in troubled areas like Lebanon, the Balkans, and the Persian Gulf, where he sought to avert the Gulf War of 1991. He advocated religious liberty and human rights during pastoral visits to many countries, including Cuba and Nigeria in 1998. Among the notable ecumenical and interreligious events of the pontificate was the World Day of Prayer for Peace on Oct. 27, 1986, which he convoked in Assisi and attended along with representatives of numerous other churches and religious groups.

In 1984 the Holy See and the U.S. established diplomatic relations. (The pope has met with Presidents Jimmy Carter, Ronald Reagan, George Bush, Bill Clinton, and George W. Bush.) Relations with Poland were re-established in 1989. Diplomatic relations were established with the Soviet Union in 1990 and with the Russian Federation in 1992.

Administration: Under Pope John Paul II the long-term financial problems of the Holy See were addressed and brought under control. Finances were on the agenda at the first plenary assembly of the College of Cardinals, Nov. 5-9, 1979, and subsequent meetings of that body. A council of cardinals for the study of organizational and economic problems of the Holy See was established in 1981. In 1988, the Holy See's financial report (for 1986) was published for the first time, along with the 1988 budget. In Apr. 1991, a meeting of the presidents of episcopal conferences was held to discuss ways of increasing the Peter's Pence Collection taken in support of the Pope.

A reorganization of responsibilities of Vatican offices was carried out in 1984, and in 1988 an apostolic constitution, *Pastor Bonus*, on reform of the Roman Curia was issued. A Vatican labor office was instituted in 1989. Pope John Paul established a new Pontifical Academy of Social Sciences in 1994 and Pontifical Academy for Life in 1995. On Apr. 8, 1994, he celebrated Mass in the Sistine Chapel for the unveiling of the Michelangelo frescoes, which had been painstakingly cleaned and restored. The opening presentation of the Holy See's Internet site took place on Mar. 24, 1997.

Canonizations: John Paul II proclaimed 1,338 Blesseds in 147 ceremonies and had proclaimed 482 Saints in 51 liturgical celebrations; his 17 predecessors from Pope Clement VIII to Pope Paul VI canonized a total of 302 people.

BENEDICT XVI

See separate entry, p. 232.

PAPAL ENCYCLICALS — BENEDICT XIV (1740) TO FRANCIS (2013-)

(*Source:* The Papal Encyclicals *[5 vols.], Claudia Carlen, I.H.M.; Pieran Press, Ann Arbor, MI. Used with permission.*)

An encyclical letter is a pastoral letter addressed by a pope to the whole Church. In general, it concerns matters of doctrine, morals or discipline, or significant commemorations. Its formal title consists of the first few words of the official text. Some encyclicals, notably *Pacem in Terris* by John XXIII, *Ecclesiam Suam* by Paul VI and several by John Paul II, have been addressed to people of good will in general as well as to bishops and the faithful in communion with the Church.

An encyclical epistle resembles an encyclical letter but is addressed only to part of the Church. The authority of encyclicals was stated by Pius XII in the encyclical *Humani Generis* Aug. 12, 1950: "Nor must it be thought that what is contained in encyclical letters does not of itself demand assent, on the pretext that the popes do not exercise in them the supreme power of their teaching authority. Rather, such teachings belong to the ordinary magisterium, of which it is true to say: 'He who hears you, hears me' (Lk 10:16); for the most part, too, what is expounded and inculcated in encyclical letters already appertains to Catholic doctrine for other reasons."

The Second Vatican Council declared: "Religious submission of will and of mind must be shown in a special way to the authentic teaching authority of the Roman Pontiff, even when he is not speaking *ex cathedra*. That is, it must be shown in such a way that his supreme magisterium is acknowledged with reverence, the judgments made by him are sincerely adhered to, according to his manifest mind and will. His mind and will in the matter may be known chiefly either from the character of the documents (one of which could be an encyclical), from his frequent repetition of the same doctrine, or from his manner of speaking" (Dogmatic Constitution on the Church, *Lumen Gentium*, No. 25).

The following list contains the titles and indicates the subject matter of encyclical letters and epistles. The latter are generally distinguishable by the limited scope of their titles or contents.

Benedict XIV (1740-58)

1740: *Ubi primum* (On the duties of bishops), Dec. 3.
1741: *Quanta cura* (Forbidding traffic in alms), June 30.
1743: *Nimiam licentiam* (To the bishops of Poland, on validity of marriages), May 18.
1745: *Vix pervenit* (To the bishops of Italy, on usury and other dishonest profit), Nov. 1.
1748: *Magnae Nobis* (To the bishops of Poland, on marriage impediments and dispensations), June 29.
1749: *Peregrinantes* (To all the faithful, proclaiming a Holy Year for 1750), May 5.
Apostolica Constitutio (On preparation for the Holy Year), June 26.
1751: *A quo primum* (To the bishops of Poland, on Jews and Christians living in the same place), June 14.
1754: *Cum Religiosi* (To the bishops of the States of the Church, on catechesis), June 26.
Quod Provinciale (To the bishops of Albania, on Christians using Mohammedan names), Aug. 1.
1755: *Allatae sunt* (To missionaries of the Orient, on the observance of Oriental rites), July 26.
1756: *Ex quo primum* (To bishops of the Greek rite, on the Euchologion), Mar. 1.
Ex omnibus (To the bishops of France, on the apostolic constitution, *Unigenitus*), Oct. 16.

Clement XIII (1758-69)

1758: *A quo die* (Unity among Christians), Sept. 13.
1759: *Cum primum* (On observing canonical sanctions), Sept. 17.
Appetente Sacro (On the spiritual advantages of fasting), Dec. 20.
1761: *In Dominico agro* (On instruction in the faith), June 14.
1766: *Christianae republicae* (On the dangers of anti-Christian writings), Nov. 25.
1768: *Summa quae* (To the bishops of Poland, on the Church in Poland), Jan. 6.

Clement XIV (1769-74)

1769: *Decet quam maxime* (To the bishops of Sardinia, on abuses in taxes and benefices), Sept. 21.
Inscrutabili divinae sapientiae (To all Christians,

proclaiming a universal jubilee), Dec.12.
Cum summi (Proclaiming a universal jubilee), Dec. 12.
1774: *Salutis nostra* (To all Christians, proclaiming a universal jubilee), Apr. 30.

Pius VI (1775-99)

1775: *Inscrutabile* (On the problems of the pontificate), Dec. 25.
1791: *Charitas* (To the bishops of France, on the civil oath in France), Apr. 13.

Pius VII (1800-1823)

1800: *Diu satis* (To the bishops of France, on a return to Gospel principles), May 15.

Leo XII (1823-29)

1824: Ubi primum (To all bishops, on Leo XII's assuming the pontificate), May 5.
Quod hoc ineunte (Proclaiming a universal jubilee), May 24.
1825: *Charitate Christi* (Extending jubilee to the entire Church), Dec. 25.

Pius VIII (1829-30)

1829: *Traditi humilitati* (On Pius VIII's program for the pontificate), May 24.

Gregory XVI (1831-46)

1832: *Summo iugiter studio* (To the bishops of Bavaria, on mixed marriages), May 27.
Cum primum (To the bishops of Poland, on civil obedience), June 9.
Mirari vos (On liberalism and religious indifferentism), Aug. 15.
1833: *Quo graviora* (To the bishops of the Rhineland, on the "pragmatic Constitution"), Oct. 4.
1834: *Singulari Nos* (On the errors of Lammenais), June 25.
1835: *Commissum divinitus* (To clergy of Switzerland, on Church and State), May 17.
1840: *Probe nostis* (On the Propagation of the Faith), Sept. 18.
1841: *Quas vestro* (To the bishops of Hungary, on mixed marriages), Apr. 30.
1844: *Inter praecipuas* (On biblical societies), May 8.

Pius IX (1846-78)

1846: *Qui pluribus* (On faith and religion), Nov. 9.
1847: *Praedecessores Nostros* (On aid for Ireland), Mar. 25.
Ubi primum (To religious superiors, on discipline for religious), June 17.
1849: *Ubi primum* (On the Immaculate Conception), Feb. 2.
Nostis et Nobiscum (To the bishops of Italy, on the Church in the Pontifical States), Dec. 8.
1851: *Exultavit cor Nostrum* (On the effects of jubilee), Nov. 21.
1852: *Nemo certe ignorat* (To the bishops of Ireland, on the discipline for clergy), Mar. 25.
Probe noscitis Venerabiles (To the bishops of Spain, on the discipline for clergy), May 17.
1853: *Inter multiplices* (To the bishops of France, pleading for unity of spirit), Mar. 21.
1854: *Neminem vestrum* (To clergy and faithful of Constantinople, on the persecution of Armenians), Feb. 2.
Optime noscitis (To the bishops of Ireland, on the proposed Catholic university for Ireland), Mar. 20.
Apostolicae Nostrae caritatis (Urging prayers for

peace), Aug. 1.

1855: *Optime noscitis* (To the bishops of Austria, on episcopal meetings), Nov. 5.

1856: *Singulari quidem* (To the bishops of Austria, on the Church in Austria), Mar. 17.

1858: *Cum nuper* (To the bishops of the Kingdom of the Two Sicilies, on care for clerics), Jan. 20.

Amantissimi Redemptoris (On priests and the care of souls), May 3.

1859: *Cum sancta mater Ecclesia* (Pleading for public prayer), Apr. 27.

Qui nuper (On Pontifical States), June 18.

1860: *Nullis certe verbis* (On the need for civil sovereignty), Jan. 19.

1862: *Amantissimus* (To bishops of the Oriental rite, on the care of the churches), Apr. 8.

1863: Quanto conficiamur moerore (To the bishops of Italy, on promotion of false doctrines), Aug. 10.

Incredibili (To the bishops of Bogota, on persecution in New Granada), Sept. 17.

1864: *Maximae quidem* (To the bishops of Bavaria, on the Church in Bavaria), Aug. 18.

Quanta cura (Condemning current errors), Dec. 8.

1865: *Meridionali Americae* (To the bishops of South America, on the seminary for native clergy), Sept. 30.

1867: *Levate* (On the afflictions of the Church), Oct. 27.

1870: *Respicientes* (Protesting the taking of the Pontifical States), Nov. 1.

1871: *Ubi Nos* (To all bishops, on Pontifical States), May 15.

Beneficia Dei (On the 25th anniversary of his pontificate), June 4.

Saepe Venerabiles Fratres (On thanksgiving for 25 years of pontificate), Aug. 5.

1872: *Quae in Patriarchatu* (To bishops and people of Chaldea, on the Church in Chaldea), Nov. 16.

1873: *Quartus supra* (To bishops and people of the Armenian rite, on the Church in Armenia), Jan. 6.

Etsi multa (On the Church in Italy, Germany and Switzerland), Nov. 21.

1874: *Vix dum a Nobis* (To the bishops of Austria, on the Church in Austria), Mar. 7.

Gravibus Ecclesiae (To all bishops and faithful, proclaiming a jubilee for 1875), Dec. 24.

1875: *Quod nunquam* (To the bishops of Prussia, on the Church in Prussia), Feb. 5.

Graves ac diuturnae (To the bishops of Switzerland, on the Church in Switzerland), Mar. 23.

Leo XIII (1878-1903)

1878: *Inscrutabili Dei consilio* (On the evils of society), Apr. 21.

Quod Apostolici muneris (On socialism), Dec. 28.

1879: *Aeterni Patris* (On the restoration of Christian philosophy), Aug. 4.

1880: *Arcanum* (On Christian marriage), Feb. 10.

Grande munus (On Sts. Cyril and Methodius), Sept. 30.

Sancta Dei civitas (On mission societies), Dec. 3.

1881: *Diuturnum* (On the origin of civil power), June 29.

Licet multa (To the bishops of Belgium, on Catholics in Belgium), Aug. 3.

1882: *Etsi Nos* (To the bishops of Italy, on conditions in Italy), Feb. 15.

Auspicato concessum (On St. Francis of Assisi), Sept. 17.

Cum multa (To the bishops of Spain, on conditions in Spain), Dec. 8.

1883: *Supremi Apostolatus officio* (On devotion to the Rosary), Sept. 1.

1884: *Nobilissima Gallorum gens* (To the bishops of France, on the religious question), Feb. 8.

Humanum genus (On Freemasonry), Apr. 20.

Superiore anno (On the recitation of the Rosary), Aug. 30.

1885: *Immortale Dei* (On the Christian constitution of states), Nov. 1.

Spectata fides (To the bishops of England, on Christian education), Nov. 27.

Quod auctoritate (Proclamation of extraordinary Jubilee), Dec. 22.

1886: *Iampridem* (To the bishops of Prussia, on Catholicism in Germany), Jan. 6.

Quod multum (To the bishops of Hungary, on the liberty of the Church), Aug. 22.

Pergrata (To the bishops of Portugal, on the Church in Portugal), Sept. 14.

1887: *Vieben noto* (To the bishops of Italy, on the Rosary and public life), Sept. 20.

Officio sanctissimo (To the bishops of Bavaria, on the Church in Bavaria), Dec. 22.

1888: *Quod anniversarius* (On his sacerdotal jubilee), Apr. 1.

In plurimis (To the bishops of Brazil, on the abolition of slavery), May 5.

Libertas (On the nature of human liberty), June 20.

Saepe Nos (To the bishops of Ireland, on boycotting in Ireland), June 24.

Paterna caritas (To the Patriarch of Cilicia and the archbishops and bishops of the Armenian people, on reunion with Rome), July 25.

Quam aerumnosa (To the bishops of America, on Italian immigrants), Dec. 10.

Etsi cunctas (To the bishops of Ireland, on the Church in Ireland), Dec. 21.

Exeunte iam anno (On the right ordering of Christian life), Dec. 25.

1889: *Magni Nobis* (To the bishops of the United States, on the Catholic University of America), Mar. 7.

Quamquam pluries (On devotion to St. Joseph), Aug. 15.

1890: *Sapientiae Christianae* (On Christians as citizens), Jan. 10.

Dall'alto Dell'Apostolico seggio (To the bishops and people of Italy, on Freemasonry in Italy), Oct. 15.

Catholicae Ecclesiae (On slavery in the missions), Nov. 20.

1891: *In ipso* (To the bishops of Austria, on episcopal reunions in Austria), Mar. 3.

Rerum novarum (On capital and labor), May 15.

Pastoralis (To the bishops of Portugal, on religious union), June 25.

Pastoralis officii (To the bishops of Germany and Austria, on the morality of dueling), Sept. 12.

Octobri mense (On the Rosary), Sept. 22.

1892: *Au milieu des sollicitudes* (To the bishops, clergy and faithful of France, on the Church and State in France), Feb. 16.

Quarto abeunte saeculo (To the bishops of Spain, Italy, and the two Americas, on the Columbus quadricentennial), July 16.

Magnae Dei Matris (On the Rosary), Sept. 8.

Inimica vis (To the bishops of Italy, on Freemasonry), Dec. 8.

Custodi di quella fede (To the Italian people, on Freemasonry), Dec. 8.

1893: *Ad extremas* (On seminaries for native clergy), June 24.

Constanti Hungarorum (To the bishops of Hungary, on the Church in Hungary), Sept. 2. *Laetitiae sanctae* (Commending devotion to the Rosary), Sept. 8.

Non mediocri (To the bishops of Spain, on the Spanish College in Rome), Oct. 25.

Providentissimus Deus (On the study of Holy Scripture), Nov. 18.

1894: *Caritatis* (To the bishops of Poland, on the Church in Poland), Mar. 19.

Inter graves (To the bishops of Peru, on the Church in Peru), May 1.

Litteras a vobis (To the bishops of Brazil, on the clergy in Brazil), July 2.

Iucunda semper expectatione (On the Rosary), Sept. 8.

Christi nomen (On the propagation of the Faith and Eastern churches), Dec. 24.

1895: *Longinqua* (To the bishops of the United States, on Catholicism in the United States), Jan. 6.

Permoti Nos (To the bishops of Belgium, on social conditions in Belgium), July 10.

Adiutricem (On the Rosary), Sept. 5.

1896: *Insignes* (To the bishops of Hungary, on the Hungarian millennium), May 1.

Satis cognitum (On the unity of the Church), June 29.

Fidentem piumque animum (On the Rosary), Sept. 20.

1897: *Divinum illud munus* (On the Holy Spirit), May 9.

Militantis Ecclesiae (To the bishops of Austria, Germany, and Switzerland, on St. Peter Canisius), Aug. 1.

Augustissimae Virginis Mariae (On the Confraternity of the Holy Rosary), Sept. 12.

Affari vos (To the bishops of Canada, on the Manitoba school question), Dec. 8.

1898: *Caritatis studium* (To the bishops of Scotland, on the Church in Scotland), July 25.

Spesse volte (To the bishops, priests, and people of Italy, on the suppression of Catholic institutions), Aug. 5.

Quam religiosa (To the bishops of Peru, on civil marriage law), Aug. 16.

Diuturni temporis (On the Rosary), Sept. 5.

Quum diuturnum (To the bishops of Latin America, on Latin American bishops' plenary council), Dec. 25.

1899: *Annum Sacrum* (On consecration to the Sacred Heart), May 25.

Depuis le jour (To the archbishops, bishops, and clergy of France, on the education of the clergy), Sept. 8.

Paternae (To the bishops of Brazil, on the education of the clergy), Sept. 18.

1900: *Omnibus compertum* (To the Patriarch and bishops of the Greek-Melkite rite, on unity among the Greek Melkites), July 21.

Tametsi futura prospicientibus (On Jesus Christ the Redeemer), Nov. 1.

1901: *Graves de communi re* (On Christian democracy), Jan. 18.

Gravissimas (To the bishops of Portugal, on religious orders in Portugal), May 16.

Reputantibus (To the bishops of Bohemia and Moravia, on the language question in Bohemia), Aug. 20.

Urbanitatis Veteris (To the bishops of the Latin church in Greece, on the foundation of a seminary in Athens), Nov. 20.

1902: *In amplissimo* (To the bishops of the United States, on the Church in the United States), Apr. 15.

Quod votis (To the bishops of Austria, on the proposed Catholic University), Apr. 30.

Mirae caritatis (On the Holy Eucharist), May 28.

Quae ad Nos (To the bishops of Bohemia and Moravia, on the Church in Bohemia and Moravia), Nov. 22.

Fin dal principio (To the bishops of Italy, on the education of the clergy), Dec. 8.

Dum multa (To the bishops of Ecuador, on marriage legislation), Dec. 24.

St. Pius X (1903-14)

1903: *E supremi* (On the restoration of all things in Christ), Oct. 4.

1904: *Ad diem illum laetissimum* (On the Immaculate Conception), Feb. 2.

Iucunda sane (On Pope Gregory the Great), Mar. 12.

1905: *Acerbo nimis* (On teaching Christian doctrine), Apr. 15.

Il fermo proposito (To the bishops of Italy, on Catholic Action in Italy), June 11.

1906: *Vehementer Nos* (To the bishops, clergy, and people of France, on the French Law of Separation), Feb. 11.

Tribus circiter (On the Mariavites or Mystic Priests of Poland), Apr. 5.

Pieni l'animo (To the bishops of Italy, on the clergy in Italy), July 28.

Gravissimo officio munere (To the bishops of France, on French associations of worship), Aug. 10.

1907: *Une fois encore* (To the bishops, clergy, and people of France, on the separation of Church and State), Jan. 6.

Pascendi dominici gregis (On the doctrines of the Modernists), Sept. 8.

1909: *Communium rerum* (On St. Anselm of Aosta), Apr. 21.

1910: *Editae saepe* (On St. Charles Borromeo), May 26.

1911: *Iamdudum* (On the Law of Separation in Portugal), May 24.

1912: *Lacrimabili statu* (To the bishops of Latin America, on the Indians of South America), June 7.

Singulari quadam (To the bishops of Germany, on labor organizations), Sept. 24.

Benedict XV (1914-22)

1914: *Ad beatissimi Apostolorum* (Appeal for peace), Nov. 1.

1917: *Humani generis Redemptionem* (On preaching the Word of God), June 15.

1918: *Quod iam diu* (On the future peace conference), Dec. 1.

1919: *In hac tanta* (To the bishops of Germany, on St. Boniface), May 14.

Paterno iam diu (On children of central Europe), Nov. 24.

1920: *Pacem, Dei munus pulcherrimum* (On peace and Christian reconciliation), May 23.

Spiritus Paraclitus (On St. Jerome), Sept. 15.

Principi Apostolorum Petro (On St. Ephrem the Syrian), Oct. 5.

Annus iam plenus (On children of central Europe), Dec. 1.

1921: *Sacra propediem* (On the Third Order of St. Francis), Jan. 6.

In praeclara summorum (To professors and students of fine arts in Catholic institutions of learning,

on Dante), Apr. 30.
Fausto appetente die (On St. Dominic), June 29.

Pius XI (1922-39)

1922: *Ubi arcano Dei consilio* (On the peace of Christ in the Kingdom of Christ), Dec. 23.

1923: *Rerum omnium perturbationem* (On St. Francis de Sales), Jan. 26.

Studiorum Ducem (On St. Thomas Aquinas), June 29.

Ecclesiam Dei (On St. Josaphat), Nov. 12.

1924: *Maximam gravissimamque* (To the bishops, clergy, and people of France, on French diocesan associations), Jan. 18.

1925: *Quas primas* (On the feast of Christ the King), Dec. 11.

1926: *Rerum Ecclesiae* (On Catholic missions), Feb. 28.

Rite expiatis (On St. Francis of Assisi), Apr. 30.

Iniquis afflictisque (On the persecution of the Church in Mexico), Nov. 18.

1928: *Mortalium animos* (On religious unity), Jan. 6.

Miserentissimus Redemptor (On reparation to the Sacred Heart), May 8.

Rerum Orientalium (On the promotion of Oriental Studies), Sept. 8.

1929: *Mens Nostra* (On the promotion of Spiritual Exercises), Dec. 20.

Quinquagesimo ante (On his sacerdotal jubilee), Dec. 23.

Rappresentanti in terra (On Christian education), Dec. 31. [Latin text, *Divini illius magistri*, published several months later with minor changes.]

1930: *Ad salutem* (On St. Augustine), Apr. 20.

Casti connubii (On Christian Marriage), Dec. 31.

1931: *Quadragesimo anno* (Commemorating the fortieth anniversary of Leo XIII's *Rerum novarum*, on reconstruction of the soical order), May 15.

Non abbiamo bisogno (On Catholic Action in Italy), June 29.

Nova impendet (On the economic crisis), Oct. 2.

Lux veritatis (On the Council of Ephesus), Dec. 25.

1932: *Caritate Christi compulsi* (On the Sacred Heart), May 3.

Acerba animi (To the bishops of Mexico, on persecution of the Church in Mexico), Sept. 29.

1933: *Dilectissima Nobis* (To the bishops, clergy, and people of Spain, on oppression of the Church in Spain), June 3.

1935: *Ad Catholici sacerdotii* (On the Catholic priesthood), Dec. 20.

1936: *Vigilanti cura* (To the bishops of the United States, on motion pictures), June 29.

1937: *Mit brennender Sorge* (To the bishops of Germany, on the Church and the German Reich), Mar. 14.

Divini Redemptoris (On atheistic communism), Mar. 19.

Nos es muy conocida (To the bishops of Mexico: on the religious situation in Mexico), Mar. 28

Ingravescentibus malis (On the Rosary) Sept. 29.

Pius XII (1939-58)

1939: *Summi Pontificatus* (On the unity of human society), Oct. 20.

Sertum laetitiae (To the bishops of the United States, on the 150th anniversary of the establishment of the hierarchy in the United States), Nov. 1.

1940: *Saeculo exeunte octavo* (To the bishops of Portugal and its colonies, on the eighth centenary of the independence of Portugal), June 13.

1943: *Mystici Corporis Christi* (On the Mystical Body of Christ), June 29.

Divino afflante Spiritu (On promoting biblical studies, commemorating the 50th anniversary of *Providentissimus Deus*), Sept. 30.

1944: *Orientalis Ecclesiae* (On St. Cyril, Patriarch of Alexandria), Apr. 9.

1945: *Communium interpretes dolorum* (To the bishops of the world, appealing for prayers for peace during May), Apr. 15.

Orientales omnes Ecclesias (On the 350th anniversary of the reunion of the Ruthenian Church with the Apostolic See), Dec. 23.

1946: *Quemadmodum* (Pleading for the care of the world's destitute children), Jan. 6.

Deiparae Virginis Mariae (To all bishops, on the possibility of defining the Assumption of the Blessed Virgin Mary as a dogma of faith), May 1.

1947: *Fulgens radiatur* (On St. Benedict), Mar. 21.

Mediator Dei (On the sacred liturgy), Nov. 20.

Optatissima pax (Prescribing public prayers for social and world peace), Dec. 18.

1948: *Auspicia quaedam* (On public prayers for world peace and solution of the problem of Palestine), May 1.

In multiplicibus curis (On prayers for peace in Palestine), Oct. 24.

1949: *Redemptoris nostri cruciatus* (On the holy places in Palestine), Apr. 15.

1950: *Anni Sacri* (On the program for combating atheistic propaganda throughout the world), Mar. 12.

Summi maeroris (On public prayers for peace), July 19.

Humani generis (Concerning some false opinions threatening to undermine the foundations of Catholic doctrine), Aug. 12.

Mirabile illud (On the crusade of prayers for peace), Dec. 6.

1951: *Evangelii praecones* (On the promotion of Catholic missions), June 2.

Sempiternus Rex Christus (On the Council of Chalcedon), Sept. 8.

Ingruentium malorum (On reciting the Rosary), Sept. 15.

1952: *Orientales Ecclesias* (On the persecuted Eastern Church), Dec. 15.

1953: *Doctor Mellifluus* (On St. Bernard of Clairvaux, the last of the fathers), May 24.

Fulgens corona (Proclaiming a Marian Year to commemorate the centenary of the definition of the dogma of the Immaculate Conception), Sept. 8.

1954: *Sacra virginitas* (On consecrated virginity), Mar. 25.

Ecclesiae fastos (To the bishops of Great Britain, Germany, Austria, France, Belgium, and Holland, on St. Boniface), June 5.

Ad Sinarum gentem (To the bishops, clergy, and people of China, on the supranationality of the Church), Oct. 7.

Ad Caeli Reginam (Proclaiming the Queenship of Mary), Oct. 11.

1955: *Musicae sacrae* (On sacred music), Dec. 25.

1956: *Haurietis aquas* (On devotion to the Sacred Heart), May 15.

Luctuosissimi eventus (Urging public prayers for peace and freedom for the people of Hungary), Oct. 28.

Laetamur admodum (Renewing exhortation for prayers for peace for Poland, Hungary, and especially for the Middle East), Nov. 1.

Datis nuperrime (Lamenting the sorrowful events in Hungary and condemning the ruthless use of force), Nov. 5.

1957: *Fidei donum* (On the present condition of the Catholic missions, especially in Africa), Apr. 21.

Invicti athletae (On St. Andrew Bobola), May 16.

Le pelerinage de Lourdes (Warning against materialism on the centenary of the apparitions at Lourdes), July 2.

Miranda prorsus (On the communications field, motion picture, radio, television), Sept. 8.

1958: *Ad Apostolorum Principis* (To the bishops of China, on Communism and the Church in China), June 29.

Meminisse iuvat (On prayers for persecuted Church), July 14.

St. John XXIII (1958-63)

1959: *Ad Petri Cathedram* (On truth, unity, and peace, in a spirit of charity), June 29.

Sacerdotii Nostri primordia (On St. John Vianney), Aug. 1.

Grata recordatio (On the Rosary, prayer for the Church, missions, international and social problems), Sept. 26.

Princeps Pastorum (On the missions, native clergy, lay participation), Nov. 28.

1961: *Mater et Magistra* (On Christianity and social progress), May 15.

Aeterna Dei sapientia (On the 15th centenary of the death of Pope St. Leo I, the see of Peter as the center of Christian unity), Nov. 11.

1962: *Paenitentiam agere* (On the need for the practice of interior and exterior penance), July 1.

1963: *Pacem in terris* (On establishing universal peace in truth, justice, charity, and liberty), Apr. 11.

Bl. Paul VI (1963-78)

1964: *Ecclesiam Suam* (On the Church), Aug. 6.

1965: *Mense maio* (On prayers during May for the preservation of peace), Apr. 29.

Mysterium Fidei (On the Holy Eucharist), Sept. 3.

1966: *Christi Matri* (On prayers for peace during Oct.), Sept. 15.

1967: *Populorum progressio* (On the development of peoples), Mar. 26.

Sacerdotalis caelibatus (On the celibacy of the priest), June 24.

1968: *Humanae vitae* (On the regulation of birth), July 25.

St. John Paul II (1978-2005)

1979: *Redemptor hominis* (On redemption and dignity of the human race), Mar. 4

1980: *Dives in misericordia* (On the mercy of God), Nov. 30.

1981: *Laborem exercens* (On human work), Sept. 14.

1985: *Slavorum Apostoli* (Commemorating Sts. Cyril and Methodius, on the 11th centenary of the death of St. Methodius), June 2.

1986: *Dominum et Vivificantem* (On the Holy Spirit in the life of the Church and the world), May 18.

1987: *Redemptoris Mater* (On the role of Mary in the mystery of Christ and her active and exemplary presence in the life of the Church), Mar. 25.

Sollicitudo Rei Socialis (On social concerns, on the 20th anniversary of *Populorum progressio*), Dec. 30.

1991: *Redemptoris missio* (On the permanent validity of the Church's missionary mandate), Jan. 22.

Centesimus annus (Commemorating the centenary of *Rerum novarum* and addressing the social question in a contemporary perspective), May 1.

1993: *Veritatis Splendor* (On fundamental questions on the Church's moral teaching), Aug. 6.

1995: *Evangelium Vitae* (On the value and inviolability of human life), Mar. 25.

Ut Unum Sint (On commitment to ecumenism), May 25.

1998: *Fides et Ratio* (On faith and reason), Oct. 1.

2003: *Ecclesia de Eucharistia* (Church of the Eucharist), April 17.

Benedict XVI (2005-13)

2005: *Deus Caritas Est* (God is Love), Dec. 25.

2007: *Spe Salvi* (Saved by Hope), Nov. 30.

2009: *Caritas in Veritate* (Charity in Truth), June 29.

Francis (2013-)

2013: *Lumen Fidei* (The Light of Faith), June 29.

CANONIZATIONS BY LEO XIII AND HIS SUCCESSORS

"Canonization" (*see* **Glossary**) is an infallible declaration by the pope that a person who suffered martyrdom and/or practiced Christian virtue to a heroic degree is in glory with God in heaven and is worthy of public honor by the universal Church and of imitation by the faithful.

Biographies of some of the saints listed below are given elsewhere in the **Almanac**; *see* **Index**; for biographies of all new saints for 2012-13, *see* **Saints**.

Leo XIII (1878-1903)

1881: Clare of Montefalco (d. 1308); John Baptist de Rossi (1698-1764); Lawrence of Brindisi (d. 1619).

1883: Benedict J. Labre (1748-83).

1888: Seven Holy Founders of the Servite Order; Peter Claver (1581-1654); John Berchmans (1599-1621); Alphonsus Rodriguez (1531-1617).

1897: Anthony M. Zaccaria (1502-39); Peter Fourier of Our Lady (1565-1640).

1900: John Baptist de La Salle (1651-1719); Rita of Cascia (1381-1457).

St. Pius X (1903-14)

1904: Alexander Sauli (1534-93); Gerard Majella (1725-55).

1909: Joseph Oriol (1650-1702); Clement M. Hofbauer (1751-1820).

Benedict XV (1914-22)

1920: Gabriel of the Sorrowful Mother (1838-62); Margaret Mary Alacoque (1647-90); Joan of Arc (1412-31).

Pius XI (1922-39)

1925: Thérèse of Lisieux (1873-97); Peter Canisius (1521-97); Mary Magdalen Postel (1756-1846); Mary Magdalen Sophie Barat (1779-1865); John Eudes (1601-80); John Baptist Vianney (Curé of Ars) (1786-1859).

1930: Lucy Filippini (1672-1732); Catherine Tomas (1533-74); Jesuit North American Martyrs; Robert Bellarmine (1542-1621); Theophilus of Corte (1676-1740).

1931: Albert the Great (1206-80) (equivalent canonization).

1933: Andrew Fournet (1752-1834); Bernadette Soubirous (1844-79).

1934: Joan Antida Thouret (1765-1826); Mary Michaeli (1809-65); Louise de Marillac (1591-1660); Joseph Benedict Cottolengo (1786-1842); Pompilius M. Pirotti, priest (1710-56); Teresa Margaret Redi (1747-70); John Bosco (1815-88); Conrad of Parzham (1818-94).

1935: John Fisher (1469-1535); Thomas More (1478-1535).

1938: Andrew Bobola (1592-1657); John Leonardi (c. 1550-1609); Salvatore of Horta (1520-67).

Pius XII (1939-58)

1940: Gemma Galgani (1878-1903); Mary Euphrasia Pelletier (1796-1868).

1943: Margaret of Hungary (d. 1270) (equivalent canonization).

1946: Frances Xavier Cabrini (1850-1917).

1947: Nicholas of Flüe (1417-87); John of Britto (1647-93); Bernard Realini (1530-1616); Joseph Cafasso (1811-60); Michael Garicoits (1797-1863); Jeanne Elizabeth des Ages (1773-1838); Louis Marie Grignon de Montfort (1673-1716); Catherine Labouré (1806-76).

1949: Jeanne de Lestonnac (1556-1640); Maria Josepha Rossello (1811-80).

1950: Emily de Rodat (1787-1852); Anthony Mary Claret (1807-70); Bartolomea Capitanio (1807-33); Vincenza Gerosa (1784-1847); Jeanne de Valois (1461-1504); Vincenzo M. Strambi (1745-1824); Maria Goretti (1890-1902); Mariana Paredes of Jesus (1618-45).

1951: Maria Domenica Mazzarello (1837-81); Emilie de Vialar (1797-1856); Anthony M. Gianelli (1789-1846); Ignatius of Laconi (1701-81); Francis Xavier Bianchi (1743-1815).

1954: Pope Pius X (1835-1914); Dominic Savio (1842-57); Maria Crocifissa di Rosa (1813-55); Peter Chanel (1803-41); Gaspar del Bufalo (1786-1837); Joseph M. Pignatelli (1737-1811).

1958: Herman Joseph, O. Praem. (1150-1241) (equivalent canonization).

St. John XXIII (1958-63)

1959: Joaquina de Vedruna de Mas (1783-1854); Charles of Sezze (1613-70).

1960: Gregory Barbarigo (1625-97) (equivalent canonization); John de Ribera (1532-1611).

1961: Bertilla Boscardin (1888-1922).

1962: Martin de Porres (1579-1639); Peter Julian Eymard (1811-68); Anthony Pucci, priest (1819-92); Francis Mary of Camporosso (1804-66).

1963: Vincent Pallotti (1795-1850).

Bl. Paul VI (1963-78)

1964: Charles Lwanga and Twenty-one Companions, Martyrs of Uganda (d. between 1885-87).

1967: Benilde Romacon (1805-62).

1969: Julia Billiart (1751-1816).

1970: Maria Della Dolorato Torres Acosta (1826-87); Leonard Murialdo (1828-1900); Therese Couderc (1805-85); John of Ávila (1499-1569); Nicholas Tavelic, Deodatus of Aquitaine, Peter of Narbonne and Stephen of Cuneo, martyrs (d. 1391); Forty English and Welsh Martyrs (d. 16th cent.).

1974: Teresa of Jesus Jornet Ibars (1843-97).

1975: Vicenta Maria Lopez y Vicuna (1847-90); Elizabeth Bayley Seton (1774-1821); John Masias (1585-1645); Oliver Plunket (1629-81); Justin de Jacobis (1800-60); John Baptist of the Conception (1561-1613).

1976: Beatrice da Silva (1424 or 1426-90); John Ogilvie (1579-1615).

1977: Rafaela Maria Porras y Ayllon (1850-1925); John Nepomucene Neumann (1811-60); Sharbel Makhlouf (1828-98).

St. John Paul II (1978-2005)

1982: Crispin of Viterbo (1668-1750); Maximilian Kolbe (1894-1941); Marguerite Bourgeoys (1620-1700); Jeanne Delanoue (1666-1736).

1983: Leopold Mandic (1866-1942).

1984: Paola Frassinetti (1809-92); 103 Korean Martyrs (d. between 1839-67); Miguel Febres Cordero (1854-1910).

1986: Francis Anthony Fasani (1681-1742); Giuseppe Maria Tomasi (1649-1713).

1987: Giuseppe Moscati (d. 1927); Lawrence (Lorenzo) Ruiz and 15 Companions, Martyrs of Japan (d. 1630s).

1988: Eustochia Calafato (1434-85); 117 Martyrs of Vietnam (96 Vietnamese, 11 Spanish, 10 French, included 8 bishops, 50 priests, 1 seminarian, 58 lay persons); Roque Gonzalez (1576-1628), Alfonso Rodriguez (1598-1628) and Juan de Castillo (1596-1628), Jesuit martyrs of Paraguay; Rose Philippine Duchesne (1796-1852); Simon de Rojas (1552-1624); Magdalen of Canossa (1774-1835); Maria Rosa Molas y Vollve (d. 1876).

1989: Clelia Barbieri (1847-70); Gaspar Bertoni (1777-1853); Richard Pampuri, religious (1897-1930); Agnes of Bohemia (1211-82); Albert Chmielowski (1845-1916); Mutien-Marie Wiaux (1841-1917).

1990: Marguerite D'Youville (1701-77).

1991: Raphael (Jozef) Kalinowski (1835-1907).

1992: Claude La Colombiere (1641-82); Ezequiel Moreno y Diaz (1848-1905).

1993: Marie of St. Ignatius (Claudine Thevenet) (1774-1837); Teresa "de los Andes" (Juana Fernandez Solar) (1900-20); Enrique de Ossó y Cervelló (1840-96).

1995: Jan Sarkander (1576-1620); Zdislava of Lemberk (d. 1252); Marek Krizin (1588-1619), Stefan Pongracz (1582-1619), Melichar Grodziecky (1584-1619), martyrs of Kosice; Eugene de Mazenod (1782-1861).

1996: Jean-Gabriel Perboyre (1802-40); Juan Grande Roman (1546-1600); Bro. Egidio Maria of St. Joseph (1729-1812).

1997: Hedwig (1371-99); John Dukla, O.F.M. (d. 1484).

1998: Edith Stein (d. 1942).

1999: Marcellin Joseph Benoit Champagnat (1789-1840); Giovanni Calabria (1873-1954); Agostina Livia Pietrantonio (1864-94); St. Cunegunda Kinga (1224-92); Cirilo Bertrán and Eight Companion Brothers of the Christian Schools (d. Oct. 9, 1934); Inocencio de la Immaculada (d. Oct. 9, 1934); St. Jaime Hilario Barbal (1889-1937); Benedetto Menni (1841-1914); Tommaso da Cori (1655-1729).

2000: Mary Faustina Kowalska (1905-38); María Josefa of the Heart of Jesus Sancho de Guerra (1842-1912); Cristóbal Magallanes and 24 Companions (d. 1915-28); José Maria de Yermo y Parres (1851-1904); Maria de Jesús Sacramentado Venegas (1868-1959); 120 Martyrs of China (17th-20th centuries); Katherine Drexel (1858-1955); Josephine Bakhita (d. 1947).

2001: Luigi Scrosoppi (1804-84); Agostino Roscelli

(1818-1902); Bernardo da Corleone (1605-67); Teresa Eustochio Verzeri (1801-52); Rafqa Petra Choboq Ar-Rayes (1832-1914); Giuseppe Marello (1844-95); Paula Montal Fornés de San José de Calasanz (1799-1889); Léonie Françoise de Sales Aviat (1844-1914); Maria Crescentia Höss (1682-1744).

2002: Alonso de Orozco (1500-91); Ignazio da Santhia (Lorenzo Maurizio Belvisotti) (1686-1770); Umile da Bisignano (Luca Antonio Pirozzo) (1582-1637); Paulina do Coracao Agonizante de Jesus (Amabile Visintainer) (1865-1942); Benedetta Cambiagio Frassinello (1791-1858); Pio da Pietrelcina (Padre Pio,1887-1968); Juan Diego Cuauhlatoatzin (16th century); Pedro de San Jose de Betancur (1619-67); Josemaria Escriva (1902-75).

2003: Pedro Poveda Castroverde (1874-1936); José María Rubio y Peralta (1864-1929); Genoveva Torres Morales (1870-1956); Angela de la Cruz (1846-1932); María Maravillas de Jesus (1891-1974); Jozef Sebastian Pelczar (1842-1924); Urszula Ledochowska (1865-1939); Maria de Mattias (1805-66); Virginia Centurione Bracelli (1587-1651); Daniel Comboni (1831-1881); Arnold Janssen (1837-1909); Josef Freinademetz (1852-1908).

2004: Gianna Beretta Molla (1922-1962); Nimatullah Kassab al-Hardini (1828-1858); Josep Manyanet Vives (1833-1901); Luigi Orione (1872-1940); Annibale Di Francia (1851-1927); Paola Elisabetta Cerioli (1816-1865).

Benedict XVI (2005-13)

2005: Józef Bilczewski (1860-1923); Gaetano Catanoso (1879-1963); Zygmunt Gorazdowski (1845-1920); Alberto Hurtado Cruchaga (1901-1952); Felix of Nicosia (1715-1787).

2006: Rafael Guízar Valencia (1878-1938); Filippo Smaldone (1848-1923); Rosa Venerini (1656-1728); Theodore Guérin (1798-1856).

2007: Antoñio de Sant Anna Galváo (1739-1822); George Preca (1880-1962); Simon of Lipnica

(c. 1435-1482); Karel Van Sint Andres Houben (1821-1893); Anne Marie Eugenie (1817-1898)

2008: Gaetano Errico (1791-1860); Mary Bernard (Verena) Bütler (1848-1924); Alphonsa of the Immaculate Conception (1910-1946); Narcisa de Jesús Martillo Morán (1832-1869).

2009: Arcangelo Tadini (1846-1912); Bernardo Tolomei (1272-1348); Nuno de Santa Maria Álvares Pereira (1360-1431); Geltrude Comensoli (1847-1903); Caterina Volpicelli (1839-1894); Zygmunt Szcznsny Felinski (1822-1895); Francisco Coll y Guitart (1812-1875) ; Josef Damien de Veuster (1840-1889); Rafael Arnáiz Barón (1911-1938); Jeanne Jugan (1792-1879).

2010: Stanislao Soltys (Kazimierczyk) (1433-1489); Andre Bessette (1845-1937); Candida Maria de Jesus Cipitria y Barriola (1845-1912); Mary of the Cross MacKillop (1842-1909); Giulia Salzano (1846-1929); Battista da Varano (1458-1524).

2011: Guido Conforti (1865-1931); Luigi Guanella (1842-1915); Bonifacia Rodriguez Castro (1837-1905).

2012: Marianne Cope (1838-1918); Kateri Tekakwitha (1656-1680); Giovanni Battista Piamarta (1841-1913); Jacques Berthieu (1838-1896); Carmen Salles y Barangueras (1848-1911); Peter Calungsod (1654-1672); Anna Schaffer (1882-1925).

Francis (2013-)

2013: Martyrs of Otranto (Antonio Primaldo and Companions, d. 1480); Laura Montoya Upegui (1874-1949); María Guadalupe García Zavala (1878–1963); Angela of Foligno (1248-1309); Peter Faber (1506-1546).

2014: José de Anchieta (1534–1597); Marie of the Incarnation (1599-1672); François-Xavier de Montmorency-Laval (1623-1708); Pope John XXIII (1881-1963); Pope John Paul II (1920-2005).

BEATIFICATIONS BY POPE ST. JOHN PAUL II, 1979-2004

1979: Margaret Ebner (Feb. 24); Francis Coll, O.P., Jacques Laval, S.S.Sp. (Apr. 29); Enrique de Ossó y Cervelló (Oct. 14; canonized June 16, 1993).

1980: José de Anchieta, Peter of St. Joseph Betancurt (canonized July 30, 2002), Francois de Montmorency Laval, Kateri Tekakwitha, Marie Guyart of the Incarnation (June 22); Don Luigi Orione (canonized May 16, 2004), Bartolomea Longo, Maria Anna Sala (Oct. 26).

1981: Sixteen Martyrs of Japan (Lorenzo Ruiz and Companions) (Feb 18; canonized Oct. 18, 1987); Maria Repetto, Alan de Solminihac, Richard Pampuri (canonized Nov. 1, 1989), Claudine Thevenet (canonized Mar. 21, 1993), Aloysius (Luigi) Scrosoppi (canonized June 10, 2001) (Oct. 4).

1982: Peter Donders, C.SS.R., Marie Rose Durocher, Andre Bessette, C.S.C., Maria Angela Astorch, Marie Rivier (May 23); Fra Angelico (equivalent beatification) (July); Jeanne Jugan, Salvatore Lilli and 7 Armenian Companions (Oct. 3); Sr. Angela of the Cross (Nov. 5; canonized May 3, 2003).

1983: Maria Gabriella Sagheddu (Jan. 25); Luigi Versiglia, Callisto Caravario (May 15); Ursula Ledochowska (canonized May 18, 2003) (June 20); Raphael (Jozef) Kalinowski (canonized Nov. 17, 1991), Bro. Albert (Adam Chmielowski), T.O.R. (June 22; canonized Nov. 12, 1989); Giacomo Cusmano, Jeremiah of Valachia, Domingo Iturrate Zubero (Oct. 30); Marie of Jesus

Crucified (Marie Bouardy) (Nov. 13).

1984: Fr. William Repin and 98 Companions (Martyrs of Angers during French Revolution), Giovanni Mazzucconi (Feb. 19); Marie Leonie Paradis (Sept. 11); Federico Albert, Clemente Marchisio, Isidore of St. Joseph (Isidore de Loor), Rafaela Ybarra de Villalongo (Sept. 30); José Manyanet y Vives (canonized May 16, 2004), Daniel Brottier, C.S.Sp., Sr. Elizabeth of the Trinity (Elizabeth Catez) (Nov. 25).

1985: Mercedes of Jesus (Feb. 1); Ana de los Angeles Monteagudo (Feb. 2); Pauline von Mallinckrodt, Catherine Troiani (Apr. 14); Benedict Menni (canonized Nov. 21, 1999), Peter Friedhofen (June 23); Anwarite Nangapeta (Aug. 15); Virginae Centurione Bracelli (canonized May 18, 2003) (Sept. 22); Diego Luis de San Vitores, S.J., Jose M. Rubio y Peralta, S.J. (canonized May 4, 2003), Francisco Garate, S.J. (Oct. 6); Titus Brandsma, O.Carm. (Nov. 3); Pio Campidelli, C.P., Marie Teresa of Jesus Gerhardinger, Rafqa Ar-Reyes (canonized June 10, 2001) (Nov. 17).

1986: Alphonsa Mattathupandatu of the Immaculate Conception, Kuriakose Elias Chavara (Feb. 8); Antoine Chevrier (Oct. 4); Teresa Maria of the Cross Manetti (Oct. 19).

1987: Maria Pilar of St. Francis Borgia, Maria Angeles of St. Joseph, Card. Marcellis Spinola y Maestre, Emmanuel

Domingo y Sol (Mar. 29); Teresa of Jesus "de los Andes" (canonized Mar. 21, 1993) (Apr. 3); Edith Stein (Teresa Benedicta of the Cross) (May 1; canonized, Oct. 11, 1998); Rupert Meyer, S.J. (May 3); Pierre-Francois Jamet, Cardinal Andrea Carlo Ferrari, Benedicta Cambiagio Frassinello, Louis Moreau (May 10); Carolina Kozka, Michal Kozal (June 10); George Matulaitis (Matulewicz) (June 28); Marcel Callo, Pierino Morosini, Antonia Mesina (Oct. 4); Blandina Marten, Ulricke Nische, Jules Reche (Bro. Arnold) (Nov. 1); 85 Martyrs (d. between 1584-1689) of England, Scotland and Wales (Nov. 22).

1988: Giovanni Calabria (canonized April 18, 1999), Joseph Nascimbeni (Apr. 17); Pietro Bonilli, Kaspar Stangassinger, Francisco Palau y Quer, Savina Petrilli (Apr. 24), Laura Vicuna (Sept. 3); Joseph Gerard (Sept. 11); Miguel Pro, Giuseppe Benedetto Dusmet, Francisco Faa di Bruno, Junipero Serra, Frederick Jansoone, Josefa Naval Girbes (Sept. 25); Bernardo Maria Silvestrelli, Charles Houben, Honoratus Kozminski (Oct. 16); Niels Stensen (Nicolaus Steno) (Oct. 23); Katharine Drexel (canonized Oct. 1, 2000), 3 Missionary Martyrs of Ethiopia (Liberato Weiss, Samuel Marzorati, Michele Pio Fasoli) (Nov. 20).

1989: Martin of St. Nicholas, Melchior of St. Augustine, Mary of Jesus of the Good Shepherd, Maria Margaret Caiani, Maria of Jesus Siedliska, Maria Catherine of St. Augustine (Apr. 23); Victoria Rasoamanarivo (Apr. 30); Bro. Scubilionis (John Bernard Rousseau) (May 2); Elizabeth Renzi, Antonio Lucci (June 17); Niceforo de Jesus y Maria (Vicente Diez Tejerina and 25 Companions (martyred in Spain), Lorenzo Salvi, Gertrude Caterina Comensoli, Francisca Ana Cirer Carbonell (Oct. 1); 7 Martyrs from Thailand (Philip Sipong, Sr. Agnes Phila, Sr. Lucia Khambang, Agatha Phutta, Cecilia Butsi, Bibiana Khampai, Maria Phon), Timothy Giaccardo, Mother Maria of Jesus Deluil-Martiny (Oct. 22); Giuseppe Baldo (Oct. 31).

1990: 9 Martyrs of Astoria during Spanish Civil War (De la Salle Brothers Cirilo Bertran, Marciano Jose, Julian Alfredo, Victoriano Pio, Benjamin Julian, Augusto Andres, Benito de Jesus, Aniceto Adolfo; and Passionist priest Innocencio Inmaculada; canonized Nov. 21, 1999), Mercedes Prat, Manuel Barbal Cosan (Bro. Jaime), Philip Rinaldi, Tommaso da Cori (canonized Nov. 21, 1999) (Apr. 29); Juan Diego (confirmation of Apr. 9 decree; canonized July 31, 2002), 3 Child Martyrs (Cristobal, Antonio and Juan), Fr. Jose Maria de Yermo y Parres (May 6; canonized May 21, 2001); Pierre Giorgio Frassati (May 20); Hanibal Maria Di Francia (canonized May 16, 2004), Joseph Allamano (Oct. 7); Marthe Aimee LeBouteiller, Louise Therese de Montaignac de Chauvance, Maria Schinina, Elisabeth Vendramini (Nov. 4).

1991: Annunciata Cocchetti, Marie Therese Haze, Clara Bosatta (Apr. 21); Jozef Sebastian Pelczar (June 2; canonized May 18, 2003); Boleslava Lament (June 5); Rafael Chylinski (June 9); Angela Salawa (Aug. 13); Edoardo Giuseppe Rosaz (July 14, Susa, Italy); Pauline of the Heart of Jesus in Agony Visentainer (canonized May 19, 2002) (Oct. 18, Brazil); Adolph Kolping (Oct. 27).

1992: Josephine Bakhita (canonized Oct. 1, 2000), Josemaria Escriva de Balaguer (May 17; canonized Oct. 6, 2000); Francesco Spinelli (June 21, Caravaggio, Italy); 17 Irish Martyrs, Rafael Arnáiz Barón, Nazaria Ignacia March Mesa, Léonie Françoise de Sales Aviat (canonized Nov. 25, 2001), and Maria Josefa Sancho de Guerra (canonized Oct. 1, 2000) (Sept. 27); 122 Martyrs of Spanish Civil War, Narcisa Martillo Morán (Oct.

25); Cristóbal Magellanes and 24 companions, Mexican martyrs (Nov. 22), and Maria de Jesús Sacramentado Venegas (Nov. 22; canonized May 21, 2000).

1993: Dina Belanger (Mar. 20); John Duns Scotus (Mar. 20, cult solemnly recognized); Mary Angela Truszkowska, Ludovico of Casoria, Faustina Kowalska (canonized Apr. 30, 2000), Paula Montal Fornés (canonized Nov. 25, 2001) (Apr. 18); Stanislaus Kazimierczyk (Apr. 18, cult solemnly recognized); Maurice Tornay, Marie-Louise Trichet, Columba Gabriel and Florida Cevoli (May 16); Giuseppe Marello (Sept. 26; canonized Nov. 25, 2001); Eleven martyrs of Almeria, Spain, during Spanish Civil War (2 bishops, 7 brothers, 1 priest, 1 lay person); Victoria Diez y Bustos de Molina, Maria Francesca (Anna Maria) Rubatto; Pedro Castroverde (canonized May 4, 2003), Maria Crucified (Elisabetta Maria) Satellico (Oct. 10).

1994: Isidore Bakanja, Elizabeth Canori Mora; Dr. Gianna Beretta Molla (Apr. 24; canonized May 16, 2004); Nicolas Roland, Alberto Hurtado Cruchaga, Maria Rafols, Petra of St. Joseph Perez Florida, Josephine Vannini (Oct. 16); Magdalena Caterina Morano (Nov. 5); Hyacinthe Marie Cormier, Marie Poussepin, Agnes de Jesus Galand, Eugenia Joubert, Claudio Granzotto (Nov. 20).

1995: Peter ToRot (Jan. 17); Mother Mary of the Cross MacKillop (Jan. 19); Joseph Vaz (Jan. 21); Rafael Guizar Valencia, Modestino of Jesus and Mary, Genoveva Torres Morales (canonized May 4, 2003), Grimoaldo of the Purification (Jan. 29); Johann Nepomuk von Tschiderer (Apr. 30); Maria Helena Stollenwerk, Maria Alvarado Cordozo, Giuseppina Bonino, Maria Domenica Brun Barbantini, Agostino Roscelli (May 7; canonized June 10, 2001); Damien de Veuster (June 4); 109 Martyrs (64 from French Revolution – Martyrs of La Rochelle – and 45 from Spanish Civil War), Anselm Polanco Fontecha, Felipe Ripoll Morata, and Pietro Casini (Oct. 1); Mary Theresa Scherer, Maria Bernarda Butler and Marguerite Bays (Oct. 29).

1996: Daniel Comboni (canonized Oct. 5, 2003) and Guido Maria Conforti (Mar. 17); Card. Alfredo Ildefonso Schuster, O.S.B., Filippo Smaldone and Gennaro Sarnelli (priests) and Candida Maria de Jesus Cipitria y Barriola, Maria Raffaella Cimatti, Maria Antonia Bandres (religious) (May 12); Bernhard Lichtenberg and Karl Leisner (June 23), Wincenty Lewoniuk and 12 companions, Edmund Rice, Maria Ana Mogas Fontcuberta and Marcelina Darowska (Oct 6); Otto Neururer, Jakob Gapp and Catherine Jarrige (Nov. 24).

1997: Bp. Florentino Asensio Barroso, Sr. Maria Encarnacion Rosal of the Sacred Heart, Fr. Gaetano Catanoso, Fr. Enrico Rebuschini and Ceferino Gimenez Malla, first gypsy beatified (May 4); Bernardina Maria Jablonska, Maria Karlowska (June 6); Frédéric Ozanam (Aug. 22); Bartholomew Mary Dal Monte (Sep. 27); Elías del Socorro Nieves, Domenico Lentini, Giovanni Piamarta, Emilie d'Hooghvorst, Maria Teresa Fasce (Oct. 12); John Baptist Scalabrini, Vilmos Apor, María Vicenta of St. Dorothy Chávez Orozco (Nov. 9).

1998: Bp. Vincent Bossilkov, María Sallés, Brigida of Jesus (Mar. 15); Fr. Cyprian Tansi (Mar. 22); Nimatullah al-Hardini (canonized May 16, 2004), 11 Spanish nuns (May 10); Secondo Polla (May 23); Giovanni Maria Boccardo, Teresa Grillo Chavez, Teresa Bracco (May 24); Jakob Kern, Maria Restituta Kafka, and Anton Schwartz (June 21); Giuseppe Tovini (Sept. 20); Card. Alojzije Stepinac (Oct. 3);

Antônio de Sant'Anna Galvão, Faustino Miguez, Zeferino Agostini, Mother Theodore Guérin (Oct. 25).

1999: Vicente Soler, and six Augustinian Recollect Companions, Manuel Martin Sierra, Nicolas Barre, Anna Schaeffer (Mar. 7); Padre Pio (May 2; canonized June 16, 2002); Fr. Stefan Wincenty Frelichowski (June 7); 108 Polish Martyrs, Regina Protmann, Edmund Bojanowski (June 13); Bp. Anton Slomsek (Sept. 19); Ferdinando Maria Baccilieri, Edward Maria Joannes Poppe, Arcangelo Tadini, Mariano da Roccacasale, Diego Oddi, Nicola da Gesturi (Oct. 3).

2000: André de Soveral, Ambrósio Francisco Ferro and 28 Companions, Nicolas Bunkerd Kitbamrung, Maria Stella Mardosewicz and 10 Companions, Pedro Calungsod and Andrew of Phú Yên (Mar. 5); Mariano de Jesus Euse Hoyos, Francis Xavier Seelos, Anna Rosa Gattorno, Maria Elisabetta Hesselblad, Mariam Thresia Chiramel Mankidiyan (Apr. 9); Jacinta and Francisco Marto of Fatima (May 13); Pope Pius IX, Pope John XXIII, Tommaso Reggio, Guillaume-Joseph Chaminade, Columba Marmion (Sept. 3).

2001: José Aparicio Sanz and 232 Companions of the Spanish Civil War (Mar. 11); Manuel Gonzalez Garcia, Marie-Anne Blondin, Caterina Volpicelli, Caterina Cittadini, Carlos Manuel Cecilio Rodriguez Santiago (Apr. 29); George Preca, Ignatius Falzon, Maria Adeodata Pisani (May 9); Abp. Józef Bilczewski and Fr. Sygmunt Gorazdowski, Ukrainian martyrs (June 27).

2002: Gaetano Errico, Lodovico Pavoni, Luigi Variara, Maria del Transito de Jesus Sacramentado, Artemide Zatti, Maria Romero Meneses (Apr. 14); Kamen Vitchev, Pavel Djidjov, Josaphat Chichkov (May 26); Juan Bautista and Jacinto de Los Angeles (Aug. 1); Zygmunt Szczêsny Feliñski, Jan Balicki, Jan Beyzym, Sancja Szymkowiak (Aug. 18); Daudi Okelo, Jildo Irwa, Andrea Giacinto Longhin, O.F.M. Cap., Marcantonio Durando, Marie de la Passion Hélène Marie de Chappotin de Neuville, Liduina Meneguzzi (Oct. 20).

2003: Pierre Bonhomme, María Dolores Rodríguez Sopeña, María Caridad Brader, Juana María Condesa Lluch, László Batthyány-Strattmann (Mar. 23); Eugenia Ravasco, Giacomo Alberione, Giulia Salzano, Marco d'Aviano, Maria Cristina Brando, Maria Domenica Mantovani (Apr. 27); Maria of Jesus Crucified Petkovic (June 6); Ivan Merz (June 22); Vasil' Hopko, Zdenka Schelingová (Sept. 14); Mother Teresa of Calcutta (Oct. 19); Juan Nepomuceno Zegrí y Moreno, Valentin Paquay, Luigi Maria Monti, Bonifacia Rodríguez Castro, Rosalie Rendu (Nov. 9).

2004: Luigi Talamoni, Matilde del Sagrado Corazón Téllez Robles, Piedad de la Cruz Ortiz Real, Maria Candida of the Eucharist (Mar. 21); Augusto Czartoryski, Laura Montoya, María Guadalupe García Zavala, Giulia Nemesia Valle, Eusebia Palomino Yenes, Alexandrina Maria da Costa (Apr. 25); Pere Tarrés i Claret, Alberto Marvelli, Pina Suriano (Sept. 5); Peter Vigne, Joseph-Marie Cassant, Anna Katharina Emmerick, Maria Ludovica De Angelis, Charles of Austria (Oct. 3).

BEATIFICATIONS UNDER POPE BENEDICT XVI (2005-13)

For biographical details of all those beatified in 2010-2011, please *see* under **Saints**.

2005: Ascensión of the Heart of Jesus, Marianne Cope (May 14); Wladyslaw Findysz, Bronislaw Markiewicz, Ignacy Klopotowski (June 19); Cardinal Clemens August von Galen (Oct. 9); Charles de Foucauld, Maria Pia Pastena, Maria Crocifissa Curcio, Eurosia Fabris (Nov. 13); María De Los Ángeles Ginard Martí, Josep Tàpies and six Companions (Oct. 29); Anacleto González Flores and 8 Companions, José Trinidad Rangel, Andrés Solá Molist, Leonardo Pérez, Darío Acosta Zurita (Nov. 20).

2006: Agostino Thevarparampil Kunjachan, Luigi Biraghi, Luigi Monza (Apr. 30); Maria Teresa of Saint Joseph (May 13); Sr. Maria of the Passion (May 14); Rita Amada of Jesus (May 28); Eustáquio von Lieshout (June 15); Sára Salkaházi, Moses Tovini (Sept. 17); Maria Teresa of Jesus (Oct. 8); Paul Josef Nardini, Margarita Maria López de Maturana (Oct. 22); Mariano de la Mata Aparicio (Nov. 5); Euphrasia of the Sacred Heart of Jesus Eluvathingal (Dec. 3).

2007: Luigi Boccardo (Apr. 14); Maria Maddalena of the Passion (Apr. 15); Francesco Spoto (Apr. 21) Maria Rosa Pellesi (Apr. 29); Carmen del Niño Jesús González Ramos García Prieto (May 6); Carlo Liviero (May 27); Basile-Antoine Marie Moreau (Sept. 15); Marie-Céline de la Présentation (Jeanne Germaine Castang), Stanislaw of Jesus and Mary (Jana Papczynski) (Sept. 16), Maria Luisa Merkert (Sept. 30), Albertina Berkenbrock (Oct. 20), Emmanuel Gómez González, Adílio Daronch (Oct. 21), Franz Jägerstätter (Oct. 26), Celina Chludzinska v. Borzecka (Oct. 27), Zepherin Namuncurá (Nov. 11), Antonio Rosmini (Nov. 18),

Lindalva Justo de Oliveira (Dec. 2).

2008: Sr. Giuseppina Nicoli (Feb. 3); Celestina of the Mother of God (Marianna Donati) (Mar. 30); Candelaria of St. Joseph (Apr. 27); Mary Magdalene of the Incarnation (May 3); Margaret Flesch (May 4); Martha Wiecka (May 24); Maria Giuseppina di Gesù Crocifisso (June 1); Jacques Ghazir Haddad (June 22); Josepha Hendrina Stenmanns (June 29); Vincenza Maria Poloni (Sept. 21); Michał Sopoko (Sept. 28); Giovanni Francesco Bonifacio (Oct. 4); Luís Martin and Zélia Guérin (Oct. 19); Peter Kibe Kasui and 187 Companions (Nov. 24); José Olallo Valdés (Nov. 29).

2009: Raphael Rafiringa (June 7); Émilie de Villeneuve (July 5); Eustachio Kugler (Oct. 4); Ciriaco Maria Sancha y Hervas (Oct. 18); Carlo Gnocchi (Oct. 25); Zoltan Lajos Meszlenyi (Oct. 31); Maria Alfonsina Danil (Nov. 22);

2010: Josep Samsó y Elias (Jan. 23); Bernardo Francisco de Hoyos (Apr. 18); Angelo Paoli (Apr. 25); José Tous y Soler (Apr. 25); Teresa Manganiello (May 22); Maria Pierina De Micheli; Jerzy Popieluszko (June 6); Manuel Lozano Garrido (June 12); John Henry Newman (Sept. 19); Chiara Badano (Sept. 25); Alfona Clerici (Oct. 23); Szilárd Ignác Bogdánffy (Oct. 30); Barbara Maix (Nov. 6).

2011: John Paul II (Karol Wojtyla) (May 1); Giustino Maria Russolillo (May 7); Georg Häfner (May 15); Maria Clara Galvão Meixa de Moura Telles (May 21); Dulce Lopes Pontes de Souza Brito (May 22); Maria Serafina Micheli (May 28); Juan de Palafox Mendoza (June 5); Alois Andritzki (June 13); Marguerite Rutan (June 19); Johannes Prassek and Two Companions (June 25); Serafino Morazzone, Clemente Vismara, Enrichetta Alfieri (June 26); Janos Scheffler (July 3); Elena Aiello (Sept. 14); Francesco Paleari (Sept. 17); Maria Jula Ivanisevic and Four Companions (Sept. 24); Antonia

Maria Verna (Oct. 2); Anna Maria Janer Anglarill (Oct. 8); Maria Catalina Echegeray (Oct. 29); Carl Lampert (Nov. 13); Francisco Esteban Lacal and 21 Companions (Dec. 17).
2012: Hildegard Burjan (Jan. 29); Maria Ines Teresa Arias Espinosa (Apr. 21); Giuseppe Toniolo (Apr. 29); Pierre-Adrien Toulorge (Apr. 29); Louise-Elisabeth de

Lamoignon (My 27); Jean-Jospeh Lataste (June 3); Cecilia Eusepi (June 17); Mariano Arciero (June 24); Louis Brisson (Sept. 22); Gabriele Maria Allegra (Sept. 29); Gabriele Maria Allegra (Sept. 29); Bedrich Bachstein and 13 Companions (Oct. 13); Maria Luisa Prosperi (Nov. 10); María Crescencia Pérez (Nov. 17); Maria Troncatti (Nov. 24); Devasahayam (Lazarus) Pillai (Dec. 2).

BEATIFICATIONS UNDER POPE FRANCIS (2013-)

2013: Cristóbal of Saint Catherine Fernández de Valladolid (Apr. 7); Luca Passi (Apr. 13); Nicolò Rusca (Apr. 21); Francisca de Paula de Jesus (May 4); Luigi Novarese (May 11); Giuseppe Puglisi (May 25); Zofia Czeska-Maciejowska (June 9); Margaret Lucja Szewczyk (June 9); Odoardo Focherini (June 15); Vladimir Ghika (Aug. 31); Antonio Franco (Sept. 2); Maria Bolognesi (Sept. 7); José Gabriel del Rosario Brochero (Sept. 14); Tommaso Olera (Sept. 21); Miroslav Bulešic (Sept. 28); Rolando Rivi (Oct. 5); Martyrs of the Religious Persecution

during the Spanish Civil War (Oct. 13); Sándor Istvan (Oct. 19); Maria Theresia Bonzel (Nov. 10).
2014: Maria Cristina of Savoy (Jan. 25); Giuseppe Girotti (Apr. 26); Anton Durcovici (May 17); Mario Vergara (May 24); Isidore Ngei Ko Lat (May 24); Maria Esperanza Alhama (May 31); Paul Yun Ji-Chung and 123 companions (Aug. 15); Giovannina Franks (Sept. 20); Alvaro del Portillo (Sept. 27); Teresa Demjanovich (Oct. 4); Francesco Zirano (Oct. 12); Pope Paul VI (Oct. 19); Maria Assunta Caterina Marchetti (Oct. 25).

ROMAN CURIA

The Roman Curia is the Church's network of central administrative agencies (called dicasteries) serving the Vatican and the local churches, with authority granted by the Pope.

The Curia evolved gradually from advisory assemblies or synods of the Roman clergy with whose assistance the popes directed church affairs during the first 11 centuries. Its original office was the Apostolic Chancery, established in the fourth century to transmit documents. The antecedents of its permanently functioning agencies and offices were special commissions of cardinals and prelates. Its establishment in a form resembling what it is now dates from the second half of the 16th century.

Pope Paul VI initiated a four-year reorganization study in 1963 that resulted in the constitution *Regimini Ecclesiae Universae.* The document was published Aug. 18, 1967, and went into full effect in March 1968. Pope John Paul II, in the apostolic constitution *Pastor Bonus,* published June 28, 1988, and effective Mar. 1, 1989, ordered modifications of the Curia based on the broad outline of Paul VI's reorganization.

In accordance with Pope John Paul II's reform effective Mar. 1, 1989, and later revisions, the Curia consists of the Secretariat of State, nine congregations (governing agencies), three tribunals (judicial agencies), 11 councils (promotional agencies) and three offices (specialized service agencies). All have equal juridical status with authority granted by the pope.

SECRETARIAT OF STATE

The Secretariat of State, *Palazzo Apostolico Vaticano,* Vatican City. Card. Pietro Parolin, Secretary of State; Most Rev. Giovanni Angelo Becciu, Deputy for General Affairs; Most Rev. Dominique Mamberti, Secretary for Relations with States.

The Secretariat of State provides the pope with the closest possible assistance in the care of the universal Church. It consists of two sections:

• The Section for General Affairs assists the pope in expediting daily business of the Holy See. It coordinates curial operations, prepares drafts of documents entrusted to it by the pope, has supervisory duties over the *Acta*

Apostolicae Sedis, Annuario Pontificio, the Vatican Press Office and the Central Statistics Office.

• The Section for Relations with States (formerly the Council for Public Affairs of the Church, a separate body) handles diplomatic and other relations with civil governments. Attached to it is a council of Cardinals and Bishops.

Background: Evolved gradually from secretarial offices (dating back to the 15th century) and the Congregation for Extraordinary Ecclesiastical Affairs (dating back to 1793; restructured as the Council for the Public Affairs of the Church by Paul VI in 1967). John Paul II gave it its present form in his June 28, 1988, reform of the Curia.

CONGREGATIONS

Congregation for the Doctrine of the Faith: Piazza del S. Uffizio 11, 00193 Rome, Italy. Card. Gerhard Ludwig Müller, prefect; Most Rev. Luis F. Ladaria Ferrer, S.J., secretary; Most Rev. Augustine Di Noia, O.P., adjunct secretary.

Has responsibility to safeguard the doctrine of faith and morals. Accordingly, it examines doctrinal questions and promotes studies thereon; evaluates theological opinions and, when necessary and after prior consultation with concerned bishops, reproves those regarded as opposed to principles of the faith; examines books on doctrinal matters and can reprove such works, if the contents so warrant, after giving authors the opportunity to defend themselves. It examines matters pertaining to the Privilege of Faith (Petrine Privilege) in marriage cases, and safeguards the dignity of the sacrament of penance. Attached to the congregation are the Pontifical Biblical Commission and the Theological Commission.

Background: At the beginning of the 13th century, legates of Innocent III were commissioned as the Holy Office of the Inquisition to combat heresy; the same task was entrusted to the Dominican Order by Gregory IX in 1231 and to the Friars Minor by Innocent IV from 1243 to 1254. On July 21, 1542 (apostolic constitution *Licet*), Paul III instituted a permanent congregation of cardinals with supreme and universal competence over matters concerning heretics and those suspected of heresy. Pius

IV, St. Pius V and Sixtus V further defined the work of the congregation. St. Pius X changed its name to the Congregation of the Holy Office. Paul VI (*motu proprio Integrae Servandae,* Dec. 7, 1965), began reorganization of the Curia with this body, to which he gave the new title, Congregation for the Doctrine of the Faith. Its orientation is not merely negative, in the condemnation of error, but positive, in the promotion of orthodox doctrine.

Congregation for the Oriental Churches: Palazzo del Bramante, Via della Conciliazione 34, 00193 Rome, Italy. Card. Leonardo Sandri, prefect; Most Rev. Cyril Vasil', S.J., secretary. Members include all patriarchs of the Eastern Catholic Churches and major archbishops.

Has competence in matters concerning the persons and discipline of Eastern Catholic Churches. It has jurisdiction over territories in which the majority of Christians belong to Eastern Churches (i.e., Egypt, the Sinai Peninsula, Eritrea, Northern Ethiopia, Southern Albania, Bulgaria, Cyprus, Greece, Iran, Iraq, Lebanon, Palestine, Syria, Jordan, Turkey, Afghanistan); also, over minority communities of Eastern Church members no matter where they live.

Background: Established by Pius IX Jan. 6, 1862 (apostolic constitution Romani Pontifices), and united with the Congregation for the Propagation of the Faith. The congregation was made autonomous by Benedict XV May 1, 1917 (motu proprio Dei Providentis), and given wider authority by Pius XI Mar. 25, 1938 (motu proprio Sancta Dei Ecclesia).

Congregation for Divine Worship and the Discipline of the Sacraments: Piazza Pio XII 10, 00193 Rome, Italy. Vacant, prefect; Most Rev. Arthur Roche, secretary.

Supervises everything pertaining to the promotion and regulation of the liturgy, primarily the sacraments, without prejudice to the competencies of the Congregation for the Doctrine of the Faith. Attached to the congregation are special commissions treating causes of nullity of sacred ordinations and dispensations from obligations of sacred ordination of deacons and priests.

Background: Originally two separate congregations: the Congregation for Divine Worship (instituted by Paul VI, May 8, 1969) and the Congregation for the Discipline of the Sacraments (established by St. Pius X, June 29, 1908, to replace the Congregation of Rites instituted by Pope Sixtus V in 1588). They were united by Paul VI, July 11, 1975, as the Congregation for the Sacraments and Divine Worship; reestablished as separate congregations by John Paul II in an autograph letter of Apr. 5, 1984, and reunited anew by the same Pope, June 28, 1988 (apostolic constitution Pastor Bonus), as the Congregation for Divine Worship and the Discipline of the Sacraments.

Congregation for the Causes of Saints: Piazza Pio XII 10, 00193 Rome, Italy. Card. Angelo Amato, S.D.B., prefect; Most Rev. Marcello Bartolucci, secretary.

Handles matters connected with beatification and canonization causes (in accordance with revised procedures decreed in 1983), and the preservation of relics.

Background: Established by Sixtus V in 1588 as the Congregation of Rites; affected by legislation of Pius XI in 1930; title changed and functions defined by Paul VI, 1969 (apostolic constitution Sacra Rituum Congregatio). It was restructured and canonization procedures were revised by John Paul II in 1983 (apostolic constitution Divinus Perfectionis Magister).

Congregation for Bishops: Piazza Pio XII 10, 00193 Rome, Italy. Card. Marc Ouellet P.S.S., prefect; Most Rev.

Ilson de Jesus Montanari, secretary.

Has functions related in one way or another to bishops and the jurisdictions in which they serve. It supervises the Pontifical Commission for Latin America. Attached to the congregation are a central coordinating office for Military Vicars (established Feb. 2, 1985) and an office for coordinating ad limina visits (established June 29, 1988).

Background: Established by Sixtus V Jan. 22, 1588 (apostolic constitution Immensa); given an extension of powers by St. Pius X June 20, 1908, and Pius XII Aug. 1, 1952 (apostolic constitution Exsul Familia); given present title (was known as Consistorial Congregation) by Paul VI (Aug. 1, 1967); competencies redefined by John Paul II, June 28, 1988.

Congregation for the Evangelization of Peoples: Piazza di Spagna 48, 00187 Rome, Italy. Card. Fernando Filoni, prefect; Most Rev. Savio Hon Tai-Fai, S.D.B., secretary; Most Rev. Protase Rugambwa, adjunct secretary.

Directs and coordinates missionary work throughout the world. Accordingly, it has competence over those matters which concern all the missions established for the spread of Christ's kingdom without prejudice to the competence of other congregations. These include: fostering missionary vocations; assigning missionaries to fields of work; establishing ecclesiastical jurisdictions and proposing candidates to serve them as bishops and in other capacities; encouraging the recruitment and development of indigenous clergy; mobilizing spiritual and financial support for missionary activity. To promote missionary cooperation, the congregation has a Supreme Council for the Direction of Pontifical Missionary Works composed of the Missionary Union of the Clergy and Religious, the Society for the Propagation of the Faith, the Society of St. Peter the Apostle for Native Clergy, the Society of the Holy Childhood, and the International Center of Missionary Animation.

Background: Originated as a commission of cardinals by St. Pius V and Gregory XII for missions in East and West Indies, Italo-Greeks and for ecclesiastical affairs in Protestant territories of Europe; Clement VIII instituted a Congregation of the Propagation of the Faith in 1599 which ceased to exist after several years. Erected as a stable congregation by Gregory XV June 22, 1622 (apostolic constitution Inscrutabili Divinae); its functions were redefined by John Paul II, June 28, 1988.

Congregation for the Clergy: Piazza Pio XII 3, 00193 Rome, Italy. Card. Beniamino Stella, prefect; Most Rev. Celso Morga Iruzubieta, secretary.

Has three offices with competencies concerning the life, discipline, rights and duties of the clergy; the preaching of the Word, catechetics, norms for religious education of children and adults; preservation and administration of the temporal goods of the Church. Attached to it are the International Council for Catechetics (established in 1973 by Paul VI) and the Institute Sacrum Ministerium for the permanent formation of the clergy (established in line with John Paul II's 1992 apostolic exhortation Pastores Dabo Vobis).

Background: Established by Pius IV Aug. 2, 1564 (apostolic constitution Alias Nos), under the title Congregation of the Cardinals Interpreters of the Council of Trent; affected by legislation of Gregory XIII and Sixtus V; known as Congregation of the Council until Aug. 15, 1967, when Paul VI renamed it the Congregation for the Clergy and redefined its competency; John Paul II gave it added responsibilities June 28, 1988.

Congregation for Institutes of Consecrated Life and Societies of Apostolic Life: Piazza Pio XII 3, 00193 Rome, Italy. Card. João Bráz de Aviz, prefect; Most Rev. Jose Rodriguez Carballo, O.F.M., secretary.

Has competence over institutes of Religious, secular institutes, societies of the apostolic life and third (secular) orders. With two sections, the congregation has authority in matters related to the establishment, general direction and suppression of the various institutes; general discipline in line with their rules and constitutions; the movement toward renewal and adaptation of institutes in contemporary circumstances; the setting up and encouragement of councils and conferences of major religious superiors for intercommunication, etc.

Background: Founded by Sixtus V May 27, 1586, with the title, Congregation for Consultations of Regulars; confirmed by the apostolic constitution Immensa Jan. 22, 1588; made part of the Congregation for Consultations of Bishops and other Prelates in 1601; made autonomous by St. Pius X in 1908 as Congregation of Religious; title changed to Congregation for Religious and Secular Institutes by Paul VI in 1967; given present title by John Paul II, June 28, 1988.

Congregation for Catholic Education (for Seminaries and Institutes of Study): Piazza Pio XII 3, 00193 Rome, Italy. Card. Zenon Grocholewski, prefect; Most Rev. Angelo Zani, secretary.

Has supervisory competence over institutions and works of Catholic education. It carries on its work through three offices. One office handles matters connected with the direction, discipline and temporal administration of seminaries, and with the education of diocesan clergy, religious and members of secular institutes. A second office oversees Catholic universities, faculties of study and other institutions of higher learning inasmuch as they depend on the authority of the Church; encourages cooperation and mutual assistance among Catholic institutions, and the establishment of Catholic hospices and centers on campuses of non-Catholic institutions. A third office is concerned in various ways with all Catholic schools below the college-university level, with general questions concerning education and studies, and with the cooperation of conferences of bishops and civil authorities in educational matters. The congregation supervises Pontifical Works for Priestly Vocations.

Background: The title (Congregation of Seminaries and Universities) and functions of the congregation were defined by Benedict XV Nov. 4, 1915; Pius XI, in 1931 and 1932, and Pius XII, in 1941 and 1949, extended its functions; Paul VI changed its title to Congregation for Catholic Education in 1967; given its present title by Pope John Paul II, June 28, 1988. Its work had previously been carried on by two other congregations erected by Sixtus V in 1588 and Leo XII in 1824.

Inter-Agency Curia Commissions

In accordance with provisions of the apostolic constitution *Pastor Bonus,* John Paul II established the following interdepartmental permanent commissions to handle matters when more than one agency of the Curia is involved in activities:

• For matters concerning appointments to local Churches and the setting up and alteration of them and their constitution (Mar. 22, 1989). Members include officials of the Secretariat of State and Congregation for Bishops. President, Card. Pietro Parolin, Secretary

of State.

• For matters concerning members, individually or as a community, of Institutes of Consecrated Life founded or working in mission territories (Mar. 22, 1989). Members include officials of the Congregations for the Evangelization of Peoples and for Institutes of Consecrated Life and Societies of Apostolic Life. President, Card. Fernando Filoni, prefect of the Congregation for the Evangelization of Peoples.

• For the formation of candidates for Sacred Orders (Mar. 22, 1989). Members include officials of the Congregations for Catholic Education, for Institutes of Consecrated Life and Societies of Apostolic Life, for Evangelization of Peoples, for Oriental Churches. President, Card. Zenon Grocholewski, prefect of the Congregation for Catholic Education.

• For promoting a more equitable distribution of priests throughout the world (July 20, 1991). Members include secretaries of congregations for Evangelization of Peoples, for the Clergy, Catholic Education, for the Institutes of Consecrated Life and Societies of Apostolic Life; and vice-president of Commission for Latin America. President, Card. Zenon Grocholewski, Prefect of the Congregation for Catholic Education.

• For the Church in Eastern Europe (Jan. 15, 1993), replacing the Pontifical Commission for Russia which was terminated. The commission is concerned with both Latin and Eastern-rite churches in territories of the former Soviet Union and other nations affected by the historical circumstances resulting from atheistic communism. It is responsible for promoting the apostolic mission of the Church and fostering ecumenical dialogue with the Orthodox and other Churches of the Eastern tradition. Members, under presidency of Cardinal Secretary of State, include the secretary and undersecretary of the Section for Relations with States and secretaries of Congregations for the Oriental Churches, for the Clergy, for Institutes of Consecrated Life and Societies of Apostolic Life, secretary of the Pontifical Council for Promoting Christian Unity. President, Card. Pietro Parolin.

Tribunals

Apostolic Penitentiary: Piazza della Cancelleria 1, 00186 Rome, Italy. Card. Mauro Piacenza, major penitentiary; regent, Most Rev. Krzysztof Jozef Nykiel.

Has jurisdiction for the internal forum only (sacramental and non-sacramental). It issues decisions on questions of conscience; grants absolutions, dispensations, commutations, sanations and condonations; has charge of non-doctrinal matters pertaining to indulgences.

Background: Origin dates back to the 12th century; affected by the legislation of many popes; radically reorganized by St. Pius V in 1569; jurisdiction limited to the internal forum by St. Pius X; Benedict XV annexed the Office of Indulgences to it Mar. 25, 1917.

Apostolic Signatura: Piazza della Cancelleria 1, 00186 Rome, Italy. Card. Raymond L. Burke, prefect; Most Rev. Frans Daneels, O. Praem., secretary.

The principal concerns of this supreme court of the Church are to resolve questions concerning juridical procedure and to supervise the observance of laws and rights at the highest level. It decides the jurisdictional competence of lower courts and has jurisdiction in cases involving personnel and decisions of the Rota. It is the supreme court of the State of Vatican City.

Background: A permanent office of the Supreme

Tribunal of the Apostolic Signatura has existed since the time of Eugene IV in the 15th century; affected by the legislation of many popes; reorganized by St. Pius X in 1908 and made the supreme tribunal of the Church.

Roman Rota: Piazza della Cancelleria 1, 00186 Rome, Italy. Msgr. Pio Vito Pinto, Dean.

The ordinary court of appeal for cases appealed to the Holy See. It is best known for its competence and decisions in cases involving the validity of marriage.

Background: Originated in the Apostolic Chancery; affected by the legislation of many popes; reorganized by St. Pius X in 1908; further revised by Pius XI in 1934; new norms approved and promulgated by John Paul II in 1982 and 1987.

PONTIFICAL COUNCILS

Pontifical Council for the Laity: Piazza S. Calisto 16, 00153 Rome, Italy. Card. Stanislaw Rylko, president; Most Rev. Josef Clemens, secretary.

Its competence covers the apostolate of the laity and their participation in the life and mission of the Church. Members are mostly lay people from different parts of the world and involved in different apostolates.

Background: Established on an experimental basis by Paul VI Jan. 6, 1967; given permanent status Dec. 10, 1976 (*motu proprio Apostolatus Peragendi*).

Pontifical Council for Promoting Christian Unity: Via dell' Erba 1, 00193 Rome, Italy. Card. Kurt Koch, president; Most Rev. Brian Farrell, L.C., secretary.

Handles relations with members of other Christian ecclesial communities; deals with the correct interpretation and execution of the principles of ecumenism; initiates or promotes Catholic ecumenical groups and coordinates on national and international levels the efforts of those promoting Christian unity; undertakes dialogue regarding ecumenical questions and activities with churches and ecclesial communities separated from the Apostolic See; sends Catholic observer-representatives to Christian gatherings, and invites to Catholic gatherings observers of other churches; orders into execution conciliar decrees dealing with ecumenical affairs. The **Commission for Religious Relations with the Jews** is attached to the secretariat.

Background: Established by John XXIII June 5, 1960, as a preparatory secretariat of the Second Vatican Council; raised to commission status during the first session of the council in the fall of 1962; status as a secretariat confirmed and functions defined by Paul VI in 1966 and 1967; made a pontifical council by John Paul II, June 28, 1988.

Pontifical Council for the Family: Piazza S. Calisto 16, 00153 Rome, Italy. Most Rev. Vincenzo Paglia, president; Most Rev. Jean Laffitte, secretary.

Is concerned with promoting the pastoral care of families so they may carry out their educative, evangelizing and apostolic mission and make their influence felt in areas such as defense of human life and responsible procreation according to the teachings of the Church. Members, chosen by the Pope, are married couples and men and women from all parts of the world and representing different cultures. They meet in general assembly at least once a year.

Background: Instituted by John Paul II May 9, 1981, replacing the Committee for the Family established by Paul VI Jan. 11, 1973.

Pontifical Council for Justice and Peace: Piazza S. Calisto 16, 00153 Rome, Italy. Card. Peter Turkson, president; Most Rev. Mario Toso, secretary.

Its primary competence is to promote justice and peace in the world according to the Gospels and social teaching of the Church.

Background: Instituted by Paul VI Jan. 6, 1967, on an experimental basis; reconstituted and made a permanent commission Dec. 10, 1976; its competence was redefined and it was made a pontifical council June 28, 1988, by John Paul II.

Pontifical Council "Cor Unum": Piazza S. Calisto 16, 00153 Rome, Italy. Card. Robert Sarah, president; secretary, Msgr. Giovanni Pietro Dal Toso.

Its principal aims are to provide informational and coordinating services for Catholic aid and human development organizations and projects on a worldwide scale. Attached to the council are the John Paul II Foundation for the Sahel and "Populorum Progressio."

Background: Instituted by Paul VI July 15, 1971.

Pontifical Council for Pastoral Care of Migrants and Itinerant Peoples: Piazza S. Calisto 16, 00153 Rome, Italy. Card. Antonio Maria Vegliò, president; Most Rev. Joseph Kalathiparambil, secretary.

Is concerned with pastoral assistance to migrants, nomads, tourists, sea, and air travelers.

Background: Instituted by Paul VI and placed under general supervision of Congregation for Bishops, Mar. 19, 1970; made autonomous as a pontifical council and renamed by John Paul II, June 28, 1988.

Pontifical Council for Pastoral Assistance to Health Care Workers: Via della Conciliazione 3, 00193 Rome, Italy. Most Rev. Zygmunt Zimowski, president; Rev. Jean-Marie Mate Musivi Mupendawatu, secretary.

Its functions are to stimulate and foster the work of formation, study and action carried out by various international Catholic organizations in the health care field.

Background: Established in 1985 as a commission by John Paul II; made a council June 28, 1988.

Pontifical Council for the Interpretation of Legislative Texts: Piazza Pio XII 10, 00193 Rome, Italy. Card. Francesco Coccopalmerio, president; Most Rev. Juan Ignacio Arrieta Ochoa de Chinchetru, secretary.

Primary function is the authentic interpretation of the universal laws of the Church.

Background: Established by John Paul II, Jan. 2, 1984, as the Pontifical Commission for the Authentic Interpretation of the Code of Canon Law; name changed and given additional functions June 28, 1988. Its competency was extended in 1991 to include interpretation of Code of Canon Law of Oriental Church that was promulgated in 1990.

Pontifical Council for Interreligious Dialogue: Via dell' Erba 1, 00193 Rome, Italy. Card. Jean-Louis Tauran, president; Most Rev. Miguel Ángel Ayuso Guixot, M.C.C.I, secretary.

Its function is to promote studies and dialogue for the purpose of increasing mutual understanding and respect between Christians and non-Christians. The Commission for Religious Relations with Muslims is attached to the council.

Background: Established by Paul VI May 19, 1964, as the Secretariat for Non-Christians; given present title and functions by John Paul II, June 28, 1988.

Pontifical Council for Culture: Piazza S. Calisto 16, 00153 Rome, Italy. Card. Gianfranco Ravasi, president; Most Rev. Barthélemy Adoukonou, secretary.

Its functions are to foster the Church's and the Holy See's relations with the world of culture and to establish dialogue with those who do not believe in God or who profess no religion provided these are open to sincere cooperation. It consists of two sections: (1) faith and culture; (2) dialogue with cultures. Attached to it is the **Coordinating Council for Pontifical Academies.**

Background: Present council with expanded functions was instituted by John Paul II (*motu proprio* of Mar. 25, 1993) through the merger of the Pontifical Council for Culture (established May 20, 1982, by John Paul II) and the Pontifical Council for Dialogue with Non-Believers (established by Paul VI Apr. 9, 1965, as the secretariat for Non-Believers).

Pontifical Council for Social Communications: Palazzo S. Carlo, 00120 Vatican City. Most Rev. Claudio Maria Celli, president; Msgr. Paul Tighe, secretary; Msgr. Giuseppe Antonio Scotti, adjunct secretary.

Engaged in matters pertaining to instruments of social communication so that through them the message of salvation and human progress is fostered and carried forward in civil culture and mores.

Background: Instituted on an experimental basis by Pius XII in 1948; reorganized three times in the 1950s; made permanent commission by John XXIII Feb. 22, 1959; established as council and functions restated by John Paul II June 28, l988.

Pontifical Council for Promoting the New Evangelization: Via della Conciliazione 5, 00193 Rome, Italy. Most Rev. Salvatore Fisichella, president; Most Rev. Jose Octavio Ruiz Arenas, secretary.

Intended to help rekindle the faith in the West, with a particular focus placed on the United States, Europe and South America; the title was first coined under Pope John Paul II to mean a reawakening of the faith in regions where the long-established Christian community faces declines in practice and zeal.

Background: Created by Pope Benedict XVI on June 30, 2010. The new dicastery was officially established on Oct. 12, 2010 through the *motu proprio, Ubicumque et semper.*

OFFICES

Apostolic Camera: Palazzo Apostolico, 00120 Vatican City. Card. Tarcisio Bertone, S.D.B., chamberlain of the Holy Roman Church; Abp. Pier Luigi Celata, vice-chamberlain.

Administers the temporal goods and rights of the Holy See between the death of one pope and the election of another (*sede vacante*), in accordance with special laws.

Background: Originated in the 11th century; reorganized by Pius XI in 1934; functions redefined (especially of *camerlengo*) by subsequent legislation in 1945, 1962 and 1975.

Administration of the Patrimony of the Apostolic See: Palazzo Apostolico, 00120 Vatican City. Card. Domenico Calcagno, president; Mons. Luigi Misto, secretary.

Handles the estate of the Apostolic See under the direction of papal delegates acting with ordinary or extraordinary authorization.

Background: Some of its functions date back to 1878; established by Paul VI Aug. 15, 1967.

Prefecture for the Economic Affairs of the Holy See: Largo del Colonnato 3, 00193 Rome, Italy. Card. Giuseppe Versaldi, president; Mons. Lucio Angel Vallejo Balda, secretary.

A financial office that coordinates and supervises administration of the temporalities of the Holy See. Background: Established by Paul VI Aug. 15, 1967; functions redefined by John Paul II, June 28, 1988.

Secretariat for the Economy: Established by Pope Francis on Feb. 24, 2014 to assist with the economic oversight and reform of the Holy See. Card. George Pell, pres.

OTHER CURIA AGENCIES

Prefecture of the Papal Household: Most Rev. Georg Gänswein, prefect; Most Rev. Leonardo Sapienza, regent.

Oversees the papal chapel — which is at the service of the pope in his capacity as spiritual head of the Church, and the pontifical family — which is at the service of the pope as a sovereign. It arranges papal audiences, has charge of preparing non-liturgical elements of papal ceremonies, makes all necessary arrangements for papal visits and trips, and settles questions of protocol connected with papal audiences and other formalities.

Background: Established by Paul VI, Aug. 15, 1967, under the title Prefecture of the Apostolic Palace; it supplanted the Sacred Congregation for Ceremonies founded by Sixtus V, Jan. 22, 1588. The office was updated and reorganized under the present title by Paul VI, Mar. 28, 1968.

Office for Liturgical Celebrations of the Supreme Pontiff: Palazzo Apostolico Vaticano, 00120 Vatican City. Msgr. Guido Marini, Master of Ceremonies.

Prepares everything necessary for liturgical and other sacred celebrations by the Pope or in his name; directs everything in accordance with prescriptions of liturgical law.

Background: Evolved gradually from the early office of Apostolic Master of Ceremonies; affected by legislation of Pope Paul IV in 1563 and Benedict XV in 1917; restructured by Paul VI in 1967; given its present title (formerly known as Prefecture of Pontifical Ceremonies) and constituted as an autonomous agency of the Roman Curia by John Paul II, June 28, 1988.

Vatican Press Office: Via della Conciliazione 54, 00120 Vatican City. Rev. Federico Lombardi, S.J., director; Rev. Ciro Benedettini, C.P., vice-director.

Established Feb. 29, 1968, to replace service agencies formerly operated by *L'Osservatore Romano* and an office created for press coverage of the Second Vatican Council. New directives were issued in 1986.

Vatican Information Service (VIS): Via della Conciliazione 54, 00120 Vatican City.

Established Mar. 28, 1990, within the framework but distinct from the Vatican Press Office. Furnishes information, in English, French and Spanish, on pastoral and magisterial activity of the Pope through use of electronic mail and fax.

Central Statistics Office: Palazzo Apostolico, 00120 Vatican City.

Established by Paul VI, Aug. 15, 1967; attached to the Secretariat of State. Compiles, systematizes and analyzes information on the status and condition of the Church.

COMMISSIONS AND COMMITTEES

Listed below are non-curial institutes that assist in the work of the Holy See. Some are attached to curial agencies, as indicated. Other institutes are listed elsewhere in the *Almanac*; see *Index*.

Pontifical Commission for the Cultural Heritage of the Church: Established by John Paul II, June 28, 1988, as Pontifical Commission for Preserving the Church's Patrimony of Art and History and attached to the Congregation for the Clergy; made autonomous and given present title Mar. 25, 1993. Card. Gianfranco Ravasi, president.

Pontifical Commission for Sacred Archeology: Instituted by Pius IX Jan, 6, 1852. Card. Gianfranco Ravasi, president.

Pontifical Biblical Commission: Instituted by Leo XIII Oct. 30, 1902; completely restructured by Paul VI June 27, 1971; attached to the Congregation for the Doctrine of the Faith. Card. Gerhard Müller, president.

Pontifical Commission for Latin America: Instituted by Pius XII Apr. 19, 1958; attached to the Congregation for Bishops July, 1969; restructured by John Paul II in 1988. Card. Marc Ouellet, P.S.S., president; Prof. Guzmán Carriquiry, secretary.

Pontifical Commission for the Revision and Emendation of the Vulgate: Established in 1984 by John Paul II to replace the Abbey of St. Jerome instituted by Pius XI in 1933. Rev. Jean Mallet, O.S.B., director.

Pontifical Commission "Ecclesia Dei": Established by John Paul II, July 2, 1988, to facilitate the return to full ecclesial communion of priests, seminarians and religious who belonged to the fraternity founded by Marcel Lefebvre; attached to the Congregation for the Doctrine of the Faith in 2009. Card. Gerhard Müller, president.

Pontifical Commission for Reference on the Institute for Works of Religion: Established by Pope Francis on June 24, 2013, to gather accurate information on the legal status and various activities of the Institute to permit, when necessary, a better harmonization of the said Institute with the universal mission of the Apostolic See. Card. Raffaele Farina, president.

Pontifical Commission for Reference on the Organisation of the Economic-Administrative Structure of the Holy See: Established by Pope Francis, July 18, 2013, to gather information, report to the Holy Father and co-operate with the Council of Cardinals for the study of the organizational and economic problems of the Holy See. Dr. Joseph F.X. Zahra, president.

Pontifical Commission for the Protection of Minors: Established on Mar. 22, 2014 by Pope Francis to assist the Church's response to the clergy sex abuse scandal and to continue reforms in institutional life for the protection of minors; the eight members include Card. Sean O'Malley of Boston and Marie Collins, an abuse victim from Ireland.

Council of Cardinals to assist in the governance of the Universal Church and to reform the Roman Curia: Established officially on April 13, 2013 to assist Pope Francis with the reform of the Roman Curia. The eight members include Card. Sean O'Malley of Boston and Card. George Pell, Sec. for the Economy. Card. Oscar Andrés Rodríguez Maradiaga, S.D.B., coordinator.

Council for the Economy: Established on Feb. 24, 2014 to assist with the financial oversight and reforms of the Holy See's finances. Card. Reinhard Marx, coordinator.

International Theological Commission: Instituted by Paul VI, Apr. 11, 1969, as an advisory adjunct of no more than 30 theologians to the Congregation for the Doctrine of the Faith; definitive statutes promulgated by John Paul II, Aug. 6, 1982. Card. Gerhard Müller, president; Rev. Serge Thomas Bonino, O.P., general secretary.

Commission for Religious Relations with the Jews: Instituted by Paul VI, Oct. 22, 1974, to promote and foster relations of a religious nature between Jews and Christians; attached to the Council for Promoting Christian Unity. Card. Kurt Koch, president.

Commission for Religious Relations with Muslims: Instituted by Paul VI, Oct. 22, 1974, to promote, regulate and interpret relations between Catholics and Muslims; attached to the Council for Interreligious Dialogue. Card. Jean-Louis Tauran, president.

Pontifical Committee for International Eucharistic Congresses: Instituted, 1879, by Pope Leo XIII; established as a pontifical committee with new statutes by John Paul II, Feb. 11, 1986. Most Rev. Piero Marini, president.

Pontifical Committee for Historical Sciences: Instituted by Pius XII, Apr. 7, 1954, as a continuation of a commission dating from 1883. Very Rev. Bernard Ardura, O. Praem., president.

Vatican II Archives: Preserves the documents of the Second Vatican Council.

Financial Security Committee: Established Aug. 8, 2013, for the prevention and contrast of laundering activities, financing of terrorism and proliferation of weapons of mass destruction. Msgr. Peter Wells, president.

Disciplinary Commission of the Roman Curia: Most Rev. Giorgio Corbellini, president.

Institute for Works of Religion: Instituted by Pius XII June 27, 1942, to bank and administer funds for works of religion; replaced an earlier administration established by Leo XIII in 1887; reorganized by John Paul II (chirograph of Mar. 1, 1990). Headed by a commission of cardinals, including Cards. Tarcisio Bertone, Telesphore Toppo, Jean-Louis Tauran. Ernst von Freyburg, president.

Fabric of St. Peter: Administration, care and preservation of Vatican Basilica. Card. Angelo Comastri, president.

Office of Papal Charities (Apostolic Almoner): Distributes alms and aid to those in need in the name of the pope. Most Rev. Konrad Krajewski, almoner.

Labor Office of the Apostolic See (ULSA - *Ufficio del Lavoro della Sede Apostolica*): Has competence in regard to those who work for the Apostolic See; charged with settling labor issues. Instituted by John Paul II (*motu proprio* of Jan. 1, 1989); functions reaffirmed and definitive text of statutes approved by John Paul II (*motu proprio* of Sept. 30, 1994). Most Rev. Giorgio Corbellini, president.

Papal Basilicas:
• **Papal Basilica of St. Peter in the Vatican**: Archpriest, Card. Angelo Comastri.
• **Papal Archbasilica of St. John in the Lateran**: Archpriest, Card. Agostino Vallini.
• **Papal Basilica of St. Paul Outside the Walls**: Archpriest, Card. James Harvey.
• **Papal Basilica of Saint Mary Major**: Archpriest, Card. Abril y Castello Santos.

Internationalization

As of July 1, 2014, principal officials of the Roman Curia were from the following countries: Italy (Cards. Amato, Antonelli, Baldelli, Baldisseri, Bertello, Bertone, Cacciavillan, Calcagno, Cheli, Coccopalmerio, Comastri, de Paolis, Filoni, Martino, Monterisi, Nicora, Parolin, Piacenza, Pompedda, Ravasi, Sardi, Sebastiani, Silvestrini, Sodano, Vallini, Vegliò, Versaldi; Abps. Becciu, Celata, Celli, Cunial, de Magistris, del Blanco Prieto, di Ruberto, Fisichella, Gardin, Girotti, Marchetto, Marini, Nesti, Paglia, Salerno, Toso, Vachelli, Bps. Bertagna, Corbellini, de Nicolò, Girotti, Pastore, Sciacca); France (Cards. Etchegaray, Poupard, Tauran,

Abp. Bruguès, Mamberti); United States (Cards. Baum, Burke, Harvey, O'Brien, Stafford, Abps. DiNoia); Spain (Cards. Abril y Castello, Martinez Somalo, Herranz; Abps. Arrieta Ochoa de Chinchetru, Gil Hellín, Ladaria, Morga Iruzubieta, Redrado Marchite); Argentina (Card. Sandri); Germany (Card. Cordes, Müller; Abp. Clemens); Poland (Cards. Grocholewski, Rylko, Abps. Hoser, Kaszak, Nowak, Stankiewicz, Zimowski, Bp. Nykiel); Brazil (Cards. Cañizares Llovera, João Bráz de Aviz; Abp. Montanari); Chile (Card. Medina Estévez); China (Abp. Hon Tai-Fai); Australia (Card. Pell); French Guinea (Card. Sarah); Ghana (Card. Turkson); Great Britain (Roche); Ireland (Bp. Farrell); Mexico (Card. Lozano Barrágan); Nigeria (Card. Arinze); Portugal (Cards. Saraiva Martins, Monteiro de Castro); India (Card. Dias; Bp. Kalathiparambil); Slovakia (Card. Tomko, Abp. Vasil'); Ukraine (Abp. Marusyn); Tanzania (Bp. Rugambwa); Croatia (Abp. Eterovic); Canada (Card. Ouellet); Switzerland (Card. Koch); Belgium (Bp. Daneels); Colombia (Abp. Ruiz Arenas).

VATICAN CITY STATE

The State of Vatican City (*Stato della Città del Vaticano*) is the territorial seat of the papacy. The smallest sovereign state in the world, it is situated within the city of Rome, embraces an area of 108.7 acres, and includes within its limits the Vatican Palace, museums, art galleries, gardens, libraries, radio station, post office, bank, astronomical observatory, offices, apartments, service facilities, St. Peter's Basilica, and neighboring buildings between the Basilica and Viale Vaticano. The extraterritorial rights of Vatican City extend to more than 10 buildings in Rome, including the major basilicas and office buildings of various congregations of the Roman Curia, and to the papal villas at Castel Gandolfo 15 miles southeast of the City of Rome. Castel Gandolfo is the summer residence of the Holy Father.

The government of Vatican City is in the hands of the reigning pope, who has full executive, legislative and judicial power. The administration of affairs, however, is handled by the **Pontifical Commission for the State of Vatican City** under Card. Giuseppe Bertello. The legal system is based on Canon Law; in cases where this code does not obtain, the laws of the City of Rome apply. The City is an absolutely neutral state and enjoys all the rights and privileges of a sovereign power. The citizens of Vatican City, and they alone, owe allegiance to the pope as a temporal head of state. On Nov. 26, 2000, Pope John Paul II promulgated the new Fundamental Law of the Vatican City State. The new law replaced that first established in 1929 by Pope Pius XI. A further change was introduced on Mar. 2, 2011, when Pope Benedict XVI issued a new law that regulates Vatican citizenship and restricts vehicle access to Vatican grounds. The new law extends the possibility of having official Vatican "residents" – those living on the grounds of Vatican City without being citizens. Vatican citizenship is usually held by cardinals, archbishops, and officials who serve in various posts in the Roman Curia and administration of the Vatican City State. Cardinals of the Roman Curia residing outside Vatican City enjoy the privileges of extraterritoriality. The Secretary General for the Governorate of the Vatican City State is Most Rev. Fernando Vergez Alzaga, L.C.

The normal population is approximately 1,000. While the greater percentage is made up of priests and religious, there are several hundred laypersons living in Vatican City. They are housed in their own apartments in the City and are engaged in secretarial, domestic, trade and service occupations. Approximately 3,400 laypersons are employed by the Vatican.

Services of honor and order are performed by the Swiss Guards, who have been charged with responsibility for the personal safety of popes since 1506. The current Captain of the Swiss Guards is Col. Daniel Rudolf Anrig, who was appointed on Aug. 19, 2008. Additional police and ceremonial functions are under the supervision of a special office. These functions were formerly handled by the Papal Gendarmes, the Palatine Guard of Honor, and the Guard of Honor of the Pope (Pontifical Noble Guard); the units were disbanded by Pope Paul VI on Sept. 14, 1970.

The **Basilica of St. Peter**, built between 1506 and 1626, is the largest church in Christendom (with the exception of the Basilica of Our Lady Queen of Peace in Ivory Coast) and the site of most papal ceremonies. The pope's own patriarchal basilica, however, is **St. John Lateran**, whose origins date back to 324.

St. Ann's, staffed by Augustinian Fathers, is the parish church of Vatican City. Its pastor is appointed by the pope, following the recommendation of the prior general of the Augustinians and the archpriest of the Vatican Basilica.

The Church of **Santa Susanna** was designated as the national church for Americans in Rome by Pope Benedict XV Jan. 10, 1922, and entrusted to the Paulist Fathers, who have served there continuously since then except for several years during World War II.

Pastoral care in Vatican City State, which is separate from the diocese of Rome, is entrusted to the archpriest of St. Peter's Basilica, who is also vicar general for Vatican City and the papal villas at Castel Gandolfo (chirograph of Pope John Paul II, Jan. 14, 1991). Cardinal Angelo Comastri succeeded to the post of Archpriest of St. Peter's Basilica, vicar general for Vatican City, and President of the Fabric of St. Peter on Oct. 31, 2006.

The Vatican Library (00120 Vatican City; Msgr. Cesare Pasini, prefect; Dr. Ambrogio Piazzoni, vice-prefect) has among its holdings 150,000 manuscripts, about 1,000,000 printed books, and 7,500 incunabula. The **Vatican Secret Archives** (00120 Vatican City; Most Rev. Sergio Pagano, prefect), opened to scholars by Leo XIII in 1881, contain central church documents dating back to the time of Innocent III (1198-1216). Abp. Jean-Louis Brugues O.P., is librarian and archivist of the Holy Roman Church.

The independent temporal power of the pope, which is limited to the confines of Vatican City and small areas outside, was for many centuries more extensive than it is now. As late as the 19th century, the pope ruled 16,000 square miles of Papal States across the middle of Italy, with a population of over 3,000,000. In 1870 forces of the Kingdom of Italy occupied these lands that, with the exception of the small areas surrounding the Vatican and Lateran in Rome and the Villas of Castel Gandolfo, became part of the Kingdom by the Italian law of May 13, 1871.

The **Roman Question**, occasioned by this seizure and the voluntary confinement of the pope to the Vatican, was settled with ratification of the Lateran Agreement June 7, 1929, by the Italian government and Vatican City. The agreement recognized Catholicism as the religion of Italy and provided, among other things, a financial indemnity to the Vatican in return for the former Papal States; it became Article 7 of the Italian Constitution, Mar. 26, 1947. The Lateran Agreement was superseded by a new concordat given final approval by the Italian Chamber of Deputies Mar. 20 and formally ratified June 3, 1985.

Papal Flag

The papal flag consists of two equal vertical stripes of yellow and white, charged with the insignia of the papacy on the white stripe — triple crown or tiara over two crossed keys, one of gold and one of silver, tied with a red cord and two tassels. The divisions of the crown represent the teaching, sanctifying and ruling offices of the pope. The keys symbolize his jurisdictional authority.

The papal flag is a national flag inasmuch as it is the standard of the Supreme Pontiff as the sovereign of the state of Vatican City. It is also universally accepted by the faithful as a symbol of the supreme spiritual authority of the Holy Father.

Vatican Radio

The declared purpose of Vatican radio station HVJ is "that the voice of the Supreme Pastor may be heard throughout the world by means of the ether waves, for the glory of Christ and the salvation of souls." Designed by Guglielmo Marconi, the inventor of radio, and supervised by him until his death, the station was inaugurated by Pope Pius XI in 1931. The original purpose has been extended to a wide variety of programming.

Vatican Radio operates on international wave lengths, transmits programs in 37 languages, and serves as a channel of communication between the Vatican, church officials and listeners in general in many parts of the world. The station broadcasts about 400 hours a week throughout the world.

The daily English-language program for North America is broadcast on 6095, 7305, 9600 Khz as well as via satellite INTELSAT 325,5° East (Atlantic) – 4097.75 Mhz – LHCP polarization.

Frequencies, background information and audio files can be obtained at www.radiovaticana.org and www.vatican.va.

The staff of 415 broadcasters and technicians includes 30 Jesuits. Studios and offices are at Palazzo Pio, Piazza Pia, 3, 00193 Rome. The transmitters are situated at Santa Maria di Galeria, a short distance north of Rome. Rev. Federico Lombardi, S.J., director-general.

2014 Vatican Stamps and Coins

The Vatican Philatelic and Numismatic Office (00120 Vatican City) published the following list of stamps and coins for the Year 2014:

Stamps
1. Easter of Resurrection
2. Pope Francis II Year - MMXIV
3. 25th Anniversary of the fall of the Berlin Wall
4. Europa 2014 — "Instruments of national music"
5. Canonization of John XXIII and John Paul II
6. Centenary of the death of St. Pius X

7. 400th Anniversary of the death of El Greco
8. 500th Anniversary of the death of Bramante
9. 450th Anniversary of the death of Michelangelo
10. 1200th Anniversary of the death of Charlemagne
11. 150th Anniversary of the birth of Richard Strauss
12. 125th Anniversary of the birth of Charlie Chaplin
13. The international Journeys of Pope Francis in 2013
14. 400th Anniversary of the death of St. Camillo de Lellis
15. 400th Anniversary of the death of William Shakespeare
16. Holy Christmas

Postal Stationery
• Postcards
• Aerogramme
• Philatelic Cover 2014
• Envelope Postal Stationery

Philatelic and Numismatic Covers
• Philatelic and Numismatic Cover "25th Anniversary of the fall of the Berlin Wall"
• Stamp and Coin Card "Canonization of John Paul II"

Year Book
• Vaticano 2014

Coins
• Euro coin set BU Version
• Euro Coin Set Proof Version with a 20 Euro silver coin "Canonization of John XXIII"
• Euro Coin Set Proof Version with a 50 Euro gold coin "Canonization of John Paul II"
• Commemorative silver and bronze medals "Canonization of John XXIII and John Paul II"
• 2 Euro Bimetallic Commemorative Coin "25th Anniversary of the fall of the Berlin Wall"
• 5 Euro Silver Commemorative Coin "57th World Day of Peace"
• 10 Euro silver Commemorative Coin "50th World Day of Social communications"
• 10 Euro gold Commemorative Coin "Baptism - MMXIV"
• 20 Euro gold Commemorative Coin "450th Anniversary of the death of Michelangelo"
• 50 Euro gold Commemorative Coin "450th Anniversary of the death of Michelangelo"
• 100 Euro gold Commemorative Coin "The Evangelists: Mark"
• 200 Euro gold Commemorative Coin "The theological virtues: Charity"

Papal Audiences

General audiences are scheduled weekly, on Wednesday. In Vatican City, they are held in the Audience Hall on the south side of St. Peter's Basilica or, weather permitting, in St. Peter's Square. The hall, which was opened in 1971, has a seating capacity of 6,800 and a total capacity of 12,000. Audiences have been held during the summer at Castel Gandolfo when the pope is there on a working vacation.

General audiences last from about 60 to 90 minutes, during which the pope gives a talk and his blessing. A résumé of the talk, which is usually in Italian, is given in several languages. Arrangements for papal audiences are handled by an office of the Prefecture of the Apostolic Household.

American visitors can obtain passes for general audiences by applying to the Bishops' Office for United States Visitors to the Vatican, Casa Santa Maria, Via dell'Umilita, 30, 00187 Rome. Private and group audiences are reserved for dignitaries of various categories and for special occasions.

Publications

Acta Apostolicae Sedis, 00120 Vatican City: The only "official commentary" of the Holy See, was established in 1908 for the publication of activities of the Holy See, laws, decrees and acts of congregations and tribunals of the Roman Curia. The first edition was published in Jan. 1909. St. Pius X made AAS an official organ in 1908. Laws promulgated for the Church ordinarily take effect three months after the date of their publication in this commentary. The publication, mostly in Latin, is printed by the Vatican Press. The immediate predecessor of this organ was *Acta Sanctae Sedis*, founded in 1865 and given official status by the Congregation for the Propagation of the Faith in 1904.

Annuario Pontificio, 00120 Vatican City: The yearbook of the Holy See. It is edited by the Central Statistics Office of the Church and is printed in Italian, with some portions in other languages, by the Vatican Press. It covers the worldwide organization of the Church, lists members of the hierarchy, and includes a wide range of statistical information. The publication of a statistical yearbook of the Holy See dates back to 1716, when a volume called *Notizie* appeared. Publication under the present title began in 1860, was suspended in 1870, and resumed again in 1872 under the title Catholic Hierarchy. This volume was printed privately at first, but has been issued by the Vatican Press since 1885. The title *Annuario Pontificio* was restored in 1912, and the yearbook was called an "official publication" until 1924.

L'Osservatore Romano, Via del Pellegrino, 00120 Vatican City: The daily newspaper of the Holy See. It began publication July 1, 1861, as an independent enterprise under the ownership and direction of four Catholic laymen headed by Marcantonio Pacelli, vice minister of the interior under Pope Pius IX and a grandfather of the late Pius XII. Leo XIII bought the publication in 1890, making it the "pope's" own newspaper.

The only official material in *L'Osservatore Romano* is what appears under the heading, "*Nostre Informazioni*." This includes notices of appointments by the Holy See, the texts of papal encyclicals and addresses by the Holy Father and others, various types of documents, accounts of decisions and rulings of administrative bodies, and similar items. Additional material includes news and comment on developments in the Church and the world. Italian is the language most used. The editorial board is directed by Prof. Giovanni Maria Vian. A staff of about 15 reporters covers Rome news sources. A corps of correspondents provides foreign coverage.

A weekly roundup edition in English was inaugurated in 1968. Other weekly editions are printed in French (1949), Italian (1950), Spanish (1969), Portuguese (1970) and German (1971). The Polish edition (1980) is published monthly. *L'Osservatore della Domenica* is published weekly as a supplement to the Sunday issue of the daily edition.

Vatican Television Center (*Centro Televisivo Vaticano*, CTV), Palazzo Belvedere, 00120 Vatican City: Instituted by John Paul II Oct. 23, 1983, with the rescript, *Ex Audentia*. Most Rev. Claudio Maria Celli, pres. of the Pontifical Council for Social Communications, is president of the administrative council.

Vatican Press, 00120 Vatican City: The official printing plant of the Vatican. The Vatican press was conceived by Marcellus II and Pius IV but was actually founded by Sixtus V on Apr. 27, 1587, to print the Vulgate and the writings of the Fathers of the Church and other authors. A Polyglot Press was established in 1626 by the Congregation for the Propagation of the Faith to serve the needs of the Oriental Church. St. Pius X merged both presses under the title Vatican Polyglot Press. It was renamed Vatican Press July 1, 1991, by John Paul II following restructuring. The plant has facilities for the printing of a wide variety of material in about 30 languages. Dir., Rev. Sergio Pellini, S.D.B.

Vatican Publishing House (Libreria Editrice Vaticana), Piazza S. Pietro, 00120 Vatican City: Formerly an office of the Vatican Press to assist in the circulation of the liturgical and juridical publications of the Apostolic See, the congregations and later the *Acta Apostolicae Sedis*. In 1926, with the expansion of publishing activities and following the promulgation of the 1917 Code, the office was made an independent entity. An administrative council and editorial commission were instituted in 1983; in 1988 *Pastor Bonus* listed it among institutes joined to the Holy See; new statutes were approved by the Secretariat of State July 1, 1991. President, Msgr. Giuseppe Scotti.

Activities of the Holy See: An annual documentary volume covering the activities of the pope and of the congregations, commissions, tribunals and offices of the Roman Curia.

Statistical Yearbook of the Church (*Annuarium Statisticum Ecclesiae*): Issued by the Central Statistics Office of the Church, it contains principal data concerning the presence and work of the Church in the world. The first issue was published in 1972 under the title Collection of Statistical Tables, 1969. It is printed in corresponding columns of Italian, French, and Latin. Some of the introductory material is printed in other languages.

DIPLOMATIC ACTIVITIES OF THE HOLY SEE

REPRESENTATIVES OF THE HOLY SEE

Representatives of the Holy See and their functions were the subject of a document entitled *Sollicitudo Omnium Ecclesiarum* which Pope Paul VI issued on his own initiative under the date of June 24, 1969. As of Aug. 1, 2014 the Holy See maintained full diplomatic relations with 179 states around the world.

Delegates and Nuncios

Papal representatives "receive from the Roman Pontiff the charge of representing him in a fixed way in the various nations or regions of the world.

"When their legation is only to local churches, they are known as apostolic delegates. When to this legation, of a religious and ecclesial nature, there is added diplomatic legation to states and governments, they receive the title of nuncio, pro-nuncio, and internuncio." An apostolic nuncio has the diplomatic rank of ambassador extraordinary and plenipotentiary. Traditionally, because the diplomatic service of the Holy See has the longest uninterrupted history in the world, a nuncio has precedence among diplomats in the country to which he is accredited and serves as dean of the diplomatic corps on state occasions. Since 1965 pro-nuncios, also of ambassadorial rank, have been assigned to countries in which this prerogative is not recognized. In recent years, the Vatican has phased out the title of pro-nuncio. The title of nuncio (with an asterisk denoting he is not dean of the diplomatic corps) has been given to the majority of appointments of ambassadorial rank. *See* **Other Representatives**.

Service and Liaison

Representatives, while carrying out their general and special duties, are bound to respect the autonomy of local churches and bishops. Their service and liaison responsibilities include the following:

- Nomination of Bishops: To play a key role in compiling, with the advice of ecclesiastics and lay persons, and submitting lists of names of likely candidates to the Holy See with their own recommendations.
- Bishops: To aid and counsel local bishops without interfering in the affairs of their jurisdictions.
- Episcopal Conferences: To maintain close relations with them and to assist them in every possible way. (Papal representatives do not belong to these conferences.)
- Religious Communities of Pontifical Rank: To advise and assist major superiors for the purpose of promoting and consolidating conferences of men and women religious and to coordinate their apostolic activities.
- Church-State Relations: The thrust in this area is toward the development of sound relations with civil governments and collaboration in work for peace and the total good of the whole human family. The mission of a papal representative begins with appointment and assignment by the pope and continues until termination of his mandate. He acts "under the guidance and according to the instructions of the cardinal secretary of state to whom he is directly responsible for the execution of the mandate entrusted to him by the

Supreme Pontiff." Normally representatives are required to retire at age 75.

NUNCIOS AND DELEGATES

(*Sources:* Annuario Pontificio, L'Osservatore Romano, Acta Apostolicae Sedis, *Catholic News Service.*) As of July 30, 2014. *Country, rank of legation (corresponding to rank of legate unless otherwise noted), name of legate (archbishop unless otherwise noted) as available. An asterisk indicates a nuncio who is not presently dean of the diplomatic corps.*

Delegate for Papal Legations: Abp. Luciano Suriani. The post was established in 1973 to coordinate papal diplomatic efforts throughout the world. The office entails responsibility for "following more closely through timely visits the activities of papal representatives … and encouraging their rapport with the central offices" of the Secretariat of State.

Albania: Tirana, Nunciature; Ramiro Moliner Inglés.*

Algeria: Algiers, Nunciature; Thomas Yeh Sheng-nan* (also Nuncio* to Tunisia).

Andorra: Nunciature; Renzo Fratini (also Nuncio to Spain).

Angola: Luanda, Nunciature; Novatus Rugambwa* (also Nuncio* to São Tome and Principe). (Diplomatic relations established in 1997.)

Antigua and Barbuda: Nunciature; Nicola Girasoli* (resides in Port of Spain, Trinidad).

Antilles: Apostolic Delegation; Nicola Girasoli (resides in Port of Spain, Trinidad).

Arabian Peninsula: Apostolic Delegation; Petar Rajic. (also nuncio in Kuwait, Qatar, United Arab Emirates, and Yemen.

Argentina: Buenos Aires, Nunciature; Emil Paul Tscherrig.

Armenia: Nunciature; Marek Solczynski* (resides in Tbilisi, Georgia; also nuncio* to Georgia and Azerbaijan). (Diplomatic relations established in 1992.)

Australia: Canberra, Nunciature; Paul Richard Gallagher.

Austria: Vienna, Nunciature; Peter Stephan Zurbriggen.

Azerbaijan: Nunciature; Marek Soczynski* (resides in Tbilisi, Georgia; also nuncio* to Georgia and Armenia). (Diplomatic relations established in 1992.)

Bahamas: Nunciature; Nicola Girasoli* (resides in Port of Spain, Trinidad).

Bahrain: Manama; Nunciature; Petar Rajic. (Diplomatic relations established Jan. 12, 2000; also nuncio in Kuwait, Qatar, United Arab Emirates, and Yemen).

Bangladesh: Dhaka, Nunciature; George Kocherry.*

Barbados: Nunciature; Nicola Girasoli* (resides in Port of Spain, Trinidad).

Belarus: Nunciature; Claudio Gugerotti.*

Belgium: Brussels, Nunciature; Giacinto Berloco (also Nuncio to Luxembourg).

Belize: Nunciature; Leon Kalenga Badikebele* (resides in Port of Spain, Trinidad).

Benin (formerly Dahomey): Nunciature; Brian Udaigwe.* (resides in Accra, Ghana).

Bolivia: La Paz, Nunciature; Giambattista Diquattro.

Bosnia and Herzegovina: Sarajevo; Nunciature; Luigi Pezzuto.*

Botswana: Nunciature (Diplomatic relations established in November 2008); Mario Cassari (resides in Pretoria, South Africa; also Nuncio* to Lesotho, Namibia, South Africa, and Swaziland.).

Brazil: Brasilia, Nunciature; Vacant.

Brunei Darussalam: See Malaysia and Brunei.

Bulgaria: Sofia, Nunciature (reestablished in 1990); Anselmo Guido Pecorari (also nuncio to Macedonia).*

Burkina Faso: Ouagadougou, Nunciature; Vito Rallo* (also Nuncio* to Niger).

Burma: See Myanmar.

Burundi: Bujumbura, Nunciature; Franco Coppola.*

Cambodia: Nunciature (Diplomatic relations established in 1994); Paul Tschang In-Nam* (resides in Bangkok, Thailand).

Cameroon: Yaounde, Nunciature; Piero Pioppo (also Nuncio to Equatorial Guinea).

Canada: Ottawa, Nunciature; Luigi Bonazzi.*

Cape Verde, Republic of: Nunciature; Luis Mariano Montemayor* (resides in Dakar, Senegal).

Central African Republic: Bangui, Nunciature; Franco Coppola* (also Nuncio* to Chad).

Chad: Nunciature; Franco Coppola* (resides in Bangui, Central African Republic).

Chile: Santiago, Nunciature; Ivo Scapolo.

China, Republic of: Taipei (Taiwan), Nunciature; Vacant.

Colombia: Bogota, Nunciature; Ettore Balestrero.

Comoros: See Madagascar: (formerly Zaire)

Congo (formerly Zaire): Kinshasa-Gombe, Nunciature; Jan Romeo Pawlowski.*

Congo: Brazzaville, Nunciature; Adolfo Tito Yllana* (also Nuncio* to Gabon).

Costa Rica: San Jose, Nunciature; Antonio Arcari.

Côte d'Ivoire (Ivory Coast): Abidjan, Nunciature; Joseph Spiteri.

Croatia: Zagreb, Nunciature; Alessandro D'Errico (also nuncio to Bosnia and Herzegovina).

Cuba: Havana, Nunciature; Bruno Musarò.*

Cyprus: Nicosia, Nunciature; Giuseppe Lazzarotto (also Nuncio to Israel).

Czech Republic: Prague, Nunciature; Giueseppe Leanza.

Denmark: Copenhagen, Nunciature; Vacant* (also Nuncio* to Finland, Iceland, Norway and Sweden).

Djibouti: Nunciature (established May 2000); Vacant (resides in Addis Ababa, Ethiopia).

Dominica: Nunciature; Nicola Girasola* (resides in Port-of-Spain, Trinidad).

Dominican Republic: Santo Domingo, Nunciature; Jude Thaddeus Okolo (also serves as Apostolic Delegate to Puerto Rico).

East Timor: Díli, Nunciature (diplomatic relations established on May 20, 2002); Joseph Marino (also Nuncio* to Indonesia).

Ecuador: Quito, Nunciature; Giacomo Ottonello.

Egypt: Cairo, Nunciature; Jean-Paul Gobel (also delegate to the Organization of the League of Arab States).*

El Salvador: San Salvador, Nunciature; Leon Kalenga Badikebele.

Equatorial Guinea: Santa Isabel, Nunciature; Piero Pioppo* (resides in Yaounde, Cameroon).

Eritrea: Nunciature; Hubertus Van Megen.* (Diplomatic relations established in 1995.)

Estonia: Nunciature; Pedro Lopez Quintana* (resides in Vilnius, Lithuania).

Ethiopia: Addis Ababa, Nunciature; Vacant* (also Nuncio* to Djibouti and apostolic delegate to Somalia).

European Union: Brussels, Belgium, Nunciature; Alain Lebeaupain.

Fiji: Nunciature; Martin Krebs* (resides in Wellington, New Zealand).

Finland: Helsinki, Nunciature; Henryk Jozef Nowacki* (resides in Denmark).

France: Paris, Nunciature; Luigi Ventura.

Gabon: Libreville, Nunciature; Jan Romeo Pawlowski* (resides in Congo).

Gambia: Nunciature; Miroslaw Adamczyk* (resides in Freetown, Sierra Leone).

Georgia: Tbilisi, Nunciature; Marek Solczynski* (also Nuncio* to Armenia and Azerbaijan). (Diplomatic relations established in 1992.)

Germany: Bonn, Nunciature; Nikola Eterovic.

Ghana: Accra, Nunciature; Jean-Marie Speich.*

Great Britain: London, Nunciature; Antonio Mennini* (also papal representative to Gibraltar).

Greece: Athens, Nunciature; Edward Joseph Adams.*

Grenada: Nunciature; Nicola Girasoli* (resides in Port of Spain, Trinidad). **Guatemala:** Guatemala City, Nunciature; Nicolas Thevenin.

Guinea: Conakry, Nunciature; Santo Rocco Gangemi* (resides in Freetown, Sierra Leone).

Guinea Bissau: Nunciature; Luis Mariano Montemayor* (resides at Dakar, Senegal).

Guyana: Nunciature; Nicola Girasola (resides in Port of Spain, Trinidad).

Haiti: Port-au-Prince, Nunciature; Vacant.

Honduras: Tegucigalpa, Nunciature; Luigi Bianco.

Hungary: Budapest, Nunciature; Alberto Bottari de Castello (also Nuncio* to Moldova).

Iceland: Nunciature; Henryk Jozef Nowacki* (resides in Denmark).

India: New Delhi, Nunciature; Salvatore Pennacchio* (also Nuncio* to Nepal).

Indonesia: Jakarta, Nunciature; Antonio Guido Filipazzi (also nuncio to East Timor).*

Iran: Teheran, Nunciature; Leo Boccardi.*

Iraq: Baghdad, Nunciature; Giorgio Lingua* (also Nuncio to Jordan).

Ireland: Dublin, Nunciature; Charles Brown.

Israel: Nunciature; Giuseppe Lazzarotto (also Nuncio to Cyprus). (Diplomatic relations established June 1994.)

Italy: Rome, Nunciature; Adriano Bernardini (also Nuncio to San Marino).

Ivory Coast: See Côte d'Ivoire.

Jamaica: Nunciature; Nicola Girasoli (resides in Port of Spain, Trinidad).

Japan: Tokyo, Nunciature; Joseph Chennoth*.

Jerusalem and Palestine: Apostolic Delegation (also Nuncio to Israel): Antonio Franco.

Jordan: Nunciature; Giorgio Lingua* (also Nuncio to Iraq).

Kazakstan: Almaty, Nunciature; Miguel Maury Buendía* (also Nuncio* to Kyrgyzstan and Tajikistan).

Kenya: Nairobi, Nunciature; Charles D. Balvo* (also nuncio to South Sudan).

Kiribati: Nunciature; Martin Krebs* (resides in Wellington, New Zealand).

Korea: Seoul, Nunciature; Osvaldo Padilla* (also Nuncio* to Mongolia).

Kuwait: Al Kuwait, Nunciature; Petar Rajic * (also nuncio in Qatar, Bahrain, the United Arab Emirates, and Yemen).

Kyrgyzstan: Nunciature; Miguel Maury Buendía* (resides in

Kazakhstan; also Nuncio* to Kyrgyzstan and Tajikistan).

Laos: Apostolic Delegation; Paul Tschang In-Nam (resides in Bangkok, Thailand; also apostolic delegate to Myanmar).

Latvia: Nunciature; Pedro Lopez Quintana* (resides in Vilna, Lithuania).

Lebanon: Beirut, Nunciature; Gabriele Giordano Caccia.

Lesotho: Maseru, Nunciature; Mario Cassari (also Nuncio to Botswana, South Africa, Namibia, and Swaziland; resides in Pretoria, South Africa).

Liberia: Monrovia, Nunciature; Vacant* (resides in Freetown, Sierra Leone).

Libya: Nunciature; Aldo Cavalli* (resides in Malta). (Diplomatic relations established in 1997.)

Liechtenstein: Nunciature; Diego Causero (resides in Bern, Switzerland).

Lithuania: Vilnius, Nunciature; Pedro Lopez Quintana* (also Nuncio to Estonia and Latvia.).

Luxembourg: Nunciature; Giacinto Berloco (resides in Brussels, Belgium).

Macedonia: Nunciature; Anselmo Guido Pecorari* (also Nuncio to Slovenia; resides in Slovenia).

Madagascar: Antananarivo, Nunciature; Eugene Nugent* (also Nuncio* to Seychelles, and Mauritius and Apostolic Delegate to Comoros and Reunion).

Malawi: Lilongwe, Nunciature; Julio Murat* (resides in Lusaka, Zambia).

Malaysia and Brunei: Nunciature (diplomatic relations established in 2011); Joseph Marino (resides in Indonesia).

Mali: Nunciature; Santo Rocco Coppola* (resides in Dakar, Senegal, also nuncio to Guinea).

Malta: La Valletta, Nunciature; Aldo Cavalli(also Nuncio* to Libya).

Marshall Islands: Nunciature; Martin Krebs* (resides in Wellington, New Zealand).

Mauritania: Nouakchott, Apostolic Delegation; Luis Mariano Montemayor (resides in Dakar, Senegal).

Mauritius: Port Louis, Nunciature; Eugene Nugent* (resides in Antananarivo, Madagascar).

Mexico: Mexico City, Nunciature; Christophe Pierre.* (Diplomatic relations established in 1992).

Micronesia, Federated States of: Nunciature; Martin Krebs* (resides in Wellington, New Zealand).

Moldova: Nunciature; Francisco-Javier Lozano Sebastian* (resides in Bucharest, Romania). (Diplomatic relations established in 1992.)

Monaco, Principality of: Nunciature; Luigi Travaglino.

Mongolia: Nunciature; Osvaldo Padilla* (resides in Seoul, South Korea).

Montenegro: Podgorica, Nunciature; Luigi Pezzuto (Diplomatic relations established Dec. 17, 2006).

Morocco: Rabat, Nunciature; Antonio Sozzo.*

Mozambique: Maputo, nunciature; Vacant.* (Diplomatic relations established in 1995.)

Myanmar (formerly Burma): Apostolic Delegation; Paul Tschang In-Nam (resides in Bangkok, Thailand).

Namibia: Nunciature; Mario Cassari* (resides in Pretoria, South Africa).

Nauru: Nunciature; Martin Krebs* (resides in Wellington, New Zealand).

Nepal: Nunciature; Salvatore Pennacchio* (resides in New Delhi, India).

Netherlands: The Hague, Nunciature; Andre Dupuy.*

New Zealand: Wellington, Nunciature; New Zealand* (also Nuncio* to Fiji, Kiribati, Marshall Islands,

Federated States of Micronesia, Tonga, Vanuatu and Western Samoa; Apostolic Delegate to Pacific Islands).

Nicaragua: Managua, Nunciature; Fortunatus Nwachukwu.

Niger: Niamey, Nunciature; Vito Rallo* (also Nuncio* to Burkina Faso.)

Nigeria: Lagos, Nunciature; Augustine Kasujja.*

Norway: Nunciature; Henryk Jozef Nowacki* (resides in Denmark).

Pacific Ocean: Nunciature; Martin Krebs (resides in Wellington, New Zealand).

Pakistan: Islamabad, Nunciature; Edgar Pena Parra.

Palau, Republic of: Palau, Nunciature; Martin Krebs.*

Panama: Panama City, Nunciature; Andrés Carrascosa Coso.

Papua New Guinea: Port Moresby; Nunciature; Michael W. Banach* (also Nuncio* to Solomon Islands).

Paraguay: Asuncion, Nunciature; Eliseo Antonio Ariotti.

Peru: Lima, Nunciature; James P. Green.

Philippines: Manila, Nunciature; Giuseppe Pinto.

Poland: Warsaw; Nunciature; Celestino Migliore.

Portugal: Lisbon, Nunciature; Rino Passigato.

Puerto Rico: See Dominican Republic.

Qatar: Dawhah, Nunciature; Petar Rajic (Diplomatic relations established in Nov. 2002; also nuncio in Kuwait, Bahrain, United Arab Emirates, and Yemen).

Reunion: See Madagascar.

Romania: Bucharest, Nunciature. Francisco-Javier Lozano.*

Russia (Federation of): Moscow, Nunciature; Ivan Jurkovic. Nuncio appointed Representative of the Holy See to Russian Federation, 1994.

Rwanda: Kigali, Nunciature. Vacant.

St. Vincent and the Grenadines: Nunciature; Nicola Girasoli, Nuncio (resides in Port of Spain, Trinidad).

Samoa: Nunciature; Martin Krebs* (resides in Wellington, New Zealand).

San Marino: Nunciature; Adriano Bernardini (also nuncio to Italy).

Santa Lucia: Nunciature; Nicola Girasoli* (resides in Port of Spain, Trinidad).

São Tome and Principe: Nunciature; Novatus Rugambwa* (also Nuncio* to Angola, where he resides).

Senegal: Dakar, Nunciature; Luis Mariano Montemayor* (also Nuncio* to Cape Verde, Guinea-Bissau and Mali; Apostolic Delegate to Mauritania.)

Serbia: Belgrade, Nunciature; Orlando Antonini.

Seychelles Islands: Nunciature; Eugene Nugent* (resides in Antananrivo, Madagascar).

Sierra Leone: Freetown, Nunciature (1996); Miroslav Adamczyk* (also Nuncio* to Gambia and Liberia).

Singapore: Nunciature; Leopoldo Girelli* (He is also apostolic delegate to Malaysia and Brunei, and non-residential pontifical representative to Vietnam.)

Slovakia: Nunciature; Mario Giordana.

Slovenia: Ljubljana, Nunciature; Anselmo Guido Pecorari (also Nuncio to Macedonia and Kosovo).

Solomon Islands: Nunciature; Michael W. Banach (resides in Port Moresby, Papua New Guinea).

Somalia: Apostolic Delegation (est. 1992); Vacant (resides in Sudan).

South Africa: Pretoria, Nunciature; Mario Cassari* (also Nuncio* to Botswana, Namibia, and Swaziland.)

South Sudan: Nunciature; Daniel Balvo (also nuncio to Kenya).

Spain: Madrid, Nunciature; Renzo Fratini.

Sri Lanka: Colombo, Nunciature; Pierre Nguyên Van Tot.*

Sudan: Khartoum, Nunciature; Hubertus Van Megen.*

Suriname: Nunciature; Nicola Girasoli* (resides in Port of Spain, Trinidad).

Swaziland: Nunciature; Mario Cassari* (resides in Pretoria, South Africa).

Sweden: Nunciature; Henryk Jozef Nowacki* (resides in Denmark).

Switzerland: Bern, Nunciature; Diego Causero (also Nuncio to Liechtenstein).

Syria: (Syrian Arab Republic): Damascus, Nunciature, Mario Zenari.*

Tajikistan: Nunciature (1996); Miguel Maury Buendía* (resides in Kazakstan; also Nuncio* to Kyrgyzstan and Kazakstan).

Tanzania: Dar-es-Salaam, Nunciature; Francesco Padilla.*

Thailand: Bangkok, Nunciature; Paul Tschang In-Nam* (also Nuncio* to Cambodia and Apostolic Delegate to Laos and Myanmar).

Togo: Lome, Nunciature; Brian Udaigwe* (resides in Accra, Ghana).

Tonga: Nunciature; Martin Krebs* (resides in Wellington, New Zealand).

Trinidad and Tobago: Port of Spain, Trinidad, Nunciature; Nicola Girasoli, Nuncio (also Nuncio to Antigua and Barbuda, Bahamas, Barbados, Belize, Dominica, Grenada, Jamaica, Saint Lucia, Saint Vincent and the Grenadines, Suriname and Apostolic Delegate to Antilles).

Tunisia: Tunis, Nunciature; Thomas Yeh Sheng-nan* (resides in Algiers, Algeria).

Turkey: Ankara, Nunciature; Antonio Lucibello.*

Turkmenistan: Nunciature (1996); Antonio Lucibello* (resides in Ankara, Turkey).

Uganda: Kampala, Nunciature; Pro-Nuncio, Michael A. Blume, S.V.D.

Ukraine: Kiev, Nunciature; Thomas E. Gullickson.*

United Arab Emirates: Abu Dhabi, Nunciature (diplomatic relations established May 31, 2007): Petar Rajic* (also nuncio to Kuwait, Bahrain, Qatar, and Yemen).

United States of America: Washington, DC, Nunciature; Carlo Maria Viganó.*

Uruguay: Montevideo, Nunciature; George Panikulam.

Uzbekistan: Nunciature; Ivan Jurkovic* (resides in Kazakstan; also Nuncio* to Kazakstan, Kyrgyzstan, and Tajikistan).

Vanuatu: Nunciature; Martin Krebs* (resides in Wellington, New Zealand).

Venezuela: Caracas, Nunciature; Aldo Giordano.

Vietnam: Apostolic Delegation; Leopoldo Girelli (resides in Indonesia).

Western Samoa: Nunciature; Charles D. Balvo* (resides in Wellington, New Zealand).

Yemen: San'a, Nunciature; Petar Rajic* (relations established in 1998, also nuncio in Kuwait, Bahrain, United Arab Emirate, and Qatar).

Yugoslavia: Belgrade, Nunciature; Eugenio Sbarbaro.

Zaire: See Congo: Lusaka, Nunciature; Giuseppe Leanza* (also Nuncio* to Malawi).

Zambia: Lusaka, Nunciature; Vacant* (also Nuncio* to Malawi).

Zimbabwe: Harare, Nunciature; Marek Zalewski.*

The Current Nuncio to the U.S.

The post of nuncio to the United States is currently held by Abp. Carlo Maria Viganó (b. Jan. 16, 1941) who was named nuncio to the United States on Oct. 19, 2011. A native of Varese, Italy, Viganò was ordained a priest on Mar. 24, 1968 and earned a doctorate *utroque iure* (both canon and civil law). He entered the diplomatic service of the Holy See in 1973 and worked at the papal diplomatic mission in Iraq and Great Britain, and from 1978 to 1989, was an official of the Secretariat of State in Rome. He was named Special Envoy and Permanent Observer of the Holy See to the Council of Europe in Strasbourg in 1989. In 1992, he was appointed titular abp. of Ulpiana and apostolic nuncio to Nigeria and was consecrated a bishop on Apr. 26, 1992. He returned to the Secretariat of State in 1998 and served there until 2009 when he was appointed Secretary-General of the Governatorate of Vatican City State.

The U.S. Apostolic Nunciature is located at 3339 Massachusetts Ave., N.W., Washington, D.C. 20008-3687; (202) 333-7121.

A Nuncio represents the Holy Father to both the hierarchy and Church of a particular nation and to that nation's civil government.

From 1893 to 1984, papal representatives to the Church in the U.S. were apostolic delegates (all archbishops): Francesco Satolli (1893-96), Sebastiano Martinelli, O.S.A., (1896-1902), Diomede Falconio, O.F.M. (1902-1911), Giovanni Bonzano (1911-22), Pietro Fumasoni-Biondi (1922-33), Amleto Cicognani (1933-58), Egidio Vagnozzi (1958-67), Luigi Raimondi (1967-73), Jean Jadot (1973-80), and Pio Laghi (1980-90) who was the first to hold the title Pro-Nuncio, beginning in 1984 (*See* Index, **U.S.-Vatican Relations**). Abp. (now Card.) Agostino Cacciavillan was Pro-Nuncio and permanent observer to the Organization of American States from 1990–998. Abp. Gabriel Montalvo was nuncio and permanent observer to the Organization of American States from 1998–2005. Abp. Pietro Sambi served as nuncio to the United States and permanent observer to the Organization of American States from Dec. 17, 2005 until his passing after an illness on July 27, 2011.

Other Representatives

(*Sources:* Annuario Pontificio; *Catholic News Service.*)

The Holy See has representatives to or is a regular member of a number of quasi-governmental and international organizations. Most Rev. Ernesto Gallina was first appointed delegate to International Governmental Organizations Jan. 12, 1991.

Governmental Organizations: U.N. (Abp. Bernardito Auza, permanent observer); U.N. Office in Geneva and Specialized Institutions (Abp. Silvano Maria Tomasi, permanent observer); African Union (Vacant); League of Arab States (Abp. Jean-Paul Gobel); International Atomic Energy Agency (Vacant, permanent representative); U.N. Office at Vienna and U.N. Organization for Industrial Development (Vacant, permanent observer); U.N. Food and Agriculture Organization (Abp. Luigi Travaglino, permanent observer); U.N. Educational, Scientific and Cultural Organization (Msgr. Francesco Follo, permanent observer); World Trade Organization (Abp. Silvano Maria Tomasi); Council of Europe (Vacant, special representative with function of permanent observer); Council for Cultural Cooperation of the Council of Europe (Vacant, delegate); Organization of American States (Abp. Carlo Maria Viganó, permanent observer, with personal title of Apostolic Nuncio); Organization for Security and Cooperation in Europe (Vacant, permanent representative); International Institute for the Unification of Private Law (Prof. Giuseppe dalla Torre del Tiempo di Sanguinetto Conte, delegate); International Committee of Military Medicine (Msgr. Robrecht Boone, delegate), World Organization of Tourism (Abp. Renzo Fratini, permanent observer).

Non-Governmental Organizations: International Committee of Historical Sciences (Rev. Bernard Ardura, O.Praem.); International Committee of the History of Art (Dr. Antonio Paolucci); International Committee of Anthropological and Ethnological Sciences; Committee for the Neutrality of Medicine; International Center of Study for the Preservation and Restoration of Cultural Goods (Dr. Francesco Buranelli); International Council of Monuments and Sites (Msgr. Francesco Follo, delegate); International Alliance on Tourism; World Association of Jurists (Vacant); International Commission of the Civil State (Msgr. Paul Richard Gallagher); International Astronomical Union; International Institute of Administrative Sciences; International Technical Committee for Prevention and Extinction of Fires; World Medical Association; International Archives Council; World Trade Organization.

DIPLOMATS TO THE HOLY SEE

(*Sources:* Annuario Pontificio, L'Osservatore Romano).

Listed below are countries maintaining diplomatic relations with the Holy See, dates of establishment (in some cases) and names of Ambassadors (as of Aug. 30, 2014). Leaders (.....) indicate the post was vacant.

Albania (1991): Rrok Logu.
Algeria (1972): Boudjemaa Delmi.
Andorra: Jaume Serra Serra.
Angola (1997): Vieira Armindo Fernandes do Espirito Santo.
Antigua and Barbuda (1986): David Shoul.
Argentina: Juan Pablo Cafiero.
Armenia (1992): Viguen Tchitetchian.
Australia (1973): John McCarthy.
Austria: Alfons M. Kloss.
Azerbaijan (1992): Elchin Oktyabr Oglu Amirbayov.
Bahamas (1979): .....
Bahrain (2000): Naser Muhamed Youssef al Belooshi.
Bangladesh (1972): Abdul Hannan.
Barbados (1979): Peter Patrick Kenneth Simmons.
Belarus (1992): Sergei F. Aleinik.
Belgium (1835): Charles Ghislain.
Belize (1983): Lawrence H. Llewellyn.
Benin (formerly Dahomey) (1971): Theodore C. Loko.
Bolivia: Carlos Federico de la Riva Guerra.
Bosnia and Herzegovina (1992): .....
Botswana: Lameck Nthekela.
Brazil: Franco de Sa Barbuda Almir.
Bulgaria (1990): .....
Burkina Faso (1973): Eric Yemdaogo Tiare.
Burundi (1963): Edouard Bizimana.
Cambodia (1994): .....
Cameroon (1966): Antoine Zanga.
Canada (1969): .....
Cape Verde (1976): Emanuel Antero Garcia da Veiga.
Central African Republic (1975): .....
Chad (1988): Hissein Brahim Taha. **Chile:** Fernando Zegers Santa Cruz.
China, Republic of (Taiwan) (1966): Wang Larry Yu-yuan.
Colombia: German Cardona Gutierrez.
Congo (formerly Zaire) (1963): Jean-Pierre Hamuli Mupenda.
Congo (1977): Henri Marie Joseph Lopes.
Costa Rica: Fernando Sanchez Campos.
Côte d'Ivoire (Ivory Coast) (1971): Joseph Tebah-Klah.
Croatia (1992): Filip Vucak.
Cuba: Eduardo Delgado Bermúdez.
Cyprus (1973): Georgios F. Poulides.
Czech Republic (1929-50, reestablished, 1990, with Czech and Slovak Federative Republic; reaffirmed, 1993): Pavel Vosalík.
Denmark (1982): Lars Vissing.
Djibouti: (2000): Barkat Gourad Hamadou. (Diplomatic relations established May 20, 2000.)
Dominica (1981): .....
Dominican Republic: Victor Manuel Grimaldi Céspedes.
East Timor (2002): ..... (Diplomatic relations established on May 20, 2002.)
Ecuador: Luis Dositeo Latorre Tapia.
Egypt (1966): .....
El Salvador: Manuel Roberto Lopez Barrera.
Equatorial Guinea (1981): Narciso Ntugu Abeso Oyana.
Eritrea (1995): Petros Tseggai Asghedom.
Estonia (1991): Jüri Seilenthal.
Ethiopia (1969): Nega Tsegaye Tessema.
European Union: Laurence Argimon-Pistre.
Fiji (1978): Naivakarurubalavu Solo Mara.
Finland (1966): .....
France: Bruno Joubert.
Gabon (1967): Firmin Mboutsou.
Gambia, The (1978): Elizabeth Ya Eli Harding.
Georgia (1992): Princess Khétévane Bagration de Moukhrani.
Germany: Reinhard Scweppe.
Ghana (1976): Genevieve Delali Tsegah.
Great Britain (1982): Nigel M. Baker.
Greece (1980): Georgios Papadopoulos
Grenada (1979): .....
Guatemala: Alfonso Roberto Matta Fahsen.
Guinea (1986): Ibrahima Sow.
Guinea-Bissau (1986): Hilia Garez Gomes Lima Barber.
Guyana (Cooperative Republic of): Laleshwar Kumar Narayan Singh.
Haiti: Carl-Henri Guiteau.
Honduras: Alejandro Emilio Valladares Lanza.
Hungary (1990): Gábor Gyoriványi.
Iceland (1976): Martin Eyjolfsson.
India: Mysore Kapanalah Lokesh.
Indonesia (1965): Budiarman Badar
Iran (1966): .....
Iraq (1966): Mohammed Hadi Ali Al-Sadr Habbeb.
Ireland: David Cooney.
Israel (1994): Zion Evrony.
Italy: Francesco Maria Greco.
Ivory Coast: See Côte d'Ivoire.
Jamaica (1979): Margaret Ann Louise Jobson.
Japan (1966): Hidekazu Yamaguchi.
Jordan (1994): Makram Mustafa Al Queisi.
Kazakhstan (1992): Mukhtar Tileuberdi.
Kenya (1965): .....
Kiribati (1995): .....
Korea (1966): Thomas Han Hong-soon.
Kuwait (1969): Bader Saleh Al-Tunaib.
Kyrgyzstan (1992): Bolot Iskovich Otunbaev.
Latvia (1991): Einars Semanis.
Lebanon (1966): Georges Chakib El Khoury.
Lesotho (1967): Lineo Lydia Khechane-Ntoane.
Liberia (1966): Rudolf P. von Balimoos.
Libya: (1997): .....
Liechtenstein (1985): Prince Nikolaus de Liechtenstein.
Lithuania: Irena Vaisvilaite.
Luxembourg (1955): Jean-Paul Senninger.
Macedonia (1994): Gioko Gjorgjevski.
Madagascar (1967): .....
Malawi (1966): Isaac Chikwekwere Lamba.
Malaysia: Dato' Ho May Young.

Mali (1979): Boubacar Sidiki Toure.
Malta (1965): George Gregory Buttigieg.
Marshall Islands (1993): . . . . .
Mauritius: Mohunlall Goburdhun.
Mexico (personal representative, 1990; diplomatic relations, 1992): Mariano Palacios Alcocer.
Micronesia, Federated States (1994): . . . . .
Moldova (1992): Stefan Gorda.
Monaco: Jean-Claude Michel.
Mongolia (1992): Luvsantersen Orgil.
Montenegro: (Diplomatic relations established Dec. 17, 2006): Antun Sbutega.
Morocco: . . . . .
Mozambique (diplomatic relations, 1995): Amadeus Paulo Samuel da Conceicao.
Namibia: (diplomatic relations established Sept. 1995): Neville Melvin Gertze.
Nauru (1992): . . . . .
Nepal (1983): Suresh Prasad Pradhan.
Netherlands (1967): Joseph Weterings.
New Zealand (1973): George Robert Furness Troup.
Nicaragua: José Cuadra Chamorro.
Niger (1971): Aminatou Batoure Gaoh.
Nigeria (1976): Francis Okeke.
Norway (1982): Thomas Hauff.
Order of Malta (see Index): Alberto Leoncini Bartoli.
Pakistan (1965): Aman Rashid.
Palau, Republic of (1998): . . . . .
Panama: Lawrence Christie Delia Cardenas.
Papua New Guinea (1977): . . . . .
Paraguay: Esteban Kriskovic.
Peru: . . . . .
Philippines (1951): Mercedes Arrastia Tuason.
Poland (1989): Hanna Suchocka.
Portugal: . . . . .
Qatar: (Diplomatic relations established Nov. 2002): Mohamad Jaham Abdulaziz Al-Kuwari.
Romania (1920; broken off, 1948; reestablished, 1990): Bogadan Tataru-Cazaban.
Russia (Federation of) (1989; formal diplomatic relations established in 2009): . . . . .
Rwanda (1964): Joseph Bonesha.
Saint Lucia (1984): Gilbert Ramez Chagoury.
Saint Vincent and the Grenadines (1990): . . . . .
San Marino (1986): Sante Canducci.
São Tome and Principe (1984): . . . . .
Senegal (1966): Félix Oudiane.
Serbia: Mirko Jelic.
Seychelles (1984): Vivianne Fock Tave.
Sierra Leone: (Diplomatic relations established July 1996): Ibrahim Sorie.
Singapore (1981): Barry Desker.
Slovak Republic (1993; when it became independent republic): Jozef Dravecký.
Slovenia (1992): Maja Lovrencic Svetek.
Solomon Islands (1984): . . . . .
South Africa (1994): Claudinah Ntini Ramosepele.
South Sudan (2013): . . . . .
Spain: Eduardo Gutierrez Saenz de Buruaga.
Sri Lanka (1975): Tamara Kunanayakam.
Sudan (1972): Nasreldin Ahmed Wali Abdeltif.
Suriname (1994): . . . . .
Swaziland (1992): H.R.H. Prince David M. Dlamini.
Sweden (1982): Lars-Hjalmar Wide.
Switzerland (1992): Pierre Yves Fux, Ambassador with special mission to Holy See.

Syria (Arab Republic) (1966): Edin Aala Hussam.
Tajikistan (1996): . . . . .
Tanzania (1968): . . . . .
Thailand (1969): Chalermpol Thanchitt.
Togo (1981): Félix Kodjo Sagbo.
Tonga (1994): . . . . .
Trinidad and Tobago (1978): Margaret King-Rousseau.
Tunisia (1972): . . . . .
Turkey (1966): Kenan Gürsoy.
Turkmenistan (1996): . . . . .
Uganda (1966): Marcel R. Tibaleka.
Ukraine (1992): Tetiana Izhevska.
United Arab Emirates (2007): Hissa Abdulla Ahmed Al-Otaiba.
United States (1984): Ken Hackett.
Uruguay: Daniel Edgardo Ramada Piendibene.
Uzbekistan (1992): . . . . .
Vanuatu (1994): . . . . .
Venezuela: . . . . .
Western Samoa (1994): . . . . .
Yemen: (1998): . . . . .
Yugoslavia: Darko Tanaskovic.
Zaire: See Congo.
Zambia (1965): Paul William Lumbi.
Zimbabwe (1980): David Douglas Hamadziripi.

Special Representatives

United Nations (Center of Information of UN at the Holy See): Shalini Dewan, director.
Office of the League of Arab States: Ahmed Al-Shibli Ghanim Taha (a Memorandum of Understanding between the Vatican Secretariat of State and the League of Arab States was signed on Apr. 23, 2009.)
United Nations High Commission for Refugees: Laurens Jolles, delegate.
State of Palestine: Issa Jamil Kassissieh.

U.S.-HOLY SEE RELATIONS

The U.S. and the Holy See announced Jan. 10, 1984, the establishment of full diplomatic relations, thus ending a period of 117 years in which there was no formal diplomatic relationship. The announcement followed action by the Congress in Nov. 1983 to end a prohibition on diplomatic relations enacted in 1867.

William A. Wilson, President Reagan's personal representative to the Holy See from 1981, was confirmed as the U.S. ambassador by the Senate, on Mar. 7, 1984. He presented his credentials to Pope John Paul II on Apr. 9, 1984, and served until May 1986, when he resigned. He succeeded by Frank Shakespeare, 1986-89, and Thomas P. Melady, 1989-93. Raymond L. Flynn, Mayor of Boston, was appointed by Bill Clinton and confirmed by the Senate in July 1993. He served until 1997 when he was succeeded by Corinne Claiborne "Lindy" Boggs. She was succeeded by James Nicholson who served until 2005. On Aug. 1, 2005, Pres. George W. Bush nominated as Nicholson's successor L. Francis Rooney III, an Oklahoma and Florida businessman. On Nov. 5, 2007, President Bush nominated Mary Ann Glendon to become Ambassador to the Holy See. The U.S. Senate voted to confirm her on Dec. 19, 2007. On May 27, 2009, Barack Obama chose Miguel Diaz, a theology professor, as Ambassador to the Holy See. On June 14, 2013, Barack Obama noninated Ken Hackett, retired president of Catholic Relief Services, to be U.S. ambassador to the Holy See. He was approved by the U.S. Senate on Aug. 1, 2013.

Abp. (later Cardinal) Pio Laghi, apostolic delegate to the U.S. since 1980, was named first pro-nuncio by the Pope on Mar. 26, 1984. He served until 1990, when he was named prefect of the Congregation for Catholic Education. Abp. (now Cardinal) Agostino Cacciavillan was appointed pro-nuncio on June 13, 1990. He served until he was named president of the Administration of the Patrimony of the Apostolic See (APSA) and was succeeded on Dec. 7, 1998, by Abp. Gabriel Montalvo. Abp. Montalvo served as nuncio from 1998 to 2005. He was succeeded by Abp. Pietro Sambi, who served from 2005-2011. The current nuncio is Abp. Carlo Maria Viganó, who was named nuncio to the United States on Oct. 19, 2011.

Nature of Relations

The nature of relations was described in nearly identical statements by John Hughes, a State Department spokesman, and the Holy See. Hughes said: "The United States of America and the Holy See, in the desire to further promote the existing mutual friendly relations, have decided by common agreement to establish diplomatic relations between them at the level of embassy on the part of the United States of America, and nunciature on the part of the Holy See, as of today, Jan. 10, 1984."

The Holy See statement said: "The Holy See and the United States of America, desiring to develop the mutual friendly relations already existing, have decided by common accord to establish diplomatic relations at the level of apostolic nunciature on the side of the Holy See and of embassy on the side of the United States beginning today, Jan. 10, 1984."

The establishment of relations was criticized as a violation of the separation-of-church-and-state principle by spokesmen for the National Council of Churches, the National Association of Evangelicals, the Baptist Joint Committee on Public Affairs, Seventh Day Adventists, Americans United for Separation of Church and State, and the American Jewish Congress.

Legal Challenge Dismissed

U.S. District Judge John P. Fullam, ruling May 7, 1985, in Philadelphia, dismissed a legal challenge to U.S.-Holy See relations brought by Americans United for Separation of Church and State. He stated that Americans United and its allies in the challenge lacked legal standing to sue, and that the courts did not have jurisdiction to intervene in foreign policy decisions of the executive branch of the U.S. government. Parties to the suit brought by Americans United were the National Association of Laity, the National Coalition of American Nuns and several Protestant church organizations. Bishop James W. Malone, president of the U.S. Catholic Conference, said in a statement: "This matter has been discussed at length for many years. It is not a religious issue but a public policy question which, happily, has now been settled in this context."

Russell Shaw, a conference spokesman, said the decision to send an ambassador to the Holy See was not a church-state issue and "confers no special privilege or status on the Church."

Earlier Relations

Official relations for trade and diplomatic purposes were maintained by the U.S. and the Papal States while the latter had the character of and acted like other sovereign powers in the international community.

Consular relations developed in the wake of an announcement, made by the papal nuncio in Paris to the American mission there Dec. 15, 1784, that the Papal States had agreed to open several Mediterranean ports to U.S. shipping.

U.S. consular representation in the Papal States began with the appointment of John B. Sartori, a native of Rome, in June 1797. Sartori's successors as consuls were: Felix Cicognani, also a Roman, and Americans George W. Greene, Nicholas Browne, William C. Sanders, Daniel LeRoy, Horatio V. Glentworth, W.J. Stillman, Edwin C. Cushman, David M. Armstrong.

Consular officials of the Papal States who served in the U.S. were: Count Ferdinand Lucchesi, 1826 to 1829, who resided in Washington; John B. Sartori, 1829 to 1841, who resided in Trenton, NJ; Daniel J. Desmond, 1841 to 1850, who resided in Philadelphia; Louis B. Binsse, 1850 to 1895, who resided in New York.

U.S. recognition of the consul of the Papal States did not cease when the states were absorbed into the Kingdom of Italy in 1871, despite pressure from Baron Blanc, the Italian minister. Binsse held the title until his death Mar. 28, 1895. No one was appointed to succeed him.

Diplomatic Relations

The U.S. Senate approved a recommendation, made by President James K. Polk in Dec. 1847 for the establishment of a diplomatic post in the Papal States. Jacob L. Martin, the first charge d'affaires, arrived in Rome Aug. 2, 1848, and presented his credentials to Pius IX Aug. 19. Martin, who died within a month, was succeeded by Lewis Cass, Jr. Cass became minister resident in 1854 and served in that capacity until his retirement in 1858.

John P. Stockton, who later became a U.S. Senator from New Jersey, was minister resident from 1858 to 1861. Rufus King was named to succeed him but, instead, accepted a commission as a brigadier general in the Army. Alexander W. Randall of Wisconsin took the appointment. He was succeeded in Aug. 1862 by Richard M. Blatchford who served until the following year. King was again nominated minister resident and served in that capacity until 1867 when the ministry was ended because of objections from some quarters in the U.S. and failure to appropriate funds for its continuation. J. C. Hooker, a secretary, remained in the Papal States until the end of March, 1868, closing the ministry and performing functions of courtesy.

Personal Envoys

Myron C. Taylor was appointed by President Franklin D. Roosevelt in 1939 to serve as his personal representative to Pope Pius XII and continued serving in that capacity during the presidency of Harry S. Truman until 1951. Henry Cabot Lodge was named to the post by President Richard M. Nixon in 1970, served also during the presidency of Gerald Ford, and represented President Carter at the canonization of St. John Neumann in 1977. Miami attorney David Walters served as the personal envoy of President Jimmy Carter to the Pope from July 1977 until his resignation Aug. 16, 1978. He was succeeded by Robert F. Wagner who served from Oct. 1978 to the end of the Carter presidency in Jan. 1981. William A. Wilson, appointed by President Ronald Reagan in Feb. 1981, served as his personal envoy until 1984 when he was named ambassador to the Holy See.

None of the personal envoys had diplomatic status.

President Harry S. Truman nominated Gen. Mark Clark to be ambassador to the Holy See in 1951, but withdrew the nomination at Clark's request because of controversy over the appointment. None of Truman's three immediate successors — Dwight D. Eisenhower, John F. Kennedy and Lyndon B. Johnson — had a personal representative to the pope.

PONTIFICAL ACADEMIES

Pontifical Academy of Sciences

(*Sources:* Annuario Pontificio, *Catholic News Service.*)
The Pontifical Academy of Sciences was constituted in its present form by Pius XI Oct. 28, 1936, in virtue of *In Multis Solaciis*, a document issued on his own initiative.

The academy is the only supranational body of its kind in the world with a pope-selected, life-long membership of outstanding mathematicians and experimental scientists regardless of creed from many countries. The normal complement of 70 members was increased to 80 in 1985-86 by John Paul II. There are additional honorary and supernumerary members.

The academy traces its origin to the *Linceorum Academia* (Academy of the Lynxes, its symbol) founded in Rome Aug. 17, 1603. Pius IX reorganized this body and gave it a new name, *Pontificia Accademia dei Nuovi Lincei,* in 1847. It was taken over by the Italian state in 1870 and called the *Accademia Nazionale dei Lincei.* Leo XIII reconstituted it with a new charter in 1887. Pius XI designated the Casina of Pope Pius IV in the Vatican Gardens as the site of academy headquarters in 1922 and gave it its present title and status in 1936. In 1940, Pius XII gave the title of Excellency to its members; John XXIII extended the privilege to honorary members in 1961.

Members in U.S.

Scientists in the U.S. who presently hold membership in the Academy are listed below according to year of appointment. Nobel prize-winners are indicated by an asterisk.

Christian de Duve,* professor of biochemistry at the International Institute of Cellular and Molecular Pathology at Brussels, Belgium, and Rockefeller University, NY (Apr. 10, 1970);

Marshall Warren Nirenberg,* director of Laboratory on genetics and biochemistry at the National Institutes of Health, Bethesda, MD (June 24, 1974).

George Palade,* professor of cellular biology at University of California, San Diego and Victor Weisskopf, professor of physics at the Massachusetts Institute of Technology, Cambridge, Mass. (Dec. 2, 1975); David Baltimore,* professor of biology at the Massachusetts Institute of Technology, Cambridge, MA; Har Gobind Khorana,* professor of biochemistry, and Alexander Rich, professor of biophysics, both at the Massachusetts Institute of Technology, Cambridge, MA (Apr. 17, 1978).

Charles Townes,* professor emeritus of physics at the University of California at Berkeley (Jan. 26, 1983); Beatrice Mintz, senior member of the Cancer Research Institute of Philadelphia and Maxine Singer, biochemist, president of Carnegie Institution, Washington, DC (June 9, 1986). Roald Z. Sagdeev, professor of physics at University of Maryland, College Park and Peter Hamilton Raven, professor of biology at the Missouri Botanical Garden of St. Louis, MO (Oct. 4, 1990); Luis Angel Caffarelli, professor of mathematics at New York University and Luigi

Luca Cavalli-Sforza, professor of genetics at Stanford University (Aug. 2, 1994). Joshua Lederberg, professor of genetics at Rockefeller University, NY (Mar. 4, 1996); Joseph Edward Murray, professor of plastic surgery at Harvard Medical School, Cambridge, MA; Paul Berg, professor of biochemistry at Stanford Univ. and Vera C. Rubin, professor of astronomy at Carnegie Institution of Washington (June 25, 1996); Gary S. Becker,* professor of economics at the University of Chicago (Mar. 3, 1997); Chen-ning Yang,* professor of physics and director of the Institute of Theoretical Physics at the State University of NY at Stony Brook (Apr. 18,1997); Frank Press, professor of geophysics and director of the Washington Advisory Group (Sept. 3, 1999); Ahmed Zewail, professor of Chemistry and Physics, California Institute of Technology, Pasadena (Sept. 3, 1999); Mario Jose Molina, professor of atmospheric chemistry at the Massachusetts Institute of Technology (Nov. 9, 2000); Günter Blobel,* professor of cellular biology of the Rockefeller University, NY (Sept. 28, 2001); Fotis C. Kafatos, professor of molecular biology at Harvard University (Jan. 23, 2003); Tsung-Dao Lee, professor of Physics at Columbia University in New York (Apr. 14, 2003); William D. Phillips,* professor of physics at the University of Maryland and the National Institute of Standards and Technology, Gaithersburg, PA (Oct. 23, 2004); Veerabhadran (Ram) Ramanathan, professor of atmospheric science at the University of California, San Diego, and director of the Center for Atmospheric Science at Scripps Institution of Oceanography, La Jolla (Oct. 23, 2004); Edward Witten, professor of Physics at the Institute for Advanced Study, Princeton, NJ (June 21, 2006); Francis S. Collins, director of the National Institutes of Health, Bethesda, MD (Oct. 10, 2009); Edward M. De Robertis, professor of chemical biology at the Howard Hughes Institute of Medicine of the University of California, CA (Oct. 10, 2009); Miguel A. L. Nicolelis, professor of neuroscience at Duke University, NC (Jan. 5, 2011).

There is also one honorary member from the U.S.: Robert J. White, professor of neurosurgery at Case Western Reserve University, Cleveland (Mar. 29, 1994).

Members in Other Countries

Listing includes place and date of selection. Nobel prize winners are indicated by an asterisk.

Argentina: Antonio M. Battro (Sept. 21, 2002).

Armenia: Rudolf M. Muradian (Oct. 16, 1994).

Austria: Hans Tuppy (Apr. 10, 1970); Walter Thirring (June 9, 1986).

Belgium: Paul Adriaan Jan Janssen (June 25, 1990); Thierry Boon-Falleur (April 9, 2002).

Brazil: Carlos Chagas, former president of the academy (Aug. 18, 1961); Johanna Döbereiner (Apr. 17, 1978); Crodowaldo Pavan (Apr. 17, 1978); Rudolf Muradian (Oct. 16, 1994).

Canada: John Charles Polanyi* (June 9, 1986).

Chile: Héctor Rezzio Croxatto (Dec. 2, 1975); Rafael Vicuna (Nov. 10, 2000).

Congo (formerly Zaire): Felix wa Kalengo Malu (Sept. 26, 1983).

Denmark: Aage Bohr* (Apr. 17, 1978).
France: André Blanc-LaPierre (Apr. 17, 1978); Paul Germain (June 9, 1986); Jacques-Louis Lions (Oct. 4, 1990); Jean-Marie Lehn (May 30, 1996); Claude Cohen-Tannoudji (May 17, 1999); Nicole M. Le Douarin (Sept. 3, 1999); Pierre Jean Léna (Jan. 18, 2001); Yves Quéré (Dec. 20, 2003).
Germany: Rudolf L. Mössbauer* (Apr. 10, 1970); Manfred Eigen* (May 12, 1981); Wolf Joachim Singer (Sept. 18, 1992); Paul Joseph Crutzen (June 25, 1996); Yuri Ivanovich Manin (June 26, 1996); Jürgen Mittelstrass (Sept. 21, 2002); Theodor Wolfgang Hänsch (June 21, 2006); Klaus von Klitzing (Oct. 9, 2007).
Ghana: Daniel Adzei Bekoe (Sept. 26, 1983).
Great Britain: Hermann Alexander Brück (Apr. 5, 1955); George Porter* (June 24, 1974); Max Ferdinand Perutz* (May 12, 1981); Stephen William Hawking (Jan. 9, 1986); Martin John Rees (June 25, 1990); Sir Richard Southwood (Sept. 18, 1992); Raymond Hide (June 25, 1996).
India: Mambillikalathil Govind Kumar Menon (May 12, 1981); Chintamani N.R. Rao (June 25, 1990).
Israel: Michael Sela (Dec. 2, 1975); Aaron J. Ciechanover (March 13, 2007).
Italy: Giampietro Puppi (Apr. 17, 1978); Nicola Cabibbo (June 9, 1986), President; Nicola Dallaporta (Oct. 5, 1989), honorary member; Bernardo Maria Colombo (Sept. 18, 1992); Antonino Zichichi (Nov. 9, 2000); Enrico Berti (Sept. 28, 2001).
Japan: Minoru Oda (Sept. 18, 1992); Ryoji Noyori* (Oct. 1, 2002); Takashi Gojobori, Jan. 31, 2008.
Kenya: Thomas R. Odhiambo (May 12, 1981).
Mexico: Marcos Moshinsky (June 9, 1986).
Nigeria: Thomas Adeoye Lambo (June 24, 1974).
Poland: Stanislaw Lojasiewicz (Jan. 28, 1983); Czeslaw Olech (June 9, 1986); Michal Heller (Oct. 4, 1990); Andrzej Szezeklik (Oct. 16, 1994).
Russia: Vladimir Isaakovich Keilis-Borok (Oct. 16, 1994); Sergei Petrovich Novikov (June 25, 1996), also teaches at University of Maryland).
Spain: Manuel Lora-Tamayo (Sept. 24, 1964); Garcia-Bellido, Antonio (June 24, 2003).
Sweden: Sune Bergström* (Dec. 14, 1985); Kai Siegbahn* (Dec. 14, 1985).
Switzerland: Werner Arber* (May 12, 1981); Carlo Rubbia* (Dec. 14, 1985); Albert Eschenmoser (June 9, 1986).
Taiwan: Te-tzu Chang (Apr. 18, 1997); Yuan Tseh Lee (Oct. 9, 2007).
Vatican City State: Cottier, Card. George, O.P. (Oct. 28, 1992; honorary member); Rev. Enrico do Rovasenda, O.P. (Nov. 13, 1968), honorary member.
Venezuela: Marcel Roche (Apr. 10, 1970); Ignacio Rodríguez-Iturbe (Jan. 10, 2008).
Ex officio members: Rev. George V. Coyne, S.J., director of Vatican Observatory (Sept. 2, 1978); Raffaele Cardinal Farina, S.D.B., prefect of the Vatican Library (May 24, 1997); Most Rev. Sergio B. Pagano, prefect of the Secret Vatican Archives (Jan. 7, 1997). President: Werner Arber, professor emeritus of microbiology at the

University of Basel, Switzerland (app. Jan. 13, 2011). Chancellor: Most Rev. Marcelo Sánchez Sorondo.
Honorary members: Rev. Jean-Michel Maldame, O.P., Dean of Faculty, Catholic Institute of Toulouse.

Pontifical Academy of Social Sciences

Founded by John Paul II, Jan. 1, 1994 (*motu proprio Socialium Scientiarum Investigationes*), to promote the study and the progress of social sciences, to advise the Vatican on social concerns and to foster research aimed at improving society. The number of members is not less than 20 nor more than 40. Five of the 32 members of the Academy (as of Jan. 1, 2014) were from the United States: Kenneth J. Arrow of Stanford University, Mary Ann Glendon of Harvard University, Kevin Ryan of Boston University, Joseph Stiglitz of Columbia University, and Russell Hittinger of the University of Tulsa. President, Prof. Margaret Scotford Archer; Chancellor, Most Rev. Marcelo Sánchez Sorondo. Address: Casino Pio IV, Vatican Gardens.

Pontifical Academy for Life

Established by John Paul II, Feb. 11, 1994 (*motu proprio Vitae Mysterium*), "to fulfill the specific task of study, information and formation on the principal problems of biomedicine and law relative to the promotion and defense of life, especially in the direct relationship they have with Christian morality and the directives of the Church's magisterium."

Members, appointed by the pope without regard to religion or nationality, represent the various branches of "the biomedical sciences and those that are most closely related to problems concerning the promotion and protection of life." Membership, as of Jan. 1, 2014, included the following from the United States:

Prof. Carl Anderson, Vice-President of the Pontifical John Paul II Institute for Studies of Marriage and the Family; Mrs. Mercedes Arzu-Wilson, founder and president of the Foundations Family of the Americas and founder and director of the Commission at the World Organization for the Family; Dr. Thomas Hilgers, founder and director of the Institute "Paul VI," Omaha, NE; Mrs. Christine de Vollmer, president of the World Organization for the Family; Prof. Denis Cavanagh, professor of obstetrics and gynecology, University of South Florida College of Medicine; Prof. John M. Finnis, professor of philosophy of law, University of Oxford and the University Notre Dame; Dr. A.J. Luke Gormally, director emeritus of Linacre Centre for Health Care Ethics in England and research professor at Ave Maria School of Law; Prof. John Haas, professor of Moral Theology and the Pontifical College Josephinum, president of the National Catholic Bioethics Center and the International Institute of Culture. President: Msgr. Ignacio Carrasco de Paula.

Hierarchy of the Catholic Church

ORGANIZATION AND GOVERNMENT

As a structured society, the Catholic Church is organized and governed along lines corresponding mainly to the jurisdictions of the pope and bishops. The pope is the supreme head of the Church. He has primacy of jurisdiction as well as honor over the entire Church. Bishops, in union with and in subordination to the pope, are the successors of the Apostles for care of the Church and for the continuation of Christ's mission in the world. They serve the people of their own dioceses, or particular churches, with ordinary authority and jurisdiction. They also share, with the pope and each other, common concern and effort for the general welfare of the whole Church.

Bishops of exceptional status are patriarchs of Eastern Catholic Churches who, subject only to the pope, are heads of the faithful belonging to their rites throughout the world.

Subject to the Holy Father and directly responsible to him for the exercise of their ministry of service to people in various jurisdictions or divisions of the Church throughout the world are: resident archbishops and metropolitans (heads of archdioceses), diocesan bishops, vicars and prefects apostolic (heads of vicariates apostolic and prefectures apostolic), certain abbots and prelates, and apostolic administrators. Each of these, within his respective territory and according to the provisions of canon law, has ordinary jurisdiction over pastors (who are responsible for the administration of parishes), priests, religious and lay persons. Also subject to the Holy Father are titular archbishops and bishops, religious orders and congregations of pontifical right, pontifical institutes and faculties, papal nuncios and apostolic delegates. Assisting the pope and acting in his name in the central government and administration of the Church are cardinals and other officials of the Roman Curia.

THE HIERARCHY

The ministerial hierarchy is the orderly arrangement of the ranks and orders of the clergy to provide for the spiritual care of the faithful, the government of the Church, and the accomplishment of the Church's total mission in the world. Persons belong to this hierarchy by virtue of ordination and canonical mission.

The term hierarchy is also used to designate an entire body or group of bishops; for example, the hierarchy of the Church, the hierarchy of the United States.

Hierarchy of Order: Consists of the pope, bishops, priests and deacons. Their purpose, for which they are ordained to holy orders, is to carry out the sacramental and pastoral ministry of the Church.

Hierarchy of Jurisdiction: Consists of the pope and bishops by divine institution, and other church officials by ecclesiastical institution and mandate, who have authority to govern and direct the faithful for spiritual ends.

The Pope

His Holiness the Pope is the Bishop of Rome, Vicar of Jesus Christ, successor of St. Peter, Prince of the Apostles, Supreme Pontiff of the Universal Church, Primate of Italy, Archbishop and Metropolitan of the Roman Province, Sovereign of the State of Vatican City, Servant of the Servants of God.

Cardinals

(*See* **p. 276**, and **Index**)

Patriarchs

Patriarch, a term which had its origin in the Eastern Church, is the title of a bishop who, second only to the pope, has the highest rank in the hierarchy of jurisdiction. He is the incumbent of one of the sees listed below. Subject only to the pope, a patriarch of the Eastern Church is the head of the faithful belonging to his rite throughout the world. The patriarchal sees are so called because of their special status and dignity in the history of the Church.

The Council of Nicaea (325) recognized three patriarchs — the Bishops of Alexandria and Antioch in the East, and of Rome in the West. The First Council of Constantinople (381) added the bishop of Constantinople to the list of patriarchs and gave him rank second only to that of the pope, the bishop of Rome and patriarch of the West; this action was seconded by the Council of Chalcedon (451) and was given full recognition by the Fourth Lateran Council (1215). The Council of Chalcedon also acknowledged patriarchal rights of the bishop of Jerusalem.

Eastern patriarchs are as follows: one of Alexandria, for the Copts; three of Antioch, one each for the Syrians, Maronites and Greek Melkites (the latter also has the personal title of Greek Melkite patriarch of Alexandria and of Jerusalem). The patriarch of Babylonia, for the Chaldeans, and the patriarch of Sis, or Cilicia, for the Armenians, should be called, more properly, *Katholikos* — that is, a prelate delegated for a universality of causes. These patriarchs are elected by bishops of their churches; they receive approval and the pallium, symbol of their office, from the pope.

Latin Rite patriarchates were established for Antioch, Jerusalem, Alexandria and Constantinople during the Crusades; afterwards, they became patriarchates in name only. Jerusalem, however, was reconstituted as a patriarchate by Pius IX, in virtue of the bull *Nulla Celebrior* of July 23, 1847. In 1964, the Latin titular patriarchates of Constantinople, Alexandria and Antioch, long a bone of contention in relations with Eastern Churches, were abolished.

As of Aug. 15, 2014, the patriarchs in the Church were: Ibrahim Isaac Sidrak, of Alexandria, for the Copts; Card. Gregory III Laham, of Antioch, for the Greek Melkites (the patriarch also has personal titles of Alexandria and Jerusalem for the Greek Melkites); Card. Bechara Rai, of Antioch, for the Maronites; Nerses

Bedros XIX Tarmouni, of Cilicia, for the Armenians; Louis Raphaël I Sako, of Babylon of the Chaldeans; Ignace Joseph III Younan, of Antioch, for the Syrians. (For biographical information on the patriarchs, see **Eastern Catholics**, p. 343.)

The titular patriarchs (in name only) of the Latin Rite were: Patriarch of Lisbon (currently vacant); Abp. Francesco Moraglia of Venice; Abp. Filipe Neri António do Rosário Ferrão of the East Indies (archbishop of Goa and Damao, India); and Abp. Fouad Twal of Jerusalem. The patriarchate of the West Indies has been vacant since 1963.

Major Archbishops

A major archbishop has the prerogatives but not the title of a patriarch. As of May 15, 2014, there were four major archbishops: Abp. Sviatoslav Schevchuk, of the major archbishopric of Kiev and Halych of the Ukrainian Catholic Church (Ukraine); Card. George Alencherry, of the major archbishopric of Ernakulam-Angomaly of the Syro-Malabar Church (India); Card. Isaac Mar Cleemis Thottunkal of the major archbishopric of Trivandrum of the Syro-Malankara Catholic Church (India), whose election was confirmed on Feb. 8, 2007, by Pope Benedict XVI); and Card. Lucian Muresan of the major archbishopric of Fagaras and Alba Julia for the Romanian Greek Catholic Church (Romania) who was promoted to the rank of major archbishop on Dec. 16, 2005.

Archbishops, Metropolitans

Archbishop: A bishop with the title of an archdiocese.

Coadjutor Archbishop: An assistant archbishop with right of succession.

Metropolitan: Archbishop of the principal see, an archdiocese, in an ecclesiastical province consisting of several dioceses. He has the full powers of bishop in his own archdiocese and limited supervisory jurisdiction and influence over the other (suffragan) dioceses in the province. The pallium, conferred by the pope, is the symbol of his status as a metropolitan.

Titular Archbishop: Has the title of an archdiocese that formerly existed in fact but now exists in title only. He does not have ordinary jurisdiction over an archdiocese. Examples are archbishops in the Roman Curia, papal nuncios, apostolic delegates.

Archbishop *ad personam:* A title of personal honor and distinction granted to some bishops. They do not have ordinary jurisdiction over an archdiocese.

Primate: A title of honor given to the ranking prelate of some countries or regions.

Bishops

Diocesan Bishop: A bishop in charge of a diocese.

Coadjutor Bishop: An assistant (auxiliary) bishop to a diocesan bishop, with right of succession to the see.

Titular Bishop: A bishop with the title of a diocese that formerly existed in fact but now exists in title only; an assistant (auxiliary) bishop to a diocesan bishop.

Episcopal Vicar: An assistant, who may or may not be a bishop, appointed by a residential bishop as his deputy for a certain part of a diocese, a determined type of apostolic work, or the faithful of a certain rite.

Eparch, Exarch: Titles of bishops of Eastern churches.

Nomination of Bishops: Nominees for episcopal ordination are selected in several ways. Final appointment and/or approval in all cases is subject to decision by the pope.

In the U.S., bishops periodically submit the names of candidates to the archbishop of their province. The names are then considered at a meeting of the bishops of the province, and those receiving a favorable vote are forwarded to the nuncio for transmission to the Holy See and consideration for possible vacancies. Bishops are free to seek the counsel of priests, religious and lay persons with respect to nominees. For the selection of diocesan bishops or archbishops, the nuncio consults with appropriate bishops of the ecclesiastical province and all other relevant officials. Normally, three names are submitted on what is termed a *terna* from the nuncio to the Congregation for Bishops. The bishop members of the Congregation, including the Cardinals, will study the *terna* and submit a complete dossier to the Holy Father for each along with their preference. The pope makes the final decision on the appointment.

Eastern Catholic churches have their own procedures and synodal regulations for nominating and making final selection of candidates for episcopal ordination. Such selection is subject to approval by the pope. The Code of Canon Law concedes no rights or privileges to civil authorities with respect to the election, nomination, presentation or designation of candidates for the episcopate.

Ad Limina Visit: Diocesan bishops and apostolic vicars are obliged to make an ad limina visit ("to the threshold" of the Apostles) every five years to the tombs of Sts. Peter and Paul, have audience with the Holy Father and consult with appropriate Vatican officials. They are required to send a report on conditions in their jurisdiction to the Cong. for bishops approximately six — and not less than three — months in advance of the scheduled visit.

Others with Ordinary Jurisdiction

Ordinary: One who has the jurisdiction of an office: the pope, diocesan bishops, vicars general, prelates of missionary territories, vicars apostolic prefects apostolic, vicars capitular during the vacancy of a see, superiors general, abbots primate and other major superiors of men religious.

Some prelates and abbots, with jurisdiction like that of diocesan bishops, are pastors of the people of God in territories (prelatures and abbacies) not under the jurisdiction of diocesan bishops.

Vicar Apostolic: Usually a titular bishop who has ordinary jurisdiction over a mission territory.

Prefect Apostolic: Has ordinary jurisdiction over a mission territory.

Apostolic Administrator: Usually a bishop appointed to administer an ecclesiastical jurisdiction temporarily. Administrators of lesser rank are also appointed on occasion and have more restricted supervisory duties.

Vicar General: A bishop's deputy for the administration of a diocese; does not have to be a bishop.

Prelates Without Jurisdiction

The title of protonotary apostolic was originally given by the fourth century or earlier to clergy who collected accounts of martyrdom and other church documents, or who served the Church with distinction in other ways. Other titles — e.g., domestic prelate, papal chamberlain, prelate of honor — are titles of clergy in service to the pope and the papal household, or of clergy honored for particular reasons. All prelates without jurisdiction are appointed by the pope, and have designated ceremonial privileges and the title of Rev. Monsignor.

SYNOD OF BISHOPS

The Synod of Bishops was chartered by Pope Paul VI Sept. 15, 1965, in a document he issued on his own initiative under the title *Apostolica Sollicitudo*. Provisions of this *motu proprio* are contained in Canons 342 to 348 of the Code of Canon Law. According to major provisions of the Synod charter:

• The purposes of the Synod are "to encourage close union and valued assistance between the Sovereign Pontiff and the bishops of the entire world; to insure that direct and real information is provided on questions and situations touching upon the internal action of the Church and its necessary activity in the world of today; to facilitate agreement on essential points of doctrine and on methods of procedure in the life of the Church."

• The Synod is a central ecclesiastical institution, permanent by nature.

• The Synod is directly and immediately subject to the pope, who has authority to assign its agenda, to call it into session, and to give its members deliberative as well as advisory authority.

• In addition to a limited number of ex officio members and a few heads of male religious institutes, the majority of the members are elected by and representative of national or regional episcopal conferences. The pope reserved the right to appoint the general secretary, special secretaries and no more than 15 percent of the total membership.

The pope is president of the Synod. The secretary general is Cardinal Lorenzo Baldisseri. Address: Palazzo del Bramante, Via delia Conciliazione 34, 00193 Rome, Italy.

Assemblies

1. First Assembly: The first assembly was held from Sept. 29 to Oct. 29, 1967. Its objectives, as stated by Pope Paul VI, were "the preservation and strengthening of the Catholic faith, its integrity, its force, its development, its doctrinal and historical coherence."

2. Pope-Bishop Relations: The second assembly, held Oct. 11 to 28, 1969, was extraordinary in character. It opened the way toward greater participation by bishops with the pope and each other in the governance of the Church.

3. Priesthood and Justice: The ministerial priesthood and justice in the world were the principal topics under discussion at the second ordinary assembly, Sept. 30 to Nov. 6, 1971.

4. Evangelization: The assembly of Sept. 27 to Oct. 26, 1974, produced a general statement on evangelization of the modern world, covering the need for it and its relationship to efforts for total human liberation from personal and social evil.

5. Catechetics: The fourth ordinary assembly, Sept. 30 to Oct. 29, 1977, focused attention on catechetics, with special reference to children and young people.

6. Family: "A Message to Christian Families in the Modern World" and a proposal for a "Charter of Family Rights" were produced by the assembly held Sept. 26 to Oct. 25, 1980.

7. Reconciliation: Penance and reconciliation in the mission of the Church was the theme of the assembly held Sept. 29 to Oct. 29, 1983.

8. Vatican II Review: The second extraordinary assembly was convened Nov. 24 to Dec. 8, 1985, for the purposes of: (1) recalling the Second Vatican Council; (2) evaluating the implementation of its enactments during the 20 years since its conclusion; (3) seeking ways and means of promoting renewal in the Church in accordance with the spirit and letter of the council.

9. Vocation and Mission of the Laity in the Church and in the World 20 years after the Second Vatican Council: The seventh ordinary assembly, Oct. 1–30, 1987, produced a set of 54 propositions which were presented to the pope for consideration in the preparation of a document of his own on the theme of the assembly. He responded with the apostolic exhortation, *Christifideles Laici*, "The Christian Faithful Laity," released by the Vatican Jan. 30, 1989.

10. Formation of Priests in Circumstances of the Present Day: The eighth general assembly, Sept. 30 – Oct. 28, 1990, dealt principally with the nature and mission of the priesthood. Pope John Paul issued an apostolic exhortation entitled *Pastores Dabo Vobis* ("I Will Give You Shepherds") Apr. 7, 1992.

11. The Consecrated Life and Its Role in the Church and in the World: The ninth general assembly was held Oct. 2 – 29, 1994. Pope John Paul's reflections on the proceedings of the assembly and the recommendations of the bishops were the subjects of his apostolic exhortation entitled *Vita Consecrata* ("Consecrated Life"), issued Mar. 25, 1996.

12. The Bishop: Servant of the Gospel of Jesus Christ for the Hope of the World: The 10th ordinary general assembly was held from Sept. 30 – Oct. 27, 2001. Pope John Paul II's reflections on the proceedings of the assembly and the recommendations of the bishops was the subject of the apostolic exhortation *Ecclesia in Europa*, issued on June 28, 2003.

13. The Eucharist: Source and Summit of the Life and Mission of the Church: The 11th ordinary general assembly was held from Oct. 2 – Oct. 23, 2005. Pope Benedict XVI's reflections on the proceedings of the assembly and the recommendations of the bishops were the subject of an apostolic exhortation, *Sacramentum Caritatis* issued on Mar. 13, 2007.

14. The Word of God in the Life and Mission of the Church: The 12th ordinary general assembly was from Oct. 5 – Oct. 26, 2008. Pope Benedict XVI's reflections on the proceedings of the assembly and the recommendations of the Bishops was the subject of an apostolic exhortation, *Verbum Domini*, issued on Nov. 11, 2010.

15. The New Evangelization for the Transmission of the Christian Faith: The 13th ordinary general assembly was held in Oct. 2012. [See under **Special Reports**.]

Special Synods have been held for Europe (Nov. 28 – Dec. 14, 1991, on the theme "So that we might be witnesses of Christ who has set us free"); for Africa (Apr. 10 – May 8, 1994, on the theme "The Church in Africa and Her Evangelizing Mission Toward the Year 2000: 'You Shall Be My Witnesses' (Acts 1:8)"); for Lebanon (Nov. 27 – Dec. 14, 1995, on the theme "Christ is Our Hope: Renewed by His Spirit, in Solidarity We Bear Witness to His Love"); the Americas (Nov. 16 – Dec. 12, 1997, on the theme, "Encounter with the Living Jesus Christ: Way to Conversion, Community and Solidarity"); for Asia (Apr. 19 – May 14, 1998, on the theme "Jesus Christ the Savior and His Mission of Love and Service in Asia: '...That They May Have Life, and Have it Abundantly' (Jn 10:10)"; for Oceania (Nov. 12 – Dec. 12, 1998, on the theme "Jesus Christ and the Peoples of Oceania: Walking His Way, Telling His Truth, Living His Life"; a special assembly for Europe (Oct. 1–23, 1999), on the theme "Jesus Christ, Alive in His Church, Source of Hope for Europe"; a Second Special Assembly for Africa (Oct. 5–25, 2009); and a Special Assembly for the Middle East (Oct. 10–24, 2010). An Extraordinary Synod on the Family is scheduled for Oct. 2014., and an Ordinary Synod on the Family is scheduled for Oct. 2015.

COLLEGE OF CARDINALS

Cardinals are chosen by the pope to serve as his principal assistants and advisers in the central administration of church affairs. Collectively, they form the College of Cardinals. Provisions regarding their selection, rank, roles and prerogatives are detailed in Canons 349 to 359 of the Code of Canon Law.

History of the College

The College of Cardinals was constituted in its present form and categories of membership in the 12th century. Before that time the pope had a body of advisers selected from among the bishops of dioceses neighboring Rome, priests and deacons of Rome. The college was given definite form in 1150, and in 1179 the selection of cardinals was reserved exclusively to the pope. Sixtus V fixed the number at 70, in 1586. Bl. John XXIII set aside this rule when he increased membership at the 1959 and subsequent consistories. The number was subsequently raised by Paul VI. The number of cardinals entitled to participate in papal elections was limited to 120 by Paul VI in 1973. The limit on the number of cardinals was set aside by Pope John Paul II three times, in 1998, 2001 and 2003. *As of Aug. 1, 2014,* **117 of the 210** *cardinals were eligible to vote.*

In 1567 the title of cardinal was reserved to members of the college; previously it had been used by priests attached to parish churches of Rome and by the leading clergy of other notable churches. The Code of Canon Law promulgated in 1918 decreed that all cardinals must be priests. Previously there had been cardinals who were not priests (e.g., Card. Giacomo Antonelli, d. 1876, Secretary of State to Pius IX, was a deacon). John XXIII provided in the *motu proprio Cum Gravissima* Apr. 15, 1962, that cardinals would henceforth be bishops; this provision is included in the revised Code of Canon Law.

Age Limits

Pope Paul VI placed age limits on the functions of cardinals in the apostolic letter *Ingravescentem Aetatem,* dated Nov. 21, 1970, and effective Jan. 1, 1971. At 80, they cease to be members of curial departments and offices, and become ineligible to take part in papal elections. They retain membership in the College of Cardinals, however, with relevant rights and privileges.

Three Categories

All cardinals except Eastern patriarchs are aggregated to the clergy of Rome. This aggregation is signified by the assignment to each cardinal, except the patriarchs, of a titular church in Rome. The three categories of members of the college are cardinal bishops, cardinal priests and cardinal deacons.

Cardinal bishops include the six titular bishops of the suburbicarian sees and Eastern patriarchs. First in rank are the titular bishops of the suburbicarian sees neighboring Rome: Ostia, Palestrina, Porto-Santa Rufina, Albano, Velletri-Segni, Frascati, Sabina-Poggio Mirteto. The dean of the college holds the title of the See of Ostia as well as his other suburbicarian see. These cardinal bishops are engaged in full-time service in the central administration of church affairs in departments of the Roman Curia.

Full recognition is given in the revised Code of Canon Law to the position of Eastern patriarchs as the heads of sees of apostolic origin with ancient liturgies. They are assigned rank among the cardinals in order of seniority, following the suburbicarian titleholders.

Cardinal priests, who were formerly in charge of leading churches in Rome, are bishops whose dioceses are outside Rome.

Cardinal deacons, who were formerly chosen according to regional divisions of Rome, are titular bishops assigned to full-time service in the Roman Curia.

The dean and sub-dean of the college are elected by the cardinal bishops — subject to approval by the pope — from among their number. The dean, or the sub-dean in his absence, presides over the college as the first among equals. Cardinals Angelo Sodano and Roger Etchegeray were elected dean and vice-dean, respectively, on Apr. 30, 2005. The Secretary to the College of Cardinals is Abp. Ilson de Jesus Montanari, sec. of the Cong. for Bishops.

Selection and Duties

Cardinals are selected by the pope and are inducted into the college in appropriate ceremonies. Cardinals under the age of 80 elect the pope when the Holy See becomes vacant (*see* **Index: Papal Election,** *see also below under* **Conclave**); and are major administrators of church affairs, serving in one or more departments of the Roman Curia. Cardinals in charge of agencies of the Roman Curia and Vatican City are asked to submit their resignation from office to the pope on reaching the age of 75. All cardinals enjoy a number of special rights and privileges. Their title, while symbolic of high honor, does not signify any extension of the powers of holy orders. They are called princes of the Church.

A cardinal *in pectore (petto)* is one whose selection has been made by the pope but whose name has not been disclosed; he has no title, rights or duties until such disclosure is made, at which time he takes precedence from the time of the secret selection.

BIOGRAPHIES OF CARDINALS

Biographies of the cardinals, as of Sept. 15, 2014, are given below in alphabetical order. For historical notes, order of seniority and geographical distribution of cardinals, see separate entries. An * asterisk indicates cardinals ineligible to take part in papal elections.

Abril y Castello, Santos: b. Sept. 21, 1935, Alfambra, diocese of Teruel, Spain; Rome; ord. priest, Mar. 19, 1960; entered the diplomatic service of the Holy See in 1967 and served in the nunciatures in Pakistan and Turkey and in the Secretariat of State; ord. titular abp. of Tamada and app. nuncio in Bolivia, Apr. 29, 1985; pro-nuncio in Cameroon, Gabon and Equatorial Guinea, Oct. 2, 1989; nuncio in the Federal Republic of Yugoslavia, Feb. 24, 1996; nuncio to Argentina, Mar. 4, 2000; nuncio to Slovenia, Bosnia and Hercegovina, and Macedonia in 2003; app. vice camerlengo of the Holy Roman Church, Jan. 22, 2011; app. archpriest of the papal Liberian basilica, Rome, Nov. 21, 2011; app. pres. Comm. of Cardinals Overseeing the Works of Religion, Mar. 4, 2014; card., Feb. 18, 2012, with the deaconry of S. Ponziano.

Curial membership: Bishops, Education, Evangelization, Saints (Congregation); Works of Religion (Commission); Eucharistic Congresses.

Agustoni,* **Gilberto:** b. July 26, 1922, Schaffhausen,

Switzerland; ord., Apr. 20, 1946; called to Rome in 1950 to work under Card. Ottaviani in the Cong. for the Holy Office; a Prelate Auditor of the Roman Rota, 1970-86; ord. titular abp. of Caorle Jan. 6, 1987; sec. of the Cong. for the Clergy, 1986-92; pro-prefect of the Apostolic Signatura, 1992-94; card. deacon, Nov. 26, 1994; titular church Sts. Urban and Laurence at Prima Porta. Prefect of Supreme Tribunal of Apostolic Signatura, 1994-98.

Alencherry, George: b. Apr. 19, 1945, Kottayam, archiepiscopal of Changanacherry of the Syro-Malabars, India; ord. priest, Nov. 19, 1972; ord. first eparch of Thuckalay of the Syro-Malbars, Feb. 2, 1997; elected abp. major of Ernakulam-Changanacherry by the Syro-Malabar Synod, May 24, 2011; election was confirmed by Pope Benedict XVI, May 25, 2011; card., Feb. 18, 2012, with the title of S. Bernardo alle Terme Diocleziane.

Curial membership: Doctrine of the Faith, Oriental Churches (Congregations).

Álvarez Martínez,* Francisco: b. July 14, 1925, Santa Eulalia de Ferroñes Llanera, Spain; ord., June 11, 1950; app. bp. of Tarazona, Apr. 13, 1973; cons., June 3, 1973; bp. of Calahorra and La Calzado-Logroño, Dec. 20, 1976; transferred to Orihuela-Alicante, May 12, 1989; abp. of Toledo, 1995-2002; member of the Standing Committee and the Executive Committee of the Spanish Episcopal Conference; card., Feb. 21, 2001; titular church, St. Mary Regina Pacis in Monte Verde.

Amato, S.D.B., Angelo: b. June 8, 1938, Molfetta, Italy; studied at the Pontifical Salesian Univ. and the Pontifical Gregorian Univ. in Rome and the Salesian Univ. in Brindisi; ord. Dec. 22, 1967, for the Salesians; ord. titular abp. of Sila, Jan. 6, 2003; sec. of the Cong. for the Doctrine of the Faith, 2002-2008; prefect of the Cong. for the Causes of the Saints, July 9, 2008; created card. deacon, Nov. 20, 2010; deaconry of S. Maria in Aquiro.

Curial membership: Divine Worship, Doctrine (congregations); Christian Unity (council).

Amigo Vallejo,* O.F.M., Carlos: b. Aug. 23, 1934, Medina de Rioseco, Spain; joined Order of Friars Minor and ord. Aug. 17, 1960; ord. abp. of Tanger, Morocco, Apr. 28, 1974; abp. of Toledo, 1974-84; abp. of Seville, 1984-2009; card., Oct. 21, 2003; titular church, St. Mary of Monserrat of the Spanish.

Curial membership: Health Care Workers (council); Latin America (commission).

Angelini,* Fiorenzo: b. Aug. 1, 1916, Rome, Italy; ord., Feb. 3, 1940; master of pontifical ceremonies, 1947-54; ord. bp. (titular see of Messene) July 29, 1956, and head of Rome Vicariate's section for apostolate to health care workers; abp, 1985; pres. of newly established Curia agency for health care workers; card. deacon, June 28, 1991, deaconry, Holy Spirit (in Sassio). President of Pontifical Council for Pastoral Assistance to Health Care Workers, 1989-96.

Antonelli, Ennio: b. Nov. 18, 1936, Todi, Italy; ord., Apr. 2, 1960; bp. of Gubbio, Aug. 29, 1982; abp. of Perugia-Città della Pieve, 1988-2001; secretary-general of the Italian Episcopal Conference, 1995; abp. of Florence, Mar. 21, 2001-June 7, 2008; pres. of the Pont. Council for the Family, 2008-2012; card., Oct. 21, 2003; titular church, St. Andrew delle Fratte.

Curial membership: Laity, Social Communications (councils).

Arinze,* Francis: b. Nov. 1, 1932, Eziowelle, Nigeria; ord., Nov. 23, 1958; ord. titular bp. of Fissiana and aux. bp. of Onitsha, Aug. 29, 1965; abp. of Onitsha, 1967-84; pro-president of Secretariat for Non–Christians (now the Council for Interreligious Dialogue), 1984; card. deacon, May 25, 1985; deaconry, St. John (della Pigna); transferred to the order of card. priests, Jan. 29, 1996; transferred to the order of card. bishops, Apr. 25, 2005, with Suburbicarian See of Veletri-Segni; President of Council for Interreligious Dialogue, 1985-2002; Prefect of the Cong. for Divine Worship and the Discipline of the Sacraments, 2002-2008.

Curial membership: Doctrine of the Faith, Oriental Churches, Evangelization of Peoples, Causes of Saints (congregations); Laity, Christian Unity (councils); International Eucharistic Congresses (committee).

Arns,* O.F.M., Paulo Evaristo: b. Sept. 14, 1921, Forquilhinha, Brazil; ord., Nov. 30, 1945; held various teaching posts; director of *Sponsa Christi,* monthly review for religious, and of the Franciscan publication center in Brazil; ord. titular bp. of Respetta and aux. bp. of São Paulo, July 3, 1966; abp. of São Paulo, 1970-98; card., Mar. 5, 1973; titular church, St. Anthony of Padua (in Via Tuscolana).

Assis, Raymundo Damasceno: b. Feb. 15, 1937, Capela Nova, Brazil; studied at the Major Seminary of Mariana, Pontifical Gregorian Univ., Rome, the Superior Institute of Catechesis in Münich, Germany, and the Univ. of Brasília and the Pontifical Catholic Univ. of Mina Gerais; ord. Mar. 19, 1968; ord. titular bp. of Novapietra and aux. bp. of Brasília, Sept. 15, 1986; sec. general of the Episcopal Council of Latin America (CELAM) 1991-1995; app. abp. of Aparecida, Jan. 28, 2004; pres. of CELAM, 2007-2011; created card. priest, Nov. 20, 2010; titular church of Immacolata al Tiburtino.

Curial membership: Social Communications (council); Latin America (commission).

Backis, Audrys Juozas: b. Feb. 1, 1937, Kaunas, Lithuania; ord., Mar. 18, 1961; entered Holy See diplomatic service in 1964 and posted to the Philippines, Costa Rica, Turkey, Nigeria, and the Council for the Public Affairs of the Church; underscretary to the Council for the Public Affairs of the Church, 1979-88; app. titular abp. of Meta and nuncio to the Netherlands, Aug. 5, 1988; app. abp. of Vilnius Dec. 24, 1991; pres. of the Lithuanian Bishops' Conference; card., Feb. 21, 2001; titular church, Nativity of Our Lord Jesus Christ in Via Gallia.

Curial membership: Education (congregation); Social Communication (council).

Bagnasco, Angelo: b. Feb. 14, 1943, Pontevico, Italy; ord. June 29, 1966; earned a doctorate in philosophy from the State Univ. of Genoa in 1979 and served in pastoral ministry from 1966-1985; professor of metaphysics and contemporary atheism at the Theological Faculty of Northern Italy, 1980-1998; cons. bp. of Pesaro, Feb. 7, 1998; promoted to abp. when the diocese was elevated to the rank of metropolitan see, Mar. 11, 2000; app. military ordinary for Italy, June 20, 2003; app. abp. of Genoa, Aug. 29, 2006; app. by Pope Benedict XVI president of the Italian Episcopal Conference on Mar. 7, 2007 (re-appointed, Mar. 17, 2012); card., Nov. 24, 2007, titular church, Great Mother of God.

Curial membership: Bishops, Oriental Churches, Sacraments (congregation).

Baldisseri, Lorenzo: b. Sept. 29, 1940, San Pietro in Campo, Barga, Italy; ord. June 29, 1963; studied at the seminary of Pisa, the Pontifical Lateran Univ., Rome, for a licentiate in theology and doctorate in canon law, the Pontifical Ecclesiastical Academy, and the Univ. of Perugia; entered the diplomatic service of the Holy See in 1973 and served in the nunciatures in Guatemala, El Salvador, Brazil, Japan, Paraguay, Zimbabwe, and Haiti; taught canon law and international law at the Salesian International Theological Institute and at the Francisco Marroquín University in Guatemala; app. titular abp. of Diocleziana and nuncio to Haiti, Jan. 15, 1992; ord. Mar. 7, 1992; nuncio to Paraguay, 1995-1999; nuncio to India and Nepal, 1999-2002; nuncio to Brazil, 2002-2012; app. sec. of the Cong. for Bishops, Jan. 11, 2012 and sec. of the College of Cardinals, Mar. 7, 2012; sec. of the 2013 conclave; app. sec. general of the Synod of Bishops, Sept. 21, 2013; created a card., Feb. 22, 2014 with the the deaconry of S. Anselmo all'Aventino.

Curial membership: Bishops (congregation).

Barbarin, Philippe: b. Oct. 17, 1950, Rabat, Morocco; ord. Dec. 17, 1977; from 1994 to 1998, served in Madagascar as pastor and professor in the island's seminary; ord. bp. of Moulins, France, Nov. 22, 1998; abp. of Lyon, July 16, 2002, card., Oct. 21, 2003; titular church, Most Holy Spirit al Monte Pincio.

Curial membership: Sacraments, Consecrated Life and Societies of Apostolic Life (congregations).

Bassetti, Gualtiero: b. Apr. 7, 1942, Popolano di Marradi, Italy; ord. June 29, 1966; studied at the Archiepiscopal Seminary of Florence; cons. bp. of Massa Marittima-Piombino, Sept. 8, 1994; app. bp. of Arezzo-Cortona-Sansepolcro, Nov. 21, 1998; app. abp. of Perugia-Città della Pieve, July 16, 2009; created card. priest, Feb. 22, 2014 with the title of S. Cecilia.

Curial membership: Bishops (congregation), Christian Unity (commission).

Baum,* William Wakefield: b. Nov. 21, 1926, Dallas, TX; moved to Kansas City, MO, at an early age; ord. (Kansas City-St. Joseph diocese), May 12, 1951; executive director of U.S. Bishops' Commission for Ecumenical and Interreligious Affairs, 1964-69; attended Second Vatican Council as *peritus* (expert adviser); ord. bp. of Springfield-Cape Girardeau, MO, Apr. 6, 1970; abp. of Washington, DC, 1973-80; card., May 24, 1976; titular church, Holy Cross on the Via Flaminia; prefect of Cong. for Catholic Education (Seminaries and Institutes of Study), 1980-90. Major Penitentiary, 1990-2001; res., Nov. 22, 2001.

Becker,* S.J., Karl Josef: b. Apr. 18, 1928, Cologne, Germany; entered the Society of Jesus (Jesuits) and ord. priest July 31, 1958, for the Society; served as professor of dogmatic theology at the Pontifical Gregorian University, Rome, from 1969 to 2003; consultor of the Cong. for the Doctrine of the Faith from 1977; cardinal, Feb. 18, 2012, but was exempted from episcopal consecration; deaconry of S. Giuliano Martire.

Bertello, Giuseppe: b. Oct. 1, 1942, Foglizzo, Italy; earned a doctorate in canon law and studied diplomacy at the Pontifical Ecclesiastical Academy, Rome; ord. priest, June 29, 1966, and entered the diplomatic service of the Holy See in 1971; served in Sudan, Turkey, Venezuela and in the Office of the Organization of the United Nations in Geneva; ord. titular abp. of Urbisaglia and named pro-nuncio in Ghana, Togo and Benin, Oct. 17, 1987; nuncio in Rwanda, 1991; app. permanent Observer of Office of the United Nations and Specialized Institutions in Geneva in 1995; nuncio to Mexico in 2000; nuncio in Italy and in the Republic of San Marino in 2007; app. president of the Pontifical Commission for Vatican City State and of the Governorate of Vatican City State, Sept. 3, 2011; Council of Cardinals, Apr. 13, 2014; card. Feb. 18, 2012 with the deaconry of Ss. Vito, Modesto e Crescenzia.

Curial membership: Bishops, Evangelization (congregations); Justice and Peace (council).

Bertone,* S.D.B., Tarcisio: b. Dec. 2, 1934, Romano Canavese, entered the Society of St. Francis de Sales of St. John Bosco (Salesians); ord., July 1, 1960; prof. of Special Moral Theology, Pontifical Salesian Athenaeum (later Pontifical Salesian Univ. in 1973), 1967-76; prof. of Canon Law, 1976-1991; vice-rector, Pontifical Salesian Univ. of Rome, 1987–1989; ord. abp. of Vercelli, Aug. 1, 1991; sec. of the Cong. for the Doctrine of the Faith, 1995-2002; abp. of Genoa, Dec. 10, 2002; card., Oct. 21, 2003; titular church, St. Mary, Helper in Via Tuscolana; transferred to the order

of card. bishops (with the suburbicarian see of Frascati), May 10, 2008; Secretary of State, Sept. 15, 2006-Aug. 31, 2013; app. Chamberlain (Camerlengo) of the Holy Roman Church, Apr. 4, 2007.

Curial membership: Bishops, Clergy, Doctrine of the Faith, Eastern Churches, Evangelization, Sacraments (congregations); Institute for Works of Religion (commission).

Betori, Giuseppe: b. Feb. 25, 1947, Foligno, Italy; earned a doctorate in Sacred Scripture from the Pontifical Biblical Institute; ord. priest, Sept. 26, 1970; ord. titular bp. of Falerone, May 6, 2001, and served as sec. general of the Italian Bishops' Conference; app. abp. of Florence, Sept. 8, 2008; survived an assassination attempt in November 2011; cardinal on Feb. 18, 2012, with the title of S. Marcello.

Curial membership: Education (congregation); Culture (council).

Biffi,* Giacomo: b. June 13, 1928, Milan, Italy; ord., Dec. 23, 1950; ord. titular bp. of Fidene and aux. of Milan, Jan. 11, 1976; abp. of Bologna, 1984-2003; card., May 25, 1985; titular church, Sts. John the Evangelist and Petronius.

Bozanic, Josip: b. Mar. 20, 1949, Rijeka, Yugoslavia; ord., June 29, 1975; prof. of canon law and dogmatic theology in the Seminary of Rijeka, 1988-1997; ord. bp. of Krk, Veglia, June 25, 1989; abp. of Zagreb, Croatia, July 5, 1997; pres. of the Croatian Conference of Bishops and vice-pres. of the Council of European Bishops' Conferences; card., Oct. 21, 2003; titular church, St. Jerome of the Croatians. Abp. of Zagreb.

Curial membership: Sacraments (congregation); Laity (council).

Brady, Seán Baptist: b. Aug. 16, 1939, Drumcalpin, diocese of Kilmore, Ireland; ord. Feb. 22, 1964; served from 1964-1993 as a faculty member in the Minor Seminary, Kilmore and then vice-rector and rector of the Pontifical Irish College in Rome; cons. coadj. abp. of Armagh, Ireland, Feb. 19, 1995 and acceded to the metropolitan and primatial see of Armagh, Oct. 1, 1996; has been a leading voice for peace in Northern Ireland and has warned against secularism in the country; card., Nov. 24, 2007, titular church, Sts. Quirico and Giulitta.

Curial membership: Christian Unity (council); Culture (commission).

Brandmüller,* Walter: b. Jan. 5, 1929, Ansbach, Germany; studied at the Ludwig-Maximilians Univ., Münich; ord. July 26, 1953; served as a professor of Church History and Patrology; app. canon of the chapter of St. Peter's Basilica, 1997, and pres. of the Pontifical Committee for Historical Sciences, 1998-2009; ord. titular abp. of Cesarea di Mauretania, Nov. 13, 2010; created card. deacon, Nov. 20, 2010; deaconry of S. Giuliano dei Fiaminghi.

Bráz de Aviz, João: b. Apr. 24, 1947, Mafra, Brazil; earned a doctorate in theology at the Pontifical Lateran University, Rome; ord. priest, Nov. 26, 1972; ord. titular bp. of Flenucleta and aux. bp. of Vitória, Apr. 6, 1994; app. bp. of Ponta Grossa, Aug. 12, 1998; took possession on Oct. 15, 1999 and abp. of Maringa, July 17, 2002; app. abp. of Brasília, Jan. 28, 2004; app. prefect of the Congregation for the Institutes of Consecrated Life and the Societies of Apostolic Life, Jan. 4, 2011; card., Feb. 18, 2012, with the deaconry of S. Elena fuori Porta Prenestina.

Curial membership: Clergy (congregation).

Brenes Solórzano, Leopoldo José: b. Mar. 7, 1949, Ticuantepe, Nicaragua; ord. Aug. 16, 1974; studied at the National Seminary Nuestra Señora de Fátima of Managua, the Superior Institute of Ecclesiastical Studies (ISEE), Méxio (theology), the Pontifical Gregorian Univ. and Pontifical Lateran Univ., Rome; ord. titular bp. of Maturba and aux. of

Managua, Mar. 19, 1988; app. bp. of Matagalpa, Nov. 2, 1991; app. abp. of Managua, Apr. 1, 2005; created card. priest, Feb. 22, 2014 with the title of S. Gioacchino ai Prati di Castello.

Burke, Raymond Leo: b. June 30, 1948, Richland Center, WI; studied at Holy Cross Seminary, La Crosse, WI, Catholic Univ., Washington, DC, North American College and Gregorian Univ., Rome; holds a diploma in Latin Letters and a doctorate in Canon Law; ord. (La Crosse diocese), June 29, 1975; served in the Supreme Tribunal of the Apostolic Signatura (the highest court in the Church) and was the first American to hold the position of Defender of the Bond of the Supreme Tribunal of the Apostolic Signatura; app. bp. of La Crosse, Dec. 10, 1994; ord. Jan. 6, 1995, pres. of the board of directors, National Catholic Rural Life Conference, 1996-2001; app. abp. of St. Louis, Dec. 2, 2003; app. prefect of the Supreme Tribunal of the Apostolic Signatura, June 27, 2008; he is considered one of the greatest living experts on canon law; created card. deacon, Nov. 20, 2010; deaconry of S. Agatha of the Goths.

Curial membership: Secretariat of State; Divine Worship (congregations); Texts (council).

Cacciavillan,* Agostino: b. Aug. 14, 1926, Novale de Valdagno (Vicenza), Italy; ord., June 26, 1949; attended Pont. Ecclesiastical Academy; entered Holy See diplomatic service; posted to the Philippines, Spain, Portugal, and Secretariat of State; pro-nuncio in Kenya and apostolic delegate to Seychelles, 1976; titular abp. of Amiternum, Feb. 28, 1976; nuncio to India, 1981; pro-nuncio to Nepal, 1985; nuncio to United States and permanent observer at the Org. of American States, 1990; pres. Admin. of the Patrimony of the Apostolic See (APSA), 1998-2002; card. deacon, Feb. 21, 2001; protodeacon, Mar. 2, 2008; deaconry, Holy Guardian Angels in Città Giardino.

Caffarra, Carlo: b. June 1, 1938, Samboseto di Busseto, in the province of Parma, Italy; ord. July 2, 1961; studied at the Pontifical Lombard Seminary, Gregorian Univ., for a doctorate in canon law, and the Pontifical Accademia Alfonsiana, with a diploma for a specialization in Moral Theology; after holding a variety of teaching positions, he was named to the International Theological Commission in 1974; founded in 1981 the John Paul II Pontifical Institute for Studies on Marriage and the Family; consultor to the Cong. for the Doctrine of the Faith, 1983- 88; app. Sept. 8, 1995, abp. of Ferrara-Comacchio; app. Dec. 16, 2003, abp. of Bologna; pres. of the Episcopal Conference of Emilia Romagna; card. Mar. 24, 2006; titular church, San Giovanni Battista dei Fiorentini.

Curial membership: Evangelization of People (con gregation); Family (council); Pontifical Academy of Life; Apostolic Signatura.

Calcagno, O.F.M., Domenico: b. Feb. 3, 1943, Parodi Ligure, province of Alessandria, Italy; earned a doctorate in Sacred Theology from the Pontifical Gregorian Univ., Rome; ord. priest, Feb. 25, 1967, ord. bp. of Savona-Noli, Mar. 9, 2002; app. sec. of the Administration of the Patrimony of the Apostolic See, Aug. 31, 2007 and elevated to abp.; app. president of the Administration of the Patrimony of the Apostolic See, July 7, 2011; card., Feb. 18, 2012, with the deaconry of Annunciazione della Beata Vergine Maria a Via Ardeatina.

Curial membership: Evangelization (congregation); Health Care (council); Vatican City State (commission).

Canestri,* Giovanni: b. Sept. 30, 1918, Castelspina, Italy; ord., Apr. 12, 1941; spiritual director of Rome's seminary, 1959; ord. titular bp. of Tenedo and aux. to the card. vicar of Rome, July 30, 1961; bp. of Tortona, 1971–75; titular bp. of Monterano (personal title of abp.) and vice regent of Rome, 1975–84; abp. of Cagliari, 1984–87; abp. of Genoa, July 6, 1987–95; card., June

28, 1988; titular church, St. Andrew of the Valley.

Cañizares Llovera, Antonio: b. Oct. 10, 1945, Utiel, Spain; after studies in the diocesan seminary of Valencia, he earned a doctorate in theology from the Pontifical Univ. of Salamanca in 1971; ord. June 21, 1970; sec. of the Episcopal Commission for the Doctrine of the Faith, 1985-92; founder and first presdent of the Spanish Assoc. of Catechists, 1977-89; app. bp. of Ávila, Mar. 6, 1992; contributed to the compilation of the Spanish-language edition of the *Catechism of the Catholic Church*; app. abp. of Granada, Dec. 10, 1996; founder, first grand chancellor of the Catholic Univ., "Santa Teresa de Jesús" in Ávila, 1994-97; app. metropolitan abp. of Toledo and primate of Spain, Oct. 24, 2002; card., Mar. 24, 2006; titular church, di San Pancrazio; app. Prefect of the Cong. for Divine Worship and the Discipline of the Sacraments, Dec. 9, 2008; app. abp. of Valencia, Aug. 28, 2014.

Curial membership: Bishops, Doctrine of the Faith (congregations); Ecclesia Dei, Latin America (commissions).

Capovilla, Loris Francesco: b. Oct. 14, 1915, Pontelongo, Italy; ord. May 23, 1940; studied at the Patriarchal Seminary of Venice; served as secretary to Angelo Giuseppe Roncalli, patriarch of Venice, and later Pope John XXIII, from Mar. 15, 1953 to June 3, 1963; app. canon of the Vatican basilica in 1960; app. abp. of Chieti, June 25, 1967; ord. July 15, 1967; transferred to the titular see of Messembria (the titular see of **Archbishop Roncalli**) and named prelate of Loreto and pontifical delegate to the Lauretano Shrine, Sept. 25, 1971; ret. Dec. 10, 1988; created card. priest, Feb. 22, 2014 with the title of S. Maria in Trastevere.

Cassidy,* Edward Idris: b. July 5, 1924, Sydney, Australia; ord., July 23, 1949; entered Vatican diplomatic service in 1955; served in nunciatures in India, Ireland, El Salvador and Argentina; ord. titular bp. of Amantia with personal title of abp., Nov. 15, 1970; pro-nuncio to Republic of China (Taiwan), 1970-79 and pro-nuncio to Bangladesh and apostolic delegate in Burma, 1973-79; pro-nuncio to Lesotho and apostolic delegate to southern Africa, 1979-84; pro-nuncio to the Netherlands, 1984-88; substitute of the Secretary of State for General Affairs, 1988-89; pres. of Pontifical Council for Promoting Christian Unity, 1989-2001; card. deacon, June 28, 1991; deaconry, St. Mary (in via Lata).

Castrillón Hoyos,* Darío: b. July 4, 1929, Medellín, Colombia; ord.; Oct. 26, 1952; dir. local Cursillo Movement; delegate for Catholic Action; taught canon law at the Free Civil Univ.; gen. sec. of the Colombian Bishops' Conference; coadj. bp. of Pereira, June 2, 1971; bp. of Pereira, 1976-1992; gen. sec. of Latin American Episcopal Council (CELAM), 1983-87; pres. CELAM, 1987-91; abp. of Bucaramanga, 1992-96; pro-prefect Cong. for the Clergy, 1996-98; Pref. Cong. for the Clergy, 1998-2006; Protodeacon, 2007- 2008; card. deacon, Feb. 21, 1998; card. priest, Mar. 2, 2008; titular church, Holy Name of Mary on the Forum Traiani.

Curial membership: Bishops, Education, Evangelization of Peoples, Sacraments (congregations); Texts (councils); Latin America (commission).

Cheong-Jin-Suk,* Nicolas: b. Dec. 7, 1931, Supyo Dong, near Seoul, Korea; raised in the faith, he survived the tumult of the Korean War and then entered the Major Seminary of Song Shin; ord. Mar. 18, 1961; after pastoral service, he was sent to Rome for studies in canon law; app. bp. of Cheongju, June 25; member of the Executive Committee of the Korean Episcopal Conference, 1975-99; pres. of the Korean Episcopal Conference, 1996-99; abp. of Seoul, 1998-2012 and administrator of the diocese of P'yong-yang; card., Mar. 24, 2006; titular church, Sta. Maria Immacolata di Lourdes a Boccea.

Curial membership: Family, Social Communications (councils).

Cipriani Thorne, Juan Luis: b. Dec. 28, 1943, Lima, Peru; champion basketball player and student in industrial engineering, he joined Opus Dei in 1962; ord. for the prelature, Aug. 21, 1977; after a doctorate in theology at the Univ. of Navarre and pastoral work in Lima, he taught moral theology at the Pontifical Faculty of Theology, Lima, and was regional vicar for Peru and vice-chancellor of the Univ. of Piura; app. titular bp. of Turuzi and aux. bp. of Ayacucho, May 23, 1988; cons. July 3, 1988; app. abp. of Ayacucho, May 13, 1995; tried to negotiate a peaceful resolution to the siege of the Japanese ambassador's residence in Lima, Dec. 1996-Apr. 1997 and ministered to Japanese and Peruvian hostages; app. abp. of Lima, Jan. 9, 1999; card., Feb. 21, 2001; titular church St. Camillus de Lellis.

Curial membership: Causes of Saints, Sacraments (congregation); Economy, Latin America (commission); Economic Affairs (prefecture).

Coccopalmerio, Francesco: b. Mar. 6, 1938, San Giuliano Milanese, Italy; earned a doctorate in canon law from the Pontifical Gregorian Univ. and a doctorate in jurisprudence at the Catholic Univ. of the Sacred Heart in Milan; ord. priest, June 29, 1962 and served as a professor of canon law at the Theological Faculty of Northern Italy from 1966-1999; ord. titular bishop of Celiana and appointed aux. bp. of Milan, Apr. 8, 1993; app. pres. of the Pontifical Council of Legislative Texts and promoted to the rank of archbishop, Feb. 15, 2007; card. Feb. 18, 2012, with the deaconry of S. Giuseppe dei Falegnami.

Curial membership: Doctrine of the Faith (congregation); Christian Unity (council); Signatura (tribunal)

Collins, Thomas C.: b. Jan. 16, 1947, Guelph, Ontario; earned a doctorate in theology at the Pontifical Gregorian Univ., Rome; ord. priest, May 5, 1973 and served as rector of St. Peter's Seminary, London, Ontario, 1995 until 1997; cons. coadjutor bp. of St. Paul in Alberta, May 14, 1997; acceded to the see of St. Paul in Alberta, June 30, 1997; app. coadj. abp. of Edmonton, Feb. 18, 1999; acceded to the see of Edmonton, June 7, 1999; app. metropolitan abp. of Toronto, Dec. 16, 2006; cardinal, Feb. 18, 2012 with the title of S. Patrizio.

Curial membership: Education (congregation); Social Communications (council).

Comastri, Angelo: b. Sept. 17, 1943, Sorano, diocese of Sovana-Pitigliano (now Pitigliano-Sovana-Orbetello), Italy; ord. Mar. 11, 1967; after many years of pastoral work, served as bp. of Massa Marittima-Piombo, 1990-1994; pres. of the National Italian Committee for the Jubilee of the year 2000; app. prelate of Loreto and pontifical delegate for the Lauretano shrine, and promoted to abp., Nov. 9, 1996; app. coadj. of the archpriest of the papal basilica of St. Peter in the Vatican, vicar general of His Holiness for the State of Vatican City, and pres. of the Fabric of St. Peter's, Feb. 5, 2005; succeeded to the post of archpriest of the papal Vatican basilica, Oct. 31, 2006; card., Nov. 24, 2007, deaconry, San Salvatore in Lauro.

Curial membership: Saints (congregation).

Connell,* Desmond: b. Mar. 24, 1926, Phibsboro, Ireland; ord., May 19, 1951; taught at Univ. College Dublin, 1953-72; dean of the faculty of Philosophy and Sociology, 1983; chaplain to the Poor Clares in Donnybrook and Carmelites in Drumcondra and Blackrock; app. abp. of Dublin, Jan. 21, 1988; cons., Mar. 6, 1988; ret. Apr. 26, 2004; card., Feb. 21. 2001; titular church, St. Sylvester in Capite.

Coppa,* Giovanni: b. Nov. 9, 1925, Alba, Italy; ord. Jan. 2, 1949; entered the Roman Curia in 1952 and held various posts; app. titular abp. of Serta and delegate for the pontifical representations in the Secretariat of State, Dec. 1, 1979; cons. Jan. 6, 1980; nuncio to the Czech Republic and Slovakia, Jan. 1, 1993; ceased in his functions of nuncio in Slovakia, Mar. 2,

1994; resigned as nuncio the Czech Republic, May 19, 2001; card., Nov. 24, 2007; deaconry, St. Linus.

Cordero Lanza di Montezemolo,* Andrea: b. Aug. 27, 1925, Turin, Italy; ord. Mar. 13, 1954; entered diplomatic service after studies at the Pontifical Ecclesiastical Academy in 1959; served for 42 years in various diplomatic posts; app. undersecretary and secretary of the Pont. Comm. Justice and Peace; app. nuncio and titular abp. of Anglona, Apr. 5, 1977; nuncio to Papau New Guinea and apostolic delegate to Solomon Islands, 1977; app. apostolic delegate in Jerusalem, Palestine, and Jordan, Apr. 28, 1990; transf. to see of Tuscania, Apr. 13, 1991, and first nuncio to Israel, 1994-98; nuncio to Italy and San Marino, 1998-2001; app. archpriest of the basilica of St. Paul Outside-the-Walls, 2005-2009; an expert ecclesiastical herald, he assisted the design of the papal coat-of-arms for Pope Benedict XVI in 2005; card., Mar. 24, 2006; titular church, Diaconia di Santa Maria in Portico.

Cordes,* Paul-Josef: b. Sept. 5, 1934, Kirchhundem, Paderborn, Germany; ord. Dec. 21, 1961; served in the seminary for the dioceses of Paderborn and Münster, 1962-1969, and after doctoral studies was in the secretariat of the Episcopal Conference of Germany; titular bp of Naisso and aux. bp. of Paderborn, Oct. 27, 1975; cons., Feb. 1, 1976, vice-president of the Pontifical Council for the Laity, 1980-1995; promoted to abp., 1995; pres. Pontifical Council Cor Unum, 1995-2010; card., Nov. 24, 2007, deaconry, San Lorenzo in Piscibus.

Curial membership: Clergy, Evangelization, Saints (congregations); Justice and Peace (council).

Cottier,* O.P., Georges: b. Apr. 25, 1922; ord. July 2, 1951; theologian of the Papal Household theologian, 1989; secretary general of the International Theological Commission, 1989-2004; cons. titular abp. of Tullia, Oct. 20, 2003; card., Oct. 21, 2003; titular church, Sts. Dominic and Sixtus.

Danneels,* Godfried: b. June 4, 1933, Kanegem, Belgium; ord., Aug. 17, 1957; professor of liturgy and sacramental theology at Catholic Univ. of Louvain, 1969-77; ord. bp. of Antwerp, Dec. 18, 1977; abp. of Mechelen-Brussel, 1979-2010; installed, Jan. 4, 1980; card., Feb. 2, 1983; titular church, St. Anastasia.

Curial membership: Secretariat of State (second section); Divine Worship and Sacraments, Education, Evangelization of Peoples, Oriental Churches (congregations).

Darmaatmadja, S.J., Julius Riyadi: b. Dec. 20, 1934, Muntilan, Mageland, Central Java, Indonesia; entered Society of Jesus in 1957; ord., Dec. 18, 1969; ord. abp. of Semarang, June 29, 1983; abp. of Jakarta, 1996-2010; card., Nov. 26, 1994; titular church, Sacred Heart of Mary.

Curial membership: Interreligious Dialogue (councils).

De Giorgi,* Salvatore: b. Sept. 6, 1930 Vernole, Italy; ord., June 28, 1953; diocesan chaplain to the Teachers' Movement of Catholic Action; dir. Diocesan Pastoral Office; app. titular bp. of Tulana and aux. bp. of Oria, Nov. 21, 1973; bp. of Oria, Mar. 17, 1978; abp. of Foggia, Apr. 4, 1981; abp. of Taranto, Oct. 10, 1987 (resigned, 1990); general president of Catholic Action, 1990-96; abp. of Palermo, 1996-2006; president of the Sicilian Episcopal Conference; card., Feb. 21, 1998; titular church, St. Mary in Ara Caeli.

Curial membership: Bishops, Sacraments (congregations); Laity, Family (councils).

De Paolis, C.S., Velasio: b. Sept. 19, 1935, Sonnino, Italy; made his profession for the Cong. of the Missionaries of St. Charles Borromeo (Scalabrinians) in 1955 and studied at the Pontifical Gregorian Univ., the Univ. of St Thomas (Angelicum), La Sapienza Univ., and Alphonsianum, Rome; ord. Mar. 18, 1961; held various academic posts; respected expert in canon law; app. titular bp. of Telepte and sec. of the Supreme Tribunal of the Apostolic Signatura,

Dec. 30, 2003; ord., Feb. 21, 2004; app. pres. of the prefecture for the Economic Affairs of the Holy See and promoted to the rank of abp., Apr. 12, 2008; pontifical delegate for the Cong. of the Legionaries of Christ, 2010-2014; created card. deacon, Nov. 20, 2010; deaconry of Gesù Buon Pastore alla Montagnola.

Curial membership: Divine Worship, Saints (congregation); Legislative Texts (council); Signatura (tribunal).

Dias, Ivan: b. Apr. 14, 1936, Bandra, India; ord., Dec. 8, 1958; entered the Holy See diplomatic service and was posted to Indonesia, Madagascar, Reunion, the Comorros, Mauritius, and Secretariat of State; app. titular abp. of Rusubisir and pro-nuncio in Ghana, Togo and Benin, May 8, 1982; cons., June 19, 1982; nuncio in Korea, 1987-91; nuncio in Albania, 1991-97; abp. of Bombay, Jan. 22, 1997-May 22, 2006; cons., Mar. 13, 1997; card., Feb. 21, 2001; titular church, Holy Spirit in Ferratella; app. Prefect of the Cong. for the Evang. of Peoples, May 20, 2006.

Curial membership: Doctrine of the Faith, Eastern Churches, Education, Sacraments, (congregations); Christian Unity, Culture, Interreligious Dialogue, Legislative Texts, Social Comm. (councils); Cultural Heritage of the Church, Latin America (commission).

DiNardo, Daniel N.: b. May 23, 1949, Steubenville, OH; ord. July 16, 1977; studied at the Catholic Univ. of America, in Washington, DC, the North American College, Pontifical Gregorian Univ., and the Augustinianum in Rome; served at the Cong. for Bishops in the Roman Curia, 1984 to 1991 and also as director of Villa Stritch and adjunct professor at the Pontifical North American College; app. coadj. bp. of Sioux City, Aug. 19, 1997, cons., Oct. 7, 1997; acceded as bp. of Sioux City, Nov. 28, 1998; app. coadj. bp. of Galveston-Houston, Jan. 16, 2004; inst. Mar. 26, 2004; app. coadj. abp. of Galveston-Houston, Dec. 29, 2004; abp. of Galveston-Houston, Feb. 28, 2006; card., Nov. 24, 2007; titular church, St. Eusebius.

Curial membership: Cultural Heritage, Economy, Migrants (councils).

Dolan, Timothy M.: b. Feb. 6, 1950, St. Louis, MO; studied at St. Louis Preparatory Seminary, Cardinal Glennon College, the North American College, Rome, and the Pontifical Univ. of St. Thomas Aquinas (Rome); earned a doctorate in Church History from The Catholic Univ. of America in Washington, DC; ord. priest for the archdiocese of St. Louis, June 19, 1976; served on the staff of apostolic nunciature (Washington, DC); rector, North American College, Rome, 1994-2001; app. titular bp. of Natchez and aux. bp. of St. Louis, June 19, 2001; ord., Aug. 15, 2001; app. abp. of Milwaukee, June 25, 2002; inst., Aug. 28, 2002; app. abp. of New York, Feb. 23, 2009; inst. Apr. 15, 2009; elected pres of the USCCB, Nov. 2011; card., Feb. 18, 2012, with the titular church of Nostra Signora di Guadalupe a Monte Mario.

Curial membership: Evangelization of Peoples (congregation); New Evangelization, Social Communications (councils).

do Nascimento,* Alexandre: b. Mar. 1, 1925, Malanje, Angola; ord., Dec. 20, 1952, in Rome; forced into exile in Lisbon, Portugal, 1961-71; returned to Angola, 1971; active with student and refugee groups; professor at Pius XII Institute of Social Sciences; ord. bp. of Malanje, Aug. 31, 1975; abp. of Lubango and apostolic administrator of Onjiva, 1977-86; held hostage by Angolan guerrillas, Oct. 15 to Nov. 16, 1982; card., Feb. 2, 1983; titular church, St. Mark in Agro Laurentino. Abp. of Luanda, 1986.

Duka, O.P., Dominik: b. Apr. 26, 1943, Hradec Králové, East Bohemia, Czech Republic (then Czechoslovakia); entered the Order of Preachers (Dominicans) secretly in 1968 and took the name Dominik; ord. priest, June 22, 1970,

and made his solemn profession in the Order of Preachers in 1971; deprived of the state authorization to exercise his priestly ministry by the Czech communist government and worked in a factory for 15 years but served secretly as vicar provincial and master of the novices; arrested in 1981-1982 and imprisoned; ord. bp. of Hradec Králové, Sept. 26, 1998, awarded the First Grade Medal of Merit for the Czech Republic, 2001; app. metropolitan abp. of Prague, Feb. 13, 2010; elected pres. of the Czech Bishops Conference, 2010; card., Feb. 18, 2012 with the title of Ss. Marcellino e Pietro.

Curial membership: Consecrated Life (congregation); Justice and Peace (council).

Dziwisz, Stanislaw: b. Apr. 27, 1939, in Raba Wyzna, Poland; ord. June 23, 1963; secretary to Card. Karol Wojtyla, 1966-78; with election of Wojtyla as Pope John Paul II in 1978, he became papal secretary, a post he held until John Paul II's death in 2005; named a prelate of his holiness in 1985, titular bishop of San Leone e Prefetto and adjunct prefect of the Papal Household on Feb. 7, 1998, and named titular abp. on Sept. 29, 2003; app. abp. of Cracow, June 3, 2005; card. Mar. 24, 2006; titular church, Titolo di Santa Maria del Popolo.

Curial membership: Education (congregation); Laity, Social Communications (councils).

Egan,* Edward Michael: b. Apr. 2, 1932, Oak Park, IL; ord., Dec. 15, 1957, in Rome; sec. to Card. Albert Meyer, 1958-60; assistant vice-rector of the North American College, 1960-64; vice-chancellor of the archdiocese of Chicago, 1964-68; co-chancellor for human relations and ecumenism, 1968-72; judge of Roman Rota, 1972-85; ord. titular bp. of Allegheny and aux. bp. of New York, May 22, 1985; app. bp. of Bridgeport, Nov. 5, 1988; abp. of New York, May 11, 2000, inst., June 19, 2000; ret. Feb. 23, 2009; card., Feb. 21, 2001; titular church, Ss. John and Paul.

Curial membership: Eastern Churches (congregation), Family (council); Signatura (tribunal); Economic Affairs (office); Cultural Heritage (commission).

Eijk, Willem J.: b. June 22, 1953, Duivendrecht, Netherlands; earned doctorates in medicine at the University of Leiden and moral philosophy at the Pontifical University of St. Thomas Aquinas, Rome; ord. priest, June 1, 1985; professor of moral theology, 1997 to 1999; member of the International Theological Commission; ord. bp. of Groningen-Leeuwarden, Nov. 6, 1999; app. abp. of Utrecht, Dec. 11, 2007; card., Feb. 18, 2012, with the title of S. Callisto.

Curial membership: Clergy, Education (congregations).

Erdö, Peter: b. June 25, 1952, Budapest, Hungary; ord. June 18, 1975 and earned doctorates in Theology and Canon Law from the Lateran Univ., Rome; professor of Theology and Canon Law, seminary of Esztergom, 1980-1988; guest professor, in Canon Law, Pontifical Gregorian Univ., 1986; rector of the Catholic Univ. Péter Pázmány, 1998; ord. Jan. 6, 2000, titular bp. of Puppi and aux. bp. of Szikesfehirvar; abp. of Esztergom-Budapest, Dec. 7, 2002; card., Oct. 21, 2003; titular church, St. Balbina.

Curial membership: Education, Sacraments (congregation); Culture, Legislative Texts (council); Signatura (tribunal).

Errázuriz Ossa,* Francisco Javier: b. Sept. 5, 1933, Santiago, Chile; ord. for the Schönstatt Fathers, July 16, 1961; chaplain to students and professionals of the Schönstatt Movement and regional superior; elected superior general of the Schönstatt Fathers, 1974; app. titular abp. of Hólar and sec. of the Cong. For Institutes of Consecrated Life and Societies of Apostolic Life, Dec. 22, 1990; app. abp. of Valparaiso, Sept. 24, 1996; transferred to archdio. of Santiago, Apr. 24, 1998; pres. of the Episcopal Conference of Chile and first vice-pres. of CELAM; Council of Cardinals, Apr. 13, 2014;

card., Feb. 21, 2001; titular church, St. Mary of Peace.
Curial membership: Consecrated Life (congregation); Culture, Family (council); Latin America (commission).

Estepa Llaurens,* José Manuel: b. Jan. 1, 1926, Andújar, Spain; ord. Jan. 27, 1954; ord. titular bp. of Tisili and aux. bp. of Madrid, Oct. 15, 1972; app. general military vicar of Spain and promoted to titular abp. of Velebusdo, July 30, 1983; transf. to the titular see of Italica, with personal title of abp., Nov. 18, 1989; res. Oct. 30, 2003; created card. priest, Nov. 20, 2010; titular church of S. Gabriele Arcangelo all'Acqua Traversa.

Etchegaray,* Roger: b. Sept. 25, 1922, Espelette, France; ord., July 13, 1947; deputy director, 1961-66, and secretary general, 1966-70, of French Episcopal Conference; ord. titular bp. of Gemelle di Numidia and aux. of Paris, May 27, 1969; abp. of Marseilles, 1970-84; prelate of Mission de France, 1975-82; president of French Episcopal Conference, 1979-81; card., June 30, 1979; titular church, St. Leo I. President of Council Cor Unum, 1984-95; pres. of Council for Justice and Peace (1984-98) and president of Central Committee for the Jubilee of the Holy Year 2000 (1994-98); transferred to order of card. bishops, June 24, 1998 (suburbicarian see of Porto-Santa Rufina); Vice-dean of the Sacred College of Cardinals, Apr. 30, 2005.

Ezzati Andrello, Ricardo, S.D.B.: b. Jan. 7, 1942, Campiglia dei Berici, Italy; ord. Mar. 18, 1970; entered the Congregation of St. John Bosco of St. Francis de Sales (Salesians) in 1961; studied at the Catholic Univ. of Valparaíso, the Pontifical Salesian Univ. in Rome, and the Institut de Pastorale Catéchetique, Strasbourg, France; he took his perpetual vows in 1966; app. bp. of Valdivia, June 28, 1996; ord. Sept. 8, 1996; app. titular bp. of La Imperial and aux. of Santiago and apostolic administrator of Valdivia; app. abp. of Concepción, Dec. 27, 2006; app. abp. of Santiago, Dec. 15, 2010; card. priest, Feb. 22, 2014 with the title of SS. Redentore a Val Melaina.

Falcão,* José Freire: b. Oct. 23, 1925, Erere, Brazil; ord., June 19, 1949; ord. titular bp. of Vardimissa and coadj. of Limoeiro do Norte, June 17, 1967; bp. of Limoeiro do Norte, Aug. 19, 1967; abp. of Teresina, Nov. 25, 1971; abp. of Brasília, 1984-2004; res. Jan. 28, 2004; card., June 28, 1988; titular church, St. Luke (Via Prenestina).

Farina,* S.D.B., Raffaele: b. Sept. 24, 1933, Buonalbergo, Italy; ord. July 1, 1958; entered the Salesians in 1949, final vows in 1954; doctorate in Ecclesiastical History from the Pontifical Gregorian Univ. in Rome and served as a prof. of Church History and rector at the Theological Faculty of the Pontifical Salesian Univ.; sec. of the Pontifical Committee of Historical Science and under-sec. of the Pontifical Council for Culture; app. prefect of the Apostolic Vatican Library, May 25, 1997; cons. titular bp. of Oderzo, Dec. 16, 2006; app. archivist and librarian of the Holy Roman Church, June 25, 2007; app. pres. of the Pontifical Commission for Reference to the IOR, June 24, 2013; card., Nov. 24, 2007; deaconry, San Giovanni della Pigna.
Curial membership: Education, Saints (congregation); Cultural Heritage (commission).

Felix, Kelvin Edward: b. Feb. 15, 1933, Roseau, Dominica; ord. Apr. 8, 1956; studied at St. John Vianney Seminary in Port of Spain, Trinidad and Tobago, St. Francis Xavier Univ., Nova Scotia, Canada, Univ. of Notre Dame, and the Univ. of Bradford, Yorkshire, England; he was the first Catholic priest to be ordained in Dominica; app. abp. of Castries, St. Lucia, July 17, 1981; cons. Oct. 5, 1981; pres. of the Caribbean Conference of Churches, 1981-1986 and pres. of the Antilles Episcopal Conference, 1991-1997; awarded the Order of the British Empire (OBE) by Queen Elizabeth II in 1992; res. Feb. 15, 2008; card. priest, Feb. 22, 2014, with the title of S. Maria della Salute a Primavalle.

Fernandes de Araújo,* Serafim: b. Aug. 13, 1924, Minas Novas, Brazil; ord., Mar. 12, 1949; taught canon law at provincial seminary of Diamantina; titular bp. of Verinopolis and aux. bp. of Belo Horizonte, Jan. 19, 1959; co-adjutor abp. of Belo Horizonte, 1982; abp. Belo Horizonte, 1986-2004; res. Jan. 28, 2004; co-president of the Fourth General Conference of the Latin American Episcopate, 1992; card., Feb. 21, 1998; titular church, St. Louis Marie Grignion de Montfort.

Filoni, Fernando: b. Apr. 15, 1946, Manduria, Italy; earned a doctorate in canon law from the Pontifical Lateran Univ., Rome, and a doctorate in philosophy at the State Univ. La Sapienza, in Rome; ord. priest, July 3, 1970 and entered diplomatic service of the Holy See on Apr. 3, 1981; served in Sri Lanka, Iran, Brazil, and Hong Kong; ord. titular abp. of Volturno and appointed nuncio in Jordan and Iraq, Jan. 17, 2001; app. nuncio in Philippines, Feb. 25, 2006; app. sostituto for the General Affairs of the Church of the Secretariat of State, June 9, 2007, app. prefect of the Congregation for the Evangelization of Peoples on May 10, 2011; card., Feb. 18, 2012, with the deaconry of Nostra Signora di Coromoto in S. Giovanni di Dio.
Curial membership: Doctrine of the Faith, Education, Oriental Churches

Furno,* Carlo: b. Dec. 2, 1921, Bairo Canavese, Italy; ord., June 25, 1944; entered diplomatic service of the Holy See in the 1950s; served in Colombia, Ecuador and Jerusalem; worked in Secretariat of State for 11 years; ord. titular bp. of Abari with personal title of abp., Sept. 16, 1973; nuncio in Peru, 1973-78, Lebanon, 1978-82, Brazil, 1982-92, Italy, 1992-94; card. deacon, Nov. 26, 1994; deaconry, Sacred Heart of Christ the King. Grand Master of the Equestrian Order of the Holy Sepulchre, 1995-2007; pontifical delegate for Patriarchal Basilica of St. Francis in Assisi, 1996; archpriest emeritus of the patriarchal basilica of Santa Maria Maggiore, Rome, 1998-2004.

George, O.M.I., Francis E.: b. Jan. 16, 1937, Chicago, IL; ord., Dec. 21, 1963; provincial of central region of Oblates of Mary Immaculate, 1973-74, vicar general, 1974-86; ord. bp. of Yakima, Sept. 21, 1990; abp. of Portland, OR, Apr. 30, 1996, installed, May 27, 1996; abp. of Chicago, Apr. 8, 1997, installed, May 7, 1997; card., Feb. 21, 1998; titular church, St. Bartholomew on Tiber Island.
Curial membership: Divine Worship and the Discipline of the Sacraments, Institutes of Consecrated Life, Oriental Churches, Evangelization (congregations); Cor Unum, Culture (council); Cultural Heritage of the Church (commission).

Gracias, Oswald: b. Dec. 24, 1944, Bombay (now Mumbai), India; ord. Dec. 20, 1970; doctorate in canon law and a diploma in jurisprudence from the Pontifical Urbanian Univ. in Rome, 1982; served as chancellor and secretary to the bishop of Jamshedpur, 1971-1976; chancellor, judge of the metropolitan tribunal, and judicial vicar of Bombay from 1982-1997; cons. titular bp. of Bladia and aux. bp. of Bombay, Sept. 16, 1997; abp. of Agra, 2000-2006; app. abp. of Bombay, Oct. 14, 2006; Council of Cardinals, Apr. 13, 2014; card., Nov. 24, 2007; titular church, St. Paul of the Cross at Corviale.
Curial membership: Sacraments (congregation); Texts (council)

Grech,* O.S.A., Prosper: b. Dec. 24, 1925, Vittoriosa, Malta; entered the Augustinians in 1943; doctorate a doctorate in theology at the Pontifical Gregorian Univ., Rome and a licentiate in Sacred Scriptures from the Pontifical Biblical Institute, Rome; ord. priest, Mar. 25, 1950; served as a professor of Scripture from 1971 to 1989 at the Pontifical Lateran Univ.; member of the Pontifical Theological Academy and the Pontifical Biblical Commission; cons. titular abp. of San Leone, Feb. 8, 2012; card., Feb. 18, 2012, with the deaconry of S. Maria Goretti.

Grocholewski, Zenon: b. Oct. 11, 1939, Bródki, Poland; ord., May 26, 1963; doctorate in canon law; served in the Supreme

Tribunal of the Apostolic Signatura, 1972-1999; prefect of the Supreme Tribunal of the Apostolic Signatura; member of the commission studying the 1983 Code of Canon Law; titular bp. of Agropoli, Dec. 21, 1982; titular abp., Dec. 16, 1991; prefect of the Cong. for Catholic Education, Nov. 15, 1999; card. deacon, Feb. 21, 2001; titular church, deaconry, St. Nicholas in Carcere. Prefect of the Cong. for Catholic Education.

Curial membership: Bishops, Doctrine of the Faith, Evangelization, Sacraments (congregations); Texts (council); Apostolic Signatura (tribunal).

Gulbinowicz,* Henryk Roman: b. Oct. 17, 1923, Szukiszki, Poland; ord., June 18, 1950; ord. titular bp. of Acci and apostolic administrator of Polish territory in Lithuanian archdio. of Vilnius (Vilna), Feb. 8, 1970; abp. of Wroclaw, Poland, 1976-2004; card., May 25, 1985; titular church, Immaculate Conception of Mary (a Grottarosa).

Herranz Casado,* Julián: b. Mar. 31, 1930, Baena, Spain; joined the personal prelature of Opus Dei and ord. Aug. 7, 1955; ord. titular bp. of Vertara, Jan. 6, 1991; pres. of the Pontifical Council for the Interpretation of the Legislative Texts, 1994-2007; president of the Disciplinary Commission of the Roman Curia, Dec. 3, 1999; card. deacon, Oct. 21, 2003; titular church, St. Eugene.

Curial membership: Bishops, Causes of Saints, Doctrine of the Faith, Evangelization of Peoples (congregations); Apostolic Signatura (Tribunal); Laity (Council); Ecclesia Dei (commission).

Harvey, James M.: b. Oct. 20, 1949, Milwaukee, Wisc.; studied at De Sales Preparatory Seminary in Milwaukee, St. Francis Seminary of Milwaukee, the Pontifical North American College and Pontifical Gregorian Univ. in Rome; and studied at the Pontifical Ecclesiastical Academy; ord. , June 29, 1975; entered diplomatic service of the Holy See in 1980 and served in various posts; assessor of the Secretariat of State, July 22, 1997; elected titular bp. of Memfi and app. prefect of the Pontifical Household, Feb. 7, 1998; cons. a bp., Mar. 19, 1998, promoted to the rank of abp., Sept. 20, 2003; app. archpriest of the papal basilica of S. Paolo fuori le mura on Nov. 23, 2012; card. deacon Nov. 24, 2012, with the deaconry of S. Pio V a Villa Carpegna.

Curial membership: Causes of the Saints, Evangelization of Peoples (Congregations); Administration of the Patrimony of the Apostolic See (APSA).

Hummes,* O.F.M., Cláudio: b. Aug. 8, 1934, Montenegro, Brazil; ord., priest for the Franciscans, Aug. 3, 1958; specialist in ecumenism; taught philosophy at the Franciscan seminary in Garibaldi, at the major seminary of Viamão and the Pontifical Catholic Univ. of Porto Alegre; adviser for ecumenical affairs to the National Bishops' Conference of Brazil; Provincial of Rio Grande do Sul, 1972-75; pres. of the Union of Latin American Conferences of Franciscans; app. coadj. bp. of Santo André, Mar. 22, 1975; cons., May 25, 1975; succeeded to see, Dec. 29, 1975; app. abp. of Fortaleza, July 21, 1996; Abp. of São Paulo, 1998-2006; card., Feb. 21, 2001; titular church, St. Anthony of Padua in Via Merulana; prefect of the Cong. for Clergy, 2006-2010.

Curial membership: Bishops, Doctrine of the Faith, Education, Evangelization, Sacraments (congregation); Cor Unum, Culture, Family, Interreligious Dialogue, Laity (councils); Latin America (commission).

Husar,* M.S.U., Lubomyr: b. Feb. 26, 1933, Lviv, Ukraine; family fled to Austria because of the war and then to the U.S.; ord. for the eparchy of Stamford for Ukrainians, U.S., Mar. 30, 1958; entered the Studite Monks after completing a doctorate in theology in Rome; superior of the Studion in Grottaferrata, Italy; ord. bp. Apr. 2, 1977; app. archiman-

drite of Studite Monks residing outside Ukraine; organized a new Studite monastery in Ternopil, Ukraine, 1994; elected exarch of Kyiv-Vyshorod, 1995; app. aux. bp. to major abp. of Lviv, 1996; elected major abp. of Lviv for Ukrainians, Jan. 25, 2001; title changed to major abp. of Kiev and Halych, Aug. 21, 2005; ret. Feb. 10, 2011; card., Feb. 21, 2001; titular church, Holy Wisdom in Via Boccea.

Curial membership: Oriental Churches (congregation); Christian Unity, Culture, Texts (councils).

Jaworski,* Marian: b. Aug. 21, 1926, Lwów, Poland (modern Lviv, Ukraine); ord., June 25, 1950; taught at the Catholic Theological Academy of Warsaw and Pontifical Theological faculty of Kraków; first rector of the Pontifical Theological Academy, Kraków, 1981-87; app. titular bp. of Lambaesis and apostolic admin. of Lubaczów, May 21, 1984; cons., June 23, 1984; app. abp. of Lviv for Latins, Jan. 16, 1991; ret. Oct. 21, 2008; pres. of the Ukrainian Episcopal Conference, 1992; card. (in pectore), Feb. 21, 1998; titular church, St. Sixtus.

Curial membership: Clergy (congregation); Family (council).

Karlic,* Estanislao Esteban: b. Feb. 7, 1926; Oliva, Argentina; ord. Dec. 8, 1954; ord. titular bp. of Castro, Aug. 15, 1977; promoted to coadj. abp. and apostolic administrator of Paraná, Jan. 19, 1983; acceded to the see of Paraná, Apr. 1, 1986; pres. of the Episcopal Conference of Argentina, 1996-1999 and 1999-2002; ret., Apr. 29, 2003; card., Nov. 24, 2007; titular church, Santa Maria Addolorata on Piazza Buenos Aires.

Kasper,* Walter: b. Mar. 5, 1933, Heidenheim/Brenz, Germany; ord., Apr. 6, 1957; taught theology and later dean of the theological faculty in Münster and Tübingen; app. bp. of Rottenburg-Stuttgart, Apr. 17, 1989, cons., June 17, 1989; co-chair of the International Commission for Lutheran/Catholic Dialogue, 1994; sec. of the Pontifical Council for Promoting Christian Unity, June 1, 1999; pres. Pontifical Council for Promoting Christian Unity, 2001-2010; card. deacon, Feb. 21, 2001; deaconry, All Saints in Via Appia Nuova.

Curial membership: Doctrine of the Faith, Oriental Churches (congregations); Interreligious Dialogue (council); Apostolic Signatura (tribunal); Culture, Legislative Texts (council).

Keeler,* William Henry: b. Mar. 4, 1931, San Antonio, TX; ord., (Harrisburg diocese) July 17, 1955; secretary to Bp. Leech at Vatican II, named peritus by Pope John XXIII; ord. titular bp. of Ulcinium and aux. bp. of Harrisburg, Sept. 21, 1979; bp. of Harrisburg, 1983-1989, abp. of Baltimore, 1989-2007; card., Nov. 26, 1994; titular church, St. Mary of the Angels.

Curial membership: Oriental Churches (congregation); Christian Unity (council).

Kitbunchu,* Michael Michai: b. Jan. 25, 1929, Samphran, Thailand; ord., Dec. 20, 1959, in Rome; rector of metropolitan seminary in Bangkok, 1965-72; ord. abp. of Bangkok, June 3, 1973; card., Feb. 2, 1983, the first from Thailand; ret. May 14, 2009, titular church, St. Laurence in Panisperna.

Curial membership: Evangelization of Peoples (congregation).

Koch, Kurt: b. Mar. 15, 1950, Emmenbrücke, Switzerland; studied at the Univ. of Lucerne, Switzerland and Ludwig-Maximilians-Universität, Münich, Germany; dissertation on philosophy of history in Wolfhart Pannenberg; ord. June 20, 1982, held various academic posts; ord. bp. of Basel, Jan. 6, 1996; member of the International Catholic-Orthodox Theological Commission and a member of the International Catholic-Lutheran Dialogue Commission; pres. of the Swiss Bishops Conference, 2007-2010; app. pres. of the Pontifical Council for the Promotion of Christian Unity and promoted to the rank of abp., July 1, 2010; created card. deacon, Nov. 20, 2010; deaconry of Nostra Signora del Sacro Cuore in Circo Agonale.

Curial membership: Doctrine, Oriental Churches, Saints (congregations); Interreligious Dialogue (council).

Korec,* S.J., Ján Chryzostom: b. Jan. 22, 1924, Bosany, Slovakia; entered Society of Jesus in 1939; ord., Oct. 1, 1950; ord. bp. secretly, Aug. 24, 1951; sentenced to 12 years in prison in 1960 for helping seminarians with their study and ordaining priests; paroled in 1968; appointed bp. of Nitra, Feb. 6, 1990; ret. June 9, 2005; card., June 28, 1991; titular church, Sts. Fabian and Venantius (a Villa Forelli).

Kutwa, Jean-Pierre: b. Dec. 22, 1945, Blockhauss, Abidjan, Ivory Coast; ord. July 11, 1971; studied at the Grand Seminary of Anyama, Catholic Institute of Occidental Africa (I.C.A.O.), and the Pontifical Urbanian Univ., Rome, earned doctorate in biblical theology; app. abp. of Gagnoa, May 15, 2001; ord. Sept. 16, 2001; app. abp. of Abidjan, May 2, 2006; card. priest, Feb. 22, 2014 with the title of S. Emerenziana a Tor Fiorenza.

Lacroix, Gérald Cyprien: b. July 27, 1957, Saint-Hilaire de Dorset, Canada; ord. Oct. 8, 1988; entered the Secular Institute of Pius X in 1975 and took his perpetual vows in 1982; studied at Saint-Anselme College, in Manchester and worked in a restaurant and as a graphic designer in a publishing house before entering the Institute; studied theology at Université de Laval; served in Colombia from 1990-2000; ord. titular bp. of Ilta and aux. of Québec, May 24, 2009; app. abp. of Québec, Feb. 22, 2011; card. priest, Feb. 22, 2014 with the title of S. Giuseppe all'Aurelio.

Lajolo, Giovanni: b. Jan. 3, 1935, Novara, Italy; ord., Apr. 29, 1960; studied at the Pontifical Gregorian Univ. in Rome, for doctorate in canon law from the Univ. of Munich, and studied at Pontifical Ecclesiastical Academy; entered service of Secretariat of State in 1970 and served in nunciature of Germany and then Secretariat of State; named titular abp. of Cesariana and sec. of the Admin. of the Patrimony of the Apostolic See, Oct. 3, 1988; cons. Jan. 6, 1989; nuncio in Germany from 1995-2003; sec. of the secretariat of State for the Relations with the States, 2003-2006; pres. of the Pontifical Commission for the State of Vatican City and president of the Governatorato, June 22, 2006; card., Nov. 24, 2007; deaconry, Sta. Maria Liberatrice on Monte Testaccio.

Curial membership: Bishops (congregation); Culture (council), APSA, Signatura (offices).

Langlois, Chibly: b. Nov. 29, 1958, La Vallée, Haiti; ord. Sept. 22, 1991; studied at the Grand Seminary of Notre-Dame of Port-au-Prince and the Pontifical Lateran Univ. in Rome; app. bp. of Fort-Liberté, April 8, 2004; ord. June 6, 2004; app. bp. of Les Cayes, July 15, 2011; card. priest, Feb. 22, 2014, with the title of S. Giacomo in Augusta.

Law,* Bernard F.: b. Nov. 4, 1931, Torreon, Mexico, the son of U.S. Air Force colonel; ord., (Jackson diocese), May 21, 1961; editor of Natchez-Jackson, MS, diocesan paper, 1963-68; director of NCCB Committee on Ecumenical and Interreligious Affairs, 1968-71; ord. bp. of Springfield-Cape Girardeau, MO, Dec. 5, 1973; abp. of Boston, Jan. 11, 1984; card., May 25, 1985; titular church, St. Susanna; res, Dec.13, 2002; archpriest of the patriarchal basilica of Sta. Maria Maggiore, Rome, 2004-2012.

Curial membership: Bishops, Clergy, Consecrated Life and Societies of Apostolic Life, Divine Worship and Sacraments, Education, Evangelization of Peoples, Oriental Churches; (congregations); Family (council).

Lehmann, Karl: b. May 16, 1936, Sigmaringen, Germany; ord., Oct. 10, 1963; doctorates in theology and philosophy; assistant to Fr. Karl Rahner at Univ. of Münster; taught dogmatic theology at the Johannes Gutenberg Univ., Mainz; member of the Central Committee of German Catholics and the Jaeger-Stählin Ecumenical Circle; taught at the Albert Ludwig Univ., Freiburg im Breisgau; member of the

International Theological Commission; edited the official publication of the documents of the Joint Synod of the Dioceses in the Federal Republic of Germany, Synod of Würzburg, 1971-75; app. bp. of Mainz, June 21, 1983; cons., Oct. 2, 1983; pres. of the German Bishops' Conference; card., Feb. 21, 2001; titular church, St. Leo I.

Curial membership: Bishops, Oriental Churches (congregations); Christian Unity (council); APSA (office).

Levada, William J.: b. June 15, 1936, Long Beach, CA; studied at St. John's College, Camarillo, CA, and the Gregorian Univ. in Rome; ord., Dec. 20, 1961; ord. titular bp. of Capri and aux. bp. of Los Angeles, May 12, 1983; app. abp. of Portland, OR, July 3, 1986; coadj. abp. of San Francisco, Aug. 17, 1995; abp. of San Francisco, Dec. 27, 1995; ret. and app. Prefect for the Cong. for the Doctrine of the Faith, May 13, 2005; ret., July 2, 2012; card., Mar. 24, 2006; titular church, Diaconia di Sta. Maria in Dominica.

Curial membership: Bishops, Causes of Saints, Eastern Churches, Education, Evangelization (congregations); Christian Unity (council); Ecclesial Dei, Latin America (commissions); Synod of Bishop (special council).

López Rodríguez, Nicolás de Jesús: b. Oct. 31, 1936, Barranca, Dominican Republic; ord., Mar. 18, 1961; sent to Rome for advanced studies at Angelicum and Gregorian Univ.; served in various diocesan offices after returning to home diocese of La Vega; ord. first bp. of San Francisco de Macoris, Feb. 25, 1978; abp. of Santo Domingo and Military Ordinary for Dominican Republic, Nov. 15, 1981; card., June 28, 1991; titular church, St. Pius X (alla Balduina).

Curial membership: Clergy, Institutes of Consecrated Life and Societies of Apostolic Life (congregations); Social Communications (council); Latin America (commission).

Lozano Barragán,* Javier: b. Jan. 26, 1933, Toluca, Mexico; ord. Oct. 30, 1955; pres. of the Mexican Theological Society and dir. of the Institute of Pastoral Theology of the Episcopal Conference of Latin America (CELAM); ord. titular bp. of Tinisia di Numidia and aux. bp. of Mexico, Aug. 15, 1979; bp. of Zacatecas, 1984-96; pres. of Pontifical Council for Health Care Workers, 1996-2009; named abp. 1997; card. deacon, Oct. 21, 2003, deaconry, St. Michael the Archangel. Pres. emeritus of Pontifical Council for Health Care Workers.

Curial membership: Bishops, Causes of Saints, Evangelization (congregations); Eucharistic Congresses, Latin America (commissions).

McCarrick,* Theodore E.: b. July 7, 1930, New York, NY; ord., May 31, 1958; dean of students Catholic Univ. of America, 1961-63; pres., Catholic Univ. of Puerto Rico, 1965-69; secretary to Card. Cooke, 1970; ord. titular bp. of Rusubisir and aux. bp. of New York, June 29, 1977; app. first bp. of Metuchen, NJ, Nov. 19, 1981, installed, Jan. 31, 1982; app. abp. of Newark, June 3, 1986, installed, July 25, 1986; abp. of Washington, Nov. 21, 2000; ins, Jan. 3, 2001, card. priest, Feb. 21, 2001; titular church, Sts. Nereus and Achilleus; ret. May 16, 2006.

Curial membership: Christian Unity (council); APSA (office).

Macharski,* Franciszek: b. May 20, 1927, Kraków, Poland; ord., Apr. 2, 1950; engaged in pastoral work, 1950-56; abp. of Kraków, 1979-2005; card., June 30, 1979; titular church, St. John at the Latin Gate. Abp. emeritus of Kraków.

Curial membership: Secretariat of State (second sec tion); Bishops, Clergy, Consecrated Life and Societies of Apostolic Life, Education, Evangelization of Peoples (congregations).

Mahony, Roger M.: b. Feb. 27, 1936, Hollywood, CA; ord., (Fresno diocese) May 1, 1962; ord. titular bp. of Tamascani and aux. bp. of Fresno, Mar. 19,1975; bp. of Stockton, Feb. 15, 1980, installed, Apr. 25, 1980; abp. of Los Angeles, July 16, 1985, installed, Sept. 5, 1985; ret. Mar. 1, 2011; card., June 28, 1991; titular church, Four Crowned Saints.

Curial membership: Eastern Churches (congregation), Social Communications (council); Economic Affairs (office).

Maida,* Adam Joseph: b. Mar. 18, 1930, East Vandergrift, PA; ord., (Pittsburgh diocese), May 26, 1956; ord. bp. of Green Bay, Jan. 25, 1984; app. abp. of Detroit, Apr. 28, 1990, installed, June 12, 1990; ret. Jan. 5, 2009; card., Nov. 26, 1994; titular church, Sts. Vitalis, Valeria, Gervase and Protase.

Curial membership: Education (congregation); Migrants and Itinerant Peoples (council); Institute for Works of Religion (commission).

Majella Agnelo,* Geraldo: b. Oct. 19, 1933, Juiz de Fora, Brazil; ord. June 29, 1957; taught at the seminary of Aparecida, Immaculate Conception Seminary, and Pius XI Theological Institute; rector of Our Lady of the Assumption Seminary; bp. of Toledo, May 5, 1978; cons., Aug. 6, 1978; app. abp. of Londrina, Oct. 27, 1982; pres. of the Brazilian Bishops' Liturgical Commission; app. sec. of the Cong. For Divine Worship and the Discipline of Sacraments, Sept. 16, 1991; app. abp. of São Salvador da Bahia, Jan. 13, 1999; card., Feb. 21, 2001; titular church, St. Gregory the Great in Magliana Nuova.

Curial membership: Pastoral Care of Migrants and Itinerant People (council); Cultural Heritage of the Church (commission).

Martínez Sistach, Lluís: b. Apr. 29, 1937, Barcelona, Spain; ord. Sept. 17, 1961; doctorate in utroque iure, both canon and civil law, from the Pontifical Lateran Univ., Rome, in 1967; professor of canon law at the Theological Faculty of Catalonia and at the Superior Institute of Religious Sciences of Barcelona, 1975-1987; cons. titular bp. of Aliezira and aux. bp. of Barcelona, Dec. 27, 1987; bp. of Tortosa, 1991-1997; abp. of Tarragona, 1997-2004; app. abp. of Barcelona, June 15, 2004; card., Nov. 24, 2007; titular church, St. Sebastian in the Catacombs.

Curial membership: Laity, Texts (councils); Signatura (tribunal); Economic Affairs (prefecture).

Martínez Somalo,* Eduardo: b. Mar. 31, 1927, Baños de Rio Tobia, Spain; ord., Mar. 19, 1950; ord. titular bp. of Tagora with personal title of abp., Dec. 13, 1975; in secretariat of state from 1956; substitute (assistant) secretary of state, 1979-88; card. deacon, June 28, 1988; deaconry, Most Holy Name of Jesus (raised pro hac vice to presbyteral title); card. priest, Jan. 9, 1999; prefect of Cong. for Divine Worship and Sacraments, 1988-92. Prefect of Cong. for Institutes of Consecrated Life and Societies of Apostolic Life, 1992-2004; Chamberlain (Camerlengo) of the Holy Roman Church, 1993-2007; Protodeacon, 1996-99.

Curial membership: Secretariat of State (second section); Bishops, Causes of Saints, Clergy, Divine Worship and Sacraments, Education, Evangelization of Peoples (congregations); Legislative Texts (council); Latin America, Institute for Works of Religion (commissions).

Martino,* Renato: b. Nov. 23, 1932, Salerno, Italy; ord. June 27, 1957; diplomatic service of the Holy See, July 1, 1962; served in various diplomatic postings, 1962-80; ord. titular abp. of Segerme, Dec. 14, 1980; pro-nuncio in Thailand and apostolic delegate in Laos, Malaysia and Singapore, 1980-86; permanent observer of the Holy See to the U.N., 1986-2002; pres. of the Pontifical Council Justice and Peace, 2002-2006; card. deacon, Oct. 21, 2003, titular church, St. Francis of Paola ai Monti; Pres. of the Pontifical for Council for Pastoral Care of Migrants and Itinerants, Mar. 11, 2006; protodeacon, June 12, 2014.

Curial membership: Evangelization of Peoples (congrega-

tion); "Cor Unum" (council); Vatican City State (commission); Admin. of the Patrimony of the Apostolic See (APSA).

Marx, Reinhard: b. Sept. 21, 1953, Geseke, Germany; studied at the Theological Faculty of Paderborn, Institut Catholique de Paris, Ruhr-Universität Bochum, and Westfälische Wilhelms-Universität Münster; ord. June 2, 1979; ord. titular bp. of Pedena and aux. bp. of Paderborn, Sept. 21, 1996; app. bp. of Trier, Dec. 20, 2001; app. abp. of München und Freising, Nov. 30, 2007; author of a number of books and ranked among the foremost European social scientists; app. Coord. for Council on the Economy, Mar. 8, 2014; card. priest, Nov. 20, 2010; titular church of S. Corbiniano.

Curial membership: Education, Oriental Churches (congregations); Justice (council).

Mazombwe,* Medardo Joseph: b. Sept. 24, 1931, Chundamira, Northern Rhodesia (modern Zambia); studied at St. Mary's Seminar in Kasina, Nyasaland (modern Malawi), the Regional Major Seminary of Kachebere, Nyasaland, Lovanium Univ., Leopoldville (modern Kinshasa), and Univ. of Lusaka; ord. Sept. 4, 1960; ord. bp. of Chipata, Feb. 7, 1971; chair of the regional conferences under the Association of Member Episcopal Conferences in Eastern Africa (A.M.E.C.E.A.), 1979-1986; app. abp. of Lusaka, Nov. 30 1996; ord. Oct. 28, 2006; card. priest, Nov. 20, 2010; titular church of S. Emerenziana a Tor Fiorenza.

Curial membership: Evangelization (congregation); Cor Unum (council).

Medina Estévez,* Jorge Arturo: b. Dec. 23, 1926, Santiago, Chile; ord., June 12, 1954; ord. abp., Jan. 6, 1985, Santiago, Chile; appointed pro-Prefect, Cong. for Divine Worship and the Discipline of the Sacraments, 1996-98; prefect of the Cong. for Divine Worship and the Discipline of the Sacraments, 1998-2002; card. deacon, Feb. 21, 1998; card. priest, Mar. 2, 2008; titular church, St. Sabas; Protodeacon, 2005-2007.

Meisner,* Joachim: b. Dec. 25, 1933, Breslau, Silesia, Germany (present-day Wroclaw, Poland); ord., Dec. 22, 1962; regional director of Caritas; ord. titular bp. of Vina and aux. of apostolic administration of Erfurt-Meiningen, E. Germany, May 17, 1975; bp. of Berlin, 1980-88; card., Feb. 2, 1983; titular church, St. Prudenziana. Abp. of Cologne, Dec. 20, 1988; res., Feb. 28, 2014.

Curial membership: Bishops, Clergy, Divine Worship and Sacraments (congregations); Legislative Texts (council); Economic Affairs of Holy See (office).

Mejía,* Jorge María: b. Jan. 31, 1923, Buenos Aires, Argentina; ord., Sept. 22, 1945; peritus at Second Vatican Council; sec. of CELAM's Depart. of Ecumenism, 1967-77; sec. of Pontifical Commission for Religious Relations with Jews, 1977-86; vice-president of the Pontifical Commission Justice and Peace and titular bp. of Apollonia, Apr. 12, 1986; sec. of the Cong. for Bishops and titular abp., Mar. 1994; Archivist and Librarian of the Holy Roman Church, 1998-2003; card. deacon, Feb. 21, 2001; deaconry, St. Jerome della Carità.

Monsengwo Pasinya, Laurent: b. Oct. 7, 1939, Mongobele, Congo (modern Democratic Republic of Congo); he is a member of the royal lines of Basakata; studied at the Major Seminary of Kabwe, Pontifical Urban Univ., Pontifical Biblical Institute, Rome, and the Pontifical Biblical Institute in Jerusalem; he was the first African to obtain a doctorate in biblical studies; ord. Dec. 21, 1963; ord. titular bishop of Acque nuove di Proconsulare and aux. bp. of Inongo, May 4, 1980; transferred to aux. bp. of Kisangani, Apr. 7, 1981; app. abp. of Kisangani, Sept. 1, 1988, and was noted for his efforts to help guide his country during a civil war and the dictatorship of Mobutu Sese Seko into a democracy; app. abp. of

Kinshasa, Dec. 2007; Council of Cards., Apr. 13, 2014; card. priest, Nov. 20, 2010; titular church of S. Maria Regina Pacis in Ostra mare.

Curial membership: Education (congregation); Justice (council).

Monteiro de Castro, Manuel: b. Mar. 29, 1938, Santa Eufémia de Prazins, Guimarães, Portugal; doctorate in canon law at Pontifical Gregorian Univ., Rome, and a diploma in diplomacy from the Pontifical Ecclesiastical Academy, Rome; ord. priest, July 9, 1961; entered the diplomatic service of the Holy See in 1967 and served in Panama, Guatemala, Vietnam and Cambodia, Australia, Mexico, and Belgium; ord. titular abp. of Benevento and app. pro-nuncio to Trinidad and Tobago, Bahamas, Barbados, Belize, Dominica, Jamaica, Grenada, St. Lucia; and apostolic delegate in The Antilles, Feb. 16, 1985; app. nuncio to El Salvador and Honduras, Aug. 21, 1990; app. nuncio to South Africa, Nambia and Swaziland, Feb. 2, 1998 and nuncio to Lesotho, Mar. 7, 1998; app. nuncio to Spain and Andorra, Mar. 1, 2000; permanent observer of the Holy See at the World Tourism Organization, 1997-2009; app. sec. of the Congregation for Bishops, July 3, 2009 and sec. of the College of Cardinals, Oct. 21, 2009; app. penitentiary major on Jan. 5, 2012; res. Sept. 21, 2013; card. Feb. 18, 2012 with the deaconry of S. Domenico di Guzman.

Curial membership: Bishops, Saints (congregations); Migrants (council).

Monterisi,* Francesco: b. May 28, 1934, Barletta, Italy; studied at the Pontifical Major Seminary and the Pontifical Lateran Univ., Rome; later studied diplomacy at the Pontifical Ecclesiastical Academy; ord. Mar. 16, 1957 and entered the diplomatic service of the Holy See in 1964; served in various diplomatic posts and was named titular abp. of Alba marittima and nuncio in South Korea, Dec. 24, 1982; ord. Jan. 6, 1983; delegate for the pontifical representations on Aug. 28, 1990; nuncio to Bosnia-Herzegovina 1993-1998; app. sec. of the Cong. for Bishops and of the College of Cardinals, Mar. 7, 1998; sec. of the 2005 conclave; app. archpriest of the papal basilica of S. Paolo fouri le Mura, July 3, 2009; card. deacon, Nov. 20, 2010; deaconry of S. Paolo alla Regola.

Curial membership: Oriental Churches, Saints (congregation); Latin America (commission).

Müller, Gerhard Ludwig: b. Dec. 31, 1947, Mainz-Finthen, Germany; ord. Feb. 11, 1878; studied at Johannes-Gutenberg-Univ., Mainz, Ludwig-Maximilians-Univ., Münich, and Albert-Ludwigs-Univ., Freiburg im Breisgau; doctorate in theology in 1977; qualified as professor of theology in 1985 in Freiburg im Breisgau and appointed professor of Catholic dogmatics at the Ludwig-Maximilian Univ. in Munich; he is the author more than 400 academic writings; member of the International Theological Commission from 1998 to 2002; app. bp. of Regensburg, Oct. 1, 2002; ord. Nov. 11, 2002; founded the Pope Benedict XVI Institute in Regensburg in 2008 and was app. editor of the *Collected Writings of Joseph Ratzinger;* app. prefect of the Congregation for the Doctrine of the Faith, July 2, 2012; card. deacon, Feb. 22, 2014, with the deaconry of S. Agnese in Agone.

Curial membership: Oriental Churches (congregation); Legislative Texts (commission).

Muresan,* Lucian: b. May 23, 1931, village of Ferneziu, eparchy of Maramures, Romania; endured severe persecution under the Romanina Communist regime and worked in various jobs as religion was banned by the government; ord. priest, Dec. 19, 1964, and served in secret; elected eparch of Maramures of the Romanians, Mar. 14, 1990, and cons., May 27, 1990; opened the Baia Mare Theological Institute, 1990-1991; app. abp. of Fagaras si Alba Iulia of the Romanians,

July 4, 1994; welcomed Pope John Paul II during his visit to Romania in 1999; abp. major on Dec. 16, 2005; card. Feb. 18, 2012, with the title of S. Atanasio.

Curial membership: Oriental Churches (congregation).

Murphy-O'Connor,* Cormac: b. Aug. 24, 1932, Reading, Great Britain; ord., Oct. 28, 1956; dir. of vocations and secretary to the bp.; rector of the Venerable English College, Rome, 1971-77; app. bp. of Arundel and Brighton, Nov. 17, 1977; cons., Dec. 21, 1977; co-chairman of the Anglican-Roman Catholic International Commission (ARCIC), 1982-2000; chairman of several committees of the Bishop's Conference of England and Wales; app. abp. of Westminster, Feb. 15, 2000; ret. Apr. 3, 2009; card., Feb. 21, 2001; titular church, St. Mary sopra Minerva.

Naguib, Antonios: b. Mar. 18, 1935, Samalout, eparchy of Minya of the Copts, Egypt; studied Pontifical Urban College and the Pontifical Biblical Institute, Rome; ord. Oct. 30, 1960 and ord. bp. of Minya of the Copts, Sept. 9, 1977; elected patriarch of Alexandria of the Copts, Mar. 30, 2006 and granted ecclesiastical communio, Apr. 7, 2006; pres. of the Synod of the Coptic-Catholic Church in Egypt and president of the Catholic Bishops Conference of Egypt; card. patriarch, Nov. 20, 2010.

Curial membership: Oriental Churches (congregation); Migrants (council).

Napier, O.F.M., Wilfrid Fox: b. Mar. 8, 1941, Swartberg, South Africa; ord., for the Franciscans, July 25, 1970; app. apostolic admin. of Kokstad, 1978; app. bp. of Kokstad, Nov. 29, 1980; cons., Feb. 28, 1981; deeply involved in the mediation and negotiations surrounding the ending of apartheid in South Africa and subsequent South African politics; pres. of the Southern African Catholic Bishops' Conference, 1987-94; app. abp. of Durban, May 29, 1992; apostolic admin. sede vacante et ad nutum Sanctae Sedis of Umzimkulu, 1994; card., Feb. 21, 2001; titular church, St. Francis of Assisi in Acilia.

Curial membership: Evangelization, Consecrated Life (congregations); Culture (council); Economy, Health Care (commissions); Economic Affairs (office).

Nichols, Vincent Gerard: b. Nov. 8, 1945, Crosby, England; ord. Dec. 21, 1969; studied at the Venerable English College in Rome and the Pontifical Gregorian Univ. and at the Univ. of Manchester and Loyola Univ., Chicago; app. gen. sec. of the Bishops' Conference in England and Wales, 1984; ord. titular bp. of Othona and aux. of Westminster, Jan. 24, 1992; app. abp. of Birmingham, Feb. 15, 2000; transferred to the metropolitan see of Westminster, Apr. 3, 2009; card. priest, Feb. 22, 2014 with the title of Santissimo Redentore e Sant Alfonso in via Merulana.

Curial membership: Bishops, Oriental Churches (congregations).

Nicora, Attilio: b. Mar. 16, 1937, Varese, Italy; ord. June 27, 1964; ord. titular bp. of Fornos minore and aux. bp. of Milan, May 28, 1977; bp. of Verona, 1992-2002; pres. of the Administration of the Patrimony of the Apostolic See (APSA) and abp., Sept. 2002; card. deacon, Oct. 21, 2003; deaconry, St. Philip Neri in Eurosia. Pres. of the Administration of the Patrimony of the Apostolic See.

Curial membership: Secretariat of State (second section), Bishops, Evangelization of Peoples (congregation); Apostolic Signatura (tribunal); Texts (council); Vatican City, Works of Religion (commission).

Njue, John: b. 1944, Embu, Kenya; ord. Jan. 6, 1973; after studies in Rome, he served as a professor of philosophy and rector at the National Seminary of Bungoma, diocese of Kakmega, 1975; cons. the first bp. of Embu, Sept. 20, 1986; app. coadj. abp. of Nyeri, Jan. 23, 2002; app. abp. of Nairobi,

Oct. 6, 2007; card., Nov. 24, 2007; titular church, Most Precious Blood of Our Lord Jesus Christ.

Curial Membership: Clergy, Evangelization (congregation).

Nycz, Kazimierz: b. Feb. 1, 1950, Stara Wies, Poland; studied at the Major Seminary of Kraków, Pontifical Academy of Theology of Kraków, and the Catholic Univ. of Lublin; ord., May 20, 1973; ord. titular bp. of Villa del re and aux. bp. of Kraków, June 4, 1988; app. bp. of Koszalin-Kołobrzeg, June 9, 2004; app. abp. of Warsaw, Mar. 3, 2007; card. priest, Nov. 20, 2010; titular church of Ss. Silvestro e Martino ai Monti.

Curial membership: Clergy, Divine Worship (congregation).

Obando Bravo,* S.D.B., Miguel: b. Feb. 2, 1926, La Libertad, Nicaragua; ord., Aug. 10, 1958; ord. titular bp. of Puzia di Bizacena and aux. of Matagalpa, Mar. 31, 1968; abp. emeritus of Managua, 1970-2005; card., May 25, 1985; titular church, St. John the Evangelist (a Spinaceta).

Curial membership: Clergy, Consecrated Life and Societies of Apostolic Life, Divine Worship and Sacraments, (congregations).

O'Brien, Edwin F.: b. Apr. 8, 1939, Bronx, NY; earned a doctorate in Sacred Theology at the Pontifical Univ. of St. Thomas Aquinas, Rome; ord. priest for New York archdio., May 29, 1965; served as a military chaplain; rector of the Pontifical North American College, Rome, 1990-1994; ord. titular bp. of Tizica and aux. bp. of New York, Mar. 25, 1996; app. coadjutor abp. for Military Services Archdio., Apr. 8, 1997; abp. of Military Services Archdio., Aug. 12, 1997; app. abp. of Baltimore, July 12, 2007; app. grand master of the Equestrian Order of the Holy Sepulchre of Jerusalem, Aug. 29, 2011; card., Feb. 18, 2012, with the deaconry of S. Sebastiano al Palatino.

Curial membership: Education, Oriental Churches (congregations); "Cor Unum" (council).

O'Brien, Keith Michael Patrick: b. Mar. 17, 1938, Ballycastle, Ireland; ord. Apr. 3, 1965; ord. abp. of St. Andrews and Edinburgh, May 30, 1985; card., Oct. 21, 2003; titular church, Sts. Joachim and Anne at the Tuscolano.

Curial membership: Migrants and Itinerant People, Social Communications (councils).

Okogie, Anthony Olubunmi: b. June 16, 1935, Lagos, Nigeria; ord. Dec. 11, 1966; ord. titular bp. of Mascula, June 5, 1971; abp. of Lagos, Apr. 13, 1973; card., Oct. 21, 2003; titular church, Blessed Virgin Mary of Mt. Carmel of Mostacciano.

Curial membership: Evangelization of Peoples (congregation); Social Communications (council).

O'Malley, O.F.M. Cap., Sean P.: b. June 29, 1944, Lakewood, OH; studied at St. Fidelis Seminary, Capuchin College, and Catholic Univ., Washington, DC; ord. Aug. 29, 1970; episcopal vicar of priests serving Spanish speaking in Washington archdio., 1974-84; executive director of Spanish Catholic Center, Washington, from 1973; ord. coadj. bp. of St. Thomas, Virgin Islands, Aug. 2, 1984; bp. of St. Thomas, Oct. 16, 1985; app. bp. of Fall River, June 16, 1992; app. bp. of Palm Beach, Sept. 3, 2002; app. abp. of Boston, July 1, 2003; Comm. for the Protection of Minors, Mar. 22, 2014; Council of Cardinals, Apr. 13, 2014; card., Mar. 24, 2006; titular church, Sta. Maria della Vittoria.

Curial membership: Clergy; Consecrated Life (congregation).

Onaiyekan, John Olorunfemi: b. Jan. 29, 1944, Kabba, Nigeria; studied at Ss. Peter and Paul Major Seminary, in Bodija, Ibadan, Pontifical Urbanian Univ., in Rome, and Pontifical Biblical Institute, Rome; doctorate in 1976 from the Urbanian Univ.; ord. priest, Aug. 3, 1969; app. titular bp. of Tunusuda and aux. bp. of Ilorin, Sept. 10, 1982; cons. on Jan. 6, 1983; app. bp. of Ilorin, Oct. 20, 1984; app. coadj. of Abuja, July 7, 1990; acceded to the see of Abuja, Sept. 28, 1992; promoted to metropolitan abp. of Abuja, Mar. 26, 1995; in 2012,

he was a nominee for the Nobel Peace Prize, with the Muslim Sultan of Sokoto, Alhaji Muhammed Sa'ad Abubakar III; card. priest Nov. 24, 2012, with the title of S. Saturnino.

Curial membership: Doctrine of the Faith (congregation), Family (council).

Ortega y Alamino, Jaime Lucas: b. Oct. 18, 1936, Jagüey Grande, Cuba; ord., Aug. 2, 1964 detained in work camps (UMAP), 1966-67; parish priest; ord. bp. of Pinar del Rio, Jan. 14, 1979; app. abp. of Havana, Nov. 20, 1981; card., Nov. 26, 1994; titular church, Sts. Aquila and Priscilla.

Curial membership: Clergy (congregation); Health Care Workers (council); Latin America (commission).

Ouédraogo, Philippe Nakellentuba: b. Jan. 25, 1945, Konéan, Burkina Faso; ord. July 14, 1973; studied at the Grand Séminaire Régional de Koumi and the Pontifical Urbanian Univ., Rome, obtained doctorate in canon law; app. bp. of Ouahigouya, July 5, 1996; ord. Nov. 23, 1996; app. abp. of Ouagadougou, May 13, 2009; card. priest, Feb. 22, 2014 with the title of S. Maria Consolatrice al Tiburtino.

Ouellet, P.S.S., Marc: b. June 8, 1944, Lamotte, Canada; ord. May 25, 1968; entered the Society of Priests of Saint-Sulpice, 1972; rector and prof., Major Seminary of Montréal, 1989-1994 and Major Seminary of Edmonton, 1994-1997; prof., John Paul II Institute of Studies on Marriage and the Family, 1997-2001; ord. titular bp. of Agropoli, Mar. 19, 2001; sec. of the Pont. Council for the Promotion of Christian Unity, 2001-2002; abp. of Québec, Nov. 15, 2002-June 30, 2010; card., Oct. 21, 2003; titular church, St. Mary in Traspontina; prefect of the Cong. of Bishops and pres. of the Pont. Comm. for Latin America, June 30, 2010.

Curial membership: Clergy, Education, Oriental Churches, Sacraments (congregation); Culture, Legislative Texts (councils); Latin America, Eucharistic Congresses (commissions); Economic Affairs (office).

Panafieu,* Bernard: b. Jan. 26, 1931, Châtellerault, France; ord. Apr. 22, 1956; ord. titular bp. of Tibili, June 9, 1974, and aux. bp. of Annecy, 1974-78; abp. of Aix, 1978-94; coadj. abp. of Marseilles, Aug. 24, 1994; abp. of Marseilles, 1995-2006; metropolitan abp. when Marseille was elevated to that rank, Dec. 16, 2002; card., Oct. 21, 2003; titular church, St. Gregory Barbarigo alle Tre Fontane.

Curial membership: Interreligious Dialogue, Justice and Peace (councils).

Parolin, Pietro: b. Jan. 17, 1955, Schiavon, diocese of Vicenza, Italy; ord. Apr. 27, 1980; studied in the seminary of Vicenza; later, earned a doctorate in canon law at the Pontifical Gregorian Univ., Rome, and diplomacy at the Pontifical Ecclesiastical Academy; entered the diplomatic service of the Holy See on July 1, 1986 and worked in the nunciatures in Nigeria, México, and the section for the Relations with the States of the Secretariat of State; under-sec. of the section for the Relations with the States on 2002-2009; app. titular abp. of Acquapendente and nuncio in Venezuela, Aug. 17, 2009; ord. Sept. 12, 2009; app. secretary of State, Aug. 31, 2013; card. priest, Feb. 22, 2014, with the title of Ss. Simone e Giuda Taddeo a Torre Angela.

Curial membership: Bishops (congregation); Works of Religion (commission).

Paskai,* O.F.M., László: b. May 8, 1927, Szeged, Hungary; ord., Mar. 3, 1951; ord., titular bp. of Bavagaliana and apostolic administrator of Veszprem, Apr. 5, 1978; bp. of Veszprem, Mar. 31, 1979; coadj. abp. of Kalocsa, Apr. 5, 1982; abp. of Esztergom (renamed Esztergom–Budapest, 1993), 1987-2002; card., June 28, 1988; titular church, St. Theresa (al Corso d'Italia).

Curial membership: Consecrated Life and Societies of

Apostolic Life, Oriental Churches (congregations).

Patabendige Don, Albert Malcolm Ranjith: b. Nov. 15, 1947, Polgahawela, Sri Lanka; studied at the National Seminary in Kandy, Pontifical Urban Univ. and the Pontifical Biblical Institute, Rome, and the Hebrew Univ. of Jerusalem; ord. June 29, 1975; ord. titular bp. of Cabarsussi and aux. of Colombo, Aug. 31, 1991; app. nuncio to Indonesia and East Timor and transferred to the titular see of Umbriatica, Apr. 29, 2004; app. sec. of the Cong. for Divine Worship and the Discipline of the Sacraments, Dec. 10, 2005; app. abp. of Colombo, June 16, 2009; created card. priest, Nov. 20, 2010; titular church of S. Lorenzo in Lucina.

Curial membership: Divine Worship, Evangelization (congregations)

Pell, George: b. Apr. 8, 1941, Ballarat, Australia; ord. Dec. 16, 1966; episcopal vicar for Education, diocese of Ballarat, 1973-1984; rector of Corpus Christi College, the Provincial Seminary for Victoria and Tasmania, 1985-1987; ord. titular bp. of Scala, May 21, 1987; aux. bp. of Melbourne, 1987-96; abp. of Melbourne, 1996-2001; abp. of Sydney, Mar. 26, 2001; grand prior of the Equestrian Order of the Holy Sepulchre of Jerusalem, Australian Lieutenancy, Southern, 1998; app. member of the Council of Cardinals; app. pres. of the Secretariat for the Economy, Feb. 24, 2014; card., Oct. 21, 2003; titular church, St. Mary Dominic Mazzarello.

Curial membership: Sacraments (congregation); Family, Justice and Peace (councils).

Pengo, Polycarp: b. Aug. 5, 1944, Mwayze, Tanzania; ord., Aug. 5, 1971; taught moral theology at the major seminary in Kipalapala, Tanzania, 1977; rector of the major seminary in Segerea, 1978-83; ord. bp. of Nachingwea, Jan. 6, 1984; bp. of Tunduru-Masasi 1986-90; coadj. abp. of Dar-es-Salaam, Jan. 22, 1990; abp. of Dar-es-Salaam, July 22, 1992, in succession to Laurean Card. Rugambwa; card., Feb. 21, 1998; titular church, Our Lady of La Salette.

Curial membership: Clergy, Doctrine of the Faith, Evangelization of Peoples (congregation); Culture, Family, Interreligious Dialogue (council).

Pham Minh Man,* Jean Baptiste: b. 1934, Ca Mau, Vietnam; ord. May 25, 1965; ord. coadj. bp. of My Tho, Aug. 11, 1993; abp. of Thàn-Phô Hô Chi Minh (Hô Chi Minh City), Mar. 1, 1998; res., Mar. 2. 2014; card., Oct. 21, 2003; titular church, St. Justin.

Curial membership: Sacraments, Evangelization of Peoples (congregation).

Piacenza, Mauro: b. Sept. 15, 1944, Genoa, Italy; studied at the Major Archiepiscopal Seminary of Genoa and the Pontifical Lateran Univ.; ord. Dec. 21, 1969; professor of canon law and theology and entered Roman Curia in 1990; app. titular bp. of Vittoriana and pres. of the Pontifical Commission for the Cultural Heritage of the Church, Oct. 13, 2003; ord. Nov. 15, 2003; app. pres. of the Pontifical Commission for Sacred Archeology, Aug. 28, 2004; app. sec. of the Cong. for the Clergy and abp., May 7, 2007; prefect of the Cong. for the Clergy 2010-2013; app. Major Penitentiary, Sept. 21, 2013; card. deacon, Nov. 20, 2010; deaconry of S. Paolo alle Tre Fontane.

Curial membership: Clergy, Divine Worship, Education (congregations); Social Communications (council)

Piovanelli,* Silvano: b. Feb. 21, 1924, Ronta di Mugello, Italy; ord., July 13, 1947; ord. titular bp. of Tubune di Mauretania and aux. of Florence, June 24, 1982; abp. of Florence, 1983-2001; card., May 25, 1985; titular church, St. Mary of Graces (Via Trionfale).

Poletto,* Severino: b. Mar. 18, 1933, Salgareda (Treviso),

Italy; ord., June 29, 1957; pref. of discipline at the diocesan seminary and vocation director; founded Diocesan Centre for Family Ministry, 1973; coordinated city mission for the 500th anniversary of the foundation of the diocese of Casale Monferrato; app. coadj. bp. of Fossano, Apr. 3, 1980; cons., May 17, 1980; succeeded to see on Oct. 29, 1980; app. bp. of Asti, Mar. 16, 1989; app. abp. of Turin, June 19, 1999; card., Feb. 21, 2001; titular church, St. Joseph in Via Trionfale.

Curial membership: Economic Affairs of the Holy See (office).

Poli, Mario Aurelio: b. Nov. 29, 1947, Buenos Aires, Argentina; ord. Nov. 25, 1978; studied at the Univ. of Buenos Aires, Metropolitan Seminary of the Immaculate Conception, Buenos Aires, and the Pontifical Catholic Univ. of Argentina; app. titular bp. of Abidda and aux. of Buenos Aires, Feb. 8, 2002; ord. Apr. 20, 2002; app. bp. of Santa Rosa, June 24, 2008; app. abp. of Buenos Aires, Mar. 28, 2013; card. priest, Feb. 22, 2014 with the title of S. Roberto Bellarmino.

Curial membership: Oriental Churches (congregation).

Poupard,* Paul: b. Aug. 30, 1930, Bouzille, France; ord., Dec. 18, 1954; ord. titular bp. of Usula and aux. of Paris, Apr. 6, 1979; title of abp. and pro-president of the Secretariat for Non-Believers, 1980; card. deacon, May 25, 1985; card. priest, Jan. 29, 1996; titular church, St. Praxedes; president of Pontifical Council for Dialogue with Non-Believers, 1985-93. President of Pontifical Council for Culture, 1988; President of the Pontifical Council for Interreligious Dialogue, 2006-2007.

Curial membership: Divine Worship and Sacraments, Education, Evangelization of Peoples (congregations); Christian Unity, Interreligious Dialogue, Laity (council).

Pujats,* Janis: b. Nov. 14, 1930, the Rezekne district of Latvia; ord., Mar. 29, 1951; taught art history and liturgy at the Catholic Theological Seminary, Riga; vicar general in the Metropolitan Curia, Riga, 1979-84; declared persona non grata by the KGB, 1984; abp. of Riga, 1991-2010; pres. of the Latvian Bishops' Conference; card. (in pectore), Feb. 21, 1998, titular church, St. Sylvia.

Puljic, Vinko: b. Sept. 8, 1945, Prijecani, Bosnia–Herzegovina; ord., June 29, 1970; spiritual director of minor seminary of Zadar, 1978-87; parish priest; app. vice–rector of Sarajevo major seminary, 1990; ord. abp. of Vrhbosna (Sarajevo), Jan. 6, 1991, in Rome; card., Nov. 26, 1994; titular church, St. Clare in Vigna Clara.

Curial membership: Evangelization of Peoples (congregation); Interreligious Dialogue (council).

Quevedo, Orlando Beltran, O.M.I.: b. Mar. 11, 1939, Laoag, Philippines; ord. June 5, 1964 in Washington, D.C.; entered the Order of the Oblates of Mary Immaculate in 1954 and studied at San Jose Seminary, Quezon City, St. Peter's Novitiate, Mission, TX, The Catholic Univ. of America, Washington, DC, the Univ. of Santo Tomas, Manila, and St. Louis Univ., MO; app. bp. of Kidapawan, July 23, 1980; ord. Oct. 28, 1980; app. abp. of Nueva Segovia, Mar. 22, 1986; one of the great voices for peace in the Philippines; created card. priest, Feb. 22, 2014 with the title of S. Maria Regina Mundi a Torre Spaccata.

Rai, O.M.M., Béchara Boutros: b. Feb. 25, 1940, Himlaya, Lebanon; studied at the Pontifical Lateran Univ., Rome, for licentiate in theology and a doctorate in canon law; entered the Maronite Order of the Blessed Virgin Mary (Mariamita) (O.M.M.); ord., Sept. 3, 1967; elected patriarchal vicar and titular bp. of Cesarea di Filippo by the Maronite Patriarchal Synod, May 2, 1986; app. eparch of Jbeil (Byblos), June 9, 1990; elected patriarch of Antioch of the Maronites, Mar. 15, 2011; confirmed by Pope Benedict XVI on Mar. 25, 2011; card. patriarch Nov. 24, 2012.

Curial membership: Oriental Churches (congregation); Supreme Tribunal of the Apostolic Signatura; Migrants and Itinerants, Social Communications (councils).

Ravasi, Gianfranco: b. Oct. 18, 1942, Merate, Italy; studied at the Major Seminary of Milan, Pontifical Gregorian Univ. and Pontifical Biblical Institute; ord. June 28, 1966, and served as a professor of Scripture; prefect of the Ambrosian Library, Milan, 1989-2007; app. member of the Pontifical Biblical Commission, 1995; wrote the meditations for the Way of the Cross on Good Friday 2007; app. titular abp. of Villamagna di Proconsolare and president of the Pontifical Council of Culture and president of the Pontifical Commission for the Cultural Patrimony of the Church, and of the Pontifical Commission for Sacred Archeology, Sept. 3, 2007; ord. Sept. 29, 2007; prolific author and renowned biblical scholar; card. deacon, Nov. 20, 2010; deaconry of S. Giorgio in Velabro.

Curial membership: Education (congregation); Interreligious Dialogue, New Evangelization (councils).

Re,* Giovanni Battista: b. Jan. 30, 1934, Borno (Brescia), Italy; ord., Mar. 3, 1957; earned doctorate in canon law and taught in the Brescia Seminary; entered Holy See diplomatic service, served in Panama and Iran; recalled for service in Secretariat of State; sec. for Cong. for Bishops, 1987; titular abp., Nov. 7, 1987; sostituto for Secretariat of State, 1989; prefect of the Cong. of Bishops and pres. of the Pont. Comm. for Latin America, 2000-2010; card., Feb. 21, 2001; titular church, Twelve Holy Apostles; card. bishop as titular bp. of suburbicarian see of Sabina-Poggio Mirteto.

Curial membership: Secretariat of State (second section); Doctrine of the Faith, Eastern Churches, Evangelization (congregations); Texts (council); Vatican City State (commission); APSA (office).

Ricard, Jean-Pierre: b. Sept. 26, 1944, Marseille, France; studied at Institut Catholique in Paris; ord. Oct. 5, 1968; app. titular bp. of Pulcheriopoli and aux. bp. of Grenoble, Apr. 17, 1993; app. coadj. bp. of Montpellier, July 4, 1996; bp. of Montpellier, Sept. 6, 1996; promoted close relations with the Church in Africa and visited Peru in 1999 to meet a *fidei donum* priest of the diocese; visited Lebanon in 2000; major supporter of dialogue with the Jews; elected pres. of the Episcopal Conference of France, Nov. 6, 2001; app. abp. of Bordeaux, Dec. 21, 2001; in 2003 authored book, *Sept défis pour l'Eglise* (Seven Challenges for the Church); app. member of the Council for the Economy, Mar. 8, 2014; card., Mar. 24, 2006; titular church, Sant'Agostino.

Curial membership: Doctrine of the Faith, Sacraments (congregations); Culture, Economy (councils); Ecclesia dei (commission).

Rigali, Justin Francis: b. Apr. 19, 1935, Los Angeles, CA; educ. St. John's Seminary (Camarillo, CA); ord. priest (Los Angeles*), Apr. 25, 1961; in Vatican diplomatic service from 1964; ord. titular abp. of Bolsena, Sept. 14, 1985, by Pope John Paul II; president of the Pontifical Ecclesiastical Academy, 1985-89; secretary of Cong. for Bps., 1989-94, and College of Cardinals, 1990-94; app. abp. of St. Louis, Jan. 25, 1994, inst., Mar. 16, 1994; app. abp. of Philadelphia, July 15, 2003; ret. July 19, 2011; card., Oct. 21, 2003; titular church, St. Prisca.

Curial membership: Sacraments (congregation); APSA (office).

Rivera Carrera, Norberto: b. June 6, 1942, La Purísima, Mexico; ord., July 3, 1966; taught dogmatic theology at major seminary of Mexico City; professor of ecclesiology at Pontifical Univ. of Mexico; bp. of Tehuacán, Nov. 5, 1985; abp. of Mexico City, June 13,1995; app. member of the Council for the Study of the Organizational and Economic Problems of the Holy See, Oct. 23, 2010; card., Feb. 21, 1998; titular church, St. Francis of Assisi at Ripa Grande.

Curial membership: Clergy, Divine Worship and the Discipline of Sacraments (congregation); Family (council); Economy, Latin America (commissions).

Robles Ortega, Francisco: b. Mar. 2, 1949, Mascota, México; ord. July 20, 1976; vicar general of Autlán and prof. of philosophy and theology at its seminary; cons. titular bp. of Bossa and aux. bp. of Toluca, June 5, 1991; bp. of Toluca, 1996-2003; app. abp. of Monterrey, Jan. 25, 2003; card., Nov. 24, 2007; app. abp. of Guadalajara, Dec. 7, 2011; titular church, St. Mary of the Presentation.

Curial membership: Latin America (commission).

Rodé,* C.M., Franc: b. Sept. 23, 1934, Jarse, Ljubljana, Slovenia; the family left for Austria and then Argentina during World War II; entered the Cong. of the Missions (Vincentians), Mar. 6, 1952 and took perpetual vows in 1957; studied at the Gregorian Univ., Rome and the Institut Catholique in Paris; ord. June 29, 1960; returned to Slovenia and after parish ministry, he taught at the Faculty of Theology in Ljubljana; his work in support of Catholic education caused him to be placed under surveillance by state authorities; app. undersec. of the Secretariat for Non-Believers and then sec. of the Pont. Council for Culture; app. abp. of Ljubljana, Mar. 5, 1997; prefect of the Cong. for the Institutes of Consecrated Life and Societies of Apostolic Life, 2004-2010; card. Mar. 24, 2006; titular church, Diaconia di San Francesco Saverio alla Garbatella.

Curial membership: Bishops, Doctrine of the Faith, Education, Evangelization, Sacraments (congregations); Culture (council); Ecclesia Dei (commission).

Rodríguez Maradiaga, S.D.B., Oscar Andrés: b. Dec. 29, 1942, Tegucigalpa, Honduras; ord., for the Salesians June 28, 1870; taught Salesian colleges in El Salvador, Honduras and Guatemala; prof. at the Salesian Theological Institute, Guatemala, and rector Salesian Philosophical Institute, Guatemala; app. titular bp. of Pudentiana and aux. bp. of Tegucigalpa, Oct. 28, 1978; app. abp. of Tegucigalpa, Jan. 8, 1993; pres. of CELAM, 1995-99; pres. of the Episcopal Conference of Honduras; coord. for the Council of Cardinals, Apr. 13, 2014; card. priest, Feb. 21, 2001; titular church, St. Mary of Hope.

Curial membership: Clergy (congregation); Justice and Peace, Social Communication (councils); Latin America (commission).

Romeo, Paolo: b. Feb. 20, 1938, Acireale, Italy; studied at the Seminary of Acireale, Pontifical Gregorian Univ., and Pontifical Lateran Univ., Rome; ord. Mar. 18, 1961, studied at the Pontifical Ecclesiastical Academy, entered the Holy See diplomatic service in 1967; ord. titular abp. of Vulturia, Jan. 6, 1984; nuncio to Haiti, 1983-1990, Colombia, 1990-1999, Canada, 1999-2001, and Italy and San Marino, 2001-2006; app. abp. of Palermo, Dec. 19, 2006; card. priest, Nov. 20, 2010; titular of S. Maria Odigitria dei Siciliani, deaconry elevated pro hac vice to titular church.

Curial membership: Laity (council); Latin America (commission).

Rosales,* Gaudencio: b. Aug. 10, 1932, Batangas City; ord. Mar. 23, 1958; app. titular bp. of Esco and aux. bp. of Manila, Aug. 12, 1974; app. coadj. bp. of Malaybalay, June 9, 1982; bp. of Malaybalay, Sept. 14, 1984; app. abp. of Lipa, Dec. 30, 1992; app. abp. of Manila, Sept. 15, 2003; card., Mar. 24, 1006, titular church, Santissimo Nome di Maria a Via Latina.

Curial membership: Interreligious Dialogue; Social Communications (councils).

Rouco Varela, Antonio María: b. Aug. 24, 1936, Villalba, Spain; ord.; Mar. 28, 1959; taught fundamental theology and canon law at the Mondoñedo seminary; adjunct prof. at the Univ. of Munich; taught ecclesiastical law at Pontifical Univ. of Salamanca; vice-rector of Pontifical Univ. of Salamanca;

titular bp. of Gergis and aux. bp. of Santiago de Compostela, Sept. 17, 1976; abp. of Santiago de Compostela, May 9,1984; abp. of Madrid June 29, 1994; card., Feb. 21, 1998, titular church, St. Laurence in Damaso.

Curial membership: Bishops, Clergy, Education (congregations); "Cor Unum," Culture, Texts (councils); Supreme Tribunal of the Apostolic Signatura (tribunal); Economic Affairs (office).

Rubiano Sáenz,* Pedro: b. Sept. 13, 1932, Cartago, Colombia; ord., July 8, 1956; chaplain to Marco Fidel Suárez Air Force Academy, St. Liberata National College, and Our Lady of Remedies Clinic; app. bp. of Cúcuta, June 2, 1971; cons., June 11, 1971; app. coadj. abp. of Cali, Mar. 26, 1983; abp. of Cali, 1985-1994; apost. admin. of Popayán; abp. of Bogota, 1994-2010; card. priest, Feb. 21, 2001; titular church, Transfiguration of Our Lord Jesus Christ.

Curial membership: Education (congregation); Migrants and Itinerant Peoples (council).

Ruini,* Camillo: b. Feb. 19, 1931, Sassuolo, Italy; ord., Dec. 8, 1954; taught at seminaries in central Italy; ord. titular bp. of Nepte and aux. bp. of Reggio Emilia and Guastella, June 29, 1983; secretary general of Italian Bishops' Conference, 1986–91; abp. Jan. 17, 1991 and pro-vicar general of the Pope for the Rome diocese; pro–Archpriest of Patriarchal Lateran Archbasilica; card., June 28, 1991; titular church, St. Agnes outside the Wall. Vicar General of the Pope for the Diocese of Rome and Archpriest of Patriarchal Lateran Basilica, and grand chancellor of Pontifical Lateran Univ., 1991-2008; President of the Peregrinatio ad Petri Sedem, 1992–96.

Curial membership: Bishops (congregation); Laity (council).

Rylko, Stanisław: b. July 4, 1945, Andrychów, Poland; ord. Mar. 30, 1969; doctorate in social sciences from Pontifical Gregorian Univ., Rome and served as a professor at the Pontifical Theological Academy of Kraków; app. titular bp. of Novica and sec. of the Pontifical Council for the Laity, Dec. 20, 1995; pres. of the Pont. Council for the Laity and abp., Oct. 4, 2003; card., Nov. 24, 2007; deaconry, Sacred Heart of Christ the King.

Curial Membership: Bishops, Saints (congregation); Latin America (commission).

Salazar Gomez, Rubén: b. Sept. 22, 1942, Bogotá, Colombia; studied at San Joaquín of Ibagué Minor Seminary, Pontifical Gregorian Univ., Rome, and Pontifical Biblical Institute, Rome; ord. a priest, May 20, 1967; app. bp. of Cúcuta, Feb. 11, 1992; ord. Mar. 25, 1992; app. metropolitan abp. of Barranquilla, Mar. 18, 1999; pres. of the episcopal conference of Colombia for the triennium 2008-2011; app. metropolitan abp. of Bogotá, July 8, 2010; card. priest in the consistory of Nov. 24, 2012, with the title of S. Gerardo Maiella.

Curial membership: Latin America (commission), Justice and Peace (council).

Sandoval Íñiguez,* Juan: b. Mar. 28, 1933, Yahualica, Mexico; ord., Oct. 27, 1957; ord. coadj. bp. of Ciudad Juárez, Apr. 30, 1988; bp. of Ciudad Juarez, July 11, 1992; app. abp. of Guadalajara, Apr. 21, 1994; card., Nov. 26, 1994; ret., Dec. 7, 2011; titular church, Our Lady of Guadalupe and St. Philip the Martyr on Via Aurelia.

Curial membership: Institutes of Consecrated Life and Societies of Apostolic Life, Catholic Education (congregations); Culture, Latin America (commission); Economic Affairs of the Holy See (office); Works of Religion (commission).

Sandri, Leonardo: b. Nov. 18, 1943, Buenos Aires, Argentina; ord., Dec. 2, 1967; doctorate in canon law at the Pontifical Gregorian Univ., Rome and studied at the Pontifical Ecclesiastical Academy; entered the Holy See diplomatic service in 1974 and served in nunciatures in Madagascar, Maurice and the U.S.; held several posts in the Secretariat of State; titular

abp. of Cittanova and nuncio in Venezuela, July 22, 1997; cons., Oct. 11, 1997; nuncio to México, Mar. 1, 2000; sostituto of the Secretariat of State for General Affairs, Sept. 16, 2000; card. Nov. 24, 2007; deaconry, Sts. Biagio and Carlo at Catinari; Prefect of Cong. for Oriental Churches, June 9, 2007.

Curial membership: Doctrine, Evangelization (congregations), Christian Unity, Vatican City (commission)

Santos,* O.F.M., Alexandre José Maria dos: b. Mar. 18, 1924, Zavala, Mozambique; ord., July 25, 1953; first Mozambican black priest; ord. abp. of Maputo, Mar. 9, 1975; card., June 28, 1988; titular church, St. Frumentius (ai Prati Fiscali).

Sarah, Robert: b. June 15, 1945, Ourous, Guinea; studied at the Grand Seminary of Nancy, France, the Pontifical Gregorian Univ., Rome, and Studium Biblicum Franciscanum of Jerusalem; ord. July 20, 1969, app. abp. of Conakry, Aug. 13, 1979 and ord. Dec. 8, 1979; app. sec. of the Cong. for the Evangelization of Peoples, Oct. 1, 2001; app. pres. of the Pontifical Council Cor Unum, Oct. 7, 2010; card. deacon, Nov. 20, 2010 with the deaconry of S. Giovanni Bosco in via Tuscolana.

Curial membership: Evangelization (congregation); Justice, Laity (council).

Saraiva Martins,* C.M.F., José: b. Jan. 6, 1932, Gagos do Jarmelo, Portugal; ord., for the Claretians, Mar. 16, 1957; taught at Claretian seminary in Marino, Italy; Claretianum, Rome; and the Pontifical Urbanian Univ. and served as rector, 1977-80, 1980-83, 1986-88; sec. of the Cong. for Catholic Education and titular abp. of Thuburnica, May 26, 1988; cons. abp., July 2, 1988; pref. of Cong. for the Causes of Saints, 1998-2008; card. deacon, Feb. 21, 2001; deaconry of Our Lady of the Sacred Heart; card. bishop, Feb. 24, 2009, suburbicarian see of Palestrina.

Curial membership: Bishops, Sacraments (congregations); Health Care (council); Vatican City (commission).

Sardi,* Paolo: b. Sept. 1, 1934, Ricaldone, Italy; studied at the Major Seminary in Torino, Pontifical Gregorian Univ., Rome, and Università Cattolica del Sacro Cuore, Milan; ord. June 29, 1958; appointed to the Secretariat of State, 1976; app. titular abp. of Sutri and apostolic nuncio with special responsibilities, Dec. 10, 1996; ord. Jan. 6, 1997; vice-camerlengo of the Holy Roman Church, 2004-2011; app. pro-patron of the Sovereign Military and Hospitaller Order of St. John of Jerusalem of Rhodes and of Malta, June 6, 2009 and patron Nov. 30, 2010; created card. deacon, Nov. 20, 2010; deaconry of S. Maria Ausiliatrice in via Tuscolana.

Curial membership: Consecrated Life, Saints (congregations); Laity (council).

Sarr, Théodore-Adrien: b. Nov. 28, 1936, Fadiouth, Sénégal; ord. May 28, 1964; pastoral ministry and prof. of the Minor Seminary of N'Gasobil and superior, 1970-1974; cons. bp. of Kaolack, Nov. 24, 1974; app. abp. of Dakar, June 2, 2000; well known voice for peace in western Africa; card., Nov. 24, 2007; titular church, St. Lucy at the Piazza d'Armi.

Curial membership: Evangelization, Sacraments (congregation); Culture (council).

Scheid, Eusebio Oscar: b. Dec. 8, 1932, Luzerna, Brazil; ord. July 3, 1960; joined the Cong. of Priests of the Sacred Heart of Jesus (S.C.J.); ord. bp. of São José dos Campos, May 1, 1981; app. abp. of Florianapolis, Jan. 23, 1991; app. abp. of São Sebastião do Rio de Janeiro, July 25, 2001; ret. Feb. 27, 2009; card., Oct. 21, 2003; titular church, Sts. Boniface and Alexis.

Curial membership: Latin America (commission).

Scherer, Odilo: b. Sept. 21, 1949, São Francisco, Brazil; ord. Dec. 7, 1976; doctorate in theology Pontifical Gregorian Univ. in Rome; rector and professor in several seminaries and universities; 1994-2001 Cong. for Bishops; cons. titular bp. of Novi and aux. bp. of São Paulo, Nov. 28, 2001; elected sec. general of the National Conference of Bishops of Brazil, 2003; app. abp. of São Paulo, Mar. 21, 2007; card., Nov. 24, 2007; titular church, St. Andrea at the Quirinale.

Curial membership: Clergy (congregation); Latin America, Works of Religion (commission); Economic Affairs (office).

Schönborn, O.P., Christoph: b. Jan. 22, 1945, Skalsko, Bohemia (fled to Austria in Sept. 1945); entered Dominican Order in 1963; ord., 1970; student pastor in Graz Univ., 1973-75; assoc. professor of dogma in the Univ. of Fribourg, 1976; professor theology, 1978; professor dogmatic theology, 1981-91; Orthodox-Roman Catholic Dialogue Commission of Switzerland, 1980–87; International Theological Commission, 1980–; foundation, "Pro Oriente" since 1984; secretary for the draft commission of the *Catechism of the Catholic Church*, 1987–1992; ord. aux. bp. (Sutri) of Vienna, Sept. 29, 1991; coadj. of Vienna, Apr. 13, 1995; abp. Vienna, Sept. 14, 1995; card., Feb. 21, 1998; titular church, Jesus the Divine Worker.

Curial membership: Doctrine of the Faith, Education, Oriental Churches (congregations); Culture (council); Cultural Heritage of the Church, Works of Religion (commissions).

Schwery,* Henri: b. June 14, 1932, Saint-Leonard, Switzerland; ord., July 7, 1957; director of minor seminary and later rector of the College in Sion; bp. of Sion, 1977–95; card., June 28, 1991; titular church, Protomartyrs (a via Aurelia Antica).

Scola, Angelo: b. Nov. 7, 1941, Malgrate, Italy; ord., July 18, 1970; professor of theological anthropology Pontifical John Paul II Institute for Studies on Marriage and the Family at the Pontifical Lateran Univ., Rome; later, professor of Contemporary Christology at the Faculty of Theology, Pontifical Lateran Univ., Rome; ord. bp. of Grosseto, Sep. 21, 1991; rector of the Pontifical Lateran Univ., 1995-2002; patriarch of Venice, Jan. 5, 2002; card., Oct. 21, 2003; titular church, the Seven Most Holy Apostles; app. abp. of Milan, June 28, 2011.

Curial membership: Clergy, Doctrine of the Faith, Oriental Churches, Sacraments (congregations); Culture, Family, Laity(council); Economic Affairs (office).

Sebastián Aguilar, Fernando, C.M.F.: b. Dec. 14, 1929; Calatayud, Spain; ord. June 28, 1953; entered the Congregation of the Missionary Sons of the Immaculate Heart of Mary (Claretians) in 1945 and was professed in 1946; studied at the Instituto de Enseñanza Media, Calatayud, the Catholic Univ. of Louvain, and the Pontifical Athenaeum of St. Thomas Aquinas in Rome where he earned a doctorate in theology; app. bp. of León, Aug. 22, 1979; cons. Sept. 29, 1979; res. July 38, 1983; app. abp. of Pamplona and bp. of Tudela, Mar. 26, 1993; res. July 31, 2007; card. priest Feb. 22, 2014 with the title of S. Angela Merici.

Sebastiani,* Sergio: b. Apr. 11, 1931, Montemonaco (Ascoli Piceno), Italy; ord., 1956; entered Holy See diplomatic service and posted to Peru, Brazil, and Chile; recalled to Secretariat of State; app. titular abp. of Caesarea in Mauretania and pro-nuncio in Madagascar and Mauritius and apostolic delegate to Reunion and Comorros; nuncio to Turkey, 1985; sec. to Central Committee for the Great Jubilee of the Year 2000, 1994; pres. Prefecture for the Economic Affairs of the Holy See, Nov. 3, 1997; card., Feb. 21, 2001; titular church, Deaconry of St. Eustace. Pres. of the Prefecture for the Economic Affairs of the Holy See.

Curial membership: Bishops, Causes of Saints, Clergy, Evangelization (congregations); Christian Unity (council); Apostolic Signatura (tribunal).

Sepe, Crescenzio: b. June 2, 1943, Carinaro (Caserta), Italy; ord., Mar. 12, 1967; taught at Lateran and Urbanian Univs.; studied at Pontifical Ecclesiastical Academy; entered Holy See diplomatic service and posted to Brazil; recalled to Secretariat of State, 1987; pres. of Commission for Vatican

Telecommunications; app. titular abp. of Grado and sec. of the Cong. for the Clergy, Apr. 2, 1992; cons. Apr. 26, 1992; General Secretary of the Central Committee for the Great Jubilee of the Year 2000, 1997-2001; Pref. Cong. for the Evangelization of Peoples, 2001-2006; card. deacon, Feb. 21, 2001; deaconry, God the Merciful Father; app. abp. of Naples, May 20, 2006.

Curial membership: Clergy, Doctrine of the Faith (congregation); Legislative Texts (councils).

Sfeir,* Nasrallah Pierre: b. May 15, 1920, Reyfoun, in Maronite diocese of Sarba, Lebanon; ord., May 7, 1950; sec. of Maronite patriarchate, 1956-61; taught Arabic literature and philosophy at Marist Fathers College, Jounieh, 1951–61; ord. titular bp. of Tarsus for the Maronites, July 16, 1961; elected Patriarch of Antioch for Maronites, Apr. 19, 1986; granted ecclesial communion by John Paul II May 7, 1986; card., Nov. 26, 1994. Patriarch of Antioch for Maronites.

Curial membership: Oriental Churches (congregation).

Sgreccia,* Elio: b. June 6, 1928, Nidastore Arcevia, Italy; studied at the Theological Seminary of Fano and the Univ. of Bologna; ord. June 29, 1951; direc. of Bioethics Center of the Catholic Univ. Sacro Cuore of Milan, 1985-2006; ord. titular bp. of Zama Minor, Jan. 6, 1993; sec. of the Pontifical Council for the Family, 1992-1996; vice-pres. of the Pontifical Academy for Life, 1994-2005; pres. of the Academy, 2005-2008; key voice for responsible bioethics in modern era; card. deacon, Nov. 20, 2010; deaconry of S. Angelo in Pescheria.

Silvestrini,* Achille: b. Oct. 25, 1923, Brisighella, Italy; ord., July 13, 1946; official in Secretariat of State from 1953; ord. titular bp. of Novaliciana with personal title of abp., May 27, 1979; undersecretary, 1973-79, and secretary, 1979-88, of the Council for Public Affairs of the Church (now the second section of the Secretariat of State); card., June 28, 1988; deaconry, St. Benedict Outside St. Paul's Gate, card. priest, Jan. 9, 1999; prefect of Apostolic Signatura, 1988-91. Prefect of Cong. for Oriental Churches, 1991-2001; Grand Chancellor of Pontifical Oriental Institute.

Simonis,* Adrianus J.: b. Nov. 26, 1931, Lisse, Netherlands; ord., June 15, 1957; ord. bp. of Rotterdam, Mar. 20, 1971; coadj. abp. of Utrecht, June 27, 1983; abp. of Utrecht, 1983-2007; card., May 25, 1985; titular church, St. Clement.

Curial membership: Consecrated Life and Societies of Apostolic Life, Education (congregations); Christian Unity (council).

Sodano,* Angelo: b. Nov. 23, 1927, Isola d'Asti, Italy; ord., Sept. 23, 1950; entered diplomatic service of the Holy See in 1959; served in Ecuador and Uruguay; ord. titular abp. of Nova di Cesare, Jan. 15, 1978; nuncio to Chile, 1978-88; secretary of the Council for Relations with States, 1988-90; pro-Secretary of State, 1990-1991; card. June 28, 1991; titular church, S. Maria Nuova; card. bishop, Jan. 10, 1994, as titular bp. of suburbicarian see of Albano (while retaining title to S. Maria Nuova). Secretary of State, June 29, 1991-Sept. 15, 2006; Vice-dean of the Sacred College of Cardinals, 2002-05; dean of the College of Cardinals (Apr. 30, 2005).

Stafford,* James Francis: b. July 26, 1932, Baltimore, MD; ord., (Baltimore*) Dec. 15, 1957; ord. titular bp. of Respetta and aux. bp. of Baltimore, Feb. 29, 1976; app. bp. of Memphis, Nov. 17, 1982; app. abp. of Denver, June 3, 1986, installed July 30, 1986; app. President of Pontifical Council for the Laity, 1996-2003; Major Penitentiary of the Apostolic Penitentiary, Oct. 4, 2003-June 2, 2009; card. deacon, Feb. 21, 1998; card. priest, Mar. 2, 2008; titular church, S. Pietro in Montorio.

Curial membership: Bishops, Doctrine of the Faith, Causes of Saints, Evangelization of Peoples (congregations); Texts (council).

Stella, Beniamino: b. Aug. 18, 1941, Pieve di Soligno,

Italy; ord. Mar. 19, 1966; studied at the Major Roman Seminary, the Pontifical Lateran Univ., and the Pontifical Ecclesiastical Academy, Rome; entered the diplomatic service of the Holy See in 1970 and served in nunciatures in the Dominican Republic, Zaire, the Second Section of the Secretariat of State, Malta; app. titular abp. of Midila and nuncio in the Central African Republic, Congo and Chad, Aug. 21, 1987; ord. Sept. 5, 1987; nuncio in Cuba, 1992-1999, Colombia, 1999-2007; app. president of the Pontifical Ecclesiastical Academy, Oct. 13, 2007; app. prefect of the Congregation for the Clergy, Sept. 21, 2013; card. deacon, Feb. 22, 2014 with the deaconry of Ss. Cosma e Damiano.

Curial membership: Bishops, Catholic Education (congregation).

Tagle, Luis Antonio Gokim: b. June 21, 1957, Manila, Philippines; has the nickname "Chito"; studied at St. Jose Seminary, Manila, Ateneo de Manila University, and The Catholic Univ. of America, Washington, D.C., where he earned a doctorate in theology, summa cum laude; ord. priest, for Manila, Feb. 27, 1982, member of the International Theological Commission, 1997-2002, and on editorial board of the Bologna-based "History of Vatican II" project founded by Giuseppe Alberigo; app. bp. of Imus, Oct. 22, 2001; ord. bp., Dec. 12, 2001; app abp of Manila, Oct. 13, 2011; card. priest Nov. 24, 2012, with the title of S. Felice da Cantalice a Centocelle.

Curial membership: Family and Pastoral of Migrants and Itinerants (councils).

Tauran, Jean-Louis: b. Apr. 3, 1943, Bordeaux, France; ord. Sep. 20, 1969; entered the diplomatic service of the Holy See in 1975; app. titular abp. of Telepte and appointed secretary of the Secretariat of State for the Relations with the States, 1990-2003; Archivist and Librarian of the Holy Roman Church, 2003; card. deacon, Oct. 21, 2003, titular church, St. Apollinaris alle Terme Neroniane-Alessandrine; Pres. of the Pont. Council for Interreligious Dialogue, 2007.

Curial membership: Secretariat of State (second section), Bishops, Doctrine of the Faith, Oriental Churches (Congregations); Culture (council); Supreme Tribunal of the Apostolic Signatura (tribunal); Vatican City State, Works of Religion (commission); APSA (office).

Tempesta, Orani João, O. Cist.: b. June 23, 1950, São José do Rio Pardo, Brazil; ord. Dec. 7, 1974; entered the Order of the Cistercians in 1968 and took solemn vows in 1972; studied at the monastery of São Bento, in São Paulo, the Theological Institute "Pio IX" in São Paulo, and the Faculty of Philosophy Dom Bosco, São João Del Rei, Minas Gerais; elected first abbot of the monastery of Nossa Senhora de São Bernardo, in São José do Rio Pardo, in 1996; app. bp. of São José do Rio Preto, Feb. 26, 1997; cons. Sep. 25, 1997; app. abp. of Belém do Pará, Oct. 13, 2004; app. abp. of São Sebastião do Rio de Janeiro, Feb. 27, 2009; created cardinal priest, Feb. 22, 2014 with the title of S. Maria Madre della Provvidenza a Monte Verde.

Terrazas Sandoval, C.SS.R., Julio: b. Mar. 7, 1936, Vallegrande, Bolivia; ord., for the Redemptorists July 29, 1962; superior of the Redemptorist community in Vallegrande and vicar forane; app. aux. bp. of La Paz and cons., Apr. 15, 1978; transferred to the see of Oruro, Jan. 9, 1982; pres. of the Bolivian Episcopal Conference in 1985 and 1988; app. abp. of Santa Cruz, Feb. 6, 1991; ret., Mar. 25, 2013; card., Feb. 21, 2001; titular church, St. John Baptist Rossi.

Curial membership: Laity (council); Latin America (commission).

Tettamanzi,* Dionigi: b. Mar. 14, 1934, Renate, Italy; ord., June 28, 1957; taught fundamental theology at the major seminary of Lower Venegono, pastoral theology at the Priestly Institute of Mary Immaculate and the Lombard Regional Institute of Pastoral Ministry, Milan; rector of the Pontifical Lombard Seminary, Rome; abp. of Ancona-Osimo, July 1,1989 (res. 1991); general secretary of the Italian Episcopal Conference, 1991-95; Vice-President of the Italian Episcopal Conference, May 25, 1995; abp. of Genoa Apr. 20, 1995; card., Feb. 21, 1998; titular church, Sts. Ambrose and Charles; app. abp. of Milan, July 11, 2002; ret. June 28, 2011.

Curial membership: Clergy, Education, Oriental Churches (congregations).

Thottunkal, Baselios Cleemis: b. June 15, 1959, Nedungadappally, India; studied at the Infant Jesus Minor Seminary of the Eparchy of Tiruvalla, St. Berchman's College, Changanacherry, St. Joseph's Pontifical Seminary, Aluva, Pontifical Seminary of Pune, Dharmaram College, Bangalore, Pontifical Univ. of St. Thomas Aquinas, Rome, where he earned a doctorate in theology; ord. a priest, June 11, 1986, for the eparchy of Battery; app. titular bp. of Chayal of the Syro-Malankars and aux. of Trivandrum of the Syro-Malankars, June 18, 2001; cons. Aug. 15, 2001; app. bp. of Tiruvalla of the Syro-Malankars, Sept. 11, 2003; app. first metropolitan of Tiruvalla, May 15, 2006; unanimously elected abp. major, Feb. 8, 2007; confirmed on Feb. 10, by Pope Benedict XVI; card. priest in the consistory of Nov. 24, 2012, with the title of S. Gregorio VII.

Curial membership: Oriental Churches (congregation), Inter-religious Dialogue (council).

Tomko,* Jozef: b. Mar. 11, 1924, Udavske, Slovakia; ord., Mar. 12, 1949; ord. titular abp. of Doclea, Sept. 15, 1979; secretary-general of the Synod of Bishops, 1979-85; card. deacon, May 25, 1985; card. priest, Jan. 29, 1996; titular church, St. Sabina. Prefect of the Cong. for the Evangelization of Peoples, 1985-2001; Grand Chancellor of Pontifical Urban Univ.; President of Pontifical Committee for International Eucharistic Congresses, 2001.

Tong Hon, John: b. July 31, 1939, Hong Kong; earned a doctorate in theology at the Pontifical Urbanian Univ.; ord, priest, Jan. 6, 1966; ord. titular bp. of Bossa and aux. of Hong Kong, Dec. 9, 1996; app. coadj. bp. of Hong Kong, Jan. 30, 2008; acceded to the see of Hong Kong, Apr. 15, 2009; card., Feb. 18, 2012 with the title of Regina Apostolorum.

Curial membership: Evengelization (congregation); Interreligious Dialogue (council).

Toppo, Telesphore Placidus: b. Oct. 15, 1939, Chainpur, India, to tribal family that had converted to Christianity; ord. May 3, 1969; ord. bp. of Dumka, June 8, 1979; abp. of Ranchi, Aug. 7, 1985; supported programs to assist tribes in Jharkhand; card., Oct. 21, 2003; titular church, Sacred Heart of Jesus in Agony at Vitinia.

Curial membership: Evangelization of Peoples (congregation); Culture, Interreligious Dialogue (councils).

Tucci,* S.J., Roberto: b. Apr. 19, 1921, Naples, Italy; ord., for the Jesuits, Aug. 24, 1950; editor of La Civiltà Cattolica; member of the Preparatory Commission on the Apostolate of the Laity for Vatican II and peritus involved in drafting Ad Gentes and Gaudium et Spes; consultor to the Pontifical Council for Social Communications, 1965-89; vice-pres. of the Italian Catholic Union of the Press, 1961–82; general sec. of the Italian Province of the Jesuits, 1967–69; app. general manager of Vatican Radio, 1973; since 1982, he has been responsible for all papal visits outside Italy; app. chairman of the Administrative Committee of Vatican Radio, 1986; card., Feb. 21, 2001; titular church, Deaconry of St. Ignatius Loyola in Campo

Marzio. Chairman of the Administrative Committee of Vatican Radio.

Tumi,* Christian Wiyghan: b. Oct. 15, 1930, Kikaikelaki, Cameroon; ord., Apr. 17, 1966; ord. bp. of Yagoua, Jan. 6, 1980; coadj. abp. of Garoua, Nov. 19, 1982; abp. of Garoua, 1984–91; abp. of Douala, Aug. 31, 1991; card., June 28, 1988; titular church, Martyrs of Uganda (a Poggio Ameno).

Curial membership: Divine Worship and Sacraments, Education, Evangelization of Peoples (congregations); Cor Unum, Family (councils).

Turcotte, Jean–Claude: b. June 26, 1936, Montreal, Canada; ord., May 24, 1959; ord. titular bp. of Suas and aux. of Montreal, June 29, 1982; abp. of Montreal, Mar. 17, 1990; card., Nov. 26, 1994; titular church, Our Lady of the Blessed Sacrament and the Holy Canadian Martyrs.

Curial membership: Evangelization, Causes of Saints (congregation); Social Communications (council).

Turkson, Peter Kodwo Appiah: b. Oct. 11, 1948, Wassaw Nsuta, Ghana; ord. July 20, 1975; abp. of Cape Coast, Jan. 6, 1992-Oct. 24, 2009; pres. of the Catholic Bishops' Conference and Chancellor of the Catholic Univ. College of Ghana; card. priest, Oct. 21, 2003; titular church, St. Liborius; pres. of the Pontifical Council for Justice and Peace, Oct. 24, 2009.

Curial membership: Evangelization, Sacraments (congregation); Christian Unity (council); Cultural Heritage of the Church (commission).

Urosa Savino, Jorge Liberato: b. Aug. 28, 1942, Caracas, Venezuela; ord. Aug. 15, 1967; doctorate in theology Gregorian Univ., 1971; rector several Venezuelan seminaries, 1974–82 and prof. of philosophical anthropology and dogmatic theology; pres. of the organization of Venezuelan Seminaries, 1974–77; vice-pres. of Organization of Latin American Seminaries, 1976–82; app. titular bp. of Vegesela in Byzacena and aux. bp. of Caracas, July 13, 1982; app. abp. of Valencia in Venezuela, Mar. 17, 1990; app. abp. of Caracas, Sept. 19, 2005; card., Mar. 24, 2006, titular church, Sta. Maria ai Monti.

Curial membership: Clergy (congregation); Culture, Justice and Peace (council); Latin America (commission); Economic Affairs (office).

Vallini, Agostino: b. Apr. 17, 1940, Poli, Italy; ord. July 19, 1964; study of canon law Pontifical Lateran Univ.; doctorate in utroque iure; taught in Naples, 1969–71; called back to Rome 1971 to teach public ecclesiastical law at the Lateran, with the task of reorganizing the field in keeping with the Second Vatican Council; rector Major Seminary of Naples, 1978; app. titular bp. of Tortibulum and aux. bp. of Naples, Mar. 23, 1989; app. suburbicarian bp. of Albano, Nov. 13, 1999; app. prefect of the Supreme Tribunal of the Apostolic Signatura, 2004–2008; pres. of the Court of Causation of the Vatican City State, 2004–2008; card., Mar. 24, 2006; titular church, Diaconia di San Pier Damiani ai Monti di San Paolo; card. priest, retaining titular church, pro hac vice, Feb. 24, 2009; app. Vicar General of Rome, Archpriest of the Archbasilica of St. John Lateran, and grand chancellor of the Pontifical Lateran Univ., June 27, 2008.

Curial membership: Consecrated Life, Evangelization, Saints (Congregation); Economy, Texts (councils); APSA; Economic Affairs (office).

Vanhoye,* S.J., Albert: b. July 24, 1923, Hazebrouck, France; entered the Jesuits, Sept. 11, 1941 and ord. July 24, 1954; professor at Pontifical Biblical Institute, the Biblicum, Rome 1963–; dean of biblical faculty, 1969–75 and rector, 1984–90; taught at Gregorian Univ. and Lateran Univ., Rome; assisted in the preparation of the apostolic constitution, Sapientia Christiana; served as member of the Pontifical Biblical Commission, 1984–2001 and sec. of the commission, 1990–2001; consultor to the Congs. of Catholic Education from 1978 and Doctrine of the Faith from 1990; card., Mar. 24, 2006; titular church, diaconia di Sta. Maria della Mercede e Sant'Adriano a Villa Albani.

Vegliò, Antonio Maria: b. Feb. 3, 1938, Macerata Feltria, Italy; earned a doctorate in canon law and studied at the Pontifical Ecclesiastical Academy, Rome; ord. priest, Mar. 18, 1962; entered the diplomatic service of the Holy See in 1968 and served in the nunciatures in Peru, Philippines, Senegal, and Great Britain; ord. titular abp. of Eclano and app. pro-nuncio in Papua New Guinea and Solomon Islands, July 27, 1985; app. pro-Nuncio in Cape Verde, Guinea-Bissau, Mali and Senegal in 1989, nuncio in Cape Verde, Guinea-Bissau, Mali and Senegal in 1994, nuncio in Kuwait in 1998, and nuncio in Lebanon, 1997-2001; ap. sec. of Congregation for the Oriental Churches, Apr. 11, 2001; app. president of the Pontifical Council for the Pastoral Care of Migrants and Itinerant Peoples, Feb. 28, 2009; cardinal Feb. 18, 2012 with the deaconry of S. Cesareo in Palatio.

Curial membership: Divine Worship (congregation); Family, Laity (councils).

Vela Chiriboga,* Raúl Eduardo: b. Jan. 1, 1934, Riobamba, Ecuador; studied at the Major Seminary of Quito; ord. July 28, 1957, general sec. of the episcopal conference of Ecuador, 1970-1975; ord. titular bp. Ausafa and aux. bp. Guayaquil, May 21, 1972; bp. Azogues, 1975-1989; transf. to the titular see of Pauzera and app. military ordinary of Ecuador, July 8, 1989; app. abp. of Quito, Mar. 21, 2003; res., Sept. 11, 2010; created card. priest, Nov. 20, 2010; titular church of S. Maria in Via.

Curial membership: Family (council); Latin America (commission).

Versaldi, Giuseppe: b. July 30, 1943, Villarboit, Italy; earned a doctorate in canon law from the Pontifical Gregorian Univ. and was advocate at the Sacred Roman Rota; ord. priest June 29, 1967; ord. bp. of Alessandria, May 26, 2007; app. apostolic visitor to the Legionaires of Christ, June 27, 2009; app. president of the Prefecture for the Economic Affairs of the Holy See and named abp. Sept. 21, 2010; card., Feb. 18, 2012, with the deaconry of Sacro Cuore di Gesù a Castro Pretorio.

Curial membership: Bishops, Consecrated Life (congregations); Signatura (tribunal).

Vidal,* Ricardo J.: b. Feb. 6, 1931, Mogpoc, Philippines; ord., Mar. 17, 1956; ord. titular bp. of Claterna and coadj. of Melalos, Nov. 30, 1971; abp. of Lipa, 1973-81; coadj. abp. of Cebu, Apr. 13, 1981; abp. of Cebu, Aug. 24, 1982; card., May 25, 1985; titular church, Sts. Peter and Paul (in Via Ostiensi).

Curial membership: Education, Evangelization of Peoples (congregations); Family, Health Care Workers (councils).

Vingt-Trois, André: b. Nov. 7, 1942, Paris, France; ord. June 28, 1969; served as professor of theology and in a variety of pastoral positions, including diocesan formation; cons. titular bp. of Tibili and aux. of Paris, Oct. 14, 1988; abp. of Tours, 1999-2005; app. abp. of Paris and ordinary of the Catholics of Oriental rite in France, Feb. 11, 2005; elected pres. Episcopal Conference of France, Nov. 5, 2007; card., Nov. 24, 2007; titular church, St. Louis of the French.

Curial membership: Bishops, Clergy, Oriental Churches (congregations); Family, Migrants (councils).

Vlk,* Miloslav: b. May 17, 1932, Lisnice, Czech Republic; during communist persecution when theological studies were impossible he studied archival science at Charles Univ. and worked in various archives in Bohemia; ord., June 23, 1968, during "Prague Spring"; sent to isolated parishes in Bohemian Forest by State authorities in 1971; state authorization to exercise his priestly ministry was cancelled in 1978; from then until 1986 he worked as a window-washer in Prague, carrying out his priestly ministry secretly; the situation changed with the "velvet revolution"; ord. bp. Ceske Budejovice, Mar. 31, 1990; abp. Prague, 1991–2010; card., Nov. 26, 1994; titular church, Holy Cross in Jerusalem; President of the Council of European Episcopal Conferences, 1993–.
Curial membership: Oriental Churches (congregation); Social Communications (council).

Wamala,* Emmanuel: b. Dec. 15, 1926, Kamaggwa, Uganda; ord., Dec. 21, 1957; ord. bp. of Kiyinda-Mityana, Nov. 22, 1981; coadj. abp. Kampala, June 21, 1988; abp. Kampala, 1990-2006; card., Nov. 26, 1994; titular church, St. Hugh.

Wetter,* Friedrich: b. Feb. 20, 1928, Landau, Germany; ord., Oct. 10, 1953; ord. bp. of Speyer, June 29, 1968; abp. of Munich and Freising, 1982-2007; card., May 25, 1985; titular church, St. Stephen (al Monte Celio).

Williams,* Thomas Stafford: b. Mar. 20, 1930, Wellington, New Zealand; ord., Dec. 20, 1959, in Rome; studied in Ireland after ordination, receiving degree in social sciences; served in various pastoral assignments on his return to New Zealand; missionary in Western Samoa to 1976; abp. of Wellington, New Zealand, 1979-2005; ret. Mar. 20, 2005; card., Feb. 2, 1983; titular church, Jesus the Divine Teacher (at Pineda Sacchetti).
Curial membership: Evangelization of Peoples (congregation).

Woelki, Rainer Maria: b. Aug. 18, 1956, Cologne-Mülheim, Germany; earned a doctorate in theology from the Pontifical University della Santa Croce, Rome; ord. priest, June 14, 1985, for the archdiocese of Cologne; ord. titular bp. of Scampa and aux. bp. of Cologne, Mar. 30, 2003; app. abp. of Berlin, July 2, 2011; app. abp. of Cologne, July 11, 2014; card., Feb. 18, 2012, with the title of S. Giovanni Maria Vianney.
Curial membership: Education (congregation); Christan Unity (council).

Wuerl, Donald W.: b. Nov. 12, 1940, Pittsburgh, PA; studied at Catholic Univ., Washington, DC), North American College, Pontifical Gregorian Univ., and Pontifical Univ. of St. Thomas Aquinas (Angelicum), Rome; earned doctorate in theology from the Angelicum; ord. for Pittsburgh, Dec. 17, 1966, in Rome; ord. titular bp. of Rosemarkie Jan. 6, 1986, in Rome; served as aux. bp. of Seattle, 1986 87; app. bp. of Pittsburgh, Feb. 11, 1988, inst., Mar. 25, 1988; app. abp. of Washington, May 16, 2006; a prolific writer, he has authored numerous books; created card. priest, Nov. 20, 2010; titular church of S. Pietro in Vincoli.
Curial membership: Bishops, Clergy, Doctrine of the Faith (congregations); Christian Unity (council).

Yeom Soo jung, Andrew: b. Dec. 5, 1943, Ansong, Korea; a descendant of several Korean Martyrs; ord. Dec. 8, 1973; studied at the Seminary of Seoul, the Catholic University of Korea, and the East Asian Pastoral Institute in the Philippines; app. titular bp. of Tibiuca and auxiliary of Seoul, Dec. 1, 2001; cons. Jan. 25, 2002; app. abp. of Seoul, May 10, 2012; created cardinal priest, Feb. 24, 2014 with the title of S. Crisogono.

Zen Ze-Kiun,* S.D.B., Joseph: b. Jan. 13, 1932, Yang King-pang, Shanghai, China; parents were converts and survived great hardships during World War II; profession in the Salesians, Aug. 16, 1949, perpetual vows, Aug. 16, 1955; ord. in Turin, Italy, Feb. 11, 1961; app, coadj. bp. Hong Kong, Sept. 13, 1996; bp. Hong Kong, Sept. 23, 2002; card. Mar. 24, 2006; titular church, Sta. Maria Madre del Redentore a Tor Bella Monaca.
Curial membership: Evangelization; Sacraments (congregations); Synod of Bishops.

Zubeir Wako, Gabriel: b. Feb. 27, 1941, Mboro, diocese of Wau, Sudan; ord. July 21, 1963; ord. bp. of Wau, Apr. 6, 1975; coadj. abp. of Khartoum, Oct. 30, 1979; abp. of Khartoum, Oct. 10, 1981; card., Oct. 21, 2003; titular church, St. Anthanasius in Via Tiburtina. Abp. of Khartoum.
Curial membership: Evangelization of Peoples (congregation); "Cor Unum," Migrants (councils).

CATEGORIES OF CARDINALS

(As of Sept. 1, 2014.) Information below includes categories of cardinals listed according to seniority or order of precedence. Seniority or precedence usually depends on order of elevation. It is customary for cardinal deacons to be promoted eventually to the rank of cardinal priest.

Order of Bishops

Titular Bishops of Suburbicarian Sees: Angelo Sodano, dean (June 28, 1991, Albano and Ostia); Roger Etchegaray (June 24, 1998, Porto-Santa Rufina; vice-dean); Giovanni Battista Re (Oct. 1, 2002, Sabina-Poggio Mirteto); Francis Arinze (Apr. 25, 2005, Velletri-Segni); Tarcisio Bertone, (May 10, 2008, Frascati); José Saraiva Martins (Feb. 24, 2009, Palestrina). Eastern Rite Patriarchs: Nasrallah Pierre Sfeir (Nov. 26, 1994); Antonios Naguib (Nov. 20, 2010); Bechara Rai, O.M.M. (Nov. 24, 2012).

Order of Priests

Paulo Evaristo Arns, O.F.M., William W. Baum, Franciszek Macharski, Michael Michai Kitbunchu, Alexandre do Nascimento, Godfried Danneels, Thomas Stafford Williams, Joachim Meisner, Miguel Obando Bravo, S.D.B., Ricardo Vidal, Henryk Roman Gulbinowicz, Jozef Tomko, Andrzej Maria Deskur, Paul Poupard, Louis-Albert Vachon, Friedrich Wetter, Silvano Piovanelli, Adrianus J. Simonis, Bernard F. Law, Giacomo Biffi, Eduardo Martinez Somalo, Achille Silvestrini, José Freire Falcão, Alexandre José Maria dos Santos, O.F.M., Giovanni Canestri, Antonio Maria Javierre Ortas, S.D.B., Edward Bede Clancy, László Paskai, O.F.M., Christian Wiyghan Tumi, Edward I. Cassidy, Frédéric Etsou-Nzabi-Bamungwabi, C.I.C.M., Nicolás de Jesús López Rodriguez, Virgilio Noè, Fiorenzo Angelini, Roger Mahony, Camillo Ruini, Ján Chryzostom Korec, S.J., Henri Schwery, Miloslav Vlk, Carlo Furno, Julius Riyadi Darmaatmadja, S.J., Jaime Lucas Ortega y Alamino, Gilberto Agustoni,Emmanuel Wamala, William Henry Keeler, Jean-Claude Turcotte, Ricardo Maria Carles Gordó, Adam Joseph Maida, Vinko Puljic, Juan Sandoval Íñiguez, Kazimierz Swiàtek, Ersilio Tonino, Salvatore de Giorgi, Serafim Fernandes de Araújo, Antonio Maria Rouco Varela, Dionigi Tettamanzi, Polycarp Pengo, Christoph Schönborn, O.P., Norberto Rivera Carrera, Francis George, O.M.I., Marian Jaworski, Janis Pujats, Agostino Cacciavillan, Sergio Sebastiani, Zenon Grocholewski, Crescenzio Sepe, Jorge María Mejía, Walter Kasper, Roberto Tucci, S.J., Ivan Dias, Geraldo Majella Agnelo, Pedro Rubiano

Sáenz, Theodore E. McCarrick, Desmond Connell, Audrys Juozas Backis, Francisco Javier Errázuriz Ossa, Juan Julio Terrazas Sandoval, C.SS.R., Wilfrid Fox Napier, O.F.M., Oscar Andres Rodríguez Maradiaga, S.D.B., Luis Cipriani Thorne, Francisco Álvarez Martínez, Cláudio Hummes, O.F.M., José Da Cruz Policarpo, Severino Poletto, Cormac Murphy-O'Connor, Edward Michael Egan, Lubomyr Husar, Karl Lehmann, Angelo Scola, Anthony Olubunmi Okogie, Bernard Panafieu, Gabriel Zubeir Wako, Carlos Amigo Vallejo, Justin Francis Rigali, Keith Michael O'Brien, Eusebio Oscar Scheid, Ennio Antonelli, Tarcisio Bertone, Peter Kodwo Appiah Turkson, Telesphore Placidus Toppo, George Pell, Josip Bozanic, Jean Baptiste Pham Minh Man, Philippe Barbarin, Peter Erdö, Marc Ouellet, P.S.S., Urosa Savino, Rosales, Ricard, Cañizares Llovera, Cheong-Jin-Suk, O'Malley, Dziwisz, Caffara, Zen Ze-Kiun, Seán Brady, Lluís Martínez Sistach, André Vingt-Trois, Angelo Bagnasco, Théodore-Adrien Sarr, Oswald Gracias, Francisco Lopez Ortega, Daniel Nicholas DiNardo, Odilo Scherer, John Njue, Darío Castrillón Hoyos, Jorge Medina Estévez, James Francis Stafford, Estanislao Esteban Karlic, Medardo Joseph Mazombwe, Raúl Eduardo Vela Chiriboga, Monsengwo Pasinya, Paolo Romeo, Donald Wuerl, Raymundo Damasceno Assis, Kazimierz Nycz, Albert Malcolm Ranjith Patabendige Don, Reinhard Marx, José Manuel Estepa Llaurens, José Manuel Estepa Llaurens, George Alencherry, Thomas C. Collins, Dominik Duka, Willem J. Eijk, Giuseppe Betori, Timothy M. Dolan, Rainer Maria Woelki, John Tong Hon, Lucian Muresan, Baselios Cleemis Thottunkal, John Onaiyekan, Ruben Salazar Gomez, Luis Tagle, Jean-Louis Tauran, Francesco Marchisano, Attilio Nicora,Julián Herranz, Javier Lozano Barragán, Georges Cottier, O.P., Pietro Parolin, Vincent Gerard Nichols, Leopoldo José Brenes Solórzano, Gérald Cyprien Lacroix, Jean-Pierre Kutwa, Orani João Tempesta, O. Cist., Gualtiero Bassetti, Mario Aurelio Poli, Andrew Yeom Soo jung, Ricardo Ezzati Andrello, S.D.B., Philippe Nakellentuba Ouédraogo, Orlando Beltran Quevedo, O.M.I., Chibly Langlois, Loris Francesco Capovilla, Fernando Sebastián Aguilar, C.M.F., Kelvin Edward Felix.

Order of Deacons

Renato Martino, Levada, Rodé, Vallini, Montezemolo, Vanhoye, Leonardo Sandri Giovanni Lajolo, Paul-Josef Cordes, Stanislaw Rylko, Angelo Comastri, Raffaele Farina S.D.B. Giovanni Coppa, Angelo Amato, Antonios Naguib, Robert Sarah, Francesco Monterisi, Raymond Leo Burke, Kurt Koch, Paolo Sardi, Mauro Piacenza,Velasio De Paolis, Gianfranco Ravasi, Elio Sgreccia, Walter Brandmuller, Domenico Bartolucci, Fernando Filoni, Manuel Monteiro de Castro, Santos y Abril Castello, Antonio Maria Veglio, Giuseppe Bertello, Francesco Coccopalmerio, Joao Braz de Aviz, Edwin F. O'Brien, Domenico Calcagno, Giuseppe Versaldi, Prosper Grech, Karl Josef Becker, James M. Harvey, Lorenzo Baldisseri, Gerhard Ludwig Müller, Beniamino Stella.

CONSISTORIES

(As of Sept. 1, 2014.) Information below includes dates of consistories at which the current cardinals were created.

They are listed according to seniority. Of these 210 cardinals, 2 were named by Paul VI (consistories of Mar. 5, 1973 and May 24, 1976); 109 by John Paul II (consistories of June 30, 1979, Feb. 2, 1983, May 25, 1985, June 28, 1988, June 28, 1991, Nov. 26, 1994, Feb. 21, 1998, Feb. 21,

2001, and Oct. 21, 2003), 80 by Benedict XVI (Mar. 24, 2006, Nov. 24, 2007, Nov. 20, 2010, Feb. 19, 2012, Nov. 24, 2012), and 19 by Francis (Feb. 22, 2014).

POPE PAUL VI
1973 (Mar. 5): Paulo Evaristo Arns, O.F.M.
1976 (May 24): William W. Baum.

POPE JOHN PAUL II
1979 (June 30): Roger Etchegaray, Franciszek Macharski.
1983 (Feb. 2): Michael Michai Kitbunchu, Alexandre do Nascimento, Godfried Danneels, Thomas Stafford Williams, Carlo Maria Martini, Józef Glemp, Joachim Meisner.
1985 (May 25): Francis A. Arinze, Miguel Obando Bravo, S.D.B., Ricardo Vidal, Henryk Roman Gulbinowicz, Jozef Tomko, Andrzej Maria Deskur, Paul Poupard, Friedrich Wetter, Silvano Piovanelli, Adrianus J. Simonis, Bernard F. Law, Giacomo Biffi.
1988 (June 28): Eduardo Martinez Somalo, Achille Silvestrini, José Freire Falcão, Alexandre José Maria dos Santos, O.F.M., Giovanni Canestri, László Paskai, O.F.M., Christian Wiyghan Tumi.
1991 (June 28): Angelo Sodano, Edward I. Cassidy, Nicolás de Jesús López Rodriguez, Fiorenzo Angelini Roger Mahony, Camillo Ruini, Ján Chryzostom Korec, S.J., Henri Schwery.
1994 (Nov. 26): Nasrallah Pierre Sfeir, Miloslav Vlk, Carlo Furno, Julius Riyadi Darmaatmadja, S.J., Jaime Lucas Ortega y Alamino, Gilberto Agustoni, Emmanuel Wamala, William Henry Keeler, Jean-Claude Turcotte, Ricardo Maria Carles Gordó, Adam Joseph Maida, Vinko Puljic, Juan Sandoval Íñiguez.
1998 (Feb. 21): Jorge Medina Estévez, Darío Castrillón Hoyos, James F. Stafford, Salvatore de Giorgi, Serafim Fernandes de Araújo, Antonio Maria Rouco Varela, Dionigi Tettamanzi, Polycarp Pengo, Christoph Schönborn, O.P., Norberto Rivera Carrera, Francis George, O.M.I., Giovanni Cheli, Marian Jaworski, Janis Pujats.
2001 (Feb. 21): Giovanni Battista Re, Agostino Cacciavillan, Sergio Sebastiani, Zenon Grocholewski, José Saraiva Martins, C.M.F., Crescenzio Sepe, Jorge María Mejía, Walter Kasper, Ivan Dias, Geraldo Majella Agnelo, Pedro Rubiano Sáenz, Theodore E. McCarrick, Desmond Connell, Audrys Juozas Backis, Francisco Javier Errázuriz Ossa, Juan Julio Terrazas Sandoval, C.SS.R., Wilfrid Fox Napier, O.F.M., Oscar Andres Rodríguez Maradiaga, S.D.B., Luis Cipriani Thorne, Francisco Álvarez Martínez, Cláudio Hummes, Jorge Mario Bergoglio, S.J., José Da Cruz Policarpo, Severino Poletto, Cormac Murphy-O'Connor, Edward M. Egan, Lubomyr Husar, Karl Lehmann, Jean Honoré, O.F.M., Roberto Tucci, S.J.
2003 (Oct. 21): Jean-Louis Tauran, Renato Martino, Julián Herranz, Javier Lozano Barragán, Attilio Nicora, Angelo Scola, Anthony Olubunmi Okogie, Bernard Panafieu, Gabriel Zubeir Wako, Carlos Amigo Vallejo, Justin Francis Rigali, Keith Michael O'Brien, Eusebio Oscar Scheid, Ennio Antonelli, Tarcisio Bertone, Peter Kodwo Appiah Turkson, Telesphore Placidus Toppo, George Pell, Josip Bozanic, Jean Baptiste Pham Minh Man, Philippe Barbarin, Peter Erdö, Marc Ouellet, P.S.S., Georges Cottier, O.P.

POPE BENEDICT XVI
2006 (Mar. 24): William Levada, Franc Rodé, C.M., Agostino Vallini, Jorge Liberato Urosa Savino, Gaudencio Rosales, Jean-Pierre Ricard, Antonio Cañizares Llovera, Cheong Jin-Suk, Sean Patrick

O'Malley, O.F.M. Cap., Stanislaw Dziwisz, Carlo Caffarra, Joseph Zen Ze-Kiun, S.D.B., Andrea Cordero Lanza di Montezemolo, Albert Vanhoye, S.J.
2007 (Nov. 24): Leonardo Sandri, John P. Foley, Giovanni Lajolo, Paul-Josef Cordes, Stanislaw Rylko, Angelo Comastri, Raffaele Farina SDB, Seán Brady, Lluís Martínez Sistach, André Vingt-Trois, Angelo Bagnasco, Théodore-Adrien Sarr, Oswald Gracias, Francisco Lopez Ortega, Daniel Nicholas DiNardo, Odilo Scherer, John Njue, Giovanni Coppa, Estanislao Esteban Karlic.
2010 (Nov. 20): Angelo Amato, Antonios Naguib, Robert Sarah, Francesco Monterisi, Fortunato Baldelli, Raymond Leo Burke, Kurt Koch, Paolo Sardi, Mauro Piacenza, Velasio De Paolis, Gianfranco Ravasi, Medardo Joseph Mazombwe, Raúl Eduardo Vela Chiriboga, Monsengwo Pasinya, Paolo Romeo, Donald Wuerl, Raymundo Damasceno Assis, Kazimierz Nycz, Albert Malcolm Ranjith Patabendige Don, Reinhard Marx, José Manuel Estepa Llaurens, Elio Sgreccia, Walter Brandmuller, Domenico Bartolucci.
2012 (Feb. 19): Fernando Filoni, Manuel Monteiro de Castro, Santos Abril Castello, Antonio Maria Veglio, Giuseppe Bertello, Francesco Coccopalmerio, Joao Braz de Aviz, Edwin F. O'Brien, Domenico Calcagno, Giuseppe Versaldi, George Alencherry, Thomas C. Collins, Dominik Duka, Willem J. Eijk, Giuseppe Betori, Timothy M. Dolan, Rainer Maria Woelki, John Tong Hon, Lucian Muresan, Julien Ries, Prosper Grech, Karl Josef Becker; (Nov. 24): James M. Harvey, Bechara Boutros Rai, O.M.M., Baselios Cleemis Thottunkal, John Onaiyekan, Ruben Salazar Gomez, Luis Tagle.

POPE FRANCIS
2014 (Feb. 22) Pietro Parolin, Lorenzo Baldisseri, Gerhard Ludwig Müller, Beniamino Stella, Vincent Gerard Nichols, Leopoldo José Brenes Solórzano, Gérald Cyprien Lacroix, Jean-Pierre Kutwa, Orani João Tempesta, O. Cist., Gualtiero Bassetti, Mario Aurelio Poli, Andrew Yeom Soo jung, Ricardo Ezzati Andrello, S.D.B., Philippe Nakellentuba Ouédraogo, Orlando Beltran Quevedo, O.M.I., Chibly Langlois, Loris Francesco Capovilla, Fernando Sebastián Aguilar, C.M.F., Kelvin Edward Felix.

DISTRIBUTION OF CARDINALS
As of Aug. 15, 2014, there were 210 cardinals from 68 countries or areas. Listed below are areas, countries, number and last names. Names with asterisks are cardinals ineligible to vote.

Europe — 113
Italy (49): Amato, Angelini,* Antonelli, Bagnasco, Baldisseri, Bartolucci,* Bassetti, Bertello, Bertone,* Betori, Biffi,* Cacciavillan,* Caffarra, Calcagno, Canestri,* Capovilla,* Coccopalmerio, Comastri, Coppa,* Cordero Lanza di Montezemolo,* de Giorgi,* De Paolis, Farina, Filoni, Furno,* Lajolo, Martino, Monterisi,* Nicora, Noè,* Parolin, Piacenza, Piovanelli,* Poletto, Ravasi, Re,* Romeo, Ruini,* Sardi,* Scola, Sebastiani,* Sepe, Sgreccia,* Silvestrini,* Sodano,* Stella, Tettamanzi,* Tucci,* Vallini, Veglio, Versaldi.
Germany (10): Becker,* Brandmüller,* Cordes,* Kasper, Lehmann, Marx, Meisner, Müller, Wetter,* Woelki.
Spain (10): Abril Castello, Alvarez Martinez,* Amigo Vallejo, Cañizares Llovera, Carles Gordó,* Estepa Llaurens,* Herranz Casado,* Martínez Sistach, Martinez Somalo,* Rouco Varela, Sebastián Aguilar.*

France (8): Barbarin, Etchegaray,* Panafieu,* Poupard,* Ricard, Tauran, Vanhoye,* Vingt-Trois.
Poland (6): Dziwisz, Grocholewski, Gulbinowicz,* Macharski,* Nycz, Rylko.
Switzerland (4): Agustoni,* Cottier,* Koch, Schwery.
Portugal (2): Policarpo, Monteiro de Castro, Saraiva Martins*
Czech Republic (2): Duka, Vlk*
England (2), Murphy-O'Connor*; Nichols.
Hungary (2): Erdö, Paskai.*
Ireland (2): Brady, Connell.*
Netherlands (2): Eijk, Simonis*
Slovakia (2): Korec,* Tomko.*
Ukraine (2): Husar, Jaworski.*
One from each of the following countries: **Austria,** Schönborn; **Belgium,** Danneels; **Bosnia Herzegovina,** Puljic; Croatia, Bozanic; **Latvia,** Pujats*; **Lithuania,** Backis; **Malta,** Grech*; **Romania,** Murasyn*; **Scotland,** O'Brien; **Slovenia,** Rodé.*

Asia — 19
India (5): Alencherry, Dias, Gracias, Thottunkal, Toppo.
Philippines (4): Quevedo, Rosales, Tagle, Vidal.*
Hong Kong (2): Tong Hon, Zen Ze-kiun.*
Korea (2): Cheong Jin-Suk,* Yeom Soo jung.
Lebanon (2), Bechara Rai, Sfeir.*
One from each of the following countries: **Indonesia,** Darmaatmadja*; **Sri Lanka,** Ranjith Patabendige; **Thailand,** Kitbunchu*; **Vietnam,** Pham Minh Man.*

Oceania — 4
Australia (2): Cassidy,* Pell.
One from **New Zealand,** Williams.*

Africa — 18
Nigeria (3): Arinze,* Okogie, Onaiyekan.
One from each of the following countries: **Angola,** do Nascimento*; **Burkina Faso,** Ouédraogo; **Cameroon,** Tumi*; **Congo,** Pasinya; **Egypt,** Naguib; **Ghana,** Turkson; **Guinea,** Sarah; **Ivory Coast,** Kutwa; **Kenya,** Njue; **Mozambique,** Santos*; **Senegal,** Sarr; **South Africa,** Napier; **Sudan,** Wako; **Tanzania,** Pengo; **Uganda,** Wamala.*

North America – 27
United States (18): Baum,* Burke, DiNardo, Dolan, Egan,* George, Harvey, Keeler,* Law,* Levada, McCarrick,* Mahony, Maida,* O'Brien, O'Malley, Rigali, Stafford,* Wuerl.
Mexico (4): Lozano Barragán, Rivera Carrera, Robles Ortega, Sandoval Iñiguez.
Canada (4): Collins, Lacroix, Ouellet, Turcotte.

Central and South America – 24
Brazil (10): Arns,* Braz de Aviz, Damasceno Assis, Falcão,* Fernandes de Araújo,* Hummes,* Majella Agnelo, Scheid,* Scherer, Tempesta.
Argentina (4): Karlic,* Mejia,* Poli, Sandri.
Colombia (3): Castrillón Hoyos,* Rubiano Saenz, Salazar Gomez.
Chile (2): Errazuriz Ossa, Ezzati Andrello, Medina Estévez.*
Nicaragua (2): Brenes Solórzano, Obando Bravo.*
One each from the following countries: **Bolivia,** Sandoval; **Cuba,** Ortega y Alamino; **Dominican Republic,** Lopez Rodriguez; **Ecuador,** Vela Chiriboga*; **Haiti,** Langlois; **Honduras,** Rodriguez Maradiaga; **Peru,** Cipriani Thorne; **Saint Lucia,** Felix*; **Venezuela,** Urosa Savino

Cardinal Electors

As of Aug. 15, 2014, there were 117 cardinal-electors: 58 are from Europe, 17 from North America, 11 from South America, 5 from Central America, 16 from Africa, 9 from Asia and 1 from Oceania. The electors are from 53 countries.

Total Cardinals

As of Aug. 1, 2014, there were 211 cardinals: 113 are from Europe, 27 from North America, 24 from South America, 7 from Central America, 18 from Africa, 19 from Asia and 3 from Oceania. The cardinals are from 68 countries.

Ineligible to Vote

As of Aug. 1, 2014, 93 of the 210 cardinals were ineligible to take part in a papal election in line with the apostolic letter *Ingravescentem Aetetem* effective Jan. 1, 1971, which limited the functions of cardinals after completion of their 80th year.

Cardinals affected are: Agustoni, Álvarez Martínez, Angelini, Araujo Sales, Arinze, Arns, Bartolucci, Baum, Becker, Biffi, Brandmüller, Cacciavillan, Canestri, Carles Gordó, Cassidy, Castrillón Hoyos, Cheli, Cheong Jin-suk, Connell, Coppa, Cordero Lanza di Montezemolo, Cottier, Danneels, De Giorgi, do Nascimento, Egan, Errázuriz Ossa, Estepa Llaurens, Etchegaray, Falcão, Farina, Furno, Glemp, Grech, Gulbinowicz, Herranz Casado, Husar, Jaworski, Karlic, Kasper, Keeler. Kitbunchu, Korec, Law, Lozano Barragán, McCarrick, Macharski, Maida, Majella Agnelo, Martinez Somalo, Martino, Mazombwe, Medina Estévez, Meisner, Mejia, Muresan, Murphy-O'Connor, Obando Bravo, Panafieu, Paskai, Piovanelli, Poletto, Poupard, Pujats, Ries, Rosales, Rubiano Saenz, Ruini, Sandoval Íñiguez, Santos, Saraiva Martins, Scheid; Schwery, Sebastiani, Sfeir, Sgreccia, Silvestrini, Simonis, Sodano, Stafford, Tomko, Tucci, Tumi, Vanhoye, Vidal, Vlk, Wamala, Wetter, Williams, Zen.

Cardinals who complete their 80th year in 2014-15 and who become ineligible to vote: 2014: Bertone, Cordes, Darmaatmadja, Hummes, Monterisi, Pham Minh Man, Re, Rodé, Sardi, Tettamanzi, Vela Chiriboga; 2015: Abril y Castello, De Paolis, Lajolo, Naguib, Okogie, Rigali.

Cardinals of the United States

As of Aug. 15, 2014, the following cardinals were in service, according to their years of elevation (for biographies, see College of Cardinals above):

1976: **William W. Baum** (major penitentiary emeritus); 1985: **Bernard F. Law** (abp. emeritus of Boston); 1991: **Roger M. Mahony** (abp. emeritus of Los Angeles); 1994: **William H. Keeler** (abp. emeritus of Baltimore); **Adam J. Maida** (abp. emeritus of Detroit); 1998: **Francis E. George, O.M.I.** (abp. of Chicago), **James F. Stafford** (Major Penitentiary emeritus of the Apostolic Penitentiary); 2001: **Edward M. Egan** (abp. emeritus of New York), **Theodore E. McCarrick** (abp. emeritus of Washington); 2003: **Justin F. Rigali** (abp. emeritus of Philadelphia); 2006: **William J. Levada** (prefect emeritus of the Cong. for the Doctrine of the Faith), **Sean P. O'Malley, O.F.M. Cap.** (abp. of Boston). 2007: **Daniel N. DiNardo** (abp. of Galveston-Houston); 2010: **Raymond L. Burke** (prefect of the Apostolic Signatura); **Donald W. Wuerl** (abp. of Washington, D.C.); 2012: **Timothy M. Dolan** (abp. of New York); **Edwin F. O'Brien** (Grand Master of the Knights of the Holy Sepulchre); **James M. Harvey** (archpriest of the papal basilica of S. Paolo fuori le mura, Rome). **Lubomyr Husar, M.S.U.,** major abp. emeritus of Lviv for Ukrainians, is also an American citizen.

U.S. Cardinals of the Past (according to year of elevation; for biographical data, see **American Catholics of the Past** at www.catholicalmanac.com):

1875: John McCloskey; 1886: James Gibbons; 1911: John Farley, William O'Connell; 1921: Dennis Dougherty; 1924: Patrick Hayes, George Mundelein; 1946: John Glennon, Edward Mooney, Francis Spellman, Samuel Stritch; 1953: James F. McIntyre; 1958: John O'Hara, C.S.C., Richard Cushing; 1959: Albert Meyer, Aloysius Muench; 1961: Joseph Ritter; 1965: Lawrence J. Shehan; 1967: Francis Brennan, John P. Cody, Patrick A. O'Boyle, John J. Krol; 1969: John J. Wright, Terence J. Cooke, John F. Dearden, John J. Carberry; 1973: Humberto S. Medeiros, Timothy Manning; 1983: Joseph L. Bernardin; 1985: John J. O'Connor; 1988: James A. Hickey, Edmund Szoka; 1994: Anthony J. Bevilacqua; 2001: Avery Dulles, S.J.; 2007: John P. Foley. (Myroslav Lubachivsky, major abp. of Lviv of the Ukrainians (Ukraine), was made a card. in 1985. He was a citizen of the United States and metropolitan of the Philadelphia Ukrainian Rite Archeparchy, from 1979-81.)

Prelates who became cardinals after returning to their native countries: John Lefebvre de Chevrus, first bp. of Boston (1808-23) and apostolic administrator of New York (1810-15), elevated to the cardinalate, 1836, in France. Ignatius Persico, O.F.M. Cap., bp. of Savannah (1870-72), elevated to the cardinalate, 1893, in Italy; Diomede Falconio, O.F.M. ord. a priest in Buffalo, NY, missionary in U.S., apostolic delegate to the U.S. (1902-11), elevated to cardinalate, 1911, in Italy.

Deceased Cardinals 2013-2014

The following Cardinals died between Aug. 2013 and Aug. 2014.

Agre, Cardinal Bernard Agre, 88, June 9, 2014, abp. of Abidjan from 1994-2006.

Bartolucci, Cardinal Domenico, 96, Nov. 11, 2013, long-time director of the Sistine Chapel Choir.

Carles Gordo, Cardinal Ricardo, 87, Dec. 17, 2013, abp. of Barcelona from 1990-2004.

Ce, Cardinal Marco, 88, May 12, 2014, patriarch of Venice from 1978-2002.

Clancy, Cardinal Edward Bede, 90, Aug. 3, 2014, abp. of Sydney, Australia, from 1988-2001.

Delly, Cardinal Emmanuel-Karim, 86, Apr. 8, 2014, Patriarch of the Chaldeans from 2003-2012.

Lourdusamy, Cardinal D., Simon, 90, June 2, 2014, Indian Cardinal, the first Asian to hold a major post in the Roman Curia, and prefect of the Congregation for the Oriental Churches from 1985-1991.

Marchisano, Cardinal Francesco, 85, July 27, 2014, Italian Cardinal and one of the great caretakers of the Vatican's artistic and cultural patrimony.

Mazombwe, Cardinal Medardo, 81, Aug. 29, 2013, abp. of Lusaka from 1996-2006.

Policarpo, Cardinal Jose da Cruz, 78, Mar. 12, 2014, patriarch of Lisbon, from 1998-2013.

Szoka, Edmund C., 86, Aug. 20, 2014, abp. of Detroit, 1981-1990 and long-time Vatican official.

The Universal Church

THE CHURCH IN COUNTRIES THROUGHOUT THE WORLD

(Principal sources for statistics: *Annuarium Statisticum Ecclesiae*, Statistical Yearbook of the Church, 2012 — the most recent edition; *Annuario Pontificio*, 2014; and Agenzia Internazionale FIDES. Figures are as of Jan. 1, 2013, except for cardinals [as of Aug. 30, 2014] and others which are indicated. For 2013-2014 developments, see **Index** entries for individual countries.)

An asterisk indicates that the country has full diplomatic relations with the Holy See (see **Diplomats to the Holy See** in the **Holy See** section, p. 264).

Abbreviations (in order in which they appear): archd. – archdiocese; dioc. – diocese; ap. ex. – apostolic exarchate; prel. – prelature; abb. – abbacy; v.a. – apostolic vicariate; p.a. – apostolic prefecture; a.a. – apostolic administration; mil. ord. – military ordinariate; card. – cardinal; abp. – archbishops; bp. – bishops (diocesan and titular); priests (dioc. – diocesan or secular priests; rel. – those belonging to religious orders); p.d. – permanent deacons; sem. – major seminarians, diocesan and religious; bros. – brothers; srs. – sisters; bap. – baptisms; Caths. – Catholic population; tot. pop. – total population; (AD) – apostolic delegate (see **Index**: Papal Representatives.)

Afghanistan

Republic in south-central Asia; capital, Kabul. Christianity antedated Muslim conquest in the seventh century but was overcome by it. All inhabitants are subject to the law of Islam (Shariah). Under Afghan's Taliban regime, religious freedom was severely restricted, and proselytizing was forbidden. In January 2002, Italian and English chaplains celebrated the first public Mass in nearly 10 years in Kabul, at the Italian Embassy.

Albania*

Archd., 2; dioc., 3; a.a., 1; abp., 3; bp., 5; parishes, 122; priests, 149 (50 dioc., 99 rel.); p.d., 1; sem., 36; bros., 19; srs., 481; bap., 4,265; Caths., 517,000 (15.9%); tot. pop., 3,234,000.

Republic in the Balkans, bordering the Adriatic Sea; capital, Tirana. Christianity was introduced in apostolic times. The northern part of the country remained faithful to Rome while the South broke from unity following the schism of 1054. A large percentage of the population became Muslim following the invasion (15th century) and long centuries of occupation by the Ottoman Turks. Many Catholics fled to southern Italy, Sicily and Greece. In 1945, at the time of the communist takeover, an estimated 68 percent of the population was Muslim; 19 percent was Orthodox and 13 percent Roman Catholic. The Catholic Church prevailed in the north. During 45 years of communist dictatorship, the Church fell victim, as did all religions, to systematic persecution.

In 1967, the government, declaring it had eliminated all religion in the country, proclaimed itself the first atheist state in the world. The right to practice religion was restored in late 1990. In March 1991, a delegation from the Vatican was allowed to go to Albania; later in the year diplomatic relations were established with the Holy See at the request of the Albanian prime minister. Pope John Paul II made a one-day visit to the country Apr. 25, 1993, during which he ordained four bishops appointed by him in December 1992 to fill long-vacant sees. The first Albanian cardinal was named in November 1994. Albanians welcomed hundreds of thousands of ethnic Albanians from Kosovo during Yugoslav persecution in 1999.

Algeria*

Archd., 1; dioc., 3; abp., 3; bp., 4; parishes, 36; priests, 77 (23 dioc., 54 rel.); p.d., 1; sem., 4; bros., 17; srs., 152; bap., 7; Caths., 9,000 (.024%); tot. pop., 37,495,000.

Republic in northwest Africa; capital, Algiers. Christianity, introduced at an early date, succumbed to Vandal devastation in the fifth century and Muslim conquest in 709, but survived in small communities into the 12th century. Missionary work was unsuccessful except in service to traders, military personnel and captives along the coast. Church organization was established after the French gained control of the territory in the 1830s. A large number of Catholics were among the estimated million Europeans who left the country after it secured independence from France, July 5, 1962. Islam is the state religion. Armed Islamic militants and guerrillas have caused terror and unrest in Algeria since 1992. Among the more than 80,000 people killed were seven Trappist monks and the Catholic bishop of Oran, all in 1996.

Andorra*

Parishes, 7; priests, 16 (10 dioc., 6 rel.); srs., 10; bap., 331; Caths., 75,000 (96%); tot. pop., 78,000.

Parliamentary state (1993) in the Pyrenees; capital, Andorra la Vella. From 1278-1993, it was a co-principality under the rule of the French head of state and the bishop of Urgel, Spain, who retain their titles. Christianity was introduced at an early date. Catholicism is the state religion. Ecclesiastical jurisdiction is under the Spanish Diocese of Urgel. The constitution calls for freedom of religion, but also guarantees "the Roman Catholic Church free and public exercise of its activities and the preservation of the relations of special cooperation with the state."

Angola*

Archd., 5; dioc., 14; card., 1; abp., 5; bp., 21; parishes, 442; priests, 918 (530 dioc., 388 rel.); sem., 1,292; bros., 89; srs., 2,238; catechists, 41,033; bap., 169,512; Caths., 9,834,000 (55.5%); tot. pop., 17,694,000.

Republic in southwest Africa; capital, Luanda. Evangelization by Catholic missionaries from Portugal, dating from 1491, reached high points in the 17th and 18th centuries. Independence from Portugal in 1975 and the long civil war that followed (peace accord signed in 1991) left the Church with a heavy loss of personnel resulting from the departure of about half the foreign missionaries and the persecution and martyrdom experienced by the Church during the war. Renewed fighting following elections in late 1992 brought repeated appeals for peace from the nation's bishops and religious in 1993 and 1994.

Despite another peace accord signed by the rebels and the government in late 1994, conditions have remained unsettled. One effect of the fighting was to cut off Church leaders from large groups of the faithful. In an attempt to encourage peace efforts, the Vatican established diplomatic relations with Angola in 1997. Attacks on Church workers, however, continued in 1998 and 1999. In 2000, Church leaders began an active peace movement, holding national and diocesan congresses and beginning a consultation with Angolan political leaders. Government and rebel representatives signed a peace agreement in 2002, after the government killed rebel leader Jonas Savimbi, and the Church offered humanitarian aid and helped to rebuild the country.

Antigua and Barbuda*

Dioc., 1; bp., 1; parishes, 2; priests, 10 (5 dioc., 5 rel.); p.d, 5; sem., 1; srs., 9; bap., 69; Caths., 9,000 (10.46%); tot. pop., 86,000.

Independent (1981) Caribbean island nation; capital, St. John's, Antigua. The Diocese of St. John's-Basseterre includes Antigua and Barbuda, St. Kitts and Nevis, Anguilla, the British Virgin Islands and Montserrat.

Argentina*

Archd., 14; dioc., 51; prel., 4; ap. ex., 3 (for Armenians of Latin America); mil. ord., 1; card., 3; abp., 20; bp., 93; parishes, 2,793; priests, 5,970 (4,070 dioc., 1,900 rel.); p.d., 839; sem., 1,485; bros., 758; srs., 7,654; bap., 547,926; catechists, 99,421; Caths., 38,401,000 (92%); tot. pop., 41,666,000.

Republic in southeast South America, bordering on the Atlantic; capital, Buenos Aires. Priests were with the Magellan exploration party and the first Mass in the country was celebrated Apr. 1, 1519. Missionary work began in the 1530s, diocesan organization in the late 1540s, and effective evangelization about 1570. Independence from Spain was proclaimed in 1816. Since its establishment in the country, the Church has been influenced by Spanish cultural and institutional forces, antagonistic liberalism, government interference and opposition; the latter reached a climax during the last five years of the first presidency of Juan Peron (1946-55).

Widespread human rights violations, including the disappearance of thousands of people, marked the "Dirty War," the period of military rule from 1976 to December 1983, when an elected civilian government took over. In 1996 the Argentine bishops said they did not do enough to stop human rights violations during the "Dirty War." In the late 1990s, the bishops spoke out against government corruption and have worked to find solutions to the country's crises. In 2013, Card. Jorge Mario Bergoglio of Buenos Aires was elected Pope Francis.

Armenia*

Ord., 1 (for Catholic Armenians of Eastern Europe, with seat in Armenia); parishes, 11; abp., 2; priests, 11 (7 dioc., 4 rel.); sem., 10; bros., 5; srs., 26; bap., 220; Caths., 200,000 (6%); tot. pop., 3,280,000.

Republic in Asia Minor; capital Yerevan. Part of the USSR from 1920 until it declared its sovereignty in September 1991. Ancient Armenia, which also included territory annexed by Turkey in 1920, was Christianized in the fourth century. Diplomatic relations were established with the Holy See on May 23, 1992. Pope John Paul II visited Armenia in late September 2001 to help mark the 1,700th anniversary of Christianity in the nation. The small Catholic community in Armenia has good relations with the predominant Armenian Apostolic Church, an Oriental Orthodox Church.

Australia*

Archd., 7; dioc., 25; mil. ord., 1; card., 3; abp., 10; bp., 52; parishes, 1,370; priests, 3,073 (1,848 dioc., 1,224 rel.); p.d., 133; sem., 325; bros., 984; srs., 5,958; catechists, 7,097; bap., 69,075; Caths., 6,196,000 (27.3%); tot. pop. 22,684,000.

Commonwealth; island continent southeast of Asia; capital, Canberra. The first Catholics in the country were Irish under penal sentence, 1795-1804; the first public Mass was celebrated May 15, 1803. Official organization of the Church dates from 1820. The country was officially removed from mission status in March 1976.

Near the end of the 20th century, the Church in Australia was rocked by allegations of sexual abuse from previous decades. In 1996 the Australian bishops published a plan for dealing with such cases. In 1998 the bishops also apologized to aboriginal children their support of harsh government policy in the 1970s.

In an unusual move, in mid-November 1998, just before the Synod of Bishops for Oceania and after the Australian bishops' ad limina visits, Vatican officials met with Church leaders from Australia to discuss doctrinal and pastoral issues. In December 1998, the Vatican and representatives of Australian Church leaders signed a document, later endorsed by the Australian bishops' conference, that spoke of a "crisis of faith" in the Catholic Church on the continent. The Australian Church, like many others in the late 20th and early 21st century, struggled with cases of clergy sexual abuse. Pope Benedict XVI made a memorable visit in 2008.

Austria*

Archd., 2; dioc., 7; abb., 1; ord., 1; mil. ord., 1; card., 1; abp., 3; bp., 21; parishes, 3,052; priests, 4,137 (2,529 dioc., 1,608 rel.); p.d., 639; sem., 275; bros., 545; srs., 4,385; catechists, 2,086; bap., 48,916; Caths., 6,154,000 (72.7%); tot. pop., 8,466,000.

Republic in central Europe; capital, Vienna. Christianity was introduced by the end of the third century, strengthened considerably by conversion of the Bavarians from about 600, and firmly established in the second half of the eighth century. Catholicism survived and grew stronger as the principal religion in the country in the post-Reformation period, but suffered from Josephinism in the 18th century. Although liberated from much government harassment in the aftermath of the Revolution of 1848, the Church came under pressure again some 20 years later in the Kulturkampf. The Church faced strong opposition from Socialists after WW I and suffered persecution from 1938 to 1945 during the Nazi regime. Some Church-state matters are regulated by a concordat originally concluded in 1934.

At the turn of the century, the Church in Austria was beset by internal difficulties, including a seminary pornography scandal and the launch of a global movement seeking more lay participation in Church decision-making and changes in Church policy on ordination of women and priestly celibacy. In 1995, Card. Hans Hermann Gröer resigned as archbishop of Vienna amid charges of sexual misconduct. His successor,

Card. Christoph Schönborn, has worked to restore a sense of unity to the Church and to bring healing.

Azerbaijan*

Mission. Independent republic (1991) on the Caspian Sea; formerly part of the USSR; capital, Baku. Islam is the prevailing religion. Soviet rulers destroyed Baku's one Catholic church in the late 1930s; in the 21st century, the church was rebuilt and was dedicated in 2007. A small Catholic community of Polish and Armenian origin near the capital is ministered to by two missionaries. Latin-rite Catholics are under the apostolic administration of Caucasus (seat in Georgia), established in December 1993. The Holy See reached an agreement with the government in 2011 to regulate relations.

Bahamas*

Dioc., 1; bp., 1; parishes, 30; priests, 29 (14 dioc., 15 rel.); p.d., 1; sem., 5; srs., 18; catechists, 235; bap., 430; Caths., 50,000 (14.7%); tot. pop., 340,000.

Independent (July 10, 1973) island group consisting of some 700 (30 inhabited) small islands southeast of Florida and north of Cuba; capital, Nassau. On Oct. 12, 1492, Columbus landed on one of these islands, where the first Mass was celebrated in the New World. Organization of the Catholic Church in the Bahamas dates from about the middle of the 19th century. The Church was under the jurisdiction on the Archdiocese of New York until 1960, when Nassau became a diocese. From 1891 to 1981, Benedictines from St. John's Abbey in Collegeville, MN, were responsible for episcopal leadership. After that time, Benedictine priests and brothers continued working in the Bahamas until 2005; local Benedictine nuns continue their work there. Nassau became an archdiocese in 1999.

Bahrain*

Parish, 1; priests, 7 (1 dioc., 6 rel.); srs., 6 bap., 143; Caths., 100,000 (4.3%); tot. pop., 1,235,000. (AD)

Island state in Persian Gulf; capital, Manama. Population is Muslim; Catholics are foreign workers, under ecclesiastical jurisdiction of Arabia apostolic vicariate. Diplomatic relations were established between Bahrain and the Holy See in January 2000.

Bangladesh*

Archd., 1; dioc., 5; abp., 3; bp., 9; parishes, 97; priests, 360 (196 dioc., 164 rel.); p.d., 2; sem., 105; bros., 101 srs., 1,100; catechists, 1,546; bap., 8,088; Caths., 344,000 (.22%); tot. pop. 152,629,000.

Formerly the eastern portion of Pakistan. Officially constituted as a separate nation Dec. 16, 1971; capital, Dhaka. Jesuit, Dominican and Augustinian missionaries were in the area in the 16th century. An apostolic vicariate (of Bengali) was established in 1834; the hierarchy was erected in 1950. Islam, the principal religion, was declared the state religion in 1988; freedom of religion is granted. Church-run humanitarian and development agencies have been instrumental in responding to natural disasters, such as flooding. The bishops have emphasized inculturation and Church social doctrine.

Barbados*

Dioc., 1; bp., 2; parishes, 6; priests, 11 (4 dioc., 7 rel.); p.d., 1; srs., 9; bap., 99; sem., 1; Caths., 11,000 (3.4%); tot. pop., 277,000.

Parliamentary democracy (independent since 1966), easternmost of the Caribbean islands; capital, Bridgetown. About 70 % of the population are Anglican.

Belarus*

Archd., 1; dioc., 3; card., 1; abp., 2; bp., 4; parishes, 629; priests, 480 (288 dioc., 192 rel.); sem., 129; bros., 6; srs., 314; bap., 7,787; Caths., 1,415,000 (13.7%); tot. pop., 10,309,000.

Independent republic (1991) in Eastern Europe; former Soviet republic (Byelorussia); capital, Minsk. Slow recovery of the Church was reported after years of repression in the Soviet Union, although in the mid-1990s under the authoritarian rule of President Alexander Lukashenka, the Church encountered tensions, especially in refusal of permits for foreign religious workers. In December 2000, the nation's bishops asked forgiveness for the "human weaknesses" of Church members throughout the centuries and said the Church forgave acts of Soviet-era persecution. In October 2002, Belarus adopted one of the most restrictive religion laws in the former Soviet Union, but by April 2003 government officials had granted the Catholic Church full legal status.

Belgium*

Archd., l; dioc., 7; mil. ord., 1; card., 2; abp., 3; bp., 17; parishes, 3,846; priests, 5,600 (3,220 dioc., 2,380 rel.); p.d., 599; sem., 227; bros., 836; srs., 8,921; catechists, 8,415; bap., 77,157; Caths., 8,029,000 (72%); tot. pop., 11,139,000.

Constitutional monarchy in northwestern Europe; capital, Brussels. Christianity was introduced about the first quarter of the fourth century and major evangelization was completed about 730. During the rest of the medieval period the Church had flourishing diocesan and parochial organization, generally vigorous monastic life and influential monastic and cathedral schools. Lutherans and Calvinists made some gains during the Reformation period but there was a strong Catholic restoration in the first half of the 17th century, when the country was under Spanish rule. Jansenism disturbed the Church from about 1640 into the 18th century. Josephinism, imposed by an Austrian regime, hampered the Church late in the same century. Repressive and persecutory measures were enforced during the Napoleonic conquest. Freedom came with separation of Church and state in the wake of the Revolution of 1830, which ended the reign of William I. Thereafter, the Church encountered serious problems with philosophical liberalism and political socialism.

Catholics have long been engaged in strong educational, social and political movements. In 1990, in an unprecedented political maneuver, King Baudouin temporarily gave up his throne, saying his Catholic conscience would not allow him to sign a law legalizing abortion. In the mid- and late-1990s, Church leaders expressed concern that Belgians dissented from Church teachings. Therapeutic in vitro fertilization for stable married couples continued at a leading Belgian Catholic hospital despite Vatican objections. The bishops fought a losing battle against the 2002 legalization of euthanasia and faced new allegations of sexual abuse of minors by clergy. Controversy surrounded the massive seizure of records and files from the residence and chancery of the Abp. of Mechelen-Brussels in 2010.

Belize*

Dioc., 1; abp.; bp., 2; parishes, 14; priests, 44 (11 dioc., 33 rel.); p.d., 7; sem., 2; bros., 5; srs., 53 catechists, 495; bap., 2,431; Caths., 162,000 (49.4%); tot. pop., 328,000.

Independent (Sept. 21, 1981) constitutional monarchy on eastern coast of Central America; capital, Belmopan. Its history has points in common with Guatemala, where evangelization began in the 16th century. The Church in Belize worked with refugees during the decades of Central American civil wars.

Benin*

Archd., 2; dioc., 8; abp., 4; bp., 7; parishes, 370; priests, 890 (742 dioc., 148 rel.); sem., 536; bros., 115; srs., 1,323; catechists, 11,756; bap., 50,180; Caths., 3,167,000 (33.8%); tot. pop., 9,364,000.

Democratic republic in West Africa, bordering on the Atlantic; capital, Porto Novo. Missionary work was very limited from the 16th to the 18th centuries. Effective evangelization dates from 1861. The hierarchy was established in 1955. In the 1970s, Benin's Marxist-Leninist government nationalized Catholic schools, expelled foreign missionaries and jailed some priests. After the government dropped the one-party system in 1989, Abp. Isidore de Souza of Cotonou presided over the 1990 national conference that drew up a new constitution and prepared the way for elections. One challenge facing the Church as it entered the 21st century was maintaining peace with people of other faiths. Pope Benedict XVI visited the country in November 2011.

Bermuda

Dioc., 1; bp., 1; parishes, 6; priests, 8 (1 dioc., 7 rel.); sem., 7; srs., 2; bap., 94; Caths., 9,000 (14%); tot. pop., 64,000. (AD)

British dependency, consisting of 360 islands (20 of them inhabited), nearly 600 miles east of Cape Hatteras; capital, Hamilton. Catholics were not permitted until about 1800. Occasional pastoral care was provided the few Catholics there by visiting priests during the 19th century. Early in the 1900s priests from Nova Scotia began serving the area. An apostolic prefecture was set up in 1953. The first bishop assumed jurisdiction in 1956, when it was made an apostolic vicariate; diocese established, 1967.

Bhutan

Parish; bap., 1; Caths., 1,000 (approx.); tot. pop., 721,000.

Kingdom in the Himalayas, northeast of India; capital, Thimphu. Buddhism is the state religion; Christians, including Catholics, are free to worship in private homes but cannot erect religious buildings, proselytize or congregate in public. Jesuits (1963) and Salesians (1965) were invited to the country to direct schools. Salesians were expelled in February 1982, on disputed charges of proselytism. The only Catholic missionary allowed to stay in the country was Canadian Jesuit Father William Mackey, who served Catholics there from 1963 until his death in 1995. Ecclesiastical jurisdiction is under the Darjeeling (India) Diocese, which ordained the first indigenous Bhutanese priest in 1995.

Bolivia*

Archd., 4; dioc., 6; prel., 2; mil. ord., 1; v.a., 5; card., 1; abp., 6; bp., 23; parishes, 597; priests, 1,219 (615 dioc., 604 rel.); p.d., 105; sem., 639; bros., 229; srs., 2,434; catechists, 17,933; bap., 153,745; Caths., 9,241,000 (85.4%); tot. pop., 10,825,000.

Republic in central South America; capital, Sucre; seat of government, La Paz. Catholicism, the official religion, was introduced in the 1530s, and the first diocese was established in 1552. Effective evangelization among the Indians, slow to start, reached high points in the middle of the 18th and the beginning of the 19th centuries and was resumed about 1840. Independence from Spain was proclaimed in 1825, at the end of a campaign that started in 1809. Church-state

relations are regulated by a 1951 concordat with the Holy See. Catholics have worked against social poverty and corruption. Early in the 21st century, amid social and economic turmoil, surveys showed the Catholic Church was seen as the most credible institution in the country.

Bosnia and Herzegovina*

Archd., 1; dioc., 2; card., 1; abp., 2; bp., 3; parishes, 303; priests, 651 (306 dioc., 345 rel.); sem., 141; bros., 18; srs., 536; bap., 4,734; Caths., 444,000 (11.6%); tot. pop., 3,837,000.

Independent republic (1992) in southeastern Europe; formerly part of Yugoslavia; capital, Sarajevo. During the three years of fighting that erupted after Bosnia-Herzegovina declared its independence, some 450,000 Catholics were driven from their homes; many fled to Croatia or southern Bosnia. Sarajevo Card. Vinko Puljic, named a cardinal in 1994, has led the bishops in calls for the safe return of all refugees from the war and acknowledged that in some areas Croatian Catholics were responsible for atrocities. Although the bishops worked to rebuild the Church, they said ethnic discrimination and violence still plagued the nation more than a decade after the war ended.

Botswana

Dioc., 1; v.a., 1; bp., 2; parishes, 40; priests, 63 (14 dioc., 49 rel.); p.d., 5; sem., 20; bros., 5; srs., 82; catechists, 362; bap., 1,300; Caths., 101,000 (5%); tot. pop., 1,877,000.

Republic (independent since 1966) in southern Africa; capital, Gaborone. The first Catholic mission was opened in 1928 near Gaborone; earlier attempts at evangelization dating from 1879 were unsuccessful. The Church in Botswana gave strong support to tens of thousands of South African refugees from apartheid. As Botswana's diamond industry grew, Church leaders worked to minimize the effects of social changes such as pockets of unemployment and competition for jobs.

Brazil*

Archd., 44; dioc., 215; prel., 12; abb., 1; exarch., 1; mil. ord., 1; card., 9; abp., 75; bp., 370; parishes, 11,012; priests, 21,066 (13,496 dioc., 7,570 rel.); p.d., 3,182; sem., 8,779; bros., 2,674; srs., 29,868; catechists, 490,564; bap., 1,520,168; Caths., 166,097,000 (84.5%); tot. pop., 196,600,000.

Federal republic in northeastern South America; capital, Brasilia. One of several priests with the discovery party celebrated the first Mass in the country Apr. 26, 1500. Evangelization began some years later, and the first diocese was erected in 1551. During the colonial period, which lasted until 1822, evangelization made some notable progress — especially in the Amazon region between 1680 and 1750 — but was seriously hindered by government policy and the attitude of colonists regarding Amazon Indians the missionaries tried to protect from exploitation and slavery. The Jesuits were suppressed in 1782 and other missionaries expelled as well. Liberal anti-Church influence grew in strength. The government exercised maximum control over the Church. After the proclamation of independence from Portugal in 1822 and throughout the regency, government control was tightened and the Church suffered greatly from dissident actions of ecclesiastical brotherhoods, Masonic anticlericalism and general decline in religious life. Church and state were separated by the constitution of 1891, proclaimed two years after the end of the empire.

The Church carried into the 20th century problems associated with increasingly difficult political, economic and social conditions affecting the majority of the population. Many Afro-Brazilians indiscriminately mixed African-based rites such as candomble with Catholic rituals. In the second half of the 20th century, the bishops became known for their liberal stances on social and some theological issues. In the 1980s, Vatican officials had a series of meetings with Brazilian bishops to discuss liberation theology and other issues. The Brazilian bishops' conference took the lead in advocating for land reform in the country. Members of the Church's Pastoral Land Commission often faced threats, harassment and murder. The Church-founded Indigenous Missionary Council worked for the rights of the country's Indians. Pope Francis visited Brazil in July 2013 for World Youth Day in Rio de Janeiro.

Brunei

P.a., 1; parishes, 3; priests, 4 (3 dioc., 1 rel); sem., 1; srs. 1; bap., 200; Caths., 1,900 (0.4%); tot. pop., 428,000.

Independent state (1984) on the northern coast of Borneo; formal name, Brunei Darussalam; capital, Bandar Seri Begawan. Islam is the official religion; other religions are allowed with some restrictions. Most of the Catholics are technicians and skilled workers from other countries who are not permanent residents; under ecclesiastical jurisdiction of Miri Diocese, Malaysia.

Bulgaria*

Dioc., 2; ap. ex., 1; abp., 1; bp., 3; parishes, 56; priests, 67 (25 dioc., 42 rel.); sem., 5; bros., 7; srs., 85; bap., 360; Caths., 73,000 (1%); tot. pop., 7,305,000.

Republic in southeastern Europe on the eastern part of the Balkan peninsula; capital, Sofia. Most of the population is Orthodox. Christianity was introduced before 343 but disappeared with the migration of Slavs into the territory. The baptism of Boris I about 865 ushered in a new period of Christianity, which soon became involved in switches of loyalty between Constantinople and Rome. Through it all the Byzantine, and later Orthodox, element remained stronger and survived under the rule of Ottoman Turks into the 19th century.

In 1947 the constitution of the new republic decreed the separation of Church and state. Catholic schools and institutions were abolished and foreign religious banished in 1948. A year later the apostolic delegate was expelled. Ivan Romanoff, vicar general of Plovdiv, died in prison in 1952. Bp. Eugene Bossilkoff, imprisoned in 1948, was sentenced to death in 1952; his fate remained unknown until 1975, when the Bulgarian government informed the Vatican that he had died in prison shortly after being sentenced. He was beatified in 1998. Although Church leaders were permitted to attend the Second Vatican Council, all Church activity was under surveillance and/or control by the government, which professed to be atheistic. Pastoral and related activities were strictly limited. There was some improvement in Bulgarian-Vatican relations in 1975. In 1979, the Sofia-Plovdiv apostolic vicariate was raised to a diocese, and a bishop was appointed for the vacant see of Nicopoli.

Diplomatic relations with the Holy See were established in 1990. In the late 1990s, the government instituted religion classes in state schools, but Church leaders had no input into the curriculum and that teachers were mostly Orthodox. In 2002, Pope John Paul II visited Bulgaria.

Burkina Faso*

Archd., 3; dioc., 11; abps., 6; bp., 13; parishes, 162; priests, 968 (796 dioc., 172 rel.); sem., 439; bros., 339; srs., 1,457; catechists, 7,389; bap., 74,587; Caths., 2,460,000

(14.68%); tot. pop., 16,758,000.

Republic inland in West Africa; capital, Ouagadougou. Missionaries of Africa started the first missions in 1900 and 1901. Their sisters began work in 1911. A minor and a major seminary were established in 1926 and 1942, respectively. The hierarchy was established in 1955. The first indigenous bishop in modern times from West Africa was ordained in 1956 and the first cardinal created in 1965. In 1980 and 1990, Pope John Paul II's visits to the country were used to launch appeals for an end to desertification of sub-Saharan Africa and an end to poverty in the region. In later years, the pope encouraged increased evangelization and interreligious harmony.

Burma

(See **Myanmar**, p. 320.)

Burundi*

Archd., 2; dioc., 6; abp., 3; bp., 8; parishes, 164; priests, 696 (600 dioc., 96 rel.); sem., 609; bros., 203; srs., 1,733; catechists, 5,187; bap., 186,091; Caths., 5,945,000 (67.2%); tot. pop., 8,841,000.

Republic (1966), near the equator in east-central Africa; capital, Bujumbura. The first permanent Catholic mission station was established late in the 19th century. Large numbers were received into the Church following the ordination of the first Burundian priests in 1925. The first indigenous bishop was appointed in 1959.

In 1972-73, the country was torn by tribal warfare between the Tutsis, the ruling minority, and the Hutus. In 1979, the government began expelling foreign missionaries, and in 1986, seminaries were nationalized. A gradual resumption of Church activity since 1987 has been hampered by continuing ethnic violence, which began in 1993 and left more than 150,000 Burundians dead. The bishops repeatedly have called for peace and for an end to sanctions imposed by the Organization of African Unity in 1996. Missionaries continued to be the target of violent attacks, and the papal nuncio was killed after being shot in an ambush in 2003.

Cambodia*

V.a., 1; p.a., 2; bp., 2; parishes, 39 (there were also 28 mission stations without resident priests); priests, 96 (38 dioc., 58 rel.); sem., 9; bros., 26; srs., 99; catechists, 253; baptisms, 583; Caths., 21,000 (.16%); tot. pop., 15,602,000.

Constitutional monarchy in Southeast Asia; capital, Phnom Penh. Evangelization dating from the second half of the 16th century had limited results, more among Vietnamese than Khmers. Thousands of Catholics of Vietnamese origin were forced to flee in 1970 because of Khmer hostility. Most indigenous priests and nuns were killed under the 1975-79 Pol Pot regime. During those years, the Vietnamese invasion in 1979 and the long civil war that followed, foreign missionaries were expelled, local clergy and religious were sent to work the land and a general persecution followed. Religious freedom was re-established in 1990. Diplomatic relations with the Holy See were established in March 1994. Despite a lack of vocations, many Catholics maintain their faith through small Christian communities led by lay catechists. In the 21st century, Church leaders described their congregations as young and vibrant, involved in such things as AIDS ministry.

Cameroon*

Archd., 5; dioc., 19; card., 1; abp., 7; bp., 24; parishes, 1,009; priests, 2,128 (1,480 dioc., 648 rel.); p.d., 24; sem.,

1,685; bros., 430; srs., 2,556; catechists, 26,100; bap., 128,103; Caths., 5,799,000 (28.4%); tot. pop., 20,387,000.

Republic in West Africa; capital, Yaounde. Effective evangelization began in 1890, although Catholics had been in the country long before that time. In the 40-year period from 1920 to 1960, the number of Catholics increased from 60,000 to 700,000. The first black priests were ordained in 1935. Twenty years later the first indigenous bishops were ordained and the hierarchy established. The first Cameroonian cardinal (Christian Wiyghan Tumi) was named in 1988. Around that same time, unknown people began persecuting Church personnel. Among those murdered was Abp. Yves Plumy of Garoua in 1991. Some felt the government did not do enough to investigate.

Canada*
(See **Catholic Church in Canada, p. 441**; see also **Statistics of the Church in Canada**, p. 447).

Cape Verde*
Dioc., 2; bp., 2; parishes, 35; priests, 62 (21 dioc., 41 rel.); sem., 27; bros., 5; srs., 115; catechists, 2,768; bap., 5,573; Caths., 540,000 (93.7%); tot. pop., 576,000.

Independent (July 5, 1975) island group in the Atlantic 300 miles west of Senegal; formerly a Portuguese overseas province; capital, Praia, São Tiago Island. Evangelization began some years before the establishment of a diocese in 1532. The Church languished from the 17th to the 19th centuries, and for two long periods there was no resident bishop. Portugal's anti-clerical government closed the only minor seminary in 1910. Missionaries returned in the 1940s. Cape Verde has faced massive emigration of youth because of perennial drought and a weak economy.

Central African Republic*
Archd., 1; dioc., 8; abp., 2; bp., 11; parishes, 116; priests, 324 (185 dioc., 139 rel.); sem., 218; bros., 37; srs., 371; catechists, 4,227; bap., 20,786; Caths., 1,626,000 (36.5%); tot. pop., 4,459,000.

Former French colony (independent since 1960) in central Africa; capital, Bangui. Effective evangelization dates from 1894. The region was organized as a mission territory in 1909. The first indigenous priest was ordained in 1938. The hierarchy was organized in 1955. The Church in the country has expressed concern about the growing number of sects. Frequent military coups and attempted coups have left the nation divided, and church leaders have worked for reconciliation; including heading the national dialogue coordination team. Hundreds of thousands of people remain displaced, and sporadic fighting continues.

Chad*
Archd., 1; dioc., 6; v.a., 1; abp., 2; bp., 7; parishes, 122; priests, 266 (151 dioc., 115 rel.); sem., 127; p.d.; bros., 41; srs., 379; catechists, 6,991; bap., 19,450; Caths., 1,090,000 (9.6%); tot. pop., 11,323,000.

Republic (independent since 1960) in north-central Africa; former French possession; capital, N'Djamena. Evangelization began in 1929, leading to firm organization in 1947 and establishment of the hierarchy in 1955. Many catechists, who often were local community leaders, were killed during Chad's 1982-87 civil war. The Vatican established diplomatic relations with Chad in 1988. After the government established more freedoms in the early 1990s, the Church worked to teach people, including Catholics, that solidarity must extend across religious, ethnic and regional boundaries. Church workers were involved in ministering to hundreds of thousands of refugees displaced during the conflict in the Darfur region of Sudan.

Chile*
Archd., 5; dioc., 19; prel., 1; v.a., 1; mil. ord., 1; card., 2; abp., 8; bp., 39; parishes, 954; priests, 2,415 (1,182 dioc., 1,233 rel.); p.d., 1,029; sem., 659; bros., 384; srs., 4,303; catechists, 46,282; bap., 131,995; Caths., 12,883,000 (74%); tot. pop., 17,403,000.

Republic on the southwest coast of South America; capital, Santiago. Priests were with the Spanish on their entrance into the territory early in the 16th century. The first parish was established in 1547 and the first diocese in 1561. Overall organization of the Church took place later in the century. By 1650, most of the peaceful Indians in the central and northern areas were evangelized. Missionary work was more difficult in the southern region. Church activity was hampered during the campaign for independence, 1810-18, and through the first years of the new government, to 1830. Later, Church activity increased but was hampered by shortages of indigenous personnel and attempts by the government to control Church administration through the patronage system. Separation of Church and state was decreed in the constitution of 1925.

Church-state relations were strained during the regime of Marxist President Salvador Allende (1970-73). In the mid-1970s, the Adio. of Santiago established the Vicariate of Solidarity to counter human-rights abuses under the rule of Gen. Augusto Pinochet. The Chilean bishops issued numerous statements strongly critical of human rights abuses by the military dictator, who remained in power until 1990, when an elected president took office. The Church was praised for its role in educating and registering voters in the 1988 plebiscite that rejected another term for Pinochet. In 1999, when a British court ruled that Pinochet could be extradited from Britain to Spain to face trial for torture and murder, Chilean bishops said the ruling damaged Chilean democracy.

China, People's Republic of
Archd., 20; dioc., 92; p.a., 29. No Roman Catholic statistics are available. In 1949 there were between 3,500,000-4,000,000 Catholics, about .7% of the total population; current total is unknown. Tot. pop. 1,346,028,000. **Hong Kong:** Dioc., 1; card., 2; bps., 2; parishes, 51; priests, 317 (75 dioc., 242 rel.); p.d., 16; sem., 42; bros., 54; srs., 489; catechists, 1,456; bap., 6,249; Caths., 547,000 (5.2%); tot. pop., 7,155,000. **Macau:** Dioc., 1; bp., 2; parishes, 9; priests, 77 (26 dioc., 51 rel.); sem., 21; bros., 25; srs., 194; bap., 360; catechists, 128; Caths., 30,000; tot. pop. 582,000.

People's republic in eastern part of Asia; capital, Beijing. Christianity was introduced by the Church of the East monks called "Nestorians," who had some influence on part of the area from 635 to 845 and again from the 11th century until 1368. John of Monte Corvino started a Franciscan mission in 1294; he was ordained an archbishop about 1307. Missionary activity involving more priests increased for a while thereafter, but the Franciscan mission ended in 1368. Jesuit Matteo Ricci initiated a remarkable period of activity in the 1580s. In what became known as the Chinese rites controversy, the Jesuits argued that Confucian veneration of ancestors was compatible with Catholicism, but Dominican and Franciscan missionaries viewed it as idolatry. The controversy even was debated in Europe throughout the 17th century, and the Vatican ruled against the rites in the early 1800s.

In the mid-19th century, the Opium War forced China to open its doors, accept free trade and allow Christian missionaries in. Progress in evangelization resumed with an extension of legal and social tolerance. At the turn of the 20th century, however, Christian missionary activity helped provoke the Boxer Rebellion against foreign influence in China.

Missionary work in the 20th century reached a new high. The hierarchy was instituted by Pope Pius XII, Apr. 11, 1946 (Apostolic Constitution *Quotidie Nos*). Then followed persecution initiated by communists, before and especially after they established the republic in 1949. The government outlawed missionary work and pastoral activity; expelled more than 5,000 foreign missionaries; arrested, imprisoned and harassed Chinese Church officials; closed more than 4,000 schools, clinics and social service institutions; denied the free exercise of religion; detained hundreds of priests, religious and lay people in jail or in slave labor; proscribed Catholic movements for "counterrevolutionary activities" and "crimes against the new China."

The government formally established the Chinese Catholic Patriotic Association, independent of the Holy See, in July 1957. Initially, relatively few priests and lay people joined the organization, which was condemned by Pius XII in 1958. Many of the Catholics who then joined the Patriotic Association indicated they chose to cooperate with the government and work within its restrictions, but remained loyal to the Vatican. The government formed the nucleus of what it hoped might become the hierarchy of a national Chinese Catholic Church in 1958 by "electing" 26 bishops and having them consecrated validly but illicitly between Apr. 13, 1958, and Nov. 15, 1959. Additional bishops were subsequently ordained. Catholics continued to practice the faith clandestinely and face persecution.

From 1966 to 1978, the Cultural Revolution declared religions to be dangerous and illegal in China. The Catholic registered communities were forbidden to exist. Total persecution of the Catholics followed for more than 10 years.

In the 1980s, although bishops on the mainland were asked to register with the government and join the Patriotic Association, many began to reconcile secretly with the Vatican. Gradually, and in some regions more than others, clandestine and registered Catholic communities began to mingle. By the early 21st century, nearly all of the government-approved bishops in the Patriotic Association had reconciled with the Vatican. Although Chinese officials continued to insist on the right to name bishops, in most cases bishops also were approved by the Vatican.

In 2007, Pope Benedict XVI issued a historic letter to Chinese Catholics urging reconciliation between the clandestine and registered Catholic communities. The letter said registration with the government was permissible as long as it did not compromise the faith. It also formally revoked all Vatican pastoral directives and special faculties previously granted to address pastoral necessities in difficult times. However, it said the Patriotic Association's idea of an independent Chinese church that self-manages itself democratically was "incompatible with Catholic doctrine," and it criticized government limits on the church's activities. The last years have also brought a sharp increase in the persecution of the Church.

Colombia*

Archd., 13; dioc., 52; v.a., 10; mil. ord., 1; card., 3; abp., 24; bp., 83; parishes, 4,042; priests, 9,210 (6,801 dioc., 2,409 rel.); p.d., 515; sem., 4,041; bros., 1,174 srs., 14,727; catechists, 55,628; bap., 602,595; Caths., 44,045,000 (93.3%); tot. pop., 47,186,000.

Republic in northwest South America; capital, Bogotá. Evangelization began in 1508. The first two dioceses were established in 1534. Vigorous development of the Church was reported by the middle of the 17th century despite obstacles posed by the multiplicity of Indian languages, government interference through patronage rights, rivalry among religious orders and the small number of native American priests among the predominantly Spanish clergy. Some persecution, including the confiscation of property, followed in the wake of the proclamation of independence from Spain in 1819. Guerrilla warfare aimed at Marxist-oriented radical social reform and redistribution of land, along with violence related to drug traffic, has plagued the country since the 1960s, posing problems for the Church, which backed reforms but rejected actions of radical groups. In the late 20th and early 21st centuries, the Church worked as a mediator between the government and guerrillas, but Church leaders suffered threats, attacks, and sometimes death, including from paramilitaries. For example, on Mar. 16, 2002, Abp. Isaias Duarte Cancino of Cali was shot to death for speaking out about the political situation; he was one of at least 10 Church workers killed in 2002.

Comoros

A.a., 1; bp.; parishes, 4; missions, 4; priests, 4 (1 dioc.; 3 rel.); bros., 1; srs., 7; catechists, 20; bap., 28; Caths., 6,000 (.07%); tot. pop., 893,000. (AD)

Consists of main islands of Grande Comore, Anjouan and Moheli in Indian Ocean off southeast coast of Africa; capital, Moroni, Grande Comore Island. Former French territory; independent (July 6, 1975). The majority of the population is Muslim. An apostolic administration was established in 1975.

Congo, Democratic Republic of *

Archd., 6; dioc., 41; Card., 1; abp., 8; bp., 41; parishes, 1,421; priests, 5,540 (3,532 dioc., 2,008 rel.); p.d., 4, sem., 3,398; bros., 1,529; srs., 9,181; catechists, 80,958; bap., 466,802; Caths., 39,691,000 (52.5%); tot. pop., 75,588,000.

Republic in south central Africa; capital, Kinshasa. Christianity was introduced in 1484 and evangelization began about 1490. The first bishop from black Africa was ordained in 1518. Subsequent missionary work was hindered by factors including 18th- and 19th-century anti-clericalism. Modern evangelization started in the second half of the 19th century. The hierarchy was established in 1959. In the civil disorders that followed independence in 1960, some missions and other Church installations were abandoned, thousands of people reverted to tribal religions and many priests and religious were killed.

Church-state tensions developed in the late 1980s and 1990s because of the Church's criticism of President Mobutu Sese Seko. In 1992, Abp. Laurent Monswengo Pasinya was named president of a council charged with drafting a new constitution and overseeing a transition to democracy, but Mobutu supporters blocked effective change, and the archbishop resigned in 1994. In the long years of civil war, Church personnel worked to meet humanitarian needs and to promote peace. The Church today is the only stable institution in a country ravaged by civil strife, corruption, and endmic poverty.

Congo, Republic of *

Archd., 1; dioc., 6; p.a., 1; abp., 2; bp., 5; parishes, 160;

priests, 440 (328 dioc., 102 rel.); p.d., 1; sem., 339; bros., 109; srs., 479; catechists, 3,695; bap., 27,984; Caths., 2,813,000 (55%); tot. pop., 5,108,000.

Republic (independent since 1960) in west central Africa; former French possession; capital, Brazzaville. Small-scale missionary work with little effect preceded modern evangelization dating from the 1880s. The work of the Church has been affected by political instability, communist influence, tribalism and hostility to foreigners. The hierarchy was established in 1955. In 1992 Bp. Ernest Kombo of Owando was appointed chief organizer of the country's parliamentary elections. In 1994, the Church canceled independence day celebrations after more than 142 Catholics, mostly children, were crushed or suffocated in a rain-induced stampede at a Catholic church in Brazzaville. During renewed violence in the late 1990s, the bishops appealed for peace and stability.

Costa Rica*

Archd., 1; dioc., 7; abp., 2; bp., 9; parishes, 292; priests, 785 (595 dioc., 190 rel.); sem., 269; p.d., 5; bros., 82; srs., 830; catechists, 23,538; bap., 40,870; Caths., 3,859,000 (82.7%); tot. pop., 4,667,000.

Republic in Central America; capital, San José. Evangelization began about 1520 and proceeded by degrees to real development and organization of the Church in the 17th and 18th centuries. The republic became independent in 1838. Twelve years later Church jurisdiction also became independent with the establishment of a diocese in the present capital.

Côte d'Ivoire (Ivory Coast)*

Archd., 4; dioc., 11; card., 1; abp., 5; bp., 16; parishes, 476; priests, 1,407 (1,102 dioc., 305 rel.); p.d., 6; sem., 677; bros. 427; srs., 1,098; catechists, 17,755; bap., 67,822; Caths., 5,641,000 (24.4%); tot. pop., 23,138,000.

Republic in western Africa; capital, Abidjan. The Holy Ghost Fathers began systematic evangelization in 1895. The first priests from the area were ordained in 1934. The hierarchy was set up in 1955; the first indigenous cardinal (Bernard Yago) was named in 1983. In 1990 Pope John Paul II consecrated the continent's biggest, most costly and most controversial cathedral in Yamoussoukro. The pope only agreed to accept the cathedral after convincing the country's president to build an adjacent hospital and youth center.

Croatia*

Archd., 5; dioc., 11; mil. ord., 1; card., 1; abp., 6; bp., 16; parishes, 1,621; priests, 2,390 (1,599 dioc., 791 rel.); p.d., 22; sem., 406; bros., 65; srs., 3,400; catechists, 1,122; bap., 37,727; Caths., 3,856,000 (90.3%); tot. pop., 4,268,000.

Independent (1991) republic in southeastern Europe; capital Zagreb; formerly a constituent republic of Yugoslavia. Christianity was introduced in the seventh century. On-again, off-again fighting from 1991 to 1995 pitted mostly Catholic Croats against mostly Orthodox Serbs. In 1995, Croatian bishops issued guidelines for rebuilding the nation including suppressing feelings of vengeance toward Serbs. However, in 1996 the head of Croatia's Helsinki human rights committee criticized the bishops for taking a weak stance on Croat abuses after the 1995 Croatian recapture of the Serb-occupied Krajina region. The 1998 beatification of Croatian Cardinal Alojzije Stepinac generated controversy among some Serb and Jewish leaders, who considered the cardinal a Nazi sympathizer. Pope Benedict XVI visited in June 2011.

Cuba*

Archd., 3; dioc., 8; card., 1; abp., 4; bp., 13; parishes, 305; priests, 376 (201 dioc., 175 rel.); p.d., 78; sem., 78; bros., 37; srs., 618; catechists, 4,212; bap., 81,639; Caths. 6,771,000 (60.2%); tot. pop., 11,248,000.

Republic under Communist dictatorship, south of Florida; capital, Havana. Effective evangelization began about 1514, leading eventually to the predominance of Catholicism on the island. Vocations to the priesthood and religious life were unusually numerous in the 18th century but declined in the 19th. The island became independent of Spain in 1902 following the Spanish-American War.

Fidel Castro took control of the government Jan. 1, 1959. In 1961, after Cuba was officially declared a socialist state, the University of Villanueva was closed, 350 Catholic schools were nationalized and 136 priests expelled. A greater number of foreign priests and religious had already left the country. Freedom of worship and religious instruction were limited to Church premises and no social action was permitted by the Church, which survived under surveillance. A new constitution approved in 1976 guaranteed freedom of conscience but restricted its exercise. Small improvements in Church-state relations occurred in the late 1980s and early 1990s. In December 1997, just before Pope John Paul II's historic visit, the government allowed public celebration of Christmas, banned for 30 years. Although the pope's January 1998 visit was seen as a new dawn for the Church on the islands, Cuban Catholics say change has come slowly. Church leaders say the government has made concessions on public worship and restoration of church buildings. Some progress has been made on visas for foreign Church personnel and in Church-run media. In 2007, representatives of the Latin American bishops' council (CELAM) met on the island for the first time. Pope Benedict XVI visited in March 2012; after his trip, Cuba declared Good Friday a national holiday, and it was hoped that further progress would be achieved in the areas of human rights and economic freedom.

Cyprus*

Archd., 1 (Maronite); abp., 2; parishes, 16; priests, 42 (11 dioc., 31 rel.); sem., 1; bros., 10; srs., 47; bap., 89; Caths., 20,000 (2.4%); tot. pop., 839,000.

Republic in the eastern Mediterranean; capital, Nicosia. Christianity was preached on the island in apostolic times and has a continuous history from the fourth century. Latin and Eastern rites were established but the latter prevailed and became Orthodox after the schism of 1054. Christians have suffered under many governments, particularly during the period of Turkish dominion from late in the 16th to late in the 19th centuries, and from differences between the 80 percent Greek majority and the Turkish minority. About 80 percent of the population are Orthodox.

Czech Republic*

Archd., 2; dioc., 6; ap. ex., 1; card., 2; abp., 3; bp., 17; parishes, 2,438; priests, 1,887 (1,328 dioc., 559 rel.); p.d., 201; sem., 166; bros., 132; srs., 1,327; catechists, 1,122; bap., 22,782; Caths., 3,308,000 (31.5%); tot. pop., 10,511,000.

Independent state (Jan. 1, 1993); formerly part of Czechoslovakia; capital, Prague. The martyrdom of Prince Wenceslaus in 929 triggered the spread of Christianity. Prague has had a continuous history as a diocese since 973. A parish system was organized about the 13th century in Bohemia and Moravia. Mendicant orders strengthened relations with the Latin rite in the 13th century. In the following century the teachings of John Hus in Bohemia brought trouble to the Church in the forms of schism and heresy and initiated a series of religious wars that continued for decades following his death at the stake in 1415. So many of the faithful joined the Bohemian Brethren that Catholics became a minority.

In the 1560s, a Counter-Reformation got under way and led to a gradual restoration through the thickets of Josephinism, the Enlightenment, liberalism and troubled politics. St. Jan Sarkander, a priest accused of helping an invading Polish army, was killed by Protestants in 1620. (His 1995 canonization caused strains with the Protestant community.)

In 1920, two years after the establishment of the Republic of Czechoslovakia, the schismatic Czechoslovak Church was proclaimed at Prague, resulting in numerous defections from the Catholic Church in the Czech region. Following the accession of the Gottwald regime to power early in 1948, perse cution began in the Czech part of Czechoslovakia. A number of theatrical trials of bishops and priests were staged in 1950. Pressure was applied on Eastern Catholics in Slovakia to join the Orthodox Church. Diplomatic relations with the Holy See were terminated in 1950. In the following decade, thousands of priests were arrested and hundreds were deported, and attempts were made to force government-approved "peace priests" on the people. Pope Pius XII granted the Czech Church emergency powers to appoint clergy during the communist persecution.

From January to October 1968, Church-state relations improved to some extent under the Dubcek regime: a number of bishops were reinstated; some priests were still barred from priestly work; the "peace priests" organization was disbanded. The Eastern Catholic Church was re-established. In 1969, rehabilitation trials for priests and religious ended, but there was no wholesale restoration of priests and religious to their proper ways of life and work. Government restrictions continued to hamper the work of priests and nuns. Signatories of the human rights declaration Charter 77 were particular objects of government repression and retribution.

In December 1983, the Czechoslovakian foreign minister met with the pope at Vatican City; it was the first meeting of a high Czech official with a pope since the country had been under communist rule. In 1988, three new bishops were ordained in Czechoslovakia, the first since 1973. The communist government fell in late 1989. In 1990, bishops were appointed to fill vacant sees; diplomatic relations between the Holy See and Czechoslovakia were re-established, and Pope John Paul II visited the country. In 1997 the issue of married Czech priests secretly ordained under communist rule was resolved when they began work in the country's new Eastern Catholic jurisdiction. Under a 1949 communist decree declaring priests Culture Ministry employees, Czech priests were still paid by the state. A Church spokesman said confiscation of Church property under communist rule left priests still financially dependent on the state. Pope Benedict XVI visited in Sept. 2009.

Denmark*

Dioc., 1; bp., 2; parishes, 47; priests, 72 (39 dioc., 33 rel.); p.d., 5; sem., 20; bros., 2; srs., 187; bap., 646; Caths., 38,000 (.7%); tot. pop., 5,587,000.

Includes the Faroe Islands and Greenland. Constitutional monarchy in northwestern Europe; capital, Copenhagen. Christianity was introduced in the ninth century and the first diocese for the area was established in 831. Intensive evangelization and full-scale organization of the Church occurred from the second half of the 10th century and ushered in a period of great development and influence in the 12th and 13th centuries. Decline followed, resulting in almost total loss to the Church during the Reformation, when Lutheranism became the national religion. A few Catholic families practiced the faith secretly until religious freedom was legally assured in the mid-1800s. Since then, immigration has increased the number of Catholics. About 95 percent of the population are Evangelical Lutherans.

Catholicism was introduced in Greenland, a Danish island province northeast of North America, about 1000. The first diocese was established in 1124 and a line of bishops dated from then until 1537. The first known churches in the Western Hemisphere, dating from about the 11th century, were on Greenland. The departure of Scandinavians and spread of the Reformation reduced the Church to nothing. The Moravian Brethren evangelized the Inuit from the 1720s to 1901. By 1930 the Danish Church — Evangelical Lutheran — was in full possession. Since 1930, priests have been in Greenland, which is part of the Copenhagen Dio.

Djibouti*

Dioc., 1; bp., 1; parishes, 5; priests, 3 (1 dioc., 2 rel.); bros., 6; srs., 25; catechists, 10; sem., 1; bap., 15; Caths., 5,000 (0.6%); tot. pop., 850,000. (AD)

Independent (1977) republic in East Africa; capital, Djibouti. Christianity in the area, formerly part of Ethiopia, antedated but was overcome by the Arab invasion of 1200. Modern evangelization, begun in the latter part of the 19th century, had meager results. The hierarchy was established in 1955. Formal diplomatic relations with the Holy See were established in May 2000.

Dominica*

Dioc., 1; bp., 1; parishes, 15; priests, 23 (12 dioc., 11 rel.); sem., 10; bros., 5; srs., 14; catechists, 315; bap., 512; Caths., 42,000 (60.9%); tot. pop., 69,000.

Independent (Nov. 3, 1978) state in Caribbean; capi tal, Roseau. Evangelization began in 1642.

Dominican Republic*

Archd., 2; dioc., 9; mil. ord., 1; v.a., 1; card., 1; abp., 3; bp., 17; parishes, 648; priests, 1,073 (624 dioc., 449 rel.); p.d., 530; sem., 621; bros., 267; srs., 3,125; catechists, 50,114; bap., 85,844; Caths., 8,934,000 (88%); tot. pop., 10,135,000.

Caribbean republic on the eastern two-thirds of the island of Hispaniola, bordering on Haiti; capital, Santo Domingo. Evangelization began shortly after discovery by Columbus in 1492 and Church organization, the first in America, was established by 1510. Catholicism is the state religion. Pope John Paul II visited the country in 1992 to mark the quincentennial celebrations of Columbus' discovery. The pope also opened the Fourth General conference of the Latin American Episcopate there. Church leaders worked to end social injustices, including the plight of mistreated sugar cane workers.

East Timor*

Dioc., 2; bp., 2; parishes, 56; priests, 199 (90 dioc., 109 rel.); sem., 191; p.d., 1; bros., 50; srs., 499; catechists, 1,555; bap., 22,275; Caths., 1,122,000 (96%); tot. pop., 1,167,000.

Independent (May 2002) state; capital, Dili. The predominantly Catholic former Portuguese colony was invaded by Indonesia in 1975 and annexed the following year. Most countries did not recognize the annexation. The Catholic Church worked to bring peace between the Indonesian government and guerrilla forces seeking independence. Bp. Carlos Filipe Ximenes Belo, former apostolic administrator of Dili, was a co-winner of the 1996 Nobel Peace Prize for his peace efforts. In 1999, dozens of civilians— including more than two dozen at a Catholic church — were killed during a terror campaign waged by pro-Indonesia paramilitaries in the run-up to an August vote on independence for East Timor. Indonesian troops withdrew, and in August 2001, East Timor held elections for a transitional government. The Church has worked on peace and reconciliation issues to raise awareness of social issues.

Ecuador*

Archd., 4; dioc., 12; v.a., 8; mil. ord., 1; Card., 1; abp., 8; bp., 38; parishes, 1,243; priests, 2,152 (1,339 dioc., 813 rel.); p.d., 84; sem., 587; bros., 488; srs., 5,128; catechists, 48,716; bap., 259,057; Caths., 13,573,000 (87.6%); tot. pop., 15,495,000.

Republic on the west coast of South America, includes Galápagos Islands; capital, Quito. Evangelization began in the 1530s. The first diocese was established in 1545. Multi-phased missionary work, spreading from the coastal and mountain regions into the Amazon, made the Church highly influential during the colonial period. The Church was practically enslaved by the constitution enacted in 1824, two years after Ecuador, as part of Colombia, gained independence from Spain. Some change for the better took place later in the century, but from 1891 until the 1930s the Church labored under serious liabilities imposed by liberal governments. Foreign missionaries were barred from the country for some time; the property of religious orders was confiscated; education was taken over by the state; traditional state support was refused; legal standing was denied; attempts to control Church offices were made through insistence on rights of patronage. A period of harmony and independence for the Church began after agreement was reached on Church-state relations in 1937. In 1998, the Church was actively involved in peace talks that ended a border dispute of some 170 years with Peru. At the beginning of the 21st century, Ecuador's bishops were working to fight social turmoil and the results of severe economic austerity measures. They also were working to support family members left behind as up to 2.5 million of the country's residents emigrated to foreign lands for work.

Egypt*

Patriarchates, 2 (Alexandria for the Copts and for the Melkites); dioc., 11; v.a., 1; ex., 1; patriarch, 1; Card., 1; abp., 3; bp., 15; parishes, 204; priests, 497 (237 dioc., 260 rel.); p.d., 8; sem., 94; bros., 73; srs., 1,135; catechists, 1,929; bap., 2,139; Caths., 228,000 (.28%); tot. pop., 82,541,000.

Arab Republic in northeastern Africa; capital, Cairo. Alexandria was the influential hub of a Christian community established by the end of the second century; it became a patriarchate and the center of the Coptic Church and had great influence on the spread of Christianity in various parts of Africa. Monasticism developed from desert communities of hermits in the third and fourth centuries. Arianism was first preached in Egypt in the 320s. In the fifth century, the Coptic Church went Monophysite through failure to accept doctrine formulated by the Council of Chalcedon in 451 with respect to the two natures of Christ. The country was thoroughly Arabized after 640 and was under the rule of Ottoman Turks from 1517 to 1798.

Islam, the religion of some 90 percent of the population, is the state religion. The Christian population faced the upheaval that toppled Pres. Hosni Mubarak in early 2011 with fear given the increase in anti-Christian violence. Concern continues to grow about the safety of Christians as Islamic extremists have expanded their attacks on Christian churches and houses.

El Salvador*

Archd., 1; dioc., 7; mil. ord., 1; abp., 3; bp., 11 parishes, 471, priests, 896 (660 dioc., 236 rel.); p.d., 3; sem., 525; bros., 71; srs., 1,668; catechists, 16,683; bap., 64,278; Cath., 4,993,000 (80%); tot. pop., 6,251,000.

Republic in Central America; capital, San Salvador. Evangelization affecting the whole territory followed Spanish occupation in the 1520s. The country was administered by the captaincy general of Guatemala until 1821, when independence from Spain was declared and it was annexed to Mexico. El Salvador joined the Central American Federation in 1825, declared independence in 1841 and became a republic formally in 1856.

During the country's 1980-92 civil war, Church leaders worked to achieve social justice. The San Salvador Archdiocese's human rights office, Tutela Legal, documented abuses and political killings and offered legal support to victims, despite Church persecution. Abp. Oscar Romero of San Salvador, peace advocate and outspoken champion of human rights, was murdered Mar. 24, 1980, while celebrating Mass. Four U.S. Church women were murdered the same year. Six Jesuits and two lay women were assassinated Nov. 16, 1989, at Central American University in El Salvador. Church leaders, particularly Abp. Romero's successor, Abp. Arturo Rivera Damas, were active in the peace process. In the 1990s, Church-government relations cooled. Church leaders often urged the U.S. government not to deport the hundreds of thousands of Salvadoran refugees who lived, often illegally, in the United States, and sent money to their families in El Salvador. The situation worsened after the destruction caused by Hurricane Mitch in 1998.

England*

Archd., 4; dioc., 15; ap. ex., 1; mil. ord. (Great Britain), 1; card., 2; abp., 6; bp., 26; parishes, 2,886; priests, 5,347 (4012 dioc., 1,335 rel.); p.d., 866; sem., 252; bros., 2,377; srs., 5,870; catechists, 30,860; bap., 71,471; Caths., 5,800,000 10.5% (10.47%; tot. Catholic pop. for Great Britain: 6,009,000); tot. pop., 54,996,000 (tot. pop. for Great Britain: 58,050,000). Note: England and Wales share a joint Episcopal Conference; see also **Scotland** and **Wales**.

Center of the United Kingdom of Great Britain (England, Scotland, Wales) and Northern Ireland, off the northwestern coast of Europe; capital, London. The arrival of St. Augustine of Canterbury and a band of monks in 597 marked the beginning of evangelization. Real organization of the Church took place some years after the Synod of Whitby, held in 663. Heavy losses were sustained in the wake of the Danish invasion in the 780s, but recovery starting from the time of Alfred the Great and dating especially from the middle of the 10th century led to Christianization of the whole country and close Church-state relations. The Norman Conquest of 1066 opened the Church in England to European influence. The Church began to decline in numbers in the 13th century. In the 14th century, John Wycliff presaged the

Protestant Reformation.

Henry VIII, failing in 1529 to gain annulment of his marriage to Catherine of Aragon, refused to acknowledge papal authority over the Church in England, had himself proclaimed its head, suppressed all houses of religious, and persecuted people — Sts. Thomas More and John Fisher, among others — for not subscribing to the Oath of Supremacy and Act of Succession. He held the line on other-than-papal doctrine, however, until his death in 1547. Doctrinal aberrations were introduced during the reign of Edward VI (1547-53), through the Order of Communion, two books of Common Prayer, and the Articles of the Established Church. Mary Tudor's attempted Catholic restoration (1553-58) was a disaster, resulting in the deaths of more than 300 Protestants. Elizabeth (1558-1603) firmed up the established Church with the aid of Matthew Parker, archbishop of Canterbury, with formation of a hierarchy, legal enactments and multi-phased persecution. More than 100 priests and 62 lay persons were among the casualties of persecution during the underground Catholic revival that followed the return to England of missionary priests from France and the Lowlands.

Several periods of comparative tolerance ensued after Elizabeth's death. The first of several apostolic vicariates was established in 1685; this form of Church government was maintained until the restoration of the hierarchy and diocesan organization in 1850. The revolution of 1688 and subsequent developments to about 1781 subjected Catholics to a wide variety of penal laws and disabilities in religious, civic and social life. The situation began to improve in 1791, and from 1801 Parliament frequently considered proposals for the repeal of penal laws against Catholics.

The Act of Emancipation restored citizenship rights to Catholics in 1829. Restrictions remained in force for some time afterward, however, on public religious worship and activity. The hierarchy was restored in 1850. Since then the Catholic Church, existing side by side with the established Churches of England and Scotland, has followed a general pattern of growth and development. After the Church of England began ordaining women priests in 1994, hundreds of Anglican priests and four Anglican bishops have been received into the Catholic Church, although many said ordination of women was not their primary reason for leaving. In the late 20th and early 21st centuries, the Church was active in the prolife movement and was outspoken on bioethical issues. Pope Benedict XVI visited in Sept. 2010 for the beatification of John Henry Cardinal Newman. Recent studies have revealed that nearly a quarter of Britons now profess no reigious affiliation, a mark of secularization in the country. (See also **Ireland, Northern**)

Equatorial Guinea*

Archd., 1; dioc., 2; abp., 1; bp., 1; parishes, 72; priests, 150 (84 dioc., 66 rel.); p.d. 1; sem., 53; bros., 28; srs., 225; catechists, 1,114; bap., 21,385; Caths., 684,000 (96.6%); tot. pop., 708,000.

Republic on the west coast of Africa, consisting of Rio Muni on the mainland and the islands of Bioko and Annobon in the Gulf of Guinea: capital, Malabo. Evangelization began in 1841. The country became independent of Spain in 1968. The Church was severe ly repressed during the 11-year rule of President Macias Nguema. Developments since his overthrow in 1979 indicated some measure of improvement. An ecclesiastical

province was established in October 1982.

In the 1990s, bishops worked to educate Catholics about the need for social justice and respect for human rights. In mid-1998, the government expelled three foreign missionaries involved in development programs partially funded by the United States.

Eritrea*

Dioc., 3; bp., 4; parishes, 121; priests, 507 (101 dioc., 406 rel); sem., 549; p.d., 3, bros., 107; srs., 999; catechists, 183; bap., 3,806; Caths., 196,000 (3.5%); tot. pop., 5,539,000.

Independent state (May 24, 1993) in northeast Africa; formerly a province of Ethiopia. Christianity was introduced in the fourth century. Population is evenly divided between Christians and Muslims. Catholics form a small minority; most of the population is Orthodox or Muslim. In 1995, two new dioceses were established, but because of three decades of civil war, the dioceses had no facilities and little staffing. In 1998 the government announced plans to take over private schools and health clinics, most of which were run by the Church. Eritrean bishops form an episcopal conference with Ethiopia, and the bishops of the two countries frequently appealed for peace during their governments' border war.

Estonia*

A.a., 1; abp., 1 (nuncio is apostolic administrator); parishes, 9; priests, 14 (12 dioc., 2 rel); sem., 1; srs., 20; bap., 66; Caths., 6,000 (.45%); tot. pop., 1,340,000.

Independent (1991) Baltic republic; capital, Tallinn. (Forcibly absorbed by the USSR in 1940, it regained independence in 1991.) Catholicism was introduced in the 11th and 12th centuries. Jurisdiction over the area was made directly subject to the Holy See in 1215. Lutheran penetration was general in the Reformation period, and Russian Orthodox influence was strong from early in the 18th century until 1917, when independence was attained. The first of several apostolic administrators was appointed in 1924. The small Catholic community was hard-hit during the 1940-91 Soviet occupation (not recognized by the Holy See or the United States). Since its independence, the small Catholic community in Estonia has worked to re-establish Catholic theology and education. In 1999 the Holy See and government of Estonia reached agreement on a number of issues, including guarantees that the Church could name its own bishops and that priests from abroad would be able to continue to work in the country.

Ethiopia*

Archd., 1; dioc., 2; v.a., 8; abp., 2; bp., 12; parishes, 297; priests, 581 (279 dioc., 302 rel.); p.d., 3; sem., 275; bros., 95; srs., 766; catechists, 2,676; bap., 27,072; Caths., 926,000 (1%); tot. pop., 87,993,000.

People's capital in northeast Africa; capital, Addis Ababa. The country was evangelized by missionaries from Egypt in the fourth century and had a bishop by about 340. Following the lead of its parent body, the Egyptian (Coptic) Church, the Church in the area succumbed to the Monophysite heresy in the sixth century. An apostolic delegation was set up in Addis Ababa in 1937 and several jurisdictions were organized, some under Vatican congregations. The northern Church jurisdictions follow the Alexandrian rite, while the southern part of the country is Latin rite. The small Church has good relations with Orthodox and Protestant Churches, all of which face the task of helping people move from a rural society to a more modern society without losing Christian identity. Although the constitution calls for religious freedom, treatment of the churches can vary in different localities.

Falkland Islands

P.a., 1; parish, 1; srs., 1; bap., 1; priest, 1; Caths., 300 (approx.) (10%); tot. pop., 3,000 (approx).

British colony off the southern tip of South America; capital, Port Stanley. The islands are called Islas Malvinas by Argentina, which also claims sovereignty.

Fiji*

Archd., 1; abp., 1; parishes, 35; priests, 133 (35 dioc., 98 rel.); p.d., sem., 55; bros., 51; srs., 140; bap., 2,000; catechists, 550; Caths., 106,000 (8%); tot. pop., 1,321,000.

Independent island group (100 inhabited) in the south-west Pacific; capital, Suva. Marist missionaries began work in 1844 after Methodism had been firmly established. An apostolic prefecture was organized in 1863. The hierarchy was established in 1966.

Finland*

Dioc., 1; bp., 1; parishes, 7; priests, 23 (13 dioc., 10 rel.); p.d., 1; sem., 14; srs., 34; bap., 250; Caths., 12,000 (.02%); tot. pop., 5,442,000.

Republic in northern Europe; capital, Helsinki. Swedes evangelized the country in the 12th century. The Reformation swept the country, resulting in the prohibition of Catholicism in 1595, general reorganization of ecclesiastical life and affairs, and dominance of the Evangelical Lutheran Church. Catholics were given religious liberty in 1781 but missionaries and conversions were forbidden by law. The first Finnish priest since the Reformation was ordained in 1903 in Paris. An apostolic vicariate for Finland was erected in 1920 (made a diocese in 1955). A law on religious liberty, enacted in 1923, banned the foundation of monasteries.

France*

Archd., 24; dioc., 72; prel., 1; ap. ex., 2; mil. ord., 1; card., 8; abp., 38; bp., 144; parishes, 15,406; priests, 18,207 (13,562 dioc., 4,645 rel.); p.d., 2,538; sem., 1,283; bros., 2,905; srs., 33,040; catechists, 53,698; bap., 290,591; Caths., 47,583,000 (75%); tot. pop., 63,556,000.

Republic in Western Europe; capital, Paris. Christianity was known around Lyons by the middle of the second century. By 250 there were 30 dioceses. The hierarchy reached a fair degree of organization by the end of the fourth century. Vandals and Franks subsequently invaded the territory and caused barbarian turmoil and doctrinal problems because of their Arianism. The Frankish nation was converted following the baptism of Clovis about 496. Christianization was complete by some time in the seventh century. From then on the Church, its leaders and people, figured in virtually every important development — religious, cultural, political and social — through the periods of the Carolingians, feudalism, the Middle Ages and monarchies to the end of the 18th century. The University of Paris became one of the intellectual centers of the 13th century. Churchmen and secular rulers were involved with developments surrounding the Avignon residence of the popes and curia from 1309 until near the end of the 14th century and with the disastrous Western Schism that followed.

Strong currents of Gallicanism and conciliarism ran through ecclesiastical and secular circles in France; the former was an ideology and movement to restrict papal control of the Church in the country, the latter sought to make the pope subservient to a general council. Calvinism entered the country about the middle of the 16th century and won a strong body of converts. Jansenism appeared in the next century, to be followed by the highly influential Enlightenment. The Revolution, which started in 1789 and was succeeded by the Napoleonic period, completely changed the status of the Church, taking a toll of numbers by persecution and defection and disenfranchising the Church in practically every way. Throughout the 19th century the Church was caught up in the whirl of imperial and republican developments and was made the victim of official hostility, popular indifference and liberal opposition. In the 20th century, the Church struggled with problems involving the heritage of the Revolution and its aftermath. In the 1990s, French bishops fought a racist backlash that resulted from large-scale emigration from Africa. Pope Benedict XVI visited in Sept. 2008.

Gabon*

Archd., 1; dioc., 4; p.a., 1; abp., 1; bp., 4; parishes, 70; priests, 171 (89 dioc., 82 rel.); p.d., 2; sem., 185; bros., 43; srs., 186; catechists, 2,242; bap., 12,044; Caths., 823,000 (51%); tot. pop., 1,611,000.

Republic on the west coast of central Africa; capital Libreville. Sporadic missionary effort took place before 1881 when effective evangelization began. The hierarchy was established in 1955. In 1993, Gabon's president defeated a Catholic priest in presidential elections. In the late 1990s, the government and the Holy See signed an agreement setting out the rights of the Church in society.

Gambia*

Dioc., 1; bp., 3; parishes, 39; priests, 26 (16 dioc., 10 rel.); sem., 9; bros., 1; srs., 57; bap., 1,076; Caths., 43,000 (2.2%); tot. pop., 1,980,000.

Republic (1970) on the northwestern coast of Africa; capital, Banjui. Christianity was introduced by Portuguese explorers in the 15th century; effective evangelization began in 1822. The country was under the jurisdiction of an apostolic vicariate until 1931. The hierarchy was established in 1957.

Georgia*

A.a., 1; parishes, 31; abp., 1; bp., 1; priests, 24 (13 dioc., 11 rel); sem., 12; brs. 4; srs., 40; bap 112; Caths., 110,000 (2.4%); tot. pop., 4,491,000.

Independent (1991) state in the Caucasus; former Soviet republic; capital, Tbilisi. Christianity came to the area under Roman influence and, according to tradition, was spread through the efforts of St. Nino (or Christiana), a maiden who was brought as a captive to the country and is venerated as its apostle. The apostolic administration of the Caucasus (with seat in Georgia) was established in December 1993 for Latin-rite Catholics of Armenia, Azerbaijan and Georgia. Chaldean- and Armenian-rite Catholics also are present. Differences between Catholicism and Orthodoxy often are blurred on the parish level. The Catholic Church and the Armenian Orthodox Church have been unable to secure the return of Churches closed during the Soviet period, many of which were later given to the Georgian Orthodox Church. Early in the 21st century, many denominations, including Catholics, reported attacks and harassment from Orthodox mobs.

Germany*

Archd., 7; dioc., 20; ap. ex., 1; mil. ord., 1; card., 9; abp., 9; bp., 100; parishes, 11,157; priests, 17,007 (12,857 dioc., 4,150 rel.); p.d., 3,118; sem., 1,076; bros., 1,515; srs., 26,085; catechists, 9,345; bap., 167,704; Caths., 25,177,000 (30.7%); tot. pop., 81,932,000.

Country in northern Europe; capital, Berlin. From 1949-90 it was partitioned into the Communist German Democratic Republic in the East (capital, East Berlin) and the German Federal Republic in the West (capital, Bonn). Christianity was introduced in the third century, if not earlier. Trier, which became a center for missionary activity, had a bishop by 400. Visigoth invaders introduced Arianism in the fifth century but were converted in the seventh century by the East Franks, Celtic and other missionaries. St. Boniface, the apostle of Germany, established real ecclesiastical organization in the eighth century.

Beginning in the Carolingian period, bishops began to act in dual roles as pastors and rulers, a state of affairs that inevitably led to confusion and conflict in Church-state relations and perplexing problems of investiture. The Church developed strength and vitality through the Middle Ages but succumbed to abuses that antedated and prepared the ground for the Reformation. Martin Luther's actions from 1517 made Germany a confessional battleground. Religious strife continued until the conclusion of the Peace of Westphalia at the end of the Thirty Years' War in 1648. Nearly a century earlier the Peace of Augsburg (1555) had been designed, without success, to assure a degree of tranquility by recognizing the legitimacy of different religious confessions in different states, depending on the decisions of princes. The implicit principle that princes should control the churches emerged in practice into the absolutism and Josephinism of subsequent years. St. Peter Canisius and his fellow Jesuits spearheaded a Counter Reformation in the second half of the 16th century. Before the end of the century, however, 70 percent of the population of north and central Germany were Lutheran. Calvinism also had established a strong presence.

The Church suffered some impoverishment as a result of shifting boundaries and the secularization of property shortly after 1800. It came under direct attack in the Kulturkampf of the 1870s but helped to generate the opposition that resulted in a dampening of the campaign of Bismarck against it. Despite action by Catholics on the social front and other developments, discrimination against the Church spilled over into the 20th century and lasted beyond World War I. Catholics in politics struggled with others to pull the country through numerous postwar crises. The dissolution of the Center Party, agreed to by the bishops in 1933 without awareness of the ultimate consequences, contributed in part to the rise of Hitler to supreme power. Church officials protested the Nazi anti-Church and anti-Semitic actions, but to no avail.

After World War II East Germany, compelled to com munism under Soviet domination, initiated a program of control and repression of the Church. The regime eliminated religious schools, curtailed freedom for religious instruction and formation, and restricted the religious press. Beginning in the mid-1950s, the communists substituted youth initiation and Communist ceremonies for many sacraments. Bishops were generally forbidden to travel outside the Republic. The number of priests decreased, partly because of reduced seminary enrollments ordered by the East German government.

The official reunification of Germany took place Oct. 3, 1990, and the separate episcopal conferences were merged to form one conference in November. During the 1990s, the united German bishops fought against introduction of the former East Germany's more liberal abortion law. When a high-court decision allowed a woman to obtain an abortion after visiting a state-approved counseling center and obtaining proof she had been counseled, German Church leaders searched for a compromise position, since they ran more than 250 such centers. In 1999, Pope John Paul II asked the German bishops to include a line on the proof-of-counseling certificate that said it could not be used for abortion, but some German states said they would not consider the line valid. Eventually, most of the bishops withdrew their centers from the system. As the 20th century came to an end, German Church leaders also spoke on behalf of immigrants, refugees and asylum seekers and against a surge in racist and anti-Semitic attacks. Early in the 21st century, a change in the country's tax rate and growing unemployment led to a severe budget crisis for many German dioceses. Recent sexual abuse cases caused a major scandal in the country, compounded by the controversial resignation of Bp. Walter Mixa of Ausgburg. Pope Benedict XVI visited Germany in 2011 in his first official trip as pope.

Ghana*

Archd., 4; dioc., 15; p.a.; Card., 1; abp., 8; bp., 15; parishes, 503; priests, 1,421 (1,160 dioc., 261 rel.); p.d., 2; sem., 768; bros., 226; srs., 1,027; catechists, 6,342; bap., 57,580; Caths., 3,292,000 (13%); tot. pop., 25,111,000.

Republic on the western coast of Africa; capital, Accra. Priests visited the country in 1482, 11 years after discovery by the Portuguese, but missionary effort, hindered by the slave trade and other factors, was slight until 1880 when systematic evangelization began. An apostolic prefecture was set up in 1879. The hierarchy was established in 1950.

In 1985, the government shut down the Church's newspaper, *The Catholic Standard*, for criticizing the government; in 1989 the government ordered religious bodies to register. However, in 1992 the paper resumed publication, and five new dioceses were established in 1995. In 1997 the bishops issued a pastoral letter urging an end to political corruption and ethnic tension.

Gibraltar

Dioc., 1; bp., 2; parishes, 5; priests, 12 (12 dioc.); sem., 1; bros., 2; srs., 5; bap., 354; Caths., 23,000 (79%); tot. pop., 29,000.

British dependency on the tip of the Spanish Peninsula on the Mediterranean. Evangelization took place after the Moors were driven out near the end of the 15th century. The Church was hindered by the British, who acquired the colony in 1713. Most of the Catholics were, and are, Spanish and Italian immigrants and their descendants. An apostolic vicariate was organized in 1817. The diocese was erected in 1910.

Great Britain

(See separate entries for **England, Scotland, Wales, Northern Ireland.**)

Greece*

Archd., 4; dioc., 4; v.a., 1; ap. ex., 2; abp., 4; bp., 4; parishes, 81; priests, 100 (61 dioc., 39 rel.); p.d., 3; sem., 3; bros., 28; srs., 118; bap., 686; Caths., 140,000 (1.2%); tot. pop., 11,290,000.

Republic in southeastern Europe on the Balkan

Peninsula; capital, Athens. St. Paul preached the Gospel at Athens and Corinth on his second missionary journey and visited the country again on his third tour. Other Apostles may have passed through. Two bishops from Greece attended the First Council of Nicaea. After the division of the Roman Empire, the Church remained Eastern in rite and later broke ties with Rome as a result of the schism of 1054. A Latin-rite jurisdiction was set up during the period of the Latin Empire of Constantinople, 1204-61, but crumbled afterward. Unity efforts of the Council of Florence had poor results and failed to save the Byzantine Empire from conquest by the Ottoman Empire in 1453. The country now has Latin, Byzantine and Armenian rites. The Greek Orthodox Church is predominant. The Catholic Church continues to work to obtain full legal rights. In May 2001, during the first papal visit to Greece since the eighth century, Pope John Paul II apologized for past wrongs against the Orthodox, including the 13th-century sack of Constantinople.

Greenland

(Statistics for Greenland are included in **Denmark**)

Grenada*

Dioc., 1; bp., 2; parishes, 20; priests, 32 (10 dioc., 22 rel.); p.d., 4; sem., 3; bros., 4; srs., 33; catechists, 102; bap., 373; Caths., 46,000 (45%); tot. pop., 102,000.

Independent island state in the West Indies; capital, St. George's.

Guam

Archd., 1; abp., 1; parishes, 24; priests, 49 (39 dioc., 10 rel.); p.d., 21; sem., 37; srs., 108; bap., 1,953; catechists, 471; Caths., 144,000 (85%); tot. pop., 169,000.

Outlying area of U.S. in the southwest Pacific; capital, Agana. The first Mass was offered in the Mariana Islands in 1521. The islands were evangelized by the Jesuits, from 1668, and other missionaries. The first Micronesian bishop was ordained in 1970. The Agana Diocese, which had been a suffragan of San Francisco, was made a metropolitan see in 1984.

Guatemala*

Archd., 2; dioc., 10; prel., 1; v.a., 2; abp., 3; bp., 18; parishes, 486; priests, 1,178 (636 dioc., 542 rel.); p.d., 10; sem., 483; bros., 216; srs., 2,733; catechists, 53,970; bap., 163,605; Caths. 12,039,000 (80%); tot. pop. 15,082,000.

Republic in Central America; capital, Guatemala City. Evangelization dates from the beginning of Spanish occupation in 1524. The first diocese, for all Spanish American territories administered by the captaincy general of Guatemala, was established in 1534. The country became independent in 1839, following annexation to Mexico in 1821, secession in 1823 and membership in the Central American Federation from 1825. In 1870, a government installed by a liberal revolution repudiated the concordat of 1853 and took active measures against the Church. Separation of Church and state was decreed; religious orders were suppressed and their property seized; priests and religious were exiled; schools were secularized. Full freedom was subsequently granted.

During the nation's 36-year civil war, which ended in 1996, Church officials spoke out against atrocities and illegal drafting of youths and often were persecuted. The Guatemala City archbishop's human rights office, established after decades of war, was one of the few agencies able to document abuses. Bishops participated in the country's peace process, at times withdrawing in an effort to force government and guerrilla leaders back to the table.

After the war, the archbishop's human rights office began an extensive project to help document abuses during the war. Two days after the report was released in April 1998, Aux. Bp. Juan Gerardi Conedera of Guatemala City, who headed the project, was murdered. In 2001, a priest who lived with the bishop and three military officers were convicted of involvement in the murder, but said they would appeal the decision. One of the three officers was killed in a Guatemala City prison riot in 2003. Church leaders mobilized to help Guatemalans after mudslides and flooding from Hurricane Stan in 2005 made it the country's worst natural disaster in nearly 30 years.

Guinea*

Archd., 1; dioc., 2; Card., 1; abp. 2; bp., 3; parishes, 64; priests, 137 (115 dioc., 22 rel.); sem., 68; bros., 27; srs., 76; catechists, 519; bap., 2,385; Caths., 253,000 (2.3%); tot. pop., 11,115,000.

Republic on the west coast of Africa; capital, Conakry. Occasional missionary work followed exploration by the Portuguese about the middle of the 15th century; organized effort dates from 1877. The hierarchy was established in 1955. Following independence from France in 1958, Catholic schools were nationalized, youth organizations banned and missionaries restricted. Foreign missionaries were expelled in 1967. Abp. Raymond-Marie Tchidimbo of Conakry, sentenced to life imprisonment in 1971 on a charge of conspiring to overthrow the government, was released in August 1979; he resigned his see. Private schools, suppressed by the government for more than 20 years, again were authorized in 1984.

Guinea-Bissau*

Dioc., 2; bp., 2; parishes, 33; priests, 88 (20 dioc., 68 rel.); sem., 32; bros., 15; srs., 144; bap., 1,817; catechists, 1,150; Caths., 204,000 (12.8%); tot. pop., 1,594,000.

Independent state on the west coast of Africa; capital, Bissau. Catholicism was introduced in the second half of the 15th century but limited missionary work, hampered by the slave trade, had meager results. Missionary work in the 20th century began in 1933. An apostolic prefecture was made a diocese in 1977. In 1998, Bp. Settimio Ferrazzetta of Bissau worked to mediate a crisis between the government and military leaders.

Guyana*

Dioc., 1; bp., 2; parishes, 24; priests, 31 (4 dioc., 27 rel.); p.d., 3; sem., 8; bros., 3; srs., 56; catechists, 580; bap., 1,022; Caths., 63,000 (7.9%); tot. pop., 796,000.

Republic on the north coast of South America; capital, Georgetown. In 1899 the Catholic Church and other churches were given equal status with the Church of England and the Church of Scotland. Most of the Catholics are Portuguese. The Georgetown Diocese was established in 1956, 10 years before Guyana became independent of England. The first indigenous bishop was appointed in 1971. Schools were nationalized in 1976. In the late 1970s and in the 1980s, *The Catholic Standard* newspaper was cited by the Inter-American Press Association as the "sole independent voice" in Guyana.

Haiti*

Archd., 2; dioc., 8; abp., 4; bp., 12; parishes, 397; priests,

899 (578 dioc., 321 rel.); p.d., 3; sem., 506; bros., 332; srs., 2,006; catechists, 3,289; bap., 117,171; Caths., 7,443,000 (74%); tot. pop., 10,413,000.

Caribbean republic on the western third of Hispaniola adjacent to the Dominican Republic; capital, Port-au-Prince. Evangelization followed discovery by Columbus in 1492. Capuchins and Jesuits did most of the missionary work in the 18th century. From 1804, when independence was declared, until 1860, the country was in schism. Relations were regularized by a concordat concluded in 1860, when an archdiocese and four dioceses were established.

In the second half of the 20th century, the Church worked to develop the small nation, considered among the poorest in the Western Hemisphere. In the 1980s and 1990s, priests and religious often were targets of political violence, which resulted in a series of coups. The Church was sometimes seen as the lone voice for the people and, at times, was seen as backing the government. A Salesian priest, Fr. Jean-Bertrand Aristide, known for his fiery, anti-government sermons, won the December 1990 president election, considered the first genuinely democratic vote in Haitian history. A 1991 military coup forced him into exile for three years and resulted in an international trade embargo against Haiti. Aristide was laicized by the Vatican and married in January 1996. In the late 1990s, the Church continued its service in the social field through programs in basic literacy and operation of schools and health facilities. On Jan. 12, 2010, a 7.0 magnitude earthquake struck Haiti and devastated Port-au-Prince. More than 150,000 people were killed, with exact numbers still unknown. Bp. Chibly Langlois of Les Cayes was named the first Haitian Cardinal in 2014.

Honduras*

Archd., 1; dioc., 8; card., 1; abp., 1; bp., 12; parishes, 224; priests, 461 (276 dioc., 185 rel.); sem., 189; bros., 33; srs., 916; catechists, 19,514; bap., 60,915; Caths., 6,768,000 (80.7%); tot. pop., 8,388,000.

Republic in Central America; capital, Tegucigalpa. Evangelization preceded establishment of the first diocese in the 16th century. Under Spanish rule and after independence from 1823, the Church held a favored position until 1880, when equal legal status was given to all religions. Harassment of priests and nuns working among indigenous peasants and Salvadoran refugees was reported during the years of Central American civil unrest in the late 20th century. In 1998 Hurricane Mitch killed more than 6,000 Hondurans and forced more than 2 million in the country to evacuate their homes. The Church took a lead role in post-hurricane relief and development efforts.

Hungary*

Archd., 4; dioc., 9; abb., 1; ap. ex., 1; mil. ord. 1; card., 2; abp., 8; bp., 23; parishes, 2,184; priests, 2,205 (1,792 dioc., 413 rel.); p.d., 118; sem., 327; bros., 72; srs., 883; catechists, 2,926; bap., 39,116; Caths., 6,069,000 (61%); tot. pop., 9,919,000.

Republic in east central Europe; capital, Budapest. The early origins of Christianity in the country, whose territory was subject to a great deal of change, is not known. Magyars accepted Christianity about the end of the 10th century. St. Stephen I promoted its spread and helped to organize some of its historical dioceses. Bishops became influential in politics as well as in the Church.

For centuries the country served as a buffer for the Christian West against barbarians from the East, notably the Mongols in the 13th century. Hussites and Waldensians prepared the way for the Reformation, which struck at almost the same time as the Turks. The Reformation made considerable progress after 1526, resulting in the conversion of large numbers to Lutheranism and Calvinism by the end of the century. Turks repressed the Churches, Protestant as well as Catholic, during a reign of 150 years, but they managed to survive. Domination of the Church was one of the objectives of government policy during the reigns of Maria Theresa and Joseph II in the second half of the 18th century; their Josephinism affected Church-state relations until World War I.

Secularization increased in the second half of the 19th century, which also witnessed the birth of many new Catholic organizations and movements. Catholics were involved in the social chaos and anti-religious atmosphere of the years following World War I, struggling with their compatriots for religious as well as political survival.

After World War II, the communist campaign against the Church started with the disbanding of Catholic organizations in 1946. In 1948, Caritas, the Catholic charitable organization, was taken over, and all Catholic institutions were suppressed. Interference in Church administration and attempts to split the bishops preceded the arrest of Card. Jozsef Mindszenty Dec. 26, 1948, and his sentence to life imprisonment in 1949. (He was free for a few days during the unsuccessful uprising of 1956. He then took up residence at the U.S. Embassy in Budapest, where he remained until September 1971, when he was permitted to leave the country. He died in 1975 in Vienna.)

In 1950, religious orders and congregations were suppressed and 10,000 religious were interned. Several dozen priests and monks were assassinated, jailed or deported. About 4,000 priests and religious were confined in jail or concentration camps. The government sponsored a national "Progressive Catholic" Church and captive organizations for priests. Despite a 1964 agreement with the Holy See regarding episcopal appointments, bishops remained subject to government surveillance and harassment.

On Feb. 9, 1990, an accord was signed between the Holy See and Hungary re-establishing diplomatic relations. Pope John Paul II reorganized the ecclesiastical structure of the country in May 1993. In 1997, the Vatican and Hungary signed an agreement that restored some Church property confiscated under communism and provided some sources of funding for Church activities. Hungary's bishops have said social conflicts, political changes and economic strains have put new pressures on the Church.

Iceland*

Dioc., 1; bp., 1; parishes, 5; priests, 14 (4 dioc., 10 rel.); sem., 1; bros., 1; srs., 34; bap., 183; Caths., 11,000 (3.4%); tot. pop., 322,000.

Island republic between Norway and Greenland; cap ital, Rekjavik. Irish hermits were there in the eighth century. Missionaries subsequently evangelized the island and Christianity was officially accepted about 1,000. The first bishop was ordained in 1056. The Black Death had dire effects, and spiritual decline set in during the 15th century. Lutheranism was introduced from Denmark between 1537 and 1552 and made the official religion. Some Catholic missionary work was done in the 19th century. Religious freedom was granted to the few Catholics in 1874. A vicariate was erected in 1929 and was made a diocese in 1968.

India*

Patriarchate, 1 (titular of East Indies); major archbishoprics (Syro-Malabar and Syro-Malankara), 2; archd., 30; dioc., 137; Card., 7; patr., 2; abp., 41; bp., 171; parishes, 10,056; priests, 27,983 (14,703 dioc., 13,280 rel.); p.d., 33; sem., 15,329; bros., 4,282; srs., 99,330; catechists, 114,175; bap., 318,612; Caths., 19,762,000 (1.6%); tot. pop. 1,213,370,000.

Republic on the subcontinent of south central Asia; capital, New Delhi. Long-standing tradition credits the Apostle Thomas with the introduction of Christianity in the Kerala area. Evangelization followed the establishment of Portuguese posts and the conquest of Goa in 1510. Jesuits, Franciscans, Dominicans, Augustinians and members of other religious orders figured in the early missionary history. An archdio. for Goa, with two suffragan sees, was set up in 1558.

Missionaries had some difficulties with the British East India Co., which exercised virtual government control from 1757 to 1858. They also had trouble because of a conflict that developed between policies of the Portuguese government, which pressed its rights of patronage in episcopal and clerical appointments, and the Vatican Congregation for the Propagation of the Faith, which sought greater freedom of action in the same appointments. This struggle resulted in the schism of Goa between 1838 and 1857. In 1886, when the number of Catholics was estimated to be 1 million, the hierarchy for India and Ceylon was restored.

Jesuits contributed greatly to the development of Catholic education from the second half of the 19th century. A large percentage of the Catholic population is located around Goa and Kerala and farther south. The country is predominantly Hindu. Anti-conversion laws in effect in several states have had a restrictive effect on pastoral ministry and social service.

Recent years have seen tensions within the Syro-Malabar rite over liturgy and tradition. In addition, there have been tensions between the Latin-rite and Eastern-rite Catholic churches in India over the care of Catholics outside the traditional boundaries of their rites. In the late 20th and early 21st centuries, Church leaders campaigned for the rights of low-caste Indians. Religious also faced a series of attacks, including murders, by extremist Hindus who claimed they were trying to convert people to Christianity.

Indonesia*

Archd., 10; dioc., 27; mil. ord. 1; card., 1; abp., 13; bps., 34; parishes, 1,234; priests, 4,140 (1,819 dioc., 2,321 rel.); p.d., 12; sem., 3,936; bros., 1,328; srs., 9,091; catechists, 26,588; bap., 192,065; Caths., 7,534,000 (3%); tot. pop., 247,214,000.

Republic in the Malay Archipelago, consisting of some 3,000 islands; capital, Jakarta. Evangelization by the Portuguese began about 1511. St. Francis Xavier spent some 14 months in the area. Christianity was strongly rooted in some parts of the islands by 1600. Islam's rise to dominance began at this time. The Dutch East Indies Co., which gained effective control in the 17th century, banned evangelization by Catholic missionaries for some time, but Dutch secular and religious priests managed to resume the work. A vicariate of Batavia for all the Dutch East Indies was set up in 1841. About 90 percent of the population is Muslim. The hierarchy was established in 1961.

From 1981 to about 1996, Catholics and Protestants clashed more than 40 times over what Catholics perceived as Communion host desecration. At least three Protestants died from beatings by Catholics after the incidents.

In the late 1990s, as the Indonesian economy took a nose-dive, Muslim-Christian violence increased, especially in the Molucca Islands. Church leaders continued to urge calm and dialogue, and at one point a bishop sought U.N. intervention to prevent what he saw as a potential genocide of Christians. A militant Muslim group charged with inciting much of the violence disbanded in late 2002, Church leaders expressed hope for peace. The Church worked for years to help victims of the December 2004 tsunami and subsequent earthquakes and tsunamis, offering its services to people regardless of religious affiliation.

Iran*

Archd., 4; dioc., 2; abp., 4; parishes, 18; priests, 15 (8 dioc., 7 rel.); p.d., 3; sem., 3; srs., 26; bap., 41; Caths., 5,000 (.007%); tot. pop., 76,725,000.

Islamic republic (Persia until 1935) in southwestern Asia; capital, Teheran. Some of the earliest Christian communities were established in this area outside the Roman Empire. They suffered persecution in the fourth century and were then cut off from the outside world. Nestorianism was generally professed in the late fifth century. Islam became dominant after 640. Some later missionary work was attempted but without success. Religious liberty was granted in 1834, but Catholics were the victims of a massacre in 1918. Islam is the religion of perhaps 98 percent of the population. Catholics belong to the Latin, Armenian and Chaldean rites.

After Iran nationalized many Church-run social institutions in 1980, about 75 Catholic missionaries left the country, by force or by choice. In recent years, however, Iranian authorities have shown more cooperation regarding entry visas for Church personnel. Although freedom of worship is guaranteed in Iran, Church sources said Catholic activities are monitored carefully by authorities. Since Pope John Paul II and Iranian President Mohammed Khatami met in 1999, the Holy See and Iran have had several high-level diplomatic exchanges.

Iraq*

Patriarchate, 1; archd., 9; dioc., 5; ap. ex., 2; card, 1; patriarch, 1; abp., 9; bp., 3; parishes, 114; priests, 174 (123 dioc., 51 rel.); sem., 63; bros., 10; srs., 286; catechists, 784; bap., 2,565; Caths., 318,000 (1%); tot. pop., 33,913,000.

Republic in southwestern Asia; capital, Baghdad. Some of the earliest Christian communities were established in the area, whose history resembles that of Iran. Catholics belong to the Armenian, Chaldean, Latin and Syrian rites; Chaldeans are most numerous. Islam is the religion of some 90 percent of the population. Iraq's Chaldean Catholic patriarch was outspoken against the international embargo against Iraq, saying it especially hurt children and the sick. In early 2003, Vatican officials met separately with U.S. and Iraqi leaders in an effort to prevent the U.S.-led war; the Vatican embassy in Baghdad remained open throughout the conflict, and Church aid agencies treated wounded. Catholic aid organizations geared up relief efforts after the war but were frustrated by lawlessness and looting. According to estimates, the Christian population in Iraq has declined from a prewar population of 1.2 million to a current estimate of several hundred thousand. Refugee agencies said Christians, including Catholics, were targeted for persecution marked by violence, murder and restrictions on religious freedom;

some Christians in Baghdad were told to convert to Islam, pay higher taxes or leave their homes. The U.N. High Commissioner for Refugees reported over 40% of Iraqi refugees are Christian even though they represent only about 4% of Iraq's total population. After the war, Catholic leaders were among those expressing alarm at the growing number of Christians leaving the country or fleeing to northern Iraq, where Christians banded together in an effort to gain more of a political voice. 2014 brought staggering violence against Christians owing to the rise of the IS, Islamic State, including the massacre of Christians in Mosul and the Nineveh Plain.

Ireland*

Archd., 4; dioc., 22; card., 2; abp., 7; bp., 42; parishes, 1,359; priests, 4,688 (2,800 dioc., 1,888 rel.); p.d., 16; sem., 181; bros., 628; srs., 6,912; bap., 72,900 (preceding figures include **Northern Ireland**); Caths., 5,387,000 (76%); tot. 7,078,000 (population numbers include **Northern Ireland**; in **Republic of Ireland**, Catholics comprise 95% of the pop.).

Republic in the British Isles; capital, Dublin. St. Patrick, who is venerated as the apostle of Ireland, evangelized parts of the island for some years after the middle of the fifth century. Conversion of the island was not accomplished, however, until the seventh century or later. Celtic monks were the principal missionaries. The Church was organized along monastic lines at first, but a movement developed in the 11th century for the establishment of jurisdiction along episcopal lines. The Church gathered strength during the period from the Norman Conquest of England to the reign of Henry VIII despite a wide variety of rivalries, wars, and other disturbances.

Henry introduced an age of repression of the faith, which continued for many years under several of his successors. The Irish suffered from proscription of the Catholic faith, economic and social disabilities, subjection to absentee landlords and a plantation system designed to keep them from owning property, and actual persecution which took an uncertain toll of lives up until about 1714. Some penal laws remained in force until emancipation in 1829. Nearly 100 years later Ireland was divided in two, making Northern Ireland, consisting of six counties, part of the United Kingdom (1920) and giving dominion status to the Irish Free State, made up of the other 26 counties (1922). This state (Eire, in Gaelic) was proclaimed the Republic of Ireland in 1949. The Catholic Church pre dominates but religious freedom is guaranteed for all. The Irish Republic and Northern Ireland share a bishops' conference, which has worked for peace in Northern Ireland. Recent years have witnessed a decrease in vocations and growing turmoil over issues such as priestly pedophilia, divorce, and abortion. Ireland was also convulsed in 2009 and 2010 by the Murphy and Ryan reports detailing the extent of sex abuse among schools run by religious communities and the archdiocese of Dublin. Pope Benedict summoned the Irish bishops to the Vatican in early 2010 and in March 2010 issued the "Letter to the Catholics of Ireland" in which he apologized to the victims and promised reform and renewal for the Church in the country. (See **News in Depth for updates**.) In 2012, the Irish Parliament defeated by a vote of 109-20 a bill that would have expanded the availiability of abortions in the country.

Ireland, Northern

Tot. pop., 1,610,000; Catholics comprise more than one third. (Other statistics are included in **Ireland**).

Part of the United Kingdom, it consists of six of the nine counties of Ulster in the northeast corner of Ireland; capital, Belfast. Early history is given under **Ireland**.

Nationalist-unionist tensions fall primarily along Catholic-Protestant lines, with nationalists, mainly Catholics, advocating an end to British rule. Violence and terrorism began in the late 1960s and, by the late 1990s, more than 3,000 people had been killed.

On Apr. 10, 1998, the governments of the Irish Republic and Great Britain and the political parties of Northern Ireland reached an agreement known as the Good Friday agreement. Irish bishops supported it, and it was endorsed by the voters in Ireland and Northern Ireland. However, the agreement or the coalition government established as a result of the agreement was suspended several times, and Northern Ireland's bishops spoke out in support of continuing democratic structures.

For years, Catholics claimed discrimination in the workplace and harassment from the Royal Ulster Constabulary, Northern Ireland's police force that was disbanded and reformed as the Police Service of Northern Ireland. In 2002 some 40 percent of the new force was Catholic, compared to 8 percent in 2001.

Israel*

Patriarchates, 2 (Jerusalem for Latins; patriarchal vicariate for Greek-Melkites); archd., 2; ap.ex., 5; patriarch, 2; abp., 5; bp., 3; parishes, 87; priests, 408 (97 dioc., 311 rel.); p.d., 11; sem., 148; bros., 187; srs., 1,077; bap., 1,806; Caths., 266,000 (3.4%); tot. pop., 7,901,000.

Parliamentary democracy in the Middle East; capitals, Jerusalem and Tel Aviv (diplomatic). Israel was the birthplace of Christianity, the site of the first Christian communities. Some persecution was suffered in the early Christian era and again during the several hundred years of Roman control. Muslims conquered the territory in the seventh century and, except for the period of the Kingdom of Jerusalem established by Crusaders, remained in control most of the time up until World War I. The Church survived in the area, sometimes just barely, but it did not prosper greatly or show any notable increase in numbers. The British took over the protectorate of the area after World War I.

Partition into Israel for the Jews and Palestine for the Arabs was approved by the United Nations in 1947. War broke out a year later with the proclamation of the Republic of Israel. The Israelis won the war and 50 percent more territory than they had originally been ceded. War broke out again for six days in June 1967, and in October 1973.

Judaism is the faith professed by about 85 percent of the inhabitants; approximately one-third of them are considered observant. Israeli-Holy See relations improved in 1994 with the implementation of full diplomatic relations, and the Church gained legal status in 1997, although some taxation issues remained unresolved.

The Holy See repeatedly has asked for an internationally guaranteed statute to protect the sacred nature of Jerusalem, which is holy to Christians, Muslims and Jews. It has underlined that this means more than access to specific holy places and that the political and religious dimensions of Jerusalem are interrelated. During the Palestinian intifada, the Vatican and Holy Land Church leaders defended Israeli rights to live without the threat of terrorism and the Palestinians' right to a homeland, saying both would only be achieved through a negotiated settlement. Pope Francis visited in May 2014 and made a passionate plea for peace; he also called for renewed negotiations between the Israelis and Palestinians.

Italy*

Patriarchate, 1 (Venice); archd. 60 (40 are metropolitan sees); dioc., 156; prel., 3; abb., 6; mil. ord. 1; pat., 1 (Venice); card., 48; abp., 175; bps., 536 (hierarchy includes 213 residential, 15 coadjutors or auxiliaries, 126 in Curia offices, remainder in other offices or retired); parishes, 25,701; priests, 48,291 (32,619 dioc., 15,672 rel.); p.d., 4,191; sem., 5,866; bros., 3,391; srs., 86,431; catechists, 245,179; bap., 407,262; Caths., 58,049,000 (95%); tot. pop., 61,077,000.

Republic in southern Europe; capital, Rome. A Christian community was formed early in Rome, probably by the middle of the first century. St. Peter established his see there. He and St. Paul suffered death for the faith in the 60s. The early Christians were persecuted at various times, as in other parts of the empire, but the Church developed in numbers and influence, gradually spreading out from towns and cities in the center and south to rural areas and the north.

Church organization began in the second century. The Church emerged from underground in 313, with the Edict of Milan, and rose to a position of prestige and lasting influence on politics and culture until well into the 19th century. In the 1870s, the Papal States were annexed by the Kingdom of Italy. The 1929 Lateran Pacts included a treaty recognizing the Vatican as an independent state, a financial agreement by which Italy agreed to compensate the Vatican for loss of the papal states, and a concordat regulating Church-state relations. In 1984 the Vatican and Italy signed a revised concordat, reducing some of the Church's privileges and removing Catholicism as the state religion.

The Church strongly opposed Italy's abortion law in 1978 and forced a 1981 referendum on the issue. Abortion remained legal, and the Italian Church has taken a more low-profile stance. The Church has been active in social issues, including helping unprecedented numbers of illegal immigrants in the late 1990s. Church leaders have expressed concern about Italy's low birth rate.

Jamaica*

Archd., 1; dioc., 2; abp., 3; bp., 3; parishes, 61; priests, 102 (74 dioc., 28 rel.); p.d., 47; sem., 10; bros., 188; srs., 131; catechists, 480; bap., 842; Caths., 72,000 (2.7%); tot. pop., 2,708,000.

Republic in the West Indies; capital, Kingston. Franciscans and Dominicans evangelized the island from about 1512 until 1655. Missionary work was interrupted after the English took possession but was resumed by Jesuits about the turn of the 19th century. An apostolic vicariate was organized in 1837. The hierarchy was established in 1967. In the late 1990s, Church leaders spoke out against violence; more than 800 people were murdered in Jamaica in 1997 alone.

Japan*

Archd., 3; dioc., 13; abp., 6; bp., 18; parishes, 893; priests, 1,505 (525 dioc., 980 rel.); p.d., 27; sem., 132; bros., 212; srs., 5,791; catechists, 1,840; bap., 6,302; Caths., 542,000 (.4%); tot. pop., 127,606,000.

Archipelago in the northwest Pacific; capital, Tokyo. Jesuits began evangelization in the middle of the 16th century and about 300,000 converts, most of them in Kyushu,

were reported at the end of the century. The Nagasaki Martyrs were victims of persecution in 1597. Another persecution took some 4,000 lives between 1614 and 1651. Missionaries, banned for two centuries, returned about the middle of the 19th century and found Christian communities still surviving in Nagasaki and other places in Kyushu. A vicariate was organized in 1866. Religious freedom was guaranteed in 1889. The hierarchy was established in 1891. Several Japanese bishops at the 1998 Synod of Bishops for Asia said Catholicism has grown slowly in the region because the Church is too Western.

Since the 1980s, on several occasions Church leaders have apologized and asked forgiveness for the Church's complicity in the nation's aggression during the 1930s and 1940s. At the end of the 20th century, bishops and religious superiors suggested that during the 21st century the Japanese Church focus on pastoral care for migrant workers, concern for the environment and interreligious dialogue.

Japan's Catholic prime minister, Taro Aso, met with Pope Benedict XVI in a private audience at the Vatican on July 7, 2009. He is the third Catholic prime minister; the others were Hara Takashi (1918-1921) and Hosokowa Morihiro (1993-94). In March 2009, Abp. Dominique Mamberti, the Vatican secretary for relations with states, met his counterpart in Tokyo, marking the first time a Vatican foreign minister had visited the country since diplomatic relations were established in 1942. The earthquake that struck in early 2011 caused immense damage; Catholic resources were used to help the victims.

Jordan*

Archd., 1; ex. pat., 2; abp., 2; bp., 1; parishes, 65; priests, 131 (55 dioc., 76 rel.); sem., 3; bros., 9; srs., 158; bap., 877; Caths., 107,000 (1.7%); tot. pop., 6,388,000.

Constitutional monarchy in the Middle East; capital, Amman. Christianity there dates from apostolic times. Survival of the faith was threatened many times under the rule of Muslims from 636 and Ottoman Turks from 1517 to 1918, and in the Islamic Emirate of Trans-Jordan from 1918 to 1949. In the years following the creation of Israel, some 500,000 Palestinian refugees, including Christians, moved to Jordan. Islam is the state religion, but religious freedom is guaranteed for all. The Greek Melkite Archdiocese of Petra and Filadelfia is located in Jordan. Latin-rite Catholics are under the jurisdiction of the Latin Patriarchate of Jerusalem. Jordan established diplomatic relations with the Holy See in 1994. In the late 20th and especially in the early 21st centuries, an influx of Iraqi refugees strained the resources of the Jordanian Catholic community, which offered aid, including housing, counseling and schooling.

Kazakhstan

Archd. 1, dioc., 2; a.a.; 1; abp., 3; bp., 3; parishes, 68; priests, 91 (48 dioc., 43 rel.); sem., 11; bros., 9; srs., 134; bap., 596; Caths., 133,000 (0.8%); tot. pop., 16,673,000.

Independent republic (1991); formerly part of USSR; capital, Astana. About 47 percent of the population is Muslim, and about 44 percent is Orthodox. The Catholic population is mainly of German, Polish and Ukrainian origin, descendants of those deported during the Stalin regime. A Latin-rite apostolic administration was established in 1991. In 1998, the Vatican and the Kazakh government signed an agreement guaranteeing the Church legal rights. Diocesan structure was established in 1999, and the Vatican created the first archdiocese and diocese in 2003. The country had its first priestly ordinations on Kazakh soil in 2006.

Kenya*

Archd. 4; dioc., 20; v.a., 1; mil. ord., 1; card. 1; abp. 6; bp., 20; parishes, 879; priests, 2,492 (1,655 dioc., 837 rel.); p.d., 5; sem., 1,569; bros., 697; srs., 4,821; catechists, 11,785; bap., 379,371; Caths., 12,181,000 (28.7%); tot. pop., 42,436,000.

Republic in East Africa on the Indian Ocean; capital, Nairobi. Systematic evangelization by the Holy Ghost Missionaries began in 1889, nearly 40 years after the start of work by Protestant missionaries. The hierarchy was established in 1953. Three metropolitan sees were established in 1990. Kenyan Catholics were in the forefront of ministering to victims of the 1998 explosion at the U.S. Embassy in Nairobi. The Kenyan bishops have been outspoken against ethnic violence, poverty, government corruption and mismanagement, and the need for a constitutional review. In some rural areas, Church workers, including foreign missionaries, were targeted for their work with the poor.

Kiribati*

Dioc., 1; bp., 1; parishes, 22; priests, 29 (19 dioc., 10 rel.); p.d. 2; sem., 13; bros., 12; srs., 96; catechists, 220; bap., 1,894; Caths., 60,000 (54.5%); tot. pop., 110,000.

Former British colony (Gilbert Islands) in Oceania; became independent July 12, 1979; capital, Bairiki on Tarawa. French Missionaries of the Sacred Heart began work in the islands in 1888. A vicariate for the islands was organized in 1897. The hierarchy was established in 1966.

Korea, North

Tot. pop., 24,136,000. No recent Catholic statistics available; there were an estimated 100,000 Catholics reported in 1969.

Northern part of peninsula in eastern Asia; formal name Democratic People's Republic of Korea (May 1, 1948); capital, Pyongyang. See **South Korea** for history before country was divided. After liberation from Japan in 1945, the Soviet regime in the North systematically punished all religions. After the 1950-53 Korean war, Christian worship was not allowed outside of homes until 1988, when the country's one Catholic Church was built in Pyongyang. A 1999 South Korean government report said North Korea clearly restricts religious practices and churches in the North exist only for show.

Korea, South*

Archd., 3; dioc., 12; mil. ord. 1; card., 1; abp., 6; bp., 24; parishes, 1,646; priests, 4,165 (3,524 dioc., 641 rel.); sem., 1,739; p.d., 3; bros., 588; srs., 9,363; catechists, 16,451; bap., 132,837; Caths., 5,310,000 (10.5%); tot. pop., 50,345,000.

Southern part of peninsula in eastern Asia; formal name, Republic of Korea (1948); capital, Seoul. Some Catholics may have been in Korea before it became a "hermit kingdom" toward the end of the 16th century and closed its borders to foreigners. The modern introduction to Catholicism came in 1784 through lay converts. A priest arriving in the country in 1794 found 4,000 Catholics there who had never seen a priest. A vicariate was erected in 1831 but was not manned for several years thereafter. There were 15,000 Catholics by 1857. Four persecutions in the 19th century took a terrible toll; several thousand died in the last one, 1866-69. (In 1984, 103 of

these martyrs were canonized.) Freedom of religion was granted in 1883, when Korea opened its borders. During World War II, most foreign priests were arrested and expelled, seminaries were closed and churches were taken over. After liberation from Japan in 1945, the Church in the South had religious freedom. Since the 1950-53 Korean war, the Church in South Korea has flourished. Church leaders in the South have worked to alleviate famine in the North. Pope Francis visited in Aug. 2014.

Kuwait*

V.a., 1; pat. ex., 1; abp., 1; bp., 1; parishes, 4; priests, 23 (7 dioc., 16 rel.); p.d., 1; bros., 12; bap., 549; Caths., 350,000 (10.7%); tot. pop., 3,268,000.

Constitutional monarchy (sultanate or sheikdom) in southwest Asia bordering on the Persian Gulf. Remote Christian origins probably date to apostolic times. Islam is the predominant and official religion. Catholics are mostly foreign workers; the Church enjoys religious freedom.

Kyrgyzstan*

A.a., 1; parishes, 3; priests, 8 (2 dioc., 6 rel.); sem., 1; bros., 1; srs., 6; bap., 10; Caths., 1,000; tot. pop., 5,326,000.

Independent republic bordering China; former Soviet republic; capital, Bishkek (former name, Frunze). Most of the people are Sunni Muslim. Established diplomatic relations with the Holy See in August 1992; became apostolic administration in March 2006. The country received its first bishop in July 2006.

Laos

V.a., 4; bp., 3; parishes, 67; priests, 17 (17 dioc.); p.d., 1; sem., 20; srs., 93; catechists, 294; bap., 909; Caths., 46,000 (.7%); tot. pop., 6,385,000. (AD)

People's republic in southeast Asia; capital, Vientiane. Systematic evangelization by French missionaries started about 1881; earlier efforts ended in 1688. The first mission was established in 1885; an apostolic vicariate was organized in 1899. Most of the foreign missionaries were expelled following the communist takeover in 1975. Catholic schools remain banned, and the government lets foreign missionaries into the country only as "social workers." A Laotian bishop at the 1998 Synod of Bishops for Asia said religious practice was nearly normal in two of the country's four apostolic vicariates, but elsewhere was more controlled and sometimes difficult. Buddhism is the state religion.

Latvia*

Archd., 1; dioc., 3; card., 1; bp., 5; parishes, 274; priests, 149 (124 dioc., 25 rel.); p.d., 1; sem., 24; srs., 95; catechist, 327; bap., 5,763; Caths., 419,000 (20%); tot. pop., 2,103,000.

Independent (1991) Baltic republic; capital, Riga. (Forcibly absorbed by the USSR in 1940; it regained independence in 1991). Catholicism was introduced late in the 12th century. Lutheranism became the dominant religion after 1530. Catholics were free to pracice their faith during the long period of Russian control and during independence from 1918 to 1940. The relatively small Catholic community in Latvia was repressed during the 1940-91 Soviet takeover. After Latvia declared its independence, the Church began to flourish, including among people who described themselves as nonreligious. In the late 1990s, one archbishop urged the Russian government not to interfere in disputes over citizenship for the country's ethnic Russians, who make up about one-third of the country's population.

Lebanon*

Patriarchates, 3; archd., 12 (1 Armenian, 4 Maronite, 7 Greek Melkite); dioc., 8 (1 Chaldean, 6 Maronite); v.a., 1 (Latin); card., 2 (patriarch and emeritus of the Maronites); patriarchs, 4 (patriarchs of Antioch of the Maronites, Antioch of the Syrians and Cilicia of the Armenians who reside in Lebanon); abp., 24; bp., 18; parishes, 1,078; priests, 1,576 (850 dioc., 726 rel.); p.d., 34; sem., 390; bros., 168; srs., 2,543; catechists, 449; bap., 11,069; Caths., 2,138,000 (52.4%); tot. pop., 4,082,000.

Republic in the Middle East; capital, Beirut. Christianity, introduced in apostolic times, was firmly established by the end of the fourth century and has remained so despite heavy Muslim influence since early in the seventh century. The country is the center of the Maronite rite, and the presidency is reserved for a Maronite Catholic. In the 1980s, the country was torn by violence and often heavy fighting among rival political-religious factions drawn along Christian-Muslim lines. A 1995 Synod of Bishops for Lebanon provoked controversy by directly criticizing Israeli occupation of southern Lebanon and Syria's continued deployment of troops in the area. After Syria withdrew the majority of its troops in 2005, Lebanon's bishops were outspoken in calling for free and fair elections. The Catholic Church has multiple rites in Lebanon and has been seen as influential with politicians.

Lesotho*

Archd., 1; dioc., 3; abp., 1; bp., 3; parishes, 95; priests, 249 (92 dioc., 157 rel.); sem., 70; bros., 26; srs., 624; catechists, 1,194; bap., 15,211; Caths., 1,280,000 (54.5%); tot. pop., 2,348,000.

Constitutional monarchy, an enclave in the southeastern part of South Africa; capital, Maseru. Oblates of Mary Immaculate, the first Catholic missionaries in the area, started evangelization in 1862. Fr. Joseph Gerard, beatified in 1988, worked 10 years before he made his first conversion. An apostolic prefecture was organized in 1894. The hierarchy was established in 1951. Under the military government of the late 1980s, Lesotho's Catholics pressed for democratic reforms. In the 1990s, they gave special pastoral care to families whose breadwinners had to travel to South Africa to work, often for weeks at a time.

Liberia*

Archd., 1; dioc., 2; abp., 1; bp., 2; parishes, 56; priests, 63 (42 dioc., 21 rel.); sem., 44; bros., 14; srs., 67; catechists, 207; bap. 1,784; Caths., 314,000 (8%); tot. pop., 3,917,000.

Republic in West Africa; capital, Monrovia. Missionary work and influence, dating intermittently from the 16th century, were slight before the Society of African Missions undertook evangelization in 1906. The hierarchy was established in 1982. Fighting within the country, which began in 1989, culminated in 1996 and resulted in the evacuation of most Church workers and the archbishop of Monrovia. The war claimed the lives of 150,000 and made refugees of or displaced another million. Most Church institutions in Monrovia were destroyed. Monrovia Archbp. Michael Francis was among leaders calling for U.S.-led intervention to quell chaos in the country in mid-2003.

Libya*

V.a., 3; p.a.; bp., 2; parishes, 7; priests, 14 (2 dioc., 13 rel.); srs., 62; bap., 85; Caths., 56,000 (0.75%);

tot. pop., 7,458,000.

Arab state in North Africa; capital, Tripoli. Christianity was probably preached in the area at an early date but was overcome by the spread of Islam from the 630s. Islamization was complete by 1067, and there has been no Christian influence since then. Almost all Catholics are foreign workers. Islam is the state religion. After implementation of a U.N. embargo against the country in 1992, the government removed most limitations on entry of Catholic religious orders, especially health care workers. Libya established diplomatic relations with the Holy See in 1997. Vatican officials called for peace in the face of the country's severe civil upheaval in 2011, and Christians have been under attack in the chaotic political climate that followed the fall and execution of Muammar Qadafi.

Liechtenstein*

Archd. 1; abp., 1; parishes, 10; priests, 35 (24 dioc., 11 rel); sem., 8; srs., 52; bap., 298; Caths., 28,000 (75.6%); tot. pop., 37,000.

Constitutional monarchy in central Europe; capital, Vaduz. Christianity in the country dates from the fourth century. The Reformation had hardly any influence in the country. Catholicism is the state religion, but religious freedom for all is guaranteed by law.

Lithuania*

Archd., 2; dioc., 5; mil. ord., 1; card., 1; abp., 1; bp., 10; parishes, 712; priests, 835 (729 dioc., 106 rel.); sem., 94; bros., 25; srs., 633; catechists, 1,231; bap., 29,946; Caths., 2,701,000 (78%); tot. pop., 3,455,000.

Baltic republic forcibly absorbed and under Soviet domination from 1940; regained independence, 1991; capital, Vilnius. Catholicism was introduced in 1251 and a short-lived diocese was established by 1260. Effective evangelization took place between 1387 and 1417, when Catholicism became the state religion. Efforts of czars to "russify" the Church between 1795 and 1918 were strongly resisted. Concordat relations with the Vatican were established in 1927, nine years after independence from Russia and 13 years before Russia annexed Lithuania. The Russians closed convents and seminaries; in Kaunas, men needed government approval to attend the seminary. Priests were restricted in pastoral ministry and subject to appointment by government officials; no religious services were allowed outside churches; religious press and instruction were banned. Some bishops and hundreds of priests and laity were imprisoned or detained in Siberia between 1945 and 1955. Two bishops — Vincentas Sladkevicius and Julijonas Steponavicius — were forbidden to act as bishops and relegated to remote parishes in 1957 and 1961, respectively. Despite such conditions, a vigorous underground Church flourished in Lithuania.

In the 1980s, government pressure eased, and some bishops were allowed to return to their dioceses. In 1989, Pope John Paul II appointed bishops in all six Lithuanian dioceses. The Church strongly supported the 1990 independence movement, and Lithuanian independence leaders urged young men to desert the Russian army and seek sanctuary in churches. However, communist rule had nearly destroyed the Church's infrastructure. In 2000 the Church and government signed a series of agreements regularizing the Church's position.

Luxembourg*

Archd., 1; abp., 2; parishes, 275; priests, 207 (151 dioc.,

56 rel.); p.d., 6; sem., 5; bros., 21; srs., 566; bap., 2,641; Caths. 411,000 (76.5%); tot. pop., 537,000.

Constitutional monarchy in Western Europe; capital, Luxembourg. Christianity, introduced in the fifth and sixth centuries, was firmly established by the end of the eighth century. A full-scale parish system was in existence in the ninth century. Monastic influence was strong until the Reformation, which had minimal influence in the country. The Church experienced some adverse influence from the currents of the French Revolution. In recent years, the Church has restructured its adult formation program to involve more lay workers.

Macedonia*

Dioc., 1; bp., 2; parishes, 9; priests, 21 (14 dioc., 7 rel.); sem., 13; srs., 31; bap., 82; Caths., 15,000 (.6%); tot. pop., 2,350,000.

Former Yugoslav Republic of Macedonia; declared independence in 1992; capital, Skopje. The Diocese of Skopje-Prizren includes the Yugoslav province of Kosovo, so the Macedonian Church helped with ethnic Albanians during the period of ethnic cleansing by Serb forces and retaliatory NATO air strikes.

Madagascar*

Archd., 5; dioc., 16; abp., 8; bp., 24; parishes, 328; priests, 1,529 (725 dioc., 804 rel.); p.d., 2; sem., 1,087; bros., 551; srs., 4,509; catechists, 13,874; bap., 167,197; Caths., 6,752,000 (30%); tot. pop. 21,265,000.

Republic (Malagasy Republic) off the eastern coast of Africa; capital, Antananarivo. Missionary efforts were gener ally fruitless from early in the 16th century until the Jesuits were permitted to start open evangelization about 1845. An apostolic prefecture was set up in 1850 and an apostolic vicariate in the North was under the charge of the Holy Ghost Fathers in 1898. There were 100,000 Catholics by 1900. The first indigenous bishop was ordained in 1936. The hierarchy was established in 1955. In the late 1980s and early 1990s, the Church joined opposition calls for renewal of social institutions. Today, the Church in Madagascar runs hundreds of schools and dozens of orphanages and is active in the island's social justice concerns; some consider it the largest landowner, after the government.

Malawi*

Archd., 2; dioc., 6; abp., 1; bp., 11 parishes, 149; priests, 443 (323 dioc., 120 rel.); sem., 327; bros., 70; srs., 898; catechists, 2,240; bap., 119,361; Caths., 5,060,000 (32.6%); tot. pop., 15,531,000.

Republic in the interior of East Africa; capital, Lilongwe. Missionary work, begun by Jesuits in the late 16th and early 17th centuries, was generally ineffective until the end of the 19th century. The Missionaries of Africa (White Fathers) arrived in 1889 and later were joined by others. A vicariate was set up in 1897. The hierarchy was established in 1959. In the late 1980s, the Church in Malawi helped hundreds of thousands of refugees from the war in Mozambique. Malawi's churches, especially the Catholic Church, was instrumental in bringing about the downfall of President Hastings Kamuzu Banda, who ruled for 30 years. A 1992 bishops' pastoral letter criticized Banda's rule and the nation's poverty and galvanized Malawians into pro-democracy protests. Banda responded by summoning the country's bishops, seizing copies of the letter and expelling an Irish member of the Malawi hierarchy. Western donors called off aid, and in 1994 Banda was forced to call multi-party elections, which he

lost. In 2002, Church officials were outspoken against plans by Banda's successor, President Bakili Muluzi, to seek a third term of office; Church officials said they were threatened and attacked for that criticism.

Malaysia

Archd., 3; dioc., 6; abp., 6; bp., 8; parishes, 168; priests, 270 (207 dioc., 63 rel.); p.d., 10; sem., 68; bros., 81; srs., 509; catechists, 2,812; bap., 19,289; Caths., 1,095,000 (3.7%); tot. pop., 29,337,000. (AD)

Parliamentary democracy and elective monarchy in Southeast Asia; capital, Kuala Lumpur. Christianity, introduced by Portuguese colonists about 1511, was confined almost exclusively to Malacca until late in the 18th century. The effectiveness of evangelization increased from then on because of the recruitment and training of indigenous clergy. Singapore (see separate entry), founded in 1819, became a center for missionary work. Effective evangelization in Sabah and Sarawak began in the second half of the 19th century. The hierarchy was established in 1973. In accordance with government wishes for Bahasa Malaysia to be the national language, the Church has tried to introduce it into its liturgies. For more than a decade, Church leaders campaigned against the Internal Security Act, which allows renewable 30-day detentions without trial. Proselytizing Muslims is illegal, but the government allows conversions from other religions. In 2011, Malaysia normalized relations with the Holy See.

Maldives

Republic, an archipelago 400 miles southwest of India and Ceylon; capital, Male. No serious attempt was ever made to evangelize the area, which is completely Muslim. Population, 310,000.

Mali*

Archd., 1; dioc., 5; abp., 1; bp., 5; parishes, 43; priests, 177 (117 dioc., 60 rel.); sem., 72; bros., 14; srs., 270; catechists, 1,098; bap., 4,034; Caths., 220,000 (1.3%); tot. pop., 16,570,000.

Republic, inland in western Africa; capital, Bamako. Catholicism was introduced late in the second half of the 19th century. Missionary work made little progress in the midst of the predominantly Muslim population. A vicariate was set up in 1921. The hierarchy was established in 1955. In recent years, the Church has promoted the role of women in society. Catholics have cordial relations with Muslims.

Malta*

Archd., 1; dioc., 1; card., 1; abp., 6; bp., 4; parishes, 85; priests, 794 (431 dioc., 363 rel.); sem., 83; bros., 74; srs., 977; catechists, 11,218; bap., 3,105; Caths., 408,000 (92%); tot. pop., 444,000.

Republic south of Sicily; capital, Valletta. Catacombs and inscriptions are evidence of the early introduction of Christianity. St. Paul was shipwrecked on Malta in 60. Saracens controlled the islands from 870 to 1090, a period of difficulty for the Church. The line of bishops extends from 1090 to the present. Late in the 20th century, Church-state conflict developed over passage of government-sponsored legislation affecting Catholic schools and Church-owned property. An agreement reached in 1985 ended the dispute. An influx of several thousand African migrants early in the 21st century strained Maltese hospitality, and Jesuit priests were targeted with arson because of their advocacy for the groups. Pope Benedict XVI visited in April 2010.

Marshall Islands*

P.a., 1; parishes, 4; priests, 6 (5 dioc., 1 rel.); p.d., 1; sem., 2; brs., 1; srs., 12; bap., 211; Caths., 5,000 (8.8%); tot. pop., 57,000.

Island republic in central Pacific Ocean; capital, Majura. Formerly administered by United States as part of U.N. Trust Territory of the Pacific; independent nation, 1991. An apostolic prefecture was erected May 25, 1993 (formerly part of Carolines-Marshall Diocese), with Fr. James Gould, a U.S. Jesuit, as its first apostolic prefect.

Mauritania*

Dioc., 1; bp., 1; parishes, 6; priests, 12 (3 dioc., 9 rel.); brs. 1; srs., 36; sem., 2; bap., 34; Caths., 5,000 (.14%); tot. pop., 3,637,000. (AD)

Islamic republic on the northwest coast of Africa; capital, Nouakchott. With few exceptions, the Catholics in the country are foreign workers. At the 1994 Synod of Bishops for Africa, a bishop from Mauritania reported increasing problems with fundamentalist Muslims, but cautioned Church leaders against generalizing about Muslims.

Mauritius*

Dioc., 1; v.a., 1; bp., 2; parishes, 51; priests, 101 (52 dioc., 49 rel.); sem., 12; bros., 25; srs., 225; catechists, 1,509; bap., 5,520; Caths., 348,000 (26%); tot. pop., 1,291,000.

Island republic in the Indian Ocean; capital, Port Louis. Catholicism was introduced by Vincentians in 1722. Port Louis, made a vicariate in 1819 and a diocese in 1847, was a jumping-off point for missionaries to Australia, Madagascar and South Africa. During a 1989 visit to Mauritius, Pope John Paul II warned against sins that accompanied its rapid economic development and booming tourism industry.

Mexico*

(See **Catholic Church in Mexico**, p. 449; see also **Statistics of the Church in Mexico**, p. 455.)

Micronesia*

Dioc., 1; bp., 1; parishes, 26; priests, 19 (9 dioc., 10 rel.); p.d., 40; sem., 10; bros. 1; srs., 55; catechists, 541; bap., 1,604; Caths., 76,000 (59%); tot. pop., 129,000.

Federated States of Micronesia (Caroline archipel ago) in southwest Pacific; capital, Palikir; former U.N. trust territory under U.S. administration; became independent nation September 1991. Effective evangelization began in the late 1880s. The government established diplomatic relations with the Holy See in 1994.

Moldova*

Dioc., 1; bp., 1; parishes, 17; priests, 34 (17 dioc., 17 rel.); p.d., 2; sem., 11; bros., 2; srs., 40; bap., 68; Caths., 20,000 (.6%); tot. pop., 3,560,000.

Independent republic, former constituent republic of the USSR; capital, Kishinev. The majority of people belong to the Orthodox Church. Catholics are mostly of Polish or German descent.

Monaco*

Archd., 1; abp., 1; parishes, 6; priests, 21 (15 dioc., 6 rel.); p.d., 3; sem., 2; srs., 9; bap., 176; Caths., 30,000 (90%); tot. pop., 36,000.

Constitutional monarchy, an enclave on the Mediterranean coast of France; capital, Monaco. Christianity was introduced before 1000. Catholicism is the official religion but religious freedom is guaranteed for all.

Mongolia*

Bp., 1; parishes, 4; priests, 20 (5 dioc., 20 rel.); sem., 4; bros., 6; srs., 58; bap., 118; Caths., 1,000 (.04%); tot. pop., 2,804,000.

Republic in north central Asia; formerly under com munist control; capital, Ulan Bator. Christianity was introduced by Oriental Orthodox. Some Franciscans were in the country in the 13th and 14th centuries, en route to China. Freedom of worship is guaranteed under the new constitution, which went into effect in 1992. The government established relations with the Holy See in 1992 and indicated that missionaries would be welcome to help rebuild the country. The first Catholic parish was established in 1994, and by 1997 the Church had extended its work beyond the capital. In 2003 a missionary from the Philippines became Mongolia's first bishop.

Montenegro

Archd., 1, Dioc. 1; abp., 1; bp., 1; parishes, 44; priests, 37 (25 dioc., 12 rel.); sem., 2; brs. 1; srs., 150; bap., 241; Caths., 22,000 (3%); tot. pop., 738,000.

Independent nation (July 2006) in southeastern Europe; formerly part of Yugoslavia and Serbia and Montenegro; capital Podgorica. Church history coincides with much of Serbia. Montenegro and the Vatican announced diplomatic ties in December 2006.

Morocco*

Archd., 2; abp., 4; bp., 14; parishes, 36; priests, 42 (13 dioc., 29 rel.); bros., 12; srs., 222; bap., 58; Caths., 23,000 (.07%); tot. pop., 32,597,000.

Constitutional monarchy in North Africa; capital, Rabat. Christianity was known in the area by the end of the third century. Bishops from Morocco attended a council at Carthage in 484. Catholic life survived under Visigoth and, from 700, Arab rule; later it became subject to influence from the Spanish, Portuguese and French. Islam is the state religion. The hierarchy was established in 1955.

Mozambique*

Archd., 3; dioc., 9; card., 1; abp. 4; bp., 13; parishes, 308; priests, 641 (254 dioc., 387 rel.); p.d. 2, sem., 479; bros., 109; srs., 1,165; catechists, 42,620; bap., 114,704; Caths., 6,056,000 (24.3%); tot. pop., 24,898,000. (AD)

Republic in southeast Africa; capital, Maputo. Christianity was introduced by Portuguese Jesuits about the middle of the 16th century. Evangelization continued from then until the 18th century, when it went into decline largely because of the Portuguese government's expulsion of the Jesuits. Conditions worsened in the 1830s, improved after 1881, but deteriorated again during the anticlerical period from 1910 to 1925.

Conditions improved in 1940, the year Portugal concluded a new concordat with the Holy See and the hierarchy was established. Missionaries' outspoken criticism of Portuguese policies in Mozambique resulted in Church-state tensions in the years immediately preceding independence. The first two indigenous bishops were ordained Mar. 9, 1975. Two ecclesiastical provinces were established in 1984. Mozambican bishops and members of the Rome-based Sant' Egidio Community were official mediators in the talks that ended 16 years of civil war in 1992. Since then, Church participation has flourished, with high attendance at Mass, a boom in vocations and active catechists at the parish level.

Myanmar

Archd., 3; dioc., 13; abp., 4; bp., 19; parishes, 358; priests, 793 (714 dioc., 79 rel.); sem., 393; bros., 139; srs., 1,819; catechists, 3,180; bap., 17,456; Caths., 675,000 (1.1%); tot. pop., 60,976,000. (AD)

Socialist republic in Southeast Asia, formerly Burma; name changed to Myanmar in 1989; capital, Yangon (Rangoon). Christianity was introduced about 1500. Small-scale evangelization had limited results from the middle of the 16th century until the 1850s, when effective organization of the Church began. The hierarchy was established in 1955. Buddhism was declared the state religion in 1961, but the state is now officially secular. In 1965, Church schools and hospitals were nationalized. In 1966, all foreign missionaries who had entered the country for the first time after 1948 were forced to leave when the government refused to renew their work permits. The Church is involved primarily in pastoral and social activities.

Namibia*

Archd., 1; dioc., 1; v.a., 1; abp., 1; bp., 2; parishes, 102; priests, 94 (22 dioc., 72 rel.); p.d., 49; sem., 32; bros., 21; srs., 509; catechists, 1,393; bap., 7,836; Caths., 444,000 (20%); tot. pop., 2,220,000. (AD)

Independent (March 21, 1990) state in southern Africa; capital, Windhoek. The area shares the history of South Africa. The hierarchy was established in 1994. The Church is hindered by a lack of priests.

Nauru*

Parishes, 2; priest, 1 (rel); p.d., 2; srs., 3; bap., 154; Caths., 5,000 (35.7%); tot. pop., 14,000.

Independent republic in western Pacific; capital, Yaren. Forms part of the Tarawa and Nauru Diocese (Kiribati). Established diplomatic relations with the Holy See in 1992.

Nepal*

P.a., 1; parishes, 8; priests, 67 (14 dioc.; 53 rel.); sem., 24; bros., 13; srs., 160; bap., 201; Caths., 8,000 (.02%); tot. pop., 29,129,000.

Constitutional monarchy in central Asia; capital, Katmandu. Little is known of the country before the 15th century. Some Jesuits passed through from 1628 and some sections were evangelized in the 18th century, with minimal results, before the country was closed to foreigners. Conversions from Hinduism, the state religion, are not recognized in law and are punishable by imprisonment. The Church has established an effective charitable network in Nepal, which officially declared itself a secular state in 2006.

Netherlands*

Archd., 1; dioc., 6; mil ord., 1; card., 2; abp., 2; bp., 14; parishes, 1,122; priests 2,400 (1,083 dioc., 1,317 rel.); p.d., 374; sem., 179; bros., 735; srs., 5,669; bap., 24,213; Caths., 4,659,000 (27.8%); tot. pop., 16,767,000.

Constitutional monarchy in northwestern Europe; capital, Amsterdam (seat of government, The Hague). Evangelization, begun about the turn of the sixth century by Irish, Anglo-Saxon and Frankish missionaries, resulted in Christianization of the country by 800 and subsequent strong influence on the Lowlands. Invasion by French Calvinists in 1572 brought serious losses to the Catholic Church and made the Reformed Church dominant. Catholics suffered a practical persecution of official repression and social handicap in the 17th century. The schism of Utrecht occurred in 1724. Only one-third of the population was Catholic in 1726. The Church had only a skeletal organization from 1702 to 1853, when the hierarchy was re-established.

Despite this upturn, cultural isolation was the experience of Catholics until about 1914. From then on new vigor came into the life of the Church, and a whole new climate of interfaith relations began to develop. Before and for some years following the Second Vatican Council, the thrust and variety of thought and practice in the Dutch Church moved it to the vanguard position of "progressive" renewal. A synod of Dutch bishops held at the Vatican in January 1980 discussed ideological differences among Catholics with the aim of fostering unity and restoring some discipline within the nation's Church. However, even into the 1990s Church leaders spoke of a polarization among Catholics over issues such as sexual morality, ministries for women and priestly celibacy. The bishops also spoke out against permissive laws on euthanasia and assisted suicide.

New Zealand*

Archd., 1; dioc., 5; mil. ord., 1; card., 1; abp., 2; bp., 10; parishes, 271; priests, 499 (317 dioc., 182 rel.); p.d., 22; sem., 27; bros., 138; srs., 828; bap., 8,188; Caths. 553,000 (12.5%); tot. pop., 4,433,000.

Parliamentary democracy in southwestern Pacific Ocean; capital, Wellington. Protestant missionaries were the first evangelizers. On North Island, Catholic missionaries started work before the establishment of two dioceses in 1848; their work among the Maoris was not organized until about 1881. On South Island, whose first resident priest arrived in 1840, a diocese was established in 1869. These three jurisdictions were joined in a province in 1896. The Marists were the predominant Catholic missionaries in the area. The first Maori bishop was named in 1988. In 1998, Pope John Paul II urged New Zealand's bishops not to allow the Church to fall prey to the practices and values of prevailing culture.

Nicaragua*

Archd., 1; dioc., 6; v.a., 1; card., 1; abp., 3; bp., 12; parishes, 322; priests, 585 (425 dioc., 160 rel.); p.d., 32; sem., 302; bros., 62; srs., 860; catechists, 44,911; bap., 58,288; Caths., 5,408,000 (89%); tot. pop., 6,071,000.

Republic in Central America: capital, Managua. Evangelization began shortly after the Spanish conquest, about 1524, and eight years later the first bishop took over jurisdiction of the Church in the country. Jesuits were leaders in missionary work during the colonial period, which lasted until the 1820s. Evangelization increased after establishment of the republic in 1838 and extended to the Atlantic coastal area, where Protestant missionaries began work about the middle of the 1900s.

Many Church leaders, clerical and lay, supported the aims but not necessarily all the methods of the Sandinista revolution, which forced the resignation and flight July 17, 1979, of Anastasio Somoza, whose family had controlled the government since the early 1930s. During the Sandinista period that followed, four priests accepted government posts. Some Nicaraguan Catholics threw their energies behind the Sandinista program of land reform and socialism, forming what some called a "popular church" based on liberation theology, while others strongly opposed the government. Managua Card. Miguel Obando Bravo helped mediate cease-fire talks during the war between the Sandinistas and U.S.-backed guerrillas. Land distribution, exacerbated by a wide gap in incomes, continued to be an issue, and in the late 1990s the Nicaraguan bishops continued to call for compromise between the government and former government officials. Despite an influx of aid after Hurricane Mitch killed more than 2,500 Nicaraguans and forced 900,000 to evacuate in 1998, Church leaders still cited poverty as a major issue.

Niger*

Archd., 1; dioc.; 1; bp., 2; parishes, 21; priests, 60 (28 dioc., 32 rel.); p.d., 1; sem., 10; bros., 9; srs., 96; catechists, 248; bap., 440; Caths., 22,000 (.13%); tot. pop., 16,275,000.

Republic in west central Africa; capital, Niamey. The first mission was set up in 1831. An apostolic prefecture was organized in 1942, and the first diocese was established in 1961. The country is predominantly Muslim. The Church is active in the fields of health and education.

Nigeria*

Archd., 9; dioc., 43; v.a., 2; card., 3; abp., 13; bp., 43; parishes, 3,217; priests, 6,610 (5,608 dioc., 1,002 rel.); p.d., 4; sem., 6,352; bros., 448; srs., 5,331; catechists, 17,209; bap., 4423,648; Caths., 25,500,000 (15.9%); tot. pop., 160,527,000.

Republic in West Africa; capital, Lagos. The Portuguese introduced Catholicism to the coastal region in the 15th century. Capuchins did some evan gelization in the 17th century but systematic mission ary work did not get under way along the coast until about 1840. A vicariate for this area was organized in 1870. A prefecture was set up in 1911 for missions in the northern part of the country, where Islam was strongly entrenched. The hierarchy was established in 1950. From 1967, when Biafra seceded, until early in 1970 the country was torn by civil war. Under the 1993-99 rule of Gen. Sani Abacha, Church leaders spoke out on behalf of human rights and democracy. After Abacha announced elections, the bishops said the country needed "new leading actors and fresh vision." As the 21st century began, bishops spoke out against imposition of Islamic law in individual states within the country. Recent years have seen a severe increase in attacks on Christians by Islamic extremist groups, including Boko Haram.

Norway*

Dioc., 1; prel., 2; bp., 3; parishes, 37; priests, 83 (47 dioc., 36 rel.); p.d., 2; sem., 7; bros., 5; srs., 143; bap., 1,053; Caths., 136,000 (2.7%); tot. pop., 5,054,000.

Constitutional monarchy in northern Europe; capital, Oslo. Evangelization begun in the ninth century by missionaries from England and Ireland put the Church on a firm footing about the turn of the 11th century. The first diocese was set up in 1153 and development of the Church progressed until the Black Death in 1349 inflicted losses from which it never recovered. Lutheranism, introduced from outside in 1537 and furthered cautiously,

gained general acceptance by about 1600 and was made the state religion. Legal and other measures crippled the Church, forcing priests to flee the country and completely disrupting normal activity. Changes for the better came in the 19th century, with the granting of religious liberty in 1845 and the repeal of many legal disabilities in 1897. Norway was administered as a single apostolic vicariate from 1892 to 1932, when it was divided into three jurisdictions.

Oman

Parishes, 4; priests, 9 (1 dioc., 8 rel.); bap., 157; Caths., 80,000 (2.6%); tot. pop., 3,028,000.

Independent monarchy in eastern corner of Arabian Peninsula; capital, Muscat. Under ecclesiastical jurisdiction of Arabia apostolic vicariate.

Pakistan*

Archd., 2; dioc., 4; p.a., 1; abp., 2; bp., 7; parishes, 123; priests, 280 (153 dioc., 127 rel.); sem., 175; bros., 65; srs., 803; catechists, 663; bap., 21,311; Caths., 1,221,000 (.07%); tot. pop., 174,442,000.

Islamic republic in southwest Asia; capital, Islamabad. Islam, firmly established in the eighth century, is the state religion. Christian evangelization of the native population began about the middle of the 19th century, years after earlier scattered attempts. The hierarchy was established in 1950. A series of death sentences against Christians accused of blasphemy resulted in acquittals during appeal processes, but in 1998 Bp. John Joseph of Faisalabad committed suicide to protest the strict blasphemy laws, which continued to be used as reasons for Christian arrests. In early 2002, the government did away with the system under which religious minorities, such as Catholics, could only vote in elections for members of their religious group. Pakistani Christians, including Catholics, have been the target of several terrorist incidents since the United States attacked Afghanistan in October 2001 and have grown more violent in the last few years.

Palau*

Parishes, 3; priests, 4 (2 dioc., 2 rel.); p.d., 1; srs., 5; bap., 327; Caths., 13,000 (56.5%); tot. pop., 23,000.

Independent (1994) nation in western Pacific; capital, Koror; part of Caroline chain of Islands. Under ecclesiastical jurisdiction of diocese of Caroline Islands, Federated States of Micronesia.

Panama*

Archd., 1; dioc., 5; prel., 1; v.a., 1; abp., 3; bp., 10; parishes, 199; priests, 424 (223 dioc., 201 rel.); p.d., 65; sem., 152; bros., 52; srs., 457; catechists, 2,840; bap., 34,034; Caths., 3,310,000 (87%); tot. pop., 3,788,000.

Republic in Central America; capital, Panama City. Catholicism was introduced by Franciscan missionaries and evangelization started in 1514. The Panama Diocese, oldest in the Americas, was set up at the same time. The Catholic Church has favored status and state aid for missions, charities and parochial schools, but freedom is guaranteed to all religions. In May 1989, Panama's bishops accused the government of thwarting the presidential elections and of attempting to intimidate the Church. The elections' legitimate leader, Guillermo

Endara, temporarily sought refuge at the Vatican Embassy in Panama City. After increasing unrest and violence, on Dec. 24, 1989, the country's dictator, Gen. Manuel Noriega, sought refuge at the Vatican Embassy. Ten days later, after U.S. troops spent days blasting the embassy with loud rock music and after meetings with Church diplomatic officials, Noriega surrendered.

Papua New Guinea*

Archd., 4; dioc., 15; abp., 2; bp., 25; parishes, 390; priests, 617 (265 dioc., 352 rel.); p.d., 4; sem., 457; bros., 198; srs., 914; catechists, 3,668; bap., 34,452; Caths., 2,044,000 (31%); tot. pop., 6,554,000.

Independent (Sept. 16, 1975) republic in southwest Pacific; capital, Port Moresby. Marists began evangelization about 1844 but were handicapped by many factors, including "spheres of influence" laid out for Catholic and Protestant missionaries. An apostolic prefecture was set up in 1896 and placed in charge of the Divine Word Missionaries. The territory suffered greatly during World War II. Hierarchy was established for New Guinea and adjacent islands in 1966. A decade-long war that began in the Bougainville area in the late 1980s left many churches, schools and health centers destroyed. At the end of the century, the Church fought social disintegration marked by violence, poverty and corruption.

Paraguay*

Archd., 1; dioc., 11; v.a., 2; mil. ord. 1; abp., 2; bp., 18; parishes, 363; priests, 776 (337 dioc., 439 rel.); p.d., 168; sem., 488; bros., 149; srs., 1,538; bap., 100,989; catechists, 48,060; Caths., 6,222,000 (93%); tot. pop., 6,673,000.

Republic in central South America; capital, Asunción. Catholicism was introduced in 1542, evangelization began almost immediately. A diocese erected in 1547 was occupied for the first time in 1556. On many occasions thereafter, dioceses in the country were left unoccupied because of political and other reasons. Jesuits who came into the country after 1609 devised the reductions system for evangelizing the Indians, teaching them agriculture, husbandry, trades and other arts, and giving them experience in property use and community life. The reductions were communes of Indians only, and had an average population of 3,000-4,000, under the direction of the missionaries. At their peak, some 30 reductions had a population of 100,000. Political officials regarded the reductions with disfavor because politicians did not control them and feared that the Indians trained in them might foment revolt and upset the established colonial system under Spanish control. The reductions lasted until about 1768, when the Jesuits were expelled.

Church-state relations following independence from Spain in 1811 were often tense because of government efforts to control the Church through continued exercise of Spanish patronage rights and by other means. The Church as well as the whole country suffered during the War of the Triple Alliance, 1865-70. After that time, the Church had the same kind of experience in Paraguay as in the rest of Latin America, with forces of liberalism, anticlericalism, massive educational needs, poverty, and a shortage of priests and other personnel.

In the 1980s, Church-state tensions increased as Catholic leaders spoke out against President Alfredo Stroessner's decades of one-man rule. A 1988 papal visit seemed to increase the Church's confidence, as bishops repeatedly spoke out against Stroessner. The army general who overthrew Stroessner in 1989 said he did so in part to defend the Catholic Church.

Retired Bp. Fernando Lugo, who campaigned on a platform of equality for Paraguay's poor farmers and indigenous people, was elected president of Paraguay in 2008, ending the six-decade rule of the Colorado Party.

Peru*

Archd., 7; dioc., 19; prel., 10; v.a., 8; mil. ord. 1; card., 1; abp., 12; bp., 58; parishes, 1,587; priests, 3,260 (1,937 dioc., 1,323 rel.); p.d., 61; sem., 1,826; bros., 542; srs., 5,697; catechists, 55,963; bap., 364,330; Caths., 27,010,000 (88.6%); tot. pop., 30,478,000.

Republic on the west coast of South America; capital, Lima. An effective diocese became operational in 1537, five years after the Spanish conquest. Evangelization, already under way, developed for some time after 1570 but deteriorated before the end of the colonial period in the 1820s. The first American saint of the new world was a Peruvian, Rose of Lima, a Dominican tertiary who died in 1617 and was canonized in 1671.

In the new republic founded after the wars of independence the Church experienced problems of adjustment, government efforts to control it through continuation of the patronage rights of the Spanish crown; suppression of houses of religious and expropriation of Church property; religious indifference and outright hostility. In the 20th century, liberation theology was born in Peru under the leadership of Father Gustavo Gutierrez. In the 1980s and early 1990s, the Maoist Sendero Luminoso guerrillas often targeted Church workers, who also found themselves prone to false charges of terrorism. A Peruvian cardinal was credited with much of the success of an early 1990s government effort to win the surrender of the rebels. When the government initiated a drastic economic program in 1990, Peruvian Church leaders worked to help feed and clothe the poor. In the late '90s, the Church successfully fought a government program of sterilization. Early in the 21st century, Church leaders became more outspoken on environmental issues and took the lead in reconstruction after the 2007 earthquake hit coastal areas.

Philippines*

Archd., 16; dioc., 58; prel., 4; v.a., 7; mil. ord. 1; card., 3; abp., 24; bp., 133; parishes, 3,214; priests, 9,213 (6,111 dioc., 3,102 rel.); p.d.,14; sem., 8,097; bros., 1,515; srs., 12,813 catechists, 99,026; bap., 1,582,139; Caths., 80,241,000 (82.3%); tot. pop., 97,463,000.

Republic, an archipelago of 7,000 islands off the southeast coast of Asia; capital, Manila. Systematic evangelization was begun in 1564 and resulted in firm establishment of the Church by the 19th century. During the period of Spanish rule, which lasted from the discovery of the islands by Magellan in 1521 to 1898, the Church experienced difficulties with the patronage system under which the Spanish crown tried to control ecclesiastical affairs through episcopal and other appointments. This system ended in 1898 when the United States gained possession of the islands and instituted a policy of separation of Church and state. Anticlericalism flared late in the 19th century. The Aglipayan schism, an attempt to set up a nationalist Church, occurred in 1902.

Church leaders and human rights groups constantly criticized abuses under former president and dictator Ferdinand Marcos. Church newspapers were among those censored or closed after he declared martial law, and religious and lay people were arrested and held without formal charges for long periods of time. After Marcos declared himself the victor in the 1986 elections and international observers declared his win a fraud, the Philippine bishops' call for a nonviolent struggle for justice was seen as the catalyst for the nation's "people power" revolution. Corazon Aquino, Marcos's successor, took refuge with Carmelite nuns during the revolution. At the turn of the century, Church workers often found themselves unintentional victims of violence spurred by Muslim separatists' fight for autonomy in the southern Philippines. Church social action focused on the poor, overseas workers, ecology, corruption, and a fight against the death penalty. There was also much controversy over a proposed changes to the contraception laws.

Poland*

Archd., 15; dioc., 28; mil. ord., 1; ordinariate, 1; cards., 6; abps., 26; bps., 103; parishes, 10,330; priests, 30,229 (23,624 dioc., 6,605 rel.); p.d., 14; sem., 4,097; bros., 1,061; srs., 21,180; catechists, 14,081; bap., 378,356; Caths., 37,037,000 (96%); tot. pop., 38,550,000.

Republic in Eastern Europe; capital, Warsaw. The first traces of Christianity date from the second half of the ninth century. Its spread was accelerated by the union of the Slavs in the 10th century. The first diocese was set up in 968. The Reformation, supported mainly by city dwellers and the upper classes, peaked from about the middle of the 16th century, resulting in numerous conversions to Lutheranism, the Reformed Church and the Bohemian Brethren.' A successful Counter-Reformation, with the Jesuits in a position of leadership, was completed by about 1632. The movement served a nationalist as well as religious purpose; in restoring religious unity to a large degree, it united the country against potential invaders, the Swedes, Russians and Turks. The Counter-Reformation had bad side effects, leading to the repression of Protestants long after it was over and to prejudice against Eastern-rite Catholics. The Church, in the same manner as the entire country, was adversely affected by the partitions of the 18th and 19th centuries. Russification hurt the Eastern- and Latin-rite Catholics.

In the republic established after World War I the Church reorganized itself, continued to serve as a vital force in national life, and enjoyed generally harmonious relations with the state. Progressive growth was strong until 1939, when German and Russian forces invaded and World War II began. In 1945, seven years before the adoption of a Soviet-type of constitution, the communist-controlled

government initiated a policy that included a constant program of atheistic propaganda; a strong campaign against the hierarchy and clergy; the imprisonment in 1948 of 700 priests and even more religious; rigid limitation on the activities of the Catholic press and religious movements.

Regular contacts on a working level were initiated by the Vatican and Poland in 1974; regular diplomatic relations were established in 1989. Cardinal Karol Wojtyla of Krakow was elected to the papacy in 1978. Church and papal support was strong for the independent labor movement, Solidarity, which was recognized by the government in August 1980 but outlawed in December 1981, when martial law was imposed (martial law was suspended in 1982). In May 1989, following recognition of Solidarity and a series of political changes, the Catholic Church was given legal status for the first time since the communists took control of the government in 1944. In 1990, a new constitution was adopted, declaring Poland a democratic state. In 1992, the pope restructured the Church in Poland, adding 13 new dioceses. A new concordat between the Polish government and the Holy See was signed in 1993.

Since the end of communist rule, Poland's Church has struggled with anti-Semitism among some clergy. A dispute over a Carmelite convent outside the former Nazi death camp at Auschwitz resulted in the convent's removal, but several years later the Church was forced to speak against Catholic protesters who posted hundreds of crosses outside the camp. A nearly eight-year national synod process concluded in 1999 with calls for priests to live less luxurious lifestyles and to keep parishes finances open. The Polish Church continued to be a source of missionary priests in more than 90 countries. Church leaders also were dogged by allegations of spying under the communist regime, a charge that led the newly appointed archbishop of Warsaw to resign in early 2007 shortly before his installation. The country celebrated Pope John Paul II's beatification in May 2011.

Portugal*

Patriarchate (Lisbon), 1; archd., 2; dioc., 17; mil. ord., 1; patriarch, 1; card., 3; abp., 6; bp., 36; parishes, 4,415; priests, 3,600 (2,659 dioc., 941 rel.); p.d., 330; sem., 474; bros., 261; srs., 5,032; catechists, 61,325; bap., 61,963; Caths., 9,322,000 (88.4%); tot. pop., 10,542,000.

Republic in the western part of the Iberian peninsula; capital, Lisbon. Christianity was introduced before the fourth century. From the fifth century to early in the eighth century the Church experienced difficulties from the physical invasion of barbarians and the intellectual invasion of doctrinal errors in the forms of Arianism, Priscillianism and Pelagianism. The Church survived under the rule of Arabs from about 711 and of the Moors until 1249. Ecclesiastical life was fairly vigorous from 1080 to 1185, and monastic influence became strong. A decline set in about 1450. Several decades later Portugal became the jumping-off place for many missionaries to newly discovered colonies. The Reformation had little effect in the country.

In the early 1700s, King John V broke relations with Rome and required royal approval of papal acts. His successor, Joseph I, expelled the Jesuits from Portugal and the colonies. Liberal revolutionaries with anti-Church policies made the 19th century a difficult one for the Church. Similar policies prevailed in Church-state relations in the 20th century until the accession to power of Premier Antonio de Oliveira Salazar in 1928; the hierarchy was seen as closely aligned with him. In 1940 Salazar concluded a concordat with the Holy See that regularized Church-state relations but still left the Church in a subservient condition.

In 1930, after lengthy investigation, the Church authorized devotion to Our Lady of Fátima, who appeared to three Portuguese children in 1917. Pope John Paul II, who credited Our Lady of Fátima with saving his life during a 1981 assassination attempt on her feast day, visited Portugal several times, including in May 2000 to beatify two of the Fátima visionaries. At that time, he had his Secretary of State, Cardinal Angelo Sodano, announce that the so-called third secret of Fátima would be published. The following month, the Vatican published the secret and said the message predicted the struggles of the Church with Nazism and communism and foretold the shooting of Pope John Paul.

Puerto Rico

Archd., 1; dioc., 5; abp., 1; bp., 8; parishes, 329; priests, 676 (350 dioc., 326 rel.); p.d., 455; sem., 93; bros., 49; srs., 885; catechists, 6,614; bap., 21,109; Caths., 3,106,000 (84.7%); tot. pop., 3,667,000. (AD)

A U.S. commonwealth, the smallest of the Greater Antilles, 885 miles southeast of the southern coast of Florida; capital, San Juan. Following its discovery by Columbus in 1493, the island was evangelized by Spanish missionaries and remained under Spanish ecclesiastical as well as political control until 1898, when it became a possession of the United States. The original diocese, San Juan, was erected in 1511. The present hierarchy was established in 1960.

Qatar

Parish; priest, 7 (1 dioc., 6 rel.); p.d., 1; bap., 348; Caths., 350,000 (19%); tot. pop., 1,844,000.

Independent state in the Persian Gulf; capital, Doha. Under ecclesiastical jurisdiction of Arabia apostolic vicariate.

Réunion

Dioc., 1; bp., 1; parishes, 71; priests, 127 (65 dioc., 62 rel.); p.d., 20; sem., 16; bros., 12; srs., 293; catechists, 2,890; bap., 9,821; Caths., 664,000 (79%); tot. pop., 838,000. (AD)

French overseas department, 450 miles east of Madagascar; capital, Saint-Denis. Catholicism was introduced in 1667 and some intermittent missionary work was done through the rest of the century. An apostolic prefecture was organized in 1712. Vincentians began work there in 1817 and were joined later by Holy Ghost Fathers. In 1998 the bishops joined their counterparts in Guadeloupe, French Guiana and Martinique to call slavery "an immense collective sin."

Romania*

Archd., 3; dioc., 8; ord., 1; ex., 1; abp., 5; bp., 14; parishes, 1,907; priests, 2,033 (1,752 dioc., 281 rel.); p.d., 3; sem., 606; bros., 136; srs., 1,213; catechists, 516; bap., 10,482; Caths., 1,612,000 (7.5%); tot. pop., 21,358,000.

Republic in southeastern Europe; capital, Bucharest. Latin Christianity, introduced in the third century, all but disappeared during the barbarian invasions. The Byzantine rite was introduced by the Bulgars about the beginning of the eighth century and established firm roots. It eventually became Orthodox, but a large number of its adherents returned later to union with Rome.

Communists took over the government following World War II, forced the abdication of Michael I in 1947, and enacted a Soviet type of constitution in 1952. By that time a campaign against religion was already in progress. In 1948 the government denounced a concordat concluded in 1929, nationalized all schools and passed a law on religions that resulted in the disorganization of Church administration. The 1.5 million-member Romanian Byzantine-rite Church, by government decree, was incorporated into the Romanian Orthodox Church, and Catholic properties were given to the Orthodox. Five of the six Latin-rite bishops were immediately disposed of by the government, and the last was sentenced to 18 years' imprisonment in 1951. Religious orders were suppressed in 1949.

Some change for the better in Church-state relations was reported after the middle of the summer of 1964, although restrictions were still in effect. The Eastern Church regained liberty in 1990 with the change of government. The hierarchy was restored and diplomatic relations with the Holy See were re-established. Today, most Latin-rite Catholics are ethnic Hungarians residing in Transylvania. Pope John Paul II visited Romania May 7-9, 1999. Church leaders said the historic visit led to a deeper openness and understanding between Catholics and Orthodox.

Russia*

Archd., 2; dioc. 3 (2 for European Russia, 1 for Siberia); ap. ex., 1; abp., 2; bp., 2; parish, 235; priests, 320 (114 dioc., 206 rel.); p.d., 3; sem., 63; bros., 23; srs, 412; bap., 1,174; Caths., 932,000 (.65%); tot. pop., 143,151,000.

Federation in Europe and Asia; capital, Moscow. The Orthodox Church has been predominant in Russian history. It developed from the Byzantine Church before 1064. Some of its members subsequently established communion with Rome as the result of reunion movements, but most remained Orthodox. The government has always retained some kind of general or particular control of this Church.

From the beginning of the Communist government in 1917, all churches of whatever kind became the targets of official campaigns designed to negate their influence on society and/or to eliminate them entirely. An accurate assessment of the situation of the Catholic Church in Russia was difficult to make. Research by a Polish priest, reported in 1998, documented the arrests, trials and fabricated confessions of priests in the 1920s and 1930s. A report by a team of research specialists made public by the Judiciary Committee of the U.S. House of Representatives in 1964 said: "The fate of the Catholic Church in the USSR and countries occupied by the Russians from 1917 to 1959 shows the following: (a) the number killed: 55 bishops; 12,800 priests and monks; 2.5 million Catholic believers; (b) imprisoned or deported: 199 bishops; 32,000 priests and 10 million believers; (c) 15,700 priests were forced to abandon their priesthood and accept other jobs; and (d) a large number of seminaries and religious communities were dissolved." Despite repression, Lithuania and Ukraine remained strongholds of Catholicism. During his 1985-91 presidency, Soviet President Mikhail Gorbachev met twice with Pope John Paul II — meetings later credited with the return of religious freedom in the Soviet Union. In 1991, the pope established two Latin-rite apostolic administrations in the Russian Republic: one in Moscow and one based in Novosibirsk, Siberia. Catholic communities in Europe and the United States have been instrumental in helping to rebuild the Church in Russia. Under a 1997 religion law, every religious organization in Russia had to register on a national level, then re-register each parish by the end of 1999 to enjoy full legal benefits such as owning property and publishing religious literature. The apostolic administrations registered with no problems, but after the Russian government rejected the Jesuits' registration application, they were forced to take the matter to the country's constitutional court, which ruled that they qualified.

The Vatican's upgrading of Russia's four apostolic administrations to dioceses in early 2002 provoked new tensions with the Orthodox, who accused the Catholic Church of trying to convert its members. Russian authorities refused to readmit five prominent Church leaders, including one bishop, after they left the country. The Vatican eventually appointed a new bishop for the vacant Russian diocese and transferred the expelled bishop. Formal diplomatic relations were established between Russia and the Holy See in 2009.

Rwanda*

Archd., 1; dioc., 8; abp., 2; bp., 9; parishes, 162; priests, 743 (590 dioc., 153 rel.); sem., 553; bros., 210; srs., 1,819; catechists, 4,136; bap., 119,111; Caths., 5,168,000 (47%); tot. pop., 11,033,000.

Republic in east central Africa; capital, Kigali. Catholicism was introduced about the turn of the 20th century. The hierarchy was established in 1959. Intertribal warfare between the ruling Hutus (90 percent of the population) and the Tutsis (formerly the ruling aristocracy) plagued the country for a number of years. In April 1994, the deaths of the presidents of Rwanda and Burundi in a suspicious plane crash sparked the outbreak of a ferocious civil war. Among the thousands of victims — mostly Tutsis — were three bishops and about 25 percent of the clergy. Thousands more fled the country.

Although in 1996 Pope John Paul II said that all members of the Church who participated in the genocide must face the consequences, in 1997 the Vatican donated $50,000 to help ensure that certain people — including priests and religious — received fair trials. Two nuns accused of participating in the genocide were sent to prison in Belgium, but a bishop was acquitted after a nine-month trial in Rwanda. The bishop later said Marian apparitions in his diocese in the 1980s foretold the genocide.

Saint Lucia*

Archd., 1; abp., 1; parishes, 22; priests, 28 (17 dioc., 11 rel.); sem., 3; bros., 4; srs., 46; catechists, 262; bap., 1,505; Caths., 106,000 (67%); tot. pop., 159,000.

Independent (Feb. 22, 1979) island state in West Indies; capital, Castries.

Saint Vincent and the Grenadines*

Dioc., 1; bp., 1; parishes, 9; priests, 12 (7 dioc., 5 rel.); sem., 1; srs., 15; catechists, 31; bap., 97; Caths., 15,000 (12.7%); tot. pop., 118,000.

Independent state (1979) in West Indies; capital, Kingstown. The Kingstown diocese (St. Vincent) was established in 1989; it was formerly part of Bridgetown-Kingstown Diocese with see in Barbados. The Vatican established diplomatic relations with St. Vincent and the Grenadines in 1990. The Church is recognized for its role in education and health care.

Samoa, American

Dioc., 1; bp., 1; parishes, 17; priests, 20 (17 dioc., 3 rel.); p.d., 32; sem., 6; srs., 11; bap., 521; Caths., 15,000 (23%); tot. pop., 65,000.

Unincorporated U.S. territory in southwestern Pacific, consisting of six small islands; seat of government, Pago Pago on the Island of Tutuila. Samoa-Pago Pago Diocese established in 1982.

Samoa, Western*

Archd., 1; abp., 1; parishes, 38; priests, 52 (35 dioc., 17 rel.); p.d., 19; sem., 10; bros., 14; srs., 70; catechists, 146; bap., 1,332; Caths., 43,000 (23%); tot. pop., 189,000.

Independent state in the southwestern Pacific; capital, Apia. Catholic missionary work began in 1845. Most of the missions now in operation were estab lished by 1870 when the Catholic population num bered about 5,000. Additional progress was made in missionary work from 1896. The first Samoan priest was ordained in 1892. A diocese was established in 1966; elevated to a metropolitan see in 1982.

San Marino*

Parishes, 12; priests, 23 (8 dioc., 14 rel.); p.d. 1; bros., 1; srs 19; bap., 243; Caths., 30,000 (94%); tot. pop., 32,000.

Republic, a 24-square-mile enclave in northeastern Italy; capital, San Marino. The date of initial evangelization is not known, but a diocese was established by the end of the third century. Ecclesiastically, it forms part of the Diocese of San Marino-Montefeltro in Italy.

São Tome and Principe*

Dioc., 1; bp., 2; parishes, 12; priests, 13 (6 dioc., 7 rel.); sem. 8; bros., 3; srs., 34; catechists, 545; bap., 3,549; Caths., 125,000 (66%); tot. pop., 190,000.

Independent republic (July 12, 1975), consisting of two islands off the western coast of Africa in the Gulf of Guinea; former Portuguese territory; capital, São Tome. Evangelization was begun by the Portuguese who discovered the islands in 1471-72. The São Tome Diocese was established in 1534. In a 1992 visit to São Tome, a major transport center for slaves until the mid-1800s, Pope John Paul II condemned slavery as "a cruel offense" to African dignity.

Saudi Arabia

Parishes, 3; priests, 7 (1 dioc., 6 rel.); p.d., bap., 406; Caths., 1,530,000; total pop., 26,417,000.

Monarchy occupying four-fifths of Arabian peninsula; capital, Riyadh. Population is Muslim; all other religions are banned. Christians in the area are workers from other countries. The Church falls under the ecclesiastical jurisdiction of the Arabian apostolic vicariate. In May 1999, Pope John Paul II met with the crown prince of Saudi Arabia at the Vatican. In 2007, Pope Benedict XVI met with King Abdullah in the Vatican; human rights and religious freedom were major topics of discussion.

Scotland*

Archd., 2; dioc., 6; card., 1; abp., 4; bp., 11; parishes, 392; priests, 561 (426 dioc., 135 rel.); p.d., 44; sem., 32; bros., 174; srs., 390; bap., 6,600; Caths., 650,866 (14%); tot. pop., 4,614,000.

Part of the United Kingdom, in the northern British Isles; capital, Edinburgh. St. Ninian's arrival in 397 marked the beginning of Christianity in Scotland. The arrival of St. Columba and his monks in 563 inaugurated a new era of evangelization that reached into remote areas by the end of the sixth century. He was extremely influential in determining the character of the Church, which was tribal, monastic, and in union with Rome. Considerable disruption of Church activity resulted from Scandinavian invasions in the late eighth and ninth centuries. By 1153 the Scottish Church took a turn away from its insularity and was drawn into closer contact with the European community. Anglo-Saxon religious and political relations, com plicated by rivalries between princes and ecclesiastical superiors, were not always the happiest.

From shortly after the Norman Conquest of England to 1560 the Church suffered adverse effects from the Hundred Years' War, the Black Death, the Western Schism and other developments. In 1560 Parliament abrogated papal supremacy over the Church in Scotland and committed the country to Protestantism in 1567. The Catholic Church was proscribed, to remain that way for more than 200 years, and the hierarchy was disbanded. Defections made the Church a minority religion from that time on. Presbyterian Church government was ratified in 1690. Priests launched the Scottish Mission in 1653, incorporating themselves as a mission body under an apostolic prefecture and working underground to serve the faithful in much the same way their confreres did in England. Catholics got some relief from legal disabilities in 1793 and more relief later. Many left the country about that time. Some of their numbers were filled subsequently by immigrants from Ireland. About 100 heather priests, trained in clandestine places, were ordained by the early 19th century. The hierarchy was restored in 1878. Pope Benedict XVI visited in 2010. The Church in Scotland was rocked by the resignation of Cardinal Keith O'Brien in 2013 amid allegations of sexual impropriety.

Senegal*

Archd., 1; dioc., 6; card. 1; abp., 1; bp., 6; parishes, 133; priests, 472 (349 dioc., 123 rel.); p.d., 1; sem., 183; bros., 190; srs., 804; catechists, 1,980; bap., 11,003; Caths., 705,000 (5.3%); tot. pop., 13,208,000.

Republic in West Africa; capital, Dakar. The country had its first contact with Catholicism through the Portuguese some time after 1460. Some incidental missionary work was done by Jesuits and Capuchins in the 16th and 17th centuries. A vicariate for the area was placed in charge of the Holy Ghost Fathers in 1779.

More effective evangelization efforts were accomplished after the Senegambia vicariate was erected in 1863; the hierarchy was established in 1955. During a 1992 trip to the predominantly Muslim country, Pope John Paul II praised the small Catholic community for its contributions, especially in the areas of health care and education.

Serbia*

Archd., 2; dioc., 3; ex., 1; a.a., 1; abp., 2; bp., 4; parishes, 241; priests, 273 (237 dioc., 36 rel.); p.d., 11; sem., 51; bros., 49; srs., 255; bap., 3,425; Caths., 456,000 (6.3%); tot. pop., 7,223,000.

Independent nation in southeastern Europe; part of the former Yugoslavia; capital, Belgrade.

Christianity was introduced from the seventh to ninth centuries in the regions combined to form Yugoslavia after World War I. Since these regions straddled the original line of demarcation for the Western and Eastern Empires (and churches), and since the Reformation had little lasting effect, the Christians are nearly all either Latin- or Eastern-rite Catholics or Orthodox. Yugoslavia was proclaimed a Socialist republic in 1945, and persecution of the Catholic Church began. In an agreement signed June 25, 1966, the government recognized the Holy See's spiritual jurisdiction over the Church in the country and guaranteed to bishops the possibility of maintaining contact with Rome in ecclesiastical and religious matters. During early 1990s the split of the Yugoslav republic, Catholic leaders joined Orthodox and, in some cases, Muslim leaders in calling for peace.

Seychelles*

Dioc., 1; bp., 1; parishes, 19; priests, 24 (10 dioc., 14 rel.); p.d., 1; sem., 3; bros. 5; srs., 57; catechists, 209; bap., 1,098; Caths., 67,000 (76%); tot. pop., 88,000.

Independent (1976) group of 92 islands in the Indian Ocean; capital, Victoria. Catholicism was introduced in the 18th century. An apostolic vicariate was organized in 1852. All education in the islands was conducted under Catholic auspices until 1954. In 1991, Bp. Felix Paul of Port Victoria said the country's one-party socialist government was an affront to the rights and dignity of its people, but President France-Albert René continued to lead the government into the 21st century. Pope John Paul II warned Seychelles to beware of the dark side of tourism, a main industry in the country.

Sierra Leone*

Archd., 1; dioc., 2; abp., 1; bp., 3; parishes, 70; priests, 161 (95 dioc., 66 rel.); sem., 62; bros., 50; srs., 101; catechists, 659; bap., 10,493; Caths., 307,000 (5%); tot. pop., 6,038,000.

Republic on the west coast of Africa; capital, Freetown. Catholicism was introduced in 1858. Members of the African Missions Society, the first Catholic missionaries in the area, were joined by Holy Ghost Fathers in 1864. Protestant missionaries were active in the area before their Catholic counterparts. Educational work had a major part in Catholic endeavor. The hierarchy was established in 1950. Most of the inhabitants are followers of traditional African religions.

Church leaders suffered at the hands of rebel soldiers in the late 1990s, when a military coup ousted the country's democratically elected government. Although some Church workers fled to neighboring Guinea, some remained. Rebels kidnapped several foreign missionaries and, shortly before West African intervention forces ousted them from power in 1998, rebels forced the archbishop of Freetown to strip naked while they plundered his office. As the war lessened and later ended, the Church worked for reconciliation, to rehabilitate child soldiers and to rebuild damaged Church property.

Singapore*

Archd., 1; abp., 2; parishes, 31; priests, 138 (75 dioc., 63 rel.); sem., 27; bros., 92; srs., 188; catechists, 1,805; bap., 3,886; Caths., 196,000 (3.7%); tot. pop., 5,270,000.

Independent island republic off the southern tip of the Malay Peninsula; capital, Singapore. Christianity was introduced in the area by Portuguese colonists about 1511. Singapore was founded in 1819; the first parish Church was built in 1846. Freedom of religion is generally respected, although in the late 1980s nearly a dozen people involved in Catholic social work were arrested and detained without trial under the Internal Security Act.

Slovakia*

Archd., 4; dioc., 7; mil. ord.; card., 2; abp., 7; bp., 19; parishes, 1,554; priests, 2,902 (2,290 dioc., 612 rel.); p.d., 16; sem., 476; bros., 186, srs., 2,297; catechists, 1,588; bap., 42,450; Caths., 4,027,000 (74%); tot. pop., 5,464,000.

Independent state (Jan. 1, 1993); formerly part of Czechoslovakia; capital, Bratislava. Christianity was introduced in Slovakia in the eighth century by Irish and German missionaries, and the area was under the jurisdiction of German bishops. In 863, Sts. Cyril and Methodius began pastoral and missionary work in the region, ministering to the people in their own language. A diocese established at Nitra in 880 had a continuous history (except for one century ending in 1024). The Church in Slovakia was severely tested by the Reformation and political upheavals. After World War I, when it became part of the Republic of Czechoslovakia, it was 75 percent Catholic.

Vigorous persecution of the Church began in Slovakia in 1944, when communists mounted an offensive against bishops, priests and religious. Msgr. Josef Tiso, a Catholic priest who served as president of the Slovak Republic from 1939-45, was tried for "treason" in December 1946 and was executed the following April.

In 1972, the government ordered the removal of nuns from visible but limited apostolates to farms and mental hospitals. In 1973, the government allowed the ordination of three bishops in the Slovak region.

When Slovakia split from Czechoslovakia in 1993, the country slid into economic difficulties. Church-state tensions increased, and the Slovakian government eventually apologized to Bp. Rudolf Balaz of Banska Bystrica, whose house had been raided in a government investigation of stolen art. In an attempt to fight the effects of decades of communism, in 1996 the bishops said all adult Catholics who had not received confirmation must undergo a special two-year catechism course. In 2000, the government and Vatican signed an accord establishing

the Church's legal status. The country is remarkably pro-life, including the celebration of an annual Day of the Unborn Child.

Slovenia*

Archd., 2; dioc., 4; abp., 2; bp., 6; parishes, 786; priests, 1,063 (772 dioc., 291 rel.); p.d., 31; sem., 97; bros., 43; srs., 547; catechists, 628; bap., 13,747; Caths., 1,560,000 (76%); tot. pop., 2,057,000.

Independent republic (1991) in southeastern Europe; formerly part of Yugoslavia; capital, Ljubljana. Established diplomatic relations with the Holy See in 1992. After independence, Church leaders found themselves in repeated skirmishes with Slovenia's governing coalition over religious education, restitution of Church property and the Church's proper social role.

Solomon Islands*

Archd., 1; dioc., 2; abp., 1; bp., 3; parishes, 30; priests, 72 (39 dioc., 33 rel.); sem., 72; bros., 24; srs., 98; catechists, 775; bap., 4,177; Caths., 111,000 (20%); tot. pop., 558,000.

Independent (July 7, 1978) island group in Oceania; capital, Honiara, on Guadalcanal. After violence interrupted the Marists' evangelization of the Southern Solomons, they resumed their work in 1898. An apostolic vicariate was organized in 1912. A similar jurisdiction was set up for the Western Solomons in 1959. World War II caused a great deal of damage to mission installations.

Somalia

Dioc., 1; parish, 1; priests, 3 (1 dioc., 2 rel.); srs., 4; Caths., 100; tot. pop., 8,695,000. (AD)

Republic on the eastern coast of Africa; capital, Mogadishu. The country has been Muslim for centuries. Pastoral activity has been confined to immigrants. Schools and hospitals were nationalized in 1972, resulting in the departure of some foreign missionaries.

South Africa*

Archd., 5; dioc., 20; v.a., 1; mil. ord., 1; card., 1; abp., 8; bp., 20; parishes, 796; priests, 1,239 (568 dioc., 671 rel.); p.d., 239; sem., 413; bros., 144; srs., 2,104; catechists, 11,750; bap., 59,213; Caths., 3,687,000 (7.2%); tot. pop., 51,146,000.

Republic in the southern part of Africa; capitals, Cape Town (legislative), Pretoria (administrative) and Bloemfontein (judicial). Christianity was introduced by the Portuguese who discovered the Cape of Good Hope in 1488. Boers, who founded Cape Town in 1652, expelled Catholics from the region. There was no Catholic missionary activity from that time until the 19th century. A bishop established residence in 1837, and evangelization got under way thereafter among the Bantus and white immigrants. The hierarchy was established in 1951.

Under South Africa's apartheid regime, the Church found itself the victim of attacks, from the parish level to the headquarters of the bishops' conference in Pretoria. Some Church leaders were detained, tortured and deported, particularly in the 1970s and 1980s. However, in a 1997 statement to South Africa's Truth Commission, the Catholic Church said the complicity of some Catholics with apartheid was an "act of omission rather than commission." Since the end of apartheid, Catholic leaders have spoken out against an increase in violence and anti-Muslim sentiment and have worked to combat the growing AIDS problem. Reports of clergy sexual abuse became public in 2003.

South Sudan*

Archd., 1; dioc., 6; abp., 1; bp., 8; parishes, 89; priests, 256 (184 dioc., 72 rel.); sem., 368; bros., 45; srs., 159; catechists, 3,512; bap., 57,457; Caths., 5,549,000 (40%); tot. pop., 13,886,000.

Republic in North Africa, previously known as Southern Sudan, in east-central Africa; capital, Juba. It was established officially in 2011 after breaking off from Sudan, the result of two civil wars.

The Holy See and the Republic of South Sudan established diplomatic relations in Feb. 2013, including the establishment of an apostolic nunciature. The Republic of South Sudan is also a UN member state, as well as a member state of the African Union and the Intergovernmental Authority on Development. The country is majority Christian, with Catholics comrpising the largest religious group; Muslims comprise 18% of the population.

Spain*

Archd., 14; dioc., 55; mil. ord., 1; card., 10; abp., 22; bp., 98; parishes, 22,912; priests, 24,044 (16,355 dioc., 7,689 rel.); p.d., 404; sem., 1,940; bros., 3,723; srs., 46,962; catechists, 95,157; bap., 277,932; Caths., 43,048,000 (93.3%); tot. pop., 46,163,000.

Constitutional monarchy on the Iberian peninsula in southwestern Europe; capital, Madrid. Christians were on the peninsula by 200; some of them suffered martyrdom during persecutions of the third century. A council held in Elvira about 305 enacted the first legislation on clerical celibacy in the West. Vandals invaded the peninsula in the fifth century, bringing with them an Arian brand of Christianity that they retained until their conversion following the baptism of their king, Reccared, in 589.

In the seventh century, Toledo was established as the primatial see. The Visigoth kingdom lasted to the time of the Arab invasion, 711-14. The Church survived under Muslim rule but experienced some doctrinal and disciplinary irregularities as well as harassment. Re-evangelization of most of the peninsula was accomplished by 1248; unification was achieved during the reign of Ferdinand and Isabella. The discoveries of Columbus and other explorers ushered in an era of colonial expansion in which Spain became one of the greatest missionary-sending countries in history. In 1492, in repetition of anti-Semitic actions of 694, the expulsion of unbaptized Jews was decreed, leading to mass baptisms but a questionable number of real conversions in 1502. Activity by the Inquisition followed. Spain was not seriously affected by the Reformation. Ecclesiastical decline set in about 1650.

Anti-Church actions authorized by a constitution enacted in 1812 resulted in the suppression of religious and other encroachments on the leaders, people and goods of the Church. Political, religious and cultural turmoil recurred during the 19th century and into the 20th. A revolutionary republic was proclaimed in 1931, triggering a series of developments that led to civil war from 1936 to 1939. During the conflict, which pitted leftist Loyalists against the forces of Francisco Franco, more than 6,600 priests and religious and an unknown number of lay people were massacred. One-man, one-party rule, established after the civil war and with rigid control policies with respect to personal liberties and social and economic issues, continued for more than 35 years before giving way after the death of Franco to democratic reforms. Since the 1970s, the Catholic Church has not been the established religion; the constitution guarantees freedom for other religions as well. In the late 20th century, Spanish Church leaders fought a growing feeling of indifference among many Catholics. After the March 2004 al-Qaida bombings led to the election of a Socialist government, Spanish Church leaders were appalled by the series of social policy changes being proposed. Pope Benedict XVI visited in 2010 and 2011.

Sri Lanka*

Archd., 1; dioc., 10; card., 1; abp., 3; bp., 14; parishes, 428; priests, 1,286 (813 dioc., 473 rel.); p.d., 1; sem., 480; bros., 190; srs., 2,660; catechists, 13,324; bap., 25,129; Caths., 1,536,000 (7.3%); tot. pop., 21,004,000.

Independent socialist republic, island southeast of India; capital, Colombo. The Portuguese began evangelizing in the 16th century. In 1638, the Dutch began forcing Portuguese from the coastal areas. The Dutch outlawed Catholicism, banished priests and confiscated buildings, forcing people to become Calvinists. Blessed Joseph Vaz, an Oratorian priest, is credited with almost single-handedly reviving the Catholic Church toward the end of the 17th century.

Anti-Catholic laws were repealed by the British in 1806. The hierarchy was established in 1886; the country gained independence in 1948. In an unusual move in January 1998, Archbp. Nicholas M. Fernando of Colombo, authorized by the Vatican Congregation for the Doctrine of the Faith, lifted the excommunication of a prominent Sri Lankan theologian, Oblate Father Tissa Balasuriya. Sri Lankan bishops repeatedly called for reconciliation in the decades-long war between the Liberation Tigers of Tamil Eelam and the Sinhalese-dominated government.

Sudan*

Archd., 2; dioc., 7; ap. ex., 1; card., 1; abp., 2; bp., 14; parishes, 44; priests, 407 (277 dioc., 130 rel.); p.d., 5; sem., 245; bros., 82; srs., 357; catechists, 4,637; bap., 59,963; Caths., 1,075,000 (3.9%); tot. pop., 27,692,000

Republic in northeastern Africa, the largest country on the continent; capital Khartoum. Christianity was introduced from Egypt and gained acceptance in the sixth century. Under Arab rule, it was eliminated in the northern region. No Christians were in the country in 1600.

Evangelization attempts begun in the 19th century in the south yielded hard-won results. By 1931 there were nearly 40,000 Catholics there, and considerable progress was made by missionaries after that time. In 1957, a year after the republic was established, Catholic schools were nationalized. An act restrictive of religious freedom went into effect in 1962, resulting in the harassment and expulsion of foreign missionaries. By 1964 all but a few Sudanese missionaries had been forced out of the southern region. The northern area, where Islam predominates, is impervious to Christian influence.

Late in 1971 some missionaries were allowed to return to work in the South. The hierarchy was established in 1974. The most recent fighting, which began in 1983, originally pitted the mostly Arab and Muslim North against the mostly black African Christian and animist South, but it has since evolved into a nationwide conflict fueled by religion, ethnicity, oil and ideology. The imposition of Islamic penal codes in 1984 was a cause of concern to all Christian Churches. Recent government policies have denied Christians the right to places of worship and authorization to gather for prayer. Bishops from the South have condemned human rights violations — aggravated by famine and war — in their area. They have said they want peace but cannot accept an Islamic state and were hopeful that terms of a 2005 peace agreement would hold. The agreement would allow southerners to vote on independence after a six-year period of power-sharing. A widespread conflict in the western Darfur region resulted in a massive exodus of Sudanese, who were cared for in neighboring countries by international – including church-run – agencies.

Surinam*

Dioc., 1; bp., 1; parishes, 33; priests, 22 (6 dioc., 16 rel.); sem., 1; bros., 4; srs., 9; bap., 1,444; Caths., 135,000 (24.2%); tot. pop., 557,000.

Independent (Nov. 25, 1975) state in northern South America; capital, Paramaribo. Catholicism was introduced in 1683. Evangelization began in 1817.

Swaziland*

Dioc., 1; bp., 1; parishes, 17; priests, 30 (14 dioc., 16 rel.); sem., 15; bros., 3; srs., 49; bap., 664; Caths., 59,000 (5.2%); tot. pop., 1,130,000.

Monarchy in southern Africa, almost totally surrounded by South Africa; capital, Mbabane. Missionary work was entrusted to the Servites in 1913. An apostolic prefecture was organized in 1923. The hierarchy was established in 1951. Swaziland established diplomatic relations with the Holy See in 1992. In the 1990s, Swazi Catholics worked to help transform the country to a democracy but to retain the traditions of the people.

Sweden*

Dioc., 1; abp., 1; bp., 3; parishes, 44; priests, 178 (83 dioc., 95 rel.); p.d., 22; sem., 16; bros., 12; srs., 217 catechists, 347; bap., 1,376; Caths., 104,000 (1.1%); tot. pop., 9,519,000.

Constitutional monarchy in northwestern Europe; capital, Stockholm. Christianity was introduced by St. Ansgar, a Frankish monk, in 829-830. The Church became well-established in the 12th cen-

tury and was a major influence at the end of the Middle Ages. Political and other factors favored the introduction and spread of the Lutheran Church, which became the state religion in 1560. The Augsburg Confession of 1530 was accepted by the government; all relations with Rome were severed; monasteries were suppressed; the very presence of Catholics in the country was forbidden in 1617. A decree of tolerance for foreign Catholics was issued about 1781. Two years later an apostolic vicariate was organized for the country. In 1873 Swedes were given the legal right to leave the Lutheran church and join another Christian church. Membership in the Lutheran church is presumed by law unless notice is given of membership in another church.

Since 1952 Catholics have enjoyed almost complete religious freedom. The hierarchy was re-established in 1953. Hindrances to growth of the Church are the strongly entrenched established church, limited resources, a clergy shortage and the size of the country. In the 1960s, an influx of guest workers increased the number of Catholics, and in the 1970s and 1980s, refugees helped increase Church numbers. In 1998, the pope named the first Swedish bishop in more than 400 years. In the early 21st century, the government worked to give the Church and other minority faiths the right to operate as legal entities, including owning property.

Switzerland*

Dioc., 6; abb., 2; card., 4; abp., 3; bp., 17; parishes, 1,627; priests, 2,552 (1,545 dioc., 1,007 rel.); p.d., 247; sem., 186; bros., 341; srs., 5,042; catechists, 1,630; bap., 28,260; Caths., 3,488,000 (43.6%); tot. pop., 7,996,000.

Confederation in central Europe; capital, Bern. Christianity was introduced in the fourth century or earlier and was established on a firm footing before the barbarian invasions of the sixth century. Constance, established as a diocese in the seventh century, was a stronghold of the faith against the pagan Alamanni, in particular, who were not converted until some time in the ninth century. During this period of struggle with the barbarians, a number of monasteries of great influence were established.

The Reformation in Switzerland was triggered by Zwingli in 1519 and furthered by him at Zurich until his death in battle against the Catholic cantons in 1531. Calvin set in motion the forces that made Geneva the international capital of the Reformation and transformed it into a theocracy. Catholics mobilized a Counter-Reformation in 1570, six years after Calvin's death. Struggle between Protestant and Catholic cantons was a fact of Swiss life for several hundred years. The Helvetic Constitution enacted at the turn of the 19th century embodied anti-Catholic measures and consequences, among them the dissolution of 130 monasteries. The Church was reorganized later in the century to meet the threats of liberalism, radicalism and the Kulturkampf. In the process, the Church, even though on the defensive, gained the strength and cohesion that characterizes it to the present time. In 1973, constitutional articles banning Jesuits from the country and prohibiting the establishment of convents and monasteries were repealed. In the 1990s, Swiss bishops battled internal divisions and sought forgiveness for any anti-Semitism on behalf of the Church.

Syria*

Patriarchates, 1 (Greek Melkites; patriarchs of Antioch of Maronites and Syrians reside in Lebanon); archd., 12 (1 Armenian, 2 Maronite, 5 Greek Melkite, 4 Syrian); dioc., 3 (Armenian, Chaldean, Maronite); v.a., 1 (Latin); ap.ex., 1; patriarch, 1; card., 1; abp., 15; bp., 4; parishes, 216; priests, 286 (208 dioc., 78 rel.); p.d., 15; sem., 71; bros., 33; srs., 520; catechists, 1,148; bap., 2,158; Caths., 432,000 (2%); tot. pop., 21,641,000.

Arab socialist republic in southwest Asia; capital, Damascus. Christian communities were formed in apostolic times. It is believed that St. Peter established a see at Antioch before going to Rome. Damascus became a center of influence. The area was the place of great men and great events in the early history of the Church. Monasticism developed there in the fourth century; so did the Monophysite and Monothelite heresies to which a portion of the Church succumbed. Byzantine Syrians who remained in communion with Rome were given the name Melkites. Christians of various persuasions — Jacobites, Orthodox and Melkites — were subject to various degrees of harassment from the Arabs who took over in 638 and from the Ottoman Turks who isolated the country and remained in control from 1516 to the end of World War II.

Syrian Catholics are members of the Armenian, Chaldean, Greek-Melkite, Latin, Maronite and Syrian rites. During a visit to Syria in May 2001, Pope John Paul II became the first pontiff in history to enter a mosque. Early in the 21st century, growing instability in neighboring countries, including Iraq, led to an influx of Christians and challenges for the small but flourishing Catholic community. Christians have faced severe violence in the country over the last year owing to the bloody civil war in the country, with rebel groups committing attacks and massacres of Christian villages. Many fear for the future of the Christian population in the country.

Taiwan*

Archd., 2; dioc., 8; card., 1; abp., 3; bp., 9; parishes, 449; priests, 639 (231 dioc., 408 rel.); p.d., 1; sem., 59; bros., 61; srs., 1,050; catechists, 279; bap., 3,298; Caths., 243,000 (1.03%); tot. pop., 23,529,000.

Democratic island state, 100 miles off the southern coast of mainland China; capital, Taipei. Attempts to introduce Christianity in the 17th century were unsuccessful. Evangelization in the 19th century resulted in some 1,300 converts in 1895. Missionary endeavor was hampered by the Japanese, who occupied the island following the Sino-Japanese war of 1894-95. Great progress was made in missionary endeavor among the Chinese who emigrated to the island (seat of the Nationalist Government of the Republic of China) following the Communist takeover of the mainland in 1949. The hierarchy was established in 1952. Many Taiwanese Catholics have worked to form a bridge to Catholics in mainland China.

Tajikistan*

Mission, 3; parishes, 3; priests, 4 (4 rel.); srs., 8; bap., 14; Cath., 4,000 (0.05%); tot. pop. 7,638,000.

Independent republic (1992) in Asia; formerly part of the USSR; capital, Dushanbe. The majority of the population is Sunni Muslim. When the Vatican established diplomatic relations in 1996, Church officials estimated most of the country's Catholics had fled. In 1997, the Vatican established a mission in the country.

Tanzania*

Archd., 5; dioc., 29; card., 1; abp., 5; bp., 37; parishes, 977; priests, 2,791 (1,805 dioc., 986 rel.); p.d. 1; sem., 1,284; bros., 775; srs., 10,537; catechists, 15,073; bap., 339,770; Caths., 13,900,000 (30.3%); tot. pop., 45,798,000.

Republic on and off the eastern coast of Africa; capital, Dar es Salaam. The first Catholic mission in the former Tanganyikan portion of the republic was manned by Holy Ghost Fathers in 1868. The hierarchy was established there in 1953. Zanzibar was the landing place of Augustinians with the Portuguese in 1499. Some evangelization was attempted between then and 1698 when the Arabs expelled all priests from the territory. There was no Catholic missionary activity from then until the 1860s. The Holy Ghost Fathers arrived in 1863 and were entrusted with the mission in 1872. Zanzibar was important as a point of departure for missionaries to Tanganyika, Kenya and other places in East Africa. A vicariate for Zanzibar was set up in 1906.

In the late 20th century the Church in Tanzania saw an increase in vocations and an active Church life. The bishops assisted hundreds of thousands of refugees from Rwanda, Burundi and Mozambique. More recently, Church leaders worked to stem the AIDS pandemic and to improve education.

Thailand*

Archd., 2; dioc., 8; card., 1; abp., 3; bp., 14; parishes, 479; priests, 830 (519 dioc., 311 rel.); sem., 347; bros., 149; srs., 1,450; catechists, 1,661; bap., 7,250; Caths., 361,000 (.5%); tot. pop., 68,252,000.

Constitutional monarchy in southeast Asia; capital, Bangkok. The first Christians in the region were Portuguese traders who arrived early in the 16th century. A number of missionaries began arriving in the mid-1500s, but pastoral care was confined mostly to the Portuguese until the 1660s, when evangelization began. A seminary was organized in 1665, a vicariate was set up four years later, and a point of departure was established for China. Persecution and death for some of the missionaries ended evangelization efforts in 1688. It was resumed, however, and made progress from 1824 onward. In 1881 missionaries were sent from Siam to neighboring Laos. The hierarchy was established in 1965. Archbp. Michael Michai Kitbunchu was named the first Thai cardinal in 1983. The Church is recognized for its social justice efforts, including work with refugees.

Togo*

Archd., 1; dioc., 6; abp., 3; bp., 8; parishes, 207; priests, 651 (491 dioc., 160 rel.); sem., 572; bros., 216; srs., 901; catechists, 5,926; bap., 31,285; Caths.,

1,843,000 (30%); tot. pop., 6,150,000.

Republic on the west coast of Africa; capital, Lome. The first Catholic missionaries in the area, where slave raiders operated for nearly 200 years, were members of the African Missions Society who arrived in 1563. They were followed by Divine Word Missionaries in 1914, when an apostolic prefecture was organized. At that time the Catholic population numbered about 19,000. The African Missionaries returned after their German predecessors were deported following World War I. The first indigenous priest was ordained in 1922. The hierarchy was established in 1955. In the early 1990s, Archbp. Philippe Fanoko Kossi Kpodzro of Lome served as president of the transitional legislative assembly.

Tonga*

Dioc., 1; bp., 1; parishes, 14; priests, 36 (29 dioc., 7 rel.); sem., 27; bros., 2; srs., 37; bap., 523; Caths., 14,000 (13.7%); tot. pop., 102,000.

Polynesian monarchy in the southwestern Pacific, consisting of about 150 islands; capital, Nuku'alofa. Marists started missionary work in 1842, some years after Protestants had begun evangelization. By 1880 the Catholic population numbered about 1,700. A vicariate was organized in 1937. The hierarchy was established in 1966. Tonga established diplomatic relations with the Holy See in 1994.

Trinidad and Tobago*

Archd., 1; abp., 2; bp., 1; parishes, 61; priests, 109 (48 dioc., 61 rel.); sem., 19; bros., 5; srs., 152; catechists, 700; bap., 3,812; Caths., 337,000 (25.6%); tot. pop., 1,318,000.

Independent nation, consisting of two islands in the Caribbean; capital, Port-of-Spain. The first Catholic Church in Trinidad was built in 1591, years after several missionary ventures had been launched and a number of missionaries killed. Capuchins were there from 1618 until about 1802. Missionary work continued after the British gained control early in the 19th century. Cordial relations have existed between the Church and state, both of which have manifested their desire for the development of indigenous clergy. In 1999, Church leaders protested reinstatement of the death penalty.

Tunisia*

Dioc., 1; abp., 1; parishes, 10; priests, 32 (10 dioc., 22 rel.); bros., 5; sem., 2; srs., 121; bap., 42; Caths., 25,000 (.02%); tot. pop., 10,778,000.

Republic on the northern coast of Africa; capital, Tunis. Ancient Carthage, now a site outside the capital city of Tunis, hosted early Church councils and was home to Church fathers like St. Augustine. Carthage was devastated by Vandals in the fifth century and invaded by Muslims in the seventh century, after which it had few Christians until the 19th century. An apostolic vicariate was organized in 1843, and the Carthage Archdiocese was established in 1884. The Catholic population in 1892 consisted of most of the approximately 50,000 Europeans in the country. When Tunis became a republic in 1956, most of the Europeans left the country. A 1964 agreement with the Vatican and Holy See suppressed the Archdiocese of Carthage and replaced it with the Territorial Prelature of Tunis. In 1995 the prelature was made a diocese.

Today Tunisia's Catholics are predominantly foreign nationals. The Church's social presence is seen in schools, hospitals and institutions for the disabled.

Turkey*

Archd., 3; v.a., 2; ord., 1; ap. ex., 1; abp., 2; bp., 3; parishes, 56; priests, 72 (13 dioc., 59 rel.); p.d., 3; sem., 5; bros., 15; srs., 61; bap., 132; Caths., 47,000 (.06%); tot. pop., 75,176,000.

Republic in Asia Minor and southeastern Europe; capital, Ankara. Christian communities were established in apostolic times, as attested in the Acts of the Apostles, some of the Letters of St. Paul, and Revelation. The territory was the scene of heresies and ecumenical councils, the place of residence of Fathers of the Church, and the area in which ecclesiastical organization reached the dimensions of more than 450 sees in the middle of the seventh century. The region remained generally Byzantine except for the period of the Latin occupation of Constantinople from 1204 to 1261, but was conquered by the Ottoman Turks in 1453 and remained under their domination until establishment of the republic in 1923. Christians, always a minority, numbered more Orthodox than Catholics; they all were under some restrictions during the Ottoman period. They suffered persecution in the 19th and 20th centuries, the Armenians being the most numerous victims. Turkey is overwhelmingly Muslim. Catholics are tolerated to a degree.

Turkmenistan*

Mission, 1; parish, 1; priests, 2 (rel.); bap., 6; Caths., 1,000 (0.02%); tot. pop., 5,216,000.

Former constituent republic of USSR; independent, 1991; capital, Ashgabat. Almost all the population is Sunni Muslim. The Vatican established diplomatic relations with the country in 1996 and set up a mission in 1997.

Tuvalu

Mission, 1; parish, 1; priest, 2 (rel.); bap., 2; Caths., 100; tot. pop., 10,000.

Independent state (1978) in Oceania, consisting of 9 islands; capital, Funafuti.

Uganda*

Archd., 4; dioc., 15; mil. ord., 1; card., 1; abp., 6; bp., 27; parishes, 508; priests, 2,061 (1,728 dioc., 333 rel.); p.d., 2; sem., 1,470; bros., 602; srs., 3,581; catechists, 15,063; bap., 552,352; Caths., 15,346,000 (45%); tot. pop., 34,131,000.

Republic in East Africa; capital, Kampala. The Missionaries of Africa (White Fathers) were the first Catholic missionaries, starting in 1879. Persecution broke out from 1885 to 1887, taking a toll of 22 Catholic martyrs, who were canonized in 1964, and a number of Anglican victims. (Pope Paul VI honored all those who died for the faith during a visit to Kampala in 1969.) By 1888, there were more than 8,000 Catholics. Evangelization was resumed in 1894, after being interrupted by war, and proceeded thereafter. The first African bishop was ordained in 1939. The hierarchy was established in 1953.

The Church was suppressed during the erratic regime of President Idi Amin, who was deposed in the spring of 1979. Guerrilla activity in northern and southwestern Uganda has hampered Church workers. The Church has devoted much of its resources to caring for the many victims of HIV/ AIDS in the country. In northern Uganda as a guerrilla war continued, church officials worked to protect children from being inducted into military or guerrilla service.

Ukraine*

Major archbishopric, 2 (Ukrainian); archd., 4 (Metropolitans); dioc., 12; pat. ex., 3; card., 2; abp., 3; bp., 32; parishes, 4,632; priests, 3,744 (3,130 dioc., 614 rel.); p.d., 27; sem., 1,075; bros., 261; srs., 1,267; catechists, 2,288; bap., 39,224; Caths., 4,847,000 (10.6%); tot. pop., 45,779,000.

Independent republic bordering on the Black Sea; former USSR republic; capital, Kiev. The baptism of Vladimir and his people in 988 marked the beginning of Christianity in the territory of Kievan Rus, which is included in today's Ukraine. The 1596 Union of Brest brought the Ukrainian Byzantine- rite community back into communion with Rome. The Eastern Catholic Church was officially suppressed and underground in the USSR from the late 1940s; all of its bishops were killed or imprisoned and its property seized by the government and given to the Orthodox. Some Catholic priests continued to minister clandestinely under communist rule.

As the Eastern Church regained its legal status under Soviet President Mikhail Gorbachev, serious tensions arose with the Orthodox over ownership of property and the allegiance of priests and lay people. Latin-rite dioceses were re-established in 1991. In the late 1990s, rising inflation and weakening currency, aggravated by the government's and some companies' failure to pay wages, led Ukrainian Church leaders to fight homelessness and hunger. Despite opposition from Ukraine's largest Orthodox Church, Pope John Paul II visited Ukraine in June 2001. Despite Russian Orthodox objections, the Ukrainian Catholic Church moved its headquarters from Lviv to Kiev and Halych in 2005. Catholics share in the deep concern for the future of Ulraine in the face of Russian aggression in 2014.

United Arab Emirates*

V.a, 1; bp., 2; parishes, 8; priests, 32 (4 dioc., 28 rel.); srs., 38; bap., 1,997; Caths., 800,000 (9.4%); tot. pop., 8,495,000.

Independent state along Persian Gulf; capital, Abu Dhabi. The apostolic vicariate of Arabia has its seat in Abu Dhabi. It includes the states of Bahrain, Oman, Qatar, Saudi Arabia and Yemen (see separate entries) as well as United Arab Emirates. Diplomatic relations with the Holy See were established in May 2007.

United States*

(See **Catholic Church in the U.S.**, p. 352; see also **U.S. Catholic History**, p. 358; and **Statistics of the Church in the U.S.**, p. 432).

Uruguay*

Archd., 1; dioc., 9; abp., 2; bp., 13; parishes, 235; priests, 501 (257 dioc., 244 rel.); p.d., 103; sem., 75; bros., 92; srs., 876; catechists, 4,257; bap., 20,489; Caths., 2,603,000 (77%); tot. pop., 3,381,000.

Republic on the southeast coast of South America; capital, Montevideo. The Spanish established a settle ment in 1624 and evangelization followed. Missionaries followed the reduction pattern to reach the Indians, form them in the faith and train them in agriculture, husbandry, other arts, and the experience of managing property and living in community. The constitution of 1830 made Catholicism the religion of the state and subsidized some of its activities, principally the missions to the Indians. Separation of Church and state was provided for in the constitution of 1917. In 1997, despite a court decision halting further investigations, the Church pledged to make one last effort to help search for people who remained missing from the 1973-85 military dictatorship.

Uzbekistan*

A.a, 1; parishes, 5; priests, 9 (1 dioc., 8 rel.); bros., 2; sem., 1; srs.,10; bap., 16; Caths. 4,000 (0.01%); tot. pop. 29,736,000.

Former republic of USSR; independent, 1991; capital, Tashkent. The communist government confiscated Catholic properties in 1917 and severely repressed the practice of religion in the country. The country won its independence in 1991. The majority of the population is Sunni Muslim. A small number of Catholics live in Tashkent. The Vatican established a mission in 1997. In 2005 the Church became an apostolic administration and received its first Catholic bishop.

Vanuatu*

Dioc., 1; bp., 1; parishes, 31; priests, 30 (20 dioc., 10 rel.); p.d.; sem., 14; bros., 13; srs., 46; catechists, 300; bap., 530; Caths., 29,000 (12%); tot. pop., 240,000.

Independent (July 29, 1980) island group in the southwest Pacific; capital, Vila. Effective, though slow, evangelization by Catholic missionaries began about 1887. An apostolic vicariate was set up in 1904. The hierarchy was established in 1966.

Vatican City State

(See separate entry, p. 261)

Venezuela*

Archd., 9; dioc., 24; ord.; v.a., 4; ap. ex., 2; mil. ord. 1; card., 1; abp., 11; bp., 42; parishes, 1,378; priests, 2,774 (1,882 dioc., 892 rel.); p.d.,204; sem., 1,160; bros., 202; srs., 3,293; catechists, 28,980; bap., 404,684; Caths., 26,095,000 (88%); tot. pop., 29,718,000.

Republic in northern South America; capital, Caracas. Evangelization began in 1513-14 and involved members of a number of religious orders who worked in assigned territories, developing missions into pueblos or villages of Indian converts. Nearly 350 towns originated as missions. The first diocese was established in 1531. Fifty-four missionaries met death by violence from the start of missionary work until 1817. Missionary work was seriously hindered during the wars of independence in the second decade of the 19th century and continued in decline through the rest of the century as dictator followed dictator in a period of political turbulence. Restoration of the missions got under way in 1922. In mid-2005, amid increasing poverty, several surveys found the Catholic Church had the highest respect of any of the nation's institutions. The Church faced hostility from the late Pres. Hugo Chavez, including attacks on the offices of the papal nuncio.

Vietnam

Archd., 3; dioc., 23; card., 1; abp., 2; bp., 40; parishes, 2,675; priests, 4,493 (3,299 dioc., 1,194 rel.); p.d., 2; sem., 3,172; bros., 2,179; srs., 14,797; catechists, 56,203; bap., 173,596, Caths., 6,573,000 (7.4%); tot. pop., 88,773,000.

Country in southeast Asia, reunited officially July 2, 1976, as the Socialist Republic of Vietnam; capital, Hanoi.

Catholicism was introduced in 1533, but missionary work was intermittent until 1615, when Jesuits arrived to stay. Two vicariates were organized in 1659. A seminary was set up in 1666, and two Vietnamese priests were ordained two years later. A congregation of native women religious formed in 1670 is still active. Severe persecution broke out in 1698, three times in the 18th century, and again in the 19th. Up to 300,000 people suffered in some way from persecution during the 50 years before 1883, when the French moved in to secure religious liberty for the Catholics. Most of the 117 beatified Martyrs of Vietnam were killed during this 50-year period. After the French were forced out of Vietnam in 1954, the country was partitioned at the 17th parallel. The North became Communist and the Viet Cong, joined by North Vietnamese regular army troops in 1964, fought to gain control of the South. In 1954 there were approximately 1.1 million Catholics in the North and 480,000 in the South. More than 650,000 fled to the South to avoid the government repression. In South Vietnam, the Church continued to develop during the war years.

After the end of the war in 1975, the government exercised control over virtually all aspects of Church life. In the late 1980s, bishops noted some softening of the government's hard line. In the 1990s, the Vatican and Vietnam held intermittent talks on Church-state issues, with sporadic progress reported, but in 1997, the government censored the section of the "Catechism of the Catholic Church" that dealt with human rights. Although at times the Vatican was forced to wait years for government approval of bishops' appointments, in the late 20th and early 21st century, Vatican delegations made regular visits to Vietnam to discuss the appointments and other Church-related issues. Early in the 21st century, the government approved a series of bishops'

appointments in northern Vietnam, and Church leaders said they saw a rejuvenation of the faith there. Recent years have also seen government seizures of Catholic property, including the old nunciature. Catholic protests have resulted in arrests and threats. The Vietnam-Holy See Joint Working Group has held several meetings in the Vatican to strengthen and develop bilateral relations between Vietnam and the Holy See. In Jan. 2013, then-Pope Benedict XVI met with the head of the Vietnamese Communist Party in the Vatican.

Virgin Islands (U.S.)

Dioc., 1 (St. Thomas, suffragan of Washington, DC); bp., 2; parishes, 8; priests, 23 (15 dioc., 8 rel.); p.d., 27; sem., 6; bros., 3; srs., 24; bap., 256; Caths., 30,000 (27.5%); tot. pop., 109,000.

Organized unincorporated U.S. territory in Atlantic Ocean; capital, Charlotte Amalie on St. Thomas (one of the three principal islands). The islands were discovered by Columbus in 1493 and named for St. Ursula and her virgin companions. Missionaries began evangelization in the 16th century. A church on St. Croix dates from about 1660; another, on St. Thomas, from 1774. The Baltimore archdiocese had jurisdiction over the islands from 1804 to 1820, when it was passed on to the first of several places in the Caribbean area. Some trouble arose over a pastoral appointment in the 19th century, resulting in a small schism. The Redemptorists took over pastoral care in 1858; normal conditions have prevailed since.

Wales*

Archd., 1; dioc., 2; abp., 1; bp., 4; parishes, 156; priests, 193 (119 dioc., 74 rel.); p.d., 33; sem., 8; bros., 84; srs., 319; bap, 2,159; Caths., 208,779 (.7%); tot. pop., 3,073,000.

Part of the United Kingdom, on the western part of the island of Great Britain. Celtic missionaries completed evangelization by the end of the sixth century, the climax of what has been called the age of saints. Welsh Christianity received its distinctive Celtic character at this time. Some conflict developed when attempts were made — and proved successful later — to place the Welsh Church under the jurisdiction of Canterbury; the Welsh opted for direct contact with Rome.

The Church made progress despite the depredations of Norsemen in the eighth and ninth centuries. Norman infiltration occurred near the middle of the 12th century, resulting in a century-long effort to establish territorial dioceses and parishes to replace the Celtic organizational plan of monastic centers and satellite churches. The Western Schism produced split views and allegiances. Actions of Henry VIII in breaking away from Rome had serious repercussions. Proscription and penal laws crippled the Church, resulted in heavy defections and touched off a 150-year period of repression. Methodism prevailed by 1750. Modern Catholicism came to Wales with Irish immigrants in the 19th century, when the number of Welsh Catholics was negligible. Catholic emancipation was granted in 1829. The hierarchy was restored in 1850. Wales shares a bishops' conference with England.

Yemen*

Parishes, 4; priests, 4 (rel.); srs., 22; bap., 2; Caths., 3,000 (0.01%); tot. pop., 24,527,000.

Republic on southern coast of Arabian peninsula; capital, Sana. Formerly North Yemen (Arab Republic of Yemen) and South Yemen (People's Republic of Yemen); formally reunited in 1990. Christians perished in the first quarter of the sixth century. Muslims have been in control since the seventh century. The state religion is Islam; the Church is under the ecclesiastical jurisdiction of Arabia apostolic vicariate. In the early 1990s, Salesians reported some harassment of Church workers in the South. In early 1998, three Missionaries of Charity nuns were murdered. The Vatican established diplomatic relations with Yemen in October 1998.

Zambia*

Archd., 2; dioc., 9; Card., 1; abp., 3; bp., 9; parishes, 316; priests, 860 (462 dioc., 398 rel.); sem., 567; bros., 201; srs., 2,021; catechists, 7,117; bap., 46,533; Caths., 4,602,000 (33%); tot. pop., 13,983,000.

Republic in central Africa; capital, Lusaka. Portuguese priests did some evangelizing in the 16th and 17th centuries but no results of their work remained in the 19th century. Jesuits began work in the South in the 1880s and White Fathers in the North and East in 1895. Evangelization of the western region began for the first time in 1931. The number of Catholics doubled in the 20 years following World War II. Zambian Catholics have welcomed tens of thousands of refugees from the region. In the 1990s, Zambian Church leaders worked caring for victims of HIV/AIDS and spoke out against foreign debt. In 2003, the bishops urged parishes to set up civic education programs to help with the nation's constitutional review process.

Zimbabwe*

Archd., 2; dioc., 6; abp., 4; bp., 6; parishes, 238; priests, 491 (280 dioc., 211 rel.); p.d., 22; sem., 494; bros., 96; srs., 1,010; catechists, 5,919; bap., 24,658; Caths., 1,812,000 (11.2%); tot. pop., 16,138,000.

Independent republic (1980) in south central Africa; capital, Harare. Earlier unsuccessful missionary ventures preceded the introduction of Catholicism in 1879. Missionaries began to make progress after 1893. The hierarchy was established in 1955; the first black bishop was ordained in 1973.

In 1969, four years after the government of Ian Smith made a unilateral declaration of independence from England, a new constitution was enacted for the purpose of assuring continued white supremacy over the black majority. Catholic and Protestant prelates in the country protested. The Smith regime was ousted in 1979 after seven years of civil war in which at least 25,000 people were killed.

In 1997, the bishops published a report detailing more than 7,000 cases of killings, torture and human rights abuses by government troops in western Zimbabwe from 1981-87. As the Church entered the 21st century, it was devoting tremendous resources toward palliative care of AIDS victims and work with AIDS orphans. Some lay Church leaders were outspoken against government-backed campaigns of violence against white landowners and the poor; Bp. Pius Ncube of Bulawayo was targeted for speaking against government abuses. In 2007, the bishops issued a strong pastoral letter condemning Robert Mugabe's regime, and, after Mugabe failed to win a majority in the 2008 presidential election, spoke out against post-election violence.

CATHOLIC WORLD STATISTICS

(Principal sources: *Statistical Yearbook of the Church*, 2012 (the latest edition); figures are as of Jan. 1, 2013, unless indicated otherwise.)

	Africa	North America[1]	South America	Asia	Europe	Oceania	WORLD TOTALS
Patriarchates[2]	2	–	–	8	2	–	12
Archdioceses	94	91	102	124	181	18	610
Dioceses	406	365	450	350	513	56	2,113
Prelatures		7	27	4	6	–	44
Abbacies		–	–		10	–	10
Exarchates/Ords.		2	6	1	15	1	25
Military Ords.	3	4	9	3	15	2	36
Vicariates Apostolic	22	5	38	21	1	–	87
Prefectures	4	–	1	4	1	1	11
Apostolic Admin.	–	–	1	3	4	–	8
Independent Missions	1	2	–	3	–	2	8
Cardinals[3]	18	24	27	19	113	3	210
Patriarchs[2]	1	–	–	8	2	–	11
Archbishops	143	158	167	199	372	29	1,068[4]
Bishops	542	768	787	541	1,104	103	3,845[4]
Priests	40,133	73,472	49,452	60,042	186,489	4,725	414,313
Diocesan	27,493	50,900	31,964	34,731	131,742	2,731	279,561
Religious	12,640	22,572	17,488	25,311	54,747	1,994	134,752
Perm. Deacons	419	20,950	6,308	230	13,826	371	42,104
Brothers	8,645	9,249	6,704	11,688	17,574	1,454	55,314
Sisters	68,590	110,868	75,527	169,590	269,532	8,422	702,529
Maj. Seminarians	27,728	16,189	19,652	35,476	19,928	1,085	120,051
Sec. Inst. Mbrs. (Men)	77	42	212	72	367	1	771
Sec. Inst. Mbrs. (Women)	851	1,620	4,355	1,839	15,993	44	24,702
Lay Missionaries	7,195	58,399	259,004	31,344	6,456	90	362,488
Catechists	393,580	941,351	904,756	365,720	549,878	15,358	3,170,643
Parishes	15,217	33,455	24,314	24,169	122,159	2,426	221,740[5]
Kindergartens	14,711	10,192	6,860	14,064	23,959	1,402	71,188
Students	1,444,069	602,289	779,779	1,875,272	1,954,799	72,462	6,728,670
Elem./PrimarySchools	36,613	13,133	10,062	16,097	15,884	3,457	95,246
Students	16,472,059	3,312,361	3,209,505	5,675,312	2,939,700	690,732	32,299,669
Secondary Schools	12,060	4,637	6,328	10,450	9,633	675	43,783
Students	5,241,057	1,659,517	2,079,024	5,801,336	3,660,559	427,744	18,869,237
Students, Higher Insts[6]	106,957	627,450	342,473	1,472,056	345,396	13,232	2,907,573
Social Service Facilities	15,419	18,567	20,327	21,425	37,442	2,172	115,352
Hospitals	1,298	878	615	1,137	1,039	200	5,167
Dispensaries	5,256	2,947	2,190	3,760	2,637	532	17,322
Leprosaria	229	26	46	322	21	4	648
Homes for Aged/Handic.	632	1,924	1,891	2,520	8,200	532	15,699
Orphanages	1,398	836	1,582	3,980	2,194	110	10,124
Nurseries	2,099	1,048	2,613	3,661	2,284	110	11,596
Matrimonial Advice Ctrs.	1,728	3,458	2,178	933	6,173	274	14,744
Social Educ. Ctrs.	223	688	863	581	1,141	167	3,663
Other Institutions	2,556	6,762	8,349	4,751	13,752	219	36,389
Baptisms	3,839,544	3,578,084	4,107,528	2,581,901	2,170,870	130,375	16,408,302
Under Age 7	2,577,280	3,261,043	3,527,000	2,147,877	2,083,521	116,000	13,712,721
Over Age 7	1,262,264	317,041	580,528	434,024	87,349	14,375	2,695,581
Marriages	354,096	529,266	549,345	626,380	648,540	21,399	2,728,026
Between Catholics	310,728	478,817	533,962	562,442	585,594	13,943	2,485,486
Mixed Marriages	43,368	50,449	15,383	63,938	62,946	7,456	243,540
Catholic Pop[7]	198,587,000	252,263,000	346,556,000	134,641,000	286,868,000	9,706,000	1,228,621,000
World Population	1,066,140,000	545,930,000	401,041,000	4,254,259,000	718,706,000	37,301,000	7,023,377,000

1. Includes Central America. 2. For listing and description, see Index. 3. As of Aug. 30, 2014. 4. Figures for the hierarchy (cardinals, abps. and bps.) include 2,729 ordinaries, 548 coadjutors or aux., 292 with offices in the Roman Curia, 17 in other offices, 1,547 ret.5. 172,587 have parish priests; 45,668 are administered by other priests; 528 are entrusted to perm. deacons; 208 to bros; 575 to women rel.; 1,089 to lay people; 1,085 vacant. 6. There are also approximately 526,236 in univs. for ecclesiastical studies and 3,103,072 other univ. students. 7. Percentages of Catholics in world pop.: Africa, 18.6; North America (Catholics 86,452,000; tot. pop., 348,921,000), 24.7; Central America (Catholics, 165,811,000; tot. pop., 197,009,000), 84; South America, 86; Asia, 3.1; Europe, 40; Oceania, 26; world, 17.5 (Catholic totals do not include those in areas that could not be surveyed, est. to be approx. 9 million).

EPISCOPAL CONFERENCES

(*Principal sources:* Annuario Pontificio *and* Catholic Almanac *survey.*)

Episcopal conferences, organized and operating under general norms and particular statutes approved by the Holy See, are official bodies in and through which the bishops of a given country or territory act together as pastors of the Church. Listed according to countries or regions are titles and addresses of conferences, telephone numbers (where possible), and names and sees of presidents.

Africa, Northern: Conference Episcopale Regionale du Nord de l'Afrique (CERNA), 13 rue KhelifaBoukhalfa, 16000 Algiers, Algeria; (021) 63-35-62. Abp. Vincent Landel (Rabat).

Africa, Southern: Southern African Catholic Bishops' Conference (SACBC), 140 Visagie St., P.O. Box 941, Pretoria 0001, S. Africa; (021) 65-35-62. Abp. Stephen Brislin (Cape Town).

Albania: Conferenza Episcopale dell'Albania, Tirane, Rruga Don Bosco 1, Kulia Postare 2950; (042) 47-159. Abp. Angelo Massafra, O.F.M. (Shkodre-Pult).

Angola and São Tome: Conferencia Episcopal de Angola e HR Tome (CEAST), C.P. 3579 Luanda, Angola; (02) 44-36-86. Abp. Gabriel Mbilingi (Lubango).

Antilles: Antilles Episcopal Conference (AEC), P.O. Box 3086, St. James (Trinidad and Tobago), W.I.; (868) 622-2932. Abp. Patrick Pinder (Nassau).

Arab Countries: Conférence des Evêques Latins dans les Régions Arabes (CELRA), Latin Patriarchate, P.O. Box 14152, Jerusalem (Old City); (02) 628-85-54. Patriarch Fouad Twal (Jerusalem).

Argentina: Conferencia Episcopal Argentina (CEA), C1008AAV, Calle Suipacha 1034, 1008 Buenos Aires; (011) 4328-95-70. Abp. Jose Maria Arancedo (Santa Fe de la Vera Cruz).

Australia: Australian Catholic Bishops' Conference, 63 Currong St., Braddon, A.C.T. 2601; (02) 6201-9845; www.catholic.org.au. Abp. Denis Hart (Melbourne).

Austria: Österreichische Bischofskonferenz, Wollzeile 2, A1010 Vienna; 01-516-11-32.80. Christoph Card. Schönborn, O.P. (Vienna).

Balkans: Int'l. Conference of Bishops of Sts. Cyril and Methodius, 11000 Beograd (Srbija), Visegradska 23; (011) 303-22-46. Abp. Zef Gashi, S.D.B. (Bar).

Bangladesh: Catholic Bishops' Conference of Bangladesh (CBCB), P.O. Box 3, Dhaka1000; (02) 40-88-79. Abp. Patrick D'Rozario, C.S.C. (Dhaka).

Belgium: Bisschoppenconferentie van België — Conférence Épiscopale de Belgique, Rue Guimard 1, B1040 Brussels; (02) 509-96-93; www.catho. be, www.kerknet.be. Abp. Andre-Joseph Leonard (Mechelen-Brussel).

Belarus: Conferentia Episcoporum Catholicorum, 220030 Minsk, pl. Swobody 9; (017) 26.61.27. Bp. Aleksander Kaszkiewicz (Grodno).

Benin: Conférence Episcopale du Bénin, Cotonou, 01 B.P. 491; 30.01.45. Abp. Antoine Ganye (Cotonou).

Bolivia: Conferencia Episcopal Boliviana (CEB), Casilla 2309, Calle Potosi 814, La Paz; (02) 40-67-98. Bp. Oscar Aparicio Cespedes (Military Ordinary).

Bosnia and Herzegovina: Biskupska Konferencija Bosne i Hercegovine (B.K. B.i.H.), Nadbiskupski Ordinariat, Kaptol 7, 71000 Sarajevo; (071) 47-21-78. Bp. Franjo Komarica (Banja Luka).

Brazil: Conferência Nacional dos Bispos do Brasil (CNBB), C.P. 02067, SE/Sul Quadra 801, Conjunto "B," 70259970 Brasilia, D.F.; (061) 313-8300. Card. Raymondo Damasceno Assis (Aparecida).

Bulgaria: Mejduritual Episcopska Konferenzia vâv Bâlgaria, Ul. Liulin Planina 5, 1606 Sofia; (0) 540-406. Bp. Christo Proykov (Briula, titular see).

Burkina Faso and Niger: Conférence des Evêques de Burkina Faso et du Niger, B.P. 1195, Ouagadougou, Burkina Faso; 30-60-26. Abp. Seraphim François Rouamba (Koupela).

Burma: See **Myanmar**.

Burundi: Conférence des Evêques catholiques du Burundi (C.E.CA.B.), B. P. 1390, 5 Blvd. de l'Uprona, Bujumbura; 223-263. Bp. Gervais Banshimiyubusa (Ngozi).

Cameroon: Conférence Episcopale Nationale du Cameroun (CENC), BP 1963, Yaoundé; 231-15-92. Abp. Joseph Atanga, S.J. (Bertoua).

Canada: See **Canadian Conference of Catholic Bishops** in **Catholic Church in Canada**, p. 441.

Central African Republic: Conférence Episcopale Centrafricaine (CECA), B.P. 1518, Bangui; 50-24-84. Abp. Paulin Pomodimo (Bangui).

Chad: Conférence Episcopale du Tchad, B.P. 456, N'Djaména; (235) 51-74-44. Bp. Jean-Claude Bouchard, O.M.I. (Pala).

Chile: Conferencia Episcopal de Chile (CECH), Casilla 517V, Correo 21, Cienfuegas 47, Santiago; (02) 671-77-33. Abp. Andrello Ricardo Ezzati, S.D.B. (Santiago de Chile).

China: Chinese Regional Episcopal Conference, 34 Lane 32, KuangFu South Rd., Taipeh 10552, Taiwan; (02) 578-2355. Abp. John Hung Shan-chuan (Taipei).

Colombia: Conferencia Episcopal de Colombia, Apartado 7448, Carrera 8ª 47, N. 8485, Santafé de Bogotá D.E.; (91) 311-42-77. Card. Rubén Salazar Gómez (Barranquila).

Congo: Conférence Episcopale du Congo, B.P. 200, Brazzaville; (83) 06-29. Bp. Louis Portella Mbuyu (Kinkala).

Congo, Democratic Republic (formerly Zaire): Conférence Episcopale du Zaïre (CEZ), B.P. 3258, KinshasaGombe; 012-33-992. Bp. Nicolas Djomo Lola (Tshumbe).

Costa Rica: Conferencia Episcopal de Costa Rica (CECOR), Apartado 497, 1000 San Jose; 221-30-53. Abp. Hugo Barrantes Ureña (San Jose de Costa Rica).

Côte d'Ivoire: Conference Episcopale de la Côte d'Ivoire, B.P. 1287, Abidjan 01. Bp. Alexis Touabli Youlo (Agboville).

Croatia: Hrvatska Biskupska Konferencija, Kaptol 22, HR10000 Zagreb; 385-01-481-18-93; www.hbk.hr. Bp. Marin Srakic (Djakovo-Osijek).

Cuba: Conferencia de Obispos Católicos de Cuba (COCC), Apartado 594, Calle 26 n. 314 Miramar, 10100 Havana 1; (07) 22-3868. Abp. Guillermo Garcia Ibanez Dionisio (Santiago de Cuba).

Czech Republic: Ceská Biskupská Konference, Sekretariat, Thakurova 3, 160 00 Praha (Prague) 6; (02) 33-15-421. Card. Dominik Duca, O.P. (Prague).

Dominican Republic: Conferencia del Episcopado Dominicano (CED), Apartado 186, Santo Domingo; (809) 685-3141. Nicolas de Jesus Card. Lopez Rodriguez (Santo Domingo).

Ecuador: Conferencia Episcopal Ecuatoriana, Apartado 1081, Avenida América 1805 y Lagasca, Quito; (02) 23-82-21. Abp. Antonio Arregui Yarza (Guayaquil).

El Salvador: Conferencia Episcopal de El Salvador (CEDES). 15 Av. Norte 1420, Col. Layco, Apartado 1310, San Salvador; 25-8997. Abp. Jose Luis Escobar Alas (San Salvador).

Equatorial Guinea: Conferencia Episcopal de Guinea Ecuatorial, Apartado 106, Malabo. Abp. Ildefonso Obama Obono (Malabo).

Ethiopia: Ethiopian Episcopal Conference, P.O. Box 21322, Addis Ababa; (01) 55-03-00. Abp. Berhaneyesus Demerew Souraphiel, C.M. (Addis Ababa).

France: Conférence des Evêques de France, 106 rue du Bac, 75341 Paris CEDEX 07; 33-01-45-49-69-70; www. cef.fr. André Cardinal Vingt-Trois (Paris).

Gabon: Conférence Episcopale du Gabon, B.P. 2146, Libreville; 72-20-73. Bp. Timothée Modibo-Nzockena (Franceville).

Gambia, Liberia and Sierra Leone: InterTerritorial Catholic Bishops' Conference of the Gambia, Liberia and Sierra Leone (ITCABIC), Santanno House, P.O. Box 893, Freetown, Sierra Leone; (022) 22-82-40. Bp. Daniel Koroma (Kenema).

Germany: Deutsche Bischofskonferenz, Postfach 2962, Kaiserstrasse 163, D53019 Bonn; (0049) 228-103-290. Abp. Robert Zollitsch (Freiburg im Breisgau).

Ghana: Ghana Bishops' Conference, National Catholic Secretariat, P.O. Box 9712 Airport, Accra; (021) 500-491. Bp. Joseph Osei-Bonsu (Konongo-Mampong).

Great Britain: Bishops' Conference of England and Wales, General Secretariat, 39 Eccleston Square, London, SWIV IBX; (020) 7630-8220. Card. Vincent Nichols (Westminster).

Greece: Conferentia Episcopalis Graeciae, Odos Homirou 9, 106 72 Athens; (01) 3642-311. Bp. Fragkiskos Papamanolis, O.F.M. Cap, (Syros, Santorini, and Milos).

Guatemala: Conferencia Episcopal de Guatemala (CEG), Apartado 1698, 01901 Ciudad de Guatemala; 543-18-27/8. Bp. Rodolfo Valenzuela Nunez (Vera Paz).

Guinea: Conférence Episcopale de la Guinée, B.P. 1006 bis, Conkary. Bp. Emmanuel Felemou (Kankan).

Guinea Bissau: See **Senegal**.

Haiti: Conférence Episcopale de Haïti (CEH). B.P. 1572, Angle rues Piquant et Lammarre, Port-au-Prince; 222-5194. Bp. Chibly Langlois (Les Cayes).

Honduras: Conferencia Episcopal de Honduras (CEH), Apartado 847, Blvd. Estadio Suyapa, Tegucigalpa; (504) 32-40-43. Oscar Andrés Card. Rodríguez Maradiaga (Tegucigalpa).

Hungary: Magyar Katolikus Püspöki Konferencia, H-1071 Budapest VII, Városligeti fasor 45; 1-342-69-59. Peter Card. Erdö (Esztergom-Budapest).

India: Catholic Bishops' Conference of India (CBCI), CBCI Centre, Ashok Place, Goldakkhana, New Delhi110001; (011) 334-44-70. Vard. Baselios Thottunkal (Trivandrum).

Conference of Catholic Bishops of India – Latin Rite (CCBI L.R.), Bangalore-560084, Karnataka, D'Costa Lay out, 2nd Cross, Wheeler's Rd., St. Mary's Town; (080)

2549.8081. Card. Oswald Gracias (Mumbai).

Indian Ocean: Conférence Episcopale de l'Océan Indien (CEDOI) (includes Islands of Mauritius, Seychelles, Comore and La Réunion), 13 rue Msgr. Gonin, Port Louis, Mauritius; (230) 208-3068. Bp. Denis Wiehe (Victoria).

Indonesia: Konperensi Waligereja Indonesia (KWI), Jl. Cut Mutiah 10, Tromolpos 3044, Jakarta 10002; (021) 33-64-22. Ignatius Suharyo Hardjoatmodjo (Jakarta).

Ireland: Irish Episcopal Conference, "Ara Coeli," Armagh BT61 7QY; 028-3752-2045. Sean Card. Brady (Armagh).

Italy: Conferenza Episcopale Italiana (CEI), Circonvallazione Aurelia, 50, 00165 Rome; 06-663-981. Angelo Card. Bagnasco (Genoa).

Ivory Coast: See **Côte d'Ivoire**.

Japan: Catholic Bishops' Conference of Japan, Shiomi 21010, KotoKu, Tokyo, 135; (03) 56324411. Abp. Leo Jun Ikenaga, S.J. (Osaka).

Kazakstan: Episcopal Conference of Kazakstan, 473003 Astana, 3 Tashenova St., P.O. Box 622; (3172) 37.29.35. Abp. Tomash Peta (Most Blessed Mary, Astana).

Kenya: Kenya Episcopal Conference (KEC), The Kenya Catholic Secretariat, P.O. Box 13475, Nairobi; (020) 444-3133. John Card. Njue (Nairobi).

Korea: Catholic Bishops' Conference of Korea, Box 16, Seoul 100600; (02) 466-3417. Bp. Peter Kang U-il (Cheju).

Laos and Cambodia: Conférence Episcopale du Laos et du Cambodge, c/o Msgr. Pierre Bach, Paris Foreign Missions, 254 Silom Rd., Bangkok 10500; (02) 234-1714. Louis-Marie Ling Mangkhanekoun (Acque nuove di Proconsolare).

Latvia: Latvijas Biskapu Konference, Maza Pils iela 2/a, LV-1050, Riga; (7) 22-72-66. Bp. Janis Bulis (Rezekne-Aglona).

Lesotho: Lesotho Catholic Bishops' Conference, Catholic Secretariat, P.O. Box 200, Maseru 100; (0501) 31-25-25. Abp. Gerard Tlali Lerotholi, O.M.I. (Maseru).

Liberia: Catholic Bishops' Conference of Liberia, 1000 Monrovia 10, P.O. Box 10-2078; 227-245. Bp. Lewis Zeigler (Gbarnga).

Lithuania: Conferentia Episcopalis Lituaniae, Sventaragio, 4, 2001 Vilnius; (5) 212-54-55. Abp. Sigitas Tamkevicius, S.J. (Kaunas).

Madagascar: Conférence Episcopale de Madagascar, 102 bis Av. Maréchal Joffre, Antanimena, B. P 667, Antananarivo; (02) 2220-478. Abp. Desire Tsarahazana (Toamasina).

Malawi: Episcopal Conference of Malawi, Catholic Secretariat of Malawi, P.O. Box 30384, Lilongwe 3; 782-066. Bp. Joseph Mukasa Zuza (Mzuzu).

Malaysia-Singapore-Brunei: Catholic Bishops' Conference of Malaysia, Singapore and Brunei (BCMSB), Xavier Selangor Darul Ehsan, 46000 Petaling Jaya, Malaysia; (03) 758-1371. Abp. John Ha Tiong Hock (Kuching).

Mali: Conférence Episcopale du Mali, B.P. 298, Bamako; 225-499. Bp. Jean-Baptiste Tiama (Sikasso).

Malta: Konferenza Episkopali Maltija, Archbishop's Curia, Floriana; (356) 234317; www.maltachurch.org.mt. Abp. Mario Grech (Malta).

Mexico: See the Conferencia del Episcopado Mexicano (CEM), in the section on the **Catholic**

Church in Mexico, p. 449.

Mozambique: Conferência Episcopal de Moçambique (CEM), Av. Paulo Samuel Kankhomba 188/RC, C.P. 286; (01) 49-07-66. Bp. Lucio Andrice Muandula (Xai-Xai).

Myanmar: Myanmar Catholic Bishops' Conference (MCBC), 292 Pyi Rd., P.O. Box 1080, Yangon; (01) 23-71-98. Bp. John Hsane Hgyi (Pathein).

Namibia: Namibian Catholic Bishops' Conference (NCBC). P.O. Box 11525 W., Windhoek; (061) 22-47-98. Abp. Ndumbukuti Nashenda Liborius, O.M.I. (Windhoek).

Netherlands: Nederlandse Bisschoppenconferentie, Postbus 13049, NL3507 LA, Utrecht; (31)-30-232-69-00; www.omroep.nl/rkk. Card. Willem Eijk (Utrecht).

New Zealand: New Zealand Catholic Bishops Conference, P.O. Box 1937, Wellington 6015; (04) 496-1747. Abp. John Dew (Wellington).

Nicaragua: Conferencia Episcopal de Nicaragua (CEN), Apartado Postal 2407, de Ferretería Lang 1 cuadro al Norte y 1 cuadro al Este, Managua; (02) 666-292. Bp. Rene Jiron Socrates (Juigalpa).

Niger: See Burkina Faso.

Nigeria: Catholic Bishops Conference of Nigeria, P.O. Box 951, 6 Force Rd., Lagos; (01) 263-58-49. Abp. Ignatius Ayau Kaigama (Jos).

Pacific: Conferentia Episcopalis Pacifici (CE PAC), P.O. Box 289, Suva (Fiji); 300-340. Bp. Mafi Soane Patita Paini (Togo).

Pakistan: Pakistan Episcopal Conference, P.O. Box 909, Lahore 54000; (042) 6366-137. Abp. Lawrence J. Saldanha (Lahore).

Panama: Conferencia Episcopal de Panamá (CEP), Apartado 870033, Panama 7; 223-0075. Bp. José Luis Lacunza Maestrojuán, O.A.R. (Goroka).

Papua New Guinea and Solomon Islands: Catholic Bishops' Conference of Papua New Guinea and Solomon Islands, P.O. Box 398, Waigani, N.C.D., Papua New Guinea; 25-9577. Abp. John Ribat, M.S.C. (Port Moresby).

Paraguay: Conferencia Episcopal Paraguaya (CEP), Alberdi 782, Casilla Correo 1436, Asunción; (021) 490-920. Bp. Claudio Gimenez Medina Catalino (Caacupe).

Peru: Conferencia Episcopal Peruana, Apartado 310, Rio de Janeiro 488, Lima 100; (01) 463-10-10. Abp. Salvador Pineiro Garcia-Calderon (Ayacucho).

Philippines: Catholic Bishops' Conference of the Philippines (CBCP), P.O. Box 3601, 470 General Luna St., 1099 Manila; (02) 527-4054. Abp. Socrates Villegas (Lingayen-Dagupan).

Poland: Konferencja Episkopatu Polski, Skwer Kardynala Stefana Wyszynskiego 6, 01015 Warsaw; (022) 838-92-51. Jozef Michalik (Przemysl of the Latins).

Portugal: Conferência Episcopal Portuguesa, Campo dos Mártires da Pátria, 431 Esq., 1100 Lisbon; 21-885-21-23. Card. Jose da Cruz Policarpo (Lisbon).

Puerto Rico: Conferencia Episcopal Puertorriqueña (CEP), P.O. Box 40682, Estacion Minillas, San Juan 009400682; (787) 728-1650. Abp. Roberto Octavio Gonzalez Nieves, O.F.M. (San Juan).

Romania: Conferinte Episcopala România, Via Popa Tatu 58, Bucharest; (01) 311-12-89. Abp. Ioan Robu (Bucharest).

Russian Federation: Conference of Catholic Bishops of the Russian Federation (C.V.C.F.R.), 101031 Moskva, Via Pietrovka, d. 19 str., 5Kv. 35; (095) 923-16-97. Bp. Joseph Werth, S.J. (Transfiguration at Novosibirsk).

Rwanda: Conférence Episcopale du Rwanda (C.Ep.R.), B.P. 357, Kigali; 75439. Bp. Smaragde Mbonyintege (Kabgayi).

Scandinavia: Conferentia Episcopalis Scandiae, Trollbärsvägen 16, S426 55 Västra Frölunda (Sweden); (031) 709-64-87. Bp. Anders Arborelius, O.C.D. (Stockholm).

Scotland: Bishops' Conference of Scotland, 64 Aitken St., Airdrie, ML6; 44-1236-764-061. Abp. Philip Tartaglia (Glasgow).

Senegal, Mauritania, Cape Verde and Guinea Bissau: Conférence des Evêques du Sénégal, de la Mauritanie, du CapVert et de GuinéeBissau, B.P. 941, Dakar, Senegal. Bp. Benjamin Ndiaye (Kaolack).

Serbia and Montenegro: Biskupska konferecija Srbije I Crne Gore, 11000 Beograd, Visegradska 23; (011) 303.22.46. Bp. Stanslav Hocevar, S.D.B. (Beograd).

Sierra Leone: See Gambia, Liberia and Sierra Leone.

Slovakia: Biskupská Konferencia Slovenska, Kapitulská 11, 81521 Bratislava; (07) 733-54-50. Abp. Stanislav Zvolensky (Bratislava).

Slovenia: Slovenska Skofovska Konferenca, CirilMetodov trg 4, p.p.1990, 1001 Ljubljana; (386) 1-2342612. Abp. Anton Stres, C.M. (Ljubljana).

Spain: Conferencia Episcopal Española, Apartado 29075, Calle Añastro 1, 28080 Madrid; 91-343-96-15. Antonio Maria Card. Rouco Varela (Madrid).

Sri Lanka: Catholic Bishops' Conference of Sri Lanka, 19 Balcombe Place, Cotta Rd., Borella, Colombo 8; (01) 95-091; 59-70-62. Albert Ranjith Card. Patabendige (Colombo).

Sudan: Sudan Catholic Bishops' Conference (SCBC), P.O. Box 6011, Khartoum; (011) 225-075-9. Card. Zubeir Wako (Khartoum).

Switzerland: Conférence des Evêques Suisses, Secretariat, C.P. 22, av. Moléson 21, CH1706 Fribourg; (026) 322-47-94; www.kath.ch. Bp. Marcus Buchel (Sankt Gallen).

Tanzania: Tanzania Episcopal Conference (TEC), P.O. Box 2133, Mansfield St., DaresSalaam; (022) 51-075. Bp. Ngalalekumtwa Tarcisius (Iringa).

Thailand: Bishops' Conference of Thailand, 122-67 Soi Naaksuwan, Nonsi Road, Yannawa, Bangkok; 02-6815361-8. Abp. Louis Chamniern Santisukniran (Thare and Nonseng).

Togo: Conférence Episcopale du Togo, B.P. 348, Lomé; 21-22-72. Bp. Comlan Messan Alowonou Benoit (Kpalime).

Turkey: Turkish Episcopal Conference, Ölçek Sokak 83, Harbiye, 80230 Istanbul; (212) 248-07-75. Abp. Ruggero Franceschini, O.F.M. Cap. (Izmir).

Uganda: Uganda Episcopal Conference, P.O. Box 2886, Kampala; (041) 510-398. Abp. John Baptist Odama (Gulu).

Ukraine: Ukraine Episcopal Conference, 79008 Lviv, Mytropolycha Kuria Latynskoho Obriadu, Pl. Katedralna 1; (0322) 76-94-15. Abp. Mieczyslaw

Mokrzycki (Lviv of the Latins).

United States: See **The United States Conference of Catholic Bishops**, p. 420.

Uruguay: Conferencia Episcopal Uruguaya (CEU), Avenida Uruguay 1319, 11100 Montevideo; (02) 900-26-42. Bp. Rodolfo Pedro Wirz Kraemer (Maldonado-Punta del Este).

Venezuela: Conferencia Episcopal de Venezuela (CEV), Apartado 4897, Torre a Madrices, Edificio Juan XXIII, Piso 4, Caracas 1010A; (0212) 4432-23-65. Abp. Rafael Padron Sanchez Diego (Cumana).

Vietnam: Conferenza Episcopale del Viêt Nam, Nha Trang, Khán Hoà, 22 Tran Phu; (058) 822-842. Bp. Pierre Nguyen Van Nhon (Da Lat).

Yugoslavia: Biskupska Konferencija Savezne Republike Jugoslavije, 11000 Beograd, Visegradska 23; (011) 642-280. Abp. Stanislav Hocevar, S.D.B. (Beograd).

Zambia: Zambia Episcopal Conference, P.O. Box 31965, 20201 Lusaka; (01) 212-070. Bp. George Cosmas Zumaire Lungu (Chipata).

Zimbabwe: Zimbabwe Catholic Bishops' Conference (ZCBC), Causeway, P.O. Box 8135, Harare; (14) 705-368. Angel Floro Martinez, I.E.M.E. (Gokwe).

Regional Conferences (*Sources:* Almanac *survey*; Annuario Pontificio.)

Africa: Symposium of Episcopal Conferences of Africa and Madagascar (SECAM) (Symposium des Conférences Episcopales d'Afrique et de Madagascar, SCEAM): Gabriel Mbilingi, C.S.Sp., abp. of Lubango, president. Address: Secretariat, P.O. Box 9156 Airport, Accra, Ghana.

Association of Episcopal Conferences of Central Africa (Association des Conférences Episcopales de l'Afrique Centrale, ACEAC): Comprises Burundi, Rwanda and Zaire. Smaragde Mbonyintege, bp. of Kabgayi, president. Address: B.P. 20511, Kinshasa, Democratic Republic of Congo.

Association of Episcopal Conferences of the Region of Central Africa (Association des Conférences Episcopales de la Région de l'Afrique Central, ACERAC): Comprises Cameroon, Chad, Congo, Equatorial Guinea, Central African Republic and Gabon. Bp. Timothée Modibo-Nzockena, bp. of Franceville, president. Address: Secretariat, B.P. 200, Brazzaville, Republic of the Congo.

Association of Episcopal Conferences of Anglophone West Africa (AECAWA): Comprises Gambia, Ghana, Liberia, Nigeria and Sierra Leone. Card. John Olorunfemi Onaiyekan, abp. of Abuja, president. Address: P.O. Box 11, Santasi, Ghana.

Association of Member Episcopal Conferences in Eastern Africa (AMECEA): Represents Eritrea, Ethiopia, Kenya, Malawi, Sudan, Tanzania, Uganda and Zambia. Affiliate members: Seychelles (1979), Somalia (1994). Abp. Tarcisius Gervazio Ziyaye, Abp. of Blantyre, president. Address: P.O. Box 21191, Nairobi, Kenya.

Regional Episcopal Conference of French Speaking West Africa (Conférence Episcopale Régionale de l'Afrique de l'Ouest Francophone, CERAO): Comprises Benin, Burkina Faso, Cape Verde, Côte d'Ivoire, Guinea, Guinea Bissau, Mali, Mauritania, Niger, Senegal and Togo. Peter Card. Turkson, abp. of Cape Town, president. Address: Secretariat General, B.P.470 CIDEX 1, Abidjan — Côte d'Ivoire.

InterRegional Meeting of Bishops of Southern Africa (IMBISA): Bishops of Angola, Botswana, Lesotho, Mozambique, Namibia, São Tome e Principe, South Africa, Swaziland and Zimbabwe. Abp. Gabriel Mbilingi, C.S.Sp., abp. of Lubango, president. Address: 88 Broadlands Rd., Avondale, Harare, Zimbabwe.

Asia: Federation of Asian Bishops' Conferences (FABC): Represents 14 Asian episcopal conferences and four independent jurisdictions (Hong Kong, Macau, Nepal, Mongolia) as regular members (excluding the Middle East). Established in 1970; statutes approved experimentally Dec. 6, 1972. Abp. Orlando B. Quevedeo, O.M.B., abp. of Cotabato, secretary general. Address: 16 Caine Road, Hong Kong; 25258021; www.fabc.org.ph.

Oceania: Federation of Catholic Bishops' Conferences of Oceania (FCBCO). Statutes approved Dec. 25, 1997. Bp. Peter Ingham, bp. of Wollongong in Australia, president. Address: P.O. Box 1937, 22-30 Hill St., Wellington, New Zealand 6015.

Europe: Council of European Bishops' Conferences (Consilium Conferentiarum Episcoporum Europae, CCEE): Reorganized in 1993 in accordance with suggestions made during the 1991 Synod of Bishops on Europe. Peter Card. Erdö, abp. of Esztergom-Budapest, president. Address of secretariat: Gallusstrasse 24, CH9000 Sankt Gallen, Switzerland; (0041) 71-227-33-74; www.kath.ch/ccee.

Commission of the Episcopates of the European Community (Commissio Episcopatuum Communitatis Europaeae, COMECE): Established in 1980; represents episcopates of states belonging to European Community. Card. Reinhard Marx, abp. of Munich-Freising, president. Address of secretariat: 42, Rue Stévin, B1000 Brussels, Belgium; (02) 230-73-16.

Central and South America: Latin American Bishops' Conference (Consejo Episcopal Latino-Americano, CELAM): Established in 1956; statutes approved Nov. 9, 1974. Represents 22 Latin American national bishops' conferences. Abp. Carlos Aguiar Retes, president. Address of the secretariat: Carrera 5 No. 11831, Usaquén, Bogotá, Colombia; (91) 612-16-20.

Episcopal Secretariat of Central America and Panama (Secretariado Episcopal de America Central y Panama, SEDAC): Statutes approved experimentally Sept. 26, 1970. Abp. José Francisco Ulloa, abp. of Panama, president. Address of secretary general: Calle 20 y Av Mexico 24-45, Apartado 6386, Panama 5, Panama; 262-7802.

INTERNATIONAL CATHOLIC ORGANIZATIONS

(Principal sources: Sr. Dorothy Farley, Executive Director, ICO Information Center; Pontifical Council for the Laity; Catholic Almanac *survey.)*

Guidelines

International organizations wanting to call themselves "Catholic" are required to meet standards set by the Vatican's Council for the Laity and to register with and get the approval of the Papal Secretariat of State, according to guidelines dated Dec. 3 and published in *Acta Apostolicae Sedis* under the date of Dec. 23, 1971.

Among conditions for the right of organizations to "bear the name Catholic" are:

• leaders "will always be Catholics," and candidates for office will be approved by the Secretariat of State

• adherence by the organization to the Catholic Church, its teaching authority and the teachings of the Gospel

• evidence that the organization is really international with a universal outlook and that it fulfills its mission through its own management, meetings and accomplishments.

The guidelines also stated that leaders of the organizations "will take care to maintain necessary reserve as regards taking a stand or engaging in public activity in the field of politics or trade unionism. Abstention in these fields will normally be the best attitude for them to adopt during their term of office."

The guidelines were in line with a provision stated by the Second Vatican Council: "No project may claim the name 'Catholic' unless it has obtained the consent of the lawful Church authority."

They made it clear that all organizations are not obliged to apply for recognition, but that the Church "reserves the right to recognize as linked with her mission and her aims those organizations or movements which see fit to ask for such recognition."

Conference of International Catholic Organizations

A permanent body for collaboration among various organizations the conference seeks to promote the development of international life along the lines of Christian principles. Eleven international Catholic organizations participated in its foundation and first meeting in 1927 at Fribourg, Switzerland. In 1951, the conference established its general secretariat and adopted governing statutes that were approved by the Vatican Secretariat of State in 1953.

The permanent secretariat is located at 3739 rue de Vermont, CH1202 Geneva, Switzerland. Other office addresses are: 1 rue Varembe, CH1211 Geneva 20, Switzerland (International Catholic Center of Geneva); 9, rue Cler, F75007 Paris, France (International Catholic Center for UNESCO); ICO Information Center, 323 East 47th St., New York, NY 10017.

Charter

According to its charter (adopted in November 1997), the conference "responds to the challenge of *Christifideles Laici*: Open to the saving power of Christ the frontiers of States, economic and political systems, the vast domains of culture, civilization and development (No. 34)."

In a universal vision of those problems, these organizations have the following responsibilities to their members:

• to make them increasingly aware of the compexities of the situations in which they live and work

• to help them to grow in discernment and critical analysis

• to facilitate the search for solutions to concrete difficulties.

The Conference is open to any organization which is acting and is involved recognizably Catholic in its work in the international world, which accepts the present Charter, respects its principles in practice and adheres to its Statutes. The Conference witnesses to the organized presence of Catholics in the international world.

Fundamental Convictions

• Their desire to announce Jesus Christ to the women and men of our time, and their vocation to serve the world, are indivisible; faith calls for action

• Their wish to contribute to the building of the Kingdom of God is demonstrated by solidarity with all women and men of good will

• Their desire for participation in decision-making in the Church in areas which concern their competence and in which they are involved.

A Unique Spirituality

In its desire to live fully its faith in Jesus Christ, the Conference stresses:

• The need to be rooted in reality, through a relationship with God lived out in the world

• An experience of community nourished by group sharing and exchange

• Openness to the international dimension, validated by experiences at the local level to which it gives meaning

• Adaptation to different human groups and to different sensibilities

• The witness of Christian freedom to initiate, as well as willingness to live in "solid and strong communion" with the Church

• Desire to serve the universal Church through insertion in the local Churches by respecting diverse pastoral programs, but also to participate in major events in the life of the universal Church.

Members

Members of the Conference of International Catholic Organizations are listed below. Information includes name, date and place of establishment (when available), address of general secretariat. Approximately 30 of the organizations have consultative status with other international or regional non-governmental agencies.

Caritas Internationalis (1951, Rome, Italy): Piazza San Calisto 16, I00153, Rome, Italy. Coordinates and represents its 146 national member organizations (in 194 countries) operating in the fields of development, emergency aid, social action.

Catholic International Education Office (1952): 60, rue des Eburons, B1000 Brussels, Belgium.

Catholic International Union for Social Service (1925, Milan, Italy): rue de la Poste 111, B1210 Brussels, Belgium (general secretariat).

Christian Life Community (CVX) (1953): Borgo Santo Spirito 8, C.P. 6139, I00195 Rome, Italy. First Sodality of Our Lady founded in 1563.

International Ascent, The: 84, rue Charles Michels, F93206 Saint Denis Cedex, France. Member of ICO.

International Association of Charities (1617, Chatillon les Dombes, France): Rue Joseph Brand, 118, B1030 Brussels, Belgium.

International Catholic Child Bureau (1948, in Paris): 63, rue de Lausanne, CH1202 Geneva, Switzerland.

International Catholic Committee of Nurses and MedicoSocial Assistants (ICCN) (1933): Square Vergote, 43, B1040 Brussels, Belgium.

International Catholic Conference of Scouting (1948): Piazza Pasquale Paoli, 18, I-00186 Rome, Italy.

International Catholic Migration Commission (1951): 3739 rue de Vermont, C.P. 96, CH1211 Geneva 20, Switzerland. Coordinates activities worldwide on behalf of refugees and migrants, both administering programs directly and supporting the efforts of national affiliated agencies.

International Catholic Organization for Cinema and Audiovisual (1928, The Hague, The Netherlands): Rue du Saphir, 15, B1040 Brussels, Belgium (general secretariat). Federation of National Catholic film offices.

International Catholic Society for Girls (1897): 3739, rue de Vermont, CH1202 Geneva, Switzerland.

International Catholic Union of the Press: 3739 rue de Vermont, Case Postale 197, CH1211 Geneva 20 CIC, Switzerland. Coordinates and represents at the international level the activities of Catholics and Catholic federations or associations in the field of press and information. Has seven specialized branches: International Federation of Catholic Journalists; International Federation of Dailies; International Federation of Periodicals; International Federation of Catholic News Agencies; International Catholic Federation of Teachers and Researchers in the Science and Techniques of Information; International Federation of Church Press Associations; and International Federation of Book Publishers.

International Conference of Catholic Guiding (1965): c/o Mlle Francoise Parmentier, rue de la Tour 64, 75016 Paris. Founded by member bodies of interdenominational World Association of Guides and Girl Scouts.

International Coordination of Young Christian Workers (YCYCW): via dei Barbieri 22, I-00186 Rome, Italy.

International Council of Catholic Men (ICCM) (Unum Omnes) (1948): Wahringer Str. 24, A.1090 Vienna IX, Austria.

International Federation of Catholic Medical Associations (1954): Palazzo San Calisto, I-00120 Vatican City.

International Federation of Catholic Parochial Youth Communities (1962, Rome, Italy): St. Kariliquai 12, 6000 Lucerne 5, Switzerland.

International Federation of Catholic Pharmacists (1954): Bosdorf 180, 9190 Stekene, Belgium.

International Federation of Rural Adult Catholic Movements (1964, Lisbon, Portugal): Rue Jaumain 15, B5330 Assesse, Belgium.

International Federation of Catholic Universities (1949): 21, rue d'Assas, F75270 Paris 06, France.

International Federation of the Catholic Associations of the Blind: Avenue Dailly 90, B1030 Brussels, Belgium. Coordinates actions of Catholic groups and associations for the blind and develops their apostolate.

International Independent Christian Youth (IICY): 11, rue Martin Bernard, 75013 Paris, France.

International Military Apostolate (1967): Breite Strasse 25, D53111 Bonn, Germany. Comprised of organizations of military men.

International Movement of Apostolate of Children (1929, France): 24, rue Paul Rivet, F92350 Le Plessis Robinson, France.

International Movement of Apostolate in the Independent Social Milieux (MIAMSI) (1963): Piazza San Calisto 16, 00153 Rome, Italy.

International Movement of Catholic Agricultural and Rural Youth (1954, Annevoie, Belgium): 53, rue J. Coosemans, B1030 Brussels, Belgium (permanent secretariat).

International Young Catholic Students (1946, Fribourg, Switzerland; present name, 1954): 171 rue de Rennes, F75006 Paris, France.

Pax Romana (1921, Fribourg, Switzerland, divided into two branches, 1947): **Pax Romana IMCS (International Movement of Catholic Students)** (1921): 171, rue de Rennes, F-75006, Paris, France, for undergraduates; **Pax Romana ICMICA (International Catholic Movement for Intellectual and Cultural Affairs)** (1947): rue du Grand Bureau 15, CH-1227 Geneva, Switzerland, for Catholic intellectuals and professionals.

Society of St. Vincent de Paul (1833, Paris): 5, rue du Pré-aux-Clercs, F-75007 Paris, France.

Unda: International Catholic Association for Radio and Television (1928, Cologne, Germany): rue de l'Orme, 12, B-1040 Brussels, Belgium.

World Movement of Christian Workers (1961): Blvd. du Jubilé 124, 1080 Brussels, Belgium.

World Organization of Former Pupils of Catholic Education (1967, Rome): 48, rue de Richelieu, F-75001 Paris, France.

World Union of Catholic Teachers (1951): Piazza San Calisto 16, 00153 Rome, Italy.

World Union of Catholic Women's Organizations (1910): 18, rue Notre Dame des Champs, F-75006 Paris, France.

Other Catholic Organizations

Apostleship of Prayer (1849): Borgo Santo Spirito 5, I-00193 Rome, Italy. National secretariat in most countries.

Apostolatus Maris (Apostleship of the Sea) (1922, Glasgow, Scotland): Pontifical Council for

Migrants and Itinerant People, Piazza San Calisto 16, 00153 Rome, Italy. (See **Index**.)

L'Arche Communities: B.P. 35, 60350 Cuise Lamotte, France.

Associationes Juventutis Salesianae (Associations of Salesian Youth) (1847): Via della Pisana, 1111, 00163 Rome, Italy.

Blue Army of Our Lady of Fatima: P.O. Box 976, Washington, NJ, 07882.

Catholic International Federation for Physical and Sports Education (1911; present name, 1957): 5, rue Cernuschi, 75017 Paris, France.

Christian Fraternity of the Sick and Handicapped: 9, Avenue de la Gare, CH1630, Bulle, Switzerland.

"Communione e Liberazione" Fraternity (1955, Milan, Italy): Via Marcello Malpighi 2, 00161 Rome, Italy. Catholic renewal movement.

"Focolare Movement" (Work of Mary) (1943, Trent, Italy): Via di Frascati, 306, I-00040 Rocca di Papa (Rome), Italy.

Foi et Lumiere: 8 rue Serret, 75015 Paris, France.

Franciscans International: 345 E. 47th St., New York, NY 10017. A nongovernmental organization at the UN.

Inter Cultural Association (ICA, 1937, Belgium) and **Association Fraternelle Internationale** (AFI): 91, rue de la Servette, CH-1202 Geneva, Switzerland.

International Association of Children of Mary (1847): 67 rue de Sèvres, F-75006 Paris, France.

International Catholic Rural Association (1962, Rome): Piazza San Calisto, 00153 Rome, Italy. International body for agricultural and rural organizations. Invited member of ICO.

International Catholic Union of Esperanto: Via Berni 9, 00185 Rome, Italy.

International Centre for Studies in Religious Education LUMEN VITAE (193435, Louvain, Belgium, under name Catechetical Documentary Centre; present name, 1956): 184, rue Washington, B1050 Brussels, Belgium. Also referred to as Lumen Vitae Centre; concerned with all aspects of religious formation.

International Young Christian Workers (1925, Belgium): 11, rue Plantin, B1070 Brussels, Belgium. Associate member of ICO.

Legion of Mary (1921, Dublin, Ireland): De Montfort House, North Brunswick St., Dublin, Ireland. (See **Index**.)

Medicus Mundi Internationalis (1964, Bensberg, Germany FR): P.O. Box 1547, 6501 BM Nijmegen, Netherlands. To promote health and medicosocial services, particularly in developing countries; recruit essential health and medical personnel for developing countries; contribute to training of medical and auxiliary personnel; undertake research in the field of health.

NOVALIS, Marriage Preparation Center: University of St. Paul, 1 rue Stewart, Ottawa 2, ON, Canada.

Our Lady's Teams (Equipes NotreDame) (1937, France): 49, rue de la Glacière, 75013 Paris, France. Movement for spiritual formation of couples.

Pax Christi International (1950): rue du Vieux Marché aux grains 21, B1000 Brussels, Belgium. International Catholic peace movement. Originated in Lourdes, France, in 1948 by French and German Catholics to reconcile enemies from World War II; spread to Italy and Poland and acquired its international title when it merged with the English organization Pax. Associate member of ICO.

Pro Sanctity Movement: Piazza S. Andrea della Valle 3, 00166 Rome, Italy.

St. Joan's International Alliance (1911, in England, as Catholic Women's Suffrage Society): Quai Churchill 19, Boite 061, B4020 Liège, Belgium. Associate member of ICO.

Salesian Cooperators (1876, Turin, Italy): **Salesian Cooperators**: Founded by St. John Bosco; for lay men and women and diocesan clergy. A public association of the faithful, members commit themselves to apostolates in the local Church, especially on behalf of the young, in the Salesian spirit and style. Address: 174 Filors Lane, Stony Point, NY 10980-2645; (845) 947-2200.

Secular Franciscan Order (1221, first Rule approved): Via Piemonte, 70, 00187, Rome, Italy.

Secular Fraternity of Charles de Foucauld: Katharinenweg 4, B-4700 Eupen, Belgium.

Serra International (1953, in U.S.): 65 E. Wacker Pl. Suite 1210, Chicago, IL 60601.

Unio Internationalis Laicorum in Servitio Ecclesiae (1965, Aachen, Germany): Postfach 990125, Am Kielshof 2, 5000 Cologne, Germany 91. Consists of national and diocesan associations of persons who give professional services to the Church.

Union of Adorers of the Blessed Sacrament (1937): Largo dei Monti Parioli 3, I-00197, Rome, Italy.

World Catholic Federation for the Biblical Apostolate (1969, Rome): Mittelstrasse, 12, P.O. Box 601, D-7000, Stuttgart 1, Germany.

Regional Organizations

European Federation for Catholic Adult Education (1963, Lucerne, Switzerland): Hirschengraben 13, P.B. 2069, CH-6002 Lucerne, Switzerland.

European Forum of National Committees of the Laity (1968): 169, Booterstown Av., Blackrock, Co. Dublin, Ireland.

Movimiento Familiar Cristiano (194950, Montevideo and Buenos Aires): Carrera 17 n. 4671, Bogotá, D.E., Colombia. Christian Family Movement of Latin America.

Eastern Catholic Churches

Sources: Fr. Ronald Roberson, C.S.P., Associate Director, Ecumenical and Interreligious Affairs, USCCB.; Annuario Pontificio; Official Catholic Directory.

The Second Vatican Council, in its Decree on Eastern Catholic Churches (*Orientalium Ecclesiarum*), stated the following points regarding Eastern heritage, patriarchs, sacraments and worship.

Venerable Churches: The Catholic Church holds in high esteem the institutions of the Eastern Churches, their liturgical rites, ecclesiastical traditions, and Christian way of life. For, distinguished as they are by their venerable antiquity, they are bright with that tradition which was handed down from the Apostles through the Fathers, and which forms part of the divinely revealed and undivided heritage of the universal Church (No. 1). That Church, Holy and Catholic, which is the Mystical Body of Christ, is made up of the faithful who are organically united in the Holy Spirit through the same faith, the same sacraments, and the same government and who, combining into various groups held together by a hierarchy, form separate Churches or rites. It is the mind of the Catholic Church that each individual Church or rite retain its traditions whole and entire, while adjusting its way of life to the various needs of time and place (No. 2).

Such individual Churches, whether of the East or of the West, although they differ somewhat among themselves in what are called rites (that is, in liturgy, ecclesiastical discipline, and spiritual heritage) are, nevertheless, equally entrusted to the pastoral guidance of the Roman Pontiff, the divinely appointed successor of St. Peter in supreme government over the universal Church. They are consequently of equal dignity, so that none of them is superior to the others by reason of rite (No. 3).

Eastern Heritage: Each and every Catholic, as also the baptized of every non-Catholic Church or community who enters into the fullness of Catholic communion, should everywhere retain his proper rite, cherish it, and observe it to the best of his ability (No. 4). The Churches of the East, as much as those of the West, fully enjoy the right, and are in duty bound, to rule themselves. Each should do so according to its proper and individual procedures (No. 5). All Eastern rite members should know and be convinced that they can and should always preserve their lawful liturgical rites and their established way of life, and that these should not be altered except by way of an appropriate and organic development (No. 6).

Patriarchs: The institution of the patriarchate has existed in the Church from the earliest times and was recognized by the first ecumenical Synods. By the name Eastern Patriarch is meant the bishop who has jurisdiction over all bishops (including metropolitans), clergy, and people of his own territory or rite, in accordance with the norms of law and without prejudice to the primacy of the Roman Pontiff (No. 7). Though some of the patriarchates of the Eastern Churches are of later origin than others, all

are equal in patriarchal dignity. Still the honorary and lawfully established order of precedence among them is to be preserved (No. 8). In keeping with the most ancient tradition of the Church, the Patriarchs of the Eastern Churches are to be accorded exceptional respect, since each presides over his patriarchate as father and head.

This sacred Synod, therefore, decrees that their rights and privileges should be re-established in accord with the ancient traditions of each Church and the decrees of the ecumenical Synods. The rights and privileges in question are those which flourished when East and West were in union, though they should be somewhat adapted to modern conditions.

The Patriarchs with their synods constitute the superior authority for all affairs of the patriarchate, including the right to establish new eparchies and to nominate bishops of their rite within the territorial bounds of the patriarchate, without prejudice to the inalienable right of the Roman Pontiff to intervene in individual cases (No. 9).

What has been said of Patriarchs applies as well, under the norm of law, to major archbishops, who preside over the whole of some individual Church or rite (No. 10).

Sacraments: This sacred Ecumenical Synod endorses and lauds the ancient discipline of the sacraments existing in the Eastern Churches, as also the practices connected with their celebration and administration (No. 12).

With respect to the minister of holy chrism (confirmation), let that practice be fully restored which existed among Easterners in most ancient times. Priests, therefore, can validly confer this sacrament, provided they use chrism blessed by a Patriarch or bishop (No. 13).

In conjunction with baptism or otherwise, all Eastern-Rite priests can confer this sacrament validly on all the faithful of any rite, including the Latin; licitly, however, only if the regulations of both common and particular law are observed. Priests of the Latin rite, to the extent of the faculties they enjoy for administering this sacrament, can confer it also on the faithful of Eastern Churches, without prejudice to rite. They do so licitly if the regulations of both common and particular law are observed (No. 14).

The faithful are bound on Sundays and feast days to attend the divine liturgy or, according to the regulations or custom of their own rite, the celebration of the Divine Praises. That the faithful may be able to satisfy their obligation more easily, it is decreed that this obligation can be fulfilled from the Vespers of the vigil to the end of the Sunday or the feast day (No. 15). Because of the everyday intermingling of the communicants of diverse Eastern Churches in the same Eastern region or territory, the faculty for hearing confession, duly and unrestrictedly granted by his proper bishop to a priest of any rite, is applicable to the entire territory of the grantor, also to the places and the faithful belonging to any other rite in the same territory, unless an Ordinary of the place explicitly decides otherwise with respect to the places pertaining to his rite (No. 16).

This sacred Synod ardently desires that where it has fallen into disuse the office of the permanent diaconate be restored. The legislative authority of each individual church should decide about the subdiaconate and the minor orders (No. 17).

By way of preventing invalid marriages between Eastern Catholics and baptized Eastern non-Catholics, and in the interests of the permanence and sanctity of marriage and of domestic harmony, this sacred Synod decrees that the canonical 'form' for the celebration of such marriages obliges only for lawfulness. For their validity, the presence of a sacred minister suffices, as long as the other requirements of law are honored (No. 18).

Worship: Henceforth, it will be the exclusive right of an ecumenical Synod or the Apostolic See to establish, transfer, or suppress feast days common to all the Eastern Churches. To establish, transfer, or suppress feast days for any of the individual Churches is within the competence not only of the Apostolic See but also of a patriarchal or archiepiscopal synod, provided due consideration is given to the entire region and to other individual Churches (No. 19). Until such time as all Christians desirably concur on a fixed day for the celebration of Easter, and with a view meantime to promoting unity among the Christians of a given area or nation, it is left to the Patriarchs or supreme authorities of a place to reach a unanimous agreement, after ascertaining the views of all concerned, on a single Sunday for the observance of Easter (No. 20). With respect to rules concerning sacred seasons, individual faithful dwelling outside the area or territory of their own rite may conform completely to the established custom of the place where they live. When members of a family belong to different rites, they are all permitted to observe sacred seasons according to the rules of any one of these rites (No. 21). From ancient times the Divine Praises have been held in high esteem among all Eastern Churches. Eastern clerics and religious should celebrate these Praises as the laws and customs of their own traditions require. To the extent they can, the faithful too should follow the example of their forebears by assisting devoutly at the Divine Praises (No. 22).

Restoration of Ancient Practices

An "Instruction for the Application of the Liturgical Prescriptions of the Code of Canons of the Eastern Churches" was published by the Congregation for the Oriental Churches in January 1996. It has been published in several languages. Msgr. Alan Detscher, then executive director of the U.S. bishops' Secretariat for the Liturgy, said it was the first instruction on liturgical renewal of the Eastern Catholic Churches since the Second Vatican Council (1962-65).

JURISDICTIONS AND FAITHFUL OF THE EASTERN CATHOLIC CHURCHES

Introduction

The Church originated in Palestine, whence it spread to other regions of the world where certain places became key centers of Christian life with great influence on the local churches in their respective areas. These centers developed into the ancient patriarchates of Constantinople, Alexandria, Antioch and Jerusalem in the East, and Rome in the West. The main lines of Eastern Church patriarchal organization and usages were drawn before the Roman Empire became two empires, East (Byzantine) and West (Roman), in 292. Other churches with distinctive traditions grew up beyond the boundaries of the Roman Empire in Persia, Armenia, Syria, Egypt, Ethiopia, and India. The "nestorian" church in Persia, known today as the Assyrian Church of the East, broke communion with the rest of the church in the wake of the Council of Ephesus (431) whose teachings it did not accept. The "monophysite" churches of Armenia, Syria, Egypt, Ethiopia, Eritrea and India (known today as the Oriental Orthodox Churches) did not accept the christological teachings of the Council of Chalcedon (451) and so broke away from the church within the Roman Empire. And finally, in the wake of the mutual excommunications of 1054 between the Patriarch of Constantinople and the papal legate, the church within the empire divided into what would become the Catholic Church in the West and the Orthodox Church in the East. This was a lengthy process of estrangement that culminated only in 1204 and the sack of Constantinople by the Latin Crusaders.

In the following centuries, attempts to overcome these divisions took place, most notably at the Second Council of Lyons in 1274 and the Council of Ferrara-Florence in 1438-39. Both failed. Subsequently, the Catholic Church began to send missionaries to work with separated Eastern Christians, and some groups within those churches spontaneously asked to enter into full communion with Rome. Thus began the formation of the Eastern Catholic Churches, which retained most of the liturgical, canonical, spiritual and theological patrimony of their non-Catholic counterparts.

The Code of Canons of the Eastern Churches groups these churches today into four categories: patriarchal, major archiepiscopal, metropolitan, and other churches *sui iuris*. In common usage, an eparchy is equivalent to a diocese in the Latin rite.

STATISTICS

Principal source: 2014 Annuario Pontificio.

The following statistics are the sum of those reported for Eastern Catholic jurisdictions only, and do not include Eastern Catholics under the jurisdiction of Latin bishops. Some of the figures reported are only approximate. The churches are grouped according to their liturgical traditions.

PATRIARCHS

The current Patriarchs of the Eastern Catholic Churches (as of July 15, 2014) are as follows:

Sidrak, Ibrahim Isaac: b. Aug. 19, 1955; ord. Feb. 7, 1980; cons. bp. Nov. 15, 2002; Patriarch of Alexandria of the Copts, Jan. 15, 2013; granted "ecclesiastical communion" with Pope Benedict XVI, Jan. 18, 2013.

Sako, Louis Raphael I: b. July 4, 1948; ord. June 1, 1974; cons. bp. Nov. 14, 2003; Patriarch of Babylon of the Chaldeans, Jan. 31, 2013; granted "ecclesiastical communion" with Pope Benedict XVI, Feb. 1, 2013.

Laham, Gregory III: b. Dec. 15, 1933; ord. Feb. 15, 1959; cons. bp. Nov. 27, 1981; patriarch of Greek Melkites, Nov. 29, 2000; granted "ecclesiastical communion" with Pope John Paul II, Dec. 5, 2000.

Bechara Rai: b. Feb. 25, 1940; ord. Sept. 3, 1967; cons. bp. July 12, 1986; patriarch of Antioch, for the Maronites, Mar. 15, 2011; granted "ecclesiastical communion" with Pope Benedict XVI, Mar. 24, 2011.

Tarmouni, Nerses XIX Bedros: b. Jan. 17, 1940, in Cairo, Egypt; ord. Aug. 15, 1965; cons. bp. Feb. 18, 1990; patriarch of Cilicia of the Armenians, Oct. 7, 1999; granted "ecclesiastical communion" with the Pope John Paul II, Oct. 13, 1999.

Younan, Joseph: b. Nov. 11, 1944; ord. Sept. 12, 1971; cons. bp. Jan. 7, 1996; patriarch of Antioch of the Syrians, Jan. 20, 2009; granted "ecclesiastical communion" with Pope Benedict XVI, Jan. 23, 2009.

ALEXANDRIAN

The liturgical tradition of Egypt, in particular that of the early Patriarchate of Alexandria. In the Egyptian desert monasteries the rite evolved in a distinctive way and eventually became that of the Coptic Orthodox Church. The Greek Patriarchate of Alexandria adopted the Byzantine rite by the 12th century. The Coptic rite, with its Alexandrian origins, spread to Ethiopia in the fourth century where it underwent substantial modifications under strong Syrian influence. The Catholic Churches in this group are:

The Coptic Catholic Church (Patriarchate): Seven eparchies in Egypt; 167,108. Catholic missionaries were present since the 17th century. The Patriarchate was established first in 1824 and renewed in 1895. Liturgical languages are Coptic and Arabic.

The Ethiopian Catholic Church (Metropolitanate): Three eparchies in Ethiopia and three in Eritrea; 206,067. Catholic missionary activity began in the 19th century, and the present ecclesiastical structure dates from 1961. The liturgical languages are Ge'ez and Amharic.

ANTIOCHIAN

The liturgical tradition of Antioch, one of the great centers of the early Christian world, also known as West Syrian. In Syria it developed under strong influence of Jerusalem, especially the Liturgy of St. James, into the form used by today's Syrian Orthodox and Catholics in the Middle East and India. The Maronites of Lebanon developed their own variation of the West Syrian rite which later came under Latin influence.

The Catholic Churches of this group are:

The Syro-Malankara Catholic Church (Major Archbishopric): Eight eparchies in India and one Apostolic Exarchate in the United States; 439,818. Began in 1930 when two bishops, a priest, a deacon and a layman of the Malankara Orthodox Church were received into full communion with Rome. Raised to Major Archiepiscopal status in 2005. The liturgical language is Malayalam.

The Maronite Catholic Church (Patriarchate): Ten eparchies in Lebanon, three in Syria, two in the United States, and one each in Cyprus, Egypt, Argentina, Brazil, Australia, the Holy Land, Canada, and Mexico, plus patriarchal exarchates in Jordan and Jerusalem; 3,388,543.

Founded by followers of St. Maron in the fourth century, the Maronites claim to have always been in communion with Rome. They have no counterpart among the separated Eastern churches. The patriarchate dates to the eighth century, and was confirmed by Pope Innocent III in 1216. Liturgical language is Arabic.

The Syrian Catholic Church (Patriarchate): Four eparchies in Syria, two in Iraq, and one each in Lebanon, Egypt, and North America, and patriarchal exarchates in Turkey, Venezuela, and Iraq/Kuwait; 265,582.

Catholic missionary activity among the Syrian Orthodox began in the 17th century, and there has been an uninterrupted series of Catholic patriarchs since 1783. The liturgical languages are Syriac/Aramaic and Arabic.

ARMENIAN

The liturgical tradition of the Armenian Apostolic and Armenian Catholic Churches. It contains elements of the Syriac, Jerusalem, and Byzantine rites. From the fifth to the seventh centuries there was strong influence from Syria and Jerusalem. More Byzantine usages were adopted later, and in the Middle Ages elements of the Latin tradition were added.

Three eparchies in Syria, one each in Lebanon, Iran, Iraq, Egypt, Turkey, Ukraine, France, Argentina and the United States/Canada, and Ordinariates in Greece, Romania, and Eastern Europe (Armenia); 566,176.

Catholic missionaries had been working among the Armenians since the 14th century, and an Armenian Catholic patriarchate was established in Lebanon in 1742. The liturgical language is classical Armenian. His Beatitude Nerses Bedros XIX Tarmouni, canonically elected as patriarch of Cilicia of the Armenians, by the Synod of Bishops of the Armenian Catholic Church was approved by Pope John Paul II on Oct. 18, 1999.

BYZANTINE

The tradition of the Eastern Orthodox and Byzantine Catholic Churches which originated in the Orthodox Patriarchate of Constantinople (Byzantium). Its present form is a synthesis of Constantinopolitan and Palestinian elements that took place in the monasteries between the ninth and 14th centuries. It is by far the most widely used Eastern liturgical tradition. The Catholic Churches of this group are:

Belarusans (formerly Byelorussian, also known as White Russian): No hierarchy, Apostolic Visitator. Most Belarusan Orthodox became Catholic with the Union of Brest in 1595-6, but this union was short lived. A modest revival has taken place since the end of communism. The liturgical language is Belarusan.

The Bulgarian Catholic Church: One apostolic exarchate in Bulgaria; 10,000. Originated with a group of Bulgarian Orthodox who became Catholic in 1861; liturgical language is Old Slavonic.

Greek Catholics in Former Yugoslavia: One eparchy (Krizevci) located in Zagreb with jurisdiction over Slovenia, Croatia, and Bosnia-Herzegovina; Apostolic Exarchates in Serbia-Montenegro and in Macedonia; 54,660. A bishop for former Serbian Orthodox living in Catholic Croatia was first appointed in 1611; liturgical languages are Old Slavonic and Croatian.

The Greek Catholic Church: Apostolic exarchates in Greece and Turkey; 6,020. Catholic missionaries in Constantinople formed a small group of Byzantine Catholics there in the mid-19th century. Most of them moved to Greece in the 1920s. The liturgical language is Greek.

The Hungarian Catholic Church: One eparchy and one apostolic exarchate in Hungary; 326,200.

Descendants of groups of Orthodox in Hungary who became Catholic in the 17th century and after. The liturgical language is Hungarian.

The Italo-Albanian Catholic Church: Two eparchies, one territorial abbey in Italy; 62,012.

Descended mostly from Albanian Orthodox who came to southern Italy and Sicily in the 15th century and eventually became Catholic; liturgical languages are Greek and Italian.

The Melkite Greek Catholic Church (Patriarchate): Five eparchies in Syria, seven in Lebanon, one each in Jordan, Israel, Brazil, U.S., Canada, Mexico, and Australia. Apostolic Exarchates in Venezuela and Argentina, and patriarchal exarchates in Iraq and Kuwait; 1,670,160.

Catholic missionaries began work within the Greek Orthodox Patriarchate of Antioch in the mid-17th century. In 1724 it split into Catholic and Orthodox counterparts, the Catholics becoming known popularly as Melkites. Liturgical languages are Greek and Arabic.

The Romanian Greek Catholic Church (Major Archbishopric): Five eparchies in Romania and one in the US and Canada; 512,950.

Romanian Orthodox in Transylvania formally entered into union with Rome in 1700; the liturgical language is Romanian. In December 2005, the Romanian Greek Catholic Church was raised to the rank of Major Archbishopric.

Russians: An apostolic exarchate was established for Russia in 1917 and for Russians in China in 1928, but neither is functioning today. There are now at least eight parishes in Russia and 13 in the diaspora. In 2004 Pope John Paul II appointed Bp. Joseph Werth of the Diocese of the Transfiguration in Novosibirsk as Ordinary Bishop for Catholics of the Byzantine rite throughout Russia, but no other ecclesial structures were established.

The Ruthenian Catholic Church (Metropolitanate in the United States): One eparchy in Ukraine, one Archeparchy and three eparchies in the United States, and an apostolic exarchate in the Czech Republic. Originated with the reception of 63 Orthodox priests into the Catholic Church at the Union of Uzhhorod in 1646. Liturgical languages are Old Slavonic and English; 573,661.

The Slovak Catholic Church (Metropolitanate): Three eparchies in Slovakia, and one eparchy in Canada; 233,916.

Also originated with the Union of Uzhhorod in 1646; eparchy of Presov was established for them in 1818. Liturgical languages are Old Slavonic and Slovak. Organized as a Metropolitan church on Jan. 30, 2008.

The Ukrainian Greek Catholic Church (Major Archbishopric): Nine eparchies and three archepiscopal exarchates in Ukraine, two eparchies in Poland, five eparchies in Canada, four in the United States, one each in France, Great Britain, Australia, Brazil and Argentina, apostolic exarchate in Germany; 4,468,630.

Originated with the Union of Brest between the Orthodox Metropolitanate of Kiev and the Catholic Church in 1595-6. Liturgical languages are Old Slavonic and Ukrainian.

CHALDEAN

Also called East Syrian, the liturgical tradition of the Chaldean Catholic and Syro-Malabar Catholic Churches as well as the Assyrian Church of the East. Descends from the ancient rite of the church of Mesopotamia in the Persian Empire. It is celebrated in the eastern dialect of classical Syriac. The Catholic Churches of this tradition are:

The Chaldean Catholic Church (Patriarchate): Ten eparchies in Iraq, three in Iran, two in the U.S., one each in Lebanon, Egypt, Syria, and Turkey; 536,680.

A group of disaffected members of the ("Nestorian") Assyrian Church of the East asked for union with Rome in 1553. In that year Pope Julius III ordained their leader a bishop and named him Patriarch; liturgical languages are Syriac, Arabic.

The Syro-Malabar Catholic Church (Major Archbishopric): 28 eparchies in India, one in the U.S.; 3,899,579.

Descended from Thomas Christians of India who became Catholic in the wake of Portuguese colonization; the diocese of Ernakulam-Angamaly was raised to Major Archepiscopal status in 1993; the liturgical language is Malayalam.

EASTERN JURISDICTIONS

For centuries Eastern Churches were identifiable with a limited number of nationality and language groups in certain countries of the Middle East, Eastern Europe, Asia and Africa. The persecution of religion in the former Soviet Union since 1917 and in communist-controlled countries for more than 40 years following World War II — in addition to decimating and destroying the Church in those places — resulted in the emigration of many Eastern Catholics from their homelands. This forced emigration, together with voluntary emigration, has led to the spread of Eastern Churches to many other countries.

Europe

Bp. Krikor Ghabroyan, of the Armenian Eparchy of Sainte-Croix-de-Paris, France, is apostolic visitator for Armenian Catholics in Western Europe who do not have their own bishop. **Bp. Youssef Ibrahim Sarraf** of Cairo of the Chaldeans is apostolic visitator for Chaldeans in Europe. **Bp. Samis Mazloum** is apostolic visitator for Maronites in Western and Northern Europe. **Archimandrite Jan Sergiusz Gajek** is Apostolic Visitator for Greek Catholics in Belarus.

Austria: Byzantine ordinariate.

Bulgaria: Bulgarian apostolic exarchate.

Croatia: Eparchy of Krizevci.

Czech Republic: Ruthenian apostolic exarchate.

France: Ukrainian eparchy (2013). Armenian eparchy (1986). Maronite eparchy (2012). Ordinariate for all other Eastern Catholics.

Germany: Ukrainian apostolic exarchate.

Great Britain: Ukrainian eparchy (2013).

Greece: Byzantine apostolic exarchate. Armenian ordinariate.

Hungary: Hungarian Byzantine eparchy, apostolic exarchate.

Italy: Two Italo-Albanian eparchies, one abbacy.

Macedonia: One apostolic exarchate.

Poland: Ukrainian metropolitan see (1996), one epar-

chy. Ordinariate for all other Eastern Catholics.
Romania: Romanian Byzantine major archbishopric, four eparchies; Armenian ordinariate.
Russia: Russian apostolic exarchate (for Byzantine Catholics).
Serbia and Montenegro: One apostolic exarchate.
Slovakia: Slovak Byzantine metropolitan see, two eparchies.
Ukraine: Armenian archeparchy; Ruthenian eparchy; Ukrainian major archbishopric, eight eparchies, two archepiscopal exarchates.

Asia
Armenia: Armenian ordinariate (for Armenians of Eastern Europe).
China: Russian Byzantine apostolic exarchate.
Cyprus: Maronite archeparchy.
India: Syro-Malankara metropolitan see, five eparchies. Syro-Malabar major archbishopric (1993), four metropolitan sees, 24 eparchies.
Iran: Two Chaldean metropolitan sees, one archeparchy, one eparchy; Armenian eparchy.
Iraq: Two Syrian archeparchies; Melkite patriarchal exarchate; Chaldean patriarchate, two metropolitan sees, three archeparchies and five eparchies; Armenian archeparchy.
Israel (including Jerusalem): Syrian patriarchal exarchate; Maronite archeparchy; Melkite archeparchy, patriarchal exarchate; Chaldean patriarchal exarchate; Armenian patriarchal exarchate.
Jordan: Melkite archeparchy.
Kuwait: Melkite patriarchal exarchate; Syrian patriarchal exarchate.
Syria: Two Maronite archeparchies, one eparchy; two Syrian metropolitan and two archeparchal sees; Melkite patriarchate, four metropolitan sees, one archeparchy; Chaldean eparchy; Armenian archeparchy, one eparchy .
Turkey: Syrian patriarchal exarchate; Greek apostolic exarchate; Chaldean archeparchy; Armenian archeparchy.

Oceania
Australia: Ukrainian eparchy; Melkite eparchy (1987); Maronite eparchy.

Africa
Egypt: Coptic patriarchate, six eparchies; Maronite eparchy; Syrian eparchy; Melkite patriarchal dependency; Chaldean eparchy; Armenian eparchy.
Eritrea: Three Ethiopian eparchies.
Ethiopia: Ethiopian metropolitan see, two eparchies.
Sudan: Melkite patriarchal dependency.

North America
Canada: One Ukrainian metropolitan, four eparchies; Slovak eparchy; Melkite eparchy; Armenian eparchy for Canada and the U.S. (New York is see city); Maronite eparchy.
United States: Two Maronite eparchies; Syrian eparchy (1995); one Ukrainian metropolitan see, three eparchies; one Ruthenian metropolitan see, three eparchies; Melkite eparchy; Romanian eparchy; Syro-Malabar eparchy based in Chicago;

Belarusan apostolic visitator; Armenian eparchy for Canada and U.S. (New York is see city); two Chaldean eparchies; other Eastern Catholics are under the jurisdiction of local Latin bishops. See **Eastern Catholics in the United States.**)
Mexico: Melkite eparchy; Maronite eparchy (1995).

South America
Armenian Catholics in Latin America (including Mexico and excluding Argentina) are under the jurisdiction of an apostolic exarchate.
Argentina: Ukrainian eparchy; Maronite eparchy; Armenian eparchy; Melkite apostolic exarchate; ordinariate for all other Eastern Catholics.
Brazil: Maronite eparchy; Melkite eparchy; Ukrainian eparchy; ordinariate for all other Eastern Catholics.
Venezuela: Melkite apostolic exarchate.

Synods, Assemblies
These assemblies are collegial bodies that have pastoral authority over members of the Eastern Catholic Churches. (Canons 102-113, 152-153, 322 of Oriental Code of Canon Law.)
Patriarchal Synods:
Synod of the Coptic Catholic Church: Antonios Naguib, patriarch of Alexandria of the Copts.
Synod of the Greek-Melkite Catholic Church: Gregory III Laham, patriarch of Antioch of the Greek Catholics-Melkites.
Synod of the Syrian Catholic Church: Joseph Younan, patriarch of Antioch of the Syrians.
Synod of the Maronite Church: Card. Bechara Rai, patriarch of Antioch of the Maronites.
Synod of the Chaldean Church: Louis Raphael Sako, patriarch of Babylonia of the Chaldeans.
Synod of the Armenian Catholic Church: Nerses Bedros XIX Tarmouni, patriarch of Cilicia of the Armenians.

Major Archiepiscopal Synods:
The Synod of the Ukrainian Greek Catholic Church (raised to major archiepiscopal status Dec. 23, 1963): Sviatoslav Schevchuk, major archbishop of Kiev and Halych, president.
The Synod of the Syro-Malabar Catholic Church (raised to major archiepiscopal status, Jan. 29, 1993): Card. Mar George Alencherry, major archbishop of Ernakulam-Angamaly of the Syro-Malabars, president.
The Synod of the Syro-Malankara Catholic Church (raised to major archiepiscopal status Feb. 10, 2005): Card. Isaac Mar Cleemis Thottunkal of Trivandrum of the Syro-Malankarese, president.
The Synod of the Romanian Greek Catholic Church (raised to major archiepiscopal status Dec. 16, 2005): Card. Lucian Muresan of Fagaras and Alba Julia, president.

Councils, Assemblies, Conferences
Council of Ethiopian Churches: Most Rev. Berhane-Yesus Demerew Souraphiel, C.M., Archbishop of Addis Ababa, president.
Council of Ruthenian Churches, U.S.A.: Abp. William C. Skurla, Metropolitan of Pittsburgh of the Byzantines, president.

Assembly of the Catholic Hierarchy of Egypt (Dec. 5, 1983): His Beatitude Ibrahim Isaac Sidrak, Patriarch of Alexandria of the Copts, president.

Assembly of Catholic Patriarchs and Bishops of Lebanon: His Beatitude Bechara Rai, patriarch of Antioch of the Maronites, president.

Assembly of Ordinaries of the Syrian Arab Republic: His Beatitude Gregory III Laham, patriarch of Antioch of the Greek Melkites, president.

Assembly of Catholic Ordinaries of the Holy Land (Jan. 27, 1992): His Beatitude Fouad Twal, patriarch of Jerusalem of the Latins, president.

Interritual Union of the Bishops of Iraq: His Beatitude Louis Raphael Sako, patriarch of Babylonia of the Chaldeans, president.

Iranian Episcopal Conference (Aug. 11, 1977): Most Rev. Ignatius Bedini, SDB, Archbishop of Ispahan of the Latins, president.

Episcopal Conference of Turkey (Nov. 30, 1987): Most Rev. Ruggero Franceschini, O.F.M.Cap., Archbishop of Izmir, president.

EASTERN CATHOLIC CHURCHES IN THE U.S.

Statistics, from the 2014 Annuario Pontificio *unless noted otherwise, are membership figures reported by Eastern jurisdictions. Additional Eastern Catholics are included in statistics for Latin dioceses.*

Byzantine Tradition

Ukrainians: There were 50,332 reported in four jurisdictions in the U.S.: the metropolitan see of Philadelphia (1924, metropolitan 1958) and the suffragan sees of Stamford, CN (1956), St. Nicholas of Chicago (1961) and St. Josaphat in Parma (1983).

Ruthenians: There were 83,661 reported in four jurisdictions in the U.S.: the metropolitan see of Pittsburgh (est. 1924 at Pittsburgh; metropolitan and transferred to Munhall, 1969; transferred to Pittsburgh, 1977) and the suffragan sees of Passaic, NJ (1963), Parma, OH (1969) and Holy Mary of Protection in Phoenix, AZ (est. 1981 at Van Nuys, transferred to Phoenix, 2009). Hungarian and Croatian Byzantine Catholics in the U.S. are also under the jurisdiction of Ruthenian bishops.

Melkites: There were 24,000 reported under the jurisdiction of the Melkite eparchy of Newton, MA (established as an exarchate, 1965; eparchy, 1976).

Romanians: There were 6,200 reported in 15 Romanian Catholic Byzantine Rite parishes in the U.S., under the jurisdiction of the Romanian eparchy of St. George Martyr, Canton, OH (established as an exarchate, 1982; eparchy, 1987).

Russians: In the United States, there are parishes in New York City (St. Michael) and in El Segundo in the Los Angeles area (St. Andrew). They are under the jurisdiction of local Latin bishops.

Alexandrian Tradition

Copts: Have a Catholic Chapel—Resurrection, in Brooklyn, NY, and St. Mary's Coptic Catholic parish, Los Angeles, CA.

Antiochian Tradition

Maronites: There were 85,800 reported in two jurisdictions in the U.S.: the eparchy of St. Maron, Brooklyn (established at Detroit as an exarchate, 1966; eparchy, 1972; transferred to Brooklyn, 1977) and the eparchy of Our Lady of Lebanon of Los Angeles (resident in St. Louis, MO, established Mar. 1, 1994).

Syrians: The eparchy of Our Lady of the Deliverance of Newark with 25,000 faithful was established in 1995 for Syrian Catholics of the U.S. and Canada.

Syro-Malankarese: A new Apostolic Exarchate was established for the 10,000 Syro-Malankara faithful in the United States in 2010. It has 13 parishes served by 15 priests. The headquarters is in New Hyde Park, New York.

Armenian Tradition

An apostolic exarchate for Canada and the United States was established July 3, 1981; raised to status of eparchy on Sept. 12, 2005; 36,000 in the two countries.

Chaldean Tradition

Chaldeans: There were 170,000 reported under the jurisdictions of the eparchy of St. Thomas the Apostle of Detroit (established as an exarchate, 1982; eparchy, 1986) and the eparchy of St. Peter the Apostle of San Diego (established on May 21, 2002).

Syro-Malabarese (Malabar): The eparchy of Saint Thomas the Apostle in Chicago (established Feb. 16, 2001) has eight parishes around the country. Estimated 87,000 faithful with 43 diocesan priests.

Eastern Catholic Associates

Eastern Catholic Associates is the association of all Eastern Catholic bishops and their equivalents in law in the United States, representing the Armenian, Chaldean, Maronite, Melkite, Syriac, Romanian, Ruthenian, Syro-Malabar and Ukrainian churches. President: Abp. William C. Skurla, Metropolitan Archbishop of Pittsburgh of the Byzantines. Vice President: Most Rev. John Kudrick, Bishop of Parma of the Byzantines.

The association meets at the same time as the United States Conference of Catholic Bishops in the fall of each year.

BYZANTINE DIVINE LITURGY

The Divine Liturgy in all rites is based on the consecration of bread and wine by the narration-reactualization of the actions of Christ at the Last Supper, and the calling down of the Holy Spirit. Aside from this fundamental usage, there are differences between the Roman (Latin) Rite and Eastern Rites, and among the Eastern Rites themselves. Following is a general description of the Byzantine Divine Liturgy which is in widest use in the Eastern Churches.

In the Byzantine, as in all Eastern Rites, the bread and wine are prepared at the start of the Liturgy. The priest does this in a little niche or at a table in the sanctuary. Taking a round loaf of leavened bread stamped with religious symbols, he cuts out a square host and other particles while reciting verses expressing the symbolism of the action. When the bread and wine are ready, he says a prayer of offering and incenses the oblations, the altar, the icons and the people.

Liturgy of the Catechumens: At the altar a litany for all classes of people is sung by the priest. The congregation answers, "Lord, have mercy." The Little Entrance comes next. In procession, the priest leaves the sanctuary carrying the Book of the Gospels, and then returns. He sings prayers especially selected for the day and the feast. These are followed by the solemn singing of the prayer, "Holy God, Holy Mighty One, Holy Immortal One." The Epistle follows. The Gospel is sung or read by the priest facing the people at the middle door of the sanctuary.

An interruption after the Liturgy of the Catechumens, formerly an instructional period for those learning the faith, is clearly marked. Catechumens, if present, are dismissed with a prayer. Following this are a prayer and litany for the faithful.

Great Entrance: The Great Entrance or solemn Offertory Procession then takes place. The priest first says a long silent prayer for himself, in preparation for the great act to come. Again he incenses the oblations, the altar, the icons and people. He goes to the table on the Gospel side for the veil-covered paten and chalice. When he arrives back at the sanctuary door, he announces the intention of the Mass in the prayer: "May the Lord God remember all of you in his kingdom, now and forever." After another litany, the congregation recites the Nicene Creed.

Consecration: The most solemn portion of the sacrifice is introduced by the preface, which is very much like the preface of the Roman Rite. At the beginning of the last phrase, the priest raises his voice to introduce the singing of the Sanctus. During the singing he reads the introduction to the words of consecration. The words of consecration are sung aloud, and the people sing "Amen" to both consecrations. As the priest raises the Sacred Species in solemn offering, he sings: "Thine of Thine Own we offer unto Thee in behalf of all and for all." A prayer to the Holy Spirit is followed by the commemorations, in which special mention is made of the all-holy, most blessed and glorious Lady, the Mother of God and ever-Virgin Mary. The dead are remembered and then the living.

Holy Communion: A final litany for spiritual gifts precedes the Our Father. The Sacred Body and Blood are elevated with the words, "Holy Things for the Holy." The Host is then broken and commingled with the Precious Blood. The priest recites preparatory prayers for Holy Communion, consumes the Sacred Species, and distributes Holy Communion to the people under the forms of both bread and wine. During this time the choir or congregation sings a communion verse.

The Liturgy closes quickly after this. The consecrated Species of bread and wine are removed to the side table to be consumed later by the priest. A prayer of thanksgiving is recited, a prayer for all the people is said in front of the icon of Christ, a blessing is invoked upon all, and the people are dismissed.

BYZANTINE CALENDAR

The Byzantine calendar has many distinctive features of its own, although it shares common elements with the Roman calendar — e.g., general purpose, commemoration of the mysteries of faith and of the saints, identical dates for some feasts. Among the distinctive things are the following. The liturgical year begins on Sept. 1, the Day of Indiction, in contrast with the Latin or Roman start on the First Sunday of Advent late in November or early in December. The Advent season begins on Dec. 10.

Cycles of the Year

As in the Roman usage, the dating of feasts follows the Gregorian Calendar. Formerly, until well into this century, the Julian Calendar was used. (The Julian Calendar, which is now about 13 days late, is still used by some Eastern Churches.) The year has several cycles, which include proper seasons, the feasts of saints, and series of New Testament readings. All of these elements of worship are contained in liturgical books of the rite. The ecclesiastical calendar, called the *Menologion*, explains the nature of feasts, other observances and matters pertaining to the liturgy for each day of the year. In some cases, its contents include the lives of saints and the history and meaning of feasts.

The Divine Liturgy (Mass) and Divine Office for the proper of the saints, fixed feasts, and the Christmas season are contained in the Menaion. The *Triodion* covers the pre-Lenten season of preparation for Easter; Lent begins two days before the Ash Wednesday observance of the Roman Rite. The *Pentecostarion* contains the liturgical services from Easter to the Sunday of All Saints, the first after Pentecost. The *Evangelion* and *Apostolos* are books in which the Gospels, and Acts of the Apostles and the Epistles, respectively, are arranged according to the order of their reading in the Divine Liturgy and Divine Office throughout the year.

The cyclic progression of liturgical music throughout the year, in successive and repetitive periods of eight weeks, is governed by the *Oktoechos*, the *Book of Eight Tones*.

Sunday Names

Many Sundays are named after the subject of the Gospel read in the Mass of the day or after the name of a feast falling on the day — e.g., Sunday of the Publican and Pharisee, of the Prodigal Son, of the Samaritan Woman, of St. Thomas the Apostle, of the Fore-Fathers (Old Testament Patriarchs).

Other Sundays are named in the same manner as in the Roman calendar, e.g., numbered Sundays of Lent and after Pentecost.

Holy Days

The calendar lists about 28 holy days. Many of the major holy days coincide with those of the Roman calendar, but the feast of the Immaculate Conception is observed on Dec. 9 instead of Dec. 8, and the feast of All Saints falls on the Sunday after Pentecost rather than on Nov. 1. Instead of a single All Souls' Day, there are five All Souls' Saturdays. According to regulations in effect in the Byzantine

(Ruthenian) Archeparchy of Pittsburgh and its suffragan sees of Passaic, Parma and Van Nuys, holy days are obligatory, solemn and simple, and attendance at the Divine Liturgy is required on five obligatory days — the feasts of the Epiphany, the Ascension, Sts. Peter and Paul, the Assumption of the Blessed Virgin Mary, and Christmas. Although attendance at the liturgy is not obligatory on 15 solemn and seven simple holy days, it is recommended. In the Byzantine (Ukrainian) Archeparchy of Philadelphia and its suffragan sees of St. Josaphat in Parma, St. Nicholas (Chicago) and Stamford, the obligatory feasts are the Epiphany, Annunciation, Ascension, Sts. Peter & Paul, Dormition, and Christmas.

Lent

The first day of Lent — the Monday before Ash Wednesday of the Roman Rite — and Good Friday are days of strict abstinence for persons in the age bracket of obligation. No meat, eggs, or dairy products may be eaten on these days. All persons over the age of 14 must abstain from meat on Fridays during Lent, Holy Saturday, and the vigils of the feasts of Christmas and Epiphany; abstinence is urged, but is not obligatory, on Wednesdays of Lent. The abstinence obligation is not in force on certain "free" or "privileged" Fridays.

Synaxis

An observance without a counterpart in the Roman calendar is the synaxis. This is a commemoration, on the day following a feast, of persons involved with the occasion for the feast — e.g., Sept. 9, the day following the feast of the Nativity of the Blessed Virgin Mary, is the Synaxis of Joachim and Anna, her parents.

Holy Week

In the Byzantine Rite, Lent is liturgically concluded with the Saturday of Lazarus, the day before Palm Sunday, which commemorates the raising of Lazarus from the dead. On the following Monday, Tuesday and Wednesday, the Liturgy of the Presanctified is prescribed.

On Holy Thursday, the Liturgy of St. Basil the Great is celebrated together with Vespers.

The Divine Liturgy is not celebrated on Good Friday. On Holy Saturday, the Liturgy of St. Basil the Great is celebrated along with Vespers.

BYZANTINE FEATURES

Art: Named for the empire in which it developed, Byzantine art is a unique blend of imperial Roman and classic Hellenic culture with Christian inspiration. The art of the Greek Middle Ages, it reached a peak of development in the 10th or 11th century. Characteristic of its products, particularly in mosaic and painting, are majesty, dignity, refinement and grace. Its sacred paintings, called icons, are reverenced highly in all the Eastern Churches of the Byzantine tradition.

Church Building: The classical model of Byzantine church architecture is the Church of the Holy Wisdom (*Hagia Sophia*), built in Constantinople in the first half of the sixth century and still standing.

The square structure, extended in some cases in the form of a cross, is topped by a distinctive onion-shaped dome and surmounted by a triple-bar cross. The altar is at the eastern end of building, where the wall bellies out to form an apse. The altar and sanctuary are separated from the body of the church by a fixed or movable screen, the iconostas, to which icons or sacred pictures are attached (see below).

Clergy: The Byzantine Churches have married as well as celibate priests. In places other than the U.S., where married candidates have not been accepted for ordination since about 1929, men already married can be ordained to the diaconate and priesthood and can continue in marriage after ordination. Celibate deacons and priests cannot marry after ordination; neither can a married priest remarry after the death of his wife. Bishops must be unmarried.

Iconostasis: A large screen decorated with sacred pictures or icons that separates the sanctuary from the nave of a church; its equivalent in the Roman Rite, for thus separating the sanctuary from the nave, is an altar rail. An iconostas has three doors through which the sacred ministers enter the sanctuary during the Divine Liturgy: smaller (north and south) Deacons' Doors and a large central Royal Door. The Deacons' Doors usually feature the icons of Sts. Gabriel and Michael; the Royal Door, the icons of the Evangelists — Matthew, Mark, Luke and John. To the right and left of the Royal Door are the icons of Christ the Teacher and of the Blessed Virgin Mary with the Infant Jesus. To the extreme right and left are the icons of the patron of the church and St. John the Baptist (or St. Nicholas of Myra). Immediately above the Royal Door is a picture of the Last Supper. To the right are six icons depicting the major feasts of Christ, and to the left are six icons portraying the major feasts of the Blessed Virgin Mary. Above the picture of the Last Supper is a large icon of Christ the King. Some icon screens also have pictures of the 12 Apostles and the major Old Testament prophets surmounted by a crucifixion scene.

Liturgical Language: In line with Eastern tradition, Byzantine practice has favored the use of the language of the people in the liturgy. Two great advocates of the practice were Sts. Cyril and Methodius, apostles of the Slavs, who devised the Cyrillic alphabet and pioneered the adoption of Slavonic in the liturgy.

Sacraments: Baptism is administered by immersion, and confirmation (Chrismation) is conferred at the same time. The Eucharist is administered by intinction, i.e., by giving the communicant a piece of consecrated leavened bread that has been dipped into the consecrated wine. When giving absolution in the sacrament of penance, the priest holds his stole over the head of the penitent. Distinctive marriage ceremonies include the crowning of the bride and groom. Ceremonies for anointing the sick closely resemble those of the Roman Rite. Holy orders are conferred by a bishop.

Sign of the Cross: The sign of the cross in conjunction with a deep bow expresses reverence for the presence of Christ in the Blessed Sacrament. (*See* entry in **Glossary**, p. 156.)

VESTMENTS, APPURTENANCES

Antimension: A silk or linen cloth laid on the altar for the Liturgy; it may be decorated with a picture of the burial of Christ and the instruments of his passion; the relics of martyrs are sewn into the front border.

Asteriskos: Made of two curved bands of gold or silver which cross each other to form a double arch; a star depends from the junction, which forms a cross; it is placed over the diskos holding the consecrated bread and is covered with a veil.

Diskos: A shallow plate, which may be elevated on a small stand, corresponding to the Roman-Rite paten.

Eileton: A linen cloth that corresponds to the Roman-Rite corporal.

Epimanikia: Ornamental cuffs; the right cuff symbolizing strength, the left, patience and good will.

Epitrachelion: A stole with ends sewn together, having a loop through which the head is passed; its several crosses symbolize priestly duties.

Lance: A metal knife used for cutting up the bread to be consecrated during the Liturgy.

Phelonion: An ample cape, long in the back and sides and cut away in front; symbolic of the higher gifts of the Holy Spirit.

Poterion: A chalice or cup that holds the wine and Precious Blood.

Spoon: Used in administering Holy Communion by intinction; consecrated leavened bread is dipped into consecrated wine and spooned onto the tongue of the communicant.

Sticharion: A long white garment of linen or silk with wide sleeves and decorated with embroidery; formerly the vestment for clerics in minor orders, acolytes, lectors, chanters, and subdeacons; symbolic of purity.

Veils: Three are used, one to cover the poterion, the second to cover the diskos, and the third to cover both.

Zone: A narrow clasped belt made of the same material as the *epitrachelion*; symbolic of the wisdom of the priest, his strength against enemies of the Church and his willingness to perform holy duties.

CODE OF CANONS OF THE EASTERN CHURCHES

The **Code of Canons of the Eastern Churches** serves as the legal corpus for the Eastern Churches, providing the legal principles for the preservation of the rich heritage of these Churches. The overarching theological structure for the Code was enunciated by the Second Vatican Council in its declaration in *Orientalium Ecclesiarum* (3):

These individual Churches, whether of the East or the West, although they differ somewhat among themselves in rite (to use the current phrase), that is, in liturgy, ecclesiastical discipline, and spiritual heritage, are, nevertheless, each as much as the others, entrusted to the pastoral government of the Roman Pontiff, the divinely appointed successor of St. Peter in primacy over the universal Church. They are consequently of equal dignity, so that none of them is superior to the others as regards rite and they enjoy the same rights and are under the same obligations, also in respect of preaching the Gospel to the whole world (cf. Mark 16:15) under the guidance of the Roman Pontiff.

Background

The creation and promulgation of the Code for the Eastern Churches began during the pontificate of Pope Pius XI (1922-39) when he established a commission of cardinals in 1929 to examine the requirements for a code. This preparatory commission was succeeded in 1935 by a new commission with the task of undertaking the actual composition of the Code. What followed was a gradual process of promulgations. Pope Pius XII (1939-58) issued a series of apostolic letters as different elements of the Eastern Code were completed. This method of promulgation continued until 1972 when Pope Paul VI (1963-78) established the Pontifical Commission for the Revision of the Code of Eastern Canon Law.

The commission approached the initial stages of its work quite deliberately. Extensive consultation was made with canonists as well as many bishops of the Eastern Churches. These efforts culminated in November 1988 with the unanimous vote of the commission's members accepting the draft of the new Code. On Oct. 18, 1990, Pope John Paul II officially promulgated the Code of Canons of the Eastern Churches. The Code became effective on Oct. 1, 1991. As the decree makes clear, in accordance with this universal legislation, each Eastern Catholic Church is to develop its own particular law. This stands in contrast to the Code of Canon Law that applies only to the single Latin Church.

Contents and Structure

The Code of Canons of the Eastern Churches marked a significant milestone in the history of Church law. It represented the long process in the development of Canon Law for the Eastern Churches throughout the 20th century and was an eloquent means of both respecting and preserving the proper discipline of those Churches. It was noted from the start that the Code for the Eastern Catholics was organized differently in comparison with the Code of Canon Law for the Latin Rite. There are different elements to Eastern Law, and the Code presents the independence of these laws from the Latin Rite, save, of course, for those canons that give reference to the Pope. Nevertheless, while safeguarding the centuries' old traditions and heritage of the Eastern Catholic Churches, the differences are not disruptive to the unity of the Church. Rather, the Code is an instrument in moving toward appropriate unity. As the 1996 document, "Applying the Liturgical Prescriptions of the Code of Canons of the Eastern Catholic Churches" (9), by the Congregation for the Eastern Churches states:

The Code of Canons of the Eastern Churches, in can. 28 § 1 which refers to *Lumen Gentium*, No. 23, and *Orientalium Ecclesiarum*, No. 3, elucidates the important areas which articulate the heritage of each of the Churches *sui iuris*: liturgy, theology, spirituality and discipline. It is necessary to note that these particular fields penetrate and condition one another in turn inside a global vision of divine revelation which pervades all life and which culminates in the praise of the most holy Trinity.

The Catholic Church in the United States

CHRONOLOGY OF U.S. CATHOLIC HISTORY

The following are key dates in U.S. Catholic History. Reprinted from Our Sunday Visitor's Encyclopedia of American Catholic History.

1492 Christopher Columbus sailed to the New World and reached San Salvador (probably Watlings Island in the Bahamas). He subsequently made three voyages and established a Spanish presence on Santo Domingo (Hispaniola).

1497 John Cabot, a Genoese sailing under the English flag, reached the coasts of Labrador and Newfoundland.

1499 Alonso de Ojeda and Amerigo Vespucci reached Venezuela and explored the South American coast.

1500 Pedro Cabral reached Brazil.

1511 Diocese of Puerto Rico established as suffragan of Seville, Spain. Bishop Alonso Manso, sailing from Spain in 1512, became first bishop to take up residence in New World.

1513 Juan Ponce de León reached Florida and sailed as far north as the Carolinas.

1519 Hernando Cortes began the conquest of Mexico; by the next year, the Aztec Empire had been conquered and the Spanish rule over Mexico was established.

1521 Missionaries accompanying Ponce de León and other explorers probably said first Masses within present limits of US.

1526 Lucas Vázquez de Ayllón attempted to establish a colony in South Carolina; it later failed.

1534-36 Jacques Cartier explored the Newfoundland area and sailed up the St. Lawrence River.

1539 Hernando de Soto journeyed through Florida and as far north as Arkansas.

1540 Francisco Coronado set out to find the Seven Cities of Gold, journeying through Texas, Kansas and New Mexico. Franciscans Juan de Padilla and Marcos de Niza accompanied Coronado expedition through the territory. They celebrated the first Mass within territory of 13 original colonies.

c. 1540 Juan de Padilla, the first martyr of the United States, was murdered on the plains of Kansas by local Indians.

1565 City of St. Augustine, oldest in U.S., founded by Pedro Menendez de Aviles, who was accompanied by four secular priests. America's oldest mission, Nombre de Dios, was established. Fr. Martin Francisco Lopez de Mendoza Grajales became the first parish priest of St. Augustine, where the first parish in the U.S. was established.

1602 Carmelite Anthony of the Ascension offered first recorded Mass in Calif. on shore of San Diego Bay.

1608 Samuel de Champlain established the first permanent French colony at Québec.

1606 Bishop Juan de las Cabeyas de Altamirano, O.P., conducted the first episcopal visitation in the U.S.

1609 Henry Hudson entered New York Bay and sailed up the Hudson River. Santa Fe established as a mission in New Mexico. It later served as a headquarters for missionary efforts in the American Southwest.

1611 Pierre Biard, S.J., and Ennémond Massé, S.J., began missionary labors among the Indians of Maine.

1612 First Franciscan province in U.S. erected under title of Santa Elena; it included Georgia, South Carolina and Florida.

1613 Four Jesuits attempted to establish permanent French settlement near mouth of Kennebec River, Maine.

1619 French Franciscans began work among settlers and Indians. They were driven out by English in 1628.

1620 The Mayflower Compact drawn up by the Pilgrims. The chapel of *Nombre de Dios* was dedicated to *Nuestra Senora de la Leche y Buen Parto* (Our Nursing Mother of the Happy Delivery) in Florida; oldest shrine to the Blessed Mother in the U.S.

1622 Pope Gregory XV established the Congregation de Propaganda Fide to oversee all mission territories. The Catholics of America remained under its jurisdiction until 1908.

1630 New England made a prefecture apostolic in charge of French Capuchins.

1634 Ark and Dove reached Maryland with the first settlers. Maryland established by Lord Calvert; two Jesuits were among first colonists. First Mass offered on Island of St. Clement in Lower Potomac by Jesuit Fr. Andrew White.

1638 Jean Nicolet discovered the water route to the Mississippi.

1642 Jesuits Isaac Jogues and René Goupil were mutilated by Mohawks; Goupil was killed shortly afterwards. Dutch Calvinists rescued Fr. Jogues. The colony of Virginia outlawed priests and disenfranchised Catholics.

1646 Jesuit Isaac Jogues and John Lalande were martyred by Iroquois at Ossernenon, now Auriesville.

1647 Massachusetts Bay Company enacted an anti-priest law.

1649 The General Assembly of Maryland passed an act of religious toleration for the colony.

1653 Jesuits opened a school at Newton Manor, the first school in the American English colonies.

1654 Following the English Civil War and the deposition of King Charles I, the installed Puritan regime in Maryland repealed the act of religious toleration in Maryland.

1656 Church of St. Mary erected on Onondaga Lake, in first French settlement within the state. Kateri Tekakwitha, "Lily of the Mohawks," was born at Ossernenon, now Auriesville (d. in Canada, 1680). She was beatified in 1980; canonized Oct. 21, 2012.

1660 Jesuit René Menard opened first regular mission in Lake Superior region.

1668 Fr. Marquette founded Sainte Marie Mission at Sault Sainte Marie.

1671 Sieur de Lusson and Claude Allouez, S.J., arrived at Mackinac Island and claimed possession of the western country in the name of France.

1673 Louis Joliet and Jacques Marquette, S.J., began their expedition down the Mississippi River.

1674 Fr. Marquette set up a cabin for saying Mass in what later became the city of Chicago.

1675 Fr. Marquette established Mission of the Immaculate Conception among Kaskaskia Indians, near present site of Utica; transferred to Kaskaskia, 1703.

1678 Franciscan Recollect Louis Hennepin, first white man to describe Niagara Falls, celebrated Mass there.

1680 Louis Hennepin followed the Mississippi to its source. The missions of New Mexico destroyed by a local Indian uprising.

1682 Mission Corpus Christi de Isleta (Ysleta) founded by Franciscans near El Paso, first mission in present-day Texas.

1682 Religious toleration extended to members of all faiths in Pennsylvania.

1683 The New York colony passed the Charter of Liberties providing for religious freedom for believers in Christ.

1687 Eusebio Kino, S.J., launched the missions in Arizona at Pimería Alta.

1688 Maryland became royal colony as a result of the so-called Glorious Revolution in England; Anglican Church became the official religion (1692). Toleration Act repealed; Catholics disenfranchised and persecuted until 1776. Hanging of Ann Glover, an elderly Irish-Catholic widow, who refused to renounce her Catholic religion.

1689 Jesuit Claude Allouez died after 32 years of missionary activity among Indians of midwest; he had evangelized Indians of 20 different tribes. Jesuit Jacques Gravier succeeded Allouez as vicar general of Illinois.

1690 Mission San Francisco de los Tejas founded in east Texas.

1692 The Church of England officially established in Maryland. New Mexico re-subjugated by the Spanish and the missions re-opened.

1697 Religious liberty granted to all except "papists" in South Carolina.

1700 Jesuit Eusebio Kino, who first visited the area in 1692, established mission at San Xavier del Bac, near Tucson. In 1783, under Franciscan administration, construction was begun of the Mission Church of San Xavier del Bac near the site of the original mission; it is still in use as a parish church. Although the New York Assembly enacted a bill calling for religious toleration for all Christians in 1683, other penal laws were now enforced against Catholics; all priests were ordered out of the province.

1701 Tolerance granted to all except "papists" in New Jersey.

1703 Mission San Francisco de Solano founded on Rio Grande; rebuilt in 1718 as San Antonio de Valero, or the Alamo.

1704 Destruction of Florida's northern missions by English and Indian troops led by Governor James Moore of South Carolina. Franciscans Juan de Parga, Dominic Criodo, Tiburcio de Osorio, Augustine Ponze de León, Marcos Delgado and two Indians, Anthony Enixa and Amador Cuipa Feliciano, were slain by the invaders.

1709 French Jesuit missionaries obliged to give up their central New York missions.

1716 Antonio de Margil, O.F.M., began his missionary labors in Texas.

1718 The Catholics in Maryland officially disenfranchised. City of New Orleans founded by Jean Baptiste Le Moyne de Bienville.

1727 Ursuline Nuns founded convent in New Orleans, oldest convent in what is now U.S.; they conducted a school, hospital and orphan asylum.

1735 Bishop Francis Martinez de Tejadu Diaz de Velasco, auxiliary of Santiago, was the first bishop to take up residence in U.S., at St. Augustine.

1740s The First Great Awakening among Protestants.

1741 Because of an alleged popish plot to burn the city of New York, four whites were hanged and 11 blacks burned at the stake.

1744 Mission church of the Alamo built in San Antonio.

1751 First Catholic settlement founded among Huron Indians near Sandusky, Ohio, by Jesuit Fr. de la Richardie.

1754-63 The French and Indian War (The Seven Years War in Europe), the first world war; the conflict ended with the defeat of France and the loss of their American colonies.

1755 Fifty-six Catholics of Acadia expelled to the American colonies; those landing in Boston were denied the services of a Catholic priest.

1763 The Jesuits banished from the territories of Louisiana and Illinois. Spain ceded Florida to England. The English also gained control of all French territories east of the Mississippi following the cessation of the French and Indian War.

1765 The Quartering Act imposed on the colonies by the British as a means of paying the cost of colonial defense. It was followed by the Stamp Act, sparking the rise of the Sons of Liberty and the convening of the Stamp Act Congress.

1767 Jesuits expelled from Spanish territory. Spanish Crown confiscated their property, including the Pious Fund for Missions. Upper California missions entrusted to Franciscans.

1769 Franciscan Junípero Serra, missionary in Mexico for 20 years, began establishment of Franciscan missions in California, in present San Diego. He was beatified in 1988.

1770 The Boston Massacre resulted in the deaths of five colonists in Boston.

1773 The Tea Act sparked the Boston Tea Party. The British responded with the Intolerable Acts in 1774. Charles Carroll of Carrollton published the "First Citizen" letter in defense of the Church and Catholics against Daniel Dulany and the royal colonial government in Maryland.

1774 Elizabeth Bayley Seton, foundress of the American Sisters of Charity, was born in New York City on Aug. 28. She was canonized in 1975. The British Parliament passed the Quebec Act granting the French in the region the right to their own religion, language and customs. The first Continental Congress is convened.

1775-1781 The American Revolution, in which Catholics played a major role. In 1790, newly elected President George Washington wrote to American Catholics to thank them for their instrumental role in the war for American freedom.

1775 The Continental Congress denounced the rampant anti-Catholicism of the colonies to King George III. General Washington discouraged Guy Fawkes Day procession, in which pope was carried in effigy.

1776 Charles Carroll received appointment with Samuel Chase and Benjamin Franklin to a commission of the Continental Congress seeking aid from Canada; Fr. John Carroll accompanied them on their mission. Virginia became the first state to vote for full religious freedom in the new state's bill of rights. Similar provisions were passed by Maryland and Pennsylvania. The Continental Congress passed the Declaration of Independence (Charles Carroll was also the longest surviving signer). The New Jersey State Constitution tacitly excluded Catholics from office.

1777 The New York State Constitution gave religious liberty, but the naturalization law required an oath to renounce allegiance to any foreign ruler, ecclesiastical as well as civil.

1778 Fr. Gibault aided George Rogers Clark in campaign against British in conquest of Northwest Territory.

1780 The Massachusetts State Constitution granted religious liberty, but required a religious test to hold public office and provided for tax to support Protestant teachers of piety, religion and morality.

1781 Expedition from San Gabriel Mission founded present city of Los Angeles, Pueblo "de Nuestra Senora de los Angeles." British General Cornwallis surrendered at Yorktown, ending the Revolutionary War.

1783 The Treaty of Paris ended the American Revolution; Great Britain recognized the independence of the United States.

1784 The Vatican appointed Fr. John Carroll to the post of superior of the American Catholic missions. The State Constitution of New Hampshire included a religious test that barred Catholics from public office; local support was provided for public Protestant teachers of religion.

1787 Daniel Carroll of Maryland and Thomas FitzSimons of Pennsylvania signed the Constitution of the United States.

1788 First public Mass said in Boston on Nov. 2 by Abbé de la Poterie, first resident priest.

1789 Pope Pius VI erected the first United States diocese, Baltimore; John Carroll is named the first bishop.

1790 Catholics given right to vote in South Carolina.

1791 French Sulpicians opened the first seminary in the United States, St. Mary's in Baltimore.

Georgetown Academy is established and begins holding classes. Bishop Carroll convoked the first synod of the clergy of the diocese. The Bill of Rights ratified by the Congress. Pierre Charles L'Enfant designed the Federal City of Washington. His plans were not fully implemented until the early 1900s.

1792 James Hoban designed the White House.

1793 Rev. Stephen T. Badin first priest ordained by Bishop Carroll; he soon began missionary work in Kentucky.

1799 Prince Demetrius Gallitzin (Fr. Augustine Smith) arrived in the Allegheny Mountains. He labored there for the next 40 years and established the Church in western Pennsylvania, at Loretto.

1800 Jesuit Leonard Neale became first bishop consecrated in present limits of U.S.

1801 Start of the Second Great Awakening among Protestants.

1802 First mayor of Washington, appointed by President Jefferson, was Catholic Judge Robert Brent.

1803 The Louisiana Purchase resulted in the acquisition by the United States of all French lands from the Mississippi River to the Rocky Mountains for $15 million.

1804-06 President Jefferson sponsored the expedition of Lewis and Clark into the Louisiana Territory.

1806 New York anti-Catholic 1777 Test Oath for naturalization repealed.

1808 Pope Pius VII declared Baltimore the first metropolitan see of the United States, erecting at the same time the new dioceses of Bardstown (KY), Boston, New York, and Philadelphia as suffragans.

1809 Mother Elizabeth Ann Seton established the first native American congregation of sisters, at Emmitsburg, Maryland.

1810 The United States annexed West Florida under the pretext that it was included in the Louisiana Purchase.

1811 Catholic Canadian trappers and traders with John J. Astor expedition founded first American settlement, Astoria. Fr. Guy I. Chabrat becomes first priest ordained west of the Allegheny Mountains.

1812 The War of 1812; it was ended by the Treaty of Ghent in 1814.

1814 St. Joseph's Orphanage, Philadelphia, opened, the first Catholic asylum for children in the United States.

1818 Religious freedom established by new constitution in Connecticut, although the Congregational Church remained, in practice, the state church. Bp. Dubourg arrived at St. Louis, with Vincentians Joseph Rosati and Felix de Andreis. Rose Philippine Duchesne arrived at St. Charles; founded first American convent of the Society of the Sacred Heart. She was beatified in 1940 and canonized in 1988.

1822 Bp. John England founded the *United States Catholic Miscellany*, the first Catholic newspaper in the country of a strictly religious nature. The Society for the Propagation of the Faith is founded in France; it sent missionaries throughout the world. Vicariate Apostolic of Mississippi and Alabama established.

1823 President Monroe proposed the Monroe Doctrine of foreign policy. Fr. Gabriel Richard elected delegate to Congress from Michigan territory; he was the first priest elected to the House of Representatives.

1828 New York State Legislature enacted a law upholding sanctity of seal of confession. The first hospital opened west of the Mississippi in St. Louis, staffed by the Sisters of Charity from Emmitsburg, Maryland.

1829 The First Provincial Council of Baltimore convoked. The Oblate Sisters of Providence, the first African-American congregation of women religious in the United States was established in Baltimore.

1831 Xavier University founded.

1833 Fr. Frederic Baraga celebrated first Mass in present Grand Rapids.

1834 First native New Yorker to become a secular priest, Rev. John McCloskey, was ordained. Indian missions in Northwest entrusted to Jesuits by Holy See. A mob of Nativists attacked and burned down the Ursuline Convent at Charlestown, Mass.

1835 Samuel F.B. Morse published *The Foreign Conspiracy Against the Liberties of the United States.*

1836 Texans under Stephen F. Austin declared their independence from Mexico; the Battle of the Alamo in San Antonio resulted in the deaths of 188 Texans, including the commander William B. Travis and perhaps Davy Crockett. Texas soon won its independence and was annexed in 1845. John Nepomucene Neumann arrived from Bohemia and was ordained a priest in Old St. Patrick's Cathedral, New York City. He was canonized in 1977. The infamous work of Maria Monk's *Awful Disclosures of the Hotel Dieu Nunnery of Montreal,* detailing supposed scandals of Catholic religious, was published. President Jackson nominated Roger Brooke Taney as chief justice of the Supreme Court.

1838 Fathers Blanchet and Demers, "Apostles of the Northwest," sent to territory by Abp. of Québec.

1839 Pope Gregory XVI condemned the slave trade in his decree *In Supremo Apostolatus.*

1840 Mother Theodore Guérin founded the Sisters of Providence of St.-Mary-of-the-Woods in Indiana.

1842 Fr. Augustine Ravoux began ministrations to French and Indians at Fort Pierre, Vermilion and Prairie du Chien; printed devotional book in Sioux language the following year. Henriette Delille and Juliette Gaudin began the Sisters of the Holy Family in New Orleans, the second African-American community of women religious. University of Notre Dame founded by Holy Cross Fr. Edward Sorin and Brothers of St. Joseph on land given the diocese of Vincennes by Fr. Stephen Badin.

1844 Thirteen persons killed, two churches and a school burned in Know-Nothing riots at Philadelphia. Orestes Brownson received into the Church; he subsequently founded *Brownson's Quarterly Review.*

1845 Nativists opposed to Catholics and Irish immigration, established the Native American Party. Issac Hecker received into the Church. The potato famine began in Ireland, causing in part the mass migration of Irish to the United States. The St. Vincent de Paul Society founded in the United States.

1846-48 The Mexican-American War was caused by a border dispute between the United States and Mexico. Catholic chaplains were appointed to the army, to minister to Mexican Catholics.

1846 Peter H. Burnett, who became first governor of California in 1849, received into Catholic Church. First Benedictine Abbey in New World founded near Latrobe by Fr. Boniface Wimmer.

1847 The Bishops of the United States requested Pope Pius IX to name the Immaculate Conception patron of the United States.

1848 The first permanent American Trappist foundation established, in Kentucky. Jacob L. Martin named the first American representative to the Vatican.

1852 The First Plenary Council of Baltimore held. Redemptorist John Nepomucene Neumann became fourth bishop of Philadelphia. He was beatified in 1963 and canonized in 1977.

1853 Calling for the exclusion of Catholics and foreigners from office and a 21-year residence requirement, the American Party was founded, known also as the Know-Nothing Party.

1854 Members of the Benedictine Swiss-American congregation established a community at St. Meinrad in southern Indiana.

1855 The German Catholic Central Verein founded. The "Bloody Monday" Riots in Louisville, Kentucky, leave 20 dead.

1857 The Supreme Court issued the Dred Scott Decision; Chief Justice Roger Taney stated that Congress could not exclude slavery from the territories since, according to the Constitution, slaves were property and could be transported anywhere. The American College at Louvain opened; closed June 2011.

1858 Jesuit Fr. De Smet accompanied General Harney as chaplain on expedition sent to settle troubles between Mormons and U.S. government. The Paulists, the first native religious community for men, established. Cornerstone of second (present) St. Patrick's Cathedral, New York City, was laid; the cathedral was completed in 1879.

1859 The North American College founded in Rome as a training center for American seminarians.

1860 South Carolina seceded from the Union.

1861-65 The American Civil War. Catholics participated in large numbers on both sides. There were approximately 40 Catholic chaplains in the Union army and 28 in the Confederate army. More than 500 Catholic nuns ministered to the sick and wounded. Over 20 generals in the Union army and 11 generals in the Confederate army were Catholics.

1861 The Confederacy was formed after 11 states seceded from the Union. Jefferson Davis was elected president of the Confederacy.

1865 *Catholic World* founded. A Test Oath law passed by state legislature (called Drake Convention) to crush Catholicism in Missouri. Law declared unconstitutional by Supreme Court in 1866. Rev. H. H. Spalding, a Protestant missionary, published the Whitman Myth to hinder work of Catholic missionaries in Oregon. President Lincoln was assassinated. The murder sparked anti-Catholicism, including charges that Jesuits orchestrated his death. Congress passed the Thirteenth Amendment abolishing slavery.

1866 The Second Plenary Council of Baltimore.

1867 Reconstruction launched in the South; the presence of Federal troops did not end until 1877. The Ku Klux Klan founded to defeat

Reconstruction, oppose Catholicism, and establish white supremacy in the post-war South. The U.S. purchased Alaska for $7.2 million; organized by Secretary of State William Seward, the purchase was called "Seward's Folly."

1869-70 The Fist Vatican Council convoked. Most of the bishops of the United States took part in the deliberations of the council.

1869 The Transcontinental Railroad completed, with the two tracks meeting at Promontory, near Ogden, Utah. The Knights of Labor founded.

1870 The Holy Name Society organized in the U.S.

1873 Blessed Fr. Damien de Veuster of the Sacred Hearts Fathers arrived in Molokai and spent the remainder of his life working among lepers. He was beatified in 1995.

1875 James A. Healy, first bishop of Negro blood consecrated in U.S., became second Bishop of Portland, Maine. Abp. John McCloskey of New York became the first American prelate to be elevated to the College of Cardinals.

1876 George Armstrong Custer killed at the Battle of Little Bighorn (in the Second Sioux War) in Montana. *The American Catholic Quarterly Review* is established. James Gibbons publishes *Faith of Our Fathers*.

1878 Franciscan Sisters of Allegany becomes first native American community to send members to foreign missions.

1880 William R. Grace becomes the first Catholic mayor of New York City.

1882 Knights of Columbus founded by Fr. Michael J. McGivney.

1884 The Third Plenary Council of Baltimore held. John Gilmary Shea began the U.S. Catholic Historical Society.

1886 Abp. Charles J. Seghers, "Apostle of Alaska," was murdered by a guide; he had surveyed southern and northwest Alaska in 1873 and 1877. Abp. James Gibbons of Baltimore is named the second American cardinal. Augustus Tolton is ordained the first African-American priest for the United States. The Knights of St. John was established.

1887 The American Protective Association (APA) was established to resist the growth of immigration. The Dawes Act was passed, dissolving all Indian tribes and distributing their lands among their former members, who were not permitted to dispose of their property for 25 years.

1889 The Catholic University of America opened. The first African-American Lay Congress was held in Washington, D.C.; subsequent congresses held in Cincinnati (1890), Philadelphia (1892), Chicago (1893), and Baltimore (1894). Mother Frances Xavier Cabrini arrived in New York City to begin work among Italian immigrants. She was canonized in 1946. *American Ecclesiastical Review* begun.

1890 Archbishop Ireland delivered an address on public and private schools at the gathering of the National Education Association in St. Paul, Minnesota.

1891 Vicariate Apostolic of Oklahoma and Indian Territory was established. Katharine Drexel founded Sisters of Blessed Sacrament for Indians and Colored Peoples. She was canonized in 2000. The Rosary Society organized.

1893 The Apostolic Delegation under Abp. Francesco Satolli established in Washington, D.C.; it became an Apostolic Nunciature in 1984 with the establishment of full diplomatic relations between the U.S. and the Holy See. The first Catholic college for women in the United States, College of Notre Dame of Maryland, was established. *St. Anthony Messenger* launched.

1898 Puerto Rico ceded to U.S. (became self-governing Commonwealth in 1952); inhabitants granted U.S. citizenship in 1917. The United States annexed Hawaii; the monarchy had been overthrown in 1897.

1898 The Spanish-American War.

1899 Pope Leo XIII issued *Testem Benevolentiae*.

1901 President McKinley assassinated.

1904 The National Catholic Education Association (NCEA) founded. First publication of the *Catholic Almanac*.

1905 The Catholic Church Extension Society for home missions established.

1907 The first volume of the *Catholic Encyclopedia* was published by the Catholic University of America.

1908 Pope St. Pius X published *Pascendi Domini Gregis* against Modernism. Pope Pius issued the bull *Sapienti Consilio*, by which the Church in the U.S. was removed from mission status and the jurisdiction of the Congregation de Propaganda Fide. First American Missionary Congress held in Chicago.

1909 The Holy Name Society was established. *America* Magazine founded by the Jesuits.

1911 The Catholic Foreign Mission Society of America (Maryknoll) founded. Katharine Drexel founded the Sisters of the Blessed Sacrament.

1912 *Our Sunday Visitor* founded.

1914-18 World War I.

1917 The United States entered the First World War. The National Catholic War Council was founded. Over one million Catholics served in the Armed Forces (over 20% of the total U.S. military).

1919 The Bishops' *Program of Social Reconstruction* published. The National Catholic Welfare Council was founded. Peter Guilday began the American Catholic Historical Association.

1920 The National Catholic News Service (NC, now the Catholic News Service, CNS) was established.

1924 The Federated Colored Catholics of the United States was established. *Commonweal* magazine was founded by Michael Williams.

1925 The Supreme Court declares the Oregon school law unconstitutional. The Scopes Trial, also called the Dayton Monkey Trial, took place in Dayton, Ohio.

1926 The Twenty-Eighth International Eucharistic Congress was held in Chicago.

1928 Alfred E. Smith of New York nominated for president by the Democratic Party; he was the first Catholic ever chosen to head a major-party national ticket. He was defeated by Herbert Hoover, in part because of his opposition to Prohibition and his faith.

1929 The stockmarket crash signaled the start of the Great Depression. The Catholic Church devoted enormous resources to alleviating the suffering of those afflicted by the global Depression.

1932 Franklin Delano Roosevelt was elected president, launching the New Deal period (1933-45).

1933 The Catholic Worker Movement was established by Dorothy Day and Peter Maurin.

1934 John LaFarge, S.J., begins the first Catholic Interracial Council in New York.

1937 The Association of Catholic Trade Unionists (ACTU) established.

1939 Myron C. Taylor named personal representative of President Roosevelt to Pope Pius XII.

1939-45 World War II.

1941 Pearl Harbor was attacked by Japan; the U.S. entered World War II. Catholics comprised over 25% of the Armed Forces.

1945 End of World War II. Delegates from 50 nations established the Charter of the United Nations.

1947 The Christian Family Movement was begun by Pat and Patty Crowley. The Supreme Court issued the decision *Everson v. Board of Education* approving the use of public school buses to carry Catholic students to parochial schools.

1948 Protestants and Other Americans for Separation of Church and State (POAU) founded.

1951 President Truman nominates General Mark Clark as Ambassador to Vatican City. The nomination later withdrawn in the face of anti-Catholic protests.

1954 The Sisters Formation Conference was founded. The Supreme Court decided *Brown v. Board of Education of Topeka*; the decision declared that segregation in the public schools was unconstitutional.

1955 John Tracy Ellis published *American Catholics and the Intellectual Life.*

1956 Leadership Conference of Women Religious and Conference of Major Superiors of Men was founded.

1957 The Civil Rights Act was passed, the first since 1875.

1958 Christopher Dawson was named the first holder of the Chauney Stillman Chair of Roman Catholic Studies at the Harvard Divinity School.

1959 Pope John XXIII announced his intention to convoke the Second Vatican Council.

1960 John F. Kennedy elected president of the United States; he was the first Catholic president.

1962-65 The Second Vatican Council.

1962 Gustave Weigel, S.J., appointed by the Vatican to be one of the five Catholic observers at the third general assembly of the World Council of Churches at New Delhi. Archbishop Joseph Rummel of New Orleans announced the integration of archdiocesan Catholic schools.

1963 The Catholic University of America prohibited Hans Küng, John Courtney Murray, S.J., Gustave Weigel, S.J., and Godfrey Diekmann, O.S.B., from speaking at the school. Elizabeth Ann Seton, the first American to be beatified. President Kennedy assassinated in Dallas.

1964 The Civil Rights Act passed.

1965 Pope Paul VI visited the United Nations, the first pope to visit the U.S. Gommar A. De Pauw organizes the Catholic Traditionalist movement.

1966 The National Conference of Catholic Bishops and the United States Catholic Conference were organized. Harold Perry, S.V.D., became the second African-American to be named a bishop.

1967 The Land O' Lakes Statement issued. The Catholic Charismatic Movement began. The Catholic Committee on Urban Ministry (CCUM) was established.

1968 Pope Paul VI issued *Humanae Vitae*. The National Black Catholic Clergy Caucus, the National Black Sisters' Conference, the National Black Catholic Seminarians Association, and the National Federation of Priests' Council were formed. Catholics United for the Faith established.

1969 The Organization of Priests Associated for Religious, Educational, and Social Rights (PADRES) established. The Campaign for Human Development established.

1970 Patricio Flores, the first modern Latino bishop, ordained.

1971 The Leadership Conference of Women Religious established.

1972 Religious Brothers Conference established.

1973 Roe v. Wade Decision handed down by the Supreme Court, legalizing abortion.

1975 Pope Paul VI canonized the first American saint, Elizabeth Ann Seton.

1976 The U.S. celebrated the Bicentennial. The 41st International Eucharistic Congress in Philadelphia.

1977 Fellowship of Catholic Scholars established.

1979 Pope John Paul II visited the U.S.

1983 The NCCB issued *Challenge of Peace*.

1986 The NCCB issued *Economic Justice for All*. The Vatican and Catholic University of America removed Fr. Charles Curran from teaching theology at the university.

1987 Pope John Paul II visited the U.S. for the second time. The National Black Catholic Congress convoked in Washington, D.C.

1991 The U.S. played a major role in the Gulf War.

1992 Council of Major Superiors of Women Religious founded.

1993 World Youth Day held in Denver.

1995 Pope John Paul II visited the United Nations, Baltimore, and New York.

1997 U.S. Bishops took part in a special assembly of the Synod of Bishops on the Church in the Americas.

1999 Pope John Paul II visited St. Louis.

2001 The U.S. attacked on Sept. 11. The NCCB and USSC merged to form the United States Conference of Catholic Bishops (USCCB); Bishop Wilton Gregory of Belleville was elected the first black president of the USCCB.

2002 The pedophilia crisis erupted across the country; the USCCB passed a series of protective norms.

2003 The U.S. launched the Iraq War to topple Saddam Hussein.

2004 Pres. George W. Bush re-elected president. The Democratic nominee, Sen. John Kerry, a Catholic, caused considerable controversy because of his pro-abortion position. The issue sparked a national debate over the issue of Catholic politicians and abortion.

2008 Pope Benedict XVI visited Washington, D.C. and New York, his first apostolic voyage to the United States as pope. Sen. Barack Obama elected the first African-American president; his running-mate, Sen. Joseph Biden of Delaware became the first nominally Catholic vice-president.

2012 The Bishops of the United States speak out publicly against the Mandate issued by the Obama Administration that would require Catholic employers to provide their employees with insurance that includes contraception, sterilization, and abortion-inducing drugs. The mandate is the cause of immense conteoversy over the limitations being placed upon religious liberty.

U.S. CATHOLIC HISTORY

Courtesy Rev. Clyde Crews, Ph.D.

The starting point of the mainstream of Catholic history in the U.S. was in Baltimore at the end of the Revolutionary War. Long before that time, however, Catholic explorers had traversed much of the country and missionaries had done considerable work among Indians in the Southeast, Northeast and Southwest. (*See* Index, Chronology of Church in U.S.)

Spanish and French Missions

Missionaries from Spain evangelized Indians in Florida (which included a large area of the Southeast), New Mexico, Texas and California. Franciscan Juan de Padilla, killed in 1542 in what is now central Kansas, was the first of numerous martyrs among the early missionaries. The city of St. Augustine, settled by the Spanish in 1565, was the first permanent settlement in the United States and also the site of the first parish, established the same year with secular Fr. Martin Francisco Lopez de Mendoza Grajales as pastor. Italian Jesuit Eusebio Kino (1645-1711) established Spanish missions in lower California and southern Arizona, where he founded San Xavier del Bac mission in 1700. Bl. Junípero Serra (1713-84), who established nine of the famous chain of 21 Franciscan missions in California, was perhaps the most noted of the Spanish missionaries. He was beatified in 1988.

French missionary efforts originated in Canada and extended to parts of Maine, New York and areas around the Great Lakes and along the Mississippi River as far south as Louisiana. Sts. Isaac Jogues, René Goupil and John de Brébeuf, three of eight Jesuit missionaries of New France martyred between 1642 and 1649 (canonized in 1930), met their deaths near Auriesville, New York. Jesuit explorer Jacques Marquette (1637-75), who founded St. Ignace Mission at the Straits of Mackinac in 1671, left maps and a diary of his exploratory trip down the Mississippi River with Louis Joliet in 1673. Claude Allouez (1622-89), another French Jesuit, worked for 32 years among Indians in the Midwest, baptizing an estimated 10,000. French Catholics founded the colony in Louisiana in 1699. In 1727, Ursuline nuns from France founded a convent in New Orleans, the oldest in the United States.

English Settlements

Catholics were excluded by penal law from English settlements along the Atlantic coast.

The only colony established under Catholic leadership was Maryland, granted to George Calvert (Lord Baltimore) as a proprietary colony in 1632; its first settlement at St. Mary's City was established in 1634 by a contingent of Catholic and Protestant colonists who had arrived from England on the *Ark and the Dove*. Jesuits Andrew White and John Altham, who later evangelized Indians of the area, accompanied the settlers. The principle of religious freedom on which the colony was founded was enacted into law in 1649 as the Act of Toleration. It was the first such measure passed in the colonies and, except for a four-year period of Puritan control, remained in effect until 1688, when Maryland became a royal colony and the Anglican Church was made the official religion in 1692. Catholics were disenfranchised and persecuted until 1776.

The only other colony where Catholics were assured some degree of freedom was Pennsylvania, founded by the Quaker William Penn in 1681.

One of the earliest permanent Catholic establishments in the English colonies was St. Francis Xavier Mission, Old Bohemia, in northern Maryland, founded by the Jesuits in 1704 to serve Catholics of Delaware, Maryland and southeastern Pennsylvania. Its Bohemia Academy, established in the 1740s, was attended by sons of prominent Catholic families in the area.

Catholics and the Revolution

Despite their small number, which accounted for about one percent of the population, Catholics made significant contributions to the cause for independence from England.

Fr. John Carroll (1735-1815), who would later become the first bishop of the American hierarchy, and his cousin, Charles Carroll (1737-1832), a signer of the Declaration of Independence, were chosen by the Continental Congress to accompany Benjamin Franklin and Samuel Chase to Canada to try to secure that country's neutrality. Fr. Pierre Gibault (1737-1804) gave important aid in preserving the Northwest Territory for the revolutionaries. Thomas FitzSimons (1741-1811) of Philadelphia gave financial support to the Continental Army, served in a number of campaigns and later, with Daniel Carroll of Maryland, became one of the two Catholic signers of the Constitution. John Barry (1745-1803), commander of the *Lexington*, the first ship commissioned by Congress, served valiantly and is considered a founder of the U.S. Navy. There is no record of the number of Catholics who served in Washington's armies, although 38 to 50 percent had Irish surnames.

Casimir Pulaski (1748-79) and Thaddeus Kosciusko (1746-1817) of Poland served the cause of the Revolution. Assisting also were the Catholic nations of France, with a military and naval force, and Spain, with money and the neutrality of its colonies.

Acknowledgment of Catholic aid in the war and the founding of the Republic was made by General Washington in his reply to a letter from prominent Catholics seeking justice and equal rights: "I presume your fellow citizens of all denominations will not forget the patriotic part which you took in the accomplishment of our Revolution and the establishment of our government or the important assistance which they received from a nation [France] in which the Roman Catholic faith is professed."

In 1789, religious freedom was guaranteed under the First Amendment to the Constitution. Discriminatory laws against Catholics remained in force in many of the states, however, until well into the 19th century.

Beginning of Organization

Fr. John Carroll's appointment as superior of the American missions on June 9, 1784, was the first step toward organization of the Church in this country. According to a report he made to Rome the following year, there were 24 priests and approximately 25,000 Catholics, mostly in Maryland and Pennsylvania, in a general population of four million. Many of them had been in the Colonies for several generations. For the most part, however, they were an unknown minority laboring under legal and social handicaps.

Establishment of the Hierarchy

Fr. Carroll was named the first American bishop in 1789 and placed in charge of the Diocese of Baltimore, whose boundaries were coextensive with those of the United States. He was ordained in England on Aug. 15, 1790, and installed in his see the following Dec. 12.

Ten years later, Fr. Leonard Neale became his coadjutor and the first bishop ordained in the U.S. Bishop Carroll became an archbishop in 1808 when Baltimore was designated a metropolitan see and the new dioceses of Boston, New York, Philadelphia and Bardstown (now Louisville) were established. These jurisdictions were later subdivided, and by 1840 there were, in addition to Baltimore, 15 dioceses, 500 priests and 663,000 Catholics in the general population of 17 million.

Priests and First Seminaries

The original number of 24 priests noted in Bishop Carroll's 1785 report was gradually augmented with the arrival of others from France and other countries. Among arrivals from France after the Civil Constitution of the Clergy went into effect in 1790 were Jean Louis Lefebvre de Cheverus and Sulpicians Ambrose Maréchal, Benedict Flaget and William Dubourg, who later became bishops.

The first seminary in the country was St. Mary's, established in 1791 in Baltimore and placed under the direction of the Sulpicians. French seminarian Stephen T. Badin (1768-1853), who fled to the U.S. in 1792 and became a pioneer missionary in Kentucky, Ohio and Michigan, was the first priest ordained (1793) in the U.S. Demetrius Gallitzin (1770-1840), a Russian prince and convert to Catholicism who did pioneer missionary work in western Pennsylvania, was ordained to the priesthood in 1795; he was the first to receive all his orders in the U.S. By 1815, St. Mary's Seminary had 30 ordained alumni.

Two additional seminaries, Mt. St. Mary's at Emmitsburg, Maryland, and St. Thomas at Bardstown, Kentucky, were established in 1809 and 1811, respectively. These and similar institutions founded later played key roles in the development and growth of the American clergy.

Early Schools

Early educational enterprises included the establishment in 1791 of a school at Georgetown that later became the first Catholic university in the U.S.; the opening of a secondary school for girls, conducted by Visitation Nuns, in 1799 at Georgetown; and the start of a similar school in the first decade of the 19th century at Emmitsburg, Maryland, by St. Elizabeth Ann Seton.

By the 1840s, which saw the beginnings of the present public school system, more than 200 Catholic elementary schools, half of them west of the Alleghenies, were in operation. From this start, the Church subsequently built the greatest private system of education in the world.

Sisterhoods

Institutes of women Religious were largely responsible for the development of educational and charitable institutions. Among them were Ursuline Nuns in Louisiana from 1727 and Visitation Nuns at Georgetown in the 1790s.

The first contemplative foundation in the country was established in 1790 at Fort Tobacco, Maryland, by three American-born Carmelites trained at an English convent in Belgium.

The first community of American origin was the Sisters of Charity of St. Joseph, founded in 1808 at Emmitsburg, Maryland, by Mother Elizabeth Ann Bayley Seton (canonized in 1975). Other early American communities were the Sisters of Loretto and the Sisters of Charity of Nazareth, both founded in 1812 in Kentucky, and the Oblate Sisters of Providence, a black community founded in 1829 in Baltimore by Mother Mary Elizabeth Lange.

Among pioneer U.S. foundresses of European communities were Mother Rose Philippine Duchesne (canonized in 1980), who established the Religious of the Sacred Heart in Missouri in 1818, and Mother Theodore Guérin, who founded the Sisters of Providence of St.-Mary-of-the-Woods in Indiana in 1840.

The number of sisters' communities, most of them branches of European institutes, increased apace with needs for their missions in education, charitable service and spiritual life.

Trusteeism

The initial lack of organization in ecclesiastical affairs, nationalistic feeling among Catholics and the independent action of some priests were factors involved in several early crises.

In Philadelphia, some German Catholics, with the reluctant consent of Bp. Carroll, founded Holy Trinity, the first national parish in the U.S. They refused to accept the pastor appointed by the bishop and elected their own. This and other abuses led to formal schism in 1796, a condition that existed until 1802, when they returned to canonical jurisdiction. Philadelphia was also the scene of the Hogan Schism, which developed in the 1820s when Fr. William Hogan, with the aid of lay trustees, seized control of St. Mary's Cathedral. His movement, for churches and parishes controlled by other than canonical procedures and run in extralegal ways, was nullified by a decision of the Pennsylvania Supreme Court in 1822.

Similar troubles seriously disturbed the peace of the Church in other places, principally New York, Baltimore, Buffalo, Charleston and New Orleans.

Dangers arising from the exploitation of lay control were gradually diminished with the extension and enforcement of canonical procedures and with changes in civil law about the middle of the century.

Anti-Catholicism

Bigotry against Catholics waxed and waned during the 19th century and into the 20th. The first major campaign of this kind, which developed in the wake of the panic of 1819 and lasted for about 25 years, was mounted in 1830 when the number of Catholic immigrants began to increase to a noticeable degree. Nativist anti-Catholicism generated a great deal of violence, represented by loss of life and property in Charlestown, Massachusetts, in 1834, and in Philadelphia 10 years later. Later bigotry was fomented by the Know-Nothings, in the 1850s; the Ku Klux Klan, from 1866; the American Protective Association, from 1887; and the Guardians of Liberty. Perhaps the last eruption of virulently overt anti-Catholicism occurred during the campaign of Alfred E. Smith for the presidency in 1928. Observers feel the issue was muted to a considerable extent in the political area with the election of John F. Kennedy to the presidency in 1960.

The Catholic periodical press had its beginnings in response to the attacks of bigots. The *U.S. Catholic Miscellany* (1822-61), the first Catholic newspaper in the U.S., was founded by Bishop John England of Charleston to answer critics of the Church. This remained the character of most of the periodicals published in the 19th and into the 20th century.

Growth and Immigration

Between 1830 and 1900, the combined factors of natural increase, immigration and conversion raised the Catholic population to 12 million. A large percentage of the growth figure represented immigrants: some 2.7 million, largely from Ireland, Germany and France, between 1830 and 1880; and another 1.25 million during the 1880s when Eastern and Southern Europeans came in increasing numbers. By the 1860s the Catholic Church, with most of its members concentrated in urban areas, was probably the largest religious body in the country.

The efforts of progressive bishops to hasten the acculturation of Catholic immigrants occasioned a number of controversies, which generally centered around questions concerning national or foreign-language parishes. One of them, called Cahenslyism, arose from complaints that German Catholic immigrants were not being given adequate pastoral care.

Eastern Rite Catholics

The immigration of the 1890s included large numbers of Eastern Rite Catholics with their own liturgies and tradition of a married clergy, but without their own bishops. The treatment of their clergy and people by some of the U.S. (Latin Rite) hierarchy and the prejudices they encountered resulted in the defection of thousands from the Catholic Church.

In 1907, Basilian monk Stephen Ortynsky was ordained the first bishop of Byzantine Rite Catholics in the U.S. Eventually jurisdictions were established for most Byzantine and other Eastern Rite Catholics in the country.

Councils of Baltimore

The bishops of the growing U.S. dioceses met at Baltimore for seven provincial councils between 1829 and 1849.

In 1846, they proclaimed the Blessed Virgin Mary patroness of the United States under the title of the Immaculate Conception, eight years before the dogma was proclaimed in Rome.

After the establishment of the Archdiocese of Oregon City in 1846 and the elevation to metropolitan status of St. Louis, New Orleans, Cincinnati and New York, the first of the three plenary councils of Baltimore was held.

The first plenary assembly was convoked on May 9, 1852, with Abp. Francis P. Kenrick of Baltimore as papal legate. The bishops drew up regulations concerning parochial life, matters of church ritual and ceremonies, the administration of church funds and the teaching of Christian doctrine.

The second plenary council, meeting from Oct. 7 to 21, 1866, under the presidency of Abp. Martin J. Spalding, formulated a condemnation of several current doctrinal errors and established norms affecting the organization of dioceses, the education and conduct of the clergy, the management of ecclesiastical property, parochial duties and general education.

Abp. (later Cardinal) James Gibbons called into session the third plenary council which lasted from Nov. 9 to Dec. 7, 1884. Among highly significant results of actions taken by this assembly were the preparation of the line of Baltimore catechisms that became a basic means of religious instruction in this country; legislation that fixed the pattern of Catholic education by requiring the building of elementary schools in all parishes; the establishment of the Catholic University of America in Washington, D.C., in 1889; and the determination of six holy days of obligation for observance in this country.

The enactments of the three plenary councils have had the force of particular law for the Church in the U.S.

The Holy See established the Apostolic Delegation in Washington, D.C., on Jan. 24, 1893.

Slavery

In the Civil War period, as before, Catholics reflected attitudes of the general population with respect to the issue of slavery. Some supported it, some opposed it, but none were prominent in the Abolition Movement. Pope Gregory XVI had condemned the slave trade in 1839, but no contemporary pope or American bishop published an official document on slavery itself. The issue did not split Catholics in schism as it did Baptists, Methodists and Presbyterians.

Catholics fought on both sides in the Civil War. Five hundred members of 20 or more sisterhoods served the wounded of both sides.

One hundred thousand of the four million slaves emancipated in 1863 were Catholics; the highest concentrations were in Louisiana, about 60,000, and Maryland, 16,000. Three years later, their pastoral care was one of the subjects covered in nine decrees issued by the Second Plenary Council of Baltimore. The measures had little practical effect with respect to integration of the total Catholic community, predicated as they were on the proposition that individual bishops should handle questions regarding segregation in churches and related matters as best they could in the pattern of local customs.

Long-entrenched segregation practices continued in force through the rest of the 19th century and well into the 20th. The first effective efforts to alter them were initiated by Card. Joseph Ritter of St. Louis in 1947, Card. (then Abp.) Patrick O'Boyle of Washington in 1948, and Bp. Vincent Waters of Raleigh in 1953.

Friend of Labor

The Church became known during the 19th century as a friend and ally of labor in seeking justice for the working man. Cardinal Gibbons journeyed to Rome in 1887, for example, to defend and prevent a condemnation of the Knights of Labor by Leo XIII. The encyclical *Rerum Novarum* (1891) was hailed by many American bishops as a confirmation, if not vindication, of their own theories. Catholics have always formed a large percentage of union membership, and some have served unions in positions of leadership.

Americanism

Near the end of the century some controversy developed over what was characterized as Americanism or the phantom heresy. It was alleged that Americans were discounting the importance of contemplative virtues, exalting the practical virtues, and watering down the purity of Catholic doctrine for the sake of facilitating convert work.

The French translation of Fr. Walter Elliott's *Life of Isaac Hecker*, which fired the controversy, was one of many factors that led to the issuance of Leo XIII's *Testem Benevolentiae* in January 1899, in an attempt to end the matter. It was the first time the orthodoxy of the Church in the U.S. was called into question.

Schism

In the 1890s, serious friction developed between Poles and Irish in Scranton, Buffalo and Chicago, resulting in schism and the establishment of the Polish National Catholic Church. A central figure in the affair was Fr. Francis Hodur, who was excommunicated by Bp. William O'Hara of Scranton in 1898. Nine years later, his ordination by an Old Catholic Abp. of Utrecht gave the new church its first bishop.

Another schism of the period led to formation of the American Carpatho-Russian Orthodox Greek Catholic Church.

Coming of Age

In 1900, there were 12 million Catholics in the total U.S. population of 76 million, 82 dioceses in 14 provinces, and 12,000 priests and members of about 40 communities of men Religious. Many sisterhoods, most of them of European origin and some of American foundation, were engaged in Catholic educational and hospital work, two of their traditional apostolates.

The Church in the U.S. was removed from mission status with promulgation of the apostolic constitution *Sapienti Consilio* by Pope St. Pius X on June 29, 1908.

Before that time, and even into the early 1920s, the Church in this country received financial assistance from mission-aid societies in France, Bavaria and Austria. Already, however, it was making increasing contributions of its own. At the present time, it is one of the major national contributors to the worldwide Society for the Propagation of the Faith.

American foreign missionary personnel increased from 14 or less in 1906 to an all-time high in 1968 of 9,655 priests, brothers, sisters, seminarians, and lay persons. The first missionary seminary in the U.S. was in operation at Techny, Illinois, in 1909, under the auspices of the Society of the Divine Word. Maryknoll, the first American missionary society, was established in 1911 and sent its first priests

to China in 1918. Despite these contributions, the Church in the U.S. has not matched the missionary commitment of some other nations.

Bishops' Conference

A highly important apparatus for mobilizing the Church's resources was established in 1917 under the title of the National Catholic War Council. Its name was changed to National Catholic Welfare Conference several years later, but its objectives remained the same: to serve as an advisory and coordinating agency of the American bishops for advancing works of the Church in fields of social significance and impact — education, communications, immigration, social action, legislation, youth and lay organizations.

The forward thrust of the bishops' social thinking was evidenced in a program of social reconstruction they recommended in 1919. By 1945, all but one of their 12 points had been enacted into legislation — including many later social security programs.

The NCWC was renamed the United States Catholic Conference (USCC) in November 1966, when the hierarchy also organized itself as a territorial conference with pastoral-juridical authority under the title, National Conference of Catholic Bishops. The USCC carried on the functions of the former NCWC until July 2001, when it merged with the National Conference of Catholic Bishops to create the USCCB.

Catholic Press

The establishment of the National Catholic News Service (NC) — now the Catholic News Service (CNS) — in 1920 was an important event in the development of the Catholic press, which had its beginnings about 100 years earlier. Early in the 20th century there were 63 weekly newspapers. The 2014 *Catholic Press Directory*, published by the Catholic Press Association, reported a total of 231 periodicals in North America, with a circulation of 10,444,933.

Lay Organizations

A burst of lay organizational growth occurred from the 1930s onwards with the appearance of Catholic Action types of movements and other groups and associations devoted to special causes, social service and assistance for the poor and needy. Several special apostolates developed under the aegis of the National Catholic Welfare Conference (now the U.S. Catholic Conference); the outstanding one was the Confraternity of Christian Doctrine.

Nineteenth-century organizations of great influence included: The St. Vincent de Paul Society, whose first U.S. office was set up in 1845 in St. Louis; the Catholic Central Union (*Verein*), dating from 1855; the Knights of Columbus, founded in 1882; the Holy Name Society, organized in the U.S. in 1870; the Rosary Society (1891); and scores of chapters of the Sodality of the Blessed Virgin Mary.

Pastoral Concerns

The potential for growth of the Church in this country by immigration was sharply reduced but not entirely curtailed after 1921 with the passage of restrictive federal legislation. As a result, the

Catholic population became more stabilized and, to a certain extent and for many reasons, began to acquire an identity of its own.

Some increase from outside has taken place in the past 50 years, however, from Canada, from Central and Eastern European countries, and from Puerto Rico and Latin American countries since World War II. This influx, while not as great as that of the 19th century and early 20th, has enriched the Church here with a sizable body of Eastern Rite Catholics for whom 12 ecclesiastical jurisdictions have been established. It has also created a challenge for pastoral care of millions of Hispanics in urban centers and in agricultural areas where migrant workers are employed.

The Church continues to grapple with serious pastoral problems in rural areas, where about 600 counties have no priests in ministry. The National Catholic Rural Life Conference was established in 1922 in an attempt to make the Catholic presence felt on the land, and the Glenmary Society since its foundation in 1939 has devoted itself to this single apostolate. Religious communities and diocesan priests are similarly engaged.

Other challenges lie in the cities and suburbs, where 75 percent of the Catholic population lives. Conditions peculiar to each segment of the metropolitan area have developed in recent years as the flight to the suburbs has not only altered some traditional aspects of parish life but has also, in combination with many other factors, left behind a complex of special problems in inner city areas.

A Post-War World

In the years after the Second World War, Catholics increasingly assumed a mainline role in American life. This was evidenced especially in the 1960 election of John F. Kennedy as the nation's first Catholic president. Catholic writers and thinkers were making a greater impact in the nation's life. One example of this was Trappist Thomas Merton's runaway best-selling book of 1948, *The Seven Storey Mountain*; another was the early television success of Bp. Fulton Sheen's "Life is Worth Living" series, begun in 1952. Meanwhile, lay leader Dorothy Day, founder of the Catholic Worker movement, continued to challenge American society with her views on pacifism and evangelical poverty.

A Post-Conciliar World

Catholic life in the United States was profoundly affected by the Second Vatican Council (1962-65). In the post-conciliar generation, American Catholicism grew both in numbers and complexity. Lay ministry and participation expanded; extensive liturgical changes (including the use of English) were implemented; and the numbers of priests, vowed religious and seminarians declined.

The Church has taken a high profile in many social issues. This has ranged from opposition to abortion, capital punishments and euthanasia to support for civil rights, economic justice and international peace and cooperation. Meanwhile Catholics have been deeply involved in inter-faith and ecumenical relationships. The bishops have issued landmark pastoral statements, including "The Challenge of Peace" (1983) and "Economic Justice for All" (1986).

In these years after the Council, the Catholics in America have known something of alienation, dissent and polarity. They also found new intensity and maturity. New U.S. saints have been declared by the universal church, such as Elizabeth Ann Seton (1975), John Nepomucene Neumann (1977), and Rose Philippine Duchesne (1988). Especially at the time of visits to America by Pope John Paul II (e.g., in 1979, 1987, 1993, 1995, and 1999), U.S. Catholics have given evidence – in their personal and corporate lives – of the ongoing power of faith, liturgy and the primal call of the Gospel in its many dimensions.

Modern U.S. Catholicism

In the decades after Vatican Council II, the American Church confronted a variety of challenges, including the increasing age of American religious, especially in the Religious Institutes of Women; the decline in vocations; the presence of nominally Catholic organizations that nevertheless work to counter or alter Catholic teaching on such issues as abortion, contraception, papal supremacy, collegiality, women's ordination, clerical celibacy, and homosexuality; the societal decay precipitated by a proliferation of an abortion culture; the weakening of the family structure and the destructive effects of unrestrained materialism and secular humanism; the spread of religious apathy and indifferentism; the needs of Catholic immigrants; and the lamentable state of American education. The varied difficulties, however, were overshadowed from late 2001 by the sexual scandal involving child molestation by a small number of priests in the country and the resulting legal cases, lawsuits, and media frenzy. While perpetrated by only a few hundred priests over nearly 40 years, the cases of child molestation (the vast majority of cases involved teenage boys) created the most severe scandal faced by the Church in the U.S. in the previous century. Compounding the legal and financial problems caused by the actions of the priests was the failure on the part of many bishops to recognize the severity of the scandal and the willingness of some bishops to move pedophile priests from one pastoral assignment to another.

At the summer meeting of the USCCB, the American bishops drafted a series of documents to insure the safety of children and to improve oversight of the situation. The bishops approved a Charter for the Protection of Children and Young People and Essential Norms for Diocesan/ Eparchial Policies Dealing With Allegations of Sexual Abuse of Minors by Priests, Deacons, or Other Church Personnel. Officials of the Holy See rejected initially certain elements of canonical details of the norms, but the subsequent changes made by the bishops were given full Vatican approval. Nevertheless, the scandal created crushing financial difficulties for many dioceses facing a host of lawsuits, as well as a crisis of confidence among American Catholics.ears have also brought significant controversies regarding restrictions on religious liberty, including the mandate issued by the Department of Health and Human Services compelling all religious-based employers (with a very narrow exception) to provide insurance coverage to employees that includes contraception, sterilization, and abortion-inducing drugs. In May 2012, 43 Catholic institutions began lawsuits against the

HHS Mandates.

Even in the face of these problems, there are a number of positive developments that give reason for guarded optimism: the progress in ecumenism; the rise of new religious congregations; the increase in conversions (over 400,000 a year); the marked sophistication of Catholic communications, centered in the USCCB; the Church's active role in social issues (human rights, poverty, health care, race relations, abortion and economic justice); and the greater involvement of the laity – especially women – in the life of the Church. Today, the membership in the U.S. is approximately 23% (70 million) of the U.S. population.

MISSIONARIES TO THE AMERICAS

An asterisk with a feast date indicates that the saint or blessed is listed in the General Roman Calendar or the proper calendar for U.S. dioceses.

Allouez, Claude Jean (1622-89): French Jesuit; missionary in Canada and midwestern U.S.; preached to 20 different tribes of Indians and baptized over 10,000; vicar general of Northwest.

Altham, John (1589-1640): English Jesuit; missionary among Indians in Maryland.

Amadeus of the Heart of Jesus (1846-1920): Provincial Superior of the Ursulines in the United States and missionary in Montana, Wyoming, and Alaska; founded 12 Ursuline missions for the Native Americans.

Anchieta, José de, Bl. (1534-97): Portuguese Jesuit, born Canary Islands; missionary in Brazil; writer; beatified 1980; feast, June 9.

Andreis, Felix de (1778-1820): Italian Vincentian; missionary and educator in western U.S.

Aparicio, Sebastian, Bl. (1502-1600): Franciscan brother, born Spain; settled in Mexico, c. 1533; worked as road builder and farmer before becoming Franciscan at about the age of 70; beatified, 1787; feast, Feb. 25.

Badin, Stephen T. (1768-1853): French missioner; came to U.S., 1792, when Sulpician seminary in Paris was closed; ordained, 1793, Baltimore, the first priest ordained in U.S.; missionary in Kentucky, Ohio and Michigan; bought land on which Notre Dame University now stands; buried on its campus.

Baraga, Frederic (1797-1868): Slovenian missionary bishop in U.S.; studied at Ljubljana and Vienna, ordained, 1823; came to U.S., 1830; missionary to Indians of Upper Michigan; first bishop of Marquette, 1857-1868; wrote Chippewa grammar, dictionary, prayer book and other works.

Bauer, Benedicta (1803-65): Missionary Dominican sister who helped establish convents and schools for German-speaking immigrants in New Jersey, California, Missouri, Washington and Kansas.

Bertran, Louis, St. (1526-81): Spanish Dominican; missionary in Colombia and Caribbean, 1562-69; canonized, 1671; feast, Oct. 9.

Betancur, Pedro de San José, Bl. (1626-67): Secular Franciscan, born Canary Islands; arrived in Guatemala, 1651; established hospital, school and homes for poor; beatified 1980; feast, Apr. 25.

Bourgeoys, Marguerite, St. (1620-1700): French foundress, missionary; settled in Canada, 1653; founded Congregation of Notre Dame, 1658; beati-

fied, 1950; canonized 1982; feast, Jan. 12.

Brébeuf, Jean de, St. (1593-1649): French Jesuit; missionary among Huron Indians in Canada; martyred by Iroquois, Mar. 16, 1649; canonized, 1930; one of Jesuit North American martyrs; feast, Oct. 19* (U.S.).

Cancer de Barbastro, Louis (1500-49): Spanish Dominican; began missionary work in Middle America, 1533; killed at Tampa Bay, Florida.

Castillo, John de, St. (1596-1628): Spanish Jesuit; worked in Paraguay Indian mission settlements (reductions); martyred; beatified, 1934; canonized, 1988; feast, Nov. 16.

Catala, Magin (1761-1830): Spanish Franciscan; worked in California mission of Santa Clara for 36 years.

Chabanel, Noel, St. (1613-49): French Jesuit; missionary among Huron Indians in Canada; murdered by renegade Huron, Dec. 8, 1649; canonized, 1930; one of Jesuit North American martyrs; feast, Oct. 19* (U.S.).

Chaumonot, Pierre Joseph (1611-93): French Jesuit; missionary among Indians in Canada.

Clarke, Mary Frances (1803-87): Founder of the Sisters of Charity of the Blessed Virgin Mary; went to Iowa to start schools for children of white farmers and Native Americans; in Iowa Women's Hall of Fame.

Claver, Peter, St. (1581-1654): Spanish Jesuit; missionary among Negroes of South America and West Indies; canonized, 1888; patron of Catholic missions among black people; feast, Sept. 9*.

Cope, Marianne, St. (1838-1918): German-born immigrant; entered Sisters of St. Francis; led sisters to Hawaii to take over a hospital and then to Molokai to care for lepers, including Bl. Damien de Veuster; she cared for women and young girls with the disease; she was beatified in May 2005 and canonized in Oct. 2012; feast, Jan. 23.

Daniel, Anthony, St. (1601-48): French Jesuit; missionary among Huron Indians in Canada; martyred by Iroquois, July 4, 1648; canonized, 1930; one of Jesuit North American martyrs; feast, Oct. 19* (U.S.).

De Smet, Pierre Jean (1801-73): Belgian-born Jesuit; missionary among Indians of northwestern U.S.; served as intermediary between Indians and U.S. government; wrote on Indian culture.

Duchesne, Rose Philippine, St. (1769-1852): French nun; educator and missionary in the U.S.; established first convent of the Society of the Sacred Heart in the U.S., at St. Charles, Missouri; founded schools for girls; did missionary work among Indians; beatified, 1940; canonized, 1988; feast, Nov. 18* (U.S.).

Farmer, Ferdinand (family name, Steinmeyer) (1720-86): German Jesuit; missionary in Philadelphia, where he died; one of the first missionaries in New Jersey.

Flaget, Benedict J. (1763-1850): French Sulpician bishop; came to U.S., 1792; missionary and educator in U.S.; first bishop of Bardstown, Kentucky (now Louisville), 1810-32; 1833-50.

Frances Xavier Cabrini: *See under* **Saints**, p 207.

Friess, Caroline (1824-92): Mother Superior of the School Sisters of Notre Dame in America from 1850-92; through her labors, the sisters opened 265 parochial schools in 29 diocese and four institutes of higher education for women.

Gallitzin, Demetrius (1770-1840): Russian prince, born The Hague; convert, 1787; ordained priest at Baltimore, 1795; frontier missionary, known as Fr. Smith; Gallitzin, PA, named for him; his cause for canonization was opened in 2007.

Garnier, Charles, St. (c. 1606-49): French Jesuit; missionary among Hurons in Canada; martyred by Iroquois, Dec. 7, 1649; canonized, 1930; one of Jesuit North American martyrs; feast, Oct. 19* (U.S.).

Gibault, Pierre (1737-1804): Canadian missionary in Illinois and Indiana; aided in securing states of Ohio, Indiana, Illinois, Michigan and Wisconsin for the Americans during Revolution.

Gonzalez, Roch, St. (1576-1628): Paraguayan Jesuit; worked in Paraguay Indian mission settlements (reductions); martyred; beatified, 1934; canonized, 1988; feast, Nov. 16.

Goupil, René, St. (1607-42): French lay missionary; had studied surgery at Orleans, France; missionary companion of St. Isaac Jogues among the Hurons; martyred, Sept. 29, 1642; canonized, 1930; one of Jesuit North American martyrs; feast, Oct. 19* (U.S.).

Gravier, Jacques (1651-1708): French Jesuit; missionary among Indians of Canada and midwestern U.S.

Guérin, St. Theodore (1798-1856): Pioneer educator and Sister of Providence; arrived in U.S. in 1830 and founded St. Mary-of the-Woods in Vincennes, Indiana. Canonized on Oct. 15, 2006; feast, Oct. 3.

Hennepin, Louis (d. c. 1701): Belgian-born Franciscan missionary and explorer of Great Lakes region and Upper Mississippi, 1675-81, when he returned to Europe.

Ireland, Seraphine (1842-1930): Mother Superior of the Sisters of St. Joseph in the upper Midwest; opened 30 schools, five hospitals, and the College of St. Catherine, the second Catholic college for women in the U.S.

Jesuit North American Martyrs: Isaac Jogues, Anthony Daniel, John de Brébeuf, Gabriel Lalemant, Charles Garnier, Noel Chabanel (Jesuit priests), and René Goupil and John Lalande (lay missionaries) who were martyred between Sept. 29, 1642, and Dec. 9, 1649, in the missions of New France; canonized June 29, 1930; feast, Oct. 19* (U.S.). See separate entries.

Jogues, Isaac, St. (1607-46): French Jesuit; missionary among Indians in Canada; martyred near present site of Auriesville, NY, by Mohawks, Oct. 18, 1646; canonized, 1930; one of Jesuit North American Martyrs; feast, Oct. 19* (U.S.).

Kino, Eusebio (1645-1711): Italian Jesuit; missionary and explorer in U.S.; arrived Southwest, 1681; established 25 Indian missions, took part in 14 exploring expeditions in northern Mexico, Arizona and southern California; helped develop livestock raising and farming in the area. He was selected in 1965 to represent Arizona in Statuary Hall.

Lalande, John, St. (d. 1646): French lay missionary, companion of Isaac Jogues; martyred by Mohawks at Auriesville, NY, Oct. 19, 1646; canonized, 1930; one of Jesuit North American Martyrs; feast, Oct. 19* (U.S.).

Lalemant, Gabriel, St. (1610-49): French Jesuit; missionary among the Hurons in Canada; martyred by the Iroquois, Mar. 17, 1649; canonized, 1930; one of Jesuit North American Martyrs; feast, Oct. 19* (U.S.).

Lalor, Teresa (d. 1846): Co-founder, with Bp. Neale of Baltimore, of the Visitation Order in the U.S.; helped establish houses in Mobile, Kaskaskia, and Baltimore.

Lamy, Jean Baptiste (1814-88): French prelate; came to U.S., 1839; missionary in Ohio and Kentucky; bishop in Southwest from 1850; first bishop (later Abp.) of Santa Fe, 1850-85. He was nominated in 1951 to represent New Mexico in Statuary Hall.

Las Casas, Bartolome (1474-1566): Spanish Dominican; missionary in Haiti, Jamaica and Venezuela; reformer of abuses against Indians and black people; bishop of Chalapas, Mexico, 1544-47; historian.

Laval, Françoise de Montmorency, Bl. (1623-1708): French-born missionary bishop in Canada; named vicar apostolic of Canada, 1658; first bishop of Québec, 1674; jurisdiction extended over all French-claimed territory in New World; beatified 1980; feast, May 6.

Manogue, Patrick (1831-95): Missionary bishop in U.S., born Ireland; migrated to U.S.; miner in California; studied for priesthood at St. Mary's of the Lake, Chicago, and St. Sulpice, Paris; ordained, 1861; missionary among Indians of California and Nevada; coadj. bishop, 1881-84, and bishop, 1884-86, of Grass Valley; first bishop of Sacramento, 1886-95, when see was transferred there.

Margil, Antonio, Ven. (1657-1726): Spanish Franciscan; missionary in Middle America; apostle of Guatemala; established missions in Texas.

Marie of the Incarnation, St. (Marie Guyard Martin) (1599-1672): French widow; joined Ursuline Nuns; arrived in Canada, 1639; first superior of Ursulines in Québec; missionary to Indians; writer; beatified 1980; feast, Apr. 30.

Marquette, Jacques (1637-75): French Jesuit; missionary and explorer in America; sent to New France, 1666; began missionary work among Ottawa Indians on Lake Superior, 1668; accompanied Joliet down the Mississippi to mouth of the Arkansas, 1673, and returned to Lake Michigan by way of Illinois River; made a second trip over the same route; his diary and map are of historical significance. He was selected in 1895 to represent Wisconsin in Statuary Hall.

Massias (Macias), John de, St. (1585-1645): Dominican brother, a native of Spain; entered Dominican Friary at Lima, Peru, 1622; served as doorkeeper until his death; beatified, 1837; canonized 1975; feast, Sept. 16.

Mazzuchelli, Samuel C. (1806-64): Italian Dominican; missionary in midwestern U.S.; called builder of the West; writer. A decree advancing his beatification cause was promulgated July 6, 1993.

Membre, Zenobius (1645-87): French Franciscan; missionary among Indians of Illinois; accompanied LaSalle expedition down the Mississippi (1681-82) and Louisiana colonizing expedition (1684) that landed in Texas; murdered by Indians.

Mozcygemba, Leopold (1824-91): Polish Franciscan priest and missionary, the patriarch of American Polonia; labored as a missionary in Texas and 11 other states for nearly 40 years; co-founded the Polish seminary of Sts. Cyril and Methodius in Detroit (1885) and served as confessor at Vatican Council I.

Nerinckx, Charles (1761-1824): Belgian priest; missionary in Kentucky; founded Sisters of Loretto at the Foot of the Cross.

Nobrega, Manoel (1517-70): Portuguese Jesuit; leader of first Jesuit missionaries to Brazil, 1549.

Padilla, Juan de (d. 1542): Spanish Franciscan; missionary among Indians of Mexico and southwestern U.S.; killed by Indians in Kansas; protomartyr of the U.S.

Palou, Francisco (c. 1722-89): Spanish Franciscan; accompanied Junípero Serra to Mexico, 1749;

founded Mission Dolores in San Francisco; wrote history of the Franciscans in California.

Pariseau, Mary Joseph (1833-1902): Canadian Sister of Charity of Providence; missionary in state of Washington from 1856; founded first hospitals in Northwest Territory; artisan and architect. Represents Washington in National Statuary Hall.

Peter of Ghent (d. 1572): Belgian Franciscan brother; missionary in Mexico for 49 years.

Porres, Martin de, St. (1579-1639): Peruvian Dominican oblate; his father was a Spanish soldier and his mother a black freedwoman from Panama; called wonder worker of Peru; beatified, 1837; canonized, 1962; feast, Nov. 3*.

Quiroga, Vasco de (1470-1565): Spanish missionary in Mexico; founded hospitals; bishop of Michoacan, 1537.

Ravalli, Antonio (1811-84): Italian Jesuit; missionary in far-western U.S., mostly Montana, for 40 years.

Raymbaut, Charles (1602-43): French Jesuit; missionary among Indians of Canada and northern U.S.

Richard, Gabriel (1767-1832): French Sulpician; missionary in Illinois and Michigan; a founder of University of Michigan; elected delegate to Congress from Michigan, 1823; first priest to hold seat in the House of Representatives.

Riepp, Benedicta (1825-62): Founder of the first Benedictine community of nuns in the U.S.; by the time of her death, the order had founded convents in Illinois, Kentucky, Minnesota, and New Jersey.

Rodriguez, Alfonso, St. (1598-1628): Spanish Jesuit; missionary in Paraguay; martyred; beatified, 1934; canonized, 1988; feast, Nov. 16.

Rosati, Joseph (1789-1843): Italian Vincentian; missionary bishop in U.S. (vicar apostolic of Mississippi and Alabama, 1822; coadj. of Louisiana and the Two Floridas, 1823-26; administrator of New Orleans, 1826-29; first bishop of St. Louis, 1826-1843).

Russell, Mary Baptist (1829-98): Mother Superior of the Sisters of Mercy in San Francisco from 1854-98; founded St. Mary's Hospital in 1857, schools, and homes the aged and former prostitutes.

Sahagun, Bernardino de (c. 1500-90): Spanish Franciscan; missionary in Mexico for over 60 years; expert on Aztec archaeology.

Seelos, Bl. Francis X. (1819-67): Redemptorist missionary, born Bavaria; ordained, 1844, at Baltimore; missionary in Pittsburgh and New Orleans. Beatified by Pope John Paul II on April 8, 2000.

Seghers, Charles J. (1839-86): Belgian missionary bishop in North America; Apostle of Alaska; Abp. of Oregon City (now Portland), 1880-84; murdered by berserk companion while on missionary journey.

Serra, Junipero, Bl. (1713-84): Spanish Franciscan, born Majorca; missionary in America; arrived Mexico, 1749, where he did missionary work for 20 years; began work in Upper California in 1769 and established nine of the 21 Franciscan missions along the Pacific coast; baptized some 6,000 Indians and confirmed almost 5,000; a cultural pioneer of California Represents California in Statuary Hall. He was declared venerable May 9, 1985, and was beatified Sept. 25, 1988; feast, July 1* (U.S.).

Solanus, Francis, St. (1549-1610): Spanish Franciscan; missionary in Paraguay, Argentina and Peru; wonder worker of the New World; canonized,

1726; feast, July 14.

Sorin, Edward F. (1814-93): French priest; member of Congregation of Holy Cross; sent to U.S. in 1841; founder and first president of the University of Notre Dame; missionary in Indiana and Michigan.

Todadilla, Anthony de (1704-46): Spanish Capuchin; missionary to Indians of Venezuela; killed by Motilones.

Turibius de Mogrovejo, St. (1538-1606): Spanish Abp. of Lima, Peru, c. 1580-1606; canonized 1726; feast, Mar. 23*.

Twelve Apostles of Mexico (early 16th century): Franciscan priests who arrived in Mexico, 1524: Fathers Martin de Valencia (leader), Francisco de Soto, Martin de la Coruna, Juan Suares, Antonio de Ciudad Rodrigo, Toribio de Benevente, Garcia de Cisneros, Luis de Fuensalida, Juan de Ribas, Francisco Ximenes; Brothers Andres de Coroboda, and Juan de Palos.

Valdivia, Luis de (1561-1641): Spanish Jesuit; defender of Indians in Peru and Chile.

Vasques de Espiñosa, Antonio (early 17th century): Spanish Carmelite; missionary and explorer in Mexico, Panama and western coast of South America.

Vieira, Antonio (1608-87): Portuguese Jesuit; preacher; missionary in Peru and Chile; protector of Indians against exploitation by slave owners and traders; considered foremost prose writer of 17th-century Portugal.

Ward, Mary Francis Xavier (1810-84): Established the Sisters of Mercy in U.S.; arrived in Pittsburgh in 1843; founded convents in 10 states to care for the sick and poor and provide education.

White, Andrew (1579-1656): English Jesuit; missionary among Indians in Maryland.

Wimmer, Boniface (1809-87): German Benedictine; missionary among German immigrants in the U.S.

Youville, Marie Marguerite d', St. (1701-71): Canadian widow; foundress of Sisters of Charity (Grey Nuns), 1737, at Montréal: beatified, 1959; canonized 1990, first native Canadian saint; feast, Dec. 23.

Zumarraga, Juan de (1468-1548): Spanish Franciscan; missionary; first bishop of Mexico; introduced first printing press in New World, published first book in America, a catechism for Aztec Indians; extended missions in Mexico and Central America; vigorous opponent of exploitation of Indians; approved of devotions at Guadalupe; leading figure in early church history in Mexico.

FRANCISCAN MISSIONS

The 21 Franciscan missions of Upper California were established during the 54-year period from 1769 to 1822. Located along the old El Camino Real, or King's Highway, they extended from San Diego to San Francisco and were the centers of Indian civilization, Christianity and industry in the early history of the state.

Junípero Serra (beatified 1988) was the great pioneer of the missions of Upper California He and his successor as superior of the work, Fermin Lasuen, each directed the establishment of nine missions. One hundred and 46 priests of the Order of Friars Minor, most of them Spaniards, labored in the region from 1769 to 1845; 67 of them died at their posts, two as martyrs. The regular time of mission service was 10 years.

The missions were secularized by the Mexican government in the 1830s but were subsequently restored to the Church by the U.S. government. They are now variously used as the sites of parish churches, a university, houses of study and museums.

The names of the missions and the order of their establishment were as follows:

San Diego de Alcala, San Carlos Borromeo (El Carmelo), San Antonio de Padua, San Gabriel Arcangel, San Luis Obispo de Tolosa, San Francisco de Asis (Dolores), San Juan Capistrano; Santa Clara de Asis, San Buenaventura, Santa Barbara, La Purisima Concepcion de Maria Santisima, Santa Cruz, Nuestra Señora de la Soledad, San José de Guadalupe, San Juan Bautista, San Miguel Arcangel, San Fernando Rey de España, San Luis Rey de Francia, Santa Iñes, San Rafael Arcangel, San Francisco Solano de Sonoma (Sonoma).

Find more material at: www.CatholicAlmanac.com.

CHURCH-STATE RELATIONS IN THE UNITED STATES

CHURCH-STATE DECISIONS OF THE SUPREME COURT

Among sources of this selected listing of U.S. Supreme Court decisions was *The Supreme Court on Church and State*, Joseph Tussman, editor; Oxford University Press, New York, 1962.

Watson v. Jones, 13 Wallace 679 (1872): The Court declared that a member of a religious organization may not appeal to secular courts against a decision made by a church tribunal within the area of its competence.

Reynolds v. United States, 98 US 145 (1879): Davis v. Beason, 133 US 333 (1890); Church of Latter-Day Saints v. United States, 136 US 1 (1890). The Mormon practice of polygamy was at issue in three decisions and was declared unconstitutional.

Bradfield v. Roberts, 175 US 291 (1899): The Court denied that an appropriation of government funds for an institution (Providence Hospital, Washington, DC) run by Roman Catholic sisters violated the No Establishment Clause of the First Amendment.

Pierce v. Society of Sisters, 268 US 510 (1925): The Court denied that a state can require children to attend public schools only. The Court held that the liberty of the Constitution forbids standardization by such compulsion, and that the parochial schools involved had claims to protection under the Fourteenth Amendment.

Cochran v. Board of Education, 281 US 370 (1930): The Court upheld a Louisiana statute providing textbooks at public expense for children attending public or parochial schools. The Court held that the children and state were beneficiaries of the appropriations, with incidental secondary benefit going to the schools.

United States v. MacIntosh, 283 US 605 (1931): The Court denied that anyone can place allegiance to the will of God above his allegiance to the government since such a person could make his own interpretation of God's will the decisive test as to whether he would or would not obey the nation's law. The Court stated that the nation, which has a duty to survive, can require citizens to bear arms in its defense.

Everson v. Board of Education, 330 US 1 (1947): The Court upheld the constitutionality of a New Jersey statute authorizing free school bus trans-portation for parochial as well as public school students. The Court expressed the opinion that the benefits of public welfare legislation, included under such bus transportation, do not run contrary to the concept of separation of Church and State.

McCollum v. Board of Education, 333 US 203 (1948): The Court declared unconstitutional a program for releasing children, with parental consent, from public school classes so they could receive religious instruction on public school premises from representatives of their own faiths.

Zorach v. Clauson, 343 US 306 (1952): The Court upheld the constitutionality of a New York statute permitting, on a voluntary basis, the release during school time of students from public school classes for religious instruction given off public school premises.

Torcaso v. Watkins, 367 US 488 (1961): The Court declared unconstitutional a Maryland requirement that one must make a declaration of belief in the existence of God as part of the oath of office for notaries public.

McGowan v. Maryland, 81 Sp Ct 1101; Two Guys from Harrison v. McGinley, 81 Sp Ct 1135; Gallagher v. Crown Kosher Super Market, 81 Sp Ct 1128; Braunfeld v. Brown, 81 Sp Ct 1144 (1961): The Court ruled that Sunday closing laws do not violate the No Establishment of Religion Clause of the First Amendment, even though the laws were religious in their inception and still have some religious overtones. The Court held that, "as presently written and administered, most of them, at least, are of a secular rather than of a religious character, and that presently they bear no relationship to establishment of religion as those words are used in the Constitution of the United States."

Engel v. Vitale, 370 US 42 (1962): The Court declared that the voluntary recitation in public schools of a prayer composed by the New York State Board of Regents is unconstitutional on the ground that it violates the No Establishment of Religion Clause of the First Amendment.

Abington Township School District v. Schempp and Murray v. Curlett, 83 Sp Ct 1560 (1963): The Court ruled that Bible reading and recitation of the Lord's Prayer in public schools, with voluntary participation by students, are unconstitutional on the ground that they violate the No Establishment of Religion Clause of the First Amendment.

Chamberlin v. Dade County, 83 Sp Ct 1864 (1964): The Court reversed a decision of the Florida Supreme Court concerning the constitutionality of prayer and devotional Bible reading in public schools during the school day, as sanctioned by a state statute which specifically related the practices to a sound public purpose.

Board of Education v. Allen, No. 660 (1968): The Court declared constitutional the New York schoolbook-loan law that requires local school boards to purchase books with state funds and lend them to parochial and private school students.

Walz v. Tax Commission of New York (1970): The Court upheld the constitutionality of a New York statute exempting church-owned property from taxation.

Earle v. DiCenso, Robinson v. DiCenso, Lemon v. Kurtzman, Tilton v. Richardson (1971): In Earle v. DiCenso and Robinson v. DiCenso, the Court ruled unconstitutional a 1969 Rhode Island statute that provided salary supplements to teachers of secular subjects in parochial schools; in Lemon v. Kurtzman, the Court ruled unconstitutional a 1968 Pennsylvania statute that authorized the state to purchase services for the teaching of secular subjects in nonpublic schools. The principal argument against constitutionality in these cases was that the statutes and programs at issue entailed excessive entanglement of government with religion. In Tilton v. Richardson, the Court held that this argument did not apply to a prohibitive degree with respect to federal grants, under the Higher Education Facilities Act of 1963, for the construction of facilities for nonreligious purposes by four church-related institutions of higher learning, three of which were Catholic, in Connecticut.

Yoder, Miller and Yutzy (1972): In a case appealed on behalf of Yoder, Miller and Yutzy, the Court ruled that Amish parents were exempt from a Wisconsin statute requiring them to send their children to school until the age of 16. The Court said in its decision that secondary schooling exposed Amish children to attitudes, goals and values contrary to their beliefs, and substantially hindered "the religious development of the Amish child and his integration into the way of life of the Amish faith-community at the crucial adolescent state of development."

Committee for Public Education and Religious Liberty, et al., v. Nyquist, et al., No. 72-694 (1973): The Court ruled that provisions of a 1972 New York statute were unconstitutional on the grounds that they were violative of the No Establishment Clause of the First Amendment and had the "impermissible effect" of advancing the sectarian activities of church-affiliated schools. The programs ruled unconstitutional concerned: (1) maintenance and repair grants, for facilities and equipment, to ensure the health, welfare and safety of students in nonpublic, nonprofit elementary and secondary schools serving a high concentration of students from low income families; (2) tuition reimbursement ($50 per grade school child, $100 per high school student) for parents (with income less than $5,000) of children attending nonpublic elementary or secondary schools; tax deduction from adjusted gross income for parents failing to qualify under the above reimbursement plan, for each child attending a nonpublic school.

Sloan, Treasurer of Pennsylvania, et al., v. Lemon, et al., No. 72-459 (1973): The Court ruled unconstitutional a Pennsylvania Parent Reimbursement Act for Nonpublic Education which provided funds to reimburse parents (to a maximum of $150) for a portion of tuition expenses incurred in sending their children to nonpublic schools. The Court held that there was no significant difference between this and the New York tuition reimbursement program (above), and declared that the Equal Protection Clause of the Fourteenth Amendment cannot be relied upon to sustain a program held to be violative of the No Establishment Clause.

Levitt, et al., v. Committee for Public Education and Religious Liberty, et al., No. 72-269 (1973): The Court ruled unconstitutional the Mandated Services Act of 1970 under which New York provided $28 million ($27 per pupil from first to seventh grade, $45 per pupil from seventh to 12th grade) to reimburse nonpublic schools for testing, recording and reporting services required by the state. The Court declared that the act provided "impermissible aid" to religion in contravention of the No Establishment Clause.

In related decisions handed down June 25, 1973, the Court: (1) affirmed a lower-court decision against the constitutionality of an Ohio tax credit law benefiting parents with children in nonpublic schools; (2) reinstated an injunction against a parent reimbursement program in New Jersey; (3) affirmed South Carolina's right to grant construction loans to church-affiliated colleges, and (4) dismissed an appeal contesting its right to provide loans to students attending church-affiliated colleges (Hunt v. McNair, Durham v. McLeod).

Wheeler v. Barrera (1974): The Court ruled that nonpublic school students in Missouri must share in federal funds for educationally deprived students on a comparable basis with public school students under Title I of the Elementary and Secondary Education Act of 1965.

Norwood v. Harrison 93 S. Ct. 2804: The Court ruled that public assistance that avoids the prohibitions of the "effect" and "entanglement" tests (and which therefore does not substantially promote the religious mission of sectarian schools) may be confined to the secular functions of such schools.

Wiest v. Mt. Lebanon School District (1974): The Court upheld a lower court ruling that invocation and benediction prayers at public high school commencement ceremonies do not violate the principle of separation of Church and State.

Meek v. Pittenger (1975): The Court ruled unconstitutional portions of a Pennsylvania law providing auxiliary services for students of nonpublic schools; at the same time, it ruled in favor of provisions of the law permitting textbook loans to students of such schools. In denying the constitutionality of auxiliary services, the Court held that they had the "primary effect of establishing religion" and involved "excessive entanglement" of Church and state officials with respect to supervision; objection was also made against providing such services only on the premises of nonpublic schools and only at the request of such schools.

TWA, Inc., v. Hardison, 75-1126; International Association of Machinists and Aero Space Workers v. Hardison, 75-1385 (1977): The Court ruled that federal civil-rights legislation does not require employers to make more than minimal efforts to accommodate employees who want a particular working day off as their religion's Sabbath Day, and that an employer cannot accommodate such an employee by violating seniority systems determined by a union collective bargaining agreement. The Court noted that its ruling was not a constitutional judgment but an interpretation of existing law.

Wolman v. Walter (1977): The Court ruled constitutional portions of an Ohio statute providing tax-paid textbook loans and some auxiliary services (standardized and diagnostic testing, therapeutic and remedial services, off school premises) for nonpublic school students. It decided that other portions of the law, providing state funds for nonpublic school field trips and instructional materials (audio-visual equipment, maps, tape recorders), were unconstitutional.

Byrne v. Public Funds for Public Schools (1979): The Court decided against the constitutionality of a 1976 New Jersey law providing state income tax deductions for tuition paid by parents of students attending parochial and other private schools.

Student Bus Transportation (1979): The Court upheld a Pennsylvania law providing bus transportation at public expense for students to nonpublic schools up to 10 miles away from the boundaries of the public school districts in which they lived.

Reimbursement (1980): The Court upheld the constitutionality of a 1974 New York law providing direct cash payment to nonpublic schools for the costs of state-mandated testing and record-keeping.

Ten Commandments (1980): The Court struck down a 1978 Kentucky law requiring the posting of the Ten Commandments in public school classrooms in the state.

Widmar v. Vincent (1981): The Court ruled that the University of Missouri at Kansas City could not deny student religious groups the use of campus facilities for worship services. The Court also, in Brandon v. Board of Education of Guilderland Schools, declined without comment to hear an appeal for reversal of lower court decisions denying a group of New York high school students the right to meet for prayer on public school property before the beginning of the school day.

Lubbock v. Lubbock Civil Liberties Union (1983): By refusing to hear an appeal in this case, the Court upheld a lower court ruling against a public policy of permitting student religious groups to meet on public school property before and after school hours.

Mueller v. Allen (1983): The Court upheld a Minnesota law allowing parents of students in public and nonpublic (including parochial) schools to take a tax deduction for the expenses of tuition, textbooks and transportation. Maximum allowable deductions were $500 per child in elementary school and $700 per child in grades seven through 12.

Lynch v. Donnelly (1984): The Court ruled 5-to-4 that the First Amendment does not mandate "complete separation of church and state," and that, therefore, the sponsorship of a Christmas nativity scene by the City of Pawtucket, RI, was not unconstitutional. The case involved a scene included in a display of Christmas symbols sponsored by the city in a park owned by a non-profit group. The majority opinion said "the Constitution (does not) require complete separation of church and state; it affirmatively mandates accommodation, not merely tolerance, of all religions and forbids hostility toward any. Anything less" would entail callous indifference not intended by the Constitution. Moreover, "such hostility would bring us into 'war with our national tradition as embodied in the First Amendment's guaranty of the free exercise of religion.'" (The additional quotation was from the 1948 decision in McCollum v. Board of Education.)

Christmas Nativity Scene (1985): The Court upheld a lower court ruling that the Village of Scarsdale, NY, must make public space available for the display of privately sponsored nativity scenes.

Wallace v. Jaffree, No. 83-812 (1985): The Court ruled against the constitutionality of a 1981 Alabama law calling for a public-school moment of silence that specifically included optional prayer.

Grand Rapids v. Ball, No. 83-990, and **Aguilar v. Felton, No. 84-237** (1985): The Court ruled against the constitutionality of programs in Grand Rapids and New York City allowing public school teachers to teach remedial entitlement subjects (under the Elementary and Secondary Education Act of 1965) in private schools, many of which were Catholic.

Bender v. Williamsport Area School District (1986): The Court let stand a lower federal-court decision allowing a public high school Bible study group the same "equal access" to school facilities as that enjoyed by other extra-curricular clubs. A similar decision was handed down in 1990 in Board of Education v. Mergens, involving Westside High School in Omaha.

County of Allegheny v. American Civil Liberties Union (1989): The Court ruled (1) that the display of a Christmas nativity scene in the Allegheny County Courthouse in Pittsburgh, PA, violated the principle of separation of church and state because it appeared to be a government-sponsored endorsement of Christian belief; (2) and that the display of a Hanukkah menorah outside the Pittsburgh-Allegheny city-county building was constitutional because of its "particular physical setting" with secular symbols.

Unemployment Division v. Smith (1990): The Court ruled that religious use of the hallucinogenic cactus peyote is not covered by the First Amendment protection of religious freedom.

Lee v. Weisman (1992): The Court banned officially organized prayer at public school graduation ceremonies.

Lamb's Chapel v. Center Moriches Union School District (1993): The Court reversed a ruling by the 3rd U.S. Circuit Court of Appeals, declaring that the school district was wrong in prohibiting the congregation of Lamb's Chapel from using public school meeting space after hours to show a film series addressing family problems from a religious perspective. In view of the variety of organizations permitted to use school property after school hours, said the Court's opinion: "There would have been no realistic danger that the community would think that the district was endorsing religion or any particular creed, and any benefit to religion or to the church would have been no more than incidental."

5th U.S. Circuit Court of Appeals (1993): The Court let stand a ruling by the 5th U.S. Circuit Court of Appeals, permitting students in Texas, Mississippi and Louisiana to include student-organized and student-led prayers in graduation exercises.

Church of Lukumi Babalu Aye v. City of Hialeah (1993): The Court ruled that municipal laws that effectively prohibit a single church from performing its religious rituals are unconstitutional. The ordinances at issue singled out one religion, Santeria, for the purpose of restricting its members from the practice of ritual animal sacrifices.

Zobrest v. Catalina Foothills School District (1993): The Court ruled that a public school district may provide a sign-language interpreter for a deaf student attending a Catholic school without violating constitutional separation of church and state. The majority opinion said: "Handicapped children, not sectarian schools are the primary beneficiaries of the Disabilities Education Act; to the extent sectarian schools benefit at all from (the act), they are only incidental beneficiaries."

Fairfax County, Va., school district (1994): The Court upheld lower court rulings against a Fairfax County, VA, school district's practice of charging churches more rent than other entities for the use of school buildings.

Board of Education of Kiryas Joel Village School District v. Grumet (1994): The Court ruled in 1994 that a school district created to meet the special education needs of an Hasidic Jewish community violated the Establishment Clause of the Constitution. The Court said the New York Legislature effectively endorsed a particular religion when it established a public school district for the Satmar Hasidic Village of Kiryas Joel.

Agostino v. Felton (1997): The court reversed, 5 to 4, its 1985 Aguilar v. Felton ruling, which had declared it unconstitutional for teachers employed by public school districts to hold Title I remedial programs for low-income students on the property of church-related schools.

Boerne v. Flores (1997): The court ruled, 6 to 3, that the Religious Freedom Restoration Act (1993) was unconstitutional because Congress overstepped its constitutional authority in enacting the law. Congress "has been given the power to 'enforce,' not the power to determine what constitutes a constitutional violation," said the majority opinion.

Mitchell v. Helms (2000): The court ruled, 6 to 3, that a Louisiana parish can distribute money for instructional equipment — including computers, books, maps, and film strip projectors — to private schools as long as it is done in a "secular, neutral and non-ideological" way. The court's decision overturns two previous Supreme Court bans on giving public materials to parochial schools.

Santa Fe Independent School District v. Doe (2000): The court affirmed a lower court ruling that said prayer in public schools must be private and that such prayers at high school football games violate the constitutionally required separation of church and state. At issue in the Santa Fe case was a Texas school policy which permitted students selected by their peers to deliver an inspirational message of their own design at football games and the graduation ceremony. In 1999, the Santa Fe policy was struck down by the U.S. Court of Appeals for the Fifth Circuit. The Court of Appeals held that the policy violated the Establishment Clause of the First Amendment, even though the government played no role in creating the message or selecting the messenger.

Chandler v. Siegelman (2001): The court let stand a lower court ruling that students may participate in group prayers at school functions such as football games or graduations.

The Good News Club v. Milford Central Schools (2001): The court ruled that if the Boy Scouts and 4-H can use a public school as a meeting hall, a children's Bible study class can also.

Brown v. Gilmore (2001): The court declined to hear a challenge to Virginia's mandatory minute of silence in schools.

Children's Health Care is a Legal Duty Inc. v. McMullan (2001): The court turned down an appeal that claimed Medicare and Medicaid payments to church-run health centers violate the constitutional separation of church and state.

Gentala v. Tucson (2001): The court ordered a federal appeals court to take another look at a case that asked whether taxpayers must cover $340 in expenses from a prayer rally in a city park, saying it should be reconsidered in light of the high court's earlier ruling that a Bible club cannot be excluded from meeting at a public school so long as other groups with a moral viewpoint are allowed to gather there.

Cleveland Voucher Program (2002): By a 5-4 ruling, the court upheld the Cleveland voucher program that had been implemented in 1995 to assist the improvement of one of the worst public school systems in the country.

Ten Commandments (2005): By a 5-4 vote, the court prohibited the posting of the Ten Commandments in court houses; at the same time, the court permitted their posting in state houses.

Gonzales v. Carhart and Gonzales v. Planned Parenthood (2007): By a 5-4 vote, the court upheld the Partial Birth Abortion Ban Act that Congress passed and President George W. Bush signed into law in 2003, saying that the prohibition does not violate the constitutional right to an abortion.

RELIGION IN PUBLIC SCHOOLS

Based on a Catholic News Service article by Carol Zimmermann.

A diverse group of religious and civil rights organizations issued a joint statement Apr. 13, 1995, in an effort to clarify the confusing issue of prayer and religious observances or discussions in public schools. Their six-page statement outlines what is and what is not currently permissible in expressing religious beliefs in public schools.

The statement says, for example: "Students have the right to pray individually or in groups, or to discuss their religious views with their peers so long as they are not disruptive." But, the statement specifies that such prayers or discussions do not include "the right to have a captive audience listen or to compel other students to participate."

Prayer at Graduations

Regarding prayer at graduation ceremonies, the document says school officials may not mandate or organize prayer, but fails to set the record straight about student-led prayer at these services.

"The courts have reached conflicting conclusions under the federal Constitution" in this area, says the statement, recommending that schools consult their lawyers for the rules that apply to them, "until the issue is authoritatively resolved."

Since the Supreme Court's 1992 Lee v. Weisman opinion prohibited school authorities from even arranging for a speaker to present a prayer, lower courts in different states have made various rulings about student-led prayer at commencement exercises.

In Virginia, the state's Attorney General and the Board of Education proposed guidelines in mid-April to allow student-led prayer at graduations, despite a 1994 ruling by a U.S. district judge banning all prayer at graduations.

Religion in the Classroom

"It is both permissible and desirable to teach objectively about the role of religion in the history of the United States and other countries," but public school teachers may not specifically teach religion.

The same rules apply to the recurring controversy surrounding theories of evolution. Teachers may discuss explanations of the beginnings of life, but only within the confines of classes on religion or social studies. Public school teachers are required, according to the statement, to teach only scientific explanations of life's beginnings in science classes. And, just as teachers may not advance a religious view, they should not ridicule a student's religious belief.

Constitutional Protection

The statement says that students' expressions of religious beliefs in reports, homework or artwork are constitutionally protected. Likewise, students have the right to speak to and attempt to persuade their peers on religious topics. "But school officials should intercede to stop student religious speech if it turns into religious harassment aimed at a student or a small group of students."

The statement also says:

• Students have the right to distribute religious literature to their schoolmates, subject to reasonable restrictions for any non-school literature.

• Student religious clubs in secondary schools "must be permitted to meet and to have equal access" to school media for announcing their events.

• Religious messages on T-shirts and the like cannot be singled out for suppression.

• Schools can use discretion about dismissing students for off-site religious instruction.

The 35 organizations that endorsed the statement included the National Association of Evangelicals, the American Jewish Congress, the Christian Legal Society, the National Council of Churches, the Baptist Joint Committee on Public Affairs, the American Muslim Council, the Presbyterian Church (USA) and the American Civil Liberties Union.

Purpose of the Statement

"By making this document available," said Phil Baum, executive director of the American Jewish Congress, "the organizations are attempting to clarify what has become one of the most divisive issues of our time: religion in the public schools."

He said the document attempts to "ensure that the rights of all students are respected in the public schools."

Baum noted that the American Jewish Congress, which initiated the effort to draft the statement, had a long-standing commitment to ensuring that public schools are themselves religiously neutral.

"We believe, however, that it is inconsistent with that historic commitment to ask the public schools to root out private expressions of religious faith."

CHURCH TAX EXEMPTION

The exemption of church-owned property was ruled constitutional by the U.S. Supreme Court May 4, 1970, in the case of Walz v. The Tax Commission of New York.

Suit in the case was brought by Frederick Walz, who purchased in June 1967, a 22-by-29-foot plot of ground in Staten Island valued at $100 and taxable at $5.24 a year. Shortly after making the purchase, Walz instituted a suit in New York State, contending that the exemption of church property from taxation authorized by state law increased his own tax rate and forced him indirectly to support churches in violation of his constitutional right to freedom of religion under the First Amendment. Three New York courts dismissed the suit, which had been instituted by mail. The Supreme Court, judging that it had probable jurisdiction, then took the case.

In a 7-1 decision affecting Church-state relations in every state in the nation, the Court upheld the New York law under challenge.

For and Against

Chief Justice Warren E. Burger, who wrote the majority opinion, said that Congress from its ear-liest days had viewed the religion clauses of the Constitution as authorizing statutory real estate tax exemption to religious bodies. He declared: "Nothing in this national attitude toward religious tolerance and two centuries of uninterrupted freedom from taxation has given the remotest sign of leading to an established church or religion, and on the contrary it has operated affirmatively to help guarantee the free exercise of all forms of religious beliefs."

Justice William O. Douglas wrote in dissent that the involvement of government in religion as typified in tax exemption may seem inconsequential but: "It is, I fear, a long step down the establishment path. Perhaps I have been misinformed. But, as I read the Constitution and the philosophy, I gathered that independence was the price of liberty."

Burger rejected Douglas' "establishment" fears. If tax exemption is the first step toward establishment, he said, "the second step has been long in coming."

The basic issue centered on the following question: Is there a contradiction between federal constitutional provisions against the establishment of religion, or the use of public funds for religious purposes, and state statutes exempting church property from taxation? In the Walz decision, the Supreme Court ruled that there is no contradiction.

Legal Background

The U.S. Constitution makes no reference to tax exemption. There was no discussion of the issue in the Constitutional Convention nor in debates on the Bill of Rights.

In the Colonial and post-Revolutionary years, some churches had established status and were state-supported. This changed with enactment of the First Amendment, which laid down no-establishment as the federal norm. This norm was adopted by the states which, however, exempted churches from tax liabilities.

No establishment, no hindrance, was the early American view of Church-State relationships.

This view, reflected in custom law, was not generally formulated in statute law until the second half of the 19th century, although specific tax exemption was provided for churches in Maryland in 1702, in Virginia in 1800, and in North Carolina in 1806.

The first major challenge to church property exemption was initiated by the Liberal League in the 1870s. It reached the point that President Grant included the recommendation in a State of the Union address in 1875, stating that church property should bear its own proportion of taxes. The plea fell on deaf ears in Congress, but there was some support for the idea at state levels. The exemption, however, continued to survive various challenges.

About 36 state constitutions contain either mandatory or permissive provisions for exemption. Statutes provide for exemption in all other states.

There has been considerable litigation challenging this exemption, but most of it focused on whether a particular property satisfied statutory requirements. Few cases before Walz focused on the strictly constitutional question, whether directly under the First Amendment or indirectly under the Fourteenth.

Objections

Objectors to the tax exempt status of churches feel that churches should share, through taxation, in the cost of the ordinary benefits of public services they enjoy, and/or that the amount of "aid" enjoyed through exemption should be proportionate to the amount of social good they do.

According to one opinion, exemption is said to weaken the independence of churches from the political system that benefits them by exemption.

In another view, exemption is said to involve the government in decisions regarding what is and what is not religion.

The Wall of Separation

Thomas Jefferson, in a letter written to the Danbury (Connecticut) Baptist Association Jan. 1, 1802, coined the metaphor, "a wall of separation between Church and State," to express a theory concerning interpretation of the religion clauses of the First Amendment: "Congress shall make no law respecting an establishment of religion or prohibiting the free exercise thereof."

The metaphor was cited for the first time in judicial proceedings in 1879, in the opinion by Chief Justice Waite in Reynolds v. United States. It did not, however, figure substantially in the decision.

Accepted as Rule

In 1947 the wall of separation gained acceptance as a constitutional rule, in the decision handed down in Everson v. Board of Education. Associate Justice Black, in describing the principles involved in the No Establishment Clause, wrote:

"Neither a state nor the Federal Government can set up a church. Neither can pass laws which aid one religion, aid all religions, or prefer one religion over another. Neither can force nor influence a person to go to or to remain away from church against his will or force him to profess a belief or disbelief in any religion. No person can be punished for entertaining or professing religious beliefs or disbeliefs, for church attendance or non-attendance. No tax in any amount, large or small, can be levied to support any religious activities or institutions, whatever they may be called, or whatever form they may adopt to teach or practice religion. Neither a state nor the Federal Government can, openly or secretly, participate in the affairs of any religious organizations or groups and vice versa. In the words of Jefferson, the clause against establishment of religion by law was intended to erect 'a wall of separation between Church and State.' "

Mr. Black's associates agreed with his statement of principles, which were framed without reference to the Freedom of Exercise Clause. They disagreed, however, with respect to application of the principles, as the split decision in the case indicated. Five members of the Court held that the benefits of public welfare legislation — in this case, free bus transportation to school for parochial as well as public school students — did not run contrary to the concept of separation of Church and State embodied in the First Amendment.

(For coverage of the recent Supreme Court decision pertaining to vouchers, *see* **Education**.)

CATHOLICS IN THE U.S. GOVERNMENT

CATHOLICS IN PRESIDENTS' CABINETS

From 1789 to 1940, nine Catholics were appointed to cabinet posts by six of 32 presidents. The first was Roger Brooke Taney (later named first Catholic Supreme Court Justice) who was appointed in 1831 by Andrew Jackson. Catholics have been appointed to cabinet posts from the time of Franklin D. Roosevelt to the present. Listed below in chronological order are presidents, Catholic cabinet officials, posts held, dates.

Andrew Jackson: Roger B. Taney, Attorney General, 1831-33, Secretary of Treasury, 1833-34.

Franklin Pierce: James Campbell, Postmaster General, 1853-57.

James Buchanan: John B. Floyd, Secretary of War, 1857-61.

William McKinley: Joseph McKenna, Attorney General, 1897-98.

Theodore Roosevelt: Robert J. Wynne, Postmaster General, 1904-05; Charles Bonaparte, Secretary of Navy, 1905-06, Attorney General, 1906-09.

Franklin D. Roosevelt: James A. Farley, Postmaster General, 1933-40; Frank Murphy, Attorney General, 1939-40; Frank C. Walker, Postmaster General, 1940-45.

Harry S. Truman: Robert E. Hannegan, Postmaster General, 1945-47; J. Howard McGrath, Attorney General, 1949-52; Maurice J. Tobin, Secretary of Labor, 1948-53; James P. McGranery, Attorney General, 1952-53.

Dwight D. Eisenhower: Martin P. Durkin, Secretary of Labor, 1953; James P. Mitchell, Secretary of Labor, 1953-61.

John F. Kennedy: Robert F. Kennedy, Attorney General, 1961-63; Anthony Celebrezze, Secretary of Health, Education and Welfare, 1962-63; John S. Gronouski, Postmaster General, 1963.

Lyndon B. Johnson: Robert F. Kennedy, 1963-64; Anthony Celebrezze, 1963-65, and John S. Gronouski, 1963-65, reappointed to posts held in Kennedy Cabinet; John T. Connor, Secretary of Commerce, 1965-67; Lawrence O'Brien, Postmaster General, 1965-68.

Richard M. Nixon: Walter J. Hickel, Secretary of Interior, 1969-71; John A. Volpe, Secretary of Transportation, 1969-72; Maurice H. Stans, Secretary of Commerce, 1969-72; Peter J. Brennan, Secretary of Labor, 1973-74; William E. Simon, Secretary of Treasury, 1974.

Gerald R. Ford: Peter J. Brennan, 1974-75, and William E. Simon, 1974-76, reappointed to posts held above.

Jimmy Carter: Joseph Califano, Jr., Secretary of Health, Education and Welfare, 1977-79; Benjamin Civiletti, Attorney General, 1979-81; Moon Landrieu, Secretary of Housing and Urban Development, 1979-81; Edmund S. Muskie, Secretary of State, 1980-81.

Ronald Reagan: Alexander M. Haig, Secretary of State, 1981-82; Raymond J. Donovan, Secretary of Labor, 1981-84; Margaret M. Heckler, Secretary of Health and Human Services, 1983-85; William J. Bennett, Secretary of Education, 1985-88; Ann Dore McLaughlin, Secretary of Labor, 1988-89; Lauro F. Cavazos, Secretary of Education, 1988-89; Nicholas F. Brady, Secretary of

Treasury, 1988-89.

George Bush: Lauro F. Cavazos (reappointed), Secretary of Education, 1989-90; Nicholas F. Brady (reappointed), Secretary of Treasury, 1989-93; James D. Watkins, Secretary of Energy, 1989-93; Manuel Lujan, Jr., Secretary of Interior, 1989-93; Edward J. Derwinski, Secretary of Veteran Affairs, 1989-92; Lynn Martin, Secretary of Labor, 1990-93; Edward Madigan, Secretary of Agriculture, 1991-93; William P. Barr, Attorney General, 1991-93.

Bill Clinton: Henry G. Cisneros, Secretary of Housing and Urban Development, 1993-97; Federico F. Peña, Secretary of Transportation, 1993-97; Donna Shalala, Secretary of Health and Human Services, 1993-2001; William M. Daley, Secretary of Commerce, 1997-2000; Andrew Cuomo, Secretary of Housing and Urban Development, 1997-2001; Alexis H. Herman, Secretary of Labor, 1997-2001.

George W. Bush: Paul O'Neill, Secretary of the Treasury, 2001-03; Tommy Thompson, Secretary of Health and Human Services, 2001-05; Mel Martinez, Secretary of Housing and Urban Development, 2001-05; Anthony Principi, Secretary of Veterans Affairs, 2001-05; Jim Nicholson, Secretary of Veterans Affairs, 2005-07; Alberto Gonzalez, Attorney General, 2005-07; Carlos Gutierrez, Commerce Secretary, 2005-08.

Barack H. Obama: Sen. John Kerry, Sec. of State, 2013-; Thomas Perez, Sec. of Labor, 2013-; Julian Castro, Sec. of Housing and Urban Development, 2009-14; Tom Vilsack, Secr. of Agriculture, 2009-; Ray Lahood, Sec. of Transportation, 2009-13; Janet Napolitano, Sec. of Homeland Security, 2009-13; Sen. Ken Salazar, Sec. of the Interior, 2009-12; Hilda Solis, Sec. of Labor, 2009-12; Kathleen Sebelius, Sec. of Health and Human Services, 2009-14; Leon Panetta, Sec. of Defense, 2011-13; Shaun Donovan, Sec. of Housing and Urban Development, 2009-14.

[It is noted that Catholic members of the Obama Cabinet uniformly hold positions that are in opposition to the Church's teachings, particularly on abortion.]

Cabinet members who became Catholics after leaving their posts were: Thomas Ewing, Secretary of Treasury under William H. Harrison and Secretary of Interior under Zachary Taylor; Luke E. Wright, Secretary of War under Theodore Roosevelt; Albert B. Fall, Secretary of Interior under Warren G. Harding.

Catholics in the 113th Congress

As of the start of the 113th Congress in 2013, there were 163 Catholic members, comprising approximately 25% of the total Congressional membership and therefore the largest faith group in that body (Baptists were second, with 73 House and Senate members; there are also 46 Methodists). There are presently 136 Catholics in the House (61 Republicans and 75 Democrats) and 27 Catholics in the Senate (18 Democrats and 9 Republicans), according to the Pew Forum and Congressional Quarterly. In the 112th Congress, there were 63 Republicans and 69 Democrats, meaning that the number of Catholic Republicans in the House has declined. Among congressional leaders, three are Catholics (Speaker of the House John Boehner, R-Ohio; and House Minority Leader Nancy Pelosi, D-Calif.; Senate Majority Whip Richard Durbin, D-Ill.). It is noted, however, that Catholic representatives and senators do not vote as a bloc, nor do many

vote consistently in line with the teachings of the Church.

There are also 34 members who are of the Jewish faith, as well as three practicing Buddhists, and two Muslims, and one Hindu. In addition, there are 43 Presbyterians, 39 Episcopalians, 23 Lutherans, 15 Mormons, and five members of the Orthodox Churches.

Catholic Supreme Court Justices

Roger B. Taney, Chief Justice 1836-64; app. by Andrew Jackson.

Edward D. White, Associate Justice 1894-1910, app. by Grover Cleveland; Chief Justice 1910-21; app. by William H. Taft.

Joseph McKenna, Associate Justice 1898-1925; app. by William McKinley.

Pierce Butler, Associate Justice 1923-39; app. by Warren G. Harding.

Frank Murphy, Associate Justice 1940-49; app. by Franklin D. Roosevelt.

William Brennan, Associate Justice 1956-90; app. by Dwight D. Eisenhower.

Antonin Scalia, Associate Justice 1986-; app. by Ronald Reagan.

Anthony M. Kennedy, Associate Justice 1988-; app. by Ronald Reagan.

Clarence Thomas, Associate Justice 1991-; app. by George H. W. Bush.

John Roberts, Chief Justice 2005-; app. by George W. Bush.

Samuel Alito, Associate Justice 2005-; app. George W. Bush.

Sonia Sotomayor, Associate Justice 2009-; app. Barack Obama.

Sherman Minton, Associate Justice from 1949 to 1956; became a Catholic several years before his death in 1965.

Catholics in Statuary Hall

Statues of 13 Catholics deemed worthy of national commemoration are among those enshrined in National Statuary Hall and other places in the U.S. Capitol. The Hall, formerly the chamber of the House of Representatives, was erected by Act of Congress July 2, 1864.

Donating states, names and years of placement are listed.

Arizona: Rev. Eusebio Kino, S.J., missionary, 1965.

California: Rev. Junípero Serra, O.F.M. missionary, 1931. (Beatified 1988.)

Hawaii: Fr. Damien, missionary, 1969. (Canonized 2009.)

Illinois: Gen. James Shields, statesman, 1893.

Louisiana: Edward D. White, Justice of the U.S. Supreme Court (1894-1921), 1955.

Maryland: Charles Carroll, statesman, 1901.

Nevada: Patrick A. McCarran, statesman, 1960.

New Mexico: Dennis Chavez, statesman, 1966. (Abp. Jean B. Lamy, pioneer prelate of Santa Fe, was nominated for Hall honor in 1951.)

North Dakota: John Burke, U.S. treasurer, 1963.

Oregon: Dr. John McLoughlin, pioneer, 1953.

Washington: Mother Mary Joseph Pariseau, pioneer missionary and humanitarian.

West Virginia: John E. Kenna, statesman, 1901.

Wisconsin: Rev. Jacques Marquette, S.J., missionary, explorer, 1895.

United States Hierarchy

U.S. CATHOLIC JURISDICTIONS, HIERARCHY, STATISTICS

According to the United States Conference of Catholic Bishops, the organizational structure of the Catholic Church in the United States consists of 195 archdioceses/dioceses, one Apostolic Exarchate, and one Personal Ordinariate. Specifically, there are: 145 Latin Catholic dioceses, 33 Latin Catholic archdioceses, 15 Eastern Catholic dioceses, 2 Eastern Catholic archdioceses, one Apostolic Exarchate for the Syro-Malankara Catholic Church, one Personal Ordinariate of the Chair of St. Peter. The current number of archdioceses reflects the creation of the archdiocese of Galveston-Houston on Dec. 29, 2004. The eparchy of Our Lady of Deliverance of Newark for Syrian-rite Catholics in the U.S. and Canada has its seat in Newark, NJ. The Armenian apostolic eparchy for the United States and Canada has its seat in New York. On Jan. 1, 2012, Pope Benedict XVI established the Personal Ordinariate of the Chair of St. Peter. On April 23, 2013, Pope Francis extended the jurisdiction of the Romanian Catholic Eparchy of St. George the Martyr in Canton, Ohio, over all the Romanian Greek-Catholics residing in Canada. On Nov. 14, 2006, the Bishops of the USCCB approved a new non-geographic 15th USCCB region, composed of the bishops of Eastern-rite Catholic Churches. The structure includes the territorial episcopal conference known as the United States Conference of Catholic Bishops (USCCB). The representative of the Holy See to the Church in the United States is an Apostolic Nuncio (presently Abp. Carlo Maria Viganò, J.C.D.).

ECCLESIASTICAL PROVINCES

(Sources: The Official Catholic Directory, *Catholic News Service.)*

The 34 ecclesiastical provinces bear the names of archdioceses, i.e., of metropolitan sees.

Anchorage: Archdiocese of Anchorage and suffragan sees of Fairbanks, Juneau. Geographical area: Alaska.

Atlanta: Archdiocese of Atlanta (GA) and suffragan sees of Savannah (GA); Charlotte and Raleigh (NC), Charleston (SC). Geographical area: Georgia, North Carolina, South Carolina.

Baltimore: Archdiocese of Baltimore (MD) and suffragan sees of Wilmington (DE); Arlington and Richmond (VA); Wheeling-Charleston (WV). Geographical area: Maryland (except five counties), Delaware, Virginia, West Virginia.

Boston: Archdiocese of Boston (MA) and suffragan sees of Fall River, Springfield and Worcester (MA); Portland (ME); Manchester (NH); Burlington (VT). Geographical area: Massachusetts, Maine, New Hampshire, Vermont.

Chicago: Archdiocese of Chicago and suffragan sees of Belleville, Joliet, Peoria, Rockford, Springfield. Geographical area: Illinois.

Cincinnati: Archdiocese of Cincinnati and suffragan sees of Cleveland, Columbus, Steubenville, Toledo, Youngstown. Geographical area: Ohio.

Denver: Archdiocese of Denver (CO) and suffragan sees of Colorado Springs and Pueblo (CO); Cheyenne (WY). Geographical area: Colorado, Wyoming.

Detroit: Archdiocese of Detroit and suffragan sees of Gaylord, Grand Rapids, Kalamazoo, Lansing, Marquette, Saginaw. Geographical area: Michigan.

Dubuque: Archdiocese of Dubuque and suffragan sees of Davenport, Des Moines, Sioux City. Geographical area: Iowa.

Galveston-Houston: Archdiocese of Galveston-Houston and suffragan sees of Austin, Beaumont, Brownsville, Corpus Christi, Tyler, and Victoria. Geographical area: Southeast Texas.

Hartford: Archdiocese of Hartford (CT) and suffragan sees of Bridgeport and Norwich (CT); Providence (RI). Geographical area: Connecticut, Rhode Island.

Indianapolis: Archdiocese of Indianapolis and suffragan sees of Evansville, Fort Wayne-South Bend, Gary, Lafayette. Geographical area: Indiana.

Kansas City (KS): Archdiocese of Kansas City and suffragan sees of Dodge City, Salina, Wichita. Geographical area: Kansas.

Los Angeles: Archdiocese of Los Angeles and suffragan sees of Fresno, Monterey, Orange, San Bernardino, San Diego. Geographical area: Southern and Central California.

Louisville: Archdiocese of Louisville (KY) and suffragan sees of Covington, Lexington and Owensboro (KY); Knoxville, Memphis and Nashville (TN). Geographical area: Kentucky, Tennessee.

Miami: Archdiocese of Miami and suffragan sees of Orlando, Palm Beach, Pensacola-Tallahassee, St. Augustine, St. Petersburg, Venice. Geographical area: Florida.

Milwaukee: Archdiocese of Milwaukee and suffragan sees of Green Bay, La Crosse, Madison, Superior. Geographical area: Wisconsin.

Mobile: Archdiocese of Mobile, AL, and suffragan sees of Birmingham (AL); Biloxi and Jackson (MS). Geographical area: Alabama, Mississippi.

Newark: Archdiocese of Newark and suffragan sees of Camden, Metuchen, Paterson, Trenton. Geographical area: New Jersey.

New Orleans: Archdiocese of New Orleans and suffragan sees of Alexandria, Baton Rouge, Houma-Thibodaux, Lafayette, Lake Charles and Shreveport. Geographical area: Louisiana.

New York: Archdiocese of New York and suffragan sees of Albany, Brooklyn, Buffalo, Ogdensburg, Rochester, Rockville Centre, Syracuse. Geographical area: New York.

Oklahoma City: Archdiocese of Oklahoma City (OK) and suffragan sees of Tulsa (OK) and Little Rock (AR). Geographical area: Oklahoma, Arkansas.

Omaha: Archdiocese of Omaha and suffragan sees of Grand Island, Lincoln. Geographical area: Nebraska.

Philadelphia: Archdiocese of Philadelphia and suffragan sees of Allentown, Altoona-Johnstown, Erie, Greensburg, Harrisburg, Pittsburgh, Scranton. Geographical area: Pennsylvania.

Philadelphia (Byzantine, Ukrainians): Metropolitan See of Philadelphia (Byzantine) and Eparchies of St. Josaphat in Parma (OH), St. Nicholas of the Ukrainians in Chicago and Stamford, CT The jurisdiction extends to all Ukrainian Catholics in the U.S. from the ecclesiastical province of Galicia in the Ukraine.

Pittsburgh (Byzantine, Ruthenians): Metropolitan See of Pittsburgh, PA and Eparchies of Passaic (NJ), Parma (OH), Van Nuys (CA).

Portland: Archdiocese of Portland (OR) and suffragan sees of Baker (OR); Boise (ID); Great Falls-Billings and Helena (MT). Geographical area: Oregon, Idaho, Montana.

St. Louis: Archdiocese of St. Louis and suffragan sees of Jefferson City, Kansas City-St. Joseph, Springfield-Cape Girardeau. Geographical area: Missouri.

St. Paul and Minneapolis: Archdiocese of St. Paul and Minneapolis (MN) and suffragan sees of Crookston, Duluth, New Ulm, St. Cloud and Winona (MN); Bismarck and Fargo (ND); Rapid City and Sioux Falls (SD). Geographical area: Minnesota, North Dakota, South Dakota.

San Antonio: Archdiocese of San Antonio (TX) and suffragan sees of Amarillo, Dallas, El Paso, Fort Worth, Laredo, Lubbock, and San Angelo. Geographical area: Texas.

San Francisco: Archdiocese of San Francisco (CA) and suffragan sees of Oakland, Sacramento, San Jose, Santa Rosa and Stockton (CA); Honolulu (HI); Reno (NV); Las Vegas (NV); Salt Lake City (UT). Geographical area: Northern California, Nevada, Utah, Hawaii.

Santa Fe: Archdiocese of Santa Fe (NM) and suffragan sees of Gallup and Las Cruces (NM); Phoenix and Tucson (AZ). Geographical area: New Mexico, Arizona.

Seattle: Archdiocese of Seattle and suffragan sees of Spokane, Yakima. Geographical area: Washington.

Washington: Archdiocese of Washington, DC, and suffragan see of St. Thomas (VI). Geographical area: District of Columbia, five counties of Maryland, Virgin Islands.

ARCHDIOCESES, DIOCESES, ARCHBISHOPS, BISHOPS

(Sources: *Official Catholic Directory*; Catholic News Service; *L'Osservatore Romano*. As of Aug. 20, 2014.)

Information includes name of diocese, year of foundation (as it appears on the official document erecting the see), present ordinaries (year of installation), auxiliaries and former ordinaries (for biographies, *see* Index).

Archdioceses are indicated by an asterisk.

Albany, NY (1847): Edward B. Scharfenberger, bishop, 2014.

Former bishops: John McCloskey, 1847-64; John J. Conroy, 1865-77; Francis McNeirny, 1877-94; Thomas M. Burke, 1894-1915; Thomas F. Cusack, 1915-18; Edmund F. Gibbons, 1919-54; William A. Scully, 1954-69; Edwin B. Broderick, 1969-76; Howard J. Hubbard, 1977-2014.

Alexandria, LA (1853): Ronald P. Herzog, bishop, 2004.

Established at Natchitoches, transferred to Alexandria, 1910; title changed to Alexandria-Shreveport, 1977; redesignated Alexandria, 1986, when Shreveport was made a diocese.

Former bishops: Augustus M. Martin, 1853-75; Francis X. Leray, 1877-79, administrator, 1879-83; Anthony Durier, 1885-1904; Cornelius Van de Ven, 1904-32; Daniel F. Desmond, 1933-45; Charles P. Greco, 1946-73; Lawrence P. Graves, 1973-82; William B. Friend, 1983-86; John C. Favalora, 1986-89; Sam G. Jacobs, 1989-2003.

Allentown, PA (1961): John O. Barres, bishop, 2009.

Former bishop: Joseph McShea, 1961-83; Thomas J. Welsh, 1983-97; Edward P. Cullen, 1997-2009.

Altoona-Johnstown, PA (1901): Mark L. Bartchak, bishop, 2011.

Established as Altoona, name changed, 1957.

Former bishops: Eugene A. Garvey, 1901 20; John J. McCort, 1920 36; Richard T. Guilfoyle, 1936 57; Howard J. Carroll, 1958 60; J. Carroll McCormick, 1960 66; James J. Hogan, 1966 86; Joseph V. Adamec, 1987-2011.

Amarillo, TX (1926): Patrick J. Zurek, bishop, 2008.

Former bishops; Rudolph A. Gerken, 1927-33; Robert E. Lucey, 1934-41; Laurence J. Fitzsimon, 1941-58; John L. Morkovsky, 1958-63; Lawrence M. De Falco, 1963-79; Leroy T. Matthiesen, 1980-97; John W. Yanta, 1997-2008.

Anchorage,* Alaska (1966): Roger Lawrence Schwietz O.M.I., archbishop, 2001.

Former archbishop: Joseph T. Ryan, 1966-75; Francis T. Hurley, 1976-2001.

Arlington, VA (1974): Paul S. Loverde, bishop, 1999.

Former bishop: Thomas J. Welsh, 1974-83; John R. Keating, 1983-98.

Atlanta,* GA (1956; archdiocese, 1962): Wilton Daniel Gregory, archbishop, 2004. Luis R. Zarama, David P. Talley, auxiliaries.

Former ordinaries: Francis E. Hyland, 1956-61; Paul J. Hallinan, first archbishop, 1962-68; Thomas A. Donnellan, 1968-87; Eugene A. Marino, S.S.J., 1988-90; James P. Lyke, 1991-92; John F. Donoghue, 1993-2004.

Austin, TX (1947): Joe Steve Vazquez, bishop, 2010.

Former bishops: Louis J. Reicher, 1947-71; Vincent M. Harris, 1971-86; John E. McCarthy, 1986-2001; Gregory Michael Aymond, 2001-2009.

Baker, OR (1903): Liam S. Cary, bishop, 2012.

Established as Baker City, name changed, 1952.

Former bishops: Charles J. O'Reilly, 1903 18; Joseph F. McGrath, 1919 50; Francis P. Leipzig, 1950 71; Thomas J. Connolly, 1971-99; Robert Vasa, 1999-2011.

Baltimore,* MD (1789; archdiocese, 1808): William Edward Lori, archbishop, 2012; Denis James Madden, auxiliary.

Former ordinaries: John Carroll, 1789-1815, first archbishop; Leonard Neale, 1815-17; Ambrose Marechal, S.S., 1817-28; James Whitfield, 1828-34; Samuel Eccleston, S.S., 1834-51; Francis P. Kenrick, 1851-63; Martin J. Spalding, 1864-72; James R. Bayley, 1872-77; Cardinal James Gibbons, 1877-1921; Michael J. Curley, 1921-47; Francis P.

Keough, 1947-61; Cardinal Lawrence J. Shehan, 1961-74; William D. Borders, 1974-89; Cardinal William H. Keeler, 1989-2007; Cardinal Edwin F. O'Brien, 2007-2011.

Baton Rouge, LA (1961): Robert W. Muench, bishop, 2001.

Former bishops: Robert E. Tracy, 1961-74; Joseph V. Sullivan, 1974-82; Stanley J. Ott, 1983-93; Alfred C. Hughes, 1993-2001.

Beaumont, TX (1966): Curtis J. Guillory, S.V.D., bishop, 2000.

Former bishops: Vincent M. Harris, 1966-71; Warren L. Boudreaux, 1971-77; Bernard J. Ganter, 1977-93; Joseph A. Galante, 1994-2000.

Belleville, IL (1887): Edward Braxton, bishop, 2005.

Former bishops: John Janssen, 1888-1913; Henry Althoff, 1914-47; Albert R. Zuroweste, 1948-76; William M. Cosgrove, 1976-81; John N. Wurm, 1981-84; James P. Keleher, 1984-93; Wilton D. Gregory, 1994-2004.

Biloxi, MS (1977): Roger Paul Morin, 2009.

Former bishop: Joseph Lawson Howze, 1977-2001; Thomas John Rodi, 2001-2008.

Birmingham, AL (1969): Robert J. Baker, bishop, 2007.

Former bishops: Joseph G. Vath, 1969-87; Raymond J. Boland, 1988-93; David E. Foley, 1994-2005.

Bismarck, ND (1909): David D. Kagan, bishop, 2011.

Former bishops: Vincent Wehrle, O.S.B., 1910-39; Vincent J. Ryan, 1940-51; Lambert A. Hoch, 1952-56; Hilary B. Hacker, 1957-82; John F. Kinney, 1982-95; Paul A. Zipfel, 1996-2011.

Boise, ID (1893): Michael P. Driscoll, 1999.

Former bishops: Alphonse J. Glorieux, 1893-1917; Daniel M. Gorman, 1918-27; Edward J. Kelly, 1928-56; James J. Byrne, 1956-62; Sylvester Treinen, 1962-88; Tod David Brown, 1989-98.

Boston,* MA (1808; archdiocese, 1875): Sean O'Malley, O.F.M. Cap., 2003. John A. Dooher, Robert F. Hennessey, Arthur L. Kennedy, Peter J. Uglietto, auxiliaries.

Former ordinaries: John L. de Cheverus, 1810-23; Benedict J. Fenwick, S.J., 1825-46; John B. Fitzpatrick, 1846-66; John J. Williams, 1866-1907, first archbishop; Cardinal William O'Connell, 1907-44; Cardinal Richard Cushing, 1944-70; Cardinal Humberto Medeiros, 1970-83; Cardinal Bernard F. Law, 1984-2002.

Bridgeport, CT (1953): Frank Caggiano, bishop, 2013.

Former bishops: Lawrence J. Shehan, 1953-61; Walter W. Curtis, 1961-88; Edward M. Egan, 1988-2000; William Edward Lori, 2001-2012.

Brooklyn, NY (1853): Nicholas A. DiMarzio, 2003. Octavio Cisneros, Raymond Chappetto, Paul R. Sanchez, auxiliaries.

Former bishops: John Loughlin, 1853-91; Charles E. McDonnell, 1892-1921; Thomas E. Molloy, 1921-56; Bryan J. McEntegart, 1957-68; Francis J. Mugavero, 1968-90; Thomas V. Daily, 1990-2003.

Brownsville, TX (1965): Daniel E. Flores, bishop, 2010.

Former bishops: Adolph Marx, 1965; Humberto S. Medeiros, 1966-70; John J. Fitzpatrick, 1971-91; Enrique San Pedro, S.J., 1991-94; Raymundo J. Peña, 1995-2010.

Buffalo, NY (1847): Richard Joseph Malone, bishop, 2012. Edward M. Grosz, auxiliary.

Former bishops: John Timon, C.M., 1847-67; Stephen V. Ryan, C.M., 1868-96; James E. Quigley, 1897-1903; Charles H. Colton, 1903-15; Dennis J. Dougherty,

1915-18; William Turner, 1919-36; John A. Duffy, 1937-44; John F. O'Hara, C.S.C., 1945-51; Joseph A. Burke, 1952-62; James McNulty, 1963-72; Edward D. Head, 1973-95 Henry J. Mansell, 1995-2003; Edward U. Kmiec, 2004-2012.

Burlington, VT (1853): Vacant.

Former bishops: Louis De Goesbriand, 1853-99; John S. Michaud, 1899-1908; Joseph J. Rice, 1910-38; Matthew F. Brady, 1938-44; Edward F. Ryan, 1945-56; Robert F. Joyce, 1957-71; John A. Marshall, 1972-91. Kenneth A. Angell, bishop, 1992-2005; Salvatore R. Matano, 2005-13.

Camden, NJ (1937): Dennis J. Sullivan, bishop, 2013.

Former bishops: Bartholomew J. Eustace, 1938-56; Justin J. McCarthy, 1957-59; Celestine J. Damiano, 1960-67; George H. Guilfoyle, 1968-89; James T. McHugh, 1989-98; Nicholas A. DiMarzio, 1999-2003; Joseph Galante, 2004-2012.

Charleston, SC (1820): Robert E. Guglielmone, bishop, 2009.

Former bishops: John England, 1820-42; Ignatius W. Reynolds, 1844-55; Patrick N. Lynch, 1858-82; Henry P. Northrop, 1883-1916; William T. Russell, 1917-27; Emmet M. Walsh, 1927-49; John J. Russell, 1950-58; Paul J. Hallinan, 1958-62; Francis F. Reh, 1962-64; Ernest L. Unterkoefler, 1964-90; David B. Thompson, 1990-99; Robert J. Baker, 1999-2007.

Charlotte, NC (1971): Peter J. Jugis, bishop, 2003.

Former bishops: Michael J. Begley, 1972-84; John F. Donoghue, 1984-93; William G. Curlin, 1994-2002.

Cheyenne, WY (1887): Paul D. Etienne, bishop, 2009.

Former bishops: Maurice F. Burke, 1887-93; Thomas M. Lenihan, 1897-1901; James J. Keane, 1902-11; Patrick A. McGovern, 1912-51; Hubert M. Newell, 1951-78; Joseph Hart, 1978-2001; David Laurin Ricken, 2001-2008.

Chicago,* IL (1843; archdiocese, 1880): Cardinal Francis E. George, archbishop, 1997. John R. Manz, Joseph N. Perry, Francis J. Kane, George J. Rassas, Alberto Rojas, Andrew P. Wypych, auxiliaries.

Former ordinaries: William Quarter, 1844-48; James O. Van de Velde, S.J., 1849-53; Anthony O'Regan, 1854-58; James Duggan, 1859-70; Thomas P. Foley, administrator, 1870-79; Patrick A. Feehan, 1880-1902, first archbishop; James E. Quigley, 1903-15; Cardinal George Mundelein, 1915-39; Cardinal Samuel Stritch, 1939-58; Cardinal Albert Meyer, 1958-65; Cardinal John Cody, 1965-82; Cardinal Joseph L. Bernardin, 1982-96.

Cincinnati,* OH (1821; archdiocese, 1850): Dennis M. Schnurr, co-adjutor, 2008, archbishop, 2009. Joseph R. Binzer, auxiliary.

Former ordinaries: Edward D. Fenwick, O.P., 1822-32; John B. Purcell, 1833-83, first archbishop; William H. Elder, 1883-1904; Henry Moeller, 1904-1925; John T. McNicholas, O.P., 1925-50; Karl J. Alter, 1950-69; Paul F. Leibold, 1969-72; Joseph L. Bernardin, 1972-82; Daniel E. Pilarczyk, 1982-2009.

Cleveland, OH (1847): Richard Gerard Lennon, bishop, 2006.

Former ordinaries: L. Amadeus Rappe, 1847-70; Richard Gilmour, 1872-91; Ignatius F. Horstmann, 1892-1908; John P. Farrelly, 1909-21; Joseph Schrembs, 1921-45; Edward F. Hoban, 1945-66; Clarence G. Issenmann, 1966-74; James A. Hickey, 1974-80; Anthony M. Pilla, 1980-2006.

Colorado Springs, CO (1983): Michael J. Sheridan, bishop, 2003.

Former ordinaries: Richard C. Hanifen, 1984-2003.

Columbus, OH (1868): Frederick Francis Campbell, bishop, 2004.

Former bishops: Sylvester H. Rosecrans, 1868-78; John A. Watterson, 1880-99; Henry Moeller, 1900-03; James J. Hartley, 1904-44; Michael J. Ready, 1944-57; Clarence Issenmann, 1957-64; John J. Carberry, 1965-68; Clarence E. Elwell, 1968-73; Edward J. Herrmann, 1973-82; James A. Griffin, 1983-2004.

Corpus Christi, TX (1912): William M. Mulvey, bishop, 2010.

Former bishops: Paul J. Nussbaum, C.P., 1913-20; Emmanuel B. Ledvina, 1921-49; Mariano S. Garriga, 1949-65; Thomas J. Drury, 1965-83; Rene H. Gracida, 1983-97. Roberto O. Gonzalez, O.F.M., 1997-99; Edmond Carmody, 2000-2010

Covington, KY (1853): Roger J. Foys, bishop, 2002.

Former bishops: George A. Carrell, S.J., 1853-68; Augustus M. Toebbe, 1870-84; Camillus P. Maes, 1885-1914; Ferdinand Brossart, 1916-23; Francis W. Howard, 1923-44; William T. Mulloy, 1945-59; Richard Ackerman, C.S.Sp., 1960-78; William A. Hughes, 1979-95; Robert W. Muench, 1996-2001.

Crookston, MN (1909): Michael J. Hoeppner, bishop, 2007.

Former bishops: Timothy Corbett, 1910-38; John H. Peschges, 1938-44; Francis J. Schenk, 1945-60; Laurence A. Glenn, 1960-70; Kenneth J. Povish, 1970-75; Victor H. Balke, 1976-2007.

Dallas, TX (1890): Kevin J. Farrell, bishop, 2007. John D. Deshotel, auxiliary.

Established 1890, as Dallas, title changed to Dallas-Ft. Worth, 1953; redesignated Dallas, 1969, when Ft. Worth was made a diocese.

Former bishops: Thomas F. Brennan, 1891-92; Edward J. Dunne, 1893-1910; Joseph P. Lynch, 1911-54; Thomas K. Gorman, 1954-69; Thomas Tschoepe, 1969-90; Charles V. Grahmann, 1990-2007.

Davenport, IA (1881): Martin John Amos, bishop, 2006.

Former bishops: John McMullen, 1881-83; Henry Cosgrove, 1884-1906; James Davis, 1906-26; Henry P. Rohlman, 1927-44; Ralph L. Hayes, 1944-66; Gerald F. O'Keefe, 1966-93; William E. Franklin, 1993-2006.

Denver,* CO (1887; archdiocese, 1941): Samuel J. Aquila, archbishop, 2012.

Former ordinaries: Joseph P. Machebeuf, 1887-89; Nicholas C. Matz, 1889-1917; J. Henry Tihen, 1917-31; Urban J. Vehr, 1931-67, first archbishop; James V. Casey, 1967-86; J. Francis Stafford, 1986-96; Charles J. Chaput, O.F.M. Cap., 1997-2011.

Des Moines, IA (1911): Richard Edmund Pates, bishop, 2008.

Former bishops: Austin Dowling, 1912-19; Thomas W. Drumm, 1919-33; Gerald T. Bergan, 1934-48; Edward C. Daly, O.P., 1948-64; George J. Biskup, 1965-67; Maurice J. Dingman, 1968-86; William H. Bullock, 1987-93; Joseph L. Charron, C.PP.S., 1993-2007.

Detroit,* MI (1833; archdiocese, 1937): Allen H. Vigneron, archbishop, 2009. Francis R. Reiss, Michael J. Byrnes, Donald F. Hanchon, José A. Cepeda Escobedo, auxiliaries.

Former ordinaries: Frederic Rese, 1833-71; Peter P. Lefevere, administrator, 1841-69; Caspar H. Borgess, 1871-88; John S. Foley, 1888-1918; Michael J. Gallagher, 1918-37; Cardinal Edward Mooney, 1937-58, first archbishop; Cardinal John

F. Dearden, 1958-80; Cardinal Edmund C. Szoka, 1981-90; Cardinal Adam J. Maida, 1990-2009.

Dodge City, KS (1951): John B. Brungardt, bishop, 2010.

Former bishops: John B. Franz, 1951 59; Marion F. Forst, 1960 76; Eugene J. Gerber, 1976 82; Stanley G. Schlarman, 1983-98; Ronald M. Gilmore, 1998-2010.

Dubuque,* Iowa (1837; archdiocese, 1893): Michael O. Jackels, archbishop, 2013.

Former ordinaries: Mathias Loras, 1837-58; Clement Smyth, O.C.S.O., 1858-65; John Hennessy, 1866-1900, first archbishop; John J. Keane, 1900-11; James J. Keane, 1911-29; Francis J. Beckman, 1930-46; Henry P. Rohlman, 1946-54; Leo Binz, 1954-61; James J. Byrne, 1962-83; Daniel W. Kucera, O.S.B., 1984-95; Jerome Hanus, O.S.B., 1995-2013.

Duluth, MN (1889): Paul D. Sirba, bishop, 2009.

Former bishops: James McGolrick, 1889-1918; John T. McNicholas, O.P., 1918-25; Thomas A. Welch, 1926-59; Francis J. Schenk, 1960-69; Paul F. Anderson, 1969-82; Robert H. Brom, 1983-89; Roger L. Schwietz, O.M.I., 1990-2000; Dennis M. Schnurr, 2001-2008.

El Paso, TX (1914): Mark J. Seitz, bishop, 2013.

Former bishops: Anthony J. Schuler, S.J., 1915-42; Sidney M. Metzger, 1942-78; Patrick F. Flores, 1978-79; Raymundo J. Pena, 1980-95; Armando X. Ochoa, 1996-2011.

Erie, PA (1853): Lawrence T. Persico, bishop, 2012.

Former bishops: Michael O'Connor, 1853-54; Josue M. Young, 1854-66; Tobias Mullen, 1868-99; John E. Fitzmaurice, 1899-1920; John M. Gannon, 1920-66; John F. Whealon, 1966-69; Alfred M. Watson, 1969-82; Michael J. Murphy, 1982-90; Donald W. Trautman, 1990-2012.

Evansville, IN (1944): Charles C. Thompson, 2011, bishop.

Former bishops: Henry Joseph Grimmelsman, 1944-1965; Paul Francis Leibold, 1966-1969; Francis Raymond Shea, 1969-1989; Gerald Andrew Gettelfinger, 1989-2011.

Fairbanks, Alaska (1962): Vacant.

Former bishops: Francis D. Gleeson, S.J., 1962-68; Robert L. Whelan, S.J., 1968-85; Michael J. Kaniecki, S.J., 1985-2000, Donald Kettler, 2002-2013.

Fall River, MA (1904): Edgar M. da Cunha, S.D.V., bishop, 2014.

Former bishops: William Stang, 1904-07; Daniel F. Feehan, 1907-34; James E. Cassidy, 1934-51; James L. Connolly, 1951-70; Daniel A. Cronin, 1970-91; Sean O'Malley, O.F.M. Cap., 1992-2002; George William Coleman, 2003-2014.

Fargo, ND (1889): John F. Folda, bishop, 2013. Established at Jamestown, transferred, 1897.

Former bishops: John Shanley, 1889-1909; James O'Reilly, 1910-34; Aloysius J. Muench, 1935-59; Leo F. Dworschak, 1960-70; Justin A. Driscoll, 1970-84; James S. Sullivan, 1985-2002; Samuel J. Aquila, 2002-2012.

Fort Wayne-South Bend, IN (1857): Kevin C. Rhoades, bishop, 2009.

Established as Fort Wayne, name changed, 1960.

Former bishops: John H. Luers, 1858-71; Joseph Dwenger, C.Pp.S., 1872-93; Joseph Rademacher, 1893-1900; Herman J. Alerding, 1900-24; John F. Noll, 1925-56; Leo A. Pursley, 1957-76; William E. McManus, 1976-85; John M. D'Arcy, 1985-2009.

Fort Worth, TX (1969): Michael F. Olson, bishop, 2013.
Former bishop: John J. Cassata, 1969-80; Joseph P. Delaney, 1981-2005; Kevin W. Vann, 2005-2012.

Fresno, CA (1967): Armando X. Ochoa, bishop, 2011. Formerly Monterey-Fresno, 1922.
Former bishops (Monterey-Fresno): John J. Cantwell, administrator, 1922-24; John B. MacGinley, first bishop, 1924-32; Philip G. Sher, 1933-53; Aloysius J. Willinger, 1953-67.
Former bishops (Fresno): Timothy Manning, 1967-69; Hugh A. Donohoe, 1969-80; Joseph J. Madera, M.Pp.S., 1980-91. John T. Steinbock, 1991-2010.

Gallup, NM (1939): James S. Wall, bishop, 2009.
Former bishops: Bernard T. Espelage, O.F.M., 1940-69; Jerome J. Hastrich, 1969-90; Donald Pelotte, S.S.S., 1990-2008.

Galveston-Houston, TX * (1847; archdiocese, 2004): Card. Daniel N. DiNardo, archbishop, 2006. George A. Sheltz, auxiliary.
Established as Galveston, name changed, 1959.
Former bishops: John M. Odin, C.M., 1847-61; Claude M. Dubuis, 1862-92; Nicholas A. Gallagher, 1892-1918; Christopher E. Byrne, 1918-50; Wendelin J. Nold, 1950-75; John L. Morkovsky, 1975-84; Joseph A. Fiorenza, 1985-2004, first archbishop, 2004-2006.

Gary, IN (1956): Dale J. Melczek, bishop, 1996.
Former bishops: Andrew G. Grutka, 1957-84; Norbert F. Gaughan, 1984-96.

Gaylord, MI (1971): Steven J. Raica, 2014.
Former bishops: Edmund C. Szoka, 1971-81; Robert J. Rose, 1981-89; Patrick R. Cooney, 1989-2009; Bernard A. Hebda, 2009-13

Grand Island, NE (1912): William J. Dendinger, bishop, 2004.
Established at Kearney, transferred, 1917.
Former bishops: James A. Duffy, 1913-31; Stanislaus V. Bona, 1932-44; Edward J. Hunkeler, 1945-51; John L. Paschang, 1951-72; John J. Sullivan, 1972-77; Lawrence J. McNamara, 1978-2004.

Grand Rapids, MI (1882): David J. Walkowiak, bishop, 2013.
Former bishops: Henry J. Richter, 1883-1916; Michael J. Gallagher, 1916-18; Edward D. Kelly, 1919-26; Joseph G. Pinten, 1926-40; Joseph C. Plagens, 1941-43; Francis J. Haas, 1943-53; Allen J. Babcock, 1954-69; Joseph M. Breitenbeck, 1969-89; Robert J. Rose, 1989-2003; Kevin M. Britt, 2003-2004; Walter A. Hurley, 2005-2013.

Great Falls-Billings, MT (1904): Michael W. Warfel, bishop, 2007.
Established as Great Falls, name changed, 1980.
Former bishops: Mathias C. Lenihan, 1904-30; Edwin V. O'Hara, 1930-39; William J. Condon, 1939-67; Eldon B. Schuster, 1968-77; Thomas J. Murphy, 1978-87; Anthony M. Milone, 1988-2006.

Green Bay, WI (1868): David Laurin Ricken, bishop, 2008.
Former bishops: Joseph Melcher, 1868-73; Francis X. Krautbauer, 1875-85; Frederick X. Katzer, 1886-91; Sebastian G. Messmer, 1892-1903; Joseph J. Fox, 1904-14; Paul P. Rhode, 1915-45; Stanislaus V. Bona, 1945-67; Aloysius J. Wycislo, 1968-83; Adam J. Maida, 1984-90. Robert J. Banks, 1990-2003; David A. Zubic, 2003-2007.

Greensburg, PA (1951): Lawrence E. Brandt, bishop, 2004.
Former bishops: Hugh L. Lamb, 1951-59; Willam G. Connare, 1960-87; Anthony G. Bosco, 1987-2004.

Harrisburg, PA (1868): Ronald W. Gainer, bishop, 2014.
Former bishops: Jeremiah F. Shanahan, 1868-86; Thomas McGovern, 1888-98; John W. Shanahan,1899-1916; Philip R. McDevitt, 1916-35; George L. Leech, 1935-71; Joseph T. Daley, 1971-83; William H. Keeler, 1984-89; Nicholas C. Dattilo, 1990-2004; Kevin C. Rhoades, 2004-2009; Joseph Patrick McFadden, 2010-2013.

Hartford, * **CT** (1843; archdiocese, 1953): Leonard P. Blair, archbishop, 2013. Christie A. Macaluso, auxiliary.
Former ordinaries: William Tyler, 1844-49; Bernard O'Reilly, 1850-56; F. P. MacFarland, 1858-74; Thomas Galberry, O.S.A., 1876-78; Lawrence S. McMahon, 1879-93; Michael Tierney, 1894-1908; John J. Nilan, 1910-34; Maurice F. McAuliffe, 1934-44; Henry J. O'Brien, 1945-68, first archbishop; John F. Whealon, 1969-91; Daniel A. Cronin, 1991-2003; Henry J. Mansell, 2003-13.

Helena, MT (1884): George L. Thomas, bishop, 2004.
Former bishops: John B. Brondel, 1884-1903; John P. Carroll, 1904-25; George J. Finnigan, C.S.C., 1927-32; Ralph L. Hayes, 1933-35; Joseph M. Gilmore, 1936-62; Raymond Hunthausen, 1962-75; Elden F. Curtiss, 1976-93; Alexander J. Brunett, 1994-97; Robert C. Morlino, 1999-2003.

Honolulu, HI (1941): Clarence L. Silva, bishop, 2005.
Former bishops: James J. Sweeney, 1941-68; John J. Scanlan, 1968-81; Joseph A. Ferrario, 1982-93; Francis X. DiLorenzo (apostolic administrator, 1993), 1994-2004.

Houma-Thibodaux, LA (1977): Shelton Fabre, bishop, 2013.
Former bishop: Warren L. Boudreaux, 1977-92; C. Michael Jarrell, 1993-2002; Sam G. Jacobs, 2003-2013

Indianapolis, * **IN** (1834; archdiocese, 1944): Joseph W. Tobin, C.Ss.R., archbishop; Christopher J. Coyne, auxiliary.
Established at Vincennes, transferred, 1898.
Former ordinaries: Simon G. Bruté, 1834-39; Celestine de la Hailandiere, 1839-47; John S. Bazin, 1847-48; Maurice de St. Palais, 1849-77; Francis S. Chatard, 1878-1918; Joseph Chartrand, 1918-33; Joseph E. Ritter, 1934-46, first archbishop; Paul C. Schulte, 1946-70; George J. Biskup, 1970-79; Edward T. O'Meara, 1980-92; Daniel M. Buechlein, O.S.B., 1992-2011.

Jackson, MS (1837): Joseph R. Kopacz, bishop, 2013.
Established at Natchez, title changed to Natchez-Jackson, 1956; transferred to Jackson, 1977 (Natchez made titular see).
Former bishops: John J. Chanche, S.S., 1841-52; James Van de Velde, S.J., 1853-55; William H. Elder, 1857-80; Francis A. Janssens, 1881-88; Thomas Heslin, 1889-1911; John E. Gunn, S.M., 1911-24; Richard O. Gerow, 1924-67; Joseph B. Brunini, 1968-84; William R. Houck, 1984-2003; Joseph Latino, bishop, 2003-13.

Jefferson City, MO (1956): John R. Gaydos, bishop, 1997.
Former bishops: Joseph Marling, C.Pp.S., 1956-69; Michael F. McAuliffe, 1969-97.

Joliet, IL (1948): Robert D. Conlon, bishop, 2011. Joseph Siegel, auxiliary.
Former bishops: Martin D. McNamara, 1949-66; Romeo Blanchette, 1966-79; Joseph L. Imesch, 1979-2006; James Peter Sartain, 2006-2010.

Juneau, Alaska (1951): Edward J. Burns, bishop, 2009.

Former bishops: Dermot O'Flanagan, 1951-68; Joseph T. Ryan, administrator, 1968-71; Francis T. Hurley, 1971-76, administrator, 1976-79; Michael H. Kenny, 1979-95; Michael W. Warfel, 1996-2007.

Kalamazoo, MI (1971): Paul J. Bradley, bishop, 2009.

Former bishop: Paul V. Donovan, 1971-94; Alfred J. Markiewicz, 1995-97; James A. Murray, 1997-2009.

Kansas City,* KS (1877; archdiocese, 1952): Joseph F. Naumann, archbishop, 2005.

Established as vicariate apostolic, 1850, became Diocese of Leavenworth, 1877, transferred to Kansas City, 1947.

Former ordinaries: J. B. Miege, vicar apostolic, 1851-74; Louis M. Fink, O.S.B., vicar apostolic, 1874-77, first bishop; Thomas F. Lillis, 1904-10; John Ward, 1910-29; Francis Johannes, 1929-37; Paul C. Schulte, 1937-46; George J. Donnelly, 1946-50; Edward Hunkeler, 1951-69, first archbishop; Ignatius J. Strecker, 1969-93; James P. Keleher, 1993-2005.

Kansas City-St. Joseph, MO (Kansas City, 1880, St. Joseph, 1868, united 1956): Robert W. Finn, bishop, 2005.

Former bishops: John J. Hogan, 1880-1913; Thomas F. Lillis, 1913-38; Edwin V. O'Hara, 1939-56; John P. Cody, 1956-61; Charles H. Helmsing, 1962-77; John J. Sullivan, 1977-93; Raymond J. Boland, 1993-2005.

Former bishops (St. Joseph): John J. Hogan, 1868-80, administrator, 1880-93; Maurice F. Burke, 1893-1923; Francis Gilfillan, 1923-33; Charles H. Le Blond, 1933-56.

Knoxville, TN (1988): Richard Stika, bishop, 2009.

Former bishops: Anthony J. O'Connell, bishop, 1988-98; Joseph E. Kurtz, 1999-2007.

La Crosse, WI (1868): William Callahan, OFM Conv., 2010.

Former bishops: Michael Heiss, 1868-80; Kilian C. Flasch, 1881-91; James Schwebach, 1892-1921; Alexander J. McGavick, 1921-48; John P. Treacy, 1948-64; Frederick W. Freking, 1965-83; John J. Paul, 1983-94; Raymond L. Burke, 1995-2003; Jerome E. Listecki, 2004-2009.

Lafayette, IN (1944): Timothy Doherty, bishop, 2010.

Former bishops: John G. Bennett, 1944-57; John J. Carberry, 1957-65; Raymond J. Gallagher, 1965-82; George A. Fulcher, 1983-84 William L. Higi, 1984-2010.

Lafayette, LA (1918): C. Michael Jarrell, bishop, 2002.

Former bishops: Jules B. Jeanmard, 1918-56; Maurice Schexnayder, 1956-72; Gerard L. Frey, 1973-89; Harry J. Flynn, 1989-94; Edward J. O'Donnell, 1994-2002.

Lake Charles, LA (1980): Glen J. Provost, bishop, 2007

Former bishop: Jude Speyrer, 1980-2000; Edward Braxton, 2000-2005.

Lansing, MI (1937): Earl Boyea, bishop, 2008.

Former bishops: Joseph H. Albers, 1937-65; Alexander Zaleski, 1965-75; Kenneth J. Povish, 1975-95; Carl F. Mengeling, 1995-2008.

Laredo, Tx. (2000): James A. Tamayo, bishop, 2000.

Las Cruces, NM (1982): Oscar Cantu, bishop, 2013.

Former bishops: Ricardo Ramirez, C.S.B., 1982-2013.

Las Vegas, NV (1995): Joseph Pepe, 2001.

Formerly Reno-Las Vegas, 1976; made separate diocese 1995.

Former bishops: Daniel F. Walsh, 1995-2000.

Lexington, KY (1988): Vacant.

Former bishops: James Kendrick Williams, 1988-2002; Ronald William Gainer, 2002-14.

Lincoln, NE (1887): James Douglas Conley, bishop, 2012.

Former bishops: Thomas Bonacum, 1887-1911; J. Henry Tihen, 1911-17; Charles J. O'Reilly, 1918-23; Francis J. Beckman, 1924-30; Louis B. Kucera, 1930-57; James V. Casey, 1957-67; Glennon P. Flavin, 1967-92; Fabian W. Bruskewitz, 1992-2012

Little Rock, AR (1843): Anthony Basil Taylor, bishop, 2008.

Former bishops: Andrew Byrne, 1844-62; Edward Fitzgerald, 1867-1907; John Morris, 1907-46; Albert L. Fletcher, 1946-72; Andrew J. McDonald, 1972-2000; James Peter Sartain, 2000-2006.

Los Angeles,* CA (1840; archdiocese, 1936): José H. Gomez, archbishop, 2011. Thomas J. Curry, Gerald E. Wilkerson, Edward William Clark, Oscar Azarcon Solis, Alexander Salazar, auxiliaries.

Founded as diocese of Two Californias, 1840; became Monterey diocese, 1850; Baja California detached from Monterey diocese, 1852; title changed to Monterey Los Angeles, 1859, Los Angeles San Diego, 1922; became archdiocese under present title, 1936 (San Diego became separate see).

Former ordinaries: Francisco Garcia Diego y Moreno, O.F.M., 1840 46; Joseph S. Alemany, O.P., 1850-53; Thaddeus Amat, C.M., 1854-78; Francis Mora, 1878-96; George T. Montgomery, 1896-1903; Thomas J. Conaty, 1903-15; John J. Cantwell, 1917-47, first archbishop; Cardinal James McIntyre, 1948-70; Cardinal Timothy Manning, 1970-85; Cardinal Roger M. Mahony, 1985-2011.

Louisville,* KY (1808; archdiocese, 1937): Joseph E. Kurtz, archbishop, 2007.

Established at Bardstown, transferred, 1841.

Former ordinaries: Benedict J. Flaget, S.S., 1810-32; John B. David, S.S., 1832-33; Benedict J. Flaget, S.S., 1833-50; Martin J. Spalding, 1850-64; Peter J. Lavialle, 1865-67; William G. McCloskey, 1868-1909; Denis O'Donaghue, 1910-24; John A. Floersh, 1924-67, first archbishop; Thomas J. McDonough, 1967-81; Thomas C. Kelly, O.P., 1982-2007.

Lubbock, TX (1983): Placido Rodriguez, C.M.F., bishop, 1994.

Former bishop: Michael J. Sheehan, 1983-93.

Madison, WI (1946): Robert C. Morlino, bishop, 2003.

Former bishops: William P. O'Connor, 1946-67; Cletus F. O'Donnell, 1967-92, William H. Bullock, 1993-2003.

Manchester, NH (1884): Peter A. Libasci, bishop, 2011; Francis J. Christian, auxiliary.

Former bishops: Denis M. Bradley, 1884-1903; John B. Delany, 1904-06; George A. Guertin, 1907-32; John B. Peterson, 1932-44; Matthew F. Brady, 1944-59; Ernest J. Primeau, 1960-74; Odore J. Gendron, 1975-90; Leo E. O'Neil, 1990-97; John B. McCormack, 1998-2011.

Marquette, MI (1857): John F. Doerfler, 2013.

Founded as Sault Ste. Marie and Marquette; changed to Marquette, 1937.

Former bishops: Frederic Baraga, 1857-68; Ignatius Mrak, 1869-78; John Vertin, 1879-99; Frederick Eis, 1899-1922; Paul J. Nussbaum, C.P., 1922-35; Joseph C. Plagens, 1935-40; Francis Magner, 1941-47; Thomas L. Noa, 1947-68;

Charles A. Salatka, 1968-77; Mark F. Schmitt, 1978-92; James H. Garland, 1992-2005; Alexander K. Sample, 2005-2013.

Memphis, TN (1970): J. Terry Steib, S.V.D., bishop, 1993.

Former bishops: Carroll T. Dozier, 1971-82; J. Francis Stafford, 1982-86; Daniel M. Buechlein, O.S.B.,1987-92.

Metuchen, NJ (1981): Paul G. Bootkoski, bishop, 2002.

Former bishops: Theodore E. McCarrick, 1981-86; Edward T. Hughes, 1987-97; Vincent DePaul Breen, 1997-2002.

Miami,* FL (1958; archdiocese, 1968): Thomas G. Wenski, archbishop, 2010. Peter Baldacchino, auxiliary.

Former ordinaries: Coleman F. Carroll, 1958-77, first archbishop; Edward A. McCarthy, 1977-94; John C. Favalora, 1994-2010.

Milwaukee,* WI (1843; archdiocese, 1875): Jerome E. Listecki, archbishop, 2009. Donald J. Hying, auxiliary.

Former ordinaries: John M. Henni, 1844-81, first archbishop; Michael Heiss, 1881-90; Frederick X. Katzer, 1891-1903; Sebastian G. Messmer, 1903-30; Samuel A. Stritch, 1930-39; Moses E. Kiley, 1940-53; Albert G. Meyer, 1953-58; William E. Cousins, 1959-77; Rembert G. Weakland, O.S.B., 1977-2002; Timothy M. Dolan, 2002-2009.

Mobile,* AL (1829; archdiocese, 1980): Thomas John Rodi, archbishop, 2008.

Founded as Mobile, 1829, title changed to Mobile-Birmingham, 1954; redesignated Mobile, 1969.

Former bishops: Michael Portier, 1829-59; John Quinlan, 1859-83; Dominic Manucy, 1884; Jeremiah O'Sullivan, 1885-96; Edward P. Allen, 1897-1926; Thomas J. Toolen, 1927-69; John L. May, 1969-80; Oscar H. Lipscomb, first archbishop, 1980-2008.

Monterey in California (1967): Richard J. Garcia, bishop, 2006.

Formerly Monterey-Fresno, 1922. (Originally established in 1850, see Los Angeles listing.)

Former bishops (Monterey-Fresno): John J. Cantwell, administrator, 1922-24; John B. MacGinley, first bishop, 1924-32; Philip G. Sher, 1933-53; Aloysius J. Willinger, 1953-67.

Former bishops (Monterey): Harry A. Clinch, 1967-82; Thaddeus A. Shubsda, 1982-91; Sylvester D. Ryan, 1992-2006

Nashville, TN (1837): David Choby, bishop, 2005.

Former bishops: Richard P. Miles, O.P., 1838-60; James Whelan, O.P., 1860-64; Patrick A. Feehan, 1865-80; Joseph Rademacher, 1883-93; Thomas S. Byrne, 1894-1923; Alphonse J. Smith, 1924-35; William L. Adrian, 1936-69; Joseph A. Durick, 1969-75; James D. Niedergeses, 1975-92; Edward U. Kmiec, 1992-2004.

Newark,* NJ (1853; archdiocese, 1937): John J. Myers, 2001; Bernard A. Hebda, coadjutor, 2013. Thomas A. Donato, John W. Flesey, Manuel Cruz, auxiliaries.

Former ordinaries: James R. Bayley, 1853-72; Michael A. Corrigan, 1873-80; Winand M. Wigger, 1881-1901; John J. O'Connor, 1901-27; Thomas J. Walsh, 1928-52, first archbishop; Thomas A. Boland, 1953-74; Peter L. Gerety, 1974-86; Theodore E. McCarrick, 1986-2000.

New Orleans,* LA (1793; archdiocese, 1850): Gregory Michael Aymond, archbishop, 2009.

Former ordinaries: Luis Penalver y Cardenas, 1793-1801; John Carroll, administrator, 1805-15; W. Louis Dubourg, S.S., 1815-25; Joseph Rosati, C.M., administrator, 1826-29; Leo De Neckere, C.M., 1829-33; Anthony Blanc, 1835-60, first archbishop; Jean Marie Odin, C.M., 1861-70; Napoleon J. Perche, 1870-83; Francis X. Leray, 1883-87; Francis A. Janssens, 1888-97; Placide L. Chapelle, 1897-1905; James H. Blenk, S.M., 1906-17; John W. Shaw, 1918-34; Joseph F. Rummel, 1935-64; John P. Cody, 1964-65; Philip M. Hannan, 1965-88; Francis B. Schulte, 1988-2002; Alfred Hughes, 2002-2009.

Newton, MA (Melkite) (1966; eparchy, 1976): Nicholas J. Samra, eparch, 2011.

Former ordinaries: Justin Najmy, exarch, 1966-68; Joseph Tawil, exarch, 1969-76, first eparch, 1976-89; Ignatius Ghattas, B.S.O., 1990-92; John A. Elya, B.S.O., 1993-2004; Cyrille Salim Bustros, S.M.S.P., 2004.

New Ulm, MN (1957): John LeVoir, bishop, 2008.

Former bishop: Alphonse J. Schladweiler, 1958-75; Raymond A. Lucker, 1975-2000; John Clayton Nienstedt, 2001-2007.

New York,* NY (1808; archdiocese, 1850): Cardinal Timothy M. Dolan, archbishop, 2009. Dominick J. Lagonegro, Gerald T. Walsh, Peter Byrne, John Jenik, John O'Hara, auxiliaries.

Former ordinaries: Richard L. Concanen, O.P., 1808-10; John Connolly, O.P., 1814-25; John Dubois, S.S., 1826-42; John J. Hughes, 1842-64, first archbishop; Cardinal John McCloskey, 1864-85; Michael A. Corrigan, 1885-1902; Cardinal John Farley, 1902-18; Cardinal Patrick Hayes, 1919-38; Cardinal Francis Spellman, 1939-67; Cardinal Terence J. Cooke, 1968-83; Cardinal John J. O'Connor, 1984-2000; Cardinal Edward M. Egan, 2000-2009.

Norwich, CT (1953): Michael R. Cote, bishop, 2003.

Former bishops: Bernard J. Flanagan, 1953-59; Vincent J. Hines, 1960-75; Daniel P. Reilly, 1975-94; Daniel A. Hart, 1995-2003.

Oakland, CA (1962): Michael C. Barber, S.J., bishop, 2013.

Former bishop: Floyd L. Begin, 1962-77; John S. Cummins, 1977-2003; Allen H. Vigneron, 2003-2009; Salvatore Cordileone, 2009-2012.

Ogdensburg, NY (1872): Terry R. LaValley, bishop, 2010.

Former bishops: Edgar P. Wadhams, 1872-91; Henry Gabriels, 1892-1921; Joseph H. Conroy, 1921-39; Francis J. Monaghan, 1939-42; Bryan J. McEntegart, 1943-53; Walter P. Kellenberg, 1954-57; James J. Navagh, 1957-63; Leo R. Smith, 1963; Thomas A. Donnellan, 1964-68; Stanislaus J. Brzana, 1968-93; Paul S. Loverde, 1993-99; Gerald M. Barbarito, 1999-2003; Robert Joseph Cunningham, 2004-2009.

Oklahoma City,* OK (1905; archdiocese, 1972): Paul S. Coakley, archbishop, 2010.

Former ordinaries: Theophile Meerschaert, 1905-24; Francis C. Kelley, 1924-48; Eugene J. McGuinness, 1948-57; Victor J. Reed, 1958-71; John R. Quinn, 1971-77, first archbishop; Charles A. Salatka, 1977-92; Eusebius J. Beltran, 1993-2011.

Omaha,* NE (1885; archdiocese, 1945): George J. Lucas, archbishop, 2009.

Former ordinaries: James O'Gorman, O.C.S.O., 1859-74, vicar apostolic; James O'Connor, vicar apostolic, 1876-85, first bishop, 1885-90; Richard Scannell, 1891-1916; Jeremiah J. Harty, 1916-27; Francis Beckman, administrator, 1926-28; Joseph

F. Rummel, 1928-35; James H. Ryan, 1935-47, first archbishop; Gerald T. Bergan, 1948-69; Daniel E. Sheehan, 1969-93; Elden F. Curtiss, 1993-2009

Orange, CA (1976): Kevin W. Vann, bishop, 2012; Dominic Mai Luong, auxiliary.

Former bishop: William R. Johnson, 1976-86; Norman F. McFarland, 1986-98; Tod D. Brown, 1998-2012

Orlando, FL (1968): John G. Noonan, bishop, 2010.

Former bishops: William Borders, 1968-74; Thomas J. Grady, 1974-89; Thomas G. Wenski, 2005-2010.

Our Lady of Deliverance of Newark (for Syrian-rite Catholics of the U.S. and Canada, 1995): Yousif Benham Habash, bishop, 2010.

Former bishops: Joseph Younan, 1996-2009.

Our Lady of Lebanon of Los Angeles, CA (Maronite) (1994): Abdallah E. Zaidan, M.L., bishop, 2013.

Former eparch: John G. Chedid, 1994-2000; Robert J. Shaheen, 2000-2013.

Our Lady of Nareg (Apostolic Eparchy for Armenian Catholics in the United States and Canada), New York, NY (1981, eparchy, 2005): Mikael A. Mouradian, I.C.P.B., 2011.

Former exarchs: Nerses Mikael Setian, 1981-93; Hovhannes Tertzakian, O.M. Ven., 1995-2000; Manuel Batakian, 2000; first eparch, 2005.

Owensboro, KY (1937): William F. Medley, bishop, 2009.

Former bishops: Francis R. Cotton, 1938-60; Henry J. Soenneker, 1961-82; John J. McRaith, 1982-2009.

Palm Beach, FL (1984): Gerald Michael Barbarito, 2003.

Former bishop: Thomas V. Daily, 1984-90; J. Keith Symons, 1990-98; Anthony J. O'Connell, 1998-2002; Sean O'Malley, O.F.M. Cap., 2002-2003.

Parma, OH (Byzantine, Ruthenian) (1969): John Kudrick, bishop, 2002.

Former bishops: Emil Mihalik, 1969-84; Andrew Pataki, 1984-95; Basil Schott, O.F.M., 1996-2002.

Passaic, NJ (Byzantine, Ruthenian) (1963): Kurt R. Burnette, 2013.

Former bishops: Stephen Kocisko, 1963-68; Michael J. Dudick, 1968-95; Andrew Pataki, 1996-2007; William C. Skurla, 2007-2012.

Paterson, NJ (1937): Arthur J. Serratelli, bishop, 2004.

Former bishops: Thomas H. McLaughlin, 1937-47; Thomas A. Boland, 1947-52; James A. McNulty, 1953-63; James J. Navagh, 1963-65; Lawrence B. Casey, 1966-77; Frank J. Rodimer, 1978-2004.

Pensacola-Tallahassee, FL (1975): Gregory L. Parkes, bishop, 2012.

Former bishops: Rene H. Gracida, 1975-83; J. Keith Symons, 1983-90; John M. Smith, 1991-95; John H. Ricard, S.S.J., 1997-2011.

Peoria, IL (1877): Daniel R. Jenky, C.S.C., bishop, 2002.

Former bishops: John L. Spalding, 1877-1908; Edmund M. Dunne, 1909-29; Joseph H. Schlarman, 1930-51; William E. Cousins, 1952-58; John B. Franz, 1959-71; Edward W. O'Rourke, 1971- 90; John J. Myers, 1990-2001.

Philadelphia,* PA (1808; archdiocese, 1875): Charles J. Chaput, archbishop, 2011. Timothy C. Senior, John J. McIntyre, Michael J. Fitzgerald, auxiliaries.

Former ordinaries: Michael Egan, O.F.M., 1810-14; Henry Conwell, 1820-42; Francis P. Kenrick, 1842-51; John N. Neumann, C.SS.R., 1852-60; James F. Wood, 1860-83, first archbishop; Patrick J. Ryan, 1884-1911; Edmond F. Prendergast, 1911-18; Cardinal Dennis Dougherty, 1918-51; Cardinal John O'Hara, C.S.C., 1951-60; Cardinal John Krol, 1961-88; Cardinal Anthony J. Bevilacqua, 1988-2003; Cardinal Justin F. Rigali, 2003-2011.

Philadelphia,* PA (Byzantine, Ukrainian) (1924; metropolitan, 1958): Stephen Soroka, archbishop, 2001. John Bura, auxiliary.

Former ordinaries: Stephen Ortynsky, O.S.B.M., 1907-16; Constantine Bohachevsky, 1924-61; Ambrose Senyshyn, O.S.B.M., 1961-76; Joseph Schmondiuk, 1977-78; Myroslav J. Lubachivsky, 1979-80, apostolic administrator, 1980-81; Stephen Sulyk, 1981-2000.

Phoenix, AZ (1969): Thomas J. Olmsted, bishop, 2003. Eduardo A. Nevares, auxiliary.

Former bishops: Edward A. McCarthy, 1969-76; James S. Rausch, 1977-81; Thomas J. O'Brien, 1982-2003.

Pittsburgh,* PA (Byzantine, Ruthenian) (1924; metropolitan, 1969): William C. Skurla, achbishop, 2012.

Former ordinaries: Basil Takach 1924-48; Daniel Ivancho, 1948-54; Nicholas T. Elko, 1955-67; Stephen J. Kocisko, 1968-91, first metropolitan; Thomas V. Dolinay, 1991-93; Judson M. Procyk, 1995-2001; Basil Schott, O.F.M., 2002-2010.

Pittsburgh, PA (1843): David A. Zubic, bishop, 2007. William J. Walterscheid, auxiliary.

Former bishops: Michael O'Connor, 1843-53, 1854-60; Michael Domenec, C.M., 1860-76; J. Tuigg, 1876-89; Richard Phelan, 1889-1904; J.F. Regis Canevin, 1904-20; Hugh C. Boyle, 1921-50; John F. Dearden, 1950-58; John J. Wright, 1959-69; Vincent M. Leonard, 1969-83; Anthony J. Bevilacqua, 1983-88; Donald W. Wuerl, 1988-2006.

Portland, ME (1853): Robert P. Deeley, bishop, 2013.

Former bishops: David W. Bacon, 1855-74; James A. Healy, 1875-1900; William H. O'Connell, 1901-06; Louis S. Walsh, 1906-24; John G. Murray, 1925-31; Joseph E. McCarthy, 1932-55; Daniel J. Feeney, 1955-69; Peter L. Gerety, 1969-74; Edward C. O'Leary, 1974-88, Joseph J. Gerry, O.S.B., 1989-2004; Richard Joseph Malone, 2004-2012.

Portland,* OR (1846): Alexander K. Sample, 2013. Peter L. Smith, auxiliary.

Established as Oregon City, name changed, 1928.

Former ordinaries: Francis N. Blanchet, 1846-80 vicar apostolic, first archbishop; Charles J. Seghers, 1880-84; William H. Gross, C.SS.R., 1885-98; Alexander Christie, 1899-1925; Edward D. Howard, 1926-66; Robert J. Dwyer, 1966-74; Cornelius M. Power, 1974-86; William J. Levada, 1986-95; Francis E. George, 1996-97; John G. Vlazny, 1997-2013.

Providence, RI (1872): Thomas J. Tobin, bishop, 2005. Robert E. Evans, auxiliary.

Former bishops: Thomas F. Hendricken, 1872-86; Matthew Harkins, 1887-1921; William A. Hickey, 1921-33; Francis P. Keough, 1934-47; Russell J. McVinney, 1948-71; Louis E. Gelineau, 1972-97; Robert E. Mulvee, 1997-2005.

Pueblo, CO (1941): Stephen J. Berg, bishop, 2014.

Former bishops: Joseph C. Willging, 1942-59; Charles A. Buswell, 1959-79; Arthur N. Tafoya, 1980-2009; Fernando Isern, 2009-2013.

Raleigh, NC (1924): Michael F. Burbidge, bishop, 2006. Former bishops: William J. Hafey, 1925-37; Eugene J. McGuinness, 1937-44; Vincent S. Waters, 1945-75; F. Joseph Gossman, 1975-2006.

Rapid City, SD (1902): Robert D. Gruss, bishop, 2011. Established at Lead, transferred, 1930.

Former bishops: John Stariha, 1902-09; Joseph F. Busch, 1910-15; John J. Lawler, 1916-48; William T. McCarty, C.SS.R., 1948-69; Harold J. Dimmerling, 1969-87; Charles J. Chaput, O.F.M., Cap., 1988-97; Blase Cupich, 1998-2010.

Reno, NV (1931): Randolph R. Calvo, bishop, 2005. Established at Reno, 1931; title changed to Reno-Las Vegas, 1976, redesignated Reno, 1995, when Las Vegas was made a separate diocese.

Former bishops (Reno/Reno-Las Vegas): Thomas K. Gorman, 1931-52; Robert J. Dwyer, 1952-66; Joseph Green, 1967-74; Norman F. McFarland, 1976-86; Daniel F. Walsh, 1987-95; Phillip F. Straling, 1995-2005.

Richmond, VA (1820): Francis X. DiLorenzo, 2004. Former bishops: Patrick Kelly, 1820-22; Ambrose Marechal, S.S., administrator, 1822-28; James Whitfield, administrator, 1828-34; Samuel Eccleston, S.S., administrator, 1834-40; Richard V. Whelan, 1841-50; John McGill, 1850-72; James Gibbons, 1872-77; John J. Keane, 1878-88; Augustine Van de Vyver, 1889-1911; Denis J. O'Connell, 1912-26; Andrew J. Brennan, 1926-45; Peter L. Ireton, 1945-58; John J. Russell, 1958-73; Walter F. Sullivan, 1974-2003.

Rochester, NY (1868): Salvatore Matano, bishop, 2013. Former bishops: Bernard J. McQuaid, 1868-1909; Thomas F. Hickey, 1909-28; John F. O'Hern, 1929-33; Edward F. Mooney, 1933-37; James E. Kearney, 1937-66; Fulton J. Sheen, 1966-69; Joseph L. Hogan, 1969-78; Matthew H. Clark, 1979-2012.

Rockford, IL (1908): David J. Malloy, bishop, 2012. Former bishops: Peter J. Muldoon, 1908-27; Edward F. Hoban, 1928-42; John J. Boylan, 1943-53; Raymond P. Hillinger, 1953-56; Loras T. Lane, 1956-68; Arthur J. O'Neill, 1968-94; Thomas G. Doran, 1994-2012.

Rockville Centre, NY (1957): William Francis Murphy, bishop, 2001. Paul H. Walsh, Robert J. Brennan, Nelson J. Perez, Andrzej J. Zglejszewski, auxiliaries.

Former bishop: Walter P. Kellenberg, 1957-76; John R. McGann, 1976-2000; James McHugh, 2000.

Sacramento, CA (1886): Jaime Soto, coadjutor bishop, 2007, bishop, 2008. Myron J. Cotta, auxiliary.

Former bishops: Patrick Manogue, 1886-95; Thomas Grace, 1896-1921; Patrick J. Keane, 1922-28; Robert J. Armstrong, 1929-57; Joseph T. McGucken, 1957-62; Alden J. Bell, 1962-79; Francis A. Quinn, 1979-93; William K. Weigand, 1993-2008.

Saginaw, MI (1938): Joseph Robert Cistone, bishop, 2009.

Former bishops: William F. Murphy, 1938-50; Stephen S. Woznicki, 1950-68; Francis F. Reh, 1969-80; Kenneth E. Untener, 1980-2004; Robert J. Carlson, 2004-09.

St. Augustine, FL (1870): Felipe de Jesús Estevez, bishop, 2011.

Former bishops: Augustin Verot, S.S., 1870-76; John Moore, 1877-1901; William J. Kenny, 1902-13; Michael J. Curley, 1914-21; Patrick J. Barry, 1922-40; Joseph P. Hurley, 1940-67; Paul F. Tanner, 1968-79; John J. Snyder, 1979-2000; Victor Benito Galeone, 2001-2011.

St. Cloud, MN (1889): Donald Kettler, bishop, 2013. Former bishops: Otto Zardetti, 1889-94; Martin Marty, O.S.B., 1895-96; James Trobec, 1897-1914; Joseph F. Busch, 1915-53; Peter Bartholome, 1953-68; George H. Speltz, 1968-87; Jerome Hanus, O.S.B.,1987-94, John F. Kinney, 1995-2013

St. George's in Canton, OH (Byzantine, Romanian) (1982; eparchy, 1987): John Michael Botean, bishop, 1996.

Former bishop: Vasile Louis Puscas, 1983-93.

St. Josaphat in Parma, OH (Byzantine eparchy, Ukrainians) (1983): Bohdan J. Danylo, bishop, 2014.

Former bishops: Robert M. Moskal, 1984-2009.

St. Louis,* MO (1826; archdiocese, 1847): Robert J. Carlson, archbishop, 2009. Edward Rice, auxiliary.

Former ordinaries: Joseph Rosati, C.M., 1827-43; Peter R. Kenrick, 1843-95, first archbishop; John J. Kain, 1895-1903; Cardinal John Glennon, 1903-46; Cardinal Joseph Ritter, 1946-67; Cardinal John J. Carberry, 1968-79; John L. May, 1980-92; Justin F. Rigali, 1994-2003; Raymond L. Burke, 2003-2008.

St. Maron, Brooklyn, NY (Maronite) (1966; diocese, 1971): Gregory John Mansour, eparch, 2004. Established at Detroit, transferred to Brooklyn, 1977.

Former eparchs: Francis Zayek, exarch 1966-72, first eparch 1972-97; Hector Y. Doueihi, 1997-2004.

St. Nicholas in Chicago (Byzantine Eparchy of St. Nicholas of the Ukrainians) (1961): Richard Stephen Seminack, 2003.

Former bishops: Jaroslav Gabro, 1961-80; Innocent H. Lotocky, O.S.B.M., 1981-93; Michael Wiwchar, C.SS.R., 1993-2000.

St. Paul and Minneapolis,* MN (1850; archdiocese, 1888): John C. Nienstedt, coadjutor, 2007, archbishop, 2008. Lee Anthony Piché, Andrew H. Cozzens, auxiliaries.

Former ordinaries: Joseph Crétin, 1851-57; Thomas L. Grace, O.P., 1859-84; John Ireland, 1884-1918, first archbishop; Austin Dowling, 1919-30; John G. Murray, 1931-56; William O. Brady, 1956-61; Leo Binz, 1962-75; John R. Roach, 1975-95; Harry J. Flynn, 1995-2008.

St. Peter the Apostle of San Diego (Chaldean) (2002, eparchy): Sarhad Jammo, first eparch, 2002. Bawai Soro, auxiliary.

St. Petersburg, FL (1968): Robert N. Lynch, bishop, 1996.

Former bishops: Charles McLaughlin, 1968-78; W. Thomas Larkin, 1979-88; John C. Favalora, 1989-94.

St. Thomas the Apostle of Detroit (Chaldean) (1982; eparchy, 1985): Frank Kalabat, 2014.

Former bishops: Ibrahim N. Ibrahim, exarch, 1982-1985, first eparch, 1985-2014.

St. Thomas of the Syro-Malabars of Chicago (Syro-Malabars) (2001, eparchy): Jacob Angadiath, first eparch, 2001. John Alappat, auxiliary.

Salina, KS (1887): Edward J. Weisenburger, bishop, 2012.

Established at Concordia, transferred, 1944.

Former bishops: Richard Scannell, 1887-91; John J. Hennessy, administrator, 1891-98; John F. Cunningham, 1898-1919; Francis J. Tief, 1921-38; Frank A. Thill, 1938-57; Frederick W. Freking, 1957-64; Cyril J. Vogel, 1965-79; Daniel W. Kucera, O.S.B., 1980-84; George K. Fitzsimons, 1984-2004, Paul S. Coakley, 2004-11.

Salt Lake City, UT (1891): John C. Wester, bishop, 2007.

Former bishops: Lawrence Scanlan, 1891-1915; Joseph S. Glass, C.M., 1915-26; John J. Mitty, 1926-32; James E. Kearney, 1932-37; Duane G. Hunt, 1937-60; J. Lennox Federal, 1960-80; William K. Weigand, 1980-93; George H. Niederauer, 1995-2005.

San Angelo, TX (1961): Michael J. Sis, 2013.

Former bishops: Thomas J. Drury, 1962-65; Thomas Tschoepe, 1966-69; Stephen A. Leven, 1969-79; Joseph A. Fiorenza, 1979-84; Michael D. Pfeifer, O.M.I., 1985-2013.

San Antonio,* TX (1874; archdiocese, 1926): Gustavo Garcia-Siller, M.Sp.S., 2010.

Former ordinaries: Anthony D. Pellicer, 1874-80; John C. Neraz, 1881-94; John A. Forest, 1895-1911; John W. Shaw, 1911-18; Arthur Jerome Drossaerts, 1918-40, first archbishop; Robert E. Lucey, 1941-69; Francis Furey, 1969-79; Patrick F. Flores, 1979-2004; José H. Gomez, 2004-2010.

San Bernardino, CA (1978): Gerald R. Barnes, bishop, 1995. Rutilio J. Del Riego, auxiliary.

Former bishop: Phillip F. Straling, 1978-95.

San Diego, CA (1936): Robert H. Brom, bishop, 1990; Cirilo Flores, coadjutor, 2012.

Former bishops: Charles F. Buddy, 1936-66; Francis J. Furey, 1966-69; Leo T. Maher, 1969-90.

San Francisco,* CA (1853): Salvatore J. Cordileone, archbishop, 2012. William J. Justice, Robert W. McElroy, auxiliaries.

Former ordinaries: Joseph S. Alemany, O.P., 1853-84; Patrick W. Riordan, 1884-1914; Edward J. Hanna, 1915-35; John Mitty, 1935-61; Joseph T. McGucken, 1962-77; John R. Quinn, 1977-95; William J. Levada, 1995-2005; George H. Niederauer, 2005-2012.

San Jose, CA (1981): Patrick J. McGrath, bishop, 1999. Thomas A. Daly, auxiliary

Former ordinaries: R. Pierre DuMaine, 1981-98.

Santa Fe*, NM (1850; archdiocese, 1875): Michael J. Sheehan, archbishop, 1993.

Former ordinaries: John B. Lamy, 1850-85; first archbishop; John B. Salpointe, 1885-94; Placide L. Chapelle, 1894-97; Peter Bourgade, 1899-1908; John B. Pitaval, 1909-18; Albert T. Daeger, O.F.M., 1919-32; Rudolph A. Gerken, 1933-43; Edwin V. Byrne, 1943-63; James P. Davis, 1964-74; Robert F. Sanchez, 1974-93.

Santa Rosa, CA (1962): Robert Francis Vasa, coadjutor bp., 2010, bishop, 2011.

Former bishops: Leo T. Maher, 1962 69; Mark J. Hurley, 1969 86; John T. Steinbock, 1987 91; G. Patrick Ziemann, 1992-99; Daniel Walsh, 2000-2011.

Savannah, GA (1850): Gregory J. Hartmayer, O.F.M. Conv., bishop, 2011.

Former bishops: Francis X. Gartland, 1850-54; John Barry, 1857-59; Augustin Verot, S.S., 1861-70; Ignatius Persico, O.F.M. Cap., 1870-72; William

H. Gross, C.SS.R., 1873-85; Thomas A. Becker, 1886-99; Benjamin J. Keiley, 1900-22; Michael Keyes, S.M., 1922-35; Gerald P. O'Hara, 1935-59; Thomas J. McDonough, 1960-67; Gerard L. Frey, 1967-72; Raymond W. Lessard, 1973-95; John Kevin Boland, 1995-2011.

Scranton, PA (1868): Joseph C. Bambera, bishop, 2010.

Former bishops: William O'Hara, 1868-99; Michael J. Hoban, 1899-1926; Thomas C. O'Reilly, 1928-38; William J. Hafey, 1938-54; Jerome D. Hannan, 1954-65; J. Carroll McCormick, 1966-83; John J. O'Connor, 1983-84; James C. Timlin, 1984-2003; Joseph F. Martino, 2003-2009.

Seattle,* WA (1850; archdiocese, 1951): James Peter Sartain, archbishop, 2010. Eusebio Elizondo, M.Sp.S., auxiliary.

Established as Nesqually, name changed, 1907.

Former ordinaries; Augustin M. Blanchet, 1850-79; Aegidius Junger, 1879-95; Edward J. O'Dea, 1896-1932; Gerald Shaughnessy, S.M., 1933-50; Thomas A. Connolly, first archbishop, 1950-75; Raymond G. Hunthausen, 1975-91; Thomas J. Murphy, 1991-97; Alexander J. Brunett, 1997-2011

Shreveport, LA (1986): Michael G. Duca, bishop, 2008.

Former bishops: William B. Friend, 1986-2006.

Sioux City, IA (1902): Ralph W. Nickless, bishop, 2005.

Former bishops: Philip J. Garrigan, 1902-19; Edmond Heelan, 1919-48; Joseph M. Mueller, 1948-70; Frank H. Greteman, 1970-83; Lawrence D. Soens, 1983-98; Daniel N. DiNardo, 1998-2004.

Sioux Falls, SD (1889): Paul J. Swain, bishop, 2006.

Former bishops: Martin Marty, O.S.B., 1889-94; Thomas O'Gorman, 1896-1921; Bernard J. Mahoney, 1922-39; William O. Brady, 1939-56; Lambert A. Hoch, 1956-78; Paul V. Dudley, 1978-95; Robert J. Carlson, 1995-2004.

Spokane, WA (1913): Blase Cupich, bishop, 2010.

Former bishops: Augustine F. Schinner, 1914-25; Charles D. White, 1927-55; Bernard J. Topel, 1955-78; Lawrence H. Welsh, 1978-90. William S. Skylstad, 1990-2010.

Springfield, IL (1853): Thomas J. Paprocki, bishop, 2010.

Established at Quincy, transferred to Alton, 1857; transferred to Springfield, 1923.

Former bishops: Henry D. Juncker, 1857-68; Peter J. Baltes, 1870-86; James Ryan, 1888-1923; James A. Griffin, 1924-48; William A. O'Connor, 1949-75; Joseph A. McNicholas, 1975-83; Daniel L. Ryan, bishop, 1984-99.

Springfield, MA (1870): Mitchell Thomas Rozanski, bishop, 2014.

Former bishops: Patrick T. O'Reilly, 1870-92; Thomas D. Beaven, 1892-1920; Thomas M. O'Leary, 1921-49; Christopher J. Weldon, 1950-77; Joseph F. Maguire, 1977-91; John A. Marshall, 1991-94; Thomas L. Dupre, 1995-2004; Timothy A. McDonnell, 2004-2014.

Springfield-Cape Girardeau, MO (1956): James Vann Johnston, Jr., bishop, 2008.

Former bishops: Charles Helmsing, 1956-62; Ignatius J. Strecker, 1962-69; William Baum, 1970-73; Bernard F.

Law, 1973-84; John J. Leibrecht, 1984-2008.

Stamford, CT (Byzantine, Ukrainian) (1956): Paul P. Chomnycky, O.S.B.M., eparch, 2006.

Former eparchs: Ambrose Senyshyn, O.S.B.M., 1956-61; Joseph Schmondiuk, 1961-77; Basil Losten, 1977-2006.

Steubenville, OH (1944): Jeffrey M. Monforton, 2012.

Former bishops: John K. Mussio, 1945-77; Albert H. Ottenweller, 1977-92; Gilbert I. Sheldon, 1992-2002; Robert Daniel Conlon, 2002-11.

Stockton, CA (1962): Stephen E. Blaire, bishop, 1999.

Former bishops: Hugh A. Donohoe, 1962-69; Merlin J. Guilfoyle, 1969-79; Roger M. Mahony, 1980-85; Donald W. Montrose, 1986-99.

Superior, WI (1905): Peter F. Christensen, bishop, 2007.

Former bishops: Augustine F. Schinner, 1905-13; Joseph M. Koudelka, 1913-21; Joseph G. Pinten, 1922-26; Theodore M. Reverman, 1926-41; William P. O'Connor, 1942-46; Albert G. Meyer, 1946-53; Joseph Annabring, 1954-59; George A. Hammes, 1960-85; Raphael M. Fliss, 1985-2007.

Syracuse, NY (1886): Robert Joseph Cunningham, bishop, 2009.

Former bishops: Patrick A. Ludden, 1887-1912; John Grimes, 1912-22; Daniel J. Curley, 1923-32; John A. Duffy, 1933-37; Walter A. Foery, 1937-70; David F. Cunningham, 1970-76; Frank J. Harrison, 1976-87; Joseph T. O'Keefe, 1987-95; James M. Moynihan, 1995-2009.

Toledo, OH (1910): Daniel E. Thomas, bishop, 2014.

Former bishops: Joseph Schrembs, 1911-21; Samuel A. Stritch, 1921-30; Karl J. Alter, 1931-50; George J. Rehring, 1950-67; John A. Donovan, 1967-80; James R. Hoffman, 1980-2003; Leonard P. Blair, 2003-13.

Trenton, NJ (1881): David M. O'Connell, C.M., bishop, 2010.

Former bishops: Michael J. O'Farrell, 1881-94; James A. McFaul, 1894-1917; Thomas J. Walsh, 1918-28; John J. McMahon, 1928-32; Moses E. Kiley, 1934-40; William A. Griffin, 1940-50; George W. Ahr, 1950-79; John C. Reiss, 1980-97; John M. Smith, 1997-2010.

Tucson, AZ (1897): Gerald F. Kicanas, bishop, 2003.

Former bishops: Peter Bourgade, 1897-99; Henry Granjon, 1900-22; Daniel J. Gercke, 1923-60; Francis J. Green, 1960-81; Manuel D. Moreno, 1982-2003.

Tulsa, OK (1972): Edward J. Slattery, bishop, 1993.

Former bishops: Bernard J. Ganter, 1973-77; Eusebius J. Beltran, 1978-92.

Tyler, TX (1986): Vacant.

Former bishop: Charles E. Herzig, 1987 91; Edmond Carmody, 1992-2000; Alvaro Corrada del Rio, S.J., 2000-11.

Van Nuys, CA (Byzantine, Ruthenian) (1981): Gerald N. Dino, eparch, 2007.

Former bishop: Thomas V. Dolinay, 1982-90; George M. Kuzma, 1991-2000; William C. Skurla, 2002-2007.

Venice, FL (1984): Frank J. Dewane, bishop, 2007.

Former bishops: John J. Nevins, 1984-2007.

Victoria, TX (1982): David E. Fellhauer, bishop, 1990.

Former bishop: Charles V. Grahmann, 1982-89.

Washington,* DC (1939): Cardinal Donald W. Wuerl, archbishop. Martin D. Holley, Barry C. Knestout, auxiliaries.

Former ordinaries: Michael J. Curley, 1939-47; Cardinal Patrick O'Boyle, 1948-73; Cardinal William Baum, 1973-80; Cardinal James A. Hickey, 1980-2000; Cardinal Theodore E. McCarrick, 2000-2006

Wheeling-Charleston, WV (1850): Michael J. Bransfield, bishop, 2004.

Established as Wheeling, name changed, 1974.

Former bishops: Richard V. Whelan, 1850-74; John J. Kain, 1875-93; Patrick J. Donahue, 1894-1922; John J. Swint, 1922-62; Joseph H. Hodges, 1962-85; Francis B. Schulte, 1985-88; Bernard W. Schmitt, 1989-2004.

Wichita, KS (1887): Carl Kemme, bishop, 2014.

Former bishops: John J. Hennessy, 1888-1920; Augustus J. Schwertner, 1921-39; Christian H. Winkelmann, 1940-46; Mark K. Carroll, 1947-67; David M. Maloney, 1967-82; Eugene J. Gerber, 1982-2001; Thomas J. Olmsted, 2001-2003; Michael Owen Jackels, 2005-2013.

Wilmington, DE (1868): William Francis Malooly, bishop, 2008.

Former bishops: Thomas A. Becker, 1868-86; Alfred A. Curtis, 1886-96; John J. Monaghan, 1897-1925; Edmond Fitzmaurice, 1925-60; Michael Hyle, 1960-67; Thomas J. Mardaga, 1968-84; Robert E. Mulvee, 1985-95; Michael A. Saltarelli, 1995-2008.

Winona, MN (1889): John M. Quinn, co-adjutor, 2008, bishop, 2009.

Former bishops: Joseph B. Cotter, 1889-1909; Patrick R. Heffron, 1910-27; Francis M. Kelly, 1928-49; Edward A. Fitzgerald, 1949-69; Loras J. Watters, 1969-86; John G. Vlazny, 1987-97; Bernard J. Harrington, 1998-2009.

Worcester, MA (1950): Robert McManus, bishop, 2004.

Former bishops: John J. Wright, 1950-59; Bernard J. Flanagan, 1959-83; Timothy J. Harrington, 1983-94; Daniel P. Reilly, 1994-2004.

Yakima, WA (1951): Joseph J. Tyson, bishop, 2011.

Former bishops: Joseph P. Dougherty, 1951-69; Cornelius M. Power, 1969-74; Nicolas E. Walsh, 1974-76; William S. Skylstad, 1977-90; Francis E. George, O.M.I., 1990-96; Carlos A. Sevilla, S.J., 1996-2011.

Youngstown, OH (1943): George V. Murry, S.J., bishop, 2007

Former bishops: James A. McFadden, 1943-52; Emmet M. Walsh, 1952-68; James W. Malone, 1968-95; Thomas J. Tobin, 1995-2005.

Apostolic Exarchate for the Syro-Malankara Catholics in the United States (created July 14, 2010): Thomas Naickamparampil, first exarch.

Archdiocese for the Military Services, U.S.A., Washington, DC (1957; restructured, 1985): Timothy M. Broglio, archbishop, 2007. Richard Brendan Higgins, Joseph Walter Estabrook, F. Richard Spencer, Neal J, Buckon, Robert J. Coyle, auxiliaries.

Military vicar appointed, 1917; canonically established, 1957, as U.S. Military Vicariate under jurisdiction of New York archbishop; name changed, restructured as independent jurisdiction, 1985.

Former military vicars: Cardinal Patrick Hayes, 1917-38; Cardinal Francis Spellman, 1939-67; Cardinal Terence J. Cooke, 1968-83; Cardinal John J. O'Connor, apostolic administrator, 1984-85.

Former military ordinaries: Archbishop Joseph T. Ryan, 1985-91; Joseph T. Dimino, 1991-97; Edwin F. O'Brien, 1997-2007.

(Note: For coverage of **Missionary Bishops**, *see* under **Missionary Activity of the Church in the U.S.**)

CHANCERY OFFICES OF U.S. ARCHDIOCESES AND DIOCESES

A chancery office, under this or another title, is the central administrative office of an archdiocese or dio cese. (Archdioceses are indicated by asterisk.) As of Aug. 15, 2014.

Albany, NY: Pastoral Center, 40 N. Main Ave., 12203. (518) 453-6611; www.rcda.org.

Alexandria, LA: The Chancery Office, P.O. Box 7417, 71306. (318) 445-2401; www.diocesealex.org.

Allentown, PA: The Chancery Office, P.O. Box F, 18105-1538. (610) 437-0755; www.allentown diocese.org.

Altoona-Johnstown, PA: The Chancery, 927 S. Logan Blvd., Hollidaysburg, 16648. (814) 695-5579; www.dioceealtjtn.org.

Amarillo, TX: Pastoral Center, 1800 N. Spring St., P.O. Box 5644, 79117-5644. (806) 383-2243; www.amarillodiocese.org.

Anchorage,* AK: The Chancery Office, 225 Cordova St., 99501. (907) 297-7700; www.archdioceseofanchorage.org

Arlington, VA: The Chancery Office, Suite 914, 200 N. Glebe Rd., 22203. (703) 841-2500; www.arlington diocese.org.

Atlanta,* GA: Catholic Center, 680 W. Peachtree St. N.W., 30308. (404) 888-7802; www.archatl.com.

Austin, TX: The Chancery Office, 1600 N. Congress Ave., P.O. Box 13327, 78711. (512) 476-4888; www.austindiocese.org.

Baker, OR: Diocesan Pastoral Office, P.O. Box 5999, Bend, 97708. (541) 388-4004; www.dioceseof baker.org.

Baltimore,* MD: The Chancery Office, 320 Cathedral St., 21201. (410) 547-5446; www.archbalt.org.

Baton Rouge, LA: Catholic Life Center, P.O. Box 2028. 70821-2028. (225) 387-0561; www.diobr.org.

Beaumont, TX: Diocesan Pastoral Office, 70 Archie St., P.O. Box 3948, 77704-3948. (409) 838-0451; www.dioceseofbmt.org.

Belleville, IL: The Chancery, 222 S. Third St. 62220-1985, (618) 277-8181; www.diobelle.org.

Biloxi, MS: Administration Offices, P.O. Box 6489, 39522-6489. (228) 702-2100; www.biloxidiocese.org.

Birmingham, AL: Catholic Life Center, P.O. Box 12047, 35202-2047. (205) 838-8322; www.bhmdiocese.org.

Bismarck, ND: The Chancery Office, 420 Raymond St., Box 1575, 58502-1575. (701) 223-1347; www.bismarckdiocese.org.

Boise, ID: The Chancery Office, 303 Federal Way, 83705-5925. (208) 342-1311; www.catholicidaho.org.

Boston,* MA: The Chancery Office, 2121 Commonwealth Ave., Brighton, 02135. (617) 254-0100; www.rcab.or.

Bridgeport, CT: The Catholic Center, 238 Jewett Ave., 06606-2892. (203) 372-4301; www.bridgeportdiocese.com

Brooklyn, NY: The Chancery Office, 75 Greene Ave., P.O. Box C, 11238. (718) 399-5970; www.dioceseofbrooklyn. org.

Brownsville, TX: The Catholic Pastoral Center, P.O. Box 2279, 1910 E. Elizabeth St., 78522-2279. (956) 542-2501; www.cdob.org.

Buffalo, NY: The Chancery Office, 795 Main St., 14203. (716) 847-5500; www.buffalodiocese.org.

Burlington, VT: The Chancery Office, P.O. Box 489, Buirlington, VT.05402-0489. (802) 658-6110; www.vermontcatholic.org.

Camden, NJ: Camden Diocesan Center, 631 Market St., P.O. Box 708, 08102. (856) 756-7900; www.camden diocese.org.

Charleston, SC: The Chancery Office, 119 Broad St., P.O. Box 818, 29402. (843) 723-3488; www.catholic-doc.org.

Charlotte, NC: The Pastoral Center, P.O. Box 36776, 28236. (704) 370-6299; www.charlottedio cese.org.

Cheyenne, WY: The Chancery Office, Box 1468, 82003-0426. (307) 638-1530; www.dioceseof cheyenne.

Chicago,* IL: Pastoral Center, P.O. Box 1979, 60690. (312) 751-7999; www.archdiocese-chgo.org

Cincinnati,* OH: The Chancery Office, 100 E. 8th St. 45202. (513) 421-3131; www.catholiccincinnati.org.

Cleveland, OH: The Chancery Office, 1027 Superior Ave., 44114. (216) 696-6525; www.dioceseofcleveland.org

Colorado Springs, CO: Pastoral Center, 228 N. Cascade Ave., 80903-1498; (719) 636-2345; www.diocs.org.

Columbus, OH: Chancery Office, 198 E. Broad St., 43215. (614) 224-2251; www.colsdioc.org

Corpus Christi, TX: The Chancery Office, 620 Lipan St., P.O. Box 2620, 78403-2620. (512) 882-6191; www.diocesecc.org.

Covington, KY: Catholic Center, P.O. Box 15550, 41015. (859) 392-1500; www.covingtondiocese.org.

Crookston, MN: Chancery Office, 1200 Memorial Dr., 56716. (218) 281-4533; www.crookston.org.

Dallas, TX: Chancery Office, 3725 Blackburn St., 75219. (214) 528-2240; www.cathdal.org.

Davenport, IA: Chancery Office, 2706 N. Gaines St., 52804-1998. (563) 324-1911; www.davenport diocese.org.

Denver,* CO: Catholic Pastoral Center, 1300 South Steele St., 80210. (303) 722-4687; www.archden.org.

Des Moines, IA: Chancery Office, 601 Grand Ave., 50309;. (515) 243-7653; www.dmdiocese.org.

Detroit,* MI: Chancery Office, 1234 Washington Blvd., 48226. (313) 237-5800; www.aodonline.org.

Dodge City, KS: Chancery Office, 910 Central Ave., 67801-4905. (620) 227-1500; www.dcdiocese.org.

Dubuque,* IA: Chancery Office, 1229 Loretta Ave., 52003; (563) 556-2580; www.arch.pvt.k12.ia.us/home.

Duluth, MN: Pastoral Center, 2830 E. 4th St., 55812. (218) 724-9111; www.dioceseduluth.org.

El Paso, TX: The Chancery Office, 499 St. Matthews St., 79907. (915) 872-8400; www.elpasodi ocese.org.

Erie, PA: St. Mark Catholic Center, P.O. Box 10397, 16514-0397. (814) 824-1135; www.eriecd.org.

Evansville, IN: Chancery Office, P.O. Box 4169, 47724-0169. (812) 424-5536; www.evansville-diocese.org.

Fairbanks, AK: Chancery Office, 1316 Peger Rd., 99709. (907) 374-9500; www.cbna.info.

Fall River, MA: Chancery Office, 450 Highland Ave., Box 2577, 02722. (508) 675-1311.

Fargo, ND: Chancery, 5201 Bishop Blvd., Suite A, 58104-7605; (701) 356-7900; www.fargodiocese.org.

Fort Wayne-South Bend, IN: Chancery, 1103 S. Calhoun St., Fort Wayne, 46801. (260) 422-4611; South Bend Chancery, 114 W. Wayne St., South Bend, 46601; (574) 234-0687;www.diocesefwsb.org.

Fort Worth, TX: Catholic Center, 800 W. Loop 820 South, 76108. (817) 560-3300; www.fwdioc.org.

Fresno, CA: Chancery Office, 1550 N. Fresno St., 93703-3788. (559) 488-7400; www.dioceseoffresno.org.

Gallup, NM: Chancery, 711 S. Puerco Dr., P.O. Box 1338, 87305. (505) 863-4406; www.dioceseofgallup.org.

Galveston-Houston, TX: Chancery Office, 1700 San Jacinto, 77002-8291; (713) 659-5461; www.diogh.org.

Gary, IN: The Chancery Office, 9292 Broadway, Merrillville, 46410. (219) 769-9292; www.dcgary.org.

Gaylord, MI: Diocesan Pastoral Center, 611 North St., 49735. (989) 732-5147; www.dioceseofgaylord.org.

Grand Island, NE: Chancery Office, P.O. Box 5131, 2708 Old Fair Rd., 68802. (308) 382-6565; www.gidiocese.org.

Grand Rapids, MI: Chancery, 360 Division Ave. S., 49503. (616) 243-0491; www.dioceseofgrandrapids.org.

Great Falls-Billings, MT: Chancery, P.O. Box 1399, Great Falls, 59401. (406) 727-6683; www.dioceseofgfb.org.

Green Bay, WI: Chancery, P.O. Box 23825, 1910 S. Webster Ave., 54305-3825. (920) 437-7531; www.gbdioc.org.

Greensburg, PA: Chancery, 723 E. Pittsburgh St., 15601. (724) 837-0901; www.dioceseofgreensburg.org.

Harrisburg, PA: Chancery, 4800 Union Deposit Rd., 17111-3710. (717) 657-4804; www.hbgdiocese.org.

Hartford,* CT: Chancery, 134 Farmington Ave., 06105-3784. (860) 541-6491; www.archdioceseofhartford.org.

Helena, MT: Chancery, 515 N. Ewing, P.O. Box 1729, 59624-1729. (406) 442-5820; www.diocesehelena.org.

Honolulu, HI: Chancery, 1184 Bishop St., 96813; (808) 585-3300; www.catholichawaii.com.

Houma-Thibodaux, LA: Pastoral Center, 2779 Highway 311, Schriever, 70395-3273. (985) 868-7720; www.htdiocese.org.

Indianapolis,* IN: Archbishop Edward T. O'Meara Catholic Center, 1400 N. Meridian St., 46202. (317) 236-1405; www.archindy.org.

Jackson, MS: Chancery, 237 E. Amite St., P.O. Box 2248, 39225-2248. (601) 969-1880; www.jacksondiocese.org.

Jefferson City, MO: Chancery, 2207 W. Main St., P.O. Box 104900, 65110-4900. (573) 635-9127; www.diojeffcity.org.

Joliet, IL: Chancery, 425 Summit St., 60435. (815) 722-6606; www.dioceseofjoliet.org.

Juneau, AK: Chancery, 414 6th St., No. 300, 99801; (907) 586-2227; www.dioceseofjuneau.org.

Kalamazoo, MI: Chancery, 215 N. Westnedge Ave., 49007-3760. (269) 349-8714; www.dioceseofkalamazoo.

Kansas City,* KS: Chancery, 12615 Parallel Pkwy., 66109. (913) 721-1570; www.archkck.org.

Kansas City-St. Joseph, MO: The Chancery Office, P.O. Box 419037, Kansas City, 64141-6037. (816) 756-1850; www.diocese-kcsj.org.

Knoxville, TN: Chancery, 805 Northshore Dr., SW, P.O. Box 11127; 37939-1127. (865) 584-3307;

www.dioceseofknoxville.org.

La Crosse, WI: The Chancery Office, 3710 East Ave. S., Box 4004, 54602-4004. (608) 788-7700; www.dioceseoflacrosse.com

Lafayette, IN: Bishop's Office, P.O. Box 260, 610 Lingle Ave.,47901. (765) 742-0275; www.dioceseoflafayette. org.

Lafayette, LA: Chancery, 1408 Carmel Ave., 70501. (337) 261-5652; www.diolaf.org.

Lake Charles, LA: Chancery, 414 Iris St., 70601. (318) 439-7400; www.lcdiocese.org.

Lansing, MI: Chancery, 300 W. Ottawa St., 48933-1577. (517) 342-2440; www.dioceseoflansing.org.

Laredo, TX: Chancery, 1901 Corpus Christi St., 78043. (956) 727-2140; www.thedioceseoflaredo.org.

Las Cruces, NM: Chancery, 1280 Med Park Dr., 88005-3239. (575) 523-7577; www.dioceseoflascruces.org.

Las Vegas, NV: Chancery, 336 Cathedral Way, [P.O. Box 18316, 89114-8316]. (702) 735-3500; www.lasvegas-diocese.org.

Lexington, KY: Catholic Center, 1310 Main St., 40508-2048. (859) 253-1993; www.cdlex.org.

Lincoln, NE: Chancery, 3400 Sheridan Blvd. [P.O. Box 80328, 68501-0328]. (402) 488-0921; www.dioceseoflincoln.org

Little Rock, AR: Chancery, 2500 N. Tyler St., [P.O. Box 7565; 72217-7565]. (501) 664-0340; www.dolr.org

Los Angeles,* CA: Archdiocesan Catholic Center, 3424 Wilshire Blvd., 90010-2202. (213) 637-7000; www.archdiocese.la

Louisville,* KY: Chancery, 212 E. College St., [P.O. Box 1073, 40201-1073]. (502) 585-3291; www.archlou.org.

Lubbock, TX: The Catholic Center, P.O. Box 98700, 79499. (806) 792-3943; www.catholiclubbock.org.

Madison, WI: Bishop O'Connor Catholic Pastoral Center, 3577 High Point Rd., [P.O. Box 44983, 53719-4983]. (608) 821-3000; www.madisondiocese.org.

Manchester, NH: Chancery, 153 Ash St., [P.O. Box 310, 03105-0310]. (603) 669-3100; www.diocesemanch.org.

Marquette, MI: Chancery, 117 W. Washington St., P.O. Box 1000, 49855. (906) 227-9111; www.dioceseofmarquette.org.

Memphis, TN: The Catholic Center, 5825 Shelby Oaks Dr., 38134. (901) 373-1200; www.cdom.org.

Metuchen, NJ: Chancery, 146 Metlars Ln., Piscataway, NJ 08854-4303; [P.O. Box 191, 08840-0191]; (732) 562-1990; www.diometuchen.org.

Miami,* FL: Chancery, 9401 Biscayne Blvd., Miami Shores, 33138. (305) 757-6241; www.miamiarch.org.

Milwaukee,* WI: Archbishop Cousins Catholic Center, P.O. Box 70912, 53207-0912. (414) 769-3300; www.archmil.org.

Mobile,* AL: Chancery, 400 Government St., P.O. Box 1966, 36633. (251) 434-1585; www.mobilearchdiocese.org

Monterey, CA: Chancery, P.O. Box 2048, 93942-2048. (831) 373-4345; www.dioceseofmonterey.org.

Nashville, TN: Chancery, 2400 21st Ave. S., 37212-5387. (615) 383-6393; www.dioceseofnashville.com

Newark,* NJ: Chancery, 171 Clifton Ave., P.O. Box 9500, 07104-0500. (973) 497-4000; www.rcan.org.

New Orleans,* LA: Chancery, 7887 Walmsley Ave., 70125. (504) 861-9521; www.arch-no.org

Newton, MA (Melkite): Chancery, 3 VFW Pkwy., Roslindale, 02131. (617) 323-9922; www.melkite.org.

New Ulm, MN: Catholic Pastoral Center, 1400 Sixth St. N., 56073-2099. (507) 359-2966; www.dnu.org.

New York,* NY: Chancery, 1011 First Ave., 10022-4134. (212) 371-1000; www.ny-archdiocese.org.

Norwich, CT: Chancery, 201 Broadway, 06360-4328. (860) 887-9294; www.norwichdiocese.org

Oakland, CA: Chancery, 2121 Harrison St. Suite 100, 94612; (510) 893-4711; www.oakdiocese.org

Ogdensburg, NY: Chancery, 604 Washington St., P.O. Box 369, 13669. (315) 393-2920; www.dioogdensburg.org

Oklahoma City,* OK: Pastoral Center, 7501 NW Expressway, 73132. (405) 721-5651; www.catharch dioceseokc.org

Omaha,* NE: Chancery, 100 N. 62nd St., 68132-2795. (402) 558-3100; www.archomaha.com

Orange, CA: Chancery, 2811 E. Villa Real Dr., 92867, [P.O. Box 14195, 92863-1595]. (714) 282-3000; www.rcbo.org.

Orlando, FL: Chancery, P.O. Box 1800, 32802-1800. (407) 246-4800; www.orlandodiocese.org

Our Lady of Deliverance of Newark, for Syrian rite Catholics of the U.S. and Canada: P.O. Box 8366, Union City, NJ, 07087-8262. (201) 583-1067; www.syriac-catholic.org.

Our Lady of Lebanon, Eparchy, USA (Maronite): Chancery, 1021 South Tenth St., St. Louis, MO 63104; (314) 231-1021; www.usamaronite.org.

Owensboro, KY: Catholic Pastoral Center, 600 Locust St., 42301-2130. (270) 683-1545; www.owensborodio.org.

Palm Beach, FL: Pastoral Center, 9995 N. Military Trail, Palm Beach Gardens, 33410. (561) 775-9500; www.diocesepb.org.

Parma, OH (Byzantine): Chancery, 1900 Carlton Rd., 44134-3129. (216) 741-8773; www.parma.org.

Passaic, NJ (Byzantine): Chancery, 445 Lackawanna Ave., West Paterson, 07424. (973) 890-7777; www.eparchyof passaic.com

Paterson, NJ: Diocesan Pastoral Center, 777 Valley Rd., Clifton, 07013. (973) 777-8818; www.paterson diocese.org.

Pensacola-Tallahassee, FL: Pastoral Center, 11 N. B. St., Pensacola, 32501. (850) 435-3500; www.ptdiocese.org

Peoria, IL: Chancery, 607 N.E. Madison Ave., 61603. (309) 671-1550; www.cdop.org

Philadelphia,* PA: Chancery, 222 N. 17th St., 19103. (215) 587-3600; www.archphila.org.

Philadelphia,* PA (Byzantine): Chancery, 827 N. Franklin St., 19123-2097. (215) 627-0143; www. ukrarcheparchy.us.

Phoenix, AZ: Chancery, 400 E. Monroe St., 85004-2376. (602) 354-2000; www.diocesephoenix.org.

Pittsburgh,* PA (Byzantine): Chancery, 66 Riverview Ave., 15214. (412) 231-4000; www.archeparchy.org

Pittsburgh, PA: Pastoral Center, 111 Blvd. of the Allies, 15222. (412) 456-3000; www.diopitt.org.

Portland, ME: Chancery, 510 Ocean Ave., P.O. Box 11559, 04103. (207) 773-6471; www.portlanddiocese.net.

Portland, OR*: Pastoral Center, 2838 E. Burnside St., 97214. (503) 234-5334; www.archdpdx.org.

Providence, RI: Chancery, One Cathedral Sq., 02903. (401) 278-4500; www.dioceseofprovidence.org

Pueblo, CO: Catholic Pastoral Center, 1001 N. Grand Ave., 81003. (719) 544-9861; www.dioceseofpueblo.com.

Raleigh, NC: Catholic Center, 715 Nazareth St., 27606. (919) 821-9700; www.dioceseofraleigh.org

Rapid City, SD: Chancery, 606 Cathedral Dr., P.O. Box 678, 57709. (605) 343-3541; www.rapidcitydiocese.org

Reno, NV: Pastoral Center, 290 Arlington Ave., Suite 200, 89501. (775) 329-9274; www.catholi creno.org

Richmond, VA: Pastoral Center, 7800 Carousel Lane, 23294-4201. (804) 359-5661; www.richmonddiocese.org

Rochester, NY: The Pastoral Center, 1150 Buffalo Rd., 14624. (585) 328-3210; www.dor.org

Rockford, IL: Chancery, 555 Colman Center Drive, 61108, [P.O. Box 7044, 61125-7044]. (815) 399-4300; www.rockforddiocese.org.

Rockville Centre, NY: Chancery, 50 N. Park Ave., P.O. Box 9023, 11571-9023. (516) 678-5800; www. drvc.org.

Sacramento, CA: Pastoral Center, 2110 Broadway, 95818. (916) 733-0100; www.diocese-sacramento. org.

Saginaw, MI: Chancery, 5800 Weiss St., 48603-2799. (989) 799-7910; www. saginaw.org

St. Augustine, FL: Catholic Center, 11625 Old St. Augustine Rd., Jacksonville, 32258. (904) 262-3200; www.dosafl.com

St. Cloud, MN: Chancery, 214 Third Ave. S., 56301; [P.O. Box 1248, 56302-1248]. (320) 251-2340; www.stclouddiocese.org

St. George's in Canton, OH (Byzantine, Romanian): Chancery 1123 44th St. N.E., 44714, [P.O. Box 7189, 44705-0189]. (330) 493-9355; www.romaniancatholic.org.

St. Josaphat in Parma, OH (Byzantine): Chancery, P.O. Box 347180, 44134-7180. (440) 888-1522; www.stjosaphateparchy.org

St. Louis,* MO: Catholic Center, 4445 Lindell Blvd., 63108-2497. (314) 633-2222; www.archstl. org.

St. Maron of Brooklyn (Maronite): Pastoral Center, 109 Remsen St., 11201. (718) 237-9913; www.stmaron.org

St. Nicholas in Chicago (Byzantine): Chancery, 2245 W. Rice St., 60622. (773) 276-5080; www.stni cholaseparchy.org

St. Paul and Minneapolis,* MN: Chancery, 226 Summit Ave., St. Paul, 55102-2197. (651) 291-4400; www.archspm.org

St. Peter the Apostle of San Diego (Chaldean): Chancery Office, 1627 Jamacha Way, El Cajon, CA 92019. (619) 590-9028; www.kaldu.org

St. Petersburg, FL: Chancery, 6363 9th Ave. N, 33710, [P.O. Box 40200, 33743-0200]. (727) 344-1611; www.dioceseofstpete.org.

St. Thomas of Chicago (Syro-Malabar): Diocesan Office, 717 N. Eastland, Elmhurst, IL 60126. (630) 530-8399; www.stthomasdiocese.org

St. Thomas the Apostle of Detroit (Chaldean Catholic Diocese – USA): Chancery, 25603 Berg Rd., Southfield, MI 48034. (248) 351-0440; www..

Salina, KS: Chancery, 103 N. 9th St., 67401, [P.O. Box 980, 67402-0980]. (785) 827-8746; www.salinadiocese.org

Salt Lake City, UT: Pastoral Center, 27 C St., 84103. (801) 328-8641; www.utahcatholicdiocese. org

San Angelo, TX: Chancery, P.O. Box 1829, 76902-1829. (915) 651-7500; www.san-angelo-diocese.org.

San Antonio,* TX: Chancery, 2718 W. Woodlawn, [P.O. Box 28410, 78228-0410]. (210) 734-2620; www.archdiosa.org.

San Bernardino, CA: Chancery, 1201 E. Highland Ave., 92404. (909) 475-5300; www.sbdiocese.org.

San Diego, CA: Pastoral Center, 3888 Paducah Dr., 92117 [P.O. Box 85728, 92186-5728], (858) 490-8200; www.diocese-sdiego.org.

San Francisco,* CA: Chancery, One Peter Yorke Way 94109. (415) 614-5500; www.sfarchdiocese.org

San Jose, CA: Chancery, 1150 N. First St., Suite 100, 95112-4966. (408) 983-0100; www.dsj.org.

Santa Fe,* NM: Catholic Center, 4000 St. Joseph's Pl. N.W., Albuquerque, 87120-1741. (505) 831-8100.

Santa Rosa, CA: Chancery, P.O. Box 1297, 95402-1297. (707) 545-7610; www.santarosacatholic.org.

Savannah, GA: Pastoral Center, 601 E. Liberty St., 31401-5196. (912) 201-4100; www.diosav.org.

Scranton, PA: Chancery, 300 Wyoming Ave., 18503-1279. (570) 207-2216; www.dioceseofscranton.org.

Seattle,* WA: Chancery, 910 Marion St., 98104-1299. (206) 382-4560; www.seattlearch.org.

Shreveport, LA: Catholic Center, 3500 Fairfield Ave. 71104. (318) 868-4441; www.dioshpt.org.

Sioux City, IA: Chancery, 1821 Jackson St., P.O. Box 3379, 51102-3379. (712) 255-7933; www.scdiocese.org.

Sioux Falls, SD: Pastoral Center, 523 N. Duluth Ave., 57104-2714. (605) 334-9861; www.sfcatholic.org.

Spokane, WA: Pastoral Center, 1023 W. Riverside Ave., P.O. Box 1453, 99201. (509) 358-7300; www.dioceseofspokane.org.

Springfield, IL: Pastoral Center, 1615 W. Washington, P.O. Box 3187, 62708-3187. (217) 698-8500; www.dio.org.

Springfield, MA: Chancery, P.O. Box 1730, 01102. (413) 732-3175; www.diospringfield.org.

Springfield-Cape Girardeau, MO: The Catholic Center, 601 S. Jefferson Ave., Springfield. 65806-3143. (417) 866-0841; home.catholicweb.com/diocspfdcape/index.cfm

Stamford, CT (Byzantine): Chancery, 14 Peveril Rd., 06902-3019. (203) 324-7698

Steubenville, OH: Chancery, 422 Washington St., P.O. Box 969, 43952. (740) 282-3631; www.diosteub.org.

Stockton, CA: Chancery, 1125 N. Lincoln St., 95203. (209) 472-1008; www.stocktondiocese.org

Superior, WI: Chancery, 1201 Hughitt Ave., Box 969, 54880. (715) 392-2937; www.catholicdos.org.

Syracuse, NY: Chancery, 240 E. Onondaga St., P.O. Box 511, 13201-0511. (315) 422-7203; wwwsyrdioc.org.

Toledo, OH: Chancery, 1933 Spielbusch Ave., 43604 [P.O. Box 985, 43697-0895]. (419) 244-6711; www.toledodiocese.org

Trenton, NJ: Chancery, 701 Lawrenceville Rd., P.O. Box 5147, 08638. (609) 406-7400; www.dioceseoftrenton.org.

Tucson, AZ: Pastoral Center, 111 S. Church Ave., Box 31, 85702. (520) 792-3410; www.diocesetucson.org

Tulsa, OK: Chancery, 12300 E. 91st St. S, Broken Arrow, 74102 [P.O. Box 690240, Tulsa 74169]. (918) 294-1904; www.dioceseoftulsa.org

Tyler, TX: Chancery, 1015 E.S.E. Loop 323, 75701-9663. (903) 534-1077; www.dioceseoftyler.org

Van Nuys, CA (Byzantine): Chancery, 8105 N. 16th St., Phoenix, AZ 85020. (602) 861-9778; www.eparchy-of-vannuys.org.

Venice, FL: Catholic Center, P.O. Box 2006, 34284. (941) 484-9543; www.dioceseofvenice.org.

Victoria, TX: Chancery, 1505 E. Mesquite Ln., 77901 [P.O. Box 4070, 77903]. (361) 573-0828; www.victoriadiocese.org

Washington,* DC: Pastoral Center, 5001 Eastern Ave., Hyattsville, MD 20782 [P.O. Box 29260, DC 20017-0260]. (301) 853-4500; www.adw.org

Wheeling-Charleston, WV: Chancery, 1300 Byron St., P.O. Box 230, Wheeling, 26003. (304) 233-0880; www.dwc.org.

Wichita, KS: Chancery, 424 N. Broadway, 67202. (316) 269-3900; www.cdowk.org

Wilmington, DE: Chancery, 1925 Delaware Ave., P.O. Box 2030, 19899-2030. (302) 573-3100; www.cdow.org.

Winona, MN: Chancery, 55 W. Sanborn St., P.O. Box 588, 55987. (507) 454-4643; www.dow.org.

Worcester, MA: Chancery, 49 Elm St., 01609-2597. (508) 791-7171; www.worcesterdiocese.org.

Yakima, WA: Chancery, 5301-A Tieton Dr., 98908-3493. (509) 965-7119; www.yakimadiocese.org.

Youngstown, OH: Chancery, 144 W. Wood St., 44503. (330) 744-8451; www.doy.org.

Military Archdiocese: P.O. Box 4469, Washington, DC 20017-0469; 3311 Toledo Terrace, Suite A201, Hyattsville, MD 20782-4135. (202) 269-9100; www.milarch.org.

Armenian Apostolic Exarchate for the United States and Canada: 110 E. 12th St., New York, NY 10003. (212) 477-2030.

Apostolic Exarchate for the Syro-Malankara Catholics in the United States: Mar Ivanios Malankara Catholic Centre, 950 Hill Side Avenue, New Hyde Park, New York 11004.

CATHEDRALS, BASILICAS, AND SHRINES IN THE U.S.

CATHEDRALS IN THE UNITED STATES

A cathedral is the principal church in a diocese, the one in which the bishop has his seat (cathedra). He is the actual pastor, although many functions of the church, which usually serves a parish, are the responsibility of a priest serving as the rector. Because of the dignity of a cathedral, the dates of its dedication and its patronal feast are observed throughout a diocese. The pope's cathedral, the Basilica of St. John Lateran, is the highest-ranking church in the world.

(Archdioceses are indicated by asterisk.)

Albany, NY: Immaculate Conception.

Alexandria, LA: St. Francis Xavier.

Allentown, PA: St. Catherine of Siena.

Altoona-Johnstown, PA: Blessed Sacrament (Altoona); St. John Gualbert (Johnstown).

Amarillo, TX: St. Laurence.

Anchorage,* AK: Holy Family.

Arlington, Va: St. Thomas More.

Atlanta,* GA: Christ the King.

Austin, TX: St. Mary (Immaculate Conception).

Baker, OR: St. Francis de Sales.

Baltimore,* MD: Mary Our Queen; Basilica of the National Shrine of the Assumption of the Blessed Virgin Mary (Co-Cathedral).

Baton Rouge, LA: St. Joseph.

Beaumont, TX: St. Anthony (of Padua).

Belleville, IL: St. Peter.

Biloxi, MS: Nativity of the Blessed Virgin Mary.

Birmingham, AL: St. Paul.

Bismark, N.D.: Holy Spirit.

Boise, Id.: St. John the Evangelist.
Boston,* MA: Holy Cross.
Bridgeport, CT: St. Augustine.
Brooklyn, NY: St. James (Minor Basilica).
Brownsville, TX: Immaculate Conception.
Buffalo, NY: St. Joseph.
Burlington, VT: Immaculate Conception; St. Joseph (Co-Cathedral).
Camden, NJ: Immaculate Conception.
Charleston, SC: St. John the Baptist.
Charlotte, NC: St. Patrick.
Cheyenne, WY: St. Mary.
Chicago,* IL: Holy Name (of Jesus).
Cincinnati,* OH: St. Peter in Chains.
Cleveland, OH: St. John the Evangelist.
Colorado Springs, Colo: St. Mary.
Columbus, OH: St. Joseph.
Corpus Christi, TX: Corpus Christi.
Covington, KY: Basilica of the Assumption.
Crookston, MN: Immaculate Conception.
Dallas, TX: Cathedral-Santuario de Guadalupe.
Davenport, IA: Sacred Heart.
Denver,* CO: Immaculate Conception (Minor Basilica).
Des Moines, IA: St. Ambrose.
Detroit,* MI: Most Blessed Sacrament.
Dodge City, KS: Our Lady of Guadalupe.
Dubuque,* IA: St. Raphael.
Duluth, MN: Our Lady of the Rosary.
El Paso, TX: St. Patrick.
Erie, PA: St. Peter.
Evansville, IN: Most Holy Trinity (Pro-Cathedral).
Fairbanks, AK: Sacred Heart.
Fall River, MA: St. Mary of the Assumption.
Fargo, N.D.: St. Mary.
Fort Wayne-S. Bend, IN: Immaculate Conception (Fort Wayne); St. Matthew (South Bend).
Fort Worth, TX: St. Patrick.
Fresno, CA: St. John (the Baptist).
Gallup, NM: Sacred Heart.
Galveston-Houston, TX: St. Mary (Minor Basilica, Galveston); Sacred Heart Co-Cathedral (Houston).
Gary, IN: Holy Angels.
Gaylord, MI: St. Mary, Our Lady of Mt. Carmel.
Grand Island, NE: Nativity of Blessed Virgin Mary.
Grand Rapids, MI: St. Andrew.
Great Falls-Billings, MT: St. Ann (Great Falls); St. Patrick Co-Cathedral (Billings).
Green Bay, WI: St. Francis Xavier.
Greensburg, PA: Blessed Sacrament.
Harrisburg, PA: St. Patrick.
Hartford,* CT: St. Joseph.
Helena, MT: St. Helena.
Honolulu, HI: Our Lady of Peace; St. Theresa of the Child Jesus (Co-Cathedral).
Houma-Thibodaux, LA: St. Francis de Sales (Houma); St. Joseph Co-Cathedral (Thibodaux).
Indianapolis,* IN: Sts. Peter and Paul.
Jackson, MS: St. Peter.
Jefferson City, MO: St. Joseph.
Joliet, IL: St. Raymond Nonnatus.
Juneau, AK: Nativity of the Blessed Virgin Mary.
Kalamazoo, MI: St. Augustine.
Kansas City,* KS: St. Peter the Apostle.
Kansas City-St. Joseph, MO: Immaculate

Conception (Kansas City); St. Joseph Co-Cathedral (St. Joseph).
Knoxville, TN: Sacred Heart of Jesus.
La Crosse, WI: St. Joseph the Workman.
Lafayette, IN: St. Mary.
Lafayette, LA: St. John the Evangelist.
Lake Charles, LA: Immaculate Conception.
Lansing, MI: St. Mary.
Laredo, TX: San Augustin.
Las Cruces, NM: Immaculate Heart of Mary.
Las Vegas, NV: Guardian Angel.
Lexington, KY: Christ the King.
Lincoln, NE: Cathedral of the Risen Christ.
Little Rock, AR: St. Andrew.
Los Angeles,* CA: Cathedral of Our Lady of the Angels of Los Angeles (opened in 2002).
Louisville,* KY: Assumption.
Lubbock, TX: Christ the King.
Madison, WI: St. Raphael.
Manchester, NH: St. Joseph.
Marquette, MI: St. Peter.
Memphis, TN: Immaculate Conception.
Metuchen, NJ: St. Francis (of Assisi).
Miami,* FL: St. Mary (Immaculate Conception).
Milwaukee,* WI: St. John.
Mobile,* AL: Immaculate Conception (Minor Basilica).
Monterey, CA: San Carlos Borromeo.
Nashville, TN: Incarnation.
Newark,* NJ: Sacred Heart (Minor Basilica).
New Orleans,* LA: St. Louis. (Minor Basilica)
Newton, MA (Melkite): Our Lady of the Annunciation (Boston).
New Ulm, MN: Holy Trinity.
New York,* NY: St. Patrick.
Norwich, CT: St. Patrick.
Oakland, CA: St. Francis de Sales.
Ogdensburg, NY: St. Mary (Immaculate Conception).
Oklahoma City,* OK: Our Lady of Perpetual Help.
Omaha,* NE: St. Cecilia.
Orange, CA: Holy Family.
Orlando, FL: St. James.
Our Lady of Deliverance of Newark, New Jersey for Syrian Rite Catholics in the U.S. and Canada: Our Lady of Deliverance.
Our Lady of Lebanon of Los Angeles, CA (Maronite): Our Lady of Mt. Lebanon-St. Peter.
Owensboro, KY: St. Stephen.
Palm Beach, FL: St. Ignatius Loyola, Palm Beach Gardens.
Parma, OH (Byzantine): St. John the Baptist.
Passaic, NJ (Byzantine): St. Michael.
Paterson, NJ: St. John the Baptist.
Pensacola-Tallahassee, FL: Sacred Heart (Pensacola); Co-Cathedral of St. Thomas More (Tallahassee).
Peoria, IL: St. Mary.
Philadelphia,* PA: Sts. Peter and Paul (Minor Basilica).
Philadelphia,* PA (Byzantine): Immaculate Conception of Blessed Virgin Mary.
Phoenix, AZ: Sts. Simon and Jude.
Pittsburgh,* PA (Byzantine): St. John the Baptist, Munhall.
Pittsburgh, PA: St. Paul.

Portland, ME: Immaculate Conception.
Portland,* OR: Immaculate Conception.
Providence, RI: Sts. Peter and Paul.
Pueblo, CO: Sacred Heart.
Raleigh, NC: Sacred Heart.
Rapid City, SD: Our Lady of Perpetual Help.
Reno, NV: St. Thomas Aquinas.
Richmond, VA: Sacred Heart.
Rochester, NY: Sacred Heart.
Rockford, IL: St. Peter.
Rockville Centre, NY: St. Agnes.
Sacramento, CA: Blessed Sacrament.
Saginaw, MI: St. Mary.
St. Augustine, FL: St. Augustine (Minor Basilica).
St. Cloud, MN: St. Mary.
St. George's in Canton, OH (Byzantine, Romanian): St. George.
St. Josaphat in Parma, OH (Byzantine): St. Josaphat.
St. Louis,* MO: St. Louis.
St. Maron, Brooklyn, NY (Maronite): Our Lady of Lebanon.
St. Nicholas in Chicago (Byzantine): St. Nicholas.
St. Paul and Minneapolis,* MN: St. Paul (St. Paul); Basilica of St. Mary Co-Cathedral (Minneapolis).
St. Petersburg, FL: St. Jude the Apostle.
St. Thomas the Apostle of Detroit (Chaldean): Our Lady of Chaldeans Cathedral (Mother of God Church), Southfield, MI
St. Thomas of Chicago (Syro-Malabar): Mar Thoma Shleeha Church.
Salina, KS: Sacred Heart.
Salt Lake City, UT: The Madeleine.
San Angelo, TX: Sacred Heart.
San Antonio,* TX: San Fernando.
San Bernardino, CA: Our Lady of the Rosary.
San Diego, CA: St. Joseph.
San Francisco,* CA: St. Mary (Assumption).
San Jose, CA: St. Joseph (Minor Basilica); St. Patrick, Proto-Cathedral.
Santa Fe,* NM: San Francisco de Asis (Minor Basilica).
Santa Rosa, CA: St. Eugene.
Savannah, GA: St. John the Baptist.
Scranton, PA: St. Peter.
Seattle,* WA: St. James.
Shreveport, LA: St. John Berchmans.
Sioux City, IA: Epiphany.
Sioux Falls, SD: St. Joseph.
Spokane, WA: Our Lady of Lourdes.
Springfield, IL: Immaculate Conception.
Springfield, MA: St. Michael.
Springfield-Cape Girardeau, MO: St. Agnes (Springfield); St. Mary (Cape Girardeau).
Stamford, CT (Byzantine): St. Vladimir.
Steubenville, OH: Holy Name.
Stockton, CA: Annunciation.
Superior, WI: Christ the King.
Syracuse, NY: Immaculate Conception.
Syro-Malankara Exarchate: St. John Chrysostom Pro-Cathedral
Toledo, OH: Queen of the Most Holy Rosary.
Trenton, NJ: St. Mary (Assumption).
Tucson, AZ: St. Augustine.
Tulsa, OK: Holy Family.
Tyler, TX: Immaculate Conception.

Van Nuys, CA (Byzantine): St. Mary (Patronage of the Mother of God), Van Nuys; St. Stephen's (Pro-Cathedral), Phoenix, AZ
Venice, Fla: Epiphany.
Victoria, TX: Our Lady of Victory.
Washington,* DC: St. Matthew.
Wheeling-Charleston, WV: St. Joseph (Wheeling); Sacred Heart (Charleston).
Wichita, KS: Immaculate Conception.
Wilmington, DE: St. Peter.
Winona, MN: Sacred Heart.
Worcester, MA: St. Paul.
Yakima, WA: St. Paul.
Youngstown, OH: St. Columba.
Apostolic Exarchate for Armenian Catholics in the U.S. and Canada: St. Ann (110 E. 12th St., New York, NY 10003).

BASILICAS IN THE UNITED STATES

Basilica is a title assigned to certain churches because of their antiquity, dignity, historical importance or significance as centers of worship. Major basilicas have the papal altar and holy door, which is opened at the beginning of a Jubilee Year; minor basilicas enjoy certain ceremonial privileges.

Among the major basilicas are the patriarchal basilicas of St. John Lateran, St. Peter, St. Paul Outside the Walls and St. Mary Major in Rome; St. Francis and St. Mary of the Angels in Assisi, Italy. The patriarchal basilica of St. Lawrence, Rome, is a minor basilica. The dates in the listings below indicate when the churches were designated as basilicas.

Minor Basilicas in U.S., Puerto Rico, Guam

Alabama: Mobile, Cathedral of the Immaculate Conception (Mar. 10, 1962).

Arizona: Phoenix, St. Mary's (Immaculate Conception) (Sept. 2, 1985).

California: San Francisco, Mission Dolores (Feb. 6, 1952); Carmel, Old Mission of San Carlos (Feb. 5, 1960); Alameda, St. Joseph (Jan. 21, 1972); San Diego, Mission San Diego de Alcala (Nov. 17, 1975); San Jose, St. Joseph (Jan. 28, 1997); San Juan Capistrano, Mission Basilica of San Juan Capistrano (Feb. 14, 2000).

Colorado: Denver, Cathedral of the Immaculate Conception (Nov. 3, 1979).

Connecticut: Waterbury, Basilica of the Immaculate Conception (Feb. 9, 2008); Stamford, Basilica of St. John the Evangelist (June 16, 2009).

District of Columbia: National Shrine of the Immaculate Conception (Oct. 12, 1990).

Florida: St. Augustine, Cathedral of St. Augustine (Dec. 4, 1976); Daytona Beach, Basilica of St. Paul (Jan. 25, 2006); Orlando, Basilica of the National Shrine of Mary, Queen of the Universe (June 3, 2009).

Illinois: Chicago, Our Lady of Sorrows (May 4, 1956); Queen of All Saints (Mar. 26, 1962); Basilica of St. Hyacinth (Nov. 30, 2003).

Indiana: Vincennes, Old Cathedral (Mar. 14, 1970); Notre Dame, Basilica of the Most Sacred Heart, Univ. of Notre Dame (Nov. 23, 1991).

Iowa: Dyersville, St. Francis Xavier (May 11, 1956); Des Moines, St. John the Apostle (Aug. 10,

1989).

Kentucky: Trappist, Our Lady of Gethsemani (Mar. 22, 1949); Covington, Cathedral of Assumption (Oct. 19, 1953); Bardstown, St. Joseph Proto-Cathedral Basilica (2001).

Louisiana: Alexandria, Basilica of the Immaculate Conception (Feb. 22, 2009); New Orleans, St. Louis King of France (Dec. 9, 1964).

Maine: Lewiston, Basilica of Sts. Peter and Paul (May 22, 2005).

Maryland: Baltimore, Assumption of the Blessed Virgin Mary (July 14, 1937; designated national shrine, 1993); Emmitsburg, Shrine of St. Elizabeth Ann Seton (Feb. 13, 1991).

Massachusetts: Boston, Perpetual Help ("Mission Church") (Sept. 8, 1954); Chicopee, St. Stanislaus (June 25, 1991); Webster, St. Joseph (Oct. 1998).

Michigan: Grand Rapids, St. Adalbert (Aug. 22, 1979).

Minnesota: Minneapolis. St. Mary (Jan. 18, 1926).

Mississippi: Natchez, St. Mary Basilica (Sept. 8, 1998).

Missouri: Conception, Basilica of Immaculate Conception (Aug. 8, 1940); St. Louis, St. Louis King of France (Jan. 27, 1961).

New Jersey: Newark, Cathedral Basilica of the Sacred Heart (Dec. 22, 1995).

New Mexico: Mesilla, Basilica of San Albino (June 2008); Santa Fe, Cathedral Basilica of St. Francis of Assisi (Oct. 4, 2005).

New York: Brooklyn, Our Lady of Perpetual Help (Sept. 5, 1969), Cathedral-Basilica of St. James (May 6, 1982); Buffalo, St. Adalbert's Basilica (Aug. 11, 1907); Lackawanna, Our Lady of Victory (July 14, 1926); Youngstown, Blessed Virgin Mary of the Rosary of Fatima (Oct. 7, 1975); Syracuse, Sacred Heart of Jesus (Aug. 27, 1998).

North Carolina: Asheville, St. Lawrence (Apr. 6, 1993; ceremonies, Sept. 5, 1993); Belmont, Our Lady Help of Christians (July 27, 1998).

North Dakota: Jamestown, St. James (Oct. 26, 1988).

Ohio: Carey, Shrine of Our Lady of Consolation (Oct. 21, 1971).

Pennsylvania: Latrobe, St. Vincent Basilica, Benedictine Archabbey (Aug. 22, 1955); Conewago, Basilica of the Sacred Heart (June 30, 1962); Philadelphia, Sts. Peter and Paul (Sept. 27, 1976); Danville, Sts. Cyril and Methodius (chapel at the motherhouse of the Sisters of Sts. Cyril and Methodius) (June 30, 1989); Loretto, St. Michael the Archangel (Sept. 9, 1996); Scranton, National Shrine of St. Ann (Oct. 18, 1997).

Texas: Galveston, St. Mary Cathedral (Aug. 2, 1979); San Antonio, Basilica of the National Shrine of the Little Flower (Sept. 27, 1931); Basilica of Our Lady of San Juan del Valle-National Shrine (May 2, 1954); Beaumont, Saint Anthony Cathedral Basilica (August 2006).

Virginia: Norfolk, St. Mary of the Immaculate Conception (July 9, 1991).

West Virginia: Wheeling, Basilica of the Co-Cathedral of the Sacred Heart (Nov. 9, 2009).

Wisconsin: Milwaukee, St. Josaphat (Mar. 10, 1929); Hubertus, Holy Hill National Shrine of Mary, Help of Christians (Nov. 19, 2006).

Puerto Rico: San Juan, Cathedral of San Juan

(Jan. 25, 1978).

Guam: Agana, Cathedral of Dulce Nombre de Maria (Sweet Name of Mary) (1985).

BASILICA OF THE NATIONAL SHRINE OF THE IMMACULATE CONCEPTION

The Basilica of the National Shrine of the Immaculate Conception is dedicated to the honor of the Blessed Virgin Mary, declared patroness of the United States under this title in 1846, eight years before the proclamation of the dogma of the Immaculate Conception. The church was designated a minor basilica by Pope John Paul II Oct. 12, 1990. The church is the eighth largest religious building in the world and the largest Catholic church in the Western Hemisphere, with numerous special chapels and with normal seating and standing accommodations for 6,000 people. Open daily, it is adjacent to The Catholic University of America, at Michigan Ave. and Fourth St. N.E., Washington, DC 20017; (202) 526-8300; www.nationalshrine.com. Rev. Msgr. Walter R. Rossi is the rector.

SHRINES AND PLACES OF HISTORIC INTEREST IN THE U.S.

(Principal source: Catholic Almanac *survey.)*

Listed below, according to state, are shrines, other centers of devotion and some places of historic interest with special significance for Catholics. The list is necessarily incomplete because of space limitations.

Information includes, where possible: name and location of shrine or place of interest, date of foundation, sponsoring agency or group, and address for more information.

Alabama: Our Lady of the Angels, Hanceville; Birmingham Diocese. Address: Our Lady of the Angels Monastery, 3222 County Road 548, Hanceville, 35077; (256) 352-6267.

• St. Jude Church of the City of St. Jude, Montgomery (1934; dedicated, 1938); Mobile Archdiocese. Address: 2048 W. Fairview Ave., Montgomery, 36108; (334) 265-1390.

• Shrine of the Most Blessed Trinity, Holy Trinity (1924); Missionary Servants of the Most Blessed Trinity. Address: Holy Trinity, 36859.

Arizona: Chapel of the Holy Cross, Sedona (1956); Phoenix Diocese: P.O. Box 1043, W. Sedona 86339.

• Mission San Xavier del Bac, near Tucson (1692); National Historic Landmark; Franciscan Friars and Tucson Diocese; Address: 1950 W. San Xavier Rd., Tucson, 85746-7409; (520) 294-2624.

• Shrine of St. Joseph of the Mountains, Yarnell (1939); erected by Catholic Action League; currently maintained by Board of Directors. Address: P.O. Box 267, Yarnell, 85362.

California: Mission San Diego de Alcala (July 16, 1769); first of the 21 Franciscan missions of Upper California; Minor Basilica; National Historic Landmark; San Diego Diocese. Address: 10818 San Diego Mission Rd., San Diego, 92108; (619) 283-7319.

• Carmel Mission Basilica (Mission San Carlos Borromeo del Rio Carmelo), Carmel by the Sea (June 3, 1770); Monterey Diocese. Address: 3080 Rio Rd., Carmel, 93923; (831) 624-1271.

• Old Mission San Luis Obispo de Tolosa, San

Luis Obispo (Sept. 1, 1772); Monterey Diocese (Parish Church). Address: Old Mission Church, 751 Palm St., San Luis Obispo, 93401.

• San Gabriel Mission, San Gabriel (Sept. 8, 1771); Los Angeles Archdiocese (Parish Church, staffed by Claretians). Address: 537 W. Mission, San Gabriel, 91776.

• Mission San Francisco de Asis (Oct. 9, 1776) and Mission Dolores Basilica (1860s); San Francisco Archdiocese. Address: 3321 Sixteenth St., San Francisco, 94114.

• Old Mission San Juan Capistrano, San Juan Capistrano (Nov. 1, 1776); Orange Diocese. Address: P.O. Box 697, San Juan Capistrano, 92693; (949) 248-2026; www.missionsjc.com.

• Old Mission Santa Barbara, Santa Barbara (Dec. 4, 1786); National Historic Landmark; Parish Church, staffed by Franciscan Friars. Address: 2201 Laguna St., Santa Barbara, 93105; (805) 682-4713.

• Old Mission San Juan Bautista, San Juan Bautista (June 24, 1797); National Historic Landmark; Monterey Diocese (Parish Church). Address: P.O. Box 400, San Juan Bautista, 95045.

• Mission San Miguel, San Miguel (July 25, 1797); Parish Church, Monterey diocese; Franciscan Friars. Address: P.O. Box 69, San Miguel, 93451; (805) 467-3256.

• Old Mission Santa Inés, Solvang (1804); Historic Landmark; Los Angeles Archdiocese (Parish Church, staffed by Capuchin Franciscan Friars). Address: P.O. Box 408, Solvang, 93464; (805) 688-4815; www.missionsantaines.org.

Franciscan Friars founded 21 missions in California. (See Index: **Franciscan Missions**.)

• Shrine of Our Lady of Sorrows, Sycamore (1883); Sacramento Diocese. Address: c/o Our Lady of Lourdes Church, 745 Ware Ave., Colusa, 95932.

Colorado: Mother Cabrini Shrine, Golden; Missionary Sisters of the Sacred Heart. Address: 20189 Cabrini Blvd., Golden, 80401.

Connecticut: Shrine of Our Lady of Lourdes, Litchfield (1958); Montfort Missionaries. Address: P.O. Box 667, Litchfield, 06759.

• Shrine of the Infant of Prague, New Haven (1945); Dominican Friars. Address: P.O. Box 1202, 5 Hillhouse Ave., New Haven, 06505.

District of Columbia: Mount St. Sepulchre, Franciscan Monastery of the Holy Land (1897; church dedicated, 1899); Order of Friars Minor. Address: 1400 Quincy St. N.E., Washington, DC 20017.

• Basilica of the National Shrine of the Immaculate Conception. See Index for separate entry.

Florida: Mary, Queen of the Universe Shrine, Orlando (1986, temporary facilities; new shrine dedicated, 1993); Orlando diocese. Address: 8300 Vineland Ave., Orlando, 32821; (407) 239-6600; www.maryqueenoftheuniverse.org.

• Our Lady of La Leche Shrine (Patroness of Mothers and Mothers-to-be) and Mission of Nombre de Dios, Saint Augustine (1565); Angelus Crusade Headquarters; St. Augustine Diocese. Address: 30 Ocean Ave., St. Augustine 32084.

Illinois: Holy Family Log Church, Cahokia (1799; original log church erected 1699); Belleville Diocese (Parish Church). Address: 116 Church St., Cahokia, 62206; (618) 337-4548.

• Marytown/Shrine of St. Maximilian Kolbe

and Retreat Center, Libertyville; Our Lady of the Blessed Sacrament Sanctuary of Perpetual Eucharistic Adoration (1930) and Archdiocesan Shrine to St. Maximilian Kolbe (1989), conducted by Conventual Franciscan Friars, 1600 West Park Ave., Libertyville, 60048; (847) 367-7800.

• National Shrine of Our Lady of the Snows, Belleville (1958); Missionary Oblates of Mary Immaculate. Address: 442 S. De Mazenod Dr., Belleville, 62223.

• National Shrine of St. Jude, Chicago (1929); located in Our Lady of Guadalupe Church, founded and staffed by Claretians. Address: 3200 E. 91st St., Chicago, 60617; (312) 236-7782.

• National Shrine of St. Therese and Museum, Darien (1930), at St. Clara's Church, Chicago; new shrine, 1987, after original destroyed by fire); Carmelites of Most Pure Heart of Mary Province. Address: Carmelite Visitor Center, 8501 Bailey Rd., Darien, 60561; (630) 969-3311; www.saint-therese.org.

• Shrine of St. Jude Thaddeus, Chicago (1929) located in St. Pius V Church; staffed by Dominicans, Central Province. Address: 1909 S. Ashland Ave., Chicago, 60608; (312) 226-0020; www.op.org/dom-central/places/stjude.

Indiana: Our Lady of Monte Cassino Shrine, St. Meinrad (1870); Benedictines. Address: Saint Meinrad Archabbey, Highway 62, St. Meinrad, 47577; (812) 357-6585; www.saintmeinrad.edu/abbey/shrine.

• Old Cathedral (Basilica of St. Francis Xavier), Vincennes (1826, parish records go back to 1749); Evansville Diocese. Minor Basilica, 1970. Address: 205 Church St., Vincennes, 47591; (812) 882-5638.

Iowa: Grotto of the Redemption, West Bend (1912); Sioux City Diocese. Life of Christ in stone. Mailing address: P.O. Box 376, West Bend, 50597; (515) 887-2371; www.aw-cybermail.com/grotto.htm.

Louisiana: National Votive Shrine of Our Lady of Prompt Succor, New Orleans (1810); located in the Chapel of the Ursuline Convent (a National Historic Landmark). Address: 2635 State St., New Orleans, 70118.

• Shrine of St. Ann. Mailing address: 4920 Loveland St., Metaire, 70006; (504) 455-7071.

• Shrine of St. Roch, New Orleans (1876); located in St. Roch's Campo Santo (Cemetery); New Orleans Archdiocese. Address: 1725 St. Roch Ave., New Orleans, 70117.

Maryland: Basilica of the National Shrine of the Assumption of the Blessed Virgin Mary, Baltimore (1806). Mother Church of Roman Catholicism in the U.S. and the first metropolitan cathedral. Designed by Benjamin Henry Latrobe (architect of the Capitol) it is considered one of the finest examples of neoclassical architecture in the world. The church hosted many of the events and personalities central to the growth of Roman Catholicism in the U.S. Address: Cathedral and Mulberry Sts., Baltimore, MD 21201.

• National Shrine Grotto of Our Lady of Lourdes, Emmitsburg (1809, Grotto of Our Lady; 1875, National Shrine Grotto of Lourdes); public oratory, Archdiocese of Baltimore. Address: Mount St. Mary's College and Seminary, Emmitsburg, 21727; (301) 447-5318; www.msmary.edu/grotto/.

• National Shrine of St. Elizabeth Ann Seton, Emmitsburg. Foundation of Sisters of Charity (1809); first parochial school in America (1810);

dedicated as Minor Basilica (1991). Address: 333 South Seton Ave., Emmitsburg, 21727; (301) 447-6606; www.setonshrine.org.

• St. Francis Xavier Shrine, "Old Bohemia," near Warwick (1704); located in Wilmington Diocese; restoration under aupices of Old Bohemia Historical Society, Inc. Address: P.O. Box 61, Warwick, 21912.

• St. Jude Shrine (1873), Archdiocese of Baltimore. Address: 308 N. Paca St., P.O. Box 1455, Baltimore, 21203.

Massachusetts: National Shrine of Our Lady of La Salette, Ipswich (1945); Missionaries of Our Lady of La Salette. Address: 251 Topsfield Rd., Ipswich, 01938.

• Our Lady of Fatima Shrine, Holliston (1950); Xaverian Missionaries. Address: 101 Summer St., Holliston, 01746; (508) 429-2144.

• St. Anthony Shrine, Boston (1947); downtown Service Church with shrine; Boston Archdiocese and Franciscans of Holy Name Province. Address: 100 Arch St., Boston, 02107.

• St. Clement's Eucharistic Shrine, Boston (1945); Boston Archdiocese, staffed by Oblates of the Virgin Mary. Address: 1105 Boylston St., Boston, 02215.

• National Shrine of The Divine Mercy, Stockbridge (1960); Congregation of Marians. Address: National Shrine of The Divine Mercy, Eden Hill, Stockbridge, 01262.

Michigan: Cross in the Woods-Parish, Indian River (1947); Gaylord diocese; staffed by Franciscan Friars of Sacred Heart Province, St. Louis. Address: 7078 M-68, Indian River, 49749; (231) 238-8973; www.rc.net/gaylord/crossinwoods.

• Shrine of the Little Flower, Royal Oak (c. 1929, by Father Coughlin); Detroit archdiocese. Address: 2123 Roseland, Royal Oak, 48073.

Minnesota: National Shrine of St. Odilia; St. Cloud Diocese. Address: P.O. Box 500, Onamia, 56359.

Missouri: Memorial Shrine of St. Rose Philippine Duchesne, St. Charles; Religious of the Sacred Heart of Jesus. Address: 619 N. Second St., St. Charles, 63301; (314) 946-6127.

• National Shrine of Our Lady of the Miraculous Medal, Perryville; located in St. Mary of the Barrens Church (1837); Vincentians. Address: 1811 W. St. Joseph St., Perryville, 63775; (573) 547-8343; www.amm.org.

• Old St. Ferdinand's Shrine, Florissant (1819, Sacred Heart Convent; 1821, St. Ferdinand's Church); Friends of Old St. Ferdinand's, Inc. Address: No. 1 Rue St. Francois, Florissant, 63031.

• Shrine of Our Lady of Sorrows, Starkenburg (1888; shrine building, 1910); Jefferson City Diocese. Address: c/o Church of the Risen Savior, 605 Bluff St., Rhineland, 65069; (573) 236-4390.

Nebraska: The Eucharistic Shrine of Christ the King (1973); Lincoln Diocese and Holy Spirit Adoration Sisters. Address: 1040 South Cotner Blvd., Lincoln, 68510; (402) 489-0765.

New Hampshire: Shrine of Our Lady of Grace, Colebrook (1948); Missionary Oblates of Mary Immaculate. Address: R.R. 1, Box 521, Colebrook, 03576-9535; (603) 237-5511.

• Shrine of Our Lady of La Salette, Enfield (1951); Missionaries of Our Lady of La Salette. Address: Rt. 4A, P.O. Box 420, Enfield, 03748.

New Jersey: Blue Army Shrine of the Immaculate Heart of Mary (1978); National Center of the Blue Army of Our Lady of Fatima, USA, Inc. Address: Mountain View Rd. (P.O. Box 976), Washington, 07882-0976; (908) 689-1701; www.bluearmy.com

• Shrine of St. Joseph, Stirling (1924); Missionary Servants of the Most Holy Trinity. Address: 1050 Long Hill Rd., Stirling, 07980; (908) 647-0208; www.STShrine.org.

New Mexico: St. Augustine Mission, Isleta (1613); Santa Fe Archdiocese. Address: P.O. Box 463, Isleta, Pueblo, 87022.

• Santuario de Nuestro Senor de Esquipulas, Chimayo (1816); Santa Fe archdiocese, Sons of the Holy Family; National Historic Landmark, 1970. Address: Santuario de Chimayo, P.O. Box 235; Chimayo, 87522.

• Shrine of St. Bernadette (2003); Santa Fe archdiocese, St. Bernadette parish. Address: 1800 Martha St., N.E., Albuquerque, NM 87112-3161; (505) 298-7557; www.shrineofstbernadette.com.

New York: National Shrine of Bl. Kateri Tekakwitha, Fonda (1938); Order of Friars Minor Conventual. Address: P.O. Box 627, Fonda, 12068.

• Marian Shrine (National Shrine of Mary Help of Christians), West Haverstraw (1953); Salesians of St. John Bosco. Address: 174 Filors Lane, Stony Point, NY 10980-2645; (845) 947-2200; www.MarianShrine.org.

• National Shrine Basilica of Our Lady of Fatima, Youngstown (1954); designated a national shrine in 1994; Barnabite Fathers. Address: 1023 Swann Rd., Youngstown, 14174; (716) 754-7489.

• Original Shrine of St. Ann in New York City (1892); located in St. Jean Baptiste Church; Blessed Sacrament Fathers. Address: 184 E. 76th St., NY 10021; (212) 288-5082.

• Our Lady of Victory National Shrine, Lackawanna (1926); Minor Basilica. Address: 767 Ridge Rd., Lackawanna, 14218.

• Shrine Church of Our Lady of Mt. Carmel, Brooklyn (1887); Brooklyn Diocese (Parish Church). Address: 275 N. 8th St., Brooklyn, 11211; (718) 384-0223.

• Shrine of Our Lady of Martyrs, Auriesville (1885); Society of Jesus. Address: Auriesville, 12016; (518) 853-3033; www.klink.net/~jesuit.

• Shrine of Our Lady of the Island, Eastport (1975); Montfort Missionaries. Address: Box 26, Eastport, 11941; (516) 325-0661.

• Shrine of St. Elizabeth Ann Seton, New York City (1975); located in Our Lady of the Rosary Church. Address: 7 State St., NY 10004.

• Shrine of St. Frances Xavier Cabrini, New York (1938; new shrine dedicated 1960); Missionary Sisters of the Sacred Heart. Address: 701 Fort Washington Ave., 10040; (212) 923-3536; www.cabrinishrineny.org

Ohio: Basilica and National Shrine of Our Lady of Consolation, Carey (1867); Minor Basilica; Toledo Diocese; staffed by Conventual Franciscan Friars. Address: 315 Clay St., Carey, 43316; (419) 396-7107.

• National Shrine of Our Lady of Lebanon, North Jackson (1965); Eparchy of Our Lady of Lebanon of Los Angeles. Address: 2759 N. Lipkey Rd., N. Jackson, 44451; (330) 538-3351; www.

nationalshrine.org.
• National Shrine and Grotto of Our Lady of Lourdes, Euclid (1926); Sisters of the Most Holy Trinity. Address: 21281 Chardon Rd., Euclid, 44117-2112; (216) 481-8232.
• National Shrine of St. Dymphna, Massillon (1938), Youngstown diocese. Address: 3000 Erie St. S., Massillon, 44648-0004.
• Our Lady of Czestochowa Shrine, Garfield Heights (1939); Sisters of St. Joseph, Third Order of St. Francis. Address: 12215 Granger Rd., Garfield Hts., 44125; (216) 581-3535.
• Our Lady of Fatima, Ironton (1954); Address: Old Rt. 52, Haverhill, OH. Mailing address: St. Joseph Church, P.O. Box 499, Ironton, 45638-0499; (740) 429-2144.
• St. Anthony Shrine, Cincinnati (1888); Franciscan Friars, St. John Baptist Province. Address: 5000 Colerain Ave., Cincinnati, 45223.
• Shrine and Oratory of the Weeping Madonna of Mariapoch, Burton (1956); Social Mission Sisters. Parma Diocese (Byzantine). Address: 17486 Mumford Rd., Burton, 44021.
• Shrine of the Holy Relics (1892); Sisters of the Precious Blood. Address: 2291 St. Johns Rd., Maria Stein, 45860; (419) 925-4532.
• Sorrowful Mother Shrine, Bellevue (1850); Society of the Precious Blood. Address: 4106 State Rt. 269, Bellevue, 44811; (419) 483-3435.
Oklahoma: National Shrine of the Infant Jesus of Prague, Prague (1949); Oklahoma City Archdiocese. Address: P.O. Box 488, Prague ,74864.
Oregon: The Grotto (National Sanctuary of Our Sorrowful Mother), Portland (1924); Servite Friars. Address: P.O. Box 20008, Portland, 97294; www.thegrotto.com.
Pennsylvania: Basilica of the Sacred Heart of Jesus, Conewago Township (1741; present church, 1787); Minor Basilica; Harrisburg Diocese. Address: 30 Basilica Dr., Hanover, 17331.
• National Shrine Center of Our Lady of Guadalupe, Allentown (1974); located in Immaculate Conception Church; Allentown Diocese. Address: 501 Ridge Ave., Allentown, 18102; (610) 433-4404.
• National Shrine of Our Lady of Czestochowa (1955); Order of St. Paul the Hermit (Pauline Fathers). Address: P.O. Box 2049, Doylestown, 18901.
• National Shrine of St. John Neumann, Philadelphia (1860); Redemptorist Fathers, St. Peter's Church. Address: 1019 N. 5th St., Philadelphia, 19123.
• National Shrine of the Sacred Heart, Harleigh (1975); Scranton Diocese. Address: P.O. Box 500, Harleigh (Hazleton), 18225; (570) 455-1162.
• Old St. Joseph's National Shrine, Philadelphia (1733); Philadelphia Archdiocese (Parish Church). Address: 321 Willings Alley, Philadelphia, 19106; (215) 923-1733; www.oldstjoseph.org.
• St. Ann's Basilica Shrine, Scranton (1902);

Passionist Community. Designated a minor basilica Aug. 29, 1996. Address: 1230 St. Ann's St., Scranton, 18504; (570) 347-5691.
• St. Anthony's Chapel, Pittsburgh (1883); Pittsburgh Diocese. Address: 1700 Harpster St., Pittsburgh, 15212.
• Shrine of St. Walburga, Greensburg (1974); Sisters of St. Benedict. Address: 1001 Harvey Ave., Greensburg, 15601; (724) 834-3060.
South Dakota: Fatima Family Shrine, Alexandria; St. Cloud Diocese. Address: St. Mary of Mercy Church, Box 158, Alexandria, 57311.
Texas: Mission Espiritu Santo de Zuniga, Goliad (1749). Victoria Diocese.
• Mission Nuestra Senora de la Purisma Concepcion, San Antonio. San Antonio Archdiocese. Address: 807 Mission Rd., 78210.
• Mission San Francisco de la Espada, San Antonio (1731); San Antonio Archdiocese. Address: 10040 Espada Rd., 78214; (210) 627-2064.
• Mission San Jose y San Miguel de Aguayo, San Antonio (1720); San Antonio Archdiocese. Address: 701 E. Pyron Ave., 78214; (210) 922-0543.
• Mission San Juan Capistrano, San Antonio (1731); San Antonio Archdiocese. Address: 9101 Graf Rd., 78214.
• National Shrine of Our Lady of San Juan Del Valle, San Juan (1949); Brownsville Diocese; staffed by Oblates of Mary Immaculate. Address: P.O. Box 747, San Juan, 78589; (956) 787-0033.
• Nuestra Senora de la Concepcion del Socorro, Socorro, El Paso (1692).
• Oblate Lourdes Grotto Shrine of the Southwest, Tepeyac de San Antonio, San Antonio Archdiocese. Address: P.O. Box 96, San Antonio, 78291-0096; (210) 342-9864; www.oblatemissions.org.
• Old Mission San Francisco de los Tejas, Weches (1690); San Antonio Archdiocese.
• Presidio La Bahia, Goliad (1749); Victoria Diocese. Address: P.O. Box 57, Goliad, 77963; (361) 645-3752.
• San Elizario Presidio Chapel, El Paso (1789); El Paso Diocese. Address: El Paso Co., San Elceario, P.O. Box 398, 79855.
• Ysleta Mission (Nuestra Senora del Carmen), Ysleta, El Paso (1744). El Paso Diocese.
Vermont: St. Anne's Shrine, Isle La Motte (1666); Burlington Diocese, conducted by Edmundites. Address: West Shore Rd., Isle La Motte, 05463; (802) 928-3362.
Wisconsin: Holy Hill — National Shrine of Mary, Help of Christians (1857); Discalced Carmelite Friars. Address: 1525 Carmel Rd., Hubertus, 53033.
• National Shrine of St. Joseph, De Pere (1889); Norbertine Fathers. Address: 1016 N. Broadway, De Pere, 54115.
• Shrine of Mary, Mother Thrice Admirable Queen and Victress of Schoenstatt (1965), Address: W284 N698 Cherry Lane, Waukesha, 53188-9402; (414) 547-7733.

Biographies of American Bishops

(*Sources:* Catholic Almanac *survey,* The Official Catholic Directory, Annuario Pontificio, *Catholic News Service. As of Aug. 20, 2014. For notable former bishops of the U.S., see* **American Catholics of the Past** *at www. CatholicAlmanac.com.*)

Information includes: date and place of birth; educational institutions attended; date of ordination to the priesthood with, where applicable, name of archdiocese (*) or diocese in parentheses; date of episcopal ordination; episcopal appointments; date of resignation/retirement.

A

Adamec, Joseph V.: b. Aug. 13, 1935, Bannister, MI; educ. Michigan State Univ. (East Lansing), Nepomucene College and Lateran Univ. (Rome); ord. priest (for Nitra diocese, Slovakia), July 3, 1960; served in Saginaw diocese; ord. bp. of Altoona-Johnstown, May 20, 1987; ret. Jan. 14, 2011.

Adams, Edward J.: b. Aug. 24, 1944, Philadelphia, PA; educ. St. Charles Borromeo Seminary (Philadelphia), Pontifical Ecclesiastical Academy (Rome); ord. priest (Philadelphia*), May 16, 1970; in Vatican diplomatic service from 1976; ord. titular abp. of Scala, Oct. 23, 1996; app. papal nuncio to Greece, Feb. 22, 2011.

Allué, Emilio S., S.D.B.: b. Feb. 18, 1935, Huesca, Spain; educ. Salesain schools (Huesca, Spain) Don Bosco College/Seminary (Newton, NJ); Salesian Pontifical Univ. (Rome), Fordham Univ. (New York); ord. priest Dec. 22, 1966, in Rome; ord. titular bp. of Croe and aux. bp. of Boston, Sept. 17, 1996; ret. June 30, 2010.

Amos, Martin J.: b. Dec. 8, 1941, Cleveland; educ. St. Mary Seminary Cleveland; ord. priest (Cleveland), May 25, 1968; app. aux. bp. of Cleveland April 3, 2001, ord., June 7, 2001, app. bp. of Davenport Oct. 12, 2006.

Anderson, Moses B., S.S.E.: b. Sept. 9, 1928, Selma, AL; educ. St. Michael's College (Winooski, VT), St. Edmund Seminary (Burlington, VT), Univ. of Legon (Ghana); ord. priest, May 30, 1958; ord. titular bp. of Vatarba and aux. bp. of Detroit, Jan. 27, 1983; ret. Oct. 24, 2003.

Angadiath, Jacob: b. Oct. 26, 1945, Periappuram, Kerala, India; educ. St. Thomas Apostolic Seminary, Vadavathoor, Kottayam, India, Univ. of Kerala, India, Univ. of Dallas (U.S.); ord. priest (Palai, Kerala) Jan. 5, 1972; Director, Syro-Malabar Catholic Mission, Archdiocese of Chicago, 1999-2001; app. bp. of Eparchy of St. Thomas of Chicago of the Syro-Malabarians and Permanent Apostolic Visitator in Canada, Mar. 13, 2001; inst., July 1, 2001.

Angell, Kenneth A.: b. Aug. 3, 1930, Providence, RI; educ. St. Mary's Seminary (Baltimore, MD); ord. priest (Providence) May 26, 1956; ord. titular bp. of Septimunicia and aux. bp. of Providence, RI, Oct. 7, 1974; bp. of Burlington, Oct. 6, 1992; inst., Nov. 9, 1992; ret. Nov. 9, 2005.

Apuron, Anthony Sablan, O.F.M. Cap.: b. Nov. 1, 1945, Agana, Guam; educ. St. Anthony College and Capuchin Seminary (Hudson, NH), Capuchin Seminary (Garrison, NY), Maryknoll Seminary (New York), Univ. of Notre Dame (Notre Dame, IN); ord. priest, Aug. 26, 1972, in Guam; ord. titular bp. of Muzuca in Proconsulari and aux. bp. of Agana, Guam (unicorporated U.S. territory), Feb. 19, 1984; abp. of Agana, Mar. 10, 1986.

Aquila, Samuel J.: b. Sept. 24, 1950, Burbank, CA; educ. St. Thomas Seminary, Denver, San Anselmo (Rome); ord. priest (Denver*), June 5, 1976; rector, St. John Vianney Seminary (Denver), 1999-2001; app. coadjutor bp. of Fargo, June 12, 2001; ord., Aug. 24, 2001; bp. of Fargo, Mar. 19, 2002; app. abp. of Denver, May 29, 2012; inst. July 18, 2012.

Arias, David, O.A.R.: b. July 22, 1929, Leon, Spain; educ. St. Rita's College (San Sebastian, Spain), Our Lady of Good Counsel Theologate (Granada, Spain), Teresianum Institute (Rome, Italy); ord. priest, May 31, 1952; ord. titular bp. of Badie and aux. bp. of Newark, Apr. 7, 1983; episcopal vicar for Hispanic affairs; ret. May 21, 2004.

Aymond, Gregory M.: b. Nov. 12, 1949, New Orleans, LA; educ. St. Joseph Seminary College, Notre Dame Seminary (New Orleans, LA); ord. priest (New Orleans*), May 10, 1975; ord. titular bp. of Acolla and aux. bp. of New Orleans, Jan. 10, 1997; co-adjutor bp. of Austin, June 2, 2000, ins., Aug. 3, 2000; bp. of Austin, Jan. 2, 2001; app. abp. of New Orleans, June 12, 2009; inst. Aug. 20, 2009.

Azarcon Solis, Oscar: b. Oct. 13, 1953, San Jose, Philippines; educ: Divine Word Seminary, Tagaytay City, Univ. of St. Thomas Seminary, Manila; ord. Apr. 28, 1979 (Cabanatuan, Philippines); incard. Houma-Thibodaux 1992; app. tit. bp. of Urci and aux. bp. of Los Angeles, Dec. 1, 2003; ord. Feb. 10, 2004.

B

Baker, Robert J.: b. June 4, 1944, Fostoria, OH; educ. Pontifical College Josephinum, Columbus, OH, Gregorian Univ., Rome; ord. (St. Augustine), Mar. 21, 1970; app. bp of Charleston, July 13, 1999; ord., Sept. 29, 1999; app. bp. of Birmingham; inst. Oct. 23, 2007.

Baldacchino, Peter: b. Dec. 5, 1960, Sliema, Malta; educ. Seton Hall Univ.; ord. priest (Newark*), May 25, 1996.; app. titular bp. of Vatarba and aux. bp. of Miami, Feb. 20, 2014; ord. bp., Mar. 19, 2014.

Balke, Victor H.: b. Sept. 29, 1931, Meppen, IL; educ. St. Mary of the Lake Seminary (Mundelein, IL), St. Louis Univ. (St. Louis, MO); ord. priest (Springfield, IL), May 24, 1958; ord. bp. of Crookston, Sept. 2, 1976; ret. Sept. 28, 2007.

Baltakis, Paul Antanas, O.F.M.: b. Jan. 1, 1925, Troskunai, Lithuania; educ. seminaries of the Franciscan Province of St. Joseph (Belgium); ord. priest, Aug. 24, 1952, in Belgium; served in U.S. as director of Lithuanian Cultural Center, New York, and among Lithuanian youth; head of U.S. Lithuanian Franciscan Vicariate, Kennebunkport, ME, from 1979; ord. titular bp. of Egara, Sept. 24, 1984; assigned to pastoral assistance to Lithuanian Catholics living outside Lithuania (resides in Brooklyn).

Balvo, Charles Daniel: b. June 29, 1951, Brooklyn, NY; educ. North American College and Pontifical Gregorian

Univ. (Rome) and Catholic Univ. of America (Washington, DC); ord. priest (New York*), June 6, 1976; studied at the Pontifical Ecclesiastical Academy and entered the diplomatic service of the Holy See; served in nunciatures in Africa, South America, and Eastern Europe; ord. titular abp. of Castello, June 29, 2005 and appointed apostolic nuncio to New Zealand, Cook Islands, Fiji, Marshall Islands, Kiribati, Fed. States Micronesia, Nauru, Western Samoa, Tonga, Palau and Vanuatu, and Apostolic Delegate to the Pacific Ocean, Apr. 1, 2005; app. nuncio to Kenya, Jan. 17, 2013.

Bambera, Joseph C.: b. Mar. 21, 1956, Carbondale, PA; educ., Univ. of Pittsburgh (Pittsburgh, PA); St. Pius X Seminary (Dalton, PA), Mary Immaculate Seminary (Northhampton, PA), St. Paul Univ. (Ottawa) ord. priest, Nov. 5, 1983 (Scranton); app. bp. of Scranton, Feb. 23, 2010; ord. bp., Apr. 26, 2010.

Banach, Michael W.: b. Nov. 19, 1962, Worcester, Mass.; educ. College of the Holy Cross (Mass.), Pontifical North American College and Pontifical Gregorian Univ. (Rome); ord. priest July 2, 1988 (Worcester, Mass.); entered papal diplomatic corps and served in numerous nunciatures and as the Holy See permanent representative to the International Atomic Energy Agency (AIEA), to the Organization for Security and Cooperation in Europe (OSCE), and to the Preparatory Commission for the Comprehensive Nuclear-Test-Ban Treaty Organization (CTBTO) and Holy See permanent observer to the United Nations Organization for Industrial Development (ONUDI) and to the Office of the United Nations in Vienna, Austria; app. apostolic nuncio and titular abp. of Memphis, Feb. 22, 2013.

Banks, Robert J.: b. Feb. 26, 1928, Winthrop, MA; educ. St. John's Seminary (Brighton, MA), Gregorian Univ., Lateran Univ. (Rome); ord. priest (Boston*), Dec. 20, 1952, in Rome; rector of St. John's Seminary, Brighton, MA, 1971 81; vicar general of Boston, 1984; ord. titular bp. of Taraqua and aux. bp. of Boston, Sept. 19, 1985; bp. of Green Bay, Oct. 16, 1990, inst., Dec. 5, 1990; ret. Oct. 10, 2003.

Barbarito, Gerald M.: b. Jan. 4, 1950, Brooklyn, NY; educ. Cathedral College (Douglaston, NY), Immaculate Conception Seminary (Huntington, NY), Catholic Univ. (Washington, DC); ord. priest (Brooklyn), Jan. 31, 1976; ord. titular bp. of Gisipa and aux. bp. of Brooklyn, Aug. 22, 1994; bp. of Ogdensburg, Oct. 27, 1999; inst., Jan. 7, 2000; app. bp. of Palm Beach, July 1, 2003.

Barber, S.J., Michael C.: b. July 13, 1954, Salt Lake City, UT; educ. Loyola Marymount Univ., Gonzaga Univ. (Spokane, WA), Regis College at the Univ. of Toronto, Pontifical Gregorian Univ. (Rome); ord. priest for the Society of Jesus, June 8, 1985; held posts in Western Samoa, the Gregorian, the Univ. of Oxford, England, St. Patrick's Seminary in Menlo Park, CA, and St. John's Seminary, Brighton, MA; app. bp. of Oakland, May 3, 2013; ord. bp., May 25, 2013.

Barnes, Gerald R.: b. June 22, 1945, Phoenix, AZ, of Mexican descent; educ. St. Leonard Seminary (Dayton, OH), Assumption St. John's Seminary (San Antonio, TX); ord. priest (San Antonio*), Dec. 20, 1975; ord. titular bp. of Montefiascone and aux. bp. of San Bernardino, Mar. 18, 1992; bp. of San Bernardino, Dec. 28, 1995.

Barres, John O.: b. Sept. 20, 1960, Port Chester, NY; educ. Princeton Univ. (Princeton, NJ), New York Univ. Graduate School of Business (New York, NY), Catholic Univ. of America (Washington, D.C.), Pontifical Univ. della Santa Croce (Rome); ord priest, Oct. 21, 1989 (Wilmington); app. bp. of Allentown, May 27, 2009; ord. bp. July 30, 2009.

Bartchak, Mark L.: b. Jan. 1, 1955, Cleveland, OH; educ.

St. Mark Seminary and Gannon Univ. (Erie, PA), Christ the King Seminary (East Aurora, NY), The Catholic Univ. of America (Washington, D.C.); ord. priest (Erie), May 15, 1981; app. consultant for the USCCB Committee on Canonical Affairs and Church Governance, 2007; judge for the Congregation for the Doctrine of the Faith; visiting judge in various diocesan tribunals; lecturer on canon law at Catholic Univ. of America, The Catholic Univ. of Lublin, Poland, and St. Paul Univ., Ottawa, Canada; pres. of the Canon Law Society of America; app. bp. of Altoona-Johnstown, Jan. 14, 2011; ord. Apr. 19, 2011.

Batakian, Manuel: b. Nov. 5, 1929, Greece; moved with his family to Lebanon during World War II; educ. philosophy and theology studies in Rome; ord. priest (as a member of the Institute of the Clergy of Bzommar, an Armenian patriarchal religious order), Dec. 8, 1954; patriarchal vicar of the Institute and superior of its motherhouse in Bzommar, 1978-84; pastor of the Armenian Catholic Cathedral, Paris, 1984-90; rector of the Armenian Pontifical College, Rome, 1990-94; elected auxiliary of the patriarchate, Dec. 8, 1994, ordained bp., Mar. 12, 1995; trans. Our Lady of Nareg in New York Sept. 12, 2005; ret. May 21, 2011.

Baum, William W.: (See **Cardinals, Biographies.**)

Beltran, Eusebius J.: b. Aug. 31, 1934, Ashley, PA; educ. St. Charles Seminary (Philadelphia, PA); ord. priest (Atlanta*), May 14, 1960; ord. bp. of Tulsa, Apr. 20, 1978; app. abp. of Oklahoma City, Nov. 24, 1992; inst., Jan 22, 1993; ret. Dec. 16, 2010.

Bennett, Gordon D., S.J.: b. Oct. 21, 1946, Denver; educ. Mount St. Michael's (Spokane, WA), Jesuit School of Theology (Berkeley, CA), Fordham Univ. (NY); entered Society of Jesus, 1966; ord priest, June 14, 1975; app. titular bp. of Nesqually and aux. bp. of Baltimore, Dec. 23, 1997, ord. Mar. 3, 1998; app. bp. of Mandeville (Jamaica), July 6, 2004; ret. Aug. 6, 2006.

Berg, Stephen J.: b. Mar. 3, 1951, Miles City, MT; educ. University of Colorado, Boulder, Eastern New Mexico Univ., Assumption Seminary, San Antonio, TX; ord. priest (Fort Worth), May 15, 1999; app. bp. of Pueblo, Jan. 15, 2014; ord. bp., Feb. 27, 2014.

Bevard, Herbert A.: b. Feb. 24, 1946, Baltimore; educ. St. Charles Borromeo Seminary (Wynnewood, PA), Dickinson College (Carlisle, PA); ord. pr. May 20, 1972 (Philadelphia); app. bp. of St. Thomas, July 7, 2008; ord. bp. Sept. 3, 2008.

Binzer, Joseph R.: b. Apr. 26, 1955, Cincinnati, OH; educ. Miami Univ. (Ohio), Mount St. Mary's Seminary of the West (Cincinnati), Athenaeum of Ohio, The Catholic Univ. of America (Washington, D.C.); ord priest (Cincinnati*), June 4, 1994; app. titular bp. Subbur and aux. bp. of Cincinnati, Apr. 6, 2011; ord. bp., June 9, 2011.

Blair, Leonard P.: b. Apr. 12, 1949, Detroit; educ. Sacred Heart Seminary, Detroit, MI; Pontifical North American College, Gregorian Univ., and the Angelicum, Rome; ord. priest (Detroit*), June 26, 1976; at Vatican Secretariat of State, 1986-1991; Secretary to the President of the Prefecture for the Economic Affairs of the Holy See, 1994-1997; app. aux. of Detroit, July 9, 1999, ord., Aug. 24, 1999; app. bp. of Toledo, Oct. 7, 2003; app. abp. of Hartford, Oct. 29, 2013.

Blaire, Stephen E.: b. Dec. 22, 1941, Los Angeles, CA; educ. St. John's Seminary (Camarillo, CA); ord. priest (Los Angeles*), Apr. 29, 1967; ord. titular bp. of Lamzella and aux. of Los Angeles, May 31, 1990; app. bp. of Stockton, Jan. 19, 1999, inst., Mar. 16, 1999.

Blume, Michael A., S.V.D.: b. May 30, 1946, South Bend,

IN; educ. Gregorian Univ. (Rome); ord. priest Dec. 23, 1972 (Divine Word Fathers); Under-Sec. of the Pont. Council for the Pastoral Care of Migrants and Itinerants, Apr. 6, 2000; app. abp. (nuncio to Benin and Togo) and titular abp. of Alessano, Alexanum Aug. 24, 2005; cons. Sept. 30, 2005; app. nuncio to Uganda, Feb. 2, 2013.

Boland, Ernest B., O.P.: b. July 10, 1925, Providence, RI; educ. Providence College (RI), Dominican Houses of Study (Somerset, OH; Washington, DC); ord. priest, June 9, 1955; ord. bp. of Multan, Pakistan, July 25, 1966; res., Oct. 20, 1984.

Boland, J.(John) Kevin: b. Apr. 25, 1935, Cork, Ireland (brother of Bp. Raymond J. Boland); educ. Christian Brothers School (Cork), All Hallows Seminary (Dublin); ord. priest (Savannah), June 14, 1959; ord. bp. of Savannah, Apr. 18, 1995; ret. July 19, 2011.

Boles, John P.: b. Jan. 21, 1930, Boston, MA; educ. St. John Seminary, Boston College (Boston, MA); ord. priest (Boston*), Feb. 2, 1955; ord. titular bp. of Nova Sparsa and aux. bp. of Boston, May 21, 1992; ret. Oct. 12, 2006.

Bootkoski, Paul G.: b. July 4, 1940, Newark, NJ; educ. Seton Hall Univ. (South Orange, NJ), Immaculate Conception Seminary (Darlington, NJ); ord. priest, (Newark*), May 29, 1966; ord. titular bp. of Zarna and aux. bp. of Newark, Sept. 5, 1997; app. bp. of Metuchen, Jan. 4, 2002.

Botean, John Michael: b. July 9, 1955, Canton, OH; educ. St. Fidelis Seminary (Herman, PA), Catholic Univ. of America (Washington, DC), St. Gregory Melkite Seminary (Newton Centre, MA), Catholic Theological Union (Chicago, IL); ord. priest (Romanian rite St. George's in Canton), May 18, 1986; ord. bp. of St. George's in Canton for Romanians, Aug. 24, 1996.

Boyea, Earl: b. Apr. 10, 1951, Pontiac, MI; educ. Sacred Heart Seminary (Detroit), North American College and Pontifical Gregorian Univ. (Rome), Wayne State Univ. (Detroit), Catholic Univ. of America (Washington, DC); ord., May 20, 1978 (Detroit*); rector and president of the Pontifical College Josephinum (Columbus, OH), 2000-2002; app. titular bp. of Siccenna and aux. bp. of Detroit, July 22, 2002, ord., Sept. 13, 2002; app. bp. of Lansing, Feb. 27, 2008; inst. Apr. 29, 2008.

Bradley, Paul J.: b. Oct. 18, 1945, Glassport, PA; educ. St. Meinrad Seminary (St. Meinrad, IN); ord. priest May 1, 1971 (Pittsburgh); app. aux. bp. of Pittsburgh and tit. bp. of Afufenia Dec. 16, 2004; ord. Feb. 2, 2005; app. bp. of Kalamazoo, Apr. 6, 2009, inst. June 5, 2009.

Brandt, Lawrence E.: b. Mar. 27, 1939, Charleston, WV; educ. Pontifical College Josephinum (Worthington, Ohio), North American College (Rome), Univ. of Innsbruck (Austria), Pontifical Lateran Univ. (Rome); ord. priest (Rapid City), Dec. 19, 1969; after studies in the Pontifical Ecclesiastical Academy, entered into the diplomatic service of the Holy See, 1973 and held posts in Madagascar, Germany, Ecuador and Algeria; incardinated in Erie diocese in 1981; app. bp. of Greensburg of Jan. 2, 2004.

Bransfield, Michael J.: b. Sept. 8, 1943; educ. St. Charles Borromeo Sem. (Wynnewood, PA), Catholic Univ. of America (Washington); ord. priest May 15, 1971 (Philadelphia); app. bp. of Wheeling-Charleston Dec. 9, 2004; ord. Feb. 22, 2005.

Braxton, Edward K.: b. June 28, 1944, Chicago, IL; educ. Loyola Univ. of Chicago, Univ. of St. Mary of the Lake and Mundelein Seminary (Chicago), Louvain Univ. (Belgium); ord. priest (Chicago*), May 13, 1970; ord. titular bp. of Macomades rusticiana and aux. bp. of St. Louis, May 17, 1995; app. bp. of Lake Charles, Dec. 11, 2000; inst., Feb. 22, 2001; app. bp. of Belleville, Mar. 16, 2005; inst. June 22, 2005.

Brennan, Robert J.: b. June 7, 1962, Bronx, NY; educ. Saint John's University, Seminary of the Immaculate Conception (Huntington, NY); ord. priest (Rockville Center), May 27, 1989; Secretary to the Bishop (1994-2002); Vicar General and Moderator of the Curia, 2002-2010; app. aux. bp. of Rockville Center and titular bp. of Erdonia, June 8, 2012; ord. bp., July 25, 2012.

Broglio, Timothy M.: b. Dec. 22, 1951, Cleveland, OH; educ. Boston College (Boston, MA), North American College and Gregorian Univ. (Rome); ord. May 19, 1977; graduate of the Pontifical Ecclesiastical Academy; entered the diplomatic corps in 1983; chief of staff to the Vatican Secretary of State; app. titular abp. (Amiternum) and papal nuncio to the Dominican Republic and apostolic delegate to Puerto Rico, Feb. 27, 2001; ord., Mar. 19, 2001; app. abp. for Military Services, Nov. 19, 2007; inst. Jan. 25, 2008.

Brom, Robert H.: b. Sept. 18, 1938, Arcadia, WI; educ. St. Mary's College (Winona, MN), Gregorian Univ. (Rome); ord. priest (Winona), Dec. 18, 1963, in Rome; ord. bp. of Duluth, May 23, 1983; coadj. bp. of San Diego, May, 1989; bp. of San Diego, July 10, 1990; ret. Sept. 18, 2013.

Brown, Charles J.: Oct. 13, 1959, New York, N.Y.; educ. Univ. of Notre Dame (Notre Dame, IN), Univ. of Oxford (Oxford, England), Univ. of Toronto (Toronto, Canada), Pontifical Univ. of St. Anselmo (Rome, Italy); ord. priest, May 13, 1989 (New York*); official of the Congregation for the Doctrine of the Faith, 1994-2011; app. nuncio to Ireland, Nov. 26, 2011; ord. titular abp. of Aquileia, Jan. 6, 2012.

Brown, Tod D.: b. Nov. 15, 1936, San Francisco, CA; educ. St. John's Seminary (Camarillo, CA), North American College (Rome); ord. priest (Monterey-Fresno), May 1, 1963; ord. bp. of Boise, Apr. 3, 1989; app. bp. of Orange, June 30, 1998; ret. Sept. 21, 2012.

Brucato, Robert A.: b. Aug. 14, 1931, New York, NY; educ. Cathedral College (Douglaston, NY), St. Joseph's Seminary (Dunwoodie, NY), Univ. of Our Lady of the Lake (San Antonio, TX); ord. priest (New York*), June 1, 1957; air force chaplain for 22 years; ord. titular bp. of Temuniana and aux. of New York, Aug. 25, 1997; ret. Oct. 31, 2006.

Brunett, Alexander J.: b. Jan. 17, 1934, Detroit, MI; educ. Gregorian Univ. (Rome), Sacred Heart Seminary, Univ. of Detroit (Detroit, MI), Marquette Univ. (Milwaukee, WI); ord. priest (Detroit*), July 13, 1958; ord. bp. of Helena, July 6, 1994; app. abp. of Seattle, Oct. 28, 1997, inst., Dec. 18, 1997.

Brungardt, John B.: b. July 10, 1958, Salina, KS; educ. Benedictine College (Atchison, KS), Kansas State Univ.; Pontifical College Josephinum (Columbus, OH); ord. priest (Wichita), May 23, 1998; app. bp. of Dodge City, Dec. 15, 2010; ord. Feb. 2, 2011.

Bruskewitz, Fabian W.: b. Sept. 6, 1935, Milwaukee, WI; educ. North American College, Gregorian Univ. (Rome); ord. priest (Milwaukee*), July 17, 1960; ord. bp. of Lincoln, May 13, 1992; ret. Sept. 14, 2012.

Buckon, Neal J.: b. Sept. 3, 1953, Columbus, OH; educ. John Carroll Univ. (Univ. Heights, OH), Cleveland State Univ., Borromeo College (Wycliffe, OH), St. Mary's Seminary (Cleveland, OH); ord. priest (Cleveland), May 25, 1995; served in the U.S. Army, 1975-1982; Army chaplain from 1998; app. titular bp. of Vissalsa and aux. bp. of the Archdio. for the Military Services, Jan. 3, 2011; ord. Feb. 22, 2011.

Buechlein, Daniel M., O.S.B.: b. Apr. 20, 1938; educ. St. Meinrad College and Seminary (St. Meinrad, IN), St. Anselm Univ. (Rome); solemn profession as Benedictine monk, Aug. 15, 1963; ord. priest (St. Meinrad Archabbey)

May 3, 1964; ord. bp. of Memphis, Mar. 2, 1987; app. abp. of Indianapolis, July 14, 1992; inst., Sept. 9, 1992; res. Sept. 21, 2011.

Bura, John: b. June 12, 1944, Wegeleben, Germany; educ. St. Basil College Seminary (Stamford), St. Josaphat Ukrainian Catholic Seminary, The Catholic Univ. of America, Washington; ord. priest Feb. 14, 1971 (Philadelphia/Ukrainian); ap. aux. bp. Ukrainian Arch. of Philadelphia and tit. bp. of Limisa Jan. 3, 2006; inst. Feb. 21, 2006; Apostolic Admin. of St. Josaphat in Parma (Ukrainians), July 29, 2009.

Burbidge, Michael F.: b. June 16, 1957, Philadelphia; educ. St. Charles Borromeo Seminary; ord. priest (Philadelphia*), May 19, 1984; app. titular bp. of Cluain Iraird and aux. bp. of Philadelphia, June 21, 2002, ord., Sept. 5, 2002; app. bp. of Raleigh, June 8, 2006.

Burke, John J., O.F.M.: b. Mar. 16, 1935, River Edge, NJ; educ. St. Joseph Seminary (Callicoon, NY), St. Bonaventure Univ. (St. Bonaventure, NY), Holy Name College (Washington, DC); solemnly professed in Franciscan Order, Aug. 20, 1958; ord. priest, Feb. 25, 1961; missionary in Brazil from 1964; ord. coadjutor bp. of Miracema do Tocantins, Brazil, Mar. 25, 1995; bp. of Miracema do Tocantins, Feb. 14, 1996.

Burke, Raymond L.: (See **Cardinals' Biographies**).

Burnette, Kurt R.; b. Nov 7, 1955, Fakenham, England; educ. Rice Univ., Houston, TX, Univ. of Utah, Pontifical Oriental Institute, Rome; ord. priest (Van Nuys, Ruthenian), Apr. 26, 1989; rector of the Byzantine Catholic Seminary of SS. Cyril and Methodius (2012-2013); app. bp. of Passaic of the Ruthenians, Oct. 29, 2013; ord. bp., Dec. 12, 2013.

Burns, Edward J.: b. Oct. 7, 1957, Pittsburgh, PA; educ. Duquesne Univ. (Pittsburgh, PA), Mount St. Mary Seminary (Emmitsburg, MD); ord. priest (Pittsburgh), June 25, 1983; Exec. Dir. of the Secretariat for Clergy, Consecrated Life and Vocations, USCCB (1999-2008); app. bp. of Juneau, Jan. 19, 2009; ord. bp. Mar. 3, 2009; inst. Apr. 2, 2009.

Bustros, Cyrille Salim, S.M.S.P.: b. Jan. 26, 1939, Ain-Bourday, Lebanon; educ. Missionaries of St. Paul and Seminary of St.e-Anne of Jerusalem (Jerusalem), Univ. of Louvain (Louvain, Belgium); ord. June 29, 1962 (Society of the Missionaries of St. Paul); elected abp. of Baalbeck, Lebanon, Oct. 25, 1988; app. eparch of Newton, June 22, 2004; confirmed as abp. of Beirut, June 15, 2011.

Byrne, Peter: b. July 24, 1951, Manhattan, NY; educ. Fordham Univ., St. Joseph's Seminary, Yonkers, N.Y.; ord. priest (New York*), Dec. 1, 1984; app. titular bp. of Cluain Iraird and aux. bp. of New York, June 14, 2014; ord. Aug. 4, 2014.

Byrnes, Michael J.: b. Aug. 23, 1958; educ. Univ. of Michigan, Sacred Heart Seminary (Detroit), Pontifical Gregorian Univ. (Rome); faculty of Sacred Heart Seminary, 2003; vice-rector and dean of formation, Sacred Heart Seminary, and pastor Presentation/Our Lady of Victory Parish, 2004-11; app. titular bp. of Eguga and aux. bp. of Detroit, Mar. 22, 2011; ord. May 5, 2011.

C

Caggiano, Frank J.: b. Mar. 29, 1959, Brooklyn; educ. Immaculate Conception Seminary (Huntington, NY), Gregorian Univ. (Rome); ord. priest May 16, 1987 (Brooklyn); appointed aux. bp. of Brooklyn and tit. bp. of Inis Cathaig June 6, 2006; ord. Aug. 22, 2006; app. bp. of Bridgeport, July 31, 2013; inst. Sept. 19, 2013.

Callahan, William P., O.F.M. Conv.: b. June 17, 1950, Chicago, Ill.; educ. St. Mary Minor Seminary (Crystal Lake, Ill.), Loyola Univ. (Chicago), Univ. of St. Michael's College,

Univ. of Toronto (Toronto, Canada); entered the Conventual Franciscans and made his first profession, Aug. 11, 1970; ord. priest, Apr. 30, 1977; spiritual director of the North American College, 2005-2007; app. titular bp. of Lares and aux. bp. of Milwaukee, Oct. 30, 2007; cons. bp. Dec. 21, 2007; app. bp. of La Crosse, June 11, 2010; inst. Aug. 11, 2010.

Calvo, Randolph R.: b. Aug. 28, 1950, Agana, Guam; educ. St. Patrick's Seminary and Univ. (Menlo Park, CA), Angelicum (Rome); ord. priest May 21, 1977 (San Francisco); app. bp of Reno Dec. 23, 2005; ord. bp. Feb. 17, 2006.

Camacho, Tomas Aguon: b. Sept. 18, 1933, Chalon Kanoa, Saipan; educ. St. Patrick's Seminary (Menlo Park, CA); ord. priest, June 14, 1961; ord. first bp. of Chalan Kanoa, Northern Marianas (U.S. Commonwealth), Jan. 13, 1985.

Campbell, Frederick F.: b. Aug. 5, 1943, Elmira, NY; educ. Ohio State Univ., St. Paul Seminary, St. Paul, MN; ord. priest (St. Paul and Minneapolis*), May 31, 1980; app. titular bp. of Afufenia and aux. bp. of St. Paul and Minneapolis, Mar. 2, 1999, ord., May 14, 1999; app. bp. of Columbus, Oct. 14, 2004; inst. Jan. 13, 2005.

Cantú, Oscar: b. Dec. 5, 1966, Houston, TX; educ. Holy Trinity Seminary and Univ. of Dallas (Dallas, TX), St. Mary's Seminary, (Houston, TX), Gregorian Univ. (Rome); ord. priest, May 21, 1994 (Galveston-Houston*); app. titular bp. of Dardano and aux. bp. of San Antonio, Apr. 10, 2008; ord. bp., June 2, 2008; app. bp. of Las Cruces, Jan. 10, 2013.

Carlson, Robert J.: b. June 30, 1944, Minneapolis, MN; educ. Nazareth Hall and St. Paul Seminary (St. Paul, MN), Catholic Univ. (Washington, DC); ord. priest (St. Paul Minneapolis*), May 23, 1970; ord. titular bp. of Avioccala and aux. bp. of St. Paul and Minneapolis, Jan. 11, 1984; app. coadjutor bp. of Sioux Falls, Jan. 13, 1994; succeeded as bp. of Sioux Falls, Mar. 21, 1995; app. bp. of Saginaw, Dec. 29, 2004; inst. Feb. 24, 2005; app. abp. of St. Louis, Apr. 21, 2009; inst. June 10, 2009.

Carmody, Edmond: b. Jan. 12, 1934, Ahalena, Kerry, Ireland; educ. St. Brendan's College (Killarney), St. Patrick Seminary (Carlow); ord. priest (San Antonio*), June 8, 1957; missionary in Peru 1984 89; ord. titular bp. of Mortlach and aux. bp. of San Antonio, Dec. 15, 1988; app. bp. of Tyler, 1992-2000; app. bp. of Corpus Christi, Feb. 3, 2000; inst., Mar. 17, 2000.

Carmon, Dominic, S.V.D.: b. Dec. 13, 1930, Opelousas, LA; entered Society of Divine Word, 1946; ord. priest, Feb. 2, 1960; missionary in Papua New Guinea, 1961 68; ord. titular bp. of Rusicade and aux. bp. of New Orleans, Feb. 11, 1993; ret. Dec. 13, 2006.

Cary, Liam S.: b. Aug. 21, 1947, Portland, OR; educ. Mount Angel Seminary and St. Patrick Seminary (Portland, OR), Pontifical North American College and Pontifical Gregorian Univ. (Rome, Italy); ord. priest, Sept. 5, 1992 (Portland*); app. bp. of Baker, Mar. 8, 2012; ord. bp. May 18, 2012.

Casey, Luis Morgan: b. June 23, 1935, Portageville, MO; ord. priest (St. Louis*), Apr. 7, 1962; missionary in Bolivia from 1965; ord. titular bp. of Mibiarca and aux. bp. of La Paz, Jan. 28, 1984; vicar apostolic of Pando, Bolivia, Jan. 18, 1988, and apostolic administrator (1995) of La Paz.

Cepeda Escobedo, José A.: b. San Luis Potosi, Mexico, May 15, 1969; educ., Seminario Arquidiocesano Guadalupano Josefino (San Luis Potosi), Our Lady of the Lake Univ. (San Antonio), College Seminary of the Immaculate Heart of Mary (Santa Fe, NM), St. Mary's University (San Antonio), Pontifical Univ. of St. Thomas Aquinas (Rome); ord. priest (San Antonio*), June 1, 1996; rector, Assumption Seminary, San Antonio, 2010; app. titular bp. of Tagase and aux. bp. Detroit, Apr. 18, 2011; ord. May 5, 2011.

Chappetto, Raymond F.: b. Aug. 20, 1945, Astoria, NY;

educ. Our Lady of Angels Seminary (Albany, NY), St. John's Univ.; ord. priest (Brooklyn), May 29, 1971; served in various pastoral assignments and was named by the National Catholic Education Association Pastor of the Year in 2008; app. aux. bp. of Brooklyn and titular bp. of Citium, May 2, 2012; ord. bp., July 11, 2012.

Chaput, Charles J., O.F.M. Cap.: b. Sept. 26, 1944, Concordia, KS; educ. St. Fidelis College (Herman, PA), Capuchin College and Catholic Univ. (Washington, DC), Univ. of San Francisco; solemn vows as Capuchin, July 14, 1968; ord. priest, Aug. 29, 1970; ord. bp. of Rapid City, SD, July 26, 1988, the second priest of Native American ancestry (member of Prairie Band Potawatomi Tribe) ordained a bp. in the U.S.; app app. abp. of Denver, inst., Apr. 7, 1997; app. abp. of Philadelphia, July 19, 2011; inst., Sept. 8, 2011.

Charron, Joseph L., C.P.P.S.: b. Dec. 30, 1939, Redfield, SD; educ. St. John's Seminary (Collegeville, MN); ord. priest, June 3, 1967; ord. titular bp. of Bencenna and aux. bp. of St. Paul and Minneapolis, Jan. 25, 1990; app. bp. of Des Moines, Nov. 12, 1993; res. Apr. 10, 2007.

Chavez, Gilbert Espinosa: b. May 9, 1932, Ontario, CA; educ. St. Francis Seminary (El Cajon, CA), Immaculate Heart Seminary (San Diego), Univ. of CA; ord. priest (San Diego). Mar. 19, 1960; ord. titular bp. of Magarmel and aux. of San Diego, June 21, 1974; ret. June 1, 2007.

Choby, David R.: b. Jan. 17, 1947, Nashville, TN; educ. St. Ambrose College (Davenport, IA), Catholic Univ. of America (Washington), and the Angelicum (Rome); ord. priest Sept. 6, 1974 (Nashville); app. bp of Nashville Dec. 20, 2005; ord. bp. Feb. 27, 2006.

Chomnycky, Paul P.: b. May 19, 1954, Vancouver, B.C; educ. Univ. of British Columbia (Vancouver), Pont. St. Anselm Univ., Pont. Gregorian Univ. (Rome); ord. Oct. 1, 1988 (Basilians); app. bp for Ukrainian Catholics living in Great Britain April 5, 2002; ord. bp. June 11, 2002; trans. Ukrainian Dio. of Stamford Jan. 3, 2006; inst. Feb. 20, 2006.

Christensen, Peter F.: b. Dec. 24, 1952, Pasadena, CA; educ. College of the Redwoods (Eureka, CA), Univ. of Montana (Missoula, MT), St. John Vianney Seminary, Univ. of St. Thomas, and St. Paul Seminary (St. Paul, MN); ord. May 25, 1985 (St. Paul and Minneapolis*); app. bp. of Superior, June 28, 2007; ord. Sept. 14, 2007.

Christian, Francis J.: b. Oct. 8, 1942, Peterborough, NH; educ. St. Anselm College (Manchester, NH), St. Paul Seminary (Ottawa), American College in Louvain (Belgium); ord. priest (Manchester), June 29, 1968; ord titular bp. of Quincy and aux. of Manchester, May 14, 1996.

Cisneros, Octavio: b. July 19, 1945, Cuba; educ.: Immaculate Conception Sem. (Huntington, N.Y.); ord. priest Mary 29, 1971; app. aux. bp. of Brooklyn and tit. bp. of Eanach Duin June 6, 2006; ord. Aug. 22, 2006.

Cistone, Joseph R.: b. May 18, 1949, Philadelphia, PA; educ. St. Charles Borromeo Seminary (Overbrook, PA); ord. priest (Philadelphia*), May 17, 1975; app. titular bp. of Case mediane and aux. bp. of Philadelphia, June 8, 2004; ord. July 28, 2004; app. bp. of Saginaw, May 20, 2009; inst. July 28, 2009.

Clark, Edward W.: b. Nov. 30, 1946, Minneapolis; educ. Our Lady Queen of Angels Seminary (San Fernando, CA), St. John's Seminary College (Camarillo, CA), Gregorian Univ. (Rome); ord. priest (Los Angeles*), May 9, 1972; President/Rector, St. John's Seminary College (Camarillo, CA), 1994-2001; app. titular bp. of Gardar and aux. bp. of Los Angeles, Jan. 16, 2001, ord., Mar. 26, 2001.

Clark, Matthew H.: b. July 15, 1937, Troy, NY; educ. St. Bernard's Seminary (Rochester, NY), Gregorian Univ. (Rome); ord. priest (Albany) Dec. 19, 1962; ord. bp. of Rochester, May 27, 1979; inst., June 26, 1979; ret. Sept. 21, 2012.

Coakley, Paul S.: b. June 3, 1955, Norfolk, VA; educ. Univ. of Kansas (Lawrence), St. Pius X Seminary (Erlanger, KY), Mount St. Mary's Seminary (Emmitsburg, MD); ord. Priest May 21, 1983 (Wichita); app. bp. of Salina Oct. 21, 2004; ord. Dec. 28, 2004; app. abp. of Oklahoma City, Dec. 16, 2010; inst. Feb. 11, 2011.

Coleman, George W.: b. Feb. 1, 1939, Fall River, MA; educ. Holy Cross College (Worcester, MA), Fall River, St. John's Seminary (Boston, MA), North American College and Gregorian Univ. (Rome), Brown Univ. (Providence, RI); ord. priest, Dec. 16, 1964; app. bp. of Fall River, Apr. 30, 2003; ord. bp., July 22, 2003; ret. July 3, 2014.

Conley, James Douglas: b. Mar. 19, 1955, Kansas City, MO; educ., Univ. of Kansas (Lawrence, KS), St. Pius X Seminary (Erlanger, KY), Mt. St. Mary's Seminary (Emmitsburg, MD), Pont. North American College and Accademia Alfonsiana (Rome); ord. priest May 18, 1985 (Wichita); served in Congregation for Bps. in Rome, 1996-2006; Chaplain of His Holiness, Feb. 9, 2001; app. titular bp. of Cissa and aux. bp. of Denver, Apr. 10, 2008; ord. bp., May 30, 2008; app. bp. of Lincoln, Sept. 14, 2012; inst. Nov. 20, 2012.

Conlon, Robert D.: b. Dec. 4, 1948, Cincinnati; educ. Mount St. Mary's Seminary of the West, Univ. of St. Paul, Ottawa; ord. priest (Cincinnati*), Jan. 15, 1977; app. bp. of Steubenville, May 31, 2002; app. bp. of Joliet, May 17, 2011; inst. July 14, 2011.

Connolly, Thomas J.: b. July 18, 1922, Tonopah, NV; educ. St. Patrick's Seminary (Menlo Park, CA), Catholic Univ. (Washington, DC), Lateran Univ. (Rome); ord. priest (Reno Las Vegas), Apr. 8, 1947; ord. bp. of Baker, June 30, 1971; res., Nov. 19, 1999.

Cooney, Patrick R.: b. Mar. 10, 1934, Detroit, MI; educ. Sacred Heart Seminary (Detroit), Gregorian Univ. (Rome), Univ. of Notre Dame (Notre Dame, IN); ord. priest (Detroit*), Dec. 20, 1959; ord. titular bp. of Hodelm and aux. bp. of Detroit, Jan. 27, 1983; app. bp. of Gaylord, Nov. 6, 1989; inst., Jan. 28, 1990; ret. Oct. 3, 2009.

Cordileone, Salvatore: b. June 5, 1956, San Diego, CA.; educ. St. Francis Seminary (San Diego), Univ. of San Diego (San Diego), North American College (Rome), Pontifical Gregorian Univ. (Rome); ord. July 9, 1982; official of the Supreme Tribunal of the Apostolic Signatura in Roma, 1995-2002 and vice-director of Villa Stritch in Rome; app. titular bp. of Natchez and aux. bp. of San Diego, July 5, 2002, ord., Aug. 21, 2002; app. bp. of Oakland, Mar. 23, 2009; inst. May 5, 2009; app. abp. of San Francisco, July 27, 2012; inst. Oct. 4, 2012.

Corrada del Rio, Alvaro, S.J.: b. May 13, 1942, Santurce, Puerto Rico; entered Society of Jesus, 1960, at novitiate of St. Andrew on Hudson (Poughkeepsie, NY); educ. Jesuit seminaries, Fordham Univ. (New York), Institut Catholique (Paris); ord. priest, July 6, 1974, in Puerto Rico; pastoral coordinator of Northeast Catholic Hispanic Center, New York, 1982-85; ord. titular bp. of Rusticiana and aux. bp. of Washington, DC, Aug. 4, 1985; app. apostolic administrator of Caguas, Puerto Rico, Aug. 5, 1997 (retained his title as aux. bp. of Washington); app. bp. of Tyler, Dec. 5, 2000; inst., Jan. 30, 2001; app. bp. of Mayaguez, Puerto Rico, July 6, 2011.

Costello, Thomas J.: b. Feb. 23, 1929, Camden, NY; educ. Niagara Univ. (Niagara Falls, NY), St. Bernard's Seminary (Rochester, NY), Catholic Univ. (Washington, DC); ord. priest (Syracuse), June 5, 1954; ord. titular bp. of Perdices and aux. bp. of Syracuse, Mar. 13, 1978; ret. Mar. 23, 2004.

Cote, Michael R.: b. June 19, 1949, Sanford, ME; educ. Our Lady of Lourdes Seminary (Cassadaga, NY), St. Mary's Seminary College (Baltimore, MD); Gregorian Univ. (Rome), Catholic Univ. (Washington, DC); ord. priest (Portland, ME), June 29, 1975, by Pope Paul VI in Rome; secretary, 1989-94 at apostolic nunciature, Washington; ord. titular bp. of Cebarades and aux. of Portland, ME, July 27, 1995; app. bp. of Norwich, Mar. 11, 2003; inst., May 13, 2003.

Cotey, Arnold R., S.D.S.: b. June 15, 1921, Milwaukee, WI; educ. Divine Savior Seminary (Lanham, MD), Marquette Univ. (Milwaukee, WI); ord. priest, June 7, 1949; ord. first bp. of Nachingwea (now Lindi), Tanzania, Oct. 20, 1963; ret., Nov. 11, 1983.

Cotta, Myron J.: b. Mar. 21, 1953, Dos Palos, CA; educ. West Hills Community College, Coalinga, CA, St. John's Seminary, Camarillo, CA; ord. priest (Los Angeles*); app. titular bp. of Muteci and aux. bp. of Sacramento, Jan. 24, 2014; ord. bp. Mar. 25, 2014.

Coyle, Robert J.: b: Sept. 23, 1964, Brooklyn, N.Y.; educ. Fordham Univ. (New York), Immaculate Conception Seminary (Huntington, N.Y.); ord. priest May 25, 1991 (Rockville Centre); joined the U.S. Navy, June 3, 1988 and served for 24 years; app. titular bp. of Zabi and aux. bp. of the Military Archdio., Feb. 11, 2013; ord. bishop Apr. 25, 2013.

Coyne, Christopher J.: b. June 17, 1958, Woburn, MA; educ. Univ. of Mass. (Lowell), St. John Seminary (Brighton), Pont. Liturgical Institute (Rome); ord. priest (Boston*), June 7, 1986; app. aux. bp. of Indianapolis and titular bp. of Mopta, Jan. 14, 2011; ord. Mar. 2, 2011.

Cozzens, Andrew H.: b. Aug. 3, 1968, Stamford, CT; educ. Benedictine College (Atchison, KS), St. Paul Seminary (Minneapolis, MN); ord. priest (St. Paul and Minneapolis*), May 31, 1997; app. titular bp. of Bisica and aux. of Minneapolis-St. Paul, Oct. 10, 2013; ord. bp. Dec. 9, 2013.

Cronin, Daniel A.: b. Nov. 14, 1927, Newton, MA; educ. St. John's Seminary (Boston, MA), North American College and Gregorian Univ. (Rome); ord. priest (Boston*), Dec. 20, 1952; attaché apostolic nunciature (Addis Ababa), 1957 61; served in papal Secretariat of State, 1961 68; ord. titular bp. of Egnatia and aux. bp. of Boston, Sept. 12, 1968; bp. of Fall River, Dec. 16, 1970; abp. of Hartford, Dec. 10, 1991; ret. Oct. 23, 2003.

Cruz, Manuel A.: b. Dec. 2, 1953, Havana, Cuba; educ. Seton Hall Univ. (South Orange, NJ), Immaculate Conception Seminary (South Orange, NJ); ord. priest, May 31, 1980 (Newark*); app. aux. bp. of Newark and titular bp. of Gaguari, June 9, 2008; ord. bp. Sept. 9, 2008.

Cullen, Edward P.: b. Mar. 15, 1933, Philadelphia, PA; educ. St. Charles Borromeo Seminary (Overbrook, PA), Univ. of Pennsylvania and LaSalle Univ. (Philadelphia), Harvard Graduate School of Business; ord. priest (Philadelphia*), May 19, 1962; ord. titular bp. of Paria in Proconsolare and aux. of Philadelphia, Feb. 8, 1994; app. bp. of Allentown, Dec. 16, 1997, inst., Feb. 9, 1998; res. May 27, 2009.

Cummins, John S.: b. Mar. 3, 1928, Oakland, CA; educ. St. Patrick's Seminary (Menlo Park, CA), Catholic Univ. (Washington, DC), Univ. of CA; ord. priest (San Francisco*), Jan. 24, 1953; exec. dir. of the CA Catholic Conference 1971-76; ord. titular bp. of Lambaesis and aux. bp. of Sacramento, May 16, 1974; app. bp. of Oakland, inst., June 30, 1977; ret. Oct. 1, 2003.

Cunningham, Robert J.: b. June 18, 1943, Buffalo, N.Y.; educ. St. John Vianney Seminary (East Aurora, N.Y.), Catholic Univ. of America (Washington, D.C.); ord. May 24, 1969 (Buffalo); bp. of Ogdensburg Mar. 9, 2004; ord. May 18, 2004; app. bp. of Syracuse, Apr. 21, 2009; inst. May 26, 2009.

Cupich, Blase: b. Mar. 19, 1949, Omaha, NE; educ. College of St. Thomas (St. Paul, MN), Gregorian Univ. (Rome), Catholic Univ. of America (Washington, DC); ord. priest (Omaha*), Aug. 16, 1975; service at the apostolic nunciature, Washington, DC, 1981-87; rector, Pontifical College Josephinum (Columbus, OH), 1989-97; app. bp. of Rapid City, SD, July 7, 1998; ord., Sept. 21, 1998.

Curlin, William G.: b. Aug. 30, 1927, Portsmouth, VA; educ. Georgetown Univ. (Washington, DC), St. Mary's Seminary (Baltimore, MD); ord. priest (Washington*), May 25, 1957; ord. titular bp. of Rosemarkie and aux. bp. of Washington, Dec. 20, 1988; app. bp. of Charlotte, Feb. 22, 1994, ret., Sept. 16, 2002.

Curry, Thomas J.: b. Jan. 17, 1943, Drumgoon, Ireland; educ. Patrician College (Ballyfin), All Hallows Seminary (Dublin); ord. priest (Los Angeles*), June 17, 1967; ord. titular bp. of Ceanannus Mór and aux. of Los Angeles, Mar. 19, 1994.

Curtiss, Elden F.: b. June 16, 1932, Baker, OR; educ. St. Edward Seminary College and St. Thomas Seminary (Kenmore, WA); ord. priest (Baker), May 24, 1958; ord. bp. of Helena, MT, Apr. 28, 1976; app. abp. of Omaha, NE, May 4, 1993; ret. June 3, 2009.

D

Da Cunha, Edgar M., S.D.V.: b. Aug. 21, 1953, Riachão do Jacuípe Bahia, Brazil; educ. Catholic Univ. of Salvador (Brazil), Immaculate Conception Seminary (Newark, NJ); professed perpetual vows, Feb. 11, 1979, and ord., priest Mar. 27, 1982; app. titular bp. of Ucres and aux. of Newark, June 27, 2003; app. bp. of Fall River, July 3, 2014; inst. Sept. 24, 2014.

Daily, Thomas V.: b. Sept. 23, 1927, Belmont, MA; educ. Boston College, St. John's Seminary (Brighton, MA); ord. priest (Boston*), Jan. 10, 1952; missionary in Peru for five years as a member of the Society of St. James the Apostle; ord. titular bp. of Bladia and aux. bp. of Boston, Feb. 11, 1975; app. first bp. of Palm Beach, FL, July 17, 1984; app. bp. of Brooklyn, Feb. 20, 1990; inst., Apr. 18, 1990; ret., Aug. 1, 2003.

Daly, Thomas: b. Apr. 30, 1960, San Francisco, CA; educ. Univ. of San Francisco, St. Patrick's Seminary (Menlo Park, CA), Boston College; ord. priest, May 9, 1987 (San Francisco*); app. titular bp. of Tabalta and aux. bp. of San Jose, Mar. 16, 2011; ord. May 25, 2011.

Deeley, Robert: b. June 18, 1946, Cambridge, Mass.; Catholic Univ. of Americ (Washington, D.C.), Pontifical Gregorian Univ. (Rome); ord. priest July 14, 1973 (Boston*); app. titular bp. of Kearney and aux. bp. of Boston, Nov. 9, 2012; ord. bishop, Jan. 4, 2013; app. bp. of Portland in Maine, Dec. 18, 2013.

Del Riego, Rutilio: b. Sept. 21, 1940, Valdesandinas (Leon), Spain; educ. Diocesan Laborer Priests seminary (Salamanca, Spain), Catholic Univ. of America); ord. priest June 5, 1965, (Diocesan Laborer Priests); app. aux. bp. San Bernardino and tit. bp. of Daimlaig July 26, 2005; ord. Sept. 20, 2005.

Dendinger, William J.: b. May 20, 1939, Omaha; educ. Conception College Seminary (Conception, MO), Aquinas Institute (Iowa); ord. priest May 29, 1965; U.S. Air Force chaplain, 1970-2002, achieving the rank of Major General; app. bp. of Grand Island Oct. 14, 2004; ord. Dec. 13, 2004.

Deshotel, John D.: b. Jan. 6, 1952, Basile, LA; educ. Univ. of Dallas (Dallas, TX); ord. priest (Dallas), May 13, 1978; app. titular bp. of Cova and aux. bp. of Dallas, Mar. 13, 2010; ord. bp., Apr. 27, 2010.

De Simone, Louis A.: b. Feb. 21, 1922, Philadelphia, PA; educ. Villanova Univ. (Villanova, PA), St. Charles Borromeo

Seminary (Overbrook, PA); ord. priest (Philadelphia*), May 10, 1952; ord. titular bp. of Cillium and aux. bp. of Philadelphia, Aug. 12, 1981; ret., Apr. 5, 1997.

DeWane, Frank J.: b. March 9, 1950, Green Bay, Wis.; educ. Univ. of Wisconsin (Oshkosh), American Univ., George Washington Univ. (Washington, DC), North American College, Pont. Gregorian Univ., Angelicum (Rome); ord. priest July 16, 1988 (Green Bay); app. coadj. bp. of Venice April 25, 2006; ord. bp. July 25, 2006; bp. of Venice, Jan. 19, 2007.

Di Lorenzo, Francis X.: b. Apr. 15, 1942, Philadelphia, PA; educ. St. Charles Borromeo Seminary (Philadelphia), Univ. of St. Thomas (Rome); ord. priest (Philadelphia*), May 18, 1968; ord. titular bp. of Tigia and aux. bp. of Scranton, Mar. 8, 1988; app. apostolic administrator of Honolulu, Oct. 12, 1993; bp. of Honolulu, Nov. 29, 1994; app. bp. of Richmond, Mar. 31, 2004.

DiMarzio, Nicholas: b. June 16, 1944, Newark, NJ; educ. Seton Hall Univ. (South Orange, NJ), Immaculate Conception Seminary (Darlington, NJ), Catholic Univ. (Washington, DC), Fordham Univ. (New York), Rutgers Univ. (New Brunswick, NJ); ord. priest (Newark*), May 30, 1970; ord. titular bp. of Mauriana and aux. bp. of Newark, Oct. 31, 1996, app. Bp. of Camden, June 8, 1999, inst., July 22, 1999; app. bp. of Brooklyn, Aug. 1, 2003.

Dimino, Joseph T.: b. Jan. 7, 1923, New York, NY; educ. Cathedral College (Douglaston, NY), St. Joseph's Seminary (Yonkers, NY), Catholic Univ. (Washington, DC); ord. priest (New York*), June 4, 1949; ord. titular bp. of Carini and aux. bp. of the Military Services archdiocese, May 10, 1983; app. ordinary of Military Services archdiocese, May 14, 1991; ret., Aug. 12, 1997.

DiNardo, Daniel N.: (See **Cardinals' Biographies**).

DiNoia, Joseph Augustine, O.P.: b. July 10, 1943, New York, NY; educ. Dominican House of the Studies in Washington, DC, Yale Univ., New Haven, CT; ord. priest for the Dominicans, June 4, 1970; served as exec. dir. of the Secretariat for Doctrine and Pastoral Practices for the NCCB; member of the Int. Theol. Comm., 1997-2002 and undersec. of the Cong. for the Doctrine of the Faith, 2002-2009; in 1998 he was granted the title Magister in Sacra Theologia by the Dominicans; app. sec. of the Congr. of Divine Worship and Discipline of the Sacraments, June 16, 2009; ord. titular abp. of Oregon City, July 11, 2009; app. Vice Pres. of the Pntifical Commission "Eclesia Dei," June 26, 2012.

Dino, Gerald N.: b. Jan. 11, 1940, Binghamton, NY; educ. Duquesne Univ. (Pittsburgh, PA), Byzantine Catholic Seminary of Sts. Cyril and Methodius (Pittsburgh, PA), Pontifical Oriental Inst. (Rome); ord. priest, Mar. 21, 1965 (Passaic); app. protosincellus of the eparchy of Passaic of the Ruthenians, U.S.A., and pastor in Linden, New Jersey; app. bp. of the eparchy of Van Nuys of the Ruthenians, Dec. 6, 2007; ord. bp. Mar. 27, 2008.

Doerfler, John F.: b. Nov. 2, 1964, Appleton, WI; educ. College of St. Thomas (St. Paul, MN), Gregorian University (Rome), The Catholic Univ. of America and John Paul II Institute for Marriage and the Family (Washington, DC); ord. priest, July 13, 1991; app. bp. of Marquette, Dec. 17, 2013; ord. bp., Feb. 11, 2014.

Doherty, Timothy L.: b. Sept. 29, 1950, Rockford, IL; educ.: St. Mary's Minor Seminary (Crystal Lake, IL), St. Ambrose College (Davenport, IA), North American College and Pontifical Lateran Univ. (Rome), Loyola Univ. (Chicago, IL); ord. priest (Rockford), 1976; diocesan ethicist for health care, 1995-2010; app bp. of Lafayette, IN, May 12, 2010.

Dolan, Timothy M.: (See **Cardinals' Biographies**).

Donato, Thomas A.: b. Oct. 1, 1940, Jersey City, NJ;

educ. Seton Hall Univ. (South Orange, NJ), Immaculate Conception Seminary (Darlington, NJ); ord. priest (Newark*), May 29, 1965; app. aux. bp. of Newark and tit. bp of Jamestown, May 21, 2004; ord. Aug. 4, 2004.

Dooher, John A.: b. May 3, 1943, Dorchester, MA; educ. St. John's Seminary (Brighton, MA); ord. May 21, 1969 (Boston); app. aux. bp. of Boston and titular bp. of Teveste Oct. 12, 2006; ord. Dec. 12, 2006.

Doran, Thomas George: b. Feb. 20, 1936, Rockford, IL; educ. Loras College (Dubuque, IA), Gregorian Univ. (Rome), Rockford College (Rockford, IL); ord. priest (Rockford), Dec. 20, 1961; ord. bp. of Rockford, June 24, 1994; ret. Mar. 20, 2012.

Doueihi, Stephen Hector: b. June 25, 1927, Zghorta, Lebanon; educ. Univ. of St. Joseph (Beirut, Lebanon), Propaganda Fide, Gregorian Univ. and Institute of Oriental Study (Rome); ord. priest, Aug. 14, 1955; came to U.S. in 1973; ord. eparch of Eparchy of St. Maron of Brooklyn, Jan 11, 1997; ret. Jan. 10, 2004.

Dougherty, John Martin: b. Apr. 29, 1932, Scranton, PA; educ. St. Charles College (Catonsville, MD), St. Mary's Seminary (Baltimore), Univ. of Notre Dame (South Bend, IN); ord. priest (Scranton), June 15, 1957; ord. titular bp. of Sufetula and aux. bp. of Scranton, Mar. 7, 1995; ret. Aug. 31, 2009.

Driscoll, Michael P.: b. Aug. 8, 1939, Long Beach, CA; educ. St. John Seminary (Camarillo, CA), Univ. of Southern CA; ord. priest (Los Angeles*), May 1, 1965; ord. titular bp. of Massita and aux. bp. of Orange, Mar. 6, 1990; app. bp. of Boise, Jan. 19, 1999, inst., Mar. 18, 1999.

Duca, Michael Gerard: b. June 5, 1952, Dallas, TX; educ. Holy Trinity Seminary, Irving, TX, Pontifical Univ. of St. Thomas Aquinas, Rome; ord. priest, Apr. 29, 1978 (Dallas); rector of Holy Trinity Seminary (1996-2008); app. bp. of Shreveport, Apr. 1, 2008; ord. bp. May 19, 2008.

Duffy, Paul, O.M.I.: b. July 25, 1932, Norwood, MA; educ Oblate houses of study in Canada and Washington, DC; ord. priest, 1962; missionary in Zambia from 1984; app. first bp. of Mongu, Zambia, July 1, 1997; ret. Feb. 15, 2011.

DuMaine, (Roland) Pierre: b. Aug. 2, 1931, Paducah, KY; educ. St. Joseph's College (Mountain View, CA), St. Patrick's College and Seminary (Menlo Park, CA), Univ. of CA (Berkeley), Catholic Univ. (Washington, DC); ord. priest (San Francisco), June 15, 1957; ord. titular bp. of Sarda and aux. bp. of San Francisco, June 29, 1978; app. first bp. of San Jose, Jan. 27, 1981; inst., Mar. 18, 1981; res., Nov. 27, 1999.

Dunne, John C.: b. Oct. 30, 1937, Brooklyn, NY; educ. Cathedral College (Brooklyn, NY). Immaculate Conception Seminary (Huntington, NY), Manhattan College (New York); ord. priest (Rockville Centre), June 1, 1963; ord. titular bp. of Abercorn and aux. bp. of Rockville Centre, Dec. 13, 1988; ret. June 22, 2013.

Dupre, Thomas L.: b. Nov. 10, 1933, South Hadley Falls, MA; educ. College de Montreal, Assumption College (Worcester, MA), Catholic Univ. (Washington, DC), ord. priest (Springfield, MA), May 23, 1959; ord. titular bp. of Hodelm and aux. bp. of Springfield, MA, May 31, 1990; bp. of Springfield, Mar. 14, 1995; res. Feb.11, 2004.

E

Edyvean, Walter J.: b. Oct. 18, 1938, Medford, MA; educ. Boston College, St. John's Seminary (Brighton, MA), the North American College and the Gregorian Univ. (Rome); ord. priest (Boston*), Dec. 16, 1964; served on staff of Congregation for Catholic Education, 1990-2001; app. titular bp. of Elie and aux. bp. of Boston, June 29, 2001, ord., Sept. 14, 2001; ret. June 29, 2014.

Egan, Edward M.: (See **Cardinals, Biographies**).

Elizondo, Eusebio: b. Aug. 8, 1954, Victoria, Mexico; educ. Missionaries of the Holy Spirit seminary, (Jalisco, Mexico), Gregorian Univ. (Rome); ord. priest (Missionaries of Holy Spirit) Aug. 18, 1984; app. auxiliary bp. of Seattle and titular bp. of Acolla May 12, 2005; ord. bp. June 6, 2005.

Elya, John A., B.S.O.: b. Sept. 16, 1928, Maghdouche, Lebanon; educ. diocesan monastery (Sidon, Lebanon), Gregorian Univ. (Rome, Italy); professed as member of Basilian Salvatorian Order, 1949; ord. priest, Feb. 17, 1952, in Rome; came to U.S., 1958; ord. titular bp. of Abilene of Syria and aux. bp. of Melkite diocese of Newton, MA, June 29, 1986; app. bp. of Newton (Melkites), Nov. 25, 1993, res. Jun. 22, 2004.

Estevez, Felipe de Jesus: b. Feb. 5, 1946, Betancourt, Cuba; educ: Grand Seminary, Montreal, Gregorian Univ., Rome; ord. May 30, 1970 (Matanzas, Cuba); incard. Miami Feb. 1979; app. aux. bp. of Miami and tit. bp. of Kearney Nov. 21, 2003; ord. Jan. 7, 2004; app. bp. of St. Augustine, Apr. 27, 2011; inst. June 2, 2011.

Etienne, Paul D.: b. June 15, 1959, Tell City, IN; educ. Bellarmine College (Louisville, KY), Univ. of St. Thomas/St. John Vianney College Seminary (St. Paul, MN), North American College and Pontifical Gregorian Univ. (Rome); ord. priest, June 27, 1992 (Indianapolis*); app. bp. of Cheyenne, Oct. 19, 2009; ord. Dec. 9, 2009.

Evans, Robert C.: b. Sept. 2, 1947, Moultri, GA; educ. Our Lady of Providence (Warwick, RI), North American College, Pontifical Gregorian Univ., and Pontifical Univ. of St. Thomas Aquinas (Rome); ord. priest (providence), July 2, 1973; sec. at the apostolic nunciature in Washington, DC (2005-2007); app. aux. bp. of Providence, titular bp. of Aquae Regiae, Oct. 15, 2009; ord. Jan. 5, 2010.

F

Fabre, Shelton J.: b. Oct. 25, 1963, New Roads, LA; educ. St. Joseph Seminary College (Covington, LA) and American College (Louvain, Belgium);ord. Aug. 5, 1989 (Baton Rouge, LA); app. aux. bp. of New Orleans and tit. bp. of Pudenzuana Dec. 13, 2006; ord. Feb. 28, 2007; app. bp. of Houma-Thibodaux, Sept. 23, 2013.

Farrell, Kevin J.: b. Dublin, Ireland, Sept. 2, 1947; educ. Univ. of Salamanca (Spain), Gregorian Univ. and Univ. of St. Thomas Aquinas (Rome), Univ. of Notre Dame (South Bend, IN); ord. priest (of the Legionaries of Christ), Dec. 24, 1978; incardinated into Archdio. of Washington, 1984; app. titular bp. of Rusucccuru and aux. bp. of Washington, Dec. 28, 2001; app. bp. of Dallas, Mar. 6, 2007.

Favalora, John C.: b. Dec. 5, 1935, New Orleans, LA; educ. St. Joseph Seminary (St. Benedict, LA), Notre Dame Seminary (New Orleans), Gregorian Univ. (Rome), Catholic Univ. of America (Washington, DC), Xavier Univ. and Tulane Univ. (New Orleans); ord. priest (New Orleans*), Dec. 20, 1961; ord. bp. of Alexandria, LA, July 29, 1986; bp. of St. Petersburg, Mar. 14, 1989; app. abp. of Miami, inst., Dec. 20, 1994; ret. Apr. 20, 2010.

Fellhauer, David E.: b. Aug. 19, 1939, Kansas City, MO; educ. Pontifical College Josephinum (Worthington, OH), St. Paul Univ. (Ottawa); ord. priest (Dallas), May 29, 1965; ord. bp. of Victoria, May 28, 1990.

Finn, Robert W.: b. April 2, 1953, St. Louis; educ. Kenrick-Glennon Seminary (St. Louis), North American College and Angelicum Univ. (Rome); ord. July 7, 1979 (St. Louis); coad. bp. Kansas City-St. Joseph, Mo., Mar. 9, 2004; ord. May 3, 2004; bp. of Kansas City-St. Joseph, Mo., May 24, 2005.

Fiorenza, Joseph A.: b. Jan. 25, 1931, Beaumont, TX; educ. St. Mary's Seminary (LaPorte, TX); ord. priest (Galveston Houston), May 29, 1954; ord. bp. of San Angelo, Oct. 25, 1979; app. bp. of Galveston Houston, Dec. 18, 1984, inst., Feb. 18, 1985; vice president, NCCB/USCC, 1995-1998, President, 1998-2001; app. first abp. of Galveston Houston, Dec. 29, 2004; ret. Feb. 28, 2006.

Fitzgerald, Michael J.: b. May 23, 1948, Montclair, NJ; educ. Temple Univ. (Philadelphia, PA), Villanova Univ. (Philadelphia, PA), St. Charles Borromeo Seminary (Overbrook, PA), Catholic Univ. of America (Washington, D.C.), Gregorian Univ. (Rome); ord. priest, May 17, 1980 (Philadelphia*); app. titular bp. of Tamallula and aux. bp. of Philadelphia, June 22, 2010; ord. bp., Aug. 6, 2010.

Flanagan, Thomas Joseph: b: Oct. 23, 1930, Rathmore, Ireland; educ. St. Patrick's College, Thurles, Ireland; ord priest (San Antonio*), June 10, 1956; app. titular bp. of Bavagaliana and aux. bp. of San Antonio, Jan. 5, 1998, ord., Feb. 16, 1998; ret. Dec. 15, 2005.

Flesey, John W.: b. Aug. 6, 1942, Jersey City (NJ); educ. St. Peter's College (Jersey City), Immaculate Conception Seminary (South Orange, NJ), Catholic Univ. of America (Washington, DC), Iona College (New Rochelle, NY), Pontifical Gregorian Univ., Pontifical Univ. of St. Thomas Aquinas (Rome); ord. priest (Newark*), May 31, 1969; dean of the School of Theology, Seton Hall Univ.; app. aux. bp. of Newark and tit. bp. of Allegheny May 21, 2004; ord. Aug. 4, 2004.

Fliss, Raphael M.: b. Oct. 25, 1930, Milwaukee, WI; educ. St. Francis Seminary (Milwaukee, WI), Catholic Univ. (Washington, DC), Pontifical Lateran Univ. (Rome); ord. priest (Milwaukee*), May 26, 1956; ord. coadj. bp. of Superior with right of succession, Dec. 20, 1979; bp. of Superior, June 27, 1985; ret. June 28, 2007.

Flores, Cirilo: b. June 20, 1948, Corona, CA; educ. Loyola Marymount Univ. (Los Angeles, CA), Stanford Univ. (Palo Alto, CA); St. John's Seminary (Camarillo, CA); ord. priest (Orange), June 8, 1991; app. titular bp. of Quiza and aux. bp. of Orange, Jan. 5, 2009; ord. bp. Mar. 19, 2009; app. coadjutor bp. of San Diego, Jan. 4, 2012; acceded to see, Sept. 18, 2013.

Flores, Daniel E.: b. Aug. 28, 1961, Palacios, Texas; educ. Univ. of Dallas, Holy Trinity Seminary (Dallas), Pont. Univ. of St. Thomas Aquinas (Rome); ord. priest Jan. 30, 1988 (Corpus Christi); app. aux. bp. of Detroit and tit. bp. of Cozila Oct. 28, 2006; ord. Nov. 29, 2006; app. bp. of Brownsville, Dec. 29, 2009; inst. Feb. 2, 2010.

Flores, Patrick F.: b. July 26, 1929, Ganado, TX; educ. St. Mary's Seminary (Houston, TX); ord. priest (Galveston Houston), May 26, 1956; ord. titular bp. of Itolica and aux. bp. of San Antonio, May 5, 1970 (first Mexican American bp.); app. bp. of El Paso, Apr. 4, 1978, inst., May 29, 1978; app. abp. of San Antonio, 1979; inst., Oct. 13, 1979; ret. Dec. 29, 2004.

Flynn, Harry J.: b. May 2, 1933, Schenectady, NY; educ. Siena College (Loudonville, NY), Mt. St. Mary's College (Emmitsburg, MD); ord. priest (Albany), May 28, 1960; ord. coadjutor bp. of Lafayette, LA, June 24, 1986; bp. of Lafayette, LA, May 15, 1989; app. coadj. abp. of St. Paul and Minneapolis Feb. 24, 1994, inst., Apr. 27, 1994; abp. of St. Paul and Minneapolis, Sept. 8, 1995; ret. May 2, 2008.

Folda, John T.: b. August 8, 1961, Omaha, Neb.; educ.: Univ. of Nebraska, St. Charles Borromeo Seminary (Philadelphia), Pontifical Univ. of St. Thomas Aquinas (Rome); ord. priest (Lincoln), May 27, 1989; app. bp. of Fargo, Apr. 8, 2013; ord. bp. June 19, 2013.

Foley, David E.: b. Feb. 3, 1930, Worcester, MA; educ. St. Charles College (Catonsville, MD), St. Mary's

Seminary (Baltimore, MD); ord. priest (Washington*), May 26, 1952; ord. titular bp. of Octaba and aux. bp. of Richmond, June 27, 1986; app. bp. of Birmingham, Mar. 22, 1994; ret. May 10, 2005.

Foys, Roger J.: b. July 27, 1945, Chicago; educ. Univ. of Steubenville, St. John Vianney Seminary, (Bloomingdale, OH), Catholic Univ. of America, Washington, DC; ord. priest (Steubenville), May 16, 1973; Knight Commander of the Equestrian Order of the Holy Sepulchre of Jerusalem, 1986; app. bp. of Covington, May 31, 2002.

Franklin, William Edwin: b. May 3, 1930, Parnell, IA; educ. Loras College and Mt. St. Bernard Seminry (Dubuque, IA); ord. priest (Dubuque*), Feb. 4, 1956; ord. titular bp. of Surista and aux. bp. of Dubuque, Apr. 1, 1987; app. bp. of Davenport, Nov. 12, 1993, inst., Jan. 20, 1994; ret. Oct. 12, 2006.

Friend, William B.: b. Oct. 22, 1931, Miami, FL; educ. St. Mary's College (St. Mary, KY), Mt. St. Mary Seminary (Emmitsburg, MD), Catholic Univ. (Washington, DC), Univ. of Notre Dame (South Bend, IN); ord. priest (Mobile*), May 7, 1959; ord. titular bp. of Pomaria and aux. bp. of Alexandria Shreveport, LA, Oct. 30, 1979; app. bp. of Alexandria Shreveport, Nov. 17, 1982, inst., Jan 11, 1983; app. first bp. of Shreveport, June, 1986; inst., July 30, 1986; ret. Dec. 20, 2006.

G

Gainer, Ronald W.: b. Aug. 24, 1947, Pottsville, PA; educ. St. Charles Borromeo Seminary (Philadelphia), Gregorian Univ. (Rome); ord. priest (Allentown), May 19, 1973; app. bp. of Lexington, KY, ord. bp., Feb. 22, 2003; app. bp. of Harrisburg, Jan. 24, 2014; inst. Mar. 19, 2014.

Galante, Joseph A.: b. July 2, 1938, Philadelphia, PA; educ. St. Joseph Preparatory School, St. Charles Seminary (Philadelphia, PA); Lateran Univ., Angelicum, North American College (Rome); ord. priest (Philadelphia*), May 16, 1964; on loan to diocese of Brownsville, TX, 1968-72, where he served in various diocesan posts; returned to Philadelphia, 1972; assistant vicar (1972 79) and vicar (1979 87) for religious; undersecretary of Congregation for Institutes of Consecrated Life and Societies of Apostolic Life (Rome), 1987 92; ord. titular bp. of Equilium and aux. bp. of San Antonio, Dec. 11, 1992; app. bp. of Beaumont, Apr. 5, 1994; app. co-adjutor bp. of Dallas, Nov. 23, 1999; app. bp. of Camden, Mar. 23, 2004; ret. Jan. 8, 2013.

Galeone, Victor Benito: b. Sept. 13, 1935, Philadelphia; educ. St. Charles College (Baltimore), North American College, Pontifical Gregorian Univ. (Rome), ord. priest (Baltimore*), Dec. 18, 1960; served as missionary in Peru, 1970-75, 1978-85; app. bp. of St. Augustine, June 25, 2001, ord., Aug. 21, 2001; ret. Apr. 27, 2011.

Garcia, Richard J.: b. Apr. 24, 1947, San Francisco; educ. St. Patrick's Seminary (Menlo Park, CA), Pontifical Univ. of St. Thomas Aquinas (Rome); ord priest (San Francisco*), May 13, 1973; app. Titular bp. of Bapara and aux. bp. of Sacramento, Nov. 25, 1997, ord., Jan. 28, 1998; app. bp. of Monterey in California, Dec. 19, 2006.

Garcia-Siller, Gustavo, M.Sp.S.: b. Dec. 21, 1956, San Luis Potosi, Mexico, educ. St. John's Seminary (Camarillo, Calif.), Western Jesuit Univ. (Guadalajara, Mexico), Gregorian Univ. (Rome); ord. priest, June 22, 1984; app. aux. bp of Chicago and titular bp. of Esco, Jan. 24, 2003; ord., Mar. 19, 2003; app. abp. of San Antonio, Oct. 14, 2010; inst. Nov. 23, 2010.

Garland, James H.: b. Dec. 13, 1931, Wilmington, OH; educ. Wilmington College (OH), Ohio State Univ. (Columbus, OH); Mt. St. Mary's Seminary (Cincinnati, OH), Catholic Univ. (Washington, DC); ord. priest (Cincinnati*),

Aug. 15, 1959; ord. titular bp. of Garriana and aux. bp. of Cincinnati, July 25, 1984; app. bp. of Marquette, Oct. 6, 1992; inst., Nov. 11, 1992; ret. Dec. 13, 2005.

Gaydos, John R.: b. Aug. 14, 1943, St. Louis, MO; educ Cardinal Glennon College (St. Louis, MO), North American College, Gregorian Univ. (Rome); ord. priest (St. Louis*), Dec. 20, 1968; ord. bp. of Jefferson City, Aug. 27, 1997.

Gelineau, Louis E.: b. May 3, 1928, Burlington, VT; educ. St. Michael's College (Winooski, VT), St. Paul's Univ. Seminary (Ottawa), Catholic Univ. (Washington, DC); ord. priest (Burlington), June 5, 1954; ord. bp. of Providence, RI, Jan. 26, 1972; ret., June 11, 1997.

Gendron, Odore J.: b. Sept. 13, 1921, Manchester, NH; educ. St. Charles Borromeo Seminary (Sherbrooke, QC), Univ. of Ottawa, St. Paul Univ. Seminary (Ottawa, Ont., Canada); ord. priest (Manchester), May 31, 1947; ord. bp. of Manchester, Feb. 3, 1975; res., June 12, 1990.

George, Cardinal Francis E., O.M.I.: (See **Cardinals, Biographies**).

Gerber, Eugene J.: b. Apr. 30, 1931, Kingman, KS; educ. St. Thomas Seminary (Denver, CO), Wichita State Univ.; Catholic Univ. (Washington, DC), Angelicum (Rome); ord. priest (Wichita), May 19, 1959; ord. bp. of Dodge City, Dec. 14, 1976; app. bp. of Wichita, Nov. 17, 1982, inst., Feb. 9, 1983; res. Oct. 4, 2001.

Gerety, Peter L.: b. July 19, 1912, Shelton, CT; educ. Sulpician Seminary (Paris, France); ord. priest, (Hartford*), June 29, 1939; ord. titular bp. of Crepedula and coadjutor bp. of Portland, ME, with right of succession, June 1, 1966; app. apostolic administrator of Portland, 1967; bp. of Portland, ME, Sept. 15, 1969; app. abp. of Newark, Apr. 2, 1974; inst., June 28, 1974; ret., June 3, 1986.

Gerry, Joseph J., O.S.B.: b. Sept. 12, 1928, Millinocket, ME; educ. St. Anselm Abbey Seminary (Manchester, NH), Univ. of Toronto (Canada), Fordham Univ. (New York); ord. priest, June 12, 1954; abbot of St. Anselm Abbey, Manchester, NH, 1972; ord. titular bp. of Praecausa and aux. of Manchester, Apr. 21, 1986; bp. of Portland, ME, Dec. 27, 1988, inst., Feb. 21, 1989; ret. Feb. 10, 2004.

Gettelfinger, Gerald A.: b. Oct. 20, 1935, Ramsey, IN; educ. St. Meinrad Seminary (St. Meinrad, IN), Butler Univ. (Indianapolis, IN); ord. priest (Indianapolis*), May 7, 1961; ord. bp. of Evansville, Apr. 11, 1989; ret. Apr. 26, 2011.

Gilbert, Edward J., C.SS.R.: b. Dec. 26, 1936, Brooklyn, NY; educ. Mt. St. Alphonsus Seminary (Esopus, NY), Catholic Univ. (Washington, DC); ord. priest (Redemptorists, Baltimore Province), June 21, 1964; ord. bp. of Roseau, Dominica, Sept. 7, 1994; ret. Dec. 26, 2011.

Gilmore, Ronald W.: b. Apr. 23, 1942, Wichita, KS; educ. Univ. Seminary (Ottawa), St. Paul Univ. (Ottawa); ord. priest (Wichita), June 7, 1969; app. Bp. of Dodge City, May 11, 1998, ord., July 16, 1998; ret. Dec. 15, 2010.

Goedert, Raymond E.: b. Oct. 15, 1927, Oak Park, IL; educ. Quigley Preparatory Seminary (Chicago, IL), St. Mary of the Lake Seminary and Loyola Univ. (Chicago, IL), Gregorian Univ. (Rome); ord. priest (Chicago*), May 1, 1952; ord. titular bp. of Tamazeni and aux. bp. of Chicago, Aug. 29, 1991; ret., Jan. 24, 2003.

Gomez, José H.: b. Dec. 26, 1951, Monterrey, Mexico (became U.S. citizen 1995); educ. National Univ., Mexico, Univ. of Navarre (Spain); ord. priest of the Prelature of Opus Dei, Aug. 15, 1978; Vicar of Opus Dei for State of Texas, 1999-2001; app. titular bp. of Belali and aux. bp of Denver, Jan. 23, 2001, ord., Mar. 26, 2001; app. abp. of San Antonio, Dec. 29, 2004; inst. Feb. 15, 2005; app. coadjutor abp. of Los Angeles, Apr. 6, 2010; acceded to the see, Mar. 1, 2011.

Gonzalez, Roberto O., O.F.M., b. June 2, 1950, Elizabeth, NJ; educ. St. Joseph Seminary (Callicoon, NY), Siena College, (Loudonville, NY), Washington Theological Union (Silver Spring, MD), Fordham Univ. (New York, NY); solemnly professed in Franciscan Order, 1976; ord. priest, May 8, 1977; ord. titular bp. of Ursona and aux. bp. of Boston, Oct. 3, 1988; app. coadj. bp. of Corpus Christi, May 16, 1995; bp. of Corpus Christi, Apr. 1, 1997; app. abp. of San Juan de Puerto Rico, Mar. 26, 1999, inst., May 8, 1999.

Gonzalez Valer, S.F., Francisco: b. Arcos de Jalon, Spain, May 22, 1939; educ. Missionary Seminary of the Holy Family, Barcelona (Spain), Catholic Univ. of America (Washington, DC); ord. priest (of the Congregation of the Sons of the Holy Family), May 1, 1964; Episcopal Vicar for Hispanic Catholics, Archdiocese of Washington, 1997; app. titular bp. of Lamfua and aux. bp. of Washington, Dec. 28, 2001; ret. May 27, 2014.

Gorman, John R.: b. Dec. 11, 1925, Chicago, IL; educ. St. Mary of the Lake Seminary (Mundelein, IL), Loyola Univ. (Chicago, IL); ord. priest (Chicago*), May 1, 1956; ord. titular bp. of Catula and aux. bp. of Chicago, Apr. 11, 1988; ret., Jan. 24, 2003.

Gracida, Rene H.: b. June 9, 1923, New Orleans, LA; educ. Rice Univ. and Univ. of Houston (Houston, TX), Univ. of Fribourg (Switzerland); ord. priest (Miami*), May 23, 1959; ord. titular bp. of Masuccaba and aux. bp. of Miami, Jan. 25, 1972; app. first bp. of Pensacola Tallahassee, Oct. 1, 1975, inst., Nov. 6, 1975; app. bp. of Corpus Christi, May 24, 1983, inst., July 11, 1983; ret., Apr. 1, 1997.

Grahmann, Charles V.: b. July 15, 1931, Halletsville, TX; educ. The Assumption St. John's Seminary (San Antonio, TX); ord. priest (San Antonio*), Mar. 17, 1956; ord. titular bp. of Equilium and aux. bp. of San Antonio, Aug. 20, 1981; app. first bp. of Victoria, TX, Apr. 13, 1982; app. coadj. bp. of Dallas, Dec. 9, 1989; bp. of Dallas, July 14, 1990; ret. Mar. 6, 2007.

Green, James P.: b. May 30, 1950, Philadelphia, PA; educ. St. Charles Borromeo Seminary (Overbrook, PA), Pontifical Ecclesiastical Academy (Rome); ord. priest (Philadelphia*), May 15, 1976; after studies at the Pontifical Ecclesiastical Academy, entered the diplomatic service of the Holy See in 1987 and served in Papua New Guinea, Korea, the Netherlands, Spain, Scandinavia, and Taiwan; head of the English-language section in the Secretariat of State 2002-2006; app. nuncio to South Africa, Lesotho, and Namibia, and apostolic delegate in Botswana, Aug. 17, 2006; cons. Sept. 6, 2006; app. nuncio to Peru, Oct. 15, 2011.

Gregory, Wilton D.: b. Dec. 7, 1947, Chicago, IL; educ. Quigley Preparatory Seminary South, Niles College of Loyola Univ. (Chicago, IL), St. Mary of the Lake Seminary (Mundelein, IL), Pontifical Liturgical Institute, Sant'Anselmo (Rome); ord. priest, (Chicago*), May 9, 1973; ord. titular bp. of Oliva and aux. bp. of Chicago, Dec. 13, 1983; app. bp. of Belleville, Dec. 29, 1993; inst., Feb. 10, 1994 vice president, NCCB/USCC, 1998-2001; president, USCCB, 2001-2004; app. abp. of Atlanta, Dec. 9, 2004; inst. Jan. 17, 2005.

Gries, Roger W., O.S.B.: b. Mar. 26, 1937, Cleveland; educ. St. John Univ., (Collegeville, MN), St. Joseph's Seminary, Cleveland, Loyola Univ., Chicago; ord. priest (Order of St. Benedict), May 16, 1963; Abbot, St. Andrew Abbey, Cleveland, 1981-2001; app. aux. bp. of Cleveland, April 3, 2001, ord., June 7, 2001; res. Nov. 1, 2013.

Griffin, James A.: b. June 13, 1934, Fairview Park, OH; educ. St. Charles College (Baltimore, MD), Borromeo College (Wicklife, OH); St Mary Seminary (Cleveland, OH); Lateran Univ. (Rome); Cleveland State Univ.; ord. priest (Cleveland), May 28, 1960; ord. titular bp. of Holar

and aux. bp. of Cleveland, Aug. 1, 1979; app. bp. of Columbus, Feb. 8, 1983; ret. Oct. 14, 2004.

Grosz, Edward M.: b. Feb. 16, 1945, Buffalo, NY; educ. St. John Vianney Seminary (East Aurora, NY), Univ. of Notre Dame (Notre Dame, IN); ord. priest (Buffalo), May 29, 1971; ord. titular bp. of Morosbisdus and aux. bp. of Buffalo, Feb. 2, 1990.

Gruss, Robert D.: b. June 25, 1955, Texarkana, AR; Madison Area Technical College (Madison, WI), Spartan School of Aeronautics (Tulsa, OK), St. Ambrose University (Davenport, IA), Pontifical North American College and Pontifical Univ. of St. Thomas (Rome); ord. priest, July 2, 1994 (Davenport); vice-rector, North American College, Rome, 2007-2010; app. bp. of Rapid City, May 26, 2011; ord. bp. July 28, 2011.

Guglielmone, Robert E.: b. Dec. 30, 1945, New York, NY; St. John's Univ. (Jamaica, NY); Seminary of the Immaculate Conception (Huntington, NY); ord. priest, Apr. 8, 1978; app. bp. of Charleston, Jan. 24, 2009; ord. bp. Mar. 25, 2009.

Guillory, Curtis J., S.V.D.: b. Sept. 1, 1943, Mallet, LA; educ. Divine Word College (Epworth, IA), Chicago Theological Union (Chicago), Creighton Univ. (Omaha, NE); ord. priest, Dec. 16, 1972; ord. titular bp. of Stagno and aux. bp. of Galveston-Houston, Feb. 19, 1988; bp. of Beaumont, June 2, 2000, inst., July 28, 2000.

Gullickson, Thomas E.: b. Aug. 14, 1950, Sioux Falls, SD; educ. North American College and Pontifical Gregorian Univ. (Rome, Italy); ord. priest, June 27, 1976 (Sioux Falls); after studies in the Pontifical Ecclesiastical Academy, he entered the diplomatic service of the Holy See in 1985 and served in the nunciatures in Rwanda, Austria, Czechoslovakia, Jerusalem, and Germany; app. titular abp. of Bomarzo, Oct. 2, 2004; cons. Nov. 11, 2004; Apostolic Nuncio to Trinidad and Tobago, Bahamas, Dominica, St. Kitts and Nevis, Santa Lucia, San Vincenzo and Grenadine; app. nuncio to Ukraine, May 21, 2011.

Gumbleton, Thomas J.: b. Jan. 26, 1930, Detroit, MI; educ. St. John Provincial Seminary (Detroit, MI), Pontifical Lateran Univ. (Rome); ord. priest (Detroit*), June 2, 1956; ord. titular bp. of Ululi and aux. bp. of Detroit, May 1, 1968; ret. Feb. 8, 2006.

H

Habash, Yousif Benham: b. June 1, 1951, Qaraqosh, Iraq; educ. Seminary of St. John of the Dominicans (Mosul), Seminary of Charfet (Lebanon), Pontifical Univ. of the Holy Spirit (Kaslik, Lebanon); ord. priest, Aug. 31, 1975; served in the U.S. in the mission for Our Lady of Deliverance of Newark and then in Chicago and Los Angeles; app. Our Lady of Deliverance of Newark, Apr. 12, 2010.

Hanchon, Donald F.: b. Oct. 9, 1947, Wayne, MI educ. St. John Provincial Seminary, Univ. of Detroit, Univ. of Notre Dame; ord. priest (Detroit*), Oct. 19, 1974; app. titular bp. of Horreomargum and aux. bp. of Detroit, Mar. 22, 2011; ord. May 5, 2011.

Hanifen, Richard C.: b. June 15, 1931, Denver, CO; educ. Regis College and St. Thomas Seminary (Denver, CO), Catholic Univ. (Washington, DC), Lateran Univ. (Rome); ord. priest (Denver*), June 6, 1959; ord. titular bp. of Abercorn and aux. bp. of Denver, Sept. 20, 1974; app. first bp. of Colorado Springs, Nov. 10, 1983; inst., Jan. 30, 1984; ret., Jan. 30, 2003.

Hanus, Jerome George, O.S.B.: b. May 25, 1940, Brainard, NE; educ. Conception Seminary (Conception, MO), St. Anselm Univ. (Rome), Princeton Theological Seminary

(Princeton, NJ); ord. priest (Conception Abbey, MO), July 30, 1966; abbot of Conception Abbey, 1977-87; president of Swiss American Benedictine Congregation, 1984 87; ord. bp. of St. Cloud, Aug. 24, 1987; app. coadjutor abp. of Dubuque, Aug. 23, 1994; abp. of Dubuque, Oct. 16, 1995; ret. Apr. 8, 2013.

Harrington, Bernard J.: b. Sept. 6, 1933, Detroit, MI; educ. Sacred Heart Seminary (Detroit), St. John's Provincial Seminary (Plymouth, MI), Catholic Univ. of America (Washington, DC), Univ. of Detroit; ord. priest (Detroit*), June 6, 1959; ord. titular bp. of Uzali and aux. bp. of Detroit, Jan. 6, 1994; app. Bp. of Winona, Nov. 5, 1998, inst., Jan. 6, 1999; ret. May 7, 2009.

Hart, Joseph: b. Sept. 26, 1931, Kansas City, MO; educ. St. John Seminary (Kansas City, MO), St. Meinrad Seminary (Indianapolis, IN); ord. priest (Kansas City St. Joseph), May 1, 1956; ord. titular bp. of Thimida Regia and aux. bp. of Cheyenne, WY, Aug. 31, 1976; app. bp. of Cheyenne, inst., June 12, 1978; ret., Sept. 26, 2001.

Hartmayer, Gregory J., O.F.M. Conv.: b. Nov. 21, 1951, Buffalo, NY; educ. Franciscan novitiate in Ellicott City (MD), St. Hyacinth College and Seminary (MA); St. Anthony-on-Hudson (Rensselaer, NY), Emmanuel College (Boston), Boston College; solemn profession in the Conventual Franciscans, Aug. 15, 1973; ord. priest, May 5, 1979; app. bp. of Savannah, July 19, 2011; ord. Oct. 18, 2011.

Harvey, James M.: (See Cardinals' Biographies).

Hebda, Bernard A.: b. Sept. 3, 1959, Pittsburgh, PA; educ. Harvard Univ. (Cambridge, MA), Columbia Law School, Parker School of Foreign and Comparative Law, St. Paul Seminary (Pittsburgh, PA), North American College and Gregorian Univ. (Rome); ord. priest, July 1, 1989 (Pittsburgh); served in the Pontifical Council for Legislative Texts (1996-2003) and assistant spiritual director at the North American College; app. bp. of Gaylord, Oct. 7, 2009; ord. Dec. 1, 2009; app. coadj. abp. of Newark, Sept. 24, 2013.

Heim, Capistran F., O.F.M.: b. Jan. 21, 1934, Catskill, NY; educ. Franciscan Houses of Study; ord. priest, Dec. 18, 1965; missionary in Brazil; ord. first bp. of prelature of Itaituba, Brazil, Sept. 17, 1988; inst., Oct. 2, 1988.

Hennessey, Robert F.: b. April 20, 1952 (Boston); educ. St. John's Seminary (Brighton, Mass.), Moreau Seminary (Notre Dame, Ind.); ord. May 20, 1978 (Boston); app. aux. bp. of Boston and tit. bp. of Tigia Oct. 12, 2006; ord. Dec. 12, 2006.

Hermann, Robert J.: b. Aug. 12, 1934, Weingarten, MO; educ. Cardinal Glennon College (Shrewsbury, MO.), St. Louis Univ.; ord. priest (St. Louis), Mar. 30, 1963; aux. bp. St. Louis and tit. bp. of Zerta, Oct. 16, 2002; ord., Dec. 12, 2002; ret. Dec. 1, 2010.

Hermes, Herbert, O.S.B.: b. May 25, 1933, Scott City, KS; ord. priest (St. Benedict Abbey, Atchison, KS), May 26, 1960; missionary in Brazil; ord. bp. of territorial prelature of Cristalandia, Brazil, Sept. 2, 1990; ret. Feb. 25, 2009.

Herzog, Ronald P.: b. April 22, 1942, Akron, OH; educ. St. Joseph Seminary (St. Benedict, LA), Pontifical College Josephinum (Worthington, OH); ord. priest June 1, 1968 (Natchez-Jackson, MS; now Biloxi); app. bp. of Alexandria Nov. 4, 2004; ord. Jan. 5, 2005.

Higgins, Richard B.: b. Feb. 22, 1944, Longford, Ireland; educ. Pontifical Lateran Univ. (Rome); ord. priest (Sacramento), Mar. 9, 1968; entered the Air Force as a chaplain, 1974; app. titular bp. of Case Calane and aux. bp. of the Archdiocese for the Military Services, May 7, 2004.

Higi, William L.: b. Aug. 29, 1933, Anderson, IN; educ. Our Lady of the Lakes Preparatory Seminary (Wawasee,

IN), Mt. St. Mary of the West Seminary and Xavier Univ. (Cincinnati, OH); ord. priest, (Lafayette, IN) May 30, 1959; ord. bp. of Lafayette, IN, June 6, 1984; ret. May 12, 2010.

Hoeppner, Michael J.: b. June 1,1949, Winona, MN; educ. Immaculate Heart of Mary Seminary (Winona), Pontifical North American College and Pontifical Gregorian Univ. (Rome), St. Paul Univ. (Ottawa, Canada), Winona State Univ. (Winona); ord. priest, June 29, 1975 (Winona); app. bp. of Crookston, Sept. 28, 2007; inst. Nov. 30, 2007.

Holley, Martin D.: b. Dec. 31, 1954, Pensacola, FL; educ. Alabama State Univ. (Montgomery, AL), Catholic Univ. of America (Washington, DC), St. Vincent de Paul Regional Seminary (Boynton Beach); ord. priest (Pensacola-Tallahassee), May 8, 1987; app. titular bp. of Rusibisir and aux. bp. of Washington, May 18, 2004; ord. July 2, 2004.

Houck, William Russell: b. June 26, 1926, Mobile, AL; educ. St. Bernard Jr. College (Cullman, AL), St. Mary's Seminary College and St. Mary's Seminary (Baltimore, MD), Catholic Univ. (Washington, DC); ord. priest (Mobile*), May 19, 1951; ord. titular bp. of Alessano and aux. bp. of Jackson, MS, May 27, 1979, by Pope John Paul II; app. bp. of Jackson, Apr. 11, 1984, inst., June 5, 1984; ret., Jan. 3, 2003.

Howze, Joseph Lawson: b. Aug. 30, 1923, Daphne, AL; convert to Catholicism, 1948; educ. St. Bonaventure Univ. (St. Bonaventure, NY); ord. priest (Raleigh), May 7, 1959; ord. titular bp. of Massita and aux. bp. of Natchez Jackson, Jan. 28, 1973; app. first bp. of Biloxi, Mar. 8, 1977; inst., June 6, 1977; res. May 15, 2001.

Hubbard, Howard J.: b. Oct. 31, 1938, Troy, NY; educ. St. Joseph's Seminary (Dunwoodie, NY); North American College and Gregorian Univ. (Rome), Catholic Univ. (Washington, DC); ord. priest (Albany), Dec. 18, 1963; ord. bp. of Albany, Mar. 27, 1977; res. Feb. 11, 2014.

Hughes, Alfred C.: b. Dec. 2, 1932, Boston, MA; educ. St. John Seminary (Brighton, MA), Gregorian Univ. (Rome); ord. priest (Boston*), Dec. 15, 1957, in Rome; ord. titular bp. of Maximiana in Byzacena and aux. bp. of Boston, Sept. 14, 1981; app. bp. of Baton Rouge, Sept. 7, 1993; coadj. abp. of New Orleans, Feb. 16, 2001; abp. of New Orleans, Jan. 3, 2002; ret. June 12, 2009.

Hughes, Edward T.: b. Nov. 13, 1920, Lansdowne, PA; educ. St. Charles Seminary, Univ. of Pennsylvania (Philadelphia); ord. priest (Philadelphia*), May 31, 1947; ord. titular bp. of Segia and aux. bp. of Philadelphia, July 21, 1976; app. bp. of Metuchen, Dec. 11, 1986, inst., Feb. 5, 1987; ret., July 8, 1997.

Hunthausen, Raymond G.: b. Aug. 21, 1921, Anaconda, MT; educ. Carroll College (Helena, MT), St. Edward's Seminary (Kenmore, WA), St. Louis Univ. (St. Louis, MO), Catholic Univ. (Washington, DC), Fordham Univ. (New York City), Univ. of Notre Dame (Notre Dame, IN); ord. priest (Helena), June 1, 1946; ord. bp. of Helena, Aug. 30, 1962; app. abp. of Seattle, Feb. 25, 1975; ret., Aug. 21, 1991.

Hurley, Francis T.: b. Jan. 12, 1927, San Francisco, CA; educ. St. Patrick's Seminary (Menlo Park, CA), Catholic Univ. (Washington, DC); ord. priest (San Francisco*), June 16, 1951; assigned to NCWC in Washington, DC, 1957; assistant (1958) and later (1968) associate secretary of NCCB and USCC; ord. titular bp. of Daimlaig and aux. bp. of Juneau, AK, Mar. 19, 1970; app. bp. of Juneau, July 20, 1971, inst., Sept. 8, 1971; app. abp. of Anchorage, May 4, 1976, inst., July 8, 1976; res., Mar. 3, 2001.

Hurley, Walter A.: b. May 30, 1937, Fredericton, New Brunswick; educ. Sacred Heart Seminary, St. John Provincial Seminary, Catholic Univ. of America; ord. priest, June 5, 1965 (Detroit); app. aux. bp. of Detroit and titular bp. of Cunavia, July 7, 2003; app. bp. of Grand Rapids, June 21, 2005; inst. Aug. 5, 2005; ret. Apr. 18, 2013.

Hying, Donald J.: b. Aug. 18, 1963, West Allis, WI; educ. Marquette Univ. (Marquette), St. Francis de Sales Seminary (St. Francis, WI); St. Mary of the Lake Seminary (Mundelein, IL); ord. priest, May 20, 1989 (Milwaukee*); rector, St. Francis de Sales Seminary, 2007-2011; app. titular bp. of Regiae and aux. bp. of Milwaukee, May 26, 2011; ord. bp. July 20, 2011.

I J

Ibrahim, Ibrahim N.: b. Oct. 1, 1937, Telkaif, Mosul, Iraq.; educ. Patriarchal Seminary (Mosul, Iraq), St. Sulpice Seminary (Paris, France); ord. priest, Dec. 30, 1962, in Baghdad, Iraq; ord. titular bp. of Anbar and apostolic exarch for Chaldean Catholics in the United States, Mar. 8, 1982, in Baghdad; inst., in Detroit, Apr. 18, 1982; app. first eparch, Aug. 3, 1985, when exarchate was raised to eparchy of St. Thomas Apostle of Detroit; ret., May 3, 2014.

Imesch, Joseph L.: b. June 21, 1931, Detroit, MI; educ. Sacred Heart Seminary (Detroit, MI), North American College, Gregorian Univ. (Rome); ord. priest (Detroit*), Dec. 16, 1956; ord. titular bp. of Pomaria and aux. bp. of Detroit, Apr. 3, 1973; app. bp. of Joliet, June 30, 1979; ret. May 16, 2006.

Iriondo, Robert J.: b. Dec. 19, 1938, Legazti, Spain; educ. Collegio San Vittore and Pontifical Gregorian Univ., Rome; ord. priest (of the Canons Regular of the Lateran), Dec. 22, 1962; incardinated into Archdio. of New York, 1996; Vicar for Hispanics, 1997; ord. titular bp. of Alton and aux. of New York, Dec. 12, 2001; res., Feb. 1, 2014.

Irwin, Francis X.: b. Jan 9, 1934, Medford, MA; educ. Boston College High School, Boston College, St. John's Seminary (Brighton, MA), Boston College School of Social Service; ord. priest (Boston*), Feb. 2, 1960; ord. titular bp. of Ubaza and aux. bp. of Boston, Sept. 17, 1996; ret. Oct. 20, 2009.

Isern, Fernando: b. Sept. 22, 1958, Havana, Cuba; educ. Florida International Univ. (Miami, FL), St. John Vianney College Seminary (Miami), St. Vincent De Paul Regional Seminary (Boynton Beach); ord. priest (Miami*), Apr. 16, 1993; app. bp. of Pueblo, Oct. 15, 2009; ord. Dec. 10, 2009; res. June 13, 2013.

Jackels, Michael O.: b. April 13, 1954, Rapid City, S.D.; educ. Univ. of Nebraska-Lincoln, St. Pius X Seminary (Erlanger, KY), Mt. St. Mary's (Emmitburg, MD); ord. priest May 30, 1981 (Lincoln, NE); app. bp. of Wichita Jan. 29, 2005; ord. Apr. 4, 2005; app. abp. of Dubuque, Apr. 8, 2013; inst. May 30, 2013.

Jacobs, Sam Gallip: b. Mar. 4, 1938, Greenwood, MS; educ. Immaculata Seminary (Lafayette, LA), Catholic Univ. (Washington, DC); ord. priest (Lafayette), June 6, 1964; became priest of Lake Charles diocese, 1980, when that see was established; ord. bp. of Alexandria, LA, Aug. 24, 1989; app. bp. of Houma-Thibodaux, Aug. 1, 2003; res. Sept. 23, 2013.

Jammo, Sarhad: b. Mar. 14, 1941, Baghdad, Iraq; educ. Patriarchal Seminary of Mosul, Urban College of the Propaganda Fide Pontifical Oriental Institute (Rome); ord. priest (Baghdad*), Dec. 19, 1964; rector, Chaldean Seminary, Baghdad; after service in Iraq, transferred in 1977 to the Eparchy of St. Thomas the Apostle of Detroit for Chaldeans; app. first eparch of the eparchy of St. Peter the Apostle of San Diego (Chaldean), May 21, 2002.

Jarrell, C. Michael: b. May 15, 1940, Opelousas, LA; educ. Immaculata Minor Seminary (Lafayette, LA);

Catholic Univ. (Washington, DC); ord. priest (Lafayette, LA), June 3, 1967; ord. bp. of Houma-Thibodaux, Mar. 4, 1993; app. bp. of Lafayette, Nov. 8, 2002.

Jenik, John J.: b. Mar. 7, 1944, Manhattan, NY; educ. Cathedral College and Saint Joseph's Seminary (NY), Fordham University (Bronx, NY); ord. priest (New York*), May 30, 1970; app. titular bp. of Druas and aux. bp. of New York, June 14, 2014; ord. Aug. 4, 2014.

Jenky, Daniel R., C.S.C.: b. Mar. 3, 1947, Chicago; educ. Univ. of Notre Dame; ord. priest, Apr. 6, 1974; Religious Superior of the Holy Cross religious at Notre Dame, 1985-1990; app. titular bp. of Amanzia and aux. of Ft. Wayne-South Bend, Oct. 21, 1997, ord., Dec. 16, 1997, bp. of Peoria, Feb. 12, 2002, inst. Apr. 10, 2002.

Johnston, James Vann: b. Oct. 16, 1959, Knoxville, TN; educ. Univ. of Tennessee (Knoxville, TN), St. Meinrad Seminary (St.Meinrad, IN), Catholic Univ. of America (Washington, DC.); ord. priest, June 9, 1990 (Knoxville); app. bp. of Springfield-Cape Girardeau, Jan. 24, 2008; ord. bp., Mar. 31, 2008.

Jugis, Peter J.: b. March 3, 1957, Charlotte, NC; educ. Univ. of North Carolina at Charlotte, North American College and Gregorian Univ. (Rome), Catholic Univ. of America (Washington, DC); ord. priest, June 12, 1983; app. bp. of Charlotte, Aug. 1, 2003; ord. Oct. 24, 2003.

Justice, William J.: b. May 8, 1942; educ., St. Patrick Seminary (Menlo Park, CA), Univ. of San Francisco (San Francisco, CA); ord. priest, May 17, 1968 (San Francisco*); app. titular bp. of Matara di Proconsolare and aux. bp. of San Francisco, Apr. 10, 2008; ord. bp., May 28, 2008.

K

Kagan, David D.: b. Nov. 9, 1949, Waukegan, IL; educ. Loras College/St. Pius X Seminary (Dubuque, IA), Pontifical North American College and Gregorian Univ. (Rome, Italy); ord. priest, June 14, 1975 (Rockford); app. Protonotary Apostolic, 2011; app. bp. of Bismarck. Oct. 19, 2011; ord. bp. Nov. 30, 2011; res. Apr. 8, 2013.

Kalabat, Frank Yohanna: b. May 13, 1970, San Diego, CA; educ. St. Francis Seminary (San Diego, CA), the first born U.S. Chaldean to enter an American seminary, Sacred Heart Major Seminary (Detroit, MI); ord. priest, July 5, 1995 (St. Thomas the Apostle); app. bp. of St. Thomas the Apostle of Detroit (Chaldean), May 3, 2014; ord. June 14, 2014.

Kane, Francis Joseph: b. Oct. 30, 1942, Chicago, IL; educ. Quigley Preparatory Seminary (Chicago, IL), Niles College Seminary (Chicago, IL), St. Mary of the Lake Seminary (Chicago, IL); ord. priest, May 14, 1969 (Chicago*); app. aux. bp. of Chicago and titular bp. of Sault Ste Marie, MI Jan. 24, 2003; ord., Mar. 19, 2003.

Keeler, Cardinal William Henry: (See **Cardinals, Biographies.**)

Keleher, James P.: b. July 31, 1931, Chicago, IL; educ. Quigley Preparatory Seminary (Chicago, IL), St. Mary of the Lake Seminary (Mundelein, IL); ord. priest (Chicago*), Apr. 12, 1958; ord. bp. of Belleville, Dec. 11, 1984; app. abp. of Kansas City, KS, June 28, 1993; ret. Jan. 15, 2005.

Kemme, Carl: b. Aug. 14, 1960, Effingham, IL; educ. Cardinal Glennon College Seminary and Kenrick Seminary (St. Louis, MO); ord. priest (Springfield), May 10, 1986; app. bp. of Wichita, Feb. 20, 2014; ord. bp., May 1, 2014.

Kennedy, Arthur L.: b. Jan. 9, 1942, Boston, MA; educ., St. John Seminary (Brighton, MA), Pontifical North American College and Pontifical Gregorian Univ. (Rome), Boston Univ. (Boston, MA); ord. priest (Boston*); rector of St. John Seminary in Brighton, 2007-2010; app. titular bp. of Timidana and aux. bp. of Boston, June 30, 2010.

Kettler, Donald J.: b. Nov. 26, 1944, Minneapolis: educ. St. John's Seminary Collegeville, MN; ord. priest (Sioux Falls), May 29, 1970; app. bp. of Fairbanks, AK, June 7, 2002, ord., Aug. 22, 2002; app. bp. of St. Cloud, Sept 20, 2013.

Kicanas, Gerald F.: b. Aug. 18, 1941, Chicago, IL; educ. Quigley Preparatory Seminary, St. Mary of the Lake Seminary and Loyola Univ. in Chicago; ord. priest (Chicago*), Apr. 27, 1967; ord. titular bp. of Bela and aux. of Chicago, Mar. 20, 1995; app. coadj. bp. of Tucson, Oct. 30, 2001; inst. as coadj. bp. of Tuscon, Jan. 17, 2002; bp. of Tucson, Mar. 7, 2003.

Kinney, John F.: b. June 11, 1937, Oelwein, IA; educ. Nazareth Hall and St. Paul Seminaries (St. Paul, MN); Pontifical Lateran Univ. (Rome); ord. priest (St. Paul Minneapolis*), Feb. 2, 1963; ord. titular bp. of Caorle and aux. bp. of St. Paul and Minneapolis, Jan. 25, 1977; app. bp. of Bismarck June 30, 1982; app. bp. of St. Cloud, May 9, 1995; res. Sept. 20, 2013.

Kmiec, Edward U.: b. June 4, 1936, Trenton, NJ; educ. St. Charles College (Catonsville, MD), St. Mary's Seminary (Baltimore, MD), Gregorian Univ. (Rome); ord. priest (Trenton), Dec. 20, 1961; ord. titular bp. of Simidicca and aux. bp. of Trenton, Nov. 3, 1982; app. bp. of Nashville, Oct. 13, 1992; inst., Dec. 3, 1992; app. bp. of Buffalo, Aug. 12, 2004; ret. May 29, 2012.

Knestout, Barry C.: b. June 11, 1962, Cheverly (MD), Univ. of Maryland (College Park, MD), Mount St. Mary's Seminary (Emmitsburg, MD); ord. priest (Washington*), June 24, 1989; app. titular bp. of Leavenworth and aux. bp. of Washington, Nov. 18, 2008; ord. bp. Dec. 29, 2008.

Kopacz, Joseph R.: b. Sept. 16, 1950, Dunmore, PA; St. Pius X Seminary (Dalton, PA), University of Scranton (Scranton, PA), Christ the King Seminary (East Aurora, NY); ord. priest (Scranton), May 7, 1977; app. bp. of Jackson, Dec. 12, 2013; ord. bp., Feb. 6, 2014.

Kucera, Daniel W., O.S.B.: b. May 7, 1923, Chicago, IL; educ. St. Procopius College (Lisle, IL), Catholic Univ. (Washington, DC); professed in Order of St. Benedict, June 16, 1944; ord. priest, May 26, 1949; abbot, St. Procopius Abbey, 1964 71; pres. Illinois Benedictine College, 1959 65 and 1971 76; ord. titular bp. of Natchez and aux. bp. of Joliet, July 21, 1977; app. bp. of Salina, Mar. 5, 1980; app. abp. of Dubuque, inst., Feb. 23, 1984; ret., Oct. 16, 1995.

Kudrick, John M.: b. Dec. 23, 1947, Lloydell, PA; educ. Third Order Regular of St. Francis, 1967; ord. priest, May 3, 1975; granted bi-ritual faculties for service in the Byzantine Rite, 1978; app. bp. of Parma, May 3, 2002.

Kurtz, Joseph E.: b. Aug. 18, 1946, Shenandoah, PA.; educ. St. Charles Borromeo Seminary, Philadelphia, Marywood College, Scranton; ord. priest (Allentown), Mar. 18, 1972; app. bp. of Knoxville, Oct. 26, 1999, ord., Dec. 8, 1999; app. abp. of Louisville, June 12, 2007; elected pres. of the USCCB, Nov. 14, 2013.

Kurtz, Robert, C.R.: b. July 25, 1939, Chicago, IL; ord. priest, Mar. 11, 1967; ord. bp. of Hamilton, Bermuda, Sept. 15, 1995; inst. Aug. 15, 2007.

L

LaValley, Terry R.: b. Mar. 26, 1956, Plattsburgh, NY; educ. State Univ. of New York (Plattsburgh, NY), Wadhams Hall Seminary (Ogdensburg, NY), Christ the King Seminary (East Aurora, NY), St. Paul Univ. (Ottawa); ord. priest, Sept. 24, 1988 (Ogdensburg); app. bp. of Ogdensburg, Feb. 23, 2010; ord. bp. Apr. 30, 2010.

Lagonegro, Dominick J.: b. Mar. 6, 1943, White Plains, NY;

educ. Cathedral College, (Douglaston), St. Joseph Seminary, Yonkers; ord. priest (New York*), May 31, 1969; ord. titular bp. of Modrus and aux. of New York, Dec. 12, 2001.

Latino, Joseph: b. Oct. 21, 1937, New Orleans, LA; educ. St. Joseph College Seminary (Covington, LA), Notre Dame Seminary (New Orleans, LA); ord. priest, May 25, 1963; app. bp. Jackson, Jan. 3, 2003; ord., Mar. 7, 2003; ret., Dec. 12, 2013.

Law, Bernard F.: (See **Cardinals, Biographies.**)

Leibrecht, John J.: b. Aug. 30, 1930, Overland, MO; educ. Catholic Univ. (Washington, DC); ord. priest (St. Louis*), Mar. 17, 1956; superintendent of schools of St. Louis archdiocese, 1962 1981; ord. bp. of Springfield Cape Girardeau, MO, Dec. 12, 1984; ret. Jan. 24, 2008.

Lennon, Richard G.: b. Mar. 26, 1947, Arlington, (MA); educ. St. John's Seminary, Brighton; ord. priest (Boston*), May 19, 1973; rector, St. John's Seminary 1999-2001; app. titular bp. of Sufes and aux. bp. of Boston, June 29, 2001, ord., Sept. 14, 2001; apost. admin. of Boston, 2002-03; app. bp. of Cleveland, Apr. 4, 2006.

Lessard, Raymond W.: b. Dec. 21, 1930, Grafton, ND; educ. St. Paul Seminary (St. Paul, MN), North American College (Rome); ord. priest (Fargo), Dec. 16, 1956; served on staff of the Congregation for Bps. in the Roman Curia, 1964 73; ord. bp. of Savannah, Apr. 27, 1973; ret., Feb. 7, 1995.

Levada, William J.: (See **Cardinals, Biographies**).

LeVoir, John: b. Feb. 7, 1946, Minneapolis, MN; educ., Univ. of St. Thomas (Houston, TX), Dallas Univ. (Dallas, TX), St. Paul Seminary (St. Paul and Minneapolis, MN); ord. priest, May 30, 1981 (St. Paul and Minneapolis*); co-author of *Covenant of Love: John Paul II on Sexuality, Marriage, and Family in the Modern World, Faith for Today*, and the series *Image of God*; app. bp. of New Ulm, July 14, 2008.

Libasci, Peter A.: b. Nov. 9, 1951, Jackson Heights (NY); educ. St. John's Univ. (Queens, NY), St. Meinrad School of Theology (St. Meinrad, IN); ord. priest (Rockville Center, NY), Apr. 1, 1978; app. titular bp. of Satafis and aux. bp. of Rockville Center, Apr. 3, 2007; app. bp. of Manchester, Sept. 19, 2011; inst. Dec. 8, 2011.

Lippert, Donald, O.F.M. Cap.: b. June 12, 1957, Pittsburgh, PA; professed perpetual vows for the Capuchin Franciscans, Aug. 20, 1983; ord. priest, June 8, 1985, for the Capuchin Franciscans; app. bp. pf Mendi, Paula, New Guinea, Nov. 22, 2011; ord. bp., Feb. 4, 2012.

Lipscomb, Oscar H.: b. Sept. 21, 1931, Mobile, AL; educ. McGill Institute, St. Bernard College (Cullman, AL), North American College and Gregorian Univ. (Rome), Catholic Univ. (Washington, DC); ord. priest (Mobile*), July 15, 1956; ord. first abp. of Mobile, Nov. 16, 1980; ret. Apr. 2, 2008.

Listecki, Jerome E.: b. Mar. 12, 1949, Chicago; educ. Loyola Univ. and St. Mary of the Lake Seminary, Mundelein, IL, De Paul Univ. College of Law, Univ. of St. Thomas Aquinas and Pontifical Gregorian Univ., Rome; ord. priest (Chicago*), June 1, 1975, app. titular bp. of Nara and aux bp. of Chicago, Nov. 7, 2000, ord., Jan. 8, 2001; app. bp. of La Crosse, Dec. 29, 2004; inst. Mar. 1, 2005; app. abp. of Milwaukee, Nov. 14, 2009; inst. Jan. 15, 2010.

Lohmuller, Martin N.: b. Aug. 21, 1919, Philadelphia, PA; educ. St. Charles Borromeo Seminary (Philadelphia, PA), Catholic Univ. (Washington, DC); ord. priest (Philadelphia*), June 3, 1944; ord. titular bp. of Ramsbury and aux. bp. of Philadelphia, Apr. 2, 1970; ret., Oct. 11, 1994.

Lori, William E.: b. May 6, 1951, Louisville, KY; educ. St. Pius X College (Covington, KY), Mount St.

Mary's Seminary (Emmitsburg, MD), Catholic Univ. (Washington, DC); ord. priest (Washington*), May 14, 1977; ord. titular bp. of Bulla and aux. bp. of Washington, DC, Apr. 20, 1995; app. bp. of Bridgeport, Jan. 23, 2001; inst., Mar. 19, 2001; app. abp. of Baltimore, Mar. 20, 2012; inst. May 16, 2012.

Losten, Basil: b. May 11, 1930, Chesapeake City, MD; educ. St. Basil's College (Stamford, CT), Catholic Univ. (Washington, DC); ord. priest (Philadelphia* Ukrainian Byzantine), June 10, 1957; ord. titular bp. of Arcadiopolis in Asia and aux. bp. of Ukrainian archeparchy of Philadelphia, May 25, 1971; app. apostolic administrator of archeparchy, 1976; app. bp. of Ukrainian eparchy of Stamford, Sept. 20, 1977; ret. Jan. 3, 2006.

Loverde, Paul S.: b. Sept. 3, 1940, Framingham, MA; educ. St. Thomas Seminary (Bloomfield, CT), St. Bernard Seminary (Rochester, NY), Gregorian Univ. (Rome), Catholic Univ. (Washington, DC); ord. priest (Norwich), Dec. 18, 1965; ord. titular bp. of Ottabia and aux. bp. of Hartford, Apr. 12, 1988; app. bp. of Ogdensburg, Nov. 11, 1993; inst., Jan. 17, 1994; app. bp. of Arlington, Jan. 25, 1999, inst., Mar. 25, 1999.

Lucas, George J.: b. June 12, 1949, St. Louis, MO; educ. Major Seminary of St. Louis, Univ. of St. Louis; ord. priest (St. Louis*), May 24, 1975; rector, Kenrick-Glennon Seminary, 1995-1999; app. bp. of Springfield in Illinois, Oct. 19, 1999, ord., Dec. 14, 1999; app. abp. of Omaha, June 3, 2009; inst. July 26, 2009.

Luong, Dominic Dinh Mai: b. Dec. 20, 1940, Minh Cuong, Vietnam; educ. seminary (Buffalo, NY), and St. Bernard Seminary (Rochester, NY), Canisius College (Buffalo); ord. priest in Buffalo for Diocese of Danang, Vietnam, May 21, 1966; incardinated into New Orleans 1986; named aux. bp. of Orange, CA, and titular bp. of Cebarades, April 25, 2003; ord., June 11, 2003.

Lynch, Robert N.: b. May 27, 1941, Charleston, WV; educ. Pontifical College Josephinum (Columbus, OH); John XXIII National Seminary (Weston, MA); ord. priest (Miami*), May 13, 1978; assoc. gen. secretary (1984 89) and gen. secretary (1989 95) of the NCCB/USCC; app. bp. of St. Petersburg, Dec. 5, 1995; ord. and inst., Jan. 26, 1996; app. apostolic administrator of Palm Beach (while continuing as bp. of St. Petersburg), June 2, 1998.

M

Macaluso, Christie Albert: b. June 12, 1945, Hartford, CT; educ. St. Thomas Seminary (Bloomfield, CT), St. Mary's Seminary (Baltimore, MD), Trinity College (Hartford, CT), New York Univ.; ord. priest (Hartford*), May 21, 1971; ord. titular bp. of Grass Valley and aux. bp. of Hartford, June 10, 1997.

McCarrick, Theodore E.: (See **Cardinals, Biographies**.)

McCarthy, James F.: b. July 9, 1942, Mount Kisco, NY; educ. Cathedral College and St. Joseph's Seminary, New York; ord. priest (New York*), June 1, 1968; app. titular bp. of Veronna and aux. bp. of New York, May 11, 1999, inst., June 29, 1999; res., June 12, 2002.

McCarthy, John E.: b. June 21, 1930, Houston, TX; educ. Univ. of St. Thomas (Houston, TX); ord. priest (Galveston Houston), May 26, 1956; assistant director Social Action Dept. USCC, 1967 69; executive director Texas Catholic Conference; ord. titular bp. of Pedena and aux. bp. of Galveston Houston, Mar. 14, 1979; app. bp. of Austin, Dec. 19, 1985, inst., Feb. 25, 1986; res., Jan. 2, 2001.

McCormack, John B.: b Aug. 12, 1935, Winthrop, MA; educ. St. John Seminary College and St. John Seminary

Theologate (Boston, MA); ord. priest (Boston*), Feb. 2, 1960; ord. titular bp. of Cerbali and aux. bp. of Boston, Dec. 27, 1995; app. bp. of Manchester, NH, July 21, 1998, inst., Sept. 22, 1998.

McDonnell, Charles J.: b. July 7, 1928, Brooklyn, NY; educ. Seton Hall Univ. (South Orange, NJ), Immaculate Conception Seminary (Darlington, NJ), Long Island Univ. (Brooklyn, NY); ord. priest (Newark*), May 29, 1954; U.S. Army Chaplain, 1965 89; ret., from active duty with rank of Brigadier General; ord. titular bp. of Pocofelto and aux. bp. of Newark, May 12, 1994; ret. May 21, 2004.

McDonnell, Timothy A.: b. Dec. 23, 1937, New York City; educ. St. Joseph Seminary, Yonkers, Iona College, New Rochelle; ord. priest (New York*), June 1, 1963; ord. titular bp. of Semina and aux. bp. of New York, Dec. 12, 2001; app. bp. of Springfield in Massachusetts, Mar. 9, 2004; ret. June 19, 2014.

McElroy, Robert W.: b. Feb. 5, 1954, San Francisco, CA; educ. St. Patrick Seminary (Menlo Park, CA), Harvard Univ. (Cambridge, MA), Stanford Univ. (Palo Alto, CA), Jesuit School of Theology (Berkeley, CA), North American College (Rome); ord. priest, Apr. 12, 1980 (San Francisco*); app. titular bp. of Gemellae in Byzacena and aux. bp. of San Francisco, July 6, 2010; ord. bp. Sept. 7, 2010.

McGrath, Patrick J.: b. July 11, 1945, Dublin, Ire.; educ. St. John's College Seminary (Waterford), Lateran Univ. (Rome, Italy); ord. priest in Ireland, June 7, 1970; came to U.S. same year and became San Francisco archdiocesan priest; ord. titular bp. of Allegheny and aux. bp. of San Francisco, Jan. 25, 1989; app. coadj. bp. of San Jose, June 30, 1998; bp. of San Jose, Nov. 29, 1999.

McIntyre, John J.: b. Aug. 20, 1963, Philadelphia, PA; educ. St. Alphonsus Seminary (Suffield, CT), St. Charles Borromeo Seminary (Obervbrook, PA); ord. priest, May 16, 1992 (Philadelphia*); sec. to Card. Justin Rigali, 1999-2010; app. titular bp. of Bononia and aux. bp. of Philadelphia, June 8, 2010; ord. bp. Aug. 6, 2010.

McLaughlin, Bernard J.: b. Nov. 19, 1912, Buffalo, NY; educ. Urban Univ. (Rome, Italy); ord. priest (Buffalo), Dec. 21, 1935, at Rome; ord. titular bp. of Mottola and aux. bp. of Buffalo, Jan. 6, 1969; res., Jan. 5, 1988.

McManus, Robert J.: b. July 5, 1951, Warwick, RI; educ. Our Lady of Providence Seminary, Catholic Univ. (Washington, DC), Seminary of Toronto, Canada, Pontifical Gregorian Univ. (Rome); ord. priest (Providence), May 27, 1978; diocesan Vicar for Education and Rector of Our Lady of Providence; app. titular bp. of Allegheny and aux. of Providence, Dec. 1, 1998, ord., Feb. 22, 1999; app. bp. of Worcester, Mar. 9, 2004.

McNabb, John C., O.S.A.: b. Dec. 11, 1925, Beloit, WI; educ. Villanova Univ. (Villanova, PA), Augustinian College and Catholic Univ. (Washington, DC), De Paul Univ. (Chicago, IL); ord. priest, May 24, 1952; ord. titular bp. of Saia Maggiore, June 17, 1967 (resigned titular see, Dec. 27, 1977); prelate of Chulucanas, Peru, 1967; first bp. of Chulucanas, Dec. 12, 1988; ret. Oct. 28, 2000.

McNaughton, William J., M.M.: b. Dec. 7, 1926, Lawrence, MA; educ. Maryknoll Seminary (Maryknoll, NY); ord. priest, June 13, 1953; ord. titular bp. of Thuburbo Minus and vicar apostolic of Inchon, Korea, Aug. 24, 1961; first bp. of Inchon, Mar. 10, 1962, when vicariate was raised to diocese; ret. Apr. 25, 2002.

McRaith, John Jeremiah: b. Dec. 6, 1934, Hutchinson, MN; educ. St. John Preparatory School (Collegeville, MN), Loras College, St. Bernard Seminary (Dubuque, IA); ord. priest (New Ulm), Feb. 21, 1960; exec. dir. of

Catholic Rural Life Conference, 1971 78; ord. bp. of Owensboro, KY, Dec. 15, 1982; ret. Jan. 5, 2009.

Madden, Denis J.: b. Mar. 8, 1940, Carbondale, Pa.; educ. Univ. of Notre Dame, Univ. of Maryland; ord. priest Apr. 1, 1967 (Benedictines); inc. Baltimore Nov. 4, 1976; app. aux. bp. of Baltimore and tit. bp. of Baia, May 10, 2005; ord. bp. Aug. 24, 2005.

Madera, Joseph J., M.Sp.S.: b. Nov. 27, 1927, San Francisco, CA; educ. Domus Studiorum of the Missionaries of the Holy Spirit (Coyoacan, D.F. Mexico); ord. priest, June 15, 1957; ord. coadj. bp. of Fresno, Mar. 4, 1980; bp. of Fresno, July 1, 1980; app. titular bp. of Orte and aux. of Military Services archdiocese, June 30, 1991; ret. Sept. 15, 2004.

Maginnis, Robert P.: b. Dec. 22, 1933, Philadelphia, PA; educ. St. Charles Borromeo Seminary (Overbrook, PA); ord. priest (Philadelphia*), May 13, 1961; ord. titular bp. of Siminina and aux. bp. of Philadelphia, Mar. 11, 1996.

Maguire, Joseph F.: b. Sept. 4, 1919, Boston, MA; educ. Boston College, St. John's Seminary (Boston, MA); ord. priest (Boston*), June 29, 1945; ord. titular bp. of Macteris and aux. bp. of Boston, Feb. 2, 1972; app. coadj. bp. of Springfield, MA, Apr. 13, 1976; succeeded as bp. of Springfield, MA, Oct. 15, 1977; ret., Dec. 27, 1991.

Mahony, Roger M.: (See **Cardinals, Biographies.**)

Maida, Adam J.: (See **Cardinals, Biographies.**)

Malloy, David J.: b. Feb. 3, 1956, Milwaukee, WI; educ. St. Francis de Sales Seminary (Milwaukee, WI), North American College, Pontifical Univ. of St. Thomas, and Pontifical Gregorian Univ. (Rome, Italy); ord. priest (Milwaukee*), July 1, 1983; entered the Pontifical Ecclesiastical Academy and served as secretary to the apostolic nunciatures in Pakistan and Syria and the Mission of the Holy See to the United Nations in New York; served in the Prefecture of the Papal Household in Rome, 1998-2001; USCCB Associate General Secretary, 2001-2006; USCCB General Secretary, 2006-2011; app. bp. of Rockford, Mar. 20, 2012; ord. bp., May 14, 2012.

Malone, Richard J.: b. Mar. 19, 1946, Salem, MA; educ. St. John's Seminary, Brighton, Boston Univ., ord. priest (Boston*), May 20, 1972; app. titular bp. of Aptuca and aux. bp. of Boston, Jan. 27, 2000, ord., Mar. 1, 2000; app. bp. of Portland, ME, Feb. 10, 2004; app. bp. of Buffalo, May 29, 2012.

Malooly, William Francis: b. Jan. 18, 1944, Baltimore; educ. St. Charles Minor Seminary, St. Mary's Seminary (Baltimore) ord priest (Baltimore*), May 7, 1970, app. titular bp. of Flumenzer and aux. bp. of Baltimore, Dec. 12, 2000, ord., Mar. 1, 2001; app. bp. of Wilmington, July 7, 2008.

Manning, Elias (James), O.F.M. Conv.: b. Apr. 14, 1938, Troy, NY; educ. Sao José Seminary (Rio de Janeiro, Brazil); ord. priest, Oct. 30, 1965, in New York; ord. bp. of Valenca, Brazil, May 13, 1990; ret. Feb. 2, 2014.

Manning, Thomas R., O.F.M.: b. Aug. 29, 1922, Baltimore, MD; educ. Duns Scotus College (Southfield, MI), Holy Name College (Washington, DC); ord. priest, June 5, 1948; ord. titular bp. of Arsamosata, July 14, 1959 (res. titular see, Dec. 30, 1977); prelate of Coroico, Bolivia, July 14, 1959; became first bp., 1983, when prelature was raised to diocese; ret., Oct. 9, 1996.

Mansell, Henry J.: b. Oct. 10, 1937, New York, NY; educ. Cathedral College, St. Joseph's Seminary and College (New York); North American College, Gregorian Univ. (Rome); ord. priest (New York*), Dec. 19, 1962; ord. titular bp. of Marazane and aux. bp. of New York, Jan. 6, 1993, by John Paul II in Vatican City; app. bp. of

Buffalo, Apr. 18, 1995; inst., June 12, 1995; app. abp. of Hartford, Oct. 20, 2003; ret. Oct. 29, 2013.

Mansour, Gregory John: b. Nov. 11, 1955, Flint, MI; educ. Univ. of Michigan (Kalamazoo, MI), Catholic Univ, of America (Washington, DC), North American College and Pontifical Gregorian Univ. (Rome); ord. priest (Eparchy of St. Maron of Brooklyn), Sept. 18, 1982; app. bp. of the Eparchy of St. Maron, Brooklyn, NY, Jan. 10, 2004.

Manz, John R.: b. Nov. 14, 1945, Chicago, IL; educ. Niles College Seminary (Niles, IL), Univ. of St. Mary of the Lake Mundelein Seminary (Chicago); ord. priest (Chicago*), May 12, 1971; ord. titular bp. of Mulia and aux. bp. of Chicago, Mar. 5, 1996.

Marconi, Dominic A.: b. Mar. 13, 1927, Newark, NJ; educ. Seton Hall Univ. (S. Orange, NJ), Immaculate Conception Seminary (Darlington, NJ), Catholic Univ. (Washington, DC); ord. priest (Newark*), May 30, 1953; ord. titular bp. of Bure and aux. bp. of Newark, June 25, 1976; res., July 1, 2002.

Marino, Joseph: b. Jan. 23, 1953, Birmingham, AL; educ. Pontifical North American College and Pontifical Gregorian Univ. (Rome); ord. priest, Aug. 25, 1979 (Birmingham); studies at the Pontifical Ecclesiastical Academy, entered papal diplomatic service in 1988; diplomatic posts in the Philippines, Uruguay, Nigeria, Great Britain, and the Secretariat of State in Rome; app. apostolic nuncio to Bangladesh and titular abp. of Natchitoches, Jan. 12, 2008; ord. Mar. 29, 2008; app. nuncio to Malaysia, East Timor, and Brunei.

Martino, Joseph F.: b. May 1, 1946, Philadelphia, PA; educ. St. Charles Borromeo Seminary (Overbrook, PA), Gregorian Univ. (Rome); ord. priest (Philadelphia*), Dec. 18, 1970; ord. titular bp. of Cellae in Mauretania and aux. bp. of Philadelphia, Mar. 11, 1996; app. bp. of Scranton, July 25, 2003; res. Aug. 31, 2009.

Matano, Salvatore R.: b. Sept. 15, 1946, Providence, RI; educ. Our Lady of Providence Seminary College (Warwick, RI), Gregorian Univ. (Rome); ord. priest Dec. 17, 1971 (Providence); served on staff of apostolic nunciature (Washington, DC); app. coadj. bp. of Burlington, Mar. 3, 2005; ord. Apr. 19, 2005; bp. of Burlington, Nov. 9, 2005; app. bp. of Rochester, Nov. 6, 2013.

Medley, William F.: b. Sept. 17, 1952, Marion County, Kentucky; educ. Bellarmine Univ. (Louisville, KY), St. Meinrad School of Theology (St. Meinrad, IN); ord. priest (Louisville), May 22, 1982; app. bp. of Owensboro, Dec. 15, 2009; ord. Feb. 10, 2010.

Melczek, Dale J.: b. Nov. 9, 1938, Detroit, MI; educ. St. Mary's College (Orchard Lake, MI), St. John's Provincial Seminary (Plymouth, MI), Univ. of Detroit; ord. priest (Detroit*), June 6, 1964; ord. titular bp. of Trau and aux. bp. of Detroit, Jan. 27, 1983; apostolic administrator of Gary, Aug. 19, 1992; coadjutor bp. of Gary, Oct. 28, 1995; bp. of Gary, June 1, 1996.

Mengeling, Carl F.: b. Oct. 22, 1930, Hammond, IN; educ. St. Meinrad College and Seminary (St. Meinrad, IN), Alphonsianum Univ. (Rome); ord. priest (Gary), May 25, 1957; ord. bp. of Lansing, Jan. 25, 1996; ret. Feb. 27, 2008.

Michaels, James E., S.S.C.: b. May 30, 1926, Chicago, IL; educ. Columban Seminary (St. Columban, NE), Gregorian Univ. (Rome); ord. priest, Dec. 21, 1951; ord. titular bp. of Verbe and aux. bp. of Kwang Ju, Korea, Apr. 14, 1966; app. aux. bp. of Wheeling, Apr. 3, 1973 (title of see changed to Wheeling-Charleston, 1974); res., Sept. 22, 1987.

Miller, J. Michael, C.S.B.: b. July 9, 1946, Ottawa, Canada; educ. St. Michael's College, Univ. of Toronto

(Toronto, Canada), Gregorian Univ. (Rome); ord. priest (Congregation of St. Basil), June 29, 1975, Congregation of St. Basil; official in Secretariat of State, Rome, 1992-97; pres. of Univ. of St. Thomas Aquinas, Houston, Texas, 1997-2004; 2004; app. titular abp. of Vertara and sec. of the Cong. for Catholic Education, Rome, Nov. 25, 2003; app. coadj. abp. of Vancouver, June 1, 2007.

Milone, Anthony M.: b. Sept. 24, 1932, Omaha, NE; educ. North American College (Rome); ord. priest (Omaha*), Dec. 15, 1957, in Rome; ord. titular bp. of Plestia and aux. bp. of Omaha, Jan. 6, 1982; app. bp. of Great Falls Billings, Dec. 14, 1987, inst., Feb. 23, 1988; ret. July 12, 2006.

Monforton, Jeffrey M.: b. May 5, 1963, Detroit, MI; educ. Wayne State Univ., Sacred Heart Major Seminary (Detroit, MI), Pontifical North American College and Pontifical Gregorian Univ. (Rome); ord. priest (Detroit*), June 25, 1994; sec. to Cardinal Adam Maida, 1998-2005; served as an apostolic visitor by the Congregation for Catholic Education in the apostolic visitation of U.S. seminaries and houses of formation, 2005-2006; rector of Sacred Heart Major Seminary, 2006; app. bp. of Steubenville, July 3, 2012; ord., Sept. 12, 2012.

Morin, Roger Paul: b. Mar. 7, 1941, Lowell, MA; educ. Notre Dame Seminary (New Orleans, LA), Tulane Univ. (New Orleans, LA); ord. priest, Apr. 15, 1971 (New Orleans*); app. aux. bp. of New Orleans and titular bp. of Aulona, Feb. 11, 2003; ord., Apr. 22, 2003; bp. of Biloxi, Mar. 2, 2009.

Morlino, Robert C.: b. Dec. 31, 1946, Scranton, PA; educ. Fordham Univ., Univ. of Notre Dame, Weston School of Theology, Cambridge, MA, Gregorian Univ., Rome; ord. priest for the Society of Jesus, Maryland Province, June 1, 1974, incardinated into the Diocese of Kalamazoo, MI, Oct. 26, 1983, app. bp. of Helena, July 6, 1999, inst,. Sept. 21, 1999; app. bp. of Madison, May 23, 2003.

Morneau, Robert F.: b. Sept. 10, 1938, New London, WI; educ. St. Norbert's College (De Pere, WI), Sacred Heart Seminary (Oneida, WI), Catholic Univ. (Washington, DC); ord. priest (Green Bay), May 28, 1966; ord. titular bp. of Massa Lubrense and aux. bp. of Green Bay, Feb. 22, 1979; ret. Oct. 10, 2013.

Moskal, Robert M.: b. Oct. 24, 1937, Carnegie, PA; educ. St. Basil Minor Seminary (Stamford, CT), St. Josaphat Seminary and Catholic Univ. (Washington, DC); ord. priest (Philadelphia*, Byzantine Ukrainian), Mar. 25, 1963; ord. titular bp. of Agatopoli and aux. bp. of the Ukrainian archeparchy of Philadelphia, Oct. 13, 1981; app. first bp. of St. Josaphat in Parma, Dec. 5, 1983; ret. July 29, 2009.

Mouradian, Mikael A.: b. July 5, 1961, Beirut, Lebanon; ord. priest, (Institute of the Patriarchal Clergy of Bzommar, Oct. 24, 1987; app. eparch of Our Lady of Nareg, May 21, 2011; ord. bp. Oct. 2, 2011; inst. Oct. 2, 2011.

Moynihan, James M.: b. July 16, 1932, Rochester, NY; educ. St. Bernard's Seminary (Rochester, NY), North American College and Gregorian Univ. (Rome); ord. priest (Rochester), Dec. 15, 1957, in Rome; ord. bp. of Syracuse, May 29, 1995; ret. Apr. 21, 2009.

Muench Robert W.: b. Dec. 28, 1942, Louisville, KY; educ. St. Joseph Seminary and Notre Dame Seminary (New Orleans, LA), Catholic Univ. (Washington, DC); ord. priest (New Orleans*), June 18, 1968; ord. titular bp. of Mactaris and aux. bp. of New Orleans, June 29, 1990; app. bp. of Covington Jan. 5, 1996; inst., Mar. 19, 1996; app. bp. of Baton Rouge, Dec. 15, 2001.

Mulvee, Robert E.: b. Feb. 15, 1930, Boston, MA; educ. St. Thomas Seminary (Bloomfield, CT), Univ. Seminary (Ottawa, ON), American College (Louvain, Belgium), Lateran Univ. (Rome); ord. priest (Manchester), June 30, 1957; ord. titular bp. of Summa and aux. bp. of Manchester, NH, Apr. 14, 1977; app. bp. of Wilmington, Del., Feb. 19, 1985; app. coadj. bp. of Providence, Feb. 9, 1995; bp. of Providence, June 11, 1997; ret. Mar. 31, 2005.

Mulvey, William M.: b. Aug. 23, 1949, (Houston, TX); educ. St. Edward's Univ. (Austin, TX), North American College, Pontifical Univ. of St. Thomas Aquinas, and Pontifical Gregorian Univ. (Rome); ord. priest (Austin), July 29, 1975; app. bp. of Corpus Christi, Jan. 10, 2010; ord. Mar. 25, 2010.

Murphy, William F.: b. May 14, 1940, Boston MA; educ. Boston Latin School (Boston), Harvard College, St. John's Seminary (Boston), Gregorian Univ. (Rome); ord. priest (Boston*), Dec. 16, 1964; ord. titular bp. of Saia Maggiore and aux. bp. of Boston, Dec. 27, 1995; app. bp. of Rockville Centre, June 25, 2001, inst., Sept. 5, 2001.

Murray, James A.: b. July 5, 1932, Jackson, MI; educ. Sacred Heart Seminary Detroit, St. John Provincial Seminary (Plymouth, MI), Catholic Univ. of America; ord. priest (Lansing), June 7, 1958; app. bp. of Kalamazoo, Nov. 18, 1997, ord., Jan. 27, 1998; ret. Apr. 6, 2009.

Murry, George V., S.J.: b. Dec. 28, 1948, Camden, NJ; educ. St. Joseph's College (Philadelphia, PA), St. Thomas Seminary (Bloomfield, CT), St. Mary Seminary (Baltimore, MD), Jesuit School of Theology (Berkeley, CA), George Washington Univ. (Washington, DC); entered Jesuits 1972; ord. priest, June 9, 1979; ord. titular bp. of Fuerteventura and aux. bp. of Chicago, Mar. 20, 1995; app. co-adjutor of St. Thomas in the Virgin Islands, May 5, 1998; bp. of St. Thomas in the Virgin Islands, June 30, 1999; bp. of Youngstown, Jan. 30, 2007.

Myers, John Joseph: b. July 26, 1941, Ottawa, IL; educ. Loras College (Dubuque, IA), North American College and Gregorian Univ. (Rome), Catholic Univ. of America (Washington, DC); ord. priest (Peoria), Dec. 17, 1966, in Rome; ord. coadj. bp. of Peoria, Sept. 3, 1987; bp. of Peoria, Jan. 23, 1990; app. abp. of Newark, July 24, 2001.

N

Naickamparampil, Thomas: b. Mylapra, India, June 6, 1961; educ. St. Aloysious Minor Seminary, (Pattom, Trivandrum, India), Papal Seminary of Pune (Pune, India); Gregorian Univ. (Rome); ord. priest (Trivandrum*), Dec. 29, 1986; app. first apostolic exarchate for the Syro-Malankara Catholic Church in the United States and apostolic visitor for the Syro-Malankara Catholics in Canada and Europe; ord. bp. Sept. 21, 2010.

Naumann, Joseph F.: b. June 4, 1949, St. Louis, MO; educ. Cardinal Glennon Seminary College and Kenrick Seminary (St. Louis, MO); ord. priest (St. Louis*), 1975; app. titular bp. of Caput Cilla and aux. bp. of St. Louis, July 9, 1997; app. coadj. abp. of Kansas City, Jan. 7, 2004; abp. of Kansas City, Jan. 15, 2005.

Nevares, Eduardo: b. Feb. 19, 1954, San Antonio, TX; educ.: LaSalette Minor Seminary (Jefferson City, MO), St. Henry Preparatory Seminary (Belleville, IL), LaSalette Junior College Seminary and LaSalette Senior College Seminary (Ipswich, MA), Univ. of St. Thomas (Houston, TX); entered the novitiate of the Missionaries of Our Lady of LaSalette in 1976, professed first vows in 1977, and final vows in 1980; ord. priest, July 18, 1981; app. auxiliary bp. of Phoenix and titular bp. of Natchez, May 11, 2010.

Nevins, John J.: b. Jan. 19, 1932, New Rochelle, NY; educ. Iona College (New Rochelle, NY), Catholic Univ.

(Washington, DC); ord. priest (Miami*), June 6, 1959; ord. titular bp. of Rusticana and aux. bp. of Miami, Mar. 24, 1979; app. first bp. of Venice, FL, July 17, 1984; inst., Oct. 25, 1984; ret. Jan. 19, 2007.

Newman, William C.: b. Aug. 16, 1928, Baltimore, MD; educ. St. Mary Seminary (Baltimore, MD), Catholic Univ. (Washington, DC), Loyola College (Baltimore, MD); ord. priest (Baltimore*), May 29, 1954; ord. titular bp. of Numluli and aux. bp. of Baltimore, July 2, 1984; ret. Aug. 28, 2003.

Nickless, R. Walker: b. May 28, 1947, Denver; educ. St. Thomas Seminary, Univ. of Denver, Gregorian Univ. (Rome); ord. priest Aug. 4, 1973 (Denver); app. bp. of Sioux City, Iowa, Nov. 10, 2005; ord. bp. Jan. 20, 2006.

Niederauer, George H.: b. June 14, 1936, Los Angeles, CA; educ. St. John's Seminary (Camarillo, CA), Catholic Univ. (Washington, DC), Loyola Univ. of Los Angeles, Univ. of Southern CA, Loretta Heights College (Denver, CO); ord. priest (Los Angeles*), Apr. 30, 1962; app. bp. of Salt Lake City, Nov. 3, 1994, ord., Jan. 25, 1995; app. Abp. of San Francisco, Dec. 15, 2005; ret. July 27, 2012.

Nienstedt, John C.: b. Mar. 18, 1947, Detroit, MI; educ. Sacred Heart Seminary (Detroit), North American College, Gregorian Univ., Alphonsianum (Rome); ord. priest (Detroit*), July 27, 1974; served in Vatican Secretariat of State, 1980 86; rector of Sacred Heart Seminary (Detroit), 1988 94; pastor of the Shrine of the Little Flower (Royal Oak, MI), 1994; ord. titular bp. of Alton and aux. bp. of Detroit, July 9, 1996; app. bp. of New Ulm, June 12, 2001, inst., Aug. 6, 2001; app. coadj. abp. of St. Paul-Minneapolis, Apr. 24, 2007; acceded to the see, May 2, 2008.

Noonan, John G.: b. Feb. 26, 1951, Limerick, Ireland; educ. St. John Vianney College Seminary (Miami), St. Vincent de Paul Seminary (Boynton Beach, Fla.); app. aux. bp. Miami June 21, 2005; ord. bp. Aug. 24, 2005; app. bp. Of Orlando, Dec. 16, 2010.

Novak, Alfred, C.Ss.R.: b. June 2, 1930, Dwight, NE; educ. Immaculate Conception Seminary (Oconomowoc, WI); ord. priest, July 2, 1956; ord. titular bp. of Vardimissa and aux. bp. of Sao Paulo, Brazil, May 25, 1979; bp. of Paranagua, Brazil, Mar. 14, 1989; ret. Aug. 2, 2006.

O

O'Brien, Edwin F.: (See **Cardinals' Biographies**).

O'Brien, Thomas Joseph: b. Nov. 29, 1935, Indianapolis, IN; educ. St. Meinrad High School Seminary, St. Meinrad College Seminary (St. Meinrad, IN); ord. priest (Tucson), May 7, 1961; ord. bp. of Phoenix, Jan. 6, 1982; res., June 18, 2003.

Ochoa, Armando: b. Apr. 3, 1943, Oxnard, CA; educ. Ventura College (Ventura, CA), St. John's College and St. John's Seminary (Camarillo, CA); ord. priest (Los Angeles*), May 23, 1970; ord. titular bp. of Sitifi and aux. bp. of Los Angeles, Feb. 23, 1987; app. bp. of El Paso, Apr. 1, 1996; inst., June 26, 1996; app. bp. of Fresno, Dec. 1, 2011; inst. Feb. 2, 2012.

O'Connell, C.M., David M.: b.: Apr. 21, 1955, Philadelphia, PA; educ.: Niagara Univ. (Niagara, NY), Mary Immaculate Seminary (Northhampton, PA); Catholic Univ. of America (Washington, D.C.); ord. priest for the Congregation of the Missions, May 29, 1982; held various academic posts at Mary Immaculate Seminary and St. John's Univ.; president of Catholic Univ. of America 1998-2010; app. coadj. bp. of Toledo, June 4, 2010; acceded to see, Dec. 1, 2010.

O'Hara, John J.: b. Feb. 7, 1946, Jersey City, NJ; educ. Seton Hall University (South Orange, NJ), St. Joseph's Seminary (NY); ord. priest (New York*), Dec. 1, 1984; app. titular bp. of Ath Truim and aux. bp. of New York, June 14, 2014; ord. Aug. 4, 2014.

Olivier, Leonard J., S.V.D.: b. Oct. 12, 1923, Lake Charles, LA; educ. St. Augustine Major Seminary (Bay St. Louis, MS), Catholic Univ. (Washington, DC), Loyola Univ. (New Orleans, LA); ord. priest, June 29, 1951; ord. titular bp. of Leges in Numidia and aux. bp. of Washington, Dec. 20, 1988; ret. May 18, 2004.

Olmsted, Thomas J.: b. Jan. 21, 1947, Oketo, KS; educ. St. Thomas Seminary (Denver), North American College and Pontifical Gregorian Univ. (Rome); ord. priest (Lincoln), July 2, 1973; served in Vatican Secretariat of State, 1979-1988; Dean of Formation, Pontifical College Josephinum, Columbus, OH, 1993, President and Rector, Pontifical College, Josephinum, 1997; app. coadjutor bp. of Wichita, Feb. 16, 1999, ord., Apr. 20, 1999; bp. of Wichita, Oct. 4, 2001; app. bp. of Phoenix, Nov. 25, 2003.

O'Malley, Sean, O.F.M.Cap.: (See **Cardinals' Biographies**).

Olson, Michael F.: b. June 29, 1966, Park Ridge, IL; educ. Quigley Preparatory Seminary North (Chicago, IL), The Catholic University of America (Washington, DC), Univ. of St. Thomas (Houston), St. Louis Univ. (St. Louis), Academia Alfonsiana (Rome); ord. priest (Fort Worth), June 3, 1994; app. bp. of Fort Worth, Nov. 19, 2013; ord. bp. Jan. 29, 2014.

Ottenweller, Albert H.: b. Apr. 5, 1916, Stanford, MT; educ. St. Joseph's Seminary (Rensselaer, IN), Catholic Univ. (Washington, DC); ord. priest (Toledo), June 19, 1943; ord. titular bp. of Perdices and aux. bp. of Toledo, May 29, 1974; app. bp. of Steubenville, OH, Oct. 11, 1977, inst., Nov. 22, 1977; ret., Jan. 28, 1992.

P

Paprocki, Thomas J.: b. Aug. 5, 1952, Chicago, IL; educ. Niles College of Loyola (Chicago, IL), St. Mary of the Lake Seminary (Chicago, IL), DePaul Univ. College of Law (Chicago, IL), Gregorian Univ. (Rome); ord. priest, May 10, 1978 (Chicago*); app. aux. bp. of Chicago and titular bp. of Vulturara, Jan. 24, 2003; ord., Mar. 19, 2003; app. bp. of Springfield, Apr. 20, 2010; inst. June 22, 2010.

Parkes, Gregory L.: b. Apr. 2, 1964, Mineola, NY; educ. Florida State Univ. (Tallahassee, FL), St. Vincent de Paul Seminary (Boynton Beach, FL), Pontifical North American College and Pontifical Gregorian Univ. (Rome, Italy); ord. priest (Orlando), June 26, 1999; app. bp. of Pensacola-Tallahassee, Mar. 20, 2012; ord. bp., June 12, 2012.

Pates, Richard E.: b. Feb. 12, 1943, St. Paul; educ. St. Paul Seminary, North American College (Rome); ord. priest (St. Paul and Minneapolis*), Dec. 20, 1968; staff, Apostolic Nunciature, Washington, 1975-81; app. titular bp. of Suacia and aux. bp. of St. Paul and Minneapolis, Dec. 22, 2000, ord., Mar. 26, 2001; app. bp. of Des Monies, Apr. 10, 2008; inst. May 29, 2008.

Pearce, George H., S.M.: b. Jan. 9, 1921, Brighton, MA; educ. Marist College and Seminary (Framington, MA); ord. priest, Feb. 2, 1947; ord. titular bp. of Attalea in Pamphylia and vicar apostolic of the Samoa and Tokelau Islands, June 29, 1956; title changed to bp. of Apia, June 21, 1966; app. abp. of Suva, Fiji Islands, June 22, 1967; res., Apr. 10, 1976.

Peña, Raymundo J.: b. Feb. 19, 1934, Robstown, TX; educ. Assumption Seminary (San Antonio, TX); ord. priest (Corpus Christi), May 25, 1957; ord. titular bp. of Trisipa and aux. bp. of San Antonio, Dec. 13, 1976; app. bp. of El Paso, Apr. 29, 1980; app. bp. of Brownsville, May 23, 1995; ret. Dec. 9, 2009.

Pepe, Joseph A.: b. June 18, 1942, Philadelphia; educ. St. Charles Borromeo Seminary, Univ. of St. Thomas (Rome); ord. priest (Philadelphia*), May 16, 1970; app. bp. of Las Vegas, April 6, 2001, ord., May 31, 2001.

Perez, Nelson J.: b. Miami, FL, June 16, 1961; educ. Montclair State College, St. Charles Borromeo Seminary (Philadelphia, PA); ord. priest. (Philadelphia*), May 20, 1989; app. aux. bp. of Rockville Centre and titular bp. of Catrum, June 8, 2012; ord. bp., July 25, 2012.

Perry, Joseph N.: b. Apr. 18, 1948, Chicago, IL; educ. Capuchin Seminary of St. Lawrence, (Milwaukee), St. Mary Capuchin Seminary, Crown Point, (IN), St. Francis Seminary (Milwaukee), Catholic Univ. of America (Washington, DC); ord. priest (Milwaukee*), May 24, 1975; app. titular bp. of Lead and aux. bp. of Chicago, May 5, 1998; ord., June 29, 1998.

Persico, Lawrence T.: b. Monessesn, PA, Nov. 21, 1950; educ. Seminary of St. Pius X (Erlanger, KY), St. Vincent Seminary (Latrobe, PA), The Catholic University of America, Washington, DC; ord. priest, Apr. 30, 1977 (Greensburg); served as chancellor and vicar general of Greensburg and also vice-president of the Pennsylvania Catholic Conference (2006-2012); app. bp. of Erie, July 31, 2012; ord., Oct. 1, 2012.

Pevec, A. Edward: b. Apr. 16, 1925, Cleveland, OH; educ. St. Mary's Seminary, John Carroll Univ. (Cleveland, OH); ord. priest (Cleveland), Apr. 29, 1950; ord. titular bp. of Mercia and aux. bp. of Cleveland, July 2, 1982; res., Apr. 3, 2001.

Pfeifer, Michael, O.M.I.: b. May 18, 1937, Alamo, TX; educ. Oblate school of theology (San Antonio, TX); ord. priest, Dec. 21, 1964; provincial of southern province of Oblates of Mary Immaculate, 1981; ord. bp. of San Angelo, July 26, 1985; ret., Dec. 12, 2012.

Piché, Lee Anthony: b. May 8, 1958, Minneapolis, MN; educ. St. Paul Seminary and St. Thomas College (St. Paul, MN), St. Joseph Seminary (Princeton, NJ), Columbia Univ. (New York); ord. priest, May 26, 1984 (St. Paul and Minneapolis*); app. aux. bp. of Minneapolis and St. Paul and titular bp. of Tamata, May 27, 2009; ord. June 29, 2009.

Pilarczyk, Daniel E.: b. Aug. 12, 1934, Dayton, OH; educ. St. Gregory's Seminary (Cincinnati, OH), Urban Univ. (Rome), Xavier Univ. and Univ. of Cincinnati (Cincinnati, OH); ord. priest (Cincinnati*), Dec. 20, 1959; ord. titular bp. of Hodelm and aux. bp. of Cincinnati, Dec. 20, 1974; app. abp. of Cincinnati, Oct. 30, 1982; inst., Dec. 20, 1982; president of NCCB/USCC, 1989 92; ret. Dec. 21, 2009.

Pilla, Anthony M.: b. Nov. 12, 1932, Cleveland, OH; educ. St. Gregory College Seminary (Cincinnati, OH), Borromeo College Seminary (Wickliffe, OH), St. Mary Seminary and John Carroll Univ. (Cleveland, OH); ord. priest (Cleveland), May 23, 1959; ord. titular bp. of Scardona and aux. bp. of Cleveland, Aug. 1, 1979; app. apostolic admin. of Cleveland, 1980; bp. of Cleveland, Nov. 13, 1980. President of NCCB/USCC, 1995 98; res. Apr. 4, 2006.

Potocnak, Joseph J., S.C.J.: b. May 13, 1933, Berwick, PA; educ. Dehon Seminary (Great Barrington, MA), Kilroe Seminary (Honesdale, PA), Sacred Heart (Hales Corners, WI); ord. priest, Sept 21, 1966; missionary in South Africa from 1973; ord. bp. of De Aar, South Africa, May 1, 1992.

Provost, Glen J.: b. Aug. 9, 1949, Lafayette, La.; educ. Immaculata Seminary (Lafayette), St. Joseph Seminary College (St. Benedict, La.), Pontifical North American College (Rome), Univ. of South Louisiana (Lafayette, La.); ord. June 29, 1975 (Lafayette); app. bp. of Lake Charles, Mar. 6, 2007; ord. bp. Apr. 23, 2007.

Q

Quinn, Francis A.: b. Sept. 11, 1921, Los Angeles, CA; educ. St. Joseph's College (Mountain View, CA), St. Patrick's Seminary (Menlo Park, CA), Catholic Univ. (Washington, DC); Univ. of CA (Berkeley); ord. priest (San Francisco*), June 15, 1946; ord. titular bp. of Numana and aux. bp. of San Francisco, June 29, 1978; app. bp. of Sacramento, Dec. 18, 1979; ret., Nov. 30, 1993.

Quinn, John M.: b. Dec. 17, 1945, Detroit; educ. Sacred Heart Seminary, St. John Provincial Seminary, Univ. of Detroit and Catholic Univ. of America (Washington, DC); ord. priest, Mar. 17, 1972; app. aux. bp. of Detroit and titular bp. of Ressiana, July 7, 2003; app. coadj. bp. of Winona, Oct. 15, 2008; bp. of Winona, May 7, 2009.

Quinn, John R.: b. Mar. 28, 1929, Riverside, CA; educ. St. Francis Seminary (El Cajon, CA), North American College (Rome); ord. priest (San Diego), July 19, 1953; ord. titular bp. of Thisiduo and aux. bp. of San Diego, Dec. 12, 1967; bp. of Oklahoma City and Tulsa, Nov. 30, 1971; first abp. of Oklahoma City, Dec. 19, 1972; app. abp. of San Francisco, Feb. 22, 1977, inst., Apr. 26, 1977; president NCCB/USCC, 1977 80; res., see Dec. 27, 1995.

R

Raica, Steven J.: b. Nov. 8, 1952, Munising, MI; educ. Michigan State Univ. (Lansing, MI), St. John Provincial Seminary (Plymouth, MI), Pontifical North American College (Rome, Italy); ord. priest (Lansing), Oct. 14, 1978; app. bp. of Gaylord, June 27, 2014; ord. Aug. 28, 2014.

Ramirez, Ricardo, C.S.B.: b. Sept. 12, 1936, Bay City, TX; educ. Univ. of St. Thomas (Houston, TX), Univ. of Detroit (Detroit, MI), St. Basil's Seminary (Toronto, ON), Seminario Concilium (Mexico City, Mexico), East Asian Pastoral Institute (Manila, Philippines); ord. priest, Dec. 10, 1966; ord titular bp. of Vatarba and aux. of San Antonio, Dec. 6, 1981; app. first bp. of Las Cruces, NM, Aug. 17, 1982; inst., Oct. 18, 1982; ret. Jan. 10, 2013.

Rassas, George J.: b. Baltimore May 26, 1942; educ. Univ. of St. Mary of the Lake (Mundelein, IL), Loyola Univ. (Chicago); ord. priest May 2, 1968 (Chicago); app. aux. bp. Chicago and tit. bp. of Reperi Dec. 1, 2005; ord. bp. Feb. 2, 2006.

Reichert, Stephen J., O.F.M. Cap.: b. May 14, 1943, Leoville, KS; educ. Capuchin minor seminary (Victoria, KS), St. Fidelis College (Hermann, PA), Capuchin College (Washington, DC); ord. priest, Sept. 27, 1969; missionary in Papua New Guinea since 1970; ord. bp. of Mendi, Papua New Guinea, May 7, 1995; app. abp. of Madang, Papua New Guinea, Nov. 30, 2010; inst. Feb. 2, 2011.

Reilly, Daniel P.: b. May 12, 1928, Providence, RI; educ. Our Lady of Providence Seminary (Warwick, RI), St. Brieuc Major Seminary (Cotes du Nord, France); ord. priest (Providence), May 30, 1953; ord. bp. of Norwich, Aug. 6, 1975; app. bp. of Worcester, Oct. 27, 1994, inst., Nov. 8, 1994; ret. Mar. 9, 2004.

Reiss, Francis R.: b. Nov. 11, 1940, Detroit; educ. Sacred Heart Seminary, St. John Provincial Seminary, Univ. of Detroit, Gregorian Univ.; ord. priest, June 4, 1966; app. aux. bp. of Detroit and titular bp. of Remesiana, July 7, 2003.

Rhoades, Kevin C.: b. Nov. 26, 1957, Mahanoy City, PA; educ. Mt. St. Mary's College (Emmitsburg, MD), St. Charles Borromeo Seminary (Wynnewood, PA); Gregorian Univ. (Rome); ord. priest July 9, 1983 (Harrisburg); app. bp. of Harrisburg Oct. 14, 2004; ord. Dec. 9, 2004; app. bp. of Ft. Wayne-South Bend, Nov. 14, 2009; inst. Jan. 13, 2010.

Riashi, Georges, B.C.O.: b. Nov. 25, 1933, Kaa el Rim,

Lebanon; ord. priest, Apr. 4, 1965; parish priest of Our Lady of Redemption Parish, Warren, MI (Newton Greek Catholic Melkite eparchy); U.S. citizen; ord. first bp. of eparchy of St. Michael's of Sydney (Australia) for Greek Catholic Melkites, July 19, 1987; app. abp. of archeparchy of Tripoli of Lebanon for Greek-Melkites, Aug. 5, 1995.

Ricard, John H., S.S.J.: b. Feb. 29, 1940, Baton Rouge, LA; educ. St. Joseph's Seminary (Washington, DC); Tulane Univ. (New Orleans, LA); ord. priest, May 25, 1968; ord. titular bp. of Rucuma and aux. of Baltimore, July 2, 1984; urban vicar, Baltimore; app. bp. of Pensacola Tallahassee, Jan 21, 1997; ret. Mar. 11, 2011.

Rice, Edward M.: b. July 28, 1960, St. Louis, MO; educ. Cardinal Glennon College and Kenrick-Glennon Seminary, St. Louis, MO; ord. priest Jan. 3, 1987 (St. Louis*); titular bp. of Sufes and aux. bp. of St. Louis, Dec. 1, 2010; ord. Jan. 13, 2011.

Ricken, David L.: b. Nov. 9, 1952, Dodge City, KS; educ. Conception Seminary College, MO, Univ. of Louvain (Belgium), Pontifical Gregorian Univ., Rome; ord. priest (Pueblo), Sept. 12, 1980; official of the Congregation for the Clergy, 1996-1999; app. coadj. Bp. of Cheyenne, Dec. 14, 1999, ord. bp. by Pope John Paul II at the Vatican, Jan. 6, 2000; bp. of Cheyenne, Sept. 26, 2001; app. bp. of Green Bay, July 9, 2008; inst. Aug. 28, 2008.

Rigali, Justin F.: (See Cardinals, Biographies.)

Rizzotto, Vincent M.: b. Sept. 9, 1931, Houston, TX; educ. St. Mary Seminary (Houston), the Catholic Univ. of America (Washington, DC), ord. priest, (Galveston, now Galveston-Houston) May 26, 1956; Vicar General of Galveston-Houston, 1994; app. titular bp. of Lamasba and aux. bp. of Galveston-Houston June 22, 2001, ord., July 31, 2001; ret. Oct. 30, 2006.

Rodi, Thomas J: b. Mar. 27, 1949, New Orleans, LA; educ. Georgetown Univ. (Washington, D.C.), Tulane Univ. School of Law (New Orleans), Notre Dame Seminary (New Orleans); ord. priest, (New Orleans*), May 20, 1978; app. bp. of Biloxi, May 15, 2001, ord., July 2, 2001; app. abp. of Mobile, Apr. 2, 2008; inst. June 6, 2008.

Rodimer, Frank J.: b. Oct. 25, 1927, Rockaway, NJ; educ. Seton Hall Prep (South Orange, NJ), St. Charles College (Catonsville, MD), St. Mary's Seminary (Baltimore, MD), Immaculate Conception Seminary (Darlington, NJ), Catholic Univ. (Washington, DC); ord. priest (Paterson), May 19, 1951; ord. bp. of Paterson, Feb. 28, 1978; ret. June 1, 2004.

Rodriguez, Miguel, C.SS.R.: b. Apr. 18, 1931, Mayaguez, P.R.; educ. St. Mary's Minor Seminary (North East, PA), Mt. St. Alphonsus Major Seminary (Esopus, NY); ord. priest, June 22, 1958; ord. bp. of Arecibo, P.R., Mar. 23, 1974; res., Mar. 20, 1990.

Rodriguez, Placido, C.M.F.: b. Oct. 11, 1940, Celaya, Guanajuato, Mexico; educ. Claretian Novitate (Los Angeles, CA), Claretville Seminary College (Calabasas, CA), Catholic Univ. (Washington, DC), Loyola Univ. (Chicago, IL); ord. priest, May 23, 1968; ord. titular bp. of Fuerteventura and aux. bp. of Chicago, Dec. 13, 1983; app. bp. of Lubbock, TX, Apr. 5, 1994.

Roque, Francis X.: b. Oct. 9, 1928, Providence RI; educ. St. John's Seminary (Brighton, MA); ord. priest, (Providence) Sept. 19, 1953; became chaplain in U.S. Army 1961; ord. titular bp. of Bagai and aux. bp. of Military Services archdiocese, May 10, 1983; ret. Sept. 15, 2004.

Rosazza, Peter Anthony: b. Feb. 13, 1935, New Haven, CT; educ. St. Thomas Seminary (Bloomfield, CT), Dartmouth College (Hanover, NH), St. Bernard's Seminary (Rochester, NY), St. Sulpice (Issy, France); ord. priest (Hartford*), June

29, 1961; ord. titular bp. of Oppido Nuovo and aux. bp. of Hartford, June 24, 1978; ret., June 30, 2010.

Rose, Robert John: b. Feb. 28, 1930, Grand Rapids, MI; educ. St. Joseph's Seminary (Grand Rapids, MI), Seminaire de Philosophie (Montreal, Canada), Urban Univ. (Rome), Univ. of Michigan; ord. priest (Grand Rapids), Dec. 21, 1955; ord. bp. of Gaylord, Dec. 6, 1981; app. bp. of Grand Rapids, inst., Aug. 30, 1989; ret. Oct. 13, 2003.

Rozanski, Mitchell Thomas: b. Aug. 6, 1958, Baltimore, MD; educ. Catholic Univ. of America (Washington, DC); ord. priest (Baltimore*), Nov. 24, 1984; app. titular bp. of Walla Walla and aux. bp. of Baltimore, July 2, 2004; ord. Aug. 24, 2004; app. bp. of Springfield, June 19, 2014; inst. Aug. 12, 2014.

Rueger, George E.: b. Sept. 3, 1933, Framingham, MA; educ. Holy Cross College (Worcester, MA), St. John's Seminary (Brighton), Harvard Univ. (Cambridge, MA); ord. priest (Worcester), Jan. 6, 1958; ord. titular bp. of Maronana and aux. bp. of Worcester, Feb. 25, 1987; ret. Jan. 25, 2005.

Ryan, Daniel L.: b. Sept. 28, 1930, Mankato, MN; educ. St. Procopius Seminary (Lisle, IL), Lateran Univ. (Rome); ord. priest (Joliet), May 3, 1956; ord. titular bp. of Surista and aux. bp. of Joliet, Sept. 30, 1981; app. bp. of Springfield, IL, Nov. 22, 1983, inst., Jan. 18, 1984; res. Oct. ,19, 1999.

Ryan, Sylvester D.: b. May 3, 1930, Catalina Is., CA; educ. St. John's Seminary (Camarillo, CA); ord. priest (Los Angeles*), May 3, 1957; ord. titular bp. of Remesiana and aux. bp. of Los Angeles, May 31, 1990; app. bp. of Monterey, Jan. 28, 1992; ret. Dec. 19, 2006.

S

Salazar, Alexander: b. Nov. 28, 1949, San Jose, Costa Rica; educ. California State Univ. and Immaculate Heart College (Los Angeles), St. John's Seminary (Camarillo, CA); ord. priest June 16, 1984; appointed aux. bp. of Los Angeles and titular bp. of Nesqually Sept. 7, 2004; ord. Nov. 4, 2004.

Sample, Alexander K.: b. Nov. 7, 1960, Kalispell, Mont.; educ. Michigan Technological Univ. (Houghton), St. Thomas College (St. Paul, MN), Pontifical College Josephinum (Columbus, OH), Angelicum (Rome); ord. priest June 1, 1990 (Marquette); app. bp of Marquette Dec. 13, 2005; ord. bp. Jan. 25, 2006; app. abp. of Portland in Oregon, Jan. 29, 2013; inst. Apr. 2, 2013.

Samra, Nicholas J.: b. Aug. 15, 1944, Paterson, NJ; educ. St. Anselm College (Manchester, NH), St. Basil Seminary (Methuen, MA), St. John Seminary (Brighton, MA); ord. priest (Newton), May 10, 1970; ord. titular bp. of Gerasa and aux. bp. of Melkite diocese of Newton, July 6, 1989; res. Jan. 11, 2005; app. eparch of Newton, June 15, 2011.

Sanchez, Paul R.: b. Nov. 26, 1946, Brooklyn, NY; educ. St. Bonaventure's Univ. (New York), Univ. of Notre Dame (South Bend, IN), Pontifical Gregorian Univ. (Rome); ord. priest (Brooklyn), Dec. 17, 1971; served in various pastoral assignments and was an adjunct faculty member at St. John's Univ. and the Seminary of the Immaculate Conception, Huntington, NY; app. aux. bp. of Brooklyn and titular bp. of Coeliana, May 2, 2012; ord. bp., July 11, 2012

Sansaricq, Guy A.: b. Oct. 6, 1934, Jeremie, Haiti; educ. St. Paul College (Ottawa); ord. priest June 29, 1960 (Les Cayes, Haiti); incard. Brooklyn 1991; appointed aux. bp. of Brooklyn and tit. bp. of Glenndalocha June 6, 2006; ord. Aug. 22, 2006.

Sartain, James P.: b. June 6, 1952, Memphis, TN; educ. St. Meinrad Seminary, (IN), North American College,

(Rome), Pontifical Univ. of St. Thomas (the Angelicum), Pontifical Institute of St. Anselm (Rome); ord. priest (Memphis), July 15, 1978; app. bp. of Little Rock, Jan. 4, 2000, ord., Mar. 6, 2000; app. bp. of Joliet, May 16, 2006; app. abp. of Seattle, Dec. 1, 2010.

Sartoris, Joseph M.: b. July 1, 1927, Los Angeles, CA; educ. St. John's Seminary (Camarillo, CA); ord. priest (Los Angeles*), May 30, 1953; ord. titular bp. of Oliva and aux. bp. of Los Angeles, Mar. 19, 1994; ret., Dec. 31, 2002.

Scarpone Caporale, Gerald, O.F.M.: b. Oct. 1, 1928, Watertown, MA; ord. priest, June 24, 1956; ord. coadj. bp. of Comayagua, Honduras, Feb. 21, 1979; succeeded as bp. of Comayagua, May 30, 1979.

Scharfenberger, Edward B.: b. May 29, 1948, Brooklyn, NY; educ. Cathedral College of the Immaculate Conception, North American College and Pontifical Gregorian Univ. (Rome), Alphonsian Academy (Rome), The Catholic Univ. of America (Washington, DC); ord. priest (Brooklyn), July 2, 1973; app. bp. of Albany, Feb. 11, 2014; ord. bp., Apr. 10, 2014.

Schlarman, Stanley Gerard: b. July 27, 1933, Belleville, IL; educ. St. Henry Prep Seminary (Belleville, IL), Gregorian Univ. (Rome), St. Louis Univ. (St. Louis, MO); ord. priest (Belleville), July 13, 1958, Rome; ord. titular bp. of Capri and aux. bp. of Belleville, May 14, 1979; app. bp. of Dodge City, Mar. 1, 1983; res., May 12, 1998.

Schmitz Simon, Paul, O.F.M. Cap.: b. Dec. 4, 1943, Fond du Lac, WI; ord. priest, Sept. 3, 1970; missionary in Nicaragua from 1970; superior of vice province of Capuchins in Central America (headquartered in Managua), 1982-84; ord. titular bp. of Elepla and aux. of the vicariate apostolic of Bluefields, Nicaragua, Sept. 17, 1984; app. bp. of vicariate apostolic of Bluefields, Aug. 17, 1994.

Schnurr, Dennis M.: b. June 21, 1948, Sheldon, IA; educ. Loras College (Dubuque), Gregorian Univ. (Rome), Catholic Univ. of America (Washington, DC); ord. priest (Sioux City), July 20, 1974; Staff, Apostolic Nunciature, Washington, DC, 1985-1989; Assoc. Gen. Secretary, National Conference of Catholic Bps./United States Catholic Conference (NCCB/USCC), 1989-1995; National Executive Director, World Youth Day 1993, Denver, 1991-1993; General Secretary, NCCB/USCC, 1995-2001; app. bp. of Duluth, Jan. 18, 2001, ord., Apr. 2, 2001; app. co-adj. abp. of Cincinnati, Oct. 17, 2008; acceded to the see, Dec. 21, 2009.

Schulte, Francis B.: b. Dec. 23, 1926, Philadelphia, PA; educ. St. Charles Borromeo Seminary (Overbrook, PA); ord. priest (Philadelphia*), May 10, 1952; ord. titular bp. of Afufenia and aux. bp. of Philadelphia, Aug. 12, 1981; app. bp. of Wheeling-Charleston, June 4, 1985; abp. of New Orleans, Dec. 6, 1988, inst., Feb. 14, 1989; ret., Jan. 3, 2002.

Schwietz, Roger L., O.M.I.: b. July 3, 1940, St. Paul, MN; educ. Univ. of Ottawa (Canada), Gregorian Univ. (Rome); ord. priest, Dec. 20, 1967; ord. bp. of Duluth Feb. 2, 1990; bp. of Duluth, 1990-2000; coadj. abp. of Anchorage, Jan. 18, 2000; abp. of Anchorage, Mar. 3, 2001.

Seitz, Mark J.: b. Jan. 10, 1954, Milwaukee, WI; educ. Univ. of Dallas (Dallas, TX), St. John's Univ. (Collegeville, MN), National Catholic Bioethics Center (Philadelphia, PA); ord. priest (Dallas), May 17, 1980; app. titular bp. of Cozila and aux. bp. of Dallas, Mar. 11, 2010; ord. bp. Apr. 27, 2010; app. bp. of El Paso, May 6, 2013; inst. July 9, 2013.

Seminack, Richard: b. Mar. 3, 1942, Philadelphia; educ. St. Basil Seminary College (Stamford, CT), St. Josaphat Major Seminary and Catholic Univ. of America (Washington), Oriental Institute (Rome); ord. priest, May 25, 1967 (archeparchy of Philadelphia); incard. Eparchy of St. Josaphat (Parma) 1983; app. bp. of St. Nicholas of Chicago for Ukrainians, Mar. 25, 2003; ord., June 4, 2003.

Senior, Timothy C.: b. Mar. 22, 1960, Philadelphia, PA; educ. St. Charles Seminary Overbrook, PA), Boston College (Boston, MA); ord. priest (Philadelphia*), May 18, 1985; sec. for archdiocesan Catholic Human Services (1997-2004); app. titular bp. of Floriana and aux. bp. of Philadelphia, June 8, 2009; ord. bp. July 31, 2009.

Serratelli, Arthur J.: b. Apr. 18, 1944, Newark, NJ; educ. Seton Preparatory School (NJ), Seton Hall Univ. (NJ), North American College and Gregorian Univ. (Rome), Pontifical Biblical Institute (Rome); ord. priest (Newark*), Dec. 20, 1968; prof. of Sacred Scripture, Immaculate Conception Seminary; rector of the College Seminary, Seton Hall Univ.; prelate of honor, 1998; app. titular bp. of Enera and aux. bp. of Newark, July 3, 2000; app. bp. of Paterson, June 1, 2004.

Sevilla, Carlos A., S.J.: b. Aug. 9, 1935, San Francisco, CA; entered Jesuits Aug. 14, 1953; educ. Gonzaga Univ. (Spokane, WA), Santa Clara Univ. (Santa Clara, CA), Jesuitenkolleg (Innsbruck, Austria), Catholic Institute of Paris (France); ord. priest, June 3, 1966; ord. titular bp. of Mina and aux. bp. of San Francisco, Jan. 25, 1989; bp. of Yakima, Dec. 31, 1996; ret. Apr. 12, 2011.

Shaheen, Robert J.: b. June 3, 1937, Danbury, CT; ord., May 2, 1964; elected eparch of Our Lady of Lebanon of Los Angeles of the Maronites (U.S.A.), Dec. 5, 2000; ret. July 10, 2013.

Sheehan, Michael J.: b. July 9, 1939, Wichita, KS; educ. Assumption Seminary (San Antonio, TX), Gregorian Univ. and Lateran Univ. (Rome); ord. priest (Dallas), July 12, 1964; ord. first bp. of Lubbock, TX, June 17, 1983; apostolic administrator of Santa Fe, Apr. 6, 1993; app. abp. of Santa Fe, Aug. 17, 1993.

Sheldon, Gilbert I.: b. Sept. 20, 1926, Cleveland, OH; educ. John Carroll Univ. and St. Mary Seminary (Cleveland, OH); ord. priest (Cleveland), Feb. 28, 1953; ord. titular bp. of Taparura and aux. bp. of Cleveland, June 11, 1976; app. bp. of Steubenville, Jan. 28, 1992, ret., May 31, 2002.

Sheltz, George A.: b. Apr. 20, 1946, Houston, TX; educ. of St. Thomas and St. Mary's Seminary (Houston, TX); ord. priest, May 15, 1971 (Galveston-Houston*); app. titular bp. of Hirina and aux. bp. of Galveston-Houston, Feb. 21, 2012; ord. bp., May 2, 2012.

Sheridan, Michael J.: b. Mar. 4, 1945, St. Louis, MO; educ. Glennon College, Kenrick Seminary (St. Louis, MO), Angelicum (Rome); ord. priest (St. Louis*), 1971; app. titular bp. of Thibiuca and aux. bp. of St. Louis, July 9, 1997; coadj. bp. of Colorado Springs, Dec. 4, 2001; bp. of Colorado Springs, Jan. 30, 2003.

Silva, Clarence: b. Aug. 6, 1949, Honolulu; educ. St. Patrick Seminary (Menlo Park, Calif.); ord. priest May 2, 1975 (Oakland); app. bp. of Honolulu May 17, 2005; ord. bp. July 21, 2005.

Siegel, Joseph M.: b. July 18, 1963, Joliet, IL; educ. St. Meinrad Seminary College, North American College, Pontifical Univ. of St. Thomas Aquinas and Pontifical Gregorian Univ. (Rome), Univ. of St. Mary of the Lake/Mundelein Seminary; ord. priest (Joliet), June 4, 1988; app. aux. bp. of Joliet and titular bp. of Pupiana, Oct. 28, 2009; ord. Jan. 19, 2010.

Sirba, Paul D.: b. Sept. 2, 1960, St. Paul, MN; educ. Archdiocesan Seminary (St. Paul and Minneapolis), Notre Dame Institute for Catechetics (Alexandria, VA); ord. priest (St. Paul and Minneapolis*), May 31, 1986;

app. bp. of Duluth, Oct. 15, 2009; ord. Dec. 14, 2009.

Sis, Michael J.: b. Jan. 9, 1960, Bryan, TX; educ. University of Notre Dame (South Bend, IN), North American College, Pontifical Gregorian Univ., and Pontifical Lateran Univ. (Rome); ord. priest (Austin), July 19, 1986; app. bp. of San Angelo, Dec. 12, 2013; ord. bp., Jan. 27, 2014.

Sklba, Richard J.: b. Sept. 11, 1935, Racine, WI; educ. Old St. Francis Minor Seminary (Milwaukee, WI), North American College, Gregorian Univ., Pontifical Biblical Institute, Angelicum (Rome); ord. priest (Milwaukee*), Dec. 20, 1959; ord. titular bp. of Castra and aux. bp. of Milwaukee, Dec. 19, 1979; ret. Oct. 18, 2010.

Skurla, William C.: b. June 1, 1956, Duluth; educ. Columbia Univ., New York, Mary Immaculate Seminary, Northhampton, PA; ord. priest (Franciscan), 1987; incardinated into Eparchy of Van Nuys, 1996; app. bp. of Van Nuys Byzantine Catholic Eparchy in California, Feb. 19, 2002; app. bp. of Ruthenian Byzantine diocese of Passaic, Dec. 6, 2007; app. abp. of Pittsburgh for the Ruthenians, Jan. 19, 2012; inst. Apr. 18, 2012.

Skylstad, William S.: b. Mar. 2, 1934, Omak, WA; educ. Pontifical College Josephinum (Worthington, OH), Washington State Univ. (Pullman, WA), Gonzaga Univ. (Spokane, WA); ord. priest (Spokane), May 21, 1960; ord. bp. of Yakima, May 12, 1977; app. bp. of Spokane, Apr. 17, 1990; vice-pres. of USCCB, 2001-2004; pres. of USCCB, 2004-2007; app. apostolic admin. of Baker, Jan. 24, 2011.

Slattery, Edward J.: b. Aug. 11, 1940, Chicago, IL; educ. Quigley Preparatory, St. Mary of the Lake Seminary (Mundelein, IL), Loyola Univ. (Chicago); ord. priest (Chicago*), Apr. 26, 1966; vice president, 1971-76, and president, 1976-94, of the Catholic Church Extension Society; ord. bp. of Tulsa, Jan. 6, 1994.

Smith, John M.: b. June 23, 1935, Orange, NJ; educ. Immaculate Conception Seminary (Darlington, NJ), Seton Hall Univ. (South Orange, NJ), Catholic Univ. (Washington, DC); ord. priest (Newark*), May 27, 1961; ord. titular bp. of Tre Taverne and aux. bp. of Newark, Jan. 25, 1988; app. bp. of Pensacola-Tallahassee, FL, June 25, 1991; app. coadj. bp. of Trenton, Nov. 21, 1995; bp. of Trenton, July 1, 1997; ret. Dec. 1, 2010.

Smith, Peter L.: b. Feb. 8, 1958, Pietermaritzburg, South Africa; educ. Mount Angel Seminary (Mount Angel, OR), The Catholic Univ. of America (Washington, DC); ord. priest (Portland*), June 9, 2001; titular bp. of Tubunae in Mauretania and aux. bp. of Portland in Oregon, Mar. 4, 2014; ord. bp., Apr. 29, 2014.

Snyder, John J.: b. Oct. 25, 1925, New York, NY; educ. Cathedral College (Brooklyn, NY), Immaculate Conception Seminary (Huntington, NY); ord. priest (Brooklyn), June 9, 1951; ord. titular bp. of Forlimpopli and aux. bp. of Brooklyn, Feb. 2, 1973; app. bp. of St. Augustine, inst., Dec. 5, 1979; res., Dec. 11, 2000.

Soens, Lawrence D.: b. Aug. 26, 1926, Iowa City, IA; educ. Loras College (Dubuque, IA), St. Ambrose College (Davenport, IA), Kenrick Seminary (St. Louis, MO), Univ. of Iowa; ord. priest (Davenport), May 6, 1950; ord. bp. of Sioux City, Aug. 17, 1983, res., Nov. 28, 1998.

Soro, Bawai: b. Mar. 3, 1954, Kerkuk, Iraq; originally ord. a priest in 1982 and a bp. in 1984 for the Assyrian Church of the East; in 2008 he and 1,000 Assyrian families were received into full communion with the Chaldean Catholic Church; app. titular bp. of Foratiana and aux. bp. of St. Peter the Apostle of San Diego of the Chaldeans, Jan. 11, 2014.

Soroka, Stephen: b. Nov. 13, 1951, Winnipeg, Manitoba; educ. Univ. of Manitoba, Ukrainian Seminary, Washington, DC, Catholic Univ. of America, ordained (Ukrainian Archdiocese of Winnipeg*), June 13, 1982; Chancellor and financial administrator of the Winnipeg archdiocese, 1994, auxiliary bp., Winnipeg, 1996; metropolitan abp. of Philadelphia for the Ukrainians, Nov. 29, 2000; inst., Feb. 27, 2001.

Soto, Jaime: b. Dec. 31, 1955, Inglewood, CA; educ. St. John's Seminary, Camarillo, CA, Columbia Univ. School of Social Work, New York; ord. priest (Orange), June 12, 1982; Episcopal Vicar for Hispanic Ministry, 1989; app. titular bp. of Segia and aux. bp. of Orange, Mar. 23, 2000, ord., May 31, 2000; app. coadj. bp. of Sacramento, Oct. 11, 2007; inst. Nov. 19, 2007; bp. of Sacramento, Nov. 29, 2008.

Sowada, Alphonse A., O.S.C.: b. June 23, 1933, Avon, MN; educ. Holy Cross Scholasticate (Ft. Wayne, IN), Catholic Univ. (Washington, DC), ord. priest, May 31, 1958; missionary in Indonesia from 1958; ord. bp. of Agats, Indonesia, Nov. 23, 1969; ret. May 9, 2001.

Spencer, F. Richard: b. June 10, 1951, Sylacauga, AL; educ.: Jacksonville State Univ., (AL), Univ. of Wisconsin (LaCrosse, WI), St. Mary's Seminary and Univ. (Baltimore, MD), and military training courses; ord. priest, May 14, 1988 (Baltimore*); commissioned an Army Officer in 1973 and began serving active duty in 1974; returned to active duty ministry in Jan. 1999; selected to attend the National War College, Class 2010; app. titular bp. of Auzia and auxiliary bp. of the Archdiocese for the Military Services, May 22, 2010.

Stafford, James Francis: (See Cardinals, Biographies).

Steib, J. (James) Terry, S.V.D.: b. May 17, 1940, Vacherie, LA; educ. Divine Word seminaries (Bay St. Louis, MS, Conesus, NY, Techny, IL), Xavier Univ. (New Orleans, LA); ord. priest, Jan. 6, 1967; ord. titular bp. of Fallaba and aux. bp. of St. Louis, Feb. 10, 1984; app. bp. of Memphis, Mar. 24, 1993.

Steiner, Kenneth Donald: b. Nov. 25, 1936, David City, NE; educ. Mt. Angel Seminary (St. Benedict, OR), St. Thomas Seminary (Seattle, WA); ord. priest (Portland,* OR), May 19, 1962; ord. titular bp. of Avensa and aux. bp. of Portland, Mar. 2, 1978; ret. Nov. 25, 2011.

Stika, Richard F.: b. July 4, 1957, St. Louis, MO; educ. St. Louis Univ. (St. Louis, MO), Cardinal Glennon College (St. Louis), Kenrick Seminary (St. Louis); ord. priest (St. Louis), Dec. 14, 1985; possesses bi-ritual faculties of the Maronite Church; in 1999 he coordinated for the archdiocese the visit of Pope John Paul II to St. Louis; app. bp. of Knoxville, Jan. 12, 2009; ord. bp., Mar. 19, 2009.

Straling, Phillip F.: b. Apr. 25, 1933, San Bernardino, CA; educ. Immaculate Heart Seminary, St. Francis Seminary, Univ. of San Diego and San Diego State Univ. (San Diego, CA), North American College (Rome); ord. priest (San Diego), Mar. 19, 1959; ord. first bp. of San Bernardino, Nov. 6, 1978; app. first bp. of Reno, Mar. 21, 1995, when Reno Las Vegas diocese was made two separate dioceses; res. Jun. 21, 2005.

Sullivan, Dennis J.: b. Mar. 17, 1945, New York, NY; educ. Iona College (New Rochelle, NY), St. Joseph Seminary (Dunwoodie, NY); ord. May 29, 1971; app. titular bp. of Enera and aux. bp. of New York, June 28, 2004; ord. Sept. 21, 2004; app. bp. of Camden, Jan. 8, 2013; inst. Feb. 12, 2013.

Sulyk, Stephen: b. Oct. 2, 1924, Balnycia, Western Ukraine; migrated to U.S. 1948; educ. Ukrainian Catholic Seminary of the Holy Spirit (Hirschberg, Germany), St. Josaphat's Seminary and Catholic Univ. (Washington, DC); ord. priest (Philadelphia,* Byzantine), June 14, 1952; ord. abp. of the Ukrainian archeparchy of Philadelphia, Mar. 1, 1981; res., Nov. 29, 2000.

Swain, Paul J.: b. Sept. 12, 1943, Newark, NY; educ. Univ. of Wisc.-Madison, Univ. of Wisc. Law School, John XXIII Seminary (Weston, Mass.); ord. May 27, 1988 (Madison); app. bp. of Sioux Falls, SD, Aug. 31, 2006; ord. Oct. 26, 2006.

Symons, J. Keith: b. Oct. 14, 1932, Champion, MI; educ. St. Thomas Seminary (Bloomfield, CT), St. Mary Seminary (Baltimore, MD); ord. priest (St. Augustine), May 18, 1958; ord. titular bp. of Siguitanus and aux. bp. of St. Petersburg, Mar. 19, 1981; app. bp. of Pensacola Tallahassee, Oct. 4, 1983, inst., Nov. 8, 1983; app. bp. of Palm Beach, June 12, 1990; res., June 2, 1998.

T

Tafoya, Arthur N.: b. Mar. 2, 1933, Alameda, NM; educ. St. Thomas Seminary (Denver, CO), Conception Seminary (Conception, MO); ord. priest (Santa Fe*), May 12, 1962; ord. bp. of Pueblo, Sept. 10, 1980; ret. Oct. 15, 2009.

Talley, David P.: b. Sept. 11, 1950, Columbus, GA; educ. St. Meinrad Seminary (IN), Pontifical Gregorian Univ. (Rome); app. titular bp. of Lambaesis and aux. bp. of Atlanta, Jan. 3, 2013; ord. bishop Apr. 2, 2013.

Tamayo, James A.: b. Oct. 23, 1949, Brownsville, TX; educ. Del Mar College (Corpus Christi, TX), Univ. of St. Thomas and Univ. of St. Thomas School of Theology (Houston); ord. priest (Corpus Christi), June 11, 1976; ord. titular bp. of Ita and aux. bp. of Galveston Houston, Mar. 10, 1993; app. first bp. of Laredo, TX, July 3, 2000, ins., Aug. 9, 2000.

Taylor, Anthony Basil: b. Apr. 24, 1954, Forth Worth, TX; educ. Univ. of Oklahoma (Enid, OK), St. Meinrad Seminary (IN), Pontifical North American College and Gregorian Univ. (Rome, Italy), Fordham Univ. (New York, NY); ord. priest (Oklahoma City*), Aug. 2, 1980; app. bp. of Little Rock, Apr. 10, 2008; inst. June 5, 2008.

Thomas, Daniel E.: b. June 11, 1959, Philadelphia; educ. St. Charles Borromeo Sem. (Philadelphia), Gregorian Univ. (Rome); ord. priest May 18, 1985 (Philadelphia); appointed aux. bp. of Philadelphia and titular bp. of Bardstown June 8, 2006; ord. July 26, 2006; app. bp. of Toledo, Aug. 25, 2014.

Thomas, Elliott G.: b. July 15, 1926, Pittsburgh, PA; educ. Howard Univ. (Washington, DC), Gannon Univ. (Erie, PA), St. Vincent de Paul Seminary (Boynton Beach, FL); ord. priest (St. Thomas, Virgin Islands), June 6, 1986; ord. bp. of St. Thomas in the Virgin Islands, Dec. 12, 1993; res., June 30, 1999.

Thomas, George L.: b. May 19, 1950, Anaconda, MT; educ. St. Thomas Seminary, Seattle, Univ. of Washington, Seattle; ord. priest (Seattle*), May 22, 1976; chancellor and vicar general, 1988-1999, diocesan administrator of Seattle, 1996-1997; app. titular bp. of Vagrauta and aux. bp. of Seattle, Nov. 19, 1999, inst., Jan. 28, 2000; app. bp. of Helena, Mar. 23, 2004.

Thompson, Charles C.: b. Apr. 11, 1961, Louisville, KY; educ. Bellarmine College (Louisville), St. Meinrad School of Theology (Meinrad, IN), St. Paul University (Ottawa); ord. priest (Louisville), May 30, 1987; app. bp. of Evansville, Apr. 26, 2011; ord. bp. June 29, 2011.

Tiedemann, Neil, C.P.: b. Mar. 5, 1948, Brooklyn, NY; educ. Passionist seminary; entered Congregation of the Passionists in 1970 and took his perpetual vows on Aug. 22, 1974; ord. priest, May 16, 1975; app. bp. of Mandeville, Jamaica, May 20, 2008.

Timlin, James C.: b. Aug. 5, 1927, Scranton, PA; educ. St. Charles College (Catonville, MD), St. Mary's Seminary (Baltimore, MD), North American College (Rome); ord. priest (Scranton), July 16, 1951; ord. titular bp. of Gunugo and aux. bp. of Scranton, Sept. 21, 1976; app. bp. of Scranton, Apr. 24, 1984; ret., July 25, 2003.

Tobin, Joseph William, C.SS.R.: b. May 3, 1952, Detroit, MI,; educ. Holy Redeemer College (Waterford, WI), Mount St. Alphonsus Major Seminary (New York); ord. priest, Redemptorists, June 1, 1978; Superior General of the Redemptorists, 1997-2009; app. titular abp. of Obba and Sec. of the Congregation for Institutes of Consecrated Life and Societies of Apostolic Life, Aug. 2, 2010; app. abp. of Indianapolis, Oct. 18, 2012; inst. Dec. 3, 2012.

Tobin, Thomas J.: b. Apr. 1, 1948, Pittsburgh, PA; educ. St. Mark Seminary High School, Gannon Univ. (Erie, PA), St. Francis College (Loretto, PA), North American College (Rome); ord. priest (Pittsburgh), July 21, 1973; ord. titular bp. of Novica and aux. bp. of Pittsburgh, Dec. 27, 1992; app. bp. of Youngstown Dec. 5, 1995; inst., Feb. 2, 1996; app. bp. of Providence, Mar. 31, 2005; inst. May 31, 2005.

Trautman, Donald W.: b. June 24, 1936, Buffalo, NY; educ. Our Lady of Angels Seminary (Niagara Falls, NY), Theology Faculty (Innsbruck, Austria), Pontifical Biblical Institute (Rome), Catholic Univ. (Washington, DC); ord. priest (Buffalo), Apr. 7, 1962, in Innsbruck; ord. titular bp. of Sassura and aux. of Buffalo, Apr. 16, 1985; app. bp. of Erie, June 12, 1990; ret. July 31, 2012.

Turley Murphy, Daniel T. , O.S.A.: b. Jan. 25, 1943, Chicago, IL; ord. priest, Dec. 21, 1961; ord. coadj. bp. of Chulucanas, Peru, Aug. 17, 1996.

Tyson, Joseph J.: b. Oct. 16, 1957, Moses Lake, Wash.; educ. Univ. of Washington, Catholic Univ. of America; ord. priest June 10, 1989 (Seattle); app. aux. bp. of Seattle and titular bp. of Migirpa May 12, 2005; ord. bp. June 6, 2005, app. bp. of Yakima, Apr. 12, 2011; inst. May 31, 2011.

U V

Uglietto, Peter J.: b. Sept. 24, 1951, Cambridge, MA; educ., St. John Seminary (Brighton, MA), Creighton Univ. (Omaha, NE), John Paul II Institute for Marriage and Family (Washington, DC); ord. priest, May 21, 1977 (Boston*); rector, Blessed John XXIII National Seminary, 2005-2010; app. titular bp. of Thubursicum and aux. bp. of Boston, June 30, 2010.

Valero, René A.: b. Aug. 15, 1930, New York, NY; educ. Cathedral College, Immaculate Conception Seminary (Huntington, NY), Fordham Univ. (New York); ord. priest (Brooklyn), June 2, 1956; ord. titular bp. of Turris Vicus and aux. bp. of Brooklyn, Nov. 24, 1980; ret. Oct. 27, 2005.

Vann, Kevin W.: b. May 10, 1951, Springfield, IL; educ. Milikin Univ. (Decatur, IL), Immaculate Conception Seminary (Springfield), Kenrick Seminary (St. Louis), Univ. of St. Thomas Aquinas (Rome); ord. May 30, 1981 (Springfield); app. coadjutor bp. Forth Worth May 17, 2005; ord. bp. July 13, 2005; app. bp. of Orange, Sept. 21, 2012; inst. Dec. 12, 2012.

Vasa, Robert F.: b. May 7, 1951, Lincoln, NE, educ. St. Thomas Seminary, Denver, Holy Trinity Seminary, Dallas, Pontifical Gregorian Univ. (Rome); ord. priest (Lincoln), May 22,1976; Vicar General and Moderator of the Curia, 1996; app. bp. of Baker, OR Nov. 19, 1999, inst., Jan. 26, 2000; app. coadjutor bp. of Santa Rosa, Jan. 24, 2011; inst. Mar. 6, 2011; acceded to see June 30, 2011.

Vasquez, José S.: b. July 9, 1957, Stamford, Texas; educ. St. Mary Seminary, Houston, Univ. of St. Thomas, North American College and Pontifical Gregorian Univ. (Rome); ord. priest (San Angelo), June 30, 1984; app. titular bp. of Cova and aux. of Galveston-Houston, Nov. 30, 2001, ord., Jan. 23, 2002; app. bp. of Austin, Jan. 26, 2010; inst. Mar. 8, 2010.

Vigneron, Allen H.: b. Oct. 21, 1948, Detroit, MI; educ. Sacred Heart Seminary (Detroit, MI), North American College, Gregorian Univ. (Rome), Catholic Univ. (Washington, DC); ord. priest (Detroit*), July 26, 1975; served in Vatican Secretariat of State, 1991 94; rector of Sacred Heart Seminary (Detroit), 1994; ord. titular bp. of Sault Ste Marie and aux. bp. of Detroit, July 9, 1996; app. coadj. bp. of Oakland, Jan. 10, 2003; bp. of Oakland Oct. 1, 2003; app. abp. of Detroit, Jan. 5, 2009; inst. Jan. 28, 2009.

Vlazny, John G.: b. Feb. 22, 1937, Chicago, IL; educ. Quigley Preparatory Seminary (Chicago, IL), St. Mary of the Lake Seminary (Mundelein, IL), Gregorian Univ. (Rome), Univ. of Michigan, Loyola Univ. (Chicago, IL); ord. priest (Chicago*), Dec. 20, 1961; ord. titular bp. of Stagno and aux. bp. of Chicago, Dec. 13, 1983; app. bp. of Winona, MN, May 19, 1987; app. abp. of Portland in Oregon, Oct. 28, 1997, inst., Dec. 19, 1997; ret. Jan. 29, 2013.

W

Walkowiak, David J.: b. June 18, 1953, Cleveland, OH; educ. Univ. of Notre Dame, St. Mary Seminary (Wickliffe, OH), The Catholic Univ. of America (Washington, DC); ord. priest June 9, 1979 (Cleveland); app. bp. of Grand Rapids, Apr. 18, 2013; ord. bp. June 18, 2013.

Wall, James S.: b. Oct. 11, 1964, Ganado, AZ; educ. Arizona State Univ. (Phoenix, AZ); St. John's Seminary (Camarillo, CA), Mundelein Seminary (Chicago, IL); ord. priest (Phoenix), June 6, 1998; member of the National Advisory Council of the USCCB, 2003-2007; app. bp. of Gallup, Feb. 5, 2009; ord. bp. Apr. 23, 2009.

Walsh, Daniel Francis: b. Oct. 2, 1937, San Francisco, CA; educ. St. Joseph Seminary (Mountain View, CA), St. Patrick Seminary (Menlo Park, CA) Catholic Univ. (Washington, DC); ord. priest (San Francisco*), Mar. 30, 1963; ord. titular bp. of Tigia and aux. bp. of San Francisco, Sept. 24, 1981; app. bp. of Reno-Las Vegas, June 9, 1987; app. first bp. of Las Vegas, Mar. 21, 1995, when the Reno-Las Vegas diocese was made two separate dioceses; app. bp. Santa Rosa, Apr. 11, 2000; ret. June 30, 2011.

Walsh, Gerald T.: b. Apr. 25, 1942, New York, NY; educ. Iona College (New Rochelle, NY), St. Joseph Seminary (Dunwoodie, NY), Fordham Univ. (New York, NY); ord. May 27, 1967; app. titular bp. of Altiburo and aux. bp. of New York, June 28, 2004; ord. Sept. 21, 2004.

Walsh, Paul H., O.P.: b. Aug. 17, 1937, Brooklyn; educ. Providence College (R.I.), St. Stephen's College (Dover, MA), Dominican House of Studies (Washington); ord. Dominican, June 9, 1966; incard. Rockville Centre, Dec. 13, 1984; app. aux. bp. of Rockville Centre and titular

bp. of Abtugni, Apr. 3, 2003; ord. bp., May 29, 2003; ret. Aug. 17, 2012.

Walterscheid, William J.: b. Nov. 18, 1956, Ashland, PA; educ. St. John Seminary College (Brighton, MA), Pontifical Gregorian Univ. (Rome); ord. priest (Harrisburg), July 11, 1992; dir. of Pastoral Formation, North American College, Rome, 1999-2000; vice rector, North American College, 2000-2003; app. aux. bp. of Pittsburgh and titular bp. of California, Feb. 25, 2011; ord. Apr. 25, 2011.

Wang, Ignatius: b. Feb. 27, 1934, Beijing, China; educ. Urbanian Univ. and Gregorian Univ. (Rome); ord. priest (for apostolic vicariate in southern China) July 4, 1959; unable to return home, he served in the Antilles and transferred to San Francisco in 1974; aux. bp. of San Francisco and titular bp. of Sitipa, Dec. 13, 2002; ord., Jan. 30, 2003; ret. May 16, 2009.

Warfel, Michael William: b. Sept 16, 1948, Elkhart, IN; educ. Indiana Univ, St. Gregory's College Seminary, Mt. St. Mary's Seminary of the West (Cincinnati, OH); ord. priest, Apr. 26, 1980; ord. bp. of Juneau, Dec. 17, 1996; app. bp. of Great-Fall-Billings, Nov. 20, 2007.

Wcela, Emil A.: b. May 1, 1931, Bohemia, NY; educ. St. Francis College (Brooklyn, NY), Immaculate Conception Seminary (Huntington, NY), Catholic Univ. (Washington, DC), Pontifical Biblical Institute (Rome, Italy); ord. priest (Brooklyn), June 2, 1956; ord. titular bp. of Filaca and aux. bp. of Rockville Centre, Dec. 13, 1988; ret. Apr. 3, 2007.

Weakland, Rembert G., O.S.B.: b. Apr. 2, 1927, Patton, PA; joined Benedictines, 1945; ord. priest, June 24, 1951; abbot primate of Benedictine Confederation, 1967-77; ord. abp. of Milwaukee, Nov. 8, 1977; res., May 24, 2002.

Weigand, William K.: b. May 23, 1937, Bend, OR; educ. Mt. Angel Seminary (St. Benedict, OR), St. Edward's Seminary and St. Thomas Seminary (Kenmore, WA); ord. priest (Boise), May 25, 1963; ord. bp. of Salt Lake City, Nov. 17, 1980; app. bp. of Sacramento, Nov. 30, 1993, inst., Jan. 27, 1994; ret. Nov. 29, 2008

Weisenburger, Edward J.: b. Dec. 23, 1960, Alton, IL; educ. Conception Seminary College (Conception, MO), American College Seminary at the Catholic Univ. of Louvain (Leuven, Belgium), Univ. of St. Paul (Ottawa, Canada); ord. priest, Dec. 19, 1987 (Oklahoma City*); aside from pastoral service and duties in the archdiocese, he served as on-site chaplain in 1995 during the recovery after the Oklahoma City Bombing; app. bp. of Salina, Feb. 6, 2012; ord. bp., May 1, 2012.

Weitzel, John Quinn, M.M.: b. May 10, 1928, Chicago, IL; educ. Maryknoll Seminary (Maryknoll, NY); ord. priest, Nov. 5, 1955; missionary to Samoa, 1979; ord. bp. of Samoa-Pago Pago, American Samoa, Oct. 29, 1986; ret. May 31, 2013.

Wenski, Thomas G.: b. Oct. 18, 1950, West Palm Beach, FL; educ. St. John Vianney College Seminary, St. Vincent de Paul Regional Seminary, Fordham Univ.; ord. priest (Miami*), May 15, 1976; director of Miami Haitian Apostolate; app. titular bp. of Kearney and aux. of Miami, June 24, 1997; app. coadj. bp. of Orlando, July 1, 2003; bp. of Orlando, Nov. 13, 2004; app. abp. of Miami, Apr. 20, 2010.

Wester, John Charles: b. Nov. 5, 1950, San Francisco; educ. St. John's Seminary, Camarillo, CA, St. Patrick's Seminary, Menlo Park, CA, Univ. of San Francisco; ord. priest (San Francisco*), May 15, 1976; app. titular bp. of Lamiggiga and aux. bp. of San Francisco, June 30, 1998;

app. bp. of Salt Lake City, Jan. 8, 2007.

Wilkerson, Gerald E.: b. Oct. 21, 1939, Des Moines, IA; educ. St. John's Seminary (Camarillo, CA); ord. priest (Los Angeles*), Jan. 5, 1965; app. titular bp. of Vincennes and aux. bp. of Los Angeles, Nov. 5, 1997, ord., Jan. 21, 1998.

Williams, James Kendrick: b. Sept. 5, 1936, Athertonville, KY; educ. St. Mary's College (St. Mary's, KY), St. Maur's School of Theology (South Union, KY); ord. priest (Louisville*), May 25, 1963; ord. titular bp. of Catula and aux. bp. of Covington, June 19, 1984; first bp. of Lexington, KY, inst., Mar. 2, 1988; res., June 11, 2002.

Winter, William J.: b. May 20, 1930, Pittsburgh, PA; educ. St. Vincent College and Seminary (Latrobe, PA), Gregorian Univ. (Rome, Italy); ord. priest (Pittsburgh), Dec. 17, 1955; ord. titular bp. of Uthina and aux. bp. of Pittsburgh, Feb. 13, 1989; ret. May 20, 2005.

Wiwchar, Michael, C.Ss.R.: b. May 9, 1932, Komarno, Manitoba, Canada; educ. Redemptorist Seminary (Windsor, Ontario); made solemn vows as Redemptorist, 1956; ord. priest, June 28, 1959; pastor St. John the Baptist Parish, Newark, NJ, 1990-93; ord. bp. of St. Nicholas of Chicago for the Ukrainians, Sept. 28, 1993; bp. of Saskatoon of Ukrainians, Nov. 29, 2000.

Wuerl, Donald W.: (See **Cardinals' Biographies**).

Y Z

Yanta, John W.: b. Oct. 2, 1931, Runge, TX; educ. St. John's Preparatory Seminary and Assumption Seminary (San Antonio); ord. priest (San Antonio*), Mar. 17, 1956; ord. titular bp. of Naratcata and aux. bp. of San Antonio, Dec. 30, 1994; app. bp. of Amarillo, Jan. 21,1997, inst., Mar. 17, 1997; ret. Jan. 3, 2008.

Younan, Joseph: b. Nov. 15, 1944, Hassakeh, Syria; educ. Our Lady of Deliverance Seminary (Charfet, Lebanon), Pontifical College of the Propagation of the Faith (Rome); ord. priest, Sept. 12, 1971; came to U.S., 1986; served Syrian Catholics in U.S.; ord. first bp. Our Lady of Deliverance of Newark for Syrian Catholics in the U.S. and Canada, Jan. 7, 1996, in Kamisly, Syria; ret. Jan. 20, 2009; elected patriarch of Antioch for the Syrians, Jan. 20, 2009; inst. Feb. 15, 2009.

Zaidan, Abdallah E.: b. March 10, 1963, Kseibe, Lebanon; educ. Holy Spirit Univ. (Kaslik, Lebanon), St. John's Univ. (NY), Pepperdine Univ. (CA); entered the Congregation of Maronite Lebanese Missionaries and ord. priest, July 20, 1986; contributed to the establishment of Maronite missions in Dallas and Houston; app. eparch of the Maronite Eparchy of Our Lady of Lebanon of Los Angeles, July 10, 2013; ord. bp. Sept. 28, 2013.

Zarama Pasqualetto, Luis R.: b. Nov. 28, 1958, Pasto, Colombia; educ. Seminary of Pasto, Universidad Mariana (Pasto, Colombia), Universidad Javeriana (Bogota, Colombia); ord. priest (Atlanta*), Nov. 27, 1993; became an American citizen on July 4, 2004; app. aux. bp. of Atlanta and titular bp. of Baranus, July 27, 2009; ord. bp. Sept. 29, 2009.

Zavala, Gabino: b. Sept. 7, 1951, Guerrero, Mexico; became U.S. citizen, 1976; educ. St. John's Seminary (Los Angeles), Catholic Univ. (Washington, DC); ord. priest (Los Angeles*), May 28, 1977; ord. titular bp. of Tamascani and aux. bp. of Los Angeles, Mar. 19, 1994; ret. Jan. 4, 2012.

Zayek, Francis: b. Oct. 18, 1920, Manzanillo, Cuba; ord. priest, Mar. 17, 1946; ord. titular bp. of Callinicum and aux. bp. for Maronites in Brazil, Aug. 5, 1962; named apostolic exarch for Maronites in U.S., with headquarters in Detroit; inst., June 11. 1966; first eparch of St. Maron of Detroit,

Mar. 25, 1972; see transferred to Brooklyn, June 27, 1977; given personal title of abp., Dec. 22, 1982; ret., Nov. 23, 1996.

Zglejszewski, Andrzej J.: b. Dec. 18, 1961, Czarna Bialostocka, Poland; educ. College seminary in Bialystok and Warsaw; Seminary of the Immaculate Conception (Huntington, NY), Fordham Univ. (New York); ord. priest (Rockville Centre), May 26, 1990; app. titular bp. of Nicives and aux. bp. of Rockville Centre, Feb. 11, 2014; ord. bp. Mar. 25, 2014.

Zipfel, Paul A.: b. Sept. 22, 1935, St. Louis, MO; educ. Cardinal Glennon College, Kenrick Seminary (St. Louis, MO), Catholic Univ. (Washington, DC), St. Louis Univ. (St. Louis, MO); ord. priest (St. Louis*), Mar. 18, 1961; ord. titular bp. of Walla Walla and aux. bp. of St. Louis, June 29, 1989; app. bp. of Bismarck, Dec. 31, 1996; ret. Oct. 19, 2012.

Zubic, David A.: b. Sept. 4, 1949, Sewickley, PA; educ. St. Paul Seminary Duquesne Univ. (Pittsburgh), St. Mary's Seminary (Baltimore), Duquesne Univ. (Pittsburgh); ord. priest (Pittsburgh), May 3, 1975; ord. titular bp. of Jamestown and aux. of Pittsburgh, Apr. 6, 1997; app. bp. of Green Bay, Oct. 10, 2003; app. bp. of Pittsburgh, July 18, 2007.

Zurek, Patrick J.: b. Aug. 17, 1948, Wallis, TX; educ. Univ. of St. Thomas (Houston), Angelicum and Alphonsian Academy (Rome); ord priest (Austin), June 29, 1975; app. titular bp. of Tamugadi and aux. bp. of San Antonio, Jan. 5, 1998, ord., Feb. 16, 1998; app. bp. of Amarillo, Jan. 3, 2008.

BISHOP-BROTHERS

(The asterisk indicates brothers who were bishops at the same time.)

There have been 10 pairs of brother-bishops in the history of the U.S. hierarchy.

Living: Francis T. Hurley,* abp. of Anchorage and Mark J. Hurley,* bp. emeritus of Santa Rosa (deceased). Raymond J. Boland,* bp. emeritus of Kansas City-St. Joseph, MO and John Kevin Boland,* bp. of Savannah.

Deceased: Francis Blanchet* of Oregon City (Portland) and Augustine Blanchet* of Walla Walla; John S. Foley of Detroit and Thomas P. Foley of Chicago; Francis P. Kenrick,* apostolic administrator of Philadelphia, bp. of Philadelphia and Baltimore, and Peter R. Kenrick* of St. Louis; Matthias C. Lenihan of Great Falls and Thomas M. Lenihan of Cheyenne; James O'Connor, vicar apostolic of Nebraska and bp. of Omaha, and Michael O'Connor of Pittsburgh and Erie; Jeremiah F. and John W. Shanahan, both of Harrisburg; Sylvester J. Espelage, O.F.M.* of Wuchang, China, who died 10 days after the ordination of his brother, Bernard T. Espelage, O.F.M.* of Gallup; Coleman F. Carroll* of Miami and Howard Carroll* of Altoona-Johnstown.

U.S. BISHOPS OVERSEAS

Edwin Cardinal O'Brien, Grand Master of the Equestrian Order of the Holy Sepulchre of Jerusalem; Raymond Leo Cardinal Burke, Prefect of the Apostolic Signatura, Roman Curia; James Michael Cardinal Harvey, Archpriest of the Basilica of St. Paul Outside the Walls; James Francis Cardinal Stafford, Major Penitentiary Emeritus of the Apostolic Penitentiary, Roman Curia; Lubomyr Cardinal Husar, Major Archbishop emeritus of Kyiv-Halyc, Kiev, Ukraine. Abp. Joseph Augustine Di Noia, O.P., Adjunct Secretary of the Congregation for the Doctrine of the Faith, Roman Curia.

Abp. Edward J. Adams, apostolic nuncio to Greece;

Abp. Charles Balvo, nuncio to Kenya and South Sudan; Abp. Michael August Blume, S.V.D., Apostolic Nuncio to Uganda; Abp. Thomas Edward Gullickson, Apostolic Nuncio to Ukraine; Abp. Joseph Salvador Marino, Apostolic Nuncio to Malaysia, East Timor, and Brunei; Abp. James P. Green, nuncio to Peru; Abp. Charles Brown, nuncio to Ireland; Abp. Edward Joseph Gilbert, C.SS.R., Archbishop emeritus of Port of Spain, Trinidad and Tobago, Antilles; Abp. Roberto Octavio González Nieves, O.F.M., Archbishop of San Juan de Puerto Rico; Abp Abp. George Hamilton Pearce, S.M., Archbishop Emeritus of Suva, Fiji, Pacific (Oceania); Abp. George Riashi, B.C.O., Archbishop of archeparchy of Tripoli of Lebanon (Lebanon) for Greek Catholic Melkites; Abp. Rrok Kola Mirdita, Archbishop of Tiranë-Durrës, Albania; Abp. Stephen Joseph Reichert, O.F.M. Cap., archbishop of Madang, Papua New Guinea; Abp. Ignace Joseph III (Ephrem) Younan, Patriarch of Antioch, Lebanon; Abp. Cyril Bustros, S.M.S.P., abp. of Beirut; Abp. Michael Banach, Holy See permanent representative to the International Atomic Energy Agency (AIEA), to the Organization for Security and Cooperation in Europe (OSCE), and to the Preparatory Commission for the Comprehensive Nuclear-Test-Ban Treaty Organization (CTBTO) and Holy See permanent observer to the United Nations Organization for Industrial Development (ONUDI) and to the Office of the United Nations in Vienna, Austria.

Bp. Gordon Dunlap Bennett, S.J., Bishop Emeritus of Mandeville, Jamaica, Antilles; Bp. Herbert Armstrong Bevard, Bishop of Saint Thomas, American Virgin Islands; Bp. Ernest Bertrand Boland, O.P., Bishop Emeritus of Multan, Pakistan; Bp. Christopher Cardone, O.P., Bishop of Auki, Solomon Islands; Bp. Luis Morgan Casey, Vicar Apostolic emeritus of Pando, Bolivia; Bp. Nicholas D'Antonio Salza, O.F.M., Prelate Emeritus of Inmaculada Concepción de la B.V.M. en Olancho, Honduras; Bp. Paul Francis Duffy, O.M.I., Bishop emeritus of Mongu, Zambia; Bp. Daniel Fernández Torres, Auxiliary Bishop of San Juan de Puerto Rico; Bp. Capistran Heim, O.F.M., Bishop of the Prelacy of Itaituba; Bp. Robert Bever, aux. bp. of Cochabamba, Bolivia; Bp. Hlib Lonchyna, M.S.U., bp. of Holy Family, London (Ukrainian); Bp. Boris Gudziak, bp. of Saint Wladimir-le-Grand de Paris (Ukrainian);

Bp. Heriberto Hermes, O.S.B., Prelate Emeritus of Cristalândia, Goias, Brazil; Bp. Henry Theophilus Howaniec, O.F.M., Bishop of Santissima Trinità in Almaty, Kazakhstan; Bp. Antons Justs, Bishop of Jelgava, Latvia; Bp. Robert Joseph Kurtz, C. R., Bishop of Hamilton in Bermuda, Antilles; Bp. Miguel La Fay Bardi, O. Carm., Prelate of Sicuani, Peru; Bp. Hlib Lonchyna, M.S.U., Auxiliary Bishop of Lviv (Ukrainian), Ukraine; Bp. Elias James Manning, O.F.M. Conv., Bishop of Valença, Brazil; Bp. Adalberto Martínez Flores, Bishop of San Pedro, Paraguay; Bp. Juan Conway McNabb, O.S.A., Bishop Emeritus of Chulucanas, Peru; Bp. William John McNaughton, M.M., Bishop Emeritus of Inchon, South Korea; Bp. William Dermott Molloy McDermott, Bishop Emeritus of Huancavélica, Peru; Bp. Tomás Andrés Mauro Muldoon, O.F.M., Bishop of Juticalpa, Honduras; Bp. Alfredo Ernest Novak, C.SS.R., Bishop Emeritus of Paranaguá, Parana, Brazil; Bp. Donald Joseph Leo Pelletier, M.S., Bishop of Morondava, Madagascar; Bp. Miguel Romano Gómez, Auxiliary Bishop of Guadalajara, Jalisco, México; Bp. Geraldo Scarpone Caporale, O.F.M., Bishop Emeritus of Comayagua, Honduras; Bp. Pablo Ervin Schmitz Simon, O.F.M. Cap., Vicar Apostolic of Bluefields, Nicaragua; Bp. Alphonsus Augustus Sowada, O.S.C., Bishop Emeritus of Agats, Indonesia; Bp. Neil Tiedemann, C.P., Bishop of Mandeville, Jamaica, Antilles; Bp. Daniel Thomas Turley Murphy, O.S.A., Bishop of Chulucanas, Peru; Bp. David Albin Zywiec Sidor, O.F.M. Cap., Auxiliary Bishop of Bluefields, Nicaragua; Bp. William Fey, O.F.M. Cap., Bishop of Kimbe, Papua New Guinea; Bp. Henry Theophilus Howaniec, O.F.M., Bishop emeritus of Santissima Trinita in Almaty; Christopher J. Glancy, C.S.V., aux. bp. of Belize City-Belmopan, Belize. (See **Missionary Bishops**.)

DECEASED BISHOPS, 2013-2014

Boland, Bp. Raymond J., 82, Feb. 27, 2014, bishop of Kansas City St. Joseph from 1993 to 2005.

Donnelly, Bp. Robert W., 83, July 21, 2014, auxiliary bishop of Toledo from 1984 to 2006.

Daly, Bp. James, 92, Oct. 14, 2013, auxiliary bishop of Rockville Centre from 1977 to 1996.

Lyne, Bp. Timothy J., 94, Sept. 25, 2013, auxiliary bishop of Chicago from 1983 to 1995.

McCormack, Bp. William J., 89, Nov. 23, 2013, auxiliary bishop of New York from 1987 to 2001.

McDonald, Bp. Andrew J., 91, bishop of Little Rock from 1972 to 2000.

Popp, Bp. Bernard F., 97, auxiliary bishop of San Antonio from 1983 to 1993.

Quinn, Bp. Alexander J., 81, Oct. 18, 2013, auxiliary bishop of Cleveland from 1983 to 2008.

Szoka, Card. Edmund C., 86, Aug. 20. 2014, abp. of Detroit from 1981-1990 and Vatican official from 1990-2006.

Thompson, Bp. David B., 90, Nov. 24, 2013, bishop of Charleston from 1990 to 1999.

RETIRED/RESIGNED U.S. PRELATES

Information, as of Aug. 20, 2014, includes name of the prelate and see held at the time of retirement or resignation; abps. are indicated by an asterisk. Most of the prelates listed below resigned their sees because of age in accordance with church law. See Index: Biographies, U.S. Bishops

Forms of address of retired residential prelates (unless they have a titular see): Abp. or Bp. Emeritus of (last see held); Former Abp. or Bp. of (last see held).

Joseph V. Adamec (Altoona-Johnstown), Emilio S. Allue S.D.B. (Boston, aux.), Kenneth A. Angell (Burlington), Juan Arzube (Los Angeles, aux.), Victor H. Balke (Crookston), Robert J. Banks (Green Bay), Eusebius J. Beltran* (Oklahoma City), Gordon D. Bennett (Mandeville, Jamaica), Ernest B. Boland, O.P. (Multan, Pakistan), Kevin Boland (Savannah), Raymond J. Boland (Kansas-City-St. Joseph), John P. Boles (Boston, aux.), William D. Borders* (Baltimore), Paul M. Boyle, C.P. (Mandeville, Jamaica), Joseph M. Breitenbeck (Grand Rapids), Robert Brom (San Diego), Tod Brown (Orange), Robert A. Brucato (New York, aux.), Fabian Bruskewitz (Lincoln), Daniel Buechlein, O.S.B.* (Indianapolis).

Edmond Carmody (Corpus Christi), Dominic Carmon (New Orleans, aux.), Joseph L. Charron, C.PP.S. (Des Moines), Gilbert E. Chavez (San Diego, aux.), Matthew Clark (Rochester), George Coleman (Fall River), John W. Comber, M.M. (Foratiano, titular see), Thomas Connolly (Baker), Ronald G. Connors, C.SS.R. (San Juan de la Maguana, Dominican Republic), Patrick Cooney (Gaylord), Thomas J. Costello (Syracuse, aux.), Arnold

R. Cotey, S.D.S. (Nachingwea, now Lindi, Tanzania), Daniel A. Cronin* (Hartford), Edward Cullen (Allentown), John Stephen Cummins (Oakland), William G. Curlin (Charlotte), Thomas V. Daily (Brooklyn), Nicholas D'Antonio, O.F.M. (Olancho, Honduras).

Louis A. DeSimone (Philadelphia, aux.), Joseph T. Dimino* (Military Services archdiocese), Thomas G. Doran (Rockford), Stephen Hector Doueihi (St. Maron of Brooklyn), John Dougherty (aux. Scranton), Michael J. Dudick (Passaic, Byzantine rite), Paul Duffy (Mongu, Zambia), Roland Pierre DuMaine (San Jose), Thomas L. Dupre (Springfield), Dennis V. Durning, C.S.Sp. (Arusha, Tanzania), Walter Edyvean (aux. Boston), Edward Cardinal Egan* (New York), John Elya (Newton), John Favalora (Miami*), J. Lennox Federal (Salt Lake City), Joseph A. Fiorenza* (Galveston-Houston), Thomas J. Flanagan (San Antonio, aux.), Raphael M. Fliss (Superior), Patrick F. Flores* (San Antonio), Harry Flynn* (St. Paul-Minneapolis), David E. Foley (Birmingham), Marion F. Forst (Dodge City), William E. Franklin (Davenport), William B. Friend (Shreveport).

Joseph Galante (Camden), Victor Galeone (St. Augustine), James H. Garland (Marquette), Louis E. Gelineau (Providence), Odore Gendron (Manchester), Peter L. Gerety* (Newark), Joseph J. Gerry, O.S.B. (Portland, ME), Gerald Gettelfinger (Evansville), Ronald Gilmore (Dodge City), Raymond E. Goedert (Chicago, aux.), Francisco Gonzalez Valer (aux. Washington, D.C.), John R. Gorman (Chicago, aux.), Rene H. Gracida (Corpus Christi), Charles V. Grahmann (Dallas), Roger W. Gries (Cleveland, aux.), James Griffin (Columbus), Thomas J. Gumbleton (Detroit, aux.), Richard C. Hanifen (Colorado Springs), Jerome Hanus (Dubuque*), Bernard Harrington (Winona), Joseph Hart (Cheyenne), Edward D. Head (Buffalo), Herbert Hermes, O.S.B. (Cristalandia, Brazil), William Higi (Lafayette), Josu Iriondo (New York, aux.).

Joseph L. Hogan (Rochester), William Russell Houck (Jackson), Henry Howaniec, O.F.M. (Santissima Trinita in Almaty), Joseph Lawson Howze (Biloxi), Howard Hubbard (Albany), Alfred Hughes* (New Orleans), Edward T. Hughes (Metuchen), Raymond G. Hunthausen* (Seattle), Walter A. Hurley (Grand Rapids), Ibrahim Ibrahim (St. Thomas the Apostle), Joseph L. Imesch (Joliet), Francis Irwin (Boston, aux.), Fernando Isern (Pueblo), Sam Jacobs (Houma-Thibodaux), Cardinal William Keeler* (Baltimore), James P. Keleher* (Kansas City), Thomas C. Kelly, O.P.* (Louisville), John Kinney (St. Cloud), Edward Kmiec (Buffalo), Daniel W. Kucera, O.S.B.* (Dubuque), Bernard Cardinal Law* (Boston), John J. Leibrecht (Springfield-Cape Girardeau), Raymond W. Lessard (Savannah), Card. William J. Levada (prefect for the Cong. of the Doctrine of the Faith), Oscar Lipscomb* (Mobile), Martin N. Lohmuller (Philadelphia, aux.), Basil Losten (Stamford).

Robert P. Maginnis (Philadelphia, aux.), Cardinal Adam Maida* (Detroit), Cardinal Theodore McCarrick* (Washington, D.C.), James F. McCarthy (New York, aux.) John McCarthy (Austin), Charles J. McDonnell (Newark, aux.), Timothy McDonnell (Springfield), John B. McDowell

(Pittsburgh, aux.), Norman McFarland (Orange, CA), Bernard J. McLaughlin (Buffalo, aux.), John C. McNabb, O.S.A. (Chulucanas), William J. McNaughton (Inchon), John J. McRaith (Owensboro), Joseph Madera (Military Archdiocese, aux.), Joseph F. Maguire (Springfield, MA), Cardinal Roger Mahony* (Los Angeles), Elias Manning (Valenca, Brazil), Thomas R. Manning, O.F.M. (Coroico, Bolivia), Henry Mansell* (Hartford), Dominic Anthony Marconi (Newark, aux.), Joseph Martino (Scranton), Leroy T. Matthiesen (Amarillo), Carl F. Mengeling (Lansing), Anthony F. Mestice (New York, aux.), James E. Michaels (Wheeling Charleston, aux.), Anthony M. Milone (Great Falls-Billings), Robert Morneau (Green Bay, aux.), Michail Moskal (St. Josaphat), James M. Moynihan (Syracuse), Robert E. Mulvee (Providence), James A. Murray (Kalamazoo), John J. Nevins (Venice), William C. Newman (Baltimore, aux.), Alfredo Ernest Novak, C.SS.R. Paranaguá, Brazil), Thomas Joseph O'Brien (Phoenix), Leonard James Olivier, S.V.D. (Washington, aux.).

George H. Pearce, S.M.* (Suva, Fiji Islands), Raymundo J. Peña (Brownsville), Edward Pevec (Cleveland, aux.), Daniel Pilarczyk (Cincinnati*), Anthony M. Pilla (Cleveland), Francis A. Quinn (Sacramento), John R. Quinn* (San Francisco), Ricardo Ramirez (Las Cruces), Daniel P. Reilly (Worcester), John Ricard, S.S.J. (Pensacola), Cardinal Justin Rigali* (Philadelphia), Vincent M. Rizzotto (Galveston-Houston, aux.), Francis X. Roque (Military Archdiocese, aux.), Peter A. Rosazza (aux. Hartford), Robert John Rose (Grand Rapids), George E. Rueger (Worcester, aux.), Daniel Ryan (Springfield, IL), Sylvester Ryan (Monterey).

Michael A. Saltarelli (Wilmington), Nicholas J. Samra (Melkite eparchy of Newton, aux.), Joseph Sartoris (Los Angeles, aux.), Stanley G. Schlarman (Dodge City), Walter J. Schoenherr (Detroit, aux.), Francis B. Schulte* (New Orleans), Carlos A. Sevilla (Yakima), Daniel E. Sheehan* (Omaha), Robert J. Shaheen (Our Lady of Lebanon), Gilbert I. Sheldon (Steubenville), William Skylstad (Spokane), John Snyder (St. Augustine), Kenneth D. Steiner (Portland, aux.), Philip Straling (Reno), Stephen Sulyk* (Philadelphia, Ukrainians), J. Keith Symons (Palm Beach).

Arthur Tafoya (Pueblo), Elliott Thomas (Virgin Islands), James C. Timlin (Scranton), Donald Trautman (Erie), René A. Valero (Brooklyn, aux.), George Vlazny (Portland*), Daniel Walsh (Santa Rosa), Ignatius Wang (San Francisco, aux.), Emil A. Wcela (Rockville Center, aux.), Rembert G. Weakland, O.S.B.* (Milwaukee), William K. Weigand (Sacramento), James Kendrick Williams (Lexington), George O. Wirz (Madison, aux.), John W. Yanta (Amarillo), Joseph Younan (Our Lady of Deliverance), Gabino Zavala (Los Angeles, aux.), Francis Zayek (St. Maron of Brooklyn), Paul A. Zipfel (Bismarck).

American Bishops of the Past: For coverage of the deceased bishops who served in the United States, please visit www.CatholicAlmanac.com.

The United States Conference of Catholic Bishops

Courtesy USCCB

According to the United States Conference of Catholic Bishops, the USCCB is an assembly of the hierarchy of the United States and the U.S. Virgin Islands who jointly exercise certain pastoral functions on behalf of the Christian faithful of the United States. The purpose of the Conference is to promote the greater good which the Church offers humankind, especially through forms and programs of the apostolate fittingly adapted to the circumstances of time and place. This purpose is drawn from the universal law of the Church and applies to the episcopal conferences which are established all over the world for the same purpose.

The bishops themselves constitute the membership of the Conference and are served by a staff of over 350 lay people, priests, deacons, and religious located at the Conference headquarters in Washington, DC. There is also a small Office of Film and Broadcasting in New York City and a branch office of Migration and Refugee Services in Miami.

The Conference is organized as a corporation in the District of Columbia. Its purposes under civil law are: "To unify, coordinate, encourage, promote and carry on Catholic activities in the United States; to organize and conduct religious, charitable and social welfare work at home and abroad; to aid in education; to care for immigrants; and generally to enter into and promote by education, publication and direction the objects of its being."

History

When the bishops merged their two national organizations into the United States Conference of Catholic Bishops (USCCB) on July 1, 2001, it marked the latest chapter in the evolution of the bishops' national structure, which was established 82 years ago in the aftermath of the First World War. Like its immediate predecessors — the National Conference of Catholic Bishops (NCCB) and United States Catholic Conference (USCC) — the USCCB is an organization staffed by lay people, priests, and members of religious orders, but whose members are the bishops of the United States, and it is the bishops who direct its activities.

The concept of the bishops acting together on matters of mutual interest can be traced back to 1919 when, in their first national meeting since 1884, they agreed to meet annually and to form the National Catholic Welfare Council (NCWC) to serve as their organized voice on the national scene. The word "Council" was replaced by the word "Conference" in 1922.

In 1966, following the Second Vatican Council, NCWC was reorganized into two parallel conferences. The National Conference of Catholic Bishops — sometimes referred to as the canonical arm — would deal with matters connected to the internal life of the Church, such as liturgy and priestly life and ministry. The U.S. Catholic Conference — in effect the civil arm — would represent the bishops as they related to the "secular" world, in areas such as social concerns, education, communications and public affairs. During the period from 1992 to 1996, a Conference committee on mission and structure, headed by the late Card. Joseph L. Bernardin of Chicago, led the bishops in extensive consultation on restructuring. A primary purpose of this undertaking was to provide more of the nation's approximately 300 bishops with an opportunity to be directly involved in the work of the Conference, which operates primarily through a committee structure.

In 1997 the bishops voted to combine NCCB-USCC into one conference, to be called the U.S. Conference of Catholic Bishops. They decided that in the future only bishops would be voting members of committees, but non-bishops could serve on some committees as consultants or advisers. A new committee on statutes and bylaws, headed by Abp. Daniel E. Pilarczyk of Cincinnati, which was formed to lead the rest of the reorganization process, completed its work last year. The new statutes and bylaws were subsequently approved by the Holy See.

It is unlikely that persons outside the bishops' conference will notice any immediate difference in the new structure. Many of the same concerns that motivated the bishops in 1919 — like the welfare of immigrants, communicating through the Catholic press, and defending the legal rights of the Church — are still pressing today, as evidenced in the departments which carry out these functions, though many others have been added as well. In a May 23, 2001, letter sent to organizations which have dealings with the Conference, its General Secretary, Msgr. William P. Fay, said the renaming "will not affect any change in the activities or programs of the Conference but simply how the Conference is identified."

USCCB Restructuring

At their fall general meeting on Nov. 14, 2006, the bishops of the USCCB approved a plan to restructure national operations of the USCCB and to cut diocesan assessments by 16 percent, eliminate more than 60 jobs at the USCCB headquarters in Washington and satellite offices, and trim the number of USCCB committees. The comprehensive plan of reorganization and strategic planning for 2008-2011 was approved by a 213-19 vote. Diocesan heads then voted 158-6 to adopt the proposal to reduce diocesan funding of the USCCB in 2008 by 16 percent. Diocesan assessments, covering nearly $11.9 million of the USCCB's overall budget of $139.5 million in 2007, was reduced in 2008 to just under $10 million.

The restructuring plan was overseen by the bishops' Committee on Priorities and Plans, in the last few years under the chairmanship of Archbishop Michael J. Sheehan of Santa Fe, NM, who also served as secretary of the conference.

Central to the reorganization was the plan for the conference to concentrate on top priorities discerned by the bishops. Those chosen for the 2008-2011 planning cycle:

• Implementation of the pastoral initiative on marriage.
• Faith formation focused on sacramental practice.
• Priestly and religious vocations.
• The Life and dignity of the human person.
• Recognition of cultural diversity, with special emphasis on Hispanic ministry, "in the spirit of Encuentro."

Mission Statement

Preamble

Evangelizing is in fact the grace and vocation proper to the Church, her deepest identity. She exists to evangelize. (*Evangelii Nuntiandi*, No. 14)

The mission of evangelization is entrusted by Christ to his Church to be carried out in all her forms of ministry, witness, and service. By evangelizing, the Church seeks to bring about in all Catholics such an enthusiasm for their faith that, in living their faith in Jesus and strengthened by the sacraments, most especially the celebration of the Eucharist, they freely share that faith with others to transform the world. (Based on Go and Make Disciples, A National Plan and Strategy for Catholic Evangelization in the United States, 1990).

Mission

The mission of the United States Conference of Catholic Bishops (see CIC, c. 447) is to support the ministry of bishops with an emphasis on evangelization, by which the bishops exercise in a communal and collegial manner certain pastoral functions entrusted to them by the Lord Jesus of sanctifying, teaching, and governing (see *Lumen Gentium*, No. 21).

This mission calls the Conference to:

-Act collaboratively and consistently on vital issues confronting the Church and society (see *Christus Dominus*, No. 38.1)

-Foster communion with the Church in other nations, within the Church universal, under the leadership of its supreme pastor, the Roman Pontiff

-Offer appropriate assistance to each bishop in fulfilling his particular ministry in the local Church (Cf. *Apostolos Suos*, 1998.)

Administration

The principal officers of the conference are: Abp. Joseph Kurtz, president; Cardinal Daniel DiNardo, vice president; Bp. Kevin J. Farrell, treasurer; Abp. Peter Sartain, secretary; ; Msgr. Ronny Jenkins, J.C.D., general secretary. Headquarters of the conferences are located at 3211 Fourth St. N.E., Washington, D.C. 20017; (202) 541-3000; www.usccb.org.

USCCB REGIONS

I. Maine, Vermont, New Hampshire, Massachusetts, Rhode Island, Connecticut. II. New York. III. New Jersey, Pennsylvania. IV. Delaware, District of Columbia, Maryland, Virgin Islands, Virginia, West Virginia, Military Archdiocese. V. Alabama, Kentucky, Louisiana, Mississippi, Tennessee. VI. Michigan, Ohio. VII. Illinois, Indiana, Wisconsin. VIII. Minnesota, North Dakota, South Dakota. IX. Iowa, Kansas, Missouri, Nebraska. X. Arkansas, Oklahoma, Texas. XI. California, Hawaii, Nevada. XII. Idaho, Montana, Alaska, Washington, Oregon. XIII. Utah, Arizona, New Mexico, Colorado, Wyoming, including El Paso. XIV. Florida, Georgia, North Carolina, South Carolina. XV: Eastern Catholic Churches (non-geographic; approved on Nov. 14, 2006).

Pastoral Council

The conference, one of many similar territorial conferences envisioned in the conciliar Decree on the Pastoral Office of Bishops in the Church (No. 38), is "a council in which the bishops of a given nation or territory [in this case, the United States] jointly exercise their pastoral office to promote the greater good which the Church offers mankind, especially through the forms and methods of the apostolate fittingly adapted to the circumstances of the age."

Its decisions, "provided they have been approved legitimately and by the votes of at least two-thirds of the prelates who have a deliberative vote in the conference, and have been recognized by the Apostolic See, are to have juridically binding force only in those cases prescribed by the common law or determined by a special mandate of the Apostolic See, given either spontaneously or in response to a petition of the conference itself."

All bishops who serve the Church in the U.S., its territories and possessions, have membership and voting rights in the USCCB. Retired bishops cannot be elected to conference offices nor can they vote on matters that by law are binding by two-thirds of the membership. Only diocesan bishops can vote on diocesan quotas, assessments or special collections.

Officers, Committees

The conference operates through a number of bishops' committees with functions in specific areas of work and concern. Their basic assignments are to prepare materials on the basis of which the bishops, assembled as a conference, make decisions, and to put suitable action plans into effect.

The officers, with several other bishops, hold positions on executive-level committees — Administrative, Executive, the Committee on Budget and Finance, the Committee on Personnel, and the Committee on Priorities and Plans. They also, with other bishops, serve on the USCCB Administrative Committee.

STANDING COMMITTEES

The standing committees and their chairmen (Cardinals, Archbishops, and Bishops), as of Aug. 15, 2014 are as follows (chairmen elect are in parentheses):

Canonical Affairs and Church Governance – Abp. Timothy P. Broglio

Catholic Education – Abp. George Lucas

Child and Youth Protection – Bp. R. Daniel Conlon

Clergy, Consecrated Life, and Vocations – Bp. Michael F. Burbidge

Committee on Communications – Bp. John Wester

Cultural Diversity in the Church – Bp. Jaime Soto
• Subcommittee on African American Affairs (Permanent) – Bp. Shelton Fabre
• Subcommittee on Asian and Pacific Island Affairs (Permanent) – Bp. Randolph R. Calvo
• Subcommittee on Hispanics Affairs – Bp. Gerald R. Barnes
• Subcommittee on Native American Catholics (Permanent) – Abp. Charles J. Chaput, O.F.M. Cap.
• Subcommittee on Pastoral Care of Migrants, Refugees, and Travelers (Permanent) – Bp. Rutilio J. Del Riego

Divine Worship – Bp. Arthur Serratelli
• Subcommittee on Hispanics and the Liturgy (Permanent) – Bp. Octavio Cisneros

Doctrine – Abp. John Nienstedt
• Subcommittee on the Translation of Scripture Text (Permanent) – Bp. Arthur J. Serratelli

Domestic Justice and Human Development – Abp. Thomas Wenski
• Subcommittee on the Catholic Campaign for Human Development (Permanent) – Bp. Jaime Soto

Ecumenical and Interreligious Affairs – Bp. Denis J. Madden

Evangelization and Catechesis – Abp, Leonard P. Blair
• Subcommittee on the Catechism (Permanent) – Abp. Leonard P. Blair

International Justice and Peace – Bp. Richard Pates (Bp. Oscar Cantú)

Laity, Marriage, Family Life, and Youth – Bp. Richard Malone

Migration – Bp. Eusebio Elizondo, M.Sp.S.

National Collections – Abp. Dennis Schnurr
• Subcommittee on Catholic Home Missions (Permanent) – Bp. Michael Warfel
• Subcommittee on the Church in Africa (Permanent) – Bp. John H. Ricard, S.S.J.
• Subcommittee on the Church in Central and Eastern Europe (Permanent) – Cardinal Justin Rigali
• Subcommittee on the Church in Latin America (Permanent) – Abp. José H. Gomez

Pro-Life Activities – Cardinal Sean O'Malley

Ad Hoc Committee for the Defense of Marriage – Abp. Salvatore Cordileone

Executive Level and Management Committees

Administrative Committee – Abp. Joseph Kurtz

Budget and Finance – Bp. Kevin J. Farrell
• Audit Subcommittee– Bp. Kevin J. Farrell

Priorities and Plans – Bp. George V. Murry, S.J.

Executive Committee – Abp. Joseph Kurtz

Task Forces, Boards and Related Organizations

Task Force on Health Care – Bp. Kevin C. Rhoades

Task Force on Spanish Language Bible – Abp. José H. Gomez

North American College, Rome – Abp. John J. Myers

Board of Directors: Catholic Legal Immigration Network, INC – Bp. Jaime Soto

Board of Directors: Catholic Relief Services – Bp.William P. Callahan, OFM Conv.; Bp. Frank Dewane; Bp. Cirilo B. Flores.

Board of Trustees: CCD, INC – Card. Timothy M. Dolan

National Review Board – Francesco Cesareo, Ph.D.

STATE CATHOLIC CONFERENCES

These conferences are agencies of bishops and dioceses in the various states. Their general purposes are to develop and sponsor cooperative programs designed to cope with pastoral and common-welfare needs, and to represent the dioceses before governmental bodies, the public, and in private sectors. Their membership consists of representatives from the dioceses in the states — bishops, clergy and lay persons in various capacities.

The National Association of State Catholic Conference Directors maintains liaison with the general secretariat of the United States Conference of Catholic Bishops.

Alaska Catholic Conference, 225 Cordova St., Anchorage. AK 99501; (907) 297-7700; Exec. Dir., Mary Gore.

Arizona Catholic Conference, 400 E. Monroe St., Phoenix, AZ 85004-2376; (602) 354-2391; Exec. Dir., Ron Johnson.

California Catholic Conference, 1119 K St., 2nd Floor, Sacramento, CA 95814; (916) 443-4851; Exec. Dir., Edward Dolejsi.

Colorado Catholic Conference, 1535 Logan St., Denver, CO 80203; (303) 894-8808; Exec. Dir. Jennifer Kraska.

Connecticut Catholic Conference, 134 Farmington Ave., Hartford, CT 06105; (860) 524-7882; Exec. Dir., Michael Culhane.

Florida Catholic Conference, 201 W. Park Ave., Tallahassee, FL 32301; (850) 222-3803; Exec. Dir., Michael Sheedy.

Georgia Catholic Conference, Office Bldg., 3200 Deans Bridge Rd., Augusta, GA 30906; (706) 798-1719; Exec. Dir., Francis J. Mulcahy, Esq.

Hawaii Catholic Conference, Stephen Diocesan Center, 6301 Pali Hwy., Kaneohe, HI 96744; (808) 585-3341; Exec. Dir., Dcn. Walter Yoshimitsu.

Illinois, Catholic Conference of, 65 E. Wacker Pl., Ste. 1620, Chicago, IL 60601; (312) 368-1066. 108 E. Cook, Springfield, IL 62701; (217) 528-9200; Exec. Dir., Robert Gilligan.

Indiana Catholic Conference, 1400 N. Meridian St., P.O. Box 1410, Indianapolis, IN 46206; (317) 236-1455; Exec. Dir., Glenn Tebbe.

Iowa Catholic Conference, 530-42nd St., Des Moines, IA 50312-2707; (515) 243-6256; Exec. Dir., Thomas Chapman.

Kansas Catholic Conference, 6301 Antioch, Merriam, KS 66202; (913) 722-6633; Exec. Dir.,

Michael Schuttloffel.

Kentucky, Catholic Conference of, 1042 Burlington Lane, Frankfort, KY 40601; (502) 875-4345; Interim Exec. Dir., Rev. Patrick Delahanty.

Louisiana Catholic Conference, 3423 Hundred Oaks Ave., Baton Rouge, LA 70808; (225) 344-7120; Exec. Dir., Daniel J. Loar.

Maryland Catholic Conference, 188 Duke of Gloucester St., Annapolis, MD 21401; (410) 269-1155; Exec. Dir., Mary Ellen Russell.

Massachusetts Catholic Conference, 150 Staniford St., West End Pl., Boston, MA 02114-2511; (617) 367-6060; Acting Exec. Dir., James F. Driscoll.

Michigan Catholic Conference, 510 N. Capitol Ave., Lansing, MI 48933; (517) 372-9310; President and CEO, Paul Long.

Minnesota Catholic Conference, 475 University Ave. W., St. Paul, MN 55103; (651) 227-8777; Interim Exec. Dir., Jason Adkins.

Missouri Catholic Conference, P.O. Box 1022, 600 Clark Ave., Jefferson City, MO 65102; (573) 635-7239; Exec. Dir., J. Micheal Hoey.

Montana Catholic Conference, P.O. Box 1708, Helena, MT 59624; (406) 442-5761; Exec. Dir., James Ziegler.

Nebraska Catholic Conference, 215 Centennial Mall South, Suite 410, Lincoln, NE 68508-1890; (402) 477-7517; Exec. Dir., James R. Cunningham.

Nevada Catholic Conference, 290 South Arlington Ave., Ste. 200, Reno, NV 89501-1713; (775) 322-7412; Exec. Dir., Vacant.

New Jersey Catholic Conference, 149 N. Warren St., Trenton, NJ 08608; (609) 989-1120; Exec. Dir., Patrick R. Brannigan.

New York State Catholic Conference, 465 State St., Albany, NY 12203; (518) 434-6195; www.nyscatholicconference.org; Exec. Dir., Richard E. Barnes.

North Dakota Catholic Conference, 103 3rd St., Ste. 2, Bismarck, ND 58501; (701) 223-2519; www.ndcatholic.org; Exec. Dir., Christopher T. Dodson.

Ohio, Catholic Conference of, 9 E. Long St., Suite 201, Columbus, OH 43215; (614) 224-7147; Exec. Dir., Carolyn Jurkowitz.

Oregon Catholic Conference, 2838 E. Burnside, Portland, OR 97214; (503) 233-8387; General Counsel and Exec. Dir., Msgr. Denis O'Donovan.

Pennsylvania Catholic Conference, 223 North St., Box 2835, Harrisburg, PA 17105; (717) 238-9613; (717) 238-9613; Exec. Dir., Dr. Robert J. O'Hara, Jr.

Texas Catholic Conference, 1625 Rutherford Lane, Bldg. D, Austin, TX 78754; (512) 339-9882; Exec. Dir., Jeffery Patterson.

Washington State Catholic Conference, 508 2nd Ave. West, Seattle, WA 98119-3928; (206) 301-0556; Exec. Dir., Sr. Sharon Park, O.P.

West Virginia State Catholic Conference, P.O. Box 230, Wheeling, WV 26003; (304) 233-0880; Dir., Rev. Brian P. O'Donnell, S.J., Ph.D.

Wisconsin Catholic Conference, 30 W. Mifflin St., Suite 302, Madison, WI 53703; (608) 257-0004; Exec. Dir., John A. Huebscher.

Background

The National Conference of Catholic Bishops (NCCB), was established by action of the U.S. hierarchy Nov. 14, 1966, as a strictly ecclesiastical body with defined juridical authority over the Church in this country. It was set up with the approval of the Holy See and in line with directives from the Second Vatican Council. Its constitution was formally ratified during the November 1967 meeting of the U.S. hierarchy. The NCCB was a development from the Annual Meeting of the Bishops of the United States, whose pastoral character was originally approved by Pope Benedict XV, Apr. 10, 1919.

The USCC, as of Jan. 1, 1967, took over the general organization and operations of the former National Catholic Welfare Conference, Inc., whose origins dated back to the National Catholic War Council of 1917. The council underwent some change after World War I and was established on a permanent basis on Sept. 24, 1919, as the National Catholic Welfare Council to serve as a central agency for organizing and coordinating the efforts of U.S. Catholics in carrying out the social mission of the Church in this country. In 1923, its name was changed to National Catholic Welfare Conference, Inc., and clarification was made of its nature as a service agency of the bishops and the Church rather than as a conference of bishops with real juridical authority in ecclesiastical affairs.

The Official Catholic Directory stated that the USCC assisted "the bishops in their service to the Church in this country by uniting the people of God where voluntary collective action on a broad interdiocesan level is needed. The USCC provided an organizational structure and the resources needed to insure coordination, cooperation, and assistance in the public, educational and social concerns of the Church at the national, regional, state and, as appropriate, diocesan levels."

CATHOLIC RELIEF SERVICES

Catholic Relief Services is the official overseas aid and development agency of U.S. Catholics; it is a separately incorporated organization of the U.S. Conference of Catholic Bishops.

CRS was founded in 1943 by the bishops of the United States to help civilians in Europe and North Africa caught in the disruption and devastation of World War II. As conditions in Europe improved in the late 1940s and early 1950s, the works conducted by CRS spread to other continents and areas — Asia, Africa and Latin America.

Although best known for its record of disaster response, compassionate aid to refugees and commitment to reconstruction and rehabilitation, CRS places primary focus on long-term development projects designed to help people to help themselves and to determine their own future. Administrative funding for CRS comes largely from the American Bishops' Overseas Appeal (ABOA). Major support is derived from private, individual donors and through programs such as Operation Rice Bowl and the new Global Village Project.

Carolyn Y. Woo is Executive Director. CRS headquarters are located at 209 W. Fayette St., Baltimore, MD 21201; (410) 625-2220; www.catholicrelief.org.

Cultural Diversity in the Church

The increasing and vibrant diversity of the Catholic Church in the United States is both a vital strength and immense pastoral challenge to the American Catholic community. Much as the history of American Catholicism in the 19th and 20th centuries was profoundly shaped by the contributions of immigrants from Ireland, Germany, Italy, and Eastern Europe, so too will the Church in the United States be impacted significantly by the contributions of Hispanics, African Americans, Asians and Pacific Islanders, Europeans, and Native Americans in the 21st century and beyond.

Secretariat of Cultural Diversity in the Church

The Secretariat of Cultural Diversity in the Church of the United States Conference of Catholic Bishops is the primary instrument for the U.S. bishops in organizing pastoral care for the many different groups of Catholics in the country. The Secretariat has four subcommittees: Hispanic Catholics, African American Catholics, Native American Catholics, Asian Catholics, African Catholics, Pacific Islander Catholics, Catholic migrants and refugees. It was created officially on Jan. 1, 2008 as part of the wider reorganization of the USCCB by uniting several different secretariats.

According to its own stated mandate, the Secretariat of Cultural Diversity in the Church assists the bishops in instilling the vision of *Encuentro* 2000 and *Ecclesia in America* throughout the Church by working collaboratively with all the committees of the Conference and with bishops and their dioceses to bring Catholics from various culturally diverse communities into a fuller participation in the faith, life, and evangelizing mission of the Church. The committee especially works to promote an awareness of cultural diversity within all the committees and offices of the USCCB. This mandate includes the following responsibilities: Pastoral care of Hispanic Catholics, African American Catholics, Native American Catholics, Asian Catholics, African Catholics, Pacific Islander Catholics, Catholic migrants and refugees. Most Rev. Daniel Flores, Bp. of Brownsville, is current Chairman of the Secretariat. María del Mar Muñoz-Visoso is the Executive Director, assisted by Alejandro Aguilera-Titus, Assistant Director of Hispanic Affairs; Donna Toliver Grimes, Assistant Director of African American Affairs; Sr. Anna Nguyen, S.C.C., Assistant Director of Asian Pacific Affairs, and Sr. Myrna Tordillo, MSCS, Program Coordinator for Pastoral Care for Migrants, Refugees, and Travelers. Contact information: 3211 Fourth St. N.E., Washington, DC, 20017, (202) 541-3000, www.usccb.org.

HISPANIC CATHOLICS IN THE UNITED STATES

The nation's Hispanic population totaled 50.5 million in 2010, according to figures reported by the U.S. Census Bureau. It is estimated that 71 percent of the Hispanics were baptized Catholics. Perhaps 100,000 Catholic Hispanics a year are departing the Faith.

Subcommittee on Hispanic Affairs

The national secretariat for Hispanics was established by the U.S. Catholic Conference for service promoting and coordinating pastoral ministry to the Spanish-speaking. Its basic orientation is toward integral evangelization, combining religious ministry with development efforts in programs geared to the culture and needs of Hispanics. Its concerns are urban and migrant Spanish-speaking people; communications and publications in line with secretariat purposes and the service of people; bilingual and bicultural religious and general education; liaison for and representation of Hispanics with church, civic and governmental agencies.

The mandate of the subcommittee declares that the subcommittee on Hispanic Affairs is under the direction of and assists the Committee on Cultural Diversity within the Church by working collaboratively with the committee and other USCCB committees to affirm the gifts and contributions of Hispanic Catholics and to provide more opportunities for Hispanic Catholics to engage in the life of the Church and help shape its evangelization mission. This mandate includes the following areas of responsibility: The subcommittee is directly responsible for outreach to Hispanic communities and to work closely with the subcommittee on Pastoral Care of Migrants and Refugees.

The Subcommittee states that its key mission priorities are:

• Promote the vision for Hispanic/Latino(a) ministry articulated in the National Pastoral Plan for Hispanic Ministry.

• Promote the implementation of Encuentro and Mission: A New Pastoral Framework for Hispanic Ministry at the national and local level.

• Provide support and technical assistance to dioceses, key national Catholic organizations, and institutions on issues related to the Hispanic/Latino presence and the Encuentro process.

• Collaborate with USCCB committees, secretariats, and offices in the implementation of the five priorities as they relate to Hispanics/Latinos(as) in the area of vocations, marriage and family life, faith formation, life and dignity of the human person, and cultural diversity.

• Develop means to share news and information periodically with the Hispanic ministry network through a newsletter and/or website.

• Follow up on the National Encuentro for Hispanic Youth and Young Adult Ministry and the National

Symposium on Lay Ecclesial Ministry.

• Continue ongoing relationship with CELAM, particularly in regard to the implementation of Ecclesia in America and the conclusions of the Fifth Conference of the Latin-American Episcopate and of the Caribbean held in Aparecida, Brazil.

Bp. Gerald Barnes is currently the Chairman of the Subcommittee of Bishops for Hispanic/Latino Affairs. Alejandro Aguilera-Titus is the assistant director of the subcommittee. Address: 3211 Fourth St. N.E., Washington, DC, 20017, (202) 541-3000, www. usccb.org.

Pastoral Patterns

Pastoral ministry to Hispanics varies, depending on cultural differences and the availability of personnel to carry it out. The pattern in cities with large numbers of Spanish-speaking people is built around special and bilingual churches, centers or other agencies where pastoral and additional forms of service are provided in a manner suited to the needs, language and culture of the people. Pastoral ministry to Hispanics was the central concern of three national meetings, Encuentros, held in 1972, 1977 and 1985. The third national Encuentro in 1985 produced a master pastoral plan for ministry which the National Conference of Catholic Bishops approved in 1987. Its four keys are collaborative ministry; evangelization; a missionary option regarding the poor, the marginalized, the family, women and youth; and the formation of lay leadership. A National Encuentro was held in 2000. In 2002, the Secretariat published *Encuentro and Mission: A New Pastoral Framework for Hispanic Ministry.*

The U.S. bishops, at their annual meeting in November 1983, approved and subsequently published a pastoral letter on Hispanic Ministry under the title, "The Hispanic Presence: Challenge and Commitment." (For text, see pp. 46-49 of the *1985 Catholic Almanac.*)

Bishops

As of Aug. 1, 2014, there were 42 (28 active) bishops of Hispanic origin in the United States; all were named since 1970 (for biographies, see Index). Fifteen were heads of archdioceses or dioceses: Abp. José H. Gomez (Los Angeles) and Abp. Gustavo Garcia-Siller, M.Sp.S. (San Antonio); Bishops Gerald R. Barnes (San Bernardino), Oscar Cantú (Las Cruces), Edgar M. Da Cunha, S.D.V. (Fall River), Felipe de Jesús Estevez (St. Augustine), Daniel E. Flores (Brownsville), Richard J. Garcia (Monterey in California), Fernando Isern (Pueblo), Armando X. Ochoa (Fresno), Placido Rodriguez, C.M.F. (Lubbock), Jaime Soto (Sacramento), James A. Tamayo (Laredo), José S. Vasquez (Austin); Cirilo B. Flores (San Diego).

Thirteen were auxiliary bishops: Octavio Cisneros (Brooklyn), Manuel Cruz (Newark), Rutilio del Riego (San Bernardino), Eusebio Elizondo, M.Sp.S. (Seattle), José Cepeda Escobedo (Detroit), Francisco Gonzalez Valer, S.F. (Washington, DC), Robert J. Iriondo (New York), Eduardo Nevares (Phoenix), Nelson Perez (Rockville Center), Alberto Rojas (Chicago), Alexander Salazar (Los Angeles), Paul Sanchez (Brooklyn), Luis Zarama (Atlanta), and Paul Sanchez (Brooklyn).

Resigned/retired prelates: Abp. Patrick F. Flores (San Antonio); Bps. Emilio Simeon Allué (Boston),

Bishop David Arias, O.A.R. (Newark), Bishop Joseph J. Madera (Military Services), Bishop Raymundo J Peña (Brownsville), Bishop Rene H. Gracida (Corpus Christi), Bishop Agustin Roman (Miami), Bishop Rene Valero (Brooklyn), Gilbert Espinoza Chavez (San Diego), Carlos A. Sevilla, S.J. (Yakima), Arthur N. Tafoya (Pueblo), Ricardo Ramirez, C.S.B. (Las Cruces), and Gabino Zavala (Los Angeles), Bishop Roberto O. Gonzalez, O.F.M. (Corpus Christi), was appointed archbishop of San Juan de Puerto Rico on Mar. 26, 1999, by Pope John Paul II. Bp. Alvaro Corrada del Rio, S.J. (Tyler) was appointed bp. of Mayaguez, Puerto Rico, on July 6, 2011.

Hispanic priests and nuns in the U.S. number about 1,600 and 3,000, respectively, according to recent estimates.

The National Pastoral Plan for Hispanic Ministry

The National Pastoral Plan for Hispanic Ministry was approved by the NCCB in November 1987. This plan is addressed to the entire Church in the United States. It focuses on the pastoral needs of the Hispanic Catholic, but it challenges all Catholics as members of the Body of Christ.

General Objective: To live and promote by means of a Pastoral de Conjunto, a model of Church that is: communitarian, evangelizing, and missionary, incarnate in the reality of the Hispanic people and open to the diversity of cultures, a promoter and example of justice ... that develops leadership through integral education ... that is leaven for the Kingdom of God in society.

Catholic Hispanic Organizations

Academy of Catholic Hispanic Theologians of the United States – ACHTUS. Dr. Carmen Nanko-Fernández, Assistant Professor of Pastoral Ministry, Catholic Theological Union, 5401 S. Cornell Ave., Chicago, Il 60615; (773) 371-5533.

Asociación Nacional de Diáconos Hispanos – ANDH. Deacon Jorge Benavente, 818 N. East Ave., Waukesha, WI 53186; (262) 542-2589.

Asociación Nacional de Sacerdotes Hispanos – ANSH Rev. Heberto M. Diaz, Diocese of Brownsville, 1910 University Blvd., Brownsville, TX 78522-2279; (956) 550-1517.

Catholic Association of Latino Leaders – CALL. Mr. Mario Paredes, 2718 W. Woodlawn Ave., P. O. Box 28410, San Antonio, TX; (210) 734-2620.

Catholic Migrant Farmworker Network – CMFN. Sr. Karen Bernhardt HM, CMFN President, P.O. Box 50026, Boise, ID 83705.

Federación de Institutos Pastorales – FIP. Sr. Ruth Bolarte, President, 7700 SW 56 St., Miami, FL 33155; (305) 279-2333.

Instituto Nacional Hispano de Liturgia – INHL. Rev. Juan J. Sosa, St. Catherine of Siena, 9200 SW 107th Ave., Miami. FL 33176; (305) 274-6333.

Mexican American Catholic College – MACC. Dr. Arturo Chavez, 3115 W Ashby, San Antonio, TX 78228; (210) 732-2156.

National Catholic Association of Diocesan Directors for Hispanic Ministry – NCADDHM Rev. Hector Madrigal, President, Diocese of Amarillo, TX.

National Catholic Network de Pastoral Juvenil Hispana – NCNPJH, Diocese of Beaumont, P. O. Box 3948; Beaumont, TX 77701; (409) 838-0451.

National Catholic Council for Hispanic Ministry (NCCHM)

The council is a volunteer federation of Roman Catholic organizations, agencies and movements committed to the development of Hispanics/Latinos in Church and society. It was established June 17, 1990, at a gathering at Mundelein College, Chicago; its by-laws were adopted in January 1991 at Mercy Center, Burlingame, CA. Currently, there are 56 members. Carmen F. Aguinaco, Pres., 205 W. Monroe, Chicago, IL 60606; (312) 544-8153; www.ncchm.org.

Statistics

(*Courtesy, Secretariat for Hispanic Affairs, USCCB.*)

According to the most recent official Census estimates (as of 2010), there is a population of 50.5 million Hispanics, or about 16 percent of the total population. They are the fastest growing minority group in the United States, and the Hispanic population in the country is the second largest one in the world, after only Mexico. The nation's Hispanic Catholic population (not including Puerto Rico) has increased by 71 percent since 1960, and approximately 68 percent are Catholic. Hispanics also account for 71 percent of the U.S. Catholic population growth since 1960. The total Hispanic Catholic population as a percentage of the U.S. Catholic population is approximately 40 percent. Of these Hispanic Catholics, 64 percent attend church services regularly.

According to statistics based on the 2010 Census, 4,800 U.S. parishes have Hispanic ministry; approximately 21 percent of U.S. parishes have a majority Hispanic presence. There are approximately 3,000 Hispanic priests (7.45 percent of the total) and 29 active Hispanic bishops. Over the past few years, 20% of all new priests ordained in the United States have been of Hispanic/Latino(a) descent. Hispanics/Latinos(as) constitute 43% of all laypeople engaged in diocesan ministry programs. The 10 metropolitan areas with the largest Hispanic populations are: Los Angeles, New York, Chicago, Miami, Houston, Riverside-San Bernardino, Orange County, Phoenix, San Antonio, and Dallas. Eight states in 2011 had more than one million Hispanic residents: Arizona, California, Colorado, Florida, Illinois, New Jersey, New York, and Texas. Approximately one half of the Hispanic population lived in just two states: California and Texas. In New Mexico, Hispanics made up 47 percent of the state's total population, the highest for any state.

Current U.S. Census figures reveal that Hispanics accounted for 56 percent of the nation's increase in population over the decade from 2000-2010. Data demonstrate that the Hispanic population in the U.S. is young. The median age of the Hispanic population in 2009 is 27.4 years, compared with 36.8 years for the general population. The Hispanic population comprises 26 percent of the children under the age of five; Hispanics comprise 22 percent of children younger than 18. Only 4.8 percent of Hispanics are older than 65. More than 50% of all Millennial Catholics in the United States under age 25 are of Hispanic/Latino(a) descent. The poverty rate in the general population in 1999 was 7.7 percent among non-Hispanic whites; the poverty rate among Hispanics was 21.2 percent or 7.2 million people. This is a record low matching that of the 1970s. It is projected that Hispanics/Latinos(as) will surpass the 132.8 million mark by the year 2050. Hispanics will comprise 30 percent of the total population.

AFRICAN-AMERICAN CATHOLICS IN THE UNITED STATES

The Subcommittee for African-American Catholics reports that there are presently approximately three million African-American Catholics in the United States out of 36 million total African-Americans (13 percent of the total population).

Subcommittee on African-American Catholics

(*Courtesy, Subcommittee for African-American Catholics, USCCB.*)

The Subcommittee on African American Affairs is the officially recognized voice of the African-American Catholic community as it articulates the needs and aspirations regarding ministry, evangelization, social justice issues, and worship. According to the Subcommittee:

The subcommittee attends the needs and aspirations of African American Catholics in regard to issues of ministry, evangelization, social justice, worship and other areas of concern. The subcommittee also seeks to be a resource for the all the Bishops and the entire Catholic Church in the U.S. It aims to articulate the socio-cultural dimension of the African American Catholic community and identify or create resources that would allow for an authentic integration of the richness of the African American Catholic culture and the Catholic Church in the United States.

The Subcommittee for African-American Catholics was established initially as a committee and secretariat by the National Conference of Catholic Bishops in 1987. It was reorganized as a subcommittee in Jan. 2008 and is part of the Bishop's Committee for Cultural Diversity in the Church. The purpose of the subcommittee is to assist the bishops in their evangelization efforts to the African-American community. The subcommittee is under the direction of and assists the Committee on Cultural Diversity in the Church by working collaboratively with the committee and other USCCB committees to affirm the gifts and contributions of African American Catholics and to provide more opportunities for African American Catholics to engage in the life of the Church and help shape its evangelizing mission. This mandate includes the following areas of responsibility: The subcommittee is directly responsible for outreach to the African American communities and to work closely with the subcommittee on Pastoral Care of Migrants and Refugees.

The subcommittee is chaired by Bp. Martin D. Holley, aux. bp. of Washington. Beverly Carroll is the assistant director of the subcommittee. Address: 3211 Fourth St. N.E., Washington, DC, 20017, (202) 541-3000, www. usccb.org.

Bishops

There were 15 (8 active) black bishops as of Sept. 1, 2014. Five were heads of dioceses: Abp. Wilton D. Gregory (Atlanta, president of the USCCB, 2001-2004); Bishops Curtis J. Guillory, S.V.D. (Beaumont), George V. Murry, S.J. (Youngstown), Edward K. Braxton (Belleville), J. Terry Steib, S.V.D. (Memphis). Four were auxiliary bishops: Shelton J. Fabre (New Orleans), Joseph N. Perry (Chicago), and Martin D. Holley (Washington). Elliott G. Thomas, of St. Thomas, Virgin Islands (res., June 30, 1999), Joseph L. Howze of Biloxi (res., May 15, 2001), Leonard J. Olivier, S.V.D., Washington aux. (ret., May 18, 2004), John H. Ricard, S.S.J (ret. Mar. 11, 2011), Gordon D. Bennett (ret. Aug. 8, 2006), and Dominic Carmon,

S.V.D., New Orleans aux. (ret., Dec. 13, 2006), and Guy A. Sansaricq, Brooklyn (ret. Oct. 6, 2010), are retired. African-American Bishops of the Past: James August Healy (1830-1900); Joseph A. Francis, S.V.D. (1923-1997); Eugene A. Marino, S.S.J. (1934-2000); Raymond Rodly Caeser, S.V.D. (1932-1987); James Lyke, O.F.M. (1939-1992); Carl A. Fisher, S.S.J. (1945-1993); Emerson J. Moore (1938-1995); Harold R. Perry, S.V.D. (1916-1991), and Moses Anderson, S.S.E. (1928-2013),

Statistics

The Subcommittee for African-American Catholics reports that there are presently approximately three million African-American Catholics in the United States out of 36 million total African-Americans. They are served by 798 parishes, 75 African-American pastors, and 71 Diocesan Offices for African American Catholic Ministry. There are approximately 250 African-American priests, 400 African-American sisters, 50 African-American brothers, 437 African-American deacons, and 26 African-American Seminarians. It is projected that the Black population will increase to 62 million by 2050, or 16% of the total population.

African-American Catholic Organizations

Black Catholic Catechetical Network A network intended to assist and revitalize catechesis for Black Catholics throughout the United States. Address: Mrs. Therese Wilson Favors, Office of African American Catholic Ministries, Archdiocese of Baltimore, 320 Cathedral St., Baltimore, Maryland 21201; (410) 625-8471.

Black Catholic Theological Symposium A national interdisciplinary theological society of the Roman Catholic tradition that was established "to foster among Black Catholics an ethical community of scholarly dialogue; to publish reports, the Symposium's discussions, and the research of Symposium members; to encourage the teaching and discussion of Black Catholic religious and cultural experiences." Address: Dr. M. Shawn Copeland, Convener, Associate Professor, Theology Department, Boston College, 140 Commonwealth Ave., Chestnut Hill, MA 02467; www.bcts.org.

Institute for Black Catholic Studies Founded in 1980, the IBCS of Xavier University of Louisiana offers programs in pastoral ministries, religious education and pastoral theology taught from the perspective of the Christian faith expressed in the Black religious community. Address: Sr. Jamie Phelps, OP, Ph.D., Dir., Xavier University, 1 Drexel Dr., New Orleans, LA 70125; (504) 483-7691; www.xula.edu/IBCS.html.

Josephite Fathers and Brothers The Josephite Pastoral Center was established in Sept. 1968 as an educational and pastoral service agency for the Josephites in their mission work, specifically in the black community, subsequently to all those who minister in the African-American community. St. Joseph's Society of the Sacred Heart, the sponsoring body, has about 134 priests and 11 brothers in 64 mostly southern parishes in 17 dioceses. Contact: 1130 N. Calvert St., Baltimore, MD 21202; (410) 727-3386; www.josephite.com and Josephite Pastoral Center, St. Joseph Seminary, 1200 Varnum St. NE, Washington, DC 20017; (202) 526-9270.

Knights of Peter Claver and Knights of Peter Claver, Ladies Auxiliary. The largest Black Catholic organization in the United States, the Knights are a fraternal and aid society. The Knights were begun in 1909 and the Ladies Auxiliary was authorized and their constitution adopted in August 1922; it was recognized as a Division of the National Council in 1926. The Junior Daughters was established in 1930 and the Junior Knights were established in 1935. Address: Mr. Anthanase Jones, Exec. Dir., 1825 Orleans Ave., New Orleans, LA 70116; (504) 821-4225; www.knightsofpeterclaver.com.

National African American Catholic Youth Ministry Network An affiliate of the National Federation for Catholic Youth Ministry, the NAACYMN provides assists the needs of youth and youth ministers in the African American community. The National African American Catholic Youth Ministry Network was founded in 1986. Address: Mr. Michael Youngblood, Office of Black Catholic Ministries, 1933 Spielbusch Ave., P.O. Box 958, Toledo, OH 43697-0985; (419) 244-6711; www.nbccongress.org.

National Association of African American Catholic Deacons Founded in 1993, (NAAACD) promotes unity among African American deacons, assists the professional spiritual growth of its members, and develops relationships with the National Black Catholic Congress, the National Black Catholic Clergy Caucus, and the Bishops' Committee on the Diaconate in relevant matters. Address: Rev. Mr. Marvin T. Threatt, Ph.D.,10125 Fabled Water Ct., Spring Valley, CA 91977; (619) 670-8339.

National Association of Black Catholic Administrators Established in 1976, the NABCA works to address issues and concerns facing African American communities and promote and support African American leadership. Address: Mrs. Annette Turner, President, Office of Multicultural Ministry, Archdiocese of Louisville, 1200 South Shelby St., Louisville, KY 40203-2600; (502) 636-0296.

The National Black Catholic Apostolate for Life Founded in 1997, the National Black Catholic Apostolate for Life is a ministry committed to promote the culture of life and defending unconditionally human life from the moment of conception to natural death. Address: Fr. James E. Goode, OFM, Ph.D., Pres., 440 West 36th St., New York, NY 10018-6326; (212) 868-1847; www.blackcatholicsforlife.org

National Black Catholic Clergy Caucus The National Black Catholic Clergy Caucus, founded in 1968 in Detroit, is a fraternity of several hundred black priests, permanent deacons and brothers pledged to mutual support in their vocations and ministries. Address: Deacon Dunn Cumby, DDS, President, 603 North East 17, Oklahoma City, OK 73105; (405) 524-7214.

National Black Catholic Congress The National Black Catholic Congress, Inc., was formed in 1985 exclusively to assist in the development of the Roman Catholic Church in the African-American community and to devise effective means of evangelization of African-American peoples in the United States. Address: Valerie E. Washington, President, Archdiocese of Baltimore Catholic Center, 320 Cathedral St., 3rd Floor, Baltimore, MD 21201, (410) 547-8496, www.nbccongress.org.

National Black Catholic Seminarians Association The NBCSA promotes the bonds of brotherhood among Black Catholic Seminarians and focuses on vocations of Black men and those who work with Black persons. Address: Br. Damian Harris, SVD, President, Divine Word Seminary, P.O. Box 0380, Epworth, IA 52045; (563) 876-3057; www.bcvp.org.

National Black Sisters' Conference The NBSC provides support to its membership of Black Catholic women religious through prayer, study, solidarity, and programs. Address: Sr.

Patricia Haley, SCN, President, National Office,101 Q St., NE, Washington, DC 20002; (202) 529-9520.

National Office for Black Catholics The National Office for Black Catholics, organized in July 1970, is a central agency with the general purposes of promoting active and full participation by black Catholics in the Church and of making more effective the presence and ministry of the Church in the black community. Address: The Paulist Center, 3025 Fourth St. N.E., Washington, DC, 20017; (202) 635-1778.

Xavier University of Louisiana Founded by Saint Katherine Drexel and the Sisters of Blessed Sacrament in 1925, Xavier University of Louisiana is the only predominately Black Catholic university in the world. Dr. Norman C. Francis, President,1 Drexel Dr., New Orleans, LA 70125; (504) 520-7541; www.xula.edu.

ASIAN AND PACIFIC ISLANDER CATHOLICS IN THE UNITED STATES

One of the most challenging areas of ministry in the United States today is meeting the pastoral needs of Asian and Pacific Islander communities in the United States. As of 2010, 14.6 million (5% of the total U.S. population) people are Asian and 540,000 Pacific Islanders, including Hawaiians (0.3% of total U.S. population.)

Subcommittee on Asian and Pacific Islanders

The pastoral care of Asian and Pacific communities was coordinated nationally from the 1980s through the Office for the Pastoral Care of Migrants and Refugees (PCMR) of the Migration and Refugee Services Department at USCCB. When, however, the USCCB underwent its restructuring, a permanent bishops' subcommittee on Asian and Pacific Affairs was formed in 2008 as part of the Committee on Cultural Diversity in the Church. The subcommittee states that its priorities include:

• Assist dioceses in building capacities to welcome and integrate Asian and Pacific Catholics in parish life.

• Increase availability of sacraments, pastoral services, and appropriate religious education materials in the languages and cultural idioms of Asian and Pacific Island communities who cannot sufficiently make use of the common and ordinary pastoral services of local parishes.

• Promote the formation of Asian and Pacific Island Catholic pastoral leaders so they become evangelizers of their families, ethnic communities, and local churches.

• Assist Asian and Pacific Island Catholics in strengthening their faith communities and building communion with each other, with diverse members of the Church, and with their local bishops and pastors through diocesan, regional, and national gatherings.

• Promote the implementation of recommendations in Asian and Pacific Presence: Harmony in Faith at the local and national level.

The subcommittee is currently chaired by Bp. Raldolph Calvo, Bishop of Reno. Sister Anna Nguyen, S.C.C., is the assistant director of the subcommittee. Address: 3211 Fourth St. N.E., Washington, DC, 20017, (202) 541-3000, www. usccb.org.

Statistics

The Subcommittee for Asians and Pacific Islanders reports that there are presently approximately 14.6 million (5% of the total U.S. population) people in the United States who are Asian and 540,000 Pacific Islanders, including Hawaiians (0.3% of total U.S. population.) The largest Asian U.S. populations are Chinese (including mainland China, Hong Kong and Taiwan), Filipino, Indian, Vietnamese, followed by Korean, and Japanese. The largest Pacific Islander populations in the U.S. are Hawaiian, Micronesian, Guamanian, Samoan and Tongan. Except for the Filipinos, the majority of Asian and Pacific people in the U.S. are followers of Buddhism, Hinduism, and Islam.

The U.S. Asian Pacific populations with the largest number of Catholics are the Filipinos, followed by the Vietnamese, Chinese, Indian and Korean. The USCCB estimated in 1999 that Asian Pacific Catholics made up the third largest group of people of color, accounting for about 2.6% of all Catholics in the U.S.The Subcommittee also states that Asian Catholics also include members of Eastern Catholic Churches of the Syro-Malabar, Syro-Malankara, and Midle-Eastern Catholic rites.

In 2001 the USCCB issued a pastoral statement, Asian and Pacific Presence: Harmony in Faith. It was notable for being the first time that the bishops of the United States collectively issued a letter devoted to Asian and Pacific people in the Church. The full text of the document is available at: www.usccb.org/apa/statement.shtml.

NATIVE-AMERICAN CATHOLICS IN THE UNITED STATES

According to the United States Conference of Catholic Bishops' report, "Native American Catholics at the Millennium," there are nearly half a million Native American Catholics in the U.S. They are served by a variety of ministries, including the Bureau of Catholic Indian Missions and the USCCB Subcommittee of Native American Catholics.

Bureau of Catholic Indian Missions

Established in 1874 as the representative of Catholic Indian missions before the federal government and the public, the bureau was made a permanent organization in 1884 by the Third Plenary Council of Baltimore. After a remarkable history of rendering important services to the Indian people, the bureau continues to represent the Catholic Church in the U.S. in her apostolate to the American Indian. Its primary concerns are evangelization, catechesis, liturgy, family life, education, and advocacy. Address: 2021 H Street N.W., Washington, DC, 20006-4207, (202) 331-8542.

Subcommittee of Native American Catholics

The Subcommittee on Native American Affairs is part of the USCCB Committee on Cultural Diversity within the Church and works directly with the standing committee and other USCCB committees to address the pastoral needs of Native American Catholics. The key mission priorities are:

• Continue to support and collaborate with key national organizations, including the Bureau of Catholic Indian Missions and the Tekakwitha Conference.

• Continue to identify and/or develop culturally and ethnically specific resources in the areas of catechesis, lay ministry formation, liturgy, evangelization, and the diaconate.

• Continue to collaborate with other USCCB offices, including Laity, Marriage, Family Life, and Youth; Education; Evangelization and Catechesis;

Vocations; Liturgy; and Pastoral Practices.

The subcommittee is currently chaired by Abp. Charles J. Chaput of Philadelphia. Address: 3211 Fourth St. N.E., Washington, DC, 20017, (202) 541-3000, www. usccb.org.

Kateri Tekakwitha Conference

The Kateri Tekakwitha Conference is so named in honor of Blessed Kateri Tekakwitha, "Lily of the Mohawks," who was born in 1656 at Ossernenon (Auriesville), NY, in 1656, baptized in 1676, lived near Montreal, died in 1680, and was beatified in 1980. The conference was established in 1939 as a missionary-priest advisory group in the Diocese of Fargo. It was a missionary-priest support group from 1946 to 1977. Since 1977 it has been a gathering of Catholic Native peoples and the men and women — clerical, religious and lay persons — who minister to Native Catholic communities.

Conferences and local Kateri Circles serve as occasions for the exchange of ideas, prayer and mutual support. Since 1980, the national center has promoted and registered 130 Kateri Circles in the U.S. and Canada. Publications include a quarterly newsletter.

The conference has a board of 12 directors, the majority of whom are Native people. Abp. Charles Chaput, O.F.M. Cap., is the episcopal moderator. Address: Tekakwitha Conference National Center, P.O. Box 6768, Great Falls, MT, 59406, (406) 727-0147.

Statistics

On June 19, 2003, the United States Conference of Catholic Bishops issued a report, "Native American Catholics at the Millennium," on the current state of Native American Catholics in the U.S. There are 4.1 million people who identify themselves as Native American. Of these, 493,615 Native Americans, or 12% of the total population, are considered Catholic. Native Americans comprise 3.5% of all Catholics in the U.S. More than 340 parishes in the United States serve predominantly Native American congregations.

Bishops

There is presently one Native American bishop in the United States: Abp. Charles J. Chaput, O.F.M. Cap. of Philadelphia.

PASTORAL CARE OF MIGRANTS, REFUGEES, AND TRAVELERS

As a result of globalization, modern travel, and economic and political unrest, men, women, and children are forced to be constantly on the move. They are still in need of pastoral care, and the Church has a long history of reaching out to all of the populations of migrants, refugees, and travelers. There are two primary bodies charged with the immediate pastoral needs of these groups. The first is the Pontifical Council for the Pastoral Care of Migrants and Itinerant Peoples and the other is the Subcommittee on the Pastoral Care of Migrants, Refugees and Travelers.

Pontifical Council for Pastoral Care of Migrants and Itinerant Peoples

For details, see under the Roman Curia in the section on the Holy See.

The Subcommittee on the Pastoral Care of Migrants, Refugees and Travelers

The Subcommittee on the Pastoral Care of Migrants, Refugees and Travelers is part of the Committee on Cultural Diversity within the Church by and works both with the other subcommittees and other USCCB committees to support the pastoral care of migrants, refugees and travelers. According to the subcommittee, People on the Move ministries include:

Airport and airline workers and travelers; Circus and Carnival Workers; Gypsies and Irish Travelers; Port and ship chaplains, seafarers and fishers; Migrant Farm Workers; Race Car drivers in conjunction with Championship Auto Racing Team Ministries; Tourism – National Parks, Tourist Centers, pilgrimage groups, and workers in the Tourist industry; Truckers, highway travelers and workers at truck stops, bus stations and rest stops in conjunction with the National Diaconate Office.

The subcommittee is currently chaired by Bp. Rutilio Del Riego, aux. bp. of San Bernardino. Sr. Myrna Tordillo, MSCS, is the assistant director of the subcommittee. Address: 3211 Fourth St. N.E., Washington, DC, 20017, (202) 541-3000, www. usccb.org.

MISSIONARY ACTIVITY OF THE U.S. CHURCH

Sources: U.S. Catholic Mission Handbook 2010: Mission Inventory 2008-2009 *(the most recent issue), reproduced with permission of the United States Catholic Mission Council, 3029 Fourth St. N.E., Washington, DC.*

OVERSEAS MISSIONS

Field Distribution, 2008-2009

Africa: 418 (213 men; 205 women). Largest numbers in Kenya, 112; Tanzania, 60; Zambia, 35; Uganda, 35; Ghana, 25; South Africa, 25; Nigeria, 21.

Asia: 395 (254 men; 141 women). Largest numbers in Philippines, 86; Japan, 62; Taiwan, 52; China PRC Hong Kong SAR, 48; India, 43; Korea, 21; Bangladesh, 19; Thailand, 12. (Those present in China were there for professional services.)

Caribbean: 154 (63 men; 91 women). Largest numbers in Puerto Rico, 36; Jamaica, 34; Dominican Republic 23; Belize, 26; Haiti, 11.

Eurasia (Kazakhstan, Russia, Siberia): 6 (5 men; 1 women). Largest group, Russia, 3.

Europe: 85 (25 men; 60 women). Largest numbers in Italy, 33; Ireland, 15; England, 10; Germany, 4.

Latin America: 567 (215 men; 352 women). Largest numbers in Peru, 106; Mexico, 77; Brazil, 90; Bolivia, 55; Guatemala, 60; Chile, 55.

Middle East: 11 (7 men; 4 women). Largest numbers in Jordan, 4; Israel, 3; Lebanon, 3.

North America (Canada and United States): 1,629 (313 men; 1,316 women). Largest number in the United States, 1,605.

Oceania: 87 (56 men; 31 women). Largest numbers in

Papua New Guinea, 26; Micronesia, 23; Marshall Island, 8; Australia, 6; Guam, 4.

TOTAL: 3,352 (1,151 men; 2,201 women).

Missionary Personnel, 2008-2009

Bishops: 22.

Religious Priests: 50 mission sending groups had 784 priests in overseas assignments. Listed below are those with 15 or more members abroad.

Jesuits, 169; Maryknoll Fathers and Brothers, 152; Oblates of Mary Immaculate, 113; Society of Divine Word, 72; Order of Friars Minor, 54; Holy Cross Fathers, 41; Columbans, 29; Franciscans (O.F.M. Cap), 29; Oblates of Francis de Sales, 26; Glenmary Home Missoners, 26; Dominicans, 16; Marianists, 15.

Diocesan Priests: There were 49 priests from 25 dioceses. The majority were in Latin American countries.

Religious Brothers: 34 mission sending groups had 171 brothers in overseas assignments. Those with 15 or more members: Jesuits, 314; Marianists, 36; Franciscans (O.F.M.), 20; Holy Cross Congregation, 17.

Religious Sisters: 130 mission sending communities of women Religious had 1,962 sisters in overseas missions. Those with 15 or more members: Maryknoll Mission Sisters, 185; Franciscan Missionaries of Mary, 130; School Sisters of Notre Dame, 112; Missionaries of Charity, 92; Medical Mission Sisters, 51; Dominicans, 45; Congregation of Sisters of St. Agnes, 45; St. Joseph Sisters, 45; Franciscan Sisters, 39; Sisters of Charity of the BVM, 38; Ursulines, 37; Providence Sisters, 37; Daughters of Charity, 34; Holy Cross, Cong. of Sisters, 30; Sisters of Mercy (various communities), 25; Sisters of Notre Dame de Namur, 24; Medical Missionaries of Mary, 22; Franciscan Sisters of Little Falls, 21; IHM Sisters of Immaculata, 21; Little Sisters of the Poor, 20; Sisters of St. Joseph of Carondelet, 17; Apostles of the Sacred Heart, 18; Mission Sisters of the Immaculate Heart of Mary, 17; Franciscan Sisters of Atonement, 16.

Lay Persons: 45 mission-sending groups had 358 members in overseas missions. Those with 15 or more members:

Jesuit Volunteer Corps, 98; Jesuit Volunteers International, 40; Salesian Lay Missionaries, 24; Catholic Medical Mission Board, 22; Mercy Corps, 20; LAMP Ministries, 17; Red Cloud Volunteers, 16.

Seminarians: There were 9 from 2 groups. Jesuits, 7; Maryknoll, 2.

U.S. MISSIONARY BISHOPS

The following is a list of missionary bishops from the United States in active service around the world. This list does not include retired bishops. As of July 15, 2011:

Africa

Madagascar: Morondava (diocese), Donald Pelletier, M.S.
Zambia: Mongu (diocese), Paul F. Duffy, O.M.I.

Asia

Kazakhstan: Almaty (diocese), Henry Howaniec, O.F.M.

Central America, West Indies

Honduras: Juticalpa (diocese), Thomas Maurus Muldoon, O.F.M.

Nicaragua: Bluefields (vicariate apostolic), Paul Simon Schmitz, O.F.M.Cap., David Albin Zywiec Sidor, O.F.M. Cap. (aux. bp.).

Puerto Rico: San Juan (archdiocese), Roberto Octavio González Nieves, O.F.M., Daniel Fernández Torres (aux. bp.); Mayaguez (diocese), Alvaro Corrado del Rio, S.J.

Trinidad and Tobago: Port of Spain (archdiocese), Edward J. Gilbert, C.SS.R.

North America

Bermuda: Hamilton (diocese), Robert Kurtz, C.R.
Jamaica: Mandeville (diocese), Neil Tiedemann, C.P.
Mexico: Nuevo Laredo (diocese), Ricardo Watty Urquidi, M.Sp.S., first bishop; Guadalajara; Miguel Romano Gómez (aux. bp.).

St. Thomas, American Virgin Islands: Hamilton: Herbert Armstrong Bevard.

United States: Gallup (diocese), James S. Wall.

Oceania

American Samoa: Samoa-Pago Pago (diocese), John Quinn Weitzel, M.M. (emeritus, May 31, 2013); successor: Peter Brown, C.Ss.R., ord. bp. Aug. 22, 2013.

Papua New Guinea: Kimbe (diocese), William Fey, O.F.M. Cap.; Mendi (diocese), Stephen J. Reichert, O.F.M.Cap.

Solomon Islands: Gizo (diocese), Christopher Cardone, O.P., aux. bp.

South America

Bolivia: Pando (vicariate apostolic), Luis Morgan Casey.
Brazil: Itaituba (prelacy), Capistran Heim, O.F.M.; Miracema do Tocantins (diocese); Valença (diocese), Elias James Manning, O.F.M. Conv.

Paraguay: San Pedro: Adalberto Martínez Flores;
Peru: Chulucanas (diocese), Daniel Thomas Turley Murphy, O.S.A.; Sicuani (prelacy), Michael La Fay Bardi, O.Carm.

U.S. CATHOLIC MISSION ASSOCIATION

This is a voluntary association of individuals and organizations for whom the missionary presence of the universal Church is of central importance. It is a nonprofit religious, educational and charitable organization which exists to promote global missions. Its primary emphasis is on cross-cultural evangelization and the promotion of international justice and peace. The association is also responsible for gathering and publishing annual statistical data on U.S. missionary personnel overseas. President: Rev. Gregory Gallagher, OMI; Executive Director, Rev. John R. Nuelle, MS. Address: 3029 Fourth St. N.E., Washington, DC, 20017, (202) 832-3112, www.uscatholicmission.org.

Mission Statement

In its 1996-97 handbook, the association included the following in a mission statement.

"In the Church, our understanding of the mission of evangelization is evolving to embrace dialogue, community building, struggles for justice, efforts to model justice and faith in our lifestyles, activities and structures, in addition to the teaching/preaching/witnessing role traditionally at the heart of the mission enterprise. Still, the contemporary 'identity-confusion' about 'mission' stands forth as a major challenge for USCMA as we move toward the 21st century.

"The larger context of mission is the Spirit moving in

the Signs of our Times: the liberation movements, the women's movements, the economy movements, the rising awareness and celebration of cultural diversity, the search for ways to live peacefully and creatively with great pluralism, rapid technological change, the emergence of the global economy, the steady increase in poverty and injustice, the realigning of the global political order - and the many ripples radiating out from each of these."

Home Missions

The expression "home missions" is applied to places in the U.S. where the local church does not have its own resources, human and otherwise. These areas share the name "missions" with their counterparts in foreign lands because they too need outside help to provide the personnel and means for making the Church present and active there in carrying out its mission for the salvation of people.

Dioceses in the southeast, the southwest, and the far west are most urgently in need of outside help to carry on the work of the Church. Millions of people live in counties in which there are no resident priests. Many others live in rural areas beyond the reach and influence of a Catholic center. According to recent statistics compiled by the Glenmary Research Center, there are more than 500 priestless counties in the United States.

Mission Workers

A number of forces are at work to meet the pastoral needs of these missionary areas and to establish permanent churches and operating institutions where they are required. In many dioceses, one or more missions and stations are attended from established parishes and are gradually growing to independent status. Priests, brothers and sisters belonging to scores of religious institutes are engaged full-time in the home missions. Lay persons, some of them in affiliation with special groups and movements, are also involved.

The Society for the Propagation of the Faith, which conducts an annual collection for mission support in all parishes, allocates 40% of this sum for disbursement to home missions through the American Board of Catholic Missions.

Various mission-aid societies frequently undertake projects on behalf of the home missions.

The Glenmary Home Missioners, founded by Fr. W. Howard Bishop in 1939, is the only home mission society established for the sole purpose of carrying out the pastoral ministry in small towns and rural districts of the U.S. Glenmary serves in many areas where at least 20 per cent of the people live in poverty and less than one per cent are Catholic. With 61 priests and 19 professed brothers as of January 1998 the Glenmary Missioners had missions in the archdioceses of Atlanta and Cincinnati, and in the dioceses of Birmingham, Charlotte, Covington, Jackson, Lexington, Little Rock, Nashville, Owensboro, Richmond, Savannah, Tulsa, Tyler and Wheeling-Charleston. National headquarters are located at 4119 Glenmary Trace, Fairfield, OH. The mailing address is P.O. Box 465618, Cincinnati, OH, 45246, (513) 874-8900.

Organizations

Black and Indian Mission Office (The Commission for Catholic Missions among the Colored People and the Indians): Organized officially in 1885 by decree of the Third Plenary Council of Baltimore. Provides financial support for religious works among Blacks and Native Americans in 133 archdioceses and dioceses through funds raised by an annual collection in all parishes of the U.S. on the first Sunday of Lent, the designated Sunday.

Bureau of Catholic Indian Missions See under Native American Catholics above.

Catholic Negro-American Mission Board (1907): Supports priests and sisters in southern states and provides monthly support to sisters and lay teachers in the poorest black schools.

Address: 2021 H St. N.W., Washington, DC, 20006-4207, (202) 331-8542.

The Catholic Church Extension Society (1905): Established with papal approval for the purpose of preserving and extending the Church in rural and isolated parts of the U.S. and its dependencies through the collection and disbursement of funds for home mission work. Since the time of its founding, more than $400 million has been received and distributed for church construction, religious education and seminary formation, campus and outreach ministries, evangelization, and salaries for missionaries. The Society celebrated its 100th anniversary in 2005. Works of the society are supervised by a 14-member board of governors: Card. Francis George of Chicago, chancellor; Fr. John Wall, president; three archbishops, three bishops and six lay people. Headquarters: 150 S. Wacker Dr., 20th Floor, Chicago, IL, 60601, (312) 236-7240; www.catholicextension.org.

National Catholic Rural Life Conference: Founded in 1923 through the efforts of Bp. Edwin V. O'Hara. Applies the Gospel message to rural issues through focus on rural parishes and the provision of services including distribution of educational materials development of prayer and worship resources, advocacy for strong rural communities. Bp. Frank J. Dewane, president; James F. Ennis, exec. dir. National headquarters: 4625 Beaver Ave., Des Moines, IA, 50310, (515) 270-2634, www.ncrlc.com.

Bishops' Committee On The Home Missions

Established in 1924, the Committee on the Home Missions of the U.S. Conference of Catholic Bishops provides financial support for missionary activities that strengthen and extend the presence of the Church in the United States and its island territories in the Caribbean and the Pacific. Funding for mission dioceses and national organizations engaged in home mission work is provided through the annual Catholic Home Missions Appeal, which is nationally scheduled on the last weekend of April. For 2006-2007, $8.4 million was allocated to mission dioceses and mission organizations thanks to the faithfulness and sustained generosity of Catholics. Since 1924, close to $300 million has been collected and disbursed for home missions. The committee's work is supervised by seven bishops and a small national staff. Bp. Peter F. Christensen, Bishop of Superior, is chairperson; Mary Mencarini Campbell, Dir. National headquarters: U. S. Conference of Catholic Bishops, 3211 4th NE, Washington, DC, 20017-1194, (202) 541-3450, www.usccb.org.

U.S. Catholic Statistics

U.S. STATISTICAL SUMMARY

(Principal sources: The Official Catholic Directory, 2014, Almanac survey comparisons, where given, are with figures reported in the previous edition of the Directory. Totals below do not include statistics for Outlying Areas of U.S. unless otherwise noted. These are given in tables on the preceding pages and elsewhere in the Catholic Almanac; see Index.)

Catholic Population: 69,470,686; increase, 34,026 Percent of total population: 22%.

Jurisdictions: In the United States, there are 196 archdioceses and dioceses: 33 Latin Catholic archdioceses, 145 Latin Catholic dioceses, 15 Eastern Catholic dioceses, and 2 Eastern Catholic archdioceses; there is also 1 apostolic exarchate (New York based Armenian exarchate for U.S. and Canada) and 1 personal ordinariate of the Chair of St. Peter. The current number of dioceses reflects the elevation of the diocese of Galveston-Houston to an archdiocese on Dec. 29, 2004, and the creation on July 3, 2000, of the new diocese of Laredo. There are also the eparchies of St. Maron and Our Lady of Lebanon of Los Angeles (Maronites), Newton (Melkites), St. Thomas Apostle of Detroit (Chaldeans), St. George Martyr of Canton, Ohio (Romanians), St. Thomas of Chicago (Syro-Malabars), the Eparchy of St. Peter the Apostle of San Diego, and the creation of the Syro-Malankara apostolic exarchate on June 14, 2010. The personal ordinariate of the Chair of St. Peter was established on Jan. 1, 2012. The eparchy of Our Lady of Deliverance of Newark has its seat in Newark, NJ. The Armenian apostolic exarchate for the United States and Canada has its seat in New York. Vacant jurisdictions (as of Aug. 15, 2014): Burlington, Fairbanks, Lexington.

Cardinals: 18 (5 head archiepiscopal sees in U.S.; three are Roman Curia officials; 10 are retired). As of July 10, 2014.

Archbishops: 55. Diocesan, in U.S., 30 (does not include 5 cardinals and military archbishop); retired, 25; there are also 9 archbishops serving outside U.S. As of July 15, 2014.

Bishops: 447. Diocesan, in U.S. (and Virgin Islands), 156; auxiliaries, 76; retired, 175; there are also 20 bishops serving outside U.S. As of Jul. 15, 2014.

Priests: 39,022; decrease, 346. Diocesan, 26,696 (decrease, 283); religious order priests (does not include those assigned overseas), 12,326 (decrease, 63). There were 508 newly ordained priests; increase, 37.

Permanent Deacons: 18,089; decrease, 32.

Brothers: 4,349; decrease, 110

Sisters: 50,836; decrease, 1,721.

Seminarians: 5,046. Diocesan seminarians, 3,598; religious order seminarians, 1,448.

Receptions into Church: 836,656. Includes 730,171 infant baptisms; 39,654 adult baptisms and 66,831 already baptized persons received into full communion with the Church.

First Communions: 775,645.

Confirmations: 583,358.

Marriages: 157,755.

Deaths: 411,322.

Parishes: 17,900.

Seminaries, Diocesan: 74.

Religious Seminaries: 85.

Colleges and Universities: 233. Students, 810,201.

High Schools: 1,303. Students, 612,400.

Elementary Schools: 5,547. Students, 1,401,323

Non Residential Schools for Handicapped: 50. Students, 5,391.

Teachers: 163,979 (priests, 1,259; brothers, 744; scholastics, 97; sisters, 3,515; laity, 158,364).

Public School Students in Religious Instruction Programs: 3,356,206. High school students, 640,585; elementary school students, 2,715,621.

Hospitals: 554; patients treated, 88,867,803.

Health Care Centers: 423; patients treated, 5,615,216.

Specialized Homes: 1,426; patients assisted, 545,876.

Residential Care of Children (Orphanages): 103; children assisted, 20,187.

Day Care and Extended Day Care Centers: 893; children assisted, 105,742.

Special Centers for Social Services: 3,250; assisted annually, 32,517,698.

PERCENTAGE OF CATHOLICS IN TOTAL POPULATION IN U.S.

(Source: The Official Catholic Directory, 2014; *figures are as of Jan. 1, 2014. Total general population figures at the end of the table are U.S. Census Bureau estimates for Jan. 1 of the respective years. Archdioceses are indicated by an asterisk; for dioceses marked +, see Dioceses with Interstate Lines.)*

State Diocese	Catholic Pop.	Total Pop.	Cath. Pct.	State Diocese	Catholic Pop.	Total Pop.	Cath. Pct.
Alabama	**162,627**	**4,819,646**	**3.4**	**Illinois**, cont.			
*Mobile	70,077	1,783,780	4	Springfield	145,189	1,146,638	13
Birmingham	92,550	3,035,866	3	**Indiana**	**755,096**	**6,508,645**	**12**
Alaska	**48,353**	**639,355**	**8**	*Indianapolis	218,505	2,621,455	8
*Anchorage	27,345	400,000	7	Evansville	79,504	510,626	16
Fairbanks	11,008	164,355	8	Ft.Wayne S.Bend	159,812	1,275,094	13
Juneau	10,000	75,000	13	Gary	185,100	793,759	23
Arizona	**1,082,972**	**6,344,972**	**17**	Lafayette	112,175	1,307,711	9
Phoenix	736,271	4,494,151	18	**Iowa**	**478,101**	**3,061,026**	**16**
Tucson	346,701	1,850,293	19	*Dubuque	200,058	1,000,130	20
Arkansas				Davenport	93,824	763,844	12
Little Rock	140,753	2,949,131	5	Des Moines	101,558	837,773	12
California	**12,468,704**	**38,472,373**	**32**	Sioux City	82,661	459,279	18
*Los Angeles	4,276,930	11,852,427	36	**Kansas**	**414,755**	**2,877,404**	**14**
*San Francisco	442,752	1,776,095	25	*Kansas City	204,662	1,339,351	15
Fresno	1,200,000	2,808,697	43	Dodge City	48,264	215,895	22
Monterey	205,045	1,025,226	20	Salina	41,327	334,858	12
Oakland	440,065	2,642,214	17	Wichita	120,502	987,300	12
Orange	1,319,262	3,090,132	43	**Kentucky**	**374,791**	**4,355,853**	**9**
Sacramento	987,727	3,550,864	28	*Louisville	192,485	1,368,911	14
San Bernardino	1,622,829	4,350,096	37	Covington	91,904	513,971	18
San Diego	998,127	3,236,492	31	Lexington	41,914	1,588,319	3
San Jose	590,000	1,890,909	31	Owensboro	48,488	884,652	5
Santa Rosa	175,443	945,402	19	**Louisiana**	**1,242,206**	**4,529,870**	**27**
Stockton	210,524	1,303,819	16	*New Orleans	500,818	1,252,044	40
Colorado	**794,657**	**5,187,359**	**15**	Alexandria	42,929	383,421	11
*Denver	563,441	3,472,884	16	Baton Rouge	197,069	975,750	20
Colo. Springs	167,502	1,046,889	16	Houma-			
Pueblo	63,714	667,586	10	Thibodaux	95,556	202,000	47
Connecticut	**1,220,499**	**3,590,636**	**34**	Lafayette	291,991	602,334	48
*Hartford	571,979	1,947,602	29	Lake Charles	72,238	294,447	25
Bridgeport	420,000	933,835	45	Shreveport	41,605	819,874	5
Norwich+	228,520	709,199	32	**Maine**			
Delaware+				Portland	169,198	1,329,000	13
Wilmington	240,338	1,369,080	18	**Maryland**			
District of Columbia				*Baltimore	485,167	3,199,194	15
*Washington+	630,823	2,867,377	22	**Massachusetts**	**2,709,482**	**6,582,301**	**41**
Florida	**2,284,212**	**19,242,439**	**12**	*Boston	1,904,863	4,146,381	46
*Miami	765,804	4,480,981	17	Fall River	288,845	823,654	35
Orlando	393,271	4,320,834	9	Springfield	217,274	827,274	26
Palm Beach	233,685	1,989,000	12	Worcester	298,500	784,992	38
Pensacola				**Michigan**	**1,968,402**	**9,814,609**	**20**
Tallahassee	64,714	1,425,502	5	*Detroit	1,271,588	4,263,954	30
St. Augustine	170,924	2,051,250	8	Gaylord	55,893	505,498	11
St. Petersburg	432,209	2,958,926	15	Grand Rapids	191,100	1,283,717	15
Venice	223,605	2,015,946	11	Kalamazoo	108,946	949,165	11
Georgia	**1,078,394**	**9,932,399**	**11**	Lansing	195,858	1,792,681	11
*Atlanta	1,000,000	6,998,399	13	Marquette	43,868	310,787	14
Savannah	78,394	2,934,000	3	Saginaw	101,149	708,837	14
Hawaii				**Minnesota**	**1,234,067**	**5,371,854**	**23**
Honolulu	162,288	1,392,313	12	*St. Paul and			
Idaho				Minneapolis	825,000	3,238,832	25
Boise	175,530	1,595,728	11	Crookston	32,936	259,516	13
Illinois	**3,546,282**	**12,873,621**	**28**	Duluth	54,771	446,483	12
*Chicago	2,203,000	5,955,220	37	New Ulm	58,717	281,707	21
Belleville	90,000	860,658	10	St. Cloud	127,989	559,865	23
Joliet	605,870	1,906,348	32	Winona	134,654	585,451	23
Peoria	111,723	1,492,335	7	**Mississippi**	**106,745**	**2,923,539**	**9**
Rockford	390,500	1,512,422	26	Biloxi	58,257	811,946	7

State / Diocese	Catholic Pop.	Total Pop.	Cath. Pct.
Mississippi, cont.			
Jackson	48,491	2,111,593	2
Missouri	**785,378**	**6,015,898**	**13**
*St. Louis	521,804	2,222,774	23
Jefferson City	68,955	914,936	8
Kansas City			
St. Joseph	128,364	1,524,329	8
Springfield			
C. Girardeau	66,255	1,353,859	5
Montana	**85,844**	**1,010,361**	**8**
Great Falls			
Billings	40,654	422,344	10
Helena	45,190	588,017	8
Nebraska	**374,197**	**1,863,672**	**20**
*Omaha	230,866	957,784	24
Grand Island	45,744	307,587	15
Lincoln	97,587	598,301	16
Nevada	**661,802**	**2,749,122**	**24**
Las Vegas	574,000	2,059,944	28
Reno	87,802	689,178	13
New Hampshire			
Manchester	275,641	1,316,470	21
New Jersey	**3,761,209**	**8,865,160**	**42**
*Newark	1,352,000	2,859,850	47
Camden	511,822	1,443,274	35
Metuchen	636,280	1,383,217	46
Paterson	425,000	1,149,326	37
Trenton	836,107	2,029,493	41
New Mexico	**620,400**	**2,328,528**	**27**
*Santa Fe	323,850	1,295,074	25
Gallup	62,000	475,000	13
Las Cruces	234,550	558,454	42
New York	**7,111,359**	**20,100,103**	**35**
*New York	2,613,420	5,807,600	45
Albany	330,000	1,392,464	24
Brooklyn	1,403,137	4,838,406	29
Buffalo	630,650	1,540,269	41
Ogdensburg	96,650	501,414	19
Rochester	311,781	1,513,796	21
Rockville Ctr.	1,467,221	3,308,154	44
Syracuse	258,500	1,198,000	22
North Carolina	**407,445**	**9,801,384**	**4**
Charlotte	184,774	5,011,622	4
Raleigh	222,671	4,789,762	5
North Dakota	**131,573**	**699,628**	**19**
Bismarck	58,684	301,124	19
Fargo	72,889	398,504	18
Ohio	**1,964,274**	**11,288,817**	**17**
*Cincinnati	454,918	3,000,051	15
Cleveland	701,219	2,772,156	25
Columbus	269,126	2,356,877	11
Steubenville	35,603	508,406	7
Toledo	319,907	1,465,561	22
Youngstown	183,501	1,185,766	15
Oklahoma	**178,229**	**3,946,614**	**5**
*Oklahoma City	115,078	2,296,614	5
Tulsa	63,151	1,650,000	4
Oregon	**457,813**	**3,989,949**	**11**
*Portland	421,852	3,386,023	12
Baker	35,961	603,926	6
Pennsylvania	**3,244,201**	**12,750,398**	**25**
*Philadelphia	1,455,927	4,050,793	36
Allentown	263,243	1,272,212	21
Altoona J'town	87,592	650,389	13

State / Diocese	Catholic Pop.	Total Pop.	Cath. Pct.
Pennsylvania, cont.			
Erie	184,000	855,252	22
Greensburg	144,169	665,682	22
Harrisburg	243,227	2,242,629	11
Pittsburgh	634,910	1,921,225	33
Scranton	231,133	1,092,216	21
Rhode Island			
Providence	619,672	1,050,292	59
South Carolina			
Charleston	186,084	4,723,723	4
South Dakota	**141,273**	**797,173**	**18**
Rapid City	24,057	227,211	11
Sioux Falls	117,216	569,962	21
Tennessee	**210,686**	**6,444,202**	**3**
Knoxville	66,844	2,393,404	3
Memphis	64,064	1,562,650	4
Nashville	79,778	2,488,148	3
Texas	**7,440,623**	**26,288,405**	**28**
*Galveston			
Houston	1,188,876	6,402,824	19
*San Antonio	728,001	2,458,351	30
Amarillo	46,650	435,408	11
Austin	549,420	2,974,659	18
Beaumont	73,672	628,794	12
Brownsville	1,074,477	1,264,001	85
Corpus Christi	398,706	574,137	69
Dallas	1,236,944	3,923,052	32
El Paso+	689,032	877,940	78
Fort Worth	700,000	3,437,062	20
Laredo	320,967	352,439	91
Lubbock	136,894	494,455	28
San Angelo	73,028	768,389	10
Tyler	120,528	1,408,700	9
Victoria	103,428	288,101	36
Utah			
Salt Lake City	277,000	2,817,222	10
Vermont			
Burlington	117,000	625,000	19
Virginia	**675,028**	**8,703,653**	**8**
Arlington	440,028	3,103,653	14
Richmond	235,000	5,600,000	4
Washington	**754,914**	**6,862,242**	**11**
*Seattle	572,450	5,350,045	11
Spokane	107,983	830,641	13
Yakima	74,481	681,556	11
West Virginia			
Wheeling			
Charleston	77,810	1,852,994	4
Wisconsin	**1,443,969**	**5,705,369**	**25**
*Milwaukee	591,890	2,332,085	25
Green Bay	333,711	1,011,244	33
La Crosse	162,117	901,157	18
Madison	283,442	1,023,584	28
Superior	72,809	437,299	17
Wyoming			
Cheyenne	57,248	576,412	10
East. Churches	**617,230**	**–**	**–**
Military Arch. ('99)	**1,194,000**	**–**	**–**
Outlying Areas	**2,740,606**	**4,162,055**	**66**
Total 2014	**69,470,686**	**319,304,410**	**22**
Total 2013	68,436,660	317,235,394	22
Total 2004	67,828,393	296,799,389	23

CATHOLIC POPULATION OF THE UNITED STATES

(Source: The Official Catholic Directory, 2014*; figures as of Jan. 1, 2014. Archdioceses are indicated by an asterisk; for dioceses marked +, see Dioceses with Interstate Lines.)*

State Diocese	Cath. Pop.	Dioc. Priests	Rel. Priests	Total Priests	Perm. Deac.	Bros.	Sisters	Par ishes
Alabama	**162,627**	**178**	**62**	**240**	**136**	**40**	**220**	**130**
*Mobile	70,077	90	32	122	69	9	108	76
Birmingham	92,550	88	30	118	67	31	112	54
Alaska	**48,353**	**51**	**19**	**70**	**47**	**2**	**36**	**78**
*Anchorage	27,345	25	11	36	13	–	23	23
Fairbanks	11,008	16	7	23	31	2	11	46
Juneau	10,000	10	1	11	3	–	2	9
Arizona	**1,082,972**	**231**	**172**	**403**	**425**	**33**	**310**	**171**
Phoenix	736,271	134	99	233	235	12	132	93
Tucson	346,701	97	73	170	190	21	178	78
Arkansas, Little Rock	**140,753**	**75**	**28**	**103**	**110**	**28**	**148**	**89**
California	**12,468,704**	**2,069**	**1,499**	**3,568**	**1,340**	**350**	**3,805**	**1,070**
*Los Angeles	4,276,930	502	547	1,049	380	82	1,503	287
*San Francisco	442,752	265	159	424	85	32	613	90
Fresno	1,200,000	140	36	176	60	1	96	89
Monterey	205,045	78	18	96	2	32	17	53
Oakland	440,065	163	169	332	119	87	324	83
Orange	1,319,262	179	84	263	120	9	326	57
Sacramento	987,727	165	64	229	141	8	163	102
San Bernardino	1,622,829	104	114	218	115	21	133	91
San Diego	998,127	164	85	249	164	21	229	98
San Jose	590,000	159	197	356	37	44	285	50
Santa Rosa	175,443	80	13	93	42	26	31	41
Stockton	210,524	70	13	83	45	2	49	36
Colorado	**794,657**	**290**	**144**	**434**	**285**	**22**	**337**	**214**
*Denver	563,441	195	110	305	180	17	211	123
Colo. Springs	167,502	41	18	59	57	4	83	39
Pueblo	63,714	54	16	70	48	1	43	52
Connecticut	**1,220,499**	**632**	**167**	**799**	**461**	**52**	**1,043**	**372**
*Hartford	571,979	298	89	387	307	30	596	213
Bridgeport	420,000	230	29	259	8	91	–	294
Norwich+	228,520	104	49	153	63	22	153	76
Delaware, Wilmington+	**240,338**	**125**	**60**	**185**	**111**	**20**	**201**	**57**
D.C.,*Washington+	**630,823**	**289**	**351**	**640**	**265**	**106**	**489**	**139**
Florida	**2,284,212**	**916**	**341**	**1,257**	**681**	**111**	**799**	**465**
*Miami	765,804	232	37	269	148	46	249	102
Orlando	393,271	138	69	207	96	3	78	79
Palm Beach	233,685	111	27	138	101	4	92	50
Pensacola Tallahassee	64,714	74	9	83	70	5	23	49
St. Augustine	170,924	93	21	114	65	2	109	52
St. Petersburg	432,209	155	115	270	114	36	172	74
Venice	223,605	113	63	176	87	15	76	59
Georgia	**1,078,394**	**272**	**101**	**373**	**323**	**22**	**161**	**143**
*Atlanta	1,000,000	187	80	267	246	20	78	88
Savannah	78,394	85	21	106	77	2	83	55
Hawaii, Honolulu	**162,288**	**54**	**58**	**112**	**60**	**31**	**160**	**66**
Idaho, Boise	**175,530**	**74**	**15**	**89**	**80**	**4**	**69**	**52**
Illinois	**3,546,282**	**1,521**	**967**	**2,488**	**1,239**	**329**	**3,079**	**981**
*Chicago	2,203,000	769	680	1,449	652	235	1,677	356
Belleville	90,000	101	39	140	–	8	65	114
Joliet	605,870	176	122	298	223	55	422	120
Peoria	111,723	179	40	219	147	12	205	157
Rockford	390,500	191	41	232	136	6	101	104
Springfield	145,189	105	45	150	44	13	609	130
Indiana	**755,096**	**503**	**404**	**907**	**214**	**150**	**1,317**	**407**
*Indianapolis	218,505	142	84	226	43	27	543	127
Evansville	79,504	70	5	75	59	1	228	69
Ft. Wayne South Bend	159,812	80	268	348	22	108	450	81
Gary	185,100	96	37	133	69	12	66	68
Lafayette	112,175	115	10	125	21	2	30	62

State Diocese	Cath. Pop.	Dioc. Priests	Rel. Priests	Total Priests	Perm. Deac.	Bros.	Sisters	Par ishes
Iowa	**478,101**	**486**	**44**	**530**	**291**	**22**	**870**	**438**
*Dubuque	200,058	176	32	208	113	21	622	166
Davenport	93,824	97	3	100	51	1	137	80
Des Moines	101,558	83	9	92	85	–	50	81
Sioux City	82,661	130	–	130	42	–	61	111
Kansas	**414,755**	**306**	**75**	**381**	**46**	**18**	**900**	**329**
*Kansas City	204,662	105	53	158	26	17	460	105
Dodge City	48,264	30	4	34	–	–	71	48
Salina	41,327	55	17	72	16	1	129	86
Wichita	120,502	116	1	117	4	–	240	90
Kentucky	**374,791**	**347**	**90**	**437**	**271**	**54**	**1,101**	**276**
*Louisville	192,485	140	39	179	136	46	580	102
Covington	91,904	83	14	97	42	6	292	47
Lexington	41,914	53	18	71	70	2	60	48
Owensboro	48,488	71	19	90	2	23	171	79
Louisiana*	**1,242,206**	**626**	**273**	**899**	**494**	**109**	**699**	**450**
*New Orleans	500,818	191	135	326	228	65	405	108
Alexandria	42,929	57	11	68	19	3	28	50
Baton Rouge	197,069	72	26	98	73	19	81	67
Houma Thibodaux	95,556	58	7	65	37	5	20	39
Lafayette	291,991	168	63	231	95	11	131	121
Lake Charles	72,238	46	14	60	25	1	9	38
Shreveport	41,605	34	17	51	17	5	25	27
Maine, Portland	**169,198**	**134**	**32**	**166**	**42**	**17**	**234**	**55**
Maryland, *Baltimore	**485,167**	**230**	**208**	**438**	**168**	**61**	**789**	**145**
Massachusetts	**2,709,482**	**1,143**	**679**	**1,822**	**563**	**225**	**2,396**	**557**
*Boston	1,904,863	670	471	1,141	270	135	1,707	289
Fall River	288,845	147	83	230	96	15	139	85
Springfield	217,274	147	37	184	87	13	333	81
Worcester	298,500	179	88	267	110	62	217	102
Michigan	**1,968,402**	**924**	**280**	**1,204**	**489**	**67**	**1,985**	**682**
*Detroit	1,271,588	362	190	552	215	63	850	239
Gaylord	55,893	63	6	69	18	–	22	80
Grand Rapids	191,100	106	19	125	38	1	350	82
Kalamazoo	108,946	66	8	74	46	1	202	46
Lansing	195,858	164	45	209	114	2	433	81
Marquette	43,868	73	7	80	44	–	44	72
Saginaw	101,149	90	5	95	14	–	84	82
Minnesota	**1,243,067**	**789**	**188**	**977**	**344**	**121**	**1,551**	**659**
*St.Paul & Minneapolis	825,000	394	73	467	182	48	580	188
Crookston	32,936	47	3	50	20	–	65	66
Duluth	54,771	74	6	80	51	–	89	84
New Ulm	58,717	63	–	63	15	–	45	76
St. Cloud	127,989	103	96	199	48	54	427	131
Winona	134,654	108	10	118	28	19	345	114
Mississippi	**106,748**	**103**	**54**	**157**	**41**	**15**	**183**	**115**
Biloxi	58,257	55	22	77	38	10	36	42
Jackson	48,491	48	32	80	3	5	147	73
Missouri	**785,378**	**583**	**533**	**1,116**	**402**	**204**	**1,726**	**442**
*St. Louis	521,804	339	380	719	252	134	1,424	194
Jefferson City	68,955	87	6	93	66	2	46	95
Kansas City-St. Joseph	128,364	99	77	176	61	24	191	87
Springfield-Cape Girardeau	66,255	58	70	128	23	44	65	66
Montana	**85,844**	**139**	**17**	**156**	**52**	**3**	**73**	**109**
Great Falls Billings	40,654	58	12	70	10	1	39	51
Helena	45,190	81	5	86	42	2	34	58
Nebraska	**374,197**	**393**	**86**	**479**	**239**	**22**	**454**	**301**
*Omaha	230,866	181	77	258	230	22	265	131
Grand Island	45,744	62	–	62	7	–	50	36
Lincoln	97,587	150	9	159	8	2	139	134
Nevada	**661,802**	**73**	**24**	**97**	**70**	**6**	**23**	**57**
Las Vegas	574,000	39	18	57	39	3	–	29
Reno	87,802	34	6	40	31	3	23	28
New Hampshire, Manchester	**275,641**	**161**	**49**	**210**	**44**	**19**	**389**	**88**

State Diocese	Cath. Pop.	Dioc. Priests	Rel. Priests	Total Priests	Perm. Deac.	Bros.	Sisters	Par- ishes
New Jersey	**3,761,209**	**1,655**	**390**	**2,045**	**1,030**	**221**	**2,313**	**602**
*Newark	1,352,000	726	148	874	236	90	853	218
Camden	511,822	251	35	286	143	12	252	70
Metuchen	636,280	178	36	214	159	15	256	94
Paterson	425,000	261	117	378	198	50	642	111
Trenton	836,107	239	54	293	294	54	310	109
New Mexico	**620,400**	**210**	**128**	**338**	**284**	**63**	**241**	**191**
*Santa Fe	323,850	139	83	222	215	55	130	93
Gallup	62,000	37	12	49	25	6	76	52
Las Cruces	234,550	34	33	67	44	2	35	46
New York	**7,111,359**	**2,406**	**1,135**	**3,541**	**1,135**	**654**	**6,677**	**1,300**
*New York	2,613,420	584	679	1,263	383	354	2,727	368
Albany	330,000	195	68	263	107	56	604	127
Brooklyn	1,403,137	482	158	640	218	98	769	186
Buffalo	630,650	308	92	400	134	35	819	164
Ogdensburg	96,650	112	4	116	77	7	96	97
Rochester	311,781	170	41	211	146	30	423	95
Rockville Centre	1,467,221	337	54	391	–	68	1,026	134
Syracuse	258,500	218	39	257	70	6	213	129
North Carolina	**407,445**	**209**	**85**	**294**	**162**	**13**	**169**	**151**
Charlotte	184,774	120	42	162	104	7	129	73
Raleigh	222,671	89	43	132	58	6	40	78
North Dakota	**131,573**	**205**	**27**	**232**	**124**	**20**	**172**	**230**
Bismarck	58,684	73	19	92	79	20	81	98
Fargo	72,889	132	8	140	45	–	91	132
Ohio	**1,964,274**	**1,176**	**432**	**1,608**	**814**	**204**	**2,662**	**773**
*Cincinnati	454,918	268	228	496	212	114	774	213
Cleveland	701,219	383	92	475	206	51	949	185
Columbus	269,126	150	29	179	104	9	233	106
Steubenville	35,603	74	33	107	12	7	52	58
Toledo	319,907	165	31	196	189	11	450	124
Youngstown	183,501	136	19	155	91	12	204	87
Oklahoma	**178,229**	**149**	**49**	**198**	**170**	**37**	**127**	**140**
*Oklahoma City	115,078	77	25	102	106	9	81	63
Tulsa	63,151	72	24	96	64	28	46	77
Oregon	**457,813**	**202**	**166**	**368**	**82**	**68**	**384**	**159**
*Portland	421,852	166	160	326	73	68	368	124
Baker	35,961	36	6	42	–	9	16	35
Pennsylvania	**3,244,201**	**1,875**	**733**	**2,608**	**726**	**199**	**5,153**	**1,032**
*Philadelphia	1,455,927	523	305	828	286	97	2,543	235
Allentown	263,243	191	64	255	102	15	340	104
Altoona Johnstown	87,592	113	59	172	38	10	64	87
Erie	184,000	179	7	186	63	–	312	116
Greensburg	144,169	109	104	213	2	32	198	78
Harrisburg	243,227	134	37	171	68	1	283	89
Pittsburgh	634,910	365	109	474	100	37	996	203
Scranton	231,132	261	48	309	67	7	417	120
Rhode Island, Providence	**619,672**	**270**	**91**	**361**	**92**	**65**	**431**	**142**
South Carolina, Charleston	**186,084**	**85**	**48**	**133**	**123**	**18**	**99**	**94**
South Dakota	**141,273**	**151**	**32**	**183**	**66**	**4**	**292**	**226**
Rapid City	24,057	37	14	51	27	3	33	83
Sioux Falls	117,216	114	18	132	39	1	259	143
Tennessee	**210,686**	**171**	**61**	**232**	**179**	**37**	**92**	**142**
Knoxville	66,844	62	20	82	55	11	46	47
Memphis	64,064	64	14	78	55	24	44	42
Nashville	79,778	45	27	72	69	2	2	53
Texas	**7,440,623**	**1,302**	**738**	**2,040**	**1,674**	**260**	**1,968**	**1,065**
*Galveston Houston	1,188,876	199	201	400	416	10	438	146
*San Antonio	728,001	152	173	325	343	93	673	139
Amarillo	46,650	42	5	47	57	–	–	38
Austin	549,420	138	53	191	169	40	95	102
Beaumont	73,672	41	24	65	39	2	17	44
Brownsville	1,074,477	80	33	113	3	92	19	88
Corpus Christi	398,706	120	25	145	97	7	153	69

State Diocese	Cath. Pop.	Dioc. Priests	Rel. Priests	Total Priests	Perm. Deac.	Bros.	Sisters	Par ishes
Texas, cont.								
Dallas	1,236,944	101	82	183	172	8	101	69
El Paso	689,032	73	42	115	25	12	106	57
Fort Worth	700,000	73	51	124	–	5	74	89
Laredo	320,967	24	19	43	26	5	56	32
Lubbock	136,894	50	9	59	71	–	23	62
San Angelo	73,028	60	5	65	83	–	17	46
Tyler	120,528	101	8	109	102	–	51	51
Victoria	103,428	48	8	56	39	1	76	50
Utah, Salt Lake City	**277,000**	**56**	**18**	**74**	**75**	–	**29**	**48**
Vermont, Burlington	**117,000**	**85**	**36**	**121**	**43**	**18**	**90**	**73**
Virginia	**675,028**	**324**	**89**	**413**	**205**	**16**	**274**	**211**
Arlington	440,028	170	59	229	69	8	132	68
Richmond	235,000	154	30	184	136	8	142	143
Washington	**754,914**	**339**	**158**	**497**	**219**	**26**	**524**	**269**
*Seattle	572,450	191	92	283	117	18	363	147
Spokane	107,983	78	63	141	60	6	135	81
Yakima	74,481	70	3	73	42	2	26	41
West Virginia, Wheeling Charleston	**77,810**	**98**	**45**	**143**	**44**	**6**	**129**	**110**
Wisconsin	**1,443,969**	**854**	**443**	**1,297**	**463**	**97**	**2,216**	**739**
*Milwaukee	591,890	326	313	639	180	73	935	202
Green Bay	333,711	178	98	276	142	14	480	157
La Crosse	162,117	148	9	157	60	2	387	162
Madison	283,442	133	18	151	15	7	350	114
Superior	72,809	69	5	74	66	1	64	104
Wyoming, Cheyenne+	**57,248**	**55**	**3**	**58**	**37**	–	**15**	**34**
EASTERN CHURCHES	**594,626**	**644**	**101**	**745**	**343**	**20**	**276**	**603**
*Philadelphia	14,299	52	3	55	7	–	43	67
*Pittsburgh	57,686	51	7	58	22	1	60	75
St. Nicholas	10,400	46	10	56	–	11	–	38
Stamford	14,180	56	10	66	10	2	38	51
St. Josaphat (Parma)	8,378	45	–	45	12	2	2	38
Parma	8,525	37	–	37	16	–	6	28
Passaic	13,367	64	10	74	25	1	14	84
Holy Prot. of Mary	2,254	23	1	24	8	2	5	19
St. Maron (Maronites)	33,000	52	11	63	19	8	2	34
Our Lady of Lebanon (Maronites)	46,000	38	11	49	20	–	6	32
Newton (Melkites)	22,041	49	–	49	60	–	5	43
St. Peter the Apostle of San Diego	65,000	19	–	19	12	–	7	7
St. Thomas Apostle of Detroit (Chaldean)	170,000	24	–	24	120	–	12	11
St. Thomas (Syro-Malabrs)	87,000	46	13	59	–	–	–	21
St. George Martyr (Romanian)	5,000	21	2	23	7	5	4	14
Our Lady of Deliverance (Syrians, U.S. Canada)	22,600	11	–	11	4	–	–	9
Armenian Ex.(U.S. Canada)	37,500	6	–	6	–	–	–	9
Syro-Malankara Ex. (U.S.)	–	16	1	17	–	–	33	13
Military Archd. ('99)[1]	**1,194,000**	–	–	–	–	–	–	–
Outlying Areas								
Puerto Rico	2,524,177	345	283	628	519	28	823	329
Samoa-Pago Pago	14,030	15	2	17	22	–	–	18
Caroline Islands	77,733	13	15	28	65	2	34	29
Chalan Kanoa (N. Mariana Is.)	32,249	13	1	14	–	–	–	12
Guam, *Agana	135,150	44	10	54	18	1	85	24
Marshall Islands	5,000	1	5	6	1	–	11	5
Virgin Islands, St. Thomas	30,000	15	4	19	31	1	19	8
TOTAL 2014	**69,470,686**	**26,696**	**12,326**	**39,022**	**18,089**	**4,349**	**50,836**	**17,900**
TOTAL 2013	69,436,660	26,979	12,389	39,368	18,121	4,459	52,557	17,990
TOTAL 2004	66,407,105	29,715	14,772	44,487	14,106	5,568	74,698	19,484

[1] 307 diocesan and 52 religious-order chaplains are on loan to the military (*2014 Annuario Pontificio*).

RECEPTIONS INTO THE CHURCH IN THE UNITED STATES

(Source: The Official Catholic Directory, 2014*; figures as of Jan. 1, 2014. Archdioceses are indicated by an asterisk; for dioceses marked +, see Dioceses with Interstate Lines. Information includes infant and adult baptisms and those received into full communion.)*

State Diocese	Infant Baptisms	Adult Bapts.	Rec'd into Full Com.	State Diocese	Infant Baptisms	Adult Bapts.	Rec'd into Full Com.
Alabama	**2,899**	**384**	**748**	**Indiana**, cont.			
*Mobile	1,071	194	274	Lafayette	1,652	180	271
Birmingham	1,828	190	474	**Iowa**	**6,361**	**406**	**827**
Alaska	**778**	**60**	**101**	*Dubuque	1,997	84	213
*Anchorage	447	38	52	Davenport	1,253	137	111
Fairbanks	284	16	40	Des Moines	1,716	114	318
Juneau	47	6	9	Sioux City	1,395	71	185
Arizona	**11,722**	**549**	**2,417**	**Kansas**	**7,470**	**528**	**1,050**
Phoenix	7,522	306	1,918	*Kansas City	3,406	218	468
Tucson	4,200	243	499	Dodge City	911	25	60
Arkansas, Lit. Rock	**2,555**	**171**	**440**	Salina	918	66	112
California	**155,905**	**4,587**	**11,403**	Wichita	2,235	219	410
*Los Angeles	67,887	1,345	4,652	**Kentucky**	**4,755**	**518**	**783**
*San Francisco	4,978	214	385	*Louisville	2,170	168	391
Fresno	16,520	405	572	Covington	988	186	90
Monterey	5,501	134	616	Lexington	749	77	126
Oakland	7,567	279	288	Owensboro	848	87	176
Orange	12,139	569	1,004	**Louisiana**	**11,943**	**560**	**1,779**
Sacramento	7,968	439	1,080	*New Orleans	3,383	151	526
San Bernardino	9,569	329	524	Alexandria	524	31	96
San Diego	8,914	362	656	Baton Rouge	2,007	148	305
San Jose	6,994	291	649	Houma Thibodaux	1,316	44	139
Santa Rosa	2,746	123	290	Lafayette	3,300	93	282
Stockton	5,122	97	687	Lake Charles	947	70	326
Colorado	**10,754**	**591**	**925**	Shreveport	466	23	105
*Denver	8,607	419	626	**Maine**, Portland	**1,228**	**68**	**91**
Colorado Springs	1,082	89	140	**Maryland**,*Baltimore	**5,381**	**444**	**481**
Pueblo	1,065	83	159	**Massachusetts**	**19,290**	**227**	**892**
Connecticut	**10,341**	**349**	**544**	*Boston	12,529	–	412
*Hartford	5,236	154	258	Fall River	2,492	56	77
Bridgeport	3,652	122	137	Springfield	2,063	73	10
Norwich+	1,453	73	149	Worcester	2,206	98	302
Delaware, Wilm.+	**2,174**	**109**	**489**	**Michigan**	**15,125**	**1,212**	**2,388**
D.C., *Washington+	**3,751**	**690**	**402**	*Detroit	7,765	484	950
Florida	**27,883**	**2,205**	**3,854**	Gaylord	432	65	94
*Miami	10,387	492	1,181	Grand Rapids	2,229	153	295
Orlando	5,142	244	537	Kalamazoo	1,035	114	177
Palm Beach	3,255	218	530	Lansing	2,128	247	505
Pensacola				Marquette	494	40	69
Tallahassee	864	129	218	Saginaw	1,042	109	298
St. Augustine	1,813	249	460	**Minnesota**	**12,536**	**415**	**625**
St. Petersburg	3,009	702	548	*St. Paul and			
Venice	3,413	171	380	Minneapolis	7,679	269	–
Georgia	**10,021**	**530**	**1,592**	Crookston	525	10	62
*Atlanta	8,471	382	1,124	Duluth	566	34	127
Savannah	1,604	148	468	New Ulm	739	9	82
Hawaii, Honolulu	**2,242**	**182**	**151**	St. Cloud	1,690	41	222
Idaho, Boise	**2,271**	**222**	**299**	Winona	1,337	52	132
Illinois	**46,369**	**2,540**	**2,946**	**Mississippi**	**1,685**	**180**	**396**
*Chicago	29,829	1,797	1,172	Biloxi	887	99	181
Belleville	1,000	104	200	Jackson	798	81	215
Joliet	7,074	158	582	**Missouri**	**8,963**	**798**	**1,268**
Peoria	1,594	163	252	*St. Louis	5,242	313	480
Rockford	5,193	174	435	Jefferson City	1,035	150	291
Springfield	1,679	144	305	Ks. City-St. Joe	1,855	206	333
Indiana	**9,718**	**951**	**1,460**	Springfield-			
*Indianapolis	3,853	391	563	Cape Girardeau	831	129	164
Evansville	1,123	98	125	**Montana**	**1,169**	**58**	**197**
Ft. Wayne S. Bend	1,792	176	351	Great Falls Billings	561	58	136
Gary	1,298	106	150	Helena	608	–	61

State / Diocese	Infant Baptisms	Adult Bapts.	Rec'd into Full Com.
Nebraska	**5,780**	**328**	**797**
*Omaha	3,882	155	453
Grand Island	795	77	126
Lincoln	1,103	96	218
Nevada	**6,799**	**284**	**1,080**
Las Vegas	5,084	163	878
Reno	1,715	121	202
New Hampshire			
Manchester	2,047	41	134
New Jersey	**34,321**	**1,694**	**1,241**
*Newark	12,793	313	129
Camden	5,018	465	245
Metuchen	4,022	114	228
Paterson	5,871	113	179
Trenton	6,617	689	460
New Mexico	**5,703**	**353**	**764**
*Santa Fe	3,793	205	338
Gallup	472	89	168
Las Cruces	1,438	59	258
New York	**64,716**	**2,497**	**2,473**
*New York	21,516	1,309	1,115
Albany	2,927	70	124
Brooklyn	15,502	582	315
Buffalo	3,717	185	249
Ogdensburg	822	31	42
Rochester	2,382	190	–
Rockville Centre	14,973	–	293
Syracuse	2,877	130	335
North Carolina	**9,891**	**406**	**973**
Charlotte	5,501	253	573
Raleigh	4,390	153	400
North Dakota	**2,090**	**114**	**294**
Bismarck	984	81	186
Fargo	1,106	33	108
Ohio	**18,453**	**1,615**	**3,082**
*Cincinnati	5,341	388	748
Cleveland	5,869	321	870
Columbus	3,190	405	397
Steubenville	278	53	412
Toledo	2,282	304	361
Youngstown	1,493	144	294
Oklahoma	**3,784**	**284**	**931**
*Okla. City	2,263	175	591
Tulsa	1,521	109	340
Oregon	**5,551**	**461**	**1,226**
*Portland	4,800	407	1,089
Baker	751	54	128
Pennsylvania	**26,359**	**1,186**	**1,869**
*Philadelphia	11,851	335	302
Allentown	2,440	–	121
Altoona Johnstn.	829	54	164
Erie	1,300	92	80
Greensburg	1,119	57	157
Harrisburg	1,794	325	390
Pittsburgh	4,818	226	448
Scranton	2,208	97	207
Rhode Island, Providence	**3,197**	**134**	**424**
South Carolina			
Charleston	2,832	156	365
South Dakota	**2,001**	**21**	**396**
Rapid City	451	21	64
Sioux Falls	1,550	–	332
Tennessee	**4,030**	**290**	**831**
Knoxville	1,094	83	206
Tennessee, cont.			
Memphis	1,240	85	259
Nashville	1,696	122	366
Texas	**70,918**	**5,469**	**5,093**
*Galv. Houston	10,048	1,952	1,173
*San Antonio	8,434	530	605
Amarillo	962	40	89
Austin	7,389	407	747
Beaumont	1,410	106	–
Brownsville	7,786	222	698
Corpus Christi	2,074	164	284
Dallas	13,596	856	369
El Paso	4,094	137	218
Fort Worth	6,310	380	–
Laredo	3,028	65	101
Lubbock	832	130	242
San Angelo	1,660	325	169
Tyler	2,044	85	218
Victoria	1,251	70	180
Utah, Salt Lake City	**5,042**	**269**	**1,210**
Vermont, Burlington	**658**	**70**	**74**
Virginia	**9,984**	**606**	**1,866**
Arlington	6,934	372	897
Richmond	3,050	234	969
Washington	**9,958**	**560**	**744**
*Seattle	6,075	394	409
Spokane	1,181	83	181
Yakima	2,702	83	154
West Virginia			
Wheeling Chas.	855	148	156
Wisconsin	**14,060**	**521**	**1,188**
*Milwaukee	5,758	194	360
Green Bay	3,487	136	194
La Crosse	1,686	66	383
Madison	2,303	89	165
Superior	826	36	86
Wyoming, Chey.+	**839**	**87**	**108**
Eastern Churches	**4,301**	**75**	**206**
*Philadelphia	183	5	16
*Pittsburgh	111	5	36
St. Nicholas	190	–	–
Stamford	204	5	3
St. Josaphat (Parma)	34	1	3
Parma	47	–	9
Passaic	135	3	19
Holy Protect. of Mary	60	12	17
St. Maron (Maronites)	360	7	23
Our Lady of Lebanon (Maronites)	409	6	22
Newton (Melkites)	295	13	20
St. Peter the Apostle	401	1	10
St. Thomas Apostle of Detroit (Chaldeans)	1,217	4	–
St. Thomas (Syro-Mal.)	283	3	36
St. George Martyr (Romanian)	19	1	2
Our Lady of Deliverance (Syrians, U.S. Can.)	179	6	3
Arme. Ex. (U.S. Can.)	183	–	–
Syro-Malankara Ex. (U.S.)			
Military Archd.	**3,362**	**837**	**311**
Outlying Areas	**17,342**	**1,614**	**447**
Total 2014	**730,171**	**39,654**	**66,831**
Total 2013	763,208	41,918	71,582

The Catholic Church in Canada

Background

The first date in the remote background of the Catholic history of Canada is July 7, 1534, when a priest in the exploration company of Jacques Cartier celebrated Mass on the Gaspe Peninsula.

Successful colonization and the significant beginnings of the Catholic history of the country date from the foundation of Québec in 1608 by Samuel de Champlain and French settlers. Montréal was established in 1642.

The earliest missionaries were Franciscan Récollets (Recollects) and Jesuits who arrived in 1615 and 1625, respectively. They provided some pastoral care for the settlers but worked mainly among the 100,000 Indians — Algonquins, Hurons and Iroquois — in the interior and in the Lake Ontario region. Eight of the Jesuit missionaries, killed in the 1640s, were canonized in 1930. (*See* **Index: Jesuit North American Martyrs.**) Sulpician Fathers, who arrived in Canada late in the 1640s, played a part in the great missionary period, which ended about 1700.

St. Kateri Tekakwitha, "Lily of the Mohawks," who was baptized in 1676 and died in 1680, was declared "Blessed" in 1980 and canonized in 2012.

The communities of women religious with the longest histories in Canada are the Canonesses of St. Augustine and the Ursulines, since 1639; and the Hospitallers of St. Joseph, since 1642. Communities of Canadian origin are the Congregation of Notre Dame, founded by St. Marguerite Bourgeoys in 1658, and the Grey Nuns, formed by St. Marie Marguerite d'Youville in 1737. Mother Marie (Guyard) of the Incarnation, an Ursuline nun, was one of the first three women missionaries to New France; called "Mother of the Church in Canada," she was declared "Blessed" in 1980 and given an equivalent canonization by Pope Francis in Apr. 2014.

Start of Church Organization

Ecclesiastical organization began with the appointment in 1658 of François De Montmorency-Laval, "Father of the Church in Canada," as vicar apostolic of New France. He was the first bishop of Québec from 1674 to 1688, with jurisdiction over all French-claimed territory in North America. He was declared "Blessed" in 1980 and given an equivalent canonization by Pope Francis in Apr. 2014.

In 1713, the French Canadian population numbered 18,000. In the same year, the Treaty of Utrecht ceded Acadia, Newfoundland and the Hudson Bay Territory to England. The Acadians were scattered among the American colonies in 1755.

The English acquired possession of Canada and its 70,000 French-speaking inhabitants by virtue of the Treaty of Paris in 1763. Anglo-French and Anglican-Catholic differences and tensions developed. The pro-British government at first refused to recognize the titles of church officials, hindered the clergy in their work and tried to install a non-Catholic educational system. Laws were passed that guaranteed religious liberties to Catholics (Québec Act of 1774, Constitutional Act of 1791, legislation approved by Queen Victoria in 1851), but it took some time before actual respect for these liberties matched the legal enactments. The initial moderation of government antipathy toward the Church was caused partly by the loyalty of Catholics to the Crown during the American Revolution and the War of 1812.

Growth

The 15 years following the passage in 1840 of the Act of Union, which joined Upper and Lower Canada, were significant. New communities of men and women religious joined those already in the country. The Oblates of Mary Immaculate, missionaries par excellence in Canada, advanced the penetration of the West that had been started in 1818 by Abbé Provencher. New jurisdictions were established, and Québec became a metropolitan see in 1844. The first Council of Québec was held in 1851. The established Catholic school system enjoyed a period of growth.

Laval University was inaugurated in 1854 and canonically established in 1876.

Archbishop Elzear-Alexandre Taschereau of Québec was named Canada's first cardinal in 1886.

The apostolic delegation to Canada was set up in 1899. It became a nunciature October 16, 1969, with the establishment of diplomatic relations with the Vatican. The present Apostolic Nuncio is Archbishop Luigi Bonazzi, appointed on Dec. 18, 2013.

Early in this century, Canada had eight ecclesiastical provinces, 23 dioceses, three vicariates apostolic, 3,500 priests, 2 million Catholics, about 30 communities of men religious, and 70 or more communities of women religious. The Church in Canada was phased out of mission status and removed from the jurisdiction of the Congregation for the Propagation of the Faith in 1908.

Diverse Population

The greatest concentration of Catholics is in the eastern portion of the country. In the northern and western portions, outside metropolitan centers, there are some of the most difficult parish and mission areas in the world. Bilingual (English-French) differences in the general population are reflected in the Church; for example, in the parallel structures of the Canadian Conference of Catholic Bishops, which was established in 1943. Québec is the center of French cultural influence. Many language groups are represented among Catholics, who include more than 257,000 members of Eastern Rites in one metropolitan see, seven eparchies and an apostolic exarchate.

Education, a past source of friction between the Church and the government, is administered by the civil provinces in a variety of arrangements authorized by the Canadian Constitution. Denominational schools have tax support in one way in Québec and Newfoundland, and in another way in Alberta, Ontario and Saskatchewan. Several provinces provide tax support only for public schools, making private financing necessary for separate church-related schools.

ECCLESIASTICAL JURISDICTIONS OF CANADA

Provinces

Names of ecclesiastical provinces and metropolitan sees in bold face; suffragan sees in parentheses.

Edmonton (Calgary, St. Paul).

Gatineau-Hull (Amos, Mont-Laurier, Rouyn Noranda).

Grouard-McLennan (Mackenzie-Ft. Smith, Prince George, Whitehorse).

Halifax (Antigonish, Charlottetown).

Keewatin-LePas (Churchill-Hudson Bay, Labrador-Schefferville, Moosonee).

Kingston (Alexandria-Cornwall, Peterborough, Sault Ste. Marie).

Moncton (Bathurst, Edmundston, St. John).

Montréal (Joliette, St. Jean-Longueuil, St. Jerome, Valleyfield).

Ottawa (Hearst, Pembroke, Timmins).

Québec (Chicoutimi, Ste.-Anne-de-la-Pocatiere, Trois Rivieres).

Regina (Prince Albert, Saskatoon, Abbey of St. Peter).

Rimouski (Baie-Comeau, Gaspe).

St. Boniface (no suffragan).

St. John's (Grand Falls, St. George).

Sherbrooke (Nicolet, St. Hyacinthe).

Toronto (Hamilton, London, St. Catharines, Thunder Bay).

Vancouver (Kamloops, Nelson, Victoria).

Winnipeg-Ukrainian (Edmonton, New Westminster, Saskatoon, Toronto).

Jurisdictions immediately subject to the Holy See: Roman-Rite Archdiocese of Winnipeg, Byzantine Eparchy of Sts. Cyril and Methodius for Slovaks, Byzantine Eparchy of St. Sauveur de Montréal for Greek Melkites; Antiochene Eparchy of St. Maron of Montréal for Maronites.

JURISDICTIONS, HIERARCHY

(Principal sources: Information office, Canadian Conference of Catholic Bishops; Rev. Mr. William Kokesch, Dir., Communications Service, Canadian Conference of Catholic Bishops; Annuaire, Conférence des Évêques Catholiques du Canada; Catholic Almanac *survey;* Annuario Pontificio; L'Osservatore Romano; *Catholic News Service. As of June 1, 2014.)*

Information includes names of archdioceses (indi-

cated by asterisk) and dioceses, date of foundation, present ordinaries and auxiliaries; addresses of chancery office/bishop's residence; cathedral.

Alexandria-Cornwall, ON (1890 as Alexandria; name changed to Alexandria-Cornwall, 1976): Marcel Damphousse, bishop, 2012.

Diocesan Center: 220, chemin Montréal, C.P. 1388, Cornwall, ON K6H 5V4; (613) 933-1138; www.alexandria-cornwall.ca/. Cathedral: St. Finnans (Alexandria); Nativity Co-Cathedral (Cornwall).

Amos, QC (1938): Gilles Lemay, bishop, 2011.

Bishop's Residence: 450, rue Principale Nord, Amos, QC J9T 2M1; (819) 732-6515; www.dioceseamos.org. Cathedral: St. Teresa of Ávila.

Antigonish, NS (Arichat, 1844; transferred, 1886): Brian J. Dunn, bishop, 2010.

Chancery Office: 168 Hawthorne St., P.O. Box 1330, Antigonish, NS B2G 2L7; (902) 863-3335; www.antigonishdiocese.com/title.htm. Cathedral: St. Ninian.

Baie-Comeau, QC (p.a., 1882; v.a., 1905; diocese Gulf of St. Lawrence, 1945; name changed to Hauterive, 1960; present title, 1986): Jean Pierre Blais, bishop.

Bishop's Residence: 639, rue de Bretagne, Baie-Comeau, QC G5C 1X2; (418) 589-5744; www.diocese-bc.org. Cathedral: Paroisse St. Jean-Eudes.

Bathurst, NB (Chatham, 1860; transferred, 1938): Daniel Jodoin, bishop, 2013.

Bishop's Residence: 645, avenue Murray, C.P. 460, Bathurst, NB E2A 3Z4; (506) 546-1420; www.diocesebathurst.com. Cathedral: Sacred Heart of Jesus.

Calgary, AB (1912): Frederick Henry, bishop, 1997.

Address: Room 290, The Iona Building, 120 17 Ave. SW, Calgary, AB T2S 2T2; (403) 218-5526; www.rcdiocese-calgary.ab.ca. Cathedral: St. Mary.

Charlottetown, PEI (1829): Richard Grecco, bishop, 2009.

Bishop's Residence: P.O. Box 907, Charlottetown, PEI C1A 7L9; (902) 368-8005; www.dioceseofcharlottetown/com. Cathedral: St. Dunstan's.

Chicoutimi, QC (1878): André Rivest, bishop, 2004. Roch Pedneault, aux.

Bishop's Residence: 602, Racine Est, Chicoutimi, QC G7H 6J6; (418) 543-0783; www.evechedechicoutimi.qc.ca. Cathedral: St. Francois-Xavier.

Churchill-Hudson Bay, MB (p.a., 1925; v.a. Hudson Bay, 1931; diocese of Churchill, 1967; present title, 1968): Anthony W. Krotki, O.M.I, bishop, 2013.

Diocesan Office: P.O. Box 10, Churchill, MB R0B 0E0; (204) 675-2252. Cathedral: Holy Canadian Martyrs.

Corner Brook and Labrador, QC (formerly Labrador City-Schefferville; v.a. Labrador, 1946; diocese, 1967): Peter Joseph Hundt, bishop, 2011.

Bishop's Residence: Sutton House, 320 avenue Elizabeth, C.P. 545, Labrador City, Labrador, NL A2V 2L3; (709) 944-2046; www.labdiocese.com. Cathedral: Our Lady of Perpetual Help.

Edmonton,* AB (St. Albert, 1871; archdiocese, transferred Edmonton, 1912): Richard W. Smith, archbishop, 2007. Gregory Bittman, auxiliary.

Archdiocesan Office: 8421-101 Avenue, Edmonton, Alta. T6A 0L1; (780) 469-1010; www.edmontoncatholicchurch.com. Cathedral: Basilica of St. Joseph.

Edmonton, AB (Ukrainian Byzantine) (ap. ex. of western Canada, 1948; eparchy, 1956): David Motiuk, bishop, 2007.

Eparch's Residence: 9645 108th Ave., Edmonton, Alta. T5H 1A3; (780) 424-5496. Cathedral: St. Josaphat.

Edmundston, NB (1944): Claude Champagne, O.M.I., bishop, 2009.

Diocesan Center: 60, rue Bouchard, Edmundston, NB E3V 3K1; (506) 735-5578; www.diocese-edmunston.ca. Cathedral: Immaculate Conception.

Gaspé, QC (1922): Jean Gagnon, bishop, 2002.

Bishop's House: 172, rue Jacques-Cartier, Gaspé, QC G4X 1M9; (418) 368-2274; www.gaspesie.net/diocesegaspe. Cathedral: Christ the King.

Gatineau,* QC (1963, as Hull; name changed, 1982; archdiocese, 1990): Paul-André Durocher, archbishop, 2011.

Diocesan Center: 180 Boulevard Mont-Bleu, Hull, QC J8Z 3J5; (819) 771-8391; www.diocesegatineau-hull.qc.ca.

Grand Falls, NL (Harbour Grace, 1856; present title, 1964): Robert Anthony Daniels, bishop, 2013.

Chancery Office: 8A Church Rd., P.O. Box 771, Grand Falls-Windsor, NL A2A 2M4; (709) 489-2778; www.rcdiocesegrandfalls.ca/. Cathedral: Immaculate Conception.

Grouard-McLennan,* AB (v.a. Athabaska-Mackenzie, 1862; Grouard, 1927; archdiocese Grouard-McLennan, 1967); Gerard Pettipas, C.Ss.R., archbishop, 2006.

Archbishop's Residence: 210-1 Street West, C.P. 388, McLennan, AB T0H 2L0; (780) 324-3820. Cathedral: St. Jean-Baptiste (McLennan).

Halifax-Yarmouth,* NS (1842; archdiocese, 1852; united with Yarmouth diocese, 2009): Anthony Mancini, archbishop, 2007; archbishop of Halifax-Yarmouth, 2009.

Chancery Office: 1531 Grafton St., P.O. Box 1527, Halifax, NS B3J 2Y3; (902) 429-9800; www.catholichalifax.org.

Hamilton, ON (1856): David Crosby, O.M.I., bishop, 2010. Daniel Miehm, auxiliary.

Chancery Office: 700 King St. West, Hamilton, ON L8P 1C7; (905) 528-7988; www.hamiltondiocese.com/. Cathedral: Christ the King.

Hearst, ON (p.a., 1918; v.a., 1920; diocese, 1938): Vincent Cadieux, O.M.I., bishop, 2007.

Bishop's Residence: 76 7e rue, C.P. 1330, Hearst, ON P0L 1N0; (705) 362-4903; www.hearstdiocese.com. Cathedral: Notre Dame of the Assumption.

Joliette, QC (1904): Gilles Lussier, bishop, 1991.

Bishop's Residence: 2 rue Saint-Charles-Borromée Nord, C.P. 470, Joliette, QC J6E 6H6; (450) 753-7596; www.diocesedejoliette.org. Cathedral: St. Charles Borromeo.

Kamloops, BC (1945): David Monroe, bishop, 2002.

Bishop's Residence: 635-A Tranquille Rd., Kamloops, BC V2B 3H5; (250) 376-3351. Cathedral: Sacred Heart.

Keewatin-Le Pas,* MB (v.a., 1910; archdiocese, 1967): Murray Chatlain, archbishop, 2012.

Archbishop's Residence: 76 1st St. W., P.O. Box 270, The Pas, MB R9A 1K4; (204) 623-6152.

Cathedral: Our Lady of the Sacred Heart.

Kingston,* ON (1826; archdiocese, 1889): Brendan Michael O'Brien, archbishop, 2007.

Chancery Office: 390 Palace Rd., Kingston, ON K7L 4T3; (613) 548-4461; www.romancatholic.kingston.on.ca. Cathedral: St. Mary of the Immaculate Conception.

London, ON (1855; transferred Sandwich, 1859; London, 1869): Ronald P. Fabbro, C.S.B., bishop, 2002. Robert Anthony Daniels, auxiliary.

Bishop's Residence: 1070 Waterloo St., London, ON N6A 3Y2; (519) 433-0658; www.rcec.london.on.ca. Cathedral: St. Peter's Cathedral Basilica.

Mackenzie-Fort Smith, NT (v.a. Mackenzie, 1902; diocese Mackenzie-Fort Smith, 1967): Mark Hagemoen, bishop, 2013.

Diocesan Office: 5117-52nd St., Yellowknife, NT XIA 1T7; (867) 920-2129. Cathedral: St. Joseph (Ft. Smith).

Moncton,* NB (1936): Valery Vienneau, archbishop, 2012.

Archbishop's Residence: 452, rue Amirault, Dieppe, NB E1A 1G3; (506) 857-9531. Cathedral: Our Lady of the Assumption.

Mont-Laurier, QC (1913): Paul Lortie, bishop, 2012.

Bishop's Residence: 435, rue de la Madone, Mont-Laurier, QC J9L 1S1; (819) 623-5530. Cathedral: Notre Dame de Fourvières.

Montréal,* QC (1836; archdiocese, 1886): Christian Lépine, archbishop, 2012. Thomas Dowd, auxiliary.

Archbishop's Residence: 2000, rue Sherbrooke Ouest, Montréal, QC H3H 1G4; (514) 931-7311; www.diocesemontreal.org. Cathedral: Basilica of Mary Queen of the World and Saint James.

Montréal, QC (Sauveur de Montréal, Eparchy of Greek Melkites) (ap. ex. 1980; eparchy, 1984): Ibrahim M. Ibrahim, 2003.

Address: 34 rue Maplewood, Montréal, QC H2V 2MI; (514) 272-6430.

Montréal, QC (St. Maron of Montréal, Maronites) (1982): Paul-Marwan Tabet, C.M.L., bishop, 2013.

Chancery Office: 12 475 rue Grenet, Montréal, QC H4J 2K4; (514) 331-2807. Cathedral: St. Maron.

Moosonee, ON (v.a. James Bay, 1938; diocese Moosonee, 1967): Vincent Cadieux, O.M.I., bishop, 1992.

Bishop's Residence: 2 Bay Rd., C.P. 40, Moosonee, ON P0L 1Y0; (705) 336-2908. Cathedral: Christ the King.

Nelson, BC (1936): John Corriveau, O.F.M. Cap., bishop, 2007.

Bishop's Residence: 402 West Richards St., Nelson, BC VIL 3K3; (250) 354-6921; www.diocese.nelson.bc.ca/. Cathedral: Mary Immaculate.

New Westminster, BC (Ukrainian Byzantine) (1974): Kenneth Nowakowski, eparch, 2007

Eparch's address: 502 5th Ave., New Westminster, BC V3L 1S2; (604) 524-8824; www.vcn.bc.ca/ucepnw.

Nicolet, QC (1885): André Gazaille, bishop, 2011.

Bishop's Residence: 49, rue Mgr Brunault, Nicolet, QC J3T 1X7; (819) 293-4696. Cathedral: St. Jean-Baptiste.

Ottawa,* ON (Bytown, 1847, name changed,

1854; archdiocese, 1886): Terrence Prendergast, S.J., archbishop, 2007. Christian Riesbeck, C.C., aux.

Archbishop's Residence: 1247 Place Kilborn, Ottawa, ON K1H 6K9; (613) 738-5025; www. ecclesia-ottawa.org. Cathedral: Basilica of Notre Dame-of-Ottawa.

Pembroke, ON (v.a. 1882; diocese, 1898): Michael Mulhall, bishop, 2007. Bishop's Residence: 188 Renfrew St., P.O. Box 7, Pembroke, ON K8A 6X1; (613) 732-7933; www.diocesepembroke.org. Cathedral: St. Columbkille.

Peterborough, ON (1882): Nicola De Angelis, C.F.I.C., bishop 2002.

Bishop's Residence: 350 Hunter St. West, P.O. Box 175, Peterborough, ON K9J 6Y8; (705) 745-5123; www.peterboroughdiocese.org. Cathedral: St. Peter-in-Chains.

Prince Albert, SK (v.a., 1890; diocese, 1907): Albert Thévenot, M. Afr., bishop, 2008.

Address: 1415 4th Ave. West, Prince Albert, SK S6V 5H1; (306) 922-4747; www.padiocese.sk.ca. Cathedral: Sacred Heart.

Prince George, BC (p.a., 1908; v.a. Yukon and Prince Rupert, 1944; diocese Prince George, 1967): Stephen A. Jensen, bishop, 2013.

Chancery Office: 6500 Southbridge Ave., P.O. Box 7000, Prince George, BC V2N 3Z2; (250) 964-4424; www.pgdiocese.bc.ca. Cathedral: Sacred Heart.

Québec,* QC (v.a., 1658; diocese, 1674; archdiocese, 1819; metropolitan, 1844; primatial see, 1956): Cardinal Gérard Cyprien Lacroix, I.S.P.X., archbishop, 2011. Denis Grondin, Gaetan Proulx, O.S.M., auxiliaries.

Chancery Office: 1073, boul. René-Lévesque ouest, Québec, QC G1S 4R5; (418) 688-1211; www. diocesequebec.qc.ca/. Cathedral: Notre-Dame-de-Québec (Basilica).

Regina,* SK (1910; archdiocese, 1915): Daniel Bohan, archbishop, 2005.

Chancery Office: 445 Broad St. North, Regina, SK S4R 2X8; (306) 352-1651; www.archregina.sk.ca. Cathedral: Our Lady of the Most Holy Rosary.

Rimouski,* QC (1867; archdiocese, 1946): Pierre-André Fournier, archbishop, 2008.

Archbishop's Residence: 34, rue de l'Évêché Ouest, C.P. 730, Rimouski, QC G5L 7C7; (418) 723-3320; www.dioceserimouski.com.

Rouyn-Noranda, QC (1973): Dorylas Moreau, bishop, 2001.

Bishop's Residence: 515, avenue Cuddihy, C.P. 1060, Rouyn-Noranda, QC J9X 4C5; (819) 764-4660; www.dioc-cath-rouyn-noranda.org. Cathedral: St. Michael the Archangel.

Saint-Boniface,* MB (1847; archdiocese, 1871): Albert LeGatt, archbishop, 2009.

Archbishop's Residence: 151, avenue de la Cathédrale, Saint-Boniface, MB R2H 0H6; (204) 237-9851. Cathedral: Basilica of St. Boniface.

St. Catharine's, ON (1958): Gerard P. Bergie, bishop, 2010.

Bishop's Residence: P.O. Box 875, St. Catharines, ON L2R 6Y3; (905) 684-0154; www.romancatholic.niagara.on.ca. Cathedral: St. Catherine of Alexandria.

Saint-Hyacinthe, QC (1852): François Lapierre, P.M.E., bishop, 1998.

Bishop's Residence: 1900, rue Girouard Ouest, C.P. 190, Saint-Hyacinthe, QC J2S 7B4; (450) 773-8581; www.diocese-st-hyacinthe.qc.ca. Cathedral: St. Hyacinthe the Confessor.

Saint-Jean-Longueuil, QC (1933 as St.-Jean-de-Québec; named changed, 1982): Lionel Gendron, P.S.S., bishop, 1996. Louis Dicaire, auxiliary.

Bishop's Residence: 740, boulevard Sainte-Foy, C.P. 40, Longueuil, QC J4K 4X8; (450) 679-1100; www.diocese-st-jean-longueuil.org. Cathedral: St. John the Evangelist.

St. Jérôme, QC (1951): Pierre Morissette, bishop, 2008.

Bishop's Residence: 355, Place du Curé Labelle, Saint-Jerome, QC J7Z 5A9; (450) 432-9742; www. diocese-stjerome.qc.ca. Cathedral: St. Jerome.

Saint John, NB (1842): Robert Harris, bishop, 2007; Raymond Poisson, auxiliary.

Chancery Office: 1 Bayard Dr., Saint John, NB E2L 3L5; (506) 653-6800; www.dioceseofsaintjohn.org. Cathedral: Immaculate Conception.

St. John's,* NL (p.a., 1784; v.a., 1796; diocese, 1847; archdiocese, 1904): Martin W. Currie, archbishop, 2007.

Chancery Office: P.O. Box 37, St. John's, NL. A1C 5N5; (709) 726-3660; www.stjohnsarchdiocese.nf.ca. Cathedral: St. John the Baptist.

St. Paul in AB (1948): Paul Terrio, bishop.

Bishop's Residence: 4410, 51e avenue, Saint Paul, AB T0A 3A2; (780) 645-3277. Cathedral: St. Paul.

Sainte-Anne-de-la-Pocatière, QC (1951): Yvon-Joseph Moreau, O.C.S.O., bishop, 2008.

Bishop's Residence: 1200, 4e avenue, C.P. 430, La Pocatière, QC G0R 1Z0; (418) 856-1811. Cathedral: St. Anne.

Saskatoon, SK (1933): Donald Bolen, bishop, 2009.

Chancery Office: 100-5th Ave. North, Saskatoon, SK S7K 2N7; (306) 242-1500; www.saskatoonrcdiocese.com. Cathedral: St. Paul.

Saskatoon, SK (Ukrainian Byzantine) (ap. ex., 1951; diocese, 1956): P. Bryan Bayda, C.SS.R, 2008.

Address: 866 Saskatchewan Crescent East, Saskatoon, SK S7N 0L4; (306) 653-0138.

Sault Ste. Marie, ON (1904): Jean-Louis Plouffe, bishop, 1990, Noël Simard, auxiliary.

Chancery Office: 30, chemin Ste. Anne, Sudbury, ON P3C 5E1, (705) 674-2727; www.isys.ca/cathcom.htm. Cathedral: Pro-Cathedral of the Assumption, North Bay.

Sherbrooke,* QC (1874; archdiocese, 1951); Luc Cyr, archbishop, 1996.

Archbishop's Residence: 130, rue de la Cathédrale, C.P. 430, Sherbrooke, QC J1H 5K1; (819) 563-9934; www.diosher.org. Cathedral: St. Michel.

Thunder Bay, ON (Ft. William, 1952; transferred, 1970): Frederick J. Colli, bishop, 1999.

Bishop's Office: 1222 Reaume St., P.O. Box 10400, Thunder Bay, ON P7B 6T8; (807) 343-9313; www. dotb.ca. Cathedral: St. Patrick.

Timmins, ON (v.a. Temiskaming, 1908; diocese Haileybury, 1915; present title, 1938): Serge Poitras, bishop, 2012.

Address: 65, Ave. Jubilee Est, Timmins, ON P4N 5W4; www.nt.net/~dioctims/. Cathedral: St. Anthony of Padua.

Toronto,* ON (1841; archdiocese, 1870): Cardinal

Thomas C. Collins, archbishop, 2006. John A. Boissonneau, Peter Joseph Hundt, Vincent Nguyen, William Terrence McGrattan, Wayne J. Kirkpatrick, auxiliaries.

Chancery Office: Catholic Pastoral Centre, 1155 Yonge St., Toronto, ON M4T 1W2; (416) 934-0606; www.archtoronto.org. Cathedral: St. Michael.

Toronto, ON (Eparchy for Slovakian Byzantine) (1980): John Pazak, C.Ss.R., 2000.

Eparch's Residence: 223 Carlton Rd., Unionville, ON L3R 3M2; (905) 477-4867.

Toronto, ON (Eparchy for Ukrainian Byzantine) (ap. ex., 1948; eparchy, 1956): Stephen Victor Chmilar eparch, 2003.

Chancery Office: 3100-A Weston Rd., Weston, ON M9M 2S7; (416) 746-0154; www.ucet.ca. Cathedral: St. Josaphat.

Trois-Rivières, QC (1852): Joseph Luc André Bouchard, bishop, 2012.

Bishop's Residence: 362, rue Bonaventure, C.P. 879, Trois-Rivières, QC G9A 5J9; (819) 374-9847; www.diocese-tr.qc.ca/. Cathedral: The Assumption.

Valleyfield, QC (1892): Noel Simard, bishop, 2011.

Bishop's Residence: 11, rue de l'Eglise, Salaberry-de-Valleyfield, QC J6T 1J5; (450) 373-8122; www.rocler.qc.ca/diocese-valleyfield/. Cathedral: St. Cecilia.

Vancouver,* BC (v.a. British Columbia, 1863; diocese New Westminster, 1890; archdiocese Vancouver, 1908): J. Michael Miller, C.S.B., archbishop, 2009.

Chancery Office: 150 Robson St., Vancouver, BC V6B 2A7; (604) 683-0281; www.rcav.bc.ca. Cathedral: Holy Rosary.

Victoria, BC (diocese Vancouver Is., 1846; archdiocese, 1903; diocese Victoria, 1908): Vacant.

Chancery Office: Diocesan Pastoral Centre, #1-4044 Nelthorpe St., Victoria, BC V8X 2A1; (250) 479-1331; www.rcdvictoria.org. Cathedral: St. Andrew.

Whitehorse, YT (v.a., 1944; diocese 1967): Gary Gordon, bishop, 2006.

Chancery Office: 5119 5th Ave., Whitehorse, YT Y1A 1L5; (867) 667-2052. Cathedral: Sacred Heart.

Winnipeg,* MB (1915): Joseph Gagnon, archbishop, 2013.

Chancery Office: Catholic Centre, 1495 Pembina Highway, Winnipeg, MB R3T 2C6; (204) 452-2227; www.archwinnipeg.ca. Cathedral: St. Mary.

Winnipeg,* MB (Ukrainian Byzantine) (Ordinariate of Canada, 1912; ap. ex. Central Canada, 1948; ap. ex. Manitoba, 1951; archeparchy Winnipeg, 1956): Lawrence Huculak, O.S.B.M., archeparch, 1993. Archeparchy Office: 233 Scotia St., Winnipeg, MB R2V 1V7; (204) 338-7801; www.archeparchy.ca. Cathedral: Sts. Vladimir and Olga.

Military Ordinariate of Canada (1951): Donald J. Thériault, bishop, 1998.

Address: Canadian Forces Support Unit (Ottawa), Uplands Site – Bldg. 469, Ottawa, ON K1A 0K2; (613) 990-7824.

An Apostolic Exarchate for Armenian-Rite Catholics in Canada and the United States was established in July 1981 with headquarters in New York City (110 E. 12th St., New York, NY 10003); (212) 477-2030. Manuel Batakian, exarch, 1995.

The Eparchy of Our Lady of Deliverance of Newark for Syrian-rite Catholics in the United States and Canada was established Nov. 6, 1995. Address: 502 Palisade Ave., Union City, NJ 08087-5213; (201) 583-1067; www.Syriac-Catholic.org. Vacant.

The Eparchy for Canada, Mar Addai of Toronto for Chaldeans was established June 10, 2011. Address N/A. Hanna Zora, first eparch.

Hungarian Emigrants throughout the world, resides in Canada: Most Rev. Attila Mikloshazy, S.J., titular bishop of Cast`el Minore. Address: 2661 Kingston Rd., Scarborough, ON M1M 1M3; (416) 261-7207.

Note: The diocese of **Gravelbourg**, in Saskatchewan, was dissolved in September 1998 as part of a reorganization of Canadian dioceses. The regions under the jurisdiction of **Gravelbourg** were integrated into the neighboring dioceses of **Regina** and **Saskatoon**. The **Territorial Abbacy of St. Peter**, Muenster, SK, was also dissolved.

Dioceses with Interprovincial Lines

The following dioceses, indicated by + in the table, have interprovincial lines.

Churchill-Hudson Bay includes part of Northwest Territories.

Keewatin-LePas includes part of Manitoba and Saskatchewan provinces.

Corner Brook and Labrador includes the Labrador region of Newfoundland and the northern part of Québec province.

Mackenzie-Fort Smith, Northwest Territories, includes part of Alberta and Saskatchewan provinces.

Moosonee, Ontario, includes part of Québec province.

Pembroke, Ontario, includes one county of Québec province.

Whitehorse, Yukon Territory, includes part of British Columbia.

CANADIAN CONFERENCE OF CATHOLIC BISHOPS

The Canadian Conference of Catholic Bishops was established Oct. 12, 1943, as a permanent voluntary association of the bishops of Canada, was given official approval by the Holy See in 1948, and acquired the status of an episcopal conference after the Second Vatican Council.

The CCCB acts in two ways: (1) as a strictly ecclesiastical body through which the bishops act together with pastoral authority and responsibility for the Church throughout the country; (2) as an operational secretariat through which the bishops act on a wider scale for the good of the Church and society.

At the top of the CCCB organizational table are the president, an executive committee, a permanent council and a plenary assembly. The membership consists of all the bishops of Canada.

Departments and Offices

The CCCB's work is planned and coordinated by the Programmes and Priorities Committee composed of the six chairmen of the national episcopal commissions and the two general secretaries. It is chaired by the vice-president of the CCCB.

The CCCB's 12 episcopal commissions undertake study

and projects in special areas of pastoral work. Six serve nationally (justice and peace; canon law/inter-rite; relations with associations of clergy, consecrated life and laity; evangelization of peoples; ecumenism; doctrine); three relate to French sectors (*communications sociale, éducation Chrétienne, liturgie*); and three relate to corresponding English sectors (social communications, Christian education, liturgy).

The general secretariat consists of a general secretary and assistants and directors of public relations. The current general secretary is Msgr. Patrick Powers, P.H.

Administrative services for purchasing, archives and library, accounting, personnel, publications, printing and distribution are supervised by directors who relate to the general secretaries.

Various advisory councils and committees with mixed memberships of lay persons, religious, priests and bishops also serve the CCCB on a variety of topics.

Operations

Meetings for the transaction of business are held at least once a year by the plenary assembly, six times a year by the executive committee, and four times a year by the permanent council.

Bishop Paul-Andre Durocher of Gatineau is president of the CCCB, and Archbishop Douglas Crosby of Hamilton is vice-president for the 2013-2015 term.

The Conference headquarters is located at 2500 Don Reid Dr., Ottawa, K1H 2J2, Canada; (613) 241-9461; www.cccb.ca.

CANADIAN SHRINES

Our Lady of the Cape (Cap de la Madeleine), Queen of the Most Holy Rosary: The Three Rivers, Québec, parish church, built in 1714 and considered the oldest stone church on the North American continent preserved in its original state, was rededicated June 22, 1888, as a shrine of the Queen of the Most Holy Rosary. The site increased in importance as a pilgrimage and devotional center, and in 1904 St. Pius X decreed the crowning of a statue of the Blessed Virgin which had been donated 50 years earlier to commemorate the dogma of the Immaculate Conception. In 1909, the First Plenary Council of Québec declared the church a shrine of national pilgrimage. In 1964, the church at the shrine was given the status and title of minor basilica.

St. Anne de Beaupre: The devotional history of this shrine in Québec began with the reported cure of a cripple, Louis Guimont, on Mar. 16, 1658, the starting date of construction work on a small chapel of St. Anne. The original building was successively enlarged and replaced by a stone church, which was given the rank of minor basilica in 1888. The present structure, a Romanesque-Gothic basilica, houses the shrine proper in its north transept, including an eight-foot-high oaken statue and a relic of St. Anne, a portion of her forearm.

St. Joseph's Oratory: The massive oratory basilica standing on the western side of Mount Royal and overlooking the city of Montréal had its origin in a primitive chapel erected there by Blessed André Bessette, C.S.C., in 1904. Eleven years later, a large crypt was built to accommodate an increasing number of pilgrims, and in 1924 construction work was begun on the large church. A belfry, housing a 60-bell carillon and standing on the site of the original chapel, was dedicated May 15, 1955, as the first major event of the jubilee year observed after the oratory was given the rank of minor basilica.

Martyrs' Shrine: A shrine commemorating several of the Jesuit Martyrs of North America who were killed between 1642 and 1649 in the Ontario and northern New York area is located on the former site of old Fort Sainte Marie. Before its location was fixed near Midland, ON, in 1925, a small chapel had been erected in 1907 at old Mission St. Ignace to mark the martyrdom of Fathers Jean de Brebeuf and Gabriel Lalemant. This sanctuary has a U.S. counterpart in the Shrine of the North American Martyrs near Auriesville, NY, under the care of the Jesuits.

Others

In Québec City: Basilica of Notre Dame (1650), once the cathedral of a diocese stretching from Canada to Mexico; Notre Dame des Victoires (1690); the Ursuline Convent (1720), on du Parloir St.

Near Montréal: Hermitage of St. Anthony, La Bouchette; Ste. Anne de Micmacs, Restigouche; Chapel of Atonement, Pointe aux Trembles; Our Lady of Lourdes, Rigaud; St. Benoît du Lac, near Magog.

In Montréal: Notre Dame Basilica (1829).

Near Montréal: Chapel of St. Marie Marguerite d'Youville, foundress of the Grey Nuns; Notre Dame de Lourdes, at Rigaud.

STATISTICAL SUMMARY OF THE CATHOLIC CHURCH IN CANADA

(*Principal source:* 2014 Directory of the Canadian Conference of Catholic Bishops; *figures as of Jan. 2014.*)
Catholic population statistics are those reported in the 2001 Canadian Census. Archdioceses are indicated by
an asterisk. For dioceses marked +, *see* **Canadian Dioceses with Interprovincial Lines**.

Canada's 10 civil provinces and two territories are divided into 18 ecclesiastical provinces consisting of
18 metropolitan sees (archdioceses) and 44 suffragan sees; there are also eight Oriental Rite dioceses, one
archdiocese and three eparchies immediately subject to the Holy See, and the Military Ordinariate.

This table presents a regional breakdown of Catholic statistics. In some cases, the totals are approximate
because diocesan boundaries fall within several civil provinces.

Civil Province Diocese	Cath. Pop.	Dioc. Priests	Rel. Priests	Total Priests	Perm. Deacs.	Bro- thers	Sis- ters	Lay Assts.	Par- ishes[1]
Newfoundland	**188,089**	**100**	**14**	**114**	**2**	**8**	**207**	**3**	**168**
St. John's*	111,605	41	10	51	1	8	173	2	70
Corner Brook & Lab.+	40,624	32	3	35	–	–	15	–	28
Grand Falls	35,860	27	1	28	1	–	19	1	70
Prince Edward Island									
Charlottetown	**63,240**	**48**	**2**	**50**	**1**	**1**	**108**	**18**	**52**
Nova Scotia	**327,945**	**194**	**25**	**219**	**46**	**–**	**407**	**11**	**248**
Halifax*	161,115	75	16	91	41	–	172	7	95
Antigonish	129,730	99	3	102	–	–	225	–	118
Yarmouth	37,100	20	6	26	5	–	10	4	35
New Brunswick	**385,985**	**164**	**82**	**246**	**4**	**13**	**507**	**117**	**228**
Moncton*	110,895	41	22	63	1	13	228	84	56
Bathurst	107,655	42	47	89	–	0	139	–	57
Edmundston	52,035	23	7	30	–	–	54	13	32
St. John	115,400	58	6	64	3	–	86	20	83
Québec	**5,926,191**	**2,055**	**1,318**	**3,373**	**416**	**850**	**9,668**	**749**	**1,358**
Gatineau*	234,725	44	19	63	3	5	123	18	53
Montréal*	1,494,132	467	576	1,043	88	244	3,078	89	208
Québec*	917,045	395	251	646	92	107	2,867	99	207
Rimouski*	143,640	85	6	91	15	19	512	14	103
Sherbrooke*	245,495	157	89	246	22	62	542	35	59
Amos	95,506	8	14	22	–	2	62	1	61
Baie Comeau	90,130	33	9	42	9	0	33	16	55
Chicoutimi	263,950	137	25	162	43	20	387	55	67
Gaspé	85,840	43	5	48	3	2	113	9	65
Joliette	206,981	56	50	106	7	73	119	41	41
Mont Laurier	77,340	30	5	35	2	1	28	18	19
Montréal, St. Maron (Maronites)	4,100	11	7	18	1	1	6	30	16
Montréal, St. Sauveur (Greek Melkites)	9,200	6	8	14	–	–	–	–	6
Nicolet	184,625	102	13	125	24	42	267	44	43
Rouyn Noranda	56,380	21	3	24	–	1	82	21	39
Ste Anne de la Pocatière	87,700	83	1	84	7	–	115	16	**55**
St.-Hyacinthe	336,445	92	104	206	29	115	551	52	87
St.-Jean Long	553,470	68	35	103	4	72	275	92	46
St. Jérôme	407,112	66	21	87	19	6	115	43	36
Trois Rivières	232,985	87	67	154	32	56	369	37	67
Valleyfield	199,390	64	10	74	16	22	24	19	25
Ontario	**3,930,075**	**1,177**	**838**	**2,015**	**525**	**97**	**2,444**	**225**	**1,130**
Kingston*	116,845	76	10	86	22	1	150	–	51
Ottawa*	392,635	137	54	191	86	16	572	13	107
Toronto*	1,626,465	296	419	715	131	53	564	72	244
Alexandria Corn	55,570	32	1	33	19	2	23	–	29
Hamilton	559,290	121	95	216	37	11	173	41	153

Civil Province Diocese	Cath. Pop.	Dioc. Priests	Rel. Priests	Total Priests	Perm. Deacs.	Bro- thers	Sis- ters	Lay Assts.	Par- ishes[1]
Ontario, cont.									
Hearst	31,790	25	–	25	1	–	1	17	28
London	444,310	110	167	277	47	1	473	57	116
Moosonee+	3,830	0	3	3	1	1	–	3	8
Pembroke+	67,870	46	6	52	9	3	159	2	56
Peterborough	99,785	65	13	78	6	–	79	3	64
St. Catharine's	153,565	62	38	100	16	3	30	8	46
Sault Ste. Marie	206,405	76	12	88	92	1	180	2	96
Thunder Bay	73,780	31	12	43	33	–	9	–	43
Timmins	50,605	20	4	24	7	4	14	7	27
Toronto (Ukr.)	42,330	79	4	83	18	1	17	–	57
Toronto (Slovaks)	5,000	4	–	4	–	–	–	–	5
Manitoba	**344,845**	**161**	**103**	**264**	**51**	**11**	**369**	**21**	**351**
Keewatin Le Pas*+	37,380	5	13	18	–	–	6	–	45
St. Boniface*	113,495	63	50	113	20	10	230	20	95
Winnipeg*	158,095	61	23	84	18	1	110	–	89
Winnipeg (Ukrainians)*	29,760	29	11	40	12	–	21	–	106
Churchill Hud. Bay+	6,115	3	6	9	1	–	2	1	16
Saskatchewan+	**286,625**	**175**	**68**	**243**	**6**	**17**	**297**	**55**	**416**
Regina*	126,980	82	19	101	2	8	67	–	156
Prince-Albert	55,450	38	17	55	2	–	66	9	86
Saskatoon	86,645	36	32	68	2	9	145	46	95
Saskatoon (Ukrainians)	17,550	19	10	29	3	–	19	–	79
Alberta	**783,940**	**272**	**161**	**433**	**79**	**22**	**344**	**53**	**386**
Edmonton*	333,545	91	92	183	24	14	222	41	125
Grouard McLellan*	44,470	18	8	26	2	–	12	8	60
Calgary	320,425	105	41	146	43	4	79	–	79
Edmonton (Ukrainians)	28,845	31	10	41	4	4	18	–	84
St. Paul	56,655	27	10	37	6	–	13	4	38
British Columbia	**672,515**	**200**	**132**	**332**	**5**	**24**	**210**	**5**	**292**
Vancouver*	402,310	110	97	207	1	17	108	–	89
Kamloops	51,435	14	4	18	2	1	12	–	67
Nelson	67,025	29	6	35	–	–	8	–	46
New Westminster (Ukrainians)	7,780	9	1	10	1	–	2	–	12
Prince George	49,500	16	7	23	1	4	19	5	37
Victoria	94,465	22	17	39	–	2	61	–	41
Yukon Territory									
Whitehorse+	**8,150**	**6**	**4**	**10**	**–**	**–**	**3**	**4**	**22**
Northwest Territories									
MacKenzie Ft. Smith+	**20,110**	**4**	**5**	**9**		**1**	**6**	**14**	**37**
Military Ordinariate	**13,400**	**50***	**–****	**50**	**7**	**–**	**–**	**46**	**23****
TOTALS	**12.951.110**[2]	**4.498**	**2.741**	**7.239**	**1.134**	**1.449**	**13.946**	**1.122**	**4.349**

1. Denotes both parishes and missions.
2. Catholics comprise about 43% of the total population. According to the 2012 *Annuarium Statisticum Ecclesiae* (the most recent edition), there were 104,188 baptisms and 18,174 marriages.
* The Canadian Military Ordinariate does not incardinate clerics.
** Not included in the total.

The Catholic Church in Mexico

BACKGROUND

Start of Church Organization

The history of the Catholic Church in Mexico began in 1519 with the capture of Mexico's native civilization, the Aztec Empire, by the Spanish *conquistadores* under Hernándo Cortés. The Spanish army besieged the Aztec capital of Tenochtitlan, massacred most of the inhabitants, strangled the Aztec emperor Montezuma, and crushed the rest of the empire. Mexico City became the chief city of New Spain and the cultural and religious center of colonial Mexico; it was declared a diocese in 1530.

The record of Colonial Spanish treatment of the native peoples of Mexico is a grim one. The Indians suffered exploitation, slavery, and rapid depletion of their population from disease; they were forced to labor in inhuman conditions in mines and endured servitude in the *encomienda* system.

In sharp contrast to the treatment of the natives by the government was the effort to evangelize Mexico by the religious orders, who followed the command of Pope Alexander VI in the 1494 Treaty of Tordesillas to convert all peoples who would be encountered in the coming age of exploration. A papal bull, dated Apr. 25, 1521, gave the Franciscans the permission of the Holy See to preach in New Spain. They were joined by the Dominicans and, later, by the Jesuits. The missionary orders soon distinguished themselves by their resistance to the brutal enslavement of the Indians, their mastery of native languages, and their willingness to endure enormous hardships in bringing the faith to the distant corners of Mexico.

As the Church became more established, however, the missionary priests and friars came increasingly into conflict with the secular clergy, who desired full control over ecclesiastical affairs, resented the extensive powers of religious orders, and normally identified closely with the interests of the crown. The government thus decreed that the missionaries were to have 10 years in which to convert the Indians, after which control would pass to the diocesan clergy. This was protested by the missionary orders, and the conflict was resolved in favor of the diocesan priests in 1640 thanks to the efforts of Bishop Juan de Palafox de Mendoza of Puebla.

The alliance of the secular clergy with the government was a reflection of the control enjoyed by the Spanish Crown over the Church in Mexico. The Holy See had granted to the kings of Spain royal patronage over the Church in Mexico, and the practice of the *Patronato Real* meant that the king nominated all Church officials in New Spain and held authority over the Church's temporal concerns.

A major element in this policy was the forced conversion of the local peoples. Coerced into adopting the faith, many Indians were insincere or hesitant to embrace the faith. To insure the full embrace of the faith, Spanish authorities received permission from King Philip II in 1569 to introduce the Inquisition to Mexico. Indians who had survived the mines, diseases, and brutality of the colonial rulers were now subjected to tribunals to test their faith. This practice was eventually ended when authorities decided that the natives were not culpable because of limited intelligence. Nevertheless, the close identification of the diocesan clergy with the interests and policies of the Spanish crown created a hostility toward the Church in Mexico by the lower classes that endures today.

On the positive side, the Church did much through its missionaries to save many Indians from death and enslavement and to preserve vital portions of Mesoamerican culture, art, and history. Friars also traveled to northern Mexico and beyond, bringing the faith into California, Texas, and New Mexico.

The native peoples were given a profound encouragement to embrace the Catholic faith in 1531 by the appearance of Our Lady of Guadalupe to the farmer Juan Diego (beatified in 1990 and canonized in 2002 by Pope John Paul II) on the Tepeyac hill just outside of Mexico City. The shrine built in her honor remains the most important religious site in Mexico. Enshrined within it is the mantle brought by Juan Diego to Bishop Zumaragga to convince him of the genuine nature of the apparition. Miraculously emblazoned upon it is the life-size image of the Virgin Mary.

MEXICAN INDEPENDENCE

The Spanish domination of Mexico endured for nearly three centuries, deteriorating gradually throughout the 1700s as the gulf widened between the Spanish ruling class and the native classes that were joined by the *mestizos* and *creoles* (descendants of Native Americans and Europeans). Unrest broke out into a full-scale rebellion in 1810 with the uprising of many priests led by Father Miguel Hidalgo y Costilla and, after his execution, by Father José Maria Morelos y Pavón. While suppressed in 1816 by the colonial regime with the support of the upper classes and most of the diocesan clergy, it proved only the first of several revolts, culminating in the 1821 declaration of Mexican independence. By the terms of the independence, the Church received a special status and had enormous sway in political life.

A republic was proclaimed in 1834 and various liberal regimes came to power. Anticlericalism became commonplace, made even more strident by the lingering hostility over the Church's activities with Spanish colonial government. Much influenced by the ideals of the European revolutions then taking place, the Mexican republican movements were strongly anti-Catholic. For more than a decade, power was in the hands of Antonio López de Santa Anna (also known for his victory at the Alamo) and Valentín Gómez Farías. After the Mexican-American War (1846-1848), the political instability led to the dictatorship of Santa Anna.

Santa Anna was toppled in 1855 by a liberal regime whose anti-Church legislation sparked an armed struggle called the War of the Reform (1858-1861). The laws issued by the government included the *Ley Juárez*, abolishing all ecclesiastical courts, and the *Ley Lerdo*, forcing the Church to sell all of its lands. Deprived of its properties, the Church lost control of education and schools, and Mexico's educational system became often bitterly anti-Catholic.

While the liberal forces won the War of the Reform, the conflict had so debilitated Mexico that the French were able to intervene in 1861 and install their puppet, the Austrian duke Maximilian, on the Mexican throne. As the United States was embroiled in its own civil war from 1861-1865, it was unable to respond to French imperialist ambitions in Mexico. Maximilian initially enjoyed the support of the conservative elements and the Church, but his liberal reforms alienated the mistrustful conservatives and he soon clung to power only with French support. When France finally withdrew its troops in 1867, Maximilian was deposed by republican forces and executed.

MODERN MEXICO

The fall of Emperor Maximilian signaled a restoration of the anticlerical constitution of 1857 and the elevation of Benito Juárez – the republican leader long recognized by the United States – as president. His successor, Sebastián Lerdo de Tijada, was toppled in 1876 by Porfirio Díaz, who remained dictator for 34 years. A civil war ended his regime, and more bloodshed ensued. Finally, a constitution was issued in 1917 that placed severe restrictions on the Church: there could be no criticism of the government, only Mexicans could be clergy, the Church was not permitted to own property, and any privileges were stripped away.

The situation became worse after 1923, when the papal legate was expelled. The administration of Plutarco Calles (1924-1928) launched a wave of persecution that sparked a popular but ultimately unsuccessful uprising called the Cristero Rebellion. Coupled with the repressive measures of local governments, the Calles regime and its successors forced the Church into very difficult circumstances, with only a few priests remaining in the country. The tragedy was deepened by the execution of dozens of priests and nuns by republican forces for assorted and imaginary crimes or for speaking out on behalf of the poor or oppressed Catholics. A number of the executed clergy have been beatified and canonized since the tragedy, most so during the pontificate of Pope John Paul II. The persecution prompted Pope Pius XI to issue the encyclicals *Iniquis afflictisque* (1926) and *Acerba animi* (1932).

An easing of the situation began in 1940 as the rigid anticlerical laws ceased to be enforced with enthusiasm. A rapprochement was visible in the 1958 elections, when the Church received conciliatory gestures from the ruling Revolutionary Party and its presidential candidate Adolfo López Mateos. The Church continued to exist under numerous legal disabilities and was oppressed in a number of the Mexican states.

Gradual improvement in relations between Mexico and the Holy See led to the exchange in 1990 of personal representatives between the Mexican president and Pope John Paul II. The Holy Father's efforts to build a further diplomatic bridge culminated in the establishment of full diplomatic ties in 1992. This was followed by the final easing of many of the handicaps under which the Church had long suffered.

The faith of the Mexican people is profoundly deep, as was seen in the nearly frenzied greeting given to Pope John Paul II in 1979, 1990, 1993, and 1999. However, social unrest, poverty, economic challenges, the violence of drug cartels, and corruption still plague the country. Church leaders — especially religious orders — have been outspoken in their criticism of government human rights abuses and corruption. During the mid-1990s, the Jesuits said they were the target of a "campaign of intimidation" because of their human rights work.

On May 24, 1993, Cardinal Juan Jesus Posadas Ocampo of Guadalajara was killed during a supposed shoot-out among rival drug cartels. The murder remained unsolved, although Cardinal Posadas' successor, Cardinal Juan Sandoval Íñiguez, continued to claim that high-ranking officials, including the Mexican attorney general at the time, lied to protect others involved in a plot. In 2001 Cardinal Sandoval said he would seek a reopening of the case because he had new evidence contradicting the findings of the official investigation; he also claimed he had been almost fatally poisoned in 1999 during a dinner with federal officials angry with his insistence that the murder was not accidental.

In the 1970s and 1980s, one of Mexico's most prominent proponents of liberation theology was Bishop Samuel Ruiz Garcia of San Cristobal de las Casas. In the early 1990s the Vatican began investigating his views, but because he had the trust of indigenous peasants, in 1994 he was thrown into the role of mediator between the government and the mostly native Zapatista National Liberation Army in Chiapas. He continued that role until 1998, when he resigned after accusing the government of "dismantling any possible means or effort to solve the crisis in Chiapas." Mexico's bishops said at that time that they would provide support to the peace process but would not seek to mediate the conflict.

On July 2, 2000, Vicente Fox Quesada, head of the National Action Party and a practicing Catholic, won the Mexican presidential election, marking the first time since 1929 that the country was not ruled by the Institutional Revolutionary Party. Mexico City Cardinal Norberto Rivera Carrera told reporters the election was "not a miracle, as some have suggested, but it is an extraordinary act." Church officials emphasized that they expected no special privileges from the new government, but the general climate was one of optimism for an improvement in church-state relations.

Within weeks, Fox – with news cameras flashing – received Communion in his hometown parish. However, in July 2001, the Vatican said he failed to have his first marriage annulled before marrying his spokeswoman in a civil ceremony; thus, he would be prohibited from receiving the sacraments. In June 2001, federal and state officials participated in a public Mass at the Basilica of Our Lady of Guadalupe, breaking a taboo on government officials publicly practicing their religion. On July 31, 2002, during his fifth pastoral visit to Mexico, Pope John Paul II canonized St. Juan Diego. In recent years, the country has suffered enormously from the violence of the drug cartels and the rampant corruption in the government. Pope Benedict XVI made an apostolic visit to Leon, Mexico, in March, 2012.

ORGANIZATION

Presently, the Church in Mexico is organized into 18 provinces. There are 18 archdioceses (including the promotion of Tijuana, León, Tuxtla Gutierrez, and Tulancingo as metropolitan sees), 67 dioceses, 5 prelacies, and 2 eparchs, for the Greek Melkites and Maronites. In 2014, the new diocese of Izcalli (a suffragan of Tlalnepantla) was established. As of Aug. 15, 2014, there were four Mexican members of the College of Cardinals: Norberto Rivera Carrera, Juan Sandoval Iñiguez, Javier Lozano Barragán, and Adolfo Antonio Suárez Rivera. (For statistical information on the Church in Mexico, see below.)The current apostolic delegation to Mexico was set up in 1992 as a nunciature with the establishment of renewed formal diplomatic relations with the Vatican. The present Apostolic Nuncio is Archbishop Christophe Pierre, J.C.D., who was appointed in 2007.

ECCLESIASTICAL JURISDICTIONS OF MEXICO

Provinces

Names of ecclesiastical provinces and metropolitan sees in bold face: suffragan sees in parentheses. The current listing reflects the restructuring of Mexico's provinces in 2009.

Acapulco (Chilpancingo-Chilapa, Ciudad Altamirano, Tlapa).

Antequera, Oaxaca (Puerto Escondido, Tehuantepec, Tuxtepec; Prelacies of Mixes and Huautla).

Chihuahua (Ciudad Juárez, Cuauhtémoc-Madera, Nuevos Casas Grandes, Parral, Tarahumara).

Durango (Mazatlán, Torreón, El Salto, Gómez Palacio).

Guadalajara (Aguascalientes, Autlán, Ciudad Guzmán, Colima, San Juan de los Lagos, Tepic; Prelature of Jesús Maria del Nayar).

Hermosillo (Ciudad Obregón, Culiacán).

León (Celaya, Irapuato, Querétaro

México (Atlacomulco, Cuernavaca, Tenancingo, Toluca).

Monterrey (Ciudad Victoria, Linares, Matamoros, Nuevo Laredo, Piedras Negras, Saltillo, Tampico).

Morelia (Apatzingán, Ciudad Lázaro Cárdenas, Tacámbaro, Zamora).

Puebla de los Angeles (Huajuapan de León, Tehuacán, Tlaxcala).

San Luis Potosi (Matehuala, Ciudad Valles, Zacatecas).

Tijuana (La Paz, Mexicali, Ensenada).

Tlalnepantla (Texcoco, Cuautitlán, Netzahualcóyotl, Ecatepec, Valle de Chalco, Teotihuacan).

Tulancingo (Huejutla and Tula).

Tuxtla Gutierrez (San Cristóbal de las Casas and Tapachula).

Xalapa (Papantla, San Andrés Tuxtla, Coatzacoalcos, Tuxpan, Veracruz, Orizaba, Córdoba).

Yucatán (Campeche, Tabasco, Prelacy of Cancún-

Chetumal; Eparchy of Nuestra Señora del Paraíso).

Jurisdictions, Hierarchy

(Principal sources: Information office, Mexican Conference of Catholic Bishops; Catholic Almanac survey; Annuario Pontificio; L'Osservatore Romano; Catholic News Service. As of July 1, 2014. *Addresses and phone numbers are provided by the* Annuario Pontificio.)

Information includes names of archdioceses (indicated by asterisk) and dioceses, date of foundation, present ordinaries and auxiliaries; addresses of chancery office/bishop's residence.

Acapulco* (1958; promoted to archdiocese, 1983): Carlos Garfias Merlos, archbishop, 2010; Juan Navarro Castellanos, auxiliary.

Diocesan Address: Apartado Postal 201, Quebrada 16, 39850 Acapulco, Guerrero; (748) 2-07-63.

Aguascalientes (1899): José María De la Torre Martín, bishop, 2008.

Diocesan Address: Apartado 167, Galeana 105 Norte, 20000 Aguascalientes, Aguascalientes; (449) 9-15-32-61.

Apatzingán (1962): Miguel Patiño Velázquez, M.S.F., bishop, 1981.

Diocesan Address: Calle Esteban Vaca Calderón 100, 60600 Apatzingán, Mich.; (453) 5-34-17-87.

Atlacomulco (1984): Odilón Martínez García, bishop, 2010.

Diocesan Address: Hidalgo Sur 1, Apartado 22, 50450 Atlacomulco, Méx.; (712) 1-22-05-53.

Autlán (1961): Gonzalo Galván Castillo, bishop, 2004.

Diocesan Address: Apartado 8, Hidalgo 74, 48900 Autlán, Jal., Mex.; (317) 3-82-12-28.

Campeche (1895): José Francisco González González, bishop, 2013.

Diocesan Address: Calle 53 # 1-B Entre 8 y 10 Centro Apdo. Postal # 12724000 - Campeche, Camp.; (981) 8-16-25-24.

Cancún-Chetumal, Prelacy of (1970, as Chetumal; name changed in 1996): Pedro Pablo Elizondo Cárdenas, L.C., bishop, 2004.

Diocesan Address: Apartado Postal 165, Othón P. Blanco 150, 77000 Chetumal, Quintana Roo; (983) 2-06-38.

Celaya (1973): Benjamin Castillo Plascencia, bishop, 2010.

Diocesan Address: Curia Diocesana, Apartado 207, Manuel Doblado 110, 38000 Celaya, Gto.; (461) 6-12-48-35.

Chihuahua* (1891; promoted to archdiocese, 1958): Constancio Miranda Weckmann, archbishop, 2010.

Diocesan Address: Av. Cuauhtémoc # 1828 Col. Cuauhtémoc, Apartado Postal 7, 31000 Chihuahua, Chihuahua; (614) 4-10-32-02.

Chilpancingo-Chilapa (1863 as Chilpancingo; name changed to Chilpancingo-Chilapa, 1989): Alejo Zavala Castro, bishop, 2005.

Diocesan Address: Abasolo e Hidalgo, Apartado Postal #185, 39000 Chilpancingo, Gro.; (747) 4-71-05-92.

Ciudad Altamirano (1964): Maximino Martínez Miranda, bishop, 2006.

Diocesan Address: Juárez 18 Oriente, Centro, Apdo 17, 40680 Ciudad Altamirano, Gro.; (767) 6-72-17-74.

Ciudad Guzmán (1972): Braulio Rafael León Villegas, bishop, 1999.

Diocesan Address: Ramón Corona 26, Apartado 86, 49000 Ciudad Guzman, Jal.; (341) 4-12-19-94.

Ciudad Juárez (1957): Renato Ascencio León, bishop, 1994; José Guadalupe Torres Campos, auxiliary.

Diocesan Address: Apartado Postal 188, 32000 Cuidad Juárez, Chih.; (16) 15-09-22.

Ciudad Lázaro Cárdenas (1985): Armando António Ortíz Aguirre, bishop, 2013.

Diocesan Address: Apartado 500, Andador Ciudad del Carmen #4, Fideicomiso 2° Sector, 60950 Lázaro Cardenas, Mich.; (753) 5-41-64-07.

Ciudad Obregón (1959): Felipe Padilla Cardona, bishop, 2010.

Diocesan Address: Apartado 402, Sonora 161 Norte, 85000 Ciudad Obregón, Son.; (644) 4-13-20-98.

Ciudad Valles (1960): Roberto Octavio Balmori Cinta, M.J., bishop, 2002.

Diocesan Address: 16 de Septiembre 726, Apartado 170, 79000 Ciudad Valles, S.L.P.; (138) 2-25-97

Ciudad Victoria (1964): Antonio González Sánchez, bishop, 1995.

Diocesan Address: 15 Hidalgo y Juárez, Centro, Apartado Postal #335, 87000 Ciudad Victoria, Tamps.; (834) 3-12-87-16.

Coatzacoalcos (1984): Rutilo Muñoz Zamora, bishop, 2002.

Diocesan Address: Apartado 513 y 513, Aldama 502, 96400 Coatzacoalcos, Ver.; (921) 2-12-23-99.

Colima (1881): Vacant, bishop.

Diocesan Address: Hidalgo 135, Apartado 1, 28000 Colima, Colima; (312) 3-12-02-62.

Cordoba (2000): Eduardo Porfirio Patiño Leal, bishop, 2000.

Diocesan Address: Avenida 11-1300, Esquina con Calle 13, Apartado 154, Zona Centro, 94500 Cordoba, Ver., Mexico; (271) 7-14-91-56.

Cuauhtémoc-Madera (1966): Juan Guillermo López Soto, bishop, 1995.

Diocesan Address: Reforma y 4ª # 479, Apartado Postal 209, 31500 Cuauhtemoc, Chih.; (625) 5-81-57-22.

Cuautitlán (1979): Rodrigo Guillermo Ortiz Mondragón, bishop, 2005.

Diocesan Address: Apartado 14-21, Sor Juana Inés de la Cruz 208, Anexo a Catedral, 54800 Cuautitlán de Romero Rubio; (55) 58-72-19-96.

Cuernavaca (1891): Ramon Castro Castro, bishop, 2013.

Diocesan Address: Apartado 13, Hidalgo #17, 62000 Cuernavaca, Mor.; (777) 3-18-45-90.

Culiacán (1883 as Sinaloa; name changed 1959): Jonás Guerrero Corona, bishop, 2011; Emigdio Duarte Figueroa, auxiliary.

Diocesan Address: Apartado Postal 666, Av. Las Palmas #26 Oriente, 80220 Culiacán, Sinaloa; (667) 7-12-32-72.

Durango* (1620, promoted to archdiocese, 1891): Hector González Martínez, archbishop, 2003; Enrique Sanchez Martinez, aux.

Diocesan Address: Apartado Postal 116, 34000 Durango, Durango; (618) 8-11-42-42

Ecatepec (1995): Oscar Roberto Dominguez Couttolenc, M.G., bishop, 2012.

Diocesan Address: Plaza Principal s/n, San Cristóbal Centro, Apartado Postal 95, 55000

Ecatepec de Morelos; (5) 116-09-76.

El Salto, Prelacy of (1968): Juan Maria Huerta Muro, O.F.M., bishop, 2012.

Prelature Address: Mons. Francisco Medina s/n, Apartado Postal 58, 34950 El Salto, Durango; (675) 8-76-00-70.

Ensenada (2007): Rafael Valdez Torres, bishop, 2013.

Diocesan Address: Av. Guadalupe 565, Col. Obrera, 22830 Ensenada, B.C.; [646] 176-37-40.

Gómez Palacio (Nov. 25, 2008): José Guadalupe Torres Campos, bishop, 2008.

Diocesan Address: N/A

Guadalajara* (1548; promoted to archdiocese, 1863): Cardinal Francisco Robles Ortega, archbishop, 2011; José Trinidad González Rodriguez, Miguel Romano Gómez, José Leopoldo González González, auxiliaries.

Diocesan Address: Arzobispado, Apartado Postal 1-331, Calle Liceo 17, 44100 Guadalajara, Jal.; (33) 36-14-55-04; www.arquidiocesisgdl.org.mx.

Hermosillo* (1779, as Sonora, promoted to an archdiocese, 1963): José Ulises Macias Salcedo, archbishop, 1996.

Diocesan Address: Apartado 1, Dr. Paliza 81, 83260 Hermosillo, Son.; (662) 2-13-21-38.

Huajuapan de Leon (1903): Teodoro Enrique Pino Miranda, 2000.

Diocesan Address: Apartado 43, Anexos de Catedral, 69000 Huajuapan de León, Oax.; (953) 5-32-07-97.

Huautla, Prelacy of (1972): Jose Armando Alvarez Cano, prelate, 2011.

Diocesan Address: Casa Prelaticia Calle 5 de Feb. # 15, Apartado 2, 68500 Huautla de Jiménez, Oaxaca; (236) 3-78-00-19.

Huejutla (1922): Salvador Rangel Mendoza O.F.M., bishop, 1994.

Diocesan Address: Obispado, Apartado 8, Ave. Corona del Rosal s/n, Col. Tecoluco, 43000 Huejutla, Hgo.; (789) 8-96-01-85.

Irapuato (2004): José de Jesús Martínez Zepeda, first bishop, 2004.

Diocesan Address: Juarez 138-407, Apatado 13, 36500 Irapuato, Gto.; 462-625-61-04.

Jesús María of Nayar, Prelature of (1962): José de Jesús González Hernández, O.F.M., bishop, 2010.

Diocesan Address: Curia Prelaticia de Jesús María, Belén #24, Apartado 33-B, 63150 Tepic, Nayar; (311) 2-13-88-80.

La Paz en la Baja California Sur (1988): Miguel Angel Alba Díaz, 2001.

Diocesan Address: Apartado 25, Revolución y 5 de Mayo, 23000 La Paz, B.C.S.; (112) 2-25-96.

León* (1863, promoted to archdiocese, 2006): Alfonso Cortes Contreras, archbishop, 2012; Juan Frausto Pallares, auxiliary.

Diocesan Address: Pedro Moreno #312, Apartado 108, 37000 León, Gto.; (477) 7-13-27-47; www.diocesisleon.org.mx.

Linares (1962): Ramón Calderón Batres, bishop, 1988.

Diocesan Address: Morelos y Zaragoza s/n, Apartado 70, 67700 Linares, N.L.; (821) 2-00-54.

Matamoros (1958): Ruy Rendon Leal, bishop, 2011.

Diocesan Address: Apartado 70, Calle 5 y Morelos, 87351 Matamoros, Tamps.; (88) 13-55-11; www.communion.org.mx.

Matehuala (1997): Rodrigo Aguilar Martínez, bishop, 1997.
Diocesan Address: Rayón #200 Centro, Apartado 40, 78700 Matehuala, S.L.P.; (01) 488-2-51-42.
Mazatlán (1958): Mario Espinosa Contreras, bishop, 2005.
Diocesan Address: Apartado Postal 1, Canizales y Benito Juárez s/n, 82000 Mazatlán, Sin.; (69) 81-33-52.
Mexicali (1966): José Isidro Guerrero Macías, bishop, 1997.
Diocesan Address: Av. Morelos #192, Col. Primera sécción, Apartado 3-547, 21100 Mexicali, B.C. Norte; (686) 5-52-40-09.
México* (1530, promoted to an archdiocese, 1546): Cardinal Norberto Rivera Carrera, archbishop, 1995; José de Jesús Martinez Zepeda, Marcelino Hernández Rodríguez, Luis Fletes Santana, Rogelio Esquivel Medina, Antonio Ortega Franco, C.O., Carlos Briseño Arch, O.A.R., Florencio Armando Colín Cruz, Jesús Antonio Lerma Nolasco, Andrés Vargas Peña, Adolfo Miguel Castaño Fonseca, Crispin Ojeda Marquez, Jorge Estrada Solorzano, auxiliaries.
Diocesan Address: Curia Arzobispal, Apartado Postal 24-433, Durango 90, Col. Roma, 06700 - México, D. F.; (55) 55-25-11-10; www.arzobispa-domexico.org.mx.
Mixes, Prelacy of (1964): Don Héctor Guerrero Córdova, S.D.B., bishop, 2007
Diocesan Address: Casa del Señor Obispo, 70283, Ayutla, Mixes, Oax.; (951) 5-58-20-98.
Monterrey* (1777, as Linares o Nuevo León, promoted to an archdiocese, 1891; name changed 1922): Rogelio Cabrera Lopez, archbishop, 2012; Gustavo Rodríguez Vega, Jorge Alberto Cavazos Arizpe, Alfonso Gerardo Miranda Guardiola, Juan Armando Pérez Talamantes, auxiliaries.
Diocesan Address: Apartado 7, Zuazua 1110 Sur con Ocampo, 64000 Monterrey, N.L.; (81) 83-45-24-66; www.pixel.com.mx/info-gral/info-nl/religion/catolica/arqui.html.
Morelia* (1536, as Michoacan, promoted to an archdiocese 1863, name changed in 1924): Alberto Suárez Inda, archbishop, 1995; Enrique Díaz Díaz, Octavio Villegas Aguilar, Juan Esponosa Jimenez, auxiliaries.
Diocesan Address: Apartado 17, 58000 Morelia, Mich.; (443) 3-12-05-23.
Netzahualcóyotl (1979): Héctor Luis Morales Sánchez, bishop, 2011.
Diocesan Address: Apartado 89, 4 Avenida esq. Bellas Artes, Col. Evolución, 57700 Cuidad Netzahualcóyotl; (55) 57-97-61-32.
Nuestra Señora de los Mártires del Libano, Eparchy of (Maronites, 1995): Georges M. Saad Abi Younes, O.L.M., eparch, 2003.
Diocesan Address: Ntra. Sra. de Balvarena Correo Mayor #65, 06060 — México, D. F.; (55) 55-21-20-11.
Nuestra Señora del Paraiso, Eparchy of (Greek Melkites, 1988): Vacant.
Diocesan Address: Matías Romero 1014, Dpto. 601, Col. Del Valle, 3100 Mexico, D.F.; (5) 542-0225.
Nuevo Casas Grandes (1977): Gerardo de Jesús Rojas López, bishop, 2004.

Diocesan Address: Apartado Postal 198, Av. Hidalgo #105, 31700 Nuevo Casas Grandes, Chih.; (636) 6-94-05-20.
Nuevo Laredo (1989): Jesus Herrera Quinonez, bishop, 2011.
Diocesan Address: Saltillo 206, Apartado Postal #20-B, Col. México, 88280 Nuevo Laredo, Tamps.; (867) 7-15-29-28.
Oaxaca* (Also Antequera, 1535, promoted to archdiocese, 1891): José Luis Chávez Botello, archbishop, 2003; Miguel Ángel Alba Díaz, Gonzalo Calzada Guerrero, auxiliaries.
Diocesan Address: Apartado Postal #31, Garcia Vigil #600, 68000 Oaxaca, Oax.; (951) 6-20-49.
Orizaba (2000): Marcelino Hernández Rodríguez, bishop, 2008. Diocesan Address: Templo de Ntra. Sra. del Carmen, Sur 9 # 142 esq. Oriente 4, Apdo. Postal # 151, 94300 - Orizaba, Ver.; (272) 7-24-17-33.
Papantla (1922): José Trinidad Zapata Ortiz, bishop, 2014.
Diocesan Address: Apartado 27, Juárez 1102, 73800 Teziutlán, Pue.; (231) 3-24-30.
Parral (1992): Eduardo Carmona Ortega, O.R.C., bishop, 2012.
Diocesan Address: Apartado Postal 313, Fray Bartolomé de las Casas #13, 33800 Parral, Chih.; (152) 2-03-71.
Piedras Negras (2003): Alonso Gerardo Garza Treviño, first bishop, 2003. Diocesan address: Hidalgo Sur # 404 Centro 26000 - Piedras Negras, Coah.; (878) 7-82-94-80.
Puebla de los Angeles* (1525, as Tlaxcala, renamed in 1903): Victor Sánchez Espinosa, archbishop, 2009. Eugenio Lira Rugarcia, Dagoberto Sosa Arriaga, Tomás López Durán, Rutilo Felipe Pozos Lorenzini, auxiliaries.
Diocesan Address: Apartado 235, Av. 2, Sur N. 305, 72000 Puebla, Pue.; (222) 2-32-62-12.
Puerto Escondido (2003): Pedro Vazquez Villalobos, first bishop, 2012.
Diocesan Address: Felipe Merklin s/n, Col. Centro Puerto Escondido, Oax; 954-582-36-77.
Querétaro (1863): Faustino Armendariz Jimenez, bishop, 2011.
Diocesan Address: Apartado Postal 49, Reforma #48, 76000 Querétaro, Qro.; (42) 12-10-33.
Saltillo (1891): Raul Vera López, O.P., bishop, 1999.
Diocesan Address: Hidalgo Sur 166, Apartado 25, 25000 Saltillo, Coah.; (844) 4-12-37-84.
San Andrés Tuxtla (1959): José Trinidad Zapata Ortiz, bishop, 2004.
Diocesan Address: Constitución y Morelos, 95700 San Andrés Tuxtla, Ver.; (294) 9-42-03-74.
San Cristóbal de las Casas (1539, as Chiapas, renamed in 1964): Felipe Arizmendi Esquivel, bishop, 2000; Enrique Díaz Díaz, coadjutor bishop, 2014.
Diocesan Address: 5 de Feb. y 20 de Nov. # 1 Centro 29200 — San Cristóbal las Casas, Chis; (967) 6-78-00-53; www.laneta.apc.org/curiasc.
San Juan de los Lagos (1972): Felipe Salazar Villagrana, bishop, 2008.
Diocesan Address: Morelos 30, Apartado #1, 47000 San Juan de los Lagos, Jal.; (395) 7-85-05-70; www.redial.com.mx/obispado/index.htm.
San Luis Potosí* (1854, promoted to an arch-

diocese, 1988): Jesus Cabrero Romero, archbishop, 2012.
Diocesan Address: Madero #300, Apartado N. 1, 78000 - San Luis Potosí, S.L.P.; (444) 8-12-45-55.
Tabasco (1880): Gerardo de Jesús Rojas López, bishop, 2010.
Diocesan Address: Apartado Postal 97, Fidencia 502, 86000 Villahermosa, Tab.; (93) 12-13-97.
Tacámbaro (1913): Luis Castro Medellín, M.S.F., bishop, 2002.
Diocesan Address: Apartado 4, Professor Enrique Aguilar 49, 61650 Tacámbaro, Mich.; (459) 6-00-44.
Tampico (1870, as Ciudad Victoria o Tamaulipas, renamed in 1958): José Luis Dibildox Martinez, bishop, 2003.
Diocesan Address: Apartado 545, Altamira 116 Oriente, 89000 Tampico, Tamps.; (12) 12-28-02.
Tapachula (1957): Leopoldo González González, bishop, 2005.
Diocesan Address: Apartado 70, Av. Primera Sur 1, 30700 Tapachula, Chiapas; (962) 6-15-03; www.diocesis-tapachula.org.mx.
Tarahumara (1958, as a vicariate apostolic, promoted to diocese, 1993): Rafael Sandoval Sandoval, M.N.M., bishop, 2005.
Diocesan Address: Apartado Postal 11, Av. López Mateos #7, 33190 Guachochi, Chih.; (649) 5-43-02-23.
Tehuacán (1962): Rodrigo Aguilar Martínez, bishop, 2006.
Diocesan Address: Apartado Postal 137, Agustin A. Cacho 107, 75700 Tehuacán, Pue.; (238) 3-83-14-68.
Tehuantepec (1891): Oscar Armando Campos Contreras, bishop, 2010.
Diocesan Address: Apartado Postal 93, Mina s/n. Anexos de Catedral, 70760 Tehuantepec, Oax.; (971) 7-15-00-60.
Tenancingo (2009): Raul Gomez Gonzalez, first bishop, 2009.
Diocesan Address: N/A.
Teotihuacan (2008): Francisco Escobar Galicia, bishop, 2008.
Diocesan Address: N/A.
Tepic (1891): Luis Flores Calzada, bishop, 2012.
Diocesan Address: Apartado 15, Av. de las Flores 10, Fracciónamiento Residencial La Loma, 63137 Tepic, Nay.; (311) 2-14-46-45.
Texcoco (1960): Juan Manuel Mancilla Sanchez, bishop, 2009; Víctor René Rodríguez Gómez, auxiliary.
Diocesan Address: Apartado Postal 35, Fray Pedro de Gante 2, 56100 Texcoco, Méx.; (595) 4-08-69.
Tijuana* (1963, promoted to archdiocese, 2006): Rafael Romo Muñoz, bishop, 1996-2006, first archbishop, 2006.
Diocesan Address: Apartado 226, Calle 10ª y Av. Ocampo # 1049, 22000 Tijuana, B.C.N.; (664) 6-84-84-11 y 12; www.iglesiatijuana.org.
Tlalnepantla* (1964, promoted to archdiocese, 1989): Carlos Aguiar Retes, archbishop, 2009; Francisco Ramírez Navarro, Efrain Mendoza Cruz, auxiliary.
Diocesan Address: Apartado 268 y 270, Av. Juárez 42, 54000 Tlalnepantla, Méx.; (55) 55-65-39-44.
Tlapa (1992): Dagoberto Sosa Arriaga, bishop, 2013.
Diocesan Address: Anexo Catedral, Centro, 41300 Tlapa de Comonfort, Gro.; (757) 4-76-08-35.
Tlaxcala (1959): Francisco Moreno Barrón, bishop, 2001.

Diocesan Address: Apartado 84, Lardizábal 45, 90000 Tlaxcala, Tlax.; (246) 4-62-32-43.
Toluca (1950): Francisco Javier Chavolla Ramos, bishop, 2003.
Diocesan Address: Apartado 82, Portal Reforma Norte 104, 50000 Toluca, Méx.; (72) 15-25-35; www.diocesistoluca.org.mx.
Torreón (1957): Vacant.
Diocesan Address: Apartado Postal 430, Av. Morelos 46 Poniente, 27000 Torreón, Coah.; (871) 7-12-30-43.
Tula (1961): Juan Pedro Juárez Meléndez, bishop, 2006.
Diocesan Address: 5 de Mayo, #5, Apartado 31, 42800 Tula de Allende, Hgo.; (773) 7-32-02-75.
Tulancingo* (1863, promoted to archdiocese, 2006): Domingo Díaz Martínez, archbishop, 2008.
Diocesan Address: Apartado #14, Plaza de la Constitución, 43600 Tulancingo, Hgo.; (775) 3-10-10.
Tuxpan (1962): Juan Navarro Castellanos, bishop, 2009.
Diocesan Address: Independencia #56, 92870 Tuxpan, Ver.; (783) 4-16-36.
Tuxtepec (1979): José Antonio Fernández Hurtado, bishop, 2005.
Diocesan Address: Bonfil #597, entre Juárez y Villa Col. Santa Fe Apartado Postal 9, 68320 — Tuxtepec, Oax.; (287) 5-00-42.
Tuxtla Gutiérrez* (1964, promoted to archdiocese, 2006): Fabio Martinez Castilla, archbishop, 2013. José Mendoza Corzo, auxiliary.
Diocesan Address: Uruguay #500 A Col. El Retiro Apdo. Postal # 36529040 - Tuxtla Gutiérrez, Chis.; (961) 6-04-06-44; www.chisnet.com.mx/~cosi/obispado.
Valle de Chalco (2003): Victor Rene Rodriguez Gomez, first bishop, 2012.
Diocesan Address: Calle Colorines 12, Col. Granjas, 56600 Chalco, Mex.
Veracruz (1962): Luis Felipe Gallardo Martín del Campo, S.D.B., bishop, 2006.
Diocesan Address: Insurgentes Veracruzanos #470, Paseo del Malecón, 91700 Veracruz, Ver.; (229) 9-31-24-13.
Xalapa* (1962; originally Veracruz and Xalapa, 1863; promoted to archdiocese, 1951): Hipolito Reyes Larios, archbishop, 2007.
Diocesan Address: Apartado 359, Av. Manuel Avila Camacho #73, 91000 Xalapa, Ver.; (228) 8-12-05-79.
Yucatán* (1561, promoted to archdiocese, 1906): Emilio Carlos Berlie Belaunzarán, archbishop, 1995; José Rafael Palma Capetillo, auxiliary.
Diocesan Address: Calle 58 N. 501, 97000 Mérida, Yuc.; (99) 23-79-83; www.geocities.com/SoHo/207/principa.html.
Zacatecas (1863): Sigifredo Moriega Barcelo, bishop, 2012.
Diocesan Address: Apartado #1, Miguel Auza #219, 98000 Zacatecas, Zacatecas; (492) 9-22-02-32; www.logicnet.com.mx/obispado.
Zamora (1863): Javier Navarro Rodríguez, bishop, 2007; Jaime Calderon Calderon, auxiliary.
Diocesan Address: Altos de Catedral (Calle Hidalgo), Apartado Postal #18, 59600 Zamora, Mich.; (351) 5-12-12-08.

CONFERENCIA DEL EPISCOPADO MEXICANO

(Sources: *Annuario Pontificio;* Pbro. Jorge Fco. Vázquez M., Secretario Adjunto, Conferencia del Episcopado Mexicano; *Conferencia del Episcopado Mexicano, Directorio, 2014*; translation courtesy Suzanne Lea.)

STRUCTURE

The Mexican Conference of Bishops (CEM, *Conferencia del Episcopado Mexicano*) is the permanent body of Mexican bishops. The bishops adhere to the guidelines of the conference in specific fulfillment of their pastoral labors. They do this in order to obtain the greatest good for the people that the church can achieve. The conference proposes:

1) To study the problems that occur in pastoral work, and to seek solutions. 2) To initiate, with a common end in mind and a common course of action, the forms and methods of preaching that best suit the needs of the country. 3) In regard to the collective salvific mission of the church: To look for and to teach the best way in which the respective activities of the deacons, priests, religious, and lay person will be most efficient. 4) To facilitate relations with the civil authority and with other organizations in specific cases. 5) To write to the Episcopal commission regarding patrimonial and proprietary matters, and give counsel on determined financial or labor related points.

All those elected to the body of the CEM will have three years of service and will not be reelected to the same position after two three-year sessions have been completed consecutively.

The address of the conference headquarters is: Prolongación Misterios No. 26, Col. Tepeyac Insurgentes, 07020 México, D.F. Tels. (01-55) 5577-5401; www.cem.org.mx.

Permanent Assembly

The Permanent Assembly is the representative arm of the bishops belonging to the CEM. Its function is to ensure the continuation of the works of the conference and the fulfillment of its accords.

The Permanent Assembly is comprised of the Presidential Assembly and the Assembly of Pastoral Regions. It meets four times per year in ordinary session. It meets in extraordinary sessions whenever the majority of its members or those of the Presidential Assembly determine it to be necessary.

A session is valid if two-thirds of the members are present.

Officers

President: Card. José Francisco Robles Ortega of Guadalajara.

Vice-President: Bp. Javier Navarro Rodríguez of Zamora.

Secretary General: Bp. Eugenio Andrés Lira Rugarcía, aux. bishop of Puebla.

General Treasurer: Bishop Oscar Roberto Domínguez Couttolenc of Tlapa.

Spokesmen: Bp. Oscar Roberto Domínguez Couttolenc., MG of Ecatepec; Bp. Sigifredo Noriega Barceló of Zacatecas; Abp. Carlos Garfias Merlos of Acapulco.

Commissions

Biblical Studies: Bishop Florencio Colin Cruz.

Doctrine: Bishop José Guadalupe Martin Rabago.

Culture: Bishop Felipe Arizmendi Esquivel.

Education: Bishop Alfonso Cortes Contreras.

Health Care: Bishop Emigdio Duarte Figueroa.

Liturgy: Bishop Victor Sanchez Espinosa.

Missions: Bishop Rafael Sandoval Sandoval.

Pastoral Sanctuaries: Bishop Felipe Salazar Villagrana.

Catechesis: Bishop José Antonio Fernandez Hurtado.

Social Justice: Bishop Ramon Castro.

Clergy: Bishop Marcelino Hernández.

Social Communications: Bishop Luis Artemio Calzada Flores.

Interreligious Dialogue: Card. Francisco Robles Ortega.

Consecrated Life: Bishop Roberto Balmori Cinta, M.J.

Diaconate: Bishop José Trinidad Zapata Ortiz.

Lay Apostolates: Bishop Eduardo Carmona Ortega.

Priestly Formation: Bishop José Francisco Gonzalez.

Seminaries and Vocations: Bishop José Luis Amezcua.

STATISTICAL SUMMARY OF THE CATHOLIC CHURCH IN MEXICO

(Principal sources: *Annuario Pontificio, 2014; Annuarium Statisticum Ecclesiae, 2012* (the most recent edition); Conferencia del Espiscopado Mexicano, Directorio, 2014; figures as of January 2013. Catholic population statistics are those reported in the most recent *Annuario* population estimates. Archdioceses are indicated by an asterisk.) Includes 18 provinces: 18 archdioceses, 68 dioceses, 5 prelacies, and two eparchies. There are 170 total prelates: 4 Cardinals, 26 Archbishops, 61 Bishops, 28 Auxiliary or Coadjutor Bishops, 48 Retired Bishops, and 2 Eparchs. The Catholic population of Mexico comprises approximately 92% of the overall Mexican population of 110,292,000 according to the Conferencia del Episcopado Mexicano, Directorio, 2014 (the most recent edition). In 2013, there were 1,868,754 baptisms and 280,896 marriages. This table presents a provincial breakdown of Catholic statistics. The population totals are approximate.

Province Diocese	Cath. Pop.	Dioc. Priests	Rel. Priests	Total Priests	Perm. Deacs.	Brothers	Sisters	Parishes
Acapulco	**4,973,000**	**336**	**68**	**404**	**23**	**100**	**466**	**215**
Acapulco*	2,623,000	104	30	134	22	37	132	76
Chilpancingo-Chilapa	889,000	125	16	141	1	16	188	75
Ciudad Altamirano	980,000	67	5	73	–	19	81	36
Tlapa	481,000	40	17	57	–	28	65	28
Baja California	**4,370,000**	**394**	**114**	**508**	**13**	**180**	**837**	**221**
Tijuana*	2,225,000	156	61	217	10	108	474	99
Ensenada	447,000	32	18	50	–	20	71	28

Province Diocese	Cath. Pop.	Dioc. Priests	Rel. Priests	Total Priests	Perm. Deacs.	Bro- thers	Sis- ters	Par- ishes
Baja California, con't.								
La Paz	528,000	59	19	78	1	20	151	39
Mexicali	1,170,000	147	16	163	2	32	141	55
Bajío	**7,094,000**	**744**	**342**	**1,086**	**14**	**503**	**2,202**	**373**
León*	2,437,000	230	118	348	12	197	665	123
Celaya	1,516,000	167	69	236	–	83	377	70
Irapuato	1,190,000	123	46	169	2	51	231	67
Querétaro	1,941,000	224	109	333	–	172	929	113
Chiapas	**3,814,000**	**266**	**70**	**336**	**320**	**109**	**689**	**173**
Tuxtla Gutiérrez*	1,014,000	118	18	136	–	45	347	68
San Cristobal	1,325,000	61	44	105	320	56	194	57
Tapachula	1,475,000	87	8	95	–	8	148	48
Chihuahua	**4,865,000**	**331**	**101**	**432**	**21**	**123**	**606**	**225**
Chihuahua*	1,385,000	119	27	146	8	33	161	66
Ciudad Juárez	2,318,000	91	19	110	–	29	177	73
Cuauhtémoc-Madera	351,000	32	10	42	–	11	56	26
Nuevo Casas Grandes	135,000	27	2	29	1	5	44	25
Parral	372,000	40	13	53	10	13	56	20
Tarahumara	304,000	22	30	52	2	32	112	15
Durango	**3,455,000**	**401**	**64**	**465**	**–**	**95**	**518**	**507**
Durango*	1,170,000	154	24	178	–	42	233	92
El Salto	337,000	27	–	27	–	2	19	15
Mazatlán	774,000	79	8	87	–	9	106	48
Torreón	706,000	91	31	122	–	33	93	314
Gómez Palacio	468,000	50	1	50	–	9	67	38
Guadalajara	**12,019,000**	**2,215**	**447**	**2,662**	**19**	**920**	**2,754**	**910**
Guadalajara*	5,355,000	1,116	353	1,469	3	665	821	459
Aguascalientes	1,667,000	269	39	308	1	56	668	108
Autlán	337,000	116	–	116	3	–	194	49
Ciudad Guzmán	459,000	91	19	110	–	52	110	59
Colima	627,000	119	5	124	–	9	304	53
San Juan los Lagos	1,074,000	293	15	308	–	106	413	77
Tepic	1,154,000	201	4	205	11	8	197	90
Jesús Maria of Nayar	139,000	10	12	22	1	24	47	15
Hermosillo	**3,877,000**	**426**	**21**	**447**	**5**	**114**	**451**	**225**
Hermosillo*	1,088,000	133	3	136	1	7	117	75
Ciudad Obregón	946,000	118	15	133	–	29	134	65
Culiacán	1,843,000	175	3	178	4	78	200	85
Hidalgo	**3,172,000**	**318**	**21**	**339**	**2**	**34**	**337**	**181**
Tulancingo	*1,575,000	154	6	160	1	19	179	88
Huejutla	547,000	91	7	98	–	7	62	47
Tula	1,050,000	73	8	81	1	8	96	46
Mexico	**12,937,000**	**1,132**	**1,139**	**2,271**	**151**	**2,253**	**6,104**	**791**
Mexico*	7,364,000	594	1,037	1,631	149	2,046	5,170	456
Atlacomulco	949,000	115	3	118	1	4	100	66
Cuernavaca	1,936,000	135	49	184	1	139	407	108
Tenancingo	368,000	40	17	57	–	25	97	32
Toluca	2,320,000	248	33	281	–	39	330	129
Monterrey	**10,721,000**	**935**	**334**	**1,269**	**58**	**663**	**1,512**	**506**
Monterrey*	4,512,000	384	211	595	44	499	736	188
Ciudad Victoria	412,000	51	9	60	–	14	89	35
Linares	360,000	39	3	42	–	3	55	22
Matamoros	1,826,000	104	9	113	5	12	114	55
Nuevo Laredo	884,000	52	19	71	8	26	87	44
Piedras Negras	358,000	50	13	63	–	17	87	32

Province Diocese	Cath. Pop.	Dioc. Priests	Rel. Priests	Total Priests	Perm. Deacs.	Bro- thers	Sis- sters	Par- ishes
Monterrey, cont.								
Saltillo	1,191,000	132	56	188	1	76	326	63
Tampico	1,178,000	123	14	137	–	16	18	67
Morelia	**5,479,000**	**915**	**186**	**1,101**	**–**	**302**	**2,162**	**468**
Morelia*	2,455,000	429	136	565	–	222	1,064	236
Apatzingán	373,000	59	–	59	–	–	126	27
Ciudad Lázaro Cárdenas	794,000	31	15	46	–	20	68	24
Tacámbaro	355,000	86	2	88	–	2	121	41
Zamora	1,502,000	310	33	343	–	58	783	140
Oaxaca	**4,317,000**	**310**	**94**	**403**	**50**	**107**	**399**	**253**
Oaxaca*	1,438,000	144	37	181	21	40	199	122
Huautla1	134,000	18	4	22	1	5	3	9
Mixes1	142,000	14	25	39	18	31	37	18
Puerto Escondido	483,000	41	8	49	–	8	55	29
Tehuantepec	1,389,000	52	12	63	–	15	81	47
Tuxtepec	730,000	41	8	49	10	8	24	28
Puebla de los Angeles	**7,797,000**	**727**	**186**	**913**	**4**	**238**	**1,203**	**479**
Puebla de los Angeles*	4,484,000	387	160	547	2	208	720	277
Huajuapan de León	1,225,000	112	–	112	1	–	148	72
Tehuacán	1,005,000	91	8	99	–	8	130	57
Tlaxcala	1,083,000	137	18	155	1	22	205	73
San Luis Potosi	**4,331,000**	**537**	**101**	**638**	**11**	**251**	**1,426**	**286**
San Luis Potosi*	1,892,000	226	75	301	11	218	839	113
Ciudad Valles	1,019,000	69	15	84	–	18	138	47
Matehuala	250,000	32	3	35	–	3	36	17
Zacatecas	1,170,000	210	8	218	–	12	413	109
Tlalnepantla	**15,226,239**	**952**	**141**	**1,086**	**50**	**408**	**1,031**	**616**
Tlalnepantla*	1,953,000	273	39	312	9	100	247	200
Cuautitlan	3,516,000	162	22	184	–	43	260	67
Ecatepec	1,488,000	160	13	173	23	31	72	97
Netzahualcóyotl	3,630,000	112	27	139	–	51	98	83
Teotihuacan	799,000	65	–	65	11	–	95	24
Texcoco	1,480,000	113	13	126	7	154	169	86
Valle de Chalco	2,360,000	67	27	87	–	29	90	59
Xalapa	**9,018,000**	**776**	**52**	**829**	**46**	**73**	**1,089**	**449**
Xalapa*	1,206,000	150	4	154	–	4	319	83
Coatzacoalcos	895,000	61	1	62	1	2	75	25
Cordoba	698,000	82	1	83	–	8	161	44
Orizaba	589,000	77	12	89	–	16	120	43
Papantla	1,744,000	101	–	101	1	–	134	58
San Andrés Tuxtla	1,035,000	97	3	100	33	9	100	61
Tuxpan	910,000	96	–	97	1	1	21	62
Veracruz	1,941,000	112	31	143	11	33	159	73
Yucatán	**5,015,000**	**466**	**185**	**651**	**76**	**248**	**993**	**317**
Yucatán*	1,614,000	179	49	228	34	72	540	108
Campeche	652,000	117	16	133	7	48	161	60
Tabasco	1,520,000	141	25	166	15	27	160	91
Cancún-Chetumal1	1,028,000	19	88	107	19	94	129	55
Nuestra Sra. de los Mártires2	154,000	8	4	12	1	4	–	3
Nuestra Sra. del Paraiso2	4,700	2	3	5	–	3	3	–
Totals:	**101,350,0003**	**12,181**	**3,666**	**15,847**	**863**	**6,721**	**24,779**	**7,165**

Note: 1. Prelacy. 2. Eparchy. 3. According to the Conferencia del Episcopado Mexicano and the *Annuarium Statisticum Ecclesiae.*

Consecrated Life

INSTITUTES OF CONSECRATED LIFE

Religious institutes and congregations are special societies in the Church — institutes of consecrated life — whose members, called Religious, commit them selves by public vows to observance of the evangelical counsels of poverty, chastity and obedience in a community kind of life in accordance with rules and constitutions approved by Church authority.

Secular institutes (covered in their own *Almanac* entries) are also institutes of consecrated life.

The particular goal of each institute and the means of realizing it in practice are stated in the rule and constitutions proper to the institute. Local bishops can give approval for rules and constitutions of institutes of diocesan rank. Pontifical rank belongs to institutes approved by the Holy See. General jurisdiction over all religious is exercised by the Congregation for Institutes of Consecrated Life and Societies of Apostolic Life. General legislation concerning religious is contained in Canons 573 to 709 in Book II, Part III, of the Code of Canon Law.

All institutes of consecrated life are commonly called religious orders, despite the fact that there are differences between orders and congregations. The best known orders include the Benedictines, Trappists, Franciscans, Dominicans, Carmelites and Augustinians, for men; and the Carmelites, Benedictines, Poor Clares, Dominicans of the Second Order and Visitation Nuns, for women. The orders are older than the congregations, which did not appear until the 16th century.

Contemplative institutes are oriented to divine worship and service within the confines of their communities, by prayer, penitential practices, other spiritual activities and self-supporting work. Examples are the Trappists and Carthusians, the Carmelite and Poor Clare nuns. Active institutes are geared for pastoral ministry and various kinds of apostolic work. Mixed institutes combine elements of the contemplative and active ways of life. While most institutes of men and women can be classified as active, all of them have contemplative aspects.

Clerical communities of men are those whose membership is predominantly composed of priests.

Non-clerical or lay institutes of men are the various brotherhoods.

"The Consecrated Life and Its Role in the Church and in the World" was the topic of the ninth general assembly of the Synod of Bishops held Oct. 2-29, 1994.

Societies of Apostolic Life

Some of the institutes listed below have a special kind of status because their members, while living a common life characteristic of religious, do not profess the vows of religious. Examples are the Maryknoll Fathers, the Oratorians of St. Philip Neri, the Paulists and Sulpicians. They are called societies of apostolic life and are the subject of Canons 731 to 746 of the Code of Canon Law.

RELIGIOUS INSTITUTES OF MEN IN THE UNITED STATES

Sources: Annuario Pontificio, The Official Catholic Directory; Catholic Almanac *survey. As of June 1, 2014.*

Africa, Missionaries of, M. Afr.: Founded 1868 at Algiers by Cardinal Charles M. Lavigerie; known as White Fathers until 1984. Generalate, Rome, Italy. U.S. headquarters, 1624 21st St. N.W., Washington, DC 20009, (202) 232-5154. Missionary work in Africa.

African Missions, Society of, S.M.A.: Founded 1856, at Lyons, France, by Bishop Melchior de Marion Brésillac. Generalate, Rome, Italy. American province (1941), 23 Bliss Ave., Tenafly, NJ 07670, (201) 567-9085, www.smafathers.com. Missionary work.

Alexian Brothers, C.F.A.: Founded 14th century in western Germany and Belgium during the Black Plague. Motherhouse, Aachen, Germany. Generalate, 198 James Blvd., Signal Mountain, TN 37377, (423) 886-0380. Hospital and general health work.

Apostolic Life Community of Priests in the Opus Spiritus Sancti, A.L.C.P./O.S.S. (Holy Spirit Fathers): Founded 1974 in Moshi, Tanzania, by German Fr. Bernard Bendel; In US, 1992; US address, Immaculate Heart Church, 2926 North Williams Ave. Portland, OR 97227, (503) 287-3724. educational and foreign mission work.

Assumptionists (Augustinians of the Assumption), A.A.: Founded 1845, at Nimes, France, by Rev. Emmanuel d'Alzon; in U.S., 1946. General House, Rome, Italy. U.S. province, 330 Market St., Brighton, MA 02135, (617) 783-0400, www.assumption.us. Educational, parochial, ecumenical, retreat, foreign mission work.

Atonement, Franciscan Friars of the, S.A.: Founded as an Anglican Franciscan community in 1898 at Garrison, NY, by Fr. Paul Wattson. Community corporately received into the Catholic Church in 1909. Generalate, St. Paul's Friary, Graymoor, Rte. 9, PO Box 300, Garrison, NY 10524, (914) 424-2113; www.atonementfriars.org Ecumenical, mission, retreat and charitable works.

Augustinian Recollects, O.A.R.: Founded 1588; in U.S., 1944. General motherhouse, Rome, Italy. *Monastery of St. Cloud* (formerly St. Augustine Province, 1944), 29 Ridgeway Ave., West Orange, NJ 07052-3217, (973) 731-0616, www.augustinianrecollects.us. St. Nicholas of Tolentino Province (U.S. Delegation), *St. Nicholas of Tolentino Monastery,*

3201 Central Ave., Union City, NJ 07087, (201) 422-7550. Missionary, parochial, education work.

Augustinians (Order of St. Augustine), O.S.A.: Established canonically in 1256 by Pope Alexander IV; in U.S., 1796. General motherhouse, Rome, Italy. *St. Thomas Monastery*, 800 Lancaster Ave., Villanova, PA 19085-1687, (610) 519-4674, www. augustinians.org., (1796). *Our Mother of Good Counsel Province* (1941), 5401 S. Cornell Ave., Chicago, IL 60615, (773) 595-4000, www.mid-weststaugustinians.org. *Province of St. Augustine,* (1969), 1605 28th St., San Diego, CA 92102-1417, (619) 235-0247.

Barnabites (Clerics Regular of St. Paul), C.R.S.P.: Founded 1530, in Milan, Italy, by St. Anthony M. Zaccaria; approved 1533; in U.S., 1952. Historical motherhouse, Church of St. Barnabas (Milan). Generalate, Rome, Italy. North American province, 981 Swann Rd, PO Box 167, Youngstown, NY 14174, (716) 754-7489, www.barnabites.com. Parochial, educational, mission work.

Basil the Great, Order of St. (Basilian Order of St. Josaphat), O.S.B.M.: General motherhouse, Rome, Italy. U.S. province, 29 Peacock Ln., Locust Valley, NY 11560, (516) 609-3262. Parochial work among Byzantine Ukrainian Rite Catholics.

Basilian Fathers (Congregation of the Priests of St. Basil), C.S.B.: Founded 1822, at Annonay, France. General motherhouse, Toronto, ON, Canada. U.S. address: 1910 W. Alabama, Houston, TX 77098, (713) 522-1736. Educational, parochial work.

Basilian Salvatorian Fathers, B.S.O.: Founded 1684, at Saida, Lebanon, by Eftimios Saifi; in U.S., 1953. General motherhouse, Saida, Lebanon. American headquarters, 30 East St., Methuen, MA 01844. Educational, parochial work among Eastern Rite peoples.

Benedictine Monks (Order of St. Benedict), O.S.B.: Founded 529, in Italy, by St. Benedict of Nursia; in U.S., 1846.

• **American Cassinese Congregation (1855)**. Pres., Rt. Rev. Melvin J. Valvano, O.S.B., Newark Abbey, 528 Dr. Martin Luther King Blvd., Newark, NJ 07102, (973) 733-2822. Abbeys and priories belonging to the congregation:

St. Vincent Archabbey, 300 Fraser Purchase Rd., Latrobe, PA 15650, (724) 805-2503, www. benedictine.stvincent.edu. *Saint John's Abbey*, P.O. Box 2015, Collegeville, MN 56321, (320) 363-2548, www.saintjohnsabbey.org. *St. Benedict's Abbey*, 1020 North Second St., Atchison, KS 66002, (913) 367-7853, www.kansasmonks.org. *St. Mary's Abbey*, 230 Mendham Rd., Morristown, NJ 07960, (973) 538-3231, www.osbmonks.org. *Newark Abbey*, 528 Dr. Martin Luther King, Jr., Blvd., Newark, NJ 07102, (973) 792-5700. *Belmont Abbey*, 100 Belmont Mt. Holly Rd., Belmont, NC 28012, (704) 461-6675, www.belmontabbey.org. *St. Bernard Abbey*, 1600 Saint Bernard Dr., Cullman, AL 35055, (256) 734-8291. *St. Gregory's Abbey*, 1900 W. MacArthur, Shawnee, OK 74804, (405) 878-5491, www.monksok.org. *St. Leo Abbey*, St. Leo, FL 33574, (352) 588-8624, www.saintleoabbey. org. *Assumption Abbey*, P.O. Box A, Richardton, ND 58652, (701) 974-3315. *St. Bede Abbey*, Peru, IL 61354, (815) 223-3140, www.theramp.net/stbede/

index.html. *St. Martin's Abbey*, 5000 Abbey Way, S.E., Lacey, WA 98503-3200, (360) 438-4440, www. stmartin.edu. *Holy Cross Abbey*, P.O. Box 1510, Canon City, CO 81215, (719) 275-8631, www.holy-crossabbey.org. *St. Anselm's Abbey*, 100 St. Anselm Dr., Manchester, NH, 03102, (603) 641-7651, www. anselm.edu. *Holy Trinity Priory*, P.O. Box 990, Butler, PA 16003, (724) 287-4461. *Benedictine Priory*, 6502 Seawright Dr., Savannah, GA 31406, (912) 644-7001, www.bcsav.net. *Woodside Priory*, 302 Portola Rd., Portola Valley, CA 94028, (650) 851-6133; www.prioryca.org. *Mary Mother of the Church Abbey*, 12829 River Rd., Richmond, VA 23233, (804) 784-3508, www.richmondmonks. org. *Abadia de San Antonio Abad*, P.O. Box 729, Humacao, PR 00792, (787) 852-1616; *St. Procopius Abbey*, 5601 College Rd., Lisle, IL 60532, (630) 969-6410, www.Procopius.org.

• **Swiss-American Congregation (1870)**. Abbeys and priory belonging to the congregation:

St. Meinrad Archabbey, 100 Hill Dr., St. Meinrad, IN 47577-1003, (812) 357-6514, www.saintmeinrad. edu. *Conception Abbey*, 37174 State Hwy., VV, Conception, MO 64433-0501, (660) 944-3100, www. conceptionabbey.org. *Mt. Michael Abbey*, 22520 Mt. Michael Rd., Elkhorn, NE 68022-3400, (402) 289-2541, www.mountmichael.org. *Subiaco Abbey,* Subiaco, AR 72865, (479) 934-1001, www.subi. org. *St. Joseph's Abbey*, St. Benedict, LA 70457, (504) 892-1800. *Mt. Angel Abbey*, St. Benedict, OR 97373, (503) 845-3030. *Marmion Abbey*, 850 Butterfield Rd., Aurora, IL 60502 (630) 897-7215. *St. Benedict's Abbey*, 12605 224th Ave., Benet Lake, WI 53102, (262) 396-4311, www.benetlake. org. *Glastonbury Abbey*, 16 Hull St., Hingham, MA 02043, (781) 749-2155, www.glastonburyab-bey.org. *Blue Cloud Abbey*, Marvin, SD 57251-0098, (605) 398-9200, www.bluecloud.org. *Corpus Christi Abbey*, 101 South Vista Dr., Sandia, TX 78383, (361) 547-3257, www.geocities.com/Athens/styx/8125/ccabbey.html. *Prince of Peace Abbey*, 650 Benet Hill Rd., Oceanside, CA 92054, (760) 967-4200, www.princeofpeaceabbey.org. *St. Benedict Abbey*, 254 Still River Rd., PO Box 22, Still River (Harvard), MA 01467, (978) 456-8017.

• **Congregation of St. Ottilien for Foreign Missions:** St. Paul's Abbey, PO Box 7, 289 Rt. 206 South, Newton, NJ 07860, (973) 383-2470. Christ the King Priory, PO Box 528, Schuyler, NE 68661, (402) 615-2331, www.missionmonks.com.

• **Congregation of the Annunciation**, St. Andrew Abbey, P.O. Box 40, Valyermo, CA 93563-0040, (661) 944-2178, www.valyermo.com.

• **English Benedictine Congregation**: St. Anselm's Abbey, 4501 S. Dakota Ave. N.E., Washington, DC 20017, (202) 269-2300. Abbey of St. Gregory the Great, Cory's Lane, Portsmouth, RI 02871-1352, (401) 683-2000. Abbey of St. Mary and St. Louis, 500 S. Mason Rd., St. Louis, MO 63141-8500, (314) 434-3690, www.priory.org, www.stlouisabbey.org.

• **Houses Not in Congregations**: Mount Saviour Monastery, 231 Monastery Rd., Pine City, NY 14871-9787, (607) 734-1688, www.servtech. com/~msaviour; Weston Priory, 58 Priory Hill Rd., Weston, VT 05161-6400, (802) 824-5409, www. westonpriory.org.

Benedictines, Camaldolese Hermits of America, O.S.B. Cam.: Founded 1012, at Camaldoli, near Arezzo, Italy, by St. Romuald; in U.S., 1958. General motherhouse, Arezzo, Italy. U.S. foundation, New Camaldoli Hermitage, 62475 Highway 1, Big Sur, CA 93920, (831) 667-2456, www.contemplation.org.

Benedictines, Olivetan, O.S.B.: General motherhouse, Siena, Italy. U.S. monasteries: *Our Lady of Guadalupe Abbey*, PO Box 1080, Pecos, NM 87552, (505) 757-6600, www.pecosabbey.org. *Holy Trinity Monastery*, P.O. Box 298, St. David, AZ 85630-0298, (520) 720-4642, www.holytrinitymonastery.org. *Monastery of the Risen Christ*, P.O. Box 3931, San Luis Obispo, CA 93403-3931, (805) 544-1810. *Benedictine Monastery of Hawaii*, PO Box 490, Waialua, HI 96791, (808) 637-7887, www.Hawaiibenedictines.org.

Benedictines, Subiaco Congregation, O.S.B.: Independent priory, 1983. Monastery of Christ in the Desert, Abiquiu, NM 87510, (505) 470-6668, www.christdesert.org. St. Mary's Monastery, P.O. Box 345, Petersham, MA 01366, (978) 724-3350.

Benedictines, Sylvestrine, O.S.B.: Founded 1231, in Italy, by Sylvester Gozzolini. General motherhouse, Rome, Italy. U.S. foundations: 17320 Rosemont Rd., Detroit, MI 48219, (313) 531-0140. 2711 E. Drahner Rd., Oxford, MI 48370, (248) 628-2249, www.benedictinemonks.org. 1697 State Highway 3, Clifton, NJ 07012, (201) 778-1177.

Blessed Sacrament, Congregation of the, S.S.S.: Founded 1856, at Paris, France, by St. Pierre Julien Eymard; in U.S., 1900. General motherhouse, Rome, Italy. U.S. province, 5384 Wilson Mills Rd., Cleveland, OH 44143-3092, (440) 442-6311, www.blessedsacrament.com. Eucharistic apostolate.

Brigittine Monks (Order of the Most Holy Savior), O.Ss.S.: Monastery of Our Lady of Consolation, 23300 Walker Lane, Amity, OR 97101, (503) 835-8080, www.brigittine.org.

Camaldolese Hermits of the Congregation of Monte Corona, Er. Cam.: Founded 1520, from Camaldoli, Italy, by Bl. Paul Giustiniani; in U.S., 1959; motherhouse, Frascati (Rome), Italy. U.S. foundation, Holy Family Hermitage, 1501 Fairplay Rd., Bloomingdale, OH 43910-7971, (740) 765-4511.

Camillian Fathers and Brothers (Order of St. Camillus; Order of Servants of the Sick), O.S.Cam.: Founded 1582, at Rome, by St. Camillus de Lellis; in U.S., 1923. General motherhouse, Rome, Italy. North American province, 3345 South 1st St., Milwaukee, WI 53215, (414) 481-3696, www.camillians.org.

Carmelites (Order of Our Lady of Mt. Carmel), O. Carm.: General motherhouse, Rome, Italy. Most Pure Heart of Mary Province (1864), 1317 Frontage Rd., Darien, IL 60559, (630) 971-0050. North American Province of St. Elias (1931), PO Box 3079, Middletown, NY 10940-0890, (845) 344-2225; www.carmelitefriars.org. Mt. Carmel Hermitage, Pineland, R.R. 1, Box 330 C, Bolivar, PA, 15923, (724) 238-0423. Educational, charitable work.

Carmelites, Order of Discalced, O.C.D.: Established 1562, a Reform Order of Our Lady of Mt. Carmel; in U.S., 1924. Generalate, Rome, Italy. *Western Province* (1983), 926 E. Highland Ave., P.O. Box 2178, Redlands, CA 92373, (909) 793-0424; www.ocdwest.org. *Province of*

St. Thérèse (Oklahoma,1935), 515 Marylake Dr., Little Rock AR 72206, (501) 888-5827. *Immaculate Heart of Mary Province* (1947), 1233 S. 45th St., Milwaukee, WI 53214, (414) 672-7212. *Our Lady of Mt. Carmel Monastery*, 1628 Ridge Rd., Munster, IN 46321, (219) 838-7111, www.carmelitefathers.com. Spiritual direction, retreat, parochial work.

Carmelites of Mary Immaculate, C.M.I.: Founded 1831, in India, by Bl. Kuriakose Elias Chavara and two other Syro-Malabar priests; canonically established, 1855. Generalate, Kerala, India. North American headquarters, St. Anthony Church, 862 Manhattan Ave, Brooklyn, NY 11222, (718) 383-3339.

Carthusians, Order of, O. Cart.: Founded 1084, in France, by St. Bruno; in U.S., 1951. General motherhouse, St. Pierre de Chartreuse, France. U.S., Charterhouse of the Transfiguration, Carthusian Monastery, 1084 Ave Maria Way, Arlington, VT 05250, (802) 362-2550, www.transfiguration.chartreux.org. Cloistered contemplatives; semi-eremitic.

Charity, Brothers of, F.C.: Founded 1807, in Belgium, by Canon Peter J. Triest. General motherhouse, Rome, Italy. American District (1963), 7720 Doe Lane, Laverock, PA 19038.

Charity, Servants of (Guanellians), S.C.: Founded 1908, in Italy, by Bl. Luigi Guanella. General motherhouse, Rome, Italy. U.S. headquarters, St. Louis School, 16195 Old U.S. 12, Chelsea, MI 48118, (734) 475-8430, www.stlouiscenter.org.

Christ, Society of, S.Ch.: Founded 1932. General Motherhouse, Poznan, Poland; U.S.-Canadian Province, 3000 Eighteen Mile Rd., Sterling Heights, MI 48311.

Christian Brothers, Congregation of, C.F.C. (formerly Christian Brothers of Ireland): Founded 1802 at Waterford, Ireland, by Bl. Edmund Ignatius Rice; in U.S., 1906. General motherhouse, Rome, Italy. American Province, Eastern U.S. (1916), 33 Pryer Terr., New Rochelle, NY 10804, (914) 712-7580. Brother Rice Province, Western U.S. (1966), 958 Western Ave., Joliet, IL 60435, (815) 723-5464. Educational work.

Christian Instruction, Brothers of (La Mennais Brothers), F.I.C.: Founded 1817, at Ploermel, France, by Abbe Jean Marie de la Mennais and Abbe Gabriel Deshayes. General motherhouse, Rome, Italy. American province, Notre Dame Institute, P.O. Box 159, Alfred, ME 04002, (207) 324-0067, www.ficbrothers.org.

Christian Schools, Brothers of the (Christian Brothers), F.S.C.: Founded 1680, at Reims, France, by St. Jean Baptiste de la Salle. General motherhouse, Rome, Italy. U.S. Conference, 4351 Garden City Dr., Suite 200, Landover, MD 20785, (301) 459-9410, www.cbconf.org. Baltimore Province (1845), Box 29, Adamstown, MD 21710-0029, (301) 874-5188, www.fscbaltimore.org. Brothers of the Christian Schools (Midwest Province) (1995), 7650 S. County Line Rd., Burr Ridge, IL 60527-4718, (630) 323-3725, www.cbmidwest.org. New York Province (1848), 444 A Route 35 South, Eatontown, NJ 07724, (732) 380-7926, www.fscdena.org. Long Island-New England Province (1957), Christian Brothers Center, 635 Ocean Rd., Narragansett, RI 02882-1314, (401) 789-0244, www.cbline.org. San Francisco Province (1868), P.O. Box 3720, Napa, CA 94558, (707) 252-0222, www.delasalle.org. Fe Province (1921), De La Salle Christian Brothers, 1522 Carmel Dr., Lafayette, LA 70501, (337)

234-1973. Educational, charitable work.

Cistercians, Order of, O.Cist.: Founded 1098, by St. Robert. Headquarters, Rome, Italy. *Our Lady of Spring Bank Abbey*, 17304 Havenwood Rd., Sparta, WI 54656-8177, (608) 269-8138. *Our Lady of Dallas Abbey*, 3550 Cistercian Rd., Irving, TX 75039, (972) 438-2044. *Cistercian Monastery of Our Lady of Fatima*, 564 Walton Ave., Mt. Laurel, NJ 08054, (856) 235-1330. *Cistercian Conventual Priory, St. Mary's Priory*, 70 Schuylkill Rd., New Ringgold, PA 17960, (570) 943-2645. www.cistercian.org.

Cistercians of the Strict Observance, Order of (Trappists), O.C.S.O.: Founded 1098, in France, by St. Robert; in U.S., 1848. Generalate, Rome, Italy.
Abbey of Gethsemani (1848), 3642 Monks Rd., KY 40051, (502) 549-3117. *Our Lady of New Melleray Abbey* (1849), 6632 Melleray Circle, Peosta, IA 52068-7079, (563) 588-2319. *Holy Spirit Monastery* (1944), 2625 Hwy. 212 S.W., Conyers, GA 30094-4044, (770) 483-8705 (fax), www.trappist.net. *Our Lady of Guadalupe Trappist Abbey* (1947), 9200 NE Abbey Rd., Carlton, OR 97111, (503) 852-7174, www.trappistabbey. *Abbey of Our Lady of the Holy Trinity* (1947), 1250 South 9500 East, Huntsville, UT 84317, (801) 745-3784, www.xmission.com~hta. *Abbey of the Genesee* (1951), PO Box 900, Piffard, NY 14533, (585) 243-0660, www.geneseeabbey.org. *Mepkin Abbey* (1949), 1098 Mepkin Abbey Rd., Moncks Corner, SC 29461-4796, (843) 761-8509, www.mepkinabbey.org. *Our Lady of the Holy Cross Abbey* (1950), 901 Cool Spring Lane, Berryville, VA 22611-2900, (540) 955-4383, www.heava.org. *Assumption Abbey* (1950), Rt. 5, Box 1056, Ava, MO 65608-9142, (417) 683-5110. *Abbey of New Clairvaux* (1955), 26240 7th St., Vina, CA 96092, (530) 839-2161, www.newclairvaux.org. *St. Benedict's Monastery* (1956), 1012 Monastery Rd., Snowmass, CO 81654, (970) 927-3311, www.snowmass.org.

Claretians (Missionary Sons of the Immaculate Heart of Mary), C.M.F.: Founded 1849, at Vich, Spain, by St. Anthony Mary Claret. General headquarters, Rome, Italy. Western Province, 414 S. Mission Dr., San Gabriel, CA 91776, (626) 289-2009. Eastern Province, 400 N. Euclid Ave, Oak Park, IL 60302, (708) 848-2076. Missionary, parochial, educational, retreat work.

Clerics Regular Minor (Adorno Fathers) C.R.M.: Founded 1588, at Naples, Italy, by Ven. Augustine Adorno and St. Francis Caracciolo. General motherhouse, Rome, Italy. U.S. address, 575 Darlington Ave., Ramsey, NJ 07446, (201) 327-7375, members. tripod.com/~adornofathers.

Columban, Missionary Society of St. (St. Columban Foreign Mission Society), S.S.C.: Founded 1918. General headquarters, Dublin, Ireland. U.S. headquarters., PO Box 10, St. Columbans, NE 68056, (402) 291-1920, www. columban.org. Foreign mission work.

Comboni Missionaries of the Heart of Jesus (Verona Fathers), M.C.C.J.: Founded 1867, in Italy by Bl. Daniel Comboni; in U.S., 1939. General motherhouse, Rome, Italy. North American headquarters, Comboni Mission Center, 1318 Nagel Rd., Cincinnati, OH 45255, (513) 474-4997. Mission work in Africa and the Americas.

Consolata Missionaries, I.M.C.: Founded 1901, at Turin, Italy, by Bl. Joseph Allamano. General motherhouse, Rome, Italy. U.S. headquarters, PO Box 5550, 2301 Rt. 27, Somerset, NJ 08875, (732) 297-9191.

Crosier Fathers (Canons Regular of the Order of the Holy Cross), O.S.C.: Founded 1210, in Belgium by Bl. Theodore De Celles. Generalate, Rome, Italy. U.S. Province of St. Odilia, 3510 Vivian Ave., Shoreview, MN 55126-3852, (651) 486-7456, www. crosier.org. Mission, retreat, educational work.

Cross, Brothers of the Congregation of Holy, C.S.C.: Founded 1837, in France, by Fr. Basil Moreau; U.S. province, 1841. Generalate, Rome, Italy. Midwest Province (1841), Box 460, Notre Dame, IN 46556-0460, (574) 631-2912, www.brothersofholycross.com. Southwest Province (1956), 1101 St. Edward's Dr., Austin, TX 78704-6512, (512) 442-7856, www.holycross-sw.org. Eastern Province (1956), 85 Overlook Circle, New Rochelle, NY 10804, (914) 632-4468, www.holycrossbrothers. org. Educational, social work, missions.

Cross, Congregation of Holy, C.S.C.: Founded 1837, in France; in U.S., 1841. Generalate, Rome, Italy. Indiana Province (1841), 54515 State Rd. 933, North, PO Box 1064, Notre Dame, IN 46556-1064, (574) 631-6196. Southern Province (1968), 2111 Brackenridge St., Austin, TX 78704, (512) 443-3886, www.southerncsc. org. Educational and pastoral work; home missions and retreats; foreign missions; social services and apostolate of the press.

Divine Word, Society of the, S.V.D.: Founded 1875, in Holland, by Bl. Arnold Janssen. General motherhouse, Rome, Italy. North American Province founded 1897 with headquarters in Techny, IL. Province of Bl. Joseph Freinademetz (Chicago Province) (1985, from merger of Eastern and Northern provinces), 1985 Waukegan Rd., Techny, IL 60082, (847) 272-2700. St. Augustine (Southern Province) (1940), 201 Ruella Ave., Bay St. Louis, MS 39520, (228) 467-4322, www.svdsouth.com. St. Therese of the Child Jesus (Western Province) (1964), 2737 Pleasant St., Riverside, CA 92507, (323) 735-8130.

Dominicans (Order of Friars Preachers), O.P: Founded early 13th century by St. Dominic de Guzman. General headquarters, Santa Sabina, Rome, Italy. *Eastern Province of St. Joseph* (1805), 141 E. 65th St., New York, NY 10065, (212) 737-5757, www.opEast.org.. *Most Holy Name of Jesus (Western) Province* (1912), 5877 Birch Ct., Oakland, CA 94618-1626, (510) 658-8722, www.opwest. org. *St. Albert the Great (Central) Province* (1939), 1910 S. Ashland Ave., Chicago, IL 60608, (312) 243-0011, www.domcentral.org. *St. Martin de Porres Province* (1979), 2121 N. Causeway Blvd., Suite 200, Metairie, LA 70001-4144, (504) 837-2129, www.opsouth.org. *Spanish Province*, U.S. foundation (1926), PO Box 279, San Diego, TX 78384, (512) 279-3596. Preaching, teaching, missions, research, parishes.

Edmund, Society of St., S.S.E.: Founded 1843, in France, by Fr. Jean Baptiste Muard. General motherhouse, Edmundite Generalate, 270 Winnoski Park, Colchester, VT 05439-0270, (802) 654-3400, www.sse.org. Educational, missionary work.

Eudists (Congregation of Jesus and Mary), C.J.M.: Founded 1643, in France, by St. John Eudes. General motherhouse, Rome, Italy. North American province, 6125 Premiere Ave., Charlesbourg, QC G1H 2V9, Canada, (418) 626-6494; U.S. community, 36 Flohr Ave., W. Seneca, NY 14224, (716) 825-4475; www.eudistes.org. Parochial, educational, pastoral, missionary work.

Francis, Brothers of Poor of St., C.F.P.: Founded 1857. Motherhouse, Aachen, Germany. International Office, PO Box 35, Wever, IA 52658, (319) 752-4000, brothersofthe poorofstfrancis.org. U.S. province, 239 W. Robbins

St., Covington, KY 41011, www.brothersofthepoorofstfrancis.org. Educational work, especially with poor and neglected youth.

Francis, Third Order Regular of St., T.O.R.: Founded 1221, in Italy; in U.S., 1910. General motherhouse, Rome, Italy. Most Sacred Heart of Jesus Province (1910), 128 Woodshire Dr., Pittsburgh, PA 15215-1714, (412) 781-8333. Immaculate Conception Province (1925), 3811 Emerson Ave. N., Minneapolis, MN 55412, (612) 529-7779, www.franciscanfriarstor. com. Franciscan Commissariat of the Spanish Province (1924), 301 Jefferson Ave., Waco, TX 76701-1419, (254) 752-8434. Educational, parochial, missionary work.

Francis de Sales, Oblates of St., O.S.F.S.: Founded 1871, by Fr. Louis Brisson. General motherhouse, Rome, Italy. Wilmington-Philadelphia Province (1906), 2200 Kentmere Parkway, Wilmington, DE 19806, (302) 656-8529, www.oblates.org. Toledo-Detroit Province (1966), 2043 Parkside Blvd., Toledo, OH 43607, (419) 724-9851. Educational, missionary, parochial work.

Francis Xavier, Brothers of St. (Xaverian Brothers), C.F.X.: Founded 1839, in Belgium, by Theodore J. Ryken. Generalate, 4409 Frederick Ave., Baltimore, MD, 21229, (410) 644-0034; xaverianbrothers.org. Educational work.

Franciscan Brothers of Brooklyn, O.S.F.: Founded in Ireland; established at Brooklyn, 1858. Generalate, 135 Remsen St., Brooklyn, NY 11201, (718) 858-8217, www.franciscanbros.org. Educational work.

Franciscan Brothers of the Holy Cross, F.F.S.C.: Founded 1862, in Germany. Generalate, Hausen, Linz Rhein, Germany; U.S. region, 2500 St. James Rd., Springfield, IL 62707, (217) 528-4757; www. franciscanbrothers.net. Educational work.

Franciscan Brothers of the Third Order Regular, O.S.F.: Generalate, Mountbellew, Ireland. U.S. region, 2117 Spyglass Trail W., Oxnard, CA 93030, (805) 485-5002. (Mailing address: 4522 Gainsborough Ave., Los Angeles, CA 90029.)

Franciscan Friars of the Immaculate, F.F.I: Founded 1990, Italy. General motherhouse, Benevento, Italy. U.S. addresses, 600 Pleasant St., New Bedford, MA. 02740; 22 School Hill Rd., Baltic, CT 06330, (508) 996-8274.

Franciscan Friars of the Renewal, C.F.R.: Community established under jurisdiction of the archbishop of New York. Central House, St. Crispin Friary, 420 E. 156th St., Bronx, NY 10455, (718) 402-8255, www.franciscanfriars. com.

Franciscan Missionary Brothers of the Sacred Heart of Jesus, O.S.F.: Founded 1927, in the St. Louis archdiocese. Motherhouse, St. Joseph Rd., Eureka, MO 63025, (314) 587-3661. Care of aged, infirm, homeless men and boys.

Franciscans (Order of Friars Minor), O.F.M.: A family of the First Order of St. Francis (of Assisi) founded in 1209 and established as a separate jurisdiction in 1517; in U.S., 1844. General headquarters, Rome, Italy. English-speaking conference: 1615 Vine St., Cincinnati, OH 45210-1200, (513) 721-4700.

Immaculate Conception Province (1855), 125 Thompson St., New York, NY 10012, (212) 674-4388, icprovince.org. *Sacred Heart Province,* Franciscan Missionary Union (1858), 3140 Meramec St., St. Louis, MO 63118-4339,

(314) 655-0532. *Assumption of the Blessed Virgin Mary Province* (1887), P.O. Box 100, 165 East Pulaski St., Pulaski, WI 54162-0100. *Holy Name Province* (1901), 129 W. 31st St., 2nd Floor, New York, NY 10001, (646) 473-0265, www.hnp.org. *St. Barbara Province* (1915), 1500 34th Ave., Oakland, CA 94601, (510) 536-3722, www.sbfranciscans.org.

Our Lady of Guadalupe Province (1985), 1204 Stinson. S.W., Albuquerque, NM 87121, (505) 831-9199; OLGofm.org. *Commissariat of the Holy Cross* (1912), P.O. Box 608, Lemont, IL 60439-0608, (630) 257-2494. *Mt. Alverna Friary,* 517 S. Belle Vista Ave., Youngstown, OH 44509, (330) 799-1888. *Holy Family Croatian Custody* (1926), 4851 S. Drexel Blvd., Chicago, IL 60615-1703, (773) 536-0552.

St. Casimir Lithuanian Vice-Province, PO Box 980, Kennebunkport, ME 04046, (207) 967-2011. *Holy Gospel Province* (Mexico), U.S. foundation, 2400 Marr St., El Paso, TX 79903, (915) 565-2921. *Commissariat of the Holy Land,* 1400 Quincy St. N.E., Washington, DC 20017, (202) 269-5430, myfranciscan.com. *Holy Dormition Friary,* Byzantine Slavonic Rite, PO Box 270, Rt. 93, Sybertsville, PA 18251, (570) 788-1212, www.hdbf. com. *Academy of American Franciscan History,* 1712 Euclid Ave., Berkeley, CA 94709. Preaching, missionary, educational, parochial, charitable work.

Franciscans (Order of Friars Minor Capuchin), O.F.M. Cap.: A family of the First Order of St. Francis (of Assisi) founded in 1209 and established as a separate jurisdiction in 1528. *St. Joseph Province/St. Bonaventure Monastery* (1857), 1740 Mt. Elliott Ave., Detroit, MI 48207-3427, (313) 579-2100. *Province of St. Augustine* (1873), 220 37th St., Pittsburgh, PA 15201, (412) 682-6011, www.capuchin.com. *St. Mary Province* (1952), 30 Gedney Park Dr., White Plains, NY 10605, (914) 761-3008. *Province of the Stigmata of St. Francis* (1918), P.O. Box 809, Union City, NJ 07087-0809, (201) 865-0611. *Western American Capuchin Province, Our Lady of the Angels,* 1345 Cortez Ave., Burlingame, CA 94010, (650) 342-1489, www.beafriar.com.

St. Stanislaus Friary (1948), 2 Manor Dr., Oak Ridge, NJ 07438, (973) 697-7757. *Province of Mid-America* (1977), 3613 Wyandot St., Denver, CO 80211, (303) 477-5436, www.midamcaps.org. *Vice-Province of Texas,* 604 Bernal Dr., Dallas, TX 75212, (214) 631-1937. *St. John the Baptist Vice-Province,* P.O. Box 21350, Rio Piedras, Puerto Rico 00928-1350, (787) 764-3090. General motherhouse, Rome, Italy. Missionary, parochial work, chaplaincies.

Franciscans (Order of Friars Minor Conventual), O.F.M. Conv.: A family of the First Order of St. Francis (of Assisi) founded in 1209 and established as a separate jurisdiction in 1517; first U.S. foundation, 1852. General curia, Rome, Italy. Immaculate Conception Province (1852), *Immaculate Conception Friary,* P.O. Box 629, Rensselaer, NY 12144, (518) 472-1000, www.franciscanseast. *St. Anthony of Padua Province* (1906), 12300 Folly Quarter Rd., Ellicott City, MD 21042, (410) 531-1400,www.stanthonyprovince.org. *St. Bonaventure Province* (1939), 6107 Kenmore Ave., Chicago, IL 60660, (773) 274-7681. *Our Lady of Consolation Province* (1926), 101 St. Anthony Dr., Mt. St. Francis, IN 47146, (812) 923-8444. *St. Joseph of Cupertino Province* (1981), P.O. Box 820, Arroyo Grande, CA 93421-0820, (805) 489-1012, franciscansusa.org. Missionary, educational, parochial work.

Glenmary Missioners (The Home Missioners of

America): Founded 1939, in U.S.. General headquarters, P.O. Box 465618, Cincinnati, OH 45246, (513) 881-7442, www.glenmary.org. Home mission work.

Good Shepherd, Little Brothers of the, B.G.S.: Founded 1951, by Bro. Mathias Barrett. Foundation House, P.O. Box 389, Albuquerque, NM 87103, (505) 243-4238. General headquarters, Hamilton, ON, Canada. Operate shelters and refuges for aged and homeless; homes for handicapped men and boys, alcoholic rehabilitation center.

Holy Eucharist, Brothers of the, F.S.E.: Founded in U.S., 1957. Generalate, P.O. Box 25, Plaucheville, LA 71362, (318) 922-3630. Teaching, social, clerical, nursing work.

Holy Family, Congregation of the Missionaries of the, M.S.F.: Founded 1895, in Holland, by Rev. John P. Berthier. General motherhouse, Rome, Italy. U.S. provincialate, 3014 Oregon Ave., St. Louis, MO, 63118-1498, (314) 577-6300, www.msf-america.org. Belated vocations for the missions.

Holy Family, Sons of the, S.F.: Founded 1864, at Barcelona, Spain, by Bl. Jose Mañanet y Vives; in U.S., 1920. General motherhouse, Barcelona, Spain. U.S. address, 401 Randolph Rd., P.O. Box 4138, Silver Spring, MD 20904, (301) 622-1184, www.sonsoftheholyfamily.com.

Holy Ghost Fathers, C.S.Sp.: Founded 1703, in Paris, France, by Claude Francois Poullart des Places; in U.S., 1872. Generalate, Rome, Italy. Eastern Province (1872), 6230 Brush Run Rd., Bethel Park, PA 15102, (412) 831-0302, www.spiritans.org.Western Province (1964), 1700 W. Alabama St., Houston, TX 77098-2808, (713) 522-2882, www.spiritans.org. Missions, education. **Holy Ghost Fathers of Ireland:** Founded 1971. U.S. delegates: 4849 37th St., Long Island City, NY 11101 (East); St. Dunstan's Church, 1133 Broadway, Mill Brae, CA 94030 (West).Holy Spirit, Missionaries of the, M.Sp.S.: Founded 1914, at Mexico City, Mexico, by Felix Rougier. General motherhouse, Mexico City. U.S. headquarters, 9792 Oma Place, Garden Grove, CA 92841, (714) 534-5476, www.christthepriest.org; charity work.

Immaculate Heart of Mary, Brothers of the, I.H.M.: Founded 1948, at Steubenville, Ohio, by Bishop John K. Mussio. Villa Maria Generalate, 609 N. 7th St., Steubenville, OH 43952, (740) 283-2462. Educational, charitable work.

Jesuits (Society of Jesus), S.J.: Founded 1534, in France, by St. Ignatius of Loyola; received papal approval, 1540; suppressed in 1773 and revived in 1814 by Pope Pius VII; first U.S. province, 1833. The Jesuits remain the largest single order in the Church. Generalate, Rome, Italy. U.S. national office, Jesuit Conference, 1016 16th Street, N.W., Fourth Floor, Washington, DC 20036-1420, (202) 462-0400, www.jesuit.org. *Maryland Province* (1833), 8600 La Salle Rd., Ste. 620, Towson, MD 21286, (443) 921-131039 www.mdsj.org. *New York Province* (1943), East 83rd St., New York, NY 10028, (212) 774-5500, www.nysj.org. *Missouri Province* (1863), 4511 W. Pine Blvd., St. Louis, MO 63108-2191, (314) 361-7765, www.jesuits-mis.org. *New Orleans Province* (1907), 710 Baronne St., Suite B, New Orleans, LA 70113, (504) 788-1719.

California Province (1909), 300 College Ave., P.O. Box 519, Los Gatos, CA 95031, (408) 884-1600, www.jesuitscalifornia.org. *New England Province* (1926), 85 School

St., Watertown, MA 02472; (617) 607-2800. *Chicago Province* (1928), 2050 N. Clark St., Chicago, IL 60614, (773) 975-6363, www.jesuits-chi.org. *Oregon Province* (1932), 2222 N.W. Hoyt, Portland, OR 97210, (503) 226-6977. *Detroit Province* (1955), 2050 N. Clark St., Chicago, IL 60614, (773) 975-6888, www.detprovejesuit-det.org. *Wisconsin Province* (1955), PO Box 080288, Milwaukee, WI 53208-0288, (414) 937-6949, www.jesuitwisprov.org. *Province of the Antilles* (1947), U.S. address, 12725 S.W. 6th St., Miami, FL 33184, (305) 559-9044. Missionary, educational, literary work.

John of God, Brothers of the Hospitaller Order of St., O.H.: Founded 1537, in Spain. General motherhouse, Rome, Italy. American province, 2425 S. Western Ave., Los Angeles, CA 90018, (323) 731-0233, www.hospitallers.org. Nursing and related fields.

Joseph, Congregation of St., C.S.J.: General motherhouse, Rome, Italy. U.S. vice-province, 338 North Grand Ave., San Pedro, CA 90731-2006, (310) 831-5360. Parochial, missionary, educational work.

Joseph, Oblates of St., O.S.J.: Founded 1878, in Italy, by Bl. Joseph Marello; in U.S., 1929. General motherhouse, Rome, Italy. Our Lady of Sorrows Province, 1880 Hwy 315, Pittston, PA 18640, (570) 654-7542. California Province, 544 W. Cliff Dr., Santa Cruz, CA 95060, (831) 457-1868, www.osjoseph.org. Parochial, educational work.

Josephite Fathers, C.J.: General motherhouse, Ghent, Belgium; U.S. foundation, 5075 Harp Rd., Santa Maria, CA 93455, (805) 937-4555; www.josephiteweb.org.

Josephites (St. Joseph's Society of the Sacred Heart), S.S.J.: Established 1893, in U.S. as American congregation (originally established in U.S., in 1871 by Mill Hill Josephites from England). General motherhouse, 1130 N. Calvert St., Baltimore, MD 21202-3802, (410) 727-3386, www.josephite.com. Evangelization in African-American community.

LaSalette, Missionaries of Our Lady of: Province of Mary, Mother of the Americas, P.O. Box 777, Twin Lakes, WI 53181, (262) 877-3111.

Lateran, Canons Regular of the, C.R.L.: General House, Rome, Italy. U.S. address: 2317 Washington Ave., Bronx, NY 10458, (212) 295-9600.

Legionaries of Christ, L.C.: Founded 1941, in Mexico, by Rev. Marcial Maciel; in U.S., 1965. General headquarters, Rome, Italy. U.S. headquarters, 475 Oak Ave., Cheshite, CT 06410, novitiate, 475 Oak Ave., Cheshire, CT 06410, (203) 271-0805, www.legionofchrist.org.

Little Brothers of St. Francis, L.B.S.F.: Founded 1970 in Archdiocese of Boston by Bro. James Curran. General fraternity, 785 789 Parker St., Boston, MA 02120-3021, (617) 442-2556, www.littlebrothersofstfrancis.org. Combine contemplative life with evangelical street ministry.

Mariannhill, Congregation of the Missionaries of, C.M.M.: Trappist monastery, begun in 1882 by Abbot Francis Pfanner in Natal, South Africa, became an independent modern congregation in 1909; in U.S., 1920. Generalate, Rome, Italy. U.S. Canadian province (1938), Our Lady of Grace Monastery, 23715 Ann Arbor Trail, Dearborn Hts., MI 48127-1449, (313) 561-2330, www.rc.net/detroit/marianhill. Foreign mission work.

Marians of the Immaculate Conception, Congregation of, M.I.C.: Founded 1673; U.S. foundation, 1913. General motherhouse, Rome, Italy. Mother of Mercy Province,

Eden Hill, Stockbridge, MA 01262. Educational, parochial, mission, publication work.

Marist Brothers, F.M.S.: Co-founded 1817, in France, by St. Marcellin Champagnat. Generalate, Rome, Italy. U.S. Province, 1241 Kennedy Blvd., Bayonne, NJ 07002, (201) 823-1115; www.societyofmaryusa.org. Educational, social, catechetical work.

Marist Fathers (Society of Mary), S.M.: Founded 1816, at Lyons, France, by Jean Claude Colin; in U.S., 1863. General motherhouse, Rome, Italy. United States Province: 815 Varnum St., NE, Washington, D.C. 20017, (202) 529-2821, www.societyofmaryusa.org. Educational, foreign mission, pastoral work.

Maronite Lebanese Missionaries, Congregation of, C.M.L.M.: Founded in Lebanon 1865; established in the U.S., 1991. U.S. foundation, Our Lady of the Cedars Maronite Mission, 11935 Bellfort Village, Houston, TX 77031, (281) 568-6800.

Maronite Monks of Most Holy Trinity Monastery: Founded in 1978 and canonically approved by John Paul II and established in the Eparchy of St. Maron in 1989. A community of contemplative monks dedicated to a life of prayer and Eucharistic Adoration. Most Holy Trinity Monastery, 67 Dugway Road, Petersham, MA 01366-9725, (978) 724-3347, www.maronitemonks.org.

Mary, Society of (Marianist Fathers and Brothers; Brothers of Mary), S.M.: Founded 1817, at Bordeaux, France, by Fr. William-Joseph Chaminade; in U.S., 1849. General motherhouse, Rome, Italy. Marianist Province of the U.S., 4425 West Pine Blvd., St. Louis, MO 63108, (314) 533-1207, www.marianist.com. The Marianist provinces of Cincinnati, St. Louis, Pacific, and New York have merged to form one province. Educational work.

Mary Immaculate, Missionary Oblates of, O.M.I.: Founded 1816, in France, by St. Charles Joseph Eugene de Mazenod; in U.S., 1849. General House, Rome, Italy. U.S. Province: 327 Oblate Dr., San Antonio, TX 78216-6602, (210) 349-1475, www.omiusa.org. Parochial, foreign mission, educational work, ministry to marginal.

Maryknoll (Catholic Foreign Mission Society of America), M.M.: Founded 1911, in U.S., by Frs. Thomas F. Price and James A. Walsh. General Center, Maryknoll, NY 10545, (914) 941-7590.

Mercedarians (Order of Our Lady of Mercy), O. de M.: Founded 1218, in Spain, by St. Peter Nolasco. General motherhouse, Rome, Italy. U.S. headquarters, 3205 Fulton Rd., Cleveland, OH 44109 (216) 961-8331.

Mercy, Brothers of, F.M.M.: Founded 1856, in Germany. General motherhouse, Montabaur, Germany. American headquarters, 4520 Ransom Rd., Clarence, NY 14031, (716) 759-8341. Hospital work.

Mercy, Brothers of Our Lady, Mother of, C.F.M.M.: Founded 1844, in the Netherlands by Abp. Jan Zwijsen. Generalate, Tilburg, the Netherlands. U.S. region, 7140 Ramsgate Ave., Los Angeles, CA 90045, (310) 338-5954, www.cmmbrothers.nl.

Mercy, Congregation of Priests of (Fathers of Mercy), C.P.M.: Founded 1808, in France, by Rev. Jean Baptiste Rauzan; in U.S., 1839. General mission house, Auburn, KY 42206, (270) 542-4164; www.fathersofmercy.com. Mission work.

Mill Hill Missionaries (St. Joseph's Society for Foreign Missions), M.H.M.: Founded 1866, in England, by

Cardinal Vaughan; in U.S., 1951. International headquarters, London, England. American headquarters, 222 W. Hartsdale Ave., Hartsdale, NY 10530, (914) 682-0645.

Minim Fathers, O.M.: General motherhouse, Rome, Italy. North American delegation (1970), 3431 Portola Ave., Los Angeles, CA 90032, (213) 223-1101.

Missionaries of St. Charles, Congregation of the (Scalabrinians), C.S.: Founded 1887, at Piacenza, Italy, by Bl. John Baptist Scalabrini. General motherhouse, Rome, Italy. St. Charles Borromeo Province (1888), 27 Carmine St., New York, NY 10014, (212) 675-3993. St. John Baptist Province (1903), 546 N. East Ave., Oak Park, IL 60302, (708) 386-4430.

Missionaries of the Holy Apostles, M.Ss.A.: Founded 1962, Washington, DC, by Very Rev. Eusebe M. Menard. North American headquarters, 22 Prospect Hill Rd., Cromwell, CT 06416, (860) 632-3039; www.msausa.net.

Missionarii Franciscani Verbi Aeterni, Franciscan Missionaries of the Eternal Word, 5821 Old Leeds Rd., Irondale, AL 35210, www.mfva.info.

Missionary Servants of Christ, M.S.C.: Founded 1979 in U.S. by Bro. Edwin Baker. Headquarters, P.O. Box 270, 305 S. Lake St., Aurora, IL 60507-0270, (630) 892-2371, www.misacor-usa.org.

Missionhurst-CICM (Congregation of the Immaculate Heart of Mary): Founded 1862, at Scheut, Brussels, Belgium, by Very Rev. Theophile Verbist. General motherhouse, Rome, Italy. U.S. province, 4651 N. 25th St., Arlington, VA 22207, (703) 528-3800, www.missionhurst.org. Home and foreign mission work.

Montfort Missionaries (Missionaries of the Company of Mary), S.M.M.: Founded 1715, by St. Louis Marie Grignon de Montfort; in U.S., 1948. General motherhouse, Rome, Italy. U.S. province, 101-18 104th St., Ozone Park, NY 11416, (718) 849-5885. Mission work.

Mother Co-Redemptrix, Congregation of, C.M.C.: Founded 1953 at Lein-Thuy, Vietnam (North), by Fr. Dominic Mary Tran Dinh Thu; in U.S., 1975. General house, Hochiminhville, Vietnam. U.S. provincial house, 1900 Grand Ave., Carthage, MO 64836, (417) 358-7787, www.dongcong.net. Work among Vietnamese Catholics in U.S.

Oblates of the Virgin Mary, O.M.V.: Founded 1815, in Italy; in U.S., 1976; Generalate, Rome, Italy. U.S. provincialate: 2 Ipswich St., Boston, MA 02215, (617) 536-4141.

Oratorians (Congregation of the Oratory of St. Philip Neri), C.O.: Founded 1575, at Rome, by St. 'Philip Neri. A confederation of autonomous houses. U.S. addresses: PO Box 11586, Rock Hill, SC 29731, (803) 327-2097, www.rockhilloratory.org. For Box 1688, Monterey, CA 93940, (831) 373-0476. 4450 Bayard St., Pittsburgh, PA 15213, (412) 681-3181; pittsburghoratory.com. P.O. Drawer II, Pharr, TX 78577, (956) 843-8217. 109 Willoughby St., Brooklyn, NY 11201, (718) 788-5693.

Pallottines (Society of the Catholic Apostolate), S.A.C.: Founded 1835, at Rome, by St. Vincent Pallotti. Generalate, Rome, Italy. *Immaculate Conception Province* (1953), PO Box 979, South Orange, NJ 07079, (201) 762-2926. *Mother of God Province* (1946), 5424 W. Blue Mound Rd., Milwaukee, WI 53208, (414) 259-0688. *Irish Province* (1909), U.S. address: 3352 4th St., Wyandotte, MI 48192, www.irishpallotines.com. *Queen of Apostles Province* (1909), 448 E. 116th St., New York, NY 10029, (212) 534-0681. *Christ the King Province,* 3452 Niagara Falls, Blvd., N.

Tonawanda, NY 14120, (716) 694-4313, wwww. northtonawanda.byethost7.com. Charitable, educational, parochial, mission work.

Paraclete, Servants of the, S.P.: Founded 1947, Santa Fe, NM, archdiocese. Generalate and U.S. motherhouse, 13270 Maple Dr., St. Louis, MO 63127, (314) 965-0860; www.theservants.org. Dedicated to ministry to priests and Brothers with personal difficulties.

Paris Foreign Missions Society, M.E.P.: Founded 1662, at Paris, France. Headquarters, Paris, France; U.S. establishment, 930 Ashbury St., San Francisco, CA 94117, (415) 664-6747. Mission work and training of native clergy.

Passionists (Congregation of the Passion), C.P.: Founded 1720, in Italy, by St. Paul of the Cross. General motherhouse, Rome, Italy. St. Paul of the Cross Province (Eastern Province) (1852), 80 David St., South River, NJ 08882, (732) 257-7177, www.thepassionists.org. Holy Cross Province (Western Province), 1420 Renaissance Dr., Suite 312, Park Ridge, IL 60068, (773) 631-6336; www. passionists.org.

Patrician Brothers (Brothers of St. Patrick), F.S.P.: Founded 1808, in Ireland, by Bp. Daniel Delaney. U.S. novitiate, 7820 Bolsa Ave., Midway City, CA 92655, (714) 897-8181. Educational work.

Patrick's Missionary Society, St., S.P.S.: Founded 1932, at Wicklow, Ireland, by Msgr. Patrick Whitney; in U.S., 1953. International headquarters, Kiltegan Co., Wicklow, Ireland. U.S. foundations: 70 Edgewater Rd., Cliffside Park, NJ 07010, (201) 943-6575, 19536 Eric Dr., Saratoga, CA 95070, (408) 253-3135, www.spms.org; 8422 W. Windsor Ave., Chicago, IL 60656, (773) 887-4741.

Pauline Fathers (Order of St. Paul the First Hermit), O.S.P.P.E.: Founded 1215; established in U.S., 1955. General motherhouse, Czesto-chowa, Jasna Gora, Poland; U.S. province, P.O. Box 2049, Doylestown, PA 18901, (215) 345-0600; www.czestochowa.us.

Pauline Fathers and Brothers (Society of St. Paul for the Apostolate of Communications), S.S.P.: Founded 1914, by Very Rev. James Alberione; in U.S., 1932. Motherhouse, Rome, Italy. New York province (1932), Czestochowa, Jasna Gora, Poland; U.S. province, 654 Ferry Rd., Doylestown, PA 18901, (215) 345-0600; www. czestochowa.us. Social communications work.

Paulists (Missionary Society of St. Paul the Apostle), C.S.P.: Founded 1858, in New York, by Fr. Isaac Thomas Hecker. Motherhouse: 86-11 Midland Pkwy, Jamaica Estates, NY 11432, (718) 291-5995, www.paulist.org. Missionary, ecumenical, pastoral work.

Piarists (Order of the Pious Schools), Sch.P.: Founded 1617, at Rome, Italy, by St. Joseph Calasanctius. General motherhouse, Rome, Italy. U.S. province, 363 N. Valley Forge Rd., Devon, PA 19333, (610) 688-7337, www.devonprep. com. New York-Puerto Rico vice-province (Calasanzian Fathers), P.O. Box 7760, Ponce, PR 00732-7760, (787) 840-0610. California vice province, 3940 Perry St., Los Angeles, CA 90063, (323) 261-1386. Educational work.

Pius X, Brothers of St., C.S.P.X.: Founded 1952, at La Crosse, WI, by Bishop John P. Treacy. Motherhouse, PO Box 217, De Soto, WI 54624. Education.

Pontifical Institute for Foreign Missions, P.I.M.E.: Founded 1850, in Italy, at request of Pope Pius IX. General motherhouse, Rome, Italy. U.S. province, 17330 Quincy Ave., Detroit, MI 48221, (313) 342-4066, www.pimeusa.org work.

Precious Blood, Society of, C.P.P.S.: Founded 1815, in Italy, by St. Gaspar del Bufalo. General motherhouse, Rome, Italy. Cincinnati Province, 431 E. Second St., Dayton, OH 45402, (937) 228-9263, www.cpps-preciousblood.org. Kansas City Province, P.O. Box 339, Liberty, MO 64069-0339, (816) 781-4344, www.kcprovince.org. Pacific Province, 2337 134th Ave. W., San Leandro, CA 94577, (510) 357-4982, www.rc.net/oakland/cpps. Atlantic Province 100 Pelmo Cres., Toronto, ON M9N 2Y1, (416) 614-7096, www.precious-blood.org.

Premonstratensians (Order of the Canons Regular of Premontre; Norbertines), O. Praem.: Founded 1120, at Premontre, France, by St. Norbert; in U.S., 1893. Generalate, Rome, Italy. St. Norbert Abbey, 1016 N. Broadway, DePere, WI 54114, (920) 337-4300, www.snc.edu/norbertines. Daylesford Abbey, 220 S. Valley Rd., Paoli, PA 19301, (610) 647-2530, www.daylesford.org. St. Michael's Abbey, 19292 El Toro Rd., Silverado, CA 92676, (949) 858-0222, www.abbeynews.com. Immaculate Conception Priory (1997), 3600 Philadelphia Pike, Claymont, DE 19703, (302) 792-2791. Educational, parish work.

Priestly Fraternity of St. Peter, F.S.S.P.: Founded and approved Oct. 18, 1988; first foundation in U.S., 1991. U.S. headquarters, St. Peter's House, 119 Griffin Rd., Elmhurst, PA 18444, (570) 842-4000, www.fssp.com. Pastoral and sacramental ministry using the 1962 liturgical books.

Providence, Sons of Divine, F.D.P.: Founded 1893, at Tortona, Italy, by Bl. Luigi Orione; in U.S., 1933. General motherhouse, Rome, Italy. U.S. address, 111 Orient Ave., E. Boston, MA 02128, (617) 569-2100.

Redemptorist Fathers and Brothers (Congregation of the Most Holy Redeemer), C.SS.R.: Founded 1732, in Italy, by St. Alphonsus Mary Liguori. Generalate, Rome, Italy. Baltimore Province (1850), 7509 Shore Rd., Brooklyn, NY 11209, (718) 833-1900. Redemptorist-Denver Province (1875), 1230 South Parker Rd., Denver, CO 80203-0399, (303) 370-0035, www.redemptorists-denver. org. Richmond Vice-Province (1942), 313 Hillman St., PO Box 1529, New Smyrna Beach, FL 32168, (386) 427-3094. Mission work.

Resurrectionists (Congregation of the Resurrection), C.R.: Founded 1836, in France, under direction of Bogdan Janski. Motherhouse, Rome, Italy. U.S. Province, 7050 N. Oakley Ave., Chicago, IL 60645-3426, (773) 465-8320, www.resurrectionists.com. Ontario Kentucky Province, U.S. address, 338 N. 25th St., Louisville, KY 40212, (502) 772-3694.

Rogationist Fathers, R.C.J.: Founded by Bl. Annibale (Hannibal) di Francia, 1887. General motherhouse, Rome, Italy. U.S. delegation: 2688 S. Newmark Ave., Sanger, CA 91343, (209) 875-5808. Charitable work.

Rosary, Brothers of Our Lady of the Holy, F.S.R.: Founded 1956, in U.S. motherhouse and novitiate, 232 Sunnyside Dr., Reno, NV 89503-3510, (775) 326-9429.

Rosminians (Institute of Charity), I.C.: Founded 1828, in Italy, by Antonio Rosmini-Serbati. General motherhouse, Rome, Italy. U.S. address, 2327 W. Heading Ave., Peoria, IL 61604, (309) 676-6341. Charitable work.

Sacred Heart, Brothers of the, S.C.: Founded 1821, in France, by Fr. Andre Coindre. General motherhouse, Rome, Italy. New Orleans Province (1847), 4600 Elysian Fields Ave., New Orleans, LA 70122, (504) 282-5693;

(504) 301-4758. New England Province (1945), 219 MacArthur Ave., Sayreville, NJ 08872, (732) 718-8559, www.brothersofthesacredheart.org. New York Province (1960), 141-11 123 Ave., South Ozone Park, NY 11436-1426, (718) 322-3309. Educational work.

Sacred Heart, Missionaries of the, M.S.C.: Founded 1854, by Fr. Jules Chevelier. General motherhouse, Rome, Italy. U.S. province, 305 S. Lake St., Aurora, IL 60507-0271, (630) 892-8400.

Sacred Heart of Jesus, Congregation of the (Sacred Heart Fathers and Brothers), S.C.J.: Founded 1877, in France. General motherhouse, Rome, Italy. U.S. provincial office, PO Box 289, Hales Corners, WI 53130-0289, (414) 425-6910, www.sacredheartusa.org. Educational, preaching, mission work.

Sacred Hearts of Jesus and Mary, Congregation of (Picpus Fathers), SS.CC.: Founded 1805, in France, by Fr. Coudrin. General motherhouse, Rome, Italy. Eastern Province (1946), 77 Adams St. (Box 111), Fairhaven, MA 02719, (508) 993-2442, www.sscc.org. Western Province (1970), 2150 Damien Ave., La Verne, CA 91750, (909) 593-5441. Hawaii Province, Box 797, Kaneohe, Oahu, HI 96744, (808) 247-5035. Mission, educational work.

Sacred Hearts of Jesus and Mary, Missionaries of the, M.SS.CC.: Founded 1833, in Naples, Italy, by Cajetan Errico. General motherhouse, Rome, Italy. U.S. headquarters, 2249 Shore Rd., Linwood, NJ 08221, (609) 927-5600.

Salesians of St. John Bosco (Society of St. Francis de Sales), S.D.B.: Founded 1859, by St. John (Don) Bosco. Generalate, Rome, Italy. St. Philip the Apostle Province (1902), 148 Main St., New Rochelle, NY 10802-0639, (914) 636-4225. San Francisco Province (1926), 1100 Franklin St., San Francisco, CA 94109, (415) 441-7144; www.donboscowest.org.

Salvatorians (Society of the Divine Savior), S.D.S.: Founded 1881, in Rome, by Fr. Francis Jordan; in U.S., 1896. General headquarters, Rome, Italy. U.S. province, 1735 N. Hi-Mount Blvd., Milwaukee, WI 53208-1720, (414) 258-1735, www.salvatorians.com. Educational, parochial, mission work; campus ministries, chaplaincies.

Scalabrinians: See **Missionaries of St. Charles**.

Servites (Order of Friar Servants of Mary), O.S.M.: Founded 1233, at Florence, Italy, by Seven Holy Founders. Generalate, Rome, Italy. United States Province (1967), 3121 W. Jackson Blvd., Chicago, IL 60612, (773) 533-0360. General apostolic ministry.

Somascan Fathers, C.R.S.: Founded 1534, at Somasca, Italy, by St. Jerome Emiliani. General motherhouse, Rome, Italy. U.S. address, Pine Haven Boys Center, River Rd., P.O. Box 162, Suncook, NH 03275, (603) 485-7141, www.somascans.org.

Society of Our Lady of the Most Holy Trinity, S.O.L.T.: Headquarters, Casa San Jose, 109 W. Ave. F, PO Box 152, Robstown, TX 78380, (512) 387-2754.

Sons of Mary (Sons of Mary, Health of the Sick), F.M.S.I.: Founded 1952, in the Boston archdiocese, by Fr. Edward F. Garesche, S.J. Headquarters, 567 Salem End Rd., Framingham, MA 01701-5599,

(508) 879-2541, www.sonsofmary.com.

Stigmatine Fathers and Brothers (Congregation of the Sacred Stigmata), C.S.S.: Founded 1816, by St. Gaspar Bertoni. General motherhouse, Rome, Italy. North American Province, 554 Lexington St., Waltham, MA 02452-3097, (781) 209-3100, www.stigmatines.com. Parish work.

Sulpicians (Society of Priests of St. Sulpice), S.S.: Founded 1641, in Paris, by Fr. Jean Jacques Olier. General motherhouse, Paris, France; U.S. province, 5408 Roland Ave., Baltimore, MD 21210, (410) 323-5070, www.sulpicians.org. Education of seminarians and priests.

Theatines (Congregation of Clerics Regular), C.R.: Founded 1524, in Rome, by St. Cajetan. General motherhouse, Rome, Italy. U.S. headquarters, 1050 S. Birch St., Denver, CO 80246, (303) 756-5522.

Trappists: See **Cistercians of the Strict Observance**.

Trinitarians (Order of the Most Holy Trinity), O.SS.T.: Founded 1198, by St. John of Matha; in U.S., 1911. General motherhouse, Rome, Italy. U.S. headquarters, P.O. Box 5742, Baltimore, MD 21282, (410) 486-5171.

Trinity Missions (Missionary Servants of the Most Holy Trinity), S.T.: Founded 1929, by Fr. Thomas Augustine Judge. Generalate, PO Box 7130, Silver Springs, MD 20907-7130, (301) 434-6761, www.trinitymissions.org. Home mission work.

Viatorian Fathers (Clerics of St. Viator), C.S.V.: Founded 1831, in France, by Fr. Louis Joseph Querbes. General motherhouse, Rome, Italy. Province of Chicago (1882), 1212 E. Euclid Ave., Arlington Hts., IL 60004, (847) 398-1353. Educational work.

Vincentians (Congregation of the Mission; Lazarists), C.M.: Founded 1625, in Paris, by St. Vincent de Paul; in U.S., 1818. General motherhouse, Rome, Italy. *Eastern Province* (1867), 500 E. Chelten Ave., Philadelphia, PA 19144, (215) 848-1985. *Western Province* (1888), 13663 Rider Trail North, Earth City, MO 63045, (314) 344-1184; www.vincentian.org. *New England Province* (1975), 234 Keeney St., Manchester, CT 06040-7048, (860) 643-2828. *American Italian Branch*, Our Lady of Pompei Church, 3600 Claremont St., Baltimore, MD 21224, (410) 675-7790. *American Spanish Branch* (Barcelona, Spain), 118 Congress St., Brooklyn, NY 11201-6045, (718) 624-5670. *American Spanish Branch* (Zaragoza, Spain), Holy Agony Church, 1834 3rd Ave., New York, NY 10029, (212) 289-5589. *Southern Province* (1975), 3826 Gilbert Ave., Dallas, TX 75219, (214) 526-0234, www.cmsouth.org. Educational work.

Vocationist Fathers (Society of Divine Vocations), S.D.V.: Founded 1920, in Italy; in U.S., 1962. Generalate, Rome, Italy. U.S. headquarters, 90 Brooklake Rd., Florham Park, NJ 07932, (973) 966-6262, www.vocationist.org.

Xaverian Missionary Fathers, S.X.: Founded 1895, by Bl. Guido Conforti, at Parma, Italy. General motherhouse, Rome, Italy. U.S. province, 12 Helene Ct., Wayne, NJ 07470, (973) 942-2975, www.xaviermissionaries.org. Foreign mission work.

MEMBERSHIP OF RELIGIOUS INSTITUTES OF MEN

Principal source: Annuario Pontificio. *Statistics as of Jan. 1, 2014, unless indicated otherwise.* Listed below are world membership statistics of institutes of men of pontifical right with 500 or more members; the number of priests is in parentheses. Also listed are institutes with less than 500 members with houses in the U.S.

Jesuits (12,298)	17,287
Salesians (10,524)	15,536
Franciscans (Friars Minor) (9,588)	14,043
Franciscans (Capuchins) (7,021)	10,659
Benedictines (3,777)	7,236
Dominicans (4,470)	6,058
Society of the Divine Word (4,171)	6,001
Redemptorists (4,026)	5,279
Brothers of Christian Schools	4,604
Franciscans (Conventuals) (2,942)	4,305
Oblates of Mary Immaculate (3,009)	4,094
Discalced Carmelites (O.C.D.) (2,864)	3,964
Marist Brothers	3,524
Vincentians (2,995)	3,347
Claretians (2,182)	3,076
Holy Spirit (Holy Ghost), Vincentians Congregation of (2,155)	2,973
Augustinians (2,015)	2,818
Carmelites of the BVM (1,764)	2,450
Pallottines (1,695)	2,378
Priests of the Sacred Heart (1,694)	2,291
Passionists (1,621)	2,125
Carmelites (O.Carm.) (1,320)	2,016
Trappists (770)	1,995
Legionaries of Christ (956)	1,888
Missionaries of the Sacred Heart of Jesus (1,305)	1,828
Missionaries of St. Francis de Sales of Annecy (1,009)	1,773
Cistercians (Common Observance) (735)	1,716
Combonian Missionaries of the Heart of Jesus (1,239)	1,693
Missionaries of Africa (1,271)	1,619
Holy Cross, Congregation of (741)	1,478
Piarists (978)	1,318
Premonstratensians (946)	1,281
Brothers of Christian Instruction of St. Gabriel (24)	1,246
Marianists (395)	1,228
Christian Brothers	1,194
Salvatorians (837)	1,182
Ministers of the Sick (Camillians) (681)	1,151
Augustinians (Recollects) (922)	1,141
Hospitallers of St. John of God (123)	1,134
Brothers of the Sacred Heart (30)	1,121
Society of St. Paul (548)	1,020
Consolata Missionaries (758)	1,000
LaSalette Missionaries (701)	974
Society of African Missions (777)	947
Little Workers of Divine Providence (644)	924
Marists (776)	905
Blessed Sacrament, Congregation of (596)	901
Assumptionists (533)	898
Immaculate Heart of Mary, Congregation of (Missionhurst; Scheut Missionaries) (725)	890
Montfort Missionaries (635)	881
Brothers of Christian Instruction of Ploërmel (5)	863
Missionaries of the Holy Family (650)	851
Franciscans (Third Order Regular) (573)	844
Servants of Mary (563)	830
Scalabrinians (581)	816
Xaverian Missionaries (342)	808
Sacred Hearts, Congregation of (Picpus) (646)	780
Vincentian Cong. (482)	714
Most Precious Blood (527)	700
Mercedarians (515)	691
Heralds of Good News (377)	661
Canons Regular of St. Augustine (543)	653
Trinitarians (409)	631
Brothers of Charity (Ghent)	622
Oblates of St. Joseph (411)	601
St. Joseph, Congregation of (415)	590
Missionaries of the Mill Hill (357)	571
Servants of Charity (328)	566
Pontifical Institute for Foreign Missions (437)	553
Oblates of St. Francis de Sales (425)	547
Order of St. Paul the First Hermit (366)	531
Oratorians (417)	529
Order of St. Basil the Great (Basilians of St. Josaphat) (348)	528
Blessed Sacrament, Miss. Congr. (335)	521
Rogationists (305)	510
Somascans (353)	501
Viatorians (218)	494
Eudists (351)	481
Society of Christ (396)	471
Columbans (426)	469
Marian Fathers and Brothers (341)	464
Vocationist Fathers (248)	445
Immaculate Conception, Sons of (181)	428
Stigmatine Fathers and Brothers (331)	422
Capuchin Tertiaries (198)	412
Barnabites (285)	411
Charity, Missionaries of (1)	410
Maryknollers (335)	399
Crosiers (Order of the Holy Cross) (246)	392
Priestly Fraternity of St. Peter (229)	387
Resurrection, Congregation of the (313)	364
Mariannhill Missionaries (208)	356
St. Patrick's Mission Society (294)	356
Franciscan Missionary Brothers	344
Michael the Archangel (264)	340
Missionaries of the Holy Spirit (232)	331
Brothers of the Immaculate Conception (1)	317
Carthusians (153)	304
Rosminians (201)	290
Sulpicians (271)	271
Paris Foreign Mission Society (221)	253
St. Basil, Congr. of (215)	222
Little Brothers of Jesus (58)	214
Xaverian Brothers	211
Rosarians (80)	207
Discalced Augustinians (128)	205
Minim Fathers (120)	189
Oblates of the Virgin Mary (134)	180
Brothers of St. Patrick	178
Theatines (139)	170

Sons of the Holy Family (133)	166	Josephites (St. Joseph's Society of the	
Charitable Schools (99)	159	Sacred Heart – S.S.J.) (76)	88
Canossians (112)	151	Alexian Brothers (3)	80
Mary Immaculate, Sons of (81)	147	Brothers of Our Lady Mother of Mercy (19)	76
Clerics Regular Minor (Adorno Fathers) (70)	144	St. Paul, Missionary Soc. (58)	75
Paulists (125)	139	Franciscan Brothers of Brooklyn	70
Missionary Servants of the		Glenmary Missioners (49)	70 (2008)
Most Holy Trinity (88)	127	Camaldolese Hermits of Monte Corona (28)	60
Josephites (C.J.) (84)	113	Servants of the Holy Paraclete (17)	48
Clerics Regular of the Mother of God (66)	112	Sacerdotal Fraternity, Cong. of the (18)	48
Bethlehem Missionaries (81)	110	Brothers of Mercy	36
Presentation Brothers	108	Society of St. Edmund (27)	34
Basilian Salvatorian Fathers (87)	93	Franciscan Brothers of the Holy Cross	35
Franciscan Friars of the Atonement (60)	92	Little Brothers of the Good Shepherd (3)	30

RELIGIOUS INSTITUTES OF WOMEN IN THE UNITED STATES

Sources: The Official Catholic Directory; Catholic Almanac *survey. As of June 1, 2014.*

Adorers of the Blood of Christ, A.S.C.: Founded 1834, in Italy; in U.S., 1870. General motherhouse, Rome, Italy. U.S. region: 4233 Sulphur Ave., St. Louis, MO 63109, (314) 351-6294,; 3950 Columbia Ave., Columbia, PA 17512, (717) 285-4536; www.adorers.org. Education, retreats, social services, pastoral ministry.

Africa, Missionary Sisters of Our Lady of (Sisters of Africa), M.S.O.L.A.: Founded 1869, at Algiers, Algeria, by Cardinal Lavigerie; in U.S., 1929. General motherhouse, Rome, Italy. U.S. headquarters, 47 W. Spring St., Winooski, VT 05404-1397, (802) 655-4003, www.smnda.org. Medical, educational, catechetical and social work in Africa.

Agnes, Sisters of St., C.S.A.: Founded 1858, in U.S., by Rev. Caspar Rehrl. General motherhouse, 320 County Rd., Fond du Lac, WI 54935, (920) 907-2321, www.csasisters.org. Education, health care, social services.

Ann, Sisters of St., S.S.A.: Founded 1834, in Italy; in U.S., 1952. General motherhouse, Rome, Italy. U.S. headquarters, Mount St. Ann, Ebensburg, PA 15931, (814) 472-9354.

Anne, Sisters of St., S.S.A.: Founded 1850, at Vaudreuil, QC, Canada; in U.S., 1866. General motherhouse, Lachine, QC, Canada. U.S. address, 720 Boston Post Rd., Marlborough, MA 01752, (508) 597-0204, www.sistersofsaintanne. org. Retreat work, pastoral ministry, religious education.

Anthony, Missionary Servants of St., M.S.S.A.: Founded 1929, in U.S., by Fr. Peter Basque. General motherhouse, 100 Peter Baque Rd., San Antonio, TX 78209, (210) 824-4553. Social work.

Antonine Maronite Sisters: Founded in Beirut, Lebanon. Motherhouse, Couvent Mar-Doumith, Roumieh, El-Metn, B.P. 84, Borumana, Lebanon. U.S. house, 2691 North Lipkey Rd., North Jackson, OH 44451, (330) 538-9822; www.antoinesisters.com.

Assumption, Little Sisters of the, L.S.A.: Founded 1865, in France; in U.S., 1891. General motherhouse, Paris, France. U.S. provincialate, 100 Gladstone Ave., Walden, NY 12586, (914) 778-0667, www.little sisters.org. Social work, nursing, family life education.

Assumption, Religious of the, R.A.: Founded 1839, in France; in U.S., 1919. Generalate, Paris, France. North American province, 11 Old English Rd., Worcester, MA 01609, (508) 791-2936; www.assumptionsisters.org.

Assumption of the Blessed Virgin, Sisters of the, S.A.S.V.: Founded 1853, in Canada; in U.S., 1891. General motherhouse, Nicolet, QC, Canada. U.S. province, 2 Buchanan Rd., Salem, MA 01970, (978) 744-2757. Education, mission, pastoral ministry.

Augustinian Nuns of Contemplative Life, O.S.A.: Established in Spain in 13th century. U.S. foundation, Convent of Our Mother of Good Counsel, 440 Marley Rd., New Lenox, IL, 60451, (815) 463-9662; www.lampsalight.org.

Augustinian Sisters, Servants of Jesus and Mary, Congregation of, O.S.A.: Generalate, Rome, Italy. U.S. foundation, St. John School, 513 E. Broadway, Brandenburg, KY 40108, (270) 422-2088, www.stjohnonline.org.

Basil the Great, Sisters of the Order of St. (Byzantine Rite), O.S.B.M.: Founded fourth century, in Cappadocia, by St. Basil the Great and his sister, St. Macrina; in U.S., 1911. Generalate, Rome, Italy. U.S. motherhouses: Philadelphia Ukrainian Byzantine Rite, 710 Fox Chase Rd., Philadelphia, PA 19046-4198, (215) 379-3998, www.basilianfoxchase.org. Pittsburgh Ruthenian Byzantine Rite, Mount St. Macrina, PO Box 878, Uniontown, PA 15401, (724) 438-8644. Education, health care.

Benedict, Sisters of the Order of St., O.S.B.: Our Lady of Mount Caritas Monastery (founded 1979, Ashford, CT), 54 Seckar Rd., Ashford, CT 06278, (860) 429-7457, www.mountcaritasmonastery.org. Contemplative.

Benedictine Nuns, O.S.B.: St. Scholastica Priory, Box 606, Petersham, MA 01366, (978) 724-3213; www.stscholasticapriory.org. Cloistered.

Benedictine Nuns of the Congregation of Solesmes, O.S.B.: U.S. establishment, 1981, in Burlington diocese. Monastery of the Immaculate Heart of Mary, 4103 Vt. Rte 100, Westfield, VT 05874, (802) 744-6525, www.ihmwest field.com. Cloistered, papal enclosure.

Benedictine Nuns of the Primitive Observance, O.S.B.: Founded c. 529, in Italy; in U.S., 1948. Abbey of Regina Laudis, Flanders Rd., Bethlehem, CT 06751, (203) 266-7727, www.abbeyofreginalaudis.com. Cloistered.

Benedictine Sisters, O.S.B.: Founded c. 529, in Italy; in U.S., 1852. General motherhouse, Eichstatt, Bavaria, Germany. U.S. addresses: St. Emma Monastery, motherhouse and novitiate, 1001 Harvey Ave., Greensburg, PA 15601, (724) 834-3060, www.stemma.org. Abbey of St. Walburga, 32109 N. U.S. Highway 287, Virginia Dale, CO 80536, (970) 472-0612, www.walburga.org.

Benedictine Sisters, Missionary, O.S.B.: Founded 1885. Generalate, Rome, Italy. U.S. motherhouse, 300 N. 18th St., Norfolk, NE 68701-3687, (402) 371-3438, www.norfolkosb.org.

Benedictine Sisters, Olivetan, O.S.B.: Founded 1887, in U.S. General motherhouse, Holy Angels Convent, P.O. Box 1209, Jonesboro, AR 72403- 0130, (870) 935-5810, www.olivben.org. Educational, hospital work.

Benedictine Sisters of Perpetual Adoration of Pontifical Jurisdiction, Congregation of the, O.S.B.: Founded in U.S., 1874, from Maria Rickenbach, Switzerland. General motherhouse, 8300 Morganford Rd., St. Louis, MO 63123, (314) 638-6427.

Benedictine Sisters of Pontifical Jurisdiction, O.S.B.: Founded c. 529, in Italy. No general mother house in U.S. Three federations:

• **Federation of St. Scholastica** (1922). Pres., Sister Esther Fangman, O.S.B., 3741 Forest Ave., Kansas City, MO 64109, (816) 753-2514. Motherhouses belonging to the federation:

MOUNT ST. SCHOLASTICA, 801 S. 8th St., Atchison, Kans. 66002, (913) 360-6200, www.mountosb.org. Benedictine Sisters of Elk Co., ST. JOSEPH'S MONASTERY, St. Mary's, PA 15857, (814) 834-2267, www.osbnuns.org. Benedictine Sisters of Erie, 6101 E. Lake Rd., Erie, PA 16511, (814) 899- 0614, www.eriebenedictines.org. Benedictine Sisters of Chicago, ST. SCHOLASTICA PRIORY, 7430 N. Ridge Blvd., Chicago, IL 60645, (773) 764-2413, www.osbchicago.org. Benedictine Sisters of the Sacred Heart, 1910 Maple Ave., Lisle, IL 60532-2164, (630) 725-6000, www.shmlisle.org. Benedictine Sisters of Elizabeth, ST. WALBURGA MONASTERY, 851 N. Broad St., Elizabeth, NJ 07208-2593, (201) 352-4278, www.catholic-forum.com/bensisnj. Benedictine Sisters of Pittsburgh, 4530 Perrysville Ave., Pittsburgh, PA 15229, (412) 931-2844, www.osbpgh.org.

ST. JOSEPH'S MONASTERY, 2200 S. Lewis, Tulsa, OK 74114, (918) 742-4989, www.stjosephmonastery.org. ST. GERTRUDE'S MONASTERY, 14259 Benedictine Lane, Ridgely, MD 21660, (410) 634-2497. ST. WALBURGA MONASTERY, 2500 Amsterdam Rd., Villa Hills, KY 41017, (859) 331-6771, www.stwalburg.org. SACRED HEART MONASTERY, P.O. Box 2040, Cullman, AL 35056, (256) 734-4622, www.shmon. org. Benedictine Sisters of Virginia, 9535 Linton Hall Rd., Bristow, VA 20136-1217, (703) 361-0106, www.osbva.org. ST. SCHOLASTICA MONASTERY, 416 W. Highland Dr., Boerne, TX 78006, (830) 816-8504, www.boernebenedictines.com. ST. LUCY'S PRIORY, 19045 E. Sierra Madre Ave., Glendora, CA 91741, (626) 335-1682. Benedictine Sisters of Florida, HOLY NAME MONASTERY, P.O. Box 2450, St. Leo, FL 33574-2450, (352) 588-8320, www.floridabenedictines.com. BENET HILL MONASTERY, 2555 N. Chelton Rd., Colorado Springs, CO 80909, (719) 633-0655, www.benethillmonastery.org. QUEEN OF HEAVEN MONASTERY (Byzantine Rite), 169 Kenmore Ave., #301, Warren, OH 44483, (330) 856-1813, www.benedictinebyzantine.org. QUEEN OF ANGELS MONASTERY, 23615 N.E. 100th St., Liberty, MO 64068, (816) 750-4618.

• **Federation of St. Gertrude the Great** (1937). Office: St. Benedict of Ferdinand, Indiana, 802 E. 10th St., Ferdinand, IN 47532, (812) 367-1411, www.thedo me.org. Pres., Sister Kathryn Huber, O.S.B. Motherhouses belonging to the federation:

MOTHER OF GOD MONASTERY, 110 28th Ave., S.E., Watertown, SD 57201, (605) 882-6633, www.watertown benedictines. org. SACRED HEART MONASTERY, 1005 W. 8th St., Yankton, SD 57078-3389, (605) 668-6000, www. yank tonbenedictines.org. MT. ST. BENEDICT MONASTERY, 620 E. Summit Ave., Crookston, MN 56716, (218) 281-3441, www.msb.net. SACRED HEART MONASTERY, P.O. Box 364, Richardton, ND 58652, (701) 974-2121, www.

sacredheart monastery.com. ST. MARTIN MONASTERY, 1851 City Springs Rd., Rapid City, SD 57702-9613, (605) 343-8011, www.blackhillsbenedictine.com. MONASTERY OF IMMACULATE CONCEPTION, 802 E. 10th St., Ferdinand, IN 47532, (812) 367-2313. MONASTERY OF ST. GERTRUDE, 465 Keuterville Rd., Cottonwood, ID 83522-5183, (208) 962-3224, www.stgertrudes.org.

MONASTERY OF ST. BENEDICT CENTER, Box 5070, Madison, WI 53705-0070, (608) 836-1631, www.sbcenter.org. QUEEN OF ANGELS MONASTERY, 840 S. Main St., Mt. Angel, OR 97362, (503) 845-6141, www.benedictine-srs.org. ST. SCHOLASTICA MONASTERY, P.O. Box 3489, Fort Smith, AR 72913-3489, (479) 783-4147, www.stgcho.org. OUR LADY OF PEACE MONASTERY, 3710 W. Broadway, Columbia, MO 65203, (573) 446-2300, www.benedictinesister.org. QUEEN OF PEACE MONASTERY, Box 370, Belcourt, ND 58316, (701) 477-6167. OUR LADY OF GRACE MONASTERY, 1402 Southern Ave., Beech Grove, IN 46107, (317) 787-3287, www.bene-dictine.com. SPIRIT OF LIFE MONASTERY, 10760 W. Glennon Dr., Lakewood, CO 80226, (303) 986-9234. ST. BENEDICT'S MONASTERY 225 Masters Ave., Winnipeg, MB, R4A 2A1, Canada, (204) 338-4601, www.stbens.ca.

• **Federation of St. Benedict** (1947). Pres., Sister Colleen Haggerty, O.S.B., St. Benedict Convent, 104 Chapel Lane, St. Joseph, MN 56374-0220, (320) 363- 7100, www.sbm. osb.org. Motherhouses in U.S. belonging to the federation:

ST. BENEDICT'S CONVENT, St. Joseph, MN 56374, (320) 363-7013. ST. SCHOLASTICA MONASTERY, 1001 Kenwood Ave., Duluth, MN 55811-2300, (218) 723-7001, www.dulu-thbenedictines.org. ST. BEDE MONASTERY, 1190 Priory Rd., Eau Claire, WI 54702, (715) 834-3176, www.saintbede.org. ST. MARY MONASTERY, 2200 88th Ave. W., Rock Island, IL 61201, (309) 283-2101, www.smmsis ters.org; ANNUNCIATION MONASTERY, 7520 University Dr., Bismarck, ND 58504, (701) 255-1520, www.annunciation monastery.org. ST. PAUL'S MONASTERY, 2675 Larpenteur Ave. E., St. Paul, MN 55109, (651) 777-8181, www.osb.org/spm. ST. PLACID PRIORY, 500 College St. N.E., Lacey, WA 98516, (360) 438-1771, www.stplacid.org. MOUNT BENEDICT MONASTERY, 6000 South 1075 East, Ogden, UT 84405-4945, (801) 479-6030, www.mbutah.org.

Bethany, Sisters of, C.V.D.: Founded 1928, in El Salvador; in U.S. 1949. General motherhouse, Santa Tecla, El Salvador. U.S. address: 850 N. Hobart Blvd., Los Angeles, CA 90029, (213) 669-9411.

Bethlemita Sisters, Daughters of the Sacred Heart of Jesus (Beth.): Founded 1861, in Guatemala. Motherhouse, Bogota, Colombia. U.S. address, St. Joseph Residence, 330 W. Pembroke St., Dallas, TX 75208, (214) 948-3597.

Bon Secours, Congregation of, C.B.S.: Founded 1824, in France; in U.S., 1881. Generalate, Rome, Italy. U.S. provincial house, 1525 Marriottsville Rd., Marriottsville, MD 21104, (410) 442-1333, www.bonsecours.org. Hospital work.

Brigid, Congregation of St., C.S.B.: Founded 1807, in Ireland; in U.S., 1953. U.S. regional house, 5118 Loma Linda Dr., San Antonio, TX 78201, (210) 733-0701, www.brigidine.org.au.

Brigittine Sisters (Order of the Most Holy Savior), O.SS.S.: Founded 1344, at Vadstena, Sweden, by St. Bridget; in U.S., 1957. General motherhouse, Rome, Italy. U.S. address, Vikingsborg, 4 Runkenhage Rd., Darien, CT 06820, (203) 655-1068.

Canossian Daughters of Charity (Fd.C.C.): Founded 1808 in Verona, Italy, by St. Magdalen of Canossa.

General motherhouse, Rome, Italy. U.S. provincial house, 5625 Isleta Blvd. S.W., Albuquerque, NM 87105, (505) 873-2854, www.fdcc.org.

Carmel, Congregation of Our Lady of Mount, O. Carm.: Founded 1825, in France; in U.S., 1833. Generalate, PO Box 476, Lacombe, LA 70445, (504) 882-7577, www. mountcarmel.home.mindspring.com. Education, social services, pastoral ministry, retreat work.

Carmel, Institute of Our Lady of Mount, O. Carm.: Founded 1854, in Italy; in U.S., 1947. General motherhouse, Rome, Italy. U.S. novitiate, 5 Wheatland St., Peabody, MA 01960, (978) 531-4733; www.carmeliteoreschool.com. Apostolic work.

Carmelite Community of the Word, C.C.W.: Motherhouse and novitiate, 394 Bem Rd., Gallitzin, PA 16641, (814) 886-4098 (fax).

Carmelite Nuns, Discalced, O.C.D.: Founded 1562, Spain. First foundation in U.S. in 1790, at Charles County, MD; this monastery was moved to Baltimore. Monasteries in U.S. are listed below by state.

Alabama: 716 Dauphin Island Pkwy., Mobile 36606, (334) 471-3991. Arkansas: 7201 W. 32nd St., Little Rock 72204, (501) 565-5121, www.littlerockcarmel.org.

California: 215 E. Alhambra Rd., Alhambra 91801, (626) 282-2387, www.carmelites.org/teresacarmel; 27601 Highway 1, Carmel 93923, (831) 624-3043, www.carmelitesistersbythesea.net; 6981 Teresian Way, Georgetown 95634, (530) 333-1617; 5158 Hawley Blvd., San Diego 92116, (619) 280-5424, www.carmelsandiego.com; 721 Parker Ave., San Francisco 94118, (415) 387-2640; 530 Blackstone Dr., San Rafael 94903, (415) 479-6872; 1000 Lincoln St., Santa Clara 95050-5285, (408) 296-8412, www.members.aol.com/ santaclaracarmel.

Colorado: 6138 S. Gallup St., Littleton 80120, (303) 798- 4176. Georgia: Coffee Bluff, 11 W. Back St., Savannah 31419, (912) 925-8505, www.savannahcarmel.org. Hawaii: 6301 Pali Hwy., Kaneohe 96744, (808) 261-6542; Illinois: 949 N. River Rd., Des Plaines 60016, (847) 298-4241. Indiana: 2500 Cold Spring Rd., Indianapolis 46222-2323, (317) 926-5654, www.praythenews.com; 59 Allendale Pl., Terre Haute 47802, (812) 299-1410; www.heartsawake.org. Iowa: 17937 250th St., Eldridge 52748, (319) 285-8387; 2901 S. Cecilia St., Sioux City 51106, (712) 276-1680. Kentucky: 1740 Newburg Rd., Louisville 40205, (502) 451- 6796. Louisiana: 1250 Carmel Ave., Lafayette 70501, (337) 232-4651; 73530 River Rd., Covington 70435, (985) 898-0923.

Maryland: 1318 Dulaney Valley Rd., Towson, Baltimore 21286, (410) 823-7415, www.geocities.com/baltimorecarmel; 5678 Mt. Carmel Rd., La Plata, 20646, (301) 934-1654, www.carmelofporttobacco@erols.com. Massachusetts: 61 Mt. Pleasant Ave., Roxbury, Boston 02119, (617) 442-1411, www.carmelitesofboston.org; 15 Mt. Carmel Rd., Danvers 01923, (978) 774-3008. Michigan: 4300 Mt. Carmel Dr. NE, Ada 49301, (616) 691-7625; 35750 Moravian Dr., Clinton Township 48035, (586) 790-7255, www.rc.net/detroit/carmelite; U.S. 2 Highway N 4028, PO Box 397, Iron Mountain 49801, (906) 774-0561; 3501 Silver Lake Rd., Traverse City 49684, (231) 946-4960. Minnesota: 8251 De Montreville Trail N., Lake Elmo 55042-9547, (651) 777-3882. Mississippi: 2155 Terry Rd., Jackson 39204, (601) 373-1460.

Missouri: 2201 W. Main St., Jefferson City 65101, (573) 636-3364; 9150 Clayton Rd., Ladue, St. Louis Co. 63124, (314) 993-3494, www.stormpages.com/mtcarmel; 424 E. Monastery Rd., Springfield 65807, (417) 881-2115. Nevada: 1950 La Fond Dr., Reno 89509-3099, (775) 323-

3236. *New Hampshire:* 275 Pleasant St., Concord, 03301-2590, (603) 225-5791. New Jersey: 26 Harmony School Rd., Flemington 08822-2606, www.flemingtoncarmel. org. ingtoncarmel.htm; 189 Madison Ave., Morristown 07960, (973) 538-2886. New Mexico: 49 Mt. Carmel Rd., Santa Fe 87505-0352, (505) 983-7232, carmelofsantafe. org. New York: c/o Chancery Office, Diocese of Brooklyn, 361 Highland Blvd., Brooklyn 11207, (718) 235-0422; 89 Hiddenbrook Dr., Beacon, 12508, (914) 831-5572, carmelitesbeacon.org; 75 Carmel Rd., Buffalo 14214, (716) 837-6499; 1931 W. Jefferson Rd., Pittsford, NY 14534, (585) 427-7094, www.carmelitesofrochester.org.

Ohio: 3176 Fairmount Blvd., Cleveland Heights 44118, (216) 321-6568; www.clevelandcarmel.org. Oklahoma: 20000 N. County Line Rd., Piedmont 73078, (405) 348- 3947, www.okcarmel.org. Oregon: 87609 Green Hill Rd., Eugene 97402, (541) 345-8649. Pennsylvania: 1 Maria Hall Dr., Danville 17821, (570) 275-4682, www. carmelelysburg. org; 510 E. Gore Rd., Erie 16509-3799, (814) 825-0846, erieRDC.org/Carmelites.asp; 5206 Center Dr., Latrobe 15650, (724) 539-1056, www.latrobecarmel. org; P.O. Box 57, Loretto 15940-0057, (814) 472-8620, lorettocarmel.org; Byzantine Rite, 403 West County Rd., Sugarloaf 18249-9998, (570) 788-1205; 66th and Old York Rd., Philadelphia 19126, (215) 424-6143. Rhode Island: 25 Watson Ave., Barrington 02806, (401) 245-3421. South Dakota: 221 5th St., W., Alexandria, 57311, (605) 239-4382.

Texas: 600 Flowers Ave., Dallas 75211; 5801 Mt. Carmel Dr., Arlington 76017, (817) 468-1781; 1100 Parthenon Pl., Roman Forest, New Caney 77357-3276, (281) 399-0270, www.carmelnewcaney.com; 6301 Culebra and St. Joseph Way, San Antonio 78238-4909, (210) 680-1834, www. carmelsanantonio.com. Utah: 5714 Holladay Blvd., Salt Lake City 84121, (801) 277-6075, www.carmelslc.org. Vermont: 94 Main St., Montpelier, 05601, (914) 831-5572. Washington: 2215 N.E. 147th St., Shoreline 98155, (206) 363-7150. Wisconsin: W267 N2517 Meadowbrook Rd., Pewaukee 53072, (262) 691-0336, www.geocities.com/pewaukeecarmel.org; 6100 Pepper Rd., Denmark 54208, (920) 863-5055.

Carmelite Nuns of the Ancient Observance (Calced Carmelites), O. Carm.: Founded 1452, in the Netherlands; in U.S., 1930, from Naples, Italy, convent (founded 1856). U.S. monasteries: Carmelite Monastery of St. Therese and St. Mary Magdalen di Pazzi, 3551 Lanark Rd., Coopersburg, PA 18036, (610) 797-3721. Carmel of Mary, Wahpeton, ND 58075. Our Lady of Grace Monastery, 6202 CR 339 Via Maria, Christoval, TX 76935 (325) 853-1722. Carmel of the Sacred Heart, 430 Laurel Ave., Hudson, WI 54016, (715) 862-2156, www.carmelite-nuns. com. Papal enclosure.

Carmelite Sisters (Corpus Christi), O. Carm.: Founded 1908, in England; in U.S., 1920. General motherhouse, Tunapuna, Trinidad, W.I. U.S. address: Mt. Carmel Home, 412 W. 18th St., Kearney, NE 68845, (308) 237-2287, www.corpuschristicarmelites.org. Home and foreign mission work.

Carmelite Sisters for the Aged and Infirm, O. Carm.: Founded 1929, at New York, by Mother M. Angeline Teresa, O. Carm. Motherhouse, 600 Woods Rd., Avila-on-Hudson, Germantown, NY 12526, (518) 537-5000, www.carmelitesisters.com. Social work, nursing and educating in the field of gerontology.

Carmelite Sisters of Charity, C.a.Ch.: Founded 1826 at Vich, Spain, by St. Joaquina de Vedruna.

Generalate, Rome, Italy. U.S. address, 701 Beacon Rd., Silver Spring, MD 20903, (301) 434-6344.

Carmelite Sisters of St. Therese of the Infant Jesus, C.S.T.: Founded 1917, in U.S. General mother house, 1300 Classen Dr., Oklahoma City, OK 73103, (405) 232-7926, www.oksister.com. Educational work.

Carmelite Sisters of the Divine Heart of Jesus, Carmel D.C.J.: Founded 1891, in Germany; in U.S., 1912. General motherhouse, Sittard Netherlands. U.S. provincial houses: Northern Province, 1230 Kavanaugh Pl., Milwaukee, WI 53213, (414) 453- 4040, www.carmelitedcjnorth.org. Central Province, 10341 Manchester Rd., St. Louis, MO 63122, (314) 965-7616, www.carmelitesdcj.org. South Western Province, 8585 La Mesa Blvd., La Mesa, CA 91941-3901, (619) 335-7265. Social services, mission work.

Carmelite Sisters of the Most Sacred Heart of Los Angeles, O.C.D.: Founded 1904, in Mexico. General mother house and novitiate, 920 E. Alhambra Rd., Alhambra, CA 91801-2799, (626) 289-1353, wwwcarmel-msh.org. Social services, retreat and educational work.

Carmelites, Calced, O. Carm.: Founded 1856 in Naples, Italy. U.S. address: Carmelite Monastery of St. Therese, 3551 Lanark Rd., Coopersburg, PA 18036.

Carmelites of St. Theresa, Congregation of Missionary, C.M.S.T.: Founded 1903, in Mexico. General mother-house, Mexico City, Mexico. U.S. foundation, 9548 Deer Trail Dr., Houston, TX 77038, (281) 445-5520.

Casimir, Sisters of St., S.S.C.: Founded 1907, in U.S., by Mother Maria Kaupas. General motherhouse, 2601 W. Marquette Rd., Chicago, IL 60629, (773) 776- 1324. Education, missions, social services.

Cenacle, Congregation of Our Lady of the Retreat in the, R.C.: Founded 1826, in France; in U.S., 1892. Generalate, Rome, Italy. Eastern Province, Cenacle Rd., Lake Ronkonkoma, NY 11779, (516) 471-6270. Midwestern Province, 513 W. Fullerton Pkwy., Chicago, IL 60614-6428, (773) 528-6300, www.cenaclesisters.org.

Charity, Daughters of Divine, F.D.C.: Founded 1868, at Vienna, Austria; in U.S., 1913. General moth erhouse, Rome, Italy. U.S. province: 850 Hylan Blvd., Staten Island, NY 10305, (718) 720-7365. Education, social services.

Charity, Missionaries of, M.C.: Founded 1950, in Calcutta, India, by Mother Teresa; first U.S. founda-tion, 1971. General motherhouse, 54A, A.J.C. Bose Rd., Calcutta 700016, India. U.S. address, 335 E. 145th St., Bronx, NY 10451, (718) 292-0019. Service of the poor.

Charity, Religious Sisters of, R.S.C.: Founded 1815, in Ireland; in U.S., 1953. Motherhouse, Dublin, Ireland. U.S. headquarters, 10668 St. James Dr., Culver City, CA 90230, (310) 559-1654.

Charity, Sisters of (of Seton Hill), S.C.: Founded 1870, at Altoona, PA, from Cincinnati foundation. Generalate, De Paul Center, 463 Mt. Thor Rd., Greensburg, PA 15601, (724) 836-0406, www.scsh.org. Educational, hospi-tal, social, for eign mission work.

Charity, Sisters of (Grey Nuns of Montréal), S.G.M.: Founded 1737, in Canada, by St. Marie Marguerite d'Youville; in U.S., 1855. General administration, Montréal, QC H2Y 2L7, Canada. U.S. provincial house, 10 Pelham Rd., Ste. 1000, Lexington, MA 02421, (781) 674-7407, www.sqmlex.org.

Charity, Sisters of (of Leavenworth), S.C.L.: Founded 1858, in U.S. Motherhouse, 4200 S. 4th St., Leavenworth, KS 66048, (913) 758-6508, www.scls.org/.

Charity, Sisters of (of Nazareth), S.C.N.: Founded 1812, in U.S. General motherhouse, SCN Center, P.O. Box 172, Nazareth, KY 40048, (502) 348-1561; 8200 McKnight Rd., Pittsburgh, PA 15237, (412) 364-3000, www.scnazareth.org. Education, health services. Merged with the Vincentian Sisters of Charity in Nov. 2008.

Charity, Sisters of (of St. Augustine), C.S.A.: Founded 1851, at Cleveland, Ohio. Motherhouse, 5232 Broadview Rd., Richfield, OH 44286, (330) 659-5100, www.srsofcharity.org.

Charity, Sisters of Christian, S.C.C.: Founded 1849, in Paderborn, Germany, by Bl. Pauline von Mallinckrodt; in U.S., 1873. Generalate, Rome, Italy. U.S. provinces: Mallinckrodt Convent, 350 Bernardsville Rd., Mendham, NJ 07945, (973) 543-6528, www.scceast.org. 2041 Elmwood Ave., Wilmette, IL 60091-1431, (847) 920-9341, www.sccwilmette.org. Education, health services, other apostolic work.

Charity, Vincentian Sisters of, V.S.C.: Founded 1928, at Bedford, Ohio. General motherhouse, 1160 Broadway, Bedford, OH 44146, (440) 232-4755.

Charity of Cincinnati, Ohio, Sisters of, S.C.: Founded 1809; became independent community, 1852. General motherhouse, 5900 Delhi Rd., Mt. St. Joseph, OH 45051, (513) 347-5201, www.srchari-tycinti.org. Educational, hospital, social work.

Charity of Ottawa, Sisters of (Grey Nuns of the Cross), S.C.O.: Founded 1845, at Ottawa, Canada; in U.S., 1857. General motherhouse, Ottawa, Canada. U.S. provincial house, 559 Fletcher St., Lowell, MA 01854, (978) 453-4993. Educational, hospital work, extended health care.

Charity of Our Lady, Mother of Mercy, Sisters of, S.C.M.M.: Founded 1832, in Holland; in U.S., 1874. General motherhouse, Den Bosch, the Netherlands. U.S. provincialate, 520 Thompson Ave., East Haven, CT 06512, (203) 469-7872.

Charity of Our Lady, Mother of the Church, S.C.M.C: U.S. foundation, 1970. General mother house, 520 Thompson Ave., East Haven, CT 06512, (203) 469-7872.

Charity of Our Lady of Mercy, Sisters of, O.L.M.: Founded 1829, in Charleston, SC. Generalate and motherhouse, 424 Fort Johnson Rd., P. O. Box 12410, Charleston, SC 29422, (843) 795-6083. Education, campus ministry, social services.

Charity of Quebec, Sisters of (Grey Nuns), S.C.Q.: Founded 1849, at Quebec; in U.S., 1890. General moth-erhouse, 2655 Le Pelletier St., Beauport, QC GIC 3X7, Canada. U.S. address, 359 Summer St., New Bedford, MA 02740, (508) 996-6751. Social work.

Charity of Saint Elizabeth, Sisters of (Convent Station, N.J.), S.C.: Founded 1859, at Newark, NJ. General motherhouse, P.O. Box 476, Convent Station, NJ 07961-0476, (973) 290-5450, www.scnj.org. Education, pastoral ministry, social services.

Charity of St. Hyacinthe, Sisters of (Grey Nuns), S.C.S.H.: Founded 1840, at St. Hyacinthe, Canada; in U.S., 1878. General motherhouse, 16470 Avenue Bourdages, SUD, St. Hyacinthe, QC J2T 4J8, Canada. U.S. regional house, 98 Campus Ave., Lewiston, ME 04240, (207) 797-8607.

Charity of St. Joan Antida, Sisters of, S.C.S.J.A.: Founded 1799, in France; in U.S., 1932. General moth erhouse, Rome, Italy. U.S. provincial house, 8560 N. 76th Pl., Milwaukee, WI 53223, (414) 354-9233, www.scsja.org.

Charity of St. Louis, Sisters of, S.C.S.L.: Founded

1803, in France; in U.S., 1910. Generalate, Rome, Italy. U.S. provincialate, 60 Club Rd., Unit 204, Plattsburgh, NY 12901, (518) 563-7410.

Charity of St. Vincent de Paul, Daughters of, D.C.: Founded 1633, in France; in U.S., 1809, at Emmitsburg, MD, by St. Elizabeth Ann Seton. General motherhouse, Paris, France. U.S. provinces: 333 South Seton Ave., Emmitsburg, MD 21727, (301) 447-2900, www.daughtersofcharity-emmitsburg.org. 7800 Natural Bridge Rd., St. Louis, MO 63121, (314) 382-2800. 9400 New Harmony Rd., Evansville, IN 47720-8912, (812) 963-3341, www.doc-ecp.org. 96 Menands Rd., Albany, NY 12204, (518) 462-5593, www.dc-northeast.org. 26000 Altamont Rd., Los Altos Hills, CA 94022, (650) 949-8865, www.daughtersofcharity.com.

Charity of St. Vincent de Paul, Sisters of, V.Z.: Founded 1845, in Croatia. in U.S., 1955. General motherhouse, Zagreb, Croatia; U.S. foundation, 171 Knox Ave., West Seneca, NY 14224, (716) 825-5859.

Charity of St. Vincent de Paul, Sisters of, Halifax, S.C.: Founded 1856, at Halifax, NS, from Emmitsburg foundation. Generalate, Mt. St. Vincent, Halifax, NS, Canada. U.S. addresses: Commonwealth of Massachusetts, 125 Oakland St., Wellesley Hills, MA 02481-5338, (781) 997-1165, www.schalifax.ca. Boston Province, 26 Phipps St., Quincy, MA 02169, (617) 773-6085. New York Province, 85-10 61st Rd., Rezo Park, NY 11374, (718) 651-1684. Educational, hospital, social work.

Charity of St. Vincent de Paul, Sisters of, New York, SC.: Founded 1817, from Emmitsburg foundation. General motherhouse, Mt. St. Vincent on Hudson, 6301 Riverdale Ave., Bronx, NY 10471, (718) 549-9200, www.scny.org. Educational, hospital work.

Charity of the Blessed Virgin Mary, Sisters of, B.V.M.: Founded 1833, in U.S. by Mary Frances Clarke. General motherhouse, BVM Center, 1100 Carmel Dr., Dubuque, IA 52003, (563) 588-2351, www.bvmcong.com. Education, pastoral ministry, social services.

Charity of the Immaculate Conception of Ivrea, Sisters of, S.C.I.C.: Founded 18th century, in Italy; in U.S., 1961. General motherhouse, Rome, Italy. U.S. address, Immaculate Virgin of Miracles Convent, 268 Prittstown Rd., Mt. Pleasant, PA 15666, (724) 887-6753.

Charity of the Incarnate Word, Congregation of the Sisters of, C.C.V.I.: Founded 1869, at San Antonio, TX, by Bp. C. M. Dubuis. Generalate, 3200 McCullough, San Antonio, TX 78212, (210) 734-8310, www.incarnatewordsisters.org.

Charity of the Incarnate Word, Congregation of the Sisters of (Houston, TX), C.C.V.I.: Founded 1866, in U.S., by Bp. C. M. Dubuis. General motherhouse, P.O. Box 230969, Houston, TX 77223, (713) 928-6053. Educational, hospital, social work.

Charity of the Sacred Heart, Daughters of, F.C.S.C.J.: Founded 1823, at La Salle de Vihiers, France; in U.S., 1905. General motherhouse, La Salle de Vihiers, France. U.S. address, Sacred Heart Province, 226 Grove St., PO Box 642, Littleton, NH 03561, (603) 444-3970.

Charles Borromeo, Missionary Sisters of St. (Scalabrini Srs.): Founded 1895, in Italy; in U.S., 1941. American novitiate, 1414 N. 37th Ave., Melrose Park, IL 60160; (708) 343-2162.

Child Jesus, Sisters of the Poor, P.C.J.: Founded 1844, at Aix-la-Chapelle, Germany; in U.S., 1924. General motherhouse, Simpelveld, the Netherlands.

American provincialate, 4567 Olentangy River Rd., Columbus, OH 43214, (614) 459-8285; www.ourladyofbethlehem.org.

Chretienne, Sisters of Ste., S.S.Ch.: Founded 1807, in France; in U.S., 1903. General motherhouse, Metz, France. U.S. provincial house, 297 Arnold St., Wrentham, MA 02093, (508) 384-8066, www.sistersofstchretienne.org. Educational, hospital, mission work.

Christ the King, Missionary Sisters of, M.S.C.K.: Founded 1959 in Poland; in U.S., 1978. General moth erhouse, Poznan, Poland. U.S. address, 3000 18-Mile Rd., Sterling Heights, MI 48314.

Christ the King, Sister Servants of, S.S.C.K.: Founded 1936, in U.S. General motherhouse, Loretto Convent, N8114 Calvary St., Mt. Calvary, WI 53057, (920) 753-3211. Social services.

Christian Doctrine, Sisters of Our Lady of, R.C.D.: Founded 1910, in New York. Marydell Convent, 110 Larchdale Ave., Nyack, NY 10960; (845) 727-1011.

Christian Education, Religious of, R.C.E.: Founded 1817, in France; in U.S., 1905. General motherhouse, France. U.S. provincial residence, 55 Parkwood Dr., Milton, MA 02186, (617) 696-7732, www.holyunionsisters.org.

Cistercian Nuns, O. Cist.: Headquarters, Rome, Italy. U.S. address, Valley of Our Lady Monastery, E. 11096 Yanke Dr., Prairie du Sac, WI 53578, www.nunocist.org.

Cistercian Nuns of the Strict Observance, Order of, O.C.S.O.: Founded 1125, in France, by St. Stephen Harding; in U.S., 1949. U.S. addresses: Mt. St. Mary's Abbey, 300 Arnold St., Wrentham, MA 02093, (508) 528-1282, www.msmabbey.org. 14200 E Fish Canyon Rd., Sonoita, AZ 85637, (520) 455-5595, www.santaritabbey.org. Our Lady of the Redwoods Abbey, 18104 Briceland Thorn Rd., Whitethorn, CA 95589, (707) 986-7419, www.redwoodsabbey.org. Our Lady of the Mississippi Abbey, 8400 Abbey Hill Rd., Dubuque, IA 52003, (563) 582-2595, www.mis sissippiabbey.org/. Our Lady of the Angels Monastery, 3365 Monastery Dr., Crozet, VA 22932, (434) 823-1452, www.olamonastery.org.

Clare, Sisters of St., O.S.C.: General motherhouse, Dublin, Ireland. U.S. foundation, St. Francis Convent, 1974 Cherrywood St., Vista, CA 92083, (760) 945-8040.

Claretian Missionary Sisters (Religious of Mary Immaculate), R.M.I.: Founded 1855, in Cuba; in U.S., 1956. Generalate, Rome, Italy. U.S. address, 7080 SW 99 Ave., Miami, FL 33173, (305) 274-5695 (fax), www.claretiansisters.org.

Clergy, Congregation of Our Lady, Help of the, C.L.H.C.: Founded 1961, in U.S. Motherhouse, Maryvale Convent, 2522 June Bug Rd., Vale, NC 28168, (704) 276-2626.

Clergy, Servants of Our Lady Queen of the, S.R.C.: Founded 1929, in Canada; in U.S., 1934. General mother house, 57 Jules A. Brillant, Rimouski, QC G5L 1X1 Canada, (418) 724-0508. Domestic work.

Colettines: *See* Franciscan Poor Clare Nuns.

Columban, Missionary Sisters of St., S.S.C.: Founded 1922, in Ireland; in U.S., 1930. General motherhouse, Wicklow, Ireland. U.S. region, 73 Mapleton St., Brighton, MA 02135, (617) 782-5683.

Comboni Missionary Sisters (Missionary Sisters of Verona), C.M.S.: Founded 1872, in Italy; in U.S., 1950. U.S. address, 5401 Loch-Raven Blvd., Baltimore, MD 21239, (410) 323-1469, www.combonisrs.com.

Consolata Missionary Sisters, M.C.: Founded 1910, in

Italy, by Bl. Giuseppe Allamano; in U.S., 1954. General motherhouse, Turin, Italy. U.S. headquarters, 6801 Belmont Rd., P.O. Box 97, Belmont, MI 49306 (616) 361-9609, www.consolatasisters.org.

Cross, Daughters of, of Liege, F.C.: Founded 1833, in Liege, Belgium; in U.S., 1958. U.S. address, 165 W. Eaton Ave., Tracy, CA 95376.

Cross, Sisters of the Holy, C.S.C.: Founded 1841, at Le Mans, France; established in Canada, 1847; in U.S., 1881. General motherhouse, St. Laurent, Montreal, QC, Canada. U.S. regional office, 377 Island Pond Rd., Manchester, NH 03109, (603) 622-9504. Educational work.

Cross, Sisters of the Holy, Congregation of, C.S.C.: Founded 1841, at Le Mans, France; in U.S., 1843. General motherhouse, 101 Bertrand Hall – Saint Mary's, Notre Dame, IN 46556, (574) 384-5572, www.cscsisters.org. Education, health care, social services, pastoral ministry.

Cross and Passion, Sisters of the (Passionist Sisters), C.P.: Founded 1852; in U.S., 1924. Generalate, Northampton, England. U.S. address: Holy Family Convent, One Wright Lane, N. Kingstown, RI 02852, (401) 294-3554; www.passionistsisters.org.

Cyril and Methodius, Sisters of Sts., SS.C.M.: Founded 1909, in U.S., by Rev. Matthew Jankola. General mother house, Villa Sacred Heart, Danville, PA 17821, (570) 275-4929, www.sscm.org. Education, care of aged.

Disciples of the Lord Jesus Christ, D.L.J.C.: Founded 1972; canonically erected 1991. P.O. Box 17, Channing, TX 79018, (806) 534-2312, www.dljc.org.

Divine Compassion, Sisters of, R.D.C.: Founded 1886, in U.S. General motherhouse, 52 N. Broadway, White Plains, NY 10603, (914) 949-2950. Education, other ministries.

Divine Love, Daughters of, D.D.L.: Founded 1969, in Nigeria; in U.S., 1990. General house, Enugu, Nigeria. U.S. regional house, 2601 N. Sayre Ave., Chicago, IL 60707, (773) 622-2434.

Divine Spirit, Congregation of the, C.D.S.: Founded 1956, in U.S., by Archbishop John M. Gannon. Motherhouse, 409 W. 6th St., Erie, PA 16507, (330) 453-8137. Education, social services.

Divine Zeal, Daughters of, F.D.Z.: Founded 1887 in Italy by Bl. Hannibal Maria DiFrancia; in U.S., 1951. Generalate, Rome. U.S. headquarters, Hannibal House Spiritual Center, 1526 Hill Rd., Reading, PA 19602, (610) 375-1738.

Dominicans

Dominican Nuns: Nuns of the Order of Preachers, O.P.: Founded 1206 by St. Dominic at Prouille, France. Cloistered, contemplative. Two branches in the United States:

• **Dominican Nuns having Perpetual Adoration.** First monastery established 1880, in Newark, NJ, from Oullins, France, foundation (1868). Autonomous monasteries:

St. Dominic's Monastery 2636 Monastery Rd., Linden, VA 22642, (540) 635-3259, www.lindenopnuns. org; Corpus Christi Monastery, 1230 Lafayette Ave., Bronx, NY 10474, (718) 328-6996. Blessed Sacrament, 29575 Middlebelt Rd., Farmington Hills, MI 48334-2311, (248) 626-8321, www.opnuns-fh.org. Monastery of the Angels, 1977 Carmen Ave., Los Angeles, CA 90068-4098, (323) 466-2186, www.op-stjoseph.org/ nuns/angels/. Corpus Christi Monastery, 215 Oak Grove Ave., Menlo Park, CA 94025-3272, (650) 322-1801, www.nunsmenlo. org. Infant Jesus, 1501 Lotus Lane, Lufkin, TX 75904-

2699, (936) 634-4233, www.lufkintxnuns.org.

Dominican Nuns devoted to the Perpetual Rosary. First monastery established 1891, in Union City, NJ, from Calais, France, foundation (1880). Autonomous monasteries (some also observe Perpetual Adoration):

Dominican Nuns of Perpetual Rosary, 605 14th and West Sts., Union City, NJ 07087, (201)866-7004. 217 N. 68th St., Milwaukee, WI 53213, (414) 258-0579, www.dsopr.org. Perpetual Rosary, 1500 Haddon Ave., Camden, NJ 08103, (856) 342-8340. Our Lady of the Rosary, 335 Doat St., Buffalo, NY 14211. Our Lady of the Rosary, 543 Spingfield Ave., Summit, NJ 07901, (908) 273-1228, www.op.org/nunsopsummit. Monastery of the Mother of God, 1430 Riverdale St., W. Springfield, MA 01089-4698, (413) 736-3639, www.op- stjoseph.org/nuns/ ws. Dominican Monastery of the Perpetual Rosary, 802 Court St., Syracuse, NY 13208- 1766. Monastery of the Immaculate Heart of Mary, 1834 Lititz Pike, Lancaster, PA 17601-6585, (717) 569-2104. Mary the Queen, 1310 W. Church St., Elmira, NY 14905, (607) 734-9506, www.oporg/maryqueen. St. Jude, P.O. Box 170, Marbury, AL 36051-0170, (205) 755-1322, www. stjude monastery.org. Our Lady of Grace Monastery, Monastery of Our Lady of Grace, 11 Race Hill Rd., North Guilford, CT 06437, (203) 457-1985, www.ourladyofgracemonastery.org. St. Dominic's Monastery, 4901 16th St. N.W., Washington, DC 20011, (202) 726-2107.

Dominican Sisters of Charity of the Presentation, O.P.: Founded 1696, in France; in U.S., 1906. General mother house, Tours, France. U.S. headquarters, 3012 Elm St., Dighton, MA 02715, (508) 669-5425, www. dominicansister softhepresentation.org. Hospital work.

Dominican Sisters of Hope, O.P.: Formed 1995 through merger of Dominican Sisters of the Most Holy Rosary, Newburgh, NY, Dominican Sisters of the Sick Poor, Ossining, NY, and Dominican Sisters of St. Catherine of Siena, Fall River, MA. General Offices: 299 N. Highland Ave., Ossining, NY 10562, (914) 941-4420, www.ophope.org.

Dominican Sisters of Our Lady of the Rosary and of St. Catherine of Siena (Cabra): Founded 1644 in Ireland. General motherhouse, Cabra, Dublin, Ireland. U.S. regional house, 1930 Robert E. Lee Rd., New Orleans, LA 70122, (504) 288-1593.

Dominican Sisters of Peace, O.P.: Founded in 2009 through the merger of seven Dominican communities: Eucharistic Missionaries of St. Dominic, 3801 Canal St., Suite 400, New Orleans, LA 70119, (504) 486-1133, www.emdsisters.org. St. Rose of Lima, 775 Drahner Rd., #124, Oxford, MI 48371, (248) 628-2872, www. domlife.org. St. Mary, 7300 St. Charles Ave., New Orleans, LA 70118, (504) 861-8183, www.dominicansisters.net/stmarys; Dominican Sisters of Great Bend, 3600 Broadway, Great Bend, KS 67530, (316) 792-1232, www.ksdom.org. St. Mary of the Springs, 2320 Airport Dr., Columbus, OH 43219- 2098, (614) 416-1038, www. oppeace.org; St. Catherine of Siena, 2645 Bardstown Rd., St. Catharine, KY 40061, (606) 336-9303, www. opkentucky.org. Immaculate Heart of Mary, 1929. 1230 W. Market St., Akron, OH 44313-7108, (330) 836-4908, www.akrondominicans.org.

Dominican Sisters of the Perpetual Rosary, O.P.: 217 N. 68th St., Milwaukee, WI 53213, (414) 258-0579; www.dsopr.org. Cloistered, contemplative.

Dominican Sisters of the Roman Congregation of St. Dominic, O.P.: Founded 1621, in France; in U.S., 1904. General motherhouse, Rome, Italy. U.S. province, 123

Dumont Ave., Lewiston, ME 04240, (207) 786-5058; www.crsdop.org. Educational work.

Religious Missionaries of St. Dominic, O.P.: General motherhouse, Rome, Italy. U.S. address (Spanish province), 2237 Waldron Rd., Corpus Christi, TX 78418, (361) 939-9847.

Sisters of St. Dominic, O.P.: Names of congregations are given below, followed by the date of foundation, and location of motherhouse. Most Holy Rosary, 1847. Sinsinawa, WI 53824, (608) 748-4411. Most Holy Name of Jesus, 1850. 1520 Grand Ave., San Rafael, CA 94901, (415) 453-8303, www.sanrafaelop.org. Holy Cross, 1853. 555 Albany Ave., Amityville, NY 11701, (631) 842-6000, www.amityvilleop. org. St. Cecilia, 1860. 801 Dominican Dr., Nashville, TN 37228, (615) 256-5486, www.nashville-dominican.org.

St. Catherine of Siena, 1862. 5635 Erie St., Racine, WI 53402, (262) 639-4100, www.racinedominicans.org. Sacred Heart Convent, 1873. 1237 W. Monroe St., Springfield, IL 62704, (217) 787-0481, www.springfieldop.org. Sisters of Our Lady of the Rosary, Dominican Convent, 175 Route 340, Sparkill, NY 10976, (845) 359-4088, www.sparkill.org. Dominican Sisters of Mission San Jose,. 43326 Mission Blvd., Mission San Jose, CA 94539, (510) 657-2468, www. msjdominicans.org. Most Holy Rosary, 1892. 1257 Siena Heights Dr., Adrian, MI 49221, (517) 266-3570.

Our Lady of the Sacred Heart, 1877. 2025 E. Fulton St., Grand Rapids, MI 49503, (616) 643-0130. St. Dominic, 1878. 496 Western Hwy., Blauvelt, NY 10913, (845) 359-0696, www.opblauvelt.org. St. Catherine de Ricci, 1880. 131 Copley Rd., Upper Darby, PA 19082, (215) 635-6027. Sisters of St. Dominic, 1881. 1 Ryerson Ave., Caldwell, NJ 07006, (973) 403-3331, www.caldwellop.org. Dominican Sisters of Houston, 1882. 6501 Almeda Rd., Houston, TX 77021-2095, (713) 747-3310, www.houstonop.org. Tacoma Dominican Center, 1888. 935 Fawcett Ave., Tacoma, WA 98402, (253) 272-9688.

St. Rose of Lima (Servants of Relief for Incurable Cancer) 1896. 600 Linda Ave., Hawthorne, NY 10532, (914) 769- 0114, www.hawthorne-dominicans.org. St. Catherine of Siena of Kenosha, 119 Brooks St., Taos, NM 87571, (575) 751-1237. Immaculate Conception, 1929. 9000 W. 81st St., Justice, IL 60458, (708) 458-3040. Dominican Sisters of Oakford (St. Catherine of Siena), 1889. Motherhouse, Oakford, Natal, South Africa; U.S. regional house, 1965. 980 Woodland Ave., San Leandro, CA 94577, (510) 638-2822.

Dorothy, Institute of the Sisters of St., S.S.D.: Founded 1834, in Italy, by St. Paola Frassinetti; in U.S., 1911. General motherhouse, Rome, Italy. U.S. provincialate, St. Dorothy Convent, 1305 Hylan Blvd., Si, NY, 10305; (718) 987-2604.

Eucharist, Religious of the, R.E.: Founded 1857, in Belgium; in U.S., 1900. General motherhouse, Belgium. U.S. foundation, 2907 Ellicott Terr., N.W., Washington, DC 20008, (202) 966-3111.

Felix, Congregation of the Sisters of St. (Felician Sisters), C.S.S.F.: Founded 1855, in Poland by Bl. Mary Angela Truszkowska; in U.S., 1874. General motherhouse, Rome, Italy. U.S. provinces: 36800 Schoolcraft Rd., Livonia, MI 48150, (734) 591-1730, www.feliciansisters.org. 600 Doat St., Buffalo, NY 14211, (716) 892-4141, www.cssbuffalo. org. 3800 W. Peterson Ave., Chicago, IL 60659-3116, (773) 463-3020, www.felicianschicago.org. 871 Mercer Rd., Beaver Falls, PA 15010, (724) 384-5302, www.feliciansis-

tersna.org; 1500 Woodcrest Ave., Coraopolis, PA 15108, (412) 264- 2890, www.felicianspa.org. 1315 Enfield St., Enfield, CT 06082, (860) 745-7791. 4210 Meadowlark Lane, S.E., Rio Rancho, NM 87124-1021, (505) 892-8862; southwestfeliciansisters.org.

Filippini, Religious Teachers, M.P.F.: Founded 1692, in Italy; in U.S., 1910. General motherhouse, Rome, Italy. U.S. provinces: St. Lucy Filippini Province, Villa Walsh, Morristown, NJ 07960, (973) 538-2886. Queen of Apostles Province, 474 East Rd., Bristol, CT 06010, (860) 584-2138, www.queenofapostles.com. Educational work.

Francis de Sales, Oblate Sisters of St., O.S.F.S.: Founded 1866, in France; in U.S., 1951. General motherhouse, Troyes, France. U.S. headquarters, Villa Aviat Convent, 399 Childs Rd., MD 21916, (410) 398-3699; (410) 398-3699. Educational, social work.

Franciscans

Bernardine Sisters of the Third Order of St. Francis, O.S.F.: Founded 1457, at Cracow, Poland; in U.S., 1894. Generalate, 450 St. Bernardine St., Reading, PA 19607; (484) 334-6976; www.bfrancis can.org. Educational, hospital, social work.

Capuchin Poor Clares, O.S.C. Cap: U.S. establishment, 1981, Amarillo diocese. Convent of the Blessed Sacrament and Our Lady of Guadalupe, 4201 N.E. 18th St., Amarillo, TX 79107, (806) 383-9877. Cloistered.

Congregation of the Servants of the Holy Child Jesus, O.S.F.: Founded 1855, in Germany; in U.S., 1929. General motherhouse, Würzburg, Germany. American motherhouse, Villa Maria, 641 Somerset St., North Plainfield, NJ 07060-4909, (908) 757-3050.

Congregation of the Third Order of St. Francis of Mary Immaculate, O.S.F.: Founded 1865, in U.S., by Fr. Pamphilus da Magliano, O.F.M. General mother house, 520 Plainfield Ave., Joliet, IL 60435, (815) 727-3686. Educational and pastoral work.

Daughters of St. Francis of Assisi, D.S.F.: Founded 1894, in Hungary; in U.S., 1946. Provincial mother house, 507 N. Prairie St., Lacon, IL 61540, (309) 246- 2175. Nursing, CCD work.

Eucharistic Franciscan Missionary Sisters, E.F.M.S.: Founded 1943, in Mexico. Motherhouse, 943 S. Soto St., Los Angeles, CA 90023, (323) 264-6556.

Franciscan Handmaids of the Most Pure Heart of Mary, F.H.M.: Founded 1916, in U.S. General motherhouse, 15 W. 124th St., New York, NY 10027-5634, (212) 289-5655. Educational, social work.

Franciscan Hospitaller Sisters of the Immaculate Conception, F.H.I.C.: Founded 1876, in Portugal; in U.S., 1960. General motherhouse, Lisbon, Portugal. U.S. novitiate, 300 S. 17th St., San Jose, CA 95112, (408) 998-3407.

Franciscan Missionaries of Mary, F.M.M.: Founded 1877, in India; in U.S., 1904. General motherhouse, Rome, Italy. U.S. provincialate, 3305 Wallace Ave., Bronx, NY 10467, (718) 547-4693, www.fmmusa.org. Mission work.

Franciscan Missionaries of Our Lady, O.S.F.: Founded 1854, at Calais, France; in U.S., 1913. General motherhouse, Desvres, France. U.S. provincial house, 4200 Essen Lane, Baton Rouge, LA 70809, (225) 926-1627. Hospital work.

Franciscan Missionaries of St. Joseph (Mill Hill Sisters), F.M.S.J.: Founded 1883, at Rochdale, Lancashire, England; in U.S., 1952. Generalate, Manchester, England. U.S. head quarters, Franciscan House, 1006 Madison

Ave., Albany, NY 12208, (518) 482-1991.

Franciscan Missionary Sisters for Africa, O.S.F.: American foundation, 1953. Generalate, Ireland. U.S. headquarters, 172 Foster St., Brighton, MA 02135, (617) 254-4343.

Franciscan Missionary Sisters of Assisi, F.M.S.A.: First foundation in U.S., 1961. General motherhouse, Assisi, Italy. U.S. address, St. Francis Convent, 1039 Northampton St., Holyoke, MA 01040, (413) 532-8156; www.sistersofassisi.org.

Franciscan Missionary Sisters of Our Lady of Sorrows, O.S.F.: Founded 1939, in China, by Bishop Rafael Palazzi, O.F.M.; in U.S., 1949. 3600 S.W. 170th Ave., Beaverton, OR 97006, (503) 649-7127. Educational, social, domestic, retreat and foreign mission work.

Franciscan Missionary Sisters of the Divine Child, F.M.D.C.: Founded 1927, at Buffalo, NY, by Bishop William Turner. General motherhouse, 6380 Main St., Williamsville, NY 14221, (716) 632-3144. Educational, social work.

Franciscan Missionary Sisters of the Infant Jesus, F.M.I.J.: Founded 1879, in Italy; in U.S., 1961. Generalate, Rome, Italy. U.S. provincialate, 1215 Kresson Rd., Cherry Hill, NJ 08003, (609) 428-8834.

Franciscan Missionary Sisters of the Sacred Heart, F.M.S.C.: Founded 1860, in Italy; in U.S., 1865. Generalate, Rome, Italy. U.S. provincialate, 250 South St., Peekskill, NY 10566-4419, (914) 737-5409, www.fmsc.org. Educational and social welfare apostolates.

Franciscan Poor Clare Nuns (Poor Clares, Order of St. Clare, Poor Clares of St. Colette), P.C., O.S.C., P.C.C.: Founded 1212, at Assisi, Italy, by St. Francis of Assisi; in U.S., 1875. Proto-monastery, Assisi, Italy. Addresses of autonomous motherhouses in U.S. are listed below.

8650 Russell Ave., S., Minneapolis, MN 55431, (952) 881-4766, www.poorclare.com. 3626 N. 65th Ave., Omaha, NE 68104-3299, (402) 558-4916, www.oma-hapoorclare.org. 720 Henry Clay Ave., New Orleans, LA 70118-5891, (504) 895-2019, www.poorclarenuns.com. 6825 Nurrenbern Rd., Evansville, IN 47712-8518, (812) 425-4396, www.poorclare.org. 1310 Dellwood Ave., Memphis, TN 38127-6399, (901) 357-6662, www.poorclare.org/memphis. 920 Centre St., Jamaica Plain, MA 02130-3099, (617) 524-1760, www.stanthonyshrine.org/poorclares. 327 S. Broad St., Trenton, NJ 08608, (609) 392-7673. 1271 Langhorne- Newtown Rd., Langhorne, PA 19047-1297, (215) 968-5775. 4419 N. Hawthorne St., Spokane, WA 99205, (509) 327- 4479, www.calledbyjoy.com. 86 Mayflower Ave., New Rochelle, NY, 10801-1615, (914) 632-5227, www.poorclaresny.com. 421 S. 4th St., Sauk Rapids, MN 56379-1898, (612) 251-3556. 3501 Rocky River Dr., Cleveland, OH 44111, (216) 941-2821.

1671 Pleasant Valley Rd., Aptos, CA 95001, (831) 761- 9659. 2111 S. Main St., Rockford, IL 61102, (815) 963-7343, www.poorclare.org/rockford. 215 E. Los Olivos St., Santa Barbara, CA 93105-3605, (805) 682-7670, www.poorclaressantabarbara.org. 445 River Rd., Andover, MA 01810, (978) 683-7599. 809 E. 19th St., Roswell, NM 88201-7514, (575) 622-0868, www.poorclares-roswell.org. 28210 Natoma Rd., Los Altos Hills, CA 94022, (650) 948-2947, www.chcweb. com. 37 McCauley Rd., Travelers Rest, SC 29690 (864) 834-8015. 5500 Holly Fork Rd., Barhamsville, VA 23011, (757) 566-1684, www.poorclares.org. 1175 N. 300 W., Kokomo, IN 46901-1799, (765) 457-5743, www.thepoorclares.org. 3900 Sherwood Blvd., Delray Beach, FL 33445, (561) 498-3294. 200 Marycrest Dr., St. Louis, MO 63129, (314) 846-2618. 6029 Estero

Blvd., Fort Myers Beach, FL 33931, (239) 463-5599, www. poor clares-fmb.org. 9300 Hwy 105, Brenham, TX 77833, (409) 836-2444, www.franciscanpoorclares.org.

Franciscan Sisters, Daughters of the Sacred Hearts of Jesus and Mary, O.S.F.: Founded 1860, in Germany; in U.S., 1872. Generalate, Rome, Italy. U.S. motherhouse, P.O. Box 667, Wheaton, IL 60189-0667, (630) 909-6677, www.wheatonfranciscan.org. Educational, hospital, foreign mission, social work.

Franciscan Sisters Daughters of Mercy, F.H.M.: Founded 1856, in Spain; in U.S., 1962. General moth erhouse, Palma de Mallorca, Spain. U.S. address, 612 N. 3rd St., Waco, TX 76701, (254) 753-5565.

Franciscan Sisters of Allegany, O.S.F.: Founded 1859, at Allegany, NY, by Fr. Pamphilus da Magliano, O.F.M. General motherhouse, P.O. Box W, 115 East Main St., Allegany, NY 14706, (716) 373-0200, www.alleganyfran-ciscans.org. Hospital, foreign mission work.

Franciscan Sisters of Baltimore, O.S.F.: Founded 1868, in England; in U.S., 1881. General mother house, 3725 Ellerslie Ave., Baltimore, MD 21218, (410) 235- 0139. Educational work; social services.

Franciscan Sisters of Chicago, O.S.F.: Founded 1894, in U.S., by Mother Mary Therese (Josephine Dudzik). General motherhouse, 11500 Theresa Dr., Lemont, IL 60439, (630)

243-3551. Educational work, social services.

Franciscan Sisters of Christian Charity, O.S.F.: Founded 1869, in U.S. Motherhouse, Holy Family Convent, 2409 S. Alverno Rd., Manitowoc, WI 54220, (920) 682-7728, www.fscc-calledtobe.org. Hospital work.

Francis Sisters of Dillingen, O.S.F.: Founded 1241, in Bavaria; in U.S., 1913. General motherhouse, Rome, Italy. U.S. motherhouse, 102 6th St., S.E., Hankinson, ND 58041, (701) 242-7195, www.dillingenfranciscansusa.org. Education, social services.

Franciscan Sisters of Little Falls, MN, O.S.F.: Founded 1891, in U.S. General motherhouse, 116 8th Ave., S.E., Little Falls, MN 56345, (320) 632-0612, www.fslf.org. Health, education, social services, pastoral ministry, mission work.

Franciscan Sisters of Mary, F.S.M.: Established, 1987, through unification of the Sisters of St. Mary of the Third Order of St. Francis (founded 1872, St. Louis) and the Sisters of St. Francis of Maryville, MO (founded 1894). Address of general superior: 3221 McKelvey Rd., Suite 107, Bridgeton, MO 63044, (314) 768-1833, www. fsmonline.org. Health care, social services.

Franciscan Sisters of Mary Immaculate of the Third Order of St. Francis of Assisi, F.M.I.: Founded 16th century, in Switzerland; in U.S., 1932. General motherhouse, Bogota, Colombia. U.S. provincial house, 4301 N.E. 18th Ave., Amarillo, TX 79107-7220, (806) 383-5769. Education.

Franciscan Sisters of Our Lady of Perpetual Help, O.S.F.: Founded 1901, in U.S., from Joliet, IL, founda tion. General motherhouse, 335 South Kirkwood Rd., St. Louis, MO 63122, (314) 965-3700, www.franciscansisters-olph.org. Educational, hospital work.

Franciscan Sisters of Peace, F.S.P.: Established 1986, in U.S., as archdiocesan community, from Franciscan Missionary Sisters of the Sacred Heart. Congregation Center, 20 Ridge St., Haverstraw, NY 10927, (845) 942-2527, www.fspnet.org.

Franciscan Sisters of Ringwood, F.S.R.: Merged with the Sisters of St. Francis of Philadelphia in 2003.

Franciscan Sisters of St. Elizabeth, F.S.S.E.: Founded

1866, at Naples, Italy, by Bl. Ludovico of Casorio; in U.S., 1919. General motherhouse, Rome, Italy. U.S. delegate house, 499 Park Rd., Parsippany, NJ 07054, (973) 539-3797, www.franciscansisters.com. Educational work, social services.

Franciscan Sisters of St. Joseph, F.S.S.J.: Founded 1897, in U.S. General motherhouse, 5229 South Park Ave., Hamburg, NY 14075, (716) 649-1205, www.franciscansistersofsaintjoseph.org. Educational, hospital work.

Franciscan Sisters of St. Joseph (of Mexico): U.S. foundation, St. Paul College, 3015 4th St. N.E., Washington, DC 20017, (202) 832-6262.

Franciscan Sisters of the Atonement (Graymoor Sisters), S.A.: Founded 1898, in U.S., as Anglican community; entered Church, 1909. General mother house, St. Francis Convent-Graymoor, 41 Old Highland Turnpike, Garrison, NY 10524, (914) 424- 3624, www.graymoor.org. Mission work.

Franciscan Sisters of the Immaculate Conception, O.S.F.: Founded in Germany; in U.S., 1928. General mother house, Kloster, Bonlanden, Germany. U.S. province, 291 North St., Buffalo, NY 14201, (716) 881-2323.

Franciscan Sisters of the Immaculate Conception, O.S.F.: Founded 1874, in Mexico; in U.S., 1926. U.S. provincial house, 11306 Laurel Canyon Blvd., San Fernando, CA 91340, (818) 365-2582.

Franciscan Sisters of the Immaculate Conception and St. Joseph for the Dying, O.S.F.: Founded 1919, in U.S. General motherhouse, 1249 Joselyn Canyon Rd., Monterey, CA 93940, (408) 372-3579.

Franciscan Sisters of the Poor, S.F.P.: Founded 1845, at Aachen, Germany, by Bl. Frances Schervier; in U.S., 1858. Congregational office, 133 Remsen St., Brooklyn, NY 11201, (718) 643-1919, www.franciscansisters.org. Hospital, social work and foreign missions.

Franciscan Sisters of the Sacred Heart, O.S.F.: Founded 1866, in Germany; in U.S., 1876. General motherhouse, St. Francis Woods, 9201 W. St. Francis Rd., Frankfort, IL 60423- 8335, (815) 469-4895, www.fssh.net. Education, health care, other service ministries.

Hospital Sisters of the Third Order of St. Francis, O.S.F.: Founded 1844, in Germany; in U.S., 1875. General motherhouse, Muenster, Germany. U.S. motherhouse, 4849 La Verna Rd., Springfield, IL 62707, (217) 522-3386, www. hospitalsisters.org. Hospital work.

Institute of the Franciscan Sisters of the Eucharist, F.S.E.: Founded 1973. Motherhouse, 405 Allen Ave., Meriden, CT 06451, (203) 237-0841, www.fscommunity. org.

Little Franciscans of Mary, P.F.M.: Founded 1889, in U.S. General motherhouse, Baie St. Paul, QC, Canada. U.S. region, 55 Moore Ave., Worcester, MA 01602, (508) 755- 0878. Educational, hospital, social work.

Missionary Franciscan Sisters of the Immaculate Conception, M.F.I.C.: Founded 1873, in U.S. General motherhouse, Rome, Italy. U.S. address, 790 Centre St., Newton, MA 02458, (617) 527-1004, www.mficusa.org. Educational work.

Missionary Sisters of the Immaculate Conception of the Mother of God, S.M.I.C.: Founded 1910, in Brazil; in U.S., 1922. U.S. provincialate, P.O. Box 3026, Paterson, NJ 07509, (973) 279-3790, www. smic-missionarysisters.com. Mission, educa tional, health work, social services.

Mothers of the Helpless, M.D.: Founded 1873,

in Spain; in U.S., 1916. General motherhouse, Valencia, Spain. U.S. address, Sacred Heart Residence, 432 W. 20th St., New York, NY 10011, (212) 929-5790; www.sacredheartresidence.com.

Poor Clares of Perpetual Adoration, P.C.P.A.: Founded 1854, at Paris, France; in U.S., 1921, at Cleveland, OH. U.S. monasteries: 4200 N. Market Ave., Canton, OH 44714. 2311 Stockham Lane, Portsmouth, OH 45662-3049, (740) 353-4713. 4108 Euclid Ave., Cleveland, OH 44103, (216) 361-0783. 3900 13th St. N.E., Washington, DC 20017, (202) 526- 6808, www.poorclareswdc.org. 5817 Old Leeds Rd., Birmingham, AL 35210, (205) 271-2917. 3222 County Rd. 548, Hanceville, AL 35077, (256) 352-6267, www.olamshrine.com. Contemplative, clois tered, perpetual adoration.

St. Francis Mission Community, O.S.F.: Autonomous province of Franciscan Sisters of Mary Immaculate. 4305 54th St., Lubbock, TX 79413, (806) 793-9859.

School Sisters of St. Francis, O.S.F.: Founded 1874, in U.S. General motherhouse, 1501 S. Layton Blvd., Milwaukee, WI 53215, (414) 384-4105, www.sssf.org.

School Sisters of St. Francis, (Pittsburgh, PA), O.S.F.: Established 1913, in U.S. Motherhouse, Mt. Assisi Convent, 934 Forest Ave., Pittsburgh, PA 15202-1199, (412) 761-2855, www.franciscansisters-pa.org. Education, health care servic es and related ministries.

School Sisters of the Third Order of St. Francis (Bethlehem, PA), O.S.F.: Founded in Austria, 1843; in U.S., 1913. General motherhouse, Rome, Italy. U.S. province, 395 Bridle Path Rd., Bethlehem, PA 18017, (610) 866-2597. Educational, mission work.

School Sisters of the Third Order of St. Francis (Panhandle, TX), O.S.F.: Established 1931, in U.S., from Vienna, Austria, foundation (1845). General motherhouse, Vienna, Austria. U.S. center and novitiate, P.O. Box 906, Panhandle, TX 79068, (806) 537-3182, www. panhandlefranciscans.org. Educational, social work.

Sisters of Mercy of the Holy Cross, S.C.S.C.: Founded 1856, in Switzerland; in U.S. 1912. General motherhouse, Ingenbohl, Switzerland. U.S. provincial residence, 1400 O'Day St., Merrill, WI 54452, (715) 539-1460, www.holycrosssisters.org.

Sisters of Our Lady of Mercy (Mercedarians), S.O.L.M.: General motherhouse, Rome, Italy. U.S. address: Most Precious Blood, 133-157 27th Ave., Brooklyn, NY 11214, (718) 373-7343.

Sisters of St. Francis (Clinton, IA), O.S.F.: Founded 1868, in U.S. General motherhouse, 588 N. Bluff Blvd., Clinton, IA 57232-3953, (563) 242-7611, www.clinton-franciscans.com. Educational, hospital, social work.

Sisters of St. Francis (Millvale, PA), O.S.F.: Founded 1865, Pittsburgh. General motherhouse, 146 Hawthorne Rd., Millvale PO, Pittsburgh, PA 15209, (412) 821-2200. Educational, hospital work.

Sisters of St. Francis (Hastings-on-Hudson), O.S.F.: Founded 1893, in New York. General mother house, 49 Jackson Ave., Hastings-on-Hudson, NY 10706-3217, (914) 478-3930. Education, parish ministry, social services.

Sisters of St. Francis of Assisi, O.S.F.: Founded 1849, in U.S. General motherhouse, 3221 S. Lake Dr., St. Francis, WI 53235-3799, (414) 744-3150, www.lakeosfs. org. Education, other ministries.

Sisters of St. Francis of Christ the King, O.S.F.: Founded 1864, in Austria; in U.S., 1909. General motherhouse,

Rome, Italy. U.S. provincial house, 13900 Main St., Lemont, IL 60439, (630) 257-7495. Educational work, home for aged.

Sisters of St. Francis of Penance and Christian Charity, O.S.F.: Founded 1835, in Holland; in U.S., 1874. General motherhouse, Rome, Italy. U.S. provinces: 4421 Lower River Rd., Stella Niagara, NY 14144-1001, (716) 754-2193, www.franciscans-stella-niagara.org. 5314 N. Columbine Rd., Denver, CO 80221, (303) 458-6270; 3910 Bret Harte Dr., PO Box 1028, Redwood City, CA 94064, (650) 369-1725.

Sisters of St. Francis of Philadelphia, O.S.F.: Founded 1855, at Philadelphia, by Mother Mary Francis Bachmann and St. John N. Neumann. General motherhouse, Convent of Our Lady of the Angels, Aston, PA 19014, (610) 558-7701, www.osfphila.org. Education, health care, social services.

Sisters of St. Francis of Savannah, MO, O.S.F.: Founded 1850, in Austria; in U.S., 1922. Provincial house, La Verna Heights, Box 488, 104 E. Park, Savannah, MO 64485-0488, (816) 324-3179; sistersofstfrancis.org. Educational, hospital work.

Sisters of St. Francis of the Holy Cross, O.S.F.: Founded 1881, in U.S., by Rev. Edward Daems, O.S.C. General moth erhouse, 3110 Nicolet Dr., Green Bay, WI 54311, (920) 884- 2700, www.gbfranciscans.org. Educational, nursing work, pastoral ministry, foreign missions.

Sisters of St. Francis of the Holy Eucharist, O.S.F.: Founded 1378, in Switzerland; in U.S., 1893. General motherhouse, 2100 N. Noland Rd., Independence, MO 64050, (816) 252-1673; www.osfholyeucharist.org. Education, health care, social services, foreign missions.

Sisters of St. Francis of the Holy Family, O.S.F.: U.S. foundation, 1875. Motherhouse, Mt. St. Francis, 3390 Windsor Ave., Dubuque, IA 52001, (563) 583-9786, www. osfdbq.org. Varied apostolates.

Sisters of St. Francis of the Immaculate Conception, O.S.F.: Founded 1890, in U.S. General motherhouse, 2408 W. Heading Ave., West Peoria, IL 61604-5096, (309) 674-6168, www.westpeoriasis ters.org. Education, care of aging, pastoral ministry.

Sisters of St. Francis of the Martyr St. George, O.S.F.: Founded 1859, in Germany; in U.S., 1923. General motherhouse, Thuine, Germany. U.S. provincial house, St. Francis Convent, 2120 Central Ave., Alton, IL 62002, (618) 463-2750, www.altonfranciscans.org. Education, social services, foreign mission work.

Sisters of St. Francis of the Perpetual Adoration, O.S.F.: Founded 1863, in Germany; in U.S., 1875. General mother house, Olpe, Germany. U.S. provinces: Box 766, Mishawaka, IN 46546-0766, (574) 259-5427, www.ssfpa. org. 7665 Assisi Heights, Colorado Springs, CO 80919, (719) 955-7015, www.stfrancis.org.

Sisters of St. Francis of the Providence of God, O.S.F.: Founded 1922, in U.S., by Msgr. M. L. Krusas. General motherhouse, 3603 McRoberts Rd., Pittsburgh, PA 15234, (412) 885-7407. Education, varied apostolates.

Sisters of St. Joseph of the Third Order of St. Francis, S.S.J.: Founded 1901, in U.S. Administrative office, P.O. Box 305, Stevens Pt., WI 54481-0305, (715) 341-8457, www.ssj-tosf.org. Education, health care, social services.

Sisters of the Infant Jesus, I.J.: Founded 1662, at Rouen, France; in U.S., 1950. Motherhouse, Paris, France. Generalate, Rome, Italy. U.S. address: 20 Reiner St., Colma, CA 94014.

Sisters of the Sorrowful Mother (Third Order of St. Francis), S.S.M.: Founded 1883, in Italy; in U.S., 1889. General motherhouse, Rome, Italy. U.S. address: 17600 E. 51st St., Broken Arrow, OK 74012, (918) 355-1148, www. ssmfranciscans.org. Educational, hos pital work.

Sisters of St. Franciscan of the Neumann Communities, O.S.F.: Founded 1860, at Syracuse, NY. Generalate offices, 2500 Grant Blvd., Syracuse, NY 13208, (315) 624-7000, www.sosf.org.

Sisters of the Third Order of St. Francis, O.S.F.: Founded 1877, in U.S., by Bishop John L. Spalding. Motherhouse, 1175 St. Francis Lane, E. Peoria, IL 61611-1299, (309) 699-7215, www.franciscansisterpeoria.org. Hospital work.

Sisters of the Third Order of St. Francis (Oldenburg, IN), O.S.F.: Founded 1851, in U.S. General motherhouse, Sisters of St. Francis, PO Box 100, Oldenburg, IN 47036-0100, (812) 934-2475, www.oldenburgfranciscans. org. Education, social services, pastoral ministry, foreign missions.

Sisters of the Third Order of St. Francis of Penance and Charity, O.S.F.: Founded 1869, in U.S., by Fr. Joseph Bihn. Motherhouse, 200 St. Francis Ave., Tiffin, OH 44883, (419) 447-0435, www.tiffinfranciscans.org. Education, social services.

Sisters of the Third Order of St. Francis of the Perpetual Adoration, F.S.P.A.: Founded 1849, in U.S. Generalate, 912 Market St., La Crosse, WI 54601, (608) 782-5610, www.fspa.org. Education, health care.

Sisters of the Third Order Regular of St. Francis of the Congregation of Our Lady of Lourdes, O.S.F.: Founded 1877, in U.S. General motherhouse, Assisi Heights, 1001 14th St., NW, Rochester, MN 55901, (507) 282-7441; www.rochesterfranciscan.org. Education, health care, social services.

Good Shepherd Sisters (Servants of the Immaculate Heart of Mary), S.C.I.M.: Founded 1850, in Canada; in U.S., 1882. General motherhouse, QC, Canada. In U.S., Provincial House, Bay View, 313 Seaside Ave., Saco, Maine 04072, (207) 284-6429. Educational, social work.

Good Shepherd, Sisters of the, R.G.S.: Founded 1835, in France, by St. Mary Euphrasia Pelletier; in U.S., 1843. Generalate, Rome, Italy. U.S. provinces: 2108 Hatmaker St., Cincinnati, OH 45204, (513) 921-5923. 25-30 21st Ave., Astoria, NY 11105, (718) 278-1155, www.goodshepherdsistersna.org. 504 Hexton Hill Rd., Silver Spring, MD 20904, (301) 384-1169. 7654 Natural Bridge Rd., St. Louis, MO 63121, (314) 381-3400, www.goodshepherdsisters.org. 5100 Hodgson Rd., St. Paul, MN 55126, (651) 484-0221, www.bounpastorint.org. Active and contemplative (Contemplative Sisters of the Good Shepherd, C.G.S.).

Graymoor Sisters: *See* **Franciscan Sisters of the Atonement.**

Grey Nuns of the Sacred Heart, G.N.S.H.: Founded 1921, in U.S. General motherhouse, 1750 Quarry Rd., Yardley, PA 19067-3998, (215) 968-4236, www.greynun.org.

Guadalupan Missionaries of the Holy Spirit, M.G.Sp.S.: Founded 1930 in Mexico by Rev. Felix de Jesus Rougier, M.Sp.S. General motherhouse, Mexico. U.S. delegation: 2483 S.W. 4th St. Miami, FL 33135- 2907, (305) 642-9544.

Guardian Angel, Sisters of the, S.A.C.: Founded 1839, in France. General motherhouse, Madrid, Spain. U.S. foundation, 1245 S. Van Ness, Los Angeles, CA 90019, (213) 732-7881.

Handmaids of the Precious Blood, Congregation

of, H.P.B.: Founded 1947, at Jemez Springs, NM. Motherhouse and novitiate, Cor Jesu Monastery, P.O. Box 90, Jemez Springs, NM 87025, (505) 829-3906.

Helpers, Society of, H.H.S.: Founded 1856, in France; in U.S., 1892. General motherhouse, Paris, France. American province, 3206 S. Aberdeen, Chicago, IL 60657, (773) 523-8638.

Hermanas Catequistas Guadalupanas, H.C.G.: Founded 1923, in Mexico; in U.S., 1950. General motherhouse, Mexico. 4110 S. Flores, San Antonio, TX 78214, (210) 533-9344.

Hermanas Josefinas, H.J.: General motherhouse, Mexico. U.S. foundation, Assumption Seminary, 2600 W. Woodlawn Ave., PO Box 28240, San Antonio, TX 78284, (210) 734-0039. Domestic work.

Holy Child Jesus, Society of the, S.H.C.J.: Founded 1846, in England; in U.S., 1862. General motherhouse, Rome, Italy. U.S. province, 460 Shadeland Ave., Drexel Hill, PA 19026, (610) 626-1400, www.shcj.org.

Holy Faith, Congregation of the Sisters of the, C.H.F.: Founded 1856, in Ireland; in U.S., 1953. General motherhouse, Dublin, Ireland. U.S. province, 12322 S. Paramount Blvd., Downey, CA 90242, (562) 869-6092.

Holy Family, Congregation of the Sisters of the, S.S.F.: Founded 1842, in Louisiana, by Henriette Delille and Juliette Gaudin. General motherhouse, 6901 Chef Menteur Hwy., New Orleans, LA 70126, (504) 242-8315, www.sistersoftheholyfamily.com. Hospital work.

Holy Family, Sisters of the, S.H.F.: Founded 1872, in U.S. General motherhouse, P.O. Box 3248, Fremont, CA 94539, (510) 624-4500 www.holyfamilysisters. com. Educational, social work.

Holy Family of Nazareth, Sisters of the, C.S.F.N.: Founded 1875, in Italy; in U.S., 1885. General mother house, Rome, Italy. U.S. provinces: Sacred Heart, 310 N. River Rd., Des Plaines, IL 60016-1211, (847) 298-6760. Immaculate Conception BVM, 4001 Grant Ave., Philadelphia, PA 19114, (215) 268-1035, www.philacsfn.org. St. Joseph, 285 Bellevue Rd., Pittsburgh, PA 15229-2195, (412) 931-4778, www.csfn.org. Immaculate Heart of Mary, Marian Heights, 1428 Monroe Turnpike, Monroe, CT 04648, (203) 268-7646. Bl. Frances Siedliska Provincialate, 1814 Egyptian Way, Box 530959, Grand Prairie, TX 75053, (972) 641-4496, www.csfn.org.

Holy Heart of Mary, Servants of the, S.S.C.M.: Founded 1860, in France; in U.S., 1889. General moth erhouse, Montreal, QC, Canada. U.S. province, 15 Elmwood Dr., Kankakee, IL 60901, (815) 937-2380, www.sscm-usa.org. Educational, hospital, social work.

Holy Names of Jesus and Mary, Sisters of the, S.N.J.M.: Founded 1843, in Canada by Bl. Marie Rose Durocher; in U.S., 1859. Generalate, Longueuil, QC, Canada. U.S.-Ontario Province was formed in 2006 by uniting the five predominantly English-speaking provinces of the Congregation. Address: Box 25, Marylhurst, OR 97036, (503) 675-2449, www.snjm.org.

Holy Spirit, Community of the, C.H.S.: Founded 1970 in San Diego, CA. 6151 Rancho Mission Rd., No. 205, San Diego, CA 92108, (619) 584-0809.

Holy Spirit, Daughters of the, D.H.S.: Founded 1706, in France; in U.S., 1902. Generalate, Bretagne, France. U.S. motherhouse, 72 Church St., Putnam, CT 06260-1817, (860) 928-0891. Educational work, dis trict nursing, pastoral ministry.

Holy Spirit, Mission Sisters of the, M.SS.p.: Founded 1932, at Cleveland, OH. Motherhouse, 1030 N. River Rd., Saginaw, MI 48603, (517) 781-0934.

Holy Spirit, Missionary Sisters, Servants of the: Founded 1889, in Holland; in U.S., 1901. Generalate, Rome, Italy. U.S. motherhouse, Convent of the Holy Spirit, PO Box 6026, Techny, IL 60082-6026, (847) 441-0126, www.sspsusa.org. International congregation for the spread of the Gospel *ad gentes*.

Holy Spirit, Sisters of the, C.S.Sp.: Founded 1890, in Rome, Italy; in U.S. as independent diocesan community, 1929. General motherhouse, 10102 Granger Rd., Garfield Hts., OH 44125, (216) 581-2900, www.sistersoftheholy-spirit.org. Educational, social, nursing work.

Holy Spirit, Sisters of the, S.H.S.: Founded 1913, in U.S., by Most Rev. J. F. Regis Canevin. General moth erhouse, 5246 Clarwin Ave., Ross Township, Pittsburgh, PA 15229-2208, (412) 931-1917. Educational, nursing work, care of aged.

Holy Spirit and Mary Immaculate, Sisters of, S.H.Sp.: Founded 1893, in U.S. Motherhouse, 301 Yucca St., San Antonio, TX 78203, (210) 533-5149. Education, hospital work.

Holy Spirit of Perpetual Adoration, Sister Servants of the, S.Sp.S.deA.P.: Founded 1896, in Holland; in U.S., 1915. Generalate, Bad Driburg, Germany. U.S. novitiate, 2212 Green St., Philadelphia, PA 19130, (215) 567-0123, www.adorationsisters.org.

Home Mission Sisters of America (Glenmary Sisters), G.H.M.S.: Founded 1952, in U.S. Glenmary Center, PO Box 22264, Owensboro, KY 42304-2264, (270) 686-8401; www.glenmarysisters.org.

Home Visitors of Mary, Sisters, H.V.M.: Founded 1949, in Detroit, MI. Motherhouse, 121 E. Boston Blvd., Detroit, MI 48202, (313) 869-2160.

Hospitallers of St. Joseph, Religious, R.H.S.J.: Founded in 1636, in France; in U.S., 1894. Motherhouse, 2450, Chemin de la Côte Sainte-Catherine, Montréal, Canada H3T 1B1. U.S. address: 644, Langlade Road, Antigo, WI 54409, (715) 623- 4615; www.rhsj.org.

Humility of Mary, Congregation of, C.H.M.: Founded 1854, in France; in U.S., 1864. U.S. address, Humility of Mary Center, Davenport IA, 52804, (563) 323-9466, www.chmiowa.org.

Humility of Mary, Sisters of the, H.M.: Founded 1854, in France; in U.S., 1864. U.S. address, Villa Maria Community Center, Villa Maria, PA 16155, (724) 964-8861, www.humilityofmary.org.

Immaculate Conception, Little Servant Sisters of the, L.S.I.C.: Founded 1850, in Poland; in U.S., 1926. General motherhouse, Poland. U.S. provincial house, 1000 Cropwell Rd., Cherry Hill, NJ 08003, (609) 424-1962. Education, social services, African missions.

Immaculate Conception, Sisters of the, R.C.M.: Founded 1892, in Spain; in U.S., 1962. General moth erhouse, Madrid, Spain. U.S. address, 2230 Franklin, San Francisco, CA 94109, (415) 474-0159, www.rc.net/conception.

Immaculate Conception, Sisters of the, C.I.C.: Founded 1874, in U.S. General motherhouse, P.O. Box 50426, New Orleans, LA 70185, (504) 486-7426.

Immaculate Conception of the Blessed Virgin Mary, Sisters of the (Lithuanian): Founded 1918, at Mariampole, Lithuania; in U.S., 1936. U.S. headquar ters, Immaculate Conception Convent, 600 Liberty Hwy., Putnam, CT 06260, (860) 928-7955.

Immaculate Heart of Mary, Missionary Sisters, I.C.M.: Founded 1897, in India; in U.S., 1919.

Generalate, Rome, Italy. U.S. province, 283 E. 15th St., New York, NY 10003, (212) 260-8567. Educational social, foreign mission work.

Immaculate Heart of Mary, Sisters of the, I.H.M.: Founded 1848, in Spain; in U.S., 1878. General motherhouse, Rome, Italy. U.S. province, 3820 Sabino Canyon Rd., Tucson, AZ 85750, (520) 886-4273. Educational work.

Immaculate Heart of Mary, Sisters, Servants of the, I.H.M.: Founded 1845. SSIHM Leadership Council, 610 W. Elm, Monroe, MI 48162, (734) 340- 9700, www.sistersihm.org.

Immaculate Heart of Mary, Sisters, Servants of the, I.H.M.: Founded 1845; established in Scranton, PA, 1871. General motherhouse, 2300 Adams Ave., Scranton, PA 18509, (570) 346-5404, www.sistersofihm.org.

Immaculate Heart of Mary, Sisters Servants of the, I.H.M.: Founded 1845; established in West Chester, PA, 1872. General motherhouse, Villa Maria, Immaculata, PA 19345, (610) 647-2160, www.ihmimmaculata.org.

Immaculate Heart of Mary of Wichita, Sisters of, I.H.M.: Established at Wichita, KS. 1979. Address: 145 S. Millwood St., Wichita, KS 67213, (316) 722-9316, www.sistersofwichita.org.

Incarnate Word, Religious of, C.V.I.: General motherhouse, Mexico City, Mexico. U.S. address, 153 Rainier Ct., Chula Vista, CA 92011, (619) 420-0231.

Incarnate Word and Blessed Sacrament, Congregation of, C.V.I.: Founded 1625, in France; in U.S., 1853. Incarnate Word Convent, 3400 Bradford Pl., Houston, TX 77025, (713) 668-0423; www.incarnateword.org/cvi.

Incarnate Word and Blessed Sacrament, Congregation of the, I.W.B.S.: Motherhouse, 1101 Northeast Water St., Victoria, TX 77901, (361) 575-2266, www.iwbsvictoria.org.

Incarnate Word and Blessed Sacrament, Congregation of the, I.W.B.S.: Motherhouse, 2930 S. Alameda, Corpus Christi, TX 78404, (361) 882-5413, www.iwbscc.org.

Incarnate Word and Blessed Sacrament, Sisters of the, S.I.W.: Founded 1625, in France; in U.S. 1853. Motherhouse, 6618 Pearl Rd., Parma Heights, Cleveland, OH 44130, (440) 886-6440, www.incar natewordorder.org.

Infant Jesus, Congregation of the (Nursing Sisters of the Sick Poor), C.I.J.: Founded 1835, in France; in U.S., 1905. General motherhouse, 310 Prospect Park W., Brooklyn, NY 11215, (718) 965-7300.

Institute of the Blessed Virgin Mary (Loretto Sisters), I.B.V.M.: Founded 17th century in Belgium; in U.S., 1954. Motherhouse, Rathfarnham, Dublin, Ireland. U.S. address: 2521 W. Maryland Ave., Phoenix, AZ 85017, (602) 242-2544.

Institute of the Blessed Virgin Mary (Loretto Sisters), I.B.V.M.: Founded 1609, in Belgium; in U.S., 1880. Loretto Convent, Box 508, Wheaton, IL 60189, (602) 433-0658; www.ibvm.org. Educational work.

Jesus, Daughters of (*Filles de Jesus*), F.J.: Founded 1834, in France; in U.S., 1904. General motherhouse, Kermaria, Locmine, France. U.S. address, 4209 3rd Ave. S., Great Falls, MT 59405, (406) 452-7231. Educational, hospital, parish and social work.

Jesus, Little Sisters of, L.S.J.: Founded 1939, in Sahara; in U.S., 1952. General motherhouse, Rome, Italy. U.S. headquarters, 400 N. Streeper St., Baltimore, MD 21224, www.rc.net/org/littlesisters.

Jesus, Society of the Sisters, Faithful Companions of, F.C.J.: Founded 1820, in France; in U.S., 1896. General motherhouse, Kent, England. U.S. province, St.

Philomena Convent, Cory's Lane, Portsmouth, RI 02871, (401) 683-2222, www.portsmouthabbey.org.

Jesus and Mary, Little Sisters of, L.S.J.M.: Founded 1974 in U.S. Joseph House, P.O. Box 1755, Salisbury, MD 21802, (410) 742-9590, www.thejosephhouse.org.

Jesus and Mary, Religious of, R.J.M.: Founded 1818, at Lyons, France; in U.S., 1877. General mother house, Rome, Italy. U.S. province, 821 Varnum St., NE, Washington, DC 20017, (202) 526-3203. Educational work.

Jesus Crucified, Congregation of: Founded 1930, in France; in U.S., 1955. General motherhouse, Brou, France. U.S. foundation: Benedictines of Jesus Crucified, Monastery of the Glorious Cross, 61 Burban Dr., Branford, CT 06405-4003, (203) 315- 9964, www.benedictinesjc.org.

Jesus Crucified and the Sorrowful Mother, Poor Sisters of, C.J.C.: Founded 1924, in U.S., by Rev. Alphonsus Maria, C.P. Motherhouse, 261 Thatcher St., Brockton, MA 02402. Education, nursing homes, catechetical centers.

Jesus, Mary and Joseph, Missionary Sisters of, M.J.M.J.: Founded 1942, in Spain; in U.S., 1956. General motherhouse, Madrid, Spain. U.S. regional house, 12940 Leopard St., Corpus Christi, TX 78410, (361) 241-1955.

John the Baptist, Sisters of St., C.S.J.B.: Founded 1878, in Italy; in U.S., 1906. General motherhouse, Rome, Italy. U.S. provincialate, 3308 Campbell Dr., Bronx, NY 10465, (718) 518-7820, www.home.att. net/~baptistines. Education, parish and retreat work; social services.

Joseph, Congregation of Saint, C.S.J.: Founded in 2007 through the formation of seven congregations in the central United States. 1515 W. Ogden Ave., La Grange Park, IL, 60526, (708) 354-9200. 3700 E. Lincoln St., Wichita, KS 67218, (316) 689-4040. Medaille, 4010 Executive Park Dr Ste. 320, Cincinnati, OH 45241, (513)761-2888. Mount St. Joseph, 137 Mount St. Joseph Rd., Wheeling, WV 26003, (304) 232-8160. Nazareth Community Center, 3427 Gull Road, PO Box 34, Nazareth, MI 49074- 0034, (269) 381-6290.St. Joseph Center, 3430 Rocky River Drive, Cleveland, OH 44111-2997, (216) 252- 0440.

Joseph, Poor Sisters of St., P.S.S.J.: Founded 1880, in Argentina. General motherhouse, Muniz, Buenos Aires, Argentina. U.S. addresses: Casa Belen, 305 E. 4th St., Bethlehem, PA 78015, (610) 867-4030. Casa Nazareth, 5321 Spruce St., Reading, PA 19602, (610) 378-1947. St. Gabriel Convent, 4319 Sano St., Alexandria, VA 22312, (703) 354-0395.

Joseph, Religious Daughters of St., F.S.J.: Founded 1875, in Spain. General motherhouse, Spain. U.S. foundation, 319 N. Humphreys Ave., Los Angeles, CA 90022.

Joseph, Servants of St., S.S.J.: Founded 1874, in Spain; in U.S., 1957. General motherhouse, Salamanca, Spain. U.S. address, 203 N. Spring St., Falls Church, VA 22046, (703) 533-8441.

Joseph, Sisters of St., C.S.J. or S.S.J.: Founded 1650, in France; in U.S., 1836, at St. Louis. Independent motherhouses in U.S.: 637 Cambridge St., Brighton, MA 02135, (617) 783-9090, www.csjboston.org. 480 S. Batavia St., Orange, CA 92868, (714) 633-8121, www.sistersofstjosephorange.org. St. Joseph Convent, 1725 Brentwood Rd., Brentwood, NY 11717-5587, (516) 273-4531. 23 Agassiz Circle, Buffalo, NY 14214, (716) 838-4400. 1425 Washington St., Watertown, NY 13601, (315) 782-3460, www.ssjwa tertown.org. 1020 State St., Baden, PA 15005-1342, (724) 869-2151, www.stjosephbaden.org. 5031 W. Ridge Rd., Erie, PA 16506, (814) 836-4193, www.ssjerie.org. 150 French Rd., Rochester, NY 14618, (585) 641-8119, www.ssjrochester.org. Mont Marie, 34 Lower Westfield Rd. Holyoke, MA 01040, (413) 536-0853. PO Box 279, Concordia, KS 66901, (785) 243-2149, www.csjkansas.org.

Joseph, Sisters of St., of Peace, C.S.J.P.: Founded 1884, in England; in U.S. 1885. Generalate, 399 Hudson Terrace, Englewood Cliffs, NJ 07632, (201) 608-5401. Educational, hospital, social service work.

Joseph of Carondelet, Sisters of St., C.S.J.: Founded 1650, in France; in U.S., 1836, at St. Louis, MO. U.S. headquarters, 2311 S. Lindbergh Blvd., St. Louis, MO 63131, (314) 966-4048, www.csjcarondolet.org.

Joseph of Chambery, Sisters of St.: Founded 1650, in France; in U.S., 1885. Generalate, Rome, Italy. U.S. provincial house, 27 Park Rd., West Hartford, CT 06119, (860) 233-5126. Educational, hospital, social work.

Joseph of Chestnut Hill, Sisters of St., S.S.J.: Founded 1650; Philadelphia foundation, 1847. Motherhouse, Mt. St. Joseph Convent, 9701 Germantown Ave., Philadelphia, PA 19118, 215) 248-7205, www.ssjphila.org.

Joseph of Cluny, Sisters of St., S.J.C.: Founded 1807, in France. Generalate, Paris, France. U.S. provincial house, 7 Restmere Terrace, Middletown, RI 02842, (401) 846-4826.

Joseph of Medaille, Sisters of, C.S.J.: See under Joseph, Congregation of St.

Joseph of St. Augustine, Florida, Sisters of St., S.S.J.: General motherhouse, 241 St. George St., P.O. Box 3506, St. Augustine, FL 32085, (904) 824-1752, www.ssjfl.org. Educational, hospital, pastoral, social work.

Joseph of St. Mark, Sisters of St., S.J.S.M.: Founded 1845, in France; in U.S., 1937. General motherhouse, 21800 Chardon Rd., Euclid, Cleveland, OH 44117, (216) 531-7426. Nursing homes.

Joseph the Worker, Sisters of St., S.J.W.: General motherhouse, St. William Convent, 1 St. Joseph Lane, Walton, KY 41094, (859) 485-4256.

Lamb of God, Sisters of the, A.D.: Founded 1945, in France; in U.S., 1958. General motherhouse, France. U.S. address, 2063 Wyandotte Ave., Owensboro KY 42301, (502) 281-5450.

Life, Sisters of, S.V. (*Sorer Vitae*): Founded by Cardinal John J. O'Connor, 1991, to protect life. St. Frances de Chantal Convent, 198 Hollywood Ave., Bronx, NY 10465, (718) 863-2264. Our Lady of New York, 1955 Needham Ave., Bronx, NY, 10466, (718) 881-8008. Sacred Heart Convent, 450 W. 51st St., New York, NY, (212) 397-1386.

Little Sisters of the Gospel, L.S.G.: Founded 1963 in France by Rev. Rene Voillaume; in U.S., 1972. Box 305, Mott Haven Sta., Bronx, NY 10454, (718) 292- 2867.

Little Workers of the Sacred Hearts, P.O.S.C.: Founded 1892, in Italy; in U.S., 1948. General House, Rome, Italy. U.S. address, Our Lady of Grace Convent, 635 Glenbrook Rd., Stamford, CT 06906, (203) 348- 5531.

Living Word, Sisters of the, S.L.W.: Founded 1975, in U.S. Motherhouse, Living Word Center, 800 N. Fernandez Ave. B, Arlington Heights, IL 60004-5316, (847) 577-5972, www.slw.org. Education, hospital, parish ministry work.

Loretto at the Foot of the Cross, Sisters of, S.L.: Founded 1812 in U.S., by Rev. Charles Nerinckx. General motherhouse, 4000 S. Wadsworth Blvd., Littleton, CO 80123, (303) 783-0450, www.loretto community.org. Educational work.

Louis, Juilly-Monaghan, Congregation of Sisters of St., S.S.L.: Founded 1842, in France; in U.S., 1949. General motherhouse, Monaghan, Ireland. U.S. regional house, 22300 Mulholland Dr., Woodland Hills, CA 91364, (818) 883-1678. Educational, med ical, parish, foreign mission work.

Lovers of the Holy Cross Sisters (Phat Diem), L.H.C.: Founded 1670, in Vietnam; in U.S. 1976. U.S. address, Holy Cross Convent, 14700 South Van Ness Ave., Gardena, CA 90249, (310) 516-0271.

Mantellate Sisters, Servants of Mary, of Blue Island, O.S.M.: Founded 1861, in Italy; in U.S., 1916. Generalate, Rome, Italy. U.S. motherhouse, 13811 S. Western Ave., Blue Island, IL 60406, (708) 385-2103. Educational work.

Mantellate Sisters Servants of Mary, of Plainfield, O.S.M.: Founded 1861 in Italy; in U.S., 1916. 16949 S. Drauden Rd., Plainfield, IL 60586, (815) 436-5796.

Marian Sisters of the Diocese of Lincoln: Founded 1954. Marycrest Motherhouse, 6905 N. 112th St., Waverly, NE 68462-9690, (402) 786-2750.

Marianites of Holy Cross, Congregation of the Sisters, M.S.C.: Founded 1841, in France; in U.S., 1843. Motherhouse, Le Mans, Sarthe, France. North American headquarters, 1011 Gallier St., New Orleans, LA 70117-6111, (504) 945-1620, www.marianites.org.

Marist Sisters, Congregation of Mary, S.M.: Founded 1824, in France. General motherhouse, Rome, Italy. U.S. foundation: 810 Peach, Abilene, TX 79602, (915) 675-5806.

Mary, Company of, O.D.N.: Founded 1607, in France; in U.S., 1926. General motherhouse, Rome, Italy. U.S. motherhouse, 16791 E. Main St., Tustin, CA 92680-4034, (714) 541-3125, www.companyof mary.com.

Mary, Daughters of the Heart of, D.H.M.: Founded 1790, in France; in U.S., 1851. Generalate, Paris, France. U.S. provincialate, 1339 Northampton St., Holyoke, MA 01040, (413) 533-6681, www.dhmna. org. Education, retreat work.

Mary, Missionary Sisters of the Society of (Marist Sisters), S.M.S.M.: Founded 1845, at St. Brieuc, France; in U.S., 1922. General motherhouse, Rome, Italy. U.S. provincial house, 349 Grove St., Waltham, MA 02453, (781) 893-0149, www.maristmissionary smsm.org.

Mary, Servants of, O.S.M.: Founded 13th century, in Italy; in U.S., 1893. General motherhouse, England. U.S. provincial motherhouse, 7400 Military Ave., Omaha, NE 68134, (402) 571-2547.

Mary, Servants of (Servite Sisters), O.S.M.: Founded 13th century, in Italy; in U.S., 1912. General motherhouse, Servants of Mary Convent, 1000 College Ave., Ladysmith, WI 54848, (715) 532-3364, www.servitesisters.org.

Mary, Sisters of St., of Oregon, S.S.M.O.: Founded 1886, in Oregon, by Bishop William H. Gross, C.Ss.R. General motherhouse, 4440 S.W. 148th Ave., Beaverton, OR 97007, (503) 644-9181, www.ssmo.org. Educational, nursing work.

Mary, Sisters of the Little Company of, L.C.M.: Founded 1877, in England; in U.S., 1893. Generalate, London, England. U.S. provincial house, 9350 S. California Ave., Evergreen Park, IL 60805, (708) 229-5490, www.lcmglobal.org.

Mary, Sisters Servants of (Trained Nurses), S.M.: Founded 1851, at Madrid, Spain; in U.S., 1914. General motherhouse, Rome, Italy. U.S. motherhouse, 800 N. 18th St., Kansas City, KS 66102, (913) 371-3423. Home nursing.

Mary and Joseph, Daughters of, D.M.J.: Founded

1817, in Belgium; in U.S., 1926. Generalate, Rome, Italy. American provincialate, 5300 Crest Rd., Rancho Palos Verdes, CA 90274, (310) 541-8194.

Mary Help of Christians, Daughters of (Salesian Sisters of St. John Bosco), F.M.A.: Founded 1872, in Italy, by St. John Bosco and St. Mary Dominic Mazzarello; in U.S., 1908. General motherhouse, Rome, Italy. U.S. provinces: 655 Belmont Ave., Haledon, NJ 07508, (937) 790-7963. 6019 Buena Vista St., San Antonio, TX 78237, (210) 432-0089. Education, youth work.

Mary Immaculate, Daughters of (Marianist Sisters), F.M.I.: Founded 1816, in France, by Very Rev. William-Joseph Chaminade. General mother house, Rome, Italy. U.S. foundation, 251 W. Ligustrum Dr., San Antonio, TX 78228-4092, (210) 433-5501, www.marianistsisters.org. Educational work.

Mary Immaculate, Religious of, R.M.I.: Founded 1876, in Spain; in U.S., 1954. Generalate, Rome, Italy. U.S. foundation, 719 Augusta St., San Antonio, TX 78215, (210) 226-0025.

Mary Immaculate, Sisters Minor of, S.M.M.I.: Established in U.S., 1989. 305 Washington Blvd., Stamford, CT 06902, (203) 323-4546; www.sistersminormi.org.

Mary Immaculate, Sisters of, S.M.I.: Founded 1948, in India, by Bp. Louis LaRavoire Morrow; in U.S., 1981. General motherhouse, Bengal, India. U.S. address, 118 Park Rd., Leechburg, PA 15656, (724) 845-2828.

Mary Immaculate, Sisters Servants of, S.S.M.I.: Founded 1878 in Poland. General motherhouse, Mariowka-Opoczynska, Poland; American provincialate, 1220 Tugwell Dr., Catonsville, MD 21228, (410) 747-1353.

Mary Immaculate, Sisters Servants of, S.S.M.I: Founded 1892, in Ukraine; in U.S., 1935. General motherhouse, Rome, Italy. U.S. address, 9 Emmanuel Dr., PO Box 9, Sloatsburg, NY 10974-0009, (845) 753-2840. Educational, hospital work.

Mary of Namur, Sisters of St., S.S.M.N.: Founded 1819, at Namur, Belgium; in U.S., 1863. General motherhouse, Namur, Belgium. U.S. provinces: 241 Lafayette Ave., Buffalo, NY 14213-1453, (716) 884- 8221, www.ssmn.us. 909 West Shaw St., Ft. Worth, TX 76110, (817) 923-8393, web2.airmail.net/ssmn.

Mary of Providence, Daughters of St., D.S.M.P.: Founded 1872, at Como, Italy; in U.S., 1913. General motherhouse, Rome, Italy. U.S. provincial house, 4200 N. Austin Ave., Chicago, IL 60634, (773) 545-8300. Special education for mentally handicapped.

Mary of the Immaculate Conception, Daughters of, D.M.: Founded 1904, in U.S., by Msgr. Lucian Bojnowski. General motherhouse, 314 Osgood Ave., New Britain, CT 06053, (860) 225-9406. Educational, hospital work.

Mary Queen, Congregation of, C.M.R.: Founded in Vietnam; established in U.S., 1979. U.S. region, 625 S. Jefferson, Springfield, MO 65806.

Mary Reparatrix, Society of, S.M.R.: Founded 1857, in France; in U.S., 1908. Generalate, Rome, Italy. U.S. province, 225 E. 234th St., Bronx NY 10470.

Maryknoll Sisters, M.M.: Founded in 1912 in U.S. by Mother Mary Joseph. General motherhouse: PO Box 311, Maryknoll, NY 10545-0311, (914) 941-7575, www.maryknoll.org.

Medical Mission Sisters (Society of Catholic Medical Missionaries, Inc.), M.M.S.: Founded 1925, in U.S., by Mother Anna Dengel. Generalate, London, England. U.S. headquarters, 8400 Pine Rd., Philadelphia, PA 19111,

(215) 742-6100, www.medicalmissionsisters.org. Medical work, health education, especially in mission areas.

Medical Missionaries of Mary, M.M.M.: Founded 1937, in Ireland, by Mother Mary Martin; in U.S., 1950. General motherhouse, Dublin, Ireland. U.S. headquarters, 563 Minneford Ave., City Island, Bronx, NY 10464, (718) 885-0945. Medical aid in missions.

Medical Sisters of St. Joseph, M.S.J.: Founded 1946, in India; first U.S. foundation, 1985. General motherhouse, Kerala, S. India. U.S. address, 3435 E. Funston, Wichita, KS 67218, (316) 689-5360. Health care apostolate.

Mercedarian Sisters of the Blessed Sacrament, H.M.S.S.: Founded 1910, in Mexico; first U.S. foun dation, 1926. Regional House, 227 Keller St., San Antonio, TX 78204, (210) 223-5013.

Mercy, Daughters of Our Lady of, D.M.: Founded 1837, in Italy, by St. Mary Joseph Rossello; in U.S., 1919. General motherhouse, Savona, Italy. U.S. motherhouse, Villa Rossello, 1009 Main Rd., Newfield, NJ 08344, (856) 697-2983. Educational, hospital work.

Mercy, Missionary Sisters of Our Lady of, M.O.M.: Founded 1938, in Brazil; in U.S., 1955. General motherhouse, Brazil. U.S. address, 388 Franklin St., Buffalo, NY 14202, (716) 854-5198.

Mercy, Religious Sisters of, R.S.M.: Founded 1973 in U.S. Motherhouse, 1835; 1965 Michigan Ave., Alma, MI 48801, (989) 463-6035; www.rsmofalma.com.

Mercy, Sisters of, of the Americas: Formed in July, 1991, through union of nine provinces and 16 regional communities of Sisters of Mercy which previously were independent motherhouses or houses which formed the Sisters of Mercy of the Union. Mother Mary Catherine McAuley founded the Sisters of Mercy in Dublin, Ireland, in 1831; first established in the U.S., 1843, in Pittsburgh. Administrative office: 8300 Colesville Rd., No. 300, Silver Spring, MD 20910, (301) 587-0423.

Mill Hill Sisters: *See* Franciscan Missionaries of St. Joseph.

Minim Daughters of Mary Immaculate, C.F.M.M.: Founded 1886, in Mexico; in U.S., 1926. General motherhouse, Leon, Guanajuato, Mexico. U.S. address, 555 Patagonia Hwy., Nogales, AZ 85621, (520) 287-3377.

Misericordia Sisters, S.M.: Founded 1848, in Canada; in U.S., 1887. General motherhouse, 12435 Ave. Misericorde, Montreal, QC H4J 2G3, Canada. U.S. address, 225 Carol Ave., Pelham, NY 10803. Social work with unwed mothers and their children; hospital work.

Mission Helpers of the Sacred Heart, M.H.S.H.: Founded 1890, in U.S. General motherhouse, 1001 W. Joppa Rd., Baltimore, MD 21204, (410) 823-8585, www.missionhelpers.org. Religious education, evangelization.

Missionary Catechists of the Sacred Hearts of Jesus and Mary (Violetas), M.C.S.H.: Founded 1918, in Mexico; in U.S., 1943. Motherhouse, Tlalpan, Mexico. U.S. address, 805 Liberty St., Victoria, TX 77901, (512) 578-9302.

Missionary Daughters of the Most Pure Virgin Mary, M.D.P.V.M.: Founded in Mexico; in U.S., 1916. 919 N. 9th St., Kingsville, TX 78363, (512) 595-1087.

Mother of God, Missionary Sisters of the, M.S.M.G.: Byzantine, Ukrainian Rite, Stamford. Motherhouse, 711 N. Franklin St., Philadelphia, PA 19123, (215) 627-7808.

Mother of God, Sisters Poor Servants of the, S.M.G.: Founded 1869, in London, England; in U.S., 1947. General motherhouse, Maryfield, Roehampton, London. U.S. address: Maryfield Nursing Home, Greensboro Rd., High Point, NC 27260, (336) 886-2444, www.greensboro.

com/mnh. Hospital, educational work.

Nazareth, Poor Sisters of, P.S.N.: Founded in England; U.S. foundation, 1924. General mother house, Hammersmith, London, England. U.S. novi tiate, 3333 Manning Ave., Los Angeles, CA 90064, (310) 839-2361. Social services, education.

Notre Dame, School Sisters of, S.S.N.D.: Founded 1833, in Germany; in U.S., 1847. General mother-house, Rome, Italy. U.S. province: 320 E. Ripa Ave., St. Louis, MO 63125, (314) 633-7006, www.ssndcentralpacific.org.

Notre Dame, Sisters of, S.N.D.: Founded 1850, at Coesfeld, Germany; in U.S., 1874. General mother house, Rome, Italy. U.S. provinces: 13000 Auburn Rd., Chardon, OH 44024, (440) 286-7101. 1601 Dixie Highway, Covington, KY 41011, (606) 291-2040. 3837 Secor Rd., Toledo, OH 43623, (419) 474-5485. 1776 Hendrix Ave., Thousand Oaks, CA 91360, (805) 496-3243.

Notre Dame, Sisters of the Congregation of, C.N.D.: Founded 1658, in Canada, by St. Marguerite Bourgeoys; in U.S., 1860. General motherhouse, Montréal, QC, Canada. U.S. province, 223 West Mountain Rd., Ridgefield, CT 06877-3627, (203) 438- 3115, www.cnd-m.com. Education.

Notre Dame de Namur, Sisters of, S.N.D.deN.: Founded 1804, in France; in U.S., 1840. General motherhouse, Rome, Italy. U.S. provinces: 351 Broadway, Everett, MA 02149, (617) 387-2500, www.SNDdeN. org. 30 Jeffrey's Neck Rd., Ipswich, MA 01938, (978) 356-2159. 468 Poquonock Ave., Windsor, CT 06095-2473, (860) 688-1832, www.sndden.org. 1531 Greenspring Valley Rd., Stevenson, MD 21153, (410) 486-5599. 305 Cable St., Baltimore, MD 21210, (410) 243-1993, www. sndden.org. 701 E. Columbia Ave., Cincinnati, OH 45215, (513) 761-7636. 1520 Ralston Ave., Belmont, CA 94002-1908, (650) 593-2045. SND Base Communities, 125 Michigan Ave., N.E., Washington, DC 20017, (202) 884-9750; www.snd den.org. Educational work.

Notre Dame de Sion, Congregation of, N.D.S.: Founded 1850, in France; in U.S., 1892. Generalate, Rome, Italy. U.S. province, 3823 Locust St., Kansas City, MO 64109, (816) 531-1374. Creation of better understanding between Christians and Jews.

Notre Dame Sisters: Founded 1853, in Czechoslo- vakia; in U.S., 1910. General motherhouse, Javornik, Czech Republic. U.S. motherhouse, 3501 State St., Omaha, NE 68112, (402) 455-2994, www.notredame sisters.org. Educational work.

Oblates of the Mother of Orphans, O.M.O: Founded 1945, in Italy. General motherhouse, Milan, Italy. U.S. address, 20 E. 72 St., New York, NY 10021.

Our Lady of Charity, Sisters of (Eudist Sisters, Sisters of Our Lady of Charity of the Refuge), N.A.U.-O.L.C.: Founded 1641, in Caen, France, by St. John Eudes; in U.S., 1855. Autonomous houses were federated in 1944 and in March 1979 the North American Union of the Sisters of Our Lady of Charity was established. General mother-house, 620 Roswell Rd. NW, PO Box 340, Carrollton, OH 44615-0340, (330) 627-1641; www.nauolc.org. Primarily devoted to re-education and rehabilitation of women and girls in residential and non-residential settings.

Our Lady of Sorrows, Sisters of, O.L.S.: Founded 1839, in Italy; in U.S., 1947. General motherhouse, Rome, Italy. U.S. headquarters, 9894 Norris Ferry Rd., Shreveport, LA 71106.

Our Lady of the Holy Rosary, Daughters of, F.M.S.R. (*Filiae Mariae Sacri Rosarii*): Founded 1946, in North Vietnam; foundation in U.S., 1968. General Motherhouse, Saigon, Vietnam. U.S. Province, 1492 Moss St., New Orleans, LA 70119, (504) 486-0039.

Our Lady of Victory Missionary Sisters, O.L.V.M.: Founded 1922, in U.S. Motherhouse, Victory Noll, 1900 W. Park Dr., PO Box 109, Huntington, IN 46750, (260) 356-0628, www.olvm.org. Educational, social work.

Pallottine Missionary Sisters (Missionary Sisters of the Catholic Apostolate), S.A.C.: Founded in Rome, 1838; in U.S., 1912. Generalate, Rome, Italy. U.S. provincialate, 15270 Old Halls Ferry Rd., Florissant, MO 63034, (314) 837-7100, www.geocities.com/pallottinerenewal.

Pallottine Sisters of the Catholic Apostolate, C.S.A.C.: Founded 1843, at Rome, Italy; in U.S., 1889. General motherhouse, Rome. U.S. motherhouse, St. Patrick's Villa, Harriman Heights, Harriman, NY 10926, (914) 783-9007. Educational work.

Parish Visitors of Mary Immaculate, P.V.M.I.: Founded 1920, in New York. General motherhouse, Box 658, Monroe, NY 10949, (845) 783-2251, www.parishvisitors. org. Mission work.

Passionist Nuns (Passion of Jesus Christ, Religious of), C.P.: Founded 1771, in Italy, by St. Paul of the Cross; in U.S., 1910. U.S. convents: 2715 Churchview Ave., Pittsburgh, PA 15227-2141, (412) 881-1155. 631 Griffin Pond Rd., Clarks Summit, PA 18411-8899, (570) 586-2791, www.intiques.net/ cpnuns. 8564 Crisp Rd., Whitesville, KY 42378- 9729, (270) 233-4571, www.passionistnuns.org. 1151 Donaldson Hwy., Erlanger, KY 41018, (859) 371-8568. 15700 Clayton Rd., Ellisville, MO 63011, (314) 227-5275. Contemplatives.

Passionist Sisters: See **Cross and Passion, Sisters of the**

Paul, Daughters of St. (Missionary Sisters of the Media of Communication), D.S.P.: Founded 1915, at Alba, Piedmont, Italy; in U.S., 1932. General motherhouse, Rome, Italy. U.S. provincial house, 50 St. Paul's Ave., Boston, MA 02130-3491, (617) 522-8911, www.pauline. org. Apostolate of the communications arts.

Paul of Chartres, Sisters of St., S.P.C.: Founded 1696, in France. General House, Rome, Italy. U.S. address, 2920 Third Ave., So., Escanaba, MI 49828; (906) 399-0420.

Perpetual Adoration of Guadalupe, Sisters of, A.P.G.: U.S. foundation, 2403 W. Travis, San Antonio, TX 78207, (956) 227-7785.

Peter Claver, Missionary Sisters of St., S.S.P.C.: Founded 1894 in Austria by Bl. Maria Teresa Ledochowska; in U.S., 1914. General motherhouse, Rome, Italy. U.S. address, 667 Woods Mill Rd. S., Chesterfield, MO 63006, (314) 469-4923.

Pious Disciples of the Divine Master, P.D.D.M.: Founded 1924 in Italy; in U.S., 1948. General motherhouse, Rome, Italy. U.S. headquarters, 60 Sunset Ave., Staten Island, NY 10314, (718) 494-8597.

Pious Schools, Sisters of the, Sch. P.: Founded 1829 in Spain; in U.S., 1954. General motherhouse, Rome, Italy. U.S. headquarters, 17601 Nordhoff St., Northridge, CA 91325, (818) 882-6265.

Poor, Little Sisters of the, L.S.P.: Founded 1839, in France, by Bl. Jeanne Jugan; in U.S., 1868. General moth-erhouse, St. Pern, France. U.S. provinces: 110-30 221st St., Queens Village, NY 11429, (718) 464-1800. 601 Maiden Choice Lane, Baltimore, MD 21228, (410) 744-9367;

www.littlesistersofthepoor.org. 80 W. Northwest Hwy., Palatine, IL 60067, (847) 358-5700, www.littlesistersofthe poor.org. Care of aged.

Poor Clare Missionary Sisters (Misioneras Clarisas), M.C.: Founded in Mexico. General motherhouse, Rome, Italy. U.S. novitiate, 1019 N. Newhope, Santa Ana, CA 92703-1534, (714) 554-8850.

Poor Clare Nuns: *See* **Franciscan Poor Clare Nuns**.

Poor Handmaids of Jesus Christ (Ancilla Domini Sisters), P.H.J.C.: Founded 1851, in Germany by Bl. Mary Kasper; in U.S., 1868. General motherhouse, Dernbach, Westerwald, Germany. U.S. motherhouse, Ancilla Domini Convent, Donaldson, IN 46513, (219) 936-9936. Educational, hospital work, social services.

Precious Blood, Daughters of Charity of the Most, D.C.P.B.: Founded 1872, at Pagani, Italy; in U.S., 1908. General motherhouse, Rome, Italy. U.S. convent, 1482 North Ave., Bridgeport, CT 06604, (203) 334-7000.

Precious Blood, Missionary Sisters of the, C.P.S.: Founded 1885, at Mariannhill, South Africa; in U.S., 1925. Generalate, Rome, Italy. U.S. novitiate, PO Box 97, Reading, PA 19607, (610) 777-1624. Home and foreign mission work.

Precious Blood, Sisters Adorers of the, A.P.B.: Founded 1861, in Canada; in U.S., 1890. General motherhouse, Canada. U.S. autonomous monasteries: 5400 Fort Hamilton Pkwy., Brooklyn, NY 11219, (718) 438-6371, www.sisterspreciousblood.org. 700 Bridge St., Manchester, NH 03104-5495, (603) 623-4264. 166 State St., Portland, ME 04101. 400 Pratt St., Watertown, NY 13601, (315) 782-5119, www.sisters preciousblood.org. Cloistered, contemplative.

Precious Blood, Sisters of the, C.PP.S.: Founded 1834, in Switzerland; in U.S., 1844. Generalate, 4000 Denlinger Rd., Dayton, OH 45426, (937) 837-3302. Education, health care, other ministries.

Precious Blood, Sisters of the Most, C.PP.S.: Founded 1845, in Steinerberg, Switzerland; in U.S., 1870. General motherhouse, 204 N. Main St., O'Fallon, MO 63366-2203, (636) 240-3420. Education, other ministries.

Presentation, Sisters of Mary of the, S.M.P.: Founded 1829, in France; in U.S., 1903. General motherhouse, Broons, Côtes-du-Nord, France. U.S. address, Maryvale Novitiate, 11550 River Rd., Valley City, ND 58072, (701) 845-2864, www.sistersofmaryofthepresentation.com. Hospital work.

Presentation of Mary, Sisters of the, P.M.: Founded 1796, in France by Bl. Marie Rivier; in U.S., 1873. General motherhouse, Castel Gandolfo, Italy. U.S. provincial houses: 495 Mammoth Rd., Manchester, NH 03104, (603) 669-1080, www.presentationofmary-usa.org. 209 Lawrence St., Methuen, MA 01844, (978) 687-1369, www.presmarymethuen.org.

Presentation of the B.V.M., Sisters of the, P.B.V.M.: Founded 1775, in Ireland; in U.S., 1854, in San Francisco. U.S. motherhouses: 2360 Carter Rd., Dubuque, IA 52001, (563) 588-2008, www.dubuquepresentations.org. 84 Presentation Way, New Windsor, NY 12553, (845) 564-0513; www.sistersofthepresentation.org 281 Masonic Ave, San Francisco, CA 94118, (415) 422-5013, www.presentationsisterssf.org. St. Colman's Convent, Watervliet, NY 12189, (518) 273-4911. 1101 32nd Ave., S., Fargo ND 58103, (701) 237-4857, www.presetnationsistersfargo.org.

Presentation Convent, Aberdeen, SD 57401, (605) 229-8419, Leominster, MA 01453. 419 Woodrow Rd., Staten Island, NY 10312, (718) 966- 2365.

Presentation of the Blessed Virgin Mary, Sisters of, of Union: Founded in Ireland, 1775; union established in Ireland, 1976; first U.S. vice province, 1979. Generalate, Kildare, Ireland. U.S. provincialate, 729 W. Wilshire Dr., Phoenix, AZ 85007, (602) 271-9687.

Providence, Daughters of Divine, F.D.P.: Founded 1832, Italy; in U.S., 1964. Rome, Italy. U.S. address, 386 Fir St., Laplace, LA 70068, (985) 359-3163 (fax).

Providence, Missionary Catechists of Divine, M.C.D.P.: Administrative house, 2318 Castroville Rd., San Antonio, TX 78237, (210) 432-0113.

Providence, Oblate Sisters of, O.S.P.: Founded 1829, in U.S., by Mother Mary Elizabeth Lange and Father James Joubert, S.S. First order of black nuns in U.S. General motherhouse, 701 Gun Rd., Baltimore, MD 21227, (410) 242-8500. Educational work.

Providence, Sisters of, S.P.: Founded 1861, in Canada; in U.S., 1873. General motherhouse, Our Lady of Victory Convent, 5 Gamelin St., Holyoke, MA 01040, (413) 536-7511, wwwsisofprov.org.

Providence, Sisters of, S.P.: Founded 1843, in Canada; in U.S., 1854. General motherhouse, Montreal, QC, Canada. U.S. province, Mother Joseph Province, 506 Second Ave., #1200, Seattle, WA 98104, (206) 464-3394, www.sistersofprovidence.net.

Providence, Sisters of (of St. Mary-of-the-Woods), S.P.: Founded 1806, in France; in U.S., 1 Sisters of Providence, St. Mary-of-the-Woods, IN 47876, (812) 535-3131, www. sistersofprovidence.org.

Providence, Sisters of Divine, C.D.P.: Founded 1762, in France; in U.S., 1866. Generalate, 515 SW 24th St., San Antonio, TX 78207, (210) 434-1866. Educational, hospital work.

Providence, Sisters of Divine, C.D.P.: Founded 1851, in Germany; in U.S., 1876. Generalate, Rome, Italy. U.S. provinces: 9000 Babcock Blvd., Allison Park, PA 15101-2793, (412) 931-5241, www.divineprovidenceweb. org. 3415 Bridgeland Dr., Bridgetown, MO 63044, (314) 209-9181, www.divineprovi denceweb.org. 363 Bishops Hwy., Kingston, MA 02364, (781) 585-7707. Educational, hospital work.

Providence, Sisters of Divine (of Kentucky), C.D.P.: Founded 1762, in France; in U.S., 1889. General motherhouse, Fenetrange, France. U.S. province, St. Bartholomew Parish, Cincinnati, OH 45231, (513) 728-3146, www.cdpkentucky.org. Education, social services, other ministries.

Redeemer, Oblates of the Most Holy, O.SS.R.: Founded 1864, in Spain. General motherhouse, Spain. U.S. foundation, 60-80 Pond St., Jamaica Plain, MA 02130, (617) 524-1640.

Redeemer, Order of the Most Holy, O.SS.R.: Founded 1731, by Ven. Mother Marie Celeste Crostarosa, with the help of St. Alphonsus Liguori; in U.S., 1957. U.S. addresses: Mother of Perpetual Help Monastery, PO Box 220, Esopus, NY 12429, (845) 384-6533, www.redemptoristinenunsofnewyork.org. Monastery of St. Alphonsus, 200 Ligouri Dr., Liguori, MO 63057, (636) 464-1093, www.redemptoristine nuns.org.

Redeemer, Sisters of the Divine, S.D.R.: Founded 1849, in Niederbronn, France; in U.S., 1912. General motherhouse, Rome, Italy. U.S. province, 999 Rock Run Road, Elizabeth, PA 15037, (412)

751-8600. Educational, hospital work; care of the aged.

Redeemer, Sisters of the Holy, C.S.R.: Founded 1849, in Alsace; in U.S., 1924. General motherhouse, Wurzburg, Germany. U.S. provincial house, 521 Moredon Rd., Huntingdon Valley, PA 19006, (215) 914-4101. Personalized medical care in hospitals, homes for aged, private homes; retreat work.

Reparation of the Congregation of Mary, Sisters of, S.R.C.M.: Founded 1903, in U.S. Motherhouse, St. Zita's Villa, Monsey, NY 10952, (845) 356-2011.

Reparation of the Sacred Wounds of Jesus, Sisters of, S.R.: Founded 1959 in U.S. General motherhouse, 2120 S.E. 24th Ave., Portland, OR 97214-5504, (503) 236-4207.

Resurrection, Sisters of the, C.R.: Founded 1891, in Italy; in U.S., 1900. General motherhouse, Rome, Italy. U.S. provinces: 7432 Talcott Ave., Chicago, IL 60631, (773) 792-6363. Mt. St. Joseph, 35 Boltwood Ave., Castleton-on-Hudson, NY 12033, (518) 732-2429, www.resurrectionsisters.org. Education, nursing.

Rita, Sisters of St., O.S.A.: General motherhouse, Wurzburg, Germany. U.S. foundation, St. Monica's Convent, 3920 Green Bay Rd., Racine, WI 53404, (262) 639-5050, www.srsofstrita.org.

Rosary, Congregation of Our Lady of the Holy, R.S.R.: Founded 1874, in Canada; in U.S., 1899. General motherhouse, Rimouski, QC, Canada. U.S. regional house, 20 Portland Ave., Old Orchard Beach, ME 04964, (207) 934-0592, www.soeursdu-saintrosaire.org. Educational work.

Rosary, Missionary Sisters of the Holy, M.S.H.R.: Founded 1924, in Ireland; in U.S., 1954. Motherhouse, Dublin, Ireland. In U.S., 741 Polo Rd., Bryn Mawr, PA 19010, (610) 520-1976, www.holyrosarymissionarysisters. org. African missions.

Sacrament, Missionary Sisters of the Most Blessed, M.SS.S.: General motherhouse, Madrid, Spain. U.S. foundation, 1111 Wordin Ave., Bridgeport, CT 06605.

Sacrament, Nuns of the Perpetual Adoration of the Blessed, A.P.: Founded 1807 in Rome, Italy; in U.S., 1925. U.S. monasteries: 145 N. Cotton Ave., El Paso, TX 79901, (915) 533-5323. 771 Ashbury St., San Francisco, CA 94117, (415) 566-2743.

Sacrament, Oblate Sisters of the Blessed, O.S.B.S.: Founded 1935, in U.S. Motherhouse, St. Sylvester Convent, PO Box 217, Marty, SD 57361, (605) 384-3305. Care of American Indians.

Sacrament, Servants of the Blessed, S.S.S.: Founded 1858, in France, by St. Pierre Julien Eymard; in U.S., 1947. General motherhouse, Rome, Italy. American provincial house, St. Charles Borromeo Parish, 1818 Coal Pl. SE, Albuquerque, NM 87106, (505) 242-3692. Contemplative.

Sacrament, Sisters of the Blessed, for Indians and Colored People, S.B.S.: Founded 1891, in U.S., by St. Katharine Drexel. General motherhouse, 1663 Bristol Pike, PO Box 8502, Bensalem, PA 19020, (215) 244- 9900, www.katharinedrexel.org.

Sacrament, Sisters of the Most Holy, M.H.S.: Founded 1851, in France; in U.S., 1872. Generalate, 313 Corona Dr. (P.O. Box 90037), Lafayette, LA 70509, (337) 981-8475.

Sacrament, Sisters Servants of the Blessed, S.J.S.: Founded 1904, in Mexico; in U.S., 1926. General motherhouse, Mexico. U.S. address: 215 Lomita St.,

El Segundo, CA 90245, (310) 615-0766.

Sacramentine Nuns (Religious of the Order of the Blessed Sacrament and Our Lady), O.S.S.: Founded 1639, in France; in U.S., 1912. U.S. monasteries: 235 Bellvale Lakes Rd., Warwick NY 10990. 2798 US 31 N, PO Box 86, Conway, MI 49722, (231) 347-0447. Perpetual adoration of the Holy Eucharist.

Sacred Heart, Daughters of Our Lady of the, F.D.N.S.C.: Founded 1882, in France; in U.S., 1955. General motherhouse, Rome, Italy. U.S. address, 424 E. Browning Rd., Bellmawr, NJ 08031, (609) 931- 8973. Educational work.

Sacred Heart, Missionary Sisters of the (Cabrini Sisters), M.S.C.: Founded 1880, in Italy, by St. Frances Xavier Cabrini; in U.S., 1889. General motherhouse, Rome, Italy. U.S. provincial office, 222 E. 19th St., 5B, New York, NY 10003. Educational, health, social and catechetical work.

Sacred Heart, Society Devoted to the, S.D.S.H.: Founded 1940, in Hungary; in U.S., 1956. U.S. motherhouse, 9814 Sylvia Ave., Northridge, CA 91324, (818) 831-9710; www. sacredheartsisters.com. Educational work.

Sacred Heart, Society of the, R.S.C.J.: Founded 1800, in France; in U.S., 1818. Generalate, Rome, Italy. U.S. provincial house, 4389 W. Pine Blvd., St. Louis, MO 63108, (314) 652-1500, www.rscj.org. Educational work.

Sacred Heart of Jesus, Apostles of, A.S.C.J.: Founded 1894, in Italy; in U.S., 1902. General motherhouse, Rome, Italy. U.S. motherhouse, 295 Benham St., Hamden, CT 06514, (203) 248-4225, www.ascjus.org. Pastoral ministry, nursing and health care, legal assistance, elderly day care.

Sacred Heart of Jesus, Handmaids of the, A.C.J.: Founded 1877, in Spain. General motherhouse, Rome, Italy. U.S. province, 616 Coopertown Rd., Haverford, PA 19041, (610) 642-5715, www.acjusa.org. Educational, retreat work.

Sacred Heart of Jesus, Missionary Sisters of the Most (Hiltrup), M.S.C.: Founded 1899, in Germany; in U.S., 1908. General motherhouse, Rome, Italy. U.S. province, 2811 Moyers Lane, Reading, PA 19605, (610) 929-5944; www.mscrdg.org. Education, health care, pastoral ministry.

Sacred Heart of Jesus, Oblate Sisters of the, O.S.H.J.: Founded 1894; in U.S., 1949. General motherhouse, Rome, Italy. U.S. headquarters, 50 Warner Rd., Hubbard, OH 44425, (330) 759-9329, www.oblatesister.com. Educational, social work.

Sacred Heart of Jesus, Servants of the Most, S.S.C.J.: Founded 1894, in Poland; in U.S., 1959. General motherhouse, Cracow, Poland. U.S. address, 866 Cambria St., Cresson, PA 16630, (814) 886-4223, www.sacredheartsisters.org. Education, health care, social services.

Sacred Heart of Jesus, Sisters of the, S.S.C.J.: Founded 1816, in France; in U.S., 1903. General motherhouse, St. Jacut, Brittany, France. U.S. provincial house, 11931 Radium St., San Antonio, TX 78216, (210) 344-7203. Educational, hospital, domestic work.

Sacred Heart of Jesus and of the Poor, Servants of the (Mexican), S.S.H.J.P.: Founded 1885, in Mexico; in U.S., 1907. General motherhouse, Apartado 92, Puebla, Mexico. U.S. address, 3310 S. Zapata Hwy, Laredo, TX 78046, (956) 723-3343.

Sacred Heart of Jesus and Our Lady of Guadalupe, Missionaries of the, M.S.C.Gpe.: U.S. address, 1212 E. Euclid Ave., Arlington Heights, IL 60004, (708) 398-1350.

Sacred Heart of Jesus for Reparation, Congregation of the Handmaids of the, A.R.: Founded 1918, in Italy; in

U.S., 1958. U.S. address, 36 Villa Dr., Steubenville, OH 43953, (740) 282-3801.

Sacred Heart of Mary, Religious of the, R.S.H.M.: Founded 1848, in France; in U.S., 1877. Generalate, Rome, Italy. U.S. provinces; 50 Wilson Park Dr., Tarrytown, NY 10591, (914) 631-8872, www.rshm.org. 441 N. Garfield Ave., Montebello, CA 90640, (323) 887-8821, www.rshm.org.

Sacred Hearts and of Perpetual Adoration, Sisters of the, SS.CC.: Founded 1797, in France; in U.S., 1908. General motherhouse, Rome, Italy. U.S. provinces: 1120 Fifth Ave., Honolulu, HI 96816, (808) 737-5822, www.ssccpicpus.com (Pacific). 35 Huttleston Ave., Fairhaven, MA 02719, (508) 994-9341 (East Coast). Varied ministries.

Sacred Hearts of Jesus and Mary, Sisters of the, S.H.J.M.: Established 1953, in U.S. General mother house, Essex, England. U.S. address, 2150 Lake Shore Ave., Oakland CA 94606, (510) 832-2935.

Savior, Company of the, C.S.: Founded 1952, in Spain; in U.S., 1962. General motherhouse, Madrid, Spain. U.S. foundation, 820 Clinton Ave., Bridgeport, CT 06604, (203) 368-1875.

Savior, Sisters of the Divine, S.D.S.: Founded 1888, in Italy; in U.S., 1895. General motherhouse, Rome, Italy. U.S. province, 4311 N. 100th St., Milwaukee, WI 53222, (414) 466-0810, www.salvatoriansisters.org. Educational, hospital work.

Social Service, Sisters of, S.S.S.: Founded in Hungary, 1923, by Sr. Margaret Slachta. U.S. generalate, 296 Summit Ave., Buffalo, NY 14214, (716) 834-0197, www.sistersofsocialservicebuffalo.org. Social work.

Social Service, Sisters of, S.S.S.: Founded 1908, in Hungary; in U.S., 1926. General motherhouse, 4316 Lanai Rd., Encino, CA 91436, (818) 285-3359, www.sistersofsocialservice.com

Teresa of Jesus, Society of St., S.T.J.: Founded 1876, in Spain; in U.S., 1910. General motherhouse, Rome, Italy. U.S. provincial house, 18080 St. Joseph's Way, Covington, LA 70435, (985) 893-1470, www.teresians.org.

Thomas of Villanova, Congregation of Sisters of St., S.S.T.V.: Founded 1661, in France; in U.S., 1948. General motherhouse, Neuilly-sur-Seine, France. U.S. foundation, W. Rocks Rd., Norwalk, CT 06851, (203) 847-5893.

Trinity, Missionary Servants of the Most Blessed, M.S.B.T.: Founded 1912, in U.S., by Very Rev. Thomas A. Judge. General motherhouse, 3501 Solly Ave., Philadelphia, PA 19136, (215) 335-7550, www.msbt.org. Educational, social work, health services.

Trinity, Sisters Oblates to the Blessed, O.B.T.: Founded 1923, in Italy. U.S. novitiate, Beekman Rd., P.O. Box 98, Hopewell Junction, NY 12533, (914) 226-5671.

Trinity, Sisters of the Most Holy, O.Ss.T.: Founded 1198, in Rome; in U.S., 1920. General motherhouse, Rome, Italy. U.S. address, Immaculate Conception Province, 21281 Chardon Rd., Euclid, OH 44117, (216) 481-8232, www.srstrinity.org. Educational work.

Trinity, Society of Our Lady of the Most Holy, S.O.L.T.: Motherhouse, 1200 Lantana St., Corpus Christi, TX 78407, (361) 387-9095.

Ursula of the Blessed Virgin, Society of the Sisters of St., S.U.: Founded 1606, in France; in U.S., 1902. General motherhouse, France. U.S. novitiate, 50 Linnwood Rd., Rhinebeck, NY 12572, (845) 876-2341, www.societyofstursula.org. Educational work.

Ursuline Nuns (Roman Union), O.S.U.: Founded

1535, in Italy; in U.S., 1727. Generalate, Rome, Italy. U.S. provinces: 1338 North Avenue, New Rochelle, NY 10804, (914) 712-0060. 353 S. Sappington Rd., Kirkwood, MO 63122, (314) 821-6884, www.osucentral.org. 639 Angela Dr., Santa Rosa, CA 95401, (707) 545-6811. St. Mary's Residences, 100 Campus Ave., #211, Lewiston, ME 04240, (207) 786-9312.

Ursuline Sisters of Mount Saint Joseph, O.S.U.: Founded 1535, in Italy; in U.S., 1727, in New Orleans. U.S. motherhouses: 20860 St, Rte. 251, St. Martin, OH 45518-9705, (513) 875-2020. 901 E. Miami St., Paola, KS 66071, (913) 557-2349. 8001 Cummings Rd., Maple Mount, KY 42356, (270) 229-4200, www.ursuineslou.org. 2600 Lander Rd., Cleveland, OH 44124, (440) 449-1200, www.ursulinesisters.org. 8001 Cummings Rd., Maple Mount, KY 42356, (270) 229-4200, www.ursulinesmsj.org. 4045 Indian Rd., Toledo, OH 43606, (419) 536-9587, www.toledoursulines.org. 4250 Shields Rd., Canfield, OH 44406, (330) 792-7636. 1339 E. McMillan St., Cincinnati, OH 45206, (513) 961-3410.

Ursuline Sisters of the Congregation of Tildonk, Belgium, O.S.U.: Founded 1535, in Italy; Tildonk con gregation, 1832; in U.S., 1924. Generalate, Brussels, Belgium. U.S. address, 81-15 Utopia Parkway, Jamaica, NY 11432, (718) 591-0681, www.tressy.tripod.com. Educational, foreign mission work.

Ursuline Sisters of Belleville, O.S.U.: Founded 1535, in Italy; in U.S., 1910; established as diocesan community, 1983. Central house, 1026 N. Douglas Ave., Belleville, IL 62220, (618) 235-3444. Educational work.

Venerini Sisters, Religious, M.P.V.: Founded 1685, in Italy; in U.S., 1909. General motherhouse, Rome, Italy. U.S. provincialate; 23 Edward St., Worcester, MA 01605, (508) 754-1020, www.venerinisisters.org.

Vietnamese Adorers of the Holy Cross, M.T.G.: Founded 1670 in Vietnam; in U.S. 1976. General motherhouse 7408 S.E. Adler St., Portland, OR 97215, (503) 254-3284.

Vincent de Paul, Sisters: *See* **Charity of St. Vincent de Paul, Sisters of.**

Visitation Nuns, V.H.M.: Founded 1610, in France; in U.S. (Georgetown, DC), 1799. Contemplative, educational work. Two federations in U.S:

• First Federation of North America. Major pontifical enclosure. Pres., Mother Mary Jozefa Kowalewski, Monastery of the Visitation, 2055 Ridgedale Dr., Snellville, GA 30078, (770) 972-1060. Addresses of monasteries belonging to the federation: 2300 Springhill Ave., Mobile, AL 36607, (251) 473-2321. 14 Beach Rd., Tyringham, MA, 01264, (413) 243- 3995. 12221 Bievenue Rd, Rockville, VA 23146, (804) 749-4885. 5820 City Ave., Philadelphia, PA 19131, (215) 473-5888. 1745 Parkside Blvd., Toledo, OH 43607, (419) 536-1343. 2055 Ridgedale Dr., Snellville, GA 30078-2443, (770) 972-1060.

• Second Federation of North America. Constitutional enclosure. Pres., Sr. Anne Madeleine Godefroy, Monastery of the Visitation, 3020 N. Ballas Rd., St. Louis, MO 63131, (314) 432-5353, www.visitationmonastery.org/stlouis. Addresses of monasteries belonging to the federation: 1500 35th St., Washington, DC 20007, (202) 337-0305. 3020 N. Ballas Rd., St. Louis, MO 63131, (314) 432-5353. 200 E. Second St., Frederick, MD 21701, (301) 622-3322. Mt. de Chantal Monastery of the Visitation, 410 Washington Ave., Wheeling, WV 26003,

(304) 232-1283; www.mountdechan tal.org. 8902 Ridge Blvd., Brooklyn, NY 11209, (718) 745- 5151, www.visitationsisters.org. 2455 Visitation Dr., Mendota Heights, MN 55120, (651) 683-1700.

Visitation of the Congregation of the Immaculate Heart of Mary, Sisters of the, S.V.M.: Founded 1952, in U.S. Motherhouse, 2950 Kaufmann Ave., Dubuque, IA 52001, (563) 588-7256. Educational work, parish ministry.

Vocationist Sisters (Sisters of the Divine Vocations), S.V.D.: Founded 1921, in Italy; in U.S., 1967 General motherhouse, Naples, Italy. U.S. founda tion, Perpetual Help Nursery, 172 Broad

St., Newark, NJ 07104, (973) 484-3535.

Wisdom, Daughters of, D.W.: Founded 1703, in France, by St. Louis Marie Grignion de Montfort; in U.S., 1904. General motherhouse, Vendee, France. U.S. province, 385 Ocean Ave., Islip, NY 11751, (631) 277-2660, www.daughtersofwisdom. org. Education, health care, parish ministry, social services.

Xaverian Missionary Society of Mary, Inc., X.M.M.: Founded 1945, in Italy; in U.S., 1954. General motherhouse, Parma, Italy. U.S. address, 242 Salisbury St., Worcester, MA 01609, (508) 757-0514.

MEMBERSHIP OF RELIGIOUS INSTITUTES OF WOMEN

Principal source: Annuario Pontificio. *Statistics as of Jan. 1, 2014, unless indicated otherwise.* Listed below are world membership statistics of institutes of women with 500 or more members. Numbers in parentheses reflect the number of houses. For statistical information of institutes in the United States, *see* **Statistics**.

Salesian Srs. (1,414)	13,454
Calced Carmelites (706)	8,988
Franciscan Clarist Congr. (797)	7,145
Claretians (532)	6,784
Carmel, Srs. of the Mother of (672)	6,602
Franciscan Missionaries of Mary (746)	6,345
Charity, Mission. of (765)	5,310
Ador. of the Bl. Sacrament. (611)	4,753
Charity of St. Bartholomew of Capitanio (414)	4,330
Paul of Chartres, Srs. of St. (599)	4,032
Benedictine Nuns (236)	4,019
Sacred Heart Congregation (470)	3,787
Our Lady of Charity of the Good Shepherd (490)	3,556
Holy Cross, Srs. of Mercy of the (403)	3,581
Mercy of the Americas, Srs. of (1,165)	3,478
Immaculate Heart of Mary, Mission. Srs. (163)	3,248 (2009)
Holy Spirit, Mission Servants of the (424)	3,192
Notre Dame, School Srs. of (436)	3,066
Joseph, Srs. of St. (Cluny) (418)	2,769
Dominicans (198)	2,668
Canossian Daught. of Charity (324)	2,646
Poor, Little Sisters of the (194)	2,430
Paul, Daught. of St. (234)	2,372
Sacred Heart of Jesus "Sophie Barat," Society of the (381)	2,361
Dominicans of the Presentation of the Virgin (322)	2,256
Ancianos Desamparados, Hermanitas de los (204)	2,251
Charity of St. Joan Antida, Srs. of (274)	2,241
Mercy, Srs. of (Ireland) (711)	2,240
Anne, Srs. of Charity of St. (270)	2,151
Notre Dame, Srs. of (277)	2,150
Claretian Capuchins (149)	1,943
Holy Family Sisters (227)	1,943
Visitandine Nuns (133)	1,929
Ursulines of the Roman Union (225)	1,880
Carmelites of Charity of Vedruna (248)	1,859
Cross, Srs. of the (Swiss) (242)	1,831
B.V.M., Inst. of the (English) (290)	1,818
Carmelites, Scalced (124)	1,783
Holy Family, Srs. of the (Bordeaux) (259)	1,766
Jesus, Congr. of (273)	1,761
Apostolic Carmel, Srs. of (181)	1,683

Concezioniste (Franciscan Concessionists) (143)	1,669
Joseph, Srs. of St. (Chambéry) (269)	1,634
Mission, Carmelites (241)	1,632
Joseph Benedetto, Srs. of St. (116)	1,614
Felician Srs. (200)	1,574
Wisdom, Daught. of (221)	1,553
Franciscans of the Penance and Christian Charity (210)	1,552
Mary, Minister of the Infirm, Servants of (114)	1,542
Cistercian Nuns (Strict Observance) (69)	1,507
Mary Our Lady, Company of (174)	1,474
Salesian Missionaries of Mary Immaculate (174)	1,460
Cross, Srs. of the (204)	1,460
Adorers of the Blood of Christ (226)	1,453
Destitute, Srs. of the (213)	1,447
Notre Dame de Namur, Srs. of (551)	1,432
Teresian Carmelites of Verapoly (166)	1,407
Little Flower of Bethany, Srs. of the (171)	1,403
Divine Master, Pious Disciples of (167)	1,400
Benedictines, Missionary (138)	1,393
Holy Savior, Srs. of the (159)	1,392
Comboni Missionary Srs. (178)	1,380
Dorothy, Srs. of St. (167)	1,377
Teresa of Jesus, Society of St. (204)	1,371
Elizabeth, Srs. of St. (192)	1,370
Holy Family of Nazareth, Srs. of (159)	1,328
Jesus and Mary, Religious of (186)	1,327
Heart of Mary, Soc. of Daught. of (135)	1,314
Franciscan Hospitallers of the Immaculate Conception (157)	1,312
Joseph, Srs. of St. (Carondolet) (641)	1,311
Charity of Jesus and Mary, Srs. of (184)	1,295
Immaculate Conception, Little Srs. of the (227)	1,273
Jesus, Mary, and Joseph, Society of (163)	1,269
Anne, Daughters of Saint (199)	1,243
Capuchin Tertiaries of the Holy Family (205)	1,217
Anne, Srs. of Saint (171)	1,216
Mary Help of Christians, Mission. Srs. (179)	1,207
Union of the Srs. of the Presentation (232)	1,202
Franciscans of George the Martyr (141)	1,194
Mary Immaculate, Religious of (123)	1,169
Fraternity of Little Sisters of Jesus (249)	1,174
Sacred Heart of Jesus, Apostles of (177)	1,150
Our Lady of the Sacred Heart, Daughters of (193)	1,149

Salvatorians (200)	1,136
Divine Providence, Srs. of (St. Maurice) (220)	1,127
Anne, Daught. of Saint (Ranchi) (133)	1,126
Charity, Dtrs. of Divine (162)	1,122
Servants of Mary, Srs. of Our Lady of Sorrows (156)	1,122
Presentation of Mary, Srs. of the (162)	1,118
Hospitallers of the Sacred Heart of Jesus (101)	1,114
Adorers of the Blessed Sacrament and Charity (146)	1,113
Sacred Heart of Jesus, Ancelle (123)	1,106
Ursulines of Tildonk (135)	1,103
Mary, Mother of Mercy, Daught. of (210)	1,102
Anne, Srs. of, Tiruchchirappalli (187)	1,099
Assumption, Religious of the (157)	1,077
Holy Spirit, Daughters of the (148)	1,054
Jesus, Daught. of (St. Joseph of Kermaria) (146)	1,051
Franciscans of the Family of Mary (137)	1,044
Franciscans of the Immaculate Conception (148)	1,044
Franciscan Srs. (Pondicherry) (178)	1,046
Franciscans of Christ the King (141)	1,029
Notre Dame, Srs. of the Cong. of (110)	1,014
Cross and Passion, Srs. of the (Passionist Srs.) (160)	1,002
Mercedarians of Charity (137)	1,001
Caritas Srs. of Miyazaki (168)	983
Immaculate Heart of Mary, Mother of Christ (147)	983
Holy Names of Jesus and Mary, Srs. of the (68)	980
Queen of Apostles (130)	966
Religious Dominicans of the Annunciation (139)	962
Mercy of Australia, Inst. of Srs. (483)	961
Infirm of St. Francis, Srs. of (95)	951
Immaculate, Mission. of (118)	940
Servants of Jesus of Charity (92)	934
Our Lady of the Missions, Srs. of (230)	933
Jesus, Daught. of (Salamanca) (120)	928
Mary, Daught. of (168)	928
Cistercian Nuns, O. Cist. (58)	917
Handmaids of the Holy Child Jesus (143)	909
Dorothy of Frassinetti, Srs. of St. (134)	909
School Srs. of St. Francis of Milwaukee (286)	903
Divine Love, Daughters of (175)	902
Claretian (Urban) (76)	901
Precious Blood, Mission. Srs. of the (100)	897
Joseph of the Apparition, Srs. of St. (160)	886
Ursuline Franciscans (129)	886
Clarist Franciscan Mission (139)	876
Medical Srs. of St. Joseph (80)	862
Mercy, Srs. of (Verona) (87)	862
Servants of the Imm. Hrt. Of Mary, Srs. of (76)	860
Sacramentines (Perp. Ador. of the Blessed Sacrament) (60)	860
Our Lady of Mercy, Daught. of (157)	858
Joseph, Srs. of St. (Philadelphia) (128)	857
B.V.M., Inst. of the (131)	854
Franciscan Sisters of the Presentation of Mary (141)	850
Franciscan Srs. of Notre Dame de Bon Secours of Madras (129)	845
Providence, Srs. of (Portieux) (155)	842
Carmelite Sisters of St. Teresa (120)	837
Immaculate Heart of Mary, Miss. Srs. (71)	836
Imitation of Christ, Srs. of the (180)	836

Sacred Heart of Jesus, Daught. of Charity of the (119)	833
Mary Immaculate / Catherine of Siena (149)	831
Joseph, Srs. of St. (207)	829
Charity (Ancelle della) (87)	828
Cross, Daughters of, of Liege (108)	822
Camillus, Dtrs. of St. (93)	821
Immaculate Conception, Srs. of the (169)	815
Love of God, Sisters of the (107)	811
Charity, Srs. of (Thrissur) (106)	808
Elizabethan Franciscans (93)	806
Augustinians (76)	806
Joseph of the Sacred Heart of Jesus, Srs. of St. (76)	802
Ursulines of Mary Immaculate (104)	795
Dominicans of the Most Holy Rosary (305)	794
Baptistine Srs., Srs. of St. John the Baptist (123)	792
Assumption, Little Srs. of the (118)	791
Charity, Srs. of, Our Lady of Mercy (69)	791
Missionary Srs. of Mary Imm. (135)	788
Ursulines of the Sacred Heart of Jesus (99)	783
Sacred Heart of Mary Virgin Immaculate, Srs. of the (126)	783
Joseph, Inst. of Srs. of St. (162)	779
Vincent de Paul, Srs. of Charity of (107)	778
Franciscans of Gonzaga (131)	772
Immaculate Heart of Mary (139)	771
Our Lady of Africa, Mission. Srs. of (102)	759
Immaculate Conception, Srs. of Charity (93)	757
Sacred Heart of Jesus, Mission. Srs. (141)	753
Mary Immaculate, Sisters of the B.V.M. (111)	749
Joseph, Srs. of St. (Cantaous) (137)	749
Franciscan Srs. of Dillingen (82)	749
B.V.M., Religious of the (116)	740
Poor of the Inst. Palazzolo, Srs. of the (98)	735
Our Lady of the Apostles, Missionary Sisters of (123)	734
Franciscans of the Blessed Sacrament (43)	733 (2004)
Anne, Srs. of (Chennai) (135)	730
Assisi Srs. of Mary Immaculate (100)	730
Immaculate Conc. of the B.V.M. (112)	728
Joseph, Srs. of St. (Lyon) (162)	727
Franciscans Third Order Regular (55)	720
Dominicans of the Rosary (132)	715
Benedictine Srs., Fed. of St. Scholastica (21)	711
Franciscan Mission. of Mary, Auxiliatrix (118)	710
Mary Immaculate of Guadalupe (75)	707
Our Lady Mother of Mercy (153)	701
Sacred Heart of Jesus and Mary, Sisters of (84)	690
Carmelite Nuns, Discalced, O.C.D. (67)	688
Franciscan Missionaries of the Sacred Heart (103)	686
Little Srs. of Mary Immaculate (143)	686
Holy Family, Little Srs. of the (90)	683
Providence of S. Gaetano da Thiene (81)	677
Charity, Little Mission. Srs. of (99)	674
Consolata Missionary Sisters (103)	670
Bethlemite Srs., Daughters of the Sacred Heart of Jesus (91)	669
Scalabrinians (135)	667
Benedictine Srs., Federation of St. Gertrude the Great (14)	666
Mary, Dtrs. of (65)	664
Mary, Daught. of, Bannabikira Srs. (75)	663
Ann, Srs. of St. (96)	661
Sacramentine Srs. (97)	654

Servants of Jesus Sacramentado (75)	655
Jesus Crucified, Missionary Sisters of (148)	654
Mary Immaculate, Srs. of (79)	653
Maestre Pie Filippini (96)	652
Franciscan Mission. of Baby Jesus (94)	650
Teresian Carmelite Mission. (94)	645
Pious Schools, Religious of (104)	643
Mary Most Holy of the Word, Daughters of (112)	637
Mercedarians of the Blessed Sacrament (84)	635
Sacred Heart of Jesus and the Poor, Srs. of (75)	635
Providence, Srs. of (75)	633
Charles Borromeo, Srs. of Charity of (74)	626
Jesus Christ, Poor Srs. of (105)	629
Mary Reparatrix, Society of (89)	628
Divine Providence, Daught. of Mary of the (102)	626
Mother of Mercy (141)	625
Catherine Virgin and Martyr, Srs. of St. (113)	624
Claretians, Sacramentarian (63)	623
Charity of Nazareth, Srs. of (215)	621
Providence of Gap, Srs. of the (111)	620
Servants of the Poor (90)	620
Seraphic Sisters (69)	616
Dominican Srs. of Peace (185)	615
Franciscan Missionaries of the Mother of the Divine Pastor (94)	608
Sacred Heart of Jesus and the Poor (82)	602
St. Joseph of St. Mark, Srs. of (96)	598
Enfant-Jesus, Soeurs de l' (116)	597
Dominican Missionary Srs. (68)	594
Brigid, Srs. of (52)	592
Franciscan Mission., I.H.M., of Egypt (80)	590
Pallottine Srs. of the Catholic Apostolate, Mission. (78)	590
Catholic Apostle, Srs. of (78)	590
Cross, Srs. of the Company of the (53)	589
Divine Zeal, Daughters of (77)	589
Charles Borromeo, Srs. of (87)	586
Charity of St. Louis, Srs. of (79)	585
Medical Mission Srs. (104)	584
Joseph, Servants of St. (88)	584
Reparation, Srs. of (80)	583
Marcellina, Srs. of St. (49)	582
Franciscans of Mary Imm. (107)	582
Sacred Hearts and of Perp. Ador., Srs. of the (93)	582
Our Lady of the Consolation, Srs. of (90)	581
Our Lady of Perp. Help (138)	578
Franc. Dtrs. of the Sacred Hearts (59)	576
Missionary Srs. of the Immaculate Conception (88)	576
Joseph, Srs. of (Mexico) (82)	574
Srs. of Notre Dame (121)	573
Franciscans of St. Joseph (98)	569
Imm. Conc., Sr. Servants (89)	567

Albertine Srs. (70)	565
Carmelites of Trivandrum (74)	565
Ursuline Daught. of Mary Immaculate (69)	565
Franciscan Missionaries of Assisi (89)	564
Charity of Ottawa, Srs. of (62)	561
Claretian Colettines (50)	560
Basil the Great, Srs. of the Order of St. (Byzantine Rite) (71)	558
Benedictine Srs. Fed. of St. Benedict (10)	558
Jesus the Good Shepherd, Srs. of (123)	558
Immaculate Conc., Missionary Srs. (55)	550
Auxiliatrices des Ames du Purgatoire (110)	552
Teresa of the Baby Jesus (60)	548
Joseph, Srs. of (Annecy) (74)	547
Anne de Lachine, Srs. of Saint (51)	543
Franciscan Srs. of the Imm. Heart (66)	541
Sacred Heart of Jesus (Ragusa) (59)	541
Francis of Assisi, Srs. (68)	540
Franciscan Tertiaries (63)	539
Annunciation, Little Sisters of (121)	537
Immaculate Hrt. of Mary (43)	536
Marianne of Jesus, Inst. of (108)	535
Mary of the Heart of Jesus (33)	534
Sacred Heart of Jesus, Santa Verzeri (80)	528
Imm. Conc. Srs. of the Mother of God (84)	528
Poor Baby Jesus, Srs. of....(60)	526
Sacramentary Claretians (35)	525
Holy Cross and Seven Dolors, Srs. of the (131)	524
Sacred Heart of Jesus, Srs. of the (87)	523
Carmelite Missionaries of St. Teresa (81)	522
Dominican Srs. of the Rosary (Sinsinawa) (201)	520
Oblates of the Assumption (80)	519
St. Francis, Srs. of (Glen Riddle) (178)	516
Cross, Daught. of, of St. André (97)	515
Christian Charity, Dtrs. of (48)	515
Precious Blood, Dtrs. of....(63)	515
Ann, Srs. of (50)	515
Olivetan Benedictines (109)	514
Handmaids of Mary (70)	514
Holy Redeemer, Oblate Srs. of the (80)	512
Handmaids of the Lord (62)	511
Sacred Heart of Jesus, Servants of the (71)	509
Holy Family, Srs. of the (Villefranche) (80)	508
Perpetual Adoration, Benedictines(39)	508
Guardian Angel, Srs. of (86)	508
Divine Providence, Srs. of (St.-Jean-de-Bassel) (100)	505
Srs. Servants of the Imm. Hrt. Of Mary (89)	507
Immaculate Heart of Mary (89)	507
Franciscan Missionaries of Our Lord (82)	502 (2013)
Catherine of Siena, Srs. of (88)	501
Holy Spirit Sister (65)	501
Franciscans of the Sacred Heart (57)	501

ORGANIZATIONS OF RELIGIOUS

Conferences

Conferences of major superiors of religious institutes, dating from the 1950s, are encouraged by the Code of Canon Law (Code 708) "so that joining forces they can work toward the achievement of the purpose of their individual institutes more fully, transact common business and foster suitable coordination and cooperation with conferences of bishops and also with individual bishops." Statutes of the conferences must be approved by the Holy See "by which alone they are erected" (Canon 709). Conferences have been established in 24 countries of Europe, 14 in North and Central America, 10 in South America, 35 in Africa and 19 in Asia and Oceania.

Listed below are U.S. and international conferences.

Conference of Major Superiors of Men: Founded in 1956; canonically established Sept. 12, 1957. Membership, 269 major superiors representing institutes with a combined membership of approximately 24,000. Pres., Fr. James Greenfield, O.S.F.S.; Secr. John Pavlik, O.F.M. Cap. National office: 8808 Cameron St., Silver Spring, MD 20910, (301) 588-4030, www.cmsm.org.

Leadership Conference of Women Religious: Founded in 1956; canonically established Dec. 12, 1959. Membership, nearly 1,000 (Dec. 31, 1996), representing approximately 400 religious institutes. Pres., Sr. Carol Zinn, S.S.J.; Sharon Holland, I.H.M., president-elect; exec. dir., Sr. Janet Mock, C.S.J. National office: 8808 Cameron St., Silver Spring, MD 20910, (301) 588-4955, www.lcwr.org.

Council of Major Superiors of Women Religious: Canonically erected June 13, 1992. Membership, 141 superiors of 103 religious congregations. Chairperson, Sr. Regina Marie Gorman, O.C.D. National office: PO Box 4467, Washington, DC 20017-0467, (202) 832-2575, www.cmswr.org.

International Union of Superiors General (Women): Established Dec. 8, 1965; approved, 1967. Pres., Sr. Carmen Sammut, SMNDA. Address: Piazza Ponte S. Angelo, 28, 00186, Rome, Italy, 06-684-00-20.

Union of Superiors General (Men): Established in 1957. President, Fr. Adolfo Nicolas Pachon, S.J.; general secretary, David Glenday, M.C.C.J. Address: Via dei Penitenzieri 19, 00193 Rome, Italy, 06-686-82-29.

Latin American Confederation of Religious (Confederacion Latinoamericana de Religiosos — CLAR): Established in 1959; statutes reformed in 1984. President, Mercedes Casas Sanchez, F.Sp.S.; secretary general, Gabriel Narajno Salazar, C.M. Address: Calle 64 No 10-45, Piso 5°, Apartado Aéreo 56804, Santafé de Bogotá, D.C., Colombia, 57-1-310-0481/310-0392, www.clar.org.

Union of European Conferences of Major Superiors (UCESM): Established Dec. 25, 1983. President: Rev. Giovanni Peragine. Rue de Pascal 4, B-1040, Bruxelles, Belgium, 02 230 86 22.

Other Organizations

Institute on Religious Life (1974). To foster more effective understanding and implementation of teachings of the Church on religious life, promote vocations to religious life and the priesthood, and promote growth in sanctity of all the faithful according to their state in life. Fr. Thomas Nelson, O.Praem., Nat. Dir. National office, PO Box 7500, Libertyville, IL 60048; (847) 573-8975; www.religiouslife. com. Publishes *Religious Life* magazine and *Consecrated Life* periodical.

Religious Brothers Conference (1972): To publicize the unique vocations of brothers, to further communication among brothers and provide liaison with various organizations of the Church. 5401 S. Cornell Avenue, Chicago, IL 60615; (773) 595-4023, www.brothersonline.org.

National Black Sisters' Conference (1968): Black Catholic women religious and associates networking to provide support through prayer, study, solidarity and programs. Address: 101 Q. St., N.E., Washington, DC 20002, (202) 529-9250.

National Conference of Vicars for Religious (1967): National organization of diocesan officials concerned with relations between their respective dioceses and religious communities engaged therein. 9292 Broadway, Merrillville, IN 46410; secretary, Eymard Flood, OSC. Address: 2811 East Villareal Dr., PO Box 14195, Orange, CA, 92863-1595, (714) 282-3114.

National Religious Vocation Conference (NRVC) (1988, with merger of National Sisters Vocation Conference and National Conference of Religious Vocation Directors.) Service organization of men and women committed to the fostering and discernment of vocations. Executive director, Br. Paul Bednarczyk, CSC. Address: 5401 S. Cornell Avenue, Chicago, IL 60615; (773) 363-5454, www.nrvc.net.

Religious Formation Conference (1953): Originally the Sister Formation Conference; membership includes women and men Religious and non-canonical groups. Facilitates the ministry of formation, both initial and ongoing, in religious communities. National office: 8820 Cameron St., Silver Spring, MD 20910-4152, (301) 588-4938, www.relforcon.org.

SECULAR INSTITUTES

Sources: *Catholic Almanac* survey; United States Conference of Secular Institutes; *Annuario Pontificio*.

Secular institutes are societies of men and women living in the world who dedicate themselves to observe the evangelical counsels and to carry on apostolic works suitable to their talents and opportunities in the areas of their everyday life.

"Secular institutes are not religious communities but they carry with them in the world a profession of evangelical counsels which is genuine and complete, and recognized as such by the Church. This profession confers a consecration on men and women, laity and clergy, who reside in the world. For this reason they should chiefly strive for total self-dedication to God, one inspired by perfect charity. These institutes should preserve their proper and particular character, a secular one, so that they may everywhere measure up successfully to that apostolate which they were designed to exercise, and which is both in the world and, in a sense, of the world" ("Decree on the Appropriate Renewal of Religious Life," No. 11; Second Vatican Council).

Secular institutes are under the jurisdiction of the Congregation for Institutes of Consecrated Life and Societies of Apostolic Life. General legislation concerning them is contained in Canons 710 to 730 of the Code of Canon Law.

A secular institute reaches maturity in several stages. It begins as an association of the faithful, technically called a pious union, with the approval of a local bishop. Once it has proved its viability, he can give it the status of an institute of diocesan right, in accordance with norms and permission emanating from the Congregation for Institutes of Consecrated Life and Societies of Apostolic Life. On issuance of a separate decree from this congregation, an institute of diocesan right becomes an institute of pontifical right.

Secular institutes, which originated in the latter part of the 18th century, were given full recognition and approval by Pius XII Feb. 2, 1947, in the apostolic constitution *Provida Mater Ecclesia*. On Mar. 25 of the same year a special commission for secular institutes was set up within the Congregation for Religious. Institutes were commended and confirmed by Pius XII in a motu proprio of Mar. 12, 1948, and were the subject of a special instruction issued a week later, Mar. 19, 1948.

The World Conference of Secular Institutes (CMIS) was approved by the Vatican May 23, 1974. Address: Piazza San Calisto, 16, 00153 Roma, Italy: 0039-06-69887100; cmisroma@tin.it; www.cmis-int.org.

The United States Conference of Secular Institutes (USCSI) was established following the organization of the World Conference of Secular Institutes in Rome. Its membership is open to all canonically erected secular institutes with members living in the United States. The conference was organized to offer secular institutes an opportunity to exchange experiences, to do research in order to help the Church carry out its mission, and to search for ways and means to make known the existence of secular institutes in the U.S. Address: 38 Locke St., Saco, ME 04072, (207) 284-8966, www.secularinstitutes.org; Pres.: Beatrice Caron.

Institutes in the U.S.

Apostolic Oblates: Founded in Rome, Italy, 1947; established in the U.S., 1962; approved as a secular institute of pontifical right Dec. 8, 1994; for women. To promote the universal call to holiness through the specific apostolate of the Pro Sanctity Movement. Address: Teresa Monaghen, 11002 N 204th St, Elkhorn, NE 68022; (402) 289-2670; www.prosanctity.org.

Apostolic Sodales: Founded in Rome, Italy, 1992 by Bp. Giaquinta; for priests. Established to promote a spirit of fraternity among diocesan priests gathered around their bishop in ready availability in the two-fold universal vocation—the call to holiness and brotherhood. Address: Fr. Thomas Weisbecker, 9025 Larimore Ave., Omaha, NE 68134; (402) 572-0499; www.apostolic-sodales.org.

Caritas Christi: Originated in Marseilles, 1937; for women. Established as a secular institute of pontifical right Mar. 19, 1955. To form and give to the Church women who strive to love God and make him loved where he has placed them in the midst of the world. Address: Mary Sue Brueneman, PO Box 9604, Cincinnati, OH 45209, (513) 271-7894; www.ccinfo.org.

Catechists of the Sacred Heart of Jesus (*Ukrainian*): Founded in Parana, Brazil, 1940, by Christopher Meskiv, OSBM; approved as a secular institute of pontifical right, 1971; for women. Established for religious instruction, to assist clerics in missionary work, to help the Church and to maintain the Ukrainian rite and culture. Address: Elvira Julek, 195 Glenbrook Rd, Stamford, CT 06902; (203) 327-6374; egardasz@yahoo.com.

Company of St. Paul: Originated in Milan, Italy, 1920; approved as a secular institute of pontifical right, June 30, 1950; for lay people and priests. To practice the evangelical counsels as an expression of consecration to God. Professional work becomes the main means of the apostolate. Address: Fr. Stuart Sandberg, 52 Davis Ave, White Plains, NY 10605; (914) 946-1019; jssandberg@optonline.net.

Company of St. Ursula: Founded in Brescia, Italy, 1535, by Angela Merici; an international federation linking most Companies was approved as a secular institute, 1958; began in the U.S. in 2000; for women. By life-long promises, members commit to share God's love for the world, making Christ better known, and infusing the spirit of the Gospel into our surroundings. Address: Mary-Cabrini Durkin, 2718 Hackberry St, Cincinnati, OH 45206; www.companyofstursula.org.

Don Bosco Volunteers: Founded 1917 by Bl. Philip Rinaldi; approved as a secular institute of pontifical right, Aug. 5, 1978; for women. Following the charism of St. John Bosco, in an effort to renew society from within, members bring their talents to a variety of apostolates, particularly on behalf of the youth. Address: 169 Bell Rd., Scarsdale, NY 10583; (914) 723-0239; seculardbv@aol.com.

Family of Mary of the Visitation: Founded in Saigon, Vietnam, 1976; approved as a secular institute of pontifical right, 1993; for women. As faith-filled vowed women, help people to protect their faith and meet social needs, with a preferential option for the poor. Address: Mary Lien Do, 615 S Euclid St, 1-2, Santa Anna, CA 92704; liendo2004@yahoo.com.

Father Kolbe Missionaries of the Immaculata: Founded in Bologna, Italy, in 1954, by Fr. Luigi Faccenda, OFM Conv; approved as a secular institute of pontifical right, Mar. 25, 1992; for women. Live the fullness of baptismal consecration, strive for perfect charity and promote the knowledge and veneration of Mary. Address: Rumela Camanga, 531 E Merced Ave, West Covina, CA 91790; (626) 917-0040; fkmissionaries@gmail.com; www.kolbemission.org/en.

Handmaids of Divine Mercy: Founded in Bari, Italy, 1951; approved as a secular institute of pontifical right, 1972; for women. To promote the riches, the graces, the vital life stream of Divine Mercy for our world of today. Address: 2410 Hughes Ave, Bronx, NY 10458; (718) 295-3770; Spiritual Director Rev. Msgr. John A. Ruvo (914) 632-0675.

Institute of the Heart of Jesus: Founded by a Jesuit priest in Paris, France, 1791; approved as a secular institute of pontifical right, Feb 2, 1952; for diocesan priests who wish to pursue holiness through the evangelical vows, prolonged prayer, and fraternal support. Formation is fundamentally Ignatian but priests may embrace spiritualities of other Catholic traditions. Address: Fr. Enrique Sera, St. Joachim Parish, 1964 Orange Ave, Costa Mesa, CA 92627; (949) 574-7400; CorUnumPriests@gmail.com; www.corunum-usa.org.

Institute of the Heart of Jesus (*Women*): approved as a secular institute of pontifical right in 1999. Single women or widows consecrate themselves to God through the evangelical vows, prolonged prayer, mutual support in regular gatherings for discernment and accountability. Formation is fundamentally Ignatian but members may embrace spiritualities of other Catholic traditions. Address: Karen Ceckowski, PO Box 501, Conception, MO 64433; (660) 944-2842; karen@conception.edu; www.isfcj.com.

Institute of the Heart of Jesus (*Men*): Founded by a Jesuit priest in Paris, France, 1791. The Institute was erected as a secular institute of diocesan right by Bp. William Weigand in 2008; for single men and widowers who consecrate themselves to God. Address: Karen Ceckowski, Representative, 711 Carefree Pl., Maryville, MO 64468, (660) 944-2909.

Jesus Caritas Fraternity: Founded in France, 1952; approved as a secular institute of diocesan right, 1996; for women. To form members in the contemplative tradition of Brother Charles de Foucauld, bringing God's love especially to neglected children. Members strive to live the Gospel message in their daily life. Address: Mary Christensen, 4 Curran Ct, Apt 1R, Yonkers, NY 10710; (914) 961-0050.

Lay Missionaries of the Passion (*Men*): Founded by a Passionist priest under the charism of St. Paul of the Cross, in Sicily, 1980; approved as a secular institute of diocesan right, 2001. Men take vows of poverty, chastity and obedience, together with a promise to live the spirit of the Passion of our Lord according to St. Paul of the Cross. Address: James Beers, 830 Howard Ave, Apt 3-D, Staten Island, NY 10301; (718) 720-2194; beers153@verizon.net.

Lay Missionaries of the Passion (*Women*): Founded in Catania, Sicily; approved as a secular institute of pontifical right, 1999; for women. To be fully responsible to shape this world, to transform it, and to live in the spirit of the Passion. Address: Constance Leist, 311 Leonard St, Brooklyn, NY 11211; (718) 387-3619; leo311c@aol.com.

Madonna della Strada/Society of Our Lady of the Way: Founded in Vienna, Austria, 1936; approved as a secular institute of pontifical right, 1953; for women. Members pursue individual apostolates, seeking to manifest Christ in life and work with Mary and St. Ignatius in the spirit of thanksgiving with the guidance of the Holy Spirit. Address: Mary Ann Tady, 1064 Oxford Rd., Cleveland Heights, OH 44121, (216) 381-5502; matslow@aol.com; www.saecimds.com.

Mission of Our Lady of Bethany: Founded in France in 1948; approved as a secular institute of diocesan right in 1965; for women. To bring the mystery of redemptive love to the most rejected of society – the imprisoned and the prostitute – in a true fraternity of love and hope to help the Church to build the kingdom of Christ. Address: Estelle Nichols, 109 Rollins Rd, Nottingham, NH 03290; estellenichols@comcast.net.

Missionaries of the Kingship of Christ (*Women*): Founded in Assisi, Italy, 1919, by Agostino Gemelli and Armida Barelli as a Franciscan secular institute for women; approved as a secular institute of pontifical right, 1948. To give witness to Gospel values in work, family, civic, social, and spiritual environments in the spirit of St. Francis of Assisi. Address: Angela Ricciardelli, Hecker Center for Ministry, 3025 Fourth St NE #10, Washington, DC 20017; (202) 525-1267; simKingship10@comcast.net; www.simkc.org.

Notre-Dame De Vie: In the spirit of Carmel, founded by Fr. Marie-Eugene of the Child Jesus, OCD, and Marie Pila, in Venasque, France, 1932; approved as a secular institute of pontifical right, 1962; for women, men, and priests. Address: Anne Giuliani, 1419 37th St NW #260, Washington, DC 20007; (202) 687-1912; ndv_washington@yahoo.com.

Oblate Missionaries of Mary Immaculate: Founded in Canada, 1952; approved as a secular institute of pontifical right, 1984; for women. Like Christ, to manifest the unconditional love of God the Father to everyone by revealing the signs of his presence at the heart of daily life. Address: Pauline Labbe, 56 Brookfield St, Lawrence, MA 01843; (978) 687-9399; pjlabbe1@juno.com; www.ommi-is.org.

Opus Spiritus Sancti: Founded in Germany, 1950; approved as a secular institute of diocesan right, 1970; for priests. To live our charism in fraternal community, stamped by the Easter-Pentecost event. Priests work and pray for a new Pentecost through lives shared with one another, by our hope-filled vision, reconciling love, and missionary zeal. Address: Fr. Bruce Lawler, PO Box 1106, Storm Lake, IA 50588; (712) 723-3110; www.opus-spiritus-sancti.de.

Pius X Secular Institute: Founded in New Hampshire, 1939; approved in Quebec, Canada, as a secular institute of diocesan right, 1959; for priests and single laymen; associate members are priests, single lay men and women, and married couples. Totally dedicated to the evangelization of the working class by our presence in the world through apostolic works and bringing the Gospel to all. Address: Fr. Marcel Caron, 27 Cove St, Goffstown, NH 03045; (418) 626-5882; info@ispx.org; www.ispx.org.

Schoenstatt Fathers: Founded in 1965, but with roots back to Oct. 18, 1914, founding day of the Schoenstatt Movement by Fr. Joseph Kentenich; approved as a secular institute of pontifical right, June 24, 1988; for priests. To serve the needs of the Schoenstatt Family in all their different communities, promoting and cultivating Schoenstatt's original spirituality with priestly inspiration and guidance. Addresses: Fr. Francisco Rojas, W284N746 Cherry Ln., Waukesha, WI 53188; (262) 548-9061; father.francisco@gmail.com and Fr. Christian Christensen, 225 Addie Roy Rd., Austin, TX 78746; (512) 301-8762; pchri02@sbcglobal.net.

Schoenstatt Sisters of Mary: Founded in Germany, Oct. 1, 1926, by Fr. Joseph Kentenich; approved as a secular institute of pontifical right, May 20, 1948; for women. For the moral and religious renewal of society, to be Mary for our world today. Members practice a Marian spirituality as a means of growing in love for God and consecrating the world to him. Addresses: Joanna Buckley, W284N404 Cherry Ln, Waukesha, WI 53188; (262) 522-4200; vocation@schsrsmary.org and Gabriella Maschita, 130 Front St, Rockport, TX 78382; (361) 729-1868; confprov@cobridge.tv.

Secular Institute of St Francis de Sales: Founded in Vienna, Austria, 1947; approved as a secular institute of pontifical right, 1964; for women. The personal sanctification of its members living in the world according to the spirituality of St. Francis de Sales and the application of this spirituality in institute, missionary, parish, and community apostolates depending on our different life situations. Address: Dana Elzi, 104 West Main St, Middletown, PA 17057; 717-948-5009; dana.elzi104@gmail.com; www.secularinstituteofsaintfrancisdesales.org.

Servite Secular Institute: Founded in 1947, by Joan Bartlett, OBE, in London, England; approved as a secular institute of pontifical right, 1979; for single or widowed women. To be genuine leaven in the world for strengthening and enlarging Christ's body by contemplation and service in kindness, compassion, and hospitality. Address: Mary Power, 44 Stirling Ave, Ottawa, Ontario K1Y 1P8, Canada; (613) 722-0302; mpower1661@rogers.com; www.ssi.org.uk.

Servitium Christi: Founded in Holland, 1952; approved as a secular institute of diocesan right, 1963; for women. To live the mystery of the Eucharist fully as consecrated lay persons and to make known its meaning so that the glory of God may be revealed in the world. Address: Olympia Panagatos, 1550 York Ave #17A, New York, NY 10028;

(212) 734-9748.

Stabat Mater: Founded 1947 in Madrid, Spain; approved as a secular institute of diocesan right, 1988; for men. To focus on the formation of young people toward integrating the spiritual with the secular through application of Ignatian spiritual exercises with Marian devotion. Address: Antonio Pérez-Alcalá, 2001 Great Falls St, McLean, VA 22101; (703) 536-3546. **Voluntas Dei Institute:** Founded in Trois-Rivieres, Canada, on July 2, 1958, by Fr. Louis-Marie Parent, OMI; approved as a secular institute of pontifical right, 1987; for priests, laymen, and married couples. Members share in the Church's mission that has been sent by Christ to make known and to communicate to all peoples God's unconditional love. Address: Fr. Anthony Ciorra, 244 Fifth Ave., Suite P250, NY, NY 10001; (212) 726-2286; www.voluntasdeiusa.org.

*The **Annuario Pontificio** lists the following secular institutes of pontifical right that are not established in the U.S.:*

For men: Christ the King; Institute of Our Lady of Life; Institute of Prado; Priests of the Sacred Heart of Jesus. Community of St. John and Our Lady of Altagracia

For women: Alliance in Jesus through Mary; Apostles of the Sacred Heart; Catechists of Mary, Virgin and Mother; Community of St. John; Cordimarian Filiation; Daughters of the Nativity of Mary; Daughters of the Queen of the Apostles; Daughters of the Sacred Heart; Evangelical Crusade; Faithful Servants of Jesus; Handmaids of Our Mother of Mercy; Institute of Notre Dame du Travail; Institute of Our Lady of Life; Institute of St. Boniface; Little Apostles of Charity.

Life and Peace in Christ Jesus; Missionaries of Royal Priesthood; Missionaries of the Sick; Oblates of Christ the King; Oblates of the Sacred Heart of Jesus; Our Lady of Altagracia; Servants of Jesus the Priest; Union of the Daughters of God; Workers of Divine Love; Workers of the Cross; Handmaids of Holy Church; Augustinian Auxiliary Missionaries; Heart of Jesus; Apostolic Missionaries of Charity; Combonian Secular Missionaries; Missionaries of the Gospel; Secular Servants of Jesus Christ Priest; Women of Schoenstatt; Missionaries of Infinite Love.

Aspiring to Become Secular Institutes in the U.S.:

Blessed Trinity Missionary Institute: Founded in Philadelphia, 1950, by Dr. Margaret Healy according to the inspiration of Fr. Thomas Augustine Judge, CM; approved as a pious union, 1964; for women. To preserve the faith among people who are spiritually neglected and to develop a missionary spirit in the laity. Addresses: Rosa Tirado, 154-14 Ash Ave, Flushing, NY 11355; (718) 359-5910; roniltirado@earthlink.net and Vocation Chair, 8570 Vaughn Rd, Montgomery, AL 36117; (334) 207-0324; mnpecot@aol.com; www.btmi.info.

Franciscan Missionaries of Jesus Crucified: Founded in 1987, in New York by Louise Principe; approved as an association of the faithful, 1992; for women and men. To provide an opportunity for persons with disabilities, to live a life of total consecration in the pursuit of holiness, and the apostolate of service to the Church and to those who suffer in

any way. Address: Bonnie Fagan, 11 Dahlem Blvd, Niskayuna, NY 12309; (518) 452-1696; bjffmjc@aol.com; www.fmjccommunity.com.

Holy Family Institute (aggregated to the Society of St. Paul): Founded by Fr. James Alberione in 1963 for married couples who wish to commit themselves to seeking evangelical perfection in marriage; definitively approved by the Holy See in 1993. Address: Fr. Tom Fogarty, 9531 Akron-Canfield Rd, Box 498, Canfield OH 44406; (330) 533-6646; www.hficoncord.com.

Schoenstatt Family Institute: Founded July 16, 1942, in the Dachau concentration camp by Father Joseph Kentenich for married couples, which now number 600 persons in 12 countries. Marriage is a way to holiness; a sacrament, a realization and school of Divine love. Members contribute toward the renewal of marriage and family life, the Church and society through living the three evangelical counsels according to their state of life, and through a loved covenant of love with Mary and Jesus. Address: Michael and Margaret Fenelon, 1719 Orchard Ln, McHenry IL 60050; (815) 385-3152; m.j.fenelon.ill@gmail.com; www.schoenstatt-familien.de.

Volunteers with Don Bosco: Founded in 1994, in Rome by Fr. Egidio Viganò, Rector Major of the Salesians of Don Bosco; approved as an association of the faithful in 1998; for celibate men. Drawing inspiration from the charism of St. John Bosco, members strive to imitate his pastoral style and follow Christ radically through consecration in secular life. Their aim is to build a better society following the Gospel and living the Salesian spirit. Address: Fr. John Puntino, SDB, 148 Main St., New Rochelle, NY 10802; (914) 636-4225; www.volontaricdb.altervista.org.

Associations

Association of Mary Help of Christians: Founded by St. John Bosco in Turin, Italy, in 1869, for men and women. Public association of the faithful. Members encourage participation in the liturgical life of the Church, emphasizing frequent reception of the Eucharist and the Sacrament of Reconciliation. They also live and spread devotion to Mary Help of Christians according to the spirit of St. John Bosco. Address: 148 Main St., P.O. Box 639, New Rochelle, NY 10802, (614) 440-0202.

Caritas: Originated in New Orleans, 1950; for women. Follows guidelines of secular institutes. Small self supporting groups who live and work with poor and oppressed; in Louisiana and Guatemala. Address: Box 308, Abita Springs, LA 70420, (985) 892-4345.

Daughters of Our Lady of Fatima: Originated in Lansdowne, PA, 1949; for women. Received diocesan approval, Jan. 1952. Address: Fatima House, P.O. Box 116, Bedminster 18910, (215) 795-2947.

Focolare Movement: Founded in Trent, Italy, in 1943, by Chiara Lubich; for men and women. Approved as an association of the faithful, 1962. It is not a secular institute by statute; however, vows are observed by its totally dedicated core membership of 4,000 who live in small communities called Focolare (Italian word for "hearth") centers. There are 17 resident centers in the U.S.

and four in Canada. GEN (New Generation) is the youth organization of the movement. An estimated 75,000 are affiliated with the movement in the U.S. and Canada, 2,000,000 worldwide. Publications include *Living City*, monthly; *GEN II* and *GEN III* for young people and children. Five week long summer conventions, called "Mariapolis" ("City of Mary"), are held annually. Address for information: Mariopolis Luminosa, 257 Peace Ave., Hyde Park, NY 12538, (845) 229-9712 (men's or women's branch), www.focolare.us.

Jesus-Caritas Fraternity of Priests: An international association of diocesan priests who strive to combine an active life with a contemplative calling by their membership in small fraternities. U.S. address for information: Rev. Greg Pawloski, St. Patrick's Church, P.O. Box 96, 126 E. 7th St., Imperial, NE 69033-0096, (308) 882-4995, www.rc.net/org/jesuscaritas.

Madonna House Apostolate: Originated in Toronto, Canada, 1930; for priests and lay persons. Public association of the Christian faithful. Address: Madonna House, 2888 Dafoe Rd., Combermere, ON, Canada KOJ ILO, (613) 756-3713, www.madonnahouse.org.

Pax Christi: Lay institute of men and women dedicated to witnessing to Christ, with special emphasis on service to the poor in Mississippi. Addresses: St. Francis Center, 709 Ave. I, Greenwood, MS 38930. LaVerna House, 2108 Alta Woods Blvd., Jackson, MS 39204, (601) 373-4463.

Rural Parish Workers of Christ the King: Founded in 1942; for women. A secular institute of the Archdiocese of St. Louis. Dedicated to the glory of God in service of neighbor, especially in rural areas. Address: 15540 Cannon Mines Rd., Cadet, MO 63630, (636) 586-5171; rpwck.com.

Salesian Cooperators: Founded by St. John Bosco in Turin, Italy, in 1876; for lay men and women and diocesan clergy. Public association of the faithful, members commit themselves to apostolates in the local Church, especially on behalf of the young, in the Salesian spirit and style. Address: 6400 E. Chelsea St., Tampa, FL 33610; (813) 626-6191. Contact person: Fr. Dennis Donovan.

Society of Evangelical Life of the Heart of Jesus: presently an Association of the Faithful, this society was definitively approved in 1996, developing since the 1970s with the three Secular Institutes of the Heart of Jesus. In 1996 a federation Cor Unum Family was formed of the four groups. The association (for married couples, single men and women, and priests) follows the same Rule of Life as the institutes. Members live the evangelical counsels as they pursue holiness of life in their married or celibate state, committing to prolonged prayer, communal discernment and accountability, and adopt Ignatian principles of formation. Address: Bob and Cindy Kodis; 1820 76th St, Windsor Heights IA 50324; (515) 251-3930; ckodis@ishsi.com.

Teresian Institute: Founded in Spain 1911 by Pedro Poveda. Approved as an association of the faithful of pontifical right, Jan. 11, 1924. Mailing Address: 3400 S. W. 99th Ave., Miami, FL 33165, (305) 553-8567.

THIRD ORDERS

Augustine, Third Order Secular of St.: Founded 13th century; approved Nov. 7, 1400.

Carmelites, Lay (Third Order of Our Lady of Mt. Carmel): Rule for laity approved by Pope Nicholas V, Oct. 7, 1452; new statutes, January 1991. Addresses: 8501 Bailey Rd., Darien, IL 60561. PO Box 613, Williamston, MA 01267. PO Box 27, Tappan, NY 10983-0027, (845) 359-0535. Approximately 270 communities and 10,000 members in the U.S. and Canada.

Carmelites, The Secular Order of Discalced (formerly the Third Order Secular of the Blessed Virgin Mary of Mt. Carmel and of St. Teresa of Jesus): Rule based on the Carmelite reform established by St. Teresa and St. John of the Cross; approved Mar. 23, 1594. Revised rule approved May 10, 1979. Office of National Secretariat, USA: PO Box 3079, San Jose, CA 95156-3079, (408) 251-1361. Approximately 24,445 members throughout the world; 130 groups/communities and 5,200 members in the US and Canada.

Dominican Laity (formerly known as Third Order of St. Dominic): Founded in the 13th century. Addresses of provincial promoters in the United States: St. Dominic Priory, 3601 Lindell Blvd., St. Louis, MO 63108-3393, (314) 977-2588, www.op.org /domcentral. Eastern Province, 487 Michigan Ave., N.E., Washington, DC, 20017, (202) 529-5300. Priory of St. Martin de Porres, P.O. Box 12927, Raleigh, NC 27605, (919) 833-1893. Western Province, 2005 Berryman St., Berkeley, CA 94709, (510) 526-4811. St. Albert the Great Province, 3904 Golfside Dr., Ypsilanti, MI 48197, (734) 434-0195.

Franciscan Order, Secular (SFO): Founded 1209 by St. Francis of Assisi; approved Aug. 30, 1221. Vocation Director, 37430 Stonegate Circle, Clinton Township, MI 48036, (800) FRANCIS, www.NAFRA-SFO.org. International Secretariate, Via Pomponia Grecina, 31, 00145 Rome. Tau USA, quarterly. Approximately 780,000 throughout the world; 18,000 in the U.S.

Mary, Third Order of (Marist Laity): Founded, Dec. 8, 1850; rule approved by the Holy See, 1857. Addresses of provincial directors: Marist Laity Center, 1706 Jackson Ave., New Orleans, LA 70113-1510, (504) 524-5192, www.maristlaity.org. Marist Fathers, 698 Beacon St., Boston, MA 02115, (617) 262-2271. Marist Fathers, 2335 Warring St., Berkeley, CA 94704. Approximately 14,000 in world, 5,600 in U.S.

Mary, Secular Order of Servants of (Servite): Founded 1233; approved 1304. Revised rule approved 1995. Address: National Assistant for the Secular Order, 3121 W. Jackson Blvd., Chicago, IL 60612-2729, (773) 638-5800; www.secularservites.org.

Mercy, Secular Third Order of Our Lady of (Mercedarian): Founded 1219 by St. Peter Nolasco; approved the same year.

Norbert, Third Order of St.: Founded 1122 by St. Norbert; approved by Pope Honorius II in 1126.

Oblates of St. Benedict: Lay persons affiliated with a Benedictine abbey, or monastery, who strive to direct their lives, as circumstances permit, according to the spirit and Rule of St. Benedict.

Trinity, Third Order Secular of the Most: Founded 1198; approved 1219.

Apostolates and Ministries

RIGHTS AND OBLIGATIONS OF ALL THE FAITHFUL

The following rights are listed in Canons 208-223 of the revised Code of Canon Law; additional rights are specified in other canons.

• Because of their baptism and regeneration, there is equality regarding dignity and action for the building up of the Body of Christ.

• They are bound always to preserve communion with the Church.

• According to their condition and circumstances, they should strive to lead a holy life and promote the growth and holiness of the Church.

• They have the right and duty to work for the spread of the divine message of salvation to all peoples of all times and places.

• They are bound to follow with Christian obedience those things which the bishops, as they represent Christ, declare as teachers of the faith or establish as rulers of the Church.

• They have the right to make known their needs, especially their spiritual needs, to pastors of the Church.

• They have the right, and sometimes the duty, of making known to pastors and others of the faithful their opinions about things pertaining to the good of the Church.

• They have the right to receive help from their pastors, from the spiritual goods of the Church and especially from the word of God and the sacraments.

• They have the right to divine worship performed according to prescribed rules of their rite, and to follow their own form of spiritual life in line with the doctrine of the Church.

• They have the right to freely establish and control associations for good and charitable purposes, to foster the Christian vocation in the world, and to hold meetings related to the accomplishment of these purposes.

• They have the right to promote and support apostolic action but may not call it "Catholic" unless they have the consent of competent authority.

• They have a right to a Christian education.

• They have a right to freedom of inquiry in sacred studies, in accordance with the teaching authority of the Church.

• They have a right to freedom in the choice of their state of life.

• No one has the right to harm the good name of another person or to violate his or her right to maintain personal privacy.

• They have the right to vindicate the rights they enjoy in the Church, and to defend themselves in a competent ecclesiastical forum.

• They have the obligation to provide for the needs of the Church, with respect to things pertaining to divine worship, apostolic and charitable works, and the reasonable support of ministers of the Church.

• They have the obligation to promote social justice and to help the poor from their own resources.

• In exercising their rights, the faithful should have regard for the common good of the Church and for the rights and duties of others.

• Church authority has the right to monitor the exercise of rights proper to the faithful, with the common good in view.

RIGHTS AND OBLIGATIONS OF LAY PERSONS

In addition to rights and obligations common to all the faithful and those stated in other canons, lay persons are bound by the obligations and enjoy the rights specified in these canons (224-231).

• Lay persons, like all the faithful, are called by God to the apostolate in virtue of their baptism and confirmation. They have the obligation and right, individually or together in associations, to work for the spread and acceptance of the divine message of salvation among people everywhere; this obligation is more urgent in those circumstances in which people can hear the Gospel and get to know Christ only through them (lay persons).

• They are bound to bring an evangelical spirit to bear on the order of temporal things and to give Christian witness in carrying out their secular pursuits.

• Married couples are obliged to work for the building up of the people of God through their marital and family life.

• Parents have the most serious obligation to provide for the Christian education of their children according to the doctrine handed down by the Church.

• Lay persons have the same civil liberty as other citizens. In the use of this liberty, they should take care that their actions be imbued with an evangelical spirit. They should attend to the doctrine proposed by the magisterium of the Church but should take care that, in questions of opinion, they do not propose their own opinion as the doctrine of the Church.

• Qualified lay persons are eligible to hold and perform the duties of ecclesiastical offices open to them in accord with the provisions of law.

• Properly qualified lay persons can assist pastors of the Church as experts and counselors.

• Lay persons have the obligation and enjoy the right to acquire knowledge of doctrine commensurate with their capacity and condition.

• They have the right to pursue studies in the sacred sciences in pontifical universities or facilities and in institutes of religious sciences, and to obtain academic degrees.

• If qualified, they are eligible to receive from ecclesiastical authority a mandate to teach sacred sciences.

• Laymen can be invested by liturgical rite and in a stable manner in the ministries of lector and acolyte.

• Lay persons, by temporary assignment, can fulfill the office of lector in liturgical actions; likewise, all lay persons can perform the duties of commentator or cantor.

• In cases of necessity and in the absence of the usual ministers, lay persons — even if not lectors or acolytes — can exercise the ministry of the word, lead liturgical prayers, confer baptism and distribute Communion, according to the prescripts of law.

• Lay persons who devote themselves permanently or temporarily to the service of the Church are obliged to acquire the formation necessary for carrying out their duties in a proper manner.

• They have a right to remuneration for their service which is just and adequate to provide for their own needs and those of their families; they also have a right to insurance, social security and health insurance.

(*See* **Canon Law** *for details on the* **Code**.)

DIRECTORY OF LAY GROUPS

The U.S. Conference of Catholic Bishops' Secretariat for Family, Laity, Women and Youth released its 2007-2008 *Directory of Lay Movements, Organizations, and Professional Associations* (the most recent edition).

The directory contains listings for more than 100 national lay movements, professional associations, and organizations. Each listing includes a brief description of the group and the name, address, phone number of a contact person, and web/email information if available. The groups listed are national in scope, but not all are solely lay. Some are included because their work affects the life and mission of the laity and/or because their membership has a significant lay component. The secretariat acknowledges that the listing is a partial one and welcomes suggestions for groups to be included in future editions. Copies may be ordered from the USCCB Secretariat for Family, Laity, Women and Youth, 3211 4th St., N.E., Washington, DC 20017; (202) 541-3040 (phone); (202) 541-3176 (fax).

SPECIAL APOSTOLATES AND GROUPS

Apostleship of the Sea (1920, Glasgow, Scotland; 1947 in U.S.): 1500 Jefferson Dr., Port Arthur, TX 77642; (409) 985-4545; 3211 Fourth St. N.E., Washington, DC 20017 (national office); (202) 541-3035; www.aos-usa.org. An international Catholic organization for the moral, social and spiritual welfare of seafarers and those involved in the maritime industry. Formally instituted by the Holy See in 1952 (apostolic constitution *Exul Familia*), it is a sector of the Pontifical Council for Migrants and Itinerant Peoples. Its norms were updated by Pope John Paul II in a *motu proprio* dated Jan. 31, 1997. The U.S. unit, an affiliate of the USCCB, serves port chaplains in 63 U.S. ports. Pres., Fr. Sinclair Oubre.

Auxiliaries of Our Lady of the Cenacle (1878, France): 1114 Iowa Dr., LeClaire, IA 52753; (563) 289-9975; www.cenaclesisters.org. An association of consecrated Catholic laywomen, under the direction of the Congregation of Our Lady of the Cenacle. They profess annually the evangelical counsels of celibacy, poverty and obedience and serve God through their own professions and life styles and pursue individual apostolates. Reg. Dir., Carol Gantenbein.

Catholic Central Verein (Union) of America (1855): 3835 Westminster Pl., St. Louis, MO 63108; (314) 371-1653; www.socialjusticereview.org. One of the oldest Catholic lay organizations in the U.S. and the first given an official mandate for Catholic Action by a committee of the American bishops (1936); *Social Justice Review*, bimonthly.

Catholic Medical Mission Board (1928): 10 W. 17th Street, New York, NY 10011-5765; (212) 242-7757; www. cmmb.org. A charitable, nonprofit organization dedicated to providing health care supplies and support for the medically disadvantaged in developing and transitional countries. CMMB depends upon the financial generosity of over 25,000 individual donors and through product contributions by major pharmaceutical corporations. In 2012, CMMB received support from 37,188 individuals, 47 foundations, 54 corporations, 38 trusts and estates, 190 health and religious-affiliated organizations, and administered two grants from the U.S. government. CMMB also receives substantial in-kind donations from pharmaceutical companies. "The importance of the role of faith-based organizations in delivering solutions to the HIV/AIDS pandemic in the developing countries cannot be overstated. The faith-based network within many countries is often the most trusted source of refuge for those seeking help in any way, regardless of creed or color. Zambia is a prime example. CMMB's partnership with the Churches Health Association of Zambia (CHAZ) provides it with the opportunity to partner with clinics on the ground to prevent the transmission of HIV. Similarly, in Latin America and the Caribbean, CMMB has partnered with Catholic health care networks in five countries to lower childhood mortality by teaching basic health care." Pres., Bruce Wilkinson.

Catholic Volunteer Network (1963; formerly, International Liaison of Lay Volunteers in Mission): 6930 Carroll Ave., Suite 820, Takoma Park, MD 201912; (301) 270-0900; www.cnvs.org. Membership organization of 235 faith-based volunteer programs, placing persons in all fifty states and 120 countries; *The Response*, annual directory. Exec. Dir., James Lindsay.

Catholic Volunteers in Florida (1983): P.O. Box 536476, Orlando, FL 32853-6476; (407) 382-7071; www.cvif.org. Co-sponsored by the bishops of Florida to promote values of social justice by direct service to farm workers, homeless, hungry, low-income people, single mothers and others in need. Volunteers, 20 years of age and older, serve for a one year period in urban and rural settings. Exec. Dir., Richard Galentino.

Center for Applied Research in the Apostolate (CARA): 2300 Wisconsin Ave., N.W., Suite 400, Washington, DC 20007; (202) 687-8080; www.cara.georgetown.edu. A nonprofit research center serving the planning needs of the Catholic Church. CARA gathers empirical data for use by bishops, diocesan agencies, parishes, congregations of men and women religious and Catholic organizations. The *CARA Report*, quarterly; *CARA Catholic Ministry Formation Directory*, annually. Exec. Dir., Rev. Thomas Gaunt, S.J., Ph.D.

Christian Family Movement (CFM) (1947): National office, P.O. Box 540550, Omaha, NE 68154; (800) 581-9824; www.cfm.org. Originated in Chicago to Christianize family life and create communities conducive to Christian family life. Since 1968, CFM in the U.S. has included couples from all Christian churches.

Christian Life Communities (1971, promulgation of revised norms by Pope Paul VI; originated, 1563, as Sodalities of Our Lady, at the Jesuit College in Rome): 3601 Lindell Blvd., St. Louis, MO 63108 (national office); (314) 542-1335; www.clc-usa.org. The world CLC office is in Rome. Small communities of primarily lay persons who come together to form committed individuals for service to the world and the Church.

Cursillo Movement (1949, in Spain; in U.S., 1957): National Cursillo Center, P.O. Box 210226, Dallas, TX 75211. An instrument of Christian renewal designed to form and stimulate persons to engage in evangelizing their everyday environments.

Franciscan Mission Service of North America, an Overseas Lay Ministry Program (1990): P.O. Box 29034, Washington, DC 20017; (202) 832-1762; www.franciscanmissionservice.catholic.edu. Lay missioners work with Franciscan sisters, brothers and priests for a minimum of three years in underdeveloped countries. Co-Dir. Joseph Nangle, OFM, and Megeen White.

Grail, The (1921, in The Netherlands, by Rev. Jacques van Ginneken, SJ; 1940, in U.S.): Grailville, 932 O'Bannonville Rd., Loveland, OH 45140 (U. S. headquarters); (513) 683-5750; www.grail-us.org. Duisburger Strasse 442, 45478 Mulheim, Germany, (international secretariat). An international movement of women concerned about the full development of all peoples, working in education, religious, social, cultural and ecological areas.

Jesuit Volunteer Corps (1956): 18th and Thompson Sts., Philadelphia, PA 19121 (address for information); (215) 232-0300; www.jesuitvolunteers.org. Sponsored by the Society of Jesus in the U.S. Men and women volunteers work throughout the U.S. serving the poor directly and working for structural change.

LAMP Catholic Ministries (Lay Apostolic Ministries with the Poor): 2704 Schurz Ave., Bronx, NY 10465; (718) 409-5062; www.lampministries.org. Missionary service of evangelization with the materially poor and homeless in the larger metropolitan New York–New Jersey area. Newsletter, two times a year. Directors, Drs. Tom and Lyn Scheuring.

Lay Mission-Helpers Association (1955): 3435 Wilshire Blvd., #1035, Los Angeles, CA 90010; (213) 368-1870; www.laymissionhelpers.org. Trains and assigns men and women for work in overseas apostolates for periods of two to three years. Approximately 700 members of the association have served in overseas assignments since its founding. Director, Janice England. **The Mission Doctors Association**: (same address; (213) 637-7499; www.missiondoctors.org) recruits, trains and sends Catholic physicians and their families to mission hospitals and clinics throughout the world for tours of two to three years. Additionally, MDA has a short-term program for volunteer physicians with a term of service of 12 months. Program Dir., Elise Frederick.

Legion of Mary (1921, in Dublin, Ireland, by Frank Duff): Maria Center, 326 E. Ripa, St. Louis, MO 63125 (U.S. address); (314) 631-3447. De Montfort House, Dublin 7, Ireland (headquarters). Membership: active Catholics of all ages, under the direction of local bishops and priests, for the work of conversion, conservation and consolation. Pres., Mary T. Budde.

*Movimiento Familiar Cristiano***-USA** (MFC) (1969): 1711 Vista Chula St., Edinburg, TX 78539; (956) 383-8098; www.mfccusa.com. Movement of Catholic Hispanic families united in their efforts to promote the human and Christian virtues of the family so that it may become a force that forms persons, transmits the faith and contributes to the total development of the community. Antonio Layton, national director.

Pax Christi **USA** (1972): 1225 Otis St., NE, Washington, DC 20017; (202) 635-2741; www.paxchristiusa.org. Pax Christi (see International Catholic Organizations). Founded to establish peacemaking as a priority for the American Catholic Church. *Pax Christi USA*, quarterly.

Pax Romana/Catholic Movement for Intellectual and Cultural Affairs: 3025 Fourth St., N.E., Washington, DC 20017; (202) 269-6672. The U.S. affiliate of Pax Romana-ICMICA (see International Catholic Organizations); *The Notebook*, quarterly. Pres., Joseph Kirchner.

Schoenstatt Lay Movement (1914): International Schoenstatt Center, W284 N 698 Cherry Lane, Waukesha, WI 53188; (262) 547-7733. Lay movement founded in Germany by Fr. Joseph Kentenich. A Marian and apostolic way of life, Schoenstatt is present on all continents and includes people of all ages and walks of life, men and women, young and old, priests and laity. The Schoenstatt Shrine, dedicated to Mary, Mother Thrice Admirable, Queen and Victress of Schoenstatt, is an integral part of the spirituality of Schoenstatt. There are over 160 shrines around the world, 6 of them in the U.S., in Minnesota, New York, Texas, and Wisconsin.

Volunteer Missionary Movement (1969): 5980 W. Loomis Rd., Milwaukee, WI 53129; (414) 423-8660; www.vmmusa.org. Independent lay international mission organization with origins in the Catholic tradition but ecumenical and open to all Christian denominations. *Bridges*, quarterly. Exec. Dir., Julie Pagenkopf.

CATHOLIC YOUTH ORGANIZATIONS

Camp Fire Boys and Girls: 4601 Madison Ave., Kansas City, MO 64112; (816) 756-1950; www.campfireusa.org. The National Catholic Committee for Girl Scouts and Camp Fire, a standing committee of the National Federation for Catholic Youth Ministry, cooperates with Camp Fire Boys and Girls.

Catholic Forester Youth Program, Catholic Order of Foresters: Naperville, IL 60566; (800) 552-0145. To develop Christian leadership and promote the moral, intellectual, social and physical growth of its youth members. Membership: youth up to 16 years of age; over 19,046 in 610 local courts in U.S. Catholic Forester. High Chief Ranger-Pres., Robert Ciesla.

Catholic Youth Organization (CYO): Name of parish-centered diocesan Catholic youth programs throughout the country. CYO promotes a program of spiritual, social and physical activities. The original CYO was organized in 1930 by Bishop Bernard Sheil, auxiliary bishop of Chicago.

Columbian Squires (1925): 1 Columbus Plaza, New Haven, CT 06510-3326; (203) 752-4401; www.kofc.org. The official youth organization of the Knights of Columbus. To train and develop leadership through active participation in a well-organized program of spiritual, service, social, cultural and athletic activities. Membership: Catholic young men, 12-18 years old. More than 25,000 in over 1,000 circles (local units) active in the U.S., Canada, Puerto Rico, Philippines, Mexico, the Bahamas, Virgin Islands and Guam. *Squires Newsletter*, monthly.

Girl Scouts: 830 Third Ave., New York, NY 10022. Girls from archdioceses and dioceses in the U.S. and its possessions participate in Girl Scouting through the collaboration of Girl Scouts of the U.S.A., with the National Catholic Committee for Girl Scouts and Camp Fire, a standing committee of the National Federation for Catholic Youth Ministry.

Holy Childhood Association (Pontifical Association of the Holy Childhood) (1843): 366 Fifth Ave., New York, NY 10001; (212) 563-8700; www.worldmissions-catholicchurch.org. The official children's mission-awareness society of the Church. Provides mission awareness for elementary-grade students in parochial schools and religious education programs and financial assistance to children in more than 100 developing countries. Publishes *It's Our World*, three times a year, in two grade levels. Nat. Dir., Rev. Francis W. Wright, CSSp.

The National Catholic Committee on Scouting: P.O. Box 152079, Irving, TX 75015-2079; (972) 580-2114; www.catholic-church.org/catholicscouting; www.nccs-bsa.org. Works with the Boy Scouts of America in developing the character and spiritual life of members in units chartered to Catholic and non-Catholic organizations. National Committee Chairman, Robert Runnels of Leawood, KS. Admin. Sec., Barbara Nestel.

National Catholic Forensic League (1952): 21 Nancy Rd., Milford, MA 01757; (508) 473-0431. To develop articulate Catholic leaders through an inter-diocesan program of speech and debate activities. Newsletter, quarterly. Membership: 925 schools; membership open to Catholic, private and public schools through the local diocesan league. Exec. Sec.-Treas., Richard Gaudette.

National Catholic Young Adult Ministry Association (1982): P.O. Box 32253, Washington, DC 20007; (888) NCYAMA1; www.ncyama.org. A response to the needs of young adults, an invitation to share their gifts with the larger community and a challenge to live gospel values in the world. A national network for single and married young adults. Exec. Dir., Michelle M. Miller.

National Federation for Catholic Youth Ministry, Inc. (1981): 415 Michigan Ave., N.E., Washington, DC 20017; (202) 636-3825; www.nfcym.org. To foster the development of youth ministry in the United States. Exec. Dir., Robert McCarty.

Young Christian Students: 19666 W. Dunlap Rd., Dennison, IL 62423; (217) 826-5708. A student movement for Christian personal and social change.

CAMPUS MINISTRY

Campus ministry is an expression of the Church's special desire to be present to all who are involved in higher education and to further dialogue between the Church and the academic community. In the words of the U.S. bishops' 1985 pastoral letter entitled "Empowered by the Spirit," this ministry is "the public presence and service through which properly prepared baptized persons are empowered by the Spirit to use their talents and gifts on behalf of the Church in order to be sign and instrument of the Kingdom in the academic world."

Campus ministry, carried on by lay, Religious and ordained ministers, gathers members of the Church on campus to form the faith community, appropriate the faith, form Christian consciences, educate for justice and facilitate religious development.

The dimensions and challenge of this ministry are evident from, among other things, the numbers involved: approximately 550,000 Catholics on more than 230 Catholic college and university campuses; about four million in several thousand non-Catholic private and public institutions; 1,200 or more campus ministers. In many dioceses, the activities of ministers are coordinated by a local diocesan director. Two professional organizations serve the ministry on the national level:

The National Association of Diocesan Directors of Campus Ministry: Ms. Krista Bajoka (contact), 305 Michigan Ave., Detroit, MI 48226; (313) 237-5962.

The Catholic Campus Ministry Association: 1,200 members. 1118 Pendleton St., Suite 300, Cincinnati, OH 45202; (513) 842-0167; www.ccmanet.org. Exec. Dir., Austin Fragomen, Jane G. Belford.

COLLEGE SOCIETIES

Alpha Sigma Nu (1915): Marquette University, Brooks 201, P.O. Box 1881, Milwaukee, WI 53201-1881 (national headquarters); (414) 288-7542; www.alphasigmanu.org. National honor society of the 30 Jesuit institutions of higher education in the U.S. and a chapter at Sogany University in Korea; members chosen on the basis of scholarship, loyalty and service; 1,575 student and 38,000 alumni members. Member, Association of College Honor Societies. Gamma Pi Epsilon (1925) merged with Alpha Sigma Nu in 1973 to form society for men and women. Exec. Dir., Kate Greatner.

Delta Epsilon Sigma (1939): Barry University, 11300 NE Second Ave., Miami Shores, FL 33161; (305) 899-3020; www.des.barry.edu. National scholastic honor society for students, faculty and alumni of colleges and universities with a Catholic tradition. Delta Epsilon Sigma Journal, three times a year. Membership: 60,000 in 116 chapters. Sec., Dr. J. Patrick Lee.

Kappa Gamma Pi (1926): KGP National Office, 7250 Overcliff Rd, Cincinnati, OH, 45233-1038; (305) 525-3744; www.kappagammapi.org. A national Catholic college honor society for graduates who, in addition to academic excellence, have shown outstanding leadership in extracurricular activities. Also offers Cornaro Scholarship for Graduate Studies. *Kappa Gamma Pi News*, five times a year. Membership: more than 37,000 in 139 colleges; 20 alumnae chapters in metropolitan areas. Nat. Coord. Judy Gelwicks.

Phi Kappa Theta: 3901 W. 86th St., Suite 425, Indianapolis, IN 46268. National social fraternity with a Catholic heritage. Merger (1959) of Phi Kappa Fraternity, founded at Brown University in 1889, and Theta Kappa Phi Fraternity, founded at Lehigh University in 1919. *The Temple Magazine*, semi-annually, and newsletters. Membership: 2,800 undergraduate and 50,500 alumni in 63 collegiate and 40 alumni chapters. Exec. Dir., Mark T. McSweeney.

National Catholic Student Coalition (1988); 45 Lovett Ave., Newark, DE 19717; www.catholicstudent.org. National coalition of Catholic campus ministry groups at public and private institutions of higher education. Formed after National Newman Club Federation and the National Federation of Catholic College Students dissolved in the 1960s. The U.S. affiliate of Pax Romana-IMCS (see International Catholic Organizations). *The Catholic Collegian*, four times a year. Membership: 200 campus groups. Exec. Dir., Jamie Williams; contact, Kim Zitzner.

ASSOCIATIONS, MOVEMENTS, SOCIETIES IN THE U.S.

Principal source: Catholic Almanac *survey.*

Academy of American Franciscan History (1944): 1712 Euclid Ave., Berkeley, CA 94709; (510) 548-1755; www.aafh.org. To encourage the study of the Franciscan Order in the New World. Dir., Dr. Jeffrey M. Burns.

Adoremus-Society for the Renewal of the Sacred Liturgy (1995): P.O. Box 3286, St. Louis, MO 63130; (314) 863-8385; www.adoremus.org. Promotes authentic renewal of Catholic liturgy. Publishes *Adoremus Bulletin*, 10 times a year; editor, Helen Hull Hitchcock.

Aid to the Church in Need (1947): U.S. office, 725 Leonard St., Brooklyn, N.Y. 11222; (718) 609-0939; www.churchinneed.org. Assists the pastoral activities of the church in Third World countries and Eastern Europe. *Mirror*, newsletter, 9 times a year. Pres./Exec. Dir., Joseph Donnelly.

American Benedictine Academy (1947): Saint Meinrad Archabbey, Guest House, 100 Hill Dr. Saint Meinrad, IN, 47577; (800) 581-6905. To promote Benedictine values in contemporary culture. Pres., Eugene Hensell, O.S.B.

American Catholic Correctional Chaplains Association (1952): 100 E. Eighth St., Cincinnati, OH 45202; (513) 771-1877; www.catholiccorrectionalchaplains.org. Pres., Rev. Mark. Schmieder.

American Catholic Historical Association (1919): Dealy Hall, Room 637, 441 E. Fordham Rd., Bronx, NY 10458; (718) 817-3830; www.achahistory.org. *The Catholic Historical Review*, quarterly. Sec.-Treas., Rev. Dr. R. Bentley Anderson, S.J.

American Catholic Philosophical Association (1926):

Administration Building, Fordham University, 441 E. Fordham Rd., Bronx, NY, 10458; (718) 817-3295; www.acpa-main.org. *American Catholic Philosophical Quarterly; Proceedings*, annually.

American Committee on Italian Migration (1952): 25 Carmine St., New York, NY 10014; (212) 247-5419; www.acimmmigra.org. *ACIM Newsletter* and *ACIM Nuova Via*, 6 times a year.

American Friends of the Vatican Library (1981): 3535 Indian Trail, Orchard Lake, MI 48324; (248) 683-0311. AMICI, newsletter. Sponsored by the Catholic Library Association. To assist in supporting the Vatican Library. Pres., Rev. Msgr. Charles G. Kosanke.

American Life League, Inc. (1979), P.O. Box 1350, Stafford, VA 22555; (540) 659-4171; www.all.org. *Celebrate Life*, six times a year, and the *ABAC Quarterly*, for the American Bioethics Advisory Commission. Pres., Judie Brown.

Ancient Order of Hibernians in America, Inc. (1836): 31 Logan St., Auburn, NY 13021. National *Hibernian Digest*, bimonthly. 120,000 members. Nat. Sec., Thomas McNabb.

Apostleship of Prayer (1844, France; 1861, U.S.): 1501 S. Layton Blvd., Milwaukee, WI 53215; (414) 486-1152; www.apostleshipofprayer.org. Promotes Daily Offering and Sacred Heart devotion. Contact: Rev. James Kubicki.

Apostolate for Family Consecration (1975): 3375 County Rd. 36, Bloomingdale, OH 43910; (740) 765-5500; www.familyland.org. Pope John Paul II Holy Family Center, known as Catholic Familyland. To transform families and parishes and nourish families through the Catholic faith. Pres., Jerome F. Coniker.

Archconfraternity of Christian Mothers (Christian Mothers) (1881): 220 37th St., Pittsburgh, PA 15201; (412) 683-2400; www.capuchin.com. Over 3,500 branches. Dir., Rev. Bertin Roll, O.F.M. Cap.

Archconfraternity of the Holy Ghost (1912): Holy Ghost Fathers, 6230 Brush Run Rd., Bethel Park, PA 15102; (412) 831-0302; www.spiritans.org (U.S. headquarters).

Archdiocese for the Military Services Seminary Education Fund (1988): P.O. Box 4469, Washington, D.C., 20017-0469; (202) 269-9100; www.milarch.org.

Association for Social Economics (formerly the Catholic Economic Association) (1941): Marquette University, Milwaukee, WI 53233. *Review of Social Economy*, quarterly. 1,300 members.

Association of Catholic Diocesan Archivists (1979): P.O. Box 818, Charleston, SC 29402; (843) 577-1017; www.diocesanarchivists.org. To work for establishment of an archival program in every American diocese. *ACDA Bulletin*, quarterly. Treas. Brian P. Fahey.

Association of Marian Helpers (1944): Eden Hill, 2 Prospect Rd., Stockbridge, MA 01263; (413) 298-3691; www.marian.org. *Marian Helpers Bulletin*, quarterly. 900,000 members, mostly in U.S. To promote vocations to Church service and support worldwide apostolates of Marians of the Immaculate Conception. Exec. Dir., Rev. Joseph, M.I.C.

Assumption Guild — Mass Cards: 330 Market St., Brighton, MA 02135; (617) 783-0495; www.masscardsaa.com.

Beginning Experience (1974): International

Ministry Center, 136 Dowd Ave., Canton, CT 06019; (574) 283-0279; www.beginningexperience. org. Programs to help divorced, widowed and separated. Pres., Kathleen Murphy.

Calix Society (1947): 2555 Hazelwood St., St. Paul, MN 55109; www.calixsociety.org. Association of Catholic alcoholics maintaining their sobriety through 12-step program. Sec. Jim Billigmeier.

Canon Law Society of America (1939): 3025 Fourth St., NE, Hecker Center, Suite 111, Washington, DC 20017; (202) 832-2350; www.clsa.org. To further research and study in canon law. 1,600 members. Exec. Coord., Sister Sharon Euart, R.S.M., J.C.D.

Cardinal Mindszenty Foundation (CMF) (1958): P.O. Box 11321, St. Louis, MO 63105-0121; (314) 727-6279; www.mindszenty.org. To uphold and defend the Catholic Church, family life and freedom for all under God. *The Mindszenty Report*, monthly. Sec., Liza Forshaw.

Catholic Academy for Communication Arts Professionals (2002): 1645 Brook Lynn Dr., Ste. 2, Dayton, OH 45432; (937) 229-2303; www.catholica cademy.org; the U.S. affiliate of SIGNIS, the Vatican approved organization for communication.

Catholic Answers (1982): 2020 Gillespie Way, El Cajon, CA 92020; (619) 387-7200; www.catholic.com. Apologetics and evangelization organization. Founder and dir., Karl Keating.

Catholic Association of Diocesan Ecumenical and Interreligious Officers (CADEIO): 303 S. Poplar St., Carbondale, IL 62901; (618) 457-4556. To promote the work of ecumenical officers in their efforts to foster Christian unity and interreligious dialogue. Pres., Very Rev. Robert Flannery.

Catholic Biblical Association of America (1936): The Catholic University of America, Washington, DC 20064; (202) 319-5519; www.catholicbiblical.org. The *Catholic Biblical Quarterly, Old Testament Abstracts*, CBQ monograph series. Exec. Sec., Dr. Joseph Atkinson.

Catholic Book Publishers Association, Inc. (1987): 8404 Jamesport Dr., Rockford, IL 61108; (815) 332-3245; www.cbpa.org. Exec. Dir., Terry Wessels.

Catholic Cemetery Conference (1949): 1400 S. Wolf Rd., Building 3, Hillside, IL 60162; (888) 850-8131; www.catholiccemeteryconference.org. Exec. Dir., Dennis Fairbank.

Catholic Coalition on Preaching: Madonna University, 36600 Schoolcraft Rd. Livonia, MI 48150-1173; (734) 432-5538. Pres., Rev. Francis Tebbe, OFM.

Catholic Committee of Appalachia (1970): 885 Orchard Run Rd., Spencer, WV 25276; (304) 927-5798; ccappal.org. Dir., Fr. John Rausch.

Catholic Communications Foundation (CCF): 6363 St. Charles Ave., New Orleans, LA 70118. Established to assist the communications apostolate of the Catholic Church in the U.S.

Catholic Daughters of the Americas (1903): 10 W. 71st St., New York, NY 10023; (212) 877-3041; www.catholicdaughters.org. *Share Magazine*. 125,000 members. Nat. Regent, M. Joan McKenna.

Catholic Death Row Ministry (1990): P.O. Box 1328, Howe, Texas 75459-1328; (903)892-9411; to share the Catholic Faith with Death Row Inmates; also assist victims and families of Death Row inmates. Founder and director, Michael Denson.

Catholic Familyland (1975): 3375 County Rd. 36, Bloomingdale, OH 43910; (740) 765-5500; www.family land.org. Canonically named the John Paul II Holy Family Center; functions under the auspices of the Apostolate for Family Consecration. Pres., Jerome F. Coniker.

Catholic Golden Age (1975): P.O. Box 3658, Scranton, PA 18505-0658; (800) 836-5699. *CGA World*, quarterly. For Catholics over 50 years of age.

Catholic Guardian Society and Home Bureau (1913): 1011 First Ave., New York, NY 10022; (212) 371-1000. Exec. Dir., John J. Frein.

Catholic Home Bureau (1899): 1011 First Ave., New York, NY 10022; (212) 371-1000; www.catholi chomebureau.com. Exec. Dir., Philip Georgini.

Catholic Home Study Service (1936): P.O. Box 363, Perryville, MO 63775-0363; (573) 547-4084; www. amm.org/chss. Provides instruction in the Catholic faith by mail free of charge. Dir., Rev. Oscar J. Lukefahr.

Catholic Interracial Council of New York, Inc. (1934): 899 Tenth Ave., New York, NY 10019; (212) 237-8600; www.amm.org/chss.htm. To promote racial and social justice.

Catholic Knights of America (1877): Publication Office, 1850 Dalton St., Cincinnati, OH 45214. Fraternal insurance society. *CK of A Journal*, monthly. 7,800 members.

Catholic Knights of Ohio (1891): 22005 Mastick Rd., Fairview Park, OH 44126; (440) 777-5355. Fraternal insur ance society. *The Messenger*, monthly. 8,000 members in Ohio and Kentucky. Mr. Tom Welsh, General Secretary.

Catholic Kolping Society of America (1849): 1223 Van Houten, Clifton, NJ 07013. International society concerned with spiritual and educational development of members. *Kolping Banner*, monthly. Nat. Admin., Patricia Farkas.

Catholic Lawyers' Guild: Organization usually on a diocesan basis, under different titles.

Catholic League for Religious Assistance to Poland (1943): 6002 W. Berteau Ave., Chicago, IL 60634-1630; (773) 202-7720. Exec. Dir., Most Rev. Thad Jakubowski.

Catholic League for Religious and Civil Rights (1973): 450 Seventh Ave., 34th Floor, New York, NY 10123; (212) 371-3191; www.catholicleague.org. Local chapters through out U.S. Serves Catholic community as an anti-defama tion and civil rights agency. *Catalyst*, league journal. Pres., William A. Donohue, Ph.D.

Catholic Library Association (1921): 205 W. Monroe St., Suite 314, Chicago, IL 60606. www. cathla.org; *Catholic Library World, Catholic Periodical and Literature Index*, quarterlies. Malachy McCarthy, Pres.

Catholic Marketing Network (1955): 111 Ferguson Court, #102, Irving, TX 75062; (800) 506-6333; www. catholicmarketing.com. A trade association founded to encourage the most effective production and distribu tion of Catholic goods and provide a common forum for mutual interchange of ideas. *Catholic Marketing Network*, quarterly. Exec. Dir., Cherylann Tucker.

Catholic Near East Welfare Association (1926): 1011 First Ave., Suite 1552, New York, NY 10022; (212) 826-1480; www.cnewa.org. A papal agency for humanitarian and pastoral support serving the churches and peoples of the Middle East, Northeast Africa, India and Eastern Europe, with offices in New York, Vatican City, Addis Ababa, Amman, Jerusalem and Beirut. Chair., Card. Timothy M. Dolan; pres., Msgr. John Kozar.

Catholic Order of Foresters (1883): 355 Shuman Blvd.,

P.O. Box 3012, Naperville, IL 60566; (800) 552-0145; www.catholicforester.com. Fraternal insurance society. *The Catholic Forester*, bimonthly. 136,685 members. High Chief Ranger, David Huber.

Catholic Press Association of the U.S. and Canada, Inc. (1911): 205 W. Monroe, Suite 470, Chicago, IL 60606; (312) 380-6789; www.catholic press.org. *The Catholic Journalist*, monthly; *Catholic Press Directory*, annually. Exec. Dir., Timothy Walter.

Catholic Theological Society of America (1946): John Carroll University, 20700 North Park Blvd., University Hgts., OH, 44118; (216) 397-3980; www.jcu.edu/ctsa. Proceedings, annually. Exec. Sec., Mary Jane Ponyik.

Catholic Union of Texas, The K.J.T. (1889): 214 E. Colorado St., La Grange, TX 78945-0297; (979) 968-5877; www.kjtnet.org. Fraternal and insurance society. *Nasinec*, weekly, and *K. J. T. News*, monthly. 18,226 members. Pres., Elo J. Goerig.

Catholic United Financial (1878): 3499 Lexington Ave., North, St. Paul, MN 55126; (651) 490-0170; www.catholicunited.org. Fraternal life insurance society; formerly called Catholic Aid Association. *Catholic Aid News*, monthly. Chairman of the Board, Michael McGovern.

Catholic War Veterans (1935): 441 N. Lee St., Alexandria, VA 22314; (703) 549-3622; www.cwv.org. *Catholic War Veteran*, bimonthly. 500 posts.

Catholic Worker Movement (1933): 36 E. 1st St., New York, NY 10003. Lay apostolate founded by Peter Maurin and Dorothy Day; has Houses of Hospitality in over 60 U.S. cities and several communal farms in various parts of the country. *The Catholic Worker*, 8 times a year.

Catholic Workman (Katolicky Delnik) (1891): 111 West Main St., New Prague, MN 56071; (612) 758-2229. Fraternal and insurance society. *Catholic Workman*, monthly. 16,405 members.

Catholics Against Capital Punishment (1992): P.O. Box 5706, Bethesda, MD 20824-5706; (301) 652-1125; www.cacp.org. Promotes greater awareness of papal and episcopal statements against the death penalty. *CACP News* Notes, bimonthly. Nat. Coord., Frank McNeirney.

Catholics United for the Faith (1968): 827 N. Fourth St., Steubenville, OH 43952; (740) 283-2484; www.cuf.org. 23,000 members worldwide. Lay apostolic group concerned with spiritual and doctrinal formation of members. *Lay Witness*, monthly. Mike Sullivan, Dir. of Communications.

Center of Concern (1971): 1225 Otis St., N.E., Washington, DC 20017; (202) 635-2757; www.coc.org. Exec. Dir., Rev. James E. Hug, S.J.

Central Association of the Miraculous Medal (1915): 475 E. Chelten Ave., Philadelphia, PA 19144; (800) 523-3674; www.cammonline.org. *Miraculous Medal*, quarterly. Dir., Rev. James O. Kiernan, C.M.

Chaplains' Aid Association, Inc. (1917): 3311 Toledo Terrace, Hyattsville, MD 20780. To receive and administer funds toward education of seminarians to become priest-chaplains in military services.

Christian Foundation for Children and Aging: One Elmwood Ave., Kansas City, KS 66103; (913) 384-6500; www.cfcausa.org. Grassroots movement dedicated to improving through sponsorship the lives of children and aging at Catholic mission sites around the world. Exec. Dir., Paco Wertin.

Christophers, Inc., The (1945): 12 E. 48th St., New York, NY 10017; (212) 759-4050; www.christophers.org. Founded by Rev. James Keller, M.M. The Christophers stimulate personal initiative and responsible action in line with Judeo-Christian principles through broadcast of Christopher radio and TV programs; free distribution of *Christopher News Notes*, 10 times a year; publication of a weekly Christopher column in over 200 newspapers; Spanish literature; annual media awards; youth outreach. Pres., Robert V. Okulski.

Citizens for Educational Freedom (1959): 9333 Clayton Road, St. Louis, MO 63124-1511; (314) 997-6361; www.educational-freedom.org. Nonsectarian group concerned with parents' right to educational choice by means of tuition tax credits and vouchers. Exec. Dir., Mae Duggan.

Coming Home Network (1993): P.O. Box 8290, Zanesville, OH 43702; (740) 450-1175; www.chnetwork.org. Founded by Marcus Grodi (a former presbyterian pastor), *The Coming Home Network International* (CHNetwork) provides fellowship, encouragement and support for Protestant pastors and laymen who are somewhere along the journey or have already been received into the Catholic Church. Pres. Marcus Grodi.

Conference of Slovak Clergy (1985): 126 Logan Blvd., Hollidaysburg, PA, 16648; (814) 695-5579. Founded in 1985 and incorporated in 2000, the Conference seeks to associate priests and deacons of Slovak ancestry in the United States and to assist those preparing themselves for priestly ministry in the Church; provides financial assistance to the Slovak Pontifical College of Saints Cyril and Methodius in Rome and scholarships to individual students. Chair., Bp.Joseph V. Adamec.

Confraternity of Bl. Junipero Serra (1989): P.O. Box 7125, Mission Hills, CA 91346. Founded in Monterey (CA) diocese to help promote process of canonization of Bl. Junipero Serra and increase spiritual development of members. 3,500 members in U.S. and foreign countries. Dir., Rev. Thomas L. Davis, Jr.; Spiritual Dir., Rev. Noel F. Moholy, O.F.M.

Confraternity of Catholic Clergy (1976): 4445 W. 64th St., Chicago, IL 60629; (773) 581-8904. Association of priests pledged to pursuit of personal holiness, loyalty to the pope, theological study and adherence to authentic teachings of the Catholic faith. Sec., Rev. L. Dudley Day, OSA.

Confraternity of Christian Doctrine, Inc.: 3211 Fourth St., N.E., Washington, DC 20017; (202) 541-3098; www.usccb.org/nab. A distinct entity, separately incorporated and directed by a Board of Trustees from the United States Catholic Conference of Bishops. Its purpose is to foster and promote the teaching of Christ as understood and handed down by the Roman Catholic Church. To this end it licenses use of the Lectionary for Mass and the New American Bible (NAB), the Revised Psalms of the NAB and the Revised New Testament of the NAB, translations made from the original languages in accordance with the papal encyclical *Divino Afflante Spiritu* (1943) of Pope Pius XII.

Confraternity of the Immaculate Conception of Our

Lady of Lourdes (1874): Box 561, Notre Dame, IN 46556; (574) 631-6562. Distributors of Lourdes water.

Confraternity of the Most Holy Rosary: See Dominican Rosary Apostolate.

Couple to Couple League (1971), 4290 Delhi Ave., Cincinnati, OH 45238; (513) 471-2000; www.ccli.org. Founded to teach and promote marital chastity through Natural Family Planning. Exec. Dir., Michael Manhart.

Courage (1980): c/o St. John the Baptist Church and Friary, 210 West 31st St., New York, NY 10001; (212) 268-1010; www.couragerc.org. Ministry to men and women who experience same-sex attractions and desire to live Christian chastity in accordance with the teachings of the Catholic Church. Newsletter, 4 times a year. Nat. Dir., Rev. John F. Harvey, O.S.F.S.

CUSA (Catholics United for Spiritual Action, Inc.) — An Apostolate of the Sick or Disabled (1947): 176 W. 8th St., Bayonne, NJ, 07002-1227; (201) 437-0412; www.cusan.org. A group-correspondence apostolate for the disabled and chronically ill. Admin. Ms. Anna Marie Sopko.

Damien-Dutton Society for Leprosy Aid, Inc. (1944): 616 Bedford Ave., Bellmore, NY 11710; (516) 221-5829; www.damien-duttonleprosysociety. org. Provides medicine, rehabilitation and research for conquest of leprosy. *Damien Dutton Call*, quarterly. 25,000 members. Vice Pres., Elizabeth Campbell.

Daniel Dajani, S.J., Albanian Catholic Institute (1992): University of San Francisco, Xavier Hall, 650 Parker Ave., San Francisco, CA 94118; (415) 422-6966; www.albanian-catholic-institute.org. To assist the rebuilding of the Catholic Church in Albania and to promote the dissemination of knowledge of Albania's national, religious and cultural heritage. Exec. Dir., Raymond Frost.

Daughters of Isabella (1897): P.O. Box 9585, New Haven, CT 06535; www.daughtersofisabella. To unite Catholic women into a fraternal order for spiritual benefits and to promote higher ideals within society. 100,000 members.

Disaster Response Office (1990): Catholic Charities USA, 1731 King St., Suite 200, Alexandria, VA 22314; (703) 549-1390; www.catholiccharitiesusa.org. Promotes and facilitates Catholic disaster response in the U.S. Dir., Jane A. Gallagher.

Dismas Ministry: P.O. Box 070363, Milwaukee, WI 53207; (414) 977-5064; www.dismasministry.org; outreach to inmates, their families, and the community; services include spiritual ministry to inmates, victim support, and faith-based rehabilitation.

Dominican Rosary Apostolate (1806): Dominican Province of St. Joseph, 280 N. Grant Ave., Columbus, OH 43215, (614) 240-5915. Contact: Rev. André-Joseph LaCasse, O.P., Promoter of the Rosary, Dominican Province of St. Joseph.

Edith Stein Guild, Inc. (1955): Church of St. John the Baptist, 210 W. 31st St., New York, NY 10001-2876; (914) 941-7636; edithsteinguild.org. Assists and encourages Jewish Catholics; fosters among Catholics a better understanding of their Jewish heritage; promotes spread of knowledge of life and writings of St. Edith Stein; fosters better understanding between Jews and Christians and supports the Church's spirit of ecumenism. Pres., Sr. Marie Goldstein, R.S.H.M.

Enthronement of the Sacred Heart in the Home (1907): P.O. Box 111, Fairhaven, MA 02719; (508) 999-2680.

Federation of Diocesan Liturgical Commissions (FDLC) (1969): P.O. Box 29039, Washington, DC 20017; (202) 635-6990; www.fdlc.org. Voluntary association of personnel from diocesan liturgical commissions and worship offices. The main purpose is promotion of the liturgy as the heart of Christian life, especially in the parish community. Exec. Dir., Rev. Michael J. Spillane.

Federation of Seminary Spiritual Directors (1972): Cardinal Muench Seminary, 100 35th Ave., N.E., Fargo, ND 58102; (701) 232-8969. Responsible for priestly spiritual formation in high school and college seminaries, novitiates, theologates and houses of formation in the U.S. and Canada. Pres., Dennis Skonseng.

Fellowship of Catholic Scholars (1977): Ave Maria School of Law, 3475 Plymouth Rd., Ann Arbor, Michigan 48105; (734) 827-8043. Interdisciplinary research and publications of Catholic scholars in accord with the magisterium of the Catholic Church. 1,000 members. Pres., Bernard Dobranski.

First Catholic Slovak Ladies' Association, USA (1892): 24950 Chagrin Blvd., Beachwood, OH 44122; (800) 464-4642; www.fcsla.com. *Fraternally Yours*, monthly. 102,000 members. Fraternal insurance society. Pres., Cynthia Maleski.

First Catholic Slovak Union (Jednota) (1890): FCSU Corporate Center, 6611 Rockside Rd., Independence, OH 44131; (216) 642-9406; www. fcsu.com. *Jednota*, biweekly. 96,206 members.

Foundation for the Family (1986): P.O. Box 111184, Cincinnati, OH 45211; (800) 745-8252; www.ccli. org. Established by Couple to Couple League (see entry above) to provide materials for family not relating to Natural Family Planning, Exec. Dir., Mark Hayden.

Foundations and Donors Interested in Catholic Activities, Inc. (FADICA): 1350 Connecticut Ave. N.W., Suite 303, Washington, DC 20036; (202) 223-3550; www.FADICA.org. A consortium of private foundations providing continuing education and research to members to make churchrelated philanthropy more effective. Pres., Francis J. Butler.

Franciscan Apostolate of the Way of the Cross (1949): P.O. Box 23, Boston, MA 02112; (617) 542-6659. Distributes religious materials to the sick and shut-in. Dir., Rev. Robert Lynch, O.F.M.

Free The Fathers (1983): 845 Oak St. Chattanooga, TN 37403; (423) 756-9660; www.ftf.org. To work for the freedom of bishops and priests imprisoned in China. Pres., John M. Davies.

Friends of the Holy Land, Inc. (1974): 370 Mile Square Rd., Yonkers, NY 10701. To provide spiritual and material support for the Christian communities in the Holy Land. *Friends of the Holy Land* Newsletter. 300 members. Gen. Dir., Ernest F. Russo.

Guard of Honor of the Immaculate Heart of Mary (1932): 135 West 31st St., New York, NY 10001; (212) 736-8500; www.hnp.org. An archconfraternity approved by the Holy See whose members cultivate devotion to the Blessed Virgin Mary, particularly through a daily Guard Hour of Prayer. Dir., Rev. Cassian A. Miles, O.F.M.

Holy Cross Family Ministries (formerly The Family Rosary, Inc.) (1942): 518 Washington St., North Easton, MA, 02356-1200; (508) 238-4095; www.hcfm.org. Founded by Fr. Patrick Peyton, C.S.C. Encourages family prayer, especially the Rosary. Pres., Fr. John Phalen, C.S.C.

Holy Name Society: P.O. Box 12012, Baltimore, MD 21281; (410) 325-1523; www.holynamesociety.info. Founded in 1274 by Blessed John Vercelli, master general of the Dominicans, to promote reverence for the Holy Name of Jesus; this is still the principal purpose of the society, which also develops lay apostolic programs in line with directives of the Second Vatican Council. Introduced in the U.S. in 1870-71 by Dominican Fr. Charles H. McKenna, the society has about 5 million members on diocesan and parochial levels. With approval of the local bishop and pastor, women as well as men may be members.

Holy Name Society, National Association (NAHNS) (1970): P.O. Box 12012, Baltimore, MD 21281; (410) 276-1166; www.members.aol.com/nahns. Association of diocesan and parochial Holy Name Societies. *Holy Name Newsletter*, monthly.

Hungarian Catholic League of America, Inc. (1945): One Cathedral Sq., Providence, RI 02903-3695; (401) 278-4520. Chair., Rev. Msgr. William I. Varsanyi.

International Catholic Stewardship Council (1962): 1275 K St. N.W., Suite 880, Washington, DC 20005-4083; (800) 352-3452; www.catholicstewardship.org. A professional association which fosters an environment in which stewardship is understood, accepted and practiced throughout the church. Moderator, Alex R. Carrion.

International Catholic Charismatic Renewal Services: Palazzo della Cancelleria, 00120 Vatican City; 39 06 698 87538; www.iccrs.org. The ICCRS provides leadership and vision to the Catholic Charismatic Renewal throughout the world in harmony with the Pontifical Council for the Laity which has established ICCRS as a Private Association of the Faithful. *See* National Catholic Charismatic Renewal Services.

Italian Catholic Federation (1924): 675 Hegenberger Rd., #230, Oakland, CA 94621; (888) 423-1924; www.icf.org. Fraternal organization of Italian-American Catholics. 19,000 members.

John Carroll Society, The (1951): P.O. Box 50188, Washington, DC 20091; (703) 573-3043; www.johncarrollsociety.org. Exec. Asst., Mary Ann Dmochowski, Ph.D.

Judean Society, Inc., The (1966): 1075 Space Park Way No. 336, Mountain View, CA 94043.

Knights of Peter Claver (1909), and Knights of Peter Claver, Ladies Auxiliary (1926): 1825 Orleans Ave., New Orleans, LA 70116; (504) 821-4225; www.knightsofpeterclaver.com. Fraternal and aid society. *The Claverite*, biannually. National Chaplain, Most Rev. Curtis J. Guillory, S.V.D.

Knights of St. John, International Supreme Commandery (1886): 89 So. Pine Ave., Albany, NY 12208; (518) 453-5675; www.members.tripod.com/ksji/knights/ksji.html. Supreme Sec., Maj. Gen.

Joseph Hauser, Jr.

Ladies of Charity of the United States of America (1960): PO Box 31697, St. Louis, MO 63131; (314) 344-1184; www.famvin.org/lcusa. International Association founded by St. Vincent de Paul in 1617. 25,000 members in U.S.; 250,000 worldwide.

Latin Liturgy Association (1975): P. O. Box 3017, Bethlehem, PA, 18017; www.latinliturgy.com. To promote the use of the Latin language and music in the approved rites of the Church. Quarterly journal. 850 members. Pres., James F. Pauer.

Legatus (1987): 30 Frank Lloyd Wright Dr., P.O. Box 997, Ann Arbor, MI 48106; (734) 930-3854. To apply Church's moral teaching in business and personal lives of members. *Legatus Newsletter*, monthly.

Lithuanian Groups: Ateitininkai, members of Lithuanian Catholic Federation Ateitis (1910), 1209 Country Lane, Lemont, IL 60439. *Ateitis*, bimonthly. Pres., Juozas Polikaitis. Knights of Lithuania (1913): Roman Catholic educational-fraternal organization. Vytis, monthly. Pres., Evelyn Ozelis, 2533 W. 45th St., Chicago, IL 60632.

Lithuanian Catholic Alliance (1886), 7173 S. Washington St., Wilkes-Barre, PA 18701. Fraternal insurance organization. Pres., Thomas E. Mack.

Lithuanian Roman Catholic Federation of America (1906): 4545 W. 63rd St., Chicago, IL 60629; (312) 585-9500. Umbrella organization for Lithuanian parishes and organizations. *The Observer*, bimonthly. Pres., Saulius Kuprys.

Lithuanian Catholic Religious Aid, Inc. (1961): 64-25 Perry Ave., Maspeth, NY 11378-2441; (718) 326-5202. To assist Catholics in Lithuania. Chairman and Pres., Most Rev. Paul Baltakis, O.F.M.

Lithuanian Roman Catholic Priests' League (1909): P.O. Box 1025, Humarock, MA 02047-1025; (781) 834-4079. Religious-professional association. Pres., Rev. Albert Contons.

Little Flower Mission League (1957), P.O. Box 25, Plaucheville, LA 71362; (318) 922-3630. Sponsored by the Brothers of the Holy Eucharist. Dir., Bro. André M. Lucia, F.S.E.

Little Flower Society (1923): 1313 Frontage Rd. Darien, IL 60561. 200,000 members. Nat. Dir., Rev. Robert E. Colaresi, O. Carm.

Liturgical Conference, The: 415 Michigan Ave., NE, #65, Washington, DC 20017; (202) 832-6520; www.litconf.org. Liturgy, homily service. Education, research and publication programs for renewing and enriching Christian liturgical life. Ecumenical.

Loyal Christian Benefit Association (1890): P.O. Box 13005, Erie, PA 16514; (814) 453-4331; www.icba.com. Fraternal benefit and insurance society. *The Fraternal Leader*, quarterly. Pres., Jackie Sobania-Robison.

Marian Movement of Priests (1972): P.O. Box 8, St. Francis, ME 04774; (207) 398-3375; www.mmp-usa.net. Via Mercalli, 23, 20122 Milan, Italy (international headquarters). Spiritual renewal through consecration to the Immaculate Heart of Mary. 4,000 clergy members, 53,000 religious and laity (U.S.). Contact: Tammy Ouellette.

Mariological Society of America (1949): Marian

Library, #1390, University of Dayton, Dayton, OH 45469; (937) 229-4214; www.udayton.edu/mary. Founded by Rev. Juniper B. Carol, O.F.M., to promote greater appreciation of and scientific research in Marian theology. Marian Studies, annually. Sec., Rev. Thomas A. Thompson, S.M.

Marriage Encounter, National: 4704 Jamerson Pl., Orlando, FL 32807. The national office of Worldwide Marriage Encounter is located at 2210 East Highland Ave., #106, San Bernardino, CA 92404; (909) 863-9963. Brings couples together for a weekend program of events directed by a team of several couples and a priest, to develop their abilities to communicate with each other as husband and wife.

Maryheart Crusaders, The (1964): 22 Button St., Meriden, CT 06450; (203) 239-5979; www.maryheartcrusaders.org. Pres., Louise D'Angelo.

Men of the Sacred Heart (1964): National Shrine of the Sacred Heart, P.O. Box 500, Harleigh, PA 18225; (570) 455-1162. Promotes enthronement of Sacred Heart.

Militia Immaculate National Center — Marytown (1917): 1600 W. Park Ave., Libertyville, IL 60048; (847) 367-7800; www.consecration.com. Canonically established with international headquarters in Rome. A pious association to promote total consecration to Mary in the spirit of St. Maximilian Kolbe. Pres., Fr. Patrick Greenough, OFM Conv.

Missionary Association of Catholic Women (1916): 3501 S. Lake Dr., P.O. Box 07212, Milwaukee, WI 53207-0912; (414) 769-3406.

Missionary Vehicle Association, Inc. (MIVA America) (1971): 1400 Michigan Ave., N.E., Washington, DC 20017-7234; (202) 635-3444; www.miva.org. To raise funds and distribute them annually as vehicle grants to missionaries working with the poor in Third World countries. Nat. Dir., Rev. Philip De Rea, MSC; Exec. Dir., Rev. Anthony F. Krisak.

Morality in Media, Inc. (1962): 475 Riverside Dr., Suite 1264, New York, NY 10115; (212) 870-3222; www.moralityinmedia.org. Interfaith national organization. Works by constitutional means to curb the explosive growth of hard-core pornography and to turn back the tide of grossly offensive, indecent media. A major project is the National Obscenity Law Center which provides legal information for prosecutors and other attorneys. Newsletter, bimonthly. Pres., Robert W. Peters.

National Association of African American Catholic Deacons: 1418 Glen View Rd., Yellow Springs, OH 45387; (937) 974-1588. To assist and promote permanent deacons of Africn American heritage. Pres. Deacon Paul E. Richardson.

National Assembly of Religious Women (NARW): 529 S. Wabash Ave., Suite 404, Chicago, IL 60605; (312) 663-1980. Founded as the National Assembly of Women Religious, 1970; title changed, 1980. A movement of feminist women committed to prophetic tasks of giving witness, raising awareness and engaging in public action and advocacy for justice in church and society.

National Association for Lay Ministry (1977): 6896 Laurel St., N.W., Washington, DC 20012; (202) 291-4100; www.nalm.org. Acts as advocate and support for lay people who respond to a call to ministry in the Church. Exec. Dir., Christopher Anderson.

National Association of Catholic Chaplains: 5007 S. Howell Ave., Ste. 120, Milwaukee, WI 532-7; (414) 483-4898; www.nacc.org. Supports the work and ministry of Catholic chaplains; publishes newsletter, *Vision*, and e-mail newsletter, *NACC Now*.

National Association of Catholic Family Life Ministers: 5818 Wilmington Pike, #230, Centerville, OH 45459; (937) 431-5443; www.nacflm.org. Strives to be a voice and advocate for families and family ministry in Church and society. Pres., Lorrie Gramer.

National Association of Catholic Home Educators (1993): 6102 Saints Hill Lane, Broad Run, VA 20137; (540) 349-4314; www.nache.com. Promotion of home-schooling. *The Catholic Home Educator*, quarterly.

National Association of Church Personnel Administrators (1971): 100 E. 8th St., Cincinnati, OH 45202; (513) 421-3134; www.nacpa.org. Association for human resource and personnel directors dedicated to promotion and development of just personnel practices for all church employees. Exec. Dir., Sr. Ellen Doyle, OSU.

National Association of Diaconate Directors (1977): 7625 N. High St., Columbus, OH 43215; (614) 985-2276; www.nadd.org. Deacon Thomas R. Dubois, Exec. Dir.

National Association of Diocesan Ecumenical Officers: 7800 Kenrick Rd., St. Louis, MO 63119; (314) 961-4320. Network of Catholics involved in ecumenical and interreligious work. Pres., Vincent A. Heier.

National Association of Pastoral Musicians (1976): 962 Wayne Ave., Suite 210, Silver Spring, MD 20910; (240) 247-3000; www.npm.org. 9,000 members. Dedicated to fostering the art of musical liturgy. *Pastoral Music*, six times a year. Exec. Dir., Dr. J. Michael McMahon.

National Association of Priest Pilots (1964): 481 N. Shore Dr., Apt. 301, Clear Lake IA 50428-1368; (641) 357-4539. Pres., Rev. Msgr. John Hemann.

National Catholic AIDS Network: P.O. Box 422984, San Francisco, CA 94142; (707) 874-3031; www.ncan.org. Exec. dir., Rev. Rodney DeMartini; Board Pres., Rev. Robert J. Vitillo.

National Catholic Band Association (1953): 3334 N. Normandy, Chicago, IL 60634; (773) 282-9153; www.catholicbands.org.

National Catholic Conference for Interracial Justice (NCCIJ) (1960): 1200 Varnum St. N.E., Washington, DC 20017; (202) 529-6480. Exec. Dir., Rev. Mr. Joseph M. Conrad, Jr.

National Catholic Conference for Seafarers: 4219 Constance St., New Orleans, LA 70115; (504) 891-6677. Association of chaplains and laity serving in the pastoral care of seafarers.

National Catholic Council on Addiction (NCCA): 1601 Joslyn Rd., Lake Orion, MI 48360; (800) 626-6910; www.nccatoday.com. An affiliate of the USCCB. Committed to assisting members in a greater awareness of alcoholism, other chemical addictions and prevention issues. Dir.: Louise Westcott.

National Catholic Development Conference (1968): 86 Front St., Hempstead, NY 11550; (516) 481-6000. Professional association of organizations and individuals engaged in raising funds for Catholic charitable activities. Pres., Sr. Georgette Lehmuth, OSF.

National Catholic Ministry to the Bereaved (NCMB) (1990): 28700 Euclid Ave., Wickliffe, OH, 44092-2527; (440) 943-3480; www.griefwork.org. Offers ongoing education, resources and assistance to dioceses, parishes and caregivers in their ministry to the bereaved. Coordinator: Mary Ann Wachtel, SFCC.

National Catholic Pharmacists Guild of the United States (1962): 1012 Surrey Hills Dr., St. Louis, MO 63117; (314) 645-0085. *The Catholic Pharmacist*. Co-Pres., Exec. Dir. and Editor, John P. Winkelmann.

National Catholic Society of Foresters (1891): 320 S. School St., Mt. Prospect, IL 60056; (847) 342-4500; www.ncsf.com. A fraternal insurance society. *National Catholic Forester*, quarterly. National Pres., Margaret Babinat.

National Catholic Women's Union (1916): 3835 Westminster Pl., St. Louis, MO 63108; (314) 371-1653; www.socialjusticereview.org. 7,000 members.

National Center for the Laity (1977): P.O. Box 291102, Chicago, IL 60629; (708) 974-5221; www.catholiclabor.org/ncl.htm. To promote and implement the vision of Vatican II: That the laity are the Church in the modern world as they attend to their occupational, family and neighborhood responsibilities. *Initiatives*, six times a year.

National Center for Urban Ethnic Affairs (1971): P.O. Box 20, Cardinal Station, Washington, DC 20064; (202) 232-3600. Research and action related to the Church's concern for cultural pluralism and urban neighborhoods. An affiliate of the USCCB. Pres., Dr. John A. Kromkowski.

National Christ Child Society Inc. (1887): 6900 Wisconsin Ave. N.W., Suite 604, Bethesda, MD 20815; (800) 814-2149; www.NationalChristChildSoc.org. Founder, Mary V. Merrick. A nonprofit Catholic association of volunteers of all denominations dedicated to the service of needy children and youth regardless of race or creed. Approximately 7,000 adult members in 38 chapters in U.S. Exec. Dir., Margaret Saffell.

National Committee of Catholic Laymen, The (1977): 215 Lexington Ave., Fourth Floor, New York, NY 10016; (212) 685-6666. Lobbying and publishing organization representing "orthodox" Catholics who strongly support Pope John Paul II. *Catholic Eye*, monthly; editor, Mrs. Anne Conlon.

National Conference of Catechetical Leadership (formerly, National Conference of Diocesan Directors of Religious Education) (1936): 125 Michigan Ave., N.E., Washington, DC 20017; (202) 884-9753; www.nccl.org. To promote catechetical ministry at the national diocesan and parish levels. 1,300 members. Exec. Dir., Leland Nagel.

National Conference of Catholic Airport Chaplains (1986): P.O. Box 66353, Chicago, IL 60666; (773) 686-2636; www.nccac.us. Provides support and communication for Catholics performing pastoral ministry to airport and airline workers and Catholic travelers; affiliated with Bishops' Committee on Migration, USCCB. Pres., Deacon Rev. Michael Zaniolo, STL, CAC.

National Conference of Diocesan Vocation Directors (NCDVD) (1961): 440 W. Neck Rd., Huntington, NY 11743; (631) 645-8210. Professional organization for diocesan vocation personnel providing resources and on-going education in their promoting, assessing and forming of candidates for the diocesan priesthood. Pres., Fr. Leonard Plazewski.

National Council for Catholic Evangelization (1983): 415 Michigan Ave, NE, Suite 90, Washington, DC, 20017; 1-800-786-NCCE; www.catholicevangelization.org. To promote evangelization as the "primary and essential mission of the Church," in accordance with *Evangelii Nuntiandi*, the 1975 apostolic exhortation of Pope Paul VI. Exec. Dir., Sr. Priscilla Lemire, RJM.

National Council of Catholic Women (1920): 200 N. Glebe Rd., Suite 703, Arlington, VA 22203; (703) 224-0990; www.nccw.org. A federation of some 7,000 organizations of Catholic women in the U.S. NCCW unites Catholic organizations and individual Catholic women of the U.S., develops their leadership potential, assists them to act upon current issues in the Church and society, provides a medium through which Catholic women may speak and act upon matters of common interest, and relates to other national and international organizations in the solution of presentday problems. It is an affiliate of the World Union of Catholic Women's Organizations. *Catholic Woman*, bimonthly. Exec. Dir., Sheila McCarron.

National Evangelization Teams (NET): 110 Crusader Ave., West St. Paul, MN 55118-4427; (651) 450-6833; www.netusa.org. Trains Catholic young adults to be evangelists to peers and high school/junior high youth through traveling retreat teams.

National Federation of Catholic Physicians' Guilds (1927): P.O. Box 757, Pewaukee, WI 53072; (262) 523-6201; www.cathmed.com. *Linacre* Quarterly. Exec. Dir., Robert H. Herzog.

National Federation of Priests' Councils (1968): 333 N. Michigan Ave., Ste. 1205, Chicago, IL 60601; (312) 442-9700; www.nfpc.org. To give priests' councils a representative voice in matters of presbyteral, pastoral and ministerial concern to the U.S. and the universal Church. *Touchstone*, quarterly. Pres., Rev. Richard Vega.

National Institute for the Word of God (1972): 487 Michigan Ave. N.E., Washington, DC 20017; (203) 562-6193; www.wordofgodinstitute.org. For renewed biblical preaching, Bible sharing and evangelization. Dir., Rev. John Burke, OP.

National Life Center, Inc.: 686 N. Broad St., Woodbury, NJ 08096; (856) 848-1819, (800) 848-LOVE; www.nationallifecenter.com. Interdenominational guidance and referral service organization offering pregnant women alternatives to abortion. Pres., Denise F. Cocciolone.

National Organization for Continuing Education of Roman Catholic Clergy, Inc. (1973): 333 N. Michigan Ave., Ste. 1205, Chicago, IL 60601; (312) 781-9450; www.nocercc.org. Membership: 152 dioceses, 66 religious provinces, 46 institutions, 49 individuals in U.S., 18 associates outside U.S. Pres., Fr. Mark R. Hession.

National Pastoral Life Center: 18 Bleecker St., New

York, NY 10012-2404; (212) 431-7825; www.nplc.org. *Church*, quarterly. Dir., Fr. John Hurley, CSP.

National Service Committee of the Catholic Charismatic Renewal: Charismcenter USA, PO Box 628, Locust Grove, VA 22508; (540) 972-0225; www.nsc-hariscenter.org, www.iccrs.org. The mission of the National Service Committee is "to stir into flame the grace of Pentecost within and beyond the Church, to broaden and deepen the understanding that baptism in the Holy Spirit is the Christian inheritance of all, and to strengthen the Catholic Charismatic Renewal." Exec. Dir., Walter Matthews.

NETWORK, A Catholic Social Justice Lobby (1971): 25 E St. NW, Suite 200, Washington, DC 20002; (202) 347-9797; www.networklobby.org. A national Catholic social justice lobby. *NETWORK Connection*, bimonthly. Exec. Dir., Simone Campbell.

Nocturnal Adoration Society of the United States (1882): 414 Westberry Dr., Rapid City, SD 57702; (605) 342-2294; www.sibrcc.org. Nat. Dir., Rev. Bernard Camire, S.S.S.

North American Academy of Liturgy: c/o CSSR Executive Office, Valparaiso University, Valparaiso, IN 46383. Foster ecumenical and interreligious liturgical research, publication and dialogue on a scholarly level. Proceedings, annually. Pres., Alan Barthel.

North American Conference of Separated and Divorced Catholics (1972): P.O. Box 360, Richland, OR 97870; (541) 893-6089; www.nacsdc.com. Exec. Dir., Irene Varley.

North American Forum on the Catechumenate: 125 Michigan Ave. NE, Washington, DC 20017; (202) 884-9758; www.naforum.org. An international network committed to the implementation of the Order of Christian Initiation of Adults. Exec. Dir., James Schellman.

Order of the Alhambra (1904): 4200 Leeds Ave., Baltimore, MD 21229; (410) 242-0660; www.OrderAlhambra.org. Fraternal society dedicated to assisting developmentally disabled and handicapped children. 7,000 members in US and Canada. Exec. Dir., Roger J. Reid.

Our Lady's Rosary Makers (1949): 4611 Poplar Level Rd., Louisville, KY 40233; www.olrm.org. To supply missionaries with free rosaries for distribution throughout the world. *News Bulletin*, monthly. Pres., Michael Ford.

Papal Foundation, The: 150 Monument Rd., Ste. 609, Bala Cynwyd, PA 19004; (610) 535-6340; V. Pres., James V. Coffey.

Paulist National Catholic Evangelization Association (1977): 3031 Fourth St., NE, Washington, DC 20017-1102; (202) 832-5022; www.pemdc.org. To work with unchurched and alienated Catholics; to develop, test and document contemporary ways in which Catholic parishes and dioceses can evangelize the unchurched and inactive Catholics. Share the Word, bimonthly magazine; *Evangelization Update*, bimonthly newsletter. Dir., Rev. Frank DeSiano, CSP.

Philangeli (Friends of the Angels) (1949 in England; 1956 in U.S.): Viatorian Fathers, 1115 E. Euclid St., Arlington Heights, IL 60004.

Pious Union of Prayer (1898): St. Joseph's Home, P.O. Box 288, Jersey City, NJ 07303; (201) 798-4141. St. Joseph's Messenger and *Advocate of the Blind*, quarterly.

Polish Roman Catholic Union of America (1887): 984 N. Milwaukee Ave., Chicago, IL 60622; (773) 728-2600; www.prcua.org. Fraternal benefit society. *Narod Polski*, bimonthly. Sec.-Treas. Josephine Szarowicz.

Pontifical Mission for Palestine (1949): 1011 First Ave., New York, NY 10022-4195; (212) 826-1480; www.cnewa.org. A papal relief and development agency of the Holy See for the Middle East, with offices in New York, Vatican City, Amman, Beirut and Jerusalem. Pres., Msgr. Archim; Robert L. Stern, JCD.

Pontifical Mission Societies (1916): 70 West 36th St., 8th Floor, New York, NY 10018; (212) 563-8700; www.worldmissions-catholicchurch.org. To promote mission awareness among clergy, religious, candidates, and others engaged in pastoral ministry. Nat. Dir., Fr. Andrew Small, O.M.I.

Population Research Institute (1989): 1190 Progress Drive, Suite 2D, P.O. Box 1559, Front Royal, VA 22630; (540) 622-5240; www.pop.org. Non-profit research and educational organization dedicated to objectively presenting the truth about population-related issues. *PRI Review*, a bimonthly newsletter, which reports on population news of interest from around the world. Pres., Steven W. Mosher.

Priests' Eucharistic League (1887): 5384 Wilson Mills Rd., Highland Heights, OH 44143. *Emmanuel*, 10 issues a year. Nat. Dir., Very Rev. Norman Pelletier, SSS.

Pro Ecclesia Foundation (1970): 350 Fifth Ave., New York, NY 10118. *Pro Ecclesia Magazine*. Pres., Dr. Timothy A. Mitchell.

ProLife Across America (1989): P.O. Box 18669, Minneapolis, MN 55418; (612) 781-0410; www.prolifeacrossamerica.org. A non-profit organization that uses various media to promote the culture of life. Contact: Mary Ann Kuharski.

Pro Maria Committee for Our Lady of Beauraing (1952): 112 Norris Rd. Tyngsboro, MA 01879; (978) 649-1813. Promotes devotion to Our Lady of Beauraing (*see* Index).

Pro Sanctity Movement: Pro Sanctity Spirituality Center, 205 S. Pine Dr., Fullerton, CA 92833; (714) 956-1020. 45-30 195th St., Flushing, NY 11358; (718) 649-0324. 6762 Western Ave., Omaha, NE 68132; (402) 553-4418. 11002 N. 204th St., Elkhorn, NE 68022; (402) 289-1938; www.prosanctity.org. Nat. Dir. Jessi Kary. Organized to spread God's call of all persons to holiness.

Project Children (1975): P.O. Box 933, Greenwood Lake, NY 10925; (845) 477-3472; www.interwebinc.com/children. Nonsectarian volunteer group; provides children of Northern Ireland with a six-week summer vacation with host families in the U.S.

The Providence Association of the Ukrainian Catholics in America (Ukrainian Catholic Fraternal Benefit Society) (1912): 817 N. Franklin St., Philadelphia, PA 19123; (215) 627-4984.

Queen of the Americas Guild, Inc. (1979): P.O. Box 851, St. Charles, IL 60174; (630) 584-1822; www.queenoftheamericasguild.org. To build English information center and retreat center near Basilica in Mexico City and spread the message of Guadalupe. 7,000 members. Nat. Coord. Rebecca Nichols.

Raskob Foundation for Catholic Activities, Inc. (1945): P.O. Box 4019, Wilmington, DE 19807-0019; (302) 655-4440; www.rfca.org. Exec. Pres., Frederick Perella, Jr.

Reparation Society of the Immaculate Heart of Mary, Inc. (1946): 100 E. 20th St., Baltimore, MD 21218. *Fatima Findings*, monthly.

Retrouvaille: P.O.Box 25, Kelton, PA 19346. A ministry to hurting marriages, Retrouvaille consists of a weekend experience with follow-up sessions designed to provide couples with ways and means of healing and reconciling. Emphasis is placed on communication, enabling husband and wife to rediscover each other and to examine their lives in a new and positive way. The ministry is neither a retreat nor a sensitivity group, nor does it include group dynamics or discussions. The program is conducted by trained couples and priests, with programs offered under the auspices of diocesan family life agencies. International Coordinating Team: Bill and Peg Swaan.

Sacred Heart League: 6050 Hwy 61 N, P.O. Box 190, Walls, MS 38680. Pres., Fr. Robert Hess, S.C.J.

St. Ansgar's Scandinavian Catholic League (1910): 160 Cornelison Ave., Jersey City, NJ 07304; (201) 333-2525. Prayers and financial support for Church in Scandinavia. *St. Ansgar's Bulletin*, annually. 1,000 members. Pres., Astrid M. O'Brien.

St. Anthony's Guild (1924): P.O. 2948, Paterson, NJ 07509-2948; (973) 777-3737. Promotes devotion to St. Anthony of Padua and support for formation programs, infirm friars and ministries of the Franciscans of Holy Name Province. *The Anthonian*, quarterly. Dir., Fr. Joseph Hertel, OFM.

St. Bernadette Institute of Sacred Art (1993): P.O. Box 8249, Albuquerque, NM 87198-8249; (505) 265-9126; www.nmia.com/~paulos. To promote, initiate, encourage interest and sustain projects and persons engaged in sacred art.

St. Gregory Foundation for Latin Liturgy (1989): Newman House, 601 Buhler Ct., Pine Beach, NJ 08741; (732) 914-1222; www.johnhenrynewman. org. To promote within the Church in the U.S. the use of the Latin language in the Mass in accordance with the teachings of Vatican II. Founder and Pres., Rev. Peter M.J. Stravinskas, Ph.D., S.T.D.

St. Margaret of Scotland Guild, Inc. (1938): Graymoor, P.O. Box 300, Garrison, NY 10524-0300; (845) 424-3671. Moderator, Bro. Pius MacIsaac.

St. Martin de Porres Guild (1935): 141 E. 65th St., New York, NY 10021; (212) 744-2410; www.op-stjoseph.org. Dir., Rev. Raymond F. Halligan, O.P.

Serra International (1934): 220 S. State St., Suite 1703, Chicago, IL 60604; (312) 588-0700; www.serrainternational.org. Fosters vocations to the priesthood, and religious life, trains Catholic lay leadership. Formally aggregated to the Pontifical Society for Priestly Vocations, 1951. *Serran*, bimonthly. 21,000 members in 673 clubs in 35 countries. Exec. Dir., John W. Woodward.

Slovak Catholic Federation (1911): 301 S. State St.,

Clarks Summit, PA 18411; (570) 585-7382; www. slovakcatholicfederation.org. Founded by Rev. Joseph Murgas to promote and coordinate religious activities among Slovak Catholic fraternal societies, religious communities and Slovak ethnic parishes in their effort to address themselves to the special needs of Slovak Catholics in the U.S. and Canada. Pres., Rev. Philip A. Altavilla.

Slovak Catholic Sokol (1905): 205 Madison St., Passaic, NJ 07055; (800) 886-7656; www.slovak-catholicsokol.org. Fraternal benefit society. *Slovak Catholic Falcon*, weekly. 38,000 members.

Society for the Propagation of the Faith (1822): 70 West 36th St., 8th Floor, New York, NY 10018; (212) 563-8700; www.worldmissions-catholic-church.org. Established in all dioceses. Church's principal instrument for promoting mission awareness and generating financial support for the missions. General fund for ordinary and extraordinary subsidies for all mission dioceses. Is subject to Congregation for the Evangelization of Peoples. Mission, four times a year; *Director's Newsletter*, monthly. Nat. Dir., Fr. Andrew Small, O.M.I.

Society of St. Monica (1986): 215 Falls Ave., Cuyahoga Falls, OH 44221. Confident, daily prayer for the return of inactive Catholics and Catholics who have left the Church. More than 10,000 members worldwide. Founder and Spir. Dir., Fr. Dennis M. McNeil.

Society of St. Peter Apostle (1889): 70 West 36th St., 8th Floor, New York, NY 10018; (212) 563-8700; www.world missions-catholicchurch.org. Church's central fund for support of seminaries, seminarians and novices in all mission dioceses. Nat. Dir., Fr. Andrew Small, O.M.I.

Society of the Divine Attributes (1974): 2905 Castlegate Ave., Pittsburgh, PA 15226; (412) 456-3114. Contemplative prayer society. 3,000 members worldwide (lay, clerical and religious). Spir. Dir. Rev. Ronald D. Lawler, OFM Cap.

Spiritual Life Institute of America (1960): Box 219, Crestone, CO 81131; (719) 256-4778; www.spirituallifeinstitute.org. An eremetical movement to foster the contemplative spirit in America. *Forefront*, seasonal. Founder, Fr. William McNamara, O.C.D. Second foundation: Nova Nada, Primitive Wilderness Hermitage, Kemptville, Nova Scotia, Canada B0W 1Y0. Third foundation, Holy Hill Hermitage, Skreen, Co. Sligo, Ireland.

Support Our Aging Religious (SOAR) (1986): 1400 Spring St., Suite 320, Silver Spring, MD 20910-2755; (301) 589-9811; www.soar-usa.org. Laity-led campaign to raise funds for retired religious. Pres., Timothy P. Hamer.

Theresians of the United States (1961): 1237 W. Monroe, Springfield, IL 62704; (217) 726-5484; www.theresians.org. Spiritual, educational and ministerial organization of Christian women. Exec. Dir., Victoria S. Schmidt. International division: Theresian World Ministry (1971), same address.

United Societies of U.S.A. (1903): 613 Sinclair St., McKeesport, PA 15132. *Prosvita-Enlightenment*, bimonthly newspaper. 3,755 members.

United States Catholic Historical Society (1884): St. Joseph's Seminary, 201 Seminary Ave., Yonkers, NY 10704; (914) 337-8381; www.uschs.com. Exec. Vice-Pres., John T. Gildea.

Western Catholic Union (1877): 510 Maine St., Quincy, IL 62301; (217) 223-9721; www.wculife.com. 19,000 members. A fraternal benefit society. *Western Catholic Union Record*, quarterly. Pres., Mark A. Wiewel.

Women for Faith and Family (1984): P.O. Box 8326, St. Louis, MO 63132; (314) 863-8385; www.wf-f.org. An international movement to promote Catholic teachings especially on all issues involving the family and roles for women. 60,000 signers worldwide of the Affirmation for Catholic Women. Members sign an eight-point statement of fidelity to the Church. *Voices*, quarterly. Dir., Helen Hull Hitchcock.

Word on Fire (1999): 1167 Asbury Ave, Winnetka, IL 60093; (847) 224-4670; www.wordonfire.org; a global media organization in support of Catholic evangelical preaching, particularly the work of Father Robert Barron. Contact: Nancy Ross.

World Apostolate of Fatima, USA (The Blue Army of Our Lady of Fatima, 1947): P.O. Box 976, Washington, NJ 07882; (908) 689-1700; www.bluearmy.com. Soul, bimonthly; Hearts Aflame, quarterly. U.S. branch of the World Apostolate of Fatima. Promote the Fatima Message. Fatima shrine. Exec. Dir.: Michael La Corte.

Worldwide Seminarian Support, Inc. (1993) Northeast 28th Ave. Unit C, Portland, Oregon 97232; Tel: 888-437-8508; www.SeminarianSupport.org. To raise financial support for Catholic seminarians worldwide in need of educational funding. President John L. Becker Jr.

Young Ladies' Institute (1887): 1111 Gough St., San Francisco, CA 94109-6606; (415) 346-4367. *Voice of YLI*, bimonthly. 13,000 members. Pres., Joan Vandehey.

Young Men's Institute (1883): YMI Grand Council, P.O. Box 281047 San Francisco, CA 94128-1047; (800-964-9646); www.ymiusa.org. *Institute Journal*, bimonthly. 4,500 members. Grand Sec., Mike Amato.

PERSONAL PRELATURE OF THE HOLY SEE: OPUS DEI

Founded in Madrid in 1928 by Msgr. Josemaría Escrivá de Balaguer (beatified in 1992 and canonized in October 2002), Opus Dei has the aim of spreading throughout all sectors of society a profound awareness of the universal call to holiness and apostolate (of Christian witness and action) in the ordinary circumstances of life, and, more specifically, through one's professional work. On Nov. 28, 1982, Pope John Paul II established Opus Dei as a personal prelature with the full title, Prelature of the Holy Cross and Opus Dei. The 2014 edition of the *Annuario Pontificio* reported that the prelature had 2,073 priests (38 newly ordained) and 328 major seminarians. Also, there were 90,502 lay persons – men and women, married and single, of every class and social condition — of about 80 nationalities, as well as 1,961 churches and pastoral centers.

Further, the prelature operates the Pontifical University of the Holy Cross (Pontificia Università della Santa Croce) in Rome; it was established in 1985 and received approval as a pontifical institution in 1995. Courses of study include theology, philosophy, canon law, and social communications.

In the United States, members of Opus Dei, along with cooperators and friends, conduct apostolic works corporately in major cities in the East and Midwest, Texas and on the West Coast. Elsewhere, corporate works include universities, vocational institutes, training schools for farmers and numerous other apostolic initiatives. Opus Dei information offices are located at: 99 Overlook Cir., New Rochelle, NY 10804; (914) 235-6128 (office of the New York chaplain); and 655 Levering Ave., Los Angeles, CA 90024; (310) 208-0941; www.opusdei.org.

KNIGHTS OF COLUMBUS

The Knights of Columbus, a fraternal benefit society of Catholic men, is a family service organization founded by Fr. Michael J. McGivney and chartered by the General Assembly of Connecticut on Mar. 29, 1882.

Currently, there are over 1.8 million Knights, more than ever before in the Order's history. Together with their families, the Knights are nearly 6 million strong. From the first local council in New Haven, the Order has grown to more than 13,485 councils in the United States, Canada, Mexico, the Philippines, Puerto Rico, Cuba, the Dominican Republic, Panama, the Virgin Islands, Guatemala, Guam, Saipan, and Poland. The Knights of Columbus insurance program passed a major milestone when total insurance in force exceeded $90 billion in June 2013.

In keeping with their general purpose to be of service to the Church, the Knights and their families are active in many apostolic works and community programs. The Knights cooperate with the U.S. bishops in pro-life activities and religious liberty issues. According to the Knights' Annual Survey of Fraternal Activity for the year ending Dec. 31, 2013, record amounts of money and hours — more than $170 million and 70.5 million hours — were donated to charitable causes. The Knights financial contribution for the year grew by more than $10 million. Contributions increased for the 14th consecutive year. The number of volunteer service hours 2013 by 421,071 hours over the 2012 total. At an average value of $22.55 per service hour as estimated by Independent Sector, the value of the Knights' volunteer service last year was nearly $1.6 billion. Cumulative figures show that during the past decade the Knights of Columbus donated $1.5 billion to charity and 683 million hours of volunteer service in support of charitable initiatives. In 2014, the Knights pledged an initial $500,000 and will match an additional $500,000 in donations from the public to assist persecuted Christians in Iraq.

The Knights of Columbus headquarters address is One Columbus Plaza, New Haven, CT 06510-3326; (203) 752-4350; www.kofc.org. The Grand Knight is Carl Anderson.

Catholic Social Services

Catholic Charities USA (formerly National Conference of Catholic Charities): 66 Canal Center Plaza, Ste. 600, Alexandria, VA 22314; (703) 549-1390; www.catholiccharitiesusa.org. Founded in 1910 by Most Rev. Thomas J. Shahan and Rt. Rev. Msgr. William J. Kerby in cooperation with lay leaders of the Society of St. Vincent de Paul to help advance and promote the charitable programs and activities of Catholic community and social service agencies in the United States. As the central and national organization for this purpose, it services a network of more than 1,400 agencies and institutions by consultation, information and assistance in planning and evaluating social service programs under Catholic auspices.

Diocesan member agencies provide shelter, food, counseling, services to children, teen parents and the elderly, and a variety of other services to people in need — without regard to religion, gender, age or national origin. Each year millions of people receive help from Catholic Charities; in 2005 (the latest statistics available), more than $32 million were spent in activities by Catholic Charities agencies. In addition, Catholic Charities is an advocate for persons and families in need.

Catholic Charities USA serves members through national and regional meetings, training programs, literature and social policy advocacy on the national level. It is charged by the U.S. bishops with responding to disasters in this country. Catholic Charities USA's president represents North America before *Caritas Internationalis*, the international conference of Catholic Charities, and thus maintains contact with the Catholic Charities movement throughout the world. Publications include *Charities USA*, a quarterly membership magazine, and a directory of U.S. Catholic Charities agencies and institutions. Pres., Fr. Larry Snyder.

Society of St. Vincent de Paul, Council of the United States (originally called the Conference of Charity): National Council, 58 Progress Parkway, St. Louis, MO 63043; (314) 576-3993; www.svdpuscouncil.org. An association of Catholic lay men and women devoted to personal service to the poor through the spiritual and corporal works of mercy. The first conference was formed at Paris in 1833 by Bl. Frederic Ozanam and his associates.

The first conference in the U.S. was organized in 1845 at St. Louis. There are now approximately 4,400 units of the society in this country, with a membership of more than 60,000. The society operates world wide in more than 130 countries and has more than 800,000 members.

Besides person-to-person assistance, increasing emphasis is being given to stores and rehabilitation workshops of the society through which persons with marginal income can purchase refurbished goods at minimal cost. Handicapped persons are employed in renovating goods and store operations. The society also operates food centers, shelters, criminal justice and other programs. Publications include *The Ozanam News*, a biannual membership magazine, and *The United States Councilor*, a quarterly newsletter. Exec. Dir., Roger Playwin.

Catholic Health Association of the United States (CHA): National Headquarters, 4455 Woodson Road, St. Louis, MO 63134; (314) 427-2500; www.chausa.org. Represents more than 1,200 Catholic-sponsored facilities and organizations, works with its members to promote justice and compassion in healthcare, influence public policy, shape a continuum of care through integrated delivery, and strengthen ministry presence and influence in the U.S. healthcare system. CHA supports and strengthens the Catholic health ministry by being a catalyst through research and development (leading edge tools for sustaining a faithbased ministry in price competitive markets), education and facilitation (annual assembly, conferences, and other methods for engaging the ministry), and advocacy (a unity ministry voice for public policy). CHA members make up the nation's largest group of not-for-profit healthcare facilities under a single form of sponsorship. Pres., Sr. Carol Keehan, DC.

National Association of Catholic Chaplains: 3501 S. Lake Dr., Milwaukee, WI 53207; (414) 483-4898. Founded in 1965. Membership is over 3,500.

SOCIAL SERVICE ORGANIZATIONS

(See separate article for a listing of facilities for the handicapped.)

The Carroll Center for the Blind (formerly the Catholic Guild for All the Blind): 770 Centre St., Newton, MA 02458; (617) 969-6200; www.carroll.org. The center conducts diagnostic evaluation and rehabilitation programs for blind people over 16 years of age, and provides computer training and other services. Pres., Rachel Rosenbaum.

International Catholic Deaf Association: 8002 S. Sawyer Rd., Darian, IL 60561; TTY (630) 887-9472. Established by deaf adults in Toronto, Canada, in 1949, the association has more than 8,000 members in 130 chapters, mostly in the U.S. It is the only international lay association founded and controlled by deaf Catholic adults. The ICDA publishes *The Deaf Catholic*, bimonthly, sponsors regional conferences, workshops and an annual convention. Pres., Kathleen Kush.

National Apostolate for Inclusion Ministry (NAfIM): P.O. Box 218, Riverdale, MD, 20738; (301) 699-9500; www.nafim.org. Formerly known as the National Apostolate for Persons with Mental Retardation (NAPMR). Established in 1968 to promote the full participation by persons with mental retardation in the life of the Church. Exec. Dir., Barbara Lampe.

National Catholic Office for the Deaf: 7202 Buchanan St., Landover Hills, MD 20784; (301) 577-1684; www.ncod.org. Formally established in 1971, at Washington, DC, to provide pastoral service to those who teach deaf children and adults, to the parents of deaf children, to pastors of deaf persons, and to organizations of the deaf. Publishes *Vision*, a quarterly magazine. Exec. Dir., Msgr. Glenn Nelson.

National Catholic Office Partnership on Disability (NCPD): 415 Michigan Ave., N.E., Suite 240, Washington, DC 20017; (202) 529-2933; www. ncpd.org. NCPD's mission is to provide resources and consultation to a national network of diocesan directors who oversee access and inclusion at the parish level; to collaborate with other national Catholic organizations, advocating for inclusion within all their programs and initiatives and to work with Catholic organizations addressing the concerns and needs of those with various disabilities. Established in 1982 as a result of the 1978 Pastoral Statement of the U.S. Catholic Bishops on People with Disabilities., the office continues to press for words and actions which promote meaningful participation and inclusion at all levels of the Church. Exec. Dir., Mary Jane Owen, M.S.W.

Xavier Society for the Blind: 154 E. 23rd St., New York, NY 10010-4595; (212) 473-7800; www. xaviersociety.com. Founded in 1900 by Rev. Joseph Stadelman, S.J., it is a center for publications for the blind and partially sighted. Chair. Fr. John Sheehan, S.J.

OTHER SOCIAL SERVICES

Cancer Hospitals or Homes: The following homes or hospitals specialize in the care of cancer patients. Capacities are in parentheses.

Our Lady of Perpetual Help Home, Servants of Relief for Incurable Cancer, 760 Pollard Blvd., S.W., Atlanta, GA 30315; (404) 688-9515 (52).

Rose Hawthorne Lathrop Home, Servants of Relief for Incurable Cancer, 1600 Bay St., Fall River, MA 02724; (508) 673-2322 (35).

Our Lady of Good Counsel Home, Servants of Relief for Incurable Cancer, 2076 St. Anthony Ave., St. Paul, MN 55104; (651) 646-2797.

Calvary Hospital, Inc., 1740 Eastchester Rd., Bronx, NY 10461; (718) 863-6900 (200). Operated in connection with Catholic Charities, Department of Health and Hospitals, Archdiocese of New York.

St. Rose's Home, Servants of Relief for Incurable Cancer, 71 Jackson St., New York, NY 10002; (212) 677-8132 (60).

Rosary Hill Home, Servants of Relief for Incurable Cancer, 600 Linda Ave., Hawthorne, NY 10532; (914) 769-0114 (72).

Holy Family Home, Servants of Relief for Incurable Cancer, 6753 State Rd., Parma, OH 44134; (440) 845-7700; www.cle-dioc.org (50).

Sacred Heart Free Home for Incurable Cancer, Servants of Relief for Incurable Cancer, 1315 W. Hunting Park Ave., Philadelphia, PA 19140; (215) 329-3222 (45).

Substance Abuse: Facilities for substance abuse (alcohol and other drugs) include:

Daytop Village, Inc., 54 W. 40th St., New York, NY 10018; (212) 354-6000; www.daytop.org. Twenty-eight residential and ambulatory sites in New York, New Jersey, Pennsylvania, Florida, Texas and California. Msgr. William B. O'Brien, president.

Good Shepherd Gracenter, Convent of the Good Shepherd, 1310 Bacon St., San Francisco, CA 94134; (415) 586-2822. Residential program for chemically dependent women.

New Hope Manor, 35 Hillside Rd., Barryville, NY 12719; fax (914) 557-6603. Residential substance abuse treatment center for teen-age girls and women ages 13-40. Residential; half-way house and after-care program totaling 6 months or more.

St. Joseph's Hospital, L.E. Phillips Libertas Center for the Chemically Dependent, 2661 County Road, Hwy. I, Chippewa Falls, WI 54729; (715) 723-1811 (46). Residential and outpatient. Adult and adolescent programs. Hospital Sisters of the Third Order of St. Francis.

St. Joseph's Hospital (Chippewa Falls, WI) Libertas Center for the Treatment of Chemical Dependency, 1701 Dousman St., Green Bay, WI 54302 (23). Residental and outpatient adolescent programs. Hospital Sisters of the Third Order of St. Francis.

St. Luke's Addiction Recovery Services, 7707 NW 2nd Ave., Miami, FL 33150; (305) 795-0077; www.catholiccharitiesadm.org/stluke. A program of Catholic Community Services, Miami. Adult residential and family outpatient recovery services for drug, alcohol addiction and DUI.

Miami Substance Abuse Prevention Programs, 7707 N.W. Second Ave., Miami, FL 33150; (305) 795-0077; www.catholiccharitiesadm.org/stluke. Trains parents, youth, priests and teachers as prevention volunteers in the area of substance abuse.

Transitus House, 1830 Wheaton St., Chippewa Falls, WI 54729; (715) 723-1155. Two programs for chemically dependent: adult intensive residential (15 beds, women); adolescent intensive residential (5 beds, girls 15-18 yrs.). Hospital Sisters of the Third Order of St. Francis.

Matt Talbot Inn, 2270 Professor Ave., Cleveland, OH 44113; (216) 781-0288. Two programs: Chemical dependency Residential Treatment/Halfway House (capacity 27) and outpatient treatment/aftercare. Serves male clients 18 years and over.

Sacred Heart Rehabilitation Center, Inc., 2203 St. Antoine, Detroit, MI 48201 (admissions/assessment, outpatient). 400 Stoddard Rd., P.O. Box 41038, Memphis, MI 48041 (12 beds, detoxification; 70 beds residential treatment). 28573 Schoenherr, Warren, MI 48093 (outpatient). All facilities serve male and female clients 18 and over.

Straight and Narrow, Inc., 396 Straight St.,

Paterson, NJ 07501. Facilities and services include (at various locations): Straight and Narrow Hospital (Mount Carmel Guild), substance abuse, detoxification (20 beds); Alpha House for Drug and Alcohol Rehabilitation (women; 30 beds — 25 adults, 5 children); Dismas House for Drug and Alcohol Rehabilitation (men; 78 beds); The Guild for Drug and Alcohol Rehabilitation (men, 56 beds); juvenile residential units; outpatient services and facility; three halfway houses; counseling services; employment assistance; intoxicated driver's resource center; medical day care center (available to HIV infected persons and persons diagnosed with AIDS); methadone clinic.

The National Catholic Council on Alcoholism and Related Drug Problems, Inc., 1550 Hendrickson St., Brooklyn, NY 11234. Offers educational material to those involved in pastoral ministry on ways of dealing with problems related to alcoholism and medication dependency.

Convicts: Priests serve as full- or part-time chaplains in penal and correctional institutions throughout the country. Limited efforts have been made to assist in the rehabilitation of released prisoners in Halfway House establishments.

• *Dining Rooms:* Facilities for homeless: Representative of places where meals are provided, and in some cases lodging and other services as well, are:

St. Anthony Foundation, 121 Golden Gate Ave., San Francisco, CA 94102; (415) 241-2600; www.stanthonyfdn. org. Founded in 1950 by the Franciscan Friars. Multiprogram social service agency serving people who are poor and homeless. Dining room serves up to 2,100 meals daily; more than 25 million since its founding. Other services include free clothing and furniture; free medical clinic; residential drug and alcohol rehabilitation programs; employment program; emergency shelter, housing and daytime facility for homeless women; residence for low-income senior women; free hygiene services; case management for seniors; social services.

St. Vincent de Paul Free Dining Room, 675 23rd St., Oakland, CA 94612; (510) 451-7676. Administered by Daughters of Charity of St. Vincent de Paul, under sponsorship of St. Vincent de Paul Society. Hot meals served at lunch time 7 days a week. Also provides counseling, referral/information services.

St. Vincent's Dining Room, P.O. Box 5099, Reno, NV 89513; (775) 329-5363. St. Vincent Dining Room, 1501 Las Vegas Blvd., Las Vegas, NV 89101. Structured program for 275 men in which job development office works with homeless to enable them to find employment. For non-residents, there is a hot meal every day at noon. Emergency overnight shelter facility for families, women and men.

Good Shepherd Center, Little Brothers of the Good Shepherd, 218 Iron St. S.W., P.O. Box 749, Albuquerque, NM 87103; (505) 243-2527.

Holy Name Centre for Homeless Men, Inc., 18 Bleecker St., New York, NY 10012. A shelter for alcoholic, homeless men. Provides social services and aid to transients and those in need. Affiliated with New York Catholic Charities.

St. Francis Inn, 2441 Kensington Ave., Philadelphia, PA 19125. Serves hot meals. Temporary shelter for men. Day center for women. Thrift shop.

St. John's Hospice for Men, staffed by Little

Brothers of the Good Shepherd, 1221 Race St., Philadelphia, PA 19107. Hot meals served daily; 36-bed shelter; clothing distribution, showers, mail distribution, drug/alcohol rehabilitation and work programs. Good Shepherd Program of St. John's Hospice, 1225 Race St., Philadelphia, PA 19107. Ten-bed facility for homeless men with AIDS.

Camillus House, Little Brothers of the Good Shepherd, P.O. Box 11829, Miami, FL 33101; (305) 374-1065; www.camillus.org. Free comprehensive services for the poor and homeless including daily dinner; night lodging for 70; clothing distribution; showers; mail distribution; drug/alcohol rehabilitation program. Forty-eight units of single-room housing for employed formerly homeless women and men who have completed drug and alcohol rehabilitation programs.

Camillus Health Concern, P.O. Box 12408, Miami, FL 33101; (305) 577-4840. Free comprehensive medical and social services for the homeless.

• *Shelters:* Facilities for runaways, the abused, exploited and homeless include:

Anthony House, supported by St. Anthony's Guild (*see* Index). 38 E. Roosevelt Ave., Roosevelt, NY 11575 (with St. Vincent de Paul Society — for homeless men). 128 W. 112th St., New York, NY 10026 (emergency food and clothing). 6215 Holly St., P.O. Box 880, Zellwood, FL 32798 (for migrant workers and their families).

Good Shepherd Shelter-Convent of the Good Shepherd. Office, 2561 W. Venice Blvd., Los Angeles, CA 90019; (323) 737-6111. Non-emergency long-term shelter for battered women and their children.

Covenant House, 346 W. 17th St., New York, NY 10011; (212) 727-4973. Pres., Sr. Mary Rose McGeady, D.C. Provides crisis care — food, shelter, clothing, medical treatment, job placement and counseling — for homeless youth without regard to race, creed, color and national origin. Locations: New York, New Jersey (Newark, Atlantic City), Houston, Ft. Lauderdale, New Orleans, Anchorage, Los Angeles, Detroit, Orlando, Washington, DC; Toronto (Canada), Tegucigalpa (Honduras), Guatemala City (Guatemala), Mexico City (Mexico).

Crescent House, 1000 Howard Ave., Suite 1200, New Orleans, LA 70113. Provides temporary shelter, counseling and advocacy for battered women and their children.

The Dwelling Place, 409 W. 40th St., New York, NY 10018; (212) 564-7887. For homeless women 30 years of age and over.

Gift of Hope, Missionaries of Charity, 724 N.W. 17th St., Miami, FL 33136; (305) 326-0032. Shelter for women and children; soup kitchen for men.

House of the Good Shepherd, 1114 W. Grace St., Chicago, IL 60613; (773) 935-3434. For abused women with children.

Mercy Hospice, 334 S. 13th St., Philadelphia, PA 19107; (215) 545-5153. Temporary shelter and relocation assistance for homeless women and children.

Mt. Carmel House, Carmelite Sisters, 471 G Pl., N.W., Washington, DC 20001. For homeless women.

Ozanam Inn, 843 Camp St., New Orleans, LA 70130. Under sponsorship of the St. Vincent de Paul Society. Hospice for homeless men.

St. Christopher Inn, P.O. Box 150, Graymoor,

Garrison, NY 10524; (845) 424-3616; www.atonementfriars.org. Temporary shelter (21 days) for alcohol- and drug-free homeless and needy men.

Siena-Francis House, Inc., P.O. Box 217 D.T.S., Omaha, NE 68102. Two units, both at 1702 Nicholas St., Omaha, NE 68101; (402) 341-1821. Siena House (for homeless and abused women or women with children; provides 24-hour assistance and advocacy services); and Francis House (temporary shelter for homeless men). Also at this location: a 50-bed residential substance abuse program.

• *Unwed Mothers*: Residential and care services for unwed mothers are available in many dioceses.

FACILITIES FOR RETIRED AND AGED PERSONS

Sources: *Catholic Almanac* survey, *The Official Catholic Directory.*

This list covers residence, health care and other facilities for the retired and aged under Catholic auspices. Information includes name, type of facility if not evident from the title, address, and total capacity (in parentheses); unless noted otherwise, facilities are for both men and women. Many facilities for the aged offer intermediate nursing care.

Alabama: Allen Memorial Home (skilled nursing), 735 S. Washington Ave., Mobile 36603; (251) 433-2642 (119).

Cathedral Place Apartments (retirement complex), 351 Conti St., Mobile 36602; (334) 434-1590 (184).

Mercy Medical (acute rehabilitation hospital, skilled and post-acute nursing, hospice, home Health and assisted and independent living), P.O. Box 1090, Daphne 36526; (334) 626-2694 (162). Not restricted to elderly.

Sacred Heart Residence Little Sisters of the Poor, 1655 McGill Ave., Mobile 36604; (251) 476-6335 (84).

Seton Haven (retirement complex), 3721 Wares Ferry Rd., Montgomery 36193; (334) 272-4000 (114).

Arizona: Guadalupe Senior Village, 222 W. Thomas Rd., Ste. 214, Phoenix, 85103; (602) 406-6218.

California: Alexis Apartments of St. Patrick's Parish, 756 Mission St. 94103; 390 Clementina St., San Francisco 94103; (415) 495-3690 (240).

Casa Manana Inn, 3700 N. Sutter St., Stockton 95204; (209) 466-4046 (162). Non-profit housing for low-income elderly over 62.

Cathedral Plaza, 1551 Third Ave., San Diego 92101; (619) 234-0093 (222 apartments).

Guadalupe Plaza, 4142 42nd St., San Diego 92105; (619) 584-2414 (147 apartments).

Jeanne d'Arc Manor, 85 S. Fifth St., San Jose 95112; (408) 288-7421 (145). For low income elderly and handicapped.

La Paz Villas, P.O. Box 1962, Palm Desert 92261; (760) 772-1382 (24 units).

Little Flower Haven (residential care facility for retired), 8585 La Mesa Blvd., La Mesa 91941; (619) 466-3163 (85).

Little Sisters of the Poor, St. Anne's Home, 300 Lake St., San Francisco 94118; (415) 751-6510 (90).

Little Sisters of the Poor, Jeanne Jugan Residence, 2100 South Western Ave., San Pedro 90732; (310) 548-0625 (100).

Madonna Senior Center and Residence, St. Anthony Foundation, 350 Golden Gate Ave., San Francisco 94102; (415) 592-2864; www.stanthonysf.org (37).

Mercy McMahon Terrace (residential care facility), 3865 J St., Sacramento 95816; (916) 733-6510; www.mercysacramento.org (118 units).

Mercy Retirement and Care Center, 3431 Foothill Blvd., Oakland 94601; (510) 534-8540; www.mercy-retirementcenter.org (59).

Mother Gertrude Home for Senior Citizens, 11320 Laurel Canyon Blvd., San Fernando 91340; (818) 898-1546 (98).

Nazareth House (residential and skilled care), 2121 N. 1st St., Fresno 93703; (559) 237-2257 (65 residential; 39 skilled nursing).

Nazareth House (residential and skilled nursing), 3333 Manning Ave., Los Angeles 90064; (310) 839-2361 (123).

Nazareth House (retirement home), 245 Nova Albion Way, San Rafael 94903; (415) 479-8282 (151).

Nazareth House Retirement Home, 6333 Rancho Mission Rd., San Diego 92108; (619) 563-0480 (354).

O'Connor Woods, 3400 Wagner Heights Rd., Stockton 95209; (209) 956-3400; www.oconnorwoods.org, (48).

Our Lady of Fatima Villa (skilled nursing facility), 20400 Saratoga-Los Gatos Rd., Saratoga 95070; (408) 741-2950; www.fatimavilla.org; (85).

St. Bernardine Plaza (retirement home), 550 W. 5th St., San Bernardino 92401; (909) 888-0153 (150 units).

St. John of God (retirement and care center), 2468 S. St. Andrew Place, Los Angeles 90018; (323) 731-0641; www.hospitallers.org, (215).

Vigil Light Apartments, 1945 Long Dr., Santa Rosa 95405; (707) 544-2810 (54).

Villa Scalabrini (retirement center and skilled nursing Care), 10631 Vinedale St., Sun Valley 91352; (818) 768-6500; www.villascalabrini.com (130 residence; 58 skilled nursing).

Villa Siena (residence and skilled nursing care), 1855 Miramonte Ave., Mountain View 94040; (650) 961-6484; www.villasiena.org (56, residence; 20, skilled nursing care).

Colorado: Francis Heights, Inc., 2626 Osceola St., Denver 80212; (303) 433-6268 (384 units; 411 residents).

Gardens at St. Elizabeth (congregate housing and assisted living), 2835 W. 32nd Ave., Denver 80211; (303) 964-2005 (320).

Little Sisters of the Poor, 3629 W. 29th Ave., Denver 80211; (303) 433-7221 (70).

Connecticut: Augustana Homes (residence), Simeon Rd., Bethel 06801; (203) 743-2508.

Carmel Ridge, 6454 Main St., Trumbull 06611; (203) 261-2229.

Holy Family Home and Shelter, Inc., 88 Jackson St., P.O. Box 884, Willimantic 06226; (860) 423-7719; www.holyfamilywillimantic.org (155).

Monsignor Bojnowski Manor, Inc. (skilled nursing facility), 50 Pulaski St., New Britain 06053; (860) 229-0336 (60).

Notre Dame Convalescent Home, 76 West Rocks Rd., Norwalk 06851; (203) 847-5893 (60).

St. Joseph Living Center, 14 Club Rd., Windham 06280; (860) 456-1107 (120).

St. Joseph's Manor (health care facility; home for aged), Carmelite Srs. for Aged and Infirm, 6448 Main St., Trumbull 06611; (203) 268-6204; www.harborsidehealthcare.com; (297).

St. Joseph's Residence, Little Sisters of the Poor, 1365 Enfield St., Enfield 06082; (860) 741-0791 (84).

St. Lucian's Home for the Aged, 532 Burritt St., New Britain 06053; (860) 223-2123 (42).

Saint Mary's Home (residence and health care facility) 2021 Albany Ave., W. Hartford 06117; (860) 570-8200 (26).

Delaware: The Antonian, 1701 W. 10th St., Wilmington 19805; (302) 421-3758 (136 apartments).

Jeanne Jugan Residence, Little Sisters of the Poor, 185 Salem Church Rd., Newark 19713; (302) 368-5886 (80).

Marydale Retirement Village, 135 Jeandell Dr., Newark 19713; (302) 368-2784 (118 apartments).

St. Patrick's House, Inc., 115 E. 14th St., Wilmington 19801; (302) 654-6908 (12).

District of Columbia: Jeanne Jugan Residence-St. Joseph Villa, Little Sisters of the Poor, 4200 Harewood Rd., N.E., Washington 20017; (202) 269-1831; www.littlesistersofthepoorwashingtondc.org (97).

Florida: All Saints Home, 5888 Blanding Blvd., Jacksonville 32244; (904) 772-1220; www.allsaints.org (118).

Casa Calderon, Inc. (retirement apartments), 800 W. Virginia St., Tallahassee 32304; (850) 222-4026 (111).

Haven of Our Lady of Peace (assisted living and nursing home), 5203 N. 9th Ave., Pensacola 32504; (850) 477-0531 (89).

Palmer House, Inc., 1225 S.W. 107th Ave., Miami 33174; (305) 221-9566 (120 apartments).

St. Andrew Towers (retirement apartments), 2700 N.W. 99th Ave., Coral Springs 33065 (432).

St. Catherine Labouré (skilled and intermediate care), 1750 Stockton St., Jacksonville 32204; (904) 308-4700 (239).

St. Dominic Gardens (retirement apartments), 5849 N.W. 7th St., Miami 33126 (149 apartments).

St. Elizabeth Gardens, Inc. (retirement apartments), 801 N.E. 33rd St., Pompano Beach 33064 (150).

St. John's Rehabilitation Hospital and Nursing Center, Inc., 3075 N.W. 35th Ave., Lauderdale Lakes 33311.

Stella Maris House, Inc., 8636 Harding Ave., Miami Beach 33141 (136 apartments).

Illinois: Addolorata Villa (sheltered intermediate, skilled care facility; apartments), 555 McHenry Rd., Wheeling 60090; (847) 808-6168 (100 apartments).

Alvernia Manor (sheltered care), 13950 Main St., Lemont 60439; (630) 257-7721 (50).

Bishop Conway Residence, 1900 N. Karlov Ave., Chicago 60639; (773) 252-9941.

Carlyle Healthcare Center, 501 Clinton St., Carlyle 62231; (618) 594-3112 (131).

Carmelite Carefree Village, 8419 Bailey Rd., Darien 60561; (630) 960-4060 (98).

Cortland Manor Retirement Home, 1900 N. Karlov, Chicago 60639; (773) 235-3670 (48).

Holy Family Nursing and Rehabilitation Center, 2380 Dempster, Des Plaines 60016; (847) 296-3335 (362).

Holy Family Villa (intermediate care facility), 12395 McCarthy Rd., Lemont 60439; (630) 257-7721 (50).

Jugan Terrace, Little Sisters of the Poor, 2300 N. Racine, Chicago 60614; (773) 935-9600 (50 apartments).

Little Sisters of the Poor, St. Joseph's Home for the Elderly, 80 W. Northwest Hwy., Palatine 60067; (847) 358-5700 (61).

Little Sisters of the Poor Center for the Aging, 2325 N. Lakewood Ave., Chicago 60614; (773) 935-9600 (71).

Marian Heights Apartments (elderly, handicapped), 20 Marian Heights Dr., Alton 62002; (618) 462-0363 (130).

Marian Park, Inc., 26 W. 171 Roosevelt Rd., Wheaton 60187; (630) 665-9100 (470).

Maryhaven, Inc. (skilled and intermediate care facility), 1700 E. Lake Ave., Glenview 60025; (847) 729-1300 (138).

Mayslake Village (retirement apartments), 1801 35th St., Oak Brook 60523; (630) 850-8232; www.mayslake.com (630 apartments).

Meredith Memorial Home, 16 S. Illinois St., Belleville 62220; (618) 233-8780 (86).

Merkle-Knipprath Countryside (apartments and nursing facility), 1190 E. 2900 N. Rd., Clifton 60927; (815) 694-2306 (130).

Mother Theresa Home (skilled, intermediate and sheltered care), 1270 Franciscan Dr., Lemont 60439; (630) 257-5801; www.franciscancommunities.com. (150).

Nazarethville (intermediate and sheltered care), 300 N. River Rd., Des Plaines 60016; (847) 297-5900; www.nazarethvilleshealth.com. (83).

Our Lady of Angels Retirement Home, 1201 Wyoming, Joliet 60435; (815) 725-6631; www.olaretirement.org (101).

Our Lady of the Snows, Apartment Community, 9500 West Illinois Highway 15, Belleville 62223; (618) 394-6400 (201).

Our Lady of Victory Nursing Home (intermediate and skilled care), 20 Briarcliff Lane, Bourbonnais 60914; (815) 937-2022 (107).

Pope John Paul Apartments (elderly and handicapped), 1 Pope John Paul Plaza, Springfield 62703; (217) 528-1771; www.dio.org (160).

Provena Cor Mariae Center (assisted living and nursing home), 3330 Maria Linden Dr., Rockford 61107; (815) 877-7416 (146).

Provena St. Anne Center (nursing home), 4405

Highcrest Rd., Rockford 61107; (815) 229-1999 (179).

Provena St. Joseph's Home for the Aged, 659 E. Jefferson St., Freeport 61032; (815) 232-6181 (120).

Provena Villa Franciscan (skilled care), 210 N. Springfield, Joliet 60435; (815) 725-3400; www. provenahealth.com.

Queen of Peace Center, 1910 Maple Ave., Lisle 60532; (630) 852-5360; www.qopc.net (32).

Red Bud Regional Nursing Home (skilled intermediary facility), 350 W. S. First St., Red Bud 62278; (618) 282-3891 (115).

Resurrection Nursing Pavilion (skilled care), 1001 N. Greenwood, Park Ridge 60068; (847) 692-5600 (295).

Resurrection Retirement Community, 7262 W. Peterson Ave., Chicago, 60631; (773) 792-7930; www.reshealth.org (472 apartments).

Rosary Hill Home (women), 9000 W. 81st St., Justice 60458; (708) 458-3040 (48).

St. Andrew Life Center (retirement residence), 7000 N. Newark Ave., Niles 60714; (847) 647-8332 (99).

St. Anne Place (retirement apartments), 4444 Brendenwood Rd., Rockford 61107; (815) 399-6167 (120).

St. Benedict Home, 6930 W. Touhy Ave., Niles 60714; (847) 647-0003. (99).

St. Elizabeth Home (residence), 704 W. Marion St., Joliet 60436; (815) 727-0125 (11). Group living for Senior women.

St. James Manor, 1251 East Richton Rd., Crete 60417; (708) 672-6700 (110).

St. Joseph's Home (sheltered and intermediate care), 3306 S. 6th St. Rd., Springfield 62703; (217) 529-5596 (110).

St. Joseph Home of Chicago, Inc. (skilled care), 2650 N. Ridgeway Ave., Chicago 60647; (773) 235-8600; www.franciscancommunities.com (173).

St. Patrick's Residence, 1400 Brookdale Rd., Naperville 60563-2125; (630) 416-6565; www.stpatricksresidence.org

Villa Scalabrini (sheltered, intermediate and skilled), 480 N. Wolf Rd., Northlake 60164; (708) 562-0040 (259).

Indiana: Albertine Home, 1501 Hoffman St., Hammond 46327; (219) 937-0575 (35).

Provena LaVerna Terrace, 517 N. Main St., Avilla 46710; (260) 897-2093 (51).

Provena Sacred Heart Home (comprehensive nursing), 515 N. Main St., Avilla 46710; (260) 897-2841, (133).

Regina Continuing Care Center (intermediate care Facility), 3900 Washington Ave., Evansville 47714; (812) 485-4226; www.stmarys.org (137).

St. Anne Home (Residential and Comprehensive nursing), 1900 Randallia Dr., Ft. Wayne 46805; (219) 484-5555 (264).

St. Anthony Home, Inc., 203 Franciscan Dr., Crown Point 46307; (219) 661-5100; www.stanthonyhome.com (219).

St. Augustine Home for the Aged, Little Sisters of the Poor, 2345 W. 86th St., Indianapolis 46260; (317) 872-6420 (92).

St. John's Home for the Aged, Little Sisters of the Poor, 1236 Lincoln Ave., Evansville 47714; (812)

464-3607 (70).

St. Paul Hermitage (residential and intermediate care nursing), 501 N. 17th Ave., Beech Grove 46107; (317) 786-2261; www.stpaulhermitage.org; (100).

Iowa: The Alverno Health Care Facility (nursing care), 849 13th Ave. N., Clinton 52732; (563) 242-1521; www.alvernohealthcare.com (194).

Bishop Drumm Retirement Center, 5837 Winwood Dr., Johnston 50131; (515) 270-1100 (64).

Hallmar-Mercy Medical Center, 701 Tenth St. S.E., Cedar Rapids 52403; (319) 369-4638 (57).

Holy Spirit Retirement Home (intermediate care), 1701 W. 25th St., Sioux City 51103; (712) 252-2726 (95).

Kahl Home for the Aged and Infirm (skilled and intermediate care facility), 1101 W. 9th St., Davenport 52804; (319) 324-1621; www.kahlhome-dav.com (135).

The Marian Home, 2400 6th Ave. North, Fort Dodge 50501; (515) 576-1138 (116).

St. Anthony Nursing Home (intermediate care), 406 E. Anthony St., Carroll 51401; (712) 792-3581 (79).

St. Francis Continuation Care and Nursing Home Center, Burlington 52601; (319) 752-4564 (170).

Kansas: Catholic Care Center (skilled and intermediate care facility), 6700 E. 45th St, Wichita 67226; (316) 744-2020 (294).

Mt. Joseph Senior Village (intermediate care facility), 1110 W. 11, Concordia 66901; (785) 143-1347 (16 apartments).

St. John Rest Home (nursing facility), 701 Seventh St., Victoria 67671; (785) 735-2208 (90).

St. John's New Horizons, 2225 Canterbury, Hays 67601; (785) 628-8742 (43).

Villa Maria, Inc. (intermediate care facility), 116 S. Central, Mulvane 67110; (316) 777-1129 (99).

Kentucky: Bishop Soenneker Personal Care Home, 9545 Ky. 144, Knottsville, KY 42366; (270) 281-4881 (55).

Carmel Home (residence, adult day care, respite care and nursing care), 2501 Old Hartford Rd., Owensboro 42303; (270) 683-0227 (101).

Carmel Manor (skilled, intermediate and personal care home), 100 Carmel Manor Rd., Ft. Thomas, 41075; (859) 781-5111; (145).

Madonna Manor Nursing Home, 2344 Amsterdam Rd., Villa Hills 41017; (606) 341-3981 (60).

Marian Home, 3105 Lexington Rd., Louisville 40206; (502) 893-0121 (69).

Nazareth Home, 2000 Newburg Rd., Louisville 40205; (502) 459-9681; www.nazhome.org (168).

St. Charles Care Center and Village, 500 Farrell Dr., Covington 41011; (606) 331-3224; www.stcharlescare.org (149). Nursing home; adult day health program. Independent living cottages (44); assisted living (60); independent living apartments (12).

Louisiana: Annunciation Inn, 1220 Spain St., New Orleans 70117; (504) 944-0512 (111).

Bethany M.H.S. Health Care Center (women),

P.O. Box 2308, Lafayette 70502; (337) 234-2459. (200).

Château de Notre Dame (residence and nursing home), 2832 Burdette St., New Orleans 70125; (504) 866-2741 (103).

Christopher Inn Apartments, 2110 Royal St., New Orleans 70116; (504) 949-0312 (144).

Christus St. Joseph's Home (nursing home), 2301 Sterlington Rd., Monroe 71211; (318) 323-3426 (150).

Consolata Home (nursing home), 2319 E. Main St., New Iberia 70560; (337) 365-8226 (114).

Haydel Heights Apartments, 4402 Reynes St., New Orleans 70126; (504) 242-4438 (65 units).

Lafon Nursing Home of the Holy Family, 6900 Chef Menteur Hwy., New Orleans 70126; (504) 246-1100 (171).

Metairie Manor, 4929 York St., Metairie 70001; (504) 456-1467 (287).

Nazareth Inn, 9630 Hayne Blvd., New Orleans 70127; (504) 241-9630 (158).

Ollie Steele Burden Manor (nursing home), 4250 Essen Lane, Baton Rouge 70809; (225) 926-0091 (184).

Our Lady of Prompt Succor Home, 954 East Prudhomme St., Opelousas 70570; (337) 948-3634 (80).

Our Lady's Manor, Inc., 402 Monroe St., Alexandria 71301; (318) 473-2560 (114).

Place Dubourg, 201 Rue Dubourg, LaPlace 70068; (504) 652-1981 (115).

Rouquette Lodge, 4300 Hwy 22, Mandeville 70471; (504) 626-5217 (51).

St. John Berchmans Manor, 3400 St. Anthony Ave., New Orleans 70122; (504) 943-9342 (157).

St. Margaret's Daughters Home (nursing home), 3525 Bienville St., New Orleans 70119; (504) 279-6414; www.stmargaretsno.org; (139).

St. Martin Manor, 1501 N. Johnson St., New Orleans 70116; (504) 945-7728 (145).

Villa St. Maurice 500 St. Maurice Ave., New Orleans 70117; (504) 277-8477 (193).

Villa St. Maurice II, 6101 Douglas St., New Orleans 70117; (504) 277-8731 (80).

Village du Lac, Inc., 1404 Carmel Ave., Lafayette 70501; (337) 234-5106 (200).

Wynhoven Apartments and Wynhoven II (residence for senior citizens), 1000 Howard Ave., Suite 100, New Orleans, 70113; (504) 596-3460 (375).

Maine: Deering Pavilion (apartments for senior citizens), 880 Forest Ave., Portland 04103; (207) 797-8777 (232 units).

Maison Marcotte (independent living community), 100 Campus Ave., Lewiston 04240; (207) 786-0062 (128 apartments).

Mt. St. Joseph Holistic Care Community, Highwood St., Waterville 04901; (207) 873-0705 (138).

St. Andre Health Care Facility, Inc. (nursing facility), 407 Pool St., Biddeford 04005; (207) 282-5171 (96).

St. Joseph's Rehabilitation and Residence (nursing care facility), 1133 Washington Ave., Portland 04103; (207) 797-0600; www.sjr-me.org. (200).

St. Marguerite D'Youville Pavilion, 102 Campus Ave., Lewiston 04240; (207) 777-4200 (280).

St. Xavier's Home (apartments), 199 Somerset St., Bangor 04401; (207) 942-4815 (19 units).

Seton Village, Inc., 1 Carver St., Waterville 04901;

(207) 873-0178 (140 housing units).

Maryland: Little Sisters of the Poor, St. Martin's Home (for the aged), 601 Maiden Choice Lane, Baltimore 21228; (410) 744-9367 (104).

Sacred Heart Home, 5805 Queens Chapel Rd., Hyattsville 20782; (301) 277-6500; www.sacredhearthome.org (102).

St. Joseph Nursing Home, 1222 Tugwell Dr., Baltimore 21228; (410) 747-0026 (51).

Villa Rosa Nursing Home, 3800 Lottsford Vista Rd., Mitchellville 20721; (301) 459-4700 (100).

Massachusetts: Catholic Memorial Home (nursing home), 2446 Highland Ave., Fall River 02720; (508) 679-0011 (300).

Don Orione Nursing Home, 111 Orient Ave., East Boston 02128; (617) 569-2100 (185).

D'Youville Manor (nursing home), 981 Varnum Ave., Lowell 01854; (978) 454-5681; www.dyouville.com (203).

Jeanne Jugan Pavilion, 190 Highland Ave., Somerville 02143; (617) 776-4420 (30).

Jeanne Jugan Residence, Little Sisters of the Poor (home for the elderly), 190 Highland Ave., Somerville 02143; (617) 776-4420; www.littlesistersofthepoor.org (84).

Madonna Manor (nursing home), 85 N. Washington St., N. Attleboro 02760; (508) 699-2740; www.dhfo.org (129).

Marian Manor, for the Aged and Infirm (nursing home), 130 Dorchester St., S. Boston, 02127; (617) 268-3333; www.marianmanor.org (366).

Marian Manor of Taunton (nursing home), 33 Summer St., Taunton 02780; (508) 822-4885 (184).

Maristhill Nursing Home, 66 Newton St., Waltham 02154; (781) 893-0240 (154).

MI Nursing/Restorative Center, 172 Lawrence St., Lawrence 01841; (978) 685-6321; www.mihcs.com (335).

Our Lady's Haven (nursing home), 71 Center St., Fairhaven 02719; (508) 999-4561; www.dhfo.org (158).

Sacred Heart Home (nursing home), 359 Summer St., New Bedford 02740; (508) 996-6751; www.dhfo.org (217).

St. Joseph Manor Health Care, Inc., 215 Thatcher St., Brockton 02302; (508) 583-5834 (118).

St. Joseph's Nursing Care Center, 321 Centre St., Dorchester, Boston 02122; (617) 825-6320 (191).

St. Patrick's Manor (nursing home), 863 Central St., Framingham 01701; (508) 879-8000; www.stpatricksmanor.org (460).

Michigan: Bishop Noa Home for Senior Citizens (nursing home and residence), 2900 3rd Ave. S., Escanaba 49829; (906) 786-5810 (123).

Lourdes Nursing Home (skilled facility), 2300 Watkins Lake Rd., Waterford 48328; (248) 674-2241; www.lourdescampus.com (108).

Marycrest Manor (skilled nursing facility), 15475 Middlebelt Rd., Livonia 48154; (313) 427-9175 (55).

Ryan Senior Residences of the Archdiocese of Detroit: Casa Maria, 600 Maple Vista, Imlay City 48444; (810) 724-6300 (84). Kundig Center, 3300 Jeffries Freeway, Detroit 48208; (313) 894-0555

(160). Lourdes Senior Community, 2450 Watkins Lake Rd., Waterford 48328; (248) 674-2241; www.lourdescampus.com (6). Marian-Oakland West, 29250 W. Ten Mile Rd., Farmington Hills 48336; (248) 474-7204 (87). Marian Place, 408 W. Front St., Monroe 48161; (734) 241-2414 (53). Marydale Center, 3147 Tenth Ave., Port Huron 48060; (810) 985-9683 (56). Maryhaven, 11350 Reeck Rd., Southgate 48195; (734) 287-2111 (90). Sanctuary at Clinton Villa, 17825 Fifteen Mile Rd., Clinton Twp. 48035; (586) 792-0358 (86). Stapleton Center, 9341 Agnes St., Detroit 48214; (313) 822-0397 (59). Villa Marie, 15131 Newburgh Rd., Livonia 48154; (734) 464-9494 (86). St. Ann's Home, (residence and nursing home), 2161 Leonard St. N.W., Grand Rapids 49504; (616) 453-7715; www.stannshome.com (140). St. Catherine House, 1641 Webb Ave., Detroit 48206; (313) 868-4505 (12). St. Elizabeth Briarbank (women, residence), 1315 N. Woodward Ave., Bloomfield Hills 48304; (248) 644-1011 (44).

St. Francis Home (nursing home), 915 N. River Rd., Saginaw 48609; (989) 781-3150 (100).

St. Joseph's Home, 4800 Cadieux Rd., Detroit 48224; (313) 882-3800 (104).

Minnesota: Alverna Apartments, 300 8th Ave. S.E., Little Falls 56345; (320) 632-1246; www.metroplainsmanagement.com (68).

Assumption Home, 715 North First St., Cold Spring 56320; (320) 685-4110 (34).

Benedictine Health Center, 935 Kenwood Ave., Duluth, MN 55811; (218) 723-6408; www.benedictinehealthcenter.org.

Divine Providence Community Home (skilled nursing care) and Lake Villa Maria Senior Housing, 702 Third Ave. N.W., Sleepy Eye 56085; (507) 794-5333 (58).

Franciscan Health Community, 1925 Norfolk Ave., St. Paul 55116; (651) 696-8400 (223).

John Paul Apartments, 200 8th Ave. N., Cold Spring 56320; (320) 685-4429 (61).

Little Sisters of the Poor, Holy Family Residence (skilled nursing and intermediate care), 330 S. Exchange St., St. Paul 55102; (651) 227-0336 (73). Independent living apartments (32).

Madonna Towers (retirement apartments and nursing home), 4001 19th Ave. N.W., Rochester 55901; (507) 288-3911; www.madonnatowers.org (184).

Mary Rondorf Retirement Home of Sacred Heart Parish, Inc., 222 5th St., N.E., Staples 56479; (218) 894-2124 (45). Board and lodging with special services.

Mother of Mercy Nursing Home and Retirement Center, 230 Church Ave., Box 676, Albany 56307; (320) 845-2195 (114).

Regina Nursing Home and Retirement Residence Center, 1175 Nininger Rd., Hastings 55033; (651) 480-6836; www.reginamedical.com. Nursing home (61); retirement home (43); boarding care (32). Admin., Juliane M. Saxon.

Sacred Heart Hospice (skilled nursing home, adult day care, home health care) 1200 Twelfth St. S.W., Austin 55912; (507) 433-1808 (59).

St. Ann's Residence, 330 E. 3rd St., Duluth 55805; (218) 727-8831; www.stanns.com (185).

St. Anne of Winona (skilled nursing home), 1347 W. Broadway, Winona 55987; (507) 454-3621; www.saintanneofwinona.org (74).

St. Benedict's Senior Community, 1810 Minnesota Blvd. S.E., St. Cloud 56304; (320) 654-2341; www.centracare.com (198 bed skilled nursing care; adult day care, respite care). Benedict Village(retirementt apartments), 2000 15th Ave. S.E., St. Cloud 56304; (320) 252-0010; www.centracare.com. Benedict Homes (Alzheimer residential care) and Benedict Court (assisted living), 1980 15th Ave. S.E., St. Cloud 56304; (320) 252-0010.

St. Benedict's Senior Community (independent and assisted living), 1301 East 7th St., Monticello, MN 55362; (763) 295-4051; www.centracare.com.

St. Elizabeth's Health Care Center, 1200 Grant Blvd., Wabasha 55981; (651) 565-4531; www.stelizabethswabasha.org (106).

St. Elizabeth's Medical Center, 626 Shields Ave., Wabasha, MN 55981; (651) 565-4581; www.stelizabethswabasha.org.

St. Francis Home, 2400 St. Francis Dr., Breckenridge 56520; (218) 643-3000; www.sfcare.org (124).

St. Mary's Regional Health Center, 1027 Washington Ave., Detroit Lakes 56501; (218) 847-5611 (100).

St. Otto's Care Center (nursing home), 920 S.E. 4th St., Little Falls 56345; (320) 632-9281 (150).

St. William's Nursing Home, P.O. Box 30, Parkers Prairie 56361; (218) 338-4671 (90).

Villa St. Vincent (skilled nursing home and residence), 516 Walsh St., Crookston 56716; (218) 281-3424. Skilled nursing home (80); special care unit (24); apartments (27); board and care (34).

West Wind Village, 1001 Scotts Ave., Morris 56267; (320) 589-1133; www.sfhs.org (128).

Westwood Senior Apartments, 925 Kenwood Ave., Duluth 55811; (218) 733-2238; www.westwoodduluth.org (70).

Mississippi: Notre Dame de la Mer Retirement Apartments, 292 Hwy. 90, Bay St. Louis 39520; (228) 467-2885 (61).

Santa Maria Retirement Apartments, 674 Beach Blvd., Biloxi, 39530; (228) 432-1289 (223).

Villa Maria Retirement Apartments, 921 Porter Ave., Ocean Springs 39564; (228) 875-8811 (225).

Missouri: Cathedral Square Towers, 444 W. 12th St., Kansas City 64105; (816) 471-6555 (167).

Chariton Apartments (retirement apartments), 4249 Michigan Ave., St. Louis 63111; (314) 352-7600 (122 units; 143 residents).

LaVerna Village Nursing Home, 904 Hall Ave., Savannah 64485; (816) 324-3185; lavernavillage.com (133).

Little Sisters of the Poor (home for aged), 3225 N. Florissant Ave., St. Louis 63107; (314) 421-6022; www;littlesistersofthepoorstlouis.org (114).

Mary, Queen and Mother Center (nursing care), 7601 Watson Rd., St. Louis 63119; (314) 961-8000; www.cardinalcarberry.org (230).

Mother of Good Counsel Home (skilled nursing, women), 6825 Natural Bridge Rd., Northwoods, 63121; (314) 383-4765; www.mogch.org (114).

Our Lady of Mercy Country Home, 2115 Maturana Dr., Liberty 64068; (816) 781-5711; www.ourladyofmercy.net (105).

Price Memorial skilled nursing facility, Forby Rd., P.O. Box 476, Eureka 63025; (636) 587-3200 (120).

St. Agnes Home-Assisted Living, 10341 Manchester Rd., Kirkwood 63122; (314) 965-7616; www.stagneshome.com (124).

St. Joseph Hill Infirmary, Inc., (nursing care facility, men), St. Joseph Road, Eureka 63025; (636) 587-3661 (120).

St. Joseph's Home (residential and intermediate care), 723 First Capitol Dr., St. Charles 63301; (314) 946-4140; (110).

St. Joseph's Home (residential and intermediate care facility), 1306 W. Main St., Jefferson City 65109; (573) 635-0166 (90).

Nebraska: Madonna Rehabilitation Hospital, 5401 South St., Lincoln 68506; (402) 489-7102; www.madonna.org (252).

Mercy Care Center (skilled nursing facility for chronic, complex and subacute levels of care and rehabilitation), 1870 S. 75th St., Omaha 68124; (402) 343-8500 (246).

Mercy Villa, 1845 S. 72nd St., Omaha 68124; (402) 391-6224.

Mt. Carmel Home, Keens Memorial (nursing home), 412 W. 18th St., Kearney 68847; (308) 237-2287 (75).

New Cassel Retirement Center, 900 N. 90th St., Omaha 68114; (402) 393-2277; www.newcassel.org (165).

St. Joseph's Rehabilitation and Care Center, 401 N. 18th St., Norfolk 68701; (402) 644-7375 (99).

St. Joseph's Retirement Community, 320 E. Decatur St., West Point 68788; (402) 372-3477 (90).

St. Joseph's Villa (nursing home), 927 7th St., David City 68632; (402) 367-3045; www.saintjosephvilla.org (65).

New Hampshire: Mount Carmel Healthcare Center, 235 Myrtle St., Manchester 03104; (603) 627-3811 (120).

St. Ann Home (nursing home), 195 Dover Point Rd., Dover 03820; (603) 742-2612 (54).

St. Francis Rehabilitation and Nursing Center (nursing home), 406 Court St., Laconia 03246; (603) 524-0466 (51).

St. Teresa Rehabilitation and Nursing Center (nursing home), 519 Bridge St., Manchester 03104; (603) 668-2373; www.nh-cc.org; (5).

St. Vincent de Paul Healthcare Center, 29 Providence Ave., Berlin 03570; (603) 752-1820 (80).

New Jersey: McCarrick Care Center, 15 Dellwood Lane, Somerset 08873; (732) 545-4200 (142).

Morris Hall (St. Joseph Skilled Nursing Center, St. Mary Assisted Living), 1 Bishops' Dr., Lawrenceville 08648-2050; (609) 896-0006; www.morrishall.org (100).

Mount St. Andrew Villa (residence), 55 W. Midland Ave., Paramus 07652; (201) 261-5950 (55).

Our Lady's Residence (nursing home), 1100 Clematis Ave., Pleasantville 08232; (609) 646-2450 (236).

St. Ann's Home for the Aged (akilled and intermediate nursing care home, women), 198 Old Bergen Rd., Jersey City 07305; (201) 433-0950; www.saintannshome.com; (106).

St. Francis Health Resort (residence), 122 Diamond Spring Rd., Denville 07834; (973) 627-5560; www.saintfrancisres.com (150).

St. Joseph's Home for the Elderly, Little Sisters of the Poor, 140 Shepherd Lane, Totowa 07512; (973) 942-0300 (134).

St. Joseph's Rest Home for Aged Women, 46 Preakness Ave., Paterson 07522; (973) 956-1921 (35).

St. Joseph's Assisted Living Residence, 1 St. Joseph Terr., Woodbridge, 07095; (732) 634-0004 (60).

St. Joseph's Nursing Home, 3 St. Joseph Terr., Woodbridge, 07095; (732) 750-0077.

St. Mary's, 210 St. Mary's Dr., Cherry Hill 08003; (856) 424-9521 (215).

The Manor at St. Mary's, 220 St. Mary's Dr., Cherry Hill 08003; (856) 424-5344; www.themanoratstmarys.org (739).

St. Vincent's Nursing Home, 45 Elm St., Montclair 07042; (973) 754-4800 (220).

Villa Maria (residence and infirmary, women), 641 Somerset St., N. Plainfield 07061; (908) 757-3050 (86).

New York: Bernardine Apartments, 417 Churchill Ave., Syracuse 13205; (315) 469-7786.

Brothers of Mercy Sacred Heart Home (residence) 4520 Ransom Rd., Clarence 14031; (716) 759-6985 (80). Brothers of Mercy Nursing Home, 10570 Bergtold Rd., Clarence 14031; (716) 759-6985; www.brothersofmercy.org (240). Brothers of Mercy Housing Co., Inc. (apartments), 10500 Bergtold Rd., Clarence 14031; (716) 759-2122 (110).

Carmel Richmond Nursing Home, 88 Old Town Rd., Staten Island 10304; (718) 979-5000 (300).

Archcare & Ferncliff, 21 Ferncliff Dr., Rhinebeck 12572; (845) 516-1652; www.archcare.org (328).

Franciscan Health System of New York, 2975 Independence Ave., Bronx 10463; (718) 548-1700.

Good Samaritan Nursing Home (skilled nursing), 101 Elm St., Sayville 11782; (631) 244-2400 (100).

The Heritage (apartments with skilled nursing care), 1450 Portland Ave., Rochester 14621; (716) 342-1700; www.stannsrochester.org (237)

Holy Family Home/Bensonhurst Center for Rehabilitation and Healthcare, 174084th St., Brooklyn 11214; (718) 885-8484 (200).

Kateri Residence (skilled nursing), 150 Riverside Dr., New York 10024; (646) 505-3500; www.catholichealthcaresystem.org/kateri (610).

Little Sisters of the Poor, Jeanne Jugan Residence (Skilled Nursing and Health Related; Adult Care), 3200 Baychester Ave., Bronx 10475; (718) 671-2120 (60).

Little Sisters of the Poor, Queen of Peace Residence, 110-30 221st St., Queens Village 11429; (718) 464-1800.

Mary Manning Walsh Home (nursing home), 1339 York Ave., New York 10021; (212) 628-2800 (362).

Mercy Healthcare Center (skilled nursing facility), 114 Wawbeek Ave., Tupper Lake 12986; (518) 359-3355; www.muhc.org (80).

Mt. Loretto Nursing Home, (skilled nursing home), Sisters of the Resurrection, 302 Swart Hill Rd., Amsterdam 12010; (518) 842-6790 (120).

Nazareth Nursing Home (women), 291 W. North St., Buffalo 14201; (716) 881-2323 (125).

Our Lady of Consolation Nursing and Rehabilitation Care Center (skilled nursing) 111 Beach Dr., West Islip 11795; (631) 587-1600; www.olc.chsli.org (450).

Our Lady of Hope Residence (home for the aged),

Little Sisters of the Poor, 1 Jeanne Jugan Lane, Latham 12210; (518) 785-4551 (117).

Ozanam Hall of Queens Nursing Home, Inc., 42-41 201st St., Bayside 11361; (718) 423-2000 (432).

Providence Rest , 3304 Waterbury Ave., Bronx 10465; (718) 931-30000; www.providencerest.org (242).

Resurrection Nursing Home (skilled nursing facility), Castleton 12033; (518) 732-7617 (80).

St. Ann's Community (skilled nursing facility), 1500 Portland Ave., Rochester 14621; (585) 697-6000; www.stannscommunity.com (354).

St. Cabrini Nursing Home, 115 Broadway, Dobbs Ferry 10522; (914) 693-6800 (304).

St. Clare Manor (nursing home), 543 Locust St., Lockport 14094; (716) 434-4718 (28).

St. Columban's on the Lake (retirement home), 2546 Lake Rd., Silver Creek 14136; (716) 934-4515 (50).

St. Elizabeth Home (adult home), 5539 Broadway, Lancaster 14086; (716) 683-5150 (117).

St. Francis Home (skilled nursing facility), 147 Reist St., Williamsville 14221; (716) 633-5400 (142).

St. Joseph Manor (nursing home), 2211 W. State St., Olean 14760; (716) 372-7810 (22).

St. Joseph Nursing Home, 2535 Genesee St., Utica 13501; (315) 797-1230; www.stjosephnh.org.

St. Joseph's Guest Home, Missionary Sisters of St. Benedict, 350 Cuba Hill Rd., Huntington 11743; (631) 368-9528.

St. Joseph's Home (nursing home), 420 Lafayette St., Ogdensburg 13669; (315) 393-3780; www.stjh.org (117).

St. Joseph's Villa (adult home), 38 Prospect Ave., Catskill 12414; (518) 943-5701.

St. Luke Manor, 17 Wiard St., Batavia 14020; (585) 343-8806 (20).

St. Mary's Manor, 515 Sixth St., Niagara Falls 14301; (716) 285-3236 (165).

St. Patrick's Home, 66 Van Cortlandt Park S., Bronx NY 10463; (718) 519-2800; www.stpatrickshome.org (264).

St. Teresa Nursing Home, 120 Highland Ave., Middletown 10940; (914) 342-1033 (98).

St. Vincent's Home for the Aged, 319 Washington Ave., Dunkirk 14048; (716) 366-2066 (40).

Terence Cardinal Cooke Health Care Center (skilled nursing), 1249 Fifth Ave., New York 10029; (212) 360-1000 (523).

Teresian House, 200 Washington Ave. Extension, Albany 12203; (518) 456-2000; www.teresianhouse.com (300).

Uihlein Mercy Center (nursing home), 185 Old Military Rd., Lake Placid 12946; (518) 523-2464 (220).

North Carolina: Maryfield Nursing Home, 1315 Greensboro Rd., High Point 27260; (336) 886-2444 (115).

North Dakota: Manor St. Joseph (basic care facility), 404 Fourth Ave., Edgeley 58433; (701) 493-2477 (40).

Sanford Health Marillac Manor, 1016 28th St., Bismarck 58501-3139; (701) 258-8702; www.sanfordhealth.com (78 apartments).

St. Anne's Guest Home, 524 N. 17th St., Grand Forks 58203; (701) 746-9401 (86).

St. Vincent's Care Center (nursing facility), 1021 N. 26th St., Bismarck 58501; (701) 323-1999 (101).

Ohio: Archbishop Leibold Home for the Aged, Little Sisters of the Poor, 476 Riddle Rd., Cincinnati 45220; (513) 281-8001 (100).

The Assumption Village, 9800 Market St., North Lima 44452; (330) 549-0740 (120).

Francesca Residence (retirement), 39 N. Portage Path, Akron 44303; (330) 867-6334 (40).

House of Loreto (nursing home), 2812 Harvard Ave. N.W., Canton 44709; (330) 453-8137 (76).

Jennings Center for Older Adults (nursing care), 10204 Granger Rd., Cleveland 44125; (216) 581-2900; www.jenningscenter.org (150).

Little Sisters of the Poor, Sacred Heart Home, 930 Wynn Rd. Oregon 43616; (419) 698-4331 (81).

Little Sisters of the Poor, Sts. Mary and Joseph Home for Aged, 4291 Richmond Rd., Cleveland 44122; (216) 464-1222 (125).

The Maria-Joseph Living Care Center, 4830 Salem Ave., Dayton 45416; (937) 278-2692; www.mariajoseph.org (440).

Mercy St. Theresa Center, 7010 Rowan Hill Dr., Cincinnati 45227; (513) 527-0105; www.e-mercy.com (157).

Mercy Siena Retirement Community, 6125 N. Main St., Dayton 45415; (937) 278-8211; www.mercysiena.com; (99).

Mount Alverna Village (intermediate care nursing facility), 6765 State Rd., Cleveland 44134; (440) 843-7800; www.franciscanservices.com/facilities/ (203).

Mt. St. Joseph (skilled nursing facility, dual certified), 21800 Chardon Rd., Euclid 44117; (216) 531-7426 (100).

Nazareth Towers, 300 E. Rich St., Columbus 43215; (614) 464-4780 (229).

St. Augustine Health Ministries (skilled nursing facility), 7801 Detroit Ave., Cleveland 44102; (216) 939-7602 (248).

St. Francis Health Care Centre, 401 N. Broadway St., Green Springs 44836; (419) 639-2626; www.sfhcc.org (186).

St. Francis Home, Inc. (residence and nursing care), 182 St. Francis Ave., Tiffin 44883; (419) 447-2723 (173).

St. Joseph's Care Center, 2308 Reno Dr., Louisville 44641; (330) 875-5562 (100, nursing home; 40 assisted living).

St. Margaret Hall (rest home and nursing facility), Carmelite Sisters for the Aged and Infirm, 1960 Madison Rd., Cincinnati 45206; (513) 751-5880 (133).

St. Raphael Home (nursing home), 1550 Roxbury Rd., Columbus 43212; (614) 486-0436 (78).

St. Rita's Home (skilled nursing home), 880 Greenlawn Ave., Columbus 43223; (614) 443-9433 (100).

Schroder Manor Retirement Community (residential care, skilled nursing care and independent living units), Franciscan Sisters of the Poor, 1302 Millville Ave., Hamilton 45013; (513) 867-1300 (125).

The Villa Sancta Anna Home for the Aged, Inc., 25000 Chagrin Blvd., Beachwood 44122; (216) 464-9250 (68).

The Village at St. Edward (apartments, nursing care and assisted living), 3131 Smith Rd., Fairlawn 44333; (330) 666-1183; www.vased.org (160).

Oklahoma: St. Ann's Home, 9400 St. Ann's Dr., Oklahoma City 73162; (405) 728-7888 (120).

Via Christi Village Ponca City (residence), 1601

Academy, Ponca City 74604; (580) 762-0927; via-christi.org (131).

Oregon: Evergreen Court Independent Retirement Living, 451 O'Connell St., North Bend 97459; (541) 751-7658; www.baycrest-village.com.

Maryville Nursing Home, 14645 S.W. Farmington, Beaverton 97007; (503) 643-8626; www.ssmo.org.

Mt. St. Joseph, 3060 S.E. Stark St., Portland 97214; (503) 535-4700 (347).

St. Catherine's Residence and Nursing Center, 3959 Sheridan Ave., North Bend 97459; (541) 756-4151 (200).

Pennsylvania: Antonian Towers, 1318 Spring St., Bethlehem, PA 18018; (610) 865-3963.

Ascension Manor I (senior citizen housing), 911 N. Franklin St., Philadelphia 19123; (215) 922-1116.

Ascension Manor II (senior citizen housing), 970 N. 7th St., Philadelphia 19123; (215) 922-1116.

Benetwood Apartments, Benedictine Sisters of Erie, 641 Troupe Rd., Harborcreek 16421; (814) 899-0088 (80).

Bethlehem Retirement Village, 100 W. Wissahickon Ave., Flourtown 19031; (215) 233-0998.

Catholic Senior Housing Development and Management, 1318 Spring St., Bethlehem 18018; (610) 865-3963; hfmanor.com/html/independent_living.html (50).

Christ the King Manor, 1100 W. Long Ave., Du Bois 15801; (814) 371-3180 (160).

D'Youville Manor (residential care facility), 1750 Quarry Rd., Yardley 19067; (215) 579-1750 (49).

Garvey Manor and Our Lady of the Allegheny Residence (nursing home), 128 Logan Blvd., Hollidaysburg 16648-2693; (814) 695-5571; www.garveymanor.org (150).

Grace Mansion (personal care facility), Holy Family Residential Services, 1200 Spring St., Bethlehem; (610) 865-6748; www.hfmanor.org (33).

Holy Family Home, Little Sisters of the Poor, 5300 Chester Ave., Philadelphia 19143; (215) 729-5153 (105).

Holy Family Manor (skilled and intermediate nursing facility), 1200 Spring St., Bethlehem 18018; (610) 865-5595; www.hfmanor.com (208).

Immaculate Mary Home (nursing care facility), 2990 Holme Ave., Philadelphia 19136; (215) 335-2100 (296).

John XXIII Home (skilled, intermediate and personal care), 2250 Shenango Freeway, Hermitage 16148; (724) 981-3200; www.johnxxiiihome.org (196).

Little Flower Manor (residence, women), 1215 Springfield Rd., Darby 19023; (610) 534-6000 (180).

Little Flower Manor Nursing Home (skilled nursing), 1201 Springfield Rd., Darby 19023; (610) 534-6000 (185).

Little Flower Manor of Diocese of Scranton, (long-term skilled nursing care facility), 200 S. Meade St., Wilkes-Barre 18702; (570) 823-6131.

Little Sisters of the Poor, 1028 Benton Ave., Pittsburgh 15212; (412) 307-1100; www.littlsesister-softhepoor-pittsburgh.org (40).

Little Sisters of the Poor, Holy Family Residence, 2500 Adams Ave., Scranton 18509; (570) 343-4065 (58).

Maria Joseph Manor (skilled nursing, personal care facility and independent living cottages), 875 Montour Blvd., Danville 17821; (570) 275-4221 (135).

Marian Hall Home for the Aged (women), 934 Forest Ave., Pittsburgh 15202; (412) 761-1999 (49).

Marian Manor (intermediate care), 2695 Winchester Dr., Pittsburgh 15220; (412) 563-6866 (194).

Mount Macrina Manor (skilled nursing facility), 520 W. Main St., Uniontown 15401; (724) 437-1400 (141).

Neumann Apartments (low income), 25 N. Nichols St., St. Clair 17970; (570) 429-0699 (25).

Queen of Angels Apartments, 22 Rothermel St., Hyde Park, Reading 19605; (610) 921-3115 (45 units).

Queen of Peace Apartments (low income), 1318 Spring St., Bethlehem 18018; (610) 865-3963 (65).

Redeemer Village II, 1551 Huntingdon Pike, Huntingdon Valley 19006; (215) 947-8168; www.holyredeemer.com (151).

Sacred Heart Manor (nursing home and independent living), 6445 Germantown Ave., Philadelphia 19119; (215) 438-5268 (171 nursing home; 48 personal care; 48 independent living).

St. Anne's Retirement Community, 3952 Columbia Ave., Columbia 17512; (717) 285-5443; www.stannesrc.org (121).

St. Anne Home (nursing facility), 685 Angela Dr., Greensburg 15601; (724) 837-6070 (125).

St. Ignatius Nursing Home, 4401 Haverford Ave., Philadelphia 19104; (215) 349-8800 (176).

St. John Neumann Nursing Home, 10400 Roosevelt Blvd., Philadelphia 19116; (215) 248-7200 (107).

St. Joseph Home for the Aged (Residential and skilled nursing facility), 1182 Holland Rd., Holland 18966; (215) 357-5511 (76).

St. Joseph Nursing and Health Care Center (skilled nursing facility), 5324 Penn Ave., Pittsburgh 15224; (412) 665-5100 (153).

St. Leonard's Home Inc. (personal care facility), 601 N. Montgomery St., Hollidaysburg 16648; (814) 695-9581 (30).

St. Mary of Providence Center, R.D. 2, Box 145, Elverson 19520; (610) 942-4166; www.stmaryof-prov-pa.org (52).

Saint Mary's Home of Erie, 607 E. 26th St., Erie 16504-2813; (814) 459-0621; www.stmaryshome.org (131).

St. Mary's at Asbury Ridge, 4855 West Ridge Rd., Erie, PA 16506; (814) 836-5300.

St. Mary's Manor (residential, personal care, shortterm rehabilitation and nursing care), 701 Lansdale Ave., Lansdale 19446; (215) 368-0900; www.smmphl.org (200).

St. Mary's Villa Nursing Home, 675 St. Mary's Villa Rd., Moscow 18444; (570) 842-7621 (176).

Trexler Pavilion (personal care facility), 1220 Prospect Ave., Bethlehem 18018; (610) 868-7776 (30).

Vincentian de Marillac Nursing Home, 5300 Stanton Ave., Pittsburgh 15206; (412) 361-2833 (52).

Vincentian Home (nursing facility), 111 Perrymont Rd., Pittsburgh 15237; (412) 366-5600 (217).

Rhode Island: Jeanne Jugan Residence of the Little Sisters of the Poor, 964 Main St., Pawtucket 02860; (401) 723-4314 (95).

Saint Antoine Residence (skilled nursing facility), 10 Rhodes Ave., North Smithfield 02896; (401) 767-3500; www.stantoine.net (416).

St. Clare Home (nursing facility), 309 Spring St.,

Newport 02840; (401) 849-3204; newport.org (47).

Scalabrini Villa (convalescent, rest-nursing home). 860 N. Quidnessett Rd., North Kingstown 02852; (401) 884-1802; www.freeyellow.com/members3/scalabrini (175).

South Carolina: Carter-May Home/St. Joseph Residence, 1660 Ingram Rd., Charleston 29407; (843) 556-8314 (15).

South Dakota: Avera Brady Health and Rehabilitation (skilled nursing facility), 500 S. Ohlman St., Mitchell 57301; (605) 966-7701 (83).

Mother Joseph Manor (skilled nursing facility), 1002 N. Jay St., Aberdeen 57401; (605) 622-5850 (81).

Prince of Peace Retirement Community, 4500 Prince of Peace Pl., Sioux Falls 57103; (605) 322-5600 (204).

St. William's Care Center (intermediate care), 100 South 9th St., Milbank 57252; (605) 432-5811 (60).

Tekakwitha Nursing Home (skilled and intermediate care), 6 E. Chestnut St., Sisseton 57262; (605) 698-7693 (101).

Tennessee: Alexian Village of Tennessee, 100 James Blvd., Signal Mountain 37377; (423) 886-0100 (277).

St. Mary Manor, 1771 Highway 45 Bypass, Jackson 38305; (731) 668-5633.

St. Peter Manor (retirement community), 108 N. Auburndale, Memphis 38104; (901) 278-8200. St. Peter Villa (intermediate and skilled care), 141 N. McLean, Memphis 38104; (901) 276-2021.

Villa Maria Manor, 32 White Bridge Rd., Nashville 37205; (615) 352-3084 (230).

Texas: Casa, Inc., Housing for Elderly and Handicapped, 3201 Sondra Dr., Fort Worth 76107; (817) 332-7276 (200).

Casa Brendan Housing for the Elderly and Handicapped (56 apartments) and Casa II, Inc. (30 apartments), 1300 Hyman St., Stephenville 76401; (254) 965-6964 (83).

John Paul II Nursing Home (intermediate care and personal care), 209 S. 3rd St., Kenedy 78119; (830) 583-9841.

Mother of Perpetual Help Home (intermediate care facility), 519 E. Madison Ave., Brownsville 78520; (956) 546-6745 (38).

Mt. Carmel Home (personal care home), 4130 S. Alameda St., Corpus Christi 78411; (512) 855-6243 (92).

Nuestro Hogar Housing for Elderly and Handicapped, 709 Magnolia St., Arlington 76012; (817) 261-0608 (63).

St. Ann's Nursing Home, P.O. Box 1179, Panhandle 79068; (806) 537-3194 (56).

St. Dominic Residence Hall, 2401 Holcombe Blvd., Houston 77021; (713) 741-8700 (149).

St. Francis Nursing Home (intermediate care facility), 630 W. Woodlawn, San Antonio 78212; (210) 736-3177 (152).

St. Francis Village, Inc. (retired and elderly), 1 Chapel Plaza, Crowley 76036; (817) 292-5786 (420).

San Juan Nursing Home, Inc. (skilled and intermediate care facility), P.O. Box 1238, San Juan

78589; (956) 787-1771 (127).

Villa Maria (home for aged women-men), 920 S. Oregon St., El Paso 79901; (915) 533-5152 (17 units).

Villa Maria, Inc. (apartment complex), 3146 Saratoga Blvd., Corpus Christi 78415; (361) 857-6171 (59).

Utah: Successor Healthcare, 451 Bishop Federal Lane, Salt Lake City 84115; (801) 487-7557; www.stjosephvilla.com (300).

Vermont: Loretto Home, 59 Meadow St., Rutland 05701; (802) 773-8840 (57).

Michaud Memorial Manor (residential home for elderly), Derby Line 05830; (802) 873-3152 (34).

St. Joseph's Residential Care Home, 243 N. Prospect St., Burlington 05401; (802) 864-0264 (32).

Virginia: Madonna Home (home for aged), 814 W. 37th St., Norfolk 23508; (757) 623-6662 (16).

Marian Manor (assisted living, nursing care), 5345 Marian Lane, Virginia Beach 23462; (757) 456-5018; marian-manor.com (100).

Marywood Apartments, 1261 Marywood Lane, Richmond 23229; (804) 740-5567 (126).

McGurk House Apartments, 2425 Tate Springs Rd., Lynchburg 24501; (434) 846-2425 (89).

Our Lady of the Valley Retirement Community, 650 N. Jefferson St., Roanoke 24016; (540) 345-5111.

Russell House Apartments, 900 First Colonial Rd., Virginia Beach 23454; (757) 481-0770 (126).

St. Francis Home, 2511 Wise St., Richmond 23225; (804) 231-1043 (34).

St. Joseph's Home for the Aged, Little Sisters of the Poor, 1503 Michaels Rd., Henrice 23221; (804) 288-6245; www.littlesistersofthepoorvirginia.org (72).

St. Mary's Woods (independent and assisted living apartments), 1257 Marywood Lane, Richmond 23229; (804) 741-8624; www.stmaryswood.com (118 apartments).

Seton Manor (apartments), 215 Marcella Rd., Hampton 23666; (757) 827-6512 (112).

Washington: Cathedral Plaza Apartments (retirement apartments), W. 1120 Sprague Ave., Spokane 99204 (150).

Chancery Place (retirement apartments), 910 Marion, Seattle 98104; (206) 343-9415; www.ccsww.org.

The Delaney, W. 242 Riverside Ave., Spokane 99201; (509) 747-5081 (83).

Elbert House, 16000 N.E. 8th St., Bellevue 98008; (206) 747-5111.

Emma McRedmond Manor, 7960-169th N.E., Redmond 98052; (206) 869-2424 (31).

Fahy Garden Apartments, W. 1403-11 Dean Ave., Spokane 99201; (509) 326-6759 (31).

Fahy West Apartments, W. 1523 Dean Ave., Spokane 99201 (55).

The Franciscan (apartments), 15237-21st Ave. S.W., Seattle 98166; (206) 431-8001.

Providence Mt. St. Vincent (nursing center and retirement apartments), 4831 35th Ave. S.W., Seattle 98126; (206) 937-3700 (174).

Tumwater Apartments, 5701 6th Ave. S.W.,

Tumwater 98501; (360) 352-4321.

West Virginia: Welty Home for the Aged, 21 Washington Ave., Wheeling 26003; (304) 242-5233 (46).

Wisconsin: Affinity Health System, 500 S. Oakwood Rd., Oshkosh, WI 54901; (920) 223-0110.

Alexian Village of Milwaukee (retirement community/skilled nursing home), 9301 N. 76th St., Milwaukee 53223; (414) 355-9300; www.alexian village.org (327).

Bethany-St. Joseph Health Care Center, 2501 Shelby Rd., La Crosse 54601; (608) 788-5700 (226).

Clement Manor (retirement community and skilled nursing), 3939 S. 92nd St., Greenfield 53228; (414) 321-1800 (162).

Divine Savior Nursing Home, 715 W. Pleasant St., Portage 53901; (608) 742-4131 (124).

Felician Village (independent living), 1700 S. 18th St., Manitowoc 54220; (920) 683-8811 (134 apartments).

Benedictine Living Community of Arcadia, 464 S. St. Joseph Ave., Arcadia 54612; (608) 323-3341; www.blcarcadia.org (75).

McCormick Memorial Home, 212 Iroquois St., Green Bay 54301; (920) 437-0883 (60).

Marian Catholic Home (skilled care nursing home), 3333 W. Highland Blvd., Milwaukee 53208; (414) 344-8100 (215).

Marian Franciscan Center, 9632 W. Appleton Ave., Milwaukee 53225; (414) 461-8850 (310).

Marian Housing Center (independent living), 4105 Spring St., Racine 53405; (262) 633-5807 (40).

Maryhill Manor Nursing Home (skilled nursing facility), 501 Madison Ave., Niagara 54151; (715) 251-3178 (75).

Milwaukee Catholic Home (continuing care retirement community), 2462 N. Prospect Ave., Milwaukee 53211-4462; (414) 224-9700; www.milwaukeecatholichome.org (131).

Nazareth House (skilled nursing facility), 814 Jackson St., Stoughton 53589; (608) 873-6448 (99).

St. Ann Rest Home (intermediate care facility, women), 2020 S. Muskego Ave., Milwaukee 53204; (414) 383-2630 (50).

St. Anne's Home for the Elderly, 3800 N. 92nd St., Milwaukee 53222; (414) 463-7570; www.wahsa.org/st.anne (106).

St. Camillus Campus (continuing care retirement community), 10100 West Blue Mound Road, Wauwatosa 53226; (414) 258-1814; www.stcam.com (386).

St. Elizabeth Nursing Home, 109 S. Atwood Ave., Janesville 53545; (608) 752-6709 (43).

St. Francis Home (skilled nursing facility), 1416 Cumming Ave., Superior 54880; (715) 394-5591.

St. Francis Home (skilled nursing), 33 Everett St., Fond du Lac 54935; (920) 923-7980 (106).

St. Joseph's Home, 9244 29th Ave., Kenosha 53143; (262) 925-8124; www.stjosephs.com (93).

St. Joseph's Rehabilitation Center, 2902 East Ave. S., La Crosse 54601; (608) 788-9870; www.crsinc.org (80).

St. Joseph's Nursing Home of St. Joseph Community Health Services, Inc. P.O. Box 527, Hillsboro 54634; (608) 489-8000.

St. Joseph Residence, Inc. (nursing home), 107 E. Beckert Rd., New London 54961; (920) 982-5354 (107).

St. Mary's Home for the Aged (skilled nursing, Alzheimer's unit, respite care), 2005 Division St., Manitowoc 54220; (920) 684-7171; www.felician-community.com (266).

St. Mary's Nursing Home, 3515 W. Hadley St., Milwaukee 53210; (414) 873-9250 (88).

St. Monica's Senior Citizens Home, 3920 N. Green Bay Rd., Racine 53404; (262) 639-5050; www.srsofstrita.org (110).

St. Paul Home Elder Services (intermediate and skilled nursing home), 1211 Oakridge Ave., Kaukauna 54130; (920) 766-6020; www.stpaulelders.org (129).

Villa Loretto Nursing Home, N8114 County Rd. WW, Mount Calvary 53057; (920) 753-3211; www.villalorettonh.org (52).

Villa St. Francis, Inc., 1910 W. Ohio Ave., Milwaukee 53215; (414) 649-2888 (142).

FACILITIES FOR CHILDREN AND ADULTS WITH DISABILITIES

Sources: Catholic Almanac *survey*; The Official Catholic Directory.

This listing covers facilities and programs with educational and training orientation. Information about other services for the handicapped can generally be obtained from the Catholic Charities Office or its equivalent (c/o Chancery Office) in any diocese. (See Index for listing of addresses of chancery offices in the U.S.)

Abbreviation code: b, boys; c, coeducational; d, day; g, girls; r, residential. Other information includes age for admission. The number in parentheses at the end of an entry indicates total capacity or enrollment.

Deaf and Hearing Impaired

California: St. Joseph's Center for Deaf and Hard of Hearing, 3880 Smith St., Union City 94587.

Louisiana: Chinchuba Institute (d,c; birth through 18 yrs.), 1131 Barataria Blvd., Marrero 70072.

Missouri: St. Joseph Institute for the Deaf (r,d,c; birth to 14 years), 1809 Clarkson Rd., Chesterfield, MO 63107; (636) 532-3211 (Voice/TDD).

New York: Cleary School for the Deaf (d,c; infancy through 21), 301 Smithtown Blvd., Nesconset, NY 11767-2077; (516) 588-0530; www.clearyschool.org (70).

St. Francis de Sales School for the Deaf (d,c; infant through elementary grades), 260 Eastern Parkway, Brooklyn 11225; (718) 636-4573 (150).

St. Joseph's School for the Deaf (d,c; parent-infant through 14 yrs.), 1000 Hutchinson River Pkwy, Bronx 10465; (718) 828-9000 (140).

Ohio: St. Rita School for the Deaf (r,d,c; birth to 12th grade), 1720 Glendale-Milford Rd., Cincinnati 45215; (513) 771-7600; www.srsdeaf.org (130).

Pennsylvania: Archbishop Ryan School for Hearing Impaired Children (d,c; parent-infant programs through 8th grade), 233 Mohawk Ave., Norwood, PA 19074; (610) 586-7044 (49).

De Paul Institute (d,c; birth through 21 yrs.), 2904 Castlegate Ave., Pittsburgh 15226; (412) 561-4848 (77).

Abused, Abandoned, and Neglected

This listing includes facilities for abused, abandoned and neglected as well as emotionally disturbed children and youth.

Alabama: St. Mary's Home for Children (r,c; referred from agencies), 4350 Moffat Rd., Mobile 36618; (251) 344-7733.

California: Hanna Boys Center (r,b; 10-15 yrs. at intake; school, 4th to 10th grade), Box 100, Sonoma 95476; (707)996-6767 (107). Treatment center and therapeutic special school for boys with emotional problems, behavior disorders, learning disabilities.

Rancho San Antonio (r,b; 13-17 yrs.), 21000 Plummer St., Chatsworth 91311; (818) 882-6400.

St. Vincent's (r,d,g; 12-17 yrs.), 4200 Calle Real, Santa Barbara 93110-1454; (805) 683-6381.

Colorado: Mt. St. Vincent Home (r,c; 5-13 yrs.), 4159 Lowell Blvd., Denver 80211; (303) 458-7220; www.nahse.org/member/st.vincent.

Connecticut: St. Francis Home for Children (r,d,c; 4-17 yrs.), 651 Prospect St., New Haven 06511; (203) 777-5513. Exec. Dir., Peter Salerno.

Mt. St. John Home and School for Boys (r,b; 11-16 yrs.), 135 Kirtland St., Deep River 06417; (860) 526-5391; www.mtstjohn.org (77).

Delaware: Our Lady of Grace Home for Children (r,d,c; 6-12 yrs.), 487 E. Chestnut Hill Rd., Newark 19713; (302) 738-4658.

Seton Villa, Siena Hall and Children's Home (r,c; group home; 12-18 yrs,; mothers and their children), c/o 2307 Kentmere Pkwy, Wilmington 19806; (302) 656-2183.

Florida: Boystown of Florida (r,b; 12-16 yrs.; group home), 11400 S.W. 137th Court, Miami 33186.

Georgia: Village of St. Joseph (r,c; 6-16 yrs.), 1961 Druid Hills Rd., Ste. 205-B, 30329; (404) 321-2900.

Illinois: Guardian Angel Community Services (d,c; r,b), 1550 Plainfield Rd., Joliet 60435; (815) 729-0930 (35).

Maryville Academy (r,c; 6-18 yrs.), 1150 North River Rd., Des Plaines 60016; (708) 824-1893.

Mission of Our Lady of Mercy, Mercy Home for Boys and Girls (r,d,c; 15-18 yrs.), 1140 W. Jackson Blvd., Chicago 60607; (312) 738-7560; www.mercyhome.org.

Indiana: Gibault School for Boys (r; 10-18 yrs.), 6401 South U.S. Highway 41, Terre Haute 47802; (812) 299-1156; www.gibault.org.

Campagna Academy (r; 10-18 yrs.), 7403 Cline Ave., Schererville 46375; (219) 322-8614.

Kentucky: Boys' Haven (r; 12-18 yrs.), 2301 Goldsmith Lane, Louisville 40218; (502) 458-1171; www.boyshaven.org.

Louisiana: Hope Haven Center (r,c; 5-18 yrs.), 1101 Barataria Blvd., Marrero 70072; (504) 347-5581.

Maryland: Good Shepherd Center (r,g; 13-18 yrs.), 4100 Maple Ave., Baltimore, 21227; (410) 247-2770; www.goodshepherdcenter.com.

Massachusetts: The Brightside for Families and Children (r,d,c; 6-16 yrs.), 1233 Main St., Holyoke, MA 01040; (413) 539-2484; www.brightsidecares.com.

McAuley Nazareth Home for Boys (r; 6-13 yrs.), 77 Mulberry St., Leicester 01524; (508) 892-4886; www.nazareth-home.org (16). Residential treatment center.

St. Vincent Home (r,c 5-22 yrs.), 2425 Highland Ave., Fall River 02720; (508) 679-8511.

Michigan: Don Bosco Hall (r,b; 13-17 years.), 10001 Petoskey Ave., Detroit 48204; (313) 834-8677.

Holy Cross Children's Services (r,d,c; 13-17 yrs.), 8759 Clinton-Macon Rd., Clinton 49236; (517) 423-7451; www.hccsnet.org (650). Facilities located throughout the state and northern Ohio.

Vista Maria (r,g; 11-18 yrs.), 20651 W. Warren Ave., Dearborn Heights 48127; (313) 271-6250; www.community.milive.com/cc/girls.

Minnesota: St. Cloud Children's Home (r,c; 8-18 yrs.), RTC Campus, Bld. 4-D, P.O. Box 1006, Fergus Falls, MN 56538; (218) 739-9325. Day Treatment Program (d,c; 7-14 yrs.), same address.

St. Elizabeth Home (r,c; 18 yrs. and older), 306 15th Ave. N., St. Cloud 56301; (320) 252-8350.

Missouri: Child Center of Our Lady (r,d,c; 5-14 yrs.), 7900 Natural Bridge Rd., St. Louis 63121; (314) 383-0200.

Child Center-Marygrove (r,d,c; 6-21 yrs.) (97); intense treatment unit (r,b; 13-18 yrs) (13); overnight crises care (r,d,c; birth to 18 yrs.) (8), 2705 Mullanphy Lane, Florissant, 63031; (314) 830-6201; www.marygroveservices.org.

Nebraska: Father Flanagan's Boys' Home (r,c; 10-16 yrs.), 14100 Crawford St., Boys Town 68010; (402)498-1000; www.boystown.org (556). Boys Town National Research Hospital (r,d,c; 1-18 yrs.), 555 N. 30th St., Omaha 68131; (402) 498-6362; www.boys townhospital.org. Center for abused handicapped children, diagnosis of speech, language and hearing problems in children. Boys Town also has various facilities or programs in Brooklyn, NY; Portsmouth, RI; Philadelphia, PA; Washington, DC; Tallahassee, Orlando and Delray Beach, FL; Atlanta, GA; New Orleans, LA; San Antonio, TX; Las Vegas, NV; and southern CA.

New Jersey: Catholic Community Services/Mt. Carmel Guild, 1160 Raymond Blvd., Newark 07102; (973) 596-4084.

Collier High School (d,c; 13-18 yrs.), 160 Conover Rd., Wickatunk 07765; (732) 946-4771; www.collierservices.com.

Collier Group Home, 180 Spring St., Red Bank, NJ 07701; (732) 842-8337.

Collier House (transitional living), 386 Maple Pl., Keyport, NJ 07735; (732) 264-3222.

New York: The Astor Home for Children (r,d,c; 5-12 yrs.), 6339 Mill St., P.O. Box 5005, Rhinebeck 12572-5005; (845) 871-1000; www.astorservices.org. Child Guidance Clinics/Day Treatment (Rhinebeck, Poughkeepsie, Beacon, Bronx). Head Start Day Care (Poughkeepsie, Beacon, Red Hook, Dover, Millerton).

Baker Victory Services, 780 Ridge Rd. Lackawanna 14218; (716) 828-9500; www.ourladyofvictory.org.

Good Shepherd Services (r,d,c), 305 Seventh Ave., New York, NY 10001; (212) 243-7070; www.goodshepherds. org. City-wide residential programs or adolescents (12-21 yrs.); foster care and adoption services (infant-21 yrs.); training institute for human services workers; day treatment program (13-18 yrs.); community-based neighborhood family services in South Brooklyn Community (infant-adult),

LaSalle School (r,d,b; 12-18 yrs.), 391 Western Ave., Albany 12203; (518) 242-4731.

Madonna Heights Services (r,d,g; 12-18 yrs.), 151 Burrs Lane, Dix Hills 11746; (631) 643-8800; www.sco.org (110). Also conducts group homes on Long Island and outpatient programs.

St. Anne Institute (r,d,g; 12-18 yrs.), 160 N. Main Ave., Albany 12206; (518) 437-6500; www.stanneinstitute.com.

St. Catherine's Center for Children (r,d,c; birth through 12 yrs.), 40 N. Main Ave., Albany 12203; (518) 453-6700; www.st-cath.org.

St. John's of Rockaway Beach (r,b; 9-21 yrs.), 144 Beach 111th St., Rockaway Park 11694; (718) 945-2800. Programs include diagnostic centers and independent living programs.

North Dakota: Home on the Range (r,c; 10-18 yrs.), 16351 I-94, Sentinel Butte 58654; (701) 872-3745; www.hotrnd.org (79). Residential and emergency shelter therapeutic programs.

Home on the Range-Red River Victory Ranch (r,b; 10-18 yrs.), P.O. Box 9615, Fargo 58106; (701) 293-6321; www.hotr.org (12). Residential chemical addictions program.

Ohio: St. Vincent Family Centers (d,c; preschool) Outpatient counseling program (c; 2-18 yrs.), 1490 East Main St., Columbus 43205; (614) 252-0731; www.svfc.org.

Marycrest (r,g; 13-18 yrs.), 7800 Brookside Rd., Independence 44131.

Catholic Charities Services/Parmadale (r,c; 12-18 yrs.), 6753 State Rd., Parma 44134; (440) 845-7700.

Rosemont (r,g;d,c; 11-18 yrs.), 2440 Dawnlight Ave., Columbus 43211; (614) 471-2626.

Oregon: St. Mary's Home for Boys (r; 10-18 yrs.), 16535 S.W. Tualatin Valley Highway, Beaverton 97006; (503) 649-5651; www.stmaryshomeforboys.org.

Pennsylvania: Auberle (r,c; 7-18 yrs.), 1101 Hartman St., McKeesport 15132-1500; (412) 673-5800; www.auberle.org (181). Residential treatment for boys; emergency shelter care, foster care, group home for girls and family preservation program.

De LaSalle in Towne (d,b; 14-17 yrs.), 25 S. Van Pelt St., Philadelphia 19103; (215) 567-5500.

De LaSalle Vocational (b; 15-18 yrs.), 1265 Street Rd., Bensalem 19020; (215) 464-0344.

Gannondale (r,g; 12-17 yrs.), 4635 E. Lake Rd., Erie 16511; (814) 899-7659.

Harborcreek Youth Services (r,d,c; 10-17 yrs.), 5712 Iroquois Ave., Harborcreek 16421; (814) 899-7664; www.hys-erie.org.

Holy Family Institute (r,d,c; 0-18 yrs.), 8235 Ohio River Blvd., Emsworth 15202; (412) 766-4030; www.hfi-pgh.org.

Lourdesmont Good Shepherd Youth and Family Services (r,g;d,c; 12-17 yrs.), 537 Venard Rd., Clarks Summit 18411; (507) 587-4741; www.lourdesmont.com. Sponsored by the Sisters of the Good Shepherd. John A. Antognoli.

St. Gabriel's Hall (r,b; 10-18 yrs.), P.O. Box 7280, Audubon 19407; (215) 247-2776.

St. Michael's School (r,b; d,c; 12-17 yrs.), Box 370, Tunkhannock 18657; (570) 388-6155.

Texas: St. Joseph Adolescent and Family Counseling Center (c; 13-17 yrs.), 5415 Maple Ave., #320, Dallas 75235; (214) 631-TEEN.

Washington: Morning Star Boys Ranch (Spokane Boys' Ranch, Inc.) (r,b; 10-18 yrs.), Box 8087, Spokane 99203-0087; (509) 448-1411; www.morningstarboysranch.org. Dir. Joseph M. Weitensteiner.

Wisconsin: North American Union Sisters of Our Lady of Charity Center (r,c; 10-17 yrs.), 154 Edgington Lane, Wheeling, WV 26003-1535; (304) 242-0042.

St. Charles Youth and Family Services (r,d,b; 12-18 yrs.), 151 S. 84th St., Milwaukee 53214; (414) 476-3710; www.stcharlesinc.org.

Wyoming: St. Joseph's Children's Home (r,c; 6-18 yrs.), P.O. Box 1117, Torrington 82240; (307) 532-4197.

Developmentally Challenged

This listing includes facilities for children, youth, and adults with learning disabilities.

Alabama: Father Purcell Memorial Exceptional Children's Center (r, c; birth to 10 yrs.), 2048 W. Fairview Ave., Montgomery 36108; (334) 834-5590; www.mnw.net/fpm.

California: Child Study Center of St. John's Hospital (d,c; birth-18 yrs.), 1339-20th St., Santa Monica 90404; (310) 829-8921.

St. Madeleine Sophie's Center (d,c; 18 yrs. and older), 2111 E. Madison Ave., El Cajon 92019.

Tierra del Sol Foundation (d,c; 18 yrs. and older), 9919 Sunland Blvd., Sunland 91040; (818) 352-1419. 14547 Gilmore St., Van Nuys 91411; (818) 904-9164.

Connecticut: Gengras Center (d,c; 3-21 yrs.), St. Joseph College, 1678 Asylum Ave., W. Hartford 06117.

Villa Maria Education Center (d,c; 6-14 yrs.), 161 Sky Meadow Dr., Stamford 06903-3400; (203) 322-5886; www.villamariaedu.org.

District of Columbia: Lt. Joseph P. Kennedy, Jr., Institute (c; 6 weeks to 5 yrs. for Kennedy Institute for Child Development Center; 6-21 yrs. for Kennedy School; 18 yrs. and older for training and employment, therapeutic and residential services). Founded in 1959 for people of all ages with developmental disabilities and their families in the Washington archdiocese. Heaquarters: 801 Buchanan St. N.E., Washington 20017; (202) 529-7600; www.kennedyinstitute.org. Other locations in D.C. and Maryland. No enrollment limit.

Florida: L'Arche Harbor House, (c; 20 yrs. and older; community home), 700 Arlington Rd., Jacksonville 32211; (904) 721-5992.

Marian Center Services for Developmentally Handicapped and Mentally Retarded (r,d,c; 2-21 yrs.), 15701 Northwest 37th Ave., Opa Locka 33054; (305) 625-8354; www.mariancenterschool.org. Pre-school, school, workshop residence services.

Morning Star School (d,c; 4-16 yrs.), 725 Mickler Rd., Jacksonville, 32211; (904) 421-2144.

Morning Star School (d,c; school age), 954 Leigh Ave., Orlando 32804.

Morning Star School (d,c; 6-14 yrs.), 4661-80th Ave. N., Pinellas Park 33781; (727) 544-6036; www.morningstarschool.org.

Morning Star Catholic School (d,c; 6-16 yrs.), 210 E. Linebaugh Ave., Tampa 33612; (813) 935-0232; www.morningstartampa.org..

Georgia: St. Mary's Home (r,c), 2170 E. Victory Dr., Savannah 31404; (912) 236-7164.

Illinois: Bartlett Learning Center (r,d,c; 3-21 yrs.), 801 W. Bartlett Rd., Bartlett 60103; (630) 289-4221.

Brother James Court (r, men over 18 yrs.), 2508 St. James Rd., Springfield 62707; (217) 544-4878.

Good Shepherd Manor (men; 18 yrs. and older), Little Brothers of the Good Shepherd, P.O. Box 260, Momence 60954; (815) 472-3700; www.good-shepherdmanor.org. Resident care for developmentally disabled men.

Misericordia Home South (r,c), 2916 W. 47th St., Chicago 60632; (773) 254-9595. For severely and profoundly impaired children.

Misericordia Home — Heart of Mercy Village (r,c; 6-45 yrs.), 6300 North Ridge, Chicago 60660; (773) 973-6300; www.misericordia.com.

Mt. St. Joseph (developmentally disabled women; over age 21), 24955 N. Highway 12, Lake Zurich 60047; (847) 438-5050.

Presence St. Vincent Community Living Facility (r,c; adults, over 18 yrs.) (20), and St. Vincent Supported Living Arrangement (r,c; adults, over 18 yrs.) (20), 659 E. Jefferson St., Freeport 61032; (815) 232-6181; www.presencehealth.org/stjosephcenter.

St. Coletta's of Illinois (r,d,; 6 to adult), 123rd and Wolf Rd., Palos Park 60464; (708) 448-6520.

St. Mary of Providence (r,women; 18 yrs. and older), 4200 N. Austin Ave., Chicago 60634; (773) 545-8300.

Springfield Developmental Center (m; 21 yrs. and over), 4595 Laverna Rd., Springfield 62707; (217) 525-8271.

Massachusetts: Cardinal Cushing Centers (d,c; 3-22 yrs.), 85 Washington St., Braintree 02184; (781) 848-6250; www.coletta.org.

Vocational Training

Indiana: Marian Day School (d,c; 6-16 yrs.), 700 Herndon Dr., Evansville 47711; (812) 422-5346.

Kansas: Lakemary Center, Inc. (r,d,c), 100 Lakemary Dr., Paola 66071; (913) 557-4000; www.lakemaryctr.org.

Kentucky: Pitt Academy (d,c), 6010 Preston Hwy., Louisville 40219; (502) 966-6979; www.pitt.com.

Louisiana: Department of Special Education, Archdiocese of New Orleans, St. Michael Special School (d,c; 6-21 yrs.), 1522 Chippewa St., New Orleans 70130.

Holy Angels Residential Facility (r,c; teenage, 14 yrs. and older), 10450 Ellerbe Rd., Shreveport 71106; (318) 797-8500.

Ocean Avenue Community Home, 361 Ocean Ave., Gretna 70053; (504) 361-0674.

Padua Community Services (r,c; birth-25 yrs.), 200 Beta St., Belle Chasse 70037.

St. Jude the Apostle, 1430 Claire Ave., Gretna 70053; (504) 361-8457.

St. Mary's Residential Training School (r,c: 3-22 yrs.), P.O. Drawer 7768, Alexandria 71306; (318) 445-6443.

St. Peter the Fisherman, 62269 Airport Dr., Slidell 70458; (504) 641-4914.

St. Rosalie (r; men 18 and up), 119 Kass St., Gretna 70056; (504) 361-8320.

Sts. Mary and Elizabeth, 720 N. Elm St., Metairie 70003; (504) 738-6959.

Maryland: The Benedictine School for Exceptional Children (r,c; 6-21 yrs.), 14299 Benedictine Lane, Ridgely 21660; (410) 634-2112; www.benschool.com.

Francis X. Gallagher Services (r), 2520 Pot Spring Rd., Timonium 21093.

St. Elizabeth School and Habilitation Center (d,c; 11-21 yrs.), 801 Argonne Dr., Baltimore 21218; (410) 889-5054; www.stelizabeth-school.org.

Massachusetts: Cardinal Cushing School and Training Center (r,d,c; 16-22 yrs.), Hanover 02339 (116 r; 28 d).

Mercy Centre (d,c; 3-22 yrs. and over), 25 West Chester St., Worcester 01605-1136; (508) 852-7165; www.mercycentre.com.

Michigan: Our Lady of Providence Center (r,g; 11-30 yrs., d,c; 26 yrs. and older), 16115 Beck Rd., Northville 48118; (734) 453-1300.

St. Louis Center and School (r,d,b; 6-18 yrs. child care; 18-36 yrs. adult foster care), 16195 Old U.S. 12, Chelsea 48118-9646; (734) 475-8430; www.stlouiscenter.org.

Minnesota: Mother Teresa Home (r,c; 18 yrs. and older), 101-10th Ave. N., Cold Spring 56320.

St. Francis Home (r,c; 18 yrs. and older), P.O. Box 326, Waite Park 56387; (320) 251-7630.

St. Luke's Home (r; 18 yrs. and older), 411 8th Ave. N., Cold Springs 56320.

Missouri: Department of Special Education, Archdiocese of St. Louis, 4472 Lindell Blvd., St. Louis. 63108; (314) 533-3454. Serves children with developmental disabilities, mental retardation or learning disabilities; services include special ungraded day classes in 8 parish schools.

Good Shepherd, Community of the (residential for developmentally disabled men; 18 yrs. and up), The Community of the Good Shepherd, 10101 James A. Reed Rd., Kansas City 64134; (816) 767-8090.

St.Mary's Special School (r,c; 5-21 yrs.), 4445 Lindell Blvd., St. Louis 63108; (314) 792-7320. St. Mary's Supported Living (r,c) (24); supervised homes for adolescents or adults. St. Mary's Early Intervention (d,c) (30); early intervention for toddlers.

Nebraska: Madonna School for Exceptional Children (d,c; 5-21 yrs.), 2537 N. 62nd St., Omaha 68104; (402) 556-1883; www.madonnaschool.org. Children with learning problems.

Villa Marie School and Home for Exceptional Children (r,d,c; 6-18 yrs.), 3700 Sheridan Blvd., Ste. 3, Lincoln 68506; (402) 488-2040.

New Jersey: Archbishop Damiano School (d,c; 3-21 yrs.), 1145 Delsea Dr., Westville Grove 08093.

Catholic Community Services, Archdiocese of Newark, 1160 Raymond Blvd., Newark 07102.

Department of Special Education, Diocese of Camden, 5609 Westfield Ave., Pennsauken, NJ 08110-1836; (609) 488-7123; www.catholicharities.org. Services include: Archbishop Damiano School (above), and full time programs (d,c; 6-21 yrs.) at 4 elementary (96) and 2 high schools (60) and some religious education programs.

Department for Persons with Disabilities, Diocese of Paterson, 1 Catholic Charities Way, Oak Ridge,

N.J. 07438; (973) 697-4395; www.dpd.org. Services include 8 residential programs for adults, one adult training center, family support services.

Felician School for Exceptional Children (d,c; 5-21 yrs.), 260 S. Main St., Lodi 07644; (973) 777-5355.

McAuley School for Exceptional Children (d,c; 5-21 yrs.), 107 Westervelt Ave., North Plainfield, NJ 07060; (908) 754-4114.

Mt. Carmel Guild Special Education School (d,c; 6-21 yrs.), 60 Kingsland Ave., Kearny 07032; (201) 995-3280.

St. Anthony's Special Education School (d,c), 25 N. 7th St., Belleville 07109; (973) 844-3700.

Sister Georgine School (d,c; 6-17 yrs.), 544 Chestnut Ave., Trenton 08611; (609) 396-5444.

St. Patrick's Special Education School (d,c), 72 Central Ave., Newark 07102.

New York: Baker Victory Services (r), 780 Ridge Rd., Lackawanna, N.Y. 14218; (716) 828-9500; www.bakervictoryservices.org. Residential care for handicapped and retarded children; nursery school program for emotionally disturbed pre-school children.

Bishop Patrick V. Ahern High School (d,c; 15-21 yrs.), 100 Merrill Ave., Staten Island 10314.

Cantalician Center for Learning (d,c; birth-21 yrs.), 3233 Main St., Buffalo 14214; (716) 833-5353; www.cantalician.org. Infant and pre-school; elementary and secondary; workshop (426). Three group homes. Rehabilitation, day treatment and senior rehabilitation programs.

Catholic Charities Residential Services, Rockville Centre Diocese, 269 W. Main St., Bay Shore 11706. Residences for developmentally disabled adults (88).

Cobb Memorial School (r,d,c; 5-21 yrs.), 100-300 Mt. Presentation Way, Altamont 12009; (518) 861-6446.

Joan Ann Kennedy Memorial Preschool (d,c; 3-5 yrs.), 26 Sharpe Ave., Staten Island 10302.

L'Arche Syracuse (r, adults), 1232 Teall Ave., Syracuse 13206-3468; (315) 479-8088; www.larchesyracuse.com (12). Homes where assistants and persons with developmental disabilities share life, following the philosophy of Jean Vanier. Member of International L'Arche Federation, Exec. Dir., Frank Woolever.

Maryhaven Center of Hope (r,d,c; school age to adult), 51 Terryville Rd., Port Jefferson 11776; (631) 474-4120; www.maryhaven.org.

Mercy Home for Children (r,c), 243 Prospect Park West, Brooklyn 11215; (718) 832-1075. Residences for adolescents and young adults who are developmentally disabled: Visitation, Warren, Vincent Haire, Santulli and Littlejohn residences (Brooklyn), Kevin Keating Residence (Queens).

Office for Disabled Persons, Catholic Charities, Diocese of Brooklyn, 191 Joralemon St., Brooklyn 11201; (718) 722-6000; www.ccbq.org. Services include: adult day treatment center; community residences for mentally retarded adults; special events for disabled children (from age 3) and adults.

Office for Disabled Persons, Archdiocese of New York, 1011 First Ave., New York 10022; (212) 371-1000. Services include consultation and refer-

ral, variety of services for deaf, blind, mentally retarded, mentally ill.

Seton Foundation for Learning (d,c; 5-15 yrs.), 104 Gordon St., Staten Island 10304; (718) 447-1750.

North Carolina: Holy Angels (r,c; birth to adult), 6600 Wilkinson Blvd., P.O. Box 710, Belmont 28012; (704) 825-4161; www.holyangelsnc.org.

North Dakota: Friendship, Inc. (r,d,c; all ages), 3004 11th St. South, Fargo 58103; (701) 235-8217.

Ohio: Julie Billiart School (d,c; 6-12 yrs.), 4982 Clubside Rd., Cleveland 44124; (216) 381-1191; www.juliebilliartschool.org.

OLA/St. Joseph Center (d,c; 6-16 yrs.), 2346 W. 14th St., Cleveland 44113; (216) 621-3451.

Rose Mary, The Johanna Graselli Rehabilitation and Education Center (r,c; 5 yrs. and older), 19350 Euclid Ave., Cleveland 44117.

St. John's Villa (r,c; continued care and training, 15 yrs. and over), P.O. Box 457, Carrollton 44615; (330) 627-9789.

Oregon: Providence Montessori School Early Intervention Program (d,c; 3-5 yrs.), 830 N.E. 47th Ave., Portland 97213; (503) 215-2409.

Pennsylvania: Clelian Heights School for Exceptional Children (r,d,c; 5-21 yrs.), R.D. 9, Box 607, Greensburg 15601; (724) 837-8120 (95). Also conducts resocialization program (r,d,c; young adults).

Divine Providence Village (adults), 686 Old Marple Rd., Springfield 19064; (610) 328-7730. Admin., Sr. Esther Leroux.

Don Guanella Village: Don Guanella School (r,d,b; 6-21 yrs.) and Cardinal Krol Center (r; adults, postschool age), 1797 S. Sproul Rd., Springfield 19602; (610) 543-3380. Admin. Rev. Dennis Weber, S.C.

John Paul II Center (d,c; 3-21 yrs.), 1092 Welsh Rd., Shillington, PA 19607; (610) 777-0605; www.JohnPaulIICenter.org.

McGuire Memorial (r,d,c; 18 mos. to adult.), 2119 Mercer Rd., New Brighton 15066; (724) 843-3400; www.mcguirememorial.org.

Mercy Special Learning Center (d,c; 3-21 yrs. and early intervention), 830 S. Woodward St., Allentown 18103; (610) 797-8242.

Our Lady of Confidence Day School (d,c; 4½-21 yrs.), 10th and Lycoming Sts., Philadelphia 19140.

Queen of the Universe Day Center (d,c; 4½-16 yrs.), 2479 Trenton Rd., Levittown 19056; (215) 945-6090; www.qudaycenter.org.

St. Anthony School Programs (d,c; 5-21 yrs.), 2718 Custer Ave., Pittsburgh 15227; (412) 882-1333.

St. Joseph Center for Special Learning (d,c; 4-21 yrs.), 2075 W. Norwegian St., Pottsville 17901; (570) 622-4638; www.pottsville.com/stjosephctr.

St. Joseph's Center (r,d,c; birth-10 yrs.), 2010 Adams Ave., Scranton 18509; (570) 342-8379; www.stjosephcenter.org.

St. Katherine Day School (d,c; 4½-21 yrs.), 930 Bowman Ave., Wynnewood 19096; (610) 667-3958; www.stkatherinedayschool.org.

Tennessee: Madonna Learning Center, Inc., for Retarded Children (d,c; 5-16 yrs.), 7007 Poplar Ave., Germantown 38138.

Texas: Notre Dame of Dallas School (d,c; 3-21

yrs.), 2018 Allen St., Dallas 75204; (214) 720-3911.

Virginia: St. Coletta School (d,c; 5-22 yrs.), 207 S. Peyton St., Alexandria, 22314; (703) 683-3686. For developmentally disabled. Services include: occupational, physical and language therapy; vocational program with job search, placement, training and follow-up services.

St. Mary's Infant Home (r,c; birth to 14 yrs.), 317 Chapel St., Norfolk 23504; (757) 622-2208. For multiple handicapped.

Wisconsin: St Coletta of Wisconsin, N4637 County Rd. Y, Jefferson 53549; (920) 674-4330; www.stcolettawi.org. Year-round special education programs for adolescents and adults; prevocational and vocational skills training; residential living alternatives. Young adult population. Employment opportunities for those who qualify.

St. Coletta Day School (c; 8-17 yrs.), 1740 N. 55th St., Milwaukee 53208; (414) 453-1850.

Orthopedically/Physically Challenged

Pennsylvania: St. Edmond's Home for Children (r,c; 1-21 yrs.)., 320 S. Roberts Rd., Rosemont 19010; (610) 525-8800.

Virginia: St. Joseph Villa Housing Corp. (adults), 8000 Brook Rd., Richmond 23227; (804) 553-3283.

Visually Challenged

Maine: Educational Services for Blind and Visually Impaired Children (Catholic Charities, Maine), 1066 Kenduskeag Ave., Bangor 04401. 66 Western Ave., Fairfield 04937. 15 Westminster St., Lewiston 04240. P.O. Box 378, Fairfield, ME 04937; (800) 660-5231. Itinerant teachers, instructional materials center.

New Jersey: St. Joseph's School for the Blind (r,d,c; 3-21 yrs.), 257 Baldwin Ave., Jersey City 07306; (201) 653-0578; www.sjsb.net.

New York: Lavelle School for the Blind (d,c; 3-21 yrs.), East 221st St. and Paulding Ave., Bronx 10469; (718) 882-1212. For visually impaired, multiple handicapped.

Pennsylvania: St. Lucy Day School (d,c; pre-K to 8th grade), 130 Hampden Rd., Upper Darby 19082; (610) 352-4550; www.stlucydayschool.org. For children with visual impairments.

HOUSES OF RETREAT AND RENEWAL

There is great variety in retreat and renewal programs, with orientations ranging from the traditional to teen encounters. Central to all of them are celebration of the liturgy and deepening of a person's commitment to faith and witness in life.

Features of many of the forms are as follows.

Traditional Retreats: Centered around conferences and the direction of a retreat master; oriented to the personal needs of the retreatants; including such standard practices as participation in Mass, reception of the sacraments, private and group prayer, silence and meditation, discussions.

Team Retreat: Conducted by a team of several leaders or directors (priests, religious, lay persons) with division of subject matter and activities according to their special skills and the nature and needs of the group.

Closed Retreat: Involving withdrawal for a period of time — overnight, several days, a weekend — from everyday occupations and activities.

Open Retreat: Made without total disengagement from everyday involvements, on a part-time basis.

Private Retreat: By one person, on a kind of do-it-yourself basis with the one-to-one assistance of a director.

Special Groups: With formats and activities geared to particular groups; e.g., members of Alcoholics Anonymous, vocational groups and apostolic groups.

Marriage Encounters: Usually weekend periods of husband-wife reflection and dialogue; introduced into the U.S. from Spain in 1967.

Charismatic Renewal: Featuring elements of the movement of the same name; "Spirit-oriented," communitarian and flexible, with spontaneous and shared prayer, personal testimonies of faith and witness.

Christian Community: Characterized by strong community thrust.

Teens Encounter Christ (TEC), SEARCH: Formats adapted to the mentality and needs of youth, involving experience of Christian faith and commitment in a community setting.

Christian Maturity Seminars: Similar to teen encounters in basic concept but different to suit persons of greater maturity.

RENEW International: Spiritual renewal process involving the entire parish. Office, 1232 George St., Plainfield, NJ 07062; (908) 769-5400. Director, Msgr. Thomas A. Kleissler.

Cursillo: *See separate entry.*

Conference

Retreats International Inc.: National Office, Box 1067, Notre Dame, IN 46556; (574) 247-4443. An organization for promoting retreats in the U.S. was started in 1904 in New York. Its initial efforts and the gradual growth of the movement led to the formation in 1927 of the National Catholic Laymen's Retreat Conference, the forerunner of the men's division of Retreats International. The women's division developed from the National Laywomen's Retreat Movement that was founded in Chicago in 1936. The men's and women's divisions merged July 9, 1977. The services of the organization include an annual summer institute for retreat and pastoral ministry, regional conferences for retreat center leadership and area meetings of directors and key leadership in the retreat movement. The officers are: Episcopal advisor, Auxiliary Bishop Robert Morneau of Green Bay; Pres., Sr. Mary Elizabeth Imler, O.S.F.; Exec. Dir., Anne M. Luther.

Houses of Retreat and Renewal

Principal sources: Catholic Almanac *survey*; The Official Catholic Directory.

Abbreviation code: m, men; w, women; mc, married couples; y, youth. Houses and centers without code generally offer facilities to most groups. An asterisk after an abbreviation indicates that the facility is primarily for the group designated but that special groups are also accommodated. Houses furnish information concerning the types of programs they offer.

Alabama: Blessed Trinity Shrine Retreat and Cenacle, 107 Holy Trinity Rd., Holy Trinity 36856, (334) 855-4474; Visitation Sacred Heart Retreat House, 2300 Spring Hill Ave., Mobile 36607, (334) 473-2321.

Alaska: Holy Spirit Center, 10980 Hillside Dr., Anchorage 99507, (907) 346-2343, home.gci.net/~hsrh.

Arizona: Franciscan Renewal Center, 5802 E. Lincoln Dr., Scottsdale 85253, (480) 948-7460; Holy Trinity Monastery, P.O. Box 298, St. David 85630, Benedictine community, selfdirected/Spiritdirected monastic retreat, (520) 720-4642; Mount Claret Retreat Center, 4633 N. 54th St., Phoenix 85018, (602) 840-5066; Our Lady of Solitude House of Prayer, P.O. Box 1140, Black Canyon City 85324, (623) 374-9204; Redemptorist Picture Rocks Retreat House, 7101 W. Picture Rocks Rd., Tucson 85743, (520) 744-3400, www.desertrenewal.org.

Arkansas: Brothers and Sisters of Charity, Little Portion Hermitage, 350 CR 248, Berryville, 72616-8505, (479) 253-7710, www.johnmichaeltalbot.com; Little Portion Retreat and Training Center, Rt. 4, Box 430, Eureka Springs 72632, (501) 253-7379; St. Scholastica Retreat Center, P.O. Box 3489, Ft. Smith 72913, (479) 783-1135, www. scholastica-fortsmith.org; Hesychia House of Prayer, 204 St. Scholastica Rd., New Blaine, Shoal Creek, 72851, (501) 938-7375.

California: Angela Center, 535 Angela Dr., Santa Rosa 95403, (707) 528-8578; Christ the King Retreat Center, 6520 Van Maren Lane, Citrus Heights 95621, (916) 725-4720, www.passionist.org; Claretian Retreat Center, 1119 Westchester Pl., Los Angeles 90019, (323) 737-8464; El Carmelo Retreat House, P.O. Box 446, Redlands 92373, (909) 792-1047, www.elcarmelo.org; Heart of Jesus Retreat Center, 2927 S. Greenville St., Santa Ana 92704, (714) 557-4538; Holy Spirit Retreat Center, 4316 Lanai Rd., Encino 91436, (818) 784-4515; Holy Transfiguration Monastery (m*), Monks of Mt. Tabor (Byzantine Ukrainian), 17001 Tomki Rd., P.O. Box 217, Redwood Valley 95470, (707) 485-8959; Jesuit Retreat House, 300 Manresa Way, Los Altos 94022, (650) 917-4000, www.jrclosaltos.org; Madonna of Peace Renewal Center (y), P.O. Box 71, Copperopolis 95228, (209) 785-2157; Marian Retreat Center, 535 Sacramento St., Auburn 95603, (916) 887-2019; Mary and Joseph Retreat Center, 5300 Crest Rd., Rancho Palos Verdes 90275, (310) 377-4867, www.maryjoseph.org.

Marywood Retreat Center, 2811 E. Villa Real Dr., Orange 92863-1595, (714) 282-3000, www.rcbo.org; Mater Dolorosa Retreat Center, 700 N. Sunnyside Ave., Sierra Madre 91024, (626) 355-7188, www.passionist.org; Mercy Center, 2300 Adeline Dr., Burlingame 94010, (650) 340-7474, www.mercycenter.org; Mission San Luis Rey Retreat, 4050 Mission Ave., Oceanside, 92057-6402, (760) 757-3659, www.sanluisrey.org; Mount Alverno Retreat and Conference Center, 3910 Bret Harte Dr., Redwood City 94061, (650) 369-0798, www.moun-

talverno.com; New Camaldoli Hermitage, Big Sur 93920, (831) 667-2456, www.contemplation.com; Our Lady of the Oaks Villa, P.O. Box 128, Applegate 95703, (530) 878-2776.

Poverello of Assisi Retreat House, 1519 Woodworth St., San Fernando 91340, (818) 365-1071; Presentation Education and Retreat Center, 19480 Bear Creek Rd., Los Gatos 95033, (408) 354-2346, www.prescenter.org; Prince of Peace Abbey, 650 Benet Hill Rd., Oceanside 92054, (760) 430-1305; Pro Sanctity Spirituality Center, 205 S. Pine St., Fullerton 92633 (for day use), www.caprosanctity.org; Sacred Heart Retreat House (w*), 920 E. Alhambra Rd., Alhambra 91801, (626) 289-1353; St. Andrew's Abbey Retreat House, P.O. Box 40, Valyermo 93563, (661) 944-2178, www.valyermo.com; St. Anthony Retreat, P.O. Box 249, Three Rivers 93271, (559) 561-4595, www.stanthonyretreat.org; St. Clare's Retreat, 2381 Laurel Glen Rd., Soquel 95073, (831) 423-8093, www.stclaresretreatcenter.com; St. Francis Retreat, P.O. Box 970, San Juan Bautista 95045, (831) 623-4234,www.stfrancisretreat.com; St. Francis Youth Center (y), 2400 E. Lake Ave., Watsonville 95076; St. Joseph's Salesian Youth Center, P.O. Box 1639, 8301 Arroyo Dr., Rosemead 91770, (626) 280-8622, www.stjoescenter.org; St. Mary's Seminary and Retreat House, 1964 Las Canoas Rd., Santa Barbara 93105, (805) 966-4829; San Damiano Retreat, P.O. Box 767, Danville 94526, (925) 837-9141, www.sandamiano.org.

Santa Sabina Center, 25 Magnolia Ave., San Rafael 94901, (415) 457-7727; Serra Retreat, 3401 S. Serra Rd., Box 127, Malibu 90265, (310) 456-6631, www.serraretreat.com; Starcross Community, 34500 Annapolis Rd., Annapolis 95412, (707) 886-1919, www.starcross.org; Villa Maria del Mar, Santa Cruz, 21918 E. Cliff Dr., Santa Cruz 95062, (831) 475-1236, www.villamariadelmar.org; Villa Maria – House of Prayer (w), 1252 N. Citrus Dr., La Habra 90631, (562) 691-5838.

Colorado: Benet Pines Retreat Center, 3190 Benet Lane, Colorado Springs 80921, (719) 633-0655, www.benethillmonastery.org; Camp St. Malo Religious Retreat and Conference Center, 10758, Hwy. 7, Allenspark 80510, (303) 747-2892; Sacred Heart Retreat House, Box 185, Sedalia 80135, (303) 688-4198, www.gabrielmedia.org/shjrh; Spiritual Life Institute (individuals only), Nada Hermitage, P.O. Box 219, Crestone 81131, (719) 256-4778. www.spirituallifeinstitute.org.

Connecticut: St. Edmund's Retreat, P.O. Box 399, Mystic 06355, (860) 536-0565, www.sse.org/enders; Emmaus Spiritual Life Center, 24 Maple Ave., Uncasville 06382, (860) 848-3427; Holy Family Retreat, 303 Tunxis Rd., Farmington 06107, (860) 521-0440; Immaculata Retreat House, P.O. Box 55, Willimantic 06226, (860) 423-8484, www.immaculateretreat.org; Mercy Center at Madison, P.O. Box 191, 167 Neck Rd., Madison 06443, (203) 245-0401, www.mercybythesea.org; My Father's House, Box 22, 39 North Moodus Rd., Moodus 06469, (860) 873-1906, www.myfathershouse.com; Our Lady of Calvary Retreat (w*), 31 Colton St., Farmington 06032, (860) 677-8519, www.ourladyofcalvary.com;

Trinita Retreat Center, 595 Town Hill Rd., Rt. 219, New Hartford 06057, (860) 379-4329; Villa Maria Guadalupe Retreat House, 159 Sky Meadow Dr., Stamford 06903, (203) 329-1492; Wisdom House Retreat Center, 229 E. Litchfield Rd., 06759, (860) 567-3163, www.wisdomhouse.org.

Delaware: St. Francis Renewal Center, 1901 Prior Rd., Wilmington 19809, (302) 798-1454.

District of Columbia: Washington Retreat House, 4000 Harewood Rd. N.E., Washington 20017, (202) 529-1111.

Florida: Cenacle Retreat House, 1400 S. Dixie Highway, Lantana 33462-5492, (561) 582-2534, www.cenaclesisters.org; Dominican Retreat House, Inc., 7275 S.W. 124th St., Miami 33156-5324, (305) 238-2711; Franciscan Center, 3010 Perry Ave., Tampa 33603, (813) 229-2695, www.slleganyfranciscans.org/franciscancenter.htm; John Paul II Retreat House, 720 N.E. 27th St., Miami 33137, (305) 576-2748, www.acu-adsum.org; Our Lady of Divine Providence, 702 S. Bayview Ave., Clearwater, 33759, (727) 797-7412, www.divineprovidence.org; Our Lady of Perpetual Help Retreat and Spirituality Center, 3989 S. Moon Dr., Venice 34292, (941) 486-0233, www.olph-retreat.org; Saint John Neumann Renewal Center, 685 Miccosukee Rd., Tallahassee 32308, (850) 224-2971; St. Leo Abbey Retreat Center, P.O. Box 2350, St. Leo 33574, (352) 588-2009.

Georgia: Ignatius House, 6700 Riverside Dr. N.W., Atlanta 30328, (404) 255-0503.

Idaho: Nazareth Retreat Center, 4450 N. Five Mile Rd., Boise 83713, (208) 375-2932.

Illinois: Bellarmine Jesuit Retreat House (mc), 420 W. County Line Rd, Barrington 60010, (847) 381-1261, www.bellarminehall.org; Bishop Lane Retreat House, 7708 E. McGregor Rd., Rockford 61102, (815) 965-5011; bishoplane,org; Cabrini Retreat Center, 9430 Golf Rd., Des Plaines 60016, (847) 297-6530; Carmelite Spiritual Center, 8433 Bailey Rd., Darien 60561, (630) 969-4141; Cenacle Retreat House, 513 Fullerton Parkway, Chicago 60614, (773) 528-6300; Cenacle Retreat House, P.O. Box 797, Warrenville 60555, (630) 393-1231, www.cenacle.org; King's House Retreat and Renewal Center, 700 N. 66th St., Belleville 62223-3949, (618) 397-0584;

La Salle Manor, Christian Brothers Retreat House, 12480 Galena Rd., Plano 60545, (630) 552-3224, www.lasallemanor.org; St. Mary's Retreat House, P.O. Box 608, 14230 Main St., Lemont 60439, (630) 257-5102.

Indiana: Archabbey Guest House, St. Meinrad Archabbey, St. Meinrad 47577, (800) 581-6905, www.saintmeinrad.edu; Benedict Inn Retreat and Conference Center, 1402 Southern Ave., Beech Grove 46107, (317) 788-7581, www.benedictinn.org; Bethany Retreat House, 2202 Lituanica Ave., 46312, (219) 398-5047; Fatima Retreat House, 5353 E. 56th St., Indianapolis 46226-1486, (317) 545-7681, www.archindy.org; John XXIII Retreat Center, 407 W. McDonald St., Hartford City 47348, (765) 348-4008, www.netusa1.net/~john23rd; Kordes Retreat Center, 841 E. 14th St., Ferdinand 47532, (812) 367-1411, www.thedome.org/kordes; Lindenwood, PHJC Ministry Center, P.O. Box 1, Donaldson 46513, (574) 935-1780; Mount Saint Francis Retreat Center and Friary, 101 St. Anthony Dr., Mount Saint Francis 47146, (812) 923-8817, www.mountsaintfrancis.org; Sarto Retreat House, 4200 N. Kentucky Ave., Evansville 47724, (812) 424-5536.

Iowa: American Martyrs Retreat House, 2209 N. Union Rd., P.O. Box 605, Cedar Falls 50613-0605, (319) 266-3543, www.americanmartyrs.tripod.com; Emmanuel House of Prayer Country Retreat and Solitude Center, 4427 Kotts Rd. N.E., Iowa City 52240; New Melleray Guest House, 6632 Melleray Circle, Dubuque 52068, (319) 588-2319, www.newmelleray.org; Shalom Spirituality Center, 1001 Davis Ave., Dubuque 52001, (319) 582-3592, members.aol.com/dbqshalom.

Kansas: Heartland Center for Spirituality, 3600 Broadway, Great Bend 67530, (316) 792-1232; Manna House of Prayer, 323 East 5th St., Box 675, Concordia 66901, (785) 243-4428; Spiritual Life Center, 7100 E. 45th St., N. Wichita 67226, (316) 744-0167, www.slcwichita.org.

Kentucky: Bethany Spring, 115 Dee Head Rd., New Haven, 40051, (502) 549-8277; Flaget Center, 1935 Lewiston Dr., Louisville 40216, (502) 448-8581; Marydale Retreat Center, 945 Donaldson Hwy., Erlanger 41018, (606) 371-4224; Mt. St. Joseph Retreat Center, 8001 Cummings Rd., Maple Mount 42356-9999, (229) 229-0200, www.msjcenter.org; Our Lady of Gethsemani (m, w, private), The Guestmaster, Abbey of Gethsemani, Trappist, 40051; Passionist Nuns, 8564 Crisp Rd, Whitesville 42378, (270) 233-4571.

Louisiana: Abbey Christian Life Center, St. Joseph's Abbey, St. Benedict 70457, (504) 892-3473; Ave Maria Retreat House, 8089 Barataria Blvd., Crown Point, 70072, (504) 689-3837; Cenacle Retreat House (w*), 5500 St. Mary St., P.O. Box 8115, Metairie 70006, (504) 887-1420, www.cenaclesisters.org/metairie.htm; Jesuit Spirituality Center (m,w; directed), P.O. Box C, Grand Coteau 70541-1003, (337) 662-5251, www.jesuitspiritualitycenter.org; Lumen Christi Retreat Center, 100 Lumen Christi Lane, Hwy. 311, Schriever 70395, (504) 868-1523; Magnificat Center of the Holy Spirit, 23629 Faith Rd., Ponchatoula 70454, (504) 362-4356.

Manresa House of Retreats (m), P.O. Box 89, Convent 70723, (225) 562-3596; Maryhill Renewal Center, 600 Maryhill Rd., Pineville 71360, (318) 640-1378, www.diocesealex.org; Our Lady of the Oaks Retreat House, P.O. Box D, 214 Church St., Grand Coteau 70541, (318) 662-5410; Regina Coeli Retreat Center, 17225 Regina Coeli Rd., Covington 70433, (504) 892-4110; Sophie Barat House, 1719 Napoleon Ave., New Orleans 70115, (504) 899-6027.

Maine: Bay View Villa, 187 Bay View Rd., Saco 04072, (207) 286-8762; Marie Joseph Spiritual Center, 10 Evans Rd., Biddeford 04005, (207) 284-5671, www.mariejosephspiritual.org; Mother of the Good Shepherd Monastery by the Sea, 235 Pleasant Ave., Peaks Island 04108, (207) 766-2717; Notre Dame Retreat & Spiritual Center, P.O. Box 159, Alfred 04002, (207) 324-6160; St. Paul Retreat and Cursillo Center, 136 State St., Augusta 04330, (207) 622-6235.

Maryland: Retreatand Conference Center at Bon

Secours, Marriottsville 21104, (410) 442-1320, www.rccbonsecours.com; Christian Brothers Spiritual Center (m,w,y), P.O. Box 29, 2535 Buckeyestown Pike, Adamstown 21710, (301) 874-5180; Loyola on the Potomac Retreat House, Faulkner 20632, (301) 870-3515, www.loyolaretreat.org; Msgr. Clare J. O'Dwyer Retreat House (y*), 15523 York Rd., P.O. Box 310, Sparks 21152, (410) 666-2400; Our Lady of Mattaponi Youth Retreat and Conference Center, 11000 Mattaponi Rd., Upper Marlboro 20772, (301) 952-9074; Seton Retreat Center, 333 S. Seton Ave., Emmitsburg 21727, (301) 447-6021.

Massachusetts: Boston Cenacle Society, 25 Avery St., Dedham 02026; Calvary Retreat Center, 59 South St., P.O. Box 219, Shrewsbury 01545, (508) 842-8821, www.calvaryretreat.org; Campion Renewal Center, 319 Concord Rd., Weston 02193, (781) 788-6810; Community of Teresian Carmelites, 30 Chrome St., 01613, (508) 752-5734; Don Orione Center, P.O. Box 205, Old Groveland Rd., Bradford 01835, (508) 373-0461; Eastern Point Retreat House, Gonzaga Hall, 37 Niles Pond Rd., Gloucester 01930, (978) 283-0013; Espousal Center, 554 Lexington St., Waltham 02452, (781) 209-3120, www.espousal.org; Esther House of Spiritual Renewal, Sisters of St. Anne, 1015 Pleasant St., Worcester 01602-1338.

Franciscan Center — Retreat House, 459 River Rd., Andover 01810, (978) 851-3391, www.franrcent.org; Genesis Spiritual Life Center, 53 Mill St., Westfield 01085, (413) 562-3627, www.genesisspiritualcenter.org; Glastonbury Abbey (Benedictine Monks), 16 Hull St., Hingham 02043, (701) 749-2155, www.glastonburyabbey.org; Holy Cross Fathers Retreat House, 490 Washington St., N. Easton 02356, (508) 238-2051; La Salette Retreat Center, 947 Park St., Attleboro 02703, (508) 222-8530, www.lasaletteretreatcenter.com; Marian Center, 1365 Northampton St., Holyoke 01040-1913, (413) 534-4502 (day and evening programs); Marist House, 518 Pleasant St., 01701, (508) 879-1620; Miramar Retreat Center, P.O. Box M, Duxbury, 02331-0614, (781) 585-2460, www.miramarretreat.org; Mt. Carmel Christian Life Center, Oblong Rd., Box 613, Williamstown 01267, (413) 458-3164.

Sacred Heart Retreat Center, Salesians of St. John Bosco, P.O. Box 567, Ipswich 01938; St. Benedict Abbey (Benedictine Monks), 252 Still River Rd., P.O. Box 67, Still River 01467, (978) 456-3221; St. Joseph Villa Retreat Center, Sisters of St. Joseph, 339 Jerusalem Rd., Cohasset 02025, (781) 383-6024; St. Joseph's Abbey Retreat House (m) (Trappist Monks), 167 North Spencer Rd., Spencer 01562, (508) 885-8710, www.spencerabbey.org; St. Stephen Priory Spiritual Life Center (Dominican), 20 Glen St., Box 370, Dover 02030, (508) 785-0124, www.ststephenpriory.org.

Michigan: Augustine Center Retreat House, 2798 U.S. 31 North, Box 84, Conway 49722, (231) 347-3657, www.home.catholicweb.com/augustinecenter/; Capuchin Retreat, 62460 Mt. Vernon, Box 396, Washington 48094, (248) 651-4826; Colombiere Conference and Retreat Center, 9075 Big Lake Rd., Clarkston 48346, (248) 620-2534, www.colombiere.com; Manresa Jesuit Retreat House, 1390

Quarton Rd., Bloomfield Hills 48304, (248) 644-4933; Marygrove Retreat Center, Garden 49835, (906) 644-2771; Queen of Angels Retreat, 3400 S. Washington Rd., P.O. Box 2026, Saginaw 48605, (517) 755-2149, www.rc.net/saginaw/retreat.

St. Francis Retreat Center, 703 E. Main St., De Witt 48820-9499, (517) 669-8321, www.stfrancis.ws; St. Mary's Retreat House, 775 W. Drahner Rd., Oxford 48371, (248) 628-3894, www.stmarysretreathouse.org; St. Paul of the Cross Retreat Center (m*), 23333 Schoolcraft, Detroit 48223, (313) 535-9563; Weber Retreat Center, 1257 Siena Hghts. Dr., Adrian 49221, (517) 266-4000.

Minnesota: Benedictine Center, St. Paul's Monastery, 2675 Larpenteur Ave. East, St. Paul 55106, (651) 777-7251, www.osb.org/spm; The Cenacle, 1221 Wayzata Blvd., Wayzata 55391; Center for Spiritual Development, 211 Tenth St. S., P.O. Box 538, Bird Island 55310, (320) 365-3644, www.centerbi.com; Christ the King Retreat Center, 621 First Ave. S., Buffalo 55313, (763) 682-1394, www.kingshouse.com; Dunrovin Christian Brothers' Retreat Center, 15525 St. Croix Trail North, Marine on St. Croix 55047, (651) 433-2486, www.dunrovin.org.

Franciscan Retreats, Conventual Franciscan Friars, 16385 St. Francis Lane, Prior Lake 55372, (952) 447-2182, www.franciscanretreats.net; Holy Spirit Retreat House, 3864 420th Ave., Janesville, 56048, (507) 234-5712; Jesuit Retreat House (m), 8243 DeMontreville Trail North, Lake Elmo 55042, (651) 777-1311; Maryhill (m,w*), 1988 Summit Ave., St. Paul 55105, (651) 696-2970, www.sdhm.net; Villa Maria Retreat and Conference, 29847 County 2 Blvd., Frontenac 55026, (651) 345-4582; www.villamariaretreats.org.

Missouri: Assumption Abbey, Rte. 5, Box 1056, Ava 65608, (417) 683-5110, www.assumptionabbey.org; The Cenacle, 3393 McKelvey Rd., Apt. 211, Bridgeton, 63044-2544, (314) 387-2211; Cordis House, 648 S. Assisi Way, Republic 65738, (417) 732-6684; Il Ritiro The Little Retreat, P.O. Box 38, Eime Rd., Dittmer 63023, (636) 274-0554; La Salle Institute, 2101 Rue de la Salle, Wildwood 63038, (636) 938-5374; Maria Fonte Solitude (private; individual hermitages), P.O. Box 322, High Ridge 63049, (314) 677-3235.

Marianist Retreat and Conference Center, P.O. Box 718, Eureka 63025-0718, (636) 938-5390; Mercy Center, 2039 N. Geyer Rd., St. Louis 63131, (314) 909-4629; Our Lady of Assumption Abbey (m,w), Trappists, Rt. 5, Box 1056, Ava 65608-9142, (417) 683-5110; Pallottine Renewal Center, 15270 Old Halls Ferry Rd., Florissant 63034, (314) 837-7100; members.aol.com/prcrenewal/home.html; Society of Our Mother of Peace (private, individual hermitages), 6150 Antire Rd., High Ridge 63049, (636) 677-3235; White House Retreat, 3601 Lindell Blvd., St. Louis 63108, (314) 846-2575, www.whretreat.org; Windridge Solitude, 1932 W. Linda Lane, Lonedell 63060; (636) 629-4449.

Montana: Sacred Heart Retreat Center, 26 Wyoming Ave., P.O. Box 153, Billings 59103, (406) 252-0322; Ursuline Retreat Centre, 2300 Central Ave., Great Falls 59401, (406) 452-8585.

Nebraska: Our Lady of Good Counsel retreat

House, R.R. 1, Box 110, 7303 N. 112th St., Waverly 68462, (402) 786-2705.

New Hampshire: Epiphany Monastery, 96 Scobie Rd., P.O. Box 60, New Boston 03070; La Salette Shrine (private and small groups), 410 NH, Route 4A, P.O. Box 420, Enfield 03748, (603) 632-7087.

New Jersey: Bethany Ridge, P.O. Box 241, Little York 08834, (908) 995-9758; Bethlehem Hermitage, 82 Pleasant Hill Rd., Chester 07930-2135, (908) 879-7059; Cenacle Retreat House, 411 River Rd., Highland Park 08904, (732) 249-8100, www.cenacle.sisters.org; Emmaus House, 101 Center St., Perth Amboy 08861, (732) 442-7688; Father Judge Apostolic Center (young adults), 1292 Long Hill Rd., Stirling 07980; Felician Retreat House, 35 Windemere Ave., Mt. Arlington 07856, (973) 398-9806; John Paul II Retreat Center, 414 S. 8th St., Vineland 08360; Loyola House of Retreats, 161 James St., Morristown 07960, (973) 539-0740, www.loyola.org.

Marianist Family Retreat Center (families*), 417 Yale Ave., Box 488, Cape May Point 08212-0488; Maris Stella (Retreat and Vacation Center), 7201 Long Beach Blvd., P.O. Box 3135, Harvey Cedars 08008, (609) 474-1182; www.marisstella.net; Mount Paul Retreat Center, 243 Mt. Paul Rd., Oak Ridge 07438, (973) 697-6341; Franciscan Spiritual Center, 474 Sloatsburg Rd., Ringwood 07456-1978, (973) 962-9778; Queen of Peace Retreat House, St. Paul's Abbey, P.O. Box 7, Newton 07860, (973) 383-2470, www.newtonsb.org; Sacred Heart Renewal Center, P.O. Box 68, Belvidere 07823, (908) 475-4694; Sacred Heart Retreat Center (y*, m,w), 20 Old Swartswood Rd., Newton 07860, (973) 383-2620; St. Joseph by the Sea Retreat House, 400 Rte. 35 N., South Mantoloking 08738-1309, (732) 892-8494, www.sjbsea.org.

St. Pius X Spiritual Life Center, P.O. Box 216, Blackwood 08012, (856) 227-1436; San Alfonso Retreat House, P.O. Box 3098, 755 Ocean Ave., Long Beach 07740, (732) 222-2731, www.sanalfonsoretreats.org; Sanctuary of Mary, Pilgrimage Place, Branchville 07826, (973) 875-7625; Stella Maris Retreat House, 981 Ocean Ave., Elberon 07740, (732) 229-0602, www.stellamarisretreatcenter.org; Villa Pauline Retreat House, 350 Bernardsville Rd., Mendham 07945, (973) 543-9058; Vincentian Renewal Center, 75 Mapleton Rd., P.O. Box 757, Plainsboro 08536, (609) 520-9626; Vocationist Fathers Retreat, 90 Brooklake Rd., Florham Park 07932, (973) 966-6262, www.vocationist.org; Xavier Retreat and Conference Center, P.O. Box 211, Convent Station 07961, (973) 290-5100, www.xaviercenter.org.

New Mexico: Holy Cross Retreat, Conventual Franciscan Friars, 600 Holy Cross Rd., Mesilla Park 88047, (505) 524-3688, www.zianet.com/franciscan; Immaculate Heart of Mary Retreat and Conference Center, Mt. Carmel Rd., Santa Fe 87501, (505) 988-1975; Madonna Retreat Center, Inc., 4040 St. Joseph Pl., N.W., 87120, (505) 831-8196; Pecos Benedictine Monastery, Pecos 87552, (505) 757-6600, www.pecosabbey.org; Spiritual Renewal Center, 6400 Coors Rd., NW, Albuquerque 87120; (505) 890-4110; www.spiritualretreats.com; Sacred Heart Retreat, P.O. Box 1989, Gallup 87301.

New York: Bethany Spirituality Center, 202 County Road 105, Box 1003, Highland Mills 10930, (845) 460-3061, www.bthanysiritualitycnter.org. Bethlehem Retreat House, Abbey of the Genesee, 3258 River Rd., Piffard 14533, (585) 243-2220, www.abbeyretreats.org; Bishop Molloy Retreat House, 86-45 Edgerton Blvd., Jamaica 11432, (718) 639-1229, www.bishopmolloy.org; National Kateri Tekakwitha Shrine, P.O. Box 627, Fonda 12068, (518) 853-3646, www.katerishrine.com; Cardinal Spellman Retreat House, Passionist Community, 5801 Palisade Ave., Bronx (Riverdale) 10471, (718) 549-6500, www.passionists.org; Cenacle Retreat Center, 310 Cenacle Rd., Ronkonkoma 11779-2203, (631) 588-8366, www.cenaclesisters.org.

Cenacle Retreat House, State Rd., P.O. Box 467, Bedford Village 10506, (914) 234-3344; Christ the King Retreat and Conference Center, 500 Brookford Rd., Syracuse 13224, (315) 446-2680; Cormaria Retreat House, Sag Harbor, L.I. 11963, (631) 725-4206; Dominican Retreat and Conference Center, 1945 Union St., Niskayuma, (518) 393-4169, www.dslcny.org; Marian Shrine and Don Bosco Retreat Center, 174 Filors Lane, Stony Point, 10980-2645, (845) 947-2200, www.marianshrine.org; Graymoor Spiritual Life Center, Graymoor, Route 9, P.O. Box 300, Garrison 10524, (845) 424-2111, www.graymoorcenter.org; Jesuit Retreat House, Auriesville, (518) 853-3033; Monastery of the Precious Blood (w), Ft. Hamilton Parkway and 54th St., Brooklyn 11219 (single day retreats); Mount Alvernia Retreat Center, Box 858, Wappingers Falls 12590, (845) 297-5706, www.mtalvernia.org.

Mount Irenaeus Franciscan Mountain Retreat, Holy Peace Friary, P.O. Box 100, West Clarksville, NY 14786, (716) 973-2470; Mount Manresa Retreat House, 239 Fingerboard Rd., Staten Island 10305, (718) 727-3844; Mt. St. Alphonsus Redemptorist Retreat Ministry, P.O. Box 219, Esopus 12429, (845) 384-8000, www.msaretreat.org; Notre Dame Retreat House, Box 342, 5151 Foster Rd., Canandaigua 14424, (585) 394-5700, www.notredameretreathouse.org; Our Lady of Hope Center, 434 River Rd., Newburgh 12550, (914) 568-0780; Regina Maria Retreat House, 77 Brinkerhoff St., Plattsburgh 12901-2701, (518) 561-3421; St. Andrew's House, 257 St. Andrew's Rd., Walden 12586, (845) 778-5941; St. Columban Center, Diocese of Buffalo, 6892 Lake Shore Rd., P.O. Box 816, Derby 14047, (716) 947-4708, www.stcolumbacenter.org.

St. Francis Retreat, 1 Pryer Manor Rd., Larchmont 10538, (914) 235-6839; St. Francis Center for Spirituality, 500 Todt Hill Rd., Staten Island, NY 10304, (718) 981-3131, www.st-francis-center-for-spirituality.org; St. Gabriel's Spiritual Center for Youth (y, mc), 64 Burns Rd., P.O. Box 3015, Shelter Island Heights 11965, (631) 749-3154 (fax); St. Ignatius Retreat House, 251 Searingtown Rd., Manhasset 11030, (516) 621-8300, www.inisfada.net; St. Josaphat's Retreat House, Basilian Monastery, 1 East Beach Dr., Glen Cove 11542, (516) 671-8980; St. Joseph Center (Spanish Center), 275 W. 230th St., Bronx 10463, (718) 796-4340; St. Mary's Villa, 150 Sisters Servants Lane, P.O. Box 9, Sloatsburg 10974-0009, (914) 753-5100;

St. Paul Center, 2135 Crescent St., Astoria 11105, (718) 932-0752; St. Ursula Retreat Center, 186 Middle Rd., Blue Point 11715, (631) 363-2422, www.ursulinesofbluepoint.org; Stella Maris Retreat Center, 130 E. Genesee St., Skaneateles 13152, (315) 685-6836; Tagaste Monastery, 220 Lafayette Ave., Suffern 10901; Trinity Retreat, 1 Pryer Manor Rd., Larchmont 10538, (914) 235-6839.

North Carolina: Avila Retreat Center, 711 Mason Rd., Durham 27712, (919) 477-1285; Madonna House, 424 Rose Ln., Raleigh 27610.

North Dakota: Presentation Prayer Center, 1101 32nd Ave. S., Fargo 58103, (701) 237-4857; Queen of Peace Retreat, 1310 Broadway, Fargo 58102, (701) 293-9286.

Ohio: Bergamo Center for Lifelong Learning, 4400 Shakertown Rd., Dayton 45430, (937) 426-2363, www.bergamocenter.org; Friarhurst Retreat House, 8136 Wooster Pike, Cincinnati 45227, (513) 561-2270; Jesuit Retreat House, 5629 State Rd., Cleveland 44134-2292, (440) 884-9300, www.jrh-cleveland.org; Jesuit Spiritual Center at Milford, 5361 S. Milford Rd., Milford 45150, (513) 248-3500, www.milfordspiritualcenter.org; Loyola of the Lakes, 700 Killinger Rd., Clinton 44216-9653, (330) 896-2315, www.loyolaofthelakes.com; Maria Stein Spiritual Center, 2365 St. Johns Rd., Maria Stein 45860, (419) 925-7625, www.spiritualcenter.net; Our Lady of Consolation Retreat House, 321 Clay St., Carey 43316, (419) 396-7970, www.olcshrine.com; Our Lady of the Pines, 1250 Tiffin St., Fremont 43420, (419) 332-6522, www.pinesretreat.org.

Sacred Heart Retreat and Renewal Center, 3128 Logan Ave., P.O. Box 6074, Youngstown 44501, (330) 759-9539; St. Joseph Christian Life Center, 18485 Lake Shore Blvd., Cleveland 44119, (216) 531-7370, www.enterthecenter.org; St. Francis Spirituality Center, 200 St. Francis Ave., Tiffin 44883, (419) 443-1485, www.stfrancisspiritualitycenter.org; St. Therese Retreat Center, 5277 E. Broad St., Columbus, OH 43213, (614) 866-1611, www.cathedral-bookshop.com.

Oklahoma: St. Gregory's Abbey, 1900 W. MacArthut, Shawnee 74804, (405) 878-5491, www.monksok.org.

Oregon: The Jesuit Spirituality Center, 424 S.W. Mill St., Portland 97201, (503) 242-1973; Mount Angel Abbey Retreat House, 1 Abbey Dr., St. Benedict 97373, (503) 845-3027, www.mountangelabbey.org; Our Lady of Peace Retreat, 3600 S. W. 170th Ave., Beaverton 97006, (503) 649-7127, www.geocities.com/ourladyofpeaceretreat; St. Rita Retreat Center, P.O. Box 310, Gold Hill 97525, (541) 855-1333; Shalom Prayer Center, Benedictine Sisters, 840 S. Main St., Mt. Angel 97362-9527, (503) 845-6773, www.benedict-srs.org; St. Benedict Lodge, 56630 North Bank Rd., McKenzie Bridge 97413, (541) 822-3572; Trappist Abbey Guesthouse (m,w), 9200 N.E. Abbey Rd., Lafayette 97127, (503) 852-0107; www.trappistabbey.org.

Pennsylvania: Avila Retreat Center, 61 E. High St., Union City 16438, (814) 438-7020; Dominican Retreat House, 750 Ashbourne Rd., Elkins Park 19027, (215) 782-8520; Ecclesia Center, 9101 Ridge Rd., Erie 16417, (814) 774-9691; Fatima Renewal Center, 1000 Seminary Rd., Dalton 18414, (570) 563-8500; Fatima House Retreat Center, P.O. Box 116, Bedminster 18910, (215) 579-2947.

Franciscan Spirit and Life Center, 3605 McRoberts Rd., Pittsburgh 15234, (412) 881-9207; Gilmary Diocesan Center, 601 Flaugherty Run Rd., Coraopolis 15108-3899, (412) 264-8400, www.diopitt.org.

Jesuit Center, 501 N. Church Rd., Wernersville 19565, (610) 670-3641, www.jesuitcenter.org; Kearns Spirituality Center, 9000 Babcock Blvd., Allison Park 15101, (412) 366-1124, www.divineprovidenceweb.org; Mariawald Renewal Center, P.O. Box 97 (1094 Welsh Rd.), Reading 19607, (610) 777-0135, www.hometown.aol.com/mariawald/index.html; Martina Spiritual Renewal Center, 5244 Clarwin Ave., Pittsburgh 15229, (412) 931-9766; Mt. Saint Macrina House of Prayer, 510 W. Main St., Box 878, Uniontown 15401, (724) 438-7149, www.sistersofstbasil.org; St. Emma Guest House and St. Emma Retreat House, 1001 Harvey Ave., Greensburg 15601-1494, (724) 834-3060, www.stemm.org; St. Francis Center for Renewal, Monocacy Manor, 395 Bridle Path Rd., Bethlehem 18017, (610) 867-8890, www.catholic-church.org/stfranciscfn; St. Francis Retreat House, 3918 Chipman Rd., Easton 18045, (610) 258-3053; St. Gabriel's Retreat House, 631 Griffin Pond Rd., Clarks Summit 18411-8899, (570) 586-4957, www.intiques.com/cpnuns.

St. Joseph's in the Hills, 315 S. Warren Ave., Malvern 19355-0315, (610) 644-0400, www.malvernretreat.com; St. Paul of the Cross Retreat Center, 148 Monastery Ave., Pittsburgh 15203, (412) 381-7676, www.stpaulsretreatcenterpittsburgh.org; Saint Raphaela Center, 616 Coopertown Rd., Haverford 19041, (610) 642-5715; www.straphaelacenter.org; St. Vincent Summer Retreat Program (m,w,mc; summers only), Latrobe 15650, (724) 805-2139; Urban House of Prayer, 1919 Cambridge St., Philadelphia 19130, (215) 236-8328; Villa of Our Lady Retreat Center (w, mc, y), HCR No. 1, Box 41, Mt. Pocono 18344, (570) 839-7217.

Rhode Island: Bethany Renewal Center, 397 Fruit Hill Ave., N. Providence 02911, (401) 353-5860; Father Marot CYO Center (y), P.O. Box 518, Woonsocket 02895, (401) 762-3252, www.frmaryotcyo.org; Our Lady of Peace Spiritual Life Center, 333 Ocean Rd., Box 507, Narragansett 02882, (401) 884-7676; St. Paul Priory Guest House, 61 Narrangansett Ave., Newport 02840, (401) 847-2423.

South Carolina: Sea of Peace House of Prayer, 59 Palmetto Pointe Rd., Edisto Island 29438, (843) 869-0513; Springbank Retreat for Eco-Spirituality and the Arts, 1345 Springbank Rd., Kingstree 29556, (843) 382-9777, www.springbankspirit.org.

South Dakota: Sioux Spiritual Center, 20100 Center Rd., Howes, SD 57748, (605) 985-5906.

Tennessee: Carmelites of Mary Immaculate Center of Spirituality, 610 Bluff Rd., Liberty

37095, (615) 536-5177.

Texas: Benedictine Retreat Center, HC#2, Box 6300, Sandia 78383; Bishop DeFalco Retreat Center, 2100 N. Spring, Amarillo 79107-7274, (806) 383-1811, www.bdrc.org; Bishop Rene H. Gracida Retreat Center, 3036 Saratoga Blvd., Corpus Christi 78415, (512) 851-1443; Catholic Renewal Center of North Texas, 4503 Bridge St., Ft. Worth 76103, (817) 429-2920; Cenacle Retreat House, 420 N. Kirkwood, Houston 77079, (281) 497-3131, www.cenacleretreathouse.org; Christian Renewal Center (Centro de Renovacion Cristiana), Oblates of Mary Immaculate, P.O. Box 699, Dickinson 77539, (281) 337-1312, www.retreatcentercrc.org.

Holy Family Retreat Center, 9920 N. Major Dr., Beaumont 77713-7618, (409) 899-5617, www.dioceseofbmt.org/holyfamily/index/html; Holy Name Retreat Center, 430 Bunker Hill Rd., Houston 77024, (713) 464-0211; Holy Spirit Retreat and Conference Center, 501 Century Dr. S., Laredo 78040, (956) 726-4352, www.stjean.com/laredo/hsrc/holy.htm; Lebh Shomea House of Prayer, La Parra Ranch, P.O. Box 9, Sarita 78385; Montserrat Retreat House, P.O. Box 1390, Lake Dallas 75065, (940) 321-6020, www.montserratretreat.org; Moye Center, 600 London, Castroville 78009, (830) 931-2233, www.moyecenter.org; Oblate Renewal Center, 5700 Blanco Rd., San Antonio 78216, (210) 349-4173.

Omega Retreat Center, 216 W. Highland Dr., Boerne 78006, (830) 816-8471; Our Lady of Mercy Retreat Center, P.O. Box 744, 19th & Division, Slaton 79364, (806) 828-6428; Prayer Town Emmanuel Retreat House, P.O. Box 17, Channing 79018, (806) 534-2312; San Juan Retreat House (St. Eugene de Mazenod Retreat Center), P.O. Box 747, San Juan 78589, (956) 787-0033.

Utah: Abbey of Our Lady of the Holy Trinity (m), 1250 S 9500 E, Huntsville 84317, (801) 745-3784, www.xmission.com/~hta; Our Lady of the Mountains, 1794 Lake St., Ogden 84401, (801) 392-9231.

Virginia: Benedictine Retreat and Conf. Center, Mary Mother of the Church Abbey, 12829 River Rd., 23233, (804) 784-3508; Dominican Retreat, 7103 Old Dominion Dr., McLean 22101-2799, (703) 356-4243, www.dominicanretreat.org; The Dwelling Place, 601 Holly Grove Ln., Richmond 23235, (804) 323-3360; Holy Family Retreat House, P.O. 3151, 1414 N. Mallory St., Hampton 23663, (757) 722-3997; Madonna House, 828 Campbell Ave., S.W., Roanoke 24016, (540) 343-8464.

Retreat House, Holy Cross Abbey, 901 Cool Spring Lane, Berryville 22611, (540) 955-4383; Shalom House, P.O. Box 196, Montpelier 23192, (804) 883-6149; Tabor Retreat Center, 2125 Langhorne Rd., Lynchburg 24501, (804) 846-6475; The Well, 18047 Quiet Way, Smithfield 23430, (757) 255-2366, www.thewellretreatcenter.org.

Washington: Immaculate Heart Retreat Center,

6910 S. Ben Burr Rd., Spokane 99223, (509) 448-1224, www.ihrc.net; House of the Lord Retreat Center, P.O. Box 1034, Tum Tum 99034, (509) 276-2219; KAIROS House of Prayer, 1714 W. Stearns Rd., Spokane 99208, (509) 466-2187; Palisades Retreat House, 4700 SW Dash Point Rd., #100, Federal Way 98023, (206) 748-7991, www.seattlearch.org/formationandeducation; St. Juan Diego Retreat Center, 15880 Summitview Rd., Cowiche 98923, (509) 678-4935.

West Virginia: Bishop Hodges Pastoral Center, Rt. 1, Box 9D, Huttonsville, 26273, (304) 335-2165; Good Counsel Friary, 493 Tyrone Rd., Morgantown 26508, (304) 594-1714; John XXIII Pastoral Center, 100 Hodges Rd., Charleston 25314, (304) 342-0507; Paul VI Pastoral Center, 667 Stone and Shannon Rd., Wheeling 26003, (304) 277-3300; Priest Field Pastoral Center, Rt. 51, Box 133, Kearneysville 25430, (304) 725-1435; West Virginia Institute for Spirituality, 1414 Virginia St. E., Charleston, WV 25301, (304) 345-0926, www.wvis.ws.

Wisconsin: Archdiocesan Retreat Center, 3501 S. Lake Dr., P.O. Box 07912, Milwaukee 53207, (414) 769-3491, www.archmil.org; The Dwelling Place, 528 N. 31st St., Milwaukee 53208, (414) 933-1100; Franciscan Spirituality Center, 920 Market St., La Crosse 54601, (608) 791-5295, www.fspa.org; Holy Name Retreat House, Chambers Island, mailing address: 1825 Riverside Drive, P.O. Box 23825, Green Bay 54305, (920) 437-7531; Jesuit Retreat House, 4800 Fahrnwald Rd., Oshkosh 54902, (920) 231-9060, www.jesuitretreathouse.org; Marywood Franciscan Spirituality Center (FSPA), 3560 Hwy. 51 N., Arbor Vitae 54568, (715) 385-3750, www.fspa.org.

Mount Carmel Hermitage, 897 U.S. Hwy. 8, 54001, (715) 268-9313; Mount Tabor, 522 2 St., Menasha 54952, (920) 722-8918; Norbertine Center for Spirituality, St. Norbert Abbey, 1016 N. Broadway, De Pere 54115, (920) 337-4315, www.norbertines.org; Redemptorist Retreat Center, 1800 N. Timber Trail Lane, Oconomowoc 53066-4897, (262) 567-6900, www.redemptoristretreat.org; St. Anthony Retreat Center, 300 E. 4th St., Marathon 54448, (715) 443-2236, www.sarcenter.com.

Saint Benedict Center (monastery and ecumenical retreat and conference center), P.O. Box 5070, Madison 53705-0070, (608) 836-1631, www.sbcenter.org; St. Benedict's Retreat Center, 12605 224th Avenue, Benet Lake, WI 53102-0333, (262) 396-4311, www.benetlake.org; St. Clare Center for Spirituality, 7381 Church St., Custer 54423, (715) 592-4099; St. Joseph's Retreat Center, 3035 O'Brien Rd., Bailey's Harbor 54202, (920) 839-2391, www.stjosephretreat.org; St. Vincent Pallotti Center, N6409 Bowers Rd., Elkhorn 53121, (262) 723-2108, (877) 220-3306, www.elknet.net/vpallelk; Schoenstatt Center, W. 284 N. 698 Cherry Lane, Waukesha 53188, (262) 522-4300.

Catholic Education

LEGAL STATUS OF CATHOLIC EDUCATION

The right of private schools to exist and operate in the United States is recognized in law. It was confirmed by the U.S. Supreme Court in 1925 when the tribunal ruled (Pierce v. Society of Sisters, see **Church-State Decisions of the Supreme Court**, p. 366) that an Oregon state law requiring all children to attend public schools was unconstitutional.

Private schools are obliged to comply with the education laws in force in the various states regarding such matters as required basic curricula, periods of attendance, and standards for proper accreditation.

The special curricula and standards of private schools are determined by the schools themselves. Thus, in Catholic schools, the curricula include not only the subject matter required by state educational laws but also other fields of study, principally, education in the Catholic faith.

The Supreme Court has ruled that the First Amendment to the U.S. Constitution, in accordance with the No Establishment of Religion Clause of the First Amendment, prohibits direct federal and state aid from public funds to church-affiliated schools. (See several cases in **Church-State Decisions of the Supreme Court.**)

Public Aid

This prohibition does not extend to all child-benefit and public-purpose programs of aid to students of non-public elementary and secondary schools.

Statutes authorizing such programs have been ruled constitutional on the grounds that they:
• have a "secular legislative purpose"
• neither inhibit nor advance religion as a "principal or primary effect"
• do not foster "excessive government entanglement with religion."

Aid programs considered constitutional have provided bus transportation, textbook loans, school lunches and health services, and "secular, neutral or non-ideological services, facilities and materials provided in common to all school children," public and non-public.

The first major aid to education program in U.S. history containing provisions benefiting non-public school students was enacted by the 89th Congress and signed into law by President Lyndon B. Johnson on Apr. 11, 1965. The Elementary and Secondary Education Act was designed to avoid the separation of Church and state impasse which had blocked all earlier aid proposals pertaining to non-public, and especially church-affiliated, schools. The objective of the program, under public control, is to serve the public purpose by aiding disadvantaged pupils in non-public as well as public schools.

With respect to college and university education in church-affiliated institutions, the Supreme Court has upheld the constitutionality of statutes providing student loans and, under the Federal Higher Education Facilities Act of 1963, construction loans and grants for secular-purpose facilities.

Catholic schools are exempt from real estate taxation in all of the states. Since Jan. 1, 1959, nonprofit parochial and private schools have also been exempt from several federal excise taxes.

NCEA

The National Catholic Educational Association, founded in 1904, is a voluntary organization of educational institutions and individuals concerned with Catholic education in the U.S. Its objectives are to promote and encourage the principles and ideals of Christian education and formation by suitable service and other activities. The NCEA serves approximately 200,000 Catholic educators at all levels from pre-K through university. Numerous service publications are issued to members. Archbishop Wilton Gregory of Atlanta, chairman of the Board of Directors; Dr. Karen Ristau, president. Address: 1077 30th St. N.W., Washington, DC 20007; (202) 337-6232; www.ncea.org.

Association of Catholic Colleges and Universities

The ACCU, founded in 1899, is an association intended to promote and strengthen the missions and character of Catholic higher education in the United States and to serve as its collective voice. It became an independently incorporated organization separate from the NCEA in 2000. ACCU's journal, *Current Issues in Catholic Higher Education* is published semi-annually, and its electronic newsletter, Update, quarterly. ACCU serves approximately 220 colleges/universities, and the association gathers at its annual meeting fpcused on special Catholic higher education topics. Dr. Michael Galligan-Stierle, president. Address: 1 Dupont Circle, NW, Suite 650, Washington, DC 20036; (202) 457-0650; www.accunet.org.

EDUCATIONAL VOUCHERS

Although 41 educational voucher programs funded by private philanthropy were operating in the United States by 1998-99, discussion of vouchers as a political, legal, and educational issue primarily concerns publicly-funded plans allowing parents to send their children to the school of their choice. At present there are three educational voucher programs of this kind — in Milwaukee, Cleveland, and the state of Florida.

The Vouchers Debate

Proponents of vouchers argue that they are not merely consistent with parental rights but an appropriate, even necessary, practical means of realizing them. In particular, it is said, they enable low-income parents to exercise a choice about schools. Another pro-vouchers argument is that they create an incentive for self-improvement by public schools that is lacking when they enjoy a near monopoly.

Arguments against vouchers are that they take funds away from public schools and encourage highly motivated parents and competent students to abandon failing public institutions in favor of private ones. Using vouchers at church-related schools also is said to violate the First Amendment ban on an establishment of religion. The chief opponents of educational vouchers are teacher unions — the National Education Association, the American Federation of Teachers, and their affiliates — and other public school groups, church-state separationists, and some mainline African-American organizations. Phi Delta Kappa/Gallup polls in 1998 and 1999 found 51% of the respondents, including 60% of public school parents in the latter year, were in favor of total or partial government-paid tuition for children in private or church-related schools, although support declined when vouchers were specified.

Recent Developments

On June 27, 2002, the U.S. Supreme Court upheld the Cleveland voucher program in a 5-4 ruling, saying it is "entirely neutral with respect to religion." The majority opinion, written by Chief Justice William Rehnquist, said the program is therefore "a program of true private choice" and does not violate the Establishment Clause of the First Amendment.

Cleveland established the voucher program in 1995 to help address problems in what was considered one of the worst public school systems in the country. The state Legislature created the system after a federal judge declared the schools were being mismanaged and put them under the authority of the state superintendent of public instruction. The program provides for vouchers of up to $4,000 annually for children in low-income families to attend other public or private schools or pay for tutors. The vast majority of participants use their vouchers to pay tuition at church-affiliated schools, nearly all of them Catholic.

The case came to the Supreme Court after the 6th U.S. Circuit Court of Appeals ruled in 2000 that the program was unconstitutional because the vouchers are primarily used at religious schools. The U.S. Conference of Catholic Bishops in a friend-of-the-court brief argued that the program should not be considered unconstitutional because most voucher recipients choose to attend church schools.

Opponents of the program who filed briefs included the National Association for the Advancement of Colored People, an association of Ohio school boards and several groups of public schools from around the country. Opponents call vouchers a fraud meant to siphon tax money from struggling public schools. The Ohio school boards argued that the state has ignored its responsibility to provide a good education and is merely shifting the burden to religious schools.

Central to the court's reasoning was that children in the Cleveland program have a theoretical choice of attending religious schools, secular private academies, suburban public schools, or charter schools run by parents or others outside the education establishment. The fact that only a handful of secular schools and no suburban public schools have signed up to accept voucher students is not the fault of the program itself, Ohio authorities say. "We believe that the program challenged here is a program of true private choice," Chief Justice William H. Rehnquist wrote for himself and Justices Sandra Day O'Connor, Antonin Scalia, Anthony M. Kennedy and Clarence Thomas.

The Cleveland program goes too far toward state-sponsored religion, the dissenting justices said. It does not treat religion neutrally, as Rehnquist contended, wrote Justice David H. Souter. The majority is also wrong about the question of whether parents have a true choice among schools, Souter wrote for himself and Justices John Paul Stevens, Ruth Bader Ginsburg and Stephen Breyer. "There is, in any case, no way to interpret the 96.6 percent of current voucher money going to religious schools as reflecting a free and genuine choice by the families that apply for vouchers," Souter wrote.

President George W. Bush was a staunch advocate of school vouchers, and emphasized the issue in his campaign for the White House. Congress shelved that effort, but Bush resurrected the idea, proposing in his 2003 budget to give families up to $2,500 per child in tax credits if they choose a private school rather than a failing neighborhood public school. Following the court's hearing on arguments in February 2002, Education Secretary Rod Paige said he would continue advocating on behalf of both improved public schools and school choice. Republican lawmakers in Congress agreed with Bush's stance. The Bush administration sided with Ohio, arguing that the program is constitutional because parents control where the money goes. In Cleveland, the public money flows to parents, not directly to the church-run schools, the program's supporters noted.

On April 4, 2011, the U.S. Supreme Court upheld an Arizona law that provides tax vouchers for private-school tuition. By a 5-4 decision, the high court rejected arguments that the voucher program violates the First Amendment by providing state support to religious schools. Recipients receive a $500 voucher for use in paying tuition at religious schools. Reportedly, most use it for religious high schools.

EX CORDE ECCLESIAE

On Nov. 17, 1999, the Catholic Bishops of the United States approved *The Application of Ex corde Ecclesiae for the United States*, implementing the Apostolic Constitution *Ex corde Ecclesiae*. This action received the recognitio from the Congregation for Bishops on May 3, 2000. Bp. Joseph Fiorenza, President of the National Conference of Catholic Bishops, decreed that the application would have the force of particular law for the United States on May 3, 2001. Guidelines concerning the Academic Mandatum in Catholic Universities were subsequently issued, based on Canon 812. The following is the first guidelines.

Pope John Paul II's Constitution *Ex corde Ecclesiae* of 1990 fostered a productive dialogue between the Bishops of the United States and the leaders of our Catholic colleges and universities. It is anticipated that this recently approved *Application of Ex corde Ecclesiae for the United States* would further that dialogue and build a community of trust between bishops and theologians. Both bishops and theologians are engaged in a necessary though complementary service to the Church that requires ongoing and mutually respectful conversation.

Article 4, 4, e, iv of the Application states that "a detailed procedure will be developed outlining the process of requesting and granting (or withdrawing) the mandatum." These guidelines are intended to explain and serve as a resource for the conferral of the mandatum. Only those guidelines herein which repeat a norm of the Application have the force of particular law. They were approved for distribution to the members of NCCB by the Conference's general membership.

Nature of the *mandatum*.

• The mandatum is fundamentally an acknowledgment by Church authority that a Catholic professor of a theological discipline is a teacher within the full communion of the Catholic Church (Application: Article 4,4,e,i).

• The mandatum, therefore, recognizes the professor's commitment and responsibility to teach authentic Catholic doctrine and to refrain from putting forth as Catholic teaching anything contrary to the Church's magisterium (cf. Application: Article 4,4,e, iii).

• The mandatum should not be construed as an appointment, authorization, delegation or approbation of one's teaching by Church authorities. Those who have received a mandatum teach in their own name in virtue of their baptism and their academic and professional competence, not in the name of the bishop or of the Church's magisterium (Application: Article 4,4,e,ii).

Cardinal Newman Society

The Cardinal Newman Society is a national organization established in 1993 and dedicated to the renewal of Catholic identity in Catholic higher education in the United States. CNS has more than 18,000 members nationwide who share a common concern for the future of Catholic higher education and urge fidelity to the Magisterium. The society seeks to: promote discussion and understanding of the message of the Catholic Church concerning the nature and value of Catholic higher education; assist college leaders, educators, students, and alumni in their efforts to preserve the religious identity of Catholic institutions of higher learning; and advocate the faithful implementation of *Ex Corde Ecclesiae* by facilitating an active dialogue among members of the Catholic university community. **J. Laurence McCarty,** Chairman of the Board; **Patrick J. Reilly,** president. Address: 10562 Associates Court, Manassas, VA 20109; (703) 367-0333; www.cardinalnewmansociety.org.

SUMMARY OF SCHOOL STATISTICS

Status and figures (as of Jan. 1, 2014) reported by The Official Catholic Directory.
Colleges and Universities: 233 (U.S., 226; outlying areas, 7).

College and University Students: 810,201 (U.S., 787,657; outlying areas, 22,544).

High Schools: 1,303 (723 diocesan and parochial; 580 private). U.S., 1,200 (665 diocesan and parochial; 535 private). Outlying areas, 103 (58 diocesan and parochial; 45 private).

High School Students: 612,400 (322,341 diocesan and parochial; 290,059 private). U.S., 574,697 (299,728 diocesan and parochial; 274,969 private). Outlying areas, 22,613 (15,090 diocesan and parochial; 7,523 private).

Public High School Students Receiving Religious Instruction: 640,585 (U.S., 631,856; outlying areas, 8,729).

Elementary Schools: 5,547 (5,169 diocesan and parochial; 378 private). U.S., 5,391 (5,070 diocesan and parochial; 321 private). Outlying areas, 156 (99 diocesan and parochial; 57 private).

Elementary School Students: 1,401,323 (1,310,284 diocesan and parochial; 91,039 private) U.S., 1,347,982 (1,274,480 diocesan and parochial; 73,502 private). Outlying areas, 35,804 (18,267 diocesan and parochial; 17,537 private).

Public Elementary School Students Receiving Religious Instruction: 2,715,621 (U.S., 2,694,115; outlying areas, 21,506).

Non-Residential Schools for Handicapped: 52 (U.S., 51, Outlying areas, 1). Students: 5,391 (U.S., 5,311, Outlying areas, 80).

Teachers: 163,979, U.S., 159,600 (lay persons, 154,423; sisters, 3,143; priests, 1,218; brothers, 719; scholastics, 97). Outlying areas, 4,379 (lay persons, 3,941; sisters, 372; priests, 41; brothers, 25; scholastics, 0).

Seminaries: 159 (74 diocesan; 85 religious). U.S.: 140 (67 diocesan; 73 religious). Outlying areas: 19 (7 diocesan; 12 religious).

Seminarians: 5,046 (3,598 diocesan; 1,448 religious). U.S.: 4,938 (3,517 diocesan; 1,421 religious). Outlying areas: 108 (81 diocesan; 27 religious).

CATHOLIC SCHOOLS AND STUDENTS IN THE UNITED STATES

(*Source:* Official Catholic Directory, *2014; figures as of Jan. 1, 2014; Archdioceses are indicated by an asterisk.*)

State Diocese	Universities/ Colleges	Students	High Schools	Students	Elem. Schools	Students
Alabama	**1**	**1,420**	**8**	**3,062**	**40**	**9,262**
*Mobile	1	1,420	3	1,583	22	4,562
Birmingham	–	–	5	1,479	18	4,700
Alaska	**–**	**–**	**3**	**304**	**6**	**643**
*Anchorage	–	–	2	113	4	324
Fairbanks	–	–	1	191	1	239
Juneau	–	–	–	–	1	80
Arizona	**1**	**83**	**12**	**6,770**	**55**	**13,693**
Phoenix	1	83	6	4,807	37	9,295
Tucson	–	–	6	1,963	18	4,398
Arkansas						
Little Rock	–	–	5	**1,679**	26	**3,955**
California	**12**	**48,546**	**119**	**71,772**	**549**	**145,140**
*Los Angeles	4	14,046	51	26,980	219	53,011
*San Francisco	3	11,900	14	7,879	60	17,352
Fresno	–	–	2	1,168	19	4,503
Monterey	–	–	5	1,584	14	3,312
Oakland	2	5,480	9	5,669	45	11,604
Orange	–	–	7	6,569	32	12,330
Sacramento	–	–	9	6,404	38	10,030
San Bernardino	–	–	3	1,401	27	6,138
San Diego	2	8,601	6	4,155	45	12,379
San Jose	1	8,519	6	6,782	29	9,366
Santa Rosa	–	–	6	1,868	10	2,254
Stockton	–	–	2	1,313	11	2,861
Colorado	**2**	**13,867**	**8**	**4,221**	**49**	**11,335**
*Denver	2	13,867	7	3,913	39	9,133
Colorado Springs	–	–	1	308	6	1,353
Pueblo	–	–	–	–	4	849
Connecticut	**6**	**20,194**	**22**	**10,512**	**99**	**20,221**
*Hartford	2	7,179	9	4,623	54	10,413
Bridgeport	3	12,778	7	3,573	32	7,778
Norwich	1	237	6	2,316	13	2,030
Delaware, Wilmington	**–**	**–**	**8**	**3,919**	**21**	**6,752**
District of Columbia *Wash., DC	**3**	**29,914**	**20**	**10,091**	**69**	**16,944**
Florida	**4**	**28,509**	**38**	**24,026**	**170**	**58,443**
*Miami	2	11,341	14	12,314	50	21,131
Orlando	–	–	5	2,878	31	10,248
Palm Beach	–	–	3	1,440	16	4,726
Pensacola Tallahassee	–	–	2	785	7	1,937
St. Augustine	–	–	4	2,158	27	8,303
St. Petersburg	1	16,275	6	3,029	28	9,195
Venice	1	893	4	1,422	11	2,903
Georgia	**–**	**–**	**12**	**5,963**	**32**	**10,722**
*Atlanta	–	–	7	4,261	18	7,364
Savannah	–	–	5	1,702	14	3,358
Hawaii, Honolulu	**1**	**2,650**	**7**	**2,109**	**25**	**6,123**
Idaho, Boise	**–**	**–**	**1**	**725**	**13**	**2,309**
Illinois	**11**	**68,239**	**65**	**40,314**	**404**	**94,006**
*Chicago	5	48,986	36	23,228	207	60,595
Belleville	–	–	3	1,091	28	4,203
Joliet	3	16,463	7	5,303	48	1,577
Peoria	1	390	5	2,492	39	9,092
Rockford	–	–	8	4,025	40	9,762
Springfield	2	2,400	6	2,175	42	8,777
Indiana	**11**	**36,830**	**26**	**13,320**	**156**	**42,297**
*Indianapolis	2	3,926	12	6,187	59	17,412
Evansville	–	–	4	1,418	24	5,893
Ft.Wayne S. Bend	5	17,039	4	3,212	37	9,789
Gary	1	1,275	4	1,373	17	5,221

State Diocese	Universities/ Colleges	Students	High Schools	Students	Elem. Schools	Students
Indiana, cont.						
Lafayette	3	14,590	2	1,130	19	3,982
Iowa	**6**	**10,284**	**21**	**6,747**	**89**	**21,525**
*Dubuque	3	4,573	7	2,362	44	8,976
Davenport	1	3,706	5	1,029	13	3,598
Des Moines	1	831	2	1,635	16	4,720
Sioux City	1	1,174	7	1,721	16	4,231
Kansas	**4**	**8,373**	**16**	**7,143**	**93**	**21,256**
*Kansas City	3	4,637	7	3,540	40	10,564
Dodge City	–	–	–	–	7	986
Salina	–	–	5	1,038	11	1,676
Wichita	1	3,736	4	2,565	35	8,030
Kentucky	**5**	**9,459**	**23**	**10,949**	**95**	**24,303**
*Louisville	3	6,778	9	6,106	38	11,889
Covington	1	1,761	9	3,243	29	6,910
Lexington	–	–	2	896	14	2,802
Owensboro	1	920	3	704	14	2,702
Louisiana	**4**	**10,998**	**49**	**25,118**	**143**	**55,178**
*New Orleans	3	9,245	22	13,363	60	24,090
Alexandria	–	–	3	576	7	1,754
Baton Rouge	1	1,753	8	4,232	24	10,992
Houma Thib.	–	–	3	1,890	10	3,790
Lafayette	–	–	10	3,731	32	11,332
Lake Charles	–	–	1	598	6	1,977
Shreveport	–	–	2	728	4	1,243
Maine, Portland	1	3,014	3	837	11	2,156
Maryland, *Baltimore	4	11,182	20	10,545	48	16,348
Massachusetts	11	35,414	50	21,885	137	35,914
*Boston	6	22,289	32	15,629	80	23,584
Fall River	1	2,466	5	2,773	21	4,343
Springfield	1	1,679	4	637	14	3,462
Worcester	3	8,980	9	2,846	22	4,525
Michigan	**5**	**17,340**	**44**	**15,648**	**184**	**40,238**
*Detroit	3	12,608	24	10,503	66	20,728
Gaylord	–	–	4	513	16	1,852
Grand Rapids	1	2,042	4	1,389	25	4,269
Kalamazoo	–	–	3	593	19	2,353
Lansing	1	2,690	5	2,061	34	7,131
Marquette	–	–	–	–	9	1,238
Saginaw	–	–	3	589	15	2,667
Minnesota	**6**	**24,726**	**22**	**10,855**	**170**	**34,666**
*St.Paul and Minn.	2	15,244	12	8,318	81	22,764
Crookston	–	–	1	131	8	795
Duluth	1	4,240	–	–	11	1,545
New Ulm	–	–	3	381	15	1,718
St. Cloud	2	4,029	2	945	27	3,862
Winona	1	1,213	4	1,080	28	3,982
Mississippi	**2**	**36**	**9**	**2,360**	**24**	**5,859**
Biloxi	–	–	5	1,573	10	2,522
Jackson	2	36	4	787	14	3,337
Missouri	**4**	**20,406**	**40**	**17,793**	**200**	**45,151**
*St.Louis	2	15,515	27	12,236	114	28,724
Jefferson City	–	–	3	1,060	37	5,638
Kansas City St. Joseph	2	4,891	7	3,491	26	7,367
Springfield Cape Girar.	–	–	3	1,006	23	3,522
Montana	**2**	**2,577**	**5**	**903**	**16**	**2,729**
Great Falls-Billings	1	1,075	3	584	12	1,902
Helena	1	1,502	2	319	4	827
Nebraska	**2**	**8,989**	**27**	**7,830**	**84**	**20,404**
*Omaha	2	8,989	17	5,589	52	13,424
Grand Island	–	–	4	519	6	1,031
Lincoln	–	–	6	1,722	26	5,949
Nevada	**–**	**–**	**2**	**1,990**	**10**	**3,694**

State Diocese	Universities/ Colleges	Students	High Schools	Students	Elem. Schools	Students
Nevada, cont.						
Las Vegas	–	–	1	1,371	6	2,608
Reno	–	–	1	619	4	1,086
New Hampshire, Manchester	4	4,419	5	2,210	23	4,260
New Jersey	7	20,865	60	32,892	200	53,494
*Newark	4	17,007	28	13,493	70	15,957
Camden	–	–	9	6,237	29	8,383
Metuchen	–	–	5	2,734	25	7,834
Paterson	2	1,545	7	3,583	37	8,615
Trenton	1	2,313	11	6,845	39	12,705
New Mexico	1	250	5	1,522	29	4,978
*Santa Fe	1	250	2	1,383	14	3,186
Gallup	–	–	1	128	12	1,256
Las Cruces	–	–	2	11	3	536
New York	25	97,875	110	63,236	428	117,939
*New York	9	33,840	48	24,390	170	46,777
Albany	4	10,000	7	2,143	21	4,755
Brooklyn	3	29,406	19	13,820	89	29,534
Buffalo	7	17,846	14	5,168	50	10,996
Ogdensburg	–	–	2	421	11	1,679
Rochester	–	–	5	3,111	22	4,347
Rockville Centre	1	3,444	10	12,041	47	17,202
Syracuse	1	3,339	5	2,142	18	2,649
North Carolina	1	1,549	6	3,490	45	11,884
Charlotte	1	1,549	3	2,031	16	5,554
Raleigh	–	–	3	1,459	29	6,330
North Dakota	2	3,161	4	951	22	3,430
Bismarck	1	2,910	3	637	10	1,700
Fargo	1	251	1	314	12	1,730
Ohio	13	40,964	77	38,151	336	91,423
*Cincinnati	4	20,268	23	13,200	93	29,116
Cleveland	3	7,225	20	12,919	99	32,823
Columbus	2	3,740	11	4,535	42	11,202
Steubenville	1	2,351	3	492	10	1,645
Toledo	2	3,816	14	5,075	63	11,551
Youngstown	1	3,564	6	1,930	29	5,086
Oklahoma	1	734	4	2,465	29	6,804
*Oklahoma City	1	734	2	1,084	18	4,024
Tulsa	–	–	2	1,381	10	2,772
Oregon	2	5,680	10	5,639	45	9,524
*Portland	2	5,680	10	5,639	40	9,015
Baker	–	–	–	–	5	509
Pennsylvania	26	98,670	78	38,547	383	98,835
*Philadelphia	11	45,842	35	21,689	146	50,579
Allentown	2	7,105	7	3,531	38	8,770
Altoona Johnstown	2	4,247	4	1,064	20	3,437
Erie	2	8,392	7	2,213	31	4,969
Greensburg	2	4,074	2	600	16	2,372
Harrisburg	–	–	7	3,268	36	7,814
Pittsburgh	3	13,810	11	3,936	78	15,806
Scranton	4	15,200	5	2,246	16	4,363
Rhode Island, Providence	2	7,853	8	4,671	31	7,536
South Carolina, Charleston	–	–	5	1,936	28	4,992
South Dakota	2	2,026	5	1,471	23	4,961
Rapid City	–	–	2	475	3	836
Sioux Falls	2	2,026	3	996	20	4,125
Tennessee	2	2,348	11	5,520	47	11,495
Knoxville	–	–	2	1,051	8	2,113
Memphis	1	1,584	6	2,647	22	5,223
Nashville	1	764	3	1,822	17	4,159
Texas	9	28,428	55	21,014	224	58,993
*Galveston Houston	1	3,589	10	4,783	50	14,119
*San Antonio	5	16,926	11	3,908	33	9,577

State / Diocese	Universities/ Colleges	Students	High Schools	Students	Elem. Schools	Students
Texas, cont.						
Amarillo	–	–	1	86	4	739
Austin	1	5,285	6	1,593	17	4,149
Beaumont	–	–	1	448	4	1,088
Brownsville	–	–	3	916	11	3,108
Corpus Christi	–	–	2	666	16	2,849
Dallas	1	2,598	7	4,915	30	9,688
El Paso	–	–	3	1,197	10	2,774
Fort Worth	1	30	4	1,301	20	4,427
Laredo	–	–	1	364	6	1,818
Lubbock	–	–	1	54	2	341
San Angelo	–	–	–	–	3	752
Tyler	–	–	1	281	5	810
Victoria	–	–	3	502	13	2,754
Utah, Salt Lake City	–	–	3	1,787	13	4,145
Vermont, Burlington	2	2,767	2	483	11	1,607
Virginia	4	5,230	14	5,768	65	21,039
Arlington	4	5,230	6	7,627	41	13,343
Richmond	–	–	8	1,685	24	7,696
Washington	3	16,961	15	7,563	84	22,091
*Seattle	2	9,193	11	6,237	63	16,138
Spokane	1	7,768	3	1,141	14	4,082
Yakima	–	–	1	185	7	1,871
West Virginia, Wheeling Charleston	1	1,665	7	1,386	20	4,304
Wisconsin	9	32,300	29	10,839	279	48,715
*Milwaukee	5	22,999	13	6,635	95	25,147
Green Bay	2	3,407	6	2,217	52	7,732
La Crosse	1	3,000	7	1,565	63	7,138
Madison	1	2,894	3	659	44	6,434
Superior	–	–	–	–	15	2,264
Wyoming, Cheyenne	–	–	–	–	7	954
EASTERN CHURCHES	1	862	3	856	11	1,478
*Philadelphia	1	862	1	289	2	431
St. Nicholas (Chicago)	–	–	–	–	2	321
Stamford	–	–	1	180	–	–
St. Josaphat (Parma)	–	–	–	–	–	–
*Pittsburgh	–	–	–	–	–	–
Parma	–	–	–	–	1	165
Passaic	–	–	–	–	–	–
Holy Protection	–	–	–	–	1	45
St. Maron (Maronites)	–	–	–	–	–	–
Our Lady of Deliverance (Syriacs)	–	–	–	–	–	–
Our Lady of Lebanon (Maronites)	–	–	–	–	1	39
Newton (Melkites)	–	–	–	–	–	–
St. George Martyr (Romanians)	–	–	–	–	–	–
St. Peter the Apostle (Chaldeans)	–	–	–	–	–	–
St. Thomas Apostle of Detroit (Chaldeans)	–	–	–	–	–	–
St. Thomas (Syro-Malabars)	–	–	–	–	–	–
Armenians (Ap. Ex.)	–	–	1	387	4	526
SCHOOLS AND STUDENTS IN OUTLYING AREAS						
American Samoa	–	–	1	268	2	345
Caroline Islands	–	–	4	795	4	1,221
Guam	–	–	4	1,173	7	2,957
Marshall Islands	–	–	2	185	3	585
Marianas	–	–	1	139	2	246
Puerto Rico	7	22,544	88	19,904	135	30,132
Virgin Islands	–	–	2	149	3	318
TOTAL 2014	233	810,201	1,303	612,400	5,547	1,401,323
TOTAL 2013	232	818,331	1,314	612,616	5,672	1,440,232
TOTAL 2004	234	772,767	1,378	692,767	6,736	1,846,045

CATHOLIC UNIVERSITIES AND COLLEGES IN THE UNITED STATES

(*Sources*: Catholic Almanac *survey*; The Official Catholic Directory.)

Listed below are institutions of higher learning established under Catholic auspices. Some of them are now independent.

Information includes: name of each institution; indication of male (m), female (w), coeducational (c) student body; name of founding group or group with which the institution is affiliated; year of foundation; total number of students in parentheses.

Albertus Magnus College (c): 700 Prospect St., New Haven, CT 06511; (203) 773-8550; www.albertus.edu. Dominican Sisters; 1925; independent (2,065).

Alvernia College (c): 400 Saint Bernardine St., Reading, PA 19607; (610) 796-8200; www.alvernia. edu. Bernardine Sisters; 1958 (2,457).

Alverno College (w): 3400 S. 43th St., P.O. Box 343922, Milwaukee, WI 53234; (414) 382-6000; www.alverno.edu. School Sisters of St. Francis; 1887; independent (2,000).

Anna Maria College (c): 50 Sunset Lane, Paxton, MA 01612; (508) 849-3300; www.annamaria.edu. Sisters of St. Anne;1946; independent (1,244).

Aquinas College (c): 1607 Robinson Rd. S.E., Grand Rapids, MI 49506; (616) 459-8281. Sisters of St. Dominic; 1922; independent (2,571).

Aquinas College (c): 4210 Harding Rd., Nashville, TN 37205; (615) 297-7545; www.aquinas-tn.edu. Dominican Sisters; 1961 (506).

Aquinas Institute of Theology (c): 3642 Lindell Boulevard, St. Louis, MO 63108; (314) 977-3869; www.op.org/aquinas. Dominicans, 1961; graduate theology; offers distance learning program in pastoral studies and specializations in preaching (200).

Assumption College (c): 500 Salisbury St., Worcester, MA 01615-0005; (508) 767-7000; www.assumption.edu. Assumptionist Religious; 1904 (2,766).

Augustine Institute, The (c): 3001 S. Federal Blvd. Box 1126 Denver CO, 80236 Phone: (303) 937-4420 FAX: (303) 468-293; www.augustineinstitute.org; 2005. (264). Offers graduate programs leading to the M.A., with specializations in biblical theology, sacred Scripture, and evangelization and catechesis.

Ave Maria School of Law (c): 3475 Plymouth Rd., Ann Arbor, MI 48105; (734) 930-4408.

Ave Maria University (c): 5050 Ave Maria Blvd. Ave Maria, fl 34142-9505; 877-283-8648; www.avemaria.edu

Avila University (c): 11901 Wornall Rd., Kansas City, MO 64145-1698; (816) 942-8400; www.avila.edu. Sisters of St. Joseph of Carondelet; 1916 (2,658).

Barry University (c): 11300 N.E. 2nd Ave., Miami Shores, FL 33161; (305) 899-3000; www.barry.edu. Dominican Sisters (Adrian, MI); 1940 (8,691).

Bellarmine College (c): 2001 Newburg Rd., Louisville, KY 40205; (502) 452-8211; www.bellarmine.edu. Louisville archdiocese; independent (2,323).

Belmont Abbey College (c): 100 Belmont-Mt. Holly Rd., Belmont, NC 28012; (704) 825-6700; www.belmontabbey-college.edu. Benedictine Fathers; 1876 (883).

Benedictine College (c): 1020 N. Second St., Atchison, KS 66002; (913) 367-5340; www.benedictine.edu. Benedictines; 1859; independent (1,375).

Benedictine University (formerly Illinois Benedictine College) (c): 5700 College Rd., Lisle, IL 60532-0900; (630) 829-600 0; www.ben.edu. Benedictine Monks of St. Procopius Abbey; 1887 (2,809).

Boston College (University status) (c): Chestnut Hill, MA 02167; (617) 552-8000; www.bc.edu. Jesuit Fathers; 1863 (14,297).

Brescia University (c): 717 Frederica St., Owensboro, KY 42301; (270) 685-3131; www.brescia.edu. Ursuline Sisters; 1950 (820).

Briar Cliff College (c): 3303 Rebecca St., Sioux City, IA 51104; (712) 279-5405; www.briarcliff.edu. Sisters of St. Francis of the Holy Family; 1930 (994).

Cabrini College (c): 610 King of Prussia Rd., Radnor, PA 19087; (610) 902-8100; www.cabrini.edu. Missionary Srs. of Sacred Heart; 1957; private (2,669).

Caldwell College (c): 9 Ryerson Ave., Caldwell, NJ 07006; (973) 618-3000; www.caldwell.edu. Dominican Sisters; 1939 (2,270).

Calumet College of St. Joseph (c): 2400 New York Ave., Whiting, IN 46394; (219) 473-7770; www.ccsj.edu. Society of the Precious Blood, 1951 (1,141).

Canisius College (c): 2001 Main St., Buffalo, NY 14208; (716) 883-7000; www.canisius.edu. Jesuit Fathers; 1870; independent (4,995).

Cardinal Stritch University (c): 6801 N. Yates Rd., Milwaukee, WI 53217; (414) 410-4000; www.stritch.edu. Sisters of St. Francis of Assisi; 1937 (5,855).

Carlow College (w): 3333 5th Ave., Pittsburgh, PA 15213; (412) 578-6059; www.carlow.edu. Sisters of Mercy; 1929 (2,199).

Carroll College (c): 1601 N. Benton Ave., Helena, MT 59625; (406) 447-4300. Diocesan; 1909 (1,400).

Catholic Distance University (c): 120 East Colonial Highway, Hamilton, VA 20158-9012; www.cdu.edu. Offers External Degree programs, including Masters degrees in Religious Studies (7,000).

Catholic Theological Union (c): 5401 South Cornell Ave., Chicago, IL 60615; (773) 324-8000; www.ctu.edu (348).

Catholic University of America, The (c): Michigan Ave. & Fourth St., NE, Washington, DC 20064; (202) 319-5000; www.cua.edu. Hierarchy of the United States; 1887. Pontifical University (5,777).

Chaminade University of Honolulu (c): 3140 Waialae Ave., Honolulu, HI 96816; (808) 735-4711; www.chaminade.edu. Marianists; 1955 (2,788).

Chestnut Hill College (w): 9601 Germantown Ave., Philadelphia, PA 19118; (215) 248-7000; www.chc.edu. Sisters of St. Joseph; 1924 (1,645).

Christendom College (c): 134 Christendom Dr., Front Royal, VA 22630; (540) 636-2900. Independent, 1977 (477).

Christian Brothers University (c): 650 E. Parkway S., Memphis, TN 38104; (901) 321-3000. Brothers of the Christian Schools; 1871 (2,027).

Clarke College (c): 1550 Clarke Dr., Dubuque, IA 52001; (563) 588-6300; www.clarke.edu. Sisters of Charity, BVM; 1843; independent (1,126).

Creighton University (c): 2500 California Plaza, Omaha, NE 68178; (402) 280-2700; www.creighton.edu. Jesuit Fathers; 1878; independent (6,297).

Dallas, University of (c): 1845 E. Northgate, Irving, TX 75062; (972) 721-5000. Dallas diocese; 1956; independent (3,518).

Dayton, University of (c): 300 College Park, Dayton, OH 45469-1660; (937) 229-1000; www.udayton.edu. Marianists; 1850 (10,248).

DePaul University (c): One E. Jackson Blvd., Chicago, IL 60604; (312) 362-8000; www.depaul.edu. Vincentians; 1898 (23,174).

De Sales University (c): 2755 Station Ave., Center Valley, PA 18034; (610) 282-1100; www.desales.edu. Oblates of St. Francis de Sales; 1965 (1,339).

Detroit Mercy, University of (c): 4001 W. McNichols Rd., Detroit, MI, 48221; 8200 W. Outer Dr., Detroit MI 48219; (313) 993-1000. Society of Jesus and Sisters of Mercy; 1877; independent (5,843).

Dominican College (c): 470 Western Hwy., Orangeburg, NY 10962; (845) 359-7800; www.dc.edu. Dominican Sisters; 1952; independent (1,700).

Dominican University of California (c): 50 Acacia Ave., San Rafael, CA 94901-2298; (415) 457-4440; www.dominican.edu. Dominican Sisters; 1890; independent (1,578).

Dominican University (formerly Rosary College) (c): 7900 W. Division St., River Forest, IL 60305; (708) 366-2490; www.dom.edu. Sinsinawa Dominican Sisters; 1901 (2,533).

Duquesne University (c): 600 Forbes Ave., Pittsburgh, PA 15282; (412) 396-6000; www.duq.edu. Congregation of the Holy Ghost; 1878 (9,600).

D'Youville College (c): 320 Porter Ave., Buffalo, NY 14201; (716) 881-3200; www.dyc.edu. Grey Nuns of the Sacred Heart; 1908; independent (2,453).

Edgewood College (c): 1000 Edgewood College Dr., Madison, WI 53711; (608) 663-4861. Sinsinawa Dominican Sisters; 1927 (2,258).

Emmanuel College (w): 400 The Fenway, Boston, MA 02115; (617) 735-9715; www.emmanuel.edu. Sisters of Notre Dame de Namur; 1919; independent (1,549).

Fairfield University (c): 1073 North Benson Rd., Fairfield, CT 06430; (203) 254-4000; www.fairfield.edu. Jesuits; 1942 (6,001).

Felician College (c): 262 S. Main St., Lodi, NJ 07644; (201) 559-6000; www.felician.edu. Felician Sisters; 1942; independent (1,400).

Fontbonne University (c): 6800 Wydown Blvd., St. Louis, MO 63105; (314) 862-3456; www.fontbonne.edu. Sisters of St. Joseph of Carondelet; 1917; independent (2,344).

Fordham University (c): Fordham Rd. and Third Ave., New York, NY 10458; (718) 817-3040. Society of Jesus (Jesuits); 1841; independent (13,800).

Franciscan University of Steubenville (c): 1235 University Blvd., Steubenville, OH 43952; (740) 283-3771; www.franuniv.edu. Franciscan TOR Friars; 1946 (2,208). Also offers distance learning programs.

Gannon University (c): 109 University Square, Erie, PA 16541-0001; (814) 871-7000; www.gannon.edu. Diocese of Erie; 1933 (3,404).

Georgetown University (c): 37th and O Sts. N.W., Washington, DC 20057; (202) 687-0100; www.georgetown.edu. Jesuit Fathers; 1789 (12,688).

Georgian Court College (w/c): 900 Lakewood Ave., Lakewood, NJ 08701; (732) 364-2200; www.georgian.edu. Sisters of Mercy; 1908 (3,561).

Gonzaga University (c): E. 502 Boone Ave., Spokane, WA 99258; (509) 328-4220. Jesuit Fathers; 1887 (4,515).

Graduate School of Theology (c): 5890 Birch Ct., Oakland, CA 94618; (510) 652-1651; www.satgtu.org. Affiliate of the Graduate Theological Union.

Great Falls, University of (c): 1301 20th St. S., Great Falls, MT 59405; (406) 761-8210; www.ugf.edu. Sisters of Providence; 1932; independent (825).

Gwynedd-Mercy College (c): Gwynedd Valley, PA 19437; (215) 646-7300; www.gmc.edu. Sisters of Mercy; 1948; independent (2,198).

Hilbert College (c): 5200 S. Park Ave., Hamburg, NY 14075; (716) 649-7900; www.hilbert.edu. Franciscan Sisters of St. Joseph; 1957; independent (970).

Holy Cross, College of the (c): Worcester, MA 01610; (508) 793-2011; www.holycross.edu. Jesuits; 1843 (2,811).

Holy Family College (c): Grant and Frankford Aves., Philadelphia, PA 19114 and One Campus Dr., Newtown, PA 18940; (215) 637-7700; www.hfc.edu. Sisters of Holy Family of Nazareth; 1954; independent (2,559).

Holy Names College (c): 3500 Mountain Blvd., Oakland, CA 94619; (510) 436-1000; www.hnc.edu. Sisters of the Holy Names of Jesus and Mary; 1868; independent (947).

Immaculata College (w): Immaculata, PA 19345; (610) 647-4400; www.immaculata.edu. Sisters, Servants of the Immaculate Heart of Mary; 1920 (3,062).

Incarnate Word, University of the (c): 4301 Broadway, San Antonio, TX 78209; (210) 829-6000; www.uiw.edu. Sisters of Charity of the Incarnate Word; 1881 (4,264).

Iona College (c): 715 North Ave., New Rochelle, NY 10801; (914) 633-2000; www.iona.edu. Congregation of Christian Brothers; 1940; independent (4,897).

John Carroll University (c): 20700 N. Park Blvd., Cleveland, OH 44118; (216) 397-1886; www.jcu.edu. Jesuits; 1886 (4,294).

John Paul the Great Catholic University (c): 10174 Old Grove Road, Suite 200, San Diego, CA 92131; (858) 653-6740; www.jpcatholic.com.

King's College (c): 133 North River St., Wilkes-Barre, PA 18711; (570) 208-5900; www.kings.edu. Holy Cross Fathers; 1946 (2,178).

La Roche College (c): 9000 Babcock Blvd., Pittsburgh, PA 15237; (412) 367-9300; www.laroche.edu. Sisters of Divine Providence; 1963 (1,981).

La Salle University (c): 1900 W. Olney Ave., Philadelphia, PA 19141; (215) 951-1000. Christian Brothers; 1863 (5,567).

Le Moyne College (c): 1419 Salt Springs Rd., Syracuse, NY 13214; (315) 445-4100; www.lemoyne.edu. Jesuit Fathers; 1946; independent (approx. 3,129, full-time, part-time, graduate)

Lewis University (c): Romeoville, IL 60446; (815) 838-0500; www.lewisu.edu. Christian Brothers; 1932 (4,348).

Loras College (c): 1450 Alta Vista St., Dubuque, IA 52004; (563) 588-7100. Archdiocese of Dubuque; 1839 (1,736).

Lourdes College (c): 6832 Convent Blvd., Sylvania, OH 43560; (419) 885-3211; www.lourdes.edu. Sisters of St. Francis; 1958 (1,356).

Loyola College (c): 4501 N. Charles St., Baltimore, MD 21210; (410) 617-2000; www.loyola.edu. Jesuits; 1852; combined with Mt. St. Agnes College, 1971 (6,144).

Loyola Marymount University (c): 7900 Loyola Blvd., Los Angeles, CA 90045-2699; (310) 338-2700; www.lmu. edu. Society of Jesus; Religious of Sacred Heart of Mary, Sisters of St. Joseph of Orange, 1911 (6,591).

Loyola University (c): 6363 St. Charles Ave., New Orleans, LA 70118; (504) 865-2011. Jesuit Fathers; 1912 (5,842).

Loyola University Chicago (c): 820 N. Michigan Ave., Chicago, IL 60611; (312) 915-6000; www.luc. edu. Society of Jesus; 1870 (12,604).

Madonna University (c): 36600 Schoolcraft Rd., Livonia, MI 48150; (734) 432-5300. Felician Sisters; 1947 (3,979).

Magdalen College (c): 511 Kearsarge Mountain Rd., Warner, NH 03278; (603) 456-2656; www.magdalen.edu. Magdalen College Corporation; 1973 (81).

Manhattan College (c): Manhattan College Pkwy., Bronx, NY 11201; (718) 862-7200; www.manhattan.edu. De La Salle Christian Brothers; 1835; independent (2,744). Cooperative program with College of Mt. St. Vincent.

Marian College of Fond du Lac (c): 45 S. National Ave., Fond du Lac, WI 54935; (920) 923-7600; www.mariancollege.edu. Sisters of St. Agnes; 1936 (2,558).

Marian College (c): 3200 Cold Spring Rd., Indianapolis, IN 46222; (317) 955-6000; www.marian.edu. Sisters of St. Francis (Oldenburg, IN); 1851; independent (1,425).

Marquette University (c): P.O. Box 1881, Milwaukee, WI 53201-1881; (414) 288-7250; www.marquette.edu. Jesuit Fathers; 1881; independent (10,832).

Mary, University of (c): 7500 University Dr., Bismarck, ND 58504; (701) 255-7500; www.umary. edu. Benedictine Sisters; 1959 (2,546).

Marygrove College (c): 8425 W. McNichols Rd., Detroit, MI 48221; (313) 927-1200. Sisters, Servants of the Immaculate Heart of Mary; 1905; independent (6,459).

Marylhurst College (c): P.O. Box 261, Marylhurst, OR 97036-0261; (503) 636-8141; www.marylhurst. edu. Sisters of Holy Names of Jesus and Mary; 1893; independent (1,579).

Marymount College (w): Tarrytown, NY 10591; (914) 631-3200; www.marymt.edu. Religious of the Sacred Heart of Mary; 1907; independent (842). Coed in weekend degree programs.

Marymount University (c): 2807 N. Glebe Rd., Arlington, VA 22207; (703) 522-5600; www.marymount.edu. Religious of the Sacred Heart of Mary; 1950; independent (3,672).

Marywood College (c): Scranton, PA 18509; (570) 348-6211; www.marywood.edu. Sisters, Servants of the Immaculate Heart of Mary; 1915; independent (3,087).

Mercy College of Health Sciences (c): 928-6th Ave., Des Moines, IA 50309-1239; (515) 643-3180; www.mchs.edu. Sisters of Mercy of the Americas (552).

Mercyhurst College (c): 501 E. 38th St., Erie, PA 16546; (814) 824-2000; www.mercyhurst.edu. Sisters of Mercy; 1926 (3,404).

Merrimack College (c): North Andover, MA 01845; (978) 837-5000; www.merrimack.edu. Augustinians;1947 (2,108).

Misericordia (College Misericordia) (c): 301 Lake St., Dallas, PA 18612-1098; (570) 674-6400; www.miseri.edu. Religious Sisters of Mercy of the Union; 1924 (1,983).

Molloy College (c): 1000 Hempstead Ave., P.O. Box 5002, Rockville Centre, NY 11570-5002; (516) 678-5000. Dominican Sisters; 1955; independent (2,500).

Mount Aloysius College (c): 7373 Admiral Peary Hwy., Cresson, PA 16630; (814) 886-4131; www.mtaloy.edu. Sisters of Mercy; 1939 (2,000).

Mount Marty College (c): 1105 W. 8th St., Yankton, SD 57078; (800) 658-4552; www.mtmc. edu. Benedictine Sisters; 1936 (1,168).

Mount Mary College (w): 2900 N. Menomonee River Pkwy., Milwaukee, WI 53222; (414) 258-4810. School Sisters of Notre Dame; 1913 (1,368).

Mount Mercy College (c): 1330 Elmhurst Dr. N.E., Cedar Rapids, IA 52402; (319) 363-8213; www.mtmercy.edu. Sisters of Mercy; 1928; independent (1,432).

Mount St. Clare College (c): 400 N. Bluff Blvd., Clinton, IA 52732; (319) 242-4023; www.clare.edu. Sisters of St. Francis of Clinton, Iowa; 1918 (appr. 497).

Mount St. Joseph, College of (c): 5701 Delhi Rd., Cincinnati, OH 45233-1670; (513) 244-4200; www. msj.edu. Sisters of Charity; 1920 (5,527).

Mount Saint Mary College (c): Newburgh, NY 12550; (914) 561-0800; www.msmc.edu.. Dominican Sisters; 1954; independent (2,541).

Mount St. Mary's College (c): Emmitsburg, MD 21727; (301) 447-6122; www.msmary.edu. Founded by Fr. John DuBois, 1808; independent (1,821).

Mount St. Mary's College (w/c): 12001 Chalon Rd., Los Angeles, CA 90049 and 10 Chester Pl., Los Angeles, CA 90007 (Doheny Campus); (310) 954-4010; www.msmc.la.edu. Sisters of St. Joseph of Carondelet; 1925. Coed in music, nursing and graduate programs (1,965).

Mount Saint Vincent, College of (c): 6301 Riverdale Ave., New York, NY 10471; (718) 405-3200; www.cmsv.edu. Sisters of Charity; 1847; independent (1,515). Cooperative program with Manhattan College.

Neumann College (c): One Neumann Dr., Aston, PA 19014; (610) 459-0905; www.neumann.edu. Sisters of St. Francis; 1965; independent (2,221).

Newman University (c): 3100 McCormick Ave., Wichita, KS 67213; (316) 942-4291; www.newmanu. edu. Sisters Adorers of the Blood of Christ; 1933 (1,929).

New Rochelle, College of (w/c): 29 Castle Pl., New Rochelle, NY 10805 (main campus); (914) 654-5000; www.cnr.edu. Ursuline Order; 1904; independent (6,084). Coed in nursing, graduate, new resources divisions.

Niagara University (c): Lewiston Rd. Niagara Univ., NY 14109-2015; (716) 285-1212; www.niagara.edu. Vincentian Fathers and Brothers; 1856 (3,446).

Notre Dame de Namur University (c): 1500 Ralston Ave., Belmont, CA 94002; (650) 593-1601; www. cnd.edu. Sisters of Notre Dame de Namur; 1851; independent (1,799).

Notre Dame, University of (c): (University of Notre Dame du Lac) Notre Dame, IN 46556; (219) 631-5000; www.nd.edu. Congregation of Holy Cross; 1842 (11,054).

Notre Dame College of Ohio (w): 4545 College

Rd., Cleveland, OH 44121; (216) 381-1680; www.ndc.edu. Sisters of Notre Dame; 1922 (1,093).

Notre Dame of Maryland, College of (w): 4701 N. Charles St., Baltimore, MD 21210; (410) 435-0100; www.ndm.edu. School Sisters of Notre Dame; 1873 (3,077).

Oblate School of Theology (c): 285 Oblate Dr., San Antonio, TX 78216-6693; (210) 341-1366; www.ost.edu. Oblates of Mary Immaculate; 1903 (264). Graduate theology programs.

Ohio Dominican College (c): 1216 Sunbury Rd., Columbus, OH 43219-2099; (614) 253-2741; www.odc.edu. Dominican Sisters of St. Mary of the Springs; 1911 (2,300).

Our Lady of Holy Cross College (c): 4123 Woodland Dr., New Orleans, LA 70131; (504) 394-7744; www.olhcc.edu. Congregation of Sisters Marianites of Holy Cross; 1916 (3,994).

Our Lady of the Elms, College of (w): Chicopee, MA 01013; (413) 594-2761; www.elms.edu. Sisters of St. Joseph; 1928 (866).

Our Lady of the Lake College (c): 5345 Brittany Dr., Baton Rouge, LA 70808-4398; (225) 768-1710; www.ololcollege. Independent (1,421).

Our Lady of the Lake University (c): 411 S.W. 24th St., San Antonio, TX 78207; (210) 434-6711; www.ollusa.edu. Sisters of Divine Providence; 1895 (3,324).

Our Lady Seat of Wisdom Academy: 18 Karol Wojtyla Square, P.O. Box 249, Barry's Bay, Ontario K0J 1B0, Canada; (613) 756-3082; www.seatofwisdom.org.

Pontifical Catholic University of Puerto Rico (c): 2250 Avenida de las Americas, Ponce, PR 00717-0777; (787) 841-2000; www.pucpr.edu. Hierarchy of Puerto Rico; 1948; Pontifical University (9,912).

Portland, University of (c): 5000 N. Willamette Blvd., Portland, OR 97203; (503) 943-7911; www.up.edu. Holy Cross Fathers; 1901; independent (3,234).

Presentation College (c): Aberdeen, SD 7401; (605) 225-1634. Sisters of the Presentation; 1951 (615).

Providence College (c): 549 River Ave., Providence, RI 02918; (401) 865-1000; www.providence.edu. Dominican Friars; 1917 (5,742, day, evening, and graduate).

Queen of the Holy Rosary College (c): P.O. Box 3908, Mission San Jose, CA 94539; (510) 657-2468. Dominican Sisters of Mission San Jose, independent (200).

Quincy University (c): 1800 College Ave., Quincy, IL 62301; (217) 222-8020; www.quincy.edu. Franciscan Friars; 1860 (1,146).

Regis College (w): 235 Wellesley St., Weston, MA 02493-1571; (781) 768-7000; www.regiscollege.edu. Sisters of St. Joseph; 1927; independent (1,300).

Regis University (c): 3333 Regis Blvd. Denver, CO 80221; (303) 458-4100. Jesuits; 1887 (11,240).

Rivier College (c): Nashua, NH 03060; (603) 888-1311; www.rivier.edu. Sisters of the Presentation of Mary; 1933; independent (2,572).

Rockhurst College (c): 1100 Rockhurst Rd., Kansas City, MO 64110; (816) 501-4000; www.rockhurst.edu. Jesuit Fathers; 1910 (3,536).

Rosemont College of the Holy Child Jesus (w): Rosemont, PA 19010-1699; (610) 526-2984; www.rosemont.edu. Society of the Holy Child Jesus; 1921 (1,210).

Sacred Heart University (c): 5151 Park Ave., Fairfield, CT 06432; (203) 371-7999; www.sacredheart.edu. Diocese of Bridgeport; 1963; independent (6,001).

St. Ambrose University (c): Davenport, IA 52803; (319) 333-6300; www.sau.edu. Diocese of Davenport; 1882 (3,500).

Saint Anselm College (c): Manchester NH 03102-1030; (603) 641-7000; www.anselm.edu. Benedictines; 1889 (1,985).

St. Basil College (m): 195 Glenbrook Rd., Stamford, CT 06902; (203) 324-4578; UkrCathSem@aol.com. The Ukrainian Catholic Diocese of Stamford.

Saint Benedict, College of (w): 37 S. College Ave., St. Joseph, MN 56374; (320) 363-5407; www.csbsju.edu. Benedictine Sisters; 1913 (2,072). Sister college of St. John's University, Collegeville.

St. Bonaventure University (c): St. Bonaventure, NY 14778; (716) 375-2000; www.sbu.edu. Franciscan Friars; 1858; independent (2,719).

St. Catherine, College of (w): St. Paul: 2004 Randolph Ave., St. Paul, MN 55105; (651) 690-6000; Minneapolis; www.stkate.edu. Sisters of St. Joseph of Carondelet; 1905 (4,622).

St. Edward's University (c): 3001 S. Congress Ave., Austin, TX 78704; (512) 448-8400; www.stedwards.edu. Holy Cross Brothers; 1881; independent (4,267).

Saint Elizabeth, College of (w): 2 Convent Rd., Morristown, NJ 07960-6989; (973) 290-4000; www.st-elizabeth.edu. Sisters of Charity; 1899; independent (1,766). Coed in adult undergraduate and graduate programs.

St. Francis College (c): 180 Remsen St., Brooklyn Heights, NY 11201; (718) 489-5200. Franciscan Brothers; 1884; private, independent in the Franciscan tradition (2,505).

St. Francis University (c): P.O. Box 600, Loretto, PA 15940-0600; (814) 472-3000; www.sfcpa.edu. Franciscan Friars; 1847; independent (2,012).

St. Francis, University of (c): 500 N. Wilcox, Joliet, IL 60435; (815) 740-3360; www.stfrancis.edu. Sisters of St. Francis of Mary Immaculate (3,920).

St. Francis, University of (c): 2701 Spring St., Fort Wayne, IN 46808-3994; (219) 434-3100; www.sf.edu. Sisters of St. Francis; 1890 (1,740).

St. Gregory's University (c): 1900 W. MacArthur, Shawnee, OK 74801; (405) 878-5100; www.sgc.edu. Benedictine Monks; 1876 (805).

St. John's University (c): 8000 Utopia Pkwy., Jamaica, NY 11439 (Queens Campus); 300 Howard Ave., Staten Island, NY 10301 (Staten Island Campus); (718) 990-6161; www.stjohns.edu. Vincentians; 1870 (18,523).

St. John's University (m): Collegeville, MN 56321; (320) 363-2011; www.csbsju.edu. Benedictines; 1857 (2,072). All classes and programs are coeducational with College of St. Benedict.

St. Joseph in Vermont, College of (c): 71 Clement Rd., Rutland, VT 05701; (802) 773-5900; www.csj.edu. Sisters of St. Joseph; 1950; independent (482).

Saint Joseph College (w/c): 1678 Asylum Ave., West Hartford, CT 06117-2700; (860) 232-4571; www.sjc.edu. Sisters of Mercy; 1932 (1,965). Women's college in undergraduate liberal arts. Coed in graduate school and Weekend College.

Saint Joseph's College (c): 278 Whites Bridge Rd., Standish, ME 04084-5263; (207) 893-7711; www.sjcme.edu. Sisters of Mercy; 1912 (4,197 total; 1,609 graduate). Offers extensive distance education programs.

Saint Joseph's College (c): P.O. Box 909, Rensselaer, IN 47978; (219) 866-6000; www.stjoe.edu. Society of the Precious Blood; 1891 (1,101).

St. Joseph's College (c): 245 Clinton Ave., Brooklyn, NY 11205; (718) 636-6800 and 155 W. Roe Blvd., Patchogue, NY 11772; (631) 447-3200; www.sjcny.edu. Sisters of St. Joseph; 1916; independent (3,444).

St. Joseph's University (c): 5600 City Ave., Philadelphia, PA 19131; (610) 660-1000; www.sju.edu. Jesuit Fathers; 1851 (6,850).

Saint Leo University (c): P.O. Box 6665, MC 2186, Saint Leo, FL 33574; (352) 588-8200; www.saintleo.edu. Order of St. Benedict; 1889; independent (9,931).

Saint Louis University (c): 221 N. Grand Blvd., St. Louis, MO 63103; (314) 977-2222; www.slu.edu. Society of Jesus; 1818; independent (11,274).

Saint Martin's College (c): 5300 Pacific Ave. SE, Lacey, WA 98503-1297; (360) 438-4311; www.stmartin.edu. Benedictine Monks; 1895 (1,474 main and extension campuses).

Saint Mary, College of (w): 1901 S. 72nd St., Omaha, NE 68124; (402) 399-2400; www.csm.edu. Sisters of Mercy; 1923; independent (981).

Saint Mary, University of (c): 4100 S. 4th Street, Leavenworth, KS 66048; (913) 682-5151. Sisters of Charity of Leavenworth; 1923 (888).

Saint Mary-of-the-Woods College (w): St. Mary-of-the-Woods, IN 47876; (812) 535-5151; www.smwc.edu. Sisters of Providence; 1840 (1,510).

Saint Mary's College (w): Notre Dame, IN 46556; (219) 284-4556; www.saintmarys.edu. Sisters of the Holy Cross; 1844 (1,473).

Saint Mary's College (c): 3535 Indian Trail, Orchard Lake, MI 48324; (248) 683-0521; www.stmarys-avemaria.edu. 1885 (510).

St. Mary's College (c): Moraga, CA 94575; (510) 631-4000. Brothers of the Christian Schools; 1863 (4,127).

Saint Mary's University of Minnesota (c): 700 Terrace Heights, Winona, MN 55987-1399; (507) 452-4430; www.smumn.edu. Brothers of the Christian Schools; 1912 (1,376).

St. Mary's University of San Antonio (c): One Camino Santa Maria, San Antonio, TX 78228-8607; (210) 436-3011; www.stmarytx.edu. Society of Mary (Marianists). 1852 (4,264).

Saint Meinrad School of Theology (c): 200 Hill Dr., St. Meinrad, IN 47577; (812) 357-6611; www.saintmeinrad.edu. Benedictines (91 full- and part-time lay students.) Graduate-level theological studies.

St. Michael's College (c): Winooski Park, Colchester, VT 05439; (802) 654-2211; www.smcvt.edu. Society of St. Edmund; 1904 (2,630).

St. Norbert College (c): De Pere, WI 54115; (920) 403-3181; www.snc.edu. Norbertine Fathers; 1898; independent (2,045).

Saint Peter's College (c): 2641 Kennedy Blvd., Jersey City, NJ 07306; (201) 915-9000; www.spc.

edu. Society of Jesus; 1872; independent (4,201).

Saint Rose, College of (c): 432 Western Ave., Albany, NY 12203; (518) 454-5111. Sisters of St. Joseph of Carondelet; 1920; independent (4,441).

St. Scholastica, The College of (c): 1200 Kenwood Ave., Duluth, MN 55811; (218) 723-6000. Benedictine Sisters; 1912; independent (2,518).

St. Thomas, University of (c): 2115 Summit Ave., St. Paul, MN 55105; (651) 962-5000; www.stthomas.edu. Archdiocese of St. Paul and Minneapolis; 1885 (11,366).

St. Thomas, University of (c): 3800 Montrose Blvd., Houston, TX 77006-4696; (713) 522-7911; www.stthom.edu. Basilian Fathers; 1947 (7,174).

St. Thomas Aquinas College (c): Sparkill, NY 10976; (914) 398-4000; www.stac.edu. Dominican Sisters of Sparkill; 1952; independent, corporate board of trustees (2,200).

St. Thomas More, College of (c): 3020 Lubbock Street, Fort Worth, Texas 76109; (817) 923-8459; www.cstm.edu.

St. Thomas University (c): 16400 N.W. 32nd Ave., Miami, FL 33054; (305) 625-6000; www.stu.edu. Archdiocese of Miami; 1962 (3,677).

Saint Vincent College (c): 300 Fraser Purchase Rd., Latrobe, PA 15650-2690; (724) 539-9761; www.benedictine.stvincent.edu/seminary. Benedictine Fathers; 1846 (1,222).

Saint Vincent's College (c): 2800 Main St., Bridgeport, CT 06606; (203) 576-5235; www.stvincentscollege.edu. (345).

St. Xavier University (c): 3700 W. 103rd St., Chicago, IL 60655; (773) 298-3000. Sisters of Mercy; chartered 1847 (4,100).

Salve Regina University (c): Ochre Point Ave., Newport, RI 02840-4192; (401) 847-6650; www.salve.edu. Sisters of Mercy; 1934 (1,542). Offers distance learning programs in graduate studies.

San Diego, University of (c): 5998 Alcala Park, San Diego, CA 92110; (619) 260-4600. San Diego diocese and Religious of the Sacred Heart; 1949; independent (7,062).

San Francisco, University of (c): 2130 Fulton St., San Francisco, CA 94117; (415) 422-5555. Jesuit Fathers; 1855 (8,130).

Santa Clara University (c): 500 El Camino Real, Santa Clara, CA 95053; (408) 554-4000; www.scu.edu. Jesuit Fathers; 1851; independent (7,368).

Santa Fe, College of (c): 1600 St. Michael's Dr., Santa Fe, NM 87505; (505) 473-6011. Brothers of the Christian Schools; 1947 (1,588).

Scranton, University of (c): Scranton, PA 18510; (570) 941-7533; www.uofs.edu. Society of Jesus; 1888; independent (4,728).

Seattle University (c): 900 Broadway, Seattle, WA 98122; (206) 296-6000; www.seattleu.edu. Society of Jesus; 1891 (6,337).

Seton Hall University (c): 400 South Orange Ave., South Orange, NJ 07079; (973) 761-9000. Diocesan Clergy; 1856 (9,760).

Seton Hill College (w): Seton Hill Dr., Greensburg, PA 15601-1599; (724) 834-2200; www.setonhill.edu. Sisters of Charity of Seton Hill; 1883 (1,521).

Siena College (c): 515 Loudon Rd., Loudonville, NY 12211; (518) 783-2300; www.siena.edu. Franciscan Friars; 1937 (3,379).

Siena Heights University (c): 1247 E. Siena Heights Dr., Adrian, MI 49221; (517) 263-0731; www.sienahts.edu. Adrian Dominican Sisters; 1919 (2,124).

Silver Lake College of the Holy Family (c): 2406 S. Alverno Rd., Manitowoc, WI 54220-9319; (920) 684-6691. Franciscan Sisters of Christian Charity; 1935 (2,969).

Spalding University (c): 851 S. 4th Ave., Louisville, KY 40203; (502) 585-9911; www.spalding.edu. Sisters of Charity of Nazareth; 1814; independent (1,670).

Spring Hill College (c): 4000 Dauphin St., Mobile, AL 36608; (334) 380-4000; www.shc.edu. Jesuit Fathers; 1830 (1,050).

Stonehill College (c): North Easton, MA 02357; (508) 565-1000; www.stonehill.edu. Holy Cross Fathers; 1948; independent (2,550).

Thomas Aquinas College (c): 10000 N. Ojai Rd., Santa Paula, CA 93060; (805) 525-4417; www.thomasaquinas.edu. Founded 1971 (331).

Thomas More College (c): 333 Thomas More Pkwy., Crestview Hills, Covington, KY 41017; (859) 341-5800; www.thomasmore.edu. Diocese of Covington; 1921 (1,555).

Thomas More College of Liberal Arts (c): Six Manchester Street, Merrimack, NH 03054; (603) 880-8308; www.thomasmorecollege.edu.

Trinity College (w): 125 Michigan Ave. NE, Washington, DC 20017; (202) 939-5000. Sisters of Notre Dame de Namur; 1897 (1,600). Coed graduate school.

Ursuline College (w): 2550 Lander Rd., Pepper Pike, OH 44124; (440) 449-4200; www.ursuline.edu. Ursuline Nuns; 1871 (1,319).

Villanova University (c): Villanova, PA 19085; (610) 519-7499; www.villanova.edu. Order of St. Augustine; 1842 (10,396).

Viterbo College (c): 815 S. 9th, La Crosse, WI 54601; (608) 796-3000; www.viterbo.org. Franciscan Sisters of Perpetual Adoration; 1890 (2,200).

Walsh University (c): 2020 Easton St. N.W., North Canton, Ohio 44720-3396; (330) 490-7090; www.walsh.edu. Brothers of Christian Instruction; 1958 (1,648).

Washington Theological Union (c): 6896 Laurel Street N.W., Washington, DC 20012-2016; (202) 726-8800; www.wtu.edu. Coalition of Religious Seminaries; 1968 (263).

Wheeling Jesuit University (c): 316 Washington Ave., Wheeling, WV 26003-6295; (304) 243-2000; www.wju.edu. Jesuit Fathers; 1954 (1,703).

Wyoming Catholic College (c): P.O. Box 750, Lander, WY 82520; (877) 332-2930; www.wyomingcatholiccollege.com; liberal arts college that stresses the Great Books; 2005.

Xavier University (c): 3800 Victory Pkwy., Cincinnati, OH 45207; (513) 745-3000; www.xu.edu. Jesuit Fathers; 1831 (2,631).

Xavier University of Louisiana (c): 1 Drexel Dr., New Orleans, LA 70125; (504) 486-7411; www.xula.edu. Sisters of Blessed Sacrament; 1925 (3,787).

Catholic Two-Year Colleges

Ancilla Domini College (c): P.O. Box 1, Donaldson, IN 46513; (219) 936-8898; www.ancilla.edu. Ancilla Domini Sisters; 1937 (546).

Assumption College for Sisters: Mendham, NJ 07945; (973) 543-6528. Sisters of Christian Charity; 1953 (24).

Chatfield College (c): St. Martin, OH 45118; (937) 875-3344; www.chatfield.edu. Ursulines; 1971 (273).

The College of St. Catherine-Minneapolis (c): 601 25th Ave. S., Minneapolis, MN 55454; (651) 690-7702. Sisters of St. Joseph of Carondelet (918).

Donnelly College (c): 608 N. 18th St., Kansas City, KS 66102; (913) 621-6070; www.donnelly.cc.ks.us. Archdiocesan College; 1949 (645).

Don Bosco Technical Institute (m): 1151 San Gabriel Blvd., Rosemead, CA 91770; (626) 307-6500; www.boscotech.tec.ca.us. Salesians; 1969 (994).

Holy Cross College (c): 54515 State Rd., 933 N., Notre Dame, IN 46556-0308; (219) 239-8400; www.hcc-nd.edu. Brothers of Holy Cross; 1966 (503).

Manor College (c): 700 Fox Chase Road, Jenkintown, PA 19046; (215) 885-2360; www.manor.edu. Sisters of St. Basil the Great; 1947.

Maria College (c): 700 New Scotland Ave., Albany, NY 12208. Sisters of Mercy; 1963 (1,048).

Marymount College Palos Verdes (c): 30800 Palos Verdes Dr., E., Rancho Palos Verdes, CA 90275-6299; (310) 377-5501; www.marymountpv.edu. Religious of the Sacred Heart of Mary; independent (840).

St. Catharine College (c): 2735 Bardstown Rd., St. Catharine, KY 40061; (859) 336-5082. Dominican Sisters; 1931 (742).

Springfield College in Illinois (c): 1500 N. Fifth St., Springfield, IL 62702-2694; (217) 525-1420; www.sci.edu. Ursuline Sisters; 1929 (300).

Trocaire College (c): 360 Choate Ave., Buffalo, NY 14220; (716) 827-2423; www.trocaire.edu. Sisters of Mercy; 1958; independent (780).

Villa Maria College of Buffalo (c): 240 Pine Ridge Rd., Buffalo, NY 14225; (716) 896-0700; www.villa.edu. Felician Sisters 1960; independent (475).

DIOCESAN AND INTERDIOCESAN SEMINARIES

(*Sources*: Catholic Almanac *survey*; The Official Catholic Directory; Catholic News Service.)

Information, according to states, includes names of archdioceses and dioceses, and names and addresses of seminaries. Types of seminaries, when not clear from titles, are indicated in most cases. Interdiocesan seminaries are generally conducted by religious orders for candidates for the priesthood from several dioceses. The list does not include houses of study reserved for members of religious communities. Archdioceses are indicated by an asterisk.

California: Los Angeles* – St. John's Seminary (major), 5118 Seminary Rd., Camarillo 93012-2599; (805) 482-2755; www.stjohnsem.edu.

San Diego – St. Francis Seminary (college and pretheology formation program), 1667 Santa Paula Dr.,

92111; (619) 291-7446.

San Francisco* – St. Patrick's Seminary (major), 320 Middlefield Rd., Menlo Park 94025; (650) 325-5621; www.stpatricksseminary.org..

Colorado: Denver* – St. John Vianney Theological Seminary (college and pre-theology formation program), 1300 S. Steele St., 80210; (303) 282-3427; Redemptoris Mater Archdiocesan Missionary Seminary (seminary, house of formation), 1300 S. Steele St., 80210; (303) 282-3427.

Connecticut: Hartford* – St. Thomas Seminary (college formation program), 467 Bloomfield Ave., Bloomfield 06002-2999; (860) 242-5573.

Norwich – Holy Apostles College and Seminary (adult vocations; minor and major), 33 Prospect Hill Rd., Cromwell 06416; (860) 632-3000; www.holyapostles.edu.

Stamford – Byzantine Rite: Ukrainian Catholic Seminary: St. Basil College Seminary (minor), 195 Glenbrook Rd., Stamford 06902-3099; (203) 324-4578.

District of Columbia: Washington, DC* – Theological College (national, major), The Catholic University of America, 401 Michigan Ave., N.E., 20017; (202) 756-4900; www.theologicalcollege.org.

St. Josaphat's Seminary, 201 Taylor St. N.E., 20017; (202) 529-1177. (Major house of formation serving the four Ukrainian Byzantine-rite dioceses in the U.S.)

Florida: Miami* – St. John Vianney College Seminary, 2900 S.W. 87th Ave., 33165; (305) 223-4561.

Palm Beach – St. Vincent de Paul Regional Seminary (major), 10701 S. Military Trail, Boynton Beach 33436; (561) 732-4424; www.svdp.edu.

Illinois: Chicago* – St. Joseph Seminary (college), 6551 N. Sheridan Rd., Chicago 60626; (773) 973-9700; www.stjoseph.luc.edu. University of St. Mary of the Lake Mundelein Seminary (School of Theology), 1000 E. Maple Ave., Mundelein 60060; (847) 566-6401; www.vocations.org.

Indiana: Indianapolis* – Saint Meinrad Seminary, College and School of Theology (interdiocesan), St. Meinrad 47577; (812) 357-6611; www.saintmeinrad.edu.

Iowa: Davenport – St. Ambrose University Seminary (interdiocesn), 518 W. Locust St., 52803; (319) 333-6151; www.davenportdiocese.org.

Dubuque* – Seminary of St. Pius X (interdiocesan), Loras College, 52004-0178; (319) 588-7782.

Louisiana: New Orleans* – Notre Dame Seminary Graduate School of Theology, 2901 S. Carrollton Ave., 70118; (504) 866-7426; St. Joseph Seminary College (interdiocesan), St. Benedict 70457-9999; (504) 892-1800; www.stjosephabbey.org.

Maryland: Baltimore* – Mt. St. Mary's Seminary and University, 5400 Roland Ave., 21210; (410) 864-4000; www.stmarys.edu. Mt. St. Mary's Seminary, Emmitsburg 21727-7797; (301) 447-5295; www.msmary.edu.

Massachusetts: Boston* – St. John's Seminary, School of Theology, 127 Lake St., Brighton 02135; (617) 254-2610. St. John's Seminary, College of Liberal Arts, 127 Lake St., Brighton 02135; (617) 746-5450. Pope John XXIII National Seminary (for ages 30-60), 558 South Ave., Weston 02943; (781) 899-5500; www.blessedjohnXXIII.org.

Newton – Melkite Greek Catholic: St. Gregory the Theologian Seminary, 3 VFW Parkway, Roslindale, MA 02131; (617) 323-9922. Seminary of St. Basil the Great, 30 East St., 01844; (978) 683-2471.

Michigan: Detroit* – Sacred Heart Major Seminary (college/theologate and institute for ministry), 2701 Chicago Blvd., Detroit 48206; (313) 883-8500. Sts. Cyril

and Methodius Seminary, St. Mary's College (theologate and college) independent, primarily serving Polish-American community, 3535 Indian Trail, Orchard Lake 48324; (248) 683-0311.

Grand Rapids – Christopher House, 723 Rosewood Ave., S.E., East Grand Rapids 49506; (616) 243-6538.

Minnesota: St. John's School of Theology and Seminary, St. John's University, P.O. Box 7288, Collegeville 56321-7288; (320) 363-2100; www.csbsju.edu/sot.

St. Paul and Minneapolis* – St. Paul Seminary School of Divinity, University of St. Thomas, St. Paul 55101; (612) 962-5050; www.stthomas.edu. St. John Vianney Seminary (college residence), 2115 Summit Ave., St. Paul 55105; (651) 962-6825; www.stthomas.edu/sjv.

Winona – Immaculate Heart of Mary Seminary, St. Mary's University, No. 43, 700 Terrace Heights, 55987; (507) 457-7373; www.ihmseminary.org.

Missouri: St. Louis* – Kenrick-Glennon Seminary (St. Louis Roman Catholic Theological Seminary). Kenrick School of Theology and Cardinal Glennon College, 5200 Glennon Dr., 63119; (314) 792-6100.

Nebraska: Seward – St. Gregory the Great Seminary (pre-theology), 1301 280th Rd., 68434; (402) 643-4052, www.stgregorysseminary.org. Our Lady of Guadalupe Seminary, P.O. Box 147, Denton, NE 68339; (402) 797-7700; www.fssp.com.

New Jersey: Newark* – Immaculate Conception Seminary – college seminary; major seminary; graduate school – Seton Hall University, 400 South Orange Ave., South Orange 07079; (973) 761-9575; www.shu.edu. Redemptoris Mater, Archdiocesan Missionary Seminary, 672 Passaic Ave., 07032; (201) 997-3220.

New York: Brooklyn – Cathedral Seminary Residence of the Immaculate Conception (college and pre-theology), 7200 Douglaston Parkway, Douglaston 11362; (718) 229-8001. Cathedral Preparatory Seminary, 56-25 92nd St., Elmhurst 11373; (718) 592-6800. St. Alphonsus Formation Residence, 22-04 Parsons Blvd., 11357-3440; (718) 321-1096.

Buffalo – Christ the King Seminary (interdiocesan theologate), P.O. Box 607, 711 Knox Rd., East Aurora 14052; (716) 652-8900. Pope John Paul II Residence, 217 Winston Rd., 14216; (716) 836-5526.

New York* – St. Joseph's Seminary (major), 201 Seminary Ave., Dunwoodie, Yonkers 10704; (914) 968-6200. St. John Neumann Residence (college and pre-theology), 201 Seminary Ave., Yonkers, N.Y., 10744-1896; (914) 964-3025. Cathedral Preparatory Seminary, 946 Boston Post Rd., Rye 10580; (914) 968-6200; www.cathedralprep.com.

Rockville Centre – Seminary of the Immaculate Conception (major), 440 West Neck Rd., Huntington, 11743; (631) 423-2346.

St. Maron Eparchy, Brooklyn – Our Lady of Lebanon Maronite Seminary, 7164 Alaska Ave. N.W., Washington, DC 20012; (202) 723-8831; www.maroniteseminary.org.

North Dakota: Fargo – Cardinal Muench Seminary (interdiocesan high school, college and pre-theology), 100 35th Ave. N.E., Fargo 58102; (701) 232-8969; www.cardinalmuench.org.

Ohio: Cincinnati* – Mt. St. Mary's Seminary of the West (division of the Athenaeum of Ohio), 6616 Beechmont Ave., 45230; (513) 231-2223; www.mtsm.org..

Cleveland – St. Mary Seminary and Graduate School of Theology, 28700 Euclid Ave. Wickliffe 44092; (440) 943-7600. Borromeo Seminary, 28700 Euclid Ave., 44092-2585; (440) 943-7600; www.a-full-life.com.

Columbus – Pontifical College Josephinum (national),

theologate and college, 7625 North High St., 43235-1498; (614) 885-5585; www.pcj.edu.

Oregon: Portland* – Mt. Angel Seminary (interdiocesan, college, pre-theology program, graduate school of theology), 1 Abbey Dr., St. Benedict 97373; (503) 845-3951. Felix Rougier House of Studies, 585 E. College St., 97362. Jesuit Novitiate of St. Francis Xavier, 3301 S.E. 45th Ave., 97206.

Pennsylvania: Erie – St. Mark Seminary, P.O. Box 10397, Erie 16514; (814) 824-1200.

Greensburg – St. Vincent Seminary (interdiocesan; pre-theology program; theologate; graduate programs in theology; religious education), 300 Fraser Purchase Rd., Latrobe 15650-2690; (724) 539-9761; www.stvincent.edu.

Philadelphia* – Theological Seminary of St. Charles Borromeo (College, pre-theology program, spirituality year pogram, theologate), 100 East Wynnewood Rd., Wynnewood 19096; (610) 667-3394; www.scs.edu.

Pittsburgh* (Byzantine-Ruthenian) – Byzantine Catholic Seminary of Sts. Cyril and Methodius (college, pre-theology program, theologate), 3605 Perrysville Ave., 15214; (412) 321-8383; www.byzcath.org/seminary.

Pittsburgh – St. Paul Seminary (interdiocesan, college and pre-theology), 2900 Noblestown Rd., 15205; (412) 921-5800; www.diopitt.org.

Scranton – St. Pius X Seminary (college and pre-theology formation; interdiocesan), 1000 Seminary Rd., Dalton 18414; (570) 563-1131. Affiliated with the University of Scranton.

Rhode Island: Providence — Seminary of Our Lady of Providence (House of Formation; college students and pre-theology), 485 Mount Pleasant Ave., 02908; (401) 331-1316; www.catholicpriest.com.

Texas: Dallas – Holy Trinity Seminary (college and pre-theology; English proficiency and academic foundation programs), P.O. Box 140309, Irving 75014; (972) 438-2212.

El Paso – St. Charles Seminary College, P.O. Box 17548, 79917; (915) 591-9821.

Galveston-Houston – St. Mary's Seminary (theologate), 9845 Memorial Dr., Houston 77024; (713) 686-4345.

San Antonio* – Assumption Seminary (theologate and pre-theology, Hispanic ministry emphasis), 2600 W. Woodlawn Ave., 78228; (210) 734-2324.

Washington: Spokane – Bishop White Seminary, College Formation Program, E. 429 Sharp Ave., 99202; (509) 326-3255; www.bishopwhiteseminary.org.

Wisconsin: Milwaukee* – St. Francis Seminary, 3257 S. Lake Dr., St. Francis 53235; (414) 747-6400; www.sfs.edu. College Program, 2497 N. Murray Ave., Milwaukee, 53211; (414) 964-6982. Sacred Heart School of Theology (interdiocesan seminary for second-career vocations), P.O. Box 429, Hales Corners, 53130-0429; (414) 425-8300.

North American College

Founded by the U.S. Bishops in 1859, the North American College serves as a residence and house of formation for U.S. seminarians and graduate students in Rome. The first ordination of an alumnus took place June 14, 1862. Pontifical status was granted the college by Pope Leo XIII Oct. 25, 1884. Students pursue theological and related studies principally at the Pontifical Gregorian University, the Pontifical University of Saint Thomas Aquinas, and the Pontifical University della Santa Croce. The current rector is Msgr. James F. Checcio, J.C.D., M.B.A. Address: 00120 Città del Vaticano; 011-39-06-684-931; www.pnac.org.

American College of Louvain

Founded by U.S. Bishops in 1857, the American College of Louvain, Belgium, was a seminary for U.S. students. It also served as a community for English-speaking graduate-student priests and religious priests pursuing studies at the Catholic University of Louvain (Université Catholique de Louvain, founded 1425). The college was administered by an American rector and faculty, and operated under the auspices of a committee of the national Conference of Catholic Bishops. The seminary closed in June 2011.

WORLD AND U.S. SEMINARY STATISTICS

The *2012 Statistical Yearbook of the Church* (the most recent edition) reports the following comparative statistics for the years 1997 to 2012 of candidates in Philosophy and Theology (major seminarians). World totals are given first; U.S. statistics are given in parentheses.

Year	Total Major Seminarians	Diocesan	Religious
1997	108,517 (4,729)	70,534 (3,311)	37,983 (1,418)
1998	109,171 (4,830)	70,564 (3,436)	38,607 (1,394)
1999	110,021 (5,024)	70,989 (3,428)	39,032 (1,596)
2000	110,583 (5,109)	71,756 (3,479)	38,827 (1,630)
2001	112,244 (5,080)	72,241 (3,404)	40,003 (1,676)
2002	113,199 (5,169)	72,977 (3,578)	40,222 (1,591)
2003	112,373 (4,676)	72,266 (3,181)	40,107 (1,495)
2004	113,044 (5,642)	71,841 (3,929)	41,203 (1,713)
2005	114,439 (5,180)	72,188 (3,383)	42,251 (1,797)
2006	115,480 (4,913)	71,878 (3,214)	43,602 (1,699)
2007	115,919 (4,901)	71,225 (3,366)	44,602 (1,699)
2008	117,024 (5,453)	71,176 (3,804)	45,484 (1,649)
2009	117,978 (5,181)	71,219 (3,573)	46,759 (1,608)
2010	118,890 (5,321)	71,974 (3,677)	47,016 (1,644)
2011	**120,616 (5,775)**	**72,277 (3,893)**	**48,339 (1,882)**
2012	**120,051 (5,738)**	**71,989 (3,944)**	**48,062 (1,794)**

PONTIFICAL UNIVERSITIES

(*Principal source*: Annuario Pontificio.)

These universities, listed according to country of location, have been canonically erected and authorized by the Congregation for Catholic Education to award degrees in stated fields of study. New laws and norms governing ecclesiastical universities and faculties were promulgated in the apostolic constitution *Sapientia Christiana*, issued Apr. 15, 1979. Phone numbers are listed where possible.

Argentina: Pontifical Catholic University of S. Maria of Buenos Aires (June 16, 1960): Av. Alicia Moreau de Justo 1400, 1107 Buenos Aires.

Belgium: Catholic University of Louvain (founded Dec. 9, 1425; canonically erected, 1834), with autonomous institutions for French- (Louvain) and Flemish-(Leuven) speaking: Place de l'Universite I, B-1348 Louvain-La-Neuve (French); Naamsestraat 22/b, B-3000 Leuven (Flemish).

Brazil: Pontifical Catholic University of Rio de Janeiro (Jan. 20, 1947): Rua Marquês de São Vicente 225, 22451-000 Rio de Janeiro, RJ.

Pontifical Catholic University of Minas Gerais (June 5, 1983): Av. Dom José Gaspar 500, C.P. 2686, 30161-000 Belo Horizonte, MG.; (031) 319-1127.

Pontifical Catholic University of Parana (Aug. 6, 1985): Rua Imaculada Conceição, 1155, Prado Velho, C.P. 670, 80001-000 Curitiba, PR; (041) 223-0922.

Pontifical Catholic University of Rio Grande do Sul (Nov. 1, 1950): Av. Ipiranga 6681, C.P.1429,90001-000 Porto Alegre, RS.

Pontifical Catholic University of São Paulo (Jan. 25, 1947): Rua Monte Alegre 984, 05014-901 São Paulo SP.

Pontifical University of Campinas (Sept. 8, 1956): Rua Marechal Deodoro 1099, 13020-000 Campinas, SP.; (0192) 27-001.

Canada: Laval University (Mar. 15, 1876): Case Postale 460, QC G1K 7P4.

St. Paul University (formerly University of Ottawa) (Feb. 5, 1889): 223 Rue Main, Ottawa, ON K1S 1C4;

University of Sherbrooke (Nov. 21, 1957): Chemin Ste.-Catherine, 2500, boulevard de l'Université, Sherbrooke, QC J1K 12R1.

Chile: Pontifical Catholic University of Chile (June 21, 1888): Avenida Bernardo O'Higgins, 340, Casilla 114D, Santiago.

Catholic University of Valparaíso (Nov. 1, 1961): Avenida Brasil 2950, Casilla 4059, Valparaíso.

Colombia: Bolivarian Pontifical Catholic University (Aug. 16, 1945): Circular 1a, N.70-01, Apartado 56006, Medellín.

Pontifical Xaverian University (July 31, 1937): Carrera 7, N. 40-62, Apartado 56710, Santafé de Bogota D.C.; Apartado 26239, Calle 18, N. 118-250, Cali (Cali campus).

Cuba: Catholic University of St. Thomas of Villanueva (May 4, 1957): Avenida Quenta 16,660, Marianao.

Dominican Republic: Pontifical Catholic University "Mother and Teacher" (Sept. 9, 1987): Apartado 822, Santiago de Los Caballeros.

Ecuador: Pontifical Catholic University of Ecuador (July 16, 1954): Doce de Octubre, N. 1076, Apartado 17-01-2184, Quito.

France: Catholic University of Lille (Nov. 18, 1875): Boulevard Vauban 60, 59016 Lille.

Catholic Faculties of Lyon (Nov. 22, 1875): 25, Rue du Plat, 69288 Lyon 02.

Catholic Institute of Paris (Aug. 11, 1875): 21, Rue d'Assas, 75270 Paris 06.

Catholic Institute of Toulouse (Nov. 15, 1877): Rue de la Fonderie 31, 31068 Toulouse.

Catholic University of the West (Sept. 16, 1875): 3, Place André Leroy, B.P. 808, 49005 Angers; 2-41-81-66-00.

Germany: Catholic University Eichstätt (Apr. 1, 1980): Ostenstrasse 26, D-85072, Eichstätt, Federal Republic of Germany; (08421) 201.

Guatemala: Rafael Landívar University (Oct. 18, 1961): Vista Hermosa III, Zona 16, Guatemala; (02) 69-21-51.

Hungary: Catholic University Pázmány Péter (March 25, 1999): Papnövelde Utea 7, H-1053 Budapest, Hungary; (01) 11-73-701.

Ireland: St. Patrick's College (Mar. 29, 1896): Maynooth, Co. Kildare.

Italy: Catholic University of the Sacred Heart (Dec. 25, 1920): Largo Gemelli 1, 20123 Milan.

Libera University Mary of the Assumption (Oct. 26, 1939): Via della Transpontina 21, 00193 Rome, Italy.

Japan: Jochi Daigaku (Sophia University) (Mar. 29, 1913): Chiyoda-Ku, Kioi-cho 7, Tokyo 102.

Lebanon: St. Joseph University of Beirut (Mar. 25, 1881): Rue de l'Université St.-Joseph, Boite Postale 293, Beyrouth (Beirut), Liban; (01) 42-64-56.

Netherlands: Catholic University of Nijmegen (June 29, 1923): P.B. 9102, Comeniuslaam 4, 6500 HC, Nijmegen.

Panama: University of S. Maria La Antigua (May 27, 1965): Apartado 6-1696, Panama 6.

Paraguay: Catholic University of Our Lady of the Assumption (Feb. 2, 1965): Independencia Nacional y Comuneros, Casilla 1718, Asunción; (021) 44-10-44.

Peru: Pontifical Catholic University of Peru (Sept. 30, 1942): Av. Universitaria, s/n. San Miguel, Apartado 1761, Lima 100. [Stripped of its Catholic title on July 21, 2012 by the Holy See.]

Philippines: Pontifical University of Santo Tomás (Nov. 20, 1645): España Street, 1008 Manila.

Poland: Catholic University of Lublin (July 25, 1920): Aleje Racùawickie 14, Skr. Poczt. 129, 20-950, Lublin.

Catholic Theological Academy (June 29, 1989): Ul. Dewajtis 5, 01-815, Warsaw.

Pontifical Academy of Theology of Krakow (Dec. 8, 1981): Ul. Kanonicza, 25, 31-002 Kraków; (014) 22-33-31.

Portugal: Portuguese Catholic University (Nov. 1, 1967): Palma de Cima, 1 600 Lisbon.

Puerto Rico: Pontifical Catholic University of Puerto Rico (Aug. 15, 1972): 2250 Ave. Las Américas Suite 523, Ponce, Puerto Rico 00731-6382.

Spain: Catholic University of Navarra (Aug. 6, 1960): Campus Universitario, E-31080 Pamplona.

Pontifical University "Comillas" (Mar. 29, 1904): Campus de Cantoblanco, 28049 Madrid.

Pontifical University of Salamanca (Sept. 25, 1940): Compañía 5, 37002 Salamanca.

University of Deusto (Aug. 10, 1963): Avenida de las Universidades, 28, 48007 Bilbao o Apartado 1, 48080 Bilbao; 94-445-31-00.

Taiwan (China): Fu Jen Catholic University (Nov. 15, 1923, at Peking; reconstituted at Taipeh, Sept. 8,

1961): Hsinchuang, Taipeh Hsien 24205.

United States: The Catholic University of America (Mar. 7, 1889): 620 Michigan Ave. N.E., Washington, DC 20064.

Georgetown University (Mar. 30, 1833): 37th and O Sts. N.W., Washington, DC 20057.

Niagara University (June 21, 1956): Lewiston Rd., Niagara Falls, NY 14109.

Uruguay: Catholic University of Uruguay "Dámaso Antonio Larrañaga" (Jan. 25, 1985): Avda. 8 de Octubre 2738, 11.600 Montevideo.

Venezuela: Catholic University "Andrés Bello" (Sept. 29, 1963): Esquina Jesuitas, Apartado 29068, Caracas 1021; (02) 442-21-20.

ECCLESIASTICAL FACULTIES

(*Principal source:* Annuario Pontificio.)

These faculties in Catholic seminaries and universities, listed according to country of location, have been canonically erected and authorized by the Congregation for Catholic Education to award degrees in stated fields of study.

Argentina: Faculties of Philosophy and Theology, San Miguel (Sept. 8, 1932).

Australia: Catholic Institute of Sydney, Sydney (Feb. 2, 1954).

Austria: Theological Faculty, Linz (Dec. 25, 1978). International Theological Institute for Family Studies (Oct. 1, 1996).

Brazil: Philosophical and Theological Faculties of the Company of Jesus, Belo Horizonte (July 15, 1941 and Mar. 12, 1949).

Ecclesiastical Faculty of Philosophy "John Paul II," Rio de Janeiro (Aug. 6, 1981).

Cameroon: Catholic Institute of Yaoundé (Nov. 15, 1991).

Canada: College of Immaculate Conception — Montréal Section of Jesuit Faculties in Canada (Sept. 8, 1932). Suspended.

Pontifical Institute of Medieval Studies, Toronto (Oct. 18, 1939).

Dominican Faculty of Theology of Canada, Ottawa (1965; Nov. 15, 1975).

Regis College, Toronto Section of the Jesuit Faculty of Theology in Canada, Toronto (Feb. 17, 1956; Dec. 25, 1977).

Congo (formerly Zaire): Catholic Faculties of Kinshasa, Kinshasa (theology, Apr. 25, 1957; philosophy, Nov. 25, 1987).

Côte d'Ivoire (Ivory Coast): Catholic Institute of West Africa, Abidjan (Aug. 12, 1975).

Croatia: Philosophical Faculty, Zagreb (July 31, 1989).

France: Centre Sèvres, Faculties of Theology and Philosophy of the Jesuits, Paris (Sept. 8, 1932).

Germany: Theological Faculty of the Major Episcopal Seminary, Trier (Sept. 8, 1955).

Theological Faculty, Paderborn (June 11, 1966).

Theological-Philosophical Faculty, Frankfurt (1932; June 7, 1971).

Philosophical Faculty, Munich (1932; Oct. 25, 1971).

Theological Faculty, Fulda (Dec. 22, 1978).

Philosophical-Theological School of Salesians, Benediktbeuern (May 24, 1992).

Philosphical-Theological School, Vallendar (Oct. 7, 1993).

Great Britain: Heythrop College, University of London, London (Nov. 1, 1964). Theology, philosophy.

Hungary: Faculty of Theology (1635), Institute on Canon Law (Nov. 30, 1996), Budapest.

India: Jnana Deepa Vidyapeeth (Pontifical Athenaeum), Institute of Philosophy and Religion, Poona (July 27, 1926).

Vidyajyoti, Institute of Religious Studies, Faculty of Theology, Delhi (1932; Dec. 9, 1974).

Satya Nilayam, Institute of Philosophy and Culture. Faculty of Philosophy, Madras (Sept. 8, 1932; Dec. 15, 1976).

Pontifical Institute of Theology and Philosophy at the Pontifical Interritual Seminary of St. Joseph, Alwaye, Kerala (Feb. 24, 1972).

Dharmaram Vidya Kshetram, Pontifical Athenaeum of Theology and Philosophy, Bangalore (theology, Jan. 6, 1976; philosophy, Dec. 8, 1983).

Pontifical Oriental Institute of Religious Studies, Kottayam (July 3, 1982). Faculty of Theology, Ranchi (Aug. 15, 1982).

St. Peter's Pontifical Institute of Theology, Bangalore (Jan. 6, 1985).

Indonesia: Wedabhakti Pontifical Faculty of Theology, Yogyakarta (Nov. 1, 1984).

Ireland: The Milltown Institute of Theology and Philosophy, Dublin (1932).

Israel: French Biblical and Archeological School, Jerusalem (founded 1890; approved Sept. 17, 1892; canonically approved to confer Doctorate in Biblical Science, June 29, 1983).

Italy: Theological Faculty of Southern Italy, Naples. Two sections: St. Louis Posillipo (Mar. 16, 1918) and St. Thomas Aquinas Capodimonte (Oct. 31, 1941).

Pontifical Theological Faculty of Sardinia, Cagliari, (Aug. 5, 1927).

Interregional Theological Faculty, Milan (Aug. 8, 1935; restructured 1969).

Faculty of Philosophy "Aloisianum," Gallarate (1937; Mar. 20, 1974).

Pontifical Ambrosian Institute of Sacred Music, Milan (Mar. 12, 1940).

Theological Faculty of Sicily, Palermo (Dec. 8, 1980).

Theological Institute Pugliese, Molfetta (June 24, 1992).

Theological Institute Calabro, Catanzaro (Jan. 28, 1993).

Theological Faculty of Central Italy, Florence (Sep. 9, 1997).

Japan: Faculty of Theology, Nagoya (May 25, 1984).

Kenya: Catholic Higher Institute of Eastern Africa, Nairobi (May 2, 1984).

Lebanon: Faculty of Theology, University of the Holy Spirit, Kaslik (May 30, 1982).

Madagascar: Superior Institute of Theology and Philosophy, at the Regional Seminary of Antananarivo, Ambatoroka-Antananarivo (Apr. 21, 1960).

Malta: Faculty of Theology, Tal-Virtù (Nov. 22, 1769), with Institute of Philosophy and Human Studies (Sept. 8, 1984).

Mexico: Theological Faculty of Mexico (June 29, 1982) and Philosophy (Jan. 6, 1986), Institute of Canon Law (Sept. 4, 1995), Mexico City.

Nigeria: Catholic Institute of West Africa, Port

Harcourt (May 9, 1994).

Peru: Pontifical and Civil Faculty of Theology, Lima (July 25, 1571).

Poland: Pontifical Theological Faculty, Warsaw (May 3, 1988) with two sections: St. John Baptist (1837, 1920, Nov. 8, 1962) at the Metropolitan Seminary Duchowne, and St. Andrew Bobola – Bobolanum (Sept. 8, 1932).

Philosophical Faculty, Krakow (1932; Sept. 20, 1984).

Theological Faculty, Poznan (1969; pontifical designation, June 2, 1974).

Spain: Theological Faculty, Granada (1940; July 31, 1973).

Theological Faculty of San Esteban, Salamanca (1947; Oct. 4, 1972).

Theological Faculty of the North, of the Metropolitan Seminary of Burgos and the Diocesan Seminary of Vitoria (Feb. 6, 1967).

Theological Faculty of Catalunya, (Mar. 7, 1968), with the Institutes of Fundamental Theology (Dec. 28, 1984), Liturgy (Aug. 15, 1986) and Philosophy (July 26, 1988), Barcelona.

Theological Faculty "San Vicente Ferrer" (two sections), Valencia (Jan. 23, 1974).

Theological Faculty "San Damaso" (Sept. 19, 1996), Madrid.

Switzerland: Theological Faculty, Lucerne (Dec. 25, 1973).

Theological Faculty, Chur (Jan. 1, 1974).

Theological Faculty, Lugano (Nov. 20, 1993).

United States: St. Mary's Seminary and University, School of Theology, Baltimore (May 1, 1822).

St. Mary of the Lake Faculty of Theology, Mundelein, IL (Sept. 30, 1929).

Weston Jesuit School of Theology, Cambridge, MA (Oct. 18, 1932).

The Jesuit School of Theology, Berkeley, CA (Feb. 2, 1934, as "Alma College," Los Gatos, CA).

Faculty of Philosophy and Letters, St. Louis, MO (Feb. 2, 1934).

St. Michael's Institute, Jesuit School of Philosophy and Letters, Spokane, WA (Feb. 2, 1934).

Pontifical Faculty of Theology of the Immaculate Conception, Dominican House of Studies, Washington, DC (Nov. 15, 1941).

Also located in the **United States** are:

The Marian Library/International Marian Research Institute (IMRI), U.S. branch of Pontifical Theological Faculty "Marianum," University of Dayton, Dayton, OH 45469 (affil. 1976, inc. 1983).

John Paul II Institute for Studies on Marriage and the Family, U.S. section of Pontifical John Paul II Institute for Studies on Marriage and Family at the Pontifical Lateran University, 487 Michigan Ave. N.E., Washington, DC 20017 (Aug. 22, 1988).

Pontifical College Josephinum (Theologate and College) at Columbus, OH, is a national pontifical seminary. Established Sept. 1, 1888, it is directly under the auspices of the Vatican through the Apostolic Nuncio to the U.S., who serves as the seminary's chancellor.

Vietnam: Theological Faculty of the Pontifical National Seminary of St. Pius X, Dalat (July 31, 1965). Activities suppressed.

In addition to those listed above, there are other faculties of theology or philosophy in state universities and for members of certain religious orders only. These include:

Austria: Katholisch-Theologische Fakultät (1619), Universitätsstrasse, 1, A-5010 Salzburg, Österreich.

Katholisch-Theologische Fakultät (1365), Dr. Karl-Lueger-Ring, 1, A-1010 Wien, Österreich.

Theologische Fakultät (1586), Karl-Franzens-Universität, Universitätsplatz, 3, A-8010 Graz, Österreich.

Theologische Fakultät (1669), Leopold-Franzens-Universität, Karl-Rahner-Platz 1, A-6020 Innsbruck, Österreich.

Canada: Faculté de Theologie et Institut Supérieur de Science Religieuses (1878), University of Montreal, 3034, Bd. Edouard-Montpetit, C.P. 6128, Montral, QC H3C 3J7, Canada.

Croatia: Facolta di Teologia Cattolica nell'Università Statale de Split (1999), Zrinsko-Frankopanska, 19, 21000 Split, Hrvatska.

Katolicki Bogoslovni Fakultet u Zagrebu (1669), Vlaska 38, 10000 Zagreb, Hrvatska.

Czech Republic: Cyrilometodejska teologicka fakulta (1570), Univerzitni 22, 771-11 Olomouc, Ceska Republika.

Katolicka teologicka fakulta University Karlovy (1347), Thakurova 3, 160 00 Praha 6/Dejvice, Ceska Republika.

France: Faculté de Theologie Catholique (1567), 9, Place de l'Université, 67084 Strasbourg, France.

Germany: Katholisch-Theologische Fakultät, Universität Augsburg (1970), Universitätsstrasse 10, D-86159 Augsburg, Bundesrepublik Deutschland.

Katholisch-Theologische Fakultät, Universität Bamberg (1972), An der Universität 2, D-96045 Bamberg, Bundesrepublik Deutschland.

Katholisch-Theologische Fakultät (1965), Universität Ruhr, Universitätsstrasse 150, Postfach 102148, D-44801 Bochum, Bundesrepublik Deutschland.

Katholisch-Theologische Fakultät Universität Bonn (1818), Am Hof 1, D-53113 Bonn, Bundesrepublik Deutschland.

Theologische Fakultät (1657), Albert-Ludwigs Universität, Erbprinzstrasse 13, D-79098 Freiburg im Breisgau, Bundesrepublik Deutschland.

Fachbereich Katholische Theologie (1946), Johannes Gutenberg-Universität, Saarstrasse 21, D-55122, Mainz, Bundesrepublik Deutschland.

Katholisch-Theologische Fakultät (1472), Ludwig-Maximilians-Universität, Geschw.-Scholl-Platz 1, D-80539, München, Bundesrepublik Deutschland.

Katholisch-Theologische Fakultät (1780), WestfälischeWilhelms-Universität, Johannisstrasse 8-10, D-48143, Münster, Bundesrepublik Deutschland.

Katholisch-Theologische Fakultät (1978), Michaeligasse 13, D-94032, Passau, Bundesrepublik Deutschland.

Fachbereich Katholische Theologie (1962), Universitätsstrasse 31, D-93053 Regensburg, Bundesrepublik Deutschland.

Katholisch-Theologische Fakultät (1477), Eberhard-Karls-Universität Tübingen, Libermeisterstr., 18, D-72076 Tübingen,

Bundesrepublik Deutschland.

Katholisch-Theologische Fakultät (1402), Bayerische Julius-Maximilians-Universität, Sanderring 2, D-97070 Würzburg, Bundesrepublik Deutschland.

Lithuania: Kataliku Teologijos Fakultetas (1922), Vilniaus 29, LT-3000 Kaunas, Lietuva.

Poland: Wydzial Teologiczny, Wydzial Prawa Kanonicznego, Wydzial Filozofii Chrzescijanskiej (1999), ul. Dewajtis, 5, 01-815 Warszawa, Polska.

Wydzial Teologiczny Uniwersytetu Slaskiego w Katowicach (2000), ul. Wita Stwosza 17 A, 40-042 Katowice, Polska.

Wydzial Teologii Uniwersytetu Warminsko-Mazurskiego w Olsztynie (1999), ul. Stanislawa Kard. Hozjusza, 15, 11-041 Olsztyn, Polska.

Wydzial Teologiczny (1994), ul. Drzymaly, 1/a, 45-342 Opole, Polska.

Wydzial Teologiczny Uniwersytetu Mikolaja Kopernika w. Toruniu (2001), pl. Bl. Ks. S. Freli-chowskiego 1, 87-100, Torun, Polska. **Slovakia**: Rimskokatolicka cyrilo-metodska bohoslovecka fakulta (1919), Archdiocese of Bratislava-Trnava, Kapitulska 26, 814-58 Bratislava, Slovenska Republika.

Slovenia: Teoloska Fakulteta v. Ljublana (1920), p.p. 2007, 1001 Ljubljana, Slovenia.

Switzerland: Theologische Fakultät (1889), University of Fribourg, Misericorde, CH-1700 Fribourg, Switzerland.

PONTIFICAL UNIVERSITIES AND INSTITUTES IN ROME

(*Source*: Annuario Pontificio.)

Pontifical Gregorian University (Gregorian) (1552): Piazza della Pilotta, 4, 00187 Rome. Associated with the university are: **Pontifical Biblical Institute** (May 7, 1909): Via della Pilotta, 25, 00187 Rome; **Pontifical Institute of Oriental Studies** (Oct. 15, 1917): Piazza S. Maria Maggiore, 7, 00185 Rome.

Pontifical Lateran University (1773): Piazza S. Giovanni in Laterano, 4, 00184 Rome. Attached to the university is the **Pontifical Institute of Studies of Marriage and the Family**, erected by Pope John Paul II, Oct 7, 1982; a section of the Institute was established at the Dominican House of Studies, Washington, DC, by a decree dated Aug. 22, 1988; sections were opened in Mexico in 1992 and Valencia, Spain, in 1994.

Pontifical Urbaniana University (1627): Via Urbano VIII, 16, 00165 Rome.

Pontifical University of St. Thomas Aquinas (Angelicum) (1580), of the Order of Preachers: Largo Angelicum, 1, 00184 Rome.

Pontifical University *Salesianum* (May 3, 1940; university designation May 24, 1973), of the Salesians of Don Bosco: Piazza dell' Ateneo Salesiano, 1, 00139 Rome. Associated with the university is the **Pontifical Institute of Higher Latin Studies**, known as the Faculty of Christian and Classical Letters (June 4, 1971).

Pontifical University *della Santa Croce* (of the Holy Cross) (Jan. 9, 1985), of the Personal Prelature of Opus Dei: Piazza S. Apollinare, 49, 00186 Rome.

Pontifical University *Antonianum* (of St. Anthony) (May 17, 1933), of the Order of Friars Minor: Via Merulana, 124, 00185 Rome. Pontifical University status granted in 2005.

Pontifical Athenaeum of St. Anselm (1687) of the Benedictines: Piazza Cavalieri di Malta, 5, 00153 Rome.

Pontifical Athenaeum *Regina Apostolorum* (Queen of the Apostles), of the Legionaries of Christ: Via Aurelia Antica, 460, 00165 Rome.

Pontifical Institute of Sacred Music (1911; May 24, 1931): Via di Torre Rossa, 21, 00165 Rome.

Pontifical Institute of Christian Archeology (Dec. 11, 1925): Via Napoleone III, 1, 00185 Rome.

Pontifical Theological Faculty *St. Bonaventure* (Dec. 18, 1587), of the Order of Friars Minor Conventual: Via del Serafico, 1, 00142 Rome.

Pontifical Theological Faculty, Pontifical Institute of Spirituality *Teresianum* (1935), of the Discalced Carmelites: Piazza San Pancrazio, 5-A, 00152 Rome.

Pontifical Theological Faculty *Marianum* (1398), of the Servants of Mary: Viale Trente Aprile, 6, 00153 Rome. Attached to the university is **The Marian Library/International Marian Research Institute** (IMRI), U.S. branch of Pontifical Theological Faculty Marianum, University of Dayton, Dayton, OH, 45469 (affil. 1976, inc. 1983).

Pontifical Institute of Arabic and Islamic Studies (1926), of the Missionaries of Africa: Viale di Trastevere, 89, 00153 Rome.

Pontifical Faculty of Educational Science *Auxilium* (June 27, 1970), of the Daughters of Mary, Help of Christians: Via Cremolino, 141, 00166 Rome.

Pontifical Ecclesiastical Academy

The Pontifical Ecclesiastical Academy (*Pontificia Ecclesiastica Academia*) is one of the various Roman Academies (not to be confused with the Pontifical Universities that are also in Rome). The Academy has as its purpose to prepare future Vatican diplomats for service around the world and in the Secretariat of State. The Academy was founded in 1701 by Pope Clement XI to prepare students for diplomatic service on behalf of the Holy See. It bore the original name of the Pontifical Academy of Noble Ecclesiastics and was open only to members of noble families in Europe (undisputed noble lineage was expressly required). This requirement was eventually phased out, and young men of promise from all walks of life are now eligible, providing that they meet the strict requirements of admission. The name was changed to the present title to reflect the changed circumstances of admission.

Those chosen are most often already recipients of assorted degrees, including but not limited to doctorates in the sacred sciences, especially theology, Church History, and especially canon law from pontifical universities. Once admitted, these young priests undergo a very demanding program of studies that includes all aspects of ecclesiastical diplomacy and diplomatic history, Church history, diplomatic law, and also intensive study of modern languages. The current president of the Academy is Abp. Giampiero Gloder.

Catholic Communications

CATHOLIC PRESS

Statistics
The 2014 Catholic Press Directory, published by the Catholic Press Association, reported a total of 231 periodicals in North America, with a circulation of 10,444,933. The figures included 130 newspapers, with a circulation of 4,594,368; 72 magazines, with a circulation of 4,993,474; 17 newsletters, with a circulation of 549,310; and 12 other language periodicals (newspapers and magazines), with a circulation of 307,781.

Newspapers in the U.S.
There were 126 newspapers in the United States, with a circulation of 4,479,063. Four of these had national circulation totaling 136,019; 122 were diocesan newspapers with a total circulation of 4,343,044. There was one other miscellaneous newspaper with a total circulation of 19,545.

National papers included: *National Catholic Register*, founded 1900; *Our Sunday Visitor*, founded 1912; *National Catholic Reporter*, founded 1964; *The Wanderer*, founded 1867. In addition there were *The Adoremus Bulletin*, founded 1995; and the English-language weekly edition of *L'Osservatore Romano*, established in the U.S. in 1998.

The oldest U.S. Catholic newspaper is *The Pilot* of Boston, established in 1829 (under a different title).

Magazines in the U.S.
The Catholic Press Directory reported 72 magazines in the U.S., Canada, and International with a circulation of 4,993,474. In addition, there were 17 newsletters, with a circulation of 549,310.

America and *Commonweal* are the only weekly and biweekly magazines, respectively, of general interest.

The monthly magazines with the largest circulation are *Columbia* (250,000), the official organ of the Knights of Columbus, *Catholic Digest* (285,000) and *St. Anthony's Messenger* (135,000).

Other-language publications: There were an additional 12 publications (newspapers and magazines) in the U.S. in languages other than English, with a circulation of 307,781.

Canadian Statistics
There were three newspapers in Canada with a circulation of 95,760. These included one national newspaper (*The Catholic Register*, founded 1893) with a circulation of 35,360 and two diocesan (*The B.C. Catholic* and *Western Catholic Reporter*), with a total circulation of 60,400.

CATHOLIC NEWSPAPERS, MAGAZINES, AND NEWSLETTERS IN THE U.S.

(*Sources:* Catholic Press Directory; The Catholic Journalist; Catholic Almanac *survey; Catholic News Service.*) *Abbreviation code: a, annual; bm, bimonthly; m, monthly; q, quarterly; w, weekly; bw, bi-weekly.*

Newspapers
Our Sunday Visitor, w; 200 Noll Plaza, Huntington, IN 46750; (260) 356-8400; www.osv.com; national.

Acadiana Catholic, m; 1408 Carmel Ave., Lafayette, LA 70501; (337) 261-5511; www.dollouisiana.org; Lafayette diocese.

A.D. Times, bw; P.O. Box F, Allentown, PA 18105-1538; (610) 871-5200; Allentown diocese.

Adoremus Bulletin, The, 10 times a year; P.O. Box 3286, St. Louis, MO 63130; (314) 863-8385; www.adoremus.org; national liturgical journal.

Agua Viva, m; 1280 Med Park Dr., Las Cruces, NM 88005-3239; (575) 523-7577; www.dioceseoflascruces.org; Las Cruces diocese.

Alaskan Shepherd, bm; 1312 Peger Rd., Fairbanks, AK 99709; (904) 374-9532; www.cbna.info; Fairbanks diocese.

America (Ukrainian-English), 2 times a year; 817 N. Franklin St., Philadelphia, PA 19123; (215) 627-4519; Providence Association of Ukrainian Catholics in America.

Anchor, The, w; P.O. Box 7, Fall River, MA 02722; (508) 675-7151; Fall River diocese.

Arkansas Catholic, w; P.O. Box 7417, Little Rock, AR 72217; (501) 664-0125; www.arkansas-catholic.org. Little Rock diocese.

Arlington Catholic Herald, w; 200 N. Glebe Rd., Suite 607, Arlington, VA 22203; (703) 841-2590; www.catholicherald.com; Arlington diocese.

Bayou Catholic, The, w; P.O. Box 505, Schriever, LA 70395; (985) 850-3132; www.htdiocese.org; Houma-Thibodaux diocese.

Beacon, The, w; P.O. Box 1887, Clifton, NJ 07015-1887; (973) 279-8845; www.patersondiocese.org; Paterson diocese.

Bishop's Bulletin, m; 523 N. Duluth Ave., Sioux Falls, SD 57104-2714; (605) 988-3791; www.sfcatholic.org; Sioux Falls diocese.

Bolletino, m; 675 Hegenberger Rd., Suite 110, Oakland, CA 94621; (510) 633-9058; www.icf.org; Italian Catholic Federation.

Byzantine Catholic World, bw; 66 Riverview Ave., Pittsburgh, PA 15214; (412) 231-4000; www.archeparchy.org; Pittsburgh Byzantine archdiocese.

Catholic Accent, 40 times a year; 725 E. Pittsburgh St., Greensburg, PA 15601; (724) 834-4010; www.dioceseofgreensburg.org; Greensburg diocese.

Catholic Advance, The, w; 424 N. Broadway,

Wichita, KS 67202-2377; (316) 269-3965; www.catholic advance.org; Wichita diocese.

Catholic Advocate, The, w; 171 Clifton Ave., Newark, NJ 07104-9500; (973) 497-4200; www.rcan.org/advocate; Newark archdiocese.

Catholic Aid News, m; 3499 N. Lexington Ave., St. Paul, MN 55126; (651) 490-0170; www.catholicaid.com.

Catholic Anchor, w; 225 Cordova St., Anchorage, AK 99501; (907) 297-7708; www.catholicanchor.org. Anchorage diocese.

Catholic Calendar, semi-monthly; 411 Iris St., Lake Charles, LA 70601; (337) 439-7426; www.lcdiocese.org; one page in local newspaper semi-monthly; Lake Charles diocese.

Catholic Chronicle, bw; P.O. Box 985, Toledo, OH 43697; (419) 244-6711; www.catholicchronicle.org; Toledo diocese.

Catholic Commentator, The, bw; P.O. Box 14746, Baton Rouge, LA 70898-4746; (225) 387-0983; www.diobr.com; Baton Rouge diocese.

Catholic Courier, w; P.O. Box 24379, Rochester, NY 14624-0379; (585) 529-9530; www.catholiccourier.com; Rochester diocese.

Catholic East Texas, bw; 1015 ESE Loop 323, Tyler, TX 75701-9663; (903) 534-1077; Tyler diocese.

Catholic Exponent, bw; P.O. Box 6787, Youngstown, OH 44501-6787; (330) 744-5251; www.cathexpo.org; Youngstown diocese.

Catholic Free Press, w; 51 Elm St., Worcester, MA 01609; (508) 757-6387; www.catholicfreepress.org; Worcester diocese.

Catholic Health World, semi-monthly; 4455 Woodson Rd., St. Louis, MO 63134-3797; (314) 253-3410; www.chausa.org; Catholic Health Association; national.

Catholic Herald, The Colorado, m; 228 N. Cascade Ave., Colorado Springs, CO 80903; (719) 636-2345; www.coloradocatholicherald.com; Colorado Springs diocese.

Catholic Herald, w; P.O. Box 070913, Milwaukee, WI 53207-0913; (414) 769-3500; www.chnonline.org; Milwaukee archdiocese; also publishes editions for Madison and Superior dioceses.

Catholic Herald: Madison Edition, w; 702 S. High Point Rd., Madison, WI 53719; (608) 821-3070; www.madisoncatholicherald.org; Madison diocese.

Catholic Herald: Superior Edition, w; P.O. Box 969, Superior, WI 54880; (715) 392-8268; www.catholicherald.org; Superior diocese.

Catholic Herald, bw; 5890 Newman Ct., Sacramento, CA 95819; (916) 452-3344; www.diocese-sacramento.org; Sacramento diocese.

Catholic Islander, m; P.O. Box 301825, St. Thomas, USVI, 00803-1825; (340) 774-3166; www.catholicislander.com; Virgin Islands diocese.

Catholic Journalist, The, m; 205 West Monroe St., Suite 470, Chicago, IL 60606; (312) 380-6789; www.catholicpress.org; Catholic Press Association.

Catholic Key, 44 times a year; P.O. Box 419037, Kansas City, MO 64141-6037; (816) 756-1850; www.catholickey.org; Kansas City-St. Joseph diocese.

Catholic Light, bw; 300 Wyoming Ave., Scranton, PA 18503; (570) 207-2229; www.dioceseofscranton.org; Scranton diocese.

Catholic Lighthouse, m; P.O. Box 4070, Victoria, TX 77903; (361) 573-0828; www.victoriadiocese.org; Victoria diocese.

Catholic Messenger, w; P.O. Box 460, Davenport, IA 52805; (563) 323-9959; www.catholicmessenger.org; Davenport diocese.

Catholic Mirror The, m; 601 Grand Ave., Des Moines, IA 50309; (515) 237-5046; www.dmdiocese.org; Des Moines diocese.

Catholic Miscellany, The, w; 119 Broad St., Charleston, SC 29401; (843) 724-8375; www.themiscellany.org; Charleston diocese.

Catholic Missourian, w; P.O. Box 104900, Jefferson City, MO 65110-4900; (573) 635-9127; www.diojefcity.org; Jefferson City diocese.

Catholic Moment, The, w; P.O. Box 1603, Lafayette, IN 47902; (765) 742-2050; www.thecatholicmoment.org; Lafayette diocese.

Catholic New World, The, w; 3525 S. Lake Park Ave., Chicago, IL 60653; (312) 534-7324; www.catholicnewworld.com; Chicago archdiocese.

Catholic New York, w; 1011 First Ave., New York, NY 10022; (212) 688-2399; www.cny.org; New York archdiocese.

Catholic News, w; P.O. Box 85, Independence Square, Port-of-Spain, Trinidad, West Indies; (868) 623-6093; www.catholicnews-tt.net.

Catholic News and Herald, The, w; P.O. Box 37267, Charlotte, NC 28237; (704) 370-3333; www.charlottediocese.org; Charlotte diocese.

Catholic Northwest Progress, The, w; 710 9th Ave., Seattle, WA 98104; (206) 382-4850; www.seattlee-arch.org;/progress; Seattle archdiocese.

Catholic Observer, bw; Box 1730, Springfield, MA 01101-1730; (413) 737-4744; www.iobserve.org; Springfield diocese.

Catholic Peace Voice, q.; 532 W. Eighth St., Erie, PA 16502-1343; (814) 453-4955; www.paxchristiusa.org; published by Pax Christi.

Catholic Post, The, w; P.O. Box 1722, Peoria, IL 61656; (309) 671-1550; www.thecatholicpost.com; Peoria diocese.

Catholic Register, bw; P.O. Box 413, Hollidaysburg, PA 16648; (814) 695-7563; www.cathregaj.org; Altoona-Johnstown diocese.

Catholic Review, w; P.O. Box 777, Baltimore, MD 21203; (443) 524-3150; www.catholicreview.org; Baltimore archdiocese.

Catholic San Francisco, bw; One Peter Yorke Way, San Francisco, CA 94109; (415) 614-5632; www.catholic-sf.org; San Francisco archdiocese.

Catholic Sentinel, w; P.O. Box 18030, Portland, OR 97218-0030; (503) 281-1191; www.sentinel.org; Portland archdiocese, Baker diocese.

Catholic Spirit, The, w; 244 Dayton Ave., Ste. 2, St. Paul, MN 55102-1893; (651) 291-4444; www.thecatholicspirit.com; St. Paul & Minneapolis archdiocese.

Catholic Spirit, The, w; P.O. Box 191, Metuchen, NJ 08840; (732) 562-2424; www.catholicspirit.com; Metuchen diocese.

Catholic Spirit, The, m; P.O. Box 15405, Austin, TX 78761; (512) 949-2443; www.austindiocese.org; Austin diocese.

Catholic Spirit, The, m; P.O. Box 230, Wheeling, WV 26003-0119; (304) 233-0880; www.dwc.org; Wheeling-Charleston diocese.

Catholic Standard, w; P.O. Box 4464, Washington, DC, 20017; (202) 281-2410; www.cathstan.org; Washington archdiocese.

Catholic Standard and Times, w; 222 N. 17th St., Philadelphia, PA 19103; (215) 587-3660; www.cstphl.com; Philadelphia archdiocese.

Catholic Star Herald, w; 15 North 7th St., Camden, NJ 08102; (856) 583-6142; www.catholicstarherald.org; Camden diocese.

Catholic Sun, The, semi-monthly; P.O. Box 13549,

Phoenix, AZ 85002; (602) 354-2139; www.catholic-sun.org; Phoenix diocese.

Catholic Sun, The, w; 421 S. Warren St., Syracuse, NY 13202; (315) 422-8153; www.syrdio.org; Syracuse diocese.

Catholic Telegraph, w; 100 E. 8th St., Cincinnati, OH 45202; (513) 421-3131; www.catholiccincinnati.org; Cincinnati archdiocese.

Catholic Times, w; 197 E. Gay St., Columbus, OH 43215-3229; (614) 224-5195; www.ctonline.org; Columbus diocese.

Catholic Times, The, w; P.O. Box 1405, Saginaw, MI 48605; (810) 659-4670; www.catholictimesmi.org; Lansing diocese.

Catholic Times, The, w; P.O. Box 4004, La Crosse, WI 54602-4004; (608) 788-1524; www.dioceseofla-crosse.com; La Crosse diocese.

Catholic Times, w; P.O. Box 3187, Springfield, IL 62708-3187; (217) 698-8500; www.ct.dio.org; Springfield diocese.

Catholic Transcript, w; 467 Bloomfield Ave., Bloomfield, CT 06002; (860) 286-2828; Hartford archdiocese, Bridgeport and Norwich dioceses.

Catholic Universe Bulletin, bw; 1027 Superior Ave. NE, Cleveland, OH 44114-2556; (216) 696-6525; www.catholicuniversebulletin.org; Cleveland diocese.

Catholic Virginian, bw; 7800 Carousel Lane, Richmond, VA 23294; (804) 359-5654; www.catholicvirginian.org; Richmond diocese.

Catholic Voice, The, w; 3014 Lakeshore Ave., Oakland, CA 94610; (510) 893-5339; www.catholicvoiceoakland.org; Oakland diocese.

Catholic Voice, The, bw; P.O. Box 4010, Omaha, NE 68104-0010; (402) 558-6611; www.catholicvoiceomaha.com; Omaha archdiocese.

Catholic War Veteran, bm; 441 N. Lee St., Alexandria, VA 22314-2344; (703) 549-3622; www.cwv.org.

Catholic Week, The, w; P.O. Box 349, Mobile, AL 36601; (251) 434-1544; Mobile archdiocese.

Catholic Weekly, The, w; P.O. Box 1405, Saginaw, MI 48605; (989) 793-7661; www.catholicweekly.org; Saginaw diocese.

Catholic Weekly, The, w; P.O. Box 1405, Saginaw, MI 48602; (989) 793-7661; Gaylord diocese.

Catholic Witness, The, bw; P.O. Box 2555, Harrisburg, PA 17105; (717) 657-4804; www.hbg-diocese.org; Harrisburg diocese.

Central Washington Catholic, bm; 5301-A Tieton Dr., Yakima, WA 98908; (509) 965-7117; Yakima diocese.

Chicago Catolico (Spanish), m; 721 N. La Salle St., 4th Floor, Chicago, IL 60610; (312) 655-7880; Chicago archdiocese.

Chronicle of Catholic Life, bm; 1001 North Grand Ave., Pueblo, CO 81003; (719) 685-9617; www.dioceseofpueblo.com; Pueblo diocese.

Church Today, twice a month; P.O. Box 7417, Alexandria, LA 71306-0417; (318) 445-2401; www.dioceseralex.org; Alexandria diocese.

Clarion Herald, bw; P.O. Box 53247, New Orleans, LA 70153; (504) 596-3035; www.clarionherald.org; New Orleans archdiocese.

Compass, The, w; P.O. Box 23825, Green Bay, WI 54305-3825; (920) 437-7531; www.thecompassnews.org; Green Bay diocese.

Courier, The, m; P.O. Box 949, Winona, MN 55987-0949; (507) 454-4643; www.dow.org; Winona diocese.

Criterion, The, w; P.O. Box 1717, Indianapolis, IN 46206; (317) 236-1570; www.criteriononline.com; Indianapolis archdiocese.

Cross Roads, bw; 1310 W. Main St., Lexington, KY 40508-2040; (859) 253-1993; Lexington diocese.

Dakota Catholic Action, m (except July); P.O. Box 1137, Bismarck, ND 58502-1137; (701) 222-3035; www.bismarckdiocese.com; Bismarck diocese.

Denver Catholic Register, w; 1300 S. Steele St., Denver, CO 80210-2599; (303) 715-3215; www.archden.org; Denver archdiocese.

Dialog, The, w; P.O. Box 2208, Wilmington, DE 19899; (302) 573-3109; www.cdow.org/dialog.html; Wilmington diocese.

East Tennessee Catholic, The, bw; P.O. Box 11127, Knoxville, TN 37939-1127; (865) 584-3307; www.dioceseofknoxville.org; Knoxville diocese.

East Texas Catholic, semi-monthly; P.O. Box 3948, Beaumont, TX 77704-3948; (409) 832-3944; Beaumont diocese.

Eastern Catholic Life, bw; 445 Lackawanna Ave., W. Paterson, NJ 07424; (973) 890-7777; Passaic Byzantine eparchy.

Eastern Oklahoma Catholic, bw; Box 690240, Tulsa, OK 74169-0240; (918) 294-1904; www.dioceseoftulsa.org; Tulsa diocese.

Eternal Flame (Armenian-English), 167 North 6th St., Brooklyn, NY 11211; (212) 477-2030; Armenian exarchate.

Evangelist, The, w; 40 N. Main Ave., Albany, NY 12203; (518) 453-6688; www.evangelist.org; Albany diocese.

Fairfield County Catholic, m; 238 Jewett Ave., Bridgeport, CT 06606; (203) 416-1461; www.bridgeportdiocese.org; Bridgeport diocese.

FaithLife, bw; 429 E. Grandview Blvd., Erie, PA 16504; (814) 824-1161; www.eriecd.org; Erie diocese.

Florida Catholic, The, w; P.O. Box 4993, Orlando, FL 32802-4993; (407) 373-0075; www.thefloridacatholic.org; Orlando diocese; publishes editions for Miami archdiocese and Palm Beach, Pensacola-Tallahassee, St. Petersburg and Venice dioceses.

Florida Catholic: Miami Edition, w; 9401 Biscayne Blvd., Miami, FL 33138; (305) 762-1131; www.thefloridacatholic.org.

Florida Catholic: Palm Beach Edition, w; P.O. Box 109650, Palm Beach Gardens, FL 33410; (561) 775-9528; www.thefloridacatholic.org; Palm Beach diocese.

Florida Catholic: Pensacola-Tallahassee Edition, w; 11 North B St., Pensacola, FL 32501; (850) 435-3500; www.thefloridacatholic.org.

Florida Catholic: St. Petersburg Edition, w; P.O. Box 43022, St. Petersburg, FL 33743; (727) 345-3338.

Florida Catholic: Venice Edition, w; 1000 Pinebrook Rd., Venice, FL 34292; (941) 486-4701; www.thefloridacatholic.org.

Four County Catholic, m; 31 Perkins Ave., Norwich, CT 06360; (860) 886-3613; www.norwichdiocese.org; Norwich diocese.

Georgia Bulletin, w; 680 W. Peachtree St. NW, Atlanta, GA 30308; (404) 877-5500; www.archatl.com; Atlanta archdiocese.

Glasilo KSKJ Amerikanski Slovenec (Slovenian), bw; 708 E. 159th, Cleveland, OH 44110; (216) 541-7243; American Slovenian Catholic Union.

Globe, The, w; P.O. Box 5079, Sioux City, IA 51102; (712)

255-2550; www.catholicglobe.org; Sioux City diocese.

Good News for the Diocese of Kalamazoo, The, m; 215 N. Westnedge, Kalamazoo, MI 49007-3760; (269) 349-8714; www.dioceseofkalamazoo.org; Kalamazoo diocese.

Gulf Pine Catholic, w; 1790 Popps Ferry Rd., Biloxi, MS 39532; (228) 702-2126; Biloxi diocese.

Harvest, The, 121 23rd St. South, Great Falls, MT 59405; (406) 727-6683; www.dioceseofgfb.org; Great Falls diocese.

Hawaii Catholic Herald, bw; 1184 Bishop St., Honolulu, HI 96813; (808) 585-3300; www.hawaiicatholicherald.com; Honolulu diocese.

Hlas Naroda (Voice of the Nation) (Czech-English), bw; P.O. Box 159, Berwyn, IL 60402; (708) 484-0583.

Horizons, twice a month; 1900 Carlton Rd., Parma, OH 44134-3129; (216) 741-3312; www.parma.org; Parma Byzantine eparchy.

Idaho Catholic Register, twice a month; 1501 S. Federal Way, Boise, ID 83705; (208) 342-1311; www.catholicidaho.org/icr.cfm; Boise diocese.

Inland Register, every 3 weeks; P.O. Box 48, Spokane, WA 99210; (509) 358-7340; www.dioceseofspokane.org; Spokane diocese.

Inside Passage, bw; 415 6th St., Juneau, AK 99801; (907) 586-2227; www.dioceseofjuneau.org; Juneau diocese.

Intermountain Catholic, w; P.O. Box 2489, Salt Lake City, UT 84110-2489; (801) 328-8641; www.icatholic.org; Salt Lake City diocese.

Jednota (Slovak-Eng.), w; 6611 Rockside Rd., Independence, OH 44131; (216) 642-9406; First Catholic Slovak Union.

Leaven, The, w; 12615 Parallel Parkway, Kansas City, KS 66109; (913) 721-1570; www.theleaven.com; Kansas City archdiocese.

Long Island Catholic, The, w; P.O. Box 9000, Rockville Centre, NY 11575-9000; (516) 594-1000; www.licatholic.org; Rockville Centre diocese.

L'Osservatore Romano, w; 200 Noll Plaza, Huntington, IN 46750; (800) 348-2440; www.osv.com. English edition of the Vatican newspaper (published by Our Sunday Visitor).

Maronite Voice, The, m; 4611 Sadler Rd., Glen Allen, VA 23060; (804) 270-7234; www.stmaron.org; Eparchy of St. Maron of Brooklyn.

Message, The, w; P.O. Box 4169, Evansville, IN 47724-0169; (812) 424-5536; Evansville diocese.

Messenger, The, w; 2620 Lebanon Ave., Belleville, IL 62221; (618) 233-8670; www.bellevillemessenger.org; Belleville diocese.

Messenger, The, 45 times a year; P.O. Box 15550, Erlanger, KY 41015; (859) 392-1570; www.covingtondiocese.org; Covington diocese.

Michigan Catholic, The, w; 305 Michigan Ave., 4th Floor, Detroit, MI 48226; (313) 224-8000; Detroit archdiocese.

Mirror, The, w; 601 S. Jefferson Ave., Springfield, MO 65806-3143; (417) 866-0841; www.the-mirror.org; Springfield-Cape Girardeau diocese.

Mississippi Catholic, w; P.O. Box 2130, Jackson, MS 39225-2130; (601) 969-1880; www.mississippicatholic.com; Jackson diocese.

Monitor, The, w; P.O. Box 5147, Trenton, NJ 08638; (609) 406-7404; www.dioceseoftrenton.org; Trenton diocese.

Montana Catholic, The, 16 times a year; P.O. Box 1729, Helena, MT 59624; (406) 442-5820; www.diocesehelena.org/mtcath; Helena diocese.

Narod Polski (Polish Nation) (Polish-Eng.) semi-monthly; 984 Milwaukee Ave., Chicago, IL 60622-4101; (773) 782-2600; www.prcua.com; Polish Roman Catholic Union of America.

National Catholic Register, w; 432 Washington Ave., North Haven, CT 06473; (203) 230-3800; www.ncregister.com; national.

National Catholic Reporter, w; P.O. Box 411009, Kansas City, MO 64141; (816) 531-0538; www.ncronline.org; national.

National Jesuit News, m; 1616 P St. NW, Suite 300, Washington, DC 20036; (202) 462-0400; www.jesuit.org.

New Earth, The, m; 5201 Bishops Blvd., Ste. A, Fargo, ND 58104; (701) 356-7958; www.fargidiocese.org; Fargo diocese.

New Star, The, every 3 weeks; 2208 W. Chicago Ave., Chicago, IL 60622; (312) 772-1919; St. Nicholas of Chicago Ukrainian diocese.

New Vision/La Nueva Vision, m.; P.O. Box 31, Tucson, AZ 85702; (520) 792-3410; www.newvision-online.org; Tuscon diocese.

North Country Catholic, w; P.O. Box 326, Ogdensburg, NY 13669; (315) 393-2540; www.northcountrycatholic.org; Ogdensburg diocese.

North Texas Catholic, w; 800 West Loop 820 South, Fort Worth, TX 76108; (817) 560-3300; www.fwdioc.org; Fort Worth diocese.

Northern Cross, The, m.; 2830 E. 4th St., Duluth, MN 55812; (218) 724-9111; www.dioceseduluth.org; Duluth diocese.

Northern Nevada Catholic, m; 290 S. Arlington Ave., #200, Reno, NV 89501; (775) 326-9410; Reno diocese.

Northwest Indiana Catholic, w; 9292 Broadway, Merrillville, IN 46410-7088; (219) 769-9292; www.nwicatholic.com; Gary diocese.

Oblate World, The and Voice of Hope, twice a month; P.O. Box 680, Tewksbury, MA 01876; (978) 851-7258; www.omiusa.org; published by the Missionary Oblates of Mary Immaculate.

Observer, The, m; P.O. Box 2079, Monterey, CA 93942; (831) 373-2919; www.dioceseofmonterey.org; Monterey diocese.

Observer, The, m; 4545 W. 63rd St., Chicago, IL 60629; (312) 585-9500; Lithuanian Roman Catholic Federation of America.

Observer, The, twice a month; P.O. Box 7044, Rockford, IL 61125; (815) 399-4300; www.rockford-diocese.org; Rockford diocese.

One Voice, w; P.O. Box 10822, Birmingham, AL 35202; (205) 838-8305; Birmingham diocese.

Orange County Catholic, m.; P.O. Box 14195, Orange, CA 92863-1595; (714) 282-3022; Orange diocese.

Our Northland Diocese, semi-monthly; P.O. Box 610, Crookston, MN 56716; (218) 281-4553; www.crookston.org; Crookston diocese.

People of God, m; 4000 St. Joseph Pl. NW, Albuquerque, NM 87120; (505) 831-8180; www.archdiocesesantafe.org; Santa Fe archdiocese.

Pilot, The, w; 2121 Commonwealth Ave., Brighton, MA 02135-3193; (617) 746-5889; www.thebostonpilot.com; Boston archdiocese.

Pittsburgh Catholic, w; 135 First Ave., Suite 200, Pittsburgh, PA 15222; (412) 471-1252; www.pittsburghcatholic.org; Pittsburgh diocese.

Prairie Catholic, m; 1400 6th St. North, New Ulm, MN 56073-2099; (507) 359-2966; www.dnu.org; New Ulm diocese.

Record, The, w; Maloney Center, 1200 S. Shelby St., Louisville, KY 40203-2600; (502) 636-0296; www.archlou.org; Louisville archdiocese.

Register, The, w; P.O. Box 1038, Salina, KS 67402; (785) 827-8746; www.salinadiocese.org; Salina diocese.

RI Catholic, The, w; 184 Broad St., Providence, RI 02903; (401) 272-1010; www.thericatholic.com; Providence diocese.

Rio Grande Catholic, The, m; 499 St. Matthews St., El Paso, TX 79907; (915) 872-8414; www.elpasodiocese.org; El Paso diocese.

St. Louis Review, w; 20 Archbishop May Dr., St. Louis, MO 63119; (314) 792-7500; www.stlouisreview.com; St. Louis archdiocese.

Seasons, q; 5800 Weiss St., Saginaw, MI 48603-2799; (989) 797-6666; www.dioceseofsaginaw.org; Saginaw diocese.

Slovak Catholic Falcon (Slovak-English), w; 205 Madison St., P.O.Box 899, Passaic, NJ 07055; (973) 777-4010; Slovak Catholic Sokol.

Sooner Catholic, The, bw; P.O. Box 32180, Oklahoma City, OK 73123; (405) 721-1810; www.catharchdioceseok.org; Oklahoma City archdiocese.

Sophia, q; 200 E. North Ave., Northlake, IL 60164; (708) 865-7050; Newton Melkite eparchy.

South Plains Catholic, twice a month; P.O. Box 98700, Lubbock, TX 79499-8700; (806) 792-3943; www.catholiclubbock.org; Lubbock diocese.

South Texas Catholic, twice a month; P.O. Box 2620, Corpus Christi, TX 78403-2620; (361) 882-6191; www.goccn.org; Corpus Christi diocese.

Southern Cross, semi-monthly; P.O. Box 81869, San Diego, CA 92138; (858) 490-8266; www.thesoutherncross.org; San Diego diocese.

Southern Cross, The, w; 601 E. Liberty Street, Savannah, GA 31401-5196; (912) 201-4100; www.diosav.org; Savannah diocese.

Southern Nebraska Register, w; P.O. Box 80329, Lincoln, NE 68501; (402) 488-0090; Lincoln diocese.

Southwest Catholic, The, m; P.O. 411 Iris St., Lake Charles, LA 70601; (337) 439-7426; www.lcdiocese.org; Lake Charles diocese.

Southwest Kansas Register, bw; P.O. Box 137, Dodge City, KS 67801; (620) 227-1519; www.dcdiocese.org/swkregister; Dodge City diocese.

Sower (Ukrainian and English), bw; 14 Peveril Rd., Stamford, CT 06902; (203) 324-7698; www.thesower@adcus.com; Stamford Ukrainian diocese.

Star of Chaldeans (Arabic and English), bm; 25585 Berg Rd., Southfield, MI 48034; St. Thomas the Apostle Chaldean diocese.

Steubenville Register, bw; P.O. Box 160, Steubenville, OH 43952; (740) 282-3631; www.diosteub.org; Steubenville diocese.

Tablet, The, w; 310 Prospect Park West, Brooklyn, NY 11215-6214; (718) 965-7333; www.dioceseofbrooklyn.org/tablet; Brooklyn diocese.

Tautai, bw; P.O. Box 532, Feiloaimauso Hall, Apia, Samoa; Samoa-Apia archdiocese.

Tennessee Register, The, bw; 2400 21st Ave. S., Nashville, TN 37212; (615) 783-0770; www.dioceseofnashville.org; Nashville diocese.

Texas Catholic, The, bw; P.O. Box 190346, Dallas, TX 75219; (214) 528-8792; www.texascatholic.com; Dallas diocese.

Texas Catholic Herald, The, twice a month; 1700 San Jacinto St., Houston, TX 77001-0907; (713) 659-5461; Galveston-Houston diocese.

Tidings, The, w; 3424 Wilshire Blvd, Los Angeles, CA 90010; (213) 637-7360; www.the-tidings.com; Los Angeles archdiocese.

Today's Catholic, w; P.O. Box 11169, Fort Wayne, IN 46856; (260) 456-2824; www.diocesefwsb.org; Fort Wayne-South Bend diocese.

Today's Catholic, bw; P.O. Box 28410, San Antonio, TX 78228-0410; (210) 734-1690; www.satodayscatholic.org; San Antonio archdiocese.

UNIREA (The Union) (Romanian) 10 times a year; 4309 Olcott Ave., East Chicago, IN 46312; (219) 398-3760; Romanian diocese of Canton.

U. P. Catholic, The, semi-monthly; P.O. Box 548, Marquette, MI 49855; (906) 227-9131; www.dioceseofmarquette.org; Marquette diocese.

Valley Catholic, m; 900 Lafayette St., Suite 301, Santa Clara, CA 95050-4966; (408) 983-0260; www.valleycatholiconline.com; San Jose diocese.

Vermont Catholic Tribune, bw; P.O. Box 489, Burlington, VT 05402; (802) 658-6110; www.vermontcatholic.org; Burlington diocese.

Vida Nueva; 3424 Wilshire Blvd., Los Angeles, CA 90010-2241; (213) 637-7310.

Visitor, The, w; 305 N. 7th Ave., Ste. 206, St. Cloud, MN 56303; (320) 251-3022; www.stclouddiocese.org/visitor; St. Cloud diocese.

Voice of the Southwest, m; 711 S. Puerco, Gallup, NM 87301; (505) 863-4406; www.dioceseofgallup.org; Gallup diocese.

Wanderer, The, w; 201 Ohio St., St. Paul, MN 55107; (651) 224-5733; national.

Way, The (Ukrainian-Eng.), bw; 827 N. Franklin St., Philadelphia, PA 19123; (215) 922-5231; Philadelphia archeparchy.

West Nebraska Register, w; P.O. Box 608, Grand Island, NE 68802; (308) 382-4660; Grand Island diocese.

West River Catholic, m; P.O. Box 678, Rapid City, SD 57709; (605) 343-3541; www.rapidcitydiocese.org; Rapid City diocese.

West Tennessee Catholic, w; P.O. Box 341669, Memphis, TN 38184-1669; (901) 373-1213; www.cdom.org; Memphis diocese.

West Texas Angelus, m; P.O. Box 1829, San Angelo, TX 76902; (325) 651-7500; www.sanangelodiocese.org; San Angelo diocese.

West Texas Catholic, bw; P.O. Box 5644, Amarillo, TX 79117-5644; (806) 383-2243; www.amarillodiocese.org; Amarillo diocese.

Western Kentucky Catholic, m; 600 Locust St., Owensboro, KY 42301; (270) 683-1545; Owensboro diocese.

Western New York Catholic, m; 795 Main St., Buffalo, NY 14203-1250; (716) 847-8727; www.wnycatholic.org; Buffalo diocese.

Witness, The, w; P.O. Box 917, Dubuque, IA 52004-0917; (563) 588-0556; Dubuque archdiocese.

Wyoming Catholic Register, m; P.O. Box 1468, Cheyenne, WY 82003; (307) 638-1530; www.wyocathregister.org; Cheyenne diocese.

Magazines

Abbey Banner, The, 3 times a year; Saint John's Abbey, Collegeville, MN 56321; (320) 363-2011; www.saintjohnsabbey.org/banner/index.html.

AIM: Liturgy Resources, q; 3708 River Rd., Ste. 400, Franklin Park, IL 60131; (800) 566-6150; www.wlp.jspaluch.com/8062.htm.

America, w; 106 W. 56th St., New York, NY 10019; (212) 581-4640; www.americamagazine.org; Jesuits of U.S. and Canada.

American Benedictine Review, q; Assumption Abbey, Box A, Richardson, ND 58652; (701) 974-3315; www.osb.org/abr/.

American Catholic Philosophical Quarterly (formerly *The New Scholasticism*), Philosophy Documentation Center, P. O. Box 7147, Charlottesville, Virginia 22906-7147; (800) 444-2419; www.acpa-main.org; American Catholic Philosophical Assn.

American Catholic Studies; Villanova University, 800 Lancaster Ave., Villanova, PA 19085; (610) 519-5470.

The Annals of St. Anne de Beaupre, m; 9795 Boul, Ste.Anne, St. Anne de Beaupre, Quebec, GOA 3CO; (418) 827-4538.

Anthonian, The, q; c/o St. Anthony's Guild, Paterson, NJ 07509; (212) 924-1451; www.hnp.org/publications; St. Anthony's Guild.

Apostolate of the Little Flower, bm; P.O. Box 5280, San Antonio, TX 78201-0280; (210) 736-3889; Discalced Carmelite Fathers.

Augustinian, The, q; P.O. Box 340, Villanova, PA 19085; (610) 527-3330; www.augustinian.org; published by the Province of St. Thomas of Villanova.

Barry Magazine, 2 times a year; 11300 NE 2nd Ave., Miami Shores, FL 33161; (305) 899-3188; www.barry.edu/barrymagazine. Barry University.

Benedictine Sisters and Friends, 3 times a year, 104 Chapel Lane, St. Joseph,MN 56374; (320) 363-7100; www.sbm.osb.org.

Benedictines, 44 N. Mill St., Kansas City, KS 66101; (913) 342-0938; www.mountosb.org.

Bread of Life, 6 times a year, P.O. Box 127, Burlington, Ontario, L7R 3X8, Canada; (905) 632-5433; www.thebreadoflife.ca.

Bright Ideas; P.O. Box 510817, New Berlin, WI, 53151-0817; (800) 950-9952; www.lpiresourcecenter.com.

Canticle: The Voice of Women of Grace, 6 times a year, 325 Scarlet Blvd., Oldsmar, FL 34677; (813) 854-1518; www.canticlemagazine.com.

Carmelite Digest q; Carmelite Digest, PO Box 3898, Yountville CA 94599; 707-944-9007; www.carmelitedigest.com.

Carmelite Review, q; 8501 Bailey Rd., Darien, IL, 60561; (630) 971-0724; www.carlemitereview.org; published by the Province of the Most Pure Heart of Mary of the Carmelite Order.

Catechist, The, 7 times a year; 2621 Dryden Rd., Dayton, OH 45439; (937) 293-1415; www.pflaum.com.

Catechumenate: A Journal of Christian Initiation, bm; 1800 N. Hermitage Ave., Chicago, IL 60622-1101; (773) 486-8970; www.ltp.org.

Catholic Answer, The, bm; 200 Noll Plaza, Huntington, IN 46750; (260) 356-8400; www.osv.com; Our Sunday Visitor, Inc.

Catholic Biblical Quarterly; Catholic University of America, Washington, DC 20064; (202) 319-5519; cba.cua.edu/CBQ.cfm; Catholic Biblical Assn.

Catholic Cemetery, The, m; 1400 S. Wolf Rd., Bldg. 3, Hillside,IL 60162; (708) 202-1242; National Catholic Cemetery Conference.

Catholic Connection, The, m.; 3500 Fairfield Ave., Shreveport, LA 71104; (318) 868-4441; www.dioshpt.org; diocese of Shreveport.

Catholic Digest, m; 1 Montauk Ave., Ste. 200, New London, CT 06320; (860) 437-3012; www.catholicdigest.org.

Catholic Family News, m.; MPO Box 743, Niagara Falls, NY 14302; (905) 871-6292; www.cfnews.org/cfn.htm.

Catholic Historical Review, q; 2715 North Charles Street, Baltimore, Maryland 21218; (410) 516-6989; muse.jhu.edu/journals/cat.

Catholic Lawyer, q; St. John's Law Review, St. John's University School of Law, Room 3-40, 8000 Utopia Parkway, Jamaica, NY 11439; (718) 990-6655; St. Thomas More Institute for Legal Research.

Catholic Library World, q; 100 North St., #224, Pittsfield, MA 01201-5109; (413) 443-2252; www.cathla.org; Catholic Library Association.

Catholic Missions in Canada, q; 201-1155 Yonge St., Toronto, Ontario, M4T 1W2, Canada; (416) 934-3424; www.cmic.info.

Catholic Press Directory, a; 205 W. Monroe St., Ste. 470, Chicago, IL 60606; (312) 380-6789; www.catholicpress.org; Catholic Press Assn.

Catholic Response, m.; 601 Buhler Ct., Pine Beach, NJ 08741; (732) 914-1222; www.jhcnewman.org.

Catholic Review (Braille, tape, large print), bm; 154 E. 23rd St., New York, NY 10010; (212) 473-7800; Xavier Society for the Blind.

Catholic Southwest: A Journal of History and Culture, a; 1625 Rutherford Lane, Bldg. D, Austin, TX, 78754-5105; (512) 339-9882.

Catholic Woman, bm; 200 N. Glebe Rd., Suite 703, Arlington, VA 22203; (202) 224-0990; www.nccw.org; National Council of Catholic Women.

Catholic Worker, 7 times a year; 36 E. First St., New York, NY 10003; (212) 677-8627; Catholic Worker Movement.

Catholic World Report, The, 11 times a year; P.O. Box 2512, Alexandria, VA 22301; (800) 353-2324; www.catholicworldreport.com; Ignatius Press.

Celebrate!, six times a year, Novalis, 10 Lower Spadina Ave., Ste. 400, Toronto, ON M5V 2Z2; (780) 451-2228; www.celebrate-liturgy.ca; Novalis, Saint Paul University.

Charities USA; q; 1731 King St., Suite 200, Alexandria, VA 22314; (703) 549-1390; www.catholiccharitiesusa.org.

Chesterton Review, The, q; Seton Hall University, 400 South Orange Ave., South Orange, NJ 07079; (973) 275-2431; academic.shu.edu/Chesterton. G.K. Chesterton Society.

Chicago Studies, 3 times a year; 1800 N. Hermitage Ave., Chicago, IL 60622-1101; (800) 933-1800; www.ltp.org.

Christian Renewal News, v; P.O. Box 6164, Santa Maria, CA 93456; (805) 524-5890; www.theservantsandhandmaids.net; published by The Servants and Handmaids of the Sacred Heart of Jesus.

Christianity and the Arts, q; P.O. Box 118088, Chicago,

IL 60611; (312) 642-8606; www.christianarts.net.

Church, q; 18 Bleeker St., New York, NY 10012; (212) 431-7825; www.nplc.org; National Pastoral Life Center.

CMMB Today, q., 10 West 17th St., New York, N.Y. 10011; (212) 242-7757; www.cmmb.org; Catholic Medical Mission Board publication.

CNEWA Connections, bm; 1011 First Ave., New York, NY 10022; (800) 442-6392; www.cnewa.org; Catholic Near East Welfare.

Columban Mission, 8 times a year; St. Columbans, NE 68056; (402) 291-1920; www.columban.org; Columban Fathers.

Columbia, m; One Columbus Plaza, New Haven, CT 06510; (203) 752-4398; www.kofc.org; Knights of Columbus.

Commonweal, bw; 475 Riverside Dr., Room 405, New York, NY 10115; (212) 662-4200; www.commonwealmagazine.org.

Communio: International Catholic Review, q; P.O. Box 4557, Washington, DC 20017-0557; (202) 526-0251; www.communio-icr.com.

Company, q; P.O. Box 60790, Chicago, IL 60660-0790; (773) 760-9432; www.companymagazine.com; Jesuit magazine.

CONNECT!, Liturgical Publications, Inc., P.O. Box 510817, New Berlin, WI 53151; (800) 950-9952; www.lpiresourcecenter.com.

Consecrated Life, semi-annually; P.O. Box 7500, Libertyville, IL 60048-7500; (847) 573-8975; www.religiouslife.com; Institute on Religious Life. English edition of *Informationes*, official publication of Congregation for Institutes of Consecrated Life and Societies of Apostolic Life.

Consolata Missionaries, bm; P.O. Box 5550, Somerset, NJ 08875-5550; (732) 297-9191; www.consolata.org.

Cord, The, m; Franciscan Institute, St. Bonaventure University, St. Bonaventure, NY 14778; (716) 375-2160; www.sbu.edu; Franciscan Institute.

Counseling and Values, 3 times a year; College of Educational, Southern Illinois University, Carbondale, IL 62901; (618) 537-7791.

Crisis, Morley Publishing Group Inc., 2100 M Street NW, #170-339, Washington, D.C. 20037; www.insidecatholic.com; journal of lay Catholic opinion.

Cross Currents, q; College of New Rochelle, New Rochelle, NY 10805; (914) 235-1439; www.aril.org; interreligious; Assn. for Religion and Intellectual Life.

Crusade Magazine, bm; P.O. Box 341, Hanover, PA 17331; (717) 225-7147; The American Society for the Defense of Tradition, Family and Property (TFP).

CUA Magazine, 3 times a year; 620 Michigan Ave. N.E., Washington, DC 20064; (202) 319-5600; www.cua.edu; Catholic University of America.

Culture Wars, (formerly *Fidelity Magazine*), m; 206 Marquette Ave., South Bend, IN 46617; (219) 289-9786.

Darbininkas (The Worker) (Lithuanian), w; 341 Highland Blvd., Brooklyn, NY 11207; (718) 827-1352; Lithuanian Franciscans.

Desert Call, q.; P.O. Box 219, Crestone, CO 81131-0219; (719) 256-4778; www.spirituallifeinstitute.org; published by the Spiritual Life Institute.

Diakonia, 3 times a year; University of Scranton, Scranton, PA 18510-4643; (570) 941-6141; www.nyssa.cecs.uofs.edu/diaktoc.html; Center for Eastern Christian Studies.

Dominican Torch, The, q; 141 East 65th St., N.Y.,N.Y. 10021; (212) 744-2080.

Don Bosco Alive/The Salesian Bulletin; 148 Main Street, New Rochelle, NY 10802-0639; (914) 636-4225; www.salesians.org.

Eastern Oklahoma Catholic, 10 times a year; Box 690240, Tulsa, OK 74169-0240; (918) 307-4946; www.dioceseoftulsa.org; Tulsa diocese.

Ecumenical Trends, m (except Aug.); Graymoor, Route 9, P.O. Box 306, Garrison, NY 10524-0306; (845) 424-2109; www.atonementfriars.org; Graymoor Ecumenical Institute.

Eglute (The Little Fir Tree) (Lithuanian), m; 13648 Kikapoo Trail, Lockport, IL 60441; (708) 301-6410; for children ages 5-10.

Emmanuel, 10 times a year; 5384 Wilson Mills Rd., Cleveland, OH 44143; (440) 449-2103; www.blessedsacrament.com; Congregation of Blessed Sacrament.

Envoy, bm; P.O. Box 585, Granville, OH 43023; (740) 345-2705; www.envoymagazine.com; journal of Catholic apologetics and evangelization.

EWTN Religious Catalogue, two times a year; 5817 Old Leeds Rd., Irondale, AL 35210, (205) 271-2900, www.ewtn.com, printed catalogue of select new and favorite "holy reminders" for the Easter and Christmas seasons. Circ. 700,000.

Extension, m; 150 S. Wacker Dr., 20th Floor, Chicago, IL 60606; (312) 236-7240; www.catholicextension.org; Catholic Church Extension Society.

Faith, 209 Seymour Ave., Lansing, MI 48933-1577; (517) 342-2595; www.faithmag.com.

Faith-Diocese of Erie, 429 E. Grandview Blvd., Erie, PA 16504; (814) 824-1160; www.eriecd.org.

Faith-Diocese of Grand Rapids, 360 Division Ave. S., Grand Rapids, MI 49503; (616) 475-1240; www.dioceseofgrandrapids.org.

Faith and Family, bm; 432 Washington Ave., North Haven, CT 06473; (203) 230-3800; formerly *Catholic Twin Circle*.

Family Digest, The, bm; P.O. Box 40137, Fort Wayne, IN 46804 (editorial address); (952) 929-6765.

Family Foundations Magazine, P.O. Box 111184, Cincinnati, OH 45211; (513) 471-2000; www.ccli.org; published by the Couple to Couple League.

Family Friend, q; P.O. Box 11563, Milwaukee, WI 53211; (414) 961-0500; www.cfli.org; Catholic Family Life Insurance.

Fatima Crusader, The, q; P.O. Box 602, Fort Erie, ON, L2A 4M7, Canada; (905) 871-7607; www.fatima.org.

F.M.A. Focus, q; P.O. Box 598, Mt. Vernon, NY 10551; (914) 664-5604; Franciscan Mission Associates.

Franciscan Studies, a; Franciscan Institute, St. Bonaventure, NY 14778; (716) 375-2105; www.franinst.sbu.edu; Franciscan Institute.

Franciscan Way, q; 1235 University Blvd., Steubenville, OH 43952; (740) 283-6450; www.franciscan.edu.

Fraternal Leader, q; P.O. Box 13005; Erie, PA 16514-1302; (814) 453-4331; Loyal Christian Benefit Association.

Fraternally Yours (Engish-Slovak), m; 24950 Chagrin Blvd., Beachwood, OH 44122; (216) 464-8015; First Catholic Slovak Ladies Assn.

Fuente de Misericordia, q; Eden Hill, Stockbridge, MA 01263; (413) 298-3691; www.marian.org; Congregation of Marians of the Immaculate Conception.

Glenmary Challenge, The, q; P.O. Box 465618, Cincinnati, OH 45246-5618; (513) 874-8900; www.glenmary.org; Glenmary Home Missioners.

God's Word Today, m; 1 Montauk Ave., Ste. 200, New

London, CT 06320; (860) 437-3012; www.godswordtoday. org; Daily Scripture readings.

Good News for Children, 32 times during school year; 2621 Dryden Rd., Dayton, OH 45439; (800) 543-4383; www.pflaum.com.

Good Shepherd (Dobry Pastier) (Slovak-English), a; 8200 McKnight Rd., Pittsburgh, PA 15237; (412) 364-3000.

Greyfriars Review, 3 times a year; Franciscan Institute, St. Bonventure University, St. Bonaventure, NY 14778; (716) 375-2105; www.franinst.sbu.edu; Franciscan Institute.

Growing with the Gospel, w; Liturgical Publications, P.O. Box 510817, New Berlin, WI, 53151; (800) 950-9952.

Guide to Religious Ministries for Catholic Men and Women, A, a; 210 North Ave., New Rochelle, NY 10801; (914) 632-1220; www.religiousministries.com.

Health Progress, bm; 4455 Woodson Rd., St. Louis, MO 63134-3797; (314) 427-2500; www.chausa.org; Catholic Health Association.

Heart, 4389 West Pine Blvd., St. Louis, MO 63108; (314) 652-1500; www.rscj.org.

Homiletic and Pastoral Review, m; 70 Lake Street, P.O. Box 297, Ramsey, NJ 07446; (800) 353-2324; www. hprweb.com.

Horizon, q; 5401 S. Cornell Ave., Chicago, IL 60615-5604; (773) 363-5454.

Horizons, 2 times a year; Villanova University, Villanova, PA 19085; (610) 519-7302; College Theology Society.

ICSC Resource; 1275 K St. N.W., Suite 980, Washington, DC, 20005-4006; (202) 289-1093; www. catholicstewardship.org; published by International Catholic Stewardship Council.

Immaculate Heart Messenger, q; P.O. Box 269, Hanceville, AL 35077; (800) 213-5541; www.fatimafamily.org.

In a Word, m; 199 Seminary Dr., Bay Saint Louis, MS 39520-4626; (601) 467-1097; www.inaword.com; Society of the Divine Word.

Inside the Vatican, 10 times a year; Rome office: Via della Mura Aurelio 7c, 00165 Rome, Italy; U.S. office: St. Martin de Porres Lay Dominican Community, 3050 Gap Knob Rd., New Hope, KY 40052; (270) 325-5499; www.insidethevatican.com. The only current journal that focuses exclusively on Rome, the impact of the papacy worldwide, and the functioning, travels, and activities of the Holy Father and the Roman Curia.

Jesuit Bulletin, 3 times a year; 3601 Lindell Blvd., St. Louis, MO 63108; (314) 633-4610; www.jesuitsmis.org; Jesuit Seminary Aid Association.

Jesuit Journeys, 3 times a year; 3400 W. Wisconsin Ave., Milwaukee, WI 53208-0288; (414) 727-6236; www.jesuitswisprov.org.

Josephinum Journal of Theology, twice a year; 7625 N. High St., Columbus, OH 43235; (614) 885-5585; www.pcj.edu.

Josephite Harvest, The, q; 1130 N. Calvert St., Baltimore, MD 21202-3802; (410) 727-2233; www. josephite.com; Josephite Missionaries.

Journal of Catholic Legal Studies, St. John's University, 8000 Utopia Parkway, Jamaica, NY 11439; (718) 990-6655.

Jurist, The, semi-annually; Catholic University of America, Washington, DC 20064; (202) 319-5439; canon-law.cua.edu/links. Department of Canon Law.

Kinship, q; P.O. Box 22264, Owensboro, KY 42304; (270) 686-8401; www.glenmarysisters.org; Glenmary Sisters.

Law Briefs, m; 3211 Fourth St. N.E., Washington, DC 20017; (202) 541-3300; Office of General Counsel, USCCB.

Lay Witness, m; 827 North Fourth St., Steubenville, OH, 43952; (740) 283-2484; www.cuf. org; Catholics United for the Faith.

Leaflet Missal, 16565 South State St., S. Holland, IL 60473; (708) 331-5485; www.americancatholic-press.org/leafletmissal.html.

Leaves, bm; P.O. Box 87, Dearborn, MI 48121-0087; (313) 561-2330; www.rc.net/detroit/marian-hill/leaves.htm; Mariannhill Mission Society.

Legatus, 10 times a year, 5072 Annunciation Circle, Ste. 202, Ave Maria, FL 34142; (239) 435-3852; www.legatus. org. Published by Legatus International.

Liguorian, m; 1 Liguori Dr., Liguori, MO 63057; (636) 464-2500; www.liguorian.org; Redemptorists.

Linacre Quarterly; 333 E. Lancaster Avenue, #348, Wynnewood, PA 19096; (215) 877-9099; www.cathmed. org; Catholic Medical Association (National Federation of Catholic Physicians Guilds).

Liturgia y Cancion (Spanish and English), q; 5536 NE Hassalo, Portland, OR 97213; (800) 548-8749; Oregon Catholic Press.

Liturgical Catechesis, 6 times a year; 160 E. Virginia St., #290, San Jose, CA 95112; (408) 286-8505; www.rpinet.com/lc.

Liturgy Planner, The, semi-annual; P.O. Box 13071, Portland, OR 97213; (503) 331-2965.

Living City, m; 202 Comforter Blvd., Hyde Park, NY 12538; (845) 229-0230; www.livingcitymagazine.com; Focolare Movement.

Living Faith: Daily Catholic Devotions, q; 1564 Fencorp Dr., Fenton, MO 63026-2942; (636) 305-9777; www.livingfaith.com.

Magnificat, m.; Dunwoodie, P.O. Box 834, Yonkers, NY 10702; (914) 502-1820; www.magnificat.net.

Marian Helper, q.; Eden Hill, Stockbridge, MA 01263; (413) 298-3691; www.marian.org.

Marriage, bm; 955 Lake Dr., St. Paul, MN 55120; (651) 454-7947; www.marriagemagazine; International Marriage Encounter.

Maryknoll, m; Maryknoll, NY 10545-0308; (914) 941-7590; www.maryknoll.org; Catholic Foreign Mission Society.

Matrimony, q; 215 Santa Rosa Pl., Santa Barbara, CA 93109; (805) 965-9541; Worldwide Marriage Encounter.

Ministry & Liturgy, m.; 160 E. Virginia St., #290, San Jose, CA 95112; (408) 286-8505; www.rpinet.com.

Mission, q; 1663 Bristol Pike, Bensalem, PA 19020-8502; (215) 244-9900; www.katharinedrexel. org; Sisters of the Blessed Sacrament.

Mission, q., 10582 Associates Court, Manassas, VA 20109; (703) 367-0333; www.cardinalnewmansociety.org; Cardinal Newman Society to promote Catholic higher education.

Mission, 300 College Ave., Los Gatos, CA 95031; (408) 884-1634; www.jesuitscalifornia.org.

MISSION Magazine, q; 366 Fifth Ave., New York, NY 10001; (212) 563-8700; www.onefamilymission.org; Society for Propagation of the Faith.

Mission Helper, The, q; 1001 W. Joppa Rd., Baltimore, MD 21204-3787; (410) 823-8585; Mission Helpers of the Sacred Heart.

Missionhurst, bm; 4651 N. 25th St., Arlington, VA 22207; (703) 528-3804; www.missionhurst.org.

Modern Schoolman, The, q; St. Louis University, P.O. Box 56907, St. Louis, MO 63156; (314) 997-3149; St. Louis University Philosophy Department.

Momento Catolico, El; 205 W. Monroe St., Chicago, IL, 60606; (312) 236-7782; www.hmrc.claretianpubs.org.

Momentum, q; Suite 100, 1077 30th St. N.W., Washington, DC 20007-3852; (202) 337-6232; www.ncea. org; National Catholic Educational Association.

Mountain Spirit, The, bm; P.O. Box 55911, Lexington, KY 40555-5911; (866) 270-4227; www. chrisapp.org; Christian Appalachian Project.

My Daily Visitor, bm; 200 Noll Plaza, Huntington, IN 46750; (260) 356-8400; www.osv.com; Our Sunday Visitor, Inc.

National Apostolate for Inclusion Ministry, q; P.O. Box 218, Riverdale, MD, 20738-0218; (301) 699-9500; www.nafim.org.

National Catholic Forester, q; 320 S. School St., Mt. Prospect, IL 60056; (847) 342-4500; www.ncsf.com.

National Catholic Rural Life, bi-annual; 4625 Beaver Ave., Des Moines, IA 50310; (515) 270-2634; www.ncrlc. com.

NC Catholics, 715 Nazareth, Raleigh, NC 27606; (919) 821-9736; www.nccatholics.org; diocese of Raleigh.

NETWORK Connection, bm; 25 E St. NW, Washington, DC 20001; (202) 347-9797; www.net-worklobby.org; Network.

New England Province of Jesuits, P.O. Box 9199, Watertown, MA 02471; (617) 607-2895; www.sjnen. org; New England Province of the Society of Jesus.

New Oxford Review, 10 issues a year; 1069 Kains Ave., Berkeley, CA 94706; (510) 526-5374; www. newoxfordreview.org.

Notebook, The, q; CMICA-USA, 3049 4 St. N.E., Washington, DC 20017; (202) 269-6672; www.pax-romana.org; Catholic Movement for Intellectual and Cultural Affairs.

Nova-Voice of Ministry, bm; P.O. Box 432, Milwaukee, WI 53201; (800) 876-4574; www.execpc.com/~lpi; Liturgical Publications.

Oblates Magazine, six times a year, 9480 North De Mazenod Dr., Belleville, IL 62223-1160; (618) 398-4848; www.oblatesusa.org.

Old Testament Abstracts, 3 times a year; 320 Caldwell Hall, Catholic University of America, Washington, DC 20064; (202) 319-5519.

ONE, bm., 1011 First Ave., New York, NY 10022; (800) 442-6329; www.cnewa.org. Catholic Near East Welfare Association.

Ozanam News, The, twice a year; 58 Progress Parkway, St. Louis, MO 63043-3706; (314) 576-3993; www.svdpus-council.org; Society of St. Vincent de Paul.

Palabra Entre Nosotros, La, bm; 9639 Dr. Perry Rd., Unit 126N, Jamesville, MD, 21754; (301) 831-1262; www.wau.org.

Parable Magazine, P.O. Box 310, Manchester, NH 03105; (603) 669-0377;www.parablemag..com.

Parish Liturgy, q; 16565 S. State St., S. Holland, IL 60473; (708) 331-5485; www.parishliturgy.com.

Partners Magazine: Chicago Province of the Society of Jesus, 3 times a year; 2059 N. Sedgwick St., Chicago, IL 60614; (773) 975-8181; www.jesuits-chi.org.

Passionists Compassion, The, q; 526 Monastery Pl.,

Union City, NJ 07087; (201) 864-0018; www.cptryon.org.

Pastoral Life, m; Box 595, Canfield, OH 44406; (330) 533-5503; www.albahouse.org; Society of St. Paul.

Pastoral Music, bm; 962 Wayne Ave., Suite 210, Silver Spring, MD 20910-4433; (240) 247-3000; www.npm.org; National Association of Pastoral Musicians.

Pax Romana/CMICA-USA, q; 3049 4th St., N.E., Washington, DC 20017; (202) 269-6672; www.pax-romana.org.

Philosophy Today, q; 2352 N.Clifton Ave., Chicago, IL 60614; (773) 325-7267; Philosophy Department.

PIME World, m (except July-Aug.); 17330 Quincy St., Detroit, MI 48221; (313) 342-4066; www.pimeysa.org; PIME Missionaries.

Poverello, The, 10 times a year; 6832 Convent Blvd., Sylvania, OH 43560; (419) 824-3627; www.sistersosf; Sisters of St. Francis of Sylvania.

Prayers for Worship, q; P.O. Box 510817, New Berlin, WI 53151; (800) 950-9952; www.lpiresourcecenter.com.

Preach: Enlivening the Pastoral Art, 6 times a year, 3708 River Rd., Ste. 400, Franklin Park, IL 60131; (800) 566-6150; www.wlpmusic.com; published by World Library Publications.

Priest, The, m; 200 Noll Plaza, Huntington, IN 46750; (260) 356-8400; www.osv.com; Our Sunday Visitor, Inc.

Proceedings, a; Fordham University, Adm. Bldg., Bronx, NY 10458; (718) 817-4081; www.acpa-main.org; Journal of the American Catholic Philosophical Association.

Promise, 32 times a year; 2621 Dryden Rd., Suite 300, Dayton, OH 45439; (937) 293-1415; www.pflaum.com.

Queen of All Hearts, bm; 26 S. Saxon Ave., Bay Shore, NY 11706; (631) 665-0726; www.montfortmissionaries. com; Montfort Missionaries.

Reign of the Sacred Heart, q; 6889 S. Lovers Lane, Hales Corners, WI 53130; (414) 425-3383; www.poshusa.org.

Religion Teacher's Journal, m (Sept.-May); P.O. Box 6015, New London, CT 06320; (860) 437-3012; www.religionteachersjournal.com.

Religious Life, bm., P.O. Box 410007, Chicago, IL 60641; (773) 267-1195; www.religiouslife.com.

Renascence, q; P.O. Box 1881, Marquette University, Milwaukee, WI 53201-1881; (414) 288-6725.

Report on U.S. Catholic Overseas Mission, bi-annually; 3029 Fourth St. N.E., Washington, DC 20017; (202) 832-3112; www.catholicmission.org; United States Catholic Mission Association.

Response: Directory of Volunteer Opportunities, a; 6930 Carroll Ave., Suite 820, Takoma Park, MD 20912; (301) 270-0900; www.cnvs.org; Catholic Network of Volunteer Service.

Review for Religious, bm; 3601 Lindell Blvd., St. Louis, MO 63108; (314) 633-4610; www.reviewforreligious.org.

Review of Social Economy, q; University of Groningen, School of Economics & Business, P.O. Box 800, Groningen, 9700 AV, Netherlands; 31-50-3632789; www.socialeconomic.org.

Revista Maryknoll (Spanish-English), m; Maryknoll, NY 10545; (914) 941-7590; www.maryknoll.org; Catholic Foreign Mission Society of America.

RITE, 8 times a year; 1800 North Hermitage Ave., Chicago, IL 60622-1101; (773) 486-8970; www.ltp.org.

Roze Maryi (Polish), m; Eden Hill, Stockbridge, MA 01263; (413) 298-3691; www.marian.org; Marian Helpers Center.

Sacred Music, q; 134 Christendom Dr., c/o K. Poterack, Front Royal, VA 22630; (540) 636-2900.

St. Anthony Messenger, m; 28 W. Liberty St., Cincinnati,

OH 45210-1298; (513) 241-5615; www.americancatholic. org; Franciscan Friars.

St. Augustine Catholic, bm (Sept-May); 11625 Old St. Augustine Rd., Jacksonville, FL 32258; (904) 262-3200; www.staugcatholic.org; St. Augustine diocese.

St. Joseph's Messenger and Advocate of the Blind, bi-annual; St. Joseph Home, 537 Pavonia Ave., Jersey City, NJ 07303; (201) 798-4141.

St. Paul's Family Magazine, q; 14780 W. 159th St., Olathe, KS 66062; (913) 780-0405.

Salesian Bulletin, q; 148 Main St., New Rochelle, NY 10802; (914) 636-4225; www.salesians.org; Salesians of Don Bosco.

SALT/Sisters of Charity, BVM, q; 1100 Carmel Dr., Dubuque, IA 52001; (563) 588-2351; www.bvmcong.org.

Scalabrinians, q; 209 Flagg Pl., Staten Island, NY 10304; (718) 351-0257.

Scarboro Missions, 7 times a year, 2685 Kingston Rd., Scarborough, ON M1M 1M4, Canada; (416) 261-7135; www.scarboromissions.ca.

School Guide, a; 210 North Ave., New Rochelle, NY 10801; (914) 632-7771; www.schoolguides.com.

SCN Journey, bm; SCN Office of Communications, P.O. Box 9, Nazareth, KY 40048; (502) 348-1564; www. scnazarethky.org; Sisters of Charity of Nazareth.

Seeds, 32 times a year; 2621 Dryden Rd., Dayton, OH 45439; (937) 293-1415; www.pflaum.com.

Serenity, q; 601 Maiden Choice Lane, Baltimore, MD 21228; (410) 744-9367; Little Sisters of the Poor.

SerraUSA, The, bm; 65 E. Wacker Pl., #802, Chicago, IL 60601-7203; (312) 201-6549; www.serraus.org; Serra International.

Share Magazine, q; 10 W. 71st St., New York, NY 10023; (212) 877-3041; www.catholicdaughters.com; Catholic Daughters of the Americas.

Share the Word, bm; 3031 Fourth St. N.E., Washington, DC 20017-1102; (202) 832-5022; www.sharetheword.net; Paulist Catholic Evangelization Association.

Silent Advocate, q; St. Rita School for the Deaf, 1720 Glendale-Milford Rd., Cincinnati, OH 45215; (513) 771-7600; www.srsdeaf.org.

Social Justice Review, bm; 3835 Westminster Pl., St. Louis, MO 63108-3409; (314) 371-1653; www.socialjusti-cereview.com; Catholic Central Union of America.

SOUL Magazine, bm; P.O. Box 976, Washington, NJ 07882; (908) 213-2223; www.bluearmy.com; The Blue Army of Our Lady of Fatima, USA, Inc.

Spirit, w; 1884 Randolph Ave., St. Paul, MN 55105; (612) 690-7012; www.goodgroundpress.com; for teens.

Spirit, bi-annually; Seton Hall University, South Orange, NJ 07079; (201) 761-9000.

Spirit & Life, bm; 800 N. Country Club Rd., Tucson, AZ 85716; (520) 325-6401; www.benedictinesisters.org; Benedictine Srs. of Perpetual Adoration.

Spiritan Missionary News, q; 121 Victoria Park Ave., Toronto, ON, M4E 3S2, Canada; (416) 691-9319; www. spiritans.com.

Spiritual Life, q; 2131 Lincoln Rd. N.E., Washington, DC 20002; (888) 616-1713; Discalced Carmelite Friars.

Star, 10 times a year; 22 W. Kiowa, Colorado Springs, CO 80903.

Studies in the Spirituality of Jesuits, 5 times a year; 3601 Lindell Blvd., St. Louis, MO 63108; (314) 633-4622.

Sunday by Sunday, w; 1884 Randolph Ave., St. Paul, MN 55105; (651) 690-7012; www.goodgroundpress.com.

Sword Magazine, 2 times a year; 2097 Town Hall

Terrace, #3, Grand Island, NY 14072-1737; (716) 773-0992; Carmelite Fathers.

Take Out, 10 times a year; Our Sunday Visitor, 200 Noll Plaza, Huntington, IN 46750; (800) 348-2440; www. osv.com.

Theological Studies, q; Marquette University, 100 Coughlin Hall, Milwaukee, WI 53201-1881; (414) 288-3164; www.ts.mu.edu.

Theology Digest, q; P.O. Box 56907, St. Louis, MO 63156-0907; (314) 977-3410; St. Louis University.

This Rock Magazine, 10 times a year; 2020 Gillespie Way, El Cajon, CA 92020; (619) 387-7200; www.catholic. com; Catholic apologetics.

Thomist, The, q; 487 Michigan Ave. N.E., Washington, DC 20017; (202) 529-5300; www.thomist.org; Dominican Fathers.

Today's Catholic Teacher, m (Sept.-April); 2621 Dryden Rd., Dayton, OH 45439; (937) 293-1415; www.catholic-teacher.com.

Today's Liturgy, q; 5536 NE Hassalo, Portland, OR 97213; (800) 548-8749; www.ocp.org.

Today's Parish Minister, m (Sept.-May); 1 Montauk Ave., New London, CT 06320; (860) 437-3012; www.twentythirdpublications.com.

Together in the Word, bi-annual; Box 577, Techny, IL 60082-0577; (708) 272-2700; www.divineword. org; Chicago province, Society of Divine Word.

The Tower, w; The Catholic University of America, University Center, 127 Pryzbyla Center, Washington, DC 20064; (202) 319-5778.

Traces, m; 125 Maiden Lane, 15th Floor, N.Y., N.Y. 10038; (212) 337-3580; www.traces-cl.com.

Tracings, q; 5 Gamelin St., Holyoke, MA 01040; (413) 536-7511; www.sisofprov.org; Sisters of Providence.

Ultreya Magazine, bm; 4500 W. Davis St., P.O. Box 210226, Dallas, TX 75211; (214) 339-6321; Cursillo Movement.

L'Union (French and English), q; P.O. Box F, Woonsocket, RI 02895; (401) 769-0520.

Universitas, q; 221 N. Grand, Room 39, St. Louis, MO 63103; (314) 977-2537; www.slu.edu; St. Louis University.

U.S. Catholic, m; 205 W. Monroe St., Chicago, IL 60606; (312) 236-7782; www.uscatholic.org; Claretians.

Venture, 32 times during school year; 2621 Dryden Rd., Suite 300, Dayton, OH 45439; (937) 293-1415; www. pflaum.com; intermediate grades.

Vida Catolica, La, m.; 40 Green St., Lynn, MA 01902; (781) 586-0197; www.la-vida.org/catolica; Boston arch-diocese Hispanic community.

Vincentian Heritage, twice a year; 2233 N. Kenmore Ave., Chicago, IL 60614; (773) 325-7348; www.depaul.edu/~vstudies.

Vision, a, 205 W. Monroe St., Chicago, IL 60606; (312) 236-7782; www.visionguide.org; Claretian Publications in conjunction with National Religious Vocation Conference.

Vision, 3 times a year; 7202 Buchanan St., Landover Hills, MD 20784; (301) 577-1684; www. ncod.org; National Catholic Office for the Deaf.

Vision (Spanish-English), P.O. Box 28185, San Antonio, TX 78228; (210) 732-2156; www.maccsa.org; Mexican American Cultural Center.

Visions, 32 times during school year; 2621 Dryden Rd., Suite 300, Dayton, OH 45439; (937) 293-1415; www. pflaum.com; for students in grades 7-9.

Vocations and Prayer, q; 6635 Tobias Ave., Van Nuys, CA 91405; (818) 782-1765; www.vocationsandprayer.com; Rogationist Fathers.

Voice Crying in the Wilderness, A, q; 4425 Schneider Rd., Filmore, NY 14735; (716) 567-4433; Most Holy Family Monastery.

Waif's Messenger, q; 1140 W. Jackson Blvd., Chicago, IL 60607; (312) 738-9522; Mission of Our Lady of Mercy.

Way of St. Francis, bm; 1500 34th Ave., Oakland, CA 94601; (916) 443-5717; www.sbfranciscans.org; Franciscan Friars of California, Inc.

Wheeling Jesuit University Chronicle, 3 times a year; 316 Washington Ave., Wheeling, WV 26003; (304) 243-2296.

Word Among Us, The, m; 9639 Dr. Perry Rd., No. 126N, Jamesville, MD 21754; (301) 831-1262; www.wau.org.

Word and Witness, P.O. Box 510817, Wisconsin, WI, 53151-0817; (800) 950-9952; www.lpiresourcecenter.com.

World Lithuanian Catholic Directory, P.O. Box 1025, Humarock , MA 02407; (781) 834-4079.

Worship, bm; St. John's Abbey, Collegeville, MN 56321; (612) 363-3883.

Newsletters

ACT, 10 times a year; Box 925, Evansville, IN 47706-0925; (812) 962-5508; www.cfm.org; Christian Family Movement.

Action News, q; Pro-Life Action League, 6160 N. Cicero Ave., Chicago, IL 60646; (773) 777-2900; www.prolifeaction.org.

Annual Report, The, 2021 H St. N.W., Washington, DC 20006; (202) 331-8542; Black and Indian Mission Office.

Archdiocesan Bulletin, bm; 827 N. Franklin St., Philadelphia, PA 19123; (215) 627-0143; Philadelphia archeparchy.

Baraga Bulletin, The, q; P.O. Box 550, Marquette, MI 49855; (906) 227-9117; www.dioceseofmarquette.org; Bishop Baraga Association.

Bringing Home the Word, w; 28 W. Liberty St., Cincinnati, OH 45202; (513) 241-5615; www.americancatholic.org; lectionary-based resource from St. Anthony's Messenger Press.

Brothers' Voice, 5420 South Cornell Ave., #205, Chicago, IL 60615-5604; (773) 493-2306.

Called By Joy, three times a year; 4419 N. Hawthorne St., Spokane, WA 99205; (509) 327-4479; Franciscan Monastery of St. Clare.

Campaign Update, bm; 1513 Sixteenth St. N.W., Ste. 400, Washington, DC 20036; (202) 833-4999; www.cathcamp.org; Catholic Campaign for America.

Canticle, The, four times a year, 146 Hawthorne Rd., Pittsburgh, PA 15209; (412) 821-2200; www.millvalefranciscans.org; Sisters of St. Francis of Millvale.

Capuchin Chronicle, q; P.O. Box 15099, Pittsburgh, PA 15237-0099; (412) 367-2222; www.capuchin.org.

CARA Report, The, bm; Georgetown University, Washington, DC 20057-1203; (202) 687-8080; www.cara.georgetown.edu; Center for Applied Research in the Apostolate.

Caring Community, the, m; 115 E. Armour Blvd., Kansas City, MO 64111; (816) 968-2278; www.ncrpub.com.

Catalyst, 10 times a year; 450 Seventh Ave., New York, NY, 10123; (212) 371-3191; www.catholicleague.org; Catholic League for Civil and Religious Rights.

Catechist's Connection, The, 10 times a year; 115 E. Armour Blvd., Kansas City, MO 64111; (816) 968-2278; www.ncrpub.com.

Catholic Communicator, The, q; 120 East Colonial Hgwy., Hamilton, VA 20158-9012; (540) 338-2700; Catholic Distance University Newsletter.

Catholic Indian Missions, 10 times a year; 2021 H St., NW, Washington, DC 20006; (202) 331-8542. Bureau of Catholic Indian Missions.

Catholic Trends, bw; 3211 Fourth St. N.E., Washington, DC 20017; (202) 541-3290; Catholic News Service.

Catholic Update, m; 28 W. Liberty St., Cincinnati, OH 45202-6498; (513) 241-5615; www.americancatholic.org.

CCHD News, q; 3211 Fourth St. N.E., Washington, DC 20017-1194; (202) 541-3210; www.povertyusa.org; Catholic Campaign for Human Development.

Celebration, Sisters of Charity of Seaton Hill, q; DePaul Center, 463 Mount Thor Rd., Greensburg, PA 15601; (724) 836-0406; www.scsh.org.

Christ the King Seminary Newsletter, 3 times a year; 711 Knox Rd., Box 607, E. Aurora, NY 14052; (716) 652-8900.

Christian Brothers Today, twice a year; 33 Pryor Terrace, New Rochelle, NY 10804; (914) 712-7580. Christian Brothers.

Christian Response Newsletter, P.O. Box 125, Staples, MN 56479-0125; (218) 894-1165.

Christopher News Notes, 10 times a year; 12 E. 48th St., New York, NY 10017; (212) 759-4050; www.christophers.org; The Christophers.

Clarion, The, 5 times a year; Box 159, Alfred, ME 04002-0159; (207) 324-0067; Brothers of Christian Instruction.

CMSM Bulletin, m; 8808 Cameron St., Silver Spring, MD 20910; (301) 588-4030; www.cmsm.org.

Comboni Mission Newsletter, q; 1318 Nagel Rd., Cincinnati, OH 45255-3194; (513) 474-4997; www.combonimissionaries.org.

Connections, five times a year, 610 W. Elm, Monroe, MI 48161; (734) 240-9745; IHM Sisters.

Context, 22 issues a year; 205 W. Monroe St., Chicago, IL 60606; (312) 236-7782; www.contextonline.org; Claretians.

CPN Newsletter, twice a month; 1318 Nagel Rd., Cincinnati, OH, 45255-3120; (513) 474-4997; www.combonimissionaries.org.

Cross and Feathers (Tekakwitha Conference Newsletter), q; P.O. Box 6768, Great Falls, MT 59406; (406) 727-0147; www.tekconf.org; Tekakwitha Conference.

Crossroads, 8 times a year; 1118 Pendleton St., #300, Cincinnati, OH 45202; (888) 714-0171; www.ccmanet.org; Catholic Campus Ministry Association.

CrossRoads, q; 370 W. Camino Gardens Blvd., Boca Raton, FL 33432; www.crossinternational.org. Cross International Catholic Outreach.

CRUX of the News, w; P.O. Box 758, Latham, NY 12110-0758; (518) 783-0058.

Cycles of Faith, P.O. Box 510817, New Berlin, WI 53201; (800) 950-9952; www.lpiresourcecenter.com.

Damien-Dutton Call, q; 616 Bedford Ave., Bellmore, NY 11710.

Dimensions, m; 86 Front St., Hempstead, NY 11550; (516) 481-6000; www.ncdc.org; National Catholic Development Conference.

Diocesan Dialogue, two times a year; 16565 South State St., South Holland, IL 60473; (708) 331-5485; www.americancatholicpress.org.

Diocesan Newsletter, The, m; P.O. Box 2147, Harlingen, TX

78551; (956) 421-4111; www.cdob.org; Brownsville diocese.

Environment and Art Letter, m; 1800 N. Hermitage Ave., Chicago, IL 60622-1101; (773) 486-8970; www.ltp.org; Liturgy Training Publications.

E-Proclaim, 10 times a year; 3211 Fourth St., N.E., Washington, DC, 20017-1194; (202) 541-3204; www.usccb.org/ccc.

Ethics and Medics, m; 6399 Drexel Rd., Philadelphia, PA 19151; (215) 877-2660; www.ncbcenter.org; National Catholic Bioethics Center.

Eucharistic Minister, m; 115 E. Armour, Kansas City, MO 64111; (816) 968-2278; www.ncrpub.com.

Every Day Catholic, m; 28 W. Liberty St., Cincinnati, OH 45202-6498; (513) 241-5615; www.everydaycatholic.org; St. Anthony Messenger Press.

EWTN Family Newsletter, 13 times a year; 5817 Leeds Rd., Irondale, AL 35210; (205) 271-2900; www.ewtn.com; Eternal Word Television Network.

EWTN Monthly Programming Guide, 13 times a year for each satellite; 5817 Old Leeds Road, Irondale, AL 35210, 205-271-2900; www.ewtn.com; EWTN Global Catholic Network, lists monthly programming and schedule for each satellite coverage area, including special end-of-year Christmas schedule.

Explorations, q; American Interfaith Institute, 321 Chestnut St., Philadelphia, PA, 19106; (215) 238-5345.

Faith Extra, 26 times a year; P.O. Box 10668, Erie, PA 16514; www.eriecd.org; diocese of Erie.

Family Connection, The, bm; 3753 MacBeth Dr., San Jose, CA 95127; (408) 258-8534.

Father Flood, q; P.O. Box 51087, New Berlin, WI 53151-0817; (800) 950-9952; www.lpireseourcecenter.com; Liturgical Publications.

Fellowship of Catholic Scholars Newsletter Quarterly, P.O. Box 495, Notre Dame, IN 46556; www.catholicscholars.org.

Fonda Tekakwitha News, P.O. Box 627, Fonda, NY 12068; (518) 853-3636; www.katerishrine.com; Order Minor Conventuals.

Food for the Poor, 3 times a year; 550 SW 12th Ave., Deerfield Beach, FL 33442; (954) 427-2222; www.foodforthepoor.org.

FOOTSTEPS: Walking with Edmund, q; 145 Huguenot Ave., Ste. 402; (914) 712-7580; Christian Brothers Foundation.

Forum Focus, q; P.O. Box 542, Hudson, WI 54016; (651) 276-1429; www.focusonfaith.org; The Wanderer Forum Foundation.

Foundations Newsletter for Newly Married Couples, bm; P.O. Box 1632, Portland, ME, 04104-1632; (207) 775-4757.

Franciscan Foundation for the Holy Land, three or four times a year; 9924 Cedar Ridge Dr., Carmel, IN 46032; (317) 574-4191; www.ffhl.org.

Franciscan World Care, q; P.O. Box 29034, Washington, DC 20017; (202) 832-1762; www.franciscanmissionservice.catholic.edu; Franciscan Mission Service.

Frontline Report, bm; 23 Bliss Ave., Tenafly, NJ 07670; (201) 567-0450; www.smafathers.org; Society of African Missions.

Graymoor Today, m; P.O. Box 301, Garrison, NY 10524-0301; (845) 424-3671; www.atonementfriars.org.

Happiness, q; 567 Salem End Rd., Framingham, MA 01702-5599; (508) 879-2541; www.sonsofmary.com; Sons of Mary, Health of the Sick.

Harmony, 3 times a year; 800 N. Country Club Rd., Tucson, AZ 85716; (520) 325-6401; Benedictine Srs. of Perpetual Adoration.

Healing & Hope, 9480 North De Mazenod Dr., Belleville, IL 62223-1160; (618) 398-4848; www.snows.org.

Heart Beats, 169 Cummins Hwy., Roslindale, MA 02131; (617) 325-3322.

Heart to Heart, twice a year; St. Vincent Archabbey, 300 Fraser Purchase Rd., Latrobe, PA 15650; (724) 805-2601; www.stvincentstore.com; Benedictines of St. Vincent Archabbey.

HLI Reports, m; 4 Family Life, Front Royal, VA 22630; Human Life International.

HN People, bm; 158 W. 27th St., New York, NY 10001; (212) 924-1451; www.hnp.org/publications; Franciscans of Holy Name Province.

HNP Today, w; 158 W. 27th St., New York, NY 10001; (212) 924-1451; www.hnp.org/publications; Franciscans of Holy Name Province.

ICSC Commitment, 1275 K St. N.W., Suite 980, Washington, DC 20005-4006; (202) 289-1093; www.catholicstewardship.org.

Immaculate Heart of Mary Shrine Bulletin, 3 times a year; Mountain View Road, P.O. Box 976, Washington, NJ 07882-0976; (908) 689-1700; www.ewtn.com/bluearmy.

Initiatives, bm; P.O. Box 291102, Chicago, IL 60629; (773) 776-9036; www.catholiclabor.org/ncl.htm; National Center for the Laity.

Interchange, Assisi Heights, 1001 14 St., NW, #100, Rochester, MN 55901-2525; (507) 529-3523; www.rochesterfranciscan.org; Rochester Franciscan Sisters.

It's Our World, 4 times during school year; 366 Fifth Ave., New York, NY 10001; (212) 563-8700; www.hcakids.org; Young Catholics in Mission.

Journey, The, q; 210 W. 31st St., New York, NY 10001-2876; (212) 714-0950; www.capuchin.org; Province of St. Mary of Capuchin Order.

Joyful Noiseletter, The, m; P.O. Box 895, Portage, MI 49081-0895; (616) 324-0990; www.joyfulnoiseletter.com; Fellowship of Merry Christians.

Jubilee, q; 3900 Harewood Rd., NE, Washington, DC 20017; (202) 635-5400; www.jp2cc.org; John Paul II Cultural Center.

Knightline, 18 times a year; 1 Columbus Plaza, New Haven, CT 06510-3326; (203) 772-2130; www.kofc.org; Knights of Columbus Supreme Council.

Laity and Family Life Updates, bm; 20 Archbishop May Dr., St. Louis, MO, 63119; (314) 792-7173; www.stlcatholics.org.

Land of Cotton, q; 2048 W. Fairview Ave., Montgomery, AL 39196; (205) 265-6791; City of St. Jude.

Law Reports, q; 4455 Woodson Rd., St. Louis, MO 63134; (314) 427-2500; Catholic Health Association.

LCWR Update, m; 8808 Cameron St., Silver Spring, MD 20910; (301) 588-4955; www.lcwr.org; Leadership Conference of Women Religious.

Legatus, m; P.O. Box 511, Ann Arbor, MI 48106; (734) 930-3854; www.legatus.org; Legatus.

Let's Talk! (English edition), **Hablemos!** (Spanish edition), bm; 3031 Fourth St. N.E., Washington, DC 20017-1102; (202) 832-5022; www.prison-ministry.org; prison ministries of Paulist National Catholic Evangelization Assn.

Letter to the Seven Churches, bm; 1516 Jerome St., Lansing, MI 48912; (517) 372-6222; Catholic Charismatics.

Life at Risk, 10 times a year; 3211 Fourth St. N.E., Washington, DC 20017; (202) 541-3070; Pro-Life Activities Committee, USCCB.

Life Insight, m; 3211 Fourth St. N.E., Washington, DC 20017; (202) 541-3070; Committee for Pro-Life Activities, USCCB.

Liturgical Images, m; P.O. Box 2225, Hickory, NC 28603; (828) 327-3225.

Loyola World, 22 times a year; 820 North Michigan Ave., Chicago, IL, 60611; (312) 915-6157; www.luc.edu.

Magnificat, three times a year; 6559 State Hwy. M-26, Eagle Harbor, MI, 49950; (906) 289-4388 (fax); www.societystjohn.com.

Malvern Retreat House, q; P.O. Box 315, Malvern, PA 19355-0315; (610) 644-0400; www.malvernretreat.org; Laymen's Retreat League.

Maronite Voice, The, annual; 4611 Salder Rd. Glen Allen, VA 23060; (804) 270-7234; www.stmaron.org. Maronite eparchies of Brooklyn and Our Lady of Lebanon.

Maronites Today, m; P.O. Box 1891, Austin, TX 78767-1891; (512) 458-3693; www.eparchyla.org; Eparchy of Our Lady of Los Angeles.

Martyrs' Shrine Message, twice a year; P.O. Box 7, Hwy. 12, Midland, ON L4R 4K6, Canada; www.martyrs-shrine.com.

Medical Mission Sisters News, q; 8400 Pine Road, Philadelphia, PA 19111; (215) 742-6100; www.medicalmissionsisters.org.

Messenger of St. Joseph's Union, The, 3 times a year; 108 Bedell St., Staten Island, NY 10309; (718) 984-9296.

Mission, The, three times a year; 90 Cherry Lane, Hicksville, NY 11801-6299; (516) 733-7042; www.catholiccharities.cc; Catholic Charities.

Mission Messenger, The, q; P.O. Box 610, Thoreau, NM, 87323; (505) 862-7847; www.stbonaventuremission.org; St. Bonaventure Indian Mission and School.

Missionaries of Africa Report, q; 1624 21st St. N.W., Washington, DC 20009; (202) 232-5154; Society of Missionaries of Africa (White Fathers).

Mission Update, bm; 3029 Fourth St. N.E., Washington, DC 20017; (202) 832-3112; www.uscatholicmission.org.

Mountain View, q.; 8501 Bailey Rd., Darien, IL 60561; (630) 969-5050; Lay Carmelite Headquarters.

National Holy Name Newsletter, bm; 53 Laux Street, Buffalo, NY 14206-2218; (716) 847-6419; www.members.aol.com/nahns.

NCPD National Update, q; 415 Michigan Ave. N.E., #240, Washington, DC 20017; (202) 529-2933; www.ncpd.org; National Catholic Office for Persons with Disabilities.

Neighbors, Committee on Home Missions, q.; 3211 Fourth St. N.E., Washington, D.C. 20017; (202) 541-5400; Bishops' Committee on Home Missions.

News and Ideas, q.; 9480 North De Mazenod Dr., Belleville, IL 62223; (618) 398-4848; www.snows.org; Missionary Oblates of Mary Immaculate.

News and Views, q; 3900 Westminster Pl., St. Louis, MO 63108; (314) 533-0320; www.sacredheartprogram.org; Sacred Heart Program.

Newsletter of the Bureau of Catholic Indian Missions, 10 times a year; 2021 H St. N.W., Washington, DC 20006; (202) 331-8542.

North Coast Catholic, bi-monthly; P.O. Box 1297, Santa Rosa, CA 95402; (707) 566-3302; www.santarosacatholic.org; Santa Rosa diocese.

Nuestra Parroquia (Spanish-English), m; 205 W. Monroe St., Chicago, IL 60606; (312) 236-7782; www.hmrc.claretianpubs.org; Claretians.

Oblates Mission Friendship Club News, q; 9480 North De Mazenod Dr., Belleville, IL 62223-1160; (618) 398-4848; www.oblatesusa.org; Missionary Oblates of Mary Immaculate.

Origins, 48 times a year; 3211 Fourth St. N.E., Washington, DC 20017; (202) 541-3284; Catholic News Service.

Overview, m; 205 W. Monroe St., 6th Floor, Chicago, IL 60606; (312) 609-8880; Thomas More Assn.

Paulist, Today, q; 415 W. 59th St., New York, NY 10019; (212) 265-3209; www.paulist.org.

Peace Times, 3-4 times a year; P.O. Box 248, Bellevue, WA 98009-0248; (425) 451-1770.

Pentecost Today, q; P.O. Box 628, Locust Grove, VA 22508-0628; (540) 972-0225; www.nsc-chariscenter.org.

Perspectives, q; 912 Market St., La Crosse, WI 54601; (608) 791-5289; www.fspa.org.

Pilgrim, The, q; 136 Shrine Rd., Auriesville, NY 12016; (518) 853-3033; Shrine of North American Martyrs.

Poverello, q; 220 37th St., Pittsburgh, PA 15201; (412) 682-1300; www.capuchin.com; Capuchin Franciscans.

Priests for Life, bm; P.O. Box 141172, Staten Island, NY 10314; (718) 980-4400; www.priestsforlife.org.

Proclaim, 10 times a year; 3211 Fourth St. N.E., Washington, DC 20017-1194; (202) 541-3237; www.usccb.org.

Quarterly, The, q; 209 W. Fayette St., Baltimore, MD 21201; (410) 951-7455; www.catholicrelief.org; Catholic Relief Services.

Religious Life, m (bm, May-Aug.); P.O. Box 41007, Chicago, IL 60641; (312) 267-1195; www.ewtn.com/religious life; Institute on Religious Life.

RSCJ Newsletter, m; 1235 Otis St. N.E., Washington, DC 20017-2516; (202) 526-6258; www.rscj.org; Religious of Sacred Heart.

St. Anthony's Newsletter, m; 103 St. Francis Blvd., Mt. St. Francis, IN 47146; (812) 923-5250; Conventual Franciscans.

St. Joseph's Parish Life Quarterly, q; 1382 Highland Ave., Needham, MA 02192; (617) 444-0245.

Sacred Ground, three times a year; 1 Elmwood Ave., Kansas City, KS 66103-3719; (913) 384-6500; www.cfcusa.org; Christian Foundation for Children and Aging.

San Francisco Charismatics, m; 2555 17th Ave., San Francisco, CA 94116; (415) 664-8481; www.sfspirit.com.

SCJ News, 9 times a year; P.O. Box 289, Hales Corners, WI 53130-0289; (414) 427-4266; www.scjusa.net. Sacred Heart Fathers and Brothers.

SCRC Spirit, The, bm; 9795 Cabrini Dr., #105, Burbank, CA, 91504-1739; (818) 771-1361; www.scrc.org.

Sharing & Caring, q; 4960 Salem Ave., Dayton,

OH 45416; (937) 274-2707; www.preciousbloodsistersdayton.org. Precious Blood Sisters.

Shrine Advocates Newsletter, q; 9480 N. De Mazenod Dr., Belleville, IL 62223; (618) 398-4848; www.oblatesusa.org.

Spirit & The Bide, The, m; 8300 Morganford Rd., St. Louis, MO 63123; (314) 792-7070; www.stlcharismatic.org.

Spiritual Book Associates, 8 times a year; Notre Dame, IN 46556-0428; (219) 287-2838; www.spiritualbookassoc.org.

Squires Newsletter, m; One Columbus Plaza, New Haven, CT 06510-3326; (203) 752-4402; Columbian Squires.

SSpS Mission, q; P.O. Box 6026, Techny, IL 60082-6026; (847) 441-0126; www.ssps-usa.org; Holy Spirit Missionary Sisters.

Tidings, Washington Theological Union, 3 times a year; 6896 Laurel St. N.W., Washington, DC 20012; (202) 726-8800; www.wtu.edu.

Touchstone, q; NFPC Office, 333 N. Michigan Ave., Suite 1205, Chicago, IL 60601; (312) 442-9700; www.nfpc.org; National Federation of Priests' Councils.

Trinity Missions Report, q; 9001 New Hampshire Ave., Silver Spring, MD 20903; (301) 434-6761.

Triumph of the Past, m.; P.O. Box 29535, Columbus, OH 43229; (614) 261-1300.

Unda USA Newsletter, q; 901 Irving Ave., Dayton, OH 45409-2316; (937) 229-2303; www.undausa.org.

Vision: National Association of Catholic Chaplains, 10 times a year; P.O. Box 070473, Milwaukee, WI 53207-0473; (414) 483-4898; www.nacc.org.

Voices, 2 times a year; 1625 Rutherford Lane, Bldg. D, Austin, TX 78754-5105; (512) 339-7123; Volunteers for Educational and Social Services.

Voices in Mission and Ministry, q.; 1257 E. Siena Heights Dr., Adrian, MI 49221; (517) 266-3400; www.adriansisters.org; Adrian Dominicans.

Woodstock Report, q; Georgetown University, Box 571137, Washington, DC 20057; (202) 687-3532; www.georgetown.edu/centers/woodstock; Woodstock Theological Center.

Word One, 5 times a year; 205 W. Monroe St., Chicago, IL 60606; (312) 236-7782; www.wordone.org; Claretians.

Xaverian Missions Newsletter, bm; P.O. Box 5857, Holliston, MA 01746; (508) 429-2144; Xaverian Missionary Fathers.

Your Edmundite Missions Newsletter, bm; 1428 Broad St., Selma, AL 36701; (334) 872-2359; www.edmunditemissions.com; Southern Missions of Society of St. Edmund.

Youth Update, m; 28 W. Liberty St., Cincinnati, OH 45210; (513) 241-5615; www.americancatholic.org.

Zeal Newsletter, 3 times a year; P.O. Box 86, Allegany, NY 14706; (716) 373-1130; Franciscan Sisters of Allegany.

BOOKS

The Catholic Almanac, a; Our Sunday Visitor, Inc., 200 Noll Plaza, Huntington, IN 46750, publisher; editorial offices, 200 Noll Plaza, Huntington, IN 46750; (260) 444-4398; www.catholicalmanac.com; first edition, 1904.

The Official Catholic Directory, a; P.J. Kenedy & Sons in association with R.R. Bowker, a Reed Reference Publishing Company, 121 Chanlon Rd., New Providence, NJ 07974; (847) 966-8278; first edition, 1817.

BOOK CLUBS

Catholic Book Club (1928), 106 W. 56th St., New York, NY 10019; (212) 581-4640; www.americapress.org/cbc.htm; sponsors the Campion Award.

Catholic Digest Book Club (1954), 2115 Summit Ave., St. Paul, MN 55105-1081; (651) 962-6748.

Spiritual Book Associates (1934), Ave Maria Press Building, P.O. Box 428, Notre Dame, IN 46556; (219) 287-2838.

Thomas More Book Club (1939), Thomas More Association, 205 W. Monroe St., Sixth Floor, Chicago, IL 60606; (312) 609-8880.

General Publishers

(*Source:* Catholic Press Directory, Almanac *Survey.*)

Our Sunday Visitor Publishing: 200 Noll Plaza, Huntington IN 46750; (800) 348-2440, (260) 356-8400; e-mail: booksed@osv.com.

Abbey Press: One Caring Place, Saint Meinrad, IN 47577; (812) 357-8215; www.carenotes.com.

Abingdon Press: 201 8th Ave. South, Nashville, TN 37202; (615) 749-6615; www.abingdonpress.com.

ACTA Publications: 5559 Howard St., Skokie, IL 60077; (847) 676-2282; www.actapublications.com.

Alba House/St. Pauls: 2187 Victory Blvd. Staten Island, NY 10314; (718) 698-2759; www.alba-house.com

Alleluia Press: P.O. Box 103, Allendale, NJ 07401; (201) 327-3513.

American Catholic Press: 16565 South State St., South Holland, IL 60473; (708) 331-5485; www.acpress.org.

AMI Press, The Blue Army of Our Lady of Fatima: Mountain View Rd., Washington, NJ 07882; (908) 213-2223.

Apostolate for Family Consecration: 3375 County Rd. 36, Bloomingdale, OH 43910; (740) 765-5500; www.familyland.org.

Ascension Press: P.O. Box 1990, West Chester, PA 19380; 610-696-7795; www.ascensionpress.com

Ave Maria Press, Inc.: PO Box 428, Notre Dame IN 46556; (574) 287-2831; e-mail: avemariapress.1@nd.edu.

Angelus Press: 2915 Forest Ave., Kansas City, MO 64109; (816) 753-3150; www.anguspress.org.

BlueBridge: 240 W. 35th St., Suite 509, N.Y., N.Y. 10001; (212) 244-4166; www.bluebridgebooks.com.

Cathedral Foundation Press: P.O. Box 777, Baltimore, MD 21203; (443) 263-0248; www.catholicfoundation.org.

Catholic Health Assoc.: 4455 Woodson Rd., St. Louis, MO 63134; (314) 253-3477; www.chusa.org.

Catholic Library Assoc.: 100 N. St., Suite 224, Pittsfield, MA 01201; (413) 443-2252; www.cathla.org.

Catholic News Agency: 1300 S. Steele St., Denver, CO 80210; (303) 715-3265; www.catholicnewsagency.com.

Catholic News Service: 3211 Fourth St N.E., Washington DC 20017; (202) 541-3250; www.catholicnews.com.

Catholic Relief Services: 209 West Fayette St., Baltimore MD 21201; (410) 625-2220.

Catholic University of America Press: 620 Michigan Ave. NE, Washington, DC 20064; (202) 319-5052; www.cuapress.cua.edu.

The Christophers: 5 Hanover Sq., 11th Floor, New York NY 10004; (212) 759-4050; www.christophers.org.

Cistercian Publ.: St. John's Abbey, P.O. Box 7500, Collegeville, MN 56321; (320) 363-3096; www.cistercian-publications.org.

Claretian Publications: 205 West Monroe St., Chicago IL 60606; (800) 328-6515, (312) 236-7782; e-mail: editors@uscatholic.org.

Clarity Publishing, Inc.: PO Box 758, Latham NY 12110-3510; (518) 783-0058.

Couple to Couple League: P.O. Box 111184, Cincinnati, OH 45211; (513) 471-2000; www.ccli.org.

Doubleday: 1540 Broadway, New York, NY 10036; (212) 782-9392; www.randomhouse.com.

Eerdmans: 255 Jefferson Ave., SE, Grand Rapids, 49503; (616) 459-4591; www.eerdmans.com.

Emmaus Road: 827 N. Fourth St., Steubenville, OH 43952; (740) 283-2880.

Franciscan Mission Associates: PO Box 598, Mount Vernon NY 10551-0598; (914) 664-5604.

Franciscan Press: Quincy University, 1800 College Ave., Quincy, IL 62301; (217) 228-5670; www.qufranciscanpress.com.

Georgetown University Press: 3240 Prospect St., NW, Washington, DC 20007; (202) 687-5889; www.press.georgetown.edu.

Gingerbread House: 602 Montauk Hwy., Westhampton Beach, NY 11978; (631) 288-5119; www.gingerbreadbooks.com.

ICS Publ.: 2131 Lincoln Rd. NE, Washington, DC 20002; (202) 832-8489; www.icspublications.org.

Ignatius Press: 2515 McAllister St., San Francisco, CA 94118; (415) 387-2324; www.ignatius.com.

Liguori Publications: One Liguori Drive, Liguori MO 63057; (636) 464-2500; www.liguori.org.

Liturgical Press: St. John's Abbey, P.O. Box 7500, Collegeville, MN 56321; (320) 363-2213; www.litpress.org.

Little Books: P.O. Box 6009, Saginaw, MI 48608; (989) 797-6653; www.littlebooks.org.

Liturgical Press: St. John's Abbey, P.O. Box 7500, Collegeville, MN 56321; (320) 363-2213; www.litpress.org.

Liturgical Publications Inc. Resource Center: 2875 S. James Dr., New Berlin, WI 53151; (262) 785-2469; www.4lpi.com.

Loyola Press: 3441 North Ashland Avenue, Chicago, IL 60657; (800) 621-1008; www.loyolapress.org.

Marquette University Press: 1415 West Wisconisn Ave., Milwaukee, WI 53233; (414) 288-1564; www.marquette.edu/mupress/.

Missionary Oblates of Mary Immaculate: 9480 North De Mazenod Dr., Belleville, IL 62223-1160; (888) 330-6264; e-mail: mami@oblatesusa.org.

National Catholic Bioethics Center (NCBC): 6399 Drexel Rd., Philadelphia, PA 19151; (215) 877-2660; www.ncbcenter.org.

Notre Dame Press, University of: 310 Flanner Hall, Notre Dame, IN 46556; (219) 631-6346; www.undpress.edu.

Orbis Books: P.O. Box 308, Maryknoll, NY 10545; (914) 941-7636; www.orbisbooks.com.

Pauline Books & Media: 50 St. Paul's Avenue, Boston MA 02130; (617) 522-8911; www.pauline.org.

Paulist National Catholic Evangelization Association: 3031 Fourth Street N.E., Washington DC 20017; (800) 237-5515, (202) 832-5022; e-mail: pncea@pncea.org.

Paulist Press: 997 Macarthur Blvd. Mahwah, NJ 07430; (201) 825-7300; www.paulistpress.com.

Pittsburgh Press, University of: 3400 Forbes Ave., 5th Floor Eureka, Pittsburgh, PA 15260; (412) 383-2456; www.pitt.edu/~press.

Pontifical Mission Societies in the United States: 366 Fifth Ave., New York NY 10001; (800) 431-2222, (212) 563-8700; e-mail: propfaith@aol.com.

Resource Publications, Inc.: 160 E. Virginia St., #290,

San Jose, CA 95112; (408) 286-8505; www.rpinet.com.

Resurrection Press: 77 West End Rd., Totowa, NJ 07512; (973) 890-2400; www.catholicbookpublishing.com.

St. Anthony Messenger Press: 28 W Liberty St, Cincinnati OH 45202; (513) 241-5615; www.americancatholic.org.

St. Joseph's University Press: 5600 City Ave., Philadelphia, PA 19131; (610) 660-3400; www.sju.edu/sjupress.

Scepter: P.O. Box 211, New York, NY 10018; (212) 354-0670; www.scepterpublishers.org.

Servant Publications: 1143 Highland Dr., Suite E, Ann Arbor, MI 48108; (734) 677-6490; www.servantpub.com.

Sophia Institute Press: Box 5284, Manchester, NH 03108; (603) 641-9344; www.sophiainstitute.com.

Twenty-Third Publications: P.O. Bix 180, Mystic, CT 06355; (860) 437-3012; www.twentythirdpublications.com.

USCCB Publishing: 3211 Fourth St. NE, Washington, DC 20017; (202) 541-3090; www.usccb.org.

CANADIAN CATHOLIC PUBLICATIONS

(*Principal source: 2012 Catholic Press Directory.*)

Newspapers

B. C. Catholic, The, w; 150 Robson St., Vancouver, BC V6B 2A7; (604) 683-0281; www.bcc.rcav.org.

Catholic Register, The (national), w; 1155 Younge St., Suite 401, Toronto, ON M4T 1W2; (416) 934-3410; www.catholicregister.org; lay edited.

Western Catholic Reporter, w.; 8421 101 Ave. NW, Edmonton, AB T6A 0L1; (780) 465-8030; www.wcr.ab.ca.

Magazines, Other Periodicals

L'Almanach Populaire Catholique, a; 9795 St. Anne Blvd., St. Anne de Beaupre, QC G0A3C0; (418) 827-4538.

ANNALS of St. Anne de Beaupre, The, m; Box 1000, Ste. Anne de Beaupre, QC G0A 3C0; (418) 827-4538; Basilica of St. Anne.

Apostolat, bm; 8844 Notre-Dame Est, Montréal, QC H1L 3M4; (514) 351-9310; Oblates of Mary Immaculate, CMO (*Centre Missionnaire Oblat*).

Bread of Life, The, bm; P.O. Box 395, Hamilton, ON L8N 3H8; (905) 529-4496; www.breadoflife.ca.

Canadian Catholic Review, The, St. Joseph's College, University of Alberta, Edmonton, AB T6G 2J5; (403) 492-7681.

Canadian League, The, q; 1-160 Murray Park Rd., Winnipeg, MB R3J 3X5; (204) 927-2310; www.cwl.ca; Catholic Women's League of Canada.

Caravan, q; 90 Parent Ave., Ottawa, ON K1N 7B1; (613) 241-9461; www.cccb.ca; Canadian Conference of Catholic Bishops.

Celebrate! (Novalis), bm; St. Paul University, 223 Main St., Ottawa, ON K1S 1C4; (780) 451-2228.

Companion Magazine, m; 695 Coxwell Ave., Suite 600, Toronto, ON M4C 5R6; (416) 690-5611; www.franciscan.on.ca; Conventual Franciscan Fathers.

Compass — A Jesuit Journal, bm (Jan.-Nov.); Box 400, Stn. F, 50 Charles St. East, Toronto, ON M4Y 2L8; (416) 921-0653; www.io.org/ngvanv/compass/com-phome.html.

CRC Bulletin (French-English), q; 219 Argyle Ave., Ottawa, ON K2P 2H4; (613) 236-0824; www.crcn.ca; Canadian Religious Conference.

L'Église Canadienne (French), 11 times a year; 6255 rue Hutchison, Bureau 103, Montreal, QC H2V 4C7; (514)

278-3020; www.novalis.ca.

Fatima Crusader, q; P.O. Box 602, Fort Erie, ON L2A 4M7; (905) 871-7607; www.fatima.org.

Global Village Voice, The, q; 10 St. Mary St., Suite 420, Toronto, ON M4Y 1P9; (416) 922-1592; Canadian Organization for Development and Peace.

Kateri (English-French), q; P.O. Box 70, Kahnawake, QC J0L 1B0; (450) 638-1546.

Le Messager de Saint Antoine (French), 10 times a year; Lac-Bouchette, QC G0W 1V0; (418) 348-6344.

Messenger of the Sacred Heart, m; 661 Greenwood Ave., Toronto, ON M4J 4B3; (416) 466-1195; Apostleship of Prayer.

Mission Canada, q; 201-1155 Younge St., Toronto, ON M4T 1W2; (416) 934-3424; www.missioncanada.ca.

Missions Étrangères (French), bm; 180 Place Juge-Desnoyers, Laval, QC H7G 1A4; (450) 667-4190; www.smelaval.org.

Nouvel Informateur Catholiqué, Le, semi-monthly; 6550 Rte 125, Rawdon, QC J0K 1S0; (450) 834-8503.

Oratory, bm; 3800 Ch. Queen Mary, Montreal, QC H3V 1H6; (514) 733-8211; www.saint-joseph.org.

Our Family, m; P.O. Box 249, Battleford, SK; S0M 0E0; (306) 937-7771; www.ourfamilymagazine.com; Oblates of Mary Immaculate.

Prêtre et Pasteur (French), m; 4450 St. Hubert St., #500, Montreal, QC H2J 2W9; (514) 525-6210.

Prieres Missionaires, m; Missionaires de la Consolata, 2505 Boulevard Gouin ouest, Montréal, QC H3M 1B5; (514) 334-1910; www.consolata.org.

Relations (French), 10 times a year; 25 Rue Jarry Ouest, Montreal, QC H2P 1S6; (514) 387-2541.

Reveil Missionaire, bm; Missionaire de la Consolata, 2505 Boulevard Gouin ouest, Montréal, QC H3M 1B5; (514) 334-1910; www.consolata.org.

La Revue d'Sainte Anne de Beaupre (French), m; P.O. Box 1000, Ste. Anne de Beaupre, Québec G0A 3C0; (418) 827-4538.

Scarboro Missions, 9 times a year; 2685 Kingston Rd., Scarboro, ON M1M 1M4; (416) 261-7135; www.web.net/~sfms.

Spiritan Missionary News, q; 121 Victoria Park Ave., Toronto, ON M4E 3S2; (416) 698-2003; www.spiritans.com.

Unity, q; 308 Young St., Montréal, QC H3C 2G2; (514) 937-5973.

INTERNATIONAL CATHOLIC PERIODICALS

(Principal source: Catholic Almanac *survey. Included are English-language Catholic periodicals published outside the U.S.)*

African Ecclesial Review (AFER), bm; Gaba Publications, P.O. Box 4002, Eldoret, Kenya.

Australasian Catholic Record, q; 99 Albert Rd., Strathfield 2135, New South Wales, Australia.

Christ to the World, 5 times a year; Via di Propaganda 1-C, 00187, Rome, Italy.

Christian Orient, q; P.B. 1 Vadavathoor, Kottayam 686010, Kerala, India.

Doctrine and Life, m; Dominican Publications, 42 Parnell Sq., Dublin 1, Ireland.

Downside Review, q; Downside Abbey, Stratton on the Fosse, Bath, BA3 4RH, England.

East Asian Pastoral Review, q; East Asian Pastoral Institute, P.O. Box 221, U.P. Campus, 1101 Quezon City, Philippines.

Furrow, The, m; St. Patrick's College, Maynooth, Ireland.

Heythrop Journal, q; Heythrop College, Kensington Sq., London W8 5HQ, England (editorial office); published by Blackwell Publishers, 108 Cowley Rd., Oxford, OX4 1JF, England.

Holy Land Magazine, q; P.O. Box 186, 91001 Jerusalem, Israel; illustrated.

Irish Biblical Studies, The, q; Union Theological College, 108 Botanic Ave., Belfast BT7 1JT, N. Ireland.

Irish Journal of Sociology, The, a; St. Patrick's College, Maynooth, Ireland.

Irish Theological Quarterly, q; St. Patrick's College, Maynooth, Ireland.

L'Osservatore Romano, w; Vatican City. (*See above* under **U.S. Newspapers.**)

Louvain Studies, q; Peeters Publishers, Bondgenotenlaan 153, B-3000, Leuven, Belgium.

Lumen Vitae (French, with English summaries), q; International Center for Studies in Religious Education, 186, rue Washington, B-1050 Brussels, Belgium.

Mediaeval Studies, a; Pontifical Institute of Mediaeval Studies, 59 Queen's Park Crescent East, Toronto, ON M5S 2C4, Canada.

Month, m; 114 Mount St., London WIY 6AH, England.

Music and Liturgy, bm; The Editor, 33 Brockenhurst Rd., Addiscombe Croydan, Surrey CRO 7DR, England.

New Blackfriars, m; edited by English Dominicans, Blackfriars, Oxford OX1 3LY, England.

Omnis Terra (English Edition), m; Pontifical Missionary Union, Congregation for the Evangelization of Peoples, Via di Propaganda 1/c, 00187 Rome, Italy.

One in Christ, q; Edited at Turvey Abbey, Turvey, Bedfordshire MK43 8DE, England.

Priests & People (formerly **The Clergy Review**), 11 times a year; Blackfriars, Buckingham Rd., Cambridge CB3 0DD, England.

Recusant History, bi-annual; Catholic Record Society, 12 Melbourne Pl., Wolsingham, Durham DL13 3EH, England.

Religious Life Review, bm; Dominican Publications, 42 Parnell Sq., Dublin 1, Ireland.

Scripture in Church, q; Dominican Publications, 42 Parnell Sq., Dublin 1, Ireland.

Southwark Liturgy Bulletin, q; The Editor, 10 Claremont Rd., Maidstone, Kent ME14 5L2, England.

Spearhead, 5 times a year; Gaba Publications, P.O. Box 4002, Eldoret, Kenya.

Spirituality, bm; Dominican Publications, 42 Parnell Sq., Dublin 1, Ireland.

Tablet, The, w; 1 King Street Cloisters, Clifton Walk, London W60QZ, England; 44(1)-20-8748-8484.

Way, The, q; 114 Mount St., London W1Y6AN, England.

CATHOLIC NEWS AGENCIES

(Sources: International Catholic Union of the Press, Geneva; Catholic Press Association, U.S.)

Argentina: *Agencia Informativa Catolica Argentina* (AICA), av. Rivadavia, 413, 40 Casilla de Correo Central 2886, 1020 Buenos Aires.

Austria: *Katholische Presse-Agentur* (Kathpress), Singerstrasse 7/6/2, 1010 Vienna 1.

Belgium: *Centre d'Information de Presse* (CIP), 35 Chaussée de Haecht, 1030 Brussels.

Bolivia: *Agencia Noticias Fides*, ANF, Casilla 5782, La Paz. *ERBOL*, Casilla 5946, La Paz.

Chile: *Agencia informativa y de comunicaciones* (AIC Chile), Brasil 94, Santiago.

Croatia: *Christian Information Service*, Marulicev 14, PP 434, 410001 Zagreb.

Germany: *Katholische Nachrichten Agentur* (KNA), Adenauer Allee 134, 5300 Bonn 1.

Greece: *Agence TYPOS*, Rue Acharnon 246, Athens 815.

Hong Kong: *UCA-News*, P.O. Box 69626, Kwun Tong (Hong Kong).

Hungary: *Magyar Kurir*, Milkszath ter 1, 1088, Budapest.

India: *South Asian Religious News* (SAR-News), PB 6236, Mazagaon, Bombay 400 010.

Italy: *Servizio Informazioni Religiosa* (SIR), Via di Porta Cavalleggeri 143, I-00165 Roma.

Centrum Informationis Catolicae (CIC-Roma), via Delmonte de la Farina, 30/4, 00186 Roma.

Rome Reports: a private and independent international television news agency based in Rome, Italy, specializing in covering the Pope and the Vatican; produces a weekly program called "Rome Reports, The World seen from the Vatican." Address: Via della Conciliazione 44, 00193, Rome, Italy; www.romereports.com.

Zenit, a non-profit international news agency that covers the life of the Church. Innovative Media Inc. is listed officially as the publisher and editor of ZENIT in all language-editions.

Peru: ACI-PRENSA, A.P. 040062, Lima.

Switzerland: *Katholische Internationale Presse-Agentur* (KIPA), Case Postale 1054 CH 1701, Fribourg.

Centre International de Reportages et d'Information Culturelle (CIRIC), Chemin Clochetons 8, P.O. Box 1000, Lausanne.

United States of America: *Catholic News Service* (CNS), 3211 Fourth St. N.E., Washington, DC 20017; (202) 541-3250; www.catholicnews.com.

Catholic News Agency (CNA), 3392 S. Broadway, Englewood, CO 80113; (303) 997-8563; www.catholicnewsagency.com

Vatican City State: Vatican Information Service (VIS), a news service, established by the Holy See Press Office in 1991, that provides information on the activities of the Holy Father and the Roman Curia. The VIS transmits news from Monday through Friday throughout the year, except during the month of August. It is available in English, Italian, Spanish, and French; press.catholica.va.

U.S. PRESS SERVICES

Catholic News Service (CNS), established in 1920 (NC News Service), provides a worldwide daily news report by satellite throughout the U.S. and Canada and by wire and computer links into several foreign countries, and by mail to other clients, serving Catholic periodicals and broadcasters including Vatican Radio in about 40 countries. CNS also provides feature and photo services and publishes "Origins," a weekly documentary service and Catholic Trends, a fortnightly newsletter, the weekly TV and Movie Guide and Movie Guide Monthly. CNS maintains a full time bureau in Rome. It is a division of the United States Catholic Conference. Address: 3211 Fourth St. N.E., Washington, DC 20017; (202) 541-3250; www.catholicnews.com.

Catholic News Agency (CNA), established in 2004 in response to Pope John Paul II's call for a "New Evangelization. CNA provides coverage of events in the life of the Church and offers free access to Catholic dioceses, parishes, and websites. The agency is funded chiefly by donations and gifts from readers and benefactors. Address: 3392 S. Broadway, Englewood, CO 80113; (303) 997-8563; www.catholicnewsagency.com

EWTNews, 5817 Old Leeds Road, Irondale, AL 35210; 205-271-2900; www.ewtn.com. Exclusive interviews, investigative reports, live coverage of special events and cultural reporting weekly on the World Over Live newsmagazine. Daily coverage of world news from a Catholic perspective.

Spanish-Language Service, A weekly news summary provided by Catholic News Service, used by a number of Catholic newspapers. Some papers carry features of their own in Spanish.

Religion News Service (RNS) provides coverage of all religions as well as ethics, spirituality and moral issues. Founded in 1934 (as the Religious News Service) by the National Conference of Christian and Jews as an independent agency, RNS became an editorially independent subsidiary of the United Methodist Reporter, an interfaith publishing company, in 1983. It was acquired by Newhouse News Service in 1994. Address: 1930 18th Street NW, Suite B2, Washington, DC 20009; (202) 463.8777; www.religionnews.com.

RADIO, TELEVISION, THEATER

(The following listings are as of June 1, 2013. Sources, Catholic Almanac survey. Telephone and web addresses are listed as available.)

Radio

Catholic Radio Association: an association comprised primarily of the majority of Catholic radio stations in the United States and Catholic program providers united to advance the apostolate of Catholic radio. The Mission Statement states: "The Catholic Radio Association seeks to bring together Catholic radio apostolates, program providers and the hierarchy of the Catholic Church in order that this means of social communication be used effectively and in obedience to the decrees of the Second Vatican Council and the magisterium of the Church, especially as expressed in the words of Pope John Paul II." The Catholic Radio Association, 121 Broad St., Charleston, SC 29401; 843) 853-2300; www.catholicradioassociation.org.

Ave Maria Radio: Ave Maria Radio employs radio, internet and other media to offer news, analysis, teaching, devotions and music. Programs include Teresa Tomeo and Al Kresta. Ave Maria Radio, P.O. Box 504, Ann Arbor, MI 48106; (734) 930-5200; www.avemariaradio.com.

Catholic Answers Radio: Produced by Catholic Answers; programming includes "Catholic Answers Live" is a two hour, daily, call-in radio program, hosted by Patrick Coffin. Catholic Answers, 2020 Gillespie Way, El Cajon, CA 92020 USA Main: 619-387-7200; www.catholic.com.

EWTN Global Catholic Radio Network (formerly known as WEWN), 5817 Old Leeds Road, Irondale, AL 35210; 205-271-2900; www.ewtn.com; the first 24-hour U.S. Catholic radio network, launched in 1996.

Relevant Radio: Relevant Radio exists to assist the Church in the New Evangelization by providing relevant programming through a media platform to help people bridge the gap between faith and everyday life. Programming includes "Morning Air" and the "The Drew Mariani Show." Relevant Radio PO Box 10707, Green Bay, WI 54307-0707; (920) 884-1460; www.relevantradio.com.

Immaculate Heart Radio: A network of approximately 30 radio stations in the western part of the United States; started in 1997 with K-IHM, named for the Immaculate Heart of Mary, in Reno, Nevada. Programming includes an extensive array of EWTN programs. Immaculate Heart Radio, 3256 Penryn Road, Suite 100, Loomis, CA 95650-8052; (888) 887-7120; (916) 535-0500, ihradio.com

Radio Maria: Part of the international Radio Maria Association founded in Milan, Italy, in 1987. Radio Maria in the U.S. began in 2000 with a station in Alexandria, LA; it has grown to more than ten stations and offers a variety of programming. Radio Maria, 601 Washington St., Alexandria, LA 71301; 888-408-0201; radiomaria.us.

Vatican Radio: *See* under **Vatican City State**.

Stations and Programs

Christopher Radio Program: 14-minute interview series, "Christopher Closeup" weekly and "Christopher Minutes" daily, on 400 stations. 12 E. 48th St., New York, NY 10017; (212) 759-4050; www.christophers.org.

Journeys Thru Rock: Produced in cooperation with the Department of Communication, USCCB. A 15-minute weekly program currently employing a youth-oriented music and commentary format (ABC).

Sirius Satellite Radio: Offers the Catholic Channel (Channel 129) through the Archdiocese of New York; programs include, "Busted Halo with Father Dave Dwyer," "The Catholic Guy with Lino Rulli," and "Conversation with Cardinal Dolan."

Television and Communications Services

Catholic Familyland: A ministry of the Apostolate for Family Consecration. Established in 1975, FL-TV produces television and video programs and operates in Asia, Latin America, Europe and Africa. Familyland Television Network, 3375 County Rd. 36, Bloomingdale, OH 43910; (740) 765-5500; www.familyland.org.

Catholic Academy for Communication Arts Professionals: The U.S. affiliate of SIGNIS, a Vatican-approved organization for Catholic communication professionals; membership is open to those professionally involved in Catholic church-related communications and to Catholic communicators working in secular organizations. President: Sally Oberski, Catholic Academy for Communication Arts Professionals, 1645 Brook Lynn Dr., Ste 2, Dayton, OH 45432-1944; (937) 458-0265; www.catholicacademy.org.

Catholic Communication Campaign (CCC): A U.S. Catholic bishops' program that produces, distributes and supports Catholic media projects, including a weekly television talk show, "Personally Speaking," television documentaries and public service messages. Ellen McCloskey, 3211 4th St. N.E., Washington, DC 20017; (202) 541-3204; www.usccb.org/ccc.

Catholic Communications Foundation (CCF): A foundation established by the Catholic Fraternal Benefit Societies in 1966 to lend support and assistance to development of the communications apostolate of the Church. The CCF promotes diocesan communications capabilities and funds a scholarship program at the Annual Institute for Religious Communications. 303 W. Lancaster Ave., PMB 333, Wayne, PA 19087.

CatholicTV: A Catholic broadband network delivering a variety of programs. CatholicTV, PO Box 9196, 34 Chestnut St., Watertown MA 02471; catholictv.com., 617-923-0220.

Christopher TV Series, "Christopher Closeup": Originated in 1952. Half-hour interviews, weekly, on commercial TV and numerous cable outlets. 12 E. 48th St., New York, NY

10017; (212) 759-4050; www.christophers.org.

Clemons Productions, Inc.: Produces "That's the Spirit," a family show for television; "Thoughts for the Week," on the ABC Satellite Network, and "Spirituality for Today" on the internet. Available to dioceses, organizations or channels. P.O. Box 7466, Greenwich, CT 06830; www.spirituality.org.

EWTN Global Catholic Network (EWTN): 5817 Old Leeds Road, Irondale, AL 35210; 205-271-2900; www.ewtn.com. America's largest religious cable network, features 24 hours of spiritual growth programming for the entire family. Offers documentaries, weekly teaching series and talk shows, including the award-winning "Mother Angelica Live." Nightly live programs include *The Journey Home, Threshold of Hope, EWTN Live, Life on the Rock* and *The World Over.* Daily live radio programming includes the popular call-in shows, *Open Line.* Also features live Church events from around the world and devotional programs such as "The Holy Rosary." Mother M. Angelica, P.C.P.A., Foundress.

Family Theater Productions: Founded by Father Peyton. Videocassettes, films for TV. 7201 Sunset Blvd., Hollywood, CA 90046; (323) 874-6633; www.familytheater.org. Nat. Dir., Fr. Wilfred J. Raymond, C.S.C.

Franciscan Media: Producer of video and print resources for pastoral ministry; St. Anthony Messenger Press, 28 W. Liberty St., Cincinnati, OH 45210; (513) 241-5615; www.Franciscanmedia.org.

Hispanic Telecommunications Network, Inc. (HTN): Produces "Nuestra Familia," a national weekly Spanish-language TV series; 1405 N. Main, Suite 240, San Antonio, TX 78212.

Mary Productions: Originated in 1950. Offers royalty-free scripts for stage, film, radio and tape production. Audio and video tapes of lives of the saints and historical characters. Traveling theater company; Mary Productions, 212 Oakdale Dr., Tomaso Plaza, Middletown, NJ 07748; (732) 617-8144.

National Interfaith Cable Coalition: A 28-member consortium representing 64 faith groups from Roman Catholic, Jewish, Protestant and Eastern Orthodox traditions; works with faith groups to present programming on the Faith and Values Media; 74 Trinity Place, Suite 1550, New York, NY 10006; (212) 406-4121; www.faithandvalues.com.

Oblate Media and Communication Corporation: Producers, Broadcast syndicators and distributors of Catholic and value-centered video programming. 7315 Manchester Rd., St. Louis, MO 63143.

Passionist Communications, Inc.: Presents Sunday Mass on TV seen in U.S. and available to dioceses and channels; publishes "TV Prayer Guide," semi-annually. P.O. Box 440, Pelham, NY 10803-0440.

Paulist Media Works: Full service audio production in syndication to dioceses, religious communities and church groups; 3015 4th St. N.E., Washington, DC 20017; (202) 269-6064. Rev. John Geaney, exec. prod.

Paulist Productions: Producers and distributors of the INSIGHT Film Series (available for TV) and educational film series. 17575 Pacific Coast Hwy., Pacific Palisades, CA 90272; (310) 454-0688; www.paulistproductions.org.

SIGNIS (World Catholic Association for Communication): A Vatican approved non-governmental organization that includes members from 140 countries and brings together radio, television, cinema, video, media education, Internet, and new technology professionals. SIGNIS was established in November 2001 from the merger between Unda (for radio and television) and OCIC (for cinema and audiovisual); both had been created in 1928. Its varied initiatives cover fields such as the promotion of films or television programs (including juries at festivals such as Cannes, Berlin, Monte Carlo, Venice, etc.), the creation of radio, video, and television studios, production and distribution of programs, training professionals in the field, and supplying specialized equipment. General Secretariat, 15, rue du Saphir, 1030 Brussels, Belgium; 00 32 (0)2 7349708; www.signis.net/.

Telecare: non-profit, state-of-the-art television and production facility of the Diocese of Rockville Centre. Broadcasts seven days a week to almost a million homes served by Cablevision, Telecare works through a partnership with WLNY/Channel 55. Programming includes the popular *God Squad* program that reaches 12 million viewers in New York, New Jersey and Connecticut every weekday. Msgr. Thomas Hartman, Director. 1200 Glen Curtiss Blvd., Uniondale, 11553; (516) 538-4108; www.telecaretv.org.

Theater
Catholic Actors' Guild of America, Inc.: Established in 1914 to provide material and spiritual assistance to people in the theater. Has more than 500 members; publishes *The Call Board*. 1501 Broadway, Suite 510, New York, NY 10036; (212) 398-1868 (fax).

FILM

Best Films of 2013
Catholic film critic Steven Greydanus released his 2013 Best Films List in January 2013 that was published in the National Catholic Register.

"This Is Martin Bonner"; "12 Years a Slave"; "Gravity"; "The Past"; "Fill the Void"; "Fruitvale Station"; "Captain Phillips"; "From Up on Poppy Hill"; "Caesar Must Die"; "¡Vivan Las Antipodas!"

Runners-Up (in alphabetical order)

"All Is Lost"; "A Hijacking"; "Leviathan"; "Monsters University"; "Museum Hours"; "Saving Mr. Banks"; "The Hunger Games: Catching Fire"; "The Rabbi's Cat"; "To the Wonder"; "Wolf Children: Ame and Yuki."

Honorable Mention (in alphabetical order)

"42"; "Black Nativity"; "The Bling Ring"; "In a World"; "Much Ado About Nothing"; "Mud"; "The Painting"; "The Way, Way Back"; "The Wind Rises"; "The Wolverine."

Vatican List of the Greatest Films of the 20th Century
On the occasion of the 100th anniversary of cinema in 1995, the Vatican compiled this list of "great films." The 45 movies are divided into three categories: "Religion," "Values," and "Art."

Religion
"Andrei Rublev" (1969); "Babette's Feast" (1988); "Ben-Hur" (1959); "The Flowers of St. Francis" (1950); "Francesco" (1989); "The Gospel According to St. Matthew" (1966); "La Passion de Notre Seigneur Jesus-Christ" (1905); "A Man for All Seasons" (1966); "The Mission" (1986); "Monsieur Vincent" (1947); "Nazarin" (1958); "Ordet" (1954); "The Passion of Joan of Arc" (1928); "The Sacrifice" (1986); "Thérèse" (1986).

Values
"Au Revoir les Enfants" (1988); "The Bicycle Thief" (1949); "The Burmese Harp" (1956); "Chariots of Fire" (1981); "Decalogue" (1988); "Dersu Uzala" (1978); "Gandhi" (1982); "Intolerance" (1916); "It's a Wonderful Life" (1946); "On the Waterfront" (1954); "Open City" (1945); "Schindler's List" (1993); "The Seventh Seal" (1956); "The Tree of Wooden Clogs" (1978); "Wild Strawberries" (1958).

Art
"Citizen Kane" (1941); "8-1/2" (1963); "Fantasia" (1940); "Grand Illusion" (1937); "La Strada" (1956); "The Lavender Hill Mob" (1951); "The Leopard" (1963); "Little Women" (1933); "Metropolis" (1926); "Modern Times" (1936); "Napoleon" (1927); "Nosferatu" (1922); "Stagecoach" (1939); "2001: A Space Odyssey" (1968); "The Wizard of Oz" (1939).

CATHOLIC INTERNET SITES

Website addresses change periodically. Find this list online at www.CatholicAlmanac.com. Visit Our Sunday Visitor's web site at www.osv.com.

Holy See Sites
Vatican News Portal: www.news.va
Vatican: www.vatican.va
L'Osservatore Romano: www.vatican.va/news_services/or/or_eng/index.html
Vatican Radio: www.vatican.va/news_services/radio

Catholic Megasites, Directories and Links
Catholic Almanac: www.CatholicAlmanac.com
Catholic Canada: www.catholicanada.com
Catholic Community Forum: www.catholic-forum.com
Catholic Goldmine!: www.catholicgoldmine.com
Catholic Hotlinks: www.cathinsight.com
Catholic Information Center on the Internet: www.catholic.net
Catholic Information Network: www.cin.org
Catholic Internet Directory: www.catholic-church.org
Catholic Internet Yellow Pages: www.monksofadoration.org/directory.html
Catholic Kiosk: www.aquinas-multimedia.com/arch
Catholic.Net Periodicals: www.catholic.net/RCC/Periodicals
Catholic Pages: www.catholic-pages.com
Catholic Press Association: www.catholicpress.org
Catholicity Internet Directory: www.catholicity.com
Catholic Exchange: www.catholicexchange.com
Ecclesia Web Service for Catholics: www.catholic-church.org
El Directorio Catolico on Internet: www.iglesia.org
New Advent: www.newadvent.org
Our Sunday Visitor: www.OSV.com
PetersNet: www.catholicculture.org
RCNet: www.rc.net
St. Jane's: www.stjane.org
The Internet Padre: www.internetpadre.com
Theology Library Search Engines: www.shc.edu/theolibrary/engines.htm

Catholic Internet Service Providers
Catholic Families Network: www.catholicfamilies.net
Catholic Online: www.catholiconline.com
FamiLink (ISP for the family): www.familink.com

Catholic Movements and Organizations

Adoremus: www.adoremus.org
Catholic Charismatic Center: www.garg.com/ccc
Catholic Doctrinal Concordance: www.infpage.com/concordance
Catholic Family and Human Rights Institute: www.c-fam.org
Catholic Health Association USA: www.chausa.org
Catholic League: www.catholicleague.org
Focolare Movement: www.rc.net/focolare
Madonna House: www.madonnahouse.org
Nat'l Bioethics Center: www.ncbcenter.org
Opus Dei: www.opusdei.org
Pax Christi International: www.paxchristi.net
Pax Christi USA: www.paxchristiusa.org
Saints Alive: www.ichrusa.com/saintsalive
Schoenstatt (information): www.catholiclinks.org/schoenstattunitedstates.htm
Seton Home Study School: www.setonhome.org

Catholic Newspapers and Magazines

Catholic Digest: www.catholicdigest.org
Catholic New York Online: www.cny.org
Catholic Worker: www.catholicworker.org
First Things: www.firstthings.com
Houston Catholic Worker: www.cjd.org
Our Sunday Visitor: www.osv.com
The Tablet, U.K.: www.thetablet.co.uk
The Universe, U.K.: www.totalcatholic.com
The Wanderer: www.thewandererpress.com

Religious Orders and Apostolates

Apostolates/Orders: www.catholic-forum.com/links/pages/Religious_Orders
EWTN: www.ewtn.com
RCNet-Apostolates: www.rc.net/org

Colleges and Universities (Links To)

Colleges: www.shc.edu/theolibrary/edu.htm
Assocation of Catholic Colleges and Universities: www.accunet.org

Useful and Informative Sites

Mass Times: www.masstimes.org
Mass in Transit: www.massintransit.com
Christworld: www.christworld.com
Catholic-Pages: www.catholic-pages.com
PetersVoice: www.petersvoice.com
Rosary Center: www.rosary-center.org
Daily E-pistle (e-newsletter) Signup Page: www.catholic-forum.com/e-pistle.html
Grace In Action Stewardship: www.GraceInAction.org

For Kids and Families

Catholic Kids Net: www.catholickidsnet.org
Global Schoolhouse: www.gsn.org
My Friend: www.myfriendmagazine.com
Teaching Catholic Kids: www.TeachingCatholicKids.com
Apostolate for Family Consecration: www.familyland.org
Catholic Family and Human Rights Institute: www.c-fam.org
Catholic Fathers: www.dads.org
Catholic Parent Magazine: www.CatholicParent.com
Natural Family Planning: www.ccli.org
Domestic Church: www.domestic-church.com

DEVELOPMENTS IN COMMUNICATIONS 2013-14

Exceprts from the Message of His Holiness Pope Francis for the 48th World Communications Day,

issued on Jan. 24, 2014, Feast of Saint Francis de Sales: "**Communication at the Service of an Authentic Culture of Encounter**"

Today we are living in a world which is growing ever "smaller" and where, as a result, it would seem to be easier for all of us to be neighbors. Developments in travel and communications technology are bringing us closer together and making us more connected, even as globalization makes us increasingly interdependent. Nonetheless, divisions, which are sometimes quite deep, continue to exist within our human family. On the global level we see a scandalous gap between the opulence of the wealthy and the utter destitution of the poor. Often we need only walk the streets of a city to see the contrast between people living on the street and the brilliant lights of the store windows. We have become so accustomed to these things that they no longer unsettle us. Our world suffers from many forms of exclusion, marginalization and poverty, to say nothing of conflicts born of a combination of economic, political, ideological, and, sadly, even religious motives.

In a world like this, media can help us to feel closer to one another, creating a sense of the unity of the human family which can in turn inspire solidarity and serious efforts to ensure a more dignified life for all. Good communication helps us to grow closer, to know one another better, and ultimately, to grow in unity. The walls which divide us can be broken down only if we are prepared to listen and learn from one another.

This is not to say that certain problems do not exist. The speed with which information is communicated exceeds our capacity for reflection and judgment, and this does not make for more balanced and proper forms of self-expression. The variety of opinions being aired can be seen as helpful, but it also enables people to barricade themselves behind sources of information which only confirm their own wishes and ideas, or political and economic interests. The world of communications can help us either to expand our knowledge or to lose our bearings. The desire for digital connectivity can have the effect of isolating us from our neighbors, from those closest to us. We should not overlook the fact that those who for whatever reason lack access to social media run the risk of being left behind.

While these drawbacks are real, they do not justify rejecting social media; rather, they remind us that communication is ultimately a human rather than technological achievement. What is it, then, that helps us, in the digital environment, to grow in humanity and mutual understanding? We need, for example, to recover a certain sense of deliberateness and calm. This calls for time and the ability to be silent and to listen. We need also to be patient if we want to understand those who are different from us. People only express themselves fully when they are not merely tolerated, but know that they are truly accepted. If we are genuinely attentive in listening to others, we will learn to look at the world with different eyes and come to appreciate the richness of human experience as manifested in different cultures and traditions. We will also learn to appreciate more fully the important values inspired by Christianity, such as the vision of the human person, the nature of marriage and the family, the proper distinction between the religious and political spheres, the principles of solidarity and subsidiarity, and many others.

How, then, can communication be at the service of an authentic culture of encounter? What does it mean for us, as disciples of the Lord, to encounter others in the light of the Gospel? In spite of our own limitations and sinfulness, how do we draw truly close to one another? These questions are summed up in what a scribe – a communicator – once asked Jesus: "And who is my neighbor?" (Lk 10:29). This question can help us to see communication in terms of "neighborliness." We might paraphrase the question in this way: How can we be "neighborly" in our use of the communications media and in the new environment created by digital technology? I find an answer in the parable of the Good Samaritan, which is also a parable about communication. Those who communicate, in effect, become neighbors. The Good Samaritan not only draws nearer to the man he finds half dead on the side of the road; he takes responsibility for him. Jesus shifts our understanding: it is not just about seeing the other as someone like myself, but of the ability to make myself like the other. Communication is really about realizing that we are all human beings, children of God. I like seeing this power of communication as "neighborliness."

Whenever communication is primarily aimed at promoting consumption or manipulating others, we are dealing with a form of violent aggression like that suffered by the man in the parable, who was beaten by robbers and left abandoned on the road. The Levite and the priest do not regard him as a neighbor, but as a stranger to be kept at a distance. In those days, it was rules of ritual purity which conditioned their response. Nowadays there is a danger that certain media so condition our responses that we fail to see our real neighbor. It is not enough to be passersby on the digital highways, simply "connected"; connections need to grow into true encounters. We cannot live apart, closed in on ourselves. We need to love and to be loved. We need tenderness. Media strategies do not ensure beauty, goodness and truth in communication. The world of media also has to be concerned with humanity, it too is called to show tenderness. ...May the image of the Good Samaritan who tended to the wounds of the injured man by pouring oil and wine over them be our inspiration. Let our communication be a balm which relieves pain and a fine wine which gladdens hearts. May the light we bring to others not be the result of cosmetics or special effects, but rather of our being loving and merciful "neighbors" to those wounded and left on the side of the road. Let us boldly become citizens of the digital world.

PONTIFICAL HONORS AND AWARDS

Pontifical Orders

The Pontifical Orders of Knighthood are secular orders of merit whose membership depends directly on the pope.

Supreme Order of Christ (Militia of Our Lord Jesus Christ): The highest of the five pontifical orders of knighthood, the Supreme Order of Christ was approved Mar. 14,

1319, by John XXII as a continuation in Portugal of the suppressed Order of Templars. Members were religious with vows and a rule of life until the order lost its religious character toward the end of the 15th century. Since that time it has existed as an order of merit. Paul VI, in 1966, restricted awards of the order to Christian heads of state.

Order of the Golden Spur (Golden Militia): Although the original founder is not certainly known, this order is one of the oldest knighthoods. Indiscriminate bestowal and inheritance diminished its prestige, however, and in 1841 Gregory XVI replaced it with the Order of St. Sylvester and gave it the title of Golden Militia. In 1905 St. Pius X restored the Order of the Golden Spur in its own right, separating it from the Order of St. Sylvester. Paul VI, in 1966, restricted awards of the order to Christian heads of state.

Order of Pius IX: Founded by Pius IX June 17, 1847, the order is awarded for outstanding services for the Church and society, and may be given to non-Catholics as well as Catholics. The title to nobility formerly attached to membership was abolished by Pius XII in 1939. In 1957 Pius XII instituted the Class of the Grand Collar as the highest category of the order; in 1966, Paul VI restricted this award to heads of state "in solemn circumstances." The other three classes are of Knights of the Grand Cross, Knight Commanders with and without emblem, and Knights. The new class was created to avoid difficulties in presenting papal honors to Christian or non Christian leaders of high merit.

Order of St. Gregory the Great: First established by Gregory XVI in 1831 to honor citizens of the Papal States, the order is conferred on persons who are distinguished for personal character and reputation, and for notable accomplishment. The order has civil and military divisions, and three classes of knights.

Order of St. Sylvester: Instituted Oct. 31, 1841, by Gregory XVI to absorb the Order of the Golden Spur, this order was divided into two by St. Pius X in 1905, one retaining the name of St. Sylvester and the other assuming the title of Golden Militia. Membership consists of three degrees: Knights of the Grand Cross, Knight Commanders with and without emblem, and Knights.

Papal Medals

Pro Ecclesia et Pontifice: This decoration ("For the Church and the Pontiff") had its origin in 1888 as a token of the golden sacerdotal jubilee of Leo XIII; he bestowed it on those who had assisted in the observance of his jubilee and on persons responsible for the success of the Vatican Exposition. The medal, cruciform in shape, bears the likenesses of Sts. Peter and Paul, the tiara and the papal keys, the words *Pro Ecclesia et Pontifice*, and the name of the present pontiff, all on the same side; it is attached to a ribbon of yellow and white, the papal colors. Originally, the medal was issued in gold, silver or bronze. It is awarded in recognition of service to the Church and the papacy.

Benemerenti: Several medals ("To a well-deserving person") have been conferred by popes for exceptional accomplishment and service. The medals, which are made of gold, silver or bronze, bear the likeness and name of the reigning pope on one side; on the other, a laurel crown and the letter "B." These two medals may be given by the pope to both men and women. Their bestowal does not convey any title or honor of knighthood.

ECCLESIASTICAL ORDERS

Equestrian Order of the Holy Sepulchre of Jerusalem

The order traces its origin to Godfrey de Bouillon who instituted it in 1099. It took its name from the Basilica of the Holy Sepulchre where its members were knighted. After the fall of the Latin Kingdom of Jerusalem and the consequent departure of the knights from the Holy Land, national divisions were established in various countries.

The order was re-organized by Pius IX in 1847 when he reestablished the Latin Patriarchate of Jerusalem and placed the order under the jurisdiction of its patriarch. In 1888, Leo XIII confirmed permission to admit women — Ladies of the Holy Sepulchre — to all degrees of rank. Pius X reserved the office of grand master to himself in 1907; Pius XII gave the order a cardinal patron in 1940 and, in 1949, transferred the office of grand master from the pope to the cardinal patron. Pope John XXIII approved updated constitutions in 1962; the latest statutes were approved by Paul VI in 1977.

The purposes of the order are strictly religious and charitable. Members are committed to sustain and aid the charitable, cultural and social works of the Catholic Church in the Holy Land, particularly in the Latin Patriarchate of Jerusalem. The order is composed of knights and ladies grouped in three classes: class of Knights of the Collar and Ladies of the Collar; Class of Knights (in four grades); Class of Ladies (in four grades). Members are appointed by the cardinal grand master according to procedures outlined in the constitution.

Under the present constitution the order is divided into national lieutenancies, largely autonomous, with international headquarters in Rome. Then Abp. Edwin O'Brien, abp. of Baltimore since 2007, was appointed Pro-Grand Master on Aug. 29, 2011. He succeeded Card. John P. Foley, who had served as Grand Master since 2007. O'Brien was named to the College of Cardinals on Feb. 18, 2012, and became Grand Master on Mar. 12, 2012. The address of the headquarters is: Grand Magisterium of the Equestrian Order of the Holy Sepulchre of Jerusalem, Borgo Spirito Santo, 73, 00193 Roma, Italia; Tel. 39066828121; www.vatican.va/roman_curia/institutions_connected/oessh/index.htm.

As of the end of 2008 (the latest available figures), the Order had a total of 25,835 members (14,432 were Knights of all grades, 8,159 were Ladies, and 3,244 were religious. Geographical distribution: approximayely 12,500 (almost 48%) are resident in the United States; the largest Lieutenancy is that of Central Italy and Sardinia, with a total of 2,590 Members; this was followed by two US Lieutenancies: USASouthwestern with 2,540 and USA-Eastern with 2,306 Knights, Ladies and religious. The USA is the only area where the Order has more Ladies than Knights. (Source: Newsletter, *Ordo Sequestris Sancti Sepulcri Hierosolymitani*, XVII, Dec. 2009).

There are nine lieutenancies of the order in the United States and one in Puerto Rico. The U.S. lieutenancies are: USA Eastern, 1011 First Ave. - 7th Floor, New York, NY 10022; USA Middle Atlantic, P.O. Box 29260, Washington, DC, 20017-0260; USA North Central, 939 Londmeadow Ct., Lake Barrington, IL 60010; USA North Eastern, 340 Main St., Suite 906, Worcester, MA 01608; USA North Western, 8 Lenox Way, San Francisco, CA 94127; USA Northern, 848 Drakes Dream Dr., Gravois Mills, MO 65037; USA South Eastern, 2955 Ridgelake Dr., Suite 205, Metaire, LA 70002; USA South Western, 2001 Kirby Dr.,

Suite 902, Houston, TX 77019; USA Western, 8141 East Kaiser Bld., Suite 300, Anaheim Hills, CA 92808.

Order of Malta

The Sovereign Military Hospitaller Order of St. John of Jerusalem of Rhodes and of Malta traces its origin to a group of men who maintained a Christian hospital in the Holy Land in the 11th century. The group was approved as a religious order – the Hospitallers of St. John – by Paschal II in 1113.

The order, while continuing its service to the poor, principally in hospital work, assumed military duties in the 12th century and included knights, chaplains and sergeants-at-arms among its members. All the knights were professed monks with the vows of poverty, chastity and obedience. Headquarters were located in the Holy Land until the last decade of the 13th century and on Rhodes after 1308 (whence the title, Knights of Rhodes).

After establishing itself on Rhodes, the order became a sovereign power like the sea republics of Italy and the Hanseatic cities of Germany, flying its own flag, coining its own money, floating its own navy, and maintaining diplomatic relations with many nations.

The order was forced to abandon Rhodes in 1522 after the third siege of the island by the Turks under Sultan Suleyman I. Eight years later, the Knights were given the island of Malta, where they remained as a bastion of Christianity until near the end of the 18th century. Headquarters have been located in Rome since 1834.

The title of Grand Master of the Order, in abeyance for some time, was restored by Leo XIII in 1879. A more precise definition of both the religious and the sovereign status of the order was embodied in a new constitution of 1961 and a code issued in 1966.

The four main classifications of members are: Knights of Justice, who are religious with the vows of poverty, chastity and obedience; Knights of Obedience, who make a solemn promise to strive for Christian perfection; Knights of Honor and Devotion and of Grace and Devotion, all of noble lineage; and Knights of Magistral Grace. There are also chaplains, Dames and Donats of the order.

The order, with six grand priories, three sub-priories and 40 national associations, is devoted to hospital and charitable works of all kinds in some 100 countries.

Under the provisions of international law, the order maintains full diplomatic relations with the Holy See – on which, in its double nature, it depends as a religious Order, but of which, as a sovereign Order of Knighthood, it is independent – and 68 countries throughout the world.

The Grand Master, who is the head of the order, has the title of Most Eminent Highness with the rank of Cardinal. He must be of noble lineage and under solemn vows for a minimum period of 10 years, if under 50 and holds the position for life.

The present and 79th Grand Master is Fra' Matthew Festing, an Englishman. He was the Grand Prior of England since the Priory's re-establishment in 1993 after a period of 450 years. In 1977 Fra' Matthew became a member of the Order of Malta, taking solemn religious vows in 1991.

Fra' Andrew Willoughby Ninian Bertie, member of the British aristocracy who elected for life as Grand Master on Apr. 8, 1988 by the Council of State, died on Feb. 7, 2008. The patron of the Knights is Cardinal Paolo Sardi, a long-time Vatican diplomat.

The headquarters of the order is at Via Condotti, 68, Palazzo Malta, 00187 Rome, Italy; (011) 39.06.67581.1;

www.orderofmalta.org. U.S. addresses: American Association, 1011 First Ave., New York, NY 10022; (212) 371.1522, www.maltausa.org; Western Association of U.S.A., 465 California St., Suite 818, San Francisco, CA 94104, (415) 788-4550, www.orderofmaltausawestern. org; Federal Association of U.S.A., 1730 M St. N.W., Suite 403, Washington, D.C. 20036; (202) 331-2494, www. orderofmalta-federal.org.

Order of St. George

The Sacred Military Constantinian Order of St. George was established by Pope Clement XI in 1718. The purposes of the order are to work for the preaching and defense of the Catholic faith and to promote the spiritual and physical welfare of sick, disabled, homeless and other unfortunate persons. The principal officer is Prince Carlo of Bourbon-Two Sicilies, duke of Calabria. Addresses: Via Sistina 121, 00187 Rome, Italy; Via Duomo 149, 80138 Naples, Italy; American Delegation, 302 Gessner Rd., Houston, TX 77024; (713) 888-0242.

2014 CATHOLIC PRESS ASSOCIATION AWARDS

The winners of the 2014 Catholic Press Awards were announced on Friday, June 20, 2014, at the Catholic Media Convention in Charlotte, North Carolina.

Newspapers — General Excellence

National First Place: *National Catholic Reporter*, Kansas City, MO; Second Place: *Our Sunday Visitor*, Huntington, IN; Third Place: *The Catholic Register*, Toronto, Ontario, Canada; **40,000+ Diocesan paper:** First Place: *The Catholic Sun*, Phoenix, AZ; Second Place: *Catholic San Francisco*, San Francisco, CA; Third Place: *Catholic New York*, New York, NY; **17,001–40,000 Diocesan paper:** First Place: *Catholic Herald*, Madison, WI; *The New Vision*, Tucson, AZ; Third Place: *The Compass*, Green Bay, WI; **1–17,000 Diocesan paper:** First Place: *The Monitor*, Trenton, NJ; Second Place: *The Catholic Northwest Progress*, Seattle, WA; Third Place: *The Valley Catholic*, San Juan, Texas.

Magazines

National general interest First Place: *U.S. Catholic*, Chicago, IL; Second Place: *Living City Magazine*, Hyde Park, NY; Third Place: *St. Anthony Messenger*, Cincinnati, OH; Honorable Mention: America Magazine, New York, NY.

Diocesan magazines First Place: *Bayou Catholic*, Schriever, LA; Second Place: *Catholic Connection*, Shreveport, LA; Third Place: *Pittsburgh Catholic*, Pittsburgh, PA.

Mission, overseas and home First Place: *One Magazine*, New York, NY; Second Place: *Maryknoll*, Maryknoll, NY; Third Place: *Comboni Missionaries*, Cincinnati, OH; Honorable Mention: *PIME Missionaries*, Detroit, MI.

Religious order magazines First Place: *Franciscan Spirit*, Pittsburgh, PA; Second Place: *The Augustinian*, Villanova, PA; Third Place: *Heart to Heart*, Latrobe, PA.

Professional & special-interest, including clergy & religious First Place: *CHA Health Progress*, St. Louis, MO; Second Place: *Today's Catholic Teacher*, Dayton,

OH; Third Place: *HORIZON: Journal of the National Religious Vocation Conference*, Chicago, IL.

Scholarly First Place: *American Catholic Studies*, Villanova, PA; Second Place: *Horizions*, Villanova, PA; Third Place: *Catholic Southwest: Journal*, Baton Rouge, LA.

Prayer & spirituality First Place: *Magnificat*, Yonkers, NY; Second Place: S*oul - World Apostolate of Fatima*, Washington, NJ.

Books

Popular Presentation of Catholic Faith First Place: *Go to Joseph* by Br. Michael O'Neill McGrath, OSFS, Br. Micael Leach and Chrsitine Krystofczyk, World Library Publications, Franklin Park, IL; Second Place: *When Faith Feels Fragile* by R. Scott Hurd, Pauline Books and Media, Boston, MA; Third Place (Tied): *The Thorny Grace of It* by Brian Doyle, Loyola Press, Chicago, IL; Third Place (Tied): *Faith Meets World* by Barry Hudock, Liguori Publications, Liguori, MO.

Spirituality – Soft Cover First Place: *Atchison Blue* by Judith Valente, Ave Maria Press, Notre Dame, IN; Second Place: *The Art of Pausing* by Judith Valente, Br. Paul Quenon, OCSO and Michael Bever, ACTA Publications, Chicago, IL; Third Place: *Spiritual Letters* by Sr. Wendy Beckett, Orbis Books, Maryknoll, NY.

Spirituality – Hard Cover First Place: *Meditations on Vatican Art* by Mark Haydu, Liguori Publications, Liguori, MO; Second Place: *Go to Joseph* by Brother Michael O'Neill McGrath, OSFS, Michael Leach and Christine Krzystofczyk, World Library Publications, Franklin Park, IL; Third Place: *The Way of the Cross: The Path to New Life* by Joan Chittister and Janet McKenzie, Orbis Books, Maryknoll, NY; Honorable Mention: *Julian's Gospel: Illuminating the Life & Revelations of Julian of Norwich* by Veronica Mary Rolf, Orbis Books, Maryknoll, NY.

Theology First Place: *Icons of Hope: The "Last Things" in Catholic Imagination* by John E. Thiel, University of Notre Dame Press, Notre Dame, IN; Second Place: *The Catholicity of Reason* by D.C. Shindler, Wm. B. Eerdmans Publishing Co., Grand Rapids, MI; Third Place: *Moral Evil* by Andrew Michael Flescher, Georgetown University Press, Washington, DC.

Scripture – Popular Studies First Place: *Encountering Jesus in the Scriptures* by Daniel J. Harrington and Christopher R. Matthews, C21 Resources, Chestnut Hill, MA; Second Place: *Mark and Empire: Feminist Reflections* by Laurel K. Cobb, Orbis Books, Maryknoll, NY; Third Place: *Saint Paul and the New Evangelization* by Ronald D. Witherup, Liturgical Press, Collegeville, MN

Scripture - Academic Studies First Place: *The Bible in Medieval Tradition: The Letter to the Romans* by Ian Christopher Levy, Philip D.W. Krey and Thomas Ryan, Wm B. Eerdmans Publishing Company, Grand Rapids, MI; Second Place: *Word and Image: The Hermeneutics of The Saint John's Bible* by Michael Patella, OSB, Liturgical Press, Collegeville, MN; Third Place: *David Remembered: Kingship and National identity in Ancient Israel* by Joseph Blenkinsopp, William B. Eerdmans Publishing Company, Grand Rapids, MI; Honorable Mention: *Jeremiah and God's Plans of Well-Being* by Barbara Green, The University of South Carolina Press, Columbia, SC.

Liturgy First Place: *Saint Margaret Mary Sunday Missal* by Michael E. Novak and Denise C. Durand, World Library Publications, Franklin Park, IL; Second Place:

What We Have Done and What We have Failed to Do: Assessing the Liturgical Reforms of Vatican II by Msgr. Kevin W. Irwin, Paulist Press, Mahwah, NJ; Third Place: *The Passions of Holy Week* by Charles Rohrbacher, Liturgical Press, Collegeville, MN.

Pastoral Ministry First Place: *Rebuilt* by Michael White and Tom Corcoran, Ave Maria Press, Notre Dame, IN; Second Place: *Notes from the Underground: The Spiritual Journey of a Secular Priest* by Donald Cozzens, Orbis Books, Maryknoll, NY; Third Place: *Discovering Trinity in Disability* by Myroslaw Tataryn and Maria Truchan-Tataryn, Orbis Books, Maryknoll, NY.

Professional Book First Place: *Navigating Pastoral Transitions* by Graziano Marcheschi, Marti Jewell and Barbara Kerkhoff, Liturgical Press, Collegeville, MN; Second Place: *The Art of Leadership* by Notker Wolf and Enrica Rosanna, Liturgical Press, Collegeville, MN; Third Place: *Redeeming Administration* by Ann M. Garrido, Ave Maria Press, Notre Dame, IN.

Design and Production First Place: *Meditations on Vatican Art* by Mark Haydu, LC, STL, Liguori Publications, Liguori, MO; Second Place: *The Sistine Chapel: A Biblical Tour* by Christine M. Panyard, PhD, Paulist Press, Mahwah, NJ; Third Place: *Go To Joseph* by Brother Michael O'Neil McGrath, OSFS, Christine Krystofezyk and Christine Enault, World Library Publications, Franklin Park, IL; Honorable Mention: *Rebuilt: The Story of a Catholic Parish* by Michael White and Tom Corcoran, Ave Maria Press, Notre Dame, IN.

Children's Books First Place: *Shepards to the Rescue: Gospel Tim Trekkers #1* by Maria Grace Dateno, FSP, Pauline Books and Media, Boston, MA; Second Place: *The Prayer of St. Francis by St. Francis of Assisi*, Illustrated by Guiliano Ferri, Paulist Press, Mahwah, NJ; Third Place: *Francis of Assisi: Keeper of Creation* by Barbara Yoffie and Katherine A. Borgatti, Liguori Publications, Liguori, MO; Honorable Mention: *Saint Theodora and Her Promise to God* by Mary Doyle, Sisters of Providence, St. Mary-of-the-Woods, IN.

Teen and Young Adult First Place: *Prayers, Papers, and Play: Devotions for Every College Student* by Barbara Canale, Liguori Publications, Liguori, MO; Second Place: *a.k.a. genius* by Marilee Haynes, Pauline Books and Media, Boston, MA; Third Place: *The Gate* by Nancy Carabio Belanger, Harvey House Publishing, Rochester, MI; Honorable Mention: *Your College Faith . . . Own It* by Matt Swaim and Colleen Swaim, Liguori Publications, Liguori, MO.

First Time Authors First Place: *Julian's Gospel* by Veronica Mary Rolf, Orbis Books, Maryknoll, NY; Second Place: *Meditations on Vatican Art* by Mark Haydu, LC, STL, Liguori Publications, Liguori, MO; Third Place: *A Martyr's Crown* by Joyce Coronel, The Catholic Sun, Phoenix, AZ; Honorable Mention: *Act of Recovery* by Michael D. Hoffman, ACTA Publications, Chicago, IL.

Family Life First Place: *When Parents Divorce or Separate* by Lynn Cassella-Kapusinski, Pauline Books and Media, Boston, MA; Second Place: *Blessed By Less* by Susan V. Vogt, Loyola Press, Chicago, IL; Third Place: *Catholic Mom's Café* by Donna-Marie Cooper O'Boyle, Our Sunday Visitor Press, Huntington, IN; Honorable Mention: *It Is Well: Life in the Storm* by Chris Faddis, Solace Books.

History First Place: *Called to Serve: A History of Nuns in America* by Margaret M. McGuinnes, New York University Press, New York, NY; Second Place: *Thomas Aquinas and Karl Barth: An Unofficial Catholic-Protestant Dialogue* by Bruce L. McCormack and Thomas Joseph White, OP, Wm. B. Eerdmans Publishing Co., Grand Rapids, MI; Third Place: *Catholic Progressives in England After Vatican II* by Jay P. Corrin, University of Notre Dame Press, Notre Dame, IN.

Biography First Place: *Drawn from Shadows into Truth: A Memoir* by Fr. Ray Ryland, Emmaus Road Publishing, Steubenville, OH; Second Place: *Divided Friends: Portraits of the Roman Catholic Modernist Crisis in the United States* by William L. Portier, Catholic University Press, Washington, DC; Third Place: *A Worldwide Heart: The Life of Maryknoll Father John J. Considne* by Robert Hurteau, Orbis Books, Maryknoll, NY; Honorable Mentions: *Anthony deMello: The Happy Wanderer* by Bill deMello, Orbis Books, Maryknoll, NY; *The Life of Walter F. Sullivan* by Phyllis Theroux, Orbis Books, Maryknoll, NY.

Gender Issues First Place: *Religious Life at the Crossroads* by Amy Hereford, CSJ, Orbis Books, Maryknoll, NY; Second Place: *Conscience and Calling: Ethical Reflections on Catholic Women's Church Vocations* by Anne Patrick, Bloomsbury Publishing, London, UK; Third Place: *Blessed, Beautiful, and Bodacious* by Pat Gohn, Ave Maria Press, Notre Dame, IN.

Reference Books First Place: *Encyclopedia of U.S. Catholic History* by Matthew Bunson and Margaret Bunson, Our Sunday Visitor Press, Huntington, IN; Second Place: *Handbook of Roman Catholic Moral Terms* by James T. Bretzke, SJ, Georgetown University Press, Washington, DC; Third Place: *Mysticism and the Spiritual Guest: A Crosscultural Anthology* by Phyllis Zagano, Paulist Press, Mahwah, NJ; Honorable Mention: *Faith Basics: Pocket Catholic Dictionary* by Leon J. Suprenant, Jr., Emmaus Road Publishing, Steubenville, OH.

Diocesan Directory First Place: *2013 Archdiocese of Los Angeles Catholic Directory* by Hermine Lees and Chris Krause,editors; Production: Jose Velazquez and Michelle Rugel, Archdiocese of Los Angeles, Los Angeles, CA; Second Place: *Diocese of Rockford Official Directory* by Staff, Diocese of Rockford, Rockford, IL; Third Place: *2013 Catholic Directory, Diocese of Buffalo* by Staff, Diocese of Buffalo, Buffalo, NY; Honorable Mention: *2013 Diocese of Orange Catholic Directory* by Content by Mary Kay Griffing, Simona Tonti; Production: Jose Velazquez, Michelle Rugel, Diocese of Orange, Orange, CA.

Best Book from a Small Publisher First Place: *Raising Gentle Men: Lives at the Orphanage Edge* by Jay Sullivan and Kevin Atticks, Apprentice House, Baltimore, MD; Second Place: *The Ascent of Mount Carmel by St. John of the Cross: Reflections* by Marc Foley, OCD, ICS Publications, Miamisburg, OH; Third Place: *Naked and You Clothed Me* by Jim Knipper, editor; featuring Rob Bell, James Martin, SJ, Jan Richardson, Richard Rohr, OFM and Mickey McGrath, OSFS, Clear Faith Publishing, Princeton, NJ; Honorable Mention: *Young in the Spirit* by Mary Doyle, ACTA Publications, Geneva, IL.

Social Teaching First Place: *Christianity and the Political Order* by Kenneth R. Himes, Orbis Books, Maryknoll, NY; Second Place: *Preferential Option for the Poor Beyond Theology* by Daniel G. Groody and Gustavo Gutiérrez, editors, University of Notre Dame Press, Notre Dame, IN; Third Place: *Hope Sings, So Beautiful* by Christopher Pramuk, Liturgical Press, Collegeville, MN; Honorable

Mention: *The Development of Moral Theology* by Charles E. Curran, Georgetown University Press, Washington, DC.

Faith and Science First Place: *Prophets of the Posthuman: American Fiction, Biotechnology, and the Ethics of Personhood* by Christina Beiber Lake, University of Notre Dame Press, Notre Dame, IN; Second Place: *A Defense of Dignity: Creating Life, Destroying Life, and Protecting the Rights of Conscience* by Christopher Kaczor, University of Notre Dame Press, Notre Dame, IN; Third Place: *The Unbearable Wholeness of Being: God, Evolution, and the Power of Love* by Ilia Delio, Orbis Books, Maryknoll, NY; Honorable Mention: *God in the Midst of Change: Wisdom for Confusing Times* by Diarmuid O'Murchu, Orbis Books, Maryknoll, NY.

50th Anniversary of Vatican II First Place: *Visions of Hope* by Kevin J. Ahern, editor, Orbis Books, Maryknoll, NY; Second Place: *A Council that Will Never End: Lumen Gentium and the Church Today* by Paul Lakeland, Liturgical Press, Collegeville, MN; Third Place: *Do Not Quench the Spirit!: Celebrating Fifty Years of Vatican III ¡No apagues el espiritu!: Celebrando cincuenta años del Concilio Vaticano II* by Deacon William T. Ditewig, Edward Foley, Capuchin, Chris Ángel and Karla Bellinger, World Library Publications, Franklin Park, IL.

The Year of Faith First Place: *Believing* by Eugene Kennedy, Orbis Books, Maryknoll, NY; Second Place: *Giving Up God . . . to Find God: Breaking Free of Idolatry* by Kerry Walters, Orbis Books, Maryknoll, NY; Third Place: *Pope Francis: Open Mind, Faithful Heart: Reflections On Following Jesus* by Pope Francis, Jorge Mario Bergoglio, The Crossroad Publishing Company, New York, NY; Honorable Mention: *How to Share Your Faith With Anyone* by Terry Barber, Ignatius Press, San Francisco, CA.

Faithful Citizenship First Place: *Where Justice and Mercy Meet: Catholic Opposition to the Death Penalty* by Vicki Schieber, Trudy Conway and David Matzko McCarthy, editors, Liturgical Press, Collegeville, MN; Second Place: *Citizens of the World: Suffering and Solidarity in the 21st Century* by Donald H. Dunson and James A Dunson III, Orbis Books, Maryknoll, NY; Third Place: *The Ethics of Interrogation: Professional Responsibility in an Age of Terror* by Paul Lauritzen, Georgetown University Press, Washington, DC; Honorable Mention: *Robert McAfee Brown: Spiritual and Prophetic Writings* by Paul Crowley, SJ, editor, Orbis Books, Maryknoll, NY.

Papal Transition First Place: *A Call to Serve: Pope Francis and the Catholic Future* by Stefan von Kempis and Phillip Lawler, The Crossroad Publishing Company, New York, NY; Second Place: *Francis, A New World Pope* by Michel Cool, Wm. B. Eerdmans Publishing Co., Grand Rapids, MI.

Immigration First Place: *On "Strangers No Longer": Perspectives on the Historic U.S.-Mexican Catholic Bishops' Pastoral Letter on Migration* by Todd Schríbern and J. Kevin Appleby, editors, Paulist Press, Mahwah, NJ; Second Place: *Immigration and the Next America* by Archbishop Jose H. Gomez, Our Sunday Visitor Press, Huntington, IN; Third Place: *The Migrant's Way of the Cross* by Fr. Simon C. Kim, Liguori Press, Liguori, MO.

Coffee Table Book First Place: *Splendors of the Creed* by Fr. Joseph T. Leinhard, SJ and Fr. Frederic Curnier-Laroche, Magnificat, Yonkers, NY; Second Place: *History of the Diocese of Knoxville* by Dan McWilliams, The East Tennessee Catholic, Knoxville, TN; Third Place: *Purposeful Design: Understanding Creation* by Jay Schabacker, Self-Published, Lexington, SC.

Novel First Place: *The Gate* by Nancy Carbio Belanger, Harvey House Publishing; Second Place: *Rapunzel Let Down: A Fairy Tale Retold* by Regina Doman, Chesterton Press; Third Place: *Song of the Dove* by Kay Murdy, ACTA Publications, Chicago, IL; Honorable Mention: *Miram: Repentance and Redemption in Rome* by Cheryl Dickow, Bezalel Books.

Francis de Sales Award: Jim Lackey.

2014 Christopher Awards

Christopher Awards recognize the creative writers, producers and directors who have achieved artistic excellence in films, books and television specials. The 2013 awards were presented May 15, 2014, in New York.

Books: Bob Dotson, *American Story* (Viking Press/Penguin Group); Amy Andrews and Jessica Mesman Griffith, *Love & Salt* (Loyola Press); Roy Wenzl and Travis Heying, *The Miracle of Father Kapaun* (Ignatius Press); Wayne B. Drash, *On These Courts* (Touchstone Books/Simon and Schuster); Jim Ziolkowski and James S. Hirsch, *Walk In Their Shoes* (Simon and Schuster).

Books for Young People Courtney Pippin-Mathur, *Maya Was Grumpy* (Preschool and up, Flashlight Press); Suzanne Collins, *Year of the Jungle* (Kindergarten and up, Scholastic Press); Paul Fleishman and Bagram Ibatoulline, *The Matchbox Diary* (ages 6 and up, Candlewick Press); Kate DiCamillo and K.G. Campbell, *Flora & Ulysses* (ages 8 and up, Candlewick Press); Leon Leyson, with Marilyn J. Harran and Elisabeth B. Leyson, *The Boy on the Wooden Box* (ages 10 and up, Atheneum Books for Young Readers/Simon and Schuster).

Television and Cable: *ABC News 20/20: Unbreakable; Bulloch Family Ranch: Episode One* (UP TV); *Jerzy Popieluszko: Messenger of the Truth* (WTTW National Productions/PBS); *Life According to Sam* (HBO Documentary Films); *POV: Brooklyn Castle* (PBS).

Films: *42* (Warner Bros. Pictures); *Frozen* (Disney); *Gimme Shelter* (Day 28 Films/Roadside Attractions); *Gravity* (Warner Bros. Pictures).

2014 Christopher Lifetime Achievement Award: Father David T. Link; **2014 Christopher Leadership Award:** Tom Leopold.

Ecumenism and Interreligious Dialogue

ECUMENISM

Edited in consultation with the staff of the Secretariat for Ecumenical and Interreligious Affairs, USCCB.

The modern ecumenical movement, with roots in 19th-century scholars and individuals began its institutional life in 1910 among Protestants and Orthodox and led to formation of the World Council of Churches in 1948, developed outside the mainstream of Catholic interest until the 1950s. It has now become for Catholics as well one of the great religious facts of our time.

The *magna carta* of ecumenism for Catholics is a complex of several documents which include, in the first place, *Unitatis Redintegratio*, the "Decree on Ecumenism," promulgated by the Second Vatican Council Nov. 21, 1964. Other enactments underlying and expanding this decree are *Lumen Gentium* ("Dogmatic Constitution on the Church"), *Orientalium Ecclesiarum* ("Decree on Eastern Catholic Churches"), and *Gaudium et Spes* ("Pastoral Constitution on the Church in the Modern World").

The Holy See has more recently brought together Catholic ecumenical priorities in *Directory for the Application of Principles and Norms on Ecumenism* (1993) and *The Ecumenical Dimension in the Formation of Pastoral Workers* (1998). These, in addition to Pope John Paul II's encyclical letter, *Ut Unum Sint* (1995), provide a guide for Catholic ecumenical initiatives.

POPE FRANCIS (2013-)

On March 20, 2013, Pope Francis met with representatives of Christian churches, ecclesial communities and other world religions who had come to Rome for his inaugural Mass the previous day. He received them seated on an armchair at floor level, rather than on the customary raised throne.

After he was greeted by Ecumenical Patriarch Bartholomew of Constantinople, Pope Francis thanked him for his remarks, referring to him as "my brother Andrew." This was significant because Andrew is the patron saint of Constantinople and Peter is that of Rome; the two represent two ancient churches who are trying to retrieve the fraternal relationship that the two brother apostles had. This was most probably the first time ever that an ecumenical patriarch was present at the inaugural Mass of a pope.

Pope Francis recalled the significance of the Second Vatican Council for ecumenism, and quoted Pope John XXIII who said at the opening session of the council, "The Catholic Church considers it her duty to actively work so as to bring about the great mystery of that unity for which Jesus Christ prayed so ardently to His Father in heaven on the eve of his sacrifice." He went on to say that, "For my part, I wish to assure you, following in the path of my predecessors, of my firm will to continue on the path of ecumenical dialogue."

The new pope also reminded the representatives of the Jewish communities of "the very special spiritual bond" that links Jews and Christians. He quoted from Vatican II's Decree on Non-Christian Religions, which states: "The Church of Christ acknowledges that, according to God's saving design, the beginnings of her faith and her election are found already among the Patriarchs, Moses and the prophets." The pope said that he looked forward to the continuation of the fruitful dialogue that has accomplished so much in recent years.

The Holy Father then turned to the representatives of other world religions who were present, especially the Muslims who, again quoting the Council, "adore the one, living and merciful God and who call upon Him in prayer." He said that the Catholic Church is – and he repeated this twice for emphasis – "aware of the importance of the promotion of friendship and respect between men and women of different religious traditions." He went on to say that the Church "is also aware of the responsibility that we all bear to this our world, to all of creation, which we should love and protect. And we can do much for the good of the poorest, of the weak and suffering, to promote justice and reconciliation, to build peace. But, above all, we must keep alive the thirst for the Absolute in the world, not allowing a one-dimensional vision of the human person, in which humanity is reduced to that which it produces and consumes, to prevail. This is one of the most dangerous pitfalls of our times." In this brief address, Pope Francis has made it clear that he intends to continue the path of dialogue that the Catholic Church has followed since the Second Vatican Council. (Courtesy, USCCB Blog entry by Fr. Ronald Roberson, CSP, March 20, 2013.)

Address delivered by Pope Francis when he received a delegation from the Ecumenical Patriarchate of Constantinople led by Metropolitan John (Zizioulas) of Pergamon in the Vatican on June 28, 2014:

The Solemnity of the Holy Patrons of the Church of Rome, the Apostles Peter and Paul, once again gives me the joy of greeting a delegation from the sister Church of Constantinople. In extending to you a warm welcome, I express my gratitude to the Ecumenical Patriarch, His Holiness Bartholomaios I, and to the Holy Synod for having sent you to share with us in the joy of this feast.

I have vivid and moving memories of my recent meetings with my beloved brother Bartholomaios. During our common pilgrimage to the Land of Jesus, we were able to relive the gift of that embrace between our venerable predecessors, Athenagoras I and Paul VI, which took place 50 years ago in the holy city of Jerusalem. That prophetic gesture gave decisive impulse to a journey which, thank God, has never ceased. I consider it a special gift from the Lord that we were able to venerate the holy places together and to pray at each other's side at the place of Christ's burial, where we can actually touch the foundation of our hope. The joy of that meeting was then renewed when, in a certain sense, we concluded our pilgrimage here at the tomb of the Apostle Peter as we joined in fervent prayer, together with the Presidents of Israel and Palestine, for the gift of peace in the Holy Land. The Lord granted us these occasions of fraternal encounter, in which we were able to express the love uniting us in Christ, and to renew our mutual desire to walk together along the path to full unity.

We know very well that this unity is a gift of God, a gift that even now the Most High grants us the grace to attain whenever, by the power of the Holy Spirit, we choose to look at one another with the eyes of faith and to see ourselves as we truly are in God's plan, according to the designs of his eternal will, and not what we have become as a result of the historical consequences of our sins. If all of us can learn, prompted by the Spirit, to look at one another in God, our path will be even straighter and our cooperation all the more easy in the many areas of daily life which already happily unite us.

This way of "looking at one another in God" is nourished by faith, hope and love; it gives rise to an authentic theological reflection which is truly *scientia Dei*, a participation in that vision which God has of himself and of us. It is a reflection which can only bring us closer to one another on the path of unity, despite our differing starting points. I hope and I pray, then, that the work of the Joint International Commission can be a sign of this profound understanding, this theology "on its knees." In this way, the Commission's reflections on the concepts of primacy and synodality, communion in the universal Church and the ministry of the Bishop of Rome will not be an academic exercise or a mere debate about irreconcilable positions. All of us need, with courage and confidence, to be open to the working of the Holy Spirit. We need to let ourselves be caught up in Christ's loving gaze upon the Church, his Bride, in our journey of spiritual ecumenism. It is a journey upheld by the martyrdom of so many of our brothers and sisters who, by their witness to Jesus Christ the Lord, have brought about an ecumenism of blood.

Dear members of the Delegation, with sentiments of sincere respect, friendship and love in Christ, I renew my heartfelt gratitude for your presence among us. I ask you to convey my greeting to my venerable brother Bartholomaios and to continue to pray for me and for the ministry with which I have been entrusted. Through the intercession of Mary, the Most Holy Mother of God, and of Ss. Peter and Paul, the princes of the Apostles, and St. Andrew the first-called, may Almighty God bless us and fill us with every grace. Amen.

Address delivered by Pope Francis when he received His Grace Justin Welby, the Archbishop of Canterbury, in the Vatican on June 16, 2014:
"Behold, how good and how pleasant it is for brothers to dwell together in unity!" (Ps 133:1). Once again we meet, Your Grace, as co-workers in the Lord's vineyard and fellow pilgrims on the path to his Kingdom. I welcome you and the distinguished members of your delegation, and I pray that today's meeting will serve to strengthen further our bonds of friendship and our commitment to the great cause of reconciliation and communion between Christian believers.

The Lord's question – "What were you arguing about on the way?" (Mk 9:33) – might also apply to us. When Jesus put this question to his disciples they were silent; they were ashamed, for they had been arguing about who was the greatest among them. We too feel ashamed when we ponder the distance between the Lord's call and our meagre response. Beneath his merciful gaze, we cannot claim that our division is anything less than a scandal and an obstacle to our proclaiming the Gospel of salvation to the world. Our vision is often blurred by the cumulative burden of our divisions and our will is not always free of that human ambition which can accompany even our desire to preach the Gospel as the Lord commanded (cf. Mt 28:19).

The goal of full unity may seem distant indeed, it remains the aim which should direct our every step along the way. I find a source of encouragement in the plea of the Second Vatican Council's Decree on Ecumenism that we should advance in our relationship and cooperation by placing no obstacle to the ways of divine providence and by not prejudicing future promptings of the Holy Spirit (cf. *Unitatis Redintegratio*, 24). Our progress toward full communion will not be the fruit of human actions alone, but a free gift of God. The Holy Spirit gives us the strength not to grow disheartened and he invites us to trust fully in the power of his works.

As disciples who strive to follow the Lord, we realize that the faith has come to us through many witnesses. We are indebted to great saints, teachers and communities; they have handed down the faith over the ages and they bear witness to our common roots. Yesterday, on the Solemnity of the Most Holy Trinity, Your Grace celebrated Vespers in the Church of San Gregorio al Celio, from which Pope Gregory the Great sent forth Augustine and his monastic companions to evangelize the peoples of England, thus inaugurating a history of faith and holiness which in turn enriched many other European peoples. This glorious history has profoundly shaped institutions and ecclesial traditions which we share and which serve as a solid basis for our fraternal relations.

On this basis, then, let us look with confidence to the future. The Anglican-Roman Catholic International Commission and the International Anglican-Roman Catholic Commission for Unity and Mission represent especially significant forums for examining, in a constructive spirit, older and newer challenges to our ecumenical engagement.

At our first meeting, Your Grace and I discussed our shared concerns and our pain before a number of grave evils afflicting our human family. In particular, we shared our horror in the face of the scourge of human trafficking and forms of modern-day slavery. I thank you for the leadership you have shown in opposing these intolerable crimes against human dignity.

In attempting to respond to this urgent need, notable collaborative efforts have been initiated on the ecumenical level and in cooperation with civil authorities and international organizations. Many charitable initiatives have been undertaken by our communities, and they are operating with generosity and courage in various parts of the world. I think in particular of the action network against the trafficking in women set up by a number of women's religious institutes. Let us persevere in our commitment to combat new forms of enslavement, in the hope that we can help provide relief to victims and oppose this deplorable trade. I thank God that, as disciples sent to heal a wounded world, we stand together, with perseverance and determination, in opposing this grave evil.

POPE BENEDICT XVI (2005-2013)

Pope Benedict XVI reaffirmed the irreversible commitment of the Catholic Church to the ecumenical movement, and stated that ecumenism would be the "primary task" of his pontificate. This is an excerpt from his address to the Cardinals at the end of a Mass he celebrated with them the day after his election, on April 20, 2005:

"Nourished and sustained by the Eucharist, Catholics cannot but feel encouraged to strive for the full unity for which Christ expressed so ardent a hope in the Upper Room. The Successor of Peter knows that he must make himself especially responsible for his Divine Master's supreme aspiration. Indeed, he is entrusted with the task of strengthening his brethren (cf. Lk 22:32).

With full awareness, therefore, at the beginning of his ministry in the Church of Rome which Peter bathed in his blood, Peter's current Successor takes on as his primary task the duty to work tirelessly to rebuild the full and visible unity of all Christ's followers. This is his ambition, his impelling duty. He is aware that good intentions do not suffice for this. Concrete gestures that enter hearts and stir consciences are essential, inspiring in everyone that inner conversion that is the prerequisite for all ecumenical progress.

Theological dialogue is necessary; the investigation of the historical reasons for the decisions made in the past is also indispensable. But what is most urgently needed is that 'purification of memory,' so often recalled by John Paul II, which alone can dispose souls to accept the full truth of Christ. Each one of us must come before him, the supreme Judge of every living person, and render an account to him of all we have done or have failed to do to further the great good of the full and visible unity of all his disciples. The current Successor of Peter is allowing himself to be called in the first person by this requirement and is prepared to do everything in his power to promote the fundamental cause of ecumenism. Following the example of his Predecessors, he is fully determined to encourage every initiative that seems appropriate for promoting contacts and understanding with the representatives of the different Churches and Ecclesial Communities. Indeed, on this occasion he sends them his most cordial greeting in Christ, the one Lord of us all."

VATICAN II DECREE

The following excerpts from Unitatis Redintegratio *cover the broad theological background and principles and indicate the thrust of the Church's commitment to ecumenism.*

Men who believe in Christ and have been properly baptized are brought into a certain, though imperfect, communion with the Catholic Church. Undoubtedly, the differences that exist in varying degrees between them and the Catholic Church — whether in doctrine and sometimes in discipline, or concerning the structure of the Church — do indeed create many and sometimes serious obstacles to full ecclesiastical communion. These the ecumenical movement is striving to overcome (No. 3).

Elements Common to Christians

Moreover some, even very many, of the most significant elements or endowments which together go to build up and give life to the Church herself can exist outside the visible boundaries of the Catholic Church: the written word of God; the life of grace; faith, hope, and charity, along with other interior gifts of the Holy Spirit and visible elements. All of these, which come from Christ and lead back to Him, belong by right to the one Church of Christ (No. 3).

[In a later passage, the decree singled out a number of elements which the Catholic Church and other churches have in common but not in complete agreement: confession of Christ as Lord and God and as mediator between God and man; belief in the Trinity; reverence for Scripture as the revealed word of God; baptism and the Lord's Supper; Christian life and worship; faith in action; concern with moral questions.]

The brethren divided from us also carry out many of the sacred actions of the Christian religion. Undoubtedly, in ways that vary according to the condition of each church or community, these actions can truly engender a life of grace, and can be rightly described as capable of providing access to the community of salvation.

It follows that these separated Churches and Communities, though we believe they suffer from defects already mentioned, have by no means been deprived of significance and importance in the mystery of salvation. For the Spirit of Christ has not refrained from using them as means of salvation which derive their efficacy from the very fullness of grace and truth entrusted to the Catholic Church (No. 3).

Unity Lacking

Nevertheless, our separated brethren, whether considered as individuals or as Communities and Churches, are not blessed with that unity which Jesus Christ wished to bestow on all those whom he has regenerated and vivified into one body and newness of life — that unity which the holy Scriptures and the revered tradition of the Church proclaim. For it is through Christ's Catholic Church alone, which is the all-embracing means of salvation, that the fullness of the means of salvation can be obtained. It was to the apostolic college alone, of which Peter is the head, that we believe our Lord entrusted all the blessings of the New Covenant, in order to establish on earth the one Body of Christ into which all those should be fully incorporated who already belong in any way to God's People (No. 3).

In the 1995 encyclical of Pope John Paul II, *Ut Unum Sint* the language of Separate Brethren has been put aside for the designation of "fellow Christian" to speak of Christians not in full communion with the Catholic Church.

What the Movement Involves

Today, in many parts of the world, under the inspiring grace of the Holy Spirit, multiple efforts are being expended through prayer, word, and action to attain that fullness of unity which Jesus Christ desires. This sacred Synod, therefore, exhorts all the Catholic faithful to recognize the signs of the times and to participate skillfully in the work of ecumenism.

The "ecumenical movement" means those activities and enterprises which, according to various needs of the Church and opportune occasions, are started and organized for the fostering of unity among Christians. These are:

• First, every effort to eliminate words, judgments,

and actions which do not respond to the condition of separated brethren with truth and fairness and so make mutual relations between them more difficult.

• Then, "dialogue" between competent experts from different Churches and Communities [scholarly ecumenism].

• In addition, these Communions cooperate more closely in whatever projects a Christian conscience demands for the common good [social ecumenism].

• They also come together for common prayer, where this is permitted [spiritual ecumenism].

• Pope John Paul urged that the results of (now) 45 years of dialogue become a "common heritage," therefore all Catholic catechetical and ministry formation programs are to be informed by the progress of ecumenical relations [ecumenical formation].

• Finally, all are led to examine their own faithfulness to Christ's will for the Church and, wherever necessary, undertake with vigor the task of renewal and reform.

It is evident that the work of preparing and reconciling those individuals who wish for full Catholic communion is of its nature distinct from ecumenical action. But there is no opposition between the two, since both proceed from the wondrous providence of God (No. 4).

Primary Duty of Catholics

In ecumenical work, Catholics must assuredly be concerned for their separated brethren, praying for them, keeping them informed about the Church, making the first approaches toward them. But their primary duty is to make an honest and careful appraisal of whatever needs to be renewed and achieved in the Catholic household itself, in order that its life may bear witness more loyally and luminously to the teachings and ordinances which have been handed down from Christ through the Apostles.

Every Catholic must aim at Christian perfection (cf. Jas 1:4; Rom 12:1-2) and, each according to his station, play his part so that the Church may daily be more purified and renewed, against the day when Christ will present her to himself in all her glory, without spot or wrinkle (cf. Eph 5:27).

Catholics must joyfully acknowledge and esteem the truly Christian endowments from our common heritage which are to be found among our separated brethren.

Nor should we forget that whatever is wrought by the grace of the Holy Spirit in the hearts of our separated brethren can contribute to our own edification. Whatever is truly Christian never conflicts with the genuine interests of the faith; indeed, it can always result in a more ample realization of the very mystery of Christ and the Church (No. 4).

Participation in Worship

Norms concerning participation by Catholics in the worship of other Christian Churches were sketched in this conciliar decree and elaborated in a number of other documents such as: the Decree on Eastern Catholic Churches, promulgated by the Second Vatican Council in 1964; Interim Guidelines for Prayer in Common, issued June 18, 1965, by the U.S. Bishops' Committee for Ecumenical and Interreligious Affairs; a Directory on Ecumenism and Guidelines on Ecumenical Formation published in 1967, 1970, 1993 and 1998 by the Pontifical Council for Promoting Christian Unity; additional communications from the U.S. Bishops' Committee, and numerous sets of guidelines issued locally by and for dioceses throughout the U.S.

The norms encourage common prayer services for Christian unity and other intentions. Beyond that, they draw a distinction between separated churches of the Reformation tradition and of the Anglican Communion, and separated Eastern churches, in view of doctrine and practice the Catholic Church has in common with the separated Eastern churches concerning the apostolic succession of bishops, holy orders, liturgy and other creedal matters.

Full participation by Catholics in official Protestant Eucharistic liturgies is prohibited, because it implies profession of the faith expressed in the liturgy. Reception of communion by Catholics at Protestant liturgies is prohibited. Under certain conditions, Protestants may be given Holy Communion in the Catholic Church. A Catholic may stand as a witness, but not as a sponsor, in baptism, and as a witness in the marriage of separated Christians. Similarly, a Protestant may stand as a witness, but not as a sponsor, in a Catholic baptism, and as a witness in the marriage of Catholics.

The principal norms regarding liturgical participations with separated Eastern Churches are included under Eastern Ecumenism.

DIRECTORY ON ECUMENISM

A Directory for the Application of the Principles and Norms of Ecumenism *was approved by Pope John Paul II on Mar. 25, 1993, and published early in June. The Pontifical Council for Promoting Christian Unity said on release of the document that revision of Directories issued in 1967 and 1970 was necessary in view of subsequent developments. These included promulgation of the Code of Canon Law for the Latin Church in 1983 and of the Code of Canons of the Eastern Churches in 1990; publication of the* Catechism of the Catholic Church *in 1992; additional documents and the results of theological dialogues. In 1998,* The Ecumenical Dimension in the Formation of Pastoral Workers *was published by the Holy See to give practical and detailed guidance in the implementation of Chapter 3 of the* Directory.

The following excerpts are from the text published in the June 16, 1993, English edition of L'Osservatore Romano.

Address and Purpose

"The Directory is addressed to the pastors of the Catholic Church, but it also concerns all the faithful, who are called to pray and work for the unity of Christians, under the direction of their bishops."

"At the same time, it is hoped that the Directory will also be useful to members of churches and ecclesial communities that are not in full communion with the Catholic Church."

"The new edition of the Directory is meant to be an instrument at the service of the whole Church, and especially of those who are directly engaged in ecumenical activity in the Catholic Church. The Directory intends to motivate, enlighten and guide this activity, and in some particular cases also to give binding directives in accordance with the proper competence of the Pontifical Council for Promoting Christian Unity."

Outline

Principles and norms of the document are covered in five chapters.

"I. The Search for Christian Unity. The ecumenical commitment of the Catholic Church based on the doctrinal principles of the Second Vatican Council.

"II. Organization in the Catholic Church at the Service of Christian Unity. Persons and structures involved in promoting ecumenism at all levels, and the norms that direct their activity.

"III. Ecumenical Formation in the Catholic Church. Categories of people to be formed, those responsible for formation; the aims and methods of formation; its doctrinal and practical aspects.

"IV. Communion in Life and Spiritual Activity among the Baptized. The communion that exists with other Christians on the basis of the sacramental bond of baptism, and the norms for sharing in prayer and other spiritual activities, including, in particular cases, sacramental sharing.

"V. Ecumenical Cooperation, Dialogue and Common Witness. Principles, different forms and norms for cooperation between Christians with a view to dialogue and common witness in the world."

ECUMENICAL AGENCIES

Pontifical Council

The top-level agency for Catholic ecumenical efforts is the Pontifical Council for Promoting Christian Unity (formerly the Secretariat for Promoting Christian Unity), which originated in 1960 as a preparatory commission for the Second Vatican Council. Its purposes are to provide guidance and, where necessary, coordination for ecumenical endeavor by Catholics, and to establish and maintain relations with representatives of other Christian Churches for ecumenical dialogue and action.

The council, under the direction of Card. Kurt Koch (successor to Card. Walter Kasper, has established firm working relations with representative agencies of other churches, the Global Christian Forum and the World Council of Churches. It has joined in dialogue with the Eastern and Oriental Orthodox Churches, the Anglican Communion, the Lutheran World Federation, the World Alliance of Reformed Churches, the World Methodist Council, Baptist World Alliance, World Evangelical Alliance, the Pentecostals, Mennonites, Seventh-day Adventists and other religious bodies. In the past several years, staff members and representatives of the council have been involved in one way or another in nearly every significant ecumenical enterprise and meeting held throughout the world.

While the council and its counterparts in other churches have focused primary attention on common mission, theological and other related problems of Christian unity, they have also begun, and in increasing measure, to emphasize the responsibilities of the churches for greater unity of effort in areas of humanitarian need. With the Congregation of the Doctrine of the Faith, the Council carries responsibility for official Catholic action on the results of the dialogue and shepherding the process of reception in the Catholic Church.

Bishops' Committee

The Committee for Ecumenical and Interreligious Affairs of the United States Conference of Catholic Bishops was established by the American hierarchy in 1964. Its purposes are to maintain relationships with other Christian churches and religious communities at the national level, to help other offices of the Conference do their work ecumenically, to advise and assist dioceses in developing and applying ecumenical policies, and to maintain liaison with corresponding Vatican offices – the Pontifical Councils for Christian Unity and for Interreligious Dialogue and other bishops conferences when needed.

As of Nov. 2014, this standing committee of the United States Conference of Catholic Bishops is chaired by Bp. Mitchel. T. Rozanski of Springfield. Operationally, the committee is assisted by a secretariat overseen by Executive Director is Fr. John Crossin, OSFS, along with Associate Directors Fr. Ronald Roberson, CSP, and Dr. Anthony Cirelli. The committee co-sponsors several national consultations with other churches and ecclesial communities. These bring together Catholic representatives and counterparts from the Episcopal Church, the Evangelical Lutheran Church in America and Lutheran Church – Missouri Synod, the Polish National Catholic Church, the United Methodist Church, the Orthodox Churches, the Oriental Orthodox Churches, and the Reformed Churches (which include the United Church of Christ, the Presbyterian Church, the Christian Reformed Church, and the Reformed Church in America). There is also a history of engagement with the National Association of Evangelicals, the Pentecostal churches in the context of the Society for Pentecostal Studies, and – until 2001 – a 30 year conversation with the Southern Baptist Convention. (*See* **Ecumenical Dialogues.**)

The committee relates to the National Council of Churches of Christ through membership in the Faith and Order Commission and helping to produce materials for the annual Week of Prayer for Christian Unity. It also sponsored a joint study committee investigating the possibility of Roman Catholic membership in the NCCC in the 1970s. Collaboration in multiple areas of church life has proved to be more fruitful than membership given the disparity of numbers and diversity of program priorities of the Bishop's Conference and the Council. Recently the NCCC adopted a new plan and changed its structures.

The USCCB participates in a new ecumenical entity, Christian Churches Together in the USA. It includes representatives from the five major families of Christian churches in the United States which, in addition to the Catholic Church, include the historic Protestant, Orthodox, Evangelical/Pentecostal, and African American churches.

Advisory and other services are provided by the committee to ecumenical commissions and agencies in dioceses throughout the country.

Through its Section for Catholic-Jewish Relations, the committee is in contact with several national Jewish agencies and bodies. Issues of mutual interest and shared concern are reviewed for the purpose of furthering deeper understanding between the Catholic and Jewish communities.

The committee also co-sponsors interreligious activities and programs. By late 2009, there were three regional dialogues with Muslims and regular contacts with Buddhists, Hindus and Sikhs.

Offices of the committee are located at 3211 Fourth St. N.E., Washington, DC 20017; http://www.usccb.org/beliefs-and-teachings/ecumenical-and-interreligious/.

World Council of Churches

The World Council of Churches is a fellowship of churches which acknowledge "Jesus Christ as Lord and Savior." It is a permanent organization providing constituent members — 330 churches with some 450 million communicants in 100 countries — with opportunities for meeting, consultation and cooperative action with respect to doctrine, worship, practice, social mission, evangelism and missionary work, and other matters of mutual concern.

The WCC was formally established Aug. 23, 1948, in Amsterdam with ratification of a constitution by 147 communions. This action merged two previously existing movements — Life and Work (social mission), Faith and Order (doctrine) — which had initiated practical steps toward founding a fellowship of Christian churches at meetings held in Oxford, Edinburgh and Utrecht in 1937 and 1938. A third movement for cooperative missionary work, which originated about 1910 and, remotely, led to formation of the WCC, was incorporated into the council in 1961 under the title of the International Missionary Council.

Additional WCC General Assemblies that have been held since the charter meeting of 1948 include Evanston, IL (1954), New Delhi, India (1961), Uppsala, Sweden (1968), Nairobi, Kenya (1975), Vancouver, British Columbia, Canada (1983) and Canberra, Australia (1991). The 1998 general assembly was held in Harare, Zimbabwe, with the regular Catholic delegation in attendance, led by Abp. Mario Conti of Glasgow, Scotland. The Ninth General Assembly took place in Porto Alegre, Brazil, Feb. 14-23, 2006. A Catholic delegation headed by Card. Walter Kasper, President of the Pontifical Council for Promoting Christian Unity, was present. The 10th General Assembly took place in Busan, South Korea, Oct. 30-Nov. 8, 2013.

The council continues the work of the International Missionary Council, the Commission on Faith and Order, and the Commission on Church and Society. The work of the council is carried out through four program units: unity and renewal; mission, education and witness; justice, peace and creation; sharing and service.

Liaison between the council and the Vatican has been maintained since 1966 through a Joint Working Group. The Joint Commission on Society, Development and Peace (SODEPAX) was an agency of the council and the Pontifical Commission for Justice and Peace from 1968 to Dec. 31, 1980, after which another working group was formed. Roman Catholics serve as full members of the Commission on Faith and Order since 1968, the Holy See provides staff to mission, education and witness unit of the Council, and the Catholic Church is engaged in various capacities on other program committees of the council.

WCC headquarters are located in Geneva, Switzerland. The WCC also maintains fraternal relations with regional, national and local councils of churches throughout the world. Web site: http://www.oikoumene.org/

National Council of Churches

The National Council of the Churches of Christ in the U.S.A., the largest ecumenical body in the United States, is an organization of 37 Protestant, Orthodox and Anglican communions, with an aggregate membership of more than 45 million in over 100,000 congregations. The NCC, established by the churches in 1950, was structured through the merger of 12 separate cooperative agencies. Presently, the NCC carries on work in behalf of member churches in overseas ministries, Christian education, domestic social action, communications, biblical translation, theological dialogue, interfaith activities, worship and evangelism, and other areas. NCC President and General Secretary: Jim Winkler. NCC headquarters are located at 110 Maryland Avenue NE, Suite 108, Washington, DC 20002-5603; (202) 544-2350; www. nationalcouncilofchurches.us

Christian Churches Together in the USA

In early 2001, discussions began in earnest among church leaders in the United States about the possibility of forming a new ecumenical organization. There was an acute awareness that since the members of the current National Council of Churches (NCC) represent only about one third of the Christians in the United States, a much broader ecumenical witness was needed. Thus in the summer of 2001 letters were sent out to various American church leaders inviting them to attend a meeting at St. Mary's Seminary and University in Baltimore on Sept. 7-8. The letter was signed by Bp. Tod Brown, Card. William Keeler, Rev. Wesley Granberg-Michaelson (General Secretary of the Reformed Church in America), and Rev. Dr. Robert Edgar (NCC General Secretary). The meeting was to explore whether or not the time had come to "create a new, more inclusive ecumenical table and/or body." The most striking result was the unanimous strong desire among the participants for a broader structure of some kind that would include all the major groupings of churches, including the Catholic Church and major Evangelical and Pentecostal groups that do not now belong to the NCC. Subsequent organizational meetings were held in Chicago (April 2002), Pasadena (January 2003), and Navasota, Texas (January 2004). The name chosen for the new entity is "Christian Churches Together in the USA" (CCT).

In November 2004, the Catholic Bishops of the United States took an historic ecumenical step by voting to participate in CCT. Bp. Stephen E. Blaire of Stockton, CA, chairman of the Committee on Ecumenical and Interreligious Affairs, presented the proposal to the body of bishops and urged its adoption, calling CCT a "fresh and creative initiative to broaden the ecumenical table." The bishops approved the proposal to join CCT by a vote of 151-73, slightly more than a 2-to-1 margin.

From June 1-3, 2005, 67 national Christian leaders from five Christian families–Evangelical/Pentecostal, Historic Protestant, Historic Racial/Ethnic, Orthodox and Catholic–met in their fifth and largest CCT organizational meeting at the Jesuit Conference Center in Los Altos, CA. The gathering at Los Altos brought together a wider, more diverse circle of Christian church leaders than at any of the previous four meetings. Through two and a half days of sharing, prayer and worship, the participants wrestled with difficult and complex issues in a spirit of love and good will. Relationships with the Historic Black Churches were deepened through intensive dialogue and sharing.

It was decided at Los Altos to delay a formal launch planned for September 2005 in order to continue the productive and positive conversation with churches and organizations actively considering joining. Participants enthusiastically reaffirmed their commitment to "grow closer together in Christ in order to strengthen our Christian witness in the world." The Rev. Wesley Granberg-Michaelson was unanimously reelected as moderator to lead an expanded Steering Committee.

Another plenary meeting of CCT took place at Simpsonwood Conference and Retreat Center near Atlanta, GA, from Mar. 28-31, 2006. At this meeting the new By-laws of CCT were adopted and the new organization formally came into existence. Subsequent plenaries were held in February 2007 (Pasadena, CA), January 2008 (Baltimore, MD) January 2009 (Baltimore, MD), and January 2010 (Seattle, WA). The January 2011 plenary in Birmingham, AL. With 40 churches and national organizations participating, CCT is now the broadest, most inclusive fellowship of Christian churches and traditions that has ever existed in the USA. The main focus of recent meetings has been poverty in the United States, evangelization, and racism. Mass incarceration was the theme of the most recent meeting which took place in Newark, NJ, in February 2014. Moderator: Rev. Stephen Thurston (President of Historic Black Family); Catholic President: Aux. Bp. Denis J. Madden of Baltimore; Executive Director: Rev. Carlos Malave; www.christianchurchestogether.org.

Churches Uniting in Christ

Churches Uniting in Christ (CUIC) is a relationship among Christian communions that have pledged to live more closely together in expressing their unity in Christ with a primary focus upon combating racism both within the church and in society. CUIC is both an outgrowth of and successor to the Consultation on Church Union (COCU), an organization that worked for more than 40 years toward the day when Christians can become more fully reconciled to each other. After a two year pause to reassess the vision and structure of the organization, CUIC members announced their recommitment to a "New Way Forward" in 2010.

The eight marks of communion in the CUIC partnership are: mutual recognition of each other as authentic expressions of the one church of Jesus Christ, mutual recognition of members in one Baptism, mutual recognition that each affirms the apostolic faith of Scripture and tradition which is expressed in the Apostles' and Nicene Creeds, and that each seeks to give witness to the apostolic faith in its life and mission, provision for celebration of the Eucharist together with intentional regularity, engagement together in Christ's mission on a regular and intentional basis, especially a shared mission to combat racism, intentional commitment to promote unity with wholeness and to oppose marginalization and exclusion in church and society based on such things as race, age, gender, forms of disability, sexual orientation, and class, appropriate structures of accountability and appropriate means for consultation and decision making, an ongoing process of theological dialogue.

The member communions, representing 25 million Christians, are the African Methodist Episcopal Church, the Christian Church (Disciples of Christ), the Christian Methodist Episcopal Church, the Episcopal Church, the Presbyterian Church (U.S.A.), the United Church of Christ, the United Methodist Church, the Moravian Church Northern Province, and the International Council of Community Churches. The Evangelical Lutheran Church in America is a partner in mission and dialogue and the Secretariat of Ecumenical and Interreligious Affairs of the United States Conference of Catholic Bishops maintains observer status. Catholic participation includes a staff representative to the CUIC coordinating council, with a voice but no vote, and Catholic membership on the task forces, with a voice and a vote. Catholic theologians have made a significant contribution by serving on the Ministry Task Force and offering insights from the Catholic perspective.

At the January 2011 plenary meeting in Ft. Lauderdale, CUIC expressed its commitment to seek reconciliation with the African Methodist Episcopal Zion (AME Zion) Church, a member communion that suspended its membership with CUIC over concerns that the organization had not been fully committed to addressing issues of racial justice.

The final day of the 2011 plenary included consideration of recommended actions CUIC member communions might take to address racism in three specific contexts: international, national, and within the member churches.

The plenary concluded with a service of recommitment to CUIC's initial goals and marks of visible unity.

Currently the President of CUIC is Rev. Robina Winbush of the Presbyterian Church (USA), the Vice President is Mrs. Jacqueline Dupont Walker of the African Methodist Episcopal Church, the Secretary is Rev. Jean Hawxhurst of the United Methodist Church, and the Treasurer is Rev. Dr. Robert Welsh of the Disciples of Christ. churchesunitinginchrist.org

Graymoor Institute

The Graymoor Ecumenical and Interreligious Institute is a forum where issues that confront the Christian Churches are addressed, the spiritual dimensions of ecumenism are fostered, and information, documentation and developments within the ecumenical movement are published through Ecumenical Trends, a monthly journal. GEII also produces the annual materials for the Week of Prayer for Christian Unity.

Director: Fr. James Loughran, SA. Address: 475 Riverside Dr., Rm. 1960, New York, NY 10115-1999. http://www.geii.org/

INTERNATIONAL BILATERAL COMMISSIONS

Anglican Roman Catholic International Commission, sponsored by the Pontifical Council for Promoting Christian Unity and the Lambeth Conference, from 1970 to 1981; succeeded by a **Second Anglican Roman Catholic International Commission**, called into being by the Common Declaration of Pope John Paul and the Archbishop of Canterbury in 1982. It completed its work in 2005. A new International Anglican-Roman Catholic Commission for Unity and Mission, set up in 2000, has summarized the main conclusions of ARCIC and proposed ways to grow together in mission and witness. When Dr. Rowan Williams, the Archbishop of Canterbury, met with Pope Benedict XVI in Rome in November 2009, they announced preparations for the establishment of a **Third Anglican-Roman Catholic International Commission**. It met for the first time at a Catholic monastery in Bose, Italy, from May 17-27, 2011, and is examining the Church as Communion, local and universal, and how in communion the local and universal Church come to discern right ethical teaching.

The International Theological Colloquium between Baptists and Catholics, established in 1984 by the Pontifical Council for Promoting Christian Unity and the Commission for Faith and Interchurch Cooperation of the Baptist World Alliance.

The Disciples of Christ-Roman Catholic Dialogue, organized by the Council of Christian Unity of the Christian Church (Disciples of Christ) and the U.S. Bishops' Committee for Ecumenical and Interreligious Affairs, along with participation by the Disciples' Ecumenical Consultative Council and the Unity Council; since 1977.

The Evangelical-Roman Catholic Dialogue on Mission, organized by Evangelicals and the Pontifical Council for Promoting Christian Unity; from 1977. This dialogue is now sponsored by the World Evangelical Alliance, on the evangelical side.

The Lutheran-Roman Catholic Commission on Unity, established by the Pontifical Council for Promoting Christian Unity and the Lutheran World Federation; from 1967.

The Joint International Commission for Theological

Dialogue between the Orthodox Church and the Catholic Church, established by the Holy See and 14 autocephalous Orthodox Churches, began its work at a first session held at Patmos/Rhodes in 1980. Subsequent sessions have been held at Munich (1982), Crete (1984), Bari (1987), Valamo (1988), Freising (1990), Balamand (1993), and Emmitsburg, Maryland (2000); Belgrade, Serbia (2006); Ravenna, Italy (2007); Paphos, Cyprus (2009), and Vienna, Austria (2010).

Pentecostal-Roman Catholic Conversations, since 1972.

The Reformed-Roman Catholic Conversations, inaugurated in 1970 by the Pontifical Council for Promoting Christian Unity and the World Alliance of Reformed Churches.

The International Joint Commission between the Catholic Church and the Coptic Orthodox Church, since 1974. Established officially in the Common Declaration signed by Pope Paul VI and Coptic Pope Shenouda III in Rome in 1973. Superseded in 2003 by the international dialogue with the Oriental Orthodox.

The Joint International Commission between the Roman Catholic Church and the Malankara Orthodox Syrian Church, since 1989.

The Joint Commission between the Catholic Church and the Malankara Jacobite Syrian Orthodox Church, since 1990.

The Assyrian Church of the East-Roman Catholic Dialogue, officially established in the Common Declaration signed by Pope John Paul II and Mar Dinkha IV in November 1994.

Catholic Church-Oriental Orthodox Churches International Joint Commission for Dialogue was planned at a Preparatory Meeting held in Rome in January 2003. The first meeting of the Joint Commission took place in Cairo in January 2004. Subsequent meetings have taken place in Rome (2005), Etchmiadzin, Armenia (2006), Rome (2007), near Damascus, Syria (2008), Rome (2009), Antelias, Lebanon (2010), Rome (2011), Addis Ababa, Ethiopia (2012), Rome (2013), and Kerala, India (2014).

Dialogue between the World Evangelical Alliance and the Catholic Church begun in 1990 issued a statement in 2002.

Dialogue with the Mennonite World Conference begun in 1998 produced an agreed statement in 2003.

U.S. ECUMENICAL DIALOGUES

Representatives of the Bishops' Committee for Ecumenical and Interreligious Affairs, United States Conference of Catholic Bishops, have met in dialogue with representatives of other churches since the 1960s, for discussion of a wide variety of subjects related to the quest for unity among Christians. Following is a list of dialogue groups and the years in which dialogue began.

Anglican-Roman Catholic Consultation, 1965; North American Orthodox-Catholic Theological Consultation, 1965; Joint Committee of Orthodox and Catholic Bishops, 1981; Lutheran Consultation, 1965; Oriental Orthodox Consultation (with Armenian, Coptic, Ethiopian, Indian Malabar and Syrian Orthodox Churches), 1978; Polish National-Catholic Consultation, 1984; Presbyterian/Reformed Consultation, 1965; Southern Baptist Conversations, 1969; United Methodist Consultation, 1966; Faith and Order National Council of Churches, 1968; National Association of Evangelicals, 2003-2008.

COMMON DECLARATIONS OF POPES, OTHER CHURCH LEADERS

(*Source: Secretariat for Ecumenical and Interreligious Affairs, United States Conference of Catholic Bishops.*)

The following Common Declarations, issued by several popes and heads, carry the authority given them by their signators.

Paul VI and Orthodox Ecumenical Patriarch Athenagoras I, First Common Declaration, Dec. 7, 1965: They hoped the differences between the churches would be overcome with the help of the Holy Spirit, and that their "full communion of faith, brotherly concord and sacramental life" would be restored.

Paul VI and Anglican Abp. Michael Ramsey of Canterbury, Mar. 24, 1966: They stated their intention "to inaugurate between the Roman Catholic Church and the Anglican Communion a serious dialogue which, founded on the Gospels and on the ancient common traditions, may lead to that unity in truth for which Christ prayed."

Paul VI and Patriarch Athenagoras I, Second Common Declaration, Oct. 27, 1967: They wished "to emphasize their conviction that the restoration of full communion (between the churches) is to be found within the framework of the renewal of the Church and of Christians in fidelity to the traditions of the Fathers and to the inspirations of the Holy Spirit who remains always with the Church."

Paul VI and Vasken I, Orthodox Catholicos-Patriarch of All Armenians, May 12, 1970: They called for closer collaboration "in all domains of Christian life.... This collaboration must be based on the mutual recognition of the common Christian faith and the sacramental life, on the mutual respect of persons and their churches."

Paul VI and Mar Ignatius Jacob III, Syrian Orthodox Patriarch of Antioch, Oct. 27, 1971: They declared themselves to be "in agreement that there is no difference in the faith they profess concerning the mystery of the Word of God made flesh and become really man, even if over the centuries difficulties have arisen out of the different theological expressions by which this faith was expressed."

Paul VI and Shenouda III, Coptic Orthodox Pope of Alexandria, May 10, 1973: Their common declaration recalls the common elements of the Catholic and Coptic Orthodox faith in the Trinity, the divinity and humanity of Christ, the seven sacraments, the Virgin Mary, the Church founded upon the Apostles, and the Second Coming of Christ. It recognizes that the two churches "are not able to give more perfect witness to this new life in Christ because of existing divisions which have behind them centuries of difficult history" dating back to the year A.D. 451. In spite of these difficulties, they expressed "determination and confidence in the Lord to achieve the fullness and perfection of that unity which is his gift."

Paul VI and Anglican Abp. Donald Coggan of Canterbury, Apr. 29, 1977: They stated many points on which Anglicans and Roman Catholics hold the faith in common and called for greater cooperation between Anglicans and Roman Catholics.

John Paul II and Orthodox Ecumenical Patriarch Dimitrios I, First Common Declaration, Nov. 30, 1979: "Purification of the collective memory of our churches is an important fruit of the dialogue of charity and an indispensable condition of future progress." They announced the establishment of the Catholic-Orthodox Theological Commission.

John Paul II and Anglican Abp. Robert Runcie of

Canterbury, May 29, 1982: They agreed to establish a new Anglican-Roman Catholic commission with the task of continuing work already begun toward the eventual resolution of doctrinal differences.

John Paul II and Ignatius Zakka I, Syrian Orthodox Patriarch of Antioch, June 23, 1984: They recalled and solemnly reaffirmed the common profession of faith made by their predecessors, Paul VI and Mar Ignatius Jacob III, in 1971. They said: "The confusions and the schisms that occurred between the churches, they realize today, in no way affect or touch the substance of their faith, since these arose only because of differences in terminology and culture, and in the various formulae adopted by different theological schools to express the same matter. Accordingly, we find today no real basis for the sad divisions which arose between us concerning the doctrine of the Incarnation." On the pastoral level, they declared: "It is not rare for our faithful to find access to a priest of their own church materially or morally impossible. Anxious to meet their needs and with their spiritual benefit in mind, we authorize them in such cases to ask for the sacraments of penance, Eucharist and anointing of the sick from lawful priests of either of our two sister churches, when they need them."

John Paul II and Orthodox Ecumenical Patriarch Dimitrios I, Second Common Declaration, Dec. 7, 1987: Dialogue conducted since 1979 indicated that the churches can already profess together as common faith about the mystery of the Church and the connection between faith and the sacraments. They also stated that, "when unity of faith is assured, a certain diversity of expressions does not create obstacles to unity, but enriches the life of the Church and the understanding, always imperfect, of the revealed mystery."

John Paul II and Anglican Abp. Robert Runcie of Canterbury, Oct. 2, 1989: They said: "We solemnly re-commit ourselves and those we represent to the restoration of visible unity and full ecclesial communion in the confidence that to seek anything less would be to betray our Lord's intention for the unity of his people."

John Paul II and His Holiness Mar Dinkha IV, Catholicos-Patriarch of the Assyrian Church of the East, Nov. 11, 1994: Following is the text of the "Common Christological Declaration" between the Catholic Church and the Assyrian Church of the East, signed Nov. 11, 1994, by Pope John Paul II and His Holiness Mar Dinkha IV, Catholicos-Patriarch of the Assyrian Church of the East. The declaration acknowledges that, despite past differences, both churches profess the same faith in the real union of divine and human natures in the divine Person of Christ. Providing background to the declaration was the Assyrian Church's adherence to the teaching of Nestorius who, in the fifth century, denied the real unity of divine and human natures in the single divine Person of Christ.

Pope John Paul II with Ecumenical Orthodox Patriarch Bartholomew I, June 29, 1995: "Our meeting has followed other important events which have seen our Churches declare their desire to relegate the excommunications of the past to oblivion and to set out on the way to establishing full communion. "Our new-found brotherhood in the name of the Lord has led us to frank discussion, a dialogue that seeks understanding and unity. This dialogue — through the Joint International (Catholic-Orthodox) Commission — has proved fruitful and has made substantial progress.

Pope John Paul II with Anglican Abp. George Carey, Common Ecumenical Declaration, Dec. 5, 1996: The pontiff and archbishop praised the work of the Anglican-Roman Catholic International Commission and stated that "In many parts of the world Anglicans and Catholics attempt to witness together in the face of growing secularism, religious apathy and moral confusion."

Pope John Paul II with Karekin I, Catholicos of All Armenians, Dec. 13, 1996: "Pope John Paul II and Catholicos Karekin I recognize the deep spiritual communion which already unites them and the bishops and clergy and lay faithful of their churches. It is a communion which finds its roots in the common faith in the holy and life-giving Trinity proclaimed by the Apostles and transmitted down the centuries...."

Pope John Paul II with Aram I, Armenian Catholicos of Cilicia, Jan. 25, 1997: The common declaration stated, "the two spiritual leaders stress the vital importance of sincere dialogue. The Catholic Church and the Catholicate of Cilicia also have an immense field of constructive cooperation before them."

Card. Edward Cassidy with Bishop Christian Krause, President of the Lutheran World Federation, Oct. 31, 1999: "Joint Declaration on Justification by Faith."

Pope John Paul II with Karekin II, Catholicos of All Armenians, Nov. 10, 2000, in Rome: His Holiness Pope John Paul II, Bishop of Rome, and His Holiness Karekin II, Supreme Patriarch and Catholicos of All Armenians, give thanks to the Lord and Savior Jesus Christ, for enabling them to meet together on the occasion of the Jubilee of the Year 2000 and on the threshold of the 1700th anniversary of the proclamation of Christianity as the state religion of Armenia.

Pope John Paul II with Christodoulos, Archbishop of Athens, May 4, 2001: The common declaration stated: We are anguished to see that wars, massacres, torture and martyrdom constitute a terrible daily reality for millions of our brothers. We commit ourselves to struggle for the prevailing of peace throughout the whole world, for the respect of life and human dignity, and for solidarity toward all who are in need.

John Paul II and Karekin II, Catholicos of All Armenians, Sept. 27, 2001, in Etchmiadzin, Armenia: The celebration of the 1700th anniversary of the proclamation of Christianity as the religion of Armenia has brought us together – John Paul II, Bishop of Rome and Pastor of the Catholic Church, and Karekin II, the Supreme Patriarch and Catholicos of All Armenians – and we thank God for giving us this joyous opportunity to join again in common prayer, in praise of his all-holy Name. Blessed be the Holy Trinity – Father, Son and Holy Spirit – now and forever.

Pope John Paul II and Ecumenical Patriarch Bartholomew I signed a Common Declaration on Environmental Ethics, June 10, 2002: "We are gathered here today in the spirit of peace for the good of all human beings and for the care of creation. At this moment in history, at the beginning of the third millennium, we are saddened to see the daily suffering of a great number of people from violence, starvation, poverty and disease. We are also concerned about the negative consequences for humanity and for all creation resulting from the degradation of some basic natural resources such as water, air and land, brought about by an economic and technological progress which does not recognize and take into account its limits.

Pope John Paul II and Patriarch Teoctist of the Romanian Orthodox Church signed a Joint Declaration in Rome on Oct. 12, 2002: "In the deep joy of being together again in the city of Rome, close to the tombs of the holy Apostles

Peter and Paul, we exchange the kiss of peace under the gaze of the One who watches over his Church and guides our steps; and we meditate anew on these words, which the Evangelist John transmitted to us and which constitute Christ's heartfelt prayer on the eve of his Passion."

Pope John Paul II and Ecumenical Patriarch Bartholomew I, June 29, 2004: Unity and Peace! The hope kindled by that historic encounter has lit up our journey in these last decades. Aware that the Christian world has suffered the tragedy of separation for centuries, our Predecessors and we ourselves have persevered in the 'dialogue of charity,' our gaze turned to that blessed, shining day on which it will be possible to communicate with the same cup of the precious Blood and the holy Body of the Lord (cf. Patriarch Athenagoras I, Address to Pope Paul VI [Jan. 5, 1964], ibid., No. 48, p. 109).

Abp. Rowan Williams of Canterbury and Pope Benedict XVI, Nov. 23, 2006: "As Christian leaders facing the challenges of the new millennium, we affirm again our public commitment to the revelation of divine life uniquely set forth by God in the divinity and humanity of Our Lord Jesus Christ. We believe that it is through Christ and the means of salvation found in him that healing and reconciliation are offered to us and to the world."

Pope Benedict XVI and Ecumenical Patriarch Bartholomew I, on Nov. 30, 2006: "As far as relations between the Church of Rome and the Church of Constantinople are concerned, we cannot fail to recall the solemn ecclesial act effacing the memory of the ancient anathemas which for centuries have had a negative effect on relations between our Churches. We have not yet drawn from this act all the positive consequences which can flow from it in our progress toward full unity, to which the mixed Commission is called to make an important contribution. We exhort our faithful to take an active part in this process, through prayer and through significant gestures. — *From the Phanar, Nov. 30, 2006*

Pope Benedict XVI and H.B. Christolodoulos, Archbishop of Athens and All Greece, Dec. 14, 2006: "Our meeting *in charity* makes us ever more conscious of our common task: to travel together along the arduous route of a *dialogue in truth* with a view to re-establishing the full communion of faith in the bond of love. Thus, we will be obeying the divine commandment and will put into practice the prayer of Our Lord Jesus Christ. In addition, enlightened by the Holy Spirit, who accompanies Christ's Church and never abandons her, we will persevere in our commitment on this path, following the example of the Apostles and demonstrating our mutual love and spirit of reconciliation."

Pope Benedict XVI and Chrysostomos II, Archbishop of Nea Justiniana and All Cyprus, June 16, 2007: "On the happy occasion of our fraternal encounter at the tombs of Sts. Peter and Paul, the "coryphaei of the Apostles," as liturgical tradition says, we would like to declare of common accord our sincere and firm willingness, in obedience to the desire of Our Lord Jesus Christ, to intensify our search for full unity among all Christians, making every possible effort deemed useful to the life of our Communities. We desire that the Catholic and Orthodox faithful of Cyprus live a fraternal life in full solidarity, based on our common faith in the Risen Christ. We also wish to sustain and encourage the theological dialogue which is preparing through the competent International Commission to address the most demanding issues that marked the historical event of the division."

Pope Francis and Ecumenical Patriarch Bartholomew in Jerusalem, May 25, 2014:

1. Like our venerable predecessors Pope Paul VI and Ecumenical Patriarch Athenagoras who met here in Jerusalem 50 years ago, we too, Pope Francis and Ecumenical Patriarch Bartholomew, were determined to meet in the Holy Land "where our common Redeemer, Christ our Lord, lived, taught, died, rose again, and ascended into Heaven, whence he sent the Holy Spirit on the infant Church" (Common communiqué of Pope Paul VI and Patriarch Athenagoras, published after their meeting of Jan. 6, 1964). Our meeting, another encounter of the Bishops of the Churches of Rome and Constantinople founded respectively by the two Brothers the Apostles Peter and Andrew, is a source of profound spiritual joy for us. It presents a providential occasion to reflect on the depth and the authenticity of our existing bonds, themselves the fruit of a grace-filled journey on which the Lord has guided us since that blessed day of 50 years ago.

2. Our fraternal encounter today is a new and necessary step on the journey toward the unity to which only the Holy Spirit can lead us, that of communion in legitimate diversity. We call to mind with profound gratitude the steps that the Lord has already enabled us to undertake. The embrace exchanged between Pope Paul VI and Patriarch Athenagoras here in Jerusalem, after many centuries of silence, paved the way for a momentous gesture, the removal from the memory and from the midst of the Church of the acts of mutual excommunication in 1054. This was followed by an exchange of visits between the respective Sees of Rome and Constantinople, by regular correspondence and, later, by the decision announced by Pope John Paul II and Patriarch Dimitrios, of blessed memory both, to initiate a theological dialogue of truth between Catholics and Orthodox. Over these years, God, the source of all peace and love, has taught us to regard one another as members of the same Christian family, under one Lord and Savior, Jesus Christ, and to love one another, so that we may confess our faith in the same Gospel of Christ, as received by the Apostles and expressed and transmitted to us by the Ecumenical Councils and the Church Fathers. While fully aware of not having reached the goal of full communion, today we confirm our commitment to continue walking together towards the unity for which Christ our Lord prayed to the Father so "that all may be one" (Jn 17:21).

3. Well aware that unity is manifested in love of God and love of neighbour, we look forward in eager anticipation to the day in which we will finally partake together in the Eucharistic banquet. As Christians, we are called to prepare to receive this gift of Eucharistic communion, according to the teaching of St. Irenaeus of Lyon (Against Heresies, IV,18,5, PG 7,1028), through the confession of the one faith, persevering prayer, inner conversion, renewal of life and fraternal dialogue. By achieving this hoped for goal, we will manifest to the world the love of God by which we are recognized as true disciples of Jesus Christ (cf. Jn 13:35).

4. To this end, the theological dialogue undertaken by the Joint International Commission offers a fundamental contribution to the search for full communion among Catholics and Orthodox. Throughout the subsequent times of Popes John Paul II and Benedict the XVI, and Patriarch Dimitrios, the progress of our theological

encounters has been substantial. Today we express heartfelt appreciation for the achievements to date, as well as for the current endeavors. This is no mere theoretical exercise, but an exercise in truth and love that demands an ever deeper knowledge of each other's traditions in order to understand them and to learn from them. Thus we affirm once again that the theological dialogue does not seek a theological lowest common denominator on which to reach a compromise, but is rather about deepening one's grasp of the whole truth that Christ has given to his Church, a truth that we never cease to understand better as we follow the Holy Spirit's promptings. Hence, we affirm together that our faithfulness to the Lord demands fraternal encounter and true dialogue. Such a common pursuit does not lead us away from the truth; rather, through an exchange of gifts, through the guidance of the Holy Spirit, it will lead us into all truth (cf. Jn 16:13).

5. Yet even as we make this journey toward full communion we already have the duty to offer common witness to the love of God for all people by working together in the service of humanity, especially in defending the dignity of the human person at every stage of life and the sanctity of family based on marriage, in promoting peace and the common good, and in responding to the suffering that continues to afflict our world. We acknowledge that hunger, poverty, illiteracy, the inequitable distribution of resources must constantly be addressed. It is our duty to seek to build together a just and humane society in which no-one feels excluded or emarginated.

6. It is our profound conviction that the future of the human family depends also on how we safeguard – both prudently and compassionately, with justice and fairness – the gift of creation that our Creator has entrusted to us. Therefore, we acknowledge in repentance the wrongful mistreatment of our planet, which is tantamount to sin before the eyes of God. We reaffirm our responsibility and obligation to foster a sense of humility and moderation so that all may feel the need to respect creation and to safeguard it with care. Together, we pledge our commitment to raising awareness about the stewardship of creation; we appeal to all people of goodwill to consider ways of living less wastefully and more frugally, manifesting less greed and more generosity for the protection of God's world and the benefit of His people.

7. There is likewise an urgent need for effective and committed cooperation of Christians in order to safeguard everywhere the right to express publicly one's faith and to be treated fairly when promoting that which Christianity continues to offer to contemporary society and culture. In this regard, we invite all Christians to promote an authentic dialogue with Judaism, Islam and other religious traditions. Indifference and mutual ignorance can only lead to mistrust and unfortunately even conflict.

8. From this holy city of Jerusalem, we express our shared profound concern for the situation of Christians in the Middle East and for their right to remain full citizens of their homelands. In trust we turn to the almighty and merciful God in a prayer for peace in the Holy Land and in the Middle East in general. We especially pray for the Churches in Egypt, Syria, and Iraq, which have suffered most grievously due to recent events. We encourage all parties regardless of their religious convictions to continue to work for reconciliation and for the just recognition of peoples' rights. We are persuaded that it is not arms, but dialogue, pardon and reconciliation that are the only possible means to achieve peace.

9. In an historical context marked by violence, indifference and egoism, many men and women today feel that they have lost their bearings. It is precisely through our common witness to the good news of the Gospel that we may be able to help the people of our time to rediscover the way that leads to truth, justice and peace. United in our intentions, and recalling the example, 50 years ago here in Jerusalem, of Pope Paul VI and Patriarch Athenagoras, we call upon all Christians, together with believers of every religious tradition and all people of good will, to recognize the urgency of the hour that compels us to seek the reconciliation and unity of the human family, while fully respecting legitimate differences, for the good of all humanity and of future generations.

10. In undertaking this shared pilgrimage to the site where our one same Lord Jesus Christ was crucified, buried and rose again, we humbly commend to the intercession of the Most Holy and Ever Virgin Mary our future steps on the path towards the fullness of unity, entrusting to God's infinite love the entire human family. " May the Lord let his face shine upon you, and be gracious to you! The Lord look upon you kindly and give you peace!" (Num 6:25-26).

ECUMENICAL STATEMENTS

The ecumenical statements listed below, and others like them, reflect the views of participants in the dialogues which produced them. They have not necessarily been accepted by the respective churches as formulations of doctrine or points of departure for practical changes in discipline. (For other titles, see **U.S. Ecumenical Dialogues**, **Ecumenical Reports**.)

• The "Windsor Statement" on Eucharistic doctrine, published Dec. 31, 1971, by the Anglican-Roman Catholic International Commission of theologians. (For text, see pages 132-33 of the 1973 Catholic Almanac.)

• The "Canterbury Statement" on ministry and ordination, published Dec. 13, 1973, by the same commission. (For excerpts, see pages 127-30 of the 1975 *Catholic Almanac*.)

• "Papal Primacy/Converging Viewpoints," published Mar. 4, 1974, by the dialogue group sanctioned by the U.S.A. National Convention of the World Lutheran Federation and the U.S. Bishops' Committee for Ecumenical and Interreligious Affairs. (For excerpts, see pages 130-31 of the 1975 Catholic Almanac.)

• An "Agreed Statement on the Purpose of the Church," published Oct. 31, 1975, by the Anglican-Roman Catholic Consultation in the U.S.

• "Christian Unity and Women's Ordination," published Nov. 7, 1975, by the same consultation, in which it was said that the ordination of women (approved in principle by the Anglican Communion but not by the Catholic Church) would "introduce a new element" in dialogue but would not mean the end of consultation nor the abandonment of its declared goal of full communion and organic unity.

• "Holiness and Spirituality of the Ordained Ministry," issued early in 1976 by theologians of the Catholic Church and the United Methodist Church; the first statement resulting from dialogue begun in 1966.

• "Mixed Marriages," published in the spring of 1976 by the Anglican-Roman Catholic Consultation in the U.S.

• "Bishops and Presbyters," published in July, 1976, by the Orthodox-Roman Catholic Consultation in the U.S. on the following points of common understanding: (1) Ordination in apostolic succession is required for pastoral office in the Church. (2) Presiding at the Eucharistic Celebration is a task belonging to those ordained to pastoral service. (3) The offices of bishop and presbyter are different realizations of the sacrament of order. (4) Those ordained are claimed permanently for the service of the Church.

• "The Principle of Economy," published by the body named above at the same time, concerning God's plan and activities in human history for salvation.

• "Venice Statement" on authority in the Church, published Jan. 20, 1977, by the Anglican-Roman Catholic International Commission of theologians.

• "Response to the Venice Statement," issued Jan. 4, 1978, by the Anglican-Roman Catholic Consultation in the U.S.A., citing additional questions.

• "An Ecumenical Approach to Marriage," published in January, 1978, by representatives of the Catholic Church, the Lutheran World Federation and the World Alliance of Reformed Churches.

• "Teaching Authority and Infallibility in the Church," released in October 1978, by the Catholic-Lutheran dialogue group in the U.S.

• "The Eucharist," reported early in 1979, in which the Roman Catholic-Lutheran Commission indicated developing convergence of views.

• "The Holy Spirit," issued Feb. 12, 1979, by the International Catholic-Methodist Commission.

• A statement on "Ministry in the Church," published in March 1981, by the International Roman Catholic-Lutheran Joint Commission, regarding possible mutual recognition of ministries.

• The Final Report of the Anglican-Roman Catholic International Commission, 1982, on the results of 12 years of dialogue.

• "The Mystery of the Church and of the Eucharist in the Light of the Mystery of the Holy Trinity," issued by the Mixed International Commission for Theological Dialogue between the Catholic Church and the Orthodox Church at Munich, Germany, in July 1982.

• The Final Report of the Anglican-Roman Catholic International Commission, 1982, on the results of 12 years of dialogue.

• "Justification by Faith," issued Sept. 30, 1983, by the U.S. Lutheran-Roman Catholic dialogue group, claiming a "fundamental consensus on the Gospel."

• "Images of God: Reflections on Christian Anthropology," released Dec. 22, 1983, by the Anglican-Roman Catholic Dialogue in the United States.

• "The Journeying Together in Christ – The Report of the Polish National Catholic-Roman Catholic Dialogue (1984-89)."

• "Salvation and the Church," issued Jan. 22, 1987, by the Second Anglican-Roman Catholic International Commission.

• "Faith, Sacraments and the Unity of the Church," issued by the Mixed International Commission for Theological Dialogue between the Catholic Church and the Orthodox Churches in June 1987.

• "The Sacrament of Order in the Sacramental Structure of the Church, with Particular Reference to the Importance of Apostolic Succession for the Sanctification and Unity of the People of God," issued by the Mixed International Commission for Theological Dialogue between the Catholic Church and the Orthodox Church in Valamo, Finland, in 1988.

• "The Presence of Christ in Church and World" and "Toward a Common Understanding of the Church" (developed between 1984 and 1990), by the Reformed-Roman Catholic Conversations, under the auspices of the Pontifical Council for Promoting Christian Unity and the World Alliance of Reformed Churches.

• "The Church as Communion," issued by the Second Anglican-Roman Catholic International Commission, 1991.

• "Uniatism, Method of Union of the Past, and the Present Search for Full Communion," issued by the Joint International Commission for Theological Dialogue between the Catholic Church and the Orthodox Church at Balamand, Lebanon, in 1993.

• "Life in Christ: Morals, Communion and the Church," issued by the Second Anglican-Roman Catholic International Commission, 1994.

• "Common Response to the Aleppo Statement on the Date of Easter/Pacha," issued by the North American Orthodox-Catholic Theological Consultation in Washington, DC, Oct. 31, 1998.

• "The Gift of Authority," issued by the Second Anglican-Roman Catholic International Commission, May 12, 1999.

• "Baptism and 'Sacramental Economy,'" issued by the North American Orthodox-Catholic Theological Consultation at Crestwood, NY, in June 1999.

• "Guidelines Concerning the Pastoral Care of Oriental Orthodox Students in Catholic Schools," issued by the Oriental Orthodox-Roman Catholic Theological Consultation in the United States at New Rochelle, NY, in June 1999.

• "Joint Declaration of the Catholic Church and the Lutheran World Federation on the Doctrine of Justification," issued July 8, 1999, by the International Roman Catholic-Lutheran Joint Commission.

• "Agreed Report on the Local/Universal Church," issued by the United States Anglican-Roman Catholic Consultation, Nov. 12, 1999.

• "Communion in Mission" and "Action Plan to Implement 'Communion in Mission,'" issued by a special consultation of Anglican and Roman Catholic bishops in Mississauga, Ontario, Canada, May 19, 2000.

• "Sharing the Ministry of Reconciliation: A Statement on the Orthodox-Catholic Dialogue and the Ecumenical Movement," issued June 1, 2000, by the North American Orthodox-Catholic Theological Consultation in Brookline, MA.

• "Methodist-Catholic Dialogues: Thirty Years of Mission and Witness," issued by the U.S. dialogue in 2001.

• "Doing the Truth in Charity," issued in July 2001 by the World Methodist Council and the Pontifical Council for Promoting Unity's Methodist-Catholic International Commission.

• "Interchurch Families: Resources for Ecumenical Hope," issued by the Catholic/Reformed Dialogue in the United States in 2002.

• Response of the Anglican-Roman Catholic Consultation in the USA to the Anglican-Roman Catholic International Commission's "The Gift of Authority" (Mar. 29, 2003).

• "Called Together to be Peacemakes," Mennonite World Conference Catholic Dialogue 2003.

• "Church, Evangelization, and *Koinonia*," World Evangelical Alliance – Pontifical Council for Promoting Christian Unity 2003.
• "Journeying Together in Christ: The Journey Continues — The Report of the Polish National Catholic Roman Catholic Dialogue (1989-2002)."
• "The *Filioque*: A Church-Dividing Issue?" issued by the North American Orthodox-Catholic Theological Consultation, October 2003.
• "The Church as *Koinonia* of Salvation: Its Structures and Ministries," May 2004, Lutheran Catholic Dialogue in the US.
• "Mary: Grace and Hope in Christ," Anglican Roman Catholic Commission, 2004.
• "Journey in Faith: Forty Years of Reformed-Catholic Dialogue: 1965-2005," 2005.
• "Through Divine Love: The Church in Each Place and All Places," April 2005, United Methodist Roman Catholic Dialogue in the US. "Joint Declaration on Unity" by the Polish National Catholic – Roman Catholic Dialogue (May 17, 2006).
• ARCUSA Response to "Mary: Grace & Hope in Christ," October 2007, Anglican-Roman Catholic Consultation in the USA.
• "Ecclesiological and Canonical Consequences of the Sacramental Nature of the Church: Ecclesial Communion, Conciliarity and Authority," issued by the Joint International Commission for Theological Dialogue between the Catholic Church and the Orthodox Church at Ravenna, Italy, on Oct 13, 2007.
• "Nature, Constitution and Mission of the Church," International Oriental Orthodox-Roman Catholic Dialogue, Jan. 29, 2009.
• "A Common Response to the Joint International Commission for the Theological Dialogue Between the Roman Catholic Church and the Orthodox Church

Regarding the Ravenna Document: 'Ecclesiological and Canonical.
• "Consequences of the Sacramental Nature of the Church: Ecclesial Communion, Conciliarity and Authority" by the North American Orthodox-Catholic Theological Consultation, Oct. 24, 2009.
• "Celebrating Easter/Pascha Together," by the North American Orthodox-Catholic Theological Consultation, Oct. 1, 2010.
• "Steps Toward a Reunited Church: A Sketch of an Orthodox-Catholic Vision for the Future," by the North American Orthodox-Catholic Theological Consultation, Oct. 2, 2010.
• "These Living Waters," by the Catholic-Reformed Dialogue in the US, Oct. 8, 2010.
• "This Bread of Life," by the Catholic-Reformed Dialogue in the US, Oct. 8, 2010.
• "The Hope of Eternal Life," by the United States Lutheran-Catholic Dialogue, Oct. 17, 2010.
• "Heaven and Earth are Full of your Glory: A United Methodist and Roman Catholic Statement on the Eucharist and Ecology," by the U.S. United Methodist-Catholic Dialogue, April 2012.
• "The Importance of Sunday," by the North American Orthodox-Catholic Theological Consultation, Oct.27, 2012.
• "Ecclesiology and Moral Discernment: Seeking a Unified Moral Witness," by the Anglican-Roman Catholic Consultation in the USA, April 22, 2014.
• "On the Occasion of the Eighty-fifth Anniversary of the Promulgation of the decree Cum data fuerit," by the North American Orthodox-Catholic Theological Consultation, June 6, 2014.
See online: www.prounione.urbe.it/dia-int/e_dialogues. html, or http://www.usccb.org/beliefs-and-teachings/ecu-menical-and-interreligious/index.cfm

RELATIONS WITH THE ORTHODOX CHURCH

This is a group of Eastern churches of the Byzantine tradition that were in full communion with Rome during the first millennium, and which all recognize the Patriarch of Constantinople as the first Orthodox bishop. In spite of the division between Catholics and Orthodox, often symbolized by the mutual excommunications of 1054, the Catholic Church considers itself to be in almost full communion with the Orthodox Churches. According to Vatican II, they "are still joined to us in closest intimacy" in various ways, especially in the priesthood and Eucharist. The Orthodox Churches recognize the first seven ecumenical councils as normative for their faith, along with the Scriptures and other local councils that took place in later centuries.

The Orthodox Churches are organized in approximately 15 autocephalous (independent) churches that correspond in most cases to nations or ethnic groups. The Ecumenical Patriarch of Constantinople (modern Istanbul) has a primacy of honor among the patriarchs, but his actual jurisdiction is limited to his own patriarchate. As the spiritual head of worldwide Orthodoxy, he serves as a point of unity, and has the right to call Pan-Orthodox assemblies.

Top-level relations between the Churches have

improved in recent years through the efforts of Ecumenical Patriarch Athenagoras I, Bl. John XXIII, Paul VI and Patriarch Dimitrios I. Pope Paul met with Athenagoras three times before the latter's death in 1972. The most significant action of both spiritual leaders was their mutual nullification of excommunications imposed by the two Churches on each other in 1054. Development of better relations with the Orthodox was a priority of John Paul II, as well as Benedict XVI. Both Pope Benedict and Orthodox Ecumenical Patriarch Bartholomew have made known their commitment to better relations, despite contentions between Eastern Catholic and Orthodox Churches over charges of proselytism and rival property claims in places liberated from anti-religious communist control in the recent past.

The largest Orthodox body in the United States is the Greek Orthodox Archdiocese of America consisting of nine dioceses; it has an estimated membership of 1.9 million. The second largest is the Orthodox Church in America, with more than one million members; it was given autocephalous status by the Patriarchate of Moscow May 18, 1970, without the consent of the Patriarchate of Constantinople. An additional 650,000 or more Orthodox belong to smaller national and language jurisdictions.

JURISDICTIONS

The Autocephalous Orthodox Churches

Patriarchate of Constantinople (Ecumenical Patriarchate), with jurisdiction in Turkey, Crete, the Dodecanese, and Greeks in the rest of the world outside Greece and Africa. Autonomous churches linked to the Ecumenical Patriarchate exist in Finland and Estonia. Several other jurisdictions of various ethnicities in the diaspora are also directly under the Patriarchate.

Patriarchate of Alexandria, with jurisdiction in Egypt and the rest of Africa; it includes a native African Orthodox Church centered in Kenya and Uganda.

Patriarchate of Antioch, with jurisdiction in Syria, Lebanon, Iraq, Australia, the Americas.

Patriarchate of Jerusalem, with jurisdiction in Israel and Jordan. The autonomous church of Mount Sinai is linked to the Jerusalem Patriarchate.

Russian Orthodox Church, the Patriarchate of Moscow with jurisdiction over most of the former Soviet Union. Autonomous churches in Japan and China are linked to the Moscow Patriarchate, and since the breakup of the Soviet Union, a certain autonomy has been granted to the Orthodox churches in the newly independent republics of Ukraine, Belarus, Estonia, Moldova and Latvia.

The Serbian Orthodox Church, a patriarchate with jurisdiction in all of former Yugoslavia, Western Europe, North America and Australia.

The Romanian Orthodox Church, a patriarchate with jurisdiction in Romania, Western Europe and North America.

The Bulgarian Orthodox Church, a patriarchate with jurisdiction in Bulgaria, Western Europe and North America.

The Georgian Orthodox Church, a patriarchate with jurisdiction in the republic of Georgia.

The Orthodox Church of Cyprus, an archbishopric with jurisdiction in Cyprus.

The Orthodox Church of Greece, an archbishopric with jurisdiction in most of Greece.

The Orthodox Church of Poland, a metropolitanate with jurisdiction in Poland.

The Orthodox Church of Albania, an archbishopric with jurisdiction in Albania.

The Orthodox Church in the Czech and Slovak Republics, a metropolitanate with jurisdiction in the Czech and Slovak Republics. Its autocephalous status was granted by Moscow in 1951 but by Constantinople only in 1998.

The Orthodox Church in America, a metropolitanate with jurisdiction in North America and a few parishes in Latin America and Australia. Its autocephalous status was granted by Moscow in 1970; Constantinople and most other Orthodox churches have not recognized this.

Population

In 2011 the Pew Forum provided statistics that estimated 260,380,000 Orthodox Christians in the world today. This figure included the Oriental Orthodox Churches and the Assyrian Church of the East (see below). Some Orthodox claim a total membership of as many as 300 million.

Assembly of Canonical Orthodox Bishops of the United States of America

In 1960 a Standing Conference of the Canonical Orthodox Bishops in the Americas was established to promote cooperation among the various Orthodox jurisdictions in the Americas. Member churches were: Albanian Orthodox Diocese of America (Ecumenical Patriarchate), American Carpatho-Russian Orthodox Diocese in the U.S.A. (Ecumenical Patriarchate), Antiochian Orthodox Christian Archdiocese of North America, Bulgarian Eastern Orthodox Church, Greek Orthodox Archdiocese of America (Ecumenical Patriarchate), Orthodox Church in America, Romanian Orthodox Archdiocese in America and Canada, Serbian Orthodox Church in the United States and Canada, Ukrainian Orthodox Church in the United States (Ecumenical Patriarchate), and the Representation of the Moscow Patriarchate in the United States of America. At a meeting of representatives of the Orthodox Churches in Switzerland in June 2009, it was decided to establish "Episcopal Assemblies" in various parts of the Orthodox diaspora, including one for North and Central America. It replaced SCOBA as the primary structure coordinating the life of the Orthodox Churches in that region. The Assembly met in plenary for the first time in New York May 2010 and has met annually since that time. In April 2014 it was announced that separate assemblies had been created for the United States and Canada, and that Central America and Mexico had been incorporated into the Assembly for Latin America. The Assembly in the US would henceforth be known as The Assembly of Canonical Orthodox Bishops of the United States of America. A Committee for Ecumenical Relations has been established, headed by Bp. Demetrios of Mokissos, Chancellor of the Greek Orthodox Metropolis of Chicago. Assembly Office: 8-10 East 79th St., New York, NY 10021; www.assemblyofbishops.org/.

EASTERN ECUMENISM

The Second Vatican Council, in *Orientalium Ecclesiarum,* the "Decree on Eastern Catholic Churches," pointed out the special role they have to play "in promoting the unity of all Christians." The document also stated in part as follows.

The Eastern Churches in communion with the Apostolic See of Rome have a special role to play in promoting the unity of all Christians, particularly Easterners, according to the principles of this sacred Synod's Decree on Ecumenism first of all by prayer, then by the example of their lives, by religious fidelity to ancient Eastern traditions, by greater mutual knowledge, by collaboration, and by a brotherly regard for objects and attitudes (No. 24).

If any separated Eastern Christian should, under the guidance of grace of the Holy Spirit, join himself to Catholic unity, no more should be required of him than what a simple profession of the Catholic faith demands. A valid priesthood is preserved among Eastern clerics. Hence, upon joining themselves to the unity of the Catholic Church, Eastern clerics are permitted to exercise the orders they possess, in accordance with the regulations established by the competent authority (No. 25).

Divine Law forbids any common worship (communicatio in sacris) that would damage the unity of the Church, or involve formal acceptance of falsehood or the danger of deviation in the faith, of scandal, or of indifferentism. At the same time, pastoral experience clearly shows that with respect to our Eastern brethren there should and can be taken into consideration various circumstances affecting individuals, wherein the unity of the Church is not jeopardized nor are intolerable risks involved, but in which salvation itself and the spiritual profit of souls are urgently at issue.

Hence, in view of special circumstances of time, place,

and personage, the Catholic Church has often adopted and now adopts a milder policy, offering to all the means of salvation and an example of charity among Christians through participation in the sacraments and in other sacred functions and objects. With these considerations in mind, and "lest because of the harshness of our judgment we prove an obstacle to those seeking salvation," and in order to promote closer union with the Eastern Churches separated from us, this sacred Synod lays down the following policy:

In view of the principles recalled above, Eastern Christians who are separated in good faith from the Catholic Church, if they ask of their own accord and have the right dispositions, may be granted the sacraments of penance, the Eucharist, and the anointing of the sick. Furthermore, Catholics may ask for these same sacraments from those non-Catholic ministers whose Churches possess valid sacraments, as often as necessity or a genuine spiritual benefit recommends such a course of action, and when access to a Catholic priest is physically or morally impossible (Nos. 26, 27).

Again, in view of these very same principles, Catholics may for a just cause join with their separated Eastern brethren in sacred functions, things, and places (No. 28). Bishops decide when and if to follow this policy.

THE ORTHODOX CHURCHES

Pope John Paul II Returned Icon of the Mother of God of Kazan to the Russian Orthodox Church.

In August 2004 Pope John Paul II returned to the Russian Orthodox Church an icon of the Mother of God of Kazan that had hung over his desk in his personal study for 11 years. The icon was believed to have been taken out of Russia at the time of the Bolshevik Revolution, and had been given to the Holy Father by the Blue Army in 1993.

Pope John Paul II Returned Relics of Sts John Chrysostom and Gregory Nazianzen to the Patriarchate of Constantinople.

In November 2004 Pope John Paul II returned relics of Sts. John Chrysostom and Gregory Nazianzus to the Ecumenical Patriarchate. Patriarch Bartholomew traveled to Rome to receive the relics in a special service in St Peter's Basilica on Nov. 27.

Joint International Commission for Theological Dialogue.

The 12th meeting of the Joint International Commission for Theological Dialogue between the Orthodox Church and the Roman Catholic Church took place in Vienna, Austria, a city with a long history, a bridge between West and East, with a rich ecumenical life. The meeting was hosted by the Roman Catholic Archdiocese of Vienna, from Sept. 20-27, 2010, in the Kardinal König Haus.

Twenty-three Catholic members were present, a few were unable to attend. All the Orthodox churches, with the exception of the Patriarchate of Bulgaria, were represented, namely the Ecumenical Patriarchate, the Patriarchate of Alexandria, the Patriarchate of Antioch, the Patriarchate of Jerusalem, the Patriarchate of Moscow, the Patriarchate of Serbia, the Patriarchate of Romania, the Patriarchate of Georgia, the Church of Cyprus, the Church of Greece, the Church of Poland, the Church of Albania and the Church of the Czech Lands and Slovakia.

The Commission worked under the direction of its two co-presidents, Abp. Kurt Koch and Metropolitan

Prof. Dr. John of Pergamon, assisted by the co-secretaries, Metropolitan Prof. Dr Gennadios of Sassima (Ecumenical Patriarchate) and Rev. Andrea Palmieri (Pontifical Council for Promoting Christian Unity).

On the first day of the meeting, as is customary, the Roman Catholic and Orthodox members met separately to coordinate their work. The Orthodox meeting discussed among other things the unfinished draft text produced by the 11th plenary session in Paphos, Cyprus last year, and much time was given to the methodology of the dialogue. The Catholic meeting also considered the draft text, seeking specific ways to improve the text, and reflected on methodological questions. As was decided at the 10th plenary session in Ravenna, 2007, the Commission is studying the theme "The Role of the Bishop of Rome in the Communion of the Church in the First Millennium," on the basis of a draft text prepared by the Joint Coordinating Committee, which met in Aghios Nikolaos/ Crete, Greece, 2008. During its meeting in Vienna, the Commission continued the detailed consideration of the text which began at last year's plenary session at Paphos, Cyprus. At this stage, the Commission is discussing this text as a working document and it decided that the text must be further revised. It was also decided to form a sub-commission to begin consideration of the theological and ecclesiological aspects of Primacy in its relation to Synodality. The sub-commission will submit its work to the Joint Coordinating Committee of the Commission which met the next year.

North American Orthodox-Catholic Theological Consultation Issues Agreed Statement on Filioque, a Question that Divided the Two Communions for Many Centuries.

(Courtesy, USCCB.) The North American Orthodox-Catholic Theological Consultation concluded a four-year study of the Filioque on Oct. 25, 2003, when it unanimously adopted an agreed text on this difficult question that has divided the two communions for many centuries. This important development took place at the 65th meeting of the Consultation, held at St. Paul's College in Washington, DC, under the joint chairmanship of Metropolitan Maximos of the Greek Orthodox Metropolis of Pittsburgh and Abp. Daniel E. Pilarczyk of Cincinnati.

Entitled "The Filioque: A Church-Dividing Issue?," the 10,000 word text had three major sections. The first, "The Holy Spirit in the Scriptures," summarizes references to the Spirit in both the Old and New Testaments. The more lengthy second section, "Historical Considerations," provides an overview of the origins of the two traditions concerning the eternal procession of the Spirit and the slow process by which the Filioque was added to the Creed in the West. It also shows how this question concerning Trinitarian theology became entwined with disputes regarding papal jurisdiction and primacy, and reviews recent developments in the Catholic Church which point to a greater awareness of the unique and normative character of the original Greek version of the Creed as an expression of the faith that unites the Orthodox East and Catholic West. The third section, "Theological Reflections," emphasizes our limited ability to speak of the inner life of God, points out that both sides of the debate have often caricatured the positions of the other, and lists areas in which the traditions agree. It then explores the differences that have developed regarding terminology, and identifies both theological and ecclesiological divergences that have arisen over the centuries.

In a final section, the Consultation made eight recommendations to the members and bishops of the two churches. It recommends that they "enter into a new and earnest dialogue concerning the origin and person of the Holy Spirit." It also proposed that in the future both Catholics and Orthodox "refrain from labeling as heretical the traditions of the other side" on this subject, and that the theologians of both traditions make a clearer distinction between the divinity of the Spirit, and the manner of the Spirit's origin, "which still awaits full and final ecumenical resolution." The North American Orthodox-Catholic Theological Consultation is sponsored jointly by the Standing Conference of Canonical Orthodox Bishops of the Americas (SCOBA), the Bishops' Committee for Ecumenical and Interreligious Affairs of the USCCB, and the Canadian Conference of Catholic Bishops. The full text of the document is available on the USCCB website at: http://www.usccb.org/beliefs-and-teachings/ecumenical-and-interreligious/ecumenical/orthodox/filioque-church-dividing-issue-english.cfm

Orthodox-Catholic Dialogue Lays Out a Vision of Unity in Unprecedented Document

Representatives of the Orthodox and Catholic Churches issued two documents outlining immediate steps they could take to overcome their thousand-year separation. The North American Orthodox-Catholic Theological Consultation finalized these agreed statements when it met at Georgetown University in Washington, Sept. 30 to Oct. 2, 2010. The Consultation was co-chaired by Abp. Gregory M. Aymond of New Orleans and Metropolitan Maximos of Pittsburgh.

The first statement, "Steps Toward a Reunited Church: A Sketch of an Orthodox-Catholic Vision for the Future," is an unprecedented effort to begin to visualize the shape of a reunited Catholic and Orthodox Church that would result from the reestablishment of full communion. The text acknowledges that the role of the Bishop of Rome in the Church is a central point of disagreement and outlines the history of this divergence between East and West. It goes on to summarize the many elements of the Christian faith and ecclesial life that the two churches share, and emphasizes the urgency of overcoming our divisions.

"Clearly, this cannot be achieved without new, better harmonized structures of leadership on both sides: new conceptions of both synodality and primacy in the universal Church, new approaches to the way primacy and authority are exercised in both our communions," the document says.

The agreed statement lists some of the features that would characterize a fully reunited Church and then focuses on the role the papacy would play within it. This role would need to be carefully defined, "both in continuity with the ancient structural principles of Christianity and in response to the need for a unified Christian message in the world of today." The document then suggests several aspects of the Pope's ministry in a reunited Church that could be both faithful to Catholic teaching and acceptable to the Orthodox. The document also lists several "preparatory steps" that could be taken even now as a prelude to the future unity of the churches, such as shared prayer and social ministry, and enumerates several questions and problems that remain outstanding.

The text concludes that "The challenge and the invitation to Orthodox and Catholic Christians ... is now to see Christ authentically present in each other, and to find in those structures of leadership that have shaped our communities through the centuries a force to move us beyond disunity, mistrust, and competition, towards that oneness in his Body, that obedience to his Spirit, which will reveal us as his disciples before the world."

The complete text of this statement is available here: http://www.usccb.org/beliefs-and-teachings/ecumenical-and-interreligious/ecumenical/orthodox/steps-towards-reunited-church.cfm

The second statement, "Celebrating Easter/Pascha Together," is a re-affirmation of the Consultation's 1998 document, "A Common Response to the Aleppo Statement on the Date of Easter/Pascha." In this new text, the members emphasize the importance of a united witness to the Resurrection of Christ, which lies at the very center of the Christian faith, and the scandal caused by the inability to celebrate this feast day consistently on the same date.

The Consultation joins many other expressions of support for a recent proposal that would re-calculate the date of Easter for all Christians based strictly on the teaching of the First Council of Nicaea (325), which determined that Easter be celebrated on the first Sunday following the first full moon after the Spring Equinox. Determining the Equinox from the Jerusalem meridian and using the most accurate scientific instruments and astronomical data available would require a change for both traditions, but would also represent greater faithfulness to the teaching of Nicaea. The full text is available at: http://www.usccb.org/beliefs-and-teachings/ecumenical-and-interreligious/ecumenical/orthodox/celebrating-easter-together.cfm.

Orthodox-Catholic Dialogue Issues Joint Statement On The Importance Of Sunday In The Lives Of Christians

The North American Orthodox-Catholic Theological Consultation issued an agreed statement on the importance of Sunday in the lives of Christians at its Oct. 25-27, 2012 meeting at St. Paul's College in Washington. Abp. Gregory M. Aymond of New Orleans and Metropolitan Methodios of Boston jointly chaired the meeting.

The pastoral statement on the importance of Sunday calls for Orthodox and Catholic Christians to recover the theological significance of a day that for many "has become less a day of worship and family and more like an ordinary work day." It ends with a call to clergy and laity "to work cooperatively within their communities to stress the importance of Sunday for worship and family." The full text of the statement is available online: www.usccb.org/beliefs-and-teachings/dialogue-with-others/ecumenical/orthodox/the-importance-of-sunday.cfm (USCCB Press Release, Nov. 19, 2012).

Orthodox-Catholic Theological Consultation Urges Church To Lift Ban on Ordination of Married Priests in Eastern Catholic Churches in North America

The North American Orthodox-Catholic Theological Consultation voted in early June to encourage the "lifting of the restrictions regarding the ordination of married men to the priesthood in the Eastern Catholic Churches of North America. This action would affirm the ancient and legitimate Eastern Christian tradition, and would assure the Orthodox that, in the event of the restoration of full communion between the two Churches, the traditions of the Orthodox Church would not be questioned," the consultation said in a statement released June 6.

The Theological Consultation agreed to the statement at its 86th meeting, June 2-4, 2014, at the St. Methodios Faith and Heritage Center in Contoocook, New Hampshire. The meeting was hosted by the Orthodox co-chair, Metropolitan Methodios of the Greek Orthodox

Metropolis of Boston; the Catholic co-chair is Abp. Joseph W. Tobin of Indianapolis.

The Theological Consultation issued the statement on the occasion of the 85th anniversary of the promulgation of the 1929 decree Cum data fuerit from the Vatican Oriental Congregation, which oversees the Eastern Catholic churches. In the late 19th and early 20th centuries, Eastern Catholic immigrants to North America from Eastern Europe and the Middle East brought with them the tradition of a married priesthood. This Oriental Congregation decree effectively limited future ordinations to celibates, and resulted in divisions in Eastern Catholic communities and even families over this issue. The agreed statement cites two documents of the Second Vatican Council which call for Eastern Catholics to return to their authentic ancestral traditions, and exhorts those men who have received both the sacraments of priestly ordination and marriage "to persevere in their holy vocation." Consequently, the Consultation "encourages the lifting of the restrictions regarding the ordination of married men to the priesthood in the Eastern Catholic Churches of North America.

At this meeting the Consultation also continued its study of the relationship between the clergy and laity in the two Churches. The members also examined the December 2013 statement by the Patriarchate of Moscow on primacy in the Church and the response by the Ecumenical Patriarchate. The Consultation also reviewed the recent meeting between Pope Francis and Ecumenical Patriarch Bartholomew in Jerusalem. (USCCB Press Release, June 6, 2014)

RELATIONS WITH THE ORIENTAL ORTHODOX CHURCHES

The Oriental Orthodox are a family of six Churches of equal status in full communion with each other. The common element among them is that they did not accept the Christological teachings of the Council of Chalcedon (451), or any other ecumenical councils that have subsequently taken place. In the past they were erroneously referred to as "Monophysite," referring to a heresy they never accepted. Today the ancient Christological disputes are no longer considered to be church-dividing. An official international dialogue between these churches and the Catholic Church met for the first time in 2004 and has been meeting annually since that time.

The Eleventh Meeting of the International Joint Commission for Theological Dialogue between the Catholic Church and the Oriental Orthodox Churches:

The Eleventh meeting of the International Joint Commission for Theological Dialogue between the Catholic Church and the Oriental Orthodox Churches took place at the Samanvaya Retreat Centre in Pampakuda, Kerala, India, from Jan. 28 to Feb. 1, 2014. The meeting was hosted by His Holiness Baselios Marthoma Paulose II, Catholicos of the East and Malankara Metropolitan of the Malankara Orthodox Syrian Church, and was chaired jointly by Cardinal Kurt Koch, President of the Pontifical Council for Promoting Christian Unity, and by His Eminence Abp. Nareg Alemezian of the Armenian Catholicosate of Cilicia in the absence of His Eminence Metropolitan Bishoy of Damiette.

Joining delegates from the Catholic Church were representatives of the following Oriental Orthodox Churches: the Armenian Apostolic Church (Catholicosate of All Armenians), the Armenian Apostolic Church (Holy See of Cilicia), the Coptic Orthodox Church, the Ethiopian Orthodox Tewahedo Church, and the Malankara Orthodox Syrian Church. No representative of the Antiochian Syrian Orthodox Church or the Eritrean Orthodox Tewahdo Church was able to attend.

The two delegations met separately in the afternoon of Jan. 28. The Joint Commission held plenary sessions on Jan. 29, 30, 31, and Feb. 1, each of which began with a brief prayer service using material prepared for the Week of Prayer for Christian Unity.

At the beginning of the first session, Cardinal Koch announced that a number of the members had been unable to attend the meeting and that some of them had sent representatives. He also congratulated Archbishop Basilios Georges Casmoussa who was named Apostolic Visitator to the Syrian Catholic communities in Western Europe since the last meeting. The Cardinal also reported on significant ecumenical developments that had taken place since the 2013 meeting in Rome. His Holiness Pope Francis strongly reaffirmed the commitment of the Catholic Church to Christian unity in his address to heads and representatives of various churches and ecclesial communities who had come to Rome for his installation in March 2013. Since that time Pope Francis received visits from His Holiness Pope Tawadros II of the Coptic Orthodox Church on May 10, and from His Holiness Baselios Marthoma Paulose II, Catholicos of the East and Malankara Metropolitan, on Sept. 5. Cardinal Koch also reviewed the direct bilateral dialogue between the Catholic Church and the Malankara Orthodox Syrian Church which was a result of the meeting of Pope John Paul II and Catholicos Moran Mar Baselios Marthoma Mathews I in Kottayam in 1986.

At this eleventh meeting, the members continued their study of the ways in which full communion among our churches was expressed in the first five centuries with special emphasis on the development of the various Eucharistic Prayers (Anaphoras) in the early Church and the significance of pilgrimages. Thus the following papers were presented during the meeting: "The Development of the Eucharistic Prayer (anaphora) as a Case Study in the Communion and Communication among the Churches" by Fr. Columba Stewart, OSB, "Jerusalem Between Liturgy and Pilgrimage: A Case Study in the Armenian Tradition" by Very Rev. Father Shahe Ananyan, "Anaphora and Liturgy" by Metropolitan Bishoy of Damiette (read in his absence by Bp. Daniel), "Liturgy as an Element of Communion and Communication between Churches Till Mid-Sixth Century" by Fr. Baby Varghese (read in his absence by Fr. Abraham Thomas), "Pilgrimage as a Sign of Communion With a Particular Regard to the Tradition of the early Armenian Church" by Fr. Boghos Levon Zekiyan (read in his absence by Fr. Mark Sheridan, OSB), "Pilgrimages in the Early Church" by Fr. Shenouda Maher Ishak (read in his absence by Bp. Daniel), "The Role and Significance of Pilgrimage in the Ethiopian Orthodox Tewahedo Church Tradition" by Fr. Daniel SeifeMichael Feleke, "The Concept of Christian Pilgrimage" by Mor Theophilus George Saliba (read in his absence by Metropolitan Youhanon Mar Demetrios), and "The Visit of Dignitaries as an Expression of Communion between the Churches Till the End of the Fifth Century A.D." by Metropolitan Youhanon Mar Demetrios. Drawing upon the material presented in these papers, the Joint Commission's drafting committee continued its work on the proposed agreed text entitled, "The Exercise of Communion in the Life of the Early Church and its Implications for our Search for Communion Today." The latest draft was reviewed by the Joint Commission on Jan. 31.

In the evening of Jan. 29, the members of the Commission attended a festive dinner hosted by His Holiness Catholicos Baselios Marthoma Paulose II at Madaparambil River Banks in Thodupuzha. Also present were a number of other Malankara Orthodox Bishops, clergy and prominent laypeople. The Catholicos offered gifts to the members of the commission, and Cardinal Koch presented the Catholicos with a gift from His Holiness Pope Francis. The two co-chairmen spoke briefly at the end of the dinner.

In his address the Catholicos warmly welcomed those present. "I take this opportunity," he said, "to thank the Pontifical Council for Promoting Christian Unity for the extended cooperation and for all the remarkable contributions in making the ongoing dialogue fruitful, and more particularly, the department of Ecumenical Relations of our Church in hosting the meeting of the Joint Commission." Referring to the members of the Joint Commission, the Catholicos said that "we have enormous trust in your academic ability, theological commitment and ecclesial fidelity. May the Holy Spirit continue to guide you in building bridges between our ancient traditions." Recalling his visit to Rome last September, the Catholicos said, "I take this opportunity to thank Card. Kurt Koch and the Pontifical Council for their gracious hospitality in the Vatican. The life and message of His Holiness Pope Francis give us new hope in Inter-Church relations. The Ancient Christian heritage and traditions of the Oriental Orthodox and the Catholic Churches together could contribute greater things in this divided world. We would like to see the spirit of this dialogue to continue in the coming years, so that we can further explore new areas of collaboration and mutual enrichment."

In the evening of Jan. 30, the two co-chairmen of this session along with Fr. Gabriel Quicke of the staff of the Pontifical Council for Promoting Christian Unity, paid a courtesy visit to His Beatitude Baselios Thomas I, Catholicos of the Malankara Syrian Orthodox Church.

On Friday evening, Jan. 31, the members of the Joint Commission attended a cultural event which presented a number of dances native to India, portraying the rich and beautiful heritage of the country.

In the morning of Saturday, Feb. 1, the members were invited by Fr. Johns Abraham Konat to visit the Konattu Mathen Malpan Syriac Research Centre of Pampakuda containing his family's important collection of manuscripts and archives, and to visit the parish church adjacent to it.

On Sunday, Feb. 2, the members of the Joint Commission accepted an invitation from Fr. Jacob Kurian, Principal of the Orthodox Theological Seminary (Old Seminary) in Kottayam, to attend the inauguration of celebrations marking the 200th anniversary of the seminary's founding.

The twelfth meeting of the International Joint Commission will take place in Rome, hosted by the Pontifical Council for Promoting Christian Unity. Arrivals will be on Saturday, Jan. 24, 2015, and the members will be invited to attend the Vespers service presided over by Pope Francis at the Basilica of Saint Paul's Outside the Walls on Sunday evening Jan. 25. Family meetings will take place on Monday Jan. 26, followed by plenary sessions on Tuesday to Friday, Jan. 27 to 30, with departures on Saturday, Jan. 31.

The members concluded with joyful thanks to God, the Father, the Son and the Holy Spirit, for what has been accomplished at this meeting.

RELATIONS WITH THE POLISH NATIONAL CATHOLIC CHURCH

The Roman Catholic-Polish National Catholic Dialogue issued this Joint Declaration on Unity on May 17, 2006, in Fall River, Mass.:

With thankfulness to God, the members of the Roman Catholic-Polish National Catholic dialogue in the United States look back on 22 years of theological and canonical reflection concerning the nature of our division and the possibility of reaching full communion. Because of a new outpouring of the Holy Spirit that affected both our churches following the celebration of the Second Vatican Council (1962-1965) and a similar renewal within the Polish National Catholic Church, our faithful have been rediscovering one another increasingly as brothers and sisters in the Lord. At this time we wish to review the progress that we have achieved over the past two decades, and reaffirm our intention to continue our efforts to achieve that unity for which Christ prayed.

Calls for a dialogue between our churches go back as far as 1966, when Bp. Leon Grochowski, Prime Bishop of the Polish National Catholic Church, courageously proposed such a dialogue to the Roman Catholic Bishop of Scranton. Later, in 1980, Pope John Paul II of blessed memory expressed the desire that the conference of bishops of the United States examine the relationship that exists with the Polish National Catholic Church and explore the possibility of dialogue. This resulted in an exchange of correspondence between the leaders of our churches that would culminate in the first meeting of an official dialogue in Passaic, NJ, on Oct. 23, 1984.

In view of the fact that most of the ecumenical dialogues began in the 1960s and 1970s, the establishment of our dialogue was late in coming. This was the result of the particularly painful history of our relationship and the circumstances of the origins of the Polish National Catholic Church among ethnic Polish and other Roman Catholics in the United States at the end of the 19th and the beginning of the 20th century. The disputes of that time, we now realize, were more concerned with matters of church governance than points of doctrine. Nevertheless, the complicated series of events that led to our division caused much hurt and anguish even within families whose members often found themselves on opposite sides of the dispute. The consequences of those events can still be felt among us more than a century later, and must be addressed.

For this purpose, a number of highly symbolic gestures of reconciliation have taken place, perhaps most notably at the Service of Healing that was held in St. Stanislaus Polish National Catholic Cathedral in Scranton, PA, on Feb. 15, 1992. Leaders of our two churches, including Card. Edward I. Cassidy (President of the Pontifical Council for Promoting Christian Unity), His Grace John F. Swantek, Prime Bishop of the Polish National Catholic Church, and the two co-chairmen of the dialogue, asked for forgiveness, and pledged to work to overcome our divisions definitively. In 1997 Bp. James C. Timlin, then the Roman Catholic Co-Chairman of the dialogue, reiterated this request for forgiveness in a letter he issued on the occasion of the centenary of the organization of the Polish National Catholic Church.

Our dialogue has achieved much. For example, in a 1989 report summarizing the first five years of the dialogue's progress, we affirmed our agreement on the seven sacraments of the Church, in spite of some differences in practice that do not touch upon our basic common faith. The report also examined two areas of divergence – our understandings of the Word of God and the life to come – and discovered that here too there are broad areas of agreement. In sum, the report was able to look back over five years of dialogue and state that "we have thus far discovered no doctrinal obstacle that would impede the further growth of our churches toward that unity which we believe is Christ's will." A second report dealing with developments in our dialogue from 1989 to 2002 was published in 2003.

In view of this progress, concrete steps have been taken. In response to an inquiry from the Archbishop of Baltimore, Card. William Keeler, then President of the National Conference of Catholic Bishops, Card. Edward Cassidy, President of the Pontifical Council for Promoting Christian Unity, stated in 1993 that members of the Polish National Catholic Church in the United States and Canada may receive the sacraments of Penance, Holy Communion and Anointing of the Sick from Roman Catholic priests if they ask for them on their own, are properly disposed and not otherwise excluded from the sacraments in line with the provisions of canon 844 §3 of The Code of Canon Law. This was followed in 1996 by a letter by Abp. Oscar H. Lipscomb, the Chairman of the Bishops' Committee for Ecumenical and Interreligious Affairs, to the bishops of the United States spelling out in more detail the conditions under which Polish National Catholics may receive the aforementioned sacraments in the Roman Catholic Church. In 1998 the Polish National Catholic Church issued Guidelines for the Reception by Polish National Catholics of Sacraments in the Roman Catholic Church. Canon 844 §2 of The Code of Canon Law also specifies conditions under which Roman Catholics may receive the sacraments in the Polish National Catholic Church.

In light of these concrete steps toward unity, we have much for which to be thankful. Furthermore, we recognize each other's ecclesial character and sacraments, allow a certain amount of sacramental sharing, and maintain many of the same traditions. These facts bear witness to how much we have rediscovered as our common heritage. Our mutual esteem clearly rules out inappropriate actions such as proselytism among each other's faithful or the re-ordination of clergy who pass from one church to the other.

During our century-long division we have grown apart in ways that at first glance make reconciliation appear to be difficult. The Polish National Catholic Church, which during most of its existence was a member of the Union of Utrecht, has developed a strong sense of autonomy and the desire to preserve its distinctive traditions, including the vital role played by the laity in church governance. Even though the primacy and infallibility of the Bishop of Rome was not an issue at the time of our division, our churches today have different under-standings of the Pope's role in the Church. Another complicating factor is the presence of a significant number of former Roman Catholic priests in the ranks of the Polish National Catholic clergy. Such is the legacy of the divisions of the past that remain with us today.

At this point in our relationship, therefore, we the members of the Polish National Catholic-Roman Catholic dialogue wish to reaffirm our resolve to overcome what still divides us, and to state clearly that our goal is full communion between our churches. We wish to emphasize that "full communion" does not imply absorption or uniformity, but a unity that fully recognizes differing traditions that are consistent with our common apostolic faith. It must still be determined if any of our divergent traditions are truly church-dividing, or simply examples of legitimate diversity which, in the words of Pope John Paul II, "is in no way opposed to the Church's unity, but rather enhances her splendor and contributes greatly to the fulfillment of her mission" (*Ut Unum Sint*, No. 50). We plan to give further consideration to other concrete steps concerning reciprocity in regard to the sacraments, acting as godparents, and the requirement of canonical form for lawfulness only in mixed marriages. We are equally committed to a thorough examination of the theological concepts of primacy and conciliarity. This will include searching for a common understanding of the ministry of the Bishop of Rome in the Church.

As members of a commission authorized to engage in this ecumenical dialogue, our role is not to speak definitively for either of our churches. Nevertheless, we hope to propose new incremental steps that will make concrete the growing unity between us, and we wish our faithful to know of our conviction that a way can be found to overcome this regrettable division that took place among Catholics here in the United States. We know that the goal of unity is nothing less than the will of Christ for us. Therefore we ask the faithful of both our churches to join us in fervent prayer that, with a new outpouring of the Holy Spirit, the barriers between us will fall and we will one day soon find ourselves joined again in that perfect unity that befits the disciples of our Lord Jesus Christ.

The 2014 meeting of the Polish National Catholic-Roman Catholic Dialogue

The most recent session of the Polish National Catholic-Roman Catholic Dialogue took place at the Pastoral Center of the Catholic Archdiocese of Miami on Feb. 24–15, 2014. The meeting was chaired jointly by Aux. Bp. Mitchell T. Rozanski of the Archdiocese of Baltimore and Bp. John Mack of the PNCC Buffalo-Pittsburgh diocese.

During the course of the meeting the members continued their earlier reflection on the 2010 "Vision Statement" of the North American Catholic-Orthodox Theological Consultation and its possible meaning for this dialogue. Bp. Rozanski also presented Pope Francis' apostolic exhortation Evangelii Gaudium, "On the Proclamation of the Gospel in Today's World," and this was followed by a general conversation about the still unfolding ministry of Pope Francis. The members also reviewed the three "incremental steps" toward full communion that had been considered earlier in the dialogue, and assessed the future directions of the dialogue. The next meeting is scheduled to take place in Scranton, PA, in May 2015.

REFORMATION CHURCHES LEADERS AND DOCTRINES OF THE REFORMATION

Some of the leading figures, doctrines and churches of the Reformation are covered below. A companion article covers Major Protestant Churches in the U.S.

LEADERS

John Wycliff (c. 1320-1384): English priest and scholar who advanced one of the leading Reformation ideas nearly 200 years before Martin Luther — that the Bible alone is the sufficient rule of faith — but had only an indirect influence on the 16th century Reformers. Supporting belief in an inward and practical religion, he denied the divinely commissioned authority of the pope and bishops of the Church; he also denied the Real Presence of Christ in the Holy Eucharist, and wrote against the sacrament of penance and the doctrine of indulgences. Nearly 20 of his propositions were condemned by Gregory XI in 1377; his writings were proscribed more extensively by the Council of Constance in 1415. His influence was strongest in Bohemia and Central Europe.

John Hus (c. 1369-1415): A Bohemian priest and preacher of reform who authored 30 propositions condemned by the Council of Constance. Excommunicated in 1411 or 1412, he was burned at the stake in 1415. His principal errors concerned the nature of the Church and the origin of papal authority. He spread some of the ideas of Wycliff but did not subscribe to his views regarding faith alone as the condition for justification and salvation, the sole sufficiency of Scripture as the rule of faith, the Real Presence of Christ in the Eucharist, and the sacramental system. In 1457 some of his followers founded the Church of the Brotherhood which later became known as the United Brethren or Moravian Church and is considered the earliest independent Protestant body.

Martin Luther (1483-1546): An Augustinian friar, priest and doctor of theology, the key figure in the Reformation. In 1517, as a special indulgence was being preached in Germany, and in view of needed reforms within the Church, he published at Wittenberg 95 theses concerning matters of Catholic belief and practice. Leo X condemned 41 statements from Luther's writings in 1520. Luther, refusing to recant, was excommunicated the following year. His teachings strongly influenced subsequent Lutheran theology; its statements of faith are found in the Book of Concord (1580).

Luther's doctrines included the following: The sin of Adam, which corrupted human nature radically (but not substantially), has affected every aspect of man's being. Justification, understood as the forgiveness of sins and the state of righteousness, is by grace for Christ's sake through faith. Faith involves not merely intellectual assent but an act of confidence by the will. Good works are indispensably necessary concomitants of faith, but do not merit salvation. Of the sacraments, Luther retained baptism, penance and the Holy Communion as effective vehicles of the grace of the Holy Spirit; he held that in the Holy Communion the consecrated bread and wine are the Body and Blood of Christ. The rule of faith is the divine revelation in the Sacred Scriptures. He rejected purgatory, indulgences and the invocation of the saints, and held that prayers for the dead have no efficacy. Catholics clarified their positions at the Council of Trent. The 1999 Joint Declaration indicates that the condemnations of doctrine by the Council of Trent and the Book of Concord do not apply to present day Catholic and Lutheran teaching respectively.

Ulrich Zwingli (1484-1531): A priest who triggered the Reformation in Switzerland with a series of New Testament lectures in 1519, later disputations and by other actions. He held the Gospel to be the only basis of truth; rejected the Mass (which he suppressed in 1525 at Zurich), penance and other sacraments; denied papal primacy and doctrine concerning purgatory, the invocation of saints; rejected celibacy, monasticism and many traditional practices of piety. His symbolic view of the Eucharist, which was at odds with Catholic doctrine, caused an irreconcilable controversy with Luther and his followers. Zwingli was killed in a battle between the forces of Protestant and Catholic cantons in Switzerland.

John Calvin (1509-64): French leader of the Reformation in Switzerland, whose key tenet was absolute predestination of some persons to heaven and others to hell. He rejected Catholic doctrine in 1533 after becoming convinced of a personal mission to reform the Church. In 1536 he published the first edition of Institutes of the Christian Religion, a systematic exposition of his doctrine which became the classic textbook of Reformed – as distinguished from Lutheran – theology. To Luther's principal theses – regarding Scripture as the sole rule of faith, the radical corruption of human nature, and justification by faith alone – he added absolute predestination, certitude of salvation for the elect, and the incapability of the elect to lose grace. Calvin's Eucharist teaching, while affirming Christ's true presence, was not able to find agreement with that of Luther. However, in our own time, agreement has been reached between Lutherans and Reformed (Calvinists), and considerable progress has been made with Catholics and Orthodox toward a common understanding of Christ's presence in Communion.

CHURCHES AND MOVEMENTS

Adventists: Members of several Christian groups whose doctrines are dominated by belief in a more or less imminent second advent or coming of Christ upon earth for a glorious 1,000-year reign of righteousness. This reign, following victory by the forces of good over evil in a final Battle of Armageddon, will begin with the resurrection of the chosen and will end with the resurrection of all others and the annihilation of the wicked. Thereafter, the just will live forever in a renewed heaven and earth. A sleep of the soul takes place between the time of death and the day of judgment. There is no hell. The Bible, in literalist interpretation, is regarded as the only rule of faith and practice. About six churches have developed in the course of the Adventist movement which originated with William Miller (1782-1849) in the U.S. Miller, on the basis of calculations made from the Book of Daniel, predicted that the second advent of Christ would occur between 1843 and 1844. After the prophecy went unfulfilled, divisions occurred in the movement and the Seventh Day Adventists, whose actual formation dates from 1860, emerged as the largest single body. The observance of Saturday instead of Sunday as the Lord's Day dates from 1844.

Anabaptism: Originated in Saxony in the first quarter of the 16th century and spread rapidly through southern Germany. Its doctrine included several key Lutheran tenets but was not regarded with favor by Luther, Calvin or Zwingli. Anabaptists believed that baptism is for adults only and that infant baptism is invalid. Their doctrine of the Inner Light, concerning the direct influence of the Holy Spirit on the believer, implied rejection of Catholic doctrine concerning the sacraments and the nature of the Church. Eighteen artcles of faith were formulated in 1632 in Holland. Mennonites are Anabaptists.

Arminianism: A modification of the rigid predestinationism of Calvin, set forth by Jacob Arminius (1560-1609) and formally stated in the Remonstrance of 1610. Arminianism influenced some Calvinist bodies.

Baptists: So called because of their doctrine concerning baptism. They reject infant baptism and consider only baptism by immersion as valid. Leaders in the formation of the church were John Smyth (d. 1612) in England and Roger Williams (d. 1683) in America. Baptists are congregational in church government, and therefore are gathered into a variety of groupings, often called Conventions, the largest Protestant community in the US being the Southern Baptist Convention.

Congregationalists: Evangelical in spirit and seeking a return to forms of the primitive church, they uphold individual freedom in religious matters, do not require the acceptance of a creed as a condition for communion, and regard each congregation as autonomous. Robert Browne influenced the beginnings of Congregationalism.

Disciples: From a 19th century revival movement and desire for the unity of the Christian churches, a network of congregations developed which desired to be called simply "Christian churches." These churches opened their communion and membership to all, celebrated the Eucharist each Sunday and baptized only adults. From this movement the Christian Church/Disciples of Christ, the Churches of Christ and the independent Christian Churches emerged.

Methodists: A group who broke away from the Anglican Communion under the leadership of John Wesley (1703-1791), although some Anglican beliefs were retained. Doctrines include the witness of the Spirit to the individual and personal assurance of salvation. The largest Methodist body in the United States is the United Methodist Church. There are three Black Methodist bodies: African Methodist Episcopal, African Methodist Episcopal Zion, and Christian Methodist Episcopal Churches. There are also several Holiness Churches in the Wesleyan tradition: i.e., Nazarene, Free Methodist, Wesleyan Church.

Pentecostals: Churches that grew up after the 1906 enthusiastic revival, accompanied by the phenomena of speaking in foreign tongues and the experience of baptism in the Holy Spirit. From this revival churches of a Methodist or Baptist theological emphasis emerged, such as the Church of God in Christ or the Assemblies of God. In the mid-20th century, the charismatic experience began to be shared by some members of the classical churches, including Roman Catholic.

Puritans: Congregationalists who sought church reform along Calvinist lines in severe simplicity. (Use of the term was generally discontinued after 1660.)

Presbyterians: Basically Calvinistic, called Presbyterian because church polity centers around assemblies of presbyters or elders. John Knox (c. 1513-1572) established the church in Scotland.

Quakers: Their key belief is in internal divine illumination, the inner light of the living Christ, as the only source of truth and inspiration. George Fox (1624-1691) was one of their leaders in England. Called the Society of Friends, the Quakers are noted for their pacifism.

Unitarianism: A 16th century doctrine which rejected the Trinity and the divinity of Christ in favor of a uni-personal God. It claimed scriptural support for a long time but became generally rationalistic with respect to "revealed" doctrine as well as in ethics and its world-view. One of its principal early proponents was Faustus Socinus (1539-1604), a leader of the Polish Brethren. A variety of communions developed in England in the Reformation and post-Reformation periods.

Universalism: A product of 18th-century liberal Protestantism in England. The doctrine is not Trinitarian and includes a tenet that all men will ultimately be saved.

Anglican Communion: This communion, which regards itself as the same apostolic Church as that which was established by early Christians in England, derived not from Reformation influences but from the renunciation of papal jurisdiction by Henry VIII (1491-1547). His Act of Supremacy in 1534 called Christ's Church an assembly of local churches subject to the prince, who was vested with fullness of authority and jurisdiction. In spite of Henry's denial of papal authority, this Act did not reject substantially other principal articles of faith. Notable changes, proposed and adopted for the reformation of the church, took place in the subsequent reigns of Edward VI and Elizabeth, with respect to such matters as Scripture as the rule of faith, the sacraments, the nature of the Mass, and the constitution of the hierarchy. There are more than 27 provinces (national churches with their own canon law, primate and hierarchy) in the Anglican Communion. (See **Episcopal Church**, **Anglican Orders**, **Anglican-Catholic Final Report**.)

MAJOR PROTESTANT CHURCHES IN THE UNITED STATES

There are more than 250 Protestant church bodies in the U.S.

The majority of U.S. Protestants belong to the following denominations: Baptist, Methodist, Lutheran, Presbyterian, Episcopal, the United Church of Christ, the Christian Church (Disciples of Christ), Pentecostals and a variety of evangelical congregations and denominations.

See Ecumenical Dialogues, Reports and related entries for coverage of relations between the Catholic Church and other Christian churches.

Baptist Churches

Baptist churches, comprising the largest of all American Protestant denominations, were first established by John Smyth near the beginning of the 17th century in England. The first Baptist church in America was founded at Providence by Roger Williams in 1639.

Largest of the nearly 30 Baptist bodies in the U.S. are:

The Southern Baptist Convention, 901 Commerce St., Suite 750, Nashville, TN 37203, with 16 million members.

The National Baptist Convention, U.S.A., Inc., 915 Spain St., Baton Rouge, LA 70802, with 5.1 million members.

The National Baptist Convention of America, Inc., 1320 Pierre Ave., Shreveport, LA 71103, with 3.5 million members.

The American Baptist Churches in the U.S.A., P.O. Box 851, Valley Forge, PA 19482, with 1.3 million members.

The total number of U.S. Baptists is more than 29 million. The world total is 33 million.

Proper to Baptists is their doctrine on baptism. Called an "ordinance" rather than a sacrament, baptism by immersion is a sign that one has experienced and decided in favor of the salvation offered by Christ. It is administered only to persons who are able to make a responsible decision. Baptism is not administered to infants.

Baptists do not have a formal creed but generally subscribe to two professions of faith formulated in 1689 and 1832 and are in general agreement with classical Protestant theology regarding Scripture as the sole rule of faith, original sin, justification through faith in Christ, and the nature of the Church. Their local churches are autonomous.

Worship services differ in form from one congregation to another. Usual elements are the reading of Scripture, a sermon, hymns, vocal and silent prayer. The Lord's Supper, called an "ordinance," is celebrated at various times during the year.

Christian Church (Disciples of Christ)

The Christian Church (Disciples of Christ) originated early in the 1800s from two movements on the "western frontier of the expanding nation" that rejected the division of the churches that were inherited from Europe and the past, and that worked for the renewal and unity of all Christians. The movements were led by former Presbyterians, Thomas and Alexander Campbell in western Pennsylvania and Barton W. Stone in Kentucky. The two movements developed separately and grew rapidly for about 25 years before merging in 1832.

The church, which identifies itself with the Protestant mainstream, has nearly one million members in over 3,600 congregations in the U.S. and Canada. The greatest concentration of members in the U.S. is located roughly along the old frontier line, in an arc sweeping from Ohio and Kentucky through the Midwest and down into Oklahoma and Texas.

The general offices of the church are located in Indianapolis, Indiana. The church's core commitment and concern for Christian unity is based on a conviction expressed in a basic document, Declaration and Address, dating 1809 which states: "The church of Christ upon earth is essentially, intentionally and constitutionally one."

The Disciples have no official doctrine or dogma. A slogan used by the movements in their beginnings was "No creed but Christ." Their worship practices vary widely from more common informal services to what could almost be described as "high church" services. Membership is based upon the simple statement of the "Good Confession" of belief in Jesus Christ. The Lord's Supper is celebrated weekly at an "open Table," where all Christians are invited to partake, and where lay and ordained share in presiding in the service. The Disciples of Christ practice "believer's baptism" by immersion, though most congregations admit un immersed transfers from other denominations. Distinction between ordained and non ordained members is blurred somewhat because of the Disciples' emphasis on the "priesthood of all believers" that comes through the act of baptism. The Christian Church is oriented to congregational government, and has a unique structure in which three expressions (general, regional and congregational) operate as equals rather than in a hierarchy of authority. At the national or international level, the church is governed by a general assembly which has voting representation from all congregations and regions, as well as all ordained and commissioned ministers.

Episcopal Church

The Episcopal Church, which includes over 100 dioceses in the United States, Central and South America, and elsewhere overseas, regards itself as part of the same apostolic church which was established by early Christians in England. Established in this country during the colonial period, it became independent of the jurisdiction of the Church of England when a new constitution and Prayer Book were adopted at a general convention held in 1789. It has approximately two million members worldwide. Offices of the presiding bishop and the executive council are located at 815 Second Ave., New York, NY 10017.

The presiding bishop is chief pastor and primate; he or she is elected by the House of Bishops and confirmed by the House of Deputies for a term of nine years.

The Episcopal Church, which is a part of the Anglican Communion, regards the Archbishop of Canterbury as the "First among Equals," though not under his authority.

The Anglican Communion, worldwide, has 85 million members in more than 165 countries and 38 self-governing churches.

Official statements of belief and practice are found in the Book of Common Prayer. Scripture has primary importance with respect to the rule of faith, and authority is also attached to tradition. Regarding Church-wide governance, the General Convention meets every three years and consists of a House of Bishops and a House of Deputies that includes presbyters, deacons, and lay persons. During the triennium between Conventions, the Executive Council serves as the decision-making body. A similar polity is reflected on the local levels, with annual legislative meetings supplemented by, respectively, diocesan Standing Committees and parish Vestries. Dioceses elect their bishops, and congregations elect their own rectors, with the consent of the diocesan bishop.

Liturgical worship is according to the Book of Common Prayer as adopted in 1979, along with other liturgical texts authorized by General Convention, while details of ceremonial practice can vary locally with the permission of the diocesan bishop.

Lutheran Churches

The origin of Lutheranism is generally traced to Oct. 31, 1517, when Martin Luther — Augustinian friar, priest, doctor of theology — tacked "95 Theses" to the door of the castle church in Wittenberg, Germany. This call to debate on the subject of indulgences and related concerns has come to symbolize the beginning of the Reformation. Luther and his supporters intended to reform the Church they knew. Though Lutheranism has come to be visible in separate denominations and national churches, at its heart it professes itself to be a confessional movement within the one, holy, catholic and apostolic Church.

The world's 75 million Lutherans form the third largest grouping of Christians, after Roman Catholics and Orthodox. 70.5 million of them belong to church bodies which make up the Lutheran World Federation, headquartered in Geneva.

There are around 8 million Lutherans in the United States, making them the fourth largest Christian grouping, after Roman Catholics, Baptists and Methodists. There are nearly 20 U.S. Lutheran church bodies. The largest is the Evangelical Lutheran Church in America (with 3.9 million members and headquarters at 8765 W. Higgins Rd., Chicago, IL 60631), The Lutheran Church Missouri Synod (with 2.2 million members and headquarters at 1333 S. Kirkwood Rd., St. Louis, MO 63122), the Wisconsin Evangelical Lutheran Synod (with 385,000 members and headquarters at 2929 N. Mayfair Rd., Milwaukee, WI 53222) and two newer Lutheran Church bodies established after the year 2,000 (Congregations in Mission for Christ with 321,000 members, with headquarters at 7000 N Sheldon Rd, Canton, MI 48187; and the North American Lutheran Church with 125,000 members with headquarters at 3500 Mill Run Dr., Hilliard, OH 43026).

The Evangelical Lutheran Church in America and the Lutheran Church Missouri Synod carry out some work together through inter Lutheran agencies such as Lutheran World Relief, Lutheran Immigration and Refugee Services located at 700 Light Street, Baltimore, MD 21230; and Lutheran Services in America located at 100 Maryland Ave., NE Suite 500, Washington, DC 20002.

The statements of faith which have shaped the confessional life of Lutheranism are found in the Book of Concord. This 1580 collection includes the three ancient ecumenical creeds (Apostles', Nicene and Athanasian), Luther's Large and Small Catechisms (1529), the Augsburg Confession (1530) and the Apology in defense of it (1531), the Smalkald Articles (including the "Treatise on the Power and Primacy of the Pope") (1537), and the Formula of Concord (1577).

The central Lutheran doctrinal proposition is that Christians "receive forgiveness of sins and become righteous before God by grace, for Christ's sake." The Joint Declaration on the Doctrine of Justification between the Vatican and the Lutheran World Federation is valued for its ecumenical and historical agreement. Foundational work for the JDDJ was done at the ELCA-US Conference of Catholic Bishops dialogue. The Methodist World Council has also affirmed the JDDJ. In preparation for the 500th Anniversary of the Reformation, the LWF and Vatican dialogue produced "From Conflict to Communion," as a common statement on history and developing relationships between Lutherans and Catholics.

Baptism and the Lord's Supper (Holy Communion, the Eucharist) are universally celebrated among Lutherans as sacramental means of grace. Lutherans also treasure the Word proclaimed in the reading of the Scriptures, preaching and absolution.

In the ELCA, the bishop is the minister of ordination. Much of Lutheranism continues what it understands as the historic succession of bishops (though without considering the historic episcopate essential for the church). All of Lutheranism is concerned to preserve apostolic succession in life and doctrine. Lutheran churches in Scandinavia and the Baltics, in the U.S., and in Canada have moved into full communion with their Anglican counterparts.

Lutheran jurisdictions corresponding to dioceses are called districts or synods in North America. There are more than 100 of them; each of them is headed by a bishop or president. The Evangelical Lutheran Church in America moved into full communion with the three Reformed Churches (Presbyterian Church, United Church of Christ and Reformed Church in America) in 1997, and in 2000 into full communion with the Episcopal Church, all of its bishops being ordained by bishops including those in the apostolic succession as understood by Anglicans. It moved into full communion with the Moravian Church in 1999. In 2009, the ELCA and the United Methodist Church entered full communion.

Methodist Churches

John Wesley (1703 1791), an Anglican priest, was the founder of the 'Arminian' branch of Methodism (distinguished from a much smaller, parallel Calvinistic Methodism – most notably represented by the revivalistic preacher, George Whitefield (1714-1770) – that rejected Wesley's core emphases on free will and the doctrine of Christian perfection). The earliest expressions of Methodism manifested at Oxford University during Wesley's time there. Subsequently, in 1738, following a period of missionary work in America and a significant encounter with the Moravians, he had his Aldersgate conversion experience in which he received assurance of his salvation and shortly thereafter became a key leader in a religious awakening in England. By the end of the 18th century, Methodism had also taken root in America and many other parts of the world into which the British Empire was expanding. By the middle of the 19th century, the (then) Methodist Episcopal Church was the single largest denomination in the American republic.

The United Methodist Church, formed in 1968 by a merger of the Methodist Church and the Evangelical United Brethren Church, is one of the largest Protestant denominations in the U.S., with more than eight million members (and over eleven million members worldwide); its principal agencies are located in New York, Evanston, IL, Nashville, TN, and Washington, DC. The second largest Methodist body, with just under two million members, is the African Methodist Episcopal Church. Five other major Wesleyan Methodist churches in the U.S. are the African Methodist Episcopal Zion Church, Christian Methodist Episcopal Church, Free Methodist Church, Wesleyan Church, and the Salvation Army. The total Methodist membership in the U.S. is about 15.5 million.

Worldwide, there are more than 73 autonomous Methodist/Wesleyan churches in 107 countries, with a membership of more than 33 million. Many of them participate in the World Methodist Council (P.O. Box 518, Lake Junaluska, NC 28745), which serves as an ecumenical expression of similar and shared Wesleyan Methodist perspectives on the Christian faith. Significantly, Wesleyan Methodism is also a forerunner of many branches of Pentecostalism worldwide.

Wesleyan Methodism rejects predestination and maintains that Christ offers grace freely to all persons, not just to an elect. In addition to a strong emphasis upon free will and personal assurance of salvation, John Wesley stressed a doctrine of Christian perfection (in which the justified believer lived out their faith in Christ by seeking to be conformed to the image of God as embodied in the perfect love of Jesus). Thus, while Methodists expected a conversion – like many other Evangelical churches of the 18th and 19th centuries – they also placed strong emphasis upon the importance of sanctification. Methodists are in general agreement with many points of Protestant theology regarding Scripture as the sole rule of faith, original sin, justification through faith in Christ, and the sacraments of baptism and the Lord's Supper; while also stressing the significance of tradition and experience of the Holy Spirit in their role in illumining the meaning of Scripture. In The United Methodist Church, polity is a hybrid of a presbyterian conference structure (Annual Conferences over geographic areas and a General Conference to govern the denomination) with bishops who are specialized elders (presbyters) set aside for certain specific functions such as presiding over meetings of Conference, officiating at ordinations, and appointing ministers to local churches. Churches stemming from British Methodism do not have bishops but vest appointive powers within an appropriate conference. Clergy serving local congregations are generally free to choose various forms of worship services; typical elements include readings from Scripture, sermons, hymns and prayers. In 2006 the World Methodist Council signed on to the Joint Declaration on the Doctrine of Justification with Lutherans and Catholics.

Presbyterian Churches

Presbyterians are so called because of their tradition of governing the church through a system of representative bodies composed of elders (presbyters).

Presbyterianism is a part of the Reformed Family of Churches that grew out of the theological work of John Calvin following the Lutheran Reformation, to which it is heavily indebted. Countries in which it acquired early strength and influence were Switzerland, France, Holland, Scotland and England. Presbyterianism spread widely in this country in the latter part of the 18th century and afterwards. Presently, it has approximately 4.5 million communicants in nine bodies. The two largest Presbyterian bodies in the country – the United Presbyterian Church in the U.S.A. and the Presbyterian Church in the United States – were reunited in June 1983, to form the Presbyterian Church (U.S.A.), with a membership of 2.7 million. Its national offices are located at 100 Witherspoon St., Louisville, KY 40202. The church is closely allied with the Reformed Church in America, the Christian Reformed Church – both of Dutch background, the United Church of Christ, the Cumberland Presbyterian Churches, the Korean Presbyterian Church Abroad.

In Presbyterian doctrine, baptism and the Lord's Supper, viewed as seals of the covenant of grace, are regarded as sacraments. Baptism, which is not necessary for salvation, is conferred on infants and persons making a confession of faith. Baptism is only conferred once in an individual's life. In baptism, a person is admitted into the visible church and given "a sign and seal of the covenant of grace, of his ingrafting into Christ, of regeneration, of remission of sins, and of this giving up unto God, through Jesus Christ, to walk in newness of life" (Westminster Confession of Faith, 6.154). Those who are baptized have been received into God's church, set apart from other people and religions in order to be dedicated to God, and promised that God will be their God forever (Belgic Confession, art. 34). Historically, the theology and practice of the Lord's Supper have focused on Christ's atoning death. Presently, the Reformed communions celebrate the Supper in remembrance of and in gratitude for Christ's whole life, person, ministry, and work, and in recognition that this Supper is a pledge and foretaste of the eschatological feast that God prepares. Those who partake of the Lord's Supper in faith are granted and assured union with Christ, nourished in their communion with one another as members of the Body of Christ, and called to live in hope and service as Christ's thankful disciples every day.

In both sacraments, a doctrine of the real presence of Christ is considered the central theological principle. The Church is twofold, being invisible and also visible; it consists of all of the elect and all those Christians who are united in Christ as their immediate head. Presbyterians are in general agreement with classical Protestant theology regarding Scripture as the sole rule of faith and practice, salvation by grace, and justification through faith in Christ. Presbyterian congregations are governed by a council called a session composed of elders elected by the communicant membership and moderated by a teaching elder (minister of Word and Sacrament). On higher levels there are other councils called presbyteries, synods and a general assembly with various degrees of authority over local bodies; all such representative bodies are composed of elected ruling elders and teaching elders (ministers) in approximately equal numbers. The church elects a moderator every other year who presides at the General Assembly and travels throughout the church to speak to and hear from the members. Worship services, simple and dignified, include sermons, prayer, reading of the Scriptures and hymns. The Lord's Supper is celebrated at intervals. Doctrinal developments of the past several years included approval in May, 1967, by the General Assembly of the United Presbyterian Church of a contemporary confession of faith to supplement the historic Westminster Confession. A statement entitled "The Declaration of Faith" was approved in 1977 by the Presbyterian Church in the U.S. for teaching and liturgical use. The reunited church adopted "A Brief Statement of Reformed Faith" in 1991 regarding urgent concerns of the church. The Presbyterian Church (U.S.A.), along with the Reformed Church in America and the United Church of Christ, has moved into full communion with the Evangelical Lutheran Church in America in 1997. The Presbyterian Church (U.S.A.) is also in covenant or full communion with the Moravian Church (Northern and Southern provinces) and the Korean Presbyterian Church Abroad.

United Church of Christ

The 979,239 member (in 2013) United Church of Christ was formed in 1957 by a union of the Congregational Christian and the Evangelical and Reformed Churches. The former was originally established by the Pilgrims, the Puritans of the Massachusetts Bay Colony, while the latter was founded in Pennsylvania in the early 1700s by settlers from Central Europe. It considers itself "a united and uniting church" and keeps itself open to all ecumenical options. Its headquarters are located at 700 Prospect, Cleveland, OH 44115.

Its statement of faith recognizes Jesus Christ as "our crucified and risen Lord (who) shared our common lot, conquering sin and death and reconciling the world to himself." It believes in the life after death, and the fact that God "judges men and nations by his righteous will declared through prophets and apostles."

The United Church further believes that Christ calls its members to share in his baptism "and eat at his table, to join him in his passion and victory." Each local church is free to adopt its own methods of worship and to formulate its own covenants and confessions of faith. Some celebrate communion weekly; others, monthly or on another periodical basis. The United Church is governed along congregational lines, and each local church is autonomous. However, the actions of its biennial General Synod are taken with great seriousness by congregations. Between synods, a 52 member governing board oversees the work of the church. In 1989 the UCC moved into full communion with the Christian Church (Disciples of Christ) and in 1997 with the Evangelical Lutheran Church in America, Reformed Church in America and the Presbyterian Church USA in a quadrilateral agreement.

Evangelicalism

The revivalist evangelical movement, dating from 1735 in England (the Evangelical Revival) and after 1740 in the United States (the Great Awakening), has had and continues to have widespread influence in Protestant churches. It has been estimated that about 45 million American

Protestants – communicants of both large denominations and small bodies – are evangelicals.

The Bible is their rule of faith and religious practice. Being born again in a life-changing experience through faith in Christ is the promise of salvation. Missionary work for the spread of the Gospel is a normal and necessary activity.

Additional matters of belief and practice are generally of a conservative character. Fundamentalists, numbering perhaps 4.5 million, comprise an extreme right-wing sub-culture of evangelicalism. They are distinguished mainly by militant biblicism, belief in the absolute inerrancy of the Bible and emphasis on the Second Coming of Christ. Fundamentalism developed early in the 20th century in reaction against liberal theology and secularizing trends in mainstream and other Protestant denominations.

The Holiness or Perfectionist wing of evangelicalism evolved from Methodist efforts to preserve, against a contrary trend, the personal-piety and inner-religion concepts of John Wesley. There are at least 30 Holiness bodies in the U.S.

Pentecostals, probably the most demonstrative of evangelicals, are noted for speaking in tongues and the stress they place on healing, prophecy and personal testimony to the practice and power of evangelical faith. There are strong charismatic movements within many of the historic Protestant churches and Roman Catholicism.

The evangelical communities have national and international ecumenical bodies. Black and white Pentecostal churches belong to the Pentecostal and Charismatic Fellowship of North America. Over 40 Pentecostal, Holiness and evangelical churches belong to the US National Association of Evangelicals. Internationally, these national evangelical associations collaborate in the World Evangelical Alliance.

Assemblies of God

Assemblies (Churches) of God form the largest body (more than 2 million members) in the Pentecostal Movement which developed from (1) the Holiness Revival in the Methodist Church after the Civil War and (2) the Apostolic Faith Movement at the beginning of the 20th century. Members share with other Pentecostals belief in the religious experience of conversion and in the baptism by the Holy Spirit that sanctifies. Distinctive is the emphasis placed on the charismatic gifts of the apostolic church, healing and speaking in tongues, which are signs of the "second blessing" of the Holy Spirit.

The Assemblies are conservative and biblicist in theology; are loosely organized in various districts, with democratic procedures; are vigorously evangelistic. The moral code is rigid.

RELATIONS WITH ANGLICANS AND PROTESTANTS

ANGLICAN-ROMAN CATHOLIC FINAL REPORT

The Anglican Roman Catholic International Commission issued a Final Report in 1982 on 12 years of dialogue on major issues of concern, especially the Eucharist and ordained ministry.

In 1988 the Lambeth Conference called parts of the report on these two subjects "consonant in substance with the faith of Anglicans." In 1991 the Congregation for the Doctrine of the Faith and the Pontifical Council for Promoting Christian Unity called the Report a significant milestone not only in relations between the Catholic Church and the Anglican Communion but in the ecumenical movement as a whole. They said, however, that it was not yet possible to state that substantial agreement had been reached on all the questions studied by the commission, and that important differences still remained with respect to essential matters of Catholic doctrine regarding the Eucharist, ordination and other subjects. Clarifications were requested.

The Anglican Roman Catholic Commission II responded in 1994, saying that its members were in agreement regarding:

• the substantial and sacramental presence of Christ in the Eucharist;

• the propitiatory nature of the Eucharistic Sacrifice, which can also be applied to the deceased;

• institution of the sacrament of order from Christ;

• the character of priestly ordination, implying configuration to the priesthood of Christ.

In 1994 Card. Edward I. Cassidy, president of the Pontifical Council for Interreligious Dialogue addressed a letter to the Catholic and Anglican co chairmen of the commission, responding to the clarifications, stating that "no further work" seems to be necessary at this time on Eucharist and ministry. Questions still remained to be answered about a number of subjects, including the authority in the Church, ordination of women, infallibility and Marian doctrine.

THE RELATIONSHIP BETWEEN ANGLICANS AND ROMAN CATHOLICS

By Dr. John Borelli, Special Assistant to the President, Georgetown University.

Pope Francis and Abp. of Canterbury, Dr. Justin Welby, assumed office in 2013, one month apart; Dr. Welby, on 4 February 2013 and Pope Francis on 13 March 2013. Not long afterwards, in June 2013, they met for the first time when Dr. Welby made an official visit to Rome. They acknowledged a long history of relations between Anglicans and Catholics, both in communion and separated, often punctuated by challenges and that church-dividing differences remain. Still, they re-committed themselves and their churches to restoring unity and to practical efforts along the way for putting the Gospel into action.

These sentiments dominated a more sustained meeting between them a year later in June 2014. Together, they reiterated their support for the Global Freedom Network, an initiative founded by an Australian philanthropist, Andrew Forrest, to eradicate slavery and human trafficking. Mr. Forest, Pope Francis and Dr. Welby, along with Dr Mahmoud Azab, Grand Imam of Al Azhar, Egypt, established the Network in March 2014. Dr. Welby further noted the formation of a Chemin Neuf Community at Lambeth Palace, his official residence. A Roman Catholic community with an ecumenical vision, Chemin Neuf originated in Lyon and now has official status in France, the United Kingdom and Canada.

On Sunday, June 15, of his 2014 visit to Rome, Dr. Welby presided at Vespers at the Church of San Gregorio al Celio, from which Pope Gregory the Great sent the monk Augustine (later first archbishop of Canterbury) and his companions to evangelize the peoples of England in 596. In remarks the next day, June 16, Pope Francis underscored how "the Anglican-Roman Catholic International Commission and the International Anglican-Roman

Catholic Commission for Unity and Mission represent especially significant forums for examining, in a constructive spirit, older and newer challenges to our ecumenical engagement."

The Archbishop of Canterbury is head of the Anglican Communion but has no jurisdictional authority over any of its almost 40 member churches except the Church of England. Anglican unity worldwide is served further by other instruments of communion: the Lambeth Conference, a meeting, nowadays all Anglican bishops, about every ten years; the Primates Meetings, when the heads of all Anglican provinces gather; and the Anglican Consultative Council, a meeting of clergy and laity every two or three years.

The first Archbishop of Canterbury to visit Rome since the Reformation was Dr. Geoffrey Fisher in his final year as archbishop in 1960. His brief and private meeting with Pope John XXIII created a glimmer of hope that adjustments would be made to improve relations. Fisher's successor, Dr. Michael Ramsey made an official and public visit in 1966 at which time Pope Paul VI removed the episcopal finger from his ringer and put it on Dr. Ramsey's finger. Subsequently, Archbishops of Canterbury on official visits to Rome wear that ring.

In 1968, three years after the close of Vatican II and its church-wide mandate to promote Christian unity, a Joint ARC Preparatory Commission recommended topics for dialogue as well as a range of practical suggestions, which still apply today, for Catholics and Anglicans worldwide to begin growing together in unity and mission. Pope Paul and Dr. Ramsey established the first Anglican-Roman Catholic International Commission (ARCIC I) that met thirteen times from 1970 to 1981 producing seven statements on three general topics, eucharist, ministry and authority, collected into a Final Report (1981). An ARCIC II met 22 times between 1983 and 2004 producing five agreed statements on salvation, the moral life, the church, authority in the church, and the doctrines on Mary. ARCIC III has met four times since 2011 and has has two mandates: to explore the Church as Communion, local and universal, and how in communion the local and universal Church comes to discern right ethical teaching and to collect ARCIC II's five statements into a unified volume.

In 2000, after consulting widely for two years, Cardinal Edward Cassidy, President of the Vatican's Pontifical Council for Promoting Christian Unity and then Archbishop George Carey of Canterbury convened a special consultation in Mississauga, Ontario, of Catholic and Anglican bishops from thirteen regions. With ARCIC consensus stalled on the exercise of authority in the church and with the ordination of women as priests and bishops in some provinces of the Anglican Communion, this special consultation faced some risk; yet, the Mississauga meeting succeeded in recommending two short documents, "Communion in Mission" and "Action Plan to Implement 'Communion in Mission,'" and a new commission. Those at Mississauga reported that Anglican-Catholic relations had reached a significant new place, despite unresolved differences. The International Anglican-Roman Catholic Commission for Unity and Mission (IARCCUM) came into being and issued two reports in five years. One, released in 2007 and entitled Growing Together in Unity and Mission, emphasizes in detail how much Anglicans and Catholics already share.

IARCCUM's other report, Ecclesiological Reflections on the Current Situation in the Anglican Communion in the Light of ARCIC, was completed in 2004 by a sub-commission. It expressed concern about the unusual situation in the Anglican Communion where 38 member churches remain in communion while some ordain women and others will not recognize their ordination. This irregularity became more complicated in 2006 when the Episcopal Church (United States) ordained Bishop Katharine Jefferts Schori as Presiding Bishop. A more difficult challenge was already developing in 2003 when the General Convention of the Episcopal Church affirmed the election of Bishop Gene Robinson, an active homosexual. Services of blessing of homosexual unions began taking place in Anglican dioceses in Canada and in the United States. In reaction, some member churches of the Anglican Communion formed missionary outreaches within the territories of those member churches permissive of homosexual relationships, and those churches in turn charged violation of their integrity as member churches. IARCCUM's report pointed out how the serious problems, raised by these developments, strain the meaning of communion for Anglicans and undermine Anglican-Catholic agreements on the role of bishops, the nature of ecclesial communion, and the Christian moral life.

Despite tensions and disagreements, IARCCUM continues to meet and promote projects serving the real but partial communion between Anglicans and Catholics. While Dr. Welby was in Rome in June 2014, he launched IARCCUM's website (http://iarccum.org/) a rich resource on Anglican-Catholic relations and the work of IARCCUM and ARCIC. IARCCUM's Growing Together in Unity and Mission suggests much that Anglicans and Catholics can do in common now: spend more time together in prayer, study, consultation, teaching and learning, preparing educational and liturgical materials, guiding marriage preparation, and confronting injustice and poverty through common action.

In late 2009, Anglican leaders were disappointed when Pope Benedict XVI issued the apostolic constitution Anglicanorum Coetibus providing ways for communities of Anglican clergy and faithful to enter the communion of the Catholic Church as groups and retain an Anglican character to their worship and community life. There was little or no advance consultation, as the principles of Growing Together suggest. Distinctly Anglican-Catholic ordinariates, that is, juridical church structures overseen by the equivalent of a bishop, now exist in England and in the United States. Their future as continuing communities is yet to be seen and tested.

The appearance of a "Malines Conversations Group" is another development in relations worth noting. When restoration of unity seemed impossible after Pope Leo XIII in 1896 had declared the holy orders of the Church of England to be null and void in the papal bull Apostolicae Curae, a distinguished group of Catholics and Anglicans, convened by Card. Désiré Mercier, Archbishop of Mechelen (Malines, Brussels), and Edward Wood (Lord Irwin and later Earl of Halifax) began meeting in 1921 until Mercier's death in 1926. They proved that dialogue was possible even in the most adverse of times. On March 25, 2013, a group of Anglican and Catholic theologians and ecumenists, meeting at the Monastery of Chevetogne in Belgium, announced a "Malines Conversations Group." Though informal and not officially sponsored by Anglican and Catholic churches, the group has the support of the previous Archbishop of Canterbury, Dr. Rowan Williams, and the retired Archbishop of Mechelen, Card. Godfried Danneels, who serve as patrons. The group met again in 2014 reflecting on how they might serve as a theological resource for the work of ARCIC and IARRCUM.

IARRCUM has produced a national ARC (Anglican-Roman Catholic dialogue) survey which gives a window on numerous formal relationships between member churches of the Anglican Communion and Catholic conferences of bishops. Formal and informal relations also extend between Anglican and Catholic dioceses, parishes, and other institutions and their members. In the United States, an ARC dialogue began meeting in 1965 before the close of Vatican II and has produced 16 agreed statements and reports under the sponsorship of the Episcopal Church and the U. S. Conference of Catholic Bishops. Its most recent statement is "Ecclesiology and Moral Discernment: Seeking a Unified Moral Witness."

COMMUNIQUE FROM THE 2014 MEETING OF ARCIC III IN SOUTH AFRICA

The Anglican-Roman Catholic International Commission is the official body appointed by the two Communions to engage in theological dialogue in order that they may come into full communion. It held the fourth meeting of its current phase (ARCIC III), at the Vuleka Centre, Botha's Hill, Durban, South Africa (12–20 May 2014). This is the first time in its more than 40 year history that ARCIC has met in Africa. A wide range of papers was prepared for the meeting and discussed, taking the Commission further toward its goal of producing an agreed statement. The mandate for this third phase of ARCIC is to explore: the Church as Communion, local and universal, and how in communion the local and universal Church come to discern right ethical teaching.

At this meeting, ARCIC III discussed its method and agreed that it would build on that of ARCIC I and II, integrated with the method of receptive ecumenism. In the light of this work, the Schema prepared at the first meeting of ARCIC III in 2011 was revised. Discussions concentrated on the first part of the mandate, the Church as Communion, local and universal. Members reviewed texts from ARCIC II, national Anglican-Roman Catholic dialogues (ARCs), and other ecumenical material on the subject. ARCIC III decided to examine the regional level of the Church in addition to the local and universal. It considered, through papers presented, the impact of culture on the thinking of Christians and the role of the baptized in ecclesial decision-making. The ecclesiological work will be advanced by a drafting team which will bring a preliminary text back to the next meeting.

ARCIC III was also mandated to prepare a book presenting the five Agreed Statements of ARCIC II so that they can be received by the respective Communions. The Statements will be accompanied by articles on the method of ARCIC II, its use of Scripture, and major theological themes which emerged in its work, together with introductory material and commentaries. It is planned that the book will be ready for publication following the next meeting.

Members of the Commission are grateful to The Rt. Revd. Rubin Phillip, Anglican Bishop of Natal, for the generous welcome extended to them by him and his Diocese. Particular thanks are due to Mrs. Mary Robinson of the Vuleka Trust, and her colleagues at the Centre, whose mission is to equip young people for leadership in South Africa.

Bishop Rubin visited the Commission at Vuleka and participated in a discussion of local ecumenism. He and his wife Rose welcomed ARCIC members to their home to meet leaders of the local Anglican, Roman Catholic and Methodist Churches. On the Sunday the bishop presided, together with Abp. Moxon and Bp. Nicholls, at the Eucharist at the 160 year old St. Augustine's, Umlazi, where ARCIC joined in the vibrant worship of the Anglican Church of Southern Africa.

Members of the Commission visited the Hillcrest Aids Centre, and a project in Nazareth, Pinetown, run by the Diakonia Council of Churches, which works for social justice and community development with the poorest people. The next meeting will take place near Rome at the end of April 2015, when the Commission will intensify its focus on the second part of its mandate by studying ethical discernment in the Scriptures and by further developing its case study on slavery.

As the Commission welcomed the Revd. Antony Currer as the new co-secretary, replacing Msgr. Mark Langham, it was also conscious that this was the last ARCIC of Canon Alyson Barnett-Cowan. Alyson has served the Commission with great efficiency and grace, and members gave thanks for her five years of service.

The Co-Chairs of ARCIC-III are Abp. Bernard Longley of Birmingham, England, and Abp. David Moxon, the abp. of Canterbury's Representative to the Holy See.

Anglican-Roman Catholic Dialogue Releases Joint Statement: "Ecclesiology and Moral Discernment: Seeking a Unified Moral Witness."

The Anglican-Roman Catholic Dialogue in the United States (ARC-USA) has concluded a six-year round of dialogue with the release of "Ecclesiology and Moral Discernment: Seeking a Unified Moral Witness," approved at the most recent meeting Feb. 24-25, 2014, at Virginia Theological Seminary in Alexandria, VA. The meeting was chaired by Bp. John Bauerschmidt of the Episcopal Diocese of Tennessee; the Roman Catholic co-chairman, Bp. Ronald Herzog of Alexandria, LA, was unable to attend for health reasons.

In 2008 the U.S. Conference of Catholic Bishops' (USCCB) Committee on Ecumenical and Interreligious Affairs and the Most Reverend Katharine Jefferts Schori, presiding bishop of the Episcopal Church, asked the ARC-USA to address questions of ethics and the Christian life in the context of ecclesiology, in an effort to achieve greater clarity regarding areas of agreement and disagreement. They were aware that dialogue on these issues was also taking place between the Roman Catholic Church and the Anglican Communion at the international level, and also in other bilateral dialogues between churches of various traditions.

The statement reflects on the way the two churches pursue the work of teaching and learning within the Christian moral life. It examines the extent to which their respective church structures influence the way they teach and what they teach on moral questions. Inquiries and discussions about moral formation and the teaching charism of the churches guided them in addressing this topic.

With a focus on two case studies concerning migration/immigration and same sex relations, the dialogue concluded that even if the moral teachings of Anglicans and Catholics diverge on some questions, they also share important common features. The statement delves into these differences and similarities and represents progress toward a more unified Gospel witness capable of addressing contemporary concerns in ways that are useful and attractive to all Christians, as well as larger society. As Bishop Bauerschmidt said, "ARC-USA has produced some important statements in the past. This statement represents the latest landmark in our journey together as churches, and is a valuable contribution to an important topic." The full text is available online here: www.usccb.org/beliefs-and-teachings/ecumenical-and-interreligious/ecumenical/anglican/upload/arcusa-2014-statement.pdf

In the preface the co-chairmen explain the authority of the statement: "Although the members of the dialogue do not speak officially for either of our churches," they state, "we have been asked to represent them in this dialogue, and it is in that capacity that we submit this statement to the leadership of our churches and to all their faithful for their prayerful consideration as a means of hastening progress along the path to full, visible unity." The members of this round of ARC-USA hope that the statement will act as a catalyst for more intensive discussion in view of reaching a broader consensus on these moral issues. Bishop Madden affirmed this hope, saying that "this document opens new horizons in the ongoing discussion of ethical issues both between our churches and within them. I am confident that this new agreed statement will help to sharpen our understanding of where our true differences lie, and increase our awareness of how much we have in common."

JOINT DECLARATION ON JUSTIFICATION WITH THE LUTHERAN WORLD FEDERATION

By Russell Shaw

Hailed by Pope John Paul II as a "milestone" on the road to Christian unity, a Lutheran-Catholic Joint Declaration on the Doctrine of Justification was signed Oct. 31, 1999, in Augsburg, Germany, by representatives of the Catholic Church and the Lutheran World Federation.

"This document represents a sound basis for continuing the ecumenical theological research and for addressing the remaining problems with a better founded hope of resolving them in the future," Pope John Paul said the same day in Rome in a talk accompanying the recitation of the Angelus. "It is also a valuable contribution to the purification of historical memory and to our common witness."

The Joint Declaration states a "consensus" shared by the signers regarding the doctrine of justification. The key passage formulating this consensus says:

"In faith we together hold the conviction that justification is the work of the triune God. The Father sent his Son into the world to save sinners. The foundation and presupposition of justification is the incarnation, death, and resurrection of Christ. Justification thus means that Christ himself is our righteousness, in which we share through the Holy Spirit in accord with the will of the Father.

"Together we confess: By grace alone, in faith in Christ's saving work and not because of any merit on our part, we are accepted by God and receive the Holy Spirit, who renews our hearts while equipping and calling us to good works."

The signers of the Joint Declaration were Card. Edward I. Cassidy, President of the Vatican's Pontifical Council for Promoting Christian Unity, and Bp. Christian Krause, President of the Lutheran World Federation, which represents 58 million of the world's 61 million Lutherans. Most, but not all, of the churches within the federation have accepted the Joint Declaration.

Both the date and the place of the signing had symbolic significance. Oct. 31 is observed by Protestants as Reformation Day, commemorating Martin Luther's nailing of his 95 Theses on the castle church door in Wittenberg on that date in 1517. The city of Augsburg is associated with the Augsburg Confession, a document authored in 1530 by the Protestant Reformer Philipp Melanchton in an attempt to bring about reconciliation between Lutherans and Catholics.

From a theological perspective, the doctrine of justification was of central importance in the Reformation and in the mutual condemnations exchanged by Catholics and Lutherans in the 16th century via the Council of Trent and the Lutheran Confessions.

The Joint Declaration stresses that the churches "neither take the condemnations lightly nor do they disavow their own past." But, it insists, as a result of ecumenical dialogue during the last 30 years, they have come to "new insights" that transcend the mutual polemics of the Reformation era and make it clear that neither party's understanding of justification, as it is expressed in the Joint Declaration, now merits condemnation by the other, while the differences about the doctrine that continue to exist between them "are acceptable."

The Council for Promoting Christian Unity and the Lutheran World Federation reached basic agreement on the document in June 1998, but further clarifications were required on both sides before official approval was forthcoming. These clarifications are embodied in an "Annex" to the text.

In 2006 the World Methodist Council also entered into the signing of the *Joint Declaration* with the Catholic Church and the Lutheran World Federation, adding their distinctive emphasis within the internally differentiated consensus.

U.S. Lutheran-Catholic Dialogue Completes Statement on Death and Eternal Life

Members of the Lutheran-Roman Catholic Dialogue in the United States approved by unanimous consent on Oct. 17, 2010, the dialogue's final report on "The Hope of Eternal Life." The 65-page report represents the fruit of the dialogue's four-and-a-half-year study. It explores issues related to the Christian's life beyond death, such as the communion of saints, resurrection of the dead, and final judgment, as well as historically divisive issues such as purgatory, indulgences, and prayers for the dead.

U.S. Catholic-Lutheran Dialogue Begins Round XII, Theme: Ministries of Teaching

The Catholic-Lutheran dialogue began in 1965 and has continued since that time. The Twelfth Round has completed four meetings. Bp. Lee Piché, auxiliary bishop of Minneapolis-St. Paul, Minnesota is serving as the Catholic co-chairman of Round XII, the topic of which is, "Ministries of Teaching: Sources, Shapes, and Essential Contents." The topic began to come into focus during the course of the two initial meetings.

The third meeting took place Apr. 11-14, 2013, at St. Paul's College. It began with a Service of Thanksgiving in remembrance of Dr. Margaret O'Gara, a long-time Roman Catholic member of the Dialogue, who died in Aug. 2012. The Lutheran Co-Chair Rev. Dr. Lowell G. Almen offered a personal reflection on the experience of being fortuitously in Rome for the election of Pope Francis. The numerous scholarly presentations which followed led to serious and insightful discussions by the dialogue participants. Numerous formal and informal discussions characterized the four days of the meeting. The fourth meeting took place Feb. 20-23, 2014, at St. Paul's College in Washington. As usual there were numerous scholarly presentations and intense discussions. The members began discussing the possibilities for a common statement at the final session. The next meeting will take place Oct. 9-12, 2014, in Chicago.

RELATIONS WITH THE REFORMED CHURCHES

Catholics, Reformed Christians Publicly Sign Historic Agreement to Recognize Each Other's Baptisms

Representatives of the U.S. Conference of Catholic Bishops (USCCB) and four Reformed Christian denominations publicly signed an agreement on baptism on Jan. 29, 2013, in Austin, Texas. The agreement affirmed that all of the churches involved recognize the validity of each other's baptisms.

Significantly, the signing took place at the opening of the annual meeting of the ecumenical association Christian Churches Together, which includes over 40 Christian communions and groups. Each member group received a copy of the agreement, which Catholic ecumenical leaders hope will encourage them to consider how and whether they too will respond.

"There has already been a strong response from CCT members who have said this represents healing," said Fr. John Crossin, OSFS, Executive Director for the USCCB's Secretariat for Ecumenical and Interreligious Affairs. "Our hope is that this would be a model for similar agreements."

The Common Agreement on the Mutual Recognition of Baptism is the result of the seventh round of the Catholic-Reformed Dialogue in the United States, from 2003-2010, which found that the agreed formula for a valid baptism is that it include flowing water and be performed in the name of the Father, the Son and the Holy Spirit.

The signing, which occurred during a prayer service at St. Mary Cathedral, included the Presbyterian Church-USA, the Christian Reformed Church in North America, the Reformed Church in America and the United Church of Christ.

The U.S. bishops voted to accept the agreement at the annual Fall General Assembly in Baltimore in November 2010. In 2011, members of the Catholic-Reformed Dialogue privately signed the agreement. The Jan. 29 signing was a ceremonial representation of the growing unity between Christians and the progress of the ecumenical movement.

"We are overjoyed at this historic recognition of one another's baptism and are committed to move forward in a new round exploring a common vision of the church," said Bp. Denis Madden, auxiliary bishop of Baltimore and chairman of the USCCB Committee on Ecumenical and Interreligious Affairs.

More information on the Common Agreement on the Mutual Recognition of Baptism is available online: www.usccb.org/beliefs-and-teachings/ecumenical-and-interreligious/ecumenical/reformed/baptism.cfm (USCCB Press Release, Jan. 31, 2013).

Catholic-Reformed Dialogue Commences Round VIII on Mission and Identity of Church in Modern World

Participants of the Catholic-Reformed dialogue convened in Austin, Texas on Jan. 28-29 to begin a multi-year study on the mission and identity of the church in the modern world. The dialogue is chaired by Bp. Tod Brown of the Diocese of Orange, CA and the Rev. Cynthia Campbell, Ph.D., Pastor, Highland Presbyterian Church, Louisville and president emerita of McCormick Theological Seminary.

This comprehensive study, which follows an historical round in which a common agreement on Baptism was signed, will explore the Reformed and Catholic understandings of the identity of the church in terms of mission. Importantly, a major source for this study is the 2012 report "The Church—Towards a Common Vision," which was produced by the World Council of Churches (WCC), Faith and Order Commission. Topics that will be addressed in this study include unity and diversity in the church, the nature and role of authority and episcopacy (which is a direct response to Pope John Paul II's invitation in Ut Unum Sint for church leaders to help the pope think about the ministerial role of the Bishop of Rome), and the origins and current interpretations of ministry and ordination. Abp. Wilton Gregory, chairman of the USCCB's committee for ecumenical and interreligious affairs at the time of the common agreement, affirmed the work of the dialogue: "Our work together has been and will be of service to all Christian communities in ways that we cannot foresee. The Holy Spirit continues to guide us in ways unseen."

The Catholic co-chair, Bp. Brown, indicated that "there is an opportunity for greater cooperation between Catholics and Reformed in this study of the church precisely because the identity of church as a mission entails a shared understanding of identity that both are called to serve." Rev. Campbell, the Reformed co-chair, commented: "What a privilege it will be to work on this Eighth Round of the dialogue as we build on the truly historic consensus achieved on Baptism. We now have the opportunity to reflect together on what it means to be the Church – Christ's Body in and for the world. I know that this will be an opportunity for spiritual growth for the participants, and we pray, for the Church as a whole."

The significance of this round, it is hoped, will be a positive step in the direction of ecumenical unity. The next scheduled meeting will take place Sept. 16-17 in Louisville, KY.

Catholic dialogue participants included Bp. Tod Brown of Orange, CA, co-chair; Bp. Denis Madden, CEIA chair; Fr. Thomas Weinandy, Fr. John A. Radano, Kristin Colberg, Ph.D., Fr. John Crossin, Anthony Cirelli, Ph.D.

Reformed Church in America participants included Rev. Dr. Wes Granberg-Michaelson, Rev. Dr. Leanne van Dyk, and Rev. Dr. Allan Janssen; Christian Reformed Church participants included Dr. Sue Rozeboom, Rev. Peter Choi, and Rev. Dr. Ronald Feenstra; Presbyterian Church USA participants included Rev. Dr. Cynthia Campbell (co-chair), Rev. David Gambrell, and Rev. Robina Winbush. United Church of Christ participants included Rev. Dr. Sidney D. Fowler, Rev. Dr. Randi Walker, and Rev. Karen Georgia Thompson. (USCCB Press Release, Feb. 1, 2013).

INTERRELIGIOUS DIALOGUE

JUDAISM

Judaism is the religion of the Hebrew Bible and of Jews from antiquity to the present day. Divinely revealed and with a patriarchal background (Abraham and Sarah, Isaac and Jacob), Judaism emerges in full form with the Mosaic Covenant. Developed further in the reforms of Ezra and Nehemiah, it achieved distinctive form and character as the religion of the Torah (Law or the "Teaching") for Israelites. Judaism does not have a formal creed, but its principal points of teaching are clear. Basic to it is belief in the one, transcendent God who reveals himself through the Torah, the prophets, history and the life of his people. For Jews, the fatherhood of God implies the brotherhood of all humanity. Religious faith and practice are equated with righteous living according to God's Law. Moral conviction and practice are regarded as more important than precise doctrinal formulations or professions. Formal worship, whose principal act was sacrifice from Exodus times to 70 c.e., is now done by prayer, reading, preaching and meditating upon the sacred writings, and by liturgical and domestic observance of the Sabbath and festivals.

Judaism has messianic expectations of the complete fulfillment of the Covenant, the coming of God's kingdom, the ingathering of his people, and final judgment and retribution for all. Views differ regarding the manner in which these expectations will be realized — through a person, the community of God's people, an evolution of historical events, or an eschatological act of God himself. Expectations about the salvation of each individual also vary, depending on views about the nature of immortality, punishment, reward and related matters.

Sacred Books

The sacred books of biblical Judaism are the 24 of the Masoretic Hebrew text, including the Law, the Prophets and the Writings (see the **Bible**, p. 96). Together, they contain the basic instruction or norms for just living. In some contexts, the term Law or Torah refers only to the Pentateuch (Genesis, Exodus, Leviticus, Numbers, Deuteronomy); in others, it denotes all the sacred books or the whole complex of written and oral tradition.

Also of great authority are two Talmuds or books of compiled teachings, which were composed in Palestine and Babylon in the fourth and fifth centuries c.e., respectively. They consist of the Mishnah, a compilation of oral laws, and the Gemara, a collection of rabbinical commentary on the Mishnah. Midrash are collections of scriptural comments and moral counsels.

Priests were the principal religious leaders during the period of sacrificial and temple worship in ancient Judaism. With the destruction of the Jerusalem Temple in 74 c.e., Judaism was reoriented, loosing its ability to offer sacrifice in the Temple. Under the leadership of the Rabbis – who were originally teachers – a new Judaism emerged. Today, Rabbis share with cantors the function of leading prayer at Jewish liturgies. The synagogue is the place of community worship, while the family and home are focal points of many other aspects of Jewish life and practice.

Of the various categories of Jews, Orthodox are the most conservative in adhering to strict religious traditions. Others — Reformed, Conservative, Reconstructionist — are more liberal in comparison with the Orthodox. They favor greater or less modification of religious practices in accommodation to contemporary culture and living conditions.

Principal events in Jewish life include the circumcision of males, according to prescriptions of the Covenant; the bar and bat mitzvah that marks the coming of age of boys and girls in Judaism at age 13; marriage; and observance of the Sabbath and festivals. Observances of the Sabbath and festivals begin at sundown of the previous calendar day and continue until the following sundown. A list of principal Jewish observances is given here:

Sabbath: Saturday, the weekly day of rest prescribed in the Decalogue.

Sukkoth (Tabernacles): A seven-to-nine-day festival in the month of Tishri (Sept.-Oct.), marked by some Jews with Covenant-renewal and reading of The Law. It originated as an agricultural feast at the end of the harvest and got its name from the temporary shelters used by workers in the fields.

Hanukkah (The Festival of Lights, the Feast of Consecration and of the Maccabees): Commemorates the dedication of the new altar in the Temple at Jerusalem by Judas Maccabeus in 165 B.C. The eight-day festival, during which candles in an eight-branch candelabra are lighted in succession, one each day, occurs near the winter solstice, close to Christmas time.

Pesach (Passover): A seven-day festival commemorating the liberation of the Israelites from Egypt. The narrative of the Exodus, the Haggadah, is read at ceremonial Seder meals on the first and second days of the festival, which begins on the 14th day of Nisan (Mar.-Apr.).

Shavuoth, Pentecost (Feast of Weeks): Observed 50 days after Passover, commemorating the anniversary of the revelation of the Law to Moses.

Purim: A joyous festival observed on the 14th day of Adar (Feb.-Mar.), commemorating the rescue of the Israelites from massacre by the Persians through the intervention of Esther. The festival is preceded by a day of fasting. A gift- and alms-giving custom became associated with it in medieval times.

Rosh Hashana (Feast of Trumpets, New Year): Observed on the first day of Tishri (Sept.-Oct.), the festival focuses attention on the ways of life and the ways of death. It is second in importance only to the most solemn observance of Yom Kippur.

Yom Kippur (Day of Atonement): The highest holy day, observed with strict fasting. It occurs 10 days after Rosh Hashana.

Yom HaShoah (Holocaust Memorial Day): Observed in the week after Passover; increasingly observed with joint Christian-Jewish services of remembrance.

CATHOLIC-JEWISH RELATIONS

The Second Vatican Council, in addition to the Decree on Ecumenism (concerning the movement for unity among Christians, stated the mind of the Church on a similar matter in *Nostra Aetate*, a "Declaration on the Relationship of the Church to Non-Christian Religions." This document, as the following excerpts indicate, backgrounds the reasons and directions of the Church's regard for the Jews. (Other portions of the document refer to Hindus, Buddhists and Muslims.)

Excerpt from *Nostra Aetate* (No. 4) on the Spiritual Bond between Jews and Catholics

As this sacred Synod searches into the mystery of the Church, it recalls the spiritual bond linking the people of the New Covenant with Abraham's stock.

For the Church of Christ acknowledges that, according to the mystery of God's saving design, the beginnings of her faith and her election are already found among the patriarchs, Moses, and the prophets. She professes that all who believe in Christ, Abraham's sons according to faith (cf. Gal 3:7), are included in the same patriarch's call, and likewise that the salvation of the Church was mystically foreshadowed by the Chosen People's exodus from the land of bondage.

The Church, therefore, cannot forget that she received the revelation of the Old Testament through the people with whom God in his inexpressible mercy deigned to establish the Ancient Covenant. Nor can she forget that she draws sustenance from the root of that good olive tree onto which have been grafted the wild olive branches of the Gentiles (cf. Rom 11:17-24). Indeed, the Church believes that by his cross Christ, our Peace, reconciled Jew and Gentile, making them both one in himself (cf. Eph 2:14-16).

The Jews still remain most dear to God because of their fathers, for he does not repent of the gifts he makes nor of the calls he issues (cf. Rom 11:28-29). In company with the prophets and the same Apostle (Paul), the Church awaits that day, known to God alone, on which all peoples will address the Lord in a single voice and "serve him with one accord" (Zeph 3:9; cf. Is 66:23; Ps 65:4; Rom 11:11-32).

Since the spiritual patrimony common to Christians and Jews is thus so great, this sacred Synod wishes to foster and recommend that mutual understanding and respect which is the fruit above all of biblical and theological studies, and of brotherly dialogues.

True, authorities of the Jews and those who followed their lead pressed for the death of Christ (cf. Jn 19:6); still, what happened in his passion cannot be blamed upon all the Jews then living, without distinction, nor upon the Jews of today. Although the Church is the new People of God, the Jews should not be presented as repudiated or cursed by God, as if such views followed from the holy Scriptures. All should take pains, then, lest in catechetical instruction and in the preaching of God's Word they teach anything out of harmony with the truth of the Gospel and the spirit of Christ.

The Church repudiates all persecutions against any person. Moreover, mindful of her common patrimony with the Jews, and motivated by the Gospel's spiritual love and by no political considerations, she deplores the hatred, persecutions, and displays of anti-Semitism directed against the Jews at any time and from any source (No. 4).

The Church rejects, as foreign to the mind of Christ, any discrimination against men or harassment of them because of their race, color, condition of life, or religion (No. 5).

Bishops' Secretariat

The American hierarchy's first move toward implementation of the Vatican II "Declaration on the Relationship of the Church to Non-Christian Religions" (*Nostra Aetate*) was to establish, in 1965, a Subcommission for Catholic-Jewish Relations in the framework of its Commission for Ecumenical and Interreligious Affairs. Its moderator is Card. William H. Keeler of Baltimore. The Secretariat for Ecumenical and Interreligious Relations is located at 3211 Fourth St. N.E., Washington, DC 20017. Its Catholic-Jewish efforts were directed by Dr. Eugene J. Fisher from 1977 until his retirement in 2007; at present, the Executive Director of the Secretariat handles these same assignments, through a consultant appointed for this purpose.

According to the key norm of a set of guidelines issued by the secretariat Mar. 16, 1967, and updated Apr. 9, 1985, "The general aim of all Catholic-Jewish meetings (and relations) is to increase our understanding both of Judaism and the Catholic faith, to eliminate sources of tension and misunderstanding, to initiate dialogue or conversations on different levels, to multiply intergroup meetings between Catholics and Jews, and to promote cooperative social action."

Vatican Guidelines

In a document issued Jan. 3, 1975, the Vatican Commission for Religious Relations with the Jews offered a number of suggestions and directions for implementing the Christian-Jewish portion of the Second Vatican Council's Declaration on Relations with Non-Christian Religions (*Nostra Aetate*). Among "suggestions from experience" were those concerning dialogue, liturgical links between Christian and Jewish worship, the interpretation of biblical texts, teaching and education for the purpose of increasing mutual understanding, and joint social action.

Notes on Preaching and Catechesis

On June 24, 1985, the Vatican Commission for Religious Relations with the Jews promulgated its "Notes on the Correct Way to Present Jews and Judaism in Preaching and Catechesis in the Roman Catholic Church," with the intent of providing "a helpful frame of reference for those who are called upon in the course of their teaching assignments to speak about Jews and Judaism and who wish to do so in keeping with the current teaching of the Church in this area."

The document states emphatically that, since the relationship between the Church and the Jewish people is one "founded on the design of the God of the Covenant," Judaism does not occupy "an occasional and marginal place in catechesis," but an "essential" one that "should be organically integrated" throughout the curriculum on all levels of Catholic education.

The Notes discuss the relationship between the Hebrew Scriptures and the New Testament, focusing especially on typology, which is called "the sign of a problem unresolved." Underlined is the "eschatological dimension," that "the people of God of the Old and the New Testament are tending toward a like end in the future: the coming or return of the Messiah." Jewish witness to God's kingdom, the Notes declare, challenges Christians to "accept our responsibility to prepare the world for the coming of the Messiah by working together for social justice and reconciliation."

The Notes emphasize the Jewishness of Jesus' teaching, correct misunderstandings concerning the portrayal of Jews in the New Testament and describe the Jewish origins of Christian liturgy. One section addresses the "spiritual fecundity" of Judaism to the present, its continuing "witness — often heroic — of its fidelity to the one God," and mandates the development of Holocaust curricula and a positive approach in Catholic education to the "religious attachment which finds its roots in biblical tradition " between the Jewish people and the Land of Israel, affirming the "existence of the State of Israel" on the basis of "the common principles of international law."

WE REMEMBER: A REFLECTION ON THE SHOAH

On Mar. 16, 1998, the Commission for Religious Relations with the Jews under Card. Edward Idris Cassidy, issued a long-awaited white paper on the Holocaust, entitled "We Remember: Reflections on the Shoah."

The document offered repentance for the failures of many Christians to oppose the policies of Nazi Germany and to resist the extermination of the Jews during the years of the Third Reich. It analyzed the history of anti-Semitism in the Church, while distinguishing between the historical anti-Judaism of Christian teaching over the centuries and the modern, racial ideology of Nazism that climaxed with the Holocaust.

"We Remember" defends Pope Pius XII and his efforts on behalf of the Jews during World War II, and at the same time acknowledges the need for a "call to penitence" by the Church as a whole "for the failures of her sons and daughters in every age." Card. Cassidy, in an address given in May of 1998 to the American Jewish Committee responding to criticisms of the text, stated clearly that terms such as "sons and daughters" and "members of the Church" are not restricted to a single category, "but can include popes cardinals, bishops, priests and laity," and he acknowledged that Christian anti-Judaism paved the way for Nazi anti-Semitism, though distinct from it.

We Remember begins with a letter from Pope John Paul II expressing his hope that the document will indeed help to heal the wounds of past misunderstandings and injustices and enable memory to play its necessary part in the process of shaping a future in which the unspeakable iniquity of the Shoah will never again be possible."

The U.S. Conference of Catholic Bishops' Committee for Ecumenical and Interreligious Affairs in 1998 published the text of "We Remember" along with the statements of European and American bishops' conferences similarly expressing repentance for Christian sins of omission and commission during the Shoah in a volume entitled, Catholics Remember the Holocaust. In 2001 the U.S. Bishops issued Catholic Teaching on the Shoah: Implementing the Holy See's "We Remember" urging and giving guidelines for Holocaust education in all Catholic schools, from elementary through college and university level education.

Papal Statements on Jews, Judaism and the Holocaust

The following texts from papal statements are provided through the courtesy the USCCB's Secretariat for Ecumenical and Interreligious Affairs

Pope St. John Paul II

Pope St. John Paul II was deeply loved and admired by the Jewish people worldwide over his long tenure. The Jewish outpouring of grief and condolence was deep and widespread, and save for that when the beloved St. John XXIII died, entirely without precedent. The prayers and statements of Jewish groups can be seen on their websites. Pope John Paul II, in a remarkable series of addresses beginning in 1979, sought to promote and give shape to the development of dialogue between Catholics and Jews.

In a homily delivered June 7, 1979, at Auschwitz, which he called the "Golgotha of the Modern World," he prayed movingly for "the memory of the people whose sons and daughters were intended for total extermination."

In a key address delivered Nov. 17, 1980, to the Jewish community in Mainz, the Pope articulated his vision of the three "dimensions" of the dialogue: (1) "the meeting between the people of God of the Old Covenant and the people of the New Covenant"; (2) the encounter of "mutual esteem between today's Christian churches and today's people of the Covenant concluded with Moses"; (3) the "holy duty" of witnessing to the one God in the world and "jointly to work for peace and justice."

During his historic visit to the Great Synagogue in Rome Apr. 13, 1986, the Pope affirmed that God's covenant with the Jewish people is "irrevocable," and stated: "The Jewish religion is not 'extrinsic' to us, but in a certain way is 'intrinsic' to our own religion. With Judaism, therefore, we have a relationship which we do not have with any other religion."

Meeting with the Jewish community in Sydney, Australia, Nov. 26, 1986, the Holy Father termed the 20th century "the century of the Shoah" (Holocaust) and called "sinful" any "acts of discrimination or persecution against Jews."

On June 14, 1987, meeting with the Jewish community of Warsaw, the pope called the Jewish witness to the Shoah (Holocaust) a "saving warning before all of humanity" which reveals "your particular vocation, showing you (Jews) to be still the heirs of that election to which God is faithful."

Meeting with Jewish leaders Sept. 11, 1987, in Miami, the Pope praised the efforts in theological dialogue and educational reform implemented in the U.S. since the Second Vatican Council; affirmed the existence of the State of Israel "according to international law," and urged "common educational programs on the Holocaust so that never again will such a horror be possible. Never again!" On Apr. 7, 1994, the eve of Yom HaShoah, the Jewish day of prayer commemorating the victims of the Holocaust, Pope John Paul II hosted a memorial concert at the Vatican. It was, he noted, a moment of "common meditation and shared prayer," as the Kaddish, the prayer for the dead, and the Kol Nidre, the prayer for forgiveness and atonement, were recited.

Pope Benedict XVI

Because he had already built up an impressive series of positive reflections on Catholic-Jewish relations over the years, including a book, the election of Card. Joseph Ratzinger to the papacy was greeted with joy by all involved in Catholic-Jewish relations. In a major article in L'Osservatore Romano in December 2000, for example, Card. Ratzinger clarified and synthesized Catholic teaching on Jews and Judaism. With regard to the Shoah, for example, he stated: "Even if the most recent, loathsome experience of the Shoah was perpetrated in the name of an anti-Christian ideology, which tried to strike the Christian faith at its Abrahamic roots in the people of Israel, it cannot be denied that a certain insufficient resistance to this atrocity on the part of Christians can be explained by an inherited anti-Judaism present in the hearts of not a few Christians." The dialogue, he said, "must begin with a prayer to our God, first of all that he might grant to us Christians a greater esteem and love for that people, the people of Israel, to whom belong 'the adoption as sons, the glory, the covenants, the giving of the law, the worship, and the promises; theirs are the patriarchs, and from them comes Christ according to the flesh, he who is over all, God, blessed forever. Amen' (Rom 9:4-5), and this not only in the past, but still today, "for the gifts and the call of God are irrevocable" (Rom 11:29)."

In his first meeting with the International Jewish Committee for Interreligious Consultations, Benedict reassured many by affirming the direction of his predecessor: "At the very beginning of my Pontificate, I wish to assure you that the Church remains firmly committed, in her catechesis and in every aspect of her life, to implementing this decisive teaching."

Similarly, in his meeting with Jews in the Synagogue in Cologne, Benedict stated that "I make my own the words written by my venerable Predecessor on the occasion of the 60th anniversary of the liberation of Auschwitz and I too say: 'I bow my head before all those who experienced this manifestation of the mysterium iniquitatis.' The terrible events of that time must 'never cease to rouse consciences, to resolve conflicts, to inspire the building of peace' "

In his review of the year 2005 with the Vatican Curia in December of that year, the Holy Father discussed the proper understanding of the Second Vatican Council. He spoke of the "hermeneutics of continuity and discontinuity" in three key areas: faith and science, Church and State (religious freedom), and "the relationship between the Church and the faith of Israel."

Greeting the chief rabbi of Rome in January 2006, Benedict, in a remarkable formulation, emphasized God's enduring and saving love for the Jewish People: "Your visit brings me great joy, and induces me to renew with you this song of gratitude for the salvation we have received. The people of Israel have been liberated many times from the hands of their enemies and, in times of antisemitism, in the dramatic moments of the Shoah, the hand of the Almighty has supported and guided them. The favor of the God of the Covenant has always accompanied them, giving them the strength to overcome trials. To this divine loving attention your Jewish community, present in the city of Rome for more than 2,000 years, can also render testimony." While affirming the necessity of Jewish, Christian, Muslim dialogue, Benedict emphasized in meeting with the American Jewish Committee in March 2007 that "Jews and Christians have a rich common patrimony. In many ways this distinguishes our relationship as unique among the religions of the world. The Church can never forget that chosen people with whom God entered into a holy covenant (cf. *Nostra Aetate*, No. 4)."

In May 2006, Benedict visited Auschwitz. "In a place like this," he said, "words fail; in the end, there can only be a dread silence – a silence which is itself a heartfelt cry to God: Why, Lord, did you remain silent? How could you tolerate all this? In silence, then, we bow our heads before the endless line of those who suffered and were put to death here; yet our silence becomes in turn a plea for forgiveness and reconciliation, a plea to the living God never to let this happen again." Returning to Rome and reflecting on the visit at the General Audience, he stated that "At the death camp of Auschwitz-Birkenau, a place of horror and godless inhumanity, I paid homage to the victims, including over a million Jews and many Poles...

May modern humanity not forget Auschwitz and the other 'factories of death' where the Nazi regime attempted to eliminate God in order to take his place. May it not give in to the temptation of racial hatred, which is the origin of the worst forms of anti-Semitism."

MILLENNIUM EVENTS

During 2000 the London Philharmonic conducted by Maestro Gilbert Levine played a special series of concerts of Haydn's "Creation" for interreligious audiences in Baltimore, Paris, Jerusalem and, finally in Rome to celebrate the Holy Father's 80th birthday. In London, the Holy See and the World Union for Progressive Judaism sponsored a theological dialogue, wht papers of which have been published as *He Kissed Him and They Wept* (London: SCM Press) co-edited by Tony Bayfield, Sydney Brichto and Eugene Fisher. A second theological conference on Revelation and Covenant was held in London in 2003.

Pope John Paul II determined that the year marking the beginning of the 3rd millennium would be a year of repentance by the Church for the sins of its members during the 2nd millennium. On the first Sunday of Lent, during Mass in St. Peter's, he lead the Church in a liturgy of repentance in seven categories of Christian sins, one of which was the mistreatment of Jews and Judaism over the centuries including, especially the Shoah in the 20th century. A high point of the millennium year was the Pope's pilgrimage to the Holy Land. In Israel, he visited not only Christian holy places, but also those central to Jewish memory. At Yad VaShem in Jerusalem, Israel's memorial to the six million Jews murdered by Nazi Germany, he prayed for the deceased and then embraced Jewish survivors, some from his own hometown of Wadowice.

Pontifical Biblical Commission

In 2002 the Pontifical Biblical Commission issued "The Jewish People and Their Sacred Scriptures in the Christian Bible," a 205-page volume fulfilling the pope's 1997 mandate to the Commission. The first section of the report stresses, contrary to Marcionism, that the Jewish Scriptures are a fundamental part of the Christian Bible. The second section shows how the New Testament attests "conformity" (continuity) to the Jewish Bible in "fulfilling the Scriptures" but also presents a "newness" ("discontinuity, progression") in the life and certain teachings of Christ (IIA). Still, major " fundamental themes" of revelation are shared by both testaments (IIB). Jewish readings of the Bible, from rabbinic times to the present, maintain their own integrity and validity based upon the integrity and validity of the Jewish Scriptures understood in their own terms.

The third section outlines the historical setting of the New Testament as a document of "post-exilic Judaism" (IIIA) and describes the portrait of Jews in each gospel (IIIB) and of Judaism in the Pauline Letters and other apostolic writings (IIIC). The document concludes with "pastoral orientations" urging Jews and Christians to continued dialogue over the "inexhaustible riches" of our shared sacred texts.

INTERNATIONAL LIAISON COMMITTEE

The International Catholic-Jewish Liaison Committee (ILC) was formed in 1971 and is the official link between the Commission for Religious Relations with the Jewish People and the International Jewish Committee for Interreligious Consultations. The committee meets every 18 months to examine matters of common interest.

Topics under discussion have included: mission and witness (Venice, 1977), religious education (Madrid, 1978), religious liberty and pluralism (Regensburg, 1979), religious commitment (London, 1981), the sanctity of human life in an age of violence (Milan, 1982), youth and faith (Amsterdam, 1984), the Vatican Notes on Preaching and Catechesis (Rome, 1985), the Holocaust (Prague, 1990), education and social action (Baltimore, 1992), family and ecology (Jerusalem, 1994), the Catholic Church and the Shoah (Rome, 1998), theological understandings of one another and their implications for our teaching about each other (New York, 2001), Tsedek and Tsedakah – Righteousness and Charity (Buenos Aires, 2004), Healing and Health (Cape Town, 2006). The Committee continues to meet and address itself to issues of Catholic-Jewish relations. Its most recent convocation in Madrid discussed wider questions of the challenges to religion in contemporary society. In all, the committee has met twenty-two times for annual dialogues between the Catholic Church and leaders of the Jewish community from across the world.

Pope John Paul, addressing in Rome a celebration of *Nostra Aetate* (the Second Vatican Council's "Declaration on the Relationship of the Church to Non-Christian Religions") by the Liaison Committee, stated: "What you are celebrating is nothing other than the divine mercy which is guiding Christians and Jews to mutual awareness, respect, cooperation and solidarity. The universal openness of *Nostra Aetate* is anchored in and takes its orientation from a high sense of the absolute singularity of God's choice of a particular people. The Church is fully aware that Sacred Scripture bears witness that the Jewish people, this community of faith and custodian of a tradition thousands of years old, is an intimate part of the mystery of revelation and salvation."

Family Rights and Obligations

The Liaison Committee, at its May 1994, meeting in Jerusalem, issued its first joint statement, on the family, in anticipation of the UN Cairo Conference subsequently held in September.

The statement affirmed that "the rights and obligations of the family do not come from the State but exist prior to the State and ultimately have their source in God the Creator. The family is far more than a legal, social or economic unit. For both Jews and Christians, it is a stable community of love and solidarity based on God's covenant."

Caring for God's Creation

During its Mar. 23-26, 1998, meeting in the Vatican, the Liaison Committee issued its second joint statement, on the environment. Drawing deeply on the shared sacred text of Genesis, the Committee affirmed that "concern for the environment has led both Catholics and Jews to reflect on the concrete implications of their belief in God, creator of all things," especially "a recognition of the mutual dependence between the land and the human person." "Care for creation," the document concluded "is also a religious act."

In its April 2001, meeting, the Liaison Committee issued two statements, one affirming the need to preserve the sacred character of Christian and Jewish holy places, as well as the communities who give witness to them, and one urging review and revision where necessary of curriculum and course materials teaching about each other's traditions especially in institutions of theological education.

Protecting Religious Freedom and Holy Sites

At its May 2001, meeting in New York, the Liaison Committee issued a joint declaration on a subject of increasing concern, not only in the Middle East, but in Asia and Africa as well. With regard to the obligation of states, the document notes: "Government and political authorities bear special responsibility for protecting human and religious rights. Those responsible for law, order, and public security should feel themselves obligated to defend religious minorities and to use available legal remedies against those who commit crimes against religious liberty and the sanctity of holy places. Just as they are prohibited from engaging in anti-religious acts, governments must also be vigilant lest by inaction they effectively tolerate religious hatred or provide impunity for the perpetrators of anti-religious actions."

On Education in Catholic and Jewish Seminaries and Theological Schools

Also in New York, the Liaison Committee issued a statement calling on Catholic and Jewish seminaries to provide understanding of the other. In addition to expanding course work and examining existing courses for the treatment of the other, the statement concluded that "educational institutions in both our communities should make every effort to expose students to living Jewish and Christian communities through guest lecturers, field trips, involvement in local national and international dialogue groups and conferences."

Tzedeq and Tzedaqah

The 18th International Catholic-Jewish Liaison Committee Meeting was held in Buenos Aires, from July 5-8, 2004. This encounter, convened for the first time in Latin America, was devoted to the subject of Tzedeq and Tzedaqah (Justice and Charity). The group renewed its "total rejection of anti-Semitism in all its forms, including anti-Zionism as a more recent manifestation of anti-Semitism," noting that while anti-Zionism can be distinguished from anti-Semitism, it can serve as a "screen" for it and lead to it.

Healing in Our Two Traditions

The 19th International Catholic-Jewish Liaison Committee Meeting, held in Madrid, centered on Healing in the Catholic and Jewish traditions, with a special focus on the AIDS epidemic that is a scourge of the continent. Also discussed, in a spirit of frankness and trust, was the fact that the State of Israel has failed to implement its commitment in the Fundamental Agreement of 1993 to resolve issues of the legal status of the Catholic Church and consequent taxation requirements of Church properties such as hospitals and schools.

Dialogue with the Chief Rabbinate of Israel

After two meetings, in Jerusalem (June 2002) and Grottaferrata/Rome (February 2003) the respective high ranking delegations convened in Jerusalem to discuss the theme of "The Relevance of Central Teachings In the Holy Scriptures Which We Share for Contemporary Society and the Education of Future Generations Accordingly." The Feb. 27, 2003 meeting in Rome issued statements on "The Sanctity of Human Life" and "Family Values." In Jerusalem in June 2005, the Bi-Lateral Commission discussed "The Relationship between Religious and Civil Authority in the Jewish and Christian Traditions," agreeing on the following principles based upon biblical values:

At the February 2006 meeting in Rome, the Commission issued a statement on "Human Life and Technology," stating among other principle that "The conviction that we share, that life on earth is but one stage in the soul's existence, must only lead us to a greater respect for the vessel – the human form – in which the soul resides in this world. Accordingly we totally reject the idea that the temporary nature of human existence on earth allows us to instrumentalise it. In this regard we strongly condemn any kind of bloodshed to promote any ideology – especially if this is done in the name of Religion. Such action is nothing less than a desecration of the Divine Name."

The most recent meeting of the committee in Madrid (October 2013) was introduced some months earlier by an audience with Pope Francis, who greeted the group warmly and reaffirmed both its mission and the need for continued dialogue between both communities. He stated: "So I encourage you to follow this path trying, as you do so, to involve younger generations. Humanity needs our joint witness in favour of respect for the dignity of man and woman created in the image and likeness of God, and in favour of peace which is above all God's gift. As the prophet Jeremiah said, 'I know the plans I have for you, says the Lord, plans for welfare and not for evil, to give you a future of hope' (29:11). With this word, Peace – Shalom – I conclude my words, asking for your prayers and assuring you of my own."

Vatican-Israel Accord

On Dec. 30, 1993, a year of dramatic developments in the Middle East was capped by the signing in Jerusalem of a "Fundamental Agreement" between representatives of the Holy See and the State of Israel. The agreement acknowledged in its preamble that the signers were "aware of the unique nature of the relationship between the Catholic Church and the Jewish people, and of the historic process of reconciliation and growth in mutual understanding and friendship between Catholics and Jews." Abp. (later Card.) William H. Keeler, president of the National Conference of Catholic Bishops, welcomed the accord together with the Israeli Ambassador to the United States at a ceremony at the NCCB headquarters in Washington. In 1996, the Anti-Defamation League published a set of documents related to the accord, entitled "A Challenge Long Delayed," edited by Eugene Fisher and Rabbi Klenicki.

Catholic-Jewish Dialogue in the United States

The National Workshop on Christian Jewish Relations, begun in 1973 by the NCCB Secretariat, draws more than 1,000 participants from around the world. Other workshops have been held in Baltimore (1986), Minneapolis (1987), Charleston, SC (1989), Chicago (1990), Pittsburgh (1992), Tulsa (1994), Stamford (1996), and Houston (1999). In October 1987, the Bishops' Committee for Ecumenical and Interreligious Affairs began a series of twice-yearly consultations with representatives of the Synagogue Council of America. Topics of discussion have included education, human rights, respect for life, the Middle East. The consultation has issued several joint statements, for example, "On Moral Values in Public Education" (1990), "On Stemming the Proliferation of Pornography" (1993), "On Dealing with Holocaust Revisionism" (1994). Ongoing relationships are maintained by the USCCB Secretariat with such Jewish agencies as the American Jewish Committee, the Anti-Defamation League, B'nai B'rith International, and the National Jewish Council for Public Affairs.

In June 1988, the Bishops' Committee for Ecumenical and Interreligious Affairs published in Spanish and English Criteria for the Evaluation of Dramatizations of the Passion, providing for the first time Catholic guidelines for passion plays.

In January 1989, the Bishops' Committee for the Liturgy issued guidelines for the homiletic presentation of Judaism under the title, "God's Mercy Endures Forever."

When the Synagogue Council of America dissolved in 1995, the Bishops' Committee for Ecumenical and Interreligious Affairs initiated separate consultations with the new National Council of Synagogues (Reform and Conservative), chaired by Card. William H. Keeler, and the Orthodox Union/Rabbinical Council, chaired by Card. John J. O'Connor, of blessed memory. The bishops have issued several joint statements with the National Council of Synagogues: "Reflections on the Millennium" (1998), "To End the Death Penalty" (1999), and "Children and the Environment" (2001), "Filled with Sadness, Charged with Hope" (2001), and "Reflections on Covenant and Mission" (2002), More recent topics have included the relationship of the Covenant and the land of Israel (2013). Joint communiqués on issues of common concern, such as the Middle East and Catholic teaching on the Jews and the death of Jesus, have been issued since then. These documents, as well as those with Orthodox Jews can be found on the website of the USCCB on the webpage of the SEIA.

Bp. William Murphy (Diocese of Rockville Center) succeeded Card. John O' Connor as co-chair of the dialogue with Orthodox Judaism. This ongoing consultation has also issued joint communiqués and a joint statement on aid for private education.

RECENT DEVELOPMENTS

In December 1999, the Holy See's Commission and the International Jewish Committee for Interreligious Consultations announced the establishment of a committee of three Catholic and three Jewish scholars to look into the many complex historical and moral issues involving the Church and the Shoah beginning with an analysis of the thousands of archival documents for the period of World War II already made public by the Holy See in its 12 volume *Actes et Documents* (1965-80). The Committee met in New York in December 1999, in

London in May 2000, in Baltimore in July 2000, and finally in Rome in October 2000, where it issued its "Preliminary Report." The report affirmed the objectivity of the original team of four Jesuit scholars who selected the tens of thousands of texts from the Vatican archives for inclusion in the 11 volumes of the *Actes et Documents du Saint Siege Relatives a la Seconde Guerre Mondiale* (Libreria Editrice Vaticana, 1965-80), but also raised numerous questions for further study and documentation. The Joint Commission's Catholic Coordinator, Dr. Eugene Fisher praised the group's "achievement of so much consensus between Catholic and Jewish scholars on what are the questions that need to be faced today. Such solid consensus could by no means be presumed when the group started its work, so emotional and complex are the issues.... The scholarly successors of this group will be forever in their debt" (*Catholic International*, May 2002, p. 68). Card. Jorge Mejia, then Vatican Archivist, announced a major increase in the number of archivists working on preparing the remaining material for scholarly review, a process that already resulted in the release of tens of thousands of documents in 2003.

In 2004, the film, *The Passion of the Christ*, precipitated great controversy in the media. Jews, given the often violent history of Passion Plays, with which The Passion has much in common, expressed various concerns. Catholic leaders, whatever their personal feelings on the artistic merits of the movie, were strong in condemning any possible anti-Semitic use of it, pointing teachers and preachers to resources where the full and accurate teaching of the Church can be found, such as the BCEIA's *The Bible, the Jews and the Death of Jesus*.

Since then, the Secretariat for Ecumenical and Interreligious Affairs has continued to host annual and bi-annual meetings of its two official dialogues, addressing diverse topics of concern to both communities. Amongst others, these have included: an examination of seminary education about Catholic-Jewish relations; the changing face of youth membership in congregations; the role of the Ten Commandments in American life; the centrality of the land of Israel to Jewish life and identity; and, most recently, Jewish reaction to Pope Francis in Catholic-Jewish relations.

40TH ANNIVERSARY OF *NOSTRA AETATE*

Cardinal Keeler, USCCB chairman of the Catholic-Jewish dialogues, together with Rev. Arthur Kennedy, then director of the Secretariat, and Dr. Eugene Fisher represented the BCEIA at the meeting of representatives of Bishops conferences held at the Pontifical Commission on Religious Relations with the Jews on Oct. 27, 2005 in conjunction with its celebration of the 40th anniversary of Nostra Aetate. The group reported on current efforts and future hopes for the implementation of the document, especially in the area of education. The celebration that evening featured addresses by Cardinals Walter Kasper and Aaron Lustiger, and Rabbi David Rosen, International Interfaith Affairs Director of the American Jewish Committee. Ancillary to the main event were dinners hosted by the Ambassador of Great Britain to the Quirinale and the Ambassador of Israel to the Holy See.

Celebrations also took place during the anniversary year on the national level and in many dioceses throughout the country as well.

UPDATE OF GUIDELINES

In 2007, the BCEIA issued an updated version of its Guidelines for Catholic-Jewish Relations. The Guidelines were first published in 1967, and were the first guidelines issued after the Second Vatican Council. The Vatican's own Guidelines for Implementing *Nostra Aetate*, No. 4 did not come out until 1975, so the U.S. bishops' were the first such guidelines ever issued in the history of the Church. The 2007 version takes into account the numerous statements of the Holy See, Popes John Paul II and Benedict XVI, and the USCCB itself since the last update in 1985.

Pope Francis and Catholic-Jewish Relations

On Feb. 28, 2013, Pope Benedict XVI resigned the papacy and thereby opened the process for a conclave of cardinals to choose his replacement. Mar. 13, 2013 saw the election of Jose Maria Bergolio, Archbishop of Buenos Aires, as the 266th successor to St. Peter as Bishop of Rome. His choice was immediately hailed by the Jewish communities as one signaling the kind of friendship that Bergolio himself had practiced with Jews while in Argentina. Outspoken in defense of Jews, the then Archbishop of Buenos Aires had condemned the 1994 bombing of a Jewish institution by anti-Semitic terrorists. Frequently attending prayer services in synagogues, Jose Mario Bergolio was a popular figure to Jews in Argentina, befriending Rabbi Abraham Skorka with whom he co-authored, *On Heaven and Earth* (Random House, 2013) as a series of dialogues in 2010 on current issues between the two faith communities. His election has been widely acknowledged by both Jewish and Catholic groups associated with inter-religious dialogue as a positive sign of continued growth between Catholics and Jews.

ISLAM

Edited in consultation with the staff of the Secretariat for Ecumenical and Interreligious Affairs, USCCB.

Islam literally means submission (to God). As a distinct religion, Islam originated with Muhammad (A.D. 570-633) and with the revelation he is believed to have received. Muslims acknowledge that this revelation, recorded in the *Quran*, is from the one God and do not view Islam as a new religion. They profess that Muhammad was the last in a long series of prophets, most of whom are named in the Hebrew Bible and the New Testament, beginning with Adam and continuing through Noah, Abraham, Moses, Jesus and down to Muhammad. Muslims believe in the virgin birth of Jesus Christ and have great reverence for Mary, the mother of Jesus, to whom an entire chapter of the Quran is devoted.

Muslims believe in the one God, Allah in Arabic, and cognate with the Hebrew Elohim and the ancient Aramaic Elah. According to the Quran, God is one and transcendent, Creator and Sustainer of the universe, all-merciful and all-compassionate

Ruler and Judge. God possesses numerous other titles, known collectively by His 99 attributes. The profession of faith states: "There is no god but the God and Muhammad is the messenger of God."

There are five pillars of Islam, the essential duties of Muslims: to witness the faith in one God and the prophethood of Muhammad and of the prophets who came before him; to worship five times a day facing in the direction of the holy Kaaba in Mecca, a sanctuary believed to have been dedicated by Abraham to belief in one God; give alms; fast daily from dawn to dusk during the month of Ramadan; make a pilgrimage to Mecca once in a lifetime if affordable.

Muslims believe in the final judgment, the resurrection of the body, and heaven and hell. Following divinely prescribed moral norms are extremely important to Muslims. Some dietary regulations (e.g. avoiding alcoholic beverages and pork) are in effect. On Fridays, the noon prayer is a congregational (*juma*) prayer. The general themes of prayer are adoration and thanksgiving. The imam gives a sermon to the congregation, but unlike Judeo-Christian tradition, the day is not a "day of rest." Muslims do not have an ordained ministry.

The basis of Islamic belief is the Quran, believed to be the word of God revealed to Muhammad through the angel Gabriel over a period of 23 years. The contents of this sacred book are supplemented by the Sunna, a collection of sacred traditions from the life of the prophet Muhammad, and reinforced by Ijma, the consensus of scholars of Islamic Law (Shariah) which shields them against errors in matters of belief and practice.

Conciliar Statement

The attitude of the Church toward Islam was stated in the Second Vatican Council's "Constitution on the Church" (*Lumen Gentium,* No. 16): "But the plan of salvation also includes those who acknowledge the Creator, in the first place among whom are the Muslims: these profess to hold the faith of Abraham, and together with us they adore the one, merciful God, mankind's judge on the last day." The Council's "Declaration on the Relation of the Church to Non-Christian Religions" (*Nostra Aetate,* No. 3) stated the position in further detail: "The Church has a high regard for the Muslims. They worship God, who is one, living and subsistent, merciful and almighty, the Creator of heaven and earth, who has also spoken to men. They strive to submit themselves without reserve to the hidden decrees of God, just as Abraham submitted himself to God's plan, to whose faith Muslims eagerly link their own. Although not acknowledging him as God, they venerate Jesus as a prophet, his virgin Mother they also honor, and even at times devoutly invoke. Further, they await the day of judgment and the reward of God following the resurrection of the dead. For this reason, they highly esteem an upright life and worship God, especially by way of prayer, alms-deeds and fasting.

Over the centuries many quarrels and dissensions have arisen between Christians and Muslims. The sacred Council now pleads with all to forget the past, and urges that a sincere effort be made to achieve mutual understanding; for the benefit of all men, let them together preserve and promote peace, liberty, social justice and moral values."

Dialogue

Pope John Paul II met with Muslim leaders and delegations both in Rome and during his trips abroad. He addressed large gatherings of Muslims in Morocco, Indonesia, Mali and elsewhere. In 1979 on a pastoral visit to Turkey, he suggested to the Catholic community: "My brothers, when I think of the spiritual patrimony [of Islam] and of the value it has for man and for society, its capacity of offering a direction in life particularly for the young, filling the gap left by materialism, and giving a secure foundation to the social and legal order, I wonder if it is not urgent, precisely today when Christians and Muslims have entered a new period of history, to recognize and develop the spiritual bonds that unite us, in order 'to promote and defend together peace, liberty, social justice and moral values for the benefit of all men,' as the Council calls us to do (*Nostra Aetate, No.* 3). In *Tertio Millennio Adveniente* (1999), he recommended that "the dialogue with Jews and the Muslims ought to have a pre-eminent place" involving "meetings in places of significance for the great monotheistic religions." On Feb. 24, 2000, John Paul II traveled to Egypt as part of his Jubilee Year pilgrimages and was received by Grand Sheik Mohammed Sayyid Tantawi at al-Azhar University, the most influential Islamic university in the world. On a pastoral visit to Syria in May 2001, John Paul II spoke of the significant relationship that exists between Muslims and Christians citing his first letter of the new millennium: "I am thinking too of the great cultural influence of Syrian Islam, which under the Umayyad caliphs reached the farthest shores of the Mediterranean. Today, in a world that is increasingly complex and interdependent, there is a need for a new spirit of dialogue and cooperation between Christians and Muslims. Together we acknowledge the one indivisible God, the Creator of all that exists. Together we must proclaim to the world that the name of the one God is 'a name of peace and a summons to peace' (*Novo Millennio Ineunte,* No. 55)!" On the same trip to Syria, on May 6, 2001, John Paul II made the first papal visit to a mosque when he was received at the Umayyad Mosque in Damascus by the Minister of the Waqf and the Grand Mufti of Syria. On Nov. 18, 2001, John Paul II asked Catholics to fast and pray for peace on Friday, Dec. 14, the last Friday of the Ramadan fast that year. He also announced that he was intending to invite representatives of various world religions to Assisi for a day of prayer which was held on Jan. 24, 2002.

The Pontifical Council for Interreligious Dialogue holds formal dialogues with several Islamic organizations on a regular basis; these are regularly reported in the official bulletin, *Pro Dialogo* and in *Islamochristiana,* a journal published by the Pontifical Institute for Arabic and Islamic Studies.

At the beginning of the pontificate of Pope Benedict XVI, a meeting with Muslims in Cologne, France, was added to the Holy Father's participation in the 2005 World Youth Day. In a university lecture at Regensburg, Germany, on Sept. 12, 2006, Pope Benedict cited a 14th century Byzantine Emperor, Manuel Palaeologos, remarking on how the emperor had once entered into a discussion with "a startling brusqueness, a brusqueness that we find unacceptable, on the central question about the relationship between religion and violence in general, saying: 'Show me just what Mohammed brought that was new, and there you will find things only evil and inhuman, such as his command to spread by the sword the faith he preached.'" Pope Benedict concluded this reference, noting that "The emperor, after having expressed himself so forcefully, goes on to explain in detail the reasons why spreading the faith through violence is something unreasonable. Violence is incompatible with the nature of God and the nature of the soul." Although the actual subject of this lecture was an analysis of the intellectual crisis of European civilization, and the need to recover both faith and reason in contemporary discourse, unfortunately, the quote about Muhammad attracted world media attention. Violent protests broke out in Muslim-majority countries, churches were burned, and several people lost their lives, in spite of the fact that the Pope had not expressed any personal agreement with the citation. A group of 39 Muslim scholars responded to the crisis in October 2006 with an insightful written discussion of some points in the Pope's lecture. The Holy Father visited Turkey from Nov. 28–Dec. 1, 2006; in the course of his visit he met several times with Muslim leaders and prayed silently in the Blue Mosque in Istanbul. The visit to Turkey considerably improved Muslim responses to the current pontificate.

In October 2007, a group of 138 Muslim scholars convened by the Royal Academy of The Royal Aal al-Bayt Institute for Islamic Thought in Jordan, under the Patronage of H.M. King Abdullah II, composed "A Common Word Between Us and You" addressed to Christian leaders of various churches and ecclesial communities around the world. The theme of this document is the love of God and the love of neighbor, known to Christians from the words of Jesus in the New Testament. The Muslim scholars cited texts from the Quran and from the Bible to show how love of God and neighbor can constitute a common ground for Muslims and Christians to work together for mutual understanding and world peace. A number of Christian scholars have replied to "A Common Word" on the website: www.acommonword.com. The Holy See has formed The Catholic-Muslim Forum which will be meeting on Nov. 4-6, 2008 with Muslim signatories in order to formulate together an in-depth response to "A Common Word."

During the visit of Pope Benedict XVI to the United States (Apr. 15-20, 2008), the Pope John Paul II Cultural Center hosted an interreligious gathering for over 180 Jews, Muslims, Hindus, Buddhists, and Jains entitled "Peace Our Hope." The Holy Father encouraged the communities of dialogue in the United States, reminding them that "The broader purpose of dialogue is to discover the truth. What is the origin and destiny of mankind? What are good and evil? What awaits us at the end of our earthly existence? Only by addressing these deeper questions can we build a solid basis for the peace and security of the human family, for 'wherever and whenever men and women are enlightened by the splendor of truth, they naturally set out on the path of peace' (Message for the 2006 World Day of Peace, No. 3)." Pope Benedict also pointed out that dialogue not only serves the members of the respective religious communities, but also bears valuable witness to the larger society of the perennial value of religious faith.

In the U.S., the Bishops' Committee for Ecumenical and Interreligious Affairs holds regular regional bilateral dialogues with Muslims. Dialogue on a national level with the participation of Catholics and Muslims from several U.S. cities was initiated in October 1991. A series of conversations with Muslims on international and domestic issues were co-sponsored with the American Muslim Council. In the late 1990s, the Bishops' Committee initiated the following three regional dialogues with Muslims.

In 1996, an annual regional dialogue in the Midwest with the co-sponsorship of the Islamic Society of North America in Plainfield, IN, was initiated. This dialogue concluded several years of discussion on revelation with a report, Revelation: Catholic and Muslim Perspectives, published by USCCB Publishing (2006). This dialogue has continued to examine the role of virtues and values in our communities in view of the challenges that Catholics and Muslims face in American society. A mission statement was adopted in 2007:

"Catholics and Muslims engage in interreligious dialogue because it is part of our core identities as people of faith. Our common belief in the one God of mercy and love calls us into relationship with one another; therefore we see our dialogue as a spiritual journey. Common ethical concerns compel us to take responsibility for our relationship within U.S. American society. The United States Conference of Catholic Bishops and the Islamic Society of North America sponsor our annual gathering of official representatives for formal dialogue on topics of mutual concern. Our Dialogue provides a forum for Muslim-Catholic discussion, critique, and exchange of information that is supportive of the programs of our respective institutions."

In 1998, an annual dialogue in the Mid-Atlantic region with the co-sponsorship of the Islamic Circle of North America in Queens, New York, held its first meeting. The group has been working on a common document on marriage, which should be of great value for mosque and parish leaders responsible for marriage preparation. In 2007, a new round of this dialogue began work on a study of interreligious education in order to make recommendations to the education communities that serve our churches and mosques.

In 2000, the West Coast Dialogue of Muslims and Catholics began meeting in Orange, CA, with the co-sponsorship of several Islamic councils. The West Coast Dialogue issued a report in December 2003, Friends and Not Adversaries, a Catholic-Muslim Spiritual Journey. Since 2004, the West Coast dialogue has focused on a study of comparative narratives from the Bible and from the Quran; in each case, the moral, cultural, and catechetical principles of these narratives have allowed us to explore the immigrant experience of Catholics and Muslims in American society.

All three regional dialogues are co-chaired by bishops and Islamic leaders. Also in 1995 a dialogue between representatives of the ministry of W.D. Mohammed and the United States Conference of Catholic Bishops began. Since then, the relationship between Imam W.D. Mohammad's American Society of Muslims and the Catholic Church has been served by the Focolare Movement. The Pope John

Paul II Cultural Center in Washington, DC, has also been the at the service of Muslim-Catholic dialogue, hosting a dialogue on "The Primordial Relationship Between God and the Human Person in Catholicism and Islam" on Jan. 16, 2007, with Card. Angelo Scola, Patriarch of Venice, and Dr. Muzammil Siddiqi, head of the Islamic Society of Orange County, CA. On May 16, 2007, the Center sponsored a one-day dialogue on "Sin, Forgiveness, Repentance, Reparation, and Mercy" with Prof. Zeki Saritoprak of John Carroll University and Fr. Francis Tiso of the Secretariat for Ecumenical and Interreligious Affairs of the USCCB. On Oct. 3-5, 2012, a national plenary of the three regional dialogues was held at the Catholic Theological Union in Chicago, IL. The theme of the plenary was "Living our faiths together" and featured keynote addresses by Fr. Tom Michel, S.J., and Dr. Jamal Badawi.

Catholic, Muslim Leaders Celebrate Past Accomplishments, Pledge Continued Support in Public Square at National Gathering

Leading Catholic and Muslim scholars and religious leaders convened a national plenary at the Catholic Theological Union in Chicago, Oct. 3-5. Participants from the three regional Catholic-Muslim dialogues sponsored by the U.S. Conference of Catholic Bishops (USCCB) celebrated the work and public impact of the dialogues, received formal updates on the status of regional projects, and voiced a future vision for the dialogues.

In his opening address, retired Abp. Alexander Brunett of Seattle presented a narrative of the dialogues, praised the solidarity and friendship of the participants, especially following the events of 9/11, and urged his listeners to cooperate on projects of common concern in the public square. Referencing Pope John Paul II's address to Muslim youth in Morocco, he urged the audience never to lose sight of the fact that, despite the differences between religions, the unity of the human community is the more fundamental reality. In service to this unity, Catholic and Muslim leaders must advance dialogue by approaching it as a spiritual exercise that requires the cultivation of virtues, especially meekness, humility, and trust.

In response, Sayyid Syeed, Ph.D., of the Islamic Society of North America (ISNA) remarked that if the last millennium witnessed to the spilling of blood, this new period of emerging multiculturalism is an opportunity for the Catholic-Muslim dialogue in the United States to lead the way as a witness of harmony and peaceful coexistence.

A panel delivered commentary on the present status and future hopes of the dialogues. The co-chairs of the Mid-Atlantic dialogue, auxiliary Bp. Denis Madden of Baltimore (who also chairs the USCCB Committee on Ecumenical and Interreligious Affairs) and Talat Sultan, Ph.D., of the Islamic Circle of North America (ICNA) expressed gratitude to the dialogue participants for their work on the defense of family, marriage and interreligious education. Both leaders interpreted these works as important contributions to the formation of individual conscience, especially among the young.

Midwest co-chair Syeed remarked that the work of these regional dialogues is conveyed to the international Muslim community and thus serves to promote greater understanding and peace between Muslims and Christians around the world. His Catholic counterpart, aux. Bp. Francis Reiss of Detroit, emphasized this point by remarking that the reality of multiculturalism in society entails that "we live in a moment in history that is significantly and profoundly unique," to the extent that Muslims and Catholics can show the world how to live in peace and harmony with persons of different religious affiliation.

West Coast co-chair, retired Bp. Carlos Sevilla, S.J., of Yakima, Wash., encouraged dialogue participants to "cast our nets wider, so as to include in our work a wider audience, especially the youth." His Muslim co-chair, Muzammil Siddiqi, Ph.D., of the Fiqh Council of North America, urged the participants to consider publishing to a wider audience, generating more joint statements, and expanding the Catholic-Muslim network through the enhanced use of technology.

The plenary keynote addresses were delivered by scholars Jamal Badawi, Ph.D., and Jesuit Fr. Tom Michel, Ph.D. Speaking to the plenary theme of living our faiths together, Badawi drew attention to the role of language, specifically translation of religious texts and the dissemination of opinion based on particular translations, in determining the possibility and extent of harmony and/or tension between Muslims and Christians. Fr. Michel, whose address was highlighted by reflections from his experience living abroad in Muslim majority countries, argued that effective and truthful dialogue requires faithfulness to one's tradition.

West Coast Muslim-Catholic Dialogues

The 14th annual West Coast Muslim-Catholic Dialogue convened for a close study of the after-life in Christianity and Islam. Presentations focused on a comparative study of Christ's return and the judgment of nations in Mt 25:31-46 and the corresponding Muslim version of the judgment in Sahih Muslim Hadith 1172. The meeting was held at the Mary and Joseph Retreat Center in Rancho Palos Verdes, CA, on May 29-39, 2013. Bp. Carlos Sevilla, S.J., of the Diocese of Yakima, WA, and Imam Muzammil H. Siddiqi, Ph.D., of the Islamic Society of Orange County, presided.

The 15th annual West Coast Muslim-Catholic Dialogue convened for a close study of various aspects of extremism in Christianity and Islam. Presentations focused specifically on studies of jihad in Islam and just war theory in Catholicism. The meeting was co-hosted by the Islamic Society of Orange County and the Islamic Educational Center of Orange County on May 20-21, 2014. Bishop Robert McElroy of the Archdiocese of San Francisco, CA, Imam Muzammil H. Siddiqi, Ph.D., of the Islamic Society of Orange County, and Imam Mostafa Al-Qazwini, of the Islamic Educational Center of Orange County, presided.

In the first part of the meeting, a general overview on the question of jihad in both the Sunni and Shia traditions of Islam was provided by Imam Al-Qazwini and Dr. Siddiqi. In his presentation on the extremism present in certain interpretations of jihad, Imam Al-Qazwini focused his remarks on the economic realities of extreme poverty and poor education that are products of, among other phenomena, the post-colonial era in the Islamic world. While "the vast majority of Muslims despise fanaticism, radicalism, and militant Islam," nevertheless the extreme minority, especially in these marginal and poor countries, wield a powerful voice that attracts those, especially the youth and unemployed, who are looking for justice. "The world-wide Muslim population," he remarked, "suffers because of the actions of so few." Al-Qazwini then discussed the influential teaching of Ibn Taymiyyah and the rise of Wahhabism in the Muslim world, in order to provide some further historical context for Islamic extremism and the violent response of the Muslim minority to the effects of colonialism. Imam Siddiqi's presentation focused on the Sunni understanding of jihad, which he argued manifests signs of continuity with the Shia interpretation. Specifically, Siddiqi focused his attention on an exegesis of specific texts from the Qur'an, especially 2:190, which reads "Fight only against those who fight," and fight never out of sheer aggression. "In the sacred text, it is simply and clearly forbidden," he argued, "to wage war, as well as to force conversions and to conquer other countries." "Terrorism and violence and forced conversions," all of these, "are not Islamic – they are against the teachings of Islam," Siddiqi asserted. Then he shifted his remarks to the similarities between jihad and the Catholic just war theory, which he declared are nearly identical and tend more towards pacifism.

In the second part of the meeting, Bp. Robert McElroy presented the paper, "War and Peace in the Catholic Tradition: An Overview." In his address, the bishop provided a summary of the Catholic Just War Doctrine as this is presented both in the tradition, with special reference to the teaching of Augustine, as well as in canon law and the catechism. He placed considerable emphasis on the near impossible situations that give rise to a just war and provided substantial references from recent popes who have essentially taken radical pacifist approaches to international conflicts. Following Bp. McElroy, Fr. Jose Rubio presented a paper on the scriptural understanding of war entitled "War and Peace in the Bible from Genesis to Revelation." With specific emphasis on an explication of the textual evidence from both the old and new testaments, Fr. Rubio provided a scriptural foundation for understanding the rudiments of Catholic just war doctrine.

In addition to the co-chairs, those present at the meeting included Muslim participants Mr. Hussam Ayloush, Executive Director of CAIR, Greater Los Angeles Area; Ms. Sherrel A. Johnson, Community Relations Manager and Assistant to the Director of CAIR, Greater Los Angeles Area; Imam Jerrel Abdul Salaam of Paramount, CA; Mrs. Maria Khani; Ms. Fatima Saleh of the Islamic Educational Center of Orange County; Dr. Maryam Kim Kieu. Additional Catholic participants included Fr. Al Baca, Diocese of Orange; Msgr. Dennis L. Mikulanis, Diocese of San Diego; Fr. Jose A. Rubio, Diocese of San Jose; Rt. Rev. Alexei Smith, Archdiocese of Los Angeles; Fr. Michael Kiernan, Diocese of Sacramento; Fr. Quan V. Tran, Diocese of Orange; and, Dr. Anthony Cirelli, Associate Director, USCCB SEIA.

HINDUISM, BUDDHISM, AND SIKHISM

(Edited in consultation with the staff of the Secretariat for Ecumenical and Interreligious Affairs, USCCB.)

In its *Declaration on the Relation of the Church to Non-Christian Religions*, the Second Vatican Council stated: "In Hinduism men explore the divine mystery and express it both in the limitless riches of myth and the accurately defined insights of philosophy. They seek release from the trials of the present life by ascetical practices, profound meditation and recourse to God in confidence and love." (2)

Catholics, especially in India, have sought good relations with Hindus and have engaged in numerous dialogues and conferences. In visits to India, Paul VI in 1964 and John Paul II in 1986 and 1999, popes have addressed words of respect for Indian, particularly Hindu, religious leaders. Pope John Paul II said to Hindus in India in 1986: "Your overwhelming sense of the primacy of religion and of the greatness of the Supreme Being has been a powerful witness against a materialistic and atheistic view of life." In 1987, he said of Hinduism: "I hold in esteem your concern for inner peace and for the peace of the world, based not on purely mechanistic or materialistic political considerations, but on self-purification, unselfishness, love and sympathy for all."

In 1995, the Pontifical Council for Interreligious Dialogue began sending a general message to Hindus on the occasion of Diwali, a feast commemorating the victory of light over darkness. When Pope John Paul II was in India during Diwali in 1999, he addressed the religious leaders of India: "On the occasion of Diwali, the festival of lights, which symbolizes the victory of life over death, good over evil, I express the hope that this meeting will speak to the world of the things that unite us all: our common human origin and destiny, our shared responsibility for people's well-being and progress, our need of the light and strength that we seek in our religious convictions." Pope John Paul II also encouraged an intellectual exchange with Indian philosophy in his encyclical, *Fides et Ratio* (1998): "A great spiritual impulse leads Indian thought to seek an experience which would liberate the spirit from the shackles of time and space and would therefore acquire absolute value. The dynamic of this quest for liberation provides the context for great metaphysical systems" Nos. 72-73.

In the United States, dialogues between Catholics and Hindus focus on common themes of spirituality and theological philosophy. A series of informal consultations with the Vaishnava Hindu traditions over the past 10 years, since 1998, has explored the problem of evil, the mystical expression of divine love, the relationship between love and fear, and the theological rationales in our traditions for interreligious dialogue. New consultations have germinated since the Apr. 15-20, 2008, visit of Pope Benedict XVI, involving the Swadhyaya Pariwar activist movement, founded by Rev. Pandurang Shastri Athavale, and with the Vishwa Madhva Sangha in New Jersey. Leaders from the Hindu Temple Society and from the InterFaith Conference of Metropolitan Washington, DC, have been available to assist with Hindu-Catholic relations in recent years.

The Second Vatican Council, in its Declaration on the Relation of the Church to Non-Christian Religions, stated: "Buddhism in its multiple forms acknowledges the radical insufficiency of this shifting world. It teaches a path by which men, in a devout and confident spirit, can either reach a state of absolute freedom or attain supreme enlightenment by their own efforts or by higher assistance."

Numerous delegations of Buddhists and leading monks have been received by the popes, and John Paul II has met with Buddhist leaders on many of his trips. Paul VI said to a group of Japanese Buddhists in 1973: "Buddhism is one of the riches of Asia: you teach men to seek truth and peace in the kingdom of the Eternal, beyond the horizon of visible things. You likewise strive to encourage the qualities of goodness, meekness and non-violence." In 1995, while in Sri Lanka, John Paul II said to Buddhists: "I express my highest regard for the followers of Buddhism,…with its four great values of loving kindness, compassion, sympathy, and equanimity; with its 10 transcendental virtues and the joys of the Sangha [the monastic community]…. At the 1986 World Day of Prayer for Peace at Assisi, the Dalai Lama, principal teacher of the Gelugpa lineage, was placed immediately to the Holy Father's left. Numerous dialogues and good relations between Catholics and Buddhists exist in many countries.

In 1995, the Pontifical Council for Interreligious Dialogue organized a Buddhist-Christian colloquium hosted by the Fo Kuang Shan Buddhist order in Taiwan. A second colloquium was held in Bangalore, India, in 1998. A third was held in Tokyo in 2002. These grew out of the perceived need for greater ongoing contact between the Pontifical Council and Buddhist leaders and scholars. Each of these meetings has produced a report. Also in 1995, the council began sending a message to Buddhists on the feast of Vesakh, the celebration of Gautama Buddha's birth, enlightenment, and final entry into Nirvana.

A meeting of great significance between Buddhist and Catholic monastics took place at Our Lady of Gethsemani Abbey, Kentucky, in July 1996, which was organized and facilitated by Monastic Interreligious Dialogue, a network formed in 1981 mostly of monasteries of men and women following the rule of St. Benedict. The Gethsemani Encounter, the result of several formal visits and hospitality between Catholic and Buddhist monks and nuns, focused on various aspects of monastic life. There were 25 participants on each side with numerous observers. The Buddhists represented the Theravada, Tibetan, and Zen traditions. A second Gethsemani Encounter took place in April 2002, the proceedings of which have been published as Transforming Suffering: Reflections on Finding Peace in Troubled Times. In 2008, a third Gethsemani Encounter on "Monasticism and the Environment" addressed ethical concerns raised by the world ecological and food crisis, taking into consideration the witness value to the wider world of simplicity of life as practiced by monastic communities.

In 1998, an ongoing dialogue between Buddhists and Catholics in Los Angeles hosted a retreat dialogue for 50 Catholic and Buddhist participants from different regions of the U.S. The retreat/dialogue was co-planned with the Faiths in the World Committee of the National Association of Diocesan Ecumenical Officers (now called CADEIO), a network of Catholic diocesan staff responsible for ecumenical and interreligious relations. A second retreat/dialogue, co-planned by the Faiths in the World Committee, met at Graymoor, a spiritual life center at the headquarters of the Society of the Atonement, in Garrison, NY, in 2003. This second retreat/dialogue was a "two monastery dialogue," co-hosted by Graymoor and Chuang Yen Buddhist Monastery in nearby Carmel, NY.

In 1996, Card. Arinze, in a letter to "Dear Buddhist Friends," wrote: "The pluralistic society in which we live demands more than mere tolerance. Tolerance is usually thought of as putting up with the other or, at best, as a code of public conduct. Yet, this resigned, lukewarm attitude does not create the right atmosphere for true harmonious coexistence. The spirit of our religions challenges us to go beyond this. We are commanded, in fact, to love our neighbors as ourselves."

Formal dialogues continue in the Archdiocese of Los Angeles and formal relations are developing in a few other dioceses. In 1989 and 1990, the Bishops' Committee for Ecumenical and Interreligious Affairs convened its earliest national consultations on relations with Buddhists. After a series of meetings in the San Francisco area, the Bishops' Committee inaugurated a Buddhist-Catholic dialogue in March 2003, following the model of its regional dialogues, with the Dharma Realm Buddhist Association and the San Francisco Zen Center as partners. The theme of the first dialogue was "Walking the Bodhisattva Path/ Walking the Christ Path." The Northern California Chan/Zen-Catholic Dialogue met again in March 2004 to discuss the theme "Transformation of Hearts and Minds: Chan/Zen-Catholic Approaches to Precepts." In 2005, the theme was "Practice: Means Towards Transformation," at the San Francisco Zen Center. The theme of the 2006 meeting was "Meeting on the Path." The theme for the 2007 meeting was "Taking Refuge in the Buddha / Abiding in Christ," with particular attention to the stages of initiation into Buddhist and Christian life. In 2008, the dialogue topic, "Abiding in Christ; Taking Refuge in the Buddha: Then What?" focused on the stages of the spiritual life from the perspective of the training programs for lay and ordained religious teachers. Attention was directed not only to the stages formation in contemplative communities, but also in active religious orders, lay associations such as the St. Vincent de Paul Society, and the Engaged Buddhist movement.

In an effort to further the bishops' interest in interreligious dialogue, planning for a new outreach to the Sikh community began in 2005. In May 2006 the first meeting of a Sikh-Catholic Consultation comprised of representatives of the World Sikh Council–America Region and the U.S. Conference of Catholic Bishops was held in New York. At the consultation, the Sikh and Catholic communities expressed shared concerns over the challenges faced by immigrant communities in the U.S., the curtailment of religious freedom and human rights in South Asia, and the challenges of secularism to both religious communities. The consultation has also explored the spiritual teachings of Sikhism and Christianity and discussed personal paths to holiness as exemplified by Catholic saints and Sikhs revered as holy people.

The new consultation with the Sikhs arose in part from previous years of collaboration with religious organizations working together for world peace. The World Conference on Religions for Peace and Religions for Peace-USA have provided a vital forum for peace making. Religions for Peace-USA has fostered closer ties with the Sikh, Hindu, Buddhist, and Jain communities, as well as our ecumenical partners and non-governmental organizations addressing issues of the international community.

Programs for Bishops

In 2006 and 2007, on the Sunday morning before the Plenary Meeting of the United States Conference of Catholic Bishops, the Secretariat for Ecumenical and Interreligious Affairs has sponsored a breakfast for the bishops with Abp. Pietro Sambi, the Apostolic Nunzio to the United States, an expert on Middle Eastern affairs. In 2007, Abp. Sambi was joined by Dr. Sayyid M. Syeed, National Director of the Islamic Society of North America, for a Muslim-Catholic conversation that engaged questions from the Bishops in attendance.

In the recent restructuring of the USCCB, the former Subcommittee on Interreligious Dialogue will be reabsorbed into the Committee for Ecumenical and Interreligious Affairs as of 2008. In order to enhance its ability to take up interreligious concerns, the Committee has suggested the formation of an advisory group of bishops to work with the Secretariat.

INDEX

(Page numbers in bold represent the main entry for the listing)

A

Aachen, 342, 458, 461, 476
Aaron, 98, 272
Abbacies, 274, 335,
Abbacy, **128**, 298, 346, 445
Abbess, 108, **128**, 149, 210, 211
Abbot, 107, **128**, 149, 152, 167, 168, 170, 204, 205, 207, 212, 292, 402-404, 406, 416, 463
Abelard, 222
Abortion, 8, 15, 20, 24, 25, 27, 28, 32, 36, 39, 42, 44, 52, 55, 75, 76, 80, 81, 83, 84, 113-115, 117, **128**, 134, 140, 199, 200, 242, 245, 300, 310, 314, 315, 357, 362, 363, 369, 372, 504
Abraham, 21, 61, 93, 95, 98, **101**, 135, 137, 151, 605, 606, 611, 612
Abril y Castello, Card. Santos, 35, 260, **276**
Absolution, **128**, 134, 136, 137, 154, 186, 195, 222, 350, 598
Abstinence, 112, **128**, 129, 141, 160, 162, 163, 166, 171, 203, 350
Acacian Schism, 220
Academies Pontifical, 259, **271**, 272
Academy of Noble Ecclesiastics, 238, 550
Acadia, 353, 441
Accommodated Senses, 104
Acolyte, 186, **197**, 495
Act of Emancipation, 308
Act of Supremacy, 224, 596
Act of Toleration, 358
Acta Apostolicae Sedis, 113, 116, 255, **263**, 264, 340
Acta Sanctae Sedis, 263
Acts of the Apostles, 73, 96, **102**, 106, 134, 162, 331, 349
Ad Gentes, **229**, 292, 478
Ad Limina Visit, 274
Adam, 89, 98, 99, 120, **150-152**, 157, 595, 611
Adamec, Bp. Joseph V., 374, **394**, 500
Adams, Abp. Edward, 265, **394**
Addiction Recovery Services, 509
Adeodatus I, Pope, 234
Adeodatus II, Pope, 234
Adjutrix, 121
Administration of the Patrimony Apostolic See (APSA), **259**, 270, 277, 279, 287
Adoukonou, Rev. Barthelemy, 259
Adoptionism, 221
Adorno Fathers, 207, 461, 468
Adrian Dominican Sisters, 539, 544
Adrian Dominicans, 564
Adrian I, Pope, 229, 234
Adrian II, Pope, 229, 234
Adrian III, Pope, 234
Adrian IV, Pope, 235
Adrian V, Pope, 235
Adrian VI, Pope, 235, 236, 243
Adultery, 13, 39, 111, 129, 199, 201
Advent, 78, 129, **161**, 162, 164, 170, 180, 183, 185, 349, 569, 595
Aeterni Patris, **149**, 238, 247
Afghanistan, 11, 256, **298**, 321
Africa, 17, 22, 53, 58, 70, 107, 205, 206, 214, 220, 233, 234, 240, 241, 243, 244, 249, 265-267, 269, 275, 279, 284-286, 289, 290, 296-298, 301-311, 316-321, 325-331, 334-336, 339, 346, 347, 395,
403, 411, 414, 422, 423, 429, 430, 458, 461, 463, 467, 468, 474, 475, 483, 487, 489, 499, 548, 550, 563, 568, 589, 602, 609
African Missions Society, 326, 331, 458
African-American Catholics, 426-427
Agape, **129**, 147
Agapitus I, Pope, 234
Agapitus II, Pope, 234
Agatho, 229, 234
Aggiornamento, 72, **129**, 240
Agnosticism, 129
Agnus Dei, **129**, 179
Agre, Card. Bernard, 51
Aguilar, C.M.F., Card. Fernando Sebastián, 70-71, 291, 295, 296
Agustoni, Card. Gilberto, **277**, 295, 296
AIDS, 176, 302, 328, 330, 332, 334, 495, 503, 510, 602, 609
Akathist Hymn, 129
Alabama, 52, 84, 354, 365, 368, 373, 389, 390, 404, 421, 433, 435, 439, 459, 463, 470, 511, 521, 522, 526, 535
Alaska, 243, 356, 363, 365, 373, 374, 376, 378, 421, 422, 433, 435, 439, 526, 535, 545
Alb, **180**, 181
Albania, 34, 45, 214, 232, 244, 246, 256, 264, 268, 281, **298**, 336, 418, 501, 589, 590
Albertus Magnus, St., 129, 240, 539
Albigensianism, 219, 223
Alcohol Rehabilitation, 510
Alcoholism, 503, 510
Alencherry, Card. George, 274, **277**, 295, 296
Alexander I, Pope, 233
Alexander II, Pope, 226, 235
Alexander III, Pope, 204, 222, 229, 235, 237
Alexander IV, Pope, 235, 459
Alexander V (Antipope), 237, 238
Alexander VI, Pope, 144, 224, 236, 449
Alexander VII, Pope, 217, 236
Alexander VIII, Pope, 225, 236
Alexandrian Rite, 308
Alexandrian Tradition, 348
Alexian Brothers, 458, 468
Algeria, 264, 267, 268, **298**, 336, 396, 468
All Saints, 147, 162, 170, **171**, 180, 185, 283, 349, 389, 512
All Souls, 170, 171, 349
Allah, 611
Allain., Gov. William, 51
Alleluia, 129, 184, 564
Allocution, 37, 129
Allouez, Claude, 353, 358, 363
Allué, Bp. Emilio, **394**, 418
Alphonsa of the Immaculate Conception, 252
Alphonsianum, 280, 408, 410
Alphonsus Liguori, St., 107, 113, 168, 212, 213, 225, 483
Altar, 132, 135, 139, 151, 178, 179, **181**, 182, 184, 211, 215, 349-351, 389, 605
Altar Cloth, 181
Álvarez Martinez, Card. Francisco, **277**, 295, 296
Alvaro del Portillo, 216, 255
Alzheimers, 515, 520
Amato, Card. Angelo, 215-217, 256, **277**, 295, 296
Amato Ronconi, 217
Ambassadors of the Holy See, 264-268
Ambassadors to the Holy See, 268-269
Ambo, 181
Ambrose of Milan, St., 107, 109, 121
Amen, 67, 88, 109, 128, **130**, 143, 179, 187, 349, 577, 608
American College of Louvain, 546
American Friends of the Vatican Library, 498
American Samoa, 325, 416, 430, 538
Americanism, 361
Amice, 180
Amigo Vallejo, Card. Carlos, 277, 295, 296
Amos, 96, **101**
Amos, Bp. Martin, 376, 394
Anabaptism, 595
Anacletus I, Pope, 233
Anacletus II, Pope, 237
Analogy of Faith, 92, 95, 103
Anamnesis, 130
Anaphora, 130, 592
Anastasius I, Pope, 234
Anastasius II, Pope, 234
Anastasius III, Pope, 234
Anastasius IV, Pope, 235
Anathema, 130
Anchor, 215, 551, 552
Anchorite, **130**, 143
Ancient Churches of the East, 122
Ancient Order of Hibernians, 498
Anderson, Carl, 272, 507
Andorra, 264, 268, 286, 298
André Bessette, St., 163, 165, **204**, 217, 253, 446
Andrello, S.D.B., Card. Ricardo Ezzati, 70-71, **282**, 295, 296
Andrew, 105, 170, **204**, 208
Andritzki, Alois, 254
Angadiath, Bp. Jacob, 382, 394
Angel, 31, 58, 99, 119, 120, 124, **130**, 138, 173, 215, 259, 271, 339, 388, 397, 414, 416, 452, 459, 469, 477, 488, 521, 530, 546, 612
Angela of Foligno, 216, 252
Angelico, Fra, 204, 252
Angelicum, 243, 280, 284, 294, 395, 397, 398, 400-402, 412-414, 417, **550**
Angelini, Card. Fiorenzo, **277**, 295
Angell, Bp. Kenneth, 375, **394**
Angelo, Paoli, 254
Angelus, 5, 21, 25, 29, 30, 46, 49, 63, 70, 78, 79, 113, **130**, 138, 391, 555, 564, 603
Anger, **130**, 133
Anglican Church, 36, 46, 130, 226, 353, 358, **596**, 602
Anglican-Catholic Final Report, 596
Anglican-Roman Catholic Dialogue, 36, 602
Angola, 15, 37, 214, 233, 243, 264, 266, 268, 281, 296, 298, **299**, 336, 339
Anguilla, 299
Anicetus, 233
Animals, **130**, 212, 216
Anne, Srs. of St., 468, 486
Annuario Pontificio, 233, 237, 255, **263**, 264, 267, 268, 271, 298, 336, 339, 343, 344, 348, 394, 438, 442, 451, 455, 458, 467, 486, 489, 492, 507, 547, 548, 550
Annuarium Statisticum Ecclesiae, 197, 203, **263**, 298, 448, 455, 457
Annulment, 80, 81, **130**, 201, 308
Annum Sacrum, 238, 248

Annunciation, 113, **120-122**, 143, 154, 166, **171**, 174, 350, 388, 389, 459, 469, 487, 488, 513, 558
Anointing the Sick, 150, **196**, 350
Anrig, Col. Daniel, 261
Anterus, Pope, 233
Anthony of Padua, St., **107**, 167, 212-214, 277, 283, 387, 444, 462, 506
Anti-Catholicism, 354, 355, 359, 360
Antichrist, 130
Anticlericalism, **135**, 301, 304, 322, 323, 449
Antigua, 264, 267, 268, **299**, 547
Antilles Netherlands, 264, **299**, 324, 336, 416, 418, 463
Antimension, 351
Antiochene Rite, 177, 442
Antiphon, 130, 176
Antipope, 207, 219, 222, 235
Anti-Semitism, 62, **130**, 227, 228, 323, 330, 606-609
Anton Durcovici, 216, 255
Antonelli, Card. Ennio, **277**, 295, 296
Antonianum Pontifical University, 45, 550
Antonio, Rosmini Serbati, 465
Apocrypha, 97, 98
Apologetics, 76, **131**, 499, 557, 560
Apostasy, 13, 39, 43, 50, **131**, 134, 146
Apostles and Evangelists, **105**, 180
Apostles' Creed, 60, 88, **109**, 129, 154
Apostleship of Prayer, 163, 341, 498, 566
Apostleship of the Sea, 341, 495
Apostolic Almoner, 260
Apostolic Camera, 259
Apostolic Delegate, 238, 241, **265**-267, 270, 279, 280, 285, 286, 291, 297, 298, 302, 395, 396, 403
Apostolic Fathers, **106-108**, 218
Apostolic Signatura, 257, **258**, 277, 279, 280, 283, 286, 288, 290-293, 297, 398, 417
Apostolic Succession, 130, **131**, 150, 194, 579, 587, 598
Apostolicam Actuositatem, 229
Apparitions of the Blessed Virgin Mary, 3, **123**, 125, 141, 173
Apuron, Bp. Anthony, 338, **394**
Aquila, Abp. Samuel, 36, 376, 377, **394**
Aramaic, 97, 146, 147, 219, 345, 611
Archaeology, 365
Archangel, 50, **130**, 143, 171, 173, 214, 284, 390, 444, 467
Archbishop, 274
Archbishop ad personam, 274
Archconfraternity, 498, 501
Archdiocese for Military Services, 287
Archdioceses U.S., Archdioceses U.S., 384-386
Archdioceses U.S. Statistics, 432-435
Arche (L'Arche) Communities, 342, 522, 524
Archives, Secret Vatican, 261, 272
Archives, Vatican II, 260
Archpriest, 22, 53, 260, 261, 276, 280, 282-284, 286, 290, 293, 297, 417
ARCIC, 286, 582, 601, 602
Arenas, Abp. Jose Octavio Ruiz, 259, 261
Argentina, 6, 9, 18, 22, 34, 46, 63, 71, 214, 215, 228, 231, 232, 237, 243, 245, 261, 264, 268, 271, 276, 279, 283, 285, 288-290, 296, **299**, 309, 336, 345-347, 365, 479, 547, 548, 566, 611
Arianism, 107-109, 206, 209, 219, 220, 307, 309, 310, 323
Arias, O.A.R., Bp. David, **394**, 425

Arinze, Card. Francis, 261, **277**, 295, 296, 615
Arizona, 36, 54, 85, 353, 358, 364, 372, 374, 389, 390, 416, 421, 422, 426, 433, 435, 439, 511, 526, 533, 535
Ark of the Covenant, 98, **131**
Arkansas, 352, 364, 374, 421, 433, 435, 439, 470, 526, 535, 551
Armenia, 105, 207, 214, 244, 247, 264, 265, 268, 271, **299**, 309, 344, 345, 347, 583, 584
Arminianism, 596
Arns, Card. Paulo E., **277**, 295, 296
Artificial Insemination, 145
Ascension of Christ, 139, 147, 154, **171**
Ascension of the Lord, 95, 161, 162, 167, **171**
Asceticism, 131
Ash Wednesday, 128, 131, 150, 161-163, 165, **171**, 349, 350
Asia, 38, 49, 58, 63-67, 70, 77, 103, 105-108, 169, 210, 214, 240, 242, 244, 275, 296-299, 302, 303, 313, 315, 316, 318-322, 324, 330, 331, 333, 335, 339, 346, 347, 407, 423, 429, 430, 489, 568, 609, 615, 616
Aspergillum, 131
Aspersory, 131
Aspiration, 129, **131**, 578
Assemblies of God, 596, 600
Assisi, 9, 11, 55-57, 107, 137, 151, 158, 160, 169, 205-207, 212-215, 223, 231, 245, 247, 249, 282, 286, 289, 388-390, 462, 474-477, 487, 488, 491, 493, 526, 528, 539, 562, 574, 612, 616
Associations, U.S. Catholic, 498-507
Assumption of Blessed Mary, 162
Assumptionists Religious, 162
Athanasian Creed, 109
Athanasius, St., **107**-109, 167, 205
Atheism, 114, 131, 136, 215, 277
Atonement, 50, 98, 107, **131**, 151, 430, 446, 458, 468, 476, 477, 605, 607, 616
Atonement Franciscan Friars of the, 458, 468
Audiences Papal, 259, 262, 263
Augsburg Confession, 224, 329, 598, 603
Augustine of Canterbury, 167, 205, **206**, 220, 307
Augustine of Hippo, St., **107**, 212-214
Augustinian Fathers, 261, 556
Augustinian Nuns of Contemplative Life, 468
Augustinian Recollects, 458
Augustinian Sisters, 468
Augustinians, 148, 149, 261, 282, 313, 330, 458, 459, 467, 487, 541
Auschwitz, 206, 210, 323, 607, 608
Australia, 11, 28, 51, 54, 73, 74, 214, 233, 242-244, 261, 264, 268, 279, 286, 288, 296, 297, **299**, 319, 336, 339, 345-347, 412, 430, 487, 548, 566, 581, 589, 607
Austria, 6, 215, 216, 225, 233, 240, 243, 244, 247-249, 254, 264, 268, 271, 283, 289, 291, 296, **299**, 336, 341, 346, 361, 395, 396, 403, 413, 415, 418, 471, 476, 477, 482, 491, 548, 549, 566, 583, 590
Authentic Teaching, 92, 246
Authority (Magisterium), 23, 36, 72, 80, 87, 92, 93, 112, 113, 115-117, 127, 133, **148**, 198, 203, 246, 272, 494, 501, 534, 567, 572
Autocephalous Orthodox Churches, 583, 589

Autograph (Chirograph), 135, 260, 261
Auxiliary Bishop, 174
Auxiliatrix, 121, 487
Auza, Abp. Bernardito, 267
Ave Maria, 82, 132, **143**, 272, 460, 501, 527, 539, 558, 564, 567, 573, 574
Avignon Papacy, 237
Awards, 54, 500, 571-575
Awards Communications, 572-575
Aymond, Bp. Gregory, 375, 380, **394**, 422, 590
Azarcon Solis, Bp. Oscar, 378, **394**
Azerbaijan, 244, 264, 265, 268, **300**, 309

B

Babylonian Captivity, 102
Babylonian Exile, 99, 153
Bachstein, Bl. Bedrich and Companions, 255
Backis, Card. Audrys, **277**, 295, 296
Baghdad, 43, 52, 265, 313, 314, 405
Bagnasco, Card. Angelo, **277**, 295, 296, 337
Bahamas, 264, 267, 268, 286, **300**, 352, 403, 497
Bahrain, 264-268, **300**, 332
Baker, Bp. Robert, 375, **394**
Baldacchino, 132
Baldacchino, Bp. Peter, 379, **394**
Baldisseri, Card. Lorenzo, 9, 26, 38, 42, 71, 72, 75-77, 79-81, 275, **277**-78, 295, 296
Balke, Bp. Victor, 376, **394**, 418
Baltakis, Bp. Paul, **394**, 502
Baltimore, Councils of, 360
Balvo, Abp. Charles, 265-267, **394**-395, 417, 418
Bambera, Bp. Joseph C., 383, **395**
Banach, Abp. Michael W., 266, **395**
Bangladesh, 243, 264, 268, 279, **300**, 336, 408, 429
Banks, Bp. Robert J., 377, **395**, 418
Banneux, 9, 123
Baptism, 25, 30, 34, 60, 66, 88, 90, 91, 98, 109, 110, 127, **131**-135, 139, 141, 143, 144, 150, 152, 154, 158, 159, 161, 165, 171-175, 177, 182, 184, 185, 189-192, 195, 196, 201, 206, 207, 218, 219, 221, 262, 302, 309, 328, 332, 343, 350, 494, 495, 505, 534, 578-580, 582, 587, 595-600, 604
Baptism of the Lord, 161, 165, **171**
Baptists, 40, 360, 372, 582, **596**, 597
Barangueras, St. Carmen Salles y, 255
Barbados, 264, 267, 268, 286, **300**, 325
Barbarin, Card. Philippe, **278**, 295, 296
Barbarito, Bp. Gerald, 380, **395**
Barber, S.J., Abp. Michael C., 379, **395**
Barbuda, 264, 267, 268, 299
Barnabas, 105, 106, 167, 459
Barnabite Fathers, 392
Barnes, Bp. Gerald, 382, **395**, 423, 425
Barres, Bp. John, 374, **395**
Bartchak, Bp. Mark L., 374, **395**
Bartholomew, **105**, 168, 211, 213, 214
Bartolucci, Card. Domenico, 51
Bartolucci, Abp. Marcello, 256
Baruch, 96, 97, **100**, 101
Basel-Ferrara-Florence, Council of, 229
Basil the Great, Order of, Srs., 468, 488
Basilian Fathers, 459, 543
Basilian Order of St. Josaphat, 459
Basilian Salvatorian Fathers, 459, 468
Basilian Salvatorian Order, 401
Basilians, 149, 398, 467
Basilians of St. Josaphat, 467

Basilica of the National Shrine of the Immaculate Conception, 77, 390, 391
Basilicas, 144, 170, 260, 261, 387, **389**
Basilicas, U.S., 389-390
Bassetti, Card. Gualtiero, 278, 295, 296
Batakian, Bp. Manuel, 384, **395**, 445
Battista da Varano, 252
Baum, Card. William, 260, **278**, 295, 297, 371, 383, 384, 395
Beatific Vision, 130, **132**, 143, 153
Beatifications, **132**, 215-217, 232, 233, 252-255
Beatissimus Pater, 143
Beatitude, 60, 78, 110, **132**, 345, 348, 593
Becciu, Abp. Giovanni Angelo, 255, 260
Becker, Card. Josef, **278**, 295, 297
Bede the Venerable, **107**, 167, 213
Beeswax, 182
Belarus, 42, 264, 268, **300**, 336, 346, 589
Belgium, 10, 15, 28, 40, 74, 85, 123, 149, 186, 204, 206, 207, 210, 214, 228, 238, 243, 244, 247-249, 261, 264-266, 268, 271, 280, 286, 296, **300**, 325, 336, 339, 341, 342, 359, 394, 396-398, 401, 409, 412, 416, 458, 460-464, 473, 474, 479, 481, 485, 489, 546, 547, 566, 569, 601
Belize, 243, 264, 267, 268, 286, **300**, 301, 418, 429
Beltran, Abp. Eusebius, 380, 383, **395**, 418
Benedict I, Pope, 234
Benedict II, Pope, 234, 235
Benedict III, Pope, 234
Benedict IV, Pope, 234
Benedict V, Pope, 234, 235
Benedict VI, Pope, 235
Benedict VII, Pope, 235
Benedict VIII, Pope, 235
Benedict IX, Pope, 235
Benedict X, Pope, 188, 237, 257
Benedict XI, Pope, 236
Benedict XII, Pope, 236, 237
Benedict XIII, Pope, 172, 213, 214, 236-238
Benedict XIV, Pope, 123, 225, 236, 245-249
Benedict XV, Pope, 172, 188, 227, 232, 237, 239, 240, 248, 250, 256, 257, 259, 261, 423
Benedict XVI, Pope, 7-9, 11, 13, 14, 18, 21, 22, 25, 28, 29, 34, 35, 38, 51, 54, 55, 63, 67, 69-77, 80, 89, 105, 108, 115-117, 144, 147, 163, 187, 189, 195, 217, 228, 230, **232**, 233, 237, 243-245, 250, 252, 254, 259, 261, 274, 275, 277, 280, 286, 288, 292, 295, 299, 301, 304-306, 308-310, 315, 319, 326, 328, 333, 344, 345, 357, 373, 451, 578, 582, 585, 588, 601, 607, 611-613, 615
Beatifications, 233, 254
Canonizations, 233, 255
Encyclicals, 233, 250
Life, 232-233
Travels, 233
Writings, 115, 232-233
Benedict of Nursia, St., **205**, 213, 232, 459
Benedictine Confederation, 128, 416
Benedictine Fathers, 539, 543
Benedictine Nuns, 300, 468, 486
Benedictine Oblates, 207
Benedictine Sisters, 468, 469, 518, 530, 541, 542, 556
Benedictines, 128, 149, 151, 155, 176, 182, 211, 226, 300, 391, 408, 416, 458,

460, 467, 469, 479, 486, 488, 539, 542, 543, 550, 556, 562
Benediction, 5, 50, 134, 139, 141, 150, 167, 181, 367
Benin, 233, 243, 264, 268, 278, 281, **301**, 336, 339, 396
Bennett, Bp. Gordon, **395**, 417, 418
Bergoglio, Card. Jorge, See Francis
Bermuda, 77, **301**, 406, 418, 430
Bernadette Soubirous, St., 123, **205**, 250
Bernard of Clairvaux, St., **107**, 168, 212, 214, 249,
Bernardin, Card. Joseph, 376, 397, 420
Bernardine of Siena, 167, **205**, 211, 213, 214
Bernardine Sisters, 474, 539
Bernardo Francisco de Hoyos, Bl., 255
Bertagna, Abp. Bruno, 259, 260
Bertello, Card. Giuseppe, 261, **278**, 295, 297
Berthieu, St. Jacques, 217, 255
Bertie, Fra Andrew, 573
Bertone, Card. Tarcisio, 9, 10, 63, 259, **278**
Betancur, Pedro de San Jose, 363
Betori, Card. Giuseppe, **278**, 295, 296
Bethany Sisters, 469
Bethlehem, 10, 20, 37, 57-59, 148, 468, 476, 479, 502, 518, 529, 530
Bethlemita Sisters, 469
Bevard, Bp. Herbert, **395**, 418, 430
Bevilacqua, Card. Anthony, 297, 381
Bhutan, 301
Bible, 10, 18, 63, **96-105**, 107, 108, 113, 115, 132, 138, 141, 143, 149, 159, 178, 206, 218-220, 224, 366, 368, 369, 422, 500, 504, 573, 595, 600, 605, 608, 611, 613, 615
Biblical Commission, Pontifical, 105, 233, 238, 255, 260, 282, 289, 293, 608
Biblical Institute, Pontifical, 51, 105, 239, 278, 282, 285-290, 293, 413-416, 550, ,
Biblicism, 600
Biffi, Card. Giacomo, **279**, 295, 297
Biglietto, 132
Bination, 179, 185
Binzer, Bp. Joseph, 376, **395**
Bioethics, 244, 272, 291, 413, 498, 562, 565, 570
Biographies of American Bishops, 394-417
Biographies of Cardinals, 276-295
Biographies of New Blesseds and Saints, 215-217
Biretta, 132
Birth Control, 35, 242
Birth of Mary (Feast), 171
Birth of Our Lord (Feast), 170, 171
Bishop, 274
Bishop Brothers, 417,
Bishops, Biographies of U.S., 394-417
Bishops' Conferences, 11, 39, 40, 68, 79, 183, 187, 192, 193, 195, 278, 339, 580, 607, 611
Bishops, Canadian, 442-445
Bishops, Congregation of, 31, 79, 233
Bishops Mexican, 454-455
Bishops in Foreign Countries, 417-418
Bishops, National Conference of, 283, 291
Bishops, Retired/Resigned, 418-419
Bishops, Synod of, 9, 26, 38, 42, 71, 72, 75-77, 79-81, 126, 195, 233, 242, 244, 275, 278, 292, 294, 299, 315-317, 319, 339, 345, 357, 458
Bishops U.S. Overseas, 417-418
Blair, Abp. Leonard, 377, 383, **395**, 580

Blaire, Bp. Stephen, 12, 15, 383, **395**
Blasphemy, 47, **132**, 139, 321
Blessed Sacrament Exposition, 138, 141, 184, 189
Blessed Virgin Mary, See Mary Blessed Virgin, 173, 205
Blessings, 101, **132**, 141-143, 148, 159, 165, 176, 190, 196, 578
Blessings, Book of, **132**, 190
Blind Catholic Facilities and Organizations, 505, 508-509, 524-525, 556, 560
Blue Army, 342, 392, 507, 560, 564, 590
Blume, Abp. Michael, 267, **395**-396
Boland, Bp. Ernest, **396**, 418
Boland, Bp. J. Kevin, 382, **396**
Boland, Bp. Raymond, 51
Boles, Bp. John, **396**, 418
Bolivia, 5, 214, 239, 243, 264, 268, 276, 292, 296, **301**, 336, 397, 408, 418, 419, 429, 430, 566
Bollandist Acta Sanctorum, 225
Bolognesi Maria, 255
Bon Secours, Congr., 469, 527
Bonaventure, St., **107**, 149, 168, 214, 232, 397, 404, 412, 445, 462, 542, 550, 557, 558, 563
Boniface I, Pope, 234
Boniface II, Pope, 234
Boniface III, Pope, 234
Boniface IV, Pope, 234
Boniface V, Pope, 234
Boniface VI, Pope, 234
Boniface VII, Pope, 237
Boniface VIII, Pope, 144, 223, 236
Boniface IX, Pope, 236, 237
Boniface St., 167, **205**, 211, 221, 234, 248, 249, 310, 442, 444, 448, 492
Book of Blessings, **132**, 190
Book of Common Prayer, 150, 224, 597
Books of the Bible, 98-102, 220
Bootkoski, Bp. Paul, 379, 384, 418
Bosnia Herzegovina, 288, 296
Botean, Bp. John, 382, 396
Botswana, 243, 265, 266, 268, 301, 339, 403
Boyea, Bp. Earl, 378, **396**
Boy Scouts, 212, 369, 497
Boys Town, 521
Bozanic, Card. Josip, **278**, 295, 296
Brady, Card. Sean, **278**, 295, 297, 337
Bradley, Bp. Paul J., 378, 379, **396**
Brandmuller, Card. Walter, 267, **278**, 295, 296
Brandt, Bp. Lawrence, 377, **396**
Bransfield, Bp. Michael J., 384, **396**
Braxton, Bp. Edward K., 375, 378, **396**, 426
Braz de Aviz, Card. João, 257, 261, **278**, 295, 296
Brazil, 9, 22, 63, 71, 80, 214, 216, 217, 232, 233, 239, 243, 244, 247, 248, 253, 261, 265, 268, 271, 277, 278, 282, 283, 285, 290-292, 296, **301**, 302, 336, 345-347, 352, 363, 364, 397, 399, 404, 408, 410, 417-419, 425, 429, 430, 476, 481, 490, 547, 548, 581
Brenes Solórzano, Card. Leopoldo José, **278**-279, 295, 296
Brennan, Bp. Robert J., 381, **396**
Brenner, Mother Antonia, 51
Breviary, 143, **176**, 182, 189, 223, 239
Brigid, Congr. of, 469, 488
Brigittine Monks, 460
Brigittine Sisters, 469
Brigittines, 205

Brisson, Bl. Louis, 217, 255
Broglio, Abp. Timothy, 384, **396**, 422
Brom, Bp. Robert, 377, 382, **396**
Brothers, 335, 355, 357, 361, 365, 396, 417, 427, 430-432, 458, 460-468
Brothers Hospitallers of St. John of God, 208
Brothers of Charity, 460, 467
Brothers of Christian Instruction, 460, 467, 544, 561
Brothers of Christian Instruction of Ploermel, 460, 467
Brothers of Christian Schools, 460, 467
Brothers of Holy Cross, 544
Brothers of Mary, 463, 464
Brothers of Mercy, 464, 468, 516
Brothers of Our Lady, 464, 465, 468
Brothers of Our Lady Mother of Mercy, 464, 468
Brothers of St. Patrick, 465, 467
Brown, Abp. Charles, 24, 265, **396**, 418
Brown, Bp. Tod, **396**, 580, 602
Brucato, Bp. Robert, **396**, 418
Brunei, 265, 266, **302**, 337, 408, 418,
Brunett, Bp. Alexander, 378, 383, **396**, 599
Brungardt, Bp. John B., 376, **396**
Bruno of Carinthia, 235
Bruskewitz, Bp. Fabian, 378, **396**, 418
Buddhism, 35, 301, 316, 320, 428, 615, 616,
Buechlein, Abp. Daniel O.S.B., 378, 379, **396**-97, 418, 575
Bulgaria, 45, 241, 244, 256, 265, 268, **302**, 336, 345, 346, 589, 590,
Bull, 109, 129, 130, **132**, 223, 224, 226, 238, 244, 273, 356, 449, 601,
Bulla, 132, 407
Bura, Bp. John, 381, **397**
Burbidge, Bp. Michael, 381, **397**
Burial, 127, 132, 133, 137, 154, 156-158, 173, 179, 196, 351, 577
Burjan, Bl. Hildegard, 216
Burke, Card. Raymond, 258, 261, **279**, 395, 396, 297, 378, 397, 417
Burke, Bp. John, **397**, 417
Burkina Faso, 22, 71, 265, 266, 268, 287, 296, 302, 336, 338, 339
Burma, 216, 240, 265, 266, 279, **302**, 320, 336
Burnette, Bp. Kurt R., 380, **397**
Burns, Bp. Edward, 378, **397**
Burse, **132**, 181
Burundi, 53, 243, 265, 268, **302**, 325, 330, 336, 339
Bush, Pres. George W., 269, 357
Bustros, Bp. Cyrille, 380, **397**, 417
Byrne, Bp. Peter John, 379, **397**
Byrnes, Bp. Michael J., 376, **397**
Byzantine Catholics, 345, 347, 348
Byzantine Divine Liturgy, 348-350

C

Cabrini Sisters, 484
Cabrini, Mother, 205, 207, 391
Cacciavillan, Card. Agostino, 260, 267, 269, **279**, 295, 296
Caffarra, Card. Carlo, **279**, 295, 296
Caggiano, Bp. Frank J., 375, **397**
Cajetan, 168, 205, 466
Calcagno, Card. Domenico, 259, 260, **279**, 295, 296
Caldecott, Stratford, 51
Calendar Church, 161-163, 176, 242
California, 27, 54, 76, 84, 151, 168, 271, 353, 355, 358, 363-365, 372-374, 378,
379, 389-391, 402, 412, 414, 416, 421, 422, 425, 426, 433, 435, 439, 449, 452, 455, 456, 463, 465, 470, 480, 509, 511, 520-522, 526, 535, 539, 540, 544, 561, 573, 616,
Callahan, Bp. William P., 378, **397**, 422
Callistus I, Pope, 169, 205, 207, 233
Callistus II, Pope, 222, 229, 235
Callistus III, Pope, 174, 236, 237
Calumny, 132
Calungsod, St. Peter, 217
Calvary, 129, 132, 154, 157, 160, 173, 216, 472, 509, 520, 526, 528
Calvinism, 309, 310, 312
Calvo, Bp. Randolph, 8, 381, **397**
Camacho, Bp. Tomas, **397**, 454
Camaldolese, 130, 211, 222, 460, 468
Camaldolese Benedictines, 211, 460
Cambodia, 265, 267, 268, 286, **302**, 337
Camerlengo, 134, 259, 276, 278, 285
Cameroon, 22, 233, 243, 244, 265, 268, 276, 293, 296, **302**, 336, 339, 548
Camillian Fathers, 460
Campbell, Bp. Frederick, 372, 376, 397
Camp Fire Boys and Girls, 496
Campus Ministry, 4, 197, 471, 497, 498, 561
Cana, 120, 154
Canada, 22, 38, 71, 214, 217, 239, 243, 244, 248, 261, 265, 268, 271, 282, 284, 287, 289, 293, 296, **303**, 336, 342, 345-348, 353, 354, 358, 362-365, 373, 380, 386-389, 394-397, 400, 402, 404, 407-409, 412, 413, 416, 417, 429, 432, 438, 441-448, 459, 461, 463, 468, 469, 471-473, 476-478, 481-484, 491-493, 497, 500, 501, 505-508, 510, 542, 547-549, 551, 556, 557, 560, 563, 565-567, 569, 573, 581, 587, 589, 594, 597, 598, 600, 601
Canadian Catholic Publications, 565
Canadian Conference of Catholic Bishops, 336, 441, 442, 445, 447, 565, 591
Canary Islands, 363
Cancer Homes and Hospitals, 509
Candida, Maria de Jesus, 252, 253
Candlemas, 171, 173
Candles, 129, 165, 173, 176, **182**, 605
Canestri, Card. Giovanni, **279**, 295-296
Canizares Llovera, Card. Antonio, 183, **279**, 295, 296
Canon Law, 52-54, 74, **125**-128, 131, 132, 134, 135, 137, 140, 142, 143, 145, 147, 158, 177, 179, 185, 186, 190, 191, 193, 195, 200-203, 210, 222, 226-228, 239-242, 245, 258, 261, 273-290, 293, 347, 351, 395, 446, 458, 489, 494, 495, 499, 507, 548, 550, 558, 579, 594, 596
Canon Law Society of America, 395, 499
Canon of the Bible, 96, 104, 224
Canonizations by Leo XIII and His Successors, 132, 250-251
Canonizations by Benedict XVI, 252
Canonizations by Francis, 252
Canonizations by John Paul II, 251-252
Canons of Eastern Churches, 351
Canons Regular, 149, 210, 405, 461, 463, 465, 467
Canossian Daughters of Charity, 469
Canterbury, 36, 46, 107, 167, 205, 206, 211, 220-222, 224, 307, 308, 333, 513, 577, 582-586, 597, 600-602
Canticle, 108, **132**, 133, 148, 149, 174, 176, 556, 561
Cantu, Bp. Oscar, 86, 382, **397**, 422

Cape Verde, 243, 265, 266, 268, 293, **303**, 338, 339
Capital Punishment, 85, 89, **133**, 500
Capital Sins, 130, **133**, 139, 142, 147, 152, 157
Capovilla, Card. Loris Francesco, 70-71, **279**, 295, 296
Cappa Magna, 180
Capuchins, 207, 215, 224, 312, 321, 326, 331, 352, 413, 467, 486
CARA, 12, 32, 82, 197, 495, 496, 561
Cardinal Bishops, 233, 276
Cardinal Deacons, 276, 294
Cardinal in Pectore, 276
Cardinal Priests, 276
Cardinal Secretary of State, 34, 38, 41, 124, 257, 264, 324
Cardinal Virtues, **133**, 141, 143, 145, 146, 153, 158
Cardinals, 9, 17, 18, 21-23, 26, 29, 31, 33, 35, 44, 46, 54-56, 68-71, 73, 75, 77, 79, 87, 113, 132, 134, 136, 150, 159, 160, 180, 188, 222, 223, 226, 228, 232, 233, 237, 240-243, 245, 255, 256, 260, 261, 273-298, 335, 351, 356, 395, 397, 400-402, 404-408, 410, 412, 414, 417, 422, 432, 451, 455, 572, 578, 607, 611
Cardinals Biographies, 276-297
Cardinals, College of, 21, 26, 29, 54, 70, 276-297
Cardinals of the Past, U.S., 297
Caribbean, 70, 86, 282, 299, 300, 306, 312, 331, 333, 363, 425, 429, 431, 495
Caritas in Veritate, 77, 116, 117, 233, 250
Carles Gordo, Card. Ricardo, 51
Carlson, Bp. Robert, 382, 383, **397**
Carmelite Nuns, 323, 470, 487
Carmelite Order, 108, 155, 169, 556
Carmelite Sisters, 208, 470, 471, 487, 510, 517
Carmelite Sisters of Charity, 208, 470
Carmelite Sisters of St. Therese, 471
Carmelites, 42, 108, 148, 177, 217, 226, 280, 359, 391, 458, 460, 467, 470, 471, 486, 488, 493, 528, 530, 550
Carmelites of Mary Immaculate, 42, 217, 460, 530
Carmody, Bp. Edmond, 376, 383, **397**, 418
Carmon, Bp. Dominic, **397**, 418, 427
Carter, Pres. Jimmy, 236, 270
Carthusians, 149, 154, 177, 205, 222, 458, 460, 467
Cary, Bp. Liam, 374, **397**
Casa Santa Maria, 263
Casimir, 166, 205, 214, 358, 462, 471
Cassock, 180, 215
Castel Gandolfo, 29, 56, 77, 240, 261, 262, 483
Castrillon Hoyos, Card. Dario, **279**, 295-297
Casuistry, 133
Catacombs, 133, 181, 285, 318
Catechesi Tradendae, 244
Catechesis, 9, 39, 65, 66, 86-89, 110, **133**, 244-246, 277, 422, 427, 428, 455, 539, 558, 606, 608, 609
Catechism of the Catholic Church, 85, **87**-89, 110-113, 133, 227, 233, 244, 279, 291, 333, 579
Catechists World Statistics, 335
Catechumenate (RCIA), 133, 192, 505, 556
Categories of Cardinals, 294-295
Cathari, 145, 222, 223

Cathedra, 92, 133, 145, 246, 387
Cathedrals in the U.S., 31, 387-389
Cathedraticum, 133
Catherine of Siena, St., **107**, 166, 205, 206, 212-214, 387, 425, 473, 474, 487, 488
Catholic Action, 207, 212, 227, 238, 240, 248, 249, 279, 280, 341, 361, 390, 495, 553, 580
Catholic Associations, 341
Catholic Biblical Association of America, 97, 499
Catholic Book Publishers Association, 499
Catholic Charities Services, 508, 522
Catholic Church Extension Society, 356, 414, 431, 567
Catholic Daughters of the Americas, 499, 560
Catholic Organizations, 258, 312, 340-342, 362, 424, 426, 427, 496, 498, 504, 509
Catholic Population of the United States, 435-438
Catholic Population World, 335
Catholic Press Association Awards, 573-574
Catholic Relief Services, 10, 15, 86, 269, 422, 423, 563, 564
Catholic Schools and Students in the U.S., 535-545
Catholic Theological Society of America, 500
Catholic Universities and Colleges in the U.S., 539-544
Catholic University of America, 51-54, 189, 226, 247, 356, 357, 360, 390, 410, 411, 499, 539, 545, 548, 556-560, 564
Catholic World Statistics, 335
Catholic Youth Organizations, 496
Catholicos, 584, 592, 593
Causes of Saints, Congr. of the, 215-217, 256, 295, 297
Ce, Card. Marco, 51
CELAM, 277, 279, 281, 284, 285, 289, 305, 339, 425
Celata, Abp. Pier Luigi, 259
Celebret, 133
Celestine I, Pope, 229, 234
Celestine II, Pope, 235, 237
Celestine III, Pope, 235
Celestine IV, Pope, 235
Celestine V, Pope, 45, 236
Celibacy, 38, 46, 57, 103, 108, **133**, 196, 219-221, 242, 250, 299, 320, 328, 362, 495, 595
Celli, Abp. Claudio, 259, 260, 263
Cenacle, 38, 58, 62, **134**, 211, 471, 495, 526-529, 531
Censorship of Books, **134**, 144, 149
Censures, 128, **134**, 140, 152, 154, 186, 239
Centesimus Annus, 114-116, 118, 250
Central African Republic, 243, 265, 268, 292, 303, 336, 339
Central America, 44, 243, 244, 297, 300, 305, 307, 311, 312, 320, 321, 335, 339, 365, 413, 430, 489, 589
Central Statistics Office, 255, 259, 263
Cepeda Escobedo, Bp. Jose A., **397**, 425, 452
Ceylon, 214, 313, 318
Chad, 13, 265, 268, 292, **303**, 336, 339
Chair of Peter, 106, 171
Chalcedon, Council of, 108, 220, 249, 273, 307, 344, 592

Chaldean Catholics, 405
Chalice, 72, 128, 139, 143, 179, **181**, 196, 215, 349, 351
Chancery Offices of U.S. Archdioceses and Dioceses, 384-386
Chant, Gregorian, **176**, 182, 220
Chapel, 18, 29, 51, 54, 123, 124, **134**, 148, 150, 151, 182, 245, 259, 297, 348, 352, 368, 390, 391, 393, 446, 469, 514, 519, 525, 556, 574
Chaplain, 18, 21, 28, 51, **134**, 189, 210, 241, 280, 281, 287, 290, 355, 396, 398, 399, 404, 407, 412, 416, 502, 507
Chaplains'Aid Assoc., 500
Chaplet, 134
Chappetto, Bp. Raymond F., 375, **397**-398
Chaput, O.F.M. Cap., Abp. Charles, 376, 380, 381, **398**, 422, 429
Charismatic Movement, 41, 357
Charismatic Renewal, 53, **134**, 502, 505, 525
Charisms, 90, 103, 126, **135**, 160
Charities Catholic, 32, 501, 508-510, 520, 522-525, 563
Charities, Office of Papal, 260
Charity, Srs. of, 486-488
Charles Borromeo, 54, 170, **205**, 212-214, 248, 280, 394-403, 406-408, 411, 413, 415, 443, 464, 472, 484, 488, 546
Charles Borromeo, Srs. of, 488
Charron, Bp. Joseph, 376, **398**, 418
Chastity, 17, 111, 129, 133, **135**, 137, 142, 144, 149, 154, 156, 158, 160, 199, 201, 212, 458, 491, 501, 572
Chasuble, 180, 215
Chavez, Bp. Gilbert, **398**, 418, 425
Chedid, Bp. John, 380, **398**, 418
Cheong Jin-Suk, Card., **279**-280, 295-297
Chile, 22, 71, 214, 243, 245, 261, 265, 268, 271, 281, 285, 291, 296, **303**, 336, 365, 429, 547, 566
China, 8, 11, 12, 21, 214, 225-227, 238, 240, 244, 249-251, 261, 265, 268, 279, 294, **303**, 304, 316, 319, 330, 336, 346, 347, 361, 416, 417, 428, 429, 475, 501, 547, 589
Chirograph, **135**, 260, 261
Choby, Bp. David, 379, **398**
Choir, 51, 54, 130, **182**, 184, 206, 297, 349
Chomnycky, Bp. Paul, 383, **398**
Chretienne, Srs. of, 472
Chrism, 34, **135**, 150, 166, 172, 187, 192, 343
Chrism Mass, 34, 150, 166
Christ Society of, 460, 467
Christ the King (Feast), 161, 162, 170, 171
Christ the King, Missionary Sisters of, 472
Christ the King, Rural Parish Workers, 493
Christ the King, Sister Servants, 472
Christ the King, Sisters of St. Francis, 477, 487
Christensen, Bp. Peter, 383, **398**
Christian, Bp. Francis, 378, **398**
Christian Brothers, 83, 396, 460, 467, 527, 528, 539-541, 561, 562
Christian Church, U.S., 596
Christian Doctrine, Sisters of Our Lady of, 472
Christian Education, Religious of, 472
Christian Initiation, 88, 133, 166, 185,

186, 189, 191, 192, 505, 556
Christian Instruction, Brothers of, 460, 467, 544, 561
Christian Schools, Brothers of the, 208, 251, 460, 539, 543
Christian Unity, Pontifical Council for, 258, 578
Christians Baptized, Reception into, 335, 432, 439-440
Church (Defined), 210
Christifideles Laici, 244, 275, 340
Christmas, 17-21, 23, 114, 129, 144, 159, 161, 162, 165, **170**-174, 179, 180, 221, 241, 242, 262, 305, 349, 350, 368, 557, 562, 605
Christopher Awards, 575
Christophers, 500, 561, 564, 568
Christus Dominus, 229, 421
Chronicles, 96, 99
Chronology of Church History, 218-229
Chronology of U.S. Church History, 352-357
Church-State Decisions of the Supreme Court, 366, 532
Church State Relations, 366-369
Church Tax Exemption, 370
Ciborium, 181, 214
Cincture, 180
Cipitria y Barriola, 252, 253
Cipriani Thorne, Card. Luis, **280**, 295-297
Circumcision, 132, **135**, 174, 218, 605
Circumincession, 135
Cisneros, Bp. Octavio, 422
Cistercian Nuns, 472, 486, 487
Cistercian Order, 107
Cistone, Bp. Joseph, 382, **398**
Civil Rights, 16, 54, 357, 362, 369, 499, 532
Clancy, Card. Edward, 51
Clare of Assisi, 213, 215
Claretian Missionary Sisters, 472
Claretians, 205, 290, 291, 391, 461, 467, 486, 488, 560, 561, 563, 564
Claretianum, 290
Clark, Bp. Edward, 378, **398**
Clark, Bp. Matthew, 381, **398**
Clemens, Abp. Josef, 255, 258, 261
Clement I, Pope, 170, 205, 213, 218
Clement II, Pope, 222, 235
Clement III, Pope, 235, 237
Clement IV, Pope, 235
Clement V, Pope, 229, 236, 237
Clement VI, Pope, 236, 237
Clement VII, Pope, 160, 236, 237
Clement VIII, Pope, 188, 236, 245, 256
Clement IX, Pope, 236
Clement X, Pope, 236
Clement XI, Pope, 173, 225, 236, 550, 573
Clement XII, Pope, 142, 158, 225, 236, 237
Clement XIII, Pope, 174, 236, 246
Clement XIV, Pope, 225, 236, 246
Clergy, Congregation of the, 257, 289
Clergy Sex Abuse, 43, 69, 260
Clericalism, 135
Clerics of St. Viator, 466
Clerics Regular, 207, 208, 459, 461, 466, 468
Clerics Regular Minor, 207, 461, 468
Clerics Regular of St. Paul, 459
Clinton, Pres. Bill, 372
Cloister, **135**, 149
Cluny, 171, 204, 207, 221, 222, 480, 486
Coakley, Bp. Paul S., 382, **398**
Coccopalmerio, Card. Francesco, 258, 260, **280**

Coadjutor Bishop, **274**, 381, 453
Code of Canon Law, 74, **125**-128, 134, 135, 140, 142, 143, 145, 177, 179, 185, 186, 191, 193, 200, 202, 227, 228, 239, 241, 245, 258, 274-276, 283, 347, 351, 458, 489, 494, 579, 594
Code of Canon Law of Oriental Church, 258
Coins Vatican, 262
Coleman, Bp. George, 377, 379, **398**, 417
Colettines, 472, 488
Collegiality, 92, 93, 113, 127, **135**, 196, 242, 362,
Collins, Card. Thomas, 35, 39, **280**, 295-297
Colombia, 39, 77, 214, 242, 243, 261, 265, 268, 279, 282, 284, 289, 290, 292, 296, **304**, 307, 336, 339, 342, 363, 417, 469, 475, 489, 547
Colorado, 12, 36, 82, 84, 322, 373, 375, 384, 388, 389, 391, 395, 403, 413, 419, 421, 422, 426, 433, 435, 439, 469, 470, 477, 500, 511, 521, 526, 535, 545, 552, 560
Color Liturgical, 180
Colossians, 96, 103
Columban, St., Society of, 461, 462
Columban Missionary Sisters, 472
Columbian Squires, 497, 564
Columbus, Knights of, 10, 50, 356, 361, 497, 507, 551, 557, 562
Comastri, Card. Angelo, 260
Comboni Missionaries, 461, 573
Comboni Missionary Sisters, 472
Combonian Missionaries, 467
Comensoli, Geltrude, 252
Commandments of God, 149
Commissions Pontifical, 260
Communion of Saints, 88, 109, 110, 132, **135**, 204, 211, 603
Communism, **136**, 226, 227, 240, 244, 249, 250, 257, 312, 324, 327, 345
Company of Mary, 209, 464, 480
Company of St. Paul, 490
Company of St. Ursula, 204, 490
Compline, 136
Conclave, 54, 55, 70, 150, 238, 242, 276, 278, 286, 611
Concluding Rite, 179
Concordat of Worms, 136, 222
Concupiscence, 136
Confederation of Latin American Religious (CLAR), 489
Conference of Major Superiors in U.S., 489
Conference of Major Superiors of Men in U.S., 489
Conference of Major Superiors U.S., 489
Conferences Episcopal, 17, 21, 53, 68, 81, 186, 195, 245, 264, 275, 285, 294, 310, 336-339, 420
Confessional, 109, 156, 182, **195**, 310, 597, 598,
Confirmation, 86, 88, 127, 131, 135, 142, 150, 152, 185, 186, 189-**192**, 215, 223, 228, 243, 253, 327, 343, 350, 361, 494
Confraternity of Christian Doctrine, 97, 226, 238, 361, 500
Congo, 17, 243, 265, 267-269, 271, 285, 292, 296, **304**, 336, 339, 548
Congo Republic, 243, 292, **304**
Congregation of Blessed Sacrament, 460, 467, 479, 557
Congregation of Christian Brothers, 460, 540

Congregation of Clerics Regular, 466
Congregation of Divine Worship, 195
Congregation of Marians, 392, 557
Congregation of Mary, 466-468, 478, 480, 484
Congregation of Missionary, 471
Congregation of Monte Corona, 460
Congregation of Notre Dame, 363, 441
Congregation of Our Lady, 470-472, 477, 484, 495
Congregation of Our Lady of Lourdes, 477
Congregation of Sacred Heart, 466, 467
Congregation of Sisters Marianites of Holy, 542
Congregation of St. Joseph, 463, 467, 480
Congregation of St. Ottilien, 459
Congregationalists, 596
Congresses, Eucharistic, 212, 260, 276, 277, 284, 287, 292
Conjugal Covenant, 198
Conjugal Love, **198**, 199
Conley, Bp. James, 376, 395, **398**
Conlon, Bp. Robert, 378, 383, **398**, 504
Connecticut, 53, 354, 367, 371, 373, 389, 391, 421, 422, 433, 435, 439, 501, 507, 511, 521, 522, 526, 535, 545, 569
Connell, Card. Desmond, **280**, 295-297
Connolly, Bp. Thomas, 375, **398**, 418
Conscience, 5, 6, 8, 10, 19, 27, 35, 50, 58, 77, 78, 84, 92, 113, 114, 119, 126, 131, 133, **136**, 149, 155, 156, 159, 178, 195, 199, 203, 257, 300, 305, 574, 575, 579, 614,
Consecrated Life, 14, 25, 37, 86, 127, 135-137, 149, 152, 165, 167, 188, 197, 198, 244, 257, 275, 278, 281, 282, 284-287, 289-291, 293, 397, 402, 415, 422, 446, 455, 458, 489, 557
Consistory, 21, 26, 29, 70, 71, **136**, 188, 228, 243, 290, 292
Consolata Missionaries, 461, 467, 557
Consolata Missionary Sisters, 472, 487
Constantinople I, Council of, 220
Constantinople II, Council of, 220
Constantinople III, Council of, 221
Constantinople IV, Council of, 221
Consubstantiation, 136
Contemplative Sisters, 477
Contraception , 78, 82, 114, 117, **136**, 235, 323, 357, 362; see also Humanae Vitae
Contrition, **136**, 137, 141, 151, 191, 195, 196
Contumely, 137
Conventual Franciscan Fathers, 565
Conventual Franciscan Friars, 391, 392, 528, 529
Conventual Franciscans, 397, 404, 563
Cope, St. Marianne, 165, **363**
Cope, 209
Coppa, Card. Giovanni, **280**, 295-297
Coptic Catholic Church, 345, 347
Cor Unum, Pontifical Council, 41, 258, 280, 290
Cordes, Card. Paul-Josef, 261, **280**, 295-297 422
Cordileone, Abp. Salvatore, 15, 16, 20, 24, 28, 32, 380, 382, **398**, 422,
Corinthians, 96, 103, 131, 134, 218
Corporal Works of Mercy, 508
Corpus Christi (Feast), 163, 171, 173
Corpus Iuris Canonici, 137
Corpus Iuris Civilis, 220
Corrada del Rio, Bp. Alvara, 383, **398**,

425
Corsica, 214
Costa Rica, 13, 243, 265, 268, 277, **305**, 336, 412
Costello, Bp. Thomas, **398**-399, 418
Cote, Bp. Michael, 380, **399**
Côte d'Ivoire See Ivory Coast
Cotey, Bp. Arnold, **399**, 418
Cottier, O.P., Card. Georges, 272, **280**
Council of European Bishops Conferences, 11, 278, 339
Council of Major Superiors, 357, 489
Council of Major Superiors of Women, 357, 489
Counsels Evangelical, 111, 131, **137**, 149, 158, 160, 458, 489, 490, 492, 493, 495
Countries of the World Catholic Church (Statistics), 335
Countries of the World, Catholic Church, 335
Coyle, Bp. Robert J., 383, **399**
Coyne, Bp. Christopher, 272, **399**
Cozzens, Bp. Andrew H., 381, **399**
Creeds, 93, **109**, 140, 582, 598
Cremation, 132, 137
Crete, 103, 133, 237, 513, 583, 589, 590
Crib, 22, 137
Croatia, 10, 215, 233, 244, 261, 265, 268, 278, 296, 301, **305**, 336, 345, 346, 472, 548, 549, 567
Cronin, Abp. Daniel, 377, 378, **399**, 418
Crosier, **137**, 214, 215, 461
Crosier Fathers, 461
Crucifix, 63, **182**, 214, 215
Cruets, 182
Crusades, 222, 273
Cruz, Bp. Manuel, 375, **399**, 425
Cuba, 7, 35, 205, 214, 228, 233, 244, 245, 265, 268, 287, 292, 296, 300, **305**, 336, 398, 399, 401, 405, 417, 472, 507, 517, 547,
Cullen, Bp. Edward, 374, **399**, 418
Cultural Heritage Commission of the Church, 282, 285, 293
Culture, Pontifical Council for, 258, 259, 282, 288
Pontifical Council for Culture, 258, 259, 282, 288
Cummins, Bp. John, 380, **399**, 418, 562
Cunningham, Bp. Robert, 379, **399**
Cupich, Bp. Blaise, 381, 383, **399**, 422
Cura Animarum, 137
Curia, Diocesan, 137
Curia, Roman, 9, 17, 18, 21, 26, 30, 37, 53, 54, 69, 71, 74, 79, 116, 125, 131, 136-138, 144, 146, 152, 195, 238, 239, 241, 242, 245, **255**-261, 263, 273, 274, 276, 280, 281, 283, 288, 297, 335, 406, 417, 429, 432, 558, 567, 572
Curlin, Bp. William, 376, **399**, 418
Curry, Bp. Thomas, 379, **399**, 422
Cursillo Movement, 279, 496, 560,
Curtiss, Bp. Elden, 378, 380, **399**
Custos, 67, 137, 244
Cyprian, 107, 169, 206, 219, 253
Cyprus, 11, 74, 105, 106, 233, 256, 265, 268, **305**, 345, 347, 583, 585, 589, 590
Cyril and Methodius, 162, 165, **206**, 210, 212, 214, 244, 247, 250, 327, 336, 350, 364, 390, 397, 400, 442, 473, 500, 545, 546
Cyril of Alexandria, St., 107, 167, 215
Cyril of Jerusalem, St., 107, 166, 215,
Czech Republic, 233, 244, 265, 268, 280, 281, 294, 296, **305**, 336, 346, 482, 549

D

Da Cunha, Bp. Edgar M. S.V.D., 380, **399**, 425
Dachau, 211, 216, 492
Daily, Bp. Thomas, 380, **399**, 418
Dalai Lama, 616
Dalmatic, 180
Dal Toso, Msgr. Pietro, 259, 260
Daly, Bp. James, 51-52
Daly, Bp. Thomas, **399**, 418
Damasceno Assis, Card. Raymundo, **277**, 295-297, 339
Damasus I, Pope, 170, 206, 229, 234
Damasus II, Pope, 235
Damien de Veuster, St., 252, 253, 356, **363**
Dancing and Worship, 187
Danneels, Card. Godfried, **280**, 295-297
Darmaatmadja, S.J., Card. Julius, **280**, 295-297
Dates and Events in Catholic History, 218-227
Daughters of Charity, 124, 169, 430, 469, 471, 483, 510
Daughters of Charity of St. Vincent de Paul, 124, 472, 510
Daughters of Divine Love, 473, 487
Daughters of Mary, 208, 209, 211, 480, 481, 492, 550
Daughters of Mary Help of Christians, 208, 209, 481, 550
Daughters of Mary Immaculate, 211, 481
Daughters of Our Lady, 205, 209, 481, 484, 492
Daughters of Our Lady of Fatima, 492
Daughters of Our Lady of Mercy, 209, 481
Daughters of St. Francis of Assisi, 474
Day of Atonement, 605
Day of Prayer, 15, 20, 49, 163, 165, 245, 607, 612, 615
De Castro, Cardinal Manuel Monteiro, 258, 260, **286**, 295-297
De Giorgi, Card. Salvatore, 216, **280**, 295-297
De Paolis, Card. Velasio, 260, **280**-281, 295-297
De Simone, Bp. Louis, 399, 418
Deacon, 82, 107, 156, 165, 167, 168, 180, 190, 191, **196**-198, 200, 202, 206, 211, 215, 218, 276-279, 281-286, 288-292, 345, 425, 427, 503, 504, 575
Deacon U.S. Statistics, 432
Deacons Permanent, 86, **197**, 198, 298, 427, 432, 503
Dead Sea Scrolls, 98, 105
Deaf, 60, 212, 368, 370, 508, 509, 520, 524, 560
Dean of Cardinals, 292, 295
Death Penalty, 85, 133, 323, 331, 500, 575, 610
Decalogue, 39, 110, 111, 137, 569, 605
Decretals, 125, 221
Decretum, 126, 222
Deeley, Bp. Robert, 375, **399**
Dei Verbum, 93, 103, 141, 229
Delaware, 357, 358, 373, 387, 421, 433, 435, 439, 512, 521, 527, 535
Del Blanco Prieto, Abp. Felix, 260
Delegates Apostolic, 264, 267, 273, 274
Delly III, Card. Emmanuel, 52
Del Riego, Bp. Rutilio 382, **399**, 425, 429
Dendinger, Bp. William J., 377, **399**
Denmark, 40, 204, 214, 243, 265-268, 272, **306**, 311, 312, 470

Denton, Adm. Jeremiah, 52
Deposit of Faith, 87, 92, 94, **138**, 203, 230,
Deshotel, Bp. John D., 376, **399**
De Simone, B. Louis, **399**-400, 419
Deus Caritas Est, 147, 228, 233, 250
Deutero-Isaiah, 100
Deuteronomic Code, 98
Deuteronomy, 96, 98, 605
Deutero-Zechariah, 101
DeWane, Bp. Frank, 384, **400**, 431
Diabolic Obsession, 149
Diabolic Possession, 152
Diaconate, 71, 133, **196-198**, 221, 242, 344, 350, 427-429, 455, 503
Dialogue Ecumenical, *See* Ecumenical Dialogue
Dialogue Interreligious, *See* Interreligious Dialogue
Dias, Card. Ivan, 261, 268, **281**, 295, 296
Diaspora, 105, 346, 589
Diaz, Amb. Miguel, 269
Didache, 106, 110, 125, 219
Didascalia, 125
Didymus (Thomas), 106
Diego Juan, St., 170, 451
Dignitas Connubii, 203
Dignitatis Humanae, 142, 229, 243
Dilecti Amici, 244
Di Lorenzo, Bp. Francis, 377, 381, **400**
Di Marzio, Bp. Nicholas, 375, **400**
Dimino, Bp. Joseph, 384, **400**, 419
DiNardo, Card. Daniel, **281**, 295-297, 377, 382, 400, 422
Dino, Bp. Gerald N., 384, **400**
DiNoia, Abp. Augustine, 16, 256, 260, 261, **400**, 417
Diocesan and Interdiocesan Seminaries, 544-545,
Diocesan Bishops, 127, 137, 145, 172, 273, 274, 298, 421, 495
Diocesan Curia, 137
Diocesan Newspapers, 551
Diocesan Synod, 158
Dioceses, Canadian, 445, 447
Dioceses, Mexico, 451-454
Dioceses, U.S., 32, 189, 204, 360, 363,
Dioceses, World, 335
Diocletian, 206, 207, 209, 219,
Directory on Ecumenism, 191, 194, 579,
Di Ruberto, Abp. Michele, 260, 261
Disabilities, 15, 57, 76, 225-227, 308, 314, 321, 326, 368, 450, 492, 509, 520-524, 563
Discalced Augustinians, 467
Discalced Carmelite Fathers, 556
Discalced Carmelite Friars, 393, 560
Discalced Carmelites, 108, 467, 550
Disciple, 30, 75, 105, 106, 111, 120, 122, 138, 211, 218, 221
Disciples of Christ, 133, 582, 596, 597, 599
Diskos, 351
District of Columbia, 374, 389, 391, 420, 421, 433, 512, 522, 527, 535, 545
Divine Compassion Sisters, 473
Divine Love, See Daughters of Divine Love, 473, 487
Divine Office, 136, 160, 162, 166, 172, 173, 176, 182-184, 186, 188, 239, 349
Divine Zeal Daughters, 473, 488
Divino Afflante Spiritu, 97, 104, 105, 249, 500
Divorce, 80, 81, 199, **201**, 211, 212, 314, 574
Divorced and Remarried Catholics, 79-81, 202, 203

Diwali, 615
Djibouti, 265, 268, 306
Doctors of the Church, **106**-108, 114, 133, 165, 170, 185, 204
Doctrine of Justification, 587, 598, 599, 603
Doctrine of the Faith, Congr. for the, 189, 256, 260, 295, 297, 381, 382, 406, 417, 601
Doherty, Bp. Timothy L., 378, **400**
Dolan, Card. Timothy M., 8, **281**, 295-297, 379, 380, 400, 421, 422
Dominic, 107, 168, **206**, 212, 214, 215, 223, 249, 251, 280, 288, 353, 379, 380, 397, 407, 408, 418, 419, 426, 461, 464, 473, 474, 481, 493, 512, 519, 539
Dominican Nuns, 473
Dominican Nuns of Perpetual Rosary, 473
Dominican Republic, 6, 42, 70, 214, 243, 265, 266, 268, 284, 292, 296, **306**, 312, 337, 396, 418, 429, 507, 547
Dominican Sisters, 473, 474, 539-544
Dominican Sisters of Charity, 473
Dominican Sisters of Hope, 473
Dominican Sisters of Our Lady, 473
Dominican Sisters of Peace, 473
Dominican Sisters of Sparkill, 543
Dominican Sisters of St. Catherine of Siena, 473
Dominican Sisters of St. Mary, 542
Dominicans, 148, 154, 155, 168, 177, 206, 210, 216, 281, 313, 315, 391, 400, 403 430, 449, 458, 461, 467, 473, 486, 487, 502, 539, 564, 566
Do Nascimento, Card. Alexandre, **281**, 295-297
Donatism, 219, 220,
Donato, Bp. Thomas, 380, **400**
Donnelly, Bp. Robert, 52
Dooher Bp. John, 375, **400**
Doran, Bp. Thomas, 381, **400**, 575
Dormition, 350, 462,
Dorothy, Inst. of, 474
Douay-Rheims Bible, 97
Double Effect Principle, 139, 140
Doueihi, Bp. Stephen, 382, **400**, 418
Dougherty, Bp. John, **400**, 419
Doxology, **139**, 156, 178, 179, 187,
Driscoll, Bp. Michael, 375, **400**
Duca, Bp. Michael, 336, 383, **400**
Duffy, Bp. Paul, **400**, 419
Duka, Card. Dominik, **281**, 295, 296
Dulia, 139, 155,
Dulles, S.J., Card. Avery, 297, 575
Du Maine, Bp. Pierre, 382, **400**, 419
Dunne, Bp. John, 376, 381, **400**
Dupre, Bp. Thomas, 383, **400**, 419
Dziwisz, Card. Stanislaw, 45, **281**, 295, 296

E

Easter, 34, 56, 60, 72, 75, 112, 130, 139, 150, 151, 159, 161, 162, 164, 166, 167, **172**, 180, 184, 187, 192, 193, 209, 219, 221, 262, 344, 349, 557, 587, 588, 591
Easter Candle, 172
Easter Controversy, **139**, 219, 221
Easter Duty, 139
Easter Triduum, 34, **161**, 166, 172, 187
Easter Vigil, 34, 139, 150, 166, **172**, 187, 192
Eastern Catholic Churches, 3, 134, 177, 202, 229, 256, 273, 274, **343**-351, 421, 428, 576, 579, 589, 591, 592
Eastern Code of Canon Law, 351

Eastern Jurisdictions, 346, 348
Ecclesia de Eucharistia, 194, 250
Ecclesia Dei, 187-189, 233, 256, 260, 279, 283, 289
Ecclesiastes, 96, 100
Ecclesiastical Faculties, 4, 548, 549
Ecclesiasticus, 100
Economic Affairs of Holy See, 285
Economy of Salvation, 120, 138
Ecstasy, 139
Ecthesis, 221
Ecuador, 214, 243, 248, 265, 268, 282, 291, 293, 296, **307**, 337, 396, 547
Ecumenical Agencies, 580, 581
Ecumenical Councils, 59, 122, 125, 130, 137, 148, 228, 229, 331, 585, 588, 592
Ecumenical Patriarchate, 576, 589, 590, 592
Ecumenical Statements, 586, 587
Ecumenism, 34, 37, 41, 52, 57, 61, 122, 127, **139**, 159, 191, 194, 229, 230, 241, 250, 258, 281, 283, 285, 363, 446, 501, 576-616
Education, Congregation for Catholic, 25, 45, 233, 257, 270, 400, 409, 547, 548
Education, Catholic U.S., 532-547
Education, Catholic World Statistics, 335
Education, Religious (Statistics), 335, 432 Edyvean, Bp. Walter, 375, **400**-401
Egan, Card. Edward, 259, **281**, 295-297, 375, 380, 381, 401, 419
Egypt, 6, 7, 12, 23, 26, 43, 60, 98, 100, 101, 104, 106, 107, 173, 219, 244, 256, 265, 268, 286, 296, **307**, 308, 328, 344-348, 488, 586, 589, 600, 605, 612
Eijk, Card. Willem, **281**, 295-297, 338
Eileton, 351,
Ejaculation (Aspiration), 131
El Salvador, 214, 243, 244, 265, 268, 277, 279, 286, 289, **307**, 337, 469
Elijah, 99, 100
Elizabeth Ann Seton, St., 163, 165, **206**, 241, 354, 357, 359, 362, 390-392, 472
Elizondo, Bp. Eusebio, 20, 422,
Elya, Bp. John, 380, **401**, 419
Emblems of Saints, 215
Enchiridion Indulgentiarum, 145
Encyclicals, 105, 112-117, **139**, 182, 208, 227, 232, 233, 238-242, 244-249, 263, 450,
Encyclicals, Benedict XVI, 251
Encyclicals, Francis, 251
Encyclicals, John Paul II, 250-251
England, 7, 33, 45-47, 53, 54, 63, 97, 107, 125, 129, 142, 150, 151, 155, 205-207, 209, 214, 220-227, 233, 235, 237, 239, 242, 247, 253, 272, 282, 286, 296, **307**, 308, 310, 311, 314, 321, 326, 334, 337, 342, 352-354, 358-360, 375, 395-397, 429, 441, 460, 463, 464, 466, 470, 473-475, 478-482, 485, 491, 496, 505, 559, 566, 572, 574, 577, 596-602
Enthronement of the Sacred Heart, 154, 501
Envy, 133, **139**, 157
Eparch, 274, 277, 286, 288, 379-381, 383, 397, 400, 405, 409, 412, 413, 417, 443, 445, 453
Ephesians, 96, 103
Epiclesis, 139
Epikeia, 139
Epilepsy, 206, 212
Epimanikia, 351
Epiphany, 161, 162, 165, 171, **172**
Epiphany (Feast), 172

Episcopal Church, 580, 582, 596-598, 601, 602
Episcopal Conferences, 3, 17, 21, 53, 68, 81, 186, 195, 245, 264, 275, 285, 294, 310, 336-339, 420
Episcopal Vicar, 137, 274, 287, 288, 394, 403, 414
Epistles of St. Paul, 95
Equestrian Order, 282, 287, 288, 402, 417, 572
Erdö, Card. Peter, **281**, 295, 296, 337, 339
Eritrea, 256, 265, 268, **308**, 339, 344, 345, 347
Errazuriz Ossa, Card. Francisco, **281**, 295, 297
Errico Gaetano, 252, 254
Eschatology, 140
Espinosa, Bl. Maria Ines, 255
Estepa Llaurens, Card. Jose Manuel, **282**, 295, 297
Estevez, Bp. Felipe, 379, **401**, 425
Esther, 96, 97, **99**, 469, 524, 528, 605
Estonia, 11, 244, 265, 266, 268, **308**, 589
Etchegaray, Card. Roger, 260, **282**, 295-297
Eternal Word Television Network (EWTN), 82, 562
Ethiopia, 105, 106, 209, 253, 256, 265, 268, 306, **308**, 337, 339, 344, 345, 347, 583
Etienne, Bp. Paul D., 376, **401**
Eucharist, 48-50, 58, 62, 63, 67, 79, 80, 88, 103, 107, 112, 127, 129, 136, 137, 139-141, 143, 144, 146, 149-152, 154, 157, 159, 171, 172, 175, 178, 179, 181-186, 189, **192**, 196, 200, 202, 203, 217, 223, 226, 233, 239, 248, 250, 254, 275, 350, 421, 463, 474, 476, 477, 484, 491, 492, 502, 578, 582, 584, 587, 588, 590, 595, 596, 598, 600-602
Eucharist, Religious of, 474
Eucharistic Banquet, 59, 159, 178, 585
Eucharistic Celebration, 62, 186, 193, 194, 587
Eucharistic Devotion, 193
Eucharistic Franciscan Missionary Sisters, 474
Eucharistic Minister, 156, 179, 562
Eucharistic Missionaries of St. Dominic, 473
Eucharistic Prayer, 130, 139, 178, 179, 184, 187, 592
Eucharistic Sacrifice and Banquet, 178-189
Eudist Sisters, 482
Eudists, 208, 461, 467
Euphrasia Eluvathingal, 217
Europe, 10, 11, 15, 19, 27, 36, 37, 39, 42, 69, 70, 104, 107, 116, 125, 142, 168, 173, 188, 205, 206, 214, 221, 223-225, 227, 228, 232, 244, 248, 256, 257, 259, 267, 275, 296, 297, 299-303, 305-307, 309, 310, 312, 315, 317-321, 323-329, 331, 335, 339, 345-347, 353, 364, 395, 409, 418, 422-424, 429, 489, 498, 499, 550, 568, 589, 592, 595, 597, 599
Eusebio Kino, 353, 358, 364, 372
Euthanasia, 15, 19, 27, 28, 40, 85, 113, 117, **140**, 300, 320, 362
Eutychianism, 220
Evangelists, 3, 102, **104**-106, 180, 204, 262, 350, 504
Evangelium Vitae, 89, 112, 113, 133, 199, 250

Evangelization of Peoples, Congr. of, 256
Evans, Bp. Robert C., 381, **401**
Evening Prayer, 138, 148, 160-162, 174, **176**
Ex Opere Operantis, 140
Ex Opere Operatio, 140
Exarch, 42, 274, 283, 301, 379, 381, 383, 405, 417, 445
Excommunication, 59, 130, 131, 134, **140**, 142, 143, 145, 155, 156, 186, 201, 218, 220, 223, 225, 240, 328, 585
Exegesis, 42, 103, 104, 238, 239, 615
Exodus, 22, 49, 96, 98, 101, 104, 329, 605, 606
Exorcism, **140**, 152, 197
Exsultet, 172
Extension Society, 356, 414, 431, 557
Extreme Unction, 159, **196**
Ezekiel, 96, 100, **101**
Ezra, 96, 97, **99**, 101, 102, 605

F

Fabre, Bp. Shelton, 380, **401**, 422, 426
Fabric of St. Peter, 53, 260, 261, 280
Facilities for Children and Adults with Disabilities, 520-524
Facilities for Retired and Aged Persons, 4, 511-519
Falcão, Card. José Freire, **282**, 295-297
Family Pontifical Council for the, 25, 40, 258, 291,
Farina, Card. Raffaele, 43, 260, 272, **282**, 295-297, 567
Farrell, Bp. Kevin, 376, 383, **401**
Fasting, 5, 15, 112, 128, 163, 165, 171, 246, 605, 612
Fatima, 3, 9, 77, **123**, 167, 227, 254, 342, 390, 392, 393, 461, 492, 506, 507, 511, 527, 530, 557, 560, 564, 566, 573, 615
Favalora, Abp. John, 374, 379, **401**
Feast Days and Holy Days, 171-174
Federation of St. Benedict, 469
Federation of St. Gertrude, 469, 487
Federation of St. Scholastica, 469
Felician Sisters, 474, 540, 541, 544
Felix, Card. Kelvin Edward, 70-71, **282**, 295, 296
Felix, Congr. of, 474
Felix of Nicosia, 252
Fellhauer, Bp. David, 384, **401**
Fernandes de Araujo, Card. Serafim, 269, 282, 295-297
Fernández de Valladolid, Bl. Cristóbal of Saint Catherine, 216, 255
Festing, Fra Matthew, 572
Fidei Depositum, 87, 138
Fidei donum, 249, 289
Fides et Ratio, 250, 615
Fiji, 243, 265, 266, 268, **309**, 338, 395, 410, 418, 419
Filioque, 107, 588, 590
Filippini Religious, 474
Films, 51, 568-569, 575
Filoni, Card. Fernando, 49, 78, 256, 257, **282**
Finland, 214, 243, 265, 268, **309**, 587, 589
Finn, Bp. Robert, 79, 378, **401**
Fiorenza, Abp. Joseph, 286, 377, 382, **401**, 419, 533
Fisherman's Ring, 141
Fisichella, Abp. Salvatore, 259, 260
Fitzgerald, Bp. Michael J., 380, **401**
Fitzsimons Bp. George 52, 382
Five Hundred Twenty-two Spanish

Martyrs, 215-216, 255
Flanagan, Bp. Thomas, **401**, 419
Flesey, Bp. John W., 380, **401**
Fliss, Bp. Patrick, 383, **401**, 419
Flores, Bp. Cirilo, 380, **401**, 425
Flores, Bp. Daniel, 383, **401**, 424
Flores, Bp. Patrick, 382, **401**, 424
Florida, 253, 269, 272, 300, 305, 324,
  352-354, 358, 363, 366, 373, 389, 391,
  405, 410, 421, 422, 426, 433, 435, 439,
  469, 480, 495, 509, 512, 521, 522, 527,
  532, 535, 545, 553
Flynn, Abp. Harry, 83, 378, 382, **401**,
  419
Focherini Bl. Odoardo, 216, 255
Folda, Bp. John T., 377, **401**
Foley, Bp. David, 375, 376, **401**-402
Foley, Thomas, 52
Foreign Missions, 207, 213, 337, 356,
  459, 461, 464, 465, 467, 476, 477
Foreign Missions U.S. Personnel, 430
Formosus, 234
Forty Hours Devotion, 141, 208
Foys, Bp. Roger, 376, **402**
Francesco Zirano, 216, 255
Francis, Pope, 9, 19, 22, 27, 40, 41, 69,
  71-73, 74, 75, **231**, 576-577, 585, 592-
  594, 600, 604, 610, 611, 614
  Beatifications, 232, 255
  Canonizations, 7, 41, 71-73, 232, 252
  Encyclicals, 232, 250
  Life, 231-232
  Travels, 56-63, 232
Francis de Sales, St., **108**, 165, 207, 212-
  214, 225, 249, 278, 282, 387, 388, 405,
  408, 430, 462, 466, 467, 474, 491, 520,
  540, 570, 575
Francis de Sales Oblates, 462
Francis of Assisi, St., 9, 11, 55, 107, 137,
  158, 160, 169, 206, **207**, 212-215, 223,
  231, 247, 249, 286, 289, 388, 390, 462,
  474-476, 488, 491, 493, 539, 574
Francis Xavier, St., 170, **207**, 213-216,
  224, 251, 254, 282, 313, 358, 365, 387-
  389, 391, 392, 462, 546
Franciscan Brothers, 462, 468, 542
Franciscan Brothers of Brooklyn, 462,
  468
Franciscan Brothers of Christ, 462
Franciscan Handmaids, 474
Franciscan Hospitaller Sisters, 474
Franciscan Mission Service, 496, 562
Franciscan Missionaries of Jesus
  Crucified, 492
Franciscan Missionaries of Mary, 430,
  474, 486
Franciscan Missionaries of Our Lady, 474
Franciscan Missionaries of St. Joseph,
  474, 481
Franciscan Missionary Brothers, 462, 467
Franciscan Missionary Sisters, 474-476
Franciscan Missionary Sisters of Assisi,
  475
Franciscan Missionary Sisters of Our
  Lady of Sorrows, 475
Franciscan Missions, 3, 353, 358, 365,
  390, 394, 476
Franciscan Order, 42, 107, 151, 168, 169,
  174, 206, 209, 223, 224, 342, 397, 403,
  493, 498
Franciscans (Men), 462, 467-468
Franciscans (Women), 474-477, 486-488
Franciso Coll Guitart, St., 253
Franco, Bl. Antonio, 216, 253
Francois-Xavier de Montmorency-Laval,
  217, 252

Franklin, Bp. William, 376, **402**, 419
Free Will, 130, **142**, 148, 220, 598
Freemasonry, **142**, 225, 247, 248
French Guiana, 261
Friar, **142**, 215-217, 466, 595, 597
Friars Minor, Order of, See Franciscans
Friars of the Atonement, 468
Friars of the Renewal, 462
Friars Preachers, Order of, See
  Dominicans
Friend, Bp. William, 374, 382, **402**, 419
Fruits of the Holy Spirit, 142
Fruits of the Mass, 142, 158, 179
Fundamental Option, 142
Fundamentalists, 600
Funeral Mass, 179
Funeral Rites, 189
Furnishings, 154, 176, 177
Furno, Card. Carlo, **282**, 295, 297

G

Gabon, 243, 265, 268, 276, **309**, 337,
  339
Gabriel (feast), 169, 173
Gainer, Bp. Ronald W., 379, **402**
Galante, Bp. Joseph, 375, **402**
Galatians, 96, 103,
Galeone, Bp. Victor, 382, **402**, 419, 425
Gallicanism, 159, 224, 309,
Gambia, 243, 265, 266, 268, **309**,
  337-339,
Garcia, Bp. Richard, 379, **402**, 425
García Zavala, María Guadalupe, 217
Garcia Siller, Bp. Gustavo M.Sp.S., 382,
  402, 425
Garland, Bp. James, 379, **402**, 425
Gaudium et Spes, 65, 113-116, 131, 198,
  229, 243, 292, 576,
Gaydos, Bp. John, 378, **402**
Gelasius I, Pope, 220, 234
Gelasius II, Pope, 235
Gelineau, Bp. Louis, 381, **402**, 419
Gendron, Bp. Odore, 379, **402**, 419
General Instruction of the Roman Missal,
  180, 183, 184, 189
Genuflection, 142
George, Card. Francis E., 275, **282**, 295-
  297, 375, 380. 383, 402, 421
Georgia, 244, 264, 265, 268, 300, 309,
  352, 373, 421, 422, 433, 435, 439, 470,
  521, 523, 527, 535, 553, 589, 590, 604
Gerber, Bp. Eugene, 376, 384, **402**
Gerety, Bp. Peter, 380, 381, 402, 419
Germany, 17, 45, 63, 71, 74, 75, 80, 107,
  108, 149, 204-206, 211, 214, 216, 221-
  224, 227, 228, 231-233, 237, 238, 240,
  241, 243, 244, 247-249, 261, 265, 268,
  272, 277, 278, 280, 283-286, 294, 296,
  310, 337, 341, 342, 346, 360, 396, 397,
  403, 415, 424, 429, 458, 461, 462, 464,
  468, 471, 472, 474-478, 482-484, 491,
  496, 547-549, 567, 572, 587, 595, 597,
  603, 607, 608, 612
Gerry, Bp. Joseph, 381, **402**, 419
Gettelfinger, Bp. Gerald, 377, **402**, 419
Ghana, 243, 261, 264, 265, 267, 268,
  272, 278, 281, 293, 296, **310**, 337,
  339, 394, 429
Gibraltar, 214, 265, **310**
Gift of Authority, 587
Gilbert, Bp. Edward, **402**, 417
Gilmore, Bp. Ronald, 376, **402**, 419
Giovanni Antonio Farina, 217
Giovannina Franks, 216, 255
Giuseppe Girotti, 216, 255
Girl Scouts, 341, 496, 497

Glemp, Card. Jozef, 283, 295, 296
Glendon, Mary Ann, 245, 269, 272
Glenmary Home Missioners, 431, 557
Glenmary Sisters, 478, 558
Glenmary Society, 362
Gluttony, 133, 142
Gnosticism, 107, 207, 218
Goedert, Bp. Raymond, 402, 419
Gomez, Abp. Jose, 8, 12, 379, 382, **402**,
  425, 454
Gonzalez, Abp. Roberto, 376, **403**,
  425, 454
Gonzalez Valer, Bp. Francisco, 383,
  403, 425
Good Friday, 34, 35, 128, 162, 163, 166,
  172, 180, 187, 241, 289, 305, 314, 350
Good Shepherd Sisters, 477
Goods of Marriage, 143
Gorman, Bp. John, **403**, 419
Gospels, 95, 96, **102**, 106, 111, 130, 151,
  178, 209, 215, 221, 258, 349, 583, ,
Gossman, Bp. Joseph, 52
Grace, 23, 30, 44, 45, 58, 60, 61, 66,
  88-92, 95, 107, 110, 111, 120, 121,
  123, 126, 134, 135, 138, 140, **143**, 146,
  148, 150, 153, 155, 157-161, 168, 172,
  175, 176, 178, 182, 190-193, 195, 196,
  198-200, 213, 214, 217, 220, 224, 225,
  350, 356, 381, 392, 421, 443, 463, 469,
  470, 473, 480, 505, 510, 518, 521, 556,
  570, 572-574, 577-579, 588, 589, 593,
  595, 598, 599, 602, 603
Gracias, Card. Oswald 34, **282**, 295,
  296, 337
Gracida, Bp. Rene, 376, 380, **403**, 419,
  425, 530
Graduale Romanum, 185,
Grahmann, Bp. Charles, 376, 384,
  403, 419
Graymoor, 458, 476, 477, 506, 510, 529,
  557, 562, 582, 616
Graymoor Sisters, 476, 477
Great Western Schism, 23
Grech, Card. Prosper, **282**, 295, 296
Greece, 105, 106, 214, 228, 233, 234,
  241, 244, 245, 248, 256, 265, 268, 298,
  310, **311**, 337, 345, 346, 394, 395, 417,
  567, 585, 589, 590
Green, Abp. James, 264, 266, **403**, 417
Gregorian Calendar, 225, 349
Gregorian Chant, **176**, 182, 220
Gregorian University, 31, 53, 69, 215,
  239, 240, 242, 278, 400, 546, 550
Gregory I, Pope, 108, 176, 205, 213,
  215, 220, 234
Gregory II, Pope, 221, 234
Gregory III, Pope, 43, 221, 234, 273,
  344, 347, 348
Gregory IV, Pope, 171, 234
Gregory V, Pope, 235
Gregory VI, Pope, 235
Gregory VII, Pope, 125, 167, 207, 209,
  222, 235
Gregory VIII, Pope, 235, 237
Gregory VIII (Antipope), 237
Gregory IX, Pope, 126, 145, 210, 223,
  235, 255
Gregory X, Pope, 229, 235
Gregory XI, Pope, 107, 236, 237, 595
Gregory XII, Pope, 228, 229, 232, 236-
  238, 256
Gregory XIII, Pope, 225, 236, 256
Gregory XIV, Pope, 236
Gregory XV, Pope, 173, 236, 256, 352
Gregory XVI, Pope, 147, 226, 237, 246,
  355, 360, 571

Gregory III Laham, 43, 273, 344, 347, 348,
Gregory, Abp. Wilton, 374, 375, **403**, 422, 604
Grey Nuns, 365, 441, 446, 471, 477, 540
Grey Nuns of Montreal, 471, 477
Gries, Bp. Roger, 376, **403**
Griffin, Bp. James, 376, 382, **403**, 419
Grocholewski, Card. Zenon 45, 257, 258, **282**, 295, 296
Gros, Br. Jeffrey, 52
Grosz, Bp. Edward, 375, **403**
Gruss, Bp. Robert D., 381, **403**
Guadalupe, Our Lady of (Feast), 170
Guam, 243, **311**, 389, 390, 394, 397, 430, 438, 497, 507, 538
Guanella, St. Luigi, 253, 460, 524
Guardian Angel, 388, 477, 488, 521
Guardian Angels (Feast), 169, 173
Guardian Angel Sisters of, 477
Guatemala, 243, 244, 265, 268, 277, 286, 289, 300, 307, **311**, 337, 363, 364, 429, 469, 492, 507, 510, 547
Guérin, St. Théodore, 252, 355, 359, 364
Guglielmone, Bp. Robert, 375, 403
Guillory, Bp. Curtis, 375, **403**
Guinea, 11, 214, 243, 244, 261, 265, 266, 268, 269, 276, 280, 290, 293, 296, 308, **311**, 322, 325, 326, 337-339, 397, 403, 406, 411, 418, 430
Guinea Bissau, 243, 265, 337-339
Gulbinowicz, Card. Henryk, **283**, 295, 296
Gullickson, Abp. Thomas E., 266, **403**, 417
Gumbleton, Bp. Thomas, **403**, 419
Guyana, 265, 268, **311**

H

Habakkuk, 96, 98, 101
Habash, Bp. Yousif Benham, 380, **403**
Habit, 55, **143**, 155, 160, 180
Habitual Grace, 143,
Hackett Ambassador Ken, 269
Haggai, 96, 101
Hail Mary, 130, 132, **143**
Haiti, 22, 26, 45, 70, 71, 86, 243, 265, 268, 277, 284, 289, 296, 306, **311**, 312, 337, 364, 412, 429
Handmaids of Divine Mercy, 490
Hanchon, Bp. Donald, 376, 403
Hanifen, Bp. Richard, 376, **403**, 419
Hanukkah, 99, 368, **605**
Hanus, Abp. Jerome, 376, 382, **403**-404
Harrington, Bp. Bernard, 384, **404**, 419
Harrington, Fr. Daniel, 52
Hart, Bp. Joseph, 376, 380, **404**, 419
Hartmayer, Bp. Gregory, 382, **404**
Harvey, Card. James, 260, **283**, 295-297, 417
Hawaii, 16, 206, 356, 363, 372, 374, 421, 422, 433, 435, 439, 460, 466, 470, 535, 554
Hawthorne Dominicans, 474
Health Care, 8, 9, 15, 31, 35, 58, 84, 118, 258, 272, 277, 279, 284, 286, 287, 290, 293, 317, 325, 326, 363, 369, 400, 422, 432, 455, 468, 471, 473, 475-477, 481, 483, 484, 486, 495, 511-515, 517, 518, 520
Hearing Impaired Children, 520,
Hebda, Bp. Bernard A., 377, 379, **404**
Hedwig, 169, 207, 214, 251
Heim, Bp. Capistran, 418
Hell, 52, 60, 88, 108, 109, 130, 137, 140, 142, **143**, 146, 153, 595, 612

Helpers, Society of, 478
Hennessey, Bp. Robert, 375, **404**
Henoticon, 220
Hensgen, Sr. Caroleen, 52-53
Heresy, 98, 134, 140, **143**, 145, 146, 206, 208, 218-220, 224, 238, 255, 306, 308, 361, 592
Hermanas Catequistas, 478
Hermanas Josefinas, 478
Hermann, Bp. Robert J., 382, **404**
Hermeneutics, 42, 103, 104, 143, 230, 573, 608
Hermes, Bp. Herbert, **404**, 418, 419
Herranz, Card. Julian, 260, 261, **283**, 295, 296
Herzog, Bp. Ronald P., 374, **404**, 504
HHS Mandate, 8, 16, 32, 36, 43, 44, 82, 84, 86
Hierarchy of the Catholic Church, 3, 273, 567
Higgins, Bp. Richard, 384, **404**
High Schools, Catholic U.S., 432, 534-538
Higi, Bp. William, 378, **404**, 419
Hinduism, 320, 428, 615, 616
Hippolytus, 168, 184, 207, 210, 212, 219, 237
Hispanic Catholics in the United States, 424, 425
Historical Books, 96, 99, 100
Hoeppner, Bp. Michael, 376, **404**
Holland, 15, 108, 205, 214, 226, 239, 249, 461, 463, 471, 477, 478, 489, 491, 518, 558, 559, 561, 564, 596, 599
Holley, Bp. Martin, 384, **404**, 426-428
Holocaust, 38, 61, 216, 227, 241, 245, 605-607, 609, 610
Holy Cross Fathers, 430, 528, 540, 542, 544
Holy Days and Other Observances, 171-174
Holy Door, 389
Holy Family of Nazareth, Srs. of, 486
Holy Ghost Fathers, 305, 318, 324, 326, 330, 463, 498
Holy Ghost Fathers of Ireland, 463
Holy Land, 10, 18, 20, 22, 32, 37, 38, 41, 43, 46, 57-62, 67, 70, 158, 210, 222, 228, 232, 233, 242, 244, 245, 314, 345, 348, 391, 462, 501, 562, 566, 572, 577, 585, 586, 608
Holy Name Society, 356, 361, 502
Holy Names of Jesus and Mary, Srs. of, 487
Holy Office, 124, 158, 225, 255, **256**, 277
Holy Orders, 3, 34, 88, 127, 130, 131, 133, 135, 141, 146, 147, 172, 176, 186, 189-191, **196**, 197, 222, 273, 276, 350, 579, 601
Holy Saturday, 34, 166, **172**, 350
Holy See, 3, 5, 6, 9-14, 17-19, 22-27, 29-31, 33, 34, 37-39, 41, 42, 45, 46, 49, 53, 54, 56, 67-69, 71, 73-76, 79, 80, 97, 119, 124, 125, 128, 130, 134, 144, 145, 147, 150, 153, 156, 159, 162, 175, 177, 180, 182, 183, 185, 186, 189, 195, 197, 201, 202, 204, 222-224, 226, **231**-272, 274, 276-279, 281-283, 285-293, 298-302, 304, 306, 308, 309, 312-320, 323-329, 331-333, 336, 355, 356, 360, 362, 373, 395, 396, 403, 408, 418, 420, 423, 429, 442, 445, 447, 449, 450, 458, 489, 492, 493, 495, 501, 505, 507, 547, 550, 567, 569, 572, 576, 579, 581, 583, 592, 602, 607, 608, 610, 611, 613

Holy See Finances, 26, 45, 73, 74
Holy See, Representatives of the, 25, 264-267, 610
Holy See, Representatives to the, 268
Holy Sepulchre of Jerusalem, 287, 288, 402, 417, 572
Holy Sepulchre Order, 287, 572
Holy Spirit, 26, 41, 45, 56, 59, 60, 62, 65, 66, 72, 73, 75, 76, 87-96, 102, 104, 107, 109, 110, 119-122, 128, 132, 134, 135, 138, 139, 141-**144**, 146, 148, 150, 151, 154-157, 160-162, 167, 173, 174, 188, 190-192, 194-196, 200, 217-220, 248, 250, 277, 278, 281, 343, 348, 349, 351, 387, 392, 401, 403, 408, 415, 417, 458, 461, 463, 467, 477, 478, 486-488, 491, 505, 513, 526-528, 531, 548, 564, 577-579, 583-587, 589-591, 593-596, 598, 600, 603, 604
Holy Spirit Missionary Sisters, 478, 564
Holy Spirit of Perpetual Adoration, 478
Holy Thursday, 34, 150, 161, 166, **172**, 187, 194, 350
Holy Water, 131, 139, **144**, 158, 176, 182, 215
Holy Water Fonts, 182
Holy Year, 124, **144**, 228, 242, 246, 282
Home Mission Sisters, 478
Home Missions, 356, 422, 431, 461, 563
Home Visitors of Mary, Srs. of, 478
Homilist, 190
Homosexuality, 25, 55, **144**, 362
Hon Tai-Fai, Abp. Savio, 256, 261
Honduras, 243, 265, 268, 286, 289, 296, **312**, 337, 413, 418, 419, 430, 510
Hong Kong, 282, 292, 294, 296, 303, 339, 428, 429, 567
Honorius I, Pope, 221, 234
Honorius II, Pope, 235, 237, 493
Honorius III, Pope, 137, 151, 223, 235
Honorius IV, Pope, 235
Hosanna, 144
Hosea, 96, 101
Hoser, Abp. Henryk, 261
Hospice, 217, 510, 511, 515
Hospital Sisters, 476, 509
Hospitallers of St. John, 208, 467, 572
Hospitals, 8, 11, 58, 82, 134, 197, 208, 212, 213, 320, 327, 331, 335, 364, 365, 432, 484, 496, 509, 609
Houck, Bp. William, 378, **404**, 419
Howze, Bp. Joseph, 375, **404**, 419, 427
Hubbard, Bp. Howard, 374, **404**
Hughes, Abp. Alfred, 375, 379, **404**, 419
Humanae Vitae, 76, 80, 114, 117, 136, 199, 200, 242, 250, 357
Humeral Veil, 180
Humility of Mary Congr., 478
Humility of Mary, Srs., 478
Hummes, O.F.M., Card. Claudio, **283**, 295-297
Hungary, 11, 80, 170, 204, 206, 209, 211-216, 222, 243, 244, 246-249, 251, 265, 268, 281, 287, 296, **312**, 337, 346, 474, 484, 485, 547, 548, 567
Hunthausen, Abp. Raymond, 378, 383, **404**, 419
Hurley, Abp. Francis, 374, **404**, 419
Hurley, Bp. Walter A., 377, **404**-405, 419
Husar, Card. Lubomyr, **283**, 295-297, 348, 417
Hying, Bp. Donald, 379, **405**
Hymn, 17, 112, 129, 132, 146, 148-150, 158, 160, 176, 178, 179
Hyperdulia, 144,
Hypostatic Union, 144

I

Ibrahim, Bp. Ibrahim, 346, 382, **405**, 443
Iceland, 214, 243, 265, 268, **312**
Icon, **144**, 349, 350, 590
Iconoclasm, 221
Iconostasis, 350
Idaho, 374, 421, 433, 435, 439, 527, 535, 554
Idolatry, 29, 57, 61, 76, 98, 100, 101, 144, 221, 303, 575
Ignatius Loyola, 168, **207**, 213, 216, 232, 292, 388
IHM Sisters, 430, 561
Illinois, 16, 353, 361, 364, 365, 372, 373, 389, 391, 406, 407, 421, 422, 426, 433, 435, 439, 470, 512, 521, 523, 527, 535, 539, 544, 545, 557
Imesch, Bp. Joseph, 378, **405**, 419
Immaculate Conception, 17, 52, 77, 123, 124, 139, **144**, 155, 162, 170, 172, 173, 205, 206, 210, 214, 224, 226, 238, 246, 248, 249, 252, 283, 285, 288, 349, 353, 355, 360, 387-391, 393, 395-401, 403, 407, 408, 410, 412-417, 443, 444, 446, 462-465, 467, 469, 472, 474, 476-478, 481, 485-488, 498, 500, 545, 548, 549, 557
Immaculate Conception, Srs. of, 487
Immaculate Heart of Mary, Srs. of, 487
Immortality, 108, **144**, 605
Impediments, 200, **201**, 203, 246
Impotency, 201
Imprimatur, 134, 144
Imputability, 144
Incardination, 144
Incense, 134, **145**, 151
Incest, 145
Inclusive Language, 190
Inculturation, **145**, 300
Incurable Cancer, 474, 509
Index of Prohibited Books, 145
India, 10, 42, 77, 105, 106, 208, 214, 216, 238, 240-244, 261, 265, 266, 268, 272, 274, 277, 279, 281, 282, 292, 296, 301, **313**, 318, 328, 337, 344-347, 394, 409, 429, 460, 471, 474, 478, 481, 499, 548, 566, 567, 581, 583, 592, 593, 615, 616,
Indiana, 1, 355, 359, 364, 365, 373, 389, 391, 416, 421, 422, 433, 435, 439, 461, 469, 470, 513, 521, 523, 527, 535, 536, 545, 554, 597
Indissolubility of Marriage, 49, 201
Indonesia, 241, 243, 265-268, 280, 281, 288, 296, 306, **313**, 337, 414, 418, 548, 612,
Indulgence, 129, 144, **145**, 151, 152, 157, 158, 223, 595
Indult, 137, **145**, 183, 188, 197
Inerrancy, 95, 600
Infallibility, 92, **145**, 226, 587, 594, 600
Infancy Narrative, 139, 143, 148
Infused Virtues, 145
Innocent I, Pope, 96, 234
Innocent II, Pope, 229, 235, 237
Innocent III, Pope, 171, 223, 229, 235, 237, 255, 261, 345
Innocent IV, Pope, 229, 235, 255
Innocent V, Pope, 235
Innocent VI, Pope, 236, 237
Innocent VII, Pope, 236, 237
Innocent VIII, Pope, 236
Innocent IX, Pope, 236
Innocent X, Pope, 172, 225, 236
Innocent XI, Pope, 236

Innocent XII, Pope, 236
Innocent XIII, Pope, 236
Inquisition, **145**, 223, 224, 255, 328, 449
Insemination, 145, 146
Institutes of Consecrated Life, 127, 135-137, 188, 257, 278, 281, 282, 284, 285, 289, 290, 402, 415, 458, 489, 557
Inter Insigniores, 198
Inter Mirifica, 10, 229
InterAgency Curia Commissions, 257
Interdict, 146
Interment, 132
International Catholic Organizations, 340-342, 496, 498
International Catholic Periodicals, 566
International Eucharistic Congresses, 260, 277, 292
Internet, 7, 69, 75, 245, 567-570
Interpretation of the Bible, 96, **103**-105, 143, 219
Interreligious Dialogue, 22, 34, 38, 58, 258, 260, 277, 280, 281, 283, 284, 287-289, 292, 315, 455, 499, 576, 580, 600, 605, 612, 613, 615, 616
Intinction, **146**, 179, 193, 350, 351
Iowa, 24, 32, 50, 363, 373, 376, 389, 391, 399, 410, 414, 421, 422, 433, 436, 439, 470, 495, 513, 527, 536, 541, 545
Iran, 21, 23, 77, 256, 265, 268, 282, 289, 313, 345-347
Iraq, 43, 47, 49, 50, 52, 60, 77-79, 228, 256, 265, 267, 268, 282, **313**, 314, 330, 345-348, 357, 403, 405, 414, 507, 586, 589
Ireland, 19, 20, 23, 24, 45, 47, 51, 63, 69, 124, 125, 172, 205, 206, 209, 210, 214, 220-222, 224-228, 239, 243, 246, 247, 260, 261, 265, 268, 278-280, 287, 294, 296, 307, 308, 310, **314**, 321, 326, 337, 342, 355, 356, 360, 364, 381, 396, 397, 399, 401, 404, 407, 410, 418, 424, 429, 460-463, 465, 469, 471-473, 475, 478-481, 483, 484, 486, 496, 505, 506, 547, 548, 566
Irenicism, 146
Iriondo, Bp. Robert, 380, **405**, 425
Isaac, 101, 605
Isaac Jogues, 163, 169, 352, 358, 364
Isaiah, 96, 98, **100**, 101
Isern, Bp. Fernando, 381, **405**
Islam, 6, 12, 50, 58, 60, 67, 77, 78, 150, 221, 298, 300, 302, 307, 313-317, 319, 321, 329, 334, 428, 586, **611**-615
Israel, 10, 14, 17, 19, 32, 38, 41, 46, 57, 61, 62, 67, 77, 89, 90, 95, 98-102, 111, 137, 151, 245, 265, 268, 272, 280, **314**, 315, 346, 347, 429, 548, 566, 573, 577, 589, 607-611
Italo-Albanian Catholic Church, 346
Italy, 10, 13, 14, 19-23, 29, 34, 38, 42, 45-48, 50, 51, 53, 56, 70, 71, 74, 80, 107-109, 133, 144, 147, 149, 151, 156, 205-207, 209, 211, 214-217, 220, 221, 223-226, 231, 237-243, 246-249, 253, 255-262, 265-268, 270, 272, 273, 275, 277-280, 282-294, 296-298, **315**, 325, 337, 340-342, 346, 389, 394, 396, 397, 401, 403, 405, 407, 408, 410, 411, 415-417, 424, 429, 458-466, 468-486, 489-493, 502, 547, 548, 558, 566-568, 572, 573, 582, 583, 588
Ivory Coast, 22, 51, 71, 243, 261, 265, 268, 284, 296, **305**, 337, 548

J

Jackels, Abp. Michael O., 376, 384, **405**

Jacob, 17, **101**, 151, 270, 355, 381, 394, 583, 584, 593, 596, 605
Jacobs, Bp. Sam, 374, 378, **405**
Jadot, Abp. Jean, 267
Jamaica, 244, 265, 267, 268, 286, **315**, 364, 395, 403, 415, 418, 429, 430, 465, 475, 483, 485, 529, 542, 556, 558
Jammo, Bp. Sarhad, 382, **405**
Japan, 10, 41, 52, 209, 210, 214, 224, 240, 241, 243, 251, 252, 265, 268, 272, 277, **315**, 316, 337, 357, 429, 547, 548, 589
Jarrell, Bp. C. Michael, 378, **405**
Jaworski, Card. Marian, **283**, 295-296
Jeanne Jugan, St., **208**, 252, 482, 511, 512, 514, 516-518,
Jenik, Bp. John Joseph, 379, **405**
Jenkins, Msgr. Ronny, 421,
Jenky, Bp. Daniel, 380, **405**, 421
Jeremiah, 52, 96, 97, **100**, 101, 610,
Jerome, 97, 104, 107, **108**, 169
Jerusalem, 11, 14, 17, 18, 20, 32, 35, 37, 38, 52, 57-62, 67, 72, 97, 99-103, 105-107, 109, 132, 134, 142, 147, 150, 151, 155, 157, 166, 171, 173, 215, 216, 218, 222, 228, 244, 245, 265, 273, 274, 280, 282, 285, 287, 288, 290, 294, 314, 315, 336, 344, 345, 347, 348, 397, 402, 403, 417, 499, 505, 528, 548, 566, 572, 577, 585, 586, 589-592, 605, 608-610
Jerusalem Bible, 97
Jerusalem Patriarchate, 589
Jesuit Martyrs of North America, 240, 446
Jesuits (Society of Jesus), 207, 224, 278, 463, 540
Jesus Prayer, 146
Jews Judaism, 607
Joan of Arc, St., **208**, 213, 214, 223, 239, 250, 569
Job, 12, 96, **100**, 108, 510, 525
Joel, 96, **101**, 368, 369
John Chrysostom, St., 107, **108**, 169, 213, 215, 389, 590
John Damascene, St., 15, **108**, 170
John Fisher, St., 167, **208**, 211, 224, 251, 308
John Henry Newman, Bl., 113, 150, 226, 254
John I, Pope, 167, 208, 234, 242
John II, Pope, 10, 220, 234, 237
John III, Pope, 234, 235
John IV, Pope, 234, 237
John V, Pope, 234, 235, 237, 323
John VI, Pope, 234, 235
John VII, Pope, 234
John VIII, Pope, 234
John IX, Pope, 234
John X, Pope, 221, 234
John XI, Pope, 214, 234
John XII, Pope, 136, 221, 234, 235
John XIII, Pope, 235
John XIV, Pope, 235
John XV, Pope, 204, 222, 235
John XVI (Antipope), 237
John XVII, Pope, 235
John XVIII, Pope, 235
John XIX, Pope, 235
John XXI, Pope, 235,
John XXII, Pope, 129, 174, 223, 236, 237, 571
John XXIII (Antipope), 237
John XXIII, Pope St., 71-73, 227, 237, 241, 276, 588
Canonizations, 241, 251
Encyclicals, 241, 250

Life, 241
Writings, 241, 250
John XXIII National Seminary, 407, 415, 545
John Vianney, St., 168, 208, 250, 282, 394, 398, 399, 401-403, 405, 410, 416, 545
John Nepomucene Neumann, St., 208, 242, 251, 355, 362
John Paul I, 51, 227, 237, 242
John Paul II, Pope St., 7, 10, 17, 26, 33, 34, 45, 49, 51, 54, 59, 61, 67-73, 76, 80, 87, 109, 110, 112-117, 121, 123, 124, 126, 129, 132, 133, 136, 142, 145, 150, 154, 156-159, 163, 169, 180, 184, 186-189, 194, 195, 198, 199, 202-204, 206, 208, 211, 217, 227, 228, 230, 232, 233, 237, 241, 243, 245, 250-263, 269, 271, 272, 275, 276, 279, 281, 286, 287, 289, 291, 295, 298, 299, 302, 305, 306, 310-313, 317, 319, 320, 323-326, 330, 332, 344-346, 351, 357, 362, 365, 390, 400, 404, 406, 408, 412, 414, 415, 425, 449-451, 464, 495, 498, 499, 504, 507, 519, 524, 527, 529, 533, 545, 548-550, 562, 567, 576, 578, 579, 583-585, 588, 590, 592-594, 603, 604, 607, 608, 611-615
Beatifications, 245, 252-254
Canonizations, 71, 245, 251-252
Encyclicals, 112-113, 115, 121, 250
Life, 243
Pontificate, 243-245
Travels, 243-244
Writings, 112-113, 115, 121, 243-245, 250
Johnston, Bp. James, 382, **405**
Joint Declaration on Justification, 584, 603,
Jonah, 96, 101, 106
José de Anchieta, 216-217, 252
José Gabriel del Rosario Brochero, 215-216, 255
José Tous y Soler, 254
Josemaria Escriva, Balaguer St., 208, 252, 253, 507
Josep y Elias, Bl., 252, 255
Josephinism, 225, 299, 300, 306, 310, 312
Josephite Fathers, 427, 463
Joshua, 96, **98**, 146, 271
Juan Diego, 170, 451
Judah, 99-102, 106
Judaism, 60, 67, 99, 103, 150, 151, 155, 174, 314, 586, 605-608, 610
Judas Iscariot, 105
Jude, 13, 91, 96, 103, 105, **106**, 169, 212, 215, 265, 378, 388-392, 473, 523, 562
Jude Thaddeus, 13, 106, 212, 265, 391
Judges, 28, 58, 96, **98**, 99, 101, 140, 189, 198, 599
Judith, 96, 97, **99**, 573
Jugis, Bp. Peter J., 84, 376, **405**
Julian Calendar, 349
Julius I, Pope, 233
Julius II, Pope, 229, 236
Julius III, Pope, 130, 229, 236, 346
Junipero Serra, Bl., 253, 500
Jurisdictions and Faithful of the Eastern, 344-347
Just War, 118, **119**, 614, 615
Justice, Bp. William, 382, **405**
Justification, 88, 103, 109, 123, 145, **146**, 224, 584, 587, 595, 597-599, 603
Justin Martyr, 167, **209**, 215

K

Kaddish, 607,
Kagan, Bp. David, 375, **405**
Kalabat, Bp. Frank Yohana, 381, **405**
Kalathiparambil, Abp. Joseph, 258, 261
Kane, Bp. Francis, 376, **405**
Kansas, 51, 83, 278, 352, 358, 363, 364, 368, 373, 374, 378, 385, 388, 396, 398, 401, 404, 405, 409, 417-419, 421, 422, 433, 434, 436, 439, 465, 469, 480, 482, 496, 500, 513, 515, 523, 527, 536, 539, 542, 544, 552, 554-556, 561-564, 573
Kappa Gamma Pi, 498
Karekin I Catholicos, 584
Karekin II Catholicos, 584
Karlic, Card. Estanislao Esteban, 284, 295-297
Kasper, Card. Walter, **283**, 295-296, 485, 580, 581
Kateri Tekakwitha, St., 53, 163, 168, 209, 252, 353, 392, 429, 441, 529,
Katharine Drexel, St., 163, 166, 209, 253, 356, 484,
Kazakstan, 244, 265, 267, 337,
Keeler, Card. William, **283**, 295-297, 375, 378, 405, 431, 581, 594
Keleher, Bp. James, 375, 378, **405**, 419
Kennedy, Bp. Arthur L., 375, **405**-406
Kennedy, Pres. John F., 270, 357, 360, 362, 371
Kentucky, 354, 355, 359, 363-365, 368, 373, 390, 408, 421, 423, 433, 436, 439, 465, 470, 483, 499, 513, 521, 523, 527, 536, 555, 597, 616,
Kenya, 10, 243, 244, 265, 266, 268, 272, 279, 286, 296, **316**, 330, 337, 339, 395, 418, 429, 548, 566, 581, 589
Kerygma, 146
Kettler, Abp. Donald, 377, **406**
Keys, Power of the, **146**, 196
Kicanas, Bp. Gerald, 383, **406**, 422
Kings, 96, 99, 100
Kingship of Christ (Feast), 161, 162, 170, 171
Kingship of Christ, Women Missionaries, 491
Kinney, Bp. John, 375, 382, **406**
Kitbunchu, Card. Michael, **283**, 295-297
Kmiec, Bp. Edward, 375, 379, **406**, 593, 594
Knestout, Bp. Barry, 384, **406**
Knights of Columbus, 10, 50, 356, 361, 497, 507, 551, 557, 562
Knights of the Holy Sepulchre, 297
Knights of Labor, 238, 356, 361
Knights of Lithuania, 502
Knights of Malta, 573
Knights of Peter Claver, 427, 502
Knights of Rhodes, 572
Knights of St. John, 356, 502
Knights Templar, 223
Koch, Card. Kurt, 258, 260, **283**, 580, 593
Koinonia, **146**, 588
Kopacz, Bp. Joseph R., 377, **406**
Korea, 12, 22, 33, 49, 63, 64, 66, 71, 204, 214, 216, 232, 241, 243, 265, 266, 268, 279, 281, 286, 294, 296, **316**, 337, 403, 407, 408, 418, 429, 497, 581
Korec, Card. Jan, **284**, 295-297
Kucera, Bp. Daniel, 377, 379, 382, **406**, 419
Kudrick, Bp. John, 349, 380, **406**
Ku Klux Klan, 355, 360
Kulturkampf, 226, 238, 299, 310, 329
Kuriakose Elias Chavara, 217

Kurtz, Abp. Joseph, 16, 43, 44, 86, 378, 379, **406**, 422, 430
Kurtz, Bp. Robert, **406**, 419
Kutwa, Card. Jean-Pierre, 70-71, **284**, 295, 296
Kuwait, 264-268, 293, **316**, 345-347
Kyrgyzstan, 265-268, **316**

L

La Civilta Cattolica, 6, 292
La Mennais Brothers, 460
Laborem Exercens, 114-116, 250
Lacroix, Card. Gérald Cyprien, 70-71, **284**, 295, 296, 444
Ladaria Ferrer, Abp. Luis, 256, 261, 601
Laetare Sunday, 180
Laghi, Card. Pio, 267, 269
Lagonegro, Bp. Dominick, 380, **406**
Langlois, Card. Chibly, 22, 26, 70, 71, **284**, 295, 296, 312, 337
Laicization, 147
Laity, 17, 25, 48, 54, 64, 79, 91, 127, 130, 135, 175, 229, 233, 243, 258, 270, 275, 277, 278, 280, 281, 283, 285, 288-293, 317, 340, 342, 363, 422, 428, 432, 446, 489, 492, 493, 495, 496, 502-504, 562, 591, 592, 594, 601, 607
Laity, Pontifical Council for the, 17, 25, 258, 280, 290, 291, 340, 502
Lajolo, Card. Giovanni, **284**, 295-297
Lamb of God, 129, 179, 183, 480
Lambaesis, 283, 399, 415
Lambert, Bp. Francis, 375, 383
Lambeth Conference, 582, 600, 601
Lamentations, 96, 100
Languages of the Church, 147
Lanza Di Montezemolo, Card. Andrea Cordero, 23, 268, **281**, 295, 297
LaSalette Missionaries, 463, 467
Last Supper, 62, 143, 154, 172, 178, 348, 350
Lateran Basilica, 170, 290
Lateran Councils, 223, 224, 229
Lateran University, 30, 52, 53, 240, 278, 549, 550
Latin American Bishops, 248, 305, 339
Latin Liturgy, 176, 188, 222, 502, 506
Latin Patriarchate of Jerusalem, 315, 572
Latino, Bp. Joseph, 357, 378, **406**, 424-426
Latria, 129, 147, 155
Latvia, 244, 266, 268, 288, 296, **316**, 337, 418, 589
LaValley, Bp. Terry R., 406
Law, Card. Bernard, **284**, 294, 295, 297, 375, 406
Lay Ministry, 362, 428, 496, 503
Lay Mission Helpers Association, 496
Lay Organizations, 361, 495
Lazarists, 211, 466
Lazarus, 209, 255, 350
Lebanon, 20, 31, 43, 233, 244, 245, 256, 266, 268, 275, 282, 288, 289, 291, 293, 296, **317**, 330, 345, 346, 348, 367, 380, 386, 388, 389, 392, 395, 397, 400, 401, 403, 409, 412, 413, 417-419, 429, 432, 438, 440, 459, 464, 468, 538, 545, 547, 548, 554, 563, 583, 587, 589
Lectern, 181
Lectionary, 184-187, 500
Lector, 197, 495
Legal Status of Catholic Education, 532
Legion of Mary, 342, 496
Legionaries of Christ, 23, 27, 70, 281, 401, 463, 467, 550

Lehmann, Card. Karl, **284**, 295-296
Leibrecht, Bp. John, 383, **406**, 419
Lennon, Bp. Richard, 376, **406**
Lent, 30, 56, 75, 112, 128, 129, 131,
    139, 153, **161**, 162, 164-166, 171, 172,
    180, 186, 192, 195, 216, 349, 350, 431,
    441, 608
Leo I, Pope, 108, 229, 234, 250, 282, 284
Leo II, Pope, 229, 234
Leo III, Pope, 221, 234
Leo IV, Pope, 234
Leo V, Pope, 221, 234
Leo VI, Pope, 234
Leo VII, Pope, 234
Leo VIII, Pope, 234, 235
Leo IX, Pope, 222, 235
Leo X, Pope, 229, 236, 595
Leo XI, Pope, 236
Leo XII, Pope, 237, 246, 257, 263
Leo XIII, Pope, 3, 105, 114-117, 123,
    130, 132, 136, 147, 149, 172, 211, 213,
    226-228, 232, 237-239, 241, 243, 247,
    249-251, 260, 261, 263, 271, 356, 361,
    546, 571, 572, 601
Leonard of Port Maurice, 158, 209, 213
Leopold Mandic, 209, 251
Lepanto, Battle of, 173
Lesotho, 9, 214, 243, 265, 266, 268, 279,
    286, **317**, 337, 339, 403
Lessard, Bp. Raymond, 383, **406**, 419
Levada, Card. William, 189, **284**, 295-
    297, 380, 382, 406, 417, 419, 601
Leviticus, 96, 98, 605
LeVoir, Bp. John, 380, **406**
Libasci, Bp. Peter, 381, **406**
Liberation Theology, 49, **147**, 231, 244,
    302, 321, 322, 450
Liberia, 266, 268, **317**, 337-339
Liberty, Religious, 3, 8, 16, 20, 32, 48,
    50, 63, 82, 86, 245, 309, 313, 321, 333,
    353, 354, 358, 362, 367, 507, 609
Libreria Editrice Vaticana, 13, 23, 263,
    611
Libya, 266, 268, **317**
Liechtenstein, 243, 266-268, **317**
Life, Sisters of, 480
Limbo, 147
Linceorum Academia, 271
Lindalva Justo de Oliveira, 254
Linus, Pope, 233, 280
Lippert, O.F.M., Bp. Donald, 406
Lipscomb, Abp. Oscar, 379, **406**, 419,
    593
Lisbon, 39, 53, 54, 107, 266, 274, 281,
    297, 323, 338, 341, 474, 547
Listecki, Abp. Jerome, 378, 379, **406**,
    422
Litany of Saints, 140, 172
Literary Criticism, 103-105
Literary Forms, 95, 103, 230
Lithuania, 205, 208, 214, 226, 244, 265,
    266, 268, 277, 296, **317**, 325, 337, 394,
    478, 502, 550
Lithuanian Groups, 502
Little Brothers of St. Francis, 463
Little Flower Society, 502
Little Franciscans of Mary, 476
Liturgiam Authenticam, 183
Liturgical Celebrations, 21, 175, 186,
    245, 259
Liturgical Colors and Vestments, 180
Liturgical Developments, 182
Liturgical Year, 161-163, 171, 176,
    187, 349
Logos, 147
Lohmuller, Bp. Martin, **406**, 419

López Rodriguez, Card. Nicolás de
    Jesús, 268, **285**, 295-297, 337
Loretto Sisters, 479
Lori, Abp. William, 8, 15, 20, 32, 40, 48,
    357, 375, **406**
Losten, Bp. Basil, 383, **406**-407, 419
Lotocky, Bp. Hilarius, O.S.B.M., 382,
    407, 419
Louis de Montfort, St., 209
Louise de Marillac, 209, 213, 251
Louisiana, 48, 85, 353, 354, 358-360,
    364-366, 368, 369, 372, 373, 390, 391,
    411, 421, 423, 427, 428, 433, 436, 439,
    470, 478, 492, 513, 520, 521, 523, 527,
    536, 544, 545
Lourdes, 9, 122, 123, 156, 165, 205, 212,
    226, 243, 244, 250, 279, 342, 389, 391,
    393, 399, 446, 477, 501, 514, 515, 540
Lourdusamy, Card. D. Simon, 53
Louvain, 149, 207, 280, 291, 342, 355,
    396-398, 401, 409, 412, 416, 546,
    547, 566
Loverde, Bp. Paul, 375, 380, **407**
Lozano Barragan, Card. Javier, 255, 261,
    266, **284**, 295-297, 451
Lucas, Bp. George, 380, **407**
Lucia, Sr., of Fatima, 123, 124, 234, 253,
    266, 269
Lucius I, Pope, 233
Lucius II, Pope, 235
Lucius III, Pope, 223, 235
Ludovico of Casoria, 217
Lugo, Fernando, 322
Luigi Scrosoppi, 251, 252
Luigi Versiglia, 252
Luke, 30, 95, 96, **102**, 105, 106, 146,
    156, 173, 212, 213, 215, 218, 272, 282,
    350, 372, 509, 517, 523
Lumen Fidei, 72, 75, 232, 250
Lumen Gentium, 3, 89-91, 93, 119, 135,
    151, 155, 178, 190, 196, 198, 217, 228,
    229, 246, 351, 421, 575, 576, 612
Lumen Vitae Centre, 342
Luong, Bp. Dominic, 380, **407**
Luther, Martin, 104, 224, 244, 310, 459,
    595, 597, 603
Lutheran Church, 309, 329, 580, 582,
    597-599
Lutheran World Federation, 580, 582,
    584, 586, 587, 597, 598, 603
Lutheran-Catholic Joint Declaration, 603
Luxembourg, 11, 15, 40, 214, 239, 243,
    264, 266, 268, 317, **318**
Lynch, Bp. Robert, 381, **407**
Lyne, Bp. Timothy, 53

M

Macaluso, Bp. Christie, 378, **407**
Macau, 303, 339,
Maccabees, 96, 97, **99**, 102, 138, 605
Macharski, Card. Franciszek, **284**,
    295-297
Madagascar, 243, 265, 266, 268, 278,
    281, 290, 291, **318**, 319, 324, 337, 339,
    396, 418, 430, 548
Madden, Bp Denis J., 48, 375, **408**,
    422, 582
Madeleine Sophie Barat, 209
Madera, Bp. Joseph, 377, **408**, 580
Magi, 22, 120, 148, 172
Maginnis, Bp. Robert, **408**, 419
Magisterium, 23, 36, 72, 80, 87, 92, 93,
    112, 113, 115-117, 127, 133, 148, 198,
    203, 246, 272, 494, 501, 534, 567, 572
Maguire, Bp. Joseph, 383, **408**, 419

Mahony, Card. Roger, 80, 259, **284**, 295-
    297, 379, 383, 408, 419
Maida, Card. Adam, 260, **285**,295-297,
    376, 377, 408, 419
Maine, 352, 356, 358, 373, 390, 399,
    421, 433, 436, 439, 477, 507, 514, 525,
    527, 536
Maix, Barbara, 254
Majella Agnelo, Card. Geraldo, 207, 212,
    216, 251, **285**, 295-297
Major Protestant Churches in the United
    States, 596-599
Malabar Rite, 349, 581
Malachi, 96, 101,
Malankara Orthodox Church, 345
Malawi, 243, 266-268, 285, **318**, 337, 339
Malaysia, 265, 266, 268, 285, 302, **318**,
    337, 408, 418
Maldives, 318
Malloy, Bp. David, 381, **408**
Malone, Bp. Richard, 380, **408**, 422
Malooly, Bp. W. Francis, 383, **408**
Malta, 21, 35, 41, 214, 233, 243, 244,
    266, 269, 282, 290, 292, 296, **318**, 337,
    394, 548, 550, 572
Malta, Knights of, 573
Mamberti, Abp. Dominique, 5, 6, 9-11,
    13, 17, 22, 24, 25, 27, 29, 34, 35,
    41, 315,
Mandatum, 533, 534
Manichaeism, 107, 108, 219, 220, 223
Manning, Bp. Elias, **408**, 417
Manning, Bp. Thomas, **408**, 417
Manning, Timothy Cardinal, 297, 377,
    379
Mansell, Abp. Henry, 375, 378, **408**
Mansour, Abp. Gregory, 382, **408**
Mantellate Sisters, 480,
Mantellate Sisters Servants of Mary, 480
Manuel Lozano Garrido, 254
Manz, Bp. John, 376, **408**
Mar Dinkha IV, 584, 584
Mar Ignatius Jacob III, 582
Marcellin, Joseph Benoit Champagnat,
    251
Marcellus I, Pope, 233
Marcellus II, Popem 235, 236, 263
Marchetto, Abp. Agostino, 13, 260
Marchisano, Card. Francesco, 53
Marcionism, 218, 608
Marconi, Bp. Dominic, 262, **408**, 419
Margaret Clitherow, 209
Margaret Flesch, 254
Margaret Mary Alacoque, 154, 169, 174,
    205, **209**, 250
Margaret of Cortona, **209**, 212, 213
Margaret of Hungary, **209**, 251
Margaret of Scotland, 170, 208, **209**, 506
Marguerite Bourgeoys, 251, 363, 441,
    482
Maria Alfonsina Danil, 254
Maria Assunta Caterina Marchetti,
    216, 255
Maria Esperanza Alhama, 216, 255
Maria Cristina of Savoy, 216, 255
Maria Goretti, 168, **209**, 212, 251, 282
Maria Luisa Merkert, 254
Marie of the Incarnation Guyart, 217,
    252
Maria Pierina De Micheli, 254
Maria Teresa Bonzel, 216, 255
Marian Movement of Priests, 502
Marian Shrine, 35, 147, 206, 392, 529
Marian Year, 173, 249

Mariana Islands, 311
Mariana Paredes of Jesus, 209, 251
Marianist Fathers, 464
Marianist Sisters, 481
Marianists, 430, 467, 539, 540, 543
Marianites of Holy Cross, 480, 542
Marianne Cope, 165, **209**, 252, 254, 363
Mariannhill Mission Society, 558
Mariannhill Missionaries, 467
Marie Leonie Paradis, 252
Marie-Rose Durocher, 163, 169, **209**
Marini, Msgr. Guido, 259
Marini, Abp. Piero,
Marino, Bp. Joseph, 375, **408**, 417
Marinus I, Pope, 234
Marinus II, Pope, 234, 235
Mario Vergara, 216, 255
Mariological Society of America, 502
Mariology, 159
Marist Brothers, 464, 467
Marist Fathers, 291, 464, 493
Marist Missionary Sisters, 480
Marist Sisters, 480
Mark, 95, 96, **102**, 105, 106, 116
Maronites, 273, 288, 291, 317, 330, 344-
348, 413, 417, 432, 438, 440, 442, 443,
447, 451, 453, 538, 563
Marriage Doctrine, 198-199
Marriage Encounter, 53, 503, 558
Marshall Islands, 266, 269, **319**, 395,
438, 538
Martha Wiecka, 254
Martin de Porres, 170, 212, 213, 251,
365, 461, 493, 506, 558
Martin I, Pope, 166, 209, 234, 235
Martin II, Pope, See Marinus I
Martin III, Pope, See Marinus II
Martin IV, Pope, 223, 235
Martin V, Pope, 229, 236, 238
Martin of Tours, 170, 204, 209, 212, 213
Martínez Sistach, Card. Lluís, **285**,
295-296
Martinez Somalo, Card. Eduardo, 261,
285, 295-297
Martinique, 324
Martino, Bp. Joseph, 383, **408**, 419
Martino, Card. Renato, 261, **285**, 290,
295-297
Martyrdom, 12, 98, 106, 113, 191, 207,
218, 250, 274, 299, 305, 328, 446,
577, 584
Martyrology, **148**, 204
Marx, Card. Reinhard, 23, 40, 260, **285**,
295, 296, 339, 375
Mary Blessed Virgin, 31, 50, 87, 93, **119**,
123, 125, 141, 143, 144, 154, 155, 159,
166-171, 173, 180, 182, 190, 205, 214,
226, 227, 240, 249, 287, 288, 350, 360,
361, 363, 387, 388, 390, 391, 462, 472,
478, 479, 483, 493, 501
    Apparitions of, **123**, 125, 141, 173, 209
    Redemptoris Mater, 3, 121, 122, 250,
    545
    Role of Mary, 93, **119**-122, 250
Mary Faustina Kowalska, 251
Mary Help of Christians, 208, 209, 390,
392, 393, 481, 486, 492, 550
Mary Magdalen Sophie Barat, 250
Mary Magdalene, 167, 168, 209, 210,
215, 254
Mary of the Cross MacKillop, 252, 253
Mary Reparatrix, 481, 488
Maryheart Crusaders, 503
Maryknoll, 49, 227, 356, 361, 394, 407,
416, 430, 458, 464, 481, 558, 559,
565, 573-575

Maryknoll Fathers, 430, 458
Maryknoll Mission Sisters, 430
Maryknoll Priests, 464, 467
Maryknoll Sisters, 481
Maryland, 16, 54, 271, 272, 352-356,
358-360, 363, 365, 366, 370, 372-374,
390, 391, 406, 408, 409, 421, 423,
427, 433, 436, 439, 463, 470, 479, 514,
521-523, 527, 536, 542, 545, 556, 581,
583, 598
Mass, 172-190, 192-197
Mass of Chrism, 172, 187
Mass of Christian Burial, 154, 179
Mass Vestments, 180
Massachusetts, 44, 267, 271, 352, 354,
360, 373, 390, 392, 407, 421, 423, 433,
436, 439, 470, 472, 514, 521, 523, 528,
536, 545, 599
Matano, Bp. Salvatore R., 375, 381, **408**
Matrimonia Mixta, 202
Matthew, 95-97, **102**, 105, 106
Matthiesen, Bp. Leroy, 375, 419
Mauretania, 278, 288, 291, 408, 414
Mauritania, 266, **319**, 338, 339
Maximilian Kolbe, 168, 210, 212, 251,
391, 503
Mazombwe, Card. Medardo Joseph, 53
McCarrick, Card. Theodore, 32, **284**,
295-297, 379, 380, 384, 407, 419, 516
McCarthy, Bp. James, **407**, 418
McCarthy, Bp. John, **407**, 418
McCormack, Bp. John, 378, **407**
McCormack, Bp. William, 53
McDonald, Bp. Andrew J., 53
McDonnell, Bp. Charles, **407**, 418
McDonnell, Bp. Timothy, 382, **407**
McElroy, Bp. Robert W., 382, **407**
McGrath, Bp. Patrick, 382, **407**
McIntyre, Bp. John J., 380, **407**
McLaughlin, Bp. Bernard, **407**, 418
McManus, Bp. Robert, 384, **407**
McNabb, Bp. John, **407**, 418, 418
McNaughton, Bp. William, **407**, 418, 419
McRaith, Bp. John, 380, **407**-408, 419
Mediator Dei, 182, 249
Mediatrix, 121
Medical Mission Sisters, 430, 481, 563
Medical Missionaries of Mary, 430, 481
Medical Sisters of St. Joseph, 481
Medina Estévez, Card. Jorge, 261, 277,
286, 295-297
Meditations, 30, 108, 157, 289, 573, 574
Medjugorje, 23, 125
Medley, Bp. William F., 380, **408**
Meisner, Card. Joachim, **285**, 295-296
Mejía, Card. Jorge María, **285**, 295-296,
297, 610
Melady, Amb. Thomas, 53
Melczek, Bp. Dale, 377, **408**
Melkites, 248, 273, 307, 330, 344, 346,
348, 401, 412, 418, 432, 438, 440, 442,
443, 447, 451, 453, 538
Membership of Religious Institutes of
Men, 467
Membership of Religious Institutes of
Women, 486-488
Men of the Sacred Heart, 503
Men Religious, 128, 149, 165, 274, 361,
441, 489
Men Religious (Statistics), 335, 432,
467-468
Men Religious Institutes, U.S., 458-468
Menaion, 349
Mendicants, 142, 148
Mengeling, Bp. Carl, 378, **408**, 419
Menologion, 349

Mentally Retarded, 522, 524
Mercedarian Sisters, 487, 488
Mercedarians, 210, 464, 467, 476,
487, 488
Merit, 146, 148, 281, 571, 595, 603
Messiah, 89, 100-102, 106, 120, 132,
135, 149, 606
Metanoia, 148
Methodist Church, 580, 582, 586, 596,
598, 600
Methodist-Catholic International
Commission, 587
Mexico, 36, 40, 44, 75, 84, 85, 108, 123,
151, 173, 210, 214, 227, 233, 240, 243,
244, 249, 261, 266, 269, 272, 278,
284, 286, 289, 290, 296, 307, 311, 319,
337-339, 345-347, 352, 353, 355, 358,
363-365, 372, 374, 390, 392, 395, 397,
401, 402, 408, 411, 412, 417, 421, 426,
429, 430, 434, 437, 440, 446, **449-457**,
462, 463, 470, 471, 474, 476-479, 481,
483, 484, 488, 497, 506, 507, 510, 529,
537, 548, 550, 589
Micah, 96, 101
Michael (Feast), 169, 173
Michaels, Bp. James, 408
Michelangelo, 236, 245, 262
Micheli, Maria Serafina, 254
Michigan, 54, 134, 355, 359, 363-365,
373, 390, 392, 394, 397, 408, 411, 412,
416, 421, 423, 433, 436, 439, 470, 481,
482, 493, 497, 501-505, 509, 514, 515,
521, 523, 528, 536, 539, 541, 544, 545,
548, 549, 554, 557, 560, 563, 564
Micronesia, 266, 269, **319**, 321, 395, 430
Midnight Mass, 18, 170
Midrash, 605
Migliore, Abp. Celestino, 266
Migrant and Itinerant Peoples Pontifical
Council, 258
Migration, 8, 11, 12, 20, 36, 40, 81, 302,
341, 355, 420, 422, 428, 498, 504, 575
Miguel Febres Cordero, 210, 251
Miguel Pro, 210, 253
Military Services Archdiocese, 400, 408,
412, 419
Militia Immaculate, 503
Mill Hill Missionaries, 464
Miller, Abp. Michael, 367, **408**, 445
Milone, Bp. Anthony, 377, **409**, 419
Minim Daughters of Mary Immaculate,
481
Minim Fathers, 464, 467
Minim Friars, 207
Minnesota, 44, 52, 356, 365, 368, 374,
390, 392, 421, 423, 433, 436, 439, 470,
496, 515, 521, 523, 528, 536, 543,
545, 603
Miot, Abp. Joseph Serge, 312
Miracle, 7, 24, 26, 27, 32, 37, 44, 71, 72,
76, 132, **148**, 156, 204, 243, 450, 575
Miraculous Medal, 124, 205, 392, 500
Miroslav Bulesic, 215-216, 255
Misericordia Dei, 195, 244
Misericordia Sisters, 481
Missal, 16, 86, 180, 183-185, 187-189,
193, 558, 573
Missale Romanum, 178, 184
Mission Helpers, 481, 558
Mission Workers, 431
Missionaries of Africa, 302, 318, 331,
458, 467, 550, 563
Missionaries to the Americas, 209, 211,
363-365
Missionary Association of Catholic
Women, 503

Missionary Daughters, 481
Missionary Oblates of Mary Immaculate, 391, 392, 464, 554, 563, 565
Missionary Sisters of Our Lady, 468, 475, 481
Missionary Sisters of St. Benedict, 517
Missionary Sisters of Verona, 472
Missionary Society of St. Paul, 465
Mississippi, 51, 84, 352-355, 358, 364, 365, 368, 373, 390, 421, 433, 434, 436, 439, 470, 472, 493, 515, 536, 554
Missouri, 85, 271, 355, 359, 363, 367, 368, 374, 390, 392, 421, 423, 434, 436, 439, 463, 470, 515, 520, 521, 523, 528, 536, 545, 580, 597, 598
Misto, Mons. Luigi, 259
Mit Brennender Sorge, 227, 240, 249
Mitre, 180
Mixed Marriages, 200, 202, 246, 335, 586, 594
Modernism, 148, 149, 158, 226, 238, 239, 356
Molinaru, Fr. Paolo, 53
Monarchianism, 219
Monasticism, 107, 168, 205, 220, 307, 330, 595, 616
Monforton, Bp. Jeffrey M., 383, 409
Mongolia, 265, 266, 269, 319, 339
Monica, 168, 210, 211, 213, 215, 484, 506, 520, 522
Monophysitism, 108, 220
Monotheism, 149
Monothelitism, 221
Monsengwo Pasinya, Card. Laurent, 285, 295-297, 304
Monstrance, 154, 181, 215
Montalvo, Abp. Gabriel, 267, 270
Montana, 356, 363, 365, 374, 398, 421, 423, 434, 436, 439, 528, 536, 554
Monterisi, Card. Francesco, 260, 261, 286, 295-296
Montfort Missionaries, 391, 392, 464, 467, 559
Montoya Upegui, Laura, 252
Moral Teachings of the Church, 110-113
Moravian Brethren, 306
Morazzone Serafino, 254
Morga Iruzubieta, Abp. Celso, 257, 261
Morin, Bp. Roger, 375, 409
Morlino, Bp. Robert, 378, 379, 409
Morneau, Bp. Robert, 377, 409, 525
Morocco, 243, 266, 269, 277, 278, 319, 612
Mosaic Covenant, 605
Mosaic Law, 98, 103, 173, 218
Moscow Patriarchate, 589
Moses, 93, 95, 96, 98, 101, 111, 137, 151, 153-155, 254, 379, 383, 394, 415, 427, 576, 605-607, 611
Moskal, Bp. Robert, 382, 409, 419
Mother of God, 21, 119-122, 139, 143, 161, 162, 165, 173, 174, 185, 194, 208, 254, 277, 349, 389, 464, 468, 469, 473, 476, 481, 488, 577, 590
Mother of God, Sisters of, 481
Motu Proprio, 9, 14, 73, 89, 126, 149, 161, 182, 183, 187-189, 195, 202, 233, 238, 244, 256, 258-260, 272, 275, 276, 490, 495
Movimiento Familiar Cristiano, 342
Mozambique, 243, 266, 269, 290, 296, 318, 319, 330, 338, 339
Mozarabic, 177
Mozcygemba, Leopold, 364
Moynihan, Bp. James, 383, 409, 419
Muench, Bp. Robert W., 375, 409

Mulieris Dignitatem, 244
Müller, Abp. Gerhard, 70-71, 256, 260, 261, 286, 295, 296
Mulvee, Bp. Robert, 376, 409
Mulvey, Bp. William M., 376, 409
Mulieris Dignitatem, 244
Munificentissimus Deus, 240
Mupendawatu, Rev. Jean-Marie Mate Musivi, 258
Muratorian Fragment, 96
Muresan, Card. Lucian, 274, 347
Murphy, Bp. William, 409, 422, 610
Murphy-O'Connor, Card. Cormac, 286, 295-296
Murry, Bp. George, 384, 409, 421, 422, 426
Music, 26, 50, 51, 175, 176, 182, 186, 190, 239, 240, 249, 262, 322, 349, 502, 503, 541, 548, 550, 559, 566-568
Muslims, 6, 20, 41, 47, 58, 61, 62, 67, 78, 208, 210, 221, 242, 258, 260, 308, 314, 315, 318, 319, 328, 331, 334, 372, 576, 580, 605, 611-614
Myanmar, 35, 216, 265-267, 302, 320, 336, 338
Myers, Abp. John, 380, 381, 409, 475
Mystagogy, 149
Mysterium Fidei, 159, 250
Mystery of the Church, 89, 121, 123, 194, 584, 587, 606
Mystic, 107, 108, 205, 207, 210, 216, 248, 526, 565
Mystical Body of Christ, 90, 103, 160, 211, 240, 249, 343
Mystici Corporis Christi, 182, 249

N

Naguib, Card. Antonio, 273, 286, 295-297, 345, 346
Nagy, Card. Stanislas, 286, 295-296
Naickamparampil, Bp. Thomas, 348, 384, 409
Namibia, 265, 266, 269, 320, 338, 339, 403
Napier, Card. Wilfrid, O.F.M., 287, 295-297, 336
Narcisa de Jesús Martillo Morín, 252, 254
Nathan, 99, 100
Nathaniel, 105
National Assembly of Religious Women, 503
National Assembly of Women Religious, 503
National Association for Lay Ministry, 503
National Association of Catholic Family Life, 503
National Association of Catholic Home Educators, 503
National Association of Church Personnel Administrators, 503
National Association of Diaconate Directors, 197, 503
National Association of Diocesan Ecumenical Officers, 503, 616
National Association of Pastoral Musicians, 503, 559
National Association of Priest Pilots, 503
National Catholic AIDS Network, 503
National Catholic Band Association, 503
National Catholic Cemetery, 556
National Catholic Forensic League, 497
National Catholic Rural Life Conference, 279, 362, 431
National Catholic Welfare Conference,

361, 423
National Catholic Welfare Council, 356, 420, 423,
National Christ Child Society, 504
National Conference of Catholic Bishops, 88, 89, 97, 118, 137, 142, 173, 183, 185, 186, 192, 197, 202, 357, 361, 420, 423, 425, 426, 533, 546, 594, 610
National Council for Catholic Evangelization, 504
National Council of Catholic Women, 504, 556
National Federation for Catholic Youth Ministry, 427, 496, 497
National Federation of Priests' Councils, 504, 564
National Life Center, 504
National News, 82-83
National Pastoral Life Center, 504, 557
Native American Catholics in the United States,
Nativity, 17, 18, 37, 137, 161, 162, 165, 167, 169, 170, 277, 350, 368, 387, 388, 442, 492, 569
Natural Family Planning, 501, 570
Natural Law, 80, 111, 140, 147, 149, 225, 241
Naumann, Abp. Joseph, 378, 409
Nazareth, 10, 120, 123, 145, 147, 233, 359, 386, 397, 406, 471, 478, 479, 482, 486, 488, 511, 513, 514, 516, 517, 520, 521, 527, 540, 544, 559, 560, 602
Nebraska, 374, 392, 401, 417, 421, 423, 434, 436, 440, 516, 521, 523, 528, 536, 545, 555
Necromancy, 138, 149
Nehemiah, 96, 99, 101, 102, 605
Neo-Scholasticism, 149, 155, 159
Nepal, 265, 266, 269, 278, 279, 320, 339
Nerinckx, Charles, 364, 480
Nerses Bedros XIX Tarmouni, 274, 345, 347
Nestorian Churches, 107, 108, 344, 346
Nestorianism, 220, 313
Netherlands, 19, 74, 243, 266, 269, 277, 279, 281, 291, 296, 320, 338, 341, 342, 403, 464, 470-472, 496, 547, 559
NETWORK, 505
Nevada, 364, 372, 374, 421, 423, 434, 436, 440, 470, 536, 537, 554, 568
Nevares, Bp. Eduardo, 381, 409, 425
Nevins, Bp. John, 384, 409, 419
New American Bible, 97, 500
New Evangelization, 13, 14, 23, 26, 30, 55, 56, 72, 75, 79, 80, 86, 259, 275, 281, 289, 567, 573
New Hampshire, 48, 85, 354, 373, 392, 421, 434, 436, 440, 470, 491, 516, 529, 537, 564, 591
New Jersey, 86, 216, 270, 353, 354, 363, 365-367, 373, 388, 390, 392, 400, 421, 423, 426, 434, 437, 440, 470, 509, 510, 516, 521, 523, 525, 529, 537, 545, 569, 615
New Mexico, 84, 85, 352, 353, 358, 364, 372, 374, 390, 392, 395, 421, 426, 434, 437, 440, 449, 470, 529, 537
New Testament, 52, 90, 94-98, 100, 102, 104, 108, 130, 131, 134, 137, 153, 155, 174, 176, 178, 196, 218, 349, 500, 595, 606, 608, 611, 613
New Zealand, 214, 243, 265-267, 269, 294, 296, 320, 338, 339, 395
Newman, Bl. John Henry, 113, 150, 226, 255

Newsletters, 498, 551-563
Newspapers, 14, 323, 361, 500, 551-563, 565-567, 570, 573
Nicaea, Councils of, 107, 109, 139, 211, 219, 229, 273, 311, 590, 591
Nicaragua, 22, 49, 71, 243, 244, 266, 269, 278, 287, 296, **320**, 338, 413, 418, 430
Nicene Creed, 108, **109**, 192, 219, 220, 349
Nicholas I, Pope, 234
Nicholas II, Pope, 235
Nicholas III, Pope, 223, 235
Nicholas IV, Pope, 235, 236
Nicholas V, Pope, 236, 237, 493
Nicholas V (Antipope), 237
Nicholas of Flue, 210, 251
Nicholas of Longobardi, 217
Nicholas of Myra, 210, 212-214, 350
Nicholas of Tolentino, 210, 213, 458
Nicholson, Amb. James, 269
Nichols, Card. Vincent Gerard, 70-71, 286, 295, **296**
Nickless, Bp. R. Walker, 383, **410**
Nicora, Card. Attilio, 47, 260, 287, 295, **296**
Niederauer, Abp. George, 382, **410**, 419, 422
Nienstedt, Abp. John, 380, 382, **410**, 422
Niger, 265, 266, 269, **321**, 336, 338, 339
Nigeria, 24, 145, 243-245, 261, 266, 267, 269, 272, 277, 287, 296, **321**, 338, 339, 408, 429, 473, 548
Night Prayer, 136, 138, 149, 176
Nihil Obstat, 134, 149
Njue, Card. John, **286**-87, 295, 337
Noah, 137, 611
Nobel Peace Prize, 287, 307
Nomination of Bishops, 264, 274
Non Abbiamo Bisogno, 227, 240, 249
Non Expedit, 149
Non-Believers, Council for Dialogue, 259
Noonan, Bp. John G., 379, **410**
Norbertine Fathers, 393, 543
Norms of Ecumenism, 579
Norms of Judgment, 199
North American College, 37, 52, 279, 281, 283, 287, 294, 355, 394-416, 422, 546
North American Martyrs, 169, 250, 363, 364, 441, 446, 563
North Carolina, 370, 373, 390, 405, 421, 434, 437, 440, 517, 524, 530, 537, 573
North Dakota, 84, 372, 374, 390, 421, 423, 434, 437, 440, 517, 522, 524, 530, 537, 545
North Korea, 12, **316**
Norway, 204, 214, 243, 265, 266, 269, 312, **321**
Nostra Aetate, 25, 229, 605, 606, 608, 609, 611, 612
Novak, Bp. Alfred, **410**, 418, 419
NOVALIS, 342, 556, 565, 566
Novatianism, 107
Novena, 24, 149
Novice, 149, 205
Numismatic Office, 262
Nunc Dimittis, 133, 149, 176
Nuncios and Delegates, 264
Nuno de Santa Maria Álvares Pereira, 252
Nycz, Card. Kazmierz, **287**, 295-296
Nykiel, Rev. Krzysztof Jozef, 258

O

O Salutaris Hostia, 150
O'Brien, Card. Edwin, **287**, 295-297, 375, 383, 410, 573
O'Brien, Bp. Thomas, 380, **410**, 419
O'Brien, Card. Keith, 27, 28, 31, **287**, 295
O'Connell, C.M., Bp. David, 383, **410**
O'Connell, Bp. Edward, 378, **410**
O'Malley, Card. Sean, 67-70, **287**, 295-297, 375, 377, 380, 410, 422
O'Neill, Bp. Arthur, 381
Oath, 48, **149**, 151, 224, 225, 239, 246, 308, 354, 355, 366
Oath of Succession, 224
Oath of Supremacy, 308
Obadiah, 96, 101
Obama, Barack, 10, 31, 269, 357, 372
Obando Bravo, Card. Miguel, **287**, 295-297, 321
Obituaries, 51-54
Oblate Sisters, 355, 359, 474, 483, 484
Oblate Sisters of Providence, 355, 359, 483
Oblates of Mary Immaculate, 282, 288, 317, 391-393, 411, 430, 441, 467, 531, 542, 554, 563, 565, 566
Observance of Sundays, 112
Oceania, 210, 243, 275, 296, 297, 299, 316, 327, 331, 335, 339, 347, 418, 429, 430, 489
Ochoa, Bp. Armando, 377, **410**, 425, 455
Ochoa de Chinchetru, Abp. Juan, 259, 261
Octave, 21, 72, **150**, 165, 166, 170, 172-174
Office of Papal Charities, 260
Ohio, 353, 356, 359, 363, 364, 367, 373, 390, 392, 395-397, 402, 421, 423, 432, 434, 437, 440, 463, 470, 471, 499, 517, 520-522, 524, 530, 533, 537, 541, 542, 544, 545, 555, 597
Oils Holy, 150, 182
Oklahoma, 48, 50, 84, 85, 269, 356, 374, 379, 386, 388, 393, 395, 398, 411, 415, 416, 418, 421, 427, 434, 437, 440, 460, 470, 471, 517, 530, 537, 553, 555, 557, 597
Okogie, Card. Anthony, 287, 295-297
Old Testament, 8, 13, 88, 90, 95-**98**, 100-102, 108, 131, 132, 137, 138, 151-153, 155, 159, 172, 178, 218, 228, 349, 350, 499, 559, 606,
Olivetans, 459, 468, 488
Olivier, Bp. Leonard, **410**, 419, 427
Olmsted, Bp. Thomas, 381, 384, **410**
Oman, **321**, 332
Omega, 130, 151, 531
Onaiyekan, Card. John, 39, **287**, 295, 296
Ontology, 148, 150
Optatam Totius, 229
Opus Dei, 24, 151, 208, 280, 283, 402, 507, 550, 570
Oratorians, 225, 458, 464, 467
Oratory of St. Philip Neri, 464
Ordained Ministry, 9, 586, 600, 612
Order of Christian Funerals, 189
Order of Christian Initiation of Adults
   See RCIA
Order of the Alhambra, 505
Orders of Knighthood, 571
Orders Religious, 32, 38, 138, 148, 155, 177, 201, 226, 239, 240, 248, 273, 298, 304, 307, 311-313, 317, 324, 333, 420, 449, 450, 458, 544, 549, 570, 616
Orders Religious (Statistics), 335, 432, 467-468, 486-488
Orders Religious, Men, 335, 432, 467-468
Orders Religious, Women, 335, 432, 468-486
Ordinary, 273-275
Ordinatio Sacerdotalis, 198, 244
Ordination, 44, 46, 83, 98, 128, 130, 131, 133, 136, 150, 165, 184, 186, **196**-198, 200, 215, 221, 241, 244, 256, 273, 274, 294, 299, 302, 308, 327, 350, 361, 362, 394, 417, 546, 586, 587, 591, 592, 598, 600, 601, 604
Ordination of Women, 46, **198**, 299, 308, 586, 600, 601
Ordo Confirmationis, 192
Ordo Consecrationis Virginum, 160
Ordo Initiationis Christianae Adultorum, 192
Ordo Paenitentiae, 195
Oregon, 355, 356, 360, 365, 372, 374, 380, 393, 400, 412, 414, 416, 417, 421, 423, 434, 437, 440, 463, 470, 480, 507, 517-519, 522, 524, 530, 532, 537, 546, 558
Organizations, Catholic, 3, 258, 312, 340-342, 362, 424, 426, 427, 496, 498, 504, 509
Oriental Orthodox Churches, 4, 344, 580, 589, 592-594
Orientale Lumen, 244, 245
Orientalium Ecclesiarum, 229, 343, 351, 576, 589
Origen, 219
Ortega y Alamino, Card. Jaime Lucas, **287**, 295-297, 453
Orthodox Churches, 47, 191, 221, 222, 245, 344, 372, 580, 583, **588**-594
Orthodox-Roman Catholic Consultation, 587
Osservatore Romano, L', 113, 128, 259, 263, 264, 268, 374, 442, 451, 551, 554, 566, 569, 578, 605
Ostensorium, 181
Ostpolitik, 150, 242
Ouédraogo, Card. Philippe Nakellentuba, 70-71, 287, 295, 296
Ottenweller, Bp. Albert,
Ottenweller, Bp. Albert, 53, **410**, 418
Ouellet, Card. Marc, 256, 260, **287**, 295, 296
Our Father, 87, 88, 129, 140, **151**, 152, 154, 349
Overseas Missions, 429, 430

P

Pactum Callixtinum, 222
Paganism, **150**, 220
Paglia, Abp. Vincenzo, 40, 258, 261
Pago Pago, 325, 416, 430, 438
Pakistan, 11, 77, 243, 266, 269, 276, 300, **321**, 338, 396, 408, 418
Palatine Guard of Honor, 261
Palau, 253, 266, 269, **321**, 395
Palazzo Apostolico Vaticano, 255, 259
Palestine, 10, 32, 37, 67, 97, 105, 106, 122, 207, 218, 249, 256, 265, 269, 280, 314, 344, 505, 577, 605
Pallium, 180, 232, 243, 273, 274
Pallottine Sisters, 482
Palm Sunday, 161, 166, **173**, 350
Panafieu, Card. Bernard, **287**, 295-296
Panama, 243, 266, 269, 286, 289, **321**,

322, 338, 339, 365, 507, 547
Pancras, 167, 210
Pange Lingua, 150
Paola Frassinetti, 210, 251, 474
Papacy, 17, 24, 25, 56, 63, 70, 76, 106, 107, 125, 211, 220-223, 228, 231-233, 235-243, 261, 262, 323, 558, 571, 591, 607, 611
Papal Flag, 262
Papal Gendarmes, 261
Papal Household, Prefecture, 259-260
Papal Medals, 571
Papal Primacy, 13, 223, 224, 226, 586, 595
Papal Representatives, 264, 267, 298
Papal States, 225-227, 261, 262, 270, 315, 571
Papal Trips, 56-66
Paprocki, Bp. Thomas J., 383, 410, 422
Papua New Guinea, 214, 243, 244, 266, 269, 293, **322**, 338, 397, 403, 411, 418, 430,
Paraclete, 62, 139, **150**, 465, 468
Paraclete, Servants of the, 465
Paraguay, 214, 243, 251, 266, 269, 277, **322**, 338, 363-365, 418, 430, 547
Paris Foreign Mission Society, 217, 467
Parishes (Statistics), 335, 432
Parkes, Bp. Gregory, 380, 410
Parolin, Card. Pietro, 29, 31, 35, 37-39, 42, 47, 50, 67, 70-71, 255, 257, **287**, 295, 296
Parousia, 103, 150
Paschal Baylon, 210, 212
Paschal Candle, 129, 150, 182
Paschal I, Pope, 234,
Paschal II, Pope, 235, 572
Paschal III, Pope, 237
Paschal Mystery, 88, 113, 154, 161, 176, 187
Paschal Precept, 151
Paskai, Card. Laszlo, **287**-88, 295-296
Passion of Christ, 128, 151, 158, 216
Passion Sunday, 166, 173
Passionist Nuns, 482, 527
Passionist Sisters, 473, 482
Passionists, 210, 225, 415, 465, 467, 529, 559
Passover, 98, 178, 605
Pastor Aeternus, 92
Pastor Bonus, 9, 17, 26, 245, 255-257, 263
Pastoral Ministry, 30, 49, 68, 70, 115, 131, 135, 137, 143, 202, 273, 277, 290, 292, 313, 317, 424, 425, 431, 458, 468, 470-473, 475, 477, 478, 484, 505, 510, 525, 568, 574
Pastoral Office of Bishops, 421
Pastores Dabo Vobis, 244, 256, 275
Paten, 139, 179, **181**, 196, 349, 351
Pater Noster, 151
Pates, Bp. Richard, 12, 20, 24, **410**
Patriarch, 11, 14, 15, 18, 20, 35, 37, 38, 41, 43, 46, 47, 49-54, 57-60, 67, 77-79, **151**, 220-222, 240-243, 247-249, 273, 274, 279, 286, 288, 291, 297, 307, 313, 314, 317, 323, 330, 336, 343-348, 364, 417, 418, 572, 576, 583-586, 588, 592, 606, 614
Patriarchal Lateran Archbasilica, 290
Patriarchal Vatican Basilica, 53, 285
Patriarchs, Eastern Catholic, 343-346
Patriarchs, Orthodox, 581-584
Patron Saints of Places, 214
Patrons and Intercessors, 211-214
Paul, St., See Paul of Tarsus

Paul I, Pope, 51, 227, 234, 237, 242
Paul II, Pope, 233, 236, 237
Paul III, Pope, 216, 229, 236, 255
Paul IV, Pope, 130, 236, 259
Paul V, Pope, 236, 378, 382
Paul VI, Pope Bl., 18, 27, 37, 57-61, 70, 72, 76, 79, 93, 97, 108, 114-117, 124, 126, 136, 571, 572, 577, 583-586, 588, 601, 615, 633
Canonizations, 241-245, 250, 251
Encyclicals, 245, 250
Pontificate, 245-247
Paul Miki, 165, 210
Paul of Tarsus, 95, 96, 102-103, 106, 218
Paul Yun Ji-Chung and 123 companions, 216, 255
Paula de Jesus, Bl. Francisca de, 216, 255
Pauline Fathers, 393, 465
Pauline Letters, 96, 102, 608
Pauline Privilege, 201
Paulinus of Nola, 167, 210
Paulists, 355, 458, 465, 468
Pax Christi, 342, 493, 496, 552, 570
Pax Christi International, 342, 570
Pax Christi USA, 496, 570
Peace of Augsburg, 224, 225, 310
Peace of Westphalia, 225, 310
Pearce, Bp. George, **410**, 417, 419
Pectoral Cross, 151
Pedophilia, See Sex Abuse Scandal
Pedro de San Jose Betancur, 363
Pelagianism, 108, 220, 323
Pelagius I, Pope, 234
Pelagius II, Pope, 234
Pell, Card. George, 26, 73, 259, 260, **288**, 295-297
Peña, Bp. Raymundo, 375, 376, **410**, 425
Penance, 7, 50, 67, 79, 88, 90, 101, 123-125, 127-131, 136, 137, 141, 143, 144, 146, 148, 151-154, 156, 157, 161-163, 165, 171, 180, 183, 186, 189-191, **193**-196, 200, 203, 211, 219, 223, 244, 250, 255, 275, 350, 477, 486, 584, 590, 594, 595, , ,
Penance, Sacrament of, 193-196
Penitence, **151**, 607
Penitential Celebrations, 195
Penitential Rite, 178, 185, 195
Pennsylvania, 40, 43, 353, 354, 358, 359, 367, 374, 390, 393, 399, 404, 411, 421, 423, 434, 437, 440, 470, 509, 518, 520, 522, 524, 525, 530, 537, 546, 597, 599
Pentateuch, 96, **98**, 605
Pentecost, 41, 88, 89, 120, 134, 139, 151, 161, 162, 164, 167, 171, **173**, 174, 180, 184, 218, 349, 491, 505, 563, 605
Pentecost (Feast), 605
Pentecostals, 46, 580, 596, 600
Pentecostarion, 349
People of God, 30, 72, 73, 77, 89-92, 94, 121, 122, 126, 127, 131, 135, 136, **151**, 191, 196, 230, 242, 274, 423, 494, 554, 587, 606, 607
Pepe, Bp. Joseph, 378, **411**
Percentage of Catholics in Total Population, 433, 434,
Percentage of Catholics in World, 335
Perez, Bp. Nelson J., 381, **411**, 425
Pérez, María Crescencia, 215, 255
Perfectae Caritatis, 229
Permanent Deacons, 86, 197, **198**, 298, 427, 432, 503
Permanent Deacon, U.S. Statistics, 432

Permanent Deacons, World, 335
Permanent Observer, 267, 278, 279, 285, 286, 395, 418
Perpetual Eucharistic Adoration, 189, 391
Perry, Bp. Joseph, 357, 376, **411**, 427
Persecution of Christians, 11, 23, 49, 106, 218
Persian Empire, 130, 346
Persico, Bp. Lawrence, 376, **411**
Personal Envoys, 270
Personal Prelature, 151, 283, 507, 550
Peru, 41, 156, 214, 243, 248, 266, 269, 280, 282, 289, 291, 293, 296, 307, **322**, 338, 364, 365, 397, 399, 402, 403, 407, 415, 418, 429, 430, 459, 547, 549, 567
Pesach (Passover), 605
Peter, 10, 14, 16-19, 21, 26, 28, 30, 31, 34, 37, 40, 42, 44, 46, 53, 55, 59, 65, 67, 72, 79, 80, 85, 88, 90, 92, 93, 96, 98, 103, 105, 106, 108, 113, 131, 141, 144, 146, 149, 151, 157, 159, 160, 162, 163, 165-171, 173, 174, 177, 180, 189, 205, 209, 210, 212-218, 222, 228, 229, 231-233, 235, 240, 273
Peter, Primacy of, 92, 99, 104, 106, 109, 110, 115, 126, 127, 222-226, 273
Peter Canisius, **108**, 170, 240, 248, 250, 310
Peter Celestine, 212
Peter Chanel, 166, 210, 251
Peter Chrysologus, 108, 168
Peter Claver, 163, 169, 213, 214, 250, **363**, 427, 482, 502
Peter Damian, 108, 165
Peter Donders, 252
Peter Faber, 216, 252
Peter Julian Eymard, **210**, 251
Peter Lombard, 149, 222
Peter Nolasco, **210**, 464, 493
Peter of Alcantara, 210, 214
Peter of Ghent, 365
Peter of Narbonne, 210, 251
Peter of Tarentaise, 235
Petrarch, 223
Petrine Privilege, 201, 255
Pevec, Bp. A. Edward, **411**, 419
Pfeifer, Bp. Michael, 382, **411**
Pham Minh Mán Card. Jean-Baptiste, **288**, 295-297
Pharisees, 26, 111, **151**, 154, 155
Phelonion, 351
Phi Delta Kappa, 533
Phi Kappa Theta, 498
Philangeli, 505
Philemon, 96, 103
Philip, 105, 106
Philip Benizi, 210
Philip Neri, 167, **210**, 215, 286, 458, 464
Philippians, 96, 103
Philippines, 15, 22, 35, 36, 38, 45, 63, 70, 71, 77, 86, 214, 241, 243, 244, 266, 269, 277, 279, 282, 288, 292-294, 296, 319, 322, **323**, 338, 394, 408, 411, 429, 497, 507, 547, 566
Philosophy, 52, 107, 109, 128, 140, 147-149, 152, 153, 155, 159, 218, 226, 239, 243, 247, 272, 277, 280-284, 286, 289, 291, 292, 370, 395, 507, 524, 546, 548, 549, 556, 559, 615
Photian Schism, 221
Physically Challenged, 525
Piacenza, Card. Mauro, 257
Piamarta Giovanni Battista, 252
Piarists, 208, 465, 467
Piche, Lee Anthony, 381, 411

Picpus Fathers, 466
Pierce, Franklin, 371
Pilarczyk, Abp. Daniel, 376, **411**, 419, 420, 589
Pilgrimages, 189, 242, 592, 612
Pilgrims, 7, 9, 18, 21, 23, 42, 61, 62, 79, 125, 135, 158, 213, 243, 352, 446, 577, 599
Pilla, Bp. Anthony, 185, 376, **411**, 419
PIME Missionaries, 559, 573
Pio, Padre, 169, **210**, 252, 254
Pious Schools, 208, 465, 482, 488
Pious Union of Prayer, 505
Piovanelli, Card. Silvano, **288**, 295-297
Pius I, Pope, 233,
Pius II, Pope, 182, 236,
Pius III, Pope, 229, 236,
Pius IV, Pope, 109, 205, 229, 236, 256, 263, 271,
Pius V, Pope, 87, 154, 166, 188, 210, 236, 256, 257, 391,
Pius VI, Pope, 225, 236, 246, 354,
Pius VII, Pope, 173, 225, 226, 237, 246, 354, 463,
Pius VIII, Pope, 237, 246,
Pius IX, Pope, 72, 123, 136, 144, 147, 150, 158, 172-174, 210, 226, 229, 237, 243, 246, 254, 256, 260, 263, 270, 271, 273, 276, 355, 465, 571, 572,
Pius X, Pope, 123, 126, 147, 149, 155, 158, 168, 182, 188, 189, 193, 226, 237-239, 248, 250, 251, 256-258, 262, 263, 284, 356, 361, 395, 398, 405, 406, 411, 446, 465, 491, 529, 545, 546, 549, 571, 572,
Canonizations, 250
Encyclicals, 238, 248
Life, 238-239
Pius XI, 114, 115, 136, 171, 173, 213, 214, 227, 237, 239, 241, 249, 250, 256-262, 271, 285, 351, 450
Canonizations, 240, 250-251
Encyclicals, 240, 249
Life, 239-240
Pontificate, 239-240
Pius XII, 42, 70, 77, 97, 104, 105, 114, 123, 136, 160, 171-173, 182, 188, 202, 227, 237, 240-243, 245, 249, 251, 256, 257, 259, 260, 263, 270, 271, 281, 304, 306, 351, 357, 490, 500, 571, 572, 607
Canonizations, 241, 251
Encyclicals, 249
Life, 240-241
Pontificate, 240-241
PLO, 243
Poland, 9, 41, 42, 45, 69, 70, 72, 115, 204, 205, 208, 214, 221, 226, 233, 237, 239, 241, 243-246, 248, 249, 261, 266, 269, 272, 281-285, 287, 290, 296, **323**, 338, 342, 346, 358, 395, 417, 460, 465, 472, 474, 478, 481, 484, 499, 507, 547, 549, 550, 589, 590
Poletto, Card. Severino, **288**, 295-296
Poli, Card. Mario, 70-71, **288**, 295, 296
Policarpo Card. Jose, 53-54
Polish National Catholic Church, 361, 580, 593, 594
Polish National Catholic-Roman Catholic Dialogue, 587, 594
Poloni, Vincenza Maria, 254
Polycarp, 106, 165, **210**, 218, 288, 294, 295
Pontes de Souza, Brito Dulce Lopes, 254
Pontian, 168, 207, 210, 233
Pontiff, 6, 7, 9, 10, 13, 14, 17-19, 21, 22, 24-27, 29, 30, 32-34, 37, 38, 41, 42,

45, 46, 49, 55, 56, 63, 67, 69, 70, 72, 73, 76, 91-93, 117, 118, 129, 145, 159, 177, 188, 189, 193, 194, 196, 210, 228, 232, 233, 243, 244, 246, 259, 262, 264, 273, 275, 330, 343, 351, 421, 571, 584
Pontifical Academies, 3, 259, 271, 272
Pontifical Academy of Sciences, 271
Pontifical Academy of Social Sciences, 69, 245, 272
Pontifical Biblical Commission, 105, 233, 238, 255, 260, 282, 289, 293, 608
Pontifical Biblical Institute, 51, 105, 239, 278, 282, 285-290, 293, 413-416, 550
Pontifical College Josephinum, 272, 394, 396, 399, 401, 404, 407, 410, 412, 414, 545, 549
Pontifical Commissions, 260
Pontifical Councils, 233, 258, 580
Pontifical Ecclesiastical Academy, 277, 278, 280, 283, 284, 286, 287, 289-293, 394-396, 403, 408, 550
Pontifical Ecclesiastical Faculties, 548-550
Pontifical Mission Societies, 505, 565
Pontifical Missionary Union, 566,
Pontifical Noble Guard, 261
Pontifical Orders, 571
Pontifical Orders of Knighthood, 571
Pontifical Universities, 494, 547, 550
Pontificio Annuario, 233, 237, 255, 263, 264, 267, 268, 271, 298, 336, 339, 343, 344, 348, 394, 438, 442, 451, 455, 458, 467, 486, 489, 492, 507, 547, 548, 550
Pontius Pilate, 60, 109
Poor Clare Nuns, 54, 458, 472, 475, 483
Poor Clares, 128, 168, 205, 223, 280, 458, 474-476
Poor Clares of Perpetual Adoration, 476
Poor Clares of St. Colette, 475
Poor Handmaids of Jesus Christ, 483
Popes of the Roman Catholic Church, 233-237
Popish Plot, 225, 353
Popp, Bp. Bernard, 418
Population, Catholic World, 335
Population, Catholic U.S., 426
Population Research Institute, 505
Population Statistics, 447, 455
Populorum Progressio, 77, 114, 116-118, 242, 250, 258
Pornography, 83, 86, 299, 503, 610
Porphyry, 219
Portiuncula Indulgence, **151**, 223
Portugal, 9, 53, 77, 107, 123, 124, 205, 206, 214, 216, 225, 227, 233, 235, 239, 242, 243, 247-249, 261, 266, 269, 279, 281, 286, 290, 296, 298, 299, 301, 303, 319, **323**, 324, 338, 341, 365, 474, 547, 571
Potocnak, Bp. Joseph, **411**, 417
Poupard, Card. Paul, 260, **288**, 295-297
Power of the Keys, **146**, 196
Pragmatic Sanction of Bourges, 223, 224
Pragmatism, 152
Prassek, Johannes, 254
Precious Blood Sisters, 483, 564
Precious Blood Society of, 465
Prefect Apostolic, 274, 319
Prefecture of Economic Affairs of the Holy See, 54, 74, 292
Prelates, U.S. Retired, 418-419
Prelature of Opus Dei, 283, 402, 550
Premonstratensians, 210, 465, 467
Preparation of Gifts, 178
Presbyterian Churches, 598, 599
Presbyterorum Ordinis, 229

Presentation (Feast), 165, 173
Presentation (Religious), 483
Press Association Catholic, 361, 500, 551, 552, 566, 569, 573, 574
Press Association Catholic (Awards), 573, 574
Press Office Vatican, 26, 67, 255, 259
Press Catholic (Statistics), 551
Press Vatican, 10, 26, 67, 69, 72, 255, 259, 263
Preternatural Gifts, 152
Prie Dieu, 152
Priestly Celibacy, 38, 242, 299, 320
Priestly Formation, 70, 229, 455
Priestly Fraternity of St. Peter, 44, 465, 467
Primacy of St. Peter, 92, 99, 104, 106, 109, 110, 115, 126, 127, 222-226, 273
Primaldo Antonio and Companions, 252
Primary Option, 152
Primate, 38, 128, 210, 273, 274, 279, 416, 596, 597
Prior, 15, 44, 89, 96, 129, 149, **152**, 186, 193, 195, 201, 203, 233, 255, 261, 288, 527, 528, 572, 609
Priscillianism, 209, 323
Privilege of Faith (Petrine Privilege), 255
Pro-Cathedral, 152, 388, 389
Pro Ecclesia Foundation, 505
Pro Sanctity Movement, 342, 490, 505
Probabiliorism, 136, 152
Probabilism, 136, 152
Profession of Faith, 87-89, **109**, 127, 133, 178, 194, 584, 612
Pro-Life Activities, 2, 8, 84, 86, 422, 507, 563
Pro-Nuncio, 264, 267, 270, 276, 278, 279, 281, 285, 286, 291, 293
Propaganda Fide, 352, 356, 400, 405
Proportionalism, 136, **153**, 157
Protestant Churches, 146, 308, 312, **595**-600
Protestant Reformation, 126, 216, 308
Protocanonical, 97
Protodeacon, 53, 279, 285
Protomartyrs, 291
Protonotary, 21, 274, 405
Proverbs, 96, 100
Providentissimus Deus, 105, 238, 248, 249
Provost, Bp. Glen, 378, **411**
Psalms, 96, 99, **100**, 104, 130, 132, 176, 184, 500
Publications, Vatican, 262-263
Publishers, Catholic, 183
Puerto Rico, 243, 265, 266, 284, **324**, 338, 352, 356, 362, 389, 390, 396, 398, 403, 418, 425, 426, 429, 430, 438, 462, 497, 507, 538, 542, 547, 572
Pujats, Card. Janis, **288**, 295-297, 337
Puljic, Card. Vinko, **288**, 295-297, 301
Pulpit, 181, 215
Purgatory, 108, 143, 146, **153**, 224, 595, 603
Purification, 30, 101, 173, 179, 192, 253, 578, 583, 603
Purim, 99, 605
Purse, 106, 215
Pyx, 181

Q

Qatar, 264-267, 269, **324**, 332
Quadragesima, 153
Quadragesimo Anno, 114, 115, 118, 136, 227, 240, 249
Quakers, 40, 596

Quam Singulari, 193, 239
Quanta Cura, 158, 226, 246, 247
Quartodecimans, 139
Quebec, 12, 39, 85, 217, 354, 471, 491, 556
Queen of Peace, 79, 190, 261, 469, 513, 516, 518, 529, 530
Queenship of Mary, 173, 249
Quevedo, O.M.I., Card. Orlando, 70-71, **288**, 295, 296
Quinn, Abp. John, 379, 382, **411**, 418
Quinn, Bp. Alexander, 54
Quinn, Bp. Francis, 381, **411**
Quinn, Bp. John M., 383, **411**
Quinque Viae, 153
Qumran, 98

R

Racism, 153, 582
Radio, Catholic, 567, 569
Radio, Vatican, 55, 75, 262, 292, 293, 567-569
Rai, Card. Bechara Boutros, O.M.M., 273, **288**-289, 295, 296, 344-345
Raica, Bp. Steven, 377, **411**
Ramadan, 612
Ramirez, Bp. Ricardo, 378, **411**, 425
Patabendige Don, Card. Albert Malcolm Ranjith, **288**, 295, 296, 338
Raphael (Feast), 99, 130, 173, 212, 214
Rash Judgment, 153
Rassas, Bp. George, 376, **411**
Rationalism, 107, 147, 153, 222, 226
Ratzinger, Card. Joseph See Benedict XVI
Ravasi, Card. Gianfranco, 258, 260, 261, **289**, 295, 296
Ravenna, 108, 212, 235, 583, 588, 590
Raymond Nonnatus, **210**, 212, 388
Raymond of Peñafort, 126, 165, **210**, 213,
RCIA, 185-186, 574
Re, Card. Giovanni Battista, 248, **289**, 295, 296
Reader (Lector), 197, 495
Reagan Pres. Ronald, 236, 269, 270, 372
Reception of Communion, 181, 183, **193**, 579
Receptions into Church, 432
Receptions into the Church in the United States, 439, 440
Recollects, 441, 458, 467
Reconciliation, Sacrament of, See Penance
Redemptionis Donum, 244
Redemptionis Sacramentum, 184
Redemptor Hominis, 115, 244, 250
Redemptoris Custos, 244
Redemptoris Mater, 121, 122, 250, 545
Redemptoris Missio, 250
Redemptorist Fathers, 393, 465
Redemptorists, 107, 205, 208, 225, 292, 333, 402, 415, 467, 558
Reformation, Catholic, 224-225, 229
Reformation Protestant, 126, 216, 308, **595**
Rehabilitation Center, 463, 509, 512, 520
Reichert, Bp. Stephen, **411**, 417, 430
Reilly, Bp. Daniel, 379, **411**, 419
Reiss, Bp. Francis, 383, **411**, 611
Relativism, 65, 153
Relics, 77, 78, 105, 109, 127, **153**, 179, 206, 209, 221, 256, 351, 393, 590,
Religion in Public Schools, 369
Religious Freedom, 8, 9, 20, 25, 31, 32, 35, 39, 40, 43, 44, 58, 82, 138, 141,

142, 225, 229, 243, 298, 302, 306, 309, 312-317, 319, 325, 326, 329, 353, 354, 358, 368, 369, 608, 609, 616
Religious Orders, 32, 38, 138, 148, 155, 177, 201, 226, 239, 240, 248, 273, 298, 304, 307, 311-313, 317, 324, 333, 420, 449, 450, 458, 544, 549, 570, 616
Religious Orders (Statistics), 335, 432, 467-468, 486-488
Religious Orders, Men, 335, 432, 467-468
Religious Orders, Women, 335, 432, 468-486
Reliquary, 14, 154
Representatives of the Holy See, 25, 264-267, 610
Representatives to the Holy See, 268
Requiem Mass, 179
Rerum Novarum, 114-118, 136, 226, 227, 238, 240, 247, 249, 250, 361
Rescript, 154, 218, 263
Resurrection of Christ, 88, 102, 104, 144, 162, 172, 176, 182, 591, 603
Resurrectionists, 465
Retarded Children, 524
Retired Bishops, 421, 430, 455
Retired, Facilities for, 4, 511-519
Retreats, 193, 213, 461, 468, 525, 527-529
Retreats International, 525
Retrouvaille, 53, 506
Revelation, 13, 51, 56, 88, 90, 92-96, 98, 100, 103, 105, 110-112, 114, 126, 129, 136, 138, 140-143, 149, 152-159, 174, 178, 218, 226, 228, 229, 331, 351, 585, 595, 605, 606, 608, 609, 611, 613, 615
Revelation, Dogmatic Constitution, See Dei Verbum
Revelation Book of, 71, 80, **103**, 574
Revised Standard Version, 97
Rhoades, Kevin C., 376, 377, **411**, 422
Rhode Island, 53, 366, 373, 421, 434, 437, 440, 470, 518, 530, 537, 546
Riashi, Bp. Georges, **411**-412, 417
Ricard, Card. Jean-Pierre, **289**, 295-296
Ricard, Bp. John, 380, **412**, 419, 426
Ricken Bp. David 377, **412**, 422
Rigali, Card. Justin, **289**, 295-297, 381, 382, 407, 412, 419
Rights and Obligations of the Faithful, 127, 494
Rights and Obligations of the Laity, 494-495
Risen Christ, 34, 72, 87, 106, 142, 150, 388, 460, 585
Rita Amada of Jesus, 254
Rita of Cascia, 167, 210, 212, 215, 250
Rite of Christian Initiation of Adults (RCIA), 185-186, 574
Rivera Carrera, Card. Norberto, **289**, 295-297, 307, 450, 451, 453
Rizzotto, Bp. Vincent, **412**, 419
Robert Bellarmine, **108**, 169, 212, 232, 240, 250
Roberts, Chief Justice John, 372
Roche, Abp. Arthur, 256, 261
Rochet, 180,
Rodé, Card. Franc, **289**, 295-296
Rodi, Abp. Thomas, 375, 379, **412**
Rodimer, Bp. Frank, 380, **412**
Rodriguez, Bp. Miguel, **412**, 419, 425
Rodriguez, Bp. Placido, 378, **412**, 425
Rodriguez Castro, St. Bonifacia, 253
Rodríguez Maradiaga, Card. Oscar, **289**, 295-296
Rogationists, 467

Rogito, 154
Rolando Rivi, 215-216, 255
Roman Curia, 3, 9, 17, 18, 21, 26, 30, 37, 53, 54, 69, 71, 74, 79, 116, 125, 131, 136-138, 144, 146, 152, 195, 238, 239, 241, 242, 245, **255**-261, 263, 273, 274, 276, 280, 281, 283, 288, 297, 335, 406, 417, 429, 432, 558, 567, 572
Roman Empire, 125, 133, 151, 177, 219, 221, 225, 311, 313, 344
Roman Martyrology, 148, 204
Roman Missal, 180, **183-185**, 187-189, 193
Roman Question, 227, 238-240, 261
Roman Rite, 105, 106, 136, 139, 146, 154, 156, 158, 172, 174, 175, 177, 182, 188, 189, 191-193, 196, 197, 202, 227, 242, 349, 350, 442
Romani Pontifices, 256
Romania, 12, 29, 41, 216, 242, 244, 266, 269, 274, 286, 296, **324**, 338, 345-347, 589, 590
Romanian Catholics, 346, 347
Romanian Orthodox Church, 324, 584, 589
Romano Pontifici Eligendo, 297
Romans, 46, 96, 103, 134, 188, 573
Rome, 7, 9, 11, 13, 14, 17, 18, 21, 22, 24-27, 29-31, 33, 34, 37, 38, 41, 44, 45, 48, 50-55, 59, 60, 62, 63, 68, 69, 71, 77, 79, 81, 92, 96, 102, 103, 105-109, 113, 122, 129, 133, 134, 137, 139, 143, 144, 151, 155, 157, 159, 160, 162, 166, 171-173, 177, 188, 189, 204, 206-211, 213, 215, 216, 218-223, 225, 226, 228, 231-237, 239-243, 245, 247, 248, 255-259, 261-263, 265, 267, 270, 271, 273, 275-294, 297, 298, 302, 311, 315, 323, 324, 326, 329, 330, 332, 333, 337, 340-342, 344-346, 355, 358, 360, 361, 389, 394-417, 422, 458-466, 468-485, 489, 490, 492, 493, 496, 500, 503, 507, 546, 547, 550, 558, 566, 567, 572, 573, 575-578, 582-585, 588-594, 600-604, 607-612
Romeo, Card. Paolo, 47, **289**, 295-296, 378
Rooney III, L. Francis, 269
Roosevelt, Franklin D., 270, 371, 372
Roosevelt, Theodore, 371, 372
Roque, Bp. Francis, **412**, 419
Roque Gonzalez, 251
Rosales, Card. Gaudencio, **289**, 295-296
Rosary, 5, 12, 123, 134, 138, 141, **154**, 167, 169, 173, 190, 215, 238, 247-250, 356, 361, 388-390, 392, 444-446, 465, 473, 474, 482, 484, 487, 488, 501, 502, 505, 509, 513, 540, 542, 568, 570
Rosazza, Bp. Peter, **412**, 419
Rose, Bp. Robert, **412**, 419
Rose Hawthorne Lathrop Home, 509
Rose of Lima, **211**, 214, 215, 322, 473, 474
Rose Philippine Duchesne, 163, 170, 251, 354, 359, 362, 363, 392
Rosh Hashana, 605
Rosminians, 465, 467
Rota Roman, 201-203, **258**, 277, 281, 293
Rouco Varela, Card. Antonio, **289**-290, 295-297, 338
Rozanski, Bp. Mitchell, 375, 382, **412**
Rubiano Sáenz, Card. Pedro, **290**, 295-296
Rubrics, 184
Ruini, Card. Camillo, 23, 42, **290**,

295-296
Rule of St. Benedict, 188, 493, 616
Russia, 5, 14, 21, 105, 123, 210, 214,
222, 226, 227, 257, 266, 269, 272, 317,
324, 325, 346, 347, 429, 590
Russian Orthodox Church, 589, 590
Russolillo Giustino, Maria, 254
Rutan, Marguerite, 254
Ruthenian Byzantine Catholics, **346**, 350,
380, 381, 383, 410, 414, 432, 468
Rwanda, 243, 266, 269, 278, **325**, 330,
338, 339, 403
Ryan, Bp. Daniel, 382, **412**, 419
Ryan, Bp. Sylvester, 379, **412**, 419
Rylko, Card. Stanislaw, 25, 258, 261,
290, 295-296

S

Sabbath Day, 111, 367
Sabellianism, 205, 219
Sacerdotalis Caelibatus, 242, 250
Sacrae Disciplinae Leges, 245
Sacramental Economy, 88, 587
Sacramentals, 88, 127, 155, **175**-177,
196
Sacramentary, 185, 190, 488
Sacramentine Nuns, 484
Sacraments Congregation for the, 162,
184, 187, 256
Sacraments, See also individual sacra-
ments
Sacramentum Caritatis, 195, 233, 275
Sacred Heart Missionaries, 466
Sacred Heart of Jesus Oblate Sisters,
484
Sacred Heart of Jesus, Apostles of,
484, 486
Sacred Heart of Jesus, Congr. of,
465-466
Sacred Heart of Jesus, Handmaids
of, 484
Sacred Heart of Jesus Missionary, Sisters
of, 484
Sacred Heart of Jesus, Oblate Sisters,
484
Sacred Heart of Jesus, Servants of,
484, 488
Sacred Heart of Jesus, Sisters of the,
484
Sacred Heart of Jesus and the Poor,
Sisters, 488
Sacred Heart of Mary Religious, 485
Sacred Heart, Brothers of the, 462,
465, 467
Sacred Heart, 53, 54, 139, 141, 147, 154,
155, 162, 167, 173, 174, 182, 205, 207,
209, 210, 214, 238, 240, 248, 249, 253,
254, 280, 282, 290, 292, 316, 354, 359,
363, 388-393, 395-398, 404, 405, 409-
411, 416, 427, 430, 442-445, 462, 463,
465-478, 480, 481, 484-488, 490, 492,
498, 501, 503, 506, 509, 511, 513-518,
526, 528-530, 539-547, 556, 558, 559,
563, 566
Sacred Heart, Missionary Sisters of the,
207, 391, 392, 475, 484
Sacred Heart, Society of, 484
Sacred Liturgy, 87, 136, 138, 146, 147,
161, 175, **176**, 178, 181-183, 188, 229,
240, 249, 498
Sacred Music, 51, **176**, 182, 239, 240,
249, 548, 550, 559
Sacred Vessels, 154, 181, 183
Sacrilege, 31, 40, 50, 85, 139, **154**, 157
Sacristy, 6, 154
Sacrosanctum Concilium, 138, 147, 161,

175, 178, 181, 182, 229
Sadducees, 151, 154
Saints, 204-217
Saints, Patrons and Intercessors, 211-
214,
Saints, Patrons of Places, 214-215
Saints, Congregation for the Causes
of, 12, 27, 32, 37, 44, 76, 148, 152,
204, 256
Salazar, Bp. Alexander, 379, **412**, 425
Salazar Gomez, Card. Ruben, **290**,
295-296
Salesian Congregation, 208, 277, 279,
282, 293, 301, 334, 393, 466, 467, 492,
528, 544, 548, 550, 557, 560
Salesian Cooperators, 342, 493
Salesian Lay Missionaries, 430
Salesians of Don Bosco, 492, 550, 560
Salesians, See Salesian Congregation
Salvation History, 103, 104, 146, 151,
155, 161, 162, 166, 176, 179, 184
Salvation Outside the Church, 155
Salvatorians, 466, 467, 487
Salvifici Doloris, 244
Samoa, 25, 266, 267, 269, 294, **325**, 395,
410, 416, 430, 538, 555
Sample, Abp. Alexander, 379, 380, **412**
Samra, Bp. Nicholas, **412**, 419
Samuel, 96, 98-100
Sanchez, Bp. Paul R., 383, **412**, 419, 425
Sanctification, 90, 110, 175, 176, 491,
587, 598
Sanctifying Grace, 135, **143**, 145, 146,
150, 155, 157, 190
Sanctions, 33, 126, 127, 134, 246, 302
Sanctuary Lamp, 182
Sanctuary of Mary, 529
Sándor István, 215-216, 255
Sandoval Iñiguez, Card. Juan, **290**, 295-
296, 336, 450, 452, 454
Sandri Card. Leonardo 78, 256, 261,
290, 295-297, 592
Sansaricq, Bp. Guy, 375, **412**, 426
Santos, Card. Alexandre José Maria dos,
290, 295-297
Sapienti Consilio, 239, 356, 361
Sapientia Christiana, 293, 547
Sarah, Card. Robert 25, 42, 258, **290**,
295-297
Saraiva Martins, Card. Jose, 261, **290**,
295-297
Sardi, Card. Paolo, 260, **290**, 295,
296, 573
Sardinia, 6, 207, 210, 216, 226, 234, 246,
548, 572,
Sarr, Card. Theodore-Adrien, **290**,
295-297
Sartain, Bp. James, 378, 382, **412**
Sartoris, Bp. Joseph, **413**, 419
Satan, 50, 130, 138
Satanism, 155
Saturday Holy, 34, 166, 172, 350
Saudi Arabia, 325, **326**, 332
Scalabrini Srs., 472
Scalabrinians, 280, 464, 466, 467, 487,
560
Scandinavia, 204, 214, 221, 225, 338,
403, 506, 598
Scapular Medal, 155
Scapular Promise, 155
Scarpone Caporale, Bp. Gerald, **413**, 418
Scharfenberger, Bp. Edward Bernard,
374, **413**
Scheffler, Janos, 254
Scheid, Card. Oscar, **290**, 295-296
Scherer, Card. Odilo, 254, **290**-91,

295-297
Scheut Missionaries, 467
Schism, 134, **155**, 220-223, 236-238,
298, 305, 306, 309, 311-313, 320, 323,
326, 333, 359-361
Schism, Eastern, 222
Schism, Great Western, 237
Schlarman, Bp. Stanley, 376, 381, **413**,
419
Schmitz Simon, Bp. Paul O.F.M., **413**,
418, 430
Schnurr, Abp. Dennis, 376, 377, **413**, 422
Schoenstatt, 393, 491, 492, 496, 531, 570
Schoenstatt Center, 496, 531
Schoenstatt, Srs. of Mary, 491
Scholasticism, 107, 128, 149, 155, 159,
556,
Schönborn, Card. Christoph, **291**, 300,
336, 588, 589
Schönstatt Fathers, 491
Schönstatt Movement, 491, 492, 496,
531, 570
Schools Catholic, U.S., 532-546
Schools, Catholic World Statistics, 335
Schools, Religious (Statistics), 335
Schools and Students in Outlying
Areas, 538
Schulte, Abp. Francis, 378, 380, 384,
413, 419
Schwery, Card. Henry, **291**, 295-297
Schwietz, Abp. Roger O.M.I., 375, 377,
413, 422
Sciacca, Bp. Giuseppe, 260, 261
Scola, Card. Angelo, 274, **291**, 295,
296, 614
Scotland, 33, 47, 105, 170, 206, 208,
209, 214, 220, 233, 238, 248, 253, 296,
307, 308, 310, 311, **326**, 338, 341, 495,
506, 544, 581, 596, 599
Scripture, See Bible
Scripture in Church Life, 96
Scruple, 29, 155
Seal of Confession, 48, 140, **156**, 196,
355
Season of Advent, **161**, 180
Season of Lent, 131, **161**, 162, 180
Season of Ordinary Time, **161**, 180
Seasons, 138, 157, **161**, 162, 180, 195,
344, 349, 555, 557, 569
Sebastian, 71, 165, 211-213, 215, 252,
253, 266, 285, 363, 377, 379, 394
Sebastiani, Card. Sergio, 260, **291**,
295-297
Second Coming of Christ, 103, 130, 218,
583, 600
Secret Vatican Archives, 261, 272
Secretariat of State Vatican, 6, 77, 187,
269, 340, 395, 410, 416
Secular Franciscan Order, 206, 209, 223,
342, 493
Secular Franciscans, 213
Secular Institutes, 257, 458, 489-493
Secular Order, 223, 493
Secularism, 39, 144, **156**, 225, 232, 278,
584, 616
Seder, 605
Seelos, Francis Xavier, 254
Seigenthaler, John, 54
Seitz, Bp. Mark J., 376, **413**
Selection of Bishops, 274
Semi-Arians, 219,
Seminack, Bp. Richard, 382, **413**
Seminarians, 34, 37, 38, 57, 68, 156, 213,
243, 260, 284, 298, 335, 355, 357, 361,
362, 427, 430, 432, 466, 500, 506, 507,
534, 546,

Seminaries, 4, 53, 149, 156, 224, 238, 239, 248, 257, 278, 290, 293, 302, 316, 317, 359, 394, 398, 406, 409, 414, 432, 455, 501, 506, 534, 544, 545, 548, 609, ,
Seminary (Statistics), 546,
Seminary Enrollment, 546
Semi-Pelagianism, 220
Senegal, 243, 265, 266, 269, 293, 296, 303, **326**, 337-339
Sepe, Card. Crescenzio, 17, **291**, 295, 296
Septuagint, 96-98
Serbia, 266, 269, 319, **326**, 338, 347, 583, 590
Sergius I, Pope, 234
Sergius II, Pope, 222, 234
Sergius III, Pope, 234
Sergius IV, Pope, 220, 222, 235
Sermon, 129, 156, 175, 597, 612
Serra International, 342, 506, 560
Serratelli, Bp. Arthur, 86, 422
Servite Friars, 393
Servite Sisters, 480
Servites Order, 466
Seventh Day Adventists, 270, 595
Sevilla, Bp. Carlos, **413**, 614
Sexual Abuse Scandal, 67-70, 82-83
Seychelles, 243, 266, 269, 279, **326**, 337, 339
Sfeir, Card. Nasrallah, **291**, 295-297, 345, 348
Sgreccia, Card. Elio, **291**, 295-297
Shaheen, Bp. Robert, 380, **413**
Sharbel, Makhlouf, 211, 251
Sheehan, Abp. Michael, 378, 382, **413**
Sheen, Abp. Fulton, 362, 381
Shelters, 463, 508, 510, 605
Sheltz, Bp. George, 377, **413**
Sheridan, Bp. Michael, 376, **413**
Shoah, 61, 228, 245, 607-610
Shrine, 31, 35, 45, 49, 63-65, 77, 123, 124, 147, 156, 206, 279, 280, 352, 387, 389-393, 410, 446, 449, 496, 503, 507, 526, 529, 562-564
Shrines and Places of Historic Interest, 390-393
Shroud of Turin, 156
Siberia, 317, 324, **326**, 429
Sick Calls, 156,
Siegel, Bp. Joseph M., 378, **413**
Sierra Leone, 265, 266, 269, **326**, 337-339
Signatura Apostolic, 257, 258, 277, 279, 280, 283, 286, 288, 290-293, 297, 398, 417
Silva, Bp. Clarence, 378, **413**, 452
Silvestrini, Card. Achille, 260, **291**, 295-297
Simonis, Card. Adrianus, **291**, 295-297
Simony, 157
Sin, 6, 18, 23, 34, 42, 57, 59, 88, 94, 98, 104, 109, 110, 112, 114, 120, 121, 129-132, 136-138, 141-146, 148, 150-158, 160, 161, 163, 171, 172, 178, 190, 191, 193, 195, 196, 200, 218-220, 224, 324, 453, 586, 595, 597-599, 614
Sinai, 98, 111, 137, 244, 256, 589
Singapore, 41, 74, 75, 243, 266, 269, 285, 318, **327**, 337
Sirach, 96, 97, 100
Sirba, Bp. Paul D., 377, **413**-414
Sis, Bp. Michael, 382, **414**
Sisters Adorers, 483, 541
Sisters Oblates, 485
Sisters of Africa, 468

Sisters of Blessed Sacrament, 209, 356, 428, 479, 544
Sisters of Charity, 205, 206, 208, 209, 211, 225, 354, 355, 359, 363, 365, 391, 430, 470, 471, 473, 482, 526, 539-544, 560, 561
Sisters of Charity of Leavenworth, 471, 543
Sisters of Charity of Nazareth, 359, 471, 544, 560
Sisters of Charity of Seton Hill, 471, 543
Sisters of Charity of St. Joan Antida, 208, 471
Sisters of Charity of St. Vincent de Paul, 205, 472, 485
Sisters of Christian Charity, 471, 475, 544
Sisters of Divine Providence, 483, 540, 542
Sisters of Holy Family of Nazareth, 478, 540
Sisters of Holy Names of Jesus, 209, 541
Sisters of Loretto, 359, 364
Sisters of Mary, 12, 472, 475, 476, 478-480, 483-487, 491, 541
Sisters of Mercy, 365, 430, 471, 476, 481, 539-544
Sisters of Notre Dame, 52, 205, 209, 363, 430, 482, 540-542, 544
Sisters of Notre Dame de Namur, 209, 430, 482, 540, 541, 544
Sisters of Our Lady, 12, 208, 468, 472-476, 481, 482, 522
Sisters of Our Lady of Charity, 208, 482, 522
Sisters of Our Lady of Charity of Refuge, 208
Sisters of Our Lady of Mercy, 471, 476, 481
Sisters of Providence, 355, 359, 483, 540, 543, 560, 574
Sisters of St. Agnes, 430, 468, 541
Sisters of St. Anne, 208, 468, 528, 539
Sisters of St. Basil, 544
Sisters of St. Benedict, 393, 517
Sisters of St. Dominic, 474, 539
Sisters of St. Dorothy, 210, 217
Sisters of St. Francis, 216, 363, 475-477, 539-542, 559, 561
Sisters of St. Francis of Assisi, 476, 539
Sisters of St. Francis of Christ, 476
Sisters of St. Francis of Clinton, 476, 541
Sisters of St. Francis of Mary Immaculate, 542
Sisters of St. Francis of Maryville, 475
Sisters of St. Francis of Penance, 477
Sisters of St. Francis of Philadelphia, 475, 477
Sisters of St. Francis of Savannah, 477
Sisters of St. Francis of Sylvania, 559, 561
Sisters of St. Joseph, 206, 364, 393, 430, 476, 477, 479-481, 528, 539-544
Sisters of St. Joseph of Carondelet, 430, 480, 539-544
Sisters of St. Mary, 475, 480, 541, 542
Sisters of Ste. Chretienne, 472
Sisters of Sts. Cyril & Methodius, 473
Sistine Chapel, 51, 54, 245, 297, 574
Sixtus I, Pope, 233
Sixtus II, Pope, 168, 211, 233
Sixtus III, Pope, 172, 234
Sixtus IV, Pope, 145, 224, 236
Sixtus V, Pope, 126, 204, 236, 256, 257, 259, 263, 276
Skilled Care, 511-513, 517, 519, 520
Skilled Nursing Facilities, 511-520
Sklba, Bp. Richard, 379, **414**

Skurla, Bp. William, 380, 384, **414**
Skylstad, Bp. William, 383, 384, **414**, 419
Slander, 132, **157**
Slattery, Bp. Edward, 383, **414**
Slavery, 20, 31, 111, 169, 247, 301, 324, 325, 355, 360, 449, 577, 600, 602
Slavorum Apostoli, 250
Slovak Catholic Federation, 506
Slovak Catholic Sokol, 506, 555
Slovakia, 214, 244, 261, 266, 280, 284, 292, 296, 306, 327, 338, 346, 347, 394, 550, 590
Slovenia, 74, 244, 266, 269, 276, 289, 296, **327**, 338, 345, 550
Smith, Bp. John, 380, 383, **414**, 419
Smith, Bp. Peter, 380, **414**
Snyder, Bp. John, 382, **414**, 419
Social Communications, Catholic, 259, 551-575
Social Doctrine, 30, 114-117, 227, 238, 241, 300
Social Encyclicals of John Paul II, 115-117
Social Justice, 52, 53, 118, 147, 227, 307, 308, 318, 330, 426, 455, 494, 495, 499, 505, 560, 602, 606, 612
Social Service Facilities, 335
Social Service Organizations, 508
Societies of Apostolic Life, 127, 136, 188, 257, 278, 281, 284, 285, 287, 289-291, 402, 415, 458, 489, 557
Society for the Propagation of the Faith, 53, 226, 241, 256, 354, 361, 431, 506, 558
Society of African Missions, 317, 458, 467, 562
Society of Christ, 460, 467
Society of Divine Word, 397, 430, 461, 560
Society of Jesus See Jesuits
Society of Mary, 464, 486, 543
Society of Missionaries of Africa, 563
Society of Priests of St. Sulpice, 466
Society of St. Edmund, 461, 468, 543, 564
Society of St. Francis de Sales, 278, 466
Society of St. Monica, 506
Society of St. Paul, 465, 467, 492, 559
Society of St. Peter Apostle, 506
Society of St. Vincent de Paul, 226, 341, 508, 510, 559
Socio-Economic Statements by U.S. Bishops, 118
Sodalities of Our Lady, 496
Sodano, Card. Angelo, 29, 260, 277, 292, 295-297, 324
Soens, Bp. Lawrence, 383, 414
Solemnity of Christ, 14, 161
Solemnity of Mary, 21, 162, 165, 173, **174**
Solemnity of St. Joseph, 166
Sollicitudo Omnium Ecclesiarum, 264
Sollicitudo Rei Socialis, 114-118, 250
Solomon, 99-101
Soltys Stanislao, 252
Somalia, 7, 20, 265, 266, **327**, 339
Somascan Fathers, 208, 466
Song of Songs, 96, 99, **100**
Soo jung, Card. Andrew Yeom, 70-71, **294**, 296
Sorcery, 157
Soroka, Abp. Stephen, 381, **414**
Soteriology, 157
Soto, Bp. Jaime, 352, 366, 381, **414**, 422, 424, 425, 465, 474
Soul, 40, 45, 48, 61, 72, 93, 96, 108-111, 114, 120, 129, 140, 144, 154, 161, 171, 178, 191, 192, 196, 224, 507, 560, 573,

595, 610, 613
South Africa, 17, 214, 244, 265-267, 269, 286, 296, 317, 319, 320, **327**, 329, 339, 395, 403, 411, 414, 429, 463, 474, 483, 602
South America, 5, 156, 214, 247, 248, 259, 296, 297, 299, 301, 303, 304, 307, 309, 311, 322, 329, 332, 335, 339, 347, 363, 365, 395, 430, 489, 597
South Carolina, 352-355, 367, 373, 421, 434, 437, 440, 519, 530, 537, 573
South Dakota, 374, 393, 421, 434, 437, 440, 470, 519, 530, 537
South Korea, 3, 49, 63, 71, 216, 232, 243, 266, 286, **316**, 418, 581
Southern Baptist Convention, 580, 596
Sovereign Military Hospitaller Order of St. John of Jerusalem of Rhodes, 572
Soviet Union, 75, 227, 240, 244, 245, 257, 300, 325, 346, 589
Spain, 42, 51, 71, 74, 75, 105, 108, 123, 133, 145, 172, 205-210, 214-216, 219-222, 224, 225, 227, 233, 234, 239, 240, 242-244, 246-249, 253, 261, 264-267, 269, 272, 276, 277, 279, 282, 283, 285, 286, 289, 291, 296, 298, 299, 301, 303-305, 307, 308, 322, **328**, 338, 352, 353, 358, 363, 364, 394, 399, 401-403, 405, 418, 430, 449, 461, 463, 464, 466, 468, 470, 475-485, 492, 493, 496, 513, 525, 547, 549, 550, 596
Spanish Inquisition, 145, 224
Spe Salvi, 144, 233, 250
Special Apostolates and Groups, 495
Spellman, Card. Francis, 297, 380, 384, 529
Spencer, Bp. F. Richard, 384, **414**
Speyrer, Bp. Jude, 378, **414**, 419
Spiritual Exercises, 6, 30, 148, 207, 249, 492
Spiritual Renewal Programs, 252-531
Spoon, 351
Sri Lanka, 38, 63, 214, 244, 266, 269, 282, 288, 296, **328**, 338, 615
St. Ansgar's Scandinavian Catholic League, 506
St. Anthony's Guild, 97, 506
St. Jude League, 506
St. Margaret of Scotland, 170, 506
St. Martin de Porres Guild, 506
Stafford, Card. James, 260, **291**, 295-297, 376, 379, 414, 417, 498
Stamps Vatican, 262
Stanislao Soltys, 252
Stanislaw of Jesus and Mary, 254
State Catholic Conferences, 422
Stational Churches, 157
Stations of the Cross, 34, 138
Statistical Yearbook of the Church, 203, 263, 298, 335, 546
Statistics, Catholic Canada, 447, 448
Statistics, Catholic Education, 534-538
Statistics, Catholic Mexico, 455-457
Statistics, Catholic U.S., 432, 433-440
Statistics, International Church, 335
Statuary Hall, 364, 365, 372
Steib, Bp. J. Terry, 379, **414**, 426
Steiner, Bp. Kenneth, 381, **414**
Stella, Card. Beniamino, 256, **291**, 295, 296
Stephen, St., 170
Stephen I, Pope, 219, 233, 234, 312
Stephen II, Pope, 221, 234
Stephen II, Pope, 221, 234
Stephen III, Pope, 234
Stephen IV, Pope, 234

Stephen V, Pope, 234, 375
Stephen VI, Pope, 234
Stephen VII, Pope, 234
Stephen VIII, Pope, 234
Stephen IX, Pope, 235
Stewardship, 59, 130, 502, 558, 570, 586
Sticharion, 351
Stigmata, 158, 207, 214, 215, 462, 466
Stigmatine Fathers, 466, 467
Stika, Bp. Richard, 378, **414**
Stipend, **158**, 179
Stoeger, Fr. William, 54
Stole, 158, **180**, 186, 350, 351
Straling, Bp. Philip, 381, 382, **414**, 419
Strict Observance, 242, 461, 466, 472, 486
Stridon, 108
Studion, 283
Studite Monks, 283
Subaco Congregation, 460
Subdeacon, 186, 197
Subiaco Congregation, 460
Substance Abuse, 32, 509-511
Successor of Peter, 10, 16, 90, 92, 93, 113, 228, 578
Sudan, 20, 39, 47, 48, 50, 243, 265, 266, 269, 278, 294, 296, 303, 328, 338, 339, 347, 418
Suffragan See, 158, 374
Sullivan, Bp. Dennis, 379, **414**
Sulpicians, 225, 354, 359, 458, 466, 467
Sulyk, Abp. Stephen, 381, **414**, 419
Summa Theologiae, 109, 129, 153
Summary of School Statistics, 534
Summorum Pontificum, 3, 187, 189, 233
Sunday Mass, 24, 185, 568
Sundays of Lent, 349
Supererogation, 158
Support our Aging Religious, 506
Supreme Court, U.S., 16, 32, 44, 82, 84, 86, 133, 165, 366, 370, 372, 532, 533
Supreme Pontiff, 72, 91, 188, 193, 196, 259, 262, 264, 273
Supreme Tribunal of Apostolic Signatura, 277
Suriani, Abp. Luciano, 264
Suriname, 267, 269
Surplice, 180
Susannah, 101
Swain, Bp. Paul, 383, **414**
Swaziland, 243, 265-267, 269, 286, **329**, 339
Sweden, 107, 204-206, 214, 243, 265, 267, 269, 272, 329, 338, 469, 581
Swiss American Benedictine Congregation, 404
Swiss Guards, 37, 261
Switzerland, 15, 22, 77, 224, 242-244, 246-248, 261, 266, 267, 269, 272, 277, 283, 291, 296, **329**, 338-342, 403, 469, 475-477, 483, 549, 550, 567, 581, 589, 595, 599
Syllabus of Errors, 226
Sylvester I, Pope, 170, 211, 229, 233
Sylvester II, Pope, 222, 235
Sylvester III, Pope, 235
Sylvester IV, Pope, 237
Symons, Bp. J. Keith, 380, **414**, 419
Synaxis, 350
Synod of Bishops, 3, 9, 26, 38, 42, 71, 72, 75-77, 79-81, 126, 195, 233, 242, 244, 275, 278, 292, 294, 299, 315-317, 319, 339, 345, 357, 458
Synoptic Gospels, 106, 111
Synoptic Problem, 102
Syria, 5-8, 13-15, 19, 20, 28, 31, 35, 37, 41, 43, 47, 58, 60, 77, 78, 102, 105,

108, 135, 207, 228, 233, 234, 244, 245, 256, 267, 269, 317, **330**, 344-347, 401, 408, 417, 583, 586, 589, 612
Syrian Catholics, 330, 348, 417
Syrian Orthodox Church, 583, 592, 593
Syro-Malabar, 42, 274, 313, 346-348, 386, 389, 394, 428, 460
Syro-Malankara, 274, 313, 345, 347, 348, 373, 383, 387, 389, 409, 432, 438, 440
Szewczyk, Margaret Lucja, 255
Szoka, Card. Edmund, 54

T

Tabernacle, 29, 98, 142, **158**, 177, 181, 182
Table of Movable Feasts, 164
Tadini, Arcangelo, 252, 254
Tafoya, Bp. Arthur, 381, **414**, 419, 425
Tagle, Card. Luis, **292**, 295, 296
Taiwan, 265, 268, 272, 279, **330**, 336, 403, 428, 429, 547, 616
Tajikistan, 265-267, 269, **330**
Talley, Bp. David P., 374, **415**
Talmuds, 605
Tamayo, Bp. James, 378, **415**, 425
Tanzania, 214, 243, 261, 267, 269, 288, 296, **330**, 338, 339, 399, 419, 429, 458
Tarmouni Nerses XIX Bedros, 345, 347
Tauran, Card. Jean-Louis, 34, 35, 38, 259, 260, **292**, 295-296
Taylor, Bp. Anthony, 379, **415**
Te Deum, 158
Teaching Authority (Magisterium), 23, 36, 72, 80, 87, 92, 93, 112, 113, 115-117, 127, 133, 148, 198, 203, 246, 272, 494, 501, 534, 567, 572
Teaching Office, 94, 96, 127, 199
Tekakwitha, St. Kateri, 53, 168, 441
Tekakwitha Conference National Center, 429
Television, 10, 13, 82, 145, 205, 213, 250, 263, 341, 362, 562, 567-569, 575
Tempesta, O. Cist., Card. Orani, 70-71, **292**, 295, 296
Temporal Goods, 127, 257, 259
Temptation, 65, 101, 118, 150, **158**, 231, 608
Ten Commandments, 87, 88, 110-112, 131, 136, 147, 368, 369, 611
Tennessee, 36, 373, 405, 421, 434, 437, 440, 519, 524, 530, 537, 553, 555, 575, 602
Teresa of Ávila, 108
Teresa Demjanovich, 216, 255
Teresa, Mother, 7, 210, 211, 254, 471, 523
Terrazas Sandoval Card. Julio, **292**, 295-297
Tertio Millennio Adveniente, 244, 612
Tertullian, 88, 219
Test Act, 225
Testem Benevolentiae, 238, 356, 361
Tettamanzi Card. Dionigi, **292**, 295-294
Texas, 26, 44, 82, 84, 85, 352, 353, 355, 358, 364, 368, 369, 373, 374, 390, 393, 401, 402, 407, 409, 416, 421, 423, 426, 434, 437, 438, 440, 449, 462, 470, 496, 499, 500, 507, 509, 519, 522, 524, 531, 537, 538, 543, 546, 552-555, 573, 581, 597, 604
Thailand, 243, 253, 265-267, 269, 283, 285, 296, **330**, 338, 429
Theatines, 205, 466, 467
Theism, 159
Theodicy, 159
Theodore I, Pope, 234

Theodore II, Pope, 234
Theologian of the Papal Household, 280
Theological Commission, International, 198, 232, 233, 260, 279-281, 284, 286, 291, 292
Theological Virtues, 135, 138, 143, 145, 159, 191, 262
Theophany, 171, 172
Theotokos, 121, 122, **159**, 220
Thérèse of Lisieux, St., **108**, 212, 214, 215, 251
Theresians, 506
Thessalonians, 96, 103
Theta Kappa Phi Fraternity, 498
Third Order, 42, 107, 223, 248, 393, 406, 462, 467, 474-477, 487, 493, 509
Third Orders, 493
Thomas (Didymus), 106
Thomas Aquinas, 107, **109**, 113, 129, 148, 149, 153, 159, 160, 165, 171, 211-213, 215, 223, 243, 249, 281, 287, 291, 292, 294, 389, 397, 400-402, 406, 409, 413, 415, 543, 544, 546, 548, 550, 574
Thomas Becket, 170, 211, 222
Thomas, Bp. Daniel E., 380, 383, **415**
Thomas, Bp. Eliott, **415**, 419
Thomas, Bp. George, 377, **415**
Thomas Christians, 106, 346
Thomas More St., 208, **211**, 387, 388, 543, 556
Thomism, 149, 159
Thompson, Bp. Charles, 376, **415**
Thompson, Bp. David, 54
Thottunkal Card. Baselios Cleemis, **292**, 295-296
Throne, 21, 33, 176, 208, 224, 300, 450, 576
Tiedemann, Bp. Neil, 418
Timlin, Bp. James, 383, **415**, 419
Timor East, 243, 265, 268, 288, **306**, 307, 408, 418
Timothy, 96, 103
Tithing, 159
Titular Archbishop, 238, 240, 241, **274**
Titular Sees, 159
Titus, 96, **103**, 165, 211, 218, 225, 252
Titus Brandsma, 211, 252
Tobin, Abp. Joseph C.SS.R., 377, **415**
Tobin, Bp. Thomas, 372, 381, 384, **415**
Tobit, 96-99, 103
Togo, 243, 267, 269, 278, 281, **331**, 338, 339, 396
Tokelau, 410
Tolomei, Bernardo, 252
Tomko, Card. Jozef, 27, 261, **292**, 295-297
Tommaso da Olera, 215-216, 255
Tong Hon, Card. John, **292**, 295-297
Tonga, 266, 267, 269, **331**, 395
Toppo, Card. Telesphore, **292**, 295-297, 337
Torah, 96, 605
Toso, Abp. Mario, 258, 260
Tradition, 91-97
Transfiguration of Our Lord Jesus Christ, 290
Transfinalization, 159
Transignification, 159
Translation of Latin liturgical texts, 183
Translations, 16, 86, 88, 96-98, 183, 186, 189, 190, 242, 500, 614
Transubstantiation, 136, 144, 157, **159**, 193, 223, 225
Trappists, 458, 461, 466, 467, 528
Trautman, Bp. Donald, 377, **415**, 419
Travelers and Migrants Council, 258

Trent, Council of, 87, 96, 97, 104, 109, 126, 133, 137, 138, 153, 156, 159, 178, 182, 184, 185, 188, 210, 216, 220, 224, 256, 595, 603
Tribunal Action, 202
Tridentine Mass, 185, 187
Triduum, 34, 159, **161**, 166, 172, 187, 188, 194
Trination, 179, 185
Trinity Sunday, 112, 139, 162, 171
Truce of God, 222
True Cross, 207, 219, 221
Truman, Harry S., 270, 371
Trusteeism, 359
Tucci, Card. Roberto S.J., 262, **292**, 295-297
Tumi, Card. Christian, **293**, 295-297
Tunisia, 244, 264, 267, 269, **331**
Turcotte, Card. Jean-Claude, **293**, 295-297
Turkey, 77, 233, 241-243, 256, 267, 269, 276-278, 291, 299, **331**, 338, 345-348, 589, 612, 613
Turkmenistan, 267, 269, **331**
Turkson, Card. Peter, 258, **293**, 339
Turley, Bp. Murphy, **415**, 418
Typological Sense, 104
Tyson, Bp. Joseph J., 383, **415**

U

Ubi Arcano, 240, 249
Uganda, 53, 77, 205, 242, 243, 251, 267, 269, 293, 294, 296, **331**, 332, 338, 339, 396, 418, 429, 589
Uglietto, Bp. Peter J., 375, **415**
Ukraine, 15, 20, 29, 34, 226, 244, 245, 261, 267, 269, 274, 283, 296, 297, 325, **332**, 338, 345-347, 374, 403, 415, 417, 418, 481, 589
Ukrainian Byzantine Catholics, 284, 296, 332, 348
Ukrainian Orthodox Church, 589
Ultramontanism, 159
Unam Sanctam, 223
Unauthorized Eucharistic Prayers, 190
Unction, **159**, 196
Unda, 341, 564, 569
Unda-USA, 564
Uniatism, 587
Union of Brest, 244, 332, 345, 346
Union of European Conferences of Major Superiors, 489
Union of Superiors General, 489
UNIREA, 555
Unitatis Redintegratio, 229, 576-578
United Church of Christ, 580, 582, 596, 598, 599, 604
United Nations (U.N.), 269
United States Catholic Conference, 86, 357, 361, 413, 420, 500, 567
United States Catholic Historical Society, 506
United States Catholic Mission Association, 559
United States Conference of Catholic Bishops (USCCB), 183, 357, 373, 420
United States Dioceses, 373-384, 432
United States Hierarchy, 373-384, See also Bishops
United States Social Services, 508-531
United States Statistics, 432, 433-444, 534-538
United States Statistics, Catholic Education, 432, 534-538
Universi Dominici Gregis, 150, 244
Universities, 4, 22, 23, 25, 149, 156, 206,

214, 257, 290, 341, 432, 494, 497, 507, 532-539, 547, 550, 570
Universities Pontifical, 494, 547, 550
Universities, U.S. Catholic (Statistics), 534-538
Urban I, Pope, 233
Urban II, Pope, 235
Urban III, Pope, 235
Urban IV, Pope, 143, 171, 235
Urban V, Pope, 236, 237
Urban VI, Pope, 174, 236, 237
Urban VII, Pope, 236
Urban VIII, Pope, 188, 217, 236
Ursuline Nuns, 353, 358, 359, 364, 485, 544
Ursuline Order, 541
Ursuline Sisters, 485, 539, 544
Ursuline Sisters of Belleville, 485
Ursuline Sisters of Mount Saint Joseph, 485
Ursulines, 217, 363, 364, 430, 441, 486, 487, 544
Uruguay, 214, 243, 267, 269, 291, **332**, 339, 408, 454, 548
USCCB, See United States Conference of Catholic Bishops
USCCB Administrative Committee, 36, 421
USCCB Committees, 421, 424, 426, 428, 429
USCCB Regions, 421
Use of Vernacular Languages, 175, 183, 184, 241
Usury, **159**, 246
Ut Unum Sint, 61, 245, 250, 576, 578, 594, 604
Utah, 356, 374, 397, 421, 434, 438, 440, 470, 519, 531, 538
Uzbekistan, 267, 269, **332**

V

Vacchelli, Abp. Piergiuseppe, 256, 260
Vagi, 160,
Valero, Bp. René, 384, **415**, 425
Vallini, Card. Agostino, 26, 260, **293**, 295-297
Vanhoye, Card. Albert, **293**, 295-297
Vann, Bp. Kevin W., 377, 383, 405, **415**
Vanuatu, 266, 267, 269, 332, 395
Vasa, Bp. Robert, 375, **415**
Vasil', Abp. Cyril 27, 254, 261
Vasquez, Bp. Jose, 375, **415**, 425
Vatican Archives, 238, 272, 611
Vatican Bank, 22, 31, 35, 45, 46, 63, 75
Vatican City State, 3, 9, 14, 17, 37, 41, 45, 54, 73-75, 261-263, 267, 272, 278, 279, 285, 289, 292, 293, 332, 567, 568
Vatican Council I, 210, 364
Vatican Council II, 13, 87, 114, 126, 229, 242, 244, 245, 362, 570
Vatican Gardens, 22, 41, 67, 271, 272
Vatican Information Service, 124, 259, 567
Vatican Library, 239, 261, 272, 282, 498
Vatican Observatory, 54, 238, 272
Vatican Polyglot Press, 185, 263
Vatican Press Office, 26, 67, 255, 259
Vatican Publishing House, 23, 263
Vatican Radio, 55, 75, 262, 292, 293, 567-569
Vatican Secret Archives, 261, 272
Vatican Secretariat of State, 6, 77, 187, 269, 340, 395, 410, 416
Vatican Stamps, 260
Vatican Television Center, 10, 263

Vegló, Card. Antonio, 258, 261, **293**, 295-297

Vela Chiliboga, Card. Raul Eduardo, **293**, 295-297

Venerable Churches, 343

Venezuela, 31, 156, 214, 243, 267, 269, 272, 278, 287, 290, 293, 296, **332**, 339, 345-347, 352, 364, 365, 548

Veni Creator Spiritus, 160

Venial Sin, 88, 137, 153, 157, 160

Verbum Domini, 105, 233, 275

Veritatis Splendor, 112, 113, 142, 250

Vermont, 340, 341, 373, 393, 421, 434, 438, 440, 470, 519, 538, 542, 555

Verna, Bl. Antonia Maria, 255

Vernacular, 104, 147, 160, 175, 176, 183-185, 187-189, 206, 241, 242

Verona Fathers, 461

Veronica, 157, 160, 573, 574

Versaldi, Card. Giuseppe, 259

Vesakh, 34, 616

Vessels, 6, 154, 181-183

Vestments, 27, 76, 154, 177, **180**, 181, 184, 351

Viaticum, **160**, 172, 193, 196

Viator, 212, 466

Viatorian Fathers, 466, 505

Viatorians, 467

Vicar Apostolic, 217, 274, 364, 365, 378-380, 397, 407, 410, 417, 418, 441

Vicar General, 12, 13, 21, 51, 53, 137, **160**, 261, 274, 280, 282, 288-290, 293, 302, 353, 363, 395, 396, 411, 412, 415, 416

Vicar of Christ, 131, 151

Vicariates Apostolic, 273, 308, 316, 335, 441

Vidal, Card. Ricardo, **293**, 295-297

Vietnam, 11, 52, 204, 217, 241, 251, 266, 267, 286, 288, 296, **333**, 339, 407, 464, 480-482, 485, 490, 549

Viganó, Abp. Carlo M., 267, 270, 373

Vigil Mass, 34, 162

Vigilanti Cura, 249

Vigneron, Abp. Allen, 376, 380, **416**

Vincent de Paul, 124, 169, 205, 209, **211**, 212, 215, 225, 226, 341, 355, 361, 404, 405, 410, 415, 416, 466, 472, 485, 487, 502, 508, 510, 516, 545, 559, 616

Vincent Ferrer, **211**-213, 215

Vincent Pallotti, **211**, 251, 464, 531

Vincentians, 169, **211**, 225, 289, 319, 324, 354, 392, 466, 467, 540, 542

VingtTrois, Card. Andre, **293**, 295-297

Virgin Islands, 287, 299, **333**, 374, 409, 415, 418-421, 426, 430, 432, 438, 497, 507, 538, 552

Virgin Mary, See Mary Blessed Virgin, 205

Virginia, 36, 84, 86, 252, 352, 354, 369, 370, 372, 373, 390, 421, 423, 434, 438, 440, 468, 469, 512, 519, 520, 525, 531, 538, 556, 558, 565, 602

Virginity, 57, 121, **160**, 249

Virtues, 58, 65, 91, 103, 110, 121, 130, 133, 135, 138, 141, 143, 145, 146, 153, 158-**160**, 190, 191, 262, 361, 496, 613-615

Vismara, Clemente, 254

Visually Challenged, 525

Vlazny, Abp. John, 381, 384, **416**, 419, 422

Vlk, Card. Miloslav, **294**, 295-297

Vocationist Fathers, 466, 467, 529

Volpicelli, Caterina, 252, 254

Vouchers, 4, 371, 500, 532, 533

Vow, 135, 143, 149, 152, **160**, 201

Vulgate, 96, **97**, 104, 108, 220, 260, 263

W-X

Wako, Card. Gabriel, **294**, 295-297

Walburga, 211, 393, 468, 469

Waldensians, 312

Wales, 7, 33, 47, 53, 206, 209, 214, 242, 253, 286, 307, 310, **333**, 334, 337, 566

Walkowiak, Bp. David J., 377, **416**

Wall, Bp. James, 377, **416**

Walsh, Bp. Daniel, 378, 381, **416**, 419

Walsh, Bp. Gerald, **416**, 419

Walsh, Bp. Paul H., 381, **416**

Walterscheid, Bp. William, 380, **416**

Wamala, Card. Emmanuel, **294**, 295-297

Wang, Bp. Ignatius, **416**, 419

Warfel, Bp. Michael, 377, 378, **416**, 422

Washing of Hands, 179,

Washington, 10, 20, 24, 31, 32, 51-54, 77, 89, 97, 183, 185, 187, 189, 197, 226, 238, 267, 270, 271, 278, 279, 281, 284, 287, 288, 292, 294, 297, 333, 342, 354, 356-358, 360, 363, 365, 366, 372, 374, 383-387, 389-392, 395-417, 419-421, 423-431, 433-435, 438-440, 458, 459, 462-464, 470, 473, 474, 476, 479, 481, 482, 485, 489, 491, 493, 495-505, 507, 509-515, 517, 519-523, 527, 528, 531, 532, 538-540, 544-546, 548-550, 552-554, 556-568, 572-575, 580, 581, 587, 590, 591, 598, 604, 606, 610, 614, 615,

Washington, D.C., 20, 24, 31, 77, 267, 288, 292, 297, 356, 357, 360, 395, 399, 401, 410, 412, 419, 421, 435, 439, 464, 498, 557, 563, 573,

Water, 6, 47, 49, 65, 77, 90, 128, 131, 139, 141, 144, 150, 158, 172, 176, 179, 182, 191, 215, 352, 427, 479, 501, 584, 604, ,

Way of the Cross, 34, 43, 157, 158, 289, 501, 573, 575,

Wcela, Bp. Emil, **416**, 419

Weakland, Abp. Rembert, 379, **416**, 419

Weigand, Bp. William 382, **416**, 419, 491

Weisenburger, Bp. Edward J., 382, **416**

Weitzel, Bp. John, 416, 418, 430

Wenski, Abp. Thomas, 20, 24, 32, 40, 379, 380, **416**, 422

West Virginia, 84, 372, 373, 390, 421, 423, 434, 438, 440, 520, 531, 538

Wester, Bp. John, 382, **416**, 422

Wetter, Card. Friedrich, **294**, 295-297

White Fathers, 318, 331, 334, 458, 563

Whitsunday, 173

Wilkerson, Bp. Gerald, 379, **416**

Williams, Bp. James, 378, **416**, 419

Williams, Card. Thomas, **294**, 295-297

Willibrord, 212, 214,

Wilson, William A., 269, 270

Wine, 50, 128, 136, 139, 146, 157, 159, 178, 179, 181-183, 192-194, 196, 214, 222, 223, 348-351, 571, 595

Winter, Bp. William, **416**, 419

Wisconsin, 84, 270, 364, 367, 372, 373, 390, 393, 400, 414, 421, 423, 434, 438, 440, 463, 470, 495, 496, 504, 520, 522, 525, 531, 538, 546, 558, 561, 597

Wisdom Books, 96, 99

Wiseman, Card. Nicholas, 226

Wiwchar, Bp. Michael C.SSR, 382, **416**

Woelki, Card. Rainer, **294**, 295-297

Women for Faith and Family, 507

Women Missionaries, 441

Women Religious, 38, 108, 124, 125, 149, 157, 176, 194, 204, 222, 244, 264, 333, 355, 357, 359, 427, 430, 441, 489, 496, 503, 562

Women Religious, U.S., 432, 468-486

Word, Liturgy of, 178

Works of Religion, Institute for, 9, 74, 75, 260, 278, 285

World Apostolate of Fatima, 342, 392, 507, 560, 564, 590

World Communications Day, 570

World Conference of Secular Institutes, 490

World Council of Churches, 30, 241, 357, 576, 580, 604

World Day of Prayer, 49, 245, 615

World Statistics, 335

World War I, 227, 239-241, 310, 312, 314, 323, 326, 327, 331, 356, 423

World War II, 53, 77, 182, 215, 227, 232, 240-242, 245, 261, 289, 294, 310, 312, 316, 322-324, 327, 330, 334, 342, 346, 357, 362, 395, 423, 607, 610

World Youth Day, 45, 49, 56, 63, 80, 233, 302, 357, 413, 612

Wuerl, Card. Donald, **294**, 295-297

Wyoming, 363, 373, 387, 421, 434, 438, 440, 512, 522, 528, 538, 544, 552, 556

Xaverian Brothers, 462, 467

Xaverian Missionary Fathers, 466, 564

Y

Yad Va Shem, 607

Yanta, Bp. John, 375, **417**, 419

Yemen, 264-267, 269, 332, **334**

YHWH, 146

Yom HaShoah, 605, 607

Yom Kippur, 605

Younan, Patriarch Joseph, 274, 347, 348, 380, **417**

Young Ladies' Institute, 507

Young Mens' Institute, 507

Youth Day World, 45, 49, 56, 63, 80, 233, 302, 357, 413, 612

Youth Ministry, 66, 427, 496, 497

Youth Organizations, 4, 311, 496

Yugoslavia, 125, 242, 267, 269, 276, 278, 301, 305, 319, 326, 327, 339, 345, 589

Z

Zaidan, Bp. Abdallah E., 380, **417**

Zaire, 243, 265, 267-269, 271, 292, 336, 339, 548

Zambia, 53, 243, 266, 267, 269, 285, **334**, 339, 400, 418, 419, 429, 430, 495

Zarama, Bp. Luis, 375, **417**

Zavala, Bp. Gabino, **417**, 419

Zayek, Bp. Francis, 382, **417**, 419

Zeal, 26, 106, 145, **160**, 165, 188, 259, 473, 488, 491, 564

Zebedee, 105

Zechariah, 96, **101**, 132, 133, 176

Zen Zekiun, Card. Joseph, **294**, 295-297

Zephaniah, 96, **101**

Zglejszewski, Bp. Andrzej, 381, **417**

Zimbabwe, 11, 19, 243, 267, 269, 277, **334**, 339, 581

Zipfel, Bp. Paul, 375, **417**

Zoltan, Lajos Meszlanyi, Bl., 255

Zone, 44, 351

Zubic, Bp. David, 377, 381, **417**

Zucchetto, **160**, 181

Zurek, Bp. Patrick, 374, **417**

Zwingli, Huldrych, 224, 330, **594**, 595

Zygmunt, Felinski St., 252, 254